PHILIP'S

WORLD ATLAS

Philip's are grateful to the following for acting as specialist geography consultants on '*The World in Focus*' front section:

Professor D. Brunsden, Kings College, University of London, UK
Dr C. Clarke, Oxford University, UK
Dr I. S. Evans, Durham University, UK
Professor P. Haggett, University of Bristol, UK
Professor K. McLachlan, University of London, UK
Professor M. Monmonier, Syracuse University, New York, USA
Professor M-L. Hsu, University of Minnesota, Minnesota, USA
Professor M. J. Tooley, University of St Andrews, UK
Dr T. Unwin, Royal Holloway, University of London, UK

THE WORLD IN FOCUS
Cartography by Philip's

Picture Acknowledgements
NASA/GSFC page 14

Illustrations: Stefan Chabluk

WORLD CITIES
Cartography by Philip's

Page 10, Dublin: The town plan of Dublin is based on Ordnance Survey Ireland by permission of the Government Permit Number 8186. © Ordnance Survey Ireland and Government of Ireland.

Page 11, Edinburgh, and page 15, London:
This product includes mapping data licensed from Ordnance Survey® with the permission of the Controller of Her Majesty's Stationery Office. © Crown copyright 2007. All rights reserved. Licence number 100011710.

Vector data courtesy of Gräfe and Unser Verlag GmbH, München, Germany
(city-centre maps of Bangkok, Beijing, Cape Town, Jerusalem, Mexico City, Moscow, Singapore, Sydney, Tokyo and Washington D.C.)
The following city maps utilize base data supplied courtesy of MapQuest.com, Inc. (© MapQuest)
(Las Vegas, New Orleans, Orlando)

All satellite images in this section courtesy of NPA Group, Edenbridge, Kent (www.satmaps.com)

Published in Great Britain in 2007
by Philip's,
a division of Octopus Publishing Group Limited,
2–4 Heron Quays, London E14 4JP
An Hachette Livre UK Company

Copyright © 2007 Philip's

Cartography by Philip's

ISBN-13 978–0–540–09011–2
ISBN-10 0–540–09011–5

A CIP catalogue record for this book is available from the British Library.

Printed in Hong Kong

Details of other Philip's titles and services can be found on our website at: www.philips-maps.co.uk

Philip's World Atlases are published in association with The Royal Geographical Society (with The Institute of British Geographers).

The Society was founded in 1830 and given a Royal Charter in 1859 for 'the advancement of geographical science'. It holds historical collections of national and international importance, many of which relate to the Society's association with and support for scientific exploration and research from the 19th century onwards. It was pivotal in establishing geography as a teaching and research discipline in British universities close to the turn of the century, and has played a key role in geographical and environmental education ever since.

Today the Society is a leading world centre for geographical learning – supporting education, teaching, research and expeditions, and promoting public understanding of the subject.

The Society welcomes those interested in geography as members. For further information, please visit the website at: www.rgs.org

PHILIP'S

WORLD ATLAS

PAPERBACK EDITION

IN ASSOCIATION WITH
THE ROYAL GEOGRAPHICAL SOCIETY
WITH THE INSTITUTE OF BRITISH GEOGRAPHERS

Contents

World Statistics

Countries   vi
Physical Dimensions   vii
User Guide   viii

The World in Focus

Planet Earth   2–3
Restless Earth   4–5
Landforms   6–7
Oceans   8–9
Climate   10–11
Water and Vegetation   12–13
Environment   14–15
Population   16–17
The Human Family   18–19
Wealth   20–21
Quality of Life   22–23
Energy   24–25
Production   26–27
Trade   28–29
Travel and Tourism   30–31

World Cities

Amsterdam   2
Athens   2
Atlanta   3
Baghdad   3
Bangkok   3
Barcelona   4
Beijing   4
Berlin   5
Boston   6
Brussels   6
Budapest   7
Buenos Aires   7
Cairo   7
Cape Town   8
Copenhagen   8
Chicago   9
Delhi   10
Dublin   10
Edinburgh   11
Guangzhou   11
Helsinki   11
Hong Kong   12
Istanbul   12
Jakarta   12
Jerusalem   13
Johannesburg   13
Karachi   13
Kolkata   14
Lagos   14
Las Vegas   14
Lima   14
London   15
Lisbon   16
Los Angeles   16
Madrid   17
Manila   17
Melbourne   18
Mexico City   18
Miami   18
Milan   19
Moscow   19
Montréal   20
Mumbai   20
Munich   21
New Orleans   21
New York   22
Orlando   23
Osaka   23
Oslo   23
Paris   24
Prague   25
Rio de Janeiro   25
Rome   26
San Francisco   26
St Petersburg   27
Santiago   27
São Paulo   27
Seoul   27
Shanghai   28
Singapore   28
Stockholm   29
Sydney   29
Tokyo   30
Tehran   31
Toronto   31
Vienna   32
Warsaw   32
Washington   33
Wellington   33
Index to City Maps   34–39
World Cities Satellite Images   40–48

World Maps

Map Symbols   1

The World: Political
1:95 000 000   2–3

Arctic Ocean
1:35 000 000   4

Antarctica
1:35 000 000   5

Europe

Europe: Physical
1:20 000 000   6

Europe: Political
1:20 000 000   7

Scandinavia   1:6 000 000
Iceland   1:6 000 000
Færoe Islands   1:6 000 000
                                         8–9

Ireland   1:2 000 000
                                         10

Scotland   1:2 000 000
                                         11

England and Wales
1:2 000 000
                                         12–13

British Isles   1:5 000 000
                                         14

Netherlands, Belgium and
Luxembourg   1:2 500 000
                                         15

Central Europe   1:5 000 000
                                         16–17

Eastern Europe and Turkey
1:10 000 000
                                         18–19

France   1:5 000 000
                                         20

Spain and Portugal
1:5 000 000
                                         21

Italy and the Balkan States
1:5 000 000
                                         22–23

The Balearics, the Canaries and
Madeira   1:1 000 000 / 1:2 000 000
                                         24

Malta, Crete, Corfu, Rhodes
and Cyprus
1:1 000 000 / 1:1 300 000
                                         25

Asia

Asia: Physical   1:47 000 000   26

Asia: Political   1:47 000 000   27

Russia and Central Asia
1:20 000 000
                                         28–29

Japan   1:5 000 000
                                         30–31

China and the Far East
1:15 000 000
Hong Kong and Macau   1:1 000 000
                                         32–33

Northern China and Korea
1:6 000 000
                                         34–35

Indonesia and the Philippines
1:12 500 000
Java and Madura   1:7 500 000
Bali   1:2 000 000
                                         36–37

Mainland South-east Asia
1:6 000 000
Ko Phuket   1:1 000 000
Ko Samui   1:1 000 000
Pinang   1:1 000 000
Singapore   1:1 000 000
                                         38–39

South Asia   1:10 000 000
                                         40–41

Northern India, Pakistan and Nepal
1:6 000 000
Jammu and Kashmir 1:6 000 000

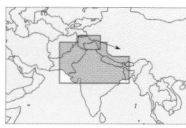

42–43

The Middle East
1:7 000 000

44–45

The Near East 1:2 500 000

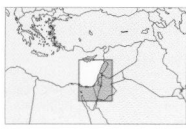

46

Arabia and the Horn of Africa 1:15 000 000

47

Africa

Africa: Physical
1:42 000 000   **48**

Africa: Political
1:42 000 000   **49**

Northern Africa
1:15 000 000
Azores 1:15 000 000
Cape Verde Islands 1:10 000 000

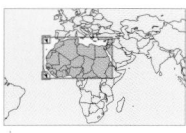

50–51

Central and Southern Africa
1:15 000 000
Seychelles 1:2 500 000
Réunion 1:2 500 000
Mauritius 1:2 500 000
Comoros 1:8 000 000

52–53

East Africa 1:8 000 000

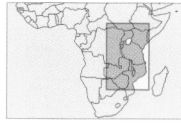

54–55

Southern Africa
1:8 000 000
Madagascar 1:8 000 000

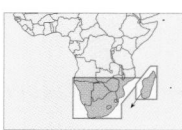

56–57

Australia and Oceania

Australia and Oceania: Physical and Political
1:50 000 000   **58**

New Zealand 1:6 000 000
Samoan Islands 1:6 000 000
Fiji 1:6 000 000
Tonga 1:6 000 000
Tahiti and Moorea 1:1 000 000

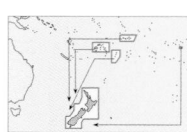

59

Western Australia
1:8 000 000

60–61

Eastern Australia
1:8 000 000
Whitsunday Islands 1:2 500 000
Tasmania 1:8 000 000

62–63

Pacific Ocean
1:54 000 000   **64–65**

North America

North America: Physical
1:35 000 000   **66**

North America: Political
1:35 000 000   **67**

Canada 1:15 000 000

68–69

Western Canada 1:7 000 000

70–71

Eastern Canada 1:7 000 000

72–73

United States 1:12 000 000
Hawai'i 1:10 000 000
Alaska 1:30 000 000

74–75

United States – West
1:6 700 000

76–77

Central and Southern California and Western Washington
1:2 500 000

78–79

United States – Midwest and North-east
1:6 700 000

80–81

North-eastern United States
1:2 500 000

82–83

United States – South
1:6 700 000

84–85

Mexico 1:8 000 000

86–87

Central America and the West Indies 1:8 000 000
Jamaica 1:3 000 000
Guadeloupe 1:2 000 000
Martinique 1:2 000 000
Puerto Rico 1:3 000 000
Virgin Islands 1:2 000 000
St Lucia 1:2 000 000
Barbados 1:2 000 000

88–89

South America

South America: Physical
1:35 000 000   **90**

South America: Political
1:35 000 000   **91**

South America – North
1:16 000 000
Trinidad and Tobago 1:2 500 000

92–93

Central South America
1:8 000 000

94–95

South America – South
1:16 000 000

96

Index to World Maps
97–176

World Statistics: Countries

This alphabetical list includes the principal countries and territories of the world. If a territory is not completely independent, the country it is associated with is named. The area figures give the total area of land, inland water and ice. The population figures are 2006 estimates where available. The annual income is the Gross Domestic Product per capita in US dollars. The figures are the latest available, usually 2006 estimates.

Country/Territory	Area km² Thousands	Area miles² Thousands	Population Thousands	Capital	Annual Income US $
Afghanistan	652	252	31,057	Kabul	800
Albania	28.7	11.1	3,582	Tirana	5,600
Algeria	2,382	920	32,930	Algiers	7,700
American Samoa (US)	0.20	0.08	58	Pago Pago	5,800
Andorra	0.47	0.18	71	Andorra La Vella	38,800
Angola	1,247	481	12,127	Luanda	4,300
Anguilla (UK)	0.10	0.04	13	The Valley	8,800
Antigua & Barbuda	0.44	0.17	69	St John's	10,900
Argentina	2,780	1,074	39,922	Buenos Aires	15,000
Armenia	29.8	11.5	2,976	Yerevan	5,400
Aruba (Netherlands)	0.19	0.07	72	Oranjestad	21,800
Australia	7,741	2,989	20,264	Canberra	32,900
Austria	83.9	32.4	8,193	Vienna	35,500
Azerbaijan	86.6	33.4	7,962	Baku	7,300
Azores (Portugal)	2.2	0.86	236	Ponta Delgada	15,000
Bahamas	13.9	5.4	304	Nassau	21,300
Bahrain	0.69	0.27	699	Manama	25,300
Bangladesh	144	55.6	147,365	Dhaka	2,200
Barbados	0.43	0.17	280	Bridgetown	18,200
Belarus	208	80.2	10,293	Minsk	7,800
Belgium	30.5	11.8	10,379	Brussels	31,800
Belize	23.0	8.9	288	Belmopan	8,400
Benin	113	43.5	7,863	Porto-Novo	1,100
Bermuda (UK)	0.05	0.02	66	Hamilton	69,900
Bhutan	47.0	18.1	2,280	Thimphu	1,400
Bolivia	1,099	424	8,989	La Paz/Sucre	3,000
Bosnia-Herzegovina	51.2	19.8	4,499	Sarajevo	5,500
Botswana	582	225	1,640	Gaborone	11,400
Brazil	8,514	3,287	188,078	Brasília	8,600
Brunei	5.8	2.2	379	Bandar Seri Begawan	25,600
Bulgaria	111	42.8	7,385	Sofia	10,400
Burkina Faso	274	106	13,903	Ouagadougou	1,300
Burma (Myanmar)	677	261	47,383	Rangoon/Naypyidaw	1,800
Burundi	27.8	10.7	8,090	Bujumbura	700
Cambodia	181	69.9	13,881	Phnom Penh	2,600
Cameroon	475	184	17,341	Yaoundé	2,400
Canada	9,971	3,850	33,099	Ottawa	35,200
Canary Is. (Spain)	7.2	2.8	1,682	Las Palmas/Santa Cruz	19,900
Cape Verde Is.	4.0	1.6	421	Praia	6,000
Cayman Is. (UK)	0.26	0.10	45	George Town	43,800
Central African Republic	623	241	4,303	Bangui	1,100
Chad	1,284	496	9,944	Ndjaména	1,500
Chile	757	292	16,134	Santiago	12,700
China	9,597	3,705	1,313,974	Beijing	7,600
Colombia	1,139	440	43,593	Bogotá	8,400
Comoros	2.2	0.86	691	Moroni	600
Congo	342	132	3,702	Brazzaville	1,300
Congo (Dem. Rep. of the)	2,345	905	62,661	Kinshasa	700
Cook Is. (NZ)	0.24	0.09	21	Avarua	9,100
Costa Rica	51.1	19.7	4,075	San José	12,000
Croatia	56.5	21.8	4,495	Zagreb	13,200
Cuba	111	42.8	11,383	Havana	3,900
Cyprus	9.3	3.6	784	Nicosia	22,700
Czech Republic	78.9	30.5	10,235	Prague	21,600
Denmark	43.1	16.6	5,451	Copenhagen	37,000
Djibouti	23.2	9.0	487	Djibouti	1,000
Dominica	0.75	0.29	69	Roseau	3,800
Dominican Republic	48.5	18.7	9,184	Santo Domingo	8,000
East Timor	14.9	5.7	1,063	Dili	800
Ecuador	284	109	13,548	Quito	4,500
Egypt	1,001	387	78,887	Cairo	4,200
El Salvador	21.0	8.1	6,822	San Salvador	4,900
Equatorial Guinea	28.1	10.8	540	Malabo	5,200
Eritrea	118	45.4	4,787	Asmara	1,000
Estonia	45.1	17.4	1,324	Tallinn	19,600
Ethiopia	1,104	426	74,778	Addis Ababa	1,000
Faroe Is. (Denmark)	1.4	0.54	47	Tórshavn	31,000
Fiji	18.3	7.1	906	Suva	6,100
Finland	338	131	5,231	Helsinki	32,800
France	552	213	60,876	Paris	30,100
French Guiana (France)	90.0	34.7	200	Cayenne	8,300
French Polynesia (France)	4.0	1.5	275	Papeete	17,500
Gabon	268	103	1,425	Libreville	7,200
Gambia, The	11.3	4.4	1,642	Banjul	2,000
Gaza Strip (OPT)*	0.36	0.14	1,429	–	1,500
Georgia	69.7	26.9	4,661	Tbilisi	3,800
Germany	357	138	82,422	Berlin	31,400
Ghana	239	92.1	22,410	Accra	2,600
Gibraltar (UK)	0.006	0.002	28	Gibraltar Town	27,900
Greece	132	50.9	10,668	Athens	23,500
Greenland (Denmark)	2,176	840	56	Nuuk	20,000
Grenada	0.34	0.13	90	St George's	3,900
Guadeloupe (France)	1.7	0.66	453	Basse-Terre	7,900
Guam (US)	0.55	0.21	171	Agana	15,000
Guatemala	109	42.0	12,294	Guatemala City	4,900
Guinea	246	94.9	9,690	Conakry	2,000
Guinea-Bissau	36.1	13.9	1,442	Bissau	900
Guyana	215	83.0	767	Georgetown	4,700
Haiti	27.8	10.7	8,309	Port-au-Prince	1,800
Honduras	112	43.3	7,326	Tegucigalpa	3,000
Hungary	93.0	35.9	9,981	Budapest	17,300
Iceland	103	39.8	299	Reykjavik	38,100
India	3,287	1,269	1,095,352	New Delhi	3,700
Indonesia	1,905	735	245,453	Jakarta	3,800
Iran	1,648	636	68,688	Tehran	8,900
Iraq	438	169	26,783	Baghdad	2,900
Ireland	70.3	27.1	4,062	Dublin	43,600
Israel	20.6	8.0	6,352	Jerusalem	26,200
Italy	301	116	58,134	Rome	29,700
Ivory Coast (Côte d'Ivoire)	322	125	17,655	Yamoussoukro	1,600
Jamaica	11.0	4.2	2,758	Kingston	4,600
Japan	378	146	127,464	Tokyo	33,100
Jordan	89.3	34.5	5,907	Amman	4,900
Kazakhstan	2,725	1,052	15,233	Astana	9,100
Kenya	580	224	34,708	Nairobi	1,200
Kiribati	0.73	0.28	105	Tarawa	2,700
Korea, North	121	46.5	23,113	Pyŏngyang	1,800
Korea, South	99.3	38.3	48,847	Seoul	24,200
Kuwait	17.8	6.9	2,418	Kuwait City	21,600
Kyrgyzstan	200	77.2	5,214	Bishkek	2,000
Laos	237	91.4	6,368	Vientiane	2,100
Latvia	64.6	24.9	2,275	Riga	15,400
Lebanon	10.4	4.0	3,874	Beirut	5,500
Lesotho	30.4	11.7	2,022	Maseru	2,600
Liberia	111	43.0	3,042	Monrovia	1,000
Libya	1,760	679	5,901	Tripoli	12,700
Liechtenstein	0.16	0.06	34	Vaduz	25,000
Lithuania	65.2	25.2	3,586	Vilnius	15,100
Luxembourg	2.6	1.0	474	Luxembourg	68,800
Macedonia (FYROM)	25.7	9.9	2,051	Skopje	8,200
Madagascar	587	227	18,595	Antananarivo	900
Madeira (Portugal)	0.78	0.30	241	Funchal	22,700
Malawi	118	45.7	13,014	Lilongwe	600
Malaysia	330	127	24,386	Kuala Lumpur/Putrajaya	12,700
Maldives	0.30	0.12	359	Malé	3,900
Mali	1,240	479	11,717	Bamako	1,200
Malta	0.32	0.12	400	Valletta	20,300
Marshall Is.	0.18	0.07	60	Majuro	2,900
Martinique (France)	1.1	0.43	436	Fort-de-France	14,400
Mauritania	1,026	396	3,177	Nouakchott	2,600
Mauritius	2.0	0.79	1,241	Port Louis	13,500
Mayotte (France)	0.37	0.14	201	Mamoundzou	4,900
Mexico	1,958	756	107,450	Mexico City	10,600
Micronesia, Fed. States of	0.70	0.27	108	Palikir	2,300
Moldova	33.9	13.1	4,467	Chişinău	2,000
Monaco	0.001	0.0004	33	Monaco	30,000
Mongolia	1,567	605	2,832	Ulan Bator	2,000
Montenegro	14.0	5.4	631	Podgorica	3,800
Montserrat (UK)	0.10	0.04	9	Plymouth	3,400
Morocco	447	172	33,241	Rabat	4,400
Mozambique	802	309	19,687	Maputo	1,500
Namibia	824	318	2,044	Windhoek	7,400
Nauru	0.02	0.008	13	Yaren District	5,000
Nepal	147	56.8	28,287	Katmandu	1,500
Netherlands	41.5	16.0	16,491	Amsterdam/The Hague	31,700
Netherlands Antilles (Neths)	0.80	0.31	222	Willemstad	16,000
New Caledonia (France)	18.6	7.2	219	Nouméa	15,000
New Zealand	271	104	4,076	Wellington	26,000
Nicaragua	130	50.2	5,570	Managua	3,000
Niger	1,267	489	12,525	Niamey	1,000
Nigeria	924	357	131,860	Abuja	1,400
Northern Mariana Is. (US)	0.46	0.18	82	Saipan	12,500
Norway	324	125	4,611	Oslo	47,800
Oman	310	119	3,102	Muscat	14,100
Pakistan	796	307	165,804	Islamabad	2,600
Palau	0.46	0.18	21	Koror	7,600
Panama	75.5	29.2	3,191	Panamá	7,900
Papua New Guinea	463	179	5,671	Port Moresby	2,700
Paraguay	407	157	6,506	Asunción	4,700
Peru	1,285	496	28,303	Lima	6,400
Philippines	300	116	89,469	Manila	5,000
Poland	323	125	38,537	Warsaw	14,100
Portugal	88.8	34.3	10,606	Lisbon	19,100
Puerto Rico (US)	8.9	3.4	3,927	San Juan	19,100
Qatar	11.0	4.2	885	Doha	29,400
Réunion (France)	2.5	0.97	788	St-Denis	6,200
Romania	238	92.0	22,304	Bucharest	8,800
Russia	17,075	6,593	142,894	Moscow	12,100
Rwanda	26.3	10.2	8,648	Kigali	1,600
St Kitts & Nevis	0.26	0.10	39	Basseterre	8,200
St Lucia	0.54	0.21	168	Castries	4,800
St Vincent & Grenadines	0.39	0.15	118	Kingstown	3,600
Samoa	2.8	1.1	177	Apia	2,100
San Marino	0.06	0.02	29	San Marino	34,100
São Tomé & Príncipe	0.96	0.37	193	São Tomé	1,200
Saudi Arabia	2,150	830	27,020	Riyadh	13,800
Senegal	197	76.0	11,987	Dakar	1,800
Serbia	88.4	34.1	9,396	Belgrade	4,400
Seychelles	0.46	0.18	82	Victoria	7,800
Sierra Leone	71.7	27.7	6,005	Freetown	900
Singapore	0.68	0.26	4,492	Singapore City	30,900
Slovak Republic	49.0	18.9	5,439	Bratislava	17,700
Slovenia	20.3	7.8	2,010	Ljubljana	23,400
Solomon Is.	28.9	11.2	552	Honiara	600
Somalia	638	246	8,863	Mogadishu	600
South Africa	1,221	471	44,188	Cape Town/Pretoria	13,000
Spain	498	192	40,398	Madrid	27,000
Sri Lanka	65.6	25.3	20,222	Colombo	4,600
Sudan	2,506	967	41,236	Khartoum	2,300
Suriname	163	63.0	439	Paramaribo	7,100
Swaziland	17.4	6.7	1,136	Mbabane	5,500
Sweden	450	174	9,017	Stockholm	31,600
Switzerland	41.3	15.9	7,524	Bern	33,600
Syria	185	71.5	18,881	Damascus	4,000
Taiwan	36.0	13.9	23,036	Taipei	29,000
Tajikistan	143	55.3	7,321	Dushanbe	1,300
Tanzania	945	365	37,445	Dodoma	800
Thailand	513	198	64,632	Bangkok	9,100
Togo	56.8	21.9	5,549	Lomé	1,700
Tonga	0.65	0.25	115	Nuku'alofa	2,200
Trinidad & Tobago	5.1	2.0	1,066	Port of Spain	19,700
Tunisia	164	63.2	10,175	Tunis	8,600
Turkey	775	299	70,414	Ankara	8,900
Turkmenistan	488	188	5,043	Ashkhabad	8,900
Turks & Caicos Is. (UK)	0.43	0.17	21	Cockburn Town	11,500
Tuvalu	0.03	0.01	12	Fongafale	1,600
Uganda	241	93.1	28,196	Kampala	1,800
Ukraine	604	233	46,711	Kiev	7,600
United Arab Emirates	83.6	32.3	2,603	Abu Dhabi	49,700
United Kingdom	242	93.4	60,609	London	31,400
United States of America	9,629	3,718	301,139	Washington, DC	43,500
Uruguay	175	67.6	3,432	Montevideo	10,700
Uzbekistan	447	173	27,307	Tashkent	2,000
Vanuatu	12.2	4.7	209	Port-Vila	2,900
Venezuela	912	352	25,730	Caracas	6,900
Vietnam	332	128	84,403	Hanoi	3,100
Virgin Is. (UK)	0.15	0.06	23	Road Town	38,500
Virgin Is. (US)	0.35	0.13	109	Charlotte Amalie	14,500
Wallis & Futuna Is. (France)	0.20	0.08	16	Mata-Utu	3,800
West Bank (OPT)*	5.9	2.3	2,460	–	1,500
Western Sahara	266	103	273	El Aaiún	N/A
Yemen	528	204	21,456	Sana'	900
Zambia	753	291	11,502	Lusaka	1,000
Zimbabwe	391	151	12,237	Harare	2,000

*OPT = Occupied Palestinian Territory   N/A = Not available

THE WORLD IN FOCUS

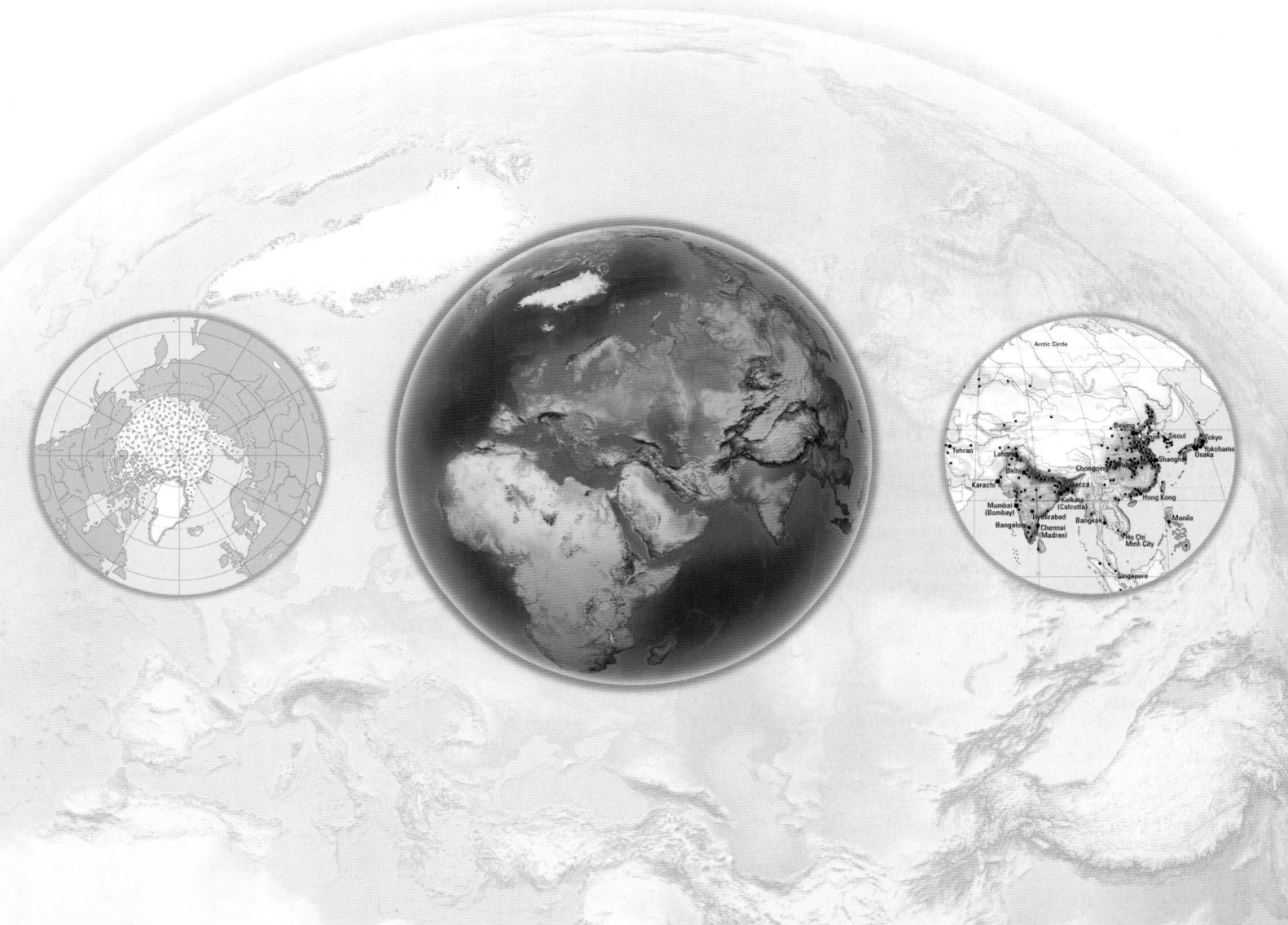

PLANET EARTH	2	WATER & VEGETATION	12	QUALITY OF LIFE	22
RESTLESS EARTH	4	ENVIRONMENT	14	ENERGY	24
LANDFORMS	6	POPULATION	16	PRODUCTION	26
OCEANS	8	THE HUMAN FAMILY	18	TRADE	28
CLIMATE	10	WEALTH	20	TRAVEL & TOURISM	30

Planet Earth

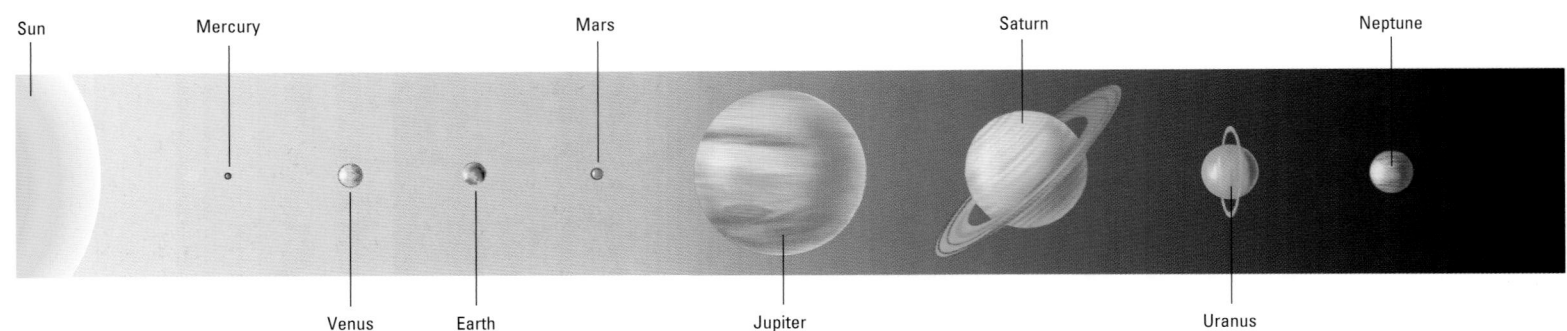

Sun   Mercury   Mars   Saturn   Neptune
Venus   Earth   Jupiter   Uranus

The Solar System

A minute part of one of the billions of galaxies (collections of stars) that populate the Universe, the Solar System lies about 26,000 light-years from the centre of our own galaxy, the 'Milky Way'. Thought to be about 5 billion years old, it consists of a central Sun with eight planets and their moons revolving around it, attracted by its gravitational pull. The planets orbit the Sun in the same direction – anti-clockwise when viewed from above the Sun's north pole – and almost in the same plane. Their orbital distances, however, vary enormously.

The Sun's diameter is 109 times that of the Earth, and the temperature at its core – caused by continuous thermonuclear fusions of hydrogen into helium – is estimated to be 15 million degrees Celsius. It is the Solar System's only source of light and heat.

Profile of the Planets

	Mean distance from Sun (million km)	Mass (Earth = 1)	Period of orbit (Earth days/years)	Period of rotation (Earth days)	Equatorial diameter (km)	Number of known satellites*
Mercury	57.9	0.06	87.97 days	58.65	4,879	0
Venus	108.2	0.82	224.7 days	243.02	12,104	0
Earth	149.6	1.00	365.3 days	1.00	12,756	1
Mars	227.9	0.11	687.0 days	1.029	6,792	2
Jupiter	778	317.8	11.86 years	0.411	142,984	63
Saturn	1,427	95.2	29.45 years	0.428	120,536	59
Uranus	2,871	14.5	84.02 years	0.720	51,118	27
Neptune	4,498	17.2	164.8 years	0.673	49,528	13

Number of known satellites at mid-2007

All planetary orbits are elliptical in form, but only Mercury follows a path that deviates noticeably from a circular one. In 2006, Pluto was demoted from its former status as a planet and is now regarded as a member of the Kuiper Belt of icy bodies at the fringes of the Solar System.

The Seasons

Seasons occur because the Earth's axis is tilted at an angle of approximately 23½°. When the northern hemisphere is tilted to a maximum extent towards the Sun, on 21 June, the Sun is overhead at the Tropic of Cancer (latitude 23½° North). This is midsummer, or the summer solstice, in the northern hemisphere.

On 22 or 23 September, the Sun is overhead at the equator, and day and night are of equal length throughout the world. This is the autumnal equinox in the northern hemisphere. On 21 or 22 December, the Sun is overhead at the Tropic of Capricorn (23½° South), the winter solstice in the northern hemisphere. The overhead Sun then tracks north until, on 21 March, it is overhead at the equator. This is the spring (vernal) equinox in the northern hemisphere.

In the southern hemisphere, the seasons are the reverse of those in the north.

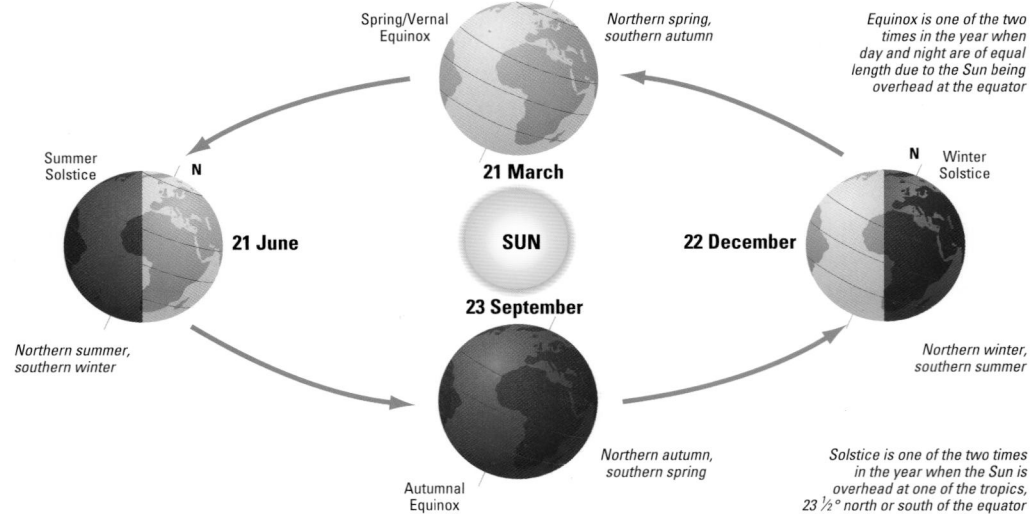

Spring/Vernal Equinox
Northern spring, southern autumn
Equinox is one of the two times in the year when day and night are of equal length due to the Sun being overhead at the equator
Summer Solstice
N
21 March
N
Winter Solstice
21 June
SUN
22 December
23 September
Northern summer, southern winter
Northern winter, southern summer
Autumnal Equinox
Northern autumn, southern spring
Solstice is one of the two times in the year when the Sun is overhead at one of the tropics, 23½° north or south of the equator

Day and Night

The Sun appears to rise in the east, reach its highest point at noon, and then set in the west, to be followed by night. In reality, it is not the Sun that is moving but the Earth rotating from west to east. The moment when the Sun's upper limb first appears above the horizon is termed sunrise; the moment when the Sun's upper limb disappears below the horizon is sunset.

At the summer solstice in the northern hemisphere (21 June), the Arctic has total daylight and the Antarctic total darkness. The opposite occurs at the winter solstice (21 or 22 December). At the equator, the length of day and night are almost equal all year.

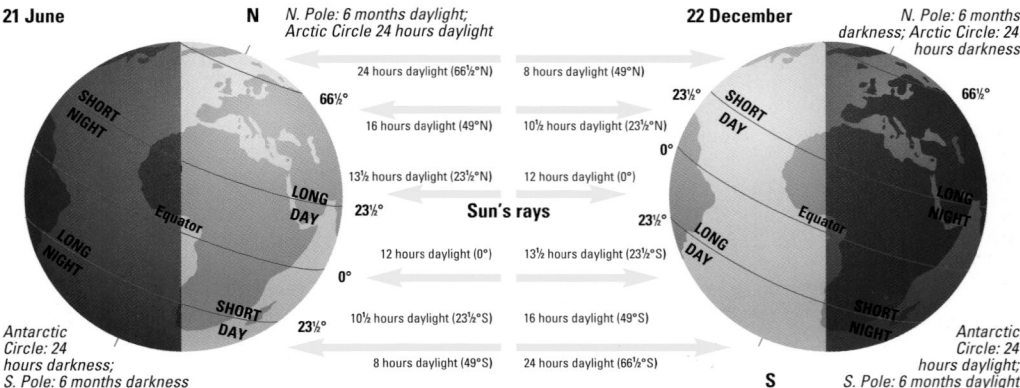

21 June
N
N. Pole: 6 months daylight; Arctic Circle 24 hours daylight
24 hours daylight (66½°N)   8 hours daylight (49°N)
66½°
16 hours daylight (49°N)   10½ hours daylight (23½°N)
13½ hours daylight (23½°N)   12 hours daylight (0°)
23½°   Sun's rays
12 hours daylight (0°)   13½ hours daylight (23½°S)
0°
10½ hours daylight (23½°S)   16 hours daylight (49°S)
23½°
Antarctic Circle: 24 hours darkness; S. Pole: 6 months darkness
8 hours daylight (49°S)   24 hours daylight (66½°S)

22 December
N. Pole: 6 months darkness; Arctic Circle: 24 hours darkness
23½°   66½°
0°
23½°
Equator
23½°
Antarctic Circle: 24 hours daylight; S. Pole: 6 months daylight
S

Time

Year: The time taken by the Earth to revolve around the Sun, or 365.24 days.

Leap Year: A calendar year of 366 days, 29 February being the additional day. It offsets the difference between the calendar and the solar year.

Month: The 12 calendar months of the year are approximately equal in length to a lunar month.

Week: An artificial period of 7 days, not based on astronomical time.

Day: The time taken by the Earth to complete one rotation on its axis.

Hour: 24 hours make one day. The day is divided into hours a.m. (ante meridiem or before noon) and p.m. (post meridiem or after noon), although most time-tables now use the 24-hour system, from midnight to midnight.

Sunrise

Sunset

The Moon

The Moon rotates more slowly than the Earth, taking just over 27 days to make one complete rotation on its axis. Since this corresponds to the Moon's orbital period around the Earth, the Moon always presents the same hemisphere towards us, and we never see the far side. The interval between one New Moon and the next is 29½ days – this is called a lunation, or lunar month. The Moon shines only by reflected sunlight, and emits no light of its own. During each lunation the Moon displays a complete cycle of phases, caused by the changing angle of illumination from the Sun.

Phases of the Moon

Mean distance from Earth: 384,401 km; Mean diameter: 3,475 km;
Mass: approximately 1/80 that of Earth; Surface gravity: one-sixth of Earth's;
Daily range of temperature at lunar equator: 280°C; Average orbital speed: 3,681 km/h

| New Moon | Waxing Crescent | First Quarter | Gibbous | Full Moon | Gibbous | Last Quarter | Waning Crescent | New Moon |

Eclipses

When the Moon passes between the Sun and the Earth, the Sun becomes partially eclipsed (1). A partial eclipse can become a total eclipse if the Moon covers the Sun completely (2) and the dark central part of the lunar shadow touches the Earth. The broad geographical zone covered by the Moon's outer shadow (P) has only a very small central area (often less than 100 km wide) that experiences totality. Totality can never last for more than 7½ minutes, and it is usually briefer than this. Lunar eclipses take place when the Moon moves through the shadow of the Earth, and can also be partial or total. Any single location on Earth can experience a maximum of four solar and three lunar eclipses in any single year, while a total solar eclipse occurs an average of once every 360 years for any given location.

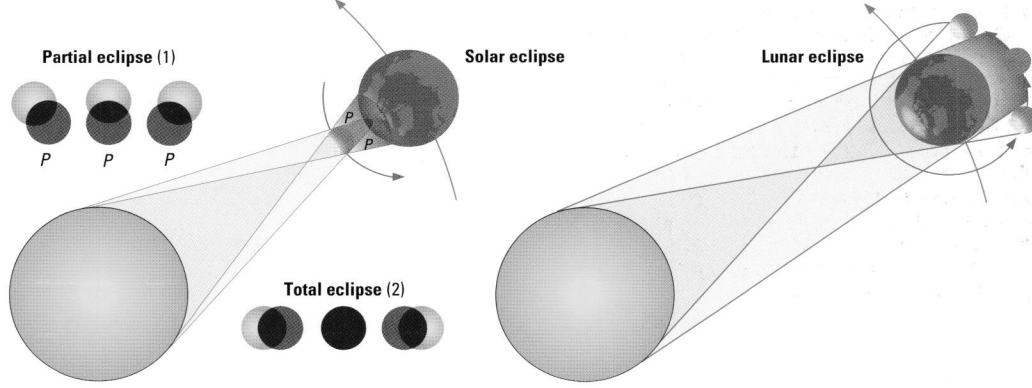

Partial eclipse (1)

Total eclipse (2)

Solar eclipse

Lunar eclipse

Tides

The daily rise and fall of the ocean's tides are the result of the gravitational pull of the Moon and that of the Sun, though the effect of the latter is not as strong as that of the Moon. This effect is greatest on the hemisphere facing the Moon and causes a tidal 'bulge'.

When the Sun, Earth and Moon are in line, spring tides occur: high tide reaches the highest values, and low tide falls to low levels. When lunar and solar forces are least coincidental with the Sun and Moon at an angle (near the Moon's first and third quarters), neap tides occur, which have a small tidal range.

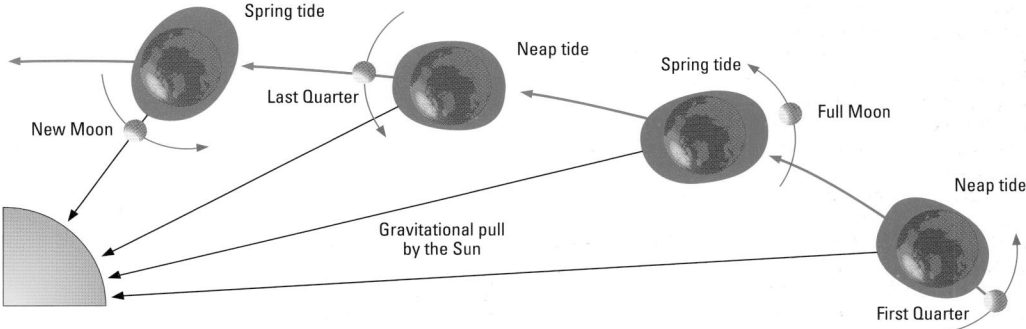

Spring tide

Neap tide

Spring tide

Last Quarter

New Moon

Full Moon

Neap tide

Gravitational pull by the Sun

First Quarter

Restless Earth

The Earth's Structure

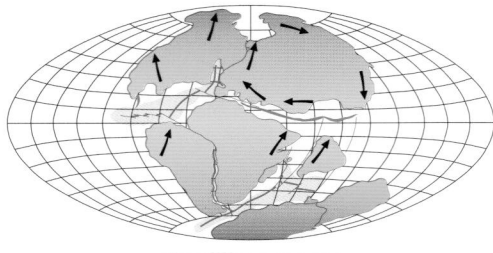

Upper mantle (*c.* 370 km)
Crust (average 5–50 km)
Transitional zone (600 km)
Outer core (2,100 km)
Lower mantle (1,700 km)
Inner core (1,350 km)

Continental Drift

About 200 million years ago the original Pangaea landmass began to split into two continental groups, which further separated over time to produce the present-day configuration.

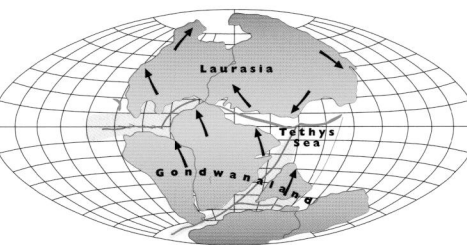

180 million years ago

135 million years ago

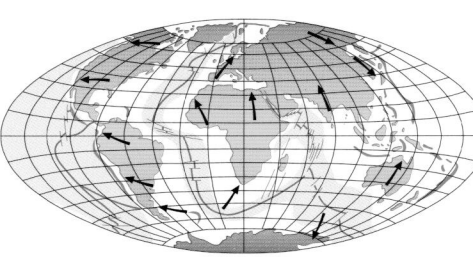

Present day

Trench
Rift
New ocean floor
Zones of slippage

Notable Earthquakes Since 1900

Year	Location	Richter Scale	Deaths
1906	San Francisco, USA	8.3	3,000
1906	Valparaiso, Chile	8.6	22,000
1908	Messina, Italy	7.5	83,000
1915	Avezzano, Italy	7.5	30,000
1920	Gansu (Kansu), China	8.6	180,000
1923	Yokohama, Japan	8.3	143,000
1927	Nan Shan, China	8.3	200,000
1932	Gansu (Kansu), China	7.6	70,000
1933	Sanriku, Japan	8.9	2,990
1934	Bihar, India/Nepal	8.4	10,700
1935	Quetta, India (*now* Pakistan)	7.5	60,000
1939	Chillan, Chile	8.3	28,000
1939	Erzincan, Turkey	7.9	30,000
1960	S. W. Chile	9.5	2,200
1960	Agadir, Morocco	5.8	12,000
1962	Khorasan, Iran	7.1	12,230
1964	Anchorage, USA	9.2	125
1968	N. E. Iran	7.4	12,000
1970	N. Peru	7.8	70,000
1972	Managua, Nicaragua	6.2	5,000
1974	N. Pakistan	6.3	5,200
1976	Guatemala	7.5	22,500
1976	Tangshan, China	8.2	255,000
1978	Tabas, Iran	7.7	25,000
1980	El Asnam, Algeria	7.3	20,000
1980	S. Italy	7.2	4,800
1985	Mexico City, Mexico	8.1	4,200
1988	N.W. Armenia	6.8	55,000
1990	N. Iran	7.7	36,000
1992	Flores, Indonesia	6.8	1,895
1993	Maharashtra, India	6.4	30,000
1994	Los Angeles, USA	6.6	51
1995	Kobe, Japan	7.2	5,000
1995	Sakhalin Is., Russia	7.5	2,000
1996	Yunnan, China	7.0	240
1997	N. E. Iran	7.1	2,400
1998	Takhar, Afghanistan	6.1	4,200
1998	Rostaq, Afghanistan	7.0	5,000
1999	Izmit, Turkey	7.4	15,000
1999	Taipei, Taiwan	7.6	1,700
2001	Gujarat, India	7.7	14,000
2002	Baghlan, Afghanistan	6.1	1,000
2003	Boumerdes, Algeria	6.8	2,200
2003	Bam, Iran	6.6	30,000
2004	Sumatra, Indonesia	9.0	250,000
2005	N. Pakistan	7.6	74,000
2006	Java, Indonesia	6.4	6,200

Earthquakes

Earthquake magnitude is usually rated according to either the Richter or the Modified Mercalli scale, both devised by seismologists in the 1930s. The Richter scale measures absolute earthquake power with mathematical precision: each step upwards represents a tenfold increase in shockwave amplitude. Theoretically, there is no upper limit, but most of the largest earthquakes measured have been rated at between 8.8 and 8.9. The 12–point Mercalli scale, based on observed effects, is often more meaningful, ranging from I (earthquakes noticed only by seismographs) to XII (total destruction); intermediate points include V (people awakened at night; unstable objects overturned), VII (collapse of ordinary buildings; chimneys and monuments fall), and IX (conspicuous cracks in ground; serious damage to reservoirs).

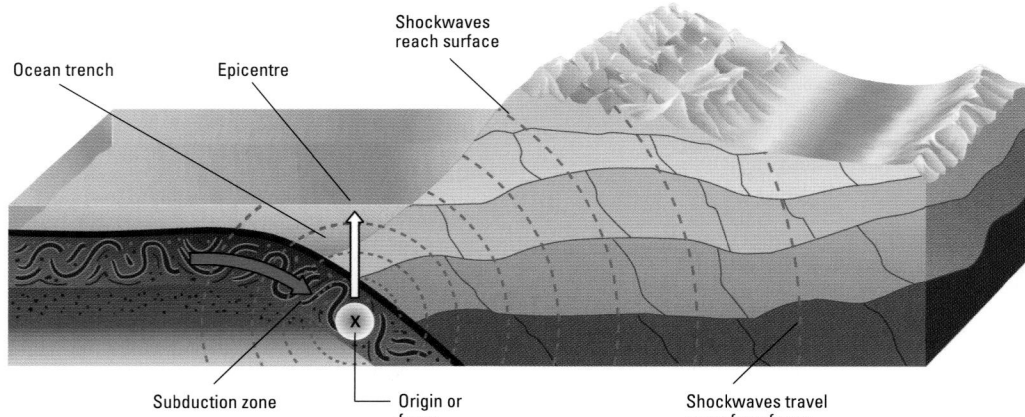

Shockwaves reach surface
Ocean trench
Epicentre
Subduction zone
Origin or focus
Shockwaves travel away from focus

Structure and Earthquakes

Mobile land areas
Submarine zones of mobile land areas
Stable land platforms
Submarine extensions of stable land platforms
Mid-oceanic volcanic ridges
Oceanic platforms

1976○ Principal earthquakes and dates (since 1900)

Earthquakes are a series of rapid vibrations originating from the slipping or faulting of parts of the Earth's crust when stresses within build up to breaking point. They usually happen at depths varying from 8 km to 30 km. Severe earthquakes cause extensive damage when they take place in populated areas, destroying structures and severing communications. Most initial loss of life occurs due to secondary causes such as falling masonry, fires and flooding.

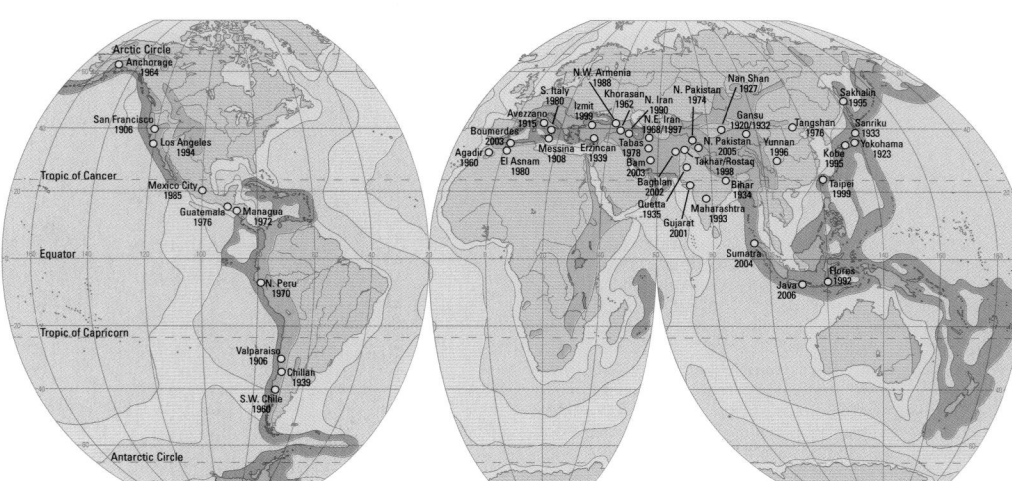

Projection: Interrupted Mollweide

Plate Tectonics

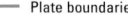

Plate boundaries   PACIFIC   Major plates

Direction of plate movements and rate of movement (cm/year)

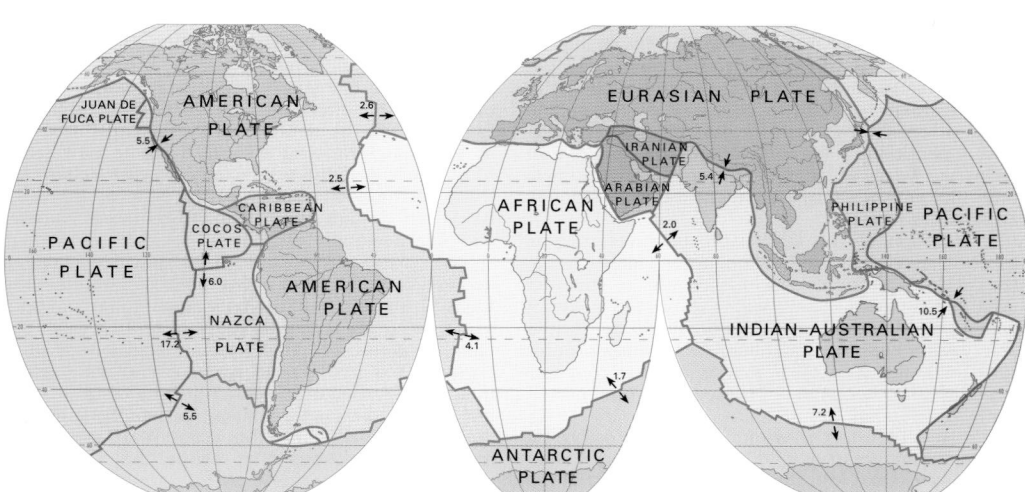

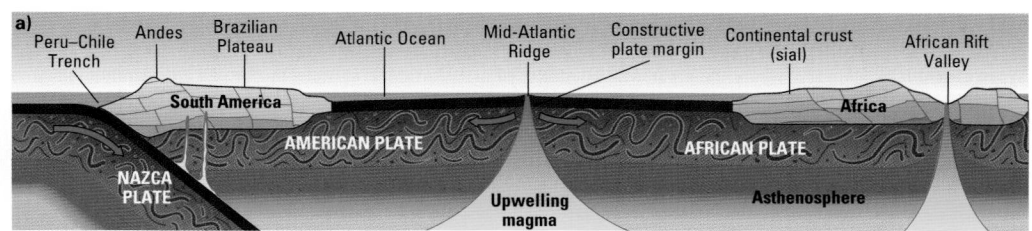

a) Peru–Chile Trench | Andes | Brazilian Plateau | Atlantic Ocean | Mid-Atlantic Ridge | Constructive plate margin | Continental crust (sial) | African Rift Valley | South America | AMERICAN PLATE | NAZCA PLATE | AFRICAN PLATE | Africa | Upwelling magma | Asthenosphere

The drifting of the continents is a feature that is unique to Planet Earth. The complementary, almost jigsaw-puzzle fit of the coastlines on each side of the Atlantic Ocean inspired Alfred Wegener's theory of continental drift in 1915. The theory suggested that the ancient super-continent, which Wegener named Pangaea, incorporated all of the Earth's landmasses and gradually split up to form today's continents.

The original debate about continental drift was a prelude to a more radical idea: plate tectonics. The basic theory is that the Earth's crust is made up of a series of rigid plates which float on a soft layer of the mantle and are moved about by continental convection currents within the Earth's interior. These plates diverge and converge along margins marked by seismic activity. Plates diverge from mid-ocean ridges where molten lava pushes upwards and forces the plates apart at rates of up to 40 mm [1.6 in] a year.

The three diagrams, left, give some examples of plate boundaries from around the world. Diagram (a) shows sea-floor spreading at the Mid-Atlantic Ridge as the American and African plates slowly diverge. The same thing is happening in (b) where sea-floor spreading at the Mid-Indian Ocean Ridge is forcing the Indian–Australian plate to collide into the Eurasian plate. In (c) oceanic crust (sima) is being subducted beneath lighter continental crust (sial).

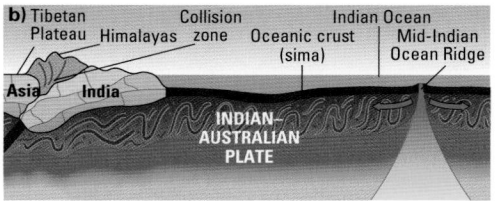

b) Tibetan Plateau | Himalayas | Collision zone | Oceanic crust (sima) | Indian Ocean | Mid-Indian Ocean Ridge | Asia | India | INDIAN–AUSTRALIAN PLATE

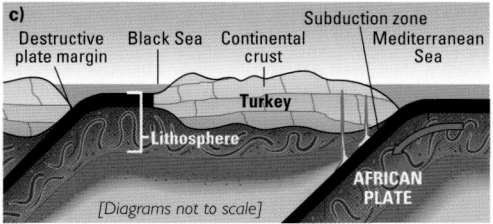

c) Destructive plate margin | Black Sea | Continental crust | Subduction zone | Mediterranean Sea | Turkey | Lithosphere | AFRICAN PLATE | [Diagrams not to scale]

Volcanoes

Volcanoes occur when hot liquefied rock beneath the Earth's crust is pushed up by pressure to the surface as molten lava. Some volcanoes erupt in an explosive way, throwing out rocks and ash, whilst others are effusive and lava flows out of the vent. There are volcanoes which are both, such as Mount Fuji. An accumulation of lava and cinders creates cones of variable size and shape. As a result of many eruptions over centuries, Mount Etna in Sicily has a circumference of more than 120 km [75 miles].

Climatologists believe that volcanic ash, if ejected high into the atmosphere, can influence temperature and weather for several years afterwards. The 1991 eruption of Mount Pinatubo in the Philippines ejected more than 20 million tonnes of dust and ash 32 km [20 miles] into the atmosphere and is believed to have accelerated ozone depletion over a large part of the globe.

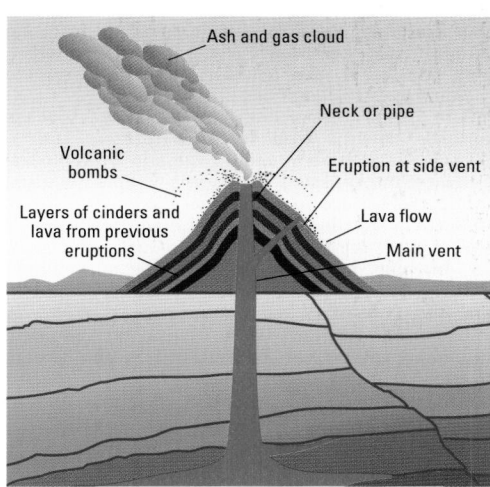

Ash and gas cloud | Neck or pipe | Volcanic bombs | Eruption at side vent | Layers of cinders and lava from previous eruptions | Lava flow | Main vent

Distribution of Volcanoes

Volcanoes today may be the subject of considerable scientific study but they remain both dramatic and unpredictable: in 1991 Mount Pinatubo, 100 km [62 miles] north of the Philippines capital Manila, suddenly burst into life after lying dormant for more than six centuries. Most of the world's active volcanoes occur in a belt around the Pacific Ocean, on the edge of the Pacific plate, called the 'ring of fire'. Indonesia has the greatest concentration with 90 volcanoes, 12 of which are active. The most famous, Krakatoa, erupted in 1883 with such force that the resulting tidal wave killed 36,000 people and tremors were felt as far away as Australia.

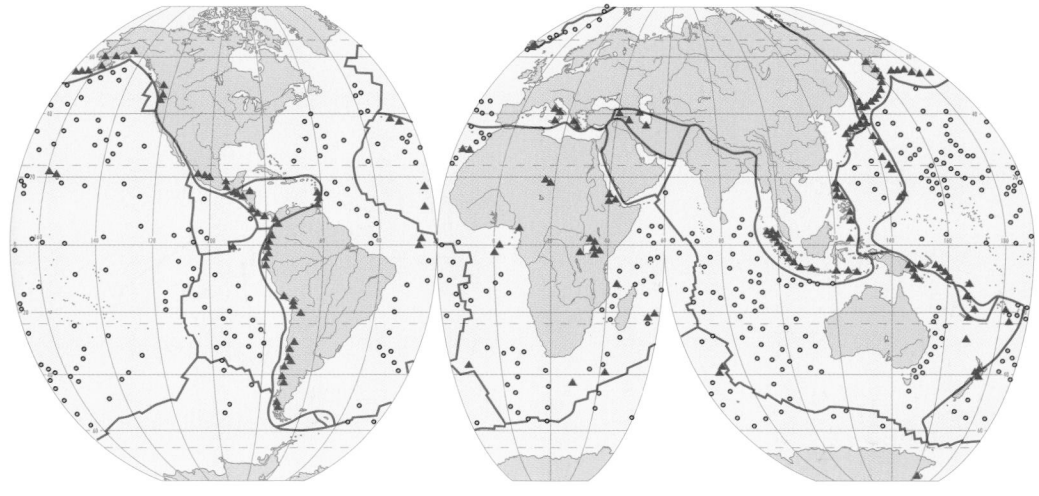

○ Submarine volcanoes

▲ Land volcanoes active since 1700

— Boundaries of tectonic plates

Landforms

The Rock Cycle

James Hutton first proposed the rock cycle in the late 1700s after he observed the slow but steady effects of erosion.

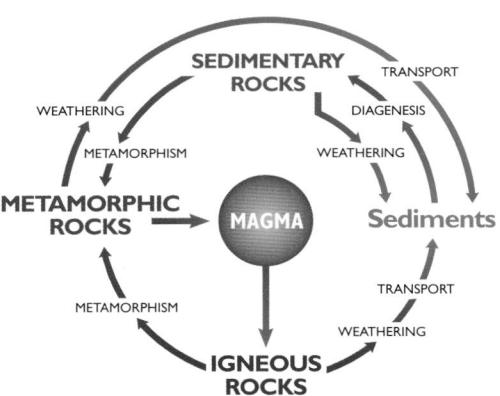

Above and below the surface of the oceans, the features of the Earth's crust are constantly changing. The phenomenal forces generated by convection currents in the molten core of our planet carry the vast segments or 'plates' of the crust across the globe in an endless cycle of creation and destruction. A continent may travel little more than 25 mm [1 in] per year, yet in the vast span of geological time this process throws up giant mountain ranges and creates new land.

Destruction of the landscape, however, begins as soon as it is formed. Wind, water, ice and sea, the main agents of erosion, mount a constant assault that even the most resistant rocks cannot withstand. Mountain peaks may dwindle by as little as a few millimetres each year, but if they are not uplifted by further movements of the crust they will eventually be reduced to rubble and transported away.

Water is the most powerful agent of erosion – it has been estimated that 100 billion tonnes of sediment are washed into the oceans every year. Three

Asian rivers account for 20% of this total; the Huang He, in China, and the Brahmaputra and Ganges in Bangladesh.

Rivers and glaciers, like the sea itself, generate much of their effect through abrasion – pounding the land with the debris they carry with them. But as well as destroying they also create new landforms, many of them spectacular: vast deltas like those of the Mississippi and the Nile, or the deep fjords cut by glaciers in British Columbia, Norway and New Zealand.

Geologists once considered that landscapes evolved from 'young', newly uplifted mountainous areas, through a 'mature' hilly stage, to an 'old age' stage when the land was reduced to an almost flat plain, or peneplain. This theory, called the 'cycle of erosion', fell into disuse when it became evident that so many factors, including the effects of plate tectonics and climatic change, constantly interrupt the cycle, which takes no account of the highly complex interactions that shape the surface of our planet.

Mountain Building

Mountains are formed when pressures on the Earth's crust caused by continental drift become so intense that the surface buckles or cracks. This happens where oceanic crust is subducted by continental crust or, more dramatically, where two tectonic plates collide: the Rockies, Andes, Alps, Urals and Himalayas resulted from such impacts. These are all known as fold mountains because they were formed by the compression of the rocks, forcing the surface to bend and fold like a crumpled rug. The Himalayas are formed from the folded former sediments of the Tethys Sea which was trapped in the collision zone between the Indian and Eurasian plates.

The other main mountain-building process occurs when the crust fractures to create faults, allowing rock to be forced upwards in large blocks; or when the pressure of magma within the crust forces the surface to bulge into a dome, or erupts to form a volcano. Large mountain ranges may reveal a combination of these features; the Alps, for example, have been compressed so violently that the folds are fragmented by numerous faults and intrusions of molten igneous rock.

Over millions of years, even the greatest mountain ranges can be reduced by the agents of erosion (most notably rivers) to a low rugged landscape known as a peneplain.

Types of faults: Faults occur where the crust is being stretched or compressed so violently that the rock strata break in a horizontal or vertical movement. They are classified by the direction in which the blocks of rock have moved. A normal fault results when a vertical movement causes the surface to break apart; compression causes a reverse fault. Horizontal movement causes shearing, known as a strike-slip fault. When the rock breaks in two places, the central block may be pushed up in a horst fault, or sink (creating a rift valley) in a graben fault.

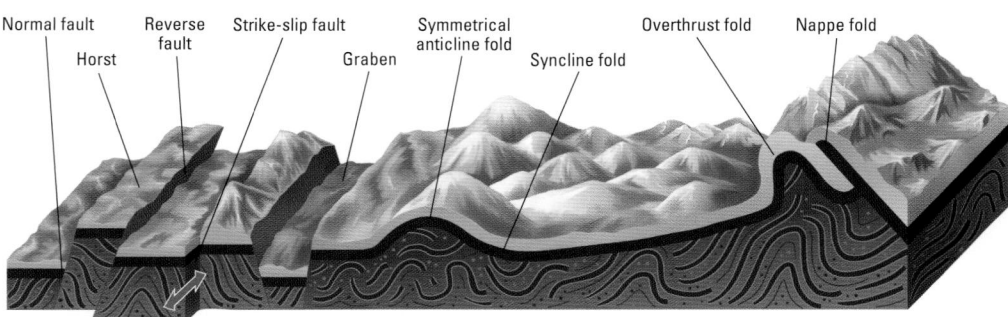

Types of fold: Folds occur when rock strata are squeezed and compressed. They are common, therefore, at destructive plate margins and where plates have collided, forcing the rocks to buckle into mountain ranges. Geographers give different names to the degrees of fold that result from continuing pressure on the rock. A simple fold may be symmetric, with even slopes on either side, but as the pressure builds up, one slope becomes steeper and the fold becomes asymmetric. Later, the ridge or 'anticline' at the top of the fold may slide over the lower ground or 'syncline' to form a recumbent fold. Eventually, the rock strata may break under the pressure to form an overthrust and finally a nappe fold.

Continental Glaciation

Ice sheets were at their greatest extent about 200,000 years ago. The maximum advance of the last Ice Age was about 18,000 years ago, when ice covered virtually all of Canada and reached as far south as the Bristol Channel in Britain.

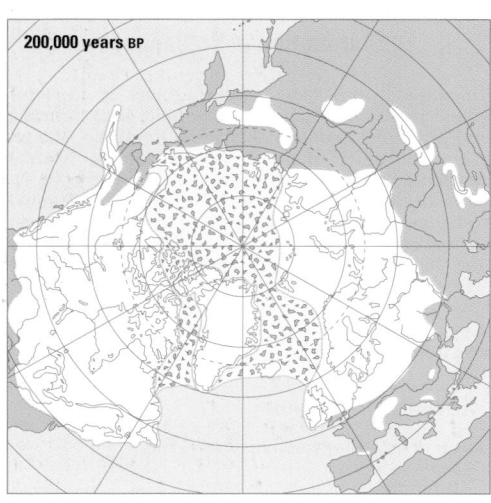

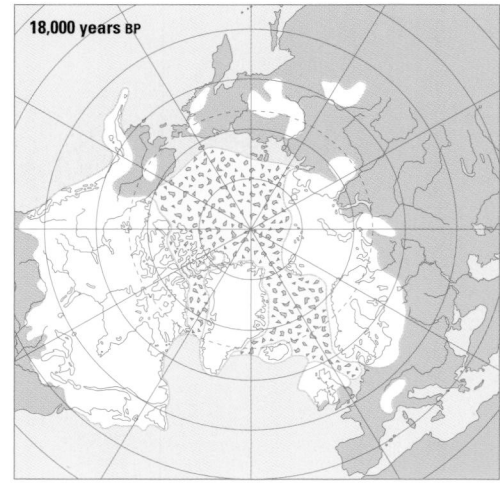

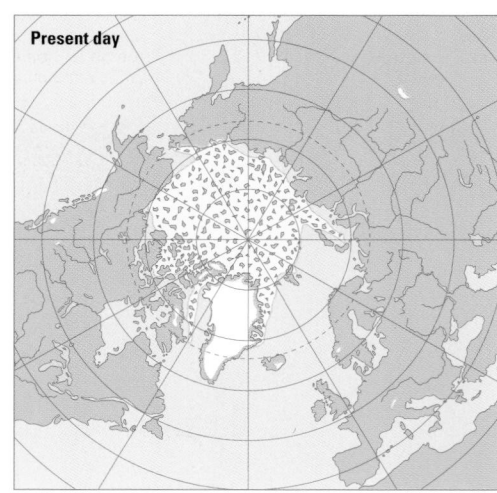

Natural Landforms

A stylized diagram to show a selection of landforms found in the mid-latitudes.

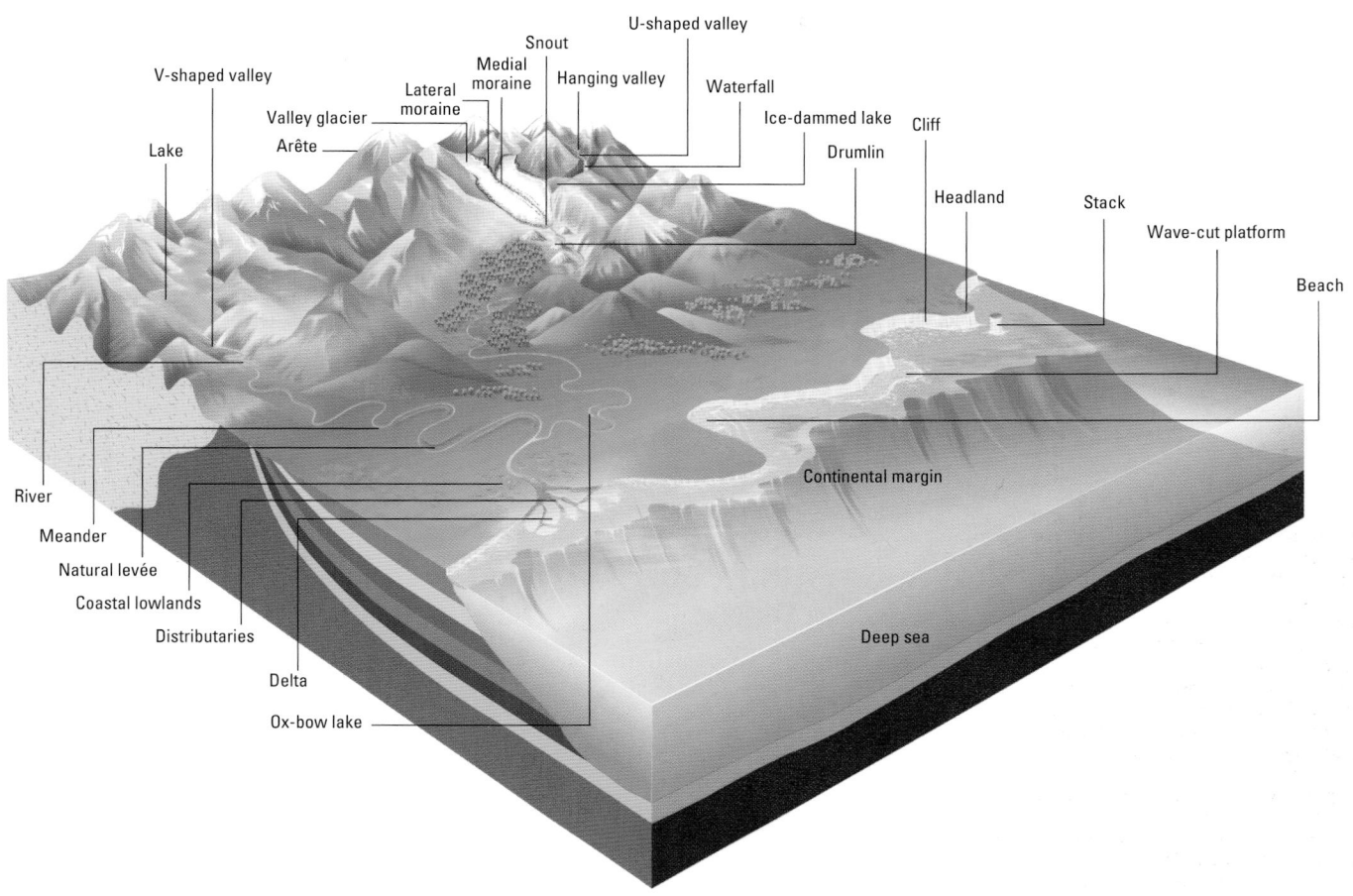

Desert Landscapes

The popular image that deserts are all huge expanses of sand is wrong. Despite harsh conditions, deserts contain some of the most varied and interesting landscapes in the world. They are also one of the most extensive environments – the hot and cold deserts together cover almost 40% of the Earth's surface.

The three types of hot desert are known by their Arabic names: sand desert, called *erg*, covers only about one-fifth of the world's desert; the rest is divided between *hammada* (areas of bare rock) and *reg* (broad plains covered by loose gravel or pebbles).

In areas of *erg*, such as the Namib Desert, the shape of the dunes reflects the character of local winds. Where winds are constant in direction, crescent-shaped *barchan* dunes form. In areas of bare rock, wind-blown sand is a major agent of erosion. The erosion is mainly confined to within 2 m [6.5 ft] of the surface, producing characteristic mushroom-shaped rocks.

Surface Processes

Catastrophic changes to natural landforms are periodically caused by such phenomena as avalanches, landslides and volcanic eruptions, but most of the processes that shape the Earth's surface operate extremely slowly in human terms. One estimate, based on a study in the United States, suggested that 1 m [3 ft] of land was removed from the entire surface of the country, on average, every 29,500 years. However, the time-scale varies from 1,300 years to 154,200 years depending on the terrain and climate.

In hot, dry climates, mechanical weathering, a result of rapid temperature changes, causes the outer layers of rock to peel away, while in cold mountainous regions, boulders are prised apart when water freezes in cracks in rocks. Chemical weathering, at its greatest in warm, humid regions, is responsible for hollowing out limestone caves and decomposing granites.

The erosion of soil and rock is greatest on sloping land and the steeper the slope, the greater the tendency for mass wasting – the movement of soil and rock downhill under the influence of gravity. The mechanisms of mass wasting (ranging from very slow to very rapid) vary with the type of material, but the presence of water as a lubricant is usually an important factor.

Running water is the world's leading agent of erosion and transportation. The energy of a river depends on several factors, including its velocity and volume, and its erosive power is at its peak when it is in full flood. Sea waves also exert tremendous erosive power during storms when they hurl pebbles against the shore, undercutting cliffs and hollowing out caves.

Glacier ice forms in mountain hollows and spills out to form valley glaciers, which transport rocks shattered by frost action. As glaciers move, rocks embedded into the ice erode steep-sided, U-shaped valleys. Evidence of glaciation in mountain regions includes cirques, knife-edged ridges, or arêtes, and pyramidal peaks.

Oceans

The Great Oceans

Relative sizes of the world's oceans

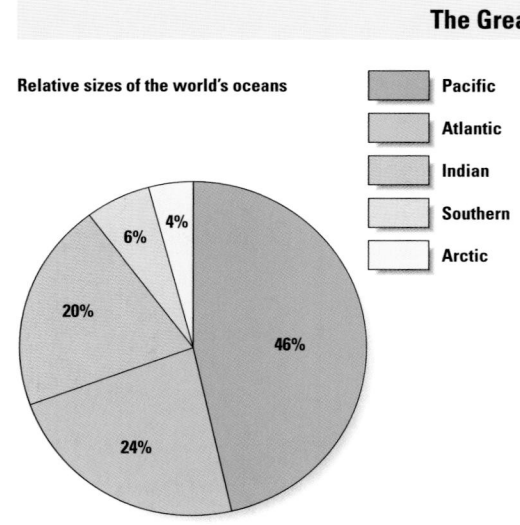

- Pacific
- Atlantic
- Indian
- Southern
- Arctic

From ancient times to about the 15th century, the legendary 'Seven Seas' comprised the Red Sea, Mediterranean Sea, Persian Gulf, Black Sea, Adriatic Sea, Caspian Sea and Indian Sea.

The Earth is a watery planet: more than 70% of its surface – over 360,000,000 sq km [140,000,000 sq miles] – is covered by the oceans and seas. The mighty Pacific alone accounts for nearly 36% of the total, and more than 46% of the sea area. Gravity holds in around 1,400 million cu. km [320 million cu. miles] of water, of which over 97% is saline.

The vast underwater world starts in the shallows of the seaside and plunges to depths of more than 11,000 m [36,000 ft]. The continental shelf, part of the landmass, drops gently to around 200 m [650 ft]; here the seabed falls away suddenly at an angle of 3° to 6° – the continental slope. The third stage, called the continental rise, is more gradual with gradients varying from 1 in 100 to 1 in 700. At an average depth of 5,000 m [16,500 ft] there begins the aptly-named abyssal plain – massive submarine depths where sunlight fails to penetrate and few creatures can survive.

From these plains rise volcanoes which, taken from base to top, rival and even surpass the tallest continental mountains in height. Mauna Kea, on Hawai'i, reaches a total of 10,203 m [33,400 ft], some 1,355 m [4,500 ft] more than Mount Everest, though scarcely 40% is visible above sea level.

In addition, there are underwater mountain chains up to 1,000 km [600 miles] across, whose peaks sometimes appear above sea level as islands, such as Iceland and Tristan da Cunha.

The Ocean Depths

Average and maximum depths of the world's great oceans, in metres

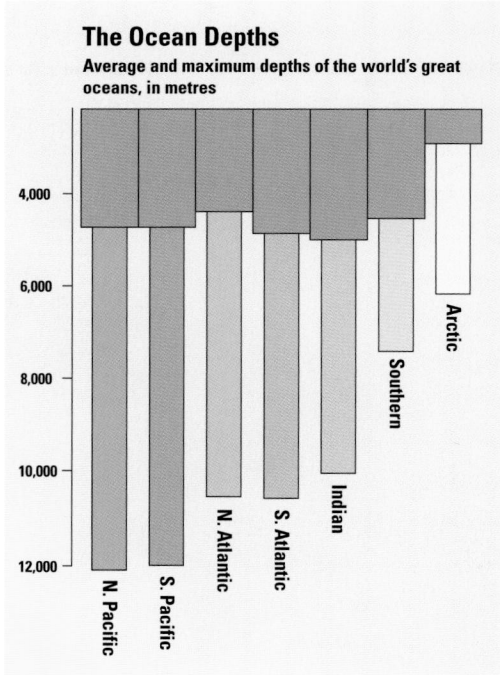

Ocean Currents

January ocean currents

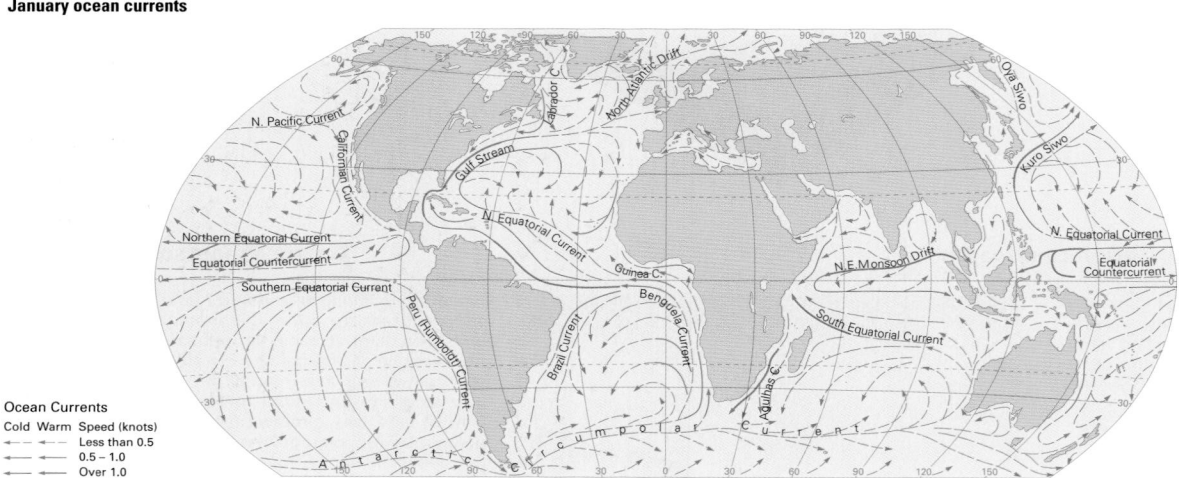

Ocean Currents

Cold Warm Speed (knots)
- Less than 0.5
- 0.5 – 1.0
- Over 1.0

July ocean currents

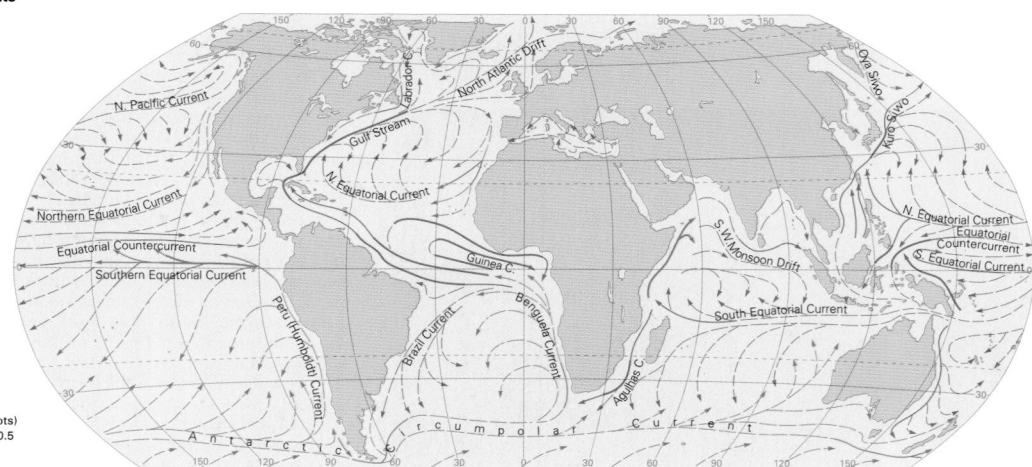

Ocean Currents

Cold Warm Speed (knots)
- Less than 0.5
- 0.5 – 1.0
- Over 1.0

Moving immense quantities of energy as well as billions of tonnes of water every hour, the ocean currents are a vital part of the great heat engine that drives the Earth's climate. They themselves are produced by a twofold mechanism. At the surface, winds push huge masses of water before them; in the deep ocean, below an abrupt temperature gradient that separates the churning surface waters from the still depths, density variations cause slow vertical movements.

The pattern of circulation of the great surface currents is determined by the displacement known as the Coriolis effect. As the Earth turns beneath a moving object – whether it is a tennis ball or a vast mass of water – it appears to be deflected to one side. The deflection is most obvious near the Equator, where the Earth's surface is spinning eastwards at 1,700 km/h [1,050 mph]; currents moving polewards are curved clockwise in the northern hemisphere and anti-clockwise in the southern.

The result is a system of spinning circles known as gyres. The Coriolis effect piles up water on the left of each gyre, creating a narrow, fast-moving stream that is matched by a slower, broader returning current on the right. North and south of the Equator, the fastest currents are located in the west and in the east respectively. In each case, warm water moves from the Equator and cold water returns to it. Cold currents often bring an upwelling of nutrients with them, supporting the world's most economically important fisheries.

Depending on the prevailing winds, some currents on or near the Equator may reverse their direction in the course of the year – a seasonal variation on which Asian monsoon rains depend, and whose occasional failure can bring disaster to millions.

World Fishing Areas

Main commercial fishing areas (numbered FAO regions)

Catch by top marine fishing areas, million tonnes (2004)

1.	Pacific, NW	[61]	21.6	22.7%
2.	Pacific, SE	[87]	15.5	16.3%
3.	Pacific, WC	[71]	11.0	11.6%
4.	Atlantic, NE	[27]	10.0	10.5%
5.	Indian, E	[57]	5.6	5.9%
6.	Indian, W	[51]	4.1	4.3%
7.	Atlantic, EC	[34]	3.4	3.6%
8.	Pacific, NE	[67]	3.1	3.3%
9.	Atlantic, NW	[21]	2.4	2.5%
10.	Atlantic, WC	[31]	2.1	2.2%

Principal fishing areas

Leading fishing nations

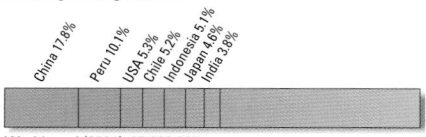

China 17.8% Peru 10.1% USA 5.3% Chile 5.2% Indonesia 5.1% Japan 4.6% India 3.8%

World total (2004): 95,000,000 tonnes
(Marine catch 90.3% Inland catch 9.7%)

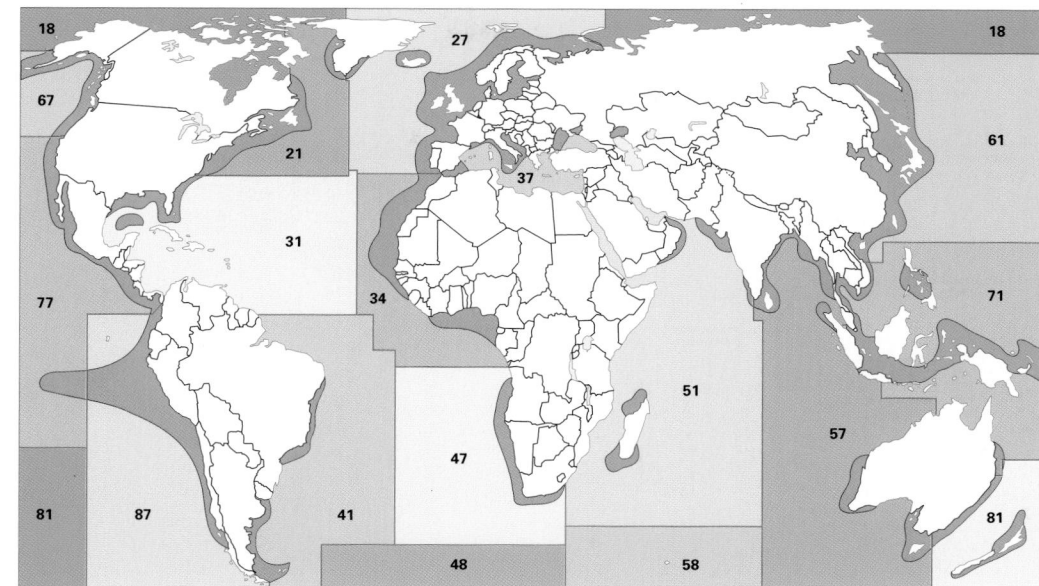

Marine Pollution

Sources of marine oil pollution

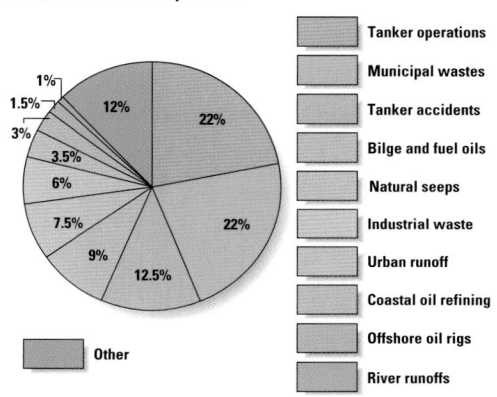

- Tanker operations
- Municipal wastes
- Tanker accidents
- Bilge and fuel oils
- Natural seeps
- Industrial waste
- Urban runoff
- Coastal oil refining
- Offshore oil rigs
- River runoffs
- Other

Oil Spills

Major oil spills from tankers and combined carriers

Year	Vessel	Location	Spill (barrels) *	Cause
1979	Atlantic Empress	West Indies	1,890,000	collision
1983	Castillo De Bellver	South Africa	1,760,000	fire
1978	Amoco Cadiz	France	1,628,000	grounding
1991	Haven	Italy	1,029,000	explosion
1988	Odyssey	Canada	1,000,000	fire
1967	Torrey Canyon	UK	909,000	grounding
1972	Sea Star	Gulf of Oman	902,250	collision
1977	Hawaiian Patriot	Hawaiian Is.	742,500	fire
1979	Independenta	Turkey	696,350	collision
1993	Braer	UK	625,000	grounding
1996	Sea Empress	UK	515,000	grounding
2002	Prestige	Spain	463,250	storm

Other sources of major oil spills

1983	Nowruz oilfield	Persian Gulf	4,250,000[†]	war
1979	Ixtoc 1 oilwell	Gulf of Mexico	4,200,000	blow-out
1991	Kuwait	Persian Gulf	2,500,000[†]	war

* 1 barrel = 0.136 tonnes/159 lit./35 Imperial gal./42 US gal. [†] estimated

River Pollution

Sources of river pollution, USA

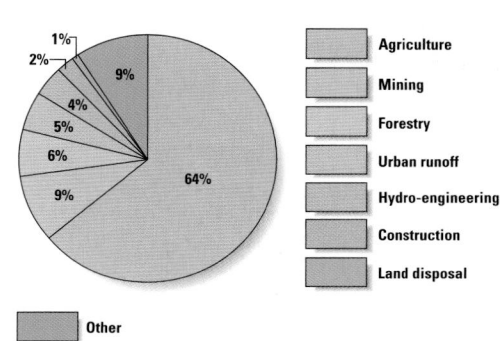

- Agriculture
- Mining
- Forestry
- Urban runoff
- Hydro-engineering
- Construction
- Land disposal
- Other

Water Pollution

- Severely polluted sea areas and lakes
- Polluted sea areas and lakes
- Areas of frequent oil pollution by shipping
- ◣ Major oil tanker spills
- ▲ Major oil rig blow-outs
- ▼ Offshore dumpsites for industrial and municipal waste
- —— Severely polluted rivers and estuaries

The most notorious tanker spillage of the 1980s occurred when the *Exxon Valdez* ran aground in Prince William Sound, Alaska, in 1989, spilling 267,000 barrels of crude oil close to shore in a sensitive ecological area. This rates as the world's 28th worst spill in terms of volume.

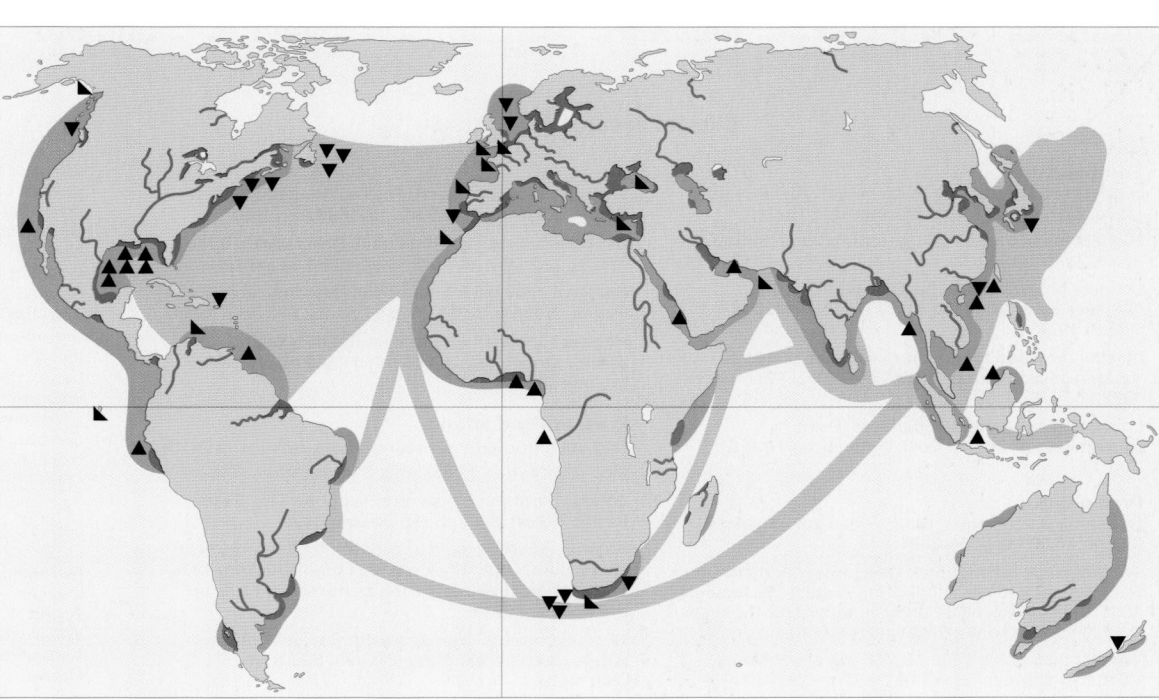

Climate

Climatic Regions

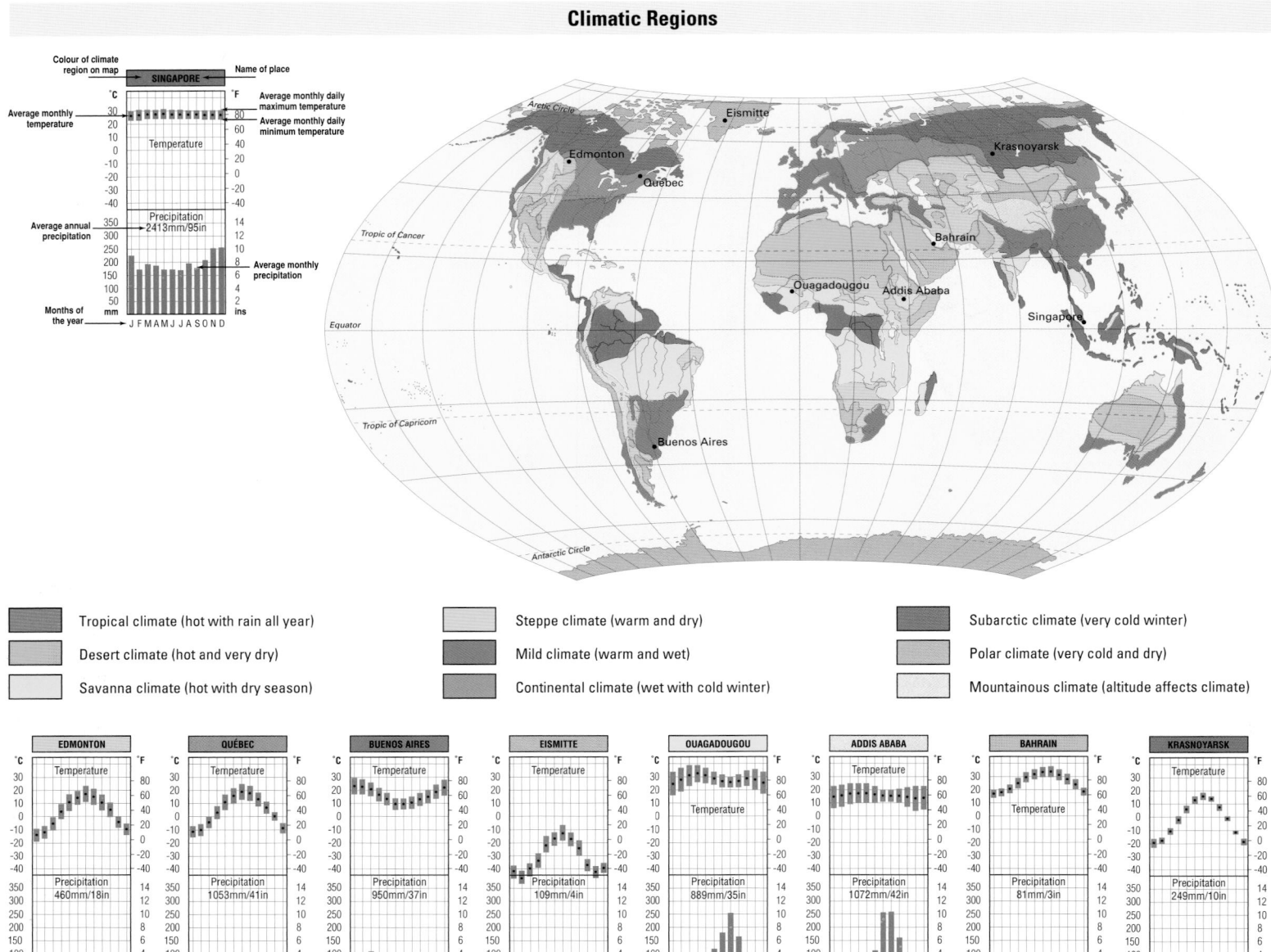

- Tropical climate (hot with rain all year)
- Desert climate (hot and very dry)
- Savanna climate (hot with dry season)
- Steppe climate (warm and dry)
- Mild climate (warm and wet)
- Continental climate (wet with cold winter)
- Subarctic climate (very cold winter)
- Polar climate (very cold and dry)
- Mountainous climate (altitude affects climate)

Climate Records

Temperature

Highest recorded shade temperature: Al Aziziyah, Libya, 57.7°C [135.9°F], 13 September 1922.

Highest mean annual temperature: Dallol, Ethiopia, 34.4°C [94°F], 1960–66.

Longest heatwave: Marble Bar, W. Australia, 162 days over 38°C [100°F], 23 October 1923 to 7 April 1924.

Lowest recorded temperature (outside poles): Verkhoyansk, Siberia, –69.8°C [–93.6°F], 7 February 1892.

Lowest mean annual temperature: Polus Nedostupnosti, Pole of Cold, Antarctica, –57.8°C [–72°F].

Precipitation

Driest place: Quillagua, Chile, mean annual rainfall 0.5 mm [0.02 in], 1964–2001.

Wettest place (12 months): Cherrapunji, Meghalaya, N. E. India, 26,461 mm [1,042 in], August 1860 to July 1861. Cherrapunji also holds the record for the most rainfall in one month: 2,930 mm [115 in], July 1861.

Wettest place (average): Mt Wai-ale-ale, Hawai'i, USA, mean annual rainfall 11,680 mm [459.8 in].

Wettest place (24 hours): Fac Fac, Réunion, Indian Ocean, 1,825 mm [71.9 in], 15–16 March 1952.

Heaviest hailstones: Gopalganj, Bangladesh, up to 1.02 kg [2.25 lb], 14 April 1986 (killed 92 people).

Heaviest snowfall (continuous): Bessans, Savoie, France, 1,730 mm [68 in] in 19 hours, 5–6 April 1969.

Heaviest snowfall (season/year): Mt Baker, Washington, USA, 28,956 mm [1,140 in], June 1998 to June 1999.

Pressure and winds

Highest barometric pressure: Agata, Siberia (at 262 m [862 ft] altitude), 1,083.8 mb, 31 December 1968.

Lowest barometric pressure: Typhoon Tip, Guam, Pacific Ocean, 870 mb, 12 October 1979.

Highest recorded wind speed: Mt Washington, New Hampshire, USA, 371 km/h [231 mph], 12 April 1934. This is three times as strong as hurricane force on the Beaufort Scale.

Windiest place: Commonwealth Bay, Antarctica, where gales frequently reach over 320 km/h [200 mph].

Climate

Climate is weather in the long term: the seasonal pattern of hot and cold, wet and dry, averaged over time (usually 30 years). At the simplest level, it is caused by the uneven heating of the Earth. Surplus heat at the Equator passes towards the poles, levelling out the energy differential. Its passage is marked by a ceaseless churning of the atmosphere and the oceans, further agitated by the Earth's diurnal spin and the motion it imparts to moving air and water. The heat's means of transport – by winds and ocean currents, by the continual evaporation and recondensation of water molecules – is the weather itself. There are four basic types of climate, each of which can be further subdivided: tropical, desert (dry), temperate and polar.

Composition of Dry Air

Nitrogen	78.09%	Sulphur dioxide	trace
Oxygen	20.95%	Nitrogen oxide	trace
Argon	0.93%	Methane	trace
Water vapour	0.2–4.0%	Dust	trace
Carbon dioxide	0.03%	Helium	trace
Ozone	0.00006%	Neon	trace

El Niño

In a normal year, south-easterly trade winds drive surface waters westwards off the coast of South America, drawing cold, nutrient-rich water up from below. In an El Niño year (which occurs every 2–7 years), warm water from the west Pacific suppresses upwelling in the east, depriving the region of nutrients. The water is warmed by as much as 7°C [12°F], disturbing the tropical atmospheric circulation. During an intense El Niño, the south-east trade winds change direction and become equatorial westerlies, resulting in climatic extremes in many regions of the world, such as drought in parts of Australia and India, and heavy rainfall in south-eastern USA. An intense El Niño occurred in 1997–8, with resultant freak weather conditions across the entire Pacific region.

Normal year

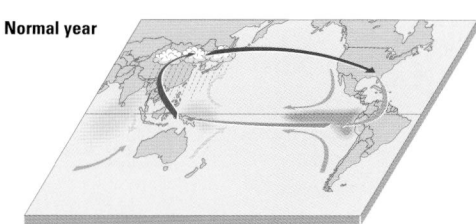

El Niño event

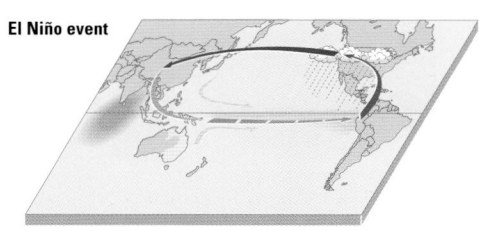

Beaufort Wind Scale

Named after the 19th-century British naval officer who devised it, the Beaufort Scale assesses wind speed according to its effects. It was originally designed as an aid for sailors, but has since been adapted for use on the land.

Scale	Wind speed km/h	mph	Effect
0	0–1	0–1	**Calm** Smoke rises vertically
1	1–5	1–3	**Light air** Wind direction shown only by smoke drift
2	6–11	4–7	**Light breeze** Wind felt on face; leaves rustle; vanes moved by wind
3	12–19	8–12	**Gentle breeze** Leaves and small twigs in constant motion; wind extends small flag
4	20–28	13–18	**Moderate** Raises dust and loose paper; small branches move
5	29–38	19–24	**Fresh** Small trees in leaf sway; wavelets on inland waters
6	39–49	25–31	**Strong** Large branches move; difficult to use umbrellas
7	50–61	32–38	**Near gale** Whole trees in motion; difficult to walk against wind
8	62–74	39–46	**Gale** Twigs break from trees; walking very difficult
9	75–88	47–54	**Strong gale** Slight structural damage
10	89–102	55–63	**Storm** Trees uprooted; serious structural damage
11	103–117	64–72	**Violent storm** Widespread damage
12	118+	73+	**Hurricane**

Conversions

°C = (°F − 32) × 5/9; °F = (°C × 9/5) + 32; 0°C = 32°F
1 in = 25.4 mm; 1 mm = 0.0394 in; 100 mm = 3.94 in

Temperature

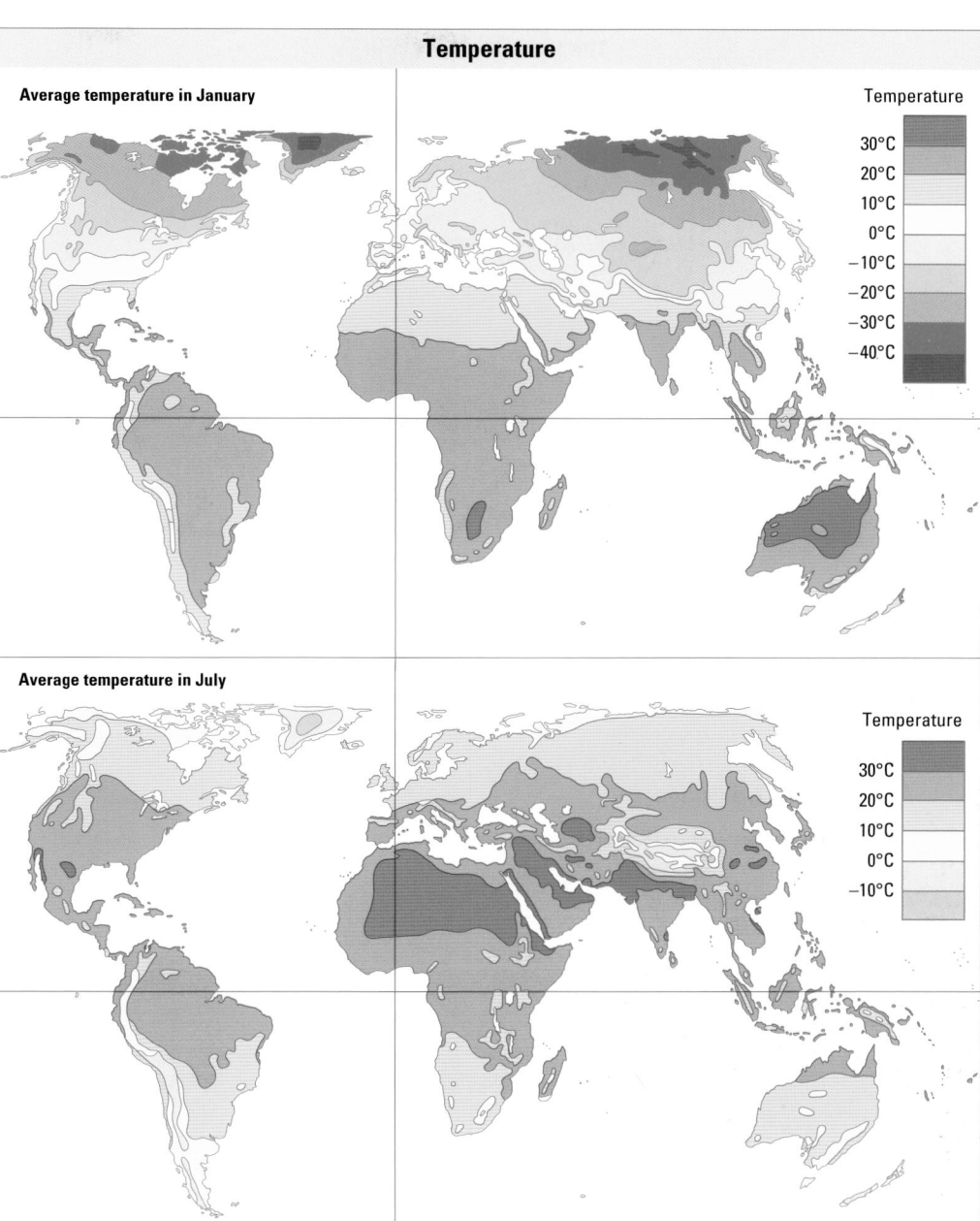

Average temperature in January

Temperature
30°C
20°C
10°C
0°C
−10°C
−20°C
−30°C
−40°C

Average temperature in July

Temperature
30°C
20°C
10°C
0°C
−10°C

Precipitation

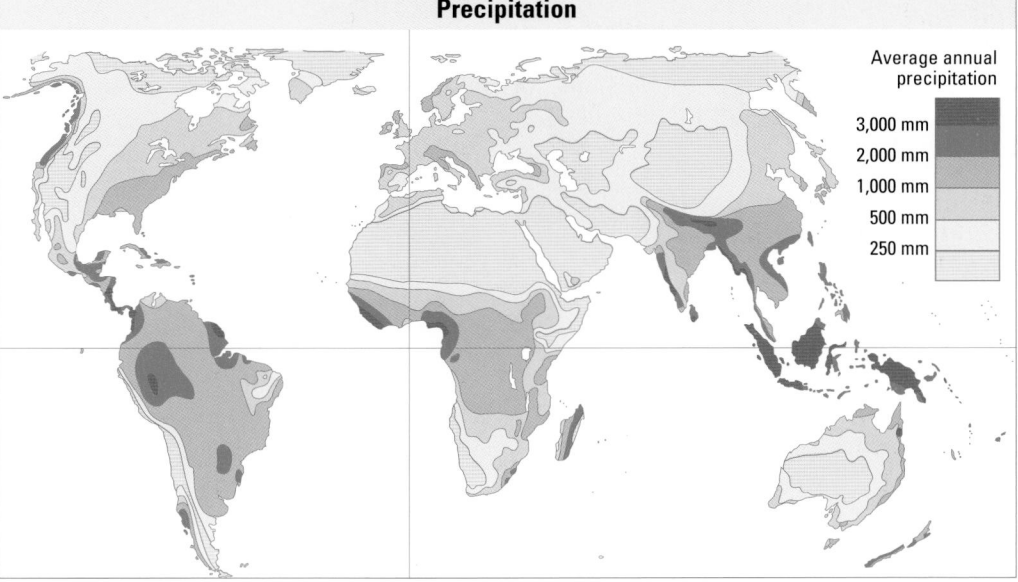

Average annual precipitation

3,000 mm
2,000 mm
1,000 mm
500 mm
250 mm

Water and Vegetation

The Hydrological Cycle

The world's water balance is regulated by the constant recycling of water between the oceans, atmosphere and land. The movement of water between these three reservoirs is known as the hydrological cycle. The oceans play a vital role in the hydrological cycle: 74% of the total precipitation falls over the oceans and 84% of the total evaporation comes from the oceans.

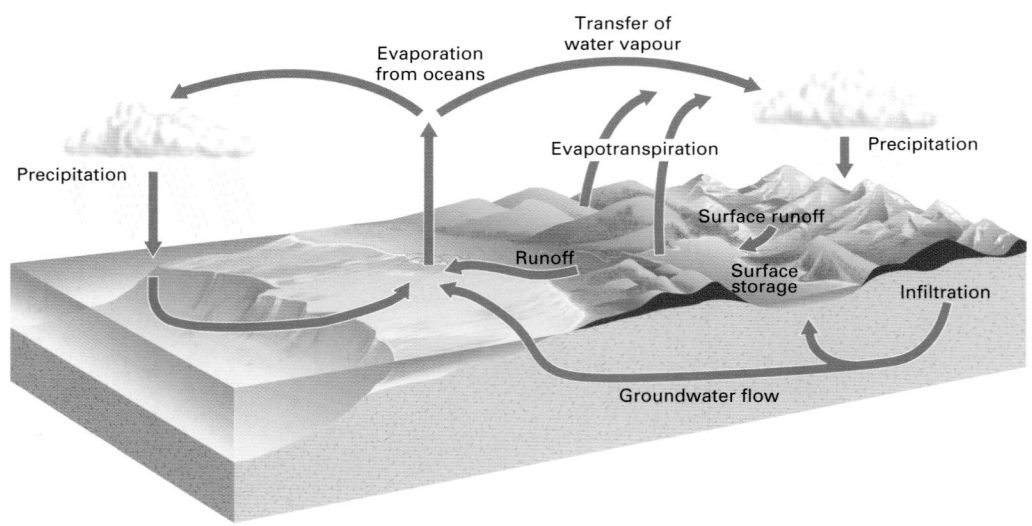

Water Distribution

The distribution of planetary water, by percentage. Oceans and ice caps together account for more than 99% of the total; the breakdown of the remainder is estimated.

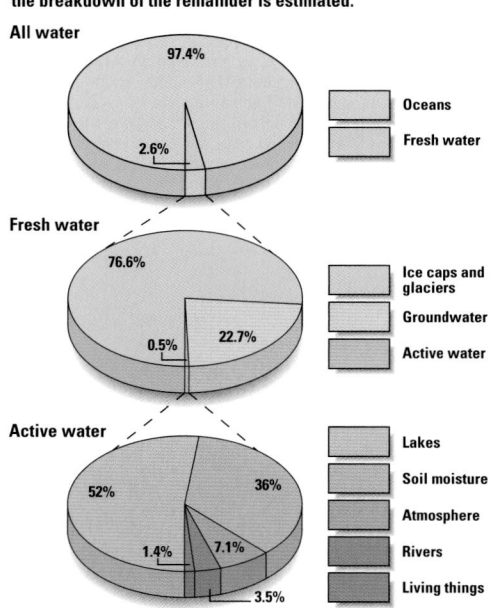

All water
97.4%
2.6%
- Oceans
- Fresh water

Fresh water
76.6%
0.5%
22.7%
- Ice caps and glaciers
- Groundwater
- Active water

Active water
52%
36%
1.4%
7.1%
3.5%
- Lakes
- Soil moisture
- Atmosphere
- Rivers
- Living things

Water Utilization

Domestic ▪ Industrial ▪ Agriculture

The percentage breakdown of water usage by sector, selected countries (2002)

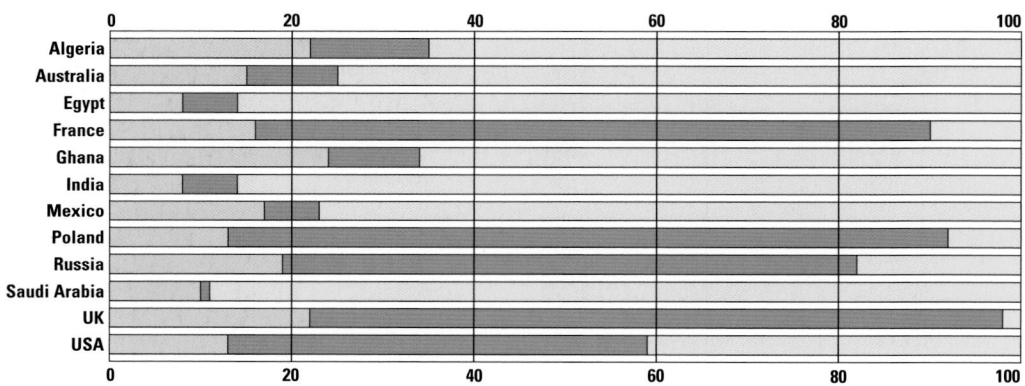

Algeria
Australia
Egypt
France
Ghana
India
Mexico
Poland
Russia
Saudi Arabia
UK
USA

Water Usage

Almost all the world's water is 3,000 million years old, and all of it cycles endlessly through the hydrosphere, though at different rates. Water vapour circulates over days, even hours, deep ocean water circulates over millennia, and ice-cap water remains solid for millions of years.

Fresh water is essential to all terrestrial life. Humans cannot survive more than a few days without it, and even the hardiest desert plants and animals could not exist without some water. Agriculture requires huge quantities of fresh water: without large-scale irrigation most of the world's people would starve. In the USA, agriculture uses 41% and industry 46% of all water withdrawals.

According to the latest figures, the average North American uses 1.3 million litres per year. This is more than six times the average African, who uses just 186,000 litres of water each year. Europeans and Australians use 694,000 litres per year.

Water Supply

Percentage of total population with access to safe drinking water (2004)

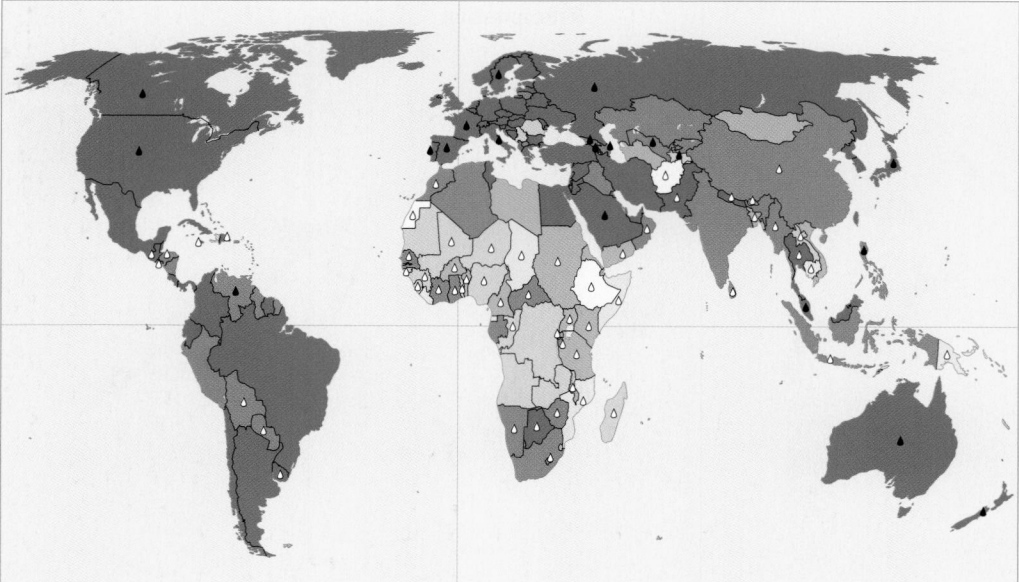

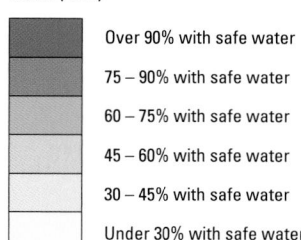

- Over 90% with safe water
- 75 – 90% with safe water
- 60 – 75% with safe water
- 45 – 60% with safe water
- 30 – 45% with safe water
- Under 30% with safe water

⌂ Under 80 litres per person per day domestic water consumption

▴ Over 320 litres per person per day domestic water consumption

NB: 80 litres of water a day is considered necessary for a reasonable quality of life.

Least well-provided countries

Afghanistan	13%	Papua New Guinea	39%
Ethiopia	22%	Cambodia	41%
Western Sahara	26%	Somalia	42%

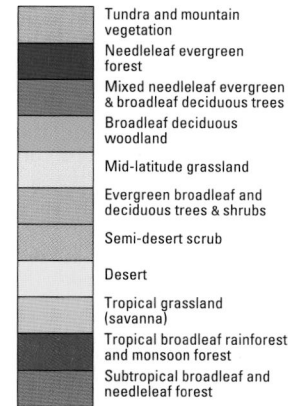

Natural Vegetation

Regional variation in vegetation

- Tundra and mountain vegetation
- Needleleaf evergreen forest
- Mixed needleleaf evergreen & broadleaf deciduous trees
- Broadleaf deciduous woodland
- Mid-latitude grassland
- Evergreen broadleaf and deciduous trees & shrubs
- Semi-desert scrub
- Desert
- Tropical grassland (savanna)
- Tropical broadleaf rainforest and monsoon forest
- Subtropical broadleaf and needleleaf forest

The map shows the natural 'climax vegetation' of regions, as dictated by climate and topography. In most cases, however, agricultural activity has drastically altered the vegetation pattern. Western Europe, for example, lost most of its broadleaf forest many centuries ago, while irrigation has turned some natural semi-desert into productive land.

Land Use by Continent (2004)

- Forest
- Permanent pasture
- Permanent crops
- Arable
- Other

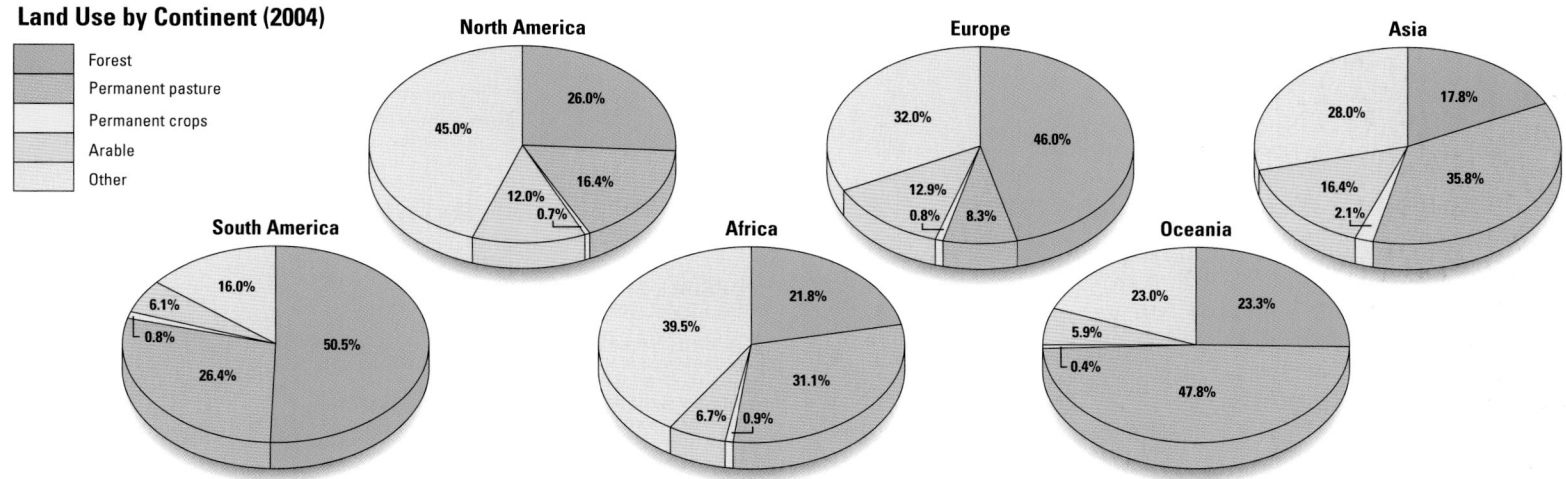

North America: 26.0%, 16.4%, 0.7%, 12.0%, 45.0%

Europe: 46.0%, 8.3%, 0.8%, 12.9%, 32.0%

Asia: 17.8%, 35.8%, 2.1%, 16.4%, 28.0%

South America: 50.5%, 26.4%, 0.8%, 6.1%, 16.0%

Africa: 21.8%, 31.1%, 0.9%, 6.7%, 39.5%

Oceania: 23.3%, 47.8%, 0.4%, 5.9%, 23.0%

Forestry: Production

	Forest and woodland (million hectares)	Annual production (2005, million cubic metres) Fuelwood	Annual production (2005, million cubic metres) Industrial roundwood*
World	*3,869.5*	*1,792.1*	*1710.6*
Europe	1,039.3	117.3	544.0
S. America	885.6	192.8	186.7
Africa	649.9	563.3	69.4
N. & C. America	549.3	130.2	623.6
Asia	547.8	779.5	237.5
Oceania	197.6	9.0	49.4

Paper and Board

Top producers (2005)**		Top exporters (2005)**	
USA	81,437	Canada	15,731
China	53,463	Germany	12,205
Japan	29,295	Finland	11,155
Germany	21,679	Sweden	10,593
Canada	19,673	USA	9,610

* roundwood is timber as it is felled
** in thousand tonnes

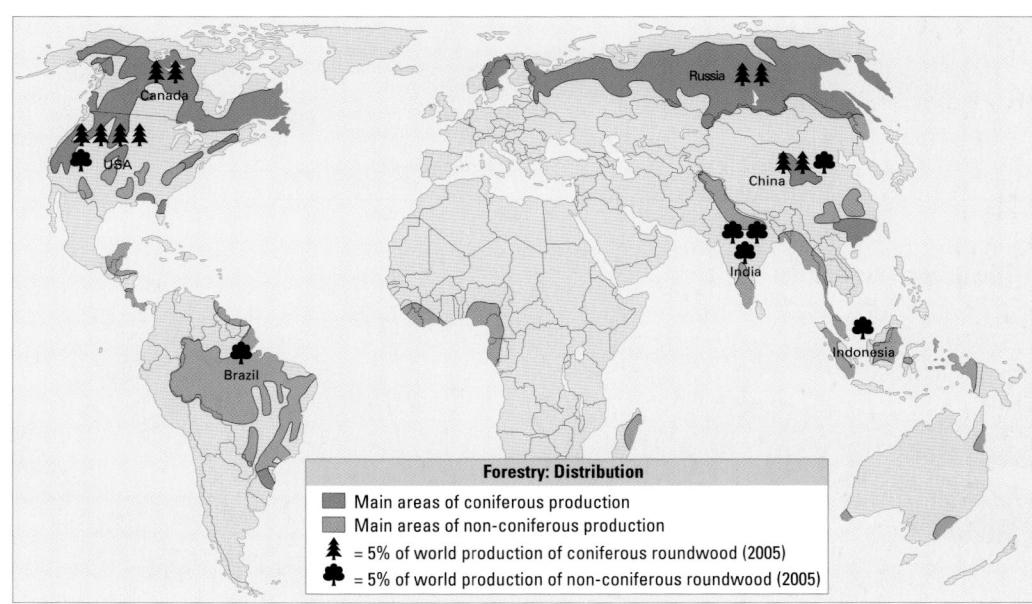

Forestry: Distribution

- Main areas of coniferous production
- Main areas of non-coniferous production
- 🌲 = 5% of world production of coniferous roundwood (2005)
- 🌳 = 5% of world production of non-coniferous roundwood (2005)

Environment

Humans have always had a dramatic effect on their environment, at least since the development of agriculture almost 10,000 years ago. Generally, the Earth has accepted human interference without obvious ill effects: the complex systems that regulate the global environment have been able to absorb substantial damage while maintaining a stable and comfortable home for the planet's trillions of lifeforms. But advancing human technology and the rapidly-expanding populations it supports are now threatening to overwhelm the Earth's ability to compensate.

Industrial wastes, acid rainfall, desertification and large-scale deforestation all combine to create environmental change at a rate far faster than the great slow cycles of planetary evolution can accommodate. As a result of overcultivation, overgrazing and overcutting of groundcover for firewood, desertification is affecting as much as 60% of the world's croplands. In addition, with fire and chain-saws, humans are destroying more forest in a day than their ancestors could have done in a century, upsetting the balance between plant and animal, carbon dioxide and oxygen, on which all life ultimately depends.

The fossil fuels that power industrial civilization have pumped enough carbon dioxide and other so-called greenhouse gases into the atmosphere to make climatic change a near-certainty. As a result of the combination of these factors, the Earth's average temperature has risen by approximately 0.5°C [1°F] since the beginning of the 20th century, and it is still rising.

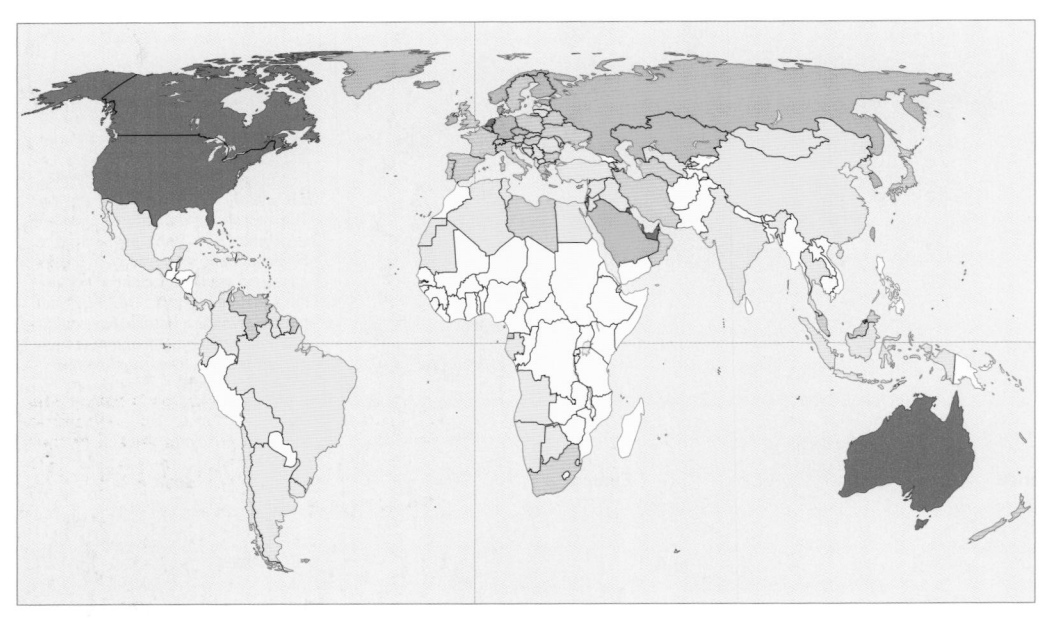

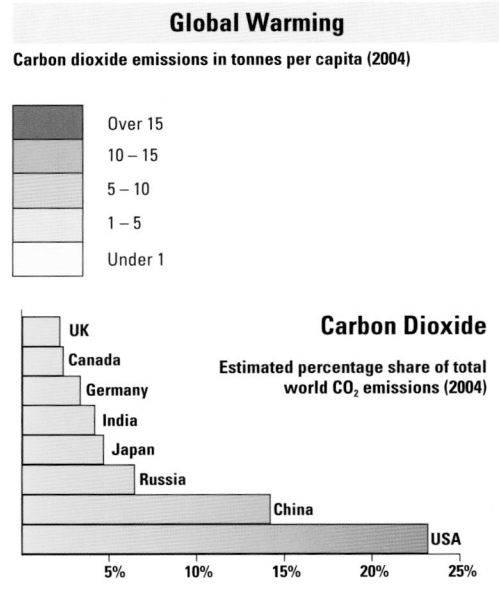

Global Warming

Carbon dioxide emissions in tonnes per capita (2004)

- Over 15
- 10 – 15
- 5 – 10
- 1 – 5
- Under 1

Carbon Dioxide

Estimated percentage share of total world CO$_2$ emissions (2004)

UK
Canada
Germany
India
Japan
Russia
China
USA

5%　10%　15%　20%　25%

Temperature Rise

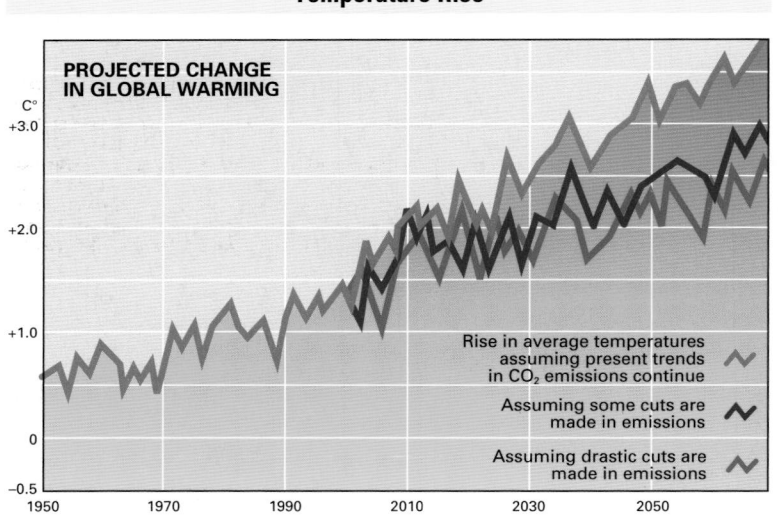

PROJECTED CHANGE IN GLOBAL WARMING

Rise in average temperatures assuming present trends in CO$_2$ emissions continue

Assuming some cuts are made in emissions

Assuming drastic cuts are made in emissions

Sea Level Rise

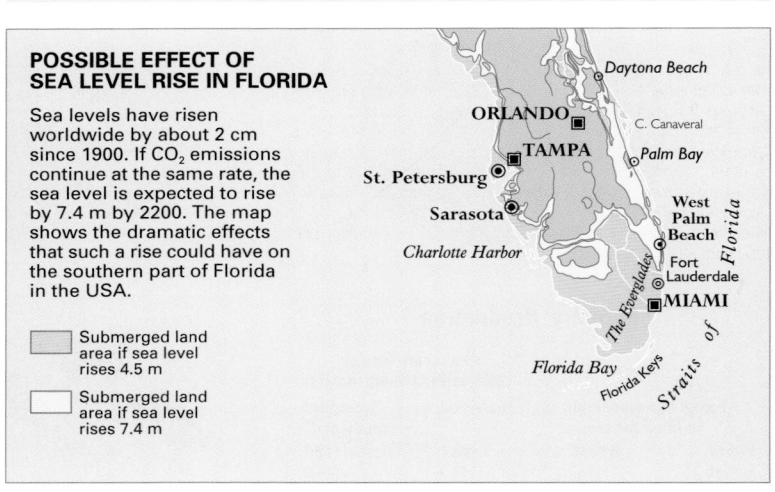

POSSIBLE EFFECT OF SEA LEVEL RISE IN FLORIDA

Sea levels have risen worldwide by about 2 cm since 1900. If CO$_2$ emissions continue at the same rate, the sea level is expected to rise by 7.4 m by 2200. The map shows the dramatic effects that such a rise could have on the southern part of Florida in the USA.

- Submerged land area if sea level rises 4.5 m
- Submerged land area if sea level rises 7.4 m

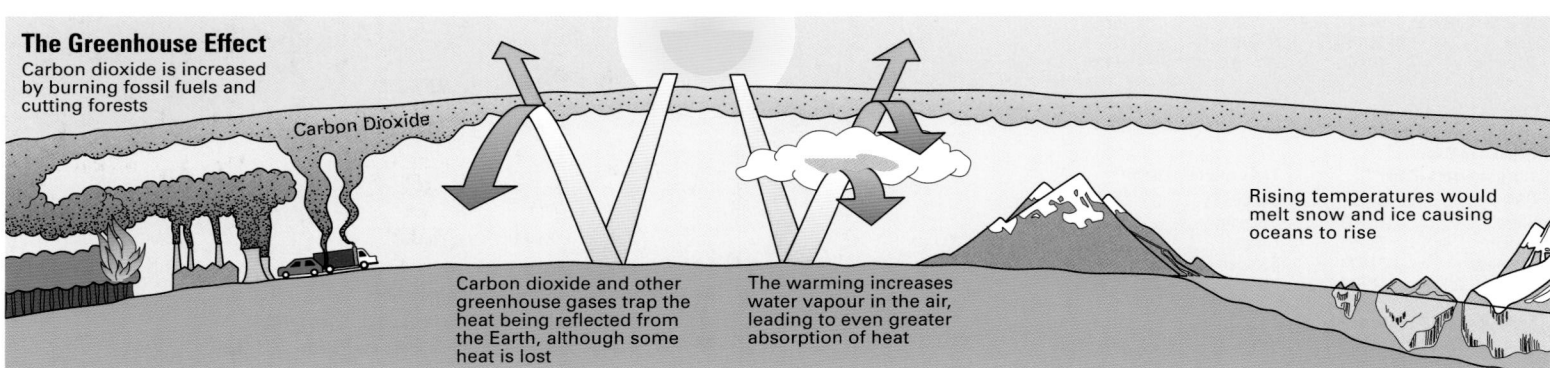

The Greenhouse Effect

Carbon dioxide is increased by burning fossil fuels and cutting forests

Carbon Dioxide

Carbon dioxide and other greenhouse gases trap the heat being reflected from the Earth, although some heat is lost

The warming increases water vapour in the air, leading to even greater absorption of heat

Rising temperatures would melt snow and ice causing oceans to rise

Desertification

- Existing deserts
- Areas with a high risk of desertification
- Areas with a moderate risk of desertification
- Former areas of rainforest
- Existing rainforest

Forest Clearance

Thousands of hectares of forest cleared annually, tropical countries surveyed 1980–85, 1990–95 and 2000–05. Loss as a percentage of remaining stocks is shown in figures on each column. Gain is indicated as a minus figure.

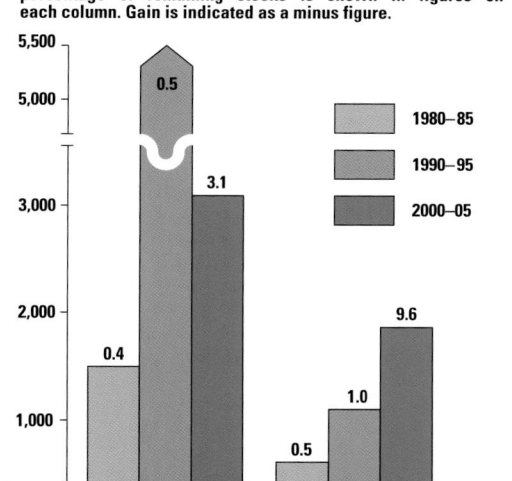

- 1980–85
- 1990–95
- 2000–05

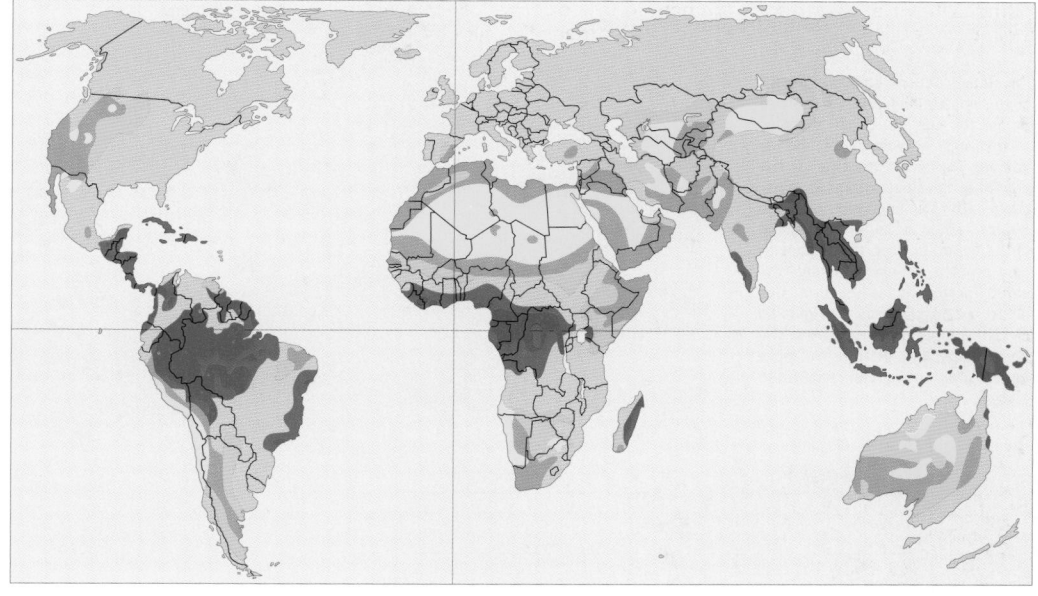

Deforestation

The Earth's remaining forests are under attack from three directions: expanding agriculture, logging, and growing consumption of fuelwood, often in combination. Sometimes deforestation is the direct result of government policy, as in the efforts made to resettle the urban poor in some parts of Brazil; just as often, it comes about despite state attempts at conservation. Loggers, licensed or unlicensed, blaze a trail into virgin forest, often destroying twice as many trees as they harvest. Landless farmers follow, burning away most of what remains to plant their crops, completing the destruction. Some countries such as Vietnam and Costa Rica have successfully implemented reafforestation programmes.

Ozone Depletion

The ozone layer, 25–30 km [15–18 miles] above sea level, acts as a barrier to most of the Sun's harmful ultra-violet radiation, protecting us from the ionizing radiation that can cause skin cancer and cataracts. In recent years, however, two holes in the ozone layer have been observed during winter: one over the Arctic and the other, the size of the USA, over Antarctica. By 1996, ozone had been reduced to around a half of its 1970 amount. The ozone (O_3) is broken down by chlorine released into the atmosphere as CFCs (chlorofluorocarbons) – chemicals used in refrigerators, packaging and aerosols.

Air Pollution

Sulphur dioxide is the main pollutant associated with industrial cities. According to the World Health Organization, at least 600 million people live in urban areas where sulphur dioxide concentrations regularly reach damaging levels. One of the world's most dangerously polluted urban areas is Mexico City, due to a combination of its enclosed valley location, 3 million cars and 60,000 factories. In May 1998, this lethal cocktail was added to by nearby forest fires and the resultant air pollution led to over 20% of the population (3 million people) complaining of respiratory problems.

Acid Rain

Killing trees, poisoning lakes and rivers, and eating away buildings, acid rain is mostly produced by sulphur dioxide emissions from industry and volcanic eruptions. By the mid 1990s, acid rain had sterilized 4,000 or more of Sweden's lakes and left 45% of Switzerland's alpine conifers dead or dying, while the monuments of Greece were dissolving in Athens' smog. Prevailing wind patterns mean that the acids often fall many hundred kilometres from where the original pollutants were discharged. In parts of Europe acid deposition has slightly decreased, following reductions in emissions, but not by enough.

World Pollution

Acid rain and sources of acidic emissions (latest available year)

Acid rain is caused by high levels of sulphur and nitrogen in the atmosphere. They combine with water vapour and oxygen to form acids (H_2SO_4 and HNO_3) which fall as precipitation.

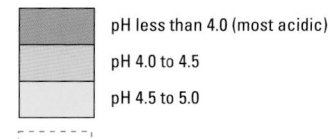

- Regions where sulphur and nitrogen oxides are released in high concentrations, mainly from fossil fuel combustion
- Major cities with high levels of air pollution (including nitrogen and sulphur emissions)

Areas of heavy acid deposition

pH numbers indicate acidity, decreasing from a neutral 7. Normal rain, slightly acid from dissolved carbon dioxide, never exceeds a pH of 5.6.

- pH less than 4.0 (most acidic)
- pH 4.0 to 4.5
- pH 4.5 to 5.0
- Areas where acid rain is a potential problem

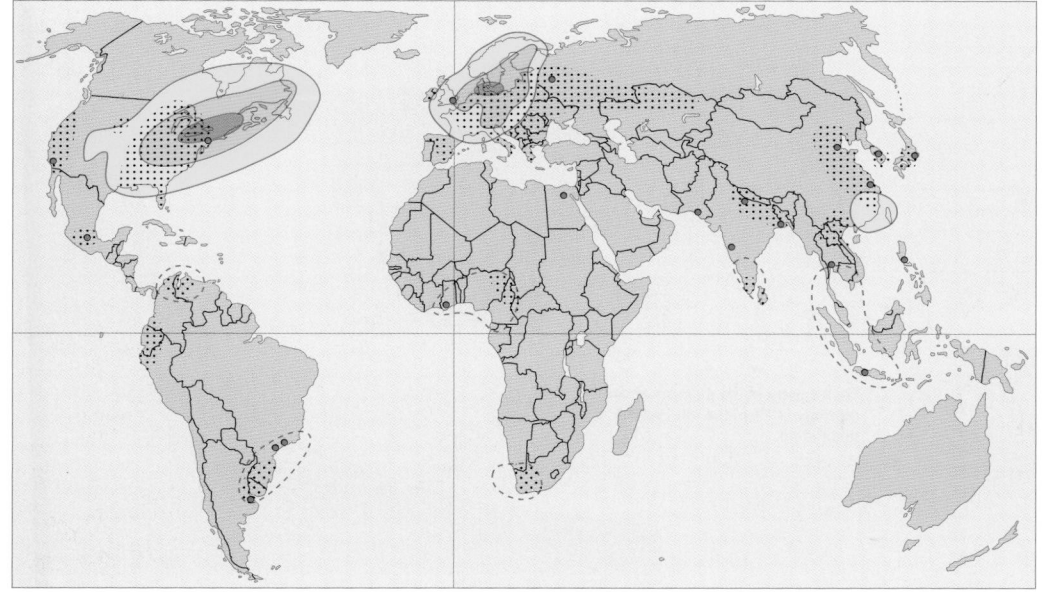

Population

Demographic Profiles

Developed nations such as the UK have populations evenly spread across the age groups and, usually, a growing proportion of elderly people. The great majority of the people in developing nations, however, are in the younger age groups, about to enter their most fertile years. In time, these population profiles should resemble the world profile (even Nigeria has made recent progress by reducing its birth rate), but the transition will come about only after a few more generations of rapid population growth.

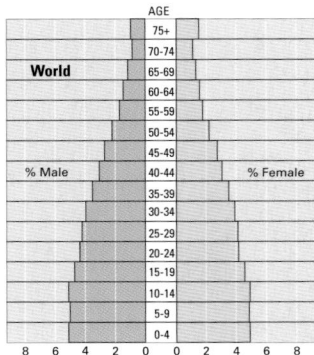

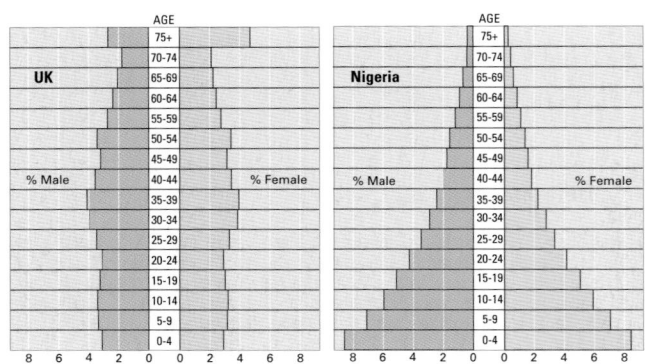

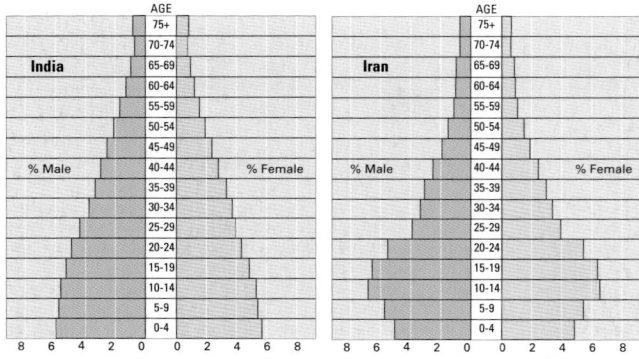

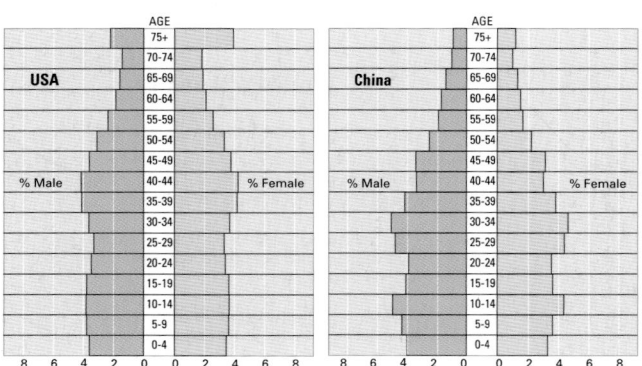

Most Populous Nations, in millions (2006 estimates)

1. China	1,314	9. Nigeria	132	17. Turkey	70
2. India	1,095	10. Japan	127	18. Iran	69
3. USA	301	11. Mexico	107	19. Thailand	65
4. Indonesia	245	12. Philippines	89	20. Congo (Dem. Rep.)	63
5. Brazil	188	13. Vietnam	84	21. France	61
6. Pakistan	166	14. Germany	82	22. UK	61
7. Bangladesh	147	15. Egypt	79	23. Italy	58
8. Russia	143	16. Ethiopia	75	24. South Korea	49

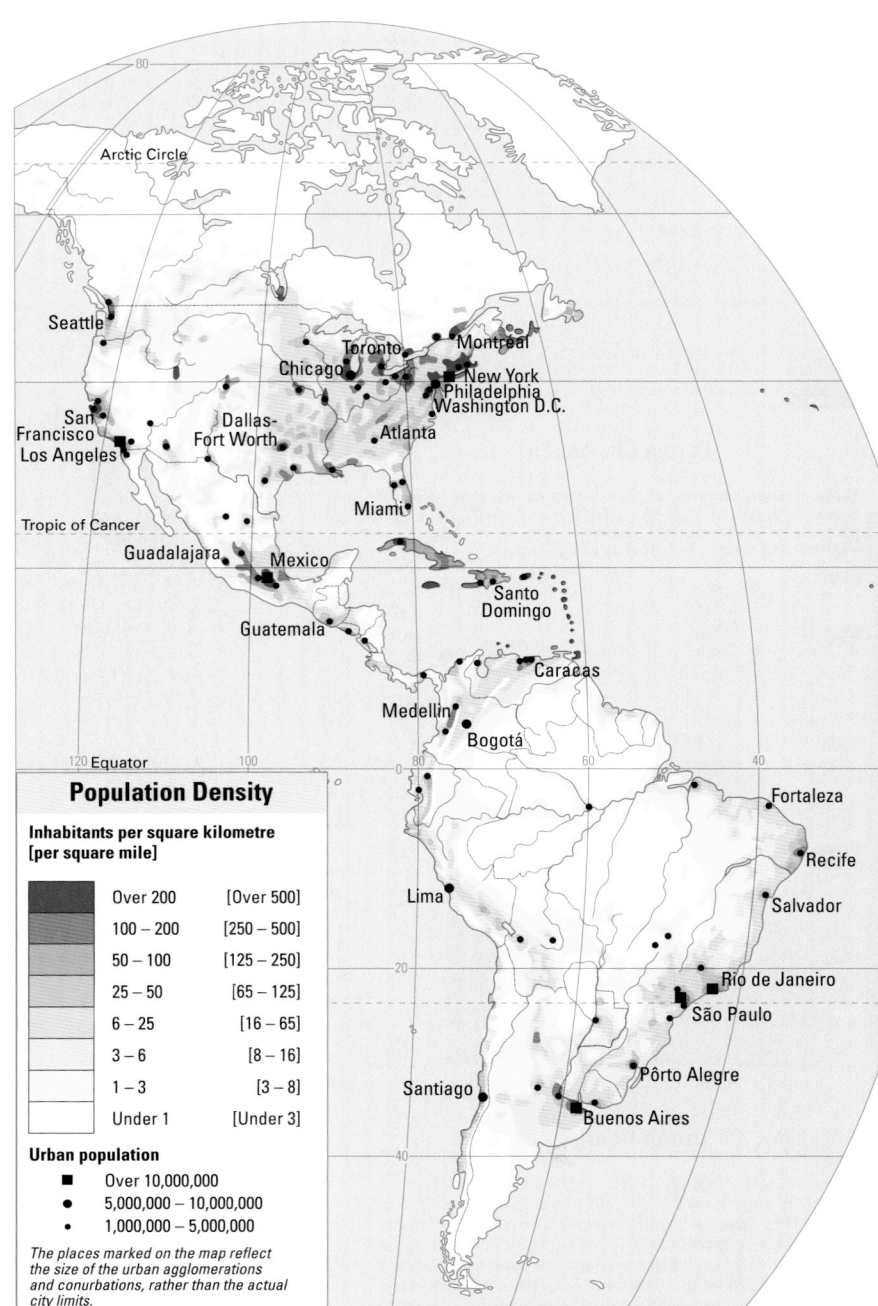

Population Density

Inhabitants per square kilometre [per square mile]

	Over 200	[Over 500]
	100 – 200	[250 – 500]
	50 – 100	[125 – 250]
	25 – 50	[65 – 125]
	6 – 25	[16 – 65]
	3 – 6	[8 – 16]
	1 – 3	[3 – 8]
	Under 1	[Under 3]

Urban population

- ■ Over 10,000,000
- ● 5,000,000 – 10,000,000
- • 1,000,000 – 5,000,000

The places marked on the map reflect the size of the urban agglomerations and conurbations, rather than the actual city limits.

Continental Comparisons

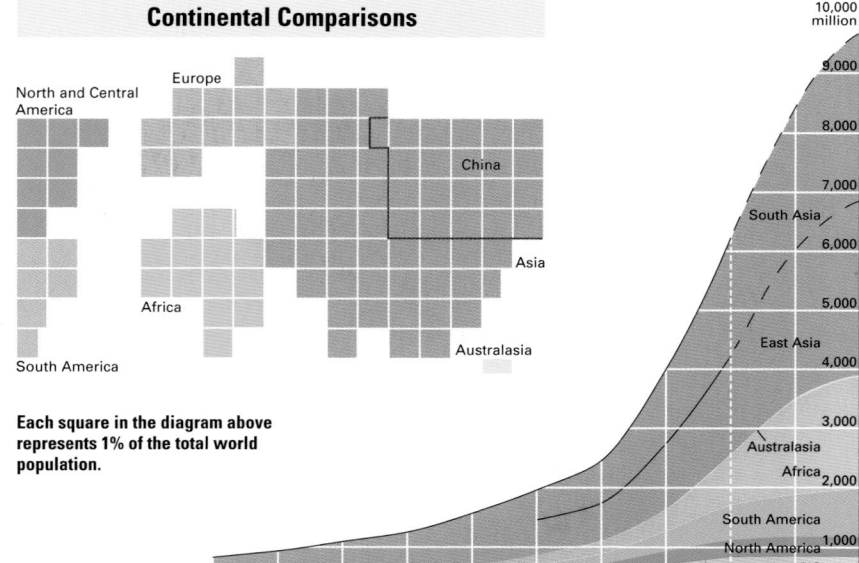

Each square in the diagram above represents 1% of the total world population.

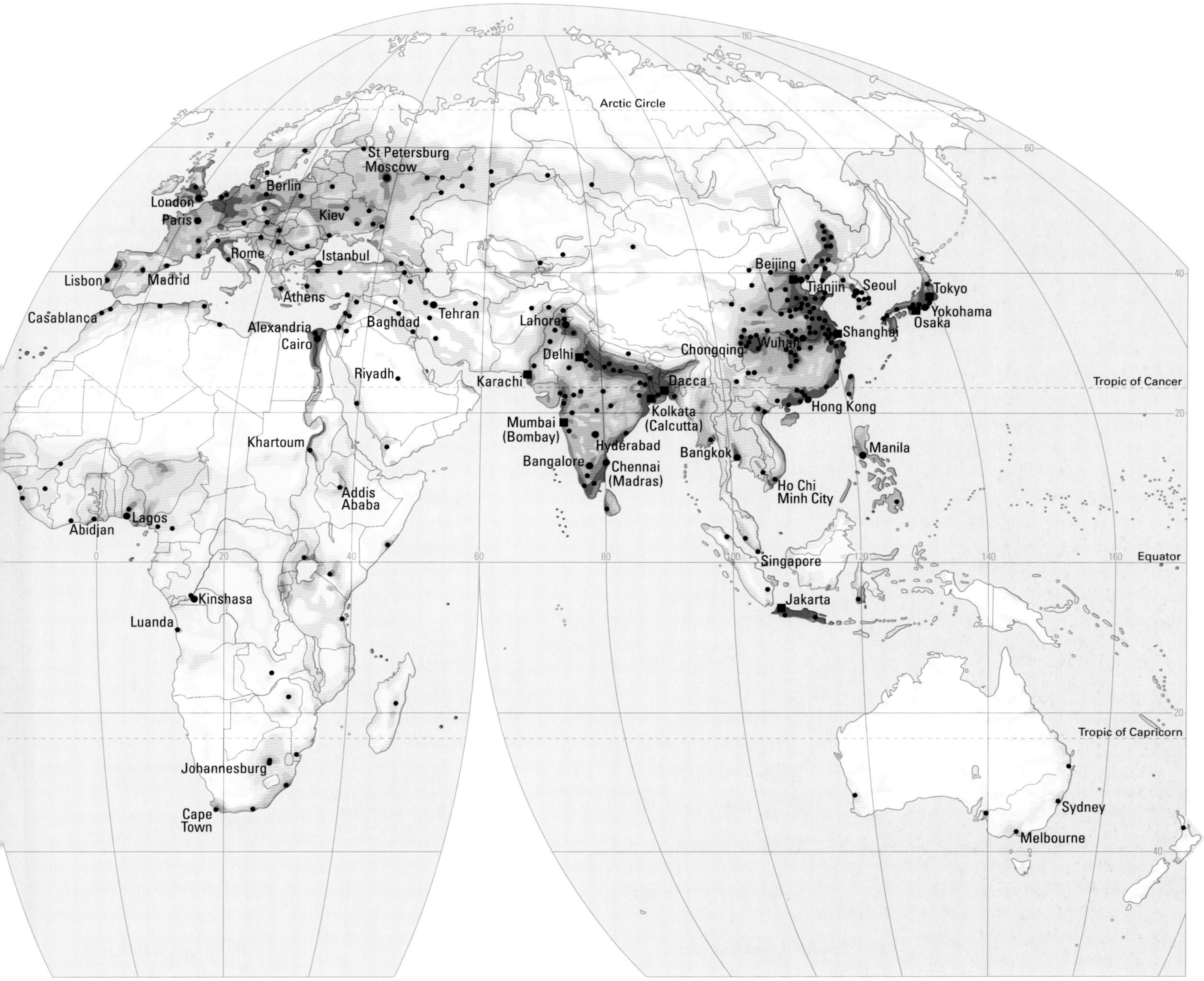

Arctic Circle

St Petersburg
Moscow
Berlin
London
Paris
Kiev
Rome
Istanbul
Lisbon
Madrid
Athens
Casablanca
Alexandria
Cairo
Baghdad
Tehran
Lahore
Riyadh
Beijing
Tianjin
Seoul
Tokyo
Yokohama
Osaka
Wuhan
Shanghai
Delhi
Chongqing
Karachi
Dacca
Tropic of Cancer
Khartoum
Mumbai
(Bombay)
Kolkata
(Calcutta)
Hong Kong
Hyderabad
Bangkok
Manila
Bangalore
Chennai
(Madras)
Addis
Ababa
Ho Chi
Minh City
Lagos
Abidjan
Singapore
Equator
Kinshasa
Jakarta
Luanda
Johannesburg
Tropic of Capricorn
Cape
Town
Sydney
Melbourne

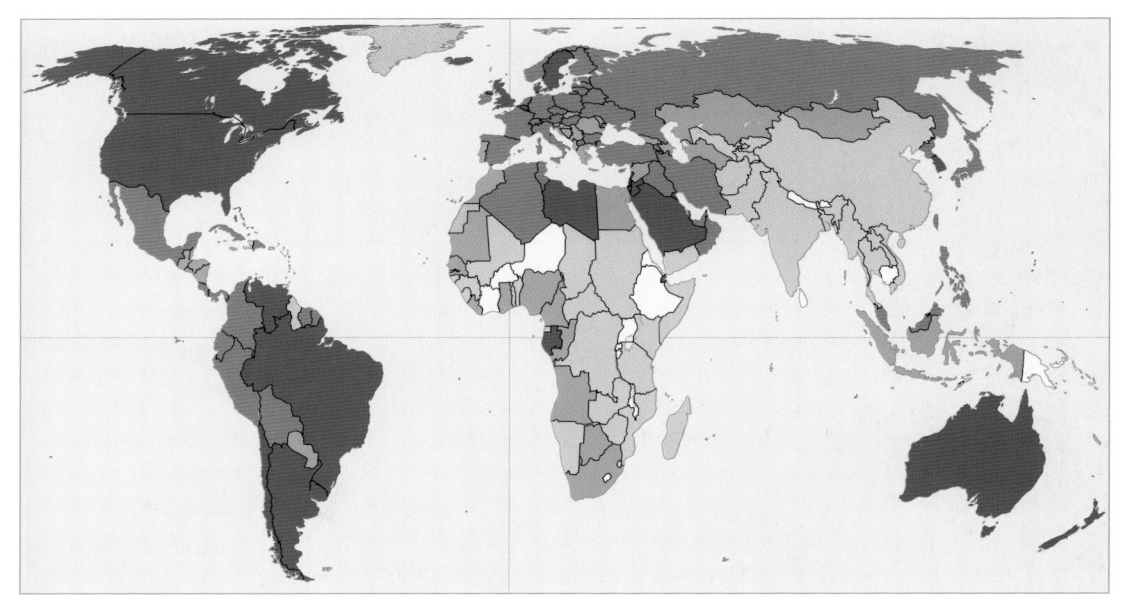

Urban Population

Percentage of total population living in towns and cities (2004)

	Over 80%
	60 – 80%
	40 – 60%
	20 – 40%
	Under 20%
	No data available

Most urbanized		Least urbanized	
Singapore	100%	Burundi	10%
Kuwait	97%	Bhutan	11%
Belgium	97%	Trinidad & Tobago	12%
Bahrain	96%	Uganda	13%
Qatar	95%	Papua New Guinea	13%

The Human Family

Predominant Languages

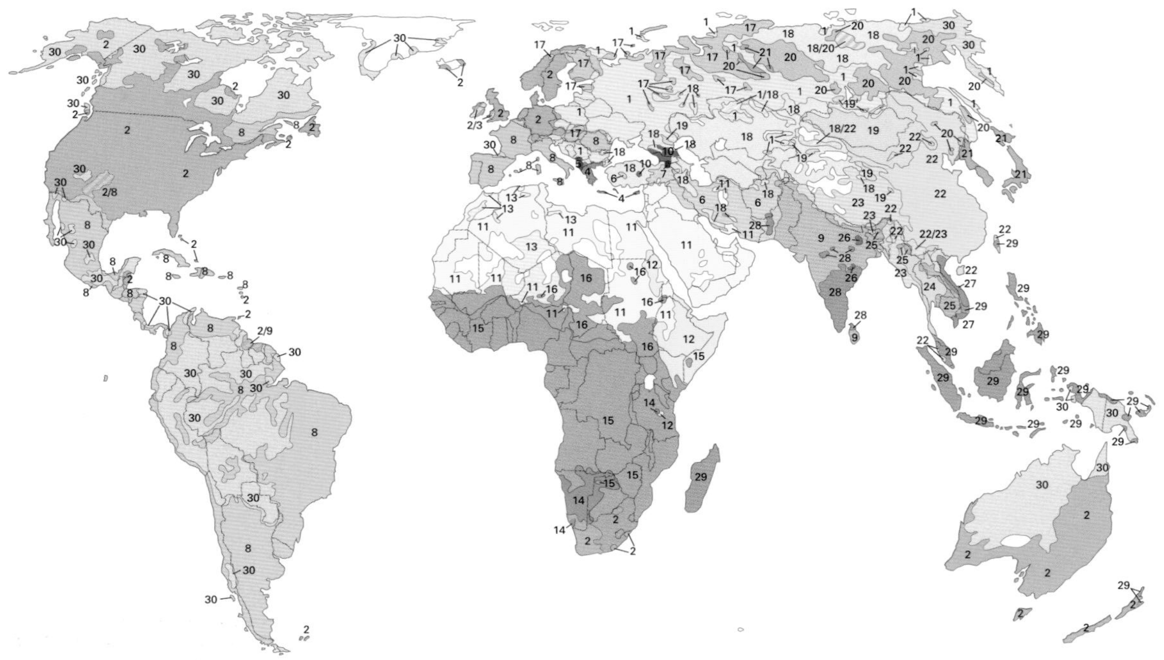

Languages of the World

Language can be classified by ancestry and structure. For example, the Romance and Germanic groups are both derived from an Indo-European language believed to have been spoken 5,000 years ago.

First-language speakers in millions (2004)
Mandarin Chinese 873, Spanish 322, English 309, Hindi 180, Portuguese 177, Bengali 171, Russian 145, Japanese 122, German 95, Wu Chinese 77, Javanese 75, Telugu 69, Marathi 68, Vietnamese 67, Korean 67, Tamil 66, French 64, Italian 61, Punjabi 60.

Distribution of Living Languages

The figures refer to the number of languages currently in use in the regions shown

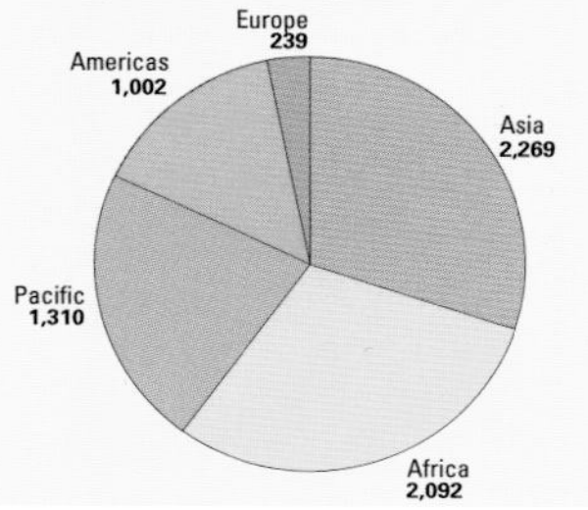

- Europe 239
- Americas 1,002
- Asia 2,269
- Pacific 1,310
- Africa 2,092

INDO-EUROPEAN FAMILY

1 Balto-Slavic group (incl. Russian, Ukrainian)
2 Germanic group (incl. English, German)
3 Celtic group
4 Greek
5 Albanian
6 Iranian group
7 Armenian
8 Romance group (incl. Spanish, Portuguese, French, Italian)
9 Indo-Aryan group (incl. Hindi, Bengali, Urdu, Punjabi, Marathi)
10 CAUCASIAN FAMILY

AFRO-ASIATIC FAMILY

11 Semitic group (incl. Arabic)
12 Kushitic group
13 Berber group

14 KHOISAN FAMILY

15 NIGER-CONGO FAMILY

16 NILO-SAHARAN FAMILY

17 URALIC FAMILY

ALTAIC FAMILY

18 Turkic group (incl. Turkish)
19 Mongolian group
20 Tungus-Manchu group
21 Japanese and Korean

SINO-TIBETAN FAMILY

22 Sinitic (Chinese) languages (incl. Mandarin, Wu, Yue)
23 Tibetic-Burmic languages

24 TAI FAMILY

AUSTRO-ASIATIC FAMILY

25 Mon-Khmer group
26 Munda group
27 Vietnamese

28 DRAVIDIAN FAMILY (incl. Telugu, Tamil)

29 AUSTRONESIAN FAMILY (incl. Malay-Indonesian, Javanese)

30 OTHER LANGUAGES

Predominant Religions

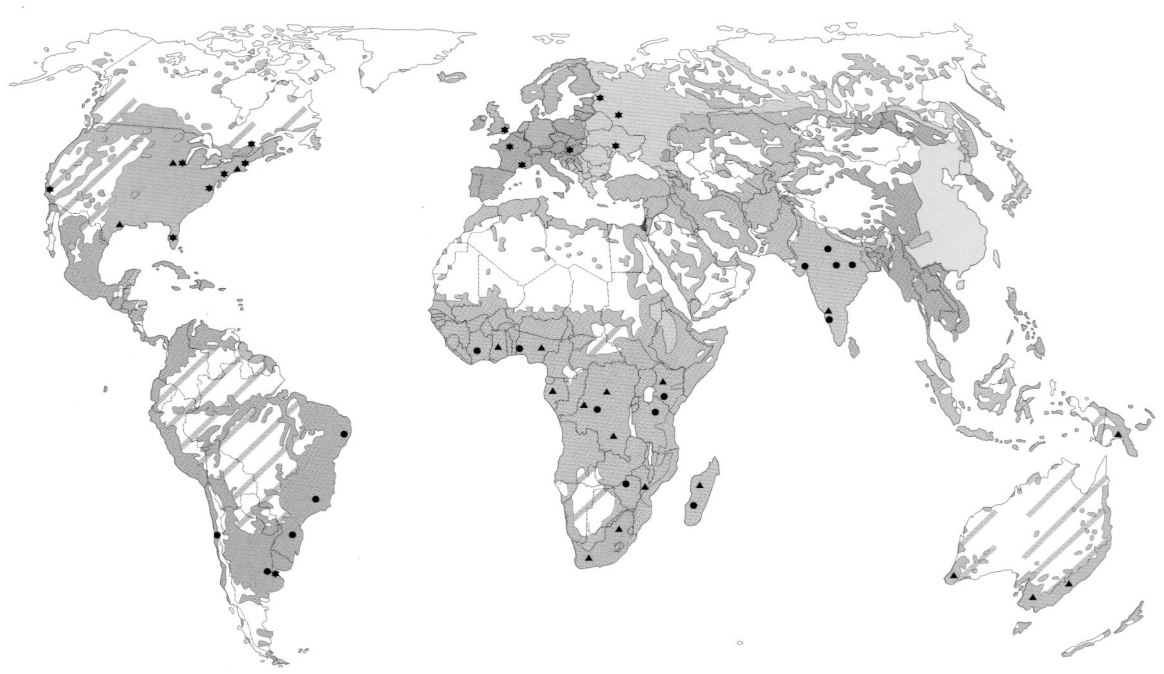

Religious Adherents

Religious adherents in millions (2005)

Christianity	2,100	Hindu	832
Roman Catholic	1,050	Chinese folk	394
Protestant	396	Buddhism	329
Orthodox	240	Ethnic religions	300
Anglican	73	New religions	103
Others	341	Sikhism	23
Islam	1,070	Judaism	15
Sunni	940	Spiritism	12
Shi'ite	120	Baha'i	6
Others	10	Confucianism	6
Non-religious/		Jainism	5
Agnostic/Atheist	1,100	Shintoism	3

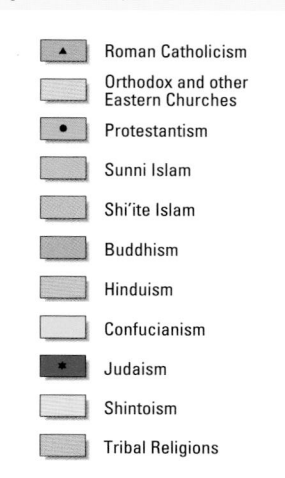

- ▲ Roman Catholicism
- Orthodox and other Eastern Churches
- • Protestantism
- Sunni Islam
- Shi'ite Islam
- Buddhism
- Hinduism
- Confucianism
- ★ Judaism
- Shintoism
- Tribal Religions

United Nations

Created in 1945 to promote peace and co-operation and based in New York, the United Nations is the world's largest international organization, with 192 members and an annual budget of US $1.9 billion (2006). Each member of the General Assembly has one vote, while the five permanent members of the 15-nation Security Council – China, France, Russia, UK and USA – hold a veto. The Secretariat is the UN's principal administrative arm. The 54 members of the Economic and Social Council are responsible for economic, social, cultural, educational, health and related matters. The UN has 16 specialized agencies – based in Canada, France, Switzerland and Italy, as well as the USA – which help members in fields such as education (UNESCO), agriculture (FAO), medicine (WHO) and finance (IFC). By the end of 1994, all the original 11 trust territories of the Trusteeship Council had become independent.

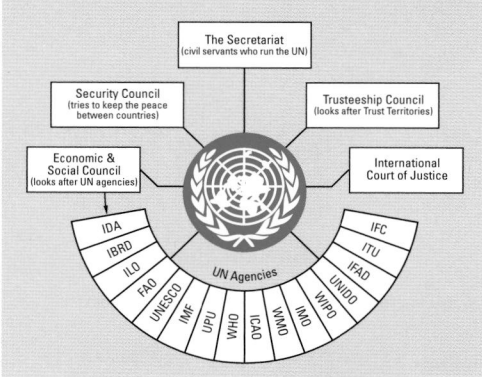

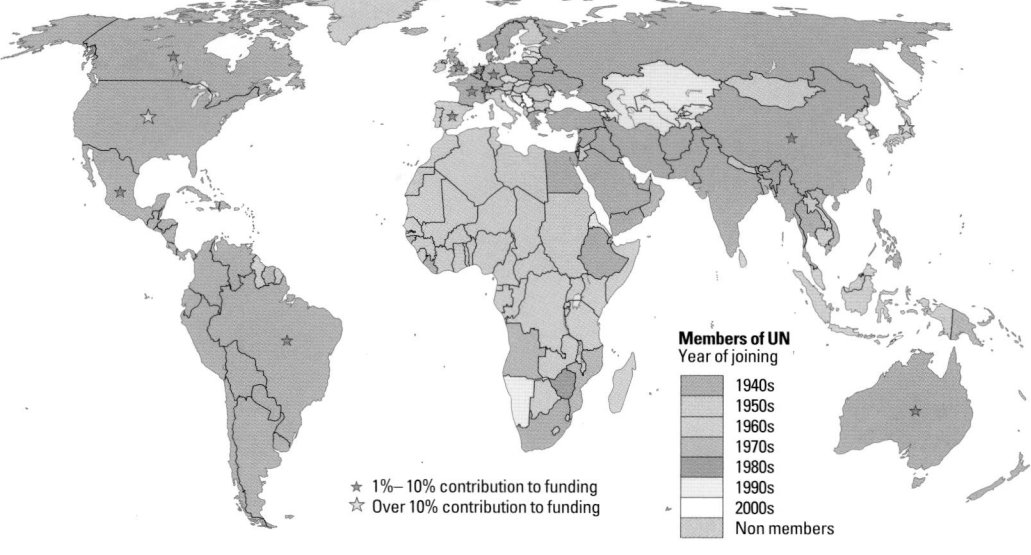

Members of UN
Year of joining

- 1940s
- 1950s
- 1960s
- 1970s
- 1980s
- 1990s
- 2000s
- Non members

★ 1%– 10% contribution to funding
☆ Over 10% contribution to funding

MEMBERSHIP OF THE UN In 1945 there were 51 members; by the end of 2006 membership had increased to 192 following the admission of East Timor, Switzerland and Montenegro. There are 2 independent states which are not members of the UN – Taiwan and the Vatican City. All the successor states of the former USSR had joined by the end of 1992. The official languages of the UN are Chinese, English, French, Russian, Spanish and Arabic.

FUNDING The UN regular budget for 2006 was US$1.9 billion. Contributions are assessed by the members' ability to pay, with the maximum 22% of the total (USA's share), the minimum 0.01%. The European Union pays over 37% of the budget.

PEACEKEEPING The UN has been involved in 61 peacekeeping operations worldwide since 1948.

International Organizations

ACP African-Caribbean-Pacific (formed in 1963). Members have economic ties with the EU.
APEC Asia-Pacific Economic Co-operation (formed in 1989). It aims to enhance economic growth and prosperity for the region and to strengthen the Asia-Pacific community. APEC is the only intergovernmental grouping in the world operating on the basis of non-binding commitments, open dialogue, and equal respect for the views of all participants. There are 21 member economies.
ARAB LEAGUE (formed in 1945). The League's aim is to promote economic, social, political and military co-operation. There are 22 member nations.
ASEAN Association of South-east Asian Nations (formed in 1967). Cambodia joined in 1999.
AU The African Union replaced the Organization of African Unity (formed in 1963) in 2002. Its 53 members represent over 94% of Africa's population. Arabic, French, Portuguese and English are recognized as working languages.
COLOMBO PLAN (formed in 1951). Its 25 members aim to promote economic and social development in Asia and the Pacific.
COMMONWEALTH The Commonwealth of Nations evolved from the British Empire. Pakistan was suspended in 1999, and Zimbabwe in 2002. In response to its continued suspension, Zimbabwe left the Commonwealth in December 2003. Pakistan was reinstated in 2004, but Fiji Islands was suspended in December 2006 following a military coup. It now comprises 16 Queen's realms, 31 republics and 6 indigenous monarchies, giving a total of 53 member states.
EU European Union (evolved from the European Community in 1993). Cyprus, the Czech Republic, Estonia, Hungary, Latvia, Lithuania, Malta, Poland, the Slovak Republic and Slovenia joined the EU in May 2004; Bulgaria and Romania joined in January 2007. The other members are Austria, Belgium, Denmark, Finland, France, Germany, Greece, Ireland, Italy, Luxembourg, Netherlands, Portugal, Spain, Sweden and the UK – together these 27 countries aim to integrate economies, co-ordinate social developments and bring about political union.
LAIA Latin American Integration Association (1980). Its aim is to promote freer regional trade.
NATO North Atlantic Treaty Organization (formed in 1949). It continues after 1991 despite the winding up of the Warsaw Pact. Bulgaria, Estonia, Latvia, Lithuania, Romania, the Slovak Republic and Slovenia became members in 2004.

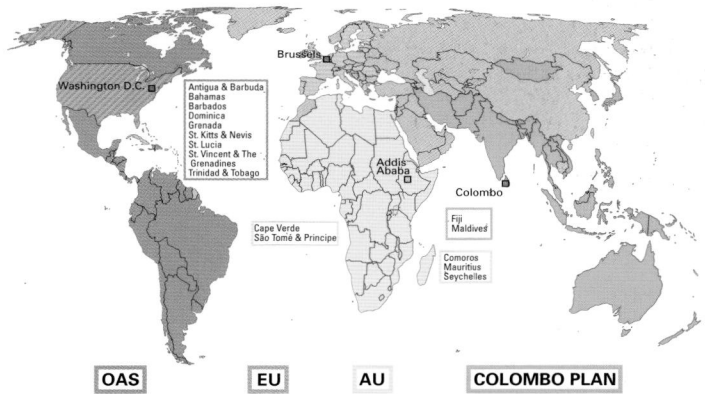

OAS | EU | AU | COLOMBO PLAN

OAS Organization of American States (formed in 1948). It aims to promote social and economic co-operation between developed countries of North America and developing nations of Latin America.
OECD Organization for Economic Co-operation and Development (formed in 1961). It comprises 30 major free-market economies. Poland, Hungary and South Korea joined in 1996, and the Slovak Republic in 2000. 'G8' is its 'inner group' of leading industrial nations, comprising Canada, France, Germany, Italy, Japan, Russia, UK and USA.
OPEC Organization of Petroleum Exporting Countries (formed in 1960). It controls about three-quarters of the world's oil supply. Gabon left the organization in 1996.

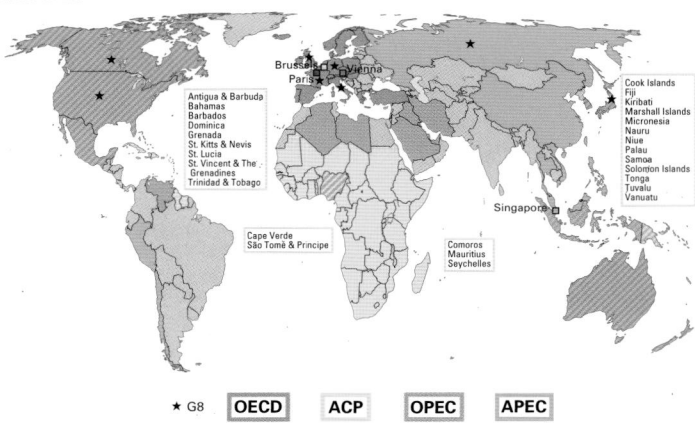

★ G8 | OECD | ACP | OPEC | APEC

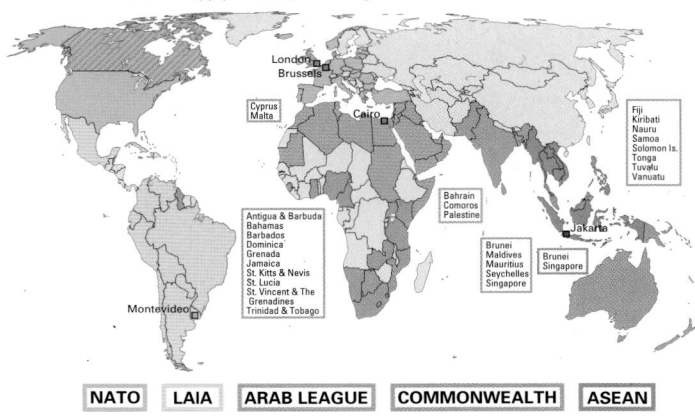

NATO | LAIA | ARAB LEAGUE | COMMONWEALTH | ASEAN

Wealth

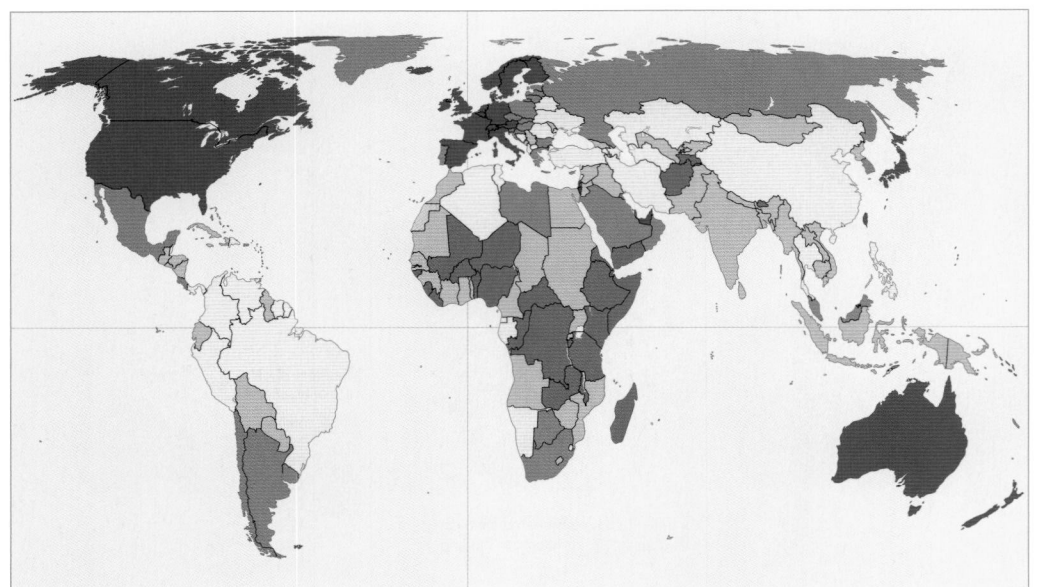

Levels of Income

Gross Domestic Product per capita: the annual value of goods and services divided by the population, using purchasing power parity (PPP) (2006)

- Over 250% of world average
- 100% – 250% of world average

[World average per person US$10,000]

- 50% – 100% of world average
- 15% – 50% of world average
- Under 15% of world average
- No data available

Wealth Creation

The Gross Domestic Product (GDP) of the world's largest economies, US$ million (2006)

1.	USA	12,980,000	23.	Poland	543,000
2.	China	10,000,000	24.	Netherlands	512,000
3.	Japan	4,220,000	25.	Philippines	443,000
4.	India	4,042,000	26.	Pakistan	427,000
5.	Germany	2,585,000	27.	Saudi Arabia	374,000
6.	UK	1,903,000	28.	Colombia	367,000
7.	France	1,871,000	29.	Ukraine	356,000
8.	Italy	1,727,000	30.	Bangladesh	331,000
9.	Russia	1,723,000	31.	Belgium	330,000
10.	Brazil	1,616,000	32.	Egypt	328,000
11.	South Korea	1,180,000	33.	Malaysia	309,000
12.	Canada	1,165,000	34.	Sweden	285,000
13.	Mexico	1,134,000	35.	Austria	280,000
14.	Spain	1,070,000	36.	Vietnam	259,000
15.	Indonesia	935,000	37.	Algeria	253,000
16.	Taiwan	686,000	38.	Hong Kong	253,000
17.	Australia	666,000	39.	Switzerland	253,000
18.	Turkey	627,000	40.	Greece	252,000
19.	Iran	610,000	41.	Czech Republic	221,000
20.	Argentina	599,000	42.	Norway	207,000
21.	Thailand	586,000	43.	Portugal	203,000
22.	South Africa	576,000	44.	Chile	203,000

The Wealth Gap

The world's richest and poorest countries, by Gross Domestic Product per capita in US $ (2006)

Richest countries		Poorest countries	
1. Luxembourg	68,800	1. Somalia	600
2. UAE	49,700	2. Malawi	600
3. Norway	47,800	3. Comoros	600
4. Ireland	43,600	4. Congo (Dem. Rep.)	700
5. USA	43,500	5. Burundi	700
6. Andorra	38,800	6. Tanzania	800
7. Iceland	38,100	7. East Timor	800
8. Denmark	37,000	8. Afghanistan	800
9. Hong Kong (China)	36,500	9. Yemen	900
10. Austria	35,500	10. Sierra Leone	900
11. Canada	35,200	11. Madagascar	900
12. San Marino	34,100	12. Guinea-Bissau	900
13. Switzerland	33,600	13. Zambia	1,000
14. Japan	33,100	14. Niger	1,000
15. Australia	32,900	15. Liberia	1,000
16. Finland	32,800	16. Ethiopia	1,000
17. Belgium	31,800	17. Eritrea	1,000
18. Netherlands	31,700	18. Djibouti	1,000
19. Sweden	31,600	19. Central African Rep.	1,100
20. Germany	31,400	20. Benin	1,100
21. UK	31,400	21. Mali	1,200

Continental Shares

Shares of population and of wealth (GNI) by continent

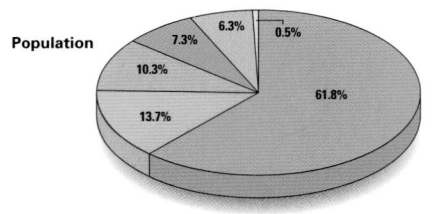

Population

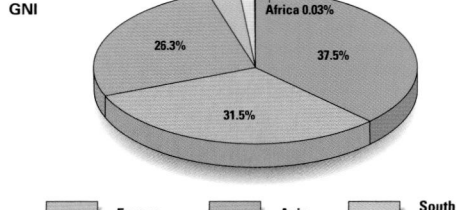

GNI

- Europe
- Asia
- South America
- Australia
- Africa
- North America

Inflation

Average annual rate of inflation (2006)

- Over 20%
- 10% – 20%
- 5% – 10%
- 2.5% – 5%
- Under 2.5%
- No data available

Highest inflation		Lowest inflation	
Zimbabwe	976%	Nauru	–3.6%
Iraq	65%	Vanuatu	–1.6%
Guinea	29%	San Marino	–1.5%
Burma (Myanmar)	21%	Barbados	–0.5%
Congo (Dem. Rep.)	18%	Dominica	–0.1%

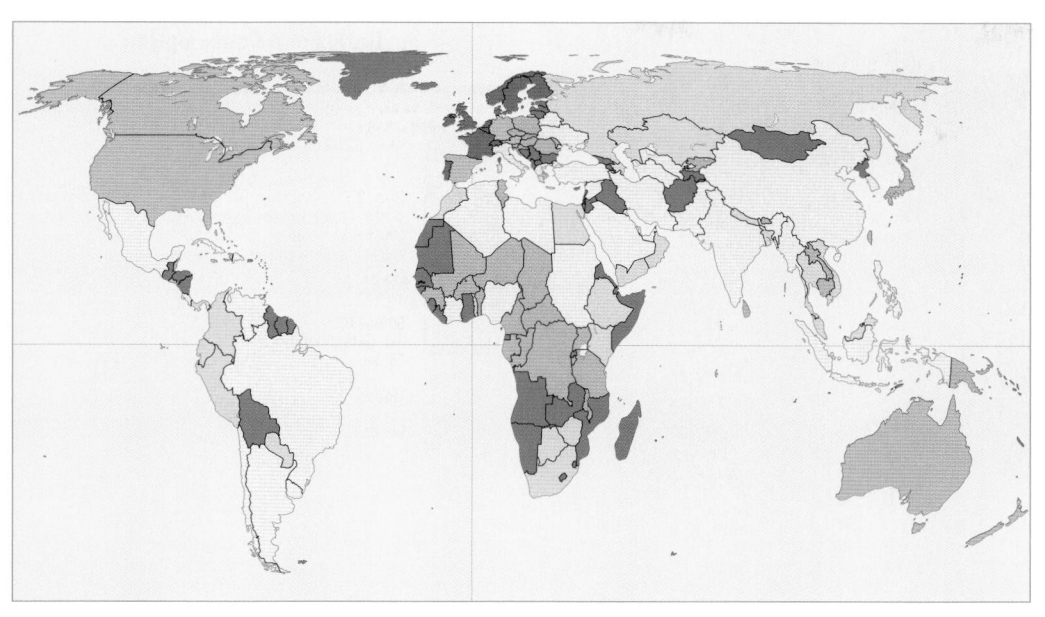

Official Development Assistance (ODA) provided and received, per capita (2004)

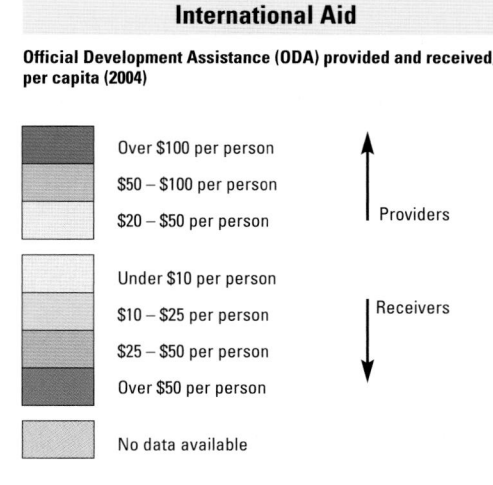

Over $100 per person

$50 – $100 per person

$20 – $50 per person

Providers

Under $10 per person

$10 – $25 per person

$25 – $50 per person

Over $50 per person

Receivers

No data available

Debt and Aid

International debtors and the aid they receive

Although aid grants make a vital contribution to many of the world's poorer countries, they are usually dwarfed by the burden of debt that the developing economies are expected to repay. It is estimated that the total debt burden of developing countries is US$523 billion.

Debt, US $ per capita (2004)

Aid, US $ per capita (2004)

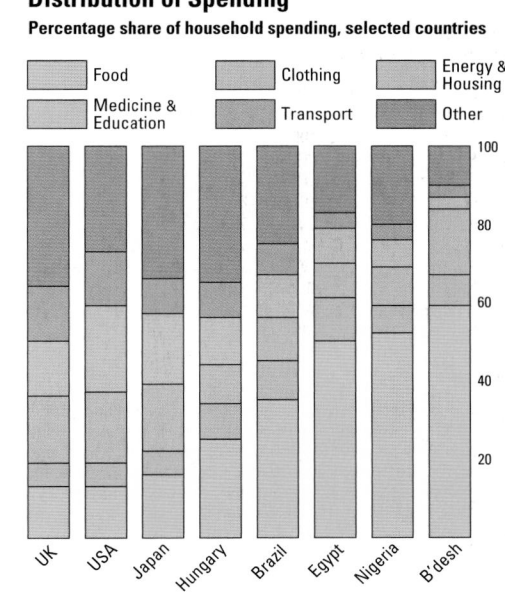

Distribution of Spending

Percentage share of household spending, selected countries

Food

Clothing

Energy & Housing

Medicine & Education

Transport

Other

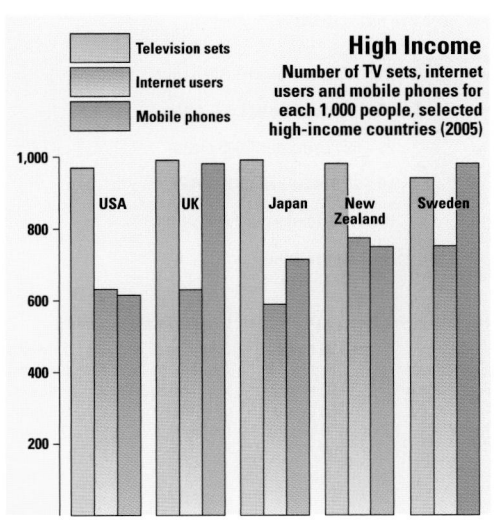

High Income

Television sets

Internet users

Mobile phones

Number of TV sets, internet users and mobile phones for each 1,000 people, selected high-income countries (2005)

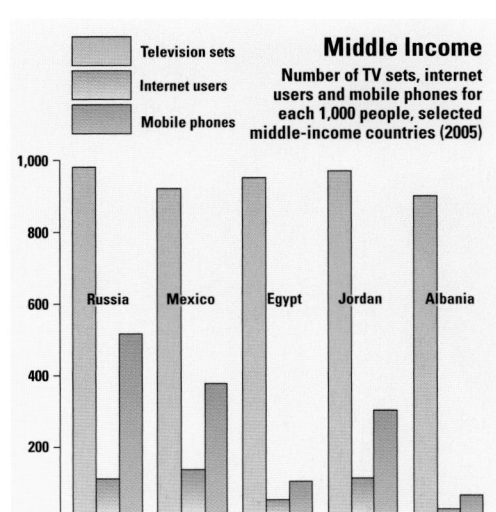

Middle Income

Television sets

Internet users

Mobile phones

Number of TV sets, internet users and mobile phones for each 1,000 people, selected middle-income countries (2005)

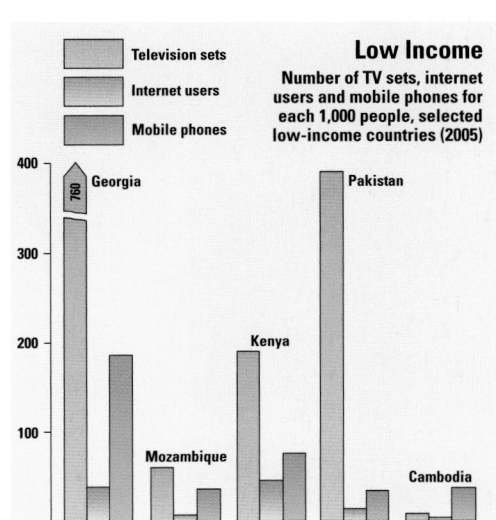

Low Income

Television sets

Internet users

Mobile phones

Number of TV sets, internet users and mobile phones for each 1,000 people, selected low-income countries (2005)

Quality of Life

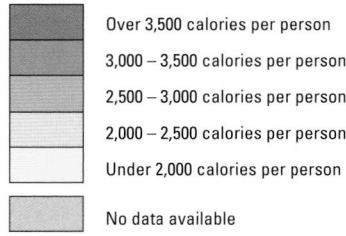

Daily Food Consumption

Average daily food intake in calories per person (2003)

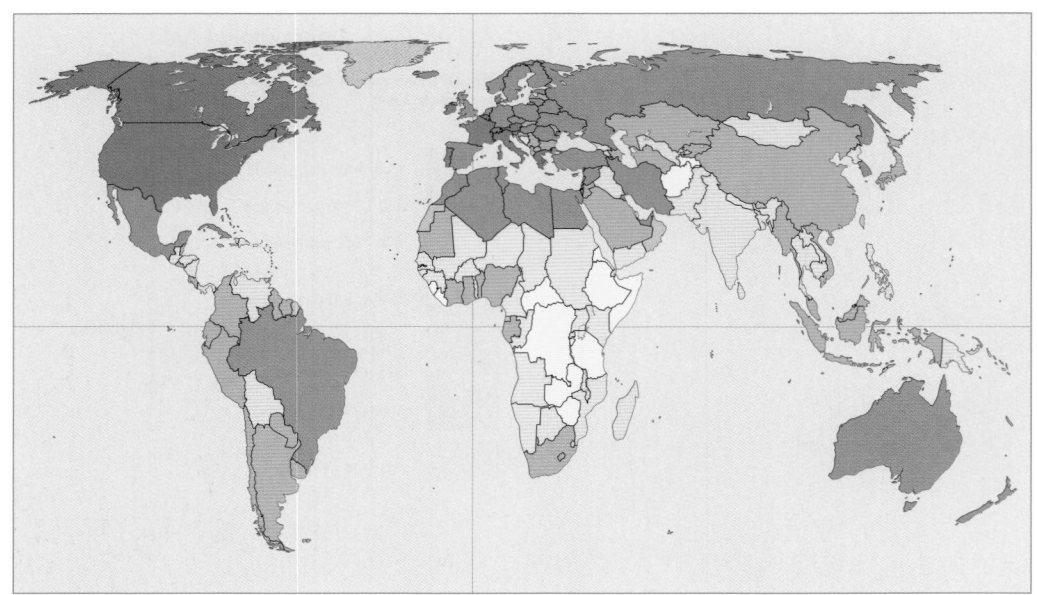

- Over 3,500 calories per person
- 3,000 – 3,500 calories per person
- 2,500 – 3,000 calories per person
- 2,000 – 2,500 calories per person
- Under 2,000 calories per person
- No data available

Hospital Capacity

Hospital beds available for each 1,000 people (2003)

Highest capacity		Lowest capacity	
Monaco	19.6	Nepal	0.2
Japan	14.7	Bangladesh	0.3
North Korea	13.6	Somalia	0.4
Niue	13.0	Afghanistan	0.4
Belarus	11.3	Guatemala	0.5
Russia	10.5	Cambodia	0.5
Germany	8.9	Yemen	0.6
Ukraine	8.8	Burma (Myanmar)	0.6
Lithuania	8.7	Sudan	0.7
Czech Republic	8.6	Pakistan	0.7

Although the ratio of people to hospital beds gives a good approximation of a country's health provision, it is not an absolute indicator. Raw numbers may mask inefficiency and other weaknesses: the high availability of beds in Belarus, for example, has not prevented infant mortality rates over three times as high as in the United Kingdom and the United States.

Life Expectancy

Years of life expectancy at birth, selected countries (2005)

The chart shows combined data for both sexes. On average, women live longer than men worldwide, even in developing countries with high maternal mortality rates. Overall, life expectancy is steadily rising, though the difference between rich and poor nations remains dramatic.

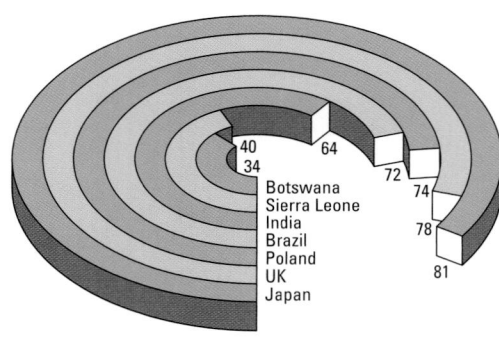

40
34
64
72
74
78
81

Botswana
Sierra Leone
India
Brazil
Poland
UK
Japan

Causes of Death

Causes of death for selected countries by percentage

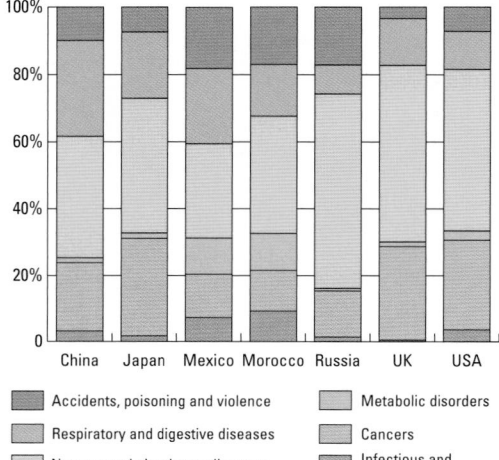

China Japan Mexico Morocco Russia UK USA

- Accidents, poisoning and violence
- Respiratory and digestive diseases
- Nervous and circulatory diseases
- Metabolic disorders
- Cancers
- Infectious and parasitic diseases

Infant Mortality

Number of babies who died under the age of one, per 1,000 live births (2006)

- Over 100 deaths per 1,000 births
- 50 – 100 deaths per 1,000 births
- 25 – 50 deaths per 1,000 births
- 10 – 25 deaths per 1,000 births
- Under 10 deaths per 1,000 births
- No data available

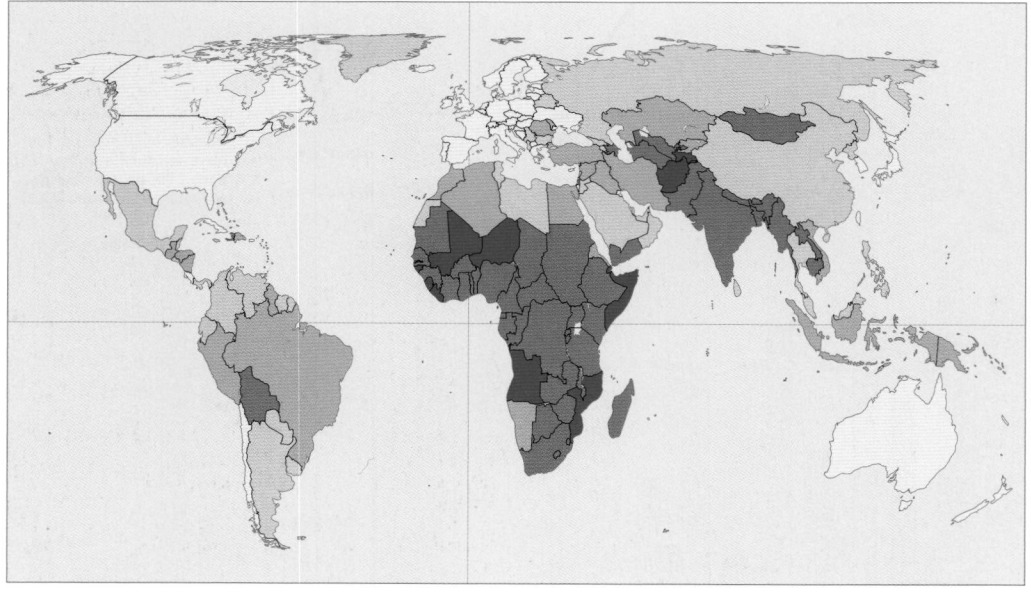

Highest infant mortality		Lowest infant mortality	
Angola	185 deaths	Singapore	2 deaths
Sierra Leone	160 deaths	Sweden	3 deaths
Afghanistan	160 deaths	Hong Kong (China)	3 deaths
Liberia	156 deaths	Japan	3 deaths
Niger	118 deaths	Iceland	3 deaths

Illiteracy

Percentage of the total adult population unable to read or write (2004)

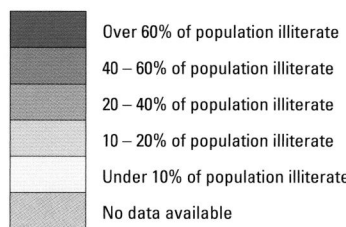

- Over 60% of population illiterate
- 40 – 60% of population illiterate
- 20 – 40% of population illiterate
- 10 – 20% of population illiterate
- Under 10% of population illiterate
- No data available

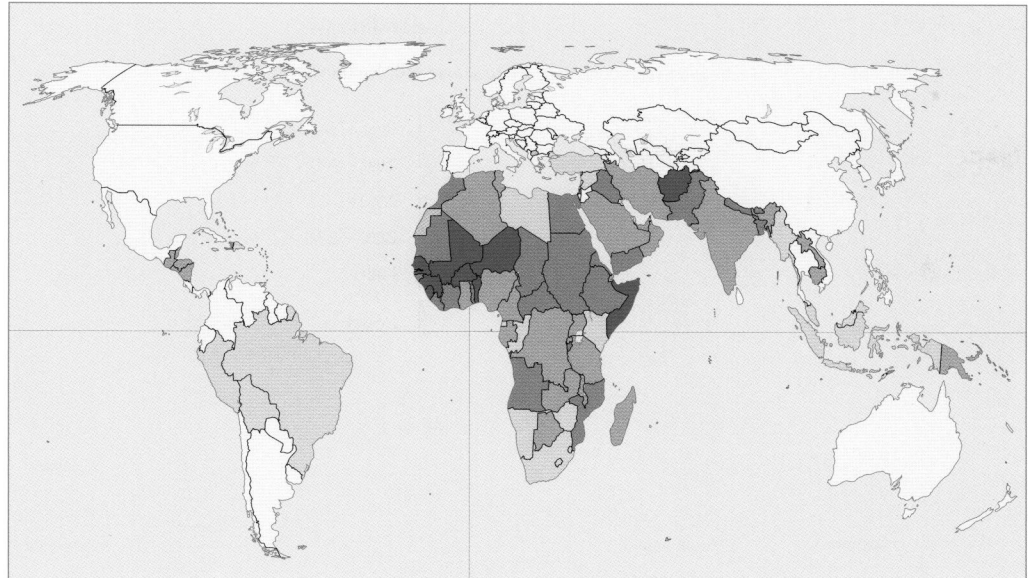

Countries with the highest and lowest illiteracy rates

Highest		Lowest	
Burkina Faso	87	Australia	0
Niger	83	Denmark	0
Mali	81	Finland	0
Sierra Leone	69	Liechtenstein	0
Guinea	64	Luxembourg	0

Fertility and Education

Fertility rates compared with female education, selected countries (2000–05)

- Percentage of females aged 12–17 in secondary education
- Fertility rate: average number of children borne per woman

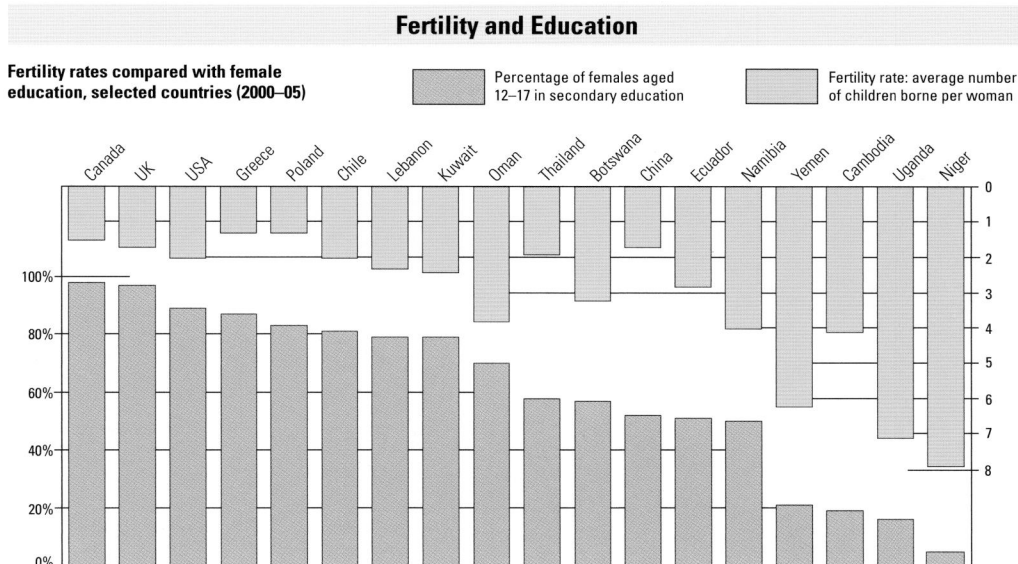

Living Standards

At first sight, most international contrasts in living standards are swamped by differences in wealth. The rich not only have more money, they have more of everything, including years of life. Those with only a little money are obliged to spend most of it on food and clothing, the basic maintenance costs of their existence; air travel and tourism are unlikely to feature on their expenditure lists. However, poverty and wealth are both relative: slum dwellers living on social security payments in an affluent industrial country have far more resources at their disposal than an average African peasant, but feel their own poverty nonetheless. A middle-class Indian lawyer cannot command a fraction of the earnings of a counterpart living in New York, London or Rome; nevertheless, he rightly sees himself as prosperous.

The rich not only live longer, on average, than the poor, they also die from different causes. Infectious and parasitic diseases, all but eliminated in the developed world, remain a scourge in the developing nations. On the other hand, more than two-thirds of the populations of OECD nations eventually succumb to cancer or circulatory disease.

Human Development Index

The Human Development Index (HDI), calculated by the UN Development Programme, gives a value to countries using indicators of life expectancy, education and standards of living (2004). Higher values show more developed countries.

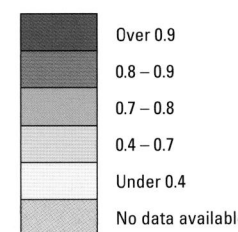

- Over 0.9
- 0.8 – 0.9
- 0.7 – 0.8
- 0.4 – 0.7
- Under 0.4
- No data available

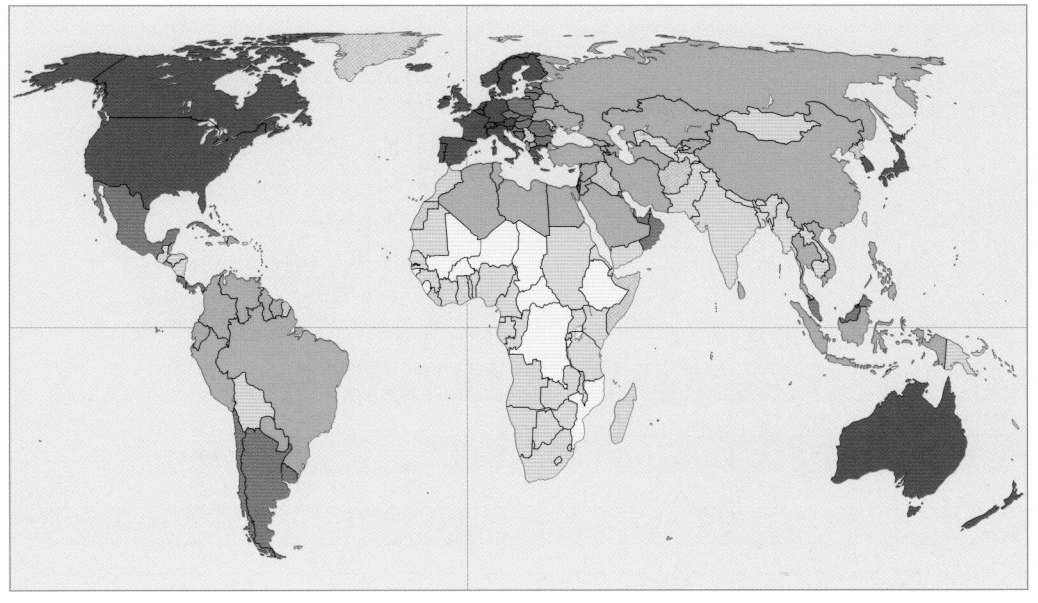

Highest values		Lowest values	
Norway	0.965	Niger	0.311
Iceland	0.960	Sierra Leone	0.335
Australia	0.957	Mali	0.338
Ireland	0.956	Burkina Faso	0.342
Sweden	0.951	Guinea-Bissau	0.349

Energy

Production

Each square represents 1% of world energy production (2005)

North America

Europe

Russia

Middle East

Asia

Japan

Africa

South America

Australasia

Consumption

Each square represents 1% of world energy consumption (2005)

North America

Europe

Russia

Middle East

Asia

Africa

South America

Japan

Australasia

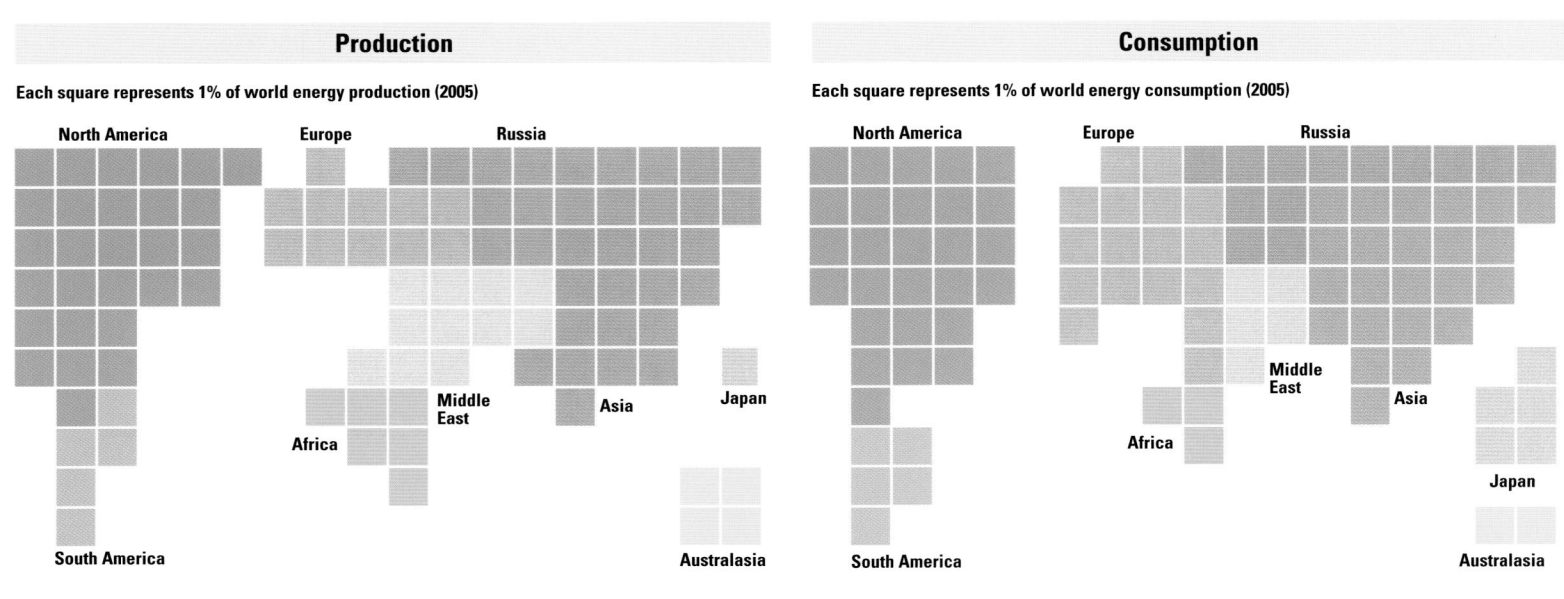

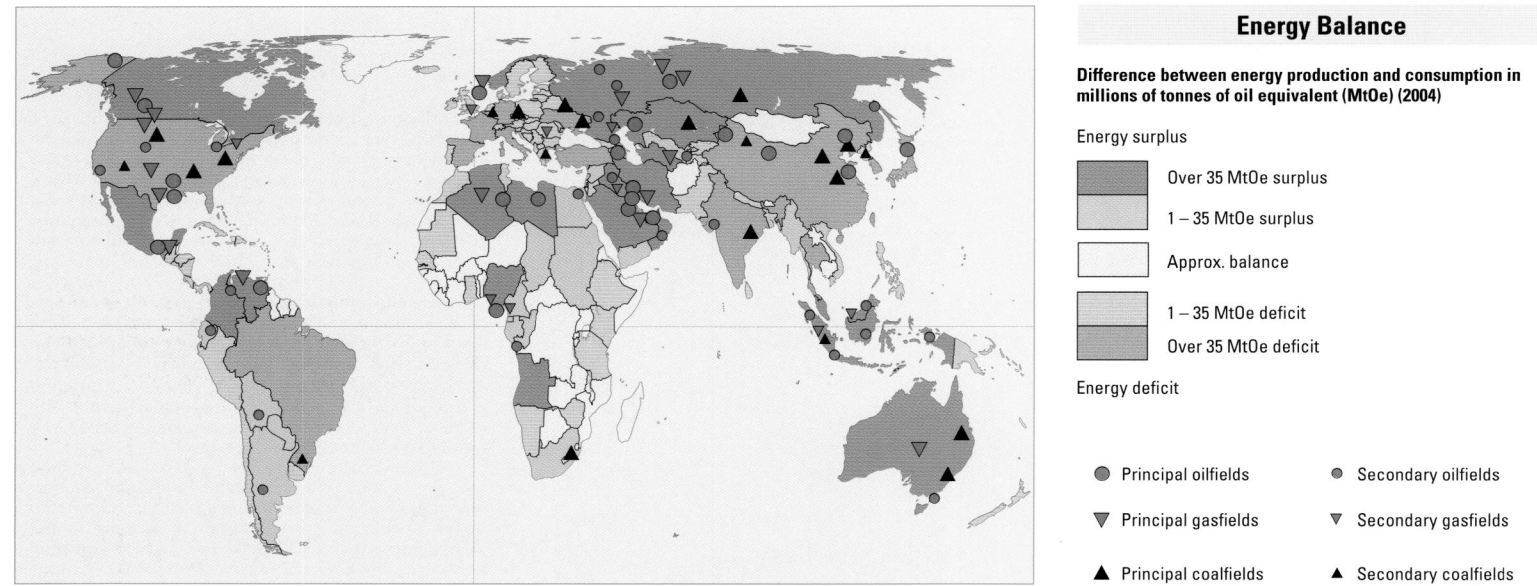

Energy Balance

Difference between energy production and consumption in millions of tonnes of oil equivalent (MtOe) (2004)

Energy surplus

Over 35 MtOe surplus

1 – 35 MtOe surplus

Approx. balance

1 – 35 MtOe deficit

Over 35 MtOe deficit

Energy deficit

- ● Principal oilfields   ● Secondary oilfields
- ▼ Principal gasfields   ▼ Secondary gasfields
- ▲ Principal coalfields   ▲ Secondary coalfields

World Energy Consumption

Energy consumed by world regions, measured in million tonnes of oil equivalent in 2005. Total world consumption was 10,537 MtOe. Only energy from oil, gas, coal, nuclear and hydroelectric sources are included. Excluded are fuels such as wood, peat, animal waste, wind, solar and geothermal which, though important in some countries, are unreliably documented in terms of consumption statistics.

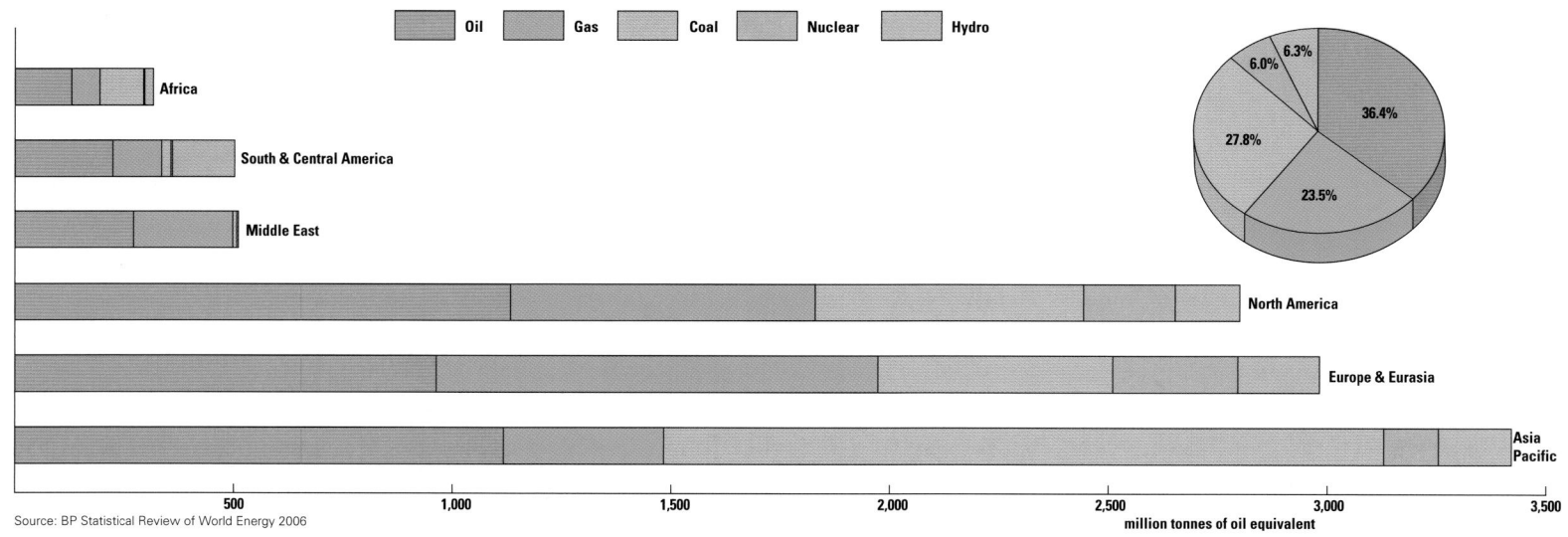

Oil   Gas   Coal   Nuclear   Hydro

Africa

South & Central America

Middle East

North America

Europe & Eurasia

Asia Pacific

6.3%
6.0%
36.4%
27.8%
23.5%

500   1,000   1,500   2,000   2,500   3,000   3,500

million tonnes of oil equivalent

Source: BP Statistical Review of World Energy 2006

Energy

Energy is used to keep us warm or cool, fuel our industries and our transport systems, and even feed us; high-intensity agriculture, with its use of fertilizers, pesticides and machinery, is heavily energy-dependent. Although we live in a high-energy society, there are vast discrepancies between rich and poor; for example, a North American consumes 13 times as much energy as a Chinese person. But even developing nations have more power at their disposal than was imaginable a century ago.

The distribution of energy supplies, most importantly fossil fuels (coal, oil and natural gas), is very uneven. In addition, the diagrams and map opposite show that the largest producers of energy are not necessarily the largest consumers. The movement of energy supplies around the world is therefore an important component of international trade. In 2005, total world movements in oil amounted to 2,462 million tonnes.

As the finite reserves of fossil fuels are depleted, renewable energy sources, such as solar, hydro-thermal, wind, tidal and biomass, will become increasingly important around the world.

Nuclear Power

Major producers by percentage of world total and by percentage of domestic electricity generation (2004)

Country	% of world total production	Country	% of nuclear as proportion of domestic electricity
1. USA	30.1%	1. Lithuania	80.6%
2. France	16.3%	2. France	78.8%
3. Japan	10.4%	3. Belgium	57.1%
4. Germany	6.1%	4. Slovak Rep.	56.2%
5. Russia	5.2%	5. Sweden	58.8%
6. South Korea	4.7%	6. Ukraine	45.9%
7. Canada	3.3%	7. Switzerland	41.3%
8. Ukraine	3.2%	8. Armenia	38.6%
9. UK	2.8%	9. Bulgaria	37.2%
= Sweden	2.8%	10. South Korea	36.0%

Although the 1980s were a bad time for the nuclear power industry (major projects ran over budget and fears of long-term environmental damage were heavily reinforced by the 1986 disaster at Chernobyl), the industry picked up in the early 1990s. Whilst the number of reactors is still increasing, however, orders for new plants have shrunk. Sixteen countries currently rely on nuclear power to supply over 25% of their electricity requirements.

Hydroelectricity

Major producers by percentage of world total and by percentage of domestic electricity generation (2004)

Country	% of world total production	Country	% of hydroelectric as proportion of domestic electricity
1. Canada	12.2%	1. Bhutan	100%
2. China	11.9%	= Paraguay	100%
3. Brazil	11.6%	= Lesotho	100%
4. USA	9.8%	4. Mozambique	99.8%
5. Russia	6.0%	5. Congo	99.7%
6. Norway	3.9%	= Congo (Dem. Rep.)	99.7%
7. Japan	3.4%	= Uganda	99.7%
8. India	3.0%	8. Nepal	99.6%
9. Sweden	2.3%	9. Zambia	99.5%
10. France	2.2%	10. Norway	98.8%

Countries heavily reliant on hydroelectricity are usually small and non-industrial: a high proportion of hydroelectric power more often reflects a modest energy budget than vast hydroelectric resources. The USA, for instance, produces only 6.7% of its power requirements from hydroelectricity; yet that 6.7% amounts to more than seven times the hydropower generated by most of Africa.

Fuel Exports

Fuels as a percentage of total value of exports (2004)

- Over 75%
- 50 – 75%
- 10 – 50%
- Under 10%
- No data available

In the 1970s, oil exports became a political issue when OPEC sought to increase the influence of developing countries in world affairs by raising oil prices and restricting production. But its power was short-lived, following a fall in demand for oil in the 1980s, due to an increase in energy efficiency and development of alternative resources. However, with the heavy energy demands of the Asian economies early in the 21st century, both oil and gas prices have risen sharply.

Conversion Rates

1 barrel = 0.136 tonnes or 159 litres or 35 Imperial gallons or 42 US gallons

1 tonne = 7.33 barrels or 1,185 litres or 256 Imperial gallons or 261 US gallons

1 tonne oil = 1.5 tonnes hard coal or 3.0 tonnes lignite or 12,000 kWh

1 Imperial gallon = 1.201 US gallons or 4.546 litres or 277.4 cubic inches

Measurements

For historical reasons, oil is traded in 'barrels'. The weight and volume equivalents (shown right) are all based on average-density 'Arabian light' crude oil.

The energy equivalents given for a tonne of oil are also somewhat imprecise: oil and coal of different qualities will have varying energy contents, a fact usually reflected in their price on world markets.

World Coal Reserves

World coal reserves (including lignite) by region and country, thousand million tonnes (2005)

World total: 901.1 thousand million tonnes

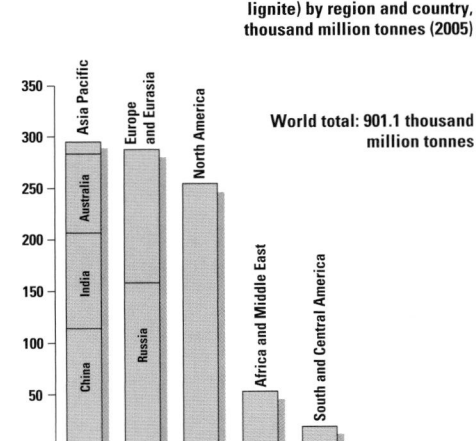

World Gas Reserves

World natural gas reserves by region and country, thousand million tonnes of oil equivalent (2005)

World total: 165.1 thousand million tonnes of oil equivalent

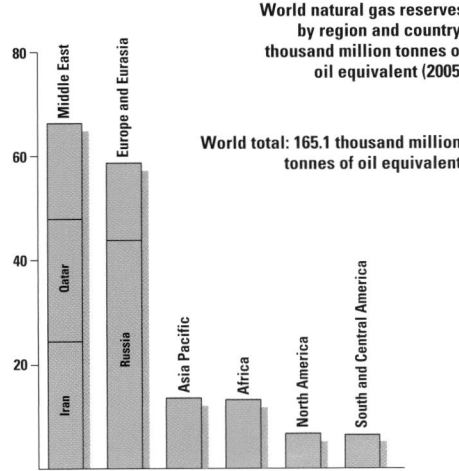

World Oil Reserves

World oil reserves by region and country, thousand million tonnes (2005)

World total: 163.6 thousand million tonnes

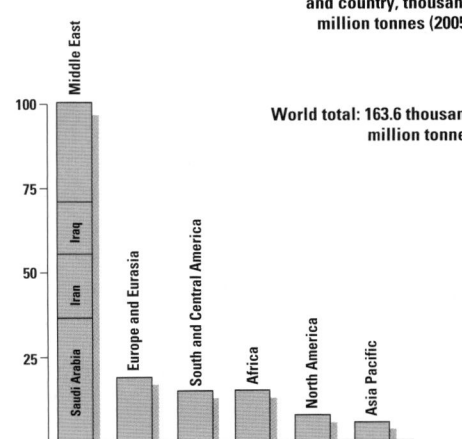

Production

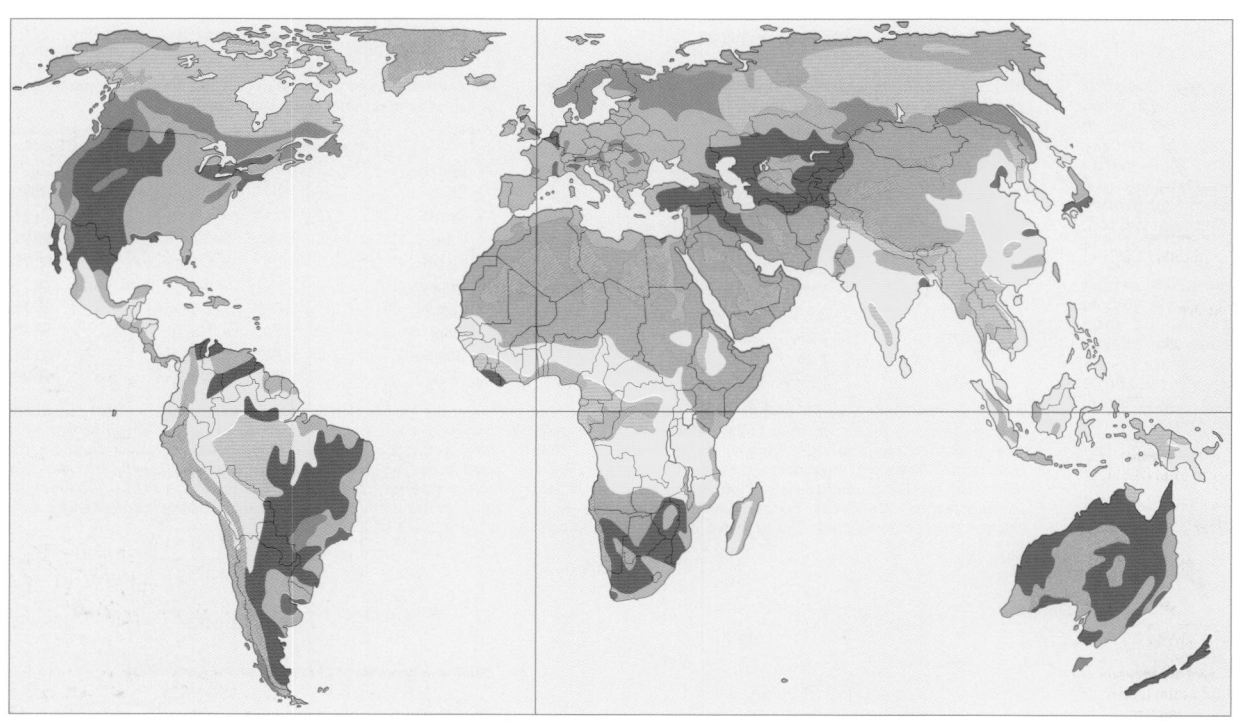

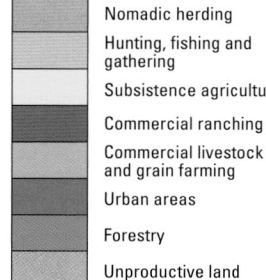
The development of agriculture has transformed human existence more than any other. The whole business of farming is constantly developing: due mainly to the new varieties of rice and wheat, world grain production has more than doubled since 1965. New machinery and modern agricultural techniques enable relatively few farmers to produce enough food for the world's 6 billion or so people.

Staple Crops

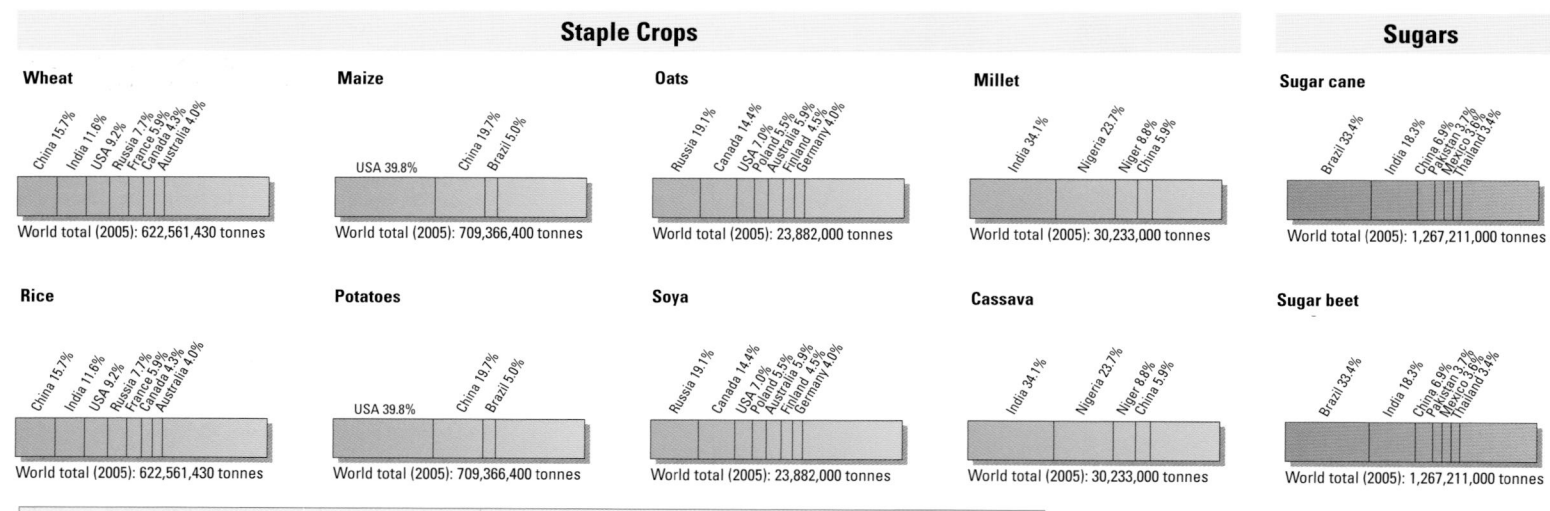

Wheat

China 15.7% | India 11.6% | USA 9.2% | Russia 7.7% | France 5.9% | Canada 4.3% | Australia 4.0%

World total (2005): 622,561,430 tonnes

Maize

USA 39.8% | China 19.7% | Brazil 5.0%

World total (2005): 709,366,400 tonnes

Oats

Russia 19.1% | Canada 14.4% | USA 7.0% | Poland 5.5% | Australia 5.9% | Finland 4.5% | Germany 4.0%

World total (2005): 23,882,000 tonnes

Millet

India 34.1% | Nigeria 23.7% | Niger 8.8% | China 5.9%

World total (2005): 30,233,000 tonnes

Rice

China 15.7% | India 11.6% | USA 9.2% | Russia 7.7% | France 5.9% | Canada 4.3% | Australia 4.0%

World total (2005): 622,561,430 tonnes

Potatoes

USA 39.8% | China 19.7% | Brazil 5.0%

World total (2005): 709,366,400 tonnes

Soya

Russia 19.1% | Canada 14.4% | USA 7.0% | Poland 5.5% | Australia 3.9% | Finland 4.5% | Germany 4.0%

World total (2005): 23,882,000 tonnes

Cassava

India 34.1% | Nigeria 23.7% | Niger 8.8% | China 5.9%

World total (2005): 30,233,000 tonnes

Sugars

Sugar cane

Brazil 33.4% | India 18.3% | China 6.9% | Pakistan 3.7% | Mexico 3.6% | Thailand 3.4%

World total (2005): 1,267,211,000 tonnes

Sugar beet

Brazil 33.4% | India 18.3% | China 6.9% | Pakistan 3.7% | Mexico 3.6% | Thailand 3.4%

World total (2005): 1,267,211,000 tonnes

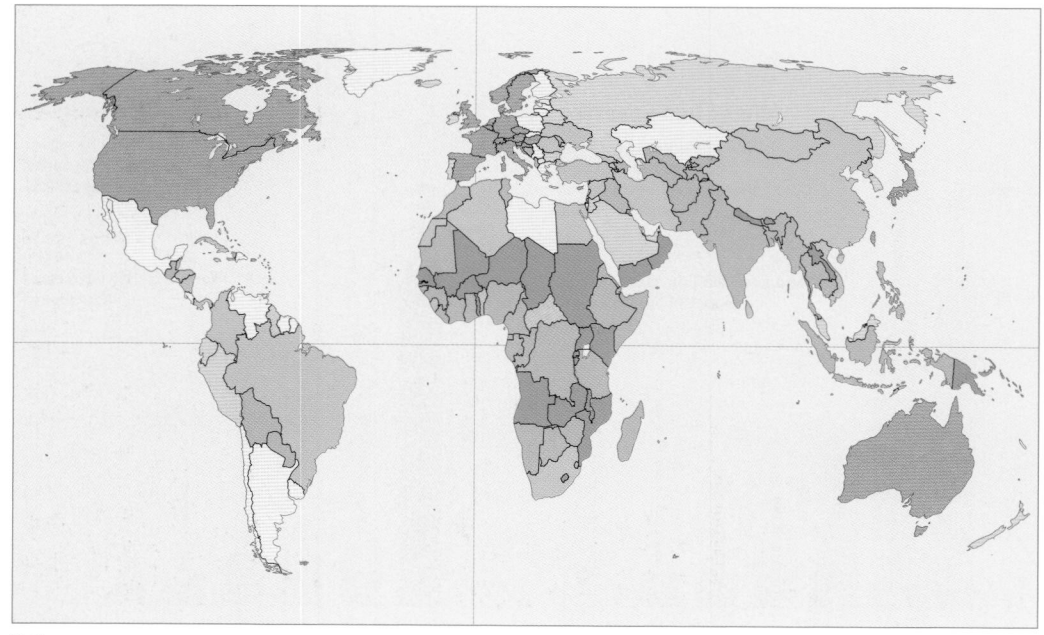

Employment

The number of workers employed in manufacturing for every 100 workers engaged in agriculture (2005)

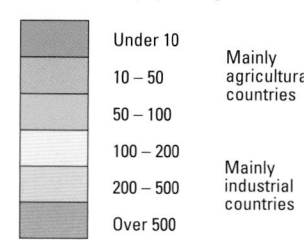

Under 10 — Mainly agricultural countries
10 – 50
50 – 100
100 – 200 — Mainly industrial countries
200 – 500
Over 500

Countries with the highest and lowest number of workers employed in manufacturing per 100 workers engaged in agriculture (2005)

Highest		Lowest	
Bahrain	7,900	Burundi	2.5
San Marino	4,200	Yemen	5.0
Micronesia	3,822	Oman	5.0
USA	3,271	Rwanda	5.6
Liechtenstein	2,350	Malawi	5.6

Mineral Production

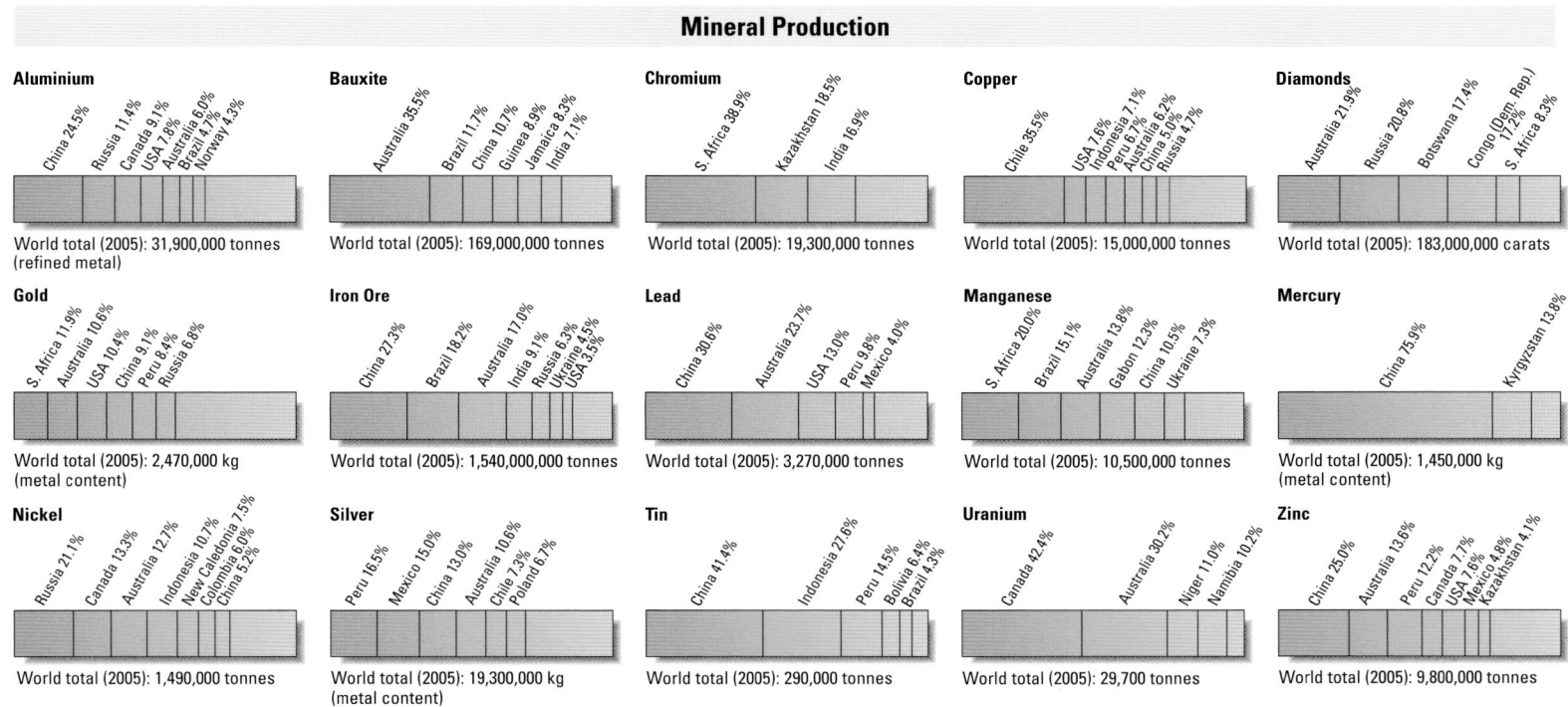

Aluminium
China 24.5% · Russia 11.4% · Canada 9.1% · USA 7.8% · Australia 6.0% · Brazil 4.7% · Norway 4.3%
World total (2005): 31,900,000 tonnes (refined metal)

Bauxite
Australia 35.5% · Brazil 11.7% · China 10.7% · Guinea 8.9% · Jamaica 8.3% · India 7.1%
World total (2005): 169,000,000 tonnes

Chromium
S. Africa 38.9% · Kazakhstan 18.5% · India 16.9%
World total (2005): 19,300,000 tonnes

Copper
Chile 35.5% · USA 7.6% · Indonesia 7.1% · Peru 6.7% · Australia 6.2% · China 5.0% · Russia 4.7%
World total (2005): 15,000,000 tonnes

Diamonds
Australia 21.9% · Russia 20.8% · Botswana 17.4% · Congo (Dem. Rep.) 11.2% · S. Africa 8.3%
World total (2005): 183,000,000 carats

Gold
S. Africa 11.9% · Australia 10.6% · USA 10.4% · China 9.1% · Peru 8.4% · Russia 6.8%
World total (2005): 2,470,000 kg (metal content)

Iron Ore
China 27.3% · Brazil 18.2% · Australia 17.0% · India 9.1% · Russia 6.3% · Ukraine 4.5% · USA 3.5%
World total (2005): 1,540,000,000 tonnes

Lead
China 30.6% · Australia 23.7% · USA 13.0% · Peru 9.6% · Mexico 4.0%
World total (2005): 3,270,000 tonnes

Manganese
S. Africa 20.0% · Brazil 15.1% · Australia 13.8% · Gabon 12.3% · China 10.5% · Ukraine 7.3%
World total (2005): 10,500,000 tonnes

Mercury
China 75.9% · Kyrgyzstan 13.8%
World total (2005): 1,450,000 kg (metal content)

Nickel
Russia 21.1% · Canada 13.3% · Australia 12.7% · Indonesia 10.7% · New Caledonia 7.5% · Colombia 6.0% · China 5.2%
World total (2005): 1,490,000 tonnes

Silver
Peru 16.5% · Mexico 15.0% · China 13.0% · Australia 10.6% · Chile 7.3% · Poland 6.7%
World total (2005): 19,300,000 kg (metal content)

Tin
China 41.4% · Indonesia 27.6% · Peru 14.5% · Bolivia 6.4% · Brazil 4.3%
World total (2005): 290,000 tonnes

Uranium
Canada 42.4% · Australia 30.2% · Niger 11.0% · Namibia 10.22%
World total (2005): 29,700 tonnes

Zinc
China 25.0% · Australia 13.6% · Peru 12.2% · Canada 7.7% · USA 7.6% · Mexico 4.6% · Kazakhstan 4.1%
World total (2005): 9,800,000 tonnes

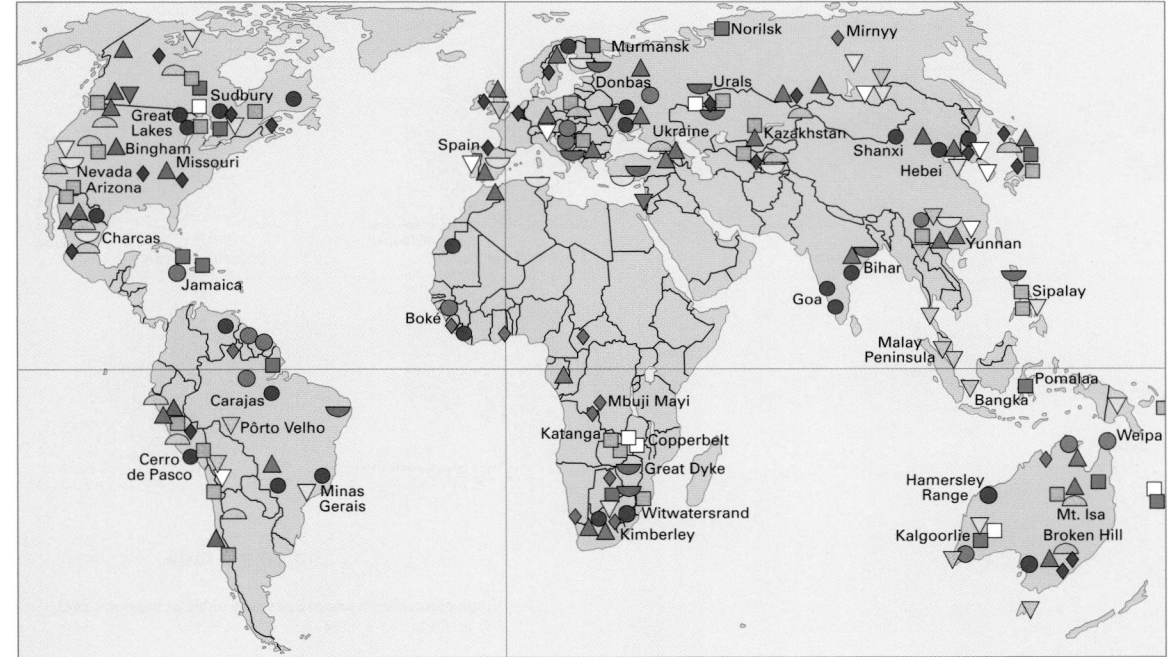

Mineral Distribution

The map shows the richest sources of the most important minerals (major mineral locations are named)

- Bauxite
- Chromium
- Cobalt
- Copper
- Diamonds
- Gold
- Iron ore
- Lead
- Manganese
- Mercury
- Molybdenum
- Nickel
- Potash
- Silver
- Tin
- Tungsten
- Zinc

The map does not show undersea deposits, most of which are considered inaccessible.

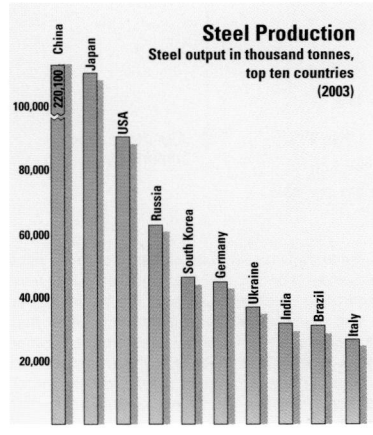

Steel Production
Steel output in thousand tonnes, top ten countries (2003)

China 220,100 · Japan · USA · Russia · South Korea · Germany · Ukraine · India · Brazil · Italy

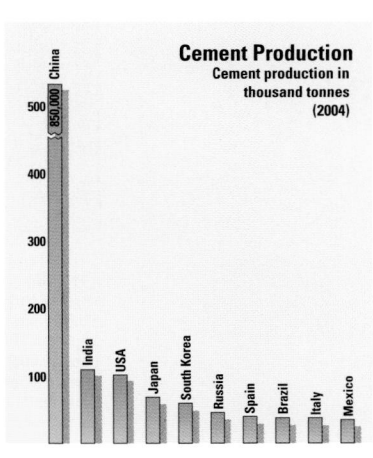

Cement Production
Cement production in thousand tonnes (2004)

China 850,000 · India · USA · Japan · South Korea · Russia · Spain · Brazil · Italy · Mexico

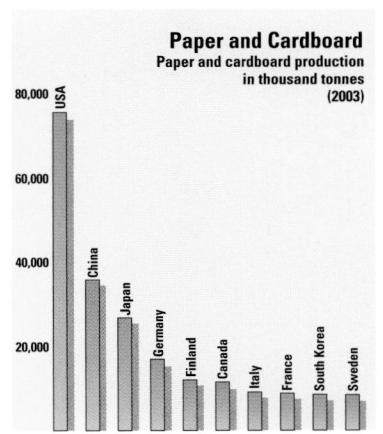

Paper and Cardboard
Paper and cardboard production in thousand tonnes (2003)

USA · China · Japan · Germany · Finland · Canada · Italy · France · South Korea · Sweden

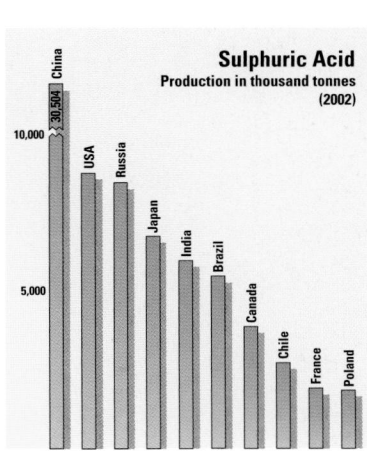

Sulphuric Acid
Production in thousand tonnes (2002)

China 30,504 · USA · Russia · Japan · India · Brazil · Canada · Chile · France · Poland

Trade

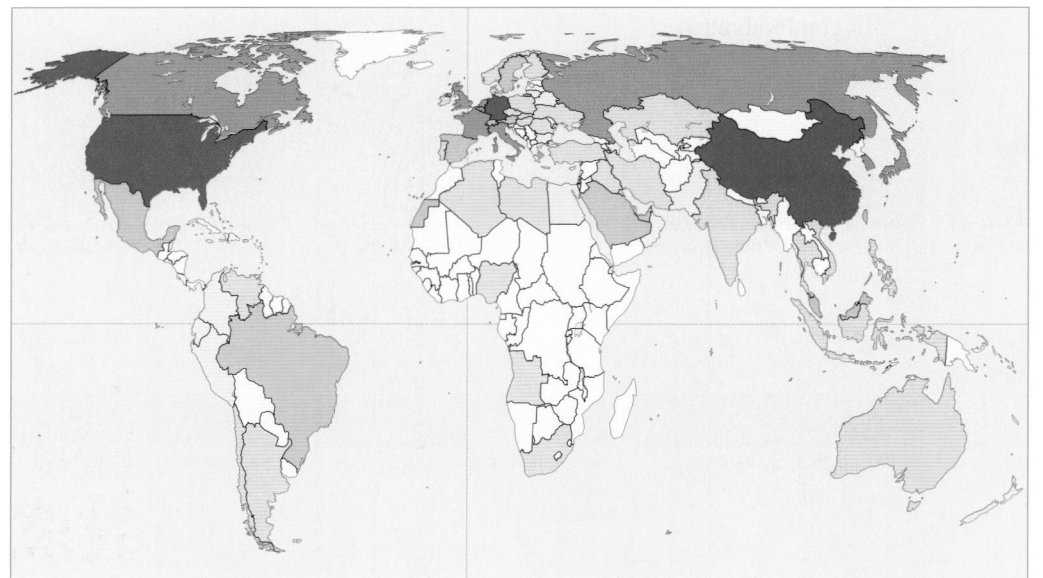

Share of World Trade

Percentage share of total world exports by value (2006)

- Over 5% of world trade
- 2.5 – 5% of world trade
- 1 – 2.5% of world trade
- 0.25 – 1% of world trade
- 0.1 – 0.25% of world trade
- Under 0.1% of world trade
- No data available

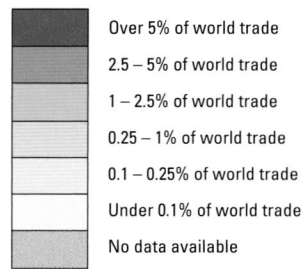

Largest share of world trade		Smallest share of world trade	
Germany	.9.1%	East Timor	.0.0%
USA	.8.2%	Eritrea	.0.0%
China	.7.8%	Burundi	.0.0%
Hong Kong (China)	.4.9%	Rwanda	.0.0%
Japan	.4.8%	Guinea-Bissau	.0.0%

The Main Trading Nations

The imports and exports of the top ten trading nations as a percentage of world trade (2006). Each country's trade in manufactured goods is shown in dark blue

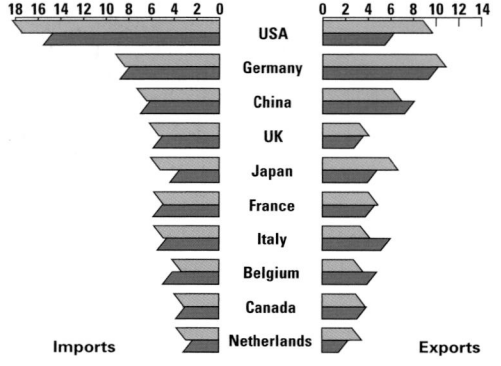

Major exports

Leading manufactured items and their exporters (2004)

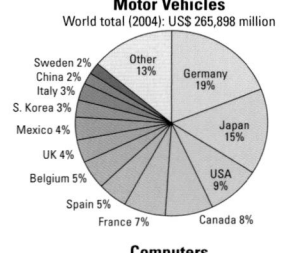

Motor Vehicles
World total (2004): US$ 265,898 million

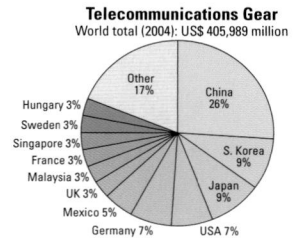

Telecommunications Gear
World total (2004): US$ 405,989 million

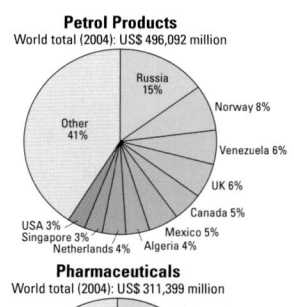

Petrol Products
World total (2004): US$ 496,092 million

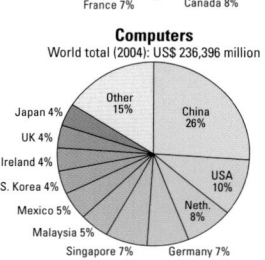

Computers
World total (2004): US$ 236,396 million

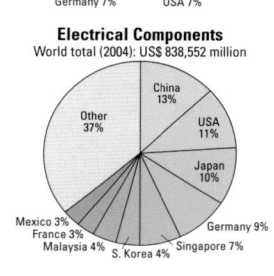

Electrical Components
World total (2004): US$ 838,552 million

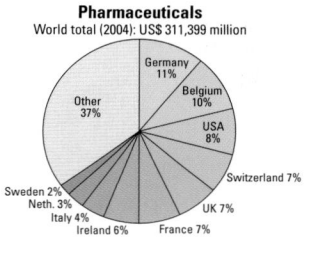

Pharmaceuticals
World total (2004): US$ 311,399 million

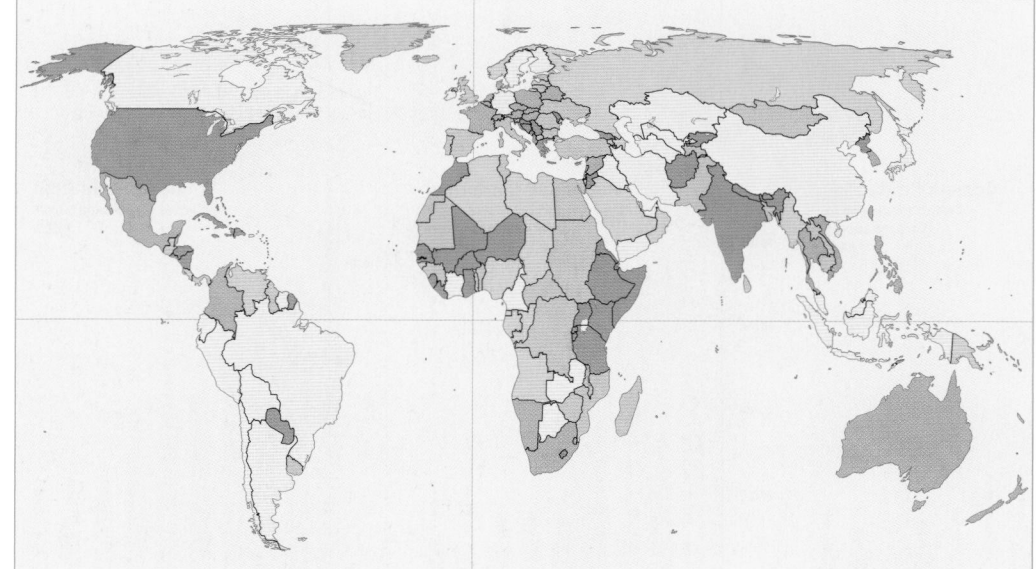

Balance of Trade

Value of exports in proportion to the value of imports (2006)

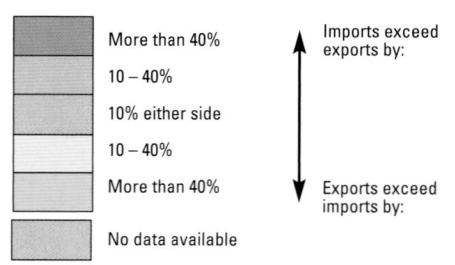

- More than 40%
- 10 – 40%
- 10% either side
- 10 – 40%
- More than 40%
- No data available

Imports exceed exports by:

Exports exceed imports by:

The total world trade balance should amount to zero, since exports must equal imports on a global scale. In practice, at least $100 billion in exports go unrecorded, leaving the world with an apparent deficit and many countries in a better position than public accounting reveals. However, a favourable trade balance is not necessarily a sign of prosperity: many poorer countries must maintain a high surplus in order to service debts, and do so by restricting imports below the levels needed to sustain successful economies.

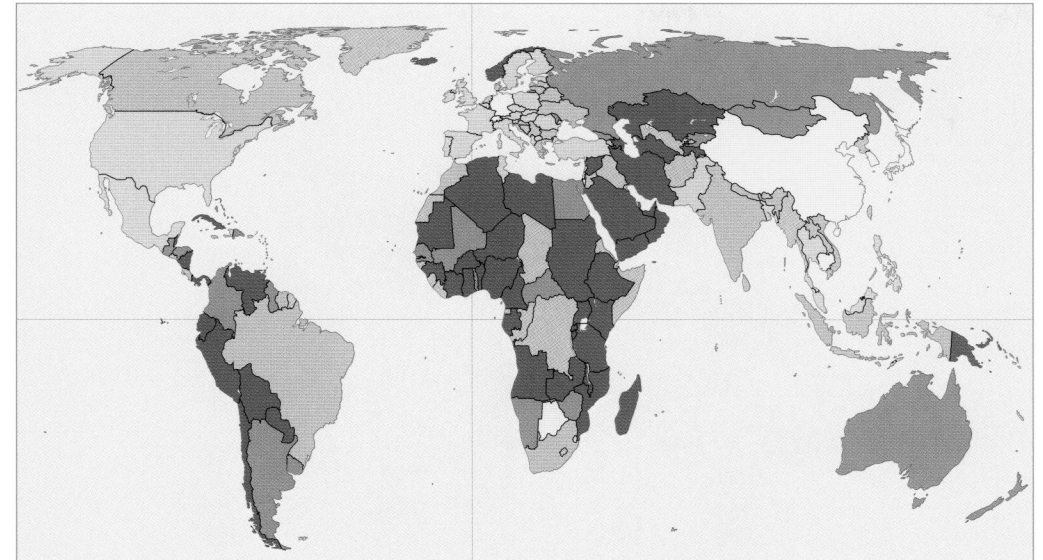

Trade in Primary Exports

Primary exports as a percentage of total export value (2004)

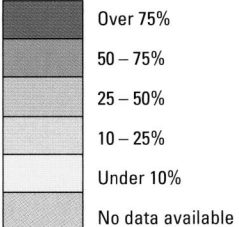

- Over 75%
- 50 – 75%
- 25 – 50%
- 10 – 25%
- Under 10%
- No data available

Primary exports are raw materials or partly processed products that form the basis for manufacturing. They are the necessary requirements of industries and include agricultural products, minerals, fuels and timber, as well as many semi-manufactured goods such as cotton, which has been spun but not woven, wood pulp or flour. Many developed countries have few natural resources and rely on imports for the majority of their primary products. The countries of South-east Asia export hardwoods to the rest of the world, while many South American countries are heavily dependent on coffee exports.

Merchant Fleets

Merchant fleets in thousand gross registered tonnage (2006). Although a large number of vessels are registered in Liberia and Panama, they are not part of the national fleet

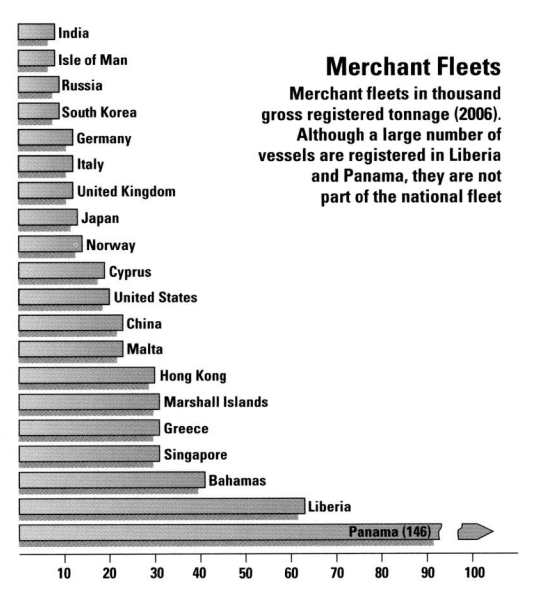

Top Ten Ports

Total container traffic, in million TEU (2004) ('TEU' stands for Twenty-foot Equivalent Unit, the equivalent of a standard container)

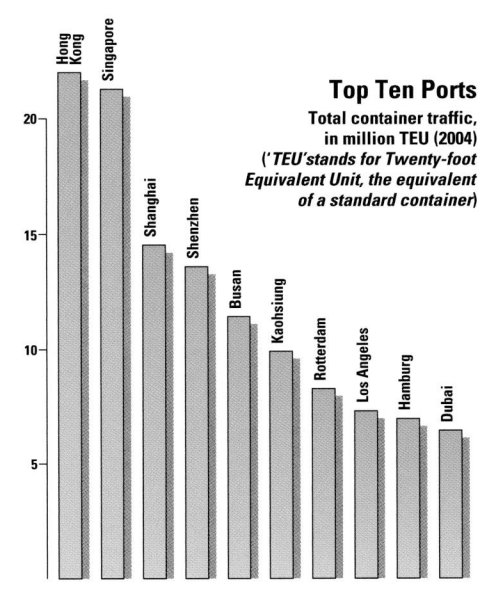

Types of Vessels

World fleet by type of vessel (2006)

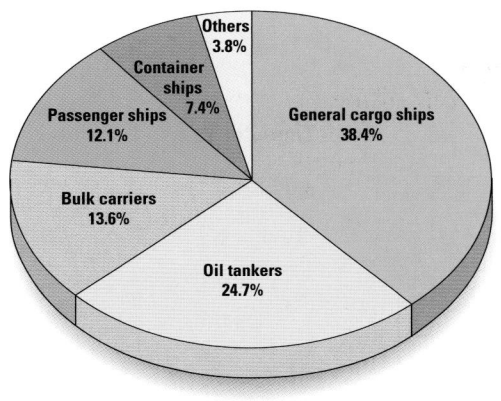

- Others 3.8%
- Container ships 7.4%
- Passenger ships 12.1%
- Bulk carriers 13.6%
- General cargo ships 38.4%
- Oil tankers 24.7%

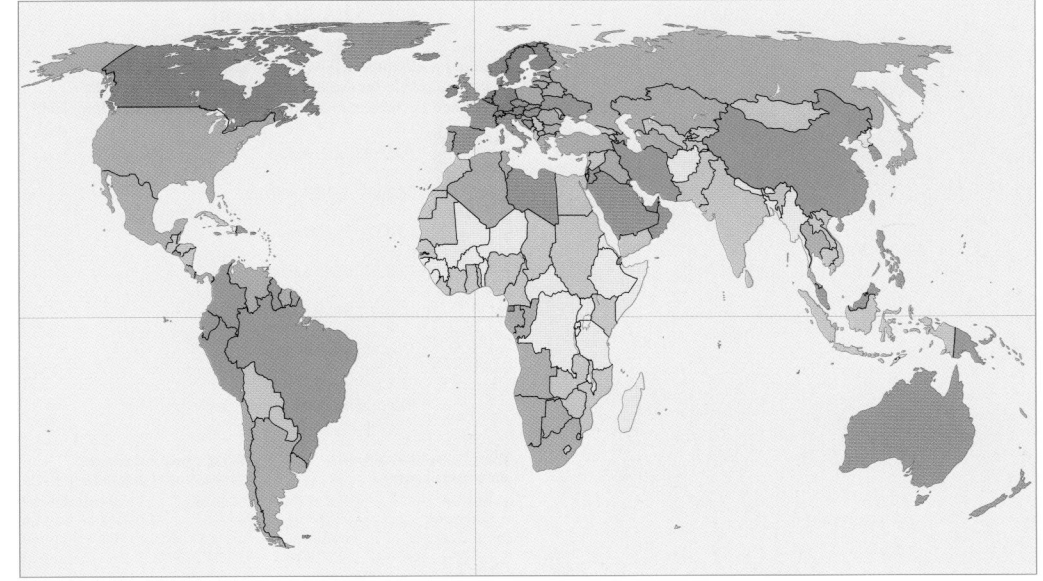

Exports Per Capita

Value of exports in US $, divided by total population (2006)

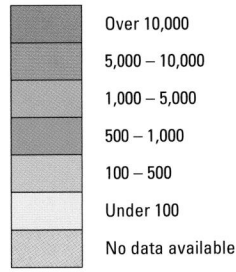

- Over 10,000
- 5,000 – 10,000
- 1,000 – 5,000
- 500 – 1,000
- 100 – 500
- Under 100
- No data available

Highest per capita

Hong Kong	$88,121
Liechtenstein	$72,675
Singapore	$63,132
United Arab Emirates	$52,676
Luxembourg	$41,209

Travel and Tourism

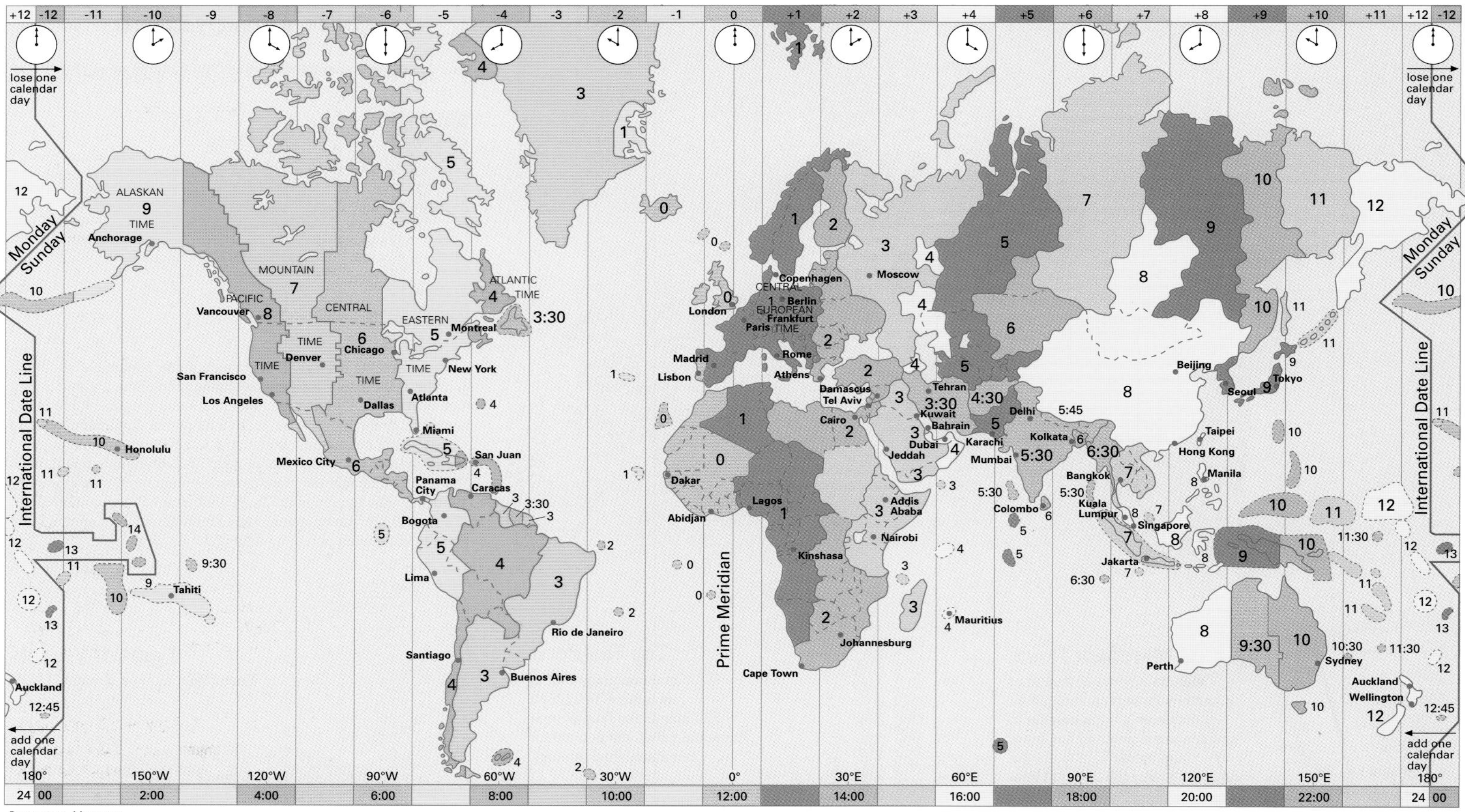

Projection: Mercator

Time Zones

Zones using UT (GMT)

Zones behind UT (GMT)

International boundaries

10 Hours fast or slow of UT or Co-ordinated Universal Time

Zones ahead of UT (GMT)

Half-hour zones

Time-zone boundaries

International Date Line

Certain time zones are affected by the incidence of daylight saving time in countries where it is adopted.

Actual solar time, when it is noon at Greenwich, is shown along the top of the map.

The world is divided into 24 time zones, each centred on meridians at 15° intervals, which is the longitudinal distance the sun travels every hour. The meridian running through Greenwich, London, passes through the middle of the first zone.

Rail and Road: The Leading Nations

Total rail network ('000 km)		Passenger km per head per year		Total road network ('000 km)		Vehicle km per head per year		Number of vehicles per km of roads	
1. USA	233.8	Japan	1,891	USA	6,378.3	USA	12,505	Hong Kong	287
2. Russia	85.5	Switzerland	1,751	India	3,319.6	Luxembourg	7,989	Qatar	284
3. Canada	73.2	Belarus	1,334	China	1,765.2	Kuwait	7,251	UAE	232
4. India	63.1	France	1,203	Brazil	1,724.9	France	7,142	Germany	195
5. China	60.5	Ukraine	1,100	Canada	1,408.8	Sweden	6,991	Lebanon	191
6. Germany	36.1	Russia	1,080	Japan	1,171.4	Germany	6,806	Macau	172
7. Argentina	34.2	Austria	1,008	France	893.1	Denmark	6,764	Singapore	167
8. France	29.3	Denmark	999	Australia	811.6	Austria	6,518	South Korea	160
9. Mexico	26.5	Netherlands	855	Spain	664.9	Netherlands	5,984	Kuwait	156
10. South Africa	22.7	Germany	842	Russia	537.3	UK	5,738	Taiwan	150
11. Brazil	22.1	Italy	811	Italy	479.7	Canada	5,493	Israel	111
12. Ukraine	22.1	Belgium	795	UK	371.9	Italy	4,852	Malta	110

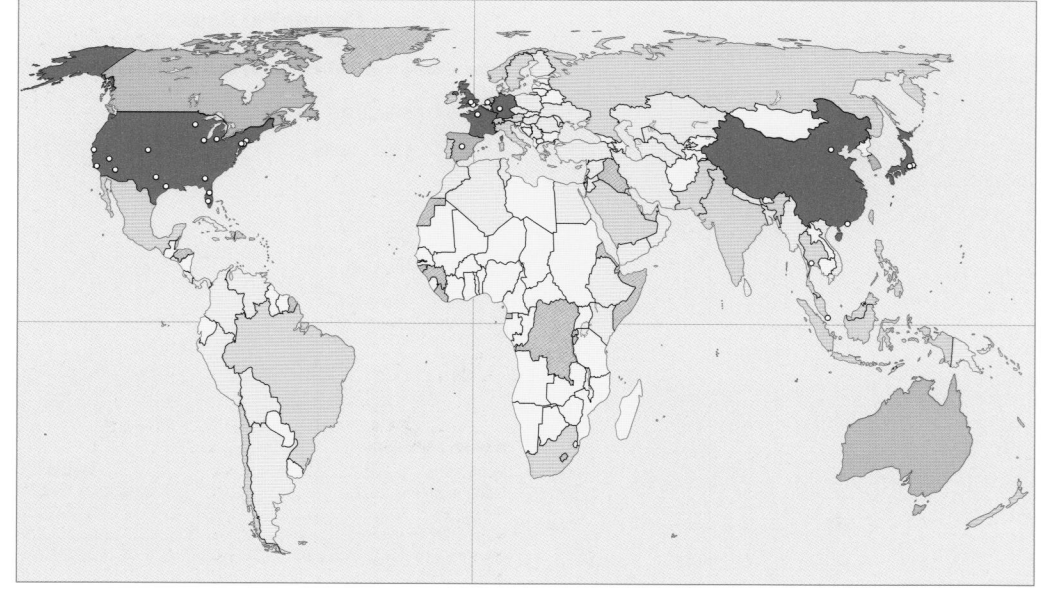

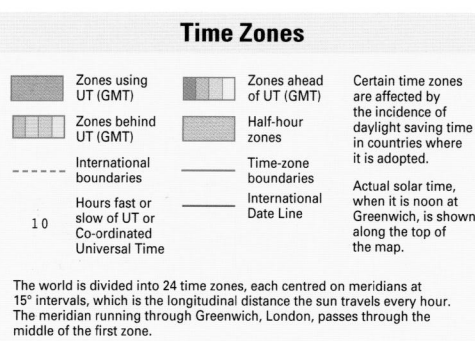

Air Travel

Passenger kilometres flown on scheduled flights (the number of passengers in thousands – international and domestic – multiplied by the distance flown from the airport of origin) (2002)

Over 100,000 million

50,000 – 100,000 million

10,000 – 50,000 million

1,000 – 10,000 million

Under 1,000 million

No data available

o Major airports (handling over 30 million passengers)

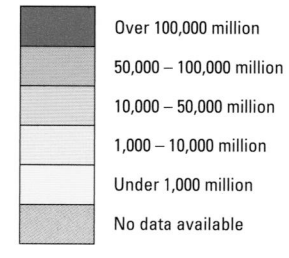

World's busiest airports (total passengers)		World's busiest airports (international passengers)	
1. Atlanta	(Hartsfield)	1. London	(Heathrow)
2. Chicago	(O'Hare)	2. Paris	(Charles de Gaulle)
3. London	(Heathrow)	3. Frankfurt	(International)
4. Tokyo	(Haneda)	4. Amsterdam	(Schipol)
5. Los Angeles	(International)	5. Hong Kong	(International)

Destinations

- Cultural and historical centres
- Coastal resorts
- Ski resorts
- Centres of entertainment
- Places of pilgrimage
- Places of great natural beauty
- Popular holiday cruise routes

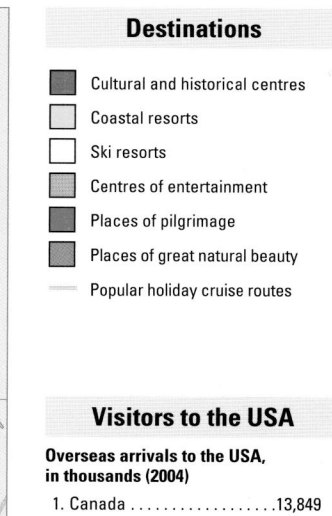

Visitors to the USA

Overseas arrivals to the USA, in thousands (2004)

1.	Canada	13,849
2.	UK	4,302
3.	Mexico	3,993
4.	Japan	3,748
5.	Germany	1,319
6.	France	775
7.	South Korea	627
8.	Australia	520
9.	Italy	470
10.	Netherlands	424

Tourist Spending

Countries spending the most on overseas tourism, US$ million (2004)

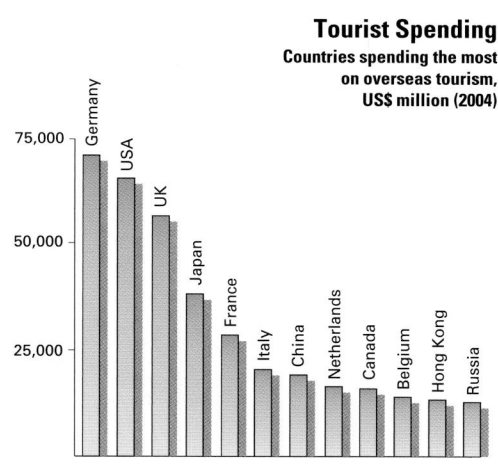

Importance of Tourism

		Arrivals from abroad (2004)	% of world total (2004)
1.	France	75,121,000	9.9%
2.	Spain	53,599,000	7.1%
3.	USA	46,077,000	6.1%
4.	China	41,761,000	5.5%
5.	Italy	37,071,000	4.9%
6.	UK	27,755,000	3.7%
7.	Hong Kong	21,811,000	2.9%
8.	Mexico	20,618,000	2.7%
9.	Germany	20,137,000	2.7%
10.	Austria	19,373,000	2.6%
11.	Canada	19,150,000	2.5%
12.	Turkey	16,826,000	2.2%

After 3 years of stagnant growth, international tourist arrivals reached an all-time record of 763 million in 2004, almost 11% more than in 2003. Growth was common to all regions, but particularly strong in Asia and the Pacific, and in the Middle East.

Tourist Earnings

Countries receiving the most from overseas tourism, US$ million (2004)

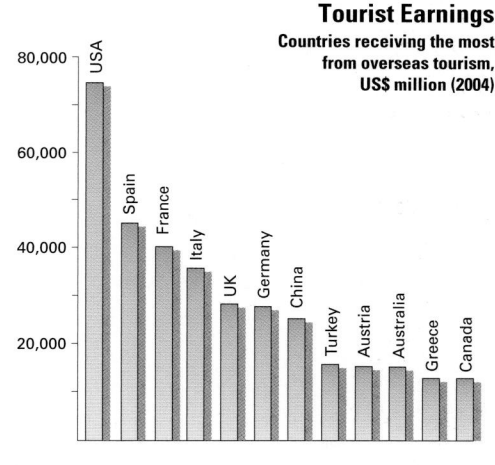

Tourism

Tourism receipts as a percentage of Gross National Income (2005)

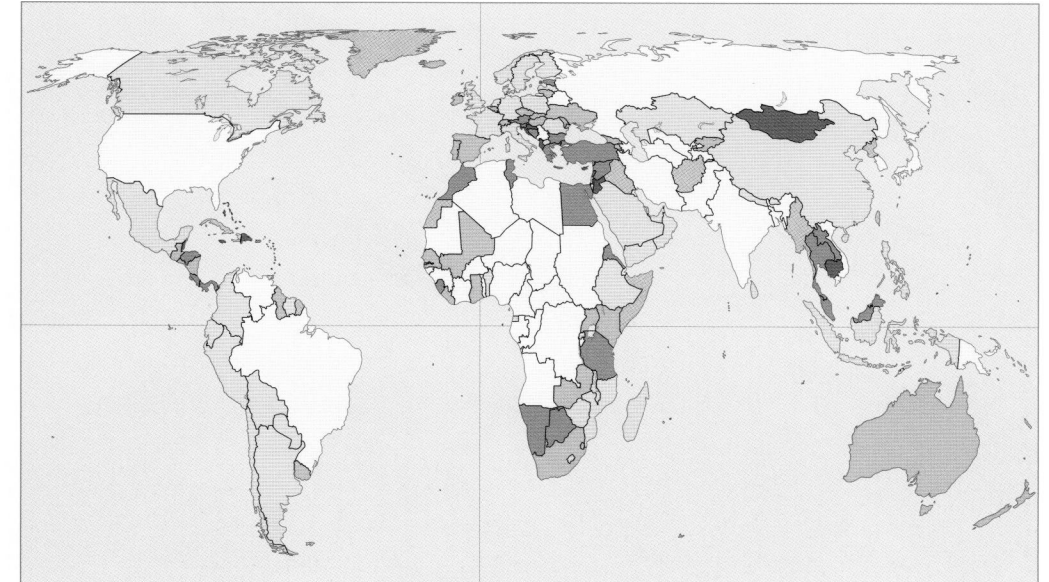

- Over 10%
- 5 – 10%
- 2.5 – 5%
- 1 – 2.5%
- Under 1%
- No data available

Percentage change in tourist arrivals from 2004 to 2005 (top six countries in total number of arrivals)

France	+1.2%
Spain	+3.7%
USA	+0.02%
China	+8.5%
Italy	–1.5%
UK	+8.0%

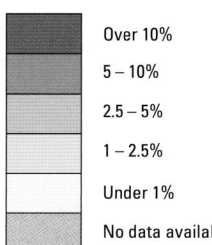

– MT EVEREST, CHINA/NEPAL –
Part of the Himalaya range, Mt Everest – the highest
mountain in the world at 8,850 m (29,035 ft) – lies just
north of centre in this image. The two arms of the Rongbuk
glacier flow away from the triangular shaded north wall, with
the Kangshung glacier due east. The international boundary
between China and Nepal bisects the peak, which was
first climbed on 28 May 1953.

WORLD CITIES

AMSTERDAM	2	HONG KONG	12	MUMBAI	20	TEHRAN	31
ATHENS	2	ISTANBUL	12	MUNICH	21	TORONTO	31
ATLANTA	3	JAKARTA	12	NEW ORLEANS	21	VIENNA	32
BAGHDAD	3	JERUSALEM	13	NEW YORK	22	WARSAW	32
BANGKOK	3	JOHANNESBURG	13	ORLANDO	23	WASHINGTON	33
BARCELONA	4	KARACHI	13	OSAKA	23	WELLINGTON	33
BEIJING	4	KOLKATA	14	OSLO	23		
BERLIN	5	LAGOS	14	PARIS	24	INDEX	34–39
BOSTON	6	LAS VEGAS	14	PRAGUE	25		
BRUSSELS	6	LIMA	14	RIO DE JANEIRO	25		
BUDAPEST	7	LONDON	15	ROME	26	WORLD CITIES	
BUENOS AIRES	7	LOS ANGELES	16	SAN FRANCISCO	26	SATELLITE IMAGES	
CAIRO	7	LISBON	16	ST PETERSBURG	27	CAPE TOWN	40
CAPE TOWN	8	MADRID	17	SANTIAGO	27	CHICAGO	41
COPENHAGEN	8	MANILA	17	SÃO PAULO	27	KARACHI	42
CHICAGO	9	MELBOURNE	18	SEOUL	27	LONDON	43
DELHI	10	MEXICO CITY	18	SHANGHAI	28	NEW YORK	44
DUBLIN	10	MIAMI	18	SINGAPORE	28	SAN FRANCISCO	45
EDINBURGH	11	MILAN	19	STOCKHOLM	29	SANTIAGO	46
GUANGZHOU	11	MOSCOW	19	SYDNEY	29	SYDNEY	47
HELSINKI	11	MONTRÉAL	20	TOKYO	30	TOKYO	48

CITY MAPS

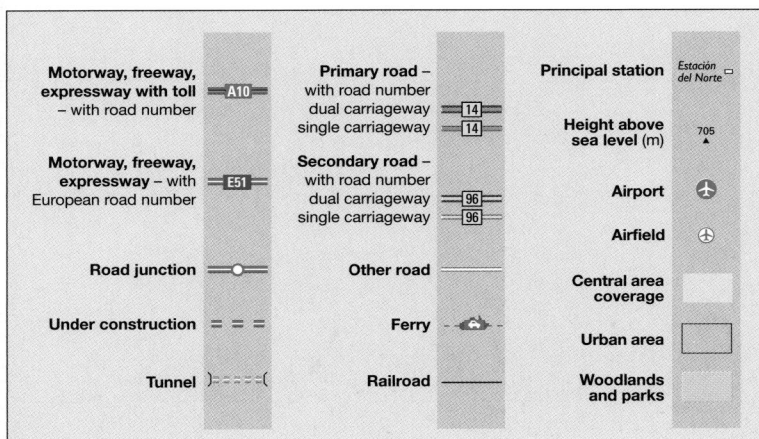

Motorway, freeway, expressway with toll – with road number	A10
Motorway, freeway, expressway – with European road number	E51
Road junction	
Under construction	= = =
Tunnel	)======(
Primary road – with road number dual carriageway single carriageway	14 / 14
Secondary road – with road number dual carriageway single carriageway	96 / 96
Other road	
Ferry	
Railroad	
Principal station	Estación del Norte
Height above sea level (m)	705 ▲
Airport	✈
Airfield	⊕
Central area coverage	
Urban area	
Woodlands and parks	

CENTRAL AREA MAPS

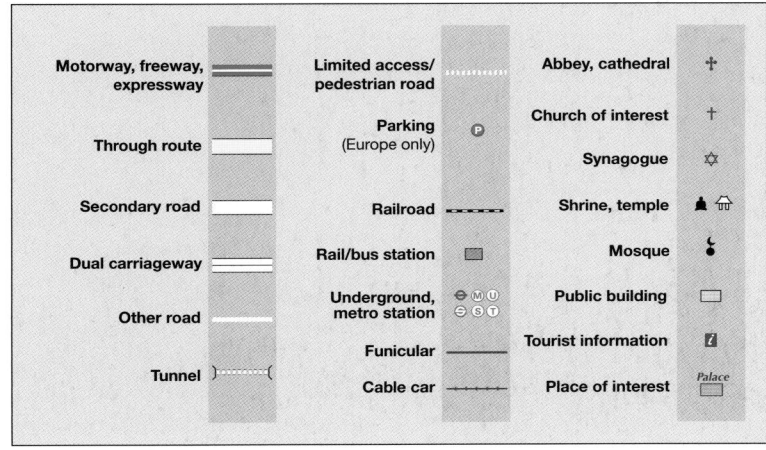

Motorway, freeway, expressway	
Through route	
Secondary road	
Dual carriageway	
Other road	
Tunnel	)======(
Limited access/ pedestrian road	
Parking (Europe only)	P
Railroad	------
Rail/bus station	
Underground, metro station	
Funicular	
Cable car	
Abbey, cathedral	†
Church of interest	†
Synagogue	✡
Shrine, temple	
Mosque	
Public building	
Tourist information	i
Place of interest	Palace

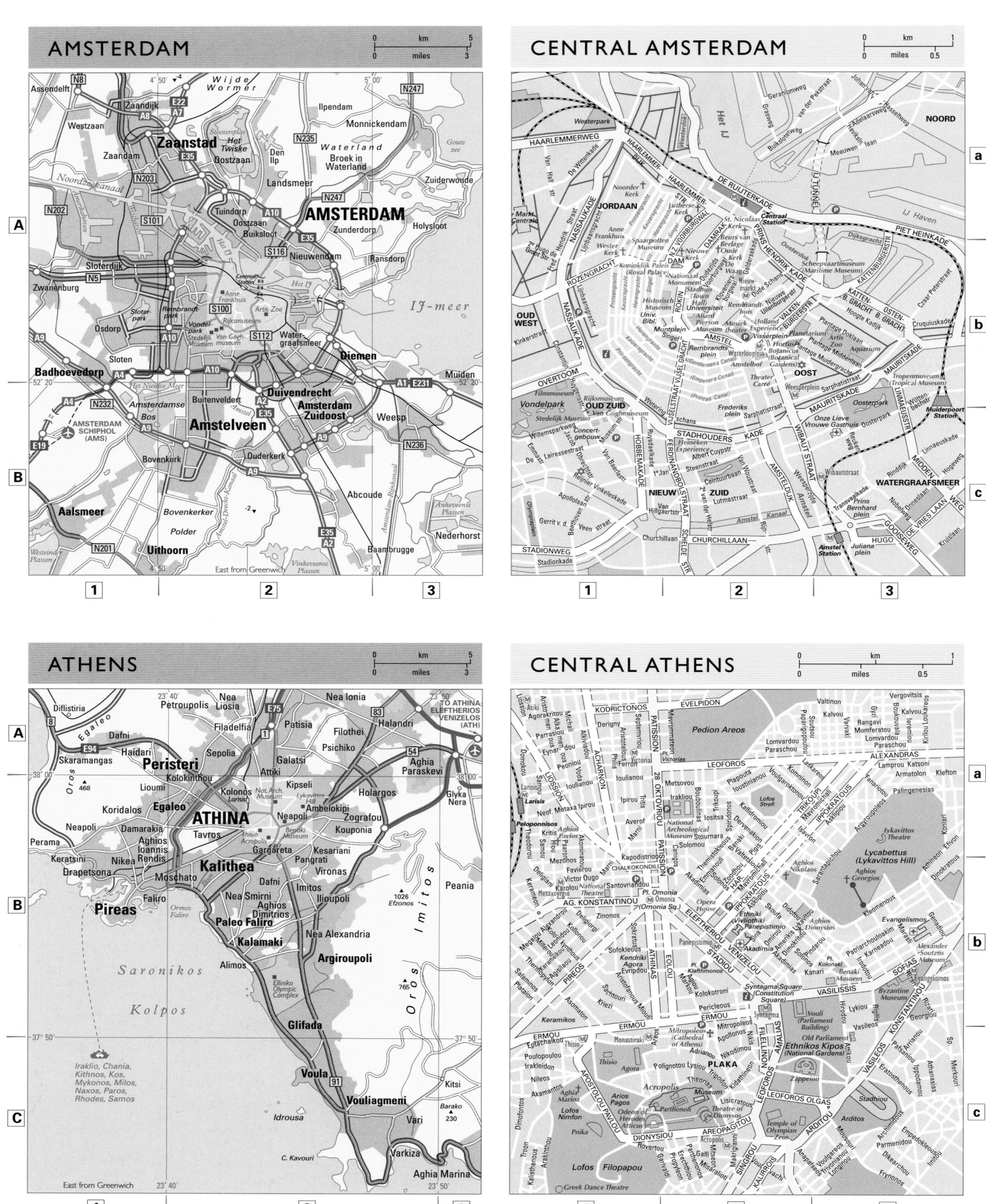

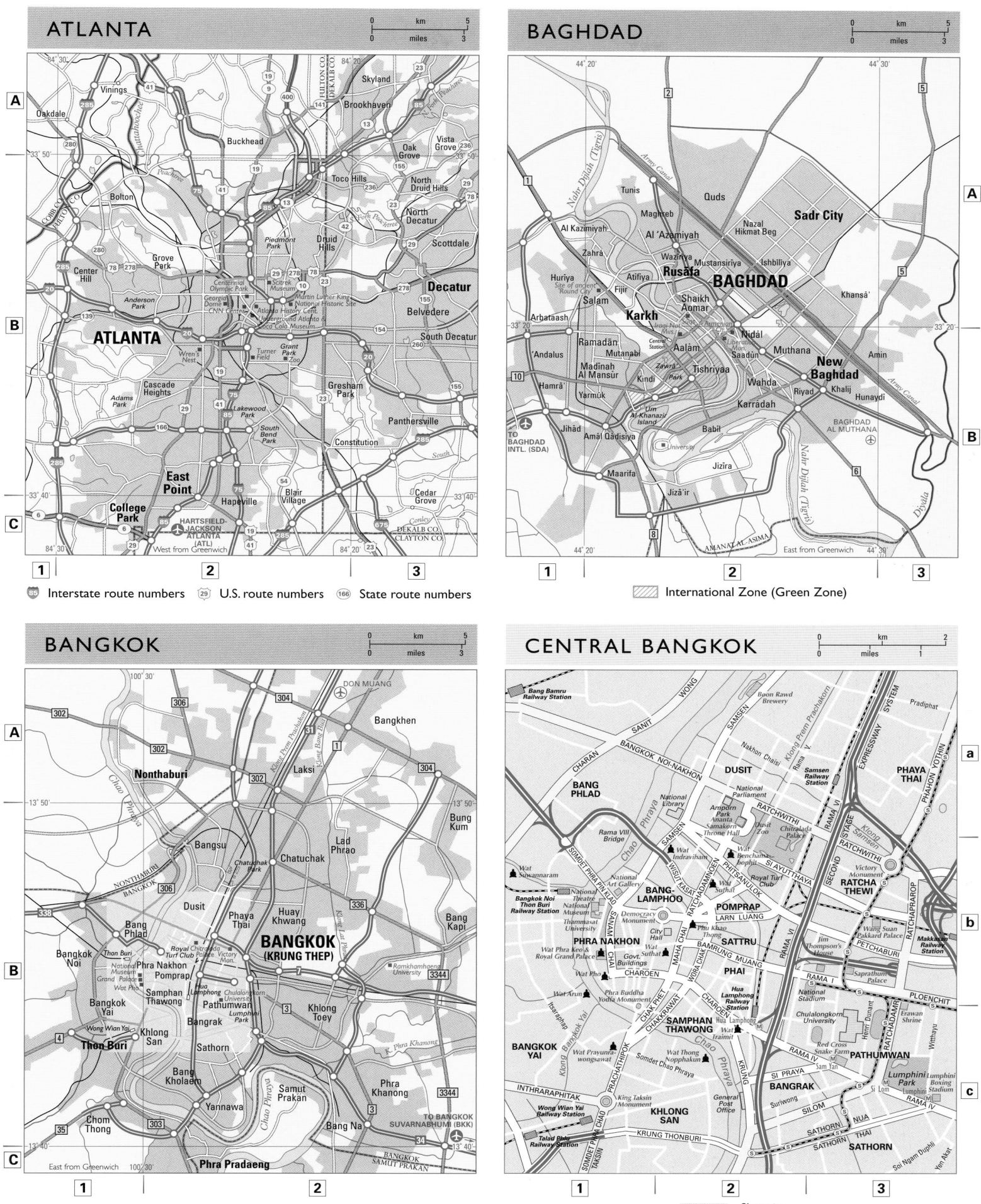

ATLANTA

BAGHDAD

⑧⑤ Interstate route numbers ㉙ U.S. route numbers ⑯⑥ State route numbers

International Zone (Green Zone)

BANGKOK

CENTRAL BANGKOK

Skytrain

COPYRIGHT PHILIP'S

BARCELONA

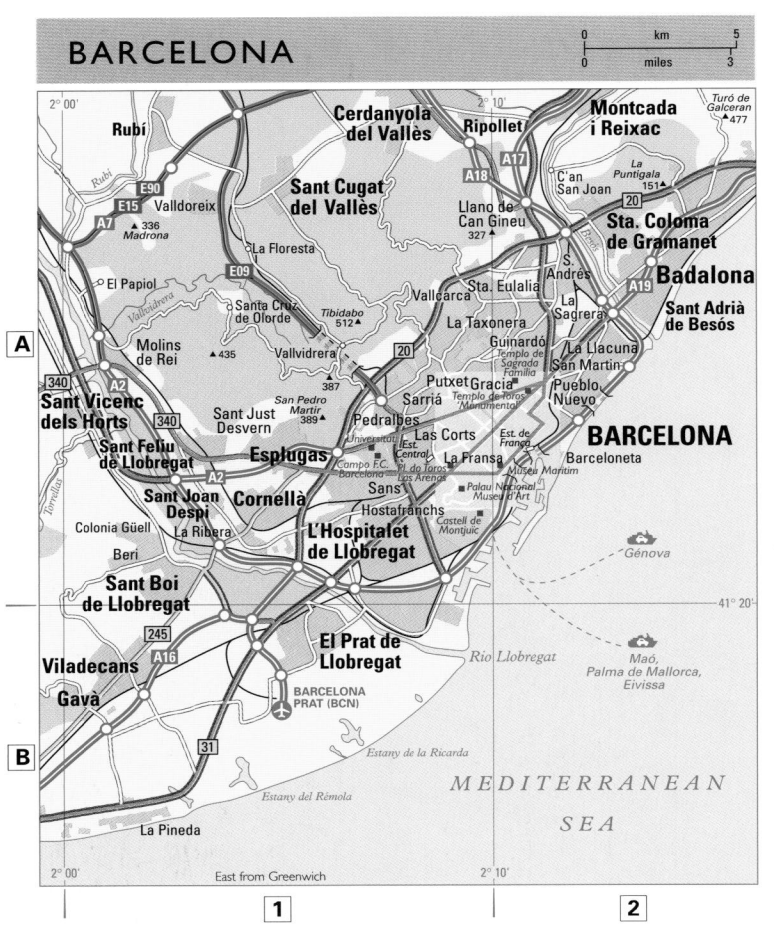

CENTRAL BARCELONA

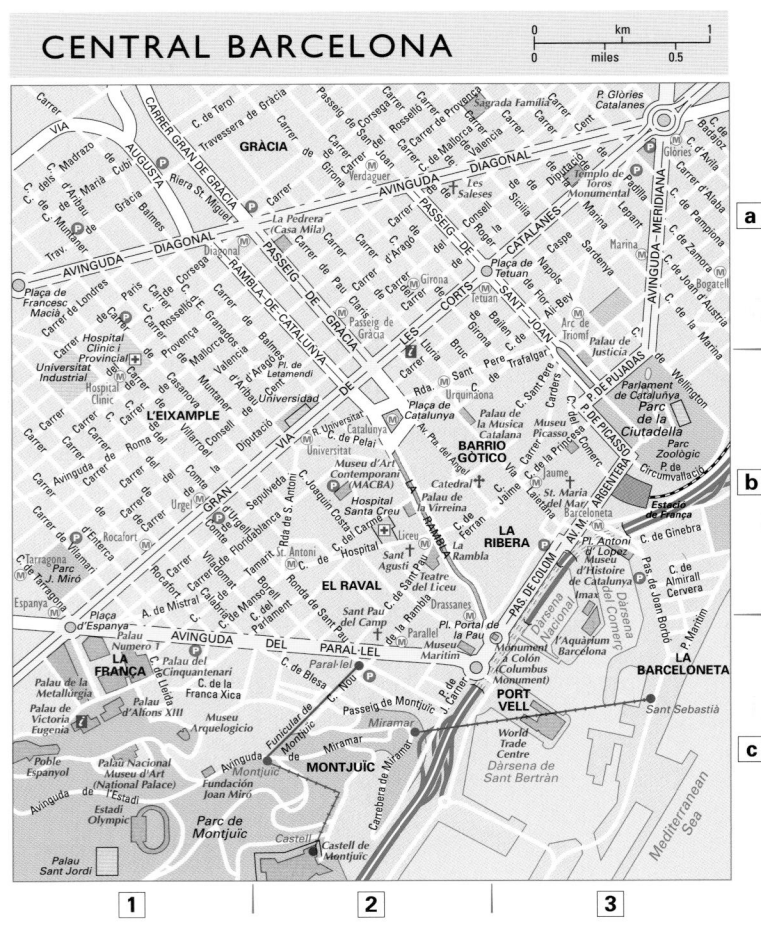

BEIJING

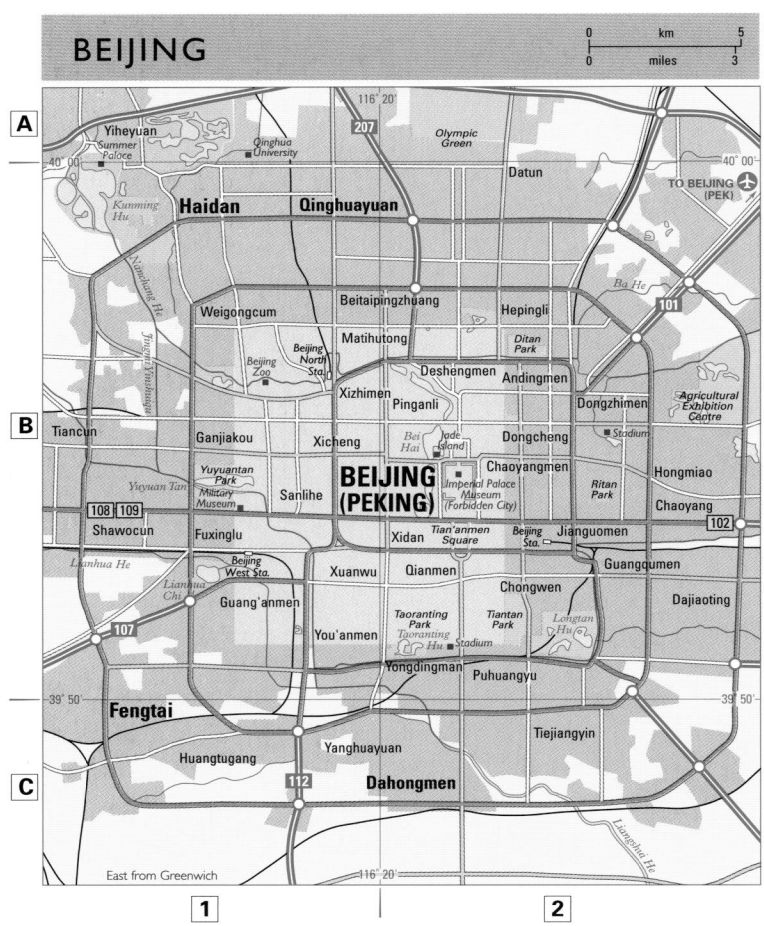

CENTRAL BEIJING

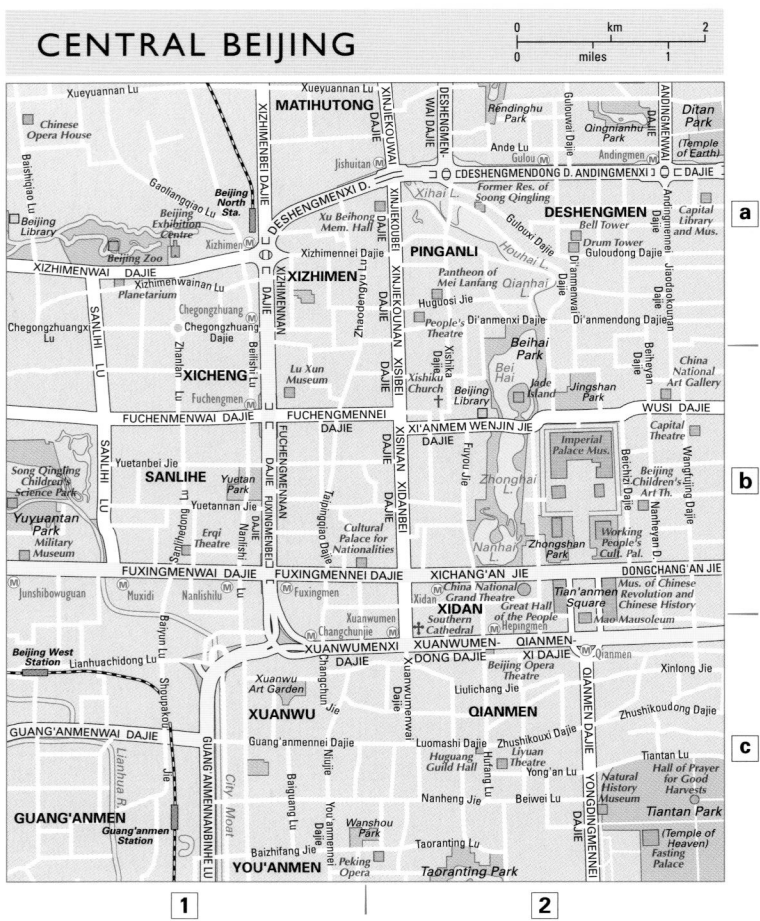

BERLIN

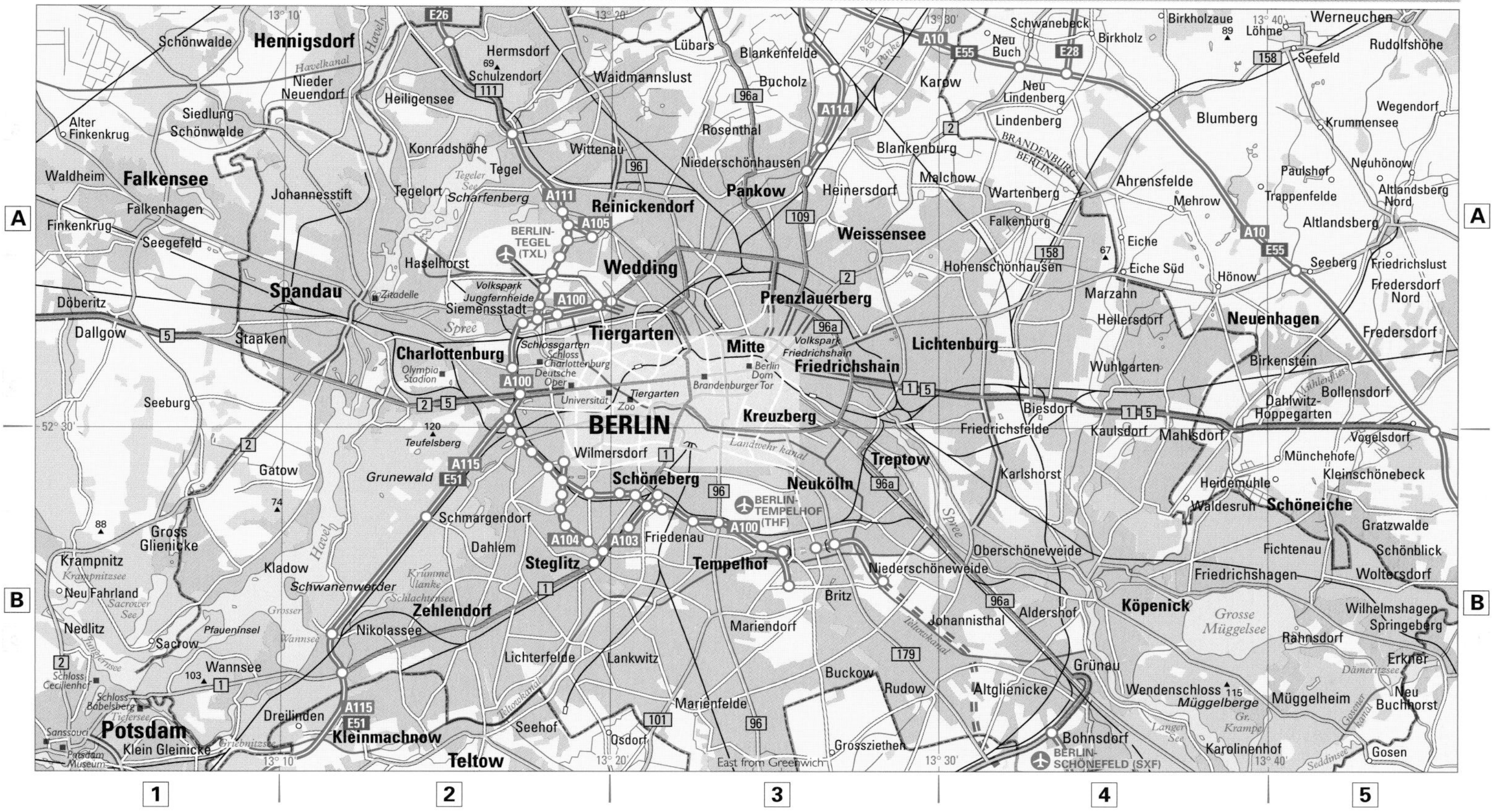

km 0 — 5
miles 0 — 3

Schönwalde Hennigsdorf Hermsdorf Schulzendorf Lübars Blankenfelde Buchholz Schwaneback Neu Buch Birkholzaue Birkholz Werneuchen Rudolfshöhe
Alter Finkenkrug Niederneuendorf Siedlung Schönwalde Heiligensee Waidmannslust Karow Neu Lindenberg Seefeld Wegendorf Neuhönow
Waldheim **Falkensee** Falkenhagen Johannesstift Scharfenberg Tegelort Tegel Wittenau Niederschönhausen Rosenthal Blankenburg Lindenberg Blumberg Krummensee
Finkenkrug Seegefeld **Pankow** Heinersdorf Malchow Wartenberg Ahrensfelde Trappenfelde Altlandsberg Nord
Spandau Haselhorst Zitadelle BERLIN-TEGEL (TXL) **Reinickendorf** **Weissensee** Hohenschönhausen Mehrow Altlandsberg
Döberitz Volkspark Jungfernheide Siemensstadt **Wedding** Marzahn Eiche Eiche Süd Hönow Seeberg Friedrichslust
Dallgow Staaken Spree Olympia Stadion **Charlottenburg** Schlossgarten Schloss Charlottenburg Deutsche Oper **Tiergarten** **Mitte** Volkspark Friedrichshain **Lichtenburg** Wuhlgarten **Neuenhagen** Frederdorf
Seeburg Universität Zoo Berlin Dom Brandenburger Tor **Friedrichshain** Biesdorf Birkenstein Frederdorf Nord
BERLIN Tiergarten **Kreuzberg** Friedrichsfelde Kaulsdorf Mahlsdorf Dahlwitz Hoppegarten Vogelsdorf
Teufelsberg Wilmersdorf Landwehr kanal **Treptow** Karlshorst Münchehofe
Grunewald **Schöneberg** **Neukölln** BERLIN-TEMPELHOF (THF) Heidemühle Kleinschönebeck Gratzwalde
Gross Glienicke Schmargendorf Dahlem Friedenau **Tempelhof** Niederschöneweide Oberschöneweide Waldesruh **Schöneiche** Fichtenau Schönblick
Krampnitz Kladow Schwanenwerder **Steglitz** Britz Johannisthal Friedrichshagen Woltersdorf
Neu Fahrland Nikolassee **Zehlendorf** Mariendorf Aldershof **Köpenick** Grosse Müggelsee Rahnsdorf Erkner
Nedlitz Sacrow Schloss Cecilienhof Lichterfelde Lankwitz Grünau Wendenschloss Müggelberge Wilhelmshagen Springeberg Neu Buchhorst
Wannsee Dreilinden Buckow Rudow Altglienicke Bohnsdorf Müggelheim Gosen
Potsdam Klein Gleinicke **Kleinmachnow** Seehof Marienfelde Qsdorf Grossziethen Grossbeeren BERLIN-SCHÖNEFELD (SXF) Karolinenhof
Sanssouci Potsdam Museum **Teltow** East from Greenwich

1 2 3 4 5
A A
B B

CENTRAL BERLIN

km 0 — 1
miles 0 — 0.5

CHARLOTTENBURG **TIERGARTEN** Hauptbahnhof Lehrter bahnhof **SCHEUNENVIERTEL** Rosa-Luxemburg-Pl.
Schwarzer Weg Waldenser Str. Bugenhagen str. Krankenhaus Moabit Fritz-Schloss-Park Hannoversche Str. Charité Krankenhaus Deutsches Th. und Kammersp. Volksbühne
Turmstrasse St. Johannis-Kirche Invalidenstr. Oranienburger Tor Oranienburger Str. Hackescher Mkt. Weinmeisterstr.
Hansatheater Alt-Moabit Bellevue Bundeskanzleramt Bodemuseum Alte Nationalgalerie **Alexanderplatz** Kongresshalle
Spree Schlosspark Bellevue Akad. d. Künste Haus der Kulturen der Welt Platz der Republik (Reichstag) Friedrichstr. Pergamonmuseum Aqua Dom & Sea Life Fernsehturm (T.V. Tower) Poliklinik
Deutsche Oper Technische Universität Tiergarten Brandenburger Tor (Brandenburg Gate) **UNTER DEN LINDEN** Altes Museum Berliner Dom (Cathedral) Rathaus **MITTE** **Museumsinsel** Märkisches Museum
Bismarckstrasse Ernst-Reuter-Pl. Siegessäule STRASSE DES 17 JUNI *Tiergarten* Komische Oper Französischer Dom Staatsoper Palast der Republik Stadtbibl. Jannowitz-brücke
Zoologischer Garten Gemäldegalerie Philharmonie Sony Centre **Holocaust Memorial** Mohrenstr. Konzerthaus Berlin Stadtmitte Deutscher Dom Spittelmarkt
Kaiser Wilhelm Gedächtniskirche KURFÜRSTENDAMM Neue Nationalgalerie Potsdamer Platz Bundesministerium der Finanzen Checkpoint Charlie Heinrich-Heine-Str. St. Michael-Kirch.
WILMERSDORF Europa-center TAUENTZIEN Staatsbibl. Martin Gropius-Bau Topography of Terror Jüdisches Museum **KREUZBERG**
Urania Anhalter Bf. Blumengrossmarkt Kottbusser Tor
Volksbühne Tempodrom Deutsches Technikmuseum Berlin Hallesches Tor GITSCHINER STRASSE SKALITZER STR.
Kleistpark YORCKSTRASSE Obentraut- Krankenhaus am Urban Böcklerpark Vivantes Klinikum am Urban Diefenbach Sporthalle
Grossgörschenstr. **Yorckstr.** GNEISENAUSTRASSE Viktoriapark HASEN-HEIDE Südstern

1 2 3 4 5
a a
b b
c c

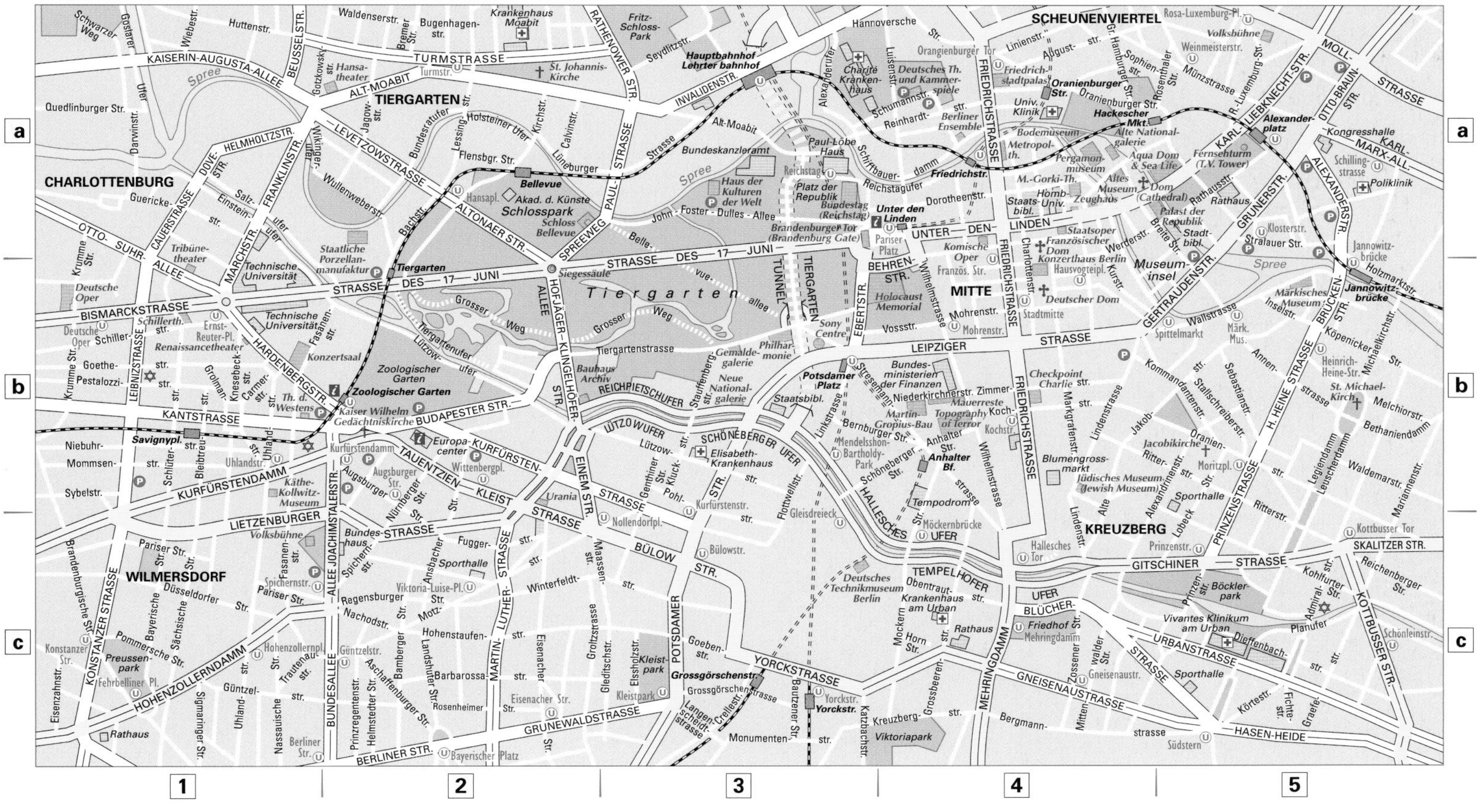

COPYRIGHT PHILIP'S

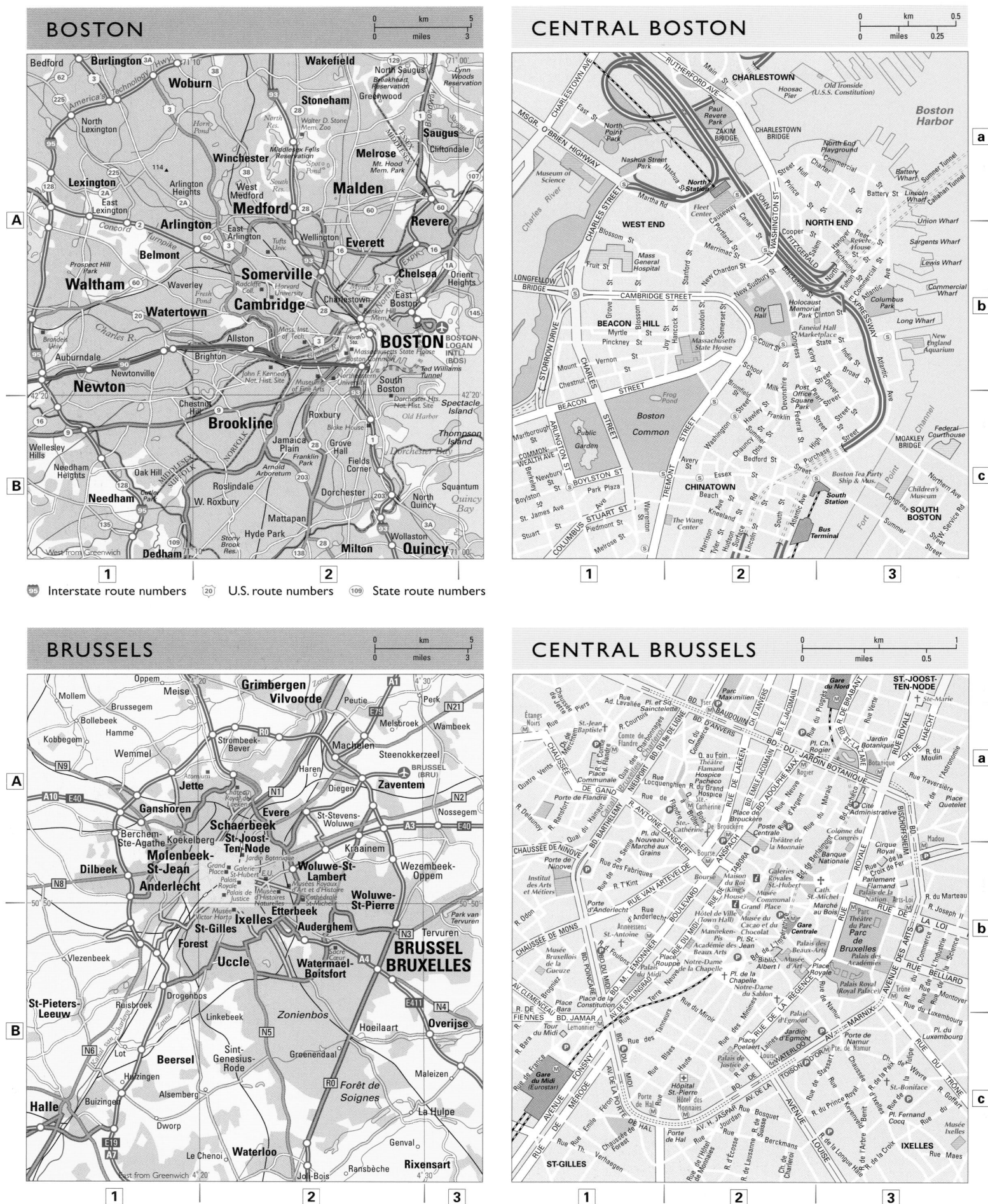

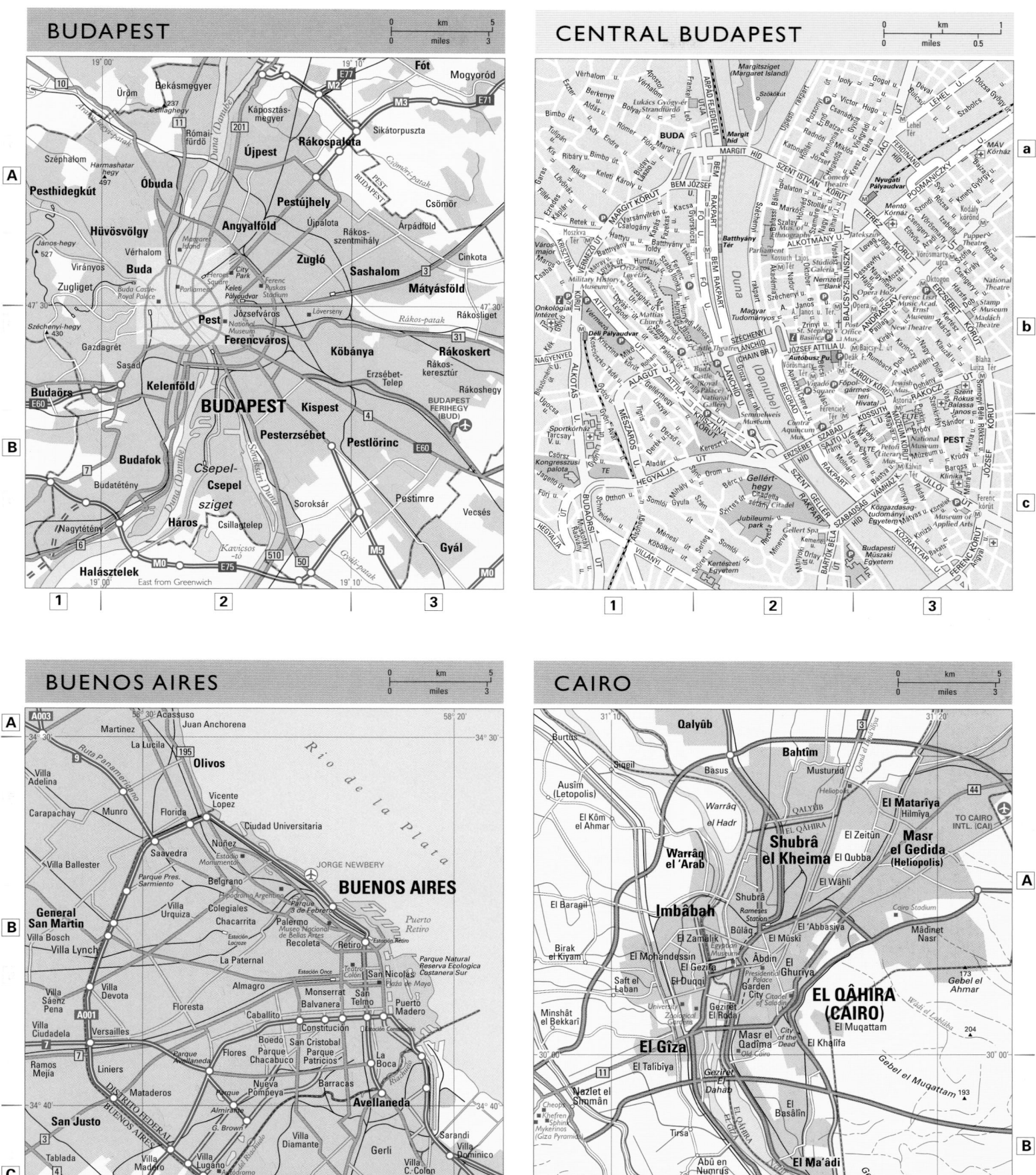

BUDAPEST

km 0 — 5
miles 0 — 3

10
19° 00'
Üröm
Békásmegyer
Csillaghegy
237
11
Római-fürdő
201
Káposztás-megyer
Sikátorpuszta
E77
M2
E71
M3
Fót
Mogyoród
Újpest
Rákospalota
Pesthidegkút
Harmashatar hegy 497
Szép halom
Óbuda
Újpalota
Rákos-szentmihály
Árpádföld
Csömör
Hüvösvölgy
Vérhalom
Pestújhely
Angyalföld
Zugló
Sashalom
János-hegy 527
Virányos
Buda
Margaret Island
City Park
Ferenc Puskás Stádium
Mátyásföld
Zugliget
Széchényi-hegy 430
Buda Castle-Royal Palace
Parliament
Józsefváros
Löversny
Rákos-patak
Rákosliget
47° 30'
Pest
National Museum
Ferencváros
Kőbánya
Rákoskert
Rákos-keresztúr
31
Gazdagrét
Keleti Pályaudvar
Sasad
Kelenföld
Erzsébet-Telep
Rákoshegy
Budaörs
E60
Kispest
4
BUDAPEST
BUDAPEST FERIHEGY (BUD)
Budafok
Pesterzsébet
Pestlőrinc
E60
7
Budatétény
Csepel-Csepel sziget
Soroksár
Pestimre
Vecsés
Nagytétény
6
Háros
Csillagtelep
Kavicsos-tó
510
M5
Gyál
Halásztelek
M0
E75
50
Gyáli-patak
M0
19° 00'
East from Greenwich
19° 10'

A   B

1   2   3

CENTRAL BUDAPEST

km 0 — 1
miles 0 — 0.5

Margitsziget (Margaret Island)
Margit híd MARGIT HÍD
BUDA
PEST
Nyugati Pályaudvar
Parliament
Danube
SZÉCHENYI LÁNCHÍD (CHAIN BR.)
Buda Castle
Royal Palace
National Gallery
Gellért-hegy Citadel
Gellért Spa
St. Stephen's Basilica
National Theatre
National Museum
ELTE
PEST
Budapesti Műszaki Egyetem
Kertészeti Egyetem
VILLÁNYI ÚT

a   b   c

1   2   3

BUENOS AIRES

km 0 — 5
miles 0 — 3

A003
Acassuso
Martinez
Juan Anchorena
34° 30'
58° 20'
9
La Lucila
Ruta Panamericana
195
Olivos
Villa Adelina
Vicente Lopez
Rio de la Plata
Carapachay
Munro
Florida
Villa Ballester
Saavedra
Núñez
Ciudad Universitaria
General San Martin
Villa Bosch
Villa Lynch
Parque Pres. Sarmiento
Estadio Monumental
JORGE NEWBERY
Villa Urquiza
Belgrano
Hipódromo Argentino
Parque 3 de Febrero
BUENOS AIRES
Colegiales
Chacarita
Palermo
Puerto Retiro
Villa Sáenz Peña
Villa Devota
Almagro
Estación Lacroze
La Paternal
Museo Nacional de Bellas Artes
Recoleta
Retiro
Estación Retiro
Parque Natural Reserva Ecológica Costanera Sur
Villa Ciudadela
A001
7
Floresta
Caballito
Estación Once
Teatro Colón
San Nicolas
Plaza de Mayo
Puerto Madero
Ramos Mejía
Liniers
Mataderos
Boedo
Flores
Parque Chacabuco
Monserrat
Balvanera
San Telmo
Constitución
Estación Constitución
San Justo
3
DISTRITO FEDERAL
BUENOS AIRES
Nueva Pompeya
Parque Patricios
San Cristobal
La Boca
Riachuelo
Avellaneda
Tablada
4
Villa Madero
Villa Lugano
Almirante G. Brown
Barracas
Sarandi
Villa Dominico
Ciudad General Belgrano
Aldo Bonzi
Tapiales
Autódromo Oscar A. Gálvez Fiorito
Caraza
Gerli
Villa C. Colon
Villa Diamante
Villa Barilari
A002
TO BUENOS AIRES EZEIZA (EZE)
Salada
Mykerinos
58° 30'
West from Greenwich
Lanús
Remedios de Escalada
Monte Chingolo
A004
58° 20'
1
2

A   B   C

1   2   3

CAIRO

km 0 — 1
miles 0 — 3

31° 10'
31° 20'
Qalyûb
Burtus
Siqeil
Bahtîm
Musturud
3
44
Ausîm (Letopolis)
Basus
El Matarîya
Hilmîya
TO CAIRO INTL. (CAI)
El Kôm el Ahmar
Warrâq el Hadr
QALYÛB
EL QÂHIRA
El Zeitûn
Masr el Gedida (Heliopolis)
Warrâq el 'Arab
Shubrâ el Kheima
El Qubba
El Wâhli
A
El Baragil
Shubrâ
Rameses Station
El 'Abbâsiya
Mâdinet Nasr
Imbâbah
Bûlâq
El Mûski
Birak el Kiyam
El Zamâlik
Egyptian Museum
El Mohandessin
El Gezira
Âbdin
El Ghurîya
Saft el Laban
El Duqqi
Presidential Palace
Garden City
Cairo Stadium
Minshât el Bekkarî
University
Zoological Gardens
Gezîret El Roda
Masr el Qadîma Old Cairo
EL QÂHIRA (CAIRO)
Citadel of Saladin
City of the Dead
El Khalîfa
El Muqattam
Gebel el Ahmar
204
173
El Gîza
El Talibîya
11
Nazlet el Simmân
Geziret El Dahab
Gebel el Muqattam 193
30° 00'
Cheops
Khefren Sphinx Mykerinos (Giza Pyramids)
Tirsa
El Basâlin
Gebel el Tura
Tura
Abû en Numrus
Zâwiyet Abû Musallam
Shabrâmant
El Ma'âdi
Tammûh
2
54
31° 10'
East from Greenwich
31° 20'

A   B

1   2   3

COPYRIGHT PHILIP'S

CAPE TOWN

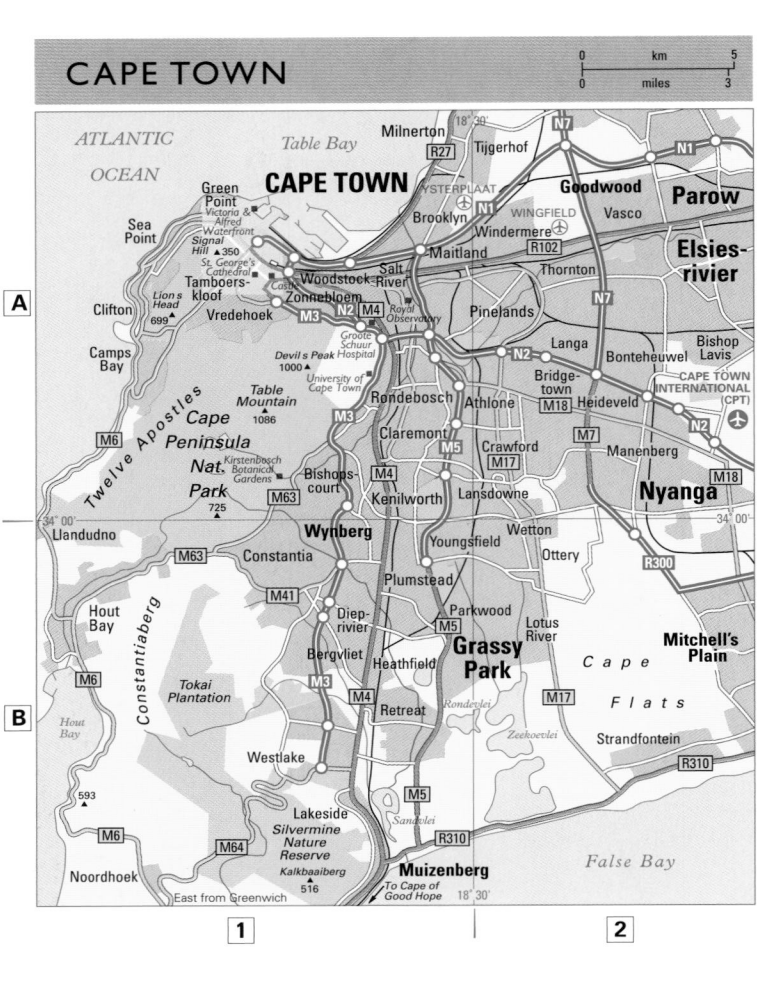

CENTRAL CAPE TOWN

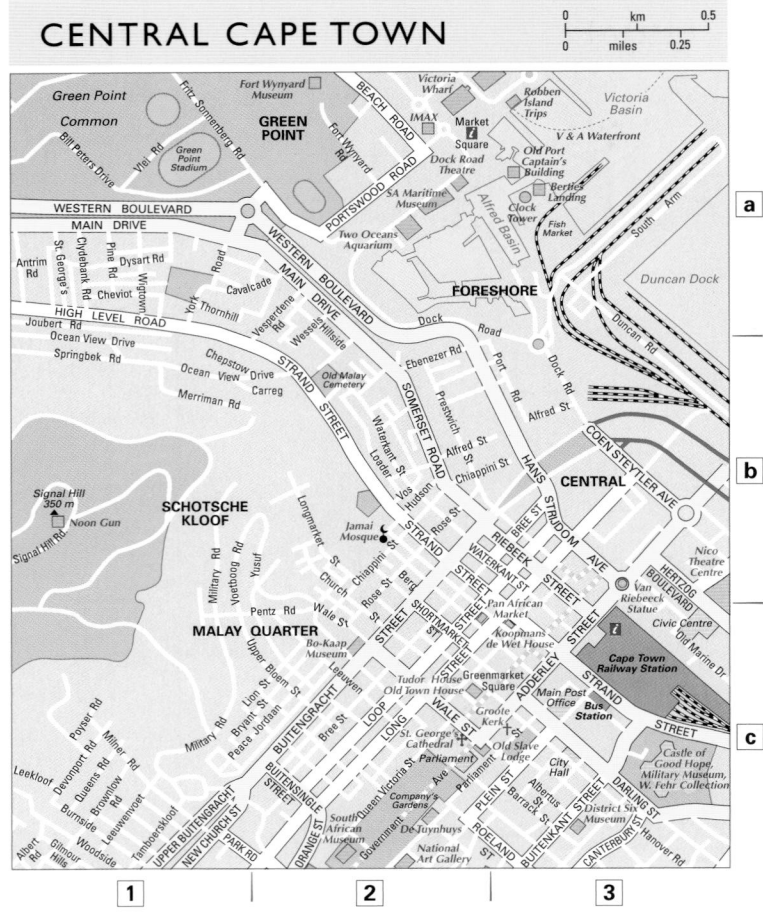

COPENHAGEN

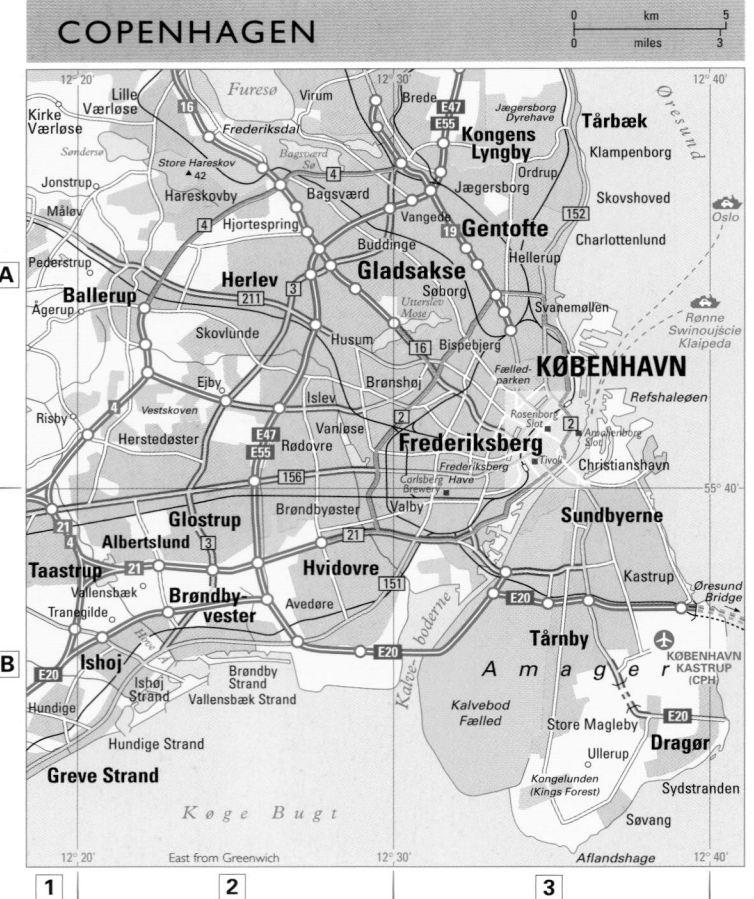

CENTRAL COPENHAGEN

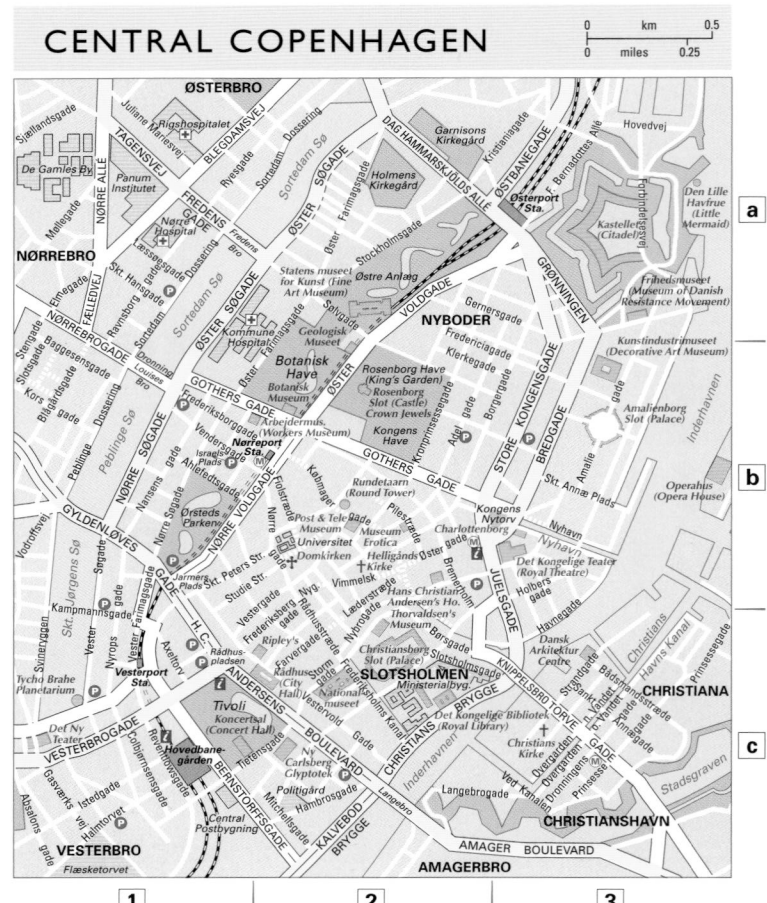

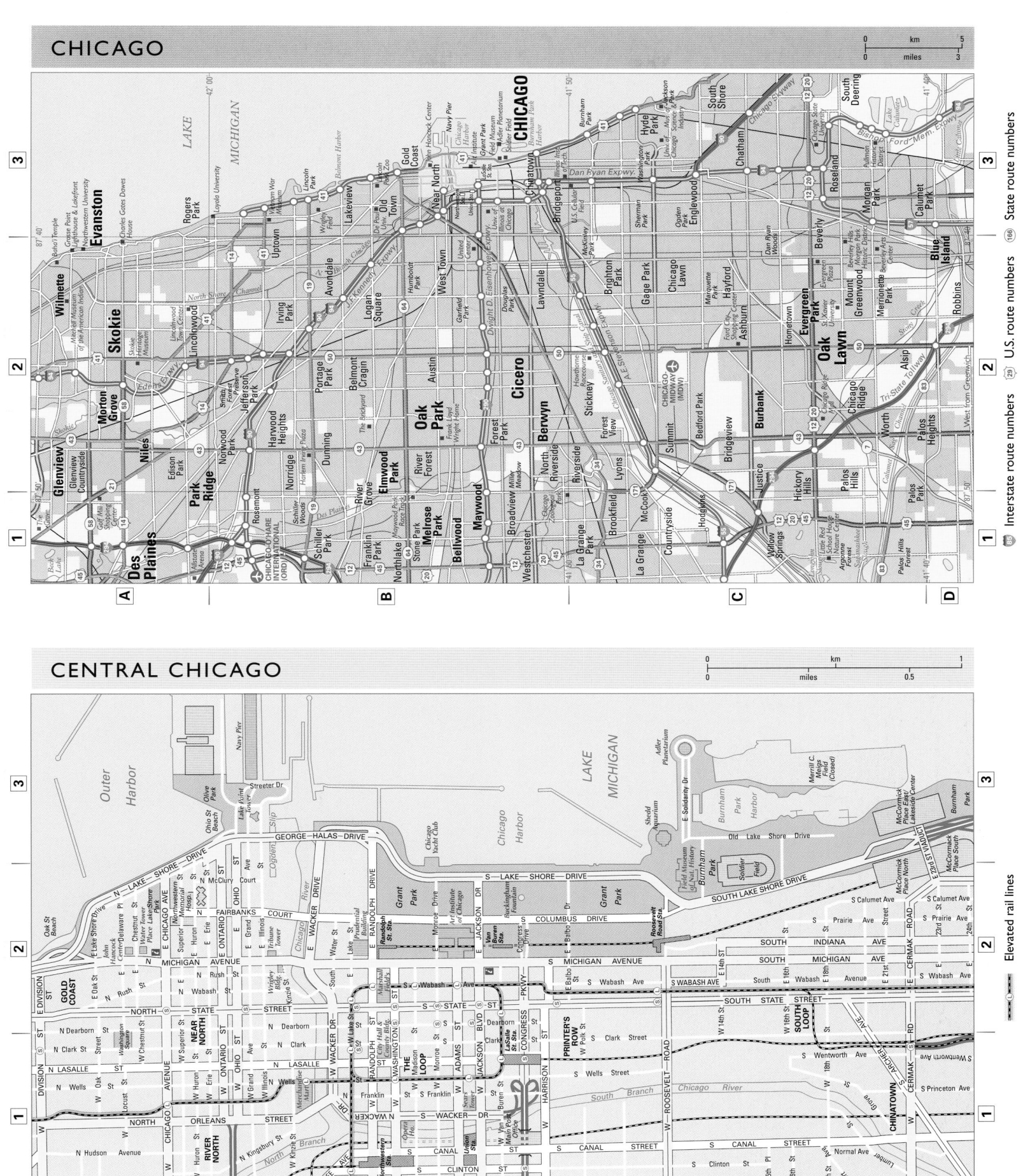

CHICAGO

CENTRAL CHICAGO

Elevated rail lines

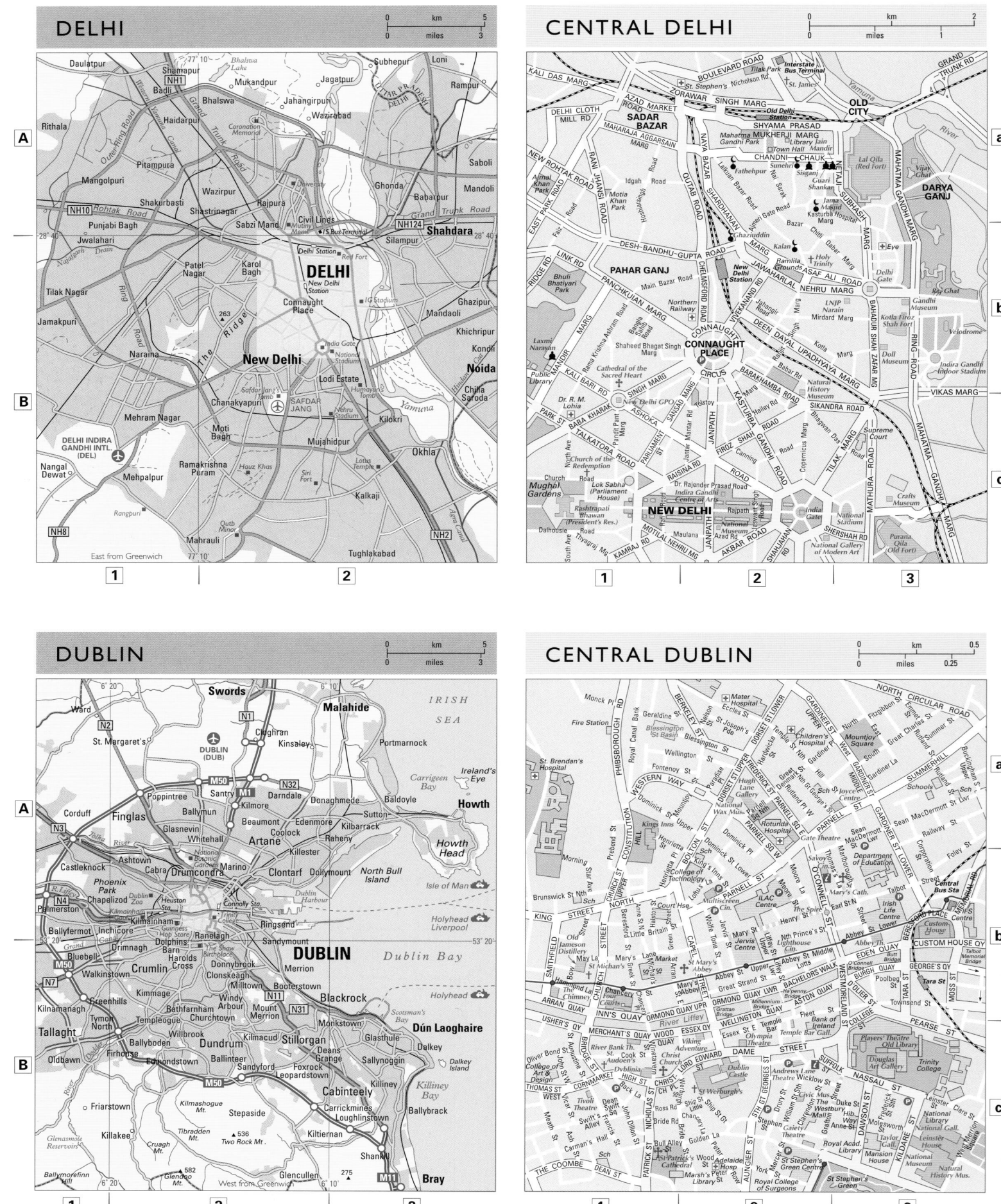

EDINBURGH

0 km 5
0 miles 3

CENTRAL EDINBURGH

0 km 0.5
0 miles 0.25

GUANGZHOU

0 km 5
0 miles 3

HELSINKI

0 km 5
0 miles 3

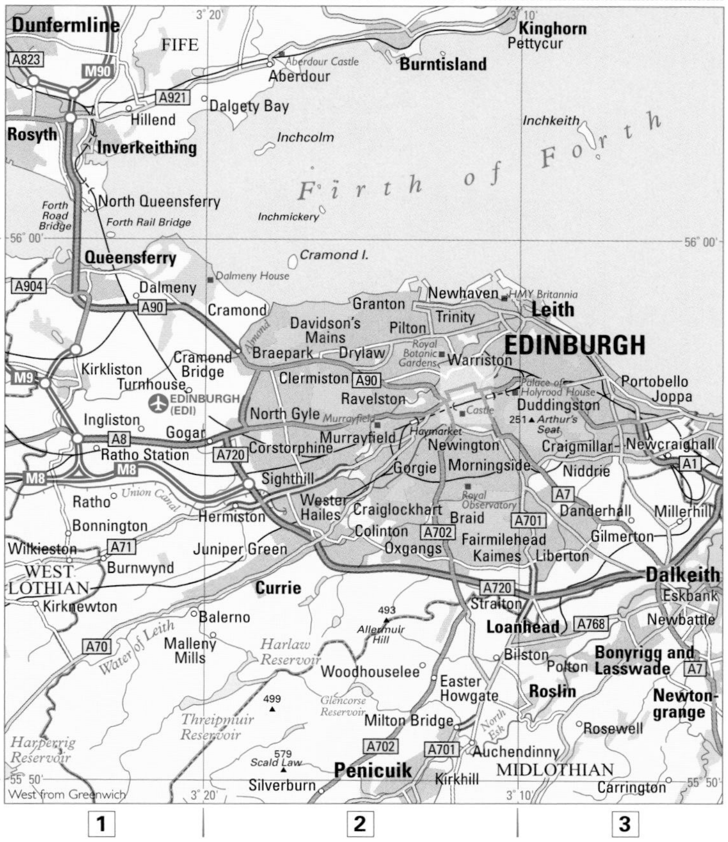

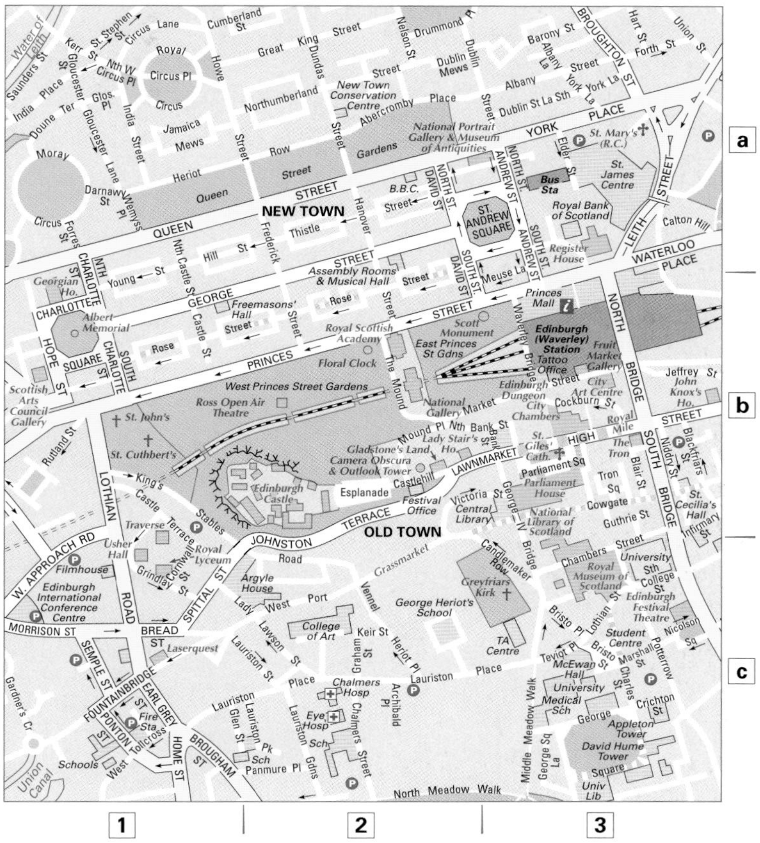

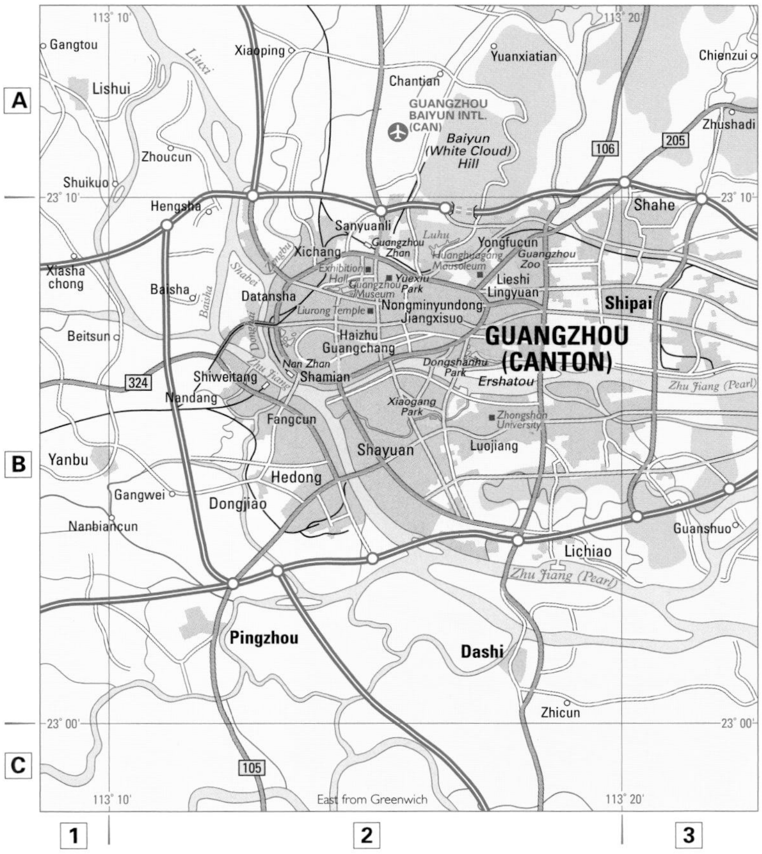

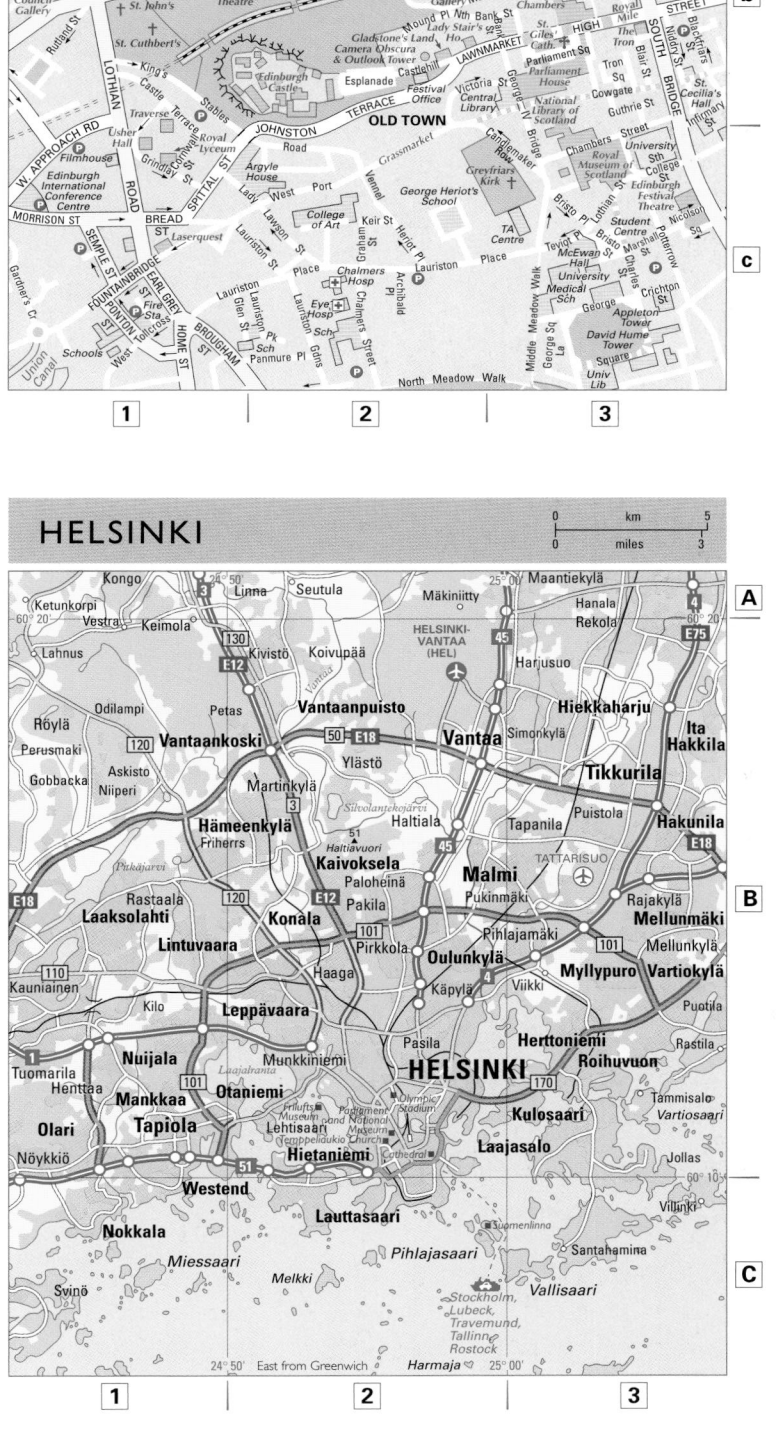

HONG KONG

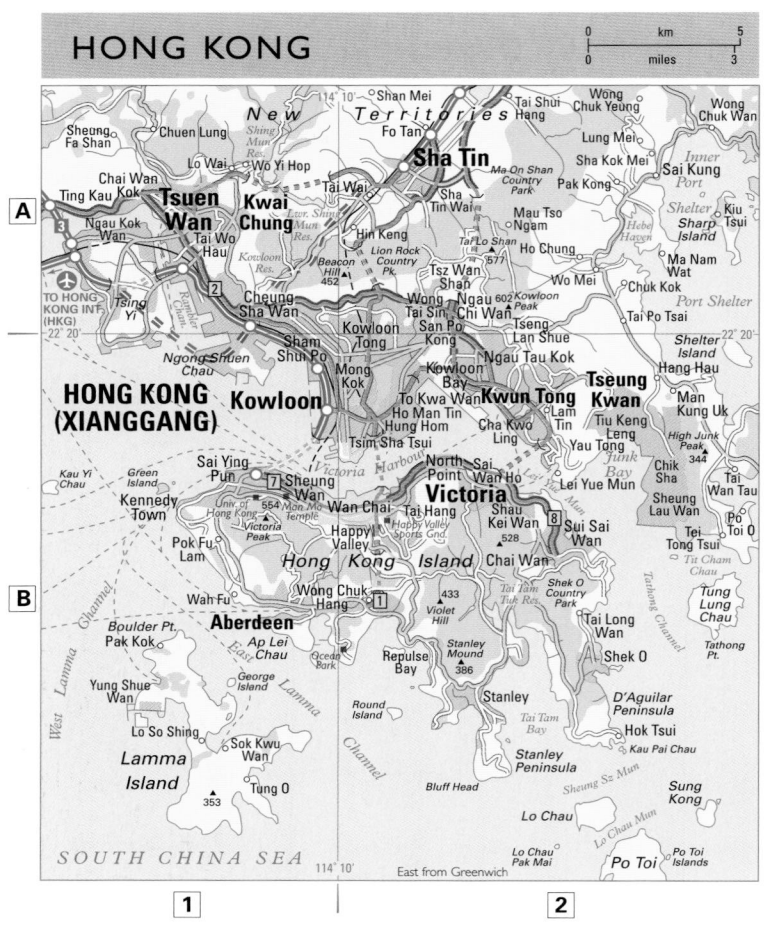

CENTRAL HONG KONG

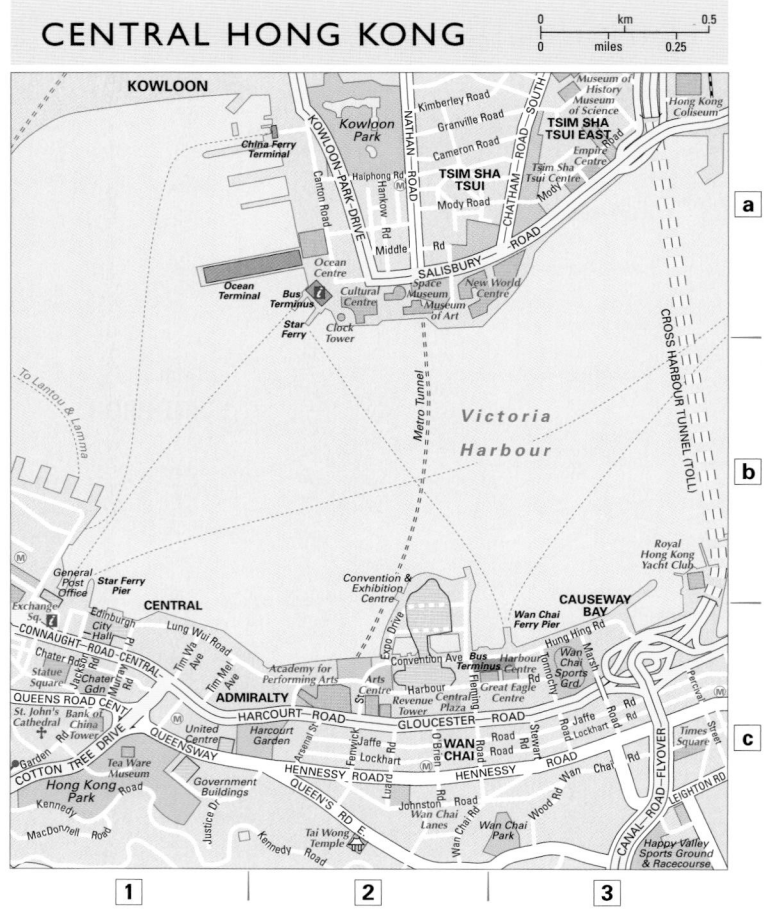

ISTANBUL

JAKARTA

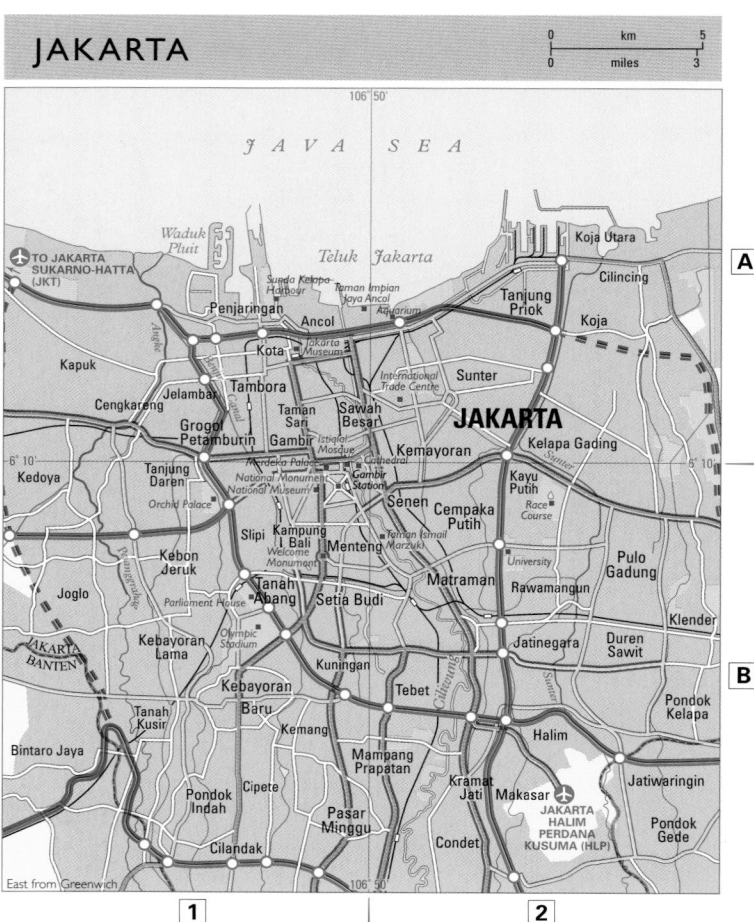

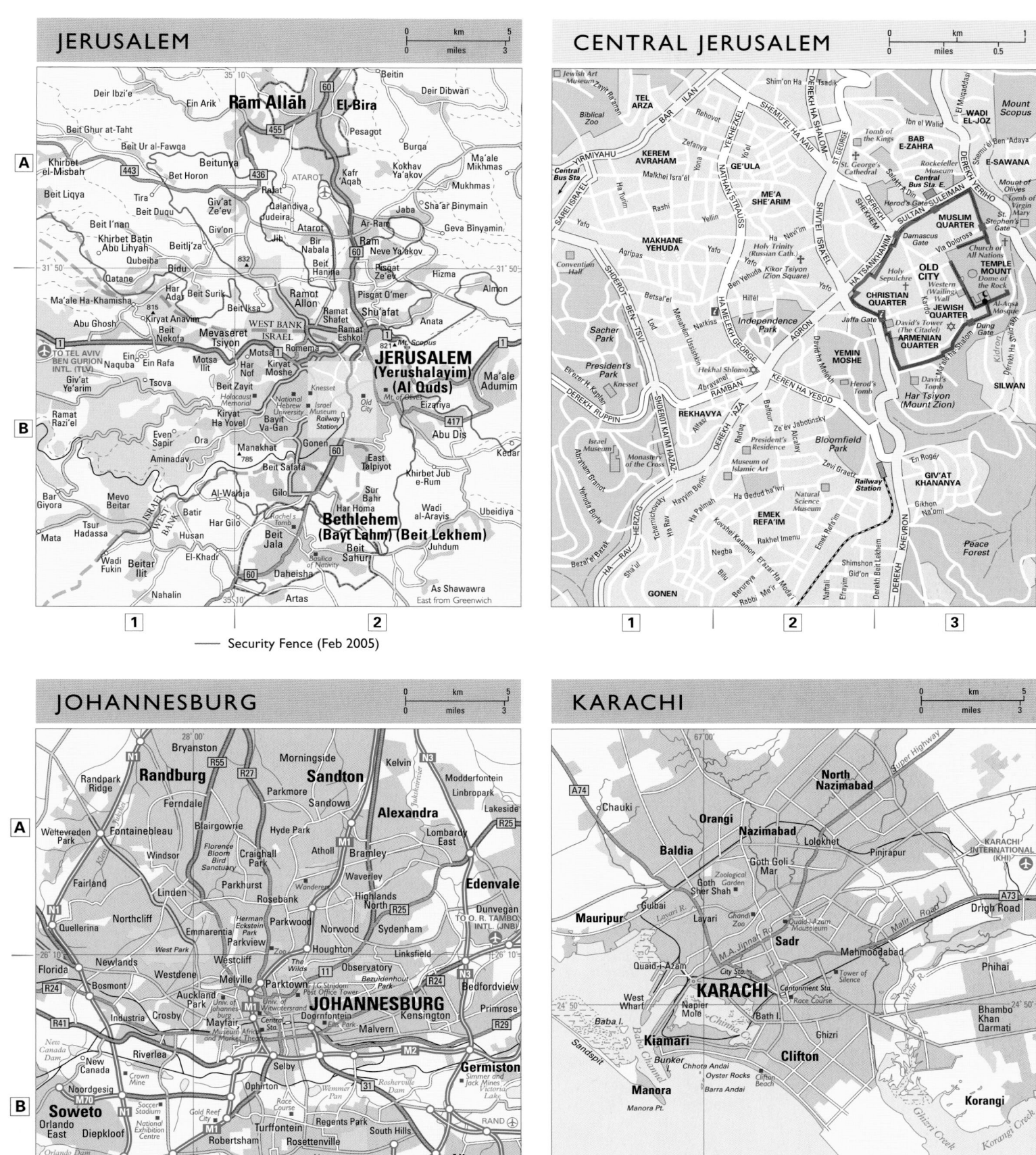

JERUSALEM

km 0 — 5
miles 0 — 3

35° 10'

Deir Ibzi'e · Ein Arik · **Rām Allāh** · El-Bira · Beitin · Deir Dibwan
Beit Ghur at-Taht · Beit Ur al-Fawqa · 455 · Pesagot · Burqa
A · Khirbet el-Misbah · Beitunya · 443 · Bet Horon · 436 · Kokhav Ya'akov · Ma'ale Mikhmas · Mukhmas
Beit Liqya · Tira · Giv'at Ze'ev · ATAROT · Kafr 'Aqab · Jaba · Sha'ar Binyamin · Geva Binyamin
Beit I'nan · Beit Duqu · Qalandiya · Judeira · Ar-Ram
Khirbet Batin · Abu Lihyah · Beitlj'za · Giv'on · Jib · Bir Nabala · Neve Ya'akov · 60
Qubeiba · 832 · Beit Hanina
Qatane · Bidu · Pisgat Ze'ev · 31° 50'
Ma'ale Ha-Khamisha · Har Adar · Beit Surik · Ramot Allon · Pisgat O'mer · Almon
Abu Ghosh · 815 · Kiryat Anavim · Beit Iksa · Ramat Shafet · Anata
Beit Nekofa · WEST BANK · Shu'afat
B · Mevaseret Tsiyon · ISRAEL · Ramat Eshkol
Ein Naquba · Motsa · Har Nof · Mt. Scopus · 1
Ein Rafa · Motsa Ilit · Kiryat Moshe · **JERUSALEM** · Ma'ale Adumim
Giv'at Ye'arim · Tsova · Kiryat Moshe · **(Yerushalayim)**
TO TEL AVIV BEN GURION INTL. (TLV) · Beit Zayit · **(Al Quds)**
Ramat Razi'el · Even Sapir · Ora · Bayit Va-Gan · Eizariya
Aminadav · Manakhat · 785 · Gonen · 60 · Abu Dis
Bar Giyora · Mevo Beitar · Batir · Al-Walaja · Gilo · East Talpiyot · 417 · Kedar
Tsur Hadassa · Har Gilo · Sur Bahr · Khirbet Jub e-Rum · Ubeidiya
Mata · Husan · Beit Jala · **Bethlehem** · Wadi al-Arayis
Wadi Fukin · Beitar Ilit · El-Khadr · **(Bayt Lahm) (Beit Lekhem)** · Juhdum
Nahalin · 60 · Daheisha · Beit Sahur · Artas · As Shawawra
35° 10' · East from Greenwich

—— Security Fence (Feb 2005)

CENTRAL JERUSALEM

km 0 — 1
miles 0 — 0.5

JOHANNESBURG

km 0 — 5
miles 0 — 3

KARACHI

km 0 — 5
miles 0 — 3

COPYRIGHT PHILIP'S

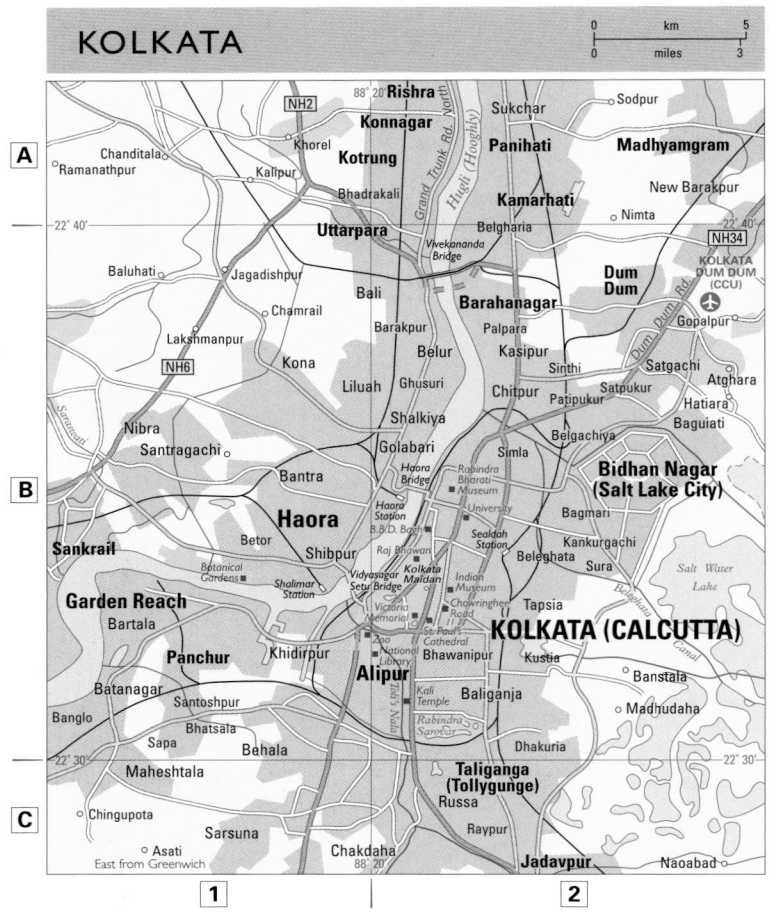

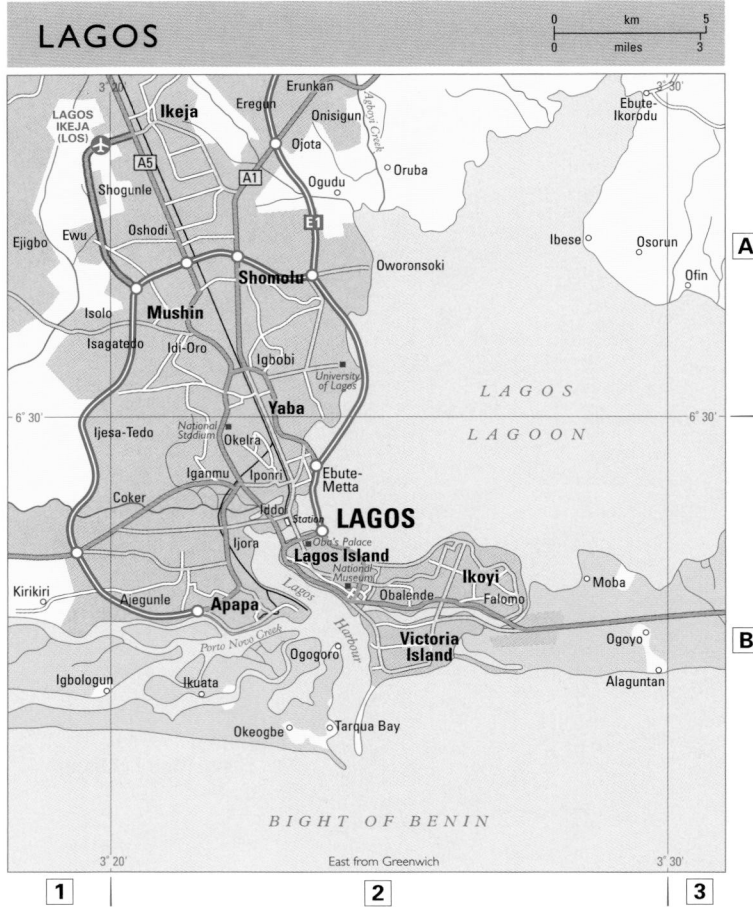

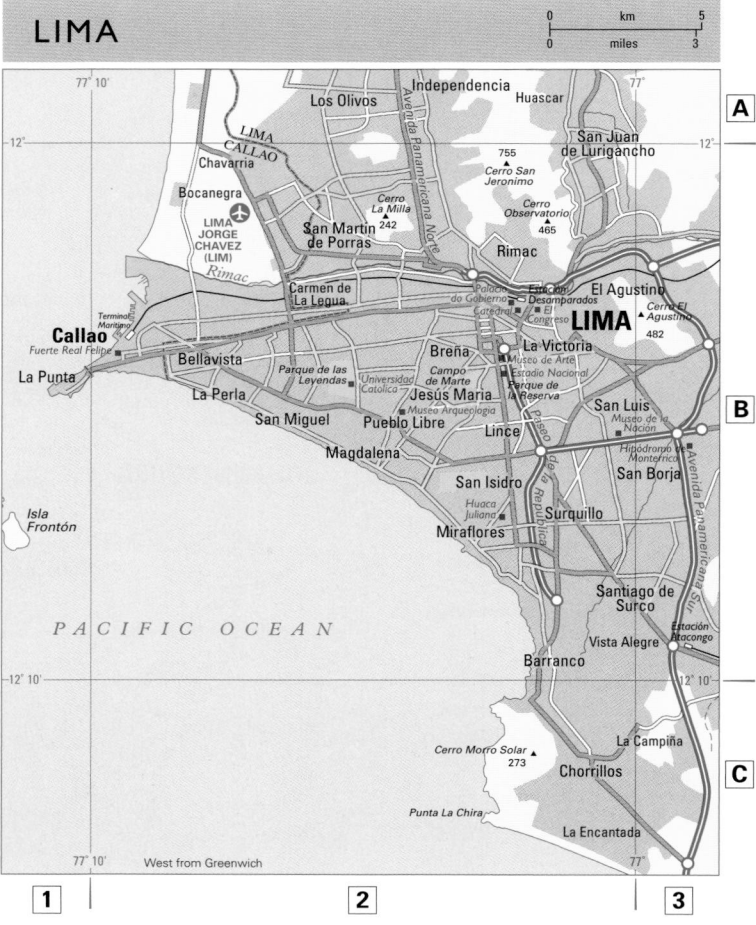

🛡️ Interstate route numbers   ⬭ U.S. route numbers   ⬭ State route numbers

LONDON

km 5
miles

A

Northwood Hatch End Harrow Weald Belmont Stanmore Mill Hill **Barnet** Finchley Colney Hatch **Waltham** Wood Green **Forest** Woodford Green To LONDON STANSTED (STN) ESSEX GREATER LONDON Hainault Havering-atte-Bower Harold Hill
Pinner Green Queensbury Colindale M1 Hendon Church End Muswell Hill Noel Park Woodford M11 Clayhall Barkingside Collier Row Gidea Park Gallows Corner Romford
Ruislip Common **Wealdstone** Greenhill Kenton Kingsbury Hampstead Garden Suburb Golders Green Highgate Hornsey **Haringey** Walthamstow Wanstead Leytonstone Gants Hill Chadwell Heath Goodmayes **Havering** Hornchurch
Eastcote West Harrow **Harrow** Harrow on the Hill East Finchley Kenwood House **Finsbury Park** Crouch End Tottenham **Redbridge** Ilford Seven Kings Becontree Rush Green Elm Park
Rayners Lane Roxeth South Harrow Wembley Dollis Hill Cricklewood Gospel Oak Kentish Town Stoke Newington Highbury Upton East Ham **Barking** **Dagenham**
A Ickenham South Ruislip Northolt Perivale Willesden Green **Camden** **Islington** Dalston **Hackney** West Ham Manor Park **A**
Hillingdon Cowley Greenford A40 **Brent** Harlesden Kilburn Maida Vale Lord's Cricket Ground Regent's Park Holborn Finsbury Shoreditch Bethnal Green A12 Bow A11 Poplar **Newham** Beckton Creekmouth Rainham
Hayes End Hayes Southall A406 **Ealing** Acton Shepherd's Bush Notting Hill Paddington **Westminster** **City** **Tower Hamlets** Limehouse Canning Town LONDON CITY (LCY) North Woolwich River Thames Thamesmead Wennington
West Drayton Harlington Cranford Heston Isleworth Brentford Chiswick A4 **Hammersmith** **Kensington** **Southwark** Bermondsey Wapping Isle of Dogs A102 Woolwich Plumstead West Heath Belvedere Erith
Sipson LONDON HEATHROW (LHR) Osterley Syon Park Kew **Chelsea** **LONDON** Camberwell Deptford **Greenwich** Greenwich Observatory Charlton Kidbrooke East Wickham Welling Northumberland Heath Barnehurst
West Bedfont A30 Feltham **Hounslow** Twickenham Richmond Park Barnes Putney **Fulham** Battersea **Lambeth** Peckham New Cross Brockley Blackheath Shooters Hill A205 Bexleyheath Crayford
Ashford SURREY Hanworth Ham **Richmond-upon-Thames** Roehampton Clapham A3 Brixton Herne Hill Dulwich Nunhead Forest Hill **Lewisham** Lee Hither Green Eltham Blackfen **Bexley** **Dartford**
B Queen Mary Res. Kempton Park Races Whitton East Sheen **Wandsworth** Southfields Balham A214 Tooting A24 Streatham Tulse Hill South Circular Road Catford A20 New Eltham A205 **B**
Sunbury-on-Thames M3 West Molesey Bushy Park Hampton Wick Wimbledon Common Kingston Vale Wimbledon Lawn Tennis Club Upper Tooting Upper Norwood South Norwood Sydenham Grove Park Southend Chislehurst Sidcup Foots Cray North Cray Coldblow Wilmington Hawley
Shepperton Q.E.II Res. Hampton Court Palace Thames Ditton **Kingston-upon-Thames** Raynes Park **Merton** Mitcham Streatham Vale Thornton Heath Crystal Palace Penge **Bromley** St. Paul's Cray Swanley Village Hextable
Walton-on-Thames Sandown Park Races Molesey Long Ditton Surbiton New Malden Morden Colliers Wood Mitcham Common Beddington Corner Selhurst Woodside **Beckenham** Elmstead Bickley Petts Wood St. Mary Cray Swanley
Weybridge **Esher** Hook Tolworth Worcester Park North Cheam **Sutton** St. Helier TO LONDON GATWICK (LGW) Addiscombe Upper Elmers End Eden Park Shortlands Southborough Orpington GREATER LONDON KENT M25 Crockenhill Farningham
A217 A23 A24 **Croydon** West from Greenwich 0° East from Greenwich M20

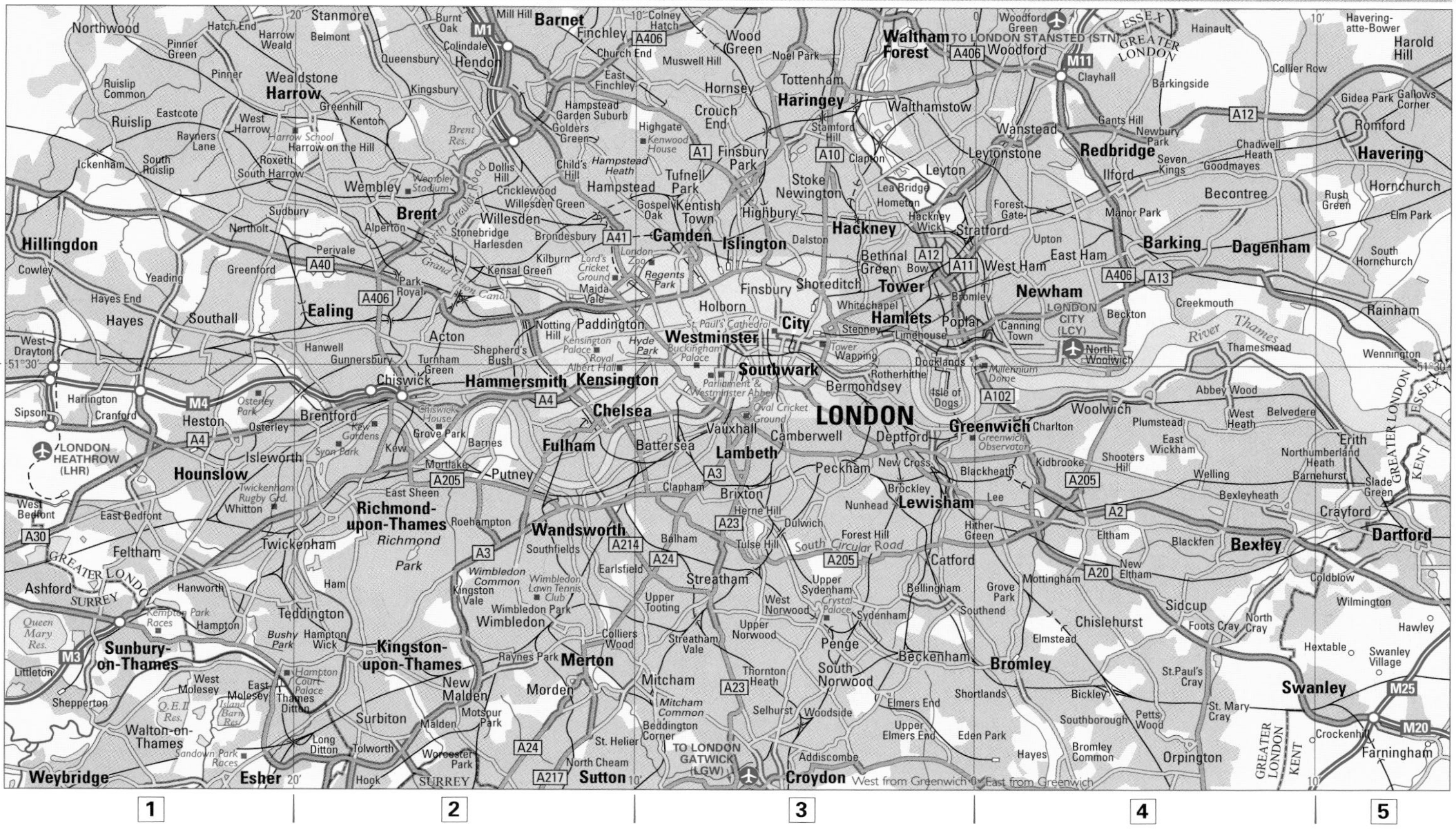

1 **2** **3** **4** **5**

CENTRAL LONDON

km 2
miles 1

a

QUEEN'S PARK WEST KILBURN Kilburn Lane HARVIST RD Queen's Park ST. JOHN'S WOOD Hospital of St. John & Elizabeth Lord's Cricket Ground King's Cross PENTONVILLE RD CITY RD HOXTON SHOREDITCH
WESTBOURNE GREEN MAIDA VALE Maida Vale Regent's Park London Zoo King's Cross Thameslink St. Pancras British Library Angel Old Street CLERKENWELL OLD ST
a PADDINGTON Little Venice London Mosque Queen Mary's Gardens Regent's College Euston Euston British Library Dickens' Ho. FARRINGDON Wesley's Chapel Barbican Mus. of London Liverpool St. **a**
St. Mary's Hospital Marylebone Madame Tussaud's Royal College of Physicians B.T. Tower BLOOMSBURY Russell Sq. British Museum HOLBORN Chancery Lane HOLBORN Barbican Moorgate St. Helen's Fenchurch St.
BAYSWATER Paddington Royal Oak Westbourne Edgware Rd. Marble Arch OXFORD STREET SOHO Covent Gdn. Old Curiosity Shop St. Barts CITY Bank Mansion House Monument Leadenhall St.
b NOTTING HILL Notting Hill Gate Kensington Gardens Hyde Park MAYFAIR Piccadilly Circus Nat. Gall. Trafalgar Sq. Royal Acad. Transport Mus. Strand Temple Ch. Somerset Ho. Tate Br. SOUTHWARK Tower of London Tower Gateway (DLR) **b**
Holland Park Kensington Palace Serpentine Gallery Albert Memorial Apsley House & Wellington Mus. Green Park ST. JAMES Charing Cross BFI London IMAX Tate Modern The Monument HMS Belfast Tower Bridge The Design Museum
KENSINGTON Commonwealth Institute Royal Albert Hall South Carriage Drive KNIGHTSBRIDGE BELGRAVIA Buckingham Palace St. James's Palace The Mall Downing Street Cabinet War Rooms Banqueting House Houses of Parliament Westminster Abbey Waterloo Waterloo East London Dungeon London Bridge Guy's Hosp. Jamaica Rd.
Olympia ADDISON Imperial Coll. Science Mus. Nat. History & Geological Mus. V. & Albert BROMPTON Brompton Oratory BELGRAVE KING'S RD St. James's Park Victoria Westminster Cath. Westminster Lambeth Palace Imperial War Mus. Waterloo International BOROUGH NEWINGTON Elephant & Castle BERMONDSEY
c WEST KENSINGTON SOUTH KENSINGTON Earl's Court Exhibition Hall Brompton Hosp. Royal Marsden Hosp. Sloane Sq. PIMLICO Victoria Coach Sta. Tate Britain Lambeth Walk St. George's R.C.C. NEW KENT ROAD WALWORTH **c**
West Brompton CHELSEA Chelsea & Westminster Hosp. National Army Mus. Chelsea Royal Hosp. River Thames Vauxhall Kennington KENNINGTON The Oval Cricket Gd. Cuming Mus. Burgess Park
West Brompton CHELSEA EMBANKMENT Chelsea Bridge Vauxhall Bridge The Oval Albany Rd.

1 **2** **3** **4** **5**

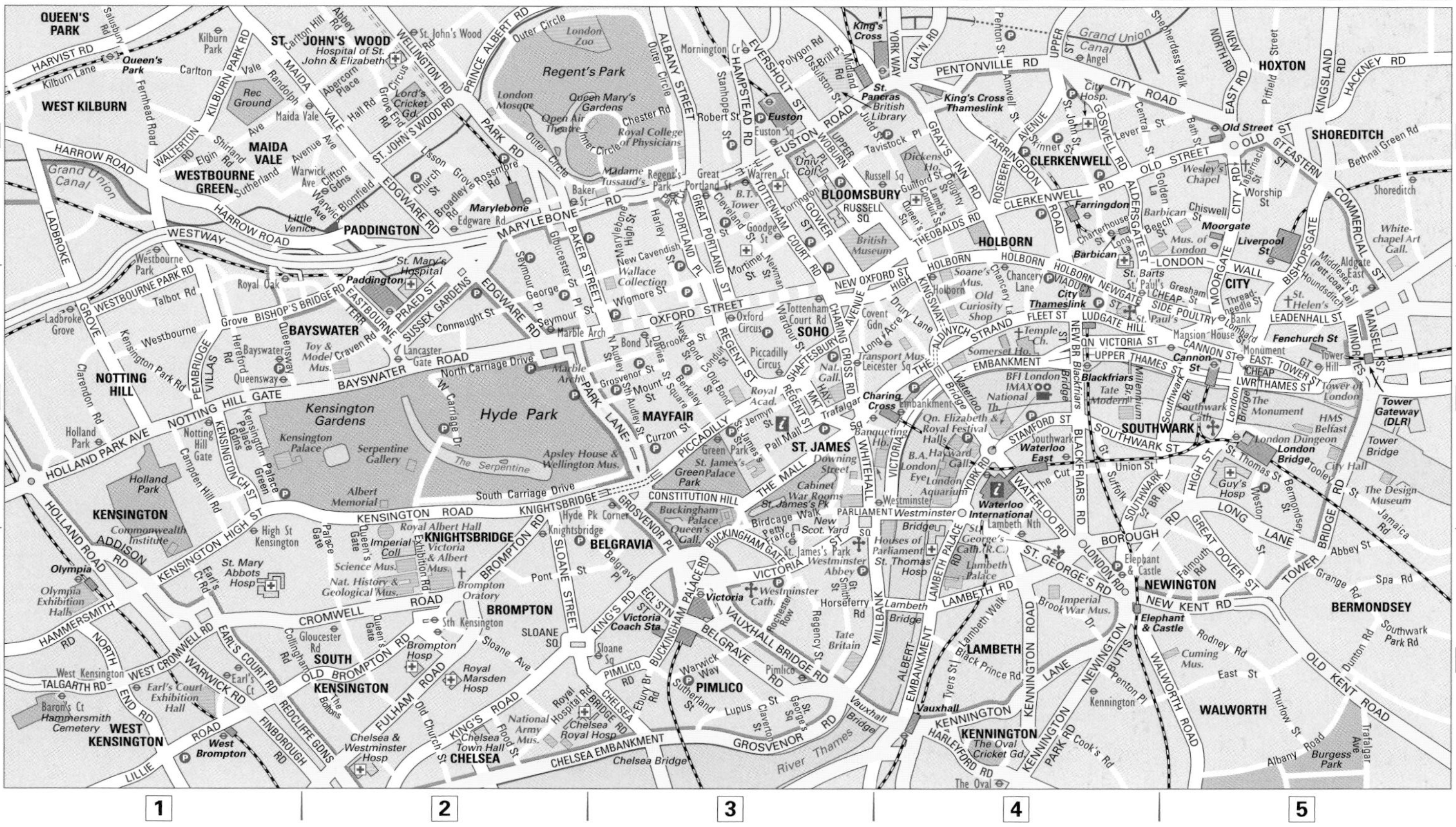

— Congestion Charging Zone

LISBON

km 5
miles 3

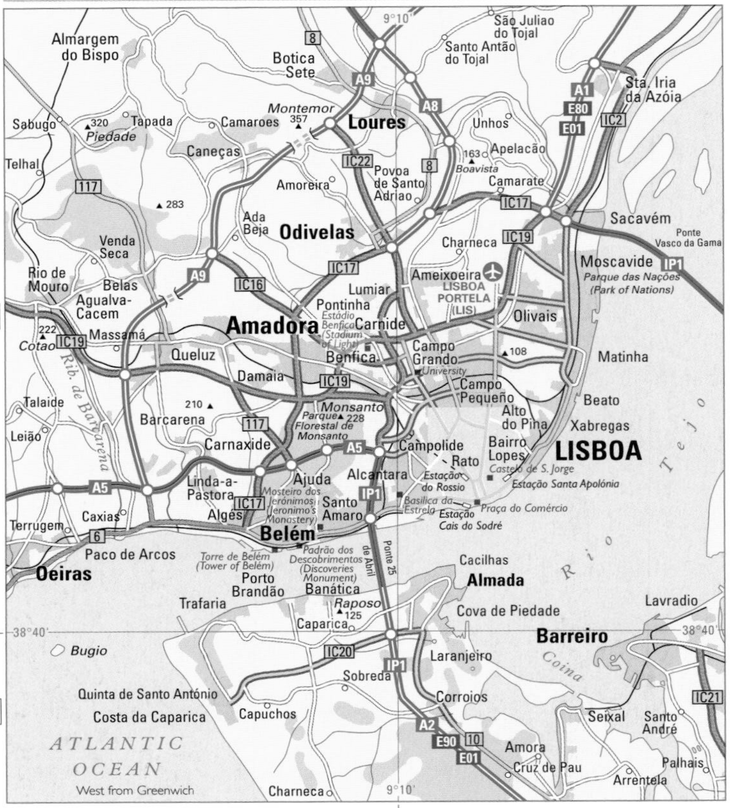

Almargem do Bispo
Botica Sete
São Julião do Tojal
Santo Antão do Tojal
Camarões
Loures
Sta. Iria da Azóia
Sabugo
Tapada
Piedade
320
357
Montemor
Unhos
Caneças
Apelação
Amoreira
Póvoa de Santo Adrião
Camarate
Telhal
283
117
Ada Beja
Odivelas
Charneca
Sacavém
Ponte Vasco da Gama
Rio de Mouro
Belas
Agualva-Cacem
Lumiar
Pontinha
Carnide
Ameixoeira
LISBOA PORTELA (LIS)
Moscavide
Parque das Nações (Park of Nations)
Talaíde
Massamá
Queluz
Benfica
Campo Grande
University
Olivais
Leião
Damaia
Campo Pequeño
108
Matinha
Carnaxide
Monsanto
Parque Florestal de Monsanto
210
228
Alto do Pina
Beato
Xabregas
Barcarena
117
Campolide
Rato
Bairro Lopes
LISBOA
Ajuda
Linda-a-Pastora
Algés
Alcântara
Estação do Rossio
Caxias
Santo Amaro
Praça do Comércio
Estação Santa Apolónia
Terrugem
Belém
Oeiras
Paço de Arcos
Porto Brandão
Banática
Cacilhas
Almada
Oeiras
Trafaria
Raposo
125
Cova de Piedade
Lavradio
Caparica
Barreiro
Bugio
Laranjeiro
Sobreda
Corroios
Seixal
Santo André
Quinta de Santo António
Costa da Caparica
Capuchos
Amora
Cruz de Pau
Palhais
Arrentela
Charneca
ATLANTIC OCEAN
West from Greenwich

CENTRAL LISBON

km 1
miles 0.5

ESTEFÂNIA
AMOREIROS
PENHA FRANÇA
ANJOS
RATO
BAIRRO LOPES
GRAÇA
BAIRRO ALTO
BAIXA
ALFAMA
Castelo de São Jorge (St. George's Castle)
Rio Tejo (Tagus)

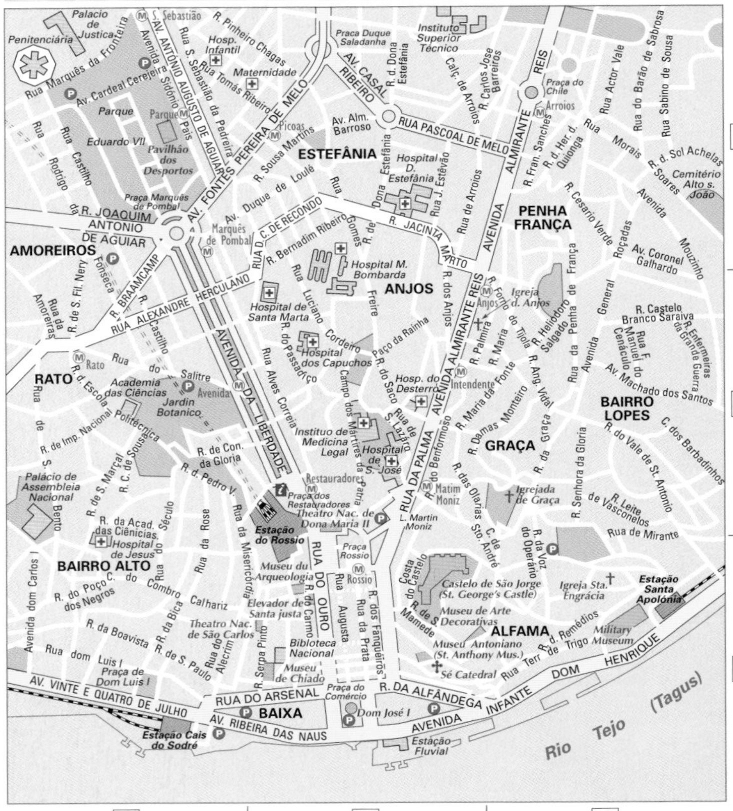

LOS ANGELES

km 5
miles 3

Tarzana
Sepulveda Dam Rec. Area
Van Nuys
San Fernando Valley
Burbank
Verdugo Mts.
Altadena
San Gabriel Mts.
Eaton Canyon Park
Encino
North Hollywood
N.B.C. Studios
Glendale
Pasadena
Sierra Madre
Sherman Oaks
Studio City
C.B.S.
Disney Studios
Eagle Rock
Monrovia
216
Fox Studios
Universal Studios
Warner Brothers Studios
Zoo
Glendale Galleria
California Institute of Technology
Santa Anita Park
Encino Reservoir
Cahuenga Peak 555
Griffith Park
Highland Park
South Pasadena
San Marino
Arcadia
Stone Canyon Reservoir
Lake Hollywood
Griffith Observatory
Garvanza
Temple City
Topanga State Park
Santa Monica Mts.
Hollywood
Southwest Museum
El Sereno
Nat. Rec. Area
459
Hollywood Bowl
Mann's Chinese Theatre
Sunset Blvd.
Silver Lake Reservoir
Arroyo Seco Park
Pasadena Fwy.
Bel Air
Beverly Glen
Franklin Reservoir
Santa Monica Blvd.
Elysian Park
Dodger Stadium
Alhambra
San Gabriel
The Getty Center
Beverly Hills
West Hollywood
Paramount Studios
Lincoln Heights
Rosemead
University of California Los Angeles
Westwood Village
405
Los Angeles County Art Museum
Wilshire Blvd.
California State University
Monterey Park
South San Gabriel
El Monte
Will Rogers State Historical Park
Brentwood Park
MacArthur Park
Civic Center
South El Monte
Whittier Narrows
Pacific Palisades
Museum of Art
LOS ANGELES
Boyle Heights
Flood Control Basin
Santa Monica
Santa Monica Fwy.
San Diego Fwy.
Convention Center
University of Southern California
California Space & Science Center
Memorial Coliseum
Exposition Park
East Los Angeles
Montebello
Montebello Town Center
Bicentennial Park
Puente Hills
Santa Monica Pier
California Heritage Museum
SANTA MONICA
Sony Picture Studio
Baldwin Hills Reservoir
Culver City
View Park
Vernon
Commerce
Pico Rivera
Pio Pico State Historic Park
Venice
Windsor Hills
Maywood
Bell
Whittier
Venice Boardwalk
Ladera Heights
Huntington Park
Walnut Park
Florence
Cudahy
Bell Gardens
Los Nietos
PACIFIC OCEAN
Marina del Rey
Westchester
Inglewood
South Gate
Downey
Santa Fe Springs
LOS ANGELES INTERNATIONAL (LAX)
Great Western Forum
Lennox
University of West Los Angeles
West from Greenwich

85 Interstate route numbers   166 State route numbers

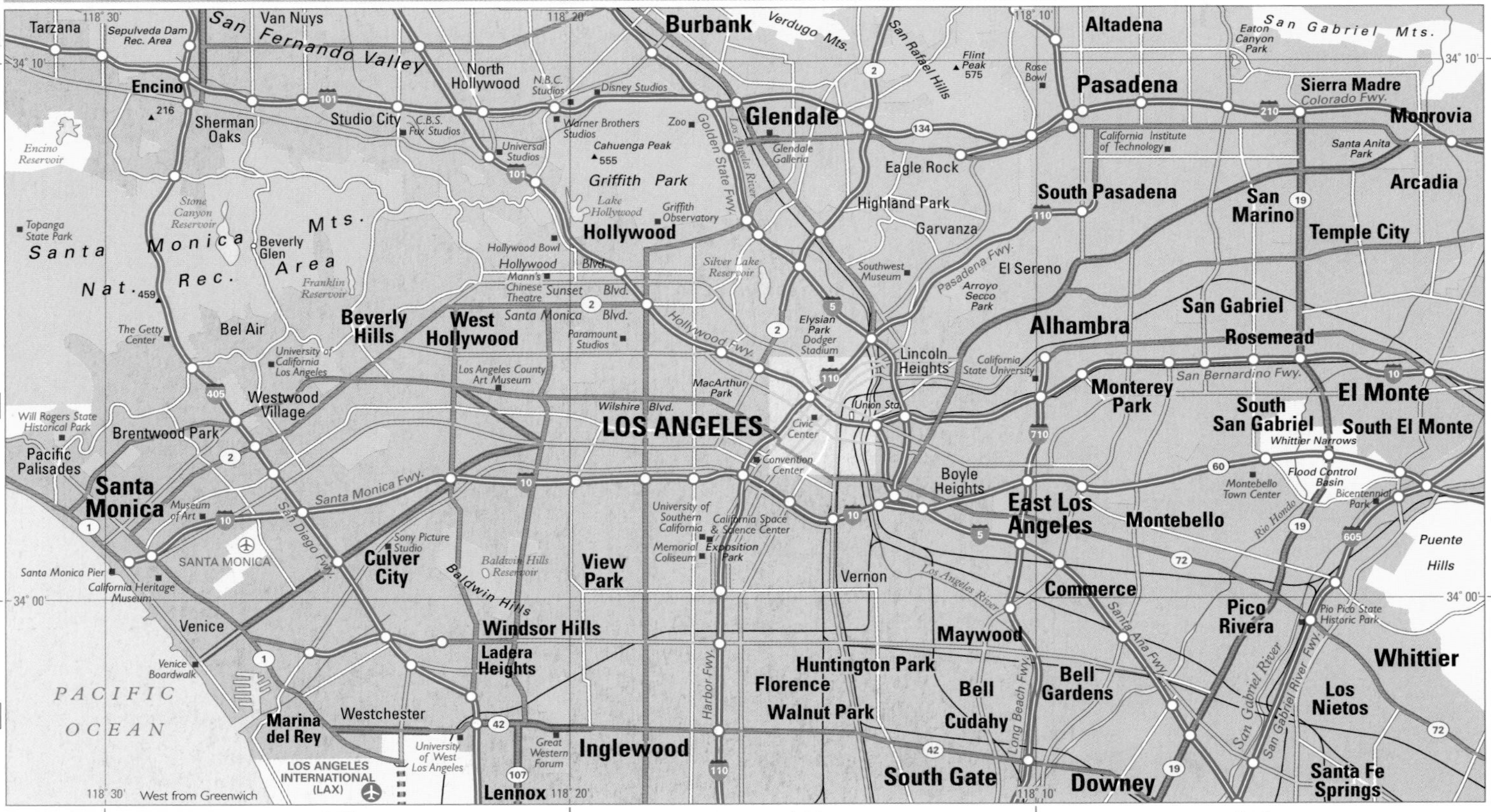

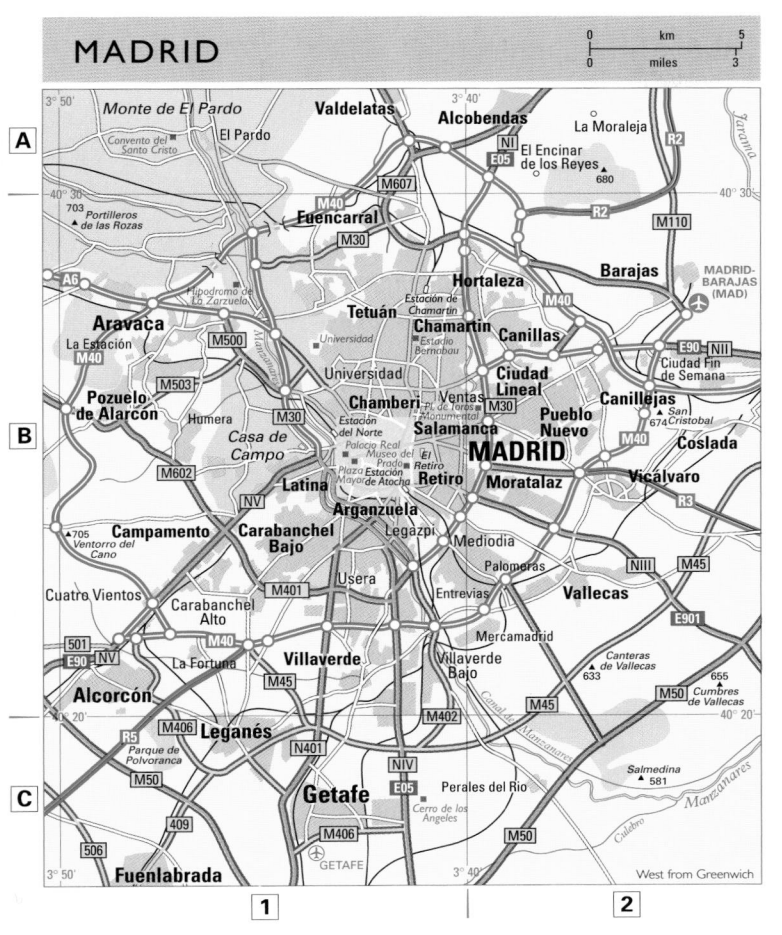

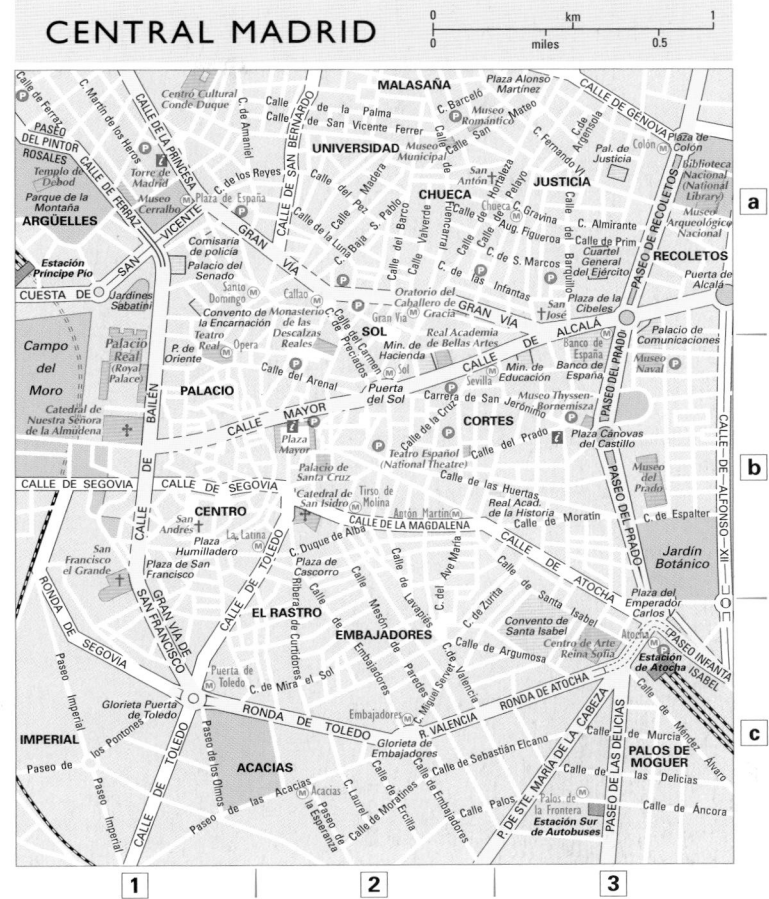

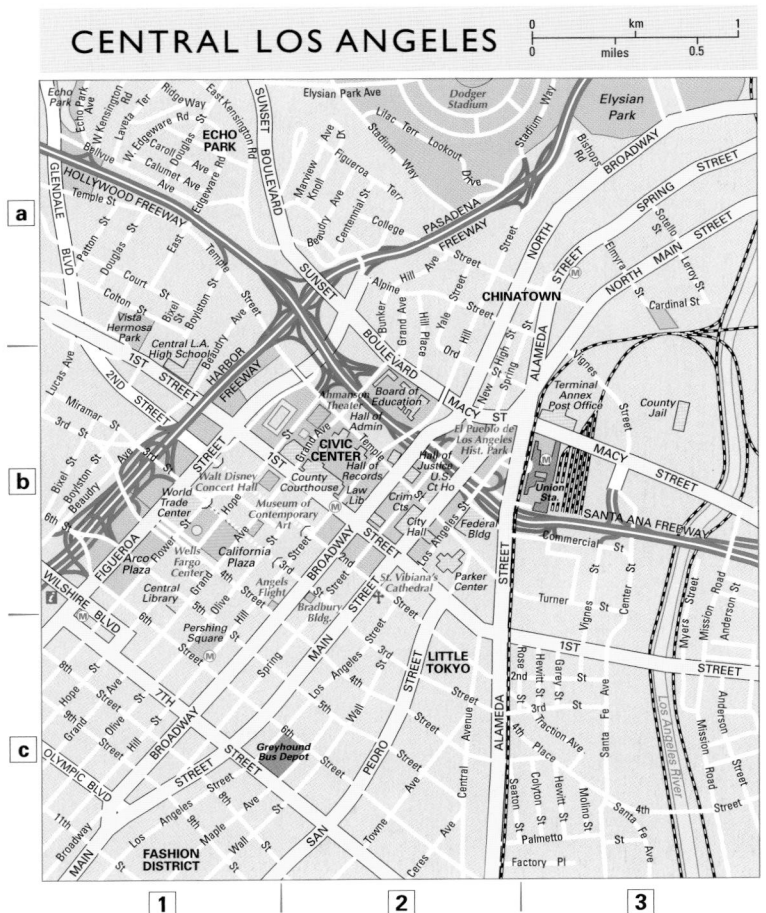

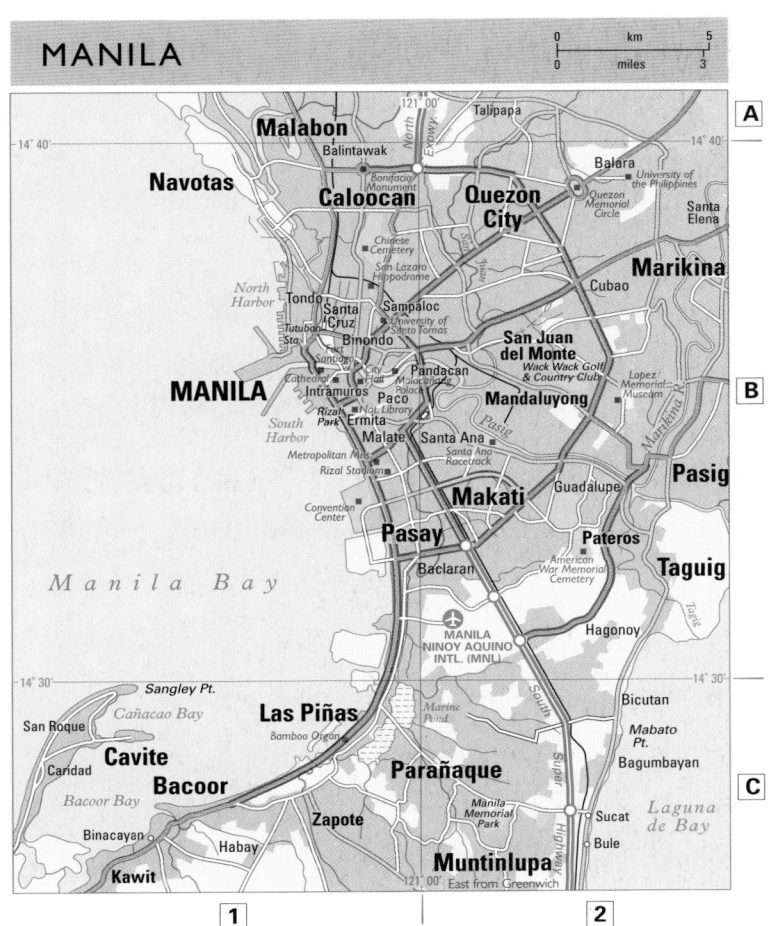

MEXICO CITY

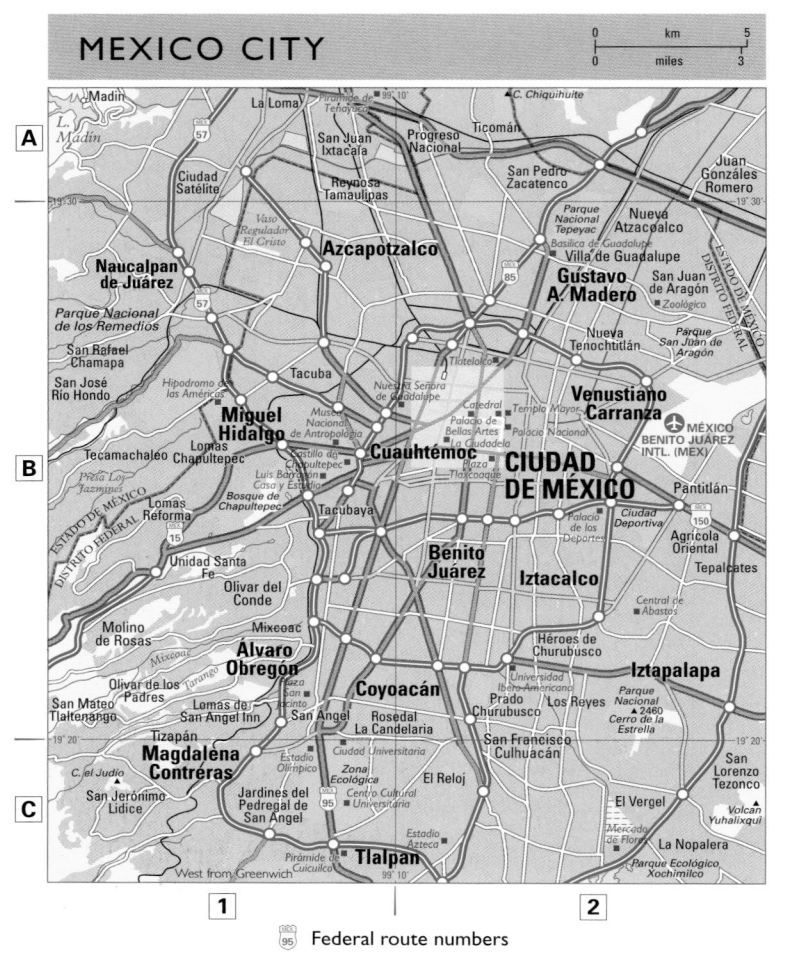

CENTRAL MEXICO CITY

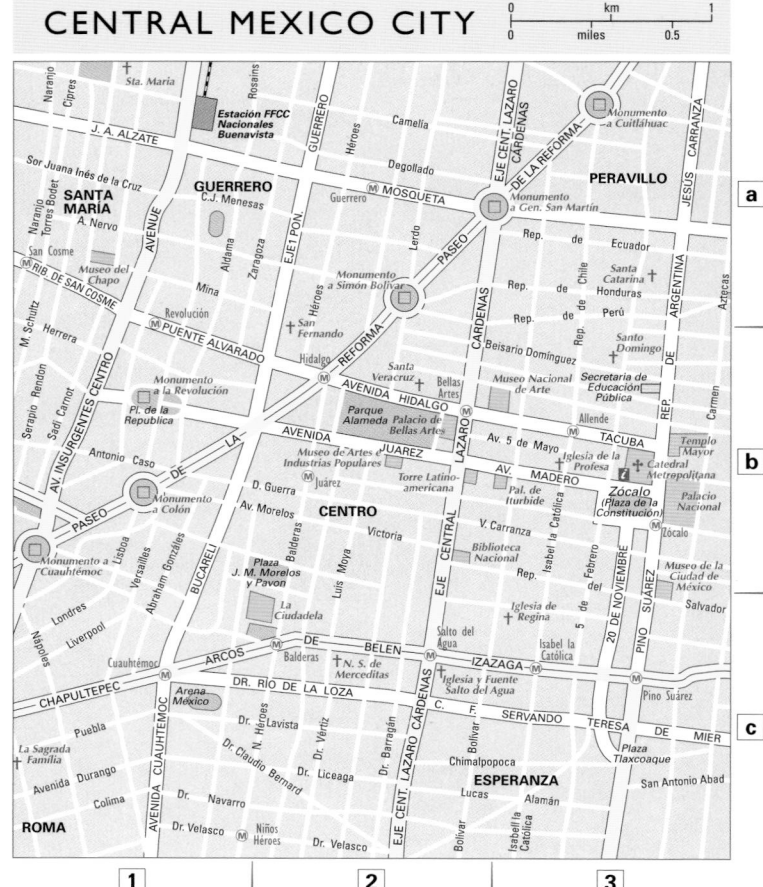

Federal route numbers

MELBOURNE

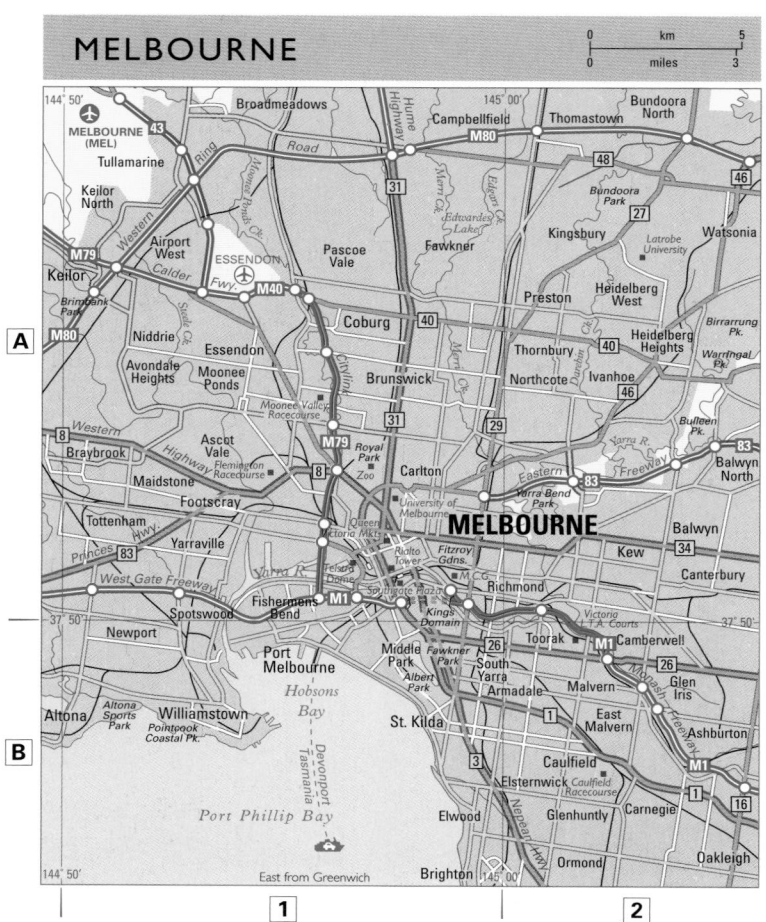

MIAMI

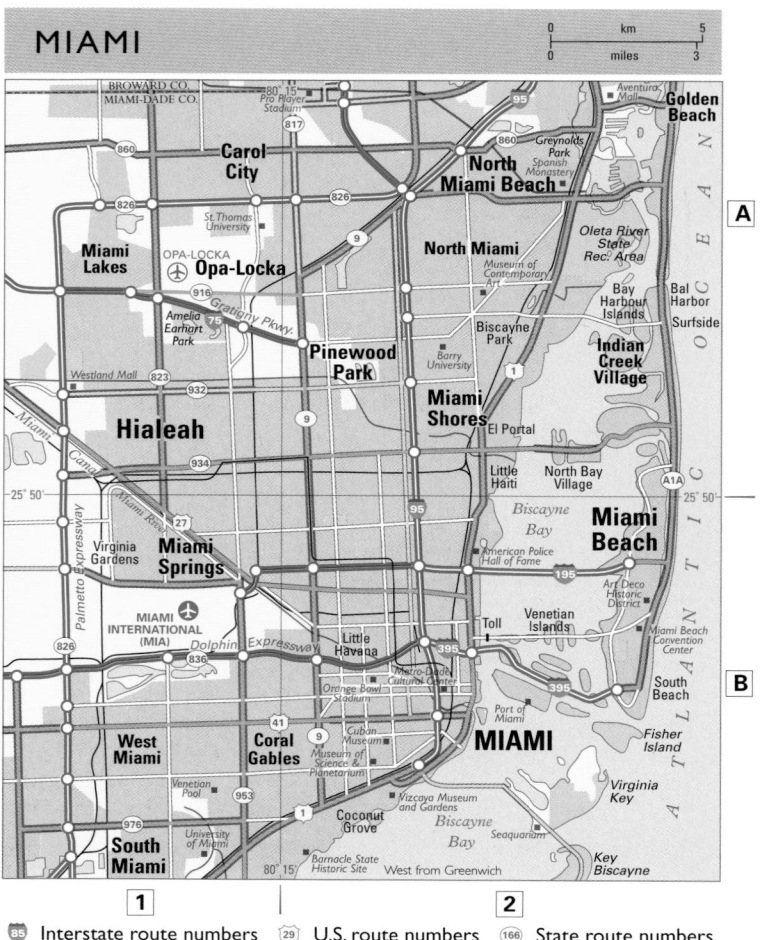

Interstate route numbers U.S. route numbers State route numbers

MILAN

km 0 — 5
miles 0 — 3

Coronno Cesate Limbiate Varedo Muggiò Concorezzo
Pertusella Garbagnate Milanese Senago Palazzolo Nova Milanese Monza
Lainate Amata Incirano San Fruttuoso Autodromo 527
Cassina Nuova Paderno Dugnano San Maurizio al Lambro Brughério A51
Valera Bollate Cusano Milanino Ciniséllo Balsamo A52 E66 A4
Passirana Arese Cormano Bresso Bruzzano Cologno Monzese
Rho Terrazzano Ospiate Novate Milanese Sesto San Giovanni Precotto Pioltello
Cornaredo Pero A4 Affori Parco Regionale Crescenzago Vimodrone
Vighignolo Figino Musocco Bovisa Greco Milano Due Segrate
Séttimo Milanese Trenno Boldinasco Loreto Lambrate Milano San Felice
Seguro MILANO Stàdio San Siro Fiera Camp. Città degli Studi Ortica Idroscala
Monzoro Quinto Romano Fiere La Scala Duomo Calvairate MILANO LINATE (LIN)
Assiano Bággio San Cristoforo Morivione Gambolóita San Bóvio
Cusago Cesano Boscone Vigentino Mezzate Peschiera Borromeo
Quartiere Zingone Córsico A7 Triulzo A51 415
Trezzano sul Naviglio Romano Banco Chiaravalle Milanese Metanopoli San Donato Milanese
Gaggiano Buccinasco Assago Gratosóglio Poasco San Giuliano Milanese
Barate Quinto de Stampi Mirasole Zivido Mediglia
San Novo E35 Sesto Ulteriano A50
Tainate San Pietro Cúsico Gudo Gamb. Opera San Brera
Noviglio Zibido San Giacomo Pontesesto Rozzano Fizzonasco Mezzano
Mairano Tolcinasco Locate di Triulzi Zúnico

CENTRAL MOSCOW

km 0 — 1
miles 0 — 0.5

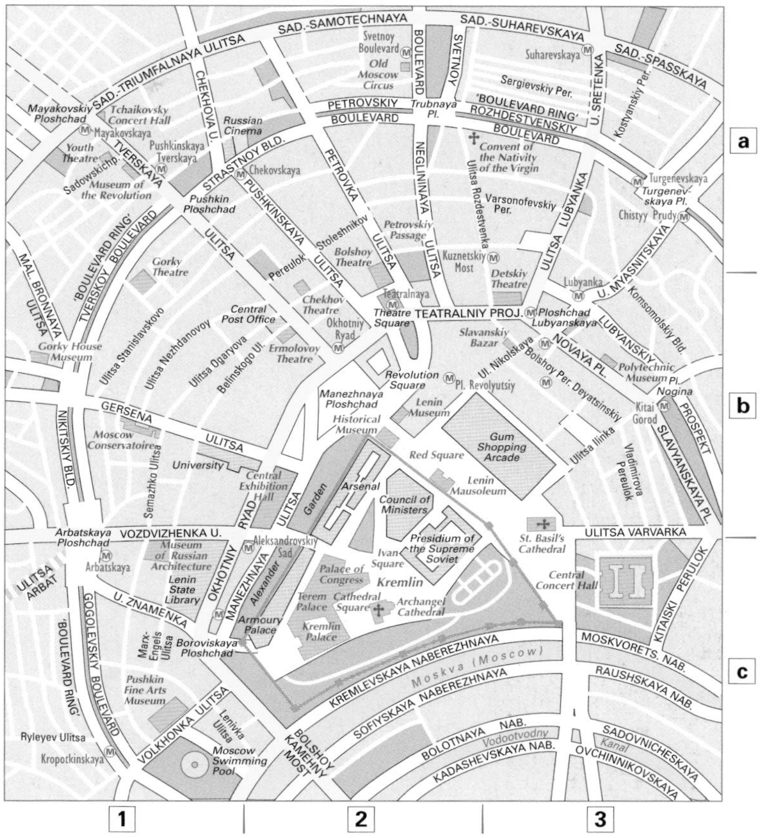

SAD.-SAMOTECHNAYA SAD.-SUHAREVSKAYA SAD.-SPASSKAYA
SAD.-TRIUMFALNAYA ULITSA CHEKHOVA UL. Old Moscow Circus Suharevskaya Sretenka
Mayakovskiy Ploshchad Tchaikovsky Concert Hall PETROVSKY BLVD. ROZHDESTVENSKY BOULEVARD Turgenevskaya
Youth Theatre Russian Cinema Pushkinskaya Pl. Convent of the Nativity of the Virgin Turgenev-skaya Pl.
Museum of the Revolution Pushkin Ploshchad Bolshoy Theatre Detskiy Mir Lubyanka Chistyy Prudy
Gorky Theatre Chekhov Theatre Theatre TEATRALNIY PROJ. Ploshchad Lubyanskaya Polytechnic Museum
Central Post Office Ermolova Theatre Revolution Square Slavyanskiy Bazar Gum Shopping Arcade Nogina
Moscow Conservatoire Manezhnaya Ploshchad Historical Museum Lenin Museum Red Square Kitai Gorod
University Central Exhibition Hall Arsenal Lenin Mausoleum St. Basil's Cathedral
Arbatskaya Ploshchad Museum of Russian Architecture Council of Ministers Presidium of the Supreme Soviet Ivan Square ULITSA VARVARKA
ULITSA ARBAT Lenin State Library Palace of Congress Terem Palace Kremlin Archangel Cathedral Central Concert Hall
Pushkin Fine Arts Museum Marx Engels Ulitsa Borovitskaya Ploshchad Armoury Palace Kremlin Palace
Ryleyev Ulitsa Moscow Swimming Pool Moskva (Moscow) RAUSHSKAYA NAB. SADOVNICHESKAYA
Kropotkinskaya VOLKHONKA BOLSHOY KAMENNY MOST SOFIYSKAYA NABEREZHNAYA KADASHEVSKAYA NAB. OVCHINNIKOVSKAYA

MOSCOW

km 0 — 5
miles 0 — 3

Putilkovo Bratsevo Degunino Vladykino Babushkin Medvezhiy Ozyora
Novonikolyskoye Mitino TO MOSCOW SHEREMETYEVO INTL. (SVO) Khimki-Khovrino Losiny Ostrov National Park Almazova
Chernyovo Penyagino Tushino Nikolskiy Petrovsko-Razumovskoye Abramtsevo Pekhra-Pokrovskoye
Krasnogorsk Pavshino Strogino Timiryazev Park Ostankino Bogorodskoye Galyanovo Vostochnyy Balashikha
Golyevo Myakinino Pokrovsko-Sresnevo Leningradskiy Prospekt Sokolniki Izmaylovo Gorenki Novaya
Arkhangelskoye Troitse-Lykovo Khorosovo Frunze Sokolniki Park Izmayloskiy Park Vishnyaki Pekhra-Yakovievskaya
Zakharkovo Rublovo Tatarovo Mnevniki Dzerzhinskiy Yaroslav Station Leportovo Nikolyskoye Saltykovka
Razdory Cherepkovo Krylatskoye MOSKVA Krasno-Presnenskaya Leningrad Station Kazan Station Bauman Novogireyevo Reutov Kutsino
Barvikha Kuntsevo Fili-Mazilovo Kiev Station Kremlin Tretyakov Art Gallery Perovo Kuskovo Serebryanka Zheleznodorozhnyy
Romashkovo Davydkovo Novodevichy Convent Pavelet Station Zhdanov Plyushchevo Veshnyaki Fenino
Poduskino Nemchinovka Gorky Park Moskvoretskiy Vykhino Kosino Kozhukhovo Temnikovo
Novoivanovskoye Ochakovo Lomonosov Moscow State University Moscow Circus Tekstilyshchik Kuzminki Zhulebino Mikhelysona Marusino
Lochino Mamonovo Bakovka Zarechie Aminyevo Leninskiye Gory Oktyabrskiy Nogatino Lyublino Lyubertsy Nekrasovka
Odintsovo Meshcherskiy Nikulino Ramenki Cheryomushki Dyakovo Maryino Koreneyo
Choboty Solntsevo Yugo-Zarad Zyuzino Volkhonka-Zil Kuryanovo Kotelniki Tomilino Malakhovka
Peredelkino Orlovo Belyayevo Bogorodskoye Bittsevsky Forest Park Lenino TO DOMODEDOVO INTL. (DME) Kapotnya Dzerzhinskiy Chkalova
Vnukovo Rasskazova Rumyantsevo Chertanovo Borisovo Tokarevo Kraskovo

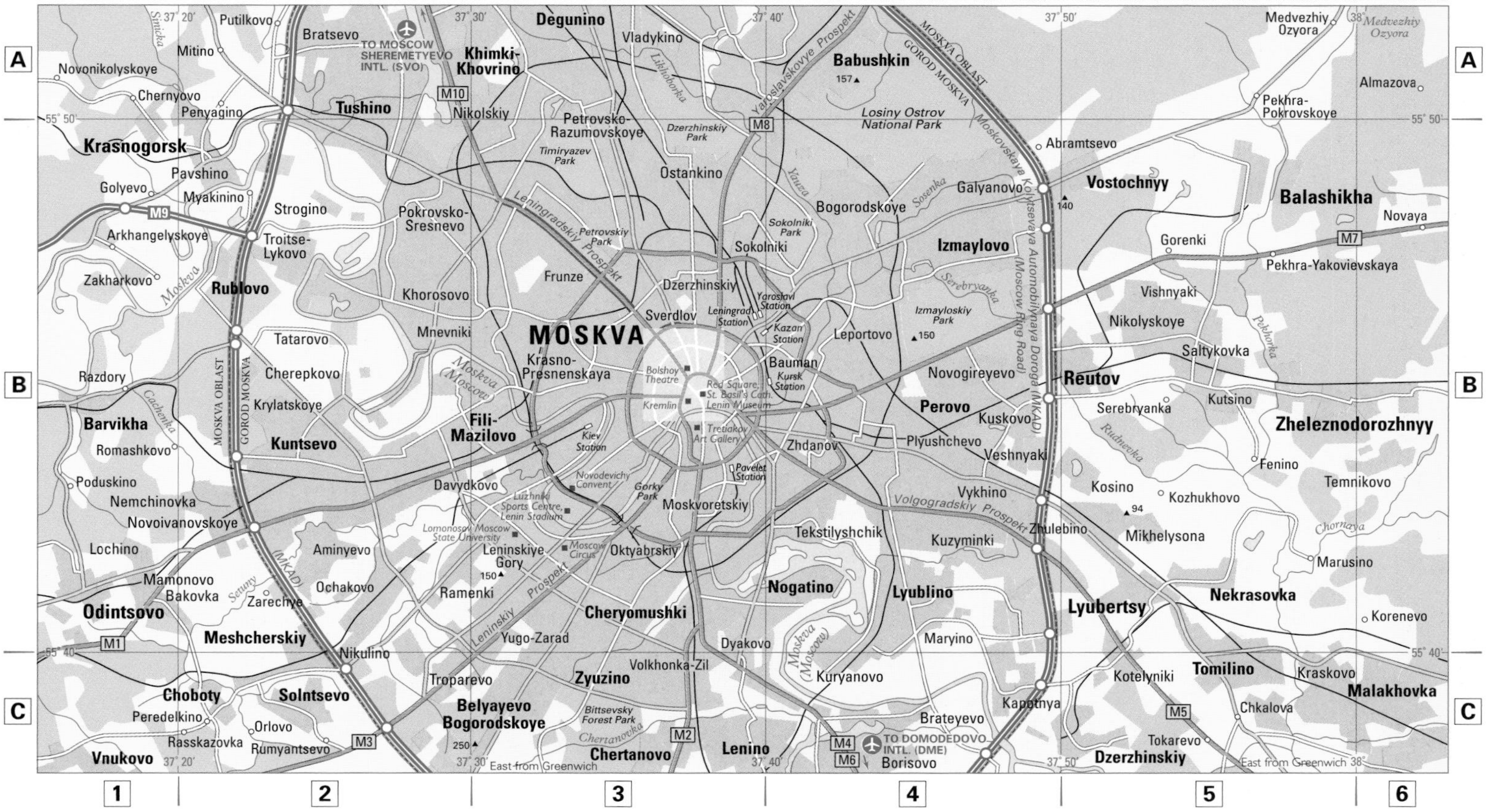

COPYRIGHT PHILIP'S

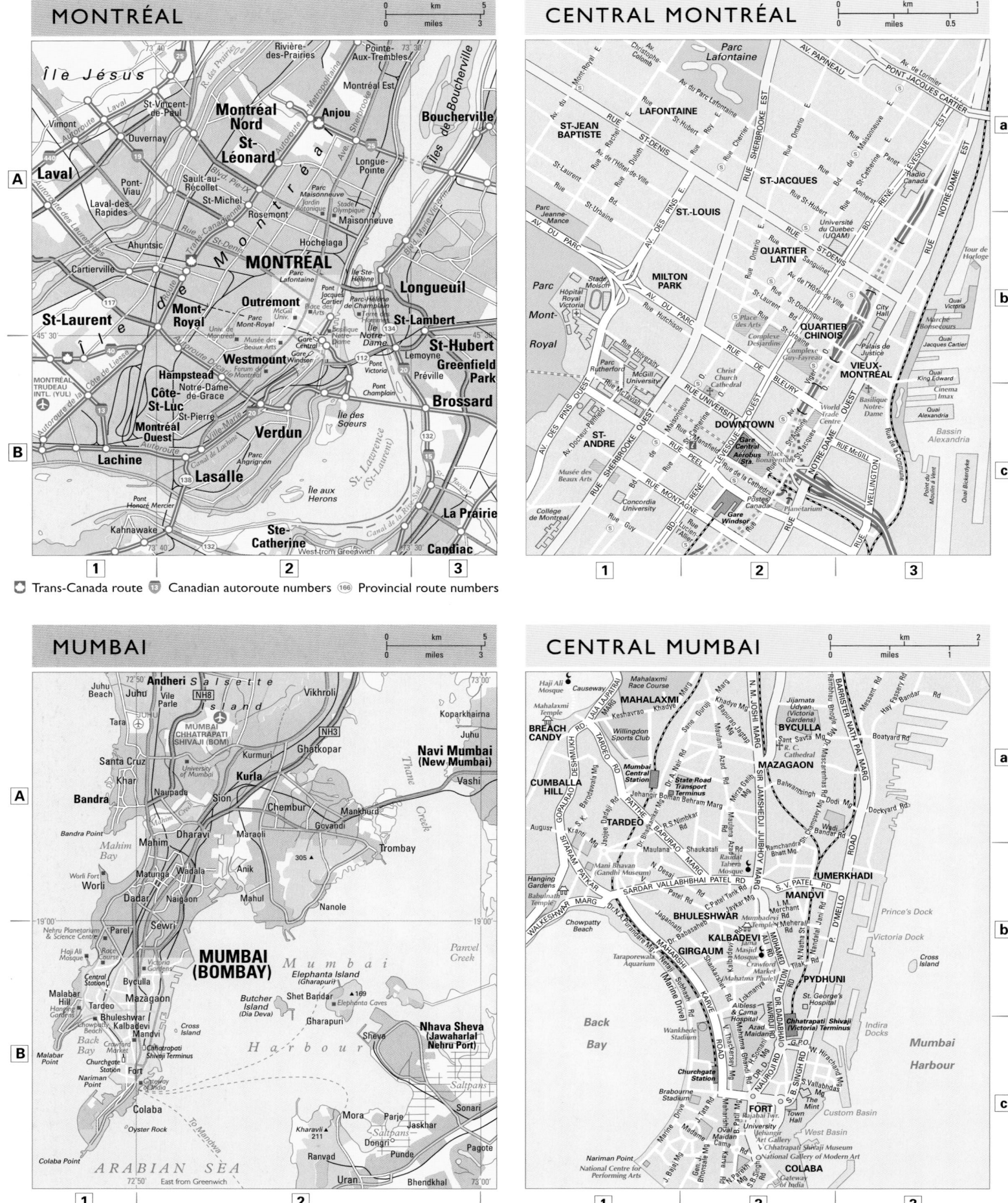

MONTRÉAL

CENTRAL MONTRÉAL

Trans-Canada route   Canadian autoroute numbers   Provincial route numbers

MUMBAI

CENTRAL MUMBAI

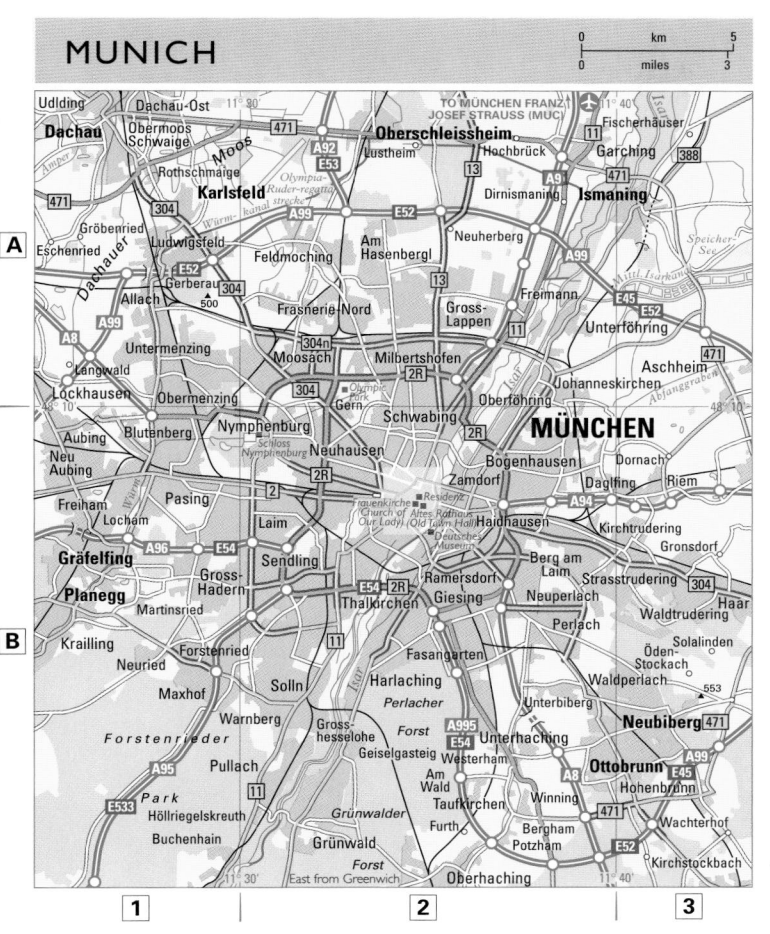

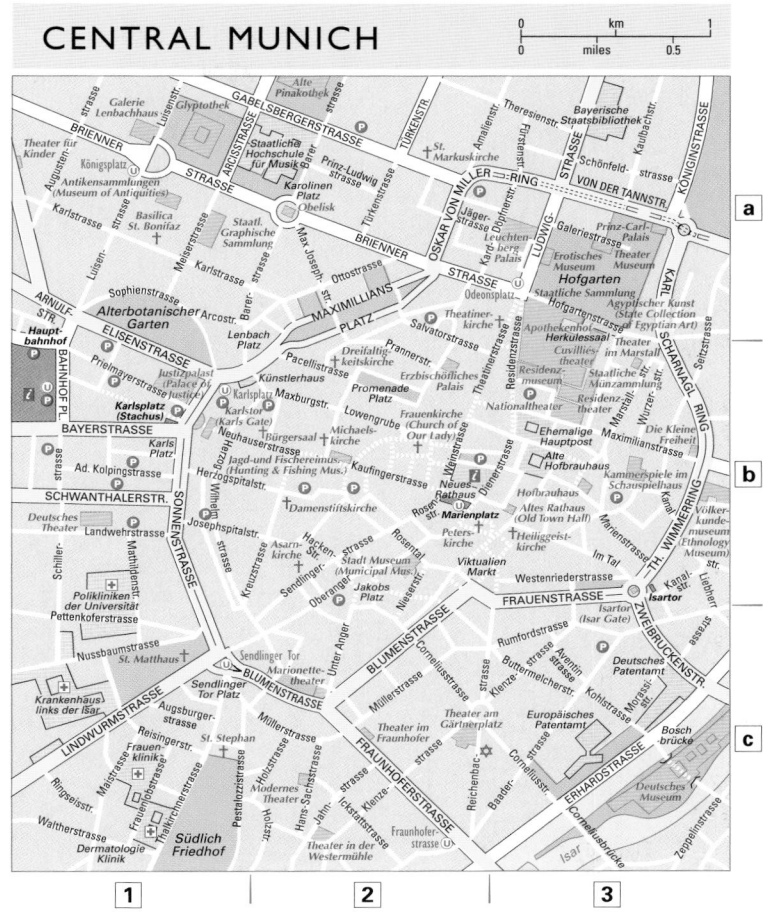

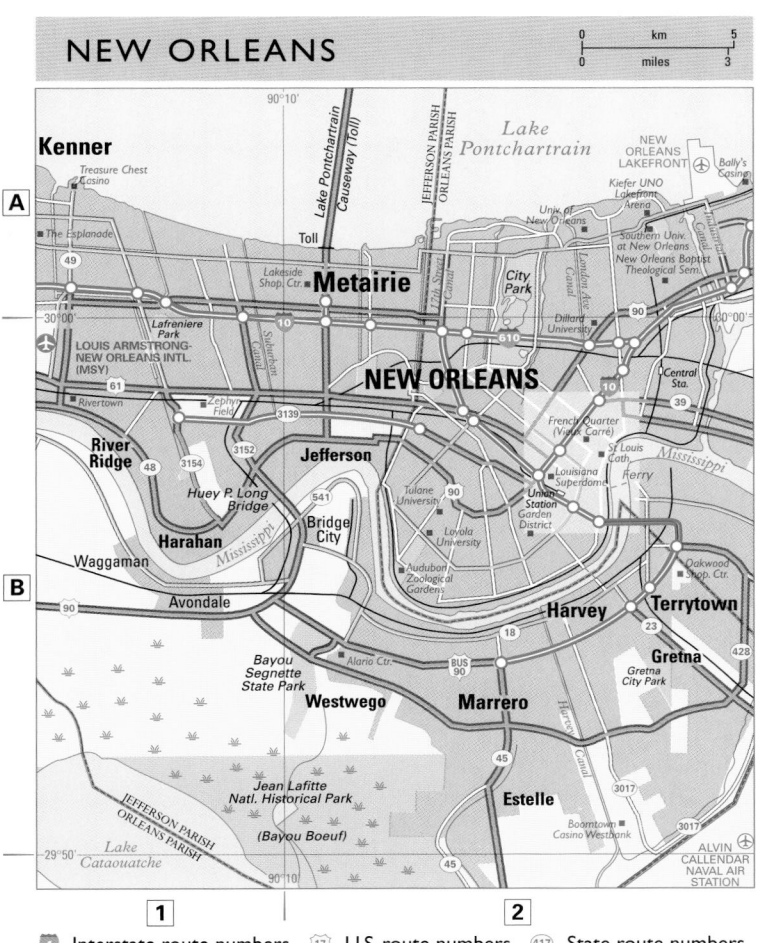

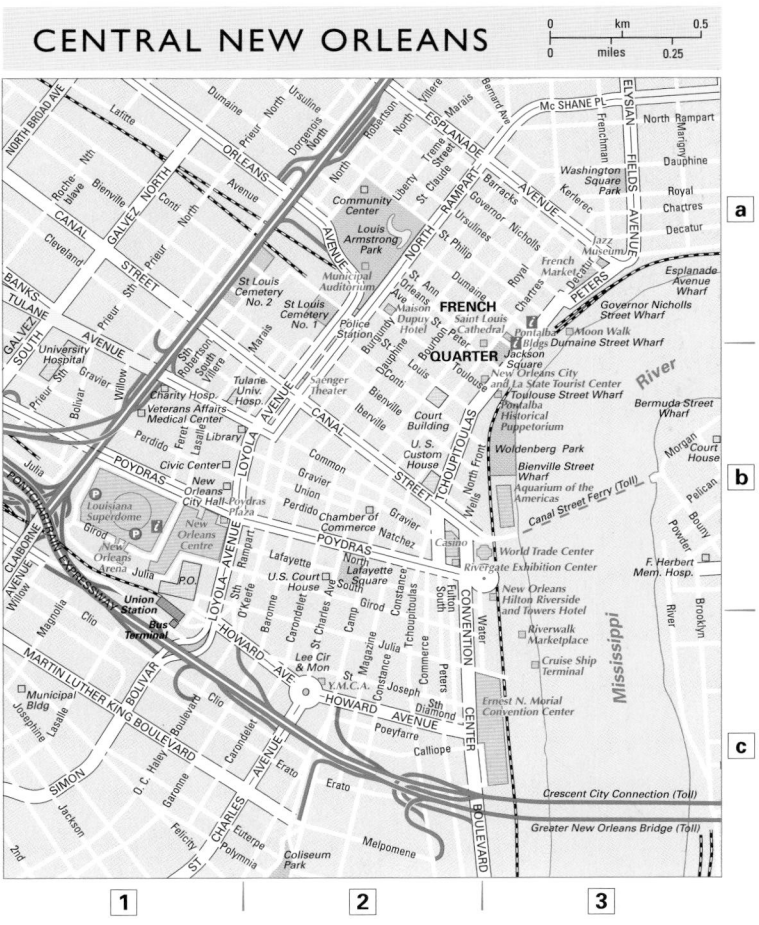

Interstate route numbers   ⑰ U.S. route numbers   ④¹⁷ State route numbers

COPYRIGHT PHILIP'S

NEW YORK

km 5
miles 3

Interstate route numbers
U.S. route numbers
State route numbers

Bronxville · Mount Vernon · Tuckahoe · Yonkers · Riverdale · Bedford Park · Williamsbridge · Westchester · Throgs Neck · Whitestone · Flushing · South Ozone Park · Rockaway Beach · Belle Harbor · Boardwalk

New Milford · Dumont · Cresskill · Haworth · Demarest · Alpine · Englewood · Englewood Cliffs · Tenafly · Bergenfield · Teaneck · Leonia · Fort Lee · Palisades Park · Ridgefield Park · Little Ferry · Ridgefield · Cliffside Park · Fairview · Edgewater · North Bergen · Guttenberg · West New York · Weehawken · Union City · Hoboken

Paramus · River Edge · Hackensack · Bogota · Lodi · Saddle Brook · Maywood · Hasbrouck Heights · Wood Ridge · Carlstadt · Moonachie · Secaucus · Teterboro · Rutherford · E. Rutherford · Lyndhurst · North Arlington

Glen Rock · Fair Lawn · Elmwood Park · Garfield · Passaic · Newark

Bronx · Manhattan · Harlem · Washington Heights · Central Park · Jackson Heights · Astoria · Long Island City · Woodside · Elmhurst · Rego Park · Forest Hills · Richmond Hill · Ridgewood · Bushwick · Williamsburg · Greenpoint · Bedford-Stuyvesant · Brooklyn · Flatbush · Kensington · Gravesend · Bensonhurst · Midwood · Flatlands · Canarsie · New Utrecht · Bay Ridge · Sunset Park · Parkville · Sheepshead Bay · Brighton Beach · Coney Island · Manhattan Beach · Breezy Point

NEW YORK · Jersey City · Bayonne · Port Richmond · Staten Island · New Dorp · Oakwood · Tottenville

ATLANTIC OCEAN

Hudson River · East River · Harlem River · Upper New York Bay · Lower New York Bay · Jamaica Bay · Rockaway

CENTRAL NEW YORK

km 2
miles 1

HARLEM · UPPER EAST SIDE · UPPER WEST SIDE · CENTRAL PARK · MIDTOWN · MANHATTAN · CHELSEA · GREENWICH VILLAGE · WEST VILLAGE · EAST VILLAGE · SOHO · LITTLE ITALY · CHINA TOWN · TRIBECA · LOWER EAST SIDE · LOWER MANHATTAN

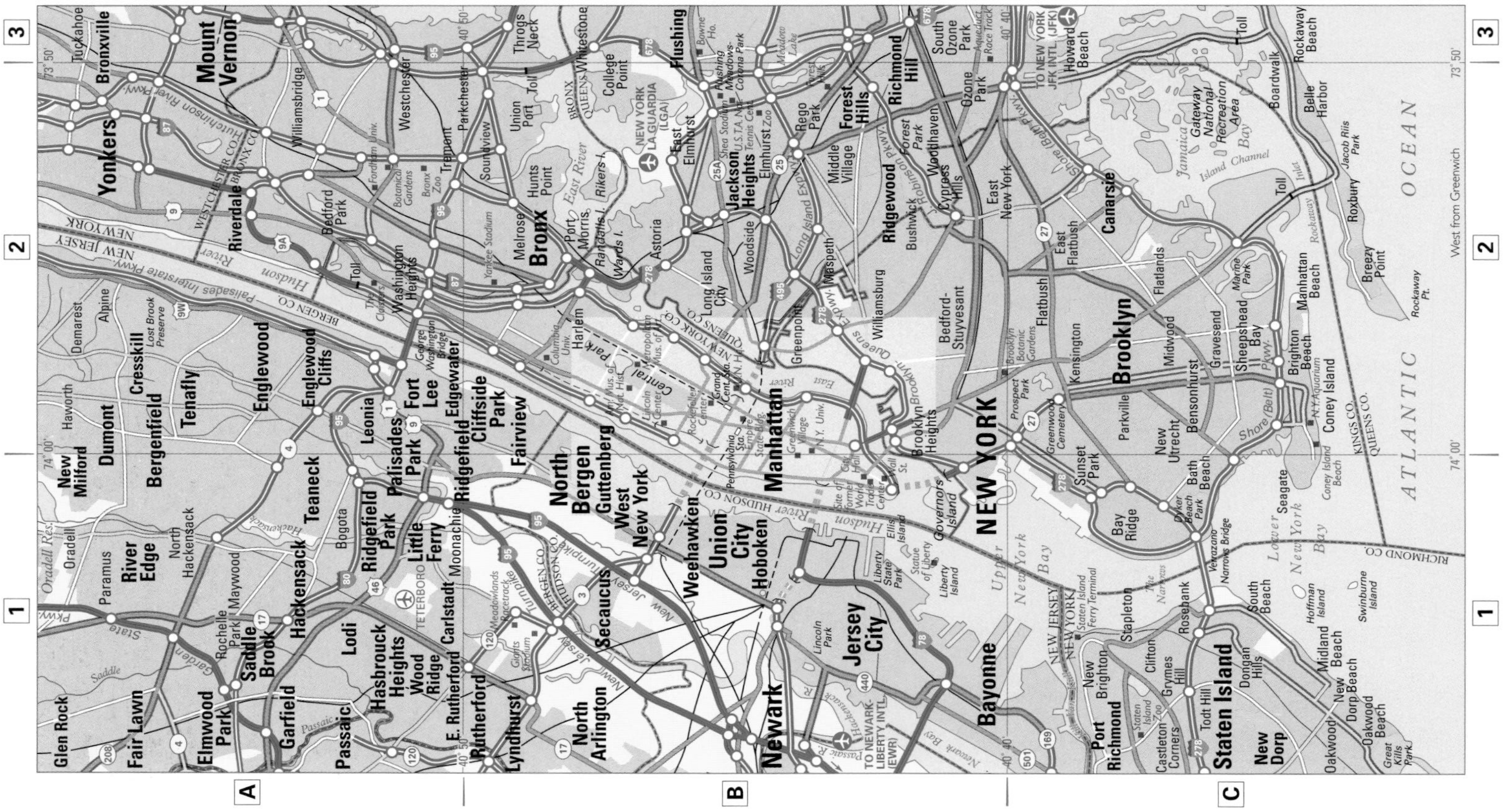

QUEENS · LONG ISLAND CITY · GREENPOINT · WILLIAMSBURG · BROOKLYN · FORT GREENE · BROOKLYN HEIGHTS

WEST NEW YORK · GUTTENBERG · WEEHAWKEN · UNION CITY · HOBOKEN

Hudson River · East River · Roosevelt Island · Governors Island · Ellis I. & Liberty I.

Central Park · The Lake · Jacqueline Kennedy Onassis Res. · Metropolitan Museum · American Museum of Natural History · Lincoln Center for the Performing Arts · United Nations Headquarters · Grand Central Sta. · St. Patrick's Cathedral · Empire State Building · Chrysler Building · Times Square · Madison Square Garden · Penn Sta. · Port Authority Bus Terminal · Intrepid Air & Space Museum · Chelsea Piers Sports and Entertainment Complex · Washington Square · World Financial Center · Ground Zero Site of former World Trade Center · Battery Park · Brooklyn-Battery Tunnel · Holland Tunnel to Newark · Lincoln Tunnel

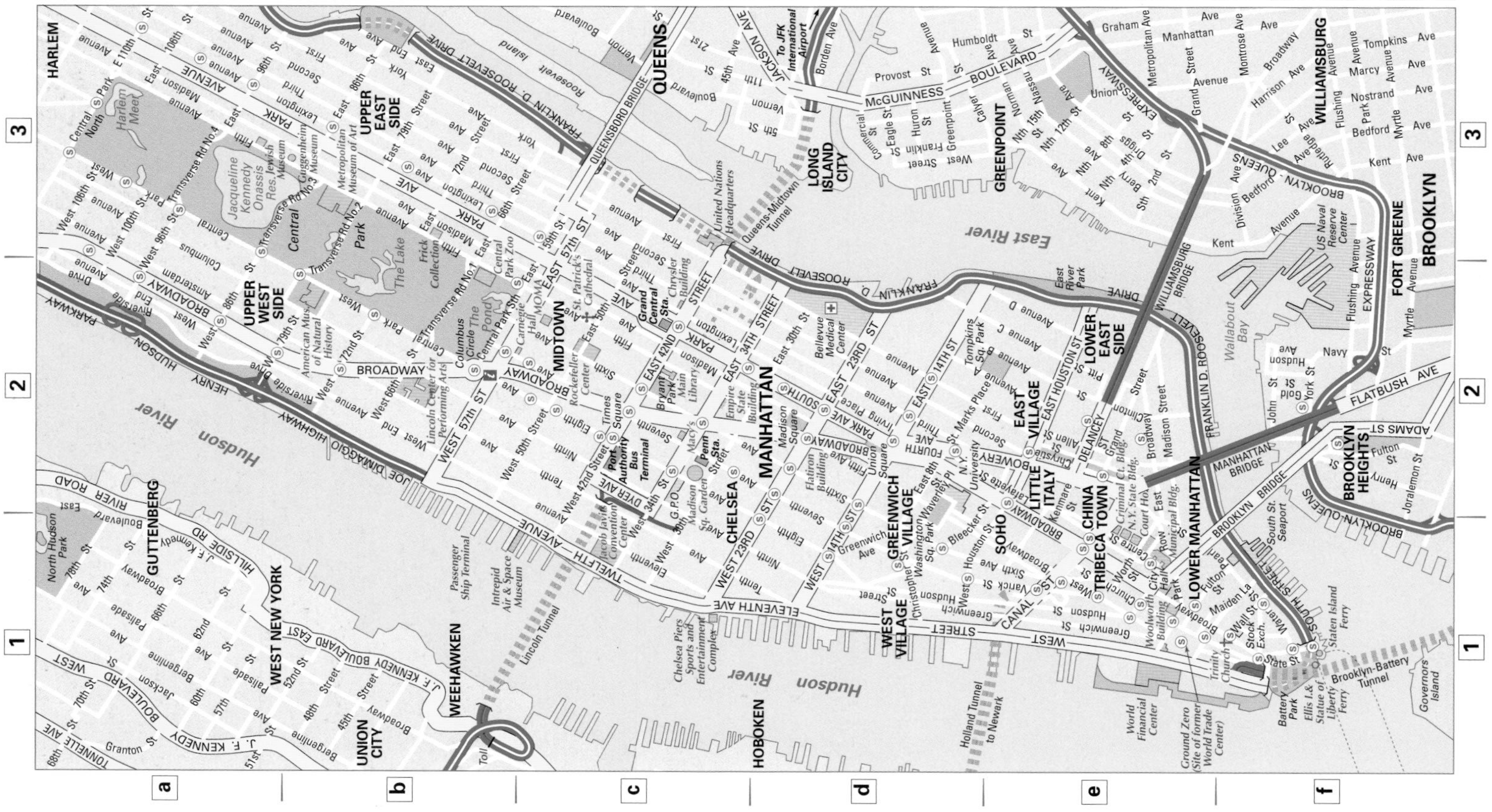

ORLANDO

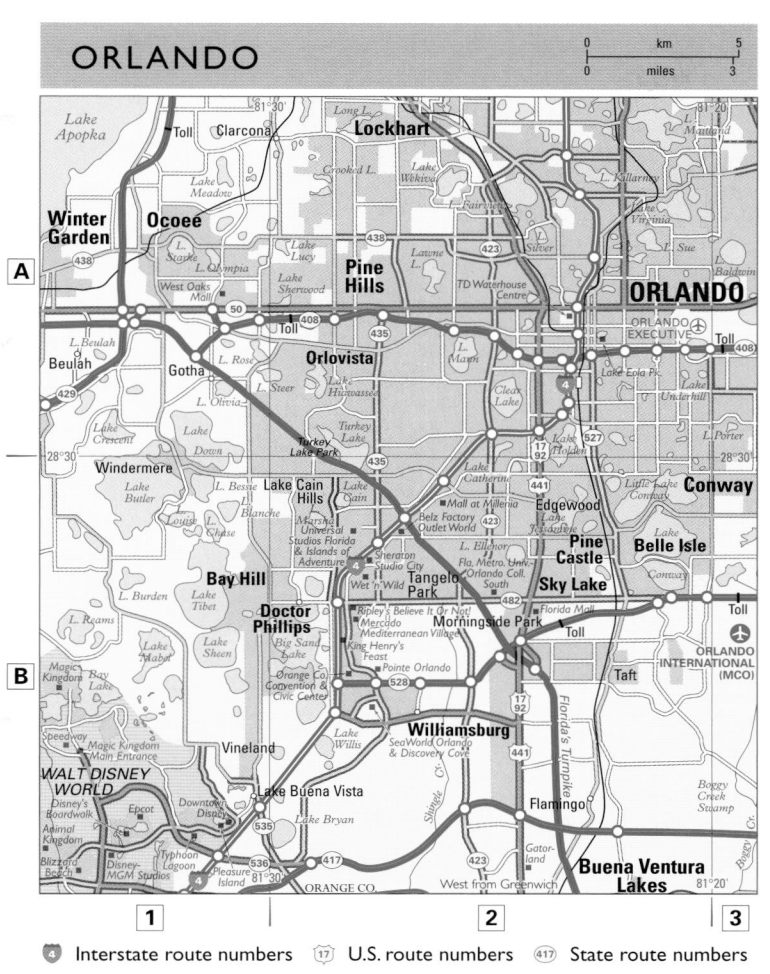

km 5 / miles 3

Interstate route numbers   U.S. route numbers   State route numbers

OSAKA

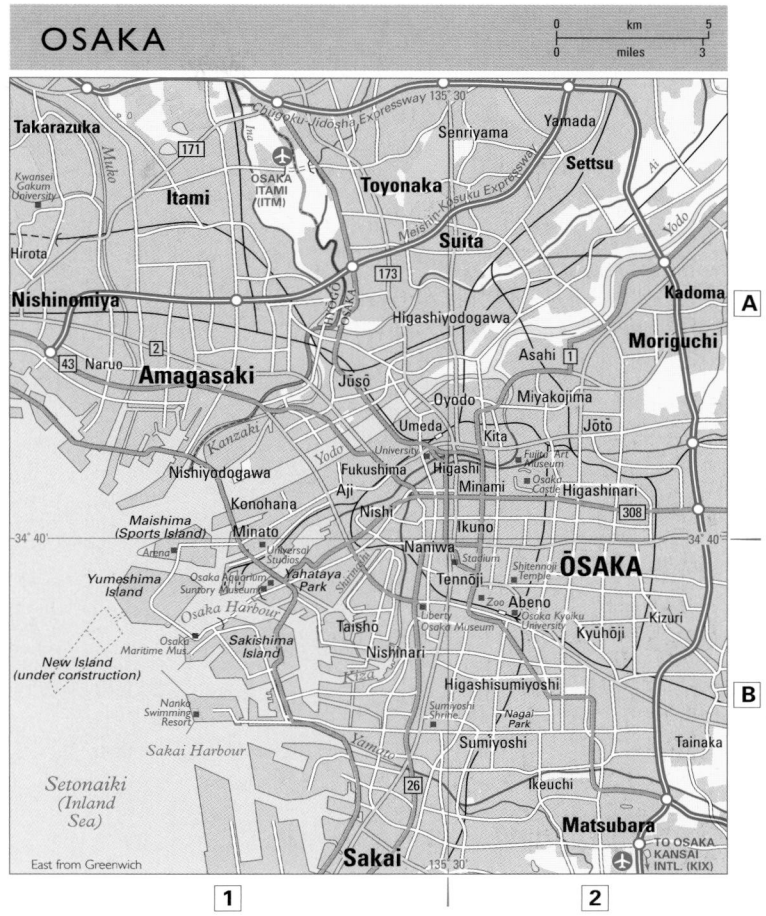

km 5 / miles 3

OSLO

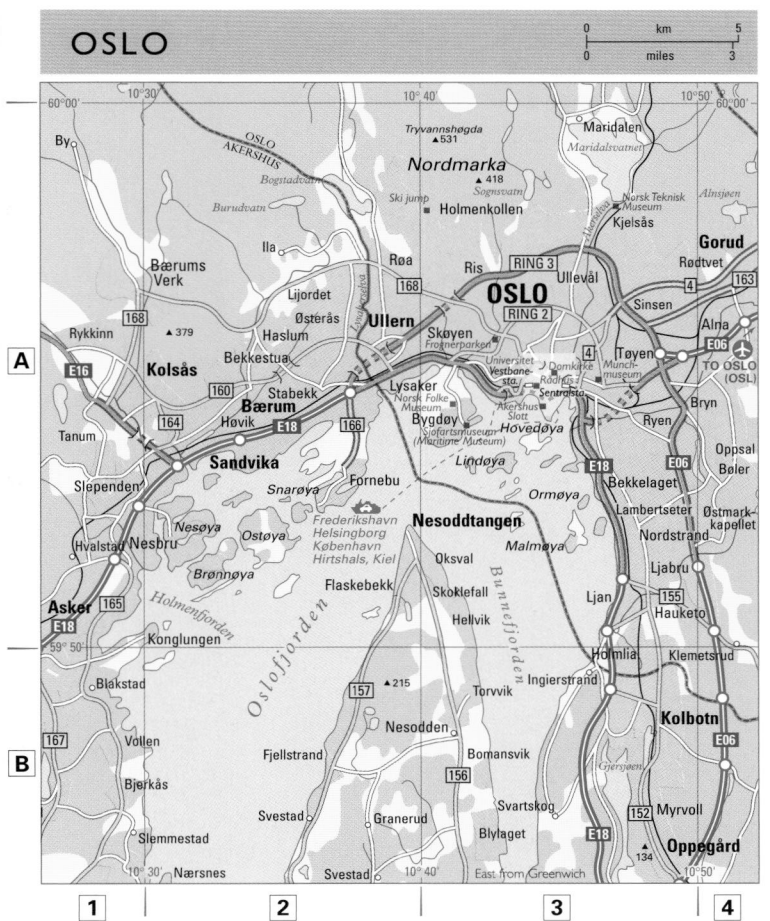

km 5 / miles 3

CENTRAL OSLO

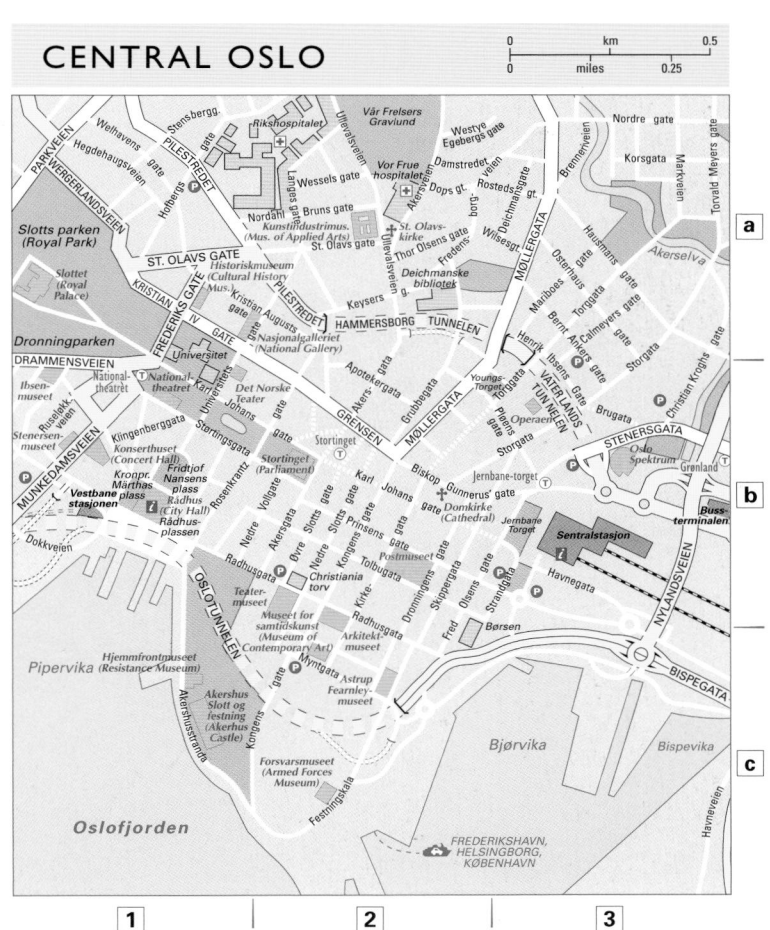

km 0.5 / miles 0.25

PARIS

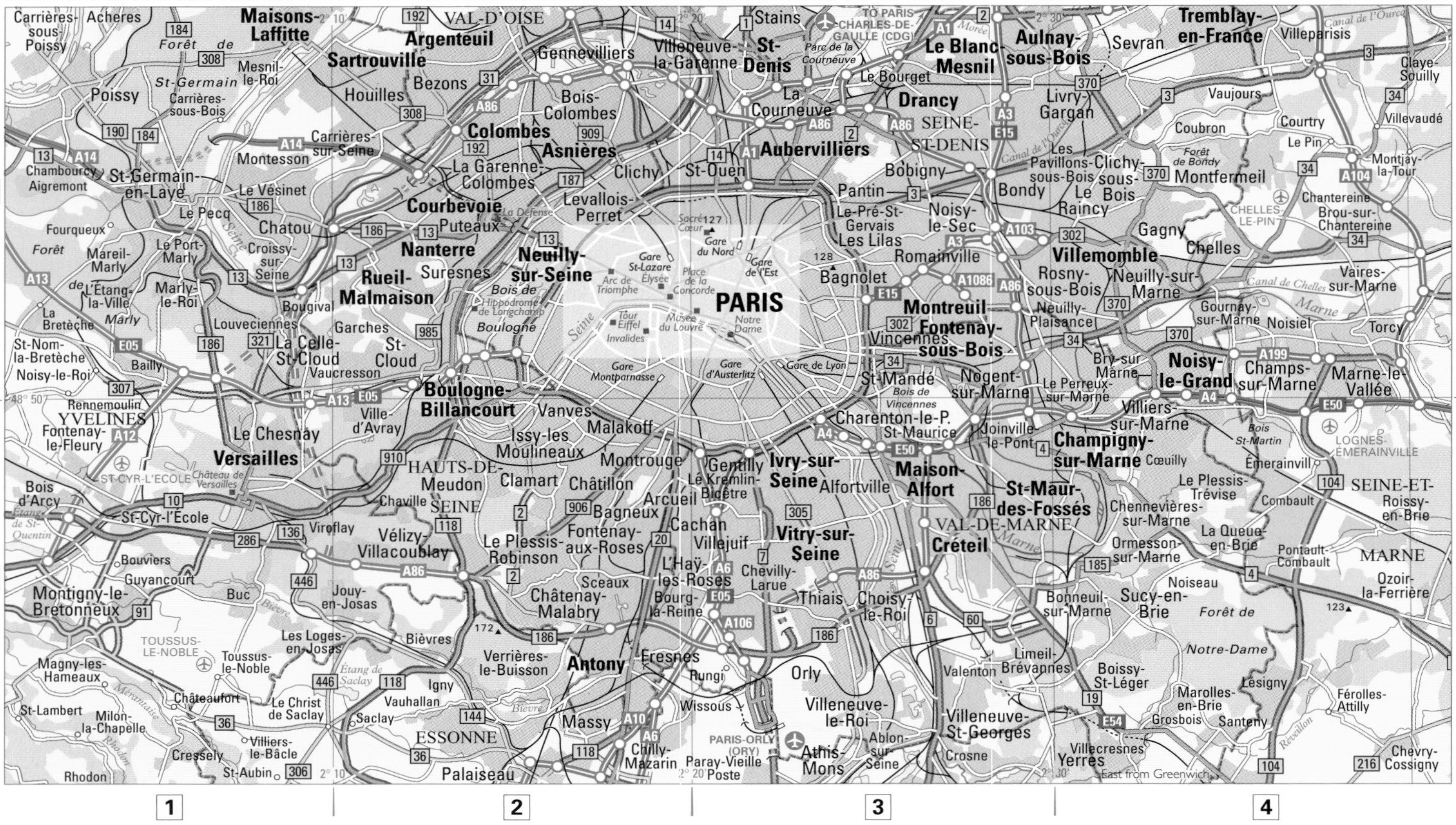

km 5
miles 3

A			**A**
B			**B**
1	2	3	4

Carrières-sous-Poissy · Achères · **Maisons-Laffitte** · Forêt de St-Germain · 192 · VAL-D'OISE · **Argenteuil** · **Sartrouville** · Gennevilliers · 14 · Stains · Parc de la Courneuve · **Le Blanc-Mesnil** · **Aulnay-sous-Bois** · Sevran · **Tremblay-en-France** · Villeparisis

Mesnil-le-Roi · **Bezons** · Houilles · Bois-Colombes · **Villeneuve-la-Garenne** · **St-Denis** · Le Bourget · **Drancy** · Livry-Gargan · Courtry · Claye-Souilly

Poissy · Carrières-sous-Bois · Montesson · **Colombes** · **Asnières** · Clichy · **St-Ouen** · **Aubervilliers** · Bobigny · SEINE-ST-DENIS · Les Pavillons-sous-Bois · Le Pin · Villevaudé

St-Germain-en-Laye · Le Vésinet · La Garenne-Colombes · Levallois-Perret · Pantin · Le Pré-St-Gervais · Les Lilas · Noisy-le-Sec · Montfermeil · Chanteureine · Montjay-la-Tour

A · Chambourcy · Aigremont · Le Pecq · Chatou · **Courbevoie** · Puteaux · La Défense · **Nanterre** · **Neuilly-sur-Seine** · Gare St-Lazare · **PARIS** · Bagnolet · Romainville · **Villemomble** · Rosny-sous-Bois · **Neuilly-sur-Marne** · Gagny · Chelles · Vaires-sur-Marne · **A**

Mareil-Marly · Le Port-Marly · Croissy-sur-Seine · Suresnes · Bois de Boulogne · Tour Eiffel · Invalides · Notre Dame · Gare du Nord · Gare de l'Est · **Montreuil** · Vincennes · **Fontenay-sous-Bois** · Bry-sur-Marne · Le Perreux-sur-Marne · Noisiel · Torcy

Marly-le-Roi · L'Étang-la-Ville · Louveciennes · Garches · **Rueil-Malmaison** · St-Cloud · Gare Montparnasse · Gare de Lyon · Gare d'Austerlitz · St-Mandé · Bois de Vincennes · Joinville-le-Pont · **Champigny-sur-Marne** · **Noisy-le-Grand** · **Champs-sur-Marne** · **Marne-la-Vallée**

La Bretèche · St-Nom-la-Bretèche · Noisy-le-Roi · Bailly · Vaucresson · **Boulogne-Billancourt** · Ville-d'Avray · Vanves · Malakoff · Montrouge · **Gentilly** · Le Kremlin-Bicêtre · **Ivry-sur-Seine** · Charenton-le-P. · St-Maurice · Alfortville · **Maisons-Alfort** · VAL-DE-MARNE · Émerainvill · SEINE-ET-MARNE

YVELINES · Fontenay-le-Fleury · Le Chesnay · **Versailles** · HAUTS-DE-SEINE · Meudon · Issy-les-Moulineaux · Châtillon · Clamart · Bagneux · Arcueil · Cachan · **Vitry-sur-Seine** · **St-Maur-des-Fossés** · **Créteil** · Chennevières-sur-Marne · Ormesson-sur-Marne · La Queue-en-Brie · MARNE

B · Bois d'Arcy · St-Cyr-l'École · Viroflay · Vélizy-Villacoublay · Le Plessis-Robinson · Fontenay-aux-Roses · Sceaux · L'Haÿ-les-Roses · Bourg-la-Reine · Villejuif · Chevilly-Larue · Thiais · Choisy-le-Roi · Bonneuil-sur-Marne · Sucy-en-Brie · Noiseau · Ozoir-la-Ferrière · **B**

Montigny-le-Bretonneux · Guyancourt · Buc · Jouy-en-Josas · Châtenay-Malabry · Bièvres · Verrières-le-Buisson · **Antony** · Fresnes · Rungis · Orly · Limeil-Brévannes · Boissy-St-Léger · Forêt de Notre-Dame

TOUSSUS-LE-NOBLE · Les Loges-en-Josas · Igny · Vauhallan · Saclay · Wissous · PARIS-ORLY (ORY) · Villeneuve-le-Roi · Valenton · Marolles-en-Brie · Grosbois · Santeny · Férolles-Attilly

Magny-les-Hameaux · Milon-la-Chapelle · Châteaufort · Le Christ de Saclay · ESSONNE · Massy · Chilly-Mazarin · Paray-Vieille-Poste · Athis-Mons · Ablon-sur-Seine · Villeneuve-St-Georges · Crosne · Villecresnes · Yerres · Chevry-Cossigny

St-Lambert · Cresselly · Villiers-le-Bâcle · St-Aubin · Palaiseau · Poste · East from Greenwich · 2°10

CENTRAL PARIS

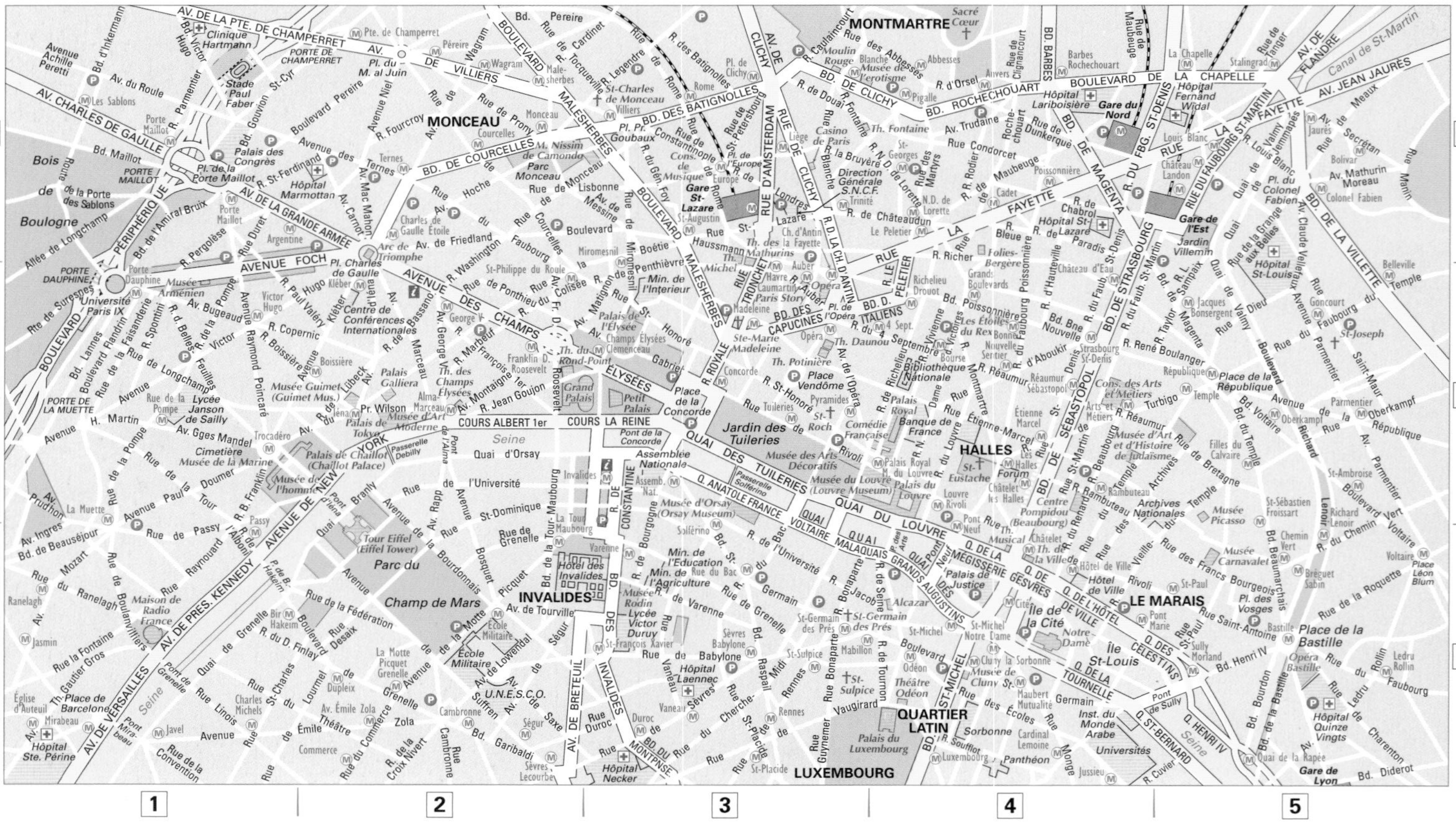

km 1
miles 0.5

a				**a**
b				**b**
c				**c**
1	2	3	4	5

MONTMARTRE · Sacré Cœur · Pte. de Champerret · PORTE DE CHAMPERRET · BOULEVARD DE LA CHAPELLE · Gare du Nord · AV. DE FLANDRE

MONCEAU · Parc Monceau · Gare St-Lazare · Gare de l'Est · BD. DE MAGENTA · AV. JEAN JAURÈS

PORTE MAILLOT · Palais des Congrès · Arc de Triomphe · Pl. Charles de Gaulle Étoile · AVENUE FOCH · AVENUE DES CHAMPS ÉLYSÉES · Pl. de la Concorde · Opéra · Bibliothèque Nationale · Place de la République · BD. DE LA VILLETTE

PORTE DAUPHINE · Université Paris IX · Musée Guimet (Guimet Mus.) · Palais Galliera · Grand Palais · Petit Palais · Jardin des Tuileries · Palais Royal · Banque de France · Musée d'Art et d'Histoire du Judaïsme · Musée Picasso

Bois de Boulogne · Palais de Chaillot (Chaillot Palace) · Musée de l'Homme · Tour Eiffel (Eiffel Tower) · Seine · QUAI D'ORSAY · Musée d'Orsay (Orsay Museum) · Assemblée Nationale · Louvre (Louvre Museum) · Centre Pompidou (Beaubourg) · **LE MARAIS** · Archives Nationales

PORTE DE LA MUETTE · Maison de Radio France · Champ de Mars · Parc du Champ de Mars · **INVALIDES** · Hôtel des Invalides · Min. de l'Éducation · Min. de l'Agriculture · Île de la Cité · Notre Dame · Île St-Louis · Place de la Bastille · Opéra de l'Est

AV. DE VERSAILLES · U.N.E.S.C.O. · École Militaire · PORT-ROYAL · Institut du Monde Arabe · Universités · **QUARTIER LATIN** · Sorbonne · Panthéon · **LUXEMBOURG** · Palais du Luxembourg · Hôpital Quinze-Vingts · Gare de Lyon

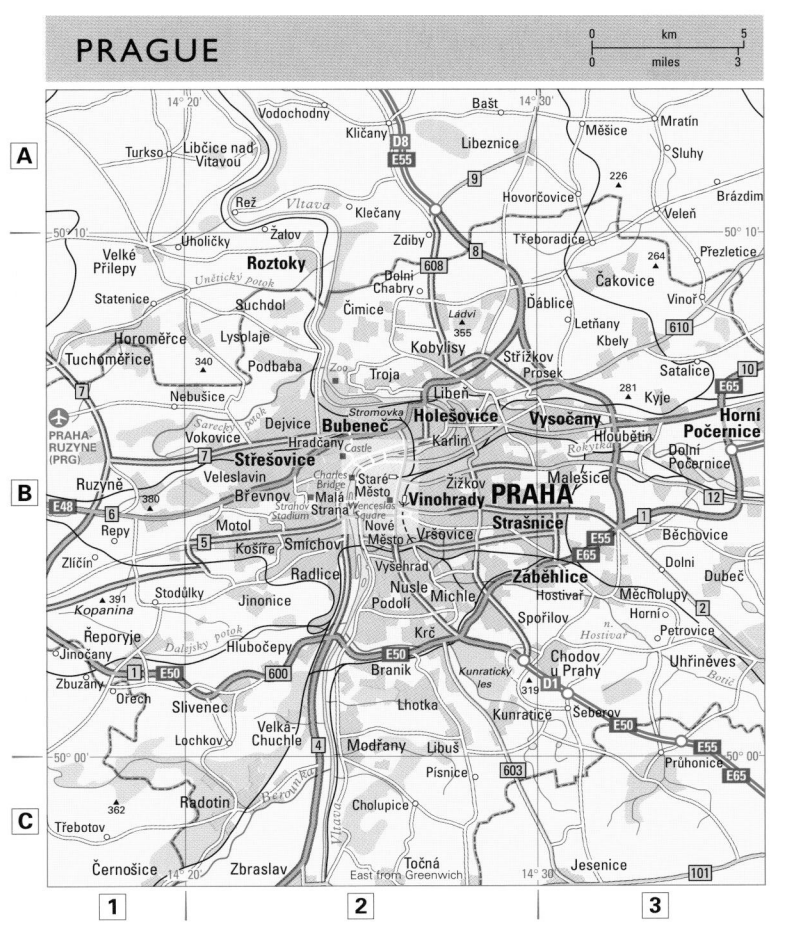

PRAGUE

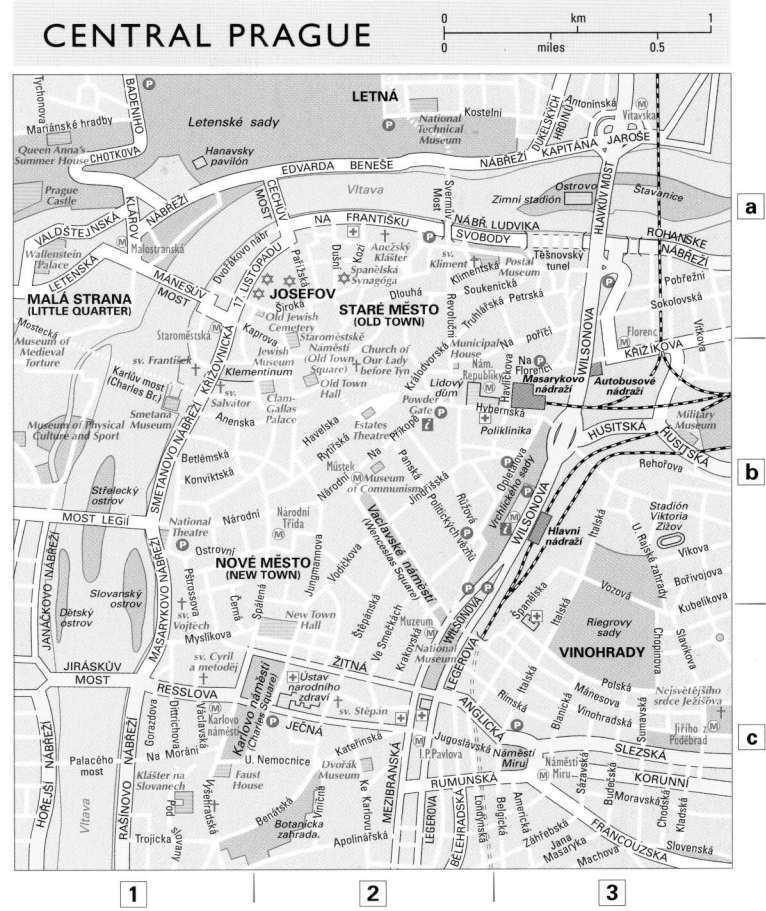

CENTRAL PRAGUE

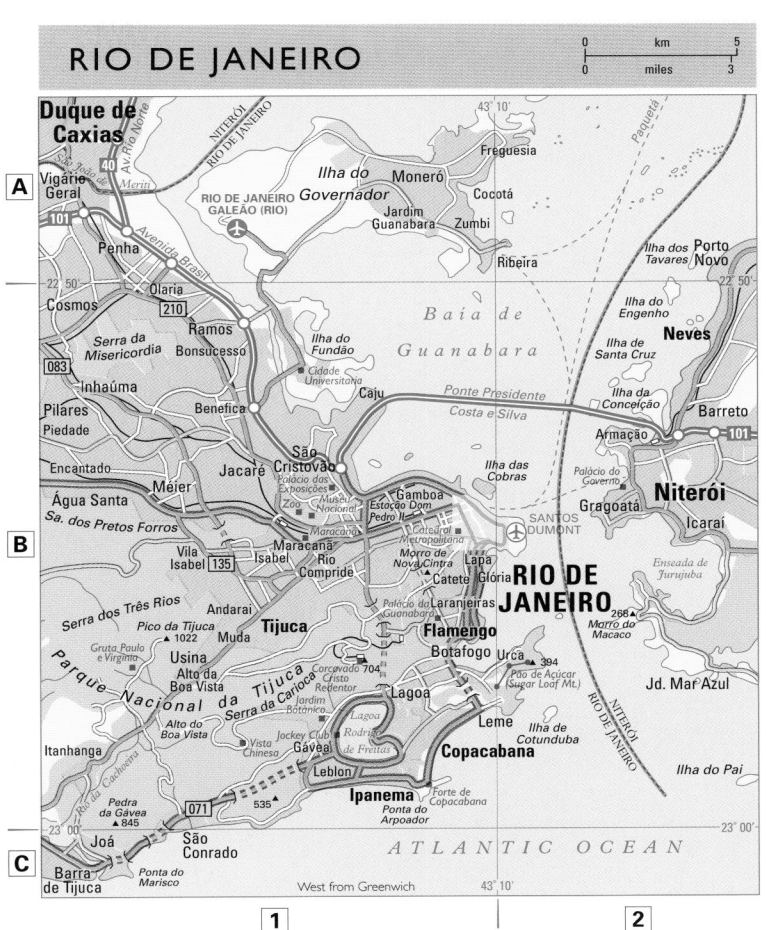

RIO DE JANEIRO

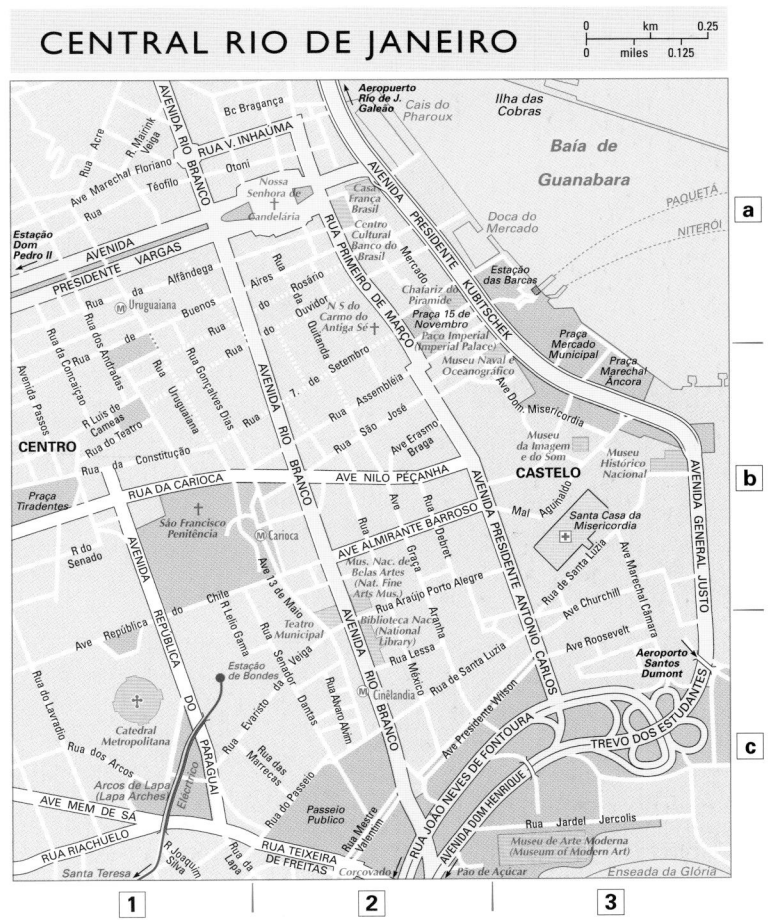

CENTRAL RIO DE JANEIRO

COPYRIGHT PHILIP'S

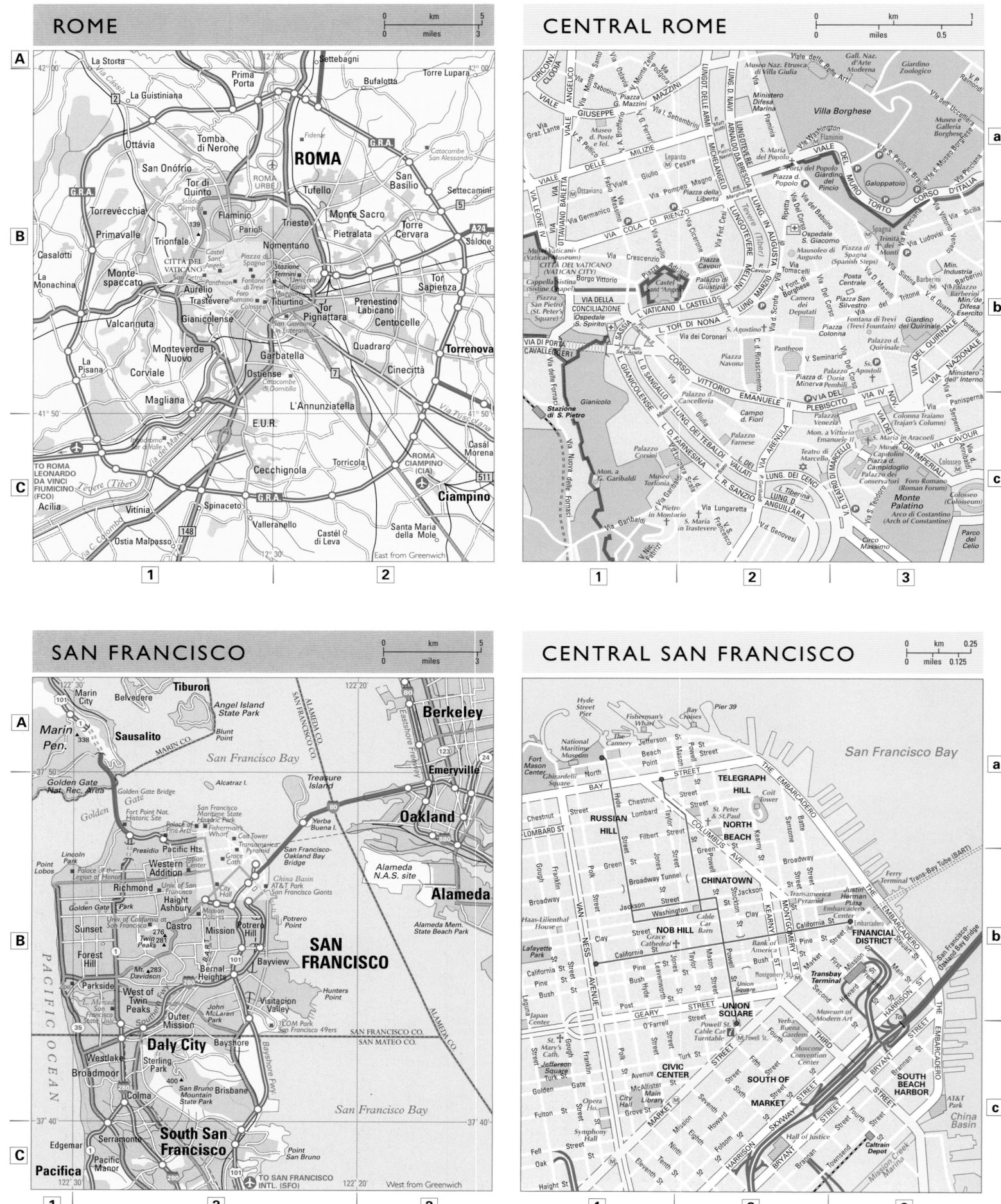

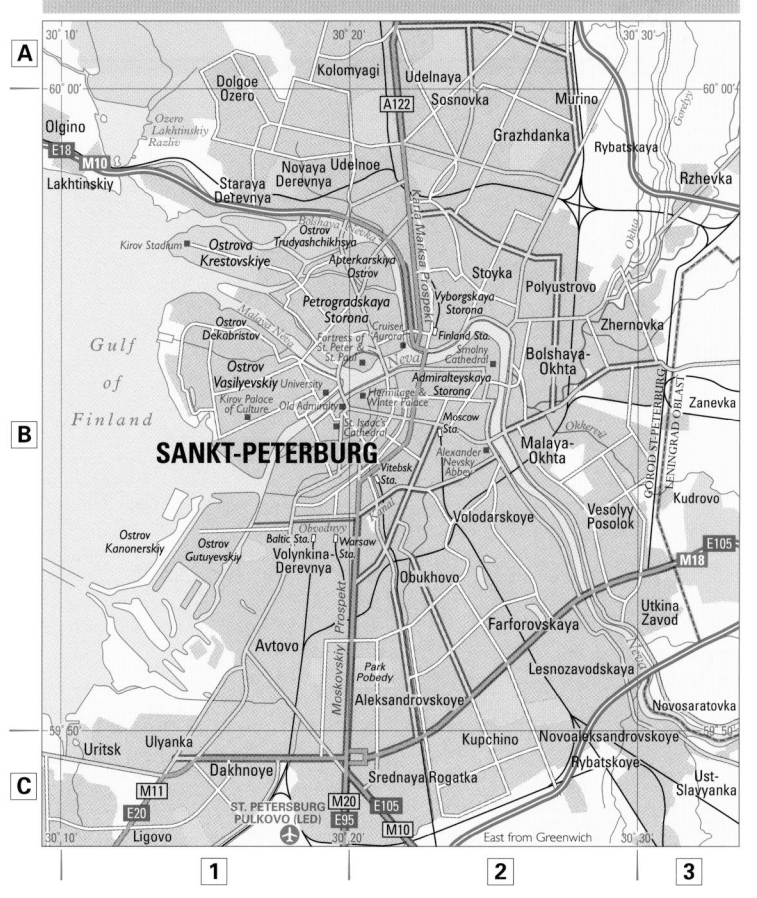

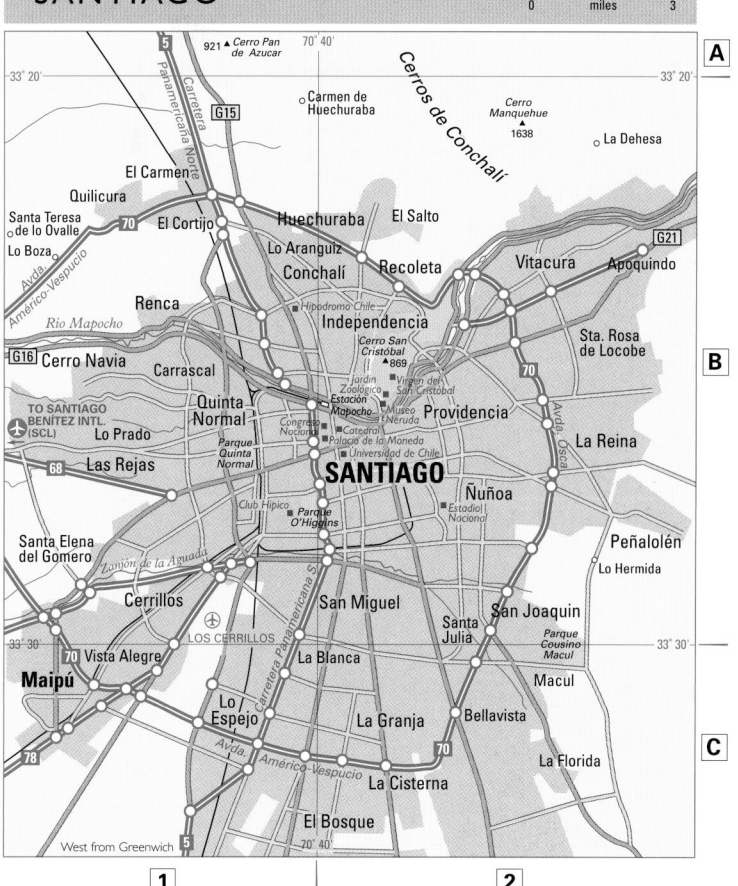

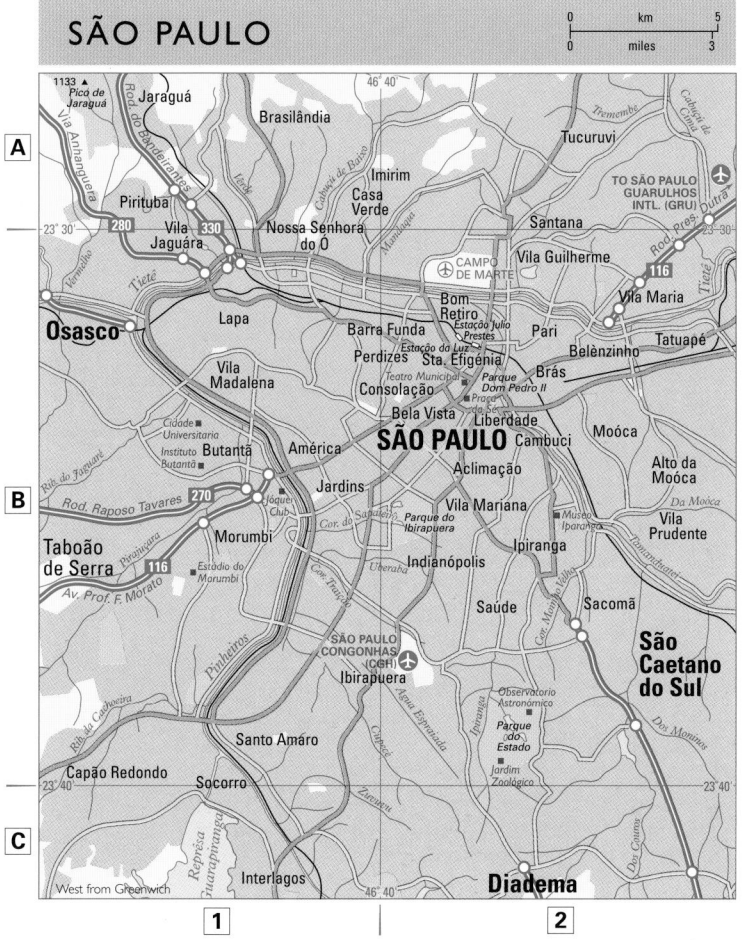

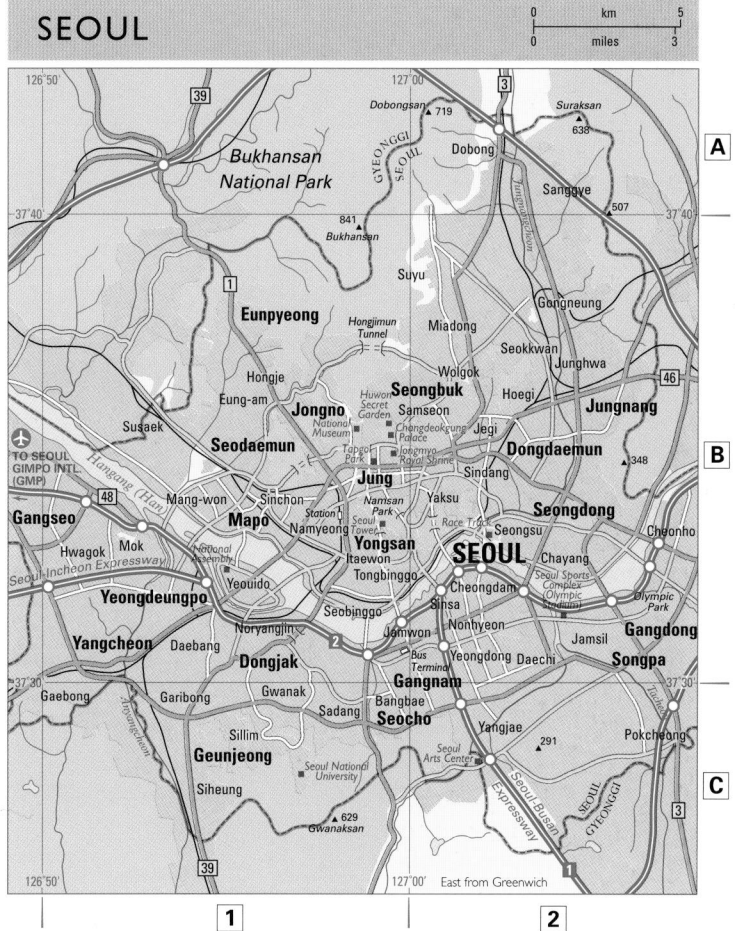

0 miles 3

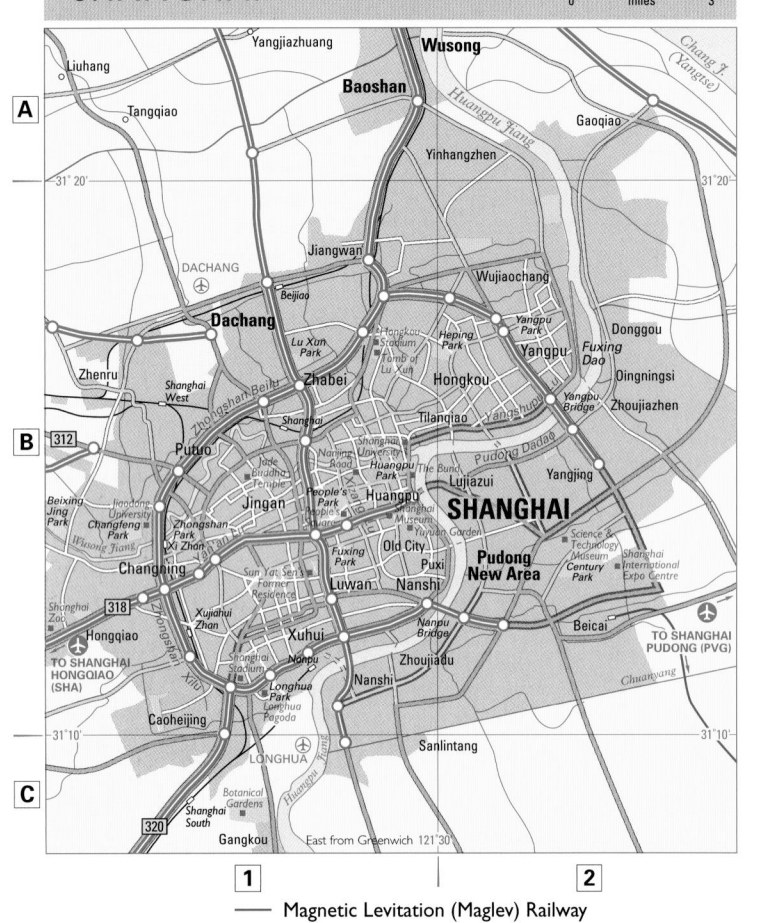

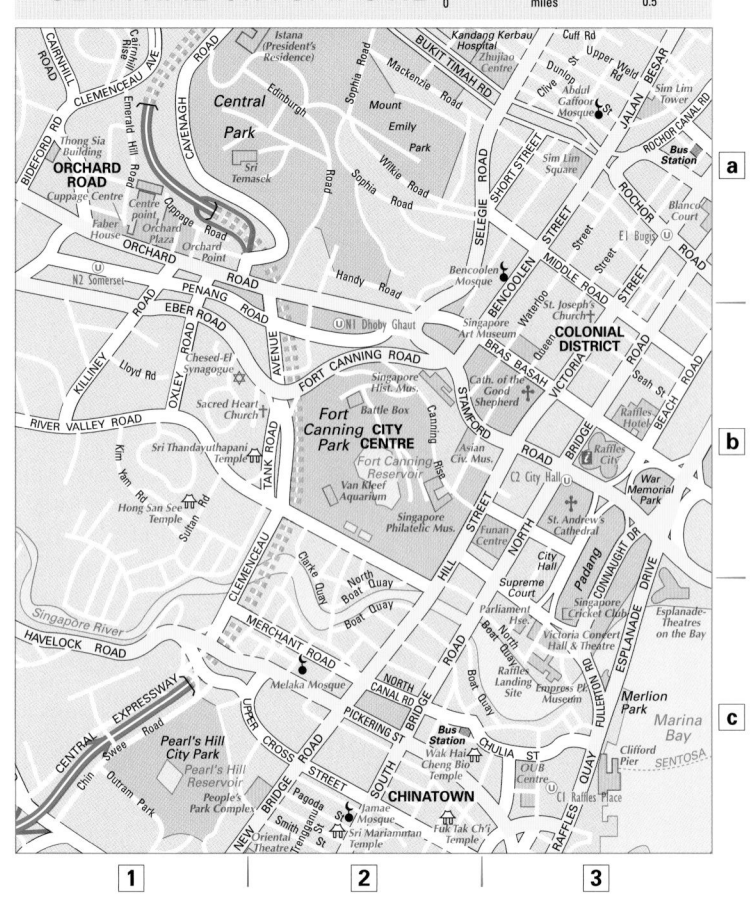

— Magnetic Levitation (Maglev) Railway

0 miles 0.5

SINGAPORE

0 km 5
0 miles 3

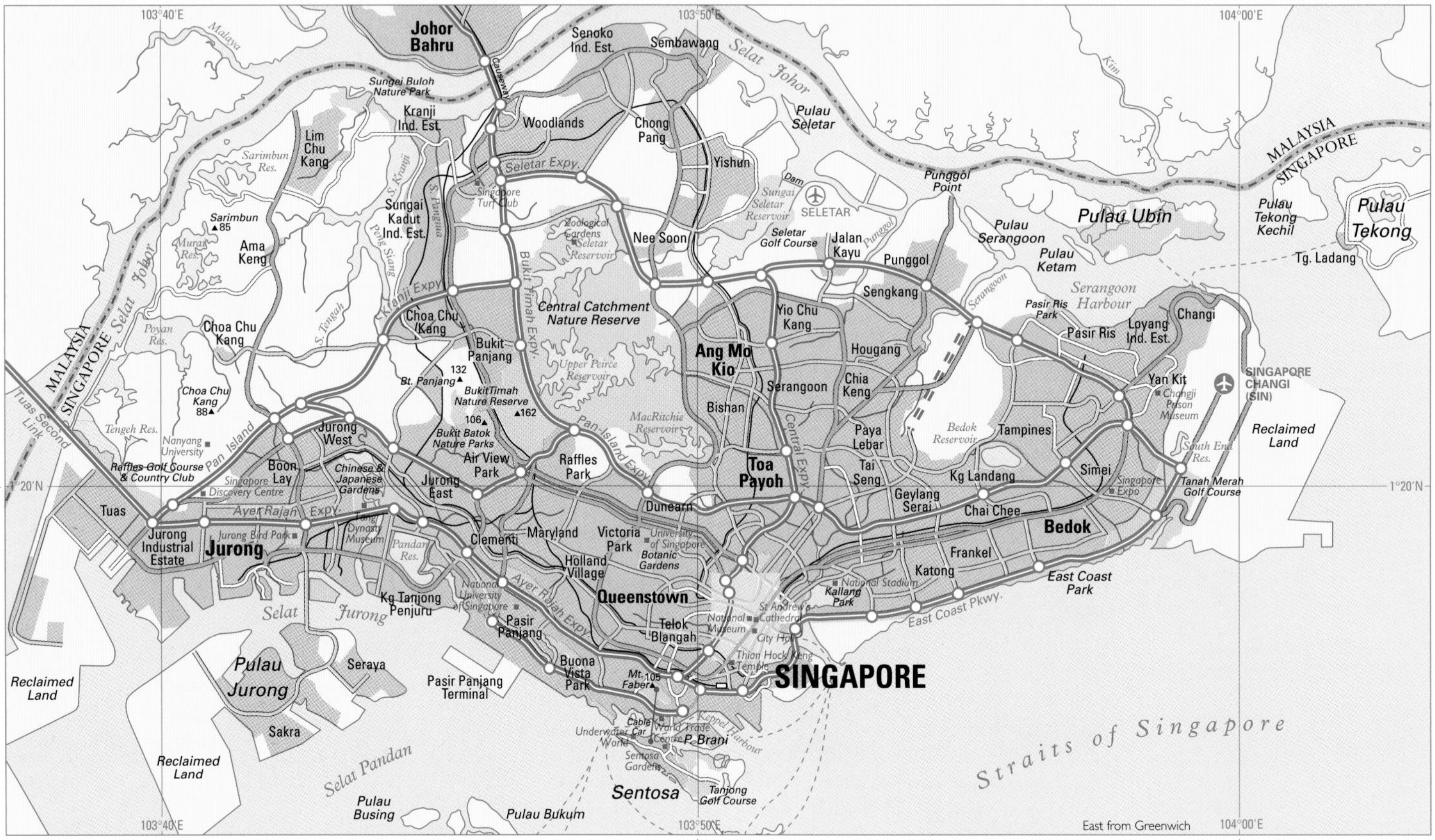

STOCKHOLM

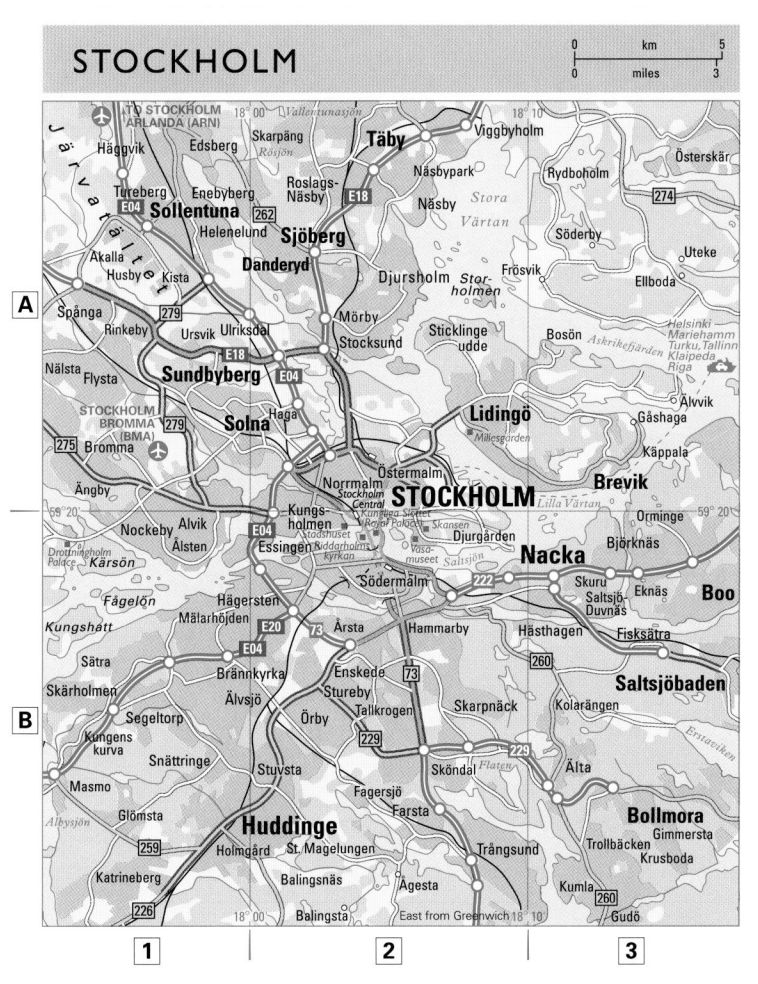

CENTRAL STOCKHOLM

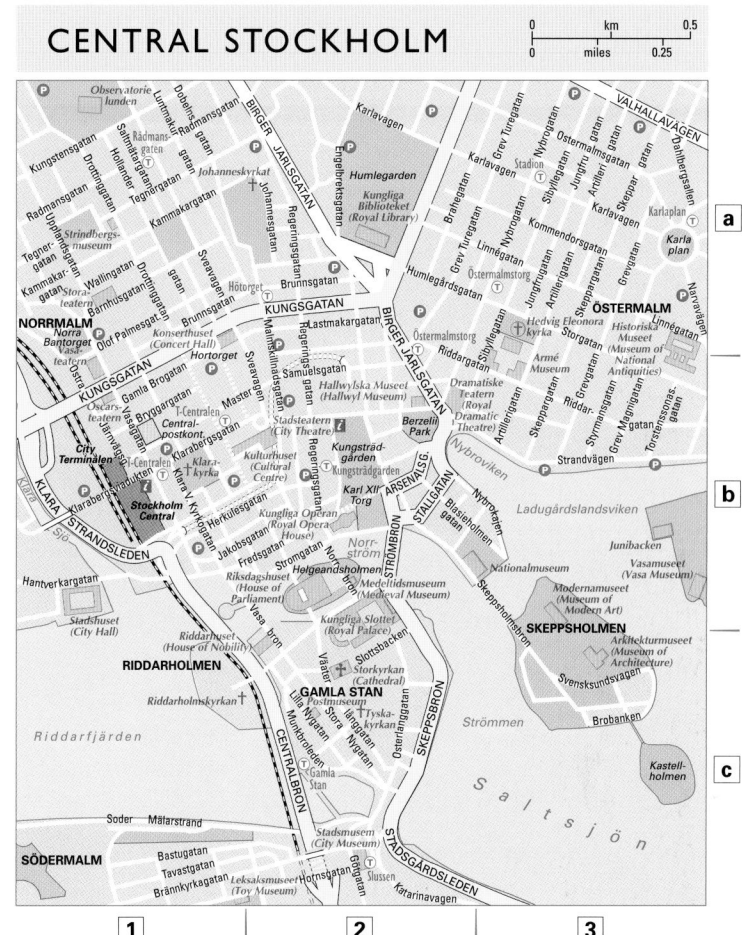

SYDNEY

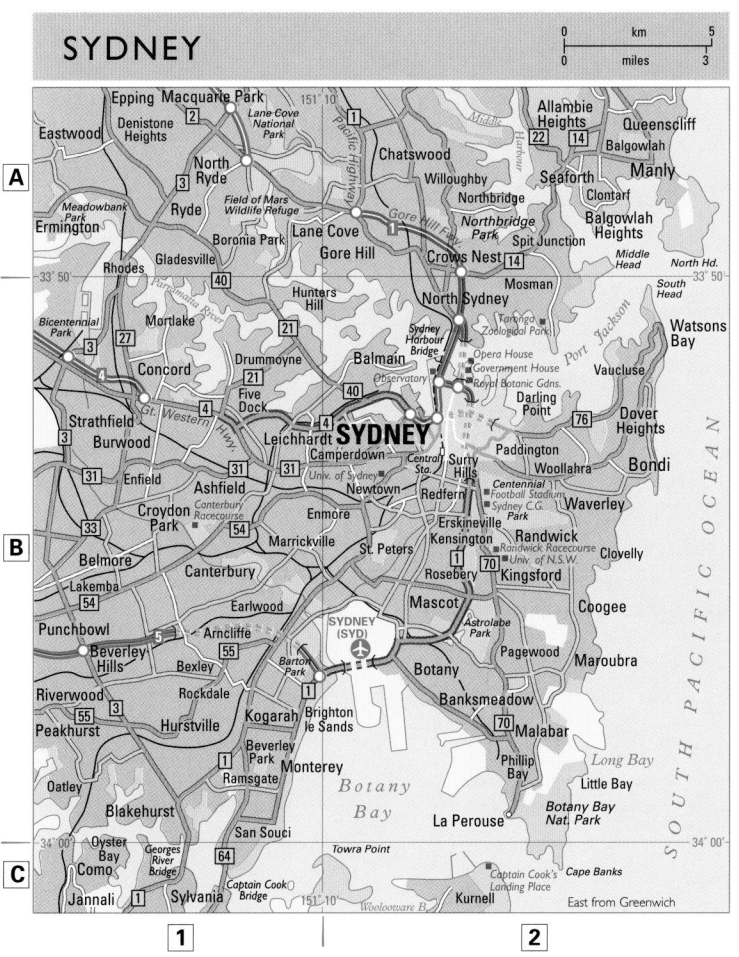

CENTRAL SYDNEY

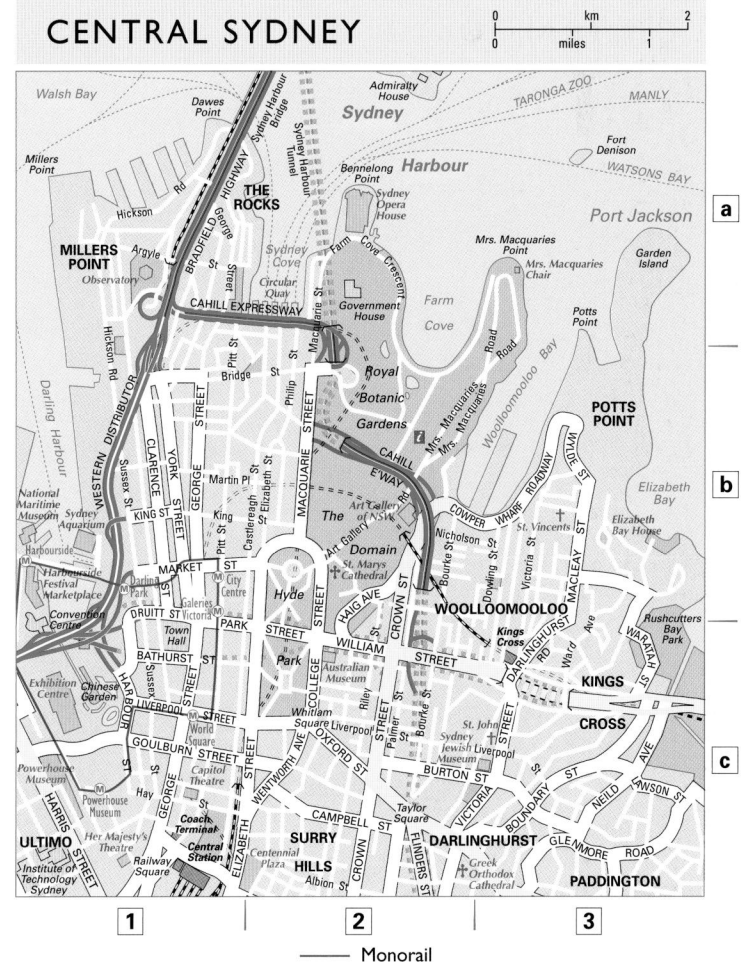

— Monorail

TOKYO

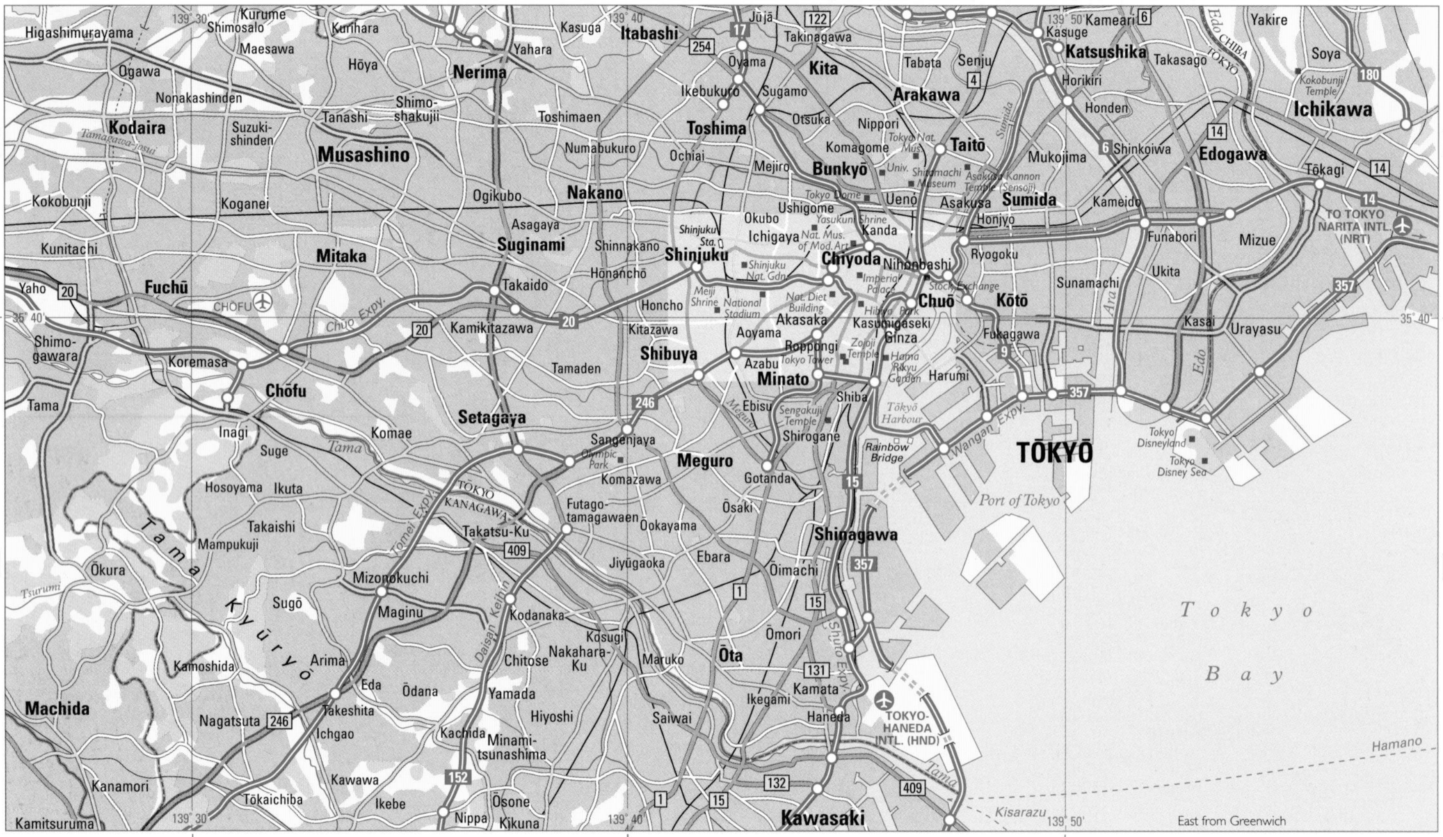

km 5
miles 3

Higashimurayama · Kurume · Shimosalo · Kurihara · Kasuga · Jūjō · 122 · Takinagawa · Kameari · 6 · Yakire · Soya

Ogawa · Shimosato · Maesawa · Yahara · 254 · Ōyama · Kita · Tabata · Senju · Horikiri · Takasago · Kokubunji Temple · 180

Itabashi · **Nerima** · Nonakashinden · Suzuki-shinden · Shimo-shakuji · Ikebukuro · Sugamo · Nippori · Honden · Shinkoiwa · Mukojima · **Ichikawa**

Kodaira · **Musashino** · Hōya · Toshimaen · **Toshima** · Otsuka · **Arakawa** · **Taitō** · Asakusa · **Sumida** · Kameido · **Edogawa** · Tōkagi · 14

Kokubunji · Koganei · Ogikubo · **Nakano** · Numabukuro · Ochiai · Mejiro · Komagome · **Bunkyō** · Ushigome · **Kanda** · Honjo · Funabori · Mizue

Kunitachi · Asagaya · Shinnakano · Okubo · Ichigaya · **Chiyoda** · Nihonbashi · Ryōgoku · Sunamachi · Ukita · TO TOKYO NARITA INTL. (NRT)

Yaho · 20 · **Mitaka** · Takaido · **Shinjuku** · Honcho · Aoyama · **Chūō** · **Kōtō** · Kasai · 357

Fuchū · Kamikitazawa · 20 · Kitazawa · **Akasaka** · Kasumigaseki · Ginza · Fukagawa · Urayasu

Shimo-gawara · Koremasa · **Shibuya** · Roppongi · Harumi

Chōfu · Tamaden · **Minato** · Ebisu · Rainbow Bridge · **TŌKYŌ**

Tama · Inagi · Suge · Komae · **Setagaya** · Sangenjaya · Shirogane · Port of Tokyo · Tokyo Disneyland · Tokyo Disney Sea

Hosoyama · Ikuta · Komazawa · **Meguro** · Gotanda · 15

Takaishi · Mampukuji · Mizonokuchi · Futago-tamagawaen · Ōkayama · Ōsaki

Machida · Sugō · Arima · Kodanaka · Nakahara-Ku · Maruko · **Ōta** · Ōmori · 357 · 15

Kamoshida · Eda · Ōdana · Chitose · Kosugi · Yamada · Ōimachi · 1 · 131

Nagatsuta · 246 · Takeshita · Hiyoshi · Saiwai · Ikegami · Kamata · Haneda · TOKYO-HANEDA INTL. (HND)

Kanamori · Ichgao · Kachida · Minami-tsunashima · 132 · 409

Kamitsuruma · Tōkaichiba · Ikebe · Nippa · Kikuna · **Kawasaki** · Kisarazu · East from Greenwich · Hamano

Tama Kyūryō · *Tokyo Bay*

1 · 2 · 3 · 4

CENTRAL TOKYO

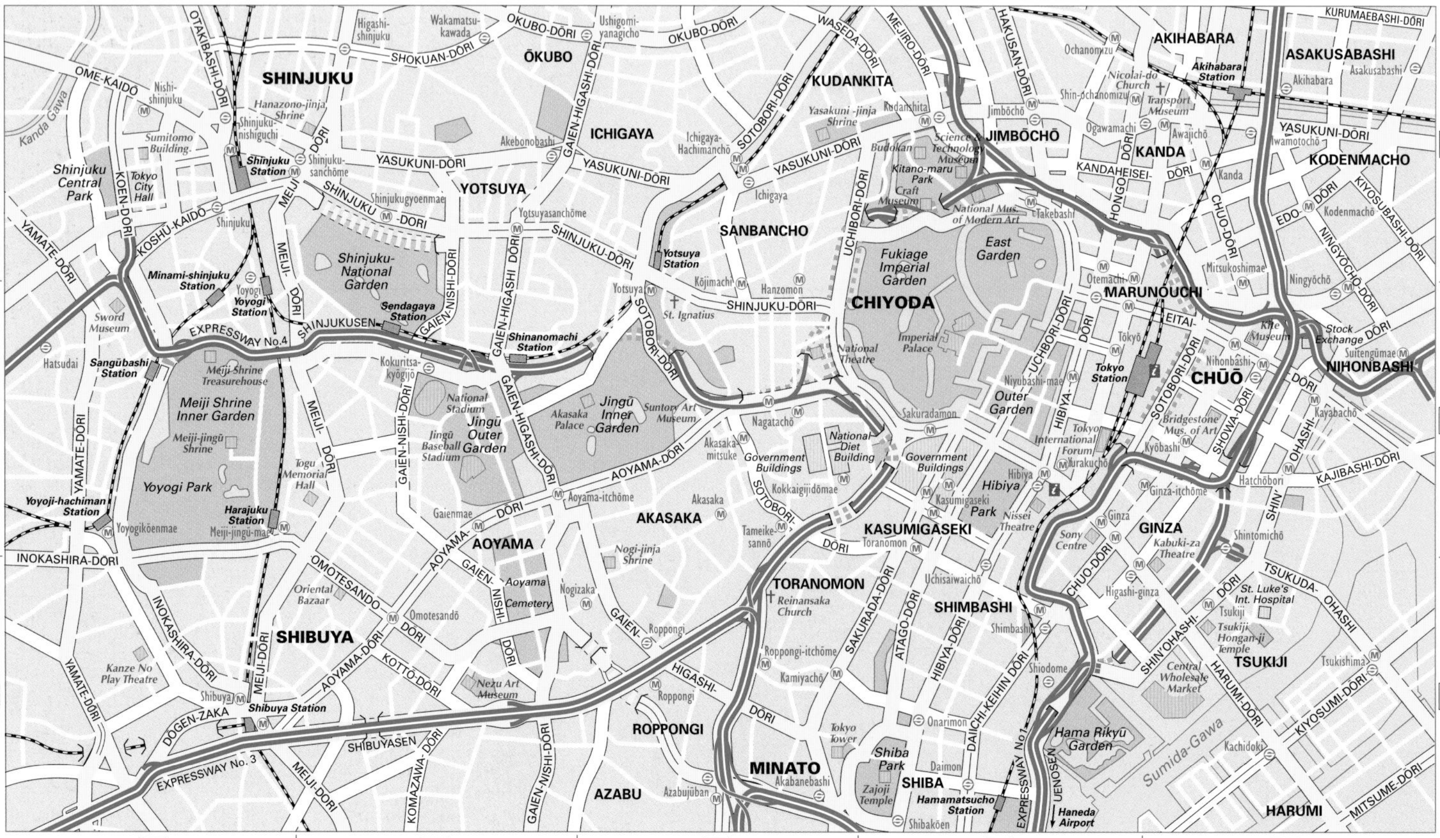

km 0.5
miles 0.25

SHINJUKU · ŌKUBO · KUDANKITA · **AKIHABARA** · **ASAKUSABASHI**

ICHIGAYA · JIMBŌCHŌ · KANDA · KODENMACHO

YOTSUYA · SANBANCHO · **CHIYODA** · **MARUNŌUCHI** · **NIHONBASHI**

Meiji Shrine Inner Garden · Yoyogi Park · Fukiage Imperial Garden · East Garden · Imperial Palace · **CHŪŌ**

SHIBUYA · Jingū Inner Garden · AKASAKA · National Diet Building · KASUMIGASEKI · **GINZA**

AOYAMA · Hibiya Park · SHIMBASHI · TSUKIJI

TORANOMON · Hama Rikyū Garden

ROPPONGI · **MINATO** · SHIBA · Hamamatsucho Station · Haneda Airport · **HARUMI**

AZABU · Tokyo Tower · Shiba Park

1 · 2 · 3 · 4 · 5

Ⓢ Toei Subway   Ⓜ Tokyo Metro

TEHRAN

km 5
0
miles 3

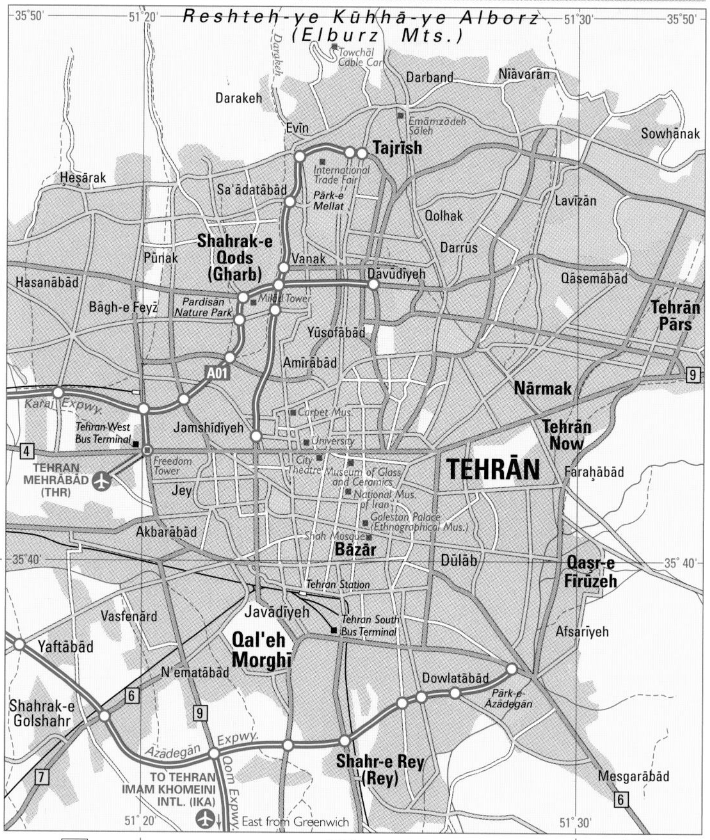

Reshteh-ye Kūhhā-ye Alborz
(Elburz Mts.)

Tōchāl Cable Car
Darband
Niāvarān
Darakeh
Darakeh
Evin
Tajrīsh
Sowhānak
Hesārak
Sa'ādatābād
Park-e Mellat
Lavīzān
Shahrak-e Qods (Gharb)
Vanak
Qolhak
Qāsemābād
Pūlnak
Dāvūdīyeh
Darrūs
Bāgh-e Feyż
Pardīsān Nature Park
Milad Tower
Amīrābād
Tehrān Pārs
Hasanābād
International Trade Fair
Yūsofābād
Nārmak
Karaj Expwy
Jamshīdīyeh
Tehrān Now
Tehrān West Bus Terminal
A01
9
Freedom Tower
University
TEHRAN MEHRĀBĀD (THR)
City Theatre
Museum of Glass and Ceramics
Farahābād
Jey
National Mus. of Iran
Golestan Palace (Ethnographical Mus.)
Akbarābād
Sipah Mosque
Bāzār
Dūlāb
Qasr-e Firūzeh
35°40'
Tehran Station
Vasfenārd
Javādīyeh
Tehran South Bus Terminal
Afsarīyeh
Yaftābād
Qal'eh Morghī
N'ematābād
Dowlatābād
Park-e Āzādegān
Shahrak-e Golshahr
6
9
Āzādegān Expwy
Shahr-e Rey (Rey)
Mesgarābād
7
Qom Expwy
TO TEHRAN IMAM KHOMEINI INTL. (IKA)
East from Greenwich
6

A · B · 1 · 2 · 3
35°50' · 51°20' · 51°30' · 35°50'
51°20' · 51°30'

CENTRAL TORONTO

km 0.5
0
miles 0.25

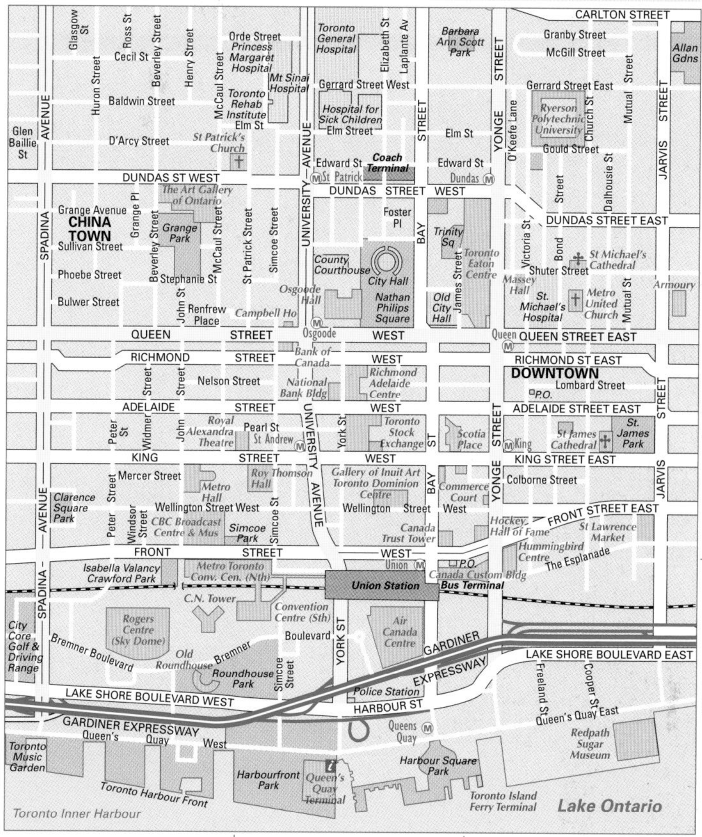

CARLTON STREET
Glasgow St
Ross St
Orde Street
Toronto General Hospital
Barbara Ann Scott Park
Granby Street
Allan Gdns
Cecil St
Beverley Street
Henry Street
Princess Margaret Hospital
Elizabeth St
Laplante Av
McGill Street
HURON
Baldwin Street
McCaul St
Mount Sinai Hospital
Hospital for Sick Children
Gerrard Street East
Gerrard Street West
Ryerson Polytechnic University
AVENUE
Glen Baillie St
D'Arcy Street
St Patrick's Church
Elm St
Elm Street
Edward St
O'Keefe Lane
Gould Street
a
DUNDAS ST WEST
Edward Street
Coach Terminal
YONGE
DUNDAS STREET WEST
DUNDAS STREET EAST
SPADINA
The Art Gallery of Ontario
Grange Avenue
Grange Pl
Grange Park
Foster Pl
Trinity Sq
BAY
Victoria St
Bond
St Michael's Cathedral
Armoury
CHINA TOWN
Sullivan Street
McCaul Street
St Patrick Street
Simcoe Street
County Courthouse
Toronto Eaton Centre
Massey Hall
Shuter Street
Metro United Church
Mutual St
Phoebe Street
Beverley Street
City Hall
Nathan Philips Square
Old City Hall
St Michael's Hospital
Bulwer Street
Osgoode Hall
Campbell Ho
QUEEN STREET WEST
Queen Street East
QUEEN STREET EAST
Bank of Canada
RICHMOND STREET WEST
RICHMOND ST EAST
DOWNTOWN
Lombard Street
Nelson Street
National Bank Bldg
Richmond Adelaide Centre
Scotia Place
ADELAIDE STREET WEST
ADELAIDE STREET EAST
Peter St
Widmer
John St
Royal Alexandra Theatre
Pearl St
St Andrew
Toronto Stock Exchange
King
St James Cathedral
St James Park
KING STREET WEST
Colborne Street
KING STREET EAST
SPADINA AVENUE
Mercer Street
Roy Thomson Hall
Gallery of Inuit Art
Toronto Dominion Centre
Commerce Court West
Clarence Square Park
Peter Street
Windsor Street
CBC Broadcast Centre & Mus
Wellington Street West
Simcoe Park
Wellington
Canada Trust Tower
Hockey Hall of Fame
St Lawrence Market
FRONT STREET WEST
Hummingbird Centre
The Esplanade
Isabella Valancy Crawford Park
Metro Toronto Conv. Cen. (Nth)
P.O.
Canada Custom Bldg
Union Station Bus Terminal
C.N. Tower
Convention Centre (Sth)
City Core Golf & Driving Range
Rogers Centre (Sky Dome)
Bremner Boulevard
Old Roundhouse
Roundhouse Park
Simcoe Street
Boulevard
Air Canada Centre
GARDINER EXPRESSWAY
LAKE SHORE BOULEVARD EAST
LAKE SHORE BOULEVARD WEST
Police Station
HARBOUR ST
Queen's Quay East
Cooper St
Freeland St
GARDINER EXPRESSWAY
Queen's Quay West
Queen's Quay
Redpath Sugar Museum
Toronto Music Garden
Harbourfront Park
Queen's Quay Terminal
Harbour Square Park
Toronto Island Ferry Terminal
Lake Ontario
Toronto Inner Harbour
Toronto Harbour Front

a · b · c
1 · 2 · 3

TORONTO

km 5
0
miles 3

Boyd Conservation Area
7 407
Thornhill
The Promenade
Concord
Markham
Brown
Metro Toronto Zoo
Rouge
2
Fairport
Rouge Hill
Vaughan
Pine Grove
Edgeley
East Don
Newtonbrook
48
Agincourt
Malvern
401
Glen Rouge Park
West Rouge
Port Union
Woodbridge
27
7
Fisherville
11
Willowdale
East Don Parkland
404
Fairview Mall
Highland Creek
2A
Humber Summit
York University
G. Ross Lord Park
Northmount
Lansing
401
Morningside Park
Woburn
West Hill
Beaumonte Heights
Black Creek Pioneer Village
North York
Scarborough Town Centre
Bendale
Highland Creek
A
Thistletown
Northwood Park
DOWNSVIEW C.A.F.B.
Armour Heights
York Mills
Wexford
Scarborough
Eastpoint Park
A
Humberwood Park
Woodbine Centre
427
Kipling Heights
Rexdale
Downsview
Yorkdale Shopping Centre
Lawrence Heights
Don Mills
York Univ.
Wilket Creek Park
Sunnybrook Health Science Centre
Ontario Science Centre
Danforth
Cliffside
Bluffers Park
Malton
Humberlea
401
11A
Thorncliffe
Weston
Forest Hill
Leaside
Dentonia Park
Scarborough Bluffs
Woodbine Race Track
409
27
York
11
Cedarvale Park
Casa Loma
Birch Cliff
Hanlon
410
401
TORONTO LESTER B. PEARSON INTL. (YYZ)
Humber Valley Village
Mount Dennis
Royal Ontario Museum
5
University of Toronto
Old City Hall
East York
Don Valley Pkwy
5
Riverdale Park
2
Kew Gardens
43°40'
Etobicoke
Lambton Mills
Swansea
High Park
Parliament Buildings
C.N. Tower & Rogers Centre
Union Sta
Gardiner Expwy
Ashbridge's Bay Park
Islington
Kingsway
Humber Bay
Parkdale
Exhibition Place
TORONTO CITY CENTRE (ISLAND)
TORONTO
Tommy Thompson Park
B
Markland Wood
427
Summerville
5
Humber Bay Park
Way
Elizabeth
Ontario Place
Toronto Harbour
LAKE ONTARIO
B
Burnhamthorpe
10
Mimico
Toronto Islands
Island Park
Dixie
Samuel Smith Park
New Toronto
403
Mississauga
Cooksville
Square One
Humber College
Long Branch
Gibraltar Point
79°40' · 79°30' · 79°20' · 79°10'
West from Greenwich

427 Provincial route numbers

1 · 2 · 3 · 4

COPYRIGHT PHILIP'S

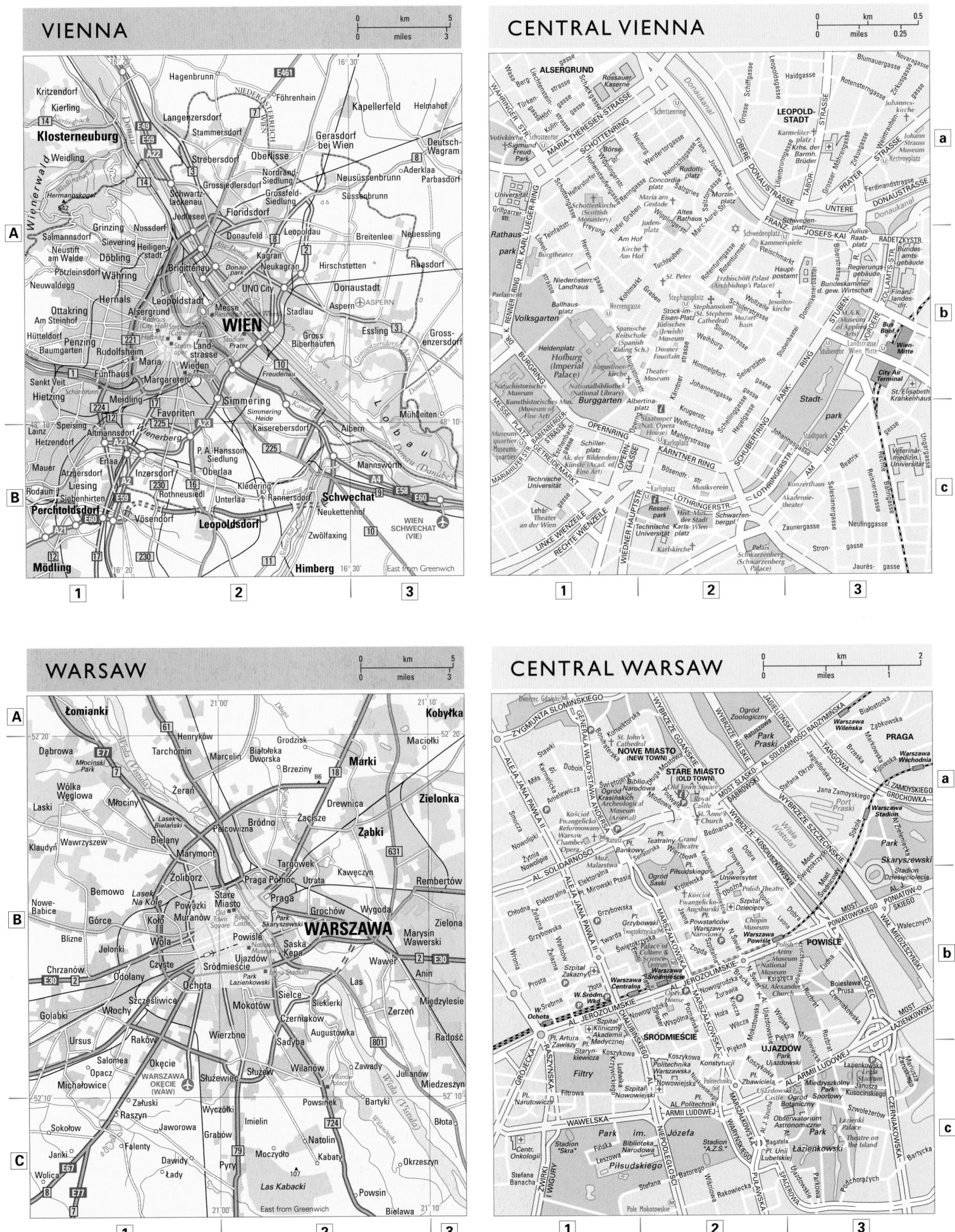

VIENNA

km 5
miles 3

Kritzendorf
Kierling
14
Klosterneuburg
Weidling
Wienerwald
Hermannskogel
542
Neustift
am Walde
Pötzleinsdorf
Neuwaldegg
Salmannsdorf
Grinzing
Nussdorf
Sievering
Döbling
Heiligen-
stadt
Währing
Hernals
Ottakring
Am Steinhof
Hütteldorf
Penzing
Baumgarten
Rudolfsheim
Hietzing
Sankt Veit
Lainz
Speising
Hetzendorf
Altmannsdorf
Meidling
Favoriten
224
112
Erlaa
Atzgersdorf
Liesing
Siebenhirten
Rodaun
Perchtoldsdorf
Vösendorf
A21
Mödling
Mauer
Inzersdorf
230
Rothneusiedl
Unterlaa
Leopoldsdorf

Hagenbrunn
Föhrenhain
E461
NIEDERÖSTERREICH
WIEN
Langenzersdorf
Stammersdorf
Streberdsorf
14
Schwartz-
lackenau
Jedlesee
A22
E59
E49
Donau
Oberlisse
Nordrand-
Siedlung
Grossjedlersdorf
Grossfeld-
Siedlung
Floridsdorf
Donaufeld
Kagran
Neukagran
Brigittenau
Donau-
park
UNO City
Leopoldstadt
Alsergrund
Messe
Reichsbrücke
WIEN
Landstrasse
Stadion
Prater
Wieden
Margareten
Fünfhaus
Maria
17
Simmering
Simmering
Heide
Kaisereberdsorf
Wienerberg
A23
225
P. A. Hansson
Siedlung
Oberlaa
Klederling
Rannersdorf
Schwechat
A4
E58
E60
9
Neukettenhof
Zwölfaxing
WIEN
SCHWECHAT
(VIE)
Himberg

Hagenbrunn
Kapellerfeld
Helmahof
Gerasdorf
bei Wien
Deutsch-
Wagram
Neusüssbrunn
Aderklaa
Parbasdorf
Leopoldau
Breitenlee
Neuessling
Hirschstetten
Raasdorf
Donaustadt
Aspern
ASPERN
Essling
Gross-
enzersdorf
Gross
Biberhäufen
Mühleiten
Albern
Mannswörth
16° 20'
16° 30'
East from Greenwich

CENTRAL VIENNA

km 0.5
miles 0.25

ALSERGRUND
Rossauer
Kaserne
LEOPOLD-
STADT
Sigmund
Freud
Park
Votivkirche
Universität
Börse
MARIA-THERESIEN-STRASSE
SCHOTTENRING
OBERE DONAUSTRASSE
Schottenkirche
(Scottish
Monastery)
Rathaus
park
Burgtheater
Parlament
Volksgarten
Heldenplatz
Hofburg
(Imperial
Palace)
Naturhistorisches
Museum
Kunsthistorisches Mus.
(Museum of
Fine Art)
Burggarten
Museums-
quartier
Technische
Universität
Ressel-
park
Lehár-
Theater
an der Wien
Technische
Universität
Karlskirche
LINKE WIENZEILE
RECHTE WIENZEILE
WIEDNER HAUPTSTR.
Karlsplatz
Stephansplatz
Stephansdom
(St. Stephens
Cathedral)
Staatsoper
Nat. Opera
House)
OPERNRING
KÄRNTNER RING
SCHUBERTRING
RING
PARK
Stadt-
park
M.A.K.
Museum
of Applied
Arts
Wien-
Mitte
City Air
Terminal
St. Elisabeth
Krankenhaus
Veterinär-
medizin.
Universität
Palais
Schwarzenberg
(Schwarzenberg
Palace)

WARSAW

km 5
miles 3

Łomianki
61
Henryków
Grodzisk
Kobyłka
52° 20'
Dąbrowa
E77
Tarchomin
Marcelin
Białołęka
Dworska
Brzeziny
Marki
Wólka
Węglowa
Młociny
Żerań
Drewnica
Zielonka
Laski
Lasek
Bielański
Bielany
Bródno
Żacisze
Klaudyn
Wawrzyszew
Marymont
Targówek
Ząbki
Żoliborz
Kawęczyn
631
Bemowo
Lasek
Na Kole
Powązki
Stare
Miasto
Praga
Rembertów
Nowe-
Babice
Górce
Koło
Muranów
Praga Północ
Grochów
Wygoda
Zielona
Blizne
Jelonki
Wola
WARSZAWA
Marysin
Wawerski
Chrzanów
Czyste
Powiśle
Saska
Kępa
Wawer
2
E30
Odolany
Ochota
Ujazdów
Śródmieście
Park
Łazienkowski
Las
Anin
Ursus
Szczęśliwice
Włochy
Sielce
Siekierki
Mokotów
Czerniaków
Zerzeń
Miedzylesie
Golabki
Raków
Wierzbno
Sadyba
Augustówka
Radość
Salomea
Opacz
Okęcie
WARSZAWA
OKĘCIE
(WAW)
Służewiec
Służew
Wilanów
Wilanów
Palace
Zawady
801
Julianów
Miedzeszyn
Michałowice
Załuski
Wyczółki
Imielin
Powsinek
Bartyki
Sokołów
Raszyn
Jaworowa
Grabów
724
Błota
Janki
Falenty
Dawidy
Natolin
Okrzeszyn
Wolica
E67
8
E77
7
Łady
Pyry
Moczydło
Kabaty
107
Las Kabacki
Powsin
Bielawa
21° 00'
21° 10'
East from Greenwich
52° 10'

CENTRAL WARSAW

km 2
miles 1

Dworzec Gdański
ZYGMUNTA SLOMINSKIEGO
GENERAŁA
WŁADYSŁAWA
ANDERSA
Ogród
Zoologiczny
PRAGA
Park
Praski
Warszawa
Wileńska
St. John's
Cathedral
NOWE MIASTO
(NEW TOWN)
STARE MIASTO
(OLD TOWN)
Old Town
Square
Royal
Castle
St. Anne's
Church
Warszawa
Wschodnia
Warszawa
Stadion
Port
Praski
AL. SOLIDARNOŚCI
Kościół
Ewangelicko
Reformowany
Warsaw
Chamber
Opera
Pl.
Bankowy
Teatralny
Grand
Theatre
Pl.
Piłsudskiego
Ogród
Saski
Uniwersytet
Polish Theatre
Park
Skaryszewski
Stadion
Dziesięciolecia
AL. JANA PAWŁA II
Kościół
Ewangelicko
Augsburski
Szpital
Dziecięcy
Powstańców
Warszawy
Chopin
Museum
Warszawa
Powiśle
POWIŚLE
Chłodna
Pl.
Grzybowski
MARSZAŁKOWSKA
Polish
Army
Museum
National
Museum
Grzybowska
Pałac
Kultury i
Nauki
(Palace
of Culture &
Science)
Warszawa
Śródmieście
Warszawa
Centralna
W.Śródm.
Ochota
AL. JEROZOLIMSKIE
Opera
House
St. Alexander
Church
SOLEC
Szpital
Zakaźny
Szpital
Kliniczny
Akademii
Medycznej
ŚRÓDMIEŚCIE
UJAZDÓW
Ujazdowski
Filtry
Pl.
Politechnika
AL. ARMII LUDOWEJ
Park
Sportowy
Filtrowa
Pl.
Narutowicza
AL. NIEPODLEGŁOŚCI
AL. ARMII LUDOWEJ
Łazienkowski
Park
WAWELSKA
Park
im.
Józefa
Piłsudskiego
Stadion
"Skra"
Biblioteka
Narodowa
Stadion
"A.Z.S."
Obserwatorium
Astronomiczne
Theatre on
the Island
Centr.
Onkologii
ŻWIRKI I WIGURY
Pole Mokotowskie
PUŁAWSKA

WASHINGTON

0 km 5
0 miles 3

85 Interstate route numbers 29 U.S. route numbers 166 State route numbers

CENTRAL WASHINGTON

0 km 1
0 miles 0.5

WELLINGTON

0 km 5
0 miles 3

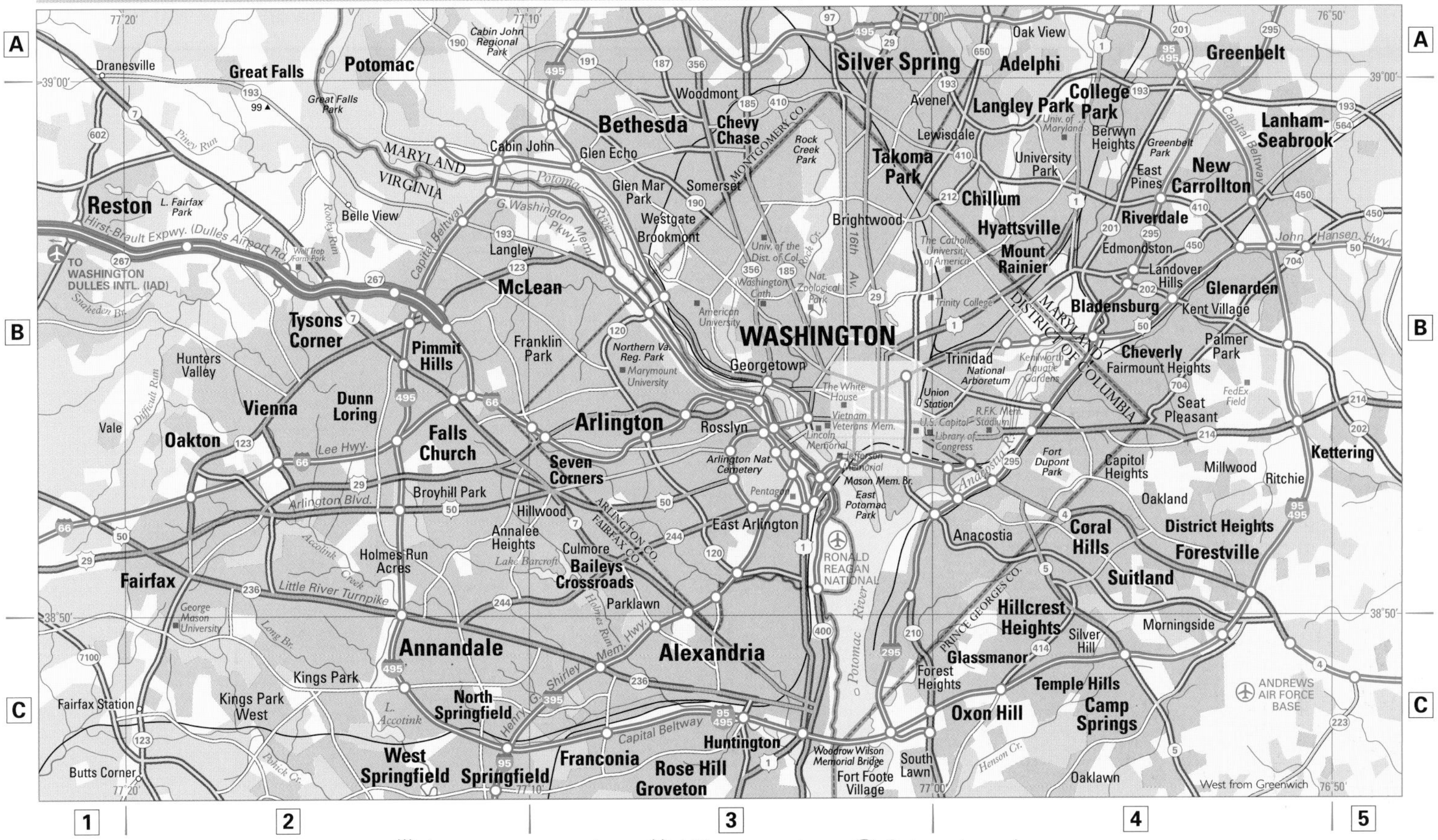

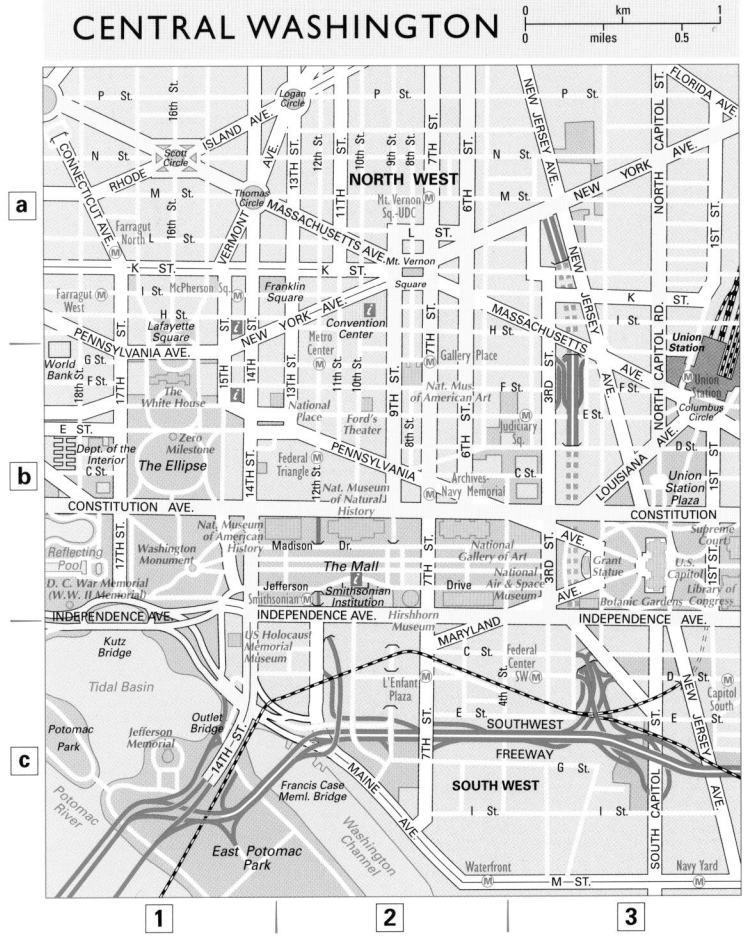

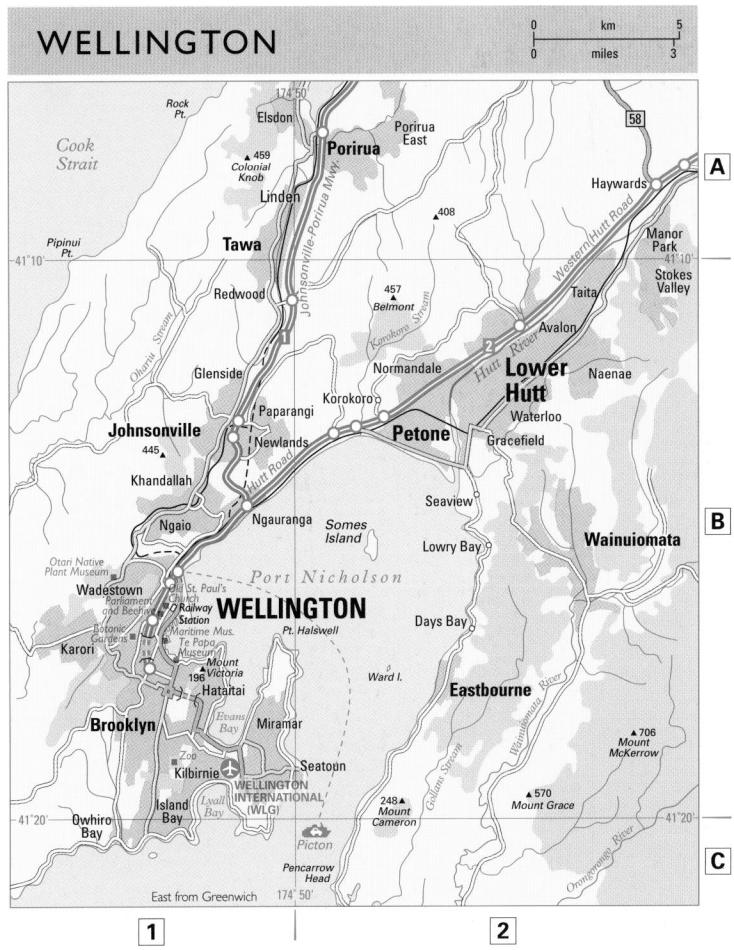

INDEX TO CITY MAPS

The index contains the names of all the principal places and features shown on the City Maps. Each name is followed by an additional entry in italics giving the name of the City Map within which it is located.

The number in bold type which follows each name refers to the number of the City Map page where that feature or place will be found.

The letter and figure which are immediately after the page number give the grid square on the map within which the feature or place is situated.

The letter represents the latitude and the figure the longitude. The full geographic reference is provided in the border of the City Maps.

The location given is the centre of the city, suburb or feature and is not necessarily the name. Rivers, canals and roads are indexed to their name. Rivers carry the symbol � after their name.

An explanation of the alphabetical order rules and a list of the abbreviations used are to be found at the beginning of the World Map Index.

A

Aalām *Baghdad* **3** B2
Abbey Wood *London* **15** B4
Abcoude *Amsterdam* **2** B2
Ābdīn *Cairo* **7** A2
Abeno *Osaka* **23** B2
Aberdeen *Hong Kong* **12** B1
Aberdour *Edinburgh* **11** A2
Aberdour Castle *Edinburgh* **11** A2
Abflanggraben ➞ *Munich* **21** A3
Ablon-sur-Seine *Paris* **24** B3
Abramtsevo *Moscow* **19** B3
Abu Dis *Jerusalem* **13** B2
Abū en Numrus *Cairo* **7** B2
Abu Ghosh *Jerusalem* **13** A1
Acassuso *Buenos Aires* **7** A1
Accotink, L. *Washington* **33** C2
Accotink Cr. ➞ *Washington* **33** B2
Achères *Paris* **24** A1
Acilia *Rome* **26** C1
Aclimação *São Paulo* **27** B2
Acropolis *Athens* **2** B2
Acton *London* **15** A2
Açúcar, Pão de *Rio de Janeiro* **25** B2
Ada Beja *Lisbon* **16** A1
Adams Park *Atlanta* **3** B2
Addiscombe *London* **15** B3
Adelphi *Washington* **33** A4
Aderklaa *Vienna* **32** A3
Adler Planetarium *Chicago* **9** B3
Admiralteyskaya Storona *St. Petersburg* **27** B2
Āffori *Milan* **19** A2
Aflandshage *Copenhagen* **8** B3
Afsariyeh *Tehran* **31** B2
Agboyi Cr. ➞ *Lagos* **14** A2
Ågerup *Copenhagen* **8** A1
Ågesta *Stockholm* **29** B2
Aghia Marina *Athens* **2** C3
Aghia Paraskevi *Athens* **2** A2
Aghios Dimitrios *Athens* **2** B2
Aghios Ioannis Rendis *Athens* **2** B1
Agincourt *Toronto* **31** A3
Agra Canal *Delhi* **10** B2
Agricola Oriental *Mexico City* **18** B2
Agua Espraiada ➞ *São Paulo* **27** B2
Agualva-Cacem *Lisbon* **16** A1
Agustino, Cerro El *Lima* **14** B3
Ahrensfelde *Berlin* **5** A4
Ahuntsic *Montreal* **20** A1
Ai ➞ *Osaka* **23** A2
Aigremont *Paris* **24** A1
Air View Park *Singapore* **28** A2
Airport West *Melbourne* **18** A1
Ajegunle *Lagos* **14** B2
Aji *Osaka* **23** A1
Ajuda *Lisbon* **16** A1
Akalla *Stockholm* **29** A1
Akasaka *Tokyo* **30** A3
Akbarābād *Tehran* **31** A2
Akershus Castle = Akershus Slott *Oslo* **23** A3
Akershus Slott *Oslo* **23** A3
Al 'Azamīyah *Baghdad* **3** A2
Al Quds = Jerusalem *Jerusalem* **13** B2
Al-Walaja *Jerusalem* **13** B1
Alaguntan *Lagos* **14** B2
Alameda *San Francisco* **26** B3
Alameda Memorial State Beach Park *San Francisco* **26** B3
Albern *Vienna* **32** B2
Albert Park *Melbourne* **18** B1
Alberton *Johannesburg* **13** B2
Albertslund *Copenhagen* **8** B2
Albysjön *Stockholm* **29** B1
Alcantara *Lisbon* **16** A1
Alcatraz I. *San Francisco* **26** B2
Alcobendas *Madrid* **17** A2
Alcorcón *Madrid* **17** B1
Aldershot *Berlin* **5** B4
Aldo Bonzi *Buenos Aires* **7** C1
Aleksandrovskoye *St. Petersburg* **27** B2
Alexander Nevsky Abbey *St. Petersburg* **27** B2
Alexandra *Johannesburg* **13** A2
Alexandra *Singapore* **28** B2
Alexandria *Washington* **33** C3
Alfortville *Paris* **24** B3
Algés *Lisbon* **16** A1
Alhambra *Los Angeles* **16** B4
Alibey ➞ *Istanbul* **12** B1
Alibey Baraji *Istanbul* **12** B1
Alibeyköy *Istanbul* **12** B1
Alimos *Athens* **2** B2
Alipur *Kolkata* **14** B1
Allach *Munich* **21** A1
Allambie Heights *Sydney* **29** A2
Allermuir Hill *Edinburgh* **11** B2
Allstate Arena *Chicago* **9** A1
Allston *Boston* **6** A3
Almada *Lisbon* **16** A2
Almargem do Bispo *Lisbon* **16** A1
Almirante G. Brown, Parque *Buenos Aires* **7** C2
Almon *Jerusalem* **13** B2
Almond ➞ *Edinburgh* **11** B2
Alna ➞ *Oslo* **23** A4
Alnsjøen *Oslo* **23** A4
Alperton *London* **15** A2

Alpine *New York* **22** A2
Alrode *Johannesburg* **13** B2
Alsemberg *Brussels* **6** B1
Alsergrund *Vienna* **32** A2
Alsip *Chicago* **9** C2
Ålsten *Stockholm* **29** B1
Älta *Stockholm* **29** B3
Altadena *Los Angeles* **16** A4
Alte-Donau ➞ *Vienna* **32** A2
Altes Rathaus *Munich* **21** B2
Altglienicke *Berlin* **5** B4
Altlandsberg *Berlin* **5** A5
Altlandsberg Nord *Berlin* **5** A5
Altmannsdorf *Vienna* **32** B1
Alto da Boa Vista *Rio de Janeiro* **25** B1
Alto da Mooca *São Paulo* **27** B2
Alto do Pina *Lisbon* **16** A2
Altona *Melbourne* **18** B1
Alvik *Stockholm* **29** B1
Älvsjö *Stockholm* **29** B2
Älvvik *Stockholm* **29** A3
Am Hasenbergl *Munich* **21** A2
Am Steinhof *Vienna* **32** A1
Am Wald *Munich* **21** B2
Ama Keng *Singapore* **28** A2
Amadora *Lisbon* **16** A1
Amagasaki *Osaka* **23** A1
Amager *Copenhagen* **8** B3
Amāl Qādisiya *Baghdad* **3** B2
Amalienborg Slot *Copenhagen* **8** A3
Amata *Milan* **19** A1
Ambelokipi *Athens* **2** B2
Ameixoeira *Lisbon* **16** A2
América *São Paulo* **27** B1
American Police Hall of Fame *Miami* **18** B2
American University *Washington* **33** B3
Amin *Baghdad* **3** B2
Aminadav *Jerusalem* **13** B1
Amīrābād *Tehran* **31** A2
Amora *Lisbon* **16** A1
Amoreira *Lisbon* **16** A1
Amper ➞ *Munich* **21** A1
Amstel-Drecht-Kanaal *Amsterdam* **2** B2
Amstelveen *Amsterdam* **2** B2
Amsterdam *Amsterdam* **2** A2
Amsterdam ✈ (AMS) *Amsterdam* **2** B1
Amsterdam-Rijnkanaal *Amsterdam* **2** B3
Amsterdam Zuidoost *Amsterdam* **2** B2
Amsterdamse Bos *Amsterdam* **2** B1
Anacosta ➞ *Washington* **33** B4
Anacostia *Washington* **33** B4
Anadoluhisarı *Istanbul* **12** B2
Anadolukavaği *Istanbul* **12** A2
Anata *Jerusalem* **13** B2
Ancol *Jakarta* **12** A1
Andaraí *Rio de Janeiro* **25** B1
Anderlecht *Brussels* **6** A1
Anderson Park *Atlanta* **3** B2
Andingmen *Beijing* **4** B2
Ang Mo Kio *Singapore* **28** A3
Ängby *Stockholm* **29** A1
Angel I. *San Francisco* **26** A2
Angel Island State Park *San Francisco* **26** A2
Angke, Kali ➞ *Jakarta* **12** A1
Angyalföld *Budapest* **7** A2
Anik *Mumbai* **20** A2
Anin *Warsaw* **32** C2
Anjou *Montreal* **20** A2
Annalee Heights *Washington* **33** B2
Annandale *Washington* **33** C2
Anne Frankhuis *Amsterdam* **2** A2
Antony *Paris* **24** B2
Aoyama *Tokyo* **30** B3
Ap Lei Chau *Hong Kong* **12** B1
Apapa *Lagos* **14** B2
Apelación *Lisbon* **16** A1
Apopka, L. *Orlando* **23** A1
Apoquindo *Santiago* **27** B2
Apterkarskiy Ostrov *St. Petersburg* **27** B2
Ar Kazimiyah *Baghdad* **3** B1
Ar Ram *Jerusalem* **13** A2
Ara ➞ *Tokyo* **30** A4
Arakawa *Tokyo* **30** A3
Arany-hegyi-patak ➞ *Budapest* **7** A2
Aravaca *Madrid* **17** B1
Arbataash *Baghdad* **3** A1
Arc de Triomphe *Paris* **24** A2
Arcadia *Los Angeles* **16** B4
Arcueil *Paris* **24** B2
Arese *Milan* **19** A1
Arganzuela *Madrid* **17** B1
Argenteuil *Paris* **24** A2
Argonne Forest *Chicago* **9** C1
Arima *Tokyo* **30** B2
Arlanda ✈ (ARN) *Stockholm* **29** A2
Arlington *Boston* **6** A1
Arlington *Washington* **33** B3
Arlington Heights *Boston* **6** A1
Arlington Nat. Cemetery *Washington* **33** B3
Armação *Rio de Janeiro* **25** B2
Armadale *Melbourne* **18** B2
Armour Heights *Toronto* **31** A2

Arncliffe *Sydney* **29** B1
Arnold Arboretum *Boston* **6** B2
Árpádföld *Budapest* **7** A3
Arrentela *Lisbon* **16** B2
Arroyo Seco Park *Los Angeles* **16** A3
Årsta *Stockholm* **29** B2
Art Institute *Chicago* **9** B3
Artane *Dublin* **10** A2
Artas *Jerusalem* **13** B2
Arthur's Seat *Edinburgh* **11** B3
Arts, Place des *Montreal* **20** A2
As Shawawra *Jerusalem* **13** B2
Asagaya *Tokyo* **30** A2
Asahi *Osaka* **23** A2
Asakusa *Tokyo* **30** A3
Asati *Kolkata* **14** C1
Aschheim *Munich* **21** A3
Ascot Vale *Melbourne* **18** A1
Ashbridge's Bay Park *Toronto* **31** B3
Ashburn *Chicago* **9** C2
Ashburton *Melbourne* **18** B2
Ashfield *Sydney* **29** B1
Ashford *London* **15** B1
Ashtown *Dublin* **10** A2
Askisto *Helsinki* **11** B1
Askrikefjärden *Stockholm* **29** A3
Asnières *Paris* **24** A2
Aspern *Vienna* **32** A2
Aspern ✈ *Vienna* **32** A3
Assago *Milan* **19** B1
Assendelft *Amsterdam* **2** A1
Assiano *Milan* **19** B1
Astoria *New York* **22** B2
Astrolabe Park *Sydney* **29** B2
Atarot *Jerusalem* **13** A2
Atarot ✈ *Jerusalem* **13** A2
Atghara *Kolkata* **14** B2
Athens = Athina *Athens* **2** B2
Athína *Athens* **2** B2
Athína ✈ (ATH) *Athens* **2** A3
Athínai = Athens *Athens* **2** B2
Athis-Mons *Paris* **24** B3
Athlone *Cape Town* **8** A2
Atholl *Johannesburg* **13** A2
Atifiya *Baghdad* **3** A2
Atişalen *Istanbul* **12** B1
Atlanta *Atlanta* **3** B2
Atlanta Hartsfield Int. ✈ (ATL) *Atlanta* **3** C2
Atlanta Zoo *Atlanta* **3** B2
Atomium *Brussels* **6** A2
Attiki *Athens* **2** A2
Atzgersdorf *Vienna* **32** B1
Aubervilliers *Paris* **24** A3
Aubing *Munich* **21** B1
Auburndale *Boston* **6** A1
Auchendinny *Edinburgh* **11** B2
Auckland Park *Johannesburg* **13** B2
Auderghem *Brussels* **6** B2
Augustdorf *Vienna* **32** B1
Augustówka *Warsaw* **32** C2
Aulnay-sous-Bois *Paris* **24** A3
Aurelio *Rome* **26** B1
Ausim *Cairo* **7** A1
Austerlitz, Gare d' *Paris* **24** A3
Austin *Chicago* **9** B2
Avalon *Wellington* **33** B2
Avedøre *Copenhagen* **8** B2
Avellaneda *Buenos Aires* **7** C2
Avenel *Washington* **33** B4
Avondale *Chicago* **9** B2
Avondale Heights *Melbourne* **18** A1
Avtovo *St. Petersburg* **27** B1
Ayazağa *Istanbul* **12** B2
Ayer Chawan, Pulau *Singapore* **28** B2
Ayer Merbau, Pulau *Singapore* **28** B2
Azabu *Tokyo* **30** B3
Azcapotzalco *Mexico City* **18** B1
Azteca, Estadia *Mexico City* **18** C2
Azucar, Cerro Pan de *Santiago* **27** A1

B

Baambrugge *Amsterdam* **2** B2
Baba Ch. *Karachi* **13** B1
Baba I. *Karachi* **13** B1
Babarpur *Delhi* **10** A2
Babushkin *Moscow* **19** A3
Back B. *Mumbai* **20** B1
Baclaran *Manila* **17** C1
Bacoor *Manila* **17** C1
Bacoor B. *Manila* **17** C1
Badalona *Barcelona* **4** A2
Badhoevedorp *Amsterdam* **2** A1
Badli *Delhi* **10** A1
Bærum *Oslo* **23** A2
Bağcılar *Istanbul* **12** B1
Bággio *Milan* **19** B1
Bāgh-e-Feyz *Tehran* **31** A1
Baghdad *Baghdad* **3** B2
Baghdad al Muthana ✈ *Baghdad* **3** B2
Baghdad Int. ✈ (SDA) *Baghdad* **3** B1
Bagmari *Kolkata* **14** B2
Bagneux *Paris* **24** B2
Bagnolet *Paris* **24** A3
Bagsværd *Copenhagen* **8** A2
Bagsværd Sø *Copenhagen* **8** A2
Baguiati *Kolkata* **14** B2
Bagumbayan *Manila* **17** C2
Baha'i Temple *Chicago* **9** A2
Bahçeköy *Istanbul* **12** A1

Bahçelievler *Istanbul* **12** B1
Bahtīm *Cairo* **7** A2
Baile Atha Cliath = Dublin *Dublin* **10** A2
Baileys Crossroads *Washington* **33** B3
Bailly *Paris* **24** A1
Bairro Lopes *Lisbon* **16** A2
Baisha *Guangzhou* **11** B2
Baiyun Hill *Guangzhou* **11** B2
Baiyun Int. ✈ (CAN) *Guangzhou* **11** A2
Bakırköy *Istanbul* **12** C1
Bal Harbor *Miami* **18** A2
Balara *Manila* **17** B2
Baldia *Karachi* **13** A1
Baldoyle *Dublin* **10** A3
Baldwin, L. *Orlando* **23** A3
Baldwin Hills *Los Angeles* **16** B2
Baldwin Hills Res. *Los Angeles* **16** B2
Balgowlah *Sydney* **29** A2
Balgowlah Heights *Sydney* **29** A2
Balham *London* **15** B3
Bali *Kolkata* **14** B2
Baliganja *Kolkata* **14** B2
Balingsås *Stockholm* **29** B2
Balingsta *Stockholm* **29** B2
Balintawak *Manila* **17** B1
Ballerup *Copenhagen* **8** A2
Ballinteer *Dublin* **10** B2
Ballyboden *Dublin* **10** B2
Ballybrack *Dublin* **10** B3
Ballyfermot *Dublin* **10** A1
Ballymorefinn Hill *Dublin* **10** B1
Ballymun *Dublin* **10** A2
Balmain *Sydney* **29** B2
Baluhati *Kolkata* **14** B1
Balvanera *Buenos Aires* **7** B2
Balwyn *Melbourne* **18** A2
Balwyn North *Melbourne* **18** A2
Banática *Lisbon* **16** A1
Bandra *Mumbai* **20** A1
Bandra Pt. *Mumbai* **20** A1
Bang Kapi *Bangkok* **3** B2
Bang Na *Bangkok* **3** B2
Bangbae *Seoul* **27** C1
Bangkhen *Bangkok* **3** A2
Bangkok *Bangkok* **3** B2
Bangkok Noi *Bangkok* **3** B1
Bangkok Yai *Bangkok* **3** B1
Banglo *Kolkata* **14** B1
Bangrak *Bangkok* **3** B2
Bangsu *Bangkok* **3** B2
Banks, C. *Sydney* **29** C2
Banksmeadow *Sydney* **29** B2
Banstala *Kolkata* **14** B2
Bantra *Kolkata* **14** B1
Baoshan *Shanghai* **28** A1
Bar Giyora *Jerusalem* **13** B1
Barahanagar *Kolkata* **14** B2
Barajas *Madrid* **17** B2
Barajas, Madrid ✈ (MAD) *Madrid* **17** B2
Barakpur *Kolkata* **14** A2
Barbarena *Lisbon* **16** A1
Barcarena, Rib. de ➞ *Lisbon* **16** A1
Barcelona *Barcelona* **4** A2
Barcelona-Prat ✈ (BCN) *Barcelona* **4** B1
Barceloneta *Barcelona* **4** A2
Barcroft, L. *Washington* **33** B3
Barking *London* **15** A4
Barkingside *London* **15** A4
Barnes *London* **15** B2
Barnet *London* **15** A2
Barra Andaí *Karachi* **13** B2
Barra Funda *São Paulo* **27** B2
Barracas *Buenos Aires* **7** B2
Barrackpur = Barakpur *Kolkata* **14** A2
Barranco *Lima* **14** B2
Barreiro *Lisbon* **16** B2
Barreto *Rio de Janeiro* **25** B2
Bartala *Kolkata* **14** B2
Barton Park *Sydney* **29** B1
Bartyki *Warsaw* **32** C2
Basus *Cairo* **7** A2
Batanagar *Kolkata* **14** B1
Bath Beach *New York* **22** C1
Bath I. *Karachi* **13** B2
Batir *Jerusalem* **13** B1
Batok, Bukit *Singapore* **28** A2
Battersea *London* **15** B3
Bauman *Moscow* **19** B3
Baumgarten *Vienna* **32** A1
Bay, L. *Orlando* **23** B1
Bay Harbour Islands *Miami* **18** A2
Bay Hill *Orlando* **23** B2
Bay Ridge *New York* **22** C1
Bayit Va-Gan *Jerusalem* **13** B2
Bayonne *New York* **22** B1
Bayrampaşa *Istanbul* **12** B1
Bayshore *San Francisco* **26** B2
Bayt Lahm *Jerusalem* **13** B2
Bayview *San Francisco* **26** B2
Bāzār *Tehran* **31** A2
Beacon Hill *Hong Kong* **12** A2
Beato *Lisbon* **16** A2
Beaumont *Dublin* **10** A2
Beaumont Heights *Toronto* **31** A1
Bebek *Istanbul* **12** B2
Béchovice *Prague* **25** B3
Beck L. *Chicago* **9** A1
Beckenham *London* **15** B3
Beckton *London* **15** A4
Becontree *London* **15** A4

Beddington Corner *London* **15** B3
Bedford *London* **6** A1
Bedford Park *Chicago* **9** C2
Bedford Park *New York* **22** A2
Bedford Stuyvesant *New York* **22** B2
Bedford View *Johannesburg* **13** B2
Bedok *Singapore* **28** B3
Bedok, Res. *Singapore* **28** A3
Beersel *Brussels* **6** B1
Behala *Kolkata* **14** B1
Bei Hai *Beijing* **4** B2
Beicai *Shanghai* **28** B2
Beijing *Beijing* **4** B1
Beit Duqu *Jerusalem* **13** A1
Beit Ghur at-Taht *Jerusalem* **13** A1
Beit Ghur el-Fawqa *Jerusalem* **13** A1
Beit Ij'za *Jerusalem* **13** A1
Beit Iksa *Jerusalem* **13** B2
Beit I'nan *Jerusalem* **13** A1
Beit Jala *Jerusalem* **13** B2
Beit Lekhem = Bayt Lahm *Jerusalem* **13** B2
Beit Liqya *Jerusalem* **13** A1
Beit Nekofa *Jerusalem* **13** B1
Beit Sahur *Jerusalem* **13** B2
Beit Sofafa *Jerusalem* **13** B2
Beit Surik *Jerusalem* **13** B1
Beit Ur al-Fawqa *Jerusalem* **13** A1
Beit Zayit *Jerusalem* **13** B1
Beitajingzhuan *Beijing* **4** B1
Beitar Ilit *Jerusalem* **13** B2
Beitin *Jerusalem* **13** A2
Beitsun *Guangzhou* **11** B2
Beitunya *Jerusalem* **13** A2
Beixing Jing Park *Shanghai* **28** B1
Békásmegyer *Budapest* **7** A2
Bekkelaget *Oslo* **23** A4
Bekkestua *Oslo* **23** A2
Bel Air *Los Angeles* **16** B2
Bela Vista *São Paulo* **27** B2
Bélanger *Montreal* **20** A1
Belas *Lisbon* **16** A1
Beleghata *Kolkata* **14** B2
Belém *Lisbon* **16** A1
Belém, Torre de *Lisbon* **16** A1
Belénzinho *São Paulo* **27** B2
Belgachia *Kolkata* **14** B2
Belgharia *Kolkata* **14** A2
Belgrano *Buenos Aires* **7** B2
Bell Gardens *Los Angeles* **16** C4
Bellavista *Lima* **14** B2
Bellavista *Santiago* **27** C2
Belle Harbor *New York* **22** C2
Belle Isle *Orlando* **23** B2
Belle View *Washington* **33** B3
Bellingham *London* **15** B3
Bellwood *Chicago* **9** B1
Belmont *Boston* **6** A1
Belmont *London* **15** A2
Belmont, Mt. *Wellington* **33** B2
Belmont Cragin *Chicago* **9** B2
Belmont Harbor *Chicago* **9** B3
Belmore *Sydney* **29** B1
Belur *Kolkata* **14** B2
Belvedere *Atlanta* **3** B3
Belvedere *London* **15** B4
Belvedere *San Francisco* **26** A2
Belyayevo-Bogorodskoye *Moscow* **19** C2
Bemowo *Warsaw* **32** B1
Benaki Museum *Athens* **2** B2
Bendale *Toronto* **31** A3
Benfica *Rio de Janeiro* **25** B1
Benfica *Lisbon* **16** A1
Benito Juárez *Mexico City* **18** B2
Benito Juárez, Int. ✈ (MEX) *Mexico City* **18** B2
Bensonhurst *New York* **22** C2
Berchem-Ste-Agathe *Brussels* **6** A1
Berg am Laim *Munich* **21** B2
Bergenfield *New York* **22** A2
Bergham *Munich* **21** B2
Bergvliet *Cape Town* **8** B1
Beri *Barcelona* **4** A1
Berkeley *San Francisco* **26** A3
Berlin *Berlin* **5** A3
Berlin Dom *Berlin* **5** A3
Berlin Tegel ✈ (TXL) *Berlin* **5** A2
Berlin Tempelhof ✈ (THF) *Berlin* **5** B3
Bermondsey *London* **15** B3
Bernabeu, Estadio *Madrid* **17** B1
Bernal Heights *San Francisco* **26** B2
Berwyn *Chicago* **9** B2
Berwyn Heights *Washington* **33** B4
Besiktas *Istanbul* **12** B2
Besòs *Barcelona* **4** A2
Bessie, L. *Orlando* **23** B1
Bet Horon *Jerusalem* **13** A1
Bethesda *Washington* **33** B3
Bethlehem = Bayt Lahm *Jerusalem* **13** B2
Bethnal Green *London* **15** A3
Betor *Kolkata* **14** B1
Beulah, L. *Orlando* **23** B1
Beverley Park *Sydney* **29** B1
Beverly Arts Center *Chicago* **9** C2
Beverly Glen *Los Angeles* **16** B2
Beverly Hills *Los Angeles* **16** B2

Beverly Hills -Morgan Park Historic District *Chicago* **9** C2
Bexley *Sydney* **29** B1
Bexley □ *London* **15** B4
Bexleyheath *London* **15** B4
Beykoz *Istanbul* **12** B2
Beylerbeyi *Istanbul* **12** B2
Beyoğlu *Istanbul* **12** B1
Bezons *Paris* **24** A2
Bezuidenhout Park *Johannesburg* **13** B2
Bhadrakali *Kolkata* **14** A2
Bhalswa *Delhi* **10** A2
Bhambo Khan Qarmati *Karachi* **13** B2
Bhatsala *Kolkata* **14** B1
Bhawanipur *Kolkata* **14** B2
Bhendkhal *Mumbai* **20** B2
Bhuleshwar *Mumbai* **20** B1
Bialoleka Dworska *Warsaw* **32** B2
Bicentennial Park *Los Angeles* **16** C4
Bicentennial Park *Sydney* **29** B1
Bickley *London* **15** B4
Bicutan *Manila* **17** C2
Bidhan Nagar *Kolkata* **14** B2
Bidu *Jerusalem* **13** A1
Bielany *Warsaw* **32** B1
Bielawa *Warsaw* **32** C2
Biesdorf *Berlin* **5** A4
Bièvre ➞ *Paris* **24** B1
Bièvres *Paris* **24** B2
Big Sand Lake *Orlando* **23** B2
Bilston *Sydney* **29** B2
Binacayan *Manila* **17** C1
Binondo *Manila* **17** B1
Bintaro Jaya *Jakarta* **12** B1
Bir Nabala *Jerusalem* **13** A2
Birak el Kiyam *Cairo* **7** A1
Birch Cliff *Toronto* **31** A3
Birkenstein *Berlin* **5** A5
Birkholz *Berlin* **5** A4
Birkholzaue *Berlin* **5** A4
Birrarrung Park *Melbourne* **18** A2
Biscayne Park *Miami* **18** A2
Bishop Lavis *Cape Town* **8** A2
Bishopscourt *Cape Town* **8** A1
Bispebjerg *Copenhagen* **8** A3
Bittsevsky Forest Park *Moscow* **19** C2
Björknas *Stockholm* **29** B3
Black Cr. ➞ *Toronto* **31** A1
Black Creek Pioneer Village *Toronto* **31** A1
Blackfen *London* **15** B4
Blackheath *London* **15** B4
Blackrock *Dublin* **10** B2
Bladensburg *Washington* **33** B4
Blair Village *Atlanta* **3** C2
Blairgowrie *Johannesburg* **13** A2
Blake House *Boston* **6** B2
Blakehurst *Sydney* **29** B1
Blakstad *Oslo* **23** B1
Blanche, L. *Orlando* **23** B1
Blankenburg *Berlin* **5** A4
Blankenfelde *Berlin* **5** A3
Blizne *Warsaw* **32** B1
Blota *Warsaw* **32** C3
Blue Island *Chicago* **9** D2
Blue Mosque = Sultanahme Camil *Istanbul* **12** B1
Bluebell *Dublin* **10** A1
Bluff Hd. *Hong Kong* **12** B2
Bluffers Park *Toronto* **31** A3
Blumberg *Berlin* **5** A4
Blunt Pt. *San Francisco* **26** A2
Blutenberg *Munich* **21** B1
Blylaget *Oslo* **23** B3
Boa Vista, Alto do *Rio de Janeiro* **25** B1
Boardwalk *New York* **22** C3
Boavista *Lisbon* **16** A2
Bobigny *Paris* **24** A3
Bocanegra *Lima* **14** B2
Boedo *Buenos Aires* **7** B2
Bogenhausen *Munich* **21** B2
Boggy Creek Swamp *Orlando* **23** B2
Bogorodskoye *Moscow* **19** B3
Bogota *New York* **22** A1
Bogstadvatnet *Oslo* **23** A2
Bohnsdorf *Berlin* **5** B4
Bois-Colombes *Paris* **24** A2
Bois-d'Arcy *Paris* **24** B1
Boissy-St-Léger *Paris* **24** B4
Boldinasco *Milan* **19** B1
Bøler *Oslo* **23** A4
Bollate *Milan* **19** A1
Bollebeek *Brussels* **6** A1
Bollensdorf *Berlin* **5** A5
Bollmora *Stockholm* **29** B3
Bolshaya Okhta *St. Petersburg* **27** B2
Bolton *Milan* **19** B1
Bom Retiro *São Paulo* **27** B2
Bombay = Mumbai *Mumbai* **20** B1
Bondi *Sydney* **29** B2
Bondy *Paris* **24** A3
Bonifacio Monument *Manila* **17** B1
Bonneuil-sur-Marne *Paris* **24** B4
Bonnington *Edinburgh* **11** B1
Bonnyrigg and Lasswade *Edinburgh* **11** B3
Bonsucesso *Rio de Janeiro* **25** B1

Bonteheuwel *Cape Town* **8** A2
Boo *Stockholm* **29** A3
Booterstown *Dublin* **10** B2
Borisovo *Moscow* **19** C3
Borle *Mumbai* **20** A2
Boronia Park *Sydney* **29** A1
Bosmont *Johannesburg* **13** B1
Bosön *Stockholm* **29** A3
Bosporus = İstanbul Boğazı *Istanbul* **12** B2
Bostancı *Istanbul* **12** C2
Boston *Boston* **6** A2
Boston Common *Boston* **6** A2
Boston Logan Int. ✈ (BOS) *Boston* **6** A2
Botafogo *Rio de Janeiro* **25** B1
Botany *Sydney* **29** B2
Botany B. *Sydney* **29** B2
Botany Bay Nat. Park △ *Sydney* **29** B2
Botič ➞ *Prague* **25** B3
Botica Sete *Lisbon* **16** A2
Boucherville *Montreal* **20** A3
Boucherville, Îs. de *Montreal* **20** A3
Bougival *Paris* **24** A1
Boulder Pt. *Hong Kong* **12** B1
Boulogne, Bois de *Paris* **24** A2
Boulogne-Billancourt *Paris* **24** A2
Bourg-la-Reine *Paris* **24** B2
Bouviers *Paris* **24** B1
Bovenkerk *Amsterdam* **2** B2
Bovenkerker Polder *Amsterdam* **2** B2
Bovisa *Milan* **19** A2
Bow *London* **15** A3
Boyacıköy *Istanbul* **12** B2
Boyd Conservation Area *Toronto* **31** A1
Boyle Heights *Los Angeles* **16** B3
Braepark *Edinburgh* **11** B2
Braid *Edinburgh* **11** B2
Bramley *Johannesburg* **13** A2
Brandeis University *Boston* **6** A1
Brandenburger Tor *Berlin* **5** A3
Brani, Pulau *Singapore* **28** B3
Branik *Prague* **25** B2
Brännkyrka *Stockholm* **29** B2
Brás *São Paulo* **27** B2
Brasilândia *São Paulo* **27** A1
Brateyevo *Moscow* **19** C3
Brazböse *Melbourne* **18** A1
Brázdim *Prague* **25** A3
Breakheart Reservation *Boston* **6** A2
Brede *Copenhagen* **8** A3
Breezy Point *New York* **22** C2
Breitenlee *Vienna* **32** A3
Breña *Lima* **14** B2
Brent □ *London* **15** A2
Brent Res. *London* **15** A2
Brentford *London* **15** B2
Brentwood Park *Los Angeles* **16** B2
Brera *Milan* **19** B2
Bresso *Milan* **19** A2
Brevik *Stockholm* **29** A3
Břevnov *Prague* **25** B2
Brickyard, The *Chicago* **9** B2
Bridgeport *Chicago* **9** C3
Bridgetown *Cape Town* **8** A2
Bridgeview *Chicago* **9** C2
Brighton *Boston* **6** A3
Brighton *Melbourne* **18** B2
Brighton Beach *New York* **22** C2
Brighton le Sands *Sydney* **29** B1
Brighton Park *Chicago* **9** C2
Brightwood *Washington* **33** B3
Brigittenau *Vienna* **32** A2
Brimbank Park *Melbourne* **18** A1
Brisbane *San Francisco* **26** B2
Brit *Berlin* **5** B3
Brixton *London* **15** B3
Broadmeadows *Melbourne* **18** A1
Broadmoor *San Francisco* **26** B2
Broadview *Chicago* **9** B1
Brockley *London* **15** B3
Bródno *Warsaw* **32** B2
Bródnowski, Kanal *Warsaw* **32** B2
Broek *Amsterdam* **2** A2
Bromley □ *London* **15** B4
Bromley Common *London* **15** B4
Bromma *Stockholm* **29** A1
Bromma ✈ *Stockholm* **29** A1
Brøndby Strand *Copenhagen* **8** B2
Brøndbyøster *Copenhagen* **8** B2
Brøndbyvester *Copenhagen* **8** B2
Brondesbury *London* **15** A2
Brønnøya *Oslo* **23** B2
Brønshøj *Copenhagen* **8** A2
Bronxville *New York* **22** A2
Brookfield *Chicago* **9** C1
Brookhaven *Atlanta* **3** A2
Brookline *Boston* **6** A3
Brooklyn *Chicago* **9** C3
Brooklyn *New York* **22** C2
Brooklyn Heights *New York* **22** B2
Brookmont *Washington* **33** B3
Brossard *Montreal* **20** B3
Brou-sur-Chantereine *Paris* **24** A4
Brown *Toronto* **31** A3
Broyhill Park *Washington* **33** B2
Brughério *Milan* **19** A2
Brunswick *Melbourne* **18** A1
Brussegem *Brussels* **6** A1

Brussel *Brussels* **6** A2
Brussel ✈ (BRU) *Brussels* **6** A2
Brussels = Brussel *Brussels* **6** A2
Bruxelles = Brussel *Brussels* **6** A2
Bruzzano *Milan* **19** A2
Bry-sur-Marne *Paris* **24** A4
Bryan, L. *Orlando* **23** B1
Bryanston *Johannesburg* **13** A1
Bryn *Oslo* **23** A1
Brzeziny *Warsaw* **32** B2
Bubeneč *Prague* **25** B2
Buc *Paris* **24** B1
Buchenhain *Munich* **21** B1
Buchholz *Berlin* **5** A3
Buckhead *Atlanta* **3** A2
Buckingham Palace *London* **15** A3
Buckow *Berlin* **5** B3
Buda *Budapest* **7** A2
Buda Castle = Budaváripalota *Budapest* **7** A2
Budafok *Budapest* **7** B2
Budaörs *Budapest* **7** B1
Budapest *Budapest* **7** A2
Budapest ✈ (BUD) *Budapest* **7** B3
Budatétény *Budapest* **7** B2
Budaváripalota *Budapest* **7** A2
Buddinge *Copenhagen* **8** A3
Buena Ventura Lakes *Orlando* **23** B2
Buena Vista *San Francisco* **26** B2
Buenos Aires *Buenos Aires* **7** B2
Bufalotta *Rome* **26** B2
Bugio *Lisbon* **16** B1
Buiksloot *Amsterdam* **2** A2
Buitenveldert *Amsterdam* **2** B2
Buizingen *Brussels* **6** B1
Bukhansan *Seoul* **27** B1
Bukit Panjang Nature Reserve *Singapore* **28** A2
Bukit Timah Nature Reserve *Singapore* **28** A2
Bukum, Pulau *Singapore* **28** B2
Bůláq *Cairo* **7** A2
Bule *Manila* **17** C2
Bulim *Singapore* **28** A2
Bullen Park *Melbourne* **18** A2
Bund, The *Shanghai* **28** B1
Bundoora North *Melbourne* **18** A2
Bundoora Park *Melbourne* **18** A2
Bunker Hill Memorial *Boston* **6** A2
Bunker I. *Karachi* **13** B1
Bunkyō *Tokyo* **30** A3
Bunnefjorden *Oslo* **23** A3
Buona Vista Park *Singapore* **28** B2
Burbank *Chicago* **9** C2
Burbank *Los Angeles* **16** A3
Burden, L. *Orlando* **23** B1
Burlington *Boston* **6** A1
Burnham Park *Chicago* **9** C3
Burnham Park Harbor *Chicago* **9** B3
Burnhamthorpe *Toronto* **31** B1
Burnt Oak *London* **15** A2
Burntisland *Edinburgh* **11** A2
Burnwynd *Edinburgh* **11** B1
Burqa *Jerusalem* **13** A2
Burtus *Cairo* **7** A1
Burudvatn *Oslo* **23** A2
Burwood *Sydney* **29** B1
Bushwick *New York* **22** B2
Bushy Park *London* **15** B1
Butantã *São Paulo* **27** B1
Butcher I. *Mumbai* **20** B2
Butler, L. *Orlando* **23** B1
Butts Corner *Washington* **33** C2
Büyükdere *Istanbul* **12** B2
Byculla *Mumbai* **20** B1
Bygdøy *Oslo* **23** A3

C

C.B.S. Fox Studios *Los Angeles* **16** B2
C.N.N. Center *Atlanta* **3** B2
C.N. Tower *Toronto* **31** B2
Caballito *Buenos Aires* **7** B2
Cabin John *Washington* **33** B2
Cabin John Regional Park ➞ *Washington* **33** A2
Cabinteely *Dublin* **10** B3
Cabra *Dublin* **10** A2
Cabuçu de Baixo ➞ *São Paulo* **27** A1
Cabuçu de Cima ➞ *São Paulo* **27** A2
Cachan *Paris* **24** B2
Cachoeira, Rib. da ➞ *São Paulo* **27** B2
Cacilhas *Lisbon* **16** A2
Cahuenga Park *Los Angeles* **16** B3
Cain, L. *Orlando* **23** B2
Cairo = El Qâhira *Cairo* **7** A2
Cairo Int. ✈ (CAI) *Cairo* **7** A3
Caju *Rio de Janeiro* **25** B1
Čakovice *Prague* **25** A3
Calcutta = Kolkata *Kolkata* **14** B2
California Inst. of Tech. *Los Angeles* **16** B4
California Los Angeles, University of *Los Angeles* **16** B2
California State University *Los Angeles* **16** B3
Callao *Lima* **14** B2
Caloocan *Manila* **17** B1
Calumet L. *Chicago* **9** C3
Calumet Park *Chicago* **9** C3

Calumet Sag Channel → Chicago 9 C2
Calvairate Milan 19 B2
Camarate Lisbon 16 A2
Camaroes Lisbon 16 A1
Camberwell London 15 B3
Camberwell Melbourne 18 B2
Cambridge Boston 6 A2
Cambuci São Paulo 27 B2
Camden □ London 15 A3
Cameron, Mt. Wellington 33 B2
Çamlıca Istanbul 12 B2
Camp Springs Washington 33 C4
Campamento Madrid 17 B1
Campbellfield Melbourne 18 A1
Camperdown Sydney 29 B2
Campo, Casa de Madrid 17 B1
Campo F.C. Barcelona Barcelona 4 A1
Campo Grando Lisbon 16 A2
Campo Pequeño Lisbon 16 A2
Campolide Lisbon 16 A2
Camps Bay Cape Town 8 A1
C'an San Joan Barcelona 4 A2
Cañacao B. Manila 17 C1
Canarsie New York 22 C2
Candiac Montreal 20 B3
Caneças Lisbon 16 A1
Canillas Madrid 17 B2
Canillejas Madrid 17 B2
Canning Town London 15 A4
Canteras de Vallecas Madrid 17 B2
Canterbury Melbourne 18 A2
Canterbury Sydney 29 B1
Canton = Guangzhou Guangzhou 11 B2
Caoheijing Shanghai 28 B1
Capão Redondo São Paulo 27 B1
Caparica Lisbon 16 A2
Caparica, Costa da Lisbon 16 B1
Cape Flats Cape Town 8 B2
Cape Peninsula △ Cape Town 8 A1
Cape Town Cape Town 8 A1
Cape Town Int. ✈ (CPT) Cape Town 8 A2
Capitol Heights Washington 33 B4
Captain Cook Bridge Sydney 29 C1
Captain Cook Landing Place Park Sydney 29 C2
Capuchos Lisbon 16 B1
Carabanchel Alto Madrid 17 B1
Carabanchel Bajo Madrid 17 B1
Carapachay Buenos Aires 7 B1
Caraza Buenos Aires 7 C2
Caridad Manila 17 C1
Carioca, Sa. da Rio de Janeiro 25 B1
Carlstadt New York 22 A1
Carlton Melbourne 18 A1
Carmen de Huechuraba Santiago 27 B1
Carmen de la Legua Lima 14 B2
Carnaxide Lisbon 16 A1
Carnegie Melbourne 18 B2
Carnide Lisbon 16 A1
Carol City Miami 18 A1
Carrascal Santiago 27 B1
Carrickmines Dublin 10 B3
Carrières-sous-Bois Paris 24 A1
Carrières-sous-Poissy Paris 24 A1
Carrières-sur-Seine Paris 24 A2
Carrigeen B. Dublin 10 A3
Cartierville Montreal 20 A1
Casa Loma Toronto 31 A2
Casa Verde São Paulo 27 A1
Casál Morena Rome 26 C2
Casalotti Rome 26 B1
Cascade Heights Atlanta 3 B2
Castèl di Leva Rome 26 C2
Castèl Sant'Angelo Rome 26 B1
Castleknock Dublin 10 A1
Castleton Corners New York 22 C1
Catete Rio de Janeiro 25 B1
Catford London 15 B3
Catherine, L. Orlando 23 B2
Caulfield Melbourne 18 B2
Cavite Manila 17 C1
Caxias Lisbon 16 A1
Cebecci Istanbul 12 B1
Cecchignola Rome 26 C2
Cecilienhof, Schloss Berlin 5 B1
Cedar Grove Atlanta 3 C3
Cedarvale Park Toronto 31 A2
Cempaka Putih Jakarta 12 B2
Çengelköy Istanbul 12 B2
Cengkareng Jakarta 12 A1
Centennial Olympic Park Atlanta 3 B2
Centennial Park Sydney 29 B2
Center Hill Atlanta 3 B2
Centocelle Rome 26 B2
Central, Gare Montreal 20 B2
Central Park New York 22 B2
Cerdanyola del Vallès Barcelona 4 A1
Cerillos Santiago 27 B1
Cerro de la Estrella, Parque Nacional △ Mexico City 18 B2
Cerro de los Angeles Madrid 17 C1
Cerro Navia Santiago 27 B1
Cesano Boscone Milan 19 B1
Cesate Milan 19 A1
Cha Kwo Ling Hong Kong 12 B2
Chacarrita Buenos Aires 7 B2
Chadwell Heath London 15 A4
Chai Chee Singapore 28 B3
Chai Wan Hong Kong 12 B2
Chai Wan Kok Hong Kong 12 A1
Chakdaha Kolkata 14 C1
Chamartin Madrid 17 B1
Chamberi Madrid 17 B1
Chambourcy Paris 24 A1
Champigny-sur-Marne Paris 24 B4
Champlain, Pont Montreal 20 B2
Champs-sur-Marne Paris 24 A4
Chamrail Kolkata 14 B1
Chanakyapuri Delhi 10 B2
Chanditala Kolkata 14 A1
Changfeng Park Shanghai 28 B1
Changhai = Shanghai Shanghai 28 B2
Changi Singapore 28 A3
Changi, Singapore ✈ (SIN) Singapore 28 A3
Changning Shanghai 28 B1
Chantereine Paris 24 A4
Chantian Guangzhou 11 A2
Chaoyang Beijing 4 B2
Chaoyangmen Beijing 4 B2
Chapelizod Dublin 10 A1
Chapultepec, Bosque de Mexico City 18 B1
Chapultepec, Castillo de Mexico City 18 B1
Charenton-le-Pont Paris 24 B3
Charleroi, Kanal de → Brussels 6 B1
Charles Bridge = Karlův most Prague 25 B2
Charles Gates Dawes House Chicago 9 A2
Charlestown Boston 6 A2
Charlottenburg Berlin 5 A2
Charlottenburg, Schloss Berlin 5 A2
Charlottenlund Copenhagen 8 A3
Charlton London 15 B4
Charneca Lisbon 16 A2
Chase, L. Orlando 23 B1
Châteaufort Paris 24 B1
Châtenay-Malabry Paris 24 B2
Chatham Chicago 9 C3
Chatillon Paris 24 B2
Chatou Paris 24 A1
Chatpur Kolkata 14 B2
Chatswood Sydney 29 A2
Chatuchak Bangkok 3 B2
Chatuchak Park Bangkok 3 B2
Chauki Karachi 13 A1
Chavarria Lima 14 B2
Chaville Paris 24 B2
Chayang Seoul 27 B2
Chelles Paris 24 A4
Chelles, Canal de Paris 24 A4
Chells-le-Pin ✈ Paris 24 A4
Chelsea Boston 6 A2
Chelsea London 15 B2
Chembur Mumbai 20 A2
Chennevières-sur-Marne Paris 24 B4
Cheongdam Seoul 27 B2
Cheonho Seoul 27 B2
Cheops Cairo 7 B1
Chertanovka → Moscow 19 C2
Chertanovo Moscow 19 C2
Cheryomushki Moscow 19 B2
Chestnut Hill Boston 6 B1
Cheung Sha Wan Hong Kong 12 A1
Cheverly Washington 33 B4
Chevilly-Larue Paris 24 B3
Chevry-Cossigny Paris 24 B4
Chevy Chase Washington 33 B3
Chhatrapati Shivaji, Mumbai ✈ (BOM) Mumbai 20 A2
Chia Keng Singapore 28 A3
Chiaravalle Milanese Milan 19 B2
Chicago Chicago 9 B3
Chicago, University of Chicago 9 C3
Chicago Harbor Chicago 9 B3
Chicago Lawn Chicago 9 C2
Chicago-Midway ✈ (MDW) Chicago 9 C2
Chicago O'Hare Int. ✈ (ORD) Chicago 9 B1
Chicago Ridge Chicago 9 C2
Chicago River, North Branch → Chicago 9 B2
Chicago Sanitary and Ship Canal Chicago 9 C2
Chicago State University Chicago 9 C3
Chicago Zoo Chicago 9 B1
Chienzui Guangzhou 11 A3
Chik Sha Hong Kong 12 B2
Child's Hill London 15 A2
Chilla Saroda Delhi 10 B2
Chillum Washington 33 B4
Chilly-Mazarin Paris 24 B2
China Basin San Francisco 26 B2
Chingupota Kolkata 14 C1
Chinna Cr. → Karachi 13 B2
Chiquihuite, Cerro Mexico City 18 A2
Chislehurst London 15 B4
Chiswick London 15 B2
Chiswick House London 15 B2
Chitose Tokyo 30 B2
Chitralada Palace Bangkok 3 B2
Chiyoda Tokyo 30 A3
Choa Chu Kang Singapore 28 A2
Chodov u Prahy Prague 25 B3
Chōfu Tokyo 30 B2
Choisy-le-Roi Paris 24 B3
Cholupice Prague 25 C2
Chom Thong Bangkok 3 B1
Chong Pang Singapore 28 A2
Chongwen Beijing 4 B2
Chorrillos Lima 14 C2
Chowpatty Beach Mumbai 20 B1
Christianshavn Copenhagen 8 A3
Chrzanów Warsaw 32 B1
Chuen Lung Hong Kong 12 A1
Chuk Kok Hong Kong 12 A2
Chulalongkom Univ. Bangkok 3 B2
Chuō Tokyo 30 A3
Church End London 15 A2
Churchtown Dublin 10 B2
Ciampino Rome 26 C2
Ciampino ✈ Rome 26 C2
Cicero Chicago 9 B2
Cilandak Jakarta 12 B1
Cilincing Jakarta 12 A2
Ciliwung → Jakarta 12 B2
Čimice Prague 25 B2
Cinecittà Rome 26 B2
Cinisello Bálsamo Milan 19 A2
Cinkota Budapest 7 A3
Cipete Jakarta 12 B1
Citta degli Studi Milan 19 B2
Città del Vaticano = Vatican City ■ Rome 26 B1
City, The London 15 A3
City of the Dead Cairo 7 A2
Ciudad de México Mexico City 18 B2
Ciudad Deportiva Mexico City 18 B2
Ciudad Fin de Semana Madrid 17 B2
Ciudad General Belgrano Buenos Aires 7 C1
Ciudad Lineál Madrid 17 B2
Ciudad Satélite Mexico City 18 A1
Ciudad Universitaria Buenos Aires 7 B2
Ciudad Universitaria Mexico City 18 C1
Claireville Res. Toronto 31 A1
Clamart Paris 24 B2
Clapham London 15 B3
Clapton London 15 A3
Claremont Cape Town 8 A1
Clayhall London 15 A4
Clear, L. Orlando 23 A2
Clermiston Edinburgh 11 B2
Clichy Paris 24 A2
Clichy-sous-Bois Paris 24 A4
Cliffside Toronto 31 A3
Cliffside Park New York 22 B2
Clifton Cape Town 8 A1
Clifton Karachi 13 B2
Clifton New York 22 C1
Clifton Beach Karachi 13 B2
Cliftondale Boston 6 A2
Cloghran Dublin 10 A2
Clonskeagh Dublin 10 B2
Clontarf Dublin 10 A2
Clontarf Sydney 29 A2
Clovelly Sydney 29 B2
Cobras, I. das Rio de Janeiro 25 B2
Coburg Melbourne 18 A1
Cocotá Rio de Janeiro 25 A1
Cœuilly Paris 24 B4
Coina Lisbon 16 B2
Coker Lagos 14 B2
Colaba Mumbai 20 B1
Colaba Pt. Mumbai 20 B1
Colegiales Buenos Aires 7 B2
Colindale London 15 A2
Colinton Edinburgh 11 B2
College Park Atlanta 3 C2
College Park Washington 33 B4
College Point New York 22 B2
Collégien Paris 24 A4
Collier Row London 15 A4
Colliers Wood London 15 B2
Colma San Francisco 26 B2
Colney Hatch London 15 A3
Cologno Monzese Milan 19 A2
Colombes Paris 24 A2
Colonia Güell Barcelona 4 A1
Colonial Knob Wellington 33 A1
Colosseo Rome 26 B1
Colosseum = Colosseo Rome 26 B1
Combault Paris 24 B4
Comércio, Praça do Lisbon 16 A2
Commerce Los Angeles 16 B4
Como Sydney 29 C1
Conceição, I. da Rio de Janeiro 25 B2
Conchali Santiago 27 B2
Concord Sydney 29 B1
Concord Toronto 31 A2
Concorde, Place de la Paris 24 A2
Concorezzo Milan 19 A2
Condet Jakarta 12 B2
Coney Island New York 22 C2
Congonhas São Paulo ✈ (CGH) São Paulo 27 B2
Conley → Atlanta 3 C3
Connaught Place Delhi 10 B2
Consolação São Paulo 27 B2
Constantia Cape Town 8 B1
Constitución Buenos Aires 7 B2
Constitution Atlanta 3 B2
Convention Center Los Angeles 16 B3
Conway Orlando 23 B2
Conway, L. Orlando 23 B2
Coogee Sydney 29 B2
Cooksville Toronto 31 B1
Coolock Dublin 10 A2
Copacabana Rio de Janeiro 25 B1
Copenhagen = København Copenhagen 8 A2
Coral Gables Miami 18 B2
Coral Hills Washington 33 B4
Corcovado, Cristo Redentor Rio de Janeiro 25 B1
Corduff Dublin 10 A1
Cormano Milan 19 A2
Cornaredo Milan 19 A1
Còrsico Milan 19 B1
Corstorphine Edinburgh 11 B2
Corviale Rome 26 B1
Coslada Madrid 17 B2
Cossigny Paris 24 B4
Cotao Lisbon 16 A1
Côte-St-Luc Montreal 20 B2
Cotunduba, I. de Rio de Janeiro 25 B2
Coubron Paris 24 A4
Countryside Chicago 9 C1
County Art Museum Los Angeles 16 B2
Courbevoie Paris 24 A2
Courtry Paris 24 A4
Cowley London 15 A1
Coyoacán Mexico City 18 B2
Craighall Park Johannesburg 13 A2
Craiglockhart Edinburgh 11 B2
Craigmillar Edinburgh 11 B3
Cramond Edinburgh 11 B2
Cramond Bridge Edinburgh 11 B1
Cramond I. Edinburgh 11 B2
Cranford London 15 B1
Crawford Cape Town 8 A2
Crayford London 15 B5
Creekmouth London 15 A4
Crescent, L. Orlando 23 A1
Crescenzago Milan 19 A2
Cressely Paris 24 B1
Cresskill New York 22 A2
Créteil Paris 24 B3
Cricklewood London 15 A2
Cristo Redentor, Estatua do Rio de Janeiro 25 B1
Crockenhill London 15 B4
Croissy-Beaubourg Paris 24 B4
Croissy-sur-Seine Paris 24 A1
Crosby Johannesburg 13 B1
Crosne Paris 24 B3
Cross I. Mumbai 20 B2
Crouch End London 15 A3
Crown Mine Johannesburg 13 B1
Crows Nest Sydney 29 A2
Croydon London 15 B3
Croydon Park Sydney 29 B1
Cruagh Mt. Dublin 10 B2
Crumlin Dublin 10 B2
Cruz de Pau Lisbon 16 B2
Crystal Palace London 15 B3
Csepel Budapest 7 B2
Csepelsziget Budapest 7 B2
Csillaghegy Budapest 7 A2
Csillagtelep Budapest 7 B2
Csömör Budapest 7 A3
Csömöri-patak → Budapest 7 A3
Cuatro Vientos Madrid 17 B1
Cuauhtémoc Mexico City 18 B2
Cuban Museum Miami 18 B2
Cubao Manila 17 B2
Çubuklu Istanbul 12 B2
Cudahy Los Angeles 16 C3
Cuicuilco, Pirámido de Mexico City 18 C1
Culmore Washington 33 B3
Culver City Los Angeles 16 B2
Cumbres de Vallecas Madrid 17 B2
Cupecê São Paulo 27 B1
Currie Edinburgh 11 B2
Cusago Milan 19 B1
Cusano Milanino Milan 19 A2
Cutler Park Boston 6 B1
Çuvuşabaşi → Istanbul 12 B1
Cypress Hills New York 22 B2
Czerniaków Warsaw 32 B2
Czyste Warsaw 32 B1

D

Da Moóca → São Paulo 27 B2
Ďáblice Prague 25 B2
Dąbrowa Warsaw 32 B1
Dachang Shanghai 28 B1
Dachang ✈ Shanghai 28 B1
Dachau Munich 21 A1
Dachau-Ost Munich 21 A1
Dachauer Moos Munich 21 A1
Dadar Mumbai 20 A1
Daebang Seoul 27 B1
Daechi Seoul 27 B2
Dafni Athens 2 B2
Dagenham London 15 A4
Daglfing Munich 21 B2
Dahab, Gezîret el Cairo 7 B2
Daheisha Jerusalem 13 B2
Dahlem Berlin 5 B2
Dahlwitz-Hoppegarten Berlin 5 A5
Dahongmen Beijing 4 C2
Dajiaoting Beijing 4 B2
Dakhnoye St. Petersburg 27 C1
Dalejsky potok → Prague 25 B2
Dalgety Bay Edinburgh 11 A1
Dalkeith Edinburgh 11 B3
Dalkey Dublin 10 B3
Dalkey I. Dublin 10 B3
Dallgow Berlin 5 A1
Dalmeny Edinburgh 11 B1
Dalston London 15 A3
Daly City San Francisco 26 B2
Damaia Lisbon 16 A1
Damarakia Athens 2 B1
Dämeritzsee Berlin 5 B5
Dan Ryan Woods Chicago 9 C2
Danderhall Edinburgh 11 B3
Danderyd Stockholm 29 A2
Danforth Toronto 31 A3
Darakeh Tehran 31 A2
Darband Tehran 31 A2
Darling Point Sydney 29 B2
Darndale Dublin 10 A2
Darrūs Tehran 31 A2
Dartford London 15 B5
Dashi Guangzhou 11 B2
Datansha Guangzhou 11 B2
Datun Beijing 4 B2
Daulatpur Delhi 10 A1
Davidson, Mt. San Francisco 26 B2
Davidson's Mains Edinburgh 11 B2
Dāvūdiyeh Tehran 31 A2
Davydkovo Moscow 19 B1
Dawidy Warsaw 32 C1
Days Bay Wellington 33 B2
Decatur Atlanta 3 B3
Dedham Boston 6 B1
Degunino Moscow 19 A2
Deir Dibwan Jerusalem 13 A2
Deir Ibzi'e Jerusalem 13 A1
Dejvice Prague 25 B2
Dekabristov, Ostrov St. Petersburg 27 B1
Delhi Delhi 10 B2
Demarest New York 22 A2
Den Ilp Amsterdam 2 A2
Denistone Heights Sydney 29 A1
Dentonia Park Toronto 31 A3
DePaul University Chicago 9 B3
Deptford London 15 B3
Des Plaines Chicago 9 A1
Deshengmen Beijing 4 B2
Deutsch-Wagram Vienna 32 A3
Deutsche Oper Berlin 5 A2
Deutscher Museum Munich 21 B2
Devil's Peak Cape Town 8 A1
Dhakuria Kolkata 14 B2
Dharavi Mumbai 20 A2
Diadema São Paulo 27 C2
Diegem Brussels 6 A2
Diemen Amsterdam 2 A2
Diepkloof Johannesburg 13 B1
Dieprivier Cape Town 8 B1
Difficult Run → Washington 33 B2
Dilbeek Brussels 6 A1
Dilli = Delhi Delhi 10 B2
Dirnismaning Munich 21 A2
Disney-M.G.M. Studios Orlando 23 B1
Disney Studios Los Angeles 16 B3
District Heights Washington 33 B4
Djakarta = Jakarta Jakarta 12 A2
Djursholm Stockholm 29 A2
Döberitz Berlin 5 A1
Döbling Vienna 32 A2
Dobong Seoul 27 B2
Dobongsan Seoul 27 A2
Docklands London 15 A3
Doctor Phillips Orlando 23 B2
Dodder → Dublin 10 B1
Dodger Stadium Los Angeles 16 B3
Dogs, Isle of London 15 B3
Dolgoe Ozero St. Petersburg 27 A1
Dollis Hill London 15 A2
Dollymount Dublin 10 A2
Dolní Prague 25 B3
Dolni Chabry Prague 25 B2
Dolni Počernice Prague 25 B3
Dolphins Barn Dublin 10 B2
Dom Pedro II, Parque São Paulo 27 B2
Don Mills Toronto 31 A2
Don Muang Int. ✈ (BKK) Bangkok 3 A2
Donaghmede Dublin 10 A3
Donau-Oder Kanal Vienna 32 A3
Donaufeld Vienna 32 A2
Donaupark Vienna 32 A2
Donaustadt Vienna 32 A2
Dongan Hills New York 22 C1
Dongcheng Beijing 4 B2
Dongdaemung Seoul 27 B2
Donggou Shanghai 28 B2
Dongjak Seoul 27 B1
Dongjiao Guangzhou 11 B2
Dongri Mumbai 20 B2
Dongshanhu Park Guangzhou 11 B2
Dongzhimen Beijing 4 B2
Donnybrook Dublin 10 B2
Doornfontein Johannesburg 13 B2
Dorchester Boston 6 B2
Dorchester B. Boston 6 B2
Dorchester Heights Nat. Historical Site ⌂ Boston 6 B2
Dornach Munich 21 B3
Dorval Int., Montréal ✈ (YUL) Montreal 20 B1
Dos Couros → São Paulo 27 C2
Dos Moninos → São Paulo 27 C2
Douglas Park Chicago 9 B2
Dover Heights Sydney 29 B2
Dowlatābād Tehran 31 B2
Down, L. Orlando 23 A1
Downey Los Angeles 16 C4
Downsview Toronto 31 A1
Downsview C.A.F.B. ✈ Toronto 31 A2
Dragør Copenhagen 8 B3
Drancy Paris 24 A3
Dranesville Washington 33 A1
Drapetsona Athens 2 B1
Dreilinden Berlin 5 B2
Drewnica Warsaw 32 B2
Drigh Road Karachi 13 A2
Drimnagh Dublin 10 B2
Drogenbos Brussels 6 B1
Druid Hills Atlanta 3 B2
Drumcondra Dublin 10 A2
Drummoyne Sydney 29 B1
Drylaw Edinburgh 11 B2
Dubeč Prague 25 B3
Dublin Dublin 10 A2
Dublin ✈ (DUB) Dublin 10 A2
Dublin B. Dublin 10 B3
Dublin Harbour Dublin 10 A2
Duddingston Edinburgh 11 B3
Dugnano Milan 19 A2
Duivendrecht Amsterdam 2 B2
Dūlāb Tehran 31 B2
Dulwich London 15 B3
Dum Dum Kolkata 14 B2
Dum Dum Int. ✈ (CCU) Kolkata 14 B2
Dumont New York 22 A2
Dún Laoghaire Dublin 10 B3
Dundrum Dublin 10 B2
Dunearn Singapore 28 B2
Dúnleary = Dún Laoghaire Dublin 10 B3
Dunn Loring Washington 33 B2
Dunning Chicago 9 B2
Dunvegan Johannesburg 13 A2
Duomo Milan 19 B2
Duque de Caxias Rio de Janeiro 25 A1
Duren Sawit Jakarta 12 A2
Dusit Bangkok 3 B2
Dworp Brussels 6 B1
Dyakovo Moscow 19 B2
Dyker Beach Park New York 22 C1
Dzerzhinskiy Moscow 19 B2
Dzerzhinskiy Park Moscow 19 B2

E

E.U.R. = Esposizione Universale di Roma Rome 26 C1
Eagle Rock Los Angeles 16 B3
Ealing □ London 15 A2
Earlsfield London 15 B2
Earlwood Sydney 29 B1
East Arlington Boston 6 A2
East Arlington Washington 33 B3
East Bedfont London 15 B1
East Boston Boston 6 A2
East Don → Toronto 31 A2
East Don Parkland Toronto 31 A2
East Elmhurst New York 22 B2
East Finchley London 15 A2
East Flatbush New York 22 C2
East Ham London 15 A4
East Humber → Toronto 31 A1
East Lamma Channel Hong Kong 12 B1
East Lexington Boston 6 A1
East Los Angeles Los Angeles 16 B3
East Molesey London 15 B1
East New York New York 22 B2
East Pines Washington 33 B4
East Point Atlanta 3 B2
East Potomac Park Washington 33 B3
East River → New York 22 B2
East Rutherford New York 22 A1
East Sheen London 15 B2
East Talpiyot Jerusalem 13 B2
East Wickham London 15 B4
East York Toronto 31 A2
Eastbourne Wellington 33 B2
Eastcote London 15 A1
Easter Howgate Edinburgh 11 B2
Eastpoint Park Toronto 31 A4
Eastwood Sydney 29 A1
Eaton Canyon Park Los Angeles 16 A4
Ebara Tokyo 30 B3
Ebisu Tokyo 30 B3
Ebute-Ikorodu Lagos 14 A2
Ebute-Metta Lagos 14 B2
Eda Tokyo 30 B2
Edendale Johannesburg 13 A2
Edenmore Dublin 10 A2
Edgars Cr. → Melbourne 18 A1
Edgeley Toronto 31 A1
Edgemar San Francisco 26 C2
Edgewater New York 22 B2
Edgewood Orlando 23 B2
Edinburgh Edinburgh 11 B2
Edinburgh ✈ (EDI) Edinburgh 11 B1
Edinburgh Castle Edinburgh 11 B2
Edison Park Chicago 9 A2
Edmondston Washington 33 B4
Edmondstown Dublin 10 B2
Edo → Tokyo 30 B4
Edogawa Tokyo 30 A4
Edsberg Stockholm 29 A1
Edwards L. Melbourne 18 A1
Efzonos Athens 2 B2
Egaleo Athens 2 B1
Egaleo, Oros Athens 2 B1
Eiche Berlin 5 A4
Eiche Sud Berlin 5 A4
Eiffel, Tour Paris 24 A2
Ein Arik Jerusalem 13 A1
Ein Naquba Jerusalem 13 B1
Ein Rafa Jerusalem 13 B1
Eizariya Jerusalem 13 B2
Ejby Copenhagen 8 A2
Ejigbo Lagos 14 A1
Ekeberg Oslo 23 A3
Eknäs Stockholm 29 B3
El 'Abbasiya Cairo 7 A2
El Agustino Lima 14 B2
El Baragil Cairo 7 A1
El Basātīn Cairo 7 B2
El Bira Jerusalem 13 A2
El Bosque Santiago 27 C2
El Carmen Santiago 27 B1
El Cortijo Santiago 27 B1
El Cristo, Vaso Regulador Mexico City 18 B1
El Duqqi Cairo 7 A2
El Encinar de los Reyes Madrid 17 A2
El Gezira Cairo 7 A2
El Ghuriya Cairo 7 A2
El Giza Cairo 7 A2
El Khadr Jerusalem 13 B1
El Khalifa Cairo 7 A2
El Kôm el Ahmar Cairo 7 A2
El Ma'ādi Cairo 7 B2
El Matarīya Cairo 7 A2
El Mohandessin Cairo 7 A2
El Monte Los Angeles 16 B4
El Muqattam Cairo 7 A2
El Mûskī Cairo 7 A2
El Pardo Madrid 17 A1
El Portal Miami 18 A2
El Prat de Llobregat Barcelona 4 B1
El Qâhira Cairo 7 A2
El Qubba Cairo 7 A2
El Reloj Mexico City 18 C2
El Retiro Madrid 17 B1
El Salto Santiago 27 B2
El Sereno Los Angeles 16 B3
El Talibīya Cairo 7 B2
El Vergel Mexico City 18 C2
El Wāhli Cairo 7 A2
El Zamālik Cairo 7 A2
El Zeitûn Cairo 7 A2
Elephanta Caves Mumbai 20 B2
Elephanta I. Mumbai 20 B2
Ellboda Stockholm 29 A3
Ellenor, L. Orlando 23 B2
Elliniko Olympic Complex Athens 2 B2
Ellis I. New York 22 B1
Elm Park London 15 A5
Elmers End London 15 B3
Elmhurst New York 22 B2
Elmstead London 15 B4
Elmwood Park Chicago 9 B2
Elmwood Park New York 22 A1
Elsdon Wellington 33 A1
Elsiesrivier Cape Town 8 A2
Elsternwick Melbourne 18 B2
Eltham London 15 B4
Elwood Melbourne 18 B1
Élysée Paris 24 A2
Elysian Park Los Angeles 16 B3
Emāmzādeh Sāleh Tehran 31 A2
Émerainville Paris 24 B4
Emeryville San Francisco 26 A3
Eminönü Istanbul 12 B1
Emirgan Istanbul 12 B2
Emmarentia Johannesburg 13 A2
Empire State Building New York 22 B2
Encantado Rio de Janeiro 25 B1
Encino Los Angeles 16 B2
Encino Res. Los Angeles 16 B1
Enebyberg Stockholm 29 A1
Enfield Sydney 29 B1
Engenho, I. do Rio de Janeiro 25 B2
Englewood Chicago 9 C3
Englewood New York 22 A2
Englewood Cliffs New York 22 A2
Enmore Sydney 29 B2
Enskede Stockholm 29 B2
Entrevias Madrid 17 B1
Epcot Orlando 23 B1
Epping Sydney 29 A1
Eregun Lagos 14 A2
Erenköy Istanbul 12 C2
Erith London 15 B5
Erlaa Vienna 32 B1
Ermington Sydney 29 A1
Ermita Manila 17 B1
Ershatou Guangzhou 11 B2
Erskineville Sydney 29 B2
Erunkan Lagos 14 A2
Erzsébet-Telep Budapest 7 B3
Eschenried Munich 21 A1
Esenler Istanbul 12 B1
Esher London 15 B1
Eskbank Edinburgh 11 B3
Esplugas Barcelona 4 A1
Esposizione Universale di Roma Rome 26 C1
Essendon Melbourne 18 A1
Essendon ✈ (MEB) Melbourne 18 A1
Essingen Stockholm 29 B1
Essling Vienna 32 A3
Est, Gare de l' Paris 24 A3
Estado, Parque do São Paulo 27 B2
Estrela, Basilica da Lisbon 16 A2
Etobicoke Toronto 31 B1
Etobicoke Cr. → Toronto 31 B1
Etterbeek Brussels 6 B2
Eung-am Seoul 27 B1
Eunpyeong Seoul 27 B1
Evanston Chicago 9 A2
Even Sapir Jerusalem 13 B1
Evere Brussels 6 A2
Everett Boston 6 A2
Evergreen Park Chicago 9 C2
Evin Tehran 31 A2
Ewu Lagos 14 A1
Exhibition Place Toronto 31 B2
Exposições, Palácio das Rio de Janeiro 25 B1
Eyüp Istanbul 12 B1
Ezeiza ✈ (EZE) Buenos Aires 7 B2

F

Fabour, Mt. Singapore 28 B2
Fælledparken Copenhagen 8 A3
Fågelön Stockholm 29 B1
Fagersjö Stockholm 29 B2
Fair Lawn New York 22 A1
Fairfax Washington 33 B2
Fairfax Station Washington 33 C2
Fairland Johannesburg 13 A1
Fairmilehead Edinburgh 11 B2
Fairmount Heights Washington 33 B4
Fairport Toronto 31 A4
Fairview New York 22 B2
Fairview, L. Orlando 23 A2
Falenty Warsaw 32 C1
Faliro Athens 2 B1
Faliro, Ormos Athens 2 B2
Falkenburg Berlin 5 A4
Falkenhagen Berlin 5 A1
Falkensee Berlin 5 A1
Falls Church Washington 33 B2
Falomo Lagos 14 B2
False Bay Cape Town 8 B2
Fangcun Guangzhou 11 B2
Farahābād Tehran 31 B2
Farforovskaya St. Petersburg 27 B2
Farningham London 15 B5
Farsta Stockholm 29 B2
Fasanerie-Nord Munich 21 A2
Fasangarten Munich 21 B2
Fatih Istanbul 12 B1
Favoriten Vienna 32 B2
Fawkner Melbourne 18 A1
Fawkner Park Melbourne 18 B1
FedEx Stadium Washington 33 B4
Feijó Lisbon 16 B2
Feldkirchen Munich 21 B3
Feldmoching Munich 21 A2
Feltham London 15 B1
Fener Istanbul 12 B1
Fenerbahçe Istanbul 12 C2
Fengtai Beijing 4 C1
Ferencváros Budapest 7 B2
Ferihegy, Budapest ✈ (BUD) Budapest 7 B3
Ferndale Johannesburg 13 A2
Férolles-Attilly Paris 24 B4
Fichtenau Berlin 5 B5
Field Museum of Natural History Chicago 9 B3
Fields Corner Boston 6 B2
Fiera Camp Milan 19 B1
Figino Milan 19 B1
Fijir Baghdad 3 A2
Filadelfia Athens 2 A2
Fili-Mazilovo Moscow 19 B1
Filothei Athens 2 A2
Finchley London 15 A2
Fine Arts, Museum of Boston 6 A2
Finglas Dublin 10 A2
Finsbury London 15 A3
Finsbury Park London 15 A3
Fiorito Buenos Aires 7 C2
Firhouse Dublin 10 B2
Fischerhäuser Munich 21 A3
Fisher Island Miami 18 B2
Fishermans Bend Melbourne 18 A1
Fisherville Toronto 31 A2
Fisksätra Stockholm 29 B3
Fitzroy Gardens Melbourne 18 A1
Five Dock Sydney 29 B1
Fjellstrand Oslo 23 B2
Flamengo Rio de Janeiro 25 B1
Flamingo Orlando 23 B2
Flaminio Rome 26 B1
Flaskebekk Oslo 23 A2
Flatbush New York 22 C2
Flaten Stockholm 29 B2
Flatlands New York 22 C2
Flemington Racecourse Melbourne 18 A1
Flint Pk. Los Angeles 16 B3
Florence Los Angeles 16 C3
Florence Bloom Bird Sanctuary ⌂ Johannesburg 13 A2
Florentia Johannesburg 13 B2
Flores Buenos Aires 7 B2
Flores, Mercado de Mexico City 18 C2
Floresta Buenos Aires 7 B2
Florida Buenos Aires 7 B2
Florida Johannesburg 13 B1
Floridsdorf Vienna 32 A2
Flushing New York 22 B3
Flushing Meadows Corona Park New York 22 B2
Flysta Stockholm 29 A1
Fo Tan Hong Kong 12 A2
Föhrenhain Vienna 32 A2
Fontainebleau Johannesburg 13 A1
Fontenay-aux-Roses Paris 24 B2
Fontenay-le-Fleury Paris 24 B1
Fontenay-sous-Bois Paris 24 A3
Foots Cray London 15 B4
Footscray Melbourne 18 A1
Forbidden City = Imperial Palace Museum Beijing 4 B2
Forest Brussels 6 B1
Forest Gate London 15 A4
Forest Heights Washington 33 C3
Forest Hill London 15 B3
Forest Hill Toronto 31 A2
Forest Hills New York 22 B2
Forest Park Chicago 9 B2
Forest Park New York 22 B2
Forest View Chicago 9 C2
Forestville Washington 33 B4
Fornebu Oslo 23 A2
Foro Romano Rome 26 B1
Forstenried Munich 21 B1
Forstenrieder Park Munich 21 B1
Fort Mumbai 20 B1
Fort Dupont Park Washington 33 B4
Fort Foote Village Washington 33 C3
Fort Lee New York 22 A2
Forth, Firth of Edinburgh 11 A2
Forth Rail Bridge Edinburgh 11 A1
Forth Road Bridge Edinburgh 11 A1
Föt Budapest 7 A3
Fourqueux Paris 24 A1
Foxrock Dublin 10 B2
Franconia Washington 33 C3
Frank Lloyd Wright Home Chicago 9 B2
Frankel Singapore 28 B3
Franklin Park Boston 6 B2
Franklin Park Chicago 9 B1
Franklin Park Washington 33 B3
Franklin Res. Los Angeles 16 B2
Frauenkirche Munich 21 B2
Frederiksberg Copenhagen 8 A3
Frederiksdal Copenhagen 8 A2
Fredersdorf Berlin 5 A5
Freguesia Rio de Janeiro 25 A1
Freidrichshain, Volkspark Berlin 5 A3
Freiham Munich 21 B1
Freimann Munich 21 A2
French Quarter New Orleans 21 B2
Fresh Pond Boston 6 A2
Fresnes Paris 24 B2
Freudenau Vienna 32 A2
Friarstown Dublin 10 B1
Friedenau Berlin 5 B3
Friedrichsfelde Berlin 5 B4
Friedrichshagen Berlin 5 B4
Friedrichshain Berlin 5 A3
Friedrichslust Berlin 5 A5
Friherrs Helsinki 11 B1
Frilufts Museum Helsinki 11 B2
Frontón, I. Lima 14 B1
Frunze Moscow 19 B2
Fūchū Tokyo 30 A1
Fuencarral Madrid 17 B1
Fuenlabrada Madrid 17 C1
Fukagawa Tokyo 30 B3
Fukushima Osaka 23 A1
Fulham London 15 B2
Funabori Tokyo 30 A4
Fundão, I. do Rio de Janeiro 25 B1
Fünfhaus Vienna 32 A2
Fureso Copenhagen 8 A2
Fürth Munich 21 B2
Futago-tamagawaen Tokyo 30 B2
Fuxing Dao Shanghai 28 B2
Fuxing Park Shanghai 28 B1
Fuxinglu Beijing 4 B1

G

G. Ross Lord Park Toronto 31 A2
Gaebong Seoul 27 C1
Gage Park Chicago 9 C2
Gagny Paris 24 A4
Galata Istanbul 12 B1
Galata Tower Istanbul 12 B1
Galatsi Athens 2 A2
Galeão, Int. de ✈ (GIG) Rio de Janeiro 25 A1
Galyanovo Moscow 19 B3
Gambir Jakarta 12 A1
Gamboa Rio de Janeiro 25 B1
Gamboloita Milan 19 B2
Gamlebyen Oslo 23 A3
Gangdong Seoul 27 B2
Gangnam Seoul 27 B1
Gangseo Seoul 27 B1
Gangtou Guangzhou 11 A1
Gangwei Guangzhou 11 B2
Ganjiakou Beijing 4 B1
Ganshoren Brussels 6 A1
Gants Hill London 15 A4
Gaoqiao Shanghai 28 A2
Garbagnate Milanese Milan 19 A1
Garbatella Rome 26 B2
Garches Paris 24 A2
Garching Munich 21 A3
Garden City Cairo 7 A2
Garden Reach Kolkata 14 B1
Garder Oslo 23 B2
Garfield New York 22 A1
Garfield Park Chicago 9 B2
Gargareta Athens 2 B2
Garibong Seoul 27 C1
Garvanza Los Angeles 16 B3
Gåshaga Stockholm 29 A3
Gateway ⌂ New York 22 C2
Gateway of India Mumbai 20 B2
Gatow Berlin 5 B1
Gavà Barcelona 4 B1
Gávea Rio de Janeiro 25 B1
Gávea, Pedra da Rio de Janeiro 25 B1
Gazdagrét Budapest 7 B1
Gaziosmanpaşa Istanbul 12 B1
Gebel el Ahmar Cairo 7 A3
Gebel el Muqattam Cairo 7 A2
Gebel el Tura Cairo 7 B2
Geiselgasteig Munich 21 B2
General San Martin Buenos Aires 7 B1
Gennevilliers Paris 24 A2
Gentilly Paris 24 B3
Gentofte Copenhagen 8 A3
Genval Brussels 6 B2
George I. Hong Kong 12 B1
Georges River Bridge Sydney 29 C1
Georgetown Washington 33 B3
Georgia Dome Atlanta 3 B2
Gerasdorf bei Wien Vienna 32 A2
Gerberau Munich 21 A1
Gerli Buenos Aires 7 C2
Germiston Johannesburg 13 B2
Gern Munich 21 B2
Getafe Madrid 17 C1
Getty Center, The Los Angeles 16 B2
Geunjeong Seoul 27 C1
Geva Binyamin Jerusalem 13 A2
Geylang Serai Singapore 28 B3
Gharapuri Mumbai 20 B2
Gharb = Shahrak-e Qods Tehran 31 A2
Ghatkopar Mumbai 20 A2
Ghazipur Delhi 10 B2
Ghizri Karachi 13 B2
Ghizri Cr. → Karachi 13 B2
Ghonda Delhi 10 A2
Ghusuri Kolkata 14 B2
Gianicolense Rome 26 B1
Giant Wheel = Riesenrad Vienna 32 A2
Gibraltar Pt. Toronto 31 B2
Gidea Park London 15 A5
Giesing Munich 21 B2
Gilmerton Edinburgh 11 B3
Gilo Jerusalem 13 B2
Gimmersta Stockholm 29 B3
Ginza Tokyo 30 B3
Giv'at Ram Jerusalem 13 B2
Giv'at Ye'arim Jerusalem 13 B1
Giv'at Ze'ev Jerusalem 13 A2
Giv'on Jerusalem 13 A1
Giza = El Giza Cairo 7 A2
Giza Pyramids Cairo 7 B1
Gjersjøen Oslo 23 B3
Gladesville Sydney 29 B1
Gladsakse Copenhagen 8 A2
Glasnevin Dublin 10 A2
Glassmanor Washington 33 C4
Glasthule Dublin 10 B3
Glen Iris Melbourne 18 B2
Glen Mar Park Washington 33 B3
Glen Rock New York 22 A1
Glen Rouge Park Toronto 31 A4
Glenarden Washington 33 B4
Glenasmole Reservoirs Dublin 10 B1
Glencorse Res. Edinburgh 11 B2
Glencullen Dublin 10 B2
Glendale Los Angeles 16 B3
Glendoo Mt. Dublin 10 B2
Glenhuntly Melbourne 18 B2
Glenside Wellington 33 B1
Glenview Chicago 9 A2
Glenview Countryside Chicago 9 A2
Glenvista Johannesburg 13 B2
Glifada Athens 2 B2
Glömsta Stockholm 29 B1
Glostrup Copenhagen 8 B2
Gogar Edinburgh 11 B2
Göktürk Istanbul 12 A1
Golabari Kolkata 14 B2
Golabki Warsaw 32 B1
Gold Coast Chicago 9 B3
Golden Gate San Francisco 26 B2
Golden Gate ⌂ San Francisco 26 A2
Golden Gate Bridge San Francisco 26 B2
Golden Gate Park San Francisco 26 B2
Golden Horn = Haliç Istanbul 12 B1
Golders Green London 15 A2
Golestan Palace Tehran 31 A2
Gollans Stream → Wellington 33 B2
Gonen Jerusalem 13 B2
Gongneung Seoul 27 B2
Goodmayes London 15 A4
Goodwood Cape Town 8 A2
Gopalpur Kolkata 14 B2
Górce Warsaw 32 B1
Gore Hill Sydney 29 A2

Gorelyy → St. Petersburg 27 A3
Gorgie Edinburgh 11 B2
Gorky Park Moscow 19 B2
Gosen Berlin 5 B5
Gosener kanal Berlin 5 B5
Gospel Oak London 15 A3
Gotanda Tokyo 30 B3
Goth Goli Mar Karachi 13 A2
Goth Sher Shah Karachi 13 A1
Gotha Orlando 23 A1
Gournay-sur-Marne Paris 24 A4
Governador, I. do Rio de Janeiro 25 A1
Governors I. New York 22 B1
Grabów Warsaw 32 C1
Grace, Mt. Wellington 33 B2
Gracefield Wellington 33 B2
Gracia Barcelona 4 A2
Gräfelfing Munich 21 B1
Gragoatá Rio de Janeiro 25 B2
Grand Bazaar = Kapali Carsi Istanbul 12 B1
Grand Central Station New York 22 B2
Grand Palace Bangkok 3 B1
Grande Place Brussels 6 A2
Grankulla = Kauniainen Helsinki 11 B1
Grant Park Chicago 9 B3
Granton Edinburgh 11 B2
Grassy Park Cape Town 8 B2
Gratosóglio Milan 19 B2
Gratzwalde Berlin 5 B5
Gravesend New York 22 C2
Grazhdanka St. Petersburg 27 B2
Great Falls Washington 33 B2
Great Falls Park Washington 33 B2
Great Western Forum Los Angeles 16 C2
Greco Milan 19 A2
Green I. Hong Kong 12 B1
Green Point Cape Town 8 A1
Greenbelt Washington 33 A4
Greenbelt Park Washington 33 B4
Greenfield Park Montreal 20 B3
Greenford London 15 A1
Greenhill London 15 A2
Greenhills Dublin 10 B1
Greenpoint New York 22 B2
Greenwich ☐ London 15 B3
Greenwich Observatory London 15 B3
Greenwich Village New York 22 B2
Greenwood Boston 6 A2
Grefsen Oslo 23 A3
Gresham Park Atlanta 3 B2
Greve Strand Copenhagen 8 B1
Griebnitzsee Berlin 5 B1
Griffith Park Los Angeles 16 B3
Grimbergen Brussels 6 A2
Grinzing Vienna 32 A2
Gröbenried Munich 21 A1
Grochów Warsaw 32 B2
Grodzisk Warsaw 32 B2
Groenendaal Brussels 6 B2
Grogol Petamburin Jakarta 12 A1
Gronsdorf Munich 21 B3
Grorud Oslo 23 A4
Gross-Glienicke Berlin 5 B1
Gross-Hadern Munich 21 B1
Gross-Lappen Munich 21 A2
Grosse Krampe Berlin 5 B5
Grosse Müggelsee Berlin 5 B4
Grosse Point Lighthouse Chicago 9 A2
Grossenzersdorf Vienna 32 A3
Grossenzersdorfer Arm → Vienna 32 A3
Grosser Biberhaufen Vienna 32 A2
Grosser Wannsee Berlin 5 B2
Grossfeld-Siedlung Vienna 32 A2
Grosshesselohe Munich 21 B2
Grossjedlersdorf Vienna 32 A2
Grossziethen Berlin 5 B3
Ground Zero New York 22 B1
Grove, The Chicago 9 A1
Grove Hall Boston 6 B2
Grove Park Atlanta 3 B2
Grove Park Hounslow, London 15 B2
Grove Park Lewisham, London 15 B4
Groveton Washington 33 C3
Grünau Berlin 5 B4
Grunewald Berlin 5 B2
Grünwald Munich 21 B2
Grünwalder Forst Munich 21 B2
Grymes Hill New York 22 C1
Guadalupe Manila 17 B2
Guadalupe, Basilica de Mexico City 18 B2
Guanabara, B. de Rio de Janeiro 25 B1
Guanabara, Jardim Rio de Janeiro 25 A1
Guanabara, Palácio da Rio de Janeiro 25 B1
Guang'anmen Beijing 4 B1
Guangqumen Beijing 4 B2
Guangzhou Guangzhou 11 B2
Guanshuo Guangzhou 11 B3
Gudö Stockholm 29 B3
Güell, Parque de Barcelona 4 A2
Guinardó Barcelona 4 A2
Gulbai Karachi 13 A1
Güngören Istanbul 12 B1
Gunnersbury London 15 B2
Gustavo A. Madero Mexico City 18 B2
Guttenberg New York 22 B1
Gutuyevskiy, Ostrov St. Petersburg 27 B1
Guyancourt Paris 24 B1
Gwanak Seoul 27 C1
Gwanaksan Seoul 27 C1
Gyál Budapest 7 B3
Gyáli-patak → Budapest 7 B2

H

Haaga Helsinki 11 B2
Haar Munich 21 B3
Habay Manila 17 C1
Hackbridge London 15 B3
Hackensack New York 22 A1
Hackensack → New York 22 B1
Hackney ☐ London 15 A3
Hackney Wick London 15 A3
Hadr, Warrâq el Cairo 7 A2
Haga Stockholm 29 A2
Hagenbrunn Vienna 32 A2
Hägersten Stockholm 29 B1
Häggvik Stockholm 29 A1
Hagonoy Manila 17 B2
Hague Park Toronto 31 A3
Haidian Beijing 4 B1
Haidari Athens 2 A1
Haidarpur Delhi 10 A1
Haidhausen Munich 21 B2
Haight-Ashbury San Francisco 26 B2
Hainault London 15 A4
Haizhu Guangchang Guangzhou 11 B2
Hakunila Helsinki 11 B3
Halandri Athens 2 A2
Halásztelek Budapest 7 B1
Haliç Istanbul 12 B1
Halim Perdana Kusuma Int. ✕ (HLP) Jakarta 12 B2
Halle Brussels 6 B1
Haltiala Helsinki 11 B2
Haltiavuori Helsinki 11 B2
Ham London 15 B2
Hämeenkylä Helsinki 11 B1
Hammarby Stockholm 29 B2
Hamme Brussels 6 A1
Hammersmith London 15 B2
Hampstead London 15 A2
Hampstead Montreal 20 B2
Hampstead Garden Suburb London 15 A2
Hampstead Heath London 15 A2
Hampton London 15 B1
Hampton Court Palace London 15 B1
Hampton Wick London 15 B2
Hamrā' Baghdad 3 B1
Hanala Helsinki 11 A3
Haneda Tokyo 30 B3
Haneda, Tōkyō ✕ (HND) Tokyo 30 B3
Hang Hau Hong Kong 12 B2
Hanging Gardens Mumbai 20 B1
Hanlon Toronto 31 B1
Hanwell London 15 A1
Hanworth London 15 B1
Haora Kolkata 14 B1
Hapeville Atlanta 3 C2
Happy Valley Hong Kong 12 B2
Har Adar Jerusalem 13 B1
Har Gilo Jerusalem 13 B2
Har Homa Jerusalem 13 B2
Har Nof Jerusalem 13 B2
Haren Brussels 6 A2
Hareskovby Copenhagen 8 A2
Haringey ☐ London 15 A3
Harjusuo Helsinki 11 B3
Harlaching Munich 21 B2
Harlaw Res. Edinburgh 11 B2
Harlem New York 22 B2
Harlesden London 15 A2
Harlington London 15 B1
Harmaja Helsinki 11 C2
Harmashatar hegy Budapest 7 A2
Harolds Cross Dublin 10 B2
Háros Budapest 7 B2
Harperrig Res. Edinburgh 11 B1
Harrow ☐ London 15 A1
Harrow on the Hill London 15 A1
Harrow School London 15 A1
Harrow Weald London 15 A1
Hartsfield-Atlanta Int. ✕ (ATL) Atlanta 3 C2
Harumi Tokyo 30 B3
Harvard University Boston 6 A2
Harwood Heights Chicago 9 B2
Ḥasanābād Tehran 31 A1
Hasbrouck Heights New York 22 A1
Haselhorst Berlin 5 A2
Hasköy Istanbul 12 B1
Hasle Oslo 23 B2
Haslum Oslo 23 A2
Hästhagen Stockholm 29 B2
Hataitai Wellington 33 B1
Hatch End London 15 A1
Hatiara Kolkata 14 B2
Hauketo Oslo 23 A3
Hauz Khas Delhi 10 B2
Havel → Berlin 5 A2
Havelkanal Berlin 5 A2
Havering ☐ London 15 A5
Havering-atte-Bower London 15 A5
Haworth New York 22 A2
Hawthorne Racecourse Chicago 9 C2
Hayes Bromley, London 15 B4
Hayes Hillingdon, London 15 A1
Hayes End London 15 A1
Hayford Chicago 9 C2
Haywards Wellington 33 A2
Heathfield Cape Town 8 B1
Heathrow, London ✕ (LHR) London 15 B1
Hebe Haven Hong Kong 12 A2
Hedong Guangzhou 11 B2
Heidelberg Heights Melbourne 18 A2
Heidelberg West Melbourne 18 A2
Heidemühle Berlin 5 B5
Heideveld Cape Town 8 A2
Heiligensee Berlin 5 A2
Heiligenstadt Vienna 32 A2
Heinersdorf Berlin 5 A3
Hélène de Champlain, Parc ⌂ Montreal 20 A2
Helenelund Stockholm 29 A1
Heliopolis = Masr el Gedida Cairo 7 A2
Hellersdorf Berlin 5 A4
Hellerup Copenhagen 8 A3
Helmahof Vienna 32 A3
Helsingfors = Helsinki Helsinki 11 B2
Helsinki Helsinki 11 B2
Helsinki-Vantaa ✕ (HEL) Helsinki 11 B2
Hendon London 15 A2
Hengsha Guangzhou 11 B2
Hennigsdorf Berlin 5 A2
Henryków Warsaw 32 B1
Henson Cr. → Washington 33 C4
Henttaa Helsinki 11 B1
Heping Park Shanghai 28 B2
Hepingli Beijing 4 B2
Herlev Copenhagen 8 A2
Herman Eckstein Park Johannesburg 13 A2
Hermannskogel Vienna 32 A1
Hermiston Edinburgh 11 B2
Hermitage and Winter Palace St. Petersburg 27 B1
Hermsdorf Berlin 5 A2
Hernals Vienna 32 A2
Herne Hill London 15 B3
Héroes de Churubusco Mexico City 18 B2
Herons, Î. aux Montreal 20 B2
Herstedøster Copenhagen 8 A2
Herttoniemi Helsinki 11 B3
Ḥeṣārak Tehran 31 A1
Heston London 15 B1
Hetzendorf Vienna 32 B1
Hextable London 15 B5
Hialeah Miami 18 A1
Hiawassa, L. Orlando 23 A2
Hickory Hills Chicago 9 C2
Hiekkaharju Helsinki 11 B3
Hietaniemi Helsinki 11 B2
Hietzing Vienna 32 A1
Higashi Osaka 23 A2
Higashimurayama Tokyo 30 A1
Higashinari Osaka 23 A2
Higashisumiyoshi Osaka 23 B2
Higashiyodogawa Osaka 23 A1
High Park Toronto 31 B2
Highbury London 15 A3
Highgate London 15 A3
Highland Cr. → Toronto 31 A3
Highland Creek Toronto 31 A3
Highland Park Los Angeles 16 B3
Highlands North Johannesburg 13 A2
Hillcrest Heights Washington 33 C4
Hillend Edinburgh 11 A1
Hillingdon ☐ London 15 A1
Hillwood Washington 33 B3
Hilmīya Cairo 7 A2
Hin Keng Hong Kong 12 A2
Hirota Osaka 23 A1
Hirschstetten Vienna 32 A2
History Center Atlanta 3 B2
Hither Green London 15 B3
Hiyoshi Tokyo 30 B2
Hizma Jerusalem 13 B2
Hjortekær Copenhagen 8 A3
Hjortespring Copenhagen 8 A2
Hlubočepy Prague 25 B2
Ho Chung Hong Kong 12 A2
Ho Man Tin Hong Kong 12 B2
Hoboken New York 22 B1
Hobsons B. Melbourne 18 B1
Hochbrück Munich 21 A2
Hochelaga Montreal 20 A2
Hodgkins Chicago 9 C1
Hoegi Seoul 27 B2
Hoeilaart Brussels 6 B2
Hofburg Vienna 32 A2
Hoffman I. New York 22 C1
Hohenbrunn Munich 21 B3
Hohenschönhausen Berlin 5 A4
Holargos Athens 2 B2
Holborn London 15 A3
Holden, L. Orlando 23 B2
Holešovice Prague 25 B2
Holland Village Singapore 28 B2
Höllriegelskreuth Munich 21 B1
Hollywood Los Angeles 16 B3
Hollywood Bowl Los Angeles 16 B2
Holmenkollen Oslo 23 A3
Holmes Run Acres Washington 33 B2
Holmgård Stockholm 29 B1
Holmlia Oslo 23 B3
Holocaust Memorial Jerusalem 13 B2
Holyrood House, Palace of Edinburgh 11 B3
Holysloot Amsterdam 2 A3
Homerton London 15 A3
Hometown Chicago 9 C2
Hōnanchō Tokyo 30 A2
Honcho Tokyo 30 A3
Honden Tokyo 30 A4
Hondo, Rio → Los Angeles 16 B4
Hong Kong Hong Kong 12 B1
Hong Kong, Univ. of Hong Kong 12 B1
Hong Kong I. Hong Kong 12 B2
Hongje Seoul 27 B1
Hongjimun Tunnel Seoul 27 B1
Hongkou Shanghai 28 B1
Hongmiao Beijing 4 B2
Hongqiao Shanghai 28 B1
Honjyo Tokyo 30 A3
Honoré Mercier, Pont Montreal 20 B1
Hönow Berlin 5 A4
Hook London 15 B2
Horikiri Tokyo 30 A4
Horn Pond Boston 6 A1
Hornchurch London 15 A5
Horni Prague 25 B3
Horni Počernice Prague 25 B3
Hornsey London 15 A3
Horoměřice Prague 25 B1
Hortaleza Madrid 17 B2
Hosoyama Tokyo 30 B2
Hostafranchs Barcelona 4 A1
Hostivař Prague 25 B3
Houbětin Prague 25 B3
Houghton Johannesburg 13 B2
Houilles Paris 24 A2
Hounslow ☐ London 15 B1
Hout Bay Cape Town 8 B1
Hove Å → Copenhagen 8 A1
Hovedøya Oslo 23 A3
Høvik Oslo 23 A2
Hovorčovice Prague 25 A3
Howard Beach New York 22 C2
Howrah = Haora Kolkata 14 B1
Howth Dublin 10 A3
Howth Hd. Dublin 10 A3
Hōya Tokyo 30 A2
Hradčany Prague 25 B2
Huanghuagang Mausoleum Guangzhou 11 B2
Huangpu Shanghai 28 B2
Huangpu Jiang → Shanghai 28 B1
Huangpu Park Shanghai 28 B1
Huangtugang Beijing 4 C1
Huascar Lima 14 A2
Huay Khwang Bangkok 3 B2
Huddinge Stockholm 29 B2
Huechuraba Santiago 27 B1
Huertas de San Beltran Barcelona 4 A1
Huizingen Brussels 6 B1
Humayun's Tomb Delhi 10 B2
Humber → Toronto 31 A1
Humber B. Toronto 31 B2
Humber Bay Toronto 31 B2
Humber Bay Park Toronto 31 B2
Humber College Toronto 31 B1
Humber Summit Toronto 31 A1
Humber Valley Village Toronto 31 A1
Humberlea Toronto 31 A1
Humberwood Park Toronto 31 A1
Humboldt Park Chicago 9 B2
Humera Madrid 17 B1
Hunaydī Baghdad 3 B2
Hundige Copenhagen 8 B1
Hundige Strand Copenhagen 8 B2
Hung Hom Hong Kong 12 B2
Hunters Hill Sydney 29 B1
Hunters Pt. San Francisco 26 B2
Hunters Valley Washington 33 B2
Huntington Washington 33 C3
Huntington Park Los Angeles 16 C3
Hurīya Baghdad 3 A1
Hurstville Sydney 29 B1
Husan Jerusalem 13 B1
Husby Stockholm 29 A1
Husum Copenhagen 8 A2
Hutt → Wellington 33 B2
Hütteldorf Vienna 32 A1
Hűvösvölgy Budapest 7 A2
Huwon Secret Garden Seoul 27 B1
Hvalstad Oslo 23 A1
Hvalstrand Oslo 23 A2
Hvidovre Copenhagen 8 B2
Hwagok Seoul 27 B1
Hyattsville Washington 33 B4
Hyde Park Boston 6 B2
Hyde Park Chicago 9 C3
Hyde Park Johannesburg 13 A2
Hyde Park London 15 A2
Hyde Park Sydney 29 B2

I

Ibese Lagos 14 A2
Ibirapuera São Paulo 27 B1
Ibirapuera, Parque do São Paulo 27 B2
Icarai Rio de Janeiro 25 B2
İçerenköy Istanbul 12 C2
Ichgao Tokyo 30 A2
Ichigaya Tokyo 30 A3
Ichikawa Tokyo 30 A4
Ickenham London 15 A1
Iddo Lagos 14 B2
Idi-Oro Lagos 14 A2
Iganmu Lagos 14 B2
Igbobi Lagos 14 A2
Igbologun Lagos 14 B1
Igny Paris 24 B2
IJ, Het → Amsterdam 2 A2
IJ-meer Amsterdam 2 A3
Ijesa-Tedo Lagos 14 B1
Ijora Lagos 14 B2
Ikebe Tokyo 30 B2
Ikebukuro Tokyo 30 A3
Ikegami Tokyo 30 B3
Ikeja Lagos 14 A2
Ikeuchi Osaka 23 B2
Ikoyi Lagos 14 B2
Ikuata Lagos 14 B2
Ikuno Osaka 23 A2
Ikuta Tokyo 30 B2
Ila Oslo 23 A2
Ilford London 15 A4
Ilioupoli Athens 2 B2
Illinois at Chicago, University of Chicago 9 B3
Illinois Institute of Technology Chicago 9 B3
Ilpendam Amsterdam 2 A2
Ilsos → Athens 2 B2
Imbābah Cairo 7 A2
Imielin Warsaw 32 C2
Imirim São Paulo 27 A2
Imitos Athens 2 B2
Imitos, Oros Athens 2 B2
Imperial Palace Museum Beijing 4 B2
Inagi Tokyo 30 B2
Inchcolm Edinburgh 11 A2
Inchicore Dublin 10 A1
Inchkeith Edinburgh 11 A3
Inchmickery Edinburgh 11 A2
Incirano Milan 19 A1
Independencia Lima 14 A2
Independencia Santiago 27 B2
India Gate Delhi 10 B2
Indian Creek Village Miami 18 A2
Indianópolis São Paulo 27 B2
Indira Gandhi Int. ✕ (DEL) Delhi 10 B1
Industria Johannesburg 13 B1
Ingierstrand Oslo 23 B3
Inglewood Los Angeles 16 C3
Ingliston Edinburgh 11 B1
Inhaúma Rio de Janeiro 25 B1
Inner Port Shelter Hong Kong 12 A2
Interlagos São Paulo 27 C1
Intramuros Manila 17 B1
Invalides Paris 24 A2
Inverkeithing Edinburgh 11 A1
Inzersdorf Vienna 32 B2
Ipanema Rio de Janeiro 25 B1
Ipiranga São Paulo 27 B2
Ipiranga → São Paulo 27 B2
Iponri Lagos 14 B2
Ireland's Eye Dublin 10 A3
Irving Park Chicago 9 B2
Isabel Rio de Janeiro 25 B1
Isagatedo Lagos 14 A1
Isar → Munich 21 A3
Ishbīlīya Baghdad 3 A2
Ishøj Strand Copenhagen 8 B2
Island Bay Wellington 33 B1
Island Park Toronto 31 B2
Islev Copenhagen 8 A2
Isleworth London 15 B2
Islington Toronto 31 B1
Islington ☐ London 15 A3
Ismaning Munich 21 A3
Ismayloskiy Park Moscow 19 B3
Isolo Lagos 14 A1
Issy-les-Moulineaux Paris 24 B2
İstanbul Istanbul 12 C1
İstanbul Boğazı Istanbul 12 B2
Istinye Istanbul 12 B2
Itä Hakkila Helsinki 11 B3
Itaewon Seoul 27 B1
Itami Osaka 23 A1
Itanhanga Rio de Janeiro 25 B1
Ivanhoe Melbourne 18 A2
Ivry-sur-Seine Paris 24 B3
Ixelles Brussels 6 B2
Izmaylovo Moscow 19 B3
Iztacalco Mexico City 18 B2
Iztapalapa Mexico City 18 B2

J

Jaba Jerusalem 13 A2
Jacaré Rio de Janeiro 25 B1
Jackson Heights New York 22 B2
Jackson Park Chicago 9 C3
Jacques-Cartier Montreal 20 A3
Jacques-Cartier, Pont Montreal 20 A2
Jadavpur Kolkata 14 C2
Jade Buddha Temple Shanghai 28 B1
Jægersborg Copenhagen 8 A3
Jægersborg Dyrehave Copenhagen 8 A3
Jagadishpur Kolkata 14 B1
Jagatpur Delhi 10 A2
Jaguaré, Rib. do → São Paulo 27 B1
Jahangirpur Delhi 10 A2
Jakarta Jakarta 12 A2
Jakarta, Teluk Jakarta 12 A1
Jalan Kayu Singapore 28 A3
Jamaica B. New York 22 C3
Jamaica Plain Boston 6 B2
Jamakpuri Delhi 10 B1
Jamshīdīyeh Tehran 31 A2
Jamsil Seoul 27 B2
Jamwon Seoul 27 B2
Janki Warsaw 32 C1
Jannali Sydney 29 C1
Jaraguá São Paulo 27 A1
Jaraguá, Pico de São Paulo 27 A1
Jardim Paulista São Paulo 27 B1
Järvatältet Stockholm 29 A1
Jaskhar Mumbai 20 B2
Jatinegara Jakarta 12 B2
Javādīyeh Tehran 31 B2
Jaworowa Warsaw 32 C1
Jedlesee Vienna 32 A2
Jefferson Memorial Washington 33 B3
Jefferson Park Chicago 9 B2
Jegi Seoul 27 B2
Jelambar Jakarta 12 A1
Jelonki Warsaw 32 B1
Jerónimos, Mosteiro dos Lisbon 16 A1
Jersey City New York 22 B1
Jerusalem Jerusalem 13 B2
Jessamine, L. Orlando 23 B2
Jésus, Î. Montreal 20 A1
Jesús María Lima 14 B2
Jette Brussels 6 A1
Jey Tehran 31 B2
Jianguomen Beijing 4 B2
Jiangwan Shanghai 28 B1
Jib Jerusalem 13 A2
Jihād Baghdad 3 B1
Jingan Shanghai 28 B1
Jinočany Prague 25 B1
Jinonice Prague 25 B2
Jiulong = Kowloon Hong Kong 12 B1
Jiyūgaoka Tokyo 30 B3
Jizā'ir Baghdad 3 B2
Jizīra Baghdad 3 B2
Joglo Jakarta 12 B1
Johannesburg Johannesburg 13 B2
Johannesburg, Univ. of Johannesburg 13 B2
Johanneskirchen Munich 21 A2
Johannestift Berlin 5 A2
Johannisthal Berlin 5 B4
John F. Kennedy Nat. Historic Site ⌂ Boston 6 A2
John McLaren Park San Francisco 26 B2
Johnsonville Wellington 33 B1
Joinville-le-Pont Paris 24 B3
Joli-Bois Brussels 6 B2
Jollas Helsinki 11 B3
Jongmyo Royal Shrine Seoul 27 B1
Jongno Seoul 27 B1
Jonstrup Copenhagen 8 A2
Joppa Edinburgh 11 B3
Jorge Chavez, Int. ✕ (LIM) Lima 14 B2
Jorge Newbery ✕ Buenos Aires 7 B2
Józefa Pilsudskiego Park Warsaw 32 B1
Jōtō Osaka 23 A2
Jouy-en-Josas Paris 24 B2
Juan Anchorena Buenos Aires 7 A2
Juan González Romero Mexico City 18 A2
Juárez Int. ✕ (MEX) Mexico City 18 B2
Judeira Jerusalem 13 A2
Juhdum Jerusalem 13 B2
Juhu Mumbai 20 A2
Jūjā Tokyo 30 A3
Jukskeirivier → Johannesburg 13 A2
Julianów Warsaw 32 B2
Jung Seoul 27 B1
Jungfernheide, Volkspark Berlin 5 A2
Jungfernsee Berlin 5 B1
Junghwa Seoul 27 B2
Jungnang Seoul 27 B2
Jungnangcheon → Seoul 27 B1
Juniper Green Edinburgh 11 B2
Junk B. Hong Kong 12 B2
Jurong Singapore 28 B2
Jurong, Selat Singapore 28 B2
Jurong Industrial Estate Singapore 28 B1
Jurujuba, Enseada de Rio de Janeiro 25 B2
Jūsō Osaka 23 A1
Justice Chicago 9 C2
Jwalahari Delhi 10 B1

K

Kaapstad = Cape Town Cape Town 8 A1
Kabaty Warsaw 32 C2
Kadıköy Istanbul 12 C2
Kadoma Osaka 23 A2
Kafr 'Aqab Jerusalem 13 A2
Kâğıthane Istanbul 12 B1
Kâğıthane → Istanbul 12 B1
Kagran Vienna 32 A2
Kahnawake Montreal 20 B1
Kaimes Edinburgh 11 B2
Kaiserebersdorf Vienna 32 B2
Kaivoksela Helsinki 11 B2
Kalamaki Athens 2 B2
Kalbadevi Mumbai 20 B1
Kalipur Kolkata 14 A1
Kalithea Athens 2 B2
Kalkaji Delhi 10 B2
Kalvebod Fælled Copenhagen 8 B3
Kalveboderne Copenhagen 8 B3
Kamarhati Kolkata 14 A2
Kamata Tokyo 30 B3
Kameari Tokyo 30 A4
Kameido Tokyo 30 A4
Kami-Itabashi Tokyo 30 A3
Kamikitazawa Tokyo 30 B2
Kamitsuruma Tokyo 30 B1
Kamoshida Tokyo 30 B2
Kampong Landang Singapore 28 A3
Kampong Tanjong Penjuru Singapore 28 B2
Kampung Bali Jakarta 12 B1
Kanamori Tokyo 30 B1
Kanda Tokyo 30 A3
Kandilli Istanbul 12 B2
Kankurgachi Kolkata 14 B2
Kanlıca Istanbul 12 B2
Kanonerskiy, Ostrov St. Petersburg 27 B1
Kanzaki → Osaka 23 A1
Kapali Carsi Istanbul 12 B1
Kapellerfeld Vienna 32 A2
Káposztásmegyer Budapest 7 A2
Kapotnya Moscow 19 C3
Käppala Stockholm 29 A3
Käpylä Helsinki 11 B2
Karachi Karachi 13 A2
Karachi Int. ✕ (KHI) Karachi 13 A2
Karkh Baghdad 3 A2
Karlin Prague 25 B2
Karlsfeld Munich 21 A1
Karlshorst Berlin 5 B4
Karlův most Prague 25 B2
Karol Bagh Delhi 10 B2
Karolinenhof Berlin 5 B4
Karori Wellington 33 B1
Karow Berlin 5 A3
Karrādah Baghdad 3 B2
Kārsön Stockholm 29 B1
Kasai Tokyo 30 B4
Kasipur Kolkata 14 B2
Kastrup Copenhagen 8 B3
Kastrup, København ✕ (CPH) Copenhagen 8 B3
Kasuga Tokyo 30 A2
Kasuge Tokyo 30 A3
Kasumigaseki Tokyo 30 B3
Katong Singapore 28 B3
Katrineberg Stockholm 29 B1
Katsushika Tokyo 30 A4
Kau Pai Chau Hong Kong 12 B2
Kau Yi Chau Hong Kong 12 B1
Kaulsdorf Berlin 5 B4
Kauniainen Helsinki 11 B1
Kawasaki Tokyo 30 B3
Kawawa Tokyo 30 B2
Kawęczyn Warsaw 32 B2
Kayu Putih Jakarta 12 B2
Kbely Prague 25 B3
Kebayoran Baru Jakarta 12 B1
Kebayoran Lama Jakarta 12 B1
Kebon Jeruk Jakarta 12 B1
Kedar Jerusalem 13 B2
Kedoya Jakarta 12 B1
Keilor Melbourne 18 A1
Keilor North Melbourne 18 A1
Keimola Helsinki 11 A2
Kelapa Gading Jakarta 12 A2
Kelenföld Budapest 7 B2
Kelvin Johannesburg 13 A2
Kemang Jakarta 12 B1
Kemayoran Jakarta 12 B2
Kemerburgaz Istanbul 12 B1
Kempton Park Races London 15 B1
Kenilworth Cape Town 8 A1
Kennedy Town Hong Kong 12 B1
Kensal Green London 15 A2
Kensington Johannesburg 13 B2
Kensington London 15 B2
Kensington New York 22 C2
Kensington Sydney 29 B2
Kensington Palace London 15 A2
Kent Village Washington 33 B4
Kentish Town London 15 A3
Kenton London 15 A2
Kenwood House London 15 A3
Kepa Warsaw 32 B2
Keppel Harbour Singapore 28 B2
Kesariani Athens 2 B2
Kettering Washington 33 B5
Kew London 15 B2
Kew Melbourne 18 A2
Kew Gardens London 15 B2
Kew Gardens Toronto 31 A3
Key Biscayne Miami 18 B2
Khalīj Baghdad 3 B2
Khandallah Wellington 33 B1
Khansā' Baghdad 3 A2
Kharavli Mumbai 20 B2
Khefren Cairo 7 B1
Khichripur Delhi 10 B2
Khidirpur Kolkata 14 B1
Khimki-Khovrino Moscow 19 A2
Khirbet Batin Abu Lihyah Jerusalem 13 A1
Khirbet el-Misbah Jerusalem 13 A1
Khirbet Jub e-Rum Jerusalem 13 B2
Khlong San Bangkok 3 B2
Khlong Toey Bangkok 3 B2
Khorel Kolkata 14 A1
Khorosovo Moscow 19 B1
Kiamari Karachi 13 B1
Kierling Vienna 32 A1
Kierlingbach → Vienna 32 A1
Kifisos → Athens 2 B2
Kikuna Tokyo 30 B2
Kilbarrack Dublin 10 A3
Kilbirnie Wellington 33 B1
Kilburn London 15 A2
Killakee Dublin 10 B2
Killester Dublin 10 A2
Killiney Dublin 10 B3
Killiney B. Dublin 10 B3
Kilmacud Dublin 10 B2
Kilmainham Dublin 10 A2
Kilmainham Gaol Dublin 10 A2
Kilmashogue Mt. Dublin 10 B2
Kilmore Dublin 10 A2
Kilnamanagh Dublin 10 B1
Kilo Helsinki 11 B1
Kilokri Delhi 10 B2
Kilternan Dublin 10 B2
Kimmage Dublin 10 B2
Kindi Baghdad 3 B2
Kinghorn Edinburgh 11 A2
Kings Domain Melbourne 18 A1
Kings Forest = Kongelunden Copenhagen 8 B3
Kings Park Washington 33 C2
Kings Park West Washington 33 C2
Kingsbury London 15 A2
Kingsbury Melbourne 18 A2
Kingsford Sydney 29 B2
Kingsford Smith, Sydney ✕ (SYD) Sydney 29 B2
Kingston-upon-Thames ☐ London 15 B2
Kingston Vale London 15 B2
Kingsway Toronto 31 B1
Kinsaley Dublin 10 A2
Kipling Heights Toronto 31 A1
Kipseli Athens 2 B2
Kirchstockbach Munich 21 B3
Kirchtrudering Munich 21 B3
Kirikiri Lagos 14 B1
Kirke Værløse Copenhagen 8 A1
Kirkhill Edinburgh 11 B2
Kirkliston Edinburgh 11 B1
Kirknewton Edinburgh 11 B1
Kirov Palace of Culture St. Petersburg 27 B1
Kiryat Anavim Jerusalem 13 B1
Kiryat Ha Yovel Jerusalem 13 B1
Kısıklı Istanbul 12 B2
Kispest Budapest 7 B2
Kista Stockholm 29 A1
Kita Osaka 23 A2
Kita Tokyo 30 A3
Kitazawa Tokyo 30 B3
Kiu Tsiu Hong Kong 12 A2
Kivistö Helsinki 11 B2
Kızıltoprak Istanbul 12 C2
Kizuri Osaka 23 B2
Kjelsås Oslo 23 A3
Kladow Berlin 5 B1
Klampenborg Copenhagen 8 A3
Klaudyń Warsaw 32 B1
Klečany Prague 25 A2
Kledering Vienna 32 B2
Klein Jukskei → Johannesburg 13 A1
Kleinmachnow Berlin 5 B2
Kleinschönebeck Berlin 5 B5
Klemetsrud Oslo 23 A4
Klender Jakarta 12 A2
Kličany Prague 25 A2
Klipriviersberg Nature Reserve Johannesburg 13 B2
Klosterneuburg Vienna 32 A1
Kőbánya Budapest 7 B2
Kobbegem Brussels 6 A1
København Copenhagen 8 A2
København ✕ (CPH) Copenhagen 8 B3
Kobylisy Prague 25 B2
Kobyłka Warsaw 32 A3
Kodaira Tokyo 30 A1
Kodanaka Tokyo 30 B2
Koekelberg Brussels 6 A1
Koganei Tokyo 30 A2
Kogarah Sydney 29 B1
Koivupää Helsinki 11 B2
Koja Jakarta 12 A2
Koja Utara Jakarta 12 A2
Kokhav Ya'akov Jerusalem 13 A2
Kokobunji Tokyo 30 A1
Kokobunji-Temple Tokyo 30 A4
Kolarängen Stockholm 29 B3
Kolbotn Oslo 23 B3
Kolkata Kolkata 14 B2
Kolkata Dum Dum Int. ✕ (CCU) Kolkata 14 A2
Kolkata Maidan Kolkata 14 B1
Koło Warsaw 32 B1
Kolokinthou Athens 2 B2
Kolomyagi St. Petersburg 27 A1
Kolonos Athens 2 B2
Kolsås Oslo 23 A2
Komae Tokyo 30 B2
Komagome Tokyo 30 A3
Komazawa Tokyo 30 B3
Kona Kolkata 14 B1
Konala Helsinki 11 B2
Kondli Delhi 10 B2
Kongelunden Copenhagen 8 B3
Kongens Lyngby Copenhagen 8 A3
Kongo Helsinki 11 A1
Konnagar Kolkata 14 A2
Konohana Osaka 23 A1
Konradshöhe Berlin 5 A2
Kopanina Prague 25 B1
Koparkhairna Mumbai 20 A2
Köpenick Berlin 5 B4
Korangi Karachi 13 B2
Koremasa Tokyo 30 B1
Koridalos Athens 2 B1
Korokoro Wellington 33 B2
Korokoro Stream → Wellington 33 B2
Kosino Moscow 19 B4
Kosugi Tokyo 30 B2
Kota Jakarta 12 A1
Kōtō Tokyo 30 A3
Kotrung Kolkata 14 A2
Kouponia Athens 2 B2
Kowloon Hong Kong 12 B1
Kowloon Peak Hong Kong 12 A2
Kowloon Res. Hong Kong 12 A1
Kowloon Tong Hong Kong 12 A2
Kraainem Brussels 6 A2
Krailling Munich 21 B1
Krampnitz Berlin 5 B1
Krampnitzsee Berlin 5 B1
Kranji, Sungei → Singapore 28 A2
Kranji Industrial Estate Singapore 28 A2
Krasno-Presnenskaya Moscow 19 B2
Krč Prague 25 B2
Kremlin Moscow 19 B2
Krestovskiye, Ostrov St. Petersburg 27 B1
Kreuzberg Berlin 5 A3
Kritzendorf Vienna 32 A1
Krumme Lanke Berlin 5 B2
Krummensee Berlin 5 A5
Krung Thep = Bangkok Bangkok 3 B2
Krusboda Stockholm 29 B3
Kuangchou = Guangzhou Guangzhou 11 B2
Küçükköy Istanbul 12 B1
Küçüksu Istanbul 12 B2
Kudrovo St. Petersburg 27 B3
Kulosaari Helsinki 11 B3
Kumla Stockholm 29 B3
Kungens kurva Stockholm 29 B1
Kungliga Slottet Stockholm 29 B2
Kungshatt Stockholm 29 B1
Kungsholmen Stockholm 29 A2
Kuningan Jakarta 12 B1
Kunitachi Tokyo 30 A1
Kunming Hu Beijing 4 B1
Kunratice Prague 25 B2
Kupchino St. Petersburg 27 B2
Kurbağalı → Istanbul 12 C2
Kurihara Tokyo 30 A2
Kurla Mumbai 20 A2
Kurmuri Mumbai 20 A2
Kurume Tokyo 30 A2
Kuryanovo Moscow 19 C3
Kuskovo Moscow 19 B3
Kustia Kolkata 14 B2
Kuzguncuk Istanbul 12 B2
Kuzyminki Moscow 19 B3
Kwai Chung Hong Kong 12 A1
Kwangchow = Guangzhou Guangzhou 11 B2
Kwun Tong Hong Kong 12 B2
Kyje Prague 25 B3
Kyūhōji Osaka 23 B2

L

La Blanca Santiago 27 C2
La Boca Buenos Aires 7 B2
La Bretèche Paris 24 A1
La Campiña Lima 14 C2
La Celle-St-Cloud Paris 24 A1
La Cisterna Santiago 27 C2
La Courneuve Paris 24 A3
La Dehesa Santiago 27 B2
La Encantada Lima 14 C2
La Estación Madrid 17 B1
La Floresta Barcelona 4 A1
La Florida Santiago 27 C2
La Fortuna Madrid 17 B1
La Fransa Barcelona 4 A1
La Garenne-Colombes Paris 24 A2
La Giustiniana Rome 26 B1
La Grange Chicago 9 C1
La Grange Park Chicago 9 C1
La Granja Santiago 27 C2
La Guardia, New York ✕ (LGA) New York 22 B2
La Hulpe Brussels 6 B2
La Llacuna Barcelona 4 A2
La Loma Mexico City 18 A1
La Lucila Buenos Aires 7 B2
La Maladrerie Paris 24 A1
La Milla, Cerro Lima 14 B2
La Monachina Rome 26 B1
La Moraleja Madrid 17 A2
La Nopalera Mexico City 18 C2
La Paternal Buenos Aires 7 B2
La Perla Lima 14 B2
La Perouse Sydney 29 B2
La Pineda Barcelona 4 B1
La Pisana Rome 26 B1
La Prairie Montreal 20 B3
La Punta Lima 14 B1
La Puntigala Barcelona 4 A2
La Queue-en-Brie Paris 24 B4
La Reina Santiago 27 B2
La Ribera Barcelona 4 A1
La Sagrera Barcelona 4 A2
La Salada Buenos Aires 7 C2
La Scala Milan 19 B2
La Storta Rome 26 A1
La Taxonera Barcelona 4 A2
La Victoria Lima 14 B2
Laajalahti Helsinki 11 B1
Laajasalo Helsinki 11 B3
Laaksolahti Helsinki 11 B1
Lablâba, W. el → Cairo 7 A2
Lachine Montreal 20 B1
Lachine, Canal de Montreal 20 B2
Lad Phrao Bangkok 3 B2
Ladera Heights Los Angeles 16 C2
Ládvi Prague 25 B2
Łady Warsaw 32 C1
Lafontaine, Parc Montreal 20 A2
Lagoa Rio de Janeiro 25 B1
Lagos Lagos 14 B2
Lagos Harbour Lagos 14 B2
Lagos-Ikeja ✕ (LOS) Lagos 14 A1
Lagos Island Lagos 14 B2
Lagos Lagoon Lagos 14 B2
Laguna de B. Manila 17 C2
Laim Munich 21 B2
Lainate Milan 19 A1
Lainz Vienna 32 B1
Lake Buena Vista Orlando 23 B1
Lake Cain Hills Orlando 23 B2
Lake Fairfax Park Washington 33 B2
Lakemba Sydney 29 B1
Lakeside Cape Town 8 B1
Lakeside Johannesburg 13 A2
Lakeview Chicago 9 B3
Lakewood Park Atlanta 3 B2
Lakhtinskiy St. Petersburg 27 B1
Lakhtinskiy Razliv, Oz. St. Petersburg 27 B1
Lakshmanpur Kolkata 14 B1
Laksi Bangkok 3 A2
Lal Qila Delhi 10 B2
Lam Tin Hong Kong 12 B2
Lambert Oslo 23 A3
Lambeth ☐ London 15 B3
Lambrate Milan 19 B2
Lambro, Parco Milan 19 B2
Lambton Mills Toronto 31 B1
Lamma I. Hong Kong 12 B1
Landover Hills Washington 33 B4
Landsmeer Amsterdam 2 A2
Landstrasse Vienna 32 A2
Landwehr kanal Berlin 5 B3
Lane Cove Sydney 29 A1
Lane Cove National Park △ Sydney 29 A1
Langa Cape Town 8 A2
Langenzersdorf Vienna 32 A2
Langer See Berlin 5 B4
Langley Washington 33 B2
Langley Park Washington 33 B4
Langwald Munich 21 A1
Lanham Washington 33 B4
Lankwitz Berlin 5 B3
L'Annunziatella Rome 26 C2
Lansdowne Cape Town 8 A2
Lansing Toronto 31 A2
Lanús Buenos Aires 7 C2
Lapa Rio de Janeiro 25 B1
Laranjeiras Rio de Janeiro 25 B1
Las Arenas Lima 14 B1
Las Barreras Rio de Janeiro 25 B1
Las Warsaw 32 B2
Las Corts Barcelona 4 A1
Las Kabacki Warsaw 32 C2
Las Pinas Manila 17 C1
Las Rejas Santiago 27 B1
Lasalle Montreal 20 B2
LaSalle Street Station Chicago 9 B3
Lasek Bielański Warsaw 32 B1
Lasek Na Kole Warsaw 32 B1
Laski Warsaw 32 B1
Latina Madrid 17 B1
Lauttasaari Helsinki 11 C2
Laval-des-Rapides Montreal 20 A1
Lavīzān Tehran 31 A2
Lavradio Lisbon 16 A2
Lawndale Chicago 9 B2
Lawne L. Orlando 23 A2
Lawrence Heights Toronto 31 A2
Layari Karachi 13 A2
Layari → Karachi 13 A1
Łazienkowski Park Warsaw 32 B2
Le Blanc-Mesnil Paris 24 A3
Le Bourget Paris 24 A3
Le Chenoi Brussels 6 B2
Le Chesnay Paris 24 B1
Le Christ de Saclay Paris 24 B2
Le Kremlin-Bicêtre Paris 24 B3
Le Mesnil-le-Roi Paris 24 A1
Le Pecq Paris 24 A1
Le Perreux Paris 24 A3
Le Pin Paris 24 A4
Le Plessis-Robinson Paris 24 B2
Le Plessis-Trévise Paris 24 B4
Le Port-Marly Paris 24 A1
Le Pré-St-Gervais Paris 24 A3
Le Raincy Paris 24 A4
Le Vésinet Paris 24 A1
Lea Bridge London 15 A3
Leaside Toronto 31 A2
Leblon Rio de Janeiro 25 B1
Lee London 15 B4
Leganés Madrid 17 C1
Legazpi Madrid 17 B1
Lehtisaari Helsinki 11 B2
Lei Yue Mun Hong Kong 12 B2
Leião Lisbon 16 A1

Leichhardt Sydney 29 B1
Leith Edinburgh 11 B3
Leme Rio de Janeiro 25 B1
Lemoyne Montreal 20 B3
Lenin Moscow 19 B2
Lenino Moscow 19 C2
Leninskiye Gory Moscow 19 B2
Lennox Los Angeles 16 C2
Leonia New York 22 A2
Leopardstown Dublin 10 B2
Leopoldau Vienna 32 A2
Leopoldsdorf Vienna 32 B2
Leopoldstadt Vienna 32 A2
Leportovo Moscow 19 B3
Leppävaara Helsinki 11 B1
Les Lilas Paris 24 A3
Les Loges-en-Josas Paris 24 B1
Les Pavillons-sous-Bois Paris 24 A4
Lésigny Paris 24 B4
Lesnozavodskaya St. Petersburg 27 B2
Lester B. Pearson Int., Toronto ✈ (YYZ) Toronto 31 A1
L'Étang-la-Ville Paris 24 A1
Letňany Prague 25 B3
Letopolis = Ausîm Cairo 7 A1
Levallois-Perret Paris 24 A2
Levent Istanbul 12 B2
Lewisdale Washington 33 B4
Lewisham □ London 15 B3
Lexington Boston 6 A1
Leyton London 15 A3
Leytonstone London 15 A4
L'Haÿ-les-Roses Paris 24 B3
L'Hospitalet de Llobregat Barcelona 4 A1
Lhotka Prague 25 B2
Liangshui He → Beijing 4 C2
Lianhua Chi Beijing 4 B1
Lianhua He → Beijing 4 B1
Libčice nad Vitavou Prague 25 A2
Libeň Prague 25 B2
Liberdade São Paulo 27 B2
Liberton Edinburgh 11 B3
Liberty I. New York 22 B1
Liberty Osaka Museum Osaka 23 B1
Liberty State Park ⌂ New York 22 B1
Libeznice Prague 25 A2
Libuš Prague 25 B2
Lichiao Guangzhou 11 B2
Lichtenburg Berlin 5 A4
Lichterfelde Berlin 5 B2
Lidingö Stockholm 29 A2
Lieshi Lingyuan Guangzhou 11 B2
Liesing Vienna 32 B1
Liesing → Vienna 32 B2
Ligovo St. Petersburg 27 C1
Lijordet Oslo 23 A2
Likhoborka → Moscow 19 A2
Lilla Värtan Stockholm 29 A3
Lille Værløse Copenhagen 8 A2
Liluah Kolkata 14 B1
Lim Chu Kang Singapore 28 A2
Lima Lima 14 B2
Limbiate Milan 19 A1
Limehouse London 15 A3
Limeil-Brévannes Paris 24 B3
Linate, Milano ✈ (LIN) Milan 19 B2
Linbro Park Johannesburg 13 A2
Lincoln Center for Performing Arts New York 22 B2
Lincoln Heights Los Angeles 16 B3
Lincoln Memorial Washington 33 B3
Lincoln Park Chicago 9 B3
Lincoln Park New York 22 B1
Lincoln Park San Francisco 26 B1
Lincoln Park Zoo Chicago 9 B3
Lincolnwood Chicago 9 A2
Linda-a-Pastora Lisbon 16 A1
Linden Johannesburg 13 A2
Linden Wellington 33 A1
Lindenberg Berlin 5 A4
Lindøya Oslo 23 A3
Liniers Buenos Aires 7 B1
Linkebeek Brussels 6 B2
Linksfield Johannesburg 13 A2
Linmeyer Johannesburg 13 B2
Linna Helsinki 11 A2
Lintuvaara Helsinki 11 B1
Lion Rock Country Park ⌂ Hong Kong 12 A2
Lion's Head Cape Town 8 A1
Lioumi Athens 2 B2
Lisboa Lisbon 16 A2
Lisboa ✈ (LIS) Lisbon 16 A2
Lisbon = Lisboa Lisbon 16 A2
Lishui Guangzhou 11 A1
Little B. Sydney 29 B2
Little Calumet → Chicago 9 D3
Little Ferry New York 22 A1
Little Lake Conway Orlando 23 B2
Little Red School House Nature Center Chicago 9 C1
Little Rouge → Toronto 31 A4
Liuhang Shanghai 28 A1
Liurong Temple Guangzhou 11 B2
Livry-Gargan Paris 24 A4
Ljan Oslo 23 A3
Llano de Can Gineu Barcelona 4 A2
Lo Aranguiz Santiago 27 B2
Lo Boza Santiago 27 B1
Lo Chau Hong Kong 12 B2
Lo Chau Pak Mai Hong Kong 12 B2
Lo Espejo Santiago 27 C1
Lo Hermida Santiago 27 B2
Lo Prado Santiago 27 B1
Lo So Shing Hong Kong 12 B1
Lo Wai Hong Kong 12 A1
Loanhead Edinburgh 11 B3
Lobau Vienna 32 A3
Lobos, Pt. San Francisco 26 B1
Locham Munich 21 B1
Lochkov Prague 25 B2
Lockhausen Munich 21 A1
Lodi New York 22 A1
Lodi Estate Delhi 10 B2
Logan Int., Boston ✈ (BOS) Boston 6 A2
Logan Square Chicago 9 B2
Lognes-Émerainville ✈ Paris 24 B4
Löhme Berlin 5 A5
Lolokhet Karachi 13 A2
Lomas Chapultepec Mexico City 18 B1
Lomas de San Angel Inn Mexico City 18 B1
Lombardy East Johannesburg 13 A2
Lomianki Warsaw 32 A1
Lomus Reforma Mexico City 18 B1
London London 15 B3
London City ✈ (LCY) London 15 A4
London Heathrow ✈ (LHR) London 15 B1
London Zoo London 15 A3
Long B. Sydney 29 B2
Long Branch Toronto 31 B1
Long Brook → Washington 33 C2
Long Ditton London 15 B2
Long Island City New York 22 B2
Longchamp, Hippodrome de Paris 24 A2
Longhua Pagoda Shanghai 28 B1
Longhua Park Shanghai 28 B1
Longjohn Slough Chicago 9 C1
Longtan Hu → Beijing 4 B2
Longue-Pointe Montreal 20 A2
Longueuil Montreal 20 A3
Longueuil-St-Hubert = St-Hubert Montreal 20 B3
Loni Delhi 10 A2
Loop, The Chicago 9 B3
Lord's Cricket Ground London 15 A2
Loreto Milan 19 B2
Los Angeles Los Angeles 16 B3
Los Angeles Int. ✈ (LAX) Los Angeles 16 C2
Los Cerrillos ✈ (ULC) Santiago 27 B1
Los Nietos Los Angeles 16 C4
Los Olivos Lima 14 A2
Los Reyes Mexico City 18 B2
Losiny Ostrov △ Moscow 19 A3
Lot Brussels 6 B1
Lotus River Cape Town 8 B2
Lotus Temple Delhi 10 B2
Loughlinstown Dublin 10 B3
Louise, L. Orlando 23 B1
Louisiana Superdome New Orleans 21 B2
Loures Lisbon 16 A1
Louveciennes Paris 24 A1
Louvre, Musée du Paris 24 A3
Lower B. New York 22 C1
Lower Hutt Wellington 33 B2
Lower New York B. = Lower B. New York 22 C1
Lower Shing Mun Res. Hong Kong 12 A1
Lowry Bay Wellington 33 B2
Loyola University Chicago 9 B3
Lu Xun, Tomb of Shanghai 28 B1
Lu Xun Park Shanghai 28 B1
Lübars Berlin 5 A3
Lucy, L. Orlando 23 A2
Ludwigsfeld Munich 21 A1
Luhu Guangzhou 11 B2
Lumiar Lisbon 16 A2
Lundtofte Copenhagen 8 A3
Lung Mei Hong Kong 12 A2
Luojiang Guangzhou 11 B2
Lustheim Munich 21 A2
Luwan Shanghai 28 B1
Luzhniki Sports Centre Moscow 19 B2
Lyndhurst New York 22 B1
Lynn Woods Res. Boston 6 A2
Lyon, Gare de Paris 24 A3
Lyons Chicago 9 C2
Lysaker Oslo 23 A2
Lysakerselva → Oslo 23 A2
Lysolaje Prague 25 B2
Lyublino Moscow 19 B3

M

Ma Nam Wat Hong Kong 12 A2
Ma On Shan Country Park ⌂ Hong Kong 12 A2
Ma'ale Adumim Jerusalem 13 B2
Ma'ale Ha Khamisha Jerusalem 13 B1
Ma'ale Mikhmas Jerusalem 13 B2
Maantiekylä Helsinki 11 A3
Maarifa Baghdad 3 B2
Mabato Pt. Manila 17 C2
Mabel, L. Orlando 23 B1
Macaco, Morro do Rio de Janeiro 25 B2
McCook Chicago 9 C2
McGill University Montreal 20 A2
Machelen Brussels 6 A2
Machida Tokyo 30 B1
Maciołki Warsaw 32 B2
McKerrow, Mt. Wellington 33 B2
McKinley Park Chicago 9 C2
McLean Washington 33 B2
Macopocho → Santiago 27 B1
McRitchie Res. Singapore 28 A2
Macul Santiago 27 C2
Madhudaha Kolkata 14 B2
Madhyamgram Kolkata 14 A2
Madîn Mexico City 18 A1
Madin, L. Mexico City 18 A1
Madînat Al Mansûr Baghdad 3 B2
Mâdinet Nasr Cairo 7 A2
Madrid Madrid 17 B1
Madrid Barajas ✈ (MAD) Madrid 17 B2
Madrona Barcelona 4 A1
Maesawa Tokyo 30 A2
Magdalena Lima 14 B2
Magdalena Contreras Mexico City 18 C1
Maghreb Baghdad 3 A2
Maginu Tokyo 30 B2
Magliana Rome 26 B1
Magny-les-Hameaux Paris 24 B1
Maheshtala Kolkata 14 C1
Mahim Mumbai 20 A2
Mahim B. Mumbai 20 A1
Mahlsdorf Berlin 5 A4
Mahmoodabad Karachi 13 A2
Mahrauli Delhi 10 B2
Mahul Mumbai 20 A2
Maida Vale London 15 A2
Maidstone Melbourne 18 A1
Maipú Santiago 27 C1
Maisonneuve, Parc Montreal 20 A2
Maisons-Alfort Paris 24 B3
Maisons-Laffitte Paris 24 A1
Maissoneuve Montreal 20 A2
Maitland Cape Town 8 A1
Makasar Jakarta 12 B2
Makati Manila 17 B2
Mäkiniitty Helsinki 11 A2
Mala Strana Prague 25 B2
Malabar Sydney 29 B2
Malabar Hill Mumbai 20 B1
Malabar Pt. Mumbai 20 B1
Malabon Manila 17 B1
Malacañang Palace Manila 17 B1
Malahide Dublin 10 A3
Malakoff Paris 24 B2
Mälarhöjaen Stockholm 29 B1
Malate Manila 17 B1
Malaya Neva St. Petersburg 27 B1
Malaya Okhta St. Petersburg 27 B2
Malchow Berlin 5 A3
Malden Boston 6 A2
Malden London 15 B2
Maleizen Brussels 6 B3
Malešice Prague 25 B3
Malir → Karachi 13 B2
Malleny Mills Edinburgh 11 B2
Malmi Helsinki 11 B2
Malmøya Oslo 23 A3
Måløv Copenhagen 8 A2
Malton Toronto 31 A1
Malvern Johannesburg 13 B2
Malvern Melbourne 18 B2
Malvern Toronto 31 A3
Mampang Prapatan Jakarta 12 B1
Mampukuji Tokyo 30 B2
Man Budrukh Mumbai 20 A2
Man Khurd Mumbai 20 A2
Manakhat Jerusalem 13 B2
Mandaluyong Manila 17 B2
Mandaoli Delhi 10 B2
Mandaqui → São Paulo 27 A2
Mandoli Delhi 10 A2
Mandvi Mumbai 20 B2
Manenberg Cape Town 8 A2
Mang Kung Uk Hong Kong 12 B2
Mang-won Seoul 27 B1
Mangolpuri Delhi 10 A1
Manguinhos ✈ Rio de Janeiro 25 B1
Manhattan New York 22 B2
Manhattan Beach New York 22 C2
Manila Manila 17 B1
Manila Ninoy Aquino Int. ✈ (MNL) Manila 17 B2
Mankkaa Helsinki 11 B1
Manly Sydney 29 A2
Mann, L. Orlando 23 A2
Mann's Chinese Theatre Los Angeles 16 B2
Mannswörth Vienna 32 B3
Manor Park London 15 A4
Manor Park Wellington 33 A2
Manora Karachi 13 B1
Manora Pt. Karachi 13 B1
Manquehue, Cerro Santiago 27 B2
Manzanares, Canal de Madrid 17 C2
Mapo Seoul 27 B1
Maracanã Rio de Janeiro 25 B1
Maraoli Mumbai 20 A2
Marcelin Warsaw 32 B1
Mareil-Marly Paris 24 A1
Margareten Vienna 32 A2
Maria Vienna 32 A2
Maridalen Oslo 23 A3
Maridalsvatnet Oslo 23 A3
Mariendorf Berlin 5 B3
Marienfelde Berlin 5 B3
Marikina Manila 17 B2
Marikina → Manila 17 B2
Marin City San Francisco 26 A1
Marin Pen. San Francisco 26 A1
Marina del Rey Los Angeles 16 C2
Marino Dublin 10 A2
Marisco, Ponta do Rio de Janeiro 25 C1
Markham Toronto 31 A2
Marki Warsaw 32 B2
Markland Wood Toronto 31 B1
Marly, Forêt de Paris 24 A1
Marly-le-Roi Paris 24 A1
Marne-la-Vallée Paris 24 A4
Marolles-en-Brie Paris 24 B4
Maroubra Sydney 29 B2
Marquette Park Chicago 9 C2
Marrickville Sydney 29 B1
Marsfield Sydney 29 A1
Marsha, L. Orlando 23 B2
Marte, Campo de São Paulo 27 B2
Martesana, Navíglio della Milan 19 A2
Martin Luther King Nat. Historic Site ⌂ Atlanta 3 B2
Martinez Buenos Aires 7 A1
Martinkylä Helsinki 11 B2
Martinsried Munich 21 B1
Maruko Tokyo 30 B3
Maryino Moscow 19 B3
Maryland Singapore 28 B2
Marymont Warsaw 32 B1
Marysin Wawerski Warsaw 32 B2
Marzahn Berlin 5 A4
Mascot Sydney 29 B2
Masmo Stockholm 29 B1
Maspeth New York 22 B2
Masr el Gedida Cairo 7 A2
Masr el Qadîma Cairo 7 A2
Massachusetts Inst. of Tech. Boston 6 A2
Massamá Lisbon 16 A1
Massey → Toronto 31 A3
Massy Paris 24 B2
Mata Jerusalem 13 B1
Matihutong Beijing 4 B1
Matinha Lisbon 16 A2
Matraman Jakarta 12 B2
Matsubara Osaka 23 B2
Mattapan Boston 6 B2
Mátyásföld Budapest 7 A3
Mau Tso Ngam Hong Kong 12 A2
Mauer Vienna 32 B1
Mauripur Karachi 13 A1
Maxhof Munich 21 B1
Mayfair Johannesburg 13 B2
Mayor, Plaza Madrid 17 B1
Maywood Chicago 9 B1
Maywood Los Angeles 16 C3
Maywood New York 22 A1
Maywood Park Race Track Chicago 9 B1
Mazagaon Mumbai 20 B2
Meadowbank Park Sydney 29 A1
Měcholupy Prague 25 B3
Měčice Prague 25 A3
Mecidiyeköy Istanbul 12 B2
Medford Boston 6 A2
Mediodia Madrid 17 B2
Meguro Tokyo 30 B3
Meguro → Tokyo 30 B3
Mehpalpur Delhi 10 B1
Mehrābād ✈ (THR) Tehran 31 A1
Mehram Nagar Delhi 10 B1
Mehrow Berlin 5 A4
Meidling Vienna 32 A2
Méier Rio de Janeiro 25 B1
Meiji Shrine Tokyo 30 A3
Meise Brussels 6 A1
Mejiro Tokyo 30 A3
Melbourne Melbourne 18 A1
Melbourne ✈ (MEL) Melbourne 18 A1
Melkki Helsinki 11 C2
Mellunkylä Helsinki 11 B3
Mellunmäki Helsinki 11 B3
Melrose Boston 6 A2
Melrose New York 22 B2
Melrose Park Chicago 9 B1
Melsbroek Brussels 6 A2
Melville Johannesburg 13 B2
Menteng Jakarta 12 B1
Mérantaise → Paris 24 B1
Mercamadrid Madrid 17 B2
Merced, L. San Francisco 26 B2
Meredale Johannesburg 13 B1
Merlimau, Pulau Singapore 28 B2
Merri Cr. → Melbourne 18 A1
Merrion Dublin 10 B2
Merrionette Park Chicago 9 C2
Merton □ London 15 B2
Mesgarābād Tehran 31 B3
Messe Vienna 32 A2
Metanópoli Milan 19 B2
Metro-Dade Cultural Centre Miami 18 B2
Metro Toronto Zoo Toronto 31 A3
Metropolitan Museum of Art New York 22 B2
Meudon Paris 24 B2
Mevaseret Tsiyon Jerusalem 13 B1
Mevo Beitar Jerusalem 13 B1
México Mexico City 18 B2
México, Ciudad de Mexico City 18 B2
Mexico City Int. ✈ (MEX) Mexico City 18 B2
Meyersdal Johannesburg 13 B2
Mezzate Milan 19 B2
Miadong Seoul 27 B2
Miami Miami 18 B2
Miami Beach Miami 18 B2
Miami Canal Miami 18 A1
Miami Int. ✈ (MIA) Miami 18 B1
Miami Shores Miami 18 A2
Miami Springs Miami 18 B1
Miasto Warsaw 32 B2
Michałowice Warsaw 32 B1
Michle Prague 25 B2
Middle Harbour Sydney 29 A2
Middle Hd. Sydney 29 A2
Middle Park Melbourne 18 B1
Middle Village New York 22 B2
Middlesex Fells Reservation Boston 6 A2
Midland Beach New York 22 C1
Midwood New York 22 C2
Miedzeszyn Warsaw 32 B3
Międzylesie Warsaw 32 B3
Miessaari Helsinki 11 C1
Miguel Hidalgo Mexico City 18 B1
Milan = Milano Milan 19 B1
Milanese, Parco Regionale ⌂ Milan 19 A1
Milano Milan 19 B1
Milano Due Milan 19 B2
Milano Linate ✈ (LIN) Milan 19 B2
Milano San Felice Milan 19 B2
Milbertshofen Munich 21 A2
Mill Hill London 15 A2
Millennium Dome London 15 A4
Miller Meadow Chicago 9 B2
Millerhill Edinburgh 11 B3
Milltown Dublin 10 B2
Millwood Washington 33 B4
Milnerton Cape Town 8 A1
Milon-la-Chapelle Paris 24 B1
Milton Boston 6 B2
Milton Bridge Edinburgh 11 B2
Mimico Toronto 31 B2
Mimico Creek → Toronto 31 B1
Minami Osaka 23 A2
Minamitsunashima Tokyo 30 B2
Minato Osaka 23 B1
Minato Tokyo 30 B3
Minshât el Bekkari Cairo 7 A1
Miraflores Lima 14 B2
Miramar Wellington 33 B1
Misericordia, Sa. da Rio de Janeiro 25 B1
Mission San Francisco 26 B2
Mississauga Toronto 31 B1
Mitaka Tokyo 30 A2
Mitcham London 15 B2
Mitcham Common London 15 B3
Mitchell Museum of the American Indian Chicago 9 A2
Mitchell's Plain Cape Town 8 B2
Mitte Berlin 5 A3
Mittel Isarkanal → Munich 21 A3
Mixcoac Mexico City 18 B1
Miyakojima Osaka 23 A2
Mizonokuchi Tokyo 30 B2
Mizue Tokyo 30 A4
Młocinski Park Warsaw 32 B1
Mlociny Warsaw 32 B1
Mnevniki Moscow 19 B1
Moba Lagos 14 B2
Moczydło Warsaw 32 C2
Modderfontein Johannesburg 13 A2
Modřany Prague 25 B2
Mogyoród Budapest 7 A3
Moinho Velho, Cor. → São Paulo 27 B2
Mok Seoul 27 B1
Mokotów Warsaw 32 B2
Molenbeek-St-Jean Brussels 6 A1
Molino de Rosas Mexico City 18 B1
Mollem Brussels 6 A1
Mollins de Rey Barcelona 4 A1
Mondeor Johannesburg 13 B2
Moneda, Palacio de la Santiago 27 B2
Moneró Rio de Janeiro 25 A1
Mong Kok Hong Kong 12 B2
Monkstown Dublin 10 B3
Monnickendam Amsterdam 2 A3
Monrovia Los Angeles 16 B4
Monsanto Lisbon 16 A1
Monsanto, Parque Florestal de Lisbon 16 A1
Mont-Royal Montreal 20 A2
Mont-Royal, Parc Montreal 20 A2
Montana de Montjuich Barcelona 4 A1
Montcada i Reixac Barcelona 4 A2
Monte Chingolo Buenos Aires 7 C2
Montebello Los Angeles 16 B4
Montemor Lisbon 16 A1
Monterey Park Los Angeles 16 B4
Montespaccato Rome 26 B1
Montesson Paris 24 A1
Monteverde Nuovo Rome 26 B1
Montfermeil Paris 24 A4
Montigny-le-Bretonneux Paris 24 B1
Montjay-la-Tour Paris 24 A4
Montparnasse, Gare Paris 24 A2
Montréal Montreal 20 A2
Montréal, Î. de Montreal 20 A2
Montréal, Université de Montreal 20 B2
Montréal Est Montreal 20 A2
Montréal-Nord Montreal 20 A2
Montréal-Ouest Montreal 20 B1
Montréal Trudeau Int. ✈ (YUL) Montreal 20 B1
Montreuil Paris 24 A3
Montrouge Paris 24 B2
Montserrat Buenos Aires 7 B2
Monza Milan 19 A2
Monzoro Milan 19 B1
Moóca São Paulo 27 B2
Moonachie New York 22 B1
Moonee Ponds Melbourne 18 A1
Moonee Valley Racecourse Melbourne 18 A1
Moosach Munich 21 A2
Mora Mumbai 20 B2
Moratalaz Madrid 17 B2
Mörby Stockholm 29 A2
Morden London 15 B2
Morée → Paris 24 A3
Morgan Park Chicago 9 C3
Moriguchi Osaka 23 A2
Morivione Milan 19 B2
Morningside Edinburgh 11 B2
Morningside Johannesburg 13 A2
Morningside Washington 33 C4
Morningside Park Orlando 23 B2
Morningside Park Toronto 31 A3
Morro Solar, Cerro Lima 14 C2
Mortlake London 15 B2
Mortlake Sydney 29 B1
Morton Grove Chicago 9 A2
Morumbi São Paulo 27 B1
Moscavide Lisbon 16 A2
Moschato Athens 2 B2
Moscow = Moskva Moscow 19 B2
Moskva Moscow 19 B2
Moskvoretskiy Moscow 19 B2
Mosman Sydney 29 A2
Móstoles Madrid 17 C1
Moti Bagh Delhi 10 B2
Motol Prague 25 B1
Motsa Jerusalem 13 B2
Motsa Illit Jerusalem 13 B1
Motspur Park London 15 B2
Mottingham London 15 B4
Mount Dennis Toronto 31 A2
Mount Greenwood Chicago 9 C2
Mount Hood Memorial Park ⌂ Boston 6 A2
Mount Merrion Dublin 10 B2
Mount Rainier Washington 33 B4
Mount Vernon New York 22 A3
Müggelberge Berlin 5 B4
Müggelheim Berlin 5 B5
Muggiò Milan 19 A2
Mühleiten Vienna 32 A3
Mühlenfliess → Berlin 5 A5
Muiden Amsterdam 2 A3
Muizenberg Cape Town 8 B1
Mujahidpur Delhi 10 B2
Mukandpur Delhi 10 A2
Mukhmas Jerusalem 13 A2
Muko → Osaka 23 A1
Mukojima Tokyo 30 A3
Mulbarton Johannesburg 13 B2
Mumbai Mumbai 20 B2
Mumbai Chhatrapati Shivaji Int. ✈ (BOM) Mumbai 20 A2
Mumbai Harbour Mumbai 20 B2
Munch Museum Oslo 23 A3
Münchehofe Berlin 5 B5
München Munich 21 B2
München Franz Josef Strauss ✈ (MUC) Munich 21 A2
Munich = München Munich 21 B2
Munkkiniemi Helsinki 11 B2
Munro Buenos Aires 7 B1
Muntinlupa Manila 17 C2
Murai Res. Singapore 28 A2
Muranów Warsaw 32 B1
Murino St. Petersburg 27 B2
Murrayfield Edinburgh 11 B2
Musashino Tokyo 30 A2
Museu Nacional Rio de Janeiro 25 B1
Mushin Lagos 14 A2
Musocco Milan 19 B1
Mustansiriya Baghdad 3 A2
Musturud Cairo 7 A2
Muswell Hill London 15 A3
Mutanabi Baghdad 3 B2
Muthana Baghdad 3 B2
Mykerinos Cairo 7 B1
Myllypuro Helsinki 11 B3
Mystic → Boston 6 A2

N

Nacka Stockholm 29 B3
Naenae Wellington 33 B2
Nærsnes Oslo 23 B1
Nagatsuta Tokyo 30 B2
Nagytétény Budapest 7 B1
Nahalin Jerusalem 13 B1
Najafgarh Drain → Delhi 10 B1
Nakahara Tokyo 30 B2
Nakano Tokyo 30 A2
Namsan Park Seoul 27 B1
Namyeong Seoul 27 B1
Nanbiancun Guangzhou 11 B1
Nanchang He → Beijing 4 B1
Nandang Guangzhou 11 B2
Nangal Dewat Delhi 10 B1
Naniwa Osaka 23 B1
Nanole Mumbai 20 A2
Nanpu Bridge Shanghai 28 B2
Nanshi Shanghai 28 B1
Nanterre Paris 24 A2
Naoabad Kolkata 14 C2
Napier Mole Karachi 13 B1
Naraina Delhi 10 B1
Nariman Point Mumbai 20 B1
Nariman Pt. Mumbai 20 B1
Närmak Tehran 31 A2
Naruo Osaka 23 A1
Näsby Stockholm 29 A2
Näsbypark Stockholm 29 A2
National Arboretum Washington 33 B3
National Zoological Park Washington 33 B3
Nativity, Basilica of Jerusalem 13 B2
Natolin Warsaw 32 C2
Naucalpan de Juárez Mexico City 18 B1
Naupada Mumbai 20 A2
Navi Mumbai Mumbai 20 A2
Navíglio di Pavia Milan 19 B1
Navíglio Grande Milan 19 B1
Navotas Manila 17 B1
Navy Pier Chicago 9 B3
Nazal Hikmat Beg Baghdad 3 A2
Nazimabad Karachi 13 A2
Nazlet el Simmân Cairo 7 B1
Nea Alexandria Athens 2 B2
Nea Ionia Athens 2 A2
Nea Liosia Athens 2 A2
Nea Smirni Athens 2 B2
Neapoli Athens 2 B2
Near North Chicago 9 B3
Nebušice Prague 25 B1
Nederhorst Amsterdam 2 B3
Nedlitz Berlin 5 B1
Nee Soon Singapore 28 A2
Needham Boston 6 B1
Needham Heights Boston 6 B1
N'ematābād Tehran 31 B2
Nerima Tokyo 30 A3
Nesodden Oslo 23 B3
Nesoddtangen Oslo 23 A3
Nesøya Oslo 23 A2
Neu Aubing Munich 21 B1
Neu Buch Berlin 5 A4
Neu Buchhorst Berlin 5 B5
Neu Fahrland Berlin 5 B1
Neu Lindenberg Berlin 5 A4
Neubiberg Munich 21 B3
Neuenhagen Berlin 5 A4
Neuessling Vienna 32 A3
Neuhausen Munich 21 B2
Neuherberg Munich 21 A2
Neuhönow Berlin 5 A5
Neuilly-Plaisance Paris 24 A4
Neuilly-sur-Marne Paris 24 A4
Neuilly-sur-Seine Paris 24 A2
Neukagran Vienna 32 A2
Neukettenhof Vienna 32 B2
Neukölln Berlin 5 B3
Neuperlach Munich 21 B2
Neuried Munich 21 B1
Neustift am Walde Vienna 32 A1
Neusüssenbrunn Vienna 32 A2
Neuwaldegg Vienna 32 A1
Neve Ya'akov Jerusalem 13 A2
Neves Rio de Janeiro 25 B2
New Baghdād Baghdad 3 B2
New Barakpur Kolkata 14 A2
New Brighton New York 22 C1
New Canada Johannesburg 13 B1
New Canada Dam Johannesburg 13 B1
New Carrollton Washington 33 B4
New Cross London 15 B3
New Delhi Delhi 10 B2
New Dorp New York 22 C1
New Dorp Beach New York 22 C1
New Malden London 15 B2
New Milford New York 22 A1
New Mumbai = Navi Mumbai Mumbai 20 A2
New Territories Hong Kong 12 A1
New Toronto Toronto 31 B1
New Utrecht New York 22 C2
New York New York 22 B3
New York La Guardia ✈ (LGA) New York 22 B2
Newark B. New York 22 B1
Newbattle Edinburgh 11 B3
Newbury Park London 15 A4
Newcraighall Edinburgh 11 B3
Newham □ London 15 A4
Newhaven Edinburgh 11 B2
Newington Edinburgh 11 B2
Newlands Johannesburg 13 B1
Newlands Wellington 33 B1
Newport Melbourne 18 B1
Newton Boston 6 B1
Newtonbrook Toronto 31 A2
Newtongrange Edinburgh 11 B3
Newtonville Boston 6 A1
Newtown Sydney 29 B2
Ngaio Wellington 33 B1
Ngau Chi Wan Hong Kong 12 B2
Ngau Tau Kok Hong Kong 12 B2
Ngauranga Wellington 33 B1
Ngong Shuen Chau Hong Kong 12 B1
Ngua Kok Wan Hong Kong 12 A1
Nhava Sheva Mumbai 20 B2
Niāvarān Tehran 31 A2
Nibra Kolkata 14 B1
Nidāl Baghdad 3 B2
Niddrie Edinburgh 11 B3
Niddrie Melbourne 18 A1
Nieder Neuendorf Berlin 5 A2
Niederschöneweide Berlin 5 B3
Niederschönhausen Berlin 5 A3
Niemeyer Rio de Janeiro 25 B1
Nieuwendam Amsterdam 2 A2
Nihonbashi Tokyo 30 A3
Niipperi Helsinki 11 B1
Nikea Athens 2 B1
Nikolassee Berlin 5 B2
Nikolskiy Moscow 19 B1
Niles Chicago 9 A2
Nimta Kolkata 14 A2
Ninoy Aquino Int. ✈ (MNL) Manila 17 B2
Nippa Tokyo 30 B2
Nippori Tokyo 30 A3
Nishi Osaka 23 A1
Nishinari Osaka 23 B1
Nishinomiya Osaka 23 A1
Nishiyodogawa Osaka 23 A1
Niterói Rio de Janeiro 25 B2
Nockeby Stockholm 29 B1
Noel Park London 15 A3
Nogatino Moscow 19 B3
Nogent-sur-Marne Paris 24 A3
Noida Delhi 10 B2
Noiseau Paris 24 B4
Noisiel Paris 24 A4
Noisy-le-Grand Paris 24 A4
Noisy-le-Roi Paris 24 A1
Noisy-le-Sec Paris 24 A3
Nokkala Helsinki 11 C1
Nomentano Rome 26 B2
Nonakashinden Tokyo 30 A2
Nongminyundong Jiangxisuo Guangzhou 11 B2
Nonhyeon Seoul 27 B2
Nonthaburi Bangkok 3 A1
Noordgesig Johannesburg 13 B1
Noordzeekanaal Amsterdam 2 A1
Nord, Gare du Paris 24 A3
Nordmarka Oslo 23 A3
Nordrand-Siedlung Vienna 32 A2
Nordstrand Oslo 23 A3
Normandale Wellington 33 B2
Norridge Chicago 9 B2
Norrmalm Stockholm 29 A2
North Arlington New York 22 B1
North Bay Village Miami 18 A2
North Bergen New York 22 B1
North Bull I. Dublin 10 A3
North Cheam London 15 B2
North Cray London 15 B4
North Decatur Atlanta 3 B3
North Druid Hills Atlanta 3 B3
North Esk → Edinburgh 11 B2
North Gyle Edinburgh 11 B2
North Hackensack New York 22 A1
North Harbor Manila 17 B1
North Hd. Sydney 29 A2
North Hollywood Los Angeles 16 B2
North Lexington Boston 6 A1
North Miami Miami 18 A2
North Miami Beach Miami 18 A2
North Nazimabad Karachi 13 A2
North Pt. Hong Kong 12 B2
North Queensferry Edinburgh 11 A1
North Quincy Boston 6 B2
North Res. Boston 6 A2
North Riverside Chicago 9 B2
North Saugus Boston 6 A2
North Shore Channel → Chicago 9 B2
North Springfield Washington 33 C2
North Station Boston 6 A2
North Sydney Sydney 29 B2
North Woolwich London 15 A4
North York Toronto 31 A2
Northbridge Sydney 29 A2
Northbridge Park Sydney 29 A2
Northcliff Johannesburg 13 A1
Northcote Melbourne 18 A2
Northeastern University Boston 6 A2
Northern Virginia Regional Park ⌂ Washington 33 B3
Northlake Chicago 9 B1
Northmount Toronto 31 A2
Northolt London 15 A1
Northumberland Heath London 15 B5
Northwestern Station Chicago 9 B3
Northwestern University Chicago 9 A2
Northwood London 15 A1
Northwood Park Toronto 31 A1
Norwood Johannesburg 13 A2
Norwood Park Chicago 9 B2
Noryangjin Seoul 27 B1
Nossa Senhora do Ó São Paulo 27 B1
Nossegem Brussels 6 A3
Notre-Dame Paris 24 A3
Notre-Dame, Basilique Montreal 20 B2
Notre-Dame, Bois Paris 24 B4
Notre-Dame-de-Grace Montreal 20 B2
Notting Hill London 15 A2
Nova Milanese Milan 19 A2
Novate Milanese Milan 19 A1
Novaya Derevnya St. Petersburg 27 A1
Nové Město Prague 25 B2
Novoaleksandrovskoye St. Petersburg 27 B2
Novodevichy Convent Moscow 19 B2
Novogireyevo Moscow 19 B3
Novosaratovka St. Petersburg 27 B3
Nowe-Babice Warsaw 32 B1
Nowe Miasto Warsaw 32 B2
Nöykkiö Helsinki 11 B1
Nueva Atzacoalco Mexico City 18 B2
Nueva Pompeya Buenos Aires 7 C2
Nueva Tenochtitlán Mexico City 18 B2
Nuijala Helsinki 11 B1
Numabukuro Tokyo 30 A2
Nuñez Buenos Aires 7 B2
Nunhead London 15 B3
Ñuñoa Santiago 27 B2
Nusle Prague 25 B2
Nussdorf Vienna 32 A2
Nyanga Cape Town 8 A2
Nymphenburg Munich 21 B2
Nymphenburg, Schloss Munich 21 B2

O

O. R. Tambo Int. ✈ (JNB) Johannesburg 13 A2
Oak Grove Atlanta 3 A3
Oak Hill Boston 6 B1
Oak Lawn Chicago 9 C2
Oak Park Chicago 9 B2
Oak View Washington 33 A4
Oakdale Atlanta 3 A2
Oakland San Francisco 26 B3
Oakland Washington 33 B4
Oaklawn Washington 33 C4
Oakleigh Melbourne 18 B2
Oakton Washington 33 B2
Oakwood Beach New York 22 C1
Oatley Sydney 29 B1
Obalende Lagos 14 B2
Oba's Palace Lagos 14 B2
Oberföhring Munich 21 B2
Oberhaching Munich 21 B2
Oberlaa Vienna 32 B2
Oberlisse Vienna 32 A2
Obermenzing Munich 21 A1
Obermoos Schwaige Munich 21 A1
Oberschleissheim Munich 21 A2
Oberschöneweide Berlin 5 B4
Observatory Johannesburg 13 B2
Óbuda Budapest 7 A2
Obukhovo St. Petersburg 27 B2
Obvodnyy Kanal St. Petersburg 27 B1
Ocean Park Hong Kong 12 B2
Ochota Warsaw 32 B1
Ocoee Orlando 23 A1
Ōdana Tokyo 30 B2
Ōden-Stockach Munich 21 B3
Odilampi Helsinki 11 B1
Odivelas Lisbon 16 A1
Odolany Warsaw 32 B1
Oeiras Lisbon 16 A1
Ofin Lagos 14 A3
Ogawa Tokyo 30 A1
Ogden Park Chicago 9 C2
Ogikubo Tokyo 30 A2
Ogogoro Lagos 14 B2
Ogoyo Lagos 14 B2
Ogudu Lagos 14 A2
O'Hare Int., Chicago ✈ (ORD) Chicago 9 B1
Ohariu Stream → Wellington 33 B1
O'Higgins, Parque Santiago 27 B2
Ōimachi Tokyo 30 B3
Ojota Lagos 14 A2
Okęcie Warsaw 32 B1
Okęcie, Warszawa ✈ (WAW) Warsaw 32 B1
Okelra Lagos 14 B2
Okeogbe Lagos 14 B2
Okhla Delhi 10 B2
Okhta → St. Petersburg 27 B2
Okkervil → St. Petersburg 27 B2
Okrzeszyn Warsaw 32 C2
Oksval Oslo 23 A3
Oktyabrskiy Moscow 19 B2
Okubo Tokyo 30 A3
Ōkura Tokyo 30 B1
Olari Helsinki 11 B1
Olaria Rio de Janeiro 25 B1
Old Admiralty St. Petersburg 27 B1
Old City Jerusalem 13 B2
Old City Shanghai 28 B1
Old City Hall Toronto 31 B2
Old Fort York Toronto 31 B2
Old Harbor Boston 6 B2
Old Town Chicago 9 B3
Old Town Hall = Altes Rathaus Munich 21 B2
Oldbawn Dublin 10 B1
Olgino St. Petersburg 27 A1
Olimpico, Estadio Mexico City 18 C1
Olivais Lisbon 16 A2
Olivar de los Padres Mexico City 18 B1
Olivar del Conde Mexico City 18 B1
Olives, Mt. of Jerusalem 13 B2
Olivia, L. Orlando 23 A1
Olivos Buenos Aires 7 B2
Olona → Milan 19 B1
Olympia, L. Orlando 23 A1
Olympic Stadium = Turner Field Atlanta 3 B2
Olympic Stadium Helsinki 11 B2
Olympique, Stade Montreal 20 A2
Ōmori Tokyo 30 B3
Onisigun Lagos 14 A2
Ontario Science Centre Toronto 31 A2
Ōokayama Tokyo 30 B3
Oostzaan Amsterdam 2 A2
Opa-Locka Miami 18 A1
Opa-Locka ✈ (OPF) Miami 18 A1
Opacz Warsaw 32 B1
Ophirton Johannesburg 13 B2
Oppegård Oslo 23 B3
Oppem Brussels 6 A1
Oppsal Oslo 23 A4
Ora Jerusalem 13 B1
Oradell New York 22 A1
Oradell Res. New York 22 A1
Orange Bowl Stadium Miami 18 B2
Orangi Karachi 13 A1
Ordrup Copenhagen 8 A3
Orech Prague 25 B1
Orient Heights Boston 6 A3
Orlando Orlando 23 A2
Orlando Dam Johannesburg 13 B1
Orlando East Johannesburg 13 B1
Orlando Executive ✈ Orlando 23 A2
Orlando Int. ✈ (MCO) Orlando 23 B3
Orlovista Orlando 23 A2
Orly Paris 24 B3
Orly, Paris ✈ (ORY) Paris 24 B3
Ormesson-sur-Marne Paris 24 B4
Ormond Melbourne 18 B2
Ormøya Oslo 23 A3
Orpington London 15 B4
Ortaköy Istanbul 12 B2
Ortica Milan 19 B2
Oruba Lagos 14 A2
Ōsaka Osaka 23 B2
Ōsaka Castle Osaka 23 A2
Ōsaka Harbour Osaka 23 B1
Ōsaka Itami Int. ✈ (ITM) Osaka 23 A1
Ōsaka Kansai ✈ (KIX) Osaka 23 B2
Ōsaki Tokyo 30 B3
Osasco São Paulo 27 B1
Osdorf Berlin 5 B3
Osdorp Amsterdam 2 A1
Oshodi Lagos 14 A2
Oslo Oslo 23 A3
Oslo ✈ (OSL) Oslo 23 A4
Ōsone Tokyo 30 B2
Osorun Lagos 14 A2
Ospiate Milan 19 A1
Ostankino Moscow 19 B2
Osterley London 15 B1
Osterley Park London 15 B1
Östermalm Stockholm 29 A2
Österskär Stockholm 29 A3
Ostia Malpasso Rome 26 C1
Ostiense Rome 26 B1
Østmarkkapellet Oslo 23 A4
Østøya Oslo 23 A2
Østre Aker Oslo 23 A3
Ōta Tokyo 30 B3
Otaniemi Helsinki 11 B1
Otari Open Air Museum Wellington 33 B1
Otsuka Tokyo 30 A3
Ottakring Vienna 32 A1
Ottávia Rome 26 B1
Ottery Cape Town 8 B2
Ottobrunn Munich 21 B3
Ouderkerk Amsterdam 2 B2
Oulunkylä Helsinki 11 B2
Ourcq, Canal de l' Paris 24 A3
Outer Mission San Francisco 26 B2
Outremont Montreal 20 A2
Overijse Brussels 6 B3
Owhiro Bay Wellington 33 C1
Oworonsoki Lagos 14 A2
Oxgangs Edinburgh 11 B2
Oxon Hill Washington 33 C4
Oyodo Osaka 23 A1
Oyster B. Sydney 29 C1
Oyster Creek Mumbai 20 A2
Oyster Rocks Karachi 13 B2
Ozoir-la-Ferrière Paris 24 B4
Ozone Park New York 22 B2

P

Pacific Heights San Francisco 26 B2
Pacific Manor San Francisco 26 C2
Pacific Palisades Los Angeles 16 B1
Pacifica San Francisco 26 C2
Paco Manila 17 B1
Paco de Arcos Lisbon 16 A1
Paddington London 15 A2

Paddington *Sydney* 29 B2
Paderno *Milan* 19 A1
Pagewood *Sydney* 29 B2
Pagote *Mumbai* 20 B2
Pai, I. do *Rio de Janeiro* 25 B2
Pak Kok *Hong Kong* 12 B1
Pak Kong *Hong Kong* 12 A2
Pakila *Helsinki* 11 B2
Palacio Real *Madrid* 17 B1
Palaiseau *Paris* 24 B2
Palazzolo *Milan* 19 A1
Paleo Faliro *Athens* 2 B2
Palermo *Buenos Aires* 7 B2
Palhais *Lisbon* 16 B2
Palisades Park *New York* 22 A1
Palmer Park *Washington* 33 B4
Palmerston *Dublin* 10 A1
Paloheinä *Helsinki* 11 B2
Palomeras *Madrid* 17 B2
Palos Heights *Chicago* 9 D2
Palos Hills *Chicago* 9 C2
Palos Hills Forest *Chicago* 9 C1
Palos Park *Chicago* 9 C1
Palpara *Kolkata* 14 B2
Panchur *Kolkata* 14 B1
Pandacan *Manila* 17 B2
Pandan, Selat *Singapore* 28 B2
Pandan Res. *Singapore* 28 B2
Pangrati *Athens* 2 B2
Pangsua, Sungei →
Singapore 28 A2
Panihati *Kolkata* 14 A2
Panjang, Bukit *Singapore* 28 A2
Panke → *Berlin* 5 A3
Pankow *Berlin* 5 A3
Pantheon *Rome* 26 B1
Panthersville *Atlanta* 3 B3
Pantin *Paris* 24 A3
Pantitlán *Mexico City* 18 B2
Panvel Cr. → *Mumbai* 20 B2
Paparangi *Wellington* 33 B1
Papiol *Barcelona* 4 A1
Paramount Studios
Los Angeles 16 B3
Paramus *New York* 22 A1
Paranaque *Manila* 17 B1
Paray-Vieille-Poste *Paris* 24 B3
Pardisān Nature Park
Tehran 31 A2
Parel *Mumbai* 20 B1
Pari *São Paulo* 27 B2
Parioli *Rome* 26 B1
Paris *Paris* 24 A3
Paris Orly ✈ (ORY) *Paris* 24 B3
Parje *Mumbai* 20 B2
Pārk-e Āzādegān *Tehran* 31 B2
Pārk-e Mellat *Tehran* 31 A2
Park Ridge *Chicago* 9 A1
Park Royal *London* 15 A2
Parkchester *New York* 22 B2
Parkdale *Toronto* 31 B2
Parkhurst *Johannesburg* 13 A2
Parklawn *Washington* 33 B3
Parkmore *Johannesburg* 13 A2
Parkside *San Francisco* 26 B2
Parktown *Johannesburg* 13 B2
Parkview *Johannesburg* 13 A2
Parkville *New York* 22 C2
Parkwood *Cape Town* 8 B1
Parkwood *Johannesburg* 13 A2
Parow *Cape Town* 8 A2
Parque Chacabuco
Buenos Aires 7 B2
Parque Patricios
Buenos Aires 7 B2
Parramatta → *Sydney* 29 A1
Paşabahçe *Istanbul* 12 B2
Pasadena *Los Angeles* 16 B4
Pasar Minggu *Jakarta* 12 B1
Pasay *Manila* 17 B1
Pascoe Vale *Melbourne* 18 A1
Pasig *Manila* 17 B2
Pasig → *Manila* 17 B2
Pasila *Helsinki* 11 B2
Pasing *Munich* 21 B1
Pasir Panjang *Singapore* 28 B2
Pasir Ris *Singapore* 28 A3
Passaic *New York* 22 A1
Passaic → *New York* 22 B1
Passirana *Milan* 19 A1
Patel Nagar *Delhi* 10 B1
Pateros *Manila* 17 B2
Pathumwan *Bangkok* 3 B2
Patipukur *Kolkata* 14 B2
Patisia *Athens* 2 A2
Paulo E. Virginia, Gruta
Rio de Janeiro 25 B1
Paulshof *Berlin* 5 A5
Paya Lebar *Singapore* 28 A3
Peakhurst *Sydney* 29 B1
Peania *Athens* 2 B3
Pearson Int. Toronto ✈
(YYZ) *Toronto* 31 A1
Peckham *London* 15 B3
Pederstrup *Copenhagen* 8 A2
Pedralbes *Barcelona* 4 A1
Pedregal de San Angel,
Jardines del *Mexico City* 18 C1
Peip'ing = Beijing *Beijing* 4 B1
Peking = Beijing *Beijing* 4 B1
Pelcowizna *Warsaw* 32 B2
Peñalolén *Santiago* 27 B2
Pencarrow Hd. *Wellington* 33 C2
Peng Siang → *Singapore* 28 A2
Penge *London* 15 B3
Penha *Rio de Janeiro* 25 A1
Penicuik *Edinburgh* 11 B2
Penjaringan *Jakarta* 12 A1
Pentagon *Washington* 33 B3
Penzing *Vienna* 32 A1
People's Park *Shanghai* 28 B1
People's Square *Shanghai* 28 B1
Perales del Rio *Madrid* 17 C2
Perchtoldsdorf *Vienna* 32 B1
Perdizes *São Paulo* 27 B2
Peristeri *Athens* 2 A2
Perivale *London* 15 A2
Perk *Brussels* 6 A2
Perlach *Munich* 21 B2
Perlacher Forst *Munich* 21 B2
Pero *Milan* 19 A1
Peropok, Bukit *Singapore* 28 B2
Perovo *Moscow* 19 B3
Pertusella *Milan* 19 A1
Pesagot *Jerusalem* 13 A2
Pesanggrahag, Kali →
Jakarta 12 B1
Peschiera Borromeo *Milan* 19 B2
Pesek, Pulau *Singapore* 28 B2
Pest *Budapest* 7 B2
Pesterzsébet *Budapest* 7 B2
Pesthidegkút *Budapest* 7 A1
Pestimre *Budapest* 7 B3
Pestlörinc *Budapest* 7 B3
Pestújhely *Budapest* 7 A2
Petas *Helsinki* 11 B2
Petone *Wellington* 33 B2
Petrogradskaya Storona
St. Petersburg 27 B2
Petroupoli *Athens* 2 A2
Petrovice *Prague* 25 B3
Petrovskiy Park *Moscow* 19 B2
Petrovsko-
Razumovskoye *Moscow* 19 B2
Pettycur *Edinburgh* 11 A2
Peutie *Brussels* 6 A2
Pfaueninsel *Berlin* 5 B1
Phaya Thai *Bangkok* 3 B2
Phihai *Karachi* 13 A2
Phillip B. *Sydney* 29 B2
Phoenix Park *Dublin* 10 A2
Phra Khanong *Bangkok* 3 B2
Phra Nakhon *Bangkok* 3 B2
Phra Pradaeng *Bangkok* 3 C2
Phranakhon *Bangkok* 3 B1
Pico Rivera *Los Angeles* 16 C4
Piedade *Lisbon* 16 A1
Piedade *Rio de Janeiro* 25 B1
Piedade, Cova da *Lisbon* 16 A2
Piedmont Park *Atlanta* 3 B2
Pierre Elliott Trudeau ✈
(YUL) *Montreal* 20 B1
Pietralata *Rome* 26 B2
Pihlajamäki *Helsinki* 11 B2
Pihlajasaari *Helsinki* 11 C2
Pilares *Rio de Janeiro* 25 B1
Pilton *Edinburgh* 11 B2
Pimmit Hills *Washington* 33 B2
Pine Castle *Orlando* 23 B2
Pine Grove *Toronto* 31 A1
Pine Hills *Orlando* 23 A2
Pinewood Park *Miami* 18 A2
Piney Run → *Washington* 33 B2
Pinganli *Beijing* 4 B2
Pingzhou *Guangzhou* 11 B2
Pinheiros → *São Paulo* 27 B1
Pinjrapur *Karachi* 13 A2
Pinner *London* 15 A1
Pinner Green *London* 15 A1
Pioltello *Milan* 19 A2
Pipinui Pt. *Wellington* 33 A1
Piræus = Pireas *Athens* 2 B1
Piraiévs = Pireas *Athens* 2 B1
Pirajuçara → *São Paulo* 27 B1
Pireas *Athens* 2 B1
Pirinççi *Istanbul* 12 B1
Pirituba *São Paulo* 27 A1
Pirkkola *Helsinki* 11 B2
Pisgat O'mer *Jerusalem* 13 B2
Pisgat Ze'ev *Jerusalem* 13 B2
Pisnice *Prague* 25 C2
Pitampura *Delhi* 10 A1
Pitkäjärvi *Helsinki* 11 B1
Planegg *Munich* 21 B1
Pleasure Island *Orlando* 23 B1
Plumstead *Cape Town* 8 B1
Plumstead *London* 15 B4
Plyushchevo *Moscow* 19 B3
Po Toi *Hong Kong* 12 B2
Po Toi O *Hong Kong* 12 B2
Poasco *Milan* 19 B2
Podbaba *Prague* 25 B2
Podoli *Prague* 25 B2
Pohick Creek →
Washington 33 C2
Pointe-Aux-Trembles
Montreal 20 A2
Poissy *Paris* 24 A1
Pok Fu Lam *Hong Kong* 12 B1
Pokcheong *Seoul* 27 C2
Pokrovsko-Sresnevo
Moscow 19 B1
Polton *Edinburgh* 11 B3
Polvoranca, Parque de
Madrid 17 C1
Polyustrovo *St. Petersburg* 27 B2
Pomprap *Bangkok* 3 B2
Pondok Gede *Jakarta* 12 A2
Pondok Indah *Jakarta* 12 B1
Pont-Viau *Montreal* 20 A1
Pontault-Combault *Paris* 24 B4
Pontinha *Lisbon* 16 A1
Poplar *London* 15 A3
Poppintree *Dublin* 10 A2
Porirua *Wellington* 33 A2
Porirua East *Wellington* 33 A2
Port Melbourne *Melbourne* 18 B1
Port Nicholson *Wellington* 33 B2
Port Richmond *New York* 22 C1
Port Shelter *Hong Kong* 12 A2
Port Union *Toronto* 31 A4
Portage Park *Chicago* 9 B2
Portela, Lisboa ✈ (LIS)
Lisbon 16 A2
Porter, L. *Orlando* 23 A3
Portmarnock *Dublin* 10 A3
Porto Brandão *Lisbon* 16 A1
Pôrto Novo *Rio de Janeiro* 25 A2
Porto Novo Cr. → *Lagos* 14 B2
Portobello *Edinburgh* 11 B3
Portrero *San Francisco* 26 B3
Potomac *Washington* 33 A2
Potrero Pt. *San Francisco* 26 B2
Potsdam *Berlin* 5 B1
Potzham *Munich* 21 B2
Pötzleinsdorf *Vienna* 32 A1
Povoa de Santo Adriao
Lisbon 16 A2
Powązki *Warsaw* 32 B1
Powiśle *Warsaw* 32 B2
Powsin *Warsaw* 32 C2
Powsinek *Warsaw* 32 C2
Poyan Res. *Singapore* 28 A2
Pozuelo de Alarcón *Madrid* 17 B1
Prado, Museo del *Madrid* 17 B1
Prado Churubusco
Mexico City 18 B2
Praga *Warsaw* 32 B2
Prague = Praha *Prague* 25 B2
Praha *Prague* 25 B2
Praha ✈ (PRG) *Prague* 25 B1
Praires, R. des → *Montreal* 20 A2
Prater *Vienna* 32 A2
Precotto *Milan* 19 A2
Prenestino Labicano *Rome* 26 B2
Prenzlauerberg *Berlin* 5 A3
Preston *Melbourne* 18 A1
Pretos Forros, Sa. dos
Rio de Janeiro 25 B1
Préville *Montreal* 20 B3
Přezletice *Prague* 25 B3
Prima Porta *Rome* 26 B1
Primavalle *Rome* 26 B1
Primrose *Johannesburg* 13 B2
Progreso Nacional
Mexico City 18 A2
Prosek *Prague* 25 B3
Prospect Hill Park *Boston* 6 A1
Providencia *Santiago* 27 B2
Průhonice *Prague* 25 C3
Psichiko *Athens* 2 A2
Pudong New Area
Shanghai 28 B2
Pueblo Libre *Lima* 14 B2
Pueblo Nuevo *Barcelona* 4 A2
Pueblo Nuevo *Madrid* 17 B2
Puerto Madero *Buenos Aires* 7 B2
Puhuangyu *Beijing* 4 B2
Puistola *Helsinki* 11 B3
Pukinmäki *Helsinki* 11 B2
Pulkovo Int. ✈ (LED)
St. Petersburg 27 C1
Pullach *Munich* 21 B1
Pullman Historic District
Chicago 9 C3
Pulo Gadung *Jakarta* 12 B2
Pūnak *Tehran* 31 A2
Punchbowl *Sydney* 29 B1
Punde *Mumbai* 20 B2
Punggol *Singapore* 28 A3
Punggol, Sungei →
Singapore 28 A3
Punggol Pt. *Singapore* 28 A3
Punjabi Bagh *Delhi* 10 A1
Puotila *Helsinki* 11 B3
Puteaux *Paris* 24 A2
Putney *London* 15 B2
Putuo *Shanghai* 28 B1
Putxet *Barcelona* 4 A1
Puxi *Shanghai* 28 B1
Pyramids *Cairo* 7 B1
Pyry *Warsaw* 32 C1

Q

Qalandiya *Jerusalem* 13 A2
Qal'eh Morghī *Tehran* 31 B2
Qanā el Ismā'ilīya *Cairo* 7 A2
Qāsemābād *Tehran* 31 A3
Qasr-e Fīrūzeh *Tehran* 31 B3
Qatane *Jerusalem* 13 B1
Qianmen *Beijing* 4 B2
Qinghuayuan *Beijing* 4 B1
Qingningsi *Shanghai* 28 B2
Qolhak *Tehran* 31 A2
Quadraro *Rome* 26 B2
Quaid-i-Azam *Karachi* 13 A1
Quartiere Zingone *Milan* 19 B1
Qubeiba *Jerusalem* 13 A1
Quds *Baghdad* 3 A2
Queen Mary Res. *London* 15 B1
Queen Victoria Market
Melbourne 18 A1
Queensbury *London* 15 A2
Queenscliffe *Sydney* 29 A2
Queensferry *Edinburgh* 11 B1
Queenstown *Singapore* 28 B2
Quellerina *Johannesburg* 13 A1
Queluz *Lisbon* 16 A1
Quezon City *Manila* 17 B2
Quilicura *Santiago* 27 B1
Quincy *Boston* 6 B2
Quincy B. *Boston* 6 B3
Quinta Normal *Santiago* 27 B1
Quinto de Stampi *Milan* 19 B2
Quinto Romano *Milan* 19 B1
Quirinale *Rome* 26 B1

R

R.F.K. Memorial Stadium
Washington 33 B4
Raasdorf *Vienna* 32 A3
Radcliffe College *Boston* 6 A2
Rådhus *Oslo* 23 A3
Radlice *Prague* 25 B2
Radość *Warsaw* 32 B3
Radotín *Prague* 25 C2
Rafat *Jerusalem* 13 A2
Raffles Park *Singapore* 28 B2
Raheny *Dublin* 10 A3
Rahnsdorf *Berlin* 5 B5
Rainham *London* 15 A5
Rajakylä *Helsinki* 11 B3
Rajpura *Delhi* 10 A2
Rákos-patak → *Budapest* 7 B3
Rákoshegy *Budapest* 7 B3
Rákoskeresztúr *Budapest* 7 B3
Rákoskert *Budapest* 7 B3
Rákosliget *Budapest* 7 B3
Rákospalota *Budapest* 7 A2
Rákosszentmihály *Budapest* 7 A2
Rakówiec *Warsaw* 32 B1
Ram *Jerusalem* 13 A2
Rām Allāh *Jerusalem* 13 A2
Ramadān *Baghdad* 3 B2
Ramakrishna Puram *Delhi* 10 B1
Rāmallāh = Rām Allāh
Jerusalem 13 A2
Ramanathpur *Kolkata* 14 A1
Ramat Allon *Jerusalem* 13 B2
Ramat Eshkol *Jerusalem* 13 B2
Ramat Razi'el *Jerusalem* 13 B1
Ramat Shafet *Jerusalem* 13 B2
Rambler Channel
Hong Kong 12 A1
Ramenki *Moscow* 19 B1
Ramersdorf *Munich* 21 B2
Rameses Station *Cairo* 7 A2
Ramos *Rio de Janeiro* 25 B1
Ramos Mejía *Buenos Aires* 7 B1
Ramot *Jerusalem* 13 B2
Rampur *Delhi* 10 A2
Ramsgate *Sydney* 29 B1
Rand ✈ (QRA)
Johannesburg 13 B2
Randalls I. *New York* 22 B2
Randburg *Johannesburg* 13 A1
Randhart *Johannesburg* 13 B2
Randpark Ridge
Johannesburg 13 A1
Randwick *Sydney* 29 B2
Ranelagh *Dublin* 10 A2
Rangpuri *Delhi* 10 B1
Rannersdorf *Vienna* 32 B2
Ransbèche *Brussels* 6 B2
Ransdorp *Amsterdam* 2 A2
Ranvad *Mumbai* 20 B2
Raposo *Lisbon* 16 A1
Rastaala *Helsinki* 11 B1
Rastila *Helsinki* 11 B3
Raszyn *Warsaw* 32 C1
Rathfarnham *Dublin* 10 B2
Ratho *Edinburgh* 11 B1
Ratho Station *Edinburgh* 11 B1
Rato *Lisbon* 16 A2
Ravelston *Edinburgh* 11 B2
Rawamangun *Jakarta* 12 B2
Rayners Lane *London* 15 A1
Raynes Park *London* 15 B2
Raypur *Kolkata* 14 C2
Real Felipe, Fuerte *Lima* 14 B2
Reams, L. *Orlando* 23 B1
Recoleta *Buenos Aires* 7 B2
Recoleta *Santiago* 27 B2
Red Fort = Lal Qila *Delhi* 10 B2
Red Square *Moscow* 19 B2
Redbridge □ *London* 15 A4
Redfern *Sydney* 29 B2
Redwood *Wellington* 33 B1
Refshaleøen *Copenhagen* 8 A3
Regents Park *Johannesburg* 13 B2
Regent's Park *London* 15 A3
Rego Park *New York* 22 B2
Reinickendorf *Berlin* 5 A3
Rekola *Helsinki* 11 B3
Rembertów *Warsaw* 32 B2
Rembrandtpark *Amsterdam* 2 A2
Remedios, Parque
Nacional de los △
Mexico City 18 B1
Remedios de Escalada
Buenos Aires 7 C2
Rémola, Estany del
Barcelona 4 B1
Renca *Santiago* 27 B1
Rennemoulin *Paris* 24 A1
Řeporyje *Prague* 25 B1
Repulse Bay *Hong Kong* 12 B2
Repy *Prague* 25 B1
Residenz *Munich* 21 B2
Reston *Washington* 33 B2
Retiro *Buenos Aires* 7 B2
Retiro *Madrid* 17 B1
Retiro, Puerto *Buenos Aires* 7 B2
Retreat *Cape Town* 8 B1
Reutov *Moscow* 19 B4
Réveillon → *Paris* 24 B4
Revere *Boston* 6 A2
Rexdale *Toronto* 31 A1
Reynosa Tamaulipas
Mexico City 18 A1
Rho *Milan* 19 A1
Rhodes *Sydney* 29 A1
Rhodon *Paris* 24 B1
Rhodon → *Paris* 24 B1
Rialto Towers *Melbourne* 18 A1
Ribeira *Rio de Janeiro* 25 A1
Ricarda, Estany de la
Barcelona 4 B1
Richmond *Melbourne* 18 A2
Richmond *San Francisco* 26 B2
Richmond Hill *New York* 22 B2
Richmond Park *London* 15 B2
Richmond-upon-
Thames □ *London* 15 B2
Ridge, The *Delhi* 10 B2
Ridgefield *New York* 22 A2
Ridgefield Park *New York* 22 A1
Ridgewood *New York* 22 B2
Riem *Munich* 21 B3
Riesenrad *Vienna* 32 A2
Rijksmuseum *Amsterdam* 2 A2
Rikers I. *New York* 22 B2
Rimac *Lima* 14 B2
Ringsend *Dublin* 10 A2
Rinkeby *Stockholm* 29 A1
Rio Comprido *Rio de Janeiro* 25 B1
Rio de Janeiro *Rio de Janeiro* 25 B1
Rio de Janeiro Galeão ✈
(GIG) *Rio de Janeiro* 25 A1
Rio de Mouro *Lisbon* 16 A1
Ripollet *Barcelona* 4 A1
Ris *Oslo* 23 A3
Risby *Copenhagen* 8 A1
Rishra *Kolkata* 14 A2
Ritchie *Washington* 33 B4
Rithala *Delhi* 10 A1
Rive Sud, Canal de la
Montreal 20 B2
River Edge *New York* 22 A1
River Forest *Chicago* 9 B2
River Grove *Chicago* 9 B1
Riverdale *New York* 22 A2
Riverdale *Washington* 33 B4
Riverdale Park *Toronto* 31 A2
Riverlea *Johannesburg* 13 B1
Riverside *Chicago* 9 C2
Riverwood *Sydney* 29 B1
Rivière-des-Prairies
Montreal 20 A2
Rixensart *Brussels* 6 B3
Riyad *Baghdad* 3 B2
Rizal Park *Manila* 17 B1
Rizal Stadium *Manila* 17 B1
Røa *Oslo* 23 A2
Robbins *Chicago* 9 D2
Robertsham *Johannesburg* 13 B2
Rochelle Park *New York* 22 A1
Rock Cr. → *Washington* 33 B3
Rock Creek Park
Washington 33 B3
Rock Pt. *Wellington* 33 A1
Rockaway Beach *New York* 22 C3
Rockaway Pt. *New York* 22 C2
Rockdale *Sydney* 29 B1
Rockefeller Center
New York 22 B2
Rocky Run → *Washington* 33 B2
Roda, Gezîret el *Cairo* 7 A2
Roda I. = Roda, Gezîret el
Cairo 7 A2
Rodaon *Vienna* 32 B1
Rødovre *Copenhagen* 8 A2
Rodrigo de Freitas, L.
Rio de Janeiro 25 B1
Roehampton *London* 15 B2
Rogers Park *Chicago* 9 A3
Roihuvuori *Helsinki* 11 B3
Roissy-en-Brie *Paris* 24 B4
Rokytka → *Prague* 25 B3
Roma *Rome* 26 B1
Roma Urbe ✈ *Rome* 26 B2
Római-Fürdö *Budapest* 7 A2
Romainville *Paris* 24 A3
Roman Forum = Foro
Romano *Rome* 26 B1
Romano Banco *Milan* 19 B1
Rome = Roma *Rome* 26 B1
Romema *Jerusalem* 13 B2
Romford *London* 15 A5
Ronald Reagan National,
Washington ✈ (DCA)
Washington 33 B3
Rondebosch *Cape Town* 8 A1
Roppongi *Tokyo* 30 B3
Rose, L. *Orlando* 23 A1
Rose Bowl *Los Angeles* 16 B4
Rose Hill *Washington* 33 C3
Rosebank *Johannesburg* 13 A2
Rosebank *New York* 22 C1
Rosebery *Sydney* 29 B2
Rosedal La Candelaria
Mexico City 18 B2
Roseland *Chicago* 9 C3
Rosemead *Los Angeles* 16 B4
Rosemont *Chicago* 9 B1
Rosemont *Montreal* 20 A2
Rosenborg Slot *Copenhagen* 8 A3
Rosenthal *Berlin* 5 A3
Rosettenville *Johannesburg* 13 B2
Rosewell *Edinburgh* 11 B3
Rosherville Dam
Johannesburg 13 B2
Rösjön *Stockholm* 29 A2
Roslags-Näsby *Stockholm* 29 A2
Roslin *Edinburgh* 11 B3
Roslindale *Boston* 6 B2
Rosny-sous-Bois *Paris* 24 A4
Rosslyn *Washington* 33 B3
Rosyth *Edinburgh* 11 A1
Rotherhithe *London* 15 B3
Rothneusiedl *Vienna* 32 B2
Rothschmaige *Munich* 21 A1
Rouge Hill *Toronto* 31 A4
Round I. *Hong Kong* 12 B2
Roxbury *Boston* 6 B2
Roxeth *London* 15 A1
Royal Botanic Gardens
Edinburgh 11 B2
Royal Observatory
Edinburgh 11 B2
Royal Palace = Kungliga
Slottet *Stockholm* 29 B2
Royal Park *Melbourne* 18 A1
Röylä *Helsinki* 11 B1
Rozas, Portilleros de las
Madrid 17 B1
Roztoky *Prague* 25 B2
Rozzano *Milan* 19 B1
Rubí → *Barcelona* 4 A1
Rudolfsheim *Vienna* 32 A2
Rudolfshöhe *Berlin* 5 A5
Rudow *Berlin* 5 B3
Rueil-Malmaison *Paris* 24 A2
Ruisbroek *Brussels* 6 B1
Ruislip *London* 15 A1
Rumelihisarı *Istanbul* 12 B2
Rungis *Paris* 24 B3
Rusāfa *Baghdad* 3 A2
Rush Green *London* 15 A5
Russa *Kolkata* 14 C2
Rutherford *New York* 22 B1
Ruzyně *Prague* 25 B1
Ruzyne, Praha ✈ (PRG)
Prague 25 B1
Rybatskaya *St. Petersburg* 27 B2
Rydboholm *Stockholm* 29 A3
Ryde *Sydney* 29 A1
Ryogoku *Tokyo* 30 A3
Rzhevka *St. Petersburg* 27 B3

S

Sa'ādatābād *Tehran* 31 A2
Saadūn *Baghdad* 3 B2
Saavedra *Buenos Aires* 7 B2
Saboli *Delhi* 10 A2
Sabugo *Lisbon* 16 A1
Sabzi Mand *Delhi* 10 A2
Sacavém *Lisbon* 16 A2
Saclay *Paris* 24 B2
Saclay, Étang de *Paris* 24 B1
Sacomã *São Paulo* 27 B2
Sacré Cœur *Paris* 24 A3
Sacrow *Berlin* 5 B1
Sacrower See *Berlin* 5 B1
Sadang *Seoul* 27 C1
Saddle → *New York* 22 A1
Saddle Brook *New York* 22 A1
Sadr *Karachi* 13 A2
Sadr City *Baghdad* 3 A2
Sadyba *Warsaw* 32 B2
Safdar Jang's Tomb *Delhi* 10 B2
Saft el Laban *Cairo* 7 A2
Saganashkee Slough
Chicago 9 C1
Sagene *Oslo* 23 A3
Sagrada Família, Templo
de *Barcelona* 4 A2
Sahar, Mumbai ✈ (BOM)
Mumbai 20 A2
Sai Kung *Hong Kong* 12 A2
Sai Wan Ho *Hong Kong* 12 B2
Sai Ying Pun *Hong Kong* 12 B1
St-Aubin *Paris* 24 B1
St-Cloud *Paris* 24 A2
St-Cyr-l'École *Paris* 24 B1
St-Cyr-l'École ✈ *Paris* 24 B1
St-Denis *Paris* 24 A3
St-Germain, Forêt de *Paris* 24 A1
St-Germain-en-Laye *Paris* 24 A1
St-Gilles *Brussels* 6 B2
St. Helier *London* 15 B2
St-Hubert *Montreal* 20 B3
St. Hubert, Galeries
Royales *Brussels* 6 A2
St. Isaac's Cathedral
St. Petersburg 27 B1
St-Jacques → *Montreal* 20 B3
St-Joost-Ten-Node *Brussels* 6 A2
St. Kilda *Melbourne* 18 B1
St-Lambert *Montreal* 20 A3
St-Lambert *Paris* 24 B1
St-Laurent *Montreal* 20 A1
St-Léonard *Montreal* 20 A2
St. Magelungen *Stockholm* 29 B2
St-Mandé *Paris* 24 A3
St. Margaret's *Dublin* 10 A2
St-Martin, Bois *Paris* 24 B4
St. Mary Cray *London* 15 B4
St-Maur-des-Fossés *Paris* 24 B3
St-Maurice *Paris* 24 B3
St-Michel *Montreal* 20 A2
St. Nikolaus-Kirken
Prague 25 B2
St-Ouen *Paris* 24 A3
St. Paul's Cray *London* 15 B4
St. Peters *Sydney* 29 B2
St. Petersburg = Sankt-
Peterburg *St. Petersburg* 27 B1
St-Pierre *Montreal* 20 B2
St-Pieters Leew *Brussels* 6 B1
St-Quentin, Étang de *Paris* 24 B1
St-Stevens-Woluwe *Brussels* 6 A2
St-Vincent-de-Paul
Montreal 20 A2
St. Xavier University
Chicago 9 C2
Ste-Catherine *Montreal* 20 B2
Ste-Hélène, Î. *Montreal* 20 A2
Saiwai *Tokyo* 30 B3
Sakai *Osaka* 23 B1
Sakai Harbour *Osaka* 23 B1
Sakra, Pulau *Singapore* 28 B2
Salam *Baghdad* 3 A2
Salamanca *Madrid* 17 B1
Sallynoggin *Dublin* 10 B3
Salmannsdorf *Vienna* 32 A1
Salmedina *Madrid* 17 C2
Salomea *Warsaw* 32 B1
Salsette I. *Mumbai* 20 A2
Salt Lake City = Bidhan
Nagar *Kolkata* 14 B2
Salt River *Cape Town* 8 A1
Salt Water L. *Kolkata* 14 B2
Saltsjö-Duvnäs *Stockholm* 29 B3
Samatya *Istanbul* 12 C1
Sampaloc *Manila* 17 B1
Samphan Thawong
Bangkok 3 B2
Samseon *Seoul* 27 B2
Samuel Smith Park
Toronto 31 B1
Samut Prakan *Bangkok* 3 B2
San Andrés *Barcelona* 4 A2
San Angel *Mexico City* 18 B1
San Basilio *Rome* 26 B2
San Borja *Lima* 14 B2
San Bóvio *Milan* 19 B2
San Bruno, Pt.
San Francisco 26 C2
San Bruno Mountain
State Park ⌂
San Francisco 26 B2
San Cristobal *Buenos Aires* 7 B2
San Cristobal *Madrid* 17 B2
San Cristóbal, Cerro
Santiago 27 B2
San Cristoforo *Milan* 19 B1
San Donato Milanese
Milan 19 B2
San Francisco *San Francisco* 26 B2
San Francisco B.
San Francisco 26 B3
San Francisco Culhuacán
Mexico City 18 C2
San Fruttuoso *Milan* 19 A2
San Gabriel *Los Angeles* 16 B4
San Gabriel → *Los Angeles* 16 C4
San Giuliano Milanese
Milan 19 B2
San Isidro *Lima* 14 B2
San Jerónimo Lídice
Mexico City 18 C1
San Joaquin *Santiago* 27 B2
San José Rio Hondo
Mexico City 18 B1
San Juan → *Manila* 17 B2
San Juan de Aragón
Mexico City 18 B2
San Juan de Aragón,
Parque *Mexico City* 18 B2
San Juan de Lurigancho
Lima 14 A2
San Juan del Monte *Manila* 17 B2
San Juan Ixtacala
Mexico City 18 A1
San Just Desvern *Barcelona* 4 A1
San Justo *Buenos Aires* 7 C1
San Lorenzo Tezonco
Mexico City 18 C2
San Luis *Lima* 14 B2
San Marino *Los Angeles* 16 B4
San Martin *Barcelona* 4 A2
San Martin de Porras *Lima* 14 B2
San Mateo Tlaltenango
Mexico City 18 B1
San Miguel *Lima* 14 B2
San Miguel *Santiago* 27 B2
San Nicolás *Buenos Aires* 7 B2
San Onófrio *Rome* 26 B1
San Pedro Martir *Barcelona* 4 A1
San Pedro Zacatenco
Mexico City 18 A2
San Pietro, Piazza *Rome* 26 B1
San Po Kong *Hong Kong* 12 A2
San Rafael Chamapa
Mexico City 18 B1
San Rafael Hills *Los Angeles* 16 A3
San Roque *Manila* 17 B2
San Siro *Milan* 19 B1
San Souci *Sydney* 29 B1
San Telmo *Buenos Aires* 7 B2
San Vicenc dels Horts
Barcelona 4 A1
Sandown *Johannesburg* 13 A2
Sandown Park Races
London 15 B1
Sandton *Johannesburg* 13 A2
Sandvika *Oslo* 23 A2
Sandyford *Dublin* 10 B2
Sandymount *Dublin* 10 B2
Sangenjaya *Tokyo* 30 B2
Sanggye *Seoul* 27 B2
Sangley Pt. *Manila* 17 C1
Sankrail *Kolkata* 14 B1
Sankt-Peterburg
St. Petersburg 27 B1
Sankt Veit *Vienna* 32 A1
Sanlihe *Beijing* 4 B1
Sanlintang *Shanghai* 28 C1
Sans *Barcelona* 4 A1
Sanssouci *Berlin* 5 B1
Sant Ambrogio, Basilica
di *Milan* 19 B2
Sant Boi de Llobregat
Barcelona 4 A1
Sant Cugat *Barcelona* 4 A1
Sant Feliu de Llobregat
Barcelona 4 A1
Sant Joan Despi *Barcelona* 4 A1
Santa Ana *Manila* 17 B2
Santa Anita Park
Los Angeles 16 B4
Santa Coloma de
Gramenet *Barcelona* 4 A2
Santa Cruz *Manila* 17 B1
Santa Cruz *Mumbai* 20 A1
Santa Cruz, I. de
Rio de Janeiro 25 B2
Santa Cruz de Olorde
Barcelona 4 A1
Santa Efigênia *São Paulo* 27 B2
Santa Elena *Manila* 17 B2
Santa Elena del Gomero
Santiago 27 B1
Santa Eulalia *Barcelona* 4 A2
Santa Fe Springs
Los Angeles 16 C4
Santa Iria da Azóia *Lisbon* 16 A2
Santa Julia *Santiago* 27 C2
Santa Monica *Los Angeles* 16 B2
Santa Monica Mts.
Los Angeles 16 B2
Santa Rosa de Locobe
Santiago 27 B2
Santa Teresa de la Ovalle
Santiago 27 B1
Santahamina *Helsinki* 11 C3
Santana *São Paulo* 27 A2
Santeny *Paris* 24 B4
Santiago *Santiago* 27 B2
Santiago Benitez ✈ (SCL)
Santiago 27 B1
Santiago de Surco *Lima* 14 B2
Santo Amaro *Lisbon* 16 A1
Santo Amaro *São Paulo* 27 B1
Santo Andre *Lisbon* 16 B2
Santo Antão do Tojal
Lisbon 16 A2
Santo António, Qta. de
Lisbon 16 B1
Santo Tomas, Univ. of
Manila 17 B1
Santos Dumont ✈ (SDU)
Rio de Janeiro 25 B2
Santoshpur *Kolkata* 14 B1
Santragachi *Kolkata* 14 B1
Santry *Dublin* 10 A2
Sanyuanli *Guangzhou* 11 B2
São Caetano do Sul
São Paulo 27 B2
São Conrado *Rio de Janeiro* 25 C1
São Cristóvão *Rio de Janeiro* 25 B1
São Jorge, Castelo de
Lisbon 16 A2
São Julião do Tojal *Lisbon* 16 A2
São Paulo *São Paulo* 27 B2
São Paulo Congonhas ✈
(CGH) *São Paulo* 27 B2
Sapa *Kolkata* 14 B1
Sapateiro, Cor. do →
São Paulo 27 B1
Sarandi *Buenos Aires* 7 C2
Saraswati → *Kolkata* 14 A1
Sarecky potok → *Prague* 25 B2
Sarimbun *Singapore* 28 A2
Sarimbun Res. *Singapore* 28 A2
Sarıyer *Istanbul* 12 A2
Sarriá *Barcelona* 4 A1
Sarsuna *Kolkata* 14 C1
Sartrouville *Paris* 24 A2
Sasad *Budapest* 7 B2
Sashalom *Budapest* 7 A3
Saska *Warsaw* 32 B2
Satalice *Prague* 25 B3
Satgachi *Kolkata* 14 B2
Satpukur *Kolkata* 14 B2
Sätra *Stockholm* 29 B1
Saúde *São Paulo* 27 B2
Saugus *Boston* 6 A2
Saugus → *Boston* 6 A2
Sault-au-Récollet *Montreal* 20 A2
Sausalito *San Francisco* 26 A2
Sawah Besar *Jakarta* 12 A1
Scald Law *Edinburgh* 11 B2
Scarborough *Toronto* 31 A3
Scarborough Bluffs *Toronto* 31 A3
Sceaux *Paris* 24 B2
Schaerbeek *Brussels* 6 A2
Scharfenberg *Berlin* 5 A2
Schiller Park *Chicago* 9 B1
Schiller Woods *Chicago* 9 B1
Schiphol, Amsterdam ✈
(AMS) *Amsterdam* 2 B1
Schlachtensee *Berlin* 5 B2
Schlossgarten *Berlin* 5 A2
Schmargendorf *Berlin* 5 B2
Schönblick *Berlin* 5 B5
Schönbrunn *Vienna* 32 A1
Schöneberg *Berlin* 5 B3
Schönefeld *Berlin* 5 B4
Schöneiche *Berlin* 5 B5
Schönwalde *Berlin* 5 A1
Schulzendorf *Berlin* 5 A2
Schwabing *Munich* 21 B2
Schwanebeck *Berlin* 5 A4
Schwanenwerder *Berlin* 5 B2
Schwarzlackenau *Vienna* 32 A2
Schwechat *Vienna* 32 B2
Schwechat, Wien ✈ (VIE)
Vienna 32 B3
Science and Industry,
Museum of *Chicago* 9 C3
Scitrek Museum *Atlanta* 3 B2
Scopus, Mt. *Jerusalem* 13 B2
Scottdale *Atlanta* 3 B3
Scutari = Üsküdar *Istanbul* 12 B2
Sea Point *Cape Town* 8 A1
Seabrook *Washington* 33 B5
Seacliff *San Francisco* 26 B2
Seaforth *Sydney* 29 A2
Seagate *New York* 22 C1
Seat Pleasant *Washington* 33 B4
Seaview *Wellington* 33 B2
SeaWorld *Orlando* 23 B2
Šeberov *Prague* 25 B3
Secaucus *New York* 22 B1
Seddinsee *Berlin* 5 B5
Seeberg *Berlin* 5 A5
Seeburg *Berlin* 5 A1
Seefeld *Berlin* 5 A5
Seegefeld *Berlin* 5 A1
Seehof *Berlin* 5 B2
Segeltorp *Stockholm* 29 B1
Segrate *Milan* 19 B2
Seguro *Milan* 19 B1
Seixal *Lisbon* 16 B2
Selby *Johannesburg* 13 B2
Seletar, Pulau *Singapore* 28 A3
Seletar Hills *Singapore* 28 A3
Seletar Res. *Singapore* 28 A2
Selhurst *London* 15 B3
Sembawang *Singapore* 28 A2
Senago *Milan* 19 A1
Sendling *Munich* 21 B2
Senju *Tokyo* 30 A3
Senriyama *Osaka* 23 A2
Sentosa *Singapore* 28 B2
Seobinggo *Seoul* 27 B1
Seocho *Seoul* 27 C1
Seodaemun *Seoul* 27 B1
Seokkwan *Seoul* 27 B2
Seongbuk *Seoul* 27 B2
Seongdong *Seoul* 27 B2
Seongsu *Seoul* 27 B2
Seoul *Seoul* 27 B2
Seoul National University
Seoul 27 C1
Seoul Tower *Seoul* 27 B1
Sepolia *Athens* 2 A2
Sepulveda Dam Rec.
Area ⌂ *Los Angeles* 16 A2
Serangoon *Singapore* 28 A3
Serangoon, Pulau
Singapore 28 A3
Serangoon, Sungei →
Singapore 28 A3
Serangoon Harbour
Singapore 28 A3
Seraya, Pulau *Singapore* 28 B2
Serebryanka → *Moscow* 19 B3
Serramonte *San Francisco* 26 C2
Sesto San Giovanni *Milan* 19 A2
Sesto Ulteriano *Milan* 19 B2
Setagaya *Tokyo* 30 B2
Seter *Oslo* 23 A3
Setia Budi *Jakarta* 12 B1
Settebagni *Rome* 26 A2
Settecamini *Rome* 26 B2
Séttimo Milanese *Milan* 19 B1
Settsu *Osaka* 23 A2
Seutula *Helsinki* 11 A2
Seven Corners *Washington* 33 B3
Seven Kings *London* 15 A4
Sévesco → *Milan* 19 A1
Sevran *Paris* 24 A4
Sewri *Mumbai* 20 B2
Sforzesco, Castello *Milan* 19 B2
Sha Kok Mei *Hong Kong* 12 A2
Sha Tin *Hong Kong* 12 A2
Sha Tin Wai *Hong Kong* 12 A2
Sha'ar Binyamin *Jerusalem* 13 A2
Shabrâmant *Cairo* 7 B2
Shah Mosque *Tehran* 31 A2
Shahdara *Delhi* 10 A2
Shahe *Guangzhou* 11 B2
Shahr-e Rey *Tehran* 31 B2
Shahrak-e Golshahr
Tehran 31 B1
Shahrak-e Qods *Tehran* 31 A2
Shaikh Aomar *Baghdad* 3 A2
Shakurbasti *Delhi* 10 A1
Shalkiya *Kolkata* 14 B2
Sham Shui Po *Hong Kong* 12 B1
Shamapur *Delhi* 10 A1
Shamian *Guangzhou* 11 B2
Shan Mei *Hong Kong* 12 A2
Shanghai *Shanghai* 28 B2
Shanghai Hongqiao ✈
(SHA) *Shanghai* 28 B1
Shanghai Pudong ✈
(PVG) *Shanghai* 28 B2
Shankill *Dublin* 10 B3
Sharp I. *Hong Kong* 12 A2
Shastrinagar *Delhi* 10 A2
Shau Kei Wan *Hong Kong* 12 B2
Shawocun *Beijing* 4 B1
Shayuan *Guangzhou* 11 B2
Sheen, L. *Orlando* 23 B1
Sheepshead Bay *New York* 22 C2
Shek O *Hong Kong* 12 B2
Shelter I. *Hong Kong* 12 B2
Shepherds Bush *London* 15 A2
Shepperton *London* 15 B1
Sheremetyevo ✈ (SVO)
Moscow 19 A2
Sherman Oaks *Los Angeles* 16 B2
Sherman Park *Chicago* 9 C2
Sherwood, L. *Orlando* 23 A2
Shet Bandar *Mumbai* 20 B2
Sheung Fa Shan *Hong Kong* 12 A1
Sheung Lau Wan
Hong Kong 12 B2
Sheung Wan *Hong Kong* 12 B1
Sheva *Mumbai* 20 B2
Sheva Nhava *Mumbai* 20 B2
Shiba *Tokyo* 30 B3
Shibpur *Kolkata* 14 B1
Shibuya *Tokyo* 30 B3
Shimogawara *Tokyo* 30 B1
Shimosalo *Tokyo* 30 A2
Shimoshakujii *Tokyo* 30 A2
Shinagawa *Tokyo* 30 B3
Shing Mun Res. *Hong Kong* 12 A1
Shinjuku *Tokyo* 30 A3
Shinjuku National
Garden *Tokyo* 30 A3
Shinkoiwa *Tokyo* 30 A4
Shinnakano *Tokyo* 30 A3
Shipai *Guangzhou* 11 B3
Shirinashi → *Osaka* 23 B1
Shirogane *Tokyo* 30 B3
Shitennoji Temple *Osaka* 23 B2
Shiweitang *Guangzhou* 11 B2
Shogunle *Lagos* 14 A2
Shomolu *Lagos* 14 A2
Shooters Hill *London* 15 B4
Shoreditch *London* 15 A3
Shortlands *London* 15 B4
Shu'afat *Jerusalem* 13 B2
Shubrâ *Cairo* 7 A2
Shubrâ el Kheima *Cairo* 7 A2
Shuikuo *Guangzhou* 11 A2
Sidcup *London* 15 B4
Siebenhirten *Vienna* 32 B1
Siedlung *Berlin* 5 A1
Siekierki *Warsaw* 32 B2
Sielce *Warsaw* 32 B2
Siemensstadt *Berlin* 5 A2
Sierra Madre *Los Angeles* 16 B4
Sievering *Vienna* 32 A2
Sighthill *Edinburgh* 11 B2
Signal Hill *Cape Town* 8 A1
Siheung *Seoul* 27 C1
Sikátorpuszta *Budapest* 7 A3
Silampur *Delhi* 10 B2
Sillim *Seoul* 27 C1
Silver, L. *Orlando* 23 A2
Silver Hill *Washington* 33 C4
Silver Spring *Washington* 33 A3
Silvermine Nature
Reserve *Cape Town* 8 B1
Silvolantekojärvi *Helsinki* 11 B2
Simei *Singapore* 28 B3
Simla *Kolkata* 14 B2
Simmering *Vienna* 32 A2
Simmering Heide *Vienna* 32 A2
Simonkylä *Helsinki* 11 B3
Sinchon *Seoul* 27 B1
Sindang *Seoul* 27 B2
Singapore ■ *Singapore* 28 B3
Singapore, Univ. of
Singapore 28 B2
Singapore Changi ✈ (SIN)
Singapore 28 A3
Sinki, Selat *Singapore* 28 B2
Sinsa *Seoul* 27 B2
Sint-Genesius-Rode *Brussels* 6 B2
Sion *Mumbai* 20 A2
Sipson *London* 15 B1
Siqeil *Cairo* 7 A1
Şişli *Istanbul* 12 B1
Site of Former World
Trade Center = Ground
Zero *New York* 22 B1
Skansen *Stockholm* 29 B2
Skärholmen *Stockholm* 29 B1
Skarpäng *Stockholm* 29 A2
Skarpnäck *Stockholm* 29 B2
Skaryszewski, Park
Warsaw 32 B2
Skokie *Chicago* 9 A2
Skokie → *Chicago* 9 A2
Skokie Heritage Museum
Chicago 9 A2
Skoklefall *Oslo* 23 A3
Sköndal *Stockholm* 29 B2
Skovlunde *Copenhagen* 8 A2
Skovshoved *Copenhagen* 8 A3
Skuru *Stockholm* 29 B3
Sky Lake *Orlando* 23 B2
Skyland *Atlanta* 3 A3
Slade Green *London* 15 B5
Slemmestad *Oslo* 23 B1
Slependen *Oslo* 23 A2
Slipi *Jakarta* 12 B1
Slivenec *Prague* 25 B2
Sloten *Amsterdam* 2 A1
Sloterdijk *Amsterdam* 2 A1
Sloterpark *Amsterdam* 2 A1
Sluhy *Prague* 25 A3
Służew *Warsaw* 32 B2
Służewiec *Warsaw* 32 B2
Smíchov *Prague* 25 B2
Smith Forest Preserve
Chicago 9 B2
Smolny *St. Petersburg* 27 B2
Smolny Cathedral
St. Petersburg 27 B2
Snake Creek Canal *Miami* 18 A2
Snakeden Branch →
Washington 33 B1
Snarøya *Oslo* 23 A2
Snättringe *Stockholm* 29 B1
Søborg *Copenhagen* 8 A2
Sobreda *Lisbon* 16 B1
Söderby *Stockholm* 29 A3
Södermalm *Stockholm* 29 B2
Sodpur *Kolkata* 14 A2
Soeurs, Î. des *Montreal* 20 B2
Sognsvatn *Oslo* 23 A3
Soignes, Forêt de *Brussels* 6 B2
Sok Kwu Wan *Hong Kong* 12 B1
Sokolniki *Moscow* 19 B3
Sokolniki Park *Moscow* 19 B3
Sokołów *Warsaw* 32 C1
Solalinden *Munich* 21 B3
Sollentuna *Stockholm* 29 A1
Solln *Munich* 21 B2
Solna *Stockholm* 29 A1
Somerset *Washington* 33 B3
Somerville *Boston* 6 A2
Somes I. *Wellington* 33 B2
Sonari *Mumbai* 20 B2
Sønderso *Copenhagen* 8 A2
Songpa *Seoul* 27 B2
Sony Picture Studio
Los Angeles 16 B2

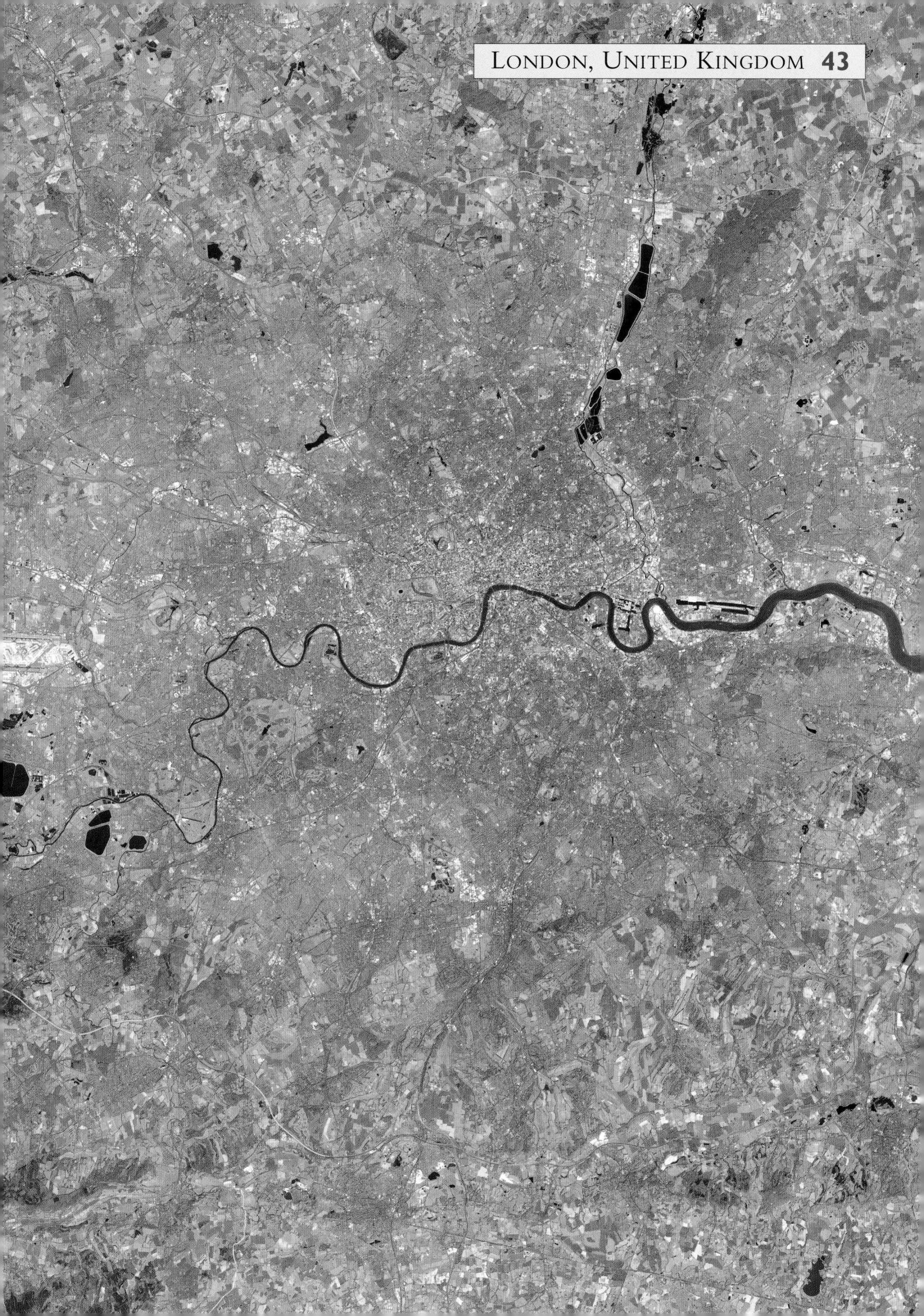

WORLD MAPS

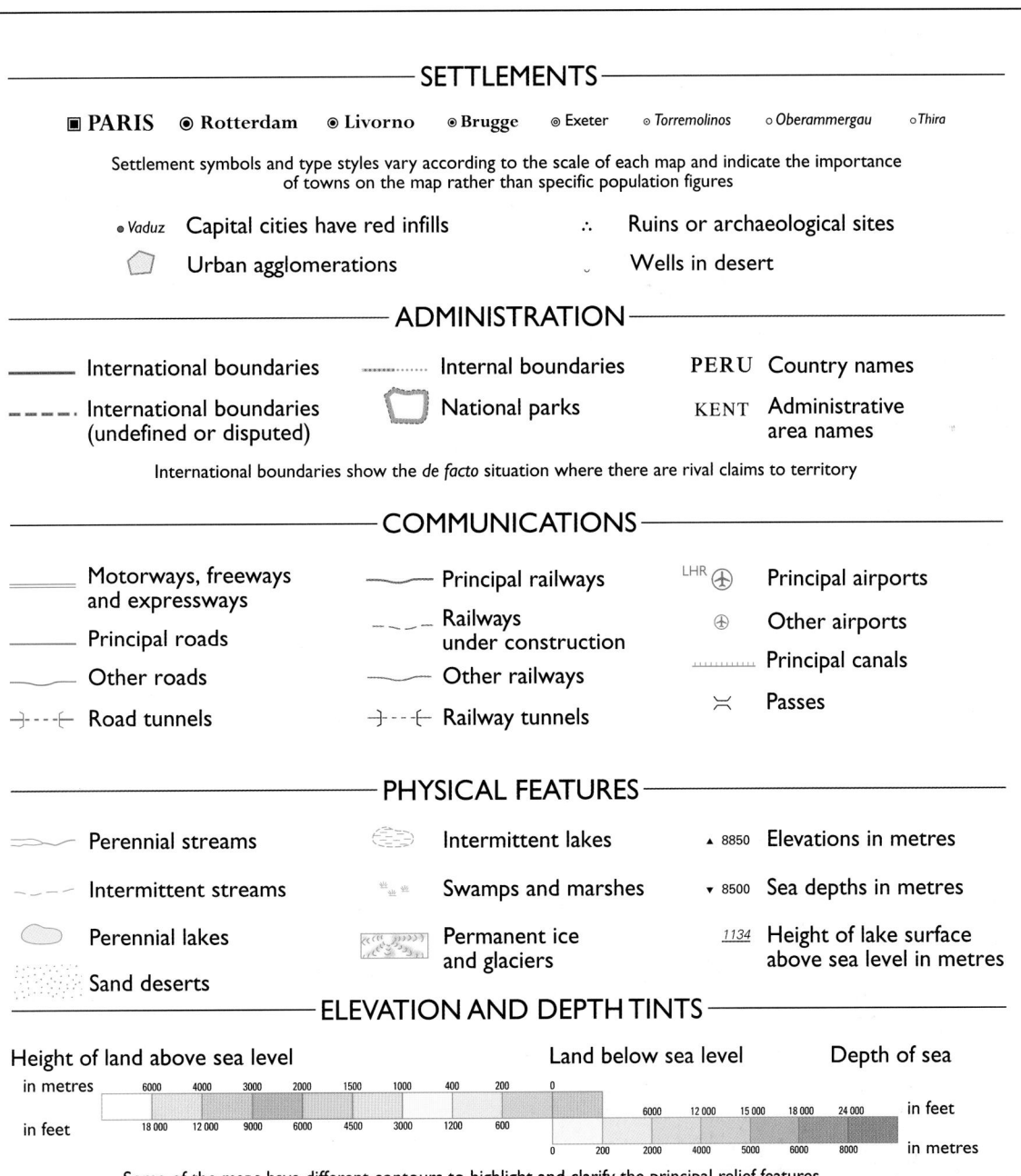

SETTLEMENTS

■ **PARIS**   ◉ **Rotterdam**   ◉ **Livorno**   ◉ **Brugge**   ◎ Exeter   ○ *Torremolinos*   ○ Oberammergau   ○ *Thira*

Settlement symbols and type styles vary according to the scale of each map and indicate the importance of towns on the map rather than specific population figures

● *Vaduz*   Capital cities have red infills   ∴   Ruins or archaeological sites

          Urban agglomerations   ᵕ   Wells in desert

ADMINISTRATION

——————   International boundaries   ···········   Internal boundaries   **PERU**   Country names

– – – – ·   International boundaries   National parks   KENT   Administrative
          (undefined or disputed)   area names

International boundaries show the *de facto* situation where there are rival claims to territory

COMMUNICATIONS

═════   Motorways, freeways   ———   Principal railways   LHR ⊕   Principal airports
          and expressways

————   Principal roads   – – –   Railways   ⊕   Other airports
                                          under construction

⌐—⌐   Other roads   —⌐—   Other railways   ··········   Principal canals

+---+   Road tunnels   +---+   Railway tunnels   ⋈   Passes

PHYSICAL FEATURES

～～   Perennial streams   ⬭   Intermittent lakes   ▲ 8850   Elevations in metres

– – –   Intermittent streams   ⁕⁕⁕   Swamps and marshes   ▼ 8500   Sea depths in metres

⬭   Perennial lakes   Permanent ice   *1134*   Height of lake surface
                                          and glaciers   above sea level in metres

⠐⠐⠐   Sand deserts

ELEVATION AND DEPTH TINTS

Height of land above sea level   Land below sea level   Depth of sea

in metres   6000 4000 3000 2000 1500 1000 400 200 0

                                                          6000 12 000 15 000 18 000 24 000   in feet

in feet   18 000 12 000 9000 6000 4500 3000 1200 600

                                                          0   200 2000 4000 5000 6000 8000   in metres

Some of the maps have different contours to highlight and clarify the principal relief features

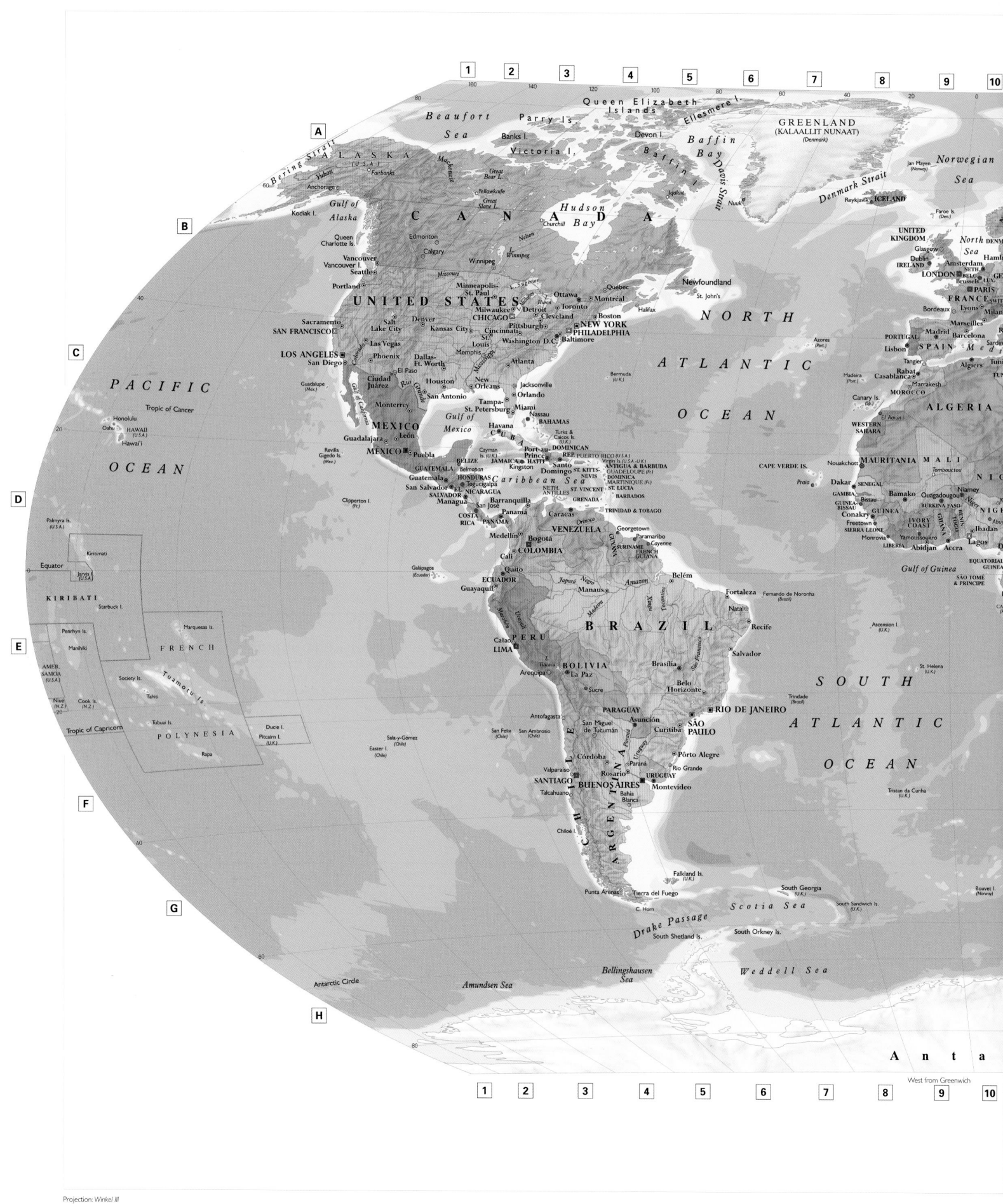

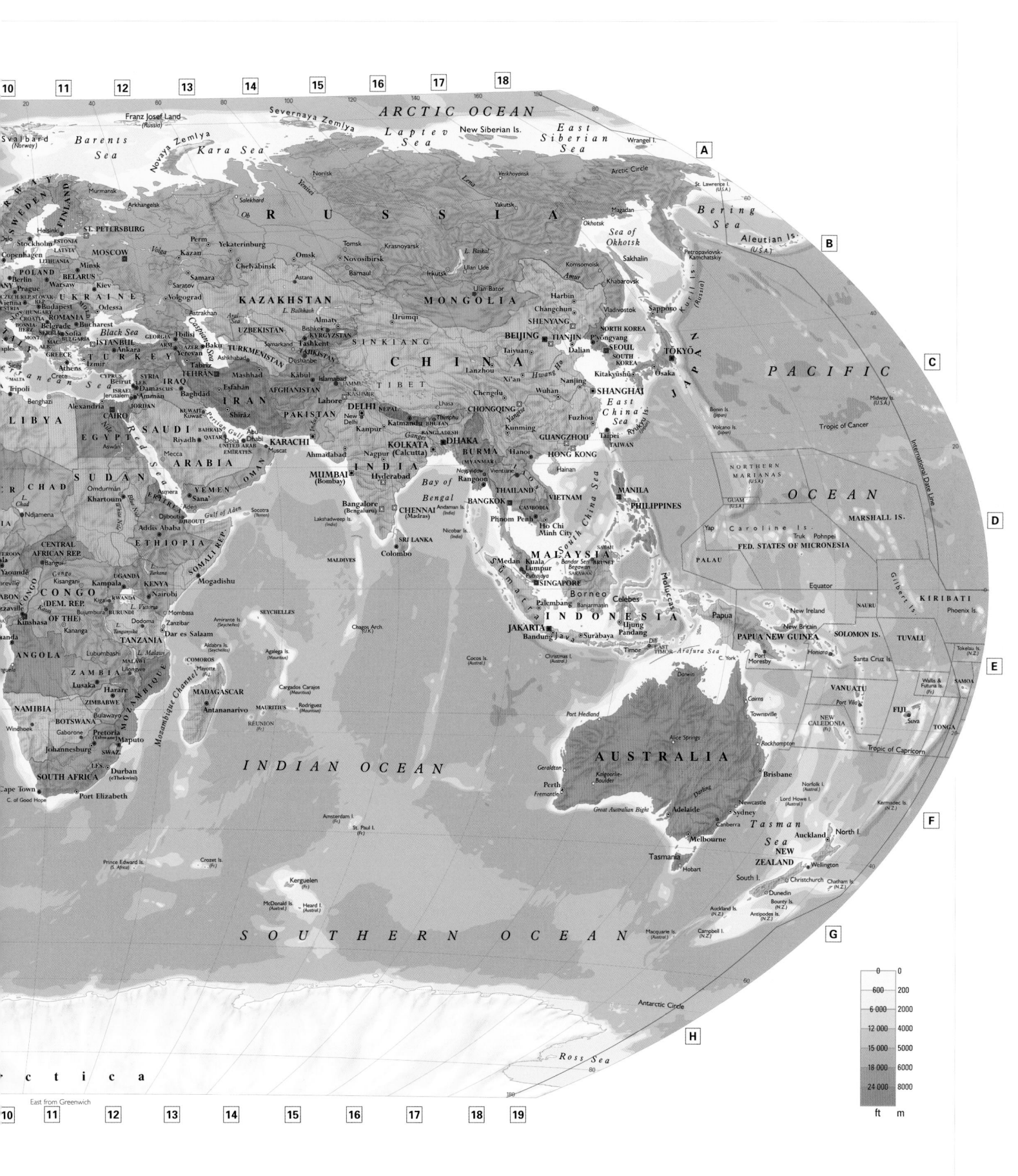

10 **11** **12** **13** **14** **15** **16** **17** **18**

20   40   60   80   100   120   140   160   180   60

ARCTIC OCEAN

Franz Josef Land
(Russia)
Severnaya Zemlya

Svalbard
(Norway)   Laptev   New Siberian Is.   East
Barents   Sea   Siberian
Novaya Zemlya   Sea
Sea   Kara Sea   Wrangel I.   **A**

Murmansk   Norilsk   Arctic Circle
St. Lawrence I.
(U.S.A.)
SWEDEN FINLAND   Salekhard   Yakutsk   Verkhoyansk
Arkhangelsk   Ob   Lena
Helsinki   Yenisey   Bering
ST. PETERSBURG   Yekaterinburg   Magadan
Stockholm ESTONIA   R U S S I A   Sea   **B**
LATVIA   Perm   Okhotsk   Petropavlovsk-
Copenhagen   Omsk   Tomsk   Krasnoyarsk   Komsomolsk   Sea of   Kamchatskiy
LITHUANIA   Kazan   Novosibirsk   Okhotsk   Aleutian Is.
Minsk   Volga   Irkutsk   Sakhalin   (U.S.A.)
POLAND   Samara   Barnaul   Ulan Ude   Amur   Khabarovsk
Berlin   BELARUS   Saratov   Astana   Harbin   Vladivostok   Sapporo   40
Warsaw   Kiev   Volgograd   KAZAKHSTAN   Changchun   SHENYANG   NORTH KOREA
Prague   UKRAINE   Astrakhan   Aral   MONGOLIA   Ulan Bator   PYONGYANG
Budapest   Sea   L. Balkhash   Almaty   SEOUL   TŌKYŌ   **C**
ROMANIA   Odessa   Caspian   Bishkek   Urumqi   BEIJING   TIANJIN   SOUTH   Osaka
Belgrade   Bucharest   Tbilisi   GEORGIA   KYRGYZSTAN   Taiyuan   Dalian   KOREA   Kitakyūshū   PACIFIC
BULGARIA   Black Sea   AZER.   Baku   Tashkent   SINKIANG   C H I N A   Lanzhou   Xi'an   Hwang Ho
ISTANBUL   ARM.   Samarkand   TAJIKISTAN   Chengdu   Nanjing
GREECE   T U R K E Y   Yerevan   Ashkhabad   TIBET   Wuhan   SHANGHAI   Bonin Is.
Athens   TURKMENISTAN   Kābul   Islamabad   Lhasa   CHONGQING   East   (Japan)
CYPRUS   SYRIA   Tabriz   Mashhad   JAMMU &   Yangtze   China   Volcano Is.
Crete   Beirut   TEHRĀN   Dushanbe   KASHMIR   Kunming   Sea   (Japan)   Tropic of Cancer
ISRAEL LEB.   Damascus   Lahore   New   Kanpur   GUANGZHOU   Fuzhou   Ryukyu Is.   20
Alexandria   Amman   Baghdād   I R A N   AFGHANISTAN   Delhi   NEPAL   Katmandu   BHUTAN   HONG KONG   TAIWAN   Taipei   NORTHERN   **D**
CAIRO   JORDAN   Esfahān   PAKISTAN   DELHI   Thimphu   BANGLADESH   Hainan   MARIANAS
LIBYA   KUWAIT   Shirāz   Ahmadābad   Nagpur   Ganges   DHAKA   Hanoi   (U.S.A.)
EGYPT   Kuwait   BAHRAIN   KARACHI   KOLKATA   BURMA   GUAM
Aswân   SAUDI   QATAR   Abu   (Calcutta)   MYANMAR   (U.S.A.)   OCEAN
Riyadh   Doha   Dhabi   MUMBAI   Naypyidaw   Rangoon   Yap   Caroline Is.   MARSHALL IS.   **E**
SUDAN   ARABIA   UNITED ARAB   (Bombay)   INDIA   Hyderabad   Bay of   THAILAND   VIETNAM   Truk   Pohnpei
Omdurman   Mecca   EMIRATES   Bangalore   Bengal   BANGKOK   CAMBODIA   PALAU   FED. STATES OF MICRONESIA
Khartoum   YEMEN   Muscat   (Bengaluru)   CHENNAI   Andaman Is.   Phnom Penh   MANILA
Sana'   OMAN   (Madras)   (India)   Ho Chi   PHILIPPINES
CHAD   Djibouti   Aden   SRI LANKA   Nicobar Is.   Minh City   PALAU   NAURU   KIRIBATI
Ndjamena   ETHIOPIA   Gulf of Aden   Socotra   MALDIVES   Colombo   (India)   MALAYSIA   SABAH   Equator   Gilbert Is.   Phoenix Is.
CENTRAL   SOMALI REP.   Lakshadweep   Medan   Kuala   Bandar Seri   New Ireland
AFRICAN REP.   Addis Ababa   (India)   Lumpur   Begawan   BRUNEI   Papua   SOLOMON IS.
Bangui   Turkana   SINGAPORE   SARAWAK   New Britain   TUVALU
UGANDA   KENYA   Putrajaya   Borneo   Celebes   PAPUA NEW GUINEA   Santa Cruz Is.   Tokelau Is.   **F**
CONGO   Kampala   Nairobi   INDONESIA   Molucca   Honiara   (N.Z.)
(DEM. REP.   RWANDA   L. Victoria   Palembang   Banjarmasin   Port   SAMOA
Kisangani   BURUNDI   JAKARTA   Moresby   Walls &
Bujumbura   TANZANIA   Bandung   Surabaya   Papua   Futuna Is.
OF THE)   Mombasa   Java   Pandang   NAURU   VANUATU   (Fr.)
Kananga   Dodoma   SEYCHELLES   Timor   DILI   Port Vila   FIJI
Dar es Salaam   Amirante Is.   Chagos Arch.   EAST   Arafura Sea   NEW   Suva
(Seychelles)   (U.K.)   TIMOR   CALEDONIA   TONGA
ANGOLA   Lubumbashi   L. Malawi   Aldabra Is.   Cocos Is.   (Fr.)
ZAMBIA   MALAWI   (Seychelles)   (Austral.)   Darwin   C. York
Lusaka   Harare   MOZAMBIQUE   Agalega Is.   Christmas I.   Cairns   Norfolk I.   Kermadec Is.   **G**
ZIMBABWE   Blantyre   (Mauritius)   (Austral.)   (Austral.)   Townsville   (Austral.)   (N.Z.)
NAMIBIA   Bulawayo   COMOROS   Cargados Carajos   Port Hedland   Lord Howe I.
BOTSWANA   Mayotte   (Mauritius)   Rockhampton   (Austral.)
Windhoek   (Fr.)   MADAGASCAR   MAURITIUS   AUSTRALIA   Brisbane   North I.
Gaborone   Antananarivo   Rodriguez   Alice Springs   Geraldton   Kalgoorlie-   Tasman   Auckland
Pretoria (Tshwane)   Maputo   (Mauritius)   Boulder   Newcastle   Sea   **F**
Johannesburg   SWAZ.   RÉUNION   Perth   Great Australian Bight   Sydney   NEW
Maseru LES.   (Fr.)   Canberra   Adelaide   Fremantle   ZEALAND   Wellington
SOUTH AFRICA   Durban (eThekwini)   INDIAN OCEAN   Melbourne   South I.   Chatham Is.
Cape Town   Port Elizabeth   Amsterdam I.   Tasmania   (N.Z.)   40
C. of Good Hope   (Fr.)   Hobart   Dunedin
St. Paul I.   Prince Edward Is.   Christchurch   Bounty Is.   (N.Z.)
(S. Afr.)   (Fr.)   Crozet Is.   Auckland Is.   Antipodes Is.   (N.Z.)
(Fr.)   Kerguelen   (N.Z.)   **G**
(Fr.)   Macquarie I.   Campbell I.
McDonald Is.   Heard I.   (Austral.)   (N.Z.)
(Austral.)   (Austral.)
S O U T H E R N   O C E A N   60

Antarctic Circle   **H**
tica   Ross Sea
East from Greenwich   180   80

10 **11** **12** **13** **14** **15** **16** **17** **18** **19**

ft	m
0	0
600	200
6 000	2000
12 000	4000
15 000	5000
18 000	6000
24 000	8000

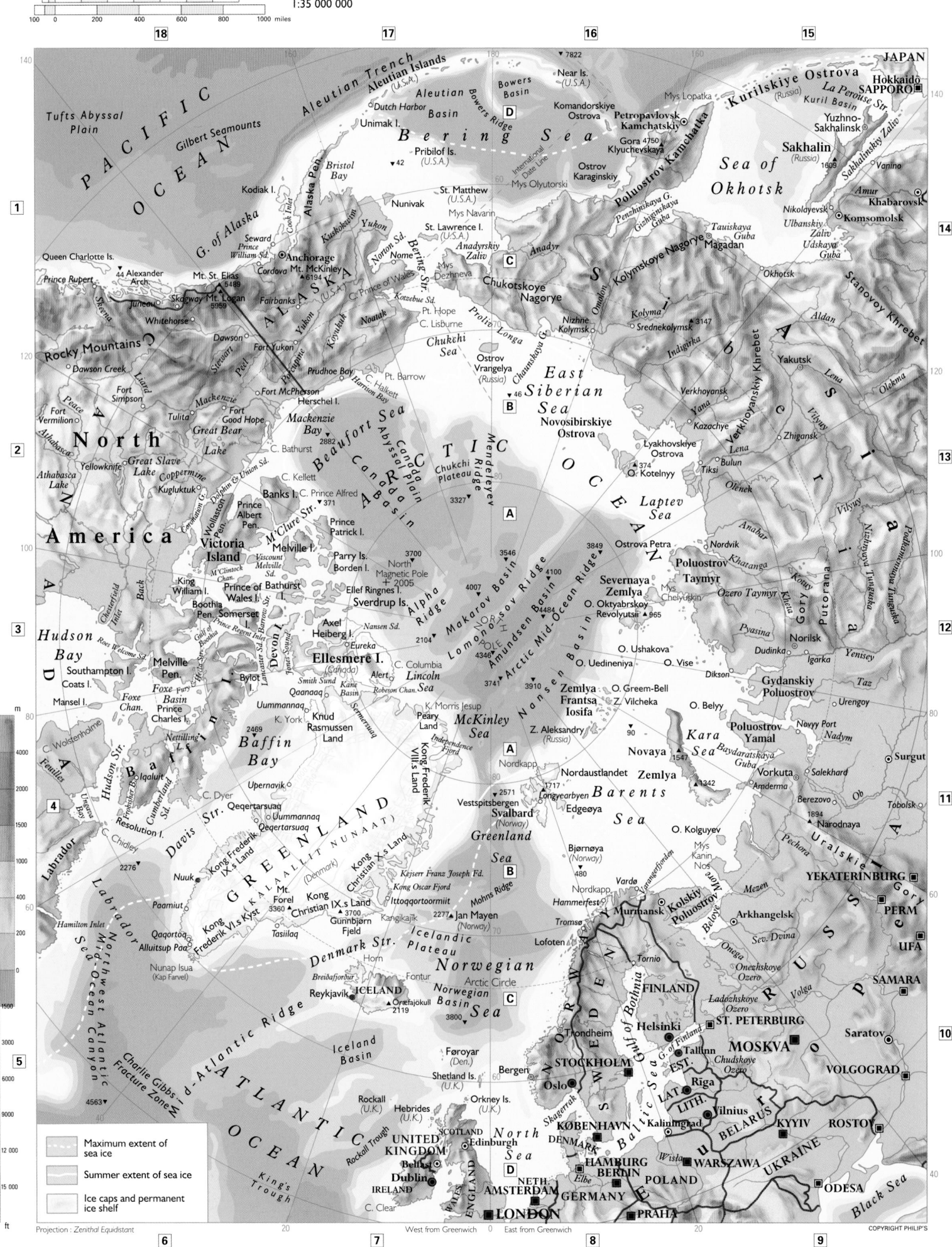

100 0   200   400   600   800   1000 1200 1400 km

1:35 000 000

100 0   200   400   600   800   1000 miles

18   17   16   15

JAPAN

PACIFIC OCEAN

Tufts Abyssal Plain

Gilbert Seamounts

Aleutian Trench
Aleutian Islands (U.S.A.)

Bowers Basin

▼7822

Mys Lopatka

Kurilskiye Ostrova (Russia)

Hokkaido
SAPPORO

1

Dutch Harbor
Unimak I.

Aleutian Basin

Bowers Ridge

D

Komandorskiye Ostrova

Petropavlovsk-Kamchatskiy

La Perouse Str.

Kuril Basin

Yuzhno-Sakhalinsk

Bristol Bay

Bering   Sea

Gora 4750 Klyuchevskaya

Sea of Okhotsk

Sakhalin (Russia)

Sakhalinskiy Zaliv

Kodiak I.

Pribilof Is. (U.S.A.)

▼42

Ostrov Karaginskiy

Poluostrov Kamchatka

▲1609

Vanino

G. of Alaska

St. Matthew (U.S.A.)

Mys Olyutorski

Amur

Khabarovsk

Seward
Prince William Sd.

Nunivak

Anchorage Mt. McKinley
Cordova ▲6194

Nome

St. Lawrence I. (U.S.A.)

Mys Navarin

Anadyrskiy Zaliv

Anadyr

Penzhinskaya G.

Gizhiginskaya Guba

Nikolayevsk

Komsomolsk

14

Queen Charlotte Is.

Alexander Arch. 44

Prince Rupert

Mt. St. Elias ▲5489

Skagway Mt. Logan 5959

Fairbanks

ALASKA (U.S.A.)

Kuskokwim

Yukon

Bering Str.
Mys Dezhneva

Chukotskoye Nagorye

Tauiskaya Guba

Magadan

Okhotsk

Ulbanskiy Zaliv

Udskaya Guba

Stanovoy Khrebet

Juneau

Whitehorse

Mt. McKinley

Prince of Wales

Kotzebue Sd.

Pt. Hope
C. Lisburne

Prolio Longa

Kolyma

Kolymskoye Nagorye

S

Okhotsk

Aldan

Rocky Mountains

Dawson

Stewart

Peel

Fort Yukon

Koyukuk

Noatak

Chukchi Sea

Nizhne-Kolymsk

Srednekolymsk

Omolon

Indigirka

i

Yakutsk

Kolyma

▲3147

Olekma

1

Dawson Creek

Liard

Fort Simpson

Prudhoe Bay

Pt. Halkett

Harrison Bay

Pt. Barrow

Ostrov Vrangelya (Russia)

▲46

East Siberian Sea

Verkhoyansk

Yana

Zhigansk

b

Lena

Verkhoyanskiy Khrebet

Vilyuy

2

Fort Vermilion

Peace

Fort Good Hope

Tulita

Mackenzie

Fort McPherson

Herschel I.

Beaufort Sea

Mackenzie Bay ▼2882

Novosibirskiye Ostrova

Kazachye

Bulun

Olenek

Tiksi

Lena

Anabar

Nizhnyaya Tunguska

13

North

Great Bear Lake

C. Bathurst

Canada Abyssal Plain

Chukchi Plateau

Lyakhovskiye Ostrova

▲374

Kotelnyy

Laptev Sea

Khatanga

Kotuy

Gory Putorana

Podkamennaya Tunguska

Athabasca Lake

Yellowknife

Great Slave Lake

Coppermine

Kuglúktuk

Dolphin & Union Sd.

C. Kellett

A R C T I C

3327▼

3546▼

Mendeleyev Ridge

Ostrova Petra

Nordvik

Poluostrov Taymyr

Ozero Taymyr

Pyasina

Norilsk

Yenisey

Taz

America

Banks I.

C. Prince Alfred

▲371

M'Clure Str.

Prince Patrick I.

3700
North Magnetic Pole + 2005

4007

Makarov Basin

Amundsen Basin

3849 ▼

4100

4484

Severnaya Zemlya

Mys Chelyuskin

Oktyabrskoy Revolyutsii ▲965

Dikson

Dudinka

Igarka

2

Victoria Island

Melville I.

Viscount Melville Sd.

Parry Is.
Borden I.

Ellef Ringnes I.

Sverdrup Is.

Alpha Ridge

O C E A N

Lomonosov Ridge

POLE

4346▼

Arctic Mid-Ocean Ridge

2104▼

Nansen Basin

O. Ushakova

O. Uedineniya

O. Vise

Urengoy

12

King William I.

Boothia Pen.

Somerset I.

M'Clintock Chan.

Prince of Bathurst I.

Wales I.

Axel Heiberg I.

Nansen Sd.

3741▼

3910▼

Zemlya Frantsa Iosifa

O. Greem-Bell

Z. Vilcheka

O. Belyy

Novyy Port

Nadym

3

Hudson Bay

Southampton I.

Coats I.

Mansel I.

Roes Welcome Sd.

Chesterfield Inlet

Back

Gulf of Prince Regent Inlet

Prince of Wales I.

Devon I.

Eureka

Ellesmere I. (Canada)

Bylot I.

C. Columbia

Alert

Lincoln Sea

Z

4346▼

McKinley Sea

Z. Aleksandry (Russia)

90 ▲

Kara Sea

Novaya

▲1547

Baydaratskaya Guba

Poluostrov Yamal

Vorkuta

Salekhard

Surgut

11

Melville Pen.

Foxe Basin

Prince Charles I.

Foxe Chan.

Fury & Hecla Str.

Baffin

Barrow Str.

Lancaster Sd.

Smith Sund

Kane Basin

K. Morris Jesup

Peary Land

Robeson Chan.

Kong Frederik VIII.s Land

K. Columbia

Nordkapp

Nordaustlandet

Zemlya

Novaya Zemlya

▲1342

Amderma

Berezovo

Narodnaya ▲1894

Ob

Tobolsk

4

C. Wolstenholme

Hudson Str.

Nettilling L.

Iqaluit

▲2469

Uummannaq

K. York

Knud Rasmussen Land

Qaanaaq

Sermersuaq

Independence Fjord

Vestspitsbergen

Longyearbyen ●

▼1717

2571▲

Barents Sea

Edgeøya

O. Kolguyev

Mys Kanin Nos

Pechora

▼

Labrador

C. Dyer

Davis Str.

Frobisher B.

Resolution I.

Cumberland Sd.

Chidley

▼2276

Upernavik

Qeqertarsuaq

Qeqertarsuaq

GREENLAND

(KALAALLIT NUNAAT)

Svalbard (Norway)

Greenland Sea

90

Bjørnøya (Norway)

480 ▼

Vardø

YEKATERINBURG

PERM

Northwest Atlantic Mid-Ocean Canyon

Nuuk

Kong Frederik IX.s Land

Kong X.s Land

Christian IX.s Land

Kejser Franz Joseph Fd.

Kong Oscar Fjord

Ittoqqortoormiit

Mohns Ridge

Nordkapp

Hammerfest

Mys Kanin Nos

Murmansk

Kolskiy Poluostrov

Beloye

Mezen

UFA

Labrador Sea

Paamiut

Mt. Forel ▲3360

Kong Christian IX.s Land

Kong Frederik VI.s Kyst

3700▲

Gunnbjørn Fjeld

Kangikajik

Greenland Sea

2277▼

Jan Mayen (Norway)

Tromsø

Lofoten

Onega

Sev. Dvina

Arkhangelsk

SAMARA

5

Qaqortoq

Alluitsup Paa

Tasiilaq

2119▲

Icelandic Plateau

Norwegian

Bodø

O. Knin

Ladozhskoye Ozero

Volga

R

VOLGOGRAD

Nunap Isua (Kap Farvel)

Breidafjordur

Horn

Fontur

Denmark Str.

Arctic Circle

Sea

Basin

3800▼

Trondheim

FINLAND

Helsinki ●

Onezhskoye Ozero

ST. PETERBURG

Saratov

10

Charlie Gibbs Fracture Zone

Mid-Atlantic Ridge

▼4563

Reykjavik ●

ICELAND

Ørǽfajökull

Iceland Basin

Norwegian Basin

Føroyar (Den.)

Bergen

Oslo ●

STOCKHOLM

Chudskoye Ozero

EST.

Tallinn

Riga

MOSKVA

Shetland Is. (U.K.)

Rockall

Hebrides (U.K.)

Orkney Is. (U.K.)

North Sea

Edinburgh

SCOTLAND

Gulf of Bothnia

G. of Finland

LAT.

LITH.

Vilnius ●

Kaliningrad

Chudskoye Ozero

VOLGOGRAD

King's Trough

Rockall Trough

UNITED KINGDOM

Belfast ●

ENGLAND

Skagerrak

KØBENHAVN

DENMARK

Baltic Sea

BELARUS

KYYIV

ROSTOV

6

ATLANTIC OCEAN

C. Clear

Dublin ●

IRELAND

LONDON ●

HAMBURG

Berlin

AMSTERDAM

NETH.

GERMANY

Elbe

POLAND

WARSZAWA

Wisła

PRAHA

UKRAINE

Black Sea

ODESA

Maximum extent of sea ice

Summer extent of sea ice

Ice caps and permanent ice shelf

Projection : Zenithal Equidistant

6   7   8   9

West from Greenwich   0   East from Greenwich

COPYRIGHT PHILIP'S

ft   m
12 000 4000
6000   2000
4500   1500
3000   1000
1200   400
600   200
0   0
500   1500
1000   3000
2000   6000
3000   9000
4000   12 000
5000   15 000
m   ft

1:35 000 000

100 0 200 400 600 800 1000 1200 1400 km
100 0 200 400 600 800 1000 miles

West from Greenwich | East from Greenwich

ATLANTIC OCEAN

Georgia Basin
South Sandwich Trench
Zavodovski I.
Visokoi I.
Candlemas I.
8325
Leskov I.
Saunders I.
Montagu I.
Bristol I. (U.K.)
South Sandwich Is. (U.K.)

King Edward Point (U.K.)
South Georgia
Bird I. (U.K.)

America-Antarctic Ridge

Maud Rise

SOUTHERN

Antarctic Circle

Lazarev Sea

Atlantic-Indian Basin

Prince Edward Fracture Zone

INDIAN OCEAN

6739
Conrad Rise

Enderby Abyssal Plain

Bases on King George Island:
Jubany (Argentina)
Com. Ferraz (Brazil)
Ten. Rodolfo Marsh (Chile)
Great Wall (China)
King Sejong (Korea)
Arctowski (Poland)
Artigas (Uruguay)
Bellingshausen (Russia)

Stanley
Falkland Is. (U.K.)

Scotia Sea

Orcadas (Arg.) 5552
Signy I. (U.K.)
Coronation I.
South Orkney Is.

Weddell Abyssal Plain

Sanae IV (S. Afr.)
Neumayer (Germany)
Fimbul Ice Shelf
Maitri (India)
Novolazarevskaya (Russia)

Riiser-Larsen Sea

Prinsesse Astrid Kyst
Prinsesse Ragnhild Kyst
Sør-Rondane
3630
Lützow Holmbukta
Syowa (Japan)
Riiser-Larsen-halvøya

Cosmonaut Sea

Kronprins Olav Kyst
Molodezhnaya (Russia)
Mizuho (Japan)

Prins Harald Kyst

C. Borley
Enderby Land 2280

Kemp Land

Stefansson Bay
Mawson (Austr.) 2645

Valdivia Abyssal Plain

ARGENTINA

Shackleton Fracture
Estr. de Le Maire
Tierra del Fuego
Ushuaia
C. de Hornos (C. Horn)
I. Hoste
CHILE

Drake Passage

Elephant I.
Clarence I.
Gen. Bernardo O'Higgins (Chile)
Joinville I.
Esperanza (Arg.)
Marambio (Arg.)
Capt. Arturo Prat (Chile)
Deception I.
James Ross I.
Robertson I.

South Shetland Is.
King George I.
Bransfield Str.

Larsen Ice Shelf

Weddell Sea

Muhlig Hofmann fjell
Kronprinsesse Martha Kyst
2717
Lyddan I.

Brunt Ice Shelf
Halley (U.K.)
Belgrano (Arg.)
Vahsel Bay

3212 3039

Coats Land
Caird Coast
Luitpold Coast

Dronning Maud Land

3318 2990

Dome Fuji (Japan)

3556 2600

MacRobertson Land

3355
Prince Charles Mts.
Lambert Glacier

Amery Ice Shelf

Prydz Bay
Zhongshan (China)
Davis (Austr.)

Amery Basin

C. Darnley

Graham Land
Palmer (U.S.A.)
Vernadsky (Ukr.)
Anvers I.
San Martin (Arg.)
Biscoe Is.
Adelaide I.
Rothera (U.K.)

Antarctic Pen.
Palmer Land

Dyer Plateau

4191
George VI Sound
3658

Filchner Ice Shelf
Berkner I.
975

Ronne Ice Shelf

Pensacola Mts. 3657

2311 1431

American Highland

1800
Ingrid Christensen Coast
Progress (Russia)

West Ice Shelf

Princess Elizabeth Land

Bellingshausen Abyssal Plain

Alexander I.
Charcot I.
C. Byrd

2987
2896

Ellsworth Mts. 4897
Vinson Massif
Patriot Hills (Chile)

Thiel Mts.

2773 2407

SOUTH POLE
Amundsen-Scott (U.S.A.)

East Antarctica

Dome Argus 4030 1040

3030 2570

Queen Mary Land

Mirny (Russia)
Davis Sea
Drygalski I.
Masson I.
Shackleton Ice Shelf
Mill I.

Peter I Øy

Siple (U.S.A.)

Ellsworth Land

West Antarctica

3022
2677
4181
1797 434

Horlick Mts.
3810

Transantarctic Mts.

4176
4528
Queen Maud Mts.

2801 3491
Beardmore Glacier

Queen Alexandra Range
Mt. Markham 4349

2407 3087

Vostok (Russia) 3488 3700

Dome C Concordia (France/Italy)

Bowman I.

Budd Coast
Casey (Austr.)
Vincennes B.

Knox Coast
Totten Glacier

Bellingshausen Sea

Thurston I. 1936

C. Flying Fish

Hudson Mts.
Walgreen Coast

Marie Byrd Land

Bentley Subglacial Trench 2080 4335

Bakutis Coast
Koler Ra.

Mt. Sidley 4181

Rockefeller Plateau 666

Edward VII Land

Getz Ice Shelf
Hobbs Coast 3496
Dart

Amundsen Sea

Amundsen Ridges

Amundsen Abyssal Plain

Sulzberger Ice Shelf

Ross Ice Shelf

Roosevelt I.

Bay of Whales
C. Colbeck

Shackleton Inlet

Mt. Lister
Scott 4023

Mt. Erebus 3743
McMurdo (U.S.A.)
Ross I.
Franklin I.
McMurdo Sd.

Ross Dep.

David Glacier 2436 4776

Scott Glacier

Denman Glacier

Sabrina Coast

Banzare Coast

Clarie Coast

Porpoise Bay

Paulding Bay

Wilhelm II Coast

Wilkes Land

Drygalski Ice Tongue
Victoria Land
Prince Albert Mts.
Mt. Murchison 3502

Coulman I.

2216 2798

Renwick Glacier 4163

Possession I.

C. Adare

Oates Land

George V Land

Terre Adélie
Dumont d'Urville (Fr.)

Commonwealth Bay
South Magnetic Pole 2005
C. Freshfield
C. Hudson

4650

Australian Basin

Ross Sea

C. Colbeck

PACIFIC OCEAN

Southeast Pacific Basin

Tharp Fracture Zone

Eltanin Fracture Zone System

Udintsev Fracture Zone

2930

Pacific-Antarctic Ridge

Antarctic Circle

Hjort Trench 6800
Macquarie Ridge

Southeast Indian Ridge

Macquarie Is. (Austr.)

International Date Line

6240

Southwest Pacific Basin

Campbell I. (N.Z.)
Auckland Is. (N.Z.)

South Tasman Rise

Tasman Sea

Hobart
Launceston
Bass Str.
Tasmania

Antipodes Is.
Campbell Plateau
Bounty Is. (N.Z.)
Stewart I.
Invercargill
Dunedin
NEW ZEALAND

MELBOURNE AUSTRALIA

COPYRIGHT PHILIP'S

Legend:
- Ice cap
- Permanent ice shelf
- Maximum extent of sea ice
- March (Summer) extent of sea ice
- ▲ 3488 3700 Surface elevation and depth of ice (in metres)
- • Stanley (U.K.) Permanent bases

Projection: Zenithal Equidistant

The Antarctic Treaty was signed in Washington in 1959 so that scientific and technical research could continue unhampered by international politics.

All territorial claims covering land areas south of latitude 60°S have been suspended. Those claims were:

Norwegian claim (Dronning Maud Land)	45°E - 20°W
Australian claims	45°E - 136°E, 142°E - 160°E
French claim (Terre Adélie)	136°E - 142°E
New Zealand claim (Ross Dependency)	160°E - 150°W
British claim	80°W - 20°W
Argentine claim	74°W - 53°W
Chilean claim	90°W - 53°W

ft m
12 000 4000
6000 2000
4500 1500
3000 1000
1200 400
600 200
0 0
500 1500
1000 3000
2000 6000
3000 9000
4000 12 000
5000 15 000
m ft

1:20 000 000

100 0 100 200 300 400 500 600 700 800 km
100 0 100 200 300 400 500 miles

Ob
Nizhniy Tagil
Chelyabinsk
Yekaterinburg
Perm
Ural
KAZAKHSTAN

UDMURTIA
BASHKORTOSTAN
Ufa
Izhevsk
Kazan
TATARSTAN
CHUVASHIA
MARI EL
Nizhniy Novgorod
Samara
Ayqoz

KOMI

Caspian Sea

Arkhangelsk
N. Dvina
Kirov
Kostroma
Yaroslavl
Ivanovo
MORDVINIA
Penza
Saratov
Volga
Volgograd
Astrakhan
Makhachkala
DAGESTAN
CHECHENIA
INGUSHETIA
NORTH OSETIA
KARACHAI-CHERKESSIA
KABARDINO-BALKARIA
ADYGEA
Krasnodar

IRAN

L. Onega
L. Ladoga
ST. PETERSBURG
Vyborg
Helsinki
Tallinn
ESTONIA
LATVIA
Riga
Pskov
L. Chudskoye
Vitebsk
Smolensk
MOSCOW
Tula
Orel
Kursk
Voronezh
Tambov
Lipetsk
Rybinsk
Res.
Vologda
R U S S I A

White Sea
Murmansk
KARELIA

Hammerfest
Tromsø
Narvik
Kirkenes
Kiruna

Don
Rostov
Taganrog
Krivoy Rog
Zaporozhye
Dnepropetrovsk
Kharkov
Donetsk
CRIMEA
Sevastopol
Simferopol
Kherson
Nikolayev
Odessa
Kiev
Dnieper
Chernihiv
Gomel
Mahilyow
Minsk
BELARUS
Brest
Pripet
Lublin
Lvov
Zhytomyr
UKRAINE
Bug
Dniester
MOLDOVA
Kishinev
Galaţi
Ploieşti
Bucharest
Danube
ROMANIA
Cluj-Napoca
Timişoara
Braşov
Constanţa

Black Sea
Bosporus
ISTANBUL
Bursa
Varna
Burgas
BULGARIA
Sofia
Plovdiv
Skopje
MACEDONIA
SERBIA
Niš
Belgrade
KOSOVO
MONTENEGRO
Podgorica
Tirana
ALBANIA
Bari

TURKEY
Ankara
Samsun
Erzurum
Kayseri
Konya
Adana
Antalya
İzmir

ARMENIA
AZERBAIJAN
GEORGIA
Baku
Tbilisi
Yerevan
Tabriz
Baghdad
IRAQ
SYRIA
Aleppo
Diyarbakır
Euphrates
Tigris

CYPRUS
Nicosia
Rhodes
Crete
GREECE
Athens
Patra
Corfu
Ionian Sea
Aegean Sea
Thessaloníki

FINLAND
Vaasa
Tampere
Turku
Oulu
Luleå
SWEDEN
Umeå
Sundsvall
Gävle
Uppsala
Stockholm
Örebro
Vänern
Vättern
Jönköping
Norrköping
Gotland
Öland
G. of Bothnia
Baltic Sea

NORWAY
Trondheim
Bergen
Stavanger
Oslo
Kristiansand
Skagerrak
Kattegat

DENMARK
Aalborg
Århus
Odense
Copenhagen
Kiel
Malmö
Gdańsk
Szczecin
Kaliningrad (Russ.)
LITHUANIA
Vilnius
Kaunas
Klaipeda
Białystok
POLAND
Warsaw
Vistula
Łódź
Poznań
Wrocław
Kraków
Katowice
Ostrava
Oder

GERMANY
Berlin
Hamburg
Bremen
Hannover
Magdeburg
Leipzig
Dresden
Halle
Chemnitz
Cologne
Essen
Dortmund
Düsseldorf
Bonn
Frankfurt am Main
Nuremberg
Stuttgart
Munich
Elbe
Rhine

CZECH REP.
Prague
SLOVAK REP.
Bratislava
Vienna
AUSTRIA
Linz
Salzburg
Graz
Innsbruck
HUNGARY
Budapest
Miskolc
Debrecen
SLOVENIA
Ljubljana
CROATIA
Zagreb
BOSNIA-HERZ.
Sarajevo
Split
Trieste
Venice
Adriatic Sea

SWITZERLAND
Zürich
Geneva
Basle
Bern
LIECH.
Meuse

NETHERLANDS
Amsterdam
The Hague
Rotterdam
Antwerp
BELGIUM
Brussels
LUX.
Luxembourg

UNITED KINGDOM
ENGLAND
London
Birmingham
Manchester
Liverpool
Leeds
Sheffield
Newcastle-upon-Tyne
Bristol
Southampton
Plymouth
WALES
Cardiff
SCOTLAND
Glasgow
Edinburgh
Dundee
Aberdeen
Newcastle
Hebrides
Orkney Is.
Shetland Is.
IRELAND
Dublin
Belfast
Cork

FRANCE
PARIS
Rouen
Le Havre
Lille
Seine
Nantes
Loire
Tours
Dijon
Lyons
St-Étienne
Grenoble
Nice
MONACO
Marseilles
Toulon
Bordeaux
Garonne
Toulouse
Limoges
Gironde
Brest
Rennes
Strasbourg
Rhône

Channel Is.
English Channel
Bay of Biscay

ITALY
Rome
Milan
Turin
Genoa
Bologna
Florence
Naples
Tiber
SAN MARINO
Corsica
Sardinia
Cagliari
Sassari
Ajaccio
Tyrrhenian Sea
Palermo
Messina
Catania
Sicily
MALTA
Valletta
Pantelleria
Taranto

SPAIN
Madrid
Barcelona
Valencia
Zaragoza
Bilbao
Seville
Málaga
Murcia
Alicante
Granada
Córdoba
Valladolid
La Coruña
Vigo
Ebro
Guadiana
Guadalquivir
Balearic Is.
Minorca
Majorca
Ibiza
Palma
ANDORRA
Andorra la Vella

PORTUGAL
Lisbon
Porto
Douro
Tagus

Melilla
Ceuta
Str. of Gibraltar
Gibraltar
Tangier
MOROCCO
ALGERIA
Algiers
Oran
Annaba
Constantine
TUNISIA
Tunis
Mediterranean Sea
A f r i c a

ATLANTIC OCEAN
Norwegian Sea
North Sea
Arctic Circle
ICELAND
Reykjavík
Faroe Is. (Den.)

■ LONDON Capital Cities

Projection: Bonne
West from Greenwich
East from Greenwich

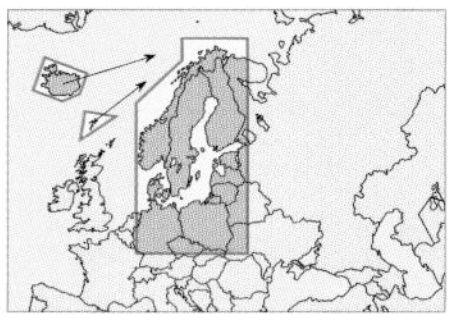

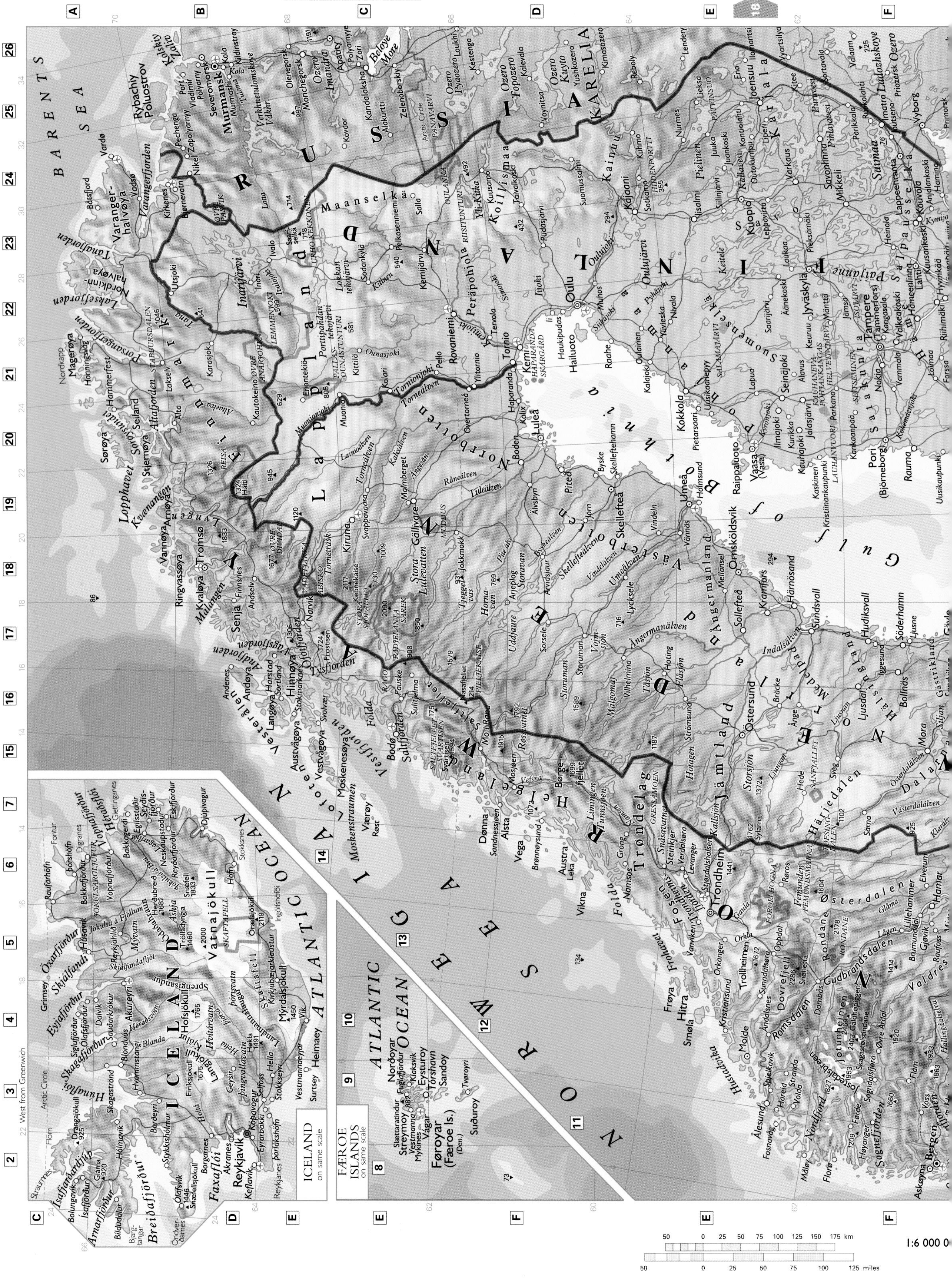

18

A B C D E F

BARENTS SEA

RUSSIA

KARELIA

FINLAND

Lappland

Finnmark

ATLANTIC OCEAN

ICELAND
on same scale

FAEROE ISLANDS
on same scale
Føroyar (Faeroe Is.) (Den.)

NORWEGIAN SEA

Gulf of Bothnia

Norrbotten

Västerbotten

Ångermanland

Jämtland

Trøndelag

Dalarna

Österdalen

Gudbrandsdalen

Murmansk

Reykjavik

Vatnajökull

Tromsø

Narvik

Luleå

Umeå

Oulu

Tampere

Trondheim

Östersund

50 0 25 50 75 100 125 150 175 km

50 0 25 50 75 100 125 miles

1:6 000 000

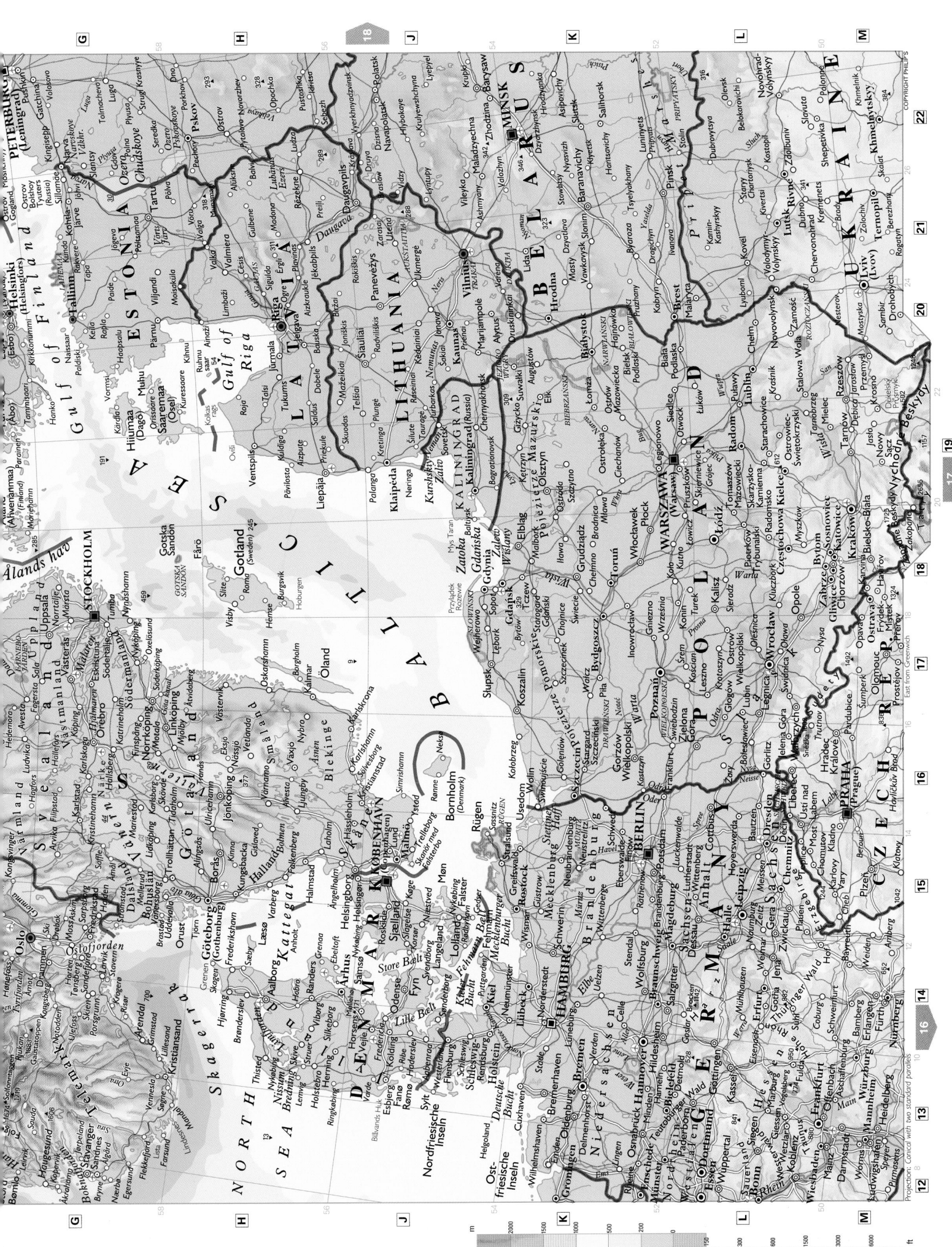

Projection: Conical with two standard parallels

10 0 10 20 30 40 50 60 70 80 km
10 0 10 20 30 40 50 miles

1:2 000 000

| 1 | 2 | 3 | 4 | 5 | 6 |

ATLANTIC OCEAN

Mull of Oa Kintyre Brodick Arran Firth of Clyde
Campbeltown
Mull of Kintyre Ailsa Craig
Trawbreaga B. Malin Inishtrahull
Malin Hd. Malin Pen. Glengad Hd. Rathlin I. Ballycastle
Sheep Haven Lough Swilly Fanad Hd. Cardonagh Giants Causeway Fair Hd. Cushendall
Mulroy B. Inishowen Pen. Moville Portstewart Portrush Cushendun
Horn Hd. Dunfanaghy Buncrana L. Foyle Coleraine Limavady Ballymoney 554 Garron Pt.
Bloody Foreland Londonderry Ballykelly Trostan GLENARIFF Carnlough
Gweedore Errigal 752 Rathmelton LONDONDERRY Roe Mts. of Antrim Larne L. Ryan
Inishfree B. The Rosses GLENVEAGH 683 Letterkenny Lifford Strabane Sawel Mt. ANTRIM Carncastle Cairnryan Stranraer
Aran I. Dungloe DONEGAL 683 Sion Mills Spurrin Mts. Magherafelt Randalstown Ballyclare 269 Portpatrick
Crohy Hd. Glenties Stranorlar Finn Newtownstewart Moneymore Antrim Carrickfergus
Gweebarra B. 601 Ardara Lavagh More 676 Castlederg Omagh TYRONE Cookstown Coalisland Lough Neagh Belfast L. Bangor
Loughros More B. Killybegs Donegal Deg Irvinestown Dungannon Craigavon Lurgan Newtownabbey Donaghadee
Rossan Pt. Slieve League Glencolumbkille Lower L. Erne Dromore Ballygawley Aughnacloy IRELAND Belfast Lisburn Newtownards
St. John's Pt. Donegal Bay Ballyshannon FERMANAGH Enniskillen Blackwater Portadown Lagan DOWN Saintfield Ards Pen.
Downpatrick Hd. Bundoran Upper Monaghan ARMAGH Banbridge Ballynahinch Portaferry
Killala B. Inishmurray I. Dromahair L. Erne Armagh Middletown Tandragee Ballyquintin Pt.
Lenadoon Pt. Manorhamilton Belturbet Clones Keady 577 Newry Dundrum St. John's Pt.
Portacloy Erris Hd. Sligo Bay Sligo Lackagh Hills MONAGHAN Annalee Slieve Gullion Mourne Mts. 852 Ardglass
Broad Haven Killala B. Dromore West Colooney L. Allen Cootehill Castleblaney Crossmaglen Slieve Donard Dundrum B. Newcastle
Mullet Pen. Belmullet 380 Ballymote LEITRIM Leitrim L. Oughter Cavan Carrickmacross Greenore Kilkeel
Inishkea North Crossmolina Killala Slieve Gamph L. Arrow Boyle Carrick-on-Shannon CAVAN L. Gowna Kingscourt LOUTH Warrenpoint Carlingford L.
Inishkea South Blacksod Bay Ballina L. Conn 544 SLIGO L. Key L. Sheelin Oldcastle Ardee Louth Clogher Hd.
Achill Hd. 672 Nephin Beg Range 806 Foxford Charlestown ROSCOMMON Ballaghaderreen Granard Ceanannus Mor (Kells) Dunleer Dundalk Bay
Achill I. Nephin Swinford L. Gara Castlerea LONGFORD Castlepollard Blackwater Slane Drogheda
Clare I. MAYO Newport Castlebar Ballyhaunis Knock Strokestown Longford Roscommon MEATH Navan Balbriggan
Inishturk Corraun Pen. Westport Claremorris Ballinrobe Tuam Roscommon Athboy Trim Dunshaughlin Rush
Inishbofin Clew Bay Louisburgh 765 Croagh Patrick L. Carra Glennamaddy IRELAND Mullingar Royal Canal Lambay I.
Inishshark Killary Harbour 819 683 L. Mask Ballinasloe WESTMEATH Moate Kilbeggan Leinster Cloncurry Swords Malahide
Clifden Mweelrea Party Mts. Lough Mask Mount Bellew Bridge Athenry Athlone Tullamore Edenderry DUB Maynooth DUBLIN Howth Hd.
CONNEMARA Connemara Lough Corrib Claregalway Loughrea Shannonbridge Clara Ferbane OFFALY Grand Canal Daingean Bog of Allen Dublin Dun Laoghaire
Slyne Hd. Roundstone Oughterard GALWAY Loughrea Aughrim Portumna Birr Tullamore Portarlington Rathangan Clane Kilcoole Killiney
Bertraghboy B. Spiddle Galway Athenry Kinvarra 368 Slieve Aughty Roscrea Mountmellick Port Laoise Monasterevin Naas KILDARE Droichead Nua Bray 123
Kilkieran B. Black Hd. Galway Bay Burren Gort Portumna Shannon Slieve Bloom 529 Arderin Athy Droichead Nua Kildare Greystones
Aran Is. Inishmore BURREN 345 Lisdoonvarna Crusheen Feakle Nenagh Borrisokane Slieve Bloom Mts. Mountrath Baltinglass Poulaphouca Res. WICKLOW 754
Inishmaan Cliffs of Moher Hags Hd. Ennistimon Tulla Killaloe Silvermine Mts. Donaghmore LAOIS Carlow Arklow Wicklow Wicklow Mts. 926
Inisheer Liscannor Bay Milltown Malbay 694 Keeper Hill Durrow Timahoe Lugnaquilla Wicklow Hd.
Mal Bay Mutton I. CLARE Ennis Lough Derg Nenagh Thurles Templemore Johnstown CARLOW Tullow Shillelagh
Loop Hd. Kilkee Sixmilebridge Limerick Golden Vale TIPPERARY Kilkenny Muine Bheag 796 Mt. Leinster Gorey
Kilrush Shannon Airport Foynes Limerick Tipperary Cashel KILKENNY Callan Blackstairs Mts. Ballycanew Cahore Pt.
Mouth of the Shannon Tarbert LIMERICK Rathkeale Thomastown WEXFORD 734 Enniscorthy
Kerry Hd. Ballybunion Newcastle West MUNSTER Kilfinnane Galtymore 920 Galty Mts. Caher Clonmel Slievenamon 722 Carrick-on-Suir New Ross Gorey
Brandon B. Ballyheige Listowel Feale Abbeyfeale 519 Mitchelstown Comeragh Mts. 795 Waterford Passage East Rosslare
Smerwick Harbour Tralee B. Ardfert Rath Luirc (Charleville) Buttevant Knockmealdown Mts. 792 WATERFORD Tramore Dunmore East Rosslare Harbour
953 Brandon Mt. Tralee Newmarket Mallow Fermoy Lismore Dungarvan Tramore B. Hook Hd. Greenore Pt. Saltee Is.
Dingle Slieve Mish Maine Castleisland Kanturk Nagles Mts. 429 Blackwater Dungarvan Harbour Waterford Harbour Carnsore Pt.
Great Blasket I. Dunmore Hd. Castlemaine Laune Killarney Millstreet Mallow Youghal St. David's Hd. St. David's
Inishvickillane Dingle Bay Glenbeigh L. Leane 646 Boggeragh Mts. Cobh Youghal B. St. Brides Bay
Valencia I. Cahirciveen Carrauntoohill 1041 707 CORK Crosshaven 115
Puffin I. L. Currane Kilgarvan Macgillycuddy's Reeks Macroom Blarney Cork St. George's Channel
Great Skellig Sneem Kenmare Caha Mts. 686 Lee Passage West Cork Harbour
Ballinskelligs B. Scariff I. Glengarriff Dunmanway Bandon Midleton
Dursey I. Castletown Bearhaven Bantry Bay Whiddy I. Bantry Timoleague Kinsale
Crow Hd. Bear I. Dunmanus B. Ballydehob Clonakilty Old Head of Kinsale
Mizen Hd. Skull Long I. Baltimore Clonakilty B.
C. Clear Clear I. Sherkin I. Galley Hd.
Fastnet Rock

CELTIC SEA

IRISH SEA

NORTHERN IRELAND

ULSTER CONNACHT LEINSTER MUNSTER

Projection: Lambert's Conformal Conic

West from Greenwich

COPYRIGHT PHILIP'S

ft	m
	1500
1500	500
600	200
300	100
0	0
50	150
100	300
200	600
500	1500
1000	3000
2000	6000

m ft

National Parks

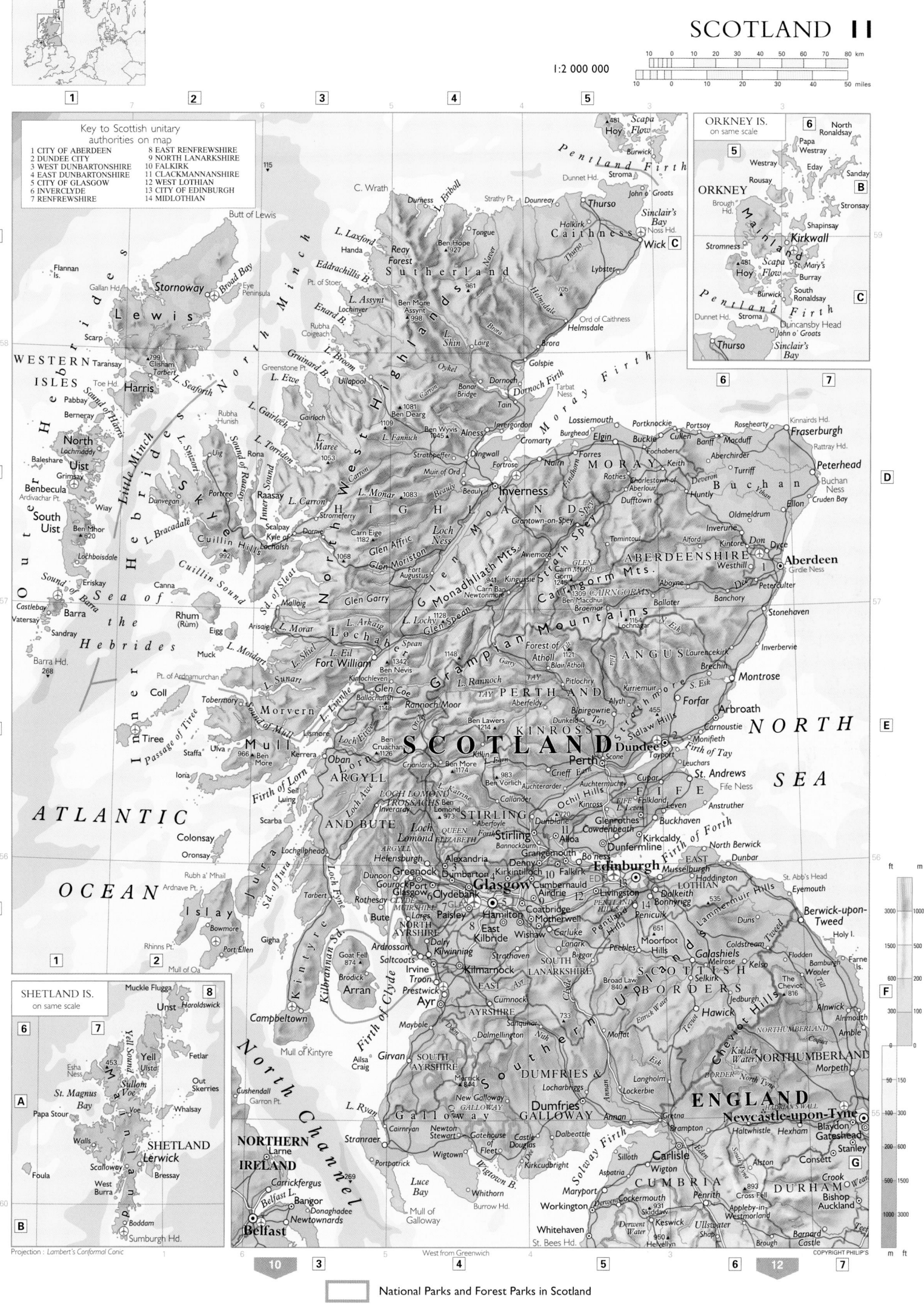

National Parks and Forest Parks in Scotland

10 0   10 20 30 40 50 60 70 80 km
10   0   10 20 30 40   50 miles

1:2 000 000

Key to English unitary
authorities on map
25 HARTLEPOOL
26 DARLINGTON
27 STOCKTON-ON-TEES
28 MIDDLESBROUGH
29 REDCAR AND CLEVELAND
30 BLACKPOOL
31 BLACKBURN WITH DARWEN
32 HALTON
33 WARRINGTON
34 KINGSTON UPON HULL
35 NORTH EAST LINCOLNSHIRE
36 STOKE-ON-TRENT
37 TELFORD AND WREKIN
38 DERBY CITY
39 CITY OF NOTTINGHAM
40 LEICESTER CITY
41 RUTLAND
42 PETERBOROUGH
43 MILTON KEYNES
44 LUTON
45 NORTH SOMERSET
46 CITY OF BRISTOL
47 BATH AND NORTH EAST SOMERSET
48 SWINDON
49 READING
50 WOKINGHAM
51 WINDSOR AND MAIDENHEAD
52 SLOUGH
53 BRACKNELL FOREST
54 THURROCK
55 SOUTHEND-ON-SEA
56 MEDWAY
57 PLYMOUTH
58 TORBAY
59 POOLE
60 BOURNEMOUTH
61 SOUTHAMPTON
62 PORTSMOUTH
63 BRIGHTON AND HOVE

Key to Welsh unitary
authorities on map
15 SWANSEA
16 NEATH PORT TALBOT
17 BRIDGEND
18 RHONDDA CYNON TAFF
19 MERTHYR TYDFIL
20 CAERPHILLY
21 BLAENAU GWENT
22 TORFAEN
23 CARDIFF
24 NEWPORT

NORTH SEA

IRISH SEA

North Channel

NORTHERN IRELAND

SCOTLAND

ENGLAND

WALES

CUMBRIA

LANCASHIRE

NORTHUMBERLAND

DURHAM

YORKSHIRE

LINCOLNSHIRE

GWYNEDD

ISLE OF MAN

The Wash

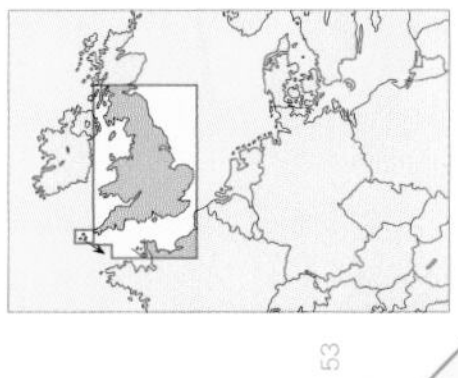

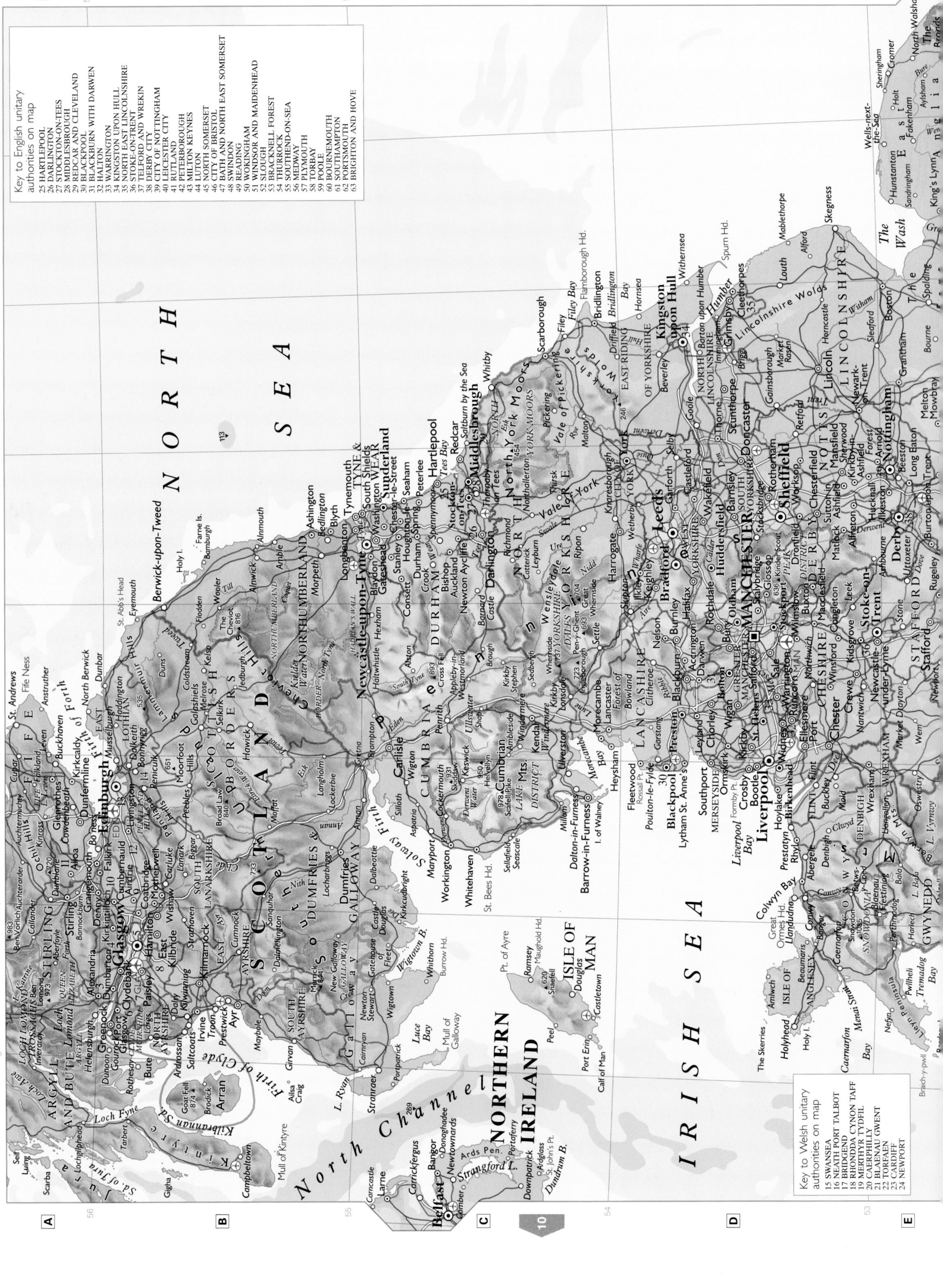

National Parks in England and Wales

Forest Parks in Scotland

ISLES OF SCILLY
on same scale

Tresco
Isles of Scilly
St. Mary's

Projection: Lambert's Conformal Conic

COPYRIGHT PHILIP'S

50 0 25 50 75 100 150 175 km
50 0 25 50 100 125 miles

1:5 000 000

ATLANTIC OCEAN

Shetland Is.
Yell
Unst
Fetlar
Mainland
Lerwick
Foula
Fair Isle

Orkney Is.
Westray
Sanday
Mainland
Stronsay
Kirkwall
Hoy
South Ronaldsay

NORWAY
Askøyna
Bergen
Osøyro
Stord
Bømlo
Leirvik
Kopervik
Åkrahamn
Haugesund
Boknafjord
Stavanger
Sandnes
Bryne
Nærbø

C. Wrath
Pentland Firth
Thurso
Wick
Helmsdale

Lewis
Stornoway
St. Kilda
Harris
North Minch
Ullapool
Lairg
Golspie
Tain
Invergordon
Dingwall
Moray Firth
Buckie
Banff
Fraserburgh
North Uist
Portree
Skye
L. Ness
Inverness
Nairn
Elgin
Peterhead
Benbecula
Glen More
Aviemore
CAIRNGORMS
Huntly
Don
Inverurie
South Uist
1182
Mts.
Aberdeen
Barra
Rhum
Mallaig
Fort William
1311
Dee
Ballater
Stonehaven
Eigg
Ben Nevis 1342
Coll
1214
Forfar
Montrose
Tiree
Mull
Oban
Tobermory
Perth
Arbroath
Dundee
St. Andrews
Colonsay
973
L. Awe
L. Lomond
Stirling
Glenrothes
Kirkcaldy
Dunbar
Jura
Greenock
Dumbarton
Dunfermline
Islay
Paisley
Glasgow
Motherwell
Edinburgh
Berwick-upon-Tweed
East Kilbride
Hamilton
Galashiels
Campbeltown
Arran
Kilmarnock
Southern Uplands
Jedburgh
816
Alnwick
Ayr
Hawick
Cheviot Hills

SCOTLAND
Grampian Mountains
North West Highlands
Sea of the Hebrides
Inner Hebrides
Outer Hebrides
789

NORTH SEA
238

Malin Hd.
Buncrana
Aran I.
Letterkenny
Coleraine
Ballymena
Larne
GLENVEAGH
Londonderry
Lifford
Antrim
Bangor
North Channel
Donegal
Omagh
Portadown
Belfast
Lisburn
Lurgan
Bundoran
Upper L.
Lough Neagh
Ballina
Sligo
Enniskillen
Armagh
Newry
Lower L. Erne
Leitrim
Clones
Castleblaney
Mull of Galloway
Whitehaven
Achill I.
L. Conn
Cavan
Castlebar
Newcastle-upon-Tyne
South Shields
Sunderland
Durham
Gateshead
Hexham
Carlisle
Workington
NORTHUMBERLAND
893
Darlington
Hartlepool
Redcar
Middlesbrough
Stockton-on-Tees
Cumbrian Mts.
978
LAKE DISTRICT
Barrow-in-Furness
Lancaster
N. YORK MOORS
Scarborough
YORKSHIRE DALES
16
Bridlington

UNITED KINGDOM

IRELAND
Westport
Roscommon
Longford
Ceanannus Mor
Drogheda
Lough Mask
Lough Corrib
Athlone
Mullingar
Boyne
Lough Ree
Connemara
Galway B.
Galway
Ballinasloe
Tullamore
Liffey
Dublin
Dun Laoghaire
Aran Is.
BURREN
Ennis
Lough Derg
Port Laoise
Athy
Bray
Galtee Mts.
Carlow
Arklow
Kilrush
Limerick
Thurles
Kilkenny
Shannon
Listowel
Tralee
Tipperary
Carrick-on-Suir
Wexford
Rosslare
953
Dingle
Mallow
Clonmel
Waterford
1041
Killarney
Blackwater
Dungarvan
Macgillycuddy's Reeks
Valencia I.
Cork
Youghal
Bantry
Bandon
Cobh
Kinsale
C. Clear
99

IRISH SEA
Anglesey
Holyhead
I. of Man
Douglas
Bangor
Colwyn Bay
Chester
1085
Snowdon
Wrexham
Crewe
PEAK DISTRICT
636
Blackpool
Preston
Blackburn
Burnley
Halifax
Bolton
Huddersfield
Oldham
MANCHESTER
Stockport
Warrington
Liverpool
Leeds
Bradford
York
Kingston upon Hull
Harrogate
Beverley
Scunthorpe
Grimsby
Doncaster
Barnsley
Rotherham
Sheffield
Lincoln
Louth
Chesterfield
Mansfield
Skegness
Boston
The Wash
Cromer
THE BROADS
Great Yarmouth
Lowestoft
Texel
Den Helder

WALES
SNOWDONIA
Pwllheli
Cardigan
Aberystwyth
Cambrian Mts.
Cardigan Bay
Welshpool
Shrewsbury
Telford
Stoke on Trent
Stafford
Derby
Nottingham
Grantham
Leicester
Nuneaton
Corby
Peterborough
Ely
Thetford
Norwich
King's Lynn
BIRMINGHAM
Coventry
Rugby
Northampton
Bedford
Cambridge
Ipswich
Bury St. Edmunds
Felixstowe
Harwich
Colchester
ENGLAND
Carmarthen
BRECON BEACONS
Brecon
886
Merthyr Tydfil
Llanelli
Neath
Rhondda
Cwmbran
Newport
Port Talbot
Swansea
Cardiff
Barry
Weston-super-Mare
Bristol
Bath
Gloucester
Cheltenham
Cotswold Hills
Oxford
High Wycombe
Luton
Harlow
Chelmsford
Basildon
Southend-on-Sea
Worcester
Redditch
Hereford
Royal Leamington Spa
Wolverhampton
Milton Keynes
Stevenage
Hemel Hempstead
Watford
LONDON
Thames
Reading
Slough
Maidstone
Canterbury
Margate
Chatham
Rochester
Reigate
Fishguard
Milford Haven
Haverfordwest
PEMBROKESHIRE COAST
Pembroke
Bristol Channel
Bridgwater
Barnstaple
Exmoor
Bude
Taunton
Yeovil
Salisbury
Newbury
Basingstoke
Guildford
Crawley
Ashford
Folkestone
Dover
Str. of Dover
Southampton
Winchester
Fareham
Portsmouth
Havant
Brighton
Worthing
Hastings
Eastbourne
36
Gris Nez
Boulogne-sur-Mer
NEW FOREST
Bournemouth
Poole
Newport
Isle of Wight
Weymouth
Le Touquet-Paris-Plage
33
618
DARTMOOR
Exeter
Exmouth
Torquay
Newquay
Truro
St. Austell
Plymouth
Falmouth
Penzance
Land's End
Isles of Scilly

CELTIC SEA

St. George's Channel

English Channel

Alderney
C. de la Hague
Pte. de Barfleur
Guernsey
St. Peter Port
Sark
Cotentin
Cherbourg
Valognes
Channel Is. (U.K.)
St. Helier
Jersey
Bayeux
Caen
Trouville-sur-Mer
Lisieux
Elbeuf
Seine

FRANCE
Dunkerque
Calais
St-Omer
Hazebrouck
Lille
Tourcoing
Tournai
Roubaix
Béthune
Lens
Bruay-la-Buissière
L'Ascq
Douai
Valenciennes
Le Tréport
Dieppe
Abbeville
Amiens
Fécamp
Le Havre
Rouen
Pays de Caux
PICARDIE
Cambrai
St-Quentin
Laon
Bolbec

BELGIUM
Brussel (Bruxelles)
Gent
Mechelen
Antwerpen
Brugge
Oostende
Zeebrugge

NETHERLANDS
's-Gravenhage (Den Haag)
ROTTERDAM
Dordrecht
Hoek van Holland
Vlissingen
Haarlem
Alkmaar

Projection: Conical with two standard parallels

East from Greenwich
West from Greenwich
COPYRIGHT PHILIP'S

316
1224

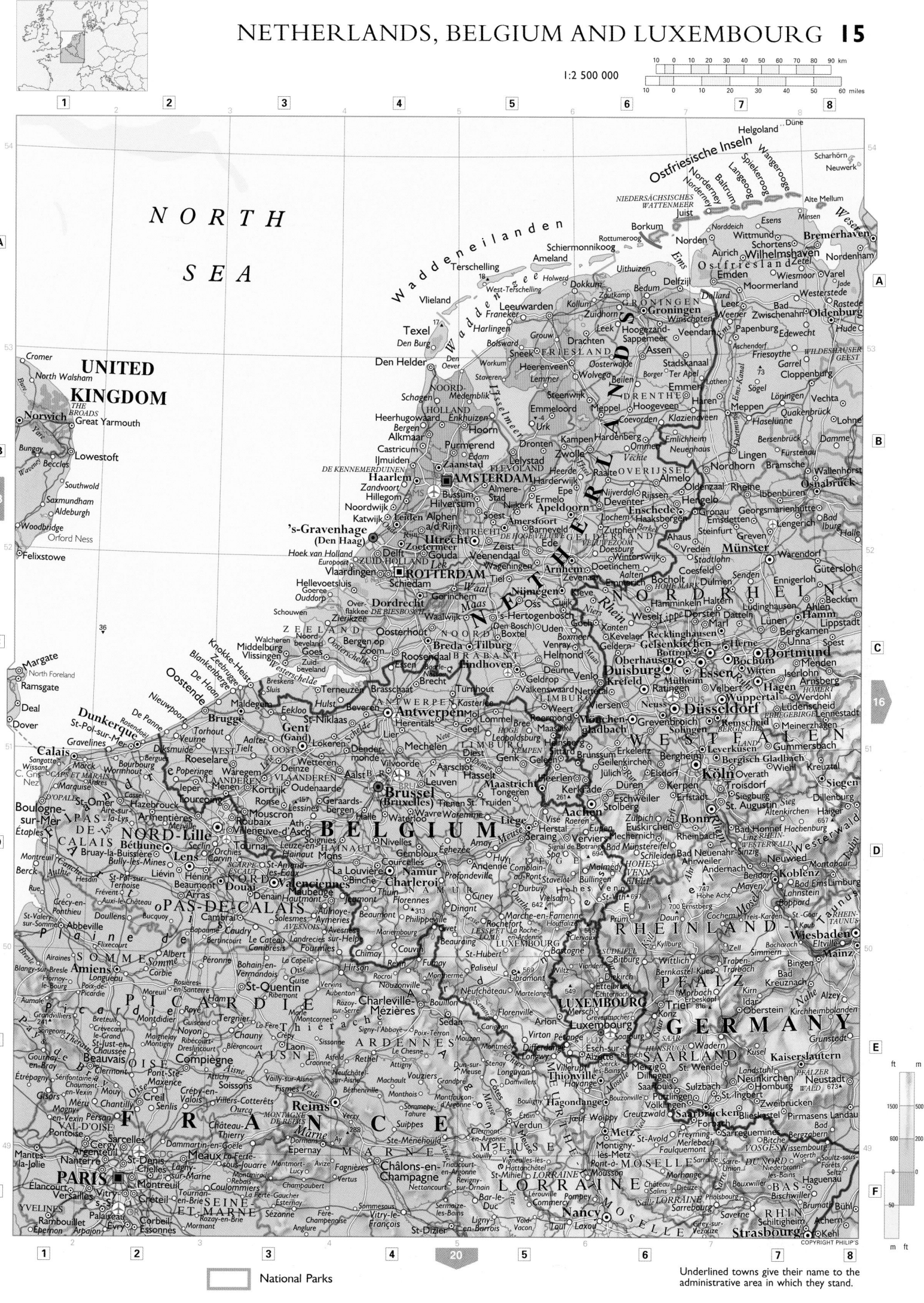

1:2 500 000

National Parks

Underlined towns give their name to the
administrative area in which they stand.

COPYRIGHT PHILIP'S

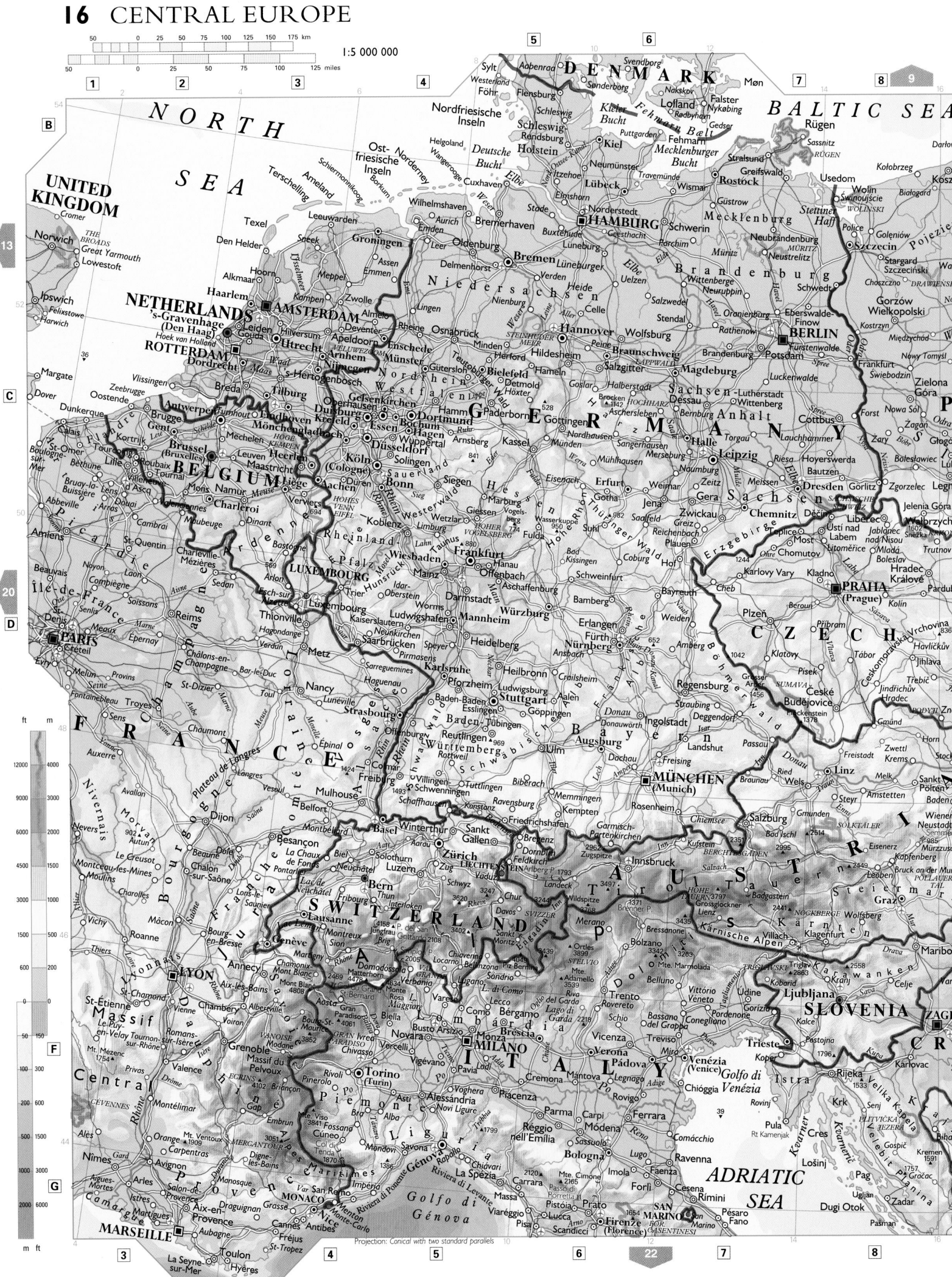

1:5 000 000

Projection: Conical with two standard parallels

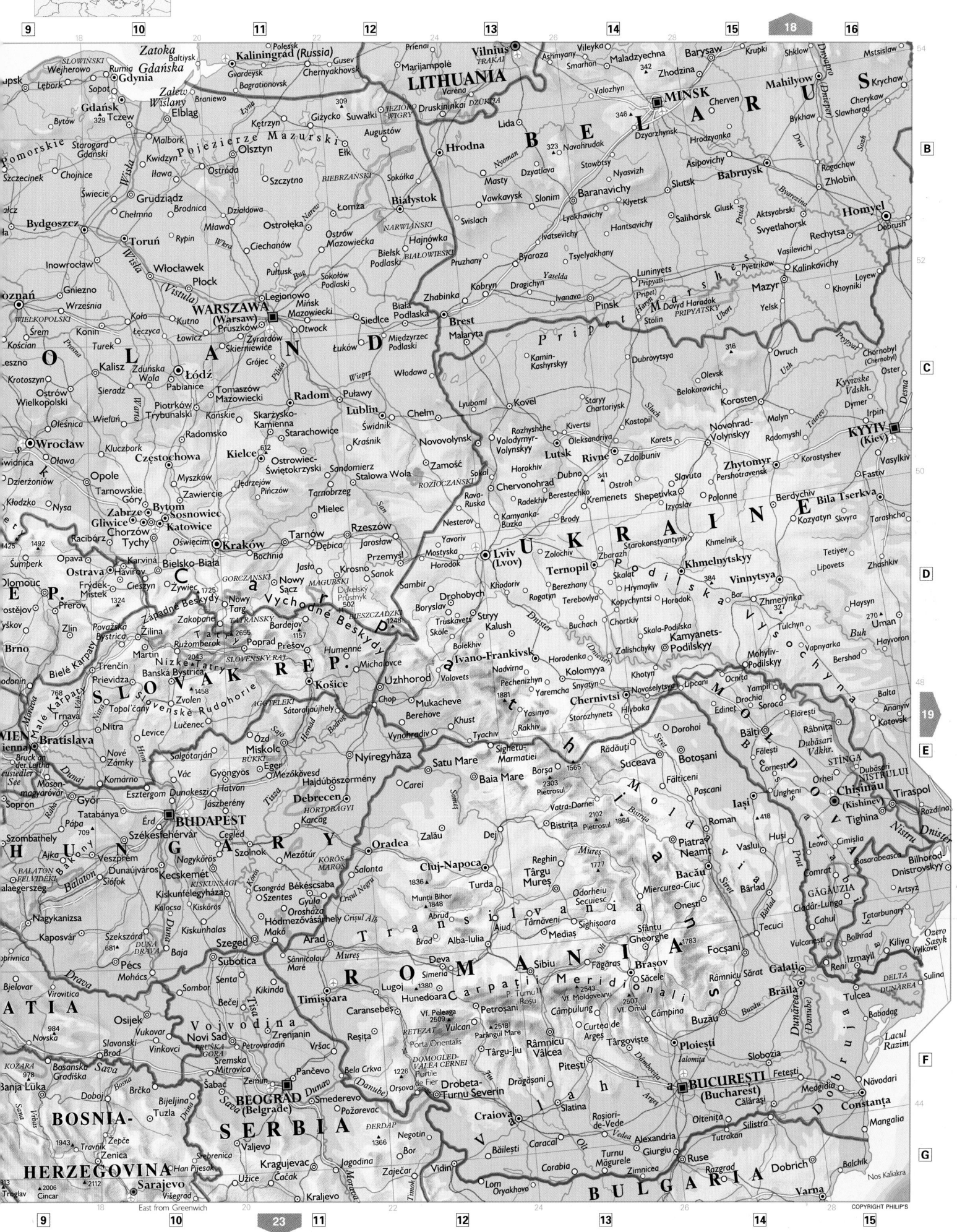

1:10 000 000

50 0 100 200 300 400 km
50 0 50 100 150 200 250 miles

28

1:5 000 000

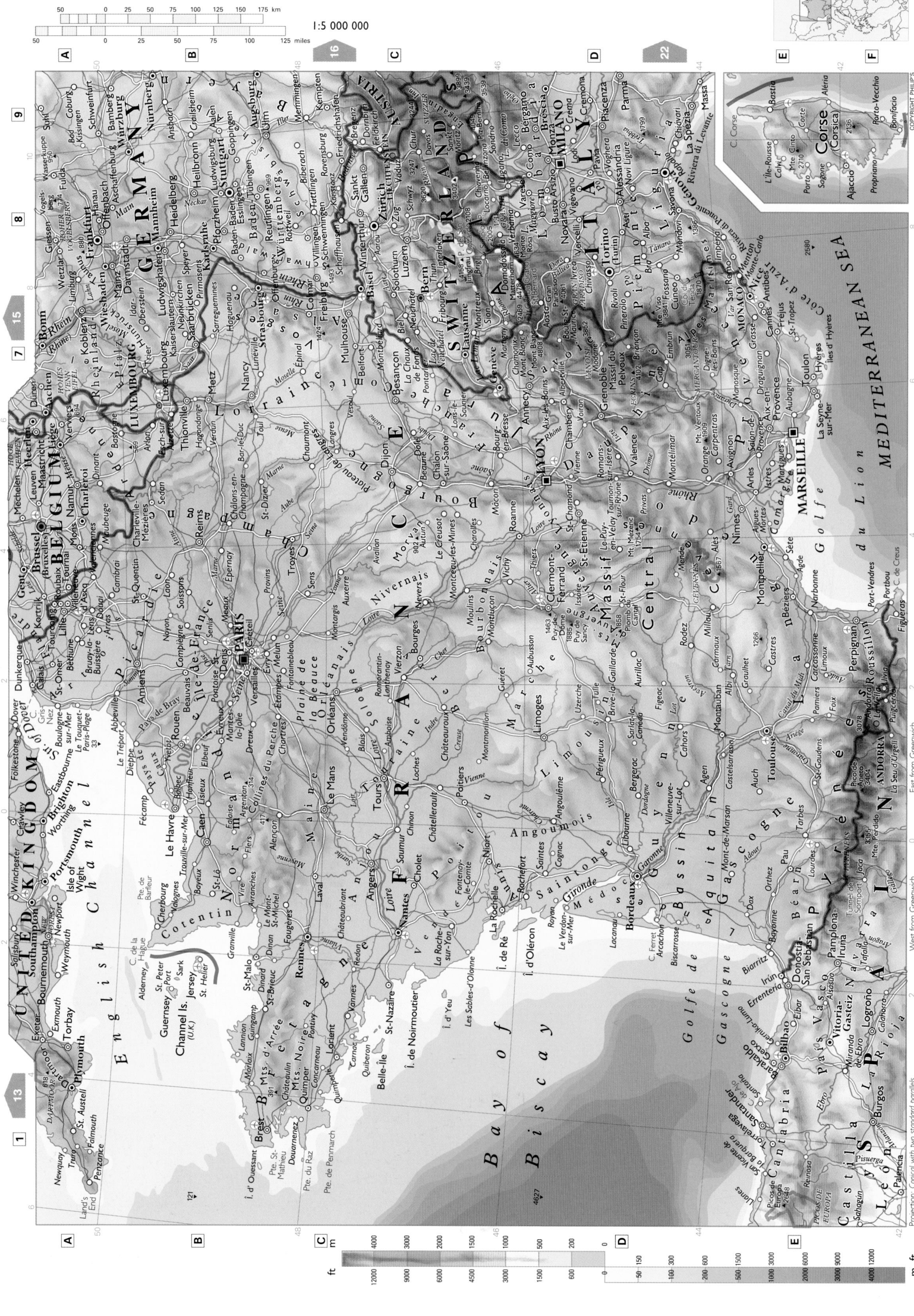

FRANCE
UNITED KINGDOM
BELGIUM
LUXEMBOURG
GERMANY
SWITZERLAND
AUSTRIA
ITALY
ANDORRA
MONACO
SPAIN
English Channel
Bay of Biscay
Golfe de Gascogne
Golfe du Lion
MEDITERRANEAN SEA
Channel Is. (U.K.)
Corse (Corsica)
PARIS
LYON
MARSEILLE
Bordeaux
Toulouse
Nantes
Lille
Strasbourg
Nice
Rennes
Brest
Dijon
Limoges
Clermont-Ferrand
Montpellier
Perpignan
Bruxelles
Bern
Torino
MILANO
Massif Central
Bretagne
Normandie
Bassin Aquitain
Pyrénées
Projection: Conical with two standard parallels
East from Greenwich
West from Greenwich
COPYRIGHT PHILIP'S

1:5 000 000

50 0 25 50 75 100 125 150 175 km
50 0 25 50 75 100 125 miles

East from Greenwich

West from Greenwich

Projection: Conical with two standard parallels

FRANCE

Montpellier · Sète · Agde · Béziers · Narbonne · Carcassonne · Limoux · Foix · Pamiers · St-Gaudens · Toulouse · Auch · Tarbes · Pau · Lourdes · Orthez · Bayonne · Dax · Biarritz · Golfe du Lion

Gascogne · **Pyrénées** · ANDORRA · Andorra la Vella · La Seu d'Urgell

Perpignan · Port-Vendres · Portbou · C. de Creus · G. de Roses · Costa Brava · Figueres · Olot · Girona · Blanes · Lloret de Mar · Sant Feliu de Guixols · Mataró · Badalona · **BARCELONA** · Santa Coloma de Gramenet · Sabadell · Terrassa · L'Hospitalet de Llobregat · El Prat de Llobregat · Sitges · Vilanova i la Geltrú

Pyrénées · Puigcerdà · Berga · Manresa · Vic · Granollers · Costa Dorada · Tarragona · Reus · Valls · G. de Sant Jordi · C. Tortosa

Pamplona · Iruña · Tudela · Jaca · Huesca · Barbastro · Monzón · Lleida (Lérida) · Cervera · Balaguer · Ebro

PAÍS VASCO · Bilbao · Barakaldo · Gernika-Lumo · Durango · Eibar · Vitoria-Gasteiz · Logroño · **La Rioja** · Miranda de Ebro · Calahorra

San Sebastián · Donostia · Errenteria · Irún · Navarra

Zaragoza · Calatayud · Tarazona · Soria · Sierra de Urbión · Sierra del Moncayo

Aragón · Teruel · Alcañiz · Caspe · Montalbán · El Maestrazgo · Morella · Vinarós · Tortosa

Cordillera Cantábrica · Santander · Torrelavega · Reinosa · Picos de Europa · Oviedo · Gijón · Avilés · Langreo · Mieres

Bay of Biscay · C. Ortegal · Ortigueira · Viveiro · Ferrol · A Coruña (La Coruña) · Betanzos · Carballo · C. Touriñán · C. Fisterra · Santiago de Compostela · Lugo · Villalba · Ribadeo

GALICIA · Pontevedra · Vigo · Ourense (Orense) · Lalín · A Estrada · Vilagarcía de Arousa · Redondela

Castilla y León · León · Astorga · Ponferrada · Zamora · Valladolid · Palencia · Burgos · Aranda de Duero · Salamanca · Ávila · Segovia · Medina del Campo · Benavente

Duero · Esla · Pisuerga

Sierra de Gredos · Sierra de Guadarrama

PORTUGAL · Bragança · Chaves · Vila Real · Viseu · Guarda · Covilhã · Castelo Branco · Coimbra · Aveiro · **Porto** · Vila Nova de Gaia · Matosinhos · Braga · Guimarães · Viana do Castelo · Douro · Minho

Figueira da Foz · Leiria · Pombal · Santarém · Torres Vedras · **LISBOA** · Sintra · Cascais · Setúbal · C. da Roca · C. Espichel · Almada

Évora · Beja · Sines · Portalegre · Elvas · Estremoz

Algarve · Faro · Lagos · Portimão · Albufeira · C. de São Vicente

ESPAÑA / SPAIN

MADRID · Alcalá de Henares · Getafe · Leganés · Móstoles · Alcorcón · Aranjuez · Toledo · Talavera de la Reina · Guadalajara · Cuenca · Montes de Toledo

Castilla–La Mancha · Albacete · Ciudad Real · Valdepeñas · Puertollano · Alcázar de San Juan · Tomelloso · Manzanares

Extremadura · Cáceres · Mérida · Badajoz · Don Benito · Villanueva de la Serena · Guadiana · Zafra

Andalucía · Sevilla · Córdoba · Jaén · Granada · Málaga · Huelva · Cádiz · Jerez de la Frontera · Almería · Úbeda · Baeza · Linares · Andújar · Utrera · Dos Hermanas · San Fernando · Algeciras · Marbella · Estepona · Torremolinos · Fuengirola · Vélez-Málaga · Motril · Guadix · Antequera · Écija · Lucena · Ronda · Osuna · Arcos de la Frontera

Sierra Morena · **Sierra Nevada** · Mulhacén 3478 · **Costa del Sol** · **Sierra de Cazorla**

Guadalquivir · G. de Cádiz · Sanlúcar de Barrameda · Chiclana de la Frontera · Medina Sidonia

Gibraltar (U.K.) · Str. of Gibraltar · C. Trafalgar · La Línea de la Concepción · San Roque · C. de Europa · Ceuta (Sp.)

Costa Blanca · Valencia · Sagunt · Gandia · Dénia · Benidorm · Alicante (Alacant) · Elche (Elx) · Elda · Villena · Alcoi · Xàtiva · Sueca · Cullera · Castelló de la Plana · Vila-real · Vila-real · Torrent · Paterna · Requena · Utiel

Golfo de Valencia · C. de la Nao · C. de San Antonio

Murcia · Cartagena · Lorca · Águilas · Mazarrón · Mar Menor · Torrevieja · Orihuela · Yecla · Jumilla · Cieza · Caravaca de la Cruz · Vélez Rubio · C. de Gata · C. de Palos

Islas Baleares · Menorca · Maó (Mahón) · Mallorca · **Palma de Mallorca** · Manacor · Sóller · Calvià · Llucmajor · C. de Formentor · Eivissa (Ibiza) · Formentera · Sant Antoni Abat · Cabrera · B. de Palma · Is. Columbretes

MEDITERRANEAN SEA

ALGERIA · **ALGER (Algiers)** · Oran · Mostaganem · Mascara · Tiaret · Relizane · Blida · Koléa · Cherchell · Ténès · Chlef · El Arbá · Médéa · Miliana · Khemis Miliana

MOROCCO · Melilla (Sp.) · Nador · Al Hoceïma · Tétouan · Tanger · Chechaouene · Ksar el Kebir · Larache · Asilah · Ceuta (Sp.) · C. Spartel

Cap des Trois Fourches · Is. Alborán (Sp.)

ATLANTIC OCEAN

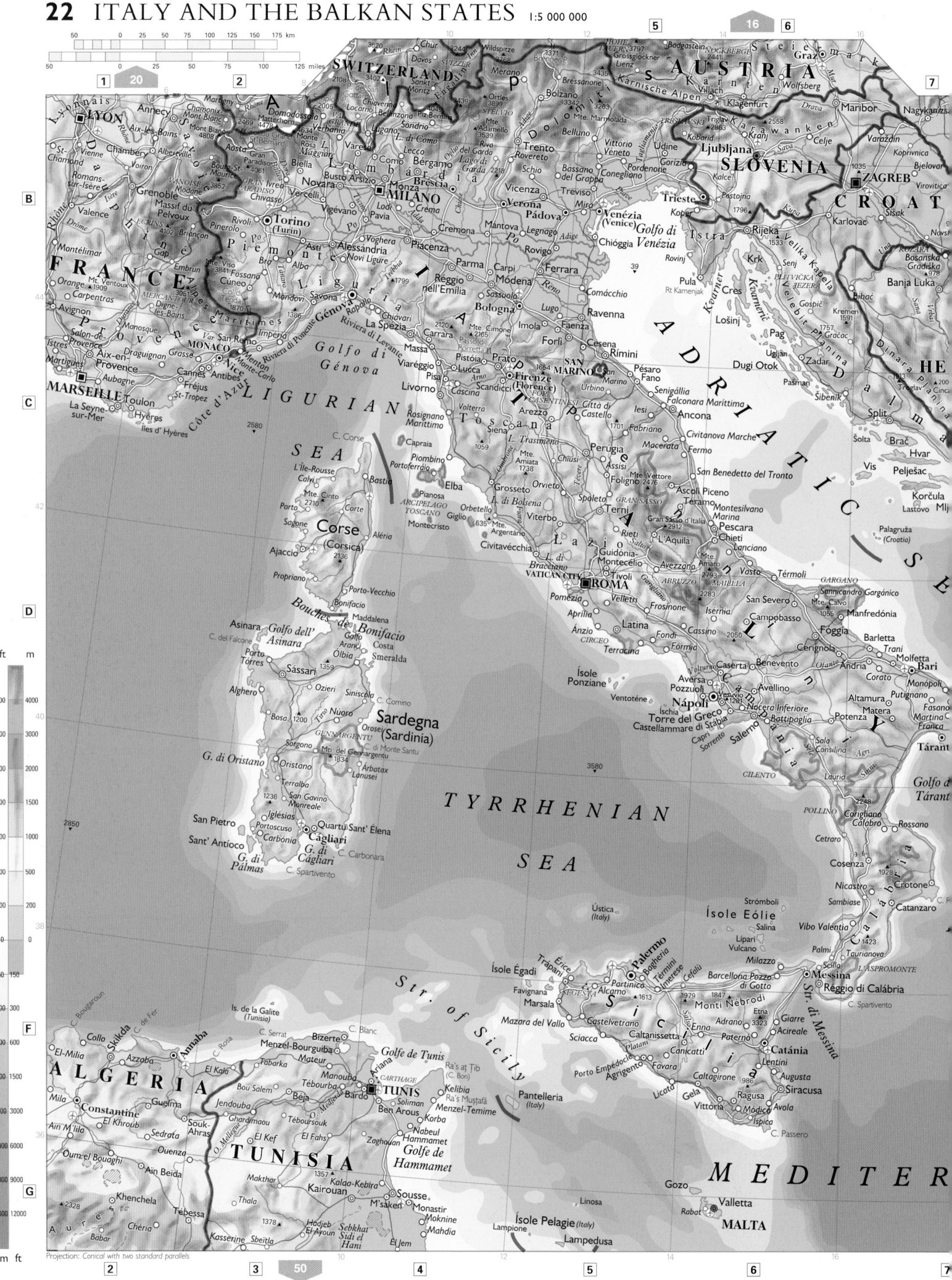

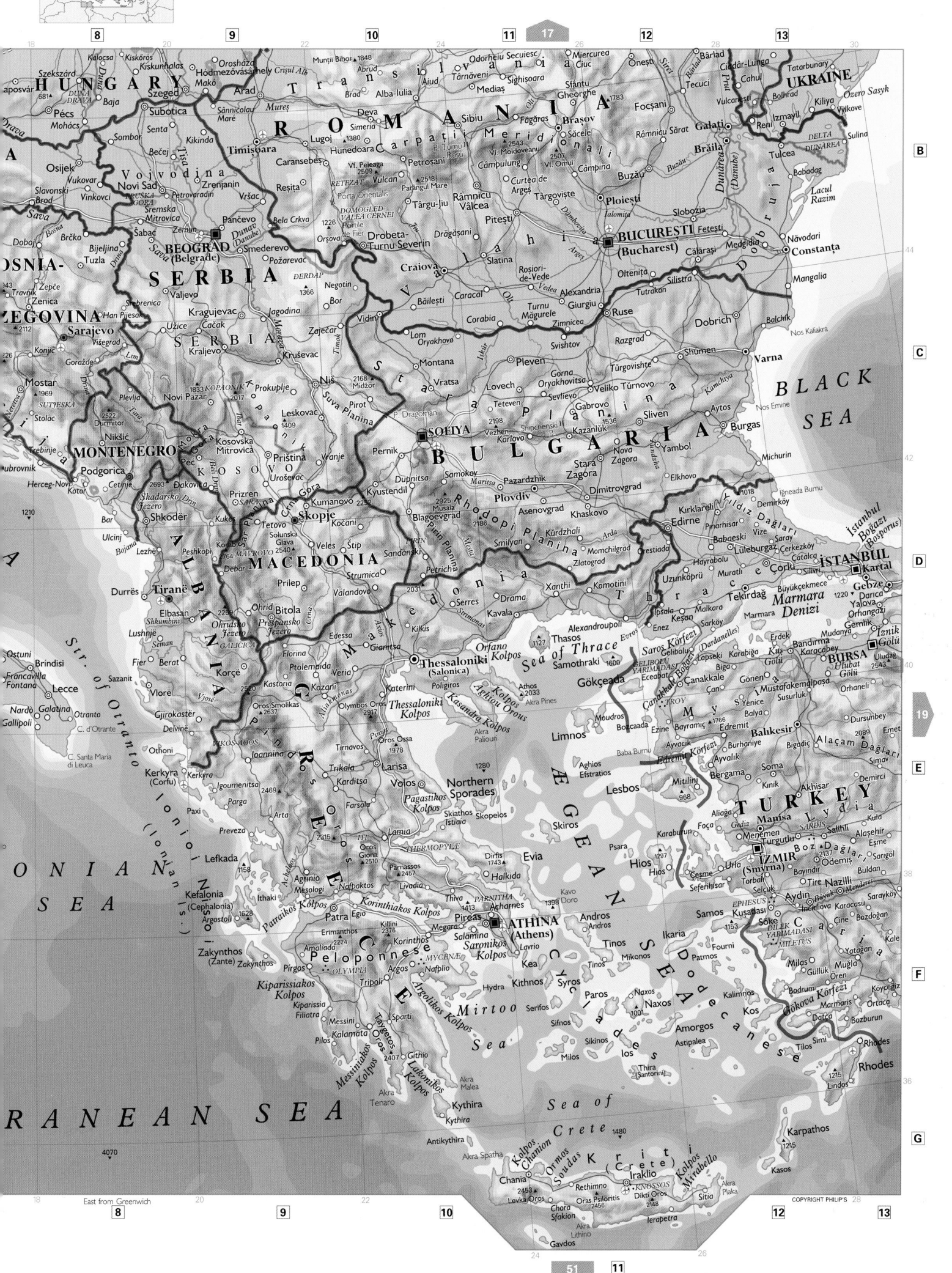

A

B

C

D

E

19

F

G

8 **9** **10** **11** **12** **13**

East from Greenwich

51

11

COPYRIGHT PHILIP'S

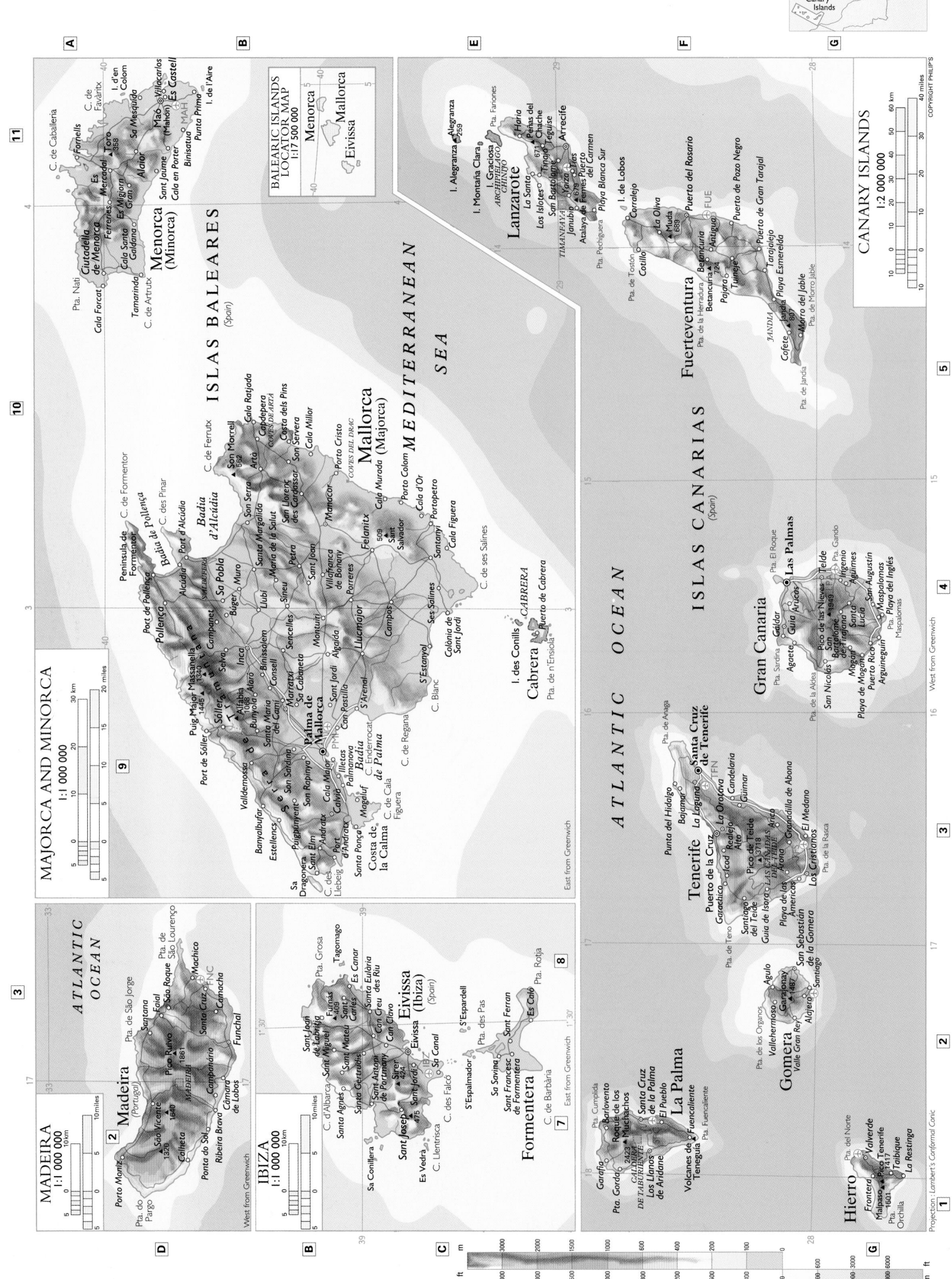

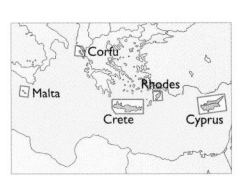

Corfu
Rhodes
Malta
Crete
Cyprus

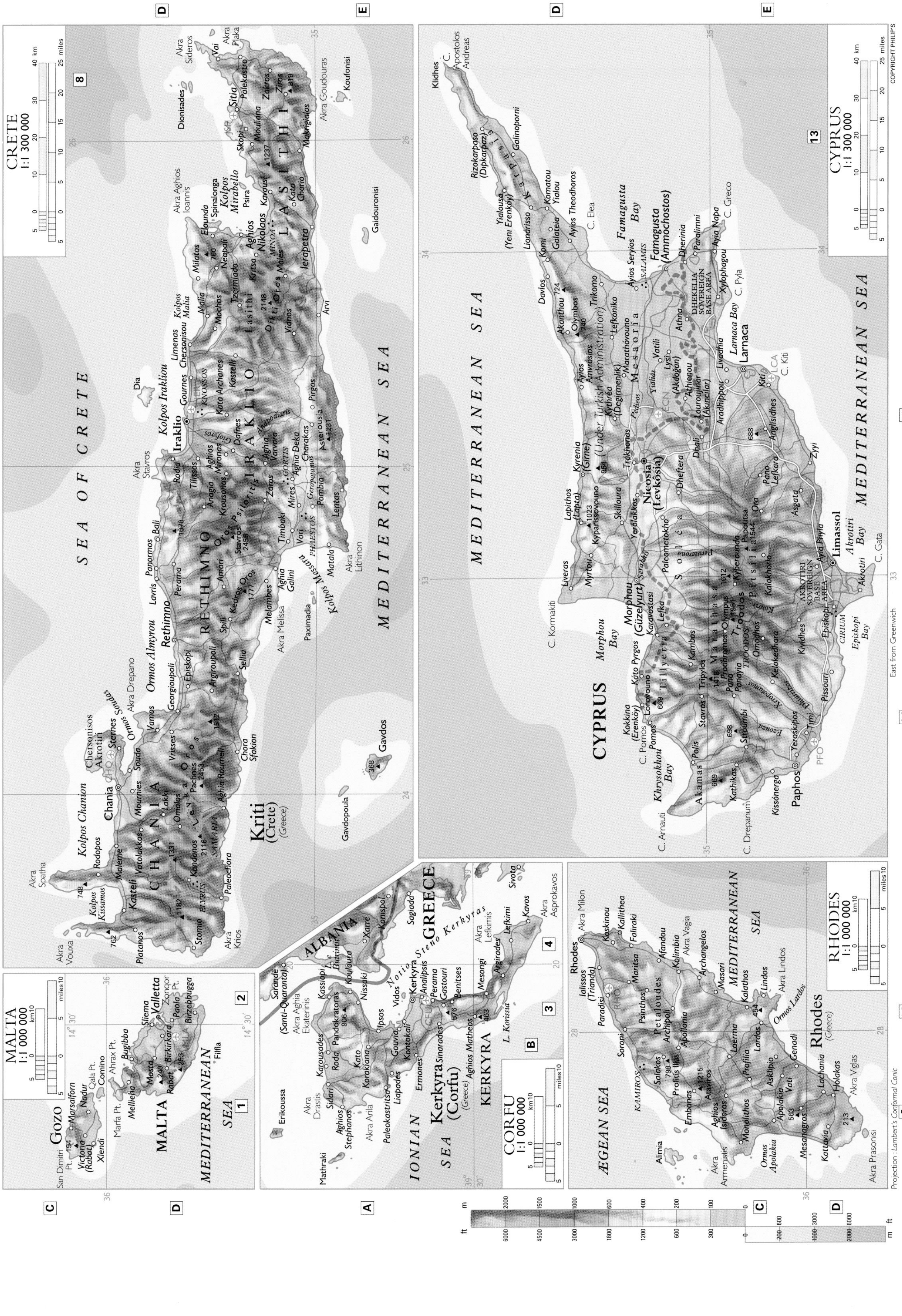

CRETE
1:1 300 000

40 km
25 miles

8

Akra Plaka
Akra Sideros
Vai
Palekastro
Ziros
Zíros
Sitia
Moúliana
Skopi
Kavoúsi
1237
Kato
Chorio
Ierapetra
Dionisades
Kolpos
Mirabello
Psira
Spinalonga
Elounda
Neapoli
780
Milatos
Aghios Nikolaos
Kritsa
Tzermiado
Lasithi
Dikti 2148
Malia
Mochos
Vianos
Arvi
Akra Aghios Ioannis
Gournes
Chersonisou
Kato Archanes
KNOSSOS
Gournia
Aghia Varvara
Aghia Deka
GORTIS
Mires
Charakas
Pombia
Lentas
Gaidouronisi
Koufonisi
Akra Goudouras

LASITHI
IRAKLIO
RETHIMNO
CHANIA

SEA OF CRETE

Dia
Kolpos Irakliou
Limenas
Iraklio
Akra Stavros
Rodia
Tilissos
Anagia
Krousonas
1078
Zaros
Timbaki
PHAESTOS
Matala
Akra Lithion
Kolpos Messara

Panormos
Bali
Perama
Spili
Kedros 1777
Melambes
Paximadia

Rethimno
Ornos Almyrou
Argyroupoli
Episkopi
Sellia
Chora Sfakion
Anopolis
2453
Omalos
Lakki
1331
Kandanos
2116
Aghia Roumeli
Paleochora

SEA OF CRETE

Akra Spatha
Kolpos Chanion
Rodopos
74B
762
Platanos
Akra Vouka
Kolpos Kissamos
Kasteli
Vatolakkos
1182
Stomio
Akra Kríos

Chania
Mournies
Souda
Akra Drepano
Ornos Souda
Stérnes
CHQ
SAMARIA
Georgioupoli
Vamos
Chersonisos
Akrotiri
Vrisses
Lavris

Kriti
(Crete)
(Greece)

368
Gavdos
Gavdopoula

MEDITERRANEAN SEA

MALTA
1:1 000 000

10 miles
km 10

1

San Dimitri Pt.
Victoria (Rabat)
Xlendi
Nadur
Marsalforn
Qala Pt.
Comino
GOZO
Marfa Pt.
Mellieha
Ahrax Pt.
Bugibba
Nadur
Mosta
Rabat
240
Birkirkara
Paola Pt.
Sliema
Valletta
Zonqor
Birzebbuga
Marsaxlokk
"Filfla"

MALTA

MEDITERRANEAN SEA

14° 30'

CORFU
1:1 000 000

10 miles
km 10

B

Erikoussa
Mathraki
Aghios Stephanos
Akra Drastis
Sidari
Paleokastritsa
Roda
Kato
Korakiana
Gouvia
Liapades
Ermones
Kerkyra
(Corfu)
(Greece)
Benitses
Perama
Vidos
Kontokali

KERKYRA

IONIAN SEA

39°

30'

Akra Aria

GREECE

ALBANIA

Sarandë (Santi-Quaranta)
Akra Aghia Ekaterini
Butrint
Kassiopi
Nissaki
Ipsos
Pandokratoras
906
Sinarades
Aghios Matheos
576
Gastouri
Mesongi
453
L. Korissía
Messongi
Andipsis
Argirades
Agirades
Korissia
Lefkimni
Kavos
Akra Lefkimis
Akra Asprokavos

2
4

Noΐto Stenó Kerkyras

RHODES
1:1 000 000

10 miles
km 10

10

AEGEAN SEA

Akra Milon
Rhodes
Ialissos (Trianda)
Kritika
Maritsa
Afandou
Psinthos
Paradisi
Soroni
Kalavarda
KAMIROS
Kalithea
Faliraki
Archangelos
Kalopetra
Kremasti
Kalamos
Masari
Malona
Petaloudes
Archipoli
Apollonia
798
Profitis Ilias
Salakos
Dimilia
Embonas
Laerma
1215
Ataviros
Aghios Isidoros
Monolithos
Lardos
Akra Lindos
Lindos
Kalathos
Asklipio
Profilia
563
Gennadi
Vati
Apolakia
Mesanagros
213
Lachania
Holakas
Kattavia
Akra Prasonisi
Akra Vglas
Armenistis
Ornos Apolakia

Rhodes
(Greece)

MEDITERRANEAN SEA

28°

36°

CYPRUS
1:1 300 000

40 km
25 miles

13

Kildhes C.
Apostolos Andreas
Rizokarpaso (Dipkarpaz)
Galinoporni
Yialousa (Yeni Erenköy)
Komi
Liondrisso
Komatou Yialou
Galateia
Ayios Theodhoros
C. Elea
Karpasia
Davlos
Akanthou
724
Komi Kebir
Trikomo
Lefkoniko
Ayios Seryios
SALAMIS
Famagusta Bay
Famagusta (Ammochostos)
Dherinia
Paralimni
Xylophagou
Ayia Napa
C. Greco

Mesaoria
(Under Turkish Administration)

C. Kormakiti
Lapithos (Lapta)
Kyrenia (Girne)
Myrtou
Liveras
Kambyli
Skilloura
Lefka
Morphou (Güzelyurt)
Karavostasi
Kazaphani
Kyparissovouno
1023
Trakhonas
Dhikomo
Nicosia (Levkosía)
ECN
Kythrea
Marathovouno
Vatili
Lysi
Athienou
Pyla
C. Pyla
Larnaca Bay
Larnaca
LCA
C. Kiti
Kiti

Morphou Bay
Akaki
Peristerona
Kambos
Tripylos
Kakopetria
1612
Troodos
Khandria
Prodhromos
Platres
Olympus 1951
Kalokhorio
Panayia
Stavros
Pano Panayia
Kannaviou
688
Kalavasos
Lefkara
Zyyi

MEDITERRANEAN SEA

CYPRUS

C. Kormakiti
Kokkina (Erenköy)
Pomos
Pyrgos
Kato Pyrgos
Loutrou
C. Pomos
Polis
Khrysokhou Bay
C. Arnauti
Akamas
Stroumbi
Kinousa
Pano Panayia
Omodhos
Kedhares
Pissouri
Episkopi Bay
Akrotiri
Akrotiri Bay
Limassol
AKROTIRI SOVEREIGN BASE AREA
C. Gata
GIRIUM

Paphos
PFO
Yeroskipos
Kouklia
Khapotami
C. Drepanum
Kissonerga
Kathikas
669
698
Stroumbi

Paphos
(Greece)

DHEKELIA SOVEREIGN BASE AREA

MEDITERRANEAN SEA

East from Greenwich

m
6000
4500
3000
1800
1200
600
300
0
ft

m
2000
1500
1000
600
400
200
100
0

ft
6000
3000
2000 - 600
0
m

100 0 200 400 600 800 1000 1200 1400 km

1:47 000 000

100 0 200 400 600 800 1000 miles

Projection: Bonne

East from Greenwich

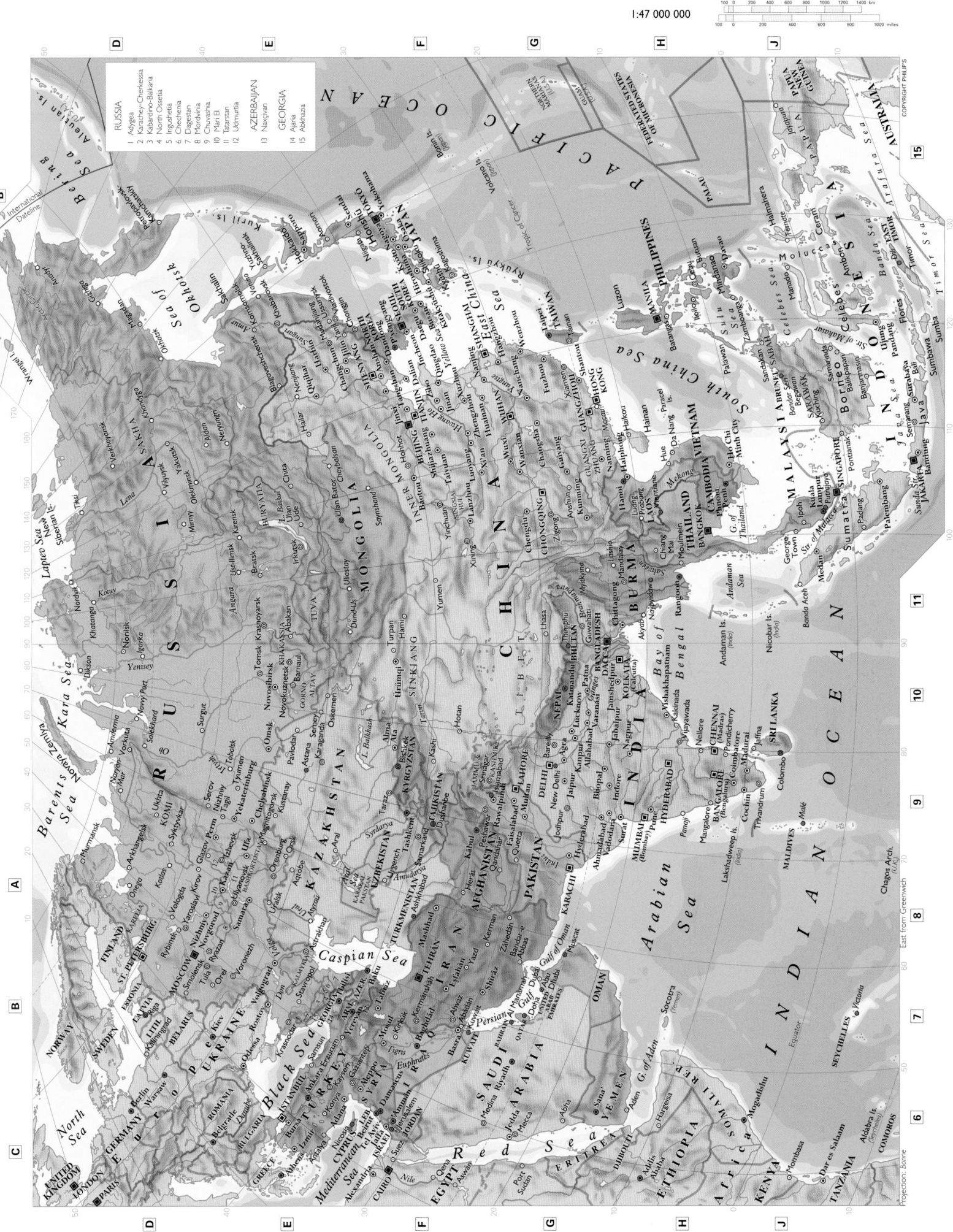

100 0 100 200 300 400 500 600 700 800 km

1:20 000 000

100 0 100 200 300 400 500 miles

	RUSSIA
1	Adygea
2	Karachey-Cherkessia
3	Kabardino-Balkaria
4	North Ossetia
5	Ingushetia
6	Chechenia
7	Dagestan
8	Mordvinia
9	Chuvashia
10	Mari El
11	Tatarstan
12	Udmurtia
13	Khakassia
	AZERBAIJAN
14	Naxçıvan
	GEORGIA UKRAINE
15	Ajaria 17 Crimea
16	Abkhazia

Projection: Conical Orthomorphic with two standard parallels

East from Greenwich

A B C D E F

OCEAN

Severnaya Zemlya

Ostrov Shmidta
Ostrov Ushakova
Ostrov Pioner
Ostrov Sergeya Kirova
Ostrov Isachenko

Mys Arkticheskiy
781 Ostrov Komsomolets
935 Ostrov Oktyabrskoy Revolyutsii
965 Ostrov Bolshevik
Ostrov Malyy Taymyr

Byrranga Gory 1146
Poluostrov
Gory Taymyr
621
Nordvik
Oz. Taymyr

Ostrov Petra
Ostrov Bolshoy Begichev
Mys Buorkhaya

Proliv Vilkitskogo
Mys Chelyuskin

Laptev Sea

Ostrova Petra

Ostrov Belkovskiy
Ostrov Kotelnyy
Lyakhovskoye
Ostrov Stolbovoy
Proliv Dmitriya Lapteva

Novosibirskiye Ostrova
Ostrov Faddeyevskiy
Ostrov Bolshoy Lyakhovskiy
Ostrov Malyy Lyakhovskiy
Novaya Sibir

Ostrov Bennetta
Ostrova Delonga
Ostrov Zhokhova
Ostrov Genriyetty
Ostrov Zhannetty

3800

East Siberian Sea

Ostrova Medvezhi
Ostrov Ayon

Ostrov Vrangelya

Chaunskaya Guba

Chukchi Sea

Mys Dezhneva (East C.)
Uelen
Vankarem
1843
Enmelen
Ugolnye Kopi
Providenya
Beringovskiy
1194

St. Lawrence I. (U.S.A.)
Mys Navarin
International Date Line
Bering Str.

Chukotskoye Nagorye
Egvekinot

Koryakskoye Nagorye
2562

Sredinnyy

Poluostrov Kamchatka
Petropavlovsk-Kamchatskiy
Yelizovo
4750
Klyuchi
3607
Vilyuchinsk

Bering Sea

Kolymskoye Nagorye

Severnaya
Zemlya

OCEAN

Lena
Verkhoyansk
2389

Khrebet Cherskogo
Gora Chen
2682
Ust-Nera
Artyk
2959

Yablonovyy Khrebet

Stanovoy Khrebet

Khrebet Dzhugdzur

Sea of Okhotsk

Sakhalin
Aleksandrovsk-Sakhalinskiy
Gora Lopatina 1609
Yuzhno-Sakhalinsk

Kurilskiye Ostrova

RUSSIA
R U S S I A

IRSKIY

Vostochnyy Sayan

Bratsk
Ust-Ilimsk
Ust-Kut
Severobaykalsk

L. Baykal

BURYATIYA

Ulan Ude
Chita

Irkutsk
Angarsk

MONGOLIA

Ulaanbaatar

Hangayn Nuruu

Hentiyn Nuruu

Aerhtai Shan

Gobi

CHINA

Da Hingan Ling
(Manchuria)
Dongbei

HARBIN
QIQIHAR
DAQING
CHANGCHUN
Mudanjiang
JILIN
Vladivostok

Khabarovsk
Komsomolsk-na-Amur
Amur
Sikhote Alin

NORTH KOREA
PYONGYANG
Hamhüng
Ch'öngjin

SOUTH KOREA
SEOUL
INCHEON
DAEJEON
DAEGU
BUSAN
GWANGJU

Sea of Japan (East Sea)

HOKKAIDŌ
SAPPORO
Hakodate

Honshū
JAPAN
KYŌTO
KŌBE
ŌSAKA

BEIJING
TANGSHAN
SHENYANG
ANSHAN
FUSHUN
CHIFENG
BAOTOU
Hohhot
Zhangjiakou
DALIAN

COPYRIGHT PHILIP'S

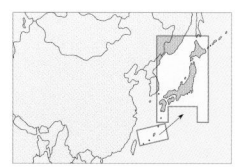

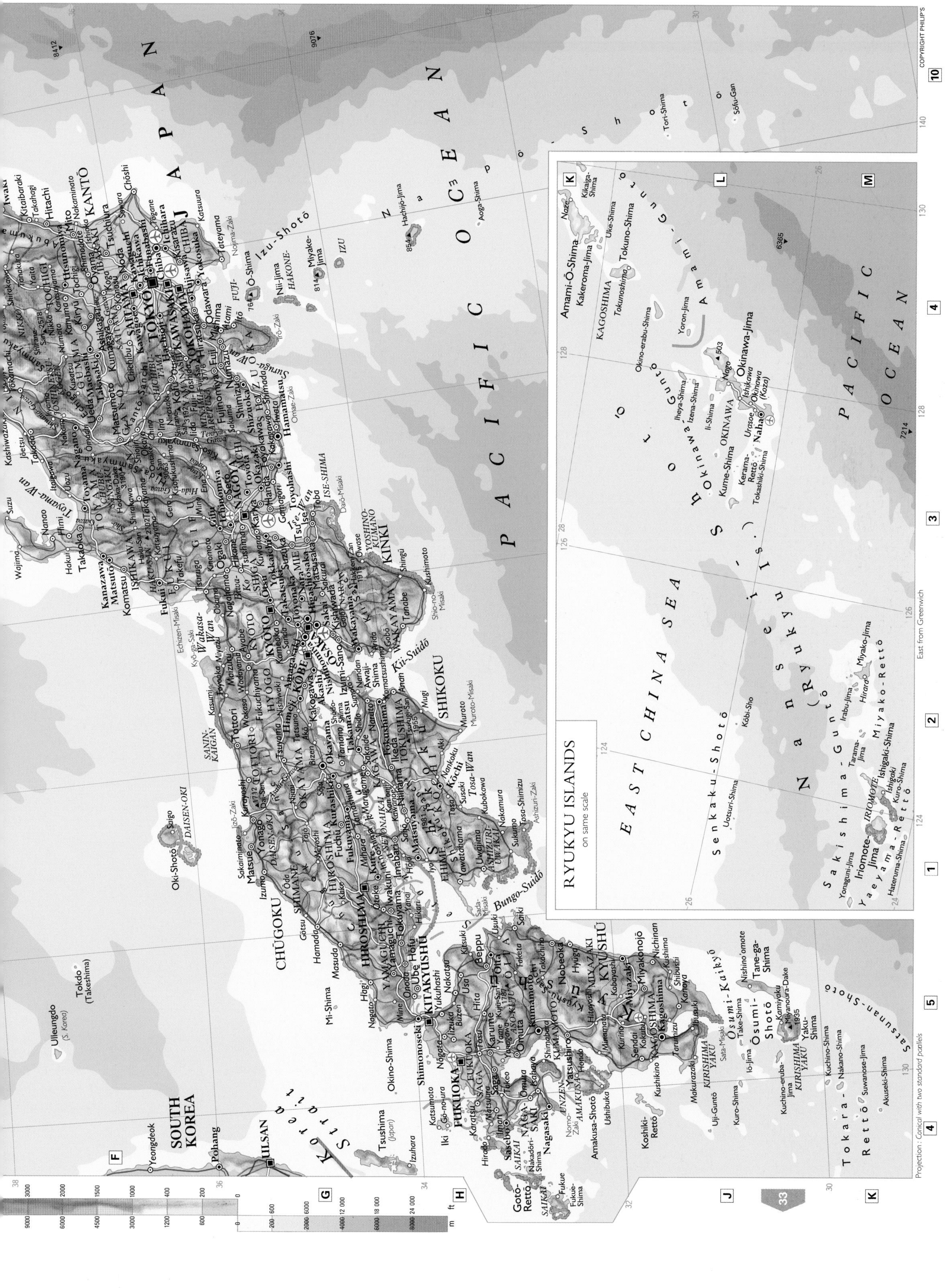

RYUKYU ISLANDS
on same scale

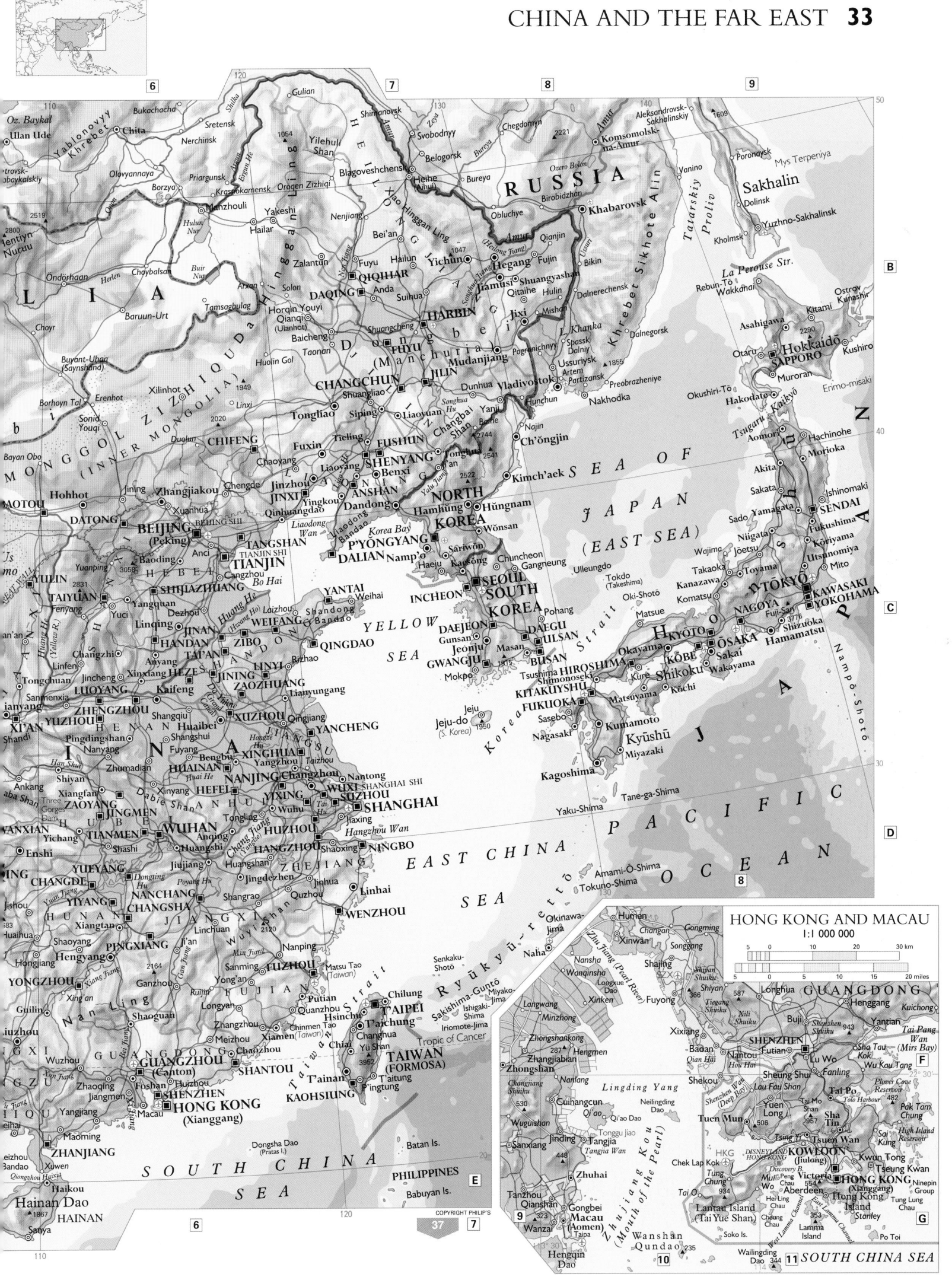

1:6 000 000

50   0   50   100   150   200 km

50   0   50   100   150 miles

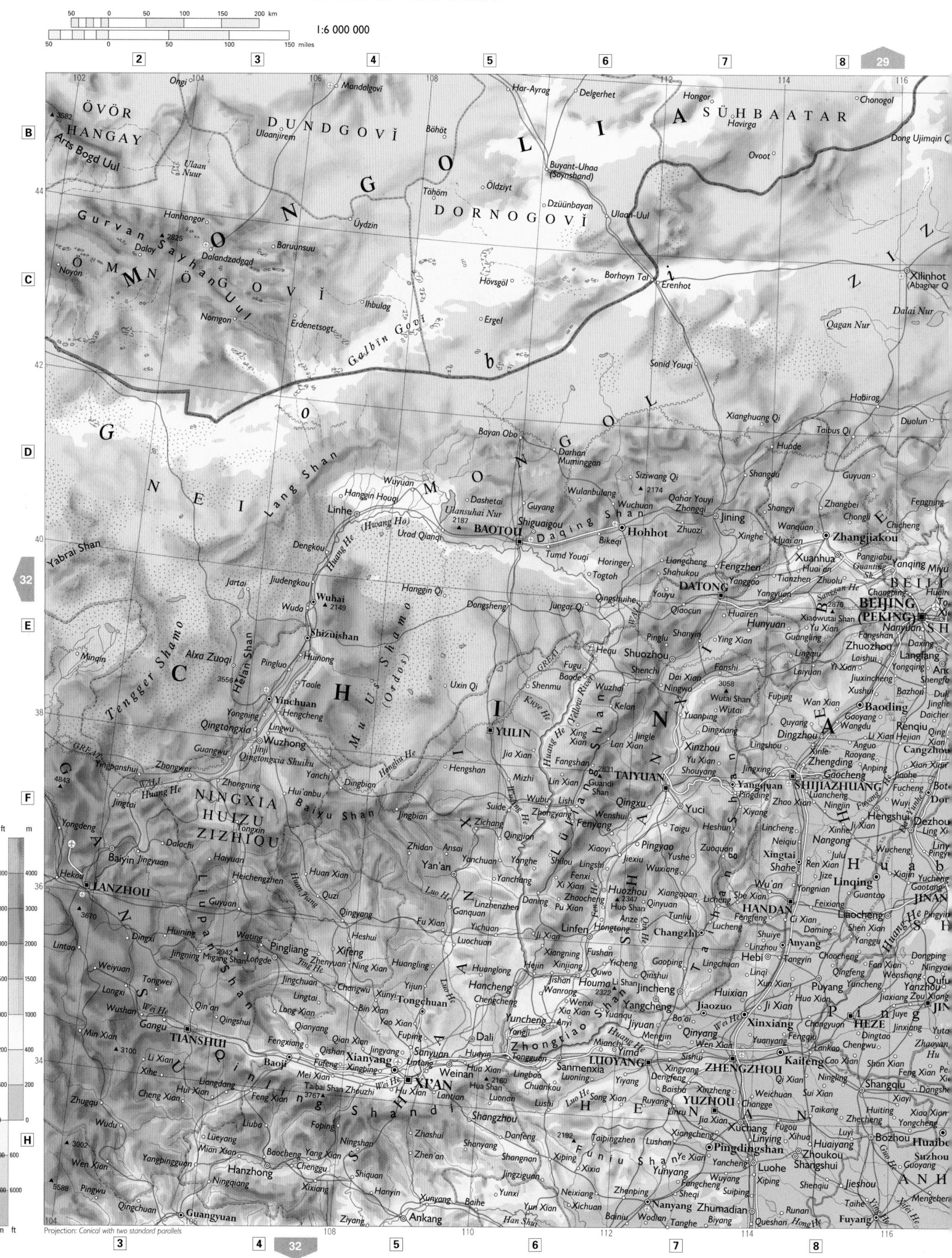

Sand deserts

Projection: Conical with two standard parallels

9　10　11　12　13　14　15　16

118　120

Horqin Youyi Qianqi
(Ulanhot)

HEILONGJIANG

Zhenlai　Maoxing Zhaoyuan Shuangcheng Acheng　Yanshou
Baicheng　Da'an
Nen　Songhua Jiang Changchunling　Lalin
Taonan　Tuquan　Anguang　Oagan Nur Qian　FUYU　Beitaolaizhao Sanchahe　Yushu　Wuchang　Shanhetun Hailin
Qian an　Shenjingzi　Kaoshan　Dehui　Shulan　Ning'an
Tongyu　Changling　Fulongquan　Nong'an
Zhanyu　Beizhengzhen

Zhangguangcai Ling

Bin Xian
HARBIN
1690　Hengdaohezi
Mudanjiang　Maqiaohe
Xiachengzi

Linkou　Jixi
Muling
Shangzhi
Yimianpo

Turiy Rog　69
Lake
Khanka

Dongjingcheng　Suiyang Suifenhe
Luozigou　Dongning
Pogranichnyy

Ussuriysk

B
44

Jarud Qi
1949
Xinkai He　Horqin Zuoyi Zhongqi　Maolin　Huaidezhen
CHANGCHUN　JILIN
JILIN
Fanjiatun
Jiaohe　Xinzhan Emu　Huangsongdian
Dunhua　Daxinggou
Wangqing
Mingyuegue
Tumen　Yanji
Helong　Longjing
Namyang Hunchun

Golenki
Razdolnoye
Tavrichanka
Artem
Vladivostok
Slavyanka

C

2029
xigten Qi　Linxi
Bairin
Zuoqi
Kailu　Tongliao
Xiliao He
Bairin Youqi
Xar Moron He
Laoha He

Shuangliao
Dongliao He
Lishu
Siping
Gongzhuling Shuangyang
Yitong
Liaoyuan
Jargalang　Bamiancheng
Xifeng

Panshi
Huadian
Huifa He
Huinan　Baishan
Dongfeng　Fusong
Quanyang　Songjianghe
Jingyu

Antu
Baihe 1677
Paektu-san
2744
Changbai

Erdao Jiang

Changbai Shan

Hoeryong
Musan　Puryong
Aoji　Unggi
Najin
Pugodong

Posyet
Khasan
Sosura

42

Ongniud Qi
2020
Wutonghaolai
Hure Qi
Xiawa

Zhangwu
Kangping
Faku
Tiefa
WALL
Kaiyuan　Shanchengzhen
WILLOW　Tieling
Qingyuan

Liuhe
Jiangyuan
Hunjiang
Shiren
Lianjiang
Chunggang-up

Kasan-dong
Huch'ang
Manp'o
Ji'an
Yalu
Wiwon
Kanggye
Puksubaek-san
2522
Pujon-ho

Ch'ongjin
Kyongsong
Odaejin

Kimch'aek
(Songjin)

D
30
40

CHIFENG
Weichang
1885
Ningcheng
Chaoyang
Beipiao　Qinghemen
Heishui
Heishan
Xinlitun Xinmin
Piao'ertun
Xinbin
Tonghua

SHENYANG
FUSHUN
Sujiatun　Qinghecheng

Huadong
Huanren 1846

Ch'osan
Pyoktong
Koin

Changjin-
ho
Changjin
Sinhung

Kilchu
Kapsan
Hapsu
Hyesan
P'ungsan

Musudan

Weichang
Longhua
Chengde
Luanne
Liugou
Shangbancheng
Kuancheng
Pingquan
Lingyuan
Yi Xian
Daling He
THE
Goubangzi
Liaoyang
Anping
Gongchangling
Tianshifu
Lianshanguan

Iwon
Tanch'on

Pukch'ong
Sinch'ang

Changjin-
ho

E

Lingyuan
Jinzhou
Beizhen
Panjin
Niuzhuang
ANSHAN
Haicheng
Kuandian

Supung
Shuiku

Pyongan
Taegwan
Pukchin

Huich'on　Oro
NORTH
Hamhung
Hungnam

SEA OF

JINXI
Huludao
Jianchang
Jianchangying
Shuangshanzi
Xingcheng
Suizhong
Yingkou
Dashiqiao
Gaizhou
Xiuyan
Fengcheng
1131
Buyun Shan
Gushan

Dandong
Langtou
Sinuiju
Donggou
Yongamp'o

Kusong
Kujang
Tokch'on

KOREA

Hongwon

Zunhua
Jixian
Yutian
Baodi
Fengrun
Luan Xian
Lulong
Qinhuangdao
Luan He
Funing
Changli
Leting
Liaodong
Wan
Liaodong
Bandao

Sokch'o
Uiju
Yalu Jiang
Sonch'on
Pakch'on
Ch'ongju

Sukch'on
Sinmi-do

Anju
P'yongsong
Sunan

Kangdong
P'yonggang
Hoeyang
1638
Changdo-ri

Pyoktong

Wonsan
Kowon
Yonghung
Tongjoson
Man
Munch'on
Anbyon
Kojo

JAPAN

B

Yanshan
TANGSHAN
Wuqing
Hangu
Jintanggang
Pulandian
(Xinjin)
Pikou

Changshan
Qundao

Korea

Jinzhou
(Jin Xian)
Lüshun

DALIAN
(Lüda)

Bay

Cho-do
Namp'o

Chunghwa
Songnim
Sariwon
Chaeryong
Sinch'on

P'YONGYANG

Kangdong
Suan
Koksan
Sepo-ri

Pyonggang
Cheorwon
Kumhwa
Hwacheon
Cheosu-ri 1708

Kosong
Sokcho
Yang-yang

(EAST SEA)

Gangseong

38

TIANJIN SHI
TIANJIN
Tanggu
Dagu
Dongya
Qingxian
Oikou
Huanghua

Bo Hai

Miaodao
Qundao

Qundao

Changyon
Ongjin
Baengnyeongdo
(S. Korea)

Haeju
Kumch'on
Kaesong
Nam-ch'on
Yonan

Panmunjom
Uijongbu

Chuncheon
Hongcheon
Gapyeong

Donghae
Samcheok

Gangneung

F

Huimin
Yanghe
Wudi
Zhanhua
Huang He
Longkou
Penglai
Daxindian
YANTAI
Weihai

Wuji
Binzhou
Laizhou
Wan
Dongying
Huang Xian
Fushan
Muping
Qixia
Wendeng
Chengshan Jiao

SEOUL
SEONGNAM
Bucheon
INCHEON
Ansan
Anyang
SUWON

Icheon
Yeoju
Wonju
Hoengseong
Jeongseon
Yeong-wol

Uljin

Ulleungdo
(S. Korea)

Shanghe
Zhangqiu
Huantai
Gaoyuan
Zhoucun
ZIBO
Hongshan
Linqu
Boshan
Anqiu
Changle
Fangzi
WEIFANG
Hanting
Pingdu
Laiyang
Rushan
923
Nanhuang
Shidao
Rongcheng

SUWON
Pyeongtaek
Cheonan
Yesan
Hongseong
Anseong

Chungju
Jecheon
Jincheon
Cheongju
Yechon

Andong
Yeongju
Uiseong
Yeongdeok
Heunghae

SOUTH

Mashang
Yidu
Jiaozhou
Laixi
Haiyang

Shandong Bandao

Anmyeondo
Seosan

KOREA

Nonsan
Gongju
Yeongdong
Sangju
Gumi
Pohang
Gyeongju

SHANDONG
24
1108
Weifang
Zhucheng
Jiaozhou
Jimo
Chengyang
QINGDAO

DAEJEON
Baryeong
Ganggyeong

Gimcheon
Waegwan
Yeongcheon
Gyeongju

TAI'AN
XINTAI
Sishui
Laiwu
Mengyin
Yishui
Wulian
Huangdao
Jiaozhou Wan

Gunsan
Iksan
Jeonju
DAEGU
Cheongdo
ULSAN

Pingyi
Yishui
Gaomi
Lancun

Gimje
Geochang
Hamyang

Miryang
Dongnae

36

Guan
Pingyi
Tanggu
YELLOW SEA

Gwanggyo
Jeong-eup
Namwon
Jirisan
Jinju
Masan
Chang-won
Gimhae
BUSAN

LINYI
Feixian
Rizhao
(Huang Hai)

GWANGJU
Damyang 1915
Hadong
Sacheon
Tong-yeong

Teng Xian
ZAOZHUANG
Tengzhou
Shijiusuo
Andongwei
Ganyu

Mokpo
Suncheon
Boseong
Beolgyo
Yeosu

Korea Strait

Tsushima
(Japan)
Izuhara

34

Guzhen
Jiawang
Pizhou
Xinyi
Haizhou
Guanyun
Chenjiagang
Lianyungang

Heuksando
(S. Korea)
Haenam
Jindo

Jindo

Iki
Karatsu

31

XUZHOU
Xiangshui
Guannan
Binhai

Jeju　Jeju-do (S. Korea)
Hallim
Hallasan
Daejeong
Namjeju
Seogwipo

JAPAN
Sasebo
Kashima
Omura
Isahaya
Nagasaki
Kuchinotsu

Nakadōri-Shima

Imari

H

SUQIAN
Suining
Da Yunhe
Lianshui
HUAI'AN
Huaiyin
Chuzhou
Baoying
Liuzhuang
YANCHENG

Funing
Sheyang

Dongtai

Fukue-Shima

Lingbi
Guzhen
Sixian
Wuhe
Hongze
Hu
XINGHUA
Dongtai

Bengbu
Fengyang
Gaoyou
Hu

118　East from Greenwich　120　122　124　126　128

9　33　10　11　12　13　14　15

COPYRIGHT PHILIP'S

1:12 500 000

Projection: Mercator

East from Greenwich

33

JAVA AND MADURA
1:7 500 000

50 0 50 100 150 200 250 300 km
50 0 50 100 150 200 miles

BALI
1:2 000 000

10 0 10 20 30 km
10 0 10 20 miles

JAKARTA Merak Tangerang Bekasi Karawang Pamanukan Kepulauan Karimunjawa Bawean Sangkapura
Anyer Serang Pandeglang Rangkasbitung Subang Indramayu Cirebon Pekalongan Jepara Muria Rembang Tuban Tg. Bugel Tanjung Pangkah Madura
Selat Sunda Pulau Rakata Panaitan Labuhan BANTEN Bogor Purwakarta Majalengka Brebes Tegal Pemalang Kendal Demak Kudus Pati Blora Kragan Bojonegoro Bangkalan Sampang Pamekasan Sumenep Tambuku
Tanjung Guhakolak Pelabuhanratu Sukabumi BANDUNG Garut Ciamis Wonosobo Salatiga Semarang Purwodadi Ngawi Mojokerto Gresik SURABAYA
Teluk Pelabuhan Ratu Pengalengan BARAT Cianjur Tasikmalaya Purwokerto Banyumas Magelang Boyolali TENGAH Surakarta Madiun Kediri Pare Pasuruan Probolinggo Situbondo
Genteng Sindangbarang Cijulang Cilacap Nusa Kambangan Kebumen Karangonyar Yogyakarta YOGYA Ponorogo Trenggalek Blitar TIMUR Malang Arjuna Bromo Semeru Jember Bondowoso Banyuwangi Bali
Pacitan Tulungagung Wlingi Pasirian Lumajang Rambipuji Nusa Barung Selat Bali

BALI SEA Tanjung Batugondang Pulau Menjangan Singaraja Kubutambahan Kepulauan
Gunung Raung Ketapang Gilimanuk Gerokgak Lovina Tejakula Kubu Tanjung
Banyuwangi Cekik Gunung Merbuk Seririt Bayun Kintamani Songan Tianyar Pamenang
Glagah Melaya BALI Busungbiu Gunung Batur Batur Penelokan Amed Tirtagangga
Jambewangi Negara Mendoyo Pupuan Baturiti Danau Batur Gunung Agung Culik Karangasem (Amlapura) Lombok
Beluki Rogojampi Srono Muncar Perancak Yehbuah Belimbing Tegallalang Rendang Saren Montongbuwoh Tanjung
Genteng Tegalsari Tjluring Pekutatan Pasar Bojera Sembung Gianyar Bangli Manggis Candi Dasa Ampenan Lombok
Jawa Bajatrejo Selat Bali Tabanan Sibang Ubud Klungkung Kusamba Mataram
Tanjung Purwo Grajagan Bali Denpasar Sukawati Badung Lembuak
Tanjung Kucur Danginpura Sanur Selat Teluk Terang Gerung
Semenanjung Blambangan Jimbaran Kuta Toyapakeh Suwana Teluk Bebera Lembar Blongas
Uluwatu Bukit Badung Nusa Dua Nusa Penida Tanjung Abah Tanjung Pangga Tanjung Tampa
INDIAN Tanjung Mebulu OCEAN

PHILIPPINES (Luzon area)
Claveria Babuyan Chan. C. Engaño Bacarra Laoog Aparri Tuao
Batac Tuguegarao Ilagan Palanan
Bangued Vigan Bontoc Bayombong Casiguran
San Fernando Baguio Baler Palanan Pt.
Bolinao Lingayen Dagupan San Jose C. San Ildefonso
Iba Tarlac Cabanatuan
Mt. Pinatubo Angeles A
San Fernando Polillo Is.
Olongapo MANILA Quezon City Lamon Bay
Cavite Santa Cruz Daet Catanduanes
Manila B. Bataan Lipa Lucena Calauag Naga Virac
Lubang Is. Batangas Calapan Marinduque Legazpi Tabaco Sorsogon
Mamburao Mindoro Sibuyan Burias Masbate Samar
Busuanga Sablayan Romblon Tablas Masbate Calbayog Catbalogan Taft
Culion San Jose Panay Roxas Cadiz Bogo Ormoc Tacloban General MacArthur
Puerto Princesa Iloilo Bacolod San Carlos Leyte Baybay Guiuan
Taytay Dumaran Negros Tanjay Cebu Mandaue Bohol Surigao Dinagat Siargao
Cuyo San Jose de Buenavista Dumaguete Siquijor Tagbilaran Talibon Camiguin Tandag
Puerto Princesa Dipolog Oroquieta Cagayan de Oro Gingoog Ilanga
Zamboanga Pagadian Ozamiz Iligan Malaybalay Cateel Baganga
Siocon Sindangan Lanao Mindanao Parang Tagum Mati
Isabela Basilan Cotabato Datu Piang Digos DAVAO
Jolo Lebak Koronadal C. San Agustin
General Santos Kiamba Tinaca Pt.
Tawi-Tawi Sarangani Is.

CELEBES SEA SULU SEA Kepulauan Nanusa Kepulauan Kawio Karakelong Beo Kepulauan Talaud Salibabu Kaburuang
Tahuna Pulau Sanghe Kepulauan Sanghe Merir (Palau) Helen Atoll (Palau) PACIFIC
Karakitang Siau OCEAN
Tahulandang Biaro Sopi Berebere Morotai
Doi Galela Ibu Tobelo Akelamo
Bunaken Kema Jailolo Halmahera Kepulauan Asia Kepulauan Mapia
Manado Amurang Tondano UTARA Ternate Tidore Teluk Buli Kepulauan Ayu Equator
GORONTALO Tilamuto Gorontalo Tanjung Flesko Makian Weda Teluk Weda Selat Gebe Waigeo Kepulauan Padaido
Tanjung Mangkalihat UTARA Kayoa Wosi Umera Raja Ampat Dampier Sorong Waibeem Kwoka Manokwari Supiori Biak
Maratua Tomini Kasiruta Labuha Gani Selat Sorong Salawati Jazirah Doberai Kironi Numfoor Warsa Biak Kepulauan Padaido
Tolitoli Buol Paleleh Sumalata Kuandang Teluk Tomini Kepulauan Bacan Mandioli Bisa Misool Klamono Ransiki Number Serui D'Urville
Palu Parigi Poh Luwuk Peleng Obilatu Kofiau Sailolof Seget Teminabuan Wasian Wariap Yapen Selat Yapen Bonoi Kumamba
TENGAH Tojo Tokala Banggai Taliabu Mangole Fluk Lenmalu Inanwatan IRIAN JAYA Wasior Sarmi Genyem
Donggala Toboli Poso Danau Poso Kolonodale Teluk Tolo Todeo Kepulauan Sula Sanana Adua Segun BARAT Teluk Nuboai Van Rees Jayapura
Lariang SULAWESI (Celebes) Kendari Monse Buru Namlea Piru Seram (Ceram) Bula Wendesi Cenderawasih Nabire Pegunungan Sentani
Mamuju Masamba Malili Mondeodo Wamulan Tifu Amahai Tehoru Waru Geser Fakfak Kwatisore Babo Puncak Waren
Mamasa Palopo Malamala Kolaka Wowoni Namrole Lima Ambon Saparua Gorong Kokas Kenian Enarotali Puncak Jaya Wamena
Makale Rantemario Mekongga Manui MALUKU Piru Kayeli Waru Manggawitu Adi Susuru Ibonma Waghete Pegunungan Maoke Puncak Trikora
Pinrang Singkang Pampana Buton Kepulauan Banda Bandanaira Kepulauan Watubela Uta Tembagapura Trikora Puncak Mandala Oksibil
Parepare Watampone Buapinang Buton Bandanaira Banda Elat Doba Amamapare Yapero Jayawijaya PAPUA NEW GUINEA
IJUNG PANDANG Sinjai Pising Raha Lawele Tual Kai Besar Kola Gumzai Teluk Flamingo Agats Mindiptana
(Makasar) Bantaeng Kabaena Baubau Wangiwangi BANDA SEA Kai Kecil Banda Elat Wokam Sewer Tanahmerah Bade
Bulukumba Benteng Binongko Tukangbesi Serua Kepulauan Kai Wangal Kepulauan Aru Pirimapun Kepi
Salayar Batuata Gunungapi Nila Teun Daya Trangan Gomogomo Pulau Dolak Muting
FLORES SEA Tanahjampea Kalao Bonerate Kalaotoa Damar Romang Barat Tepa Wuliaru Kepulauan Tanimbar Tanjung Ngabordamlu Pulau Komoran Okaba
Sunda Is. Sabalana Wetar Wesiri Kisar Moa Lakor Selu Yamdena Saumlaki Merauke
Sumbawa Sangeang Labuhanbajo Ruteng Lomblen Pantar Alor Ilwaki Leti Kepulauan Eliase Masela Selaru Tanjung Vals
Bima Raba Komodo Ende Maumere Kalabahi Dili Baucau Sermata ARAFURA SEA
NUSA TENGGARA TIMUR Aimere Atapupu Viqueque EAST TIMOR Tutuala
Sumba Waingapu Sawu Sea Pante Macassar (E. Timor) Kefamenanu Nikiniki
Waikabubak Melolo Sawu Kupang Roti Baa Raijua Dana

COPYRIGHT PHILIP'S

G H

b

d

KO SAMUI
1 : 1 000 000

Gulf of Thailand

Ko
Samui

Ang
Thong

KO PHUKET
1 : 1 000 000

Ao Phangnga

Andaman Sea

Ko
Phuket

PINANG
1 : 1 000 000

Pulau
Pinang

George Town
Butterworth

SINGAPORE
1 : 1 000 000

SINGAPORE

INDONESIA

Straits of Singapore

a

c

J

K

L

M

S O U T H   C H I N A   S E A

MALAYSIA

PENINSULAR
MALAYSIA

PHNOM
PENH

HO CHI MINH
(Saigon)

*Gulf
of
Thailand*

Kho Khot Kra
(Isthmus of Kra)

MU KO CHANG

Straits of Malacca

INDONESIA

MEDAN

KUALA LUMPUR

Johor Bahru
SINGAPORE

Kyunzu
(Mergui Archipelago)

Projection: Conical with two standard parallels

East from Greenwich

km
miles

m
ft

36

1 2 3 4 5

G H J K L M

7 8

Sand deserts

Intermittent lakes

continuation southwards on same scale

Projection: Conical with two standard parallels

1:10 000 000

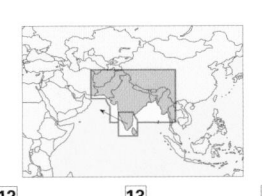

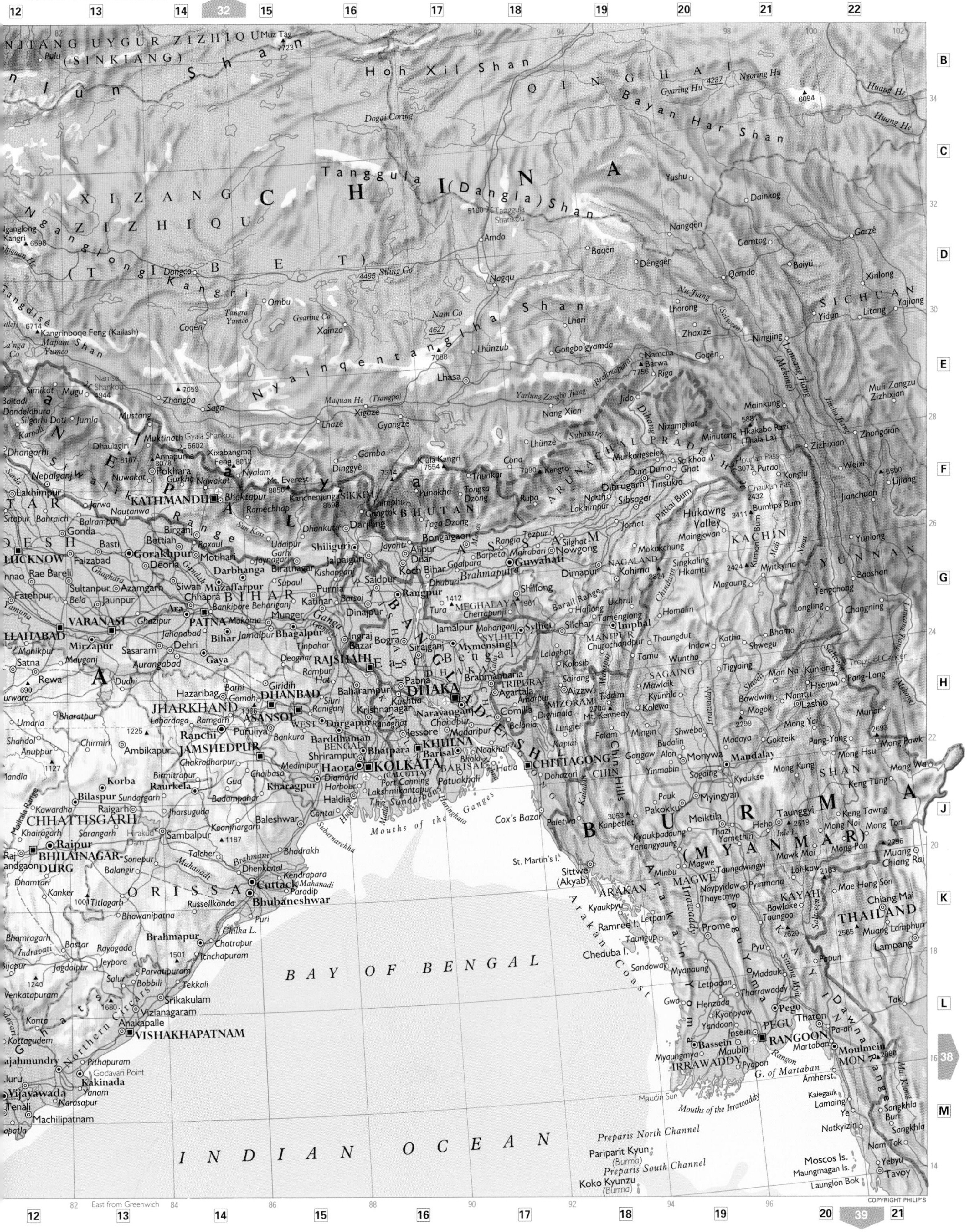

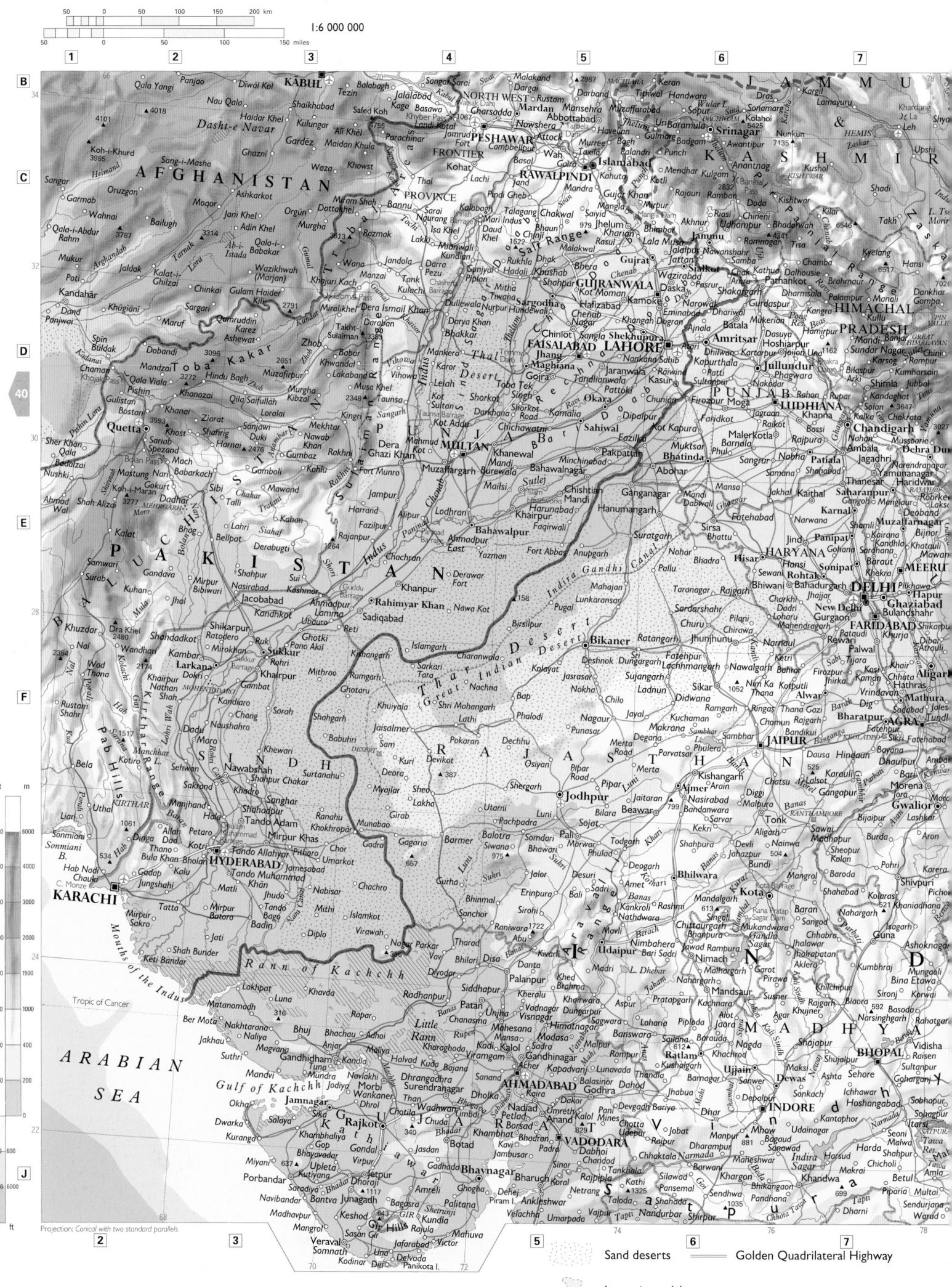

Sand deserts — Golden Quadrilateral Highway

Intermittent lakes

Projection: Conical with two standard parallels

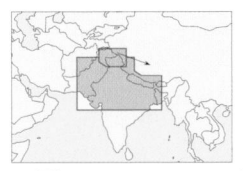

JAMMU AND KASHMIR
on same scale

COPYRIGHT PHILIP'S

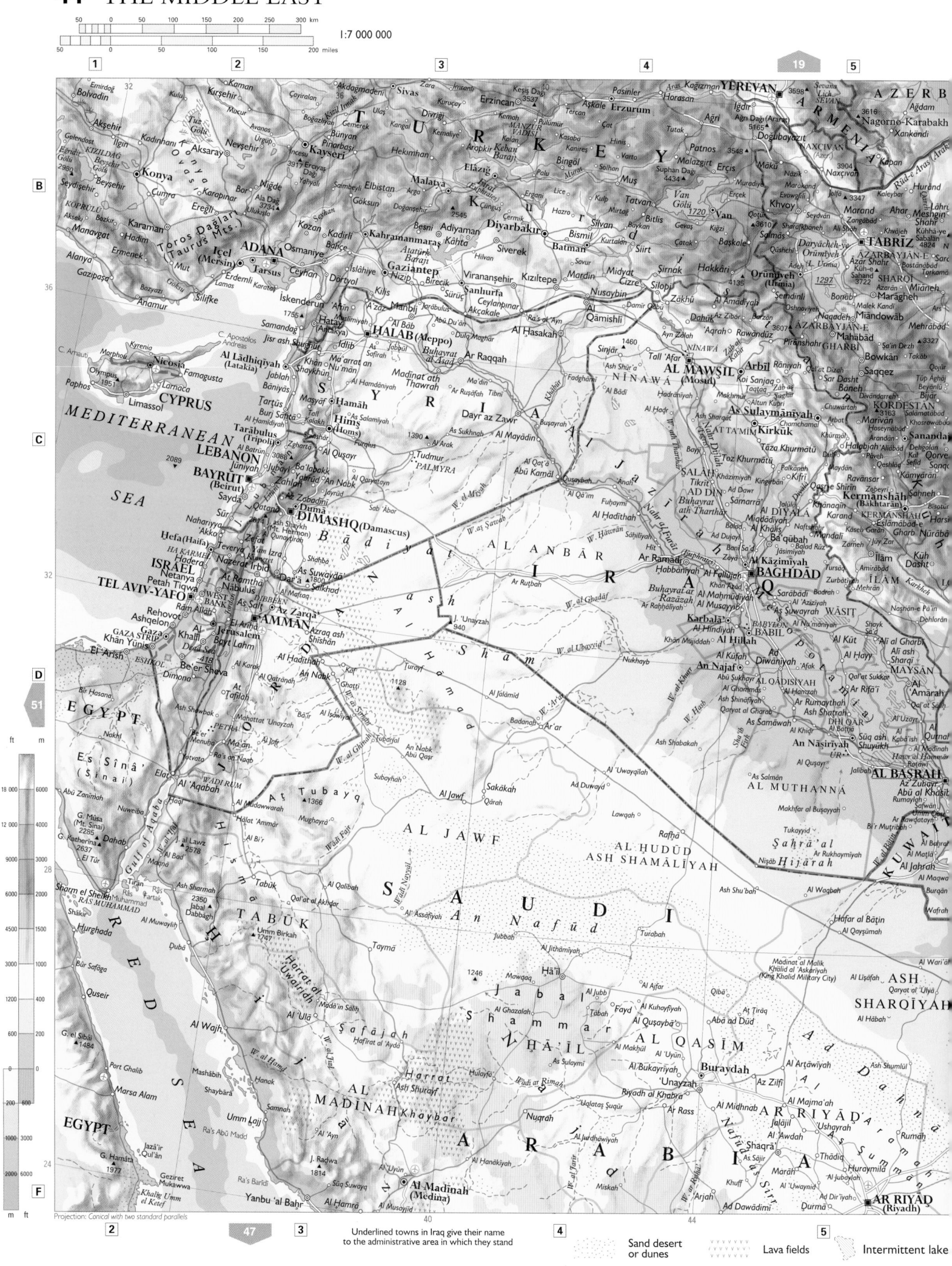

1:7 000 000

Projection: Conical with two standard parallels

Underlined towns in Iraq give their name
to the administrative area in which they stand

Sand desert
or dunes

Lava fields

Intermittent lake

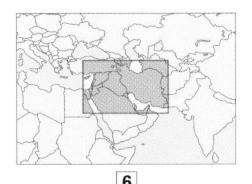

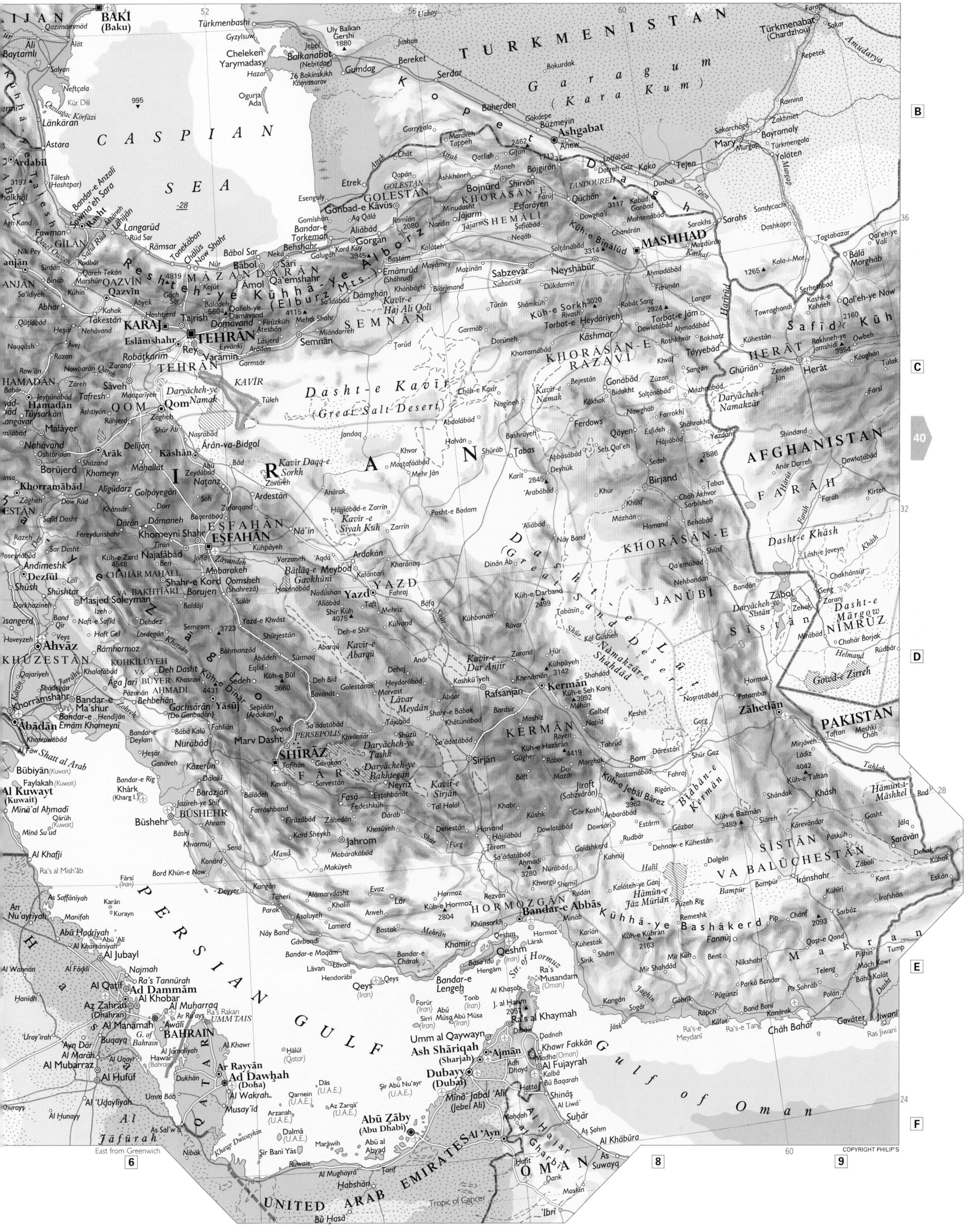

10 0 10 20 30 40 50 60 70 80 90 100 km
1:2 500 000
10 0 10 20 30 40 50 60 miles

MEDITERRANEAN SEA

CYPRUS
Paphos
Episkopi
Kividhes
Zyyi
Limassol
Akrotiri Bay
Episkopi Bay
C. Gata

2775
2089

LEBANON

Al Ḥamīdīyah
Ḥims (Homs)
Tall Kalakh
Shinshār
Furqlus
HIMṢ
Al Qusayr
Al Mīnā'
ASH SHAMÂL
Al Hirmil
Tarâbulus (Tripoli)
Zgharta
Qurnat as Sawdā' 3088
Bsharri
Al Labwah
Al Buṛayj 2464
Al Qaryatayn
Al Batrūn
Qartaba
AL BIQA 2616
Ba'labakk
An Nabk
Bi'r Ghadir
Jubayl
Ibrāhîm
2628
J. Sannîn
Yabrūd
Jūniyah
Bikfayya
BAYRŪT (Beirut)
Ash Shuwayfat
'Alayh
Zahlah
Sirghâya
SYRIA
Khān Abū Shāmat
Ad Dāmūr
JABAL LUBNÂN
1942 J. al Bārak
Az Zabdānī
Dumayr
DIMASHQ
Saydā (Sidon)
Jazzîn
Hawsh Mūssā
Al Qutayfah
Darayya
DIMASHQ (Damascus)
Dūma
Jayrūd
An Nabatîyah at Tahta
2814 J. ash Shaykh (Mt. Hermon)
Marj 'Uyūn
Qaṭana
Jaramānah
Al Ḥājānah
AL JANÛB
Al Khiyām
Al Kiswah
Sūr (Tyre)
Q. Mas'ada
Burāq
Qiryat Shemona
1197
Al Qunayṭirah
As Sanamayn
Nahariyya
Me'ona
Hagalîl (Galilee)
Ar Rafid
'Akko (Acre)
1208 Zefat
Yam Kinneret (Sea of Galilee)
Izra'
Shahbā 2464
Mifraz Hefa
Qiryat Karmi'el
HAZAFON
Fiq
Shaykh Miskîn
As Suwaydā
Hefa (Haifa)
Qiryat Ata
Teverya (Tiberias)
-210
Saham al Jawlân
Qar'ā
AD DRŪZ
1800 Salah
Dāliyat el Karmel
Nazerat (Nazareth)
Afula
Yarmūk
DAR'Â
As Suwaydā
TEL MEGIDDO
Taibe
IRBID
Umm el Fahm
Jenin
Bet She'an
Al Mafraq
Malah
CAESAREA
Shōmrōn
'AJLŪN
J. Umm ad Dara
Hadera
SAMARIA
Tūbās
'Ajlūn
1247 Jarash
Buṣrā ash Shām
Umm al Qittayn
Hanna-Karkur
Nābulus
AL MAFRAQ
ISRAEL
Ṭulkarm
JARASH
Netanya
Ra'anana
N. az Zarqā
HAMERKAZ
SHILOH
Herzliyya
Kefar Sava
AL BALQA
Bene Beraq
Peṭaḥ Tiqwa
As Salṭ
Az Zarqā
TEL AVIV-YAFO
Ramat Gan
Wādi as Sîr
Bat Yam
Holon
WEST BANK
289
Karama
AMMÂN
Lod
Ramla
Rām Allāh
Na'ûr
Rishon le Ziyyon
Yavne
Rehovot
El Arîha (Jericho)
AMM
Azraq ash Shîshân
Ashdod
Qiryat Mal'akhi
Bet Shemesh
Bayt Lahm (Bethlehem)
Jerusalem (Yerushalayim) (Al Quds)
Ma'daba
'AMMAN
Ashqelon
Qiryat Gat
MA'DABA
AZ ZARQĀ
TEL LAKHISH
Al Khalīl (Hebron)
W. al Ḥaydān
Gaza
N. Shiqma
Sederot
Dhibân
Al Ḥadîthah
GAZA STRIP
ESHKOL
Az Zāhirīyah
'En Gedi
Khān Yūnis
Dead Sea
Rafah
Be'er Sheva (Beersheba)
Bûr Sa'îd (Port Said)
Bûr Fu'ad
Arad
'En Boqeq
Ras Burûn
MASADA
Al Qatrānah
BÛR SA'ÎD
Sabkhet el Bardawîl
El Daheir
Bor Mashash
Sedom
AL KARAK
Khalîg el Tîna
Bîr el 'Abd
Dimona
1305 Al Karak
W. al Ḥasā
Români
Bîr Qaṭia
El 'Arîsh
Al Mazār
W. Bâ'ir
Qanâ es Suweis
Bîr el Garârât
W. Lahfân
-333
El Qantara
Bîr Kaseiba
HADAROM
At Ṭafîlah
Wâḥid
Bîr Madkûr
SHAMÂL SÎNÎ
Qezi'ot
Sedé Boqer
1305 Dana
JORDAN
Ismâ'ilîya
Talâta
892
Abu Aweigila
Birein
AT TAFÎLAH
Bâ'ir
ISMÂ'ILÎYA
Khamsa
Muweilih
Mizpe Ramon
Nijil
El Buheirat el Murrat el Kubra (Great Bitter L.)
Bîr Ḥasana
El Quseima
Mahattat 'Unayzah
Shawmari 1072
Gineifa
G. Yi 'Allaq 1094
Hanegev (Negev Desert)
Rujm Tal'at al Jamā'ah
MA'ÂN
El Suweis (Suez)
Bîr Beiḍa
1736
El Suweis
Adabiya
Bîr el Thamâda
PETRA
Al Jafr
Qa'el Jafr
'Uyûn Mûsa
W. el Brûk
El 'Agrûd
Wādi Mûsā
Ma'ân
EGYPT
Ain Sudr
W. el Sukra
Ma'an
ES SÎNÂ (Sinai)
Nakhl
W. Ruga
W. Mahashîm
N. Paran
Mamarr Mitlâ
948 G. el Kabrît
Bîr Abu Muhammad
N. Hiyyon
Ras Sudr
Bîr el Hisn
Bîr el Qaṭṭār
AL 'AQABAH
Ra's an Naqb 1435
Mahattat ash Shidîyah
SAUDI ARABIA
Ghubbet el Bûs
Gebel el Tih
El Thamad
'En 'Avrona
1592 Rum 1754
Baṭn al Ghûl
1272
JANÛB SÎNÎ
Bîr el Biarât
Elat
WADI RUM
Abu Sanduq
Ras Matarma
Bîr el Heisi
1165
Al 'Aqaba
Rum
At Tubayq
Al Mudawwarah
EL SUWEIS
W. Abu Ga'da
Bîr Wuseit
W. an Nira
Haql
Gulf of Aqaba

Projection: Polyconic
East from Greenwich
COPYRIGHT PHILIP'S

┅┅┅ 1974 Cease Fire Lines

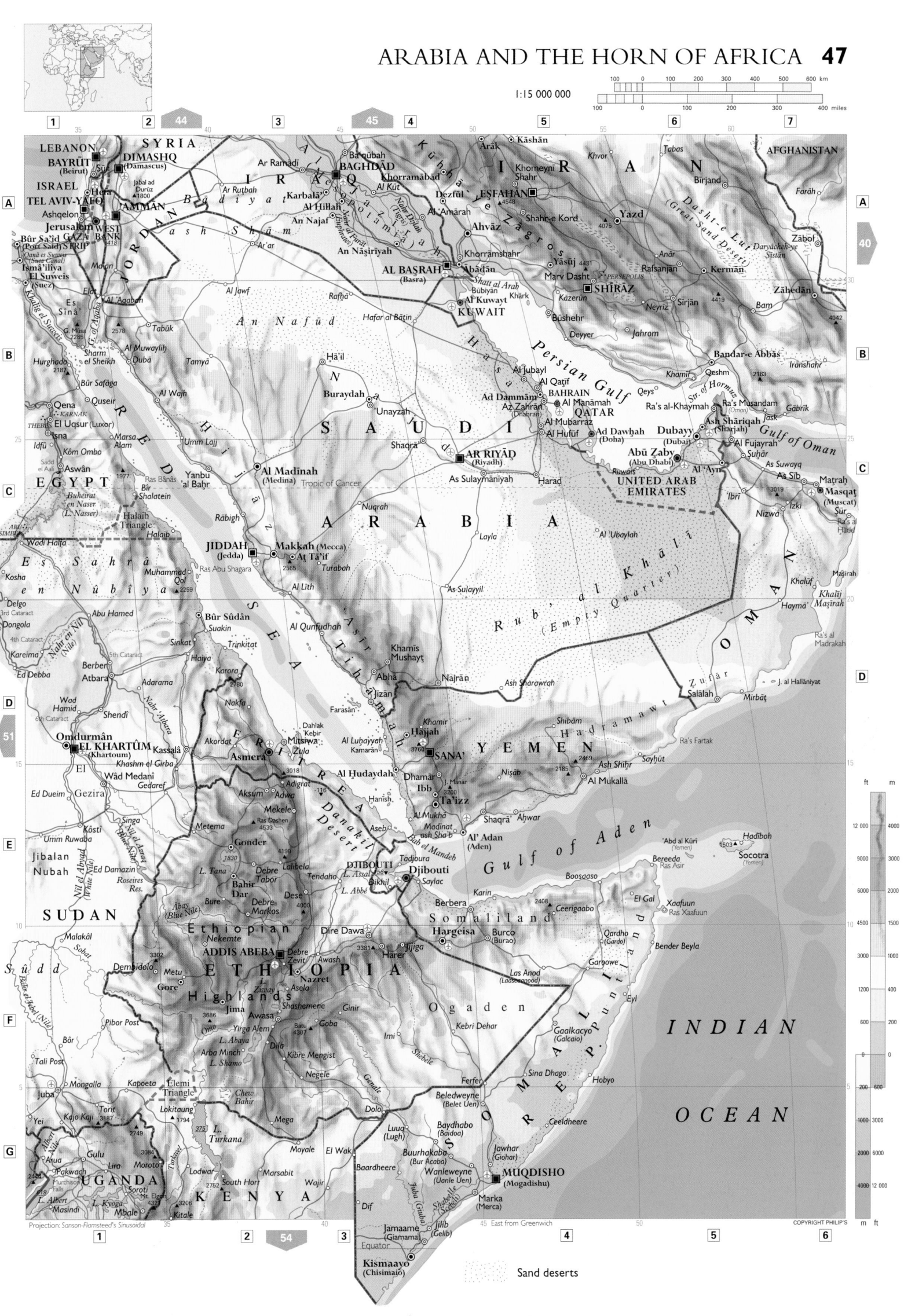

1:15 000 000

100   0   100   200   300   400   500   600 km
100   0   100   200   300   400 miles

LEBANON
BAYRŪT (Beirut)
ISRAEL
TEL AVIV-YAFO
Ashqelon
Jerusalem WEST
Bûr Sa'īd GAZA BANK
(Port Said) STRIP
Qanâ es Suweis (Suez Canal)
Ismâ'iliya
El Suweis (Suez)

SYRIA
DIMASHQ (Damascus)
Jabal ad Durūz 1800
AMMĀN
JORDAN
Ma'ān
El 'Aqaba
G. Mûsa 2285
Sharm el Sheikh
Dubā

SYRIA
Ar Ramādi
Ar Ruṭbah
Al Ḥillah
An Najaf
Ar'ar
Badiyat ash Shām

Ba'qūbah
BAGHDĀD
Karbalā'
Al Kūt
An Nāṣirīyah
Rafḥā
Hafar al Bāṭin

IRAQ
Al Jazīra
Mesopotamia
Nahr Diyala (Tigris)
Al 'Amārah
AL BAṢRAH (Basra)
Būbiyān
Al Kuwayt
KUWAIT

Khorramābād
Dezfūl
Aḥvāz
Khorramshahr
Ābādān
Shaṭṭ al Arab
Khārk

IRAN
Arāk   Kāshān
Khomeyni Shahr
EṢFAHĀN 4548
Yāsūj 4431
Būshehr
Deyyer

Tabas
Khvor
Yazd 4075
Shahr-e Kord
Marv Dasht
PERSEPOLIS
SHĪRĀZ
Kāzerūn
Neyrīz
Jahrom

Birjand
Anār
Rafsanjān
Kermān
Sirjān 4419
Bam

IRAN
AFGHANISTAN
Farāh
Zābol
Daryācheh-ye Sīstān
Zāhedān
Dasht-e Lut (Great Sand Desert)

Bandar-e Abbās
Qeshm
Khamīr
Ra's al-Khaymah
Ra's Musandam (Oman)
Ash Shāriqah (Sharjah)
 As Suwayq
Suḥār
As Sīb
Maṭrah
Masqaṭ (Muscat)

Hurghada 2187
Bûr Safâga
Quseir
Qena
KARNAK
THEBES El Uqsur (Luxor)
Isna
Idfû
Kôm Ombo
Aswân 1977
Buheirat en Naser (L. Nasser)
ABU SIMBEL
Wadi Halfa

Tabūk
Tamyā
Al Muwayliḥ
Al Wajh
Umm Lajj
Yanbu' al Bahr
Rābigh

Ḥā'il
Buraydah
Unayzah
Shaqrā'

Al Jawf
An Nafūd

SAUDI
Al Jubayl
Al Qaṭīf
Ad Dammām
Aẓ Zahrān (Dhahran)
Al Mubarraz
Al Hufūf

Persian Gulf
BAHRAIN
Al Manāmah
QATAR
Ad Dawḥah (Doha)
Dubayy (Dubai)
Abū Ẓaby (Abu Dhabi)
Riwais
UNITED ARAB EMIRATES
Al 'Ayn
'Ibrī 3019
Izki
Nizwa
Sūr
Ra's al Hadd

Gulf of Oman
Str. of Hormuz
Qeys
Gābrik
Īrānshahr 2163

AR RIYĀḌ (Riyadh)
As Sulaymānīyah
Harad
Layla
As Sulayyil
Al 'Ubaylah

ARABIA
Tropic of Cancer
Al Madīnah (Medina)
Nuqrah
Al Līth
Al Qunfudhah
At Tā'if 2565
Turabah

JIDDAH (Jedda)
MAKKAH (Mecca)
Ras Abu Shagara
Muhammad Qol 2259

EGYPT
Es Sahrâ en Nûbîya
Kosha
Delgo
Dongola
3rd Cataract
4th Cataract
Kareima
Ed Debba

Halaib
Halaib Triangle
Bîr Shalatein
Ras Bânâs

RED SEA
ḤIJĀZ
'Asīr
Tihāmah

Rub' al Khālī (Empty Quarter)
OMAN
Maşīrah
Khalūf
Khalīj Maşīrah
Haymā'
Ra's al Madrakah

SUDAN
Bûr Sûdân
Suakin
Sinkat
Haiya
Trinkitat
Karora 2780
Nakfa
Adarama
Atbara
Berber
Abu Hamed
5th Cataract
6th Cataract
Shendî
Wad Hamid
El Khartûm (Khartoum)
Omdurmân
El
Kassalā
Khashm el Girba
Wâd Medanî
Gedaref
Gezira
Ed Dueim
Kôstî
Singa
Ed Damazin
Roseires Res.
Umm Ruwaba
Jibalan Nubah
Malakâl
Sobat
Bôr
Pibor Post
Tali Post
Juba
Bahr el Abyad (White Nile)
Nahr en Nîl (Nile)
Nil el Azraq (Blue Nile)

ERITREA
Akordat
Asmera
Mitsiwa
Zula
Adigrat
Aksum
Adwa
Adigrat 116
Mekele
Ras Dashen 4533
Metema
Gonder 1830
L. Tana
Debre Tabor
Bahir Dar
Lalibela
Ābay (Blue Nile)
Bure
Debre Markos

Dahlak Kebir
Kamarān
Al Luḥayyah
Danakil Desert
Zula

YEMEN
Ḥajjah
SANA' 3760
Dhamār
Ibb
Ta'izz
Al Hudaydah
Al Mukhā
Shaqrā'
Madīnat ash Sha'b
Al' Adan (Aden)
Bab el Mandeb
J. Manār 3200
Niṣāb 2185
Ash Shiḥr
Al Mukallā 2469
Sayhūt
Khamir
Shibām
Ḥadramawt
Ra's Fartak

Abhā
Najrān
Jizān
Farasān
Hanish
Khamīs Mushayṭ
Ash Sharawrah
Ẓufār
Salālah
Mirbāṭ
J. al Ḥallāniyat

DJIBOUTI
Djibouti
Tadjoura
L. Assal 156
Dikhil
L. Abbé
Aseb
Saylac
Berbera
Karin

SOMALILAND
Hargeisa
Burco (Burao)
Ceerigaabo
Qardho (Gardo)
Bender Beyla
Boosaaso
Xaafuun
Ras Xaafuun
El Gal

Gulf of Aden
'Abd al Kūri (Yemen)
Bereeda
Ras Asir
Hadiboh
Socotra (Yemen) 1503

ETHIOPIA
ADDIS ABEBA
Debre Zeyit
Nekemte
Metu
Gore
Dembidolo
Nazret
Asela
Shashemene
Awasa
Jima
Yirga Alem
Arba Minch
Dila
Kibre Mengist
Negele
Ethiopian Highlands
Awash
Dese 4000
Debre Markos
Omo
L. Abaya
L. Shamo
Ginir
Shebele
Goba
Batu 4307
3686
3302
3381
Harer
Jijiga
Dire Dawa
Ogaden
Kebri Dehar
Imi
Gaalkacyo (Galcaio)
Garoowe
Las Anod (Laascaanood)
2408

SOMALIA
PUNTLAND
Eyl
Sina Dhago
Hobyo
INDIAN OCEAN
Ferfer
Beledweyne (Belet Uen)
Ceeldheere
Jawhar (Giohar)
MUQDISHO (Mogadishu)
Marka (Merca)

UGANDA
Arua
Pakwach
Gulu
Lira
Moroto 3084
Soroti
Mt. Elgon 4327
Mbale
L. Albert
L. Kyoga
Masindi
2414
L. Kwania

KENYA
Kapoeta
Elemi Triangle
Lokitaung 1794
Chew Bahir
Mega
L. Turkana 375
Moyale
El Wak
Yei
Kajo Kaji
Torit 3187
2749
Lodwar
South Horn 2752
Kitale 3206
Dif
Luuq (Lugh)
Buurhakaba (Bur Acaba)
Baydhabo (Baidoa)
Wanleweyne (Uanle Uen)
Dolo
Baardheere
Jamaame (Giamama)
Jilib (Gelib)
Kismaayo (Chisimaio)
Wajir
Marsabit
Garsen
Genale
Daua

Equator
East from Greenwich

Sand deserts

ft   m
12 000   4000
9000   3000
6000   2000
4500   1500
3000   1000
1200   400
600   200
0   0
200   600
1000   3000
2000   6000
4000   12 000
m   ft

200 0 200 400 600 800 1000 1200 1400 1600 1800 km

1:42 000 000

200 0 200 400 600 800 1000 1200 miles

| 1 | 2 | 3 | 4 | 5 | 6 | 7 | 8 | 9 | 10 |

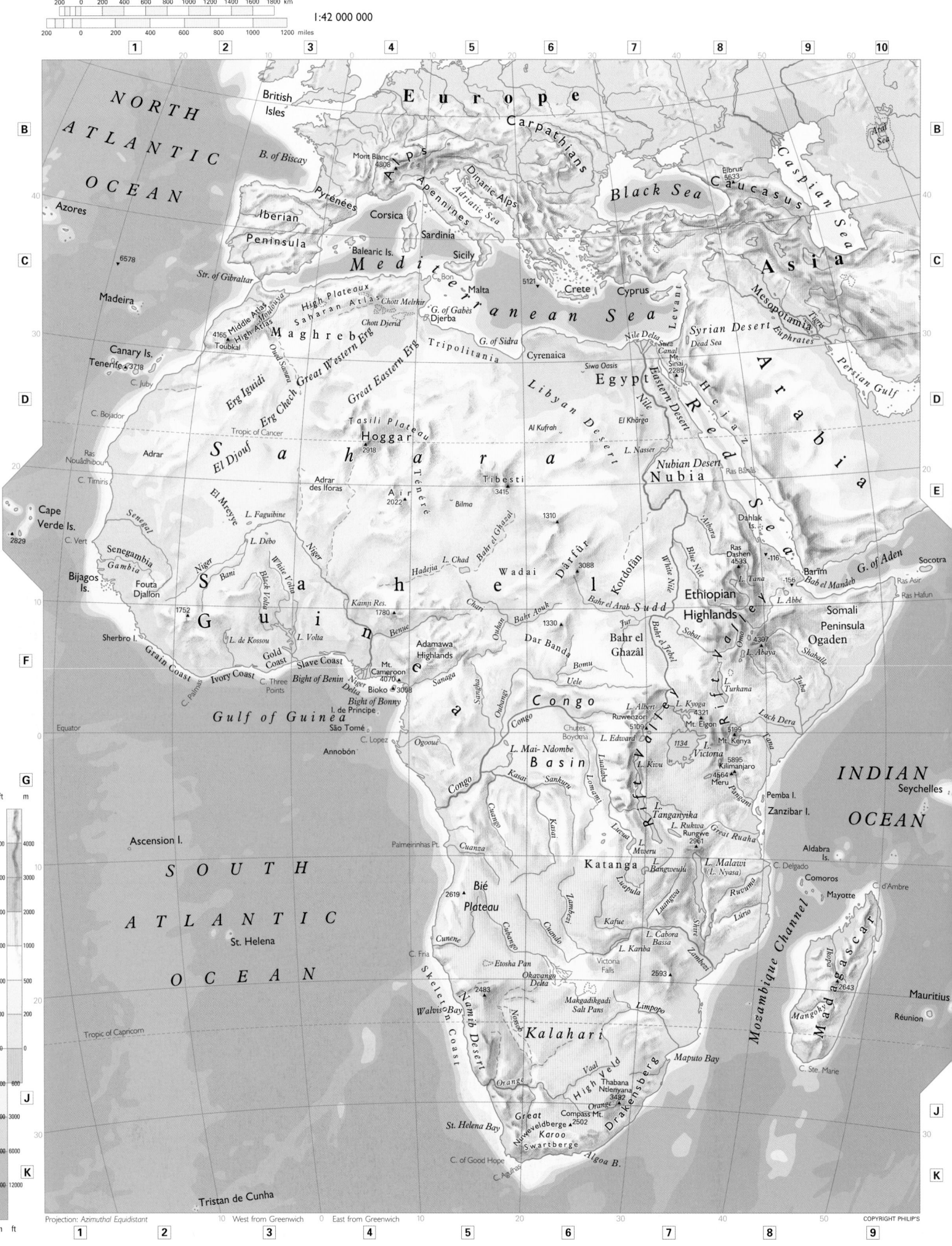

NORTH ATLANTIC OCEAN

British Isles

Europe

B. of Biscay

Carpathians

Mont Blanc 4808

Alps

Dinaric Alps

Apennines

Adriatic Sea

Black Sea

Elbrus 5633

Caucasus

Caspian Sea

Aral Sea

Iberian Peninsula

Pyrénées

Corsica

Sardinia

Sicily

Bon

Crete

Cyprus

Asia

6578

Madeira

Mediterranean Sea

Malta

5121

Levant

Mesopotamia

Tigris

Str. of Gibraltar

Middle Atlas

High Atlas

High Plateaux

Saharan Atlas

Chott Melrhir

G. of Gabès

Djerba

G. of Sidra

Cyrenaica

Tripolitania

Libyan Desert

Syrian Desert

Euphrates

Dead Sea

Canary Is.

Tenerife 3718

4165

Toubkal

Maghreb

Chott Djerid

Egypt

Suez Canal

Nile Delta

Mt. Sinai 2285

Eastern Desert

Arabia

Hejaz

Persian Gulf

C. Juby

Oued Saoura

Great Western Erg

Great Eastern Erg

Siwa Oasis

Al Khārga

Red Sea

Ras Banâs

C. Bojador

Erg Iguidi

Erg Chech

Tropic of Cancer

Tasili Plateau

Hoggar 2918

Sahara

Aïr 2022

Ténéré

Al Kufrah

Nubian Desert

Nubia

Ras Nouâdhibou

Adrar

S El Djouf

Adrar des Iforas

Bilma

Tibesti 3415

Dahlak Is.

Ras Dashen 4533

-116

Barîm

C. Timiris

El Mreyye

L. Faguibine

1310

Dârfûr

3088

Kordofân

Bab el Mandeb

Ras Asir

G. of Aden

Socotra

Cape Verde Is.

2829

C. Vert

Senegal

Niger

White Volta

L. Débo

Hadejia

L. Chad

Wadai

Bahr el Ghazâl

Blue Nile

White Nile

Athbara

L. Tana

-156

Ras Hafun

Senegambia

Gambia

Fouta Djallon

Bijagos Is.

Bani

Black Volta

S G u i n e a

Kainji Res.

1780

1752

L. de Kossou

L. Volta

Benue

Chari

Dar Banda

1330

Bahr Aouk

Jur

Bomu

Bahr el Arab

Sudd

Bahr el Jebel

Sobat

Omo

4307

Ethiopian Highlands

L. Abbé

Somali Peninsula

Ogaden

Juba

Shabelle

L. Abaya

Sherbro I.

Grain Coast

Ivory Coast

Gold Coast

Slave Coast

C. Palmas

C. Three Points

Niger Delta

Bight of Benin

Mt. Cameroon 4070

Bioko 3008

Adamawa Highlands

Sanaga

Opubu

Sangha

Ubangi

Uele

Congo

Turkana

Mt. Elgon 5199

L. Kyoga

Lach Dera

Bight of Bonny

I. de Principe

São Tomé

Gulf of Guinea

Equator

C. Lopez

Ogooué

Annobón

Congo

Kasai

L. Mai-Ndombe

Congo

Basin

Chutes Boyoma

Lualaba

Lomami

5109

Ruwenzori 4321

L. Edward

L. Albert

L. Kivu

1134

L. Victoria

Mt. Kenya 5895

Kilimanjaro 5895

Meru 4564

Pangani

Tana

INDIAN OCEAN

Seychelles

SOUTH ATLANTIC OCEAN

Ascension I.

St. Helena

Palmeirinhas Pt.

Cuanza

Congo

Kasai

Kwango

Kasai

Sankuru

Lulua

Luvua

L. Tanganyika

L. Rukwa

Rungwe 2961

Great Ruaha

Pemba I.

Zanzibar I.

Ruvuma

Lúrio

C. Delgado

Comoros

Mayotte

d'Ambre

Bié Plateau

2619

Katanga

Luapula

L. Bangweulu

L. Mweru

L. Malawi (L. Nyasa)

Cunene

Cubango

Kafue

Zambezi

Kwando

L. Cabora Bassa

Shire

Madagascar

2643

Mauritius

Réunion

Tropic of Capricorn

Etosha Pan

Okavango Delta

Victoria Falls

L. Kariba

Zambezi

2593

Mozambique Channel

Mangoky

Walvis Bay

Skeleton Coast

Namib Desert

2483

Makgadikgadi Salt Pans

Kalahari

Limpopo

Maputo Bay

Ibopa

C. Ste. Marie

St. Helena Bay

Cunene

Orange

Vaal

High Veld

Thabana Ntlenyana 3482

Orange

Compass Mt. 2502

Drakensberg

Great Nuweveldberge

Karoo

Swartberge

Maputo Bay

C. of Good Hope

C. Agulhas

Algoa B.

Tristan de Cunha

Projection: Azimuthal Equidistant

West from Greenwich 0 East from Greenwich

COPYRIGHT PHILIP'S

| 1 | 2 | 3 | 4 | 5 | 6 | 7 | 8 | 9 |

ft m
12000 4000
9000 3000
6000 2000
3000 1000
1500 500
600 200
0 0
200 600
1000 3000
2000 6000
4000 12000
m ft

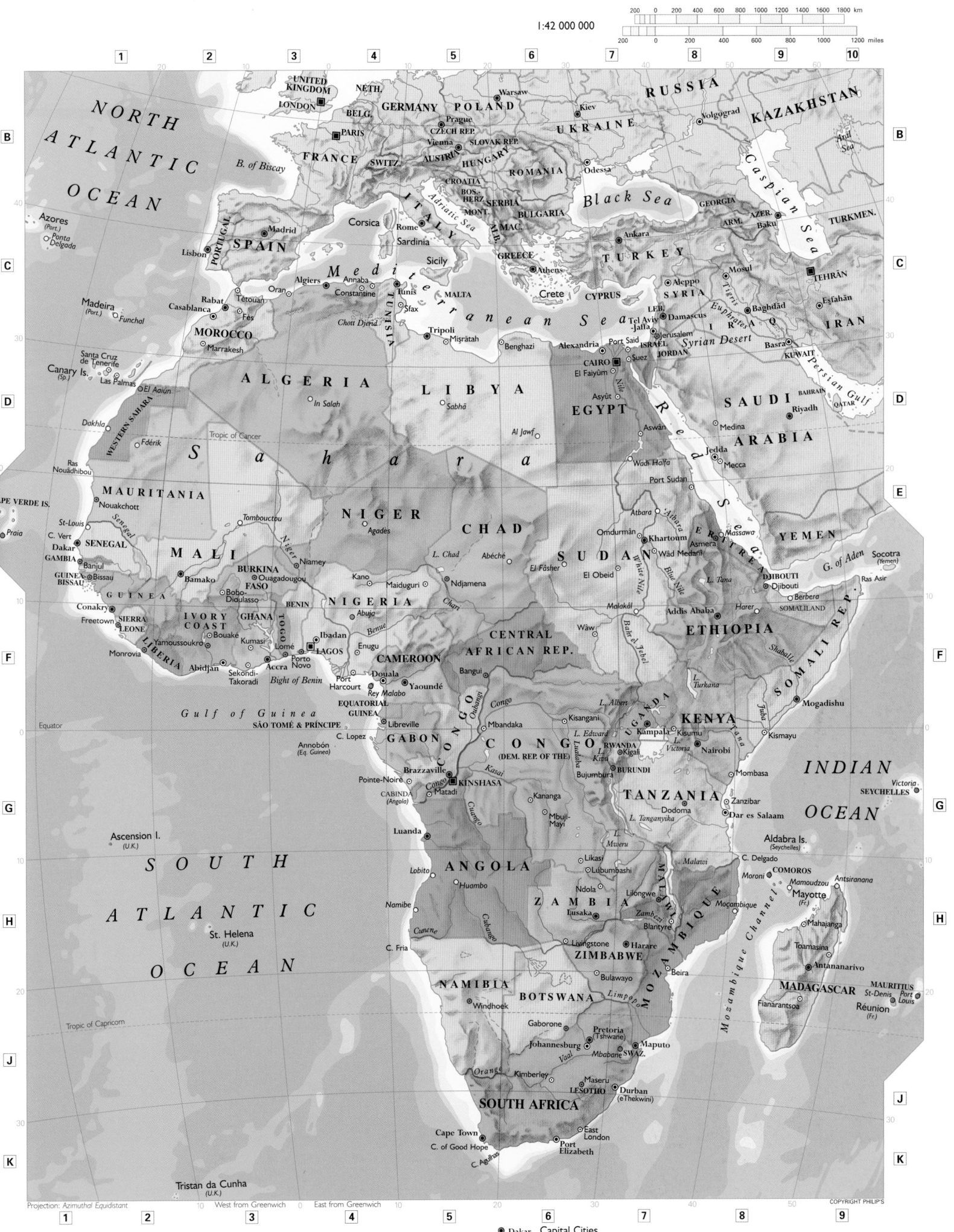

1:42 000 000

200 0 200 400 600 800 1000 1200 1400 1600 1800 km
200 0 200 400 600 800 1000 1200 miles

NORTH ATLANTIC OCEAN

UNITED KINGDOM
LONDON
NETH.
BELG.
GERMANY POLAND
PARIS
FRANCE SWITZ.
B. of Biscay
CZECH REP. Prague
Vienna
AUSTRIA SLOVAK REP.
HUNGARY
CROATIA
BOS.-
HERZ.
MONT.
SERBIA
MAC.
ITALY Adriatic Sea
Rome
Corsica
Sardinia
Sicily
MALTA
Warsaw
Kiev
Volgograd
RUSSIA
UKRAINE
Odessa
ROMANIA
BULGARIA
Black Sea
GEORGIA
ARM. AZER.
Baku
KAZAKHSTAN
Aral Sea
Caspian Sea
TURKMEN.

Azores
(Port.)
Ponta Delgada
Madrid
SPAIN
Lisbon
PORTUGAL
Madeira
(Port.) Funchal
Algiers
Oran
Constantine
Annaba
Rabat
Tétouan
Casablanca
Fes
MOROCCO
Marrakesh
Santa Cruz de Tenerife
Canary Is.
(Sp.)
Las Palmas
El Aaiún
WESTERN SAHARA
Dakhla

GREECE
Athens
Crete
TURKEY
Ankara
CYPRUS
Aleppo
SYRIA
LEB.
Tel Aviv-Jaffa
Damascus
Beirut
ISRAEL
JORDAN
Jerusalem
Port Said
Suez
Alexandria
CAIRO
El Faiyûm
Asyût
Mediterranean Sea
Tunis
Sfax
TUNISIA
Tripoli
Mişrātah
Benghazi
Chott Djerid
Mosul
TEHRĀN
Eşfahān
IRAN
Euphrates
Tigris
Baghdād
IRAQ
Basra
KUWAIT
BAHRAIN
QATAR
Persian Gulf
Riyadh
SAUDI ARABIA
Medina
Mecca
Jedda
Red Sea
Aswân
Syrian Desert

ALGERIA
In Salah
LIBYA
Sabhā
EGYPT
Al Jawf
Tropic of Cancer
Sahara
Nile

Ras Nouâdhibou
Fdérik
MAURITANIA
Nouakchott
CAPE VERDE IS.
St-Louis
C. Vert
Dakar
SENEGAL
GAMBIA
Banjul
GUINEA-BISSAU
Bissau
Bamako
MALI
Tombouctou
Niamey
NIGER
Agades
L. Chad
CHAD
Abéché
Ndjamena
Kano
Maiduguri
Maradi
NIGERIA
Abuja
Enugu
Ibadan
LAGOS
Porto Novo
Lomé
TOGO
BENIN
Kumasi
Accra
GHANA
Sekondi-Takoradi
Abidjan
IVORY COAST
Bouaké
Yamoussoukro
BURKINA FASO
Ouagadougou
Bobo-Dioulasso
Conakry
GUINEA
Freetown
SIERRA LEONE
Monrovia
LIBERIA
Senegal
Niger
Benue
Chari
El Fâsher
SUDAN
El Obeid
Omdurmân
Khartoum
Wâd Medani
Atbara
Blue Nile
White Nile
Malakâl
Wâw
Bahr el Jebel
Wadi Halfa
Port Sudan
Medina
ERITREA
Massawa
Asmera
DJIBOUTI
Djibouti
Berbera
Ras Asir
YEMEN
G. of Aden
Socotra
(Yemen)
Aden
SOMALILAND
Addis Ababa
Harer
ETHIOPIA
L. Tana
SOMALI REP.
Shabelle

Abuja
CAMEROON
Douala
Yaoundé
Rey Malabo
EQUATORIAL GUINEA
Port Harcourt
Bight of Benin
Gulf of Guinea
SÃO TOMÉ & PRÍNCIPE
Annobón
(Eq. Guinea)
C. Lopez
GABON
Libreville
CENTRAL AFRICAN REP.
Bangui
CONGO
Congo
Oubangi
Mbandaka
Kisangani
L. Albert
L. Edward
UGANDA
RWANDA
Kigali
BURUNDI
Bujumbura
L. Kivu
KENYA
Kampala
Kisumu
Nairobi
L. Victoria
Kismayu
Mombasa
L. Turkana
Juba
Mogadishu
Equator

Brazzaville
Pointe-Noire
KINSHASA
Matadi
CABINDA
(Angola)
CONGO
(DEM. REP. OF THE)
Kasai
Kananga
Mbuji-Mayi
TANZANIA
Dodoma
Zanzibar
Dar es Salaam
L. Tanganyika
INDIAN OCEAN
Victoria
SEYCHELLES

SOUTH ATLANTIC OCEAN

Ascension I.
(U.K.)
St. Helena
(U.K.)
Luanda
ANGOLA
Lobito
Huambo
Namibe
C. Fria
Likasi
Lubumbashi
Ndola
ZAMBIA
Lusaka
Lilongwe
MALAWI
Blantyre
L. Mweru
L. Malawi
Moroni
COMOROS
Mamoudzou
Mayotte
(Fr.)
Antsiranana
Mahajanga
Toamasina
Antananarivo
MADAGASCAR
Fianarantsoa
MAURITIUS
St-Denis
Port Louis
Réunion
(Fr.)
Aldabra Is.
(Seychelles)
C. Delgado
Moçambique
MOZAMBIQUE
Mozambique Channel
Zambezi
Beira
Cuando
Cunene
Cuango

NAMIBIA
Windhoek
BOTSWANA
Gaborone
ZIMBABWE
Harare
Bulawayo
Livingstone
Limpopo
Vaal
Orange
Johannesburg
Pretoria
Tshwane
Maputo
Mbabane
SWAZ.
LESOTHO
Maseru
Kimberley
SOUTH AFRICA
Cape Town
C. of Good Hope
C. Agulhas
Port Elizabeth
East London
Durban
(eThekwini)
Tropic of Capricorn

Tristan da Cunha
(U.K.)

● Dakar Capital Cities

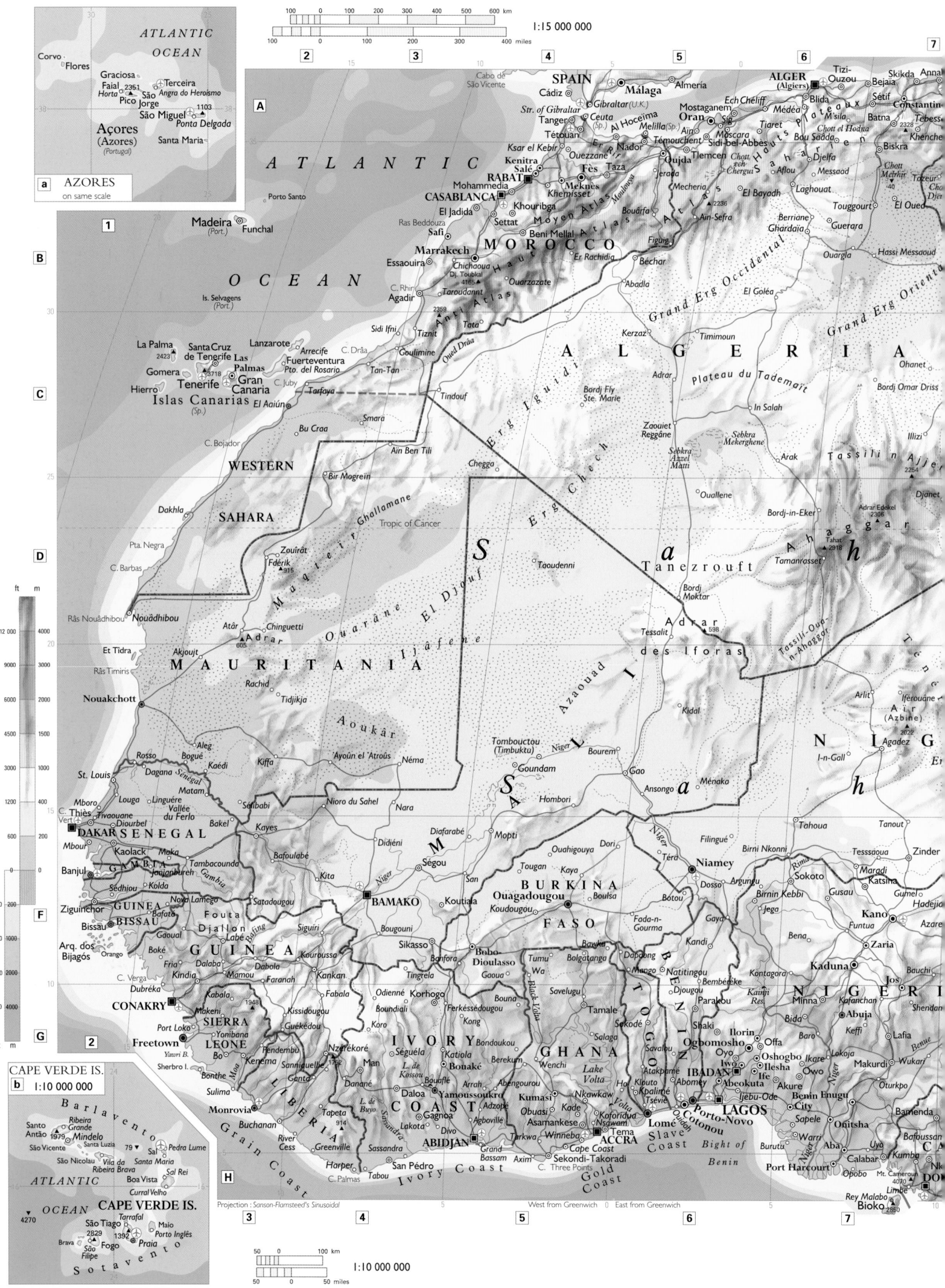

1:15 000 000

AZORES on same scale

ATLANTIC OCEAN

Corvo · Flores

Graciosa
Faial 2351 Terceira · Angra do Heroísmo
Horta ▲ São Jorge
Pico ▲ 2351
São Miguel ▲ 1103
Ponta Delgada
Santa Maria

Açores (Azores) *(Portugal)*

a AZORES on same scale

1

CAPE VERDE IS.

b 1:10 000 000

Barlavento
Santo Antão · Ribeira Grande
São Vicente · Mindelo · Santa Luzia
São Nicolau · Vila da Ribeira Brava
79 ✈ Sal · Pedra Lume
Santa Maria
Sal Rei
Boa Vista
Curral Velho

ATLANTIC OCEAN

4270

São Tiago · Tarrafal
2829 ✈ Praia
139 · Maio · Porto Inglês
Brava · São Filipe · Fogo
Sotavento

CAPE VERDE IS.

2 1:10 000 000

Projection: Sanson-Flamsteed's Sinusoidal

West from Greenwich   East from Greenwich

50 0 100 km
50 0 50 miles
1:10 000 000

a
b

A

B

47

C

D

E

F

G

H

COPYRIGHT PHILIPS

Bizerte
Ariana
CARTHAGE
Ra's at Tïb (C. Bon)
Béja
TUNIS
Nabeul
Pantelleria
Sicilia
ITALY
Peloponnese
Cyclades
Rhodes
TURKEY
Antalya
Alanya
Sifke
ADANA
Hatay
HALAB
(Aleppo)
Nahr al Furāt (Euphrates)

Kairouan
Sousse
Monastir
Mahdia
Valletta
MALTA
Lampedusa (It.)
GREECE
Chania
Kriti
Iraklio
Rhodes
CYPRUS
Paphos
Limassol
Nicosia
Al Lādhiqīyah
Hamāh
SYRIA
Hims

Mšaken
Sfax
Îles Kerkenna
Golfe de Gabès
Djerba
Zarzis
Gabès
Médenine
Ben Gardane
Zuwārah
Gharyān
TARĀBULUS (Tripoli)
Al Khums
Misrātah
Al Bayḍā
Marsā Sūsah
Darnah
Banghāzī
Al Marj
Tubruq
Bardīyah
Salūm
Marsá Maṭrūḥ
El Alamein
EL ISKANDARĪYA
(Alexandria)
Damanhūr
El Mahalla el Kubra
Būr Saʾīd (Port Saïd)
Dumyât
Tarābulus
LEBANON
Tyr
Sūr
BAYRŪT (Beirut)
ISRAEL
Hefa
TEL AVIV-YAFO
Ashqelon
Jerusalem
GAZA STRIP
WEST BANK
418
AMMAN
DIMASHQ (Damascus)
Jabal ad Durūz
IRAQ
Ar Rutbah
Bādiyat ash Shām

Tataouine
Dehibat
Mizdah
Daraj
Ghadāmis
Tarābulus (Tripolitania)
968
Surt
Ajdābiya
Khalīj Surt
Suluq
Tubruq
Ed Déffa
El Ḥamādah al al Ḥamrāʾ

LIBYA
Līḇīya
Idehan Awbāri
Birāk
Awbāri
Sabhā
Al Harūj al Aswad
1200
Sarīr Calanscio
47
Dahra
Marādah
Zillah
Tazerbo
Hūn
Awjilah
Al Joghbūb
Siwa
Es Saḥrâʾ el Gharbîya
Munkhafed el Qaṭṭâra
-133
El Faiyûm
El Gîza
PYRAMIDS
EL QÂHIRA (Cairo)
Helwân
Beni Suef
El Minyâ
Maghâgha
Mallawi
Manfalût
Asyût
Tahta
Sohâg
Girga
Qena
KARNAK
THEBES
El Uqsur (Luxor)
Isna
Idfû
Kôm Ombo
Aswân
Sadd el Aâli (Aswan High Dam)
Nahr en Nīl (Nile)
Es Sahrâ el Sharqîya
Ras Muhammad
Sharm el Sheikh
2285
G. Mûsa
Khalîg el Suweis
Es Sînâʾ
Qanâ es Suweis (Suez Canal)
El Suweis (Suez)
Madân
Elat
Al ʾAqabah
2578
Tabūk
Al Muwayliḥ
SAUDI
Al Jawf
ARABIA

EGYPT
Maṣr

Ghât
428
Fezzan
W. Barjūj
Marzūq
Al Qaṭrūn
Madama
Toummo
Chirfa
Bardai
Pic Toussidé
3265
3376
Tarso Emissi
2910
Tibesti
Zouar
Emi Koussi
3415
Bāku Bitti
2286
Aozou
Aozou Strip
Sarīr Tibastī
Ennedi
Ma'tan as Sarra
Hadabat el Gilf el Kebîr
1082
J. Uweinat
1893
El Wâḥât el Dakhla
El Wâḥât el Khârga
El Khārga
Mût
Qasr Farâfra
El Wâḥât el Selima
Wâdi Halfa
Toshka Lakes
Buheirat en Naṣer (L. Nasser)
Delgo
3rd Cataract
ABU SIMBEL
Kosha
Muhammad Qol
2259
Ras Abu Shagara
Es Saḥrâ en Nûbîya
Ras Bânâs
Bîr Shalatein
Halaib Triangle
Halaib
Ras Hadarba
RED SEA
Rābigh
Yanbu al Baḥr
Marsa Alam
1977
Bûr Safâga
Hurghada
Quseir
Al Wajh
Umm Lajj
Qena

Sahrâʾ Libîya

Sahrâʾ Rebiana

Sahrâʾ el Gharbîya

Sarīr

Al Jawf
Al Kufrah

SAHARA

NIGER
du Ténéré
Fachi
Bilma
Grand Erg de Bilma
Borkou
Faya-Largeau
Dépression du Bodélé
Erg du Djourab
Ziguéy
Mao
Lac Tchad
346
Bol
Massakory
Ati
Ounianga Kébir
Dépression du Mourdi
Fada
Zagaoua
Oum Chalouba
CHAD
Biltine
Abéché
Oum Hadjer
Mongo
Goz Beïda
Abou-Deïa
Am Timan
Birao
Malha
1954
El Wuz
El Fâsher
J. Marrah
3088
Nyâlâ
Kutum
Al Junaynah
Zalingei
Dârfûr
W. Howar (Shâu)
Bîr 'Atrun
Wâdi Halfa
3rd Cataract
Dongola
Kareima
4th Cataract
Ed Debba
Berber
Atbara
5th Cataract
Wad Hamid
Shendî
6th Cataract
El Khartûm Bahri
EL KHARTÛM (Khartoum)
Omdurmân
Abu Hamed
Adarama
Karora
Nakfa
ERITREA
Akordat
Kassalâ
Khashm el Girba
Metema
ETHIOPIA
Gonder
Bahir Dar
1830
L. Tana
Debre Markos
Âbay (Blue Nile)
Bure
Nekemte
Metu
Gore
Jima
3686
3202
Arba Minch'
L. Shamo
L. Abaya
Chew Bahir
 Filema Triangle
L. Turkana
375

SUDAN
Es Sahrâ en Nûbîya
Nahr en Nīl (Nile)
Kordofân
El Obeid
Sodiri
Umm Keddada
En Nahud
El Odaiya
Abû Zabad
Er Rahad
Umm Ruwaba
Kâdugli
Jibalan Nubah
1325
Ed Damazin
Roseires Res.
Ed Dueim
Kôstî
El Gezîra
Wâd Medanî
Gedaref
Singa
Malakâl
Sobat
Bahr el Jebel (Nile)
Sudd
Tonj
Gogriâl
Wâw
Rumbêk
Bôr
Pibor Post
Tali Post
Amadi
Jûba
Torit
Kapoeta
Lokitaung
Kajo Kaji
Yei
Faradje
Dungu
Yambiô
Obo
El Istiwa'iya
Ghazâl
Bahr el Arab
Raqa
Sa'id Bundas
Râga

Nil el Abyad (White Nile)
Nil el Azraq (Blue Nile)
Nîl el Atbara

CENTRAL AFRICAN REPUBLIC
Bangui
Bimbo
Mbaïki
Berbérati
Carnot
Bossembélé
Bozoum
Baboua
Bouar
Bossangoa
Batangafo
Kaga Bandoro
Sibut
Bambari
Ippy
Bria
Bakouma
Yalinga
Zemio
Mobaye
Zongo
Libenge
Bosobolo
Bondo
Mobayi
Bongassou
Bomu
Uele
Ango

CAMEROON
Yaoundé
Abong-Mbang
Bertoua
Nanga-Eboko
Sanaga
Batouri
Meiganga
Ngaoundéré
Garoua
Guider
Maroua
Mubi
Kumo
Biu
Goni
Chibuk
Bama
Kousseri
Ndjamena
Bongor
Pala
Kélo
Lai
Doba
Moundou
Goré
Baïbokoum
Bétaré Oya
Yoko
Tibati
Fumban
Foumban
Rés. de Mbakou
Massif de l'Adamaoua
2042
1960
2419
Gashaka
Banyo
Kumba
Numan
Yola
Jalingo
Potiskum
Nguru
Geidam
Titiwa
Gashua
Maiduguri
Nguigmi
Bosso
Bol
Moussoro
Massenya
Bitkine
Bousso
Harazé
Sarh
Koumra
Ndélé
Massakory
Mt. Toussoro
1330
Massif des Bongos
Goz Beïda

MEDITERRANEAN SEA

CYRENE
Barqa (Cyrenaica)

1:15 000 000

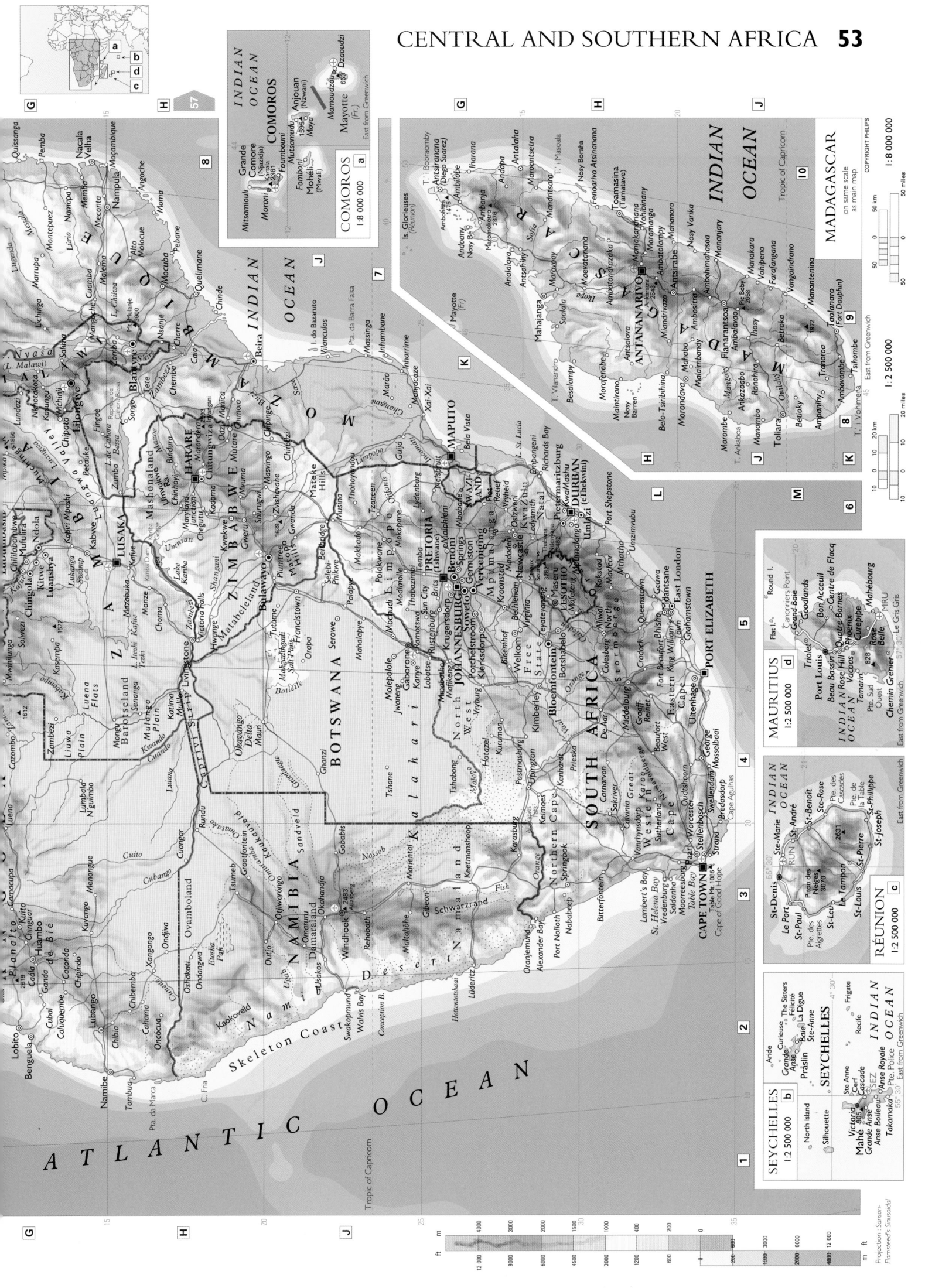

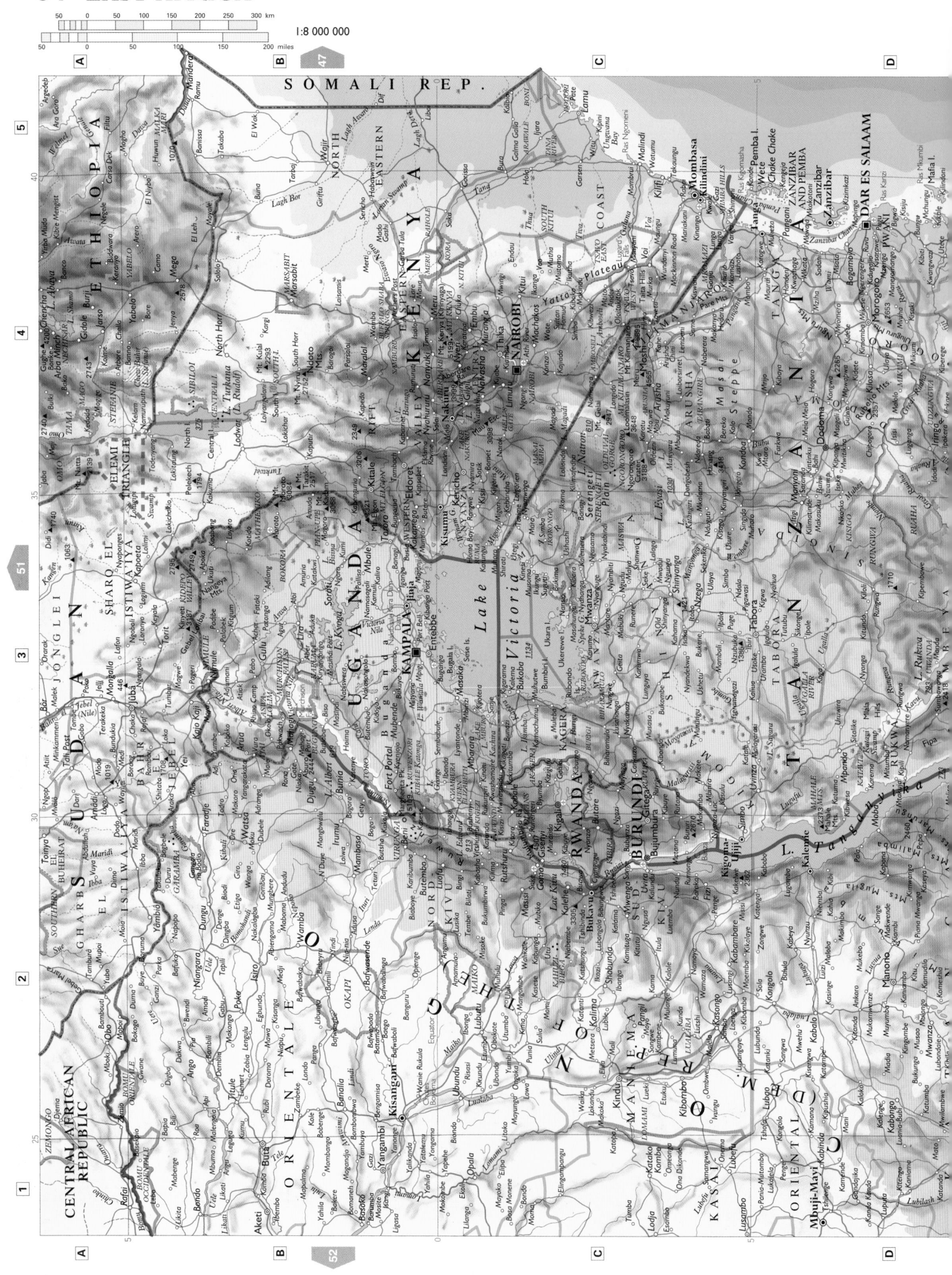

1:8 000 000

SOMALI REP.

ETHIOPIA

K E N Y A

NAIROBI

Mombasa

DAR ES SALAAM

ZANZIBAR
AND PEMBA
Zanzibar

S U D A N

U G A N D A

KAMPALA
Entebbe

Lake Victoria

RWANDA
KIGALI

BURUNDI
BUJUMBURA

T A N Z A N I A

Dodoma

L. Tanganyika

Kisangani

CENTRAL AFRICAN
REPUBLIC

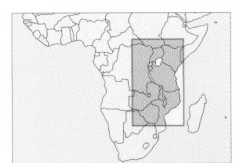

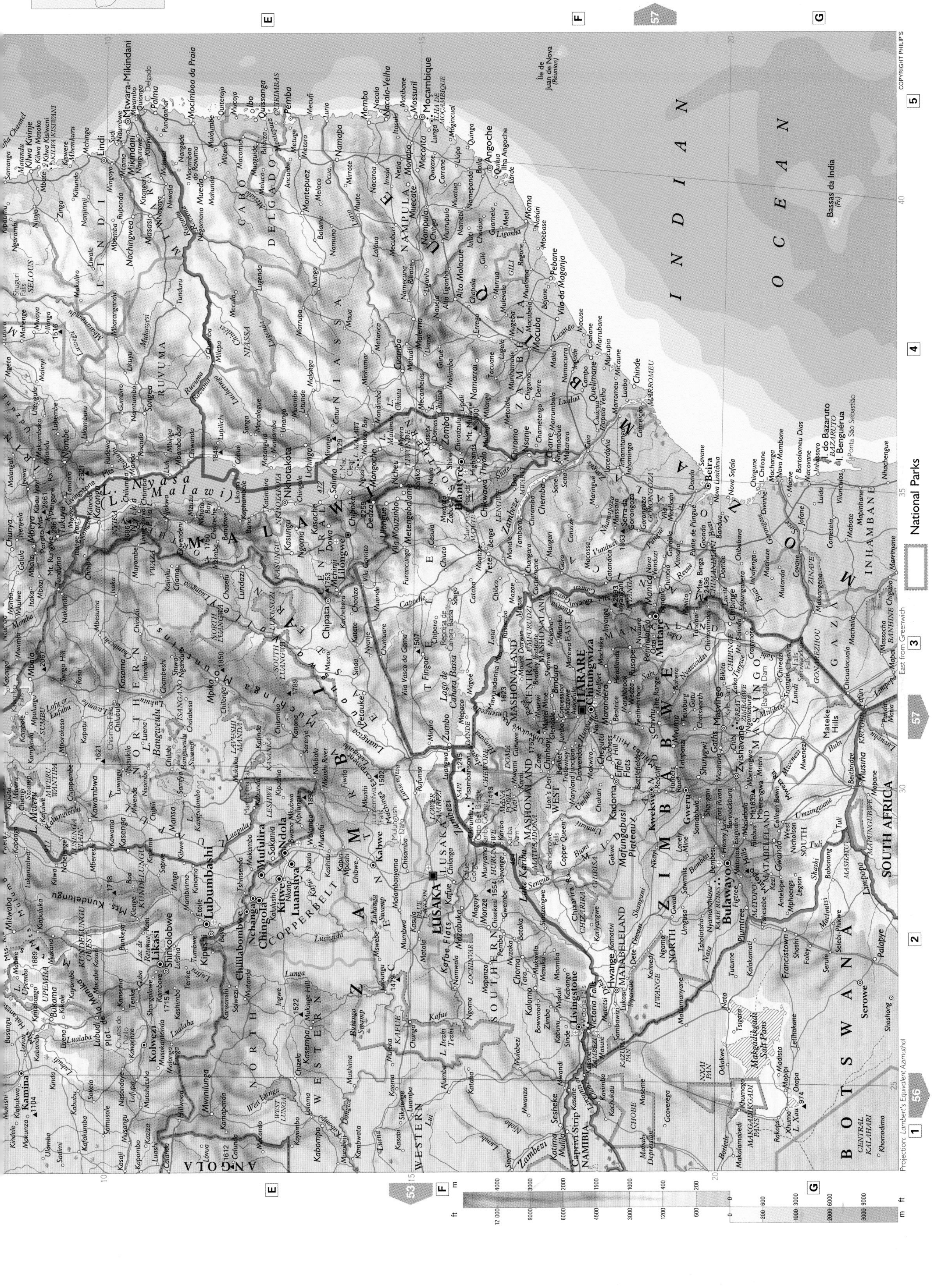

National Parks

Nature Reserves and
Game Reserves

∴ UNESCO World Heritage Sites

Projection: Lambert's Equivalent Azimuthal

East from Greenwich

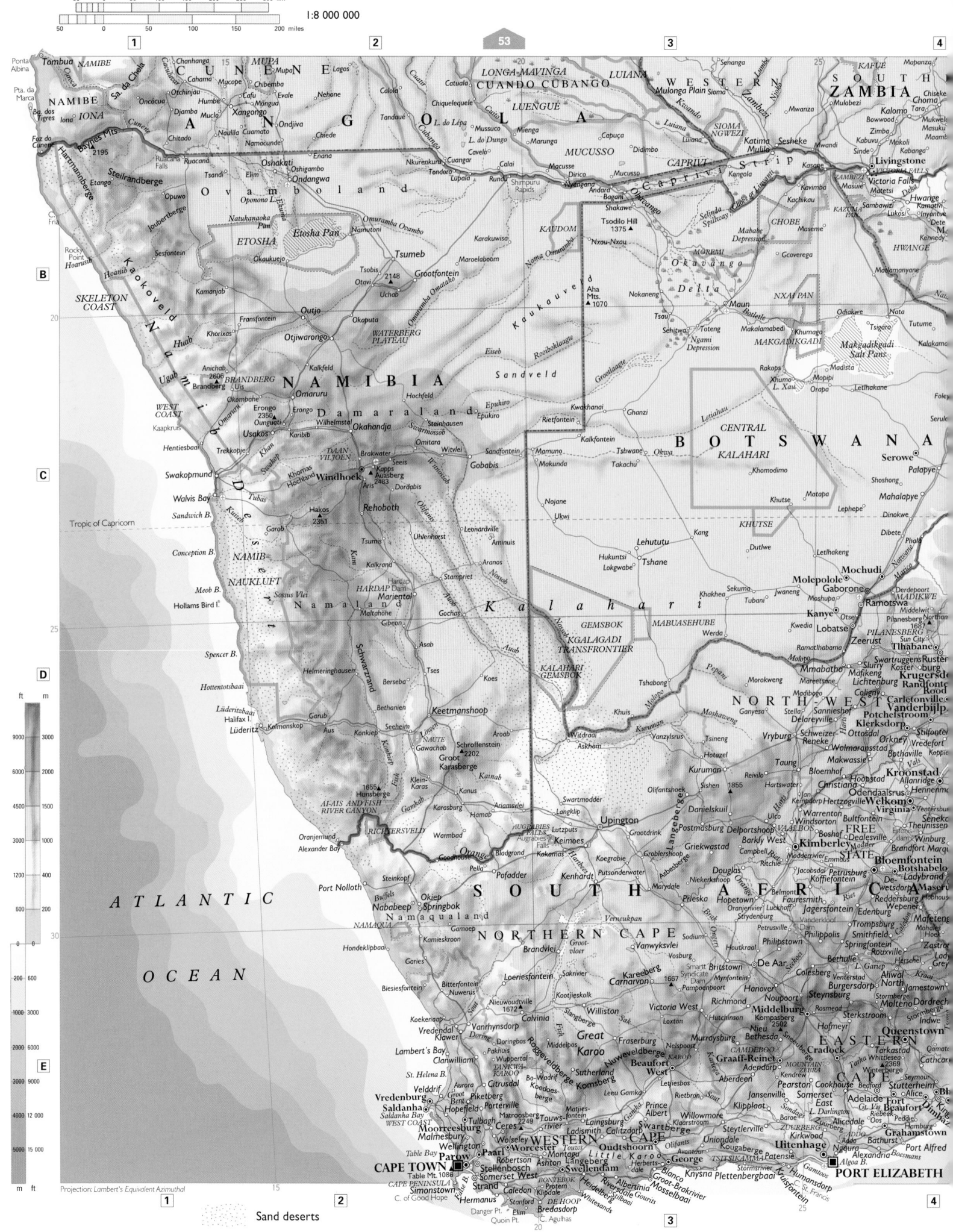

National Parks

Nature Reserves and
Game Reserves

∴ UNESCO World Heritage Sites

MADAGASCAR
1:8 000 000

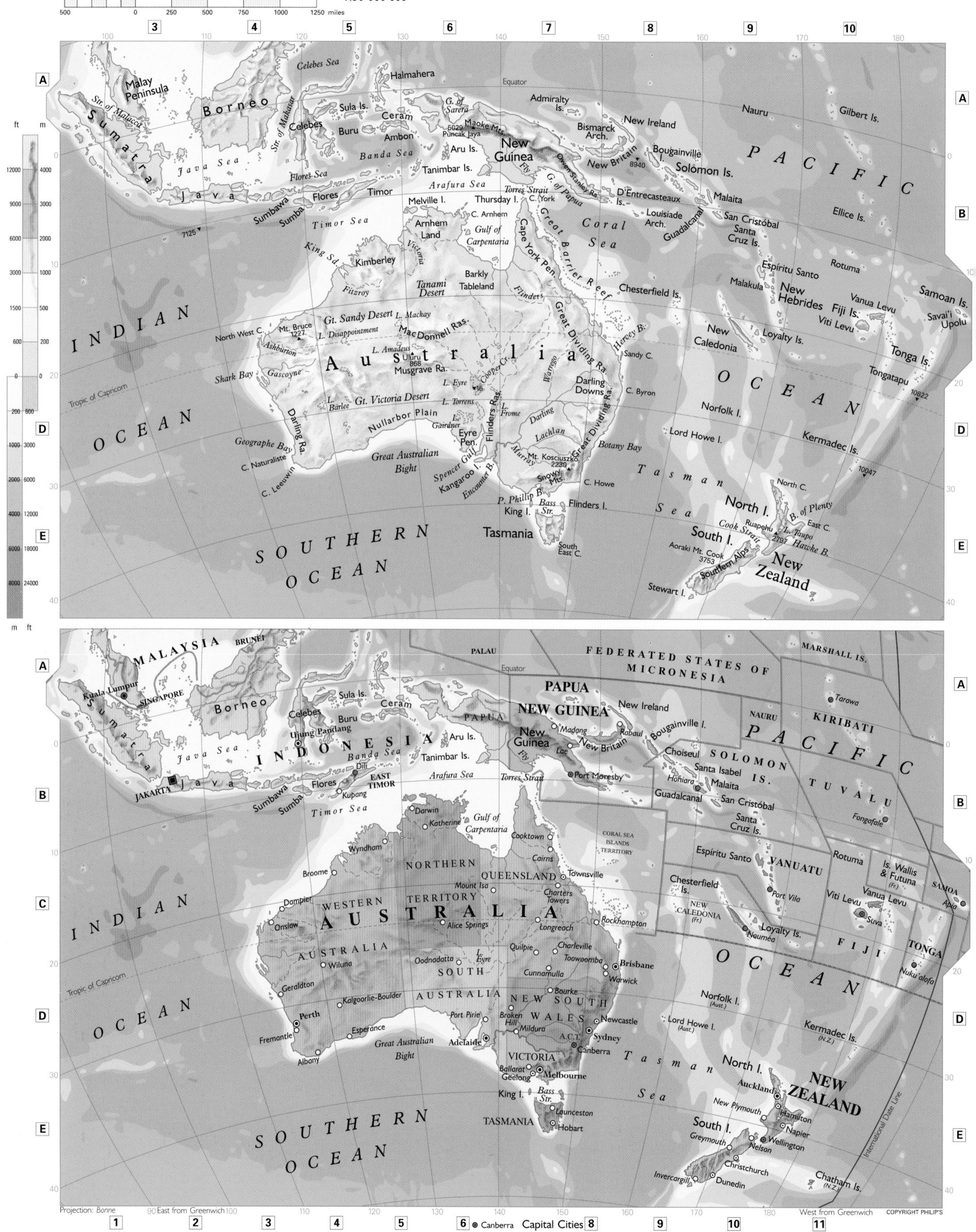

1:6 000 000

50 0 50 100 150 200 km
50 0 50 100 150 miles

4 **64** 5 6 7

FIJI [a]
on same scale

PACIFIC OCEAN

Great Sea Reef
Kia
Udu Pt.
Ringgold Is.
Yaqaga
Labasa
Nukubati Bay
Rabi
Yadua
Vanua Levu
▲1031
Buca
Somosomo
Taveuni
Yasawa Group
Yasawa
Nacula
Bua
BOUMA
Qamea
Naitaba
Nabouwalu
Namenalala
Vanua Balavu
Viwa
Naviti
Rakiraki
Nasau
Koro
Vacata
Lomaloma
Waya
Vomo
Mba
Tomanii
▲1323
Lawaki
Levuka
Wakaya
Makogai
Northern Lau Group
Vatu Vara
Mago
Vomo
Malolo
Navai
KOROYANITU
Korovou
Ovalau
Batiki
Nairai
Cicia
Tuvuca
Mamanuca Group
Nadi
Lautoka
Vunidawa
Naununu
Gau
Nayau
Lakeba Passage
Tubou
Lakeba
Oneata
Sigatoka
Korolevu
Yanuca
Beqa
Vanua Vatu
Moce
KORO SEA
Southern Lau Group
Namuka-i-Lau
Yagasa Cluster
Vatulele
Ono
Moala
Kabara
Fulaga
Ogea Levu
Ogea Driki
Kadavu Passage
Tavuki
Vunisea
Totoya
Matuku
FIJI
Suva
Kadavu
18 S
178 E 180 West from Greenwich 180 East from Greenwich 178 E

SAMOA
SAMOAN ISLANDS [b]
on same scale

PACIFIC OCEAN

Asau
Safune
Savai'i
Falelima
▲1858
Pu'apu'a
Taga
Saleleloga
Multifanua I.
Apia
Falefa
Manono
Faleolo
'Upolu
OLE PUPU PU'E
Safata B.
Amaile
14 S

AMERICAN SAMOA (U.S.A.)
AMERICAN SAMOA
Ofu
Olosega
Ta'ū
Tutuila
Pago Pago
Aunu'u
Luma
Manu'a Is.
Leone
Vaitogi
AMERICAN SAMOA
172 W 170 W West from Greenwich

2 170 3

TONGA [c]
on same scale

PACIFIC OCEAN

174 W
Fonualei
Toku
Vava'u
Neiafu
Vava'u Group
Late
Home Reef
Ofolanga
Ha'ano
Disney Reef
Tofua
Foa
Ha'apai Group
Kotu Group
Uiha
Lifuka
Nomuka
Oto Tolu Group
Fonuafo'ou
Mango
Hunga Ha'apai
Nomuka Group
Tonumea
20 S

TONGA
Nuku'alofa
Tongatapu
Tongatapu Group
Eua
West from Greenwich

1

New Zealand (main map)

PACIFIC OCEAN
C. Reinga
North C.
C. Maria van Diemen
Houhora Heads
Rangaunu B.
Doubtless B.
Whangaroa Harb.
Ahipara B.
Mangonui
Tauroa Pt.
Okaihau
Kaitaia
C. Brett
Rawene
Waitangi
B. of Islands
Opua
Hokianga Harbour
Kaikohe
Hikurangi
Whangarei
Waipoua Forest
Whangarei Harb.
Bream Hd.
Dargaville
Waipu
Bream B.
Little Barrier I.
Great Barrier I.
Kaipara Harbour
Helensville
Warkworth
C. Rodney
C. Colville
Cuvier I.
Takapuna
Coromandel
Whitianga
AUCKLAND
Manukau
Papakura
Pukekohe
Thames
Whangamata
Mayor I.
Waiuku
Mercer
Paeroa
Waihi
Te Aroha
Tauranga Harb.
Whakaari (White I.)
Whakatane
Runaway
Huntly
Morrinsville
Mount Maunganui
Raglan
Hamilton
Cambridge
Tauranga
Te Puke
Bay of Plenty
Kawhia
Te Awamutu
Whakatane
Opotiki
East C.
Kawhia Harbour
Otorohanga
Putaruru
Rotorua
Tikitere
Taneatua
Raukumara Ra.
▲Hikurangi 1763
Waipiro
North Island
Te Kuiti
Mangakino
L. Taraweta
Murupara
UREWERA
Motu
Tolaga Bay
Mokau
Mokai
Wairakei
Taupo
Rotongaio
Ormond
North Taranaki Bight
Ongarue
L. Taupo
Rangitaiki Mts.
Waikaremoana
Gisborne
New Plymouth
Inglewood
Whangamomona
Turangi
Tongariro
Nuhaka
Poverty Bay
Mt. Taranaki or Mt. Egmont
C. Egmont
EGMONT
▲2518
Stratford
Ohakune
Ruapehu ▲2797
WHANGANUI
Waiouru
Mahia Pen.
Opunake
Kaponga
Raetihi
TONGARIRO
Bay View
Hawke Bay
Hawera
Eltham
Mangaweka
Napier
Waverley
Taihape
Ruahine Ra.
C. Kidnappers
South Taranaki Bight
Patea
Hastings
Wanganui
Halcombe
Waipukurau
Bulls
Feilding
Dannevirke
Foxton
Palmerston North
Woodville
Shannon
Pahiatua
C. Turnagain
C. Farewell
Levin
Ekatahuna
Collingwood
Golden B.
D'Urville I.
Otaki
Masterton
Takaka
ABEL TASMAN
Paraparaumu
Carterton
KAHURANGI
Tasman Mts.
Tasman B.
Kapiti I.
Featherston
Greytown
Karamea
Motueka
Pelorus
Upper Hutt
Martinborough
Karamea Bight
Nelson
Richmond
Petone
Lower Hutt
Wairarapa
Seddonville
Wakefield
Picton
Wellington
L. Wairarapa
Granity
Murchison
Havelock
Cook Strait
Tadmor
NELSON LAKES
Blenheim
Westport
Lyell
Matiri Ra.
L. Rotoroa
Seddon
Inangahua
Ward
PAPAROA
Spenser Mts.
2885 Tapuae-o-Uenuku ▲
Punakaiki
Reefton
Mt. Travers ▲2337
Blackball
Hanmer Springs
Kaikoura
Runanga
Grey
Lewis
Greymouth
Kumara
Stillwater
Culverden
Waiau
Hokitika
L. Brunner
L. Jackson
ARTHUR'S PASS
Waikari
Hurunui
Ross
Arthur's
Springfield
Amberley
Waimakariri
Rangiora
Pegasus Bay
South Island
Waipara
WESTLAND
Whitecliffs
New Brighton
Southern Alps (Tiritiri o te Moana)
Aoraki
Christchurch
Mt. Cook ▲3753
Riccarton
Lyttelton
Westland Bight
Mount Cook
Banks Pen.
MT. COOK
Staveley
Lincoln
Little River
Methven
Ellesmere
Abut Hd.
Canterbury Plains
Rakaia
Ashburton
Jackson B.
MOUNT ASPIRING
Tekapo
Rangitata
Ashburton Bight
Mt. Aspiring ▲3033
L. Pukaki
Fairlie
Temuka
Okuru
Haast
L. Ohau
Canterbury Bight
Milford Sd.
Earnslaw ▲2819
Wanaka
Timaru
Sutherland Falls
Milford Sound
L. Wanaka
St. Andrews
Bligh Sound
George Sound
Arrowtown
Cromwell
Waimate
Dunstan Mts.
Kurow
Secretary I.
Queenstown
Clyde
Ngapara
Oamaru
Doubtful Sd.
FIORDLAND
Wakatipu
Alexandra
Maheno
Manapouri
Garvie Mts.
Roxburgh
Hampden
Te Anau
L. Manapouri
Mts.
Waikouaiti
Eyre Mts.
Mataura
Palmerston
Breaksea Sd.
Mossburn
Eglinton
Kingston
Naseby
Port Chalmers
Dusky Sd.
Lumsden
Clinton
Otago Harbour
Resolution I.
Southland
Ohai
Nightcaps
Kelso
Lawrence
S. Saunders
Chalky Inlet
Clifden
Winton
Gore
Balclutha
Dunedin
Tuatapere
Hedgehope
Mataura
Kaitangata
Preservation Inlet
Orepuki
Wyndham
Nugget Pt.
Riverton
Invercargill
Owaka
Solander I.
Bluff
Tahakopa
Ruapuke I.
Halfmoon Bay
Foveaux Str.
Stewart I. (Rakiura)
RAKIURA
Port Pegasus
South West C.

TASMAN SEA
PACIFIC OCEAN

34
A
36
B
38
C
64
40
D
42
E
44
F
46
G

Projection : Conical with two standard parallels
166 168 170 East from Greenwich 172
1 2 3 4

TAHITI & MOOREA [d]
1:1 000 000

Pte. Aroa
B. de Matavai
Pte. Vénus
Papetoai
Papao
Mahina
Mt. Tohiea ▲1207
Papeete
Pirae
Arué
Papenoo
Tiarei
Haapiti
Afareaitu
Faaa
Pte. Nuupere
Hitiaa
Moorea (France)
Punaauia
Paea
Mt. Aorai ▲2060
Mt. Orohena ▲2241
Faaone
Lac Vaihiria
Tahiti (France)
Mt. Tetufera ▲1799
PACIFIC OCEAN
Maraa
Papara
Mataiea
Atimaono
Taravao
Isthme de Taravao
Afaahiti
Pueu
Pte. Tatatua
Vairao
Mt. Rooniu ▲1332
Teahupoo
Presqu'île de Taiarapu
Tautira

17°30'S
17°45'S
149°45'W 149°30'W West from Greenwich 149°15'W

COPYRIGHT PHILIP'S

ft m
9000 3000
6000 2000
3000 1000
1200 400
600 200
0 0
200 600
2000 6000
4000 12 000
6000 18 000
m ft

1:1 000 000
10 0 10 km
10 0 10 miles

1:8 000 000

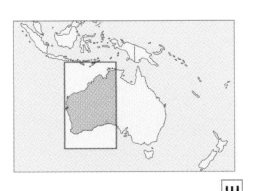

E F G

WESTERN AUSTRALIA

SOUTH AUSTRALIA

SOUTHERN OCEAN

INDIAN OCEAN

Great Victoria Desert

Nullarbor Plain

Hampton Tableland

NULLARBOR

Great Australian Bight

Archipelago of the Recherche

PETERMANN Ranges
Musgrave Ranges
CENTRAL DESERT
WARBURTON
COSMO NEWBERRY
ANANGU PITJANTJATJARA
MARALINGA TJARUTJA
WOOMERA PROHIBITED AREA

Kata Tjuta (The Olgas) 1069
Uluru (Ayers Rock) 863 ULURU KATA TJUTA
Mount Ebenezer
Curtin Springs
Mt. Woodroffe 1440
Amata
Mt. Morris 1288
Mann Ra. 1114
Mt. Aloysius 1126
Blackstone Tomkinson Ra. 1058
Mt. Buttfield
Kawlin
Mt. Forrest
Mt. Christopher
L. Christopher
Mt. Squires 705
Warburton
Barrow Ra.
YAPURARRA
Pt. Lilian 466
Macintosh Ra. 466
Saunders Pt.
Baker L.
THIRKARLI
Carnegie Ra.
J. Breaden
L. Gillen
Herbert Wash
Ernest Giles Ra.
Mt. Eureka 499
L. Throssell
Cosmo Newberry 594
Plumridge Lakes
Shell Lakes
Jubilee L.
L. Ilma
Serpentine Lakes
Nurrari Lakes
L. Maramangye
L. Dey-Dey
L. Maurice
Wynbring
Marainga
Ooldea
L. Yumbarra
Cook
L. Ifould
Penong
Bookabie
Coorabie
Ph. Fowler
Fowler B.
Yalata
Head of Bight
Nullarbor
Eucla
Wilson Bluff
Mundrabilla
Madura
Cocklebiddy
Caiguna
Pt. Culver
Pt. Dover
Red Rocks Pt.
Low Pt.
Reid
Forrest
Loongana
Naretha
Rawlinna
Zanthus
Coonana
Balladonia
Naretha
5632

Esperance
Norseman
Kalgoorlie-Boulder
Menzies
Leonora
Laverton
CAPE ARID
CAPE LE GRAND
Mt. Ragged 585
STOKES
C. Pasley
Middle I.
South East Is.
Eastern Group
Sandy Bight
C. Arid
RAVENSTHORPE
Hopetoun
Bremer Bay
Hood Pt.
PEAK CHARLES 703
FRANK HANN
Mt. Ridley
Salmon Gums
Widgiemooltha
Kambalda
Coolgardie
Kurnalpi
Goongarrie
Broad Arrow
L. Rebecca
L. Yindarlgooda
L. Lefroy
L. Dundas
L. Cowan
L. Cowan
Zanthus
Norseman
GOONGARRIE
Cue
Leinster
Leonora
Wiluna
Agnew
L. Carey
L. Rason
L. Darlot
L. Wells
L. Minigwal
L. Yeo
L. Noomie
Maynard Hills
Mt. Keith
Mt. Alexander 599
L. Ballard
Marmion
Burtle L.
Mt. Elvire
Mt. Burges 554
Marvel Loch
Southern Cross
Bullfinch
Koolyanobbing
Bonnie Rock
Mukinbudin
Merredin
WAVE ROCK
Hyden
Lake Grace
Newdegate
Lake King
Lake Magenta
FITZGERALD RIVER
Jerramungup
Ongerup
Gnowangerup
Borden
STIRLING RANGE
Mount Barker
Cranbrook
Denmark
Albany
WALPOLE NORNALUP
King George Sd.
Eclipse I.
Cape Home
C. Riche
Cheyne B.
Bald I.

PERTH
Midland
Armadale
Fremantle
Kwinana
Rockingham
Mandurah
Bunbury
Busselton
Augusta
Margaret River
CAPE NATURALISTE
CAPE LEEUWIN
LEEUWIN NATURALISTE
Pt. D'Entrecasteaux
Pemberton
Nannup
Bridgetown
Manjimup
Collie
Harvey
Pinjarra
Dwellingup
Boddington
Northam
York
Beverley
Brookton
Corrigin
Narrogin
Wagin
Katanning
Williams
Darkan
Boyup Brook
Kojonup
Tambellup
Wickepin
Kulin
Kondinin
Bruce Rock
Quairading
Kellerberrin
Tammin
Cunderdin
Goomalling
Dowerin
Wyalkatchem
Koorda
Bencubbin
Mukinbudin
Nungarin
Trayning
Wongan Hills
Dalwallinu
Wubin
Moora
Watheroo
Coorow
Carnamah
Three Springs
Mingenew
Dongara
Geraldton
Northampton
Kalbarri
Greenough
Dongara
Eneabba
Jurien Bay
Lancelin
Cervantes
Two Rocks
Yanchep
Wanneroo

MURCHISON
MOORE RIVER
NAMBUNG
LESUEUR
WATHEROO
BADGINGARRA
AVON
GREAT EASTERN HWY
GREAT SOUTHERN HWY
COOLGARDIE ESPERANCE HWY
EYRE HWY
GREAT NORTHERN HWY
NORTH WEST COASTAL HWY

L. Moore
L. Monger
Wubin
Mullewa
Morawa
Perenjori
Yalgoo
Mount Magnet
Sandstone
Paynes Find
Meekatharra
L. Austin
Cue
L. Annean
Nalbarra
Meka
L. Nabberu
Wiluna
Montague Ra.
Gascoyne Junction
Carnarvon
Shark Bay
Denham
Hamelin Pool
Monkey Mia
Useless Loop
Dirk Hartog I.
Dorre I.
Bernier I.
Steep Pt.
FRANCOIS PERON
Peron
Faure
L. MacLeod
Kennedy Ra.
KENNEDY RANGE
Minilya Roadhouse
Wooramel Roadhouse
Gascoyne Ra.
Mt. Augustus 1106
452
MOUNT AUGUSTUS
732
Godfrey Ra.
Sneeth Ra.
Waldburg Ra.
Mt. Fraser 799
Robinson Ra.
ROBINSON RANGES
Nicholson Ra.
Murchison Roadhouse
Byro
Murchison R.
Dividing Ra. 439
Tallering Peak
COLLIER RANGE
Mt. Essendon 914
Carnarvon Ra.

Aboriginal lands

Sand desert

1. NGALIWURRU / NUNGALI   5. RODNA
2. WANIMIYN   6. NTARIA
3. WARLPIRI   7. KOULPMAULPMA
4. LIALHLTUMA   8. URUNIA

m / ft scale:
3000 / 12 000
1200 / 4000
600 / 2000
400 / 1200
200 / 600
0 / 0

1 2 3 4 5

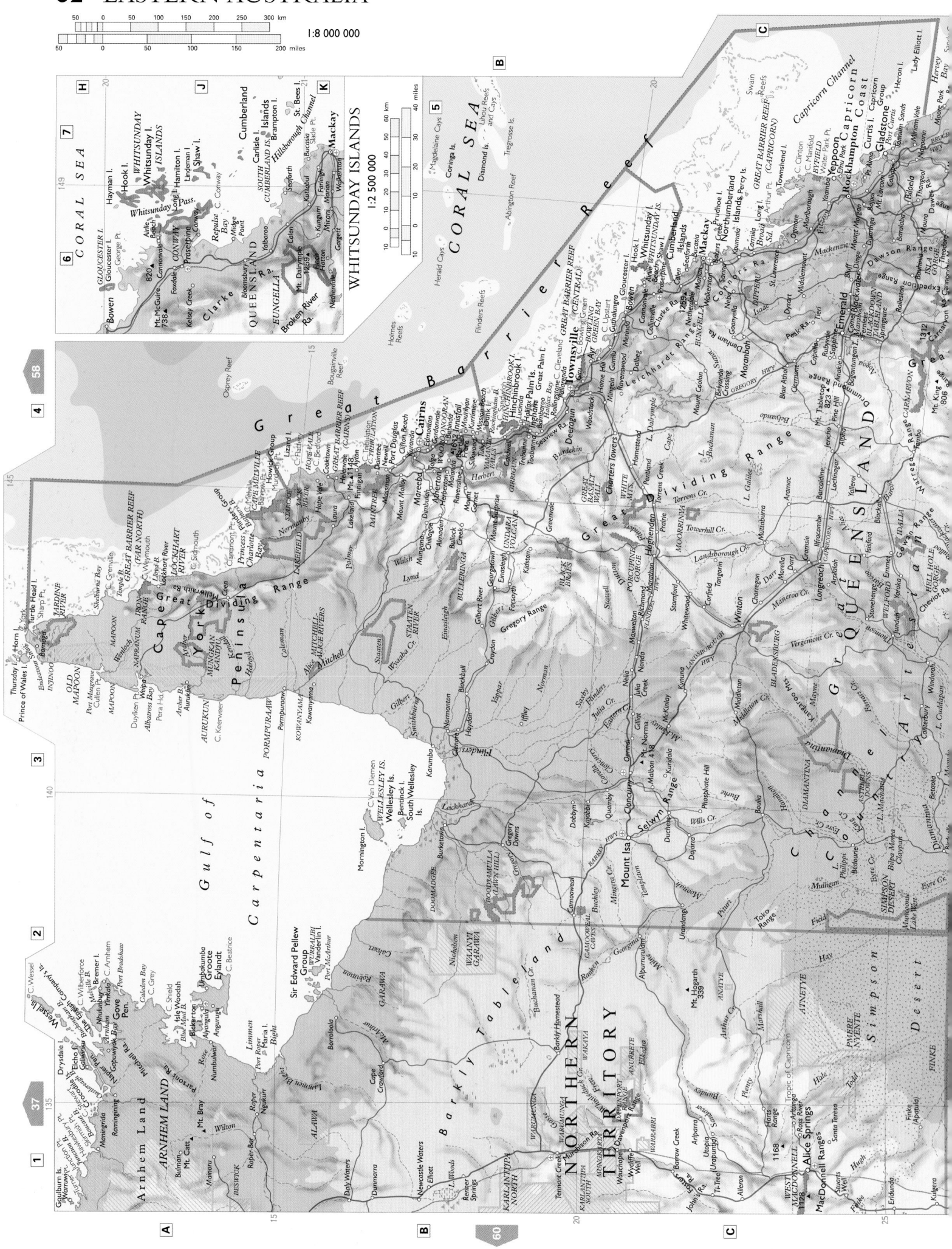

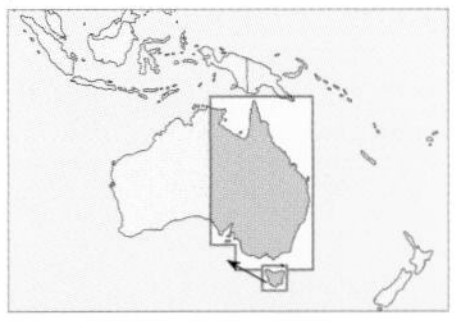

COPYRIGHT, GEORGE PHILIP LTD.

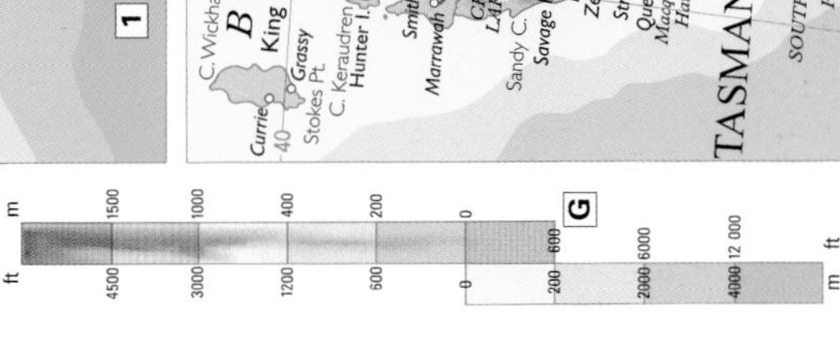

NEW SOUTH WALES

SOUTH AUSTRALIA

VICTORIA

TASMANIA

QUEENSLAND

T A S M A N   S E A

Bass Strait

Great Dividing Range

Darling Downs

Grey Range

Barrier Range

Flinders Ranges

Sturt Stony Desert

Strzelecki Desert

Tirari Desert

Simpson Desert

NULLARBOR

BRISBANE

SYDNEY

MELBOURNE

ADELAIDE

Canberra

A.C.T. (COMMONWEALTH TERRITORY)

Newcastle

Wollongong

Hobart

Launceston

Lake Eyre (North)

Lake Eyre (South)

LAKE EYRE

Lake Torrens

Lake Gairdner

Lake Frome

Lake Blanche

Sunshine Coast

Gold Coast

Port Macquarie

Coffs Harbour

Broken Hill

Wagga Wagga

Mount Gambier

Warrnambool

Geelong

Ballarat

Port Augusta

Port Pirie

Whyalla

Port Lincoln

Eyre Peninsula

Yorke Peninsula

Kangaroo I.

Spencer Gulf

Gulf St. Vincent

Fraser I.

Flinders Island

King Island

Furneaux Group

Cape Barren I.

Banks Strait

COORONG

Younghusband Peninsula

Cooper Cr.

Darling

Murray

Murrumbidgee

Lachlan

Macquarie

East from Greenwich

Projection: Bonne

Aboriginal lands

Sand desert

On same scale

m / ft

4500 3000 1500 1200 600 400 200 0
12 000 6000 4000 2000 600 200 0

61

RUSSIA
Yekaterinburg
Moskva
Volga
Tomsk
Ob
Novosibirsk
Astana (Aqmola)
Semey
Irkutsk
Os. Baykal
Chita
Lena
Sea of Okhotsk
Okhotsk
Poluostrov Kamchatka
Shirshov Ridge
Komandorskiye Ostrova (Russia)
Aleutian Basin
Bering Sea
Near Is. (U.S.A.)
Andreanof Is. (U.S.A.)

KAZAKHSTAN
Aral Sea
Balqash Köl
Altai
MONGOLIA
Ulaanbaatar
Blagoveshchensk
Amur
Khabarovsk
Sakhalin
Petropavlovsk-Kamchatskiy
7822
Aleutian
Aleutian Trench

Almaty
Ürümqi
KYRGYZSTAN
Harbin
Changchun
Vladivostok
Hakodate
La Perouse Str.
Kurilskiye Ostrova
Kuril-Kamchatka Trench
10,542
Emperor Trough
Chinook Trough

Toshkent
TAJIKISTAN
Shenyang
NORTH KOREA
Sea of Japan
Sapporo
Northwest

AFGHANISTAN
Kabul
Srinagar
Beijing
Tianjin
Taiyuan
Dalian
SOUTH KOREA
Seoul
Nagoya
Fuji-San 3776
Sendai
Tōkyō
Yokohama
Shatsky Rise
Pacific

PAKISTAN
Lahore
Delhi
CHINA
Lanzhou
Kunlun Shan
XIZANG
Xi'an
Qingdao
Kyōto
Osaka
JAPAN
Shikoku
Kyūshū
10,554
Japan Trench
Basin
Midway Is. (U.S.A.)

Kanpur
Himalaya
8850 Mt Everest
Lhasa
Chongqing
Wuhan
Shanghai
East China Sea
Iwo-Jima (Japan)
Ogasawara Gunto (Japan)
Lisianski I. (U.S.A.)

Ganga
NEPAL
Brahmaputra
Changsha
Chang J.
Hangzhou
Okinawa
Ryūkyū-rettō (Japan)
Kazan-Rettō (Japan)
Minami-Tori-Shima (Japan)

INDIA
Kolkata (Calcutta)
Dhaka
BANGLADESH
Mandalay
Irrawaddy
Kunming
Fuzhou
Taipei
TAIWAN
Kyushu-Palau Ridge
Wake I. (U.S.A.)
Mid-Pacific
Mount

Hyderabad
BURMA
Guangzhou
Macau
Hong Kong
Hainan
Hanoi
Philippine Sea
West Mariana Basin
NORTHERN MARIANAS (U.S.A.)
East Mariana Basin
MARSHALL IS.
P A

Chennai (Madras)
Bay of Bengal
Rangoon
THAILAND
Bangkok
Andaman Is. (India)
LAOS
VIETNAM
Luzon
Paracel Is.
C. Engano
Manila
Mindoro
Tinian
Saipan
GUAM (U.S.A.)
Challenger 11,022 Deep
Mariana Trench
Enewetak Atoll
Bikini Atoll
Ralik Chain
Ratak Chain
Kwajalein
Majuro

SRI LANKA
Colombo
Nicobar Is. (India)
CAMBODIA
Phnom Penh
G. of Thailand
South China Sea
Palawan
Samar
10,497
Micronesia
Yap
Caroline Is.
Chuuk
FED. STATES OF MICRONESIA
Pohnpei
Palikir
Jaluit I.
Butaritari

Ho Chi Minh
Thanh Pho
MALAYSIA
BRUNEI
SABAH
4101
Sulu Sea
Mindanao
Davao
Mindanao Trench
Koror
PALAU
West Caroline Basin
East Caroline Basin
Solomon Rise
Melanesian Basin
Tarawa
Gilbert Is.
Howland I. (U.S.A.)
Baker I. (U.S.A.)

Kuala Lumpur
PEN. MALAYSIA
SARAWAK
Celebes Sea
Maluku
Halmahera
Eauripik Rise
Melanesia
Phoenix Is.
Abariringa
Enderbury
Pacific

Singapore
Sumatera
Borneo
Sulawesi
Buru
Seram
Puncak Jaya 5029
PAPUA
PAPUA NEW GUINEA
Admiralty Is.
Bismarck Arch.
New Ireland
NAURU
Banaba
KIR

INDONESIA
Ujung Pandang
Palembang
Java Sea
Jakarta
Jawa
Surabaya
Bali
Banda Sea
Flores Sea
Flores
Dili
EAST TIMOR
Timor
Sumbawa
Sumba
7440
New Guinea
Lae
Rabaul
Bougainville
New Britain
SOLOMON IS.
Honiara
Guadalcanal
Fongafale
TUVALU
Tokelau Is. (N.Z.)
SAMOA
Apia

Ninety East Ridge
Java Trench
Selat Sunda
Christmas I. (Austral.)
North Australian Basin
C. Arnhem
Arafura Sea
Torres Strait
C. York
Port Moresby
Louisiade Arch.
Santa Cruz I. 9165
Rotuma
Vanua Levu
Viti Levu
Is. Wallis & Futuna (Fr.)
SAMOA

INDIAN
Cocos Is. (Austral.)
Darwin
Gulf of Carpentaria
Cairns
Coral Sea
Coral Sea Basin
Espíritu Santo
VANUATU
Port Vila
West Fiji Basin
Suva
FIJI
Nuku'alofa
TONGA

OCEAN
Wharton Basin
Broome
Exmouth Plateau
North West C.
Townsville
Rockhampton
Is. Chesterfield
NEW CALEDONIA (Fr.)
Is. Loyauté
Nouméa
7570
Tonga Trench
10,822

Geraldton
Perth Basin
Broken Ridge
AUSTRALIA
Alice Springs
Mount Isa
L. Eyre
Lord Howe Rise
Middleton Basin
Brisbane
Norfolk I. (Austral.)
Lord Howe Trough
Norfolk Ridge
South Fiji Basin
Kermadec Is. (N.Z.)
Kermadec Trench 10,047

Naturaliste Plateau
Perth
Great Australian Bight
Albany
Adelaide
Great Dividing Ra.
Murray
Sydney
Canberra
Mt. Kosciuszko 2230
Tasman Sea
NEW ZEALAND
Auckland
Wellington

Nouvelle Amsterdam (Fr.)
I. St. Paul (Fr.)
Melbourne
Bass Str.
Tasmania
Hobart
East Tasman Plateau
Aoraki Mt. Cook 3753
Chatham Is. (N.Z.)
Christchurch
Dunedin
Bounty Trough
Bounty Is. (N.Z.)

Is. Crozet (Fr.)
SOUTHERN
OCEAN
Heard I. (Austral.)
South Tasman Rise
Tasman Basin
Invercargill
Antipodes Is. (N.Z.)
Campbell (N.Z.) Plateau

Kerguelen
Mid-Indian Ridge
Indian Ridge
Auckland Is. (N.Z.)
Macquarie I. (Austral.)
Campbell I. (N.Z.)

ft m
12 000 4000
9000 3000
6000 2000
3000 1000
1500 500
600 200
0 0
200 600
1000 3000
2000 6000
4000 12 000
6000 18 000
8000 24 000
m ft

11 12 13 14 15

160 150 140 130

Arctic Circle

ALASKA
(U.S.A.)
6959
Anchorage

16 17 18 19 20

120 110 100 90 40

Bristol Bay

Gulf of Alaska

Is. (U.S.A.)

Prince of Wales I.
(U.S.A.) Prince Rupert
Queen Charlotte Is.
(Canada)

Juneau

C A N A D A

Edmonton

L. Winnipeg

Newfoundland

B

R
O
C
K
Y

Calgary

Regina

Winnipeg

St. Lawrence

N O R T H

50

Vancouver
Vancouver I.
Seattle
Victoria
Boise

Tufts
Abyssal
Plain

Portland

Northeast

Mendocino Fracture Zone C. Mendocino

6741

Sacramento
San Francisco

Murray Fracture Zone

4418

Pacific

Los Angeles
San Diego

Guadalupe
(Mex.)

Molokai Fracture Zone

Honolulu
Kauai Oahu
Maui HAWAIIAN IS.
4205 *(U.S.A.)*
Hilo Hawaii

Tropic of Cancer

Basin

Clarion Fracture Zone Is. Revilla Gigedo
(Mex.)

L. Superior

L. Winnipeg

Minneapolis

Missouri

Salt Lake
City

Denver

UNITED STATES

Oklahoma City

Phoenix

Ciudad
Juárez

Snake

Colorado

Kansas City

St. Louis
Memphis

Dallas

Houston

Chicago
Detroit
Pittsburgh

Cincinnati

M E X I C O

Gulf of California

C. San Lucas

Québec
Montréal
Ottawa
Toronto
L. Ontario
L. Erie
Buffalo
Boston

St. Lawrence

St. John's

New York
Philadelphia
Baltimore
Washington D.C.

Appalachian Mts.

Atlanta

C. Hatteras

Jacksonville

New
Orleans
Gulf of Mexico
Monterrey

San Antonio

Tampa
Miami

Mississippi

La Habana
Canal de Yucatán

Guadalajara
Mexico
6610
Puebla

Acapulco

Middle America Trench

Florida Str.

ATLANTIC

Bermuda
(U.K.)

Sargasso Sea

BAHAMAS

OCEAN

West Indies

CUBA

Mérida

9200

7680 HAITI DOMINICAN REP.
JAMAICA
Kingston PUERTO
RICO
(U.S.A.)

Leeward
Is.

BARBADOS

BELIZE
GUATEMALA 6662
Guatemala HONDURAS

Caribbean Sea

Windward Is.

C

D

40

E

30

F

an
Ridge

I C

Johnston I.
(U.S.A.)

Palmyra Is.
(U.S.A.)

Teraina
Tabuaeran
Kiritimati

Jarvis I.
(U.S.A.)

Malden I.

Starbuck I.

San Salvador
EL SALVADOR
NICARAGUA
Managua
Barranquilla

Coopers Ridge

Line Islands

Equator

Galápagos Fracture Zone

I. Clipperton
(Fr.)

Clipperton Fracture Zone

Guatemala
Basin

COSTA
RICA
PANAMA

Coco Ridge

San José
Colón Panamá

I. del Coco
(Costa Rica)

I. de Malpelo
(Colombia)

Galápagos
(Ecuador)

Carnegie Ridge

Maracaibo

Caracas

Panama
Basin

Orinoco

VENEZUELA

Medellín Bogotá
Cali
COLOMBIA

Quito
ECUADOR

Guayaquil

Amazonas

Iquitos

C. Paliñas

BRAZIL

G

20

H

10

KIRIBATI

MER.
MOA
U.S.A.

Manihiki
Pukapuka
Plateau
Manihiki
Suwarrow Is.

Penrhyn
(Tongareva)

Vostok I.

Nuku Hiva
Caroline I.
(Millennium I.)
Flint I.

Îs. Marquises
Hiva Oa

Marquesas Fracture Zone

East Pacific Ridge

Galápagos Ridge

Yupanqui
Basin

Mendaña
Fracture Zone

6369

Trujillo

PERU

Lima
Cuzco

J

Niue
(N.Z.)

Cook Is.
(N.Z.)
Aitutaki
Atiu

Rarotonga

Mangaia

Îs. de la
Société
Bora Bora
Huahine
Raiatea
Papeete Tahiti

Îs. Tubuai

Rangiroa

Îs. Tuamotu

FRENCH POLYNESIA

Îs. Gambier
Mururoa

Austral Seamount Chain

Tuamotu Ridge

Pacific Ridge

East Pacific Rise

Peru Basin

L. Titicaca
Arequipa 6550
Nevado Ancohuma

6866
Peru-
Arica

Iquique
Chile

Antofagasta

Nazca Ridge

La Paz
BOLIVIA

PARAGUAY

J

K

20

Oeno I.
Henderson I.
Pitcairn I. Ducie I.
(U.K.)

Rapa

Tropic of Capricorn

Easter Fracture Zone
Sala-y-Gómez
(Chile)
I. de Pascua
(Chile)

Roggeveen
Basin

Sala y Gómez Ridge

Arch. de
Juan Fernández
(Chile)

San Felix
(Chile) San Ambrosio
(Chile)

8050
Trench

San Miguel
de Tucumán

Asunción

Córdoba
Aconcagua
6962 Rosario
Valparaíso
Santiago
Buenos
Aires

Pôrto
Alegre

URUGUAY
Montevideo
Río de la Plata

L

30

Southwest

Pacific

Basin

Challenger Fracture Zone

Chile Rise

Menard Fracture Zone

Concepción

ARGENTINA

Patagonian Andes

SOUTH

ATLANTIC

OCEAN

M

40

Pacific-Antarctic Ridge

Southeast
Pacific Basin

Punta Arenas
C. de Hornos

Falkland Is.
(U.K.)

Est. de Magallanes
Tierra del Fuego

Drake Passage

6212

South Georgia
(U.K.)

N

50

West from Greenwich

COPYRIGHT PHILIP'S

11 12 13 14 15 16 17 18 19 20

160 150 140 130 120 110 100 90 80 70 60 40

100 0 200 400 600 800 1000 1200 1400 km
1:35 000 000
100 0 200 400 600 800 1000 miles

A

B

ft m
9000 3000
6000 2000
3000 1000
1500 500
600 200
0 0
200 600
1000 3000
2000 6000
4000 12000
6000 18000
8000 24000
m ft

Projection: Bonne

West from Greenwich

COPYRIGHT PHILIP'S

1:35 000 000

100 0   200   400   600   800 1000 1200 1400 km

100 0   200   400   600   800   1000 miles

RUSSIA

Asia

Bering Strait

St. Lawrence I.

Bering Sea

Kodiak I.

ALASKA (U.S.A.)

Yukon

Fairbanks

Anchorage

Gulf of Alaska

Porcupine

ARCTIC OCEAN

International Date Line

Beaufort Sea

Queen Elizabeth Is.

Ellesmere I.

Victoria I.

Baffin Bay

GREENLAND (Denmark)

Denmark Strait

ICELAND

Reykjavik

Nuuk

Davis Strait

Baffin Island

Arctic Circle

NORTHWEST

Mackenzie

Great Bear L.

Whitehorse

YUKON TERRITORY

Juneau

TERRITORIES

Yellowknife

Liard

Great Slave L.

NUNAVUT

Back

Dubawnt

Hudson Strait

Iqaluit

BRITISH COLUMBIA

Skeena

Peace

Athabasca

ALBERTA

Edmonton

CANADA

Athabasca

SASKATCHEWAN

Calgary

Saskatchewan

Regina

Churchill

MANITOBA

L. Winnipeg

Nelson

Hudson Bay

ONTARIO

Eastmain

QUÉBEC

NEWFOUNDLAND & LABRADOR

St. John's

St-Pierre et Miquelon (Fr.)

St. Lawrence

Fraser

Victoria

Vancouver

WASHINGTON

Seattle

Olympia

Portland

Salem

OREGON

Columbia

Snake

IDAHO

Boise

Helena

MONTANA

Missouri

NORTH DAKOTA

Bismarck

SOUTH DAKOTA

WYOMING

Winnipeg

MINNESOTA

Minneapolis-St. Paul

WISCONSIN

Madison

L. Superior

L. Michigan

MICHIGAN

Lansing

L. Huron

Toronto

Ottawa

Montréal

L. Ontario

Buffalo

Detroit

Cleveland

Toledo

St. Lawrence

Québec

Fredericton

NEW BRUNSWICK

MAINE

Augusta

PRINCE EDWARD

Charlottetown

NOVA SCOTIA

Halifax

VER.

N.H.

Concord

Boston

MASS.

Providence

NEW YORK

Hartford

R.I.

CONN.

NEW YORK

PHILADELPHIA

PA.

Pittsburgh

OHIO

Columbus

Sacramento

Carson City

San Francisco

San Jose

CALIFORNIA

NEVADA

Las Vegas

UTAH

Salt Lake City

COLORADO

Denver

UNITED STATES

NEBRASKA

Lincoln

IOWA

Milwaukee

CHICAGO

ILLINOIS

INDIANA

Indianapolis

KANSAS

Topeka

Kansas City

MISSOURI

St. Louis

Springfield

Cincinnati

Baltimore

Washington, D.C.

W.V.

MD.

DEL.

Richmond

VIRGINIA

Raleigh

KENTUCKY

Nashville

TENNESSEE

NORTH CAROLINA

Charlotte

Columbia

SOUTH CAROLINA

Charleston

Los Angeles

San Diego

Tijuana

Mexicali

ARIZONA

Phoenix

Tucson

Santa Fe

Albuquerque

NEW MEXICO

El Paso

Ciudad Juárez

OKLAHOMA

Oklahoma City

ARKANSAS

Little Rock

Memphis

MISSISSIPPI

Jackson

ALABAMA

Birmingham

Montgomery

GEORGIA

Atlanta

Jacksonville

Tallahassee

FLORIDA

Guadalupe (Mex.)

Tropic of Cancer

Hermosillo

MÉXICO

Culiacán

Rio Grande

Dallas-Ft. Worth

TEXAS

Austin

Houston

San Antonio

Baton Rouge

LOUISIANA

New Orleans

Florida St.

Orlando

Tampa-St. Petersburg

Miami

Nassau

BAHAMAS

Turks & Caicos Is. (U.K.)

Bermuda (U.K.)

NORTH ATLANTIC OCEAN

PACIFIC OCEAN

Monterrey

Torreón

San Luis Potosí

León

Guadalajara

Revilla Gigedo Is. (Mex.)

MÉXICO

Toluca

Puebla

Acapulco

Mérida

Gulf of Mexico

Havana

CUBA

Cayman Is. (U.K.)

JAMAICA

Kingston

HAITI

Port-au-Prince

DOMINICAN REP.

Santo Domingo

PUERTO RICO (U.S.A.)

San Juan

BELIZE

Belmopan

GUATEMALA

Guatemala

HONDURAS

Tegucigalpa

San Salvador

EL SALVADOR

NICARAGUA

Managua

L. Nicaragua

COSTA RICA

San José

PANAMA

Panamá

Caribbean Sea

Maracaibo

Barranquilla

VENEZUELA

COLOMBIA

Medellín

South America

Projection: Bonne

West from Greenwich

COPYRIGHT PHILIP'S

■ MÉXICO Capital Cities

7   8   9   10   11   12

1:15 000 000

Projection : Bonne

Devon I.
Lancaster Sound

Baffin Bay

NORTHERN CANADA
continuation northwards on same
scale as main map

ARCTIC
OCEAN

C. Columbia
2616
Alert

GREENLAND (Denmark)

Meighen

Sverdrup
Islands

Eureka

Axel Heiberg

Brodeur
Peninsula

Arctic Bay
Nanisivik
Borden
Pen.
Bylot I.
Pond Inlet

C. Adair

Clyde River

C. Raper

1890

2136

B

Brock I.
Mackenzie
King I.
Loug-
heed I.
Ellef
Ringnes I.
Amund
Ringnes I.

Prince Gustaf Adolf Sea

Norwegian
Bay

Grise
Fiord

Ellesmere Island

Hans I.

Smith Sound

Nares Str.

Grely Fd.

80

13

A

Baffin Island

Home B.

Qikiqtarjuaq

Eglinton
Prince Patrick I.

Parry Islands

Cornwall

Belcher Chan.

Jones Sound

Devon Island

4

Melville
Peninsula

Foxe
Basin

Prince
Charles
I.

Cumberland
Peninsula

2147

Pangnirtung

Cumberland Sd.

C. Mercy

C. Prince Alfred

McClure Strait

Queen
Melville I.

Elizabeth

Bathurst

Corn-
wallis

Resolute

Wellington Chan.

Lancaster Sound

Arctic
Bay
Nanisivik
Bylot I.
1951

B

Simpson
Pen.

Melville
Peninsula

Hall Beach

Igulik

Fury and Hecla Str.

Nettilling L.

Air Force I.

Dyer

Banks
Island

747

Prince Albert
Pen.

Viscount Melville
Sound

Holman

Victoria Island

M'Clintock Channel

NUNAVUT

Prince
of
Wales
Island

Somerset
Island

Brodeur
Peninsula

Pond
Inlet

Rae Isthmus
Repulse
Bay

Foxe
Pen.

Amadjuak

Meta
Incognita
Peninsula

Iqaluit

Kimmirut

Hall
Peninsula

Frobisher Bay

Resolution I.

NORTHWEST
TERRITORIES

70

C

Committee B.

Kingait

Salisbury

Hudson Strait

C. Chidley

ATLANTIC

D

Esterfield Inlet

Coats
I.

Mansel
I.

Nottingham

Ivujivik

Salluit

Kangiqsujuaq

Quaqtaq

Akpatok I.

Labrador
Sea

3809

Southampton
I.

Coral
Harbour

Bell
I.

Cratère du
Nouveau Québec 657

Kangirsuk

Puvirnituq

Ungava Bay

Kangiqsualujjuaq

Hebron

1652

257

Sleeper Is.

King George Is.

Belcher Is.

Sanikiluaq

Baker's
Dozen
Is.

Inukjuak

Péninsule

d'Ungava

L. Payne

Arnaud

Feuilles

Koksoak

Kuujjuaq

George

Baleine

Nain

Hopedale

C. Harrison

Rigolet

Cartwright

Port Hope Simpson

NEWFOUNDLAND
& LABRADOR

Belle Isle

C. Bauld
St. Anthony

50

E

Hudson

Bay

James Bay

Winisk

Peawanuck

C. Henrietta
Maria

Pte. Louis
XIV

Kuujjuarapik

Chisasibi

Grande Baleine

L. à l'Eau
Claire

Kanaaupscow

La Grande

L. Minto

Mélèze

L. Bienville

Caniapiscau

Kawawachikamach

Schefferville

Petitsikapau

Smallwood
Res.

Labrador

North West River

Happy Valley-
Goose Bay

Churchill
Falls

Churchill

Natashquan

St-Augustin

Str. of Belle Isle

Baie
Verte

Deer
Lake

Grand Falls
Windsor

Corner Brook

Lewisporte
Gander

Bonavista

Twillingate

Bonavista B.

St. John's

Carbonear

815

Big
Trout L.

Attawapiskat

Fort Albany

Charlton
I.

Akimiski I.

Wemindji

Eastmain

Eastmain

Waskaganish

Rupert

Labrador
City

Fermont

Ashuanipi

1128

Gagnon

Manicouagan

Havre-
St-Pierre

Moisie

Romaine

Natashquan

I. d'Anticosti

320

Stephenville

Channel-Port
aux Basques

Newfoundland

Marystown

Placentia

St. Race

Grand
Banks

Moosonee

Mistassini

Chibougamau

Baie-Comeau

Sept-Îles

Port-Cartier

Gulf of
St. Lawrence

Cabot Str.

St-PIERRE et MIQUELON (Fr)

O
C
E
A
N

F

Nakina

Kenogami

Hearst

Cochrane

Matagami

L. Matagami

Amos

Rés. Gouin

Roberval

St-Jean

Rimouski

Matane

Pén. de la
Gaspésie

Gaspé

Campbellton

Bathurst

Miramichi

Îs. de la Madeleine

Cape Breton I.

Sydney

Glace Bay

Greenstone

Kapuskasing

Oba

Timmins

Kirkland
Lake

Rouyn-
Noranda

Val-d'Or

La Tuque

1190

Québec

Lévis

Thetford
Mines

Grand Falls

Woodstock

Edmundston

Fredericton

NEW
BRUNSWICK

Moncton

Summerside

PR. EDWARD I.

Charlottetown

Port Hawkesbury

Antigonish

New Glasgow

NOVA SCOTIA

Marathon

Thunder Bay

Lake Superior

Houghton 183

Marquette

Sault Ste.
Marie

Elliot
Lake

Sudbury

North Bay

Pembroke

Hull

OTTAWA

MONTRÉAL

Sherbrooke

Granby

St-Hyacinthe

Shawinigan
Trois-Rivières

Joliette

Mont-
Laurier

Rés.
Cabonga

Ottawa R.

Cornwall

Montpelier

Burlington

L. Champlain

Augusta

Lewiston

Portland

Bangor

Saint
John

Amherst

B. of Fundy

Digby

Yarmouth

C. Sable

Kentville

Bridgewater

Liverpool

Dartmouth

Halifax

Truro

Sable I.
(Nova Scotia)

6309

40

Ironwood

Manistique

Escanaba
Menominee

Green
Bay

Sheboygan

MILWAUKEE

Madison

Racine
Kenosha

Rockford

CHICAGO

Gary

South Bend

INDIANA

Marathon

Wawa

Chapleau

New
Liskeard

Sault Ste.
Marie

Manitoulin
I.

Georgian
Bay

Parry
Sound

Huntsville

Barrie

Owen Sound

Peterborough

Belleville

Kingston

Syracuse

VERMONT
NEW
HAMPSHIRE

Concord

Manchester

Lowell

MASS.

BOSTON

C. Cod

Petoskey

Traverse City

Cadillac

Lake
Huron

Saginaw

Flint

Lansing

Grand
Rapids

Kalamazoo

Toledo

Windsor

Sarnia

London

Kitchener

TORONTO

Hamilton

Oshawa

L. Ontario

Niagara
Falls

Buffalo

Rochester

Elmira

Binghamton

Scranton

NEW YORK

Albany

Springfield

Hartford

CONN.

New Haven

Bridgeport

PROVIDENCE

R.I.

NEW YORK

Newark

Allentown

Trenton

DETROIT

CLEVELAND

OHIO

PENNSYLVANIA

L. Erie

Jamestown

Erie

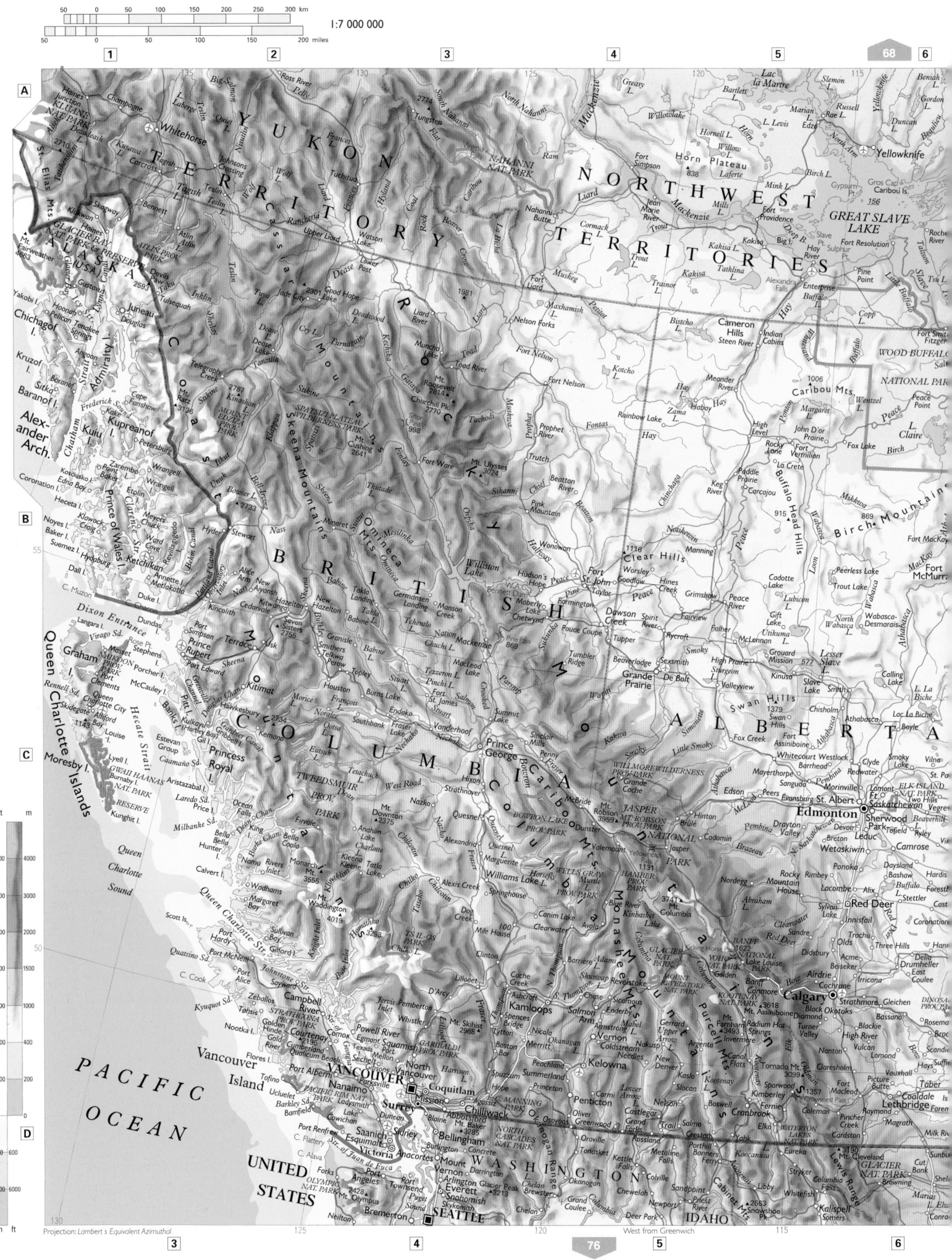

Projection: Lambert's Equivalent Azimuthal

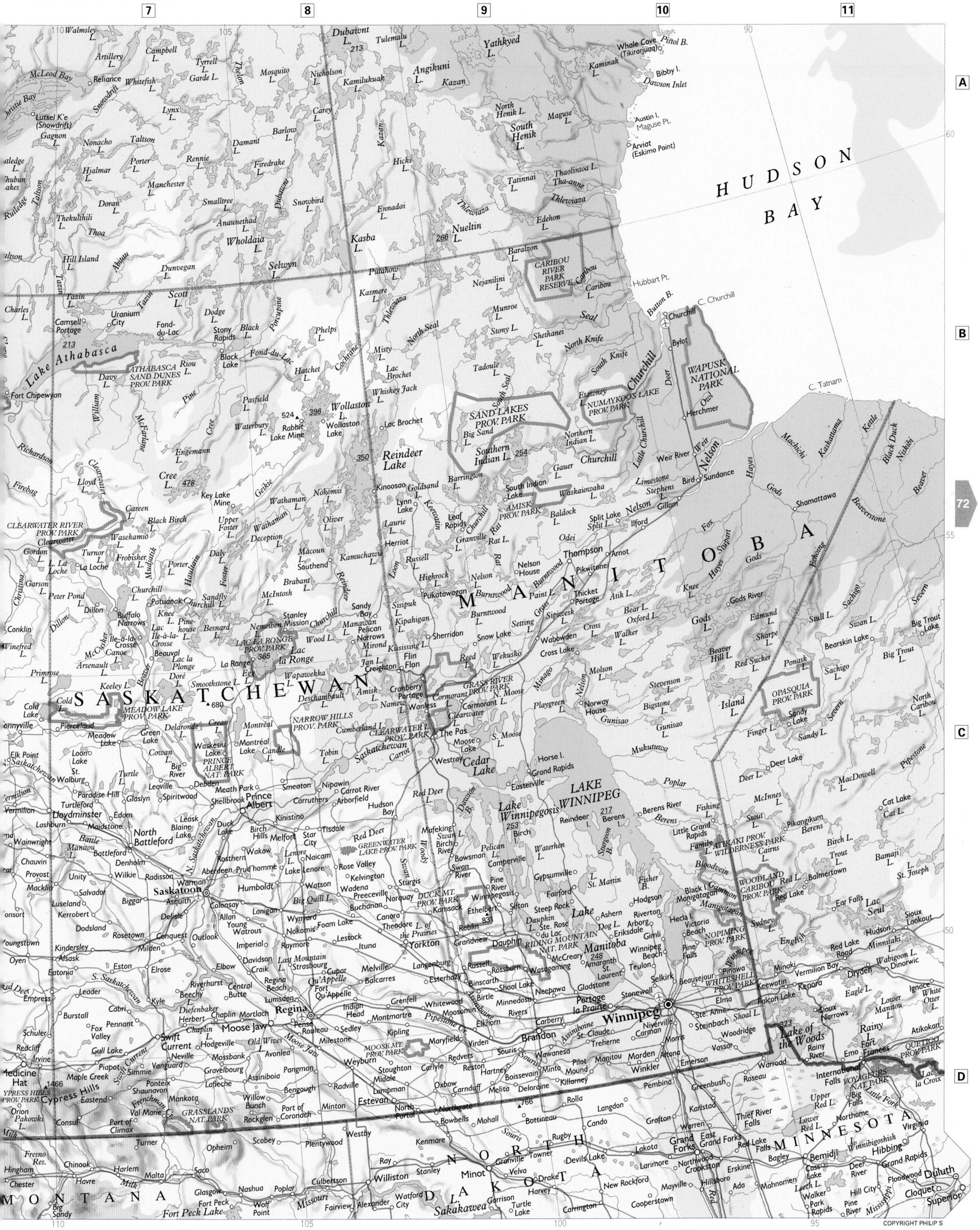

National Parks

Projection: Lambert's Equivalent Azimuthal

1:7 000 000

A

LABRADOR

SEA

South
Aulatsivik I.
Paul I.
Nain
Voisey B.
Kogaluc
Tunungayualok I.
Davis Inlet
Big Bay
Hopedale
Aillik
Makkovik
Adlavik Is.
C. Harrison
Postville
Holton
Indian Harbour
Grostwater
B.

B

L. Le
Moyne
L. Nachicapau
Balane
George
Fraser
60
L. de la
Hutte
Sauvage
Kanairiktok
North
West
River
Cartwright
Table B.
Black Tickle
Island of Ponds

Du Gué
Châteauguay
Caniapiscau
65
L. Tudor
L. Mistinibi
Mistastin
Seal L.
Nipishish
L.
Melville
1128
Paradise
River
NEWFOUNDLAND &
Square Islands
Charlottetown
Alexis
Williams Harbour

Du Gué
L. Néret
Brisay
L. Chakonipau
L. Otelnuk
Champdoré
610
L. aux
Goélands
Harp L.
Grand
L.
North West River
Goose
Happy Valley-
Goose Bay
Churchill Falls
Labrador
u
Port Hope
Simpson
Battle Harbour
Lodge Bay

L. Dalmas
Nitchequon
Attikamagen
Kawawachikamach
Scheffferville
Smallwood Reservoir
Churchill
Twin Falls
Churchill
Ossokmanuan
L.
Winokapau
L.
r
a
d
o
r
St. Lewis
Mary's
Harbour
Belle Isle

L. Nichicun
Naococane
L. Menihek
Petitsikapau
L.
Esker
Siding
Emeril
Joseph
Atikonak
L.
Minipi
L.
Little Mécatina
Natashquan
L. Brûlé
e
St-Augustin
Red
Bay
L'Anse
au Loup
Lourdes-de-
Blanc-Sablon
Forteau
Str. of Belle Isle
Cooks Harbour
L'Anse aux Meadows
St. Anthony

Mts. Otish
1128
Q
Labrador City
Fermont
Wabush
Gagnon
Rés.
Manicouagan
1049
Magpie
L.
U
É
Ashuanipi
L.
C
St-Barbe
Roddickton
Groais I.
Grey
Englee
Bell I. Is.

50

L. Plétipi
L. Opiscotéo
B
Natashquan
Romaine
St-Jean
Aguanish
Natashquan
Petit-Mécatina
St-Augustin
Olomane
Port au Choix
Hawke's Bay
Harbour
Deep
Horse Is.

C

L. Manouane
L. Manicouagan
L. Manitou
n
Sainte-
Anne
Walker
Clarke
City
Port-Cartier
Sept-Îles
Moisie
Sheldrake
Havre-St-Pierre
R. S. DE PARC NAT. DE
L'ARCHIPEL-DE-MINGAN
Musquaro
La Romaine
Kegaska
I. du
Petit-Mécatina
Harrington Harbour
Daniel's
Harbour
GROS MORNE
NAT. PARK
Rocky Harbour
Norris Point
Trout River
Springdale
La Scie
Baie
Notre Dame
Twillingate
Fogo I.
Musgrave Harbour
C. Freels
B. of Islands
Pasadena
Deer
Lake
South
Brook
Botwood
Bishop's
Falls
Lewisporte
Glenwood
Gander
Gambo

Mistassini
Dolbeau
Manouane
Rés.
Pipmuacan
Godbout
Baie-Trinité
Pte. des Monts
Cap-Chat
Ste-
Anne
Chute-aux-
Outardes
Baie-
Comeau
Betsiamites
Forestville
Mont-Louis
Grande-
Vallée
Dét. de Jacques-Cartier
Île d'Anticosti
320
Pte. Heath
Pte. du
Sud
Dét. d'Honguedo
572
GULF OF
ST. LAWRENCE
Corner
Brook
814
Stephenville
Port au Port
St-George's
George's
Long
Range
Mts.
Buchans
Grand
Falls
Windsor
Gander
Red Indian
L.
Victoria
Maelpaeg
L.
Jeddore
TERRA NOVA
NAT. PARK
Clarenville
Port Blandford
376
Trinity
Trinity B.
Bonavista
B.
Bonavista
Catalina
Old Perlican
Heart's Content
Carbonear
Conception B.
Harbour
Grace

Péribonka
L.
Péribonka
St. Lawrence
Roberval
Alma
Chicoutimi
Jonquière
La Baie
Saguenay
Les
Escoumins
Tadoussac
Betsiamites
Mts.
Chic-Chocs
Matane
Mont-
Joli
Rimouski
Le Bic
Trois-Pistoles
1268
Mt-Jacques-
PARC DE
LA GASPÉSIE
Rivière-
au-Renard
C. de Gaspé
PARC NAT. DE
FORILLON
Gaspé
Percé
Chandler
Grande-Rivière
Pén. de la Gaspésie
Cape St. George
C. St. George
St. George's B.
South Branch
Great Codroy
St. Andrew's
C. Ray
Rose Blanche
Burgeo
François
Granite
L. Grey
St. Alban's
Fortune B.
Belleoram
Terrenceville
Marystown
Argentia
Placentia
Placentia B.
St. Mary's B.
Trepassey
Torbay
St. John's
Mt
Pearl
Witless
Bay
Avalon
Peninsula
Ferryland

45

Mistassini
Alma
Tadoussac
St-Siméon
La Malbaie
Baie-
St-Paul
PARC DES
GRANDS-JARDINS
PARC PROV
DE LA
JACQUES-
CARTIER
1166
Montmagny
St-Pamphile
Matapédia
Athonlville
Campbellton
Dalhousie
Paspébiac
Bonaventure
New
Richmond
Chaleur Bay
Caraquet
Tracadie
Shippagan
Miscou I.
Î. Brion
Îs. de la
Fatima
Madeleine
(Québec)
Grande-Entrée
Cap-aux-Meules
Havre-Aubert
St. Paul
C. North
Cabot Strait
Miquelon
Fortune
St-Pierre
ST-PIERRE-
ET-MIQUELON
(France)
St. Lawrence
Grand Bank
Fortune
Burin
Miquelon
Lamèque
C. Freels
C.
Race

Québec
Lévis
Charny
Beaupré
Î. d'Orléans
Donnacona
La Pérade
Ste-Marie
Cap-de-la-Madeleine
Kedgwick
St-Quentin
Mt. Carleton
820
St-Léonard
Grand Falls
Plaster
Rock
Perth-Andover
NEW
Neguac
Miramichi B.
Miramichi
KOUGHIBOUGUAC
NAT. PARK
Newcastle
Rogersville
Richibucto
PRINCE EDWARD
ISLAND
North Cape
Tignish
Alberton
Pleasant Bay
CAPE BRETON
HIGHLANDS
NAT. PARK
532
Chéticamp
Ingonish
St. Anns B.
North Sydney
New Waterford
Sydney Mines
Glace Bay
Sydney
Cape Breton
Louisbourg
Island

Beauceville
St-Georges
Lac-
Mégantic
East Angus
Sherbrooke
Magog
Victoriaville
Plessisville
Thetford
Mines
Asbestos
Lincoln
Chamberlain
L.
Houlton
Van Buren
Fort
Edmundston
Cabano
Dégelis
St-Pascal
Rivière-du-Loup
St-Jean-Port-Joli
La Pocatière
Eagle
Lake
Caribou
Ashland
BRUNSWICK
Fredericton
Doaktown
St-Antoine
Bouctouche
Shediac
Cape
Tormentine
Summerside
Kensington
Charlottetown
Georgetown
Souris
East Pt.
St.
Peters
Murray
Hr.
Montague
Pictou
Antigonish
Mulgrave
Port
Hood
Port
Hawkesbury
Inverness
L. Bras d'Or
N. Sydney
St. Peters
Chedabucto B.
Canso
Guysborough
I. Madame

Sherbrooke
Cookshire
Coaticook
Newport
Island
Pond
Jackman
Greenville
Mooseheard
L.
1605
Patten
Millinocket
Woodstock
Hartland
Minto
Chipman
Grand L.
Oromocto
Petitcodiac
Sussex
Moncton
Sackville
Amherst
Springhill
Parrsboro
FUNDY
NAT. PARK
Hampton
Chignecto B.
Minas
Basin
Truro
Stellarton
New Glasgow
Sheet Harbour
Upper
Musquodoboit
Stewiacke
Windsor
Kentville
Enfield
Musquodoboit Harbour
NOVA
SCOTIA

MAINE
Bangor
Old Town
Brewer
Ellsworth
Skowhegan
Waterville
Belfast
Mt
Katahdin
Lincoln
Chesuncook
L.
Patten
Millinocket
Bingham
N
E
W
B
R
U
N
S
W
I
C
K
Fredericton
Junction
St. Stephen
Calais
Eastport
Machias
St. George
Blacks
Harbour
Saint
John
Bay
of
Fundy
St. John
Digby
Annapolis
Royal
Bridgetown
Middleton
KEJIMKUJIK
NAT. PARK
Weymouth
Milton
Bridgewater
Mahone
Bay
Lunenburg
Liverpool
Windsor
Dartmouth
Halifax
Sable I.
(Nova Scotia)

New
Hampshire
Mooselookmeguntic L.
Rumford
Norway
Augusta
Auburn
Lewiston
Camden
Rockland
Bath
Brunswick
Mount
Desert I.
Bar Harbor
Grand
Manan I.
St. Marys Bay
Yarmouth
Wedgeport
Rossignol
L.
Shelburne
Lockeport
Clark's Harbour
C. Sable

D

A T L A N T I C

St. Johnsbury
Berlin
Laconia
Sanford
Saco
Biddeford
Portland
Conway
Hanover
Rochester
Dover
Portsmouth
Concord
Manchester
Haverhill
Lawrence
Lowell
Nashua
Keene
Fitchburg
Newton
BOSTON
Quincy
Worcester
Brockton
Woonsocket
Lynn

UNITED STATES
C. Cod

O C E A N

100   0   100   200   300   400   500 km

1:12 000 000

100   0   50   100   150   200   250   300   350 miles

| 1 | 2 | 3 | 4 | 68 | 5 | 6 | 7 |

ALASKA
1:30 000 000 **a**

100   0   100   200   300   400   500   600 km

100   0   100   200   300   400 miles

HAWAI'I
1:10 000 000 **b**

50   0   100 km

50   0   50   100 miles

Projection: Albers' Equal Area with two standard parallels

West from Greenwich

86

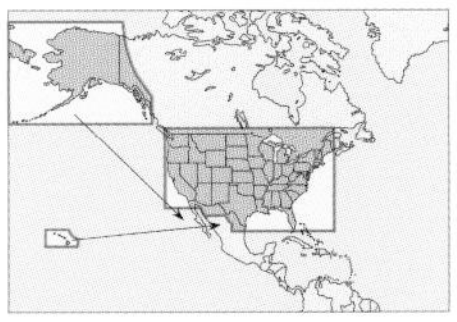

8
9
10
11
12
69
13
A
B
C
D
E
F
87
88
C A N A D A
O N T A R I O
Q U É B E C
Lake Winnipeg
Winnipeg
Lake of the Woods
Thunder Bay
Lake Superior
Sault Ste. Marie
Sudbury
North Bay
Moosonee
Timmins
Hearst
Cochrane
Chibougamau
Chicoutimi
Québec
Trois-Rivières
MONTRÉAL
OTTAWA
Kingston
TORONTO
Hamilton
London
Lake Huron
Lake Ontario
Lake Erie
Lake Michigan
Lower Pen.
Upper Pen.
Manitoulin I.
Georgian Bay
NEW BRUNSWICK
Fredericton
Saint John
Edmundston
M A I N E
Bangor
Augusta
Portland
Gulf of Maine
New England
White Mts.
VERMONT
NEW HAMPSHIRE
MASS.
CONN.
R.I.
BOSTON
PROVIDENCE
Hartford
New Haven
NEW YORK
Albany
Syracuse
Rochester
Buffalo
Adirondack Mts.
Catskill Mts.
PHILADELPHIA
Harrisburg
PITTSBURGH
P E N N S Y L V A N I A
BALTIMORE
WASHINGTON D.C.
Annapolis
Richmond
NORFOLK
Virginia Beach
WEST VIRGINIA
Charleston
Raleigh
Charlotte
N O R T H   C A R O L I N A
SOUTH CAROLINA
Columbia
Charleston
Savannah
ATLANTA
G E O R G I A
Jacksonville
Tallahassee
ORLANDO
TAMPA
St. Petersburg
MIAMI
Key West
Florida Keys
Straits of Florida
BAHAMAS
Grand Bahama I.
Abaco I.
Nassau
Andros I.
Eleuthera I.
Cat I.
Great Exuma I.
Long I.
NEW ORLEANS
Mississippi River Delta
Baton Rouge
L O U I S I A N A
Jackson
M I S S I S S I P P I
Montgomery
Birmingham
A L A B A M A
Nashville
Memphis
Knoxville
T E N N E S S E E
Louisville
Lexington
Frankfort
K E N T U C K Y
CINCINNATI
COLUMBUS
CLEVELAND
Toledo
O H I O
INDIANAPOLIS
I N D I A N A
CHICAGO
Springfield
I L L I N O I S
ST. LOUIS
Jefferson City
KANSAS CITY
M I S S O U R I
Ozark Plateau
Little Rock
A R K A N S A S
Oklahoma City
Tulsa
DALLAS
HOUSTON
Galveston
Des Moines
I O W A
MINNEAPOLIS
ST. PAUL
M I N N E S O T A
MILWAUKEE
Madison
W I S C O N S I N
DETROIT
Lansing
Grand Rapids
M I C H I G A N
Duluth
Omaha
Lincoln
Wichita
Topeka
Midwest
Appalachian Mts.
Cumberland Plateau
Allegheny Plat.
Blue Ridge
Piedmont
A T L A N T I C   O C E A N
G U L F   O F   M E X I C O
C. Cod
C. May
C. Hatteras
C. Fear
C. Romain
C. Canaveral
C. Sable
C. San Blas
Apalachee B.
Florida Bay
Tampa B.
Chesapeake Bay
Delaware B.
Pamlico Sd.
Albemarle Sd.
Long Bay
L. Okeechobee
The Everglades
95
90
85
80
75
70
45
40
35
30
25

Tallahassee ⊛ U.S. state capitals

1:6 700 000

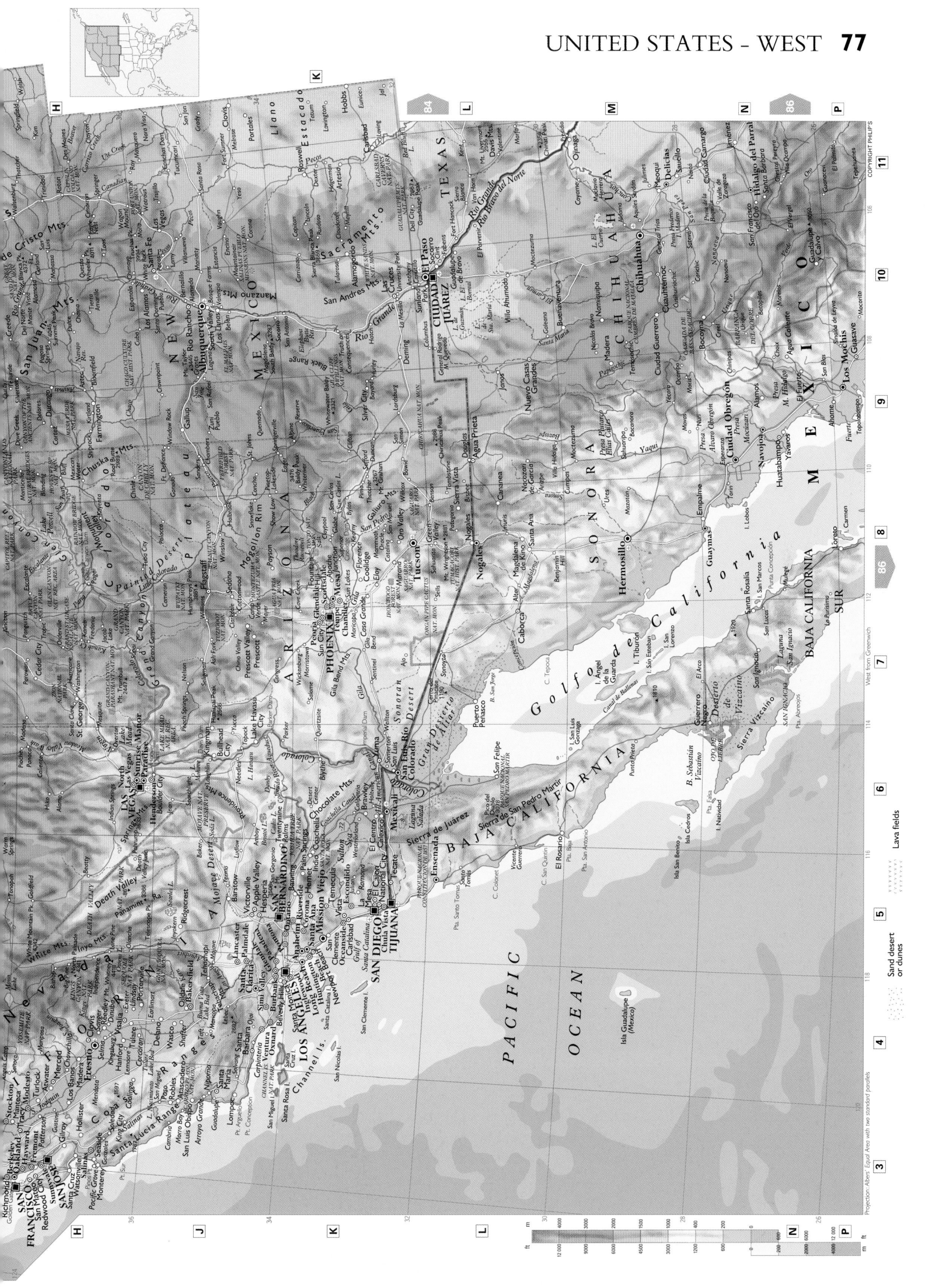

Projection: Albers' Equal Area with two standard parallels

West from Greenwich

Sand desert or dunes

Lava fields

1:2 500 000

WESTERN WASHINGTON REGION
on same scale

PACIFIC OCEAN

BRITISH COLUMBIA

Vancouver Island

Strait of Georgia

Strait of Juan de Fuca

Olympic Mountains
OLYMPIC NATIONAL PARK

WASHINGTON

OREGON

VANCOUVER

VICTORIA

SEATTLE

PORTLAND

MT RAINIER NAT PARK

MT ST HELENS NATIONAL VOLCANIC MONUMENT

Sierra Nevada

YOSEMITE NATIONAL PARK

KINGS CANYON NATIONAL PARK

SEQUOIA NATIONAL PARK

GIANT SEQUOIA NAT MON

Inyo Mts

DEATH VALLEY

Pahute Mesa

Sacramento Valley

San Joaquin Valley

CALIFORNIA

NEVADA

SACRAMENTO

SAN FRANCISCO

Oakland

SAN JOSE

Santa Clara Valley

Fresno

Reno

Carson City

Lake Tahoe

Salinas Valley

Santa Lucia Range

Coast Ranges

Diablo Range

Gabilan Range

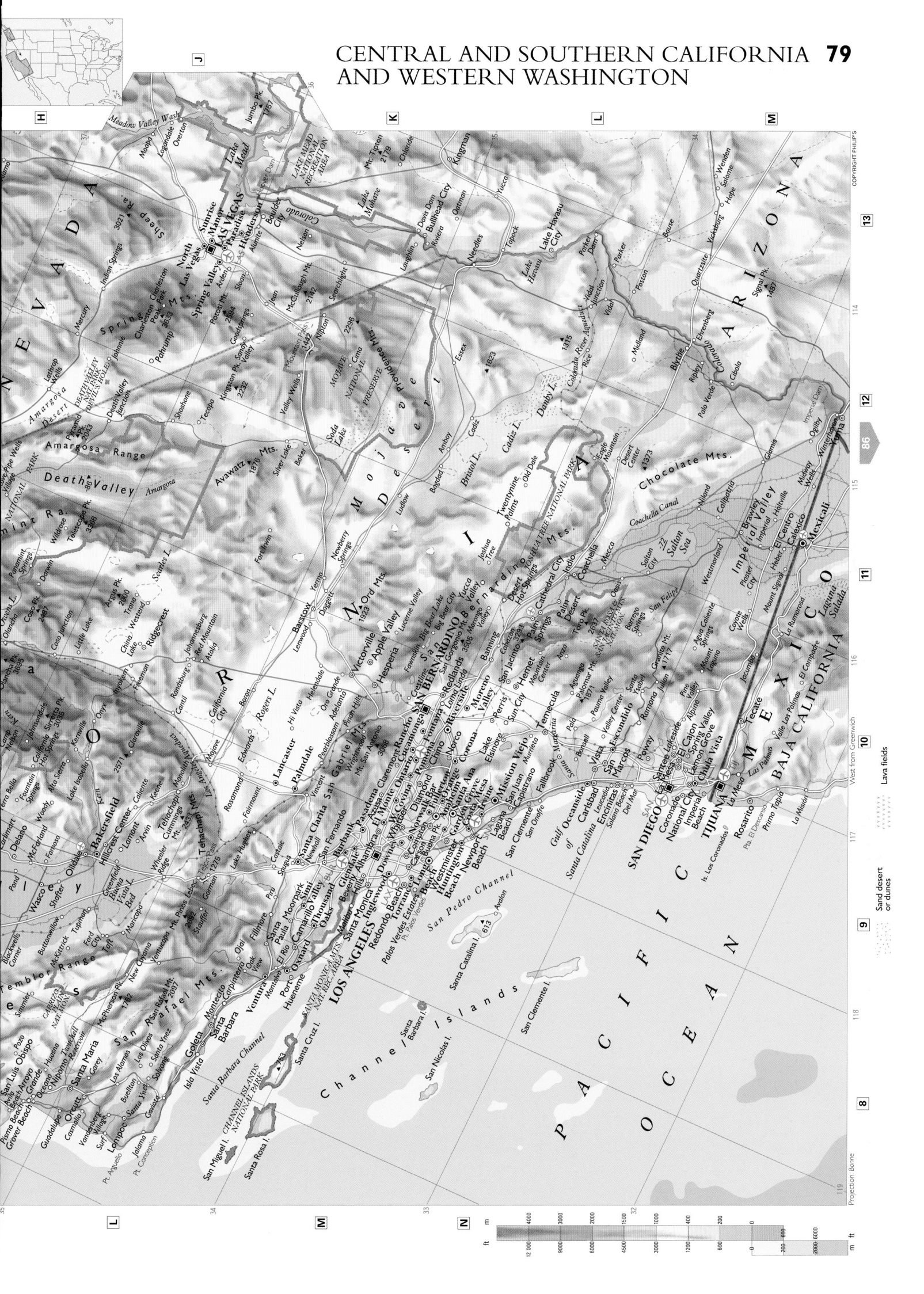

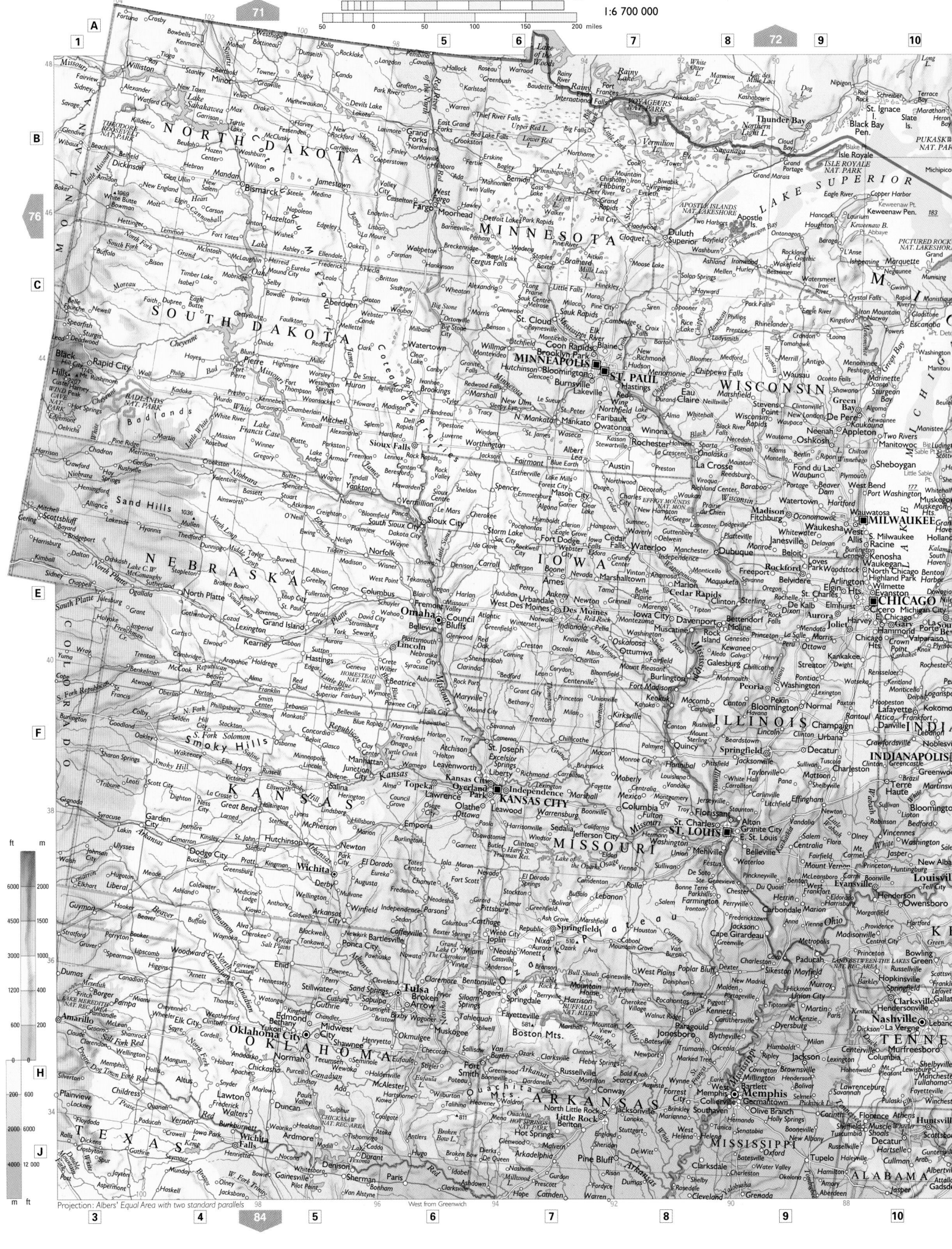

1:2 500 000

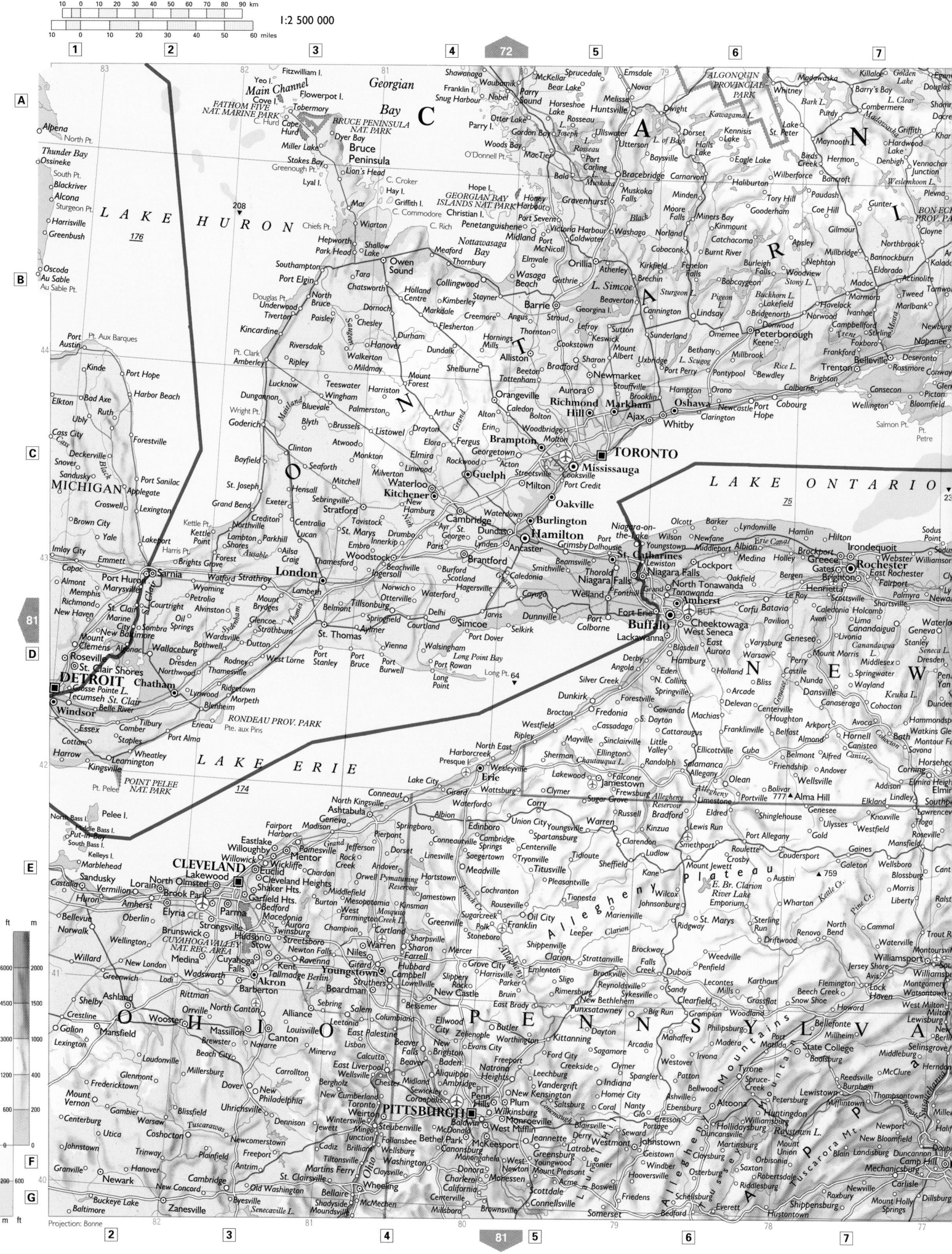

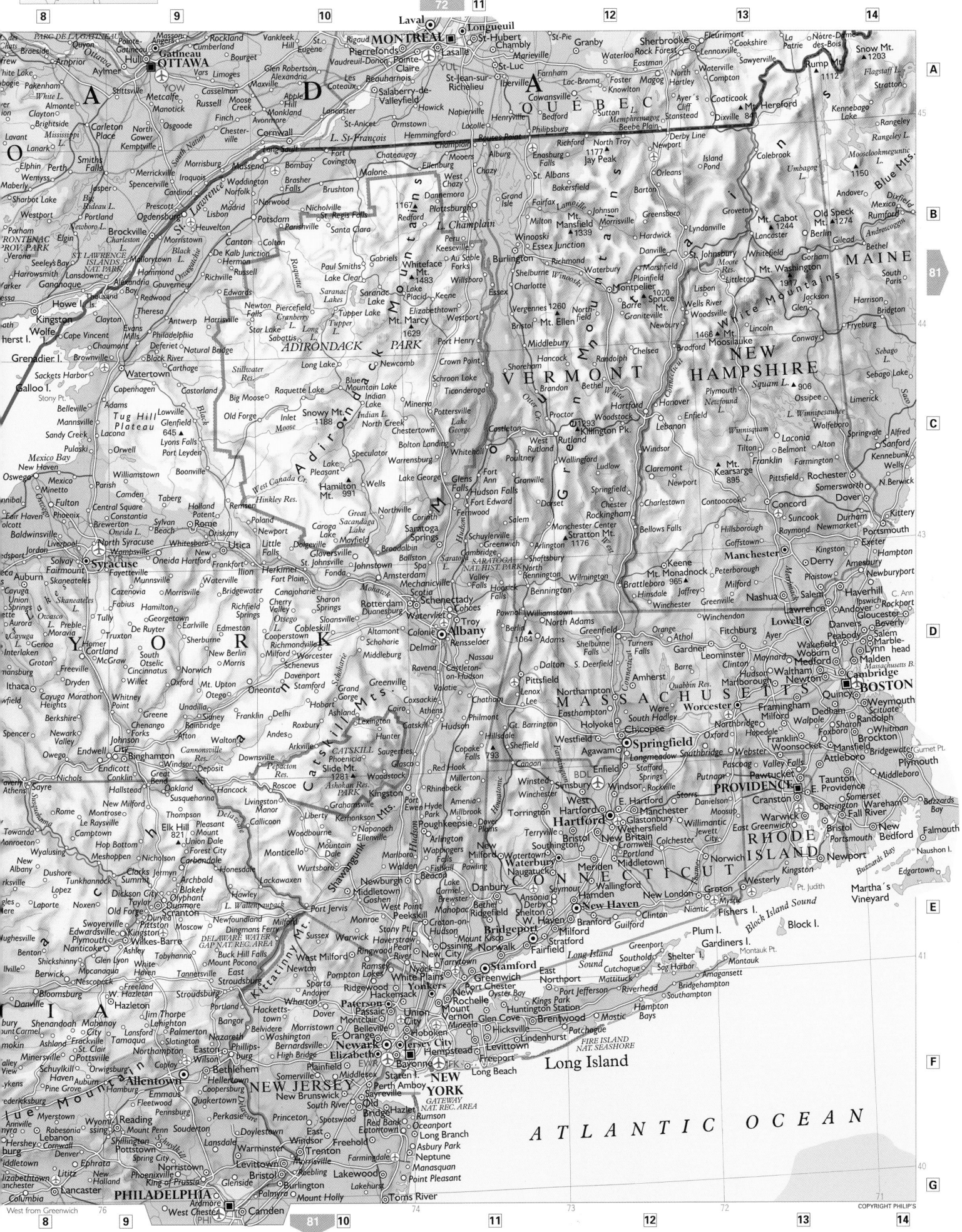

COPYRIGHT PHILIP'S

West from Greenwich

ATLANTIC OCEAN

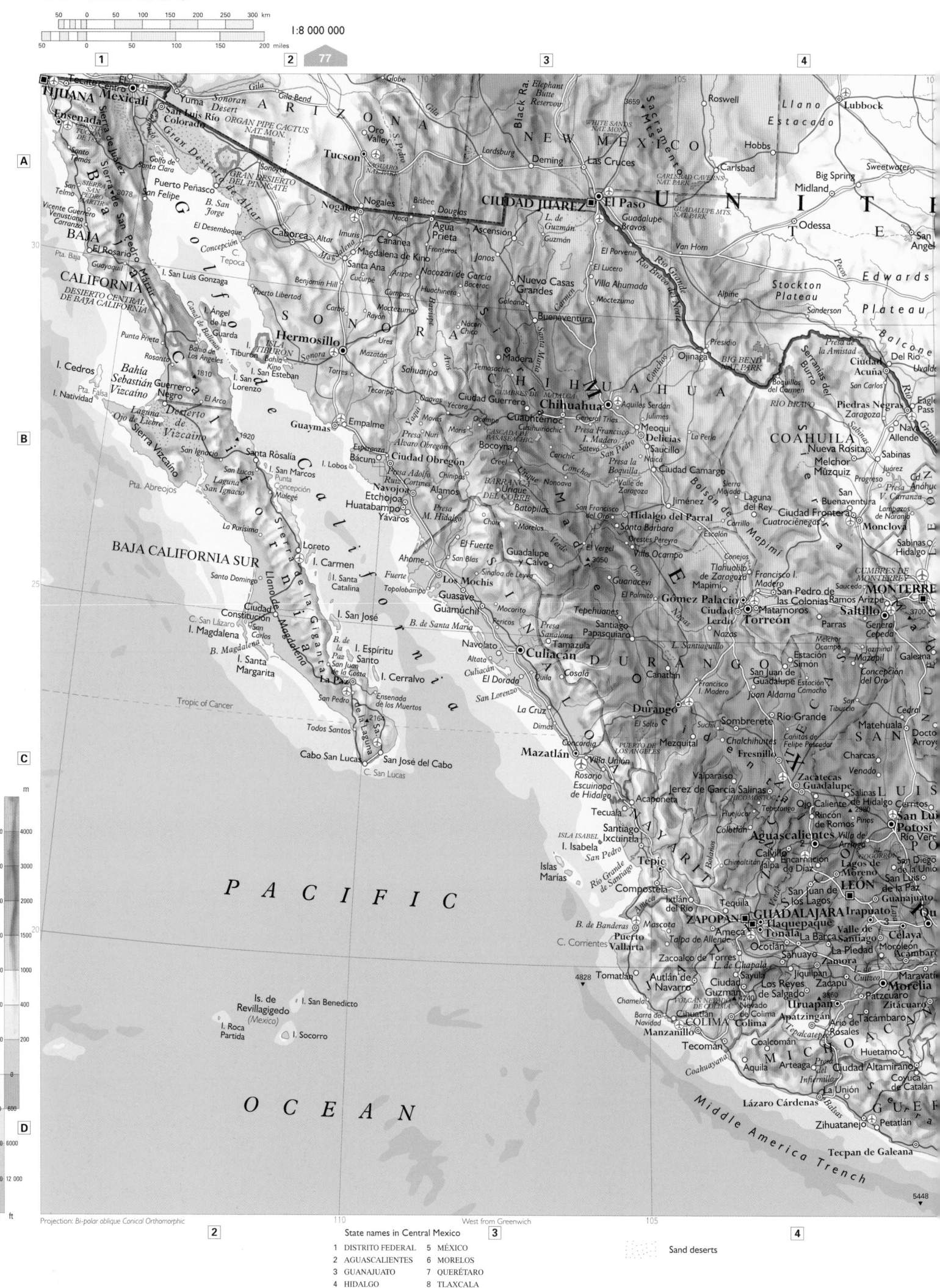

1:8 000 000

50 0 50 100 150 200 250 300 km
50 0 50 100 150 200 miles

77

| 1 | 2 | 77 | 3 | 4 |

A

B

C

D

ft   m
12 000 4000
9000   3000
6000   2000
4500   1500
3000   1000
1200   400
600   200
0   0
200   600
2000   6000
4000   12 000
m   ft

Projection: Bi-polar oblique Conical Orthomorphic

West from Greenwich

State names in Central Mexico

1 DISTRITO FEDERAL   5 MÉXICO
2 AGUASCALIENTES   6 MORELOS
3 GUANAJUATO   7 QUERÉTARO
4 HIDALGO   8 TLAXCALA

Sand deserts

1:8 000 0

JAMAICA
1:3 000 000

GUADELOUPE AND MARTINIQUE
1:2 000 000

Projection: Bi-polar oblique Conical Orthomorphic

5

ATLANTIC OCEAN

PUERTO RICO d
1:3 000 000
10 0 10 20 30 40 50 km
10 0 10 20 30 miles

PUERTO RICO
(U.S.A.)
Pta.
Isabela
Aguadilla Arecibo Manati Vega Barceloneta SAN JUAN
Baja Bayamón Rio Grande
San Utuado Carolina Fajardo Dewey
Mayagüez Sebastián Adjuntas Cordillera Central Sierra de Pta. Culebra
Cerro Luquillo Puerca Vieques
1338 de Punta Caguas Naguabo
San German Uroyan Yauco Cayey Humacao Esperanza
Mts. Coamo Yabucoa
Ponce Guayama
Guanica
Pta. Aguila I. Caja de Muertos

VIRGIN ISLANDS e
1:2 000 000
10 0 10 20 30 km
10 0 10 20 miles

Rufling Pt. The
Settlement
Anegada East
Pt.
Virgin Islands
(U.K.)
Great
Camanoe
Jost Van Guana I.
Virgin Is. Dyke I. 521 Beef I. Virgin Gorda
(U.S.A.) Hans Tortola Spanish Town
Lollik I. Road Town
Cruz Peter I.
Charlotte Bay VIRGIN IS.
Amalie St. St. John I.
Thomas I.

ST. LUCIA f
1:1 000 000
5 0 5 10 km
5 0 5 10 miles

Cap Point
Pte. Hardy
Gros Islet Esperance Bay
Castries Marquis
Girard
Anse la Raye Millet Dennery
Canaries
Soufrière Mt. Gimie Trou Gras Pt.
Soufrière 750 950 Micoud
Bay Petit Piton Vierge Pt.
Gros Piton Pt. 796
Choiseul Gros Piton ST. LUCIA
Laborie Vieux Fort
C. Moule à Chique

ATLANTIC OCEAN
Crab Hill North Point
Spring Hall
Fustic Boscobelle
Portland 245 Belleplaine
Speightstown BARBADOS
Westmoreland Bathsheba Hillcrest
Alleynes Bay Mt. Hillaby Martin's Bay
Holetown 840 Massiah
Jackson Bridgefield Street Ragged Pt.
Black Rock Ellerton Six Cross Roads
Bridgetown Ivy Edey The Crane
Carlisle Bay St. Martins
Worthing Oistins BGI
Oistins Chancery Lane
Bay South Point

BARBADOS g
1:1 000 000
5 0 5 10 km
5 0 5 10 miles

AMAS

ATLANTIC
OCEAN

Arthur's Town
New Bight
Cat I.
San Salvador I.
Conception I.
Rum Cay Tropic of Cancer
Long I.
Clarence Samana Cay
Sandy Town
Cay Crooked I.
Cay Verde Albert Snug Mayaguana I.
Town Corner
Acklins I.
Mira por vos Cay
Hogsty Reef Plana Cays
Cay Santa Little Inagua I. Turks & Caicos Is.
Domingo (U.K.)
Caicos Is. Cockburn Town
Banes Lake Rose Turks Is.
C. Lucrecia Matthew INAGUA Navidad
Antilla Town Great Bank
Mayari Inagua I. Silver
Moa Mouchoir Bank
Baracoa Bank Silver
Guantanamo Pta. de Bank
GUANTANAMO Maisí Î. de la Navidad
BAY (U.S.A.) Tortue Monte Bank
Cap- Cristi
Haitien LA ISABELA Santiago de Puerto Rico Trench
Paso de los Vientos Port-de- Cibao los Caballeros
(Windward Passage) Paix La Vega San Francisco de Macorís Milwaukee
Jean Rabel Cora 3175 Sánchez Deep
Cap-à- Fort Liberté San Juan Nagua 9200
Foux G. de la Pico Duarte Sabana de la Mar
Gonâves Gonâve ARMANDO HAITISES Aguadilla Arecibo
Hinche BERMÚDEZ Hato Mayor Bayamón SAN JUAN
St-Marc HAITI DOMINICAN Higüey C. Engaño (U.K.) Carolina
Jérémie PORT- REP. San Pedro Fajardo Anegada Virgin Is. Sombrero (U.K.)
Dame AU-PRINCE San Juan de Macorís 1338 Charlotte Amalie Road Town Anguilla (U.K.)
Î. de la Gonâve 2680 L. Enriquillo La Romana Ponce St. Thomas Virgin Is. St.-Martin
Les Cayes Massif de la Hotte SIERRA DE SANTO B. de Mayagüez Caguas (U.S.A.) St. Maarten St.-Barthélemy (Fr.)
Petit Aquin BAHORUCO DOMINGO Yuma Guayama Vieques Saba (Neth.)
Navassa I. Goave Jacmel Azua San Cristóbal Isla PUERTO Frederiksted St. Croix St. Eustatius Barbuda
(U.S.A.) Barahona Compostela Saona RICO (U.S.A.) (Neth.) ST. KITTS ANTIGUA
C. Carcasse Pedernales Baní Isla (U.S.A.) Basseterre & NEVIS & BARBUDA
Hispaniola Mona Nevis St. John's
C. Beata Antilles Redonda Antigua
I. Beata Montserrat Soufrière
(U.K.) Hills 914 Guadeloupe Passage
Beata Ridge Ste.-Rose Le Moule
Venezuelan GUADELOUPE La Désirade
(Fr.) 1467 Pointe-à-Pitre
BEAN SEA Basse-Terre Marie-Galante (Fr.)
(Fr.) Grand-Bourg
Colombian Basin I. des Saintes
I. de Aves Dominica Passage
Basin (Venezuela) Portsmouth 1447 DOMINICA
Morne MORNE
Diablotin TROIS PITONS
Roseau Martinique Passage
Mt. Pelée Ste-Marie
1397 Le François
Lesser Fort-de- Rivière-Pilote
ABC France MARTINIQUE
Islands Lesser St. Lucia Channel (Fr.)
Aruba Curaçao Castries ST. LUCIA
Oranjestad (Neth.) Soufrière
Bonaire St. Vincent Passage
NETH. Soufrière 1234 St. Vincent
ANTILLES ARC. LOS Kingstown Speightstown 340
Pen. de la C. San Román ROQUES Bequia Bridgetown
Guajira Pen. de Willemstad I. Orchila BARBADOS
Pta. Gallinas Paraguaná Canouan ST. VINCENT
MACUIRA Pta. Punto Fijo I. Blanquilla (Ven.) Carriacou & THE
Espada Is. Los Hermanos The Grenadines GRENADINES
MÉDANOS DE CORO Is. Las Aves (Ven.) St. George's GRENADA
Coro La Vela (Ven.) Is. Los Roques I. La Tortuga Tobago
CUEVA DE LA (Ven.) (Ven.) I. Los Testigos
Santa GUAJIRA Golfo de QUEBRADA NUEVA (Ven.) Scarborough
Marta Ríohacha Uribia Venezuela DEL TORO ESPARTA Port
BARRAN- TAYRONA Pta. Puerto I. de Margarita of
QUILLA ISLA DE Cardón Cumarebo La Asunción CERRO EL COPEY Spain 940
SALAMANCA Cabimas Porlamar Galera
Baranoa S.A. NEVADA DE Altagracia MARACAY Río Trinidad
Soledad STA. MARTA Mene de Mauroa MIRANDA Pen. de Paria Arima
ATLÁNTICO Sierra Nevada CARACAS Guiria Rio Claro
Ciénaga 775 Santa Rita Tucacas Maiquetía La Guaira C. Codera Carúpano San
Sabanalarga Santa Marta La Concepción Puerto ARAGUA Cumaná Caribe TRINIDAD
FALCÓN Cabello Cariaco Fernando
NA Fundación Villa del Ciudad LARA Barcelona SUCRE TRINIDAD
Valledupar Rosario Ojeda Carora San Felipe VALENCIA Río Chico Puerto Caripito & TOBAGO
El Carmen Agustín Machiques CARABOBO La Cruz Maturín Serpent's Mouth
Since- Codazzi YARACUY Villa Los Teques Barcelona
lejo CÉSAR ZULIA Barquisimeto Yaritagua de Cura San Juan Anaco MARIUSA
El Banco Betijoque PORTUGUESA de los Morros Aragua de DELTA
Magangue Ciénagas del Trujillo Acarigua Barcelona Cantaura Tucupita
Mompós CATATUMBO Trujillo EL GUACHE Valle de AMACURO
Simití Valera Guanare Portuguesa Calabozo la Pascua El Tigre
San Marcos Encontrados El Baúl GUÁRICO Santa María Ciudad Guayana
DOBA MÉRIDA San Carlos de Ipire ANZOÁTEGUI Los Barrancos
bano del Zulia Barinas Ciudad Upata
Ocaña Mérida Libertad San Fernando Maripa Ciudad Embalse de Guri
Planeta DE 4775 Ciudad de Apure Bolívar Tumeremo
Rica BOLÍVAR SANTANDER Nevada BARINAS Bolivia El Callao
NORTE Ciudad de Nutrias VENEZUELA Guasipati
Cúcuta TÁCHIRA Bruzual Achaguas Orinoco Caicara Sierra Imataca

Jamaica Channel

West from Greenwich

92

COPYRIGHT PHILIP'S

4000 3000 2000 1500 1000 500 200 0 ft
600 6000 12 000 18 000 24 000
12 000 9000 6000 4500 3000 1200 600 0 200 2000 4000 6000 8000 m

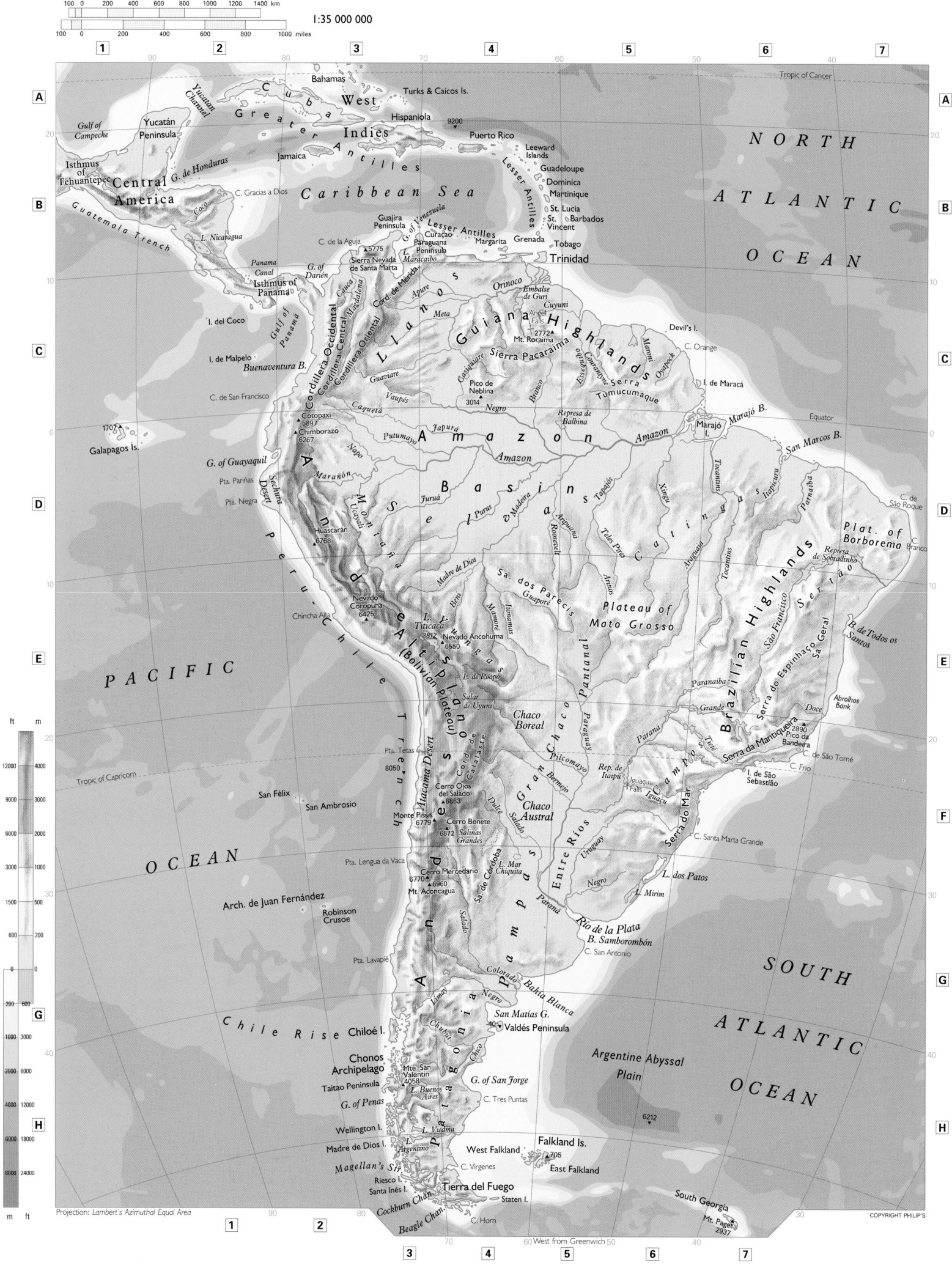

1:35 000 000

1:35 000 000

COPYRIGHT PHILIP'S

■ LIMA Capital Cities

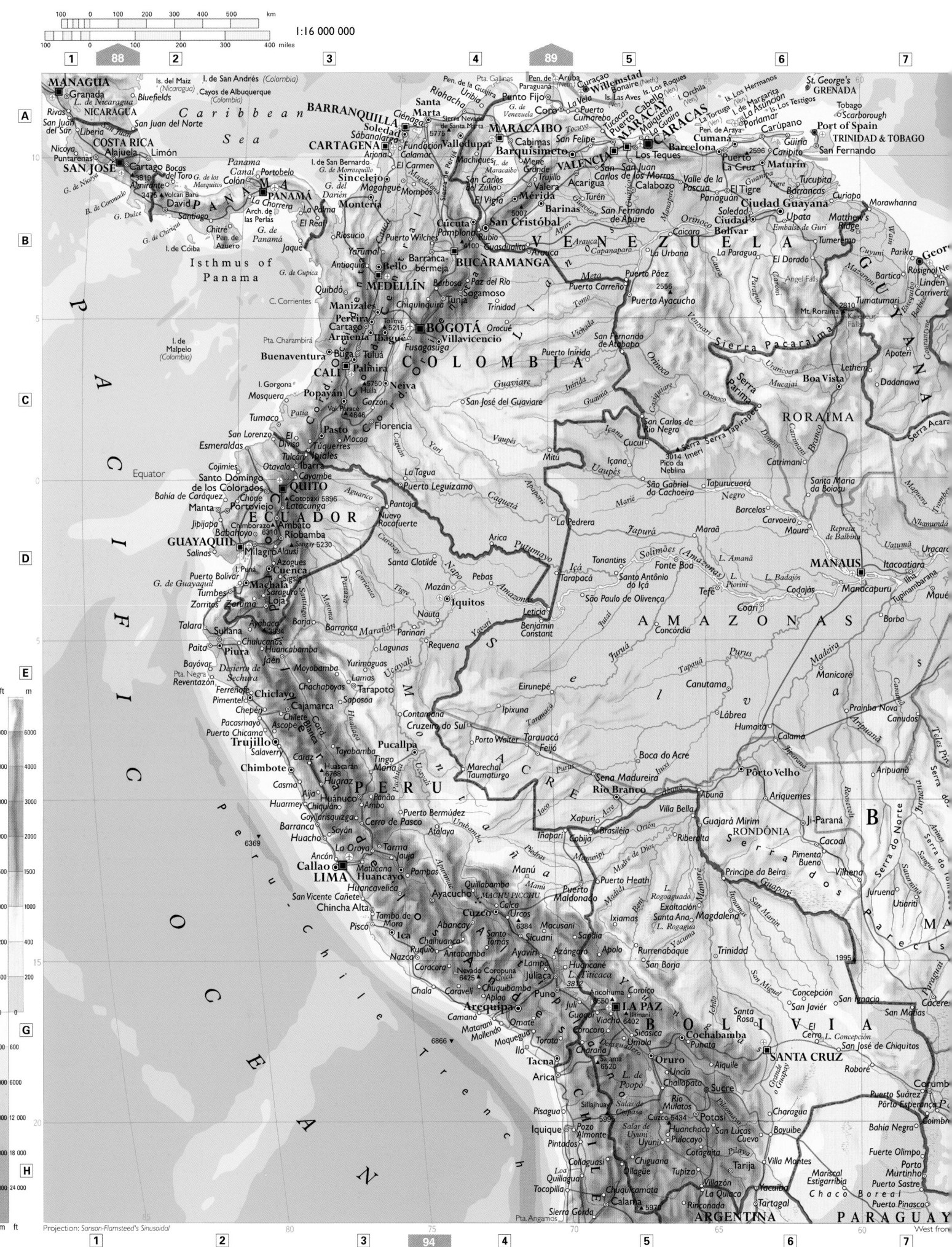

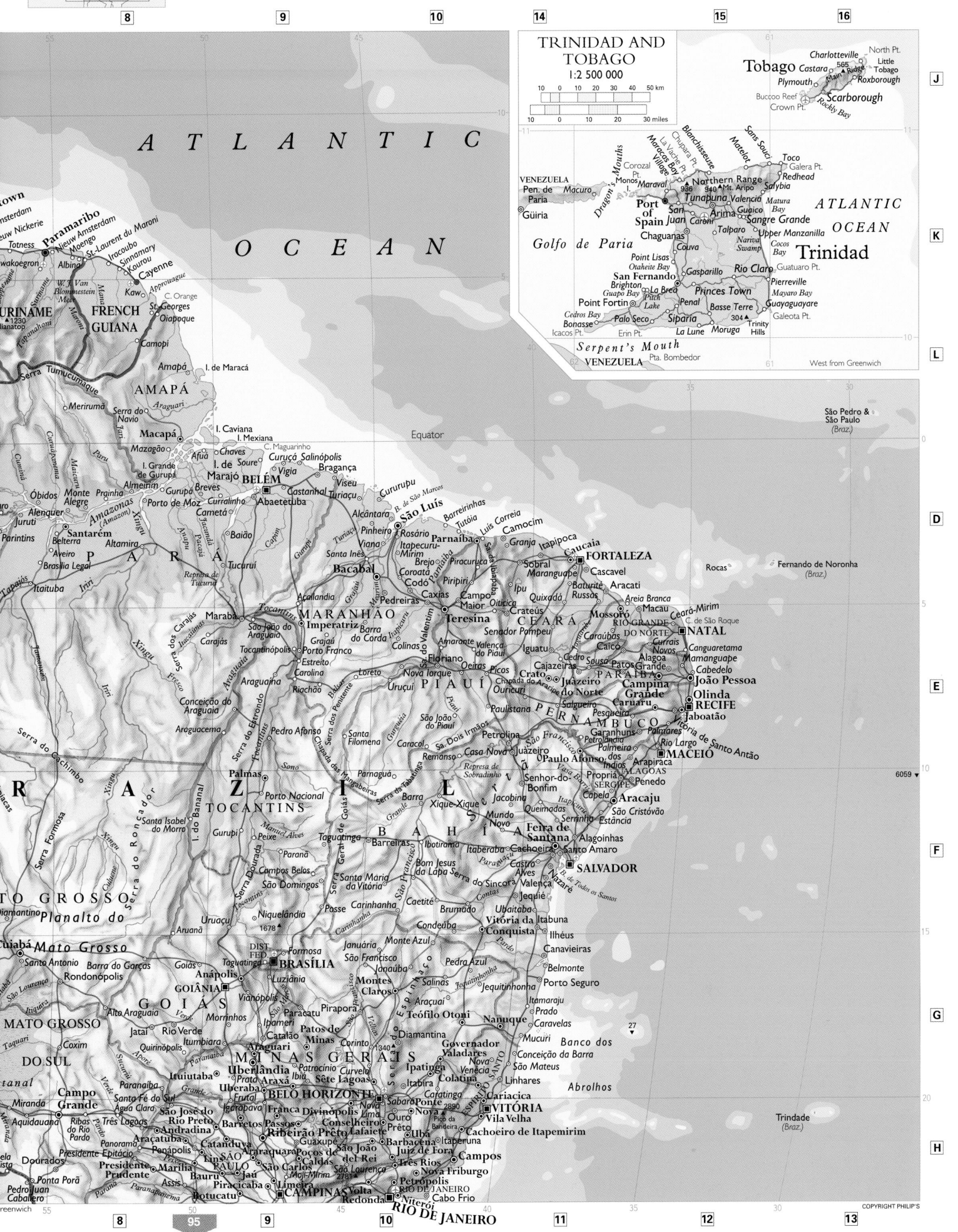

8 9 10 14 15 16

TRINIDAD AND TOBAGO
1:2 500 000
10 0 10 20 30 40 50 km
10 0 10 20 30 miles

J

Tobago Charlotteville North Pt.
Plymouth Castara 565 Little Tobago
Buccoo Reef Ridge Roxborough
Crown Pt. Rockly Bay Scarborough

Blanchisseuse Sans Souci
La Vache Pt. Matelot
Maracas Bay
Chupara Pt. Toco Galera Pt.
Corozal Village Redhead
VENEZUELA Pt. Monos Maraval Northern Range Salybia
Pen. de Macuro I. 936 940 Mt. Aripo Matura
Paria Tunapuna Valencio Bay
Güiria Port San Arima Sangre Grande ATLANTIC
of Spain Juan Caroni Guaico Upper Manzanilla OCEAN
Chaguanas Talparo Narivo
Couva Swamp Cocos
Golfo de Paria Point Lisas Bay **Trinidad**
Otaheite Bay Gasparillo Rio Claro Guataro Pt.
San Fernando Pierreville
Brighton La Brea Princes Town Mayaro Bay
Guapo Bay Pitch Penal Guayaguayare
Point Fortin Lake Basse Terre Galeota Pt.
Cedros Bay Palo Seco 304 Trinity
Bonasse Siparia Hills
Icacos Pt. Erin Pt. La Lune Moruga
Serpent's Mouth
VENEZUELA Pta. Bombedor West from Greenwich

K

L

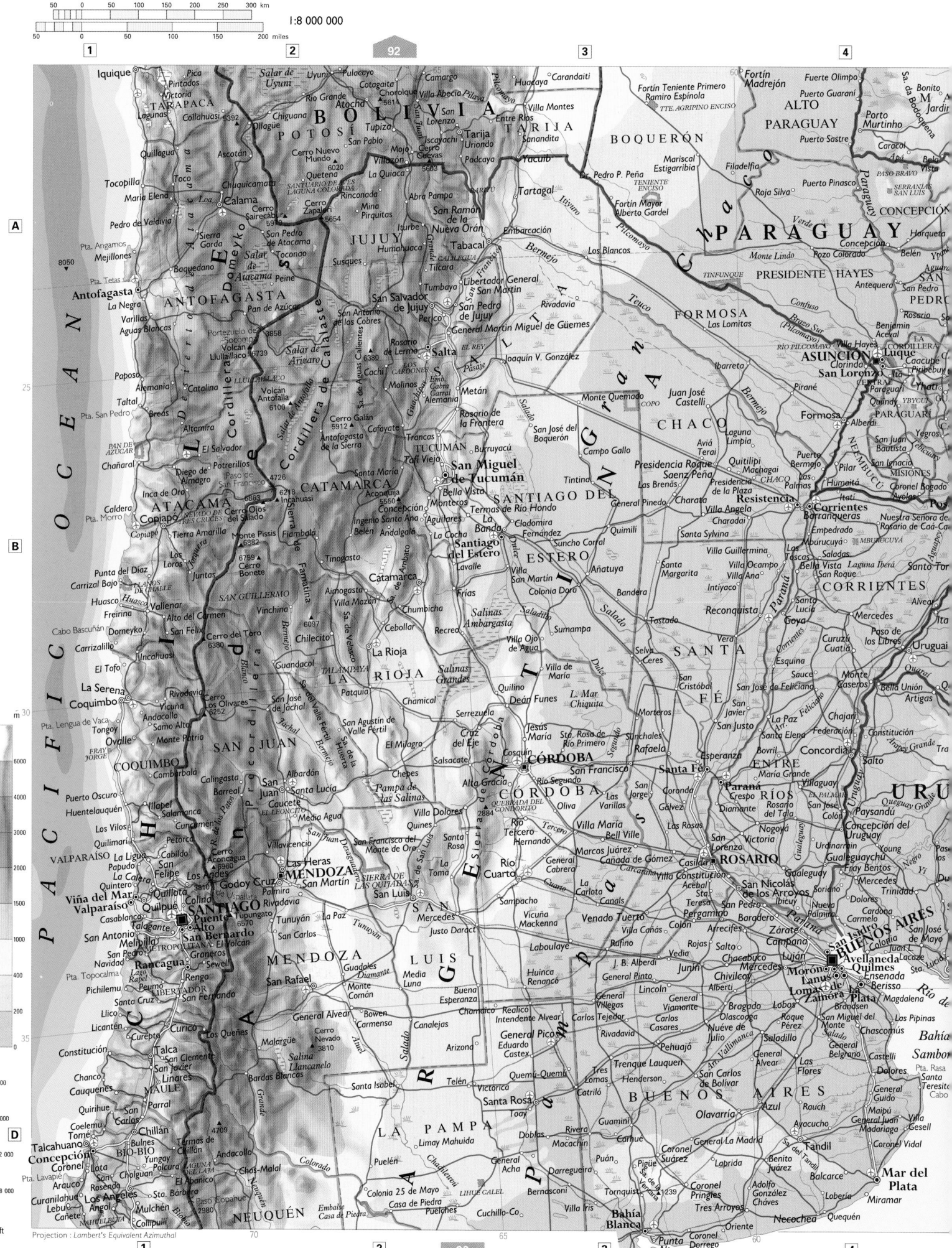

Projection : Lambert's Equivalent Azimuthal

MATO GROSSO
DO SUL
Sidrolândia
Nioaque
Maracaju
Guia Lopes
da Laguna
Dourados
Ponta Porã
Pedro Juan Caballero
CANINDEYÚ
Caruguaty
 AMAMBAY
Amambaí
Capitán Bado
Mundo Novo
CAAGUAZÚ
Oviedo
Hernandarias
Ciudad del Este
Foz do Iguaçu
PARANÁ
Abai
Francisco Beltrão
Medianeira
San Bernardo de Irigoyen
MISIONES
América
Eldorado
Montecarlo
Jardín
San Pedro
Montagudo
Obëra
Candelaria
Leandro N. Alem
Apóstoles
Santo Ángelo
Ijuí
Horizontina
Santa Rosa
Palmeira das Missões
Carazinho
Passo Fundo
Cruz Alta
Santa Maria
Santa Cruz do Sul
Cachoeira do Sul
RIO GRANDE
DO SUL
Santiago
São Borja
São Luís Gonzaga
Santa Vitória do Palmar

Três Lagoas
Andradina
Mirandópolis
Xavantina
Panorama
Araçatuba
Presidente Epitácio
Adamantina
Presidente Prudente
Martinópolis
Rancharia
Assis
Cambará
Sertanópolis
Londrina
Rolândia
Maringá
Mandaguari
Apucarana
Arapongas
Campo Mourão
PARANÁ
Pitanga
Guarapuava
Prudentópolis
União da Vitória
Porto União
Palmas
Caçador
Xanxerê
Chapecó
Concórdia
SANTA
CATARINA
Joaçaba
Campos Novos
Lages
São Joaquim
Tubarão
Laguna
Criciúma
Ararangua
Torres

Olímpia
Catanduva
Andradina
São José do Rio Preto
Bebedouro
Batatais
Ribeirão Prêto
Jaboticabal
Mococa
Araraquara
São Carlos
Rio Claro
Limeira
Americana
Sumaré
CAMPINAS
Bauru
Jaú
Araras
Moji-Guaçu
Esp. São do Pinhal
Pouso Alegre
SÃO PAULO
Itu
Jundiaí
Bragança Paulista
Atibaia
Santo André
SÃO PAULO
São Bernardo do Campo
Osasco
Guarulhos
Moji das Cruzes
São José dos Campos
SANTOS
São Vicente
Praia Grande
Itanhaém

BELO HORIZONTE
Betim
Contagem
Itabirito
Conselheiro Lafaiete
Ouro Prêto
Ponte Nova
VITÓRIA
Vila Velha
Guarapari
Oliveira
Campo Belo
São João del Rei
Ubá
Muriae
Barbacena
Cataguases
Juiz de Fora
Leopoldina
Três Rios
RIO DE JANEIRO
Volta Redonda
Barra Mansa
Nova Iguaçu
Petrópolis
Nova Friburgo
Macaé
Duque de Caxias
Niterói
São Gonçalo
Cabo Frio
Campos
Castelo
Cachoeiro de Itapemirim

ATLANTIC

OCEAN

BRAZIL

URUGUAY
MONTEVIDEO

West from Greenwich

COPYRIGHT PHILIP'S

Tropic of Capricorn

1:16 000 000

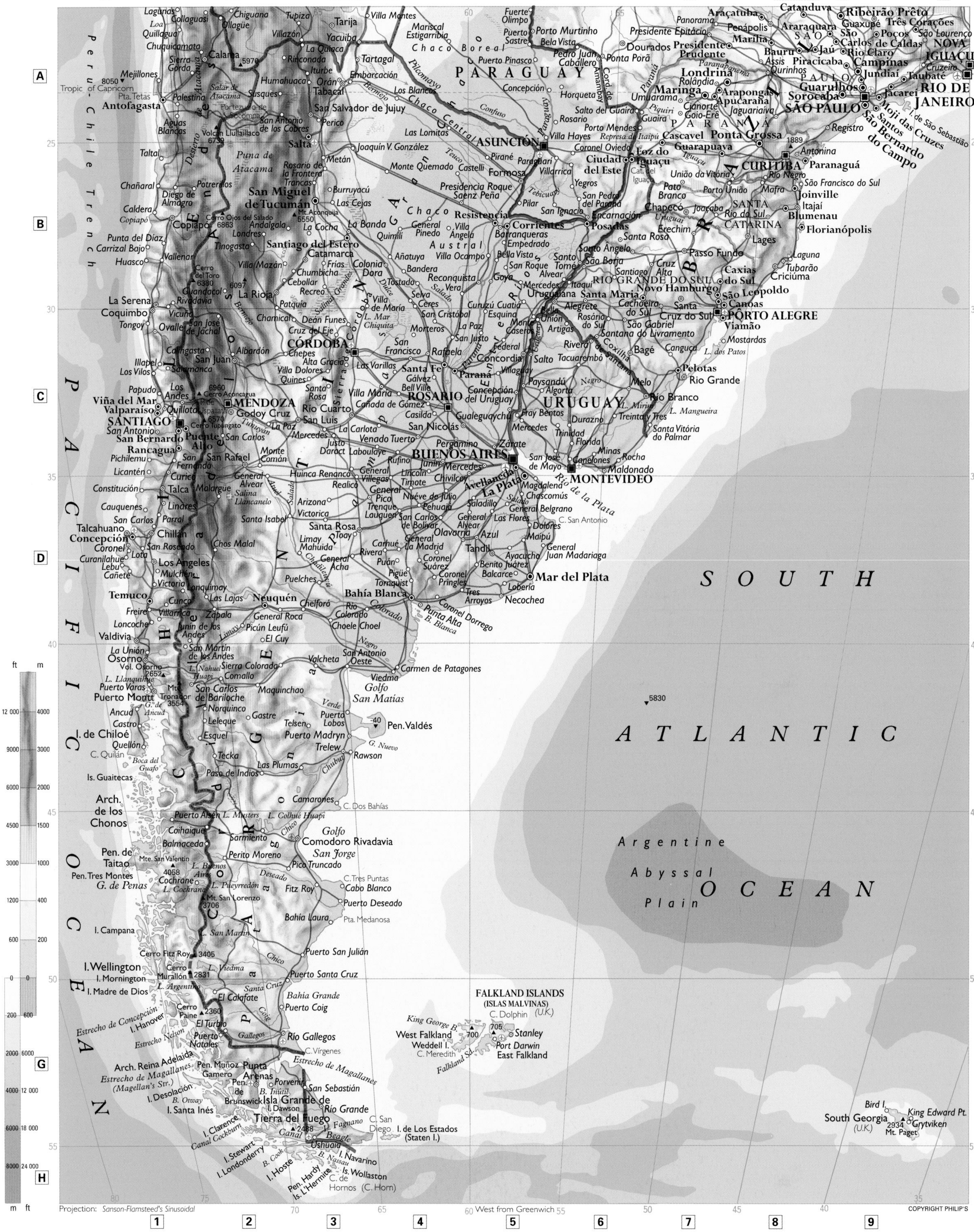

Projection: Sanson-Flamsteed's Sinusoidal

West from Greenwich

COPYRIGHT PHILIP'S

PARAGUAY

ASUNCIÓN

PARANÁ

BRAZIL

SÃO PAULO

RIO DE JANEIRO

NOVA IGUAÇU

CURITIBA

SANTA CATARINA

RIO GRANDE DO SUL

PORTO ALEGRE

URUGUAY

MONTEVIDEO

BUENOS AIRES

CÓRDOBA

ROSARIO

MENDOZA

SANTIAGO

Valparaíso

A R G E N T I N A

C H I L E

P A T A G O N I A

Mar del Plata

Bahía Blanca

Neuquén

Comodoro Rivadavia

Río Gallegos

Punta Arenas

Ushuaia

Tierra del Fuego

Isla Grande de Tierra del Fuego

I. de los Estados (Staten I.)

C. de Hornos (C. Horn)

Estrecho de Magallanes (Magellan's Str.)

P A C I F I C   O C E A N

Peru–Chile Trench

S O U T H   A T L A N T I C   O C E A N

Argentine Abyssal Plain

FALKLAND ISLANDS (ISLAS MALVINAS) (U.K.)

West Falkland
East Falkland
Stanley
Port Darwin

South Georgia (U.K.)

Grytviken
King Edward Pt.
Mt. Paget 2934
Bird I.

Tropic of Capricorn

Golfo San Matías

Pen. Valdés

Golfo San Jorge

Bahía Grande

Chaco Boreal

Chaco Central

Chaco Austral

Puna de Atacama

Salar de Atacama

Antofagasta

Salta

San Miguel de Tucumán

Santiago del Estero

Catamarca

La Rioja

San Juan

San Luis

Santa Fe

Paraná

Santa Rosa

Temuco

Valdivia

Puerto Montt

I. de Chiloé

Arch. de los Chonos

Pen. de Taitao

I. Wellington

I. Madre de Dios

Río Grande

Pelotas

Florianópolis

Blumenau

Joinville

Foz do Iguaçu

Ciudad del Este

Encarnación

Posadas

Resistencia

Corrientes

Formosa

Mar Chiquita

L. Argentino

L. Viedma

L. Buenos Aires

Cerro Aconcagua 6960

Cerro Ojos del Salado 6863

Volcán Llullaillaco 6739

Mt. Pagét 2934

INDEX TO WORLD MAPS

The index contains the names of all the principal places and features shown on the World Maps. Each name is followed by an additional entry in italics giving the country or region within which it is located. The alphabetical order of names composed of two or more words is governed primarily by the first word, then by the second, and then by the country or region name that follows. This is an example of the rule:

Mīr Kūh *Iran*	26°22N 58°55E	**45** E8
Mīr Shahdād *Iran*	26°15N 58°29E	**45** E8
Mira *Italy*	45°26N 12°8E	**22** B5
Mira por vos Cay *Bahamas*	22°9N 74°30W	**89** B5

Physical features composed of a proper name (Erie) and a description (Lake) are positioned alphabetically by the proper name. The description is positioned after the proper name and is usually abbreviated:

Erie, L. *N. Amer.*	42°15N 81°0W	**82** D4

Where a description forms part of a settlement or administrative name, however, it is always written in full and put in its true alphabetical position:

Mount Morris *U.S.A.*	42°44N 77°52W	**82** D7

Names beginning with M' and Mc are indexed as if they were spelled Mac. Names beginning St. are alphabetized under Saint, but Sankt, Sint, Sant', Santa and San are all spelt in full and are alphabetized accordingly. If the same place name occurs two or more times in the index and all are in the same country, each is followed by the name of the administrative subdivision in which it is located.

The geographical co-ordinates which follow each name in the index give the latitude and longitude of each place. The first co-ordinate indicates latitude – the distance north or south of the Equator. The second co-ordinate indicates longitude – the distance east or west of the Greenwich Meridian. Both latitude and longitude are measured in degrees and minutes (there are 60 minutes in a degree).

The latitude is followed by N(orth) or S(outh) and the longitude by E(ast) or W(est).

The number in bold type which follows the geographical co-ordinates refers to the number of the map page where that feature or place will be found. This is usually the largest scale at which the place or feature appears.

The letter and figure that are immediately after the page number give the grid square on the map page, within which the feature is situated. The letter represents the latitude and the figure the longitude. A lower-case letter immediately after the page number refers to an inset map on that page.

In some cases the feature itself may fall within the specified square, while the name is outside. This is usually the case only with features that are larger than a grid square.

Rivers are indexed to their mouths or confluences, and carry the symbol ➔ after their names. The following symbols are also used in the index: ■ country, ☒ overseas territory or dependency, □ first-order administrative area, △ national park, ⌓ other park (provincial park, nature reserve or game reserve), ✈ (LHR) principal airport (and location identifier).

Abbreviations used in the index

A.C.T. – Australian Capital Territory
A.R. – Autonomous Region
Afghan. – Afghanistan
Afr. – Africa
Ala. – Alabama
Alta. – Alberta
Amer. – America(n)
Ant. – Antilles
Arch. – Archipelago
Ariz. – Arizona
Ark. – Arkansas
Atl. Oc. – Atlantic Ocean
B. – Baie, Bahía, Bay, Bucht, Bugt
B.C. – British Columbia
Bangla. – Bangladesh
Barr. – Barrage
Bos.-H. – Bosnia-Herzegovina
C. – Cabo, Cap, Cape, Coast
C.A.R. – Central African Republic
C. Prov. – Cape Province
Calif. – California
Cat. – Catarata
Cent. – Central
Chan. – Channel
Colo. – Colorado
Conn. – Connecticut
Cord. – Cordillera
Cr. – Creek
Czech. – Czech Republic
D.C. – District of Columbia
Del. – Delaware
Dem. – Democratic
Dep. – Dependency
Des. – Desert
Dét. – Détroit
Dist. – District
Dj. – Djebel
Dom. Rep. – Dominican Republic
E. – East
El Salv. – El Salvador
Eq. Guin. – Equatorial Guinea
Est. – Estrecho
Falk. Is. – Falkland Is.
Fd. – Fjord
Fla. – Florida
Fr. – French
G. – Golfe, Golfo, Gulf, Guba, Gebel
Ga. – Georgia
Gt. – Great, Greater
Guinea-Biss. – Guinea-Bissau
H.K. – Hong Kong
H.P. – Himachal Pradesh
Hants. – Hampshire
Harb. – Harbor, Harbour
Hd. – Head
Hts. – Heights
I.(s). – Île, Ilha, Insel, Isla, Island, Isle
Ill. – Illinois
Ind. – Indiana
Ind. Oc. – Indian Ocean
Ivory C. – Ivory Coast
J. – Jabal, Jebel
Jaz. – Jazīrah
Junc. – Junction
K. – Kap, Kapp
Kans. – Kansas
Kep. – Kepulauan
Ky. – Kentucky
L. – Lac, Lacul, Lago, Lagoa, Lake, Limni, Loch, Lough
La. – Louisiana
Ld. – Land
Liech. – Liechtenstein
Lux. – Luxembourg
Mad. P. – Madhya Pradesh
Madag. – Madagascar
Man. – Manitoba
Mass. – Massachusetts
Md. – Maryland
Me. – Maine
Medit. S. – Mediterranean Sea
Mich. – Michigan
Minn. – Minnesota
Miss. – Mississippi
Mo. – Missouri
Mont. – Montana
Mozam. – Mozambique
Mt.(s) – Mont, Montaña, Mountain
Mte. – Monte
Mti. – Monti
N. – Nord, Norte, North, Northern, Nouveau, Nahal, Nahr
N.B. – New Brunswick
N.C. – North Carolina
N. Cal. – New Caledonia
N. Dak. – North Dakota
N.H. – New Hampshire
N.I. – North Island
N.J. – New Jersey
N. Mex. – New Mexico
N.S. – Nova Scotia
N.S.W. – New South Wales
N.W.T. – North West Territory
N.Y. – New York
N.Z. – New Zealand
Nac. – Nacional
Nat. – National
Nebr. – Nebraska
Neths. – Netherlands
Nev. – Nevada
Nfld & L. – Newfoundland and Labrador
Nic. – Nicaragua
O. – Oued, Ouadi
Occ. – Occidentale
Okla. – Oklahoma
Ont. – Ontario
Or. – Orientale
Oreg. – Oregon
Os. – Ostrov
Oz. – Ozero
P. – Pass, Passo, Pasul, Pulau
P.E.I. – Prince Edward Island
Pa. – Pennsylvania
Pac. Oc. – Pacific Ocean
Papua N.G. – Papua New Guinea
Pass. – Passage
Peg. – Pegunungan
Pen. – Peninsula, Péninsule
Phil. – Philippines
Pk. – Peak
Plat. – Plateau
Prov. – Province, Provincial
Pt. – Point
Pta. – Ponta, Punta
Pte. – Pointe
Qué. – Québec
Queens. – Queensland
R. – Rio, River
R.I. – Rhode Island
Ra. – Range
Raj. – Rajasthan
Recr. – Recreational, Récréatif
Reg. – Region
Rep. – Republic
Res. – Reserve, Reservoir
Rhld-Pfz. – Rheinland-Pfalz
S. – South, Southern, Sur
Si. Arabia – Saudi Arabia
S.C. – South Carolina
S. Dak. – South Dakota
S.I. – South Island
S. Leone – Sierra Leone
Sa. – Serra, Sierra
Sask. – Saskatchewan
Scot. – Scotland
Sd. – Sound
Sev. – Severnaya
Sib. – Siberia
Sprs. – Springs
St. – Saint
Sta. – Santa
Ste. – Sainte
Sto. – Santo
Str. – Strait, Stretto
Switz. – Switzerland
Tas. – Tasmania
Tenn. – Tennessee
Terr. – Territory, Territoire
Tex. – Texas
Tg. – Tanjung
Trin. & Tob. – Trinidad & Tobago
U.A.E. – United Arab Emirates
U.K. – United Kingdom
U.S.A. – United States of America
Ut. P. – Uttar Pradesh
Va. – Virginia
Vdkhr. – Vodokhranilishche
Vdskh. – Vodoskhovyshche
Vf. – Vírful
Vic. – Victoria
Vol. – Volcano
Vt. – Vermont
W. – Wadi, West
W. Va. – West Virginia
Wall. & F. Is. – Wallis and Futuna Is.
Wash. – Washington
Wis. – Wisconsin
Wlkp. – Wielkopolski
Wyo. – Wyoming
Yorks. – Yorkshire

A

A Coruña Spain 43°20N 8°25W 21 A1
A Estrada Spain 42°43N 8°27W 21 A1
A Fonsagrada Spain 43°8N 7°4W 21 A2
Aabenraa Denmark 55°3N 9°25E 9 J13
Aachen Germany 50°45N 6°6E 16 C4
Aalborg Denmark 57°2N 9°54E 9 H13
Aalen Germany 48°51N 10°6E 16 D6
Aalst Belgium 50°56N 4°2E 15 D4
Aalten Neths. 51°56N 6°35E 15 C6
Aalter Belgium 51°5N 3°28E 15 C3
Äänekoski Finland 62°36N 25°44E 8 E21
Aarau Switz. 47°23N 8°4E 20 C8
Aare → Switz. 47°33N 8°14E 20 C8
Aarhus = Århus Denmark 56°8N 10°11E 9 H14
Aarschot Belgium 50°59N 4°49E 15 D4
Aba Dem. Rep. of the Congo 3°58N 30°17E 54 B3
Aba Nigeria 5°10N 7°19E 50 G7
Abaco I. Bahamas 26°25N 77°10W 88 A4
Ābādān Iran 30°22N 48°20E 45 D6
Ābādeh Iran 31°8N 52°40E 45 D7
Abadla Algeria 31°2N 2°45W 50 B5
Abaetetuba Brazil 1°40S 48°50W 93 D9
Abagnar Qi = Xilinhot China 43°52N 116°2E 34 C9
Abah, Tanjung Indonesia 8°46S 115°38E 37 K18
Abai Paraguay 25°58S 55°54W 95 B4
Abakan Russia 53°40N 91°10E 29 D10
Abancay Peru 13°35S 72°55W 92 F4
Abariringa Kiribati 2°50S 171°40W 64 H10
Abarqū Iran 31°10N 53°20E 45 D7
Abashiri Japan 44°0N 144°15E 30 B12
Abashiri-Wan Japan 44°0N 144°30E 30 C12
Ābay = Nîl el Azraq → Sudan 15°38N 32°31E 51 E12
Abay Kazakhstan 49°38N 72°53E 28 E8
Abaya, L. Ethiopia 6°30N 37°50E 47 F2
Abaza Russia 52°39N 90°6E 28 D9
'Abbāsābād Iran 33°34N 58°23E 45 C8
Abbay = Nîl el Azraq → Sudan 15°38N 32°31E 51 E12
Abbaye, Pt. U.S.A. 46°58N 88°8W 80 B9
Abbé, L. Ethiopia 11°8N 41°47E 47 E3
Abbeville France 50°6N 1°49E 20 A4
Abbeville Ala., U.S.A. 31°34N 85°15W 85 F12
Abbeville La., U.S.A. 29°58N 92°8W 84 G8
Abbeville S.C., U.S.A. 34°11N 82°23W 85 D13
Abbeyfeale Ireland 52°23N 9°18W 10 D2
Abbot Ice Shelf Antarctica 73°0S 92°0W 5 D16
Abbotsford Canada 49°5N 122°20W 70 D4
Abbottabad Pakistan 34°10N 73°15E 42 B5
ABC Islands = Netherlands Antilles ⊠ W. Indies 12°15N 69°0W 92 A5
Abd al Kūrī Yemen 12°5N 52°20E 47 E5
Ābdar Iran 30°16N 55°19E 45 D7
'Abdolābād Iran 34°12N 56°30E 45 C8
Abdulpur Bangla. 24°15N 88°59E 43 G13
Abéché Chad 13°50N 20°35E 51 F10
Abel Tasman △ N.Z. 40°59S 173°3E 59 D4
Abengourou Ivory C. 6°42N 3°27W 50 G5
Åbenrå = Aabenraa Denmark 55°3N 9°25E 9 J13
Abeokuta Nigeria 7°3N 3°19E 50 G6
Aber Uganda 2°12N 32°25E 54 B3
Aberaeron U.K. 52°15N 4°15W 13 E3
Aberayron = Aberaeron U.K. 52°15N 4°15W 13 E3
Aberchirder U.K. 57°34N 2°37W 11 D6
Abercorn Australia 25°12S 151°5E 63 D5
Aberdare U.K. 51°43N 3°27W 13 F4
Aberdare △ Kenya 0°22S 36°44E 54 C4
Aberdare Ra. Kenya 0°15S 36°50E 54 C4
Aberdeen Australia 32°9S 150°56E 63 E5
Aberdeen Canada 52°20N 106°8W 71 C7
Aberdeen China 22°14N 114°8E 33 G11
Aberdeen S. Africa 32°28S 24°2E 56 E3
Aberdeen U.K. 57°9N 2°5W 11 D6
Aberdeen Idaho, U.S.A. 42°57N 112°50W 76 E7
Aberdeen Md., U.S.A. 39°31N 76°10W 81 F15
Aberdeen Miss., U.S.A. 33°49N 88°33W 85 E10
Aberdeen S. Dak., U.S.A. 45°28N 98°29W 80 C4
Aberdeen Wash., U.S.A. 46°59N 123°50W 78 D3
Aberdeen, City of □ U.K. 57°10N 2°10W 11 D6
Aberdeenshire □ U.K. 57°17N 2°36W 11 D6
Aberdovey = Aberdyfi U.K. 52°33N 4°3W 13 E3
Aberdyfi U.K. 52°33N 4°3W 13 E3
Aberfeldy U.K. 56°37N 3°51W 11 E5
Aberfoyle U.K. 56°11N 4°23W 11 E4
Abergavenny U.K. 51°49N 3°1W 13 F4
Abergele U.K. 53°17N 3°35W 12 D4
Abernathy U.S.A. 33°50N 101°51W 84 E4
Abert, L. U.S.A. 42°38N 120°14W 76 E3
Aberystwyth U.K. 52°25N 4°5W 13 E3
Abhā Si. Arabia 18°0N 42°34E 47 D3
Abhar Iran 36°9N 49°13E 45 B6
Abhayapuri India 26°24N 90°38E 43 F14
Abidjan Ivory C. 5°26N 3°58W 50 G5
Abilene Kans., U.S.A. 38°55N 97°13W 80 F5
Abilene Tex., U.S.A. 32°28N 99°43W 84 E5
Abingdon U.K. 51°40N 1°17W 13 F6
Abingdon U.S.A. 36°43N 81°59W 81 G13
Abington Reef Australia 18°0S 149°35E 62 B4
Abitau → Canada 59°53N 109°3W 71 B7
Abitibi → Canada 51°3N 80°55W 72 B3
Abitibi, L. Canada 48°40N 79°40W 72 C4
Abkhaz Republic = Abkhazia □ Georgia 43°12N 41°5E 19 F7
Abkhazia □ Georgia 43°12N 41°5E 19 F7
Abminga Australia 26°8S 134°51E 63 D1
Åbo = Turku Finland 60°30N 22°19E 9 F20
Abohar India 30°10N 74°10E 42 D6
Abomey Benin 7°10N 2°5E 50 G6
Abong-Mbang Cameroon 4°0N 13°8E 52 D2
Abou-Deïa Chad 11°20N 19°20E 51 F9
Aboyne U.K. 57°4N 2°47W 11 D6
Abra Pampa Argentina 22°43S 65°42W 94 A2
Abraham L. Canada 52°15N 116°35W 70 C5
Abreojos, Pta. Mexico 26°50N 113°40W 86 B2
Abrolhos, Banco dos Brazil 18°0S 38°0W 93 F11
Abrud Romania 46°19N 23°5E 17 E12
Absaroka Range U.S.A. 44°45N 109°50W 76 D9
Abu India 24°41N 72°50E 42 G5
Abū al Abyad U.A.E. 24°11N 53°50E 45 E7
Abū al Khaşīb Iraq 30°25N 48°0E 44 D5
Abū 'Alī Si. Arabia 27°20N 49°27E 45 E6
Abū 'Alī → Lebanon 34°25N 35°50E 46 A4
Abu Dhabi = Abū Ẓāby U.A.E. 24°28N 54°22E 45 E7
Abū Du'ān Syria 36°25N 38°15E 44 B3
Abu el Gaīn, W. → Egypt 29°35N 33°30E 46 F2
Abu Ga'da, W. → Egypt 29°15N 32°53E 46 F1
Abū Ḩadrīyah Si. Arabia 27°20N 48°58E 45 E6
Abu Hamed Sudan 19°32N 33°13E 51 E12
Abū Kamāl Syria 34°30N 41°0E 44 C4
Abū Madd, Ra's Si. Arabia 24°50N 37°7E 44 E3
Abū Mūsā U.A.E. 25°52N 55°3E 45 E7
Abū Qaşr Si. Arabia 30°21N 38°34E 44 D3
Abu Shagara, Ras Sudan 21°4N 37°19E 51 D13
Abu Simbel Egypt 22°18N 31°40E 51 D12
Abū Şukhayr Iraq 31°54N 44°30E 44 D5
Abu Zabad Sudan 12°25N 29°10E 51 F11
Abū Ẓāby U.A.E. 24°28N 54°22E 45 E7
Abū Zeydābād Iran 33°54N 51°45E 45 C6
Abuja Nigeria 9°5N 7°32E 50 G7
Abukuma-Gawa → Japan 38°6N 140°52E 30 E10
Abukuma-Sammyaku Japan 37°30N 140°45E 30 F10
Abunã Brazil 9°40S 65°20W 92 E5
Abunã → Brazil 9°41S 65°20W 92 E5
Aburo Dem. Rep. of the Congo 2°4N 30°53E 54 B3
Abut Hd. N.Z. 43°7S 170°15E 59 E3
Ābyek Iran 36°4N 50°33E 45 B6
Acadia △ U.S.A. 44°20N 68°13W 81 C19
Açailândia Brazil 4°57S 47°0W 93 D9
Acajutla El Salv. 13°36N 89°50W 88 D2
Acámbaro Mexico 20°2N 100°44W 86 D4
Acaponeta Mexico 22°30N 105°22W 86 C3
Acapulco Mexico 16°51N 99°55W 87 D5
Acaraí, Serra Brazil 1°50N 57°50W 92 C7
Acarigua Venezuela 9°33N 69°12W 92 B5
Acatlán Mexico 18°12N 98°3W 87 D5
Acayucán Mexico 17°57N 94°55W 87 D6
Accomac U.S.A. 37°43N 75°40W 81 G16
Accra Ghana 5°35N 0°6W 50 G5
Accrington U.K. 53°45N 2°22W 12 D5
Acebal Argentina 33°20S 60°50W 94 C3
Aceh □ Indonesia 4°15N 97°30E 36 D1
Achalpur India 21°22N 77°32E 40 J10
Acharnes Greece 38°5N 23°44E 23 E10
Acheloos → Greece 38°19N 21°7E 23 E9
Acheng China 45°30N 126°58E 35 B14
Acher India 23°10N 72°32E 42 H5
Achill Hd. Ireland 53°58N 10°15W 10 C1
Achill I. Ireland 53°58N 10°1W 10 C1
Achinsk Russia 56°20N 90°20E 29 D10
Acireale Italy 37°37N 15°10E 22 F6
Ackerman U.S.A. 33°19N 89°11W 85 E10
Acklins I. Bahamas 22°30N 74°0W 89 B5
Acme Canada 51°33N 113°30W 70 C6
Acme U.S.A. 40°8N 79°26W 82 F5
Aconcagua, Cerro Argentina 32°39S 70°0W 94 C2
Aconquija, Mt. Argentina 27°0S 66°0W 94 B2
Açores, Is. dos Atl. Oc. 38°0N 27°0W 50 a
Acornhoek S. Africa 24°37S 31°2E 57 C5
Acraman, L. Australia 32°2S 135°23E 63 E2
Acre = 'Akko Israel 32°55N 35°4E 46 C4
Acre □ Brazil 9°1S 71°0W 92 E4
Acre → Brazil 8°45S 67°22W 92 E5
Actinolite Canada 44°32N 77°19W 82 B7
Acton Canada 43°38N 80°3W 82 C4
Ad Dammām Si. Arabia 26°20N 50°5E 45 E6
Ad Dāmūr Lebanon 33°43N 35°27E 46 B4
Ad Dawādimī Si. Arabia 24°35N 44°15E 44 E5
Ad Dawḩah Qatar 25°15N 51°35E 45 E6
Ad Dawr Iraq 34°27N 43°47E 44 C4
Ad Dir'īyah Si. Arabia 24°44N 46°35E 44 E5
Ad Dīwānīyah Iraq 32°0N 45°0E 44 D5
Ad Dujayl Iraq 33°51N 44°14E 44 C5
Ad Duwayd Si. Arabia 30°15N 42°17E 44 D4
Ada Minn., U.S.A. 47°18N 96°31W 80 B5
Ada Okla., U.S.A. 34°46N 96°41W 84 D6
Adabiya Egypt 29°53N 32°28E 46 F1
Adair, C. Canada 71°30N 71°34W 69 B12
Adaja → Spain 41°32N 4°52W 21 B3
Adak I. U.S.A. 51°45N 176°45W 74 a
Adamaoua, Massif de l' Cameroon 7°20N 12°20E 51 G8
Adamawa Highlands = Adamaoua, Massif de l' Cameroon 7°20N 12°20E 51 G8
Adamello, Mte. Italy 46°9N 10°30E 20 C9
Adaminaby Australia 36°0S 148°45E 63 F4
Adams Mass., U.S.A. 42°38N 73°7W 83 D11
Adams N.Y., U.S.A. 43°49N 76°1W 83 C8
Adams Wis., U.S.A. 43°57N 89°49W 80 D9
Adams, Mt. U.S.A. 46°12N 121°30W 78 D5
Adam's Bridge Sri Lanka 9°15N 79°40E 40 Q11
Adams L. Canada 51°10N 119°40W 70 C5
Adam's Peak Sri Lanka 6°48N 80°30E 40 R12
Adana Turkey 37°0N 35°16E 44 B2
Adapazarı = Sakarya Turkey 40°48N 30°25E 19 F5
Adarama Sudan 17°10N 34°52E 51 E12
Adare, C. Antarctica 71°0S 171°0E 5 D11
Adaut Indonesia 8°8S 131°7E 37 F8
Adavale Australia 25°52S 144°32E 63 D3
Adda → Italy 45°8N 9°53E 20 D8
Addis Ababa = Addis Abeba Ethiopia 9°2N 38°42E 47 F2
Addis Abeba Ethiopia 9°2N 38°42E 47 F2
Addison U.S.A. 42°1N 77°14W 82 D7
Addo S. Africa 33°32S 25°45E 56 E4
Addo △ S. Africa 33°30S 25°50E 56 E4
Ādeh Iran 37°42N 45°11E 44 B5
Adel U.S.A. 31°8N 83°25W 85 F13
Adelaide Australia 34°52S 138°30E 63 E2
Adelaide S. Africa 32°42S 26°20E 56 E4
Adelaide I. Antarctica 67°15S 68°30W 5 C17
Adelaide Pen. Canada 68°15N 97°30W 68 C10
Adelaide River Australia 13°15S 131°7E 60 B5
Adelaide Village Bahamas 25°0N 77°31W 88 A4
Adelanto U.S.A. 34°35N 117°22W 79 L9
Adele I. Australia 15°32S 123°9E 60 C3
Adélie, Terre Antarctica 68°0S 140°0E 5 C10
Adelie Land = Adélie, Terre Antarctica 68°0S 140°0E 5 C10
Aden = Al 'Adan Yemen 12°45N 45°0E 47 E4
Aden, G. of Ind. Oc. 12°30N 47°30E 47 E4
Adendorp S. Africa 32°15S 24°30E 56 E3
Adh Dhayd U.A.E. 25°17N 55°53E 45 E7
Adhoi India 23°26N 70°32E 42 H4
Adi Indonesia 4°15S 133°30E 37 E8
Adieu, C. Australia 32°0S 132°10E 61 F5
Adieu Pt. Australia 15°14S 124°35E 60 C3
Adige → Italy 45°9N 12°20E 22 B5
Adigrat Ethiopia 14°20N 39°26E 47 E2
Adilabad India 19°33N 78°20E 40 K11
Adirondack ⌂ U.S.A. 44°0N 74°20W 83 C10
Adirondack Mts. U.S.A. 44°0N 74°0W 83 C10
Adis Abeba = Addis Abeba Ethiopia 9°2N 38°42E 47 F2
Adjumani Uganda 3°20N 31°50E 54 B3
Adjuntas Puerto Rico 18°10N 66°43W 89 d
Adlavik Is. Canada 55°0N 58°40W 73 B8
Admiralty G. Australia 14°20S 125°55E 60 B4
Admiralty I. U.S.A. 57°30N 134°30W 70 B2
Admiralty Is. Papua N. G. 2°0S 147°0E 58 B7
Adolfo González Chaves Argentina 38°2S 60°5W 94 D3
Adolfo Ruiz Cortines, Presa Mexico 27°15N 109°6W 86 B3
Adonara Indonesia 8°15S 123°5E 37 F6
Adoni India 15°33N 77°18E 40 M10
Adour → France 43°32N 1°32W 20 E3
Adra India 23°30N 86°42E 43 H12
Adra Spain 36°43N 3°3W 21 D4
Adrano Italy 37°40N 14°50E 22 F6
Adrar Algeria 27°51N 0°11E 50 C6
Adrar Mauritania 20°30N 7°30W 50 D3
Adrar des Iforas Africa 19°40N 1°40E 50 E6
Adrian Mich., U.S.A. 41°54N 84°2W 81 E11
Adrian Tex., U.S.A. 35°16N 102°40W 84 D3
Adriatic Sea Medit. S. 43°0N 16°0E 22 C6
Adua Indonesia 1°45S 129°50E 37 E7
Adwa Ethiopia 14°15N 38°52E 47 E2
Adygea □ Russia 45°0N 40°0E 19 F7
Adzhar Republic = Ajaria □ Georgia 41°30N 42°0E 19 F7
Adzopé Ivory C. 6°7N 3°49W 50 G5
Ægean Sea Medit. S. 38°30N 25°0E 23 E11
Aerhtai Shan Mongolia 46°40N 92°45E 32 B4
Afaahiti Tahiti 17°45S 149°17W 59 d
'Afak Iraq 32°4N 45°15E 44 C5
Afandou Greece 36°18N 28°12E 25 C10
Afareaitu Moorea 17°33S 149°47W 59 d
Afghanistan ■ Asia 33°0N 65°0E 40 C4
Aflou Algeria 34°7N 2°3E 50 B6
Africa 10°0N 20°0E 48 E6
'Afrīn Syria 36°32N 36°50E 44 B3
Afton N.Y., U.S.A. 42°14N 75°32W 83 D9
Afton Wyo., U.S.A. 42°44N 110°56W 76 E8
Afuá Brazil 0°15S 50°20W 93 D8
'Afula Israel 32°37N 35°17E 46 C4
Afyon Turkey 38°45N 30°33E 19 G5
Afyonkarahisar = Afyon Turkey 38°45N 30°33E 19 G5
Āgā Jarī Iran 30°42N 49°50E 45 D6
Agadès = Agadez Niger 16°58N 7°59E 50 E7
Agadez Niger 16°58N 7°59E 50 E7
Agadir Morocco 30°28N 9°55W 50 B4
Agaete Canary Is. 28°6N 15°43W 24 F4
Agalega Is. Mauritius 11°0S 57°0E 3 E12
Agar India 23°40N 76°2E 42 H7
Agartala India 23°50N 91°23E 41 H17
Agassiz Canada 49°14N 121°46W 70 D4
Agats Indonesia 5°33S 138°0E 37 F9
Agawam U.S.A. 42°5N 72°37W 83 D12
Agboville Ivory C. 5°55N 4°15W 50 G5
Ağdam Azerbaijan 40°0N 46°58E 44 B5
Agde France 43°19N 3°28E 20 E5
Agen France 44°12N 0°38E 20 D4
Āgh Kand Iran 37°15N 48°4E 45 B6
Aghia Deka Greece 35°3N 24°58E 25 D6
Aghia Ekaterinis, Akra Greece 39°50N 19°50E 25 A3
Aghia Galini Greece 35°6N 24°41E 25 D6
Aghia Varvara Greece 35°8N 25°1E 25 D7
Aghios Efstratios Greece 39°34N 24°58E 23 E11
Aghios Ioannis, Akra Greece 35°20N 25°40E 25 D7
Aghios Isidoros Greece 36°9N 27°51E 25 C9
Aghios Matheos Greece 39°30N 19°47E 25 B3
Aghios Nikolaos Greece 35°11N 25°41E 25 D7
Aghios Stephanos Greece 39°46N 19°39E 25 A3
Aghiou Orous, Kolpos Greece 40°6N 24°0E 23 D11
Aginskoye Russia 51°6N 114°32E 29 D12
Agnew Australia 28°1S 120°31E 61 E3
Agori India 24°33N 82°57E 43 G10
Agra India 27°17N 77°58E 42 F7
Ağri Turkey 39°44N 43°3E 19 G7
Agri → Italy 40°13N 16°44E 22 D7
Ağrı Dağı Turkey 39°50N 44°15E 44 B5
Ağri Karakose = Ağri Turkey 39°44N 43°3E 19 G7
Agrigento Italy 37°19N 13°34E 22 F5
Agrinio Greece 38°37N 21°27E 23 E9
Agua Caliente Mexico 32°29N 116°59W 79 N10
Agua Caliente Springs U.S.A. 32°56N 116°19W 79 N10
Água Clara Brazil 20°25S 52°45W 93 H8
Agua Fria ⌂ U.S.A. 34°14N 112°0W 77 J8
Agua Hechicera Mexico 32°28N 116°15W 79 N10
Agua Prieta Mexico 31°18N 109°34W 86 A3
Aguadilla Puerto Rico 18°26N 67°10W 89 d
Aguadulce Panama 8°15N 80°32W 88 E3
Aguanga U.S.A. 33°27N 116°51W 79 M10
Aguanish Canada 50°14N 62°2W 73 B7
Aguanish → Canada 50°13N 62°5W 73 B7
Aguapey → Argentina 29°7S 56°36W 94 B4
Aguaray Guazú → Paraguay 24°47S 57°19W 94 A4
Aguarico → Ecuador 0°59S 75°11W 92 D3
Aguaro-Guariquito △ Venezuela 8°20N 66°35W 89 E6
Aguas Blancas Chile 24°15S 69°55W 94 A2
Aguas Calientes, Sierra de Argentina 25°26S 66°40W 94 B2
Aguascalientes Mexico 21°53N 102°18W 86 C4
Aguascalientes □ Mexico 22°0N 102°20W 86 C4
Aguila, Punta Puerto Rico 17°57N 67°13W 89 d
Aguilares Argentina 27°26S 65°35W 94 B2
Águilas Spain 37°23N 1°35W 21 D5
Agüimes Canary Is. 27°58N 15°27W 24 G4
Aguja, C. de la Colombia 11°18N 74°12W 90 B3
Agujereada, Pta. Puerto Rico 18°30N 67°8W 89 d
Agulhas, C. S. Africa 34°52S 20°0E 56 E3
Agulo Canary Is. 28°11N 17°12W 24 F2
Agung, Gunung Indonesia 8°20S 115°28E 37 J18
Agur Uganda 2°28N 32°55E 54 B3
Agusan → Phil. 9°0N 125°30E 37 C7
Aha Mts. Botswana 19°45S 21°0E 56 B3
Ahaggar Algeria 23°0N 6°30E 50 D7
Ahar Iran 38°35N 47°0E 44 B5
Ahipara B. N.Z. 35°5S 173°5E 59 A4
Ahiri India 19°30N 80°0E 40 K12
Ahmad Wal Pakistan 29°18N 65°58E 42 E1
Ahmadabad India 23°0N 72°40E 42 H5
Aḩmadābād Khorāsān, Iran 35°3N 60°50E 45 C9
Aḩmadābād Khorāsān, Iran 35°49N 59°42E 45 C8
Aḩmadī Iran 27°56N 56°42E 45 E8
Ahmadnagar India 19°7N 74°46E 40 K9
Ahmadpur East Pakistan 29°12N 71°10E 42 E4
Ahmadpur Lamma Pakistan 28°19N 70°3E 42 E4
Ahmedabad = Ahmadabad India 23°0N 72°40E 42 H5
Ahmednagar = Ahmadnagar India 19°7N 74°46E 40 K9
Ahome Mexico 25°55N 109°11W 86 B3
Ahoskie U.S.A. 36°17N 76°59W 85 C16
Ahram Iran 28°52N 51°16E 45 D6
Ahrax Pt. Malta 36°0N 14°22E 25 D1
Ahuachapán El Salv. 13°54N 89°52W 88 D2
Ahvāz Iran 31°20N 48°40E 45 D6
Ahvenanmaa = Åland Finland 60°15N 20°0E 9 F19
Aḩwar Yemen 13°30N 46°40E 47 E4
Ai → India 26°26N 90°44E 43 F14
Ai-Ais Namibia 27°54S 17°59E 56 D2
Ai-Ais and Fish River Canyon △ Namibia 24°45S 17°15E 56 C2
Aichi □ Japan 35°0N 137°15E 31 G8
Aigrettes, Pte. des Réunion 21°3S 55°13E 53 c
Aiguá Uruguay 34°13S 54°46W 95 C5
Aigues-Mortes France 43°35N 4°12E 20 E6
Aihui = Heihe China 50°10N 127°30E 33 A7
Aija Peru 9°50S 77°45W 92 E3
Aikawa Japan 38°2N 138°15E 30 E9
Aiken U.S.A. 33°34N 81°43W 85 E14
Aileron Australia 22°39S 133°20E 62 C1
Aillik Canada 55°11N 59°18W 73 A8
Ailsa Craig Canada 43°8N 81°33W 82 C3
Ailsa Craig U.K. 55°15N 5°6W 11 F3
Aim Russia 59°0N 133°55E 29 D14
Aimere Indonesia 8°45S 121°3E 37 F6
Aimogasta Argentina 28°33S 66°50W 94 B2
Aïn Ben Tili Mauritania 25°59N 9°27W 50 C4
Aïn Sefra Algeria 32°47N 0°37W 50 B5
Ain Sudr Egypt 29°50N 33°6E 46 F2
Aïn Témouchent Algeria 35°16N 1°8W 50 A5
Ainaži Latvia 57°50N 24°24E 9 H21
Ainsworth U.S.A. 42°33N 99°52W 80 D4
Aiquile Bolivia 18°10S 65°10W 92 G5
Aïr Niger 18°30N 8°0E 50 E7
Air Force I. Canada 67°58N 74°5W 69 C12
Air Hitam Malaysia 1°55N 103°11E 39 M4
Airdrie Canada 51°18N 114°2W 70 C6
Airdrie U.K. 55°52N 3°57W 11 F5
Aire → U.K. 53°43N 0°55W 12 D7
Aire, I. de l' Spain 39°48N 4°16E 24 B11
Airlie Beach Australia 20°16S 148°43E 62 J6
Aisne → France 49°26N 2°50E 20 B5
Ait India 25°54N 79°14E 43 G8
Aitkin U.S.A. 46°32N 93°42W 80 B7
Aitutaki Cook Is. 18°52S 159°45W 65 J12
Aiud Romania 46°19N 23°44E 17 E12
Aix-en-Provence France 43°32N 5°27E 20 E6
Aix-la-Chapelle = Aachen Germany 50°45N 6°6E 16 C4
Aix-les-Bains France 45°41N 5°53E 20 D6
Aizawl India 23°40N 92°44E 41 H18
Aizkraukle Latvia 56°36N 25°11E 9 H21
Aizpute Latvia 56°43N 21°40E 9 H19
Aizuwakamatsu Japan 37°30N 139°56E 30 F9
Ajaccio France 41°55N 8°40E 20 F8
Ajai ⌂ Uganda 2°52N 31°16E 54 B3
Ajaigarh India 24°52N 80°16E 43 G9
Ajalpan Mexico 18°22N 97°15W 87 D5
Ajanta Ra. India 20°28N 75°50E 40 J9
Ajari Rep. = Ajaria □ Georgia 41°30N 42°0E 19 F7
Ajaria □ Georgia 41°30N 42°0E 19 F7
Ajax Canada 43°50N 79°1W 82 C5
Ajdābiyā Libya 30°54N 20°4E 51 B10
Ajka Hungary 47°4N 17°31E 17 E9
'Ajlūn Jordan 32°18N 35°47E 46 C4
'Ajlūn □ Jordan 32°18N 35°47E 46 C4
'Ajmān U.A.E. 25°25N 55°30E 45 E7
Ajmer India 26°28N 74°37E 42 F6
Ajnala India 31°50N 74°48E 42 D6
Ajo U.S.A. 32°22N 112°52W 77 K7
Ajo, C. de Spain 43°31N 3°35W 21 A4
Akabira Japan 43°33N 142°5E 30 C11
Akagera △ Rwanda 1°31S 30°33E 54 C3
Akamas Cyprus 35°3N 32°18E 25 D11
Akan △ Japan 43°20N 144°20E 30 C12
Akanthou Cyprus 35°22N 33°45E 25 D12
Akaroa N.Z. 43°49S 172°59E 59 E4
Akashi Japan 34°45N 134°58E 31 G7
Akbarpur Bihar, India 24°39N 83°58E 43 G10
Akbarpur Ut. P., India 26°25N 82°32E 43 F10
Akçakale Turkey 36°41N 38°56E 44 B3
Akdoğan = Lysi Cyprus 35°6N 33°41E 25 D12
Akelamo Indonesia 1°35N 129°40E 37 D7
Aketi Dem. Rep. of the Congo 2°38N 23°47E 52 D4
Akhisar Turkey 38°56N 27°48E 23 E12
Akhnur India 32°52N 74°45E 43 C6
Akhtyrka = Okhtyrka Ukraine 50°25N 35°0E 19 D5
Aki Japan 33°30N 133°54E 31 H6
Akimiski I. Canada 52°50N 81°30W 72 B3
Akincilar = Louroujina Cyprus 35°0N 33°28E 25 E12
Akita Japan 39°45N 140°7E 30 E10
Akita □ Japan 39°40N 140°30E 30 E10
Akjoujt Mauritania 19°45N 14°15W 50 E3
Akkeshi Japan 43°2N 144°51E 30 C12
'Akko Israel 32°55N 35°4E 46 C4
Aklavik Canada 68°12N 135°0W 68 C6
Aklera India 24°26N 76°32E 42 G7
Akō Japan 34°45N 134°24E 31 G7
Akola India 20°42N 77°2E 40 J10
Akordat Eritrea 15°30N 37°40E 47 D2
Akpatok I. Canada 60°25N 68°8W 69 C13
Åkrahamn Norway 59°15N 5°10E 9 G11
Akranes Iceland 64°19N 22°5W 8 D2
Akron Colo., U.S.A. 40°10N 103°13W 76 F12
Akron Ohio, U.S.A. 41°5N 81°31W 82 E3
Akrotiri Cyprus 34°36N 32°57E 25 E11
Akrotiri Bay Cyprus 34°35N 33°10E 25 E12
Aksai Chin China 35°15N 79°55E 43 B8
Aksaray Turkey 38°25N 34°2E 44 B2
Aksay = Aqsay Kazakhstan 51°11N 53°0E 19 D9
Akşehir Turkey 38°18N 31°30E 44 B1
Akşehir Gölü Turkey 38°30N 31°25E 19 G5
Aksu China 41°5N 80°10E 32 B3
Aksum Ethiopia 14°5N 38°40E 47 E2
Aktsyabrski Belarus 52°38N 28°53E 17 B15
Aktyubinsk = Aqtöbe Kazakhstan 50°17N 57°10E 19 D10
Akure Nigeria 7°15N 5°5E 50 G7
Akureyri Iceland 65°40N 18°6W 8 D4
Akuseki-Shima Japan 29°27N 129°37E 31 K4
Akyab = Sittwe Burma 20°18N 92°45E 41 J18
Al 'Adan Yemen 12°45N 45°0E 47 E4
Al Aḩsā = Hasa Si. Arabia 25°50N 49°0E 45 E6
Al Ajfar Si. Arabia 27°26N 43°0E 44 E4
Al Amādīyah Iraq 37°5N 43°30E 44 B4
Al 'Amārah Iraq 31°55N 47°15E 44 D5
Al Anbār □ Iraq 33°25N 42°0E 44 C4
Al 'Aqabah Jordan 29°31N 35°0E 46 F4
Al 'Aqabah □ Jordan 29°30N 35°0E 46 F4
Al Arak Syria 34°38N 38°35E 44 C3
Al 'Aramah Si. Arabia 25°30N 46°0E 44 E5
Al 'Arţāwīyah Si. Arabia 26°31N 45°20E 44 E5
Al 'Āşimah = 'Ammān □ Jordan 31°40N 36°30E 46 D5
Al 'Assāfīyah Si. Arabia 28°17N 38°59E 44 D3
Al 'Awdah Si. Arabia 25°32N 45°41E 44 E5
Al 'Ayn Si. Arabia 25°4N 38°6E 44 E3
Al 'Ayn U.A.E. 24°15N 55°45E 45 E7
Al 'Azīzīyah Iraq 32°54N 45°4E 44 C5
Al Bāb Syria 36°23N 37°29E 44 B3
Al Bad' Si. Arabia 28°28N 35°1E 44 D2
Al Bādī Iraq 35°56N 41°32E 44 C4
Al Baḩrah Kuwait 29°40N 47°52E 44 D5
Al Baḩral Mayyit = Dead Sea Asia 31°30N 35°30E 46 D4
Al Balqā' □ Jordan 32°5N 35°45E 46 C4
Al Bārūk, J. Lebanon 33°39N 35°40E 46 B4
Al Başrah Iraq 30°30N 47°50E 44 D5
Al Baţḩā Iraq 31°6N 45°53E 44 D5
Al Batrūn Lebanon 34°15N 35°40E 46 A4
Al Bayḑā Libya 32°50N 21°44E 51 B10
Al Biqā Lebanon 34°10N 36°10E 46 A5
Al Bi'r Si. Arabia 28°51N 36°16E 44 D3
Al Bukayrīyah Si. Arabia 26°9N 43°40E 44 E4
Al Burayj Syria 34°15N 36°46E 46 A5
Al Faḑilī Si. Arabia 26°58N 49°10E 45 E6
Al Fallūjah Iraq 33°20N 43°55E 44 C4
Al Fāw Iraq 30°0N 48°30E 45 D6
Al Fujayrah U.A.E. 25°7N 56°18E 45 E8
Al Ghadaf, W. → Jordan 31°26N 36°43E 46 D5
Al Ghammās Iraq 31°45N 44°37E 44 D5
Al Ghazālah Si. Arabia 26°48N 41°19E 44 E4

Al Ḥadīthah *Iraq* 34°0N 41°13E **44 C4**
Al Ḥadīthah *Si. Arabia* 31°28N 37°8E **46 D6**
Al Ḥaḍr *Iraq* 35°35N 42°44E **44 C4**
Al Ḥājānah *Syria* 33°20N 36°33E **46 B5**
Al Ḥajar al Gharbī *Oman* 24°10N 56°15E **45 E8**
Al Ḥamad *Si. Arabia* 31°30N 39°30E **44 D3**
Al Ḥamdānīyah *Syria* 35°25N 36°50E **44 C3**
Al Ḥamīdīyah *Syria* 34°42N 35°57E **46 A4**
Al Ḥammār *Iraq* 30°57N 46°51E **44 D5**
Al Ḥamrā' *Si. Arabia* 24°2N 38°55E **44 E3**
Al Ḥamzah *Iraq* 31°43N 44°58E **44 D5**
Al Ḥanākīyah *Si. Arabia* 24°51N 40°31E **44 E4**
Al Ḥarūj al Aswad *Libya* 27°0N 17°10E **51 C9**
Al Ḥasakah *Syria* 36°35N 40°45E **44 B4**
Al Ḥayy *Iraq* 32°5N 46°5E **44 C5**
Al Ḥijarah *Asia* 30°0N 44°0E **44 D4**
Al Ḥillah *Iraq* 32°30N 44°25E **44 C5**
Al Ḥillah *Si. Arabia* 23°35N 46°50E **47 B4**
Al Ḥindīyah *Iraq* 32°30N 44°10E **44 C5**
Al Ḥirmil *Lebanon* 34°26N 36°24E **46 A5**
Al Hoceïma *Morocco* 35°8N 3°58W **50 A5**
Al Ḥudaydah *Yemen* 14°50N 43°0E **47 E3**
Al Ḥudūd ash Shamālīyah □
  Si. Arabia 29°10N 42°30E **44 D4**
Al Ḥufūf *Si. Arabia* 25°25N 49°45E **45 E6**
Al Ḥumaydah *Si. Arabia* 29°14N 34°56E **44 D2**
Al Ḥunayy *Si. Arabia* 25°58N 48°45E **45 E6**
Al Īsāwīyah *Si. Arabia* 30°43N 37°59E **44 D3**
Al Jafr *Jordan* 30°18N 36°14E **46 E5**
Al Jāfūrah *Si. Arabia* 25°0N 50°15E **45 E7**
Al Jaghbūb *Libya* 29°42N 24°38E **51 C10**
Al Jahrah *Kuwait* 29°25N 47°40E **44 D5**
Al Jalāmīd *Si. Arabia* 31°20N 40°6E **44 D3**
Al Jamalīyah *Qatar* 25°37N 51°5E **45 E6**
Al Janūb □ *Lebanon* 33°20N 35°20E **46 B4**
Al Jawf *Libya* 24°10N 23°24E **51 D10**
Al Jawf *Si. Arabia* 29°55N 39°40E **44 D3**
Al Jawf □ *Si. Arabia* 29°30N 39°30E **44 D3**
Al Jazair = Algeria ■
  Africa 28°30N 2°0E **50 C6**
Al Jazirah *Iraq* 33°30N 44°0E **44 C5**
Al Jithāmīyah *Si. Arabia* 27°41N 41°43E **44 E4**
Al Jubayl *Si. Arabia* 27°0N 49°50E **45 E6**
Al Jubaylah *Si. Arabia* 24°55N 46°25E **44 E5**
Al Jubb *Si. Arabia* 27°11N 42°17E **44 E4**
Al Junaynah *Sudan* 13°27N 22°45E **51 F10**
Al Kabā'ish *Iraq* 30°58N 47°0E **44 D5**
Al Karak *Jordan* 31°11N 35°42E **46 D4**
Al Karak □ *Jordan* 31°0N 36°0E **46 E5**
Al Kāẓimīyah *Iraq* 33°22N 44°18E **44 C5**
Al Khābūrah *Oman* 23°57N 57°5E **45 F8**
Al Khafjī *Si. Arabia* 28°24N 48°29E **45 E6**
Al Khalīl *West Bank* 31°32N 35°6E **46 D4**
Al Khāliṣ *Iraq* 33°49N 44°32E **44 C5**
Al Kharsānīyah
  Si. Arabia 27°13N 49°18E **45 E6**
Al Khaṣab *Oman* 26°14N 56°15E **45 E8**
Al Khawr *Qatar* 25°41N 51°30E **45 E6**
Al Khiḍr *Iraq* 31°12N 45°33E **44 D5**
Al Khiyām *Lebanon* 33°20N 35°36E **46 B4**
Al Khobar *Si. Arabia* 26°17N 50°12E **45 E6**
Al Khums *Libya* 32°40N 14°17E **51 B8**
Al Kiswah *Syria* 33°23N 36°14E **46 B5**
Al Kūfah *Iraq* 32°2N 44°24E **44 C5**
Al Kufrah *Libya* 24°17N 23°15E **51 D10**
Al Kuhayfiyah *Si. Arabia* 27°12N 43°3E **44 E4**
Al Kūt *Iraq* 32°30N 46°0E **44 C5**
Al Kuwayt *Kuwait* 29°30N 48°0E **44 D5**
Al Labwah *Lebanon* 34°11N 36°20E **46 A5**
Al Lādhiqīyah *Syria* 35°30N 35°45E **44 C2**
Al Līth *Si. Arabia* 20°9N 40°15E **47 C3**
Al Liwā' *Oman* 24°31N 56°36E **45 E8**
Al Luḥayyah *Yemen* 15°45N 42°40E **47 D3**
Al Madīnah *Iraq* 30°57N 47°16E **44 D5**
Al Madīnah *Si. Arabia* 24°35N 39°52E **44 E3**
Al Mafraq *Jordan* 32°17N 36°14E **46 C5**
Al Mafraq □ *Jordan* 32°17N 36°15E **46 C5**
Al Maghreb = Morocco ■
  N. Afr. 32°0N 5°50W **50 B4**
Al Maḥmūdīyah *Iraq* 33°3N 44°21E **44 C5**
Al Majma'ah *Si. Arabia* 25°57N 45°22E **44 E5**
Al Makhruq, W. →
  Jordan 31°28N 37°0E **46 D6**
Al Makhūl *Si. Arabia* 26°37N 42°39E **44 E4**
Al Manāmah *Bahrain* 26°10N 50°30E **45 E6**
Al Maqwa' *Kuwait* 29°10N 47°59E **44 D5**
Al Marāḥ *Si. Arabia* 25°3N 49°35E **45 E6**
Al Marj *Libya* 32°25N 20°30E **51 B10**
Al Maṭlā *Kuwait* 29°24N 47°40E **44 D5**
Al Mawṣil *Iraq* 36°15N 43°5E **44 B4**
Al Mayādin *Syria* 35°1N 40°27E **44 C4**
Al Mazār *Jordan* 31°4N 35°41E **46 D4**
Al Midhnab *Si. Arabia* 25°50N 44°18E **44 E5**
Al Minā' *Lebanon* 34°24N 35°49E **46 A4**
Al Miqdādīyah *Iraq* 34°0N 45°0E **44 C5**
Al Mubarraz *Si. Arabia* 25°30N 49°40E **45 E6**
Al Mudawwarah *Jordan* 29°19N 36°0E **46 F5**
Al Mughayrā' *U.A.E.* 24°5N 53°32E **45 E7**
Al Muharraq *Bahrain* 26°15N 50°40E **45 E6**
Al Mukallā *Yemen* 14°33N 49°2E **47 E4**
Al Mukhā *Yemen* 13°18N 43°15E **47 E3**
Al Musayjid *Si. Arabia* 24°5N 39°5E **44 E3**
Al Musayyib *Iraq* 32°49N 44°20E **44 C5**
Al Muthannā □ *Iraq* 30°30N 45°15E **44 D5**
Al Muwayliḥ *Si. Arabia* 27°40N 35°30E **44 E2**
Al Qādisīyah □ *Iraq* 32°0N 45°0E **44 D5**
Al Qā'im *Iraq* 34°21N 41°7E **44 C4**
Al Qalībah *Si. Arabia* 28°24N 37°42E **44 D3**
Al Qāmishlī *Syria* 37°2N 41°14E **44 B4**
Al Qaryatayn *Syria* 34°12N 37°13E **46 A6**
Al Qaṣīm □ *Si. Arabia* 26°0N 43°0E **44 E4**
Al Qaṭ'a *Syria* 34°40N 40°48E **44 C4**
Al Qaṭif *Si. Arabia* 26°35N 50°0E **45 E6**
Al Qaṭrūn *Libya* 24°56N 15°3E **51 D9**
Al Qayṣūmah *Si. Arabia* 28°20N 46°7E **44 D5**
Al Quds = Jerusalem
  Israel/West Bank 31°47N 35°10E **46 D4**

Al Qunayṭirah *Syria* 32°55N 35°45E **46 C4**
Al Qunfudhah *Si. Arabia* 19°3N 41°4E **47 D3**
Al Qurnah *Iraq* 31°1N 47°25E **44 D5**
Al Quṣayr *Iraq* 30°39N 45°50E **44 D5**
Al Quṣayr *Syria* 34°31N 36°34E **46 A5**
Al Qutayfah *Syria* 33°44N 36°36E **46 B5**
Al 'Ubaylah *Si. Arabia* 21°59N 50°57E **47 C5**
Al 'Uḍaylīyah *Si. Arabia* 25°8N 49°18E **45 E6**
Al 'Ulā *Si. Arabia* 26°35N 38°0E **44 E3**
Al 'Uqayr *Si. Arabia* 25°40N 50°15E **45 E6**
Al 'Uwaynid *Si. Arabia* 24°50N 46°0E **44 E5**
Al 'Uwayqīlah *Si. Arabia* 30°30N 42°10E **44 D4**
Al 'Uyūn *Ḥijāz, Si. Arabia* 24°33N 39°35E **44 E3**
Al 'Uyūn *Najd, Si. Arabia* 26°30N 43°50E **44 E4**
Al 'Uzayr *Iraq* 31°19N 47°25E **44 D5**
Al Wajh *Si. Arabia* 26°10N 36°30E **44 E3**
Al Wakrah *Qatar* 25°10N 51°40E **45 E6**
Al Waqbah *Si. Arabia* 28°48N 45°33E **44 D5**
Al Wari'āh *Si. Arabia* 27°51N 47°25E **44 E5**
Al Yaman = Yemen ■
  Asia 15°0N 44°0E **47 E3**
Ala Dağ *Turkey* 37°44N 35°9E **44 B2**
Ala Tau *Asia* 45°30N 80°40E **28 E9**
Ala Tau Shankou = Dzungarian
  Gate *Asia* 45°10N 82°0E **32 B3**
Alabama □ *U.S.A.* 33°0N 87°0W **85 E11**
Alabama → *U.S.A.* 31°8N 87°57W **85 F11**
Alabaster *U.S.A.* 33°15N 86°49W **85 E11**
Alaçam Dağları *Turkey* 39°18N 28°49E **23 E13**
Alacant = Alicante *Spain* 38°23N 0°30W **21 C5**
Alachua *U.S.A.* 29°47N 82°30W **85 G13**
Alagoa Grande *Brazil* 7°3S 35°35W **93 E11**
Alagoas □ *Brazil* 9°0S 36°0W **93 E11**
Alagoinhas *Brazil* 12°7S 38°20W **93 F11**
Alaior *Spain* 39°57N 4°8E **24 B11**
Alajero *Canary Is.* 28°3N 17°13W **24 F2**
Alajuela *Costa Rica* 10°2N 84°8W **88 D3**
Alakamisy *Madag.* 21°19S 47°14E **57 C8**
Alaknanda → *India* 30°8N 78°36E **43 D8**
Alakurtti *Russia* 66°58N 30°25E **8 C24**
Alamarvdasht *Iran* 27°37N 52°59E **45 E7**
Alameda *Calif., U.S.A.* 37°46N 122°15W **78 H4**
Alameda *N. Mex.,*
  U.S.A. 35°11N 106°37W **77 J10**
Alamo *U.S.A.* 37°22N 115°10W **79 H11**
Alamogordo *U.S.A.* 32°54N 105°57W **77 K11**
Alamos *Mexico* 27°1N 108°56W **86 B3**
Alamosa *U.S.A.* 37°28N 105°52W **77 H11**
Åland *Finland* 60°15N 20°0E **9 F19**
Ålands hav *Europe* 60°0N 19°30E **9 G18**
Alania = North Ossetia □
  Russia 43°30N 44°30E **19 F7**
Alanya *Turkey* 36°38N 32°0E **44 B1**
Alaotra, Farihin' *Madag.* 17°30S 48°30E **57 B8**
Alapayevsk *Russia* 57°52N 61°42E **28 D7**
Alappuzha = Alleppey
  India 9°30N 76°28E **40 Q10**
Alaró *Spain* 39°42N 2°47E **24 B9**
Alarobia-Vohiposa
  Madag. 20°59S 47°9E **57 C8**
Alaşehir *Turkey* 38°23N 28°30E **23 E13**
Alaska □ *U.S.A.* 64°0N 154°0W **74 a**
Alaska, G. of *Pac. Oc.* 58°0N 145°0W **74 a**
Alaska Peninsula *U.S.A.* 56°0N 159°0W **74 a**
Alaska Range *U.S.A.* 62°50N 151°0W **74 a**
Älät *Azerbaijan* 39°58N 49°25E **45 B6**
Alatau Shan = Ala Tau
  Asia 45°30N 80°40E **28 E9**
Alatyr *Russia* 54°55N 46°35E **18 D8**
Alausi *Ecuador* 2°0S 78°50W **92 D3**
Alava, C. *U.S.A.* 48°10N 124°44W **76 B1**
Alavo = Alavus *Finland* 62°35N 23°36E **8 E20**
Alavus *Finland* 62°35N 23°36E **8 E20**
Alawoona *Australia* 34°45S 140°30E **63 E3**
'Alayh *Lebanon* 33°46N 35°33E **46 B4**
Alba *Italy* 44°42N 8°2E **20 D8**
Alba-Iulia *Romania* 46°8N 23°39E **17 E12**
Albacete *Spain* 39°0N 1°50W **21 C5**
Albacutya, L. *Australia* 35°45S 141°58E **63 F3**
Albanel, L. *Canada* 50°55N 73°12W **72 B5**
Albania ■ *Europe* 41°0N 20°0E **23 D9**
Albany *Australia* 35°1S 117°58E **61 G2**
Albany *Ga., U.S.A.* 31°35N 84°10W **85 F12**
Albany *N.Y., U.S.A.* 42°39N 73°45W **83 D11**
Albany *Oreg., U.S.A.* 44°38N 123°6W **76 D2**
Albany *Tex., U.S.A.* 32°44N 99°18W **84 E5**
Albany → *Canada* 52°17N 81°31W **72 B3**
Albarca, C. d' *Spain* 39°4N 1°22E **24 B7**
Albardón *Argentina* 31°20S 68°30W **94 C2**
Albatross B. *Australia* 12°45S 141°30E **62 A3**
Albemarle *U.S.A.* 35°21N 80°12W **85 D14**
Albemarle Sd. *U.S.A.* 36°5N 76°0W **85 C16**
Alberche → *Spain* 39°58N 4°46W **21 C3**
Alberdi *Paraguay* 26°14S 58°20W **94 B4**
Alberga → *Australia* 27°6S 135°33E **63 D2**
Albert, L. *Africa* 1°30N 31°0E **54 B3**
Albert, L. *Australia* 35°30S 139°10E **63 F2**
Albert Edward Ra.
  Australia 18°17S 127°57E **60 C4**
Albert Nile → *Uganda* 3°36N 32°2E **54 B3**
Albert Town *Bahamas* 22°37N 74°33W **89 B5**
Alberta □ *Canada* 54°40N 115°0W **70 C6**
Alberti *Argentina* 35°1S 60°16W **94 D3**
Albertinia *S. Africa* 34°11S 21°34E **56 E3**
Alberton *Canada* 46°50N 64°0W **73 C7**
Albertville *France* 45°40N 6°22E **20 D7**
Albertville *U.S.A.* 34°16N 86°13W **85 D11**
Albi *France* 43°56N 2°9E **20 E5**
Albia *U.S.A.* 41°2N 92°48W **80 E7**
Albina *Suriname* 5°37N 54°15W **93 B8**
Albina, Ponta *Angola* 15°52S 11°44E **56 B1**
Albion *Mich., U.S.A.* 42°15N 84°45W **81 D11**
Albion *Nebr., U.S.A.* 41°42N 98°0W **80 E4**
Albion *Pa., U.S.A.* 41°53N 80°22W **82 E4**
Alborán *Medit. S.* 35°57N 3°0W **21 E4**
Ålborg = Aalborg *Denmark* 57°2N 9°54E **9 H13**

Alborz, Reshteh-ye Kūhhā-ye
  Iran 36°0N 52°0E **45 C7**
Albufeira *Portugal* 37°5N 8°15W **21 D1**
Albuquerque *U.S.A.* 35°5N 106°39W **77 J10**
Albuquerque, Cayos de
  Caribbean 12°10N 81°50W **88 D3**
Alburg *U.S.A.* 44°59N 73°18W **83 B11**
Albury *Australia* 36°3S 146°56E **63 F4**
Alcalá de Henares *Spain* 40°28N 3°22W **21 B4**
Alcalá la Real *Spain* 37°27N 3°57W **21 D4**
Álcamo *Italy* 37°59N 12°55E **22 F5**
Alcañiz *Spain* 41°2N 0°8W **21 B5**
Alcântara *Brazil* 2°20S 44°30W **93 D10**
Alcántara, Embalse de
  Spain 39°44N 6°50W **21 C2**
Alcantarilla *Spain* 37°59N 1°12W **21 D5**
Alcaraz, Sierra de *Spain* 38°40N 2°20W **21 C4**
Alcaudete *Spain* 37°35N 4°5W **21 D3**
Alcázar de San Juan
  Spain 39°24N 3°12W **21 C4**
Alchevsk *Ukraine* 48°30N 38°45E **19 E6**
Alcira = Alzira *Spain* 39°9N 0°30W **21 C5**
Alcova *U.S.A.* 42°34N 106°43W **76 E10**
Alcoy *Spain* 38°43N 0°30W **21 C5**
Alcúdia *Spain* 39°51N 3°7E **24 B10**
Alcúdia, B. d' *Spain* 39°47N 3°15E **24 B10**
Aldabra Is. *Seychelles* 9°22S 46°28E **49 G8**
Aldama *Mexico* 22°55N 98°4W **87 C5**
Aldan *Russia* 58°40N 125°30E **29 D13**
Aldan → *Russia* 63°28N 129°35E **29 C13**
Aldea, Pta. de la
  Canary Is. 28°0N 15°50W **24 G4**
Aldeburgh *U.K.* 52°10N 1°37E **13 E9**
Alder Pk. *U.S.A.* 35°53N 121°22W **78 K5**
Alderney *U.K.* 49°42N 2°11W **13 H5**
Aldershot *U.K.* 51°15N 0°44W **13 F7**
Aledo *U.S.A.* 41°12N 90°45W **80 E8**
Aleg *Mauritania* 17°3N 13°55W **50 E3**
Alegranza *Canary Is.* 29°23N 13°32W **24 E6**
Alegranza, I. *Canary Is.* 29°23N 13°32W **24 E6**
Alegre *Brazil* 20°50S 41°30W **95 A7**
Alegrete *Brazil* 29°40S 56°0W **95 B4**
Aleksandriya = Oleksandriya
  Ukraine 50°37N 26°19E **17 C14**
Aleksandrov Gay *Russia* 50°9N 48°34E **19 D8**
Aleksandrovsk-Sakhalinskiy
  Russia 50°50N 142°20E **29 D15**
Aleksandry, Zemlya
  Russia 80°25N 48°0E **28 A5**
Além Paraíba *Brazil* 21°52S 42°41W **95 A7**
Alemania *Argentina* 25°40S 65°30W **94 B2**
Alemania *Chile* 25°10S 69°55W **94 B2**
Alençon *France* 48°27N 0°4E **20 B4**
Alenquer *Brazil* 1°56S 54°46W **93 D8**
'Alenuihāhā Channel
  U.S.A. 20°30N 156°0W **74 b**
Aleppo = Ḥalab *Syria* 36°10N 37°15E **44 B3**
Aléria *France* 42°5N 9°26E **20 E9**
Alert *Canada* 83°2N 60°0W **69 A13**
Alès *France* 44°9N 4°5E **20 D6**
Alessándria *Italy* 44°54N 8°37E **20 D8**
Ålesund *Norway* 62°28N 6°12E **8 E12**
Aleutian Basin *Pac. Oc.* 57°0N 177°0E **64 B9**
Aleutian Is. *Pac. Oc.* 52°0N 175°0W **74 a**
Aleutian Trench *Pac. Oc.* 48°0N 180°0E **4 D17**
Alexander *U.S.A.* 47°51N 103°39W **80 B2**
Alexander, Mt.
  Australia 28°58S 120°16E **61 E3**
Alexander Arch. *U.S.A.* 56°0N 136°0W **68 D6**
Alexander Bay *S. Africa* 28°40S 16°30E **56 D2**
Alexander City *U.S.A.* 32°56N 85°58E **85 E12**
Alexander I. *Antarctica* 69°0S 70°0W **5 C17**
Alexandra *Australia* 37°8S 145°40E **63 F4**
Alexandra *N.Z.* 45°14S 169°25E **59 F2**
Alexandra Falls *Canada* 60°29N 116°18W **70 A5**
Alexandria = El Iskandarîya
  Egypt 31°13N 29°58E **51 B11**
Alexandria *B.C.,*
  Canada 52°35N 122°27W **70 C4**
Alexandria *Ont.,*
  Canada 45°19N 74°38W **83 A10**
Alexandria *Romania* 43°57N 25°24E **17 G13**
Alexandria *S. Africa* 33°38S 26°28E **56 E4**
Alexandria *U.K.* 55°59N 4°35W **11 F4**
Alexandria *La., U.S.A.* 31°18N 92°27W **84 F8**
Alexandria *Minn.,*
  U.S.A. 45°53N 95°22W **80 C6**
Alexandria *S. Dak.,*
  U.S.A. 43°39N 97°47W **80 D5**
Alexandria *Va., U.S.A.* 38°49N 77°5W **81 F15**
Alexandria Bay *U.S.A.* 44°20N 75°55W **83 B9**
Alexandrina, L.
  Australia 35°25S 139°10E **63 F2**
Alexandroupoli *Greece* 40°50N 25°54E **23 D11**
Alexis → *Canada* 52°33N 56°8W **73 B8**
Alexis Creek *Canada* 52°10N 123°20W **70 C4**
Aleysk *Russia* 52°40N 83°0E **28 D9**
Alfabia *Spain* 39°44N 2°44E **24 B9**
Alfenas *Brazil* 21°20S 46°10W **95 A6**
Alford *Aberds., U.K.* 57°14N 2°41W **11 D6**
Alford *Lincs., U.K.* 53°15N 0°10E **12 D8**
Alfred *Maine, U.S.A.* 43°29N 70°43W **83 C14**
Alfred *N.Y., U.S.A.* 42°16N 77°48W **82 D7**
Alfreton *U.K.* 53°6N 1°24W **12 D6**
Algaida *Spain* 39°33N 2°53E **24 B9**
Ålgård *Norway* 58°46N 5°53E **9 G11**
Algarve *Portugal* 36°58N 8°20W **21 D1**
Algeciras *Spain* 36°9N 5°28W **21 D3**
Algemesí *Spain* 39°11N 0°27W **21 C5**
Alger *Algeria* 36°42N 3°8E **50 A6**
Algeria ■ *Africa* 28°30N 2°0E **50 C6**
Algha *Kazakhstan* 49°53N 57°20E **19 E10**
Alghero *Italy* 40°33N 8°19E **22 D3**
Algiers = Alger *Algeria* 36°42N 3°8E **50 A6**
Algoa B. *S. Africa* 33°50S 25°45E **56 E4**
Algoma *U.S.A.* 44°36N 87°26W **80 C10**
Algona *U.S.A.* 43°4N 94°14W **80 D6**

Algonac *U.S.A.* 42°37N 82°32W **82 D2**
Algonquin □ *Canada* 45°50N 78°30W **72 C4**
Aguarda *Uruguay* 32°25S 57°23W **96 C5**
Alhambra *U.S.A.* 34°5N 118°7W **79 L8**
Alhucemas = Al Hoceïma
  Morocco 35°8N 3°58W **50 A5**
'Alī al Gharbī *Iraq* 32°30N 46°45E **44 C5**
'Alī ash Sharqī *Iraq* 32°7N 46°44E **44 C5**
Äli Bayramlı *Azerbaijan* 39°59N 48°52E **45 B6**
'Alī Khēl *Afghan.* 33°57N 69°43E **42 C3**
Alī Shāh *Iran* 38°9N 45°50E **44 B5**
Alīābād *Iran* 36°40N 54°33E **45 B7**
'Alīābād *Khorāsān, Iran* 32°30N 57°30E **45 C8**
'Alīābād *Kordestān, Iran* 35°4N 46°58E **44 C5**
'Alīābād *Yazd, Iran* 31°41N 53°49E **45 D7**
Aliağa *Turkey* 38°47N 26°59E **23 E12**
Aliakmonas → *Greece* 40°30N 22°36E **23 D10**
Alicante *Spain* 38°23N 0°30W **21 C5**
Alice *S. Africa* 32°48S 26°55E **56 E4**
Alice *U.S.A.* 27°45N 98°5W **84 H5**
Alice → *Queens.,*
  Australia 24°2S 144°50E **62 C3**
Alice → *Queens.,*
  Australia 15°35S 142°20E **62 B3**
Alice Arm *Canada* 55°29N 129°31W **70 B3**
Alice Springs *Australia* 23°40S 133°50E **62 C1**
Alicedale *S. Africa* 33°15S 26°4E **56 E4**
Aliceville *U.S.A.* 33°8N 88°9W **85 E10**
Aliganj *India* 27°30N 79°10E **43 F8**
Aligarh *Raj., India* 25°55N 76°15E **42 G7**
Aligarh *Ut. P., India* 27°55N 78°10E **42 F8**
Alīgūdarz *Iran* 33°25N 49°45E **45 C6**
Alimia *Greece* 36°16N 27°43E **25 C9**
Alingsås *Sweden* 57°56N 12°31E **9 H15**
Alipur *Pakistan* 29°25N 70°55E **42 E4**
Alipur Duar *India* 26°30N 89°35E **41 F16**
Aliquippa *U.S.A.* 40°37N 80°15W **82 F4**
Alitus = Alytus *Lithuania* 54°24N 24°3E **9 J21**
Aliwal North *S. Africa* 30°45S 26°45E **56 E4**
Alix *Canada* 52°24N 113°11W **70 C6**
Aljustrel *Portugal* 37°55N 8°10W **21 D1**
Alkmaar *Neths.* 52°37N 4°45E **15 B4**
All American Canal
  U.S.A. 32°45N 115°15W **77 K6**
Allagash → *U.S.A.* 47°5N 69°3W **81 B19**
Allah Dad *Pakistan* 25°38N 67°34E **42 G2**
Allahabad *India* 25°25N 81°58E **43 G9**
Allan *Canada* 51°53N 106°4W **71 C7**
Allanridge *S. Africa* 27°45S 26°40E **56 D4**
Allegany *U.S.A.* 42°6N 78°30W **82 D6**
Allegheny → *U.S.A.* 40°27N 80°1W **82 F5**
Allegheny Mts. *U.S.A.* 38°15N 80°10W **81 F13**
Allegheny Plateau
  U.S.A. 41°30N 78°30W **81 E14**
Allegheny Res. *U.S.A.* 41°50N 79°0W **82 E6**
Allègre, Pte. *Guadeloupe* 16°22N 61°46W **88 b**
Allen, Bog of *Ireland* 53°15N 7°0W **10 C5**
Allen, L. *Ireland* 54°8N 8°4W **10 B3**
Allendale *U.S.A.* 33°1N 81°18W **85 E14**
Allende *Mexico* 28°20N 100°51W **86 B4**
Allentown *U.S.A.* 40°37N 75°29W **83 F9**
Alleppey *India* 9°30N 76°28E **40 Q10**
Aller → *Germany* 52°56N 9°12E **16 B5**
Alleynes B. *Barbados* 13°13N 59°39W **89 g**
Alliance *Nebr., U.S.A.* 42°6N 102°52W **80 D2**
Alliance *Ohio, U.S.A.* 40°55N 81°6E **82 F3**
Allier → *France* 46°57N 3°4E **20 C5**
Alliford Bay *Canada* 53°12N 131°58W **70 C2**
Alligator Pond *Jamaica* 17°52N 77°34W **88 a**
Alliston *Canada* 44°9N 79°52W **82 B5**
Alloa *U.K.* 56°7N 3°47W **11 E5**
Allora *Australia* 28°2S 152°0E **63 D5**
Alluitsup Paa *Greenland* 60°30N 45°35W **4 C5**
Alma *Canada* 48°35N 71°40W **73 C5**
Alma *Ga., U.S.A.* 31°33N 82°28W **85 F13**
Alma *Kans., U.S.A.* 39°1N 96°17W **80 F5**
Alma *Mich., U.S.A.* 43°23N 84°39W **81 D11**
Alma *Nebr., U.S.A.* 40°6N 99°22W **80 E4**
Alma *Wis., U.S.A.* 44°20N 91°55W **80 C8**
Alma Ata = Almaty
  Kazakhstan 43°15N 76°57E **28 E8**
Alma Hill *U.S.A.* 42°2N 78°0W **82 D7**
Almada *Portugal* 38°41N 9°8W **21 C1**
Almadén *Australia* 17°22S 144°40E **62 B3**
Almadén *Spain* 38°49N 4°52W **21 C3**
Almalyk = Olmaliq
  Uzbekistan 40°50N 69°35E **28 E7**
Almanor, L. *U.S.A.* 40°14N 121°9W **76 F3**
Almansa *Spain* 38°51N 1°5W **21 C5**
Almanzor, Pico *Spain* 40°15N 5°18W **21 B3**
Almanzora → *Spain* 37°14N 1°46W **21 D5**
Almaty *Kazakhstan* 43°15N 76°57E **28 E8**
Almazán *Spain* 41°30N 2°30W **21 B4**
Almeirim *Brazil* 1°30S 52°34W **93 D8**
Almelo *Neths.* 52°22N 6°42E **15 B6**
Almendralejo *Spain* 38°41N 6°26W **21 C2**
Almere-Stad *Neths.* 52°20N 5°15E **15 B5**
Almería *Spain* 36°52N 2°27W **21 D4**
Almirante *Panama* 9°10N 82°30W **88 E3**
Almora *India* 29°38N 79°40E **43 E8**
Almyrou, Ormos *Greece* 35°23N 24°20E **25 D6**
Alness *U.K.* 57°41N 4°16W **11 D4**
Alnmouth *U.K.* 55°24N 1°37W **12 B6**
Alnwick *U.K.* 55°24N 1°42W **12 B6**
Aloi *Uganda* 2°16N 33°10E **54 B3**
Alon *Burma* 22°12N 95°5E **41 H19**
Alor *Indonesia* 8°15N 124°30E **37 F6**
Alor Setar *Malaysia* 6°7N 100°22E **39 J3**
Alot *India* 23°56N 75°40E **42 H6**
Aloysius, Mt. *Australia* 26°0S 128°38E **61 E4**
Alpaugh *U.S.A.* 35°53N 119°29W **78 K7**
Alpena *U.S.A.* 45°4N 83°27W **81 C12**
Alpha *Australia* 23°39S 146°37E **62 C4**
Alpha Ridge *Arctic* 84°0N 118°0W **4 A2**

Alphen aan den Rijn
  Neths. 52°7N 4°40E **15 B4**
Alpine *Ariz., U.S.A.* 33°51N 109°9W **77 K9**
Alpine *Calif., U.S.A.* 32°50N 116°46W **79 N10**
Alpine *Tex., U.S.A.* 30°22N 103°40W **84 F3**
Alps *Europe* 46°30N 9°30E **20 C8**
Alpurrurulam *Australia* 20°59S 137°50E **62 C2**
Alsace □ *France* 48°15N 7°25E **20 B7**
Alsask *Canada* 51°21N 109°59W **71 C7**
Alsasua *Spain* 42°54N 2°10W **21 A4**
Alsek → *U.S.A.* 59°10N 138°12W **70 B1**
Alsta *Norway* 65°58N 12°40E **8 D15**
Alston *U.K.* 54°49N 2°25W **12 C5**
Alta *Norway* 69°57N 23°10E **8 B20**
Alta Gracia *Argentina* 31°40S 64°30W **94 C3**
Alta Sierra *U.S.A.* 35°42N 118°33W **79 K8**
Altaelva → *Norway* 69°54N 23°17E **8 B20**
Altafjorden *Norway* 70°5N 23°5E **8 A20**
Altai = Aerhtai Shan
  Mongolia 46°40N 92°45E **32 B4**
Altai = Gorno-Altay □
  Russia 51°0N 86°0E **28 D9**
Altamaha → *U.S.A.* 31°20N 81°20W **85 F14**
Altamira *Brazil* 3°12S 52°10W **93 D8**
Altamira *Chile* 25°47S 69°51W **94 B2**
Altamira *Mexico* 22°24N 97°55W **87 C5**
Altamont *U.S.A.* 42°42N 74°2W **83 D10**
Altamura *Italy* 40°49N 16°33E **22 D7**
Altanbulag *Mongolia* 50°16N 106°30E **32 A5**
Altar *Mexico* 30°43N 111°44W **86 A2**
Altar, Gran Desierto de
  Mexico 31°50N 114°10W **86 A2**
Altata *Mexico* 24°40N 107°55W **86 C3**
Altavista *U.S.A.* 37°6N 79°17W **81 G14**
Altay *China* 47°48N 88°10E **32 B3**
Altea *Spain* 38°38N 0°2W **21 C5**
Altiplano *Bolivia* 17°0S 68°0W **92 G5**
Alto Araguaia *Brazil* 17°15S 53°20W **93 G8**
Alto Cuchumatanes =
  Cuchumatanes, Sierra de los
  Guatemala 15°35N 91°25W **88 C1**
Alto del Carmen *Chile* 28°46S 70°30W **94 B1**
Alto Ligonha *Mozam.* 15°30S 38°11E **55 F4**
Alto Molocue *Mozam.* 15°50S 37°35E **55 F4**
Alto Paraguai □
  Paraguay 21°0S 58°30W **94 A4**
Alto Paraná □ *Paraguay* 25°30S 54°50W **95 B5**
Alton *Canada* 43°54N 80°5W **82 C4**
Alton *U.K.* 51°9N 0°59W **13 F7**
Alton *Ill., U.S.A.* 38°53N 90°11W **80 F8**
Alton *N.H., U.S.A.* 43°27N 71°13W **83 C13**
Altona *Canada* 49°6N 97°33W **71 D9**
Altoona *U.S.A.* 40°31N 78°24W **82 F6**
Altun Kupri *Iraq* 35°45N 44°9E **44 C5**
Altun Shan *China* 38°30N 88°0E **32 C3**
Alturas *U.S.A.* 41°29N 120°32W **76 F3**
Altus *U.S.A.* 34°38N 99°20W **84 H5**
Alucra *Turkey* 40°22N 38°47E **19 F6**
Alūksne *Latvia* 57°24N 27°3E **9 H22**
Alunite *U.S.A.* 35°59N 114°55W **79 K12**
Alusi *Indonesia* 7°35S 131°40E **37 F8**
Alva *U.S.A.* 36°48N 98°40W **84 G5**
Alvarado *Mexico* 18°46N 95°46W **87 D5**
Alvarado *U.S.A.* 32°24N 97°13W **84 E6**
Alvaro Obregón, Presa
  Mexico 27°52N 109°52W **86 B3**
Alvear *Argentina* 29°5S 56°30W **94 B4**
Alvesta *Sweden* 56°54N 14°35E **9 H16**
Alvin *U.S.A.* 29°26N 95°15W **84 G7**
Alvinston *Canada* 42°49N 81°52W **82 D3**
Älvkarleby *Sweden* 60°34N 17°26E **9 F17**
Alvord Desert *U.S.A.* 42°30N 118°25W **76 E4**
Älvsbyn *Sweden* 65°40N 21°0E **8 D19**
Alwar *India* 27°38N 76°34E **42 F7**
Alxa Zuoqi *China* 38°50N 105°40E **34 E3**
Alyangula *Australia* 13°55S 136°30E **62 A2**
Alyata = Älät *Azerbaijan* 39°58N 49°25E **45 B6**
Alyth *U.K.* 56°38N 3°13W **11 E5**
Alytus *Lithuania* 54°24N 24°3E **9 J21**
Alzada *U.S.A.* 45°2N 104°25W **76 D11**
Alzamay *Russia* 55°33N 98°39E **29 D10**
Alzira *Spain* 39°9N 0°30W **21 C5**
Am Timan *Chad* 11°0N 20°10E **51 F10**
Amadeus, L. *Australia* 24°54S 131°0E **61 D5**
Amadi
  Dem. Rep. of the Congo 3°40N 26°40E **54 B2**
Amâdi *Sudan* 5°29N 30°25E **51 G12**
Amadjuak L. *Canada* 65°0N 71°8W **69 C12**
Amagansett *U.S.A.* 40°59N 72°9W **83 F12**
Amagasaki *Japan* 34°42N 135°23E **31 G7**
Amahai *Indonesia* 3°20S 128°55E **37 E7**
Amaile *Samoa* 13°59S 171°22W **59 b**
Amakusa-Shotō *Japan* 32°15N 130°10E **31 H5**
Åmål *Sweden* 59°3N 12°42E **9 G15**
Amaliada *Greece* 37°47N 21°22E **23 F9**
Amalner *India* 21°5N 75°5E **40 J9**
Amamapare *Indonesia* 4°53S 136°38E **37 E9**
Amambaí *Brazil* 23°5S 55°13W **95 A4**
Amambaí → *Brazil* 23°22S 53°56W **95 A5**
Amambay □ *Paraguay* 23°0S 56°0W **95 A4**
Amambay, Cordillera de
  S. Amer. 23°0S 55°45W **95 A4**
Amami-Guntō *Japan* 27°16N 129°21E **31 L4**
Amami-Ō-Shima *Japan* 28°16N 129°21E **31 K4**
Aman, Pulau *Malaysia* 5°16N 100°24E **39 c**
Anamá, L. *Brazil* 2°35S 64°40W **92 D6**
Amanat → *India* 24°7N 84°4E **43 G11**
Amanda Park *U.S.A.* 47°28N 123°55W **78 C3**
Amankeldi *Kazakhstan* 50°10N 65°10E **28 D7**
Amapá *Brazil* 2°5N 50°50W **93 C8**
Amapá □ *Brazil* 1°40N 52°0W **93 C8**
Amarante *Brazil* 6°14S 42°50W **93 E10**
Amaranth *Canada* 50°36N 98°43W **71 C9**
Amargosa → *U.S.A.* 36°14N 116°51W **79 J10**
Amargosa Desert
  U.S.A. 36°40N 116°30W **79 J10**
Amargosa Range
  U.S.A. 36°20N 116°45W **79 J10**

Amari *Greece* 35°13N 24°40E **25 D6**
Amarillo *U.S.A.* 35°13N 101°50W **84 D4**
Amarkantak *India* 22°40N 81°45E **43 H9**
Amaro, Mte. *Italy* 42°5N 14°5E **22 C6**
Amarpur *India* 25°5N 87°0E **43 G12**
Amarwara *India* 22°18N 79°10E **43 H8**
Amasya *Turkey* 40°40N 35°50E **19 F6**
Amata *Australia* 26°9S 131°9E **61 E5**
Amatikulu *S. Africa* 29°3S 31°33E **57 D5**
Amatitlán *Guatemala* 14°29N 90°38W **88 D1**
Amay *Belgium* 50°33N 5°19E **15 D5**
Amazon = Amazonas →
  S. Amer. 0°5S 50°0W **93 D8**
Amazonas □ *Brazil* 5°0S 65°0W **92 E6**
Amazonas → *S. Amer.* 0°5S 50°0W **93 D8**
Ambah *India* 26°43N 78°13E **42 F8**
Ambahakily *Madag.* 21°36S 43°41E **57 C7**
Ambahita *Madag.* 24°1S 45°16E **57 C8**
Ambala *India* 30°23N 76°56E **42 D7**
Ambalavao *Madag.* 21°50S 46°56E **57 C8**
Ambanja *Madag.* 13°40S 48°27E **57 A8**
Ambararata *Madag.* 15°3S 48°33E **57 B8**
Ambarchik *Russia* 69°40N 162°20E **29 C17**
Ambarijeby *Madag.* 14°56S 47°41E **57 A8**
Ambaro, Helodranon'
  Madag. 13°23S 48°38E **57 A8**
Ambato *Ecuador* 1°5S 78°42W **92 D3**
Ambato *Madag.* 13°24S 48°29E **57 A8**
Ambato, Sierra de
  Argentina 28°25S 66°10W **94 B2**
Ambato Boeny *Madag.* 16°28S 46°43E **57 B8**
Ambatofinandrahana
  Madag. 20°33S 46°48E **57 C8**
Ambatolampy *Madag.* 19°20S 47°35E **57 B8**
Ambatomainty *Madag.* 17°41S 45°40E **57 B8**
Ambatomanoina 18°18S 47°37E **57 B8**
Ambatondrazaka
  Madag. 17°55S 48°28E **57 B8**
Ambatosoratra *Madag.* 17°37S 48°31E **57 B8**
Ambenja *Madag.* 15°17S 46°58E **57 B8**
Amberg *Germany* 49°26N 11°52E **16 D6**
Ambergris Cay *Belize* 18°0N 87°55W **87 D7**
Amberley *Canada* 44°2N 81°42W **82 B3**
Amberley *N.Z.* 43°9S 172°44E **59 E4**
Ambikapur *India* 23°15N 83°15E **43 H10**
Ambilobé *Madag.* 13°10S 49°3E **57 A8**
Ambinanindrano 20°5S 48°23E **57 C8**
Ambinanitelo *Madag.* 15°21S 49°35E **57 B8**
Ambinda *Madag.* 16°25S 45°52E **57 B8**
Amble *U.K.* 55°20N 1°36W **12 B6**
Ambleside *U.K.* 54°26N 2°58W **12 C5**
Ambo *Peru* 10°5S 76°10W **92 F3**
Amboahangy *Madag.* 24°15S 46°22E **57 C8**
Ambodifototra *Madag.* 16°59S 49°52E **57 B8**
Ambodilazana *Madag.* 18°6S 49°10E **57 B8**
Ambodiriana *Madag.* 17°55S 49°18E **57 B8**
Ambohidratrimo *Madag.* 18°50S 47°26E **57 B8**
Ambohidray *Madag.* 18°36S 48°18E **57 B8**
Ambohimahamasina
  Madag. 21°56S 47°11E **57 C8**
Ambohimahasoa *Madag.* 21°7S 47°13E **57 C8**
Ambohimanga *Madag.* 20°52S 47°36E **57 C8**
Ambohimitombo *Madag.* 20°43S 47°26E **57 C8**
Ambohitra *Madag.* 12°30S 49°10E **57 A8**
Amboise *France* 47°24N 1°2E **20 C4**
Ambon *Indonesia* 3°43S 128°12E **37 E7**
Ambondro *Madag.* 25°13S 45°44E **57 D8**
Amboseli, L. *Kenya* 2°40S 37°10E **54 C4**
Amboseli △ *Kenya* 2°37S 37°13E **54 C4**
Ambositra *Madag.* 20°31S 47°25E **57 C8**
Ambovombe *Madag.* 25°11S 46°5E **57 D8**
Amboy *U.S.A.* 34°33N 115°45W **79 L11**
Amboyna Cay
  S. China Sea 7°50N 112°50E **36 C4**
Ambridge *U.S.A.* 40°36N 80°14W **82 F4**
Ambriz *Angola* 7°48S 13°8E **52 F2**
Amchitka I. *U.S.A.* 51°32N 179°0E **74 a**
Amderma *Russia* 69°45N 61°30E **28 C7**
Amdhi *India* 23°51N 81°27E **43 H9**
Amdo *China* 32°20N 91°40E **41 C17**
Ameca *Mexico* 20°33N 104°2W **86 C4**
Ameca → *Mexico* 20°41N 105°18W **86 C3**
Amecameca de Juárez
  Mexico 19°8N 98°46W **87 D5**
Ameland *Neths.* 53°27N 5°45E **15 A5**
Amenia *U.S.A.* 41°51N 73°33W **83 E11**
America-Antarctica Ridge
  S. Ocean 59°0S 16°0W **5 B2**
American Falls *U.S.A.* 42°47N 112°51W **76 E7**
American Falls Res.
  U.S.A. 42°47N 112°52W **76 E7**
American Fork *U.S.A.* 40°23N 111°48W **76 F8**
American Highland
  Antarctica 73°0S 75°0E **5 D6**
American Samoa ☑
  Pac. Oc. 14°20S 170°0W **59 b**
American Samoa △
  Amer. Samoa 14°15S 170°28W **59 b**
Americana *Brazil* 22°45S 47°20W **95 A6**
Americus *U.S.A.* 32°4N 84°14W **85 G12**
Amersfoort *Neths.* 52°9N 5°23E **15 B5**
Amersfoort *S. Africa* 26°59S 29°53E **57 D4**
Amery Basin *S. Ocean* 68°15S 74°30E **5 C6**
Amery Ice Shelf *Antarctica* 69°30S 72°0E **5 C6**
Ames *U.S.A.* 42°2N 93°37W **80 E7**
Amesbury *U.S.A.* 42°51N 70°56W **83 D14**
Amet *India* 25°18N 73°56E **42 G5**
Amga *Russia* 60°50N 132°0E **29 C14**
Amga → *Russia* 62°38N 134°32E **29 C14**
Amgu *Russia* 45°45N 137°15E **30 B8**
Amgun → *Russia* 52°56N 139°38E **29 D15**
Amherst *Canada* 45°48N 64°8W **73 C7**
Amherst *Mass., U.S.A.* 42°23N 72°31W **83 D12**
Amherst *N.Y., U.S.A.* 42°59N 78°48W **82 D6**
Amherst *Ohio, U.S.A.* 41°24N 82°14W **82 E2**
Amherst I. *Canada* 44°8N 76°43W **83 B8**
Amherstburg *Canada* 42°6N 83°6W **72 D3**

Amiata, Mte. *Italy* 42°53N 11°37E **22 C4**
Amidon *U.S.A.* 46°29N 103°19W **80 B2**
Amiens *France* 49°54N 2°16E **20 B5**
Aminuis *Namibia* 23°43S 19°21E **56 C2**
Amīrābād *Iran* 33°20N 46°16E **44 C5**
Amirante Is. *Seychelles* 6°0S 53°0E **26 J7**
Amisk → *Canada* 56°43N 98°0W **71 C9**
Amisk L. *Canada* 54°35N 102°15W **71 C8**
Amistad, Presa de la
  Mexico 29°26N 101°3W **86 B4**
Amistad △ *U.S.A.* 29°32N 101°12W **84 G4**
Amite *U.S.A.* 30°44N 90°30W **85 F9**
Amla *India* 21°56N 78°7E **42 J8**
Amlapura = Karangasem
  Indonesia 8°27S 115°37E **37 J18**
Amlia I. *U.S.A.* 52°4N 173°30W **74 a**
Amlwch *U.K.* 53°24N 4°20W **12 D3**
'Ammān *Jordan* 31°57N 35°52E **46 D4**
'Ammān □ *Jordan* 31°40N 36°30E **46 D5**
'Ammān ✈ (AMM)
  Jordan 31°45N 36°2E **46 D5**
Ammanford *U.K.* 51°48N 3°59W **13 F4**
Ammassalik = Tasiilaq
  Greenland 65°40N 37°20W **4 C6**
Ammochostos = Famagusta
  Cyprus 35°8N 33°55E **25 D12**
Ammon *U.S.A.* 43°28N 111°58W **76 E8**
Amnat Charoen
  Thailand 15°51N 104°38E **38 E5**
Amnura *Bangla.* 24°37N 88°25E **43 G13**
Āmol *Iran* 36°23N 52°20E **45 B7**
Amorgos *Greece* 36°50N 25°57E **23 F11**
Amory *U.S.A.* 33°59N 88°29W **85 E10**
Amos *Canada* 48°35N 78°5W **72 C4**
Åmot *Norway* 59°57N 9°54E **9 G13**
Amoy = Xiamen *China* 24°25N 118°4E **33 D6**
Ampanavoana *Madag.* 15°41S 50°22E **57 B9**
Ampang *Malaysia* 3°8N 101°45E **39 L3**
Ampangalana, Lakandranon'
  Madag. 22°48S 47°50E **57 C8**
Ampanihy *Madag.* 24°40S 44°45E **57 C7**
Amparafaravola *Madag.* 17°35S 48°13E **57 B8**
Amparihinambo *Madag.* 20°31S 48°0E **57 C8**
Ampasindava, Helodranon'
  Madag. 13°40S 48°15E **57 A8**
Ampasindava, Saikanosy
  Madag. 13°42S 47°55E **57 A8**
Ampenan *Indonesia* 8°34S 116°4E **37 K18**
Amper → *Germany* 48°29N 11°55E **16 D6**
Amphoe Kathu *Thailand* 7°55N 98°21E **39 a**
Amphoe Thalang *Thailand* 8°1N 98°20E **39 a**
Ampitsikinana *Madag.* 12°57S 49°49E **57 A8**
Ampombiantambo
  Madag. 12°42S 48°57E **57 A8**
Ampotaka *Madag.* 25°3S 44°41E **57 D7**
Ampoza *Madag.* 22°20S 44°44E **57 C7**
Amqui *Canada* 48°28N 67°27W **73 C6**
Amravati *India* 20°55N 77°45E **40 J10**
Amreli *India* 21°35N 71°17E **42 J4**
Amritsar *India* 31°35N 74°57E **42 D6**
Amroha *India* 28°53N 78°30E **43 E8**
Amsterdam *Neths.* 52°23N 4°54E **15 B4**
Amsterdam *U.S.A.* 42°56N 74°11W **83 D10**
Amsterdam ✈ (AMS)
  Neths. 52°18N 4°45E **15 B4**
Amsterdam, I. = Nouvelle
  Amsterdam, Î. *Ind. Oc.* 38°30S 77°30E **3 F13**
Amstetten *Austria* 48°7N 14°51E **16 D8**
Amudarya → *Uzbekistan* 43°58N 59°34E **28 E6**
Amund Ringnes I.
  Canada 78°20N 96°25W **69 B10**
Amundsen Abyssal Plain
  S. Ocean 65°0S 125°0W **5 C14**
Amundsen Basin *Arctic* 87°30N 80°0E **4 A**
Amundsen Gulf *Canada* 71°0N 124°0W **68 B7**
Amundsen Ridges
  S. Ocean 69°15S 123°0W **5 C14**
Amundsen-Scott *Antarctica* 90°0S 166°0E **5 E**
Amundsen Sea *Antarctica* 72°0S 115°0W **5 D15**
Amuntai *Indonesia* 2°28S 115°25E **36 E5**
Amur → *Russia* 52°56N 141°10E **29 D15**
Amurang *Indonesia* 1°5N 124°40E **37 D6**
Amursk *Russia* 50°14N 136°54E **29 D14**
Amyderya = Amudarya →
  Uzbekistan 43°58N 59°34E **28 E6**
An Bien *Vietnam* 9°45N 105°0E **39 H5**
An Hoa *Vietnam* 15°40N 108°5E **38 E7**
An Nabatīyah at Tahta
  Lebanon 33°23N 35°27E **46 B4**
An Nabk *Si. Arabia* 31°20N 37°20E **44 D3**
An Nabk *Syria* 34°2N 36°44E **46 A5**
An Nafūd *Si. Arabia* 28°15N 41°0E **44 D4**
An Najaf *Iraq* 32°3N 44°15E **44 C5**
An Nāşirīyah *Iraq* 31°0N 46°15E **44 D5**
An Nhon *Vietnam* 13°55N 109°7E **38 F7**
An Nu'ayrīyah *Si. Arabia* 27°30N 48°30E **45 E6**
An Thoi, Dao *Vietnam* 9°58N 104°0E **39 H5**
An Uaimh *Ireland* 53°39N 6°41W **10 C5**
Anabar → *Russia* 73°8N 113°36E **29 B12**
Anabta *West Bank* 32°19N 35°7E **46 C4**
Anaconda *U.S.A.* 46°8N 112°57W **76 C7**
Anacortes *U.S.A.* 48°30N 122°37W **78 B4**
Anadarko *U.S.A.* 35°4N 98°15W **84 D5**
Anadolu *Turkey* 39°0N 30°0E **19 G5**
Anadyr *Russia* 64°35N 177°20E **29 C18**
Anadyr → *Russia* 64°55N 176°5E **29 C18**
Anadyrskiy Zaliv *Russia* 64°0N 180°0E **29 C19**
Anaga, Pta. de *Canary Is.* 28°34N 16°9W **24 F3**
'Ānah *Iraq* 34°25N 42°0E **44 C4**
Anaheim *U.S.A.* 33°50N 117°55W **79 M9**
Anahim Lake *Canada* 52°28N 125°18W **70 C3**
Anakapalle *India* 17°42N 83°6E **41 L13**
Anakie *Australia* 23°32S 147°45E **62 C4**
Analalava *Madag.* 14°35S 48°0E **57 A8**
Analavoka *Madag.* 22°23S 46°30E **57 C8**
Analipsis *Greece* 39°36N 19°55E **25 A3**
Anambar → *Pakistan* 30°15N 68°50E **42 D3**

Anambas, Kepulauan
  Indonesia 3°20N 106°30E **36 D3**
Anambas Is. = Anambas,
  Kepulauan *Indonesia* 3°20N 106°30E **36 D3**
Anamosa *U.S.A.* 42°7N 91°17W **80 D8**
Anamur *Turkey* 36°8N 32°58E **44 B2**
Anan *Japan* 33°54N 134°40E **31 H7**
Anand *India* 22°32N 72°59E **42 H5**
Anantapur *India* 14°39N 77°42E **40 M10**
Anantnag *India* 33°45N 75°10E **43 C6**
Ananyiv *Ukraine* 47°44N 29°58E **17 E15**
Anapodiaris → *Greece* 34°59N 25°20E **25 E7**
Anápolis *Brazil* 16°15S 48°50W **93 G9**
Anapu → *Brazil* 1°53S 50°53W **93 D8**
Anār *Iran* 30°55N 55°13E **45 D7**
Anārak *Iran* 33°25N 53°40E **45 C7**
Anas → *India* 23°26N 74°0E **42 H5**
Anatolia = Anadolu
  Turkey 39°0N 30°0E **19 G5**
Anatsogno *Madag.* 23°33S 43°46E **57 C7**
Añatuya *Argentina* 28°20S 62°50W **94 B3**
Anaunethad L. *Canada* 60°55N 104°25W **71 A8**
Anbyŏn *N. Korea* 39°1N 127°35E **35 E14**
Ancaster *Canada* 43°13N 79°59W **82 C5**
Anchor Bay *U.S.A.* 38°48N 123°34W **78 G3**
Anchorage *U.S.A.* 61°13N 149°54W **68 C5**
Anci *China* 39°20N 116°40E **34 E9**
Ancohuma, Nevado
  Bolivia 16°0S 68°50W **92 G5**
Ancón *Peru* 11°50S 77°10W **92 F3**
Ancona *Italy* 43°38N 13°30E **22 C5**
Ancud *Chile* 42°0S 73°50W **96 E2**
Ancud, G. de *Chile* 42°0S 73°0W **96 E2**
Anda *China* 46°24N 125°19E **33 B7**
Andacollo *Argentina* 37°10S 70°42W **94 D1**
Andacollo *Chile* 30°14S 71°6W **94 C1**
Andaingo *Madag.* 18°12S 48°17E **57 B8**
Andalgalá *Argentina* 27°40S 66°30W **94 B2**
Åndalsnes *Norway* 62°35N 7°43E **8 E12**
Andalucía □ *Spain* 37°35N 5°0W **21 D3**
Andalusia = Andalucía □
  Spain 37°35N 5°0W **21 D3**
Andalusia *U.S.A.* 31°18N 86°29W **85 F11**
Andaman Is. *Ind. Oc.* 12°30N 92°45E **27 G11**
Andaman Sea *Ind. Oc.* 13°0N 96°0E **36 B1**
Andamooka *Australia* 30°27S 137°9E **63 E2**
Andapa *Madag.* 14°39S 49°39E **57 A8**
Andara *Namibia* 18°2S 21°9E **56 B3**
Andenne *Belgium* 50°28N 5°5E **15 D5**
Anderson *Alaska, U.S.A.* 64°25N 149°15W **74 a**
Anderson *Calif., U.S.A.* 40°27N 122°18W **76 F2**
Anderson *Ind., U.S.A.* 40°10N 85°41W **81 E11**
Anderson *Mo., U.S.A.* 36°39N 94°27W **80 G6**
Anderson *S.C., U.S.A.* 34°31N 82°39W **85 D13**
Anderson → *Canada* 69°42N 129°0W **68 C7**
Andes *U.S.A.* 42°12N 74°47W **83 D10**
Andes, Cord. de los
  S. Amer. 20°0S 68°0W **92 H5**
Andfjorden *Norway* 69°10N 16°20E **8 B17**
Andhra Pradesh □ *India* 18°0N 79°0E **40 L11**
Andijon *Uzbekistan* 41°10N 72°15E **28 E8**
Andikíthira = Antikythira
  Greece 35°52N 23°15E **23 G10**
Andilamena *Madag.* 17°1S 48°35E **57 B8**
Andīmeshk *Iran* 32°27N 48°21E **45 C6**
Andizhan = Andijon
  Uzbekistan 41°10N 72°15E **28 E8**
Andoany *Madag.* 13°25S 48°16E **57 A8**
Andohahela △ *Madag.* 24°4S 46°44E **57 D8**
Andong *S. Korea* 36°40N 128°43E **35 F15**
Andongwei *China* 35°6N 119°20E **35 G10**
Andorra ■ *Europe* 42°30N 1°30E **20 E4**
Andorra La Vella *Andorra* 42°31N 1°32E **20 E4**
Andover *U.K.* 51°12N 1°29W **13 F6**
Andover *Maine, U.S.A.* 44°38N 70°45W **83 B14**
Andover *Mass., U.S.A.* 42°40N 71°8W **83 D13**
Andover *N.J., U.S.A.* 40°59N 74°45W **83 F10**
Andover *N.Y., U.S.A.* 42°10N 77°48W **82 D7**
Andover *Ohio, U.S.A.* 41°36N 80°34W **82 E4**
Andoya *Norway* 69°10N 15°50E **8 B16**
Andradina *Brazil* 20°54S 51°23W **93 H8**
Andrahary *Madag.* 13°37S 49°17E **57 A8**
Andramasina *Madag.* 19°11S 47°35E **57 B8**
Andranopasy *Madag.* 21°17S 43°44E **57 C7**
Andranovory *Madag.* 23°8S 44°10E **57 C7**
Andratx *Spain* 39°39N 2°25E **24 B9**
Andreanof Is. *U.S.A.* 51°30N 176°0W **74 a**
Andrews *S.C., U.S.A.* 33°27N 79°34W **85 E15**
Andrews *Tex., U.S.A.* 32°19N 102°33W **84 E3**
Ándria *Italy* 41°13N 16°17E **22 D7**
Andriamena *Madag.* 17°26S 47°30E **57 B8**
Andriandampy *Madag.* 22°45S 45°41E **57 C8**
Andriba *Madag.* 17°30S 46°58E **57 B8**
Andringitra △ *Madag.* 22°13S 46°55E **57 C8**
Androka *Madag.* 24°58S 44°2E **57 C7**
Andros *Greece* 37°50N 24°57E **23 F11**
Andros I. *Bahamas* 24°30N 78°0W **88 B4**
Andros Town *Bahamas* 24°43N 77°47W **88 B4**
Androscoggin →
  U.S.A. 43°58N 69°52W **83 C14**
Andselv *Norway* 69°4N 18°34E **8 B18**
Andújar *Spain* 38°3N 4°5W **21 C3**
Andulo *Angola* 11°25S 16°45E **52 G3**

Ånge *Sweden* 62°31N 15°35E **8 E16**
Ángel, Salto = Angel Falls
  Venezuela 5°57N 62°30W **92 B6**
Ángel de la Guarda, I.
  Mexico 29°20N 113°25W **86 B2**
Angel Falls *Venezuela* 5°57N 62°30W **92 B6**
Angeles *Phil.* 15°9N 120°33E **37 A6**
Ångelholm *Sweden* 56°15N 12°58E **9 H15**
Angels Camp *U.S.A.* 38°4N 120°32W **78 G6**
Ångermanälven →
  Sweden 64°0N 17°20E **8 E17**
Ångermanland *Sweden* 63°36N 17°45E **8 E17**
Angers *Canada* 45°31N 75°29W **83 A9**
Angers *France* 47°30N 0°35W **20 C3**
Ångesån → *Sweden* 63°36N 19°45E **8 E18**
Angikuni L. *Canada* 62°12N 99°59W **71 A9**
Angkor *Cambodia* 13°22N 103°50E **38 F4**
Anglesey *U.K.* 53°17N 4°20W **12 D3**
Anglesey, Isle of □ *U.K.* 53°16N 4°18W **12 D3**
Angleton *U.S.A.* 29°10N 95°26W **84 G7**
Anglisidhes *Cyprus* 34°51N 33°27E **25 E12**
Angmagssalik = Tasiilaq
  Greenland 65°40N 37°20W **4 C6**
Ango *Dem. Rep. of the Congo* 4°10N 26°5E **54 B2**
Angoche *Mozam.* 16°8S 39°55E **55 F4**
Angoche, I. *Mozam.* 16°20S 39°50E **55 F4**
Angol *Chile* 37°56S 72°45W **94 D1**
Angola *Ind., U.S.A.* 41°38N 85°0W **81 E11**
Angola *N.Y., U.S.A.* 42°38N 79°2W **82 D5**
Angola ■ *Africa* 12°0S 18°0E **53 G3**
Angoulême *France* 45°39N 0°10E **20 D4**
Angoumois *France* 45°50N 0°25E **20 D3**
Angra do Heroismo
  Azores 38°39N 27°13W **50 a**
Angra dos Reis *Brazil* 23°0S 44°10W **95 A7**
Angtassom *Cambodia* 11°1N 104°41E **39 G5**
Angu
  Dem. Rep. of the Congo 3°23N 24°30E **54 B1**
Anguang *China* 45°15N 123°45E **35 B12**
Anguilla ☑ *W. Indies* 18°14N 63°5W **89 C7**
Anguo *China* 38°28N 115°15E **34 E8**
Angurugu *Australia* 14°0S 136°25E **62 A2**
Angus *Canada* 44°19N 79°53W **82 B5**
Angus □ *U.K.* 56°46N 2°56W **11 E6**
Anhanduí → *Brazil* 21°46S 52°9W **95 A5**
Anholt *Denmark* 56°42N 11°33E **9 H14**
Anhui □ *China* 32°0N 117°0E **33 C6**
Anhwei = Anhui □ *China* 32°0N 117°0E **33 C6**
Anichab *Namibia* 21°0S 14°46E **56 C1**
Animas → *U.S.A.* 36°43N 108°13W **77 H9**
Anivorano *Madag.* 18°44S 48°58E **57 B8**
Anjalankoski *Finland* 60°45N 26°51E **8 F22**
Anjar *India* 23°6N 70°10E **42 H4**
Anjou *France* 47°20N 0°15W **20 C3**
Anjouan *Comoros Is.* 12°15S 44°20E **53 a**
Anjozorobe *Madag.* 18°22S 47°52E **57 B8**
Anju *N. Korea* 39°36N 125°40E **35 E13**
Ankaboa, Tanjona
  Madag. 21°58S 43°20E **57 C7**
Ankang *China* 32°40N 109°1E **34 H5**
Ankara *Turkey* 39°57N 32°54E **19 G5**
Ankarafantsika △ *Madag.* 16°0S 47°0E **57 B8**
Ankaramena *Madag.* 21°57S 46°39E **57 C8**
Ankaratra *Madag.* 19°25S 47°12E **53 H9**
Ankasakasa *Madag.* 16°21S 44°52E **57 B7**
Ankavandra *Madag.* 18°46S 45°18E **57 B8**
Ankazoabo *Madag.* 22°18S 44°31E **57 C7**
Ankazobe *Madag.* 18°20S 47°10E **57 B8**
Ankeny *U.S.A.* 41°44N 93°36W **80 E7**
Ankilimalinika *Madag.* 22°58S 43°45E **57 C7**
Ankilizato *Madag.* 20°25S 45°1E **57 C8**
Ankisabe *Madag.* 19°17S 46°29E **57 B8**
Ankoro
  Dem. Rep. of the Congo 6°45S 26°55E **54 D2**
Ankororoka *Madag.* 25°30S 45°11E **57 D8**
Anlong Veng *Cambodia* 14°14N 104°5E **38 E5**
Anmyeondo *S. Korea* 36°25N 126°25E **35 F14**
Ann, C. *U.S.A.* 42°38N 70°35W **83 D14**
Ann Arbor *U.S.A.* 42°17N 83°45W **81 D12**
Anna *U.S.A.* 37°28N 89°15W **80 G9**
Annaba *Algeria* 36°50N 7°46E **50 A7**
Annalee → *Ireland* 54°2N 7°24W **10 B4**
Annam *Vietnam* 16°0N 108°0E **38 E7**
Annamitique, Chaîne
  Asia 17°0N 106°0E **38 D6**
Annan *U.K.* 54°59N 3°16W **11 G5**
Annan → *U.K.* 54°58N 3°16W **11 G5**
Annapolis *U.S.A.* 38°59N 76°30W **81 F15**
Annapolis Royal *Canada* 44°44N 65°32W **73 D6**
Annapurna *Nepal* 28°34N 83°50E **43 E10**
Annean, L. *Australia* 26°54S 118°14E **61 E2**
Annecy *France* 45°55N 6°8E **20 D7**
Annette I. *U.S.A.* 55°9N 131°28W **70 B2**
Anning *China* 24°55N 102°26E **32 D5**
Anniston *U.S.A.* 33°39N 85°50W **85 E12**
Annobón *Atl. Oc.* 1°25S 5°36E **51 G4**
Annotto B. *Jamaica* 18°17N 76°45W **88 a**
Annville *U.S.A.* 40°20N 76°31W **83 F8**
Anogia *Greece* 35°16N 24°52E **25 D6**
Anorotsangana *Madag.* 13°56S 47°55E **57 A8**
Anosibe *Madag.* 19°26S 48°13E **57 B8**
Anping *Hebei, China* 38°15N 115°30E **34 E8**
Anping *Liaoning, China* 41°5N 123°30E **35 D12**
Anqing *China* 30°30N 117°3E **33 C6**
Anqiu *China* 36°25N 119°10E **35 F10**
Ansai *China* 36°50N 109°20E **34 F5**
Ansan *S. Korea* 37°21N 126°52E **35 F14**
Ansbach *Germany* 49°28N 10°34E **16 D6**
Anse Boileau *Seychelles* 4°43S 55°29E **53 b**
Anse Royale *Seychelles* 4°44S 55°31E **53 b**
Anshan *China* 41°5N 122°58E **35 D11**
Anshun *China* 26°18N 105°57E **32 D5**
Ansley *U.S.A.* 41°18N 99°23W **80 E4**
Anson *U.S.A.* 32°45N 99°54W **84 E5**
Anson B. *Australia* 13°20S 130°6E **60 B5**
Ansongo *Mali* 15°25N 0°35E **50 E6**

Ansonia *U.S.A.* 41°21N 73°5W **83 E11**
Anstruther *U.K.* 56°14N 2°41W **11 E6**
Ansudu *Indonesia* 2°11S 139°22E **37 E9**
Antabamba *Peru* 14°40S 73°0W **92 F4**
Antakya = Hatay *Turkey* 36°14N 36°10E **44 B3**
Antalaha *Madag.* 14°57S 50°20E **57 A9**
Antalya *Turkey* 36°52N 30°45E **19 G5**
Antalya Körfezi *Turkey* 36°15N 31°30E **19 G5**
Antambohobe *Madag.* 22°20S 46°47E **57 C8**
Antanambao-Manampotsy
  Madag. 19°29S 48°34E **57 B8**
Antanambe *Madag.* 16°26S 49°52E **57 B8**
Antananarivo *Madag.* 18°55S 47°31E **57 B8**
Antananarivo □ *Madag.* 19°0S 47°0E **57 B8**
Antanifotsy *Madag.* 19°39S 47°19E **57 B8**
Antanimbaribe *Madag.* 21°30S 44°48E **57 C7**
Antanimora *Madag.* 24°49S 45°40E **57 C8**
Antarctic Pen. *Antarctica* 67°0S 60°0W **5 C18**
Antarctica 90°0S 0°0 **5 E3**
Antelope *Zimbabwe* 21°2S 28°31E **55 G2**
Antequera *Paraguay* 24°8S 57°7W **94 A4**
Antequera *Spain* 37°5N 4°33W **21 D3**
Antero, Mt. *U.S.A.* 38°41N 106°15W **76 G10**
Antevamena *Madag.* 21°2S 44°8E **57 C7**
Anthony *Kans., U.S.A.* 37°9N 98°2W **80 G4**
Anthony *N. Mex.,*
  U.S.A. 32°0N 106°36W **77 K10**
Anti Atlas *Morocco* 30°0N 8°30W **50 C4**
Anti-Lebanon = Sharqi, Al Jabal
  ash *Lebanon* 33°40N 36°10E **46 B5**
Antibes *France* 43°34N 7°6E **20 E7**
Anticosti, Î. d' *Canada* 49°30N 63°0W **73 C7**
Antigo *U.S.A.* 45°9N 89°9W **80 C9**
Antigonish *Canada* 45°38N 61°58W **73 C7**
Antigua *Canary Is.* 28°24N 14°1W **24 F5**
Antigua *Guatemala* 14°34N 90°41W **88 D1**
Antigua *W. Indies* 17°0N 61°50W **89 C7**
Antigua & Barbuda ■
  W. Indies 17°20N 61°48W **89 C7**
Antikythira *Greece* 35°52N 23°15E **23 G10**
Antilla *Cuba* 20°40N 75°50W **88 B4**
Antilles = West Indies
  Cent. Amer. 15°0N 65°0W **89 D7**
Antioch *U.S.A.* 38°1N 121°48W **78 G5**
Antioquia *Colombia* 6°40N 75°55W **92 B3**
Antipodes Is. *Pac. Oc.* 49°45S 178°40E **64 M9**
Antlers *U.S.A.* 34°14N 95°37W **84 D7**
Antoetra *Madag.* 20°46S 47°20E **57 C8**
Antofagasta *Chile* 23°50S 70°30W **94 A1**
Antofagasta □ *Chile* 24°0S 69°0W **94 A2**
Antofagasta de la Sierra
  Argentina 26°5S 67°20W **94 B2**
Antofalla *Argentina* 25°30S 68°5W **94 B2**
Antofalla, Salar de
  Argentina 25°40S 67°45W **94 B2**
Anton *U.S.A.* 33°49N 102°10W **84 E3**
Antongila, Helodrano
  Madag. 15°30S 49°50E **57 B8**
Antonibé *Madag.* 15°7S 47°24E **57 B8**
Antonibé, Presqu'île d'
  Madag. 14°55S 47°20E **57 A8**
Antonina *Brazil* 25°26S 48°42W **95 B6**
Antonina *Brazil* 25°26S 48°42W **95 B6**
Antrim *U.K.* 54°43N 6°14W **10 B5**
Antrim *U.S.A.* 40°7N 81°21W **82 F3**
Antrim □ *U.K.* 54°56N 6°25W **10 B5**
Antrim, Mts. of *U.K.* 55°3N 6°14W **10 A5**
Antrim Plateau *Australia* 18°8S 128°20E **60 C4**
Antsakabary *Madag.* 15°3S 48°56E **57 B8**
Antsalova *Madag.* 18°40S 44°37E **57 B7**
Antsenavolo *Madag.* 21°24S 48°3E **57 C8**
Antsiafabositra *Madag.* 17°18S 46°57E **57 B8**
Antsirabe *Antananarivo,*
  Madag. 19°55S 47°2E **57 B8**
Antsirabe *Antsiranana,*
  Madag. 14°0S 49°59E **57 A8**
Antsirabe *Mahajanga,*
  Madag. 15°57S 48°58E **57 B8**
Antsiranana *Madag.* 12°25S 49°20E **57 A8**
Antsiranana □ *Madag.* 12°25S 49°17E **57 A8**
Antsohihy *Madag.* 14°50S 47°59E **57 A8**
Antsohimbondrona Seranana
  Madag. 13°7S 48°48E **57 A8**
Antu *China* 42°30N 128°20E **35 C15**

Antwerp = Antwerpen
  Belgium 51°13N 4°25E **15 C4**
Antwerp *U.S.A.* 44°12N 75°37W **83 B9**
Antwerpen *Belgium* 51°13N 4°25E **15 C4**
Antwerpen □ *Belgium* 51°15N 4°40E **15 C4**
Anupgarh *India* 29°10N 73°10E **42 E5**
Anuppur *India* 23°6N 81°41E **43 H9**
Anuradhapura *Sri Lanka* 8°22N 80°28E **40 Q12**
Anveh *Iran* 27°23N 54°11E **45 E7**
Anvers = Antwerpen
  Belgium 51°13N 4°25E **15 C4**
Anvers I. *Antarctica* 64°30S 63°40W **5 C17**
Anxi *China* 40°30N 95°43E **32 B8**
Anxious B. *Australia* 33°24S 134°45E **63 E1**
Anyang *China* 36°5N 114°21E **34 F8**
Anyang *S. Korea* 37°22N 126°55E **35 F14**
Anyer *Indonesia* 6°4S 105°53E **37 G11**
Anza *U.S.A.* 33°35N 116°39W **79 M10**
Anze *China* 36°10N 112°12E **34 F7**
Anzhero-Sudzhensk
  Russia 56°10N 86°0E **28 D9**
Ánzio *Italy* 41°27N 12°37E **22 D5**
Ao Makham *Thailand* 7°50N 98°24E **39 a**
Ao Phangnga △ *Thailand* 8°10N 98°32E **39 a**
Aoga-Shima *Japan* 32°28N 139°46E **31 H9**
Aoji *N. Korea* 42°31N 130°23E **35 C16**
Aomen = Macau
  China 22°12N 113°33E **33 G10**
Aomori *Japan* 40°45N 140°45E **30 D10**
Aomori □ *Japan* 40°45N 140°40E **30 D10**
Aonla *India* 28°16N 79°11E **43 E8**
Aorai, Mt. *Tahiti* 17°34S 149°30W **59 d**
Aoraki Mount Cook
  N.Z. 43°36S 170°9E **59 E3**

Aoral, Phnum *Cambodia* 12°N 104°15E **39 G5**
Aosta *Italy* 45°45N 7°20E **20 D7**
Aotearoa = New Zealand ■
 Oceania 40°0S 176°0E **59 D6**
Aoukâr *Mauritania* 17°40N 10°0W **50 E4**
Aozou Strip *Chad* 22°0N 19°0E **51 D9**
Apá → *S. Amer.* 22°6S 58°2W **94 A4**
Apache *U.S.A.* 34°54N 98°22W **84 D5**
Apache Junction
 U.S.A. 33°25N 111°33W **77 K8**
Apalachee B. *U.S.A.* 30°0N 84°0W **85 G13**
Apalachicola *U.S.A.* 29°43N 84°59W **85 G12**
Apalachicola →
 U.S.A. 29°43N 84°58W **85 G12**
Apaporis → *Colombia* 1°23S 69°25W **92 D5**
Aparados da Serra △
 Brazil 29°10S 50°8W **95 B5**
Aparri *Phil.* 18°22N 121°38E **37 A6**
Apatity *Russia* 67°34N 33°22E **8 C25**
Apatula = Finke
 Australia 25°34S 134°35E **62 D1**
Apatzingán *Mexico* 19°5N 102°21W **86 D4**
Apeldoorn *Neths.* 52°13N 5°57E **15 B5**
Apennines = Appennini
 Italy 44°30N 10°0E **22 B4**
Api *Nepal* 30°0N 80°57E **32 C3**
Apia *Samoa* 13°50S 171°50W **59 b**
Apiacás, Serra dos *Brazil* 9°50S 57°0W **92 E7**
Apies → *S. Africa* 25°15S 28°8E **57 D4**
Apizaco *Mexico* 19°25N 98°8W **87 D5**
Aplao *Peru* 16°0S 72°40W **92 G4**
Apo, Mt. *Phil.* 6°53N 125°14E **37 C7**
Apolakia *Greece* 36°5N 27°48E **25 C9**
Apolakia, Ormos *Greece* 36°5N 27°45E **25 C9**
Apollonia = Marsá Susah
 Libya 32°52N 21°59E **51 B10**
Apollonia *Greece* 36°15N 27°58E **25 C9**
Apolo *Bolivia* 14°30S 68°30W **92 F5**
Apopa *El Salv.* 13°48N 89°10W **88 D2**
Aporé → *Brazil* 19°27S 50°57W **93 G8**
Apostle Is. *U.S.A.* 47°0N 90°40W **80 B8**
Apostle Islands ⌒ *U.S.A.* 46°55N 91°0W **80 B8**
Apóstoles *Argentina* 28°0S 56°0W **95 B4**
Apostolos Andreas, C.
 Cyprus 35°42N 34°35E **25 D13**
Apoteri *Guyana* 4°2N 58°32W **92 C7**
Appalachian Mts. *U.S.A.* 38°0N 80°0W **81 G14**
Appennini *Italy* 44°30N 10°0E **22 B4**
Apple Hill *Canada* 45°13N 74°46W **83 A10**
Apple Valley *U.S.A.* 34°32N 117°14W **79 L9**
Appleby-in-Westmorland
 U.K. 54°35N 2°29W **12 C5**
Appledore *U.K.* 51°3N 4°13W **13 F3**
Appleton *U.S.A.* 44°16N 88°25W **80 C9**
Approuague →
 Fr. Guiana 4°30N 51°57W **93 C8**
Aprília *Italy* 41°36N 12°39E **22 D5**
Apsley *Canada* 44°45N 78°6W **82 B6**
Apucarana *Brazil* 23°55S 51°33W **95 A5**
Apure → *Venezuela* 7°37N 66°25W **92 B5**
Apurimac → *Peru* 12°17S 73°56W **92 F4**
Āq Qālā *Iran* 37°10N 54°30E **45 B7**
Aqaba = Al 'Aqaba
 Jordan 29°31N 35°0E **46 F4**
Aqaba, G. of *Red Sea* 29°0N 34°40E **44 D2**
'Aqabah, Khalīj al = Aqaba, G. of
 Red Sea 29°0N 34°40E **44 D2**
'Aqdā *Iran* 32°26N 53°37E **45 C7**
'Aqrah *Iraq* 36°46N 43°45E **44 B4**
Aqsay *Kazakhstan* 51°11N 53°0E **19 D9**
Aqtaü *Kazakhstan* 43°39N 51°12E **19 F9**
Aqtöbe *Kazakhstan* 50°17N 57°10E **19 D10**
Aqtoghay *Kazakhstan* 46°57N 79°40E **28 E8**
Aquidauana *Brazil* 20°30S 55°50W **93 H7**
Aquila *Mexico* 18°36N 103°30W **86 D4**
Aquiles Serdán *Mexico* 28°36N 105°53W **86 B3**
Aquin *Haiti* 18°16N 73°24W **89 C5**
Aquitain, Bassin *France* 44°0N 0°30W **20 D3**
Ar Rachidiya = Er Rachidia
 Morocco 31°58N 4°20W **50 B5**
Ar Rafid *Syria* 32°57N 35°52E **46 C4**
Ar Raḥḥālīyah *Iraq* 32°44N 43°23E **44 C4**
Ar Ramādī *Iraq* 33°25N 43°20E **44 C4**
Ar Ramthā *Jordan* 32°34N 36°0E **46 C5**
Ar Raqqah *Syria* 35°59N 39°8E **44 C3**
Ar Rass *Si. Arabia* 25°50N 43°40E **44 E4**
Ar Rayyān *Qatar* 25°17N 51°25E **45 E6**
Ar Rifā'ī *Iraq* 31°50N 46°10E **44 D5**
Ar Riyāḍ *Si. Arabia* 24°41N 46°42E **44 E5**
Ar Ru'ays *Qatar* 26°8N 51°12E **45 E6**
Ar Rukhaymīyah *Iraq* 29°22N 45°38E **44 D5**
Ar Rumaythah *Iraq* 31°31N 45°12E **44 D5**
Ar Ruṣāfah *Syria* 35°45N 38°49E **44 C3**
Ar Ruṭbah *Iraq* 33°0N 40°15E **44 C4**
Ara *India* 25°35N 84°32E **43 G11**
Arab *U.S.A.* 34°19N 86°30W **85 D11**
'Arab, Bahr el → *Sudan* 9°0N 29°30E **51 G11**
'Arab, Shatt al → *Asia* 29°57N 48°34E **45 D6**
'Arabābād *Iran* 33°2N 57°41E **45 C8**
Arabia *Asia* 25°0N 45°0E **26 F6**
Arabian Desert = Es Sahrâ' Esh
 Sharqiya *Egypt* 27°30N 32°30E **51 C12**
Arabian Gulf = Persian Gulf
 Asia 27°0N 50°0E **45 E6**
Arabian Sea *Ind. Oc.* 16°0N 65°0E **26 H10**
Aracaju *Brazil* 10°55S 37°4W **93 F11**
Aracati *Brazil* 4°30S 37°44W **93 D11**
Araçatuba *Brazil* 21°10S 50°30W **95 A5**
Aracena *Spain* 37°53N 6°38W **21 D2**
Araçuaí *Brazil* 16°52S 42°4W **93 G10**
'Arad *Israel* 31°15N 35°12E **46 D4**
Arad *Romania* 46°10N 21°20E **17 E11**
Arādān *Iran* 35°21N 52°30E **45 C7**
Arafura Sea *E. Indies* 9°0S 135°0E **58 B6**
Aragón □ *Spain* 41°25N 0°40W **21 B5**
Aragón → *Spain* 42°13N 1°44W **21 A5**

Araguacema *Brazil* 8°50S 49°20W **93 E9**
Araguaia → *Brazil* 5°21S 48°41W **93 E9**
Araguaína *Brazil* 7°12S 48°12W **93 E9**
Araguari *Brazil* 18°38S 48°11W **93 G9**
Araguari → *Brazil* 1°15N 49°55W **93 C9**
Araín *India* 26°27N 75°2E **42 F6**
Arak *Algeria* 25°20N 3°45E **50 C6**
Arāk *Iran* 34°0N 49°40E **45 C6**
Arakan Coast *Burma* 19°0N 94°0E **41 K19**
Arakan Yoma *Burma* 20°0N 94°40E **41 K19**
Araks = Aras, Rūd-e →
 Asia 40°5N 48°29E **44 B5**
Aral *Kazakhstan* 46°41N 61°45E **28 E7**
Aral Sea *Asia* 44°30N 60°0E **28 E7**
Aral Tengizi = Aral Sea
 Asia 44°30N 60°0E **28 E7**
Aralsk = Aral *Kazakhstan* 46°41N 61°45E **28 E7**
Aralskoye More = Aral Sea
 Asia 44°30N 60°0E **28 E7**
Aramac *Australia* 22°58S 145°14E **62 C4**
Aran I. *Ireland* 55°0N 8°30W **10 A3**
Aran Is. *Ireland* 53°6N 9°38W **10 C2**
Aranda de Duero *Spain* 41°39N 3°42W **21 B4**
Arandán *Iran* 35°23N 46°55E **44 C5**
Aranjuez *Spain* 40°1N 3°40W **21 B4**
Aranos *Namibia* 24°9S 19°7E **56 C2**
Aransas Pass *U.S.A.* 27°55N 97°9W **84 H6**
Aranyaprathet *Thailand* 13°41N 102°30E **38 F4**
Arapaho *U.S.A.* 40°18N 99°54W **80 E4**
Arapey Grande →
 Uruguay 30°55S 57°49W **94 C4**
Arapgir *Turkey* 39°5N 38°30E **44 B3**
Arapiraca *Brazil* 9°45S 36°39W **93 E11**
Arapongas *Brazil* 23°29S 51°28W **95 A5**
Ar'ar *Si. Arabia* 30°59N 41°2E **44 D4**
Araranguá *Brazil* 29°0S 49°30W **95 B6**
Araraquara *Brazil* 21°50S 48°0W **93 H9**
Ararás, Serra das *Brazil* 25°0S 53°10W **95 B5**
Ararat *Australia* 37°16S 142°58E **63 F3**
Ararat, Mt. = Ağrı Dağı
 Turkey 39°50N 44°15E **44 B5**
Araria *India* 26°9N 87°33E **43 F12**
Araripe, Chapada do
 Brazil 7°20S 40°0W **93 E11**
Araruama, L. de *Brazil* 22°53S 42°12W **95 A7**
Aras, Rūd-e → *Asia* 40°5N 48°29E **44 B5**
Arauca *Colombia* 7°0N 70°40W **92 B4**
Arauca → *Venezuela* 7°24N 66°35W **92 B5**
Arauco *Chile* 37°16S 73°25W **94 D1**
Aravalli Range *India* 25°0N 73°30E **42 G5**
Arawale ⌒ *Kenya* 1°24S 40°9E **54 C5**
Araxá *Brazil* 19°35S 46°55W **93 G9**
Araya, Pen. de *Venezuela* 10°40N 64°0W **92 A6**
Arba Minch *Ethiopia* 6°0N 37°30E **47 F2**
Arbat *Iraq* 35°25N 45°35E **44 C5**
Árbatax *Italy* 39°56N 9°42E **22 E3**
Arborea *Italy* 36°15N 44°5E **44 C5**
Arborfield *Canada* 53°6N 103°39W **71 C8**
Arboroath *U.K.* 56°34N 2°35W **11 E6**
Arborg *Canada* 50°54N 97°13W **71 C9**
Arbroath *U.K.* 56°34N 2°35W **11 E6**
Arbuckle *U.S.A.* 39°1N 122°3W **78 F4**
Arcachon *France* 44°40N 1°10W **20 D3**
Arcadia *Fla., U.S.A.* 27°13N 81°52W **85 H14**
Arcadia *La., U.S.A.* 32°33N 92°55W **84 E8**
Arcadia *Pa., U.S.A.* 40°47N 78°51W **82 F6**
Arcata *U.S.A.* 40°52N 124°5W **76 F1**
Archangel = Arkhangelsk
 Russia 64°38N 40°36E **18 B7**
Archangelos *Greece* 36°13N 28°7E **25 C10**
Archbald *U.S.A.* 41°30N 75°32W **83 E9**
Archer → *Australia* 13°28S 141°41E **62 A3**
Archer B. *Australia* 13°20S 141°30E **62 A3**
Archer Bend = Mungkan
 Kandju △ *Australia* 13°35S 142°52E **62 A3**
Archers Post *Kenya* 0°35N 37°35E **54 B4**
Arches △ *U.S.A.* 38°45N 109°25W **76 G9**
Archipel-de-Mingan △
 Canada 50°13N 63°10W **73 B7**
Archipiélago Chinijo △
 Canary Is. 29°20N 13°30W **24 E6**
Archipiélago Los Roques △
 Venezuela 11°50N 66°44W **89 D6**
Arckaringa Cr. →
 Australia 28°10S 135°22E **63 D2**
Arco *U.S.A.* 43°38N 113°18W **76 E7**
Arcos de la Frontera
 Spain 36°45N 5°49W **21 D3**
Arcot *India* 12°53N 79°20E **40 N11**
Arctic Bay *Canada* 73°1N 85°7W **69 B11**
Arctic Mid-Ocean Ridge
 Arctic 87°0N 90°0E **4 A**
Arctic Ocean *Arctic* 78°0N 160°0W **4 B18**
Arctic Red River = Tsiigehtchic
 Canada 67°15N 134°0W **68 C6**
Arctowski *Antarctica* 62°30S 58°0W **5 C18**
Arda → *Bulgaria* 41°40N 26°30E **23 D12**
Ardabīl *Iran* 38°15N 48°18E **45 B6**
Ardakān = Sepīdān *Iran* 30°20N 52°5E **45 D7**
Ardakān *Iran* 32°0N 53°59E **45 C7**
Ardara *Ireland* 54°46N 8°25W **10 B3**
Ardee *Ireland* 53°52N 6°33W **10 C5**
Arden *Canada* 44°43N 76°56W **82 B8**
Arden *Calif., U.S.A.* 38°36N 121°33W **78 G5**
Arden *Nev., U.S.A.* 36°1N 115°14W **79 J11**
Ardenne *Belgium* 49°50N 5°5E **15 D5**
Ardennes = Ardenne
 Belgium 49°50N 5°5E **15 D5**
Arderin *Ireland* 53°2N 7°39W **10 C4**
Ardestān *Iran* 33°20N 52°25E **45 C7**
Ardfert *Ireland* 52°20N 9°47W **10 D2**
Ardglass *U.K.* 54°17N 5°36W **10 B6**
Ardivachar Pt. *U.K.* 57°23N 7°26W **11 D1**
Ardlethan *Australia* 34°22S 146°53E **63 E4**
Ardmore *Okla., U.S.A.* 34°10N 97°8W **84 D6**
Ardmore *Pa., U.S.A.* 40°2N 75°17W **83 F9**

Ardnamurchan, Pt. of
 U.K. 56°43N 6°14W **11 E2**
Ardnave Pt. *U.K.* 55°53N 6°20W **11 F2**
Ardrossan *Australia* 34°26S 137°53E **63 E2**
Ardrossan *U.K.* 55°39N 4°49W **11 F4**
Ards Pen. *U.K.* 54°33N 5°34W **10 B6**
Areia Branca *Brazil* 5°0S 37°0W **93 E11**
Arena, L. *Argentina* 38°57N 123°44W **78 G3**
Arenal *Honduras* 15°21N 86°50W **88 C2**
Arendal *Norway* 58°28N 8°46E **9 G13**
Arequipa *Peru* 16°20S 71°30W **92 G4**
Arévalo *Spain* 41°3N 4°43W **21 B3**
Arezzo *Italy* 43°25N 11°53E **22 C4**
Arga *Turkey* 38°21N 37°59E **44 B3**
Arganda del Rey *Spain* 40°19N 3°26W **21 B4**
Argenta *Canada* 50°11N 116°56W **70 C5**
Argentan *France* 48°45N 0°1W **20 B3**
Argentário, Mte. *Italy* 42°24N 11°9E **22 C4**
Argentia *Canada* 47°18N 53°58W **73 C9**
Argentina ■ *S. Amer.* 35°0S 66°0W **96 D3**
Argentine Basin *Atl. Oc.* 45°0S 45°0W **96 F6**
Argentino, L. *Argentina* 50°10S 73°0W **96 G2**
Argeş → *Romania* 44°5N 26°38E **17 F14**
Arghandab → *Afghan.* 31°30N 64°15E **42 D1**
Argiroupoli *Greece* 35°17N 24°20E **25 D6**
Argolikos Kolpos *Greece* 37°20N 22°52E **23 F10**
Argos *Greece* 37°40N 22°43E **23 F10**
Argostoli *Greece* 38°11N 20°29E **23 E9**
Arguello, Pt. *U.S.A.* 34°35N 120°39W **79 L6**
Arguineguín *Canary Is.* 27°46N 15°41W **24 G4**
Argun → *Russia* 53°20N 121°28E **29 D13**
Argungu *Nigeria* 12°40N 4°31E **50 F6**
Argus Pk. *U.S.A.* 35°52N 117°26W **79 K9**
Argyle, L. *Australia* 16°20S 128°40E **60 C4**
Argyll ⌒ *U.K.* 56°6N 5°9W **11 E4**
Argyll & Bute □ *U.K.* 56°13N 5°28W **11 E3**
Århus *Denmark* 56°8N 10°11E **9 H14**
Ariadnoye *Russia* 45°8N 134°25E **30 B7**
Ariamsvlei *Namibia* 28°9S 19°51E **56 D2**
Ariana *Tunisia* 36°52N 10°12E **51 A8**
Arica *Chile* 18°32S 70°20W **92 G4**
Arica *Colombia* 2°0S 71°50W **92 D4**
Arico *Canary Is.* 28°9N 16°29W **24 F3**
Arid, C. *Australia* 34°1S 123°10E **61 F3**
Arida *Japan* 34°5N 135°8E **31 G7**
Ariège → *France* 43°30N 1°25E **20 E4**
Arila, Akra *Greece* 39°43N 19°39E **25 A3**
Arima *Trin. & Tob.* 10°38N 61°17W **89 D7**
Arinos → *Brazil* 10°25S 58°20W **92 F7**
Ario de Rosales *Mexico* 19°12N 101°43W **86 D4**
Aripo, Mt. *Trin. & Tob.* 10°45N 61°15W **93 K15**
Aripuanã *Brazil* 9°25S 60°30W **92 E6**
Aripuanã → *Brazil* 5°7S 60°25W **92 E6**
Ariquemes *Brazil* 9°55S 63°6W **92 E6**
Arisaig *U.K.* 56°55N 5°51W **11 E3**
Aristazabal I. *Canada* 52°40N 129°10W **70 C3**
Arivonimamo *Madag.* 19°1S 47°11E **57 B8**
Arizaro, Salar de
 Argentina 24°40S 67°50W **94 A2**
Arizona *Argentina* 35°45S 65°25W **94 D2**
Arizona □ *U.S.A.* 34°0N 112°0W **77 J8**
Arizpe *Mexico* 30°20N 110°10W **86 A2**
'Arjah *Si. Arabia* 24°43N 44°17E **44 E5**
Arjeplog *Sweden* 66°3N 17°54E **8 C17**
Arjepluovve = Arjeplog
 Sweden 66°3N 17°54E **8 C17**
Arjona *Colombia* 10°14N 75°22W **92 A3**
Arjuna *Indonesia* 7°49S 112°34E **37 G15**
Arka *Russia* 60°15N 142°0E **29 C15**
Arkadelphia *U.S.A.* 34°7N 93°4W **84 D8**
Arkaig, L. *U.K.* 56°59N 5°10W **11 E3**
Arkalyk = Arqalyk
 Kazakhstan 50°13N 66°50E **28 D7**
Arkansas □ *U.S.A.* 35°0N 92°30W **84 D8**
Arkansas → *U.S.A.* 33°47N 91°4W **84 E9**
Arkansas City *U.S.A.* 37°4N 97°2W **80 G5**
Arkaroola *Australia* 30°20S 139°22E **63 E2**
Arkhangelsk *Russia* 64°38N 40°36E **18 B7**
Arki *India* 31°9N 76°58E **42 D7**
Arklow *Ireland* 52°48N 6°10W **10 D5**
Arkport *U.S.A.* 42°24N 77°42W **82 D7**
Arkticheskiy, Mys
 Russia 81°10N 95°0E **29 A10**
Arkville *U.S.A.* 42°9N 74°37W **83 D10**
Arlanzón → *Spain* 42°3N 4°17W **21 A3**
Arlbergpass *Austria* 47°9N 10°12E **16 E6**
Arles *France* 43°41N 4°40E **20 E6**
Arlington *S. Africa* 28°1S 27°53E **57 D4**
Arlington *N.Y., U.S.A.* 41°42N 73°54W **83 E11**
Arlington *Oreg., U.S.A.* 45°43N 120°12W **76 D3**
Arlington *S. Dak., U.S.A.* 44°22N 97°8W **80 C5**
Arlington *Tex., U.S.A.* 32°44N 97°6W **84 E6**
Arlington *Va., U.S.A.* 38°53N 77°7W **81 F15**
Arlington *Vt., U.S.A.* 43°5N 73°9W **83 C11**
Arlington *Wash., U.S.A.* 48°12N 122°8W **78 B4**
Arlington Heights
 U.S.A. 42°5N 87°59W **80 D10**
Arlit *Niger* 19°0N 7°38E **50 E7**
Arlon *Belgium* 49°42N 5°49E **15 E5**
Arlparra *Australia* 22°11S 134°30E **62 C1**
Arltunga *Australia* 23°26S 134°41E **62 C1**
Armadale *Australia* 32°9S 116°0E **61 F2**
Armagh *U.K.* 54°21N 6°39W **10 B5**
Armagh □ *U.K.* 54°18N 6°37W **10 B5**
Armando Bermudez △
 Dom. Rep. 19°3N 71°0W **89 C5**
Armavir *Russia* 45°2N 41°7E **19 E7**
Armenia *Colombia* 4°35N 75°45W **92 C3**
Armenia ■ *Asia* 40°20N 45°0E **19 F7**
Armenistis, Akra *Greece* 36°8N 27°42E **25 C9**
Armidale *Australia* 30°30S 151°40E **63 E5**
Armour *U.S.A.* 43°19N 98°21W **80 D4**
Armstrong *B.C.,*
 Canada 50°25N 119°10W **70 C5**

Armstrong *Ont., Canada* 50°18N 89°4W **72 B2**
Arnarfjörður *Iceland* 65°48N 23°40W **8 D2**
Arnaud → *Canada* 59°59N 69°46W **69 D13**
Arnauti, C. *Cyprus* 35°6N 32°17E **25 D11**
Arnett *U.S.A.* 36°8N 99°46W **84 C5**
Arnhem *Neths.* 51°58N 5°55E **15 C5**
Arnhem, C. *Australia* 12°20S 137°30E **62 A2**
Arnhem B. *Australia* 12°20S 136°10E **62 A2**
Arnhem Land *Australia* 13°10S 134°30E **62 A1**
Arno → *Italy* 43°41N 10°17E **22 C4**
Arno Bay *Australia* 33°54S 136°34E **63 E2**
Arnold *U.K.* 53°1N 1°7W **12 D6**
Arnold *U.S.A.* 38°15N 120°21W **78 G6**
Arnot *Canada* 55°56N 96°41W **71 B9**
Arnøya *Norway* 70°9N 20°40E **8 A19**
Arnprior *Canada* 45°26N 76°21W **83 A8**
Arnsberg *Germany* 51°24N 8°5E **16 C5**
Aroa, Pte. *Moorea* 17°28S 149°46W **59 d**
Aroab *Namibia* 26°41S 19°39E **56 D2**
Aron *Russia* 57°57N 77°56E **42 G8**
Arona *Canary Is.* 28°6N 16°40W **24 F3**
Aros → *Mexico* 29°0N 107°57W **86 B3**
Arqalyk *Kazakhstan* 50°13N 66°50E **28 D7**
Arrah = Ara *India* 25°35N 84°32E **43 G11**
Arrah *Ivory C.* 6°40N 3°58W **50 G5**
Arran *U.K.* 55°34N 5°12W **11 F3**
Arras *France* 50°17N 2°46E **20 A5**
Arrecife *Canary Is.* 28°57N 13°37W **24 F6**
Arrecifes *Argentina* 34°6S 60°9W **94 C3**
Arrée, Mts. d' *France* 48°26N 3°55W **20 B2**
Arriaga *Mexico* 16°14N 93°54W **87 D6**
Arrilalah *Australia* 23°43S 143°54E **62 C3**
Arrino *Australia* 29°30S 115°40E **61 E2**
Arrow, L. *Ireland* 54°3N 8°19W **10 B3**
Arrowtown *N.Z.* 44°57S 168°50E **59 F2**
Arroyo Grande *U.S.A.* 35°7N 120°35W **79 K6**
Ars *Iran* 37°9N 47°46E **44 B5**
Arsenault L. *Canada* 55°6N 108°32W **71 B7**
Arsenev *Russia* 44°10N 133°15E **30 B6**
Arta *Greece* 39°8N 21°2E **23 E9**
Artà *Spain* 39°41N 3°21E **24 B10**
Artà, Coves de *Spain* 39°40N 3°24E **24 B10**
Arteaga *Mexico* 18°28N 102°25W **86 D4**
Artem *Russia* 43°22N 132°13E **30 C6**
Artemovsk *Russia* 54°45N 93°35E **29 D10**
Artemovsk *Ukraine* 48°35N 38°0E **19 E6**
Artesia = Mosomane
 Botswana 24°2S 26°19E **56 C4**
Artesia *U.S.A.* 32°51N 104°24W **77 K11**
Arthur *Canada* 43°50N 80°32W **82 C4**
Arthur → *Australia* 41°2S 144°40E **63 G3**
Arthur Cr. → *Australia* 22°30S 136°25E **62 C2**
Arthur Pt. *Australia* 22°7S 150°3E **62 C5**
Arthur River *Australia* 33°20S 117°2E **61 F2**
Arthur's Pass *N.Z.* 42°54S 171°35E **59 E3**
Arthur's Pass △ *N.Z.* 42°53S 171°42E **59 E3**
Arthur's Town *Bahamas* 24°38N 75°42W **89 B4**
Artigas *Antarctica* 62°30S 58°0W **5 C18**
Artigas *Uruguay* 30°20S 56°30W **94 C4**
Artillery L. *Canada* 63°9N 107°52W **71 A7**
Artois *France* 50°20N 2°30E **20 A5**
Artrutx, C. de *Spain* 39°55N 3°49E **24 B10**
Artsyz *Ukraine* 46°4N 29°26E **17 E15**
Artux *China* 39°40N 76°10E **32 C2**
Artvin *Turkey* 41°14N 41°44E **19 F7**
Artyk *Russia* 64°12N 145°6E **29 C15**
Aru, Kepulauan *Indonesia* 6°0S 134°30E **37 F8**
Aru Is. = Aru, Kepulauan
 Indonesia 6°0S 134°30E **37 F8**
Arua *Uganda* 3°1N 30°58E **54 B3**
Aruanã *Brazil* 14°54S 51°10W **93 F8**
Aruba ☑ *W. Indies* 12°30N 70°0W **89 D6**
Arucas *Canary Is.* 28°7N 15°32W **24 F4**
Arué *Tahiti* 17°31S 149°30W **59 d**
Arun → *Nepal* 26°55N 87°10E **43 F12**
Arun → *U.K.* 50°49N 0°33W **13 G7**
Arunachal Pradesh □
 India 28°0N 95°0E **41 F19**
Arusha *Tanzania* 3°20S 36°40E **54 C4**
Arusha □ *Tanzania* 4°0S 36°30E **54 C4**
Arusha △ *Tanzania* 3°16S 36°47E **54 C4**
Arusha Chini *Tanzania* 3°32S 37°20E **54 C4**
Aruwimi →
 Dem. Rep. of the Congo 1°13N 23°36E **54 B1**
Arvada *Colo., U.S.A.* 39°48N 105°5W **76 G11**
Arvada *Wyo., U.S.A.* 44°39N 106°8W **76 D10**
Arvayheer *Mongolia* 46°15N 102°48E **32 B5**
Arvi *Greece* 34°59N 25°28E **25 E7**
Arviat *Canada* 61°6N 93°59W **71 A10**
Arvidsjaur *Sweden* 65°35N 19°10E **8 D18**
Arvika *Sweden* 59°40N 12°36E **9 G15**
Arvin *U.S.A.* 35°12N 118°50W **79 K8**
Arwal *India* 25°15N 84°41E **43 G11**
Arxan *China* 47°11N 119°57E **33 B6**
Arys *Kazakhstan* 42°26N 68°48E **28 E7**
Arzamas *Russia* 55°27N 43°55E **18 C7**
Arzanah *U.A.E.* 24°47N 52°34E **45 E7**
Aş Şafā *Syria* 33°10N 37°0E **46 B6**
Aş Saffānīyah *Si. Arabia* 27°55N 48°50E **44 E5**
Aş Safirah *Syria* 36°5N 37°21E **44 B3**
Aş Sahm *Oman* 24°10N 56°53E **45 E8**
As Sājir *Si. Arabia* 25°11N 44°36E **44 E5**
Aş Salamīyah *Syria* 35°1N 37°2E **44 C3**
Aş Salmān *Iraq* 30°30N 44°32E **44 D5**
Aş Salt *Jordan* 32°2N 35°43E **46 C4**
Aş Sal'w'a *Qatar* 24°23N 50°50E **45 E6**
As Samāwah *Iraq* 31°15N 45°15E **44 D5**
As Sanamayn *Syria* 33°3N 36°10E **46 B5**
As Sohar = Şuḩār *Oman* 24°20N 56°40E **45 E8**
As Sukhnah *Syria* 34°52N 38°52E **44 C3**
As Sulaymānīyah *Iraq* 35°35N 45°29E **44 C5**
As Sulaymī *Si. Arabia* 26°17N 41°21E **44 E4**
As Sulayyil *Si. Arabia* 20°27N 45°34E **47 C4**
As Summān *Si. Arabia* 25°0N 47°0E **44 E5**
As Suwaydā' *Syria* 32°40N 36°30E **46 C5**
As Suwaydā' □ *Syria* 32°45N 36°45E **46 C5**
As Suwayq *Oman* 23°51N 57°26E **45 F8**

Aş Şuwayrah *Iraq* 32°55N 45°0E **44 C5**
Asab *Namibia* 25°30S 18°0E **56 D2**
Asad, Buḩayrat al *Syria* 36°0N 38°15E **44 C3**
Asahi-Gawa → *Japan* 34°36N 133°58E **31 G6**
Asahigawa *Japan* 43°46N 142°22E **30 C11**
Asaluyeh *Iran* 27°29N 52°37E **45 E7**
Asamankese *Ghana* 5°50N 0°40W **50 G5**
Asan → *India* 26°37N 78°24E **43 F8**
Asansol *India* 23°40N 87°1E **43 H12**
Asau *Samoa* 13°27S 172°33W **59 b**
Asbesberg *S. Africa* 29°0S 23°0E **56 D3**
Asbestos *Canada* 45°47N 71°58W **73 C5**
Asbury Park *U.S.A.* 40°13N 74°1W **83 F10**
Ascensión *Mexico* 31°6N 107°59W **86 A3**
Ascensión, B. de la
 Mexico 19°40N 87°30W **87 D7**
Ascension I. *Atl. Oc.* 7°57S 14°23W **49 G2**
Aschaffenburg *Germany* 49°58N 9°6E **16 D5**
Aschersleben *Germany* 51°45N 11°29E **16 C6**
Áscoli Piceno *Italy* 42°51N 13°34E **22 C5**
Ascope *Peru* 7°46S 79°8W **92 E3**
Ascotán *Chile* 21°45S 68°17W **94 A2**
Aseb *Eritrea* 13°0N 42°40E **47 E3**
Asela *Ethiopia* 8°0N 39°0E **47 F2**
Asenovgrad *Bulgaria* 42°1N 24°51E **23 C11**
Aşgabat = Ashgabat
 Turkmenistan 38°0N 57°50E **45 B8**
Asgata *Cyprus* 34°46N 33°15E **25 E12**
Ash Fork *U.S.A.* 35°13N 112°29W **77 J7**
Ash Grove *U.S.A.* 37°19N 93°35W **80 G7**
Ash Shabakah *Iraq* 30°49N 43°39E **44 D4**
Ash Shamāl □ *Lebanon* 34°25N 36°0E **46 A5**
Ash Shāmīyah *Iraq* 31°55N 44°35E **44 D5**
Ash Shāriqah *U.A.E.* 25°23N 55°26E **45 E7**
Ash Sharmah *Si. Arabia* 28°1N 35°16E **44 D2**
Ash Sharqāt *Iraq* 35°27N 43°16E **44 C4**
Ash Shaṭrah *Iraq* 31°30N 46°10E **44 D5**
Ash Shawbak *Jordan* 30°32N 35°34E **44 D2**
Ash Shiḩr *Yemen* 14°45N 49°36E **47 E4**
Ash Shināfīyah *Iraq* 31°35N 44°39E **44 D5**
Ash Shu'bah *Si. Arabia* 28°54N 44°44E **44 D5**
Ash Shumlūl *Si. Arabia* 26°31N 47°20E **44 E5**
Ash Shūr'a *Iraq* 35°58N 43°13E **44 C4**
Ash Shurayf *Si. Arabia* 25°43N 39°14E **44 E3**
Ash Shuwayfāt *Lebanon* 33°45N 35°30E **46 B4**
Asha *Russia* 55°0N 57°16E **18 D10**
Ashau *Vietnam* 16°6N 107°22E **38 D6**
Ashbourne *U.K.* 53°2N 1°43W **12 D6**
Ashburn *U.S.A.* 31°43N 83°39W **85 F13**
Ashburton *N.Z.* 43°53S 171°48E **59 E3**
Ashburton → *Australia* 21°40S 114°56E **60 D1**
Ashcroft *Canada* 50°40N 121°20W **70 C4**
Ashdod *Israel* 31°49N 34°35E **46 D3**
Ashdown *U.S.A.* 33°40N 94°8W **84 E7**
Asheboro *U.S.A.* 35°43N 79°49W **85 D15**
Ashern *Canada* 51°11N 98°21W **71 C9**
Asherton *U.S.A.* 28°27N 99°46W **84 G5**
Asheville *U.S.A.* 35°36N 82°33W **85 D13**
Ashewat *Pakistan* 31°22N 68°32E **42 D3**
Asheweig → *Canada* 54°17N 87°12W **72 B2**
Ashford *Australia* 29°15S 151°3E **63 D5**
Ashford *U.K.* 51°8N 0°53E **13 F8**
Ashgabat *Turkmenistan* 38°0N 57°50E **45 B8**
Ashibetsu *Japan* 43°31N 142°11E **30 C11**
Ashikaga *Japan* 36°28N 139°29E **31 F9**
Ashington *U.K.* 55°11N 1°33W **12 B6**
Ashizuri-Uwakai △
 Japan 32°56N 132°32E **31 H6**
Ashizuri-Zaki *Japan* 32°44N 133°0E **31 H6**
Ashkarkot *Afghan.* 33°3N 67°58E **42 C2**
Ashkhabad = Ashgabat
 Turkmenistan 38°0N 57°50E **45 B8**
Āshkhāneh *Iran* 37°26N 56°55E **45 B8**
Ashland *Kans., U.S.A.* 37°11N 99°46W **80 G4**
Ashland *Ky., U.S.A.* 38°28N 82°38W **81 F12**
Ashland *Maine, U.S.A.* 46°38N 68°24W **81 B19**
Ashland *Mont., U.S.A.* 45°36N 106°16W **76 D10**
Ashland *Ohio, U.S.A.* 40°52N 82°19W **82 F2**
Ashland *Oreg., U.S.A.* 42°12N 122°43W **76 E2**
Ashland *Pa., U.S.A.* 40°45N 76°22W **83 F8**
Ashland *Va., U.S.A.* 37°46N 77°29W **81 G15**
Ashland *Wis., U.S.A.* 46°35N 90°53W **80 B8**
Ashley *N. Dak., U.S.A.* 46°2N 99°22W **80 B4**
Ashley *Pa., U.S.A.* 41°12N 75°55W **83 E9**
Ashmore and Cartier Is.
 Ind. Oc. 12°15S 123°0E **60 B3**
Ashmore Reef *Australia* 12°14S 123°5E **60 B3**
Ashmyany *Belarus* 54°26N 25°52E **17 A13**
Ashokan Res. *U.S.A.* 41°56N 74°13W **83 E10**
Ashoknagar *India* 24°34N 77°43E **42 G7**
Ashqelon *Israel* 31°42N 34°35E **46 D3**
Ashta *India* 23°1N 76°43E **42 H7**
Ashtabula *U.S.A.* 41°52N 80°47W **82 E4**
Āshtiyān *Iran* 34°31N 50°0E **45 C6**
Ashton *S. Africa* 33°50S 20°5E **56 E3**
Ashton *U.S.A.* 44°4N 111°27W **76 D8**
Ashuanipi, L. *Canada* 52°45N 66°15W **73 B6**

Ashuapmushuan →
 Canada 48°37N 72°20W **72 C5**
Ashville *U.S.A.* 40°34N 78°33W **82 F6**
Asia 45°0N 75°0E **26 E9**
Asia, Kepulauan
 Indonesia 1°0N 131°13E **37 D8**
Asifabad *India* 19°20N 79°24E **40 K11**
Asinara *Italy* 41°4N 8°16E **22 D3**
Asinara, G. dell' *Italy* 41°0N 8°30E **22 D3**
Asino *Russia* 57°0N 86°0E **28 D9**
Asipovichy *Belarus* 53°19N 28°33E **17 B15**
'Asīr *Si. Arabia* 18°40N 42°30E **47 D3**
Asir, Ras *Somali Rep.* 11°55N 51°10E **47 E5**
Askham *S. Africa* 26°59S 20°47E **56 D3**
Askim *Norway* 59°35N 11°10E **9 G14**
Askja *Iceland* 65°3N 16°48W **8 D5**
Asklipio *Greece* 36°4N 27°56E **25 C9**
Askøyna *Norway* 60°29N 5°10E **8 F11**
Asmara = Asmera
 Eritrea 15°19N 38°55E **47 D2**

Asmera Eritrea 15°19N 38°55E 47 D2
Åsnen Sweden 56°37N 14°45E 9 H16
Aso Kuju △ Japan 32°53N 131°6E 31 H5
Aspatria U.K. 54°47N 3°19W 12 C4
Aspen U.S.A. 39°11N 106°49W 76 G10
Aspermont U.S.A. 33°8N 100°14W 84 E4
Aspiring, Mt. N.Z. 44°23S 168°46E 59 F2
Asprokavos, Akra Greece 39°21N 20°6E 25 B4
Aspur India 23°58N 74°7E 42 H6
Asquith Canada 52°8N 107°13W 71 C7
Assab = Aseb Eritrea 13°0N 42°40E 47 E3
Assal, L. Djibouti 11°40N 42°26E 47 E3
Assam □ India 26°0N 93°0E 41 G18
Assateague Island ⌂ U.S.A. 38°15N 75°10W 81 F16
Asse Belgium 50°24N 4°10E 15 D4
Assen Neths. 53°0N 6°35E 15 A6
Assiniboia Canada 49°40N 105°59W 71 D7
Assiniboine → Canada 49°53N 97°8W 71 D9
Assiniboine, Mt. Canada 50°52N 115°39W 70 C5
Assis Brazil 22°40S 50°20W 95 A5
Assisi Italy 43°4N 12°37E 22 C5
Assynt, L. U.K. 58°10N 5°3W 11 C3
Astana Kazakhstan 51°10N 71°30E 32 A2
Āstāneh Iran 37°17N 49°59E 45 B6
Astara Azerbaijan 38°30N 48°50E 45 B6
Astarabad = Gorgān Iran 36°55N 54°30E 45 B7
Asterousia Greece 34°59N 25°3E 25 E7
Asti Italy 44°54N 8°12E 20 D8
Astipalea Greece 36°32N 26°22E 23 F12
Astorga Spain 42°29N 6°8W 21 A2
Astoria U.S.A. 46°11N 123°50W 78 D3
Astrakhan Russia 46°25N 48°5E 19 E8
Astrebla Downs Australia 24°12S 140°34E 62 C3
Asturias □ Spain 43°15N 6°0W 21 A3
Asunción Paraguay 25°10S 57°30W 94 B4
Asunción Nochixtlán Mexico 17°28N 97°14W 87 D5
Aswa → Uganda 3°43N 31°55E 54 B3
Aswa-Lolim ⌂ Uganda 2°43N 31°35E 54 B3
Aswân Egypt 24°4N 32°57E 51 D12
Aswan High Dam = Sadd el Aali Egypt 23°54N 32°54E 51 D12
Asyût Egypt 27°11N 31°4E 51 C12
At Ţafīlah Jordan 30°45N 35°30E 46 E4
At Ţafīlah □ Jordan 30°45N 35°30E 46 E4
At Ţā'if Si. Arabia 21°5N 40°27E 47 C3
At Ta'mīm □ Iraq 35°30N 44°20E 44 C5
Aţ Ţirāq Si. Arabia 27°19N 44°33E 44 E5
Aţ Tubayq Si. Arabia 29°30N 37°0E 44 D3
Aţ Ţunayb Jordan 31°48N 35°57E 46 D4
Atacama □ Chile 27°30S 70°0W 94 B2
Atacama, Desierto de Chile 24°0S 69°20W 94 A2
Atacama, Salar de Chile 23°30S 68°20W 94 A2
Atakpamé Togo 7°31N 1°13E 50 G6
Atalaya Peru 10°45S 73°50W 92 F4
Atalaya de Femes Canary Is. 28°56N 13°47W 24 F6
Atami Japan 35°5N 139°4E 31 G9
Atamyrat Turkmenistan 37°50N 65°12E 28 F7
Atapupu Indonesia 9°0S 124°51E 37 F6
Atâr Mauritania 20°30N 13°5W 50 D3
Atari Pakistan 30°56N 74°2E 42 D6
Atascadero U.S.A. 35°29N 120°40W 78 K6
Atasū Kazakhstan 48°30N 71°0E 28 E8
Atatürk Barajı Turkey 37°28N 38°30E 19 G6
Atauro E. Timor 8°10S 125°30E 37 F7
Ataviros Greece 36°12N 27°50E 25 C9
Atbara Sudan 17°42N 33°59E 51 E12
'Atbara, Nahr → Sudan 17°40N 33°56E 51 E12
Atbasar Kazakhstan 51°48N 68°20E 28 D7
Atchafalaya B. U.S.A. 29°25N 91°25W 84 G9
Atchison U.S.A. 39°34N 95°7W 80 F6
Āteshān Iran 35°35N 52°37E 45 C7
Ath Belgium 50°38N 3°47E 15 D3
Athabasca Canada 54°45N 113°20W 70 C6
Athabasca → Canada 58°40N 110°50W 71 B6
Athabasca, L. Canada 59°15N 109°15W 71 B7
Athabasca Sand Dunes ⌂ Canada 59°4N 108°43W 71 B7
Athboy Ireland 53°37N 6°56W 10 C5
Athenry Ireland 53°18N 8°44W 10 C3
Athens = Athina Greece 37°58N 23°43E 23 F10
Athens Ala., U.S.A. 34°48N 86°58W 85 D11
Athens Ga., U.S.A. 33°57N 83°23W 85 E13
Athens N.Y., U.S.A. 42°16N 73°49W 83 D11
Athens Ohio, U.S.A. 39°20N 82°6W 81 F12
Athens Pa., U.S.A. 41°57N 76°31W 83 E8
Athens Tenn., U.S.A. 35°27N 84°36W 85 D12
Athens Tex., U.S.A. 32°12N 95°51W 84 E7
Atherley Canada 44°37N 79°20W 82 B5
Atherton Australia 17°17S 145°30E 62 B4
Athi River Kenya 1°28S 36°58E 54 C4
Athienou Cyprus 35°3N 33°32E 25 D12
Athina Greece 37°58N 23°43E 23 F10
Athínai = Athina Greece 37°58N 23°43E 23 F10
Athlone Ireland 53°25N 7°56W 10 C4
Athna Cyprus 35°3N 33°47E 25 D12
Athol U.S.A. 42°36N 72°14W 83 D12
Atholl, Forest of U.K. 56°51N 3°50W 11 E5
Atholville Canada 47°59N 66°43W 73 C6
Athos Greece 40°9N 24°22E 23 D11
Athy Ireland 53°0N 7°0W 10 C5
Ati Chad 13°13N 18°20E 51 F9
Atiak Uganda 3°12N 32°2E 54 B3
Atik L. Canada 55°15N 96°0W 71 B9
Atikaki ⌂ Canada 51°30N 95°31W 71 C9
Atikameg → Canada 52°30N 82°46W 72 B3
Atikokan Canada 48°45N 91°37W 72 C1
Atikonak L. Canada 52°40N 64°32W 73 B7
Atimaono Tahiti 17°46S 149°28W 59 d
Atitlán △ Cent. Amer. 14°38N 91°10W 87 E6
Atiu Cook Is. 20°0S 158°10W 65 J12
Atka Russia 60°50N 151°48E 29 C16
Atka I. U.S.A. 52°7N 174°30W 74 a
Atkinson U.S.A. 42°32N 98°59W 80 D4
Atlanta Ga., U.S.A. 33°45N 84°23W 85 E12
Atlanta Tex., U.S.A. 33°7N 94°10W 84 E7
Atlantic U.S.A. 41°24N 95°1W 80 E6
Atlantic City U.S.A. 39°21N 74°27W 81 F16
Atlantic-Indian Basin Antarctica 60°0S 30°0E 5 B4
Atlantic Ocean 0°0 20°0W 2 D8
Atlas Mts. = Haut Atlas Morocco 32°30N 5°0W 50 B4
Atlin Canada 59°31N 133°41W 70 B2
Atlin, L. Canada 59°26N 133°45W 70 B2
Atlin ⌂ Canada 59°10N 134°30W 70 B2
Atmore U.S.A. 31°2N 87°29W 85 F11
Atoka U.S.A. 34°23N 96°8W 84 D6
Atolia U.S.A. 35°19N 117°37W 79 K9
Atrai → Bangla. 24°7N 89°22E 43 G13
Atrak = Atrek → Turkmenistan 37°35N 53°58E 45 B8
Atrauli India 28°2N 78°20E 42 E8
Atrek → Turkmenistan 37°35N 53°58E 45 B8
Atsuta Japan 43°24N 141°26E 30 C10
Attalla U.S.A. 34°1N 86°6W 85 D11
Attapu Laos 14°48N 106°50E 38 E6
Attawapiskat Canada 52°56N 82°24W 72 B3
Attawapiskat → Canada 52°57N 82°18W 72 B3
Attawapiskat L. Canada 52°18N 87°54W 72 B2
Attica Ind., U.S.A. 40°18N 87°15W 80 E10
Attica Ohio, U.S.A. 41°4N 82°53W 82 E2
Attikamagen L. Canada 55°0N 66°30W 73 B6
Attleboro U.S.A. 41°57N 71°17W 83 E13
Attock Pakistan 33°52N 72°20E 42 C5
Attopeu = Attapu Laos 14°48N 106°50E 38 E6
Attu I. U.S.A. 52°55N 172°55E 74 a
Attur India 11°35N 78°30E 40 P11
Atuel → Argentina 36°17S 66°50W 94 D2
Åtvidaberg Sweden 58°12N 16°0E 9 G17
Atwater U.S.A. 37°21N 120°37W 78 H6
Atwood Canada 43°40N 81°1W 82 C3
Atwood U.S.A. 39°48N 101°3W 80 F3
Atyraū Kazakhstan 47°5N 52°0E 19 E9
Au Sable U.S.A. 44°25N 83°20W 82 B1
Au Sable → U.S.A. 44°25N 83°20W 81 C12
Au Sable Forks U.S.A. 44°27N 73°41W 83 B11
Au Sable Pt. U.S.A. 44°20N 83°20W 82 B1
Auas Honduras 15°29N 84°20W 88 C3
Auasberg Namibia 22°37S 17°13E 56 C2
Aubagne France 43°17N 5°37E 20 E6
Aube → France 48°34N 3°43E 20 B5
Auberry U.S.A. 37°7N 119°29W 78 H7
Auburn Ala., U.S.A. 32°36N 85°29W 85 E12
Auburn Calif., U.S.A. 38°54N 121°4W 78 G5
Auburn Ind., U.S.A. 41°22N 85°4W 81 E11
Auburn Maine, U.S.A. 44°6N 70°14W 81 C18
Auburn N.Y., U.S.A. 42°56N 76°34W 83 D8
Auburn Nebr., U.S.A. 40°23N 95°51W 80 E6
Auburn Pa., U.S.A. 40°36N 76°6W 83 F8
Auburn Wash., U.S.A. 47°18N 122°14W 78 C4
Auburn Ra. Australia 25°15S 150°30E 63 D5
Auburndale U.S.A. 28°4N 81°48W 85 G14
Aubusson France 45°57N 2°11E 20 D5
Auch France 43°39N 0°36E 20 E4
Auchterarder U.K. 56°18N 3°41W 11 E5
Auchtermuchty U.K. 56°18N 3°13W 11 E5
Auckland N.Z. 36°52S 174°46E 59 B5
Auckland Is. Pac. Oc. 50°40S 166°5E 64 N8
Aude → France 43°13N 3°14E 20 E5
Auden Canada 50°14N 87°53W 72 B2
Audubon U.S.A. 41°43N 94°56W 80 E6
Augathella Australia 25°48S 146°35E 63 D4
Aughnacloy U.K. 54°25N 6°59W 10 B5
Aughrim Ireland 53°18N 8°19W 10 C3
Augrabies Falls S. Africa 28°35S 20°20E 56 D3
Augrabies Falls △ S. Africa 28°40S 20°22E 56 D3
Augsburg Germany 48°25N 10°52E 16 D6
Augusta Australia 34°19S 115°9E 61 F2
Augusta Italy 37°13N 15°13E 22 F6
Augusta Ark., U.S.A. 35°17N 91°22W 84 D9
Augusta Ga., U.S.A. 33°28N 81°58W 85 E14
Augusta Kans., U.S.A. 37°41N 96°59W 80 G5
Augusta Maine, U.S.A. 44°19N 69°47W 81 C19
Augusta Mont., U.S.A. 47°30N 112°24W 76 C7
Augustów Poland 53°51N 23°0E 17 B12
Augustus, Mt. Australia 24°20S 116°50E 61 D2
Augustus I. Australia 15°20S 124°30E 60 C3
Aujuittuq = Grise Fiord Canada 76°25N 82°57W 69 B11
Aukštaitija △ Lithuania 55°15N 26°0E 9 J22
Aukum U.S.A. 38°34N 120°43W 78 G6
Auld, L. Australia 22°25S 123°50E 60 D3
Ault U.S.A. 40°35N 104°44W 76 F11
Aunis France 46°5N 0°50W 20 C3
Aunu'u Amer. Samoa 14°20S 170°31W 59 b
Auponhia Indonesia 1°58S 125°27E 37 E7
Aur, Pulau Malaysia 2°35N 104°10E 39 L5
Auraiya India 26°28N 79°33E 43 F8
Aurangabad Bihar, India 24°45N 84°18E 43 G11
Aurangabad Maharashtra, India 19°50N 75°23E 40 K9
Aurich Germany 53°28N 7°28E 16 B4
Aurillac France 44°55N 2°26E 20 D5
Aurora Canada 44°0N 79°28W 82 C5
Aurora S. Africa 32°40S 18°29E 56 E2
Aurora Colo., U.S.A. 39°43N 104°49W 76 G11
Aurora Ill., U.S.A. 41°45N 88°19W 80 E9
Aurora Mo., U.S.A. 36°58N 93°43W 80 G7
Aurora N.Y., U.S.A. 42°45N 76°42W 83 D8
Aurora Nebr., U.S.A. 40°52N 98°0W 80 E5
Aurora Ohio, U.S.A. 41°21N 81°20W 82 E3
Aurukun Australia 13°20S 141°45E 62 A3
Aus Namibia 26°35S 16°12E 56 D2
Ausable → Canada 43°19N 81°46W 82 C3
Auschwitz = Oświęcim Poland 50°2N 19°11E 17 C10
Austin Minn., U.S.A. 43°40N 92°58W 80 D7
Austin Nev., U.S.A. 39°30N 117°4W 76 G5
Austin Pa., U.S.A. 41°38N 78°6W 82 E6
Austin Tex., U.S.A. 30°17N 97°45W 84 F6
Austin, L. Australia 27°40S 118°0E 61 E2
Austin I. Canada 61°10N 94°0W 71 A10
Austra Norway 65°8N 11°55E 8 D14
Austral Is. = Tubuaï, Îs. French Polynesia 25°0S 150°0W 65 K13
Austral Seamount Chain Pac. Oc. 24°0S 150°0W 65 K13
Australia ■ Oceania 23°0S 135°0E 58 D6
Australian-Antarctic Basin S. Ocean 60°0S 120°0E 5 C9
Australian Capital Territory □ Australia 35°30S 149°0E 63 F4
Australind Australia 33°17S 115°42E 61 F2
Austria ■ Europe 47°0N 14°0E 16 E8
Austvågøya Norway 68°20N 14°40E 8 B16
Autlán de Navarro Mexico 19°46N 104°22W 86 D4
Autun France 46°58N 4°17E 20 C6
Auvergne □ France 45°20N 3°15E 20 D5
Auvergne, Mts. d' France 45°20N 2°55E 20 D5
Auxerre France 47°48N 3°32E 20 C5
Av-Dovurak Russia 51°17N 91°35E 29 D10
Ava U.S.A. 36°57N 92°40W 80 G7
Avallon France 47°30N 3°53E 20 C5
Avalon U.S.A. 33°21N 118°20W 79 M8
Avalon Pen. Canada 47°30N 53°20W 73 C9
Avanos Turkey 38°43N 34°51E 44 B2
Avaré Brazil 23°4S 48°58W 95 A6
Avawatz Mts. U.S.A. 35°40N 116°30W 79 K10
Aveiro Brazil 3°10S 55°5W 93 D7
Aveiro Portugal 40°37N 8°38W 21 B1
Āvej Iran 35°40N 49°15E 45 C6
Avellaneda Argentina 34°40S 58°22W 94 C4
Avellino Italy 40°54N 14°47E 22 D6
Avenal U.S.A. 36°0N 120°8W 78 K6
Aversa Italy 40°58N 14°12E 22 D6
Avery U.S.A. 47°15N 115°49W 76 C6
Aves, I. de W. Indies 15°45N 63°55W 89 C7
Aves, Is. las Venezuela 12°0N 67°30W 89 D6
Avesta Sweden 60°9N 16°10E 9 F17
Aveyron → France 44°5N 1°16E 20 D4
Avezzano Italy 42°2N 13°25E 22 C5
Aviá Terai Argentina 26°45S 60°50W 94 B3
Aviemore U.K. 57°12N 3°50W 11 D5
Avignon France 43°57N 4°50E 20 E6
Ávila Spain 40°39N 4°43W 21 B3
Avila Beach U.S.A. 35°11N 120°44W 79 K6
Avilés Spain 43°35N 5°57W 21 A3
Avis U.S.A. 41°11N 77°19W 82 E7
Avoca U.S.A. 42°25N 77°25W 82 D7
Avoca → Australia 35°40S 143°43E 63 F3
Avoca → Ireland 52°48N 6°10W 10 D5
Avola Canada 51°45N 119°19W 70 C5
Avola Italy 36°56N 15°7E 22 F6
Avon U.S.A. 42°55N 77°45W 82 D7
Avon → Australia 31°40S 116°7E 61 F2
Avon → Bristol, U.K. 51°29N 2°41W 13 F5
Avon → Dorset, U.K. 50°44N 1°46W 13 G6
Avon → Warks., U.K. 52°0N 2°8W 13 E5
Avon Park U.S.A. 27°36N 81°31W 85 H14
Avondale Zimbabwe 17°43S 30°58E 55 F3
Avonlea Canada 50°0N 105°0W 71 D8
Avonmore Canada 45°10N 74°58W 83 A10
Avonmouth U.K. 51°30N 2°42W 13 F5
Avranches France 48°40N 1°20W 20 B3
Awa-Shima Japan 38°27N 139°14E 30 E9
A'waj → Syria 33°23N 36°20E 46 B5
Awaji-Shima Japan 34°30N 134°50E 31 G7
'Awālī Bahrain 26°0N 50°30E 45 E6
Awantipur India 33°55N 75°3E 43 C6
Awasa Ethiopia 7°2N 38°28E 47 F2
Awash Ethiopia 9°1N 40°10E 47 F3
Awatere → N.Z. 41°37S 174°10E 59 D5
Awbārī Libya 26°46N 12°57E 51 C8
Awbārī, Idehan Libya 27°10N 11°30E 51 C8
Awe, L. U.K. 56°17N 5°16W 11 E3
Awjilah Libya 29°8N 21°7E 51 C10
Axe → U.K. 50°42N 3°4W 13 F5
Axel Heiberg I. Canada 80°0N 90°0W 69 B11
Axim Ghana 4°51N 2°15W 50 H5
Axios → Greece 40°57N 22°35E 23 D10
Axminster U.K. 50°46N 3°0W 13 G4
Ayabaca Peru 4°40S 79°53W 92 D3
Ayabe Japan 35°20N 135°20E 31 G7
Ayacucho Argentina 37°5S 58°20W 94 D4
Ayacucho Peru 13°0S 74°0W 92 F4
Ayaguz = Ayaköz Kazakhstan 48°10N 80°10E 32 B3
Ayaköz Kazakhstan 48°10N 80°10E 32 B3
Ayamonte Spain 37°12N 7°24W 21 D2
Ayan Russia 56°30N 138°16E 29 D14
Ayaviri Peru 14°50S 70°35W 92 F4
Aydın Turkey 37°51N 27°51E 23 F12
Aydingkol Hu China 42°40N 89°15E 32 B3
Ayer U.S.A. 42°34N 71°35W 83 D13
Ayer Hitam Malaysia 5°24N 100°16E 39 c
Ayer's Cliff Canada 45°10N 72°3W 83 A12
Ayers Rock = Uluru Australia 25°23S 131°5E 61 E5
Ayeyarwady = Irrawaddy → Burma 15°50N 95°6E 41 M19
Áyia Napa Cyprus 34°59N 34°0E 25 E13
Áyia Phyla Cyprus 34°43N 33°1E 25 E12
Áyios Amvrósios Cyprus 35°20N 33°35E 25 D12
Áyios Seryios Cyprus 35°12N 33°53E 25 D12
Áyios Theodhoros Cyprus 35°22N 34°1E 25 D13
Aykhal Russia 66°0N 111°30E 29 C12
Aykino Russia 62°15N 49°56E 18 B8
Aylesbury U.K. 51°49N 0°49W 13 F7
Aylmer Canada 42°46N 80°59W 83 D4
Aylmer, L. Canada 64°5N 108°30W 68 C9
'Ayn, Wādī al Oman 22°15N 55°28E 45 F7
Ayn Dār Si. Arabia 25°55N 49°10E 45 E7
Ayn Zālah Iraq 36°45N 42°35E 44 B4
Ayolas Paraguay 27°10S 56°59W 94 B4
Ayon, Ostrov Russia 69°50N 169°0E 29 C17
'Ayoûn el 'Atroûs Mauritania 16°38N 9°37W 50 E4
Ayr Australia 19°35S 147°25E 62 B4
Ayr Canada 43°17N 80°27W 82 C4
Ayr U.K. 55°28N 4°38W 11 F4
Ayr → U.K. 55°28N 4°38W 11 F4
Ayre, Pt. of I. of Man 54°25N 4°21W 12 C3
Ayton Australia 15°56S 145°22E 62 B4
Aytos Bulgaria 42°42N 27°16E 23 C12
Ayu, Kepulauan Indonesia 0°35N 131°5E 37 D8
Ayutla Guatemala 14°40N 92°10W 88 D1
Ayutla de los Libres Mexico 16°54N 99°13W 87 D5
Ayvacık Turkey 39°36N 26°24E 23 E12
Ayvalık Turkey 39°20N 26°46E 23 E12
Az Zabadānī Syria 33°43N 36°5E 46 B5
Az Ẓāhirīyah West Bank 31°25N 34°58E 46 D3
Az Ẓahrān Si. Arabia 26°10N 50°7E 45 E6
Az Zarqā Jordan 32°5N 36°4E 46 C5
Az Zarqā' U.A.E. 24°53N 53°4E 45 E7
Az Zarqā □ Jordan 32°5N 36°4E 46 C5
Az Zāwiyah Libya 32°52N 12°56E 51 B8
Az Zībār Iraq 36°52N 44°4E 44 B5
Az Zilfī Si. Arabia 26°12N 44°52E 44 E5
Az Zubayr Iraq 30°26N 47°40E 44 D5
Azad Kashmir □ Pakistan 33°50N 73°50E 43 C5
Azamgarh India 26°5N 83°13E 43 F10
Azangaro Peru 14°55S 70°13W 92 F4
Azaouad Mali 19°0N 3°0W 50 E5
Āzār Shahr Iran 37°45N 45°59E 44 B5
Azarān Iran 37°25N 47°16E 44 B5
Azärbayjan = Azerbaijan ■ Asia 40°20N 48°0E 19 F8
Āzarbāyjān-e Gharbī □ Iran 37°0N 44°30E 44 B5
Āzarbāyjān-e Sharqī □ Iran 37°20N 47°0E 44 B5
Azare Nigeria 11°55N 10°10E 50 F8
A'zāz Syria 36°36N 37°4E 44 B3
Azbine = Aïr Niger 18°30N 8°0E 50 E7
Azerbaijan ■ Asia 40°20N 48°0E 19 F8
Azimganj India 24°14N 88°16E 43 G13
Azogues Ecuador 2°35S 78°0W 92 D3
Azores = Açores, Is. dos Atl. Oc. 38°0N 27°0W 50 a
Azov Russia 47°3N 39°25E 19 E6
Azov, Sea of Europe 46°0N 36°30E 19 E6
Azovskoye More = Azov, Sea of Europe 46°0N 36°30E 19 E6
Azraq ash Shīshān Jordan 31°50N 36°49E 46 D5
Aztec U.S.A. 36°49N 107°59W 77 H10
Azúa de Compostela Dom. Rep. 18°25N 70°44W 89 C5
Azuaga Spain 38°16N 5°39W 21 C3
Azuero, Pen. de Panama 7°30N 80°30W 88 E3
Azul Argentina 36°42S 59°43W 94 D4
Azusa U.S.A. 34°8N 117°52W 79 L9
Azzel Matti, Sebkra Algeria 26°10N 0°43E 50 C6

B

Ba Be △ Vietnam 22°25N 105°37E 38 A5
Ba Don Vietnam 17°45N 106°26E 38 D6
Ba Dong Vietnam 9°40N 106°33E 39 H6
Ba Ngoi = Cam Lam Vietnam 11°54N 109°10E 39 G7
Ba Tri Vietnam 10°2N 106°36E 39 G6
Ba Vi △ Vietnam 21°1N 105°22E 38 B5
Ba Xian = Bazhou China 39°8N 116°22E 34 E9
Baa Indonesia 10°50S 123°0E 37 F6
Baardheere Somali Rep. 2°20N 42°27E 47 G3
Baarle-Nassau Belgium 51°27N 4°56E 15 C4
Bab el Mandeb Red Sea 12°35N 43°25E 47 E3
Bābā, Koh-i- Afghan. 34°30N 67°0E 40 B5
Baba Burnu Turkey 39°29N 26°2E 23 E12
Bābā Kalū Iran 30°7N 50°49E 45 D6
Babadag Romania 44°53N 28°44E 17 F15
Babaeski Turkey 41°26N 27°6E 23 D12
Babahoyo Ecuador 1°40S 79°30W 92 D3
Babai = Sarju → India 27°21N 81°23E 43 F9
Babar Indonesia 8°0S 129°30E 37 F7
Babar Pakistan 31°7N 69°32E 42 D3
Babarkach Pakistan 29°45N 68°0E 42 E3
Babb U.S.A. 48°51N 113°27W 76 B7
Baberu India 25°33N 80°43E 43 G9
Babi Besar, Pulau Malaysia 2°25N 103°59E 39 L4
Bābil □ Iraq 32°30N 44°30E 44 C5
Babinda Australia 17°20S 145°56E 62 B4
Babine Canada 55°22N 126°37W 70 B3
Babine → Canada 55°45N 127°44W 70 B3
Babine L. Canada 54°48N 126°0W 70 C3
Babo Indonesia 2°30S 133°30E 37 E8
Bābol Iran 36°40N 52°50E 45 B7
Bābol Sar Iran 36°45N 52°45E 45 B7
Baboua C.A.R. 5°49N 14°58E 52 C2
Babruysk Belarus 53°10N 29°15E 17 B15
Babuhri India 26°49N 69°43E 42 F3
Babusar Pass Pakistan 35°12N 73°59E 43 B5
Babuyan Chan. Phil. 18°40N 121°30E 37 A6
Babylon Iraq 32°34N 44°22E 44 C5
Bac Can Vietnam 22°8N 105°49E 38 A5
Bac Giang Vietnam 21°16N 106°11E 38 B6
Bac Lieu Vietnam 9°17N 105°43E 39 H5
Bac Ninh Vietnam 21°13N 106°4E 38 B6
Bac Phan Vietnam 22°0N 105°0E 38 B5
Bac Quang Vietnam 22°30N 104°48E 38 A5
Bacabal Brazil 4°15S 44°45W 93 D10
Bacalar Mexico 18°43N 88°27W 87 D7
Bacan, Kepulauan Indonesia 0°35S 127°30E 37 E7
Bacarra Phil. 18°15N 120°37E 37 A6
Bacău Romania 46°35N 26°55E 17 E14
Bacerac Mexico 30°18N 108°50W 86 A3
Bach Long Vi, Dao Vietnam 20°10N 107°40E 38 B6
Bach Ma △ Vietnam 16°11N 107°49E 38 D6
Bachhwara India 25°35N 85°54E 43 G11
Back → Canada 65°10N 104°0W 68 C9
Bacolod Phil. 10°40N 122°57E 37 B6
Bacuk Malaysia 6°4N 102°25E 39 J4
Bácum Mexico 27°33N 110°5W 86 B2
Bād Iran 33°41N 52°1E 45 C7
Bad → U.S.A. 44°21N 100°22W 80 C3
Bad Axe U.S.A. 43°48N 83°0W 82 C2
Bad Ischl Austria 47°44N 13°38E 16 E7
Bad Kissingen Germany 50°11N 10°4E 16 C6
Bada Barabil India 22°7N 85°24E 43 H11
Badagara India 11°35N 75°40E 40 P9
Badain Jaran Shamo China 40°23N 102°0E 32 B5
Badajós, L. Brazil 3°15S 62°50W 92 D6
Badajoz Spain 38°50N 6°59W 21 C2
Badakhshān □ Afghan. 36°30N 71°0E 40 A7
Badalona Spain 41°26N 2°15E 21 B7
Badalzai Afghan. 29°50N 65°35E 42 E1
Badampahar India 22°10N 86°10E 41 H15
Badanah Si. Arabia 30°58N 41°30E 44 D4
Badarinath India 30°45N 79°30E 43 D8
Badas, Kepulauan Indonesia 0°45N 107°5E 36 D3
Baddo → Pakistan 28°0N 64°20E 40 F4
Bade Indonesia 7°10S 139°35E 37 F9
Baden Austria 48°1N 16°13E 16 D9
Baden U.S.A. 40°38N 80°14W 82 F4
Baden-Baden Germany 48°44N 8°13E 16 D5
Baden-Württemberg □ Germany 48°20N 8°40E 16 D5
Badgam India 34°1N 74°45E 43 B6
Badgastein Austria 47°7N 13°9E 16 E7
Badger Canada 49°0N 56°4W 73 C8
Badger U.S.A. 36°38N 119°1W 78 J7
Bādghīs □ Afghan. 35°0N 63°0E 40 B3
Badgingarra △ Australia 30°23S 115°22E 61 F2
Badin Pakistan 24°38N 68°54E 42 G3
Badlands U.S.A. 43°55N 102°30W 80 D2
Badlands △ U.S.A. 43°38N 102°56W 80 D2
Badrah Iraq 33°6N 45°58E 44 C5
Badrinath India 30°44N 79°29E 43 D8
Badulla Sri Lanka 7°1N 81°7E 40 R12
Badung, Selat Indonesia 8°40S 115°22E 37 K18
Baena Spain 37°37N 4°20W 21 D3
Baengnyeongdo S. Korea 37°57N 124°40E 35 F13
Baeza Spain 37°57N 3°25W 21 D4
Bafatá Guinea-Biss. 12°8N 14°40W 50 F3
Baffin B. N. Amer. 72°0N 64°0W 69 B13
Baffin I. Canada 68°0N 75°0W 69 C12
Bafing → Mali 13°49N 10°50W 50 F3
Bafliyūn Syria 36°37N 36°59E 44 B3
Bafoulabé Mali 13°50N 10°55W 50 F3
Bafoussam Cameroon 5°28N 10°25E 52 C2
Bāfq Iran 31°40N 55°25E 45 D7
Bafra Turkey 41°34N 35°54E 19 F6
Bāft Iran 29°15N 56°38E 45 D8
Bafwasende Dem. Rep. of the Congo 1°3N 27°5E 54 B2
Bagaha India 27°6N 84°5E 43 F11
Bagamoyo Tanzania 6°28S 38°55E 54 D4
Bagan Datoh Malaysia 3°59N 100°47E 39 L3
Bagan Serai Malaysia 5°1N 100°32E 39 K3
Baganga Phil. 7°34N 126°33E 37 C7
Bagani Namibia 18°7S 21°41E 56 B3
Bagansiapiapi Indonesia 2°12N 100°50E 36 D2
Bagasra India 21°30N 71°0E 42 J4
Bagaud India 22°19N 75°53E 42 H6
Bagdad U.S.A. 34°35N 115°53W 79 L11
Bagdarin Russia 54°26N 113°36E 29 D12
Bagé Brazil 31°20S 54°15W 95 C5
Bagenalstown = Muine Bheag Ireland 52°42N 6°58W 10 D5
Baggs U.S.A. 41°2N 107°39W 76 F10
Bagh Pakistan 33°59N 73°45E 43 C5
Baghain → India 25°32N 81°1E 43 G9
Baghdād Iraq 33°20N 44°23E 44 C5
Bagheria Italy 38°5N 13°30E 22 E5
Baghlān Afghan. 32°12N 68°46E 40 A6
Baghlān □ Afghan. 36°0N 68°30E 40 B6
Bagley U.S.A. 47°32N 95°24W 80 B6
Bago = Pegu Burma 17°20N 96°29E 41 L20
Bagodar India 24°5N 85°52E 43 G11
Bagrationovsk Russia 54°23N 20°39E 9 J19
Baguio Phil. 16°26N 120°34E 37 A6
Bah India 26°53N 78°36E 43 F8
Bahadurganj India 26°16N 87°49E 43 F12
Bahadurgarh India 28°40N 76°57E 42 E7
Bahama, Canal Viejo de W. Indies 22°10N 77°30W 88 B4
Bahamas ■ N. Amer. 24°0N 75°0W 89 B5
Bahār Iran 34°54N 48°26E 45 C6
Baharampur India 24°2N 88°27E 43 G13
Baharu Pandan = Pandan Malaysia 1°32N 103°46E 39 d
Bahawalnagar Pakistan 30°0N 73°15E 42 E5
Bahawalpur Pakistan 29°24N 71°40E 42 E4
Bäherden Turkmenistan 38°25N 57°26E 45 B8
Baheri India 28°45N 79°34E 43 E8
Bahgul → India 27°45N 79°36E 43 F8
Bahi Tanzania 5°58S 35°21E 54 D4
Bahi Swamp Tanzania 6°10S 35°0E 54 D4

Bahia = Salvador Brazil 13°0S 38°30W 93 F11
Bahia □ Brazil 12°0S 42°0W 93 F10
Bahía, Is. de la Honduras 16°45N 86°15W 88 C2
Bahía Blanca Argentina 38°35S 62°13W 94 D3
Bahía de Caráquez Ecuador 0°40S 80°27W 92 D2
Bahía Kino Mexico 28°47N 111°58W 86 B2
Bahía Laura Argentina 48°10S 66°30W 96 F3
Bahía Negra Paraguay 20°5S 58°5W 92 H7
Bahir Dar Ethiopia 11°37N 37°10E 47 E2
Bahmanzād Iran 31°15N 51°47E 45 D6
Bahraich India 27°38N 81°37E 43 F9
Bahrain ■ Asia 26°0N 50°35E 45 E6
Bahror India 27°51N 76°20E 42 F7
Bāhū Kalāt Iran 25°43N 61°25E 45 E9
Bai Bung, Mui = Ca Mau, Mui Vietnam 8°38N 104°44E 39 H5
Bai Duc Vietnam 18°3N 105°49E 38 C5
Bai Thuong Vietnam 19°54N 105°23E 38 C5
Baia Mare Romania 47°40N 23°35E 17 E12
Baião Brazil 2°40S 49°40W 93 D9
Baïbokoum Chad 7°46N 15°43E 51 G9
Baicheng China 45°38N 122°42E 35 B12
Baidoa = Baydhabo Somali Rep. 3°8N 43°30E 47 G3
Baie-Comeau Canada 49°12N 68°10W 73 C6
Baie-St-Paul Canada 47°28N 70°32W 73 C5
Baie Ste-Anne Seychelles 4°18S 55°45E 53 b
Baie-Trinité Canada 49°25N 67°20W 73 C6
Baie Verte Canada 49°55N 56°12W 73 C8
Baihar India 22°6N 80°33E 43 H9
Baihe China 32°50N 110°5E 34 H6
Ba'ījī Iraq 35°0N 43°30E 44 C4
Baijnath India 29°55N 79°37E 43 E8
Baikal, L. = Baykal, Oz. Russia 53°0N 108°0E 29 D11
Baikonur = Bayqongyr Kazakhstan 45°40N 63°20E 28 E7
Baikunthpur India 23°15N 82°33E 43 H10
Baile Atha Cliath = Dublin Ireland 53°21N 6°15W 10 C5
Băileşti Romania 44°1N 23°20E 17 F12
Bainbridge Ga., U.S.A. 30°55N 84°35W 85 F12
Bainbridge N.Y., U.S.A. 42°18N 75°29W 83 D9
Bainbridge Island U.S.A. 47°38N 122°32W 78 C4
Baing Indonesia 10°14S 120°34E 37 F6
Bainiu China 32°50N 112°15E 34 H7
Bā'ir Jordan 30°45N 36°55E 46 E5
Bairiki = Tarawa Kiribati 1°30N 173°0E 64 G9
Bairin Youqi China 43°30N 118°35E 35 C10
Bairin Zuoqi China 43°58N 119°15E 35 C10
Bairnsdale Australia 37°48S 147°36E 63 F4
Baisha China 34°20N 112°32E 34 G7
Baitadi Nepal 29°35N 80°25E 43 E9
Baiyin China 36°45N 104°14E 34 F3
Baiyu Shan China 37°15N 107°30E 34 F4
Baj Baj India 22°30N 88°5E 43 H13
Baja Hungary 46°12N 18°59E 17 E10
Baja, Pta. Mexico 29°58N 115°49W 86 B1
Baja California Mexico 31°10N 115°12W 86 A1
Baja California □ Mexico 30°0N 115°0W 86 B2
Baja California Sur □ Mexico 25°50N 111°50W 86 B2
Bajag India 22°40N 81°21E 43 H9
Bajamar Canary Is. 28°33N 16°20W 24 F3
Bajana India 23°7N 71°49E 42 H4
Bajatrejo Indonesia 8°29S 114°19E 37 J17
Bajera Indonesia 8°31S 115°2E 37 J18
Bājgīrān Iran 37°36N 58°24E 45 B8
Bajimba, Mt. Australia 29°17S 152°6E 63 D5
Bajo Boquete Panama 8°46N 82°27W 88 E3
Bajo Nuevo Caribbean 15°40N 78°50W 88 C4
Bajoga Nigeria 10°57N 11°20E 51 F8
Bajool Australia 23°40S 150°35E 62 C5
Bakel Senegal 14°56N 12°20W 50 F3
Baker Calif., U.S.A. 35°16N 116°4W 79 K10
Baker Mont., U.S.A. 46°22N 104°17W 76 C11
Baker, L. Canada 64°0N 96°0W 68 C10
Baker, Mt. U.S.A. 48°50N 121°49W 76 B3
Baker City U.S.A. 44°47N 117°50W 76 D5
Baker I. Pac. Oc. 0°10N 176°35W 64 G10
Baker I. U.S.A. 55°20N 133°40W 70 B2
Baker L. Australia 26°54S 126°5E 61 E4
Baker Lake Canada 64°20N 96°3W 68 C10
Bakers Creek Australia 21°13S 149°7E 62 C4
Bakers Dozen Is. Canada 56°45N 78°45W 72 A4
Bakersfield Calif., U.S.A. 35°23N 119°1W 79 K8
Bakersfield Vt., U.S.A. 44°45N 72°48W 83 B12
Bakharden = Bäherden Turkmenistan 38°25N 57°26E 45 B8
Bākhtarān = Kermānshāh Iran 34°23N 47°0E 44 C5
Bākhtarān = Kermānshāh □ Iran 34°0N 46°30E 44 C5
Bakı Azerbaijan 40°29N 49°56E 45 A6
Bakkafjörður Iceland 66°2N 14°48W 8 C6
Bakouma C.A.R. 5°40N 22°56E 52 C4
Bakswaho India 24°15N 79°18E 43 G8
Baku = Bakı Azerbaijan 40°29N 49°56E 45 A6
Bakutis Coast Antarctica 74°0S 120°0W 5 D15
Baky = Bakı Azerbaijan 40°29N 49°56E 45 A6
Bala Canada 45°1N 79°37W 82 A5
Bala U.K. 52°54N 3°36W 12 E4
Bala, L. U.K. 52°53N 3°37W 12 E4
Balabac I. Phil. 8°0N 117°0E 36 C5
Balabac Str. E. Indies 7°53N 117°5E 36 C5
Balabagh Afghan. 34°25N 70°12E 42 B4
Ba'labakk Lebanon 34°0N 36°10E 46 B5
Balabalangan, Kepulauan Indonesia 2°20S 117°30E 36 E5
Balad Iraq 34°0N 44°9E 44 C5
Balad Rūz Iraq 33°42N 45°5E 44 C5
Bālādeh Fārs, Iran 29°17N 51°56E 45 D6
Bālādeh Māzandaran, Iran 36°12N 51°48E 45 B6
Balaghat India 21°49N 80°12E 40 J12
Balaghat Ra. India 18°50N 76°30E 40 K10
Balaguer Spain 41°50N 0°50E 21 B6
Balaklava Ukraine 44°30N 33°30E 19 F5
Balakovo Russia 52°4N 47°55E 18 D8
Balamau India 27°10N 80°21E 43 F9
Balancán Mexico 17°48N 91°32W 87 D6
Balashov Russia 51°30N 43°10E 19 D7
Balasinor India 22°57N 73°23E 42 H5
Balasore = Baleshwar India 21°35N 87°3E 41 J15
Balaton Hungary 46°50N 17°40E 17 E9
Balbina, Represa de Brazil 2°0S 59°30W 92 D7
Balboa Panama 8°57N 79°34W 88 E4
Balbriggan Ireland 53°37N 6°11W 10 C5
Balcarce Argentina 38°0S 58°10W 94 D4
Balcarres Canada 50°50N 103°35W 71 C8
Balchik Bulgaria 43°28N 28°11E 23 C13
Balclutha N.Z. 46°15S 169°45E 59 G2
Balcones Escarpment U.S.A. 29°30N 99°15W 84 G5
Bald I. Australia 34°57S 118°27E 61 F2
Bald Knob U.S.A. 35°19N 91°34W 84 D9
Baldock L. Canada 56°33N 97°57W 71 B9
Baldwin Mich., U.S.A. 43°54N 85°51W 81 D11
Baldwin Pa., U.S.A. 40°21N 79°58W 82 F5
Baldwinsville U.S.A. 43°10N 76°20W 83 C8
Baldy Peak U.S.A. 33°54N 109°34W 77 K9
Baleares, Is. Spain 39°30N 3°0E 24 B10
Balearic Is. = Baleares, Is. Spain 39°30N 3°0E 24 B10
Baleine = Whale → Canada 58°15N 67°40W 73 A6
Baleine, Petite R. de la → Canada 56°0N 76°45W 72 A4
Baler Phil. 15°46N 121°34E 37 A6
Baleshare U.K. 57°31N 7°22W 11 D1
Baleshwar India 21°35N 87°3E 41 J15
Baley Russia 51°36N 116°37E 29 D12
Balfate Honduras 15°48N 86°25W 88 C2
Balgo Australia 20°9S 127°58E 60 D4
Bali Greece 35°25N 24°47E 25 D6
Bali India 25°11N 73°17E 42 G5
Bali Indonesia 8°20S 115°0E 37 J18
Bali □ Indonesia 8°20S 115°0E 37 J18
Bali, Selat Indonesia 8°18S 114°25E 37 J17
Bali Sea Indonesia 8°0S 115°0E 37 J17
Baliapal India 21°40N 87°17E 43 J12
Balige Indonesia 2°14N 99°7E 39 L2
Balik Pulau Malaysia 5°21N 100°14E 39 c
Balikeşir Turkey 39°39N 27°53E 23 E12
Balikpapan Indonesia 1°10S 116°55E 36 E5
Balimbing Phil. 5°5N 119°58E 37 C5
Baling Malaysia 5°41N 100°55E 39 K3
Balkan Mts. = Stara Planina Bulgaria 43°15N 23°0E 23 C10
Balkanabat Turkmenistan 39°30N 54°22E 45 B7
Balkhash = Balqash Kazakhstan 46°50N 74°50E 28 E8
Balkhash, Ozero = Balqash Köli Kazakhstan 46°0N 74°50E 28 E8
Ballachulish U.K. 56°41N 5°8W 11 E3
Balladonia Australia 32°27S 123°51E 61 F3
Ballaghaderreen Ireland 53°55N 8°34W 10 C3
Ballarat Australia 37°33S 143°50E 63 F3
Ballard, L. Australia 29°20S 120°40E 61 E3
Ballater U.K. 57°3N 3°3W 11 D5
Ballenas, Canal de Mexico 29°10N 113°29W 86 B2
Balleny Is. Antarctica 66°30S 163°0E 5 C11
Ballia India 25°46N 84°12E 43 G11
Ballina Australia 28°50S 153°31E 63 D5
Ballina Ireland 54°7N 9°9W 10 B2
Ballinasloe Ireland 53°20N 8°13W 10 C3
Ballinger U.S.A. 31°45N 99°57W 84 F5
Ballinrobe Ireland 53°38N 9°13W 10 C2
Ballinskelligs B. Ireland 51°48N 10°13W 10 E1
Ballston Spa U.S.A. 43°0N 73°51W 83 D11
Ballyboghil Ireland 53°32N 6°16W 10 C5
Ballybunion Ireland 52°31N 9°40W 10 D2
Ballycanew Ireland 52°37N 6°19W 10 D5
Ballycastle U.K. 55°12N 6°15W 10 A5
Ballyclare U.K. 54°46N 6°0W 10 B5
Ballydehob Ireland 51°34N 9°28W 10 E2
Ballygawley U.K. 54°27N 7°2W 10 B4
Ballyhaunis Ireland 53°46N 8°46W 10 C3
Ballyheige Ireland 52°23N 9°49W 10 D2
Ballymena U.K. 54°52N 6°17W 10 B5
Ballymoney U.K. 55°5N 6°31W 10 A5
Ballymote Ireland 54°5N 8°31W 10 B3
Ballynahinch U.K. 54°24N 5°54W 10 B6
Ballyquintin Pt. U.K. 54°20N 5°30W 10 B6
Ballyshannon Ireland 54°30N 8°11W 10 B3
Balmaceda Chile 46°0S 71°50W 96 F2
Balmertown Canada 51°4N 93°41W 71 C10
Balmoral Australia 37°15S 141°48E 63 F3
Balmorhea U.S.A. 30°59N 103°45W 84 F3
Balochistan = Baluchistan □ Pakistan 27°30N 65°0E 40 F4
Balonne → Australia 28°47S 147°56E 63 D4
Balotra India 25°50N 72°14E 42 G5
Balqash Kazakhstan 46°50N 74°50E 28 E8
Balqash Köli Kazakhstan 46°0N 74°50E 28 E8
Balrampur India 27°30N 82°20E 43 F10
Balranald Australia 34°38S 143°33E 63 E3
Balsas → Brazil 7°15S 44°35W 93 E9
Balsas → Mexico 17°55N 102°10W 86 D4
Balsas del Norte Mexico 18°0N 99°46W 87 D5
Balta Ukraine 48°2N 29°45E 17 D15
Bălţi Moldova 47°48N 27°58E 17 E14
Baltic Sea Europe 57°0N 19°0E 9 H18
Baltimore Ireland 51°29N 9°22W 10 E2
Baltimore Md., U.S.A. 39°17N 76°36W 81 F15
Baltimore Ohio, U.S.A. 39°51N 82°36W 82 G2
Baltinglass Ireland 52°56N 6°43W 10 D5
Baltit Pakistan 36°15N 74°40E 43 A6
Baltiysk Russia 54°41N 19°58E 9 J18
Baluchistan □ Pakistan 27°30N 65°0E 40 F4
Balurghat India 25°15N 88°44E 43 G13
Balvi Latvia 57°8N 27°15E 9 H22
Balya Turkey 39°44N 27°35E 23 E12
Balykchy Kyrgyzstan 42°26N 76°12E 32 B2
Bam Iran 29°7N 58°14E 45 D8
Bama Nigeria 11°33N 13°41E 51 F8
Bamaga Australia 10°50S 142°25E 62 A3
Bamaji L. Canada 51°9N 91°25W 72 B1
Bamako Mali 12°34N 7°55W 50 F4
Bambari C.A.R. 5°40N 20°35E 52 C4
Bambaroo Australia 18°50S 146°10E 62 B4
Bamberg Germany 49°54N 10°54E 16 D6
Bamberg U.S.A. 33°18N 81°2W 85 E14
Bambili Dem. Rep. of the Congo 3°40N 26°0E 54 B2
Bamburgh U.K. 55°37N 1°43W 12 B6
Bamenda Cameroon 5°57N 10°11E 52 C2
Bamfield Canada 48°45N 125°10W 70 D3
Bāmīān □ Afghan. 35°0N 67°0E 40 B5
Bamiancheng China 43°15N 124°2E 35 C13
Bampūr Iran 27°15N 60°21E 45 E9
Bampūr → Iran 27°24N 59°0E 45 E8
Ban Ao Tu Khun Thailand 8°9N 98°20E 39 a
Ban Ban Laos 19°31N 103°30E 38 C4
Ban Bang Hin Thailand 9°32N 98°35E 39 H2
Ban Bang Khu Thailand 7°57N 98°23E 39 a
Ban Bang Rong Thailand 8°3N 98°25E 39 a
Ban Bo Phut Thailand 9°33N 100°2E 39 b
Ban Chaweng Thailand 9°32N 100°3E 39 b
Ban Chiang Klang Thailand 19°25N 100°55E 38 C3
Ban Choho Thailand 15°2N 102°9E 38 E4
Ban Dan Lan Hoi Thailand 17°0N 99°35E 38 D2
Ban Don = Surat Thani Thailand 9°6N 99°20E 39 H2
Ban Don Vietnam 12°53N 107°48E 38 F6
Ban Don, Ao → Thailand 9°20N 99°25E 39 H2
Ban Dong Thailand 19°30N 100°59E 38 C3
Ban Hong Thailand 18°18N 98°50E 38 C2
Ban Hua Thanon Thailand 9°26N 100°1E 39 b
Ban Kantang Thailand 7°25N 99°31E 39 J2
Ban Karon Thailand 7°51N 98°18E 39 a
Ban Kata Thailand 7°50N 98°18E 39 a
Ban Keun Laos 18°22N 102°35E 38 C4
Ban Khai Thailand 12°46N 101°18E 38 F3
Ban Kheun Laos 20°13N 101°7E 38 B3
Ban Khlong Khian Thailand 8°10N 98°26E 39 a
Ban Khlong Kua Thailand 6°57N 100°8E 39 J3
Ban Khuan Thailand 8°20N 98°25E 39 a
Ban Khuan Mao Thailand 7°50N 99°37E 39 J2
Ban Ko Yai Chim Thailand 11°17N 99°26E 39 G2
Ban Laem Thailand 13°13N 99°59E 38 F2
Ban Lamai Thailand 9°28N 100°3E 39 b
Ban Lao Ngam Laos 15°28N 106°10E 38 E6
Ban Le Kathe Thailand 15°49N 98°53E 38 E2
Ban Lo Po Noi Thailand 8°1N 98°34E 39 a
Ban Mae Chedi Thailand 19°11N 99°31E 38 C2
Ban Mae Nam Thailand 9°34N 100°0E 39 b
Ban Mae Sariang Thailand 18°10N 97°56E 38 C1
Ban Mê Thuôt = Buon Ma Thuot Vietnam 12°40N 108°3E 38 F7
Ban Mi Thailand 15°3N 100°32E 38 E3
Ban Muong Mo Laos 19°4N 103°58E 38 C4
Ban Na Bo Thailand 9°19N 99°41E 39 b
Ban Na Mo Laos 17°7N 105°40E 38 D5
Ban Na San Thailand 8°53N 99°52E 39 H2
Ban Na Tong Laos 20°56N 101°47E 38 B3
Ban Nam Bac Laos 20°38N 102°20E 38 B4
Ban Nam Ma Laos 22°2N 101°37E 38 A3
Ban Ngang Laos 15°59N 106°11E 38 E6
Ban Nong Bok Laos 17°5N 104°48E 38 D5
Ban Nong Boua Laos 15°40N 106°33E 38 E6
Ban Nong Pling Thailand 15°40N 100°10E 38 E3
Ban Pak Chan Thailand 10°32N 98°51E 39 G2
Ban Patong Thailand 7°54N 98°18E 39 a
Ban Phai Thailand 16°4N 102°44E 38 D4
Ban Phak Chit Thailand 8°0N 98°24E 39 a
Ban Pong Thailand 13°50N 99°55E 38 F2
Ban Rawai Thailand 7°47N 98°20E 39 a
Ban Ron Phibun Thailand 8°9N 99°51E 39 H2
Ban Sakhu Thailand 8°4N 98°18E 39 a
Ban Sanam Chai Thailand 7°33N 100°25E 39 J3
Ban Sangkha Thailand 14°37N 103°52E 38 E4
Ban Tak Thailand 17°2N 99°4E 38 D2
Ban Tako Thailand 14°5N 102°40E 38 E4
Ban Tha Dua Thailand 17°59N 98°39E 38 D2
Ban Tha Nun Thailand 8°12N 98°18E 39 a
Ban Tha Rua Thailand 7°59N 98°22E 39 a
Ban Tha Yu Thailand 8°17N 98°22E 39 a
Ban Thahine Laos 14°12N 105°33E 38 E5
Ban Thong Krut Thailand 9°25N 99°57E 39 b
Ban Xien Kok Laos 20°54N 100°39E 38 B3
Ban Yen Nhan Vietnam 20°57N 106°2E 38 B6
Banaba Kiribati 0°45S 169°50E 64 H8
Banalia Dem. Rep. of the Congo 1°32N 25°5E 54 B2
Banam Cambodia 11°20N 105°17E 39 G5
Bananal, I. do Brazil 11°30S 50°30W 93 F8
Banaras = Varanasi India 25°22N 83°0E 43 G10
Banas → Gujarat, India 23°45N 71°25E 42 H4
Banas → Mad. P., India 24°15N 81°30E 43 G9
Bânâs, Ras Egypt 23°57N 35°59E 51 D13
Banbridge U.K. 54°22N 6°16W 10 B5
Banbury U.K. 52°4N 1°20W 13 E6
Banchory U.K. 57°3N 2°29W 11 D6
Bancroft Canada 45°3N 77°51W 82 A7
Band Bonī Iran 25°30N 59°33E 45 E8
Band Qīr Iran 31°39N 48°53E 45 D6
Banda Mad. P., India 24°3N 78°57E 43 G8
Banda Ut. P., India 25°30N 80°26E 43 G9
Banda, Kepulauan Indonesia 4°37S 129°50E 37 E7
Banda Aceh Indonesia 5°35N 95°20E 36 C1
Banda Banda, Mt. Australia 31°10S 152°28E 63 E5
Banda Elat Indonesia 5°40S 133°5E 37 F8
Banda Is. = Banda, Kepulauan Indonesia 4°37S 129°50E 37 E7
Banda Sea Indonesia 6°0S 130°0E 37 F8
Bandai-Asahi △ Japan 37°38N 140°5E 30 F10
Bandai-San Japan 37°36N 140°4E 30 F10
Bandān Iran 31°23N 60°44E 45 D9
Bandanaira Indonesia 4°32S 129°54E 37 E7
Bandanwara India 26°9N 74°38E 42 F6
Bandar = Machilipatnam India 16°12N 81°8E 41 L12
Bandar-e Abbās Iran 27°15N 56°15E 45 E8
Bandar-e Anzalī Iran 37°30N 49°30E 45 B6
Bandar-e Bushehr = Būshehr Iran 28°55N 50°55E 45 D6
Bandar-e Chārak Iran 26°45N 54°20E 45 E7
Bandar-e Deylam Iran 30°5N 50°10E 45 D6
Bandar-e Emām Khomeynı Iran 30°30N 49°5E 45 D6
Bandar-e Lengeh Iran 26°35N 54°58E 45 E7
Bandar-e Maqām Iran 26°56N 53°29E 45 E7
Bandar-e Ma'shur Iran 30°35N 49°10E 45 D6
Bandar-e Rīg Iran 29°29N 50°38E 45 D6
Bandar-e Torkeman Iran 37°0N 54°10E 45 B7
Bandar Lampung Indonesia 5°20S 105°10E 36 F3
Bandar Maharani = Muar Malaysia 2°3N 102°34E 39 L4
Bandar Penggaram = Batu Pahat Malaysia 1°50N 102°56E 39 M4
Bandar Seri Begawan Brunei 4°52N 115°0E 36 D5
Bandar Sri Aman = Sri Aman Malaysia 1°15N 111°32E 36 D4
Bandawe Malawi 11°58S 34°5E 55 E3
Bandeira, Pico da Brazil 20°26S 41°47W 95 A7
Bandera Argentina 28°55S 62°20W 94 B3
Banderas, B. de Mexico 20°40N 105°25W 86 C3
Bandhavgarh India 23°40N 81°2E 43 H9
Bandi → India 26°12N 75°47E 42 F6
Bandikui India 27°3N 76°34E 42 F7
Bandırma Turkey 40°20N 28°0E 23 D13
Bandjarmasin = Banjarmasin Indonesia 3°20S 114°35E 36 E4
Bandon Ireland 51°44N 8°44W 10 E3
Bandon → Ireland 51°43N 8°37W 10 E3
Bandula Mozam. 19°0S 33°7E 55 F3
Bandundu Dem. Rep. of the Congo 3°15S 17°22E 52 E3
Bandung Indonesia 6°54S 107°36E 37 G12
Bāneh Iran 35°59N 45°53E 44 C5
Banes Cuba 21°0N 75°42W 89 B4
Banff Canada 51°10N 115°34W 70 C5
Banff U.K. 57°40N 2°33W 11 D6
Banff △ Canada 51°30N 116°15W 70 C5
Bang Fai → Laos 16°57N 104°45E 38 D5
Bang Hieng → Laos 16°10N 105°10E 38 D5
Bang Krathum Thailand 16°34N 100°18E 38 D3
Bang Lamung Thailand 13°3N 100°56E 38 F3
Bang Mun Nak Thailand 16°2N 100°23E 38 D3
Bang Pa In Thailand 14°14N 100°35E 38 E3
Bang Rakam Thailand 16°45N 100°7E 38 D3
Bang Saphan Thailand 11°14N 99°28E 39 G2
Bang Thao Thailand 7°59N 98°18E 39 a
Bangaduni I. India 21°34N 88°52E 43 J13
Bangala Dam Zimbabwe 21°7S 31°25E 55 G3
Bangalore India 12°59N 77°40E 40 N10
Banganga → India 27°6N 77°25E 42 F6
Bangaon India 23°0N 88°47E 43 H13
Bangassou C.A.R. 4°55N 23°7E 52 D4
Banggai Indonesia 1°34S 123°30E 37 E6
Banggai, Kepulauan Indonesia 1°40S 123°30E 37 E6
Banggai Arch. = Banggai, Kepulauan Indonesia 1°40S 123°30E 37 E6
Banggi, Pulau Malaysia 7°17N 117°12E 36 C5
Banghāzī Libya 32°11N 20°3E 51 B10
Bangka Sulawesi, Indonesia 1°50N 125°5E 37 D7
Bangka Sumatera, Indonesia 2°0S 105°50E 36 E3
Bangka, Selat Indonesia 2°30S 105°30E 36 E3
Bangka-Belitung □ Indonesia 2°30S 107°0E 36 E3
Bangkalan Indonesia 7°2S 112°46E 37 G15
Bangkinang Indonesia 0°18N 101°5E 36 D2
Bangko Indonesia 2°5S 102°9E 36 E2
Bangkok Thailand 13°45N 100°35E 38 F3
Bangladesh ■ Asia 24°0N 90°0E 41 H17
Bangli Indonesia 8°27S 115°21E 37 J18
Bangong Co China 33°45N 78°43E 43 C8
Bangor Down, U.K. 54°40N 5°40W 10 B6
Bangor Gwynedd, U.K. 53°14N 4°8W 12 D3
Bangor Maine, U.S.A. 44°48N 68°46W 81 C19
Bangor Pa., U.S.A. 40°52N 75°13W 83 F9
Bangued Phil. 17°40N 120°37E 37 A6
Bangui C.A.R. 4°23N 18°35E 52 D3
Banguru Dem. Rep. of the Congo 0°30N 27°10E 54 B2
Bangweulu, L. Zambia 11°0S 30°0E 55 E3
Bangweulu Swamp Zambia 11°20S 30°15E 55 E3
Banhine △ Mozam. 22°49S 32°55E 57 C5
Bani Dom. Rep. 18°16N 70°22W 89 C5
Banī Sa'd Iraq 33°34N 44°32E 44 C5
Banihal Pass India 33°30N 75°12E 43 C6
Banissa Kenya 3°55N 40°19E 54 B4
Bāniyās Syria 35°10N 36°0E 44 C3
Banja Luka Bos.-H. 44°49N 17°11E 22 B7
Banjar India 31°38N 77°21E 42 D7
Banjar → India 22°36N 80°22E 43 H9
Banjarmasin Indonesia 3°20S 114°35E 36 E4
Banjul Gambia 13°28N 16°40W 50 F2
Banka India 24°53N 86°55E 43 G12
Banket Zimbabwe 17°27S 30°19E 55 F3
Bankipore India 25°35N 85°10E 41 G14
Banks I. B.C., Canada 53°20N 130°0W 70 C3
Banks I. N.W.T., Canada 73°15N 121°30W 68 B7
Banks Pen. N.Z. 43°45S 173°15E 59 E4
Banks Str. Australia 40°40S 148°10E 63 G4
Bankura India 23°11N 87°18E 43 H12
Banmankhi India 25°53N 87°11E 43 G12
Bann → Armagh, U.K. 54°30N 6°31W 10 B5
Bann → L'derry., U.K. 55°8N 6°41W 10 A5
Bannang Sata Thailand 6°16N 101°16E 39 J3
Banning U.S.A. 33°56N 116°53W 79 M10
Bannockburn Canada 44°39N 77°33W 82 B7
Bannockburn U.K. 56°5N 3°55W 11 E5
Bannockburn Zimbabwe 20°17S 29°48E 55 G2
Bannu Pakistan 33°0N 70°18E 40 C7
Bano India 22°40N 84°55E 43 H11
Bansgaon India 26°33N 83°21E 43 F10
Banská Bystrica Slovak Rep. 48°46N 19°14E 17 D10
Banswara India 23°32N 74°24E 42 H6
Bantaeng Indonesia 5°32S 119°56E 37 F5
Banten □ Indonesia 6°30S 106°0E 37 G11
Bantry Ireland 51°41N 9°27W 10 E2
Bantry B. Ireland 51°37N 9°44W 10 E2
Bantul Indonesia 7°55S 110°19E 37 G14
Bantva India 21°29N 70°12E 42 J4
Banyak, Kepulauan Indonesia 2°10N 97°10E 36 D1
Banyalbufar Spain 39°42N 2°31E 24 B9
Banyo Cameroon 6°52N 11°45E 52 C2
Banyumas Indonesia 7°32S 109°18E 37 G13
Banyuwangi Indonesia 8°13S 114°21E 37 J17
Banzare Coast Antarctica 68°0S 125°0E 5 C9
Bao Ha Vietnam 22°11N 104°21E 38 A5
Bao Lac Vietnam 22°57N 105°40E 38 A5
Bao Loc Vietnam 11°32N 107°48E 39 G6
Bao'an = Shenzhen China 22°32N 114°5E 33 F10
Baocheng China 33°12N 106°56E 34 H4
Baode China 39°1N 111°5E 34 E6
Baodi China 39°38N 117°20E 35 E9
Baoding China 38°50N 115°28E 34 E8
Baoji China 34°20N 107°5E 34 G4
Baoshan China 25°10N 99°5E 32 D4
Baotou China 40°32N 110°2E 34 D6
Baoying China 33°17N 119°20E 35 H10
Baoyou = Ledong China 18°41N 109°5E 38 C7
Bap India 27°23N 72°18E 42 F5
Bapatla India 15°55N 80°30E 41 M12
Bāqerābād Iran 33°2N 51°58E 45 C6
Ba'qūbah Iraq 33°45N 44°50E 44 C5
Baquedano Chile 23°20S 69°52W 94 A2
Bar Montenegro 42°8N 19°6E 23 C8
Bar Ukraine 49°4N 27°40E 17 D14
Bar Bigha India 25°21N 85°47E 43 G11
Bar Harbor U.S.A. 44°23N 68°13W 81 C19
Bar-le-Duc France 48°47N 5°10E 20 B6
Bara India 25°16N 81°43E 43 G9
Bara Banki India 26°55N 81°12E 43 F9
Barabai Indonesia 2°32S 115°34E 36 E5
Baraboo U.S.A. 43°28N 89°45W 80 D9
Baracoa Cuba 20°20N 74°30W 89 B5
Baradā → Syria 33°33N 36°34E 46 B5
Baradero Argentina 33°52S 59°29W 94 C4
Baraga U.S.A. 46°47N 88°30W 80 B9
Baragoi Kenya 1°47N 36°47E 54 B4
Barah → India 27°42N 77°5E 42 F6
Barahona Dom. Rep. 18°13N 71°7W 89 C5
Barail Range India 25°15N 93°20E 41 G18
Barakaldo Spain 43°18N 2°59W 21 A4
Barakar → India 24°7N 86°14E 43 G12
Barakot India 21°33N 84°59E 43 J11
Barakpur India 22°47N 88°21E 43 H13
Baralaba Australia 24°13S 149°50E 62 C4
Baralzon L. Canada 60°0N 98°3W 71 B9
Baramula India 34°15N 74°20E 43 B6
Baran India 25°9N 76°40E 42 G7
Baran → Pakistan 25°13N 68°17E 42 G3
Baranavichy Belarus 53°10N 26°0E 17 B14
Baranof U.S.A. 57°5N 134°50W 70 B2
Baranof I. U.S.A. 57°0N 135°0W 68 D6
Barapasi Indonesia 2°15S 137°5E 37 E9
Barasat India 22°46N 88°31E 43 H13
Barat Daya, Kepulauan Indonesia 7°30S 128°0E 37 F7
Barataria B. U.S.A. 29°20N 89°55W 85 G10
Barauda India 23°33N 75°15E 42 H6
Baraut India 29°13N 77°7E 42 E7
Barbacena Brazil 21°15S 43°56W 95 A7
Barbados ■ W. Indies 13°10N 59°30W 89 g
Barbària, C. de Spain 38°39N 1°24E 24 C7
Barbas, C. W. Sahara 22°20N 16°42W 50 D2
Barbastro Spain 42°2N 0°5E 21 A6
Barberton S. Africa 25°42S 31°2E 57 D5
Barberton U.S.A. 41°1N 81°39W 82 E3
Barbosa Colombia 5°57N 73°37W 92 B4
Barbourville U.S.A. 36°52N 83°53W 81 G12
Barbuda W. Indies 17°30N 61°40W 89 C7
Barcaldine Australia 23°43S 145°6E 62 C4
Barcellona Pozzo di Gotto Italy 38°9N 15°13E 22 E6
Barcelona Spain 41°22N 2°10E 21 B7
Barcelona Venezuela 10°10N 64°40W 92 A6
Barceloneta Puerto Rico 18°27N 66°32W 89 d
Barcelos Brazil 1°0S 63°0W 92 D6
Barcoo → Australia 25°30S 142°50E 62 D3
Bardaï Chad 21°25N 17°0E 51 D9
Bardas Blancas Argentina 35°49S 69°45W 94 D2
Bardawîl, Sabkhet el Egypt 31°10N 33°15E 46 D2
Barddhaman India 23°14N 87°39E 43 H12
Bardejov Slovak Rep. 49°18N 21°15E 17 D11
Bardera = Baardheere Somali Rep. 2°20N 42°27E 47 G3
Bardīyah Libya 31°45N 25°5E 51 B10
Bardsey I. U.K. 52°45N 4°47W 12 E3

Bardstown U.S.A. 37°49N 85°28W 81 G11
Bareilly India 28°22N 79°27E 43 E8
Barela India 23°6N 80°3E 43 H9
Barents Sea Arctic 73°0N 39°0E 4 B9
Barfleur, Pte. de France 49°42N 1°16W 20 B3
Bargara Australia 24°50S 152°25E 62 C5
Bargi Dam India 22°50N 80°0E 43 H9
Barguzin Russia 53°37N 109°37E 29 D11
Barh India 25°29N 85°46E 43 G11
Barhaj India 26°18N 83°44E 43 F10
Barharwa India 24°52N 87°47E 43 G12
Barhi India 24°15N 85°25E 43 G11
Bari India 26°39N 77°39E 42 F7
Bari Italy 41°8N 16°51E 22 D7
Bari Doab Pakistan 30°20N 73°0E 42 D5
Bari Sadri India 24°28N 74°30E 42 G6
Barīdī, Ra's Si. Arabia 24°17N 37°31E 44 E3
Barīm Yemen 12°39N 43°25E 48 E8
Barinas Venezuela 8°36N 70°15W 92 B4
Baring, C. Canada 70°0N 117°30W 68 C8
Baringo, L. Kenya 0°47N 36°16E 54 B4
Barisal Bangla. 22°45N 90°20E 41 H17
Barisal □ Bangla. 22°45N 90°20E 41 H17
Barisan, Pegunungan Indonesia 3°30S 102°15E 36 E2
Barito → Indonesia 4°0S 114°50E 36 E4
Baritú △ Argentina 23°43S 64°40W 94 A3
Barjūj, Wadi → Libya 25°26N 12°12E 51 C8
Bark L. Canada 45°27N 77°51W 82 A7
Barkakana India 23°37N 85°29E 43 H11
Barker U.S.A. 43°20N 78°33W 82 C6
Barkley, L. U.S.A. 37°1N 88°14W 85 C10
Barkley Sound Canada 48°50N 125°10W 70 D3
Barkly East S. Africa 30°58S 27°33E 56 E4
Barkly Homestead Australia 19°52S 135°50E 62 B2
Barkly Tableland Australia 17°50S 136°40E 62 B2
Barkly West S. Africa 28°5S 24°31E 56 D3
Barkol Kazak Zizhixian China 43°37N 93°2E 32 B4
Bârlad Romania 46°15N 27°38E 17 E14
Bârlad → Romania 45°38N 27°32E 17 F14
Barlee, L. Australia 29°15S 119°30E 61 E2
Barlee, Mt. Australia 24°38S 128°13E 61 D4
Barletta Italy 41°19N 16°17E 22 D7
Barlovento Canary Is. 28°48N 17°48W 24 F2
Barlovento C. Verde Is. 17°0N 25°0W 50 b
Barlow L. Canada 62°0N 103°0W 71 A8
Barmedman Australia 34°9S 147°21E 63 E4
Barmer India 25°45N 71°20E 42 G4
Barmera Australia 34°15S 140°28E 63 E3
Barmouth U.K. 52°44N 4°4W 12 E3
Barna → India 25°21N 83°3E 43 G10
Barnagar India 23°7N 75°19E 42 H6
Barnala India 30°23N 75°33E 42 D6
Barnard Castle U.K. 54°33N 1°55W 12 C6
Barnaul Russia 53°20N 83°40E 28 D9
Barnesville Ga., U.S.A. 33°3N 84°9W 85 E12
Barnesville Minn., U.S.A. 46°43N 96°28W 80 B5
Barnet □ U.K. 51°38N 0°9W 13 F7
Barneveld Neths. 52°7N 5°36E 15 B5
Barnhart U.S.A. 31°8N 101°10W 84 F4
Barnsley U.K. 53°34N 1°27W 12 D6
Barnstable U.S.A. 41°42N 70°18W 81 E18
Barnstaple U.K. 51°5N 4°4W 13 F3
Barnstaple Bay = Bideford Bay U.K. 51°5N 4°20W 13 F3
Barnwell U.S.A. 33°15N 81°23W 85 E14
Baro Nigeria 8°35N 6°18E 50 G7
Baroda = Vadodara India 22°20N 73°10E 42 H5
Baroda India 25°29N 76°35E 42 G7
Baroe S. Africa 33°13S 24°33E 56 E3
Baron Ra. Australia 23°30S 127°45E 60 D4
Barotseland Zambia 15°0S 24°0E 53 H4
Barpeta India 26°20N 91°10E 41 F17
Barqa Libya 27°0N 23°0E 51 C10
Barques, Pt. Aux U.S.A. 44°4N 82°58W 82 B2
Barquísimeto Venezuela 10°4N 69°19W 92 A5
Barr Smith Range Australia 27°4S 120°20E 61 E3
Barra Brazil 11°5S 43°10W 93 F10
Barra U.K. 57°0N 7°29W 11 E1
Barra, Sd. of U.K. 57°4N 7°25W 11 D1
Barra de Navidad Mexico 19°12N 104°41W 86 D4
Barra do Corda Brazil 5°30S 45°10W 93 E9
Barra do Garças Brazil 15°54S 52°16W 93 G8
Barra do Piraí Brazil 22°30S 43°50W 95 A7
Barra Falsa, Pta. da Mozam. 22°58S 35°37E 57 C6
Barra Hd. U.K. 56°47N 7°40W 11 E1
Barra Mansa Brazil 22°35S 44°12W 95 A7
Barraba Australia 30°21S 150°35E 63 E5
Barrackpur = Barakpur India 22°47N 88°21E 43 H13
Barradale Australia 22°42S 114°58E 60 D1
Barraigh = Barra U.K. 57°0N 7°29W 11 E1
Barranca Lima, Peru 10°45S 77°50W 92 F3
Barranca Loreto, Peru 4°50S 76°50W 92 D3
Barranca del Cobre ⌂ Mexico 27°18N 107°40W 86 B3
Barrancabermeja Colombia 7°0N 73°50W 92 B4
Barrancas Venezuela 8°55N 62°5W 92 B6
Barrancos Portugal 38°10N 6°58W 21 C2
Barranqueras Argentina 27°30S 59°0W 94 B4
Barranquilla Colombia 11°0N 74°50W 92 A4
Barraute Canada 48°26N 77°38W 72 C4
Barre Mass., U.S.A. 42°25N 72°6W 83 D12
Barre Vt., U.S.A. 44°12N 72°30W 83 B12
Barreal Argentina 31°33S 69°28W 94 C2
Barreiras Brazil 12°8S 45°0W 93 F10
Barreirinhas Brazil 2°30S 42°50W 93 D10
Barreiro Portugal 38°39N 9°5W 21 C1
Barren, Nosy Madag. 18°25S 43°40E 57 B7
Barretos Brazil 20°30S 48°35W 93 H9
Barrhead Canada 54°10N 114°24W 70 C6
Barrie Canada 44°24N 79°40W 82 B5
Barrier Ra. Australia 31°0S 141°30E 63 E3
Barrier Reef Belize 17°9N 88°3W 87 D7
Barrière Canada 51°12N 120°7W 70 C4
Barrington U.S.A. 41°44N 71°18W 83 E13
Barrington L. Canada 56°55N 100°15W 71 B8
Barrington Tops Australia 32°6S 151°28E 63 E5
Barringun Australia 29°1S 145°41E 63 D4
Barron U.S.A. 45°24N 91°51W 80 C8
Barrow U.S.A. 71°18N 156°47W 74 a
Barrow → Ireland 52°25N 6°58W 10 D5
Barrow, Pt. U.S.A. 71°23N 156°29W 66 B4
Barrow Creek Australia 21°30S 133°55E 62 C1
Barrow I. Australia 20°45S 115°20E 60 D2
Barrow-in-Furness U.K. 54°7N 3°14W 12 C4
Barrow Pt. Australia 14°20S 144°40E 62 A3
Barrow Ra. Australia 26°0S 127°40E 61 E4
Barrow Str. Canada 74°20N 95°0W 4 B3
Barry U.K. 51°24N 3°16W 13 F4
Barry's Bay Canada 45°29N 77°41W 82 A7
Barsat Pakistan 36°10N 72°45E 43 A5
Barsi India 18°10N 75°50E 40 K9
Barsoi India 25°48N 87°57E 41 G15
Barstow U.S.A. 34°54N 117°1W 79 L9
Barthélemy, Col Vietnam 19°26N 104°6E 38 C5
Bartica Guyana 6°25N 58°40W 92 B7
Bartle Frere Australia 17°27S 145°50E 62 B4
Bartlesville U.S.A. 36°45N 95°59W 84 C7
Bartlett Calif., U.S.A. 36°29N 118°2W 78 J8
Bartlett Tenn., U.S.A. 35°12N 89°52W 85 D10
Bartlett, L. Canada 63°5N 118°20W 70 A5
Bartolomeu Dias Mozam. 21°10S 35°8E 55 G4
Barton U.S.A. 44°45N 72°11W 83 B12
Barton upon Humber U.K. 53°41N 0°25W 12 D7
Bartow U.S.A. 27°54N 81°50W 85 H14
Barú, Volcan Panama 8°55N 82°35W 88 E3
Barumba Dem. Rep. of the Congo 1°3N 23°37E 54 B1
Baruun Urt Mongolia 46°46N 113°15E 29 E12
Baruunsuu Mongolia 43°43N 105°35E 34 C3
Barwani India 22°2N 74°57E 42 H6
Barysaw Belarus 54°17N 28°28E 17 A15
Barzān Iraq 36°55N 44°3E 44 B5
Bāsa'idū Iran 26°35N 55°20E 45 E7
Basal Pakistan 33°33N 72°13E 42 C5
Basankusa Dem. Rep. of the Congo 1°5N 19°50E 52 D3
Basarabeasca Moldova 46°21N 28°58E 17 E15
Basarabia = Bessarabiya Moldova 47°0N 28°10E 17 E15
Basawa Afghan. 34°15N 70°50E 42 B4
Bascuñán, C. Chile 28°52S 71°35W 94 B1
Basel Switz. 47°35N 7°35E 20 C7
Bashākerd, Kūhhā-ye Iran 26°42N 58°35E 45 E8
Bashaw Canada 52°35N 112°58W 70 C6
Bāshī Iran 28°41N 51°4E 45 D6
Bashkir Republic = Bashkortostan □ Russia 54°0N 57°0E 18 D10
Bashkortostan □ Russia 54°0N 57°0E 18 D10
Basibasy Madag. 22°10S 43°40E 57 C7
Basilan Phil. 6°35N 122°0E 37 C6
Basilan Str. Phil. 6°50N 122°0E 37 C6
Basildon U.K. 51°34N 0°28E 13 F8
Basim = Washim India 20°3N 77°0E 40 J10
Basin U.S.A. 44°23N 108°2W 76 D9
Basingstoke U.K. 51°15N 1°5W 13 F6
Baskatong, Rés. Canada 46°46N 75°50W 72 C4
Basle = Basel Switz. 47°35N 7°35E 20 C7
Basoda India 23°52N 77°54E 42 H7
Basoko Dem. Rep. of the Congo 1°16N 23°40E 54 B1
Basque Provinces = País Vasco □ Spain 42°50N 2°45W 21 A4
Basra = Al Başrah Iraq 30°30N 47°50E 44 D5
Bass Str. Australia 39°15S 146°30E 63 F4
Bassano Canada 50°48N 112°20W 70 C6
Bassano del Grappa Italy 45°46N 11°44E 22 B4
Bassas da India Ind. Oc. 22°0S 39°0E 55 G4
Basse-Pointe Martinique 14°52N 61°8W 88 c
Basse-Terre Guadeloupe 16°0N 61°44W 88 b
Basse Terre Trin. & Tob. 10°7N 61°19W 93 K15
Bassein Burma 16°45N 94°30E 41 L19
Basses, Pte. des Guadeloupe 15°52N 61°17W 88 b
Basseterre St. Kitts & Nevis 17°17N 62°43W 89 C7
Bassett U.S.A. 42°35N 99°32W 80 D4
Bassi India 30°44N 76°21E 42 D7
Bastak Iran 27°15N 54°25E 45 E7
Baştām Iran 36°29N 55°4E 45 B7
Bastar India 19°15N 81°40E 41 K12
Basti India 26°52N 82°55E 43 F10
Bastia France 42°40N 9°30E 20 E8
Bastogne Belgium 50°1N 5°43E 15 D5
Bastrop La., U.S.A. 32°47N 91°55W 84 E9
Bastrop Tex., U.S.A. 30°7N 97°19W 84 F6
Basuo = Dongfang China 18°50N 108°33E 38 C7
Bat Yam Israel 32°2N 34°44E 46 C3
Bata Eq. Guin. 1°57N 9°50E 52 D1
Bataan □ Phil. 14°40N 120°25E 37 B6
Batabanó Cuba 22°41N 82°18W 88 B3
Batabanó, G. de Cuba 22°30N 82°30W 88 B3
Batac Phil. 18°3N 120°34E 37 A6
Batagai Russia 67°38N 134°38E 29 C14
Batala India 31°48N 75°12E 42 D6
Batama Dem. Rep. of the Congo 0°58N 26°33E 54 B2
Batamay Russia 63°30N 129°15E 29 C13
Batang Indonesia 6°55S 109°45E 37 G13
Batangafo C.A.R. 7°25N 18°20E 52 C3
Batangas Phil. 13°35N 121°10E 37 B6
Batanta Indonesia 0°55S 130°40E 37 E8
Batatais Brazil 20°54S 47°37W 95 A6
Batavia U.S.A. 43°0N 78°11W 82 D6
Batchelor Australia 13°4S 131°1E 60 B5
Batdambang Cambodia 13°7N 103°12E 38 F4
Batemans B. Australia 35°40S 150°12E 63 F5
Batemans Bay Australia 35°44S 150°11E 63 F5
Bates Ra. Australia 27°27S 121°5E 61 E3
Batesburg-Leesville U.S.A. 33°54N 81°33W 85 E14
Batesville Ark., U.S.A. 35°46N 91°39W 84 D9
Batesville Miss., U.S.A. 34°19N 89°57W 85 D10
Batesville Tex., U.S.A. 28°58N 99°37W 84 G5
Bath Canada 44°11N 76°47W 83 B8
Bath U.K. 51°23N 2°22W 13 F5
Bath Maine, U.S.A. 43°55N 69°49W 81 D19
Bath N.Y., U.S.A. 42°20N 77°19W 82 D7
Bath & North East Somerset □ U.K. 51°21N 2°27W 13 F5
Batheay Cambodia 11°59N 104°57E 39 G5
Bathsheba Barbados 13°13N 59°32W 89 g
Bathurst Australia 33°25S 149°31E 63 E4
Bathurst Canada 47°37N 65°43W 73 C6
Bathurst S. Africa 33°30S 26°50E 56 E4
Bathurst, C. Canada 70°34N 128°0W 68 B7
Bathurst B. Australia 14°16S 144°25E 62 A3
Bathurst Harb. Australia 43°15S 146°10E 63 G4
Bathurst I. Australia 11°30S 130°10E 60 B5
Bathurst I. Canada 76°0N 100°30W 69 B11
Bathurst Inlet Canada 66°50N 108°1W 68 C9
Batiki Fiji 17°48S 179°10E 59 a
Batlow Australia 35°31S 148°9E 63 F4
Batman Turkey 37°55N 41°5E 44 B4
Baţn al Ghūl Jordan 29°36N 35°56E 46 F4
Batna Algeria 35°34N 6°15E 50 A7
Batoka Zambia 16°45S 27°15E 55 F2
Baton Rouge U.S.A. 30°27N 91°11W 84 F9
Batong, Ko Thailand 6°32N 99°12E 39 J2
Batopilas Mexico 27°1N 107°44W 86 B3
Batouri Cameroon 4°30N 14°25E 52 D2
Båtsfjord Norway 70°38N 29°39E 8 A23
Battambang = Batdambang Cambodia 13°7N 103°12E 38 F4
Batticaloa Sri Lanka 7°43N 81°45E 40 R12
Battipáglia Italy 40°37N 14°58E 22 D6
Battle U.K. 50°55N 0°30E 13 G8
Battle → Canada 52°43N 108°15W 71 C7
Battle Creek U.S.A. 42°19N 85°11W 81 D11
Battle Ground U.S.A. 45°47N 122°32W 78 E4
Battle Harbour Canada 52°16N 55°35W 73 B8
Battle Lake U.S.A. 46°17N 95°43W 80 B6
Battle Mountain U.S.A. 40°38N 116°56W 76 F5
Battlefields Zimbabwe 18°37S 29°47E 55 F2
Battleford Canada 52°45N 108°15W 71 C7
Batu Ethiopia 6°55N 39°45E 47 F2
Batu Malaysia 3°15N 101°40E 39 L3
Batu, Kepulauan Indonesia 0°30S 98°25E 36 E1
Batu Ferringhi Malaysia 5°28N 100°15E 39 c
Batu Gajah Malaysia 4°28N 101°3E 39 K3
Batu Is. = Batu, Kepulauan Indonesia 0°30S 98°25E 36 E1
Batu Pahat Malaysia 1°50N 102°56E 39 M4
Batuata Indonesia 6°12S 122°42E 37 F6
Batugondang, Tanjung Indonesia 8°6S 114°29E 37 J17
Batukau, Gunung Indonesia 8°20S 115°5E 37 J18
Batumi Georgia 41°39N 41°44E 19 F7
Batur Indonesia 8°15S 115°20E 37 J18
Batur, Danau Indonesia 8°15S 115°24E 37 J18
Batur, Gunung Indonesia 8°14S 115°23E 37 J18
Batura Sar Pakistan 36°30N 74°31E 43 A6
Baturaja Indonesia 4°11S 104°15E 36 E2
Baturité Brazil 4°28S 38°45W 93 D11
Baturiti Indonesia 8°19S 115°11E 37 J18
Bau Malaysia 1°25N 110°9E 36 D4
Baubau Indonesia 5°25S 122°38E 37 F6
Baucau E. Timor 8°27S 126°27E 37 F7
Bauchi Nigeria 10°22N 9°48E 50 F7
Baudette U.S.A. 48°43N 94°36W 80 A6
Bauer, C. Australia 32°44S 134°4E 63 E1
Bauhinia Australia 24°35S 149°18E 62 C4
Baukau = Baucau E. Timor 8°27S 126°27E 37 F7
Bauld, C. Canada 51°38N 55°26W 69 D14
Bauru Brazil 22°10S 49°0W 95 A6
Bausi India 24°48N 87°1E 43 G12
Bauska Latvia 56°24N 24°15E 9 H21
Bautzen Germany 51°10N 14°26E 16 C8
Bavānāt Iran 30°28N 53°27E 45 D7
Bavaria = Bayern □ Germany 48°50N 12°0E 16 D6
Bavispe → Mexico 29°15N 109°11W 86 B3
Bawdwin Burma 23°5N 97°20E 41 H20
Bawean Indonesia 5°46S 112°35E 36 F4
Bawku Ghana 11°3N 0°19W 50 F5
Bawlake Burma 19°11N 97°21E 41 K20
Baxley U.S.A. 31°47N 82°21W 85 F13
Baxter U.S.A. 46°21N 94°17W 80 B6
Baxter Springs U.S.A. 37°2N 94°44W 80 G6
Baxter State ⌂ U.S.A. 46°5N 68°57W 81 B19
Bay City Mich., U.S.A. 43°36N 83°54W 81 D12
Bay City Tex., U.S.A. 28°59N 95°58W 84 G7
Bay Minette U.S.A. 30°53N 87°46W 85 F11
Bay Roberts Canada 47°36N 53°16W 73 C9
Bay St. Louis U.S.A. 30°19N 89°20W 85 F10
Bay Springs U.S.A. 31°59N 89°17W 85 F10
Bay View N.Z. 39°25S 176°50E 59 C6
Baya Dem. Rep. of the Congo 11°53S 27°25E 55 E2
Bayamo Cuba 20°20N 76°40W 88 B4
Bayamón Puerto Rico 18°24N 66°9W 89 d
Bayan Har Shan China 34°0N 98°0E 32 C4
Bayan Hot = Alxa Zuoqi China 38°50N 105°40E 34 E3
Bayan Lepas Malaysia 5°17N 100°16E 39 c
Bayan Obo China 41°52N 109°59E 34 D5
Bayan-Ovoo = Erdenetsogt Mongolia 42°55N 106°5E 34 C4
Bayana India 26°55N 77°18E 42 F7
Bayanaūyl Kazakhstan 50°45N 75°45E 28 D8
Bayandalay Mongolia 43°30N 103°29E 34 C2
Bayanhongor Mongolia 46°8N 102°43E 32 B5
Bayard N. Mex., U.S.A. 32°46N 108°8W 77 K9
Bayard Nebr., U.S.A. 41°45N 103°20W 80 E2
Baybay Phil. 10°40N 124°55E 37 B6
Baydaratskaya Guba Russia 69°0N 67°30E 28 C7
Baydhabo Somali Rep. 3°8N 43°30E 47 G3
Bayern □ Germany 48°50N 12°0E 16 D6
Bayeux France 49°17N 0°42W 20 B3
Bayfield Canada 43°34N 81°42W 82 C3
Bayfield U.S.A. 46°49N 90°49W 80 B8
Bayındır Turkey 38°13N 27°39E 23 E12
Baykal, Oz. Russia 53°0N 108°0E 29 D11
Baykan Turkey 38°7N 41°44E 44 B4
Baymak Russia 52°36N 58°19E 18 D10
Baynes Mts. Namibia 17°15S 13°0E 56 B1
Bayombong Phil. 16°30N 121°10E 37 A6
Bayonne France 43°30N 1°28W 20 E3
Bayonne U.S.A. 40°40N 74°6W 83 F10
Bayovar Peru 5°50S 81°0W 92 E2
Bayqongyr Kazakhstan 45°40N 63°20E 28 E7
Bayram-Ali = Baýramaly Turkmenistan 37°37N 62°10E 45 B9
Baýramaly Turkmenistan 37°37N 62°10E 45 B9
Bayramiç Turkey 39°48N 26°36E 23 E12
Bayreuth Germany 49°56N 11°35E 16 D6
Bayrūt Lebanon 33°53N 35°31E 46 B4
Bays, L. of Canada 45°15N 79°4W 82 A5
Baysville Canada 45°9N 79°7W 82 A5
Bayt Lahm West Bank 31°43N 35°12E 46 D4
Baytown U.S.A. 29°43N 94°59W 84 G7
Bayun Indonesia 8°11S 115°16E 37 J18
Baza Spain 37°30N 2°47W 21 D4
Bazaruto, I. do Mozam. 21°40S 35°28E 57 C6
Bazaruto △ Mozam. 21°42S 35°26E 57 C6
Bazhou China 39°8N 116°22E 34 E9
Bazmān, Kūh-e Iran 28°4N 60°1E 45 D9
Beach U.S.A. 46°58N 104°0W 80 B2
Beach City U.S.A. 40°39N 81°35W 82 F3
Beachport Australia 37°29S 140°0E 63 F3
Beachville Canada 43°5N 80°49W 82 C4
Beachy Hd. U.K. 50°44N 0°15E 13 G8
Beacon Australia 30°26S 117°52E 61 F2
Beacon U.S.A. 41°30N 73°58W 83 E11
Beaconsfield Australia 41°11S 146°48E 63 G4
Beagle, Canal S. Amer. 55°0S 68°30W 96 H3
Beagle Bay Australia 16°58S 122°40E 60 C3
Beagle G. Australia 12°15S 130°25E 60 B5
Bealanana Madag. 14°33S 48°44E 57 A8
Beals Cr. → U.S.A. 32°10N 100°51W 84 E4
Beamsville Canada 43°12N 79°28W 82 C5
Bear → Calif., U.S.A. 38°56N 121°36W 78 G5
Bear → Utah, U.S.A. 41°30N 112°8W 74 B4
Bear I. Ireland 51°38N 9°50W 10 E2
Bear L. Canada 55°8N 96°0W 71 B9
Bear L. U.S.A. 41°59N 111°21W 76 F8
Bear Lake Canada 45°27N 79°35W 82 A5
Beardmore Canada 49°36N 87°57W 72 C2
Beardmore Glacier Antarctica 84°30S 170°0E 5 E11
Beardstown U.S.A. 40°1N 90°26W 80 E8
Bearma → India 24°20N 79°51E 43 G8
Béarn France 43°20N 0°30W 20 E3
Bearpaw Mts. U.S.A. 48°12N 109°30W 76 B9
Bearskin Lake Canada 53°58N 91°2W 72 B1
Beas → India 31°10N 74°59E 42 D6
Beata, C. Dom. Rep. 17°40N 71°30W 89 C5
Beata, I. Dom. Rep. 17°34N 71°31W 89 C5
Beatrice U.S.A. 40°16N 96°45W 80 E5
Beatrice Zimbabwe 18°15S 30°55E 55 F3
Beatrice, C. Australia 14°20S 136°55E 62 A2
Beatton → Canada 56°15N 120°45W 70 B4
Beatton River Canada 57°26N 121°20W 70 B4
Beatty U.S.A. 36°54N 116°46W 78 J10
Beau Bassin Mauritius 20°13S 57°27E 53 d
Beauce, Plaine de la France 48°10N 1°45E 20 B4
Beauceville Canada 46°13N 70°46W 73 C5
Beaudesert Australia 27°59S 153°0E 63 D5
Beaufort Malaysia 5°30N 115°40E 36 C5
Beaufort N.C., U.S.A. 34°43N 76°40W 85 D16
Beaufort S.C., U.S.A. 32°26N 80°40W 85 E14
Beaufort Sea Arctic 72°0N 140°0W 66 B5
Beaufort West S. Africa 32°18S 22°36E 56 E3
Beauharnois Canada 45°20N 73°52W 83 A11
Beaulieu → Canada 62°3N 113°11W 70 A6
Beauly U.K. 57°30N 4°28W 11 D4
Beauly → U.K. 57°29N 4°27W 11 D4
Beaumaris U.K. 53°16N 4°6W 12 D3
Beaumont Belgium 50°15N 4°14E 15 D4
Beaumont U.S.A. 30°5N 94°6W 84 F7
Beaune France 47°2N 4°50E 20 C6
Beaupré Canada 47°3N 70°54W 73 C5
Beauraing Belgium 50°7N 4°57E 15 D4
Beausejour Canada 50°5N 96°35W 71 C9
Beauvais France 49°25N 2°8E 20 B5
Beauval Canada 55°9N 107°37W 71 B7
Beaver Okla., U.S.A. 36°49N 100°31W 84 C4
Beaver Pa., U.S.A. 40°42N 80°19W 82 F4
Beaver Utah, U.S.A. 38°17N 112°38W 76 G7
Beaver → B.C., Canada 59°52N 124°20W 70 B4
Beaver → Ont., Canada 55°55N 87°48W 72 A2
Beaver → Sask., Canada 55°26N 107°45W 71 B7
Beaver → U.S.A. 36°35N 99°30W 84 C5
Beaver City U.S.A. 40°8N 99°50W 80 E4
Beaver Creek Canada 63°0N 141°0W 68 C5
Beaver Dam U.S.A. 43°28N 88°50W 80 D9
Beaver Falls U.S.A. 40°46N 80°20W 82 F4
Beaver Hill L. Canada 54°5N 94°50W 71 C10
Beaver I. U.S.A. 45°40N 85°33W 81 C11
Beavercreek U.S.A. 39°43N 84°11W 81 F11
Beaverhill L. Canada 53°27N 112°32W 70 C6
Beaverlodge Canada 55°11N 119°29W 70 B5
Beaverstone → Canada 54°59N 89°25W 72 B2
Beaverton Canada 44°26N 79°9W 82 B5
Beaverton U.S.A. 45°29N 122°48W 78 E4
Beawar India 26°3N 74°18E 42 F6
Bebedouro Brazil 21°0S 48°25W 95 A6
Bebera, Tanjung Indonesia 8°44S 115°51E 37 K18
Beboa Madag. 17°22S 44°33E 57 B7
Becán Mexico 18°34N 89°31W 87 D7
Bécancour Canada 46°20N 72°26W 81 B17
Beccles U.K. 52°27N 1°35E 13 E9
Bečej Serbia 45°36N 20°3E 23 B9
Béchar Algeria 31°38N 2°18W 50 B5
Beckley U.S.A. 37°47N 81°11W 81 G13
Beddouza, Ras Morocco 32°33N 9°9W 50 B4
Bedford Canada 45°7N 72°59W 83 A12
Bedford S. Africa 32°40S 26°10E 56 E4
Bedford U.K. 52°8N 0°28W 13 E7
Bedford Ind., U.S.A. 38°52N 86°29W 80 F10
Bedford Iowa, U.S.A. 40°40N 94°44W 80 E6
Bedford Ohio, U.S.A. 41°23N 81°32W 82 E3
Bedford Pa., U.S.A. 40°1N 78°30W 82 F6
Bedford Va., U.S.A. 37°20N 79°31W 81 G14
Bedford, C. Australia 15°14S 145°21E 62 B4
Bedfordshire □ U.K. 52°4N 0°28W 13 E7
Bedok Singapore 1°19N 103°56E 39 d
Bedourie Australia 24°30S 139°30E 62 C2
Bedum Neths. 53°18N 6°36E 15 A6
Beebe Plain Canada 45°1N 72°9W 83 A12
Beech Creek U.S.A. 41°5N 77°36W 82 E7
Beechy Canada 50°53N 107°24W 71 C7
Beef I. Br. Virgin Is. 18°26N 64°30W 89 e
Beenleigh Australia 27°43S 153°10E 63 D5
Be'er Menuha Israel 30°19N 35°8E 44 D2
Be'er Sheva Israel 31°15N 34°48E 46 D3
Beersheba = Be'er Sheva Israel 31°15N 34°48E 46 D3
Beestekraal S. Africa 25°23S 27°38E 57 D4
Beeston U.K. 52°56N 1°14W 12 E6
Beeton Canada 44°5N 79°47W 82 B5
Beeville U.S.A. 28°24N 97°45W 84 G6
Befale Dem. Rep. of the Congo 0°25N 20°45E 52 D4
Befandriana Mahajanga, Madag. 15°16S 48°32E 57 B8
Befandriana Toliara, Madag. 21°55S 44°0E 57 C7
Befasy Madag. 20°33S 44°23E 57 C7
Befotaka Antsiranana, Madag. 13°15S 48°16E 57 A8
Befotaka Fianarantsoa, Madag. 23°49S 47°0E 57 C8
Bega Australia 36°41S 149°51E 63 F4
Begusarai India 25°24N 86°9E 43 G12
Behābād Iran 32°24N 59°47E 45 C8
Behala India 22°30N 88°18E 43 H13
Behara Madag. 24°55S 46°20E 57 D8
Behbehān Iran 30°30N 50°15E 45 D6
Behm Canal U.S.A. 55°10N 131°0W 70 B2
Behshahr Iran 36°45N 53°35E 45 B7
Bei Jiang → China 23°2N 112°58E 33 D6
Bei Shan China 41°30N 96°0E 32 B4
Bei'an China 48°10N 126°20E 33 B7
Beihai China 21°28N 109°6E 33 D5
Beijing China 39°53N 116°21E 34 E9
Beijing □ China 39°55N 116°20E 34 E9
Beilen Neths. 52°52N 6°27E 15 B6
Beilpajah Australia 32°54S 143°52E 63 E3
Beinn na Faoghla = Benbecula U.K. 57°26N 7°21W 11 D1
Beipiao China 41°52N 120°32E 35 D11
Beira Mozam. 19°50S 34°52E 55 F3
Beirut = Bayrūt Lebanon 33°53N 35°31E 46 B4
Beiseker Canada 51°23N 113°32W 70 C6
Beit Lekhem = Bayt Lahm West Bank 31°43N 35°12E 46 D4
Beitaolaizhao China 44°58N 125°58E 35 B13
Beitbridge Zimbabwe 22°12S 30°0E 55 G3
Beizhen = Binzhou China 37°20N 118°2E 35 F10
Beizhen China 41°38N 121°54E 35 D11
Beizhengzhen China 44°31N 123°30E 35 B12
Beja Portugal 38°2N 7°53W 21 C2
Béja Tunisia 36°43N 9°12E 51 A7
Bejaïa Algeria 36°42N 5°2E 50 A7
Béjar Spain 40°23N 5°46W 21 B3
Bejestān Iran 34°30N 58°5E 45 C8
Bekaa Valley = Al Biqā Lebanon 34°10N 36°10E 46 A5
Békéscsaba Hungary 46°40N 21°5E 17 E11
Bekily Madag. 24°13S 45°19E 57 C8
Bekisopa Madag. 21°40S 45°54E 57 C8
Bekitro Madag. 24°33S 45°18E 57 C8
Bekodoka Madag. 16°58S 45°7E 57 B8
Bekok Malaysia 2°20N 103°7E 39 L4
Bekopaka Madag. 19°9S 44°48E 57 B7
Bekuli Indonesia 8°22S 114°13E 37 J17
Bela India 25°50N 82°0E 43 G10
Bela Pakistan 26°12N 66°20E 42 F2
Bela Bela S. Africa 24°51S 28°19E 57 C4
Bela Crkva Serbia 44°55N 21°27E 23 B9
Bela Vista Brazil 22°12S 56°20W 94 A4
Bela Vista Mozam. 26°10S 32°44E 57 D5
Belan → India 24°2N 81°45E 43 G9
Belarus ■ Europe 53°30N 27°0E 17 B14
Belau = Palau ■ Palau 7°30N 134°30E 58 A6
Belavenona Madag. 24°50S 47°4E 57 C8
Belawan Indonesia 3°33N 98°32E 36 D1
Belaya → Russia 54°40N 56°0E 18 C9
Belaya Tserkov = Bila Tserkva Ukraine 49°45N 30°10E 17 D16

Belaya Zemlya, Ostrova
  Russia 81°36N 62°18E **28** A7
Belcher Chan. *Canada* 77°15N 95°0W **69** B10
Belcher Is. *Canada* 56°15N 78°45W **72** A3
Belden *U.S.A.* 40°2N 121°17W **78** E5
Belebey *Russia* 54°7N 54°7E **18** D9
Beledweyne *Somali Rep.* 4°30N 45°5E **47** G4
Belém *Brazil* 1°20S 48°30W **93** D9
Belén *Argentina* 27°40S 67°5W **94** B2
Belén *Paraguay* 23°30S 57°6W **94** A4
Belen *U.S.A.* 34°40N 106°46W **77** J10
Belet Uen = Beledweyne
  Somali Rep. 4°30N 45°5E **47** G4
Belev *Russia* 53°50N 36°5E **18** D6
Belfair *U.S.A.* 47°27N 122°50W **78** C4
Belfast *S. Africa* 25°42S 30°2E **57** D5
Belfast *U.K.* 54°37N 5°56W **10** B6
Belfast *Maine, U.S.A.* 44°26N 69°1W **81** C19
Belfast *N.Y., U.S.A.* 42°21N 78°7W **82** D6
Belfast L. *U.K.* 54°40N 5°50W **10** B6
Belfield *U.S.A.* 46°53N 103°12W **80** B2
Belfort *France* 47°38N 6°50E **20** C7
Belfry *U.S.A.* 45°9N 109°1W **76** D9
Belgaum *India* 15°55N 74°35E **40** M9
Belgium ■ *Europe* 50°30N 5°0E **15** D4
Belgorod *Russia* 50°35N 36°35E **19** D6
Belgorod-Dnestrovskiy =
  Bilhorod-Dnistrovskyy
  Ukraine 46°11N 30°23E **19** E5
Belgrade = Beograd
  Serbia 44°50N 20°37E **23** B9
Belgrade *U.S.A.* 45°47N 111°11W **76** D8
Belgrano *Antarctica* 77°52S 34°37W **5** D1
Belhaven *U.S.A.* 35°33N 76°37W **85** D16
Beli Drim → *Europe* 42°6N 20°25E **23** C9
Belimbing *Indonesia* 8°24S 115°2E **37** J18
Belinyu *Indonesia* 1°35S 105°50E **36** E3
Beliton Is. = Belitung
  Indonesia 3°10S 107°50E **36** E3
Belitung *Indonesia* 3°10S 107°50E **36** E3
Belize ■ *Cent. Amer.* 17°0N 88°30W **87** D7
Belize City *Belize* 17°25N 88°0W **87** D7
Belkovskiy, Ostrov
  Russia 75°32N 135°44E **29** B14
Bell → *Canada* 49°48N 77°38W **72** C4
Bell I. *Canada* 50°46N 55°35W **73** B8
Bell-Irving → *Canada* 56°12N 129°5W **70** B3
Bell Peninsula *Canada* 63°50N 82°0W **69** C11
Bell Ville *Argentina* 32°40S 62°40W **94** C3
Bella Bella *Canada* 52°10N 128°10W **70** C3
Bella Coola *Canada* 52°25N 126°40W **70** C3
Bella Unión *Uruguay* 30°15S 57°40W **94** C4
Bella Vista *Corrientes,*
  Argentina 28°33S 59°0W **94** B4
Bella Vista *Tucuman,*
  Argentina 27°10S 65°25W **94** B2
Bellaire *U.S.A.* 40°1N 80°45W **82** F4
Bellary *India* 15°10N 76°56E **40** M10
Bellata *Australia* 29°53S 149°46E **63** D4
Belle Fourche *U.S.A.* 44°40N 103°51W **80** C2
Belle Fourche →
  U.S.A. 44°26N 102°18W **74** B6
Belle Glade *U.S.A.* 26°41N 80°40W **85** H14
Belle-Île *France* 47°20N 3°10W **20** C2
Belle Isle *Canada* 51°57N 55°25W **73** B8
Belle Isle, Str. of *Canada* 51°30N 56°30W **73** B8
Belle Plaine *U.S.A.* 41°54N 92°17W **80** E7
Belle River *Canada* 42°18N 82°43W **82** D2
Bellefontaine *U.S.A.* 40°22N 83°46W **81** E12
Bellefonte *U.S.A.* 40°55N 77°47W **82** F7
Belleoram *Canada* 47°31N 55°25W **73** C8
Belleplaine *Barbados* 13°15N 59°34W **89** g
Bender Beyla *Somali Rep.* 9°30N 50°48E **47** F5
Belleville *Canada* 44°10N 77°23W **82** B7
Belleville *Ill., U.S.A.* 38°31N 89°59W **80** F9
Belleville *Kans., U.S.A.* 39°50N 97°38W **80** F5
Belleville *N.J., U.S.A.* 40°47N 74°9W **83** F10
Belleville *N.Y., U.S.A.* 43°46N 76°10W **83** C8
Bellevue *Idaho, U.S.A.* 43°28N 114°16W **76** E6
Bellevue *Nebr., U.S.A.* 41°9N 95°54W **80** E6
Bellevue *Ohio, U.S.A.* 41°17N 82°51W **82** E2
Bellevue *Wash., U.S.A.* 47°37N 122°12W **78** C4
Bellin = Kangirsuk
  Canada 60°0N 70°0W **69** D13
Bellingen *Australia* 30°25S 152°50E **63** E5
Bellingham *U.S.A.* 48°46N 122°29W **78** B4
Bellingshausen Abyssal Plain
  S. Ocean 64°0S 90°0W **5** C16
Bellingshausen Sea
  Antarctica 66°0S 80°0W **5** C17
Bellinzona *Switz.* 46°11N 9°1E **20** C8
Bello *Colombia* 6°20N 75°33W **92** B3
Bellows Falls *U.S.A.* 43°8N 72°27W **83** C12
Bellpat *Pakistan* 29°0N 68°5E **42** E3
Belluno *Italy* 46°9N 12°13E **22** A5
Bellwood *U.S.A.* 40°36N 78°20W **82** F6
Belmont *Canada* 42°53N 81°5W **82** D3
Belmont *S. Africa* 29°28S 24°22E **56** D3
Belmont *U.S.A.* 42°14N 78°2W **82** D6
Belmonte *Brazil* 16°0S 39°0W **93** G11
Belmopan *Belize* 17°18N 88°30W **87** D7
Belmullet *Ireland* 54°14N 9°58W **10** B2
Belo Horizonte *Brazil* 19°55S 43°56W **93** G10
Belo-sur-Mer *Madag.* 20°42S 44°0E **57** C7
Belo-Tsiribihina *Madag.* 19°40S 44°30E **57** B7
Beloha *Madag.* 25°10S 45°3E **57** D8
Belogorsk *Russia* 51°0N 128°20E **29** D13
Beloit *Kans., U.S.A.* 39°28N 98°6W **80** F4
Beloit *Wis., U.S.A.* 42°31N 89°2W **80** D9
Belokorovichi *Ukraine* 51°7N 28°2E **17** C15
Belomorsk *Russia* 64°35N 34°54E **18** B5
Belonia *India* 23°15N 91°30E **41** H17
Beloretsk *Russia* 53°58N 58°24E **18** D10
Belorussia = Belarus ■
  Europe 53°30N 27°0E **17** B14
Belovo *Russia* 54°30N 86°0E **28** D9
Beloyarskiy *Russia* 63°42N 66°40E **28** C7
Beloye, Ozero *Russia* 60°11N 37°35E **18** B6

Beloye More *Russia* 66°30N 38°0E **8** C25
Belozersk *Russia* 60°1N 37°45E **18** B6
Belpre *U.S.A.* 39°17N 81°34W **81** F13
Belrain *India* 28°23N 80°55E **43** E9
Belt *U.S.A.* 47°23N 110°55W **76** C8
Beltana *Australia* 30°48S 138°25E **63** E2
Belterra *Brazil* 2°45S 55°0W **93** D8
Belton *U.S.A.* 31°3N 97°28W **84** F6
Belton L. *U.S.A.* 31°6N 97°28W **84** F6
Beltsy = Bălți *Moldova* 47°48N 27°58E **17** E14
Belturbet *Ireland* 54°6N 7°26W **10** B4
Belukha *Russia* 49°50N 86°50E **28** E9
Belvidere *Ill., U.S.A.* 42°15N 88°50W **80** D9
Belvidere *N.J., U.S.A.* 40°50N 75°5W **83** F9
Belyando → *Australia* 21°38S 146°50E **62** C4
Belyando Crossing
  Australia 21°32S 146°51E **62** C4
Belyy, Ostrov *Russia* 73°30N 71°0E **28** B8
Belyy Yar *Russia* 58°26N 84°39E **28** D9
Belzoni *U.S.A.* 33°11N 90°29W **85** E9
Bemaraha, Lembalemban' i
  Madag. 18°40S 44°45E **57** B7
Bemarivo *Madag.* 21°45S 44°45E **57** C7
Bemarivo → *Antsiranana,*
  Madag. 14°9S 50°9E **57** A9
Bemarivo → *Mahajanga,*
  Madag. 15°27S 47°40E **57** B8
Bemavo *Madag.* 21°33S 45°25E **57** C8
Bembéréke *Benin* 10°11N 2°43E **50** F6
Bembesi *Zimbabwe* 20°0S 28°58E **55** G2
Bembesi → *Zimbabwe* 18°57S 27°47E **55** F2
Bemetara *India* 21°42N 81°32E **43** J9
Bemidji *U.S.A.* 47°28N 94°53W **80** B6
Bemolanga *Madag.* 17°44S 45°6E **57** B8
Ben *Iran* 32°32N 50°45E **45** C6
Ben Cruachan *U.K.* 56°26N 5°8W **11** E3
Ben Dearg *U.K.* 57°47N 4°56W **11** D4
Ben En △ *Vietnam* 19°37N 105°30E **38** C5
Ben Gardane *Tunisia* 33°11N 11°11E **51** B8
Ben Hope *U.K.* 58°25N 4°36W **11** C4
Ben Lawers *U.K.* 56°32N 4°14W **11** E4
Ben Lomond *N.S.W.,*
  Australia 30°1S 151°43E **63** E5
Ben Lomond *Tas.,*
  Australia 41°38S 147°42E **63** G4
Ben Lomond *U.K.* 56°11N 4°38W **11** E4
Ben Lomond △
  Australia 41°33S 147°39E **63** G4
Ben Luc *Vietnam* 10°39N 106°29E **39** G6
Ben Macdhui *U.K.* 57°4N 3°40W **11** D5
Ben Mhor *U.K.* 57°15N 7°18W **11** D1
Ben More *Argyll & Bute,*
  U.K. 56°26N 6°1W **11** E2
Ben More *Stirling, U.K.* 56°23N 4°32W **11** E4
Ben More Assynt *U.K.* 58°8N 4°52W **11** C4
Ben Nevis *U.K.* 56°48N 5°1W **11** E3
Ben Quang *Vietnam* 17°3N 106°55E **38** D6
Ben Vorlich *U.K.* 56°21N 4°14W **11** E4
Ben Wyvis *U.K.* 57°40N 4°35W **11** D4
Bena *Nigeria* 11°20N 5°50E **50** F7
Benalla *Australia* 36°30S 146°0E **63** F4
Benares = Varanasi
  India 25°22N 83°0E **43** G10
Benavente *Spain* 42°2N 5°43W **21** A3
Benavides *U.S.A.* 27°36N 98°25W **84** H5
Benbecula *U.K.* 57°26N 7°21W **11** D1
Benbonyathe Hill
  Australia 30°25S 139°11E **63** E2
Bend *U.S.A.* 44°4N 121°19W **76** D3
Bender Beyla *Somali Rep.* 9°30N 50°48E **47** F5
Bendery = Tighina
  Moldova 46°50N 29°30E **17** E15
Bendigo *Australia* 36°40S 144°15E **63** F3
Benē Beraq *Israel* 32°6N 34°51E **46** C3
Benenitra *Madag.* 23°27S 45°5E **57** C8
Benevento *Italy* 41°8N 14°45E **22** D6
Benga *Mozam.* 16°11S 33°40E **55** F3
Bengal, Bay of *Ind. Oc.* 15°0N 90°0E **41** M17
Bengalūru = Bangalore
  India 12°59N 77°40E **40** N10
Bengbu *China* 32°58N 117°20E **35** H9
Benghazi = Banghāzī
  Libya 32°11N 20°3E **51** B10
Bengkalis *Indonesia* 1°30N 102°10E **39** M4
Bengkulu *Indonesia* 3°50S 102°12E **36** E2
Bengkulu □ *Indonesia* 3°48S 102°16E **36** E2
Bengough *Canada* 49°25N 105°10W **71** D7
Benguela *Angola* 12°37S 13°25E **53** G2
Benguérua, I. *Mozam.* 21°58S 35°28E **57** C6
Beni → *Bolivia* 10°23S 65°24W **92** F5
Beni Mellal *Morocco* 32°21N 6°21W **50** B4
Beni Suef *Egypt* 29°5N 31°6E **51** C12
Beniah L. *Canada* 63°23N 112°17W **70** A6
Benidorm *Spain* 38°33N 0°9W **21** C5
Benin ■ *Africa* 10°0N 2°0E **50** G6
Benin, Bight of *W. Afr.* 5°0N 3°0E **50** H6
Benin City *Nigeria* 6°20N 5°31E **50** G7
Benito Juárez *Argentina* 37°40S 59°43W **94** D4
Benitses *Greece* 39°32N 19°55E **25** A3
Benjamin Aceval
  Paraguay 24°58S 57°34W **94** A4
Benjamin Constant
  Brazil 4°40S 70°15W **92** D4
Benjamín Hill *Mexico* 30°9N 111°7W **86** A2
Benkelman *U.S.A.* 40°3N 101°32W **80** E3
Bennett *Canada* 59°51N 135°0W **70** B2
Bennett, L. *Australia* 22°50S 131°2E **60** D5
Bennetta, Ostrov
  Russia 76°21N 148°56E **29** B15
Bennettsville *U.S.A.* 34°37N 79°41W **85** D15
Bennington *N.H., U.S.A.* 43°0N 71°55W **83** D11
Bennington *Vt., U.S.A.* 42°53N 73°12W **83** D11
Benom *Malaysia* 3°50N 102°6E **39** L4
Benoni *S. Africa* 26°11S 28°18E **57** D4

Benque Viejo *Belize* 17°5N 89°8W **87** D7
Benson *Ariz., U.S.A.* 31°58N 110°18W **77** L8
Benson *Minn., U.S.A.* 45°19N 95°36W **80** C6
Benteng *Indonesia* 6°10S 120°30E **37** F6
Bentinck I. *Australia* 17°3S 139°35E **62** B2
Bentley Subglacial Trench
  Antarctica 80°0S 115°0W **5** E15
Bento Gonçalves *Brazil* 29°10S 51°31W **95** B5
Benton *Ark., U.S.A.* 34°34N 92°35W **84** D8
Benton *Calif., U.S.A.* 37°48N 118°32W **78** H8
Benton *Ill., U.S.A.* 38°0N 88°55W **80** F9
Benton *Pa., U.S.A.* 41°12N 76°23W **83** E8
Benton Harbor *U.S.A.* 42°6N 86°27W **80** D10
Bentong *Malaysia* 3°31N 101°55E **39** L3
Bentonville *U.S.A.* 36°22N 94°13W **84** C7
Benue → *Nigeria* 7°48N 6°46E **50** G7
Benxi *China* 41°20N 123°48E **35** D12
Beo *Indonesia* 4°25N 126°50E **37** D7
Beograd *Serbia* 44°50N 20°37E **23** B9
Beolgyo *S. Korea* 34°51N 127°21E **35** G14
Beppu *Japan* 33°15N 131°30E **31** H5
Beqa *Fiji* 18°23S 178°8E **59** a
Beqaa Valley = Al Biqā
  Lebanon 34°10N 36°10E **46** A5
Ber Mota *India* 23°27N 68°34E **42** H3
Bera, Tasik *Malaysia* 3°5N 102°38E **39** L4
Berach → *India* 25°15N 75°2E **42** G6
Beraketa *Madag.* 23°7S 44°25E **57** C7
Berastagi *Indonesia* 3°11N 98°31E **39** L2
Berat *Albania* 40°43N 19°59E **23** D8
Berau, Teluk *Indonesia* 2°30S 132°30E **37** E8
Beravina *Madag.* 18°10S 45°14E **57** B8
Berber *Sudan* 18°0N 34°0E **51** E12
Berbera *Somali Rep.* 10°30N 45°2E **47** E4
Berbérati *C.A.R.* 4°15N 15°40E **52** D3
Berbice → *Guyana* 6°20N 57°32W **92** B7
Berdichev = Berdychiv
  Ukraine 49°57N 28°30E **17** D15
Berdsk *Russia* 54°47N 83°2E **28** D9
Berdyansk *Ukraine* 46°45N 36°50E **19** E6
Berdychiv *Ukraine* 49°57N 28°30E **17** D15
Berea *U.S.A.* 37°34N 84°17W **81** G11
Berebere *Indonesia* 2°25N 128°45E **37** D7
Bereeda *Somali Rep.* 11°45N 51°0E **47** E5
Berehove *Ukraine* 48°15N 22°35E **17** D12
Bereket *Turkmenistan* 39°16N 55°32E **45** B7
Berekum *Ghana* 7°29N 2°34W **50** G5
Berens → *Canada* 52°25N 97°2W **71** C9
Berens I. *Canada* 52°18N 97°18W **71** C9
Berens River *Canada* 52°25N 97°0W **71** C9
Beresford *U.S.A.* 43°5N 96°47W **80** D5
Berestechko *Ukraine* 50°22N 25°5E **17** C13
Berevo *Mahajanga,*
  Madag. 17°14S 44°17E **57** B7
Berevo Toliara, *Madag.* 19°44S 44°58E **57** B7
Berezhany *Ukraine* 49°26N 24°58E **17** D13
Berezina = Byarezina →
  Belarus 52°33N 30°14E **17** B16
Bereznik *Russia* 62°51N 42°40E **18** B7
Berezniki *Russia* 59°24N 56°46E **18** C10
Berezovo *Russia* 64°0N 65°0E **28** C7
Berga *Spain* 42°6N 1°48E **21** A6
Bergama *Turkey* 39°8N 27°11E **23** E12
Bérgamo *Italy* 45°41N 9°43E **20** D8
Bergen *Neths.* 52°40N 4°43E **15** B4
Bergen *Norway* 60°20N 5°20E **8** F11
Bergen *U.S.A.* 43°5N 77°57W **82** C7
Bergen op Zoom *Neths.* 51°28N 4°18E **15** C4
Bergerac *France* 44°51N 0°30E **20** D4
Bergholz *U.S.A.* 40°31N 80°53W **82** F4
Bergisch Gladbach
  Germany 50°59N 7°8E **15** D7
Bergville *S. Africa* 28°52S 29°18E **57** D4
Berhala, Selat *Indonesia* 1°0S 104°15E **36** E2
Berhampore = Baharampur
  India 24°2N 88°27E **43** G13
Berhampur = Brahmapur
  India 19°15N 84°54E **41** K14
Bering Sea *Pac. Oc.* 58°0N 171°0W **74** a
Bering Strait *Pac. Oc.* 65°30N 169°0W **74** a
Beringovskiy *Russia* 63°3N 179°19E **29** C18
Berisso *Argentina* 34°56S 57°50W **94** C4
Berja *Spain* 36°50N 2°56W **21** D4
Berkeley *U.S.A.* 37°51N 122°16W **78** H4
Berkner I. *Antarctica* 79°30S 50°0W **5** D18
Berkshire □ *U.K.* 42°19N 76°11W **83** D8
Berkshire Downs *U.K.* 51°33N 1°29W **13** F6
Berlin *Germany* 52°31N 13°23E **16** B7
Berlin *Md., U.S.A.* 38°20N 75°13W **81** F16
Berlin *N.H., U.S.A.* 44°28N 71°11W **83** B13
Berlin *N.Y., U.S.A.* 42°42N 73°23W **83** D11
Berlin *Wis., U.S.A.* 43°58N 88°57W **80** D9
Berlin L. *U.S.A.* 41°3N 81°0W **82** E4
Bermejo → *Formosa,*
  Argentina 26°51S 58°23W **94** B4
Bermejo → *San Juan,*
  Argentina 32°30S 67°30W **94** C2
Bermejo, Paso = Uspallata, P. de
  Argentina 32°37S 69°22W **94** C2
Bermen, L. *Canada* 53°35N 68°55W **73** B6
Bermuda ☑ *Atl. Oc.* 32°18N 64°45W **67** F13
Bern *Switz.* 46°57N 7°28E **20** C7
Bernalillo *U.S.A.* 35°18N 106°33W **77** J10
Bernardo de Irigoyen
  Argentina 26°15S 53°40W **95** B5
Bernardsville *U.S.A.* 40°43N 74°34W **83** F10
Bernasconi *Argentina* 37°55S 63°44W **94** D3
Bernburg *Germany* 51°47N 11°44E **16** C6
Berne = Bern *Switz.* 46°57N 7°28E **20** C7
Berneray *U.K.* 57°43N 7°11W **11** D1
Bernier I. *Australia* 24°50S 113°12E **61** D1
Bernina, Piz *Switz.* 46°20N 9°54E **20** C8
Beroroha *Madag.* 21°40S 45°10E **57** C8
Beroun *Czech Rep.* 49°57N 14°5E **16** D8
Berri *Australia* 34°14S 140°35E **63** E3
Berriane *Algeria* 32°50N 3°46E **50** B6

Berry *Australia* 34°46S 150°43E **63** E5
Berry *France* 46°50N 2°0E **20** C5
Berry Is. *Bahamas* 25°40N 77°50W **88** A4
Berryessa, L. *U.S.A.* 38°31N 122°6W **78** G4
Berryville *U.S.A.* 36°22N 93°34W **84** C8
Berseba *Namibia* 26°0S 17°46E **56** D2
Bershad *Ukraine* 48°22N 29°31E **17** D15
Berthold *U.S.A.* 48°19N 101°44W **80** A3
Berthoud *U.S.A.* 40°19N 105°5W **76** F11
Bertoua *Cameroon* 4°30N 13°45E **52** D2
Bertraghboy B. *Ireland* 53°22N 9°54W **10** C2
Berwick *U.S.A.* 41°3N 76°14W **83** E8
Berwick-upon-Tweed
  U.K. 55°46N 2°0W **12** B6
Berwyn Mts. *U.K.* 52°54N 3°26W **12** E4
Besal *Pakistan* 34°53N 73°56E **43** B5
Besalampy *Madag.* 16°43S 44°29E **57** B7
Besançon *France* 47°15N 6°2E **20** C7
Besar *Indonesia* 2°40S 116°0E **36** E5
Besnard L. *Canada* 55°25N 106°0W **71** B7
Besni *Turkey* 37°41N 37°52E **44** B3
Besor, N. → *Egypt* 31°28N 34°22E **46** D3
Bessarabiya *Moldova* 47°0N 28°10E **17** E15
Bessarabka = Basarabeasca
  Moldova 46°21N 28°58E **17** E15
Bessemer *Ala., U.S.A.* 33°24N 86°58W **85** E11
Bessemer *Mich., U.S.A.* 46°29N 90°3W **80** B8
Bessemer *Pa., U.S.A.* 40°59N 80°30W **82** F4
Beswick *Australia* 14°34S 132°53E **60** B5
Bet She'an *Israel* 32°30N 35°30E **46** C4
Bet Shemesh *Israel* 31°44N 35°0E **46** D4
Betafo *Madag.* 19°50S 46°51E **57** B8
Betancuria *Canary Is.* 28°25N 14°3W **24** F5
Betanzos *Spain* 43°15N 8°12W **21** A1
Bétaré Oya *Cameroon* 5°40N 14°5E **52** C2
Betatao *Madag.* 18°11S 47°52E **57** B8
Bethal *S. Africa* 26°27S 29°28E **57** D4
Bethanien *Namibia* 26°31S 17°8E **56** D2
Bethany *Canada* 44°11N 78°34W **82** B6
Bethany *Mo., U.S.A.* 40°16N 94°2W **80** E6
Bethany *Okla., U.S.A.* 35°31N 97°38W **84** D6
Bethel *Alaska, U.S.A.* 60°48N 161°45W **74** a
Bethel *Conn., U.S.A.* 41°22N 73°25W **83** E11
Bethel *Maine, U.S.A.* 44°25N 70°47W **83** B14
Bethel *Vt., U.S.A.* 43°50N 72°38W **83** C12
Bethel Park *U.S.A.* 40°19N 80°2W **82** F4
Bethlehem = Bayt Lahm
  West Bank 31°43N 35°12E **46** D4
Bethlehem *S. Africa* 28°14S 28°18E **57** D4
Bethlehem *U.S.A.* 40°37N 75°23W **83** F9
Bethulie *S. Africa* 30°30S 25°59E **56** E4
Béthune *France* 50°30N 2°38E **20** A5
Betioky *Madag.* 23°48S 44°20E **57** C7
Betong *Malaysia* 1°24N 111°31E **36** D4
Betong *Thailand* 5°45N 101°5E **39** K3
Betoota *Australia* 25°45S 140°42E **62** D3
Betpaqdala *Kazakhstan* 45°45N 70°30E **32** D2
Betroka *Madag.* 23°16S 46°0E **57** C8
Betsiamites *Canada* 48°56N 68°40W **73** C6
Betsiamites → *Canada* 48°56N 68°38W **73** C6
Betsiboka → *Madag.* 16°3S 46°36E **57** B8
Bettendorf *U.S.A.* 41°32N 90°30W **80** E8
Bettiah *India* 26°48N 84°33E **43** F11
Betul *India* 21°58N 77°59E **40** J10
Betws-y-Coed *U.K.* 53°5N 3°48W **12** D4
Beulah *Mich., U.S.A.* 44°38N 86°6W **80** C10
Beulah *N. Dak., U.S.A.* 47°16N 101°47W **80** B3
Beveren *Belgium* 51°12N 4°16E **15** C4
Beverley *Australia* 32°9S 116°56E **61** F2
Beverley *U.K.* 53°51N 0°26W **12** D7
Beverly *U.S.A.* 42°33N 70°53W **83** D14
Beverly Hills *Calif.,*
  U.S.A. 34°5N 118°24W **79** L8
Beverly Hills *Fla.,*
  U.S.A. 28°55N 82°28W **85** G13
Bevoalavo *Madag.* 25°13S 45°26E **57** D7
Bewas → *India* 23°59N 79°21E **43** H8
Bewdley *Canada* 44°5N 78°19W **82** B6
Bexhill *U.K.* 50°51N 0°29E **13** G8
Beyānlū *Iran* 36°0N 47°51E **44** C5
Beyneu *Kazakhstan* 45°18N 55°9E **19** E10
Beypazarı *Turkey* 40°10N 31°56E **19** F5
Beyşehir Gölü *Turkey* 37°41N 31°33E **44** B1
Béziers *France* 43°20N 3°12E **20** E5
Bezwada = Vijayawada
  India 16°31N 80°39E **41** L12
Bhabua *India* 25°3N 83°37E **43** G10
Bhachau *India* 23°20N 70°16E **40** H7
Bhadar → *Gujarat, India* 22°17N 72°20E **42** H5
Bhadar → *Gujarat, India* 21°27N 69°47E **42** J3
Bhadarwah *India* 32°58N 75°46E **43** C6
Bhadgaon = Bhaktapur
  Nepal 27°38N 85°24E **43** F11
Bhadohi *India* 25°25N 82°34E **43** G10
Bhadra *India* 29°8N 75°14E **42** E6
Bhadrakh *India* 21°10N 86°30E **41** J15
Bhadran *India* 22°19N 72°6E **42** H5
Bhadravati *India* 13°49N 75°40E **40** N9
Bhag *Pakistan* 29°2N 67°49E **42** E2
Bhagalpur *India* 25°10N 87°0E **43** G12
Bhagirathi → *Uttarakhand,*
  India 30°8N 78°35E **43** D8
Bhagirathi → *W. Bengal,*
  India 23°25N 88°23E **43** H13
Bhakkar *Pakistan* 31°40N 71°5E **42** D4
Bhakra Dam *India* 31°30N 76°45E **42** D7
Bhamo *Burma* 24°15N 97°15E **41** G20
Bhandara *India* 21°5N 79°42E **40** J11
Bhanpura *India* 24°31N 75°44E **42** G6
Bhanrer Ra. *India* 23°40N 79°45E **43** H8
Bhaptiahi *India* 26°19N 86°44E **43** F12
Bharat = India ■ *Asia* 20°0N 78°0E **40** K11
Bharatpur *Chhattisgarh,*
  India 23°44N 81°46E **43** H9
Bharatpur *Raj., India* 27°15N 77°30E **42** F7
Bharatpur *Nepal* 27°34N 84°10E **43** F11

Bharno *India* 23°14N 84°53E **43** H11
Bharuch *India* 21°47N 73°0E **40** J8
Bhatinda *India* 30°15N 74°57E **42** D6
Bhatpara *India* 22°50N 88°25E **43** H13
Bhattu *India* 29°36N 75°19E **42** E6
Bhaunagar = Bhavnagar
  India 21°45N 72°10E **40** J8
Bhavnagar *India* 21°45N 72°10E **40** J8
Bhawari *India* 25°42N 73°4E **42** G5
Bhayavadar *India* 21°51N 70°15E **42** J4
Bhera *Pakistan* 32°29N 72°57E **42** C5
Bhikangaon *India* 21°52N 75°57E **42** J6
Bhilai = Bhilainagar-Durg
  India 21°13N 81°26E **41** J12
Bhilainagar-Durg *India* 21°13N 81°26E **41** J12
Bhilsa = Vidisha *India* 23°28N 77°53E **42** H7
Bhilwara *India* 25°25N 74°38E **42** G6
Bhima → *India* 16°25N 77°17E **40** L10
Bhimbar *Pakistan* 32°59N 74°3E **43** C6
Bhind *India* 26°30N 78°46E **43** F8
Bhinga *India* 27°43N 81°56E **43** F9
Bhinmal *India* 25°0N 72°15E **42** G5
Bhisho *S. Africa* 32°50S 27°23E **57** E4
Bhiwandi *India* 19°20N 73°0E **40** K8
Bhiwani *India* 28°50N 76°9E **42** E7
Bhogava → *India* 22°26N 72°20E **42** H5
Bhola *Bangla.* 22°45N 90°35E **41** H17
Bholari *Pakistan* 25°19N 68°13E **42** G3
Bhopal *India* 23°20N 77°30E **42** H7
Bhubaneshwar *India* 20°15N 85°50E **41** J14
Bhuj *India* 23°15N 69°49E **42** H3
Bhumiphol Res. *Thailand* 17°20N 98°40E **38** D2
Bhusawal *India* 21°3N 75°46E **40** J9
Bhutan ■ *Asia* 27°25N 90°30E **41** F17
Biafra, B. of = Bonny, Bight of
  Africa 3°30N 9°20E **52** D1
Biak *Indonesia* 1°10S 136°6E **37** E9
Biała Podlaska *Poland* 52°4N 23°6E **17** B12
Białogard *Poland* 54°2N 15°58E **16** A8
Białystok *Poland* 53°10N 23°10E **17** B12
Biaora *India* 23°56N 76°56E **42** H7
Bīārjmand *Iran* 36°6N 55°53E **45** B7
Biaro *Indonesia* 2°5N 125°26E **37** D7
Biarritz *France* 43°29N 1°33W **20** E3
Bias *Indonesia* 8°24S 115°36E **37** J18
Bibai *Japan* 43°19N 141°52E **30** C10
Bibby I. *Canada* 61°55N 93°0W **71** A10
Biberach *Germany* 48°5N 9°47E **16** D5
Bibungwa
  Dem. Rep. of the Congo 2°40S 28°15E **54** C2
Bicester *U.K.* 51°54N 1°9W **13** F6
Bicheno *Australia* 41°52S 148°18E **63** G4
Bichia *India* 22°27N 80°42E **43** H9
Bickerton I. *Australia* 13°45S 136°10E **62** A2
Bida *Nigeria* 9°3N 5°58E **50** G7
Bidar *India* 17°55N 77°35E **40** L10
Biddeford *U.S.A.* 43°30N 70°28W **81** D18
Bideford *U.K.* 51°1N 4°13W **13** F3
Bideford Bay *U.K.* 51°5N 4°20W **13** F3
Bidhuna *India* 26°49N 79°31E **43** F8
Bīdokht *Iran* 34°20N 58°46E **45** C8
Bidyadanga *Australia* 18°45S 121°43E **60** C3
Bié, Planalto de *Angola* 12°0S 16°0E **53** G3
Bieber *U.S.A.* 41°7N 121°8W **76** F3
Biel *Switz.* 47°8N 7°14E **20** C7
Bielefeld *Germany* 52°1N 8°33E **16** B5
Biella *Italy* 45°34N 8°3E **20** D8
Bielsk Podlaski *Poland* 52°47N 23°12E **17** B12
Bielsko-Biała *Poland* 49°50N 19°2E **17** D10
Bien Hoa *Vietnam* 10°57N 106°49E **39** G6
Bienne = Biel *Switz.* 47°8N 7°14E **20** C7
Bienville, L. *Canada* 55°5N 72°40W **72** A5
Biesiesfontein *S. Africa* 30°57S 17°58E **56** E2
Big → *Canada* 54°50N 58°55W **73** B8
Big B. *Canada* 55°43N 60°35W **73** A7
Big Bear City *U.S.A.* 34°16N 116°51W **79** L10
Big Bear Lake *U.S.A.* 34°15N 116°56W **79** L10
Big Belt Mts. *U.S.A.* 46°30N 111°25W **76** C8
Big Bend *Swaziland* 26°50S 31°58E **57** D5
Big Bend △ *U.S.A.* 29°20N 103°5W **84** G3
Big Black → *U.S.A.* 32°3N 91°4W **85** F9
Big Blue → *U.S.A.* 39°35N 96°34W **80** F5
Big Creek *U.S.A.* 37°11N 119°14W **78** H7
Big Cypress △ *U.S.A.* 26°0N 81°10W **85** H14
Big Desert *Australia* 35°45S 141°10E **63** F3
Big Falls *U.S.A.* 48°12N 93°48W **80** A7
Big Fork → *U.S.A.* 48°31N 93°43W **80** A7
Big Horn Mts. = Bighorn Mts.
  U.S.A. 44°25N 107°0W **76** D10
Big I. *Canada* 61°7N 116°45W **70** A5
Big Lake *U.S.A.* 31°12N 101°28W **84** F4
Big Moose *U.S.A.* 43°49N 74°58W **83** C10
Big Muddy Cr. →
  U.S.A. 48°8N 104°36W **76** B11
Big Pine *U.S.A.* 37°10N 118°17W **78** H8
Big Piney *U.S.A.* 42°32N 110°7W **76** E8
Big Quill L. *Canada* 51°55N 104°13W **71** C8
Big Rapids *U.S.A.* 43°42N 85°29W **81** D11
Big Rideau L. *Canada* 44°40N 76°15W **83** B8
Big River *Canada* 53°50N 107°0W **71** C7
Big Run *U.S.A.* 40°57N 78°55W **82** F6
Big Sable Pt. *U.S.A.* 44°3N 86°1W **80** C10
Big Salmon → *Canada* 61°52N 134°55W **70** A2
Big Sand L. *Canada* 57°45N 99°45W **71** B9
Big Sandy *U.S.A.* 48°11N 110°7W **76** B8
Big Sandy → *U.S.A.* 38°25N 82°36W **81** F12
Big Sandy Cr. = Sandy Cr. →
  U.S.A. 41°51N 109°47W **76** F9
Big Sandy Cr. →
  U.S.A. 38°7N 102°29W **76** G12
Big Sioux → *U.S.A.* 42°29N 96°27W **80** D5
Big South Fork △
  U.S.A. 36°27N 84°47W **85** C12
Big Spring *U.S.A.* 32°15N 101°28W **84** E4
Big Stone City *U.S.A.* 45°18N 96°28W **80** C5

Big Stone Gap *U.S.A.* 36°52N 82°47W **81** G12
Big Stone L. *U.S.A.* 45°18N 96°27W **80** C5
Big Sur *U.S.A.* 36°15N 121°48W **78** J5
Big Timber *U.S.A.* 45°50N 109°57W **76** D9
Big Trout L. *Canada* 53°40N 90°0W **72** B2
Big Trout Lake *Canada* 53°45N 90°0W **72** B2
Biğa *Turkey* 40°13N 27°14E **23** D12
Bigadiç *Turkey* 39°22N 28°7E **23** E13
Biggar *Canada* 52°4N 108°0W **71** C7
Biggar *U.K.* 55°38N 3°32W **11** F5
Bigge I. *Australia* 14°35S 125°10E **60** B4
Biggenden *Australia* 25°31S 152°4E **63** D5
Biggleswade *U.K.* 52°5N 0°14W **13** E7
Biggs *U.S.A.* 39°25N 121°43W **78** F5
Bighorn *U.S.A.* 46°10N 107°27W **76** C10
Bighorn → *U.S.A.* 46°10N 107°28W **76** C10
Bighorn Canyon △
  U.S.A. 45°10N 108°0W **76** D10
Bighorn L. *U.S.A.* 44°55N 108°15W **76** D9
Bighorn Mts. *U.S.A.* 44°25N 107°0W **76** D10
Bigstone L. *Canada* 53°42N 95°44W **71** C9
Bigwa *Tanzania* 7°10S 39°10E **54** D4
Bihać *Bos.-H.* 44°49N 15°57E **16** F8
Bihar *India* 25°5N 85°40E **43** G11
Bihar □ *India* 25°0N 86°0E **43** G12
Biharamulo *Tanzania* 2°25S 31°25E **54** C3
Biharamulo △ *Tanzania* 2°24S 31°26E **54** C3
Bihariganj *India* 25°44N 86°59E **43** G12
Bihor, Munţii *Romania* 46°29N 22°47E **17** E12
Bijagós, Arquipélago dos
  Guinea-Biss. 11°15N 16°10W **50** F2
Bijaipur *India* 26°2N 77°20E **42** F7
Bijapur *Chhattisgarh,*
  India 18°50N 80°50E **41** K12
Bijapur *Karnataka, India* 16°50N 75°55E **40** L9
Bījār *Iran* 35°52N 47°35E **44** C5
Bijawar *India* 24°38N 79°30E **43** G8
Bijeljina *Bos.-H.* 44°46N 19°14E **23** B8
Bijnor *India* 29°27N 78°11E **42** E8
Bikaner *India* 28°2N 73°18E **42** E5
Bikapur *India* 26°30N 82°7E **43** F10
Bikeqi *China* 40°43N 111°20E **34** D6
Bikfayyā *Lebanon* 33°55N 35°41E **46** B4
Bikin *Russia* 46°50N 134°20E **30** A7
Bikin → *Russia* 46°51N 134°2E **30** A7
Bikini Atoll *Marshall Is.* 12°0N 167°30E **64** F8
Bikita *Zimbabwe* 20°6S 31°41E **57** C5
Bikku Bītī *Libya* 22°0N 19°12E **51** D9
Bila Tserkva *Ukraine* 49°45N 30°10E **17** D16
Bilara *India* 26°14N 73°53E **42** F5
Bilaspur *Chhattisgarh,*
  India 22°2N 82°15E **43** H10
Bilaspur *Punjab, India* 31°19N 76°50E **42** D7
Bilauk Taungdan *Thailand* 13°0N 99°0E **38** F2
Bilbao *Spain* 43°16N 2°56W **21** A4
Bilbo = Bilbao *Spain* 43°16N 2°56W **21** A4
Bildudalur *Iceland* 65°41N 23°36W **8** D2
Bílé Karpaty *Europe* 49°5N 18°0E **17** D9
Bilecik *Turkey* 40°5N 30°5E **19** F5
Bilgram *India* 27°11N 80°2E **43** F9
Bilhaur *India* 26°51N 80°5E **43** F9
Bilhorod-Dnistrovskyy
  Ukraine 46°11N 30°23E **19** E5
Bilibino *Russia* 68°3N 166°20E **29** C17
Bilibiza *Mozam.* 12°30S 40°20E **55** E5
Billabong Roadhouse
  Australia 27°25S 115°49E **61** E2
Billiluna *Australia* 19°37S 127°41E **60** C4
Billings *U.S.A.* 45°47N 108°30W **76** D9
Billiton Is. = Belitung
  Indonesia 3°10S 107°50E **36** E3
Bilma *Niger* 18°50N 13°30E **51** E8
Biloela *Australia* 24°24S 150°31E **62** C5
Biloxi *U.S.A.* 30°24N 88°53W **85** F10
Bilpa Morea Claypan
  Australia 25°0S 140°0E **62** D3
Biltine *Chad* 14°40N 20°50E **51** F10
Bima *Indonesia* 8°22S 118°49E **37** F5
Bimbo *C.A.R.* 4°15N 18°33E **52** D3
Bimini Is. *Bahamas* 25°42N 79°25W **88** A4
Bin Xian *Heilongjiang,*
  China 45°42N 127°32E **35** B14
Bin Xian *Shaanxi, China* 35°2N 108°4E **34** G5
Bina-Etawah *India* 24°13N 78°14E **42** G8
Binalbagan *Phil.* 10°12N 122°50E **37** B6
Binalong *Australia* 34°40S 148°39E **63** E4
Bīnālūd, Kūh-e *Iran* 36°30N 58°30E **45** B8
Binatang = Bintangau
  Malaysia 2°10N 111°40E **36** D4
Binche *Belgium* 50°26N 4°10E **15** D4
Bindki *India* 26°2N 80°36E **43** F9
Bindura *Zimbabwe* 17°18S 31°18E **55** F3
Bingara *Australia* 29°52S 150°36E **63** D5
Bingham *U.S.A.* 45°3N 69°53W **81** C19
Binghamton *U.S.A.* 42°6N 75°55W **83** D9
Bingöl *Turkey* 38°53N 40°29E **44** B4
Binh Dinh = An Nhon
  Vietnam 13°55N 109°7E **38** F7
Binh Khe *Vietnam* 13°57N 108°51E **38** F7
Binh Son *Vietnam* 15°20N 108°40E **38** E7
Binhai *China* 34°2N 119°49E **35** G10
Binisatua *Spain* 39°50N 4°11E **24** B11
Binissalem *Spain* 39°41N 2°50E **24** B9
Binjai *Indonesia* 3°20N 98°30E **36** D1
Binnaway *Australia* 31°28S 149°24E **63** E4
Binongko *Indonesia* 5°57S 124°2E **37** F6
Binscarth *Canada* 50°37N 101°17W **71** C8
Bintan *Indonesia* 1°0N 104°0E **36** D2
Bintangau *Malaysia* 2°10N 111°40E **36** D4
Bintuni *Indonesia* 2°7S 133°32E **37** E8
Binzert = Bizerte *Tunisia* 37°15N 9°50E **51** A7
Bío Bío □ *Chile* 37°35S 72°0W **94** D1
Bíobío → *Chile* 36°49S 73°10W **94** D1
Bioko *Eq. Guin.* 3°30N 8°40E **52** D1
Bir *India* 19°4N 75°46E **40** K9

Bîr Abu Muḥammad
  Egypt 29°44N 34°14E **46** F3
Bi'r ad Dabbāghāt *Jordan* 30°26N 35°32E **46** E4
Bi'r al Butayyihāt *Jordan* 29°47N 35°20E **46** F4
Bi'r al Mārī *Jordan* 30°4N 35°33E **46** E4
Bi'r al Qattār *Jordan* 29°47N 35°32E **46** F4
Bîr Atrun *Sudan* 18°15N 26°40E **51** E11
Bîr Beiḍa *Egypt* 30°25N 34°29E **46** E3
Bîr el 'Abd *Egypt* 31°2N 33°0E **46** D2
Bîr el Biarât *Egypt* 29°30N 34°43E **46** F3
Bîr el Duweidar *Egypt* 30°56N 32°32E **46** E1
Bîr el Garârât *Egypt* 31°3N 33°34E **46** D2
Bîr el Heisi *Egypt* 29°22N 34°36E **46** F3
Bîr el Jafir *Egypt* 30°50N 32°41E **46** E1
Bîr el Mâlhi *Egypt* 30°38N 33°19E **46** E2
Bîr el Thamâda *Egypt* 30°12N 33°27E **46** E2
Bîr Gebeil Ḥiṣn *Egypt* 30°2N 33°18E **46** E2
Bi'r Ghaḍir *Syria* 34°6N 37°3E **46** A6
Bi'r Ḥasana *Egypt* 30°29N 33°46E **46** E2
Bîr Kaseiba *Egypt* 31°0N 33°17E **46** E2
Bîr Lahfân *Egypt* 31°0N 33°51E **46** E2
Bîr Madkûr *Egypt* 30°44N 32°33E **46** E1
Bîr Mogreïn *Mauritania* 25°10N 11°25W **50** C3
Bi'r Muṭribah *Kuwait* 29°54N 47°17E **44** D5
Bîr Qaţia *Egypt* 30°58N 32°45E **46** E1
Bîr Shalateîn *Egypt* 23°5N 35°25E **51** D13
Birāk *Libya* 27°31N 14°20E **51** C8
Birawa
  Dem. Rep. of the Congo 2°20S 28°48E **54** C2
Birch → *Canada* 58°28N 112°17W **70** B6
Birch Hills *Canada* 52°59N 105°25W **71** C7
Birch I. *Canada* 52°26N 99°54W **71** C9
Birch L. *N.W.T., Canada* 62°4N 116°33W **70** A5
Birch L. *Ont., Canada* 51°23N 92°18W **72** B1
Birch Mts. *Canada* 57°30N 113°10W **70** B6
Birch River *Canada* 52°24N 101°6W **71** C8
Birchip *Australia* 35°56S 142°55E **63** F3
Bird *Canada* 56°30N 94°13W **71** B10
Bird I. = Aves, I. de
  W. Indies 15°45N 63°55W **89** C7
Bird I. *S. Georgia* 54°0S 38°3W **96** G9
Birds Creek *Canada* 45°6N 77°52W **82** A7
Birdsville *Australia* 25°51S 139°20E **62** D2
Birdum Cr. → *Australia* 15°14S 133°0E **60** C5
Birecik *Turkey* 37°2N 38°0E **44** B3
Bireun *Indonesia* 5°14N 96°39E **36** C1
Birigüi *Brazil* 21°18S 50°16W **95** A5
Bīrjand *Iran* 32°53N 59°13E **45** C8
Birkenhead *U.K.* 53°23N 3°2W **12** D4
Bîrlad = Bârlad
  Romania 46°15N 27°38E **17** E14
Birmingham *U.K.* 52°29N 1°52W **13** E6
Birmingham *U.S.A.* 33°31N 86°48W **85** E11
Birmingham Int. ✈ (BHX)
  U.K. 52°26N 1°45W **13** E6
Birmitrapur *India* 22°24N 84°46E **41** H14
Birni Nkonni *Niger* 13°55N 5°15E **50** F7
Birnin Kebbi *Nigeria* 12°32N 4°12E **50** F6
Birobidzhan *Russia* 48°50N 132°50E **29** E14
Birr *Ireland* 53°6N 7°54W **10** C4
Birrie → *Australia* 29°43S 146°37E **63** D4
Birsilpur *India* 28°11N 72°15E **42** E5
Birsk *Russia* 55°25N 55°30E **18** C10
Birtle *Canada* 50°30N 101°5W **71** C8
Birur *India* 13°30N 75°55E **40** N9
Biržai *Lithuania* 56°11N 24°45E **9** H21
Birzebbugga *Malta* 35°50N 14°32E **25** D2
Bisa *Indonesia* 1°15S 127°28E **37** E7
Bisalpur *India* 28°14N 79°48E **43** E8
Bisbee *U.S.A.* 31°27N 109°55W **77** L9
Biscarrosse *France* 44°22N 1°20W **20** D3
Biscay, B. of *Atl. Oc.* 45°0N 2°0W **20** D1
Biscayne B. *U.S.A.* 25°40N 80°12W **85** J14
Biscoe Is. *Antarctica* 66°0S 67°0W **5** C17
Biscostasing *Canada* 47°18N 82°9W **72** C3
Bishkek *Kyrgyzstan* 42°54N 74°46E **28** E8
Bishnupur *India* 23°8N 87°20E **43** H12
Bisho = Bhisho *S. Africa* 32°50S 27°23E **57** E4
Bishop *Calif., U.S.A.* 37°22N 118°24W **78** H8
Bishop *Tex., U.S.A.* 27°35N 97°48W **84** H6
Bishop Auckland *U.K.* 54°39N 1°40W **12** C6
Bishop's Falls *Canada* 49°2N 55°30W **73** C8
Bishop's Stortford *U.K.* 51°52N 0°10E **13** F8
Bisina, L. *Uganda* 1°38N 33°56E **54** B3
Biskra *Algeria* 34°50N 5°44E **50** B7
Bismarck *U.S.A.* 46°48N 100°47W **80** B3
Bismarck Arch.
  Papua N. G. 2°30S 150°0E **58** B7
Biso *Uganda* 1°44N 31°26E **54** B3
Bison *U.S.A.* 45°31N 102°28W **80** C2
Bīsotūn *Iran* 34°23N 47°26E **44** C5
Bissagós = Bijagós, Arquipélago
  dos *Guinea-Biss.* 11°15N 16°10W **50** F2
Bissau *Guinea-Biss.* 11°45N 15°45W **50** F2
Bistcho L. *Canada* 59°45N 118°50W **70** B5
Bistriţa *Romania* 47°9N 24°35E **17** E13
Bistriţa → *Romania* 46°30N 26°57E **17** E14
Biswan *India* 27°29N 81°2E **43** F9
Bitam *Gabon* 2°5N 11°25E **52** D2
Bitkine *Chad* 11°59N 18°13E **51** F9
Bitlis *Turkey* 38°20N 42°3E **44** B4
Bitola *Macedonia* 41°1N 21°20E **23** D9
Bitolj = Bitola *Macedonia* 41°1N 21°20E **23** D9
Bitter Creek *U.S.A.* 41°33N 108°33W **76** F9
Bitterfontein *S. Africa* 31°1S 18°32E **56** E2
Bitterroot → *U.S.A.* 46°52N 114°7W **76** C6
Bitterroot Range *U.S.A.* 46°0N 114°20W **76** C6
Bitterwater *U.S.A.* 36°23N 121°0W **78** J6
Biu *Nigeria* 10°40N 12°3E **51** F8
Biwa-Ko *Japan* 35°15N 136°10E **31** G8
Biwabik *U.S.A.* 47°32N 92°21W **80** B7
Bixby *U.S.A.* 35°57N 95°53W **84** D7
Biyang *China* 32°38N 113°21E **34** H7
Biysk *Russia* 52°40N 85°0E **28** D9
Bizana *S. Africa* 30°50S 29°52E **57** E4

Bizen *Japan* 34°43N 134°8E **31** G7
Bizerte *Tunisia* 37°15N 9°50E **51** A7
Bjargtangar *Iceland* 65°30N 24°30W **8** D1
Bjelovar *Croatia* 45°56N 16°49E **22** B7
Björneborg = Pori
  Finland 61°29N 21°48E **8** F19
Bjørnevatn *Norway* 69°40N 30°0E **8** B23
Bjørnøya *Arctic* 74°30N 19°0E **4** B8
Black = Da → *Vietnam* 21°15N 105°20E **38** B5
Black → *Canada* 44°42N 79°19W **82** B5
Black → *Ariz., U.S.A.* 33°44N 110°13W **77** K8
Black → *Ark., U.S.A.* 35°38N 91°20W **84** D9
Black → *La., U.S.A.* 31°16N 91°50W **84** F9
Black → *Mich., U.S.A.* 42°59N 82°27W **82** D2
Black → *N.Y., U.S.A.* 43°59N 76°4W **83** C8
Black → *Wis., U.S.A.* 43°57N 91°22W **80** D8
Black Bay Pen. *Canada* 48°38N 88°21W **72** C2
Black Birch L. *Canada* 56°53N 107°45W **71** B7
Black Braes △ *Australia* 19°10S 144°10E **62** B3
Black Canyon of the Gunnison △
  U.S.A. 38°40N 107°35W **76** G10
Black Diamond *Canada* 50°45N 114°14W **70** C6
Black Duck → *Canada* 56°51N 89°2W **72** A2
Black Forest = Schwarzwald
  Germany 48°30N 8°20E **16** D5
Black Forest *U.S.A.* 39°0N 104°43W **76** G11
Black Hd. *Ireland* 53°9N 9°16W **10** C2
Black Hills *U.S.A.* 44°0N 103°45W **80** D2
Black I. *Canada* 51°12N 96°30W **71** C9
Black L. *Canada* 59°12N 105°15W **71** B7
Black L. *Mich., U.S.A.* 45°28N 84°16W **81** C11
Black L. *N.Y., U.S.A.* 44°31N 75°36W **83** B9
Black Lake *Canada* 59°11N 105°20W **71** B7
Black Mesa *U.S.A.* 36°58N 102°58W **84** C3
Black Mt. = Mynydd Du
  U.K. 51°52N 3°50W **13** F4
Black Mts. *U.K.* 51°55N 3°7W **13** F4
Black Range *U.S.A.* 33°15N 107°50W **77** K10
Black River *Jamaica* 18°0N 77°50W **88** a
Black River *U.S.A.* 44°0N 75°47W **83** C9
Black River Falls *U.S.A.* 44°18N 90°51W **80** C9
Black Rock *Barbados* 13°7N 59°37W **89** g
Black Rock Desert
  U.S.A. 41°10N 118°50W **76** F4
Black Sea *Eurasia* 43°30N 35°0E **19** F6
Black Tickle *Canada* 53°28N 55°45W **73** B8
Black Volta → *Africa* 8°41N 1°33W **50** G5
Black Warrior →
  U.S.A. 32°32N 87°51W **85** E11
Blackall *Australia* 24°25S 145°45E **62** C4
Blackball *N.Z.* 42°22S 171°26E **59** E3
Blackbull *Australia* 17°55S 141°45E **62** B3
Blackburn *U.K.* 53°45N 2°29W **12** D5
Blackburn with Darwen □
  U.K. 53°45N 2°29W **12** D5
Blackdown Tableland △
  Australia 23°52S 149°8E **62** C4
Blackfoot *U.S.A.* 43°11N 112°21W **76** E7
Blackfoot → *U.S.A.* 46°52N 113°53W **76** C7
Blackfoot Res. *U.S.A.* 42°55N 111°39W **76** E8
Blackpool *U.K.* 53°49N 3°3W **12** D4
Blackpool □ *U.K.* 53°49N 3°3W **12** D4
Blackriver *U.S.A.* 44°46N 83°17W **82** B1
Blacks Harbour *Canada* 45°3N 66°49W **73** C6
Blacksburg *U.S.A.* 37°14N 80°25W **81** G13
Blacksod B. *Ireland* 54°6N 10°0W **10** B1
Blackstairs Mt. *Ireland* 52°33N 6°48W **10** D5
Blackstone *U.S.A.* 37°5N 78°0W **81** G14
Blackstone Ra. *Australia* 26°0S 128°30E **61** E4
Blacktown *Australia* 33°48S 150°55E **63** E5
Blackwater = West Road →
  Canada 53°18N 122°53W **70** C4
Blackwater *Australia* 23°35S 148°53E **62** C4
Blackwater → *Meath,*
  Ireland 53°39N 6°41W **10** C4
Blackwater → *Waterford,*
  Ireland 52°4N 7°52W **10** D4
Blackwater → *U.K.* 54°31N 6°35W **10** B5
Blackwell *U.S.A.* 36°48N 97°17W **84** C6
Blackwells Corner
  U.S.A. 35°37N 119°47W **79** K7
Bladensburg △
  Australia 22°30S 142°59E **62** C3
Blaenau Ffestiniog *U.K.* 53°0N 3°56W **12** E4
Blaenau Gwent □ *U.K.* 51°48N 3°12W **13** F4
Blagodarnoye = Blagodarnyy
  Russia 45°7N 43°37E **19** E7
Blagodarnyy *Russia* 45°7N 43°37E **19** E7
Blagoevgrad *Bulgaria* 42°2N 23°5E **23** C10
Blagoveshchensk
  Russia 50°20N 127°30E **29** D13
Blahkiuh *Indonesia* 8°31S 115°12E **37** J18
Blain *U.S.A.* 40°20N 77°31W **82** F7
Blaine *Minn., U.S.A.* 45°9N 93°13W **80** C7
Blaine *Wash., U.S.A.* 48°59N 122°45W **78** B4
Blaine Lake *Canada* 52°51N 106°52W **71** C7
Blair *U.S.A.* 41°33N 96°8W **80** E6
Blair Athol *Australia* 22°42S 147°31E **62** C4
Blair Atholl *U.K.* 56°46N 3°50W **11** E5
Blairgowrie *U.K.* 56°35N 3°21W **11** E5
Blairsden *U.S.A.* 39°47N 120°37W **78** F6
Blairsville *U.S.A.* 40°26N 79°16W **82** F5
Blakang Mati, Pulau
  Singapore 1°15N 103°50E **39** d
Blake Pt. *U.S.A.* 48°11N 88°25W **80** A10
Blakely *Ga., U.S.A.* 31°23N 84°56W **85** F12
Blakely *Pa., U.S.A.* 41°28N 75°37W **83** E9
Blanc, C. *Spain* 39°21N 2°51E **24** B9
Blanc, Mont *Europe* 45°48N 6°50E **20** D7
Blanca, B. *Argentina* 39°10S 61°30W **96** D4
Blanca, Cord. *Peru* 9°10S 77°35W **92** E3
Blanca Peak *U.S.A.* 37°35N 105°29W **77** H11
Blanche, C. *Australia* 33°1S 134°9E **63** E1
Blanche, L. *S. Austral.,*
  Australia 29°15S 139°40E **63** D2
Blanche, L. *W. Austral.,*
  Australia 22°25S 123°17E **60** D3

Blanchisseuse
  Trin. & Tob. 10°48N 61°18W **93** K15
Blanco *S. Africa* 33°55S 22°23E **56** E3
Blanco *U.S.A.* 30°6N 98°25W **84** G5
Blanco → *Argentina* 30°20S 68°42W **94** C2
Blanco, C. *Costa Rica* 9°34N 85°8W **88** E2
Blanco, C. *U.S.A.* 42°51N 124°34W **76** E1
Blanda → *Iceland* 65°37N 20°9W **8** D3
Blandford Forum *U.K.* 50°51N 2°9W **13** G5
Blanding *U.S.A.* 37°37N 109°29W **77** H9
Blanes *Spain* 41°40N 2°48E **21** B7
Blankenberge *Belgium* 51°20N 3°9E **15** C3
Blanquilla *Venezuela* 11°51N 64°37W **89** D7
Blanquillo *Uruguay* 32°53S 55°37W **95** C4
Blantyre *Malawi* 15°45S 35°0E **55** F4
Blarney *Ireland* 51°56N 8°33W **10** E3
Blasdell *U.S.A.* 42°48N 78°50W **82** D6
Blåvands Huk *Denmark* 55°33N 8°4E **9** J13
Blaydon *U.K.* 54°58N 1°42W **12** C6
Blayney *Australia* 33°32S 149°14E **63** E4
Blaze, Pt. *Australia* 12°56S 130°11E **60** B5
Blekinge *Sweden* 56°25N 15°20E **9** H16
Blenheim *Canada* 42°20N 82°0W **82** D3
Blenheim *N.Z.* 41°38S 173°57E **59** D5
Bletchley *U.K.* 51°59N 0°44W **13** F7
Blida *Algeria* 36°30N 2°49E **50** A6
Bligh Sound *N.Z.* 44°47S 167°32E **59** F1
Bligh Water *Fiji* 17°0S 178°0E **59** a
Blind River *Canada* 46°10N 82°58W **72** C3
Bliss *Idaho, U.S.A.* 42°56N 114°57W **76** E6
Bliss *N.Y., U.S.A.* 42°34N 78°15W **82** D6
Blissfield *U.S.A.* 40°24N 81°58W **82** F3
Blitar *Indonesia* 8°5S 112°11E **37** H15
Block I. *U.S.A.* 41°11N 71°35W **83** E13
Block Island Sd. *U.S.A.* 41°15N 71°40W **83** E13
Bloemfontein *S. Africa* 29°6S 26°7E **56** D4
Bloemhof *S. Africa* 27°38S 25°32E **56** D4
Blois *France* 47°35N 1°20E **20** C4
Blönduós *Iceland* 65°40N 20°12W **8** D3
Blongas *Indonesia* 8°53S 116°2E **37** K19
Bloodvein → *Canada* 51°47N 96°43W **71** C9
Bloody Foreland *Ireland* 55°10N 8°17W **10** A3
Bloomer *U.S.A.* 45°6N 91°29W **80** C8
Bloomfield *Canada* 43°59N 77°14W **82** C7
Bloomfield *Iowa, U.S.A.* 40°45N 92°25W **80** E7
Bloomfield *N. Mex.,*
  U.S.A. 36°43N 107°59W **77** H10
Bloomfield *Nebr., U.S.A.* 42°36N 97°39W **80** D5
Bloomington *Ill., U.S.A.* 40°28N 89°0W **80** E9
Bloomington *Ind.,*
  U.S.A. 39°10N 86°32W **80** F10
Bloomington *Minn.,*
  U.S.A. 44°50N 93°17W **80** C7
Bloomsburg *U.S.A.* 41°0N 76°27W **83** F8
Bloomsbury *Australia* 20°48S 148°38E **62** J6
Blora *Indonesia* 6°57S 111°25E **37** G14
Blossburg *U.S.A.* 41°41N 77°4W **82** E7
Blouberg *S. Africa* 23°8S 28°59E **57** C4
Blountstown *U.S.A.* 30°27N 85°3W **85** F12
Blue Earth *U.S.A.* 43°38N 94°6W **80** D6
Blue Hole △ *Belize* 17°24N 88°0W **88** C2
Blue Lagoon △ *Zambia* 15°28S 27°26E **55** F2
Blue Mesa Res. *U.S.A.* 38°28N 107°20W **76** G10
Blue Mountain Lake
  U.S.A. 43°51N 74°27W **83** C10
Blue Mountain Pk.
  Jamaica 18°3N 76°36W **88** a
Blue Mt. *U.S.A.* 40°30N 76°30W **83** F8
Blue Mts. *Jamaica* 18°3N 76°36W **88** a
Blue Mts. *Maine, U.S.A.* 44°50N 70°35W **83** B14
Blue Mts. *Oreg., U.S.A.* 45°0N 118°20W **76** D4
Blue Mud B. *Australia* 13°30S 136°0E **62** A2
Blue Nile = Nîl el Azraq →
  Sudan 15°38N 32°31E **51** E12
Blue Rapids *U.S.A.* 39°41N 96°39W **80** F5
Blue Ridge *U.S.A.* 36°40N 80°50W **81** G13
Blue River *Canada* 52°6N 119°18W **70** C5
Bluefield *U.S.A.* 37°15N 81°17W **81** G13
Bluefields *Nic.* 12°20N 83°50W **88** D3
Bluevale *Canada* 43°51N 81°15W **82** C3
Bluff *Australia* 23°35S 149°4E **62** C4
Bluff *N.Z.* 46°37S 168°20E **59** G2
Bluff *U.S.A.* 37°17N 109°33W **77** H9
Bluff Knoll *Australia* 34°24S 118°15E **61** F2
Bluff Pt. *Australia* 27°50S 114°5E **61** E1
Bluffton *U.S.A.* 40°44N 85°11W **81** E11
Blumenau *Brazil* 27°0S 49°0W **95** B6
Blunt *U.S.A.* 44°31N 99°59W **80** C4
Blyde River Canyon △
  S. Africa 24°37S 31°2E **57** C5
Blyth *Canada* 43°44N 81°26W **82** C3
Blyth *U.K.* 55°8N 1°31W **12** B6
Blythe *U.S.A.* 33°37N 114°36W **79** M12
Blytheville *U.S.A.* 35°56N 89°55W **85** D10
Bo *S. Leone* 7°55N 11°50W **50** G3
Bo Duc *Vietnam* 11°58N 106°50E **39** G6
Bo Hai *China* 39°0N 119°0E **35** E10
Bo Xian = Bozhou
  China 33°55N 115°41E **34** H8
Boa Vista *Brazil* 2°48N 60°30W **92** C6
Boa Vista *C. Verde Is.* 16°0N 22°49W **50** b
Boaco *Nic.* 12°29N 85°35W **88** D2
Bo'ai *China* 35°10N 113°3E **34** G7
Boalsburg *U.S.A.* 40°47N 77°49W **82** F7
Boane *Mozam.* 26°6S 32°19E **57** D5
Boardman *U.S.A.* 41°2N 80°40W **82** E4
Bobadah *Australia* 32°19S 146°41E **63** E4
Bobbili *India* 18°35N 83°30E **41** K13
Bobcaygeon *Canada* 44°33N 78°33W **82** B6
Bobo-Dioulasso
  Burkina Faso 11°8N 4°13W **50** F5
Bobonong *Botswana* 21°58S 28°20E **57** C4

Boby, Pic *Madag.* 22°12S 46°55E **53** J9
Boca del Río *Mexico* 19°5N 96°4W **87** D5
Boca do Acre *Brazil* 8°50S 67°27W **92** E5
Boca Raton *U.S.A.* 26°21N 80°5W **85** H14
Bocas del Dragón
  Venezuela 11°0N 61°50W **93** K15
Bocas del Toro *Panama* 9°15N 82°20W **88** E3
Bochnia *Poland* 49°58N 20°27E **17** D11
Bochum *Germany* 51°28N 7°13E **16** C4
Bocoyna *Mexico* 27°52N 107°35W **86** B3
Bodaybo *Russia* 57°50N 114°0E **29** D12
Boddam *U.K.* 59°56N 1°17W **11** B7
Boddington *Australia* 32°50S 116°30E **61** F2
Bodega Bay *U.S.A.* 38°20N 123°3W **78** G3
Boden *Sweden* 65°50N 21°42E **8** D19
Bodensee *Europe* 47°35N 9°25E **20** C8
Bodhan *India* 18°40N 77°44E **40** K10
Bodmin *U.K.* 50°28N 4°43W **13** G3
Bodmin Moor *U.K.* 50°33N 4°36W **13** G3
Bodø *Norway* 67°17N 14°24E **8** C16
Bodrog → *Hungary* 48°11N 21°22E **17** D11
Bodrum *Turkey* 37°3N 27°30E **23** F12
Boende
  Dem. Rep. of the Congo 0°24S 21°12E **52** E4
Boerne *U.S.A.* 29°47N 98°44W **84** G5
Boesmans → *S. Africa* 33°42S 26°39E **56** E4
Bogalusa *U.S.A.* 30°47N 89°52W **85** F10
Bogan → *Australia* 30°20S 146°55E **63** D4
Bogan Gate *Australia* 33°7S 147°49E **63** E4
Bogantungan *Australia* 23°41S 147°17E **62** C4
Bogata *U.S.A.* 33°28N 95°13W **84** E7
Bogda Shan *China* 43°35N 89°40E **32** B3
Boggabilla *Australia* 28°36S 150°24E **63** D5
Boggabri *Australia* 30°45S 150°5E **63** E5
Boggeragh Mts. *Ireland* 52°2N 8°55W **10** D3
Boglan = Solhan *Turkey* 38°57N 41°3E **44** B4
Bognor Regis *U.K.* 50°47N 0°40W **13** G7
Bogo *Phil.* 11°3N 124°0E **37** B6
Bogong, Mt. *Australia* 36°47S 147°17E **63** F4
Bogor *Indonesia* 6°36S 106°48E **37** G12
Bogotá *Colombia* 4°34N 74°0W **92** C4
Bogotol *Russia* 56°15N 89°50E **28** D9
Bogra *Bangla.* 24°51N 89°22E **41** G16
Boguchany *Russia* 58°40N 97°30E **29** D10
Bogué *Mauritania* 16°45N 14°10W **50** E3
Bohemian Forest = Böhmerwald
  Germany 49°8N 13°14E **16** D7
Böhmerwald *Germany* 49°8N 13°14E **16** D7
Bohol □ *Phil.* 9°50N 124°10E **37** C6
Bohol Sea *Phil.* 9°0N 124°0E **37** C6
Bohorok *Indonesia* 3°30N 98°12E **39** L2
Bohuslän *Sweden* 58°25N 12°0E **9** G15
Boi, Pta. do *Brazil* 23°55S 45°15W **95** A6
Boiaçu *Brazil* 0°27S 61°46W **92** D6
Boileau, C. *Australia* 17°40S 122°7E **60** C3
Boise *U.S.A.* 43°37N 116°13W **76** E5
Boise City *U.S.A.* 36°44N 102°31W **84** C3
Boissevain *Canada* 49°15N 100°5W **71** D8
Bojador, C. *W. Sahara* 26°0N 14°30W **50** C3
Bojana → *Albania* 41°52N 19°22E **23** D8
Bojnūrd *Iran* 37°30N 57°20E **45** B8
Bojonegoro *Indonesia* 7°11S 111°54E **37** G14
Bokaro *India* 23°46N 85°55E **43** H11
Boké *Guinea* 10°56N 14°17W **50** F3
Bokhara → *Australia* 29°55S 146°42E **63** D4
Boknafjorden *Norway* 59°14N 5°40E **9** G11
Bokor △ *Cambodia* 10°50N 104°1E **39** G5
Bokora △ *Uganda* 2°12N 31°32E **54** B3
Bokoro *Chad* 12°25N 17°14E **51** F9
Bokpyin *Burma* 11°18N 98°42E **39** G2
Bokungu
  Dem. Rep. of the Congo 0°35S 22°50E **52** E4
Bolan → *Pakistan* 28°38N 67°42E **42** E2
Bolan Pass *Pakistan* 29°50N 67°20E **40** E5
Bolaños → *Mexico* 21°12N 104°5W **86** C4
Bolbec *France* 49°30N 0°30E **20** B4
Boldājī *Iran* 31°56N 51°3E **45** D6
Bole *China* 45°11N 81°37E **32** B3
Bolekhiv *Ukraine* 49°0N 23°57E **17** D12
Bolesławiec *Poland* 51°17N 15°37E **16** C8
Bolgatanga *Ghana* 10°44N 0°53W **50** F5
Bolgrad = Bolhrad
  Ukraine 45°40N 28°32E **17** F15
Bolhrad *Ukraine* 45°40N 28°32E **17** F15
Bolívar *Mo., U.S.A.* 37°37N 93°25W **80** G7
Bolívar *N.Y., U.S.A.* 42°4N 78°10W **82** D6
Bolívar *Tenn., U.S.A.* 35°12N 89°0W **85** D10
Bolivia ■ *S. Amer.* 17°6S 64°0W **92** G6
Bolivian Plateau = Altiplano
  Bolivia 17°0S 68°0W **92** G5
Bollnäs *Sweden* 61°21N 16°24E **8** F17
Bollon *Australia* 28°2S 147°29E **63** D4
Bolmen *Sweden* 56°55N 13°40E **9** H15
Bolobo
  Dem. Rep. of the Congo 2°6S 16°20E **52** E3
Bologna *Italy* 44°29N 11°20E **22** B4
Bologoye *Russia* 57°55N 34°5E **18** C5
Bolomba
  Dem. Rep. of the Congo 0°35N 19°0E **52** D3
Bolonchén *Mexico* 20°1N 89°45W **87** D7
Boloven, Cao Nguyen
  Laos 15°10N 106°30E **38** E6
Bolpur *India* 23°40N 87°45E **43** H12
Bolsena, L. di *Italy* 42°36N 11°56E **22** C4
Bolshevik, Ostrov
  Russia 78°30N 102°0E **29** B11
Bolshoy Anyuy →
  Russia 68°30N 160°49E **29** C17
Bolshoy Begichev, Ostrov
  Russia 74°20N 112°30E **29** B12
Bolshoy Kamen *Russia* 43°7N 132°19E **30** C6
Bolshoy Kavkaz = Caucasus
  Mountains *Eurasia* 42°50N 44°0E **19** F7
Bolshoy Lyakhovskiy, Ostrov
  Russia 73°35N 142°0E **29** B15
Bolshoy Tyuters, Ostrov
  Russia 59°51N 27°13E **9** G22

Bolsward Neths. 53°3N 5°32E 15 A5
Bolt Head U.K. 50°12N 3°48W 13 G4
Bolton Canada 43°54N 79°45W 82 C5
Bolton U.K. 53°35N 2°26W 12 D5
Bolton Landing U.S.A. 43°32N 73°35W 83 C11
Bolu Turkey 40°45N 31°35E 19 F5
Bolungavík Iceland 66°9N 23°15W 8 C2
Bolvadin Turkey 38°45N 31°4E 44 B1
Bolzano Italy 46°31N 11°22E 22 A4
Bom Jesus da Lapa Brazil 13°15S 43°25W 93 F10
Boma Dem. Rep. of the Congo 5°50S 13°4E 52 F2
Bombala Australia 36°56S 149°15E 63 F4
Bombay = Mumbai India 18°56N 72°50E 40 K8
Bombay U.S.A. 44°56N 74°34W 83 B10
Bombedor, Pta. Venezuela 9°53N 61°37W 93 L15
Bomboma Dem. Rep. of the Congo 2°25N 18°55E 52 D3
Bombombwa Dem. Rep. of the Congo 1°40N 25°40E 54 B2
Bomili Dem. Rep. of the Congo 1°45N 27°5E 54 B2
Bømlo Norway 59°37N 5°13E 9 G11
Bomokandi → Dem. Rep. of the Congo 3°39N 26°8E 54 B2
Bomu → C.A.R. 4°40N 22°30E 52 D4
Bon, C. = Ra's at Tib Tunisia 37°1N 11°2E 22 F4
Bon Acceuil Mauritius 20°10S 57°39E 53 d
Bon Echo ⌓ Canada 44°55N 77°16W 82 B7
Bon Sar Pa Vietnam 12°24N 107°35E 38 F6
Bonāb Iran 36°35N 48°41E 45 B6
Bonaigarh India 21°50N 84°57E 43 J11
Bonaire Neth. Ant. 12°10N 68°15W 89 D6
Bonampak Mexico 16°44N 91°5W 87 D6
Bonang Australia 37°11S 148°41E 63 F4
Bonanza Nic. 13°54N 84°35W 88 D3
Bonaparte Arch. Australia 14°0S 124°30E 60 B3
Bonar Bridge U.K. 57°54N 4°20W 11 D4
Bonasse Trin. & Tob. 10°5N 61°54W 93 K15
Bonaventure Canada 48°5N 65°32W 73 C6
Bonavista Canada 48°40N 53°5W 73 C9
Bonavista, C. Canada 48°42N 53°5W 73 C9
Bonavista B. Canada 48°45N 53°25W 73 C9
Bondo Dem. Rep. of the Congo 3°55N 23°53E 54 B1
Bondoukou Ivory C. 8°2N 2°47W 50 G5
Bondowoso Indonesia 7°55S 113°49E 37 G15
Bone, Teluk Indonesia 4°10S 120°50E 37 E6
Bonerate Indonesia 7°25S 121°5E 37 F6
Bonerate, Kepulauan Indonesia 6°30S 121°10E 37 F6
Bo'ness U.K. 56°1N 3°37W 11 E5
Bonete, Cerro Argentina 27°55S 68°40W 94 B2
Bong Son = Hoai Nhon Vietnam 14°28N 109°1E 38 E7
Bongaigaon India 26°28N 90°34E 32 D4
Bongandanga Dem. Rep. of the Congo 1°24N 21°3E 52 D4
Bongor Chad 10°35N 15°20E 51 F9
Bongos, Massif des C.A.R. 8°40N 22°25E 52 C4
Bonham U.S.A. 33°35N 96°11W 84 E6
Boni ⌓ Kenya 1°35S 41°18E 54 C5
Bonifacio France 41°24N 9°10E 20 F8
Bonifacio, Bouches de Medit. S. 41°12N 9°15E 22 D3
Bonin Is. = Ogasawara Gunto Pac. Oc. 27°0N 142°0E 27 F16
Bonn Germany 50°46N 7°6E 16 C4
Bonne Terre U.S.A. 37°55N 90°33W 80 G8
Bonners Ferry U.S.A. 48°42N 116°19W 76 B5
Bonney, L. Australia 37°50S 140°20E 63 F3
Bonnie Rock Australia 30°29S 118°22E 61 F2
Bonny, Bight of Africa 3°30N 9°20E 52 D1
Bonnyrigg U.K. 55°53N 3°6W 11 F5
Bonnyville Canada 54°20N 110°45W 71 C6
Bonoi Indonesia 1°45S 137°41E 37 E9
Bonsall U.S.A. 33°16N 117°14W 79 M9
Bontang Indonesia 0°10N 117°30E 36 D5
Bontebok △ S. Africa 34°5S 20°28E 56 E3
Bonthe S. Leone 7°30N 12°33W 50 G3
Bontoc Phil. 17°7N 120°58E 37 A6
Bonython Ra. Australia 23°40S 128°45E 60 D4
Boodjamulla △ Australia 18°15S 138°6E 62 B2
Bookabie Australia 31°50S 132°41E 61 F5
Booker U.S.A. 36°27N 100°32W 84 C4
Booligal Australia 33°58S 144°53E 63 E3
Böön Tsagaan Nuur Mongolia 45°35N 99°9E 32 B4
Boonah Australia 27°58S 152°41E 63 D5
Boone Iowa, U.S.A. 42°4N 93°53W 80 D7
Boone N.C., U.S.A. 36°13N 81°41W 85 C14
Booneville Ark., U.S.A. 35°8N 93°55W 84 D8
Booneville Miss., U.S.A. 34°39N 88°34W 85 D10
Boonville Calif., U.S.A. 39°1N 123°22W 78 F3
Boonville Ind., U.S.A. 38°3N 87°16W 80 F10
Boonville Mo., U.S.A. 38°58N 92°44W 80 F7
Boonville N.Y., U.S.A. 43°29N 75°20W 83 C9
Boorabbin △ Australia 31°30S 120°10E 61 F3
Boorindal Australia 30°22S 146°11E 63 E4
Boorowa Australia 34°28S 148°44E 63 E4
Boosaaso Somali Rep. 11°12N 49°18E 47 E4
Boothia, Gulf of Canada 71°0N 90°0W 69 B11
Boothia Pen. Canada 71°0N 94°0W 68 B10
Bootle U.K. 53°28N 3°1W 12 D4
Booué Gabon 0°5S 11°55E 52 E2
Boquilla, Presa de la Mexico 27°31N 105°30W 86 B3
Boquillas del Carmen Mexico 29°11N 102°58W 86 B4
Bor Serbia 44°5N 22°7E 23 B10
Bôr Sudan 6°10N 31°40E 51 G12
Bor Mashash Israel 31°7N 34°50E 46 D3
Bora Bora French Polynesia 16°30S 151°45W 65 J12
Borah Peak U.S.A. 44°8N 113°47W 76 D7
Borås Sweden 57°43N 12°56E 9 H15
Borāzjān Iran 29°22N 51°10E 45 D6
Borba Brazil 4°12S 59°34W 92 D7
Borborema, Planalto da Brazil 7°0S 37°0W 90 D7
Bord Khūn-e Now Iran 28°3N 51°28E 45 D6
Borda, C. Australia 35°45S 136°34E 63 F2
Bordeaux France 44°50N 0°36W 20 D3
Borden Australia 34°3S 118°12E 61 F2
Borden-Carleton Canada 46°18N 63°47W 73 C7
Borden I. Canada 78°30N 111°30W 69 B8
Borden Pen. Canada 73°0N 83°0W 69 B11
Border Ranges △ Australia 28°24S 152°56E 63 D5
Borders = Scottish Borders □ U.K. 55°35N 2°50W 11 F6
Bordertown Australia 36°19S 140°45E 63 F3
Borðeyri Iceland 65°12N 21°6W 8 D3
Bordj Fly Ste. Marie Algeria 27°19N 2°32W 50 C5
Bordj-in-Eker Algeria 24°9N 5°3E 50 D7
Bordj Moktar Algeria 21°20N 0°56E 50 D6
Bordj Omar Driss Algeria 28°10N 6°40E 50 C7
Borehamwood U.K. 51°40N 0°15W 13 F7
Borgarfjörður Iceland 65°33N 13°47W 8 D7
Borgarnes Iceland 64°32N 21°55W 8 D3
Børgefjellet Norway 65°20N 13°45E 8 D15
Borger Neths. 52°54N 6°44E 15 B6
Borger U.S.A. 35°39N 101°24W 84 D4
Borgholm Sweden 56°52N 16°39E 9 H17
Borhoyn Tal Mongolia 43°50N 111°58E 34 C6
Borikhane Laos 18°33N 103°43E 38 C4
Borisoglebsk Russia 51°27N 42°5E 19 D7
Borisov = Barysaw Belarus 54°17N 28°28E 17 A15
Borja Peru 4°20S 77°40W 92 D3
Borkou Chad 18°15N 18°50E 51 E9
Borkum Germany 53°34N 6°40E 16 B4
Borlänge Sweden 60°29N 15°26E 9 F16
Borley, C. Antarctica 66°15S 52°30E 5 C5
Borneo E. Indies 1°0N 115°0E 36 D5
Bornholm Denmark 55°10N 15°0E 9 J16
Borogontsy Russia 62°42N 131°8E 29 C14
Borohoro Shan China 44°6N 83°10E 32 B3
Boron U.S.A. 35°0N 117°39W 79 L9
Borongan Phil. 11°37N 125°26E 37 B7
Borovichi Russia 58°25N 33°55E 18 C5
Borrego Springs U.S.A. 33°15N 116°23W 79 M10
Borrisokane Ireland 53°0N 8°7W 10 D3
Borroloola Australia 16°4S 136°17E 62 B2
Borşa Romania 47°41N 24°50E 17 E13
Borsad India 22°25N 72°54E 42 H5
Borth U.K. 52°29N 4°2W 13 E3
Borūjerd Iran 33°55N 48°50E 45 C6
Boryeong S. Korea 36°21N 126°36E 35 F14
Boryslav Ukraine 49°18N 23°28E 17 D12
Borzya Russia 50°24N 116°31E 29 D12
Bosa Italy 40°18N 8°30E 22 D3
Bosanska Gradiška Bos.-H. 45°10N 17°15E 22 B7
Boscastle U.K. 50°41N 4°42W 13 G3
Boscobelle Barbados 13°17N 59°35W 89 g
Bose China 23°53N 106°35E 32 D5
Boseong S. Korea 34°46N 127°5E 35 G14
Boshan China 36°28N 117°49E 35 F9
Boshof S. Africa 28°31S 25°13E 56 D4
Boshrūyeh Iran 33°50N 57°30E 45 C8
Bosna → Bos.-H. 45°4N 18°29E 23 B8
Bosna i Hercegovina = Bosnia-Herzegovina ■ Europe 44°0N 18°0E 22 B7
Bosnia-Herzegovina ■ Europe 44°0N 18°0E 22 B7
Bosnik Indonesia 1°5S 136°10E 37 E9
Bosobolo Dem. Rep. of the Congo 4°15N 19°50E 52 D3
Bosporus = İstanbul Boğazı Turkey 41°5N 29°3E 23 D13
Bosque Farms U.S.A. 35°51N 106°42W 77 J10
Bossangoa C.A.R. 6°35N 17°30E 52 C3
Bossier City U.S.A. 32°31N 93°44W 84 E8
Bosso Niger 13°43N 13°19E 51 F8
Bostan Pakistan 30°26N 67°2E 42 D2
Bostānābād Iran 37°50N 46°50E 44 B5
Bosten Hu China 41°55N 87°40E 32 B3
Boston U.K. 52°59N 0°2W 12 E7
Boston U.S.A. 42°22N 71°3W 83 D13
Boston Bar Canada 49°52N 121°30W 70 D4
Boston Mts. U.S.A. 35°42N 93°15W 84 D8
Boswell Canada 49°28N 116°45W 70 D5
Boswell U.S.A. 40°10N 79°2W 82 F5
Botad India 22°15N 71°40E 42 H4
Botany B. Australia 33°58S 151°11E 58 E8
Botene Laos 17°35N 101°12E 38 D3
Bothaville S. Africa 27°23S 26°34E 56 D4
Bothnia, G. of Europe 62°0N 20°0E 8 F19
Bothwell Australia 42°20S 147°1E 63 G4
Bothwell Canada 42°38N 81°52W 82 D3
Botletle → Botswana 20°10S 23°15E 56 C3
Botoşani Romania 47°42N 26°41E 17 E14
Botou Burkina Faso 12°42N 1°59E 50 F6
Botshabelo S. Africa 29°14S 26°44E 56 D4
Botswana ■ Africa 22°0S 24°0E 56 C3
Bottineau U.S.A. 48°50N 100°27W 80 A3
Bottrop Germany 51°31N 6°58E 15 C6
Botucatu Brazil 22°55S 48°30W 95 A6
Botum Sakor △ Cambodia 11°5N 103°15E 39 G4
Botwood Canada 49°6N 55°23W 73 C8
Bou Saâda Algeria 35°11N 4°9E 50 A6
Bouaflé Ivory C. 7°1N 5°47W 50 G4
Bouaké Ivory C. 7°40N 5°2W 50 G4
Bouar C.A.R. 6°0N 15°40E 52 C3
Bouârfa Morocco 32°32N 1°58W 50 B5
Boucaut B. Australia 12°0S 134°25E 62 A1
Bouctouche Canada 46°30N 64°45W 73 C7
Bougainville, C. Australia 13°57S 126°4E 60 B4
Bougainville I. Papua N. G. 6°0S 155°0E 58 B8
Bougainville Reef Australia 15°30S 147°5E 62 B4
Bougie = Bejaïa Algeria 36°42N 5°2E 50 A7
Bougouni Mali 11°30N 7°20W 50 F4
Bouillon Belgium 49°44N 5°3E 15 E5
Boulder Colo., U.S.A. 40°1N 105°17W 76 F11
Boulder Mont., U.S.A. 46°14N 112°7W 76 C7
Boulder City U.S.A. 35°58N 114°49W 79 K12
Boulder Creek U.S.A. 37°7N 122°7W 78 H4
Boulder Dam = Hoover Dam U.S.A. 36°1N 114°44W 79 K12
Boulia Australia 22°52S 139°51E 62 C2
Boulogne-sur-Mer France 50°42N 1°36E 20 A4
Boulsa Burkina Faso 12°39N 0°34W 50 F5
Boultoum Niger 14°45N 10°25E 51 F8
Bouma △ Fiji 16°50S 179°52E 59 a
Boun Neua Laos 21°38N 101°54E 38 B3
Boun Tai Laos 21°23N 101°58E 38 B3
Bouna Ivory C. 9°10N 3°0W 50 G5
Boundary Peak U.S.A. 37°51N 118°21W 78 H8
Boundiali Ivory C. 9°30N 6°20W 50 G4
Bountiful U.S.A. 40°53N 111°52W 76 F8
Bounty Is. Pac. Oc. 48°0S 178°30E 64 M9
Bounty Trough Pac. Oc. 46°0S 178°0E 64 M9
Bourbonnais France 46°28N 3°0E 20 C5
Bourdel L. Canada 56°43N 74°10W 72 A5
Bourem Mali 17°0N 0°24W 50 E5
Bourg-en-Bresse France 46°13N 5°12E 20 C6
Bourg-St-Maurice France 45°35N 6°46E 20 D7
Bourgas = Burgas Bulgaria 42°33N 27°29E 23 C12
Bourges France 47°9N 2°25E 20 C5
Bourget Canada 45°26N 75°9W 83 A9
Bourgogne □ France 47°0N 4°50E 20 C6
Bourke Australia 30°8S 145°55E 63 E4
Bourne U.K. 52°47N 0°22W 12 E7
Bournemouth U.K. 50°43N 1°52W 13 G6
Bournemouth □ U.K. 50°43N 1°52W 13 G6
Bouse U.S.A. 33°56N 114°0W 79 M13
Bousso Chad 10°34N 16°52E 51 F9
Bouvet I. = Bouvetøya Antarctica 54°26S 3°24E 2 G10
Bouvetøya Antarctica 54°26S 3°24E 2 G10
Bovill U.S.A. 46°51N 116°24W 76 C5
Bovril Argentina 31°21S 59°26W 94 C4
Bow → Canada 49°57N 111°41W 70 C6
Bow Island Canada 49°50N 111°23W 76 B8
Bowbells U.S.A. 48°48N 102°15W 80 A2
Bowdle U.S.A. 45°27N 99°39W 80 C4
Bowelling Australia 33°25S 116°30E 61 F2
Bowen Argentina 35°0S 67°31W 94 D2
Bowen Australia 20°0S 148°16E 62 J6
Bowen Mts. Australia 37°0S 147°50E 63 F4
Bowers Basin Pac. Oc. 53°45N 176°0E 4 D16
Bowers Ridge Pac. Oc. 54°0N 180°0E 4 D17
Bowie Ariz., U.S.A. 32°19N 109°29W 77 K9
Bowie Tex., U.S.A. 33°34N 97°51W 84 E6
Bowkān Iran 36°31N 46°12E 44 B5
Bowland, Forest of U.K. 54°0N 2°30W 12 D5
Bowling Green Ky., U.S.A. 36°59N 86°27W 80 G10
Bowling Green Ohio, U.S.A. 41°23N 83°39W 81 E12
Bowling Green, C. Australia 19°19S 147°25E 62 B4
Bowling Green Bay △ Australia 19°26S 146°57E 62 B4
Bowman U.S.A. 46°11N 103°24W 80 B2
Bowman I. Antarctica 65°0S 104°0E 5 C8
Bowmanville = Clarington Canada 43°55N 78°41W 82 C6
Bowmore U.K. 55°45N 6°17W 11 F2
Bowral Australia 34°26S 150°27E 63 E5
Bowraville Australia 30°37S 152°52E 63 E5
Bowron → Canada 54°3N 121°50W 70 C4
Bowron Lake ⌓ Canada 53°10N 121°5W 70 C4
Bowser L. Canada 56°30N 129°30W 70 B3
Bowsman Canada 52°14N 101°12W 71 C8
Bowwood Zambia 17°5S 26°20E 55 F2
Box Cr. → Australia 34°10S 143°50E 63 E3
Boxmeer Neths. 51°38N 5°56E 15 C5
Boxtel Neths. 51°36N 5°20E 15 C5
Boyce U.S.A. 31°23N 92°40W 84 F8
Boyd L. Canada 52°46N 76°42W 72 B4
Boyle Canada 54°35N 112°49W 70 C6
Boyle Ireland 53°59N 8°18W 10 C3
Boyne → Ireland 53°43N 6°15W 10 C5
Boyne City U.S.A. 45°13N 85°1W 81 C11
Boynton Beach U.S.A. 26°32N 80°4W 85 H14
Boyolali Indonesia 7°32S 110°35E 37 G14
Boyoma, Chutes Dem. Rep. of the Congo 0°35N 25°23E 54 B2
Boysen Res. U.S.A. 43°25N 108°11W 76 E9
Boyuibe Bolivia 20°25S 63°17W 92 G6
Boyup Brook Australia 33°50S 116°23E 61 F2
Boz Dağları Turkey 38°20N 28°0E 23 E13
Bozburun Turkey 36°43N 28°4E 23 F13
Bozcaada Turkey 39°49N 26°3E 23 E12
Bozdoğan Turkey 37°40N 28°17E 23 F13
Bozeman U.S.A. 45°41N 111°2W 76 D8
Bozen = Bolzano Italy 46°31N 11°22E 22 A4
Bozhou China 33°55N 115°41E 34 H8
Bozoum C.A.R. 6°25N 16°35E 52 C3
Bozyazı Turkey 36°6N 33°0E 44 B2
Bra Italy 44°42N 7°51E 20 D7
Brabant □ Belgium 50°46N 4°30E 15 D4
Brabant L. Canada 55°58N 103°43W 71 B8
Brač Croatia 43°20N 16°40E 22 C7
Bracadale, L. U.K. 57°20N 6°30W 11 D2
Bracciano, L. di Italy 42°7N 12°14E 22 C5
Bracebridge Canada 45°2N 79°19W 82 A5
Bräcke Sweden 62°45N 15°26E 8 E16
Brackettville U.S.A. 29°19N 100°25W 84 G4
Bracknell U.K. 51°25N 0°43W 13 F7
Bracknell Forest □ U.K. 51°25N 0°44W 13 F7
Brad Romania 46°10N 22°50E 17 E12
Bradenton U.S.A. 27°30N 82°34W 85 H13
Bradford Canada 44°7N 79°34W 82 B5
Bradford U.K. 53°47N 1°45W 12 D6
Bradford Pa., U.S.A. 41°58N 78°38W 82 E6
Bradford Vt., U.S.A. 43°59N 72°9W 83 C12
Bradley Ark., U.S.A. 33°6N 93°39W 84 E8
Bradley Calif., U.S.A. 35°52N 120°48W 78 K6
Bradley Institute Zimbabwe 17°7S 31°25E 55 F3
Brady U.S.A. 31°9N 99°20W 84 F5
Braeside Canada 45°28N 76°24W 83 A8
Braga Portugal 41°35N 8°25W 21 B1
Bragado Argentina 35°2S 60°27W 94 D3
Bragança Brazil 1°0S 47°2W 93 D9
Bragança Portugal 41°48N 6°50W 21 B2
Bragança Paulista Brazil 22°55S 46°32W 95 A6
Brahestad = Raahe Finland 64°40N 24°28E 8 D21
Brahmanbaria Bangla. 23°58N 91°15E 41 H17
Brahmani → India 20°39N 86°46E 41 J15
Brahmapur India 19°15N 84°54E 41 K14
Brahmaputra → Asia 23°40N 90°35E 43 H13
Braich-y-pwll U.K. 52°47N 4°46W 12 E3
Braidwood Australia 35°27S 149°49E 63 F4
Brăila Romania 45°19N 27°59E 17 F14
Brainerd U.S.A. 46°22N 94°12W 80 B6
Braintree U.K. 51°53N 0°34E 13 F8
Braintree U.S.A. 42°13N 71°0W 83 D14
Brak → S. Africa 29°35S 22°55E 56 D3
Brakwater Namibia 22°28S 17°3E 56 C2
Brampton Canada 43°45N 79°45W 82 C5
Brampton U.K. 54°57N 2°44W 12 C5
Bramton I. Australia 20°50S 149°17E 62 J7
Branco → Brazil 1°20S 61°50W 92 D6
Brandberg Namibia 21°10S 14°33E 56 C1
Brandberg ⌓ Namibia 21°10S 14°30E 56 C1
Brandenburg = Neubrandenburg Germany 53°33N 13°15E 16 B7
Brandenburg Germany 52°25N 12°33E 16 B7
Brandenburg □ Germany 52°50N 13°0E 16 B6
Brandfort S. Africa 28°40S 26°30E 56 D4
Brandon Canada 49°50N 99°57W 71 D9
Brandon U.S.A. 43°48N 73°6W 83 C11
Brandon B. Ireland 52°17N 10°8W 10 D1
Brandon Mt. Ireland 52°15N 10°15W 10 D1
Brandsen Argentina 35°10S 58°15W 94 D4
Brandvlei S. Africa 30°25S 20°30E 56 E3
Branford U.S.A. 41°17N 72°49W 83 E12
Braniewo Poland 54°25N 19°50E 17 A10
Bransfield Str. Antarctica 63°0S 59°0W 5 C18
Branson U.S.A. 36°39N 93°13W 80 G7
Brantford Canada 43°10N 80°15W 82 C4
Bras d'Or L. Canada 45°50N 60°50W 73 C7
Brasher Falls U.S.A. 44°49N 74°47W 83 B10
Brasil = Brazil ■ S. Amer. 12°0S 50°0W 93 F9
Brasil, Planalto Brazil 18°0S 46°30W 90 E6
Brasiléia Brazil 11°0S 68°45W 92 F5
Brasília Brazil 15°47S 47°55W 93 G9
Brasília Legal Brazil 3°49S 55°36W 93 D7
Braslaw Belarus 55°38N 27°0E 9 J22
Braşov Romania 45°38N 25°35E 17 F13
Brasschaat Belgium 51°19N 4°27E 15 C4
Brassey, Banjaran Malaysia 5°0N 117°15E 36 D5
Brassey Ra. Australia 25°8S 122°15E 61 E3
Brasstown Bald U.S.A. 34°53N 83°49W 85 D13
Brastad Sweden 58°23N 11°30E 9 G14
Bratislava Slovak Rep. 48°10N 17°7E 17 D9
Bratsk Russia 56°10N 101°30E 29 D11
Brattleboro U.S.A. 42°51N 72°34W 83 D12
Braunau Austria 48°15N 13°3E 16 D7
Braunschweig Germany 52°15N 10°31E 16 B6
Braunton U.K. 51°7N 4°10W 13 F3
Brava C. Verde Is. 15°0N 24°40W 50 b
Bravo del Norte, Rio = Grande, Rio → N. Amer. 25°58N 97°9W 84 J6
Brawley U.S.A. 32°59N 115°31W 79 N11
Bray Ireland 53°13N 6°7W 10 C5
Bray, Mt. Australia 14°0S 134°30E 62 A1
Bray, Pays de France 49°46N 1°26E 20 B4
Brazeau → Canada 52°55N 115°14W 70 C5
Brazil U.S.A. 39°32N 87°8W 80 F10
Brazil ■ S. Amer. 12°0S 50°0W 93 F9
Brazilian Highlands = Brasil, Planalto Brazil 18°0S 46°30W 90 E6
Brazo Sur → S. Amer. 25°21S 57°42W 94 B4
Brazos → U.S.A. 28°53N 95°23W 84 G7
Brazzaville Congo 4°9S 15°12E 52 E3
Brčko Bos.-H. 44°54N 18°46E 23 B8
Breaden, L. Australia 25°51S 125°28E 61 E4
Breaksea Sd. N.Z. 45°35S 166°35E 59 F1
Bream B. N.Z. 35°56S 174°28E 59 A5
Bream Hd. N.Z. 35°51S 174°36E 59 A5
Breas Chile 25°29S 70°24W 94 B1
Brebes Indonesia 6°52S 109°3E 37 G13
Brechin Canada 44°32N 79°10W 82 B5
Brechin U.K. 56°44N 2°39W 11 E6
Brecht Belgium 51°21N 4°38E 15 C4
Breckenridge Colo., U.S.A. 39°29N 106°3W 76 G10
Breckenridge Minn., U.S.A. 46°16N 96°35W 80 B5
Breckenridge Tex., U.S.A. 32°45N 98°54W 84 E5
Breckland U.K. 52°30N 0°40E 13 E8
Brecon U.K. 51°57N 3°23W 13 F4
Brecon Beacons U.K. 51°53N 3°26W 13 F4
Brecon Beacons △ U.K. 51°50N 3°30W 13 F4
Breda Neths. 51°35N 4°45E 15 C4
Bredasdorp S. Africa 34°33S 20°2E 56 E3
Bree Belgium 51°8N 5°35E 15 C5
Bregenz Austria 47°30N 9°45E 16 E5
Breiðafjörður Iceland 65°15N 23°15W 8 D2
Brejo Brazil 3°41S 42°47W 93 D10
Bremen Germany 53°4N 8°47E 16 B5
Bremer Bay Australia 34°21S 119°20E 61 F2
Bremer I. Australia 12°5S 136°45E 62 A2
Bremerhaven Germany 53°33N 8°36E 16 B5
Bremerton U.S.A. 47°34N 122°38W 78 C4
Brenham U.S.A. 30°10N 96°24W 84 F6
Brennerpass Austria 47°2N 11°30E 16 E6
Brent U.S.A. 32°56N 87°10W 85 E11
Brentwood U.K. 51°37N 0°19E 13 F8
Brentwood Calif., U.S.A. 37°56N 121°42W 78 H5
Brentwood N.Y., U.S.A. 40°47N 73°15W 83 F11
Bréscia Italy 45°33N 10°15E 20 D9
Breskens Neths. 51°23N 3°33E 15 C3
Breslau = Wrocław Poland 51°5N 17°5E 17 C9
Bressanone Italy 46°43N 11°39E 22 A4
Bressay U.K. 60°9N 1°6W 11 A7
Brest Belarus 52°10N 23°40E 17 B12
Brest France 48°24N 4°31W 20 B1
Brest-Litovsk = Brest Belarus 52°10N 23°40E 17 B12
Bretagne □ France 48°10N 3°0W 20 B2
Breton Canada 53°7N 114°28W 70 C6
Breton Sd. U.S.A. 29°35N 89°15W 85 G10
Brett, C. N.Z. 35°10S 174°20E 59 A5
Brevard U.S.A. 35°14N 82°44W 85 D13
Breves Brazil 1°40S 50°29W 93 D8
Brewarrina Australia 30°0S 146°51E 63 E4
Brewer U.S.A. 44°48N 68°46W 81 C19
Brewer, Mt. U.S.A. 36°44N 118°28W 78 J8
Brewster N.Y., U.S.A. 41°24N 73°36W 83 E11
Brewster Ohio, U.S.A. 40°43N 81°36W 82 F3
Brewster Wash., U.S.A. 48°6N 119°47W 76 B4
Brewster, Kap = Kangikajik Greenland 70°7N 22°0W 4 B6
Brewton U.S.A. 31°7N 87°4W 85 F11
Breyten S. Africa 26°16S 30°0E 57 D5
Bria C.A.R. 6°30N 21°58E 52 C4
Briançon France 44°54N 6°39E 20 D7
Bribie I. Australia 27°0S 153°10E 63 D5
Bribri Costa Rica 9°38N 82°50W 88 E3
Bridgefield Barbados 13°9N 59°36W 89 g
Bridgehampton U.S.A. 40°56N 72°19W 83 F12
Bridgend U.K. 51°30N 3°34W 13 F4
Bridgend □ U.K. 51°36N 3°36W 13 F4
Bridgenorth Canada 44°23N 78°23W 82 B6
Bridgeport Calif., U.S.A. 38°15N 119°14W 78 G7
Bridgeport Conn., U.S.A. 41°11N 73°12W 83 E11
Bridgeport N.Y., U.S.A. 43°9N 75°58W 83 C9
Bridgeport Nebr., U.S.A. 41°40N 103°6W 80 E2
Bridgeport Tex., U.S.A. 33°13N 97°45W 84 E6
Bridger U.S.A. 45°18N 108°55W 76 D9
Bridgeton U.S.A. 39°26N 75°14W 81 F16
Bridgetown Australia 33°58S 116°7E 61 F2
Bridgetown Barbados 13°6N 59°37W 89 g
Bridgetown Canada 44°55N 65°18W 73 D6
Bridgewater Australia 42°44S 147°14E 63 G4
Bridgewater Canada 44°25N 64°31W 73 D7
Bridgewater Mass., U.S.A. 41°59N 70°58W 83 E14
Bridgewater N.Y., U.S.A. 42°53N 75°15W 83 D9
Bridgewater, C. Australia 38°23S 141°23E 63 F3
Bridgnorth U.K. 52°32N 2°25W 13 E5
Bridgton U.S.A. 44°3N 70°42W 83 B14
Bridgwater U.K. 51°8N 2°59W 13 F5
Bridgwater B. U.K. 51°15N 3°15W 13 F4
Bridlington U.K. 54°5N 0°12W 12 C7
Bridlington B. U.K. 54°4N 0°10W 12 C7
Bridport Australia 40°59S 147°23E 63 G4
Bridport U.K. 50°44N 2°45W 13 G5
Brig Switz. 46°18N 7°59E 20 C7
Brigg U.K. 53°34N 0°28W 12 D7
Brigham City U.S.A. 41°31N 112°1W 76 F7
Bright Australia 36°42S 146°56E 63 F4
Brighton Australia 35°5S 138°30E 63 F2
Brighton Canada 44°2N 77°44W 82 B7
Brighton Trin. & Tob. 10°13N 61°39W 93 K15
Brighton U.K. 50°49N 0°7W 13 G7
Brighton U.S.A. 43°8N 77°34W 82 C7
Brightside Canada 45°7N 76°29W 83 A8
Brilliant U.S.A. 40°15N 80°39W 82 F4
Bríndisi Italy 40°39N 17°55E 23 D7
Brinkley U.S.A. 34°53N 91°12W 84 D9
Brinnon U.S.A. 47°41N 122°54W 78 C4
Brion, Î. Canada 47°46N 61°26W 73 C7
Brisay Canada 54°26N 70°31W 73 B5
Brisbane Australia 27°25S 153°2E 63 D5
Brisbane → Australia 27°24S 153°9E 63 D5
Bristol U.K. 51°26N 2°35W 13 F5
Bristol Conn., U.S.A. 41°40N 72°57W 83 E12
Bristol Pa., U.S.A. 40°6N 74°51W 83 F10
Bristol R.I., U.S.A. 41°40N 71°16W 83 E13
Bristol Tenn., U.S.A. 36°36N 82°11W 85 C13
Bristol Vt., U.S.A. 44°8N 73°4W 83 B11
Bristol, City of □ U.K. 51°27N 2°36W 13 F5
Bristol B. U.S.A. 58°0N 160°0W 74 a
Bristol Channel U.K. 51°18N 4°30W 13 F3
Bristol I. Antarctica 58°45S 28°0W 5 B1
Bristol L. U.S.A. 34°28N 115°41W 77 J6
Bristow U.S.A. 35°50N 96°23W 84 D6
Britain = Great Britain Europe 54°0N 2°15W 6 E5
British Columbia □ Canada 55°0N 125°15W 70 C3
British Indian Ocean Terr. = Chagos Arch. ☒ Ind. Oc. 6°0S 72°0E 26 J9
British Isles Europe 54°0N 4°0W 14 D5
British Virgin Is. ☒ W. Indies 18°30N 64°30W 89 e
Brits S. Africa 25°37S 27°48E 57 D4
Britstown S. Africa 30°37S 23°10E 56 E3
Britt Canada 45°46N 80°34W 72 C3
Brittany = Bretagne □ France 48°10N 3°0W 20 B2
Britton U.S.A. 45°48N 97°45W 80 C5

Brive-la-Gaillarde *France* 45°10N 1°32E **20 D4**
Brixen = Bressanone
  Italy 46°43N 11°39E **22 A4**
Brixham *U.K.* 50°23N 3°31W **13 G4**
Brno *Czech Rep.* 49°10N 16°35E **17 D9**
Broach = Bharuch *India* 21°47N 73°0E **40 J8**
Broad *U.S.A.* 34°1N 81°4W **85 D14**
Broad Arrow *Australia* 30°23S 121°15E **61 F3**
Broad B. *U.K.* 58°14N 6°18W **11 C2**
Broad Haven *Ireland* 54°20N 9°55W **10 B2**
Broad Law *U.K.* 55°30N 3°21W **11 F5**
Broad Pk. = Faichan Kangri
  India 35°48N 76°34E **43 B7**
Broad Sd. *Australia* 22°0S 149°45E **62 C4**
Broadalbin *U.S.A.* 43°4N 74°12W **83 C10**
Broadback *Canada* 51°21N 78°52W **72 B4**
Broadhurst Ra.
  Australia 22°30S 122°30E **60 D3**
Broads, The *U.K.* 52°45N 1°30E **12 E9**
Broadus *U.S.A.* 45°27N 105°25W **76 D11**
Brochet, L. *Canada* 58°36N 101°35W **71 B8**
Brock I. *Canada* 77°52N 114°19W **69 B8**
Brocken *Germany* 51°47N 10°37E **16 C6**
Brockport *U.S.A.* 43°13N 77°56W **82 C7**
Brockton *U.S.A.* 42°5N 71°1W **83 D13**
Brockville *Canada* 44°35N 75°41W **83 B9**
Brockway *Mont.,*
  U.S.A. 47°18N 105°45W **76 C11**
Brockway *Pa., U.S.A.* 41°15N 78°47W **82 E6**
Brocton *U.S.A.* 42°23N 79°26W **82 D5**
Brodeur Pen. *Canada* 72°30N 88°10W **69 B11**
Brodick *U.K.* 55°35N 5°9W **11 F3**
Brodnica *Poland* 53°15N 19°25E **17 B10**
Brody *Ukraine* 50°5N 25°10E **17 C13**
Brogan *U.S.A.* 44°15N 117°31W **76 D5**
Broken Arrow *U.S.A.* 36°3N 95°48W **84 C7**
Broken Bow *Nebr.,*
  U.S.A. 41°24N 99°38W **80 E4**
Broken Bow *Okla., U.S.A.* 34°2N 94°44W **84 D7**
Broken Bow Lake *U.S.A.* 34°9N 94°40W **84 D7**
Broken Hill *Australia* 31°58S 141°29E **63 E3**
Broken Ridge *Ind. Oc.* 30°0S 94°0E **64 L1**
Broken River Ra.
  Australia 21°0S 148°22E **62 K6**
Bromley □ *U.K.* 51°24N 0°2E **13 F8**
Bromo *Indonesia* 7°55S 112°55E **37 G15**
Bromsgrove *U.K.* 52°21N 2°2W **13 E5**
Brønderslev *Denmark* 57°16N 9°57E **9 H13**
Bronkhorstspruit
  S. Africa 25°46S 28°45E **57 D4**
Brønnøysund *Norway* 65°28N 12°14E **8 D15**
Brook Park *U.S.A.* 41°23N 81°48W **82 E4**
Brookhaven *U.S.A.* 31°35N 90°26W **85 F9**
Brookings *Oreg., U.S.A.* 42°3N 124°17W **76 E1**
Brookings *S. Dak.,*
  U.S.A. 44°19N 96°48W **80 C5**
Brooklin *Canada* 43°55N 78°55W **82 C6**
Brooklyn Park *U.S.A.* 45°6N 93°23W **80 C7**
Brooks *Canada* 50°35N 111°55W **70 C6**
Brooks Range *U.S.A.* 68°0N 152°0W **74 a**
Brooksville *U.S.A.* 28°33N 82°23W **85 G13**
Brookton *Australia* 32°22S 117°0E **61 F2**
Brookville *U.S.A.* 41°10N 79°5W **82 E5**
Broom, L. *U.K.* 57°55N 5°15W **11 D3**
Broome *Australia* 18°0S 122°15E **60 C3**
Brora *U.K.* 58°0N 3°52W **11 C5**
Brora → *U.K.* 58°0N 3°51W **11 C5**
Brosna → *Ireland* 53°14N 7°58W **10 C4**
Brothers *U.S.A.* 43°49N 120°36W **76 E3**
Brough *U.K.* 54°32N 2°18W **12 C5**
Brough Hd. *U.K.* 59°8N 3°20W **11 B5**
Broughton Island = Qikiqtarjuaq
  Canada 67°33N 63°0W **69 C13**
Brown, L. *Australia* 31°5S 118°15E **61 F2**
Brown, Pt. *Australia* 32°32S 133°50E **63 E1**
Brown City *U.S.A.* 43°13N 82°59W **82 C2**
Brown Willy *U.K.* 50°35N 4°37W **13 G3**
Brownfield *U.S.A.* 33°11N 102°17W **84 E3**
Browning *U.S.A.* 48°34N 113°1W **76 B7**
Brownsville *Oreg.,*
  U.S.A. 44°24N 122°59W **76 D2**
Brownsville *Pa., U.S.A.* 40°1N 79°53W **82 F5**
Brownsville *Tenn.,*
  U.S.A. 35°36N 89°16W **85 D10**
Brownsville *Tex., U.S.A.* 25°54N 97°30W **84 J6**
Brownville *U.S.A.* 44°0N 75°59W **83 C9**
Brownwood *U.S.A.* 31°43N 98°59W **84 F5**
Browse I. *Australia* 14°7S 123°33E **60 B3**
Bruas *Malaysia* 4°30N 100°47E **39 K3**
Bruay-la-Buissière *France* 50°29N 2°33E **20 A5**
Bruce, Mt. *Australia* 22°37S 118°8E **60 D2**
Bruce Pen. *Canada* 45°0N 81°30W **82 B3**
Bruce Peninsula △
  Canada 45°14N 81°36W **82 A3**
Bruce Rock *Australia* 31°52S 118°8E **61 F2**
Bruck an der Leitha
  Austria 48°1N 16°47E **17 D9**
Bruck an der Mur
  Austria 47°24N 15°16E **16 E8**
Brue → *U.K.* 51°13N 2°59W **13 F5**
Bruges = Brugge *Belgium* 51°13N 3°13E **15 C3**
Brugge *Belgium* 51°13N 3°13E **15 C3**
Bruin *U.S.A.* 41°3N 79°43W **82 E5**
Brûk, W. el → *Egypt* 30°15N 33°50E **46 E2**
Brûlé *Canada* 53°15N 117°58W **70 C5**
Brûlé, L. *Canada* 53°35N 64°4W **73 B7**
Brumado *Brazil* 14°14S 41°40W **93 F10**
Brumunddal *Norway* 60°53N 10°56E **8 F14**
Bruneau *U.S.A.* 42°53N 115°48W **76 E6**
Bruneau → *U.S.A.* 42°56N 115°57W **76 E6**
Brunei = Bandar Seri Begawan
  Brunei 4°52N 115°0E **36 D5**
Brunei ■ *Asia* 4°50N 115°0E **36 D5**
Brunner, L. *N.Z.* 42°37S 171°27E **59 E3**
Brunssum *Neths.* 50°57N 5°59E **15 D5**
Brunswick = Braunschweig
  Germany 52°15N 10°31E **16 B6**

Brunswick *Ga., U.S.A.* 31°10N 81°30W **85 F14**
Brunswick *Maine,*
  U.S.A. 43°55N 69°58W **81 D19**
Brunswick *Md., U.S.A.* 39°19N 77°38W **81 F15**
Brunswick *Mo., U.S.A.* 39°26N 93°8W **80 F7**
Brunswick *Ohio, U.S.A.* 41°14N 81°51W **82 E3**
Brunswick, Pen. de
  Chile 53°30S 71°30W **96 G2**
Brunswick B. *Australia* 15°15S 124°50E **60 C3**
Brunswick Junction
  Australia 33°15S 115°50E **61 F2**
Brunt Ice Shelf *Antarctica* 75°30S 25°0W **5 D2**
Brus Laguna *Honduras* 15°47N 84°35W **88 C3**
Brush *U.S.A.* 40°15N 103°37W **76 F12**
Brushton *U.S.A.* 44°50N 74°31W **83 B10**
Brusque *Brazil* 27°5S 49°0W **95 B6**
Brussel *Belgium* 50°51N 4°21E **15 D4**
Brussel ✈ (BRU) *Belgium* 50°54N 4°29E **15 D5**
Brussels = Brussel
  Belgium 50°51N 4°21E **15 D4**
Brussels *Canada* 43°44N 81°15W **82 C3**
Bruthen *Australia* 37°42S 147°50E **63 F4**
Bruxelles = Brussel
  Belgium 50°51N 4°21E **15 D4**
Bryan *Ohio, U.S.A.* 41°28N 84°33W **81 E11**
Bryan *Tex., U.S.A.* 30°40N 96°22W **84 F6**
Bryan, Mt. *Australia* 33°30S 139°5E **63 E2**
Bryansk *Russia* 53°13N 34°25E **18 D4**
Bryce Canyon △
  U.S.A. 37°30N 112°10W **77 H7**
Bryne *Norway* 58°44N 5°38E **9 G11**
Bryson City *U.S.A.* 35°26N 83°27W **85 D13**
Bsharri *Lebanon* 34°15N 36°0E **46 A5**
Bũ Baqarah *U.A.E.* 25°35N 56°25E **45 E8**
Bu Craa *W. Sahara* 26°45N 12°50W **50 C3**
Bũ Ḥasā *U.A.E.* 23°30N 53°20E **45 F7**
Bua *Fiji* 16°48S 178°37E **59 a**
Bua Yai *Thailand* 15°33N 102°26E **38 E4**
Buan *S. Korea* 35°44N 126°44E **35 G14**
Buapinang *Indonesia* 4°40S 121°30E **37 E6**
Bubanza *Burundi* 3°6S 29°23E **54 C2**
Bubi → *Zimbabwe* 22°20S 31°7E **55 G3**
Bũbiyān *Kuwait* 29°45N 48°15E **45 D6**
Buca *Fiji* 16°38S 179°52E **59 a**
Bucaramanga *Colombia* 7°0N 73°0W **92 B4**
Bucasia *Australia* 21°2S 149°10E **62 K7**
Buccaneer Arch.
  Australia 16°7S 123°20E **60 C3**
Buccoo Reef
  Trin. & Tob. 11°10N 60°51W **93 J16**
Buchach *Ukraine* 49°5N 25°25E **17 D13**
Buchan *U.K.* 57°32N 2°21W **11 D6**
Buchan Ness *U.K.* 57°29N 1°46W **11 D7**
Buchanan *Canada* 51°40N 102°45W **71 C8**
Buchanan *Liberia* 5°57N 10°2W **50 G3**
Buchanan, L. *Queens.,*
  Australia 21°35S 145°52E **62 C4**
Buchanan, L. *W. Austral.,*
  Australia 25°33S 123°2E **61 E3**
Buchanan, L. *U.S.A.* 30°45N 98°25W **84 F5**
Buchanan Cr. →
  Australia 19°13S 136°33E **62 B2**
Buchans *Canada* 48°50N 56°52W **73 C8**
Bucharest = București
  Romania 44°27N 26°10E **17 F14**
Bucheon *S. Korea* 37°28N 126°45E **35 F14**
Buchon, Pt. *U.S.A.* 35°15N 120°54W **78 K6**
Buck Hill Falls *U.S.A.* 41°11N 75°16W **83 E9**
Buckeye Lake *U.S.A.* 39°55N 82°29W **82 G2**
Buckhannon *U.S.A.* 39°0N 80°8W **81 F13**
Buckhaven *U.K.* 56°11N 3°3W **11 E5**
Buckhorn L. *Canada* 44°29N 78°23W **82 B6**
Buckie *U.K.* 57°41N 2°58W **11 D6**
Buckingham *Canada* 45°37N 75°24W **72 C4**
Buckingham *U.K.* 51°59N 0°57W **13 F7**
Buckingham B.
  Australia 12°10S 135°40E **62 A2**
Buckinghamshire □
  U.K. 51°53N 0°55W **13 F7**
Buckle Hd. *Australia* 14°26S 127°52E **60 B4**
Buckleboo *Australia* 32°54S 136°12E **63 E2**
Buckley *U.K.* 53°10N 3°5W **12 D4**
Buckley → *Australia* 20°10S 138°49E **62 C2**
Bucklin *U.S.A.* 37°33N 99°38W **80 G4**
Bucks L. *U.S.A.* 39°54N 121°12W **78 F5**
București *Romania* 44°27N 26°10E **17 F14**
Bucyrus *U.S.A.* 40°48N 82°59W **81 E12**
Budalin *Burma* 22°20N 95°10E **41 H19**
Budapest *Hungary* 47°29N 19°3E **17 E10**
Budaun *India* 28°5N 79°10E **43 E8**
Budd Coast *Antarctica* 68°0S 112°0E **5 C8**
Bude *U.K.* 50°49N 4°34W **13 G3**
Budge Budge = Baj Baj
  India 22°30N 88°5E **43 H13**
Budgewoi *Australia* 33°13S 151°34E **63 E5**
Budjala
  Dem. Rep. of the Congo 2°50N 19°40E **52 D3**
Buellton *U.S.A.* 34°37N 120°12W **79 L6**
Buena Esperanza
  Argentina 34°45S 65°15W **94 C2**
Buena Park *U.S.A.* 33°52N 117°59W **79 M9**
Buena Vista *Colo.,*
  U.S.A. 38°51N 106°8W **76 G10**
Buena Vista *Va., U.S.A.* 37°44N 79°21W **81 G14**
Buena Vista Lake Bed
  U.S.A. 35°12N 119°18W **79 K7**
Buenaventura *Colombia* 3°53N 77°4W **92 C3**
Buenaventura *Mexico* 29°51N 107°29W **86 B3**
Buenos Aires *Argentina* 34°36S 58°22W **94 C4**
Buenos Aires *Costa Rica* 9°10N 83°20W **88 E3**
Buenos Aires □ *Argentina* 36°30S 60°0W **94 D4**
Buenos Aires, L.
  Argentina 46°35S 72°30W **96 F2**
Buffalo *Mo., U.S.A.* 37°39N 93°6W **80 G7**
Buffalo *N.Y., U.S.A.* 42°53N 78°53W **82 D6**
Buffalo *Okla., U.S.A.* 36°50N 99°38W **84 C5**

Buffalo *S. Dak., U.S.A.* 45°35N 103°33W **80 C2**
Buffalo *Wyo., U.S.A.* 44°21N 106°42W **76 D10**
Buffalo → *Canada* 60°5N 115°5W **70 A5**
Buffalo → *S. Africa* 28°43S 30°57E **57 D5**
Buffalo △ *Canada* 36°14N 92°36W **84 C8**
Buffalo Head Hills
  Canada 57°25N 115°55W **70 B5**
Buffalo L. *Alta., Canada* 52°27N 112°54W **70 C6**
Buffalo L. *N.W.T.,*
  Canada 60°12N 115°25W **70 A5**
Buffalo Narrows
  Canada 55°51N 108°29W **71 B7**
Buffalo Springs △ *Kenya* 0°32N 37°35E **54 B4**
Buffels → *S. Africa* 29°36S 17°3E **56 D2**
Buford *U.S.A.* 34°10N 84°0W **85 D12**
Bug = Buh → *Ukraine* 46°59N 31°58E **19 E5**
Bug → *Poland* 52°31N 21°5E **17 B11**
Buga *Colombia* 4°0N 76°15W **92 C3**
Bugala I. *Uganda* 0°40S 32°20E **54 C3**
Buganda *Uganda* 0°0 31°30E **54 C3**
Buganga *Uganda* 0°3S 32°0E **54 C3**
Bugel, Tanjung *Indonesia* 6°26S 111°3E **37 G14**
Búger *Spain* 39°45N 2°59E **24 B9**
Bugibba *Malta* 35°57N 14°25E **25 D1**
Bugsuk I. *Phil.* 8°12N 117°18E **36 C5**
Bugulma *Russia* 54°33N 52°48E **18 D9**
Bugungu △ *Uganda* 2°17N 31°50E **54 B3**
Buguruslan *Russia* 53°39N 52°26E **18 D9**
Buh → *Ukraine* 46°59N 31°58E **19 E5**
Buhera *Zimbabwe* 19°18S 31°29E **57 B5**
Buhl *U.S.A.* 42°36N 114°46W **76 E6**
Builth Wells *U.K.* 52°9N 3°25W **13 E4**
Buir Nur *Mongolia* 47°50N 117°42E **33 B6**
Buji *China* 22°37N 114°5E **33 F11**
Bujumbura *Burundi* 3°16S 29°18E **54 C2**
Bukachacha *Russia* 52°55N 116°50E **29 D12**
Bukama
  Dem. Rep. of the Congo 9°10S 25°50E **55 D2**
Bukavu
  Dem. Rep. of the Congo 2°20S 28°52E **54 C2**
Bukene *Tanzania* 4°15S 32°48E **54 C3**
Bukhara = Buxoro
  Uzbekistan 39°48N 64°25E **28 F7**
Bukhoro = Buxoro
  Uzbekistan 39°48N 64°25E **28 F7**
Bukima *Tanzania* 1°50S 33°25E **54 C3**
Bukit Badung *Indonesia* 8°49S 115°10E **37 K18**
Bukit Kerajaan *Malaysia* 5°25N 100°15E **39 c**
Bukit Mertajam *Malaysia* 5°22N 100°28E **39 c**
Bukit Ni *Malaysia* 1°22N 104°12E **39 d**
Bukit Panjang *Singapore* 1°23N 103°46E **39 d**
Bukit Tengah *Malaysia* 5°22N 100°25E **39 c**
Bukittinggi *Indonesia* 0°20S 100°20E **36 E2**
Bukoba *Tanzania* 1°20S 31°49E **54 C3**
Bukum, Pulau *Singapore* 1°14N 103°46E **39 d**
Bukuya *Uganda* 0°40N 31°52E **54 B3**
Bũl, Kuh-e *Iran* 30°48N 52°45E **45 D7**
Bula *Indonesia* 3°6S 130°30E **37 E8**
Bulahdelah *Australia* 32°23S 152°13E **63 E5**
Bulan *Phil.* 12°40N 123°52E **37 B6**
Bulandshahr *India* 28°28N 77°51E **42 E7**
Bulawayo *Zimbabwe* 20°7S 28°32E **55 G2**
Buldan *Turkey* 38°2N 28°50E **23 E13**
Bulgan *Mongolia* 48°45N 103°34E **32 B5**
Bulgar *Russia* 54°57N 49°4E **18 D8**
Bulgaria ■ *Europe* 42°35N 25°30E **23 C11**
Buli, Teluk *Indonesia* 0°48N 128°25E **37 D7**
Buliluyan, C. *Phil.* 8°20N 117°15E **36 C5**
Bulim *Singapore* 1°22N 103°43E **39 d**
Bulkley → *Canada* 55°15N 127°40W **70 B3**
Bull Shoals L. *U.S.A.* 36°22N 92°35W **84 C8**
Bulleringa △ *Australia* 17°39S 143°56E **62 B3**
Bullhead City *U.S.A.* 35°8N 114°32W **79 K12**
Büllingen *Belgium* 50°25N 6°16E **15 D6**
Bullock Creek *Australia* 17°43S 144°31E **62 B3**
Bulloo → *Australia* 28°43S 142°30E **63 D3**
Bulloo L. *Australia* 28°43S 142°25E **63 D3**
Bulls *N.Z.* 40°10S 175°24E **59 D5**
Bulman *Australia* 13°39S 134°20E **62 A1**
Bulnes *Chile* 36°42S 72°19W **94 D1**
Bulsar = Valsad *India* 20°40N 72°58E **40 J8**
Bultfontein *S. Africa* 28°18S 26°10E **56 D4**
Bulukumba *Indonesia* 5°33S 120°11E **37 F6**
Bulun *Russia* 70°37N 127°30E **29 B13**
Bumba
  Dem. Rep. of the Congo 2°13N 22°30E **52 D4**
Bumbah, Khalīj *Libya* 32°20N 23°15E **51 B10**
Bumbiri I. *Tanzania* 1°40S 31°55E **54 C3**
Bumhpa Bum *Burma* 26°51N 97°14E **41 F20**
Bumi → *Zimbabwe* 17°0S 28°20E **55 F2**
Buna *Kenya* 2°58N 39°30E **54 B4**
Bunaken *Indonesia* 1°37N 124°46E **37 D6**
Bunazi *Tanzania* 1°3S 31°23E **54 C3**
Bunbury *Australia* 33°20S 115°35E **61 F2**
Bunclody *Ireland* 52°39N 6°40W **10 D5**
Buncrana *Ireland* 55°8N 7°27W **10 A4**
Bundaberg *Australia* 24°54S 152°22E **63 C5**
Bundey → *Australia* 21°46S 135°37E **62 C2**
Bundi *India* 25°30N 75°35E **42 G6**
Bundjalung △ *Australia* 29°15S 153°15E **63 D5**
Bundoran *Ireland* 54°28N 8°16W **10 B3**
Bung Kan *Thailand* 18°23N 103°37E **38 C4**
Bungay *U.K.* 52°27N 1°28E **13 E9**
Bungil Cr. → *Australia* 27°5S 149°5E **63 D4**
Bungle Bungle = Purnululu △
  Australia 17°20S 128°20E **60 C4**
Bungo-Suidō *Japan* 33°0N 132°15E **31 H6**
Bungoma *Kenya* 0°34N 34°34E **54 B3**
Bungotakada *Japan* 33°35N 131°25E **31 H5**
Bungu *Tanzania* 7°35S 39°0E **54 D4**
Bunia
  Dem. Rep. of the Congo 1°35N 30°20E **54 B3**
Bunji *Pakistan* 35°45N 74°40E **43 B6**
Bunkie *U.S.A.* 30°57N 92°11W **84 F8**
Bunnell *U.S.A.* 29°28N 81°16W **85 G14**
Buntok *Indonesia* 1°40S 114°58E **36 E4**
Bunya Mts. △ *Australia* 26°51S 151°34E **63 D5**
Bunyola *Spain* 39°41N 2°42E **24 B9**
Bunyu *Indonesia* 3°35N 117°50E **36 D5**
Buol *Indonesia* 1°15N 121°32E **37 D6**
Buon Brieng *Vietnam* 13°9N 108°12E **38 F7**
Buon Ma Thuot *Vietnam* 12°40N 108°3E **38 F7**
Buong Long *Cambodia* 13°44N 106°59E **38 F6**
Buorkhaya, Mys
  Russia 71°50N 132°40E **29 B14**
Buqayq *Si. Arabia* 26°0N 49°45E **45 E6**
Bur Acaba = Buurhakaba
  Somali Rep. 3°12N 44°20E **47 G3**
Bûr Safâga *Egypt* 26°43N 33°57E **44 E2**
Bûr Sa'îd *Egypt* 31°16N 32°18E **51 B12**
Bûr Sûdân *Sudan* 19°32N 37°9E **51 E13**
Bura *Kenya* 1°4S 39°58E **54 C4**
Burakin *Australia* 30°31S 117°10E **61 F2**
Buraq *Syria* 33°11N 36°29E **46 B5**
Burao = Burco *Somali Rep.* 9°32N 45°32E **47 F4**
Buraydah *Si. Arabia* 26°20N 43°59E **44 E4**
Burda *India* 25°50N 77°35E **42 G6**
Burdekin → *Australia* 19°38S 147°25E **62 B4**
Burdur *Turkey* 37°45N 30°17E **19 G5**
Burdwan = Barddhaman
  India 23°14N 87°39E **43 H12**
Bure *Ethiopia* 10°40N 37°4E **47 E2**
Bure → *U.K.* 52°38N 1°43E **12 E9**
Bureya → *Russia* 49°27N 129°30E **29 E13**
Burford *Canada* 43°7N 80°27W **82 C4**
Burgas *Bulgaria* 42°33N 27°29E **23 C12**
Burgeo *Canada* 47°37N 57°38W **73 C8**
Burgersdorp *S. Africa* 31°0S 26°20E **56 E4**
Burghead *U.K.* 57°43N 3°30W **11 D5**
Burgos *Spain* 42°21N 3°41W **21 A4**
Burgsvik *Sweden* 57°3N 18°19E **9 H18**
Burgundy = Bourgogne □
  France 47°0N 4°50E **20 C6**
Burhaniye *Turkey* 39°30N 26°58E **23 E12**
Burhanpur *India* 21°18N 76°14E **40 J10**
Burhi Gandak → *India* 25°20N 86°37E **43 G12**
Burhner → *India* 22°43N 80°31E **43 H9**
Burias I. *Phil.* 12°55N 123°5E **37 B6**
Burica, Pta. *Costa Rica* 8°3N 82°51W **88 E3**
Burien *U.S.A.* 47°28N 122°20W **78 C4**
Burigi, L. *Tanzania* 2°2S 31°22E **54 C3**
Burigi △ *Tanzania* 2°20S 31°6E **54 C3**
Burin *Canada* 47°1N 55°14W **73 C8**
Buriram *Thailand* 15°0N 103°0E **38 E4**
Burkburnett *U.S.A.* 34°6N 98°34W **84 D5**
Burke → *Australia* 23°12S 139°33E **62 C2**
Burke Chan. *Canada* 52°10N 127°30W **70 C3**
Burketown *Australia* 17°45S 139°33E **62 B2**
Burkina Faso ■ *Africa* 12°0N 1°0W **50 F5**
Burk's Falls *Canada* 45°37N 79°24W **72 C4**
Burleigh Falls *Canada* 44°33N 78°12W **82 B6**
Burley *U.S.A.* 42°32N 113°48W **76 E7**
Burlingame *U.S.A.* 37°35N 122°21W **78 H4**
Burlington *Canada* 43°18N 79°45W **82 C5**
Burlington *Colo.,*
  U.S.A. 39°18N 102°16W **76 G12**
Burlington *Iowa, U.S.A.* 40°49N 91°14W **80 E8**
Burlington *Kans., U.S.A.* 38°12N 95°45W **80 F6**
Burlington *N.C., U.S.A.* 36°6N 79°26W **85 C15**
Burlington *N.J., U.S.A.* 40°4N 74°51W **83 F10**
Burlington *Vt., U.S.A.* 44°29N 73°12W **83 B11**
Burlington *Wash.,*
  U.S.A. 48°28N 122°20W **78 B4**
Burlington *Wis., U.S.A.* 42°41N 88°17W **80 D9**
Burma ■ *Asia* 21°0N 96°30E **41 J20**
Burnaby I. *Canada* 52°25S 131°19W **70 C2**
Burnet *U.S.A.* 30°45N 98°14W **84 F5**
Burney *U.S.A.* 40°53N 121°40W **76 F3**
Burnham *U.S.A.* 40°38N 77°34W **82 F7**
Burnham-on-Sea *U.K.* 51°14N 3°0W **13 F5**
Burnie *Australia* 41°4S 145°56E **63 G4**
Burnley *U.K.* 53°47N 2°14W **12 D5**
Burns *U.S.A.* 43°35N 119°3W **76 E4**
Burns Junction *U.S.A.* 42°47N 117°51W **76 E5**
Burns Lake *Canada* 54°14N 125°45W **70 C3**
Burnside → *Canada* 66°51N 108°4W **68 C9**
Burnside, L. *Australia* 25°22S 123°0E **61 E3**
Burnsville *U.S.A.* 44°47N 93°17W **80 C7**
Burnt River *Canada* 44°41N 78°42W **82 B6**
Burntwood → *Canada* 56°8N 96°34W **71 B9**
Burntwood L. *Canada* 55°22N 100°26W **71 B8**
Burqān *Kuwait* 29°0N 47°57E **44 D5**
Burqin *China* 47°43N 87°0E **32 B3**
Burra *Australia* 33°40S 138°55E **63 E2**
Burray *U.K.* 58°51N 2°54W **11 C6**
Burren △ *Ireland* 53°9N 9°5W **10 C2**
Burren *Ireland* 53°1N 8°58W **10 C3**
Burren Junction
  Australia 30°7S 148°58E **63 E4**
Burrinjuck Res. *Australia* 35°0S 148°36E **63 F4**
Burro, Serranías del
  Mexico 28°56N 102°5W **86 B4**
Burrow Hd. *U.K.* 54°41N 4°24W **11 G4**
Burrum Coast △
  Australia 25°13S 152°36E **63 D5**
Burruyacú *Argentina* 26°30S 64°40W **94 B3**
Burry Port *U.K.* 51°41N 4°15W **13 F3**
Bursa *Turkey* 40°15N 29°5E **23 D13**
Burstall *Canada* 50°39N 109°54W **71 C7**
Burton *U.S.A.* 43°0N 83°40W **82 D1**
Burton, S.C. *U.S.A.* 32°26N 80°43W **85 E14**
Burton, L. *Canada* 54°45N 78°20W **72 B4**
Burton upon Trent *U.K.* 52°48N 1°38W **12 E6**
Buru *Indonesia* 3°30S 126°30E **37 E7**
Burūn, Râs *Egypt* 31°14N 33°7E **46 D2**
Burundi ■ *Africa* 3°15S 30°0E **54 C3**
Bururi *Burundi* 3°57S 29°37E **54 C2**
Burutu *Nigeria* 5°20N 5°29E **50 G7**
Burwell *U.S.A.* 41°47N 99°8W **80 E4**
Burwick *U.K.* 58°45N 2°58W **11 C5**
Bury *U.K.* 53°35N 2°17W **12 D5**

Bury St. Edmunds *U.K.* 52°15N 0°43E **13 E8**
Buryatia □ *Russia* 53°0N 110°0E **29 D12**
Busan *S. Korea* 35°5N 129°0E **35 G15**
Busango Swamp *Zambia* 14°15S 25°45E **55 E2**
Buşayrah *Syria* 35°9N 40°26E **44 C4**
Büshehr *Iran* 28°55N 50°55E **45 D6**
Büshehr □ *Iran* 28°20N 51°45E **45 D6**
Bushenyi *Uganda* 0°35S 30°10E **54 C3**
Bushire = Büshehr *Iran* 28°55N 50°55E **45 D6**
Businga
  Dem. Rep. of the Congo 3°16N 20°59E **52 D4**
Buşra ash Shām *Syria* 32°30N 36°25E **46 C5**
Busselton *Australia* 33°42S 115°15E **61 F2**
Bussum *Neths.* 52°16N 5°10E **15 B5**
Busu Djanoa
  Dem. Rep. of the Congo 1°43N 21°23E **52 D4**
Busuanga I. *Phil.* 12°10N 120°0E **37 B5**
Busungbiu *Indonesia* 8°16S 114°58E **37 J17**
Buta *Dem. Rep. of the Congo* 2°50N 24°53E **54 B1**
Butare *Rwanda* 2°31S 29°52E **54 C2**
Butaritari *Kiribati* 3°30N 174°0E **64 G9**
Bute *U.K.* 55°48N 5°2W **11 F3**
Bute Inlet *Canada* 50°40N 124°53W **70 C4**
Butembo
  Dem. Rep. of the Congo 0°9N 29°18E **54 B2**
Butere *Kenya* 0°13N 34°30E **54 B3**
Butha Qi *China* 48°0N 122°32E **33 B7**
Butiaba *Uganda* 1°50N 31°20E **54 B3**
Butler *Mo., U.S.A.* 38°16N 94°20W **80 F6**
Butler *Pa., U.S.A.* 40°52N 79°54W **82 F5**
Buton *Indonesia* 5°0S 122°45E **37 E6**
Butte *Mont., U.S.A.* 46°0N 112°32W **76 C7**
Butte *Nebr., U.S.A.* 42°58N 98°51W **80 D4**
Butte Creek → *U.S.A.* 39°12N 121°56W **78 F5**
Butterworth = Gcuwa
  S. Africa 32°20S 28°11E **57 E4**
Butterworth *Malaysia* 5°24N 100°23E **39 c**
Buttevant *Ireland* 52°14N 8°40W **10 D3**
Buttfield, Mt. *Australia* 24°45S 128°9E **61 E4**
Button B. *Canada* 58°45N 94°23W **71 B10**
Buttonwillow *U.S.A.* 35°24N 119°28W **79 K7**
Butty Hd. *Australia* 33°54S 121°39E **61 F3**
Butuan *Phil.* 8°57N 125°33E **37 C7**
Butung = Buton *Indonesia* 5°0S 122°45E **37 F6**
Buturlinovka *Russia* 50°50N 40°35E **19 D7**
Buurhakaba *Somali Rep.* 3°12N 44°20E **47 G3**
Buxa Duar *India* 27°45N 89°35E **43 F13**
Buxar *India* 25°34N 83°58E **43 G10**
Buxoro *Uzbekistan* 39°48N 64°25E **28 F7**
Buxtehude *Germany* 53°28N 9°39E **16 B5**
Buxton *U.K.* 53°16N 1°54W **12 D6**
Buy *Russia* 58°28N 41°28E **18 C7**
Buyant-Uhaa *Mongolia* 44°55N 110°11E **33 B6**
Buyo, L. de *Ivory C.* 6°16N 7°10W **50 G4**
Büyük Menderes →
  Turkey 37°28N 27°11E **23 F12**
Büyükçekmece *Turkey* 41°2N 28°35E **23 D13**
Buzău *Romania* 45°10N 26°50E **17 F14**
Buzău → *Romania* 45°26N 27°44E **17 F14**
Buzen *Japan* 33°35N 131°5E **31 H5**
Buzi → *Mozam.* 19°50S 34°43E **55 F3**
Büzmeyin *Turkmenistan* 38°3N 58°12E **45 B8**
Buzuluk *Russia* 52°48N 52°12E **18 D9**
Buzzards Bay *U.S.A.* 41°45N 70°37W **83 E14**
Bwana Mkubwe
  Dem. Rep. of the Congo 13°8S 28°38E **55 E2**
Bwindi △ *Uganda* 1°2S 29°42E **54 C2**
Byarezina → *Belarus* 52°33N 30°14E **17 B16**
Bydgoszcz *Poland* 53°10N 18°0E **17 B9**
Byelorussia = Belarus ■
  Europe 53°30N 27°0E **17 B14**
Byers *U.S.A.* 39°43N 104°14W **76 G11**
Byesville *U.S.A.* 39°58N 81°32W **82 G3**
Byfield △ *Australia* 22°52S 150°45E **62 C5**
Bykhaw *Belarus* 53°31N 30°14E **17 B16**
Bykhov = Bykhaw
  Belarus 53°31N 30°14E **17 B16**
Bylas *U.S.A.* 33°8N 110°7W **77 K8**
Bylot *Canada* 58°25N 94°8W **71 B10**
Bylot I. *Canada* 73°13N 78°34W **69 B12**
Byrd, C. *Antarctica* 69°38S 76°7W **5 C17**
Byrock *Australia* 30°40S 146°27E **63 E4**
Byron, C. *Australia* 28°43S 153°38E **63 D5**
Byron Bay *Australia* 28°43S 153°37E **63 D5**
Byrranga, Gory *Russia* 75°0N 100°0E **29 B11**
Byrranga Mts. = Byrranga, Gory
  Russia 75°0N 100°0E **29 B11**
Byske *Sweden* 64°57N 21°11E **8 D19**
Byskeälven → *Sweden* 64°57N 21°13E **8 D19**
Bytom *Poland* 50°25N 18°54E **17 C10**
Bytów *Poland* 54°10N 17°30E **17 A9**
Byumba *Rwanda* 1°35S 30°4E **54 C3**

C

C.W. McConaughy, L.
  U.S.A. 41°14N 101°40W **80 E3**
Ca → *Vietnam* 18°45N 105°45E **38 C5**
Ca Mau *Vietnam* 9°7N 105°8E **39 H5**
Ca Mau, Mui *Vietnam* 8°38N 104°44E **39 H5**
Ca Na *Vietnam* 11°20N 108°54E **39 G7**
Caacupé *Paraguay* 25°23S 57°5W **94 B4**
Caaguazú □ *Paraguay* 26°5S 55°31W **95 B4**
Caála *Angola* 12°46S 15°30E **53 G3**
Caamaño Sd. *Canada* 52°55N 129°25W **70 C3**
Caazapá *Paraguay* 26°8S 56°19W **94 B4**
Caazapá □ *Paraguay* 26°10S 56°0W **95 B4**
Caballeria, C. de *Spain* 40°5N 4°5E **24 A11**
Cabanatuan *Phil.* 15°30N 120°58E **37 A6**
Cabano *Canada* 47°40N 68°56W **73 C6**
Cabazon *U.S.A.* 33°55N 116°47W **79 M10**
Cabedelo *Brazil* 7°0S 34°50W **93 E12**
Cabildo *Chile* 32°30S 71°5W **94 C1**
Cabimas *Venezuela* 10°23N 71°25W **92 A4**

Cabinda *Angola* 5°33S 12°11E **52 F2**
Cabinda □ *Angola* 5°0S 12°30E **52 F2**
Cabinet Mts. *U.S.A.* 48°10N 115°50W **76 B6**
Cabo Blanco *Argentina* 47°15S 65°47W **96 F3**
Cabo Frio *Brazil* 22°51S 42°3W **95 A7**
Cabo Pantoja *Peru* 1°0S 75°10W **92 D3**
Cabo San Lucas *Mexico* 22°53N 109°54W **86 C3**
Cabo Verde = Cape Verde Is. ■
  Atl. Oc. 16°0N 24°0W **50 b**
Cabonga, Réservoir
  Canada 47°20N 76°40W **72 C4**
Cabool *U.S.A.* 37°7N 92°6W **80 G7**
Caboolture *Australia* 27°5S 152°58E **63 D5**
Cabora Bassa Dam = Cahora
  Bassa, Lago de *Mozam.* 15°20S 32°50E **55 F3**
Caborca *Mexico* 30°37N 112°6W **86 A2**
Cabot, L. *U.S.A.* 44°30N 71°25W **83 B13**
Cabot Hd. *Canada* 45°14N 81°17W **82 A3**
Cabot Str. *Canada* 47°15N 59°40W **73 C8**
Cabra *Spain* 37°30N 4°28W **21 D3**
Cabrera *Spain* 39°8N 2°57E **24 B9**
Cabri *Canada* 50°35N 108°25W **71 C7**
Cabriel → *Spain* 39°14N 1°3W **21 C5**
Caçador *Brazil* 26°47S 51°0W **95 B5**
Čačak *Serbia* 43°54N 20°20E **23 C9**
Caçapava do Sul *Brazil* 30°30S 53°30W **95 C5**
Cáceres *Brazil* 16°5S 57°40W **92 G7**
Cáceres *Spain* 39°26N 6°23W **21 C2**
Cache Bay *Canada* 46°22N 80°0W **72 C4**
Cache Cr. → *U.S.A.* 38°42N 121°42W **78 G5**
Cache Creek *Canada* 50°48N 121°19W **70 C4**
Cachi *Argentina* 25°5S 66°10W **94 B2**
Cachimbo, Serra do
  Brazil 9°30S 55°30W **93 E7**
Cachinal de la Sierra
  Chile 24°58S 69°32W **94 A2**
Cachoeira *Brazil* 12°30S 39°0W **93 F11**
Cachoeira do Sul *Brazil* 30°3S 52°53W **95 C5**
Cachoeiro de Itapemirim
  Brazil 20°51S 41°7W **95 A7**
Cacoal *Brazil* 11°32S 61°18W **92 F6**
Cacólo *Angola* 10°9S 19°21E **52 G3**
Caconda *Angola* 13°48S 15°8E **53 G3**
Caddo *U.S.A.* 34°7N 96°16W **84 D6**
Cader Idris *U.K.* 52°42N 3°53W **13 E4**
Cadereyta de Jiménez
  Mexico 25°36N 100°0W **86 B5**
Cadibarrawirracanna, L.
  Australia 28°52S 135°27E **63 D2**
Cadillac *U.S.A.* 44°15N 85°24W **81 C11**
Cadiz *Phil.* 10°57N 123°15E **37 B6**
Cádiz *Spain* 36°30N 6°20W **21 D2**
Cadiz *Calif., U.S.A.* 34°30N 115°28W **79 L11**
Cadiz *Ohio, U.S.A.* 40°22N 81°0W **82 F3**
Cádiz, G. de *Spain* 36°40N 7°0W **21 D2**
Cadiz L. *U.S.A.* 34°18N 115°24W **77 J6**
Cadney Park *Australia* 27°55S 134°3E **63 D1**
Cadomin *Canada* 53°2N 117°20W **70 C5**
Cadotte Lake *Canada* 56°26N 116°23W **70 B5**
Cadoux *Australia* 30°46S 117°7E **61 F2**
Caen *France* 49°10N 0°22W **20 B3**
Caernarfon *U.K.* 53°8N 4°16W **12 D3**
Caernarfon B. *U.K.* 53°4N 4°40W **12 D3**
Caernarvon = Caernarfon
  U.K. 53°8N 4°16W **12 D3**
Caerphilly *U.K.* 51°35N 3°13W **13 F4**
Caerphilly □ *U.K.* 51°37N 3°12W **13 F4**
Caesarea *Israel* 32°30N 34°53E **46 C3**
Caetité *Brazil* 13°50S 42°32W **93 F10**
Cafayate *Argentina* 26°2S 66°0W **94 B2**
Cafu *Angola* 16°30S 15°8E **56 B2**
Cagayan de Oro *Phil.* 8°30N 124°40E **37 C6**
Cagayan Is. *Phil.* 9°40N 121°16E **37 C5**
Cágliari *Italy* 39°13N 9°7E **22 E3**
Cágliari, G. di *Italy* 39°8N 9°11E **22 E3**
Caguán → *Colombia* 0°8S 74°18W **92 D4**
Caguas *Puerto Rico* 18°14N 66°2W **89 d**
Caha Mts. *Ireland* 51°45N 9°40W **10 E2**
Cahama *Angola* 16°17S 14°19E **56 B1**
Caher *Ireland* 52°22N 7°56W **10 D4**
Cahersiveen *Ireland* 51°56N 10°14W **10 E1**
Cahora Bassa, L. de
  Mozam. 15°35S 32°0E **55 F3**
Cahora Bassa, Lago de
  Mozam. 15°20S 32°50E **55 F3**
Cahore Pt. *Ireland* 52°33N 6°12W **10 D5**
Cahors *France* 44°27N 1°27E **20 D4**
Cahul *Moldova* 45°50N 28°15E **17 F15**
Caì Bau, Dao *Vietnam* 21°10N 107°27E **38 B6**
Cai Nuoc *Vietnam* 8°56N 105°1E **39 H5**
Caia *Mozam.* 17°51S 35°24E **55 F4**
Caianda *Angola* 11°2S 23°31E **55 E1**
Caibarién *Cuba* 22°30N 79°30W **88 B4**
Caicara *Venezuela* 7°38N 66°10W **92 B5**
Caicó *Brazil* 6°20S 37°0W **93 E11**
Caicos Is. *Turks & Caicos* 21°40N 71°40W **89 B5**
Caicos Passage *W. Indies* 22°45N 72°45W **89 B5**
Caiguna *Australia* 32°16S 125°29E **61 F4**
Caird Coast *Antarctica* 75°0S 25°0W **5 D1**
Cairn Gorm *U.K.* 57°7N 3°39W **11 D5**
Cairngorm Mts. *U.K.* 57°6N 3°42W **11 D5**
Cairnryan *U.K.* 54°59N 5°1W **11 G3**
Cairns *Australia* 16°57S 145°45E **62 B4**
Cairns L. *Canada* 46°45N 94°30W **71 C10**
Cairo = El Qâhira *Egypt* 30°2N 31°13E **51 B12**
Cairo *Ga., U.S.A.* 30°52N 84°13W **85 F12**
Cairo *Ill., U.S.A.* 37°0N 89°11W **80 G9**
Cairo *N.Y., U.S.A.* 42°18N 74°0W **83 D10**
Caithness *U.K.* 58°25N 3°35W **11 C5**
Caithness, Ord of *U.K.* 58°8N 3°36W **11 C5**
Caja de Muertos, I.
  Puerto Rico 17°54N 66°32W **89 d**
Cajamarca *Peru* 7°5S 78°28W **92 E3**
Cajàzeiras *Brazil* 6°52S 38°30W **93 E11**
Cala d'Or *Spain* 39°23N 3°14E **24 B10**
Cala en Porter *Spain* 39°52N 4°8E **24 B11**

Cala Figuera *Spain* 39°20N 3°10E **24 B10**
Cala Figuera, C. de *Spain* 39°27N 2°31E **24 B9**
Cala Forcat *Spain* 40°0N 3°47E **24 B10**
Cala Major *Spain* 39°33N 2°37E **24 B9**
Cala Mezquida = Sa Mesquida
  Spain 39°55N 4°16E **24 B11**
Cala Millor *Spain* 39°35N 3°22E **24 B10**
Cala Murada *Spain* 39°27N 3°17E **24 B10**
Cala Ratjada *Spain* 39°43N 3°27E **24 B10**
Cala Santa Galdana
  Spain 39°56N 3°58E **24 B10**
Calabar *Nigeria* 4°57N 8°20E **50 H7**
Calabogie *Canada* 45°18N 76°43W **83 A8**
Calabozo *Venezuela* 9°0N 67°28W **92 B5**
Calábria □ *Italy* 39°0N 16°30E **22 E7**
Calahorra *Spain* 42°18N 1°59W **21 A5**
Calais *France* 50°57N 1°56E **20 A4**
Calais *U.S.A.* 45°11N 67°17W **81 C20**
Calakmul △ *Mexico* 18°14N 89°48W **87 D7**
Calalaste, Cord. de
  Argentina 25°0S 67°0W **94 B2**
Calama *Brazil* 8°0S 62°50W **92 E6**
Calama *Chile* 22°30S 68°55W **94 A2**
Calamar *Colombia* 10°15N 74°55W **92 A4**
Calamian Group *Phil.* 11°50N 119°55E **37 B5**
Calamocha *Spain* 40°50N 1°17W **21 B5**
Calang *Indonesia* 4°37N 95°37E **36 D1**
Calanscio, Sarìr *Libya* 27°30N 21°30E **51 C10**
Calapan *Phil.* 13°25N 121°7E **37 B6**
Calatayud *Spain* 41°20N 1°40W **21 B5**
Calauag *Phil.* 13°55N 122°15E **37 B6**
Calbayog *Phil.* 12°4N 124°38E **37 B6**
Calca *Peru* 13°22S 72°0W **92 F4**
Calcasieu L. *U.S.A.* 29°55N 93°18W **84 G8**
Calcium *U.S.A.* 44°1N 75°50W **83 B9**
Calcutta = Kolkata
  India 22°34N 88°21E **43 H13**
Calcutta *U.S.A.* 40°40N 80°34W **82 F4**
Caldas da Rainha *Portugal* 39°24N 9°8W **21 C1**
Calder → *U.K.* 53°44N 1°22W **12 D6**
Caldera *Chile* 27°5S 70°55W **94 B1**
Caldera de Taburiente △
  Canary Is. 28°43N 17°52W **24 F2**
Caldwell *Idaho, U.S.A.* 43°40N 116°41W **76 E5**
Caldwell *Kans., U.S.A.* 37°2N 97°37W **80 G5**
Caldwell *Tex., U.S.A.* 30°32N 96°42W **84 F6**
Caledon *Canada* 43°51N 79°51W **82 C5**
Caledon *S. Africa* 34°14S 19°26E **56 E2**
Caledon → *S. Africa* 30°31S 26°5E **56 E4**
Caledon B. *Australia* 12°45S 137°0E **62 A2**
Caledonia *Canada* 43°7N 79°58W **82 C5**
Caledonia *U.S.A.* 42°58N 77°51W **82 D7**
Calemba *Angola* 16°0S 15°44E **56 B2**
Calen *Australia* 20°56S 148°48E **62 b**
Caletones *Chile* 34°6S 70°27W **94 C1**
Calf of Man *I. of Man* 54°3N 4°48W **12 C3**
Calgary *Canada* 51°0N 114°10W **70 C6**
Calheta *Madeira* 32°44N 17°11W **24 D2**
Calhoun *U.S.A.* 34°30N 84°57W **85 D12**
Cali *Colombia* 3°25N 76°35W **92 C3**
Calicut *India* 11°15N 75°43E **40 P9**
Caliente *U.S.A.* 37°37N 114°31W **77 H6**
California *Mo., U.S.A.* 38°38N 92°34W **80 F7**
California *Pa., U.S.A.* 40°4N 79°54W **82 F5**
California □ *U.S.A.* 37°30N 119°30W **78 H7**
California, Baja, T.N. = Baja
  California □ *Mexico* 30°0N 115°0W **86 B2**
California, Baja, T.S. = Baja
  California Sur □
  Mexico 25°50N 111°50W **86 B2**
California, G. de *Mexico* 27°0N 111°0W **86 B2**
California City *U.S.A.* 35°10N 117°55W **79 K9**
California Hot Springs
  U.S.A. 35°51N 118°41W **79 K8**
Calilegua △ *Argentina* 25°36S 64°50W **94 B3**
Calingasta *Argentina* 31°15S 69°30W **94 C2**
Calipatria *U.S.A.* 33°8N 115°31W **79 M11**
Calistoga *U.S.A.* 38°35N 122°35W **78 G4**
Calitzdorp *S. Africa* 33°33S 21°42E **56 E3**
Callabonna, L. *Australia* 29°40S 140°5E **63 D3**
Callan *Ireland* 52°32N 7°24W **10 D4**
Callander *U.K.* 56°15N 4°13W **11 E4**
Callao *Peru* 12°3S 77°8W **92 F3**
Callicoon *U.S.A.* 41°46N 75°3W **83 E9**
Calling Lake *Canada* 55°15N 113°12W **70 B6**
Calliope *Australia* 24°0S 151°16E **62 C5**
Calma, Costa de la *Spain* 39°28N 2°26E **24 B9**
Calne *U.K.* 51°26N 2°0W **13 F6**
Calola *Angola* 16°25S 17°48E **56 B2**
Caloundra *Australia* 26°45S 153°10E **63 D5**
Calpella *U.S.A.* 39°14N 123°12W **78 F3**
Calpine *U.S.A.* 39°40N 120°27W **78 F6**
Calstock *Canada* 49°47N 84°9W **72 C3**
Caltagirone *Italy* 37°14N 14°31E **22 F6**
Caltanissetta *Italy* 37°29N 14°4E **22 F6**
Calulo *Angola* 10°1S 14°56E **52 G2**
Calvert → *Australia* 16°17S 137°44E **62 B2**
Calvert I. *Canada* 51°30N 128°0W **70 C3**
Calvert Ra. *Australia* 24°0S 122°30E **60 D3**
Calvi *France* 42°34N 8°45E **20 E8**
Calvià *Spain* 39°34N 2°31E **24 B9**
Calvillo *Mexico* 21°51N 102°43W **86 C4**
Calvinia *S. Africa* 31°28S 19°45E **56 E2**
Calwa *U.S.A.* 36°42N 119°46W **78 J7**
Cam → *U.K.* 52°21N 0°16E **13 E8**
Cam Lam *Vietnam* 11°54N 109°10E **39 G7**
Cam Pha *Vietnam* 21°7N 107°18E **38 B6**
Cam Ranh *Vietnam* 11°54N 109°12E **39 G7**
Cam Xuyen *Vietnam* 18°15N 106°0E **38 C6**
Camabatela *Angola* 8°20S 15°26E **52 F3**
Camacha *Madeira* 32°41N 16°49W **24 D3**
Camacupa *Angola* 11°58S 17°22E **53 G3**
Camagüey *Cuba* 21°20N 77°55W **88 B4**
Camaná *Peru* 16°30S 72°50W **92 G4**

Camanche Res. *U.S.A.* 38°14N 121°1W **78 G6**
Camaquã *Brazil* 30°51S 51°49W **95 C5**
Camaquã → *Brazil* 31°17S 51°47W **95 C5**
Câmara de Lobos
  Madeira 32°39N 16°59W **24 D3**
Camargo *Mexico* 26°19N 98°50W **87 B5**
Camarillo *U.S.A.* 34°13N 119°2W **79 L7**
Camarón, C. *Honduras* 16°0N 85°0W **88 C2**
Camarones *Argentina* 44°50S 65°40W **96 E3**
Camas *U.S.A.* 45°35N 122°24W **78 E4**
Camas Valley *U.S.A.* 43°2N 123°40W **76 E2**
Camballin *Australia* 17°59S 124°12E **60 C3**
Cambará *Brazil* 23°2S 50°5W **95 A5**
Cambay = Khambhat
  India 22°23N 72°33E **42 H5**
Cambay, G. of = Khambhat, G. of
  India 20°45N 72°30E **40 J8**
Cambodia ■ *Asia* 12°15N 105°0E **38 F5**
Camborne *U.K.* 50°12N 5°19W **13 G2**
Cambrai *France* 50°11N 3°14E **20 A5**
Cambria *U.S.A.* 35°34N 121°5W **78 K5**
Cambrian Mts. *U.K.* 52°3N 3°57E **13 E4**
Cambridge *Canada* 43°23N 80°15W **82 C4**
Cambridge *Jamaica* 18°18N 77°54W **88 a**
Cambridge *N.Z.* 37°54S 175°29E **59 B5**
Cambridge *U.K.* 52°12N 0°8E **13 E8**
Cambridge *Mass., U.S.A.* 42°23N 71°7W **83 D13**
Cambridge *Minn., U.S.A.* 45°34N 93°13W **80 C7**
Cambridge *N.Y., U.S.A.* 43°2N 73°22W **83 C11**
Cambridge *Nebr.,
  U.S.A.* 40°17N 100°10W **80 E3**
Cambridge *Ohio, U.S.A.* 40°2N 81°35W **82 F3**
Cambridge Bay = Ikaluktutiak
  Canada 69°10N 105°0W **68 C9**
Cambridge G. *Australia* 14°55S 128°15E **60 B4**
Cambridge Springs
  U.S.A. 41°48N 80°4W **82 E4**
Cambridgeshire □ *U.K.* 52°25N 0°7W **13 E7**
Cambuci *Brazil* 21°35S 41°55W **95 A7**
Cambundi-Catembo
  Angola 10°10S 17°35E **52 G3**
Camden *Australia* 34°1S 150°43E **63 E5**
Camden *Ala., U.S.A.* 31°59N 87°17W **85 F11**
Camden *Ark., U.S.A.* 33°35N 92°50W **84 E8**
Camden *Maine, U.S.A.* 44°13N 69°4W **81 C19**
Camden *N.J., U.S.A.* 39°55N 75°7W **83 G9**
Camden *N.Y., U.S.A.* 43°20N 75°45W **83 C9**
Camden *S.C., U.S.A.* 34°16N 80°36W **85 D14**
Camden Sd. *Australia* 15°27S 124°25E **60 C3**
Camdenton *U.S.A.* 38°1N 92°45W **80 F7**
Camelford *U.K.* 50°37N 4°42W **13 G3**
Cameron *Ariz., U.S.A.* 35°53N 111°25W **77 J8**
Cameron *La., U.S.A.* 29°48N 93°20W **84 G8**
Cameron *Mo., U.S.A.* 39°44N 94°14W **80 F6**
Cameron *Tex., U.S.A.* 30°51N 96°59W **84 F6**
Cameron Highlands
  Malaysia 4°27N 101°22E **39 K3**
Cameron Hills *Canada* 59°48N 118°0W **70 B5**
Cameroon ■ *Africa* 6°0N 12°30E **52 C2**
Cameroun, Mt. *Cameroon* 4°13N 9°10E **52 D1**
Cametá *Brazil* 2°12S 49°30W **93 D9**
Camiguin I. *Phil.* 18°56N 121°55E **37 A6**
Camilla *U.S.A.* 31°14N 84°12W **85 F12**
Caminha *Portugal* 41°50N 8°50W **21 B1**
Camino *U.S.A.* 38°44N 120°41W **78 G6**
Camira Creek *Australia* 29°15S 152°58E **63 D5**
Cammal *U.S.A.* 41°24N 77°28W **82 E7**
Camocim *Brazil* 2°55S 40°50W **93 D10**
Camooweal *Australia* 19°56S 138°7E **62 B2**
Camooweal Caves △
  Australia 20°1S 138°11E **62 C2**
Camopi *Fr. Guiana* 3°12N 52°17W **93 C8**
Camp Hill *U.S.A.* 40°14N 76°55W **82 F8**
Camp Nelson *U.S.A.* 36°8N 118°39W **79 J8**
Camp Pendleton
  U.S.A. 33°13N 117°24W **79 M9**
Camp Verde *U.S.A.* 34°34N 111°51W **77 J8**
Camp Wood *U.S.A.* 29°40N 100°1W **84 G4**
Campana *Argentina* 34°10S 58°55W **94 C4**
Campana, I. *Chile* 48°20S 75°20W **96 F1**
Campanário *Madeira* 32°39N 17°2W **24 D2**
Campanet *Spain* 39°46N 2°58E **24 B9**
Campánia □ *Italy* 41°0N 14°30E **22 D6**
Campbell *S. Africa* 28°48S 23°44E **56 D3**
Campbell *Calif., U.S.A.* 37°17N 121°57W **78 H5**
Campbell *Ohio, U.S.A.* 41°5N 80°37W **82 E4**
Campbell I. *Pac. Oc.* 52°30S 169°0E **64 N8**
Campbell L. *Canada* 63°14N 106°55W **71 A7**
Campbell Plateau *S. Ocean* 50°0S 170°0E **5 A11**
Campbell River *Canada* 50°5N 125°20W **70 C3**
Campbell Town
  Australia 41°52S 147°30E **63 G4**
Campbellford *Canada* 44°18N 77°48W **82 B7**
Campbellpur *Pakistan* 33°46N 72°26E **42 C5**
Campbellton *Canada* 47°57N 66°43W **73 C6**
Campbelltown *Australia* 34°4S 150°49E **63 E5**
Campbeltown *U.K.* 55°26N 5°36W **11 F3**
Campeche *Mexico* 19°51N 90°32W **87 D6**
Campeche □ *Mexico* 19°0N 90°30W **87 D6**
Campeche, Golfo de
  Mexico 19°30N 93°0W **87 D6**
Camperdown *Australia* 38°14S 143°9E **63 F3**
Camperville *Canada* 51°59N 100°9W **71 C8**
Câmpina *Romania* 45°10N 25°45E **17 F13**
Campina Grande *Brazil* 7°20S 35°47W **93 E12**
Campinas *Brazil* 22°50S 47°0W **95 A6**
Campo Grande *Brazil* 20°25S 54°40W **93 H8**
Campo Maior *Brazil* 4°50S 42°12W **93 D10**
Campo Mourão *Brazil* 24°3S 52°22W **95 A5**
Campobasso *Italy* 41°34N 14°39E **22 D6**
Campos *Brazil* 21°50S 41°20W **95 A7**
Campos Belos *Brazil* 13°10S 47°3W **93 F9**
Campos Novos *Brazil* 27°21S 51°50W **95 B5**
Camptonville *U.S.A.* 39°27N 121°3W **78 F5**
Camptown *U.S.A.* 41°44N 76°14W **83 E8**

Câmpulung *Romania* 45°17N 25°3E **17 F13**
Camrose *Canada* 53°0N 112°50W **70 C6**
Camsell Portage
  Canada 59°37N 109°15W **71 B7**
Çan *Turkey* 40°2N 27°3E **23 D12**
Can Clavo *Spain* 38°57N 1°27E **24 C7**
Can Creu *Spain* 38°58N 1°28E **24 C7**
Can Gio *Vietnam* 10°25N 106°58E **39 G6**
Can Pastilla *Spain* 39°32N 2°42E **24 B9**
Can Tho *Vietnam* 10°2N 105°46E **39 G5**
Canaan *U.S.A.* 42°2N 73°20W **83 D11**
Canada ■ *N. Amer.* 60°0N 100°0W **68 D10**
Canada Abyssal Plain
  Arctic 80°0N 140°0W **4 B18**
Canada Basin *Arctic* 80°0N 145°0W **4 B18**
Canadian *U.S.A.* 35°55N 100°23W **84 D4**
Canadian → *U.S.A.* 35°28N 95°3W **84 D7**
Canadian Shield *Canada* 53°0N 75°0W **66 D12**
Canajoharie *U.S.A.* 42°54N 74°35W **83 D10**
Çanakkale *Turkey* 40°8N 26°24E **23 D12**
Çanakkale Boğazı
  Turkey 40°17N 26°32E **23 D12**
Canal Flats *Canada* 50°10N 115°48W **70 C5**
Canalejas *Argentina* 35°15S 66°34W **94 D2**
Canals *Argentina* 33°35S 62°53W **94 C3**
Canandaigua *U.S.A.* 42°54N 77°17W **82 D7**
Canandaigua L. *U.S.A.* 42°47N 77°19W **82 D7**
Cananea *Mexico* 31°0N 110°18W **86 A2**
Canarias, Is. *Atl. Oc.* 28°30N 16°0W **24 F4**
Canaries *St. Lucia* 13°55N 61°4W **89 f**
Canarreos, Arch. de los
  Cuba 21°35N 81°40W **88 B3**
Canary Is. = Canarias, Is.
  Atl. Oc. 28°30N 16°0W **24 F4**
Canaseraga *U.S.A.* 42°27N 77°45W **82 D7**
Canatlán *Mexico* 24°31N 104°47W **86 C4**
Canaveral, C. *U.S.A.* 28°27N 80°32W **85 G14**
Canaveral △ *U.S.A.* 28°28N 80°34W **85 G14**
Canavieiras *Brazil* 15°39S 39°0W **93 G11**
Canberra *Australia* 35°15S 149°8E **63 F4**
Canby *Calif., U.S.A.* 41°27N 120°52W **76 F3**
Canby *Minn., U.S.A.* 44°43N 96°16W **80 C5**
Canby *Oreg., U.S.A.* 45°16N 122°42W **78 E4**
Cancún *Mexico* 21°8N 86°44W **87 C7**
Candela *Argentina* 27°29S 55°44W **95 B4**
Candelaria *Canary Is.* 28°22N 16°22W **24 F3**
Candelo *Australia* 36°47S 149°43E **63 F4**
Candi Dasa *Indonesia* 8°30S 115°34E **37 J18**
Candia = Iraklio *Greece* 35°20N 25°12E **25 D7**
Candle L. *Canada* 53°50N 105°18W **71 C7**
Cando *U.S.A.* 48°32N 99°12W **80 A4**
Canea = Chania *Greece* 35°30N 24°4E **25 D6**
Canelones *Uruguay* 34°32S 56°17W **95 C4**
Cañete *Chile* 37°50S 73°30W **94 D1**
Cangas del Narcea *Spain* 43°10N 6°32W **21 A2**
Canguaretama *Brazil* 6°20S 35°5W **93 E11**
Canguçu *Brazil* 31°22S 52°43W **95 C5**
Canguçu, Serra do
  Brazil 31°20S 52°40W **95 C5**
Cangzhou *China* 38°19N 116°52E **34 E9**
Caniapiscau → *Canada* 56°40N 69°30W **73 A6**
Caniapiscau, L. *Canada* 54°10N 69°55W **73 B6**
Canicattì *Italy* 37°21N 13°51E **22 F5**
Canim Lake *Canada* 51°47N 120°54W **70 C4**
Canindeyú □ *Paraguay* 24°10S 55°0W **95 A5**
Canisteo *U.S.A.* 42°16N 77°36W **82 D7**
Canisteo → *U.S.A.* 42°7N 77°8W **82 D7**
Cañitas de Felipe Pescador
  Mexico 23°36N 102°43W **86 C4**
Çankırı *Turkey* 40°40N 33°37E **19 F5**
Cankuzo *Burundi* 3°10S 30°31E **54 C3**
Canmore *Canada* 51°7N 115°18W **70 C5**
Cann River *Australia* 37°35S 149°7E **63 F4**
Canna *U.K.* 57°3N 6°33W **11 D2**
Cannanore *India* 11°53N 75°27E **40 P9**
Cannes *France* 43°32N 7°1E **20 E7**
Canning Town = Port Canning
  India 22°23N 88°40E **43 H13**
Cannington *Canada* 44°20N 79°2W **82 B5**
Cannock *U.K.* 52°41N 2°1W **13 E5**
Cannonball → *U.S.A.* 46°26N 100°35W **80 B3**
Cannondale Mt.
  Australia 25°13S 148°57E **62 D4**
Cannonsville Res. *U.S.A.* 42°4N 75°22W **83 D9**
Cannonvale *Australia* 20°17S 148°43E **62 J6**
Canoas *Brazil* 29°56S 51°11W **95 B5**
Canoe L. *Canada* 55°10N 108°15W **71 B7**
Cañon City *U.S.A.* 38°27N 105°14W **76 G11**
Cañón de Río Blanco △
  Mexico 18°43N 97°15W **87 D5**
Cañón del Sumidero △
  Mexico 19°22N 96°24W **87 D5**
Canonniers Pt. *Mauritius* 20°2S 57°32E **53 d**
Canora *Canada* 51°40N 102°30W **71 C8**
Canowindra *Australia* 33°35S 148°38E **63 E4**
Canso *Canada* 45°20N 61°0W **73 C7**
Cantabria □ *Spain* 43°10N 4°0W **21 A4**
Cantabrian Mts. = Cantábrica,
  Cordillera *Spain* 43°0N 5°10W **21 A3**
Cantábrica, Cordillera
  Spain 43°0N 5°10W **21 A3**
Cantal, Plomb du *France* 45°3N 2°45E **20 D5**
Canterbury *Australia* 25°23S 141°53E **62 D3**
Canterbury *U.K.* 51°16N 1°6E **13 F9**
Canterbury Bight *N.Z.* 44°16S 171°55E **59 F3**
Canterbury Plains *N.Z.* 43°55S 171°22E **59 E3**
Cantil *U.S.A.* 35°18N 117°58W **79 K9**
Canton = Guangzhou
  China 23°6N 113°13E **33 D6**
Canton *Ga., U.S.A.* 34°14N 84°29W **85 D12**
Canton *Ill., U.S.A.* 40°33N 90°2W **80 E8**
Canton *Miss., U.S.A.* 32°37N 90°2W **85 E9**
Canton *Mo., U.S.A.* 40°8N 91°32W **80 E8**
Canton *N.Y., U.S.A.* 44°36N 75°10W **83 B9**

Canton *Ohio, U.S.A.* 40°48N 81°23W **82 F3**
Canton *Pa., U.S.A.* 41°39N 76°51W **82 E8**
Canton *S. Dak., U.S.A.* 43°18N 96°35W **80 D6**
Canton *S.D., U.S.A.* 36°6N 98°35W **84 C5**
Canudos *Brazil* 7°13S 58°5W **92 E7**
Canumã → *Brazil* 3°55S 59°10W **92 D7**
Canutama *Brazil* 6°30S 64°20W **92 E6**
Canutillo *U.S.A.* 31°55N 106°36W **84 F1**
Canvey *U.K.* 51°31N 0°37E **13 F8**
Canyon *U.S.A.* 34°59N 101°55W **84 D4**
Canyon De Chelly △
  U.S.A. 36°10N 109°20W **77 H9**
Canyonlands △ *U.S.A.* 38°15N 110°0W **77 G9**
Canyons of the Ancients △
  U.S.A. 37°30N 108°55W **77 H9**
Canyonville *U.S.A.* 42°56N 123°17W **76 E2**
Cao Bang *Vietnam* 22°40N 106°15E **38 A6**
Cao He → *China* 40°10N 124°32E **35 D13**
Cao Lanh *Vietnam* 10°27N 105°38E **39 G5**
Cao Xian *China* 34°50N 115°35E **34 G8**
Cap-aux-Meules *Canada* 47°23N 61°52W **73 C7**
Cap-Chat *Canada* 49°6N 66°40W **73 C6**
Cap-de-la-Madeleine
  Canada 46°22N 72°31W **72 C5**
Cap-Haïtien *Haiti* 19°40N 72°20W **89 C5**
Cap Pt. *St. Lucia* 14°7N 60°57W **89 f**
Capac *U.S.A.* 43°1N 82°56W **82 C2**
Capanaparo → *Venezuela* 7°1N 67°7W **92 B5**
Cape → *Australia* 20°59S 146°51E **62 C4**
Cape Arid △ *Australia* 33°58S 123°13E **61 F3**
Cape Barren I. *Australia* 40°25S 148°15E **63 G4**
Cape Breton Highlands △
  Canada 46°50N 60°40W **73 C7**
Cape Breton I. *Canada* 46°0N 60°30W **73 C7**
Cape Charles *U.S.A.* 37°16N 76°1W **81 G15**
Cape Coast *Ghana* 5°5N 1°15W **50 G5**
Cape Cod △ *U.S.A.* 42°0N 70°6W **81 E18**
Cape Coral *U.S.A.* 26°33N 81°57W **85 H14**
Cape Crawford *Australia* 16°41S 135°43E **62 B2**
Cape Dorset = Kingait
  Canada 64°14N 76°32W **69 C12**
Cape Fear → *U.S.A.* 33°53N 78°1W **85 E15**
Cape Girardeau *U.S.A.* 37°19N 89°32W **80 G9**
Cape Hatteras
  U.S.A. 35°30N 75°28W **85 D17**
Cape Le Grand △
  Australia 33°54S 122°26E **61 F3**
Cape Lookout △
  U.S.A. 35°45N 76°25W **85 D16**
Cape May *U.S.A.* 38°56N 74°56W **81 F16**
Cape May Point *U.S.A.* 38°56N 74°58W **81 F16**
Cape Melville △
  Australia 14°28S 144°28E **62 A3**
Cape Peninsula △
  S. Africa 34°20S 18°28E **56 E2**
Cape Range △ *Australia* 22°3S 114°0E **61 D1**
Cape St. George *Canada* 48°28N 59°14W **73 C8**
Cape Tormentine *Canada* 46°8N 63°47W **73 C7**
Cape Town *S. Africa* 33°55S 18°22E **56 E2**
Cape Tribulation △
  Australia 16°5S 145°25E **62 B4**
Cape Verde Is. ■ *Atl. Oc.* 16°0N 24°0W **50 b**
Cape Vincent *U.S.A.* 44°8N 76°20W **83 B8**
Cape York Peninsula
  Australia 12°0S 142°30E **62 A3**
Capela *Brazil* 10°30S 37°0W **93 F11**
Capella *Australia* 23°2S 148°1E **62 C4**
Capesterre-Belle-Eau
  Guadeloupe 16°4N 61°36W **88 b**
Capesterre-de-Marie-Galante
  Guadeloupe 15°53N 61°14W **88 b**
Capim → *Brazil* 1°40S 47°47W **93 D9**
Capitán Arturo Prat
  Antarctica 63°0S 61°0W **5 C17**
Capitol Reef △ *U.S.A.* 38°15N 111°10W **77 G8**
Capitola *U.S.A.* 36°59N 121°57W **78 J5**
Capoche → *Mozam.* 15°35S 33°0E **55 F3**
Capraia *Italy* 43°2N 9°50E **20 E8**
Capreol *Canada* 46°43N 80°56W **72 C3**
Capri *Italy* 40°33N 14°14E **22 D6**
Capricorn Coast
  Australia 23°16S 150°49E **62 C5**
Capricorn Group
  Australia 23°30S 151°55E **62 C5**
Capricorn Ra. *Australia* 23°20S 116°50E **60 D2**
Caprivi Game △ *Namibia* 17°55S 22°37E **56 B3**
Caprivi Strip *Namibia* 18°0S 23°0E **56 B3**
Captain's Flat *Australia* 35°35S 149°27E **63 F4**
Capulin Volcano △
  U.S.A. 36°47N 103°58W **84 C3**
Caquetá → *Colombia* 1°15S 69°15W **92 D5**
Caracal *Romania* 44°8N 24°22E **17 F13**
Caracas *Venezuela* 10°30N 66°55W **92 A5**
Caracol *Belize* 16°45N 89°6E **88 C2**
Caracol *Mato Grosso do Sul,
  Brazil* 22°18S 57°1W **94 A4**
Caracol *Piauí, Brazil* 9°15S 43°22W **93 E10**
Carajás *Brazil* 6°5S 50°30W **93 E8**
Carajás, Serra dos *Brazil* 6°0S 51°30W **93 E8**
Carangola *Brazil* 20°44S 42°5W **95 A7**
Carانsebeş *Romania* 45°28N 22°18E **17 F12**
Caراquet *Canada* 47°48N 64°57W **73 C6**
Caratasca, L. de
  Honduras 15°20N 83°40W **88 C3**
Caratinga *Brazil* 19°50S 42°10W **93 G10**
Caraúbas *Brazil* 5°43S 37°33W **93 E11**
Caravaca de la Cruz *Spain* 38°8N 1°52W **21 C5**
Caravelas *Brazil* 17°45S 39°15W **93 G11**
Caravelí *Peru* 15°45S 73°25W **92 G4**
Caravelle, Presqu'île de la
  Martinique 14°46N 60°48W **88 c**
Caraz *Peru* 9°3S 77°47W **92 E3**
Carazinho *Brazil* 28°16S 52°46W **95 B5**
Carballo *Spain* 43°13N 8°41W **21 A1**
Carberry *Canada* 49°50N 99°25W **71 D9**
Carbó *Mexico* 29°42N 110°58W **86 B2**

110 Carbonara, C. INDEX TO WORLD MAPS

Carbonara, C. *Italy* 39°6N 9°31E **22** E3
Carbondale *Colo., U.S.A.* 39°24N 107°13W **76** G10
Carbondale *Ill., U.S.A.* 37°44N 89°13W **80** G9
Carbondale *Pa., U.S.A.* 41°35N 75°30W **83** E9
Carbonear *Canada* 47°42N 53°13W **73** C9
Carbónia *Italy* 39°10N 8°30E **22** E3
Carcajou *Canada* 57°47N 117°6W **70** B5
Carcarana → *Argentina* 32°27S 60°48W **94** C3
Carcasse, C. *Haiti* 18°30N 74°28W **89** C5
Carcassonne *France* 43°13N 2°20E **20** E5
Carcross *Canada* 60°13N 134°45W **70** A2
Cardamon Hills *India* 9°30N 77°15E **40** Q10
Cardamon Mts. = Kravanh, Chuor Phnum *Cambodia* 12°0N 103°32E **39** G4
Cárdenas *Cuba* 23°0N 81°30W **88** B3
Cárdenas *San Luis Potosí, Mexico* 22°0N 99°38W **87** C5
Cárdenas *Tabasco, Mexico* 17°59N 93°22W **87** D6
Cardiff *U.K.* 51°29N 3°10W **13** F4
Cardiff ☐ *U.K.* 51°31N 3°12W **13** F4
Cardiff-by-the-Sea *U.S.A.* 33°1N 117°17W **79** M9
Cardigan *U.K.* 52°5N 4°40W **13** E3
Cardigan B. *U.K.* 52°30N 4°30W **13** E3
Cardinal *Canada* 44°47N 75°23W **83** B9
Cardona *Uruguay* 33°53S 57°18W **94** C4
Cardoso, Ilha do *Brazil* 25°8S 47°58W **95** B5
Cardston *Canada* 49°15N 113°20W **70** D6
Cardwell *Australia* 18°14S 146°2E **62** B4
Careen L. *Canada* 57°0N 108°11W **71** B7
Carei *Romania* 47°40N 22°29E **17** E12
Careme = Ciremay *Indonesia* 6°55S 108°27E **37** G13
Carey *U.S.A.* 43°19N 113°57W **76** E7
Carey, L. *Australia* 29°0S 122°15E **61** E3
Carey L. *Canada* 62°12N 102°55W **71** A8
Carhué *Argentina* 37°10S 62°50W **94** D3
Caria *Turkey* 37°20N 28°10E **23** F13
Cariacica *Brazil* 20°16S 40°25W **93** H10
Caribbean Sea *W. Indies* 15°0N 75°0W **89** D5
Cariboo Mts. *Canada* 53°0N 121°0W **70** C4
Caribou *U.S.A.* 46°52N 68°1W **81** B19
Caribou → *Man., Canada* 59°20N 94°44W **71** B10
Caribou → *N.W.T., Canada* 61°27N 125°45W **70** A3
Caribou I. *Canada* 47°22N 85°49W **72** C2
Caribou Is. *Canada* 61°55N 113°15W **70** A6
Caribou L. *Man., Canada* 59°21N 96°10W **71** B9
Caribou L. *Ont., Canada* 50°25N 89°5W **72** B2
Caribou Mts. *Canada* 59°12N 115°40W **70** B5
Caribou River ⌓ *Canada* 59°35N 96°35W **71** B9
Carichíc *Mexico* 27°56N 107°3W **86** B3
Carinda *Australia* 30°28S 147°41E **63** E4
Carinhanha *Brazil* 14°15S 44°46W **93** F10
Carinhanha → *Brazil* 14°20S 43°47W **93** F10
Carinthia = Kärnten ☐ *Austria* 46°52N 13°30E **16** E8
Caripito *Venezuela* 10°8N 63°6W **92** A6
Carleton, Mt. *Canada* 47°23N 66°53W **73** C6
Carleton Place *Canada* 45°8N 76°9W **83** A8
Carletonville *S. Africa* 26°23S 27°22E **56** D4
Carlin *U.S.A.* 40°43N 116°7W **76** F5
Carlingford L. *U.K.* 54°3N 6°9W **10** B5
Carlinville *U.S.A.* 39°17N 89°53W **80** F9
Carlisle *U.K.* 54°54N 2°56W **12** C5
Carlisle *U.S.A.* 40°12N 77°12W **82** F7
Carlisle B. *Barbados* 13°5N 59°37W **89** g
Carlisle I. *Australia* 20°49S 149°18E **62** J7
Carlos Casares *Argentina* 35°32S 61°20W **94** D3
Carlos Tejedor *Argentina* 35°25S 62°25W **94** D3
Carlow *Ireland* 52°50N 6°56W **10** D5
Carlow ☐ *Ireland* 52°43N 6°50W **10** D5
Carlsbad *Calif., U.S.A.* 33°10N 117°21W **79** M9
Carlsbad *N. Mex., U.S.A.* 32°25N 104°14W **77** K11
Carlsbad Caverns △ *U.S.A.* 32°10N 104°35W **77** K11
Carluke *U.K.* 55°45N 3°50W **11** F5
Carlyle *Canada* 49°40N 102°20W **71** D8
Carmacks *Canada* 62°5N 136°16W **68** C6
Carman *Canada* 49°30N 98°0W **71** D9
Carmarthen *U.K.* 51°52N 4°19W **13** F3
Carmarthen B. *U.K.* 51°40N 4°30W **13** F3
Carmarthenshire ☐ *U.K.* 51°55N 4°13W **13** F3
Carmaux *France* 44°3N 2°10E **20** D5
Carmel *U.S.A.* 41°26N 73°41W **83** E11
Carmel-by-the-Sea *U.S.A.* 36°33N 121°55W **78** J5
Carmel Valley *U.S.A.* 36°29N 121°43W **78** J5
Carmelo *Uruguay* 34°0S 58°20W **94** C4
Carmen *Paraguay* 27°13S 56°12W **95** B4
Carmen → *Mexico* 30°42N 106°29W **86** A3
Carmen, I. *Mexico* 25°57N 111°12W **86** B2
Carmen de Patagones *Argentina* 40°50S 63°0W **96** E4
Carmensa *Argentina* 35°15S 67°40W **94** D2
Carmi *Canada* 49°36N 119°8W **70** D5
Carmi *U.S.A.* 38°5N 88°10W **80** F9
Carmichael *U.S.A.* 38°38N 121°19W **78** G5
Carmila *Australia* 21°55S 149°24E **62** C4
Carmona *Costa Rica* 10°0N 85°15W **88** E2
Carmona *Spain* 37°28N 5°42W **21** D3
Carn Ban *U.K.* 57°7N 4°15W **11** D4
Carn Eige *U.K.* 57°17N 5°8W **11** D3
Carnamah *Australia* 29°41S 115°53E **61** E2
Carnarvon *Australia* 24°51S 113°42E **61** D1
Carnarvon *Canada* 45°3N 78°41W **82** A6
Carnarvon *S. Africa* 30°56S 22°8E **56** E3
Carnarvon △ *Australia* 24°54S 148°2E **62** C4
Carnarvon Ra. *Queens., Australia* 25°15S 148°30E **62** D4
Carnarvon Ra. *W. Austral., Australia* 25°20S 120°45E **61** E3
Carnation *U.S.A.* 47°39N 121°55W **78** C5
Carncastle *U.K.* 54°54N 5°53W **10** B6
Carndonagh *Ireland* 55°16N 7°15W **10** A4
Carnduff *Canada* 49°10N 101°50W **71** D8
Carnegie *U.S.A.* 40°24N 80°5W **82** F4
Carnegie, L. *Australia* 26°5S 122°30E **61** E3
Carnegie Ridge *Pac. Oc.* 1°0S 87°0W **65** H19
Carnic Alps = Karnische Alpen *Europe* 46°36N 13°0E **16** E7
Carniche Alpi = Karnische Alpen *Europe* 46°36N 13°0E **16** E7
Carnot *C.A.R.* 4°59N 15°56E **52** D3
Carnot, C. *Australia* 34°57S 135°38E **63** E2
Carnot B. *Australia* 17°20S 122°15E **60** C3
Carnoustie *U.K.* 56°30N 2°42W **11** E6
Carnsore Pt. *Ireland* 52°10N 6°22W **10** D5
Caro *U.S.A.* 43°29N 83°24W **81** D12
Caroga Lake *U.S.A.* 43°8N 74°28W **83** C10
Carol City *U.S.A.* 25°56N 80°14W **85** J14
Carolina *Brazil* 7°10S 47°30W **93** E9
Carolina *Puerto Rico* 18°23N 65°58W **89** d
Carolina *S. Africa* 26°5S 30°6E **57** D5
Caroline I. *Kiribati* 9°58S 150°13W **65** H12
Caroline Is. *Micronesia* 8°0N 150°0E **64** G6
Caroni *Trin. & Tob.* 10°34N 61°23W **93** K15
Caroní → *Venezuela* 8°21N 62°43W **92** B6
Caronie = Nébrodi, Monti *Italy* 37°54N 14°35E **22** F6
Caroona *Australia* 31°24S 150°26E **63** E5
Carpathians *Europe* 49°30N 21°0E **17** D11
Carpaţii Meridionali *Romania* 45°30N 25°0E **17** F13
Carpentaria, G. of *Australia* 14°0S 139°0E **62** A2
Carpentras *France* 44°3N 5°2E **20** D6
Carpi *Italy* 44°47N 10°53E **22** B4
Carpinteria *U.S.A.* 34°24N 119°31W **79** L7
Carr Boyd Ra. *Australia* 16°15S 128°35E **60** C4
Carra, L. *Ireland* 53°41N 9°14W **10** C2
Carrabelle *U.S.A.* 29°51N 84°40W **85** G12
Carranza, Presa V. *Mexico* 27°20N 100°50W **86** B4
Carrara *Italy* 44°5N 10°6E **20** D9
Carrauntoohill *Ireland* 52°0N 9°45W **10** D2
Carrick-on-Shannon *Ireland* 53°57N 8°5W **10** C3
Carrick-on-Suir *Ireland* 52°21N 7°24W **10** D4
Carrickfergus *U.K.* 54°43N 5°49W **10** B6
Carrickmacross *Ireland* 53°59N 6°43W **10** C5
Carrieton *Australia* 32°25S 138°31E **63** E2
Carrillo *Mexico* 26°54N 103°55W **86** B4
Carrington *U.S.A.* 47°27N 99°8W **80** B4
Carrizal Bajo *Chile* 28°5S 71°20W **94** B1
Carrizalillo *Chile* 29°5S 71°30W **94** B1
Carrizo Cr. → *U.S.A.* 36°55N 103°55W **77** H12
Carrizo Plain ⌓ *U.S.A.* 35°11N 119°47W **78** K7
Carrizo Springs *U.S.A.* 28°31N 99°52W **84** G5
Carrizozo *U.S.A.* 33°38N 105°53W **77** K11
Carroll *U.S.A.* 42°4N 94°52W **80** D6
Carrollton *Ga., U.S.A.* 33°35N 85°5W **85** E12
Carrollton *Ill., U.S.A.* 39°18N 90°24W **80** F8
Carrollton *Ky., U.S.A.* 38°41N 85°11W **81** F11
Carrollton *Mo., U.S.A.* 39°22N 93°30W **80** F7
Carrollton *Ohio, U.S.A.* 40°34N 81°5W **82** F3
Carron → *U.K.* 57°53N 4°22W **11** D4
Carron, L. *U.K.* 57°22N 5°35W **11** D3
Carrot → *Canada* 53°50N 101°17W **71** C8
Carrot River *Canada* 53°17N 103°35W **71** C8
Carruthers *Canada* 52°52N 109°16W **71** C7
Carson *Calif., U.S.A.* 33°49N 118°16W **79** M8
Carson *N. Dak., U.S.A.* 46°25N 101°34W **80** B3
Carson → *U.S.A.* 39°45N 118°40W **78** F8
Carson City *U.S.A.* 39°10N 119°46W **78** F7
Carson Sink *U.S.A.* 39°50N 118°25W **76** G4
Cartagena *Colombia* 10°25N 75°33W **92** A3
Cartagena *Spain* 37°38N 0°59W **21** D5
Cartago *Colombia* 4°45N 75°55W **92** C3
Cartago *Costa Rica* 9°50N 83°55W **88** E3
Cartersville *U.S.A.* 34°10N 84°48W **85** D12
Carterton *N.Z.* 41°2S 175°31E **59** D5
Carthage *Tunisia* 36°52N 10°20E **22** F4
Carthage *Ill., U.S.A.* 40°25N 91°8W **80** E8
Carthage *Mo., U.S.A.* 37°11N 94°19W **80** G6
Carthage *N.Y., U.S.A.* 43°59N 75°37W **81** D16
Carthage *Tex., U.S.A.* 32°9N 94°20W **84** E7
Cartier I. *Australia* 12°31S 123°29E **60** B3
Cartwright *Canada* 53°41N 56°58W **73** B8
Caruaru *Brazil* 8°15S 35°55W **93** E11
Carúpano *Venezuela* 10°39N 63°15W **92** A6
Caruthersville *U.S.A.* 36°11N 89°39W **80** G9
Carvoeiro *Brazil* 1°30S 61°59W **92** D6
Carvoeiro, C. *Portugal* 39°21N 9°24W **21** C1
Cary *U.S.A.* 35°47N 78°46W **85** D15
Casa de Piedra *Argentina* 38°5S 67°28W **94** D2
Casa de Piedra, Embalse *Argentina* 38°5S 67°32W **94** D2
Casa Grande *U.S.A.* 32°53N 111°45W **77** K8
Casa Nova *Brazil* 9°25S 41°5W **93** E10
Casablanca *Chile* 33°20S 71°25W **94** C1
Casablanca *Morocco* 33°36N 7°36W **50** B4
Cascada de Basaseachic △ *Mexico* 28°9N 108°15W **86** B3
Cascade *Seychelles* 4°39S 55°29E **53** b
Cascade *Idaho, U.S.A.* 44°31N 116°2W **76** D5
Cascade *Mont., U.S.A.* 47°16N 111°42W **76** C8
Cascade Locks *U.S.A.* 45°40N 121°54W **78** E5
Cascade Ra. *U.S.A.* 47°0N 121°30W **78** D5
Cascade Res. *U.S.A.* 44°32N 116°3W **76** D5
Cascades, Pte. des *Réunion* 21°9S 55°51E **53** c
Cascais *Portugal* 38°41N 9°25W **21** C1
Cascavel *Brazil* 24°57S 53°28W **95** A5
Cáscina *Italy* 43°41N 10°33E **22** C4
Casco B. *U.S.A.* 43°45N 70°0W **81** D19
Caserta *Italy* 41°4N 14°20E **22** D6
Casey *Antarctica* 66°0S 76°0E **5** C8
Caseyr, Raas = Asir, Ras *Somali Rep.* 11°55N 51°10E **47** E5
Cashel *Ireland* 52°30N 7°53W **10** D4
Casiguran *Phil.* 16°22N 122°7E **37** A6
Casilda *Argentina* 33°10S 61°10W **94** C3
Casino *Australia* 28°52S 153°3E **63** D5
Casiquiare → *Venezuela* 2°1N 67°7W **92** C5
Casma *Peru* 9°30S 78°20W **92** E3
Casmalia *U.S.A.* 34°50N 120°32W **79** L6
Caspe *Spain* 41°14N 0°1W **21** B5
Casper *U.S.A.* 42°51N 106°19W **76** E10
Caspian Depression *Eurasia* 47°0N 48°0E **19** E8
Caspian Sea *Eurasia* 43°0N 50°0E **19** F9
Cass City *U.S.A.* 43°36N 83°10W **82** C1
Cass Lake *U.S.A.* 47°23N 94°37W **80** B6
Cassadaga *U.S.A.* 42°20N 79°19W **82** D5
Casselman *Canada* 45°19N 75°5W **83** A9
Casselton *U.S.A.* 46°54N 97°13W **80** B5
Cassiar Mts. *Canada* 59°30N 130°30W **70** B2
Cassino *Italy* 41°30N 13°49E **22** D5
Cassville *U.S.A.* 36°41N 93°52W **80** G7
Castaic *U.S.A.* 34°30N 118°38W **79** L8
Castalia *U.S.A.* 41°24N 82°49W **82** E2
Castanhal *Brazil* 1°18S 47°55W **93** D9
Castara *Trin. & Tob.* 11°17N 60°42W **93** J16
Castellammare di Stábia *Italy* 40°42N 14°29E **22** D6
Castelli *Argentina* 36°7S 57°47W **94** D4
Castelló de la Plana *Spain* 39°58N 0°3W **21** C5
Castelo *Brazil* 20°33S 41°14W **95** A7
Castelo Branco *Portugal* 39°50N 7°31W **21** C2
Castelsarrasin *France* 44°2N 1°7E **20** E4
Castelvetrano *Italy* 37°41N 12°47E **22** F5
Casterton *Australia* 37°30S 141°30E **63** F3
Castile *U.S.A.* 42°38N 78°3W **82** D6
Castilla-La Mancha ☐ *Spain* 39°30N 3°30W **21** C4
Castilla y Leon ☐ *Spain* 42°0N 5°0W **21** B3
Castillos *Uruguay* 34°12S 53°52W **95** C5
Castle Dale *U.S.A.* 39°13N 111°1W **76** G8
Castle Douglas *U.K.* 54°56N 3°56W **11** G5
Castle Rock *Colo., U.S.A.* 39°22N 104°51W **76** G11
Castle Rock *Wash., U.S.A.* 46°17N 122°54W **78** D4
Castlebar *Ireland* 53°52N 9°18W **10** C2
Castlebay *U.K.* 56°57N 7°31W **11** E1
Castleblaney *Ireland* 54°7N 6°44W **10** B5
Castlederg *U.K.* 54°42N 7°35W **10** B4
Castleford *U.K.* 53°43N 1°21W **12** D6
Castlegar *Canada* 49°20N 117°40W **70** D5
Castlemaine *Australia* 37°2S 144°12E **63** F3
Castlemaine *Ireland* 52°10N 9°42W **10** D2
Castlepollard *Ireland* 53°41N 7°19W **10** C4
Castlerea *Ireland* 53°46N 8°29W **10** C3
Castlereagh → *Australia* 30°12S 147°32E **63** E4
Castlereagh B. *Australia* 12°10S 135°10E **62** A2
Castleton *U.S.A.* 43°37N 73°11W **83** C11
Castleton-on-Hudson *U.S.A.* 42°31N 73°45W **83** D11
Castletown *I. of Man* 54°5N 4°38W **12** C3
Castletown Bearhaven *Ireland* 51°39N 9°55W **10** E2
Castor *Canada* 52°15N 111°50W **70** C6
Castor → *Canada* 53°24N 78°58W **72** B4
Castorland *U.S.A.* 43°53N 75°31W **83** C9
Castres *France* 43°37N 2°13E **20** E5
Castricum *Neths.* 52°33N 4°40E **15** B4
Castries *St. Lucia* 14°2N 60°58W **89** f
Castro *Brazil* 24°45S 50°0W **95** A6
Castro *Chile* 42°30S 73°50W **96** E2
Castro Alves *Brazil* 12°46S 39°33W **93** F11
Castro Valley *U.S.A.* 37°41N 122°5W **78** H4
Castroville *U.S.A.* 36°46N 121°45W **78** J5
Castuera *Spain* 38°43N 5°37W **21** C3
Cat Ba, Dao *Vietnam* 20°50N 107°0E **38** B6
Cat Ba △ *Vietnam* 20°47N 107°3E **38** B6
Cat I. *Bahamas* 24°30N 75°30W **89** B4
Cat L. *Canada* 51°40N 91°50W **72** B1
Cat Lake *Canada* 51°40N 91°50W **72** B1
Cat Tien △ *Vietnam* 11°25N 107°17E **39** G6
Catacamas *Honduras* 14°54N 85°56W **88** D2
Cataguases *Brazil* 21°23S 42°39W **95** A7
Catalão *Brazil* 18°10S 47°57W **93** G9
Çatalca *Turkey* 41°8N 28°27E **23** D13
Catalina *Canada* 48°31N 53°4W **73** C9
Catalina *Chile* 25°13S 69°43W **94** B2
Catalina *U.S.A.* 32°30N 110°50W **77** K8
Catalonia = Cataluña ☐ *Spain* 41°40N 1°15E **21** B6
Cataluña ☐ *Spain* 41°40N 1°15E **21** B6
Catamarca *Argentina* 28°30S 65°50W **94** B2
Catamarca ☐ *Argentina* 27°0S 65°50W **94** B2
Catanduanes ☐ *Phil.* 13°50N 124°20E **37** B6
Catanduva *Brazil* 21°5S 48°58W **95** A6
Catánia *Italy* 37°30N 15°6E **22** F6
Catanzaro *Italy* 38°54N 16°35E **22** E7
Catarman *Phil.* 12°28N 124°35E **37** B6
Catatumbo-Bari △ *Colombia* 9°3N 73°12W **89** E5
Catchacoma *Canada* 44°44N 78°19W **82** B6
Cateel *Phil.* 7°47N 126°24E **37** C7
Catembe *Mozam.* 26°0S 32°33E **57** D5
Caterham *U.K.* 51°15N 0°4W **13** F7
Cathcart *S. Africa* 32°18S 27°10E **56** E4
Cathedral City *U.S.A.* 33°47N 116°28W **79** M10
Cathlamet *U.S.A.* 46°12N 123°23W **78** D3
Catlettsburg *U.S.A.* 38°25N 82°36W **81** F12
Catoche, C. *Mexico* 21°35N 87°5W **87** C7
Catriló *Argentina* 36°26S 63°24W **94** D3
Catrimani *Brazil* 0°27N 61°41W **92** C6
Catrimani → *Brazil* 0°28N 61°44W **92** C6
Catskill *U.S.A.* 42°14N 73°52W **83** D11
Catskill △ *U.S.A.* 42°8N 74°39W **83** D10
Catskill Mts. *U.S.A.* 42°10N 74°25W **83** D10
Catt, Mt. *Australia* 13°49S 134°23E **62** A1
Cattaraugus *U.S.A.* 42°20N 78°52W **82** D6
Catterick *U.K.* 54°23N 1°37W **12** C6
Catuala *Angola* 16°25S 19°2E **56** B2
Catuane *Mozam.* 26°48S 32°18E **57** D5
Catur *Mozam.* 13°45S 35°30E **55** E4
Cauca → *Colombia* 8°54N 74°28W **92** B4
Caucaia *Brazil* 3°40S 38°35W **93** D11
Caucasus Mountains *Eurasia* 42°50N 44°0E **19** F7
Caucete *Argentina* 31°38S 68°20W **94** C2
Caungula *Angola* 8°26S 18°38E **52** F3
Cauquenes *Chile* 36°0S 72°22W **94** D1
Caura → *Venezuela* 7°38N 64°53W **92** B6
Cauresi → *Mozam.* 17°8S 33°0E **55** F3
Causapscal *Canada* 48°19N 67°12W **73** C6
Cauvery → *India* 11°9N 78°52E **40** P11
Caux, Pays de *France* 49°38N 0°35E **20** B4
Cavalier *U.S.A.* 48°48N 97°37W **80** A5
Cavan *Ireland* 54°0N 7°22W **10** B4
Cavan ☐ *Ireland* 54°1N 7°16W **10** C4
Cave Creek *U.S.A.* 33°50N 111°57W **77** K8
Cavenagh Ra. *Australia* 26°12S 127°55E **61** E4
Cavendish *Australia* 37°31S 142°2E **63** F3
Caviana, I. *Brazil* 0°10N 50°10W **93** C8
Cavite *Phil.* 14°29N 120°54E **37** B6
Cawndilla L. *Australia* 32°30S 142°15E **63** E3
Cawnpore = Kanpur *India* 26°28N 80°20E **43** F9
Caxias *Brazil* 4°55S 43°20W **93** D10
Caxias do Sul *Brazil* 29°10S 51°10W **95** B5
Cay Sal Bank *Bahamas* 23°45N 80°0W **88** B4
Cayambe *Ecuador* 0°3N 78°8W **92** C3
Cayenne *Fr. Guiana* 5°5N 52°18W **93** B8
Cayey *Puerto Rico* 18°7N 66°10W **89** d
Cayman Brac *Cayman Is.* 19°43N 79°49W **88** C4
Cayman Is. ⊠ *W. Indies* 19°40N 80°30W **88** C3
Cayman Trough *Caribbean* 19°0N 81°0W **66** H11
Cayuga *Canada* 42°59N 79°50W **82** D5
Cayuga *U.S.A.* 42°54N 76°44W **83** D8
Cayuga Heights *U.S.A.* 42°27N 76°29W **83** D8
Cayuga L. *U.S.A.* 42°41N 76°41W **83** D8
Cazenovia *U.S.A.* 42°56N 75°51W **83** D9
Cazombo *Angola* 11°54S 22°56E **53** G4
Ceanannus Mor *Ireland* 53°44N 6°53W **10** C5
Ceará = Fortaleza *Brazil* 3°45S 38°35W **93** D11
Ceará ☐ *Brazil* 5°0S 40°0W **93** E11
Ceará-Mirim *Brazil* 5°38S 35°25W **93** E11
Cébaco, I. de *Panama* 7°33N 81°9W **88** E3
Cebollar *Argentina* 29°10S 66°35W **94** B2
Cebu *Phil.* 10°18N 123°54E **37** B6
Cecil Plains *Australia* 27°30S 151°11E **63** D5
Cedar → *U.S.A.* 41°17N 91°21W **80** E8
Cedar City *U.S.A.* 37°41N 113°4W **77** H7
Cedar Creek Res. *U.S.A.* 32°11N 96°4W **84** E6
Cedar Falls *Iowa, U.S.A.* 42°32N 92°27W **80** D7
Cedar Falls *Wash., U.S.A.* 47°25N 121°45W **78** C5
Cedar Key *U.S.A.* 29°8N 83°2W **85** G13
Cedar L. *Canada* 53°10N 100°0W **71** C9
Cedar Park *U.S.A.* 30°30N 97°49W **84** F6
Cedar Rapids *U.S.A.* 41°59N 91°40W **80** E8
Cedartown *U.S.A.* 34°1N 85°15W **85** D12
Cedarvale *Canada* 55°1N 128°22W **70** B3
Cedarville *S. Africa* 30°23S 29°3E **57** E4
Cedral *Mexico* 23°50N 100°45W **86** C4
Cedro *Brazil* 6°34S 39°3W **93** E11
Cedros, I. *Mexico* 28°12N 115°15W **86** B1
Cedros B. *Trin. & Tob.* 10°16N 61°54W **93** K15
Ceduna *Australia* 32°7S 133°46E **63** E1
Ceeldheere *Somali Rep.* 3°50N 47°8E **47** G4
Ceerigaabo *Somali Rep.* 10°35N 47°20E **47** E4
Cefalù *Italy* 38°2N 14°1E **22** E6
Cegléd *Hungary* 47°11N 19°47E **17** E10
Cekik *Indonesia* 8°12S 114°27E **37** J17
Celaque △ *Honduras* 14°30N 88°43W **88** D2
Celaya *Mexico* 20°31N 100°37W **86** C4
Celebes = Sulawesi *Indonesia* 2°0S 120°0E **37** E6
Celebes Sea *Indonesia* 3°0N 123°0E **37** D6
Celina *U.S.A.* 40°33N 84°35W **81** E11
Celje *Slovenia* 46°16N 15°18E **16** E8
Celle *Germany* 52°37N 10°4E **16** B6
Celtic Sea *Atl. Oc.* 50°9N 9°34W **14** F2
Cenderwasih, Teluk *Indonesia* 3°0S 135°20E **37** E9
Center *N. Dak., U.S.A.* 47°7N 101°18W **80** B3
Center *Tex., U.S.A.* 31°48N 94°11W **84** F7
Centerburg *U.S.A.* 40°18N 82°42W **82** F2
Centerville *Calif., U.S.A.* 36°44N 119°30W **78** J7
Centerville *Iowa, U.S.A.* 40°44N 92°52W **80** E7
Centerville *Pa., U.S.A.* 40°3N 79°59W **82** F5
Centerville *Tenn., U.S.A.* 35°47N 87°28W **85** D11
Centerville *Tex., U.S.A.* 31°16N 95°59W **84** F7
Central = Tsentralnyy ☐ *Russia* 52°0N 40°0E **28** D4
Central ☐ *Kenya* 0°30S 37°30E **54** C4
Central ☐ *Malawi* 13°30S 33°30E **55** E3
Central ☐ *Zambia* 14°25S 28°50E **55** E2
Central, Cordillera *Colombia* 5°0N 75°0W **92** C4
Central, Cordillera *Costa Rica* 10°10N 84°5W **88** D3
Central, Cordillera *Dom. Rep.* 19°15N 71°0W **89** C5
Central, Cordillera *Puerto Rico* 18°8N 66°35W **89** d
Central African Rep. ■ *Africa* 7°0N 20°0E **51** G9
Central America *America* 12°0N 85°0W **66** H11
Central Butte *Canada* 50°48N 106°31W **71** C7
Central City *Colo., U.S.A.* 39°48N 105°31W **76** G11
Central City *Ky., U.S.A.* 37°18N 87°7W **80** G10
Central City *Nebr., U.S.A.* 41°7N 98°0W **80** E4
Central I. *Kenya* 3°30N 36°0E **54** B4
Central Island △ *Kenya* 2°33N 36°1E **54** B4
Central Kalahari ⌓ *Botswana* 22°36S 23°58E **56** C3
Central Makran Range *Pakistan* 26°30N 64°15E **40** F4
Central Pacific Basin *Pac. Oc.* 8°0N 175°0W **64** G10
Central Patricia *Canada* 51°30N 90°9W **72** B1
Central Point *U.S.A.* 42°23N 122°55W **76** E2
Central Russian Uplands *Europe* 54°0N 36°0E **6** E13
Central Siberian Plateau *Russia* 65°0N 105°0E **26** B12
Central Square *U.S.A.* 43°17N 76°9W **83** C8
Centralia *Canada* 43°17N 81°28W **82** C3
Centralia *Ill., U.S.A.* 38°32N 89°8W **80** F9
Centralia *Mo., U.S.A.* 39°13N 92°8W **80** F7
Centralia *Wash., U.S.A.* 46°43N 122°58W **78** D4
Centre de Flacq *Mauritius* 20°12S 57°43E **53** d
Centreville *N.Y., U.S.A.* 42°28N 78°14W **82** D6
Centreville *Pa., U.S.A.* 41°44N 79°45W **82** E5
Cephalonia = Kefalonia *Greece* 38°15N 20°30E **23** E9
Cepu *Indonesia* 7°9S 111°35E **37** G14
Ceram = Seram *Indonesia* 3°10S 129°0E **37** E7
Ceram Sea = Seram Sea *Indonesia* 2°30S 128°30E **37** E7
Ceredigion ☐ *U.K.* 52°16N 4°15W **13** E3
Ceres *Argentina* 29°55S 61°55W **94** B3
Ceres *S. Africa* 33°21S 19°18E **56** E2
Ceres *U.S.A.* 37°35N 120°57W **78** H6
Cerf *Seychelles* 4°38S 55°40E **53** b
Cerignola *Italy* 41°17N 15°53E **22** D6
Cerigo = Kythira *Greece* 36°8N 23°0E **23** F10
Çerkezköy *Turkey* 41°17N 28°0E **23** D12
Cerralvo, I. *Mexico* 24°15N 109°55W **86** C3
Cerritos *Mexico* 22°25N 100°16W **86** C4
Cerro Chato *Uruguay* 33°6S 55°8W **95** C4
Cerro Cofre de Perote △ *Mexico* 19°29N 97°8W **87** D5
Cerro Corá △ *Paraguay* 22°35S 56°2W **95** A4
Cerro el Copey △ *Venezuela* 10°59N 63°53W **89** D7
Cerro Hoya △ *Panama* 7°17N 80°45W **88** E3
Cerro Saroche △ *Venezuela* 10°8N 69°38W **89** D6
Cervantes *Australia* 30°31S 115°3E **61** F2
Cervera *Spain* 41°40N 1°16E **21** B6
Cesena *Italy* 44°8N 12°15E **22** B5
Cēsis *Latvia* 57°18N 25°15E **9** H21
Česká Rep. = Czech Rep. ■ *Europe* 50°0N 15°0E **16** D8
České Budějovice *Czech Rep.* 48°55N 14°25E **16** D8
Českomoravská Vrchovina *Czech Rep.* 49°30N 15°40E **16** D8
Çeşme *Turkey* 38°20N 26°23E **23** E12
Cessnock *Australia* 32°50S 151°21E **63** E5
Cetinje *Montenegro* 42°23N 18°59E **23** C8
Cetraro *Italy* 39°31N 15°55E **22** E6
Ceuta *N. Afr.* 35°52N 5°18W **21** E3
Cévennes *France* 44°10N 3°50E **20** D5
Ceyhan *Turkey* 37°4N 35°47E **44** B2
Ceylanpınar *Turkey* 36°50N 40°2E **44** B4
Ceylon = Sri Lanka ■ *Asia* 7°30N 80°50E **40** R12
Cha-am *Thailand* 12°48N 99°58E **38** F2
Chacabuco *Argentina* 34°40S 60°27W **94** C3
Chachapoyas *Peru* 6°15S 77°50W **92** E3
Chachoengsao *Thailand* 13°42N 101°5E **38** F3
Chachran *Pakistan* 28°55N 70°30E **42** E4
Chachro *Pakistan* 25°5N 70°15E **42** G4
Chaco ☐ *Argentina* 26°30S 61°0W **94** B3
Chaco ☐ *Paraguay* 26°0S 60°0W **94** B4
Chaco → *U.S.A.* 36°46N 108°39W **77** H9
Chaco △ *Argentina* 27°0S 59°30W **94** B4
Chaco Austral *S. Amer.* 27°0S 61°30W **96** B4
Chaco Boreal *S. Amer.* 22°0S 60°0W **92** H6
Chaco Central *S. Amer.* 24°0S 61°0W **96** A4
Chaco Culture ⌓ *U.S.A.* 36°3N 107°58W **77** H10
Chacon, C. *U.S.A.* 54°42N 132°0W **70** C2
Chad ■ *Africa* 15°0N 17°15E **51** F8
Chad, L. = Tchad, L. *Chad* 13°30N 14°30E **51** F8
Chadileuvú → *Argentina* 37°46S 66°0W **94** D2
Chadiza *Zambia* 14°45S 32°27E **55** E3
Chadron *U.S.A.* 42°50N 103°0W **80** D2
Chadyr-Lunga = Ciadâr-Lunga *Moldova* 46°3N 28°51E **17** E15
Chae Hom *Thailand* 18°43N 99°35E **38** C2
Chae Son △ *Thailand* 18°42N 99°20E **38** C2
Chaem → *Thailand* 18°11N 98°38E **38** C2
Chaeryŏng *N. Korea* 38°24N 125°36E **35** E13
Chagai Hills = Chāh Gay Hills *Afghan.* 29°30N 64°0E **40** E3
Chagda *Russia* 58°45N 130°38E **29** D14
Chaghcharān *Afghan.* 34°31N 65°15E **40** B4
Chagos Arch. ⊠ *Ind. Oc.* 6°0S 72°0E **26** J9
Chagres △ *Panama* 9°33N 79°37W **88** E4
Chaguanas *Trin. & Tob.* 10°30N 61°26W **93** K15
Chāh Ākhvor *Iran* 32°41N 59°40E **45** C8
Chāh Bahar *Iran* 25°20N 60°40E **45** E9
Chāh-e Kavīr *Iran* 34°29N 56°52E **45** C8
Chāh Gay Hills *Afghan.* 29°30N 64°0E **40** E3
Chahār Borjak *Afghan.* 30°17N 62°3E **40** D3
Chahār Mahāll va Bakhtīarī ☐ *Iran* 32°0N 49°0E **45** C6
Chai Badan *Thailand* 15°12N 101°8E **38** E3
Chai Wan *China* 22°16N 114°14E **33** G11
Chaibasa *India* 22°42N 85°49E **43** H11
Chainat *Thailand* 15°11N 100°8E **38** E3
Chaiya *Thailand* 9°23N 99°14E **39** H2
Chaiyaphum *Thailand* 15°48N 102°2E **38** E4
Chaj Doab *Pakistan* 32°15N 73°0E **42** C5
Chajari *Argentina* 30°42S 58°0W **94** C4
Chak Amru *Pakistan* 32°22N 75°11E **42** C6

Chakar ➤ Pakistan 29°29N 68°2E **42 E3**
Chakari Zimbabwe 18°5S 29°51E **57 B4**
Chake Chake Tanzania 5°15S 39°45E **54 D4**
Chakhānsūr Afghan. 31°10N 62°0E **40 D3**
Chakonipau, L. Canada 56°18N 68°30W **73 A6**
Chakradharpur India 22°45N 85°40E **43 H11**
Chakrata India 30°42N 77°51E **42 D7**
Chakwal Pakistan 32°56N 72°53E **42 C5**
Chala Peru 15°48S 74°20W **92 G4**
Chalchihuites Mexico 23°29N 103°53W **86 C4**
Chalcis = Halkida
  Greece 38°27N 23°42E **23 E10**
Chaleur B. Canada 47°55N 65°30W **73 C6**
Chalfant U.S.A. 37°32N 118°21W **78 H8**
Chalhuanca Peru 14°15S 73°15W **92 F4**
Chalisgaon India 20°30N 75°10E **40 J9**
Chalk River Canada 46°1N 77°27W **72 C4**
Chalky Inlet N.Z. 46°3S 166°31E **59 G1**
Challapata Bolivia 18°53S 66°50W **92 G5**
Challenger Deep Pac. Oc. 11°30N 142°0E **64 F6**
Challenger Fracture Zone
  Pac. Oc. 35°0S 105°0W **65 L17**
Challis U.S.A. 44°30N 114°14W **76 D6**
Chalmette U.S.A. 29°56N 89°57W **85 G10**
Chalon-sur-Saône France 46°48N 4°50E **20 C6**
Chalong Thailand 7°50N 98°22E **39 a**
Châlons-en-Champagne
  France 48°58N 4°20E **20 B6**
Chálten, Cerro = Fitz Roy, Cerro
  Argentina 49°17S 73°5W **96 F2**
Chālūs Iran 36°38N 51°26E **45 B6**
Cham, Cu Lao Vietnam 15°57N 108°30E **38 E7**
Chama U.S.A. 36°54N 106°35W **77 H10**
Chamaicó Argentina 35°3S 64°58W **94 D3**
Chaman Pakistan 30°58N 66°25E **40 D5**
Chamba India 32°35N 76°10E **42 C7**
Chamba Tanzania 11°37S 37°0E **55 E4**
Chambal ➤ India 26°29N 79°15E **43 F8**
Chamberlain U.S.A. 43°49N 99°20W **80 D4**
Chamberlain ➤
  Australia 15°30S 127°54E **60 C4**
Chamberlain L. U.S.A. 46°14N 69°19W **81 B19**
Chambers U.S.A. 35°11N 109°26W **77 J9**
Chambersburg U.S.A. 39°56N 77°40W **81 F15**
Chambéry France 45°34N 5°55E **20 D6**
Chambeshi ➤ Zambia 11°53S 29°48E **52 G6**
Chambly Canada 45°27N 73°17W **83 A11**
Chambord Canada 48°25N 72°6W **73 C5**
Chamchamal Iraq 35°32N 44°50E **44 C5**
Chamela Mexico 19°32N 105°5W **86 D3**
Chamical Argentina 30°22S 66°27W **94 C2**
Chamkar Luong
  Cambodia 11°0N 103°45E **39 G4**
Chamoli India 30°24N 79°21E **43 D8**
Chamonix-Mont Blanc
  France 45°55N 6°51E **20 D7**
Chamouchouane =
  Ashuapmushuan ➤
  Canada 48°37N 72°20W **72 C5**
Champa India 22°2N 82°43E **43 H10**
Champagne Canada 60°49N 136°30W **70 A1**
Champagne France 48°40N 4°20E **20 B6**
Champaign U.S.A. 40°7N 88°15W **80 E9**
Champassak Laos 14°53N 105°52E **38 E5**
Champawat India 29°20N 80°6E **43 E9**
Champdoré, L. Canada 55°55N 65°49W **73 A6**
Champion U.S.A. 41°19N 80°51W **82 E4**
Champlain U.S.A. 44°59N 73°27W **83 B11**
Champlain, L. U.S.A. 44°40N 73°20W **83 B11**
Champotón Mexico 19°21N 90°43W **87 D6**
Champua India 22°5N 85°40E **43 H11**
Chana Thailand 6°55N 100°44E **39 J3**
Chañaral Chile 26°23S 70°40W **94 B1**
Chanārān Iran 36°39N 59°6E **45 B8**
Chanasma India 23°44N 72°5E **42 H5**
Chancery Lane Barbados 13°3N 59°30W **89 g**
Chanco Chile 35°44S 72°32W **94 D1**
Chand India 21°57N 79°7E **43 J8**
Chandan India 24°38N 86°40E **43 G12**
Chandan Chauki India 28°33N 80°47E **43 E9**
Chandannagar India 22°52N 88°24E **43 H13**
Chandausi India 28°27N 78°49E **43 E8**
Chandeleur Is. U.S.A. 29°55N 88°57W **85 G10**
Chandeleur Sd. U.S.A. 29°55N 89°0W **85 G10**
Chandigarh India 30°43N 76°47E **42 D7**
Chandil India 22°58N 86°3E **43 H12**
Chandler Australia 27°0S 133°19E **63 D1**
Chandler Canada 48°18N 64°46W **73 C7**
Chandler Ariz., U.S.A. 33°18N 111°50W **77 K8**
Chandler Okla., U.S.A. 35°42N 96°53W **84 D6**
Chandod India 21°59N 73°28E **42 J5**
Chandpur Bangla. 23°8N 90°45E **41 H17**
Chandrapur India 19°57N 79°25E **40 K11**
Chānf Iran 26°38N 60°29E **45 E9**
Chang Pakistan 26°59N 68°30E **42 F3**
Chang, Ko Thailand 12°0N 102°23E **39 G4**
Ch'ang Chiang = Chang Jiang ➤
  China 31°48N 121°10E **33 C7**
Chang Jiang ➤ China 31°48N 121°10E **33 C7**
Chang-won S. Korea 35°16N 128°37E **35 G15**
Changa India 33°53N 77°35E **43 C7**
Changan China 22°22N 113°48E **33 C7**
Changanacheri India 9°25N 76°31E **40 Q10**
Changane ➤ Mozam. 24°30S 33°30E **57 C5**
Changbai China 41°25N 128°5E **35 D15**
Changbai Shan China 42°20N 129°0E **35 C15**
Changchiak'ou = Zhangjiakou
  China 40°48N 114°55E **34 D8**
Ch'angchou = Changzhou
  China 31°47N 119°58E **33 C6**
Changchun China 43°57N 125°17E **35 C13**
Changchunling China 45°18N 125°27E **35 B13**
Changde China 29°4N 111°35E **33 D6**
Changdo-ri N. Korea 38°30N 127°40E **35 E14**
Changhai = Shanghai
  China 31°15N 121°26E **33 C7**
Changhua Taiwan 24°2N 120°30E **33 D7**

Changhǔngni
  N. Korea 40°24N 128°19E **35 D15**
Changi Singapore 1°23N 103°59E **39 d**
Changi, Singapore ✈ (SIN)
  Singapore 1°23N 103°59E **39 M4**
Changji China 44°1N 87°19E **32 B3**
Changjiang China 19°20N 108°55E **38 C7**
Changjiang Shuiku
  China 22°29N 113°27E **33 G10**
Changjin N. Korea 40°23N 127°15E **35 D14**
Changjin-ho N. Korea 40°30N 127°15E **35 D14**
Changli China 39°40N 119°13E **35 E10**
Changling China 44°20N 123°58E **35 B12**
Changlun Malaysia 6°25N 100°26E **39 J3**
Changping China 40°14N 116°12E **34 D9**
Changsha China 28°12N 113°0E **33 D6**
Changshan Qundao
  China 39°11N 122°32E **35 E12**
Changtai China 25°10N 107°45E **34 G4**
Changuinola Panama 9°26N 82°31W **88 E3**
Changwu China 35°10N 107°45E **34 G4**
Changyi China 36°40N 119°30E **35 F10**
Changyŏn N. Korea 38°15N 125°6E **35 E13**
Changyuan China 35°15N 114°42E **34 G8**
Changzhi China 36°10N 113°6E **34 F7**
Changzhou China 31°47N 119°58E **33 C6**
Chanhanga Angola 16°0S 14°8E **56 B1**
Chania Greece 35°30N 24°4E **25 D6**
Chania □ Greece 35°30N 24°0E **25 D6**
Chanion, Kolpos Greece 35°33N 23°55E **25 D5**
Channapatna India 12°40N 77°15E **40 N10**
Channel Is. U.K. 49°19N 2°24W **13 H5**
Channel Is. U.S.A. 33°40N 119°15W **79 M7**
Channel Islands △
  U.S.A. 34°0N 119°24W **79 L7**
Channel-Port aux Basques
  Canada 47°30N 59°9W **73 C8**
Channel Tunnel Europe 51°0N 1°30E **13 F9**
Channing U.S.A. 35°41N 102°20W **84 D3**
Chantada Spain 42°36N 7°46W **21 A2**
Chanthaburi Thailand 12°38N 102°12E **38 F4**
Chantrey Inlet Canada 67°48N 96°20W **68 C10**
Chanute U.S.A. 37°41N 95°27W **80 G6**
Chao Phraya ➤
  Thailand 13°40N 100°31E **38 F3**
Chao Phraya Lowlands
  Thailand 15°30N 100°0E **38 E3**
Chaocheng China 36°4N 115°37E **34 F8**
Chaoyang China 41°35N 120°22E **35 D11**
Chaozhou China 23°42N 116°32E **33 D6**
Chapaev Kazakhstan 50°25N 51°10E **19 D9**
Chapais Canada 49°47N 74°51W **72 C5**
Chapala Mozam. 15°50S 37°35E **55 F4**
Chapala, L. de Mexico 20°15N 103°0W **86 C4**
Chapayevsk Russia 53°0N 49°40E **18 D8**
Chapecó Brazil 27°14S 52°41W **95 B5**
Chapel Hill U.S.A. 35°55N 79°4W **85 D15**
Chapleau Canada 47°50N 83°24W **72 C3**
Chaplin Canada 50°28N 106°40W **71 C7**
Chaplin L. Canada 50°22N 106°36W **71 C7**
Chappell U.S.A. 41°6N 102°28W **80 E2**
Chapra = Chhapra
  India 25°48N 84°44E **43 G11**
Chara Russia 56°54N 118°20E **29 D12**
Charadai Argentina 27°35S 59°55W **94 B4**
Charagua Bolivia 19°45S 63°10W **92 G6**
Charakas Greece 35°1N 25°7E **25 D7**
Charambirá, Punta
  Colombia 4°16N 77°32W **92 C3**
Charaña Bolivia 17°30S 69°25W **92 G5**
Charanwala India 27°51N 72°10E **42 F5**
Charata Argentina 27°13S 61°14W **94 B3**
Charcas Mexico 23°8N 101°7W **86 C4**
Charcot I. Antarctica 70°0S 70°0W **5 C17**
Chard U.K. 50°52N 2°58W **13 G5**
Chardon U.S.A. 41°35N 81°12W **82 E3**
Chardzhou = Türkmenabat
  Turkmenistan 39°6N 63°34E **45 B9**
Charente ➤ France 45°57N 1°5W **20 D3**
Chari ➤ Chad 12°58N 14°31E **51 F8**
Chārīkār Afghan. 35°0N 69°10E **40 B6**
Chariton U.S.A. 41°1N 93°19W **80 E7**
Chariton ➤ U.S.A. 39°19N 92°58W **80 F7**
Chärjew = Türkmenabat
  Turkmenistan 39°6N 63°34E **45 B9**
Charkhari India 25°24N 79°45E **43 G8**
Charkhi Dadri India 28°37N 76°17E **42 E7**
Charleroi Belgium 50°24N 4°27E **15 D4**
Charleroi U.S.A. 40°9N 79°57W **82 F5**
Charles, C. U.S.A. 37°7N 75°58W **81 G16**
Charles, Peak Australia 32°52S 121°11E **61 F3**
Charles City U.S.A. 43°4N 92°41W **80 D7**
Charles L. Canada 59°50N 110°33W **71 B6**
Charles Town U.S.A. 39°17N 77°52W **81 F15**
Charlesbourg Canada 46°51N 71°16W **81 B18**
Charleston Ill., U.S.A. 39°30N 88°10W **80 F1**
Charleston Miss., U.S.A. 34°1N 90°4W **85 D9**
Charleston Mo., U.S.A. 36°55N 89°21W **80 G9**
Charleston S.C., U.S.A. 32°46N 79°56W **85 E15**
Charleston W. Va.,
  U.S.A. 38°21N 81°38W **81 F13**
Charleston L. Canada 44°32N 76°0W **83 B9**
Charleston Peak
  U.S.A. 36°16N 115°42W **79 J11**
Charlestown Ireland 53°58N 8°48W **10 C3**
Charlestown S. Africa 27°26S 29°53E **57 D4**
Charlestown Ind.,
  U.S.A. 38°27N 85°40W **81 F11**
Charlestown N.H.,
  U.S.A. 43°14N 72°25W **83 C12**
Charlestown of Aberlour
  U.K. 57°28N 3°14W **11 D5**
Charleville = Rath Luirc
  Ireland 52°21N 8°40W **10 D3**
Charleville Australia 26°24S 146°15E **63 D4**
Charleville-Mézières
  France 49°44N 4°40E **20 B6**
Charlevoix U.S.A. 45°19N 85°16W **81 C11**

Charlotte Mich., U.S.A. 42°34N 84°50W **81 D11**
Charlotte N.C., U.S.A. 35°13N 80°50W **85 D14**
Charlotte Vt., U.S.A. 44°19N 73°16W **83 B11**
Charlotte Amalie
  U.S. Virgin Is. 18°21N 64°56W **89 e**
Charlotte Harbor U.S.A. 26°57N 82°4W **85 H13**
Charlotte L. Canada 52°12N 125°19W **70 C3**
Charlottesville U.S.A. 38°2N 78°30W **81 F14**
Charlottetown Nfld. & L.,
  Canada 52°46N 56°7W **73 B8**
Charlottetown P.E.I.,
  Canada 46°14N 63°8W **73 C7**
Charlotteville
  Trin. & Tob. 11°20N 60°33W **93 J16**
Charlton Australia 36°16S 143°24E **63 F3**
Charlton I. Canada 52°0N 79°20W **72 B4**
Charny Canada 46°43N 71°15W **73 C5**
Charolles France 46°27N 4°16E **20 C6**
Charre Mozam. 17°13S 35°10E **55 F4**
Charsadda Pakistan 34°7N 71°45E **42 B4**
Charters Towers
  Australia 20°5S 146°13E **62 C4**
Chartres France 48°29N 1°30E **20 B4**
Chascomús Argentina 35°30S 58°0W **94 D4**
Chase Canada 50°50N 119°41W **70 C5**
Chasefu Zambia 11°55S 33°8E **55 E3**
Chashma Barrage
  Pakistan 32°27N 71°20E **42 C4**
Chāt Iran 37°59N 55°16E **45 B7**
Chatangay U.S.A. 44°56N 74°5W **83 B10**
Château-Chinon France 47°4N 3°56E **20 C5**
Châteaubriant France 47°43N 1°23W **20 C3**
Châteauguay, L. Canada 56°26N 70°3W **73 A5**
Châteaulin France 48°11N 4°8W **20 B1**
Châteauroux France 46°50N 1°40E **20 C4**
Châteaux, Pte. des
  Guadeloupe 16°15N 61°10W **88 b**
Châtellerault France 46°50N 0°30E **20 C4**
Chatham = Miramichi
  Canada 47°2N 65°28W **73 C6**
Chatham Canada 42°24N 82°11W **82 D2**
Chatham U.K. 51°22N 0°32E **13 F8**
Chatham U.S.A. 42°21N 73°36W **83 D11**
Chatham Is. Pac. Oc. 44°0S 176°40W **64 M10**
Chatham Rise Pac. Oc. 43°30S 180°0E **64 M10**
Chatmohar Bangla. 24°15N 89°15E **43 G13**
Chatra India 24°12N 84°56E **43 G11**
Chatrapur India 19°22N 85°2E **41 K14**
Chats, L. des Canada 45°30N 76°20W **83 A8**
Chatsu India 26°36N 75°57E **42 F6**
Chatsworth Canada 44°27N 80°54W **82 B4**
Chatsworth Zimbabwe 19°38S 31°13E **55 F3**
Chattagām = Chittagong
  Bangla. 22°19N 91°48E **41 H17**
Chattahoochee U.S.A. 30°42N 84°51W **85 F12**
Chattahoochee ➤
  U.S.A. 30°54N 84°57W **85 F12**
Chattanooga U.S.A. 35°3N 85°19W **85 D12**
Chatteris U.K. 52°28N 0°2E **13 E8**
Chau Doc Vietnam 10°42N 105°7E **39 G5**
Chaukan Pass Burma 27°8N 97°10E **41 F20**
Chaumont France 48°7N 5°8E **20 B6**
Chaumont U.S.A. 44°4N 76°8W **83 B8**
Chaunskaya G. Russia 69°0N 169°0E **29 C17**
Chautauqua L. U.S.A. 42°10N 79°24W **82 D5**
Chauvin Canada 52°45N 110°10W **71 C6**
Chaves Brazil 0°15S 49°55W **93 D9**
Chaves Portugal 41°45N 7°32W **21 B2**
Chawang Thailand 8°25N 99°30E **39 H2**
Chaykovskiy Russia 56°47N 54°9E **18 C9**
Chazy U.S.A. 44°53N 73°26W **83 B11**
Cheb Czech Rep. 50°9N 12°28E **16 C7**
Cheboksary Russia 56°8N 47°12E **18 C8**
Cheboygan U.S.A. 45°39N 84°29W **81 C11**
Chech, Erg Africa 25°0N 2°15W **50 D5**
Chechenia □ Russia 43°30N 45°29E **19 F8**
Chechen-Ingush Republic =
  Chechenia □ Russia 43°30N 45°29E **19 F8**
Chechnya = Chechenia □
  Russia 43°30N 45°29E **19 F8**
Checotah U.S.A. 35°28N 95°31W **84 D7**
Chedabucto B. Canada 45°25N 61°8W **73 C7**
Cheduba I. Burma 18°45N 93°40E **41 K18**
Cheepie Australia 26°33S 145°1E **63 D4**
Chegdomyn Russia 51°7N 133°1E **29 D14**
Chegga Mauritania 25°27N 5°40W **50 C4**
Chegutu Zimbabwe 18°10S 30°14E **55 F3**
Chehalis U.S.A. 46°40N 122°58W **78 D4**
Chehalis ➤ U.S.A. 46°57N 123°50W **78 D3**
Cheju = Jeju S. Korea 33°31N 126°32E **35 H14**
Cheju-do = Jeju-do
  S. Korea 33°29N 126°34E **35 H14**
Chekiang = Zhejiang □
  China 29°0N 120°0E **33 D7**
Chela, Sa. da Angola 16°20S 13°20E **56 B1**
Chelan U.S.A. 47°51N 120°1W **76 C3**
Chelan, L. U.S.A. 48°11N 120°30W **76 B3**
Cheleken = Hazar
  Turkmenistan 39°34N 53°16E **19 G9**
Cheleken Yarymadasy
  Turkmenistan 39°30N 53°15E **45 B7**
Chelforó Argentina 39°0S 66°33W **96 D3**
Chelkar = Shalqar
  Kazakhstan 47°48N 59°39E **28 E6**
Chelm Poland 51°8N 23°30E **17 C12**
Chelmno Poland 53°20N 18°30E **17 B10**
Chelmsford U.K. 51°44N 0°29E **13 F8**
Chelmža Poland 53°10N 18°39E **17 B10**
Chelsea Australia 38°5S 145°8E **63 F4**
Chelsea U.S.A. 43°59N 72°27W **83 C12**
Cheltenham U.K. 51°54N 2°4W **13 F5**
Chelyabinsk Russia 55°10N 61°24E **28 D7**
Chelyuskin, C. = Chelyuskin, Mys
  Russia 77°30N 103°0E **29 B11**
Chelyuskin, Mys Russia 77°30N 103°0E **29 B11**
Chemainus Canada 48°55N 123°42W **78 B3**
Chemba Mozam. 17°9S 34°53E **55 H6**

Chemin Grenier Mauritius 20°29S 57°28E **53 d**
Chemnitz Germany 50°51N 12°54E **16 C7**
Chemult U.S.A. 43°14N 121°47W **76 E3**
Chen, Gora Russia 65°16N 141°50E **29 C15**
Chenab ➤ Pakistan 30°23N 71°2E **42 D4**
Chenab Nagar Pakistan 31°45N 72°55E **42 D5**
Chenango Forks U.S.A. 42°15N 75°51W **83 D9**
Cheney U.S.A. 47°30N 117°35W **76 C5**
Chengcheng China 34°58N 109°58E **34 G5**
Chengchou = Zhengzhou
  China 34°45N 113°34E **34 G7**
Chengde China 40°59N 117°58E **35 D9**
Chengdu China 30°38N 104°2E **32 C5**
Chengele China 33°10N 107°21E **34 H4**
Chengjiang China 24°39N 103°0E **32 D5**
Chengmai China 19°50N 109°58E **38 C7**
Ch'engtu = Chengdu
  China 30°38N 104°2E **32 C5**
Chengwu China 34°58N 115°50E **34 G8**
Chengyang China 36°18N 120°21E **35 F11**
Chenjiagang China 34°23N 119°47E **35 G10**
Chennai India 13°8N 80°19E **40 N12**
Cheo, Eilean a' = Skye
  U.K. 57°15N 6°10W **11 D2**
Cheom Ksan Cambodia 14°13N 104°56E **38 E5**
Cheonan S. Korea 36°48N 127°9E **35 F14**
Cheongdo S. Korea 35°38N 128°42E **35 G15**
Cheongju S. Korea 36°39N 127°27E **35 F14**
Cheorwon S. Korea 38°15N 127°10E **35 E14**
Chepén Peru 7°15S 79°23W **92 E3**
Chepes Argentina 31°20S 66°35W **94 C2**
Chepo Panama 9°10N 79°6W **88 E4**
Chepstow U.K. 51°38N 2°41W **13 F5**
Chequamegon B. U.S.A. 46°39N 90°51W **80 B8**
Cher ➤ France 47°21N 0°29E **20 C4**
Cheraw U.S.A. 34°42N 79°53W **85 D15**
Cherbourg France 49°39N 1°40W **20 B3**
Cherdyn Russia 60°24N 56°29E **18 B10**
Cheremkhovo Russia 53°8N 103°1E **29 D11**
Cherepovets Russia 59°5N 37°55E **18 C6**
Chergui, Chott ech
  Algeria 34°21N 0°25E **50 B6**
Cherikov = Cherykaw
  Belarus 53°32N 31°20E **17 B16**
Cherkasy Ukraine 49°27N 32°4E **19 E5**
Cherkessk Russia 44°15N 42°5E **19 F7**
Cherlak Russia 54°15N 74°55E **28 D8**
Chernaya Russia 70°30N 89°10E **29 B9**
Chernigov = Chernihiv
  Ukraine 51°28N 31°20E **18 D5**
Chernigovka Russia 44°19N 132°34E **30 B6**
Chernihiv Ukraine 51°28N 31°20E **18 D5**
Chernivtsi Ukraine 48°15N 25°52E **17 D13**
Chernobyl = Chornobyl
  Ukraine 51°20N 30°15E **17 C16**
Chernogorsk Russia 53°49N 91°18E **29 D10**
Chernovtsy = Chernivtsi
  Ukraine 48°15N 25°52E **17 D13**
Chernyakhovsk Russia 54°36N 21°48E **9 J19**
Chernysheyskiy Russia 63°0N 112°30E **29 C12**
Cherokee Iowa, U.S.A. 42°45N 95°33W **80 D6**
Cherokee Okla., U.S.A. 36°45N 98°21W **84 C5**
Cherokee Village U.S.A. 36°18N 91°31W **84 C9**
Cherokees, Grand Lake O' The
  U.S.A. 36°28N 94°55W **84 C7**
Cherrapunji India 25°17N 91°47E **41 G17**
Cherry Valley U.S.A. 42°48N 74°45W **83 D10**
Cherskiy Russia 68°45N 161°18E **29 C17**
Cherskogo Khrebet
  Russia 65°0N 143°0E **29 C15**
Chersonisos Greece 35°18N 25°22E **25 D7**
Chersonisos Akrotiri
  Greece 35°30N 24°10E **25 D6**
Cherven Belarus 53°45N 28°28E **17 B15**
Chervonohrad Ukraine 50°25N 24°10E **17 C13**
Cherwell ➤ U.K. 51°44N 1°14W **13 F6**
Cherykaw Belarus 53°32N 31°20E **17 B16**
Chesapeake U.S.A. 36°49N 76°16W **81 G15**
Chesapeake B. U.S.A. 38°0N 76°10W **81 F14**
Cheshire □ U.K. 53°14N 2°30W **12 D5**
Cheshskaya Guba Russia 67°20N 47°0E **18 A8**
Cheshunt U.K. 51°43N 0°1W **13 F7**
Chesil Beach U.K. 50°37N 2°33W **13 G5**
Chesley Canada 44°17N 81°5W **82 B3**
Chester U.K. 53°12N 2°53W **12 D5**
Chester Calif., U.S.A. 40°19N 121°14W **76 F3**
Chester Ill., U.S.A. 37°55N 89°49W **80 G9**
Chester Mont., U.S.A. 48°31N 110°58W **76 B8**
Chester Pa., U.S.A. 39°51N 75°22W **81 F16**
Chester S.C., U.S.A. 34°43N 81°12W **85 D14**
Chester Vt., U.S.A. 43°16N 72°36W **83 C12**
Chester W. Va., U.S.A. 40°37N 80°34W **82 F4**
Chester-le-Street U.K. 54°51N 1°34W **12 C6**
Chesterfield U.K. 53°15N 1°25W **12 D6**
Chesterfield, Is. N. Cal. 19°52S 158°15E **58 C8**
Chesterfield Inlet
  Canada 63°30N 90°45W **68 C10**
Chesterton Ra.
  Australia 25°30S 147°27E **63 D4**
Chesterton Range △
  Australia 26°16S 147°22E **63 D4**
Chestertown U.S.A. 43°40N 73°48W **83 C11**
Chesterville Canada 45°6N 75°14W **83 A9**
Chesuncook L. U.S.A. 46°0N 69°21W **81 C19**
Chéticamp Canada 46°37N 60°59W **73 C7**
Chetumal Mexico 18°30N 88°20W **87 D7**
Chetumal, B. de
  Cent. Amer. 18°40N 88°10W **87 D7**
Chetwynd Canada 55°45N 121°36W **70 B4**
Cheviot, The U.K. 55°29N 2°9W **12 B5**
Cheviot Hills U.K. 55°20N 2°30W **12 B5**
Cheviot Ra. Australia 25°20S 143°45E **62 D3**
Chew Bahir Ethiopia 4°40N 36°50E **47 G2**
Chewelah U.S.A. 48°17N 117°43W **76 B5**
Chewore △ Zimbabwe 16°0S 29°52E **55 F2**
Cheyenne Okla., U.S.A. 35°37N 99°40W **84 D5**

Cheyenne Wyo., U.S.A. 41°8N 104°49W **76 F11**
Cheyenne ➤ U.S.A. 44°41N 101°18W **80 C3**
Cheyenne Wells
  U.S.A. 38°49N 102°21W **76 G12**
Cheyne B. Australia 34°35S 118°50E **61 F2**
Chhabra India 24°40N 76°54E **42 G7**
Chhaktala India 22°6N 74°11E **42 H6**
Chhapra India 25°48N 84°44E **43 G11**
Chhata India 27°42N 77°30E **42 F7**
Chhatarpur Jharkhand,
  India 24°23N 84°11E **43 G11**
Chhatarpur Mad. P.,
  India 24°55N 79°35E **43 G8**
Chhattisgarh □ India 22°0N 82°0E **43 J10**
Chhep Cambodia 13°45N 105°24E **38 F5**
Chhindwara Mad. P.,
  India 23°3N 79°29E **43 H8**
Chhindwara Mad. P.,
  India 22°2N 78°59E **43 H8**
Chhlong Cambodia 12°15N 105°58E **39 F5**
Chhota Tawa ➤ India 22°14N 76°36E **42 H7**
Chhoti Kali Sindh ➤
  India 24°2N 75°31E **42 G6**
Chhuikhadan India 21°32N 80°58E **43 J9**
Chhuk Cambodia 10°46N 104°28E **39 G5**
Chi ➤ Thailand 15°11N 104°43E **38 E5**
Chiai Taiwan 23°29N 120°25E **33 D7**
Chiamboni Somali Rep. 1°39S 41°35E **52 E8**
Chiang Dao Thailand 19°22N 98°58E **38 C2**
Chiang Kham Thailand 19°32N 100°18E **38 C3**
Chiang Khan Thailand 17°52N 101°36E **38 D3**
Chiang Khong Thailand 20°17N 100°24E **38 B3**
Chiang Mai Thailand 18°47N 98°59E **38 C2**
Chiang Rai Thailand 19°52N 99°50E **38 C2**
Chiang Saen Thailand 20°16N 100°5E **38 B3**
Chiapa ➤ Mexico 16°42N 93°0W **87 D6**
Chiapa de Corzo Mexico 16°42N 93°0W **87 D6**
Chiapas □ Mexico 16°30N 92°30W **87 D6**
Chiapas, Sa. Madre de
  Mexico 15°40N 93°0W **87 D6**
Chiautla de Tapia
  Mexico 18°18N 98°36W **87 D5**
Chiávari Italy 44°19N 9°19E **20 D8**
Chiavenna Italy 46°19N 9°24E **20 C8**
Chiba Japan 35°30N 140°7E **31 G10**
Chiba □ Japan 35°30N 140°20E **31 G10**
Chibabava Mozam. 20°17S 33°35E **57 C5**
Chibemba Cunene, Angola 15°48S 14°8E **53 H2**
Chibemba Huíla, Angola 16°20S 15°20E **56 B2**
Chibi Zimbabwe 20°18S 30°25E **57 C5**
Chibougamau Canada 49°56N 74°24W **72 C5**
Chibougamau, L.
  Canada 49°50N 74°20W **72 C5**
Chibuk Nigeria 10°52N 12°50E **51 F8**
Chibuto Mozam. 24°40S 33°33E **57 C5**
Chic-Chocs, Mts. Canada 48°55N 66°0W **73 C6**
Chicacole = Srikakulam
  India 18°14N 83°58E **41 K13**
Chicago U.S.A. 41°52N 87°38W **80 E10**
Chicago Heights U.S.A. 41°30N 87°38W **80 E10**
Chichagof I. U.S.A. 57°30N 135°30W **68 D6**
Chichaoua Morocco 31°32N 8°44W **50 B4**
Chichawatni Pakistan 30°32N 72°42E **42 D5**
Chichén-Itzá Mexico 20°37N 88°35W **87 C7**
Chicheng China 40°55N 115°55E **34 D8**
Chichester U.K. 50°50N 0°47W **13 G7**
Chichester Ra. Australia 22°12S 119°15E **60 D2**
Chichibu Japan 36°5N 139°10E **31 F9**
Chichibu-Tama △
  Japan 35°52N 138°42E **31 G9**
Ch'ich'iharh = Qiqihar
  China 47°26N 124°0E **33 B7**
Chicholi India 22°1N 77°40E **42 H8**
Chickasaw △ U.S.A. 34°26N 97°0W **84 D6**
Chickasha U.S.A. 35°3N 97°58W **84 D6**
Chiclana de la Frontera
  Spain 36°26N 6°9W **21 D2**
Chiclayo Peru 6°42S 79°50W **92 E3**
Chico ➤ Chubut, Argentina 43°48N 66°0W **96 E3**
Chico ➤ Santa Cruz,
  Argentina 50°0S 68°30W **96 G3**
Chicomo Mozam. 24°31S 34°6E **57 C5**
Chicomostoc Mexico 22°28N 102°46W **86 C4**
Chicontepec Mexico 20°58N 98°10W **87 C5**
Chicopee U.S.A. 42°9N 72°37W **83 D12**
Chicoutimi Canada 48°28N 71°5W **73 C5**
Chicualacuala Mozam. 22°6S 31°42E **57 C5**
Chidambaram India 11°20N 79°45E **40 P11**
Chidenguele Mozam. 24°55S 34°11E **57 C5**
Chidley, C. Canada 60°23N 64°26W **69 C13**
Chiducuane Mozam. 24°35S 34°25E **57 C5**
Chiede Angola 17°15S 16°22E **56 B2**
Chiefs Pt. Canada 44°41N 81°18W **82 B3**
Chiem Hoa Vietnam 22°12N 105°17E **38 A5**
Chiemsee Germany 47°53N 12°28E **16 E7**
Chiengi Zambia 8°45S 29°10E **55 D2**
Chiengmai = Chiang Mai
  Thailand 18°47N 98°59E **38 C2**
Chiese ➤ Italy 45°8N 10°25E **20 D9**
Chieti Italy 42°21N 14°10E **22 C6**
Chifeng China 42°18N 118°58E **35 C10**
Chignecto B. Canada 45°30N 64°40W **73 C7**
Chiguana Bolivia 21°0S 67°58E **94 A2**
Chigwell U.K. 51°37N 0°6E **13 F8**
Chihli, G. of = Bo Hai
  China 39°0N 119°0E **35 E10**
Chihuahua Mexico 28°38N 106°5W **86 B3**
Chihuahua □ Mexico 28°30N 106°0W **86 B3**
Chiili = Shieli Kazakhstan 44°20N 66°15E **28 E7**
Chik Bollapur India 13°25N 77°45E **40 N10**
Chikmagalur India 13°15N 75°45E **40 N9**
Chikwawa Malawi 16°2S 34°50E **55 F3**
Chilanga Zambia 15°33S 28°16E **55 F2**
Chilapa Mexico 17°36N 99°10W **87 D5**
Chilas Pakistan 35°25N 74°5E **43 B6**

Chilaw Sri Lanka 7°30N 79°50E 40 R11
Chilcotin → Canada 51°44N 122°23W 70 C4
Childers Australia 25°15S 152°17E 63 D5
Childress U.S.A. 34°25N 100°13W 84 D4
Chile ■ S. Amer. 35°0S 72°0W 96 D2
Chile Rise Pac. Oc. 38°0S 92°0W 65 L18
Chilecito Argentina 29°10S 67°30W 94 B2
Chilete Peru 7°10S 78°50W 92 E3
Chililabombwe Zambia 12°18S 27°43E 55 E2
Chilim Pakistan 35°5N 75°5E 43 B6
Chilin = Jilin China 43°44N 126°30E 35 C14
Chilka L. India 19°40N 85°25E 41 K14
Chilko → Canada 52°0N 123°40W 70 C4
Chilko L. Canada 51°20N 124°10W 70 C4
Chillagoe Australia 17°7S 144°33E 62 B3
Chillán Chile 36°40S 72°10W 94 D1
Chillicothe Ill., U.S.A. 40°55N 89°29W 80 E9
Chillicothe Mo., U.S.A. 39°48N 93°33W 80 F7
Chillicothe Ohio, U.S.A. 39°20N 82°59W 81 F12
Chilliwack Canada 49°10N 121°54W 70 D4
Chilo India 27°25N 73°32E 42 F5
Chiloane, I. Mozam. 20°40S 34°55E 57 C5
Chiloé, I. de Chile 42°30S 73°50W 96 E2
Chilpancingo Mexico 17°33N 99°30W 87 D5
Chiltern Hills U.K. 51°40N 0°53W 13 F7
Chilton U.S.A. 44°2N 88°10W 80 D1
Chilubi Zambia 11°5S 29°58E 55 E2
Chilubula Zambia 10°14S 30°51E 55 E3
Chilumba Malawi 10°28S 34°12E 55 E3
Chilung Taiwan 25°3N 121°45E 33 D7
Chilwa, L. Malawi 15°15S 35°40E 55 F4
Chimaltitán Mexico 21°35N 103°50W 86 C4
Chimán Panama 8°45N 78°40W 88 E4
Chimanimani Zimbabwe 19°48S 32°52E 55 F3
Chimay Belgium 50°3N 4°20E 15 D4
Chimayo U.S.A. 36°0N 105°56W 77 J11
Chimbay Uzbekistan 42°57N 59°47E 28 E6
Chimborazo Ecuador 1°29S 78°55W 92 D3
Chimbote Peru 9°0S 78°35W 92 E3
Chimkent = Shymkent
  Kazakhstan 42°18N 69°36E 28 E7
Chimoio Mozam. 19°4S 33°30E 55 F3
Chimpembe Zambia 9°31S 29°33E 55 D2
Chin □ Burma 22°0N 93°0E 41 J18
Chin Hills Burma 22°30N 93°30E 41 H18
Chin Ling Shan = Qinling Shandi
  China 33°50N 108°10E 34 H5
China Mexico 25°42N 99°14W 87 B5
China ■ Asia 30°0N 110°0E 33 C6
China, Great Plain of
  Asia 35°0N 115°0E 26 E13
China Lake U.S.A. 35°44N 117°37W 79 K9
Chinan = Jinan China 36°38N 117°1E 34 F9
Chinandega Nic. 12°35N 87°12W 88 D2
Chinati Peak U.S.A. 29°57N 104°29W 84 G2
Chincha Alta Peru 13°25S 76°7W 92 F3
Chinchaga → Canada 58°53N 118°20W 70 B5
Chinchilla Australia 26°45S 150°38E 63 D5
Chinchorro, Banco
  Mexico 18°35N 87°22W 87 D7
Chinchou = Jinzhou
  China 41°5N 121°3E 35 D11
Chincoteague U.S.A. 37°56N 75°23W 81 G16
Chinde Mozam. 18°35S 36°30E 55 F4
Chindwin → Burma 21°26N 95°15E 41 J19
Chineni India 33°2N 75°15E 43 C6
Chinga Mozam. 15°13S 38°35E 55 F4
Chingola Zambia 12°31S 27°53E 55 E2
Chingole Malawi 13°4S 34°17E 55 E3
Ch'ingtao = Qingdao
  China 36°5N 120°20E 35 F11
Chinguetti Mauritania 20°25N 12°24W 50 D3
Chingune Mozam. 20°33S 34°58E 57 C5
Chinhanguanine
  Mozam. 25°21S 32°30E 57 D5
Chinhoyi Zimbabwe 17°20S 30°8E 55 F3
Chini India 31°32N 78°15E 42 D8
Chiniot Pakistan 31°45N 73°0E 42 D5
Chínipas Mexico 27°23N 108°32W 86 B3
Chinju = Jinju S. Korea 35°12N 128°2E 35 G15
Chinko → C.A.R. 4°50N 23°53E 52 D4
Chinle U.S.A. 36°9N 109°33W 77 H9
Chinnampo = Namp'o
  N. Korea 38°52N 125°10E 35 E13
Chino Japan 35°59N 138°9E 31 G9
Chino U.S.A. 34°1N 117°41W 79 L9
Chino Valley U.S.A. 34°45N 112°27W 77 J7
Chinon France 47°10N 0°15E 20 C4
Chinook U.S.A. 48°35N 109°14W 76 B9
Chinook Trough
  Pac. Oc. 44°0N 175°0W 64 C10
Chinsali Zambia 10°30S 32°2E 55 E3
Chióggia Italy 45°13N 12°17E 22 B5
Chíos = Híos Greece 38°27N 26°9E 23 E12
Chipata Zambia 13°38S 32°28E 55 E3
Chipindo Angola 13°49S 15°48E 53 G3
Chipinge Zimbabwe 20°13S 32°28E 55 G3
Chipinge △ Zimbabwe 20°13S 32°28E 55 G3
Chipley U.S.A. 30°47N 85°32W 85 F12
Chipman Canada 46°6N 65°53W 73 C6
Chipoka Malawi 13°57S 34°28E 55 E3
Chippenham U.K. 51°27N 2°6W 13 F5
Chippewa → U.S.A. 44°25N 92°5W 80 C7
Chippewa Falls U.S.A. 44°56N 91°24W 80 C8
Chipping Norton U.K. 51°56N 1°32W 13 F6
Chiputneticook Lakes
  N. Amer. 45°35N 67°35W 81 C20
Chiquián Peru 10°10S 77°0W 92 F3
Chiquibul △ Belize 16°49N 88°52W 88 C2
Chiquimula Guatemala 14°51N 89°37W 88 D2
Chiquinquira Colombia 5°37N 73°50W 92 B4
Chirala India 15°50N 80°26E 40 M12
Chiramba Mozam. 16°55S 34°39E 55 F3
Chirawa India 28°14N 75°42E 42 E6
Chirchiq Uzbekistan 41°29N 69°35E 28 E7
Chiredzi Zimbabwe 21°0S 31°38E 57 C5

Chiricahua △ U.S.A. 32°0N 109°20W 77 K9
Chiricahua Peak
  U.S.A. 31°51N 109°18W 77 L9
Chiriquí, G. de Panama 8°0N 82°10W 88 E3
Chiriquí, L. de Panama 9°10N 82°0W 88 E3
Chirisa △ Zimbabwe 17°53S 28°15E 55 F2
Chirivira Falls Zimbabwe 21°10S 32°12E 55 G3
Chirmiri India 23°15N 82°20E 43 H10
Chirripó Grande, Cerro
  Costa Rica 9°29N 83°29W 88 E3
Chirundu Zimbabwe 16°3S 28°50E 57 B4
Chisamba Zambia 14°55S 28°20E 55 E2
Chisapani Nepal 28°37N 81°16E 43 E9
Chisasibi Canada 53°50N 79°0W 72 B4
Chisholm Canada 54°55N 114°10W 70 C6
Chisholm U.S.A. 47°29N 92°53W 80 B7
Chishtian Mandi
  Pakistan 29°50N 72°55E 42 E5
Chisimaio = Kismaayo
  Somali Rep. 0°22S 42°32E 47 H3
Chisimba Falls Zambia 10°12S 30°56E 55 E3
Chişinău Moldova 47°2N 28°50E 17 E15
Chisos Mts. U.S.A. 29°5N 103°15W 84 G3
Chistopol Russia 55°25N 50°38E 18 C9
Chita Russia 52°0N 113°35E 29 D12
Chitipa Malawi 9°41S 33°19E 55 D3
Chitose Japan 42°49N 141°39E 30 C10
Chitral Pakistan 35°50N 71°56E 40 B7
Chitré Panama 7°59N 80°27W 88 E3
Chittagong Bangla. 22°19N 91°48E 41 H17
Chittagong □ Bangla. 24°5N 91°0E 41 G17
Chittaurgarh India 24°52N 74°38E 42 G6
Chittoor India 13°15N 79°5E 40 N11
Chitungwiza Zimbabwe 18°0S 31°6E 55 F3
Chiusi Italy 43°1N 11°57E 22 C4
Chivasso Italy 45°11N 7°53E 20 D7
Chivhu Zimbabwe 19°2S 30°52E 55 F3
Chivilcoy Argentina 34°55S 60°0W 94 C4
Chiwanda Tanzania 11°23S 34°55E 55 E3
Chizarira △ Zimbabwe 17°36S 27°45E 55 F2
Chizarira △ Zimbabwe 17°44S 27°55E 55 F2
Chizela Zambia 13°8S 25°0E 55 E2
Chkalov = Orenburg
  Russia 51°45N 55°6E 18 D10
Chloride U.S.A. 35°25N 114°12W 79 K12
Cho Bo Vietnam 20°46N 105°10E 38 B5
Cho-do N. Korea 38°30N 124°40E 35 E13
Cho Phuoc Hai Vietnam 10°26N 107°18E 39 G6
Choa Chu Kang Singapore 1°22N 103°41E 39 d
Choba Kenya 2°30N 38°5E 54 B4
Chobe △ Botswana 18°37S 24°23E 56 B4
Chocolate Mts.
  U.S.A. 33°15N 115°15W 79 M11
Choctawhatchee → U.S.A. 30°25N 86°8W 85 F11
Choele Choel Argentina 39°11S 65°40W 96 D3
Choiseul St. Lucia 13°47N 61°3W 89 f
Choiseul Solomon Is. 7°0S 156°40E 58 B8
Choix Mexico 26°43N 108°17W 86 B3
Chojnice Poland 53°42N 17°32E 17 B9
Chok Chai Thailand 14°44N 102°10E 38 E4
Chōkai-San Japan 39°6N 140°3E 30 E10
Choke Canyon Res.
  U.S.A. 28°30N 98°20W 84 G5
Chokurdakh Russia 70°38N 147°55E 29 B15
Cholame U.S.A. 35°44N 120°18W 78 K6
Cholet France 47°4N 0°52W 20 C3
Cholguan Chile 37°10S 72°3W 94 D1
Choloma Honduras 15°37N 87°57W 88 C2
Choluteca Honduras 13°20N 87°14W 88 D2
Choluteca → Honduras 13°0N 87°20W 88 D2
Chom Bung Thailand 13°37N 99°36E 38 F2
Chom Thong Thailand 18°25N 98°41E 38 C2
Choma Zambia 16°48S 26°59E 55 F2
Chomolungma = Everest, Mt.
  Nepal 28°5N 86°58E 43 E12
Chomun India 27°15N 75°40E 42 F6
Chomutov Czech Rep. 50°28N 13°23E 16 C7
Chon Buri Thailand 13°21N 101°1E 38 F3
Chon Thanh Vietnam 11°24N 106°36E 39 G6
Chone Ecuador 0°40S 80°0W 92 D3
Chong Kai Cambodia 13°57N 103°35E 38 F4
Chong Mek Thailand 15°10N 105°27E 38 E5
Chong Phangan Thailand 9°39N 100°0E 39 b
Chong Samui Thailand 9°21N 99°50E 39 b
Ch'ŏngjin N. Korea 41°47N 129°50E 35 D15
Chŏngju N. Korea 39°40N 125°5E 35 E13
Chongli China 40°58N 115°15E 34 D8
Chongqing China 29°35N 106°25E 32 D5
Chongqing Shi □ China 30°0N 108°0E 32 C5
Chonguene Mozam. 25°3S 33°49E 57 C5
Chonos, Arch. de los Chile 45°0S 75°0W 96 F2
Chop Ukraine 48°26N 22°12E 17 D12
Chopim → Brazil 25°35S 53°5W 95 B5
Chor Pakistan 25°31N 69°46E 42 G3
Chora Sfakion Greece 35°15N 24°9E 25 D6
Chorbat La India 34°42N 76°37E 43 B7
Chorley U.K. 53°39N 2°38W 12 D5
Chornobyl Ukraine 51°20N 30°15E 17 C16
Chorolque, Cerro Bolivia 20°59S 66°5W 94 A2
Chorregon Australia 22°40S 143°32E 62 C3
Chorro el Indio △
  Venezuela 7°43N 72°9W 89 E5
Chortkiv Ukraine 49°2N 25°46E 17 D13
Chorzów Poland 50°18N 18°57E 17 C10
Chos-Malal Argentina 37°20S 70°15W 94 D1
Choszczno Poland 53°7N 15°25E 16 B8
Choteau U.S.A. 47°49N 112°11W 76 C7
Chotila India 22°23N 71°15E 42 H4
Chotta Udepur India 22°19N 74°1E 42 H6
Chowchilla U.S.A. 37°7N 120°16W 78 H6
Choybalsan Mongolia 48°4N 114°30E 33 B6
Choyr Mongolia 46°24N 108°30E 29 E11
Christchurch N.Z. 43°33S 172°47E 59 E4
Christchurch U.K. 50°44N 1°47W 13 G6
Christian I. Canada 44°50N 80°12W 82 B4

Christiana S. Africa 27°52S 25°8E 56 D4
Christiansted
  U.S. Virgin Is. 17°45N 64°42W 89 C7
Christie B. → Canada 62°32N 111°10W 71 A6
Christina → Canada 56°40N 111°3W 71 B6
Christmas Cr. →
  Australia 18°29S 125°23E 60 C4
Christmas I. = Kiritimati
  Kiribati 1°58N 157°27W 65 G12
Christmas I. Ind. Oc. 10°30S 105°40E 64 J2
Christopher, L.
  Australia 24°49S 127°42E 61 D4
Chtimba Malawi 10°35S 34°13E 55 E3
Chū = Shū Kazakhstan 43°36N 73°42E 28 E8
Chu → Vietnam 19°53N 105°45E 38 C5
Chu Lai Vietnam 15°28N 108°45E 38 E7
Chuadanga Bangla. 23°38N 88°51E 43 H13
Chuak, Ko Thailand 9°28N 99°41E 39 b
Ch'uanchou = Quanzhou
  China 24°55N 118°34E 33 D6
Chuankou China 34°20N 110°59E 34 G6
Chubbuck U.S.A. 42°55N 112°28W 76 E7
Chūbu □ Japan 36°45N 137°30E 31 F8
Chubu-Sangaku △
  Japan 36°30N 137°40E 31 F8
Chubut → Argentina 43°20S 65°5W 96 E3
Chuchi L. Canada 55°12N 124°30W 70 B4
Chuda India 22°29N 71°41E 42 H4
Chudskoye, Ozero
  Russia 58°13N 27°30E 9 G22
Chūgoku □ Japan 35°0N 133°0E 31 G6
Chūgoku-Sanchi Japan 35°0N 133°0E 31 G6
Chugwater U.S.A. 41°46N 104°50W 76 F11
Chuka Kenya 0°20S 37°39E 54 C4
Chukchi Plateau Arctic 78°0N 165°0W 4 B17
Chukchi Sea Russia 68°0N 175°0W 29 C19
Chukotskoye Nagorye
  Russia 68°0N 175°0E 29 C18
Chula Vista U.S.A. 32°38N 117°5W 79 N9
Chulucanas Peru 5°8S 80°10W 92 E2
Chulym → Russia 57°43N 83°51E 28 D9
Chum Phae Thailand 16°40N 102°6E 38 D4
Chum Saeng Thailand 15°55N 100°15E 38 E3
Chumar India 32°40N 78°35E 43 C8
Chumbicha Argentina 29°0S 66°10W 94 B2
Chumikan Russia 54°40N 135°10E 29 D14
Chumphon Thailand 10°35N 99°14E 39 G2
Chumuare Mozam. 14°31S 31°50E 55 E3
Chuna → Russia 57°47N 94°37E 29 D10
Chuncheon S. Korea 37°58N 127°44E 35 F14
Chunchura India 22°53N 88°27E 43 H13
Chunga Zambia 15°0S 26°2E 55 F2
Chunggang-ŭp
  N. Korea 41°48N 126°48E 35 D14
Chunghwa N. Korea 38°52N 125°47E 35 E13
Chungju S. Korea 36°58N 127°58E 35 F14
Chungking = Chongqing
  China 29°35N 106°25E 32 D5
Chungt'iaoshan = Zhongtiao
  Shan China 35°0N 111°10E 34 G6
Chunian Pakistan 30°57N 74°0E 42 D6
Chunya Tanzania 8°30S 33°27E 55 D3
Chunyang China 43°38N 129°23E 35 C15
Chupara Pt.
  Trin. & Tob. 10°49N 61°22W 93 K15
Chuquibamba Peru 15°47S 72°44W 92 G4
Chuquicamata Chile 22°15S 69°0W 94 A2
Chur Switz. 46°52N 9°32E 20 C8
Churachandpur India 24°20N 93°40E 41 G18
Church Stretton U.K. 52°32N 2°48W 13 E5
Churchill Canada 58°47N 94°11W 71 B10
Churchill → Man.,
  Canada 58°47N 94°12W 71 B10
Churchill → Nfld. & L.,
  Canada 53°19N 60°10W 73 B7
Churchill, C. Canada 58°46N 93°12W 71 B10
Churchill Falls Canada 53°36N 64°19W 73 B7
Churchill L. Canada 55°55N 108°20W 71 B7
Churchill Pk. Canada 58°10N 125°10W 70 B3
Churki India 23°50N 83°12E 43 H10
Churu India 28°20N 74°50E 42 E6
Churún Merú = Angel Falls
  Venezuela 5°57N 62°30W 92 B6
Chushal India 33°40N 78°40E 43 C8
Chuska Mts. U.S.A. 36°15N 108°50W 77 H9
Chusovoy Russia 58°22N 57°50E 18 C10
Chute-aux-Outardes
  Canada 49°7N 68°24W 73 C6
Chuuk = Truk
  Micronesia 7°25N 151°46E 64 G7
Chuvash Republic = Chuvashia □
  Russia 55°30N 47°0E 18 C8
Chuvashia □ Russia 55°30N 47°0E 18 C8
Chuwārtah Iraq 35°43N 45°34E 44 C5
Chuy Uruguay 33°41S 53°27W 95 C5
Ci Xian China 36°20N 114°25E 34 F8
Ciadâr-Lunga Moldova 46°3N 28°51E 17 E15
Ciamis Indonesia 7°20S 108°21E 37 G13
Cianjur Indonesia 6°49S 107°8E 37 G12
Cianorte Brazil 23°37S 52°37W 95 A5
Cibola U.S.A. 33°17N 114°42W 79 M12
Cicero U.S.A. 41°51N 87°44W 80 E2
Cicia Fiji 17°45S 179°18W 59 a
Ciénagas del Catatumbo △
  Venezuela 9°25N 71°54W 89 E5
Ciechanów Poland 52°52N 20°38E 17 B11
Ciego de Ávila Cuba 21°50N 78°50W 88 B4
Ciénaga Colombia 11°1N 74°15W 92 A4
Cienfuegos Cuba 22°10N 80°30W 88 B3
Cieszyn Poland 49°45N 18°35E 17 D10
Cieza Spain 38°17N 1°23W 21 C5
Cihuatlán Mexico 19°14N 104°35W 86 D4
Cijara, Embalse de Spain 39°18N 4°52W 21 C3
Cijulung Indonesia 7°42S 108°27E 37 G13
Cilacap Indonesia 7°43S 109°0E 37 G13
Cill Chainnigh = Kilkenny
  Ireland 52°39N 7°15W 10 D4

Cilo Daği Turkey 37°28N 43°55E 19 G7
Cima U.S.A. 35°14N 115°30W 79 K11
Cimarron Kans., U.S.A. 37°48N 100°21W 80 G3
Cimarron N. Mex.,
  U.S.A. 36°31N 104°55W 77 H11
Cimarron → U.S.A. 36°10N 96°16W 84 C6
Cimişlia Moldova 46°34N 28°44E 17 E15
Cimone, Mte. Italy 44°12N 10°42E 22 B4
Cinca → Spain 41°26N 0°21E 21 B6
Cincar Bos.-H. 43°55N 17°5E 22 C7
Cincinnati U.S.A. 39°9N 84°27W 81 F11
Cincinnatus U.S.A. 42°33N 75°54W 83 D9
Çine Turkey 37°37N 28°2E 23 F13
Ciney Belgium 50°18N 5°5E 15 D5
Cinto, Mte. France 42°24N 8°54E 20 E8
Circle Alaska, U.S.A. 65°50N 144°4W 74 a
Circle Mont., U.S.A. 47°25N 105°35W 76 C11
Circleville U.S.A. 39°36N 82°57W 81 F12
Cirebon Indonesia 6°45S 108°32E 37 G13
Ciremay Indonesia 6°55S 108°27E 37 G13
Cirencester U.K. 51°43N 1°57W 13 F6
Cirium Cyprus 34°40N 32°53E 25 E11
Cisco U.S.A. 32°23N 98°59W 84 E5
Citlaltépetl = Orizaba, Pico de
  Mexico 18°58N 97°15W 87 D5
Citrus Heights U.S.A. 38°42N 121°17W 78 G5
Citrusdal S. Africa 32°35S 19°0E 56 E2
Città del Vaticano = Vatican
  City ■ Europe 41°54N 12°27E 22 D5
Città di Castello Italy 43°27N 12°14E 22 C5
Ciudad Acuña Mexico 29°18N 100°55W 86 B4
Ciudad Altamirano
  Mexico 18°20N 100°40W 86 D4
Ciudad Anáhuac
  Mexico 27°14N 100°7W 86 B4
Ciudad Bolívar Venezuela 8°5N 63°36W 92 B6
Ciudad Camargo
  Mexico 27°40N 105°10W 86 B3
Ciudad Cortés Costa Rica 8°55N 84°0W 88 E3
Ciudad de México Mexico 19°24N 99°9W 87 D5
Ciudad de Valles Mexico 21°59N 99°1W 87 C5
Ciudad del Carmen
  Mexico 18°38N 91°50W 87 D6
Ciudad del Este Paraguay 25°30S 54°50W 95 B5
Ciudad Delicias = Delicias
  Mexico 28°13N 105°28W 86 B3
Ciudad Frontera
  Mexico 26°56N 101°27W 86 B4
Ciudad Guayana
  Venezuela 8°0N 62°30W 92 B6
Ciudad Guerrero
  Mexico 28°33N 107°30W 86 B3
Ciudad Guzmán
  Mexico 19°41N 103°29W 86 D4
Ciudad Juárez Mexico 31°44N 106°29W 86 A3
Ciudad Lerdo Mexico 25°33N 103°32W 86 B4
Ciudad Madero Mexico 22°19N 97°50W 87 C5
Ciudad Mante Mexico 22°44N 98°59W 87 C5
Ciudad Obregón
  Mexico 27°29N 109°56W 86 B3
Ciudad Real Spain 38°59N 3°55W 21 C4
Ciudad Rodrigo Spain 40°35N 6°32W 21 B2
Ciudad Victoria Mexico 23°44N 99°8W 87 C5
Ciudadela Spain 40°0N 3°50E 24 B10
Civitanova Marche Italy 43°18N 13°44E 22 C5
Civitavécchia Italy 42°6N 11°48E 22 C4
Cizre Turkey 37°19N 42°10E 44 B4
Clackmannanshire □
  U.K. 56°10N 3°43W 11 E5
Clacton-on-Sea U.K. 51°47N 1°11E 13 F9
Claire, L. Canada 58°35N 112°5W 70 B6
Clairton U.S.A. 40°18N 79°53W 82 F5
Clallam Bay U.S.A. 48°15N 124°16W 78 B2
Clanton U.S.A. 32°51N 86°38W 85 E11
Clanwilliam S. Africa 32°11S 18°52E 56 E2
Clara Ireland 53°21N 7°37W 10 C4
Claraville U.S.A. 35°24N 118°20W 79 K8
Clare Australia 33°50S 138°37E 63 E2
Clare U.S.A. 43°49N 84°46W 81 D11
Clare □ Ireland 52°45N 9°0W 10 D3
Clare → Ireland 53°20N 9°2W 10 C2
Clare I. Ireland 53°49N 10°0W 10 C1
Claremont Calif., U.S.A. 34°6N 117°43W 79 L9
Claremont N.H., U.S.A. 43°23N 72°20W 83 C12
Claremont Pt. Australia 14°1S 143°41E 62 A3
Claremore U.S.A. 36°19N 95°36W 84 C7
Claremorris Ireland 53°45N 9°0W 10 C3
Clarence → Australia 29°25S 153°22E 63 D5
Clarence → N.Z. 42°10S 173°56E 59 E4
Clarence, I. Chile 54°0S 72°0W 96 G2
Clarence I. Antarctica 61°10S 54°0W 5 C18
Clarence Str. Australia 12°0S 131°0E 60 B5
Clarence Town Bahamas 23°6N 74°59W 89 B5
Clarendon Pa., U.S.A. 41°47N 79°6W 82 E5
Clarendon Tex., U.S.A. 34°56N 100°53W 84 D4
Clarenville Canada 48°10N 54°1W 73 C9
Claresholm Canada 50°2N 113°33W 70 D6
Clarie Coast Antarctica 68°0S 135°0E 5 C9
Clarinda U.S.A. 40°44N 95°2W 80 E6
Clarington Canada 43°55N 78°41W 82 C6
Clarion Iowa, U.S.A. 42°44N 93°44W 80 D7
Clarion Pa., U.S.A. 41°13N 79°23W 82 E5
Clarion → U.S.A. 41°7N 79°41W 82 E5
Clarion Fracture Zone
  Pac. Oc. 20°0N 120°0W 66 H7
Clark U.S.A. 44°53N 97°44W 80 C5
Clark, Pt. Canada 44°4N 81°45W 82 B3
Clark Fork U.S.A. 48°9N 116°11W 76 B5
Clark Fork → U.S.A. 48°9N 116°15W 76 B5
Clarkdale U.S.A. 34°46N 112°3W 77 J7
Clarke City Canada 50°12N 66°38W 73 B6
Clarke I. Australia 40°32S 148°10E 63 G4
Clarke Ra. Australia 20°40S 148°30E 62 J6
Clarks Fork Yellowstone →
  U.S.A. 45°39N 108°43W 76 D9
Clark's Harbour Canada 43°25N 65°38W 73 D6
Clarks Hill L. = J. Strom
  Thurmond L. U.S.A. 33°40N 82°12W 85 E13

Clarks Summit U.S.A. 41°30N 75°42W 83 E9
Clarksburg U.S.A. 39°17N 80°30W 81 F13
Clarksdale U.S.A. 34°12N 90°35W 85 D9
Clarkston U.S.A. 46°25N 117°3W 76 C5
Clarksville Ark., U.S.A. 35°28N 93°28W 84 D8
Clarksville Tenn.,
  U.S.A. 36°32N 87°21W 85 C11
Clarksville Tex., U.S.A. 33°37N 95°3W 84 E7
Clatskanie U.S.A. 46°6N 123°12W 78 D3
Claude U.S.A. 35°7N 101°22W 84 D4
Claveria Phil. 18°37N 121°4E 37 A6
Clay U.S.A. 38°17N 121°10W 78 G5
Clay Center U.S.A. 39°23N 97°8W 80 F5
Claypool U.S.A. 33°25N 110°51W 77 K8
Claysburg U.S.A. 40°17N 78°27W 82 F6
Claysville U.S.A. 40°7N 80°25W 82 F4
Clayton Canada 45°11N 76°19W 83 A8
Clayton N. Mex.,
  U.S.A. 36°27N 103°11W 77 H12
Clayton N.Y., U.S.A. 44°14N 76°5W 83 B8
Clear, C. Ireland 51°25N 9°32W 10 E2
Clear, L. Canada 45°26N 77°12W 82 A7
Clear Hills Canada 56°40N 119°30W 70 B5
Clear I. Ireland 51°26N 9°30W 10 E2
Clear L. U.S.A. 39°2N 122°47W 78 F4
Clear Lake Iowa, U.S.A. 43°8N 93°23W 80 D7
Clear Lake S. Dak.,
  U.S.A. 44°45N 96°41W 80 C5
Clear Lake Res. U.S.A. 41°56N 121°5W 76 F3
Clearfield Pa., U.S.A. 41°2N 78°27W 82 E6
Clearfield Utah, U.S.A. 41°7N 112°2W 76 F7
Clearlake U.S.A. 38°57N 122°38W 78 G4
Clearwater Canada 51°38N 120°2W 70 C4
Clearwater U.S.A. 27°59N 82°48W 85 M4
Clearwater → Alta.,
  Canada 52°22N 114°57W 70 C6
Clearwater → Alta.,
  Canada 56°44N 111°23W 71 B6
Clearwater L. Canada 53°34N 99°49W 71 C9
Clearwater Lake △
  Canada 54°0N 101°0W 71 C8
Clearwater Mts. U.S.A. 46°5N 115°20W 76 C6
Clearwater River △
  Canada 56°55N 109°10W 71 B7
Cleburne U.S.A. 32°21N 97°23W 84 E6
Clee Hills U.K. 52°26N 2°35S 13 E5
Cleethorpes U.K. 53°33N 0°3W 12 D7
Cleeve Cloud U.K. 51°56N 2°0W 13 F6
Clemson U.S.A. 34°41N 82°50W 85 D13
Clerke Reef Australia 17°22S 119°20E 60 C2
Clermont Australia 22°49S 147°39E 62 C4
Clermont U.S.A. 28°33N 81°46W 85 G14
Clermont-Ferrand France 45°46N 3°4E 20 D5
Clervaux Lux. 50°4N 6°2E 15 D6
Clevedon U.K. 51°26N 2°52W 13 F5
Cleveland Miss., U.S.A. 33°45N 90°43W 85 E9
Cleveland Ohio, U.S.A. 41°29N 81°41W 82 E3
Cleveland Okla., U.S.A. 36°19N 96°28W 84 C6
Cleveland Tenn., U.S.A. 35°10N 84°53W 85 D12
Cleveland Tex., U.S.A. 30°21N 95°5W 84 F7
Cleveland, C. Australia 19°11S 147°1E 62 B4
Cleveland, Mt. U.S.A. 48°56N 113°51W 76 B7
Cleveland Heights
  U.S.A. 41°31N 81°33W 82 E3
Clevelândia Brazil 26°24S 52°23W 95 B5
Clew B. Ireland 53°50N 9°49W 10 C2
Clewiston U.S.A. 26°45N 80°56W 85 H14
Clifden Ireland 53°29N 10°1W 10 C1
Clifden N.Z. 46°1S 167°42E 59 G1
Cliffdell U.S.A. 46°56N 121°5W 78 D5
Cliffy Hd. Australia 35°1S 116°29E 61 G2
Clifton Australia 27°59S 151°53E 63 D5
Clifton Ariz., U.S.A. 33°3N 109°18W 77 K9
Clifton Colo., U.S.A. 39°7N 108°25W 76 G9
Clifton Tex., U.S.A. 31°47N 97°35W 84 F6
Clifton Beach Australia 16°46S 145°39E 62 B4
Clinch → U.S.A. 35°53N 84°29W 85 D12
Clingmans Dome
  U.S.A. 35°34N 83°30W 85 D13
Clint U.S.A. 31°35N 106°14W 84 F1
Clinton B.C., Canada 51°6N 121°35W 70 C4
Clinton Ont., Canada 43°37N 81°32W 82 C3
Clinton N.Z. 46°12S 169°23E 59 G2
Clinton Ark., U.S.A. 35°36N 92°28W 84 D8
Clinton Conn., U.S.A. 41°17N 72°32W 83 E12
Clinton Ill., U.S.A. 40°9N 88°57W 80 E9
Clinton Ind., U.S.A. 39°40N 87°24W 80 F10
Clinton Iowa, U.S.A. 41°51N 90°12W 80 E8
Clinton Mass., U.S.A. 42°25N 71°41W 83 D13
Clinton Miss., U.S.A. 32°20N 90°20W 85 E9
Clinton Mo., U.S.A. 38°22N 93°46W 80 F7
Clinton N.C., U.S.A. 35°0N 78°22W 85 D15
Clinton Okla., U.S.A. 35°31N 98°58W 84 D5
Clinton Tenn., U.S.A. 36°6N 84°8W 85 D12
Clinton Wash., U.S.A. 47°59N 122°21W 78 C4
Clinton Colden L.
  Canada 63°58N 107°27W 68 B9
Clintonville U.S.A. 44°37N 88°46W 80 C9
Clipperton, I. Pac. Oc. 10°18N 109°13W 65 F17
Clipperton Fracture Zone
  Pac. Oc. 19°0N 122°0W 65 G16
Clisham U.K. 57°58N 6°49W 11 D2
Clitheroe U.K. 53°53N 2°22W 12 D5
Clo-oose Canada 48°39N 124°49W 78 B2
Clocolan S. Africa 28°55S 27°34E 56 D4
Clodomira Argentina 27°35S 64°14W 94 B3
Clogher Hd. Ireland 53°48N 6°14W 10 C5
Clonakilty Ireland 51°37N 8°53W 10 E3
Clonakilty B. Ireland 51°35N 8°51W 10 E3
Cloncurry Australia 20°40S 140°28E 62 C3
Cloncurry → Australia 18°37S 140°40E 62 B3
Clondalkin Ireland 53°19N 6°25W 10 C5
Clones Ireland 54°11N 7°15W 10 B4

Clonmel *Ireland* 52°21N 7°42W **10** D4
Cloquet *U.S.A.* 46°43N 92°28W **80** B7
Clorinda *Argentina* 25°16S 57°45W **94** B4
Cloud Bay *Canada* 48°5N 89°26W **72** C2
Cloud Peak *U.S.A.* 44°23N 107°11W **76** D10
Cloudcroft *U.S.A.* 32°58N 105°45W **77** K11
Cloverdale *U.S.A.* 38°48N 123°1W **78** G4
Clovis *Calif., U.S.A.* 36°49N 119°42W **78** J7
Clovis *N. Mex., U.S.A.* 34°24N 103°12W **77** J12
Cloyne *Canada* 44°49N 77°11W **82** B7
Cluj-Napoca *Romania* 46°47N 23°38E **17** E12
Clunes *Australia* 37°20S 143°45E **63** F3
Clutha → *N.Z.* 46°20S 169°49E **59** G2
Clwyd → *U.K.* 53°19N 3°31W **12** D4
Clyde *Canada* 54°9N 113°39W **70** C6
Clyde *N.Z.* 45°12S 169°20E **59** F2
Clyde *U.S.A.* 43°5N 76°52W **82** C8
Clyde → *U.K.* 55°55N 4°30W **11** F4
Clyde, Firth of *U.K.* 55°22N 5°1W **11** F3
Clyde Muirshiel ⌂ *U.K.* 55°50N 4°40W **11** F4
Clyde River *Canada* 70°30N 68°30W **69** B13
Clydebank *U.K.* 55°54N 4°23W **11** F4
Clymer *N.Y., U.S.A.* 42°1N 79°37W **82** D5
Clymer *Pa., U.S.A.* 40°40N 79°1W **82** D5
Coachella *U.S.A.* 33°41N 116°10W **79** M10
Coachella Canal
U.S.A. 32°43N 114°57W **79** N12
Coahoma *U.S.A.* 32°18N 101°18W **84** E4
Coahuayana →
Mexico 18°41N 103°45W **86** D4
Coahuila □ *Mexico* 27°20N 102°0W **86** B4
Coal → *Canada* 59°39N 126°57W **70** B3
Coalane *Mozam.* 17°48S 37°2E **55** F4
Coalcomán *Mexico* 18°47N 103°9W **86** D4
Coaldale *Canada* 49°45N 112°35W **70** D6
Coalgate *U.S.A.* 34°32N 96°13W **84** D6
Coalinga *U.S.A.* 36°9N 120°21W **78** J6
Coalisland *U.K.* 54°33N 6°42W **10** B5
Coalville *U.K.* 52°44N 1°23W **12** E6
Coalville *U.S.A.* 40°55N 111°24W **76** F8
Coamo *Puerto Rico* 18°5N 66°22W **89** d
Coari *Brazil* 4°8S 63°7W **92** D6
Coast □ *Kenya* 2°40S 39°45E **54** C4
Coast Mts. *Canada* 55°0N 129°20W **70** C3
Coast Ranges *U.S.A.* 39°0N 123°0W **78** G4
Coatbridge *U.K.* 55°52N 4°6W **11** F4
Coatepec *Mexico* 19°27N 96°58W **87** D5
Coatepeque *Guatemala* 14°46N 91°55W **88** D1
Coatesville *U.S.A.* 39°59N 75°50W **81** F16
Coaticook *Canada* 45°10N 71°46W **83** A13
Coats I. *Canada* 62°30N 83°0W **69** C11
Coats Land *Antarctica* 77°0S 25°0W **5** D1
Coatzacoalcos *Mexico* 18°7N 94°25W **87** D6
Cobá *Mexico* 20°31N 87°45W **87** C7
Cobalt *Canada* 47°25N 79°42W **72** C4
Cobán *Guatemala* 15°30N 90°21W **88** C1
Cobar *Australia* 31°27S 145°48E **63** E4
Cóbh *Ireland* 51°51N 8°17W **10** E3
Cobija *Bolivia* 11°0S 68°50W **92** F5
Cobleskill *U.S.A.* 42°41N 74°29W **83** D10
Coboconk *Canada* 44°39N 78°48W **82** B6
Cobourg *Canada* 43°58N 78°10W **82** C6
Cobourg Pen. *Australia* 11°20S 132°15E **60** B5
Cobram *Australia* 35°54S 145°40E **63** F4
Cóbué *Mozam.* 12°0S 34°58E **55** E3
Coburg *Germany* 50°15N 10°58E **16** C6
Cocanada = Kakinada
India 16°57N 82°11E **41** L13
Cochabamba *Bolivia* 17°26S 66°10W **92** G5
Cochemane *Mozam.* 17°0S 32°54E **55** F3
Cochin *India* 9°58N 76°20E **40** Q10
Cochin China = Nam-Phan
Vietnam 10°30N 106°0E **39** G6
Cochran *U.S.A.* 32°23N 83°21W **85** E13
Cochrane *Alta., Canada* 51°11N 114°30W **70** C6
Cochrane *Ont., Canada* 49°0N 81°0W **72** C3
Cochrane *Chile* 47°15S 72°33W **96** F2
Cochrane → *Canada* 59°0N 103°40W **71** B8
Cochrane, L. *Chile* 47°10S 72°0W **96** F2
Cochranton *U.S.A.* 41°31N 80°3W **82** E4
Cockburn *Australia* 32°5S 141°0E **63** E3
Cockburn, Canal *Chile* 54°30S 72°0W **96** G2
Cockburn I. *Canada* 45°55N 83°22W **72** C3
Cockburn Ra. *Australia* 15°46S 128°0E **60** C4
Cockermouth *U.K.* 54°40N 3°22W **12** C4
Cocklebiddy *Australia* 32°0S 126°3E **61** F4
Cockpit Country, The
Jamaica 18°15N 77°45W **88** a
Coco → *Cent. Amer.* 15°0N 83°8W **88** D3
Coco, I. del *Pac. Oc.* 5°25N 87°55W **65** G19
Cocoa *U.S.A.* 28°21N 80°44W **85** G14
Cocobeach *Gabon* 0°59N 9°34E **52** D1
Cocos B. *Trin. & Tob.* 10°25N 61°2W **93** K15
Cocos Is. *Ind. Oc.* 12°10S 96°55E **64** J1
Cocos Ridge *Pac. Oc.* 4°0N 88°0W **65** G19
Cod, C. *U.S.A.* 42°5N 70°10W **81** D18
Codajás *Brazil* 3°55S 62°0W **92** D6
Codó *Brazil* 4°30S 43°55W **93** D10
Cody *U.S.A.* 44°32N 109°3W **76** D9
Coe Hill *Canada* 44°52N 77°50W **82** B7
Coelemu *Chile* 36°30S 72°48W **94** D1
Coen *Australia* 13°52S 143°12E **62** A3
Coeur d'Alene *U.S.A.* 47°41N 116°46W **76** C5
Coeur d'Alene L.
U.S.A. 47°32N 116°49W **76** C5
Coevorden *Neths.* 52°40N 6°44E **15** B6
Cofete *Canary Is.* 28°6N 14°23W **24** F5
Coffeyville *U.S.A.* 37°2N 95°37W **80** G6
Coffin B. *Australia* 34°38S 135°28E **63** E2
Coffin Bay *Australia* 34°37S 135°29E **63** E2
Coffin Bay △ *Australia* 34°34S 135°19E **63** E2
Coffin Bay Peninsula
Australia 34°32S 135°15E **63** E2
Coffs Harbour *Australia* 30°16S 153°5E **63** E5
Cognac *France* 45°41N 0°20W **20** D3
Cohocton *U.S.A.* 42°30N 77°30W **82** D7
Cohocton → *U.S.A.* 42°9N 77°6W **82** D7
Cohoes *U.S.A.* 42°46N 73°42W **83** D11
Cohuna *Australia* 35°45S 144°15E **63** F3
Coiba, I. de *Panama* 7°30N 81°40W **88** E3
Coig → *Argentina* 51°0S 69°10W **96** G3
Coigeach, Rubha *U.K.* 58°6N 5°26W **11** C3
Coihaique *Chile* 45°30S 71°45W **96** F2
Coimbatore *India* 11°2N 76°59E **40** P10
Coimbra *Brazil* 19°55S 57°48W **92** G7
Coimbra *Portugal* 40°15N 8°27W **21** B1
Coín *Spain* 36°40N 4°48W **21** D3
Coipasa, Salar de *Bolivia* 19°26S 68°9W **92** G5
Cojimies *Ecuador* 0°20N 80°0W **92** C3
Cojutepequé *El Salv.* 13°41N 88°54W **88** D2
Cokeville *U.S.A.* 42°5N 110°57W **76** E8
Colac *Australia* 38°21S 143°35E **63** F3
Colatina *Brazil* 19°32S 40°37W **93** G10
Colbeck, C. *Antarctica* 77°6S 157°48W **5** D13
Colborne *Canada* 44°0N 77°53W **82** C7
Colby *U.S.A.* 39°24N 101°3W **80** F3
Colca → *Peru* 15°55S 72°43W **92** G4
Colchester *U.K.* 51°54N 0°55E **13** F8
Colchester *U.S.A.* 41°35N 72°20W **83** E12
Cold L. *Canada* 54°33N 110°5W **71** C7
Cold Lake *Canada* 54°27N 110°10W **71** C6
Coldstream *Canada* 50°13N 119°11W **70** C5
Coldstream *U.K.* 55°39N 2°15W **11** F6
Coldwater *Canada* 44°42N 79°40W **82** B5
Coldwater *Kans., U.S.A.* 37°16N 99°20W **80** G4
Coldwater *Mich., U.S.A.* 41°57N 85°0W **81** E11
Colebrook *U.S.A.* 44°54N 71°30W **83** B13
Coleman *Canada* 49°40N 114°30W **70** D6
Coleman *U.S.A.* 31°50N 99°26W **84** F5
Coleman → *Australia* 15°6S 141°38E **62** B3
Colenso *S. Africa* 28°44S 29°50E **57** D4
Coleraine *Australia* 37°36S 141°40E **63** F3
Coleraine *U.K.* 55°8N 6°41W **10** A5
Coleridge, L. *N.Z.* 43°17S 171°30E **59** E3
Colesberg *S. Africa* 30°45S 25°5E **56** E4
Coleville *U.S.A.* 38°34N 119°30W **78** G7
Colfax *Calif., U.S.A.* 39°6N 120°57W **78** F6
Colfax *La., U.S.A.* 31°31N 92°42W **84** F8
Colfax *Wash., U.S.A.* 46°53N 117°22W **76** C5
Colhué Huapi, L.
Argentina 45°30S 69°0W **96** F3
Coligny *S. Africa* 26°17S 26°15E **57** D4
Colima *Mexico* 19°14N 103°43W **86** D4
Colima □ *Mexico* 19°10N 104°0W **86** D4
Colima, Nevado de
Mexico 19°33N 103°38W **86** D4
Colina *Chile* 33°13S 70°45W **94** C1
Colinas *Brazil* 6°0S 44°10W **93** E10
Coll *U.K.* 56°39N 6°34W **11** E2
Collahuasi *Chile* 21°5S 68°45W **94** A2
Collarenebri *Australia* 29°33S 148°34E **63** D4
Colleen Bawn *Zimbabwe* 21°0S 29°12E **55** G2
College Park *U.S.A.* 33°39N 84°27W **85** E12
College Station *U.S.A.* 30°37N 96°21W **84** F6
Collie *Australia* 33°22S 116°8E **61** F2
Collier B. *Australia* 16°10S 124°15E **60** C3
Collier Ra. *Australia* 24°45S 119°10E **61** D2
Collier Range △
Australia 24°39S 119°7E **61** D2
Collierville *U.S.A.* 35°3N 89°40W **85** D10
Collina, Passo di *Italy* 44°2N 10°56E **22** B4
Collingwood *Canada* 44°29N 80°13W **82** B4
Collingwood *N.Z.* 40°41S 172°40E **59** D4
Collins *Canada* 50°17N 89°27W **72** B2
Collins Bay *Canada* 44°14N 76°36W **83** B8
Collinsville *Australia* 20°30S 147°56E **62** C4
Collipulli *Chile* 37°55S 72°30W **94** D1
Collooney *Ireland* 54°11N 8°29W **10** B3
Colmar *France* 48°5N 7°20E **20** B7
Colo → *Australia* 33°25S 150°52E **63** E5
Cologne = Köln *Germany* 50°56N 6°57E **16** C4
Colom, I. d'en *Spain* 39°58N 4°16E **24** B11
Coloma *U.S.A.* 38°48N 120°53W **78** G6
Colomb-Béchar = Béchar
Algeria 31°38N 2°18W **50** B5
Colombia ■ *S. Amer.* 3°45N 73°0W **92** C4
Colombian Basin
S. Amer. 14°0N 76°0W **66** H12
Colombo *Sri Lanka* 6°56N 79°58E **40** R11
Colón *B. Aires, Argentina* 33°53S 61°7W **94** C3
Colón *Entre Ríos,*
Argentina 32°12S 58°10W **94** C4
Colón *Cuba* 22°42N 80°54W **88** B3
Colón *Panama* 9°20N 79°54W **88** E4
Colón, Arch. de *Ecuador* 0°0 91°0W **90** D1
Colònia de Sant Jordi
Spain 39°19N 2°59E **24** B9
Colonia del Sacramento
Uruguay 34°25S 57°50W **94** C4
Colonia Dora *Argentina* 28°34S 62°59W **94** B3
Colonial Beach *U.S.A.* 38°15N 76°58W **81** F15
Colonie *U.S.A.* 42°43N 73°50W **83** D11
Colonsay *Canada* 51°59N 105°52W **71** C7
Colonsay *U.K.* 56°5N 6°12W **11** E2
Colorado □ *U.S.A.* 39°30N 105°30W **76** G11
Colorado → *Argentina* 39°50S 62°8W **96** D4
Colorado → *N. Amer.* 31°45N 114°40W **77** L6
Colorado → *U.S.A.* 28°36N 95°59W **84** G7
Colorado City *U.S.A.* 32°24N 100°52W **84** E4
Colorado Plateau *U.S.A.* 37°0N 111°0W **77** H8
Colorado River Aqueduct
U.S.A. 33°50N 117°23W **79** L12
Colorado Springs
U.S.A. 38°50N 104°49W **76** G11
Colotlán *Mexico* 22°6N 103°16W **86** C4
Colstrip *U.S.A.* 45°53N 106°38W **76** D10
Colton *U.S.A.* 44°33N 74°56W **83** B10
Columbia *Ky., U.S.A.* 37°6N 85°18W **81** G11
Columbia *La., U.S.A.* 32°6N 92°5W **84** E8
Columbia *Miss., U.S.A.* 31°15N 89°50W **85** F10
Columbia *Mo., U.S.A.* 38°57N 92°20W **80** F7
Columbia *Pa., U.S.A.* 40°2N 76°30W **83** F8
Columbia *S.C., U.S.A.* 34°0N 81°2W **85** D14
Columbia *Tenn., U.S.A.* 35°37N 87°2W **85** D11
Columbia → *N. Amer.* 46°15N 124°5W **78** D2
Columbia, C. *Canada* 83°6N 69°57W **69** A11
Columbia, District of □
U.S.A. 38°55N 77°0W **81** F15
Columbia, Mt. *Canada* 52°8N 117°20W **70** C5
Columbia Basin *U.S.A.* 46°45N 119°5W **76** C4
Columbia Falls *U.S.A.* 48°23N 114°11W **76** B6
Columbia Mts. *Canada* 52°0N 119°0W **70** C5
Columbia Plateau
U.S.A. 44°0N 117°30W **76** E5
Columbiana *U.S.A.* 40°53N 80°42W **82** F4
Columbretes, Is. *Spain* 39°50N 0°50E **21** C6
Columbus *Ga., U.S.A.* 32°28N 84°59W **85** E12
Columbus *Ind., U.S.A.* 39°13N 85°55W **81** F11
Columbus *Kans., U.S.A.* 37°10N 94°50W **80** G6
Columbus *Miss., U.S.A.* 33°30N 88°25W **85** E10
Columbus *Mont.,*
U.S.A. 45°38N 109°15W **76** D9
Columbus *N. Mex.,*
U.S.A. 31°50N 107°38W **77** L10
Columbus *Nebr., U.S.A.* 41°26N 97°22W **80** E5
Columbus *Ohio, U.S.A.* 39°58N 83°0W **81** F12
Columbus *Tex., U.S.A.* 29°42N 96°33W **84** G6
Colusa *U.S.A.* 39°13N 122°1W **78** F4
Colville *U.S.A.* 48°33N 117°54W **76** B5
Colville → *U.S.A.* 70°25N 150°30W **74** a
Colville, C. *N.Z.* 36°29S 175°21E **59** B5
Colwood *Canada* 48°26N 123°29W **78** B3
Colwyn Bay *U.K.* 53°18N 3°44W **12** D4
Comácchio *Italy* 44°42N 12°11E **22** B5
Comalcalco *Mexico* 18°16N 93°13W **87** D6
Comallo *Argentina* 41°0S 70°5W **96** E2
Comanche *U.S.A.* 31°54N 98°36W **84** F5
Comandante Ferraz
Antarctica 62°30S 58°0W **5** C18
Comayagua *Honduras* 14°25N 87°37W **88** D2
Combahee → *U.S.A.* 32°31N 80°31W **85** E14
Combarbalá *Chile* 31°11S 71°2W **94** C1
Combe Martin *U.K.* 51°12N 4°3W **13** F3
Comber *Canada* 42°14N 82°33W **82** D2
Comber *U.K.* 54°33N 5°45W **10** B6
Combermere *Canada* 45°22N 77°37W **82** A7
Comblain-au-Pont
Belgium 50°29N 5°35E **15** D5
Comeragh Mts. *Ireland* 52°18N 7°34W **10** D4
Comet *Australia* 23°36S 148°38E **62** C4
Comilla *Bangla.* 23°28N 91°10E **41** H17
Comino *Malta* 36°1N 14°20E **25** C1
Comino, C. *Italy* 40°32N 9°49E **22** D3
Comitán de Domínguez
Mexico 16°15N 92°8W **87** D6
Commerce *Ga., U.S.A.* 34°12N 83°28W **85** D13
Commerce *Tex., U.S.A.* 33°15N 95°54W **84** E7
Committee B. *Canada* 68°30N 86°30W **69** C11
Commodore, C. *Canada* 44°47N 80°54W **82** B4
Commonwealth B.
Antarctica 67°0S 144°0E **5** C10
Commoron Cr. →
Australia 28°22S 150°8E **63** D5
Communism Pk. = imeni Ismail
Samani, Pik *Tajikistan* 39°0N 72°2E **28** F8
Como *Italy* 45°47N 9°5E **20** D8
Como, Lago di *Italy* 46°0N 9°11E **20** D8
Comodoro Rivadavia
Argentina 45°50S 67°40W **96** F3
Comorin, C. = Kanyakumari
India 8°3N 77°40E **40** Q10
Comoros ■ *Ind. Oc.* 12°10S 44°15E **53** a
Comox *Canada* 49°42N 124°55W **70** D4
Compiègne *France* 49°24N 2°50E **20** B5
Compostela *Mexico* 21°14N 104°55W **86** C4
Comprida, I. *Brazil* 24°50S 47°42W **95** A6
Compton *Canada* 45°14N 71°49W **83** A13
Compton *U.S.A.* 33°53N 118°13W **79** M8
Comrat *Moldova* 46°18N 28°40E **17** E15
Con Cuong *Vietnam* 19°2N 104°54E **38** C5
Con Dao △ *Vietnam* 8°42N 106°35E **39** H6
Con Son *Vietnam* 8°41N 106°37E **39** H6
Conakry *Guinea* 9°29N 13°49W **50** G3
Conara *Australia* 41°50S 147°26E **63** G4
Concarneau *France* 47°52N 3°56W **20** C2
Conceição *Mozam.* 18°47S 36°7E **55** F4
Conceição da Barra
Brazil 18°35S 39°45W **93** G11
Conceição do Araguaia
Brazil 8°0S 49°2W **93** E9
Concepción *Argentina* 27°20S 65°35W **94** B2
Concepción *Bolivia* 16°15S 62°8W **92** G6
Concepción *Chile* 36°50S 73°0W **94** D1
Concepción *Mexico* 18°15N 90°5W **87** D6
Concepción *Paraguay* 23°22S 57°26W **94** A4
Concepción □ *Chile* 37°0S 72°30W **94** D1
Concepción → *Mexico* 30°32N 113°2W **86** A2
Concepción, Est. de
Chile 50°30S 74°55W **96** G2
Concepción, L. *Bolivia* 17°20S 61°20W **92** G6
Concepción, Pta.
Mexico 26°53N 111°50W **86** B2
Concepción del Oro
Mexico 24°38N 101°25W **86** C4
Concepción del Uruguay
Argentina 32°35S 58°20W **94** C4
Conception, Pt. *U.S.A.* 34°27N 120°28W **79** L6
Conception B. *Canada* 47°45N 53°0W **73** C9
Conception B. *Namibia* 23°55S 14°22E **56** C1
Conception I. *Bahamas* 23°52N 75°9W **89** B4
Concession *Zimbabwe* 17°27S 30°56E **55** F3
Conchas Dam *U.S.A.* 35°22N 104°11W **77** J11
Concho *U.S.A.* 34°28N 109°36W **77** J9
Concho → *U.S.A.* 31°34N 99°43W **84** F5
Conchos → *Chihuahua,*
Mexico 29°35N 104°25W **86** B4
Conchos → *Chihuahua,*
Mexico 27°29N 106°45W **86** B3
Conchos → *Tamaulipas,*
Mexico 24°55N 97°38W **87** B5
Concord *Calif., U.S.A.* 37°59N 122°2W **78** H4
Concord *N.C., U.S.A.* 35°25N 80°35W **85** D14
Concord *N.H., U.S.A.* 43°12N 71°32W **83** C13
Concordia *Antarctica* 75°6S 123°23E **5** D17
Concordia *Argentina* 31°20S 58°2W **94** C4
Concórdia *Amazonas,*
Brazil 4°36S 66°36W **92** D5
Concórdia *Sta. Catarina,*
Brazil 27°14S 52°1W **95** B5
Concordia *Mexico* 23°17N 106°4W **86** C3
Concordia *U.S.A.* 39°34N 97°40W **80** F5
Concrete *U.S.A.* 48°32N 121°45W **76** B3
Condamine *Australia* 26°56S 150°9E **63** D5
Conde *U.S.A.* 45°9N 98°6W **80** C4
Condeúba *Brazil* 14°52S 42°0W **93** F10
Condobolin *Australia* 33°4S 147°6E **63** E4
Condon *U.S.A.* 45°14N 120°11W **76** D3
Conegliano *Italy* 45°53N 12°18E **22** B5
Conejera, I. = Conills, I. des
Spain 39°11N 2°58E **24** B9
Conejos *Mexico* 26°14N 103°53W **86** B4
Conemaugh → *U.S.A.* 40°28N 79°19W **82** F5
Confuso → *Paraguay* 25°9S 57°34W **94** B4
Congleton *U.K.* 53°10N 2°13W **12** D5
Congo (Brazzaville) = Congo ■
Africa 1°0S 16°0E **52** E3
Congo (Kinshasa) = Congo, Dem.
Rep. of the ■ *Africa* 3°0S 23°0E **52** E4
Congo ■ *Africa* 1°0S 16°0E **52** E3
Congo → *Africa* 6°4S 12°24E **52** F2
Congo, Dem. Rep. of the ■
Africa 3°0S 23°0E **52** E4
Congo Basin *Africa* 0°10S 24°30E **52** E4
Congonhas *Brazil* 20°30S 43°52W **95** A7
Congress *U.S.A.* 34°9N 112°51W **77** J7
Conills, I. des *Spain* 39°11N 2°58E **24** B9
Coniston *Canada* 46°29N 80°51W **72** C3
Conjeeveram = Kanchipuram
India 12°52N 79°45E **40** N11
Conklin *Canada* 55°38N 111°5W **71** B6
Conklin *U.S.A.* 42°2N 75°49W **83** D9
Conn, L. *Ireland* 54°3N 9°15W **10** B2
Connacht □ *Ireland* 53°43N 9°12W **10** C2
Conneaut *U.S.A.* 41°57N 80°34W **82** E4
Conneautville *U.S.A.* 41°45N 80°22W **82** E4
Connecticut □ *U.S.A.* 41°30N 72°45W **83** E12
Connecticut → *U.S.A.* 41°16N 72°20W **83** E12
Connell *U.S.A.* 46°40N 118°52W **76** C4
Connellsville *U.S.A.* 40°1N 79°35W **82** F5
Connemara *Ireland* 53°29N 9°45W **10** C2
Connemara △ *Ireland* 53°32N 9°52W **10** C2
Connersville *U.S.A.* 39°39N 85°8W **81** F11
Connors Ra. *Australia* 21°40S 149°10E **62** C4
Conoename → *Suriname* 5°48N 55°55W **93** B7
Conquest *Canada* 51°32N 107°14W **71** C7
Conrad *U.S.A.* 48°10N 111°57W **76** B8
Conrad Rise *S. Ocean* 53°0S 41°0E **5** B5
Conran, C. *Australia* 37°49S 148°44E **63** F4
Conroe *U.S.A.* 30°19N 95°27W **84** F7
Consecon *Canada* 44°0N 77°31W **82** C7
Conselheiro Lafaiete
Brazil 20°40S 43°48W **95** A7
Consell *Spain* 39°40N 2°49E **24** B9
Consett *U.K.* 54°51N 1°50W **12** C6
Consort *Canada* 52°1N 110°46W **71** C6
Constance = Konstanz
Germany 47°40N 9°10E **16** E5
Constance, L. = Bodensee
Europe 47°35N 9°25E **20** C8
Constanța *Romania* 44°14N 28°38E **17** F15
Constantine *Algeria* 36°25N 6°42E **50** A7
Constitución *Chile* 35°20S 72°30W **94** D1
Constitución *Uruguay* 31°0S 57°50W **94** C4
Constitución de 1857 △
Mexico 32°4N 115°55W **86** A1
Consul *Canada* 49°20N 109°30W **71** D7
Contact *U.S.A.* 41°46N 114°45W **76** F6
Contai *India* 21°54N 87°46E **43** J12
Contamana *Peru* 7°19S 74°55W **92** E4
Contas → *Brazil* 14°17S 39°1W **93** F11
Contoocook *U.S.A.* 43°13N 71°45W **83** C13
Contra Costa *Mozam.* 25°9S 33°30E **57** D5
Contwoyto L. *Canada* 65°42N 110°50W **68** C8
Conway = Conwy *U.K.* 53°17N 3°50W **12** D4
Conway = Conwy →
U.K. 53°17N 3°50W **12** D4
Conway *Australia* 20°24S 148°41E **62** J6
Conway *Canada* 44°6N 76°54W **82** B8
Conway *Ark., U.S.A.* 35°5N 92°26W **84** D8
Conway *N.H., U.S.A.* 43°59N 71°7W **83** C13
Conway *S.C., U.S.A.* 33°51N 79°3W **85** E15
Conway, C. *Australia* 20°34S 148°46E **62** J6
Conway, L. *Australia* 28°17S 135°35E **63** D2
Conwy *U.K.* 53°17N 3°50W **12** D4
Conwy □ *U.K.* 53°10N 3°44W **12** D4
Conwy → *U.K.* 53°17N 3°50W **12** D4
Coober Pedy *Australia* 29°1S 134°43E **63** D1
Cooch Behar = Koch Bihar
India 26°22N 89°29E **41** F16
Cooinda *Australia* 13°15S 130°5E **60** B5
Cook *Australia* 30°37S 130°25E **61** F5
Cook *U.S.A.* 47°51N 92°41W **80** B7
Cook, B. *Chile* 55°10S 70°0W **96** H3
Cook, C. *Canada* 50°8N 127°55W **70** C3
Cook, Mt. = Aoraki Mount Cook
N.Z. 43°36S 170°9E **59** E3
Cook Inlet *U.S.A.* 60°0N 152°0W **68** D4
Cook Is. *Pac. Oc.* 17°0S 160°0W **65** J12
Cook Strait *N.Z.* 41°15S 174°29E **59** D5
Cookeville *U.S.A.* 36°10N 85°30W **85** C12
Cookhouse *S. Africa* 32°44S 25°47E **56** E4
Cooks Harbour *Canada* 51°36N 55°52W **73** B8
Cookshire *Canada* 45°25N 71°38W **83** A13
Cookstown *Canada* 44°11N 79°42W **82** B5
Cookstown *U.K.* 54°39N 6°45W **10** B5
Cooksville *Canada* 43°35N 79°38W **82** C5
Cooktown *Australia* 15°30S 145°16E **62** B4
Coolabah *Australia* 31°1S 146°43E **63** E4
Cooladdi *Australia* 26°37S 145°23E **63** D4
Coolah *Australia* 31°48S 149°41E **63** E4
Coolamon *Australia* 34°46S 147°8E **63** E4
Coolgardie *Australia* 30°55S 121°8E **61** F3
Coolidge *U.S.A.* 32°59N 111°31W **77** K8
Coolidge Dam *U.S.A.* 33°10N 110°32W **77** K8
Cooma *Australia* 36°12S 149°8E **63** F4
Coon Rapids *U.S.A.* 45°9N 93°19W **80** C7
Coonabarabran
Australia 31°14S 149°18E **63** E4
Coonamble *Australia* 30°56S 148°27E **63** E4
Coonana *Australia* 31°0S 123°0E **61** F3
Coondapoor *India* 13°42N 74°40E **40** N9
Cooninnie, L. *Australia* 26°4S 139°59E **63** D2
Cooper *U.S.A.* 33°23N 95°42W **84** E7
Cooper Cr. → *Australia* 28°29S 137°46E **63** D2
Cooper Ridge *Pac. Oc.* 10°0N 150°30W **65** G12
Cooperstown *N. Dak.,*
U.S.A. 47°27N 98°8W **80** B4
Cooperstown *N.Y.,*
U.S.A. 42°42N 74°56W **83** D10
Coorabie *Australia* 31°54S 132°18E **61** F5
Coorong, The *Australia* 35°50S 139°20E **63** F2
Coorow *Australia* 29°53S 116°2E **61** E2
Cooroy *Australia* 26°22S 152°54E **63** D5
Coos Bay *U.S.A.* 43°22N 124°13W **76** E1
Coosa → *U.S.A.* 32°30N 86°16W **85** E11
Cootamundra *Australia* 34°36S 148°1E **63** E4
Cootehill *Ireland* 54°4N 7°5W **10** B4
Copahue Paso *Argentina* 37°49S 71°8W **94** D1
Copainalá *Mexico* 17°4N 93°18W **87** D6
Copake *U.S.A.* 42°7N 73°31W **83** D11
Copán *Honduras* 14°50N 89°9W **88** D2
Cope *U.S.A.* 39°40N 102°51W **76** G12
Copenhagen = København
Denmark 55°40N 12°26E **9** J15
Copenhagen *U.S.A.* 43°54N 75°41W **83** C9
Copiapó *Chile* 27°30S 70°20W **94** B1
Copiapó → *Chile* 27°19S 70°56W **94** B1
Coplay *U.S.A.* 40°44N 75°29W **83** F9
Copo △ *Argentina* 25°53S 61°41W **94** B3
Copp L. *Canada* 60°14N 114°40W **70** A6
Copper Canyon = Barranca del
Cobre △ *Mexico* 27°18N 107°40W **86** B3
Copper Harbor *U.S.A.* 47°28N 87°53W **80** B10
Copper Queen *Zimbabwe* 17°29S 29°18E **55** F2
Copperas Cove *U.S.A.* 31°8N 97°54W **84** F6
Copperbelt □ *Zambia* 13°15S 27°30E **55** E2
Coppermine = Kugluktuk
Canada 67°50N 115°5W **68** C8
Coppermine → *Canada* 67°49N 116°4W **68** C8
Copperopolis *U.S.A.* 37°58N 120°38W **78** H6
Coquet → *U.K.* 55°20N 1°32W **12** B6
Coquille *U.S.A.* 43°11N 124°11W **76** E1
Coquimbo *Chile* 30°0S 71°20W **94** C1
Coquimbo □ *Chile* 31°0S 71°0W **94** C1
Coquitlam *Canada* 49°17N 122°45W **70** D4
Corabia *Romania* 43°48N 24°30E **17** G13
Coracora *Peru* 15°5S 73°45W **92** G4
Coraki *Australia* 28°59S 153°17E **63** D5
Coral *U.S.A.* 40°29N 79°10W **82** F5
Coral Bay *Australia* 23°8S 113°46W **60** D1
Coral Gables *U.S.A.* 25°43N 80°16W **85** J14
Coral Harbour *Canada* 64°8N 83°10W **69** C11
Coral Sea *Pac. Oc.* 15°0S 150°0E **58** C8
Coral Sea Basin *Pac. Oc.* 14°0S 152°0E **64** J7
Coral Sea Islands Terr. □
Australia 20°0S 155°0E **58** C8
Coral Springs *U.S.A.* 26°16N 80°16W **85** H14
Coraopolis *U.S.A.* 40°31N 80°10W **82** F4
Corato *Italy* 41°9N 16°25E **22** D7
Corbett △ *India* 29°20N 79°0E **43** E8
Corbin *U.S.A.* 36°57N 84°6W **81** G11
Corby *U.K.* 52°30N 0°41W **13** E7
Corcaigh = Cork *Ireland* 51°54N 8°29W **10** E3
Corcoran *U.S.A.* 36°6N 119°33W **78** J7
Corcovado △ *Costa Rica* 8°33N 83°35W **88** E3
Corcubión *Spain* 42°56N 9°12W **21** A1
Cordele *U.S.A.* 31°58N 83°47W **85** F13
Cordell *U.S.A.* 35°17N 98°59W **84** D5
Córdoba *Argentina* 31°20S 64°10W **94** C3
Córdoba *Mexico* 18°53N 96°56W **87** D5
Córdoba *Spain* 37°50N 4°50W **21** D3
Córdoba □ *Argentina* 31°22S 64°15W **94** C3
Córdoba, Sierra de
Argentina 31°10S 64°25W **94** C3
Cordova *U.S.A.* 60°33N 145°45W **68** C5
Corella → *Australia* 19°34S 140°47E **62** B3
Corfield *Australia* 21°40S 143°21E **62** C3
Corfu = Kerkyra *Greece* 39°38N 19°50E **25** A3
Corfu *U.S.A.* 42°57N 78°24W **82** D6
Corfu, Str. of = Kerkyras, Notio
Steno *Greece* 39°34N 20°0E **25** A4
Coria *Spain* 39°58N 6°33W **21** C2
Corigliano Cálabro *Italy* 39°36N 16°31E **22** E7
Coringa Is. *Australia* 16°58S 149°58E **62** B4
Corinth = Korinthos
Greece 37°56N 22°55E **23** F10
Corinth *Miss., U.S.A.* 34°56N 88°31W **85** D10
Corinth *N.Y., U.S.A.* 43°15N 73°49W **83** C11
Corinth, G. of = Korinthiakos
Kolpos *Greece* 38°16N 22°30E **23** E10
Corinto *Brazil* 18°20S 44°30W **93** G10
Corinto *Nic.* 12°30N 87°10W **88** D2
Cork *Ireland* 51°54N 8°29W **10** E3
Cork □ *Ireland* 51°57N 8°40W **10** E3
Cork Harbour *Ireland* 51°47N 8°16W **10** E3
Çorlu *Turkey* 41°11N 27°49E **23** D12
Cormack L. *Canada* 60°56N 121°37W **70** A4
Cormorant *Canada* 54°14N 100°35W **71** C8
Cormorant L. *Canada* 54°15N 100°50W **71** C8
Corn Is. = Maíz, Is. del
Nic. 12°15N 83°4W **88** D3
Cornélio Procópio *Brazil* 23°7S 50°40W **95** A5
Corner Brook *Canada* 48°57N 57°58W **73** C8
Cornești *Moldova* 47°21N 28°1E **17** E15
Corning *Ark., U.S.A.* 36°25N 90°35W **85** C9

Corning Calif., U.S.A. 39°56N 122°11W 76 G2
Corning Iowa, U.S.A. 40°59N 94°44W 80 E6
Corning N.Y., U.S.A. 42°9N 77°3W 82 D7
Cornwall Canada 45°2N 74°44W 83 A10
Cornwall U.S.A. 40°17N 76°25W 83 F8
Cornwall □ U.K. 50°26N 4°40W 13 G3
Cornwall I. Canada 77°37N 94°38W 69 B10
Cornwallis I. Canada 75°8N 95°0W 69 B10
Corny Pt. Australia 34°55S 137°0E 63 E2
Coro Venezuela 11°25N 69°41W 92 A5
Coroatá Brazil 4°8S 44°0W 93 D10
Corocoro Bolivia 17°15S 68°28W 92 G5
Coroico Bolivia 16°0S 67°50W 92 G5
Coromandel N.Z. 36°45S 175°31E 59 B5
Coromandel Coast India 12°30N 81°0E 40 N12
Corona Calif., U.S.A. 33°53N 117°34W 79 M9
Corona N. Mex., U.S.A. 34°15N 105°36W 77 J11
Coronado U.S.A. 32°41N 117°10W 79 N9
Coronado, B. de Costa Rica 9°0N 83°40W 88 E3
Coronados, Is. Los Mexico 32°26N 117°19W 79 N9
Coronation Canada 52°5N 111°27W 70 C6
Coronation Gulf Canada 68°25N 110°0W 68 C9
Coronation I. Antarctica 60°45S 46°0W 5 C18
Coronation Is. Australia 14°57S 124°55E 60 B3
Coronda Argentina 31°58S 60°56W 94 C3
Coronel Chile 37°0S 73°10W 94 D1
Coronel Bogado Paraguay 27°11S 56°18W 94 B4
Coronel Dorrego Argentina 38°40S 61°10W 94 D3
Coronel Oviedo Paraguay 25°24S 56°30W 94 B4
Coronel Pringles Argentina 38°0S 61°30W 94 D3
Coronel Suárez Argentina 37°30S 61°52W 94 D3
Coronel Vidal Argentina 37°28S 57°45W 94 D4
Coropuna, Nevado Peru 15°30S 72°41W 92 G4
Corowa Australia 35°58S 146°21E 63 F4
Corozal □ Belize 18°23N 88°23W 87 D7
Corozal Pt. Trin. & Tob. 10°45N 61°37W 93 K15
Corpus Argentina 27°10S 55°30W 95 B4
Corpus Christi U.S.A. 27°47N 97°24W 84 H6
Corpus Christi, L. U.S.A. 28°2N 97°52W 84 G6
Corralejo Canary Is. 28°43N 13°53W 24 F6
Corraun Pen. Ireland 53°54N 9°54W 10 C2
Correntes, C. das Mozam. 24°6S 35°34E 57 C6
Corrib, L. Ireland 53°27N 9°16W 10 C2
Corrientes Argentina 27°30S 58°45W 94 B4
Corrientes □ Argentina 28°0S 57°0W 94 B4
Corrientes ➔ Argentina 30°42S 59°38W 94 C4
Corrientes ➔ Peru 3°43S 74°35W 92 D4
Corrientes, C. Colombia 5°30N 77°34W 92 B3
Corrientes, C. Cuba 21°43N 84°30W 88 B3
Corrientes, C. Mexico 20°25N 105°42W 86 C3
Corrigan U.S.A. 31°0N 94°52W 84 F7
Corrigin Australia 32°20S 117°53E 61 F2
Corriverton Guyana 5°55N 57°20W 92 B7
Corry U.S.A. 41°55N 79°39W 82 E5
Corse □ France 42°0N 9°0E 20 F8
Corse, C. France 43°1N 9°25E 20 E8
Corsica = Corse □ France 42°0N 9°0E 20 F8
Corsicana U.S.A. 32°6N 96°28W 84 E6
Corte France 42°19N 9°11E 20 E8
Cortés, Mar de = California, G. de Mexico 27°0N 111°0W 86 B2
Cortez U.S.A. 37°21N 108°35W 77 H9
Cortland N.Y., U.S.A. 42°36N 76°11W 83 D8
Cortland Ohio, U.S.A. 41°20N 80°44W 82 E4
Çorum Turkey 40°30N 34°57E 19 F5
Corumbá Brazil 19°0S 57°30W 92 G7
Corunna = A Coruña Spain 43°20N 8°25W 21 A1
Corvallis U.S.A. 44°34N 123°16W 76 D2
Corvette, L. de la Canada 53°25N 74°3W 72 B5
Corvo Azores 39°43N 31°8W 50 a
Corydon U.S.A. 40°46N 93°19W 80 E7
Cosalá Mexico 24°23N 106°41W 86 C3
Cosamaloapan de Carpio Mexico 18°22N 95°48W 87 D5
Cosenza Italy 39°18N 16°15E 22 E7
Coshocton U.S.A. 40°16N 81°51W 82 F3
Cosmo Newberry Australia 28°0S 122°54E 61 E3
Cosmonaut Sea S. Ocean 66°30S 40°0E 5 C5
Coso Junction U.S.A. 36°3N 117°57W 79 J9
Coso Pk. U.S.A. 36°13N 117°44W 79 J9
Cosquín Argentina 31°15S 64°30W 94 C3
Costa Blanca Spain 38°25N 0°10W 21 C5
Costa Brava Spain 41°30N 3°0E 21 B7
Costa Daurada Spain 41°12N 1°15E 21 B6
Costa del Sol Spain 36°30N 4°30W 21 D3
Costa dels Pins Spain 39°38N 3°26E 24 B10
Costa Mesa U.S.A. 33°38N 117°55W 79 M9
Costa Rica ■ Cent. Amer. 10°0N 84°0W 88 E3
Costa Smeralda Italy 41°5N 9°35E 22 D3
Cosumnes ➔ U.S.A. 38°16N 121°26W 78 G5
Cotabato Phil. 7°14N 124°15E 37 C6
Cotagaita Bolivia 20°45S 65°40W 94 A2
Côte d'Azur France 43°25N 7°10E 20 E7
Côte-d'Ivoire = Ivory Coast ■ Africa 7°30N 5°0W 50 G4
Coteau des Prairies U.S.A. 45°20N 97°50W 80 C5
Coteau du Missouri U.S.A. 47°0N 100°0W 80 B4
Cotentin France 49°15N 1°30W 20 B3
Cotillo Canary Is. 28°41N 14°1W 24 F5
Cotonou Benin 6°20N 2°25E 50 G6
Cotopaxi Ecuador 0°40S 78°30W 92 D3
Cotswold Hills U.K. 51°42N 2°10W 13 F5
Cottage Grove U.S.A. 43°48N 123°3W 76 E2
Cottam Canada 42°8N 82°45W 82 D2
Cottbus Germany 51°45N 14°20E 16 C8
Cottonwood U.S.A. 34°45N 112°1W 77 J7
Cotulla U.S.A. 28°26N 99°14W 84 G5
Coudersport U.S.A. 41°46N 78°1W 82 E6
Couedic, C. du Australia 36°5S 136°40E 63 F2
Coulee City U.S.A. 47°37N 119°17W 76 C4
Coulee Dam Nat. Recr. Area = Lake Roosevelt ⌂ U.S.A. 48°5N 118°14W 76 B4
Coulman I. Antarctica 73°35S 170°0E 5 D11
Coulonge ➔ Canada 45°52N 76°46W 72 C4
Coulterville U.S.A. 37°43N 120°12W 78 H6
Council U.S.A. 44°44N 116°26W 76 D5
Council Bluffs U.S.A. 41°16N 95°52W 80 E6
Council Grove U.S.A. 38°40N 96°29W 80 F5
Coupeville U.S.A. 48°13N 122°41W 78 B4
Courantyne ➔ S. Amer. 5°55N 57°5W 92 B7
Courcelles Belgium 50°28N 4°22E 15 D4
Courtenay Canada 49°45N 125°0W 70 D4
Courtland Canada 42°51N 80°38W 82 D4
Courtland U.S.A. 38°20N 121°34W 78 G5
Courtrai = Kortrijk Belgium 50°50N 3°17E 15 D3
Courtright Canada 42°49N 82°28W 82 D2
Coushatta U.S.A. 32°1N 93°21W 84 E8
Coutts Crossing Australia 29°49S 152°55E 63 D5
Couva Trin. & Tob. 10°25N 61°27W 93 K15
Couvin Belgium 50°3N 4°29E 15 D4
Cove I. Canada 45°17N 81°44W 82 A3
Coventry U.K. 52°25N 1°28W 13 E6
Covilhã Portugal 40°17N 7°31W 21 B2
Covington Ga., U.S.A. 33°36N 83°51W 85 E13
Covington Ky., U.S.A. 39°5N 84°30W 81 F11
Covington Tenn., U.S.A. 35°34N 89°39W 85 D10
Covington Va., U.S.A. 37°47N 79°59W 81 G14
Cowal, L. Australia 33°40S 147°25E 63 E4
Cowan, L. Australia 31°45S 121°45E 61 F3
Cowan L. Canada 54°0N 107°15W 71 C7
Cowangie Australia 35°12S 141°26E 63 F3
Cowansville Canada 45°14N 72°46W 83 A12
Coward Springs Australia 29°24S 136°49E 63 D2
Cowcowing Lakes Australia 30°55S 117°20E 61 F2
Cowdenbeath U.K. 56°7N 3°21W 11 E5
Cowell Australia 33°39S 136°56E 63 E2
Cowes U.K. 50°45N 1°18W 13 G6
Cowichan L. Canada 48°53N 124°17W 78 B2
Cowlitz ➔ U.S.A. 46°6N 122°55W 78 D4
Cowra Australia 33°49S 148°42E 63 E4
Coxilha Grande Brazil 28°18S 51°30W 95 B5
Coxim Brazil 18°30S 54°55W 93 G8
Cox's Bazar Bangla. 21°26N 91°59E 41 J17
Coyote Wells U.S.A. 32°44N 115°58W 79 N11
Coyuca de Benitez Mexico 17°2N 100°4W 87 D4
Coyuca de Catalán Mexico 18°20N 100°39W 86 D4
Cozad U.S.A. 40°52N 99°59W 80 E4
Cozumel Mexico 20°31N 86°55W 87 C7
Cozumel, Isla Mexico 20°30N 86°40W 87 C7
Crab Hill Barbados 13°19N 59°38W 89 g
Cracow = Kraków Poland 50°4N 19°57E 17 C10
Cracow Australia 25°17S 150°17E 63 D5
Cradle Mt.-Lake St. Clair △ Australia 41°49S 147°56E 63 G4
Cradock Australia 32°6S 138°31E 63 E2
Cradock S. Africa 32°8S 25°36E 56 E4
Craig U.S.A. 40°31N 107°33W 76 F10
Craigavon U.K. 54°27N 6°23W 10 B5
Craigmore Zimbabwe 20°28S 32°50E 55 G3
Craik Canada 51°3N 105°49W 71 C7
Crailsheim Germany 49°8N 10°5E 16 D6
Craiova Romania 44°21N 23°48E 17 F12
Cramsie Australia 23°20S 144°15E 62 C3
Cranberry L. U.S.A. 44°11N 74°50W 83 B10
Cranberry Portage Canada 54°35N 101°23W 71 C8
Cranbrook Australia 34°18S 117°33E 61 F2
Cranbrook Canada 49°30N 115°46W 70 D5
Crandon U.S.A. 45°34N 88°54W 80 C9
Crane Oreg., U.S.A. 43°25N 118°35W 76 E4
Crane Tex., U.S.A. 31°24N 102°21W 84 F3
Crane, The Barbados 13°6N 59°27W 89 g
Cranston U.S.A. 41°47N 71°26W 83 E13
Crater L. U.S.A. 42°56N 122°6W 76 E2
Crater Lake △ U.S.A. 42°55N 122°10W 76 E2
Craters of the Moon ⌂ U.S.A. 43°25N 113°30W 76 E7
Crateús Brazil 5°10S 40°39W 93 E10
Crato Brazil 7°10S 39°25W 93 E11
Craven, L. Canada 54°20N 76°56W 72 B4
Crawford U.S.A. 42°41N 103°25W 80 D2
Crawfordsville U.S.A. 40°2N 86°54W 80 E10
Crawley U.K. 51°7N 0°11W 13 F7
Crazy Mts. U.S.A. 46°12N 110°20W 76 C8
Crean L. Canada 54°5N 106°9W 71 C7
Crediton Canada 43°17N 81°33W 82 C3
Crediton U.K. 50°47N 3°40W 13 G4
Cree ➔ Canada 58°57N 105°47W 71 B7
Cree ➔ U.K. 54°55N 4°25W 11 G4
Cree L. Canada 57°30N 106°30W 71 B7
Creede U.S.A. 37°51N 106°56W 77 H10
Creekside U.S.A. 40°40N 79°11W 82 F5
Creel Mexico 27°45N 107°38W 86 B3
Creemore Canada 44°19N 80°6W 82 B4
Creighton Canada 54°45N 101°54W 71 C8
Creighton U.S.A. 42°28N 97°54W 80 D5
Crema Italy 45°22N 9°41E 20 D8
Cremona Italy 45°7N 10°2E 20 D9
Cres Croatia 44°58N 14°25E 16 F8
Crescent City U.S.A. 41°45N 124°12W 76 F1
Crespo Argentina 32°2S 60°19W 94 C3
Cresson U.S.A. 40°28N 78°36W 82 F6
Crestline Calif., U.S.A. 34°14N 117°18W 79 L9
Crestline Ohio, U.S.A. 40°47N 82°44W 82 F2
Creston Canada 49°10N 116°31W 70 D5
Creston Calif., U.S.A. 35°32N 120°33W 78 K6
Creston Iowa, U.S.A. 41°4N 94°22W 80 E6
Crestview Calif., U.S.A. 37°46N 118°58W 78 H8
Crestview Fla., U.S.A. 30°46N 86°34W 85 F11
Crete = Kriti Greece 35°15N 25°0E 25 D7
Crete U.S.A. 40°38N 96°58W 80 E5
Créteil France 48°47N 2°27E 20 B5
Creus, C. de Spain 42°20N 3°19E 21 A7
Creuse ➔ France 47°0N 0°34E 20 C4
Crewe U.K. 53°6N 2°26W 12 D5
Crewkerne U.K. 50°53N 2°48W 13 G5
Crianlarich U.K. 56°24N 4°37W 11 E4
Criciúma Brazil 28°40S 49°23W 95 B6
Crieff U.K. 56°22N 3°50W 11 E5
Crimea □ Ukraine 45°30N 33°10E 19 E5
Crimean Pen. = Krymskyy Pivostriv Ukraine 45°0N 34°0E 19 F5
Crişul Alb ➔ Romania 46°42N 21°17E 17 E11
Crişul Negru ➔ Romania 46°42N 21°16E 17 E11
Crna ➔ Macedonia 41°33N 21°59E 23 D9
Crna Gora = Montenegro ■ Europe 42°40N 19°20E 23 C8
Crna Gora Macedonia 42°10N 21°30E 23 C9
Crna Reka = Crna ➔ Macedonia 41°33N 21°59E 23 D9
Croagh Patrick Ireland 53°46N 9°40W 10 C2
Croatia ■ Europe 45°20N 16°0E 16 F9
Crocker, Banjaran Malaysia 5°40N 116°30E 36 C5
Crockett U.S.A. 31°19N 95°27W 84 F7
Crocodile = Umgwenya ➔ Mozam. 25°14S 32°18E 57 D5
Crocodile Is. Australia 12°3S 134°58E 62 A1
Crohy Hd. Ireland 54°55N 8°26W 10 B3
Croix, L. la Canada 48°20N 92°15W 72 C1
Croker, C. Australia 10°58S 132°35E 60 B5
Croker, C. Canada 44°58N 80°59W 82 B4
Croker I. Australia 11°12S 132°32E 60 B5
Cromarty U.K. 57°40N 4°2W 11 D4
Cromer U.K. 52°56N 1°17E 12 E9
Cromwell N.Z. 45°3S 169°14E 59 F2
Cromwell U.S.A. 41°36N 72°39W 83 E12
Crook U.K. 54°43N 1°45W 12 C6
Crooked ➔ Canada 54°50N 122°54W 70 C4
Crooked ➔ U.S.A. 44°32N 121°16W 76 D3
Crooked I. Bahamas 22°50N 74°10W 89 B5
Crooked Island Passage Bahamas 22°55N 74°35W 89 B5
Crookston Minn., U.S.A. 47°47N 96°37W 80 B5
Crookston Nebr., U.S.A. 42°56N 100°45W 80 D3
Crookwell Australia 34°28S 149°24E 63 E4
Crosby U.K. 53°30N 3°3W 12 D4
Crosby N. Dak., U.S.A. 48°55N 103°18W 80 A2
Crosby Pa., U.S.A. 41°45N 78°23W 82 E6
Crosbyton U.S.A. 33°40N 101°14W 84 E4
Cross City U.S.A. 29°38N 83°7W 85 G13
Cross Fell U.K. 54°43N 2°28W 12 C5
Cross L. Canada 54°45N 97°30W 71 C9
Cross Lake Canada 54°37N 97°47W 71 C9
Cross Sound U.S.A. 58°0N 135°0W 68 D6
Crossett U.S.A. 33°8N 91°58W 84 E9
Crosshaven Ireland 51°47N 8°17W 10 E3
Crossmaglen U.K. 54°5N 6°36W 10 B5
Crossmolina Ireland 54°6N 9°20W 10 B2
Crossville U.S.A. 35°57N 85°2W 85 D12
Croswell U.S.A. 43°16N 82°37W 82 C2
Croton-on-Hudson U.S.A. 41°12N 73°55W 83 E11
Crotone Italy 39°5N 17°8E 22 E7
Crow ➔ Canada 59°41N 124°20W 70 B4
Crow Agency U.S.A. 45°36N 107°28W 76 D10
Crow Hd. Ireland 51°35N 10°9W 10 E1
Crowell U.S.A. 33°59N 99°43W 84 E5
Crowley U.S.A. 30°13N 92°22W 84 F8
Crowley, L. U.S.A. 37°35N 118°42W 78 H8
Crown Point Ind., U.S.A. 41°25N 87°22W 80 E10
Crown Point N.Y., U.S.A. 43°57N 73°26W 83 C11
Crown Pt. Trin. & Tob. 11°18N 60°51W 93 J16
Crownpoint U.S.A. 35°41N 108°9W 77 J9
Crows Landing U.S.A. 37°23N 121°6W 78 H5
Crows Nest Australia 27°16S 152°4E 63 D5
Crowsnest Pass Canada 49°40N 114°40W 70 D6
Croydon Australia 18°13S 142°14E 62 B3
Croydon □ U.K. 51°22N 0°5W 13 F7
Crozet, Is. Ind. Oc. 46°27S 52°0E 3 G12
Crusheen Ireland 52°57N 8°53W 10 D3
Cruz, C. Cuba 19°50N 77°50W 88 C4
Cruz Alta Brazil 28°45S 53°40W 95 B5
Cruz Bay U.S. Virgin Is. 18°20N 64°48W 89 e
Cruz del Eje Argentina 30°45S 64°50W 94 C3
Cruzeiro Brazil 22°33S 45°0W 95 A7
Cruzeiro do Oeste Brazil 23°46S 53°4W 95 A5
Cruzeiro do Sul Brazil 7°35S 72°35W 92 E4
Cry L. Canada 58°45N 129°0W 70 B3
Crystal Bay U.S.A. 39°15N 120°0W 78 F7
Crystal Brook Australia 33°21S 138°12E 63 E2
Crystal City U.S.A. 28°41N 99°50W 84 G5
Crystal Falls U.S.A. 46°5N 88°20W 80 B9
Crystal River U.S.A. 28°54N 82°35W 85 G13
Crystal Springs U.S.A. 31°59N 90°21W 85 F9
Csongrád Hungary 46°43N 20°12E 17 E11
Cu Lao Hon Vietnam 10°54N 108°18E 39 G7
Cua Rao Vietnam 19°16N 104°27E 38 C5
Cuácua ➔ Mozam. 17°54S 37°0E 55 F4
Cuamato Angola 17°2S 15°7E 56 B2
Cuamba Mozam. 14°45S 36°22E 55 E4
Cuando ➔ Angola 17°30S 23°15E 53 H4
Cuando Cubango □ Angola 16°25S 20°0E 56 B3
Cuangar Angola 17°36S 18°39E 56 B2
Cuango = Kwango ➔ Dem. Rep. of the Congo 3°14S 17°22E 52 E3
Cuanza ➔ Angola 9°21S 13°9E 52 F2
Cuarto ➔ Argentina 33°25S 63°2W 94 C3
Cuatrociénegas Mexico 26°59N 102°5W 86 B4
Cuauhtémoc Mexico 28°25N 106°52W 86 B3
Cuba N. Mex., U.S.A. 36°1N 107°4W 77 H10
Cuba N.Y., U.S.A. 42°13N 78°17W 82 D6
Cuba ■ W. Indies 22°0N 79°0W 88 B4
Cubango ➔ Africa 18°50S 22°25E 56 B3
Cuc Phuong △ Vietnam 20°17N 105°38E 38 B5
Cuchumatanes, Sierra de los Guatemala 15°35N 91°25W 88 C1
Cuckfield U.K. 51°1N 0°8W 13 F7
Cucuí Brazil 1°12N 66°50W 92 C5
Cucurpé Mexico 30°20N 110°43W 86 A2
Cúcuta Colombia 7°54N 72°31W 92 B4
Cuddalore India 11°46N 79°45E 40 P11
Cuddapah India 14°30N 78°47E 40 M11
Cuddapan, L. Australia 25°45S 141°26E 62 D3
Cue Australia 27°25S 117°54E 61 E2
Cuenca Ecuador 2°50S 79°9W 92 D3
Cuenca Spain 40°5N 2°10W 21 B4
Cuenca, Serranía de Spain 39°55N 1°50W 21 C5
Cuernavaca Mexico 18°55N 99°15W 87 D5
Cuero U.S.A. 29°6N 97°17W 84 G6
Cueva de la Quebrada del Toro △ Venezuela 10°46N 69°3W 89 D6
Cuevas del Almanzora Spain 37°18N 1°58W 21 D5
Cuevo Bolivia 20°15S 63°30W 92 H6
Cuiabá Brazil 15°30S 56°0W 93 G7
Cuiabá ➔ Brazil 17°5S 56°36W 93 G7
Cuihangcun China 22°27N 113°32E 33 G10
Cuijk Neths. 51°44N 5°50E 15 C5
Cuilco Guatemala 15°24N 91°58W 88 C1
Cuillin Hills U.K. 57°13N 6°15W 11 D2
Cuillin Sd. U.K. 57°4N 6°20W 11 D2
Cuilo = Kwilu ➔ Dem. Rep. of the Congo 3°22S 17°22E 52 E3
Cuito ➔ Angola 18°1S 20°48E 56 B3
Cuitzeo, L. de Mexico 19°55N 101°5W 86 D4
Cukai Malaysia 4°13N 103°25E 39 K4
Culbertson U.S.A. 48°9N 104°31W 76 B11
Culcairn Australia 35°41S 147°3E 63 F4
Culebra Puerto Rico 18°19N 65°18W 89 d
Culgoa ➔ Australia 29°56S 146°20E 63 D4
Culgoa Flood Plain △ Australia 28°58S 147°5E 63 D4
Culiacán Mexico 24°50N 107°23W 86 C3
Culiacán ➔ Mexico 24°30N 107°42W 86 C3
Culik Indonesia 8°21S 115°37E 37 J18
Culion Phil. 11°54N 119°58E 37 B6
Cullarin Ra. Australia 34°30S 149°30E 63 E4
Cullen U.K. 57°42N 2°49W 11 D6
Cullen Pt. Australia 11°57S 141°54E 62 A3
Cullera Spain 39°9N 0°17W 21 C5
Cullman U.S.A. 34°11N 86°51W 85 D11
Cullompton U.K. 50°51N 3°24W 13 G4
Culpeper U.S.A. 38°30N 78°0W 81 F14
Culuene ➔ Brazil 12°56S 52°51W 93 F8
Culver, Pt. Australia 32°54S 124°43E 61 F3
Culverden N.Z. 42°47S 172°49E 59 E4
Cumaná Venezuela 10°30N 64°5W 92 A6
Cumberland B.C., Canada 49°40N 125°0W 70 D4
Cumberland Ont., Canada 45°29N 75°24W 83 A9
Cumberland U.S.A. 39°39N 78°46W 81 F14
Cumberland ➔ U.S.A. 37°9N 88°25W 80 G9
Cumberland, L. U.S.A. 36°52N 85°9W 81 G11
Cumberland Gap ⌂ U.S.A. 36°36N 83°40W 81 G12
Cumberland I. U.S.A. 30°50N 81°25W 85 F14
Cumberland Is. Australia 20°35S 149°10E 62 J7
Cumberland Island ⌂ U.S.A. 30°12N 81°24W 85 F14
Cumberland L. Canada 54°3N 102°18W 71 C8
Cumberland Pen. Canada 67°0N 64°0W 69 C13
Cumberland Plateau U.S.A. 36°0N 85°0W 85 D12
Cumberland Sd. Canada 65°30N 66°0W 69 C13
Cumbernauld U.K. 55°57N 3°58W 11 F5
Cumborah Australia 29°40S 147°45E 63 D4
Cumbres de Majalca △ Mexico 28°48N 106°30W 86 B3
Cumbres de Monterrey △ Mexico 25°26N 100°25W 86 B4
Cumbria □ U.K. 54°42N 2°52W 12 C5
Cumbrian Mts. U.K. 54°30N 3°0W 12 C5
Cumbum India 15°40N 79°10E 40 M11
Cuminá ➔ Brazil 1°30S 56°0W 93 D7
Cummings Mt. U.S.A. 35°2N 118°34W 79 K8
Cummins Australia 34°16S 135°43E 63 E2
Cumnock Australia 32°59S 148°46E 63 E4
Cumnock U.K. 55°28N 4°17W 11 F4
Cumpas Mexico 30°2N 109°48W 86 B3
Cumplida, Pta. Canary Is. 28°50N 17°48W 24 F2
Cunco Chile 38°55S 72°2W 96 D2
Cuncumén Chile 31°53S 70°38W 94 C1
Cunderdin Australia 31°37S 117°12E 61 F2
Cunene ➔ Angola 17°20S 11°50E 56 B1
Cúneo Italy 44°23N 7°32E 20 D7
Çüngüş Turkey 38°13N 39°17E 44 B3
Cunillera, I. = Sa Conillera Spain 38°59N 1°13E 24 C7
Cunnamulla Australia 28°2S 145°38E 63 D4
Cupar Canada 50°57N 104°10W 71 C8
Cupar U.K. 56°19N 3°1W 11 E5
Cupertino U.S.A. 37°19N 122°2W 78 H4
Cupica, G. de Colombia 6°25N 77°30W 92 B3
Curaçao Neth. Ant. 12°10N 69°0W 89 D6
Curanilahue Chile 37°29S 73°28W 94 D1
Curaray ➔ Peru 2°20S 74°5W 92 D4
Curepipe Mauritius 20°19S 57°31E 53 d
Curepto Chile 35°8S 72°1W 94 D1
Curiapo Venezuela 8°33N 61°5W 92 B6
Curicó Chile 34°55S 71°20W 94 C1
Curieuse Seychelles 4°15S 55°44E 53 b
Curitiba Brazil 25°20S 49°10W 95 B6
Curitibanos Brazil 27°18S 50°36W 95 B5
Currabubula Australia 31°16S 150°44E 63 E5
Currais Novos Brazil 6°13S 36°30W 93 E11
Curral Velho C. Verde Is. 16°8N 22°48W 50 b
Curralinho Brazil 1°45S 49°46W 93 D9
Currane, L. Ireland 51°49N 10°4W 10 E1
Currant U.S.A. 38°44N 115°28W 76 G6
Currawinya △ Australia 28°55S 144°27E 63 D3
Current ➔ U.S.A. 36°15N 90°55W 84 C9
Currie Australia 39°56S 143°53E 63 F3
Currie U.S.A. 40°16N 114°45W 76 F6
Curtea de Argeş Romania 45°12N 24°42E 17 F13
Curtin Springs Australia 25°20S 131°45E 61 E5
Curtis U.S.A. 40°38N 100°31W 80 E3
Curtis Group Australia 39°30S 146°37E 63 F4
Curtis I. Australia 23°35S 151°10E 62 C5
Curuápanema ➔ Brazil 2°25S 55°2W 93 D7
Curuçá Brazil 0°43S 47°50W 93 D9
Curuguaty Paraguay 24°31S 55°42W 95 A4
Curup Indonesia 4°26S 102°13E 36 E2
Cururupu Brazil 1°50S 44°50W 93 D10
Curuzú Cuatiá Argentina 29°50S 58°5W 94 B4
Curvelo Brazil 18°45S 44°27W 93 G10
Cusco = Cuzco Peru 13°32S 72°0W 92 F4
Cushendall U.K. 55°5N 6°4W 10 A5
Cushing U.S.A. 35°59N 96°46W 84 D6
Cushing, Mt. Canada 57°35N 126°57W 70 B3
Cusihuiriáchic Mexico 28°14N 106°50W 86 B3
Custer U.S.A. 43°46N 103°36W 80 D2
Cut Bank U.S.A. 48°38N 112°20W 76 B7
Cutchogue U.S.A. 41°1N 72°30W 83 E12
Cuthbert U.S.A. 31°46N 84°48W 85 F12
Cutler U.S.A. 36°31N 119°17W 78 J7
Cuttaburra ➔ Australia 29°43S 144°22E 63 D3
Cuttack India 20°25N 85°57E 41 J14
Cuvier, C. Australia 23°14S 113°22E 61 D1
Cuvier I. N.Z. 36°27S 175°50E 59 B5
Cuxhaven Germany 53°51N 8°41E 16 B5
Cuyahoga Falls U.S.A. 41°8N 81°29W 82 E3
Cuyahoga Valley △ U.S.A. 41°14N 81°33W 82 E3
Cuyo Phil. 10°51N 121°2E 37 B6
Cuyuni ➔ Guyana 6°23N 58°41W 92 B7
Cuzco Bolivia 20°0S 66°50W 92 H5
Cuzco Peru 13°32S 72°0W 92 F4
Cwmbran U.K. 51°39N 3°2W 13 F4
Cyangugu Rwanda 2°29S 28°54E 54 C2
Cyclades Greece 37°0N 24°30E 23 F11
Cygnet Australia 43°8S 147°1E 63 G4
Cynthiana U.S.A. 38°23N 84°18W 81 F11
Cypress Hills Canada 49°40N 109°30W 71 D7
Cypress Hills ⌂ Canada 49°40N 109°30W 71 D7
Cyprus ■ Asia 35°0N 33°0E 25 E12
Cyrenaica = Barqa Libya 27°0N 23°0E 51 C10
Cyrene Libya 32°53N 21°52E 51 B10
Czar Canada 52°27N 110°50W 71 C6
Czech Rep. ■ Europe 50°0N 15°0E 16 D8
Częstochowa Poland 50°49N 19°7E 17 C10

D

Da ➔ Vietnam 21°15N 105°20E 38 B5
Da Hinggan Ling China 48°0N 121°0E 33 B7
Da Lat Vietnam 11°56N 108°25E 39 G7
Da Nang Vietnam 16°4N 108°13E 38 D7
Da Qaidam China 37°50N 95°15E 32 C4
Da Yunhe ➔ Hopei, China 39°10N 117°10E 35 E9
Da Yunhe ➔ Jiangsu, China 34°25N 120°5E 35 G11
Da'an China 45°30N 124°7E 35 B13
Daan Viljoen ⌂ Namibia 22°2S 16°45E 56 C2
Daba Shan China 32°0N 109°0E 33 C5
Dabbagh, Jabal Si. Arabia 27°52N 35°45E 44 E2
Dabhoi India 22°10N 73°20E 42 H5
Dabo = Pasirkuning Indonesia 0°30S 104°33E 36 E2
Dabola Guinea 10°50N 11°5W 50 F3
Dabung Malaysia 5°23N 102°1E 39 K4
Dacca = Dhaka Bangla. 23°43N 90°26E 43 H14
Dacca = Dhaka □ Bangla. 24°25N 90°25E 43 G14
Dachau Germany 48°15N 11°26E 16 D6
Dachigam △ India 34°10N 75°0E 42 B6
Dacre Canada 45°22N 76°57W 82 A8
Dadanawa Guyana 2°50N 59°30W 92 C7
Dade City U.S.A. 28°22N 82°11W 85 G13
Dadhar Pakistan 29°28N 67°39E 42 E2
Ḑadnah U.A.E. 25°32N 56°22E 45 E8
Dadra & Nagar Haveli □ India 20°5N 73°0E 40 J8
Dadri = Charkhi Dadri India 28°37N 76°17E 42 E7
Dadu Pakistan 26°45N 67°45E 42 F2
Daegu S. Korea 35°50N 128°37E 35 G15
Daejeon S. Korea 36°20N 127°28E 35 F14
Daejeong S. Korea 33°8N 126°17E 35 H14
Daet Phil. 14°2N 122°55E 37 B6
Dafnes Greece 35°13N 25°3E 25 D7
Dagana Senegal 16°30N 15°35W 50 E2
Dagestan □ Russia 42°30N 47°0E 19 F8
Daggett U.S.A. 34°52N 116°52W 79 L10
Daghestan Republic = Dagestan □ Russia 42°30N 47°0E 19 F8
Dağlıq Qarabağ = Nagorno-Karabakh □ Azerbaijan 39°55N 46°45E 44 B5
Dagö = Hiiumaa Estonia 58°50N 22°45E 9 G20
Dagu China 38°59N 117°40E 35 E9
Dagupan Phil. 16°3N 120°20E 37 A6
Daguragu Australia 17°33S 130°30E 60 C5
Dahab Egypt 28°31N 34°31E 44 D2
Dahlak Kebir Eritrea 15°50N 40°10E 47 D3
Dahlonega U.S.A. 34°32N 83°59W 85 D13

INDEX TO WORLD MAPS D'Entrecasteaux, Pt. 115

Dahod *India* 22°50N 74°15E **42** H6
Dahongliutan *China* 35°45N 79°20E **43** B8
Dahra *Libya* 29°30N 17°50E **51** C9
Dahūk *Iraq* 36°50N 43°1E **44** B3
Dai Hao *Vietnam* 18°1N 106°25E **38** C6
Dai-Sen *Japan* 35°22N 133°32E **31** G6
Dai Xian *China* 39°4N 112°58E **34** E7
Daicheng *China* 38°42N 116°38E **34** E9
Daikondi = Day Kundī □ *Afghan.* 34°0N 66°0E **40** C5
Daingean *Ireland* 53°18N 7°17W **10** C4
Daintree *Australia* 16°20S 145°20E **62** B4
Daintree △ *Australia* 16°8S 145°2E **62** B4
Daiō-Misaki *Japan* 34°15N 136°45E **31** G8
Daisen-Oki △ *Japan* 35°23N 133°34E **31** G6
Daisetsu-Zan *Japan* 43°30N 142°57E **30** C11
Daisetsu-Zan △ *Japan* 43°30N 142°55E **30** C11
Dajarra *Australia* 21°42S 139°30E **62** C2
Dajiawa *China* 37°9N 119°0E **35** F10
Dak Dam *Cambodia* 12°20N 107°21E **38** F6
Dak Nhe *Vietnam* 15°28N 107°48E **38** E6
Dak Pek *Vietnam* 15°4N 107°44E **38** E6
Dak Song *Vietnam* 12°19N 107°35E **39** F6
Dak Sui *Vietnam* 14°55N 107°43E **38** E6
Dakar *Senegal* 14°34N 17°29W **50** F2
Dakhla *W. Sahara* 23°50N 15°53W **50** D2
Dakhla, El Wâhât el *Egypt* 25°30N 28°50E **51** C11
Dakor *India* 22°45N 73°11E **42** H5
Dakota City *U.S.A.* 42°25N 96°25W **80** D5
Đakovica *Serbia* 42°22N 20°26E **23** C9
Dalachi *China* 36°48N 105°0E **34** F3
Dalai Nur *China* 43°20N 116°45E **34** C9
Dālakī *Iran* 29°26N 51°17E **45** D6
Dalälven → *Sweden* 60°12N 16°43E **9** F17
Dalaman → *Turkey* 36°41N 28°43E **23** F13
Dalandzadgad *Mongolia* 43°27N 104°30E **34** C3
Dalap-Uliga-Darrit = Majuro *Marshall Is.* 7°9N 171°12E **64** G9
Dalarna *Sweden* 61°0N 14°0E **8** F16
Dālbandīn *Pakistan* 29°0N 64°23E **40** E4
Dalbeattie *U.K.* 54°56N 3°50W **11** G5
Dalbeg *Australia* 20°16S 147°18E **62** C4
Dalby *Australia* 27°10S 151°17E **63** D5
Dale City *U.S.A.* 38°38N 77°19W **81** F15
Dale Hollow L. *U.S.A.* 36°32N 85°27W **85** C12
Dalgān *Iran* 27°31N 59°19E **45** E8
Dalhart *U.S.A.* 36°4N 102°31W **84** C3
Dalhousie *Canada* 48°5N 66°26W **73** C6
Dalhousie *India* 32°38N 75°58E **42** C6
Dali *Shaanxi, China* 34°48N 109°58E **34** G5
Dali *Yunnan, China* 25°40N 100°10E **32** D5
Dalian *China* 38°50N 121°40E **35** E11
Daliang Shan *China* 28°0N 102°45E **32** D5
Daling He → *China* 40°55N 121°40E **35** D11
Dāliyat el Karmel *Israel* 32°43N 35°2E **46** C4
Dalkeith *U.K.* 55°54N 3°4W **11** F5
Dallas *Oreg., U.S.A.* 44°55N 123°19W **76** D2
Dallas *Tex., U.S.A.* 32°47N 96°48W **84** E6
Dalles, The *U.S.A.* 45°36N 121°10W **76** D3
Dalmā *U.A.E.* 24°30N 52°20E **45** E7
Dalmacija *Croatia* 43°20N 17°0E **22** C7
Dalmas, L. *Canada* 53°30N 71°50W **73** B5
Dalmatia = Dalmacija *Croatia* 43°20N 17°0E **22** C7
Dalmau *India* 26°4N 81°2E **43** F9
Dalmellington *U.K.* 55°19N 4°23W **11** F4
Dalnegorsk *Russia* 44°32N 135°33E **30** B7
Dalnerechensk *Russia* 45°50N 133°40E **30** B6
Dalnevostochnyy □ *Russia* 67°0N 140°0E **29** C14
Daloa *Ivory C.* 7°0N 6°30W **50** G4
Dalry *U.K.* 55°42N 4°43W **11** F4
Dalrymple, L. *Australia* 20°40S 147°0E **62** C4
Dalrymple, Mt. *Australia* 21°1S 148°39E **62** K6
Dalsland *Sweden* 58°50N 12°15E **9** G15
Daltenganj *India* 24°0N 84°4E **43** H11
Dalton *Ga., U.S.A.* 34°46N 84°58W **85** D12
Dalton *Mass., U.S.A.* 42°28N 73°11W **83** D11
Dalton *Nebr., U.S.A.* 41°25N 102°58W **80** E2
Dalton-in-Furness *U.K.* 54°10N 3°11W **12** C4
Dalvík *Iceland* 65°58N 18°32W **8** D4
Dálvvadis = Jokkmokk *Sweden* 66°35N 19°50E **8** C18
Dalwallinu *Australia* 30°17S 116°40E **61** F2
Daly → *Australia* 13°35S 130°19E **60** B5
Daly City *U.S.A.* 37°42N 122°27W **78** H4
Daly L. *Canada* 56°32N 105°39W **71** B7
Daly River *Australia* 13°46S 130°42E **60** B5
Daly Waters *Australia* 16°15S 133°24E **62** B1
Dam Doi *Vietnam* 8°50N 105°12E **39** H5
Dam Ha *Vietnam* 21°21N 107°36E **38** B6
Daman *India* 20°25N 72°57E **40** J8
Dāmaneh *Iran* 33°1N 50°29E **45** C6
Damanhûr *Egypt* 31°0N 30°30E **51** B12
Damant L. *Canada* 61°45N 105°5W **71** A7
Damanzhuang *China* 38°5N 116°35E **34** E9
Damar *Indonesia* 7°7S 128°40E **37** F7
Damara *C.A.R.* 4°58N 18°42E **52** D3
Damaraland *Namibia* 20°0S 15°0E **56** C2
Damascus = Dimashq *Syria* 33°30N 36°18E **46** B5
Damāvand *Iran* 35°47N 52°0E **45** C7
Damāvand, Qolleh-ye *Iran* 35°56N 52°10E **45** C7
Damba *Angola* 6°44S 15°20E **52** F3
Dâmboviţa → *Romania* 44°12N 26°26E **17** F14
Dame Marie *Haiti* 18°36N 74°26W **89** C5
Dāmghān *Iran* 36°10N 54°17E **45** B7
Damiel *Spain* 39°4N 3°37W **21** C4
Damietta = Dumyât *Egypt* 31°24N 31°48E **51** B12
Daming *China* 36°15N 115°6E **34** F8
Damīr Qābū *Syria* 36°58N 41°51E **44** B4
Dammam = Ad Dammām *Si. Arabia* 26°20N 50°5E **45** E6
Damodar → *India* 23°17N 87°35E **43** H12
Damoh *India* 23°50N 79°28E **43** H8
Dampier *Australia* 20°41S 116°42E **60** D2
Dampier, Selat *Indonesia* 0°40S 131°0E **37** E8
Dampier Arch. *Australia* 20°38S 116°32E **60** D2
Damrei, Chuor Phnum *Cambodia* 11°30N 103°0E **39** G4
Damyang *S. Korea* 35°19N 126°59E **35** G14
Dana *Indonesia* 11°0S 122°52E **37** F6
Dana *Jordan* 30°41N 35°37E **46** E4
Dana, L. *Canada* 50°53N 77°20W **72** B4
Dana, Mt. *U.S.A.* 37°54N 119°12W **78** H7
Danakil Desert *Ethiopia* 12°45N 41°0E **47** E3
Danané *Ivory C.* 7°16N 8°9W **50** G4
Danau Poso *Indonesia* 1°52S 120°35E **37** E6
Danbury *U.S.A.* 41°24N 73°28W **83** E11
Danby L. *U.S.A.* 34°13N 115°5W **77** J6
Dand *Afghan.* 31°28N 65°32E **42** D1
Dande ⌂ *Zimbabwe* 15°56S 30°16E **55** F3
Dandeldhura *Nepal* 29°20N 80°35E **43** E9
Dandeli *India* 15°5N 74°30E **40** M9
Dandenong *Australia* 38°0S 145°15E **63** F4
Dandong *China* 40°10N 124°20E **35** D13
Danfeng *China* 33°45N 110°25E **34** H6
Danger Is. = Pukapuka *Cook Is.* 10°53S 165°49W **65** J11
Danger Pt. *S. Africa* 34°40S 19°17E **56** E2
Danginpuri *Indonesia* 8°40S 115°13E **37** K18
Dangla Shan = Tanggula Shan *China* 32°40N 92°10E **32** C4
Dangrek, Phnom *Thailand* 14°15N 105°0E **38** E5
Dangriga *Belize* 17°0N 88°13W **87** D7
Dangshan *China* 34°27N 116°22E **34** G9
Daniel *U.S.A.* 42°52N 110°4W **76** E8
Daniel's Harbour *Canada* 50°13N 57°35W **73** B8
Danielskuil *S. Africa* 28°11S 23°33E **56** D3
Danielson *U.S.A.* 41°48N 71°53W **83** E13
Danilov *Russia* 58°16N 40°13E **18** C7
Daning *China* 36°28N 110°45E **34** F6
Ḑank *Oman* 23°33N 56°16E **45** F8
Dankhar Gompa *India* 32°10N 78°10E **42** C8
Danlí *Honduras* 14°4N 86°35W **88** D2
Danmark = Denmark ■ *Europe* 55°45N 10°0E **9** J14
Dannemora *U.S.A.* 44°43N 73°44W **83** B11
Dannevirke *N.Z.* 40°12S 176°8E **59** D6
Dannhauser *S. Africa* 28°0S 30°3E **57** D5
Dansville *U.S.A.* 42°34N 77°42W **82** D7
Danta *India* 24°11N 72°46E **42** G5
Dantan *India* 21°57N 87°20E **43** J12
Danube = Dunărea → *Europe* 45°20N 29°40E **17** F15
Danvers *U.S.A.* 42°34N 70°56W **83** D14
Danville *Ill., U.S.A.* 40°8N 87°37W **80** E10
Danville *Ky., U.S.A.* 37°39N 84°46W **81** G11
Danville *Pa., U.S.A.* 40°58N 76°37W **83** F8
Danville *Va., U.S.A.* 36°36N 79°23W **81** G14
Danville *Vt., U.S.A.* 44°25N 72°9W **83** B12
Danzhou *China* 19°31N 109°33E **38** C7
Danzig = Gdańsk *Poland* 54°22N 18°40E **17** A10
Dapaong *Togo* 10°55N 0°16E **50** F6
Daqing Shan *China* 40°40N 111°0E **34** D6
Daqq-e Sorkh, Kavīr *Iran* 33°45N 52°50E **45** C7
Dar Banda *Africa* 8°0N 23°0E **48** F6
Dar el Beida = Casablanca *Morocco* 33°36N 7°36W **50** B4
Dar es Salaam *Tanzania* 6°50S 39°12E **54** D4
Dar Mazār *Iran* 29°14N 57°20E **45** D8
Dar'ā *Syria* 32°36N 36°7E **46** C5
Dar'ā □ *Syria* 32°55N 36°10E **46** C5
Dārāb *Iran* 28°50N 54°30E **45** D7
Daraban *Pakistan* 31°44N 70°20E **42** D4
Daraina *Madag.* 13°12S 49°40E **57** A8
Daraj *Libya* 30°10N 10°28E **51** B8
Dārān *Iran* 32°59N 50°24E **45** C6
Dārayyā *Syria* 33°28N 36°15E **46** B5
Darband *Pakistan* 34°20N 72°50E **42** B5
Darband, Kūh-e *Iran* 31°34N 57°8E **45** D8
Darbhanga *India* 26°15N 85°55E **43** F11
D'Arcy *Canada* 50°33N 122°29W **70** C4
Dardanelle *Ark., U.S.A.* 35°13N 93°9W **84** D8
Dardanelle *Calif., U.S.A.* 38°20N 119°50W **78** G7
Dardanelles = Çanakkale Boğazı *Turkey* 40°17N 26°32E **23** D12
Dārestān *Iran* 29°9N 58°42E **45** D8
Dârfûr *Sudan* 13°40N 24°0E **51** F10
Dargai *Pakistan* 34°25N 71°55E **42** B4
Dargaville *N.Z.* 35°57S 173°52E **59** A4
Darhan *Mongolia* 49°37N 106°21E **32** B5
Darhan Muminggan Lianheqi *China* 41°40N 110°28E **34** D6
Darıca *Turkey* 40°45N 29°23E **23** D13
Darién, G. del *Colombia* 9°0N 77°0W **92** B3
Darién ⌂ *Panama* 7°36N 77°57W **88** E4
Dariganga = Ovoot *Mongolia* 45°21N 113°45E **34** B7
Darjeeling = Darjiling *India* 27°3N 88°18E **43** F13
Darjiling *India* 27°3N 88°18E **43** F13
Darkan *Australia* 33°20S 116°43E **61** F2
Darkhana *Pakistan* 30°39N 72°11E **42** D5
Darkhazīneh *Iran* 31°54N 48°39E **45** D6
Darkot Pass *Pakistan* 36°45N 73°26E **43** A5
Darling → *Australia* 34°4S 141°54E **63** E3
Darling Downs *Australia* 27°30S 150°30E **63** D5
Darling Ra. *Australia* 32°30S 116°20E **61** F2
Darlington *U.K.* 54°32N 1°33W **12** C6
Darlington *U.S.A.* 34°18N 79°52W **85** D15
Darlington □ *U.K.* 54°32N 1°33W **12** C6
Darlington, L. *S. Africa* 33°10S 25°9E **56** E4
Darlot, L. *Australia* 27°48S 121°35E **61** E3
Darłowo *Poland* 54°25N 16°25E **16** A9
Darmstadt *Germany* 49°51N 8°39E **16** D5
Darnah *Libya* 32°45N 22°45E **51** B10
Darnall *S. Africa* 29°23S 31°18E **57** D5
Darnley, C. *Antarctica* 68°0S 69°0E **5** C6
Darnley B. *Canada* 69°30N 123°30W **68** C7
Darr → *Australia* 23°39S 143°50E **62** C3
Darra Pezu *Pakistan* 32°19N 70°44E **42** C4
Darrequeira *Argentina* 37°42S 63°10W **94** D3
Darrington *U.S.A.* 48°15N 121°36W **76** B3
Dart → *U.K.* 50°24N 3°39W **13** G4
Dart, C. *Antarctica* 73°6S 126°20W **5** D14
Dartford *U.K.* 51°26N 0°13E **13** F8
Dartmoor *U.K.* 50°38N 3°57W **13** G4
Dartmoor △ *U.K.* 50°37N 3°59W **13** G4
Dartmouth *Canada* 44°40N 63°30W **73** D7
Dartmouth *U.K.* 50°21N 3°36W **13** G4
Dartmouth Res. *Australia* 26°4S 145°18E **63** D4
Dartuch, C. = Artrutx, C. de *Spain* 39°55N 3°49E **24** B10
Darvaza *Turkmenistan* 40°11N 58°24E **28** E6
Darvel, Teluk = Lahad Datu, Telok *Malaysia* 4°50N 118°20E **37** D5
Darwen *U.K.* 53°42N 2°29W **12** D5
Darwendale *Zimbabwe* 17°41S 30°33E **57** B5
Darwha *India* 20°15N 77°45E **40** J10
Darwin *Australia* 12°25S 130°51E **60** B5
Darwin *U.S.A.* 36°15N 117°35W **79** J9
Darya Khan *Pakistan* 31°48N 71°6E **42** D4
Daryācheh-ye Bakhtegān *Iran* 29°40N 53°50E **45** D7
Daryoi Amu = Amudarya → *Uzbekistan* 43°58N 59°34E **28** E6
Dās *U.A.E.* 25°20N 53°30E **45** E7
Dashen, Ras *Ethiopia* 13°8N 38°26E **47** E2
Dashetai *China* 41°0N 109°5E **34** D5
Dashköpri *Turkmenistan* 36°16N 62°8E **45** B9
Dashoguz *Turkmenistan* 41°49N 59°58E **28** E6
Dasht → *Pakistan* 25°10N 61°40E **40** G2
Daska *Pakistan* 32°20N 74°20E **42** C6
Dasuya *India* 31°49N 75°38E **42** D6
Datça *Turkey* 36°46N 27°40E **23** F12
Datia *India* 25°39N 78°27E **43** G8
Datong *China* 40°6N 113°18E **34** D7
Dattakhel *Pakistan* 32°54N 69°46E **42** C3
Datu, Tanjung *Indonesia* 2°5N 109°39E **36** D3
Datu Piang *Phil.* 7°2N 124°30E **37** C6
Datuk, Tanjong = Datu, Tanjung *Indonesia* 2°5N 109°39E **36** D3
Daud Khel *Pakistan* 32°53N 71°34E **42** C4
Daudnagar *India* 25°2N 84°24E **43** G11
Daugava → *Latvia* 57°4N 24°3E **9** H21
Daugavpils *Latvia* 55°53N 26°32E **9** J22
Daulpur *India* 26°45N 77°59E **42** F7
Dauphin *Canada* 51°9N 100°5W **71** C8
Dauphin *U.S.A.* 40°22N 76°56W **82** F8
Dauphin L. *Canada* 51°20N 99°45W **71** C9
Dauphiné *France* 45°15N 5°25E **20** D6
Dausa *India* 26°52N 76°20E **42** F7
Davangere *India* 14°25N 75°55E **40** M9
Davao *Phil.* 7°0N 125°40E **37** C7
Davao G. *Phil.* 6°30N 125°48E **37** C7
Dāvar Panāh = Sarāvān *Iran* 27°25N 62°15E **45** E9
Davenport *Calif., U.S.A.* 37°1N 122°12W **78** H4
Davenport *Iowa, U.S.A.* 41°32N 90°35W **80** E8
Davenport *Wash., U.S.A.* 47°39N 118°9W **76** C4
Davenport Ra. *Australia* 20°28S 134°0E **62** C1
Davenport Range △ *Australia* 20°36S 134°22E **62** C1
Daventry *U.K.* 52°16N 1°10W **13** E6
David *Panama* 8°30N 82°30W **88** E3
David City *U.S.A.* 41°15N 97°8W **80** E5
David Glacier *Antarctica* 75°20S 162°0E **5** D21
David Gorodok = Davyd Haradok *Belarus* 52°4N 27°8E **17** B14
Davidson *Canada* 51°16N 105°59W **71** C7
Davis *Antarctica* 68°34S 77°55E **5** C6
Davis *U.S.A.* 38°33N 121°44W **78** G5
Davis Dam *U.S.A.* 35°12N 114°34W **79** K12
Davis Inlet *Canada* 55°50N 60°59W **73** A7
Davis Mts. *U.S.A.* 30°50N 103°55W **84** F3
Davis Sea *Antarctica* 66°0S 92°0E **5** C7
Davis Str. *N. Amer.* 65°0N 58°0W **66** C14
Davlos *Cyprus* 35°25N 33°54E **25** D12
Davos *Switz.* 46°48N 9°49E **20** C8
Davy L. *Canada* 58°53N 108°18W **71** B7
Davyd Haradok *Belarus* 52°4N 27°8E **17** B14
Dawei = Tavoy *Burma* 14°2N 98°12E **38** E2
Dawes Ra. *Australia* 24°40S 150°40E **62** C5
Dawlish *U.K.* 50°35N 3°28W **13** G4
Dawna Ra. *Burma* 16°30N 98°30E **38** D2
Dawros Hd. *Ireland* 54°50N 8°33W **10** B3
Dawson *U.S.A.* 31°46N 84°27W **85** F12
Dawson, I. *Chile* 53°50S 70°50W **96** G2
Dawson B. *Canada* 52°53N 100°49W **71** C8
Dawson City *Canada* 64°10N 139°30W **68** C6
Dawson Creek *Canada* 55°45N 120°15W **70** B4
Dawson Inlet *Canada* 61°50N 93°25W **71** A10
Dawson Ra. *Australia* 24°30S 149°48E **62** C4
Dax *France* 43°44N 1°3W **20** E3
Daxian *China* 31°15N 107°23E **32** C5
Daxindian *China* 37°30N 120°50E **35** F11
Daxinggou *China* 43°25N 129°40E **35** C15
Daxue Shan *China* 30°30N 101°30E **32** C5
Day Kundī □ *Afghan.* 34°0N 66°0E **40** C5
Daylesford *Australia* 37°21S 144°9E **63** F3
Dayr az Zawr *Syria* 35°20N 40°5E **44** C4
Daysland *Canada* 52°50N 112°20W **70** C6
Dayton *Nev., U.S.A.* 39°14N 119°36W **78** F7
Dayton *Ohio, U.S.A.* 39°45N 84°12W **81** F11
Dayton *Pa., U.S.A.* 40°53N 79°15W **82** F5
Dayton *Tenn., U.S.A.* 35°30N 85°1W **85** D12
Dayton *Wash., U.S.A.* 46°19N 117°59W **76** C5
Dayton *Wyo., U.S.A.* 44°53N 107°16W **76** D10
Daytona Beach *U.S.A.* 29°13N 81°1W **85** G14
Dayville *U.S.A.* 44°28N 119°32W **76** D4
De Aar *S. Africa* 30°39S 24°0E **56** E3
De Biesbosch △ *Neths.* 51°45N 4°48E **15** C4
De Funiak Springs *U.S.A.* 30°43N 86°7W **85** F11
De Grey → *Australia* 20°12S 119°13E **60** D2
De Haan *Belgium* 51°16N 3°2E **15** C3
De Hoge Veluwe △ *Neths.* 52°5N 5°46E **15** B5
De Hoop ⌂ *S. Africa* 34°30S 20°28E **56** E3
De Kalb Junction *U.S.A.* 44°30N 75°16W **83** B9
De Kennemerduinen △ *Neths.* 52°27N 4°33E **15** B4
De Land *U.S.A.* 29°2N 81°18W **85** G14
De Leon *U.S.A.* 32°7N 98°32W **84** E5
De Panne *Belgium* 51°6N 2°34E **15** C2
De Pere *U.S.A.* 44°27N 88°4W **80** C9
De Queen *U.S.A.* 34°2N 94°21W **84** D7
De Quincy *U.S.A.* 30°27N 93°26W **84** F8
De Ruyters *U.S.A.* 42°45N 75°53W **83** D9
De Smet *U.S.A.* 44°23N 97°33W **80** C5
De Soto *U.S.A.* 38°8N 90°34W **80** F8
De Tour Village *U.S.A.* 46°0N 83°56W **81** B12
De Witt *U.S.A.* 34°18N 91°20W **84** D9
Dead Sea *Asia* 31°30N 35°30E **46** D4
Deadwood *U.S.A.* 44°23N 103°44W **80** C2
Deadwood L. *Canada* 59°10N 128°30W **70** B3
Deal *U.K.* 51°13N 1°25E **13** F9
Deal I. *Australia* 39°30S 147°20E **63** F4
Dealesville *S. Africa* 28°41S 25°44E **56** D4
Dean → *Canada* 52°49N 126°58W **70** C3
Dean, Forest of *U.K.* 51°45N 2°33W **13** F5
Dean Chan. *Canada* 52°30N 127°15W **70** C3
Deán Funes *Argentina* 30°20S 64°20W **94** C3
Dease → *Canada* 59°56N 128°32W **70** B3
Dease L. *Canada* 58°40N 130°5W **70** B2
Dease Lake *Canada* 58°25N 130°6W **70** B2
Death Valley *U.S.A.* 36°15N 116°50W **79** J10
Death Valley △ *U.S.A.* 36°29N 117°6W **79** J9
Death Valley Junction *U.S.A.* 36°20N 116°25W **79** J10
Debagram *India* 23°51N 90°33E **43** H14
Debar *Macedonia* 41°31N 20°30E **23** D9
Debden *Canada* 53°30N 106°50W **71** C7
Dębica *Poland* 50°2N 21°25E **17** C11
DeBolt *Canada* 55°12N 118°1W **70** B5
Deborah East, L. *Australia* 30°45S 119°30E **61** F2
Deborah West, L. *Australia* 30°45S 119°5E **61** F2
Debre Markos *Ethiopia* 10°20N 37°40E **47** E2
Debre Tabor *Ethiopia* 11°50N 38°26E **47** E2
Debre Zebit *Ethiopia* 11°48N 38°30E **47** F2
Debrecen *Hungary* 47°33N 21°42E **17** E11
Decatur *Ala., U.S.A.* 34°36N 86°59W **85** D11
Decatur *Ga., U.S.A.* 33°46N 84°16W **85** E12
Decatur *Ill., U.S.A.* 39°51N 88°57W **80** F9
Decatur *Ind., U.S.A.* 40°50N 84°56W **81** E11
Decatur *Tex., U.S.A.* 33°14N 97°35W **84** E6
Deccan *India* 18°0N 79°0E **40** L11
Deception Bay *Australia* 27°10S 153°5E **63** D5
Deception I. *Antarctica* 63°0S 60°15W **5** C17
Deception L. *Canada* 56°33N 104°13W **71** B8
Dechhu *India* 26°46N 72°20E **42** F5
Děčín *Czech Rep.* 50°47N 14°12E **16** C8
Deckerville *U.S.A.* 43°32N 82°44W **82** C2
Decorah *U.S.A.* 43°18N 91°48W **80** D8
Dedéagach = Alexandroupoli *Greece* 40°50N 25°54E **23** D11
Dedham *U.S.A.* 42°15N 71°10W **83** D13
Dedza *Malawi* 14°20S 34°20E **55** E3
Dee → *Aberds., U.K.* 57°9N 2°5W **11** D6
Dee → *Dumf. & Gall., U.K.* 54°51N 4°3W **11** G4
Dee → *Wales, U.K.* 53°22N 3°17W **12** D4
Deep B. *Canada* 61°15N 116°35W **70** A5
Deep Bay = Shenzhen Wan *China* 22°27N 113°55E **33** G10
Deepwater *Australia* 29°25S 151°51E **63** D5
Deer → *Canada* 58°23N 94°13W **71** B10
Deer L. *Canada* 52°40N 94°20W **71** C10
Deer Lake *Nfld. & L., Canada* 49°11N 57°27W **73** C8
Deer Lake *Ont., Canada* 52°36N 94°20W **71** C10
Deer Lodge *U.S.A.* 46°24N 112°44W **76** C7
Deer Park *U.S.A.* 47°57N 117°28W **76** C5
Deer River *U.S.A.* 47°20N 93°48W **80** B7
Deeragun *Australia* 19°16S 146°33E **62** B4
Deerdepoort *S. Africa* 24°37S 26°27E **56** C4
Defiance *U.S.A.* 41°17N 84°22W **81** E11
Degana *India* 26°50N 74°20E **42** F6
Dégelis *Canada* 47°30N 68°35W **73** C6
Deggendorf *Germany* 48°50N 12°57E **16** D7
Degh → *Pakistan* 31°3N 73°21E **42** D5
Degirmenlik = Kythréa *Cyprus* 35°15N 33°29E **25** D12
Deh Bīd *Iran* 30°39N 53°11E **45** D7
Deh Dasht *Iran* 30°47N 50°33E **45** D6
Deh-e Shīr *Iran* 31°29N 53°45E **45** D7
Dehaj *Iran* 30°42N 54°53E **45** D7
Dehak *Iran* 27°11N 62°37E **45** E9
Dehdez *Iran* 31°43N 50°17E **45** D6
Dehej *India* 21°44N 72°40E **42** J5
Dehestān *Iran* 28°30N 55°35E **45** D7
Dehgolān *Iran* 35°17N 47°25E **44** C5
Dehibat *Tunisia* 32°0N 10°47E **51** B8
Dehlorān *Iran* 32°41N 47°16E **44** C5
Dehnow-e Kūhestān *Iran* 27°58N 58°32E **45** E8
Dehra Dun *India* 30°20N 78°4E **42** D8
Dehri *India* 24°50N 84°15E **43** G11
Dehui *China* 44°30N 125°40E **35** B13
Deinze *Belgium* 50°59N 3°32E **15** D3
Dej *Romania* 47°10N 23°52E **17** E12
Deka → *Zimbabwe* 18°4S 26°42E **56** B4
DeKalb *U.S.A.* 41°56N 88°46W **80** E9
Dekese *Dem. Rep. of the Congo* 3°24S 21°24E **52** E4
Del Mar *U.S.A.* 32°58N 117°16W **79** N9
Del Norte *U.S.A.* 37°41N 106°21W **77** H10
Del Rio *U.S.A.* 29°22N 100°54W **84** G4
Delambre I. *Australia* 20°26S 117°5E **60** D2
Delano *U.S.A.* 35°46N 119°15W **79** K7
Delano Peak *U.S.A.* 38°22N 112°22W **76** G7
Delareyville *S. Africa* 26°41S 25°26E **56** D4
Delaronde L. *Canada* 54°3N 107°3W **71** C7
Delavan *U.S.A.* 42°38N 88°39W **80** D9
Delaware *U.S.A.* 40°18N 83°4W **81** E12
Delaware □ *U.S.A.* 39°0N 75°20W **81** F16
Delaware → *U.S.A.* 39°15N 75°20W **83** G9
Delaware B. *U.S.A.* 39°0N 75°10W **81** F16
Delaware Water Gap ⌂ *U.S.A.* 41°10N 74°55W **83** E10
Delay → *Canada* 56°56N 71°28W **73** A5
Delegate *Australia* 37°4S 148°56E **63** F4
Delevan *U.S.A.* 42°29N 78°29W **82** D6
Delft *Neths.* 52°1N 4°22E **15** B4
Delfzijl *Neths.* 53°20N 6°55E **15** A6
Delgado, C. *Mozam.* 10°45S 40°40E **55** E5
Delgerhet *Mongolia* 45°50N 110°30E **34** B6
Delgo *Sudan* 20°6N 30°40E **51** D12
Delhi *Canada* 42°51N 80°30W **82** D4
Delhi *India* 28°39N 77°13E **42** E7
Delhi *La., U.S.A.* 32°28N 91°30W **84** E9
Delhi *N.Y., U.S.A.* 42°17N 74°55W **83** D10
Delia *Canada* 51°38N 112°23W **70** C6
Delice *Turkey* 39°54N 34°2E **19** G5
Delicias *Mexico* 28°13N 105°28W **86** B3
Delījān *Iran* 33°59N 50°40E **45** C6
Déline *Canada* 65°11N 123°25W **68** C7
Delisle *Canada* 51°55N 107°8W **71** C7
Dell City *U.S.A.* 31°56N 105°12W **84** F2
Dell Rapids *U.S.A.* 43°50N 96°43W **80** D5
Delmar *U.S.A.* 42°37N 73°47W **83** D11
Delmenhorst *Germany* 53°3N 8°37E **16** B5
Delonga, Ostrova *Russia* 76°40N 149°20E **29** B15
Deloraine *Australia* 41°30S 146°40E **63** G4
Deloraine *Canada* 49°15N 100°29W **71** D8
Delphi *U.S.A.* 40°36N 86°41W **80** E10
Delphos *U.S.A.* 40°51N 84°21W **81** E11
Delportshoop *S. Africa* 28°22S 24°20E **56** D3
Delray Beach *U.S.A.* 26°28N 80°4W **85** H14
Delta *Colo., U.S.A.* 38°44N 108°4W **76** G9
Delta *Utah, U.S.A.* 39°21N 112°35W **76** G7
Delta Dunărea ⌂ *Romania* 45°15N 29°25E **17** F15
Delta Junction *U.S.A.* 64°2N 145°44W **68** C5
Deltona *U.S.A.* 28°54N 81°16W **85** G14
Delungra *Australia* 29°39S 150°51E **63** D5
Delvada *India* 20°46N 71°2E **42** J4
Delvinë *Albania* 39°59N 20°6E **23** E9
Demak *Indonesia* 6°53S 110°38E **37** G14
Demanda, Sierra de la *Spain* 42°15N 3°0W **21** A4
Demavend = Damāvand, Qolleh-ye *Iran* 35°56N 52°10E **45** C7
Dembia *Dem. Rep. of the Congo* 3°33N 25°48E **54** B2
Dembidolo *Ethiopia* 8°34N 34°50E **47** F1
Demchok *India* 32°42N 79°29E **43** C8
Demer → *Belgium* 50°57N 4°42E **15** D4
Deming *N. Mex., U.S.A.* 32°16N 107°46W **77** K10
Deming *Wash., U.S.A.* 48°50N 122°13W **78** B4
Demini → *Brazil* 0°46S 62°56W **92** D6
Demirci *Turkey* 39°2N 28°38E **23** E13
Demirköy *Turkey* 41°49N 27°45E **23** D12
Demopolis *U.S.A.* 32°31N 87°50W **85** E11
Dempo *Indonesia* 4°2S 103°15E **36** E2
Den Bosch = 's-Hertogenbosch *Neths.* 51°42N 5°17E **15** C5
Den Burg *Neths.* 53°3N 4°47E **15** A4
Den Chai *Thailand* 17°59N 100°4E **38** D3
Den Haag = 's-Gravenhage *Neths.* 52°7N 4°17E **15** B4
Den Helder *Neths.* 52°57N 4°45E **15** B4
Den Oever *Neths.* 52°56N 5°2E **15** B5
Denair *U.S.A.* 37°32N 120°48W **78** H6
Denali = McKinley, Mt. *U.S.A.* 63°4N 151°0W **74** a
Denau *Uzbekistan* 38°16N 67°54E **28** F7
Denbigh *Canada* 45°8N 77°15W **82** A7
Denbigh *U.K.* 53°12N 3°25W **12** D4
Denbighshire □ *U.K.* 53°8N 3°22W **12** D4
Dendang *Indonesia* 3°7S 107°56E **36** E3
Dendermonde *Belgium* 51°2N 4°5E **15** C4
Dengfeng *China* 34°25N 113°2E **34** G7
Dengkou *China* 40°18N 106°55E **34** D4
Denham *Australia* 25°56S 113°31E **61** E1
Denham, Mt. *Jamaica* 18°13N 77°32W **88** a
Denham Ra. *Australia* 21°55S 147°46E **62** C4
Denham Sd. *Australia* 25°45S 113°15E **61** E1
Denholm *Canada* 52°39N 108°1W **71** C7
Denia *Spain* 38°49N 0°8E **21** C6
Denial B. *Australia* 32°14S 133°32E **63** E1
Deniliquin *Australia* 35°30S 144°58E **63** F3
Denison *Iowa, U.S.A.* 42°1N 95°21W **80** D6
Denison *Tex., U.S.A.* 33°45N 96°33W **84** E6
Denison Plains *Australia* 18°35S 128°0E **60** C4
Denizli *Turkey* 37°42N 29°2E **19** G4
Denman Glacier *Antarctica* 66°45S 99°25E **5** C7
Denmark *Australia* 34°59S 117°25E **61** F2
Denmark ■ *Europe* 55°45N 10°0E **9** J14
Denmark Str. *Atl. Oc.* 66°0N 30°0W **66** C17
Dennery *St. Lucia* 13°55N 60°54W **89** f
Dennison *U.S.A.* 40°24N 81°19W **82** F3
Denny *U.K.* 56°1N 3°55W **11** E5
Denpasar *Indonesia* 8°39S 115°13E **37** K18
Denpasar ✈ (DPS) *Indonesia* 8°44S 115°10E **37** K18
Denton *Mont., U.S.A.* 47°19N 109°57W **76** C9
Denton *Tex., U.S.A.* 33°13N 97°8W **84** E6
D'Entrecasteaux, Pt. *Australia* 34°50S 115°57E **61** F2

D'Entrecasteaux △
  Australia 34°20S 115°33E **61 F2**
D'Entrecasteaux Is.
  Papua N. G. 9°0S 151°0E **58 B8**
Denver *Colo., U.S.A.* 39°42N 104°59W **76 G11**
Denver *Pa., U.S.A.* 40°14N 76°8W **83 F8**
Denver City *U.S.A.* 32°58N 102°50W **84 E3**
Deoband *India* 29°42N 77°43E **42 E7**
Deogarh *India* 25°32N 73°54E **42 G5**
Deoghar *India* 24°30N 86°42E **43 G12**
Deolali *India* 19°58N 73°50E **40 K8**
Deoli = Devli *India* 25°50N 75°20E **42 G6**
Deora *India* 26°22N 70°55E **42 F4**
Deori *India* 23°24N 79°1E **43 H8**
Deoria *India* 26°31N 83°48E **43 F10**
Deosai Mts. *Pakistan* 35°40N 75°0E **43 B6**
Deosri *India* 26°46N 90°29E **43 F14**
Depalpur *India* 22°51N 75°33E **42 H6**
Deping *China* 37°25N 116°58E **35 F9**
Deposit *U.S.A.* 42°4N 75°25W **83 D9**
Depuch I. *Australia* 20°37S 117°44E **60 D2**
Deputatskiy *Russia* 69°18N 139°54E **29 C14**
Dera Ghazi Khan
  Pakistan 30°5N 70°43E **42 D4**
Dera Ismail Khan
  Pakistan 31°50N 70°50E **42 D4**
Derabugti *Pakistan* 29°2N 69°9E **42 E3**
Derawar Fort *Pakistan* 28°46N 71°20E **42 E4**
Derbent *Russia* 42°5N 48°15E **19 F8**
Derby *Australia* 17°18S 123°38E **60 C3**
Derby *U.K.* 52°56N 1°28W **12 E6**
Derby *Conn., U.S.A.* 41°19N 73°5W **83 E11**
Derby *Kans., U.S.A.* 37°33N 97°16W **80 G5**
Derby *N.Y., U.S.A.* 42°41N 78°58W **82 D6**
Derby City □ *U.K.* 52°56N 1°28W **12 E6**
Derby Line *U.S.A.* 45°0N 72°6W **83 B12**
Derbyshire □ *U.K.* 53°11N 1°38W **12 D6**
Derdepoort *S. Africa* 24°38S 26°24E **56 C4**
Dereham *U.K.* 52°41N 0°57E **13 E8**
Derg → *U.K.* 54°44N 7°26W **10 B4**
Derg, L. *Ireland* 53°0N 8°20W **10 D3**
Deridder *U.S.A.* 30°51N 93°17W **84 F8**
Dermott *U.S.A.* 33°32N 91°26W **84 E9**
Derry = Londonderry
  U.K. 55°0N 7°20W **10 B4**
Derry = Londonderry □
  U.K. 55°0N 7°20W **10 B4**
Derry *N.H., U.S.A.* 42°53N 71°19W **83 D13**
Derry *Pa., U.S.A.* 40°20N 79°18W **82 F5**
Derryveagh Mts. *Ireland* 54°56N 8°11W **10 B3**
Derwent →, *Cumb., U.K.* 54°39N 3°33W **12 C4**
Derwent →, *Derby, U.K.* 52°57N 1°28W **12 E6**
Derwent →, *N. Yorks.,*
  U.K. 53°45N 0°58W **12 D7**
Derwent Water *U.K.* 54°35N 3°9W **12 C4**
Des Moines *Iowa, U.S.A.* 41°35N 93°37W **80 E7**
Des Moines *N. Mex.,*
  U.S.A. 36°46N 103°50W **77 H12**
Des Moines *Wash.,*
  U.S.A. 47°24N 122°19W **78 C4**
Des Moines → *U.S.A.* 40°23N 91°25W **80 E8**
Desaguadero →
  Argentina 34°30S 66°46W **94 C2**
Desaguadero → *Bolivia* 16°35S 69°5W **92 G5**
Desar *Malaysia* 1°31N 104°17E **39 d**
Descanso, Pta. *Mexico* 32°21N 117°3W **79 N9**
Deschaillons-sur-St-Laurent
  Canada 46°32N 72°7W **73 C5**
Deschambault L.
  Canada 54°50N 103°30W **71 C8**
Deschutes → *U.S.A.* 45°38N 120°55W **76 D3**
Dese *Ethiopia* 11°5N 39°40E **47 E2**
Deseado → *Argentina* 47°45S 65°54W **96 F3**
Deseronto *Canada* 44°12N 77°3W **82 B7**
Desert Center *U.S.A.* 33°43N 115°24W **79 M11**
Desert Hot Springs
  U.S.A. 33°58N 116°30W **79 M10**
Deshnok *India* 27°48N 73°21E **42 F5**
Desierto Central de Baja
  California △ *Mexico* 29°40N 114°50W **86 B2**
Desna → *Ukraine* 50°33N 30°32E **17 C16**
Desolación, I. *Chile* 53°0S 74°0W **96 G2**
Despeñaperros, Paso
  Spain 38°24N 3°30W **21 C4**
Dessau *Germany* 51°51N 12°14E **16 C7**
Dessye = Dese *Ethiopia* 11°5N 39°40E **47 E2**
D'Estrees B. *Australia* 35°55S 137°45E **63 F2**
Desuri *India* 25°18N 73°35E **42 G5**
Det Udom *Thailand* 14°54N 105°5E **38 E5**
Dete *Zimbabwe* 18°38S 26°50E **56 B4**
Detmold *Germany* 51°56N 8°52E **16 C5**
Detour, Pt. *U.S.A.* 45°40N 86°40W **80 C10**
Detroit *U.S.A.* 42°19N 83°12W **82 D1**
Detroit Lakes *U.S.A.* 46°49N 95°51W **80 B6**
Deua △ *Australia* 35°32S 149°46E **63 F4**
Deurne *Neths.* 51°27N 5°49E **15 C5**
Deutsche Bucht *Germany* 54°15N 8°0E **16 A5**
Deutschland = Germany ■
  Europe 51°0N 10°0E **16 C6**
Deva *Romania* 45°53N 22°55E **17 F12**
Devakottai *India* 9°55N 78°45E **40 Q11**
Devaprayag *India* 30°13N 78°35E **43 D8**
Deventer *Neths.* 52°15N 6°10E **15 B6**
Deveron → *U.K.* 57°41N 2°32W **11 D6**
Devgadh Bariya *India* 22°40N 73°55E **42 F4**
Devikot *India* 26°42N 71°12E **42 F4**
Devils Den *U.S.A.* 35°46N 119°58W **78 K7**
Devils Hole = Death Valley △
  U.S.A. 36°29N 117°6W **79 J9**
Devils Lake *U.S.A.* 48°7N 98°52W **80 A4**
Devils Paw *Canada* 58°47N 134°0W **70 B2**
Devils Postpile △ *U.S.A.* 37°37N 119°5W **78 H7**
Devils Tower *U.S.A.* 44°35N 104°42W **76 D11**
Devils Tower △
  U.S.A. 44°48N 104°55W **76 D11**
Devine *U.S.A.* 29°8N 98°54W **84 G5**
Devizes *U.K.* 51°22N 1°58W **13 F6**

Devli *India* 25°50N 75°20E **42 G6**
Devon *Canada* 53°24N 113°44W **70 C6**
Devon □ *U.K.* 50°50N 3°40W **13 G4**
Devon I. *Canada* 75°10N 85°0W **69 B11**
Devonport *Australia* 41°10S 146°22E **63 G4**
Devonport *N.Z.* 36°49S 174°49E **59 B5**
Dewas *India* 22°59N 76°3E **42 H7**
Dewetsdorp *S. Africa* 29°33S 26°39E **56 D4**
Dewey *Puerto Rico* 18°18N 65°18W **89 d**
Dexter *Maine, U.S.A.* 45°1N 69°18W **81 C19**
Dexter *Mo., U.S.A.* 36°48N 89°57W **80 G9**
Dexter *N. Mex., U.S.A.* 33°12N 104°22W **77 K11**
Dey-Dey, L. *Australia* 29°12S 131°4E **61 E5**
Deyang *China* 31°3N 104°27E **32 C5**
Deyhūk *Iran* 33°15N 57°30E **45 C8**
Deyyer *Iran* 27°55N 51°55E **45 E6**
Dez → *Iran* 31°39N 48°52E **45 D6**
Dezadeash L. *Canada* 60°28N 136°58W **70 A1**
Dezfūl *Iran* 32°20N 48°30E **45 C6**
Dezhneva, Mys *Russia* 66°5N 169°40W **29 C19**
Dezhou *China* 37°26N 116°18E **34 F9**
Dhadhar → *India* 24°56N 85°24E **43 G11**
Dhahiriya = Aẓ Ẓāhirīyah
  West Bank 31°25N 34°58E **46 D3**
Dhahran = Aẓ Ẓahrān
  Si. Arabia 26°10N 50°7E **45 E6**
Dhak *Pakistan* 32°25N 72°33E **42 C5**
Dhaka *Bangla.* 23°43N 90°26E **43 H14**
Dhaka □ *Bangla.* 24°25N 90°25E **43 G14**
Dhali *Cyprus* 35°1N 33°25E **25 D12**
Dhamār *Yemen* 14°30N 44°20E **47 E3**
Dhampur *India* 29°19N 78°33E **43 E8**
Dhamtari *India* 20°42N 81°35E **41 J12**
Dhanbad *India* 23°50N 86°30E **43 H12**
Dhangarhi *Nepal* 28°55N 80°40E **43 E9**
Dhankuta *Nepal* 26°55N 87°40E **43 F12**
Dhanpuri *India* 23°13N 81°30E **43 H9**
Dhar *India* 22°35N 75°26E **42 H6**
Dharampur *India* 22°13N 75°18E **42 H6**
Dharamsala = Dharmsala
  India 32°16N 76°23E **42 C7**
Dharan *Nepal* 26°49N 87°17E **43 F12**
Dhariwal *India* 31°57N 75°19E **42 D6**
Dharla → *Bangla.* 25°46N 89°42E **43 G13**
Dharmapuri *India* 12°10N 78°10E **40 N11**
Dharmjaygarh *India* 22°28N 83°13E **43 H10**
Dharmsala *India* 32°16N 76°23E **42 C7**
Dharni *India* 21°33N 76°53E **42 J7**
Dharwad *India* 15°30N 75°4E **40 M9**
Dhasan → *India* 25°48N 79°24E **43 G8**
Dhaulagiri *Nepal* 28°39N 83°28E **43 E10**
Dhebar, L. *India* 24°10N 74°0E **42 G6**
Dheftera *Cyprus* 35°5N 33°16E **25 D12**
Dhenkanal *India* 20°45N 85°35E **41 J14**
Dherinia *Cyprus* 35°3N 33°57E **25 D12**
Dhī Qār □ *Iraq* 31°0N 46°15E **44 D5**
Dhiarrizos → *Cyprus* 34°41N 32°34E **25 E11**
Dhībān *Jordan* 31°30N 35°46E **46 D4**
Dhilwan *India* 31°31N 75°21E **42 D6**
Dhimarkhera *India* 23°28N 80°22E **43 H9**
Dhodhekánisos = Dodecanese
  Greece 36°35N 27°0E **23 F12**
Dholka *India* 22°44N 72°29E **42 H5**
Dhoraji *India* 21°45N 70°37E **42 J4**
Dhrangadhra *India* 22°59N 71°31E **42 H4**
Dhrol *India* 22°33N 70°25E **42 H4**
Dhuburi *India* 26°2N 89°59E **41 F16**
Dhule *India* 20°58N 74°50E **40 J9**
Di Linh *Vietnam* 11°35N 108°4E **39 G7**
Di Linh, Cao Nguyen
  Vietnam 11°30N 108°0E **39 G7**
Dia *Greece* 35°28N 25°14E **25 D7**
Diablo Range *U.S.A.* 37°20N 121°25W **78 J5**
Diafarabé *Mali* 14°9N 4°57W **50 F5**
Diamante *Argentina* 32°5N 60°40W **94 C3**
Diamante → *Argentina* 34°30S 66°46W **94 C2**
Diamantina *Brazil* 18°17S 43°40W **93 G10**
Diamantina →
  Australia 26°45S 139°10E **63 D2**
Diamantina △ *Australia* 23°33S 141°23E **62 C3**
Diamantina *Brazil* 14°30S 56°30W **93 F7**
Diamond Bar *U.S.A.* 34°1N 117°48W **79 L9**
Diamond Harbour
  India 22°11N 88°14E **43 H13**
Diamond Is. *Australia* 17°25S 151°5E **62 B5**
Diamond Mts. *U.S.A.* 39°40N 115°50W **76 G6**
Diamond Springs
  U.S.A. 38°42N 120°49W **78 G6**
Diaoyu Tai = Senkaku-Shotō
  E. China Sea 25°45N 123°30E **31 M1**
Dībā *U.A.E.* 25°45N 56°16E **45 E8**
Dibai *India* 28°13N 78°15E **42 E8**
Dibaya
  Dem. Rep. of the Congo 6°30S 22°57E **52 F4**
Dibaya-Lubue
  Dem. Rep. of the Congo 4°12S 19°54E **52 E3**
Dibbeen □ *Jordan* 32°20N 35°45E **46 C4**
D'Iberville, Lac *Canada* 55°55N 73°15W **72 A5**
Dibete *Botswana* 23°45S 26°32E **56 C4**
Dibrugarh *India* 27°29N 94°55E **41 F19**
Dickens *U.S.A.* 33°37N 100°50W **84 E4**
Dickinson *U.S.A.* 46°53N 102°47W **80 B2**
Dickson *U.S.A.* 36°5N 87°23W **85 C11**
Dickson City *U.S.A.* 41°28N 75°36W **83 E9**
Didiéni *Mali* 13°53N 8°6W **50 F4**
Didsbury *Canada* 51°35N 114°10W **70 C6**
Diefenbaker, L. *Canada* 51°0N 106°55W **71 C7**
Diego de Almagro *Chile* 26°22S 70°3W **94 B1**
Diego Suarez = Antsiranana
  Madag. 12°25S 49°20E **57 A8**
Diekirch *Lux.* 49°52N 6°10E **15 E6**
Dien Ban *Vietnam* 15°53N 108°16E **38 E7**
Dien Bien *Vietnam* 21°20N 103°0E **38 B4**
Dien Khanh *Vietnam* 12°15N 109°6E **39 F7**
Dieppe *France* 49°54N 1°4E **20 B4**
Dierks *U.S.A.* 34°7N 94°1W **84 D7**

Diest *Belgium* 50°58N 5°4E **15 D5**
Dif *Somali Rep.* 0°59N 40°58E **47 G3**
Differdange *Lux.* 49°31N 5°54E **15 E5**
Dig *India* 27°28N 77°20E **42 F7**
Digba
  Dem. Rep. of the Congo 4°25N 25°48E **54 B2**
Digby *Canada* 44°38N 65°50W **73 D6**
Diggi *India* 26°22N 75°26E **42 F6**
Dighinala *Bangla.* 23°15N 92°5E **41 H18**
Dighton *U.S.A.* 38°29N 100°28W **80 F3**
Digne-les-Bains *France* 44°5N 6°12E **20 D7**
Digos *Phil.* 6°45N 125°20E **37 C7**
Digranes *Iceland* 66°4N 14°44W **8 C6**
Digul → *Indonesia* 7°7S 138°42E **37 F9**
Dihang = Brahmaputra →
  Asia 23°40N 90°35E **43 H13**
Dijlah, Nahr → *Asia* 31°0N 47°25E **44 D5**
Dijon *France* 47°20N 5°3E **20 C6**
Dikhil *Djibouti* 11°8N 42°20E **47 E3**
Dikkil = Dikhil *Djibouti* 11°8N 42°20E **47 E3**
Diksmuide *Belgium* 51°2N 2°52E **15 C2**
Dikson *Russia* 73°40N 80°5E **28 B9**
Dikti Oros *Greece* 35°8N 25°20E **25 D7**
Dila *Ethiopia* 6°21N 38°22E **47 F2**
Dili *E. Timor* 8°39S 125°34E **37 F7**
Dilley *U.S.A.* 28°40N 99°10W **84 G5**
Dilli = Delhi *India* 28°39N 77°13E **42 E7**
Dillingham *U.S.A.* 59°3N 158°28W **74 a**
Dillon *Canada* 55°56N 108°35W **71 B7**
Dillon *Mont., U.S.A.* 45°13N 112°38W **76 D7**
Dillon *S.C., U.S.A.* 34°25N 79°22W **85 D15**
Dillon → *Canada* 55°56N 108°56W **71 B7**
Dillsburg *U.S.A.* 40°7N 77°2W **82 F7**
Dilolo
  Dem. Rep. of the Congo 10°28S 22°18E **52 G4**
Dimapur *India* 25°54N 93°45E **32 D4**
Dimas *Mexico* 23°43N 106°47W **86 C3**
Dimashq *Syria* 33°30N 36°18E **46 B5**
Dimashq □ *Syria* 33°30N 36°30E **46 B5**
Dimbaza *S. Africa* 32°50S 27°14E **57 E4**
Dimboola *Australia* 36°28S 142°7E **63 F3**
Dîmbovița = Dâmbovița →
  Romania 44°12N 26°26E **17 F14**
Dimbulah *Australia* 17°8S 145°4E **62 B4**
Dimitrovgrad *Bulgaria* 42°5N 25°35E **23 C11**
Dimitrovgrad *Russia* 54°14N 49°39E **18 D8**
Dimitrovo = Pernik
  Bulgaria 42°35N 23°2E **23 C10**
Dimmitt *U.S.A.* 34°33N 102°19W **84 D3**
Dimona *Israel* 31°2N 35°1E **46 D4**
Dinagat *Phil.* 10°10N 125°40E **37 B7**
Dinajpur *Bangla.* 25°33N 88°43E **41 G16**
Dinan *France* 48°28N 2°2W **20 B2**
Dīnān Āb *Iran* 32°4N 56°49E **45 C8**
Dinant *Belgium* 50°16N 4°55E **15 D4**
Dinapur *India* 25°38N 85°5E **43 G11**
Dīnār, Kūh-e *Iran* 30°42N 51°46E **45 D6**
Dinara Planina *Croatia* 44°0N 16°30E **22 C7**
Dinard *France* 48°38N 2°6W **20 B2**
Dinaric Alps = Dinara Planina
  Croatia 44°0N 16°30E **22 C7**
Dindigul *India* 10°25N 78°0E **40 P11**
Dindori *India* 22°57N 81°5E **43 H9**
Ding Xian = Dingzhou
  China 38°30N 114°59E **34 E8**
Dinga *Pakistan* 25°26N 67°10E **42 G2**
Ding'an *China* 19°42N 110°19E **38 C8**
Dingbian *China* 37°35N 107°32E **34 F4**
Dingle *Ireland* 52°9N 10°17W **10 D1**
Dingle B. *Ireland* 52°3N 10°20W **10 D1**
Dingmans Ferry *U.S.A.* 41°13N 74°55W **83 E10**
Dingo *Australia* 23°38S 149°19E **62 C4**
Dingtao *China* 35°5N 115°35E **34 G8**
Dingwall *U.K.* 57°36N 4°26W **11 D4**
Dingxi *China* 35°30N 104°33E **34 G3**
Dingxiang *China* 38°30N 112°58E **34 E7**
Dingzhou *China* 38°30N 114°59E **34 E8**
Dinh, Mui *Vietnam* 11°22N 109°1E **39 G7**
Dinh Lap *Vietnam* 21°33N 107°6E **38 B6**
Dinin → *Ireland* 52°43N 7°18W **10 D4**
Dinira △ *Venezuela* 9°57N 70°6W **89 E6**
Dinokwe *Botswana* 23°29S 26°37E **56 C4**
Dinorwic *Canada* 49°41N 92°30W **71 D10**
Dinosaur *U.S.A.* 40°14N 109°0W **76 F9**
Dinosaur △ *U.S.A.* 40°30N 108°45W **76 F9**
Dinuba *U.S.A.* 36°32N 119°23W **78 J7**
Dionisades *Greece* 35°20N 26°10E **25 D8**
Diourbel *Senegal* 14°39N 16°12W **50 F2**
Dipalpur *Pakistan* 30°40N 73°39E **42 D5**
Dipkarpaz = Rizokarpaso
  Cyprus 35°36N 34°23E **25 D13**
Diplo *Pakistan* 24°35N 69°35E **42 G3**
Dipolog *Phil.* 8°36N 123°20E **37 C6**
Dipperu △ *Australia* 21°56S 148°42E **62 C4**
Dir *Pakistan* 35°8N 71°59E **40 B7**
Dire Dawa *Ethiopia* 9°35N 41°45E **47 F3**
Dirfis Oros *Greece* 38°40N 23°54E **23 E10**
Diriamba *Nic.* 11°51N 86°19W **88 D2**
Dirk Hartog I. *Australia* 25°50S 113°5E **61 E1**
Dirranbandi *Australia* 28°33S 148°17E **63 D4**
Disa *India* 24°18N 72°10E **42 G4**
Disappointment, C.
  U.S.A. 46°18N 124°5W **76 C1**
Disappointment, L.
  Australia 23°20S 122°40E **60 D3**
Disaster B. *Australia* 37°15S 149°58E **63 F4**
Discovery B. *Australia* 38°10S 140°40E **63 F3**
Discovery B. *China* 22°18N 114°1E **33 G11**
Disko = Qeqertarsuaq
  Greenland 69°45N 53°30W **66 C14**
Disney Reef *Tonga* 19°17S 174°7W **59 c**
Diss *U.K.* 52°23N 1°7E **13 E9**
Disteghil Sar *Pakistan* 36°20N 75°12E **43 A6**
District of Columbia □
  U.S.A. 38°55N 77°0W **81 F15**
Distrito Federal □ *Brazil* 15°45S 47°45W **93 G9**
Distrito Federal □
  Mexico 19°15N 99°10W **87 D5**

Diu *India* 20°45N 70°58E **42 J4**
Dīvāndarreh *Iran* 35°55N 47°2E **44 C5**
Divide *U.S.A.* 45°45N 112°45W **76 D7**
Dividing Ra. *Australia* 27°45S 116°0E **61 E2**
Divinópolis *Brazil* 20°10S 44°54W **93 H10**
Divnoye *Russia* 45°55N 43°21E **19 E7**
Divo *Ivory C.* 5°48N 5°15W **50 G4**
Dixie Mt. *U.S.A.* 39°55N 120°16W **78 F6**
Dixon *Calif., U.S.A.* 38°27N 121°49W **78 G5**
Dixon *Ill., U.S.A.* 41°50N 89°29W **80 E9**
Dixon Entrance *U.S.A.* 54°30N 132°0W **68 D6**
Dixville *Canada* 45°4N 71°46W **83 A13**
Diyālā □ *Iraq* 33°45N 44°50E **44 C5**
Diyālā → *Iraq* 33°13N 44°30E **44 C5**
Diyarbakır *Turkey* 37°55N 40°18E **44 B4**
Diyodar *India* 24°8N 71°50E **42 G4**
Djakarta = Jakarta
  Indonesia 6°9S 106°52E **37 G12**
Djamba *Angola* 16°45S 13°58E **56 B1**
Djambala *Congo* 2°32S 14°30E **52 E2**
Djanet *Algeria* 24°35N 9°32E **50 D7**
Djawa = Jawa *Indonesia* 7°0S 110°0E **36 F3**
Djelfa *Algeria* 34°40N 3°15E **50 B6**
Djema *C.A.R.* 6°3N 25°15E **54 A2**
Djerba, Î. de *Tunisia* 33°50N 10°48E **51 B8**
Djerid, Chott *Tunisia* 33°42N 8°30E **50 B7**
Djibouti *Djibouti* 11°30N 43°5E **47 E3**
Djibouti ■ *Africa* 12°0N 43°0E **47 E3**
Djolu *Dem. Rep. of the Congo* 0°35N 22°5E **52 D4**
Djougou *Benin* 9°40N 1°45E **50 G6**
Djoum *Cameroon* 2°41N 12°35E **52 D2**
Djourab, Erg du *Chad* 16°40N 18°50E **51 E9**
Djugu
  Dem. Rep. of the Congo 1°55N 30°35E **54 B3**
Djukbinj △ *Australia* 12°11S 131°2E **60 B5**
Djúpivogur *Iceland* 64°39N 14°17W **8 D6**
Dmitriya Lapteva, Proliv
  Russia 73°0N 140°0E **29 B15**
Dnepr = Dnipro →
  Ukraine 46°30N 32°18E **19 E5**
Dneprodzerzhinsk =
  Dniprodzerzhynsk
  Ukraine 48°32N 34°37E **19 E5**
Dnepropetrovsk =
  Dnipropetrovsk
  Ukraine 48°30N 35°0E **19 E6**
Dnestr = Dnister →
  Europe 46°18N 30°17E **17 E16**
Dnieper = Dnipro →
  Ukraine 46°30N 32°18E **19 E5**
Dniester = Dnister →
  Europe 46°18N 30°17E **17 E16**
Dnipro → *Ukraine* 46°30N 32°18E **19 E5**
Dniprodzerzhynsk
  Ukraine 48°32N 34°37E **19 E5**
Dnipropetrovsk *Ukraine* 48°30N 35°0E **19 E6**
Dnister → *Europe* 46°18N 30°17E **17 E16**
Dno *Russia* 57°50N 29°58E **9 H23**
Dnyapro = Dnipro →
  Ukraine 46°30N 32°18E **19 E5**
Do Gonbadān = Gachsārān
  Iran 30°15N 50°45E **45 D6**
Doaktown *Canada* 46°33N 66°8W **73 C6**
Doan Hung *Vietnam* 21°30N 105°10E **38 B5**
Doany *Madag.* 14°21S 49°30E **57 A8**
Doba *Chad* 8°40N 16°50E **51 G9**
Dobandi *Pakistan* 31°13N 66°50E **42 D2**
Dobbyn *Australia* 19°44S 140°2E **62 B3**
Dobele *Latvia* 56°37N 23°16E **9 H20**
Doberai, Jazirah *Indonesia* 1°25S 133°0E **37 E8**
Doblas *Argentina* 37°5S 64°0W **94 D3**
Dobo *Indonesia* 5°45S 134°15E **37 F8**
Doboj *Bos.-H.* 44°46N 18°4E **23 B8**
Dobrich *Bulgaria* 43°37N 27°49E **23 C12**
Dobruja *Europe* 44°30N 28°15E **17 F15**
Dobrush *Belarus* 52°25N 31°22E **17 B16**
Doc, Mui *Vietnam* 17°58N 106°30E **38 D6**
Docker River = Kaltukatjara
  Australia 24°52S 129°5E **61 D4**
Doctor Arroyo *Mexico* 23°40N 100°11W **86 C4**
Doctor Pedro P. Peña
  Paraguay 22°27S 62°21W **94 A3**
Doda *India* 33°10N 75°34E **43 C6**
Doda, L. *Canada* 49°25N 75°13W **72 C4**
Dodecanese *Greece* 36°35N 27°0E **23 F12**
Dodekanisa = Dodecanese
  Greece 36°35N 27°0E **23 F12**
Dodge City *U.S.A.* 37°45N 100°1W **80 G4**
Dodge L. *Canada* 59°50N 105°36W **71 B7**
Dodgeville *U.S.A.* 42°58N 90°8W **80 D8**
Dodoma *Tanzania* 6°8S 35°45E **54 D4**
Dodoma □ *Tanzania* 6°0S 36°0E **54 D4**
Dodori □ *Kenya* 1°55S 41°7E **54 C5**
Dodsland *Canada* 51°50N 108°45W **71 C7**
Dodson *U.S.A.* 48°24N 108°15W **76 B9**
Doesburg *Neths.* 52°1N 6°9E **15 B6**
Doetinchem *Neths.* 51°59N 6°18E **15 C6**
Dog Creek *Canada* 51°35N 122°14W **70 C4**
Dog L. *Man., Canada* 51°2N 98°31W **71 C9**
Dog L. *Ont., Canada* 48°48N 89°30W **72 C2**
Dogran *Pakistan* 31°48N 73°35E **42 D5**
Doğubayazıt *Turkey* 39°31N 44°5E **44 B5**
Doha = Ad Dawḩah
  Qatar 25°15N 51°35E **45 E6**
Dohazari *Bangla.* 22°10N 92°5E **41 H18**
Dohrighat *India* 26°16N 83°31E **43 F10**
Doi *Indonesia* 2°14N 127°49E **37 D7**
Doi Inthanon △ *Thailand* 18°33N 98°34E **38 C2**
Doi Khuntan △ *Thailand* 18°33N 99°14E **38 C2**
Doi Luang *Thailand* 18°30N 101°0E **38 C3**
Doi Luang △ *Thailand* 18°30N 99°30E **38 C2**
Doi Saket *Thailand* 18°52N 99°9E **38 C2**
Doi Suthep △ *Thailand* 18°48N 98°54E **38 C2**
Dois Irmãos, Sa. *Brazil* 9°0S 42°30W **93 E10**
Dokkum *Neths.* 53°20N 5°59E **15 A5**
Dokri *Pakistan* 27°25N 68°7E **42 F3**

Dolak, Pulau *Indonesia* 8°0S 138°30E **37 F9**
Dolbeau *Canada* 48°53N 72°14W **73 C5**
Dole *France* 47°7N 5°31E **20 C6**
Dolgellau *U.K.* 52°45N 3°53W **12 E4**
Dolgelley = Dolgellau
  U.K. 52°45N 3°53W **12 E4**
Dolinsk *Russia* 47°21N 142°48E **29 E15**
Dollard *Neths.* 53°20N 7°10E **15 A7**
Dolo *Ethiopia* 4°11N 42°3E **47 G3**
Dolomites = Dolomiti
  Italy 46°23N 11°51E **22 A4**
Dolomiti *Italy* 46°23N 11°51E **22 A4**
Dolores *Argentina* 36°20S 57°40W **94 D4**
Dolores *Uruguay* 33°34S 58°15W **94 C4**
Dolores *U.S.A.* 37°28N 108°30W **77 H9**
Dolores → *U.S.A.* 38°49N 109°17W **76 G9**
Dolphin, C. *Falk. Is.* 51°10S 59°0W **96 G5**
Dolphin and Union Str.
  Canada 69°5N 114°45W **68 C8**
Dom Pedrito *Brazil* 31°0S 54°40W **95 C5**
Doma △ *Zimbabwe* 16°28S 30°12E **55 F3**
Domariaganj → *India* 26°17N 83°44E **43 F10**
Domasi *Malawi* 15°15S 35°22E **55 F4**
Dombarovskiy *Russia* 50°46N 59°32E **28 D6**
Dombås *Norway* 62°4N 9°8E **8 E13**
Dome Argus *Antarctica* 80°50S 76°30E **5 E12**
Dome C. *Antarctica* 75°12S 123°37E **5 D7**
Dome Fuji *Antarctica* 77°20S 39°45E **5 D5**
Domel I. = Letsôk-aw Kyun
  Burma 11°30N 98°25E **39 G2**
Domeyko *Chile* 29°0S 71°0W **94 B1**
Domeyko, Cordillera
  Chile 24°30S 69°0W **94 A2**
Dominador *Chile* 24°21S 69°20W **94 A2**
Dominica ■ *W. Indies* 15°20N 61°20W **89 C7**
Dominica Passage
  W. Indies 15°10N 61°20W **89 C7**
Dominican Rep. ■
  W. Indies 19°0N 70°30W **89 C5**
Domodóssola *Italy* 46°7N 8°17E **20 C8**
Domville, Mt. *Australia* 28°1S 151°15E **63 D5**
Don → *Russia* 47°4N 39°18E **19 E6**
Don → *Aberds., U.K.* 57°11N 2°5W **11 D6**
Don → *S. Yorks., U.K.* 53°41N 0°52W **12 D7**
Don, C. *Australia* 11°18S 131°46E **60 B5**
Don Benito *Spain* 38°53N 5°51W **21 C3**
Don Figuerero Mts.
  Jamaica 18°5N 77°36W **88 a**
Don Sak *Thailand* 9°18N 99°41E **39 b**
Dona Ana = Nhamaabué
  Mozam. 17°25S 35°5E **55 F4**
Donaghadee *U.K.* 54°39N 5°33W **10 B6**
Donaghmore *Ireland* 52°52N 7°36W **10 D4**
Donald *Australia* 36°23S 143°0E **63 F3**
Donalsonville *U.S.A.* 31°2N 84°53W **85 F12**
Donau = Dunărea →
  Europe 45°20N 29°40E **17 F15**
Donauwörth *Germany* 48°43N 10°47E **16 D6**
Doncaster *U.K.* 53°32N 1°6W **12 D6**
Dondo *Angola* 9°45S 14°25E **52 F2**
Dondo *Mozam.* 19°33S 34°46E **55 F3**
Dondo, Teluk *Indonesia* 0°50N 120°30E **37 D6**
Dondra Head *Sri Lanka* 5°55N 80°40E **40 S12**
Donegal *Ireland* 54°39N 8°5W **10 B3**
Donegal □ *Ireland* 54°53N 8°0W **10 B4**
Donegal B. *Ireland* 54°31N 8°49W **10 B3**
Donets → *Russia* 47°33N 40°55E **19 E7**
Donets Basin *Ukraine* 49°0N 38°0E **6 E13**
Donetsk *Ukraine* 48°0N 37°45E **19 E6**
Dong Ba Thin *Vietnam* 12°8N 109°13E **39 F7**
Dong Dang *Vietnam* 21°54N 106°42E **38 B6**
Dong Giam *Vietnam* 19°25N 105°31E **38 C5**
Dong Ha *Vietnam* 16°40N 107°0E **38 D6**
Dong Hene *Laos* 16°40N 105°18E **38 D5**
Dong Hoi *Vietnam* 17°29N 106°36E **38 D6**
Dong Khe *Vietnam* 22°26N 106°27E **38 A6**
Dong Ujimqin Qi *China* 45°32N 116°55E **34 B9**
Dong Van *Vietnam* 23°16N 105°22E **38 A5**
Dong Xoai *Vietnam* 11°32N 106°55E **39 G6**
Dongara *Australia* 29°14S 114°57E **61 E1**
Dongbei *China* 45°0N 125°0E **35 D13**
Dongchuan *China* 26°8N 103°1E **32 D5**
Dongco *China* 32°8N 84°55E **41 C14**
Dongfang *China* 18°50N 108°33E **38 C7**
Dongfeng *China* 42°40N 125°34E **35 C13**
Donggala *Indonesia* 0°30S 119°40E **37 E5**
Donggou *China* 39°52N 124°10E **35 E13**
Dongguang *China* 37°50N 116°30E **34 F9**
Donghae *S. Korea* 37°29N 129°7E **35 F15**
Dongjingcheng *China* 44°0N 131°5E **35 B16**
Dongnae *S. Korea* 35°12N 129°5E **35 G15**
Dongning *China* 44°2N 131°5E **35 B16**
Dongola *Sudan* 19°9N 30°22E **51 E12**
Dongping *China* 35°55N 116°20E **34 G9**
Dongsheng *China* 39°50N 110°0E **34 E6**
Dongtai *China* 32°51N 120°21E **35 H11**
Dongting Hu *China* 29°18N 112°45E **33 D6**
Donington, C. *Australia* 34°45S 136°0E **63 E2**
Dønna *Norway* 66°6N 12°30E **8 C15**
Donna *U.S.A.* 26°9N 98°4W **84 H5**
Donnaconna *Canada* 46°41N 71°41W **73 C5**
Donnelly's Crossing
  N.Z. 35°42S 173°38E **59 A4**
Donnybrook *Australia* 33°34S 115°48E **61 F2**
Donnybrook *S. Africa* 29°59S 29°48E **57 D4**
Donora *U.S.A.* 40°11N 79°52W **82 F5**
Donostia = Donostia-San
  Sebastián *Spain* 43°17N 1°58W **21 A5**
Donostia-San Sebastián
  Spain 43°17N 1°58W **21 A5**
Donwood *Canada* 44°19N 78°16W **82 B6**
Doon → *U.K.* 55°27N 4°39W **11 F4**
Dora, L. *Australia* 22°0S 123°0E **60 D3**
Dora Báltea → *Italy* 45°11N 8°3E **20 D8**
Doran L. *Canada* 61°13N 108°6W **71 A7**

Dorchester *U.K.* 50°42N 2°27W **13** G5
Dorchester, C. *Canada* 65°27N 77°27W **69** C12
Dordabis *Namibia* 22°52S 17°38E **56** C2
Dordogne → *France* 45°2N 0°36W **20** D3
Dordrecht *Neths.* 51°48N 4°39E **15** C4
Dordrecht *S. Africa* 31°20S 27°3E **56** E4
Doré L. *Canada* 54°46N 107°17W **71** C7
Dori *Burkina Faso* 14°3N 0°2W **50** F5
Doring → *S. Africa* 31°54S 18°39E **56** E2
Doringbos *S. Africa* 31°59S 19°16E **56** E2
Dorking *U.K.* 51°14N 0°19W **13** F7
Dornbirn *Austria* 47°25N 9°45E **16** E5
Dornoch *Canada* 44°18N 80°51W **82** B4
Dornoch *U.K.* 57°53N 4°2W **11** D4
Dornoch Firth *U.K.* 57°51N 4°4W **11** D4
Dornogovĭ □ *Mongolia* 44°0N 110°0E **34** C6
Doro, Kavo *Greece* 38°9N 24°38E **23** E11
Dorohoi *Romania* 47°56N 26°23E **17** E14
Döröö Nuur *Mongolia* 48°0N 93°0E **32** B4
Dorr *Iran* 33°17N 50°38E **45** C6
Dorre I. *Australia* 25°13S 113°12E **61** E1
Dorrigo *Australia* 30°20S 152°44E **63** E5
Dorris *U.S.A.* 41°58N 121°55W **76** F3
Dorset *Canada* 45°14N 78°54W **82** A6
Dorset Ohio, *U.S.A.* 41°40N 80°40W **82** E4
Dorset Vt., *U.S.A.* 43°15N 73°5W **83** C11
Dorset □ *U.K.* 50°45N 2°26W **13** G5
Dortmund *Germany* 51°30N 7°28E **16** C4
Dörtyol *Turkey* 36°50N 36°13E **44** B3
Doruma
  Dem. Rep. of the Congo 4°42N 27°33E **54** B2
Dorūneh *Iran* 35°10N 57°18E **45** C8
Dos Bahías, C. *Argentina* 44°58S 65°32W **96** E3
Dos Hermanas *Spain* 37°16N 5°55W **21** D3
Dos Palos *U.S.A.* 36°59N 120°37W **78** J6
Dosso *Niger* 13°0N 3°13E **50** F6
Dothan *U.S.A.* 31°13N 85°24W **85** F12
Doty *U.S.A.* 46°38N 123°17W **78** D3
Douai *France* 50°21N 3°4E **20** A5
Douala *Cameroon* 4°0N 9°45E **52** D1
Douarnenez *France* 48°6N 4°21W **20** B1
Double Island Pt.
  Australia 25°56S 153°11E **63** D5
Double Mountain Fork →
  U.S.A. 33°16N 100°0W **84** E4
Doubs → *France* 46°53N 5°1E **20** C6
Doubtful Sd. *N.Z.* 45°20S 166°49E **59** F1
Doubtless B. *N.Z.* 34°55S 173°26E **59** A4
Douglas *Canada* 45°31N 76°56W **82** A8
Douglas I. of Man 54°10N 4°28W **12** C3
Douglas *S. Africa* 29°4S 23°46E **56** D3
Douglas Ariz., *U.S.A.* 31°21N 109°33W **77** L9
Douglas Ga., *U.S.A.* 31°31N 82°51W **85** F13
Douglas Wyo., *U.S.A.* 42°45N 105°24W **76** E11
Douglas Apsley △
  Australia 41°45S 148°11E **63** G4
Douglas Chan. *Canada* 53°40N 129°20W **70** C3
Douglas Pt. *Canada* 44°19N 81°37W **82** B3
Douglasville *U.S.A.* 33°45N 84°45W **85** E12
Dounreay *U.K.* 58°35N 3°44W **11** C5
Dourada, Serra *Brazil* 13°10S 48°45W **93** F9
Dourados *Brazil* 22°9S 54°50W **95** A5
Dourados → *Brazil* 21°58S 54°18W **95** A5
Dourados, Serra dos
  Brazil 23°30S 53°30W **95** A5
Douro → *Europe* 41°8N 8°40W **21** B1
Dove → *U.K.* 52°51N 1°36W **12** E6
Dove Creek *U.S.A.* 37°46N 108°54W **77** H9
Dover *Australia* 43°18S 147°2E **63** G4
Dover *U.K.* 51°7N 1°19E **13** F9
Dover Del., *U.S.A.* 39°10N 75°32W **81** F16
Dover N.H., *U.S.A.* 43°12N 70°56W **83** C14
Dover N.J., *U.S.A.* 40°53N 74°34W **83** F10
Dover Ohio, *U.S.A.* 40°32N 81°29W **82** F3
Dover, Pt. *Australia* 32°32S 125°32E **61** F4
Dover, Str. of *Europe* 51°0N 1°30E **13** G9
Dover-Foxcroft *U.S.A.* 45°11N 69°13W **81** C19
Dover Plains *U.S.A.* 41°43N 73°35W **83** E11
Dovey = Dyfi → *U.K.* 52°32N 4°3W **13** E3
Dovrefjell *Norway* 62°15N 9°33E **8** E13
Dow Rūd *Iran* 33°28N 49°4E **45** C6
Dowa *Malawi* 13°38S 33°58E **55** E3
Dowagiac *U.S.A.* 41°59N 86°6W **80** E10
Dowerin *Australia* 31°12S 117°2E **61** F2
Dowgha'i *Iran* 36°54N 58°32E **45** B8
Dowlatābād *Kermān,*
  Iran 28°20N 56°40E **45** D8
Dowlatābād *Khorāsān,*
  Iran 35°16N 59°29E **45** C8
Down □ *U.K.* 54°23N 6°2W **10** B5
Downey Calif., *U.S.A.* 33°56N 118°9W **79** M8
Downey Idaho, *U.S.A.* 42°26N 112°7W **76** E7
Downham Market *U.K.* 52°37N 0°23E **13** E8
Downieville *U.S.A.* 39°34N 120°50W **78** F6
Downpatrick *U.K.* 54°20N 5°43W **10** B6
Downpatrick Hd. *Ireland* 54°20N 9°21W **10** B2
Downton, Mt. *Canada* 52°42N 124°52W **70** C4
Dowsāri *Iran* 28°25N 57°59E **45** D8
Doyle *U.S.A.* 40°2N 120°6W **78** E6
Doylestown *U.S.A.* 40°21N 75°10W **83** F9
Dozois, Rés. *Canada* 47°30N 77°5W **72** C4
Dra Khel *Pakistan* 27°58N 66°45E **42** F2
Drâa, C. *Morocco* 28°47N 11°0W **50** C3
Drâa, Oued → *Morocco* 28°40N 11°10W **50** C3
Drac, Coves del *Spain* 39°31N 3°19E **24** B10
Drachten *Neths.* 53°7N 6°5E **15** A6
Drăgășani *Romania* 44°39N 24°17E **17** F13
Dragichyn *Belarus* 52°15N 25°8E **17** B13
Dragoman, Prokhod
  Bulgaria 42°58N 22°53E **23** C10
Dragon's Mouths = Bocas del
  Dragón *Venezuela* 11°0N 61°50W **93** K15
Draguignan *France* 43°32N 6°27E **20** E7
Drain *U.S.A.* 43°40N 123°19W **76** E2
Drake *U.S.A.* 47°55N 100°23W **80** B3

Drake Passage *S. Ocean* 58°0S 68°0W **5** B17
Drakensberg *S. Africa* 31°0S 28°0E **57** D4
Drama *Greece* 41°9N 24°10E **23** D11
Drammen *Norway* 59°42N 10°12E **9** G14
Drangajökull *Iceland* 66°9N 22°15W **8** C2
Dras *India* 34°25N 75°48E **43** B6
Drastis, Akra *Greece* 39°48N 19°40E **25** A3
Drau = Drava →
  Croatia 45°33N 18°55E **23** B8
Drava → *Croatia* 45°33N 18°55E **23** B8
Drayton *Canada* 43°46N 80°40W **82** C4
Drayton Valley *Canada* 53°12N 114°58W **70** C6
Drenthe □ *Neths.* 52°52N 6°40E **15** B6
Drepanon, Akra *Greece* 35°28N 24°14E **25** D6
Drepanum, C. *Cyprus* 34°54N 32°19E **25** E11
Dresden *Canada* 42°35N 82°11W **82** D2
Dresden *Germany* 51°3N 13°44E **16** C7
Dresden *U.S.A.* 42°41N 76°57W **82** D8
Dreux *France* 48°44N 1°23E **20** B4
Driffield *U.K.* 54°0N 0°26W **12** C7
Driftwood *U.S.A.* 41°20N 78°8W **82** E6
Driggs *U.S.A.* 43°44N 111°6W **76** E8
Drin → *Albania* 42°1N 19°38E **23** C8
Drina → *Bos.-H.* 44°53N 19°21E **23** B8
Drøbak *Norway* 59°39N 10°39E **9** G14
Drobeta-Turnu Severin
  Romania 44°39N 22°41E **17** F12
Drochia *Moldova* 48°2N 27°48E **17** D14
Drogheda *Ireland* 53°43N 6°22W **10** C5
Drogichin = Dragichyn
  Belarus 52°15N 25°8E **17** B13
Drogobych = Drohobych
  Ukraine 49°20N 23°30E **17** D12
Drohobych *Ukraine* 49°20N 23°30E **17** D12
Droichead Atha = Drogheda
  Ireland 53°43N 6°22W **10** C5
Droichead Nua *Ireland* 53°11N 6°48W **10** C5
Droitwich *U.K.* 52°16N 2°8W **13** E5
Drôme → *France* 44°46N 4°46E **20** D6
Dromedary, C. *Australia* 36°17S 150°10E **63** F5
Dromore *U.K.* 54°31N 7°28W **10** B4
Dromore West *Ireland* 54°15N 8°52W **10** B3
Dronfield *U.K.* 53°19N 1°27W **12** D6
Dronning Maud Land
  Antarctica 72°30S 12°0E **5** D3
Dronten *Neths.* 52°32N 5°43E **15** B5
Druk Yul = Bhutan ■
  Asia 27°25N 90°30E **41** F17
Drumbo *Canada* 43°16N 80°35W **82** C4
Drumcliff *Ireland* 54°20N 8°29W **10** B3
Drumheller *Canada* 51°25N 112°40W **70** C6
Drummond *U.S.A.* 46°40N 113°9W **76** C7
Drummond I. *U.S.A.* 46°1N 83°39W **81** B12
Drummond Pt. *Australia* 34°9S 135°16E **63** E2
Drummond Ra.
  Australia 23°45S 147°10E **62** C4
Drummondville *Canada* 45°55N 72°25W **72** C5
Drumright *U.S.A.* 35°59N 96°36W **84** D6
Druskininkai *Lithuania* 54°3N 23°58E **9** J20
Drut → *Belarus* 53°8N 30°5E **17** B16
Druzhina *Russia* 68°14N 145°18E **29** C15
Dry Harbour Mts.
  Jamaica 18°19N 77°24W **88** a
Dry Tortugas *U.S.A.* 24°38N 82°55W **85** F13
Dryden *Canada* 49°47N 92°50W **71** D10
Dryden *U.S.A.* 42°30N 76°18W **83** D8
Drygalski I. *Antarctica* 66°0S 92°0E **5** C7
Drygalski Ice Tongue
  Antarctica 75°24S 163°30E **5** D21
Drysdale → *Australia* 13°59S 126°51E **60** B4
Drysdale I. *Australia* 11°41S 136°0E **62** A2
Drysdale River △
  Australia 14°56S 127°2E **60** B4
Du Gué → *Canada* 57°21N 70°45W **72** A5
Du Quoin *U.S.A.* 38°1N 89°14W **80** F9
Duanesburg *U.S.A.* 42°45N 74°11W **83** D10
Duaringa *Australia* 23°42S 149°42E **62** C4
Duarte, Pico *Dom. Rep.* 19°2N 70°59W **89** C5
Dubai = Dubayy *U.A.E.* 25°18N 55°20E **45** E7
Dubāsari *Moldova* 47°15N 29°10E **17** E15
Dubāsari Vdkhr.
  Moldova 47°30N 29°0E **17** E15
Dubawnt → *Canada* 64°33N 100°6W **71** A8
Dubawnt L. *Canada* 63°8N 101°28W **71** A8
Dubayy *U.A.E.* 25°18N 55°20E **45** E7
Dubbo *Australia* 32°11S 148°35E **63** E4
Dubele
  Dem. Rep. of the Congo 2°56N 29°35E **54** B2
Dublin *Ireland* 53°21N 6°15W **10** C5
Dublin Ga., *U.S.A.* 32°32N 82°54W **85** E13
Dublin Tex., *U.S.A.* 32°5N 98°21W **84** E5
Dublin ✈ (DUB) *Ireland* 53°26N 6°15W **10** C5
Dubno *Ukraine* 50°25N 25°45E **17** C13
Dubois Idaho, *U.S.A.* 44°10N 112°14W **76** D7
Dubois Pa., *U.S.A.* 41°7N 78°46W **82** E6
Dubossary = Dubăsari
  Moldova 47°15N 29°10E **17** E15
Dubossary Vdkhr. = Dubăsari
  Vdkhr. *Moldova* 47°30N 29°0E **17** E15
Dubovka *Russia* 49°5N 44°50E **19** E7
Dubrajpur *India* 23°48N 87°25E **43** H12
Dubréka *Guinea* 9°46N 13°31W **50** G3
Dubrovitsa = Dubrovytsya
  Ukraine 51°31N 26°35E **17** C14
Dubrovnik *Croatia* 42°39N 18°6E **23** D8
Dubrovytsya *Ukraine* 51°31N 26°35E **17** C14
Dubuque *U.S.A.* 42°30N 90°41W **80** D8
Duchesne *U.S.A.* 40°10N 110°24W **76** F8
Duchess *Australia* 21°20S 139°50E **62** C2
Ducie I. *Pac. Oc.* 24°40S 124°48W **65** K15
Duck → *U.S.A.* 36°2N 87°52W **85** C11
Duck Cr. → *Australia* 22°37S 116°53E **60** D2
Duck Lake *Canada* 52°50N 106°16W **71** C7
Duck Mountain △
  Canada 51°45N 101°0W **71** C8
Duckwall, Mt. *U.S.A.* 37°58N 120°7W **78** H6

Dudhi *India* 24°15N 83°10E **43** G10
Dudinka *Russia* 69°30N 86°13E **29** C9
Dudley *U.K.* 52°31N 2°5W **13** E5
Dudwa *India* 28°30N 80°41E **43** E9
Dudwa △ *India* 28°30N 80°40E **43** E9
Duero = Douro → *Europe* 41°8N 8°40W **21** B1
Dufftown *U.K.* 57°27N 3°8W **11** D5
Dugi Otok *Croatia* 44°0N 15°3E **16** G8
Duisburg *Germany* 51°26N 6°45E **16** C4
Duiwelskloof = Modjadjiskloof
  S. Africa 23°42S 30°10E **57** C5
Dukdamın *Iran* 35°59N 57°43E **45** C8
Dukelský Průsmyk
  Slovak Rep. 49°25N 21°42E **17** D11
Dukhān *Qatar* 25°25N 50°50E **45** E6
Duki *Pakistan* 30°14N 68°25E **40** D6
Duku *Nigeria* 10°43N 10°43E **51** F8
Dulce *U.S.A.* 36°56N 107°0W **77** H10
Dulce → *Argentina* 30°32S 62°33W **94** C3
Dulce, G. *Costa Rica* 8°40N 83°20W **88** E3
Dulf *Iraq* 35°7N 45°51E **44** C5
Duliu *China* 39°2N 116°55E **34** E9
Dullewala *Pakistan* 31°50N 71°25E **42** D4
Dullstroom *S. Africa* 25°27S 30°7E **57** D5
Dulq Maghār *Syria* 36°22N 38°39E **44** B3
Duluth *U.S.A.* 46°47N 92°6W **80** B7
Dum Dum *India* 22°39N 88°26E **43** H13
Dum Duma *India* 27°40N 95°40E **41** F19
Dūmā *Syria* 33°34N 36°24E **46** B5
Dumaguete *Phil.* 9°17N 123°15E **37** C6
Dumai *Indonesia* 1°35N 101°28E **36** D2
Dumaran *Phil.* 10°33N 119°50E **37** B5
Dumas Ark., *U.S.A.* 33°53N 91°29W **84** E9
Dumas Tex., *U.S.A.* 35°52N 101°58W **84** D4
Dumayr *Syria* 33°39N 36°42E **46** B5
Dumbarton *U.K.* 55°57N 4°33W **11** F4
Dumbleyung *Australia* 33°17S 117°42E **61** F2
Dumfries *U.K.* 55°4N 3°37W **11** F5
Dumfries & Galloway □
  U.K. 55°9N 3°58W **11** F5
Dumka *India* 24°12N 87°15E **43** G12
Dumoine → *Canada* 46°13N 77°51W **72** C4
Dumoine, L. *Canada* 46°55N 77°55W **72** C4
Dumont d'Urville
  Antarctica 67°0S 110°0E **5** C10
Dumont d'Urville Sea
  S. Ocean 63°30S 138°0E **5** C9
Dumraon *India* 25°33N 84°8E **43** G11
Dumyât *Egypt* 31°24N 31°48E **51** B12
Dún Dealgan = Dundalk
  Ireland 54°1N 6°24W **10** B5
Dún Laoghaire *Ireland* 53°17N 6°8W **10** C5
Duna = Dunărea →
  Europe 45°20N 29°40E **17** F15
Dunagiri *India* 30°31N 79°52E **43** D8
Dunaj = Dunărea →
  Europe 45°20N 29°40E **17** F15
Dunakeszi *Hungary* 47°37N 19°8E **17** E10
Dunărea → *Europe* 45°20N 29°40E **17** F15
Dunaújváros *Hungary* 46°58N 18°57E **17** E10
Dunav = Dunărea →
  Europe 45°20N 29°40E **17** F15
Dunay *Russia* 42°52N 132°22E **30** C6
Dunback *N.Z.* 45°23S 170°36E **59** F3
Dunbar *U.K.* 56°0N 2°31W **11** E6
Dunblane *U.K.* 56°11N 3°58W **11** E5
Duncan *Canada* 48°45N 123°40W **78** B3
Duncan Ariz., *U.S.A.* 32°43N 109°6W **77** K9
Duncan Okla., *U.S.A.* 34°30N 97°57W **84** D6
Duncan, L. *Canada* 53°29N 77°58W **72** B4
Duncan L. *Canada* 62°51N 113°58W **70** A6
Duncan Town *Bahamas* 22°15N 75°45W **88** B4
Duncannon *U.S.A.* 40°23N 77°2W **82** F7
Duncansby Head *U.K.* 58°38N 3°1W **11** C5
Duncansville *U.S.A.* 40°25N 78°26W **82** F6
Dundalk *Canada* 44°10N 80°24W **82** B4
Dundalk *Ireland* 54°1N 6°24W **10** B5
Dundalk *U.S.A.* 39°15N 76°31W **81** F15
Dundalk Bay *Ireland* 53°55N 6°15W **10** C5
Dundas = Uummannaq
  Greenland 77°28N 69°13W **4** B4
Dundas *Canada* 43°17N 79°59W **82** C5
Dundas, L. *Australia* 32°35S 121°50E **61** F3
Dundas I. *Canada* 54°30N 130°50W **70** C2
Dundas Str. *Australia* 11°15S 131°35E **60** B5
Dundee *S. Africa* 28°11S 30°15E **57** D5
Dundee *U.K.* 56°28N 2°59W **11** E6
Dundee *U.S.A.* 42°32N 76°59W **82** D8
Dundee City □ *U.K.* 56°30N 2°58W **11** E6
Dundgovĭ □ *Mongolia* 45°10N 106°0E **34** B4
Dundrum *U.K.* 54°16N 5°52W **10** B6
Dundrum B. *U.K.* 54°13N 5°47W **10** B6
Dunedin *N.Z.* 45°50S 170°33E **59** F3
Dunedin *U.S.A.* 28°1N 82°46W **85** G13
Dunfanaghy *Ireland* 55°11N 7°58W **10** A4
Dunfermline *U.K.* 56°5N 3°27W **11** E5
Dungannon *Canada* 43°51N 81°36W **82** C3
Dungannon *U.K.* 54°31N 6°46W **10** B5
Dungarpur *India* 23°52N 73°45E **42** H5
Dungarvan *Ireland* 52°5N 7°37W **10** D4
Dungarvan Harbour
  Ireland 52°4N 7°35W **10** D4
Dungeness *U.K.* 50°54N 0°59E **13** G8
Dunglow *Ireland* 54°57N 8°21W **10** B3
Dungo, L. do *Angola* 17°15S 19°0E **56** B2
Dungog *Australia* 32°22S 151°46E **63** E5
Dungu
  Dem. Rep. of the Congo 3°40N 28°32E **54** B2
Dungun *Malaysia* 4°45N 103°25E **39** K4
Dunhua *China* 43°20N 128°14E **35** C15
Dunhuang *China* 40°8N 94°36E **32** B4
Dunk I. *Australia* 17°59S 146°29E **62** B4
Dunkeld *Australia* 37°40S 142°22E **63** F3
Dunkeld *U.K.* 56°34N 3°35W **11** E5
Dunkerque *France* 51°2N 2°20E **20** A5
Dunkery Beacon *U.K.* 51°9N 3°36W **13** F4
Dunkirk = Dunkerque
  France 51°2N 2°20E **20** A5

Dunkirk *U.S.A.* 42°29N 79°20W **82** D5
Dúnleary = Dún Laoghaire
  Ireland 53°17N 6°8W **10** C5
Dunleer *Ireland* 53°50N 6°24W **10** C5
Dunmanus B. *Ireland* 51°31N 9°50W **10** E2
Dunmanway *Ireland* 51°43N 9°6W **10** E2
Dunmarra *Australia* 16°42S 133°25E **62** B1
Dunmore *U.S.A.* 41°25N 75°38W **83** E9
Dunmore East *Ireland* 52°9N 7°0W **10** D5
Dunmore Hd. *Ireland* 52°10N 10°35W **10** D1
Dunmore Town
  Bahamas 25°30N 76°39W **88** A4
Dunn *U.S.A.* 35°19N 78°37W **85** D15
Dunnellon *U.S.A.* 29°3N 82°28W **85** G13
Dunnet Hd. *U.K.* 58°40N 3°21W **11** C5
Dunning *U.S.A.* 41°50N 100°6W **80** E3
Dunnville *Canada* 42°54N 79°36W **82** D5
Dunolly *Australia* 36°51S 143°44E **63** F3
Dunoon *U.K.* 55°57N 4°56W **11** F4
Duns *U.K.* 55°47N 2°20W **11** F6
Dunseith *U.S.A.* 48°50N 100°3W **80** A3
Dunshaughlin *Ireland* 53°31N 6°33W **10** C5
Dunsmuir *U.S.A.* 41°13N 122°16W **76** F2
Dunstable *U.K.* 51°53N 0°32W **13** F7
Dunstan Mts. *N.Z.* 44°53S 169°35E **59** F2
Dunster *Canada* 53°8N 119°50W **70** C5
Dunvegan *U.K.* 57°27N 6°35W **11** D2
Dunvegan L. *Canada* 60°8N 107°10W **71** A7
Duolun *China* 42°12N 116°28E **34** C9
Duong Dong *Vietnam* 10°13N 103°58E **39** G4
Dupree *U.S.A.* 45°4N 101°35W **80** C3
Dupuyer *U.S.A.* 48°13N 112°30W **76** B7
Duque de Caxias *Brazil* 22°46S 43°18W **95** A7
Durack → *Australia* 15°33S 127°52E **60** C4
Durack Ra. *Australia* 16°50S 127°40E **60** C4
Durance → *France* 43°55N 4°45E **20** E6
Durand *U.S.A.* 44°38N 91°58W **80** C8
Durango *Mexico* 24°3N 104°39W **86** C4
Durango *U.S.A.* 37°16N 107°53W **77** H10
Durango □ *Mexico* 24°50N 105°20W **86** C4
Durant Miss., *U.S.A.* 33°4N 89°51W **85** E10
Durant Okla., *U.S.A.* 33°59N 96°25W **84** E6
Durazno *Uruguay* 33°25S 56°31W **94** C4
Durazzo = Durrës
  Albania 41°19N 19°28E **23** D8
Durban *S. Africa* 29°49S 31°1E **57** D5
Durbuy *Belgium* 50°21N 5°28E **15** D5
Düren *Germany* 50°48N 6°29E **16** C4
Durg = Bhilainagar-Durg
  India 21°13N 81°26E **41** J12
Durgapur *India* 23°30N 87°20E **43** H12
Durham *Canada* 44°10N 80°49W **82** B4
Durham *U.K.* 54°47N 1°34W **12** C6
Durham Calif., *U.S.A.* 39°39N 121°48W **78** F5
Durham N.C., *U.S.A.* 35°59N 78°54W **85** D15
Durham N.H., *U.S.A.* 43°8N 70°56W **83** C14
Durham □ *U.K.* 54°42N 1°45W **12** C6
Durma Si. *Arabia* 24°37N 46°8E **44** E5
Durmitor *Montenegro* 43°10N 19°0E **23** C8
Durness *U.K.* 58°34N 4°45W **11** C4
Durrës *Albania* 41°19N 19°28E **23** D8
Durrow *Ireland* 52°51N 7°24W **10** D4
Dursey I. *Ireland* 51°36N 10°12W **10** E1
Dursley *U.K.* 51°40N 2°21W **13** F5
Dursunbey *Turkey* 39°35N 28°37E **23** E13
Duru
  Dem. Rep. of the Congo 4°14N 28°50E **54** B2
Durūz, Jabal ad *Jordan* 32°35N 36°40E **46** C5
D'Urville, Tanjung
  Indonesia 1°28S 137°54E **37** E9
D'Urville I. *N.Z.* 40°50S 173°55E **59** D4
Duryea *U.S.A.* 41°20N 75°45W **83** E9
Dushak *Turkmenistan* 37°13N 60°1E **45** B9
Dushanbe *Tajikistan* 38°33N 68°48E **28** F7
Dushore *U.S.A.* 41°31N 76°24W **83** E8
Dusky Sd. *N.Z.* 45°47S 166°30E **59** F1
Dussejour, C. *Australia* 14°45S 128°13E **60** B4
Düsseldorf *Germany* 51°14N 6°47E **16** C4
Dutch Harbor *U.S.A.* 53°53N 166°32W **74** a
Dutlwe *Botswana* 23°58S 23°46E **56** C3
Dutton *Canada* 42°39N 81°30W **82** D3
Dutton → *Australia* 20°44S 143°10E **62** C3
Dutywa *S. Africa* 32°8S 28°18E **57** E4
Duwayhin, Khawr
  U.A.E. 24°20N 51°25E **45** E6
Duyfken Pt. *Australia* 12°33S 141°38E **62** A3
Duyun *China* 26°18N 107°29E **32** D5
Dvina, Severnaya →
  Russia 64°32N 40°30E **18** B7
Dvinsk = Daugavpils
  Latvia 55°53N 26°32E **9** J22
Dvinskaya Guba *Russia* 65°0N 39°0E **18** B6
Dwarka *India* 22°18N 69°8E **42** H3
Dwellingup *Australia* 32°43S 116°4E **61** F2
Dwight *Canada* 45°20N 79°1W **82** A5
Dwight *U.S.A.* 41°5N 88°26W **80** E9
Dyatlovo = Dzyatlava
  Belarus 53°28N 25°28E **17** B13
Dyce *U.K.* 57°13N 2°12W **11** D6
Dyer, C. *Canada* 66°37N 61°16W **69** C13
Dyer Bay *Canada* 45°10N 81°20W **82** A3
Dyer Plateau *Antarctica* 70°45S 65°30W **5** D17
Dyersburg *U.S.A.* 36°3N 89°23W **85** C10
Dyfi → *U.K.* 52°32N 4°3W **13** E3
Dysart *U.S.A.* 22°3S 148°23E **62** C4
Dzaoudzi *Mayotte* 12°47S 45°16E **53** a
Dzavhan Gol → *Mongolia* 48°54N 93°23E **32** B4
Dzerzhinsk *Russia* 56°14N 43°30E **18** C7
Dzhalinda *Russia* 53°26N 124°0E **29** D13
Dzhambul = Taraz
  Kazakhstan 42°54N 71°22E **28** E8
Dzhankoy *Ukraine* 45°40N 34°20E **19** E5
Dzhezkazgan = Zhezqazghan
  Kazakhstan 47°44N 67°40E **28** E7
Dzhizak = Jizzax
  Uzbekistan 40°6N 67°50E **28** E7

Dzhugdzur, Khrebet
  Russia 57°30N 138°0E **29** D14
Dzhungarskiye Vorota =
  Dzungarian Gate *Asia* 45°10N 82°0E **32** B3
Działdowo *Poland* 53°15N 20°15E **17** B11
Dzibilchaltún *Mexico* 21°10N 89°35W **87** C7
Dzierżoniów *Poland* 50°45N 16°39E **17** C9
Dzilam de Bravo *Mexico* 21°24N 88°53W **87** C7
Dzūkija □ *Lithuania* 54°10N 24°30E **9** J21
Dzungaria = Junggar
  Pendi *China* 44°30N 86°0E **32** B3
Dzungarian Gate *Asia* 45°10N 82°0E **32** B3
Dzüünharaa *Mongolia* 48°52N 106°28E **32** B5
Dzüünmod *Mongolia* 47°45N 106°58E **32** B5
Dzyarzhynsk *Belarus* 53°40N 27°1E **17** B14
Dzyatlava *Belarus* 53°28N 25°28E **17** B13

E

E.C. Manning △ *Canada* 49°5N 120°45W **70** D4
Eabamet L. *Canada* 51°30N 87°46W **72** B2
Eabametoong *Canada* 51°30N 88°0W **72** B2
Eads *U.S.A.* 38°29N 102°47W **76** G12
Eagar *U.S.A.* 34°6N 109°17W **77** J9
Eagle *Alaska, U.S.A.* 64°47N 141°12W **68** C5
Eagle *Colo., U.S.A.* 39°39N 106°50W **76** G10
Eagle → *Canada* 53°36N 57°26W **73** B8
Eagle Butte *U.S.A.* 45°0N 101°10W **80** C3
Eagle Grove *U.S.A.* 42°40N 93°54W **80** D7
Eagle L. *Canada* 49°42N 93°13W **71** D10
Eagle L. *Calif., U.S.A.* 40°39N 120°45W **76** F3
Eagle L. *Maine, U.S.A.* 46°20N 69°22W **81** B19
Eagle Lake *Canada* 45°8N 78°29W **82** A6
Eagle Lake *Maine, U.S.A.* 47°3N 68°36W **81** B19
Eagle Lake *Tex., U.S.A.* 29°35N 96°20W **84** G6
Eagle Mountain
  U.S.A. 33°49N 115°27W **79** M11
Eagle Nest *U.S.A.* 36°33N 105°16W **77** H11
Eagle Pass *U.S.A.* 28°43N 100°30W **84** G4
Eagle Pk. *U.S.A.* 38°10N 119°25W **78** G7
Eagle Pt. *Australia* 16°11S 124°23E **60** C3
Eagle River *Mich., U.S.A.* 47°25N 88°18W **80** B9
Eagle River *Wis., U.S.A.* 45°55N 89°15W **80** C9
Eaglehawk *Australia* 36°44S 144°15E **63** F3
Eagles Mere *U.S.A.* 41°25N 76°33W **83** E8
Ealing □ *U.K.* 51°31N 0°20W **13** F7
Ear Falls *Canada* 50°38N 93°13W **71** C10
Earle *U.S.A.* 35°16N 90°28W **85** D9
Earlimart *U.S.A.* 35°53N 119°16W **79** K7
Earlville *U.S.A.* 42°44N 75°32W **83** D9
Earn → *U.K.* 56°21N 3°18W **11** E5
Earn, L. *U.K.* 56°23N 4°13W **11** E4
Earnslaw, Mt. *N.Z.* 44°32S 168°27E **59** F2
Earth *U.S.A.* 34°14N 102°24W **84** D3
Easley *U.S.A.* 34°50N 82°36W **85** D13
East Anglia *U.K.* 52°30N 1°0E **12** E9
East Angus *Canada* 45°30N 71°40W **73** C5
East Aurora *U.S.A.* 42°46N 78°37W **82** D6
East Ayrshire □ *U.K.* 55°26N 4°11W **11** F4
East Bengal *Bangla.* 24°0N 90°0E **41** G17
East Beskids = Vychodné Beskydy
  Europe 49°20N 22°0E **17** D11
East Brady *U.S.A.* 40°59N 79°37W **82** F5
East Branch Clarion River L.
  U.S.A. 41°30N 78°35W **82** E6
East C. = Dezhneva, Mys
  Russia 66°5N 169°40W **29** C19
East C. *N.Z.* 37°42S 178°35E **59** B7
East Caroline Basin
  Pac. Oc. 4°0N 146°45E **64** G6
East Chicago *U.S.A.* 41°38N 87°27W **80** E10
East China Sea *Asia* 30°0N 126°0E **33** D7
East Coulee *Canada* 51°23N 112°27W **70** C6
East Dereham = Dereham
  U.K. 52°41N 0°57E **13** E8
East Dunbartonshire □
  U.K. 55°57N 4°13W **11** F4
East Falkland *Falk. Is.* 51°30S 58°30W **96** G5
East Grand Forks *U.S.A.* 47°56N 97°1W **80** B5
East Greenwich *U.S.A.* 41°40N 71°27W **83** E13
East Grinstead *U.K.* 51°7N 0°0 **13** F8
East Hartford *U.S.A.* 41°46N 72°39W **83** E12
East Helena *U.S.A.* 46°35N 111°56W **76** C8
East Indies *Asia* 0°0 120°0E **26** J14
East Kilbride *U.K.* 55°47N 4°11W **11** F4
East Lamma Channel
  China 22°14N 114°9E **33** G11
East Lansing *U.S.A.* 42°44N 84°29W **81** D11
East Liverpool *U.S.A.* 40°37N 80°35W **82** F4
East London *S. Africa* 33°0S 27°55E **57** E4
East Lothian □ *U.K.* 55°58N 2°44W **11** F6
East Main = Eastmain
  Canada 52°10N 78°30W **72** B4
East Mariana Basin
  Pac. Oc. 12°0N 153°0E **64** F7
East Northport *U.S.A.* 40°53N 73°20W **83** F11
East Orange *U.S.A.* 40°46N 74°12W **83** F10
East Pacific Rise *Pac. Oc.* 15°0S 110°0W **65** J17
East Palestine *U.S.A.* 40°50N 80°33W **82** F4
East Pine *Canada* 55°48N 120°12W **70** B4
East Point *U.S.A.* 33°41N 84°27W **85** E12
East Providence *U.S.A.* 41°49N 71°23W **83** E13
East Pt. *Br. Virgin Is.* 18°40N 64°18W **89** e
East Pt. *Canada* 46°27N 61°58W **73** C7
East Renfrewshire □
  U.K. 55°46N 4°21W **11** F4
East Retford = Retford
  U.K. 53°19N 0°56W **12** D7
East Riding of Yorkshire □
  U.K. 53°55N 0°30W **12** D7
East Rochester *U.S.A.* 43°7N 77°29W **82** C7
East St. Louis *U.S.A.* 38°37N 90°9W **80** F9
East Schelde = Oosterschelde →
  Neths. 51°33N 4°0E **15** C4
East Sea = Japan, Sea of
  Asia 40°0N 135°0E **30** E7

118 East Siberian Sea
INDEX TO WORLD MAPS

East Siberian Sea Russia 73°0N 160°0E 29 B17
East Stroudsburg U.S.A. 41°1N 75°11W 83 E9
East Sussex □ U.K. 50°56N 0°19E 13 G8
East Tasman Plateau Pac. Oc. 43°30S 152°0E 64 M7
East Tawas U.S.A. 44°17N 83°29W 81 C12
East Timor ■ Asia 8°50S 126°0E 37 F7
East Toorale Australia 30°27S 145°28E 63 E4
East Walker → U.S.A. 38°52N 119°10W 78 G7
East Windsor U.S.A. 40°17N 74°34W 83 F10
Eastbourne N.Z. 41°19S 174°55E 59 D5
Eastbourne U.K. 50°46N 0°18E 13 G8
Eastend Canada 49°32N 108°50W 71 D7
Easter Fracture Zone Pac. Oc. 25°0S 115°0W 65 K16
Easter I. = Pascua, I. de Chile 27°7S 109°23W 65 K17
Eastern □ Kenya 0°0 38°30E 54 C4
Eastern Cape □ S. Africa 32°0S 26°0E 56 E4
Eastern Cr. → Australia 20°40S 141°35E 62 C3
Eastern Desert = Es Sahrâ' Esh Sharqîya Egypt 27°30N 32°30E 51 C12
Eastern Ghats India 14°0N 78°50E 40 N11
Eastern Group = Lau Group Fiji 17°0S 178°30W 59 a
Eastern Group Australia 33°30S 124°30E 61 F3
Eastern Transvaal = Mpumalanga □ S. Africa 26°0S 30°0E 57 D5
Easterville Canada 53°8N 99°49W 71 C9
Easthampton U.S.A. 42°16N 72°40W 83 D12
Eastlake U.S.A. 41°40N 81°26W 82 E3
Eastland U.S.A. 32°24N 98°49W 84 E5
Eastleigh U.K. 50°58N 1°21W 13 G6
Eastmain Canada 52°10N 78°30W 72 B4
Eastmain → Canada 52°27N 78°26W 72 B4
Eastman Canada 45°18N 72°19W 83 A12
Eastman U.S.A. 32°12N 83°11W 85 E13
Easton Md., U.S.A. 38°47N 76°5W 81 F15
Easton Pa., U.S.A. 40°41N 75°13W 83 F9
Easton Wash., U.S.A. 47°14N 121°11W 78 C5
Eastport U.S.A. 44°56N 67°0W 81 C20
Eastsound U.S.A. 48°42N 122°55W 78 B4
Eaton U.S.A. 40°32N 104°42W 76 F11
Eatonia Canada 51°13N 109°25W 71 C7
Eatonton U.S.A. 33°20N 83°23W 85 E13
Eatontown U.S.A. 40°19N 74°4W 83 F10
Eatonville U.S.A. 46°52N 122°16W 78 D4
Eau Claire U.S.A. 44°49N 91°30W 80 C8
Eau Claire, L. à l' Canada 56°10N 74°25W 72 A5
Eauripik Rise Pac. Oc. 2°0N 142°0E 64 G6
Ebano Mexico 22°13N 98°24W 87 C5
Ebbw Vale U.K. 51°46N 3°12W 13 F4
Ebeltoft Denmark 56°12N 10°41E 9 H14
Ebenezer, Mt. Australia 25°6S 132°34E 61 E5
Ebensburg U.S.A. 40°29N 78°44W 82 F6
Eberswalde-Finow Germany 52°50N 13°49E 16 B7
Ebetsu Japan 43°7N 141°34E 30 C10
Ebey's Landing ⌓ U.S.A. 48°12N 122°41W 78 B4
Ebinur Hu China 44°55N 82°55E 32 B3
Ebolowa Cameroon 2°55N 11°10E 52 D2
Ebonda Dem. Rep. of the Congo 2°12N 22°21E 52 D4
Ebre = Ebro → Spain 40°43N 0°54E 21 B6
Ebro → Spain 40°43N 0°54E 21 B6
Ecatepec de Morelos Mexico 19°36N 99°3W 87 D5
Ecbatana = Hamadān Iran 34°52N 48°32E 45 C6
Eceabat Turkey 40°11N 26°21E 23 D12
Ech Chéliff Algeria 36°10N 1°20E 50 A6
Echigo-Sammyaku Japan 36°50N 139°50E 31 F9
Echizen-Misaki Japan 35°59N 135°57E 31 G7
Echo Bay N.W.T., Canada 66°5N 117°55W 68 C8
Echo Bay Ont., Canada 46°29N 84°4W 72 C3
Echoing → Canada 55°51N 92°5W 72 B1
Echternach Lux. 49°49N 6°25E 15 E6
Echuca Australia 36°10S 144°45E 63 F3
Écija Spain 37°30N 5°10W 21 D3
Eclipse I. Australia 35°5S 117°58E 61 G2
Eclipse Is. Australia 13°54S 126°19E 60 B4
Eclipse Sd. Canada 72°38N 79°0W 69 B12
Ecuador ■ S. Amer. 2°0S 78°0W 92 D3
Ed Damazin Sudan 11°46N 34°21E 51 F12
Ed Dar el Beida = Casablanca Morocco 33°36N 7°36W 50 B4
Ed Debba Sudan 18°0N 30°51E 51 E12
Ed Déffa Egypt 30°40N 26°30E 51 B11
Ed Dueim Sudan 14°0N 32°10E 51 F12
Edam Canada 53°11N 108°46W 71 C7
Edam Neths. 52°31N 5°3E 15 B5
Eday U.K. 59°11N 2°47W 11 B6
Eddrachillis B. U.K. 58°17N 5°14W 11 C3
Eddystone U.K. 50°11N 4°16W 13 G3
Eddystone Pt. Australia 40°59S 148°20E 63 G4
Ede Neths. 52°4N 5°40E 15 B5
Edehon L. Canada 60°25N 97°15W 71 A9
Edekel, Adrar Algeria 23°56N 6°47E 50 D7
Eden Australia 37°3S 149°55E 63 F4
Eden N.C., U.S.A. 36°29N 79°53W 85 C15
Eden N.Y., U.S.A. 42°39N 78°55W 82 D6
Eden Tex., U.S.A. 31°13N 99°51W 84 F5
Eden → U.K. 54°57N 3°1W 12 C4
Edenburg S. Africa 29°43S 25°58E 56 D4
Edendale S. Africa 29°39S 30°18E 57 D5
Edenderry Ireland 53°21N 7°4W 10 C4
Edenton U.S.A. 36°4N 76°39W 85 C16
Edenville S. Africa 27°37S 27°34E 57 D4
Eder → Germany 51°12N 9°28E 16 C5
Edessa Greece 40°48N 22°5E 23 D10
Edfu = Idfû Egypt 24°55N 32°49E 51 D12
Edgar U.S.A. 40°22N 97°58W 80 E5
Edgartown U.S.A. 41°23N 70°31W 83 E14
Edge Hill U.K. 52°8N 1°26W 13 E6
Edgefield U.S.A. 33°47N 81°56W 85 E14
Edgeley U.S.A. 46°22N 98°43W 80 B4
Edgemont U.S.A. 43°18N 103°50W 80 D2
Edgeøya Svalbard 77°45N 22°30E 4 B9
Édhessa = Edessa Greece 40°48N 22°5E 23 D10
Edievale N.Z. 45°49S 169°22E 59 F2
Edina U.S.A. 40°10N 92°11W 80 E7
Edinboro U.S.A. 41°52N 80°8W 82 E4
Edinburg U.S.A. 26°18N 98°10W 84 H5
Edinburgh U.K. 55°57N 3°13W 11 F5
Edinburgh ✈ (EDI) U.K. 55°54N 3°22W 11 F5
Edinburgh, City of □ U.K. 55°57N 3°17W 11 F5
Edineţ Moldova 48°9N 27°18E 17 D14
Edirne Turkey 41°40N 26°34E 23 D12
Edison U.S.A. 48°33N 122°27W 78 B4
Edithburgh Australia 35°5S 137°43E 63 F2
Edmeston U.S.A. 42°42N 75°15W 83 D9
Edmond U.S.A. 35°39N 97°29W 84 D6
Edmonds U.S.A. 47°48N 122°22W 78 C4
Edmonton Australia 17°2S 145°46E 62 B4
Edmonton Canada 53°30N 113°30W 70 C6
Edmund L. Canada 54°45N 93°17W 72 B1
Edmundston Canada 47°23N 68°20W 73 C6
Edna U.S.A. 28°59N 96°39W 84 G6
Edremit Turkey 39°34N 27°0E 23 E12
Edremit Körfezi Turkey 39°30N 26°45E 23 E12
Edson Canada 53°35N 116°28W 70 C5
Eduardo Castex Argentina 35°50S 64°18W 94 D3
Edward → Australia 35°5S 143°30E 63 F3
Edward, L. Africa 0°25S 29°40E 54 C2
Edward VII Land Antarctica 80°0S 150°0W 5 E13
Edwards Calif., U.S.A. 34°50N 117°40W 79 L9
Edwards N.Y., U.S.A. 44°20N 75°15W 83 B9
Edwards Plateau U.S.A. 30°45N 101°20W 84 F4
Edwardsville U.S.A. 41°15N 75°56W 83 E9
Edzná Mexico 19°39N 90°19W 87 D6
Edzo Canada 62°49N 116°4W 70 A5
Eeklo Belgium 51°11N 3°33E 15 C3
Eesti = Estonia ■ Europe 58°30N 25°30E 9 G21
Effigy Mounds ⌓ U.S.A. 43°5N 91°11W 80 D8
Effingham U.S.A. 39°7N 88°33W 80 F9
Égadi, Ísole Italy 37°55N 12°16E 22 F5
Egan Range U.S.A. 39°35N 114°55W 76 G6
Eganville Canada 45°32N 77°5W 82 A7
Eger = Cheb Czech Rep. 50°9N 12°28E 16 C7
Eger Hungary 47°53N 20°27E 17 E11
Egersund Norway 58°26N 6°1E 9 G12
Egg L. Canada 55°5N 105°30W 71 B7
Éghezée Belgium 50°35N 4°55E 15 D4
Egio Greece 38°15N 22°5E 23 E10
Eglinton I. Canada 75°48N 118°30W 69 B8
Egmont Canada 49°45N 123°56W 70 D4
Egmont, C. N.Z. 39°16S 173°45E 59 C4
Egmont, Mt. = Taranaki, Mt. N.Z. 39°17S 174°5E 59 C5
Egmont △ N.Z. 39°17S 174°4E 59 C5
Egra India 21°54N 87°32E 43 J12
Eğridir Turkey 37°52N 30°51E 19 G5
Eğridir Gölü Turkey 37°53N 30°50E 44 B1
Egvekinot Russia 66°19N 179°50W 29 C19
Egypt ■ Africa 28°0N 31°0E 51 C12
Ehime □ Japan 33°30N 132°40E 31 H6
Ehrenberg U.S.A. 33°36N 114°31W 79 M12
Eibar Spain 43°11N 2°28W 21 A4
Eidsvold Australia 25°25S 151°12E 63 D5
Eidsvoll Norway 60°19N 11°14E 9 F14
Eifel Germany 50°15N 6°50E 16 C4
Eiffel Flats Zimbabwe 18°20S 30°0E 55 F3
Eigg U.K. 56°54N 6°10W 11 E2
Eighty Mile Beach Australia 19°30S 120°40E 60 C3
Eil, L. U.K. 56°51N 5°16W 11 E3
Eildon, L. Australia 37°10S 146°0E 63 F4
Eilean Sar = Western Isles □ U.K. 57°30N 7°10W 11 D1
Einasleigh Australia 18°32S 144°5E 62 B3
Einasleigh → Australia 17°30S 142°17E 62 B3
Eindhoven Neths. 51°26N 5°28E 15 C5
Eire = Ireland ■ Europe 53°50N 7°52W 10 C4
Eiríksjökull Iceland 64°46N 20°24W 8 D3
Eirunepé Brazil 6°35S 69°53W 92 E5
Eiseb → Namibia 20°33S 20°59E 56 C2
Eisenach Germany 50°58N 10°19E 16 C6
Eisenerz Austria 47°32N 14°54E 16 E8
Eivissa Spain 38°54N 1°26E 24 C7
Ejeda Madag. 24°20S 44°31E 57 C7
Ejutla Mexico 16°34N 96°44W 87 D5
Ekalaka U.S.A. 45°53N 104°33W 76 D11
Ekaterinburg = Yekaterinburg Russia 56°50N 60°30E 28 D7
Ekenäs = Tammisaari Finland 60°0N 23°26E 9 G20
Eketahuna N.Z. 40°38S 175°43E 59 D5
Ekibastuz Kazakhstan 51°50N 75°10E 28 D8
Ekoli Dem. Rep. of the Congo 0°23S 24°13E 54 C1
Eksjö Sweden 57°40N 14°58E 9 H16
Ekuma → Namibia 18°40S 16°2E 56 B2
Ekwan → Canada 53°12N 82°15W 72 B3
Ekwan Pt. Canada 53°16N 82°7W 72 B3
El Aaiún W. Sahara 27°9N 13°12W 50 C3
El Abanico Chile 37°20S 71°31W 94 D1
El 'Agrûd Egypt 30°14N 34°24E 46 E3
El 'Alamein Egypt 30°48N 28°58E 51 B11
El 'Aqaba, W. → Egypt 30°7N 33°54E 46 E2
El Arīḥā West Bank 31°52N 35°27E 46 D4
El 'Arîsh Egypt 31°8N 33°50E 46 D2
El 'Arîsh, W. → Egypt 31°8N 33°47E 46 D2
El Asnam = Ech Chéliff Algeria 36°10N 1°20E 50 A6
El Bayadh Algeria 33°40N 1°1E 50 B6
El Bluff Nic. 11°59N 83°40W 88 D3
El Cajon U.S.A. 32°48N 116°58W 79 N10
El Calafate Argentina 50°19S 72°15W 96 G2
El Campo U.S.A. 29°12N 96°16W 84 G6
El Capitan U.S.A. 37°44N 119°38E 78 H7
El Carbón Honduras 15°25N 85°32W 88 C2
El Carmen Colombia 9°43N 75°8W 92 B3
El Centro U.S.A. 32°48N 115°34W 79 N11
El Cerro Bolivia 17°30S 61°40W 92 G6
El Compadre Mexico 32°20N 116°14W 79 N10
El Cuy Argentina 39°55S 68°25W 96 D3
El Cuyo Mexico 21°31N 87°41W 87 C7
El Daheir Egypt 31°13N 34°10E 46 D3
El Descanso Mexico 32°12N 116°58W 79 N10
El Desemboque Mexico 30°33N 113°1W 86 A2
El Diviso Colombia 1°22N 78°14W 92 C3
El Djouf Mauritania 20°0N 9°0W 50 D4
El Dorado Mexico 24°17N 107°21W 86 C3
El Dorado Ark., U.S.A. 33°12N 92°40W 84 E8
El Dorado Kans., U.S.A. 37°49N 96°52W 80 G5
El Dorado Venezuela 6°55N 61°37W 92 B6
El Dorado Springs U.S.A. 37°52N 94°1W 80 G6
El Escorial Spain 40°35N 4°7W 21 B3
El Faiyûm Egypt 29°19N 30°50E 51 C12
El Fâsher Sudan 13°33N 25°26E 51 F11
El Ferrol = Ferrol Spain 43°29N 8°15W 21 A1
El Fuerte Mexico 26°25N 108°39W 86 B3
El Gal Somali Rep. 10°58N 50°20E 47 E5
El Geneina = Al Junaynah Sudan 13°27N 22°45E 51 F10
El Gezira □ Sudan 15°0N 33°0E 51 F12
El Gîza Egypt 30°0N 31°12E 51 C12
El Gogorrón △ Mexico 21°49N 100°57W 86 C4
El Goléa Algeria 30°30N 2°50E 50 B6
El Golfo de Santa Clara Mexico 31°42N 114°30W 86 A2
El Guácharo △ Venezuela 10°8N 63°21W 89 D7
El Guache △ Venezuela 9°45N 69°30W 89 E6
El Iskandarîya Egypt 31°13N 29°58E 51 B11
El Istiwa'iya Sudan 5°0N 28°0E 51 G11
El Jadida Morocco 33°11N 8°17W 50 B4
El Jardal Honduras 14°54N 88°50W 88 D2
El Kef □ Tunisia 36°0N 9°0E 51 A7
El Khârga Egypt 25°30N 30°33E 51 C12
El Khartûm Sudan 15°31N 32°35E 51 E12
El Khartûm Bahrî Sudan 15°40N 32°31E 51 E12
El Kuntilla Egypt 30°1N 34°45E 46 E3
El Leoncito △ Argentina 31°58S 69°10W 94 C2
El Lucero Mexico 30°37N 106°31W 86 A3
El Maestrazgo Spain 40°30N 0°25W 21 B5
El Mahalla el Kubra Egypt 31°0N 31°0E 51 B12
El Malpais ⌓ U.S.A. 34°53N 108°0W 77 J10
El Mansûra Egypt 31°0N 31°19E 51 B12
El Medano Canary Is. 28°3N 16°32W 24 F3
El Milagro Argentina 30°59S 65°59W 94 C2
El Minyâ Egypt 28°7N 30°33E 51 C12
El Monte U.S.A. 34°4N 118°1W 79 L8
El Obeid Sudan 13°8N 30°10E 51 F12
El Odaiya Sudan 12°8N 28°12E 51 F11
El Oro Mexico 19°51N 100°7W 87 D4
El Oued Algeria 33°20N 6°58E 50 B7
El Palmar △ Argentina 32°10S 58°31W 94 C4
El Palmito, Presa Mexico 25°40N 105°30W 86 B3
El Paso U.S.A. 31°45N 106°29W 84 F1
El Pinacate y Gran Desierto de Altar = Gran Desierto del Pinacate ⌓ Mexico 31°51N 113°32W 86 A2
El Portal U.S.A. 37°41N 119°47W 78 H7
El Porvenir Mexico 31°15N 105°51W 86 A3
El Prat de Llobregat Spain 41°19N 2°5E 21 B7
El Progreso Honduras 15°26N 87°51W 88 C2
El Pueblito Mexico 29°6N 105°7W 86 B3
El Pueblo Canary Is. 28°36N 17°47W 24 F2
El Puerto de Santa María Spain 36°36N 6°13W 21 D2
El Qâhira Egypt 30°2N 31°13E 51 B12
El Qantara Egypt 30°51N 32°20E 46 E1
El Quseima Egypt 30°40N 34°15E 46 E3
El Real de Santa María Panama 8°0N 77°40W 92 B3
El Reno U.S.A. 35°32N 97°57W 74 C7
El Rey △ Argentina 24°40S 64°34W 94 A3
El Rio U.S.A. 34°14N 119°10W 79 L7
El Roque, Pta. Canary Is. 28°10N 15°25W 24 F4
El Rosarito Mexico 28°38N 114°4W 86 B2
El Salto Mexico 23°47N 105°22W 86 C3
El Salvador ■ Cent. Amer. 13°50N 89°0W 88 D2
El Sauce Nic. 13°0N 86°40W 88 D2
El Sueco Mexico 29°54N 106°24W 86 B3
El Suweis Egypt 29°58N 32°31E 51 C12
El Tamarâni, W. → Egypt 30°7N 34°43E 46 E3
El Thamad Egypt 29°40N 34°28E 46 F3
El Tigre Venezuela 8°44N 64°15W 92 B6
El Tîh, Gebel Egypt 29°40N 33°50E 46 F2
El Tofo Chile 29°22S 71°18W 94 B1
El Tránsito Chile 28°52S 70°17W 94 B1
El Tûr Egypt 28°14N 33°36E 44 D2
El Turbio Argentina 51°45S 72°5W 96 G2
El Uqsur Egypt 25°41N 32°38E 51 C12
El Vergel Mexico 26°28N 106°22W 86 B3
El Vigía Venezuela 8°38N 71°39W 92 B4
El Wabeira Egypt 29°34N 33°6E 46 F2
El Wak Kenya 2°49N 40°56E 54 B5
El Wuz Sudan 15°5N 30°7E 51 E12
Elat Israel 29°30N 34°56E 46 F3
Elâzığ Turkey 38°37N 39°14E 44 B3
Elba Italy 42°46N 10°17E 22 C4
Elba U.S.A. 31°25N 86°4W 85 F11
Elbasan Albania 41°9N 20°9E 23 D9
Elbe U.S.A. 46°45N 122°10W 78 D4
Elbe → Europe 53°50N 9°0E 16 B5
Elbert, Mt. U.S.A. 39°7N 106°27W 76 G10
Elberton U.S.A. 34°7N 82°52W 85 D13
Elbeuf France 49°17N 1°2E 20 B4
Elbing = Elbląg Poland 54°10N 19°25E 17 A10
Elbistan Turkey 38°13N 37°15E 44 B3
Elbląg Poland 54°10N 19°25E 17 A10
Elbow Canada 51°7N 106°35W 71 C7
Elbrus Russia 43°21N 42°30E 19 F7
Elburz Mts. = Alborz, Reshteh-ye Kūhhā-ye Iran 36°0N 52°0E 45 C7
Elche Spain 38°15N 0°42W 21 C5
Elcho I. Australia 11°55S 135°45E 62 A2
Elda Spain 38°29N 0°47W 21 C5
Eldama Ravine Kenya 0°3N 35°43E 54 B4
Elde → Germany 53°7N 11°15E 16 B6
Eldon Mo., U.S.A. 38°21N 92°35W 80 F7
Eldon Wash., U.S.A. 47°33N 123°3W 78 C3
Eldora U.S.A. 42°22N 93°5W 80 D7
Eldorado Argentina 26°28S 54°43W 95 B5
Eldorado Canada 44°35N 77°31W 82 B7
Eldorado Ill., U.S.A. 37°49N 88°26W 80 G9
Eldorado Tex., U.S.A. 30°52N 100°36W 84 F4
Eldoret Kenya 0°30N 35°17E 54 B4
Eldred U.S.A. 41°58N 78°23W 82 E6
Elea, C. Cyprus 35°19N 34°4E 25 D13
Eleanora, Pk. Australia 32°57S 121°9E 61 F3
Elefantes → Africa 24°10S 32°40E 57 C5
Elektrostal Russia 55°41N 38°32E 18 C6
Elemi Triangle Africa 5°0N 35°20E 54 B4
Elephant Butte Res. U.S.A. 33°9N 107°11W 77 K10
Elephant I. Antarctica 61°0S 55°0W 5 C18
Eleuthera Bahamas 25°0N 76°20W 88 B4
Elgin Canada 44°36N 76°13W 83 B8
Elgin U.K. 57°39N 3°19W 11 D5
Elgin Ill., U.S.A. 42°2N 88°17W 80 D9
Elgin N. Dak., U.S.A. 46°24N 101°51W 80 B3
Elgin Oreg., U.S.A. 45°34N 117°55W 76 D5
Elgin Tex., U.S.A. 30°21N 97°22W 84 F6
Elgon, Mt. Africa 1°10N 34°30E 54 B3
Eliase Indonesia 8°21S 130°48E 37 F8
Elim Namibia 17°48S 15°31E 56 B2
Elim S. Africa 34°35S 19°45E 56 E2
Elista Russia 46°16N 44°14E 19 E7
Elizabeth Australia 34°42S 138°41E 63 E2
Elizabeth U.S.A. 40°39N 74°12W 83 F10
Elizabeth City U.S.A. 36°18N 76°14W 85 C16
Elizabethton U.S.A. 36°21N 82°13W 85 C13
Elizabethtown Ky., U.S.A. 37°42N 85°52W 81 G11
Elizabethtown N.Y., U.S.A. 44°13N 73°36W 83 B11
Elizabethtown Pa., U.S.A. 40°9N 76°36W 83 F8
Elk Poland 53°50N 22°21E 17 B12
Elk → Canada 49°11N 115°14W 70 C5
Elk → U.S.A. 34°46N 87°16W 85 D11
Elk City U.S.A. 35°25N 99°25W 84 D5
Elk Creek U.S.A. 39°36N 122°32W 78 F4
Elk Grove U.S.A. 38°25N 121°22W 78 G5
Elk Island △ Canada 53°35N 112°59W 70 C6
Elk Lake Canada 47°40N 80°25W 72 C3
Elk Point Canada 53°54N 110°55W 71 C6
Elk River Idaho, U.S.A. 46°47N 116°11W 76 C5
Elk River Minn., U.S.A. 45°18N 93°35W 80 C7
Elkedra → Australia 21°8S 136°22E 62 C2
Elkhart Ind., U.S.A. 41°41N 85°58W 81 E11
Elkhart Kans., U.S.A. 37°0N 101°54W 80 G3
Elkhorn Canada 49°59N 101°14W 71 D8
Elkhorn → U.S.A. 41°8N 96°19W 80 E5
Elkhovo Bulgaria 42°10N 26°35E 23 C12
Elkin U.S.A. 36°15N 80°51W 85 C14
Elkins U.S.A. 38°55N 79°51W 81 F14
Elkland U.S.A. 41°59N 77°19W 82 E7
Elko Canada 49°20N 115°10W 70 D5
Elko U.S.A. 40°50N 115°46W 76 F6
Elkton U.S.A. 43°49N 83°11W 82 C1
Ellas = Greece ■ Europe 40°0N 23°0E 23 E9
Ellef Ringnes I. Canada 78°30N 102°0W 69 B9
Ellen, Mt. U.S.A. 44°9N 72°56W 83 B12
Ellenburg U.S.A. 44°54N 73°48W 83 B11
Ellendale U.S.A. 46°0N 98°32W 80 B4
Ellensburg U.S.A. 46°59N 120°34W 76 C3
Ellenville U.S.A. 41°43N 74°24W 83 E10
Ellerton Barbados 13°7N 59°33W 89 g
Ellery, Mt. Australia 37°28S 148°47E 63 F4
Ellesmere, L. N.Z. 43°47S 172°28E 59 G4
Ellesmere I. Canada 79°30N 80°0W 69 B12
Ellesmere Port U.K. 53°17N 2°54W 12 D5
Ellice Is. = Tuvalu ■ Pac. Oc. 8°0S 178°0E 58 B10
Ellicottville U.S.A. 42°17N 78°40W 82 D6
Ellington U.S.A. 42°13N 79°6W 82 D5
Elliot Australia 17°33S 133°32E 62 B1
Elliot S. Africa 31°22S 27°48E 57 E4
Elliot Lake Canada 46°25N 82°35W 72 C3
Elliotdale = Xhora S. Africa 31°55S 28°38E 57 E4
Ellis U.S.A. 38°56N 99°34W 80 F4
Elliston Australia 33°39S 134°53E 63 E1
Ellisville U.S.A. 31°36N 89°12W 85 F10
Ellon U.K. 57°22N 2°4W 11 D6
Ellore = Eluru India 16°48N 81°8E 41 L12
Ellsworth Kans., U.S.A. 38°44N 98°14W 80 F4
Ellsworth Maine, U.S.A. 44°33N 68°25W 81 C19
Ellsworth Land Antarctica 76°0S 89°0W 5 D16
Ellsworth Mts. Antarctica 78°30S 85°0W 5 D16
Ellwood City U.S.A. 40°52N 80°17W 82 F4
Elma Canada 49°52N 95°55W 71 D9
Elma U.S.A. 47°0N 123°25W 78 D3
Elmalı Turkey 36°44N 29°56E 19 G4
Elmhurst U.S.A. 41°53N 87°56W 80 E10
Elmira Canada 43°36N 80°33W 82 C4
Elmira U.S.A. 42°6N 76°48W 82 D8
Elmira Heights U.S.A. 42°8N 76°50W 82 D8
Elmore Australia 36°30S 144°37E 63 F3
Elmshorn Germany 53°43N 9°40E 16 B5
Elmvale Canada 44°35N 79°52W 82 B5
Elora Canada 43°41N 80°26W 82 C4
Elounda Greece 35°16N 25°42E 25 D7
Eloy U.S.A. 32°45N 111°33W 77 K8
Elphin Canada 44°55N 76°37W 83 B8
Elrose Canada 51°12N 108°0W 71 C7
Elsie U.S.A. 45°52N 123°36W 78 E3
Elsinore = Helsingør Denmark 56°2N 12°35E 9 H15
Eltanin Fracture Zone System S. Ocean 54°0S 130°0W 5 B14
Eltham N.Z. 39°26S 174°19E 59 C5
Eluru India 16°48N 81°8E 41 L12
Elvas Portugal 38°50N 7°10W 21 C2
Elverum Norway 60°53N 11°34E 8 F14
Elvire → Australia 17°51S 128°11E 60 C4
Elvire, Mt. Australia 29°22S 119°36E 61 E2
Elwell, L. = Tiber Res. U.S.A. 48°19N 111°6W 76 B8
Elwood Ind., U.S.A. 40°17N 85°50W 81 E11
Elwood Nebr., U.S.A. 40°36N 99°52W 80 E4
Elx = Elche Spain 38°15N 0°42W 21 C5
Ely U.K. 52°24N 0°16E 13 E8
Ely Minn., U.S.A. 47°55N 91°51W 80 B8
Ely Nev., U.S.A. 39°15N 114°54W 76 G6
Elyria U.S.A. 41°22N 82°7W 82 E2
eMalahleni S. Africa 25°51S 29°14E 57 D4
Emāmrūd Iran 36°30N 55°0E 45 B7
Embarcación Argentina 23°10S 64°0W 94 A3
Embetsu Japan 44°44N 141°47E 30 B10
Embi Kazakhstan 48°50N 58°8E 28 E6
Embi → Kazakhstan 46°55N 53°28E 19 E9
Embonas Greece 36°13N 27°51E 25 C9
Embro Canada 43°9N 80°54W 82 C4
Embrun France 44°34N 6°30E 20 D7
Embu Kenya 0°32S 37°38E 54 C4
Emden Germany 53°21N 7°12E 16 B4
Emerald Australia 23°32S 148°10E 62 C4
Emerson Canada 49°0N 97°10W 71 D9
Emet Turkey 39°20N 29°15E 23 E13
Emi Koussi Chad 19°45N 18°55E 51 E9
Eminabad Pakistan 32°2N 74°8E 42 C6
Emine, Nos Bulgaria 42°40N 27°56E 23 C12
Emissi, Tarso Chad 21°27N 18°36E 51 D9
Emlenton U.S.A. 41°11N 79°43W 82 E5
Emmaus S. Africa 29°2S 25°15E 56 D4
Emmaus U.S.A. 40°32N 75°30W 83 F9
Emmeloord Neths. 52°44N 5°46E 15 B5
Emmen Neths. 52°48N 6°57E 15 B6
Emmet Australia 24°45S 144°30E 62 C3
Emmetsburg U.S.A. 43°7N 94°41W 80 D6
Emmett Idaho, U.S.A. 43°52N 116°30W 76 E5
Emmett Mich., U.S.A. 42°59N 82°46W 82 D2
Emmonak U.S.A. 62°47N 164°31W 74 a
Emo Canada 48°38N 93°50W 71 D10
Empalme Mexico 27°58N 110°51W 86 B2
Empangeni S. Africa 28°50S 31°52E 57 D5
Empedrado Argentina 28°0S 58°46W 94 B4
Emperor Seamount Chain Pac. Oc. 40°0N 170°0E 64 D9
Emperor Trough Pac. Oc. 43°0N 175°30E 64 C9
Emporia Kans., U.S.A. 38°25N 96°11W 80 F5
Emporia Va., U.S.A. 36°42N 77°32W 81 G15
Emporium U.S.A. 41°31N 78°14W 82 E6
Empress Canada 50°57N 110°0W 71 C7
Empty Quarter = Rub' al Khālī Si. Arabia 19°0N 48°0E 47 D4
Ems → Germany 53°20N 7°12E 16 B4
Emsdale Canada 45°32N 79°19W 82 A5
Emu China 43°40N 128°6E 35 C15
Emu Park Australia 23°13S 150°50E 62 C5
eMuziwezinto S. Africa 30°15S 30°45E 57 E5
'En 'Avrona Israel 29°43N 35°0E 46 F4
'En Boqeq Israel 31°12N 35°21E 45 D4
'En Gedi Israel 31°28N 35°25E 45 D4
En Nahud Sudan 12°45N 28°25E 51 F11
Ena Japan 35°25N 137°25E 31 G8
Enana Namibia 17°30S 16°23E 56 B2
Enard B. U.K. 58°5N 5°20W 11 C3
Enare = Inarijärvi Finland 69°0N 28°0E 8 B23
Enarotali Indonesia 3°55S 136°21E 37 E9
Encampment U.S.A. 41°12N 106°47W 76 F10
Encantadas, Serra Brazil 30°40S 53°0W 95 C5
Encarnación Paraguay 27°15S 55°50W 95 B4
Encarnación de Díaz Mexico 21°31N 102°14W 86 C4
Encinitas U.S.A. 33°3N 117°17W 79 M9
Encino U.S.A. 34°39N 105°28W 77 J11
Encounter B. Australia 35°45S 138°45E 63 F2
Endako Canada 54°6N 125°2W 70 C3
Endau Kenya 1°18S 38°31E 54 C4
Endau Rompin △ Malaysia 2°40N 103°15E 39 L4
Ende Indonesia 8°45S 121°40E 37 F6
Endeavour Str. Australia 10°45S 142°0E 62 A3
Enderbury I. Kiribati 3°8S 171°5W 64 H10
Enderby Canada 50°35N 119°10W 70 C5
Enderby Abyssal Plain S. Ocean 60°0S 40°0E 5 C5
Enderby I. Australia 20°35S 116°30E 60 D2
Enderby Land Antarctica 66°0S 53°0E 5 C5
Enderlin U.S.A. 46°38N 97°36W 80 B5
Enderrocat, C. Spain 39°28N 2°43E 24 B9
Endicott U.S.A. 42°6N 76°4W 83 D8
Endwell U.S.A. 42°6N 76°2W 83 D8
Endyalgout I. Australia 11°40S 132°35E 60 B5
Eneabba Australia 29°49S 115°16E 61 E2
Enewetak Atoll Marshall Is. 11°30N 162°15E 64 F8
Enez Turkey 40°45N 26°5E 23 D12
Enfer, Pte. d' Martinique 14°22N 60°54W 88 c
Enfield Canada 44°56N 63°32W 73 D7
Enfield Conn., U.S.A. 41°58N 72°36W 83 E12
Enfield N.C., U.S.A. 36°11N 77°41W 85 C16
Enfield N.H., U.S.A. 43°39N 72°9W 83 C12
Engadin Switz. 46°45N 10°10E 20 C9
Engaño, C. Dom. Rep. 18°30N 68°20W 89 C6
Engaño, C. Phil. 18°35N 122°23E 37 A6
Engaru Japan 44°3N 143°31E 30 B11
Engcobo = Ngcobo S. Africa 31°37S 28°0E 57 E4
Engels Russia 51°28N 46°6E 19 D8
Engemann L. Canada 58°0N 106°55W 71 B7
Enggano Indonesia 5°20S 102°40E 36 F2

England U.S.A. 34°33N 91°58W 84 D9
England □ U.K. 53°0N 2°0W 13 E5
Englee Canada 50°45N 56°5W 73 B8
Englehart Canada 47°49N 79°52W 72 C4
Englewood U.S.A. 39°38N 104°59W 76 G11
English → Canada 49°12N 91°5W 71 C10
English Bazar = Ingraj Bazar India 24°58N 88°10E 43 G13
English Channel Europe 50°0N 2°0W 13 G6
English Company's Is., The Australia 11°50S 136°32E 62 A2
English River Canada 49°14N 91°0W 72 C1
Enid U.S.A. 36°24N 97°53W 84 C6
Enkhuizen Neths. 52°42N 5°17E 15 B5
Enna Italy 37°34N 14°16E 22 F6
Ennadai L. Canada 60°58N 101°20W 71 A8
Ennedi Chad 17°15N 22°0E 51 E10
Enngonia Australia 29°21S 145°50E 63 D4
Ennis Ireland 52°51N 8°59W 10 D3
Ennis Mont., U.S.A. 45°21N 111°44W 76 D8
Ennis Tex., U.S.A. 32°20N 96°38W 84 E6
Enniscorthy Ireland 52°30N 6°34W 10 D5
Enniskillen U.K. 54°21N 7°39W 10 B4
Ennistimon Ireland 52°57N 9°17W 10 D2
Enns → Austria 48°14N 14°32E 16 D8
Eno Finland 62°47N 30°10E 8 E24
Enontekiö Finland 68°23N 23°37E 8 B20
Enosburg Falls U.S.A. 44°55N 72°48W 83 B12
Enriquillo, L. Dom. Rep. 18°20N 72°5W 89 C5
Enschede Neths. 52°13N 6°53E 15 B6
Ensenada Argentina 34°55S 57°55W 94 C4
Ensenada Mexico 31°52N 116°37W 86 A1
Ensenada de los Muertos Mexico 23°59N 109°51W 86 C2
Ensiola, Pta. de n' Spain 39°7N 2°55E 24 B9
Entebbe Uganda 0°4N 32°28E 54 B3
Enterprise Canada 60°47N 115°45W 70 A5
Enterprise Ala., U.S.A. 31°19N 85°51W 85 F12
Enterprise Oreg., U.S.A. 45°25N 117°17W 76 D5
Entre Ríos Bolivia 21°30S 64°25W 94 A3
Entre Ríos □ Argentina 30°30S 58°30W 94 C4
Entroncamento Portugal 39°28N 8°28W 21 C1
Enugu Nigeria 6°30N 7°30E 50 G7
Enumclaw U.S.A. 47°12N 121°59W 78 C5
Eólie, Ís. Italy 38°30N 14°57E 22 E6
Epe Neths. 52°21N 5°59E 15 B5
Épernay France 49°3N 3°56E 20 B5
Ephesus Turkey 37°55N 27°22E 23 F12
Ephraim U.S.A. 39°22N 111°35W 76 G8
Ephrata Pa., U.S.A. 40°11N 76°11W 83 F8
Ephrata Wash., U.S.A. 47°19N 119°33W 76 C4
Épinal France 48°10N 6°27E 20 B7
Episkopi Cyprus 34°40N 32°54E 25 E11
Episkopi Greece 35°20N 24°20E 25 D6
Episkopi Bay Cyprus 34°35N 32°50E 25 E11
Epsom U.K. 51°19N 0°16W 13 F7
Epukiro Namibia 21°40S 19°9E 56 C2
Equatoria = El Istiwa'iya Sudan 5°0N 28°0E 51 G11
Equatorial Guinea ■ Africa 2°0N 8°0E 52 D1
Er Rachidia Morocco 31°58N 4°20W 50 B5
Er Rahad Sudan 12°45N 30°32E 51 F12
Er Rif Morocco 35°1N 4°1W 50 A5
Erāwadī Myit = Irrawaddy → Burma 15°50N 95°6E 41 M19
Erāwadī Myitwanya = Irrawaddy, Mouths of the Burma 15°30N 95°0E 41 M19
Erawan △ Thailand 14°25N 98°58E 38 E2
Erbil = Arbīl Iraq 36°15N 44°5E 44 B5
Erçek Turkey 38°39N 43°36E 44 B4
Erciyaş Dağı Turkey 38°30N 35°30E 44 B2
Érd Hungary 47°22N 18°56E 17 E10
Erdao Jiang → China 42°37N 128°0E 35 C14
Erdek Turkey 40°23N 27°47E 23 D12
Erdene = Ulaan-Uul Mongolia 44°13N 111°10E 34 B6
Erdenet Mongolia 49°2N 104°5E 32 B5
Erdenetsogt Mongolia 42°55N 106°5E 34 C4
Erebus, Mt. Antarctica 77°35S 167°0E 5 D11
Erechim Brazil 27°35S 52°15W 95 B5
Ereğli Konya, Turkey 37°31N 34°4E 44 B2
Ereğli Zonguldak, Turkey 41°15N 31°24E 19 F5
Erenhot China 43°48N 112°2E 34 C7
Eresma → Spain 41°26N 4°45W 21 B3
Erfenisdam S. Africa 28°30S 26°50E 56 D4
Erfurt Germany 50°58N 11°2E 16 C6
Ergani Turkey 38°17N 39°49E 44 B3
Ergel Mongolia 43°8N 109°5E 34 C5
Ergeni Vozvyshennost Russia 47°0N 44°0E 19 E7
Ērgli Latvia 56°54N 25°38E 9 H21
Eriboll, L. U.K. 58°30N 4°42W 11 C4
Érice Italy 38°2N 12°35E 22 E5
Erie U.S.A. 42°8N 80°5W 82 D4
Erie, L. N. Amer. 42°15N 81°0W 82 D4
Erie Canal U.S.A. 43°5N 78°43W 82 C7
Erieau Canada 42°16N 81°57W 82 D3
Erikoussa Greece 39°53N 19°34E 25 A3
Eriksdale Canada 50°52N 98°7W 71 C9
Erimanthos Greece 37°57N 21°50E 23 F9
Erimo-misaki Japan 41°50N 143°15E 30 D11
Erin Canada 43°45N 80°7W 82 C4
Erin Pt. Trin. & Tob. 10°3N 61°39W 93 K15
Erinpura India 25°9N 73°3E 42 G5
Eriskay U.K. 57°4N 7°18W 11 D1
Eritrea ■ Africa 14°0N 38°30E 47 D2
Erlangen Germany 49°36N 11°0E 16 D6
Erldunda Australia 25°14S 133°12E 62 D1
Ermelo Neths. 52°18N 5°35E 15 B5
Ermelo S. Africa 26°31S 29°59E 57 D4
Ermenek Turkey 36°38N 33°0E 44 B2
Ermones Greece 39°37N 19°46E 25 A3
Ernakulam India 9°59N 76°22E 40 Q10
Erne → Ireland 54°30N 8°16W 10 B3
Erne, Lower L. U.K. 54°28N 7°47W 10 B4
Erne, Upper L. U.K. 54°14N 7°32W 10 B4
Ernest Giles Ra. Australia 27°0S 123°45E 61 E3
Erode India 11°24N 77°45E 40 P10
Eromanga Australia 26°40S 143°11E 63 D3
Erongo Namibia 21°39S 15°58E 56 C2
Erramala Hills India 15°30N 78°15E 40 M11
Errentería Spain 43°19N 1°54W 21 A5
Erri-Nundra △ Australia 37°28S 148°5E 63 F4
Errigal Ireland 55°2N 8°6W 10 A3
Erris Hd. Ireland 54°19N 10°0W 10 B1
Erskine U.S.A. 47°40N 96°0W 80 B6
Ertis = Irtysh → Russia 61°4N 68°52E 28 C7
Erwin U.S.A. 36°9N 82°25W 85 C13
Erzgebirge Germany 50°27N 12°55E 16 C7
Erzin Russia 50°15N 95°10E 29 D10
Erzincan Turkey 39°46N 39°30E 44 B3
Erzurum Turkey 39°57N 41°15E 44 B4
Es Caló Spain 38°40N 1°30E 24 C8
Es Canar Spain 39°2N 1°36E 24 B8
Es Mercadal Spain 39°59N 4°5E 24 B11
Es Migjorn Gran Spain 39°57N 4°3E 24 B11
Es Sahrâ' Esh Sharqîya Egypt 27°30N 32°30E 51 C12
Es Sînâ' Egypt 29°0N 34°0E 46 F3
Es Vedrà Spain 38°52N 1°12E 24 C7
Esambo Dem. Rep. of the Congo 3°48S 23°30E 54 C1
Esan-Misaki Japan 41°40N 141°10E 30 D10
Esashi Hokkaidō, Japan 44°56N 142°35E 30 B11
Esashi Hokkaidō, Japan 41°52N 140°7E 30 D10
Esbjerg Denmark 55°29N 8°29E 9 J13
Esbo = Espoo Finland 60°12N 24°40E 9 F21
Escalante U.S.A. 37°47N 111°36W 77 H8
Escalante → U.S.A. 37°24N 110°57W 77 H8
Escalón Mexico 26°45N 104°20W 86 B4
Escambia → U.S.A. 30°32N 87°11W 85 F11
Escanaba U.S.A. 45°45N 87°4W 80 C10
Esch-sur-Alzette Lux. 49°32N 6°0E 15 E6
Escondido U.S.A. 33°7N 117°5W 79 M9
Escuinapa de Hidalgo Mexico 22°50N 105°50W 86 C3
Escuintla Guatemala 14°20N 90°48W 88 D1
Esenguly Turkmenistan 37°37N 53°59E 28 F6
Eşfahān Iran 32°39N 51°43E 45 C6
Eşfahān □ Iran 32°50N 51°50E 45 C6
Esfarāyen Iran 37°4N 57°30E 45 B8
Esfideh Iran 33°39N 59°46E 45 C8
Esh Sham = Dimashq Syria 33°30N 36°18E 46 B5
Esha Ness U.K. 60°29N 1°38W 11 A7
Esher U.K. 51°21N 0°20W 13 F7
Eshkol △ Israel 31°20N 34°30E 46 D3
Eshowe S. Africa 28°50S 31°30E 57 D5
Esigodini Zimbabwe 20°18S 28°56E 57 C4
Esil = Ishim → Russia 57°45N 71°10E 28 D8
Esira Madag. 24°20S 46°42E 57 C8
Esk → Dumf. & Gall., U.K. 54°58N 3°2W 11 G5
Esk → N. Yorks., U.K. 54°30N 0°37W 12 C7
Eskān Iran 26°48N 63°9E 45 E9
Esker Siding Canada 53°53N 66°25W 73 B6
Eskifjörður Iceland 65°3N 13°55W 8 D7
Eskilstuna Sweden 59°22N 16°32E 9 G17
Eskimo Point = Arviat Canada 61°6N 93°59W 71 A10
Eskişehir Turkey 39°50N 30°30E 19 G5
Esla → Spain 41°29N 6°3W 21 B2
Eslāmābād-e Gharb Iran 34°10N 46°30E 44 C5
Eslāmshahr Iran 35°40N 51°10E 45 C6
Eşme Turkey 38°23N 28°58E 23 E13
Esmeraldas Ecuador 1°0N 79°40W 92 C3
Esna = Isna Egypt 25°17N 32°30E 51 C12
Esnagi L. Canada 48°36N 84°33W 72 C3
España = Spain ■ Europe 39°0N 4°0W 21 B4
Espanola Canada 46°15N 81°46W 72 C3
Espanola U.S.A. 35°59N 106°5W 77 J10
Esparza Costa Rica 9°59N 84°40W 88 E3
Esperance Australia 33°45S 121°55E 61 F3
Esperance B. Australia 33°48S 121°55E 61 F3
Esperance Harbour St. Lucia 14°4N 60°55W 89 f
Esperanza Antarctica 65°0S 55°0W 5 C18
Esperanza Argentina 31°29S 61°3W 94 C3
Esperanza Puerto Rico 18°6N 65°28W 89 d
Espichel, C. Portugal 38°22N 9°16W 21 C1
Espigão, Serra do Brazil 26°35S 50°30W 95 B5
Espinazo, Sierra del = Espinhaço, Serra do Brazil 17°30S 43°30W 93 G10
Espinhaço, Serra do Brazil 17°30S 43°30W 93 G10
Espinilho, Serra do Brazil 28°30S 55°0W 95 B5
Espírito Santo □ Brazil 20°0S 40°45W 93 H10
Espíritu Santo Vanuatu 15°15S 166°50E 58 C9
Espíritu Santo, B. del Mexico 19°20N 87°35W 87 D7
Espíritu Santo, I. Mexico 24°30N 110°22W 86 C2
Espita Mexico 21°1N 88°19W 87 C7
Espoo Finland 60°12N 24°40E 9 F21
Espungabera Mozam. 20°29S 32°45E 57 C5
Esquel Argentina 42°55S 71°20W 96 E2
Esquimalt Canada 48°26N 123°25W 78 B3
Esquina Argentina 30°0S 59°30W 94 C4
Essaouira Morocco 31°32N 9°42W 50 B4
Essebie Dem. Rep. of the Congo 2°58N 30°40E 54 B3
Essen Belgium 51°28N 4°28E 15 C4
Essen Germany 51°28N 7°2E 16 C4
Essendon, Mt. Australia 25°0S 120°29E 61 E3
Essequibo → Guyana 6°50N 58°30W 92 B7
Essex Canada 42°10N 82°49W 82 D2
Essex Calif., U.S.A. 34°44N 115°15W 79 L11
Essex N.Y., U.S.A. 44°19N 73°21W 83 B11
Essex □ U.K. 51°54N 0°27E 13 F8
Essex Junction U.S.A. 44°29N 73°7W 83 B11
Esslingen Germany 48°44N 9°18E 16 D5
Estación Camacho Mexico 24°25N 102°18W 86 C4
Estación Simón Mexico 24°42N 102°35W 86 C4
Estados, I. de Los Argentina 54°40S 64°30W 96 G4
Eşţahbānāt Iran 29°8N 54°4E 45 D7
Estância Brazil 11°16S 37°26W 93 F11
Estancia U.S.A. 34°46N 106°4W 77 J10
Estārm Iran 28°21N 58°21E 45 D8
Estcourt S. Africa 29°0S 29°53E 57 D4
Este △ Dom. Rep. 18°14N 68°42W 89 C6
Estelí Nic. 13°9N 86°22W 88 D2
Estellencs Spain 39°39N 2°29E 24 B9
Esterhazy Canada 50°37N 102°5W 71 C8
Estevan Canada 49°10N 102°59W 71 D8
Estevan Group Canada 53°3N 129°38W 70 C3
Estherville U.S.A. 43°24N 94°50W 80 D6
Eston Canada 51°8N 108°40W 71 C7
Estonia ■ Europe 58°30N 25°30E 9 G21
Estreito Brazil 6°32S 47°25W 93 E9
Estrela, Serra da Portugal 40°10N 7°45W 21 B2
Estremoz Portugal 38°51N 7°39W 21 C2
Estrondo, Serra do Brazil 7°20S 48°0W 93 E9
Esztergom Hungary 47°47N 18°44E 17 E10
Et Tîdra Mauritania 19°45N 16°20W 50 E2
Etah India 27°35N 78°40E 43 F8
Étampes France 48°26N 2°10E 20 B5
Etanga Namibia 17°55S 13°0E 56 B1
Etawah India 26°48N 79°6E 43 F8
Etawney L. Canada 57°50N 96°50W 71 B9
Etchojoa Mexico 26°55N 109°38W 86 B3
eThekwini = Durban S. Africa 29°49S 31°1E 57 D5
Ethel U.S.A. 46°32N 122°46W 78 D4
Ethelbert Canada 51°32N 100°25W 71 C8
Ethiopia ■ Africa 8°0N 40°0E 47 F3
Ethiopian Highlands Ethiopia 10°0N 37°0E 47 F2
Etive, L. U.K. 56°29N 5°10W 11 E3
Etna Italy 37°50N 14°55E 22 F6
Etoile Dem. Rep. of the Congo 11°33S 27°30E 55 E2
Etosha △ Namibia 19°0S 16°0E 56 B2
Etosha Pan Namibia 18°40S 16°30E 56 B2
Etowah U.S.A. 35°20N 84°32W 85 D12
Etrek Turkmenistan 37°36N 54°46E 45 B7
Ettelbruck Lux. 49°51N 6°5E 15 E6
Ettrick Water → U.K. 55°31N 2°55W 11 F6
Etuku Dem. Rep. of the Congo 3°42S 25°45E 54 C2
Etzná-Tixmucuy = Edzná Mexico 19°39N 90°19W 87 D6
Eua Tonga 21°22S 174°56W 59 c
Euboea = Evia Greece 38°30N 24°0E 23 E11
Eucla Australia 31°41S 128°52E 61 F4
Euclid U.S.A. 41°34N 81°32W 82 E3
Eucumbene, L. Australia 36°2S 148°40E 63 F4
Eudora U.S.A. 33°7N 91°16W 84 E9
Eufaula Ala., U.S.A. 31°54N 85°9W 85 F12
Eufaula Okla., U.S.A. 35°17N 95°35W 84 D7
Eufaula L. U.S.A. 35°18N 95°21W 84 D7
Eugene U.S.A. 44°5N 123°4W 76 D2
Eugowra Australia 33°22S 148°24E 63 E4
Eulo Australia 28°10S 145°3E 63 D4
Eungella △ Australia 20°57S 148°40E 62 C4
Eunice La., U.S.A. 30°30N 92°25W 84 F8
Eunice N. Mex., U.S.A. 32°26N 103°10W 77 K12
Eupen Belgium 50°37N 6°3E 15 D6
Euphrates = Furāt, Nahr al → Asia 31°0N 47°25E 44 D5
Eureka Canada 80°0N 85°56W 69 B11
Eureka Calif., U.S.A. 40°47N 124°9W 76 F1
Eureka Kans., U.S.A. 37°49N 96°17W 80 G5
Eureka Mont., U.S.A. 48°53N 115°3W 76 B6
Eureka Nev., U.S.A. 39°31N 115°58W 76 G6
Eureka S. Dak., U.S.A. 45°46N 99°38W 80 C4
Eureka, Mt. Australia 26°35S 121°35E 61 E3
Euroa Australia 36°44S 145°35E 63 F4
Europa, Île Ind. Oc. 22°20S 40°22E 53 J8
Europa, Picos de Spain 43°10N 4°49W 21 A3
Europa, Pt. Gib. 36°3N 5°21W 21 D3
Europe 50°0N 20°0E 6 E10
Europoort Neths. 51°57N 4°10E 15 C4
Eustis U.S.A. 28°51N 81°41W 85 G14
Eutsuk L. Canada 53°20N 126°45W 70 C3
Evale Angola 16°33S 15°44E 56 B2
Evans U.S.A. 40°23N 104°41W 76 F11
Evans, L. Canada 50°50N 77°0W 72 B4
Evans City U.S.A. 40°46N 80°4W 82 F4
Evans Head Australia 29°7S 153°27E 63 D5
Evansburg Canada 53°36N 114°59W 70 C5
Evanston Ill., U.S.A. 42°3N 87°40W 80 D10
Evanston Wyo., U.S.A. 41°16N 110°58W 76 F8
Evansville U.S.A. 37°58N 87°35W 80 G10
Evaz Iran 27°46N 53°59E 45 E7
Eveleth U.S.A. 47°28N 92°32W 80 B7
Evensk Russia 62°12N 159°30E 29 C16
Everard, L. Australia 31°30S 135°0E 63 E2
Everard Ranges Australia 27°5S 132°28E 61 E5
Everest, Mt. Nepal 28°5N 86°58E 43 E12
Everett Pa., U.S.A. 40°1N 78°23W 82 F6
Everett Wash., U.S.A. 47°59N 122°12W 78 C4
Everglades, The U.S.A. 25°50N 81°0W 85 J14
Everglades △ U.S.A. 25°30N 81°0W 85 J14
Everglades City U.S.A. 25°52N 81°23W 85 J14
Evergreen Ala., U.S.A. 31°26N 86°57W 85 F11
Evergreen Mont., U.S.A. 48°14N 114°17W 76 B6
Evesham U.K. 52°6N 1°56W 13 E6
Evia Greece 38°30N 24°0E 23 E11
Evje Norway 58°36N 7°51E 9 G12
Évora Portugal 38°33N 7°57W 21 C2
Evowghlī Iran 38°43N 45°13E 44 B5
Évreux France 49°3N 1°8E 20 B4
Evros → Greece 41°40N 26°34E 23 D12
Évry France 48°38N 2°27E 20 B5
Évvoia = Evia Greece 38°30N 24°0E 23 E11
Ewe, L. U.K. 57°49N 5°38W 11 D3
Ewing U.S.A. 42°16N 98°21W 80 D4
Ewo Congo 0°48S 14°45E 52 E2
Exaltación Bolivia 13°10S 65°20W 92 F5
Excelsior Springs U.S.A. 39°20N 94°13W 80 F6
Exe → U.K. 50°41N 3°29W 13 G4
Exeter Canada 43°21N 81°29W 82 C3
Exeter U.K. 50°43N 3°31W 13 G4
Exeter Calif., U.S.A. 36°18N 119°9W 78 J7
Exeter N.H., U.S.A. 42°59N 70°57W 83 D14
Exmoor U.K. 51°12N 3°45W 13 F4
Exmoor △ U.K. 51°8N 3°42W 13 F4
Exmouth Australia 21°54S 114°10E 60 D1
Exmouth U.K. 50°37N 3°25W 13 G4
Exmouth G. Australia 22°15S 114°15E 60 D1
Exmouth Plateau Ind. Oc. 19°0S 114°0E 64 J3
Expedition △ Australia 25°41S 149°7E 63 D4
Expedition Ra. Australia 24°30S 149°12E 62 C4
Extremadura □ Spain 39°30N 6°5W 21 C2
Exuma Sound Bahamas 24°30N 76°20W 88 B4
Eyasi, L. Tanzania 3°30S 35°0E 54 C4
Eye Pen. U.K. 58°13N 6°10W 11 C2
Eyemouth U.K. 55°52N 2°5W 11 F6
Eyjafjörður Iceland 66°15N 18°30W 8 C4
Eyl Somali Rep. 8°0N 49°50E 47 F4
Eyre (North), L. Australia 28°30S 137°20E 63 D2
Eyre (South), L. Australia 29°18S 137°25E 63 D2
Eyre, L. Australia 29°30S 137°26E 58 D6
Eyre Mts. N.Z. 45°25S 168°25E 59 F2
Eyre Pen. Australia 33°30S 136°17E 63 E2
Eysturoy Færoe Is. 62°13N 6°54W 8 E9
Eyvān = Jūy Zar Iran 33°50N 46°18E 44 C5
Eyvānkī Iran 35°24N 51°56E 45 C6
Ezine Turkey 39°48N 26°20E 23 E12
Ezouza → Cyprus 34°44N 32°27E 25 E11

F

F.Y.R.O.M. = Macedonia ■ Europe 41°53N 21°40E 23 D9
Faaa Tahiti 17°34S 149°35W 59 d
Faaone Tahiti 17°40S 149°21W 59 d
Fabala Guinea 9°44N 9°5W 50 G4
Fabens U.S.A. 31°30N 106°10W 84 F1
Fabius U.S.A. 42°50N 75°59W 83 D9
Fabriano Italy 43°20N 12°54E 22 C5
Fachi Niger 18°6N 11°34E 51 E8
Fada Chad 17°13N 21°34E 51 E10
Fada-n-Gourma Burkina Faso 12°10N 0°30E 50 F6
Faddeyevskiy, Ostrov Russia 76°0N 144°0E 29 B15
Fadghāmī Syria 35°53N 40°52E 44 C4
Faenza Italy 44°17N 11°53E 22 B4
Færoe Is. = Føroyar ☒ Atl. Oc. 62°0N 7°0W 8 F9
Făgăras Romania 45°48N 24°58E 17 F13
Fagersta Sweden 60°1N 15°46E 9 F16
Fagnano, L. Argentina 54°30S 68°0W 96 G3
Fahlīān Iran 30°11N 51°28E 45 D6
Fahraj Kermān, Iran 29°0N 59°0E 45 D8
Fahraj Yazd, Iran 31°46N 54°36E 45 D7
Faial Azores 38°34N 28°42W 50 a
Faial Madeira 32°47N 16°53W 24 D3
Faichan Kangri India 35°48N 76°34E 43 B7
Fair Haven N.Y., U.S.A. 43°18N 76°42W 83 C8
Fair Haven Vt., U.S.A. 43°36N 73°16W 81 D17
Fair Hd. U.K. 55°14N 6°9W 10 A5
Fair Isle U.K. 59°32N 1°38W 14 B6
Fair Oaks U.S.A. 38°39N 121°16W 78 G5
Fairbanks U.S.A. 64°51N 147°43W 68 C5
Fairbury U.S.A. 40°8N 97°11W 80 E5
Fairfax U.S.A. 44°40N 73°1W 83 B11
Fairfield Ala., U.S.A. 33°29N 86°55W 85 E11
Fairfield Calif., U.S.A. 38°15N 122°3W 78 G4
Fairfield Conn., U.S.A. 41°9N 73°16W 83 E11
Fairfield Idaho, U.S.A. 43°21N 114°44W 76 E6
Fairfield Ill., U.S.A. 38°23N 88°22W 80 F9
Fairfield Iowa, U.S.A. 40°56N 91°57W 80 E8
Fairfield Tex., U.S.A. 31°44N 96°10W 84 F6
Fairford Canada 51°37N 98°38W 71 C9
Fairhope U.S.A. 30°31N 87°54W 85 F11
Fairlie N.Z. 44°5S 170°49E 59 F3
Fairmead U.S.A. 37°5N 120°10W 78 H6
Fairmont Minn., U.S.A. 43°39N 94°28W 80 D6
Fairmont W. Va., U.S.A. 39°29N 80°9W 81 F13
Fairmount Calif., U.S.A. 34°45N 118°26W 79 L8
Fairmount N.Y., U.S.A. 43°5N 76°12W 83 C8
Fairplay U.S.A. 39°15N 106°2W 76 G10
Fairport U.S.A. 43°6N 77°27W 82 C7
Fairport Harbor U.S.A. 41°45N 81°17W 82 E3
Fairview Canada 56°5N 118°25W 70 B5
Fairview Mont., U.S.A. 47°51N 104°3W 76 C11
Fairview Okla., U.S.A. 36°16N 98°29W 84 C5
Fairweather, Mt. U.S.A. 58°55N 137°32W 70 B1
Faisalabad Pakistan 31°30N 73°5E 42 D5
Faith U.S.A. 45°2N 102°2W 80 C2
Faizabad India 26°45N 82°10E 43 F10
Fajardo Puerto Rico 18°20N 65°39W 89 d
Fajr, W. → Si. Arabia 29°10N 38°10E 44 D3
Fakenham U.K. 52°51N 0°51E 12 E8
Fakfak Indonesia 2°55S 132°18E 37 E8
Faku China 42°32N 123°21E 35 C12
Falaise France 48°54N 0°12W 20 B3
Falaise, Mui Vietnam 19°6N 105°45E 38 C5
Falam Burma 23°0N 93°45E 41 H18
Falcó, C. des Spain 38°50N 1°23E 24 C7
Falcón, Presa Mexico 26°35N 99°10W 87 B5
Falcon Lake Canada 49°42N 95°15W 71 D9
Falcon Res. U.S.A. 26°34N 99°10W 84 H5
Falconara Marittima Italy 43°37N 13°24E 22 C5
Falcone, C. del Italy 40°58N 8°12E 22 D3
Falconer U.S.A. 42°7N 79°12W 82 D5
Falefa Samoa 13°54S 171°31W 59 b
Falelatai Samoa 13°55S 171°59W 59 b
Falelima Samoa 13°32S 172°41W 59 b
Faleshty = Fălești Moldova 47°32N 27°44E 17 E14
Fălești Moldova 47°32N 27°44E 17 E14
Falfurrias U.S.A. 27°14N 98°9W 84 H5
Falher Canada 55°44N 117°15W 70 B5
Faliraki Greece 36°22N 28°12E 25 C10
Falkenberg Sweden 56°54N 12°30E 9 H15
Falkirk U.K. 56°0N 3°47W 11 F5
Falkirk □ U.K. 55°58N 3°49W 11 F5
Falkland U.K. 56°16N 3°12W 11 E5
Falkland Is. ☒ Atl. Oc. 51°30S 59°0W 96 G5
Falkland Sd. Falk. Is. 52°0S 60°0W 96 G5
Fall River U.S.A. 41°43N 71°10W 83 E13
Fallbrook U.S.A. 33°23N 117°15W 79 M9
Fallon U.S.A. 39°28N 118°47W 76 G4
Falls City U.S.A. 40°3N 95°36W 80 E6
Falls Creek U.S.A. 41°9N 78°48W 82 E6
Falmouth Jamaica 18°30N 77°40W 88 a
Falmouth U.K. 50°9N 5°5W 13 G2
Falmouth U.S.A. 41°33N 70°37W 83 E14
Falsa, Pta. Mexico 27°51N 115°3W 86 B1
False B. S. Africa 34°15S 18°40E 56 E2
Falso, C. Honduras 15°12N 83°21W 88 C3
Falster Denmark 54°45N 11°55E 9 J14
Falsterbo Sweden 55°23N 12°50E 9 J15
Fălticeni Romania 47°21N 26°20E 17 E14
Falun Sweden 60°37N 15°37E 8 F16
Famagusta Cyprus 35°8N 33°55E 25 D12
Famagusta Bay Cyprus 35°15N 34°0E 25 D13
Famatina, Sierra de Argentina 27°30S 68°0W 94 B2
Family L. Canada 51°54N 95°27W 71 C9
Famoso U.S.A. 35°37N 119°12W 79 K7
Fan Xian China 35°55N 115°38E 34 G8
Fanad Hd. Ireland 55°17N 7°38W 10 A4
Fandriana Madag. 20°14S 47°21E 57 C8
Fang Thailand 19°55N 99°13E 38 C2
Fangcheng China 33°18N 112°59E 34 H7
Fangshan China 38°3N 111°25E 34 E6
Fangzi China 36°33N 119°10E 35 F10
Fanjakana Madag. 21°10S 46°53E 57 C8
Fanjiatun China 43°40N 125°15E 35 C13
Fanling China 22°30N 114°8E 33 F11
Fannich, L. U.K. 57°38N 4°59W 11 D4
Fannūj Iran 26°35N 59°38E 45 E8
Fanø Denmark 55°25N 8°25E 9 J13
Fano Italy 43°50N 13°1E 22 C5
Fanshi China 39°12N 113°20E 34 E7
Fao = Al Fāw Iraq 30°0N 48°30E 45 D6
Faqirwali Pakistan 29°27N 73°0E 42 E5
Far East = Dalnevostochnyy □ Russia 67°0N 140°0E 29 C14
Far East Asia 40°0N 130°0E 26 E14
Faradje Dem. Rep. of the Congo 3°50N 29°45E 54 B2
Farafangana Madag. 22°49S 47°50E 57 C8
Farāh Afghan. 32°20N 62°7E 40 C3
Farāh □ Afghan. 32°25N 62°10E 40 C3
Farahalana Madag. 14°26S 50°10E 57 A9
Faranah Guinea 10°3N 10°45W 50 F3
Farasān, Jazā'ir Si. Arabia 16°45N 41°55E 47 D3
Farasan Is. = Farasān, Jazā'ir Si. Arabia 16°45N 41°55E 47 D3
Faratsiho Madag. 19°24S 46°57E 57 B8
Fareham U.K. 50°51N 1°11W 13 G6
Farewell, C. N.Z. 40°29S 172°43E 59 D4
Farewell C. = Nunap Isua Greenland 59°48N 43°55W 66 D15
Farghona Uzbekistan 40°23N 71°19E 28 E8
Fargo U.S.A. 46°53N 96°48W 80 B5
Fār'iah, W. al → West Bank 32°12N 35°27E 46 C4
Faribault U.S.A. 44°18N 93°16W 80 C7
Faridabad India 28°26N 77°19E 42 E6
Faridkot India 30°44N 74°45E 42 D6
Faridpur Bangla. 23°15N 89°55E 43 H13
Faridpur India 28°13N 79°33E 43 E8
Farīmān Iran 35°40N 59°49E 45 C8
Farina Australia 30°3S 138°15E 63 E2
Fariones, Pta. Canary Is. 29°13N 13°28W 24 E6
Farleigh Australia 21°4S 149°8E 62 K7
Farmerville U.S.A. 32°47N 92°24W 84 E8
Farmingdale U.S.A. 40°12N 74°10W 83 F10
Farmington Canada 55°54N 120°30W 70 B4
Farmington Calif., U.S.A. 37°55N 120°59W 78 H6
Farmington Maine, U.S.A. 44°40N 70°9W 81 C18
Farmington Mo., U.S.A. 37°47N 90°25W 80 G8
Farmington N.H., U.S.A. 43°24N 71°4W 83 C13
Farmington N. Mex., U.S.A. 36°44N 108°12W 77 H9
Farmington Utah, U.S.A. 40°59N 111°53W 76 F8
Farmington → U.S.A. 41°51N 72°38W 83 E12
Farmville U.S.A. 37°18N 78°24W 81 G14
Farne Is. U.K. 55°38N 1°37W 12 B6
Farnham Canada 45°17N 72°59W 83 A12
Farnham, Mt. Canada 50°29N 116°30W 70 C5
Faro Brazil 2°10S 56°39W 93 D7
Faro Canada 62°11N 133°22W 68 C6
Faro Portugal 37°2N 7°55W 21 D2
Fårö Sweden 57°55N 19°5E 9 H18
Farquhar, C. Australia 23°50S 113°36E 61 D1
Farrars Cr. → Australia 25°35S 140°43E 62 D3
Farrāshband Iran 28°57N 52°5E 45 D7
Farrell U.S.A. 41°13N 80°30W 82 E4
Farrokhī Iran 33°50N 59°31E 45 C8
Farruch, C. = Ferrutx, C. de Spain 39°47N 3°21E 24 B10
Farrukhabad India 27°24N 79°34E 43 F8
Fārs □ Iran 29°30N 55°0E 45 D7
Farsala Greece 39°17N 22°23E 23 E10
Fārsī Iran 27°58N 50°11E 45 E6
Farson U.S.A. 42°7N 109°26W 76 E9
Farsund Norway 58°5N 6°55E 9 G12
Fartak, Râs Si. Arabia 28°5N 34°34E 44 D2
Fartak, Ra's Yemen 15°38N 52°15E 47 D5

Fartura, Serra da *Brazil* 26°21S 52°52W **95 B5**
Fārūj *Iran* 37°14N 58°14E **45 B8**
Farvel, Kap = Nunap Isua
  Greenland 59°48N 43°55W **66 D15**
Farwell *U.S.A.* 34°23N 103°2W **84 D3**
Fāryāb □ *Afghan.* 36°0N 65°0E **40 B4**
Fasā *Iran* 29°0N 53°39E **45 D7**
Fasano *Italy* 40°50N 17°22E **22 D7**
Fastiv *Ukraine* 50°7N 29°57E **17 C15**
Fastnet Rock *Ireland* 51°22N 9°37W **10 E2**
Fastov = Fastiv *Ukraine* 50°7N 29°57E **17 C15**
Fatagar, Tanjung
  Indonesia 2°46S 131°57E **37 E8**
Fatehabad *Haryana, India* 29°31N 75°27E **42 E6**
Fatehabad *Ut. P., India* 27°1N 78°19E **43 F8**
Fatehgarh *India* 27°25N 79°35E **43 F8**
Fatehpur *Bihar, India* 24°38N 85°14E **43 G11**
Fatehpur *Raj., India* 28°0N 74°40E **42 F6**
Fatehpur *Ut. P., India* 25°56N 81°13E **43 G9**
Fatehpur *Ut. P., India* 27°10N 81°13E **43 F9**
Fatehpur Sikri *India* 27°6N 77°40E **42 F6**
Fathom Five △ *Canada* 45°17N 81°40W **82 A3**
Fatima *Canada* 47°24N 61°53W **73 C7**
Faulkton *U.S.A.* 45°2N 99°8W **80 C4**
Faure I. *Australia* 25°52S 113°50E **61 E1**
Fauresmith *S. Africa* 29°44S 25°17E **56 D4**
Fauske *Norway* 67°17N 15°25E **8 C16**
Favara *Italy* 37°19N 13°39E **22 F5**
Favárítx, C. de *Spain* 40°0N 4°15E **24 B11**
Favignana *Italy* 37°56N 12°20E **22 F5**
Fawcett, Pt. *Australia* 11°46S 130°2E **60 B5**
Fawn → *Canada* 55°20N 87°35W **72 A2**
Fawnskin *U.S.A.* 34°16N 116°56W **79 L10**
Faxaflói *Iceland* 64°29N 23°0W **8 D2**
Faya-Largeau *Chad* 17°58N 19°6E **51 E9**
Fayd *Si. Arabia* 27°1N 42°52E **44 E4**
Fayette *Ala., U.S.A.* 33°41N 87°50W **85 E11**
Fayette *Mo., U.S.A.* 39°9N 92°41W **80 F7**
Fayette *N.Y., U.S.A.* 42°48N 76°48W **83 D8**
Fayetteville *Ark., U.S.A.* 36°4N 94°10W **84 C7**
Fayetteville *N.C., U.S.A.* 35°3N 78°53W **85 D15**
Fayetteville *N.Y., U.S.A.* 43°1N 76°0W **83 C9**
Fayetteville *Tenn., U.S.A.* 35°9N 86°34W **85 D11**
Faylakah *Kuwait* 29°27N 48°20E **45 D6**
Fazilka *India* 30°27N 74°2E **42 D6**
Fazilpur *Pakistan* 29°18N 70°29E **42 E4**
Fdérik *Mauritania* 22°40N 12°45W **50 D3**
Feakle *Ireland* 52°56N 8°40W **10 D3**
Feale → *Ireland* 52°27N 9°37W **10 D2**
Fear, C. *U.S.A.* 33°50N 77°58W **85 E16**
Feather → *U.S.A.* 38°47N 121°36W **76 G3**
Feather Falls *U.S.A.* 39°36N 121°16W **78 F5**
Featherston *N.Z.* 41°6S 175°20E **59 D5**
Featherstone *Zimbabwe* 18°42S 30°55E **55 F3**
Fécamp *France* 49°45N 0°22E **20 B4**
Fedala = Mohammedia
  Morocco 33°44N 7°21W **50 B4**
Federación *Argentina* 31°0S 57°55W **94 C4**
Féderal *Argentina* 30°57S 58°48W **96 C5**
Federal Way *U.S.A.* 47°18N 122°19W **78 C4**
Fedeshkūh *Iran* 28°49N 53°50E **45 D7**
Fehmarn *Germany* 54°27N 11°7E **16 A6**
Fehmarn Bælt *Europe* 54°35N 11°20E **9 J14**
Fehmarn Belt = Fehmarn Bælt
  Europe 54°35N 11°20E **9 J14**
Fei Xian *China* 35°18N 117°59E **35 G9**
Feijó *Brazil* 8°9S 70°21W **92 E4**
Feilding *N.Z.* 40°13S 175°35E **59 D5**
Feira de Santana *Brazil* 12°15S 38°57W **93 F11**
Feixiang *China* 36°30N 114°45E **34 F8**
Felanitx *Spain* 39°28N 3°9E **24 B10**
Feldkirch *Austria* 47°15N 9°37E **16 E5**
Félicité *Seychelles* 4°19S 55°52E **53 b**
Felipe Carrillo Puerto
  Mexico 19°38N 88°3W **87 D7**
Felixburg *Zimbabwe* 19°29S 30°51E **57 B5**
Felixstowe *U.K.* 51°58N 1°23E **13 F9**
Felton *U.S.A.* 37°3N 122°4W **78 H4**
Femer Bælt = Fehmarn Bælt
  Europe 54°35N 11°20E **9 J14**
Femunden *Norway* 62°10N 11°53E **8 E14**
Fen He → *China* 35°36N 110°42E **34 G6**
Fenelon Falls *Canada* 44°32N 78°45W **82 B6**
Feng Xian *Jiangsu, China* 34°43N 116°35E **34 G9**
Feng Xian *Shaanxi,*
  China 33°54N 106°40E **34 H4**
Fengcheng *China* 40°28N 124°5E **35 D13**
Fengfeng *China* 36°28N 114°8E **34 F8**
Fengning *China* 41°10N 116°33E **34 D9**
Fengrun *China* 39°48N 118°8E **35 E10**
Fengtai *China* 39°49N 116°14E **34 E9**
Fengxiang *China* 34°29N 107°25E **34 G4**
Fengyang *China* 32°51N 117°29E **35 H9**
Fengzhen *China* 40°25N 113°2E **34 D7**
Fenoarivo *Fianarantsoa,*
  Madag. 21°43S 46°24E **57 C8**
Fenoarivo *Fianarantsoa,*
  Madag. 20°52S 46°53E **57 C8**
Fenoarivo Afovoany
  Madag. 18°26S 46°34E **57 B8**
Fenoarivo Atsinanana
  Madag. 17°22S 49°25E **57 B8**
Fens, The *U.K.* 52°38N 0°2W **12 E7**
Fenton *U.S.A.* 42°48N 83°42W **81 D12**
Fenxi *China* 36°40N 111°31E **34 F6**
Fenyang *China* 37°18N 111°48E **34 F6**
Feodosiya *Ukraine* 45°2N 35°16E **19 F5**
Ferbane *Ireland* 53°16N 7°50W **10 C4**
Ferdows *Iran* 33°58N 58°2E **45 C8**
Ferfer *Somali Rep.* 5°4N 45°9E **47 F4**
Fergana = Farghona
  Uzbekistan 40°23N 71°19E **28 E8**
Fergus *Canada* 43°43N 80°24W **82 C4**
Fergus Falls *U.S.A.* 46°17N 96°4W **80 B5**
Ferkéssédougou *Ivory C.* 9°35N 5°6W **50 G4**
Ferland *Canada* 50°19N 88°27W **72 B2**

Ferlo, Vallée du *Senegal* 15°15N 14°15W **50 E3**
Fermanagh □ *U.K.* 54°21N 7°40W **10 B4**
Fermo *Italy* 43°9N 13°43E **22 C5**
Fermont *Canada* 52°47N 67°5W **73 B6**
Fermoy *Ireland* 52°9N 8°16W **10 D3**
Fernández *Argentina* 27°55S 63°50W **94 B3**
Fernandina Beach
  U.S.A. 30°40N 81°27W **85 F14**
Fernando de Noronha
  Brazil 4°0S 33°10W **93 D12**
Fernando Póo = Bioko
  Eq. Guin. 3°30N 8°40E **52 D1**
Ferndale *Canada* 44°58N 81°17W **82 B3**
Ferndale *U.S.A.* 48°51N 122°36W **78 B4**
Fernie *Canada* 49°30N 115°5W **70 D5**
Fernlees *Australia* 23°51S 148°7E **62 C4**
Fernley *U.S.A.* 39°36N 119°15W **76 G4**
Fernwood *U.S.A.* 43°16N 73°38W **83 C11**
Ferozepore = Firozpur
  India 30°55N 74°40E **42 D6**
Ferrara *Italy* 44°50N 11°35E **22 B4**
Ferreñafe *Peru* 6°42S 79°50W **92 E3**
Ferrerías *Spain* 39°59N 4°1E **24 B11**
Ferret, C. *France* 44°38N 1°15W **20 D3**
Ferriday *U.S.A.* 31°38N 91°33W **84 F9**
Ferrol *Spain* 43°29N 8°15W **21 A1**
Ferron *U.S.A.* 39°5N 111°8W **76 G8**
Ferrutx, C. de *Spain* 39°47N 3°21E **24 B10**
Ferryland *Canada* 47°2N 52°53W **73 C9**
Fertile *U.S.A.* 47°32N 96°17W **80 B5**
Fès *Morocco* 34°0N 5°0W **50 B5**
Fessenden *U.S.A.* 47°39N 99°38W **80 B4**
Festus *U.S.A.* 38°13N 90°24W **80 F8**
Feteşti *Romania* 44°22N 27°51E **17 F14**
Fethiye *Turkey* 36°36N 29°6E **19 G4**
Fetlar *U.K.* 60°36N 0°52W **11 A8**
Feuilles → *Canada* 58°47N 70°4W **69 D12**
Fez = Fès *Morocco* 34°0N 5°0W **50 B5**
Fezzan *Libya* 27°0N 13°0E **51 C8**
Fiambalá *Argentina* 27°45S 67°37W **94 B2**
Fianarantsoa *Madag.* 21°26S 47°5E **57 C8**
Fianarantsoa □ *Madag.* 19°30S 47°0E **57 B8**
Ficksburg *S. Africa* 28°51S 27°53E **57 D4**
Field → *Australia* 23°48S 138°0E **62 C2**
Field I. *Australia* 12°5S 132°23E **60 B5**
Fier *Albania* 40°43N 19°33E **23 D8**
Fife □ *U.K.* 56°16N 3°1W **11 E5**
Fife □ *U.K.* 56°15N 3°15W **11 E5**
Fife Ness *U.K.* 56°17N 2°35W **11 E6**
Fifth Cataract *Sudan* 18°22N 33°50E **51 E12**
Figeac *France* 44°37N 2°2E **20 D5**
Figtree *Zimbabwe* 20°22S 28°20E **55 G2**
Figueira da Foz *Portugal* 40°7N 8°54W **21 B1**
Figueres *Spain* 42°18N 2°58E **21 A7**
Figuig *Morocco* 32°5N 1°11W **50 B5**
Fihaonana *Madag.* 18°36S 47°12E **57 B8**
Fiherenana *Madag.* 18°29S 48°24E **57 B8**
Fiherenana → *Madag.* 23°19S 43°37E **57 C7**
Fiji ■ *Pac. Oc.* 17°20S 179°0E **59 a**
Filabusi *Zimbabwe* 20°34S 29°20E **57 C4**
Filadelfia *Paraguay* 22°21S 60°2W **94 A3**
Filchner Ice Shelf *Antarctica* 79°0S 40°0W **5 D1**
Filey *U.K.* 54°12N 0°18W **12 C7**
Filey B. *U.K.* 54°12N 0°15W **12 C7**
Filfla *Malta* 35°47N 14°24E **25 D1**
Filiatrá *Greece* 37°9N 21°35E **23 F9**
Filingué *Niger* 14°21N 3°22E **50 F6**
Filipstad *Sweden* 59°43N 14°9E **9 G16**
Fillmore *Calif., U.S.A.* 34°24N 118°55W **79 L8**
Fillmore *Utah, U.S.A.* 38°58N 112°20W **76 G7**
Fimbul Ice Shelf *S. Ocean* 70°30S 15°0W **5 D2**
Finch *Canada* 45°11N 75°7W **83 A9**
Finch Hatton *Australia* 20°25S 148°39E **62 K6**
Findhorn → *U.K.* 57°38N 3°38N **11 D5**
Findlay *U.S.A.* 41°2N 83°39W **81 E12**
Fine *U.S.A.* 44°14N 75°8W **83 B9**
Finger L. *Canada* 53°33N 93°30W **72 B1**
Finger Lakes *U.S.A.* 42°40N 76°30W **83 D8**
Finisterre, C. = Fisterra, C.
  Spain 42°50N 9°19W **21 A1**
Finke *Australia* 25°34S 134°35E **62 D1**
Finke Gorge △ *Australia* 24°8S 132°49E **60 D5**
Finland ■ *Europe* 63°0N 27°0E **8 E22**
Finland, G. of *Europe* 60°0N 26°0E **9 G22**
Finlay → *Canada* 57°0N 125°10W **70 B3**
Finley *Australia* 35°38S 145°35E **63 F4**
Finley *U.S.A.* 47°31N 97°50W **80 B5**
Finn → *Ireland* 54°51N 7°28W **10 B4**
Finnigan, Mt. *Australia* 15°49S 145°17E **62 B4**
Finniss, C. *Australia* 33°8S 134°51E **63 E1**
Finnmark *Norway* 69°37N 23°57E **8 B20**
Finnsnes *Norway* 69°14N 18°0E **8 B18**
Finspång *Sweden* 58°43N 15°47E **9 G16**
Fiora → *Italy* 42°20N 11°34E **22 C4**
Fiordland △ *N.Z.* 45°46S 167°0E **59 F1**
Fīq *Syria* 32°46N 35°41E **46 C4**
Firat = Furāt, Nahr al →
  Asia 31°0N 47°25E **44 D5**
Fire Island △ *U.S.A.* 40°38N 73°8W **83 F11**
Firebag → *Canada* 57°45N 111°21W **71 B6**
Firebaugh *U.S.A.* 36°52N 120°27W **78 J6**
Firedrake L. *Canada* 61°25N 104°30W **71 A8**
Firenze *Italy* 43°46N 11°15E **22 C4**
Firk, Sha'ib → *Iraq* 30°59N 44°34E **44 D5**
Firozabad *India* 27°10N 78°25E **43 F8**
Firozpur *India* 30°55N 74°40E **42 D6**
Firozpur-Jhirka *India* 27°48N 76°57E **42 F7**
Fīrūzābād *Iran* 28°52N 52°35E **45 D7**
Fīrūzkūh *Iran* 35°50N 52°50E **45 C7**
Firvale *Canada* 52°27N 126°13W **70 C3**
Fish → *Namibia* 28°7S 17°10E **56 D2**
Fish → *Namibia* 31°30S 20°16E **56 E3**
Fish River Canyon
  Namibia 27°40S 17°35E **56 D2**
Fisher B. *Canada* 51°35N 97°13W **71 C9**
Fishers I. *U.S.A.* 41°15N 72°0W **83 E13**

Fishguard *U.K.* 52°0N 4°58W **13 E3**
Fishing L. *Canada* 52°10N 95°24W **71 C9**
Fishkill *U.S.A.* 41°32N 73°54W **83 E11**
Fisterra, C. *Spain* 42°50N 9°19W **21 A1**
Fitchburg *Mass., U.S.A.* 42°35N 71°48W **83 D13**
Fitchburg *Wis., U.S.A.* 42°58N 89°28W **80 D9**
Fitz Roy *Argentina* 47°0S 67°0W **96 F3**
Fitz Roy, Cerro *Argentina* 49°17S 73°5W **96 F2**
Fitzgerald *Canada* 59°51N 111°36W **70 B6**
Fitzgerald *U.S.A.* 31°43N 83°15W **85 F13**
Fitzgerald River △
  Australia 33°53S 119°55E **61 F3**
Fitzmaurice → *Australia* 14°45S 130°5E **60 B5**
Fitzroy → *Queens.,*
  Australia 23°32S 150°52E **62 C5**
Fitzroy → *W. Austral.,*
  Australia 17°31S 123°35E **60 C3**
Fitzroy Crossing
  Australia 18°9S 125°38E **60 C4**
Fitzwilliam I. *Canada* 45°30N 81°45W **82 A3**
Five Points *U.S.A.* 36°26N 120°6W **78 J6**
Fizi *Dem. Rep. of the Congo* 4°17S 28°55E **54 C2**
Flagstaff *U.S.A.* 35°12N 111°39W **77 J8**
Flagstaff L. *U.S.A.* 45°12N 70°18W **83 A14**
Flaherty I. *Canada* 56°15N 79°15W **72 A4**
Flåm *Norway* 60°50N 7°7E **8 F12**
Flambeau → *U.S.A.* 45°18N 91°14W **80 C8**
Flamborough Hd. *U.K.* 54°7N 0°5W **12 C7**
Flaming Gorge □
  U.S.A. 41°10N 109°25W **76 F9**
Flaming Gorge Res.
  U.S.A. 41°10N 109°25W **76 F9**
Flamingo, Teluk *Indonesia* 5°30S 138°0E **37 F9**
Flanders = Flandre
  Europe 50°50N 2°30E **15 B9**
Flandre *Europe* 50°50N 2°30E **15 B9**
Flandre-Occidentale = West-
  Vlaanderen □ *Belgium* 51°0N 3°0E **15 D2**
Flandre-Orientale = Oost-
  Vlaanderen □ *Belgium* 51°5N 3°50E **15 C3**
Flandreau *U.S.A.* 44°3N 96°36W **80 C6**
Flanigan *U.S.A.* 40°10N 119°53W **78 E7**
Flannan Is. *U.K.* 58°9N 7°52W **11 C1**
Flat → *Canada* 61°33N 125°18W **70 A3**
Flat I. *Mauritius* 19°53S 57°35E **53 d**
Flathead L. *U.S.A.* 47°51N 114°8W **76 C6**
Flattery, C. *Australia* 14°58S 145°21E **62 A4**
Flattery, C. *U.S.A.* 48°23N 124°29W **78 B2**
Flatwoods *U.S.A.* 38°31N 82°43W **81 F12**
Fleetwood *U.S.A.* 40°27N 75°49W **83 F9**
Flekkefjord *Norway* 58°18N 6°39E **9 G12**
Flemington *U.S.A.* 41°7N 77°28W **82 E7**
Flensburg *Germany* 54°47N 9°27E **16 A5**
Flers *France* 48°47N 0°33E **20 B3**
Flesherton *Canada* 44°16N 80°33W **82 B4**
Flesko, Tanjung
  Indonesia 0°29N 124°30E **37 D6**
Fleurieu Pen. *Australia* 35°40S 138°5E **63 F2**
Flevoland □ *Neths.* 52°30N 5°30E **15 B5**
Flin Flon *Canada* 54°46N 101°53W **71 C8**
Flinders → *Australia* 17°36S 140°36E **62 B3**
Flinders B. *Australia* 34°19S 115°19E **61 F2**
Flinders Group *Australia* 14°11S 144°15E **62 A3**
Flinders I. *S. Austral.,*
  Australia 33°44S 134°41E **63 E1**
Flinders I. *Tas., Australia* 40°0S 148°0E **63 G4**
Flinders Ranges
  Australia 31°30S 138°30E **63 E2**
Flinders Reefs *Australia* 17°37S 148°31E **62 B4**
Flint *U.K.* 53°15N 3°8W **12 D4**
Flint *U.S.A.* 43°1N 83°41W **81 D12**
Flint → *U.S.A.* 30°57N 84°34W **85 F12**
Flint I. *Kiribati* 11°26S 151°48W **65 J12**
Flintshire □ *U.K.* 53°17N 3°17W **12 D4**
Flodden *U.K.* 55°37N 2°8W **12 B5**
Floodwood *U.S.A.* 46°56N 92°55W **80 B7**
Flora *U.S.A.* 38°40N 88°29W **80 F9**
Florala *U.S.A.* 31°0N 86°20W **85 F11**
Florence = Firenze *Italy* 43°46N 11°15E **22 C4**
Florence *Ala., U.S.A.* 34°48N 87°41W **85 D11**
Florence *Ariz., U.S.A.* 33°2N 111°23W **77 K8**
Florence *Colo., U.S.A.* 38°23N 105°8W **76 G11**
Florence *Oreg., U.S.A.* 43°58N 124°7W **76 D1**
Florence *S.C., U.S.A.* 34°12N 79°46W **85 D15**
Florence, L. *Australia* 28°53S 138°9E **63 D2**
Florencia *Colombia* 1°36N 75°36W **92 C3**
Florennes *Belgium* 50°15N 4°35E **15 D4**
Florenville *Belgium* 49°40N 5°19E **15 E5**
Flores *Azores* 39°26N 31°13W **50 a**
Flores *Guatemala* 16°59N 89°50W **88 C2**
Flores *Indonesia* 8°35S 121°0E **37 F6**
Flores I. *Canada* 49°20N 126°10W **70 D3**
Flores Sea *Indonesia* 6°30S 120°0E **37 F6**
Floreşti *Moldova* 47°53N 28°17E **17 E15**
Floresville *U.S.A.* 29°8N 98°10W **84 G5**
Florianópolis *Brazil* 27°30S 48°30W **95 B6**
Florida *Cuba* 21°32N 78°14W **88 B4**
Florida *Uruguay* 34°7S 56°10W **95 C4**
Florida □ *U.S.A.* 28°0N 82°0W **85 G14**
Florida, Straits of *U.S.A.* 25°0N 80°0W **88 B4**
Florida B. *U.S.A.* 25°0N 81°20W **88 B3**
Florida Keys *U.S.A.* 24°40N 81°0W **85 J14**
Florin *U.S.A.* 38°30N 121°24W **78 G5**
Florina *Greece* 40°48N 21°26E **23 D9**
Florissant *U.S.A.* 38°47N 90°19W **80 F9**
Florø *Norway* 61°35N 5°1E **8 F11**
Flower Station *Canada* 45°10N 76°41W **83 A8**
Flowerpot I. *Canada* 45°18N 81°38W **82 A3**
Floydada *U.S.A.* 33°59N 101°20W **84 E4**
Fluk *Indonesia* 1°42S 127°44E **37 E7**
Flushing = Vlissingen
  Neths. 51°26N 3°34E **15 C3**
Fly → *Papua N. G.* 8°25S 143°0E **58 B7**

Flying Fish, C. *Antarctica* 72°6S 102°29W **5 D15**
Foa *Tonga* 19°45S 174°18W **59 c**
Foam Lake *Canada* 51°40N 103°32W **71 C8**
Foça *Turkey* 38°39N 26°46E **23 E12**
Fochabers *U.K.* 57°37N 3°6W **11 D5**
Focşani *Romania* 45°41N 27°15E **17 F14**
Fóggia *Italy* 41°27N 15°34E **22 D6**
Fogo *Canada* 49°43N 54°17W **73 C9**
Fogo *C. Verde Is.* 15°5N 24°20W **50 b**
Fogo I. *Canada* 49°40N 54°5W **73 C9**
Föhr *Germany* 54°43N 8°30E **16 A5**
Foix *France* 42°58N 1°38E **20 E4**
Folda *Nord-Trøndelag,*
  Norway 64°32N 10°30E **8 D14**
Folda *Nordland, Norway* 67°38N 14°50E **8 C16**
Foley *Botswana* 21°34S 27°21E **56 C4**
Foley *U.S.A.* 30°24N 87°41W **85 F11**
Foleyet *Canada* 48°15N 82°25E **72 C3**
Folgefonna *Norway* 60°3N 6°23E **9 F12**
Foligno *Italy* 42°57N 12°42E **22 C5**
Folkestone *U.K.* 51°5N 1°12E **13 F9**
Folkston *U.S.A.* 30°50N 82°0W **85 F13**
Follansbee *U.S.A.* 40°19N 80°35W **82 F4**
Folsom L. *U.S.A.* 38°42N 121°9W **78 G5**
Fomboni *Comoros Is.* 12°18S 43°46E **53 a**
Fond-du-Lac *Canada* 59°19N 107°12W **71 B7**
Fond du Lac *U.S.A.* 43°47N 88°27W **80 D9**
Fond-du-Lac → *Canada* 59°17N 106°0W **71 B7**
Fonda *U.S.A.* 42°57N 74°22W **83 D10**
Fondi *Italy* 41°21N 13°25E **22 D5**
Fongafale *Tuvalu* 8°31S 179°13E **58 B10**
Fonsagrada = A Fonsagrada
  Spain 43°8N 7°4W **21 A2**
Fonseca, G. de
  Cent. Amer. 13°10N 87°40W **88 D2**
Fontainebleau *France* 48°24N 2°40E **20 B5**
Fontana *U.S.A.* 34°6N 117°26W **79 L9**
Fontas → *Canada* 58°14N 121°48W **70 B4**
Fonte Boa *Brazil* 2°33S 66°0W **92 D5**
Fontenay-le-Comte
  France 46°28N 0°48W **20 C3**
Fontenelle Res. *U.S.A.* 42°1N 110°3W **76 E8**
Fontur *Iceland* 66°23N 14°32W **8 C6**
Fonuafo'ou *Tonga* 20°19S 175°25W **59 c**
Fonualei *Tonga* 18°1S 174°19W **59 c**
Foochow = Fuzhou
  China 26°5N 119°16E **33 D6**
Foping *China* 33°41N 108°0E **34 H5**
Forbes *Australia* 33°22S 148°0E **63 E4**
Forbesganj *India* 26°17N 87°18E **43 F12**
Ford City *Calif., U.S.A.* 35°9N 119°27W **79 K7**
Ford City *Pa., U.S.A.* 40°46N 79°32W **82 F5**
Førde *Norway* 61°27N 5°53E **8 F11**
Fords Bridge *Australia* 29°41S 145°29E **63 D4**
Fordyce *U.S.A.* 33°49N 92°25W **84 E8**
Forel, Mt. *Greenland* 66°52N 36°55W **66 C16**
Foremost *Canada* 49°26N 111°34W **70 D6**
Forest *Canada* 43°6N 82°0W **82 C2**
Forest *U.S.A.* 32°22N 89°29W **85 E10**
Forest City *Iowa, U.S.A.* 43°16N 93°39W **80 D7**
Forest City *N.C., U.S.A.* 35°20N 81°52W **85 D14**
Forest City *Pa., U.S.A.* 41°39N 75°28W **83 E9**
Forest Grove *U.S.A.* 45°31N 123°7W **78 E3**
Forestburg *Canada* 52°35N 112°1W **70 C6**
Foresthill *U.S.A.* 39°1N 120°49W **78 F6**
Forestier Pen. *Australia* 43°0S 148°0E **63 G4**
Forestville *Canada* 48°48N 69°2W **73 C6**
Forestville *Calif., U.S.A.* 38°28N 122°54W **78 G4**
Forestville *N.Y., U.S.A.* 42°28N 79°10W **82 D5**
Forfar *U.K.* 56°39N 2°53W **11 E6**
Forillon △ *Canada* 48°46N 64°12W **73 C7**
Forks *U.S.A.* 47°57N 124°23W **78 C2**
Forksville *U.S.A.* 41°29N 76°35W **83 E8**
Forlì *Italy* 44°13N 12°3E **22 B5**
Forman *U.S.A.* 46°7N 97°38W **80 B5**
Formby Pt. *U.K.* 53°33N 3°6W **12 D4**
Formentera *Spain* 38°43N 1°27E **24 C7**
Formentor, C. de *Spain* 39°58N 3°13E **24 B10**
Formentor, Pen. de
  Spain 39°56N 3°11E **24 B10**
Former Yugoslav Republic of
  Macedonia = Macedonia
  Europe 41°53N 21°40E **23 D9**
Fórmia *Italy* 41°15N 13°37E **22 D5**
Formosa = Taiwan ■
  Asia 23°30N 121°0E **33 D7**
Formosa *Argentina* 26°15S 58°10W **94 B4**
Formosa *Brazil* 15°32S 47°20W **93 G9**
Formosa □ *Argentina* 25°0S 60°0W **94 B4**
Formosa, Serra *Brazil* 12°0S 55°0W **93 F8**
Formosa B. = Ungwana B.
  Kenya 2°45S 40°20E **54 C5**
Fornells *Spain* 40°3N 4°7E **24 A11**
Føroyar ☑ *Atl. Oc.* 62°0N 7°0W **8 F9**
Forres *U.K.* 57°37N 3°37W **11 D5**
Forrest *Australia* 30°51S 128°6E **61 F4**
Forrest, Mt. *Australia* 24°48S 127°45E **61 D4**
Forrest City *U.S.A.* 35°1N 90°47W **85 D9**
Forsayth *Australia* 18°33S 143°34E **62 B3**
Forssa *Finland* 60°49N 23°38E **8 F20**
Forst *Germany* 51°45N 14°37E **16 C8**
Forster *Australia* 32°12S 152°31E **63 E5**
Forsyth *U.S.A.* 46°16N 106°41W **76 C10**
Fort Abbas *Pakistan* 29°12N 72°52E **42 E5**
Fort Assiniboine
  Canada 54°20N 114°45W **70 C6**
Fort Augustus *U.K.* 57°9N 4°42W **11 D4**
Fort Beaufort *S. Africa* 32°46S 26°40E **56 E4**
Fort Benton *U.S.A.* 47°49N 110°40W **76 C8**
Fort Bragg *U.S.A.* 39°26N 123°48W **76 G2**
Fort Bridger *U.S.A.* 41°19N 110°23W **76 F8**
Fort Chipewyan *Canada* 58°42N 111°8W **71 B6**
Fort Clatsop *U.S.A.* 46°8N 123°53W **78 D3**
Fort Collins *U.S.A.* 40°35N 105°5W **76 F11**
Fort-Coulonge *Canada* 45°50N 76°45W **72 C4**
Fort Covington *U.S.A.* 44°59N 74°29W **83 B10**

Fort Dauphin = Taolanaro
  Madag. 25°2S 47°0E **57 D8**
Fort Davis *U.S.A.* 30°35N 103°54W **84 F3**
Fort-de-France *Martinique* 14°36N 61°2W **88 c**
Fort Defiance *U.S.A.* 35°45N 109°5W **77 J9**
Fort Dodge *U.S.A.* 42°30N 94°11W **80 D6**
Fort Edward *U.S.A.* 43°16N 73°35W **83 C11**
Fort Erie *Canada* 42°54N 78°56W **82 D6**
Fort Fairfield *U.S.A.* 46°46N 67°50W **81 B20**
Fort Frances *Canada* 48°36N 93°24W **71 D10**
Fort Franklin = Déline
  Canada 65°11N 123°25W **68 C7**
Fort Garland *U.S.A.* 37°26N 105°26W **77 H11**
Fort George = Chisasibi
  Canada 53°50N 79°0W **72 B4**
Fort Good Hope *Canada* 66°14N 128°40W **68 C7**
Fort Hancock *U.S.A.* 31°18N 105°51W **84 F2**
Fort Hope = Eabametoong
  Canada 51°30N 88°0W **72 B2**
Fort Irwin *U.S.A.* 35°16N 116°41W **79 K10**
Fort Kent *U.S.A.* 47°15N 68°36W **81 B19**
Fort Klamath *U.S.A.* 42°42N 122°0W **76 D3**
Fort Laramie *U.S.A.* 42°13N 104°31W **76 E11**
Fort Lauderdale *U.S.A.* 26°7N 80°8W **85 H14**
Fort Liard *Canada* 60°14N 123°30W **70 A4**
Fort Liberté *Haiti* 19°42N 71°51W **89 C5**
Fort Lupton *U.S.A.* 40°5N 104°49W **76 F11**
Fort MacKay *Canada* 57°12N 111°41W **70 B6**
Fort Macleod *Canada* 49°45N 113°30W **70 D6**
Fort McMurray *Canada* 56°44N 111°7W **70 B6**
Fort McPherson
  Canada 67°30N 134°55W **68 C6**
Fort Madison *U.S.A.* 40°38N 91°27W **80 E8**
Fort Meade *U.S.A.* 27°45N 81°48W **85 H14**
Fort Morgan *U.S.A.* 40°15N 103°48W **76 F12**
Fort Myers *U.S.A.* 26°39N 81°52W **85 H14**
Fort Nelson *Canada* 58°50N 122°44W **70 B4**
Fort Nelson → *Canada* 59°32N 124°0W **70 B4**
Fort Norman = Tulita
  Canada 64°57N 125°30W **68 C7**
Fort Payne *U.S.A.* 34°26N 85°43W **85 D12**
Fort Peck *U.S.A.* 48°1N 106°27W **76 B10**
Fort Peck Dam *U.S.A.* 48°0N 106°26W **76 C10**
Fort Peck L. *U.S.A.* 48°0N 106°26W **76 C10**
Fort Pierce *U.S.A.* 27°27N 80°20W **85 H14**
Fort Pierre *U.S.A.* 44°21N 100°22W **80 C3**
Fort Plain *U.S.A.* 42°56N 74°37W **83 D10**
Fort Portal *Uganda* 0°40N 30°20E **54 B3**
Fort Providence *Canada* 61°3N 117°40W **70 A5**
Fort Qu'Appelle
  Canada 50°45N 103°50W **71 C8**
Fort Resolution *Canada* 61°10N 113°40W **70 A6**
Fort Rixon *Zimbabwe* 20°2S 29°17E **55 G2**
Fort Ross *U.S.A.* 38°32N 123°13W **78 G3**
Fort Rupert = Waskaganish
  Canada 51°30N 78°40W **72 B4**
Fort St. James *Canada* 54°30N 124°10W **70 C4**
Fort St. John *Canada* 56°15N 120°50W **70 B4**
Fort Saskatchewan
  Canada 53°40N 113°15W **70 C6**
Fort Scott *U.S.A.* 37°50N 94°42W **80 G6**
Fort Severn *Canada* 56°0N 87°40W **72 A2**
Fort Shevchenko
  Kazakhstan 44°35N 50°23E **19 F9**
Fort Simpson *Canada* 61°45N 121°15W **70 A4**
Fort Smith *Canada* 60°0N 111°51W **70 B6**
Fort Smith *U.S.A.* 35°23N 94°25W **84 D7**
Fort Stockton *U.S.A.* 30°53N 102°53W **84 F3**
Fort Sumner *U.S.A.* 34°28N 104°15W **77 J11**
Fort Thompson *U.S.A.* 44°3N 99°26W **80 C4**
Fort Union △ *U.S.A.* 35°54N 105°1W **77 J11**
Fort Valley *U.S.A.* 32°33N 83°53W **85 E13**
Fort Vermilion *Canada* 58°24N 116°0W **70 B5**
Fort Walton Beach
  U.S.A. 30°25N 86°36W **85 F11**
Fort Ware *Canada* 57°26N 125°41W **70 B3**
Fort Wayne *U.S.A.* 41°4N 85°9W **81 E11**
Fort William *U.K.* 56°49N 5°7W **11 E3**
Fort Worth *U.S.A.* 32°43N 97°19W **84 E6**
Fort Yates *U.S.A.* 46°5N 100°38W **80 B3**
Fort Yukon *U.S.A.* 66°34N 145°16W **74 a**
Fortaleza *Brazil* 3°45S 38°35W **93 D11**
Forteau *Canada* 51°28N 56°58E **73 B8**
Fortescue → *Australia* 21°0S 116°4E **60 D2**
Forth → *U.K.* 56°9N 3°50W **11 E5**
Forth, Firth of *U.K.* 56°5N 2°55W **11 E6**
Fortrose *U.K.* 57°35N 4°9W **11 D4**
Fortuna *Calif., U.S.A.* 40°36N 124°9W **76 F1**
Fortuna *N. Dak., U.S.A.* 48°55N 103°47W **80 A2**
Fortune *Canada* 47°4N 55°50W **73 C8**
Fortune B. *Canada* 47°30N 55°22W **73 C8**
Forūr *Iran* 26°17N 54°32E **45 E7**
Fosen *Norway* 63°50N 10°20E **8 E14**
Foshan *China* 23°4N 113°5E **33 D6**
Fosnavåg *Norway* 62°22N 5°38E **8 E11**
Fossano *Italy* 44°33N 7°43E **20 D7**
Fossil *U.S.A.* 45°0N 120°9W **76 D3**
Fossil Butte △ *U.S.A.* 41°50N 110°27W **76 F8**
Foster → *Canada* 55°47N 105°49W **71 B7**
Fosters Ra. *Australia* 21°35S 133°48E **62 C1**
Fostoria *U.S.A.* 41°10N 83°25W **81 E12**
Fotadrevo *Madag.* 24°3S 45°1E **57 C8**
Fougères *France* 48°21N 1°14W **20 B3**
Foul Pt. *Sri Lanka* 8°35N 81°18E **40 Q12**
Foula *U.K.* 60°10N 2°5W **11 A6**
Foulness I. *U.K.* 51°36N 0°55E **13 F8**
Foulpointe *Madag.* 17°41S 49°31E **57 B8**
Foumban *Cameroon* 5°45N 10°50E **52 C2**
Foumbouni *Comoros Is.* 11°51S 43°29E **53 a**
Fountain *U.S.A.* 38°41N 104°42W **76 G11**
Fountain Hills *U.S.A.* 33°37N 111°43W **77 K8**
Fountain Springs
  U.S.A. 35°54N 118°55W **79 K8**
Fouriesburg *S. Africa* 28°38S 28°14E **56 D4**
Fourni *Greece* 37°36N 26°32E **23 F12**
Fourth Cataract *Sudan* 18°47N 32°3E **51 E12**

Fouta Djallon Guinea 11°20N 12°10W 50 F3
Foux, Cap-à- Haiti 19°43N 73°27W 89 C5
Foveaux Str. N.Z. 46°42S 168°10E 59 G2
Fowey U.K. 50°20N 4°39W 13 G3
Fowler Calif., U.S.A. 36°38N 119°41W 78 J7
Fowler Colo., U.S.A. 38°8N 104°2W 76 G11
Fowler, Pt. Australia 32°2S 132°3E 61 F5
Fowlers B. Australia 31°59S 132°34E 61 F5
Fowman Iran 37°13N 49°19E 45 B6
Fox → Canada 56°3N 93°18W 71 B10
Fox Creek Canada 54°24N 116°48W 70 C5
Fox Lake Canada 58°28N 114°31W 70 B6
Fox Valley Canada 50°30N 109°25W 71 C7
Foxboro Canada 44°14N 77°26W 82 B7
Foxboro U.S.A. 42°4N 71°16W 83 D13
Foxdale Australia 20°22S 148°35E 62 J6
Foxe Basin Canada 66°0N 77°0W 69 C12
Foxe Chan. Canada 65°0N 80°0W 69 C12
Foxe Pen. Canada 65°0N 76°0W 69 C12
Foxford Ireland 53°59N 9°7W 10 C2
Foxton N.Z. 40°29S 175°18E 59 D5
Foyle, Lough U.K. 55°7N 7°4W 10 A4
Foynes Ireland 52°37N 9°7W 10 D2
Foz do Cunene Angola 17°15S 11°48E 56 B1
Foz do Iguaçu Brazil 25°30S 54°30W 95 B5
Frackville U.S.A. 40°47N 76°14W 83 F8
Fraile Muerto Uruguay 32°31S 54°32W 95 C5
Framingham U.S.A. 42°18N 71°24W 83 D13
Franca Brazil 20°33S 47°30W 93 H9
Francavilla Fontana
 Italy 40°32N 17°35E 23 D7
France ■ Europe 47°0N 3°0E 20 C5
Frances Australia 36°41S 140°55E 63 F3
Frances → Canada 60°16N 129°10W 70 A3
Frances L. Canada 61°23N 129°30W 70 A3
Franceville Gabon 1°40S 13°32E 52 E2
Franche-Comté ☐ France 46°50N 5°55E 20 C6
Francis Case, L. U.S.A. 43°4N 98°34W 80 D4
Francisco Beltrão Brazil 26°5S 53°4W 95 B5
Francisco Ignacio Madero
 Coahuila, Mexico 25°48N 103°18W 86 B4
Francisco Ignacio Madero Durango,
 Mexico 24°26N 104°18W 86 C4
Francisco Ignacio Madero, Presa
 Mexico 28°0N 105°37W 86 B3
Francistown Botswana 21°7S 27°33E 57 C4
François Canada 47°35N 56°45W 73 C8
François L. Canada 54°0N 125°30W 70 C3
Francois Peron △
 Australia 25°42S 113°33E 61 E1
Franeker Neths. 53°12N 5°33E 15 A5
Frank Hann △ Australia 32°52S 120°19E 61 F3
Frankford Canada 44°12N 77°36W 82 B7
Frankfort S. Africa 27°17S 28°30E 57 D4
Frankfort Ind., U.S.A. 40°17N 86°31W 80 E10
Frankfort Kans., U.S.A. 39°42N 96°25W 80 F5
Frankfort Ky., U.S.A. 38°12N 84°52W 81 F11
Frankfort N.Y., U.S.A. 43°2N 75°4W 83 C9
Frankfurt Brandenburg,
 Germany 52°20N 14°32E 16 B8
Frankfurt Hessen, Germany 50°7N 8°41E 16 C5
Fränkische Alb Germany 49°10N 11°23E 16 D6
Frankland → Australia 35°0S 116°48E 61 G2
Franklin Ky., U.S.A. 36°43N 86°35W 80 G10
Franklin La., U.S.A. 29°48N 91°30W 84 G9
Franklin Mass., U.S.A. 42°5N 71°24W 83 D13
Franklin N.H., U.S.A. 43°27N 71°39W 83 C13
Franklin N.Y., U.S.A. 42°20N 75°9W 83 D9
Franklin Nebr., U.S.A. 40°6N 98°57W 80 E4
Franklin Pa., U.S.A. 41°24N 79°50W 82 E5
Franklin Va., U.S.A. 36°41N 76°56W 81 G15
Franklin W. Va., U.S.A. 38°39N 79°20W 81 F14
Franklin B. Canada 69°45N 126°0W 68 C7
Franklin D. Roosevelt L.
 U.S.A. 48°18N 118°9W 76 B4
Franklin-Gordon Wild Rivers △
 Australia 42°35S 145°51E 63 G4
Franklin I. Antarctica 76°10S 168°30E 5 D11
Franklin I. Canada 45°24N 80°20W 82 A4
Franklin L. U.S.A. 40°25N 115°22W 76 F6
Franklin Mts. Canada 65°0N 125°0W 68 C7
Franklin Str. Canada 72°0N 96°0W 68 B10
Franklinton U.S.A. 30°51N 90°9W 85 F9
Franklinville U.S.A. 42°20N 78°27W 82 D6
Frankston Australia 38°8S 145°8E 63 F4
Fransfontein Namibia 20°12S 15°1E 56 C2
Frantsa Iosifa, Zemlya
 Russia 82°0N 55°0E 28 A6
Franz Canada 48°25N 84°30W 72 C3
Franz Josef Land = Frantsa Iosifa,
 Zemlya Russia 82°0N 55°0E 28 A6
Fraser U.S.A. 42°32N 82°57W 82 D2
Fraser → B.C., Canada 49°7N 123°11W 78 A3
Fraser → Nfld. & L.,
 Canada 56°39N 62°10W 73 A7
Fraser, Mt. Australia 25°35S 118°20E 61 E2
Fraser I. Australia 25°15S 153°10E 63 D5
Fraser Lake Canada 54°0N 124°50W 70 C4
Fraserburg S. Africa 31°55S 21°30E 56 E3
Fraserburgh U.K. 57°42N 2°1W 11 D6
Fraserdale Canada 49°55N 81°37W 72 C3
Fray Bentos Uruguay 33°10S 58°15W 94 C4
Fray Jorge △ Chile 30°42S 71°40W 94 C1
Fredericia Denmark 55°34N 9°45E 9 J13
Frederick Md., U.S.A. 39°25N 77°25W 81 F15
Frederick Okla., U.S.A. 34°23N 99°1W 84 D5
Frederick S. Dak., U.S.A. 45°50N 98°31W 80 C4
Fredericksburg Pa.,
 U.S.A. 40°27N 76°26W 83 F8
Fredericksburg Tex.,
 U.S.A. 30°16N 98°52W 84 F5
Fredericksburg Va.,
 U.S.A. 38°18N 77°28W 81 F15
Fredericktown Mo.,
 U.S.A. 37°34N 90°18W 80 G8
Fredericktown Ohio,
 U.S.A. 40°29N 82°33W 82 F2

Frederico Westphalen
 Brazil 27°22S 53°24W 95 B5
Fredericton Canada 45°57N 66°40W 73 C6
Fredericton Junction
 Canada 45°41N 66°40W 73 C6
Frederikshåb = Paamiut
 Greenland 62°0N 49°43W 4 C5
Frederikshamn = Hamina
 Finland 60°34N 27°12E 8 F22
Frederikshavn Denmark 57°28N 10°31E 9 H14
Frederiksted
 U.S. Virgin Is. 17°43N 64°53W 89 C7
Fredonia Ariz., U.S.A. 36°57N 112°32W 77 H7
Fredonia Kans., U.S.A. 37°32N 95°49W 80 G6
Fredonia N.Y., U.S.A. 42°26N 79°20W 82 D5
Fredrikstad Norway 59°13N 10°57E 9 G14
Free State ☐ S. Africa 28°30S 27°0E 56 D4
Freehold U.S.A. 40°16N 74°17W 83 F10
Freeland U.S.A. 41°1N 75°54W 83 E9
Freels, C. Nfld. & L.,
 Canada 49°15N 53°30W 73 C9
Freels, C. Nfld. & L.,
 Canada 46°37N 53°32W 73 C9
Freeman Calif., U.S.A. 35°35N 117°53W 79 K9
Freeman S. Dak., U.S.A. 43°21N 97°26W 80 D5
Freeport Bahamas 26°30N 78°47W 88 A4
Freeport Ill., U.S.A. 42°17N 89°36W 80 D9
Freeport N.Y., U.S.A. 40°39N 73°35W 83 F11
Freeport Ohio, U.S.A. 40°12N 81°15W 82 F3
Freeport Pa., U.S.A. 40°41N 79°41W 82 F5
Freeport Tex., U.S.A. 28°57N 95°21W 84 G7
Freetown S. Leone 8°30N 13°17W 50 G3
Freeville U.S.A. 42°30N 76°20W 83 D8
Frégate, L. de la Canada 53°15N 74°45W 72 B5
Fregenal de la Sierra
 Spain 38°10N 6°39W 21 C2
Freibourg = Fribourg
 Switz. 46°49N 7°9E 20 C7
Freiburg Germany 47°59N 7°51E 16 E4
Freire Chile 38°54S 72°38W 96 D2
Freirina Chile 28°30S 71°10W 94 B1
Freising Germany 48°24N 11°45E 16 D6
Freistadt Austria 48°30N 14°30E 16 D8
Fréjus France 43°25N 6°44E 20 E7
Fremantle Australia 32°7S 115°47E 61 F2
Fremont Calif., U.S.A. 37°32N 121°57W 78 H4
Fremont Mich., U.S.A. 43°28N 85°57W 81 D11
Fremont Nebr., U.S.A. 41°26N 96°30W 80 E5
Fremont Ohio, U.S.A. 41°21N 83°7W 81 E12
Fremont → U.S.A. 38°24N 110°42W 76 G8
French Camp U.S.A. 37°53N 121°16W 78 H5
French Cays = Plana Cays
 Bahamas 22°38N 73°30W 89 B5
French Creek → U.S.A. 41°24N 79°50W 82 E5
French Guiana ☐ S. Amer. 4°0N 53°0W 93 C8
French Polynesia ☐
 Pac. Oc. 20°0S 145°0W 65 J13
Frenchman Cr. →
 N. Amer. 48°31N 107°10W 76 B10
Frenchman Cr. →
 U.S.A. 40°14N 100°50W 80 E3
Fresco → Brazil 7°15S 51°30W 93 E8
Freshfield, C. Antarctica 68°25S 151°10E 5 C10
Fresnillo Mexico 23°10N 102°53W 86 C4
Fresno U.S.A. 36°44N 119°47W 78 J7
Fresno Res. U.S.A. 48°36N 109°57W 76 B9
Frew → Australia 20°0S 135°38E 62 C2
Frewsburg U.S.A. 42°3N 79°10W 82 D5
Freycinet ☐ Australia 42°11S 148°19E 63 G4
Freycinet Pen. Australia 42°10S 148°25E 63 G4
Fria Guinea 10°27N 13°38W 50 F3
Fria, C. Namibia 18°0S 12°0E 56 B1
Friant U.S.A. 36°59N 119°43W 78 J7
Frías Argentina 28°40S 65°5W 94 B2
Fribourg Switz. 46°49N 7°9E 20 C7
Friday Harbor U.S.A. 48°32N 123°1W 78 B3
Friedens U.S.A. 40°3N 78°59W 82 F6
Friedrichshafen Germany 47°39N 9°30E 16 E5
Friendship U.S.A. 42°12N 78°8W 82 D6
Friesland ☐ Neths. 53°5N 5°50E 15 A5
Frigate Seychelles 4°35S 55°56E 53 b
Frio → U.S.A. 28°26N 98°11W 84 G5
Frio, C. Brazil 22°50S 41°50W 90 F6
Friona U.S.A. 34°38N 102°43W 84 D3
Fritch U.S.A. 35°38N 101°36W 84 D4
Frobisher B. Canada 62°30N 66°0W 69 C13
Frobisher Bay = Iqaluit
 Canada 63°44N 68°31W 69 C13
Frobisher L. Canada 56°20N 108°15W 71 B7
Frohavet Norway 64°0N 9°30E 8 E13
Frome U.K. 51°14N 2°19W 13 F5
Frome → U.K. 50°41N 2°6W 13 G5
Frome, L. Australia 30°45S 139°45E 63 E2
Front Range U.S.A. 40°25N 105°45W 76 F2
Front Royal U.S.A. 38°55N 78°12W 81 F14
Frontenac ☐ Canada 44°32N 76°30W 83 B8
Frontera Canary Is. 27°47N 17°59W 24 G2
Frontera Mexico 18°32N 92°38W 87 D6
Fronteras Mexico 30°56N 109°31W 86 A3
Frosinone Italy 41°38N 13°19E 22 D5
Frostburg U.S.A. 39°39N 78°56W 81 F14
Frostisen Norway 68°14N 17°10E 8 B17
Frøya Norway 63°43N 8°40E 8 E13
Frunze = Bishkek
 Kyrgyzstan 42°54N 74°46E 28 E8
Frutal Brazil 20°0S 49°0W 93 H9
Frýdek-Místek
 Czech Rep. 49°40N 18°20E 17 D10
Fryeburg U.S.A. 44°1N 70°59W 83 B14
Fu Xian = Wafangdian
 China 39°38N 121°58E 35 E11
Fu Xian China 36°0N 109°20E 34 G5
Fucheng China 37°50N 116°10E 34 F9
Fuchou = Fuzhou China 26°5N 119°16E 33 D6
Fuchū Japan 34°34N 133°14E 31 G6
Fuencaliente Canary Is. 28°28N 17°50W 24 F2
Fuencaliente, Pta.
 Canary Is. 28°27N 17°51W 24 F2

Fuengirola Spain 36°32N 4°41W 21 D3
Fuentes de Oñoro Spain 40°33N 6°52W 21 B2
Fuerte → Mexico 25°54N 109°22W 86 B3
Fuerte Olimpo Paraguay 21°0S 57°51W 94 A4
Fuerteventura Canary Is. 28°30N 14°0W 24 F6
Fuerteventura ✈ (FUE)
 Canary Is. 28°24N 13°52W 24 F6
Fufeng China 34°22N 108°0E 34 G5
Fugou China 34°3N 114°25E 34 G8
Fugu China 39°2N 111°3E 34 E6
Fuhai China 47°2N 87°25E 32 B3
Fuhaymī Iraq 34°16N 42°10E 44 C4
Fuji Japan 35°9N 138°39E 31 G9
Fuji-Hakone-Izu △
 Japan 35°15N 138°45E 31 G9
Fuji-San Japan 35°22N 138°44E 31 G9
Fuji-Yoshida Japan 35°30N 138°46E 31 G9
Fujian ☐ China 26°0N 118°0E 33 D6
Fujinomiya Japan 35°10N 138°40E 31 G9
Fujisawa Japan 35°22N 139°29E 31 G9
Fujiyama, Mt. = Fuji-San
 Japan 35°22N 138°44E 31 G9
Fukagawa Japan 43°43N 142°2E 30 C11
Fukien = Fujian ☐ China 26°0N 118°0E 33 D6
Fukuchiyama Japan 35°19N 135°9E 31 G7
Fukue-Shima Japan 32°40N 128°45E 31 H4
Fukui Japan 36°5N 136°10E 31 F8
Fukui ☐ Japan 36°0N 136°12E 31 G8
Fukuoka Japan 33°39N 130°21E 31 H5
Fukuoka ☐ Japan 33°30N 131°0E 31 H5
Fukushima Japan 37°44N 140°28E 30 F10
Fukushima ☐ Japan 37°30N 140°15E 30 F10
Fukuyama Japan 34°35N 133°20E 31 G6
Fulaga Fiji 19°8S 178°33W 59 a
Fulda Germany 50°32N 9°40E 16 C5
Fulda → Germany 51°25N 9°39E 16 C5
Fulford Harbour
 Canada 48°47N 123°27W 78 B3
Fullerton Calif., U.S.A. 33°53N 117°56W 79 M9
Fullerton Nebr., U.S.A. 41°22N 97°58W 80 E5
Fulongquan China 44°20N 124°42E 35 B13
Fulton Mo., U.S.A. 38°52N 91°57W 80 F8
Fulton N.Y., U.S.A. 43°19N 76°25W 83 C8
Funabashi Japan 35°45N 140°0E 31 G10
Funafuti = Fongafale
 Tuvalu 8°31S 179°13E 58 B10
Funchal Madeira 32°38N 16°54W 24 D3
Funchal ✈ (FNC)
 Madeira 32°42N 16°45W 24 D3
Fundación Colombia 10°31N 74°11W 92 A4
Fundão Portugal 40°8N 7°30W 21 B2
Fundy, B. of Canada 45°0N 66°0W 73 D6
Fundy ☐ Canada 45°35N 65°10W 73 C6
Funhalouro Mozam. 23°3S 34°25E 57 C5
Funing Hebei, China 39°53N 119°12E 35 E10
Funing Jiangsu, China 33°45N 119°50E 35 H10
Funiu Shan China 33°30N 112°20E 34 H7
Funtua Nigeria 11°30N 7°18E 50 F7
Fuping Hebei, China 38°48N 114°12E 34 E8
Fuping Shaanxi, China 34°42N 109°10E 34 G5
Furano Japan 43°21N 142°23E 30 C11
Furāt, Nahr al → Asia 31°0N 47°25E 44 D5
Fürg Iran 28°18N 55°13E 45 D7
Furnås Spain 39°3N 1°32E 24 B8
Furnas, Represa de
 Brazil 20°50S 45°30W 95 A6
Furneaux Group
 Australia 40°10S 147°50E 63 G4
Furqlus Syria 34°36N 37°8E 46 A6
Fürstenwalde Germany 52°22N 14°3E 16 B8
Fürth Germany 49°28N 10°59E 16 D6
Furukawa Japan 38°34N 140°58E 30 E10
Fury and Hecla Str.
 Canada 69°56N 84°0W 69 C11
Fusagasugá Colombia 4°21N 74°22W 92 C4
Fushan Shandong,
 China 37°30N 121°15E 35 F11
Fushan Shanxi, China 35°58N 111°51E 34 G6
Fushun China 41°50N 123°56E 35 D12
Fusong China 42°20N 127°15E 35 C14
Futian China 22°32N 114°4E 33 F11
Fuxin China 42°5N 121°48E 35 C11
Fuyang China 33°0N 115°48E 34 H8
Fuyang He → China 38°12N 117°0E 34 E9
Fuyong China 22°40N 113°49E 33 F10
Fuyu Heilongjiang, China 47°49N 124°27E 35 B13
Fuyu Jilin, China 45°12N 124°43E 35 B13
Fuyun China 47°0N 89°28E 32 B3
Fuzhou China 26°5N 119°16E 33 D6
Fylde U.K. 53°50N 2°58W 12 D5
Fyn Denmark 55°20N 10°30E 9 J14
Fyne, L. U.K. 55°59N 5°23W 11 F3

G

Gaalkacyo Somali Rep. 6°30N 47°30E 47 F4
Gabela Angola 11°0S 14°24E 52 G2
Gabès Tunisia 33°53N 10°2E 51 B8
Gabès, G. de Tunisia 34°0N 10°30E 51 B8
Gabon ■ Africa 0°10S 10°0E 52 E2
Gaborone Botswana 24°45S 25°57E 56 C4
Gabriels U.S.A. 44°26N 74°12W 83 B10
Gãbrïk Iran 25°44N 58°28E 45 E8
Gabrovo Bulgaria 42°52N 25°19E 23 C11
Gãch Sãr Iran 36°7N 51°19E 45 B6
Gachsãrãn Iran 30°15N 50°45E 45 D6
Gadag India 15°30N 75°45E 40 M9
Gadap Pakistan 25°5N 67°28E 42 G2
Gadarwara India 22°50N 78°50E 43 H8
Gadhada India 22°0N 71°35E 42 J4
Gadra Pakistan 25°40N 70°38E 42 G4
Gadsden U.S.A. 34°1N 86°1W 85 D11
Gadwal India 16°10N 77°50E 40 L10
Gaffney U.S.A. 35°5N 81°39W 85 D14
Gafsa Tunisia 34°24N 8°43E 50 B7

Gagaria India 25°43N 70°46E 42 G4
Găgăuzia ☐ Moldova 46°10N 28°40E 17 E15
Gagnoa Ivory C. 6°56N 5°16W 50 G4
Gagnon Canada 51°50N 68°5W 73 B6
Gagnon, L. Canada 62°3N 110°27W 71 A6
Gahini Rwanda 1°50S 30°30E 54 C3
Gahmar India 25°27N 83°49E 43 G10
Gai Xian = Gaizhou
 China 40°22N 122°20E 35 D12
Gaidouronisi Greece 34°53N 25°41E 25 E7
Gail → U.S.A. 32°46N 101°27W 84 E4
Gaillimh = Galway Ireland 53°17N 9°3W 10 C2
Gaines U.S.A. 41°46N 77°35W 82 E7
Gainesville Fla., U.S.A. 29°40N 82°20W 85 G13
Gainesville Ga., U.S.A. 34°18N 83°50W 85 D13
Gainesville Mo., U.S.A. 36°36N 92°26W 80 G7
Gainesville Tex., U.S.A. 33°38N 97°8W 84 E6
Gainsborough U.K. 53°24N 0°46W 12 D7
Gairdner, L. Australia 31°30S 136°0E 63 E2
Gairloch U.K. 57°43N 5°41W 11 D3
Gairloch, L. U.K. 57°43N 5°45W 11 D3
Gaizhou China 40°22N 122°20E 35 D12
Gaj → Pakistan 26°26N 67°21E 42 F2
Gakuch Pakistan 36°7N 73°45E 43 A5
Galán, Cerro Argentina 25°55S 66°52W 94 B2
Galana → Kenya 3°9S 40°8E 54 C5
Galápagos = Colón, Arch. de
 Ecuador 0°0 91°0W 90 D1
Galapagos Fracture Zone
 Pac. Oc. 2°0N 110°0W 65 G17
Galapagos Rise Pac. Oc. 15°0S 95°0W 65 J18
Galashiels U.K. 55°37N 2°49W 11 F6
Galatea Cyprus 35°25N 34°4E 25 D13
Galați Romania 45°27N 28°2E 17 F15
Galatina Italy 40°10N 18°10E 23 D8
Galax U.S.A. 36°40N 80°56W 81 G13
Galcaio = Gaalkacyo
 Somali Rep. 6°30N 47°30E 47 F4
Galdhøpiggen Norway 61°38N 8°18E 8 F13
Galeana Chihuahua,
 Mexico 30°7N 107°38W 86 A3
Galeana Nuevo León,
 Mexico 24°50N 100°4W 86 A3
Galela Indonesia 1°50N 127°49E 37 D7
Galena U.S.A. 64°44N 156°56W 74 a
Galera Pt. Trin. & Tob. 10°8N 60°59W 93 K16
Galera Pt. Trin. & Tob. 10°49N 60°54W 89 D7
Galesburg U.S.A. 40°57N 90°22W 80 E8
Galeton U.S.A. 41°44N 77°39W 82 E7
Galich Russia 58°22N 42°24E 18 C7
Galicia ☐ Spain 42°43N 7°45W 21 A2
Galilee = Hagalil Israel 32°53N 35°18E 46 C4
Galilee, L. Australia 22°20S 145°50E 62 C4
Galilee, Sea of = Yam Kinneret
 Israel 32°45N 35°35E 46 C4
Galina Pt. Jamaica 18°24N 76°58W 88 a
Galinoporni Cyprus 35°31N 34°18E 25 D13
Galion U.S.A. 40°44N 82°47W 82 F2
Galiuro Mts. U.S.A. 32°30N 110°20W 77 K8
Galiwinku Australia 12°2S 135°34E 62 A2
Gallan Hd. U.K. 58°15N 7°2W 11 C1
Gallatin U.S.A. 36°24N 86°27W 85 C11
Galle Sri Lanka 6°5N 80°10E 40 R12
Gállego → Spain 41°39N 0°51W 21 B5
Gallegos → Argentina 51°35S 69°0W 96 G3
Galley Hd. Ireland 51°32N 8°55W 10 E3
Gallinas, Pta. Colombia 12°28N 71°40W 92 A4
Gallipoli = Gelibolu
 Turkey 40°28N 26°43E 23 D12
Gallipoli Italy 40°3N 17°58E 23 D8
Gallipolis U.S.A. 38°49N 82°12W 81 F12
Galloo I. U.S.A. 43°55N 76°25W 83 C8
Galloway U.K. 55°1N 4°29W 11 G4
Galloway, Mull of U.K. 54°39N 4°52W 11 G4
Galloway △ U.K. 55°3N 4°20W 11 F4
Gallup U.S.A. 35°32N 108°45W 77 J9
Galoya Sri Lanka 8°10N 80°55E 40 Q12
Galt U.S.A. 38°15N 121°18W 78 G5
Galty Mts. Ireland 52°22N 8°10W 10 D3
Galtymore Ireland 52°21N 8°11W 10 D3
Galugãh Iran 36°43N 53°48E 45 B7
Galva U.S.A. 41°10N 90°3W 80 E8
Galveston U.S.A. 29°18N 94°48W 84 G7
Galveston B. U.S.A. 29°36N 94°50W 84 G7
Gálvez Argentina 32°0S 61°14W 94 C3
Galway Ireland 53°17N 9°3W 10 C2
Galway ☐ Ireland 53°22N 9°1W 10 C2
Galway B. Ireland 53°13N 9°10W 10 C2
Gam → Vietnam 21°55N 105°12E 38 B5
Gamagõri Japan 34°50N 137°14E 31 G8
Gambat Pakistan 27°17N 68°26E 42 F3
Gambhir → India 26°58N 77°27E 42 F6
Gambia ■ W. Afr. 13°25N 16°0W 50 F2
Gambia → W. Afr. 13°28N 16°34W 50 F2
Gambier U.S.A. 40°22N 82°23W 82 F2
Gambier, C. Australia 11°56S 130°57E 60 B5
Gambier, Îs.
 French Polynesia 23°8S 134°58W 65 K14
Gambier Is. Australia 35°3S 136°30E 63 F2
Gambo Canada 48°47N 54°13W 73 C9
Gamboli Pakistan 29°53N 68°24E 42 E3
Gamboma Congo 1°55S 15°52E 52 E3
Gamka → S. Africa 33°18S 21°39E 56 E3
Gamkab → Namibia 28°4S 17°54E 56 D2
Gamlakarleby = Kokkola
 Finland 63°50N 23°8E 8 E20
Gammon → Canada 51°24N 95°44W 71 C9
Gammon Ranges △
 Australia 30°38S 139°8E 63 E2
Gamtoos → S. Africa 33°58S 25°1E 56 E4
Gan Jiang → China 29°15N 116°0E 33 D6
Ganado U.S.A. 35°43N 109°33W 77 J9
Gananoque Canada 44°20N 76°10W 83 B8
Ganãveh Iran 29°35N 50°35E 45 D6
Gãncã Azerbaijan 40°45N 46°20E 19 F8

Gancheng China 18°51N 108°37E 38 C7
Gand = Gent Belgium 51°2N 3°42E 15 C3
Ganda Angola 13°3S 14°35E 53 G2
Gandajika
 Dem. Rep. of the Congo 6°46S 23°58E 52 F4
Gandak → India 25°39N 85°13E 43 G11
Gandava Pakistan 28°32N 67°32E 42 E2
Gander Canada 48°58N 54°35W 73 C9
Gander L. Canada 48°58N 54°35W 73 C9
Ganderowe Falls
 Zimbabwe 17°20S 29°10E 55 F2
Gandhi Sagar India 24°40N 75°40E 42 G6
Gandhinagar India 23°15N 72°45E 42 H5
Gandia Spain 38°58N 0°9W 21 C5
Gando, Pta. Canary Is. 27°55N 15°22W 24 G4
Ganedidalem = Gani
 Indonesia 0°48S 128°14E 37 E7
Ganga → India 23°20N 90°30E 43 H14
Ganga Sagar India 21°38N 88°5E 43 J13
Gangan → India 28°38N 78°58E 43 E8
Ganganagar India 29°56N 73°56E 42 E5
Gangapur India 26°32N 76°49E 42 F7
Gangaw Burma 22°5N 94°5E 41 H19
Gangdisê Shan China 31°20N 81°0E 43 D9
Ganges = Ganga →
 India 23°20N 90°30E 43 H14
Ganges Canada 48°51N 123°31W 70 D4
Ganges, Mouths of the
 India 21°30N 90°0E 43 J14
Ganggyeong S. Korea 36°10N 127°0E 35 F14
Ganghwa S. Korea 37°45N 126°30E 35 F14
Gangneung S. Korea 37°45N 128°54E 35 F15
Gangoh India 29°46N 77°18E 42 E7
Gangotri India 30°50N 79°10E 43 D8
Gangotri △ India 30°50N 79°10E 43 D8
Gangseong S. Korea 38°24N 128°30E 35 E15
Gangtok India 27°20N 88°37E 41 F16
Gangu China 34°40N 105°15E 34 G3
Gangyao China 44°12N 126°37E 35 B14
Gani Indonesia 0°48S 128°14E 37 E7
Ganj India 27°45N 78°57E 43 F8
Gannett Peak U.S.A. 43°11N 109°39W 76 E9
Ganquan China 36°20N 109°20E 34 F5
Gansu ☐ China 36°0N 104°0E 34 G3
Ganta Liberia 7°15N 8°59W 50 G4
Gantheaume, C.
 Australia 36°4S 137°32E 63 F2
Gantheaume B.
 Australia 27°40S 114°10E 61 E1
Gantsevichi = Hantsavichy
 Belarus 52°49N 26°30E 17 B14
Ganyem = Genyem
 Indonesia 2°46S 140°12E 37 E10
Ganyu China 34°50N 119°8E 35 G10
Ganzhou China 25°51N 114°56E 33 D6
Gao Mali 16°15N 0°5W 50 F5
Gaomi China 36°20N 119°42E 35 F10
Gaoping China 35°45N 112°55E 34 G7
Gaotang China 36°50N 116°15E 34 F9
Gaoua Burkina Faso 10°20N 3°8W 50 F5
Gaoual Guinea 11°45N 13°25W 50 F3
Gaoxiong = Kaohsiung
 Taiwan 22°35N 120°16E 33 D7
Gaoyou Hu China 32°45N 119°20E 35 H10
Gaoyuan China 37°8N 117°58E 35 F9
Gap France 44°33N 6°5E 20 D7
Gapat → India 24°30N 82°28E 43 G10
Gapuwiyak Australia 12°25S 135°43E 62 A2
Gar China 32°10N 79°58E 32 C2
Gara, L. Ireland 53°57N 8°26W 10 C3
Garabogazköl Aylagy
 Turkmenistan 41°0N 53°30E 19 F9
Garachico Canary Is. 28°22N 16°46W 24 F3
Garachiné Panama 8°0N 78°12W 88 E4
Garafia Canary Is. 28°48N 17°57W 24 F2
Garagum Turkmenistan 39°30N 60°0E 45 B8
Garah Australia 29°5S 149°38E 63 D4
Garajonay Canary Is. 28°7N 17°14W 24 F2
Garamba △
 Dem. Rep. of the Congo 4°10N 29°40E 54 B2
Garanhuns Brazil 8°50S 36°30W 93 E11
Garautha India 25°34N 79°18E 43 G8
Garba Tula Kenya 0°30N 38°32E 54 B4
Garberville U.S.A. 40°6N 123°48W 76 F2
Garbiyang India 30°8N 80°54E 43 D9
Gard → France 43°51N 4°37E 20 E6
Garda, L. di Italy 45°40N 10°41E 22 B4
Garde L. Canada 62°50N 106°13W 71 A7
Garden City Ga., U.S.A. 32°6N 81°9W 85 E14
Garden City Kans.,
 U.S.A. 37°58N 100°53W 80 G3
Garden City Tex.,
 U.S.A. 31°52N 101°29W 84 F4
Garden Grove U.S.A. 33°47N 117°55W 79 M9
Gardēz Afghan. 33°37N 69°9E 42 C3
Gardiner Maine, U.S.A. 44°14N 69°47W 81 C19
Gardiner Mont., U.S.A. 45°2N 110°22W 76 D8
Gardiners I. U.S.A. 41°6N 72°6W 83 E12
Gardner U.S.A. 42°34N 71°59W 83 D13
Gardner Canal Canada 53°27N 128°8W 70 C3
Gardnerville U.S.A. 38°56N 119°45W 78 G7
Gardo = Qardho
 Somali Rep. 9°30N 49°6E 47 F4
Garey U.S.A. 34°53N 120°19W 79 L6
Garfield U.S.A. 47°1N 117°9W 76 C5
Garforth U.K. 53°47N 1°24W 12 D6
Gargantua, C. Canada 47°36N 85°2W 81 B11
Gargett Australia 21°9S 148°46E 62 K6
Garibaldi △ Canada 49°50N 122°40W 70 D4
Gariep, L. S. Africa 30°40S 25°40E 56 E4
Garies S. Africa 30°32S 17°59E 56 E2
Garig Gunak Barlu △
 Australia 11°26S 131°58E 60 B5
Garigliano → Italy 41°13N 13°42E 22 D5
Garissa Kenya 0°25S 39°40E 54 C4
Garland Tex., U.S.A. 32°54N 96°38W 84 E6

Garland *Utah, U.S.A.* 41°45N 112°10W **76** F7
Garmāb *Iran* 35°25N 56°45E **45** C8
Garmisch-Partenkirchen
  Germany 47°30N 11°6E **16** E6
Garmsār *Iran* 35°20N 52°25E **45** C7
Garner *U.S.A.* 43°6N 93°36W **80** D7
Garnett *U.S.A.* 38°17N 95°14W **80** F6
Garo Hills *India* 25°30N 90°30E **43** G14
Garoe = Garoowe
  Somali Rep. 8°25N 48°33E **47** F4
Garonne → *France* 45°2N 0°36W **20** D3
Garoowe *Somali Rep.* 8°25N 48°33E **47** F4
Garot *India* 24°19N 75°41E **42** G6
Garoua *Cameroon* 9°19N 13°21E **51** G8
Garrauli *India* 25°5N 79°22E **43** G8
Garrison *Mont., U.S.A.* 46°31N 112°49W **76** C7
Garrison *N. Dak., U.S.A.* 47°40N 101°25W **80** B3
Garrison Res. = Sakakawea, L.,
  U.S.A. 47°30N 101°25W **80** B3
Garron Pt. *U.K.* 55°3N 5°59W **10** A6
Garry → *U.K.* 56°44N 3°47W **11** E5
Garry, L. *Canada* 65°58N 100°18W **68** C9
Garrygala *Turkmenistan* 38°31N 56°29E **45** B8
Garsen *Kenya* 2°20S 40°5E **54** C5
Garson L. *Canada* 56°19N 110°2W **71** B6
Garstang *U.K.* 53°55N 2°46W **12** D5
Garu *India* 23°40N 84°14E **43** H11
Garub *Namibia* 26°37S 16°0E **56** D2
Garut *Indonesia* 7°14S 107°53E **37** G12
Garvie Mts. *N.Z.* 45°30S 168°50E **59** F2
Garwa = Garoua
  Cameroon 9°19N 13°21E **51** G8
Garwa *India* 24°11N 83°47E **43** G10
Gary *U.S.A.* 41°36N 87°20W **80** E10
Garzê *China* 31°38N 100°1E **32** C5
Garzón *Colombia* 2°10N 75°40W **92** C3
Gas-San *Japan* 38°32N 140°1E **30** E10
Gasan Kuli = Esenguly
  Turkmenistan 37°37N 53°59E **28** F6
Gascogne *France* 43°45N 0°20E **20** E4
Gascogne, G. de *Europe* 44°0N 2°0W **20** D2
Gascony = Gascogne
  France 43°45N 0°20E **20** E4
Gascoyne → *Australia* 24°52S 113°37E **61** D1
Gascoyne Junction
  Australia 25°2S 115°17E **61** E2
Gashaka *Nigeria* 7°20N 11°29E **51** G8
Gasherbrum *Pakistan* 35°40N 76°40E **43** B7
Gashua *Nigeria* 12°54N 11°0E **51** F8
Gasparillo *Trin. & Tob.* 10°18N 61°26W **93** K15
Gaspé *Canada* 48°52N 64°30W **73** C7
Gaspé, C. de *Canada* 48°48N 64°7W **73** C7
Gaspé Pen. = Gaspésie, Pén. de la
  Canada 48°45N 65°40W **73** C6
Gaspésie, Pén. de la
  Canada 48°45N 65°40W **73** C6
Gaspésie △ *Canada* 48°55N 66°10W **73** C6
Gasteiz = Vitoria-Gasteiz
  Spain 42°50N 2°41W **21** A4
Gastonia *U.S.A.* 35°16N 81°11W **85** D5
Gastre *Argentina* 42°20S 69°15W **96** E3
Gata, C. *Cyprus* 34°34N 33°2E **25** E12
Gata, C. de *Spain* 36°41N 2°13W **21** D4
Gata, Sierra de *Spain* 40°20N 6°45W **21** B2
Gataga → *Canada* 58°35N 126°59W **70** B3
Gatchina *Russia* 59°35N 30°9E **9** G24
Gatehouse of Fleet *U.K.* 54°53N 4°12W **11** G4
Gates *U.S.A.* 43°9N 77°42W **82** C7
Gateshead *U.K.* 54°57N 1°35W **12** C6
Gatesville *U.S.A.* 31°26N 97°45W **84** F6
Gateway *U.S.A.* 40°38N 73°51W **83** F11
Gaths *Zimbabwe* 20°2S 30°32E **55** G3
Gatineau *Canada* 45°29N 75°39W **83** A9
Gatineau → *Canada* 45°27N 75°42W **72** C4
Gatineau △ *Canada* 45°40N 76°0W **72** C4
Gatton *Australia* 27°32S 152°17E **63** D5
Gatún, L. *Panama* 9°7N 79°56W **88** E4
Gatwick, London ✈ (LGW)
  U.K. 51°10N 0°11W **13** F7
Gatyana *S. Africa* 32°16S 28°31E **57** E4
Gau *Fiji* 18°2S 179°18E **59** a
Gauer L. *Canada* 57°0N 97°50W **71** B9
Gauhati = Guwahati
  India 26°10N 91°45E **41** F17
Gauja → *Latvia* 57°10N 24°16E **9** H21
Gaujas △ *Latvia* 57°10N 24°50E **9** H21
Gaula → *Norway* 63°21N 10°14E **8** E14
Gauri Phanta *India* 28°41N 80°36E **43** E9
Gaustatoppen *Norway* 59°48N 8°40E **9** G13
Gauteng □ *S. Africa* 26°0S 28°0E **57** D4
Gāv Koshī *Iran* 28°38N 57°12E **45** D8
Gāvakān *Iran* 29°37N 53°10E **45** D7
Gavāter *Iran* 25°10N 61°31E **45** E9
Gāvbandī *Iran* 27°12N 53°4E **45** E7
Gavdopoula *Greece* 34°56N 24°0E **25** E6
Gavdos *Greece* 34°50N 24°5E **25** E6
Gaviota *U.S.A.* 34°29N 120°13W **79** L6
Gāvkhūnī, Bāţlāq-e *Iran* 32°6N 52°52E **45** C7
Gävle *Sweden* 60°40N 17°9E **8** F17
Gawachab *Namibia* 27°4S 17°55E **56** D2
Gawilgarh Hills *India* 21°15N 76°45E **40** J10
Gawler *Australia* 34°30S 138°42E **63** E2
Gawler Ranges
  Australia 32°30S 135°45E **63** E2
Gaxun Nur *China* 42°22N 100°30E **32** B5
Gay *Russia* 51°27N 58°27E **18** D10
Gaya *India* 24°47N 85°4E **43** G11
Gaya *Niger* 11°52N 3°28E **50** F6
Gaylord *U.S.A.* 45°2N 84°41W **81** C11
Gayndah *Australia* 25°35S 151°32E **63** D5
Gaysin = Haysyn
  Ukraine 48°57N 29°25E **17** D15
Gayvoron = Hayvoron
  Ukraine 48°22N 29°52E **17** D15
Gaza *Gaza Strip* 31°30N 34°28E **46** D3
Gaza □ *Mozam.* 23°10S 32°45E **57** C5
Gaza Strip ■ *Asia* 31°29N 34°25E **46** D3

Gazanjyk = Bereket
  Turkmenistan 39°16N 55°32E **45** B7
Gāzbor *Iran* 28°5N 58°51E **45** D8
Gazi *Dem. Rep. of the Congo* 1°3N 24°30E **54** B1
Gaziantep *Turkey* 37°6N 37°23E **44** B3
Gazimağusa = Famagusta
  Cyprus 35°8N 33°55E **25** D12
Gcoverega *Botswana* 19°8S 24°18E **56** B3
Gcuwa *S. Africa* 32°20S 28°11E **57** E4
Gdańsk *Poland* 54°22N 18°40E **17** A10
Gdańska, Zatoka
  Poland 54°30N 19°20E **17** A10
Gdov *Russia* 58°48N 27°55E **9** G22
Gdynia *Poland* 54°35N 18°33E **17** A10
Gebe *Indonesia* 0°5N 129°25E **37** D7
Gebze *Turkey* 40°47N 29°25E **23** D13
Gedaref *Sudan* 14°2N 35°28E **51** F13
Gediz *Turkey* 38°35N 29°48E **23** E12
Gedser *Denmark* 54°35N 11°55E **9** J14
Gedung, Pulau *Malaysia* 5°17N 100°23E **39** c
Geegully Cr. →
  Australia 18°32S 123°41E **60** C3
Geel *Belgium* 51°10N 4°59E **15** C4
Geelong *Australia* 38°10S 144°22E **63** F3
Geelvink B. = Cenderwasih, Teluk
  Indonesia 3°0S 135°20E **37** E9
Geelvink Chan. *Australia* 28°30S 114°0E **61** E1
Geesthacht *Germany* 53°26N 10°22E **16** B6
Geidam *Nigeria* 12°57N 11°57E **51** F8
Geikie → *Canada* 57°45N 103°52W **71** B8
Geikie Gorge △ *Australia* 18°3S 125°41E **60** C4
Geistown *U.S.A.* 40°18N 78°52W **82** F6
Geita *Tanzania* 2°48S 32°12E **54** C3
Gejiu *China* 23°20N 103°10E **32** D5
Gel, Meydān-e *Iran* 29°4N 54°50E **45** D7
Gela *Italy* 37°4N 14°15E **22** F6
Gelang Patah *Malaysia* 1°27N 103°35E **39** d
Gelderland □ *Neths.* 52°5N 6°10E **15** B6
Geldrop *Neths.* 51°25N 5°32E **15** C5
Geleen *Neths.* 50°57N 5°49E **15** D5
Gelib = Jilib *Somali Rep.* 0°29N 42°46E **47** G3
Gelibolu *Turkey* 40°28N 26°43E **23** D12
Gelsenkirchen *Germany* 51°32N 7°6E **16** C4
Gelugur *Malaysia* 5°22N 100°18E **39** c
Gemas *Malaysia* 2°37N 102°36E **39** L4
Gembloux *Belgium* 50°34N 4°43E **15** D4
Gemena
  Dem. Rep. of the Congo 3°13N 19°48E **52** D3
Gemerek *Turkey* 39°15N 36°10E **44** B3
Gemlik *Turkey* 40°26N 29°9E **23** D13
Gemsbok △ *Botswana* 25°5S 21°1E **56** D3
Genadi *Greece* 36°2N 27°56E **25** C9
Genale → *Ethiopia* 6°2N 39°1E **47** F2
General Acha *Argentina* 37°20S 64°38W **94** D3
General Alvear *B. Aires,*
  Argentina 36°0S 60°0W **94** D4
General Alvear *Mendoza,*
  Argentina 35°0S 67°40W **94** D2
General Artigas
  Paraguay 26°52S 56°16W **94** B4
General Belgrano
  Argentina 36°35S 58°47W **94** D4
General Bernardo O'Higgins
  Antarctica 63°0S 58°3W **5** C18
General Cabrera
  Argentina 32°53S 63°52W **94** C3
General Cepeda *Mexico* 25°21N 101°22W **86** B4
General Guido *Argentina* 36°40S 57°50W **94** D4
General Juan Madariaga
  Argentina 37°0S 57°0W **94** D4
General La Madrid
  Argentina 37°17S 61°20W **94** D3
General MacArthur
  Phil. 11°18N 125°28E **37** B7
General Martin Miguel de Güemes
  Argentina 24°50S 65°0W **94** A3
General Pico *Argentina* 35°45S 63°50W **94** D3
General Pinedo
  Argentina 27°15S 61°20W **94** B3
General Pinto *Argentina* 34°45S 61°50W **94** C3
General Roca *Argentina* 39°2S 67°35W **96** D3
General Santos *Phil.* 6°5N 125°14E **37** C7
General Treviño *Mexico* 26°14N 99°29W **87** B5
General Trías *Mexico* 28°21N 106°22W **86** B3
General Viamonte
  Argentina 35°1S 61°3W **94** D3
General Villegas *Argentina* 35°5S 63°0W **94** D3
Genesee *Idaho, U.S.A.* 46°33N 116°56W **76** C5
Genesee *Pa., U.S.A.* 41°59N 77°54W **82** E7
Genesee → *U.S.A.* 43°16N 77°36W **82** C7
Geneseo *Ill., U.S.A.* 41°27N 90°9W **80** E8
Geneseo *N.Y., U.S.A.* 42°48N 77°49W **82** D7
Geneva = Genève *Switz.* 46°12N 6°9E **20** C7
Geneva *Ala., U.S.A.* 31°2N 85°52W **85** F12
Geneva *N.Y., U.S.A.* 42°52N 76°59W **82** D7
Geneva *Nebr., U.S.A.* 40°32N 97°36W **80** E6
Geneva *Ohio, U.S.A.* 41°48N 80°57W **82** E4
Geneva, L. = Léman, L.
  Europe 46°26N 6°30E **20** C7
Genève *Switz.* 46°12N 6°9E **20** C7
Genil → *Spain* 37°42N 5°19W **21** D3
Genk *Belgium* 50°58N 5°32E **15** D5
Gennargentu, Mti. del
  Italy 40°1N 9°19E **22** D3
Genoa = Génova *Italy* 44°25N 8°57E **20** D8
Genoa *Australia* 37°29S 149°35E **63** F4
Genoa *N.Y., U.S.A.* 42°40N 76°32W **83** D8
Genoa *Nebr., U.S.A.* 41°27N 97°44W **80** E6
Genoa *Nev., U.S.A.* 39°1N 119°50W **78** F7
Génova *Italy* 44°25N 8°57E **20** D8
Génova, G. di *Italy* 44°0N 9°0E **22** C3
Genriyetty, Ostrov
  Russia 77°6N 156°30E **29** B16
Gent *Belgium* 51°2N 3°42E **15** C3
Genteng *Bali, Indonesia* 8°22S 114°9E **37** J17
Genteng *Jawa Barat,*
  Indonesia 7°22S 106°24E **37** G12

Genyem *Indonesia* 2°46S 140°12E **37** E10
Geochang *S. Korea* 35°41N 127°55E **35** G14
Geographe B. *Australia* 33°30S 115°15E **61** F2
Geographe Chan.
  Australia 24°30S 113°0E **61** D1
Georga, Zemlya *Russia* 80°30N 49°0E **28** A5
George *S. Africa* 33°58S 22°29E **56** E3
George → *Canada* 58°49N 66°10W **73** A6
George, L. *N.S.W.,*
  Australia 35°10S 149°25E **63** F4
George, L. *S. Austral.,*
  Australia 37°25S 140°0E **63** F3
George, L. *W. Austral.,*
  Australia 22°45S 123°40E **60** D3
George, L. *Uganda* 0°5N 30°10E **54** B3
George, L. *Fla., U.S.A.* 29°17N 81°36W **85** G14
George, L. *N.Y., U.S.A.* 43°37N 73°33W **83** C11
George Gill Ra.
  Australia 24°22S 131°45E **60** D5
George Pt. *Australia* 20°6S 148°36E **62** J6
George River = Kangiqsualujjuaq
  Canada 58°30N 65°59W **69** D13
George Sound *N.Z.* 44°52S 167°25E **59** F1
George Town *Australia* 41°6S 146°49E **63** G4
George Town *Bahamas* 23°33N 75°47W **88** B4
George Town *Cayman Is.* 19°20N 81°24W **88** C3
George Town *Malaysia* 5°25N 100°20E **39** c
George V Land *Antarctica* 69°0S 148°0E **5** C10
George VI Sound
  Antarctica 71°0S 68°0W **5** D17
George West *U.S.A.* 28°20N 98°7W **84** G5
Georgetown = Janjanbureh
  Gambia 13°30N 14°47W **50** F3
Georgetown *Australia* 18°17S 143°33E **62** B3
Georgetown *Ont.,*
  Canada 43°40N 79°56W **82** C5
Georgetown *P.E.I.,*
  Canada 46°13N 62°24W **73** C7
Georgetown *Guyana* 6°50N 58°12W **92** B7
Georgetown *Calif.,*
  U.S.A. 38°54N 120°50W **78** G6
Georgetown *Colo.,*
  U.S.A. 39°42N 105°42W **76** G11
Georgetown *Ky., U.S.A.* 38°13N 84°33W **81** F11
Georgetown *N.Y.,*
  U.S.A. 42°46N 75°44W **83** D9
Georgetown *Ohio,*
  U.S.A. 38°52N 83°54W **81** F12
Georgetown *S.C.,*
  U.S.A. 33°23N 79°17W **85** E15
Georgetown *Tex., U.S.A.* 30°38N 97°41W **84** F6
Georgia □ *U.S.A.* 32°50N 83°15W **85** E13
Georgia ■ *Asia* 42°0N 43°0E **19** F7
Georgia, Str. of *N. Amer.* 49°25N 124°0W **78** A3
Georgia Basin *S. Ocean* 50°45S 35°30W **5** B1
Georgian B. *Canada* 45°15N 81°0W **82** A4
Georgian Bay Islands △
  Canada 44°53N 79°52W **82** B5
Georgiyevka *Kazakhstan* 49°19N 84°34E **28** E9
Georgina → *Australia* 23°30S 139°47E **62** C2
Georgina I. *Canada* 44°22N 79°17W **82** B5
Georgioupoli *Greece* 35°20N 24°15E **25** D6
Georgiyevsk *Russia* 44°12N 43°28E **19** F7
Gera *Germany* 50°53N 12°4E **16** C7
Geraardsbergen *Belgium* 50°45N 3°53E **15** D3
Geral, Serra *Brazil* 26°25S 50°0W **95** B6
Geral de Goiás, Serra
  Brazil 12°0S 46°0W **93** F9
Geraldine *U.S.A.* 47°36N 110°16W **76** C8
Geraldton *Australia* 28°48S 114°32E **61** E1
Geraldton *Canada* 49°44N 86°59W **72** C2
Gereshk *Afghan.* 31°47N 64°35E **40** D4
Gerik *Malaysia* 5°50N 101°15E **39** K3
Gering *U.S.A.* 41°50N 103°40W **80** E2
Gerlach *U.S.A.* 40°39N 119°21W **76** F4
German Bight = Deutsche Bucht
  Germany 54°15N 8°0E **16** A5
Germansen Landing
  Canada 55°43N 124°40W **70** B4
Germantown *U.S.A.* 35°5N 89°49W **85** D10
Germany ■ *Europe* 51°0N 10°0E **16** C6
Germī *Iran* 39°1N 48°3E **45** B6
Germiston *S. Africa* 26°13S 28°10E **57** D4
Gernika-Lumo *Spain* 43°19N 2°40W **21** A4
Gero *Japan* 35°48N 137°14E **31** G8
Gerokgak *Indonesia* 8°11S 114°27E **37** J17
Gerona = Girona *Spain* 41°58N 2°46E **21** B7
Geropotamos → *Greece* 35°3N 24°50E **25** D6
Gerrard *Canada* 50°30N 117°17W **70** C5
Gertak Sanggul *Malaysia* 5°17N 100°12E **39** c
Gertak Sanggul, Tanjung
  Malaysia 5°16N 100°11E **39** c
Gerung *Indonesia* 8°43S 116°7E **37** K19
Geser *Indonesia* 3°50S 130°54E **37** E8
Getafe *Spain* 40°18N 3°43W **21** B4
Gettysburg *Pa., U.S.A.* 39°50N 77°14W **81** F15
Gettysburg *S. Dak., U.S.A.* 45°1N 99°57W **80** C4
Getxo *Spain* 43°21N 2°59W **21** A4
Getz Ice Shelf *Antarctica* 75°0S 130°0W **5** D14
Geyser *U.S.A.* 47°16N 110°30W **76** C8
Geyserville *U.S.A.* 38°42N 122°54W **78** G4
Ghadāf, W. al → *Iraq* 32°56N 43°30E **44** C4
Ghadāmis *Libya* 30°11N 9°29E **51** B8
Ghaggar → *India* 29°30N 74°53E **42** E6
Ghaghara → *India* 25°45N 84°40E **43** G11
Ghaghat → *Bangla.* 25°19N 89°38E **43** G13
Ghagra *India* 23°17N 84°33E **43** H11
Ghagra → *Zemlya* 27°29N 81°9E **43** F9
Ghallamane *Mauritania* 23°15N 10°0W **50** D4
Ghana ■ *W. Afr.* 8°0N 1°0W **50** G5
Ghansor *India* 22°39N 80°1E **43** H9
Ghanzi *Botswana* 21°50S 21°34E **56** C3
Gharb Bahr el Ghazâl □
  Sudan 7°30N 27°30E **48** F6
Ghardaïa *Algeria* 32°20N 3°37E **50** B6
Gharm *Tajikistan* 39°0N 70°20E **28** F8
Gharyān *Libya* 32°10N 13°0E **51** B8

Ghat *Libya* 24°59N 10°11E **51** D8
Ghatal *India* 22°40N 87°46E **43** H12
Ghatampur *India* 26°8N 80°13E **43** F9
Ghats, Eastern *India* 14°0N 78°50E **40** N11
Ghats, Western *India* 14°0N 75°0E **40** N9
Ghatsila *India* 22°36N 86°29E **43** H12
Ghaţţī *Si. Arabia* 31°16N 37°31E **44** D3
Ghawdex = Gozo *Malta* 36°3N 14°15E **25** C1
Ghazal, Bahr el → *Chad* 13°0N 15°47E **51** F9
Ghazâl, Bahr el →
  Sudan 9°31N 30°25E **51** G12
Ghaziabad *India* 28°42N 77°26E **42** E7
Ghazipur *India* 25°38N 83°35E **43** G10
Ghaznī *Afghan.* 33°30N 68°28E **42** C3
Ghaznī □ *Afghan.* 32°10N 68°20E **40** C6
Ghent = Gent *Belgium* 51°2N 3°42E **15** C3
Gheorghe Gheorghiu-Dej = Onești
  Romania 46°17N 26°47E **17** E14
Ghīnah, Wādī al →
  Si. Arabia 30°27N 38°14E **44** D3
Ghizar → *Pakistan* 36°15N 73°43E **43** A5
Ghotaru *India* 27°20N 70°1E **42** F4
Ghotki *Pakistan* 28°5N 69°21E **42** E3
Ghowr □ *Afghan.* 34°0N 64°20E **40** C4
Ghughri *India* 22°39N 80°41E **43** H9
Ghugus *India* 19°58N 79°12E **40** K11
Ghulam Mohammad Barrage
  Pakistan 25°30N 68°20E **42** G3
Ghūrīān *Afghan.* 34°17N 61°25E **40** B2
Gia Dinh *Vietnam* 10°49N 106°42E **39** G6
Gia Lai = Plei Ku
  Vietnam 13°57N 108°0E **38** F7
Gia Nghia *Vietnam* 11°58N 107°42E **39** G6
Gia Ngoc *Vietnam* 14°50N 108°58E **38** E7
Gia Vuc *Vietnam* 14°42N 108°34E **38** E7
Giamama = Jamaame
  Somali Rep. 0°4N 42°44E **47** G3
Gianitsa *Greece* 40°46N 22°24E **23** D10
Giant Forest *U.S.A.* 36°36N 118°43W **78** J8
Giant Sequoia △
  U.S.A. 36°10N 118°35W **78** K8
Giants Causeway *U.K.* 55°16N 6°29W **10** A5
Gianyar *Indonesia* 8°32S 115°20E **37** K18
Giarabub = Al Jaghbūb
  Libya 29°42N 24°38E **51** C10
Giarre *Italy* 37°43N 15°11E **22** F6
Gibara *Cuba* 21°9N 76°11W **88** B4
Gibb River *Australia* 16°26S 126°26E **60** C4
Gibbon *U.S.A.* 40°45N 98°51W **80** E4
Gibeon *Namibia* 25°9S 17°43E **56** D2
Gibraltar ☑ *Europe* 36°7N 5°22W **21** D3
Gibraltar, Str. of *Medit. S.* 35°55N 5°40W **21** E3
Gibraltar Range △
  Australia 29°31S 152°19E **63** D5
Gibson Desert *Australia* 24°0S 126°0E **60** D4
Gibsonville *U.S.A.* 39°46N 120°54W **78** F6
Giddings *U.S.A.* 30°11N 96°56W **84** F6
Giebnegáisi = Kebnekaise
  Sweden 67°53N 18°33E **8** C18
Giessen *Germany* 50°34N 8°41E **16** C5
Gīfān *Iran* 37°54N 57°28E **45** B8
Gift Lake *Canada* 55°53N 115°49W **70** B5
Gifu *Japan* 35°30N 136°45E **31** G8
Gifu □ *Japan* 35°40N 137°0E **31** G8
Giganta, Sa. de la
  Mexico 26°0N 111°39W **86** B2
Gigha *U.K.* 55°42N 5°44W **11** F3
Gíglio *Italy* 42°20N 10°52E **22** C4
Gijón *Spain* 43°32N 5°42W **21** A3
Gil I. *Canada* 53°12N 129°15W **70** C3
Gila → *U.S.A.* 32°43N 114°33W **77** K6
Gila Bend *U.S.A.* 32°57N 112°43W **77** K7
Gila Bend Mts. *U.S.A.* 33°10N 113°0W **77** K7
Gila Cliff Dwellings △
  U.S.A. 33°12N 108°16W **77** K9
Gīlān □ *Iran* 37°0N 50°0E **45** B6
Gilbert → *Australia* 16°35S 141°15E **62** B3
Gilbert Is. *Kiribati* 1°0N 172°0E **58** A10
Gilbert River *Australia* 18°9S 142°52E **62** B3
Gilbert Seamounts
  Pac. Oc. 52°50N 150°10W **4** D18
Gilford I. *Canada* 50°40N 126°30W **70** C3
Gilgandra *Australia* 31°43S 148°39E **63** E4
Gilgil *Kenya* 0°30S 36°20E **54** C4
Gilgit *India* 35°50N 74°15E **43** B6
Gilgit → *Pakistan* 35°44N 74°37E **43** B6
Gili *Mozam.* 16°39S 38°27E **55** F4
Gilimanuk *Indonesia* 8°10S 114°26E **37** J17
Gillam *Canada* 56°20N 94°40W **71** B10
Gillen, L. *Australia* 26°11S 124°38E **61** E3
Gilles, L. *Australia* 32°50S 136°45E **63** E2
Gillette *U.S.A.* 44°18N 105°30W **76** D11
Gilliat *Australia* 20°40S 141°28E **62** C3
Gillingham *U.K.* 51°23N 0°33E **13** F8
Gilmer *U.S.A.* 32°44N 94°57W **84** E7
Gilmore, L. *Australia* 32°29N 121°37E **61** F3
Gilmour *Canada* 44°48N 77°37W **82** B7
Gilroy *U.S.A.* 37°1N 121°34W **78** H5
Gimcheon *S. Korea* 36°11N 128°4E **35** F15
Gimhae *S. Korea* 35°14N 128°53E **35** G15
Gimie, Mt *St. Lucia* 13°54N 61°0W **89** f
Gimje *S. Korea* 35°48N 126°45E **35** G14
Gin Gin *Australia* 25°0S 151°58E **63** D5
Gingin *Australia* 31°22S 115°54E **61** F2
Gingindlovu *S. Africa* 29°2S 31°30E **57** D5
Ginir *Ethiopia* 7°6N 40°40E **47** F3
Giofyros → *Greece* 35°20N 25°6E **25** D7
Giohar = Jawhar
  Somali Rep. 2°48N 45°30E **47** G4
Giona, Oros *Greece* 38°38N 22°14E **23** E10
Gir □ *India* 21°0N 71°0E **42** J4

Gir Hills *India* 21°0N 71°0E **42** J4
Girab *India* 26°2N 70°38E **42** F4
Girâfi, W. → *Egypt* 29°58N 34°39E **46** F3
Girard *St. Lucia* 13°59N 60°57W **89** D7
Girard *Kans., U.S.A.* 37°31N 94°51W **80** G6
Girard *Ohio, U.S.A.* 41°9N 80°42W **82** E4
Girard *Pa., U.S.A.* 42°0N 80°19W **82** E4
Girdle Ness *U.K.* 57°9N 2°3W **11** D6
Giresun *Turkey* 40°55N 38°30E **19** F6
Girga *Egypt* 26°17N 31°55E **51** C12
Giri → *India* 30°28N 77°41E **42** D7
Giridih *India* 24°10N 86°21E **43** G12
Giriftu *Kenya* 1°59N 39°46E **54** B4
Giriyondo *S. Africa* 23°15S 31°40E **57** C5
Girne = Kyrenia *Cyprus* 35°20N 33°20E **25** D12
Giron = Kiruna *Sweden* 67°52N 20°15E **8** C19
Girona *Spain* 41°58N 2°46E **21** B7
Gironde → *France* 45°32N 1°7W **20** D3
Girraween △ *Australia* 28°46S 151°54E **63** D5
Girrigun △ *Australia* 18°15S 145°32E **62** B4
Ghizar → *Pakistan* 36°15N 73°43E **43** A5
Girvan *U.K.* 55°14N 4°51W **11** F4
Gisborne *N.Z.* 38°39S 178°5E **59** C7
Gisenyi *Rwanda* 1°41S 29°15E **54** C2
Gislaved *Sweden* 57°19N 13°32E **9** H15
Gitega *Burundi* 3°26S 29°56E **54** C2
Githio *Greece* 36°46N 22°34E **23** F10
Giuba = Juba →
  Somali Rep. 1°30N 42°35E **47** G3
Giurgiu *Romania* 43°52N 25°57E **17** G13
Giza = El Gîza *Egypt* 30°0N 31°12E **51** C12
Giza Pyramids *Egypt* 29°58N 31°9E **51** C12
Gizab *Afghan.* 33°22N 66°17E **42** C1
Gizhiga *Russia* 62°3N 160°30E **29** C17
Gizhiginskaya Guba
  Russia 61°0N 158°0E **29** C16
Giżycko *Poland* 54°2N 21°48E **17** A11
Gjirokastër *Albania* 40°7N 20°10E **23** D9
Gjoa Haven *Canada* 68°38N 95°53W **68** C10
Gjøvik *Norway* 60°47N 10°43E **8** F14
Glace Bay *Canada* 46°11N 59°58W **73** C8
Glacier △ *Canada* 51°15N 117°30W **70** C5
Glacier △ *U.S.A.* 48°42N 113°48W **76** B7
Glacier Bay △ *U.S.A.* 58°45N 136°30W **70** B1
Glacier Peak *U.S.A.* 48°7N 121°7W **76** B3
Gladewater *U.S.A.* 32°33N 94°56W **84** E7
Gladstone *Queens.,*
  Australia 23°52S 151°16E **62** C5
Gladstone *S. Austral.,*
  Australia 33°15S 138°22E **63** E2
Gladstone *Canada* 50°13N 98°57W **71** C9
Gladstone *U.S.A.* 45°51N 87°1W **80** C10
Gladwin *U.S.A.* 43°59N 84°29W **81** D11
Glagah *Indonesia* 8°13S 114°18E **37** J17
Glåma = Glomma →
  Norway 59°12N 10°57E **9** G14
Gláma *Iceland* 65°48N 23°0W **8** D2
Glamis *U.S.A.* 32°55N 115°5W **79** N11
Glamorgan, Vale of □
  U.K. 51°28N 3°25W **13** F4
Glasco *Kans., U.S.A.* 39°22N 97°50W **80** F5
Glasco *N.Y., U.S.A.* 42°3N 73°57W **83** D11
Glasgow *U.K.* 55°51N 4°15W **11** F4
Glasgow *Ky., U.S.A.* 37°0N 85°55W **81** G11
Glasgow *Mont., U.S.A.* 48°12N 106°38W **76** B10
Glasgow, City of □ *U.K.* 55°51N 4°12W **11** F4
Glasgow Int. ✈ (GLA)
  U.K. 55°51N 4°21W **11** F4
Glaslyn *Canada* 53°22N 108°21W **71** C7
Glastonbury *U.K.* 51°9N 2°43W **13** F5
Glastonbury *U.S.A.* 41°43N 72°37W **83** E12
Glazov *Russia* 58°9N 52°40E **18** C9
Gleichen *Canada* 50°52N 113°3W **70** C6
Gleiwitz = Gliwice
  Poland 50°22N 18°41E **17** C10
Glen *U.S.A.* 44°7N 71°11W **83** B13
Glen Affric *U.K.* 57°17N 5°1W **11** D3
Glen Canyon *U.S.A.* 37°30N 110°40W **77** H8
Glen Canyon △ *U.S.A.* 37°15N 111°0W **77** H8
Glen Canyon Dam
  U.S.A. 36°57N 111°29W **77** H8
Glen Coe *U.K.* 56°40N 5°0W **11** E3
Glen Cove *U.S.A.* 40°51N 73°38W **83** F11
Glen Garry *U.K.* 57°3N 5°7W **11** D3
Glen Innes *Australia* 29°44S 151°44E **63** D5
Glen Lyon *U.S.A.* 41°10N 76°5W **83** E8
Glen Mor *U.K.* 57°9N 4°37W **11** D4
Glen More *U.K.* 57°8N 3°40W **11** D4
Glen Moriston *U.K.* 57°11N 4°52W **11** D4
Glen Robertson *Canada* 45°22N 74°30W **83** A10
Glen Spean *U.K.* 56°53N 4°40W **11** E4
Glen Ullin *U.S.A.* 46°49N 101°50W **80** B3
Glenallen *U.S.A.* 62°7N 145°33W **68** C5
Glenariff △ *Ireland* 55°2N 6°10W **10** A5
Glenbeigh *Ireland* 52°3N 9°58W **10** D2
Glencoe *Canada* 42°45N 81°43W **82** D3
Glencoe *S. Africa* 28°11S 30°11E **57** D5
Glencoe *U.S.A.* 44°46N 94°9W **80** C6
Glencolumbkille *Ireland* 54°43N 8°42W **10** B3
Glendale *Zimbabwe* 17°22S 31°5E **55** F3
Glendale *Calif., U.S.A.* 34°9N 118°15W **79** L8
Glendive *U.S.A.* 47°7N 104°43W **76** C2
Glendo *U.S.A.* 42°30N 105°2W **76** E11
Glenelg → *Australia* 38°4S 140°59E **63** F3
Glenfield *U.S.A.* 43°43N 75°24W **83** C9
Glengad Hd. *Ireland* 55°20N 7°10W **10** A4
Glengarriff *Ireland* 51°45N 9°34W **10** E2
Glenmont *U.S.A.* 40°31N 82°6W **82** F2
Glenmorgan *Australia* 27°14S 149°42E **63** D4
Glennallen *U.S.A.* 39°31N 122°1W **78** F4
Glennamaddy *Ireland* 53°37N 8°33W **10** C3
Glenns Ferry *U.S.A.* 42°57N 115°18W **76** E6
Glenora *Canada* 44°9N 77°23W **82** B7
Glenorchy *Australia* 42°49S 147°18E **63** G4
Glenore *Australia* 17°50S 141°12E **62** B3
Glenreagh *Australia* 30°2S 153°1E **63** E5

Glenrock *U.S.A.* 42°52N 105°52W **76** E11
Glenrothes *U.K.* 56°12N 3°10W **11** E5
Glens Falls *U.S.A.* 43°19N 73°39W **83** C11
Glenside *U.S.A.* 40°6N 75°9W **83** F9
Glenties *Ireland* 54°49N 8°16W **10** B3
Glenville *U.S.A.* 38°56N 80°50W **81** F13
Glenwood *Canada* 49°0N 54°58W **73** C9
Glenwood *Ark., U.S.A.* 34°20N 93°33W **84** D8
Glenwood *Iowa, U.S.A.* 41°3N 95°45W **80** E6
Glenwood *Minn., U.S.A.* 45°39N 95°23W **80** C6
Glenwood *Wash., U.S.A.* 46°1N 121°17W **78** D5
Glenwood Springs
U.S.A. 39°33N 107°19W **76** G10
Glettinganes *Iceland* 65°30N 13°37W **8** D7
Glin *Ireland* 52°34N 9°17W **10** D2
Gliwice *Poland* 50°22N 18°41E **17** C10
Globe *U.S.A.* 33°24N 110°47W **77** K8
Głogów *Poland* 51°37N 16°5E **16** C9
Glomma → *Norway* 59°12N 10°57E **9** G14
Glorieuses, Îs. *Ind. Oc.* 11°30S 47°20E **57** A8
Glossop *U.K.* 53°27N 1°56W **12** D6
Gloucester *Australia* 32°0S 151°59E **63** E5
Gloucester *U.K.* 51°53N 2°15W **13** F5
Gloucester *U.S.A.* 42°37N 70°40W **83** D14
Gloucester I. *Australia* 20°0S 148°30E **62** J6
Gloucester Island △
Australia 20°2S 148°30E **62** J6
Gloucester Point
U.S.A. 37°15N 76°30W **81** G15
Gloucestershire □ *U.K.* 51°46N 2°15W **13** F5
Gloversville *U.S.A.* 43°3N 74°21W **83** C10
Glovertown *Canada* 48°40N 54°3W **73** C9
Glusk *Belarus* 52°53N 28°41E **17** B15
Gmünd *Austria* 48°45N 15°0E **16** D8
Gmunden *Austria* 47°55N 13°48E **16** E7
Gniezno *Poland* 52°30N 17°35E **17** B9
Gnowangerup *Australia* 33°58S 117°59E **61** F2
Go Cong *Vietnam* 10°22N 106°40E **39** G6
Gō-no-ura *Japan* 33°44N 129°40E **31** H4
Goa *India* 15°33N 73°59E **40** M8
Goa □ *India* 15°33N 73°59E **40** M8
Goalen Hd. *Australia* 36°33S 150°4E **63** F5
Goalpara *India* 26°10N 90°40E **41** F17
Goaltor *India* 22°43N 87°10E **43** H12
Goalundo Ghat *Bangla.* 23°50N 89°47E **43** H13
Goat Fell *U.K.* 55°38N 5°11W **11** F3
Goba *Ethiopia* 7°1N 39°59E **47** F2
Goba *Mozam.* 26°15S 32°13E **57** D5
Gobabis *Namibia* 22°30S 19°0E **56** C2
Gobi *Asia* 44°0N 110°0E **34** C6
Gobō *Japan* 33°53N 135°10E **31** H7
Gochas *Namibia* 24°59S 18°55E **56** C2
Godalming *U.K.* 51°11N 0°36W **13** F7
Godavari → *India* 16°25N 82°18E **41** L13
Godavari Pt. *India* 17°0N 82°20E **41** L13
Godbout *Canada* 49°20N 67°38W **73** C6
Godda *India* 24°50N 87°13E **43** G12
Goderich *Canada* 43°45N 81°41W **82** C3
Godfrey Ra. *Australia* 24°0S 117°0E **61** D2
Godhavn = Qeqertarsuaq
Greenland 69°15N 53°38W **4** C5
Godhra *India* 22°49N 73°40E **42** H5
Godoy Cruz *Argentina* 32°56S 68°52W **94** C2
Gods → *Canada* 56°22N 92°51W **72** A1
Gods L. *Canada* 54°40N 94°15W **72** B1
Gods River *Canada* 54°50N 94°5W **71** C10
Godthåb = Nuuk
Greenland 64°10N 51°35W **67** C14
Goeie Hoop, Kaap die = Good
Hope, C. of *S. Africa* 34°24S 18°30E **56** E2
Goéland, L. au *Canada* 49°50N 76°48W **72** C4
Goélands, L. aux *Canada* 55°27N 64°17W **73** A7
Goeree *Neths.* 51°50N 4°0E **15** C3
Goes *Neths.* 51°30N 3°55E **15** C3
Goffstown *U.S.A.* 43°1N 71°36W **83** C13
Gogama *Canada* 47°35N 81°43W **72** C3
Gogebic, L. *U.S.A.* 46°30N 89°35W **80** B9
Gogra = Ghaghara →
India 25°45N 84°40E **43** G11
Gogrial *Sudan* 8°30N 28°8E **51** G11
Gohana *India* 29°8N 76°42E **42** E7
Goharganj *India* 23°1N 77°41E **42** H7
Goi → *India* 22°4N 74°46E **42** H6
Goiânia *Brazil* 16°43S 49°20W **93** G9
Goiás *Brazil* 15°55S 50°10W **93** G8
Goiás □ *Brazil* 12°10S 48°0W **93** F9
Goio-Erê *Brazil* 24°12S 53°1W **95** A5
Gojō *Japan* 34°21N 135°42E **31** G7
Gojra *Pakistan* 31°10N 72°40E **42** D5
Gökçeada *Turkey* 40°10N 25°50E **23** D11
Gökova Körfezi *Turkey* 36°57N 27°50E **23** F12
Göksu → *Turkey* 36°19N 34°5E **44** B2
Gökteik *Burma* 22°26N 97°0E **41** H20
Gokurt *Pakistan* 29°40N 67°26E **42** E2
Gokwe *Zimbabwe* 18°7S 28°58E **57** B4
Gola *India* 28°3N 80°32E **43** E9
Golakganj *India* 26°8N 89°52E **43** F13
Golan Heights = Hagolan
Syria 33°0N 35°45E **46** C4
Golāshkerd *Iran* 27°59N 57°16E **45** E8
Golchikha *Russia* 71°45N 83°30E **4** B12
Golconda *U.S.A.* 40°58N 117°30W **76** F5
Gold *U.S.A.* 41°52N 77°50W **82** E7
Gold Beach *U.S.A.* 42°25N 124°25W **76** E1
Gold Coast *W. Afr.* 4°0N 1°40W **50** H5
Gold Hill *U.S.A.* 42°26N 123°3W **76** E2
Gold River *Canada* 49°46N 126°3W **70** D3
Golden *Canada* 51°20N 116°59W **70** C5
Golden B. *N.Z.* 40°40S 172°50E **59** D4
Golden Gate *U.S.A.* 37°54N 122°29W **77** H2
Golden Gate Highlands △
S. Africa 28°40S 28°40E **57** D4
Golden Hinde *Canada* 49°40N 125°44W **70** D3
Golden Lake *Canada* 45°34N 77°21W **82** A7
Golden Spike △ *U.S.A.* 41°37N 112°33W **76** F7
Golden Vale *Ireland* 52°33N 8°17W **10** D3

Goldendale *U.S.A.* 45°49N 120°50W **76** D3
Goldfield *U.S.A.* 37°42N 117°14W **77** H5
Goldsand L. *Canada* 57°2N 101°8W **71** B8
Goldsboro *U.S.A.* 35°23N 77°59W **85** D16
Goldsmith *U.S.A.* 31°59N 102°37W **84** F3
Goldthwaite *U.S.A.* 31°27N 98°34W **84** F5
Goleniów *Poland* 53°35N 14°50E **16** B8
Golestān □ *Iran* 37°20N 55°25E **45** B7
Goleta *U.S.A.* 34°27N 119°50W **79** L7
Golfito *Costa Rica* 8°41N 83°5W **88** E3
Golfo Aranci *Italy* 40°59N 9°38E **22** D3
Goliad *U.S.A.* 28°40N 97°23W **84** G6
Golra *Pakistan* 33°37N 72°56E **42** C5
Golspie *U.K.* 57°58N 3°59W **11** D5
Goma
Dem. Rep. of the Congo 1°37S 29°10E **54** C2
Gomal Pass *Pakistan* 31°56N 69°20E **42** D3
Gomati → *India* 25°32N 83°11E **43** G10
Gombari
Dem. Rep. of the Congo 2°45N 29°3E **54** B2
Gombe *Nigeria* 10°19N 11°2E **51** F8
Gombe → *Tanzania* 4°38S 31°40E **54** C3
Gomel = Homyel *Belarus* 52°28N 31°0E **17** B16
Gomera *Canary Is.* 28°7N 17°14W **24** F2
Gómez Palacio *Mexico* 25°34N 103°30W **86** B4
Gomīshān *Iran* 37°4N 54°6E **45** B7
Gomogomo *Indonesia* 6°39S 134°43E **37** F8
Gomoh *India* 23°52N 86°10E **43** H12
Gompa = Ganta *Liberia* 7°15N 8°59W **50** G4
Gonābād *Iran* 34°15N 58°45E **45** C8
Gonaïves *Haiti* 19°20N 72°42W **89** C5
Gonarezhou △ *Zimbabwe* 21°32S 31°55E **55** G3
Gonâve, G. de la *Haiti* 19°29N 72°42W **89** C5
Gonâve, Île de la *Haiti* 18°51N 73°3W **89** C5
Gonbad-e Kāvūs *Iran* 37°20N 55°25E **45** B7
Gonda *India* 27°9N 81°58E **43** F9
Gondal *India* 21°58N 70°52E **42** J4
Gonder *Ethiopia* 12°39N 37°30E **47** E2
Gondia *India* 21°23N 80°10E **40** J12
Gondola *Mozam.* 19°10S 33°37E **55** F3
Gönen *Turkey* 40°6N 27°39E **23** D12
Gongbei *China* 22°12N 113°32E **33** G10
Gonghe *China* 36°18N 100°32E **32** C5
Gongju *S. Korea* 36°27N 127°7E **35** F14
Gongming *China* 22°47N 113°53E **33** F10
Gongolgon *Australia* 30°21S 146°54E **63** E4
Gongzhuling *China* 43°30N 124°40E **35** C13
Goniri *Nigeria* 11°30N 12°15E **51** F8
Gonzales *Calif., U.S.A.* 36°30N 121°26W **78** J5
Gonzales *Tex., U.S.A.* 29°30N 97°27W **84** G6
González *Mexico* 22°48N 98°25W **87** C5
Good Hope, C. of *S. Africa* 34°24S 18°30E **56** E2
Good Hope Lake
Canada 59°16N 129°18W **70** B3
Gooderham *Canada* 44°54N 78°21W **82** B6
Goodhouse *S. Africa* 28°57S 18°13E **56** D2
Gooding *U.S.A.* 42°56N 114°43W **76** E6
Goodland *U.S.A.* 39°21N 101°43W **80** F3
Goodlands *Mauritius* 20°2S 57°39E **53** d
Goodlow *Canada* 56°20N 120°8W **70** B4
Goodooga *Australia* 29°3S 147°28E **63** D4
Goodsprings *U.S.A.* 35°49N 115°27W **79** K11
Goole *U.K.* 53°42N 0°53W **12** D7
Goolgowi *Australia* 33°58S 145°41E **63** E4
Goomalling *Australia* 31°15S 116°49E **61** F2
Goomeri *Australia* 26°12S 152°6E **63** D5
Goonda *Mozam.* 19°48S 33°57E **55** F3
Goondiwindi *Australia* 28°30S 150°21E **63** D5
Goongarrie, L. *Australia* 30°3S 121°9E **61** F3
Goongarrie △ *Australia* 30°7S 121°30E **61** F3
Goonyella *Australia* 21°47S 147°58E **62** C4
Goose → *Canada* 53°20N 60°35W **73** B7
Goose Creek *U.S.A.* 32°59N 80°2W **85** E14
Goose L. *U.S.A.* 41°56N 120°26W **76** F3
Gop *India* 22°5N 69°50E **42** H3
Gopalganj *India* 26°28N 84°30E **43** F11
Göppingen *Germany* 48°42N 9°39E **16** D5
Gorakhpur *India* 26°47N 83°23E **43** F10
Goražde *Bos.-H.* 43°38N 18°58E **23** C8
Gorda, Pta. *Canary Is.* 28°45N 18°0W **24** F2
Gorda, Pta. *Nic.* 14°20N 83°10W **88** D3
Gordan B. *Australia* 11°35S 130°10E **60** B5
Gordon *U.S.A.* 42°48N 102°12W **80** D2
Gordon → *Australia* 42°27S 145°30E **63** G4
Gordon Bay *Canada* 45°12N 79°47W **82** A5
Gordon L. *Alta., Canada* 56°30N 110°25W **71** B6
Gordon L. *N.W.T.,
Canada* 63°5N 113°11W **70** A6
Gordonvale *Australia* 17°5S 145°50E **62** B4
Goré *Chad* 7°59N 16°31E **51** G9
Gore *Ethiopia* 8°12N 35°32E **47** F2
Gore *N.Z.* 46°5S 168°58E **59** G2
Gore Bay *Canada* 45°57N 82°28W **72** C3
Gorey *Ireland* 52°41N 6°18W **10** D5
Gorg *Iran* 29°29N 59°43E **45** D8
Gorgān *Iran* 36°55N 54°30E **45** B7
Gorgona, I. *Colombia* 3°0N 78°10W **92** C3
Gorham *U.S.A.* 44°23N 71°10W **83** B13
Goriganga → *India* 29°45N 80°23E **43** E9
Gorinchem *Neths.* 51°50N 4°59E **15** C4
Goris *Armenia* 39°31N 46°22E **19** G8
Gorizia *Italy* 45°56N 13°37E **22** B5
Gorkiy = Nizhniy Novgorod
Russia 56°20N 44°0E **18** C7
Gorkovskoye Vdkhr.
Russia 57°2N 43°4E **18** C7
Gorleston *U.K.* 52°35N 1°44E **13** E9
Görlitz *Germany* 51°9N 14°58E **16** C8
Gorlovka = Horlivka
Ukraine 48°19N 38°5E **19** E6
Gorman *U.S.A.* 34°47N 118°51W **79** L8
Gorna Dzhumayo = Blagoevgrad
Bulgaria 42°2N 23°5E **23** C10
Gorna Oryakhovitsa
Bulgaria 43°7N 25°40E **23** C11

Gorno-Altay □ *Russia* 51°0N 86°0E **28** D9
Gorno-Altaysk *Russia* 51°50N 86°5E **28** D9
Gornozavodsk *Russia* 46°33N 141°50E **29** E15
Gornyatski *Russia* 67°32N 64°3E **18** A11
Gornyy *Russia* 44°57N 133°59E **30** B6
Gorodenka = Horodenka
Ukraine 48°41N 25°29E **17** D13
Gorodok = Horodok
Ukraine 49°46N 23°32E **17** D12
Gorokhov = Horokhiv
Ukraine 50°30N 24°45E **17** C13
Goromonzi *Zimbabwe* 17°52S 31°22E **55** F3
Gorong, Kepulauan
Indonesia 3°59S 131°25E **37** E8
Gorongosa △ *Mozam.* 18°50S 34°29E **57** B5
Gorongose → *Mozam.* 20°30S 34°40E **57** C5
Gorongoza *Mozam.* 18°44S 34°2E **55** F3
Gorongoza, Sa. da *Mozam.* 18°27S 34°2E **55** F3
Gorontalo *Indonesia* 0°35N 123°5E **37** D6
Gorontalo □ *Indonesia* 0°50N 122°20E **37** D6
Gort *Ireland* 53°3N 8°49W **10** C3
Gortis *Greece* 35°4N 24°58E **25** D7
Goryeong *S. Korea* 35°44N 128°15E **35** G15
Gorzów Wielkopolski
Poland 52°43N 15°15E **16** B8
Gosford *Australia* 33°23S 151°18E **63** E5
Goshen *Calif., U.S.A.* 36°21N 119°25W **78** J7
Goshen *Ind., U.S.A.* 41°35N 85°50W **81** E11
Goshen *N.Y., U.S.A.* 41°24N 74°20W **83** E10
Goshogawara *Japan* 40°48N 140°27E **30** D10
Goslar *Germany* 51°54N 10°25E **16** C6
Gospič *Croatia* 44°35N 15°23E **16** F8
Gosport *U.K.* 50°48N 1°9W **13** G6
Gosse → *Australia* 19°32S 134°37E **62** B1
Göta älv → *Sweden* 57°42N 11°54E **9** H14
Göta kanal *Sweden* 58°30N 15°58E **9** G16
Götaland *Sweden* 57°30N 14°30E **9** H16
Göteborg *Sweden* 57°43N 11°59E **9** H14
Gotha *Germany* 50°56N 10°42E **16** C6
Gothenburg = Göteborg
Sweden 57°43N 11°59E **9** H14
Gothenburg *U.S.A.* 40°56N 100°10W **80** E3
Gotland *Sweden* 57°30N 18°33E **9** H18
Gotō-Rettō *Japan* 32°55N 129°5E **31** H4
Gotska Sandön *Sweden* 58°24N 19°15E **9** G18
Gōtsu *Japan* 35°0N 132°14E **31** G6
Göttingen *Germany* 51°31N 9°55E **16** C5
Gottwaldov = Zlín
Czech Rep. 49°14N 17°40E **17** D9
Goubangzi *China* 41°20N 121°52E **35** D11
Gouda *Neths.* 52°1N 4°42E **15** B4
Goudouras, Akra *Greece* 34°59N 26°6E **25** E8
Gouin, Rés. *Canada* 48°35N 74°40W **72** C5
Goulburn *Australia* 34°44S 149°44E **63** E4
Goulburn Is. *Australia* 11°40S 133°20E **62** A1
Goulimine *Morocco* 28°56N 10°0W **50** C3
Goundam *Mali* 16°27N 3°40W **50** E5
Gourits → *S. Africa* 34°21S 21°52E **56** E3
Gournes *Greece* 35°19N 25°16E **25** D7
Gourock *U.K.* 55°57N 4°49W **11** F4
Gouverneur *U.S.A.* 44°20N 75°28W **83** B9
Gouvia *Greece* 39°39N 19°50E **25** A3
Gove Peninsula
Australia 12°17S 136°49E **62** A2
Governador Valadares
Brazil 18°15S 41°57W **93** G10
Governor's Harbour
Bahamas 25°10N 76°14W **88** A4
Govindgarh *India* 24°23N 81°18E **43** G9
Gowan Ra. *Australia* 25°0S 145°0E **62** D4
Gowanda *U.S.A.* 42°28N 78°56W **82** D6
Gower *U.K.* 51°35N 4°10W **13** F3
Gowna, L. *Ireland* 53°51N 7°34W **10** C4
Goya *Argentina* 29°10S 59°10W **94** B4
Goyder Lagoon *Australia* 27°3S 138°58E **63** D2
Goyllarisquizga *Peru* 10°31S 76°24W **92** F3
Goz Beïda *Chad* 12°10N 21°20E **51** F10
Gozo *Malta* 36°3N 14°15E **25** C1
Graaff-Reinet *S. Africa* 32°13S 24°32E **56** E3
Gračac *Croatia* 44°18N 15°57E **16** F8
Gracias a Dios, C.
Honduras 15°0N 83°10W **88** D3
Graciosa *Azores* 39°4N 28°0W **50** a
Graciosa, I. *Canary Is.* 29°15N 13°32W **24** E6
Grado *Spain* 43°23N 6°4W **21** A2
Grady *U.S.A.* 34°49N 103°19W **77** J12
Grafham Water *U.K.* 52°19N 0°18W **13** E7
Grafton *Australia* 29°38S 152°58E **63** D5
Grafton *N. Dak., U.S.A.* 48°25N 97°25W **80** A5
Grafton *W. Va., U.S.A.* 39°21N 80°2W **81** F13
Graham *Canada* 49°20N 90°30W **72** C1
Graham *U.S.A.* 33°6N 98°35W **84** E5
Graham, Mt. *U.S.A.* 32°42N 109°52W **77** K9
Graham Bell, Ostrov = Greem-
Bell, Ostrov *Russia* 81°0N 62°0E **28** A7
Graham I. *Canada* 53°40N 132°30W **70** C2
Graham Land *Antarctica* 65°0S 64°0W **5** C17
Grahamstad = Greem-
Grahamstown *S. Africa* 33°19S 26°31E **56** E4
Grahamsville *U.S.A.* 41°51N 74°33W **83** E10
Grain Coast *W. Afr.* 4°20N 10°0W **50** H3
Grajagan *Indonesia* 8°35S 114°13E **37** K17
Grajagan, Teluk
Indonesia 8°40S 114°18E **37** K17
Grajaú *Brazil* 5°50S 46°4W **93** E9
Grajaú → *Brazil* 3°41S 44°48W **93** D10
Grampian *U.S.A.* 40°58N 78°37W **82** F6
Grampian Highlands = Grampian
Mts. *U.K.* 56°50N 4°0W **11** E5
Grampian Mts. *U.K.* 56°50N 4°0W **11** E5
Grampians, The
Australia 37°15S 142°20E **63** F3
Gran Canaria *Canary Is.* 27°55N 15°35W **24** G4
Gran Chaco *S. Amer.* 25°0S 61°0W **94** B3
Gran Desierto del Pinacate △
Mexico 31°51N 113°32W **86** A2
Gran Paradiso *Italy* 45°33N 7°17E **20** D7
Gran Sasso d'Itália *Italy* 42°27N 13°42E **22** C5

Granada *Nic.* 11°58N 86°0W **88** D2
Granada *Spain* 37°10N 3°35W **21** D4
Granada *U.S.A.* 38°4N 102°19W **76** G12
Granadilla de Abona
Canary Is. 28°7N 16°33W **24** F3
Granard *Ireland* 53°47N 7°30W **10** C4
Granbury *U.S.A.* 32°27N 97°47W **84** E6
Granby *Canada* 45°25N 72°45W **83** A12
Granby *U.S.A.* 40°5N 105°56W **76** F11
Grand → *Canada* 42°51N 79°34W **82** D5
Grand → *Mo., U.S.A.* 39°23N 93°7W **80** F7
Grand → *S. Dak.,
U.S.A.* 45°40N 100°45W **80** C3
Grand Bahama I.
Bahamas 26°40N 78°30W **88** A4
Grand Baie *Mauritius* 20°0S 57°35E **53** d
Grand Bank *Canada* 47°6N 55°48W **73** C8
Grand Bassam *Ivory C.* 5°10N 3°49W **50** G5
Grand Bend *Canada* 43°18N 81°45W **82** C3
Grand-Bourg *Guadeloupe* 15°53N 61°19W **88** b
Grand Canal = Da Yunhe →
China 39°10N 117°10E **35** E9
Grand Canyon *U.S.A.* 36°3N 112°9W **77** H7
Grand Canyon △
U.S.A. 36°15N 112°30W **77** H7
Grand Canyon-Parashant ○
U.S.A. 36°30N 113°45W **77** H7
Grand Cayman
Cayman Is. 19°20N 81°20W **88** C3
Grand Coulee *U.S.A.* 47°57N 119°0W **76** C4
Grand Coulee Dam
U.S.A. 47°57N 118°59W **76** C4
Grand Erg de Bilma *Niger* 18°30N 14°0E **51** E8
Grand Falls *Canada* 47°3N 67°44W **73** C6
Grand Falls-Windsor
Canada 48°56N 55°40W **73** C8
Grand Forks *Canada* 49°0N 118°30W **70** D5
Grand Forks *U.S.A.* 47°55N 97°3W **80** B6
Grand Gorge *U.S.A.* 42°21N 74°29W **83** D10
Grand Haven *U.S.A.* 43°4N 86°13W **80** D10
Grand I. *Mich., U.S.A.* 46°31N 86°40W **80** B10
Grand I. *N.Y., U.S.A.* 43°0N 78°58W **82** D6
Grand Island *U.S.A.* 40°55N 98°21W **80** E4
Grand Isle *La., U.S.A.* 29°14N 90°0W **85** G9
Grand Isle *Vt., U.S.A.* 44°43N 73°18W **83** B11
Grand Junction *U.S.A.* 39°4N 108°33W **76** G9
Grand L. *N.B., Canada* 45°57N 66°7W **73** C6
Grand L. *Nfld. & L.,
Canada* 49°0N 57°30W **73** C8
Grand L. *Nfld. & L.,
Canada* 53°40N 60°30W **73** B7
Grand L. *U.S.A.* 29°55N 92°47W **84** G8
Grand Lake *U.S.A.* 40°15N 105°49W **76** F11
Grand Manan I. *Canada* 44°45N 66°52W **73** D6
Grand Marais *Mich.,
U.S.A.* 46°40N 85°59W **81** B11
Grand Marais *Minn.,
U.S.A.* 47°45N 90°25W **72** C1
Grand-Mère *Canada* 46°36N 72°40W **72** C5
Grand Portage *U.S.A.* 47°58N 89°41W **80** B9
Grand Prairie *U.S.A.* 32°44N 96°59W **84** E6
Grand Rapids *Canada* 53°12N 99°19W **71** C9
Grand Rapids *Mich.,
U.S.A.* 42°58N 85°40W **81** D11
Grand Rapids *Minn.,
U.S.A.* 47°14N 93°31W **80** B7
Grand St-Bernard, Col du
Europe 45°50N 7°10E **20** D7
Grand Staircase-Escalante △
U.S.A. 37°25N 111°33W **77** H8
Grand Teton *U.S.A.* 43°54N 110°50W **76** E8
Grand Teton △ *U.S.A.* 43°50N 110°50W **76** E8
Grand Union Canal *U.K.* 52°7N 0°53W **13** E7
Grande → *Jujuy,
Argentina* 24°20S 65°2W **94** A2
Grande → *Mendoza,
Argentina* 36°52S 69°45W **94** D2
Grande → *Bolivia* 15°51S 64°39W **92** G6
Grande → *Bahia, Brazil* 11°30S 44°30W **93** F10
Grande → *Minas Gerais,
Brazil* 20°6S 51°4W **93** H8
Grande, B. *Argentina* 50°30S 68°20W **96** G3
Grande, Rio → *N. Amer.* 25°58N 97°9W **84** H6
Grande Anse *Seychelles* 4°18S 55°45E **53** b
Grande Baleine, R. de la →
Canada 55°16N 77°47W **72** A4
Grande Cache *Canada* 53°53N 119°8W **70** C5
Grande Comore
Comoros Is. 11°35S 43°20E **53** a
Grande-Entrée *Canada* 47°30N 61°40W **73** C7
Grande Prairie *Canada* 55°10N 118°50W **70** B5
Grande-Rivière *Canada* 48°26N 64°30W **73** C7
Grande-Terre *Guadeloupe* 16°20N 61°25W **88** b
Grande Vallée *Canada* 49°14N 65°8W **73** C6
Grande Vigie, Pte. de la
Guadeloupe 16°32N 61°27W **88** b
Grandfalls *U.S.A.* 31°20N 102°51W **84** F3
Grandes-Jardins △
Canada 47°41N 70°51W **73** C5
Grandview *Canada* 51°10N 100°42W **71** C8
Grandview *U.S.A.* 46°15N 119°54W **76** C4
Graneros *Chile* 34°5S 70°45W **94** C1
Grangemouth *U.K.* 56°1N 3°42W **11** E5
Granger *U.S.A.* 41°35N 109°58W **76** F9
Grangeville *U.S.A.* 45°56N 116°7W **76** D5
Granisle *Canada* 54°53N 126°13W **70** C3
Granite City *U.S.A.* 38°42N 90°8W **80** F9
Granite Falls *U.S.A.* 44°49N 95°33W **80** C6
Granite L. *Canada* 48°8N 57°5W **73** C8
Granite Mt. *U.S.A.* 33°5N 116°28W **79** M10
Granite Pk. *U.S.A.* 45°10N 109°48W **76** D9
Graniteville *U.S.A.* 44°8N 72°29W **83** B12
Granity *N.Z.* 41°39S 171°51E **59** D3
Granja *Brazil* 3°7S 40°50W **93** D10
Grant *U.S.A.* 40°50N 101°43W **80** E3
Grant, Mt. *U.S.A.* 38°34N 118°48W **76** G4

Grant City *U.S.A.* 40°29N 94°25W **80** E6
Grant I. *Australia* 11°10S 132°52E **60** B5
Grant Range *U.S.A.* 38°30N 115°25W **76** G6
Grantham *U.K.* 52°55N 0°38W **12** E7
Grantown-on-Spey *U.K.* 57°20N 3°36W **11** D5
Grants *U.S.A.* 35°9N 107°52W **77** J10
Grants Pass *U.S.A.* 42°26N 123°19W **76** E2
Grantsville *U.S.A.* 40°36N 112°28W **76** F7
Granville *France* 48°50N 1°35W **20** B3
Granville *N. Dak.,
U.S.A.* 48°16N 100°47W **80** A3
Granville *N.Y., U.S.A.* 43°24N 73°16W **83** C11
Granville *Ohio, U.S.A.* 40°4N 82°31W **82** F2
Granville L. *Canada* 56°18N 100°30W **71** B8
Graskop *S. Africa* 24°56S 30°49E **57** C5
Grass → *Canada* 56°3N 96°33W **71** B9
Grass Range *U.S.A.* 47°2N 108°48W **76** C9
Grass River → *Canada* 54°40N 100°50W **71** C8
Grass Valley *Calif.,
U.S.A.* 39°13N 121°4W **78** F6
Grass Valley *Oreg.,
U.S.A.* 45°22N 120°47W **76** D3
Grasse *France* 43°38N 6°56E **20** E7
Grassflat *U.S.A.* 41°0N 78°6W **82** E6
Grasslands △ *Canada* 49°11N 107°38W **71** D7
Grassy *Australia* 40°3S 144°5E **63** G3
Graulhet *France* 43°45N 1°59E **20** E4
Gravelbourg *Canada* 49°50N 106°35W **71** D7
's-Gravenhage *Neths.* 52°7N 4°17E **15** B4
Gravenhurst *Canada* 44°52N 79°20W **82** B5
Gravesend *Australia* 29°35S 150°20E **63** D5
Gravesend *U.K.* 51°26N 0°22E **13** F8
Gravois, Pointe-à- *Haiti* 18°15N 73°56W **89** C5
Grayling *U.S.A.* 44°40N 84°43W **81** C11
Grays *U.K.* 51°28N 0°21E **13** F8
Grays Harbor *U.S.A.* 46°59N 124°1W **76** C1
Grays L. *U.S.A.* 43°4N 111°26W **76** E8
Grays River *U.S.A.* 46°21N 123°37W **78** D3
Graz *Austria* 47°4N 15°27E **16** E8
Greasy L. *Canada* 62°55N 122°12W **70** A4
Great Abaco I. = Abaco I.
Bahamas 26°25N 77°10W **88** A4
Great Artesian Basin
Australia 23°0S 144°0E **62** C3
Great Australian Bight
Australia 33°30S 130°0E **61** F5
Great Bahama Bank
Bahamas 23°15N 78°0W **88** B4
Great Barrier I. *N.Z.* 36°11S 175°25E **59** B5
Great Barrier Reef
Australia 18°0S 146°50E **62** B4
Great Barrier Reef ○
Australia 20°0S 150°0E **62** B4
Great Barrington
U.S.A. 42°12N 73°22W **83** D11
Great Basalt Wall △
Australia 19°52S 145°43E **62** B4
Great Basin *U.S.A.* 40°0N 117°0W **76** G5
Great Basin △ *U.S.A.* 38°56N 114°15W **76** G6
Great Bear → *Canada* 65°0N 124°0W **68** C7
Great Bear L. *Canada* 65°30N 120°0W **68** C8
Great Belt = Store Bælt
Denmark 55°20N 11°0E **9** J14
Great Bend *Kans., U.S.A.* 38°22N 98°46W **80** F4
Great Bend *Pa., U.S.A.* 41°58N 75°45W **83** E9
Great Blasket I. *Ireland* 52°6N 10°32W **10** D1
Great Britain *Europe* 54°0N 2°15W **6** E5
Great Camanoe
Br. Virgin Is. 18°30N 64°35W **89** e
Great Codroy *Canada* 47°51N 59°16W **73** C8
Great Divide, The = Great
Dividing Ra. *Australia* 23°0S 146°0E **62** C4
Great Divide Basin
U.S.A. 42°0N 108°0W **76** E9
Great Dividing Ra.
Australia 23°0S 146°0E **62** C4
Great Driffield = Driffield
U.K. 54°0N 0°26W **12** C7
Great Exuma I. *Bahamas* 23°30N 75°50W **88** B4
Great Falls *U.S.A.* 47°30N 111°17W **76** C8
Great Fish = Groot-Vis →
S. Africa 33°28S 27°5E **56** E4
Great Guana Cay
Bahamas 24°0N 76°20W **88** B4
Great Himalayan △
India 31°30N 77°30E **42** D7
Great Inagua I. *Bahamas* 21°0N 73°20W **89** B5
Great Indian Desert = Thar Desert
India 28°0N 72°0E **42** F5
Great Karoo *S. Africa* 31°55S 21°0E **56** E3
Great Khingan Mts. = Da
Hinggan Ling *China* 48°0N 121°0E **33** B7
Great Lake *Australia* 41°50S 146°40E **63** G4
Great Lakes *N. Amer.* 46°0N 84°0W **66** E11
Great Limpopo Transfrontier △
Africa 23°0S 31°45E **57** C5
Great Malvern *U.K.* 52°7N 2°18W **13** E5
Great Miami → *U.S.A.* 39°7N 84°49W **81** F11
Great Ormes Head *U.K.* 53°20N 3°52W **12** D4
Great Ouse → *U.K.* 52°48N 0°21E **12** E8
Great Palm I. *Australia* 18°45S 146°40E **62** B4
Great Pedro Bluff *Jamaica* 17°51N 77°44W **88** a
Great Pee Dee →
U.S.A. 33°21N 79°10W **85** E16
Great Plains *N. Amer.* 47°0N 105°0W **66** E9
Great Ruaha → *Tanzania* 7°56S 37°52E **54** D4
Great Sacandaga △
U.S.A. 43°6N 74°16W **83** C10
Great Saint Bernard Pass = Grand
St-Bernard, Col du
Europe 45°50N 7°10E **20** D7
Great Salt Desert = Kavīr, Dasht-e
Iran 34°30N 55°0E **45** C7
Great Salt L. *U.S.A.* 41°15N 112°40W **76** F7
Great Salt Lake Desert
U.S.A. 40°50N 113°30W **76** F7
Great Salt Plains L.
U.S.A. 36°45N 98°8W **84** C5

124 Great Sand Dunes
INDEX TO WORLD MAPS

Great Sand Dunes ⌓ U.S.A. 37°48N 105°45W 77 H11
Great Sandy △ Australia 26°13S 153°2E 63 D5
Great Sandy Desert Australia 21°0S 124°0E 60 D3
Great Sandy Desert U.S.A. 43°35N 120°15W 74 B2
Great Sangi = Sangihe, Pulau Indonesia 3°35N 125°30E 37 D7
Great Sea Reef Fiji 16°15S 179°0E 59 a
Great Skellig Ireland 51°47N 10°33W 10 E1
Great Slave L. Canada 61°23N 115°38W 70 A5
Great Smoky Mts. △ U.S.A. 35°40N 83°40W 85 D13
Great Stour = Stour → U.K. 51°18N 1°22E 13 F9
Great Victoria Desert Australia 29°30S 126°30E 61 E4
Great Wall Antarctica 62°30S 58°0W 5 C18
Great Wall China 38°30N 109°30E 34 E5
Great Whernside U.K. 54°10N 1°58W 12 C6
Great Yarmouth U.K. 52°37N 1°44E 13 E9
Great Zab = Zāb al Kabīr → Iraq 36°1N 43°24E 44 B4
Great Zimbabwe Zimbabwe 20°16S 30°54E 55 G3
Greater Antilles W. Indies 17°40N 74°0W 89 C5
Greater London □ U.K. 51°31N 0°6W 13 F7
Greater Manchester □ U.K. 53°30N 2°15W 12 D5
Greater St. Lucia Wetlands ⌓ S. Africa 28°6S 32°27E 57 D5
Greater Sudbury = Sudbury Canada 46°30N 81°0W 72 C3
Greater Sunda Is. Indonesia 7°0S 112°0E 36 F4
Greco, C. Cyprus 34°57N 34°5E 25 E13
Gredos, Sierra de Spain 40°20N 5°0W 21 B3
Greece U.S.A. 43°13N 77°41W 82 C7
Greece ■ Europe 40°0N 23°0E 23 E9
Greeley Colo., U.S.A. 40°25N 104°42W 76 F11
Greeley Nebr., U.S.A. 41°33N 98°32W 80 E4
Greely Fd. Canada 80°30N 85°0W 69 A11
Greem-Bell, Ostrov Russia 81°0N 62°0E 28 A7
Green → Ky., U.S.A. 37°54N 87°30W 80 G10
Green → Utah, U.S.A. 38°11N 109°53W 76 G9
Green B. U.S.A. 45°0N 87°30W 80 C10
Green Bay U.S.A. 44°31N 88°0W 80 C9
Green C. Australia 37°13S 150°1E 63 F5
Green Cove Springs U.S.A. 29°59N 81°42W 85 G14
Green Lake Canada 54°17N 107°47W 71 C7
Green Mts. U.S.A. 43°45N 72°45W 83 C12
Green River Utah, U.S.A. 38°59N 110°10W 76 G8
Green River Wyo., U.S.A. 41°32N 109°28W 76 F9
Green Valley U.S.A. 31°52N 110°56W 77 L8
Greenbank U.S.A. 48°6N 122°34W 78 B4
Greenbush Mich., U.S.A. 44°35N 83°19W 82 B1
Greenbush Minn., U.S.A. 48°42N 96°11W 80 A5
Greencastle U.S.A. 39°38N 86°52W 80 F10
Greene U.S.A. 42°20N 75°46W 83 D9
Greeneville U.S.A. 36°10N 82°50W 85 C13
Greenfield Calif., U.S.A. 36°19N 121°15W 78 J5
Greenfield Calif., U.S.A. 35°15N 119°0W 79 K8
Greenfield Ind., U.S.A. 39°47N 85°46W 81 F11
Greenfield Iowa, U.S.A. 41°18N 94°28W 80 E6
Greenfield Mass., U.S.A. 42°35N 72°36W 83 D12
Greenfield Mo., U.S.A. 37°25N 93°51W 80 G7
Greenfield Park Canada 45°29N 73°28W 83 A11
Greenland ☒ N. Amer. 66°0N 45°0W 67 C15
Greenland Sea Arctic 73°0N 10°0W 4 B7
Greenock U.K. 55°57N 4°46W 11 F4
Greenore Ireland 54°2N 6°8W 10 B5
Greenore Pt. Ireland 52°14N 6°19W 10 D5
Greenough Australia 28°58S 114°43E 61 E1
Greenough → Australia 28°51S 114°38E 61 E1
Greenough Pt. Canada 44°58N 81°26W 82 B3
Greenport U.S.A. 41°6N 72°22W 83 E12
Greensboro Ga., U.S.A. 33°35N 83°11W 85 E13
Greensboro N.C., U.S.A. 36°4N 79°48W 85 C15
Greensboro Vt., U.S.A. 44°36N 72°18W 83 B12
Greensburg Ind., U.S.A. 39°20N 85°29W 81 F11
Greensburg Kans., U.S.A. 37°36N 99°18W 80 G4
Greensburg Pa., U.S.A. 40°18N 79°33W 82 F5
Greenstone Pt. U.K. 57°55N 5°37W 11 D3
Greenvale Australia 18°59S 145°7E 62 B4
Greenville Liberia 5°1N 9°6W 50 G4
Greenville Ala., U.S.A. 31°50N 86°38W 85 F11
Greenville Calif., U.S.A. 40°8N 120°57W 78 E6
Greenville Maine, U.S.A. 45°28N 69°35W 81 C19
Greenville Mich., U.S.A. 43°11N 85°15W 81 D11
Greenville Miss., U.S.A. 33°24N 91°4W 85 E9
Greenville Mo., U.S.A. 37°8N 90°27W 80 G8
Greenville N.C., U.S.A. 35°37N 77°23W 85 D16
Greenville N.H., U.S.A. 42°46N 71°49W 83 D13
Greenville N.Y., U.S.A. 42°25N 74°1W 83 D10
Greenville Ohio, U.S.A. 40°6N 84°38W 81 E11
Greenville Pa., U.S.A. 41°24N 80°23W 82 E4
Greenville S.C., U.S.A. 34°51N 82°24W 85 D13
Greenville Tex., U.S.A. 33°8N 96°7W 84 E6
Greenwater Lake ⌓ Canada 52°32N 103°30W 71 C8
Greenwich Conn., U.S.A. 41°2N 73°38W 83 E11
Greenwich N.Y., U.S.A. 43°5N 73°30W 83 C11
Greenwich Ohio, U.S.A. 41°2N 82°31W 82 E2
Greenwich □ U.K. 51°29N 0°1E 13 F8
Greenwood Canada 49°10N 118°40W 70 D5
Greenwood Ark., U.S.A. 35°13N 94°16W 84 D7
Greenwood Ind., U.S.A. 39°37N 86°7W 80 F10
Greenwood Miss., U.S.A. 33°31N 90°11W 85 E9
Greenwood S.C., U.S.A. 34°12N 82°10W 85 D13
Greenwood, Mt. Australia 13°48S 130°4E 60 B5
Gregory U.S.A. 43°14N 99°26W 80 D4
Gregory → Australia 17°53S 139°17E 62 B2
Gregory, L. S. Austral., Australia 28°55S 139°0E 63 D2
Gregory, L. W. Austral., Australia 20°0S 127°40E 60 D4
Gregory, L. W. Austral., Australia 25°38S 119°58E 61 E2
Gregory △ Australia 15°38S 131°15E 60 C5
Gregory Downs Australia 18°35S 138°45E 62 B2
Gregory Ra. Queens., Australia 19°30S 143°40E 62 B3
Gregory Ra. W. Austral., Australia 21°20S 121°12E 60 D3
Greifswald Germany 54°5N 13°23E 16 A7
Greiz Germany 50°39N 12°10E 16 C7
Gremikha Russia 67°59N 39°47E 18 A6
Grenaa Denmark 56°25N 10°53E 9 H14
Grenada U.S.A. 33°47N 89°49W 85 E10
Grenada ■ W. Indies 12°10N 61°40W 89 D7
Grenadier I. U.S.A. 44°3N 76°22W 83 B8
Grenadines, The St. Vincent 12°40N 61°20W 89 D7
Grenen Denmark 57°44N 10°40E 9 H14
Grenfell Australia 33°52S 148°8E 63 E4
Grenfell Canada 50°30N 102°56W 71 C8
Grenoble France 45°12N 5°42E 20 D6
Grenville, C. Australia 12°0S 143°13E 62 A3
Grenville Chan. Canada 53°40N 129°46W 70 C3
Gresham U.S.A. 45°30N 122°25W 78 E4
Gresik Indonesia 7°13S 112°38E 37 G15
Gretna U.K. 55°0N 3°3W 11 F5
Gretna U.S.A. 29°54N 90°3W 85 G9
Grevenmacher Lux. 49°41N 6°26E 15 E6
Grey → Canada 47°34N 57°6W 73 C8
Grey → N.Z. 42°27S 171°12E 59 E3
Grey, C. Australia 13°0S 136°35E 62 A2
Grey Ra. Australia 27°0S 143°30E 63 D3
Greybull U.S.A. 44°30N 108°3W 76 D9
Greymouth N.Z. 42°29S 171°13E 59 E3
Greystones Ireland 53°9N 6°5W 10 C5
Greytown N.Z. 41°5S 175°29E 59 D5
Greytown S. Africa 29°1S 30°36E 57 D5
Gribbell I. Canada 53°23N 129°0W 70 C3
Gridley U.S.A. 39°22N 121°42W 78 F5
Griekwastad S. Africa 28°49S 23°15E 56 D3
Griffin U.S.A. 33°15N 84°16W 85 E12
Griffith Australia 34°18S 146°2E 63 E4
Griffith Canada 45°15N 77°10W 82 A7
Griffith I. Canada 44°50N 80°55W 82 B4
Grimaylov = Hrymayliv Ukraine 49°20N 26°5E 17 D14
Grimes U.S.A. 39°4N 121°54W 78 F5
Grimsay U.K. 57°29N 7°14W 11 D1
Grimsby Canada 43°12N 79°34W 82 C5
Grimsby U.K. 53°34N 0°5W 12 D7
Grímsey Iceland 66°33N 17°58W 8 C5
Grimshaw Canada 56°10N 117°40W 70 B5
Grimstad Norway 58°20N 8°35E 9 G13
Grinnell U.S.A. 41°45N 92°43W 80 E7
Gris-Nez, C. France 50°52N 1°35E 20 A4
Grise Fiord Canada 76°25N 82°57W 69 B11
Groais I. Canada 50°55N 55°35W 73 B8
Groblersdal S. Africa 25°15S 29°25E 57 D4
Grodno = Hrodna Belarus 53°42N 23°52E 17 B12
Grodzyanka = Hrodzyanka Belarus 53°31N 28°42E 17 B15
Groesbeck U.S.A. 31°31N 96°32W 84 F6
Grójec Poland 51°50N 20°58E 17 C11
Grong Norway 64°25N 12°8E 8 D15
Groningen Neths. 53°15N 6°35E 15 A6
Groningen □ Neths. 53°16N 6°40E 15 A6
Groom U.S.A. 35°12N 101°6W 84 D4
Groot → S. Africa 33°45S 24°36E 56 E3
Groot-Berg → S. Africa 32°47S 18°8E 56 E2
Groot-Brakrivier S. Africa 34°2S 22°18E 56 E3
Groot Karasberge Namibia 27°20S 18°40E 56 D2
Groot-Kei → S. Africa 32°41S 28°22E 57 E4
Groot-Vis → S. Africa 33°28S 27°5E 56 E4
Grootdrink S. Africa 28°33S 21°42E 56 D3
Groote Eylandt Australia 14°0S 136°40E 62 A2
Grootfontein Namibia 19°31S 18°6E 56 B2
Grootlaagte → Africa 20°55S 21°27E 56 C3
Grootvloer → S. Africa 30°0S 20°40E 56 E3
Gros C. Canada 61°59N 113°32W 70 A6
Gros Islet St. Lucia 14°5N 60°58W 89 f
Gros Morne △ Canada 49°40N 57°50W 73 C8
Gros Piton St. Lucia 13°49N 61°5W 89 f
Gros Piton Pt. St. Lucia 13°49N 61°5W 89 f
Grossa, Pta. Spain 39°6N 1°36E 24 B8
Grosse Point U.S.A. 42°23N 82°54W 82 D2
Grosser Arber Germany 49°6N 13°8E 16 D7
Grosseto Italy 42°46N 11°8E 22 C4
Grossglockner Austria 47°5N 12°40E 16 E7
Groswater B. Canada 54°20N 57°40W 73 B8
Groton Conn., U.S.A. 41°21N 72°5W 83 E12
Groton N.Y., U.S.A. 42°36N 76°22W 83 D8
Groton S. Dak., U.S.A. 45°27N 98°6W 80 C4
Grouard Mission Canada 55°33N 116°9W 70 B5
Groundhog → Canada 48°45N 82°58W 72 C3
Grouw Neths. 53°5N 5°51E 15 A5
Grove City U.S.A. 41°10N 80°5W 82 E4
Grove Hill U.S.A. 31°42N 87°47W 85 F11
Groveland U.S.A. 37°50N 120°14W 78 H6
Grover Beach U.S.A. 35°7N 120°37W 79 K6
Groves U.S.A. 29°57N 93°54W 84 G8
Groveton U.S.A. 44°36N 71°31W 83 B13
Groznyy Russia 43°20N 45°45E 19 F8
Grudziądz Poland 53°30N 18°47E 17 B10
Gruinard B. U.K. 57°56N 5°35W 11 D3
Grundy Center U.S.A. 42°22N 92°47W 80 D7
Gruver U.S.A. 36°16N 101°24W 84 C4
Gryazi Russia 52°30N 39°58E 18 D6
Gryazovets Russia 58°50N 40°10E 18 C7
Grytviken S. Georgia 54°19S 36°33W 96 G9
Gua India 22°18N 85°20E 43 H11
Gua Musang Malaysia 4°53N 101°58E 39 K3
Guacanayabo, G. de Cuba 20°40N 77°20W 88 B4
Guachípas → Argentina 25°40S 65°30W 94 B2
Guadalajara Mexico 20°40N 103°20W 86 C4
Guadalajara Spain 40°37N 3°12W 21 B4
Guadalcanal Solomon Is. 9°32S 160°12E 58 B9
Guadales Argentina 34°30S 67°55W 94 C2
Guadalete → Spain 36°35N 6°13W 21 D2
Guadalquivir → Spain 36°47N 6°22W 21 D2
Guadalupe = Guadeloupe ☒ W. Indies 16°20N 61°40W 88 b
Guadalupe Mexico 32°4N 116°32W 79 N10
Guadalupe Zacatecas, Mexico 22°45N 102°31W 86 C4
Guadalupe U.S.A. 34°58N 120°34W 79 L6
Guadalupe → U.S.A. 28°27N 96°47W 84 G6
Guadalupe, Sierra de Spain 39°28N 5°30W 21 C3
Guadalupe Bravos Mexico 31°20N 106°10W 86 A3
Guadalupe I. Pac. Oc. 29°0N 118°50W 66 G8
Guadalupe Mts. △ U.S.A. 31°40N 104°30W 84 F2
Guadalupe Peak U.S.A. 31°50N 104°52W 84 F2
Guadalupe y Calvo Mexico 26°6N 106°58W 86 B3
Guadarrama, Sierra de Spain 41°0N 4°0W 21 B4
Guadeloupe ☒ W. Indies 16°20N 61°40W 88 b
Guadeloupe △ Guadeloupe 16°10N 61°40W 88 b
Guadeloupe Passage W. Indies 16°50N 62°15W 89 C7
Guadiana → Portugal 37°14N 7°22W 21 D2
Guadix Spain 37°18N 3°11W 21 D4
Guafo, Boca del Chile 43°35S 74°0W 96 E2
Guaico Trin. & Tob. 10°35N 61°9W 93 K15
Guainía → Colombia 2°1N 67°7W 92 C5
Guaíra Brazil 24°5S 54°10W 95 A5
Guaíra □ Paraguay 25°45S 56°30W 94 B4
Guaitecas, Is. Chile 44°0S 74°30W 96 E2
Guajará-Mirim Brazil 10°50S 65°20W 92 F5
Guajira, Pen. de la Colombia 12°0N 72°0W 92 A4
Gualán Guatemala 15°8N 89°22W 88 C2
Gualeguay Argentina 33°10S 59°14W 94 C4
Gualeguaychú Argentina 33°3S 59°31W 94 C4
Gualequay → Argentina 33°19S 59°39W 94 C4
Guam ☒ Pac. Oc. 13°27N 144°45E 64 F6
Guaminí Argentina 37°1S 62°28W 94 D3
Guamúchil Mexico 25°28N 108°6W 86 B3
Guana I. Br. Virgin Is. 18°30N 64°30W 89 e
Guanabacoa Cuba 23°8N 82°18W 88 B3
Guanacaste, Cordillera de Costa Rica 10°40N 85°4W 88 D2
Guanacaste △ Costa Rica 10°57N 85°30W 88 D2
Guanaceví Mexico 25°56N 105°57W 86 B3
Guanahani = San Salvador I. Bahamas 24°0N 74°40W 89 B5
Guanaja Honduras 16°30N 85°55W 88 C2
Guanajay Cuba 22°56N 82°42W 88 B3
Guanajuato Mexico 21°1N 101°15W 86 C4
Guanajuato □ Mexico 21°0N 101°0W 86 C4
Guandacol Argentina 29°30S 68°40W 94 B2
Guane Cuba 22°10N 84°7W 88 B3
Guangdong □ China 23°0N 113°0E 33 D6
Guangling China 39°47N 114°22E 34 E8
Guangrao China 37°5N 118°25E 35 F10
Guangwu China 37°48N 105°57E 34 F3
Guangxi Zhuangzu Zizhiqu □ China 24°0N 109°0E 33 D5
Guangzhou China 23°6N 113°13E 33 D6
Guanica Puerto Rico 17°58N 66°55W 89 d
Guanipa → Venezuela 9°56N 62°26W 92 B6
Guannan China 34°8N 119°21E 35 G10
Guantánamo Cuba 20°10N 75°14W 89 B4
Guantánamo B. Cuba 19°59N 75°10W 89 C4
Guantao China 36°42N 115°25E 34 F8
Guanyun China 34°20N 119°18E 35 G10
Guapay = Grande → Bolivia 15°51S 64°39W 92 G6
Guápiles Costa Rica 10°10N 83°46W 88 D3
Guapo B. Trin. & Tob. 10°12N 61°41W 93 K15
Guaporé Brazil 28°51S 51°54W 95 B5
Guaporé → Brazil 11°55S 65°4W 92 F5
Guaqui Bolivia 16°41S 68°54W 92 G5
Guaramacal △ Venezuela 9°13N 70°12W 89 E5
Guarapari Brazil 20°40S 40°30W 95 A7
Guarapuava Brazil 25°20S 51°30W 95 B5
Guaratinguetá Brazil 22°49S 45°9W 95 A6
Guaratuba Brazil 25°53S 48°38W 95 B6
Guarda Portugal 40°32N 7°20W 21 B2
Guardafui, C. = Asir, Ras Somali Rep. 11°55N 51°10E 47 E5
Guárico □ Venezuela 8°40N 66°35W 92 B5
Guarujá Brazil 24°2S 46°25W 95 A6
Guarulhos Brazil 23°29S 46°33W 95 A6
Guasave Mexico 25°34N 108°27W 86 B3
Guasdualito Venezuela 7°15N 70°44W 92 B4
Guatemala Guatemala 14°40N 90°22W 88 D1
Guatemala ■ Cent. Amer. 15°40N 90°30W 88 C1
Guatemala Basin Pac. Oc. 11°0N 95°0W 65 F18
Guatemala Trench Pac. Oc. 14°0N 95°0W 66 H10
Guatopo △ Venezuela 10°5N 66°30W 89 D6
Guatuaro Pt. Trin. & Tob. 10°19N 60°59W 93 K16
Guaviare → Colombia 4°3N 67°44W 92 C5
Guaxupé Brazil 21°10S 47°5W 95 A6
Guayaguayare Trin. & Tob. 10°8N 61°2W 93 K15
Guayama Puerto Rico 17°59N 66°7W 89 d
Guayaquil Ecuador 2°15S 79°52W 92 D3
Guayaquil Mexico 29°59N 115°4W 86 B1
Guayaquil, G. de Ecuador 3°10S 81°0W 92 D2
Guaymas Mexico 27°56N 110°54W 86 B2
Guba Dem. Rep. of the Congo 10°38S 26°27E 55 E2
Gubkin Russia 51°17N 37°32E 19 D6
Gubkinskiy Russia 64°27N 76°36E 28 C8
Gudbrandsdalen Norway 61°33N 10°10E 8 F14
Guddu Barrage Pakistan 28°30N 69°50E 42 E3
Gudur India 14°12N 79°55E 40 M11
Guecho = Getxo Spain 43°21N 2°59W 21 A4
Guékédou Guinea 8°40N 10°5W 50 G3
Guelmine = Goulimine Morocco 28°56N 10°0W 50 C3
Guelph Canada 43°35N 80°20W 82 C4
Guerara Algeria 32°51N 4°22E 50 B6
Guéret France 46°11N 1°51E 20 C4
Guerneville U.S.A. 38°30N 123°0W 78 G4
Guernica = Gernika-Lumo Spain 43°19N 2°40W 21 A4
Guernsey U.K. 49°26N 2°35W 13 H5
Guernsey U.S.A. 42°16N 104°45W 76 E11
Guerrero □ Mexico 17°40N 100°0W 87 D5
Gūgher Iran 29°28N 56°27E 45 D8
Guhakolak, Tanjung Indonesia 6°50S 105°14E 37 G11
Guia Canary Is. 28°8N 15°38W 24 F4
Guia de Isora Canary Is. 28°12N 16°46W 24 F3
Guia Lopes da Laguna Brazil 21°26S 56°7W 95 A4
Guiana Highlands S. Amer. 5°10N 60°40W 90 C4
Guidónia-Montecélio Italy 42°1N 12°45E 22 C5
Guijá Mozam. 24°27S 33°0E 57 C5
Guildford U.K. 51°14N 0°34W 13 F7
Guilford U.S.A. 41°17N 72°41W 83 E12
Guilin China 25°18N 110°15E 33 D6
Guillaume-Delisle, L. Canada 56°15N 76°17W 72 A4
Güímar Canary Is. 28°18N 16°24W 24 F3
Guimarães Portugal 41°28N 8°24W 21 B1
Guimaras □ Phil. 10°35N 122°37E 37 B6
Guinda U.S.A. 38°50N 122°12W 78 G4
Guinea Africa 8°0N 8°0E 48 F4
Guinea ■ W. Afr. 10°20N 11°30W 50 F3
Guinea, Gulf of Atl. Oc. 3°0N 2°30E 49 F4
Guinea-Bissau ■ Africa 12°0N 15°0W 50 F3
Güines Cuba 22°50N 82°0W 88 B3
Guingamp France 48°34N 3°10W 20 B2
Güiria Venezuela 10°32N 62°18W 92 A6
Guiuan Phil. 11°5N 125°55E 37 B7
Guiyang China 26°32N 106°40E 32 D5
Guizhou □ China 27°0N 107°0E 32 D5
Gujar Khan Pakistan 33°16N 73°19E 42 C5
Gujarat □ India 23°20N 71°0E 42 H4
Gujranwala Pakistan 32°10N 74°12E 42 C6
Gujrat Pakistan 32°40N 74°2E 42 C6
Gulbarga India 17°20N 76°50E 40 L10
Gulbene Latvia 57°8N 26°52E 9 H22
Gulf, The = Persian Gulf Asia 27°0N 50°0E 45 E6
Gulf Islands ⌓ U.S.A. 30°10N 87°10W 85 F11
Gulfport U.S.A. 30°22N 89°6W 85 F10
Gulgong Australia 32°20S 149°49E 63 E4
Gulistan Pakistan 30°30N 66°35E 42 D2
Gulja = Yining China 43°58N 81°10E 32 B3
Gull Lake Canada 50°10N 108°29W 71 C7
Güllük Turkey 37°14N 27°35E 23 F12
Gulmarg India 34°3N 74°25E 43 B6
Gülshat Kazakhstan 46°38N 74°21E 28 C8
Gulu Uganda 2°48N 32°17E 54 B3
Gulwe Tanzania 6°30S 36°25E 54 D4
Gumal → Pakistan 31°40N 71°50E 42 D4
Gumbaz Pakistan 30°2N 69°0E 42 D3
Gumel Nigeria 12°39N 9°22E 50 F7
Gumi S. Korea 36°10N 128°12E 35 F15
Gumla India 23°3N 84°33E 43 H11
Gumlu Australia 19°53S 147°41E 62 B4
Gumma □ Japan 36°30N 138°20E 31 F9
Gumzai Indonesia 5°28S 134°42E 37 F8
Guna India 24°40N 77°19E 42 G7
Gunbalanya Australia 12°20S 133°4E 60 B5
Gundabooka △ Australia 30°30S 145°20E 63 E4
Gunisao → Canada 53°56N 97°53W 71 C9
Gunisao L. Canada 53°33N 96°15W 71 C9
Gunjyal Pakistan 32°20N 71°55E 42 C4
Gunnbjørn Fjeld Greenland 68°55N 29°47W 4 C6
Gunnedah Australia 30°59S 150°15E 63 E5
Gunnewin Australia 25°59S 148°33E 63 D4
Gunningbar Cr. → Australia 31°14S 147°6E 63 E4
Gunnison Colo., U.S.A. 38°33N 106°56W 76 G10
Gunnison Utah, U.S.A. 39°9N 111°49W 76 G8
Gunnison → U.S.A. 39°4N 108°35W 76 G9
Gunpowder Australia 19°42S 139°22E 62 B2
Gunsan S. Korea 35°59N 126°45E 35 G14
Guntakal India 15°11N 77°27E 40 M10
Gunter Canada 44°52N 77°32W 82 B7
Guntersville U.S.A. 34°21N 86°18W 85 D11
Guntong Malaysia 4°36N 101°3E 39 K3
Guntur India 16°23N 80°30E 41 L12
Gunungapi Indonesia 6°45S 126°30E 37 F7
Gunungsitoli Indonesia 1°15N 97°30E 36 D1
Gunza Angola 10°50S 13°50E 52 G2
Guo He → China 32°59N 117°10E 35 H9
Guoyang China 33°32N 116°12E 34 H9
Gupis Pakistan 36°15N 73°20E 43 A5
Gurbantünggüt Shamo China 45°8N 87°20E 32 B3
Gurdaspur India 32°5N 75°31E 42 C6
Gurdon U.S.A. 33°55N 93°9W 84 E8
Gurgaon India 28°27N 77°1E 42 E7
Gurgueia → Brazil 6°50S 43°24W 93 E10
Gurha India 25°12N 71°39E 42 G4
Guri, Embalse de Venezuela 7°50N 62°52W 92 B6
Gurkha Nepal 28°5N 84°40E 43 E11
Gurla Mandhata = Naimona'nyi Feng Nepal 30°26N 81°18E 43 D9
Gurley Australia 29°45S 149°48E 63 D4
Gurnet Point U.S.A. 42°1N 70°34W 83 D14
Guro Mozam. 17°26S 32°30E 55 F3
Gurué Mozam. 15°25S 36°58E 55 F4
Gurun Malaysia 5°49N 100°27E 39 K3
Gürün Turkey 38°43N 37°15E 19 G6
Gurupá Brazil 1°25S 51°35W 93 D8
Gurupá, I. Grande de Brazil 1°25S 51°45W 93 D8
Gurupi Brazil 11°43S 49°4W 93 F9
Gurupi → Brazil 1°13S 46°6W 93 D9
Guruwe Zimbabwe 16°40S 30°42E 57 B5
Gurvan Sayhan Uul Mongolia 43°50N 104°0E 32 B5
Guryev = Atyraū Kazakhstan 47°5N 52°0E 19 E9
Gusau Nigeria 12°12N 6°40E 50 F7
Gushan China 39°50N 123°35E 35 E12
Gushgy = Serhetabat Turkmenistan 35°20N 62°18E 45 C9
Gusinoozersk Russia 51°16N 106°27E 29 D11
Gustavus U.S.A. 58°25N 135°44W 70 B1
Gustine U.S.A. 37°16N 121°0W 78 H6
Güstrow Germany 53°47N 12°10E 16 B7
Gütersloh Germany 51°54N 8°24E 16 C5
Gutha Australia 28°58S 115°55E 61 E2
Guthalungra Australia 19°52S 147°50E 62 B4
Guthrie Canada 44°28N 79°32W 82 B5
Guthrie Okla., U.S.A. 35°53N 97°25W 84 D6
Guthrie Tex., U.S.A. 33°37N 100°19W 84 E4
Guttenberg U.S.A. 42°47N 91°6W 80 D8
Gutu Zimbabwe 19°41S 31°9E 57 B5
Guwahati India 26°10N 91°45E 41 F17
Guy Fawkes River △ Australia 30°0S 152°20E 63 D5
Guyana ■ S. Amer. 5°0N 59°0W 92 C7
Guyane française = French Guiana ☒ S. Amer. 4°0N 53°0W 93 C8
Guyang China 41°0N 110°5E 34 D6
Guyenne France 44°30N 0°40E 20 D4
Guymon U.S.A. 36°41N 101°29W 84 C4
Guyra Australia 30°15S 151°40E 63 E5
Guyuan Hebei, China 41°37N 115°40E 34 D8
Guyuan Ningxia Huizu, China 36°0N 106°20E 34 F4
Güzelyurt = Morphou Cyprus 35°12N 32°59E 25 D11
Guzhen China 33°22N 117°18E 35 H9
Guzmán, L. de Mexico 31°20N 107°30W 86 A3
Gwa Burma 17°36N 94°34E 41 L19
Gwaai Zimbabwe 19°15S 27°45E 55 F2
Gwaai → Zimbabwe 17°59S 26°52E 55 F2
Gwabegar Australia 30°37S 148°59E 63 E4
Gwādar Pakistan 25°10N 62°18E 40 G3
Gwaii Haanas △ Canada 52°21N 131°26W 70 C2
Gwalior India 26°12N 78°10E 42 F8
Gwanda Zimbabwe 20°55S 29°0E 55 G2
Gwane Dem. Rep. of the Congo 4°45N 25°48E 54 B2
Gwangju S. Korea 35°9N 126°54E 35 G14
Gwanju = Gwangju S. Korea 35°9N 126°54E 35 G14
Gweebarra B. Ireland 54°51N 8°23W 10 B3
Gweedore Ireland 55°3N 8°13W 10 A3
Gweru Zimbabwe 19°28S 29°45E 55 F2
Gwinn U.S.A. 46°19N 87°27W 80 B10
Gwydir → Australia 29°27S 149°48E 63 D4
Gwynedd □ U.K. 52°52N 4°10W 12 E3
Gyandzha = Gäncä Azerbaijan 40°45N 46°20E 19 F8
Gyaring Hu China 34°50N 97°40E 32 C4
Gydanskiy Poluostrov Russia 70°0N 78°0E 28 C8
Gyeongju S. Korea 35°51N 129°14E 35 G15
Gympie Australia 26°11S 152°38E 63 D5
Gyöngyös Hungary 47°48N 19°56E 17 E10
Győr Hungary 47°41N 17°40E 17 E9
Gypsum Pt. Canada 61°53N 114°35W 70 A6
Gypsumville Canada 51°45N 98°40W 71 C9
Gyula Hungary 46°38N 21°17E 17 E11
Gyumri Armenia 40°47N 43°50E 19 F7
Gyzylarbat = Serdar Turkmenistan 39°4N 56°23E 45 B8
Gyzyletrek = Etrek Turkmenistan 37°36N 54°46E 45 B7

H

Ha 'Arava → Israel 30°50N 35°20E 46 E4
Ha Coi Vietnam 21°26N 107°46E 38 B6
Ha Dong Vietnam 20°58N 105°46E 38 B5
Ha Giang Vietnam 22°50N 104°59E 38 A5
Ha Karmel △ Israel 32°45N 35°5E 46 C4
Ha Long, Vinh Vietnam 20°56N 107°3E 38 B6
Ha Tien Vietnam 10°23N 104°29E 39 G5
Ha Tinh Vietnam 18°20N 105°54E 38 C5
Ha Trung Vietnam 19°58N 105°50E 38 C5
Haaksbergen Neths. 52°9N 6°45E 15 B6
Ha'ano Tonga 19°41S 174°18W 59 c
Ha'apai Group Tonga 19°47S 174°27W 59 c
Haapiti Moorea 17°34S 149°52W 59 d
Haapsalu Estonia 58°56N 23°30E 9 G20
Haarlem Neths. 52°23N 4°39E 15 B4
Haast → N.Z. 43°50S 169°2E 59 E2
Haast Bluff Australia 23°22S 132°0E 60 D5
Hab → Pakistan 24°53N 66°41E 42 G3
Hab Nadi Chauki Pakistan 25°0N 66°50E 42 G2
Habahe China 48°3N 86°23E 32 B3

Habaswein Kenya 1°2N 39°30E 54 B4
Habay Canada 58°50N 118°44W 70 B5
Ḥabbānīyah Iraq 33°17N 43°29E 44 C4
Haboro Japan 44°22N 141°42E 30 B10
Ḥabshān U.A.E. 23°50N 53°37E 45 F7
Hachijō-Jima Japan 33°5N 139°45E 31 H9
Hachinohe Japan 40°30N 141°29E 30 D10
Hachiōji Japan 35°40N 139°20E 31 G9
Hackensack U.S.A. 40°52N 74°4W 83 F10
Hackettstown U.S.A. 40°51N 74°50W 83 F10
Hadali Pakistan 32°16N 72°11E 42 C5
Hadarba, Ras Sudan 22°4N 36°51E 51 D13
Hadarom □ Israel 31°0N 35°0E 46 E4
Ḥadd, Ra's al Oman 22°35N 59°50E 47 C6
Haddington U.K. 55°57N 2°47W 11 F6
Hadejia Nigeria 12°30N 10°5E 50 F7
Hadera Israel 32°27N 34°55E 46 C3
Hadera, N. → Israel 32°28N 34°52E 46 C3
Haderslev Denmark 55°15N 9°30E 9 J13
Hadhramaut = Ḥaḍramawt
  Yemen 15°30N 49°30E 47 D4
Hadīboh Yemen 12°39N 54°2E 47 E5
Hadong S. Korea 35°5N 127°44E 35 G14
Ḥaḍramawt Yemen 15°30N 49°30E 47 D4
Ḥadrānīyah Iraq 35°38N 43°14E 44 C4
Hadrian's Wall U.K. 55°0N 2°30W 12 B5
Hae, Ko Thailand 7°44N 98°22E 39 a
Haeju N. Korea 38°3N 125°45E 35 E13
Haenam S. Korea 34°34N 126°35E 35 G14
Haenertsburg S. Africa 24°0S 29°50E 57 C4
Haerhpin = Harbin
  China 45°48N 126°40E 35 B14
Hafar al Bāṭin Si. Arabia 28°32N 45°52E 44 D5
Hafirat al 'Aydā
  Si. Arabia 26°26N 39°12E 44 E3
Ḥafit Oman 23°59N 55°49E 45 F7
Hafizabad Pakistan 32°5N 73°40E 42 C5
Haflong India 25°10N 93°5E 41 G18
Haft Gel Iran 31°30N 49°32E 45 D6
Hagalil Israel 32°53N 35°18E 46 C4
Hagen Germany 51°21N 7°27E 16 C4
Hagerman U.S.A. 33°7N 104°20W 77 K11
Hagerman Fossil Beds △
  U.S.A. 42°48N 114°57W 76 E6
Hagerstown U.S.A. 39°39N 77°43W 81 F15
Hagersville Canada 42°58N 80°3W 82 D4
Hagfors Sweden 60°3N 13°45E 9 F15
Hagi Japan 34°30N 131°22E 31 G5
Hagolan Syria 33°0N 35°45E 46 C4
Hagondange France 49°16N 6°11E 20 B7
Hags Hd. Ireland 52°57N 9°28W 10 D2
Hague, C. de la France 49°44N 1°56W 20 B3
Hague, The = 's-Gravenhage
  Neths. 52°7N 4°17E 15 B4
Haguenau France 48°49N 7°47E 20 B7
Hai Duong Vietnam 20°56N 106°19E 38 B6
Haicheng China 40°50N 122°45E 35 D12
Haidar Khel Afghan. 33°58N 68°38E 42 C3
Haidarâbâd = Hyderabad
  India 17°22N 78°29E 40 L11
Haidargarh India 26°37N 81°22E 43 F9
Haifa = Ḥefa Israel 32°46N 35°0E 46 C4
Haikou China 20°1N 110°16E 38 B8
Ḥā'il □ Si. Arabia 26°40N 41°40E 44 E4
Hailar China 49°10N 119°38E 33 B6
Hailey U.S.A. 43°31N 114°19W 76 E6
Haileybury Canada 47°30N 79°38W 72 C4
Hailin China 44°37N 129°30E 35 B15
Hailuoto Finland 65°3N 24°45E 8 D21
Hainan □ China 19°0N 109°30E 38 C7
Hainan Dao China 19°0N 109°30E 38 C7
Hainan Str. = Qiongzhou Haixia
  China 20°10N 110°15E 38 B8
Hainaut □ Belgium 50°30N 4°0E 15 D4
Haines Alaska, U.S.A. 59°14N 135°26W 70 B1
Haines Oreg., U.S.A. 44°55N 117°56W 76 D5
Haines City U.S.A. 28°7N 81°38W 85 G14
Haines Junction
  Canada 60°45N 137°30W 70 A1
Haiphong Vietnam 20°47N 106°41E 38 B6
Haiti ■ W. Indies 19°0N 72°30W 89 C5
Haiya Sudan 18°20N 36°21E 51 E13
Haiyan China 36°53N 100°59E 32 C5
Haiyang China 36°47N 121°9E 35 F11
Haiyuan China 36°35N 105°52E 34 F3
Haizhou China 34°37N 119°7E 35 G10
Haizhou Wan China 34°50N 119°20E 35 G10
Haj Ali Qoli, Kavīr Iran 35°55N 54°50E 45 C7
Hajdúböszörmény
  Hungary 47°40N 21°30E 17 E11
Haji Ibrahim Iraq 36°40N 44°30E 44 B5
Hājjīābād Iran 33°37N 60°0E 45 C9
Hajipur India 25°45N 85°13E 43 G11
Hajjah Yemen 15°42N 43°36E 47 D3
Ḥājjīābād Iran 28°19N 55°55E 45 D7
Ḥājjīābād-e Zarrīn Iran 33°9N 54°51E 45 C7
Hajnówka Poland 52°47N 23°35E 17 B12
Hakansson, Mts.
  Dem. Rep. of the Congo 8°40S 25°45E 55 D2
Hakkâri Turkey 37°34N 43°44E 44 B4
Hakken-Zan Japan 34°10N 135°54E 31 G7
Hakodate Japan 41°45N 140°44E 30 D10
Hakos Namibia 23°13S 16°21E 56 C2
Haku-San Japan 36°9N 136°46E 31 F8
Haku-San △ Japan 36°15N 136°45E 31 F8
Hakui Japan 36°53N 136°47E 31 F8
Hala Pakistan 25°43N 68°20E 40 G6
Halab Syria 36°10N 37°15E 44 B3
Halabjah Iraq 35°10N 45°58E 44 C5
Halaib Sudan 22°12N 36°30E 51 D13
Halaib Triangle Africa 22°30N 35°20E 51 D13
Ḥalāt 'Ammār Si. Arabia 29°10N 36°4E 44 D3
Halberstadt Germany 51°54N 11°3E 16 C6
Halcombe N.Z. 40°8S 175°30E 59 D5
Halcon Phil. 13°0N 121°30E 37 B6
Halde Fjäll = Haltiatunturi
  Finland 69°17N 21°18E 8 B19

Halden Norway 59°9N 11°23E 9 G14
Haldia Bangla. 22°1N 88°3E 43 H13
Haldwani India 29°31N 79°30E 43 E8
Hale → Australia 24°56S 135°53E 62 C2
Halesowen U.K. 52°27N 2°3W 13 E5
Halesworth U.K. 52°20N 1°31E 13 E9
Haleyville U.S.A. 34°14N 87°37W 85 D11
Half Dome U.S.A. 37°44N 119°32E 78 H7
Halfmoon Bay N.Z. 46°50S 168°5E 59 G2
Halfway → Canada 56°12N 121°32W 70 B4
Halia India 24°50N 82°19E 43 G10
Haliburton Canada 45°3N 78°30W 82 A6
Halifax Australia 18°32S 146°22E 62 B4
Halifax Canada 44°38N 63°35W 73 D7
Halifax U.K. 53°43N 1°52W 12 D6
Halifax U.S.A. 40°25N 76°55W 82 F8
Halifax B. Australia 18°50S 147°0E 62 B4
Halifax I. Namibia 26°38S 15°4E 56 D2
Halīl → Iran 27°40N 58°30E 45 E8
Halkida Greece 38°27N 23°42E 23 E10
Halkirk U.K. 58°30N 3°29W 11 C5
Hall Beach = Sanirajak
  Canada 68°46N 81°12W 69 C11
Hall Pen. Canada 63°30N 66°0W 69 C13
Hall Pt. Australia 15°40S 124°23E 60 C3
Halland Sweden 57°8N 12°47E 9 H15
Hallāniyat, Jazā'ir al
  Oman 17°30N 55°58E 47 D6
Hallasan S. Korea 33°22N 126°32E 35 H14
Halle Belgium 50°44N 4°13E 15 D4
Halle Germany 51°30N 11°56E 16 C6
Hällefors Sweden 59°47N 14°31E 9 G16
Hallett Australia 33°25S 138°55E 63 E2
Hallettsville U.S.A. 29°27N 96°57W 84 G6
Halley Antarctica 75°35S 26°39W 5 D1
Hallim S. Korea 33°24N 126°15E 35 H14
Hallingdalselva →
  Norway 60°23N 9°35E 8 F13
Hallock U.S.A. 48°47N 96°57W 80 A5
Halls Creek Australia 18°16S 127°38E 60 C4
Halls Gap Australia 37°8S 142°34E 63 F3
Halls Lake Canada 45°7N 78°45W 82 A6
Hallsberg Sweden 59°5N 15°7E 9 G16
Hallstead U.S.A. 41°58N 75°45W 83 E9
Halmahera Indonesia 0°40N 128°0E 37 D7
Halmstad Sweden 56°41N 12°52E 9 H15
Hälsingborg = Helsingborg
  Sweden 56°3N 12°42E 9 H15
Hälsingland Sweden 61°40N 16°5E 8 F17
Halstead U.K. 51°57N 0°40E 13 F8
Halton □ U.K. 53°22N 2°45W 12 D5
Haltwhistle U.K. 54°58N 2°26W 12 C5
Ḥālūl Qatar 25°40N 52°40E 45 E7
Halvad India 23°1N 71°11E 42 H4
Halvān Iran 33°57N 56°15E 45 C8
Ham Tan Vietnam 10°40N 107°45E 39 G6
Ham Yen Vietnam 22°4N 105°3E 38 A5
Hamab Namibia 28°7S 19°16E 56 D2
Hamada Japan 34°56N 132°4E 31 G6
Hamadān Iran 34°52N 48°32E 45 C6
Hamadān □ Iran 35°0N 49°0E 45 C6
Hamāh Syria 35°5N 36°40E 44 C3
Hamamatsu Japan 34°45N 137°45E 31 G8
Hamar Norway 60°48N 11°7E 8 F14
Hamâta, Gebel Egypt 24°17N 35°0E 44 E2
Hambantota Sri Lanka 6°10N 81°10E 40 R12
Hamber △ Canada 52°20N 118°0W 70 C5
Hamburg Germany 53°33N 9°59E 16 B5
Hamburg Ark., U.S.A. 33°14N 91°48W 84 E9
Hamburg N.Y., U.S.A. 42°43N 78°50W 82 D6
Hamburg Pa., U.S.A. 40°33N 75°59W 83 F9
Ḥamḍ, W. al →
  Si. Arabia 24°55N 36°20E 44 E3
Hamden U.S.A. 41°23N 72°54W 83 E12
Häme Finland 61°38N 25°10E 8 F21
Hämeenlinna Finland 61°0N 24°28E 8 F21
Hamelin Pool Australia 26°22S 114°20E 61 E1
Hameln Germany 52°6N 9°21E 16 B5
Hamerkaz □ Israel 32°15N 34°55E 46 C3
Hamersley Ra. Australia 22°0S 117°45E 60 D2
Hamhŭng N. Korea 39°54N 127°30E 35 E14
Hami China 42°55N 93°25E 32 B4
Hamilton Australia 37°45S 142°2E 63 F3
Hamilton Canada 43°15N 79°50W 82 C5
Hamilton N.Z. 37°47S 175°19E 59 B5
Hamilton U.K. 55°46N 4°2W 11 F4
Hamilton Ala., U.S.A. 34°9N 87°59W 85 D11
Hamilton Mont., U.S.A. 46°15N 114°10W 76 C6
Hamilton N.Y., U.S.A. 42°50N 75°33W 83 D9
Hamilton Ohio, U.S.A. 39°24N 84°34W 81 F11
Hamilton Tex., U.S.A. 31°42N 98°7W 84 F5
Hamilton → Queens.,
  Australia 23°30S 139°47E 62 C2
Hamilton → S. Austral.,
  Australia 26°40S 135°19E 63 D2
Hamilton City U.S.A. 39°45N 122°1W 78 F4
Hamilton I. Australia 20°21S 148°56E 62 J6
Hamilton Inlet Canada 54°0N 57°30W 73 B8
Hamina Finland 60°34N 27°12E 8 F22
Hamirpur H.P., India 31°41N 76°31E 42 D7
Hamirpur Ut. P., India 25°57N 80°9E 43 G9
Hamju N. Korea 39°51N 127°26E 35 E14
Hamlet U.S.A. 34°53N 79°42W 85 D15
Hamley Bridge Australia 34°17S 138°35E 63 E2
Hamlin = Hameln
  Germany 52°6N 9°21E 16 B5
Hamlin N.Y., U.S.A. 43°17N 77°55W 82 C7
Hamlin Tex., U.S.A. 32°53N 100°8W 84 E4
Hamm Germany 51°48N 7°58E 16 C4
Hammār, Hawr al Iraq 30°50N 47°10E 44 D5
Hammerfest Norway 70°39N 23°41E 8 A20
Hammond Ind., U.S.A. 41°38N 87°30W 80 E10
Hammond La., U.S.A. 30°30N 90°28W 85 F9
Hammond N.Y., U.S.A. 44°27N 75°42W 83 B9
Hammondsport U.S.A. 42°25N 77°13W 82 D7

Hammonton U.S.A. 39°39N 74°48W 81 F16
Hampden N.Z. 45°18S 170°50E 59 F3
Hampshire □ U.K. 51°7N 1°23W 13 F6
Hampshire Downs U.K. 51°15N 1°10W 13 F6
Hampton N.B., Canada 45°32N 65°51W 73 C6
Hampton Ont., Canada 43°58N 78°45W 82 C6
Hampton Ark., U.S.A. 33°32N 92°28W 84 E8
Hampton Iowa, U.S.A. 42°45N 93°13W 80 D7
Hampton N.H., U.S.A. 42°57N 70°50W 83 D14
Hampton S.C., U.S.A. 32°52N 81°7W 85 E14
Hampton Va., U.S.A. 37°2N 76°21W 81 G15
Hampton Bays U.S.A. 40°53N 72°30W 83 F12
Hampton Tableland
  Australia 32°0S 127°0E 61 F4
Hamyang S. Korea 35°32N 127°42E 35 G14
Han Pijesak Bos.-H. 44°5N 18°57E 23 B8
Hanak Si. Arabia 25°32N 37°0E 44 E3
Hanamaki Japan 39°23N 141°7E 30 E10
Hanang Tanzania 4°30S 35°25E 54 C4
Hanau Germany 50°7N 8°56E 16 C5
Hanbogd = Ihbulag
  Mongolia 43°11N 107°10E 34 C4
Hancheng China 35°31N 110°25E 34 G6
Hancock Mich., U.S.A. 47°8N 88°35W 80 B9
Hancock N.Y., U.S.A. 41°57N 75°17W 83 E9
Hancock Vt., U.S.A. 43°55N 72°50W 83 C12
Handa Japan 34°53N 136°55E 31 G8
Handa I. U.K. 58°23N 5°11W 11 C3
Handan China 36°35N 114°28E 34 F8
Handeni Tanzania 5°25S 38°2E 54 D4
Handwara India 34°21N 74°20E 43 B6
Hanegev Israel 30°50N 35°0E 46 E4
Hanford U.S.A. 36°20N 119°39W 78 J7
Hanford Reach △
  U.S.A. 46°40N 119°30W 76 C4
Hang Chat Thailand 18°20N 99°21E 38 C2
Hang Dong Thailand 18°41N 98°55E 38 C2
Hangang → S. Korea 37°50N 126°30E 35 F14
Hangayn Nuruu Mongolia 47°30N 99°0E 32 B4
Hangchou = Hangzhou
  China 30°18N 120°11E 33 C7
Hanggin Houqi China 40°58N 107°4E 34 D4
Hanggin Qi China 39°52N 108°50E 34 E5
Hangu China 39°18N 117°53E 35 E9
Hangzhou China 30°18N 120°11E 33 C7
Hangzhou Wan China 30°15N 120°45E 33 C7
Hanhongor Mongolia 43°55N 104°28E 34 C3
Hania = Chania Greece 35°30N 24°4E 25 D6
Ḥanīdh Si. Arabia 26°35N 48°38E 45 E6
Hankinson U.S.A. 46°4N 96°54W 80 B5
Hankö Finland 59°50N 22°57E 9 G20
Hanksville U.S.A. 38°22N 110°43W 76 G8
Hanle India 32°42N 79°4E 43 C8
Hanmer Springs N.Z. 42°32S 172°50E 59 E4
Hann → Australia 17°26S 126°17E 60 C4
Hann, Mt. Australia 15°45S 126°0E 60 C4
Hanna Canada 51°40N 111°54W 70 C6
Hanna U.S.A. 41°52N 106°34W 76 F10
Hannah B. Canada 51°40N 80°0W 72 B4
Hannibal Mo., U.S.A. 39°42N 91°22W 80 F8
Hannibal N.Y., U.S.A. 43°19N 76°35W 83 C8
Hannover Germany 52°22N 9°46E 16 B5
Hanoi Vietnam 21°5N 105°55E 38 B5
Hanover = Hannover
  Germany 52°22N 9°46E 16 B5
Hanover Canada 44°9N 81°2W 82 B3
Hanover S. Africa 31°4S 24°29E 56 E3
Hanover N.H., U.S.A. 43°42N 72°17W 83 C12
Hanover Ohio, U.S.A. 40°4N 82°16W 82 F2
Hanover Pa., U.S.A. 39°48N 76°59W 83 G8
Hanover, I. Chile 51°0S 74°50W 96 G2
Hans Lollik I.
  U.S. Virgin Is. 18°24N 64°53W 89 e
Hansdiha India 24°36N 87°5E 43 G12
Hansi H.P., India 32°27N 77°50E 42 C7
Hansi Haryana, India 29°10N 75°57E 42 E6
Hanson, L. Australia 31°0S 136°15E 63 E2
Hantsavichy Belarus 52°49N 26°30E 17 B14
Hanumangarh India 29°35N 74°19E 42 E6
Hanzhong China 33°10N 107°1E 34 H4
Hanzhuang China 34°33N 117°23E 35 G9
Haora India 22°34N 88°18E 43 H13
Haparanda Sweden 65°52N 24°8E 8 D21
Happy Camp U.S.A. 41°48N 123°23W 76 F2
Happy Valley-Goose Bay
  Canada 53°15N 60°20W 73 B7
Hapsu N. Korea 41°13N 128°51E 35 D15
Hapur India 28°45N 77°45E 42 E7
Ḥaql Si. Arabia 29°10N 34°58E 46 F3
Har Indonesia 5°16S 133°14E 37 F8
Har-Ayrag Mongolia 45°47N 109°16E 34 B5
Har Hu China 38°20N 97°38E 32 C4
Har Us Nuur Mongolia 48°0N 92°0E 32 B4
Har Yehuda Israel 31°35N 34°57E 46 D3
Ḥaraḍ Si. Arabia 24°22N 49°0E 47 C4
Haramosh Pakistan 35°50N 74°54E 43 B6
Haranomachi Japan 37°38N 140°58E 30 F10
Harare Zimbabwe 17°43S 31°2E 55 F3
Harazé Chad 9°57N 20°48E 51 G10
Harbin China 45°48N 126°40E 35 B14
Harbor Beach U.S.A. 43°51N 82°39W 82 C2
Harborcreek U.S.A. 42°9N 79°57W 82 D5
Harbour Breton Canada 47°29N 55°50W 73 C8
Harbour Deep Canada 50°25N 56°32W 73 B8
Harda India 22°27N 77°5E 42 H7
Hardangerfjorden Norway 60°5N 6°0E 9 F12
Hardangervidda Norway 60°7N 7°20E 8 F12
Hardap □ Namibia 24°9S 18°0E 56 C2
Hardap Dam Namibia 24°32S 17°50E 56 C2
Hardenberg Neths. 52°34N 6°37E 15 B6
Harderwijk Neths. 52°21N 5°38E 15 B5
Hardey → Australia 22°45S 116°8E 60 D2
Hardin U.S.A. 45°44N 107°37W 76 D10
Harding S. Africa 30°35S 29°55E 57 E4

Harding Ra. Australia 16°17S 124°55E 60 C3
Hardisty Canada 52°40N 111°18W 70 C6
Hardoi India 27°26N 80°6E 43 F9
Hardwar = Haridwar
  India 29°58N 78°9E 42 E8
Hardwick U.S.A. 44°30N 72°22W 83 B12
Hardwood Lake Canada 45°12N 77°26W 82 A7
Hardy, Pen. Chile 55°30S 68°20W 96 H3
Hardy, Pte. St. Lucia 14°6N 60°56W 89 f
Hare B. Canada 51°15N 55°45W 73 B8
Hareid Norway 62°22N 6°1E 8 E12
Harer Ethiopia 9°20N 42°8E 47 F3
Hargeisa Somali Rep. 9°30N 44°2E 47 F3
Hari → Indonesia 1°16S 104°5E 36 E2
Haria Canary Is. 29°8N 13°32W 24 E6
Haridwar India 29°58N 78°9E 42 E8
Harim, Jabal al Oman 25°58N 56°14E 45 E8
Haringhata → Bangla. 22°0N 89°58E 41 J16
Harīr, W. al → Syria 32°44N 35°59E 46 C4
Harīrūd → Asia 37°24N 60°38E 45 B9
Härjedalen Sweden 62°22N 13°5E 8 E15
Harlan Iowa, U.S.A. 41°39N 95°19W 80 E6
Harlan Ky., U.S.A. 36°51N 83°19W 81 G12
Harlech U.K. 52°52N 4°6W 12 E3
Harlem U.S.A. 48°32N 108°47W 76 B9
Harlingen Neths. 53°11N 5°25E 15 A5
Harlingen U.S.A. 26°12N 97°42W 84 M6
Harlow U.K. 51°46N 0°8E 13 F8
Harlowton U.S.A. 46°26N 109°50W 76 C9
Harnai Pakistan 30°6N 67°56E 42 D2
Harney Basin U.S.A. 43°0N 119°30W 76 E4
Harney L. U.S.A. 43°14N 119°8W 76 E4
Harney Peak U.S.A. 43°52N 103°32W 80 D2
Härnösand Sweden 62°38N 17°55E 8 E17
Haroldswick U.K. 60°48N 0°50W 11 A8
Harp L. Canada 55°5N 61°50W 73 A7
Harper Liberia 4°25N 7°43W 50 H4
Harrai India 22°37N 79°13E 43 H8
Harrand Pakistan 29°28N 70°3E 42 E4
Harricana → Canada 50°56N 79°32W 72 B4
Harriman U.S.A. 35°56N 84°33W 85 D12
Harrington Harbour
  Canada 50°31N 59°30W 73 B8
Harris U.K. 57°50N 6°55W 11 D2
Harris, L. Australia 31°10S 135°10E 63 E2
Harris, Sd. of U.K. 57°44N 7°6W 11 D1
Harris Pt. Canada 43°6N 82°9W 82 C2
Harrisburg Ill., U.S.A. 37°44N 88°32W 80 G9
Harrisburg Nebr.,
  U.S.A. 41°33N 103°44W 80 E2
Harrisburg Pa., U.S.A. 40°16N 76°53W 82 F8
Harrismith S. Africa 28°15S 29°8E 57 D4
Harrison Ark., U.S.A. 36°14N 93°7W 84 C8
Harrison Maine, U.S.A. 44°7N 70°39W 83 B14
Harrison, C. Canada 54°55N 57°55W 73 B8
Harrison L. Canada 49°33N 121°50W 70 D4
Harrisonburg U.S.A. 38°27N 78°52W 81 F14
Harrisonville U.S.A. 38°39N 94°21W 80 F6
Harriston Canada 43°57N 80°53W 82 C4
Harrisville Mich., U.S.A. 44°39N 83°17W 82 B1
Harrisville N.Y., U.S.A. 44°9N 75°19W 83 B9
Harrisville Pa., U.S.A. 41°8N 80°0W 82 E5
Harrodsburg U.S.A. 37°46N 84°51W 81 G11
Harrogate U.K. 54°0N 1°33W 12 C6
Harrow Canada 42°2N 82°55W 82 D2
Harrow □ U.K. 51°35N 0°21W 13 F7
Harrowsmith Canada 44°24N 76°40W 83 B8
Harry S. Truman Res.
  U.S.A. 38°16N 93°24W 80 F7
Harsīn Iran 34°18N 47°33E 44 C5
Harstad Norway 68°48N 16°30E 8 B17
Harsud India 22°6N 76°44E 42 H7
Hart U.S.A. 43°42N 86°22W 80 D10
Hart, L. Australia 31°10S 136°25E 63 E2
Hartbees → S. Africa 28°45S 20°32E 56 D3
Hartford Conn., U.S.A. 41°46N 72°41W 83 E12
Hartford Ky., U.S.A. 37°27N 86°55W 80 G10
Hartford S. Dak., U.S.A. 43°38N 96°57W 80 D5
Hartford Vt., U.S.A. 43°40N 72°20W 83 C12
Hartford Wis., U.S.A. 43°19N 88°22W 80 D9
Hartford City U.S.A. 40°27N 85°22W 81 E11
Hartland Canada 46°20N 67°32W 73 C6
Hartland Pt. U.K. 51°1N 4°32W 13 F3
Hartlepool U.K. 54°42N 1°13W 12 C6
Hartlepool □ U.K. 54°42N 1°17W 12 C6
Hartley Bay Canada 53°25N 129°15W 70 C3
Hartmannberge Namibia 17°0S 13°0E 56 B1
Hartney Canada 49°30N 100°35W 71 D8
Harts → S. Africa 28°24S 24°17E 56 D3
Harts Range Australia 23°6S 134°55E 62 C1
Hartselle U.S.A. 34°27N 86°56W 85 D11
Hartshorne U.S.A. 34°51N 95°34W 84 D7
Hartstown U.S.A. 41°33N 80°23W 82 E4
Hartsville U.S.A. 34°23N 80°4W 85 D14
Hartswater S. Africa 27°34S 24°43E 56 D3
Hartwell U.S.A. 34°21N 82°56W 85 D13
Harunabad Pakistan 29°35N 73°8E 42 E5
Harvand Iran 28°25N 55°43E 45 D7
Harvey Australia 33°5S 115°54E 61 F2
Harvey Ill., U.S.A. 41°36N 87°50W 80 E10
Harvey N. Dak., U.S.A. 47°47N 99°56W 80 B4
Harwich U.K. 51°56N 1°17E 13 F9
Haryana □ India 29°0N 76°10E 42 E7
Haryn → Belarus 52°7N 27°17E 17 B14
Harz Germany 51°38N 10°44E 16 C6
Hasa Si. Arabia 25°50N 49°0E 45 E6
Ḥasā → Jordan 31°4N 35°29E 46 D4
Ḥasā, W. al → Jordan 31°4N 35°29E 46 D4
Ḥasanābād Iran 28°38N 52°44E 45 D7
Hasb, W. → Iraq 31°45N 44°17E 44 D5
Hasdo → India 21°44N 82°44E 43 J10
Hashimoto Japan 34°19N 135°37E 31 G7
Hashtjerd Iran 35°52N 50°40E 45 C6
Hashtpur = Tālesh Iran 37°58N 48°58E 45 B6
Haskell U.S.A. 33°10N 99°44W 84 E5
Haskovo = Khaskovo
  Bulgaria 41°56N 25°30E 23 D11

Haslemere U.K. 51°5N 0°43W 13 F7
Hasselt Belgium 50°56N 5°21E 15 D5
Hassi Messaoud Algeria 31°51N 6°1E 50 B7
Hässleholm Sweden 56°10N 13°46E 9 H15
Hastings N.Z. 39°39S 176°52E 59 C6
Hastings U.K. 50°51N 0°35E 13 G8
Hastings Mich., U.S.A. 42°39N 85°17W 81 D11
Hastings Minn., U.S.A. 44°44N 92°51W 80 C7
Hastings Nebr., U.S.A. 40°35N 98°23W 80 E4
Hastings Ra. Australia 31°15S 152°14E 63 E5
Hat Yai Thailand 7°1N 100°27E 39 J3
Hatanbulag = Ergel
  Mongolia 43°8N 109°5E 34 C5
Hatay Turkey 36°14N 36°10E 44 B3
Hatch U.S.A. 32°40N 107°9W 77 K10
Hatchet L. Canada 58°36N 103°40W 71 B8
Hateruma-Shima Japan 24°3N 123°47E 31 M1
Hatfield P.O. Australia 33°54S 143°49E 63 E3
Hatgal Mongolia 50°26N 100°9E 32 A5
Hathras India 27°36N 78°6E 42 F8
Hatia Bangla. 22°30N 91°5E 41 H17
Hato Mayor Dom. Rep. 18°46N 69°15W 89 C6
Hatta India 24°7N 79°36E 43 G8
Hatta U.A.E. 24°45N 56°4E 45 E8
Hattah Australia 34°48S 142°17E 63 E3
Hattah Kulkyne △
  Australia 34°16S 142°33E 63 E3
Hatteras, C. U.S.A. 35°14N 75°32W 85 D17
Hattiesburg U.S.A. 31°20N 89°17W 85 F10
Hatvan Hungary 47°40N 19°45E 17 E10
Hau Duc Vietnam 15°20N 108°13E 38 E7
Haugesund Norway 59°23N 5°13E 9 G11
Haukipudas Finland 65°12N 25°20E 8 D21
Haultain → Canada 55°51N 106°46W 71 B7
Hauraki G. N.Z. 36°35S 175°5E 59 B5
Haut Atlas Morocco 32°30N 5°0W 50 B4
Hautes Fagnes = Hohes Venn
  Belgium 50°30N 6°5E 15 D6
Hauts Plateaux Algeria 35°0N 1°0E 50 B6
Havana = La Habana
  Cuba 23°8N 82°22W 88 B3
Havana U.S.A. 40°18N 90°4W 80 E8
Havant U.K. 50°51N 0°58W 13 G7
Havasor = Kığzı Turkey 38°30N 43°6E 44 B4
Havasu, L. U.S.A. 34°18N 114°28W 79 L12
Havel → Germany 52°50N 12°3E 16 B7
Havelian Pakistan 34°2N 73°10E 42 B5
Havelock Canada 44°26N 77°53W 82 B7
Havelock N.Z. 41°17S 173°48E 59 D4
Havelock U.S.A. 34°53N 76°54W 85 D16
Haverfordwest U.K. 51°48N 4°58W 13 F3
Haverhill U.K. 52°5N 0°28E 13 E8
Haverhill U.S.A. 42°47N 71°5W 83 D13
Haverstraw U.S.A. 41°12N 73°58W 83 E11
Havirga Mongolia 45°41N 113°5E 34 B7
Havířov Czech Rep. 49°46N 18°20E 17 D10
Havre U.S.A. 48°33N 109°41W 76 B9
Havre-Aubert Canada 47°12N 61°56W 73 C7
Havre-St.-Pierre Canada 50°18N 63°33W 73 B7
Haw → U.S.A. 35°36N 79°3W 85 D15
Hawai'i U.S.A. 19°30N 155°30W 74 b
Hawai'i □ U.S.A. 19°30N 156°30W 74 b
Hawaiian Is. Pac. Oc. 20°30N 156°0W 74 b
Hawaiian Ridge Pac. Oc. 24°0N 165°0W 65 E11
Hawarden Canada 51°25N 106°36W 71 C7
Hawarden U.S.A. 43°0N 96°29W 80 D5
Hawea, L. N.Z. 44°28S 169°19E 59 F2
Hawera N.Z. 39°35S 174°19E 59 C5
Hawick U.K. 55°26N 2°47W 11 F6
Hawk Junction Canada 48°5N 84°38W 72 C3
Hawke B. N.Z. 39°25S 177°20E 59 C6
Hawker Australia 31°59S 138°22E 63 E2
Hawke's Bay □ N.Z. 39°45S 176°35E 59 C6
Hawkesbury Canada 45°37N 74°37W 83 A10
Hawkesbury I. Canada 53°37N 129°3W 70 C3
Hawkesbury Pt.
  Australia 11°55S 134°5E 62 A1
Hawkinsville U.S.A. 32°17N 83°28W 85 E13
Hawley Minn., U.S.A. 46°53N 96°19W 80 B5
Hawley Pa., U.S.A. 41°28N 75°11W 83 E9
Ḥawrān, W. → Iraq 33°58N 42°34E 44 C4
Hawsh Mūssá Lebanon 33°45N 35°55E 46 B4
Hawthorne U.S.A. 38°32N 118°38W 78 G4
Hay Australia 34°30S 144°51E 63 E3
Hay → Australia 24°50S 138°0E 62 C2
Hay → Canada 60°50N 116°26W 70 A5
Hay, C. Australia 14°5S 129°29E 60 B4
Hay L. Canada 58°50N 118°50W 70 B5
Hay-on-Wye U.K. 52°5N 3°8W 13 E4
Hay River Canada 60°51N 115°44W 70 A5
Haya = Tehoru Indonesia 3°23S 129°30E 37 E7
Hayachine-San Japan 39°34N 141°29E 30 E10
Hayastan = Armenia ■
  Asia 40°20N 45°0E 19 F7
Haydān, W. al → Jordan 31°29N 35°34E 46 D4
Hayden U.S.A. 40°30N 107°16W 76 F10
Hayes U.S.A. 44°23N 101°1W 80 C3
Hayes → Canada 57°3N 92°12W 72 A1
Hayes Creek Australia 13°43S 131°22E 60 B5
Hayle U.K. 50°11N 5°26W 13 G2
Hayling I. U.K. 50°47N 0°58W 13 G7
Haymen I. Australia 20°3S 148°52E 62 J6
Hays Canada 50°6N 111°48W 70 C6
Hays U.S.A. 38°53N 99°20W 80 F4
Haysyn Ukraine 48°57N 29°25E 17 D15
Hayvoron Ukraine 48°22N 29°52E 17 D15
Hayward Calif., U.S.A. 37°40N 122°4W 78 H4
Hayward Wis., U.S.A. 46°1N 91°29W 80 B8
Haywards Heath U.K. 51°0N 0°5W 13 G7
Hazafon □ Israel 32°40N 35°20E 46 C4
Hazar Turkmenistan 39°34N 53°16E 19 G9
Hazārān, Kūh-e Iran 29°35N 57°20E 45 D8

Hazard *U.S.A.* 37°15N 83°12W **81** G12
Hazaribag *India* 23°58N 85°26E **43** H11
Hazaribag Road *India* 24°12N 85°57E **43** G11
Hazelton *Canada* 55°20N 127°42W **70** B3
Hazelton *U.S.A.* 46°29N 100°17W **80** B3
Hazen *U.S.A.* 47°18N 101°38W **80** B3
Hazlehurst *Ga., U.S.A.* 31°52N 82°36W **85** F13
Hazlehurst *Miss., U.S.A.* 31°52N 90°24W **85** F9
Hazlet *U.S.A.* 40°25N 74°12W **83** F10
Hazleton *U.S.A.* 40°57N 75°59W **83** F9
Hazlett, L. *Australia* 21°30S 128°48E **60** D4
Hazro *Turkey* 38°15N 40°47E **44** B4
Head of Bight *Australia* 31°30S 131°25E **61** F5
Headlands *Zimbabwe* 18°15S 32°2E **55** F3
Healdsburg *U.S.A.* 38°37N 122°52W **78** G4
Healdton *U.S.A.* 34°14N 97°29W **84** D6
Healesville *Australia* 37°35S 145°30E **63** F4
Heany Junction *Zimbabwe* 20°6S 28°54E **57** C4
Heard I. *Ind. Oc.* 53°0S 74°0E **3** G13
Hearne *U.S.A.* 30°53N 96°36W **84** F6
Hearst *Canada* 49°40N 83°41W **72** C3
Heart → *U.S.A.* 46°46N 100°50W **80** B3
Heart's Content *Canada* 47°54N 53°27W **73** C9
Heath, Pte. *Canada* 49°8N 61°40W **73** C7
Heathrow, London ✕ **(LHR)** *U.K.* 51°28N 0°27W **13** F7
Heavener *U.S.A.* 34°53N 94°36W **84** D7
Hebbronville *U.S.A.* 27°18N 98°41W **84** H5
Hebei □ *China* 39°0N 116°0E **34** E9
Hebel *Australia* 28°58S 147°47E **63** D4
Heber *U.S.A.* 32°44N 115°32W **79** N11
Heber Springs *U.S.A.* 35°30N 92°2W **84** D8
Hebgen L. *U.S.A.* 44°52N 111°20W **76** D8
Hebi *China* 35°57N 114°7E **34** G8
Hebrides *U.K.* 57°30N 7°0W **6** D4
Hebrides, Sea of the *U.K.* 57°5N 7°0W **11** D2
Hebron = Al Khalīl *West Bank* 31°32N 35°6E **46** D4
Hebron *Canada* 58°5N 62°30W **69** D13
Hebron *N. Dak., U.S.A.* 46°54N 102°3W **80** B2
Hebron *Nebr., U.S.A.* 40°10N 97°35W **80** E5
Hecate Str. *Canada* 53°10N 130°30W **70** C2
Heceta I. *U.S.A.* 55°46N 133°40W **70** B2
Hechi *China* 24°40N 108°2E **32** D5
Hechuan *China* 30°2N 106°12E **32** C5
Hecla *U.S.A.* 45°53N 98°9W **80** C4
Hecla I. *Canada* 51°10N 96°43W **71** C9
Hede *Sweden* 62°23N 13°30E **8** E15
Hedemora *Sweden* 60°18N 15°58E **9** F16
Heerde *Neths.* 52°24N 6°2E **15** B6
Heerenveen *Neths.* 52°57N 5°55E **15** B5
Heerhugowaard *Neths.* 52°40N 4°51E **15** B4
Heerlen *Neths.* 50°55N 5°58E **15** D5
Ḥefa *Israel* 32°46N 35°0E **46** C4
Ḥefa □ *Israel* 32°40N 35°0E **46** C4
Hefei *China* 31°52N 117°18E **33** C6
Hegang *China* 47°20N 130°19E **33** B8
Hei Ling Chau *China* 22°15N 114°2E **33** G11
Heichengzhen *China* 36°24N 106°3E **34** F4
Heidelberg *Germany* 49°24N 8°42E **16** D5
Heidelberg *S. Africa* 34°6S 20°59E **56** E3
Heihe *China* 50°10N 127°30E **33** A7
Heilbron *S. Africa* 27°16S 27°59E **57** D4
Heilbronn *Germany* 49°9N 9°13E **16** D5
Heilongjiang □ *China* 48°0N 126°0E **33** B7
Heilunkiang = Heilongjiang □ *China* 48°0N 126°0E **33** B7
Heimaey *Iceland* 63°26N 20°17W **8** E3
Heinola *Finland* 61°13N 26°2E **8** F22
Heinze Kyun *Burma* 14°25N 97°45E **38** E1
Heishan *China* 41°40N 122°5E **35** D12
Heishui *China* 42°8N 119°30E **35** C10
Hejaz = Ḥijāz *Si. Arabia* 24°0N 40°0E **44** E3
Hejian *China* 38°25N 116°5E **34** E9
Hejin *China* 35°35N 110°42E **34** G6
Hekımhan *Turkey* 38°50N 37°55E **44** B3
Hekla *Iceland* 63°56N 19°35W **8** E4
Hekou *China* 22°30N 103°59E **32** D5
Helan Shan *China* 38°30N 105°55E **34** E3
Helen Atoll *Pac. Oc.* 2°40N 132°0E **37** D8
Helena *Ark., U.S.A.* 34°32N 90°36W **85** D9
Helena *Mont., U.S.A.* 46°36N 112°2W **76** C7
Helendale *U.S.A.* 34°44N 117°19W **79** L9
Helensburgh *U.K.* 56°1N 4°43W **11** E4
Helensville *N.Z.* 36°41S 174°29E **59** B5
Helenvale *Australia* 15°43S 145°14E **62** B4
Helgeland *Norway* 66°7N 13°29E **8** C15
Helgoland *Germany* 54°10N 7°53E **16** A4
Heligoland = Helgoland *Germany* 54°10N 7°53E **16** A4
Heligoland B. = Deutsche Bucht *Germany* 54°15N 8°0E **16** A5
Hell Hole Gorge △ *Australia* 25°31S 144°12E **62** D3
Hella *Iceland* 63°50N 20°24W **8** E3
Hellas = Greece ■ *Europe* 40°0N 23°0E **23** E9
Hellertown *U.S.A.* 40°35N 75°21W **83** F9
Hellespont = Çanakkale Boğazı *Turkey* 40°17N 26°32E **23** D12
Hellevoetsluis *Neths.* 51°50N 4°8E **15** C4
Hellín *Spain* 38°31N 1°40W **21** C5
Hells Canyon ⌂ *U.S.A.* 45°30N 117°45W **76** D5
Hell's Gate △ *Kenya* 0°54S 36°19E **54** C4
Helmand □ *Afghan.* 31°20N 64°0E **40** D4
Helmand → *Afghan.* 31°12N 61°34E **40** D2
Helmeringhausen *Namibia* 25°54S 16°57E **56** D2
Helmond *Neths.* 51°29N 5°41E **15** C5
Helmsdale *U.K.* 58°7N 3°39W **11** C5
Helmsdale → *U.K.* 58°8N 3°43W **11** C5
Helong *China* 42°40N 129°0E **35** C15
Helper *U.S.A.* 39°41N 110°51W **76** G8
Helsingborg *Sweden* 56°3N 12°42E **9** H15
Helsingfors = Helsinki *Finland* 60°10N 24°55E **9** F21
Helsingør *Denmark* 56°2N 12°35E **9** H15
Helsinki *Finland* 60°10N 24°55E **9** F21
Helston *U.K.* 50°6N 5°17W **13** G2
Helvellyn *U.K.* 54°32N 3°1W **12** C4
Helwân *Egypt* 29°50N 31°20E **51** C12
Hemel Hempstead *U.K.* 51°44N 0°28W **13** F7
Hemet *U.S.A.* 33°45N 116°58W **79** M10
Hemingford *U.S.A.* 42°19N 103°4W **80** D2
Hemis △ *India* 34°10N 77°15E **42** B7
Hemmingford *Canada* 45°3N 73°35W **83** A11
Hempstead *N.Y., U.S.A.* 40°42N 73°37W **83** F11
Hempstead *Tex., U.S.A.* 30°6N 96°5W **84** F6
Hemse *Sweden* 57°15N 18°22E **9** H18
Henan □ *China* 34°0N 114°0E **34** H8
Henares → *Spain* 40°24N 3°30W **21** B4
Henashi-Misaki *Japan* 40°37N 139°51E **30** D9
Henderson *Argentina* 36°18S 61°43W **94** D3
Henderson *Ky., U.S.A.* 37°50N 87°35W **80** G10
Henderson *N.C., U.S.A.* 36°20N 78°25W **85** C15
Henderson *N.Y., U.S.A.* 43°50N 76°10W **83** C8
Henderson *Nev., U.S.A.* 36°2N 114°58W **79** J12
Henderson *Tenn., U.S.A.* 35°26N 88°38W **85** D10
Henderson *Tex., U.S.A.* 32°9N 94°48W **84** E7
Henderson I. *Pac. Oc.* 24°22S 128°19W **65** K15
Hendersonville *N.C., U.S.A.* 35°19N 82°28W **85** D13
Hendersonville *Tenn., U.S.A.* 36°18N 86°37W **85** C11
Hendījān *Iran* 30°14N 49°43E **45** D6
Hendorābī *Iran* 26°40N 53°37E **45** E7
Hengcheng *China* 38°18N 106°28E **34** E4
Hengdaohezi *China* 44°52N 129°0E **35** B15
Hengduan Shan *China* 27°30N 99°0E **32** D4
Hengelo *Neths.* 52°16N 6°48E **15** B6
Henggang *China* 22°39N 114°12E **33** F11
Hengmen *China* 22°33N 113°35E **33** F10
Hengqin Dao *China* 22°7N 113°34E **33** G10
Hengshan *China* 37°58N 109°5E **34** F5
Hengshui *China* 37°41N 115°40E **34** F8
Hengyang *China* 26°59N 112°22E **33** D6
Henley-on-Thames *U.K.* 51°32N 0°54W **13** F7
Henlopen, C. *U.S.A.* 38°48N 75°6W **81** F16
Hennenman *S. Africa* 27°59S 27°1E **56** D4
Hennessey *U.S.A.* 36°6N 97°54W **84** C6
Henri Pittier △ *Venezuela* 10°26N 67°37W **89** D6
Henrietta *N.Y., U.S.A.* 43°4N 77°37W **82** C7
Henrietta *Tex., U.S.A.* 33°49N 98°12W **84** E5
Henrietta, Ostrov = Genriyetty, Ostrov *Russia* 77°6N 156°30E **29** B16
Henrietta Maria, C. *Canada* 55°9N 82°20W **72** A3
Henry *U.S.A.* 41°7N 89°22W **80** E9
Henryetta *U.S.A.* 35°27N 95°59W **84** D7
Henryville *Canada* 45°8N 73°11W **83** A11
Hensall *Canada* 43°26N 81°30W **82** C3
Hentiesbaai *Namibia* 22°8S 14°18E **56** C1
Hentiyn Nuruu *Mongolia* 48°30N 108°30E **33** B5
Henty *Australia* 35°30S 147°3E **63** F4
Henzada *Burma* 17°38N 95°26E **41** L19
Heppner *U.S.A.* 45°21N 119°33W **76** D4
Hepworth *Canada* 44°37N 81°9W **82** B3
Hequ *China* 39°20N 111°15E **34** E6
Héraðsflói *Iceland* 65°42N 14°12W **8** D6
Héraðsvötn → *Iceland* 65°45N 19°25W **8** D4
Heraklion = Iraklio *Greece* 35°20N 25°12E **25** D7
Herald Cays *Australia* 16°58S 149°9E **62** B4
Herāt *Afghan.* 34°20N 62°7E **40** B3
Herāt □ *Afghan.* 35°0N 62°0E **40** B3
Herbert *Canada* 50°30N 107°10W **71** C7
Herbert → *Australia* 18°31S 146°17E **62** B4
Herberton *Australia* 17°20S 145°25E **62** B4
Herbertsdale *S. Africa* 34°1S 21°46E **56** E3
Herceg-Novi *Montenegro* 42°30N 18°33E **23** C8
Herchmer *Canada* 57°22N 94°10W **71** B10
Herðubreið *Iceland* 65°11N 16°21W **8** D5
Hereford *U.K.* 52°4N 2°43W **13** E5
Hereford *U.S.A.* 34°49N 102°24W **84** D3
Herefordshire □ *U.K.* 52°8N 2°40W **13** E5
Herentals *Belgium* 51°12N 4°51E **15** C4
Herford *Germany* 52°7N 8°39E **16** B5
Herington *U.S.A.* 38°40N 96°57W **80** F5
Herkimer *U.S.A.* 43°2N 74°59W **83** D10
Herlong *U.S.A.* 40°8N 120°8W **78** E6
Herm *U.K.* 49°30N 2°28W **13** H5
Hermann *U.S.A.* 38°42N 91°27W **80** F8
Hermannsburg *Australia* 23°57S 132°45E **60** D5
Hermanus *S. Africa* 34°27S 19°12E **56** E2
Hermidale *Australia* 31°30S 146°42E **63** E4
Hermiston *U.S.A.* 45°51N 119°17W **76** D4
Hermon *Canada* 45°6N 77°37W **82** A7
Hermon *U.S.A.* 44°28N 75°14W **83** B9
Hermon, Mt. = Shaykh, J. ash *Lebanon* 33°25N 35°50E **46** B4
Hermosillo *Mexico* 29°10N 111°0W **86** B2
Hernád → *Hungary* 47°56N 21°8E **17** D11
Hernandarias *Paraguay* 25°20S 54°40W **95** B5
Hernandez *U.S.A.* 36°24N 120°46W **78** J6
Hernando *Argentina* 32°28S 63°40W **94** C3
Hernando *U.S.A.* 34°50N 90°0W **85** D10
Herndon *U.S.A.* 40°43N 76°51W **82** F8
Herne *Germany* 51°32N 7°14E **15** C7
Herne Bay *U.K.* 51°21N 1°8E **13** F9
Herning *Denmark* 56°8N 8°58E **9** H13
Heroica Caborca = Caborca *Mexico* 30°37N 112°6W **86** A2
Heroica Nogales = Nogales *Mexico* 31°19N 110°56W **86** A2
Heron Bay *Canada* 48°40N 86°25W **72** C2
Heron I. *Australia* 23°27S 151°55E **62** C5
Herradura, Pta. de la *Canary Is.* 28°26N 14°8W **24** F5
Herreid *U.S.A.* 45°50N 100°4W **80** C3
Herrin *U.S.A.* 37°48N 89°2W **80** G9
Herriot *Canada* 56°22N 101°16W **71** B8
Herschel I. *Canada* 69°35N 139°5W **4** C1
Hershey *U.S.A.* 40°17N 76°39W **83** F8
Herstal *Belgium* 50°40N 5°38E **15** D5
Hertford *U.K.* 51°48N 0°4W **13** F7
Hertfordshire □ *U.K.* 51°51N 0°5W **13** F7
's-Hertogenbosch *Neths.* 51°42N 5°17E **15** C5
Hertzogville *S. Africa* 28°9S 25°30E **56** D4
Hervey B. *Australia* 25°0S 152°52E **62** C5
Herzliyya *Israel* 32°10N 34°50E **46** C3
Ḥeṣār *Fārs, Iran* 29°52N 50°16E **45** D6
Ḥeṣār *Markazī, Iran* 35°50N 49°12E **45** C6
Heshui *China* 35°48N 108°0E **34** G5
Heshun *China* 37°22N 113°32E **34** F7
Hesperia *U.S.A.* 34°25N 117°18W **79** L9
Hesse = Hessen □ *Germany* 50°30N 9°0E **16** C5
Hessen □ *Germany* 50°30N 9°0E **16** C5
Hetauda *Nepal* 27°25N 85°2E **42** F11
Hetch Hetchy Aqueduct *U.S.A.* 37°29N 122°19W **78** H5
Hettinger *U.S.A.* 46°0N 102°42W **80** B2
Heuksando *S. Korea* 34°40N 125°30E **35** G13
Heunghae *S. Korea* 36°12N 129°21E **35** F15
Heuvelton *U.S.A.* 44°37N 75°25W **83** B9
Hewitt *U.S.A.* 31°28N 97°12W **84** F6
Hexham *U.K.* 54°58N 2°4W **12** C5
Hexigten Qi *China* 43°18N 117°30E **35** C9
Ḥeydarābād *Iran* 30°33N 55°38E **45** D7
Heysham *U.K.* 54°3N 2°53W **12** C5
Heywood *Australia* 38°8S 141°37E **63** F3
Heze *China* 35°14N 115°20E **34** G8
Hi Vista *U.S.A.* 34°45N 117°46W **79** L9
Hialeah *U.S.A.* 25°51N 80°16W **85** J14
Hiawatha *U.S.A.* 39°51N 95°32W **80** F6
Hibbing *U.S.A.* 47°25N 92°56W **80** B7
Hibbs B. *Australia* 42°35S 145°15E **63** G4
Hibernia Reef *Australia* 12°0S 123°23E **60** B3
Hickman *U.S.A.* 36°34N 89°11W **80** G9
Hickory *U.S.A.* 35°44N 81°21W **85** D14
Hicks, Pt. *Australia* 37°49S 149°17E **63** F4
Hicks L. *Canada* 61°25N 100°0W **71** A9
Hicksville *U.S.A.* 40°46N 73°32W **83** F11
Hida-Gawa → *Japan* 35°26N 137°3E **31** G8
Hida-Sammyaku *Japan* 36°30N 137°40E **31** F8
Hidaka-Sammyaku *Japan* 42°35N 142°45E **30** C11
Hidalgo □ *Mexico* 20°30N 99°0W **87** C5
Hidalgo, Presa M. *Mexico* 26°30N 108°35W **86** B3
Hidalgo del Parral *Mexico* 26°56N 105°40W **86** B3
Hierro *Canary Is.* 27°44N 18°0W **24** G1
Higashiajima-San *Japan* 37°40N 140°10E **30** F10
Higashiōsaka *Japan* 34°39N 135°37E **31** G7
Higgins *U.S.A.* 36°7N 100°2W **84** C4
Higgins Corner *U.S.A.* 39°2N 121°5W **78** F5
High Bridge *U.S.A.* 40°40N 74°54W **83** F10
High Island Res. *China* 22°22N 114°21E **33** G11
High Level *Canada* 58°31N 117°8W **70** B5
High Point *U.S.A.* 35°57N 80°0W **85** D15
High Prairie *Canada* 55°30N 116°30W **70** B5
High River *Canada* 50°30N 113°50W **70** C6
High Tatra = Tatry *Slovak Rep.* 49°20N 20°0E **17** D11
High Veld *Africa* 27°0S 27°0E **48** J6
High Wycombe *U.K.* 51°37N 0°45W **13** F7
Highland □ *U.K.* 57°17N 4°21W **11** D4
Highland Park *U.S.A.* 42°11N 87°48W **80** D10
Highmore *U.S.A.* 44°31N 99°27W **80** C4
Highrock L. *Canada* 55°45N 100°30W **71** B8
Higüey *Dom. Rep.* 18°37N 68°42W **89** D6
Hiiumaa *Estonia* 58°50N 22°45E **9** G20
Ḥijāz *Si. Arabia* 24°0N 40°0E **44** E3
Hijo = Tagum *Phil.* 7°33N 125°53E **37** C7
Hikari *Japan* 33°58N 131°58E **31** H5
Hiko *U.S.A.* 37°32N 115°14W **78** H11
Hikone *Japan* 35°15N 136°10E **31** G8
Hikurangi *Gisborne, N.Z.* 37°55S 178°4E **59** C6
Hikurangi *Northland, N.Z.* 35°36S 174°17E **59** A5
Hildesheim *Germany* 52°9N 9°56E **16** B5
Hill → *Australia* 30°23S 115°3E **61** F2
Hill City *Idaho, U.S.A.* 43°18N 115°3W **76** E6
Hill City *Kans., U.S.A.* 39°22N 99°51W **80** F4
Hill City *Minn., U.S.A.* 46°59N 93°36W **80** B7
Hill City *S. Dak., U.S.A.* 43°56N 103°35W **80** D2
Hill Island L. *Canada* 60°30N 109°50W **71** A7
Hillaby, Mt. *Barbados* 13°12N 59°35W **89** g
Hillcrest *Barbados* 13°13N 59°31W **89** g
Hillcrest Center *U.S.A.* 35°23N 118°57W **79** K8
Hillegom *Neths.* 52°18N 4°35E **15** B4
Hillsboro *Kans., U.S.A.* 38°21N 97°12W **80** F5
Hillsboro *N. Dak., U.S.A.* 47°26N 97°3W **80** B5
Hillsboro *Ohio, U.S.A.* 39°12N 83°37W **81** F12
Hillsboro *Oreg., U.S.A.* 45°31N 122°59W **78** E4
Hillsboro *Tex., U.S.A.* 32°1N 97°8W **84** E6
Hillsborough *Grenada* 12°28N 61°28W **89** D7
Hillsborough *U.S.A.* 43°7N 71°54W **83** C13
Hillsborough Channel *Australia* 20°56S 149°15E **62** J7
Hillsdale *Mich., U.S.A.* 41°56N 84°38W **81** E11
Hillsdale *N.Y., U.S.A.* 42°11N 73°32W **83** D11
Hillsport *Canada* 49°27N 85°34W **72** C2
Hillston *Australia* 33°30S 145°31E **63** E4
Hilo *U.S.A.* 19°44N 155°5W **74** b
Hilton *U.S.A.* 43°17N 77°48W **82** C7
Hilton Head Island *U.S.A.* 32°13N 80°45W **85** E14
Hilversum *Neths.* 52°14N 5°10E **15** B5
Himachal Pradesh □ *India* 31°30N 77°0E **42** D7
Himalaya *Asia* 29°0N 84°0E **43** E11
Himalchuli *Nepal* 28°27N 84°38E **43** E11
Himatnagar *India* 23°37N 72°57E **42** H5
Himeji *Japan* 34°50N 134°40E **31** G7
Himi *Japan* 36°50N 136°55E **31** F8
Ḥimş *Syria* 34°40N 36°45E **46** A5
Ḥimş □ *Syria* 34°30N 37°0E **46** A6
Hinche *Haiti* 19°9N 72°1W **89** C5
Hinchinbrook I. *Australia* 18°20S 146°15E **62** B4
Hinchinbrook Island △ *Australia* 18°14S 146°6E **62** B4
Hinckley *U.K.* 52°33N 1°22W **13** E6
Hinckley *U.S.A.* 46°1N 92°56W **80** B7
Hindaun *India* 26°44N 77°5E **42** F7
Hindmarsh, L. *Australia* 36°5S 141°55E **63** F3
Hindu Bagh *Pakistan* 30°56N 67°50E **42** D2
Hindu Kush *Asia* 36°0N 71°0E **40** B7
Hindupur *India* 13°49N 77°32E **40** N10
Hines Creek *Canada* 56°20N 118°40W **70** B5
Hinesville *U.S.A.* 31°51N 81°36W **85** F14
Hinganghat *India* 20°30N 78°52E **40** J11
Hingham *U.S.A.* 48°33N 110°25W **76** B8
Hingir *India* 21°57N 83°41E **43** J10
Hingoli *India* 19°41N 77°15E **40** K10
Hinna = Imi *Ethiopia* 6°28N 42°10E **47** F3
Hinnøya *Norway* 68°35N 15°50E **8** B16
Hinojosa del Duque *Spain* 38°30N 5°9W **21** C3
Hinsdale *U.S.A.* 42°47N 72°29W **83** D12
Hinthada = Henzada *Burma* 17°38N 95°26E **41** L19
Hinton *Canada* 53°26N 117°34W **70** C5
Hinton *U.S.A.* 37°40N 80°54W **81** G13
Hios *Greece* 38°27N 26°9E **23** E12
Hirado *Japan* 33°22N 129°33E **31** H4
Hirakud Dam *India* 21°32N 83°45E **41** J13
Hiran → *India* 23°6N 79°21E **43** H8
Hirapur *India* 24°22N 79°13E **43** G8
Hirara *Japan* 24°48N 125°17E **31** M2
Hiratsuka *Japan* 35°19N 139°21E **31** G9
Hiroo *Japan* 42°17N 143°19E **30** C11
Hirosaki *Japan* 40°34N 140°28E **30** D10
Hiroshima *Japan* 34°24N 132°30E **31** G6
Hiroshima □ *Japan* 34°50N 133°0E **31** G6
Hisar *India* 29°12N 75°45E **42** E6
Hisb, Sha'ib = Ḥasb, W. → *Iraq* 31°45N 44°17E **44** D5
Ḥismá *Si. Arabia* 28°30N 36°0E **44** D3
Hispaniola *W. Indies* 19°0N 71°0W **89** C5
Hīt *Iraq* 33°38N 42°49E **44** C4
Hita *Japan* 33°20N 130°58E **31** H5
Hitachi *Japan* 36°36N 140°39E **31** F10
Hitchin *U.K.* 51°58N 0°16W **13** F7
Hitiaa *Tahiti* 17°36S 149°18W **59** d
Hitoyoshi *Japan* 32°13N 130°45E **31** H5
Hitra *Norway* 63°30N 8°45E **8** E13
Hiva Oa *French Polynesia* 9°45S 139°0W **65** H14
Hixon *Canada* 53°25N 122°35W **70** C4
Ḥiyyon, N. → *Israel* 30°25N 35°10E **46** E4
Hjalmar L. *Canada* 61°33N 109°25W **71** A7
Hjälmaren *Sweden* 59°18N 15°40E **9** G16
Hjørring *Denmark* 57°29N 9°59E **9** H13
Hjort Trench *S. Ocean* 58°0S 157°30E **5** B10
Hkakabo Razi *Burma* 28°25N 97°23E **41** E20
Hlobane *S. Africa* 27°42S 31°0E **57** D5
Hluhluwe *S. Africa* 28°1S 32°15E **57** D5
Hluhluwe ⌂ *S. Africa* 22°10S 32°5E **57** C5
Hlyboka *Ukraine* 48°5N 25°56E **17** D13
Ho *Ghana* 6°37N 0°27E **50** G6
Ho Chi Minh City = Thanh Pho Ho Chi Minh *Vietnam* 10°58N 106°40E **39** G6
Ho Thuong *Vietnam* 19°32N 105°48E **38** C5
Hoa Binh *Vietnam* 20°50N 105°20E **38** B5
Hoa Da *Vietnam* 11°16N 108°40E **39** G7
Hoa Hiep *Vietnam* 11°34N 105°51E **39** G5
Hoai Nhon *Vietnam* 14°28N 109°1E **38** E7
Hoang Lien Son *Vietnam* 22°0N 104°0E **38** A4
Hoanib → *Namibia* 19°27S 12°46E **56** B2
Hoare B. *Canada* 65°17N 62°30W **69** C13
Hoarusib → *Namibia* 19°3S 12°36E **56** B2
Hobart *Australia* 42°50S 147°21E **63** G4
Hobart *U.S.A.* 35°1N 99°6W **84** D5
Hobbs *U.S.A.* 32°42N 103°8W **77** K12
Hobbs Coast *Antarctica* 74°50S 131°0W **5** D14
Hobe Sound *U.S.A.* 27°4N 80°8W **85** H14
Hoboken *U.S.A.* 40°44N 74°3W **83** F10
Hobro *Denmark* 56°39N 9°46E **9** H13
Hoburgen *Sweden* 56°55N 18°7E **9** H18
Hobyo *Somali Rep.* 5°25N 48°30E **47** F4
Hochfeld *Namibia* 21°28S 17°58E **56** C2
Hodaka-Dake *Japan* 36°17N 137°39E **31** F8
Hodeida = Al Ḥudaydah *Yemen* 14°50N 43°0E **47** E3
Hodgeville *Canada* 50°7N 106°58W **71** C7
Hodgson *Canada* 51°13N 97°36W **71** C9
Hódmezővásárhely *Hungary* 46°28N 20°22E **17** E11
Hodna, Chott el *Algeria* 35°26N 4°43E **50** A6
Hodonín *Czech Rep.* 48°50N 17°10E **17** D9
Hoek van Holland *Neths.* 52°0N 4°7E **15** C4
Hoengseong *S. Korea* 37°29N 127°59E **35** F14
Hoeryong *N. Korea* 42°30N 129°45E **35** C15
Hoeyang *N. Korea* 38°43N 127°36E **35** E14
Hof *Germany* 50°19N 11°55E **16** C6
Hofmeyr *S. Africa* 31°39S 25°50E **56** E4
Höfn *Iceland* 64°15N 15°13W **8** D6
Hofors *Sweden* 60°31N 16°15E **9** F17
Hofsjökull *Iceland* 64°49N 18°48W **8** D4
Hōfu *Japan* 34°3N 131°34E **31** G5
Hogan Group *Australia* 39°13S 147°1E **63** F4
Hogarth, Mt. *Australia* 21°48S 136°58E **62** C2
Hoge Kempen △ *Belgium* 51°6N 5°35E **15** C5
Hoggar = Ahaggar *Algeria* 23°0N 6°30E **50** D7
Hogsty Reef *Bahamas* 21°41N 73°48W **89** B5
Hoh → *U.S.A.* 47°45N 124°29W **78** C2
Hoh Xil Shan *China* 35°0N 89°0E **32** C3
Hohenwald *U.S.A.* 35°33N 87°33W **85** D11
Hoher Rhön = Rhön *Germany* 50°24N 9°58E **16** C5
Hohes Venn *Belgium* 50°30N 6°5E **15** D6
Hohhot *China* 40°52N 111°40E **34** D6
Hoi An *Vietnam* 15°30N 108°19E **38** E7
Hoi Xuan *Vietnam* 20°25N 105°9E **38** B5
Hoisington *U.S.A.* 38°31N 98°47W **80** F4
Hōjō *Japan* 33°58N 132°46E **31** H6
Hokianga Harbour *N.Z.* 35°31S 173°22E **59** A4
Hokitika *N.Z.* 42°42S 171°0E **59** E3
Hokkaidō □ *Japan* 43°30N 143°0E **30** C11
Hola *Kenya* 1°29S 40°2E **54** B4
Holakas *Greece* 35°57N 27°53E **25** D9
Holbrook *Australia* 35°42S 147°18E **63** F4
Holbrook *U.S.A.* 34°54N 110°10W **77** J8
Holcomb *U.S.A.* 42°54N 77°25W **82** D7
Holden *U.S.A.* 39°6N 112°16W **76** G7
Holdenville *U.S.A.* 35°5N 96°24W **84** D6
Holdrege *U.S.A.* 40°26N 99°23W **80** E4
Holetown *Barbados* 13°11N 59°38W **89** g
Holguín *Cuba* 20°50N 76°20W **88** B4
Hollams Bird I. *Namibia* 24°40S 14°30E **56** C1
Holland = Netherlands ■ *Europe* 52°0N 5°30E **15** C5
Holland *Mich., U.S.A.* 42°47N 86°7W **80** D10
Holland *N.Y., U.S.A.* 42°38N 78°32W **82** D6
Holland Centre *Canada* 44°23N 80°47W **82** B4
Holland Patent *U.S.A.* 43°14N 75°15W **83** C9
Hollandale *U.S.A.* 33°10N 90°51W **85** E9
Holley *U.S.A.* 43°14N 78°2W **82** C6
Hollidaysburg *U.S.A.* 40°26N 78°24W **82** F6
Hollis *U.S.A.* 34°41N 99°55W **84** D5
Hollister *Calif., U.S.A.* 36°51N 121°24W **78** J5
Hollister *Idaho, U.S.A.* 42°21N 114°35W **76** E6
Holly Hill *U.S.A.* 29°16N 81°3W **85** G14
Holly Springs *U.S.A.* 34°46N 89°27W **85** D10
Hollywood *U.S.A.* 26°0N 80°8W **85** J14
Holman *Canada* 70°44N 117°44W **68** B8
Hólmavík *Iceland* 65°42N 21°40W **8** D3
Holmen *U.S.A.* 43°58N 91°15W **80** D8
Holmes Reefs *Australia* 16°27S 148°0E **62** B4
Holmsund *Sweden* 63°41N 20°20E **8** E19
Holroyd → *Australia* 14°10S 141°36E **62** A3
Holstebro *Denmark* 56°22N 8°37E **9** H13
Holsworthy *U.K.* 50°48N 4°22W **13** G3
Holton *Canada* 54°31N 57°12W **73** B8
Holton *U.S.A.* 39°28N 95°44W **80** F6
Holtville *U.S.A.* 32°49N 115°23W **79** N11
Holwerd *Neths.* 53°22N 5°54E **15** A5
Holy I. *Anglesey, U.K.* 53°17N 4°37W **12** D3
Holy I. *Northumberland, U.K.* 55°40N 1°47W **12** B6
Holyhead *U.K.* 53°18N 4°38W **12** D3
Holyoke *Colo., U.S.A.* 40°35N 102°18W **76** F12
Holyoke *Mass., U.S.A.* 42°12N 72°37W **83** D12
Holyrood *Canada* 47°27N 53°8W **73** C9
Homa Bay *Kenya* 0°36S 34°30E **54** C3
Homalin *Burma* 24°55N 95°0E **41** G19
Homand *Iran* 32°28N 59°37E **45** C8
Homathko → *Canada* 51°0N 124°56W **70** C4
Hombori *Mali* 15°20N 1°38W **50** E5
Home B. *Canada* 68°40N 67°10W **69** C13
Home Hill *Australia* 19°43S 147°25E **62** B4
Home Reef *Tonga* 18°59S 174°47W **59** c
Homedale *U.S.A.* 43°37N 116°56W **76** E5
Homer *Alaska, U.S.A.* 59°39N 151°33W **68** D4
Homer *La., U.S.A.* 32°48N 93°4W **84** E8
Homer *N.Y., U.S.A.* 42°38N 76°10W **83** D8
Homer City *U.S.A.* 40°32N 79°10W **82** F5
Homestead *Australia* 20°20S 145°40E **62** C4
Homestead *U.S.A.* 25°28N 80°29W **85** J14
Homestead ⌂ *U.S.A.* 40°17N 96°50W **80** E5
Homoine *Mozam.* 23°55S 35°8E **57** C6
Homs = Ḥimş *Syria* 34°40N 36°45E **46** A5
Homyel *Belarus* 52°28N 31°0E **17** B16
Hon Chong *Vietnam* 10°25N 104°30E **39** G5
Hon Hai *Vietnam* 10°0N 109°0E **39** H7
Hon Me *Vietnam* 19°23N 105°56E **38** C5
Honan = Henan □ *China* 34°0N 114°0E **34** H8
Honbetsu *Japan* 43°7N 143°37E **30** C11
Honcut *U.S.A.* 39°20N 121°32W **78** F5
Honda, Bahía *Cuba* 22°54N 83°10W **88** B3
Hondeklipbaai *S. Africa* 30°19S 17°17E **56** E2
Hondo *Japan* 32°27N 130°12E **31** H5
Hondo *U.S.A.* 29°21N 99°9W **84** G5
Hondo, Río → *Belize* 18°25N 88°21W **87** D7
Honduras ■ *Cent. Amer.* 14°40N 86°30W **88** D2
Honduras, G. de *Caribbean* 16°50N 87°0W **88** C2
Hønefoss *Norway* 60°10N 10°18E **9** F14
Honesdale *U.S.A.* 41°34N 75°16W **83** E9
Honey Harbour *Canada* 44°52N 79°49W **82** B5
Honey L. *U.S.A.* 40°15N 120°19W **78** E6
Honfleur *France* 49°25N 0°13E **20** B4
Hong Gai *Vietnam* 20°57N 107°5E **38** B6
Hong He → *China* 32°25N 115°35E **34** H8
Hong Kong □ *China* 22°11N 114°14E **33** G11
Hong Kong I. *China* 22°16N 114°12E **33** G11
Hong Kong Int. ✕ **(HKG)** *China* 22°19N 113°57E **33** G10
Hongcheon *S. Korea* 37°44N 127°53E **35** F14
Hongjiang *China* 27°7N 109°59E **33** D5
Hongliu He → *China* 38°0N 109°50E **34** F5
Hongor *Mongolia* 45°45N 112°50E **34** B7
Hongsa *Laos* 19°43N 101°20E **38** C3
Hongseong *S. Korea* 36°37N 126°38E **35** F14
Hongshui He → *China* 23°48N 109°30E **33** D5
Hongtong *China* 36°16N 111°40E **34** F6
Honguedo, Détroit d' *Canada* 49°15N 64°0W **73** C7
Hongwon *N. Korea* 40°0N 127°56E **35** E14
Hongze Hu *China* 33°15N 118°35E **35** H10
Honiara *Solomon Is.* 9°27S 159°57E **58** B8
Honiton *U.K.* 50°47N 3°11W **13** G4
Honjō *Japan* 39°23N 140°3E **30** E10
Honningsvåg *Norway* 70°59N 25°59E **8** A21
Honolulu *U.S.A.* 21°19N 157°52W **74** b
Honshū *Japan* 36°0N 138°0E **30** F9
Hood, Mt. *U.S.A.* 45°23N 121°42W **76** D3
Hood, Pt. *Australia* 34°23S 119°34E **61** F2
Hood River *U.S.A.* 45°43N 121°31W **76** D3
Hoodsport *U.S.A.* 47°24N 123°9W **78** C3
Hoogeveen *Neths.* 52°44N 6°28E **15** B6
Hoogezand-Sappemeer *Neths.* 53°9N 6°45E **15** A6

Hooghly = Hugli ➤
India   21°56N 88°4E **43 J13**
Hooghly-Chinsura = Chunchura
India   22°53N 88°27E **43 H13**
Hook Hd. Ireland   52°7N 6°56W **10 D5**
Hook I. Australia   20°4S 149°0E **62 J6**
Hook of Holland = Hoek van
Holland Neths.   52°0N 4°7E **15 C4**
Hooker U.S.A.   36°52N 101°13W **84 C4**
Hooker Creek = Lajamanu
Australia   18°23S 130°38E **60 C5**
Hoonah U.S.A.   58°7N 135°27W **70 B1**
Hooper Bay U.S.A.   61°32N 166°6W **74 a**
Hoopeston U.S.A.   40°28N 87°40W **80 E10**
Hoopstad S. Africa   27°50S 25°55E **56 D4**
Hoorn Neths.   52°38N 5°4E **15 B5**
Hoover U.S.A.   33°24N 86°49W **85 E11**
Hoover Dam U.S.A.   36°1N 114°44W **79 K12**
Hooversville U.S.A.   40°9N 78°55W **82 F6**
Hop Bottom U.S.A.   41°42N 75°46W **83 E9**
Hope Canada   49°25N 121°25W **70 D4**
Hope Ariz., U.S.A.   33°43N 113°42W **79 M13**
Hope Ark., U.S.A.   33°40N 93°36W **84 E8**
Hope, L. S. Austral.,
Australia   28°24S 139°18E **63 D2**
Hope, L. W. Austral.,
Australia   32°35S 120°15E **61 F3**
Hope, Pt. U.S.A.   68°21N 166°47W **66 C3**
Hope I. Canada   44°55N 80°11W **82 B4**
Hope Town Bahamas   26°35N 76°57W **88 A4**
Hope Vale Australia   15°16S 145°20E **62 B4**
Hopedale Canada   55°28N 60°13W **73 A7**
Hopedale U.S.A.   42°8N 71°33W **83 D13**
Hopefield S. Africa   33°3S 18°22E **56 E2**
Hopei = Hebei □ China   39°0N 116°0E **34 E9**
Hopelchén Mexico   19°46N 89°51W **87 D7**
Hopetoun Vic., Australia   35°42S 142°22E **63 F3**
Hopetoun W. Austral.,
Australia   33°57S 120°7E **61 F3**
Hopetown S. Africa   29°34S 24°3E **56 D3**
Hopewell U.S.A.   37°18N 77°17W **81 G15**
Hopkins, L. Australia   24°15S 128°35E **60 D4**
Hopkinsville U.S.A.   36°52N 87°29W **80 G10**
Hopland U.S.A.   38°58N 123°7W **78 G3**
Hoquiam U.S.A.   46°59N 123°53W **78 D3**
Hordern Hills Australia   20°15S 130°0E **60 D5**
Horinger China   40°28N 111°48E **34 D6**
Horizontina Brazil   27°37S 54°19W **95 B5**
Horlick Mts. Antarctica   84°0S 102°0W **5 E15**
Horlivka Ukraine   48°19N 38°5E **19 E6**
Hormak Iran   29°58N 60°51E **45 D9**
Hormoz Iran   27°35N 55°0E **45 E7**
Hormoz, Jaz.-ye Iran   27°8N 56°28E **45 E8**
Hormozgān □ Iran   27°30N 56°0E **45 E8**
Hormuz, Küh-e Iran   27°27N 55°10E **45 E7**
Hormuz, Str. of The Gulf   26°30N 56°30E **45 E8**
Horn Austria   48°39N 15°40E **16 D8**
Horn ➤ Canada   61°30N 118°1W **70 A5**
Horn, Cape = Hornos, C. de
Chile   55°50S 67°30W **96 H3**
Horn Head Ireland   55°14N 8°0W **10 A3**
Horn I. Australia   10°37S 142°17E **62 A3**
Horn Plateau Canada   62°15N 119°15W **70 A5**
Hornavan Sweden   66°15N 17°30E **8 C17**
Hornbeck U.S.A.   31°20N 93°24W **84 F8**
Hornbrook U.S.A.   41°55N 122°33W **76 F2**
Horncastle U.K.   53°13N 0°7W **12 D7**
Hornell U.S.A.   42°20N 77°40W **82 D7**
Hornell L. Canada   62°20N 119°25W **70 A5**
Hornepayne Canada   49°14N 84°48W **72 C3**
Hornings Mills Canada   44°9N 80°12W **82 B4**
Hornitos U.S.A.   37°30N 120°14W **78 H6**
Hornos, C. de Chile   55°50S 67°30W **96 H3**
Hornsby Australia   33°42S 151°2E **63 B5**
Hornsea U.K.   53°55N 0°11W **12 D7**
Horobetsu = Noboribetsu
Japan   42°24N 141°6E **30 C10**
Horodenka Ukraine   48°41N 25°29E **17 D13**
Horodok Khmelnytskyy,
Ukraine   49°10N 26°34E **17 D14**
Horodok Lviv, Ukraine   49°46N 23°32E **17 D12**
Horokhiv Ukraine   50°30N 24°45E **17 C13**
Horqin Youyi Qianqi
China   46°5N 122°3E **35 A12**
Horqueta Paraguay   23°15S 56°55W **94 A4**
Horse Cr. ➤ U.S.A.   41°57N 103°58W **76 F12**
Horse I. Canada   53°20N 99°6W **71 C9**
Horse Is. Canada   50°15N 55°50W **73 B8**
Horsefly L. Canada   52°25N 121°0W **70 C4**
Horseheads U.S.A.   42°10N 76°49W **82 D8**
Horsens Denmark   55°52N 9°51E **9 J13**
Horseshoe Lake Canada   45°17N 79°51W **82 A5**
Horsham Australia   36°44S 142°13E **63 F3**
Horsham U.K.   51°4N 0°20W **13 F7**
Horta Azores   38°32N 28°38W **50 a**
Horten Norway   59°25N 10°32E **9 G14**
Horton U.S.A.   39°40N 95°32W **80 F6**
Horton ➤ Canada   69°56N 126°52W **68 C7**
Horwood L. Canada   48°5N 82°20W **72 C3**
Ḩoseynābād Khuzestān,
Iran   32°45N 48°20E **45 C6**
Ḩoseynābād Kordestān,
Iran   35°33N 47°8E **44 C5**
Hoshangabad India   22°45N 77°45E **42 H7**
Hoshiarpur India   31°30N 75°58E **42 D6**
Hospet India   15°15N 76°20E **40 M10**
Hoste, I. Chile   55°0S 69°0W **96 H3**
Hot Thailand   18°8N 98°29E **38 C2**
Hot Creek Range
U.S.A.   38°40N 116°20W **76 G5**
Hot Springs Ark., U.S.A.   34°31N 93°3W **84 D8**
Hot Springs S. Dak.,
U.S.A.   43°26N 103°29W **80 D2**
Hot Springs △ U.S.A.   34°31N 93°3W **84 D8**
Hotagen Sweden   63°59N 14°12E **8 E16**
Hotan China   37°25N 79°55E **32 C2**
Hotan He ➤ China   40°20N 80°56E **32 B3**
Hotazel S. Africa   27°17S 22°58E **56 D3**

Hotchkiss U.S.A.   38°48N 107°43W **76 G10**
Hotham, C. Australia   12°2S 131°18E **60 B5**
Hoting Sweden   64°8N 16°15E **8 D17**
Hotte, Massif de la Haiti   18°30N 73°45W **89 C5**
Hottentotsbaai Namibia   26°8S 14°59E **56 D1**
Hou Hai China   22°32N 113°56E **33 F10**
Houei Sai Laos   20°18N 100°26E **38 B3**
Houffalize Belgium   50°8N 5°48E **15 D5**
Houghton Mich., U.S.A.   47°7N 88°34W **80 B9**
Houghton N.Y., U.S.A.   42°25N 78°10W **82 D6**
Houghton L. U.S.A.   44°21N 84°44W **81 C11**
Houghton-le-Spring
U.K.   54°51N 1°28W **12 C6**
Houhora Heads N.Z.   34°49S 173°9E **59 A4**
Houlton U.S.A.   46°8N 67°51W **81 B20**
Houma China   35°36N 90°43W **85 G9**
Housatonic ➤ U.S.A.   41°10N 73°7W **83 E11**
Houston Canada   54°25N 126°39W **70 C3**
Houston Mo., U.S.A.   37°22N 91°58W **80 G8**
Houston Tex., U.S.A.   29°45N 95°21W **84 G7**
Hout = Mogwadi ➤
S. Africa   23°4S 29°36E **57 C4**
Houtkraal S. Africa   30°23S 24°5E **56 E3**
Houtman Abrolhos
Australia   28°43S 113°48E **61 E1**
Hovd □ Mongolia   48°2N 91°37E **32 B4**
Hove U.K.   50°50N 0°10W **13 G7**
Hovenweep △ U.S.A.   37°20N 109°0W **77 H9**
Hoveyzeh Iran   31°27N 48°4E **45 D6**
Hövsgöl Mongolia   43°37N 109°39E **34 C5**
Hövsgöl Nuur Mongolia   51°0N 100°30E **32 A5**
Howar, Wadi ➤ Sudan   17°30N 27°8E **51 E11**
Howard Australia   25°16S 152°32E **63 D5**
Howard Pa., U.S.A.   41°1N 77°40W **82 F7**
Howard S. Dak., U.S.A.   44°1N 97°32W **80 C5**
Howe U.S.A.   43°48N 113°0W **76 E7**
Howe, C. Australia   37°30S 150°0E **63 F5**
Howe, West Cape
Australia   35°8S 117°36E **61 G2**
Howe I. Canada   44°16N 76°17W **83 B8**
Howell U.S.A.   42°36N 83°56W **81 D12**
Howick Canada   45°11N 73°51W **83 A11**
Howick S. Africa   29°28S 30°14E **57 D5**
Howick Group Australia   14°20S 145°30E **62 A4**
Howitt, L. Australia   27°40S 138°40E **63 D2**
Howland I. Pac. Oc.   0°48N 176°38W **64 G10**
Howrah = Haora India   22°34N 88°18E **43 H13**
Howth Ireland   53°23N 6°6W **10 C5**
Howth Hd. Ireland   53°22N 6°4W **10 C5**
Höxter Germany   51°46N 9°22E **16 C5**
Hoy U.K.   58°50N 3°15W **11 C5**
Høyanger Norway   61°13N 6°4E **8 F12**
Hoyerswerda Germany   51°26N 14°14E **16 C8**
Hoylake U.K.   53°24N 3°10W **12 D4**
Hpa-an = Pa-an Burma   16°51N 97°40E **41 L20**
Hpunan Pass Burma   27°30N 96°55E **41 F20**
Hradec Králové
Czech Rep.   50°15N 15°50E **16 C8**
Hrodna Belarus   53°42N 23°52E **17 B12**
Hrodzyanka Belarus   53°31N 28°42E **17 B15**
Hron ➤ Slovak Rep.   47°49N 18°45E **17 E10**
Hrvatska = Croatia ■
Europe   45°20N 16°0E **16 F9**
Hrymayliv Ukraine   49°20N 26°5E **17 D14**
Hsenwi Burma   23°22N 97°55E **41 H20**
Hsiamen = Xiamen
China   24°25N 118°4E **33 D6**
Hsian = Xi'an China   34°15N 109°0E **34 G5**
Hsinchu Taiwan   24°48N 120°58E **33 D7**
Hsinhailien = Lianyungang
China   34°40N 119°11E **35 G10**
Hsüchou = Xuzhou
China   34°18N 117°10E **35 G9**
Hu Xian China   34°8N 108°42E **34 G5**
Hua Hin Thailand   12°34N 99°58E **38 F2**
Hua Xian Henan, China   34°30N 114°30E **34 G8**
Hua Xian Shaanxi, China   34°30N 109°48E **34 G5**
Huab ➤ Namibia   20°52S 13°25E **56 B2**
Huachinera Mexico   30°9N 108°55W **86 A3**
Huacho Peru   11°10S 77°35W **92 F3**
Huade China   41°55N 113°59E **34 D7**
Huadian China   43°0N 126°40E **35 C14**
Huahine, Î.
French Polynesia   16°46S 150°58W **65 J12**
Huai Hat △ Thailand   16°52N 104°17E **38 D5**
Huai He ➤ China   33°0N 118°30E **33 C6**
Huai Nam Dang △
Thailand   19°30N 98°30E **38 C2**
Huai Yot Thailand   7°45N 99°37E **39 J2**
Huai'an Hebei, China   40°30N 114°20E **34 D8**
Huai'an Jiangsu, China   33°30N 119°10E **35 H10**
Huaibei China   34°0N 116°48E **34 G9**
Huaide = Gongzhuling
China   43°30N 124°40E **35 C13**
Huaidezhen China   43°48N 124°50E **35 C13**
Huainan China   32°38N 116°58E **33 C6**
Huairen China   39°48N 113°20E **34 E7**
Huairou China   40°20N 116°35E **34 D9**
Huaiyang China   33°40N 114°52E **34 H8**
Huaiyin China   33°30N 119°2E **35 H10**
Huaiyuan China   32°55N 117°10E **35 H9**
Huajuapan de León
Mexico   17°48N 97°46W **87 D5**
Hualapai Peak U.S.A.   35°5N 113°54W **77 J7**
Huallaga ➤ Peru   5°15S 75°30W **92 E3**
Huambo Angola   12°42S 15°54E **53 G3**
Huan Jiang ➤ China   34°28N 109°0E **34 G5**
Huan Xian China   36°33N 107°7E **34 F4**
Huancabamba Peru   5°10S 79°15W **92 E3**
Huancane Peru   15°10S 69°44W **92 G5**
Huancavelica Peru   12°50S 75°5W **92 F3**
Huancayo Peru   12°5S 75°12W **92 F3**
Huanchaca Bolivia   20°15S 66°40W **92 H5**
Huang Hai = Yellow Sea
China   35°0N 123°0E **35 G12**
Huang He ➤ China   37°55N 118°50E **35 F10**
Huang Xian China   37°38N 120°30E **35 F11**
Huangling China   35°34N 109°15E **34 G5**

Huanglong China   35°30N 109°59E **34 G5**
Huangshan China   29°42N 118°25E **33 D6**
Huangshi China   30°10N 115°3E **33 C6**
Huangsongdian China   43°45N 127°25E **35 C14**
Huanren China   41°23N 125°20E **35 D13**
Huantai China   36°58N 117°56E **35 F9**
Huánuco Peru   9°55S 76°15W **92 E3**
Huaraz Peru   9°30S 77°32W **92 E3**
Huarmey Peru   10°5S 78°5W **92 F3**
Huascarán, Nevado Peru   9°7S 77°37W **92 E3**
Huasco Chile   28°30S 71°15W **94 B1**
Huasco ➤ Chile   28°27S 71°13W **94 B1**
Huasna U.S.A.   35°6N 120°24W **79 K6**
Huatabampo Mexico   26°50N 109°38W **86 B3**
Huauchinango Mexico   20°12N 98°3W **87 C5**
Huautla de Jiménez
Mexico   18°8N 96°51W **87 D5**
Huayin China   34°35N 110°5E **34 G6**
Hubbard Ohio, U.S.A.   41°9N 80°34W **82 E4**
Hubbard Tex., U.S.A.   31°51N 96°48W **84 F6**
Hubbart Pt. Canada   59°21N 94°41W **71 B10**
Hubei □ China   31°0N 112°0E **33 C6**
Hubli India   15°22N 75°15E **40 M9**
Huch'ang N. Korea   41°25N 127°2E **35 D14**
Hucknall U.K.   53°3N 1°13W **12 D6**
Huddersfield U.K.   53°39N 1°47W **12 D6**
Hudiksvall Sweden   61°43N 17°10E **8 F17**
Hudson Canada   50°6N 92°9W **72 B1**
Hudson Mass., U.S.A.   42°23N 71°34W **83 D13**
Hudson N.Y., U.S.A.   42°15N 73°46W **83 D11**
Hudson Wis., U.S.A.   44°58N 92°45W **80 C7**
Hudson Wyo., U.S.A.   42°54N 108°35W **76 E9**
Hudson ➤ U.S.A.   40°42N 74°2W **83 F10**
Hudson, C. Antarctica   68°21S 153°45E **5 C10**
Hudson Bay Nunavut,
Canada   60°0N 86°0W **69 D11**
Hudson Bay Sask.,
Canada   52°51N 102°23W **71 C8**
Hudson Falls U.S.A.   43°18N 73°35W **83 C11**
Hudson Mts. Antarctica   74°32S 99°20W **5 D16**
Hudson Str. Canada   62°0N 70°0W **69 C13**
Hudson's Hope Canada   56°0N 121°54W **70 B4**
Hue Vietnam   16°30N 107°35E **38 D6**
Huehuetenango
Guatemala   15°20N 91°28W **88 C1**
Huejúcar Mexico   22°21N 103°13W **86 C4**
Huelva Spain   37°18N 6°57W **21 D2**
Huentelauquén Chile   31°38S 71°33W **94 C1**
Huerta, Sa. de la
Argentina   31°10S 67°30W **94 C2**
Huesca Spain   42°8N 0°25W **21 A5**
Huetamo Mexico   18°35N 100°53W **86 D4**
Hugh ➤ Australia   25°1S 134°1E **62 D1**
Hughenden Australia   20°52S 144°10E **62 C3**
Hughesville U.S.A.   41°14N 76°44W **83 E8**
Hugli ➤ India   21°56N 88°4E **43 J13**
Hugo Colo., U.S.A.   39°8N 103°28W **76 G12**
Hugo Okla., U.S.A.   34°1N 95°31W **84 D7**
Hugoton U.S.A.   37°11N 101°21W **80 G3**
Hui Xian = Huixian
China   35°27N 113°12E **34 G7**
Hui Xian China   33°50N 106°4E **34 H4**
Hui'anbu China   37°28N 106°38E **34 F4**
Huichapan Mexico   20°23N 99°39W **87 C5**
Huichon N. Korea   40°10N 126°16E **35 D14**
Huifa He ➤ China   43°0N 127°50E **35 C14**
Huila, Nevado del Colombia   3°0N 76°0W **92 C3**
Huimin China   37°27N 117°28E **35 F9**
Huinan China   42°40N 126°2E **35 C14**
Huinca Renancó
Argentina   34°51S 64°22W **94 C3**
Huining China   35°38N 105°0E **34 G3**
Huinong China   39°5N 106°35E **34 E4**
Huiting China   34°5N 116°5E **34 G9**
Huixian China   35°27N 113°12E **34 G7**
Huixtla Mexico   15°9N 92°28W **87 D6**
Huize China   26°24N 103°15E **32 D5**
Hukawng Valley
Burma   26°30N 96°30E **41 F20**
Hukuntsi Botswana   23°58S 21°45E **56 C3**
Ḩulayfā' Si. Arabia   25°58N 40°45E **44 E4**
Hulin He ➤ China   45°0N 122°10E **35 B12**
Hull = Kingston upon Hull
U.K.   53°45N 0°21W **12 D7**
Hull Canada   45°26N 75°43W **83 A9**
Hull ➤ U.K.   53°44N 0°20W **12 D7**
Hulst Neths.   51°17N 4°2E **15 C4**
Hulun Nur China   49°0N 117°30E **33 B6**
Huma, Tanjung Malaysia   5°29N 100°16E **39 c**
Humacao Puerto Rico   18°9N 65°50W **89 d**
Humahuaca Argentina   23°10S 65°25W **94 A2**
Humaitá Brazil   7°35S 63°1W **92 E6**
Humaitá Paraguay   27°2S 58°31W **94 B4**
Humansdorp S. Africa   34°2S 24°46E **56 E3**
Humbe Angola   16°40S 14°55E **56 B1**
Humber ➤ U.K.   53°42N 0°27W **12 D7**
Humboldt Canada   52°15N 105°9W **71 C7**
Humboldt Iowa, U.S.A.   42°44N 94°13W **80 D6**
Humboldt Tenn., U.S.A.   35°50N 88°55W **85 D10**
Humboldt ➤ U.S.A.   39°59N 118°36W **76 G4**
Humboldt Gletscher =
Sermersuaq Greenland   79°30N 62°0W **4 B4**
Hume U.S.A.   36°48N 118°54W **78 J8**
Hume, L. Australia   36°0S 147°5E **63 F4**
Humen China   22°50N 113°40E **33 F10**
Humenné Slovak Rep.   48°55N 21°50E **17 D11**
Humphreys, Mt.
U.S.A.   37°17N 118°40W **78 H8**
Humphreys Peak
U.S.A.   35°21N 111°41W **77 J8**
Humptulips U.S.A.   47°14N 123°57W **78 C3**
Hūn Libya   29°2N 16°0E **51 C9**
Hun Jiang ➤ China   40°50N 125°38E **35 D13**
Húnaflói Iceland   65°50N 20°50W **8 D3**
Hunan □ China   27°30N 112°0E **33 D6**
Hunchun China   42°52N 130°28E **35 C16**
Hundewali Pakistan   31°55N 72°38E **42 D5**

Hundred Mile House
Canada   51°38N 121°18W **70 C4**
Hunedoara Romania   45°40N 22°50E **17 F12**
Hung Yen Vietnam   20°39N 106°4E **38 B6**
Hunga Ha'apai Tonga   20°41S 175°7W **59 c**
Hungary ■ Europe   47°20N 19°20E **17 E10**
Hungary, Plain of Europe   47°0N 20°0E **6 F10**
Hungerford Australia   28°58S 144°24E **63 D3**
Ḩ̇ŭngnam N. Korea   39°49N 127°45E **35 E14**
Hunjiang China   41°54N 126°26E **35 D14**
Hunsberge Namibia   27°45S 17°12E **56 D2**
Hunsrück Germany   49°56N 7°27E **16 D4**
Hunstanton U.K.   52°56N 0°29E **12 E8**
Hunter U.S.A.   42°13N 74°13W **83 D10**
Hunter I. Australia   40°30S 144°45E **63 G3**
Hunter I. Canada   51°55N 128°0W **70 C3**
Hunter Ra. Australia   32°45S 150°15E **63 E5**
Hunters Road Zimbabwe   19°9S 29°49E **55 F2**
Hunterville N.Z.   39°56S 175°35E **59 C5**
Huntingburg U.S.A.   38°18N 86°57W **80 F10**
Huntingdon Canada   45°5N 74°10W **83 A10**
Huntingdon U.K.   52°20N 0°11W **13 E7**
Huntingdon U.S.A.   40°30N 78°1W **82 F6**
Huntington Ind., U.S.A.   40°53N 85°30W **81 E11**
Huntington N.Y.,
U.S.A.   40°52N 73°26W **83 F11**
Huntington Oreg.,
U.S.A.   44°21N 117°16W **76 D5**
Huntington Utah,
U.S.A.   39°20N 110°58W **76 G8**
Huntington W. Va.,
U.S.A.   38°25N 82°27W **81 F12**
Huntington Beach
U.S.A.   33°40N 118°5W **79 M9**
Huntly N.Z.   37°34S 175°11E **59 B5**
Huntly U.K.   57°27N 2°47W **11 D6**
Huntsville Canada   45°20N 79°14W **82 A5**
Huntsville Ala., U.S.A.   34°44N 86°35W **85 D11**
Huntsville Tex., U.S.A.   30°43N 95°33W **84 F7**
Hunyani ➤ Zimbabwe   15°57S 30°39E **55 F3**
Hunyuan China   39°42N 113°42E **34 E7**
Hunza ➤ India   35°54N 74°20E **43 B6**
Huo Xian = Huozhou
China   36°36N 111°42E **34 F6**
Huong Khe Vietnam   18°13N 105°41E **38 C5**
Huonville Australia   43°0S 147°5E **63 G4**
Huozhou China   36°36N 111°42E **34 F6**
Hupeh = Hubei □ China   31°0N 112°0E **33 C6**
Ḩūr Iran   30°50N 57°7E **45 D8**
Ḩurand Iran   38°51N 47°22E **44 B5**
Ḩuraymīla Si. Arabia   25°8N 46°8E **44 E5**
Hurd, C. Canada   45°13N 81°44W **82 A3**
Hure Qi China   42°45N 121°45E **35 C11**
Hurghada Egypt   27°15N 33°50E **51 C12**
Hurley N. Mex., U.S.A.   32°42N 108°8W **77 K9**
Hurley Wis., U.S.A.   46°27N 90°11W **80 B8**
Huron Calif., U.S.A.   36°12N 120°6W **78 J6**
Huron Ohio, U.S.A.   41°24N 82°33W **82 E2**
Huron S. Dak., U.S.A.   44°22N 98°13W **80 C4**
Huron, L. U.S.A.   44°30N 82°40W **82 B2**
Huron East Canada   43°37N 81°18W **82 C3**
Hurricane U.S.A.   37°11N 113°17W **77 H7**
Hurungwe ☆ Zimbabwe   16°7S 29°5E **55 F2**
Hurunui ➤ N.Z.   42°54S 173°18E **59 E4**
Húsavík Iceland   66°3N 17°21W **8 C5**
Huşi Romania   46°41N 28°7E **17 E15**
Hustadvika Norway   63°0N 7°0E **8 E12**
Hustontown U.S.A.   40°3N 78°2W **82 F6**
Hutchinson Kans., U.S.A.   38°5N 97°56W **80 F5**
Hutchinson Minn.,
U.S.A.   44°54N 94°22W **80 C6**
Hutte Sauvage, L. de la
Canada   56°15N 64°45W **73 A7**
Hutton, Mt. Australia   25°51S 148°20E **63 D4**
Huy Belgium   50°31N 5°15E **15 D5**
Huzhou China   30°51N 120°8E **33 C7**
Hvammstangi Iceland   65°24N 20°57W **8 D3**
Hvar Croatia   43°11N 16°28E **22 C7**
Hvítá ➤ Iceland   64°30N 21°58W **8 D3**
Hwachon-Cheosuji
S. Korea   38°5N 127°50E **35 E14**
Hwang Ho = Huang He ➤
China   37°55N 118°50E **35 F10**
Hwange Zimbabwe   18°18S 26°30E **55 F2**
Hwange △ Zimbabwe   19°0S 26°30E **56 B4**
Hyannis Mass., U.S.A.   41°39N 70°17W **81 E18**
Hyannis Nebr., U.S.A.   42°0N 101°46W **80 E3**
Hyargas Nuur Mongolia   49°0N 93°0E **32 B4**
Hydaburg U.S.A.   55°15N 132°50W **70 B2**
Hyde Park U.S.A.   41°47N 73°56W **83 E11**
Hyden Australia   32°24S 118°53E **61 F2**
Hyder U.S.A.   55°55N 130°5W **70 B2**
Hyderabad India   17°22N 78°29E **40 L11**
Hyderabad Pakistan   25°23N 68°24E **42 G3**
Hydra Greece   37°20N 23°28E **23 F10**
Hyères France   43°8N 6°9E **20 E7**
Hyères, Îs. d' France   43°0N 6°20E **20 E7**
Hyesan N. Korea   41°20N 128°10E **35 D15**
Hyland ➤ Canada   59°52N 128°12W **70 B3**
Hymia India   33°40N 78°2E **43 C8**
Hyndman Peak U.S.A.   43°45N 114°8W **76 E6**
Hyōgo □ Japan   35°15N 134°50E **31 G7**
Hyōga Japan   32°25N 131°35E **31 H5**
Hyvinge = Hyvinkää
Finland   60°38N 24°50E **8 F21**
Hyvinkää Finland   60°38N 24°50E **8 F21**

I

I-n-Gall Niger   16°51N 7°1E **50 E7**
Iaco ➤ Brazil   9°3S 68°34W **92 E5**
Iakora Madag.   23°6S 46°40E **57 C8**
Ialissos Greece   36°24N 28°10E **25 C10**
Ialomița ➤ Romania   44°42N 27°51E **17 F14**
Iași Romania   47°10N 27°40E **17 E14**

Ib ➤ India   21°34N 83°48E **43 J10**
Iba Phil.   15°22N 120°0E **37 A6**
Ibadan Nigeria   7°22N 3°58E **50 G6**
Ibagué Colombia   4°20N 75°20W **92 C3**
Ibar ➤ Serbia   43°43N 20°45E **23 C9**
Ibaraki □ Japan   36°10N 140°10E **31 F10**
Ibarra Ecuador   0°21N 78°7W **92 C3**
Ibb Yemen   14°2N 44°10E **47 E3**
Ibembo
Dem. Rep. of the Congo   2°35N 23°35E **54 B1**
Ibenga ➤ Congo   2°19N 18°9E **52 D3**
Ibera, L. Argentina   28°30S 57°9W **94 B4**
Iberian Peninsula Europe   40°0N 5°0W **6 H5**
Iberville Canada   45°19N 73°17W **83 A11**
Ibiá Brazil   19°30S 46°30W **93 G9**
Ibiapaba, Sa. da Brazil   4°0S 41°30W **93 D10**
Ibicuí ➤ Brazil   29°25S 56°47W **95 B4**
Ibicuy Argentina   33°55S 59°10W **94 C4**
Ibiza = Eivissa Spain   38°54N 1°26E **24 C7**
Ibo Mozam.   12°22S 40°40E **55 E5**
Ibonma Indonesia   3°29S 133°31E **37 E8**
Ibotirama Brazil   12°13S 43°12W **93 F10**
Ibrāhīm ➤ Lebanon   34°4N 35°38E **46 A4**
'Ibrī Oman   23°14N 56°30E **45 F8**
Ibu Indonesia   1°35N 127°33E **37 D7**
Ibusuki Japan   31°12N 130°40E **31 J5**
Ica Peru   14°0S 75°48W **92 F3**
Iça ➤ Brazil   2°55S 67°58W **92 D5**
Icacos Pt. Trin. & Tob.   10°3N 61°57W **93 K15**
Içana Brazil   0°21N 67°19W **92 C5**
Içana ➤ Brazil   0°26N 67°19W **92 C5**
Içel Turkey   36°51N 34°36E **44 B2**
Iceland ■ Europe   64°45N 19°0W **8 D4**
Iceland Basin Atl. Oc.   61°0N 19°0W **4 C7**
Icelandic Plateau Arctic   64°0N 10°0W **4 C7**
Ich'ang = Yichang
China   30°40N 111°20E **33 C6**
Ichchapuram India   19°10N 84°40E **41 K14**
Icheon S. Korea   37°17N 127°27E **35 F14**
Ichhawar India   23°1N 77°1E **42 H7**
Ichihara Japan   35°28N 140°5E **31 G10**
Ichikawa Japan   35°43N 139°54E **31 G9**
Ichilo ➤ Bolivia   15°57S 64°50W **92 G6**
Ichinohe Japan   40°13N 141°17E **30 D10**
Ichinomiya Japan   35°18N 136°48E **31 G8**
Ichinoseki Japan   38°55N 141°8E **30 E10**
Icod Canary Is.   28°22N 16°43W **24 F3**
Icy C. U.S.A.   70°20N 161°52W **66 B3**
Ida Grove U.S.A.   42°21N 95°28W **80 D6**
Idabel U.S.A.   33°54N 94°50W **84 E7**
Idaho □ U.S.A.   45°0N 115°0W **76 D7**
Idaho City U.S.A.   43°50N 115°50W **76 E6**
Idaho Falls U.S.A.   43°30N 112°2W **76 E7**
Idalia △ Australia   24°49S 144°36E **62 C3**
Idar-Oberstein Germany   49°43N 7°16E **16 D4**
Idensalmi = Iisalmi
Finland   63°32N 27°10E **8 E22**
Idfû Egypt   24°55N 32°49E **51 D12**
Idhra = Hydra Greece   37°20N 23°28E **23 F10**
Idi, Oros = Psiloritis, Oros
Greece   35°15N 24°45E **25 D6**
Idiofa
Dem. Rep. of the Congo   4°55S 19°42E **52 E3**
Idlib Syria   35°55N 36°36E **44 C3**
Idria U.S.A.   36°25N 120°41W **78 J6**
Idutywa = Dutywa
S. Africa   32°8S 28°18E **57 E4**
Ieper Belgium   50°51N 2°53E **15 D2**
Ierapetra Greece   35°1N 25°44E **25 E7**
Iesi Italy   43°31N 13°14E **22 C5**
Ifakara Tanzania   8°8S 36°41E **54 F7**
'Ifāl, W. al ➤ Si. Arabia   28°7N 35°3E **44 D2**
Ifanadiana Madag.   21°19S 47°39E **57 C8**
Ife Nigeria   7°30N 4°31E **50 G6**
Iffley Australia   18°53S 141°12E **62 B3**
Iforas, Adrar des Africa   19°40N 1°40E **50 E6**
Ifould, L. Australia   30°52S 132°6E **61 F5**
Iganga Uganda   0°37N 33°28E **54 B3**
Igarapava Brazil   20°3S 47°47W **93 H9**
Igarka Russia   67°30N 86°33E **28 C9**
Iggesund Sweden   61°39N 17°10E **8 F17**
Iglésias Italy   39°19N 8°32E **22 E3**
Igloolik = Iglulik
Canada   69°20N 81°49W **69 C11**
Igluligaarjuk = Chesterfield Inlet
Canada   63°30N 90°45W **68 C10**
Iglulik Canada   69°20N 81°49W **69 C11**
Ignace Canada   49°30N 91°40W **72 C1**
İğneada Burnu Turkey   41°53N 28°2E **23 D13**
Igoumenítsa Greece   39°32N 20°18E **23 E9**
Igrim Russia   63°12N 64°30E **28 C7**
Iguaçu ➤ Brazil   25°36S 54°36W **95 B5**
Iguaçu, Cat. del Brazil   25°41S 54°26W **95 B5**
Iguaçu △ Brazil   25°30S 54°0W **95 B5**
Iguaçu Falls = Iguaçu, Cat. del
Brazil   25°41S 54°26W **95 B5**
Iguala Mexico   18°21N 99°32W **87 D5**
Igualada Spain   41°37N 1°37E **21 B6**
Iguassu = Iguaçu ➤
Brazil   25°36S 54°36W **95 B5**
Iguatu Brazil   6°20S 39°18W **93 E11**
Iguazú □ Argentina   25°42S 54°22W **95 B5**
Iguidi, Erg Africa   27°0N 7°0W **50 C4**
Iharana Madag.   13°25S 50°0E **57 A9**
Ihbulag Mongolia   43°11N 107°10E **34 C4**
Iheya-Shima Japan   27°4N 127°58E **31 L3**
Ihosy Madag.   22°24S 46°8E **57 C8**
Ihotry, Farihy Madag.   21°56S 43°41E **57 C7**
Ii Finland   65°19N 25°22E **8 D21**
Ii-Shima Japan   26°43N 127°49E **31 L3**
Iida Japan   35°35N 137°50E **31 G8**
Iijoki ➤ Finland   65°20N 25°20E **8 D21**
Iisalmi Finland   63°32N 27°10E **8 E22**
Iiyama Japan   36°51N 138°22E **31 F9**
Iizuka Japan   33°38N 130°42E **31 H5**
Ijâfene Mauritania   20°40N 8°0W **50 D4**

Ijebu-Ode Nigeria 6°47N 3°58E 50 G6
IJmuiden Neths. 52°28N 4°35E 15 B4
Ijo älv = Iijoki →
  Finland 65°20N 25°20E 8 D21
IJssel → Neths. 52°35N 5°50E 15 B5
IJsselmeer Neths. 52°45N 5°20E 15 B5
Ijui Brazil 28°23S 53°55W 95 B5
Ijuí → Brazil 27°58S 55°20W 95 B4
Ikalamavony Madag. 21°9S 46°35E 57 C8
Ikaluktutiak Canada 69°10N 105°0W 68 C9
Ikanga Kenya 1°42S 38°4E 54 C4
Ikare Nigeria 7°32N 5°40E 50 G7
Ikaria Greece 37°35N 26°10E 23 F12
Ikeda Japan 34°1N 133°48E 31 G6
Ikela Dem. Rep. of the Congo 1°6S 23°6E 52 E4
Iki Japan 33°45N 129°42E 31 H4
Ikimba L. Tanzania 1°30S 31°20E 54 C3
Ikongo Madag. 21°52S 47°27E 57 C8
Ikopa → Madag. 16°45S 46°40E 57 B8
Ikorongo △ Tanzania 1°50S 34°53E 54 C3
Ikparjuk = Arctic Bay
  Canada 73°1N 85°7W 69 B11
Iksan S. Korea 35°59N 127°0E 35 G14
Ikungu Tanzania 1°33S 33°42E 54 C3
Ikuntji = Haast Bluff
  Australia 23°22S 132°0E 60 D5
Ilagan Phil. 17°7N 121°53E 37 A6
Ilaka Madag. 19°33S 48°52E 57 B8
Ilâm Iran 33°36N 46°36E 44 C5
Ilam Nepal 26°58N 87°58E 43 F12
Ilâm □ Iran 33°0N 47°0E 44 C5
Ilanskiy Russia 56°14N 96°3E 29 D10
Ilawa Poland 53°36N 19°34E 17 B10
Ile → Kazakhstan 45°53N 77°10E 28 E8
Île-à-la-Crosse Canada 55°27N 107°53W 71 B7
Île-à-la-Crosse, Lac
  Canada 55°40N 107°45W 71 B7
Île-de-France □ France 49°0N 2°20E 20 B5
Ilebo Dem. Rep. of the Congo 4°17S 20°55E 52 E4
Ilek Russia 51°32N 53°21E 28 D6
Ilek → Russia 51°30N 53°22E 18 D9
Ilesha Nigeria 7°37N 4°40E 50 G6
Ilford Canada 56°4N 95°35W 71 B9
Ilfracombe Australia 23°30S 144°30E 62 C3
Ilfracombe U.K. 51°12N 4°8W 13 F3
Ilha de Moçambique
  Mozam. 15°4S 40°52E 55 F5
Ilha Grande, Represa
  Brazil 23°10S 53°5W 95 A5
Ilha Grande △ Brazil 23°10S 53°20W 95 A5
Ilhéus Brazil 14°49S 39°2W 93 F11
Ili = Ile → Kazakhstan 45°53N 77°10E 28 E8
Iliamna L. U.S.A. 59°30N 155°0W 74 a
Ilias, Profitis Greece 36°17N 27°56E 25 C9
Iligan Phil. 8°12N 124°13E 37 C6
Ilion U.S.A. 43°1N 75°2W 83 D9
Ilkeston U.K. 52°58N 1°19W 12 E6
Ilkley U.K. 53°56N 1°48W 12 D6
Illampu = Ancohuma, Nevado
  Bolivia 16°0S 68°50W 92 G5
Illana B. Phil. 7°35N 123°45E 37 C6
Illapel Chile 32°0S 71°10W 94 C1
Iller → Germany 48°23N 9°58E 16 D6
Illetas Spain 39°32N 2°35E 24 B9
Illimani, Nevado Bolivia 16°30S 67°50W 92 G5
Illinois □ U.S.A. 40°15N 89°30W 80 E9
Illinois → U.S.A. 38°58N 90°28W 80 F8
Illizi Algeria 26°31N 8°32E 50 C7
Ilma, L. Australia 29°13S 127°46E 61 E4
Ilmajoki Finland 62°44N 22°34E 8 E20
Ilmen, Ozero Russia 58°15N 31°10E 18 C5
Ilo Peru 17°40S 71°20W 92 G4
Iloilo Phil. 10°45N 122°33E 37 B6
Ilomantsi Finland 62°38N 30°57E 8 E24
Ilorin Nigeria 8°30N 4°35E 50 G6
Ilwaco U.S.A. 46°19N 124°3W 78 D2
Ilwaki Indonesia 7°55S 126°30E 37 F7
Imabari Japan 34°4N 133°0E 31 G6
Imaloto → Madag. 23°27S 45°13E 57 C8
Imandra, Ozero Russia 67°30N 33°0E 8 C25
Imanombo Madag. 24°26S 45°49E 57 C8
Imari Japan 33°15N 129°52E 31 H4
Imatra Finland 61°12N 28°48E 8 F23
imeni 26 Bakinskikh Komissarov
  = Neftçala Azerbaijan 39°19N 49°12E 45 B6
imeni 26 Bakinskikh Komissarov
  Turkmenistan 39°22N 54°10E 45 B7
imeni Ismail Samani, Pik
  Tajikistan 39°0N 72°2E 28 F8
Imeri, Serra Brazil 0°50N 65°25W 92 C5
Imerimandroso Madag. 17°26S 48°35E 57 B8
Imfolozi △ S. Africa 28°18S 31°50E 57 D5
Imi Ethiopia 6°28N 42°10E 47 F3
Imlay U.S.A. 40°40N 118°9W 76 F4
Imlay City U.S.A. 43°2N 83°5W 82 D1
Immingham U.K. 53°37N 0°13W 12 D7
Immokalee U.S.A. 26°25N 81°25W 85 H14
Ímola Italy 44°20N 11°42E 22 B4
Imperatriz Brazil 5°30S 47°29W 93 E9
Impéria Italy 43°53N 8°3E 20 E8
Imperial Canada 51°21N 105°28W 71 C7
Imperial Calif., U.S.A. 32°51N 115°34W 79 N11
Imperial Nebr., U.S.A. 40°31N 101°39W 80 E3
Imperial Beach U.S.A. 32°35N 117°6W 79 N9
Imperial Dam U.S.A. 32°55N 114°25W 79 N12
Imperial Res. U.S.A. 32°53N 114°28W 79 N12
Imperial Valley U.S.A. 33°0N 115°30W 79 N11
Imperieuse Reef
  Australia 17°36S 118°50E 60 C2
Impfondo Congo 1°40N 18°0E 52 D3
Imphal India 24°48N 93°56E 41 G18
Imroz = Gökçeada
  Turkey 40°10N 25°50E 23 D11
Imuris Mexico 30°47N 110°52W 86 A2
Imuruan B. Phil. 10°40N 119°10E 37 B5
In Salah Algeria 27°10N 2°32E 50 C6
Ina Japan 35°50N 137°55E 31 G8

Inagua △ Bahamas 21°5N 73°24W 89 B5
Inangahua N.Z. 41°52S 171°59E 59 D3
Inanwatan Indonesia 2°8S 132°10E 37 E8
Iñapari Peru 11°0S 69°40W 92 F5
Inari Finland 68°54N 27°1E 8 B22
Inarijärvi Finland 69°0N 28°0E 8 B23
Inawashiro-Ko Japan 37°29N 140°6E 30 F10
Inca Spain 39°43N 2°54E 24 B9
Inca de Oro Chile 26°45S 69°54W 94 B2
Incahuasi Argentina 27°2S 68°18W 94 B2
Incahuasi Chile 29°12S 71°5W 94 B1
İnce Burun Turkey 42°7N 34°56E 19 F5
İncesu Turkey 38°38N 35°11E 44 B2
Incheon S. Korea 37°27N 126°40E 35 F14
İncirliova Turkey 37°50N 27°41E 23 F12
Incline Village U.S.A. 39°10N 119°58W 76 G4
Incomáti → Mozam. 25°46S 32°43E 57 D5
Indalsälven → Sweden 62°36N 17°30E 8 E17
Indaw Burma 24°15N 96°5E 41 G20
Independence Calif.,
  U.S.A. 36°48N 118°12W 78 J8
Independence Iowa,
  U.S.A. 42°28N 91°54W 80 D8
Independence Kans.,
  U.S.A. 37°14N 95°42W 80 G6
Independence Ky.,
  U.S.A. 38°57N 84°33W 81 F11
Independence Mo., U.S.A. 39°6N 94°25W 80 F6
Independence Fjord
  Greenland 82°10N 29°0W 4 A6
Independence Mts.
  U.S.A. 41°20N 116°0W 76 F5
Index U.S.A. 47°50N 121°33W 78 C5
India ■ Asia 20°0N 78°0E 40 K11
Indian → U.S.A. 27°59N 80°34W 85 H14
Indian Cabins Canada 59°52N 117°40W 70 B5
Indian Harbour Canada 54°27N 57°13W 73 B8
Indian Head Canada 50°30N 103°41W 71 C8
Indian L. U.S.A. 43°46N 74°16W 83 C10
Indian Lake U.S.A. 43°47N 74°16W 83 C10
Indian Springs U.S.A. 36°35N 115°40W 79 J11
Indiana U.S.A. 40°37N 79°9W 82 F5
Indiana □ U.S.A. 40°0N 86°0W 81 F11
Indianapolis U.S.A. 39°46N 86°9W 80 F10
Indianola Iowa, U.S.A. 41°22N 93°34W 80 E7
Indianola Miss., U.S.A. 33°27N 90°39W 85 E9
Indiga Russia 67°38N 49°9E 18 A8
Indigirka → Russia 70°48N 148°54E 29 B15
Indio U.S.A. 33°43N 116°13W 79 M10
Indira Gandhi Canal India 28°0N 72°0E 42 F5
Indira Sagar India 22°15N 76°40E 42 H7
Indo-China Asia 15°0N 102°0E 26 G12
Indonesia ■ Asia 5°0S 115°0E 36 F5
Indore India 22°42N 75°53E 42 H6
Indramayu Indonesia 6°20S 108°19E 37 G13
Indravati → India 19°20N 80°20E 41 K12
Indre → France 47°16N 0°11E 20 C4
Indulkana Australia 26°58S 133°5E 63 D1
Indus → Pakistan 24°20N 67°47E 42 G2
Indus, Mouths of the
  Pakistan 24°0N 68°0E 42 H3
İnebolu Turkey 41°55N 33°40E 19 F5
Infiernillo, Presa del
  Mexico 18°35N 101°50W 86 D4
Ingenio Canary Is. 27°55N 15°26W 24 G4
Ingenio Santa Ana
  Argentina 27°25S 65°40W 94 B2
Ingersoll Canada 43°4N 80°55W 82 C4
Ingham Australia 18°43S 146°10E 62 B4
Ingleborough U.K. 54°10N 2°22W 12 C5
Inglewood Queens.,
  Australia 28°25S 151°2E 63 D5
Inglewood Vic., Australia 36°29S 143°53E 63 F3
Inglewood N.Z. 39°9S 174°14E 59 C5
Inglewood U.S.A. 33°58N 118°21W 79 M8
Ingólfshöfði Iceland 63°48N 16°39W 8 E5
Ingolstadt Germany 48°46N 11°26E 16 D6
Ingomar U.S.A. 46°35N 107°23W 76 C10
Ingonish Canada 46°42N 60°18W 73 C7
Ingraj Bazar India 24°58N 88°10E 43 G13
Ingrid Christensen Coast
  Antarctica 69°30S 76°0E 5 C6
Ingulec = Inhulec
  Ukraine 47°42N 33°14E 19 E5
Ingushetia □ Russia 43°20N 44°50E 19 F8
Ingwavuma S. Africa 27°9S 31°59E 57 D5
Inhaca Mozam. 26°1S 32°57E 57 D5
Inhafenga Mozam. 20°36S 33°53E 57 C5
Inhambane Mozam. 23°54S 35°30E 57 C6
Inhambane □ Mozam. 22°30S 34°20E 57 C5
Inhaminga Mozam. 18°26S 35°0E 55 F4
Inharrime Mozam. 24°30S 35°0E 57 C6
Inharrime → Mozam. 24°30S 35°0E 57 C6
Inhulec Ukraine 47°42N 33°14E 19 E5
Iniesta Spain 39°27N 1°45W 21 C5
Ining = Yining China 43°58N 81°10E 32 B3
Inírida → Colombia 3°55N 67°52W 92 C5
Inishbofin Ireland 53°37N 10°13W 10 C1
Inisheer Ireland 53°3N 9°32W 10 C2
Inishfree B. Ireland 55°4N 8°23W 10 A3
Inishkea North Ireland 54°9N 10°11W 10 B1
Inishkea South Ireland 54°7N 10°12W 10 B1
Inishmaan Ireland 53°5N 9°35W 10 C2
Inishmore Ireland 53°8N 9°45W 10 C2
Inishmurray I. Ireland 54°26N 8°39W 10 B3
Inishowen Pen. Ireland 55°14N 7°15W 10 A4
Inishshark Ireland 53°37N 10°16W 10 C1
Inishturk Ireland 53°42N 10°7W 10 C1
Inishvickillane Ireland 52°3N 10°37W 10 D1
Injune Australia 25°53S 148°32E 63 D4
Inklin → N. Amer. 58°50N 133°10W 70 B2
Inland Kaikoura Ra.
  N.Z. 41°59S 173°41E 59 D4
Inland Sea = Setonaikai
  Japan 34°20N 133°30E 31 G6
Inle L. Burma 20°30N 96°58E 41 J20
Inlet U.S.A. 43°45N 74°48W 83 C10
Inn → Austria 48°35N 13°28E 16 D7

Innamincka Australia 27°44S 140°46E 63 D3
Inner Hebrides U.K. 57°0N 6°30W 11 E2
Inner Mongolia = Nei Monggol
  Zizhiqu □ China 42°0N 112°0E 34 D7
Inner Sound U.K. 57°30N 5°55W 11 D3
Innerkip Canada 43°13N 80°42W 82 C4
Innetalling I. Canada 56°0N 79°0W 72 A4
Innisfail Australia 17°33S 146°5E 62 B4
Innisfail Canada 52°2N 113°57W 70 C6
In'noshima Japan 34°19N 133°10E 31 G6
Innsbruck Austria 47°16N 11°23E 16 E6
Inny → Ireland 53°30N 7°50W 10 C4
Inongo
  Dem. Rep. of the Congo 1°55S 18°30E 52 E3
Inowrocław Poland 52°50N 18°12E 17 B10
Inscription, C. Australia 25°29S 112°59E 61 E1
Insein Burma 16°50N 96°5E 41 L20
Inta Russia 66°5N 60°8E 18 A11
Intendente Alvear
  Argentina 35°12S 63°32W 94 D3
Interlaken Switz. 46°41N 7°50E 20 C7
Interlaken U.S.A. 42°37N 76°44W 83 D8
International Falls
  U.S.A. 48°36N 93°25W 80 A7
Intiyaco Argentina 28°43S 60°5W 94 B3
Inukjuak Canada 58°25N 78°15W 69 D12
Inútil, B. Chile 53°30S 70°15W 96 G2
Inuvik Canada 68°16N 133°40W 68 C6
Inveraray U.K. 56°14N 5°5W 11 E3
Inverbervie U.K. 56°51N 2°17W 11 E6
Invercargill N.Z. 46°24S 168°24E 59 G2
Inverclyde □ U.K. 55°55N 4°49W 11 F4
Inverell Australia 29°45S 151°8E 63 D5
Invergordon U.K. 57°41N 4°10W 11 D4
Inverloch Australia 38°38S 145°45E 63 F4
Invermere Canada 50°30N 116°2W 70 C5
Inverness Canada 46°15N 61°19W 73 C7
Inverness U.K. 57°29N 4°13W 11 D4
Inverness U.S.A. 28°50N 82°20W 85 G13
Inverurie U.K. 57°17N 2°23W 11 D6
Investigator Group
  Australia 34°45S 134°20E 63 E1
Investigator Str.
  Australia 35°30S 137°0E 63 F2
Inya Russia 50°28N 86°37E 28 D9
Inyanga Zimbabwe 18°12S 32°40E 55 F3
Inyangani Zimbabwe 18°5S 32°50E 55 F3
Inyantue Zimbabwe 18°33S 26°39E 56 B4
Inyo Mts. U.S.A. 36°40N 118°0W 78 J9
Inyokern U.S.A. 35°39N 117°49W 79 K9
Inza Russia 53°55N 46°25E 18 D8
Iō-Jima Japan 30°48N 130°18E 31 J5
Ioannina Greece 39°42N 20°47E 23 E9
Iola U.S.A. 37°55N 95°24W 80 G6
Iona U.K. 56°20N 6°25W 11 E2
Ione U.S.A. 38°21N 120°56W 78 G6
Ionia U.S.A. 42°59N 85°4W 81 D11
Ionian Is. = Ioioi Nisoi
  Greece 38°40N 20°0E 23 E9
Ionian Sea Medit. S. 37°30N 17°30E 23 E7
Ioioi Nisoi Greece 38°40N 20°0E 23 E9
Ios Greece 36°41N 25°20E 23 F11
Iowa □ U.S.A. 42°18N 93°30W 80 D7
Iowa → U.S.A. 41°10N 91°1W 80 E8
Iowa City U.S.A. 41°40N 91°32W 80 E8
Iowa Falls U.S.A. 42°31N 93°16W 80 D7
Iowa Park U.S.A. 33°57N 98°40W 84 E5
Ipala Tanzania 4°30S 32°52E 54 C3
Ipameri Brazil 17°44S 48°9W 93 G9
Ipatinga Brazil 19°32S 42°30W 93 G10
Ipiales Colombia 0°50N 77°37W 92 C3
Ipin = Yibin China 28°45N 104°32E 32 D5
Ipixuna Brazil 7°0S 71°40W 92 E4
Ipoh Malaysia 4°35N 101°5E 39 K3
Ippy C.A.R. 6°5N 21°7E 52 C4
İpsala Turkey 40°55N 26°23E 23 D12
Ipswich Australia 27°35S 152°40E 63 D5
Ipswich U.K. 52°4N 1°10E 13 E9
Ipswich Mass., U.S.A. 42°41N 70°50W 83 D14
Ipswich S. Dak., U.S.A. 45°27N 99°2W 80 C4
Ipu Brazil 4°23S 40°44W 93 D10
Iqaluit Canada 63°44N 68°31W 69 C13
Iquique Chile 20°19S 70°5W 92 H4
Iquitos Peru 3°45S 73°10W 92 D4
Irabu-Jima Japan 24°50N 125°10E 31 M2
Iracoubo Fr. Guiana 5°30N 53°10W 93 B8
Īrafshān Iran 26°42N 61°56E 45 E9
Iráklio Greece 35°20N 25°12E 25 D7
Iráklio □ Greece 35°10N 25°10E 25 D7
Iráklion = Iraklio Greece 35°20N 25°12E 25 D7
Irakliou, Kolpos Greece 35°23N 25°8E 25 D7
Irala Paraguay 25°55S 54°35W 95 B5
Iran ■ Asia 33°0N 53°0E 45 C7
Iran, Pegunungan
  Malaysia 2°20N 114°50E 36 D4
Iran Ra. = Iran, Pegunungan
  Malaysia 2°20N 114°50E 36 D4
Īrānshahr Iran 27°15N 60°40E 45 E9
Irapuato Mexico 20°41N 101°28W 86 C4
Iraq ■ Asia 33°0N 44°0E 44 C5
Irati Brazil 25°25S 50°38W 95 B5
Irbid Jordan 32°35N 35°48E 46 C4
Irbid □ Jordan 32°30N 35°0E 46 C4
Irebu Dem. Rep. of the Congo 0°40S 17°46E 52 E3
Ireland ■ Europe 53°50N 7°52W 10 C4
Iri = Iksan S. Korea 35°59N 127°0E 35 G14
Irian Jaya = Papua □
  Indonesia 4°0S 137°0E 37 E9
Irian Jaya Barat □
  Indonesia 2°5S 132°50E 37 E8
Iringa Tanzania 7°48S 35°43E 54 D4
Iringa □ Tanzania 7°48S 35°43E 54 D4
Iriomote △ Japan 24°29N 123°53E 31 M1
Iriomote-Jima Japan 24°19N 123°48E 31 M1
Iriona Honduras 15°57N 85°11W 88 C2

Iriri → Brazil 3°52S 52°37W 93 D8
Irish Republic ■ Europe 53°50N 7°52W 10 C4
Irish Sea Europe 53°38N 4°48W 12 D3
Irkutsk Russia 52°18N 104°20E 29 D11
Irō-Zaki Japan 34°36N 138°51E 31 G9
Iron Baron Australia 32°58S 137°11E 63 E2
Iron Knob Australia 32°46S 137°8E 63 E2
Iron Mountain U.S.A. 45°49N 88°4W 80 C9
Iron Range △ Australia 12°34S 143°18E 62 A3
Iron River U.S.A. 46°6N 88°39W 80 B9
Irondequoit U.S.A. 43°13N 77°35W 82 C7
Ironton Mo., U.S.A. 37°36N 90°38W 80 G8
Ironton Ohio, U.S.A. 38°32N 82°41W 81 F12
Ironwood U.S.A. 46°27N 90°9W 80 B8
Ironwood Forest △
  U.S.A. 32°32N 111°28W 77 K8
Iroquois Canada 44°51N 75°19W 83 B9
Iroquois Falls Canada 48°46N 80°41W 72 C3
Irpin Ukraine 50°30N 30°15E 17 C16
Irrara Cr. → Australia 29°35S 145°31E 63 D4
Irrawaddy □ Burma 17°0N 95°0E 41 L19
Irrawaddy → Burma 15°50N 95°6E 41 M19
Irrawaddy, Mouths of the
  Burma 15°30N 95°0E 41 M19
Irricana Canada 51°19N 113°37W 70 C6
Irtysh → Russia 61°4N 68°52E 28 C7
Irumu
  Dem. Rep. of the Congo 1°32N 29°53E 54 B2
Irún Spain 43°20N 1°52W 21 A5
Irunea = Pamplona-Iruña
  Spain 42°48N 1°38W 21 A5
Irvine U.K. 55°37N 4°41W 11 F4
Irvine Calif., U.S.A. 33°41N 117°46W 79 M9
Irvine Ky., U.S.A. 37°42N 83°58W 81 G12
Irvinestown U.K. 54°28N 7°39W 10 B4
Irving U.S.A. 32°48N 96°56W 84 E6
Irvona U.S.A. 40°46N 78°33W 82 F6
Irwin → Australia 29°15S 114°54E 61 E1
Irymple Australia 34°14S 142°8E 63 E3
Isa Khel Pakistan 32°41N 71°17E 42 C4
Isaac → Australia 22°55S 149°20E 62 C4
Isabel U.S.A. 45°24N 101°26W 80 C3
Isabel, I. Mexico 21°51N 105°55W 86 C3
Isabela Phil. 6°40N 121°59E 37 C6
Isabela Puerto Rico 18°30N 67°2W 89 d
Isabella, Cord. Nic. 13°30N 85°25W 88 D2
Isabella Ra. Australia 21°0S 121°4E 60 D3
Isachenko, Ostrov
  Russia 77°13N 89°72E 29 B9
Ísafjarðardjúp Iceland 66°10N 23°0W 8 C2
Ísafjörður Iceland 66°5N 23°9W 8 C2
Isagarh India 24°48N 77°51E 42 G7
Isahaya Japan 32°52N 130°2E 31 H5
Isaka Tanzania 3°56S 32°59E 54 C3
Isalo △ Madag. 22°23S 45°16E 57 C8
Isan → India 26°51N 80°7E 43 F9
Isana = Içana → Brazil 0°26N 67°19W 92 C5
Isangano △ Zambia 11°8S 30°35E 55 E3
Isar → Germany 48°48N 12°57E 16 D7
Ischia Italy 40°44N 13°57E 22 D5
Isdell → Australia 16°27S 124°51E 60 C3
Ise Japan 34°25N 136°45E 31 G8
Ise-Shima △ Japan 34°25N 136°48E 31 G8
Ise-Wan Japan 34°43N 136°43E 31 G8
Iseramagazi Tanzania 4°37S 32°10E 54 C3
Isère → France 44°59N 4°51E 20 D6
Isérnia Italy 41°36N 14°14E 22 D6
Isfahan = Eşfahān Iran 32°39N 51°43E 45 C6
Ishigaki Japan 24°26N 124°10E 31 M2
Ishigaki-Shima Japan 24°20N 124°10E 31 M2
Ishikari-Gawa →
  Japan 43°15N 141°23E 30 C10
Ishikari-Sammyaku
  Japan 43°30N 143°0E 30 C11
Ishikari-Wan Japan 43°25N 141°1E 30 C10
Ishikawa Japan 26°25N 127°49E 31 L3
Ishikawa □ Japan 36°30N 136°30E 31 F8
Ishim Russia 56°10N 69°30E 28 D7
Ishim → Russia 57°45N 71°10E 28 D8
Ishinomaki Japan 38°32N 141°20E 30 E10
Ishioka Japan 36°11N 140°16E 31 F10
Ishkoman Pakistan 36°30N 73°50E 43 A5
Ishpeming U.S.A. 46°29N 87°40W 80 B10
Isil Kul Russia 54°55N 71°16E 28 D8
Isiolo Kenya 0°24N 37°33E 54 B4
Isiro Dem. Rep. of the Congo 2°53N 27°40E 54 B2
Isisford Australia 24°15S 144°21E 62 C3
İskenderun Turkey 36°32N 36°10E 44 B3
İskenderun Körfezi
  Turkey 36°40N 35°50E 19 G6
İskŭr → Bulgaria 43°45N 24°25E 23 C11
Iskut → Canada 56°45N 131°49W 70 B2
Isla → U.K. 56°32N 3°20W 11 E5
Isla Coiba △ Panama 7°33N 81°36W 88 E3
Isla de Salamanca △
  Colombia 10°59N 74°40W 89 D5
Isla Gorge △ Australia 25°10S 149°57E 62 C4
Isla Isabel △ Mexico 21°54N 105°58W 86 C3
Isla Tiburón y San Esteban △
  Mexico 29°0N 112°27W 86 B2
Isla Vista U.S.A. 34°25N 119°53W 79 L7
Islam Headworks
  Pakistan 29°49N 72°33E 42 E5
Islamabad Pakistan 33°40N 73°10E 42 C5
Islamgarh Pakistan 27°55N 70°48E 42 F4
Islamkot Pakistan 24°42N 70°13E 42 G4
Islampur India 26°16N 88°12E 43 F13
Islampur Bihar, India 25°9N 85°12E 43 G11
Island = Iceland ■ Europe 64°45N 19°0W 8 D4
Island Lagoon Australia 31°30S 136°40E 63 E2
Island Pond U.S.A. 44°49N 71°53W 83 B13
Islands, B. of Canada 49°11N 58°15W 73 C8

Islands, B. of N.Z. 35°15S 174°6E 59 A5
Islay U.K. 55°46N 6°10W 11 F2
Isle → France 44°55N 0°15W 20 D3
Isle aux Morts Canada 47°35N 59°0W 73 C8
Isle of Wight □ U.K. 50°41N 1°17W 13 G6
Isle Royale △ U.S.A. 48°0N 88°55W 80 B9
Isleton U.S.A. 38°10N 121°37W 78 G5
Ismail = Izmayil
  Ukraine 45°22N 28°46E 17 F15
Ismâ'îlîya Egypt 30°37N 32°18E 51 B12
Isna Egypt 25°17N 32°30E 51 C12
Isoanala Madag. 23°50S 45°44E 57 C8
Isogstalo India 34°15N 78°46E 43 B8
Ísparta Turkey 37°47N 30°30E 19 G5
Íspica Italy 36°47N 14°55E 22 F6
Israel ■ Asia 32°0N 34°50E 46 D3
Issoire France 45°32N 3°15E 20 D5
Issyk-Kul = Balykchy
  Kyrgyzstan 42°26N 76°12E 32 B2
Issyk-Kul, Ozero = Ysyk-Köl
  Kyrgyzstan 42°25N 77°15E 28 E8
İstanbul Turkey 41°0N 28°58E 23 D13
İstanbul Boğazı Turkey 41°5N 29°3E 23 D13
Istiea Greece 38°57N 23°9E 23 E10
Istokpoga, L. U.S.A. 27°23N 81°17W 85 H14
Istra Croatia 45°10N 14°0E 16 F7
Istres France 43°31N 4°59E 20 E6
Istria = Istra Croatia 45°10N 14°0E 16 F7
Itá Paraguay 25°29S 57°21W 94 B4
Itaberaba Brazil 12°32S 40°18W 93 F10
Itabira Brazil 19°37S 43°13W 93 G10
Itabirito Brazil 20°15S 43°48W 95 A7
Itabuna Brazil 14°48S 39°16W 93 F11
Itacaunas → Brazil 5°21S 49°8W 93 E9
Itacoatiara Brazil 3°8S 58°25W 92 D7
Itaipú, Represa de Brazil 25°30S 54°30W 95 B5
Itaituba Brazil 4°10S 55°50W 93 D7
Itajaí Brazil 27°50S 48°39W 95 B6
Itajubá Brazil 22°24S 45°30W 95 A6
Itaka Tanzania 8°50S 32°49E 55 D3
Itala △ S. Africa 27°30S 31°7E 57 D5
Italy ■ Europe 42°0N 13°0E 22 C5
Itamaraju Brazil 17°5S 39°32W 93 G11
Itampolo Madag. 24°41S 43°57E 57 C7
Itandrano Madag. 21°47S 45°17E 57 C8
Itapecuru Mirim Brazil 3°24S 44°20W 93 D10
Itaperuna Brazil 21°10S 41°54W 95 A7
Itapetininga Brazil 23°36S 48°7W 95 A6
Itapeva Brazil 23°59S 48°59W 95 A6
Itapicuru → Bahia,
  Brazil 11°47S 37°32W 93 F11
Itapicuru → Maranhão,
  Brazil 2°52S 44°12W 93 D10
Itapipoca Brazil 3°30S 39°35W 93 D11
Itapuá □ Paraguay 26°40S 55°40W 95 B4
Itaquari Brazil 20°20S 40°25W 95 A7
Itaquí Brazil 29°8S 56°30W 94 B4
Itararé Brazil 24°6S 49°23W 95 A6
Itarsi India 22°36N 77°51E 42 H7
Itatí Argentina 27°16S 58°15W 94 B4
Itatiaia △ Brazil 22°22S 44°38W 95 A7
Itchen → U.K. 50°55N 1°22W 13 G6
Itezhi Tezhi, L. Zambia 15°30S 25°30E 55 F2
Ithaca = Ithaki Greece 38°25N 20°40E 23 E9
Ithaca U.S.A. 42°27N 76°30W 83 D8
Ithaki Greece 38°25N 20°40E 23 E9
Itiquira → Brazil 17°18S 56°44W 93 G7
Itiyuro → Argentina 22°40S 63°50W 94 A3
Itō Japan 34°58N 139°5E 31 G9
Itoigawa Japan 37°2N 137°51E 31 F8
Itonamas → Bolivia 12°28S 64°24W 92 F6
Ittoqqortoormiit Greenland 70°20N 23°0W 4 B6
Itu Brazil 23°17S 47°15W 95 A6
Itu Aba I. S. China Sea 10°23N 114°21E 36 B4
Ituiutaba Brazil 19°0S 49°25W 93 G9
Ituna Canada 51°10N 103°24W 71 C8
Itunge Port Tanzania 9°40S 33°55E 55 D3
Iturbe Argentina 23°0S 65°25W 94 A2
Ituri →
  Dem. Rep. of the Congo 1°40N 27°1E 54 B2
Iturup, Ostrov Russia 45°0N 148°0E 29 E15
Ituxi → Brazil 7°18S 64°51W 92 E6
Itzehoe Germany 53°55N 9°31E 16 B5
Ivahona Madag. 23°27S 46°10E 57 C8
Ivaí → Brazil 23°18S 53°42W 95 A5
Ivalo Finland 68°38N 27°35E 8 B22
Ivalojoki → Finland 68°40N 27°40E 8 B22
Ivanava Belarus 52°7N 25°29E 17 B13
Ivanhoe Australia 32°56S 144°20E 63 E3
Ivanhoe Canada 44°23N 77°28W 82 B7
Ivanhoe Calif., U.S.A. 36°23N 119°13W 78 J7
Ivanhoe Minn., U.S.A. 44°28N 96°15W 80 C6
Ivano-Frankivsk
  Ukraine 48°40N 24°40E 17 D13
Ivanovo = Ivanava
  Belarus 52°7N 25°29E 17 B13
Ivanovo Russia 57°5N 41°0E 18 C7
Ivato Madag. 20°37S 47°10E 57 C8
Ivatsevichy Belarus 52°43N 25°21E 17 B13
Ivdel Russia 60°42N 60°24E 18 B11
Ivinheima → Brazil 23°14S 53°42W 95 A5
Ivinhema Brazil 22°10S 53°37W 95 A5
Ivohibe Madag. 22°31S 46°57E 57 C8
Ivory Coast W. Afr. 4°20N 5°0W 50 H4
Ivory Coast ■ Africa 7°30N 5°0W 50 G4
Ivrea Italy 45°28N 7°52E 20 D7
Ivujivik Canada 62°24N 77°55W 69 C12
Ivybridge U.K. 50°23N 3°56W 13 G4
Iwaizumi Japan 39°50N 141°45E 30 E10
Iwaki Japan 37°3N 140°55E 31 F10
Iwakuni Japan 34°15N 132°8E 31 G6
Iwamizawa Japan 43°12N 141°46E 30 C10
Iwanai Japan 42°58N 140°30E 30 C10
Iwata Japan 34°42N 137°51E 31 G8
Iwate □ Japan 39°30N 141°30E 30 E10
Iwate-San Japan 39°51N 141°0E 30 E10

Iwo Nigeria 7°39N 4°9E 50 G6
Iwŏn N. Korea 40°19N 128°39E 35 D15
Ixiamas Bolivia 13°50S 68°5W 92 F5
Ixopo S. Africa 30°11S 30°5E 57 E5
Ixtepec Mexico 16°34N 95°6W 87 D5
Ixtlán del Río Mexico 21°2N 104°22W 86 C4
Iyo Japan 33°45N 132°45E 31 H6
Izabal, L. de Guatemala 15°30N 89°10W 88 C2
Izamal Mexico 20°56N 89°1W 87 C7
Izena-Shima Japan 26°56N 127°56E 31 L3
Izhevsk Russia 56°51N 53°14E 18 C9
Izhma → Russia 65°19N 52°54E 18 A9
Izmayil Ukraine 45°22N 28°46E 17 F15
İzmir Turkey 38°25N 27°8E 23 E12
İzmit = Kocaeli Turkey 40°45N 29°50E 19 F4
İznik Gölü Turkey 40°27N 29°30E 23 D13
Izra Syria 32°51N 36°15E 46 C5
Izu-Shotō Japan 34°30N 140°0E 31 G10
Izúcar de Matamoros Mexico 18°36N 98°28W 87 D5
Izumi-Sano Japan 34°23N 135°18E 31 G7
Izumo Japan 35°20N 132°46E 31 G6
Izyaslav Ukraine 50°5N 26°50E 17 C14

J

J.F.K. Int. ✕ (JFK) U.S.A. 40°38N 73°47W 83 F11
J. Strom Thurmond L. U.S.A. 33°40N 82°12W 85 E13
Jabalpur India 23°9N 79°58E 43 H8
Jabbūl Syria 36°4N 37°30E 44 B3
Jabiru Australia 12°40S 132°53E 60 B5
Jablah Syria 35°20N 36°0E 44 C3
Jablonec nad Nisou Czech Rep. 50°43N 15°10E 16 C8
Jaboatão Brazil 8°7S 35°1W 93 E11
Jaboticabal Brazil 21°15S 48°17W 95 A6
Jaca Spain 42°35N 0°33W 21 A5
Jacareí Brazil 23°20S 46°0W 95 A6
Jacarèzinho Brazil 23°5S 49°58W 95 A6
Jack River △ Australia 14°58S 144°19E 62 A3
Jackman U.S.A. 45°37N 70°15W 81 C18
Jacksboro U.S.A. 33°13N 98°10W 84 E5
Jackson Barbados 13°7N 59°36W 89 g
Jackson Ala., U.S.A. 31°31N 87°53W 85 F11
Jackson Calif., U.S.A. 38°21N 120°46W 78 G6
Jackson Ky., U.S.A. 37°33N 83°23W 81 G12
Jackson Mich., U.S.A. 42°15N 84°24W 81 D11
Jackson Minn., U.S.A. 43°37N 95°1W 80 D6
Jackson Miss., U.S.A. 32°18N 90°12W 85 E9
Jackson Mo., U.S.A. 37°23N 89°40W 80 G9
Jackson N.H., U.S.A. 44°10N 71°11W 83 B13
Jackson Ohio, U.S.A. 39°3N 82°39W 81 F12
Jackson Tenn., U.S.A. 35°37N 88°49W 85 D10
Jackson Wyo., U.S.A. 43°29N 110°46W 76 E8
Jackson B. N.Z. 43°58S 168°42E 59 E2
Jackson L. U.S.A. 43°52N 110°36W 76 E8
Jacksons N.Z. 42°46S 171°32E 59 E3
Jackson's Arm Canada 49°52N 56°47W 73 C8
Jacksonville Ala., U.S.A. 33°49N 85°46W 85 E12
Jacksonville Ark., U.S.A. 34°52N 92°7W 84 D8
Jacksonville Calif., U.S.A. 37°52N 120°24W 78 H6
Jacksonville Fla., U.S.A. 30°20N 81°39W 85 F14
Jacksonville Ill., U.S.A. 39°44N 90°14W 80 F8
Jacksonville N.C., U.S.A. 34°45N 77°26W 85 D16
Jacksonville Tex., U.S.A. 31°58N 95°17W 84 F7
Jacksonville Beach U.S.A. 30°17N 81°24W 85 F14
Jacmel Haiti 18°14N 72°32W 89 C5
Jacob Lake U.S.A. 36°43N 112°13W 77 H7
Jacobabad Pakistan 28°20N 68°29E 42 E3
Jacobina Brazil 11°11S 40°30W 93 F10
Jacques-Cartier, Dét. de Canada 50°0N 63°30W 73 C7
Jacques-Cartier, Mt. Canada 48°57N 66°0W 73 C6
Jacques-Cartier ⌂ Canada 47°15N 71°33W 73 C5
Jacuí → Brazil 30°2S 51°15W 95 C5
Jacumba U.S.A. 32°37N 116°11W 79 N10
Jacundá → Brazil 1°57S 50°26W 93 D8
Jade City Canada 59°15N 129°37W 70 B3
Jaén Peru 5°25S 78°40W 92 E3
Jaén Spain 37°44N 3°43W 21 D4
Jafarabad India 20°52N 71°22E 42 J4
Jaffa = Tel Aviv-Yafo Israel 32°4N 34°48E 46 C3
Jaffa, C. Australia 36°58S 139°40E 63 F2
Jaffna Sri Lanka 9°45N 80°2E 40 Q12
Jaffrey U.S.A. 42°49N 72°2W 83 D12
Jagadhri India 30°10N 77°20E 42 D7
Jagadishpur India 25°30N 84°21E 43 G11
Jagdalpur India 19°3N 82°0E 41 K13
Jagersfontein S. Africa 29°44S 25°27E 56 D4
Jaghīn → Iran 27°17N 57°13E 45 E8
Jagodina Serbia 44°5N 21°15E 23 C9
Jagraon India 30°50N 75°25E 42 D6
Jagtial India 18°50N 79°0E 40 K11
Jaguariaíva Brazil 24°10S 49°50W 95 A6
Jaguaribe → Brazil 4°25S 37°45W 93 D11
Jagüey Grande Cuba 22°35N 81°7W 88 B3
Jahanabad India 25°13N 84°59E 43 G11
Jahazpur India 25°37N 75°17E 42 G6
Jahrom Iran 28°30N 53°31E 45 D7
Jaijon India 31°21N 76°9E 42 D7
Jailolo Indonesia 1°5N 127°30E 37 D7
Jailolo, Selat Indonesia 0°5N 129°5E 37 D7
Jaipur India 27°0N 75°50E 42 F6
Jais India 26°15N 81°32E 43 F9
Jaisalmer India 26°55N 70°54E 42 F4
Jaisinghnagar India 23°38N 78°34E 43 H8
Jaitaran India 26°12N 73°56E 42 F5
Jaithari India 23°14N 78°37E 43 H8
Jājarm Iran 36°58N 56°27E 45 B8
Jakam → India 23°54N 74°13E 42 H6
Jakarta Indonesia 6°9S 106°52E 37 G12
Jakhal India 29°48N 75°50E 42 E6
Jakhau India 23°13N 68°43E 42 H3
Jakobstad = Pietarsaari Finland 63°40N 22°43E 8 E20
Jal U.S.A. 32°7N 103°12W 77 K12
Jalājil Si. Arabia 25°40N 45°27E 44 E5
Jalālābād Afghan. 34°30N 70°29E 42 B4
Jalalabad India 27°41N 79°42E 43 F8
Jalalpur Jattan Pakistan 32°38N 74°11E 42 C6
Jalama U.S.A. 34°29N 120°29W 79 L6
Jalapa Guatemala 14°39N 89°59W 88 D2
Jalapa Enríquez = Xalapa Mexico 19°32N 96°55W 87 D5
Jalasjärvi Finland 62°29N 22°47E 8 E20
Jalaun India 26°8N 79°25E 43 F8
Jaldhaka → Bangla. 26°16N 89°16E 43 F13
Jalesar India 27°29N 78°19E 42 F8
Jaleswar Nepal 26°38N 85°48E 43 F11
Jalgaon India 21°0N 75°42E 40 J9
Jalībah Iraq 30°35N 46°32E 44 D5
Jalingo Nigeria 8°55N 11°25E 51 G8
Jalisco □ Mexico 20°20N 103°40W 86 D4
Jalkot Pakistan 35°14N 73°24E 43 B5
Jalna India 19°48N 75°38E 40 K9
Jalón → Spain 41°47N 1°4W 21 B5
Jalor India 25°21N 72°37E 42 G5
Jalpa Mexico 21°38N 102°58W 86 C4
Jalpaiguri India 26°32N 88°46E 41 F16
Jalpan Mexico 21°14N 99°29W 87 C5
Jaluit I. Marshall Is. 6°0N 169°30E 64 G8
Jalūlā Iraq 34°16N 45°10E 44 C5
Jamaame Somali Rep. 0°4N 42°44E 47 G3
Jamaica ■ W. Indies 18°10N 77°30W 88 a
Jamalpur Bangla. 24°52N 89°56E 41 G16
Jamalpur India 25°18N 86°28E 43 G12
Jamalpurganj India 23°2N 87°59E 43 H13
Jamanxim → Brazil 4°43S 56°18W 93 D7
Jambewangi Indonesia 8°17S 114°7E 37 J17
Jambi Indonesia 1°38S 103°30E 36 E2
Jambi □ Indonesia 1°30S 102°30E 36 E2
Jambongan, Pulau Malaysia 6°45N 117°20E 36 C5
Jambusar India 22°3N 72°51E 42 H5
James → S. Dak., U.S.A. 42°52N 97°18W 80 D5
James → Va., U.S.A. 36°56N 76°27W 81 G15
James B. Canada 54°0N 80°0W 72 B3
James Ranges Australia 24°10S 132°30E 60 D5
James Ross I. Antarctica 63°58S 57°50W 5 C18
Jamesabad Pakistan 25°17N 69°15E 42 G3
Jamestown Australia 33°10S 138°32E 63 E2
Jamestown S. Africa 31°6S 26°45E 56 E4
Jamestown N. Dak., U.S.A. 46°54N 98°42W 80 B4
Jamestown N.Y., U.S.A. 42°6N 79°14W 82 D5
Jamestown Pa., U.S.A. 41°29N 80°27W 82 E4
Jamīlābād Iran 34°24N 48°28E 45 C6
Jamira → India 21°35N 88°28E 43 J13
Jamkhandi India 16°30N 75°15E 40 L9
Jammu India 32°43N 74°54E 42 C6
Jammu & Kashmir □ India 34°25N 77°0E 43 B7
Jamnagar India 22°30N 70°6E 42 H4
Jamni → India 25°13N 78°35E 43 G8
Jampur Pakistan 29°39N 70°40E 42 E4
Jamrud Pakistan 33°59N 71°24E 42 C4
Jämsä Finland 61°53N 25°10E 8 F21
Jamshedpur India 22°44N 86°12E 43 H12
Jamtara India 23°59N 86°49E 43 H12
Jämtland Sweden 63°31N 14°0E 8 E16
Jan L. Canada 54°56N 102°55W 71 C8
Jan Mayen Arctic 71°0N 9°0W 4 B7
Janakpur India 26°42N 85°55E 43 F11
Janaúba Brazil 15°48S 43°19W 93 G10
Jand Pakistan 33°30N 72°6E 42 C5
Jandaq Iran 34°3N 54°22E 45 C7
Jandía Canary Is. 28°6N 14°21W 24 F5
Jandía, Pta. de Canary Is. 28°3N 14°31W 24 F5
Jandía △ Canary Is. 28°4N 14°19W 24 F5
Jandola Pakistan 32°20N 70°9E 42 C4
Jandowae Australia 26°45S 151°7E 63 D5
Janesville U.S.A. 42°41N 89°1W 80 D9
Jangamo Mozam. 24°6S 35°21E 57 C6
Janghai India 25°33N 82°19E 43 G10
Jangheung S. Korea 34°41N 126°52E 35 G14
Janjanbureh Gambia 13°30N 14°47W 50 F3
Janjgir India 22°1N 82°34E 43 J10
Janjina Madag. 20°30S 45°50E 57 C8
Janos Mexico 30°54N 108°10W 86 A3
Januária Brazil 15°25S 44°25W 93 G10
Janūb Sīnī □ Egypt 29°30N 33°50E 46 F2
Janubio Canary Is. 28°56N 13°50W 24 F6
Jaora India 23°40N 75°10E 42 H6
Japan ■ Asia 36°0N 136°0E 31 G8
Japan, Sea of Asia 40°0N 135°0E 30 E7
Japan Trench Pac. Oc. 32°0N 142°0E 64 D6
Japen = Yapen Indonesia 1°50S 136°0E 37 E9
Japla India 24°33N 84°1E 43 G11
Japurá → Brazil 3°8S 65°46W 92 D5
Jaquarão Brazil 32°34S 53°23W 95 C5
Jaqué Panama 7°27N 78°8W 88 E4
Jarābulus Syria 36°49N 38°1E 44 B3
Jarama → Spain 40°24N 3°32W 21 B4
Jaranwala Pakistan 31°15N 73°26E 42 D5
Jarash Jordan 32°17N 35°54E 46 C4
Jarash □ Jordan 32°17N 35°54E 46 C4
Jardim Brazil 21°28S 56°2W 94 A4
Jardín América Argentina 27°3S 55°14W 95 B4
Jardine River △ Australia 11°9S 142°21E 62 A3
Jardines de la Reina, Arch. de los Cuba 20°50N 78°50W 88 B4
Jargalang China 43°5N 122°55E 35 C12
Jari → Brazil 1°9S 51°54W 93 D8
Jarīr, W. al → Si. Arabia 25°38N 42°30E 44 E4
Jarosław Poland 50°2N 22°42E 17 C12
Jarrahdale Australia 32°24S 116°5E 61 F2
Jarrahi → Iran 30°49N 48°48E 45 D6
Jarres, Plaine des Laos 19°27N 103°10E 38 C4
Jartai China 39°45N 105°48E 34 E3
Jarud Qi China 44°28N 120°50E 35 B11
Järvenpää Finland 60°29N 25°5E 8 F21
Jarvis Canada 42°53N 80°6W 82 D4
Jarvis I. Pac. Oc. 0°15S 160°5W 65 H12
Jarwa India 27°38N 82°30E 43 F10
Jasdan India 22°2N 71°12E 42 H4
Jashpurnagar India 22°54N 84°9E 43 H11
Jasidih India 24°31N 86°39E 43 G12
Jāsimīyah Iraq 33°45N 44°41E 44 C5
Jasin Malaysia 2°20N 102°26E 39 L4
Jāsk Iran 25°38N 57°45E 45 E8
Jasło Poland 49°45N 21°30E 17 D11
Jaso India 24°30N 80°29E 43 G9
Jasper Alta., Canada 52°55N 118°5W 70 C5
Jasper Ont., Canada 44°52N 75°57W 83 B9
Jasper Ala., U.S.A. 33°50N 87°17W 85 E11
Jasper Fla., U.S.A. 30°31N 82°57W 85 F13
Jasper Ind., U.S.A. 38°24N 86°56W 80 F10
Jasper Tex., U.S.A. 30°56N 94°1W 84 F7
Jasper △ Canada 52°50N 118°8W 70 C5
Jasrasar India 27°43N 73°49E 42 F5
Jászberény Hungary 47°30N 19°55E 17 E10
Jataí Brazil 17°58S 51°48W 93 G8
Jati Pakistan 24°20N 68°19E 42 G3
Jatibarang Indonesia 6°28S 108°18E 37 G13
Jatiluwih Indonesia 8°23S 115°8E 37 J18
Jatinegara Indonesia 6°13S 106°52E 37 G12
Játiva = Xátiva Spain 38°59N 0°32W 21 C5
Jaú Brazil 22°10S 48°30W 95 A6
Jauja Peru 11°45S 75°15W 92 F3
Jaunpur India 25°46N 82°44E 43 G10
Java = Jawa Indonesia 7°0S 110°0E 36 F3
Java Sea Indonesia 4°35S 107°15E 36 E3
Java Trench Ind. Oc. 9°0S 105°0E 36 F3
Jawa Indonesia 7°0S 110°0E 36 F3
Jawa Barat □ Indonesia 7°0S 107°0E 37 G12
Jawa Tengah □ Indonesia 7°0S 110°0E 37 G14
Jawa Timur □ Indonesia 8°0S 113°0E 37 G15
Jawad India 24°36N 74°51E 42 G6
Jawhar Somali Rep. 2°48N 45°30E 47 G4
Jay Peak U.S.A. 44°55N 72°32W 83 B12
Jaya, Puncak Indonesia 3°57S 137°17E 37 E9
Jayanti India 26°45N 89°40E 41 F16
Jayapura Indonesia 2°28S 140°38E 37 E10
Jayawijaya, Pegunungan Indonesia 5°0S 139°0E 37 F9
Jaynagar India 26°43N 86°9E 43 F12
Jayrūd Syria 33°49N 36°44E 44 C3
Jayton U.S.A. 33°15N 100°34W 84 E4
Jāz Mūrīān, Hāmūn-e Iran 27°20N 58°55E 45 E8
Jazīreh-ye Shīf Iran 29°4N 50°54E 45 D6
Jazminal Mexico 24°52N 101°24W 86 C4
Jazzīn Lebanon 33°31N 35°35E 46 B4
Jean U.S.A. 35°47N 115°20W 79 K11
Jean Marie River Canada 61°32N 120°38W 70 A4
Jean-Rabel Haiti 19°50N 73°5W 89 C5
Jeanerette U.S.A. 29°55N 91°40W 84 G9
Jeanette, Ostrov = Zhannetty, Ostrov Russia 76°43N 158°0E 29 B16
Jeannette U.S.A. 40°20N 79°36W 82 F5
Jebāl Bārez, Kūh-e Iran 28°30N 58°20E 45 D8
Jebel, Bahr el → Sudan 9°30N 30°25E 51 G12
Jebel Ali = Minā' Jabal 'Alī U.A.E. 25°2N 55°8E 45 E7
Jecheon S. Korea 37°8N 128°12E 35 F15
Jedburgh U.K. 55°29N 2°33W 11 F6
Jedda = Jiddah Si. Arabia 21°29N 39°10E 47 C2
Jeddore L. Canada 48°3N 55°55W 73 C8
Jędrzejów Poland 50°35N 20°15E 17 C11
Jefferson Iowa, U.S.A. 42°1N 94°23W 80 D6
Jefferson Ohio, U.S.A. 41°44N 80°46W 82 E4
Jefferson Tex., U.S.A. 32°46N 94°21W 84 E7
Jefferson, Mt. Nev., U.S.A. 38°47N 116°56W 76 G5
Jefferson, Mt. Oreg., U.S.A. 44°41N 121°48W 76 D3
Jefferson City Mo., U.S.A. 38°34N 92°10W 80 F7
Jefferson City Tenn., U.S.A. 36°7N 83°30W 85 C13
Jeffersontown U.S.A. 38°12N 85°35W 81 F11
Jeffersonville U.S.A. 38°17N 85°44W 81 F11
Jeffrey City U.S.A. 42°30N 107°49W 76 E10
Jega Nigeria 12°15N 4°23E 50 F6
Jeju S. Korea 33°31N 126°32E 35 H14
Jeju-do S. Korea 33°29N 126°34E 35 H14
Jēkabpils Latvia 56°29N 25°57E 9 H21
Jekyll I. U.S.A. 31°4N 81°25W 85 F14
Jelenia Góra Poland 50°50N 15°45E 16 C8
Jelgava Latvia 56°41N 23°49E 9 H20
Jemaja Indonesia 3°5N 105°45E 39 L5
Jemaluang Malaysia 2°16N 103°52E 39 L4
Jember Indonesia 8°11S 113°41E 37 H15
Jena Germany 50°54N 11°35E 16 C6
Jena U.S.A. 31°41N 92°8W 84 F8
Jenīn West Bank 32°28N 35°18E 46 C4
Jenkins U.S.A. 37°10N 82°38W 81 G12
Jenner U.S.A. 38°27N 123°7W 78 G3
Jennings U.S.A. 30°13N 92°40W 84 F8
Jeong-eup S. Korea 35°35N 126°50E 35 G14
Jeonju S. Korea 35°50N 127°4E 35 G14
Jepara Indonesia 7°40S 109°14E 37 G14
Jeparit Australia 36°8S 142°1E 63 F3
Jequié Brazil 13°51S 40°5W 93 F10
Jequitinhonha Brazil 16°30S 41°0W 93 G10
Jequitinhonha → Brazil 15°51S 38°53W 93 G11
Jerada Morocco 34°17N 2°10W 50 B5
Jerantut Malaysia 3°56N 102°22E 39 L4
Jerejak, Pulau Malaysia 5°19N 100°19E 39 c
Jérémie Haiti 18°40N 74°10W 89 C5
Jerez, Pta. Mexico 22°58N 97°40W 87 C5
Jerez de García Salinas Mexico 22°39N 103°0W 86 C4
Jerez de la Frontera Spain 36°41N 6°7W 21 D2
Jerez de los Caballeros Spain 38°20N 6°45W 21 C2
Jericho = El Arīḥā West Bank 31°52N 35°27E 46 D4
Jericho Australia 23°38S 146°6E 62 C4
Jerid, Chott el = Djerid, Chott Tunisia 33°42N 8°30E 50 B7
Jerilderie Australia 35°20S 145°41E 63 F4
Jermyn U.S.A. 41°32N 75°33W 83 E9
Jerome U.S.A. 42°44N 114°31W 76 E6
Jerramungup Australia 33°55S 118°55E 61 F2
Jersey U.K. 49°11N 2°7W 13 H5
Jersey City U.S.A. 40°42N 74°4W 83 F10
Jersey Shore U.S.A. 41°12N 77°15W 82 E7
Jerseyville U.S.A. 39°7N 90°20W 80 F8
Jerusalem Israel/West Bank 31°47N 35°10E 46 D4
Jervis B. Australia 35°8S 150°46E 63 F5
Jervis Inlet Canada 50°0N 123°57W 70 C4
Jesi = Iesi Italy 43°31N 13°14E 22 C5
Jessore Bangla. 23°10N 89°10E 41 H16
Jesup U.S.A. 31°36N 81°53W 85 F14
Jesús Carranza Mexico 17°26N 95°2W 87 D5
Jesús María Argentina 30°59S 64°5W 94 C3
Jetmore U.S.A. 38°4N 99°54W 80 F4
Jetpur India 21°45N 70°10E 42 J4
Jevnaker Norway 60°15N 10°26E 9 F14
Jewett U.S.A. 40°22N 81°2W 82 F3
Jewett City U.S.A. 41°36N 71°59W 83 E13
Jeyḥūnābād Iran 34°58N 48°59E 45 C6
Jeypore India 18°50N 82°38E 41 K13
Jha Jha India 24°46N 86°22E 43 G12
Jhaarkand = Jharkhand □ India 24°0N 85°50E 43 H11
Jhabua India 22°46N 74°36E 42 H6
Jhajjar India 28°37N 76°42E 42 E7
Jhal Pakistan 28°17N 67°27E 42 E2
Jhal Jhao Pakistan 26°20N 65°35E 40 F4
Jhalawar India 24°40N 76°10E 42 G7
Jhalida India 23°22N 85°58E 43 H11
Jhalrapatan India 24°33N 76°10E 42 G7
Jhang Maghiana Pakistan 31°15N 72°22E 42 D5
Jhansi India 25°30N 78°36E 43 G8
Jhargram India 22°27N 86°59E 43 H12
Jharia India 23°45N 86°26E 43 H12
Jharkhand □ India 24°0N 85°50E 43 H11
Jharsuguda India 21°56N 84°5E 41 J14
Jhelum Pakistan 33°0N 73°45E 42 C5
Jhelum → Pakistan 31°20N 72°10E 42 D5
Jhilmilli India 23°24N 82°51E 43 H10
Jhudo Pakistan 24°58N 69°18E 42 G3
Jhunjhunu India 28°10N 75°30E 42 E6
Ji-Paraná Brazil 10°52S 62°57W 92 F6
Ji Xian Hebei, China 37°35N 115°30E 34 F8
Ji Xian Henan, China 35°22N 114°5E 34 G8
Ji Xian Shanxi, China 36°7N 110°40E 34 F6
Jia Xian Henan, China 33°59N 113°12E 34 H7
Jia Xian Shaanxi, China 38°12N 110°28E 34 E6
Jiaji = Qionghai China 19°15N 110°26E 38 C8
Jiamusi China 46°40N 130°26E 33 B8
Ji'an Jiangxi, China 27°6N 114°59E 33 D6
Ji'an Jilin, China 41°5N 126°10E 35 D14
Jianchang China 40°55N 120°35E 35 D11
Jianchangying China 40°10N 118°50E 35 D10
Jiangcheng China 22°36N 101°52E 32 D5
Jiangmen China 22°32N 113°0E 33 D6
Jiangsu □ China 33°0N 120°0E 35 H11
Jiangxi □ China 27°30N 116°0E 33 D6
Jiao Xian = Jiaozhou China 36°18N 120°1E 35 F11
Jiaohe Hebei, China 38°2N 116°20E 34 E9
Jiaohe Jilin, China 43°40N 127°22E 35 C14
Jiaozhou China 36°18N 120°1E 35 F11
Jiaozhou Wan China 36°5N 120°10E 35 F11
Jiaozuo China 35°16N 113°12E 34 G7
Jiawang China 34°28N 117°26E 35 G9
Jiaxiang China 35°25N 116°20E 34 G9
Jiaxing China 30°49N 120°45E 33 C7
Jiayi = Chiai Taiwan 23°29N 120°25E 33 D7
Jibuti = Djibouti ■ Africa 12°0N 43°0E 47 E3
Jicarón, I. Panama 7°10N 81°50W 88 E3
Jiddah Si. Arabia 21°29N 39°10E 47 C2
Jido India 29°2N 94°58E 41 E19
Jieshou China 33°18N 115°22E 34 H8
Jiexiu China 37°2N 111°55E 34 F6
Jigalong Australia 23°21S 120°47E 60 D3
Jigni India 25°45N 79°25E 43 G8
Jihlava Czech Rep. 49°28N 15°35E 16 D8
Jihlava → Czech Rep. 48°55N 16°36E 17 D9
Jijiga Ethiopia 9°20N 42°50E 47 F3
Jilib Somali Rep. 0°29N 42°46E 47 G3
Jilin China 43°44N 126°30E 35 C14
Jilin □ China 44°0N 127°0E 35 C14
Jilong = Chilung Taiwan 25°3N 121°45E 33 D7
Jim Thorpe U.S.A. 40°52N 75°44W 83 F9
Jima Ethiopia 7°40N 36°47E 47 F2
Jimbaran, Teluk Indonesia 8°46S 115°9E 37 K18
Jiménez Mexico 27°10N 104°54W 86 B4
Jimo China 36°23N 120°30E 35 F11
Jin Xian = Jinzhou Hebei, China 38°2N 115°2E 34 E8
Jin Xian = Jinzhou Liaoning, China 38°55N 121°42E 35 E11
Jinan China 36°38N 117°1E 34 F9
Jinchang China 38°30N 102°10E 32 C5
Jincheng China 35°29N 112°50E 34 G7
Jind India 29°19N 76°22E 42 E7
Jindabyne Australia 36°25S 148°35E 63 F4
Jinding China 22°22N 113°33E 33 G10
Jindo S. Korea 34°28N 126°15E 35 G14
Jindřichův Hradec Czech Rep. 49°10N 15°2E 16 D8
Jing He → China 34°27N 109°4E 34 G5
Jingbian China 37°20N 108°30E 34 F5
Jingchuan China 35°20N 107°20E 34 G4
Jingdezhen China 29°20N 117°11E 33 D6
Jinggu China 23°35N 100°41E 32 D5
Jinghai China 38°55N 116°55E 34 E9
Jingle China 38°20N 111°55E 34 E6
Jingning China 35°30N 105°43E 34 G3
Jingpo Hu China 43°55N 128°55E 35 C15
Jingtai China 37°10N 104°6E 34 F3
Jingxing China 38°2N 114°8E 34 E8
Jingyang China 34°30N 108°50E 34 G5
Jingyu China 42°25N 126°45E 35 C14
Jingyuan China 36°30N 104°40E 34 F3
Jingziguan China 33°15N 111°0E 34 H6
Jinhua China 29°8N 119°38E 33 D6
Jining Nei Monggol Zizhiqu, China 41°5N 113°0E 34 D7
Jining Shandong, China 35°22N 116°34E 34 G9
Jinja Uganda 0°25N 33°12E 54 B3
Jinjang Malaysia 3°13N 101°39E 39 L3
Jinji China 37°58N 106°8E 34 F4
Jinju S. Korea 35°12N 128°2E 35 G15
Jinnah Barrage Pakistan 32°58N 71°33E 42 C4
Jinotega Nic. 13°6N 85°59W 88 D2
Jinotepe Nic. 11°50N 86°10W 88 D2
Jinsha Jiang → China 28°50N 104°36E 32 D5
Jinxi China 40°52N 120°50E 35 D11
Jinxiang China 35°5N 116°22E 34 G9
Jinzhou Hebei, China 38°2N 115°2E 34 E8
Jinzhou Liaoning, China 38°55N 121°42E 35 E11
Jinzhou Liaoning, China 41°5N 121°3E 35 D11
Jiparaná → Brazil 8°3S 62°52W 92 E6
Jipijapa Ecuador 1°0S 80°40W 92 D2
Jiquilpan Mexico 19°59N 102°43W 86 D4
Jirisan S. Korea 35°20N 127°44E 35 G14
Jishan China 35°34N 110°58E 34 G6
Jisr ash Shughūr Syria 35°49N 36°18E 44 C3
Jitarning Australia 32°48S 117°57E 61 F2
Jitra Malaysia 6°16N 100°25E 39 J3
Jiu → Romania 43°47N 23°48E 17 F12
Jiudengkou China 39°56N 106°40E 34 E4
Jiujiang China 29°42N 115°58E 33 D6
Jiulong = Kowloon China 22°19N 114°11E 33 G11
Jiuquan China 39°50N 98°20E 32 C4
Jiutai China 44°10N 125°50E 35 B13
Jiuxincheng China 39°17N 115°59E 34 E8
Jiwani Pakistan 25°1N 61°44E 40 G2
Jixi China 45°20N 130°50E 35 B16
Jiyang China 37°0N 117°12E 35 F9
Jiyuan China 35°7N 112°57E 34 G7
Jīzān Si. Arabia 17°0N 42°20E 47 D3
Jize China 36°54N 114°56E 34 F8
Jizl, Wādī al → Si. Arabia 25°39N 38°25E 44 E3
Jizō-Zaki Japan 35°34N 133°20E 31 G6
Jizzax Uzbekistan 40°6N 67°50E 28 E7
Joaçaba Brazil 27°5S 51°31W 95 B5
João Pessoa Brazil 7°10S 34°52W 93 E12
Joaquín V. González Argentina 25°10S 64°0W 94 B3
Jobat India 22°25N 74°34E 42 H6
Jodhpur India 26°23N 73°8E 42 F5
Jodiya India 22°42N 70°18E 42 H4
Joensuu Finland 62°37N 29°49E 8 E23
Jōetsu Japan 37°12N 138°10E 31 F9
Jofane Mozam. 21°15S 34°18E 57 C5
Jogbani India 26°25N 87°15E 43 F12
Jõgeva Estonia 58°45N 26°24E 9 G22
Jogjakarta = Yogyakarta Indonesia 7°49S 110°22E 37 G14
Johannesburg S. Africa 26°11S 28°2E 57 D4
Johannesburg U.S.A. 35°22N 117°38W 79 K9
Johilla → India 23°37N 81°14E 43 H9
John Crow Mts. Jamaica 18°5N 76°25W 88 a
John Day U.S.A. 44°25N 118°57W 76 D4
John Day → U.S.A. 45°44N 120°39W 76 D3
John Day Fossil Beds ⌂ U.S.A. 44°33N 119°38W 76 D4
John D'or Prairie Canada 58°30N 115°8W 70 B5
John H. Kerr Res. U.S.A. 36°36N 78°18W 85 C15
John o' Groats U.K. 58°38N 3°4W 11 C5
Johnnie U.S.A. 36°25N 116°5W 79 J10
John's Ra. Australia 21°55S 133°23E 62 C1
Johnson U.S.A. 44°38N 72°41W 83 B12
Johnson City Kans., U.S.A. 37°34N 101°45W 80 G3
Johnson City N.Y., U.S.A. 42°7N 75°58W 83 D9
Johnson City Tenn., U.S.A. 36°19N 82°21W 85 C13
Johnson City Tex., U.S.A. 30°17N 98°25W 84 F5
Johnsonburg U.S.A. 41°29N 78°41W 82 E6
Johnsondale U.S.A. 35°58N 118°32W 79 K8
Johnsons Crossing Canada 60°29N 133°18W 70 A2
Johnston, L. Australia 32°25S 120°30E 61 F3
Johnston Falls = Mambilima Falls Zambia 10°31S 28°45E 55 E2
Johnston I. Pac. Oc. 17°10N 169°8W 65 F11
Johnstone Str. Canada 50°28N 126°0W 70 C3
Johnstown Ireland 52°45N 7°33W 10 D4
Johnstown N.Y., U.S.A. 43°0N 74°22W 83 C10
Johnstown Ohio, U.S.A. 40°9N 82°41W 82 F2
Johnstown Pa., U.S.A. 40°20N 78°55W 82 F6
Johor, Selat Asia 1°28N 103°47E 39 d
Johor Bahru Malaysia 1°28N 103°46E 39 d
Jõhvi Estonia 59°22N 27°27E 9 G22
Joinville Brazil 26°15S 48°55W 95 B6
Joinville I. Antarctica 65°0S 55°30W 5 C18
Jojutla Mexico 18°37N 99°11W 87 D5
Jokkmokk Sweden 66°35N 19°50E 8 C18
Jökulsá á Bru → Iceland 65°40N 14°16W 8 D6

Jökulsá á Fjöllum →
  Iceland 66°1'N 16°30W **8 C5**
Jolfā Āzarbāijān-e Sharqī,
  Iran 38°57N 45°38E **44 B5**
Jolfā Eşfahan, Iran 32°58N 51°37E **45 C6**
Joliet U.S.A. 41°32N 88°5W **80 E9**
Joliette Canada 46°3N 73°24W **72 C5**
Jolo Phil. 6°0N 121°0E **37 C6**
Jolon U.S.A. 35°58N 121°9W **78 K5**
Jombang Indonesia 7°33S 112°14E **37 G15**
Jonava Lithuania 55°8N 24°12E **9 J21**
Jones Sound Canada 76°0N 85°0W **69 B11**
Jonesboro Ark., U.S.A. 35°50N 90°42W **85 D9**
Jonesboro La., U.S.A. 32°15N 92°43W **84 E8**
Joniškis Lithuania 56°13N 23°35E **9 H20**
Jönköping Sweden 57°45N 14°8E **9 H16**
Jonquière Canada 48°27N 71°14W **73 C5**
Joplin U.S.A. 37°6N 94°31W **80 G6**
Jora India 26°20N 77°49E **42 F6**
Jordan Mont., U.S.A. 47°19N 106°55W **76 C10**
Jordan N.Y., U.S.A. 43°4N 76°29W **83 C8**
Jordan ■ Asia 31°0N 36°0E **46 E5**
Jordan → Asia 31°48N 35°32E **46 D4**
Jordan Valley U.S.A. 42°59N 117°3W **76 E5**
Jorhat India 26°45N 94°12E **41 F19**
Jörn Sweden 65°4N 20°1E **8 D19**
Jorong Indonesia 3°58S 114°56E **36 E4**
Jørpeland Norway 59°3N 6°1E **9 G12**
Jorquera → Chile 28°3S 69°58W **94 B2**
Jos Nigeria 9°53N 8°51E **50 G7**
José Batlle y Ordóñez
  Uruguay 33°20S 55°10W **95 C4**
Joseph, L. Canada 45°10N 79°44W **82 A5**
Joseph Bonaparte G.
  Australia 14°35S 128°50E **60 B4**
Joseph L. Canada 52°45N 65°18W **73 B6**
Joshinath India 30°34N 79°34E **43 D8**
Joshinetsu-Kōgen △
  Japan 36°42N 138°32E **31 F9**
Joshua Tree U.S.A. 34°8N 116°19W **79 L10**
Joshua Tree △ U.S.A. 33°55N 116°0W **79 M10**
Jost Van Dyke I.
  Br. Virgin Is. 18°29N 64°47W **89 e**
Jostedalsbreen Norway 61°40N 6°59E **8 F12**
Jotunheimen Norway 61°35N 8°25E **8 F13**
Joubertberge Namibia 18°30S 14°0E **56 B1**
Jourdanton U.S.A. 28°55N 98°33W **84 G5**
Jovellanos Cuba 22°40N 81°10W **88 B3**
Ju Xian China 36°35N 118°20E **35 F10**
Juan Aldama Mexico 24°19N 103°21W **86 C4**
Juan Bautista Alberdi
  Argentina 34°26S 61°48W **94 C3**
Juan de Fuca, Str. of
  N. Amer. 48°15N 124°0W **78 B3**
Juán de Nova Ind. Oc. 17°3S 43°45E **57 B7**
Juan Fernández, Arch. de
  Pac. Oc. 33°50S 80°0W **90 G2**
Juan José Castelli
  Argentina 25°27S 60°57W **94 B3**
Juan L. Lacaze Uruguay 34°26S 57°25W **94 C4**
Juankoski Finland 63°3N 28°19E **8 E23**
Juárez Mexico 32°20N 115°57W **79 N11**
Juárez Coahuila, Mexico 27°37N 100°44W **86 B4**
Juárez, Sierra de Mexico 32°0N 116°0W **86 A1**
Juàzeiro Brazil 9°30S 40°30W **93 E10**
Juàzeiro do Norte Brazil 7°10S 39°18W **93 E11**
Jûbâ Sudan 4°50N 31°35E **51 H12**
Juba → Somali Rep. 1°30N 42°35E **47 G3**
Jubany Antarctica 62°30S 58°0W **5 C18**
Jubayl Lebanon 34°5N 35°39E **46 A4**
Jubbah Si. Arabia 28°2N 40°56E **44 D4**
Jubbal India 31°5N 77°40E **42 D7**
Jubbulpore = Jabalpur
  India 23°9N 79°58E **43 H8**
Jubilee L. Australia 29°0S 126°50E **61 E4**
Juby, C. Morocco 28°0N 12°59W **50 C3**
Júcar = Xúquer → Spain 39°5N 0°10W **21 C5**
Júcaro Cuba 21°37N 78°51W **88 B4**
Juchitán de Zaragoza
  Mexico 16°26N 95°1W **87 D5**
Judea = Har Yehuda
  Israel 31°35N 34°57E **46 D3**
Judith → U.S.A. 47°44N 109°39W **76 C9**
Judith, Pt. U.S.A. 41°22N 71°29W **83 E13**
Judith Gap U.S.A. 46°41N 109°45W **76 C9**
Jugoslavia = Serbia ■
  Europe 43°20N 20°0E **23 B9**
Juigalpa Nic. 12°6N 85°26W **88 D2**
Juiz de Fora Brazil 21°43S 43°19W **95 A7**
Jujuy □ Argentina 23°20S 65°40W **94 A2**
Julesburg U.S.A. 40°59N 102°16W **76 F12**
Juli Peru 16°10S 69°25W **92 G5**
Julia Cr. → Australia 20°0S 141°11E **62 C3**
Julia Creek Australia 20°39S 141°44E **62 C3**
Juliaca Peru 15°25S 70°10W **92 G4**
Julian U.S.A. 33°4N 116°38W **79 M10**
Julian, L. Canada 54°25N 77°57W **72 B4**
Julianatop Suriname 3°40N 56°30W **93 C7**
Julianehåb = Qaqortoq
  Greenland 60°43N 46°0W **4 C5**
Julimes Mexico 28°25N 105°27W **86 B3**
Jullundur India 31°20N 75°40E **42 D6**
Julu China 37°15N 115°2E **34 F8**
Jumbo Zimbabwe 17°30S 30°58E **55 F3**
Jumbo Pk. U.S.A. 36°12N 114°11W **79 J12**
Jumentos Cays Bahamas 23°0N 75°40W **88 B4**
Jumilla Spain 38°28N 1°19W **21 C5**
Jumla Nepal 29°15N 82°13E **43 E10**
Jumna = Yamuna →
  India 25°30N 81°53E **43 G9**
Jumunjin S. Korea 37°55N 128°54E **35 F15**
Junagadh India 21°30N 70°30E **42 J4**
Junction Tex., U.S.A. 30°29N 99°46W **84 F5**
Junction Utah, U.S.A. 38°14N 112°13W **77 G7**
Junction B. Australia 11°52S 133°55E **62 A1**
Junction City Kans.,
  U.S.A. 39°2N 96°50W **80 F5**

Junction City Oreg.,
  U.S.A. 44°13N 123°12W **76 D2**
Junction Pt. Australia 11°45S 133°50E **62 A1**
Jundah Australia 24°46S 143°2E **62 C3**
Jundiaí Brazil 24°30S 47°0W **95 A6**
Juneau U.S.A. 58°18N 134°25W **70 B2**
Junee Australia 34°53S 147°35E **63 E4**
Jungfrau Switz. 46°32N 7°58E **20 C7**
Junggar Pendi China 44°30N 86°0E **32 B3**
Jungshahi Pakistan 24°52N 67°44E **42 G2**
Juniata → U.S.A. 40°24N 77°1W **82 F7**
Junín Argentina 34°33S 60°57W **94 C3**
Junín de los Andes
  Argentina 39°45S 71°0W **96 D2**
Jūniyah Lebanon 33°59N 35°38E **46 B4**
Juntas Chile 28°24S 69°58W **94 B2**
Juntura U.S.A. 43°45N 118°5W **76 E4**
Jur, Nahr el → Sudan 8°45N 29°15E **51 G11**
Jura = Jura, Mts. du
  Europe 46°40N 6°5E **20 C7**
Jura = Schwäbische Alb
  Germany 48°20N 9°30E **16 D5**
Jura U.K. 56°0N 5°50W **11 F3**
Jura, Mts. du Europe 46°40N 6°5E **20 C7**
Jura, Sd. of U.K. 55°57N 5°45W **11 F3**
Jurbarkas Lithuania 55°4N 22°46E **9 J20**
Jurien Bay Australia 30°18S 115°2E **61 F2**
Jūrmala Latvia 56°58N 23°34E **9 H20**
Jurong Singapore 1°19N 103°42E **39 d**
Juruá → Brazil 2°37S 65°44W **92 D5**
Juruena Brazil 13°0S 58°10W **92 F7**
Juruena → Brazil 7°20S 58°3W **92 E7**
Juruti Brazil 2°9S 56°4W **93 D7**
Justo Daract Argentina 33°52S 65°12W **94 C2**
Jutaí → Brazil 2°43S 66°57W **92 D5**
Juticalpa Honduras 14°40N 86°12W **88 D2**
Jutland = Jylland
  Denmark 56°25N 9°30E **9 H13**
Juuka Finland 63°13N 29°17E **8 E23**
Juventud, I. de la Cuba 21°40N 82°40W **88 B3**
Jüy Zar Iran 33°50N 46°18E **44 C5**
Juye China 35°22N 116°5E **34 G9**
Jwaneng Botswana 24°45S 24°50E **53 J4**
Jylland Denmark 56°25N 9°30E **9 H13**
Jyväskylä Finland 62°14N 25°50E **8 E21**

K

K2 Pakistan 35°58N 76°32E **43 B7**
Kaakha = Kaka
  Turkmenistan 37°21N 59°36E **45 B8**
Kaap Plateau S. Africa 28°30S 24°0E **56 D3**
Kaapkruis Namibia 21°55S 13°57E **56 C1**
Kaapstad = Cape Town
  S. Africa 33°55S 18°22E **56 E2**
Kabaena Indonesia 5°15S 122°0E **37 F6**
Kabala S. Leone 9°38N 11°37W **50 G3**
Kabale Uganda 1°15S 30°0E **54 C3**
Kabalo Dem. Rep. of the Congo 6°0S 27°0E **54 D2**
Kabambare
  Dem. Rep. of the Congo 4°41S 27°39E **54 C2**
Kabango
  Dem. Rep. of the Congo 8°35S 28°30E **55 D2**
Kabanjahe Indonesia 3°6N 98°30E **36 D1**
Kabara Fiji 18°59S 178°56W **59 a**
Kabardino-Balkaria □
  Russia 43°30N 43°30E **19 F7**
Kabarega Falls = Murchison Falls
  Uganda 2°15N 31°30E **54 B3**
Kabarnet Kenya 0°30N 35°45E **54 B4**
Kabasalan Phil. 7°47N 122°44E **37 C6**
Kabat Indonesia 8°16S 114°19E **37 J17**
Kabin Buri Thailand 13°57N 101°43E **38 F3**
Kabinakagami L.
  Canada 48°54N 84°25W **72 C3**
Kabinda
  Dem. Rep. of the Congo 6°19S 24°20E **52 F4**
Kabompo Zambia 13°36S 24°14E **55 E1**
Kabompo → Zambia 14°11S 23°11E **53 G4**
Kabondo
  Dem. Rep. of the Congo 8°58S 25°40E **55 D2**
Kabongo
  Dem. Rep. of the Congo 7°22S 25°33E **54 D2**
Kabrît, G. el Egypt 29°42N 33°16E **46 F2**
Kabūd Gonbad Iran 37°5N 59°45E **45 B8**
Kābul □ Afghan. 34°28N 69°11E **42 B3**
Kābul → Pakistan 33°55N 72°14E **42 C5**
Kabunga
  Dem. Rep. of the Congo 1°38S 28°3E **54 C2**
Kaburuang Indonesia 3°50N 126°30E **37 D7**
Kabwe Zambia 14°30S 28°29E **55 E2**
Kachchh, Gulf of India 22°50N 69°15E **42 H3**
Kachchh, Rann of India 24°0N 70°0E **42 H4**
Kachchhidhana India 21°44N 78°46E **43 J8**
Kachebera Zambia 13°50S 32°50E **55 E3**
Kachikau Botswana 18°8S 24°26E **56 B3**
Kachin □ Burma 26°0N 97°30E **41 G20**
Kachira, L. Uganda 0°40S 31°7E **54 C3**
Kachiry Kazakhstan 53°10N 75°50E **28 D8**
Kachnara India 23°50N 75°6E **42 H6**
Kachot Cambodia 11°30N 103°3E **39 G4**
Kaçkar Turkey 40°45N 41°10E **19 F7**
Kadam, Mt. Uganda 1°45N 34°45E **54 B3**
Kadan Kyun Burma 12°30N 98°20E **38 F2**
Kadanai → Afghan. 31°22N 65°45E **42 D1**
Kadavu Fiji 19°0S 178°15E **59 a**
Kadavu Passage Fiji 18°45S 178°0E **59 a**
Kade Ghana 6°7N 0°56W **50 G5**
Kadhimain = Al Kāzimīyah
  Iraq 33°22N 44°18E **44 C5**
Kadi India 23°18N 72°23E **42 H5**
Kadina Australia 33°55S 137°43E **63 E2**
Kadipur India 26°10N 82°23E **43 F10**
Kadirli Turkey 37°23N 36°5E **44 B3**
Kadiyevka = Stakhanov
  Ukraine 48°35N 38°40E **19 E6**

Kadoka U.S.A. 43°50N 101°31W **80 D3**
Kadoma Zimbabwe 18°20S 29°52E **55 F2**
Kâdugli Sudan 11°0N 29°45E **51 F11**
Kaduna Nigeria 10°30N 7°21E **50 F7**
Kaédi Mauritania 16°9N 13°28W **50 E3**
Kaeng Khoï Thailand 14°35N 101°0E **38 E3**
Kaeng Krachan △
  Thailand 12°57N 99°23E **38 F2**
Kaeng Tana △ Thailand 15°25N 105°32E **38 E5**
Kaesŏng N. Korea 37°58N 126°35E **35 F14**
Kāf Si. Arabia 31°25N 37°29E **44 D3**
Kafan = Kapan Armenia 39°18N 46°27E **44 B5**
Kafanchan Nigeria 9°40N 8°20E **50 G7**
Kafinda Zambia 12°32S 30°20E **55 E3**
Kafue Zambia 15°46S 28°9E **55 F2**
Kafue → Zambia 15°30S 29°0E **53 H5**
Kafue △ Zambia 15°12S 25°33E **55 F2**
Kafue Flats Zambia 15°40S 27°25E **55 F2**
Kafulwe Zambia 9°0S 29°1E **55 D2**
Kaga Afghan. 34°14N 70°10E **42 B4**
Kaga Bandoro C.A.R. 7°0N 19°10E **52 C3**
Kagawa □ Japan 34°15N 134°0E **31 G7**
Kagera □ Tanzania 2°0S 31°30E **54 C3**
Kagera → Uganda 0°57S 31°47E **54 C3**
Kağızman Turkey 40°5N 43°10E **44 B4**
Kagoshima Japan 31°35N 130°33E **31 J5**
Kagoshima □ Japan 31°30N 130°30E **31 J5**
Kagul = Cahul Moldova 45°50N 28°15E **17 F15**
Kahak Iran 36°6N 49°46E **45 B6**
Kahama Tanzania 4°8S 32°30E **54 C3**
Kahan Pakistan 29°18N 68°54E **42 E3**
Kahang Malaysia 2°12N 103°32E **39 L4**
Kahayan → Indonesia 3°40S 114°0E **36 E4**
Kahe Tanzania 3°30S 37°25E **54 C4**
Kahemba
  Dem. Rep. of the Congo 7°18S 18°55E **52 F3**
Kahnūj Iran 27°55N 57°40E **45 E8**
Kahoka U.S.A. 40°25N 91°44W **80 E8**
Kaho'olawe U.S.A. 20°33N 156°37W **74 b**
Kahramanmaraş Turkey 37°37N 36°53E **44 B3**
Kâhta Turkey 37°46N 38°36E **44 B3**
Kahului U.S.A. 20°54N 156°28W **74 b**
Kahurangi △ N.Z. 41°10S 172°32E **59 D4**
Kahuta Pakistan 33°35N 73°24E **42 C5**
Kahuzi-Biega △
  Dem. Rep. of the Congo 1°50S 27°55E **54 C2**
Kai, Kepulauan Indonesia 5°55S 132°45E **37 F8**
Kai Besar Indonesia 5°35S 133°0E **37 F8**
Kai Is. = Kai, Kepulauan
  Indonesia 5°55S 132°45E **37 F8**
Kai Kecil Indonesia 5°45S 132°40E **37 F8**
Kaiapoi N.Z. 43°24S 172°40E **59 E4**
Kaidu He → China 41°46N 86°31E **32 B3**
Kaieteur Falls Guyana 5°1N 59°10W **92 B7**
Kaifeng China 34°48N 114°21E **34 G8**
Kaikohe N.Z. 35°25S 173°49E **59 A4**
Kaikoura N.Z. 42°25S 173°43E **59 E4**
Kailas = Kangrinboqe Feng
  China 31°0N 81°25E **43 D9**
Kailu China 43°38N 121°18E **35 C11**
Kailua U.S.A. 19°39N 155°59W **74 b**
Kaimana Indonesia 3°39S 133°45E **37 E8**
Kaimanawa Mts. N.Z. 39°15S 175°56E **59 C5**
Kaimganj India 27°33N 79°24E **43 F8**
Kaimur Hills India 24°30N 82°0E **43 G10**
Kainab → Namibia 28°32S 19°34E **56 D2**
Kainji Res. Nigeria 10°1N 4°40E **50 F6**
Kainuu Finland 64°30N 29°7E **8 D23**
Kaipara Harbour N.Z. 36°25S 174°14E **59 B5**
Kaipokok B. Canada 54°54N 59°47W **73 B8**
Kaira India 22°45N 72°50E **42 H5**
Kairana India 29°24N 77°15E **42 E7**
Kaironi Indonesia 0°47S 133°40E **37 E8**
Kairouan Tunisia 35°45N 10°5E **51 A8**
Kaiserslautern Germany 49°26N 7°45E **16 D4**
Kaitaia N.Z. 35°8S 173°17E **59 A4**
Kaitangata N.Z. 46°17S 169°51E **59 G2**
Kaithal India 29°48N 76°26E **42 E7**
Kaitu → Pakistan 33°10N 70°30E **42 C4**
Kaiyuan Liaoning, China 42°28N 124°1E **35 C13**
Kaiyuan Yunnan, China 23°40N 103°12E **32 D5**
Kajaani Finland 64°17N 27°46E **8 D22**
Kajabbi Australia 20°0S 140°1E **62 C3**
Kajana = Kajaani
  Finland 64°17N 27°46E **8 D22**
Kajang Malaysia 2°59N 101°48E **39 L3**
Kajiado Kenya 1°53S 36°48E **54 C4**
Kajo Kaji Sudan 3°58N 31°40E **51 H12**
Kaka Turkmenistan 37°21N 59°36E **45 B8**
Kakabeka Falls Canada 48°24N 89°37W **72 C2**
Kakadu △ Australia 12°0S 132°3E **60 B5**
Kakamas S. Africa 28°45S 20°33E **56 D3**
Kakamega Kenya 0°20N 34°46E **54 B3**
Kakanui Mts. N.Z. 45°10S 170°30E **59 F3**
Kakdwip India 21°53N 88°11E **43 J13**
Kake Japan 34°36N 132°19E **31 G6**
Kake U.S.A. 56°59N 133°57W **70 B2**
Kakegawa Japan 34°46N 138°1E **31 G9**
Kakeroma-Jima Japan 28°8N 129°14E **31 K4**
Kākhak Iran 34°9N 58°38E **45 C8**
Kakhovka Ukraine 46°45N 33°30E **19 E5**
Kakhovske Vdskh.
  Ukraine 47°5N 34°0E **19 E5**
Kakinada India 16°57N 82°11E **41 L13**
Kakisa Canada 60°56N 117°25W **70 A5**
Kakisa → Canada 61°3N 118°10W **70 A5**
Kakisa L. Canada 60°56N 117°43W **70 A5**
Kakogawa Japan 34°46N 134°51E **31 G7**
Kakuma Kenya 3°43N 34°33E **54 B3**
Kakwa → Canada 54°37N 118°28W **70 C5**
Kāl Gūsheh Iran 30°59N 58°12E **45 D8**
Kal Sefid Iran 34°52N 47°23E **44 C5**
Kalaallit Nunaat = Greenland ☒
  N. Amer. 66°0N 45°0W **67 C15**
Kalabagh Pakistan 33°0N 71°28E **42 C4**
Kalabahi Indonesia 8°13S 124°31E **37 F6**
Kalach Russia 50°22N 41°0E **19 D7**

Kaladan → Burma 20°20N 93°5E **41 J18**
Kaladar Canada 44°37N 77°5W **82 B7**
Kalahari Africa 24°0S 21°30E **56 C3**
Kalahari Gemsbok △
  S. Africa 25°30S 20°30E **56 D3**
Kalajoki Finland 64°12N 24°10E **8 D21**
Kalakamati Botswana 20°40S 27°25E **57 C4**
Kalakan Russia 55°15N 116°45E **29 D12**
K'alak'unlun Shank'ou =
  Karakoram Pass Asia 35°33N 77°50E **43 B7**
Kalam Pakistan 35°34N 72°30E **43 B5**
Kalama
  Dem. Rep. of the Congo 2°52S 28°35E **54 C2**
Kalama U.S.A. 46°1N 122°51W **78 E4**
Kalamata Greece 37°3N 22°10E **23 F10**
Kalamazoo U.S.A. 42°17N 85°35W **81 D11**
Kalamazoo → U.S.A. 42°40N 86°10W **80 D10**
Kalambo Falls Tanzania 8°37S 31°35E **55 D3**
Kalan Turkey 39°7N 39°32E **44 B3**
Kalannie Australia 30°22S 117°5E **61 F2**
Kalāntarī Iran 32°10N 54°8E **45 C7**
Kalao Indonesia 7°21S 121°0E **37 F6**
Kalaotoa Indonesia 7°20S 121°50E **37 F6**
Kalasin Thailand 16°26N 103°30E **38 D4**
Kālat Iran 25°29N 59°22E **45 E8**
Kalat Pakistan 29°8N 66°31E **40 E5**
Kalāteh Iran 36°33N 55°41E **45 B7**
Kalāteh-ye Ganj Iran 27°31N 57°55E **45 E8**
Kalbā U.A.E. 25°5N 56°22E **45 E8**
Kalbarri Australia 27°40S 114°10E **61 E1**
Kalbarri △ Australia 27°51S 114°30E **61 E1**
Kalce Slovenia 45°54N 14°13E **16 F8**
Kale Turkey 37°27N 28°49E **23 F13**
Kalegauk Kyun Burma 15°33N 97°35E **38 E1**
Kalehe
  Dem. Rep. of the Congo 2°6S 28°50E **54 C2**
Kalema Tanzania 1°12S 31°55E **54 C3**
Kalemie
  Dem. Rep. of the Congo 5°55S 29°9E **54 D2**
Kalewa Burma 23°1N 94°15E **41 H19**
Kaleybar Iran 38°47N 47°2E **44 B5**
Kalgoorlie-Boulder
  Australia 30°40S 121°22E **61 F3**
Kali → India 27°6N 79°53E **43 F8**
Kali Sindh → India 25°32N 76°17E **42 G6**
Kaliakra, Nos Bulgaria 43°21N 28°30E **23 C13**
Kalianda Indonesia 5°50S 105°45E **36 F3**
Kalibo Phil. 11°43N 122°22E **37 B6**
Kalima
  Dem. Rep. of the Congo 2°33S 26°32E **54 C2**
Kalimantan Indonesia 0°0 114°0E **36 E4**
Kalimantan Barat □
  Indonesia 0°0 110°30E **36 E4**
Kalimantan Selatan □
  Indonesia 2°30S 115°30E **36 E5**
Kalimantan Tengah □
  Indonesia 2°0S 113°30E **36 E4**
Kalimantan Timur □
  Indonesia 1°30N 116°30E **36 D5**
Kálimnos Greece 37°0N 27°0E **23 F12**
Kalimpong India 27°4N 88°35E **43 F13**
Kaliningrad Russia 54°42N 20°32E **9 J19**
Kalinkavichy Belarus 52°12N 29°20E **17 B15**
Kalinkovichi = Kalinkavichy
  Belarus 52°12N 29°20E **17 B15**
Kaliro Uganda 0°56N 33°30E **54 B3**
Kalispell U.S.A. 48°12N 114°19W **76 B6**
Kalisz Poland 51°45N 18°8E **17 C10**
Kaliua Tanzania 5°5S 31°48E **54 D3**
Kalix = Kalixälven →
  Sweden 65°50N 23°11E **8 D20**
Kalix Sweden 65°53N 23°12E **8 D20**
Kalixälven → Sweden 65°50N 23°11E **8 D20**
Kalka India 30°46N 76°57E **42 D7**
Kalkarindji Australia 17°30S 130°47E **60 C5**
Kalkaska U.S.A. 44°44N 85°11W **81 C11**
Kalkfeld Namibia 20°57S 16°14E **56 C2**
Kalkfontein Botswana 22°4S 20°57E **56 C3**
Kalkrand Namibia 24°1S 17°35E **56 C2**
Kallavesi Finland 62°58N 27°30E **8 E22**
Kallsjön Sweden 63°38N 13°0E **8 E15**
Kalmar Sweden 56°40N 16°20E **9 H17**
Kalmykia □ Russia 46°5N 46°1E **19 E8**
Kalmykovo Kazakhstan 49°0N 51°47E **19 E9**
Kalna India 23°13N 88°25E **43 H13**
Kalnai India 22°46N 83°30E **43 H10**
Kalocsa Hungary 46°32N 19°0E **17 E10**
Kalokhorio Cyprus 34°51N 33°2E **25 E12**
Kaloko
  Dem. Rep. of the Congo 6°47S 25°48E **54 D2**
Kalol Gujarat, India 22°37N 73°31E **42 H5**
Kalol Gujarat, India 23°15N 72°33E **42 H5**
Kalomo Zambia 17°0S 26°30E **55 F2**
Kalpi India 26°8N 79°47E **43 F8**
Kaltukatjara Australia 24°52S 129°5E **61 D4**
Kalu Pakistan 25°5N 67°39E **42 G2**
Kaluga Russia 54°35N 36°10E **18 D6**
Kalulushi Zambia 12°50S 28°3E **55 E2**
Kalumburu Australia 13°55S 126°35E **60 B4**
Kalush Ukraine 49°3N 24°23E **17 D13**
Kalutara Sri Lanka 6°35N 80°0E **40 R12**
Kalya Russia 60°15N 59°59E **18 B10**
Kalyan India 19°15N 73°9E **40 K8**
Kama Dem. Rep. of the Congo 3°30S 27°5E **54 C2**
Kama → Russia 55°45N 52°0E **18 C9**
Kamachumu Tanzania 1°37S 31°37E **54 C3**
Kamaishi Japan 39°16N 141°53E **30 E10**
Kamalia Pakistan 30°44N 72°42E **42 D5**
Kamapanda Zambia 12°5S 24°0E **55 E1**
Kamaran Yemen 15°21N 42°35E **47 D3**
Kamativi Zimbabwe 18°20S 27°6E **55 F2**
Kambalda West
  Australia 31°10S 121°37E **61 F3**
Kambar Pakistan 27°37N 68°1E **42 F3**
Kambarka Russia 56°15N 54°11E **18 C9**

Kambolé Zambia 8°47S 30°48E **55 D3**
Kambos Cyprus 35°2N 32°44E **25 D11**
Kambove
  Dem. Rep. of the Congo 10°51S 26°33E **55 E2**
Kamchatka, Poluostrov
  Russia 57°0N 160°0E **29 D17**
Kamchatka Pen. = Kamchatka,
  Poluostrov Russia 57°0N 160°0E **29 D17**
Kamchiya → Bulgaria 43°4N 27°44E **23 C12**
Kame Ruins Zimbabwe 20°7S 28°25E **55 G2**
Kamen Russia 53°50N 81°30E **28 D9**
Kamen-Rybolov Russia 44°46N 132°2E **30 B6**
Kamenjak, Rt Croatia 44°47N 13°55E **16 F7**
Kamenka Russia 65°58N 44°0E **18 A7**
Kamenka Bugskaya =
  Kamyanka-Buzka
  Ukraine 50°8N 24°16E **17 C13**
Kamensk Uralskiy Russia 56°25N 62°2E **28 D7**
Kamenskoye Russia 62°45N 165°30E **29 C17**
Kameoka Japan 35°0N 135°35E **31 G7**
Kamet India 30°55N 79°35E **43 D8**
Kamiah U.S.A. 46°14N 116°2W **76 C5**
Kamieskroon S. Africa 30°9S 17°56E **56 E2**
Kamilukuak L. Canada 62°22N 101°40W **71 A8**
Kamin-Kashyrskyy
  Ukraine 51°39N 24°56E **17 C13**
Kamina
  Dem. Rep. of the Congo 8°45S 25°0E **55 D2**
Kaminak L. Canada 62°10N 95°0W **71 A10**
Kaministiquia Canada 48°32N 89°35W **72 C1**
Kaminoyama Japan 38°9N 140°17E **30 E10**
Kamiros Greece 36°20N 27°56E **25 C9**
Kamituga
  Dem. Rep. of the Congo 3°2S 28°10E **54 C2**
Kamla → India 25°35N 86°36E **43 G12**
Kamloops Canada 50°40N 120°20W **70 C4**
Kamo Japan 37°39N 139°3E **30 F9**
Kamoke Pakistan 32°4N 74°4E **42 C6**
Kampala Uganda 0°20N 32°30E **54 B3**
Kampar Malaysia 4°18N 101°9E **39 K3**
Kampar → Indonesia 0°30N 103°8E **36 D2**
Kampen Neths. 52°33N 5°53E **15 B5**
Kamphaeng Phet
  Thailand 16°28N 99°30E **38 D2**
Kampolombo, L. Zambia 11°37S 29°42E **55 E2**
Kampong Chhnang
  Cambodia 12°20N 104°35E **39 F5**
Kampong Pengerang
  Malaysia 1°22N 104°7E **39 d**
Kampong Punggai
  Malaysia 1°27N 104°18E **39 d**
Kampong Saom
  Cambodia 10°38N 103°30E **39 G4**
Kampong Saom, Chaak
  Cambodia 10°50N 103°32E **39 G4**
Kampong Tanjong Langsat
  Malaysia 1°28N 104°1E **39 d**
Kampong Telok Ramunia
  Malaysia 1°22N 104°15E **39 d**
Kampot Cambodia 10°36N 104°10E **39 G5**
Kampuchea = Cambodia ■
  Asia 12°15N 105°0E **38 F5**
Kampung Air Putih
  Malaysia 4°15N 103°10E **39 K4**
Kampung Jerangau
  Malaysia 4°50N 103°10E **39 K4**
Kampung Raja Malaysia 5°45N 102°35E **39 K4**
Kampungbaru = Tolitoli
  Indonesia 1°5N 120°50E **37 D6**
Kamrau, Teluk Indonesia 3°30S 133°36E **37 E8**
Kamsack Canada 51°34N 101°54W **71 C8**
Kamskoye Vdkhr.
  Russia 58°41N 56°7E **18 C10**
Kamuchawie L.
  Canada 56°18N 101°59W **71 B8**
Kamuela U.S.A. 20°1N 155°41W **74 b**
Kamui-Misaki Japan 43°20N 140°21E **30 C10**
Kamyanets-Podilskyy
  Ukraine 48°45N 26°40E **17 D14**
Kamyanka-Buzka
  Ukraine 50°8N 24°16E **17 C13**
Kamyshin Russia 50°10N 45°24E **19 D8**
Kanaaupscow Canada 54°2N 76°30W **72 B4**
Kanaaupscow → Canada 53°39N 77°9W **72 B4**
Kanab U.S.A. 37°3N 112°32W **77 H7**
Kanab Cr. → U.S.A. 36°24N 112°38W **77 H7**
Kanacea Lau Group, Fiji 17°15S 179°6W **59 a**
Kanacea Taveuni, Fiji 16°59S 179°56E **59 a**
Kanagi Japan 40°54N 140°27E **30 D10**
Kanairiktok → Canada 55°2N 60°18W **73 A7**
Kananga
  Dem. Rep. of the Congo 5°55S 22°18E **52 F4**
Kanash Russia 55°30N 47°32E **18 C8**
Kanaskat U.S.A. 47°19N 121°54W **78 C5**
Kanastraíon, Ákra = Paliouri,
  Akra Greece 39°57N 23°45E **23 E10**
Kanawha → U.S.A. 38°50N 82°9W **81 F12**
Kanazawa Japan 36°30N 136°38E **31 F8**
Kanchanaburi Thailand 14°2N 99°31E **38 E2**
Kanchenjunga Nepal 27°50N 88°10E **43 F13**
Kanchipuram India 12°52N 79°45E **40 N11**
Kandaghat India 30°59N 77°7E **42 D7**
Kandahār □ Afghan. 31°0N 65°0E **40 D4**
Kandalaksha Russia 67°9N 32°30E **8 C25**
Kandalakshskiy Zaliv
  Russia 66°0N 35°0E **18 A6**
Kandangan Indonesia 2°50S 115°20E **36 E5**
Kandanghaur Indonesia 6°21S 108°6E **37 G13**
Kandanos Greece 35°19N 23°44E **25 D5**
Kandavu = Kadavu Fiji 19°0S 178°15E **59 a**
Kandavu Passage = Kadavu
  Passage Fiji 18°45S 178°0E **59 a**
Kandhkot Pakistan 28°16N 69°8E **42 E3**

Kandhla *India* 29°18N 77°19E **42** E7
Kandi *Benin* 11°7N 2°55E **50** F6
Kandi *India* 23°58N 88°5E **43** H13
Kandiaro *Pakistan* 27°4N 68°13E **42** F3
Kandla *India* 23°0N 70°10E **42** H4
Kandos *Australia* 32°45S 149°58E **63** E4
Kandreho *Madag.* 17°29S 46°6E **57** B8
Kandy *Sri Lanka* 7°18N 80°43E **40** R12
Kane *U.S.A.* 41°40N 78°49W **82** E6
Kane Basin *Greenland* 79°1N 70°0W **66** B12
Kāne'ohe *U.S.A.* 21°25N 157°48W **74** b
Kang *Botswana* 23°41S 22°50E **56** C3
Kang Krung △ *Thailand* 9°30N 98°50E **39** H2
Kangān *Fārs, Iran* 27°50N 52°3E **45** E7
Kangān *Hormozgān, Iran* 25°48N 57°28E **45** E8
Kangar *Malaysia* 6°27N 100°12E **39** J3
Kangaroo I. *Australia* 35°45S 137°0E **63** F2
Kangaroo Mts.
Australia 23°29S 141°51E **62** C3
Kangasala *Finland* 61°28N 24°4E **8** F21
Kangāvar *Iran* 34°40N 48°0E **45** C6
Kangdong *N. Korea* 39°9N 126°5E **35** E14
Kangean, Kepulauan
Indonesia 6°55S 115°23E **36** F5
Kangean Is. = Kangean, Kepulauan *Indonesia* 6°55S 115°23E **36** F5
Kanggye *N. Korea* 41°0N 126°35E **35** D14
Kangikajik *Greenland* 70°7N 22°0W **4** B6
Kangiqliniq = Rankin Inlet
Canada 62°30N 93°0W **68** C10
Kangiqsualujjuaq
Canada 58°30N 65°59W **69** D13
Kangiqsujuaq *Canada* 61°30N 72°0W **69** C12
Kangiqtugaapik = Clyde River
Canada 70°30N 68°30W **69** B13
Kangirsuk *Canada* 60°0N 70°0W **69** D13
Kangkar Chemaran
Malaysia 1°34N 104°12E **39** d
Kangkar Sungai Tiram
Malaysia 1°35N 103°55E **39** d
Kangkar Teberau
Malaysia 1°32N 103°51E **39** d
Kangping *China* 42°43N 123°18E **35** C12
Kangra *India* 32°6N 76°16E **42** C7
Kangrinboqe Feng *China* 31°0N 81°25E **43** D9
Kangto *China* 27°50N 92°35E **41** F18
Kanha △ *India* 22°15N 80°40E **43** H9
Kanhar → *India* 24°28N 83°8E **43** G10
Kaniama
Dem. Rep. of the Congo 7°30S 24°12E **54** D1
Kaniapiskau = Caniapiscau →
Canada 56°40N 69°30W **73** A6
Kaniapiskau, L. = Caniapiscau, L.
Canada 54°10N 69°55W **73** B6
Kanin, Poluostrov *Russia* 68°0N 45°0E **18** A8
Kanin Nos, Mys *Russia* 68°39N 43°32E **18** A7
Kanin Pen. = Kanin, Poluostrov
Russia 68°0N 45°0E **18** A8
Kaniva *Australia* 36°22S 141°18E **63** F3
Kanjut Sar *Pakistan* 36°7N 75°25E **43** A6
Kankaanpää *Finland* 61°44N 22°50E **8** F20
Kankakee *U.S.A.* 41°7N 87°52W **80** E10
Kankakee → *U.S.A.* 41°23N 88°15W **80** E9
Kankan *Guinea* 10°23N 9°15W **50** F4
Kankendy = Xankändi
Azerbaijan 39°52N 46°49E **44** B5
Kanker *India* 20°10N 81°40E **41** J12
Kankroli *India* 25°4N 73°53E **42** G5
Kannapolis *U.S.A.* 35°30N 80°37W **85** D14
Kannauj *India* 27°3N 79°56E **43** F8
Kannod *India* 22°45N 76°40E **40** H10
Kano *Nigeria* 12°2N 8°30E **50** F7
Kan'onji *Japan* 34°7N 133°39E **31** G6
Kanowit *Malaysia* 2°14N 112°20E **36** D4
Kanoya *Japan* 31°25N 130°50E **31** J5
Kanpetlet *Burma* 21°10N 93°59E **41** J18
Kanpur *India* 26°28N 80°20E **43** F9
Kansas □ *U.S.A.* 38°30N 99°0W **80** F4
Kansas → *U.S.A.* 39°7N 94°37W **80** F6
Kansas City *Kans., U.S.A.* 39°7N 94°38W **80** F6
Kansas City *Mo., U.S.A.* 39°6N 94°35W **80** F6
Kansenia
Dem. Rep. of the Congo 10°20S 26°0E **55** E2
Kansk *Russia* 56°20N 95°37E **29** D10
Kansu = Gansu □ *China* 36°0N 104°0E **34** G3
Kantaphor *India* 22°35N 76°34E **42** H7
Kantharalak *Thailand* 14°39N 104°39E **38** E5
Kantli → *India* 28°20N 75°30E **42** E6
Kantō □ *Japan* 36°15N 139°30E **31** F9
Kantō-Sanchi *Japan* 35°59N 138°50E **31** G9
Kanturk *Ireland* 52°11N 8°54W **10** D3
Kanuma *Japan* 36°34N 139°42E **31** F9
Kanus *Namibia* 27°50S 18°39E **56** D2
Kanyakumari *India* 8°3N 77°40E **40** Q10
Kanye *Botswana* 24°55S 25°28E **56** C4
Kanzenze
Dem. Rep. of the Congo 10°30S 25°12E **55** E2
Kanzi, Ras *Tanzania* 7°1S 39°33E **54** D4
Kao *Tonga* 19°40S 175°1W **59** c
Kao Phara *Thailand* 8°3N 98°22E **39** a
Kaohsiung *Taiwan* 22°35N 120°16E **33** D7
Kaokoveld *Namibia* 19°15S 14°30E **56** B1
Kaolack *Senegal* 14°5N 16°8W **50** F2
Kaoshan *China* 44°38N 124°50E **35** B13
Kapaa *U.S.A.* 22°5N 159°19W **74** b
Kapadvanj *India* 23°5N 73°0E **42** H5
Kapan *Armenia* 39°18N 46°27E **44** B5
Kapanga
Dem. Rep. of the Congo 8°30S 22°40E **52** F4
Kapchagai = Qapshaghay
Kazakhstan 43°51N 77°14E **28** E8
Kapedo *Kenya* 1°10N 36°6E **54** B4
Kapela = Velika Kapela
Croatia 45°10N 15°5E **16** F8
Kapema
Dem. Rep. of the Congo 10°45S 28°22E **55** E2
Kapenguria *Kenya* 1°14N 35°7E **54** B4
Kapfenberg *Austria* 47°26N 15°18E **16** E8
Kapiri Mposhi *Zambia* 13°59S 28°43E **55** E2
Kāpīsā □ *Afghan.* 35°0N 69°20E **40** B6
Kapiskau → *Canada* 52°47N 81°55W **72** B3
Kapit *Malaysia* 2°0N 112°55E **36** D4
Kapiti I. *N.Z.* 40°50S 174°56E **59** D5
Kaplan *U.S.A.* 30°0N 92°17W **84** F8
Kapoe *Thailand* 9°34N 98°32E **39** H2
Kapoeta *Sudan* 4°50N 33°35E **51** H12
Kaposvár *Hungary* 46°25N 17°47E **17** E9
Kapowsin *U.S.A.* 46°59N 122°13W **78** D4
Kapps *Namibia* 22°32S 17°18E **56** C2
Kapsabet *Kenya* 0°12N 35°6E **54** B4
Kapsan *N. Korea* 41°4N 128°19E **35** D15
Kapsukas = Marijampolė
Lithuania 54°33N 23°19E **9** J20
Kaptai L. *Bangla.* 22°40N 92°20E **41** H18
Kapuas → *Indonesia* 0°25S 109°20E **36** E3
Kapuas Hulu, Pegunungan
Malaysia 1°30N 113°30E **36** D4
Kapuas Hulu Ra. = Kapuas Hulu, Pegunungan *Malaysia* 1°30N 113°30E **36** D4
Kapulo
Dem. Rep. of the Congo 8°18S 29°15E **55** D2
Kapunda *Australia* 34°20S 138°56E **63** E2
Kapuni *N.Z.* 39°29S 174°8E **59** C5
Kapurthala *India* 31°23N 75°25E **42** D6
Kapuskasing *Canada* 49°25N 82°30W **72** C3
Kapuskasing → *Canada* 49°49N 82°0W **72** C3
Kaputar, Mt. *Australia* 30°15S 150°10E **63** E5
Kaputir *Kenya* 2°5N 35°28E **54** B4
Kara *Russia* 69°10N 65°0E **28** C7
Kara Bogaz Gol, Zaliv = Garabogazköl Aylagy
Turkmenistan 41°0N 53°30E **19** F9
Kara-Kala = Garrygala
Turkmenistan 38°31N 56°29E **45** B8
Kara Kalpak Republic = Qoraqalpoghistan □
Uzbekistan 43°0N 58°0E **28** E6
Kara Kum = Garagum
Turkmenistan 39°30N 60°0E **45** B8
Kara Sea *Russia* 75°0N 70°0E **28** B8
Karabiğa *Turkey* 40°23N 27°17E **23** D12
Karabük *Turkey* 41°12N 32°37E **19** F5
Karaburun *Turkey* 38°41N 26°28E **23** E12
Karabutak = Qarabutaq
Kazakhstan 49°59N 60°14E **28** E7
Karacabey *Turkey* 40°12N 28°21E **23** D13
Karacasu *Turkey* 37°43N 28°35E **23** F13
Karachey-Cherkessia □
Russia 43°40N 41°30E **19** F7
Karachi *Pakistan* 24°50N 67°0E **42** G2
Karad *India* 17°15N 74°10E **40** L9
Karaganda = Qaraghandy
Kazakhstan 49°50N 73°10E **28** E8
Karagayly = Qaraghayly
Kazakhstan 49°26N 76°0E **28** E8
Karaginskiy, Ostrov
Russia 58°45N 164°0E **29** D17
Karagiye, Vpadina
Kazakhstan 43°27N 51°45E **19** F9
Karagiye Depression = Karagiye, Vpadina *Kazakhstan* 43°27N 51°45E **19** F9
Karagola Road *India* 25°29N 87°23E **43** G12
Karaikal *India* 10°59N 79°50E **40** P11
Karaikkudi *India* 10°5N 78°45E **40** P11
Karaj *Iran* 35°48N 51°0E **45** C6
Karak *Malaysia* 3°25N 102°2E **39** L4
Karakalpakstan = Qoraqalpoghistan □
Uzbekistan 43°0N 58°0E **28** E6
Karakelong *Indonesia* 4°35N 126°50E **37** D7
Karakitang *Indonesia* 3°14N 125°28E **37** D7
Karakol *Kyrgyzstan* 42°30N 78°20E **32** B2
Karakoram Pass *Asia* 35°33N 77°50E **43** B7
Karakoram Ra. *Pakistan* 35°30N 77°0E **43** B7
Karakuwisa *Namibia* 18°56S 19°40E **56** B2
Karalon *Russia* 57°5N 115°50E **29** D12
Karama *Jordan* 31°57N 35°35E **46** D4
Karaman *Turkey* 37°14N 33°13E **44** B2
Karamay *China* 45°30N 84°58E **32** B3
Karambu *Indonesia* 3°53S 116°6E **36** E5
Karamea Bight *N.Z.* 41°22S 171°40E **59** D3
Karamnasa → *India* 25°31N 83°52E **43** G10
Karān *Si. Arabia* 27°43N 49°49E **45** E6
Karand *Iran* 34°16N 46°15E **44** C5
Karanganyar *Indonesia* 7°38S 109°37E **37** G13
Karangasem *Indonesia* 8°27S 115°37E **37** J18
Karanjia *India* 21°47N 85°58E **43** J11
Karasburg *Namibia* 28°0S 18°44E **56** D2
Karasino *Russia* 66°50N 86°50E **28** C9
Karasjok *Norway* 69°27N 25°30E **8** B21
Karasuk *Russia* 53°44N 78°2E **28** D8
Karasuyama *Japan* 36°39N 140°9E **31** F10
Karatau, Khrebet = Qarataū
Kazakhstan 43°30N 69°30E **28** E7
Karatax Shan *China* 35°57N 81°0E **32** C3
Karatsu *Japan* 33°26N 129°58E **31** H5
Karaul *Russia* 70°6N 82°15E **28** B9
Karauli *India* 26°30N 77°4E **42** F7
Karavostasi *Cyprus* 35°8N 32°50E **25** D11
Karawang *Indonesia* 6°30S 107°15E **37** G12
Karawanken *Europe* 46°30N 14°40E **16** E8
Karayazı *Turkey* 39°41N 42°9E **19** G7
Karazhal = Qarazhal
Kazakhstan 48°2N 70°49E **28** E8
Karbalā' *Iraq* 32°36N 44°3E **44** C5
Karcag *Hungary* 47°19N 20°57E **17** E11
Karcha → *Pakistan* 34°45N 76°10E **43** B7
Karchana *India* 25°17N 81°56E **43** G9
Karditsa *Greece* 39°23N 21°54E **23** E9
Kärdla *Estonia* 59°0N 22°45E **9** G20
Kareeberge *S. Africa* 30°59S 21°50E **56** E3
Kareha → *India* 25°44N 86°21E **43** G12
Kareima *Sudan* 18°30N 31°49E **51** E12
Karelia □ *Russia* 65°30N 32°30E **8** D25
Karelian Republic = Karelia □
Russia 65°30N 32°30E **8** D25
Karera *India* 25°32N 78°9E **42** G8
Karevāndar *Iran* 27°53N 60°44E **45** E9
Kargasok *Russia* 59°3N 80°53E **28** D9
Kargat *Russia* 55°10N 80°15E **28** D9
Kargi *Kenya* 2°31N 37°34E **54** B4
Kargil *India* 34°32N 76°12E **43** B7
Kargopol *Russia* 61°30N 38°58E **18** B6
Karhal *India* 27°1N 78°57E **43** F8
Karīān *Iran* 26°57N 57°14E **45** E8
Karianga *Madag.* 22°25S 47°22E **57** C8
Kariba *Zimbabwe* 16°28S 28°50E **55** F2
Kariba, L. *Zimbabwe* 16°40S 28°25E **55** F2
Kariba Dam *Zimbabwe* 16°30S 28°35E **55** F2
Kariba Gorge *Zambia* 16°30S 28°50E **55** F2
Karibib *Namibia* 22°0S 15°56E **56** C2
Karijini △ *Australia* 23°8S 118°15E **60** D2
Karimata, Kepulauan
Indonesia 1°25S 109°0E **36** E3
Karimata, Selat *Indonesia* 2°0S 108°40E **36** E3
Karimata Is. = Karimata, Kepulauan *Indonesia* 1°25S 109°0E **36** E3
Karimnagar *India* 18°26N 79°10E **40** K11
Karimun Kecil, Pulau
Indonesia 1°8N 103°22E **39** d
Karimunjawa, Kepulauan
Indonesia 5°50S 110°30E **36** F4
Karin *Somali Rep.* 10°50N 45°52E **47** E4
Karīt *Iran* 33°29N 56°55E **45** C8
Kariya *Japan* 34°58N 137°1E **31** G8
Kariyangwe *Zimbabwe* 18°0S 27°38E **57** B4
Karjala *Finland* 62°0N 30°25E **8** F24
Karkaralinsk = Qarqaraly
Kazakhstan 49°26N 75°30E **28** E8
Karkheh → *Iran* 31°2N 47°29E **44** D5
Karkinitska Zatoka
Ukraine 45°56N 33°0E **19** E5
Karkinitskiy Zaliv = Karkinitska Zatoka *Ukraine* 45°56N 33°0E **19** E5
Karkuk = Kirkūk *Iraq* 35°30N 44°21E **44** C5
Karleby = Kokkola
Finland 63°50N 23°8E **8** E20
Karlovac *Croatia* 45°31N 15°36E **16** F8
Karlovo *Bulgaria* 42°38N 24°47E **23** C11
Karlovy Vary *Czech Rep.* 50°13N 12°51E **16** C7
Karlsbad = Karlovy Vary
Czech Rep. 50°13N 12°51E **16** C7
Karlsena, Mys *Russia* 77°0N 67°42E **28** B7
Karlshamn *Sweden* 56°10N 14°51E **9** H16
Karlskoga *Sweden* 59°28N 14°33E **9** G16
Karlskrona *Sweden* 56°10N 15°35E **9** H16
Karlsruhe *Germany* 49°0N 8°23E **16** D5
Karlstad *Sweden* 59°23N 13°30E **9** G15
Karlstad *U.S.A.* 48°35N 96°31W **80** A5
Karmi'el *Israel* 32°55N 35°18E **46** C4
Karnak *Egypt* 25°43N 32°39E **51** C12
Karnal *India* 29°42N 77°2E **42** E7
Karnali → *Nepal* 28°45N 81°16E **43** E9
Karnaphuli Res. = Kaptai L.
Bangla. 22°40N 92°20E **41** H18
Karnaprayag *India* 30°16N 79°15E **43** D8
Karnataka □ *India* 13°15N 77°0E **40** N10
Karnes City *U.S.A.* 28°53N 97°54W **84** G6
Karnische Alpen *Europe* 46°36N 13°0E **16** E7
Kärnten □ *Austria* 46°52N 13°30E **16** E8
Karoi *Zimbabwe* 16°48S 29°45E **55** F2
Karon, Ao *Thailand* 7°51N 98°17E **39** a
Karonga *Malawi* 9°57S 33°55E **55** D3
Karoo △ *S. Africa* 32°18S 22°27E **56** E3
Karoonda *Australia* 35°1S 139°59E **63** F2
Karor *Pakistan* 31°15N 70°59E **42** D4
Karora *Sudan* 17°44N 38°15E **51** E13
Karpasia *Cyprus* 35°32N 34°15E **25** D13
Karpathos *Greece* 35°37N 27°10E **23** G12
Karpinsk *Russia* 59°45N 60°1E **18** C11
Karpogory *Russia* 64°0N 44°27E **18** B7
Karpuz Burnu = Apostolos Andreas, C. *Cyprus* 35°42N 34°35E **25** D13
Karratha *Australia* 20°53S 116°40E **60** D2
Kars *Turkey* 40°40N 43°5E **19** F7
Karsakpay *Kazakhstan* 47°55N 66°40E **28** E7
Karshi = Qarshi
Uzbekistan 38°53N 65°48E **28** F7
Karsiyang *India* 26°56N 88°18E **43** F13
Karsog *India* 31°23N 77°12E **42** D7
Kartala *Comoros Is.* 11°45S 43°21E **53** a
Kartaly *Russia* 53°3N 60°40E **28** D7
Kartapur *India* 31°27N 75°32E **42** D6
Karthaus *U.S.A.* 41°8N 78°9W **82** E6
Karufa *Indonesia* 3°50S 133°20E **37** E8
Karuma △ *Uganda* 2°5N 32°15E **54** B3
Karumba *Australia* 17°31S 140°50E **62** B3
Karumo *Tanzania* 2°25S 32°50E **54** C3
Karumwa *Tanzania* 3°12S 32°38E **54** C3
Kārūn → *Iran* 30°26N 48°10E **45** D6
Karungu *Kenya* 0°50S 34°10E **54** C3
Karviná *Czech Rep.* 49°53N 18°31E **17** D10
Karwan → *India* 27°26N 78°4E **42** F8
Karwar *India* 14°55N 74°13E **40** M9
Karwi *India* 25°12N 80°57E **43** G9
Karymskoye *Russia* 51°36N 114°21E **29** D12
Kasache *Malawi* 13°25S 34°20E **55** E3
Kasai →
Dem. Rep. of the Congo 3°30S 16°10E **52** E3
Kasai-Oriental □
Dem. Rep. of the Congo 5°0S 24°30E **54** D1
Kasaji
Dem. Rep. of the Congo 10°25S 23°27E **55** E1
Kasama *Zambia* 10°16S 31°9E **55** E3
Kasan *N. Korea* 41°18N 126°55E **35** D14
Kasandra Kolpos *Greece* 40°5N 23°30E **23** D10
Kasane *Namibia* 17°34S 24°50E **56** B3
Kasanga *Tanzania* 8°30S 31°10E **55** D3
Kasanka △ *Zambia* 11°34S 30°15E **55** E3
Kasaragod *India* 12°30N 74°58E **40** N9
Kasba L. *Canada* 60°20N 102°10W **71** A8
Kāseh Garān *Iran* 34°5N 46°2E **44** C5
Kasempa *Zambia* 13°30S 25°44E **55** E2
Kasenga
Dem. Rep. of the Congo 10°20S 28°45E **55** E2
Kasese *Uganda* 0°13N 30°3E **54** B3
Kasewa *Zambia* 14°28S 28°53E **55** E2
Kasganj *India* 27°48N 78°42E **43** F8
Kashabowie *Canada* 48°40N 90°26W **72** C1
Kashaf *Iran* 35°58N 61°7E **45** C9
Kāshān *Iran* 34°5N 51°30E **45** C6
Kashechewan *Canada* 52°18N 81°37W **72** B3
Kashgar = Kashi *China* 39°30N 76°2E **32** C2
Kashi *China* 39°30N 76°2E **32** C2
Kashimbo
Dem. Rep. of the Congo 11°12S 26°19E **55** E2
Kashipur *India* 29°15N 79°0E **43** E8
Kashiwazaki *Japan* 37°22N 138°33E **31** F9
Kashk-e Kohneh
Afghan. 34°55N 62°30E **40** B3
Kashkū'īyeh *Iran* 30°31N 55°40E **45** D7
Kāshmar *Iran* 35°16N 58°26E **45** C8
Kashmir *Asia* 34°0N 76°0E **43** C7
Kashmor *Pakistan* 28°28N 69°32E **42** E3
Kashun Noerh = Gaxun Nur
China 42°22N 100°30E **32** B5
Kasiari *India* 22°8N 87°14E **43** H12
Kasimov *Russia* 54°55N 41°20E **18** D7
Kasinge
Dem. Rep. of the Congo 6°15S 26°58E **54** D2
Kasiruta *Indonesia* 0°25S 127°12E **37** E7
Kaskaskia → *U.S.A.* 37°58N 89°57W **80** G9
Kaskattama → *Canada* 57°3N 90°4W **71** B10
Kaskinen *Finland* 62°22N 21°15E **8** E19
Kaskö = Kaskinen
Finland 62°22N 21°15E **8** E19
Kaslo *Canada* 49°55N 116°55W **70** D5
Kasmere L. *Canada* 59°34N 101°10W **71** B8
Kasongo
Dem. Rep. of the Congo 4°30S 26°33E **54** C2
Kasongo Lunda
Dem. Rep. of the Congo 6°35S 16°49E **52** F3
Kasos *Greece* 35°20N 26°55E **23** G12
Kassalâ *Sudan* 15°30N 36°0E **51** E13
Kassel *Germany* 51°18N 9°26E **16** C5
Kassiopi *Greece* 39°48N 19°53E **25** A3
Kasson *U.S.A.* 44°2N 92°45W **80** C7
Kastamonu *Turkey* 41°25N 33°43E **19** F5
Kasteli *Greece* 35°29N 23°38E **25** D5
Kastelli *Greece* 35°12N 25°20E **25** D7
Kasterlee *Belgium* 51°15N 4°59E **15** C4
Kastoria *Greece* 40°30N 21°19E **23** D9
Kasulu *Tanzania* 4°37S 30°5E **54** C3
Kasumi *Japan* 35°38N 134°38E **31** G7
Kasungu *Malawi* 13°0S 33°29E **55** E3
Kasungu △ *Malawi* 12°53S 33°9E **55** E3
Kasur *Pakistan* 31°5N 74°25E **42** D6
Kata, Ao *Thailand* 7°48N 98°18E **39** J2
Kata Archanes *Greece* 35°15N 25°10E **25** D7
Kata Tjuta *Australia* 25°20S 130°50E **61** E5
Kataba *Zambia* 16°5S 25°10E **55** F2
Katahdin, Mt. *U.S.A.* 45°54N 68°56W **81** C19
Katako Kombe
Dem. Rep. of the Congo 3°25S 24°20E **54** C1
Katale *Tanzania* 4°52S 31°7E **54** C3
Katanda *Katanga,*
Dem. Rep. of the Congo 7°52S 24°13E **54** D1
Katanda *Nord-Kivu,*
Dem. Rep. of the Congo 0°55S 29°21E **54** C2
Katanga □
Dem. Rep. of the Congo 8°0S 25°0E **54** D2
Katangi *India* 21°56N 79°50E **40** J11
Katanning *Australia* 33°40S 117°33E **61** F2
Katavi △ *Tanzania* 6°51S 31°3E **54** D3
Katavi Swamp *Tanzania* 6°50S 31°10E **54** D3
Katerini *Greece* 40°18N 22°37E **23** D10
Katghora *India* 22°30N 82°33E **43** H10
Katha *Burma* 24°10N 96°30E **41** G20
Katherîna, Gebel *Egypt* 28°30N 33°57E **44** D2
Katherine *Australia* 14°27S 132°20E **60** B5
Katherine Gorge
Australia 14°18S 132°28E **60** B5
Kathi *India* 21°47N 74°3E **42** J6
Kathiawar *India* 22°20N 71°0E **42** H4
Kathikas *Cyprus* 34°55N 32°25E **25** E11
Kathmandu *Nepal* 27°45N 85°20E **43** F11
Kathua *India* 32°23N 75°34E **42** C6
Katihar *India* 25°34N 87°36E **43** G12
Katima Mulilo *Namibia* 17°28S 24°13E **56** B3
Katimbira *Malawi* 12°40S 34°0E **55** E3
Katingan = Mendawai →
Indonesia 3°30S 113°0E **36** E4
Katiola *Ivory C.* 8°10N 5°10W **50** G4
Katmandu = Kathmandu
Nepal 27°45N 85°20E **43** F11
Katni *India* 23°51N 80°24E **43** H9
Kato Chorio *Greece* 35°3N 25°47E **25** D7
Kato Korakiana *Greece* 39°42N 19°45E **25** A3
Káto Pyrgos *Cyprus* 35°11N 32°41E **25** D11
Katompe
Dem. Rep. of the Congo 6°2S 26°23E **54** D2
Katong *Singapore* 1°18N 103°53E **39** d
Katonga → *Uganda* 0°34N 31°50E **54** B3
Katoomba *Australia* 33°41S 150°19E **63** E5
Katowice *Poland* 50°17N 19°5E **17** C10
Katrine, L. *U.K.* 56°15N 4°30W **11** E4
Katrineholm *Sweden* 59°9N 16°12E **9** G17
Katsepe *Madag.* 15°45S 46°15E **57** B8
Katsina *Nigeria* 13°0N 7°32E **50** F7
Katsumoto *Japan* 33°51N 129°42E **31** H4
Katsuura *Japan* 35°10N 140°20E **31** G10
Katsuyama *Japan* 36°3N 136°30E **31** F8
Kattavia *Greece* 35°57N 27°46E **25** D9
Kattegat *Denmark* 56°40N 11°20E **9** H14
Katumba
Dem. Rep. of the Congo 7°40S 25°17E **54** D2
Katwa *India* 23°30N 88°5E **43** H13
Katwijk *Neths.* 52°12N 4°24E **15** B4
Kaua'i *U.S.A.* 22°3N 159°30W **74** b
Kauai Channel *U.S.A.* 21°45N 158°50W **74** b
Kaudom △ *Namibia* 18°45S 20°51E **56** B3
Kaufman *U.S.A.* 32°35N 96°19W **84** E6
Kauhajoki *Finland* 62°25N 22°10E **8** E20
Kaukauna *U.S.A.* 44°17N 88°17W **80** C9
Kaukauveld *Namibia* 20°0S 20°15E **56** C3
Kaunakakai *U.S.A.* 21°6N 157°1W **74** b
Kaunas *Lithuania* 54°54N 23°54E **9** J20
Kaunia *Bangla.* 25°46N 89°26E **43** G13
Kautokeino *Norway* 69°0N 23°4E **8** B20
Kauwapur *India* 27°31N 82°18E **43** F10
Kavacha *Russia* 60°16N 169°51E **29** C17
Kavala *Greece* 40°57N 24°28E **23** D11
Kavalerovo *Russia* 44°15N 135°4E **30** B7
Kavali *India* 14°55N 80°1E **40** M12
Kavār *Iran* 29°11N 52°44E **45** D7
Kavi *India* 22°12N 72°38E **42** H5
Kavimba *Botswana* 18°2S 24°38E **56** B3
Kavīr, Dasht-e *Iran* 34°30N 55°0E **45** C7
Kavīr △ *Iran* 34°40N 52°0E **45** C7
Kavos *Greece* 39°23N 20°3E **25** B4
Kaw *Fr. Guiana* 4°30N 52°15W **93** C8
Kawagama L. *Canada* 45°18N 78°45W **82** A6
Kawagoe *Japan* 35°55N 139°29E **31** G9
Kawaguchi *Japan* 35°52N 139°45E **31** G9
Kawambwa *Zambia* 9°48S 29°3E **55** D2
Kawanoe *Japan* 34°1N 133°34E **31** G6
Kawardha *India* 22°0N 81°17E **43** J9
Kawasaki *Japan* 35°31N 139°43E **31** G9
Kawasi *Indonesia* 1°38S 127°28E **37** E7
Kawawachikamach
Canada 54°48N 66°50W **73** B6
Kawerau *N.Z.* 38°7S 176°42E **59** C6
Kawhia *N.Z.* 38°4S 174°49E **59** C5
Kawhia Harbour *N.Z.* 38°5S 174°51E **59** C5
Kawio, Kepulauan
Indonesia 4°30N 125°30E **37** D7
Kawthaung *Burma* 10°5N 98°36E **39** H2
Kawthoolei = Kayin □
Burma 18°0N 97°30E **41** L20
Kawthule = Kayin □
Burma 18°0N 97°30E **41** L20
Kaya *Burkina Faso* 13°4N 1°10W **50** F5
Kayah □ *Burma* 19°15N 97°15E **41** K20
Kayan → *Indonesia* 2°55N 117°35E **36** D5
Kaycee *U.S.A.* 43°43N 106°38W **76** E10
Kayeli *Indonesia* 3°20S 127°10E **37** E7
Kayenta *U.S.A.* 36°44N 110°15W **77** H8
Kayes *Mali* 14°25N 11°30W **50** F3
Kayin □ *Burma* 18°0N 97°30E **41** L20
Kayoa *Indonesia* 0°1N 127°28E **37** D7
Kayomba *Zambia* 13°11S 24°2E **55** E1
Kayseri *Turkey* 38°45N 35°30E **44** B2
Kaysville *U.S.A.* 41°2N 111°56W **76** F8
Kazachye *Russia* 70°52N 135°58E **29** B14
Kazakhstan ■ *Asia* 50°0N 70°0E **28** E8
Kazan *Russia* 55°50N 49°10E **18** C8
Kazan → *Canada* 64°2N 95°29W **71** A9
Kazan-Rettō *Pac. Oc.* 25°0N 141°0E **64** E6
Kazanlŭk *Bulgaria* 42°38N 25°20E **23** C11
Kazatin = Kozyatyn
Ukraine 49°45N 28°50E **17** D15
Kāzerūn *Iran* 29°38N 51°40E **45** D6
Kazi Magomed = Qazımämmäd
Azerbaijan 40°3N 49°0E **45** A6
Kazuma Pan △
Zimbabwe 18°20S 25°48E **55** F2
Kazuno *Japan* 40°10N 140°45E **30** D10
Kazym → *Russia* 63°54N 65°50E **28** C7
Kea *Greece* 37°35N 24°22E **23** F11
Keady *U.K.* 54°15N 6°42W **10** B5
Kearney *U.S.A.* 40°42N 99°5W **80** E4
Kearny *U.S.A.* 33°3N 110°55W **77** K8
Kearsarge, Mt. *U.S.A.* 43°22N 71°50W **83** C13
Keban *Turkey* 38°50N 38°50E **19** G6
Keban Barajı *Turkey* 38°41N 38°33E **44** B3
Kebnekaise *Sweden* 67°53N 18°33E **8** C18
Kebri Dehar *Ethiopia* 6°45N 44°17E **47** F3
Kebumen *Indonesia* 7°42S 109°40E **37** G13
Kechika → *Canada* 59°41N 127°12W **70** B3
Kecskemét *Hungary* 46°57N 19°42E **17** E10
Kėdainiai *Lithuania* 55°15N 24°2E **9** J21
Kedarnath *India* 30°44N 79°4E **43** D8
Kedgwick *Canada* 47°40N 67°20W **73** C6
Kediri *Indonesia* 7°51S 112°1E **37** G15
Kedros Oros *Greece* 35°11N 24°37E **25** D6
Keeler *U.S.A.* 36°29N 117°52W **78** J9
Keeley L. *Canada* 54°54N 108°8W **71** C7
Keeling Is. = Cocos Is.
Ind. Oc. 12°10S 96°55E **64** J1
Keelung = Chilung
Taiwan 25°3N 121°45E **33** D7
Keene *Canada* 44°15N 78°10W **82** B6
Keene *Calif., U.S.A.* 35°13N 118°33W **79** K8
Keene *N.H., U.S.A.* 42°56N 72°17W **83** D12
Keene *N.Y., U.S.A.* 44°16N 73°46W **83** B11
Keep River △ *Australia* 15°49S 129°8E **60** C4
Keeper Hill *Ireland* 52°45N 8°16W **10** D3
Keerweer, C. *Australia* 14°0S 141°32E **62** A3
Keeseville *U.S.A.* 44°29N 73°30W **83** B11
Keetmanshoop *Namibia* 26°35S 18°8E **56** D2
Keewatin *Canada* 49°46N 94°34W **71** D10
Keewatin → *Canada* 56°29N 100°46W **71** B8
Kefalonia *Greece* 38°15N 20°30E **23** E9
Kefamenanu *Indonesia* 9°28S 124°29E **37** F6
Kefar Sava *Israel* 32°11N 34°54E **46** C3
Keffi *Nigeria* 8°55N 7°43E **50** G7
Keflavík *Iceland* 64°2N 22°35W **8** D2
Keg River *Canada* 57°54N 117°55W **70** B5
Kegaska *Canada* 50°9N 61°18W **73** B7
Kehancha *Kenya* 1°11S 34°37E **54** C3
Keighley *U.K.* 53°52N 1°54W **12** D6
Keila *Estonia* 59°18N 24°25E **9** G21
Keimoes *S. Africa* 28°41S 20°59E **56** D3
Keitele *Finland* 63°10N 26°20E **8** E22
Keith *Australia* 36°6S 140°20E **63** F3

Keith *U.K.* 57°32N 2°57W **11** D6
Keiyasi *Fiji* 17°53S 177°46E **59** a
Keizer *U.S.A.* 44°57N 123°1W **76** D2
Kejserr Franz Joseph Fd.
  Greenland 73°30N 24°30W **4** B6
Kekri *India* 26°0N 75°10E **42** G6
Kelan *China* 38°43N 111°31E **34** E6
Kelang = Klang *Malaysia* 3°2N 101°26E **39** L3
Kelantan ➤ *Malaysia* 6°13N 102°14E **39** J4
Kelkit ➤ *Turkey* 40°45N 36°32E **19** F6
Kellerberrin *Australia* 31°36S 117°38E **61** F2
Kellett, C. *Canada* 72°0N 126°0W **69** B7
Kelleys I. *U.S.A.* 41°36N 82°42W **82** E2
Kellogg *U.S.A.* 47°32N 116°7W **76** C5
Kells = Ceanannus Mor
  Ireland 53°44N 6°53W **10** C5
Kélo *Chad* 9°10N 15°45E **51** G9
Kelokedhara *Cyprus* 34°48N 32°39E **25** E11
Kelowna *Canada* 49°50N 119°25W **70** D5
Kelsey Creek *Australia* 20°26S 148°31E **62** J6
Kelseyville *U.S.A.* 38°59N 122°50W **78** G4
Kelso *N.Z.* 45°54S 169°15E **59** F2
Kelso *U.K.* 55°36N 2°26W **11** F6
Kelso *U.S.A.* 46°9N 122°54W **78** D4
Keluang = Kluang
  Malaysia 2°3N 103°18E **39** L4
Kelvington *Canada* 52°10N 103°30W **71** C8
Kem *Russia* 65°0N 34°38E **18** B5
Kem ➤ *Russia* 64°57N 34°41E **18** B5
Kema *Indonesia* 1°22N 125°8E **37** D7
Kemah *Turkey* 39°32N 39°5E **44** B3
Kemaman *Malaysia* 4°12N 103°18E **39** K4
Kemano *Canada* 53°35N 128°0W **70** C3
Kemasik *Malaysia* 4°25N 103°27E **39** K4
Kemerovo *Russia* 55°20N 86°5E **28** D9
Kemi *Finland* 65°44N 24°34E **8** D21
Kemi älv = Kemijoki ➤
  Finland 65°47N 24°32E **8** D21
Kemi träsk = Kemijärvi
  Finland 66°43N 27°22E **8** C22
Kemijärvi *Finland* 66°43N 27°22E **8** C22
Kemijoki ➤ *Finland* 65°47N 24°32E **8** D21
Kemmerer *U.S.A.* 41°48N 110°32W **76** F8
Kemmuna = Comino
  Malta 36°1N 14°20E **25** C1
Kemp, L. *U.S.A.* 33°46N 99°9W **84** E5
Kemp Land *Antarctica* 69°0S 55°0E **5** C5
Kempas *Malaysia* 1°33N 103°42E **39** d
Kempsey *Australia* 31°1S 152°50E **63** E5
Kempt, L. *Canada* 47°25N 74°22W **72** C5
Kempten *Germany* 47°45N 10°17E **16** E6
Kempton *Australia* 42°31S 147°12E **63** G4
Kemptville *Canada* 45°0N 75°38W **83** B9
Ken ➤ *India* 25°13N 80°27E **43** G8
Kenai *U.S.A.* 60°33N 151°16W **68** C4
Kendai *India* 22°45N 82°37E **43** H10
Kendal *Indonesia* 6°56S 110°14E **37** G14
Kendal *U.K.* 54°20N 2°44W **12** C5
Kendall *Australia* 31°35S 152°44E **63** E5
Kendall *U.S.A.* 25°40N 80°19W **85** J14
Kendall ➤ *Australia* 14°4S 141°35E **62** A3
Kendallville *U.S.A.* 41°27N 85°16W **81** E11
Kendari *Indonesia* 3°50S 122°30E **37** E6
Kendawangan *Indonesia* 2°32S 110°17E **36** E4
Kendi, Pulau *Malaysia* 5°13N 100°11E **39** c
Kendrapara *India* 20°35N 86°30E **41** J15
Kendrew *S. Africa* 32°32S 24°30E **56** E3
Kene Thao *Laos* 17°44N 101°10E **38** D3
Kenedy *U.S.A.* 28°49N 97°51W **84** G6
Kenema *S. Leone* 7°50N 11°14W **50** G3
Keng Kok *Laos* 16°26N 105°12E **38** D5
Keng Tawng *Burma* 20°45N 98°18E **41** J21
Keng Tung *Burma* 21°0N 99°30E **41** J21
Kengeja *Tanzania* 5°26S 39°45E **54** D4
Kenhardt *S. Africa* 29°19S 21°12E **56** D3
Kenitra *Morocco* 34°15N 6°40W **50** B4
Kenli *China* 37°30N 118°20E **35** F10
Kenmare *Ireland* 51°53N 9°36W **10** E2
Kenmare *U.S.A.* 48°41N 102°5W **80** A2
Kenmare River *Ireland* 51°48N 9°51W **10** E2
Kennebago Lake *U.S.A.* 45°4N 70°40W **83** A14
Kennebec *U.S.A.* 43°54N 99°52W **80** D4
Kennebec ➤ *U.S.A.* 43°45N 69°46W **81** D19
Kennebunk *U.S.A.* 43°23N 70°33W **83** C14
Kennedy *Zimbabwe* 18°52S 27°10E **56** B4
Kennedy Ra. *Australia* 24°45S 115°10E **61** D2
Kennedy Range △
  Australia 24°34S 115°2E **61** D2
Kenner *U.S.A.* 29°59N 90°14W **85** G9
Kennet ➤ *U.K.* 51°27N 0°57W **13** F7
Kenneth Ra. *Australia* 23°50S 117°8E **61** D2
Kennett *U.S.A.* 36°14N 90°3W **80** G8
Kennewick *U.S.A.* 46°12N 119°7W **76** C4
Kennisis Lake *Canada* 45°13N 78°36W **82** A6
Kenogami ➤ *Canada* 51°6N 84°28W **72** B3
Kenora *Canada* 49°47N 94°29W **71** D10
Kenosha *U.S.A.* 42°35N 87°49W **80** D10
Kensington *Canada* 46°28N 63°34W **73** C7
Kent *Ohio, U.S.A.* 41°9N 81°22W **82** E3
Kent *Tex., U.S.A.* 31°4N 104°13W **84** F2
Kent *Wash., U.S.A.* 47°22N 122°14W **78** C4
Kent □ *U.K.* 51°12N 0°40E **13** F8
Kent Group *Australia* 39°30S 147°20E **63** F4
Kent Pen. *Canada* 68°30N 107°0W **68** C9
Kentaŭ *Kazakhstan* 43°32N 68°36E **28** E7
Kentland *U.S.A.* 40°46N 87°27W **80** E10
Kenton *U.S.A.* 40°39N 83°37W **81** E12
Kentucky □ *U.S.A.* 37°0N 84°0W **81** G11
Kentucky ➤ *U.S.A.* 38°41N 85°11W **81** F11
Kentucky L. *U.S.A.* 37°1N 88°16W **80** G9
Kentville *Canada* 45°6N 64°29W **73** C7
Kentwood *U.S.A.* 30°56N 90°31W **85** F9
Kenya ■ *Africa* 1°0N 38°0E **54** B4
Kenya, Mt. *Kenya* 0°10S 37°18E **54** C4
Kenyir, Tasik *Malaysia* 5°1N 102°54E **39** K4
Keo Neua, Deo *Vietnam* 18°23N 105°10E **38** C5

Keokuk *U.S.A.* 40°24N 91°24W **80** E8
Keoladeo △ *India* 27°0N 77°20E **42** F7
Keonjhargarh *India* 21°28N 85°35E **43** J11
Kep *Cambodia* 10°29N 104°19E **39** G5
Kep *Vietnam* 21°24N 106°16E **38** B6
Kepala Batas *Malaysia* 5°31N 100°26E **39** c
Kepi *Indonesia* 6°32S 139°19E **37** F9
Kerala □ *India* 11°0N 76°15E **40** P10
Kerama-Rettō *Japan* 26°5N 127°15E **31** L3
Keran *Pakistan* 34°35N 73°59E **43** B5
Kerang *Australia* 35°40S 143°55E **63** F3
Keraudren, C. *Australia* 19°58S 119°45E **60** C2
Kerch *Ukraine* 45°20N 36°20E **19** F6
Kerguelen *Ind. Oc.* 49°15S 69°10E **3** G13
Kericho *Kenya* 0°22S 35°15E **54** C4
Kerinci *Indonesia* 1°40S 101°15E **36** E2
Kerki = Atamyrat
  Turkmenistan 37°50N 65°12E **28** F7
Kerkrade *Neths.* 50°53N 6°4E **15** D6
Kerkyra *Greece* 39°38N 19°50E **25** A3
Kerkyras, Notio Steno
  Greece 39°34N 20°0E **25** A4
Kermadec Is. *Pac. Oc.* 30°0S 178°15W **58** E11
Kermadec Trench
  Pac. Oc. 30°30S 176°0W **64** L10
Kermān *Iran* 30°15N 57°1E **45** D8
Kerman *U.S.A.* 36°43N 120°4W **78** J6
Kermān □ *Iran* 30°0N 57°0E **45** D8
Kermānshāh *Iran* 34°23N 47°0E **44** C5
Kermānshāh □ *Iran* 34°0N 46°30E **44** C5
Kermit *U.S.A.* 31°52N 103°6W **84** F3
Kern ➤ *U.S.A.* 35°16N 119°18W **79** K7
Kernow = Cornwall □
  U.K. 50°26N 4°40W **13** G3
Kernville *U.S.A.* 35°45N 118°26W **79** K8
Keroh *Malaysia* 5°43N 101°1E **39** K3
Kerrera *U.K.* 56°24N 5°33W **11** E3
Kerrobert *Canada* 51°56N 109°8W **71** C7
Kerrville *U.S.A.* 30°3N 99°8W **84** F5
Kerry □ *Ireland* 52°7N 9°35W **10** D2
Kerry Hd. *Ireland* 52°25N 9°56W **10** D2
Kerulen ➤ *Asia* 48°48N 117°0E **33** B6
Kerzaz *Algeria* 29°29N 1°37W **50** C5
Kesagami ➤ *Canada* 51°40N 79°45W **72** B4
Kesagami L. *Canada* 50°23N 80°15W **72** B3
Keşan *Turkey* 40°49N 26°38E **23** D12
Kesennuma *Japan* 38°54N 141°35E **30** E10
Keshit *Iran* 29°43N 58°17E **45** D8
Kestell *S. Africa* 28°17S 28°42E **57** D4
Kestenga *Russia* 65°50N 31°45E **8** D24
Keswick *U.K.* 54°36N 3°8W **12** C4
Ket ➤ *Russia* 58°55N 81°32E **28** D9
Ketapang *Bali, Indonesia* 8°9S 114°23E **37** J17
Ketapang *Kalimantan,
  Indonesia* 1°55S 110°0E **36** E4
Ketchikan *U.S.A.* 55°21N 131°39W **70** B2
Ketchum *U.S.A.* 43°41N 114°22W **76** E6
Ketef, Khalig Umm el
  Egypt 23°40N 35°35E **44** F2
Keti Bandar *Pakistan* 24°8N 67°27E **42** G2
Ketri *India* 28°1N 75°50E **42** E6
Kętrzyn *Poland* 54°7N 21°22E **17** A11
Kettering *U.K.* 52°24N 0°43W **13** E7
Kettering *U.S.A.* 39°41N 84°10W **81** F11
Kettle ➤ *Canada* 56°40N 89°34W **71** B11
Kettle Falls *U.S.A.* 48°37N 118°3W **76** B4
Kettle Point *Canada* 43°13N 82°1W **82** C2
Kettle Pt. *Canada* 43°13N 82°1W **82** C2
Kettleman City *U.S.A.* 36°1N 119°58W **78** J7
Keuka L. *U.S.A.* 42°30N 77°9W **82** D7
Keuruu *Finland* 62°16N 24°41E **8** E21
Kewanee *U.S.A.* 41°14N 89°56W **80** E9
Keweenaw B. *U.S.A.* 47°0N 88°15W **80** B9
Keweenaw Pen. *U.S.A.* 47°15N 88°15W **80** B9
Keweenaw Pt. *U.S.A.* 47°25N 87°43W **80** B10
Key, L. *Ireland* 54°0N 8°15W **10** C3
Key Lake Mine *Canada* 57°5N 105°32W **71** B7
Key Largo *U.S.A.* 25°5N 80°27W **85** J14
Key West *U.S.A.* 24°33N 81°48W **88** B3
Keynsham *U.K.* 51°24N 2°29W **13** F5
Keyser *U.S.A.* 39°26N 78°59W **81** F14
Kezhma *Russia* 58°59N 101°9E **29** D11
Kezi *Zimbabwe* 20°58S 28°32E **57** C4
Kgalagadi Transfrontier △
  Africa 25°10S 21°0E **56** D3
Khabarovsk *Russia* 48°30N 135°5E **29** E14
Khabr *Iran* 28°51N 56°22E **45** D8
Khābūr ➤ *Syria* 35°17N 40°35E **44** C4
Khachmas = Xaçmaz
  Azerbaijan 41°31N 48°42E **19** F8
Khachrod *India* 23°25N 75°20E **42** H6
Khadro *Pakistan* 26°11N 68°50E **42** F3
Khadzhilyangar = Dahonglutan
  China 35°45N 79°20E **43** B8
Khaga *India* 25°47N 81°7E **43** G9
Khagaria *India* 25°30N 86°32E **43** G12
Khaipur *Pakistan* 29°34N 72°17E **42** E5
Khair *India* 27°57N 77°46E **42** F7
Khairabad *India* 27°33N 80°47E **43** F9
Khairagarh *India* 21°27N 81°2E **43** J9
Khairpur *Pakistan* 27°32N 68°49E **42** F3
Khairpur Nathan Shah
  Pakistan 27°6N 67°44E **42** F2
Khairwara *India* 23°58N 73°38E **42** H5
Khaisor ➤ *Pakistan* 31°17N 68°59E **42** D3
Khajuri Kach *Pakistan* 32°4N 69°51E **42** C3
Khakassia □ *Russia* 53°0N 90°0E **28** D9
Khakhea *Botswana* 24°48S 23°22E **56** C3
Khalafābād *Iran* 30°54N 49°24E **45** D6
Khalīlābād *India* 26°48N 83°5E **43** F10
Khalili *Iran* 27°38N 53°17E **45** E7
Khalkhāl *Iran* 37°37N 48°32E **45** B6

Khalturin *Russia* 58°40N 48°50E **18** C8
Khalūf *Oman* 20°30N 58°13E **47** C6
Kham Keut *Laos* 18°15N 104°43E **38** C5
Khamaria *India* 23°5N 80°48E **43** H9
Khambhaliya *India* 22°14N 69°41E **42** H3
Khambhat *India* 22°23N 72°33E **42** H5
Khambhat, G. of *India* 20°45N 72°30E **40** J8
Khamir *Iran* 26°57N 55°36E **45** E7
Khamir *Yemen* 16°2N 44°0E **47** D3
Khamīs Mushayţ
  Si. Arabia 18°18N 42°44E **47** D3
Khamsa *Egypt* 30°27N 32°23E **46** E1
Khan ➤ *Namibia* 22°37S 14°56E **56** C2
Khān Abū Shāmat *Syria* 33°39N 36°53E **46** B5
Khān Azād *Iraq* 33°7N 44°22E **44** C5
Khān Shaykhūn *Syria* 35°26N 36°38E **44** C3
Khan Tengri, Pik *Asia* 42°12N 80°10E **32** B3
Khān Yūnis *Gaza Strip* 31°21N 34°18E **46** D3
Khanai *Pakistan* 30°30N 67°8E **42** D2
Khānaqīn *Iraq* 34°23N 45°25E **44** C5
Khānbāghī *Iran* 36°10N 55°25E **45** B7
Khandwa *India* 21°49N 76°22E **40** J10
Khandyga *Russia* 62°42N 135°35E **29** C14
Khanewal *Pakistan* 30°20N 71°55E **42** D4
Khangah Dogran
  Pakistan 31°50N 73°37E **42** D5
Khanh Duong *Vietnam* 12°44N 108°44E **38** F7
Khaniá = Chania *Greece* 35°30N 24°4E **25** D6
Khaniadhana *India* 25°1N 78°8E **42** G8
Khanka, L. *Asia* 45°0N 132°24E **30** B6
Khankendy = Xankändi
  Azerbaijan 39°52N 46°49E **44** B5
Khanna *India* 30°42N 76°16E **42** D7
Khanozai *Pakistan* 30°37N 67°19E **42** D2
Khanpur *Pakistan* 28°42N 70°35E **42** E4
Khanty-Mansiysk *Russia* 61°0N 69°0E **28** C7
Khao Laem △ *Thailand* 14°56N 98°31E **38** E2
Khao Laem Res. *Thailand* 14°50N 98°30E **38** E2
Khao Lak △ *Malaysia* 8°38N 98°18E **39** H2
Khao Luang △ *Thailand* 8°34N 99°42E **39** H2
Khao Phlu *Thailand* 9°29N 99°59E **39** b
Khao Pu-Khao Ya △
  Thailand 7°26N 99°57E **39** J2
Khao Sam Roi Yot △
  Thailand 12°13N 99°57E **39** F2
Khao Sok △ *Thailand* 8°55N 98°38E **39** H2
Khao Yai △ *Thailand* 14°21N 101°29E **38** E3
Khaoen Si Nakarin △
  Thailand 14°47N 99°0E **38** E2
Khapalu *Pakistan* 35°10N 76°20E **43** B7
Khapcheranga *Russia* 49°42N 112°24E **29** E12
Khaptao △ *Nepal* 29°20N 81°10E **43** E9
Kharagpur *India* 22°20N 87°25E **43** H12
Kharan Kalat *Pakistan* 28°34N 65°21E **40** E4
Khārānaq *Iran* 32°20N 54°45E **45** C7
Kharda *India* 18°40N 75°34E **40** K9
Khardung La *India* 34°20N 77°43E **43** B7
Kharg = Khārk, Jazīreh-ye
  Iran 29°15N 50°28E **45** D6
Khârga, El Wâhât el
  Egypt 25°10N 30°35E **51** C12
Khargon *India* 21°45N 75°40E **40** J9
Khari ➤ *India* 25°54N 74°31E **42** G6
Kharian *Pakistan* 32°49N 73°52E **42** C5
Khārk, Jazīreh-ye *Iran* 29°15N 50°28E **45** D6
Kharkiv *Ukraine* 49°58N 36°20E **19** E6
Kharkov = Kharkiv
  Ukraine 49°58N 36°20E **19** E6
Kharovsk *Russia* 59°56N 40°13E **18** C7
Kharsawangarh *India* 22°48N 85°50E **43** H11
Kharta *Turkey* 40°55N 29°7E **23** D13
Khartoum = El Khartûm
  Sudan 15°31N 32°35E **51** E12
Khartum *Canada* 45°15N 77°5W **82** A7
Khasan *Russia* 42°25N 130°40E **30** C5
Khāsh *Iran* 28°15N 61°15E **45** D9
Khashm el Girba *Sudan* 14°59N 35°58E **51** F13
Khaskovo *Bulgaria* 41°56N 25°30E **23** D11
Khatanga *Russia* 72°0N 102°20E **29** B11
Khatanga ➤ *Russia* 72°55N 106°0E **29** B11
Khatauli *India* 29°17N 77°43E **42** E7
Khatra *India* 22°59N 86°51E **43** H12
Khātūnābād *Iran* 30°1N 55°25E **45** D7
Khatyrka *Russia* 62°3N 175°15E **29** C18
Khavda *India* 23°51N 69°43E **42** H3
Khawr Fakkān *U.A.E.* 25°21N 56°22E **45** E8
Khaybar, Ḥarrat
  Si. Arabia 25°45N 40°0E **44** E4
Khāzimiyah *Iraq* 34°46N 43°37E **44** C4
Khe Bo *Vietnam* 19°8N 104°41E **38** C5
Khe Long *Vietnam* 21°29N 104°46E **38** B5
Khe Sanh *Vietnam* 16°37N 106°45E **38** D6
Khed Brahma *India* 24°7N 73°5E **42** G5
Khekra *India* 28°52N 77°20E **42** E7
Khemarak Phouminville = Krong
  Kaoh Kong *Cambodia* 11°37N 102°59E **39** G4
Khemisset *Morocco* 33°50N 6°1W **50** B4
Khemmarat *Thailand* 16°10N 105°15E **38** D5
Khenāmān *Iran* 30°27N 56°29E **45** D8
Khenchela *Algeria* 35°28N 7°11E **50** A7
Khersān ➤ *Iran* 31°33N 50°22E **45** D6
Kherson *Ukraine* 46°35N 32°35E **19** E5
Kheta ➤ *Russia* 71°54N 102°6E **29** B11
Khewari *Pakistan* 26°36N 68°52E **42** F3
Khilchipur *India* 24°2N 76°34E **42** G7
Khilok *Russia* 51°30N 110°45E **29** D12
Khios = Hios *Greece* 38°27N 26°9E **23** E12
Khirsadoh *India* 22°11N 78°47E **43** H8
Khiuma = Hiiumaa
  Estonia 58°50N 22°45E **9** G20
Khiva *Uzbekistan* 41°30N 60°18E **28** E7
Khlong Khlung *Thailand* 16°12N 99°43E **38** D2
Khmelnik *Ukraine* 49°33N 27°58E **17** D14
Khmelnytskyy *Ukraine* 49°23N 27°0E **17** D14
Khmer Rep. = Cambodia ■
  Asia 12°15N 105°0E **38** F5

Khoai, Hon *Vietnam* 8°26N 104°50E **39** H5
Khodoriv *Ukraine* 49°24N 24°19E **17** D13
Khodzent = Khŭjand
  Tajikistan 40°17N 69°37E **28** E7
Khojak Pass *Afghan.* 30°51N 66°34E **42** D2
Khok Kloi *Thailand* 8°17N 98°19E **39** a
Khok Pho *Thailand* 6°43N 101°6E **39** J3
Khok Samrong *Thailand* 15°3N 100°43E **38** E3
Kholm *Russia* 57°10N 31°15E **18** C5
Kholm *Russia* 47°40N 142°5E **29** E15
Khomas Hochland
  Namibia 22°40S 16°0E **56** C2
Khomeyn *Iran* 33°40N 50°7E **45** C6
Khomeynī Shahr *Iran* 32°41N 51°31E **45** C6
Khomodino *Botswana* 22°46S 23°52E **56** C3
Khon Kaen *Thailand* 16°30N 102°47E **38** D4
Khong ➤ *Cambodia* 13°32N 105°58E **38** F5
Khong Sedone *Laos* 15°34N 105°49E **38** E5
Khonuu *Russia* 66°30N 143°12E **29** C15
Khoper ➤ *Russia* 49°30N 42°20E **19** D6
Khorāsān □ *Iran* 34°0N 58°0E **45** C8
Khorat = Nakhon Ratchasima
  Thailand 14°59N 102°12E **38** E4
Khorat, Cao Nguyen
  Thailand 15°30N 102°50E **38** E4
Khorixas *Namibia* 20°16S 14°59E **56** C1
Khorramābād *Khorāsān,
  Iran* 35°6N 57°57E **45** C8
Khorramābād *Lorestān,
  Iran* 33°30N 48°25E **45** C6
Khorrāmshahr *Iran* 30°29N 48°15E **45** D6
Khorugh *Tajikistan* 37°30N 71°36E **28** F8
Khosravi *Iran* 30°48N 51°28E **45** D6
Khosrowābād *Khuzestān,
  Iran* 30°10N 48°25E **45** D6
Khosrowābād *Kordestān,
  Iran* 35°31N 47°38E **44** C5
Khost *Pakistan* 30°13N 67°35E **42** D2
Khosūyeh *Iran* 28°32N 54°26E **45** D7
Khotyn *Ukraine* 48°31N 26°27E **17** D14
Khouribga *Morocco* 32°58N 6°57W **50** B4
Khowst *Afghan.* 33°22N 69°58E **40** C6
Khowst □ *Afghan.* 33°20N 70°0E **40** C6
Khoyniki *Belarus* 51°54N 29°55E **17** C15
Khrysokhou B. *Cyprus* 35°6N 32°25E **25** D11
Khu Khan *Thailand* 14°42N 104°12E **38** E5
Khuan Wa *Thailand* 7°53N 98°17E **39** a
Khudzhand = Khŭjand
  Tajikistan 40°17N 69°37E **28** E7
Khuff *Si. Arabia* 24°55N 44°53E **44** E5
Khŭgīānī *Afghan.* 31°34N 66°32E **42** D2
Khuis *Botswana* 26°40S 21°49E **56** D3
Khuiyala *India* 27°9N 70°25E **42** F4
Khŭjand *Tajikistan* 40°17N 69°37E **28** E7
Khujner *India* 23°47N 76°36E **42** H7
Khulna *Bangla.* 22°45N 89°34E **41** H16
Khulna □ *Bangla.* 22°25N 89°35E **41** H16
Khumago *Botswana* 20°26S 24°32E **56** C3
Khunjerab △ *Pakistan* 36°40N 75°30E **43** A6
Khunjerab Pass = Kinjirap Daban
  Asia 36°40N 75°25E **40** A9
Khŭnsorkh *Iran* 27°9N 56°7E **45** E8
Khunti *India* 23°5N 85°17E **43** H11
Khūr *Iran* 32°55N 58°18E **45** C8
Khurai *India* 24°3N 78°23E **42** G8
Khurayş *Si. Arabia* 25°6N 48°2E **45** E6
Khurja *India* 28°15N 77°58E **42** E7
Khūrmāl *Iraq* 35°18N 46°2E **44** C5
Khurr, Wādī al *Iraq* 32°3N 43°52E **44** C4
Khūsf *Iran* 32°46N 58°53E **45** C8
Khushab *Pakistan* 32°20N 72°20E **42** C5
Khust *Ukraine* 48°10N 23°18E **17** D12
Khutse △ *Botswana* 23°13S 24°12E **56** C3
Khuzdar *Pakistan* 27°52N 66°30E **42** F2
Khūzestān □ *Iran* 31°0N 49°0E **45** D6
Khvāf *Iran* 34°33N 60°8E **45** C9
Khvānsār *Iran* 32°10N 51°8E **45** C6
Khvor *Iran* 33°45N 55°0E **45** C7
Khvorgū *Iran* 27°34N 56°27E **45** E8
Khvormūj *Iran* 28°40N 51°30E **45** D6
Khvoy *Iran* 38°35N 45°0E **44** B5
Khyber Pass *Afghan.* 34°10N 71°8E **42** B4
Kia *Fiji* 16°16S 179°8E **59** a
Kiabukwa
  Dem. Rep. of the Congo 8°40S 24°48E **55** D1
Kiama *Australia* 34°40S 150°50E **63** E5
Kiamba *Phil.* 6°2N 124°46E **37** C6
Kiambi
  Dem. Rep. of the Congo 7°15S 28°0E **54** D2
Kiambu *Kenya* 1°8S 36°50E **54** C4
Kiangara *Madag.* 17°58S 47°2E **57** B8
Kiangsi = Jiangxi □
  China 27°30N 116°0E **33** D6
Kiangsu = Jiangsu □
  China 33°0N 120°0E **35** H11
Kibale △ *Uganda* 0°16N 30°18E **54** B3
Kibanga Port *Uganda* 0°10N 32°58E **54** B3
Kibara *Tanzania* 2°8S 33°30E **54** C3
Kibare, Mts.
  Dem. Rep. of the Congo 8°25S 27°10E **54** D2
Kibondo *Tanzania* 3°35S 30°45E **54** C3
Kibre Mengist *Ethiopia* 5°54N 38°59E **47** F2
Kıbrıs = Cyprus ■ *Asia* 35°0N 33°0E **25** E12
Kibumbu *Burundi* 3°32S 29°45E **54** C2
Kibungo *Rwanda* 2°10S 30°32E **54** C3
Kibuye *Burundi* 3°39S 29°59E **54** C2
Kibuye *Rwanda* 2°3S 29°21E **54** C2
Kibwesa *Tanzania* 6°30S 29°58E **54** D2
Kibwezi *Kenya* 2°27S 37°57E **54** C4
Kichha *India* 28°53N 79°30E **43** E8
Kichha ➤ *India* 28°41N 79°18E **43** E8
Kichmengskiy Gorodok
  Russia 59°59N 45°48E **18** B8

Kicking Horse Pass
  Canada 51°28N 116°16W **70** C5
Kidal *Mali* 18°26N 1°22E **50** E6
Kidderminster *U.K.* 52°24N 2°15W **13** E5
Kidepo Valley △ *Uganda* 3°52N 33°50E **54** B3
Kidete *Tanzania* 6°25S 37°17E **54** D4
Kidnappers, C. *N.Z.* 39°38S 177°5E **59** C6
Kidsgrove *U.K.* 53°5N 2°14W **12** D5
Kidston *Australia* 18°52S 144°8E **62** B3
Kidugallo *Tanzania* 6°49S 38°15E **54** D4
Kiel *Germany* 54°19N 10°8E **16** A6
Kiel Canal = Nord-Ostsee-Kanal
  Germany 54°12N 9°32E **16** A5
Kielce *Poland* 50°52N 20°42E **17** C11
Kielder Water *U.K.* 55°11N 2°31W **12** B5
Kieler Bucht *Germany* 54°35N 10°25E **16** A6
Kien Binh *Vietnam* 9°55N 105°19E **39** H5
Kien Tan *Vietnam* 10°7N 105°17E **39** G5
Kienge
  Dem. Rep. of the Congo 10°30S 27°30E **55** E2
Kiev = Kyyiv *Ukraine* 50°30N 30°28E **17** C16
Kiffa *Mauritania* 16°37N 11°24W **50** E3
Kifrī *Iraq* 34°45N 45°0E **44** C5
Kigali *Rwanda* 1°59S 30°4E **54** C3
Kigarama *Tanzania* 1°1S 31°50E **54** C3
Kigeži △ *Uganda* 0°34S 29°55E **54** C2
Kigoma □ *Tanzania* 5°0S 30°0E **54** D2
Kigoma-Ujiji *Tanzania* 4°55S 29°36E **54** C2
Kigomasha, Ras *Tanzania* 4°58S 38°58E **54** C4
Kığzı *Turkey* 38°18N 43°25E **44** B4
Kihnu *Estonia* 58°9N 24°1E **9** G21
Kii-Sanchi *Japan* 34°20N 136°0E **31** G8
Kii-Suidō *Japan* 33°40N 134°45E **31** H7
Kiira Dam *Uganda* 0°25N 33°0E **54** B3
Kikaiga-Shima *Japan* 28°19N 129°59E **31** K4
Kikinda *Serbia* 45°50N 20°30E **23** B9
Kikládhes = Cyclades
  Greece 37°0N 24°30E **23** F11
Kikwit
  Dem. Rep. of the Congo 5°0S 18°45E **52** F3
Kilar *India* 33°6N 76°25E **42** C7
Kīlauea Caldera *U.S.A.* 19°25N 155°17W **74** b
Kilbeggan *Ireland* 53°22N 7°30W **10** C4
Kilbrannan Sd. *U.K.* 55°37N 5°26W **11** F3
Kilchu *N. Korea* 40°57N 129°25E **35** D15
Kilcoy *Australia* 26°59S 152°30E **63** D5
Kildare *Ireland* 53°9N 6°55W **10** C5
Kildare □ *Ireland* 53°10N 6°50W **10** C5
Kildinstroy *Russia* 68°48N 33°6E **8** B25
Kilfinnane *Ireland* 52°21N 8°28W **10** D3
Kilgarvan *Ireland* 51°54N 9°27W **10** E2
Kilgore *U.S.A.* 32°23N 94°53W **84** E7
Kilgoris *Kenya* 1°0S 34°53E **54** C3
Kilifi *Kenya* 3°40S 39°48E **54** C4
Kilimanjaro *Tanzania* 3°7S 37°20E **54** C4
Kilimanjaro □ *Tanzania* 4°0S 38°0E **54** C4
Kilindini *Kenya* 4°4S 39°40E **54** C4
Kilis *Turkey* 36°42N 37°6E **44** B3
Kiliya *Ukraine* 45°28N 29°16E **17** F15
Kilkee *Ireland* 52°41N 9°39W **10** D2
Kilkeel *U.K.* 54°4N 6°0W **10** B5
Kilkenny *Ireland* 52°39N 7°15W **10** D4
Kilkenny □ *Ireland* 52°35N 7°15W **10** D4
Kilkieran B. *Ireland* 53°20N 9°41W **10** C2
Kilkis *Greece* 40°58N 22°57E **23** D10
Killala *Ireland* 54°13N 9°12W **10** B2
Killala B. *Ireland* 54°16N 9°8W **10** B2
Killaloe *Canada* 45°33N 77°25W **82** A7
Killaloe *Ireland* 52°48N 8°28W **10** D3
Killarney *Australia* 28°20S 152°18E **63** D5
Killarney *Canada* 49°10N 99°40W **71** D9
Killarney *Ireland* 52°4N 9°30W **10** D2
Killarney △ *Ireland* 52°0N 9°33W **10** D2
Killary Harbour *Ireland* 53°38N 9°52W **10** C2
Killdeer *U.S.A.* 47°22N 102°45W **80** B2
Killeen *U.S.A.* 31°7N 97°44W **84** F6
Killin *U.K.* 56°28N 4°19W **11** E4
Killiney *Ireland* 53°15N 6°7W **10** C5
Killington Pk. *U.S.A.* 43°36N 72°49W **83** C12
Killini *Greece* 37°54N 22°25E **23** F10
Killorglin *Ireland* 52°6N 9°47W **10** D2
Killybegs *Ireland* 54°38N 8°26W **10** B3
Kilmarnock *U.K.* 55°37N 4°29W **11** F4
Kilmore *Australia* 37°25S 144°53E **63** F3
Kilmore Quay *Ireland* 52°10N 6°36W **10** D5
Kilondo *Tanzania* 9°45S 34°20E **55** D3
Kilosa *Tanzania* 6°48S 37°0E **54** D4
Kilrush *Ireland* 52°38N 9°29W **10** D2
Kilwa Kisiwani *Tanzania* 8°58S 39°32E **54** D4
Kilwa Kivinje *Tanzania* 8°45S 39°25E **54** D4
Kilwa Masoko *Tanzania* 8°55S 39°30E **54** D4
Kilwinning *U.K.* 55°39N 4°43W **11** F4
Kim *U.S.A.* 37°15N 103°21W **77** H12
Kimaam *Indonesia* 7°58S 138°53E **37** F9
Kimamba *Tanzania* 6°45S 37°10E **54** D4
Kimba *Australia* 33°8S 136°23E **63** E2
Kimball *Minn., U.S.A.* 41°14N 103°40W **80** E2
Kimball *S. Dak., U.S.A.* 43°45N 98°57W **80** D4
Kimberley *Australia* 16°20S 127°0E **60** C4
Kimberley *B.C., Canada* 49°40N 115°59W **70** D5
Kimberley *Ont., Canada* 44°23N 80°32W **82** B4
Kimberley *S. Africa* 28°43S 24°46E **56** D3
Kimch'aek *N. Korea* 40°40N 129°10E **35** D15
Kimhae = Gimhae
  S. Korea 35°14N 128°53E **35** G15
Kimmirut *Canada* 62°50N 69°50W **69** C13
Kimpese
  Dem. Rep. of the Congo 5°35S 14°26E **52** F2
Kimry *Russia* 56°55N 37°15E **18** C6
Kinabalu, Gunung
  Malaysia 6°3N 116°14E **36** C5
Kinango *Kenya* 4°8S 39°19E **54** C4
Kinasken L. *Canada* 51°21N 118°0E **70** C5
Kinbasket L. *Canada* 52°0N 118°10W **70** C5
Kincardine *Canada* 44°10N 81°40W **82** B3
Kincolith *Canada* 55°0N 129°57W **70** C3

Kinda *Dem. Rep. of the Congo* 9°18S 25°4E **55** D2
Kinde *U.S.A.* 43°56N 83°0W **82** C2
Kinder Scout *U.K.* 53°24N 1°52W **12** D6
Kindersley *Canada* 51°30N 109°10W **71** C7
Kindia *Guinea* 10°0N 12°52W **50** F3
Kindu
　Dem. Rep. of the Congo 2°55S 25°50E **54** C2
Kineshma *Russia* 57°30N 42°5E **18** C7
Kinesi *Tanzania* 1°25S 33°50E **54** C3
King, L. *Australia* 33°10S 119°35E **61** F2
King, Mt. *Australia* 25°10S 147°30E **62** D4
King, Mt. *U.S.A.* 36°13N 121°8W **78** J5
King Cr. ➤ *Australia* 24°35S 139°30E **62** C2
King Edward ➤
　Australia 14°14S 126°35E **60** B4
King Edward Point
　S. Georgia 54°17S 36°30W **96** G9
King Frederick VI Land = Kong
　Frederik VI Kyst
　Greenland 63°0N 43°0W **4** C5
King George B. *Falk. Is.* 51°30S 60°30W **96** G4
King George I. *Antarctica* 60°0S 60°0W **5** C18
King George Is. *Canada* 57°20N 80°30W **69** D11
King George Sd. *Australia* 35°5S 118°0E **61** G2
King I. = Kadan Kyun
　Burma 12°30N 98°20E **38** F2
King I. *Australia* 39°50S 144°0E **63** F3
King I. *Canada* 52°10N 127°40W **70** C3
King Khalid Military City =
　Madinat al Malik Khālid al
　Askarīyah *Si. Arabia* 27°54N 45°31E **44** E5
King Leopold Ranges
　Australia 17°30S 125°45E **60** C4
King of Prussia *U.S.A.* 40°5N 75°23W **83** F9
King Sd. *Australia* 16°50S 123°20E **60** C3
King Sejong *Antarctica* 62°30S 58°0W **5** C18
King William I. *Canada* 69°10N 97°25W **68** C10
King William's Town
　S. Africa 32°51S 27°22E **56** E4
Kingait *Canada* 64°14N 76°32W **69** C12
Kingaok = Bathurst Inlet
　Canada 66°50N 108°1W **68** C9
Kingaroy *Australia* 26°32S 151°51E **63** D5
Kingfisher *U.S.A.* 35°52N 97°56W **84** D6
Kingirbān *Iraq* 34°40N 44°54E **44** C5
Kingisepp = Kuressaare
　Estonia 58°15N 22°30E **9** G20
Kingisepp *Russia* 59°25N 28°40E **9** G23
Kingman *Ariz., U.S.A.* 35°12N 114°4W **79** K12
Kingman *Kans., U.S.A.* 37°39N 98°7W **80** G5
Kingoonya *Australia* 30°55S 135°19E **63** E2
Kings ➤ *U.S.A.* 36°3N 119°50W **78** J7
Kings Canyon *Australia* 24°15S 131°34E **60** D5
Kings Canyon △
　U.S.A. 36°50N 118°40W **78** J8
King's Lynn *U.K.* 52°45N 0°24E **12** E8
Kings Park *U.S.A.* 40°53N 73°16W **83** F11
Kings Peak *U.S.A.* 40°46N 110°23W **76** F8
Kingsbridge *U.K.* 50°17N 3°47W **13** G4
Kingsburg *U.S.A.* 36°31N 119°33W **78** J7
Kingscote *Australia* 35°40S 137°38E **63** F2
Kingscourt *Ireland* 53°55N 6°48W **10** C5
Kingsford *U.S.A.* 45°48N 88°4W **80** C9
Kingsland *U.S.A.* 30°48N 81°41W **85** F14
Kingsport *U.S.A.* 36°33N 82°33W **85** C13
Kingston *Canada* 44°14N 76°30W **83** B8
Kingston *Jamaica* 18°0N 76°50W **88** a
Kingston *N.Z.* 45°20S 168°43E **59** F2
Kingston *N.H., U.S.A.* 42°56N 71°3W **83** D13
Kingston *N.Y., U.S.A.* 41°56N 73°59W **83** E11
Kingston *Pa., U.S.A.* 41°16N 75°54W **83** E9
Kingston *R.I., U.S.A.* 41°29N 71°30W **83** E13
Kingston Pk. *U.S.A.* 35°44N 115°55W **79** K11
Kingston South East
　Australia 36°51S 139°55E **63** F2
Kingston upon Hull *U.K.* 53°45N 0°21W **12** D7
Kingston upon Hull □
　U.K. 53°45N 0°21W **12** D7
Kingston-upon-Thames □
　U.K. 51°24N 0°17W **13** F7
Kingstown *St. Vincent* 13°10N 61°10W **89** D7
Kingstree *U.S.A.* 33°40N 79°50W **85** E15
Kingsville *Canada* 42°2N 82°45W **82** D2
Kingsville *U.S.A.* 27°31N 97°52W **84** H6
Kingussie *U.K.* 57°6N 4°2W **11** D4
Kingwood *U.S.A.* 30°2N 95°16W **84** F7
Kınık *Turkey* 39°6N 27°24E **23** E12
Kinistino *Canada* 52°57N 105°2W **71** C7
Kinjirap Daban *Asia* 36°40N 75°25E **40** A9
Kinkala *Congo* 4°18S 14°49E **52** E2
Kinki □ *Japan* 33°45N 136°0E **31** H8
Kinleith *N.Z.* 38°20S 175°56E **59** C5
Kinlochleven *U.K.* 56°43N 5°0W **11** E4
Kinmount *Canada* 44°48N 78°45W **82** B6
Kinna *Sweden* 57°32N 12°42E **9** H15
Kinnairds Hd. *U.K.* 57°43N 2°1W **11** D6
Kino Nuevo *Mexico* 28°52N 112°3W **86** B2
Kinoje ➤ *Canada* 52°8N 81°25W **72** B3
Kinomoto *Japan* 35°30N 136°13E **31** G8
Kinoni *Uganda* 0°41S 30°28E **54** C3
Kinoosao *Canada* 57°5N 102°1W **71** B8
Kinross *U.K.* 56°13N 3°25W **11** E5
Kinsale *Ireland* 51°42N 8°31W **10** E3
Kinsale, Old Hd. of
　Ireland 51°37N 8°33W **10** E3
Kinsha = Chang Jiang ➤
　China 31°48N 121°10E **33** C7
Kinshasa
　Dem. Rep. of the Congo 4°20S 15°15E **52** E3
Kinsley *U.S.A.* 37°55N 99°25W **80** G4
Kinsman *U.S.A.* 41°26N 80°35W **82** E4
Kinston *U.S.A.* 35°16N 77°35W **85** D16
Kintampo *Ghana* 8°5N 1°41W **50** G5
Kintore *Australia* 23°15S 129°38E **60** D4
Kintore Ra. *Australia* 23°15S 128°47E **60** D4
Kintyre *U.K.* 55°30N 5°35W **11** F3

Kintyre, Mull of *U.K.* 55°17N 5°47W **11** F3
Kinushseo ➤ *Canada* 55°15N 83°45W **72** A3
Kinuso *Canada* 55°20N 115°25W **70** B5
Kinvarra *Ireland* 53°8N 8°56W **10** C3
Kinyangiri *Tanzania* 4°25S 34°37E **54** C3
Kinyeti *Sudan* 3°57N 32°54E **54** B3
Kinzua *U.S.A.* 41°52N 78°58W **82** E6
Kiosk *Canada* 46°6N 78°53W **72** C4
Kiowa *Kans., U.S.A.* 37°1N 98°29W **80** G4
Kiowa *Okla., U.S.A.* 34°43N 95°54W **84** D7
Kipahigan L. *Canada* 55°20N 101°55W **71** B8
Kipanga *Tanzania* 6°15S 35°20E **54** D4
Kiparissia *Greece* 37°15N 21°40E **23** F9
Kiparissiakos Kolpos
　Greece 37°25N 21°25E **23** F9
Kipawa, L. *Canada* 46°50N 79°0W **72** C4
Kipembawe *Tanzania* 7°38S 33°27E **54** D3
Kipengere Ra. *Tanzania* 9°12S 34°15E **55** D3
Kipili *Tanzania* 7°28S 30°32E **54** D3
Kipini *Kenya* 2°30S 40°32E **54** C5
Kipling *Canada* 50°6N 102°38W **71** C8
Kippure *Ireland* 53°11N 6°21W **10** C5
Kipushi
　Dem. Rep. of the Congo 11°48S 27°12E **55** E2
Kiranomena *Madag.* 18°17S 46°2E **57** B8
Kirensk *Russia* 57°50N 107°55E **29** D11
Kirghiz Range *Asia* 42°44N 73°40E **32** B2
Kirghizia = Kyrgyzstan ■
　Asia 42°0N 75°0E **28** E8
Kirgiziya Steppe *Eurasia* 50°0N 55°0E **19** E10
Kiribati ■ *Pac. Oc.* 3°0S 180°0E **58** B10
Kırıkkale *Turkey* 39°51N 33°32E **19** G5
Kirillov *Russia* 59°49N 38°24E **18** C6
Kirin = Jilin *China* 43°44N 126°30E **35** C14
Kirinyaga = Kenya, Mt.
　Kenya 0°10S 37°18E **54** C4
Kirirom △ *Cambodia* 11°18N 104°5E **39** G5
Kirishima Yaku △
　Japan 31°24N 130°50E **31** J5
Kirkby *U.K.* 53°30N 2°54W **12** D5
Kirkby-in-Ashfield *U.K.* 53°6N 1°14W **12** D6
Kirkby Lonsdale *U.K.* 54°12N 2°36W **12** C5
Kirkby Stephen *U.K.* 54°29N 2°21W **12** C5
Kirkcaldy *U.K.* 56°7N 3°9W **11** E5
Kirkcudbright *U.K.* 54°50N 4°2W **11** G4
Kirkee *India* 18°34N 73°56E **40** K8
Kirkenes *Norway* 69°40N 30°5E **8** B24
Kirkfield *Canada* 44°34N 78°59W **82** B6
Kirkintilloch *U.K.* 55°56N 4°8W **11** F4
Kirkjubæjarklaustur
　Iceland 63°47N 18°4W **8** E4
Kirkkonummi *Finland* 60°8N 24°26E **9** F21
Kirkland *U.S.A.* 47°40N 122°12W **78** C4
Kirkland Lake *Canada* 48°9N 80°2W **72** C3
Kırklareli *Turkey* 41°44N 27°15E **23** D12
Kirksville *U.S.A.* 40°12N 92°35W **80** E7
Kirkūk *Iraq* 35°30N 44°21E **44** C5
Kirkwall *U.K.* 58°59N 2°58W **11** C6
Kirkwood *S. Africa* 33°22S 25°15E **56** E4
Kirov *Russia* 58°35N 49°40E **18** C8
Kirovabad = Gäncä
　Azerbaijan 40°45N 46°20E **19** F8
Kirovograd = Kirovohrad
　Ukraine 48°35N 32°20E **19** E5
Kirovohrad *Ukraine* 48°35N 32°20E **19** E5
Kirovsk *Russia* 67°32N 33°41E **18** A5
Kirovskiy *Kamchatka,
　Russia* 54°27N 155°42E **29** D16
Kirovskiy *Primorsk,
　Russia* 45°7N 133°30E **30** B6
Kirriemuir *U.K.* 56°41N 3°1W **11** E5
Kirsanov *Russia* 52°35N 42°40E **18** D7
Kırşehir *Turkey* 39°14N 34°5E **44** B2
Kirthar ➤ *Pakistan* 25°45N 67°30E **42** F2
Kirthar Range *Pakistan* 27°0N 67°0E **42** F2
Kirtland *U.S.A.* 36°44N 108°21W **77** H9
Kiruna *Sweden* 67°52N 20°15E **8** C19
Kirundu
　Dem. Rep. of the Congo 0°50S 25°35E **54** C2
Kiryū *Japan* 36°24N 139°20E **31** F9
Kisaga *Tanzania* 4°30S 34°23E **54** C3
Kisanga
　Dem. Rep. of the Congo 2°30N 26°35E **54** B2
Kisangani
　Dem. Rep. of the Congo 0°35N 25°15E **54** B2
Kisar *Indonesia* 8°5S 127°10E **37** F7
Kisarawe *Tanzania* 6°53S 39°0E **54** D4
Kisarazu *Japan* 35°23N 139°55E **31** G9
Kiselevsk *Russia* 54°0N 86°39E **28** D9
Kishanganga ➤
　Pakistan 34°18N 73°28E **43** B5
Kishanganj *India* 26°3N 88°14E **43** F13
Kishangarh *Raj., India* 26°34N 74°52E **42** F6
Kishangarh *Raj., India* 27°50N 70°30E **42** F4
Kishiwada *Japan* 34°28N 135°22E **31** G7
Kishtwar *India* 33°20N 75°48E **42** C6
Kisigo ➤ *Tanzania* 6°27S 34°17E **54** D3
Kisii *Kenya* 0°40S 34°45E **54** C3
Kisiju *Tanzania* 7°23S 39°19E **54** D4
Kisizi *Uganda* 1°0S 29°58E **54** C2
Kiskőrös *Hungary* 46°37N 19°20E **17** E10
Kiskunfélegyháza
　Hungary 46°42N 19°53E **17** E10
Kiskunhalas *Hungary* 46°28N 19°37E **17** E10
Kislovodsk *Russia* 43°50N 42°45E **19** F7
Kismaayo *Somali Rep.* 0°22S 42°32E **47** H3
Kiso-Gawa ➤ *Japan* 35°20N 136°45E **31** G8
Kiso-Sammyaku *Japan* 35°45N 137°45E **31** G8
Kisofukushima *Japan* 35°52N 137°43E **31** G8
Kisoro *Uganda* 1°17S 29°48E **54** C2
Kissamos = Kasteli
　Greece 35°29N 23°38E **25** D5
Kissamos, Kolpos *Greece* 35°30N 23°38E **25** D5
Kissidougou *Guinea* 9°5N 10°5W **50** G3

Kissimmee *U.S.A.* 28°18N 81°24W **85** G14
Kissimmee ➤ *U.S.A.* 27°9N 80°52W **85** H14
Kississing L. *Canada* 55°10N 101°20W **71** B8
Kissónerga *Cyprus* 34°49N 32°24E **25** E11
Kisumu *Kenya* 0°3S 34°45E **54** C3
Kiswani *Tanzania* 4°5S 37°57E **54** C4
Kiswere *Tanzania* 9°27S 39°30E **55** D4
Kit Carson *U.S.A.* 38°46N 102°48W **76** G12
Kita *Mali* 13°5N 9°25W **50** F4
Kitaibaraki *Japan* 36°50N 140°45E **31** F10
Kitakami *Japan* 39°20N 141°10E **30** E10
Kitakami-Gawa ➤
　Japan 38°25N 141°19E **30** E10
Kitakami-Sammyaku
　Japan 39°30N 141°30E **30** E10
Kitakata *Japan* 37°39N 139°52E **30** F9
Kitakyūshū *Japan* 33°50N 130°50E **31** H5
Kitale *Kenya* 1°0N 35°0E **54** B4
Kitami *Japan* 43°48N 143°54E **30** C11
Kitami-Sammyaku
　Japan 44°22N 142°43E **30** B11
Kitangiri, L. *Tanzania* 4°5S 34°20E **54** C3
Kitaya *Tanzania* 10°38S 40°8E **55** E5
Kitchener *Canada* 43°27N 80°29W **82** C4
Kitee *Finland* 62°5N 30°8E **8** E24
Kitega = Gitega *Burundi* 3°26S 29°56E **54** C2
Kitengo
　Dem. Rep. of the Congo 7°26S 24°8E **54** D1
Kitgum *Uganda* 3°17N 32°52E **54** B3
Kíthira = Kythira *Greece* 36°8N 23°0E **23** F10
Kithnos *Greece* 37°26N 24°27E **23** F11
Kiti *Cyprus* 34°50N 33°34E **25** E12
Kiti, C. *Cyprus* 34°48N 33°36E **25** E12
Kitimat *Canada* 54°3N 128°38W **70** C3
Kitinen ➤ *Finland* 67°14N 27°27E **8** C22
Kitsuki *Japan* 33°25N 131°37E **31** H5
Kittakittaooloo, L.
　Australia 28°3S 138°14E **63** D2
Kittanning *U.S.A.* 40°49N 79°31W **82** F5
Kittatinny Mt. *U.S.A.* 41°19N 74°39W **83** F10
Kittery *U.S.A.* 43°5N 70°45W **83** C14
Kittilä *Finland* 67°40N 24°51E **8** C21
Kitui *Kenya* 1°17S 38°0E **54** C4
Kitwanga *Canada* 55°6N 128°4W **70** B3
Kitwe *Zambia* 12°54S 28°13E **55** E2
Kivarli *India* 24°33N 72°46E **42** G5
Kivertsi *Ukraine* 50°50N 25°28E **17** C13
Kividhes *Cyprus* 34°46N 32°51E **25** E11
Kivu, L.
　Dem. Rep. of the Congo 1°48S 29°0E **54** C2
Kiwirrkurra *Australia* 22°49S 127°45E **60** D4
Kiyev = Kyyiv *Ukraine* 50°30N 30°28E **17** C16
Kiyevskoye Vdkhr. = Kyyivske
　Vdskh. *Ukraine* 51°0N 30°25E **17** C16
Kizel *Russia* 59°3N 57°40E **18** C10
Kiziguru *Rwanda* 1°46S 30°23E **54** C3
Kızıl Irmak ➤ *Turkey* 41°44N 35°58E **19** F6
Kizil Jilga *China* 35°26N 78°50E **43** B8
Kızıldağ △ *Turkey* 38°5N 31°20E **44** B1
Kızıltepe *Turkey* 37°12N 40°35E **44** B4
Kizimkazi *Tanzania* 6°28S 39°30E **54** D4
Kizlyar *Russia* 43°51N 46°40E **19** F8
Kizyl-Arvat = Serdar
　Turkmenistan 39°4N 56°23E **45** B8
Kjölur *Iceland* 64°50N 19°25E **8** D4
Kladno *Czech Rep.* 50°10N 14°7E **16** C8
Klaeng *Thailand* 12°47N 101°39E **38** F3
Klagenfurt *Austria* 46°38N 14°20E **16** E8
Klaipėda *Lithuania* 55°43N 21°10E **9** J19
Klaksvík *Færoe Is.* 62°14N 6°35W **8** E9
Klamath ➤ *U.S.A.* 41°33N 124°5W **76** F1
Klamath Falls *U.S.A.* 42°13N 121°46W **76** E3
Klamath Mts. *U.S.A.* 41°50N 123°20W **76** F2
Klamono *Indonesia* 1°8S 131°30E **37** E8
Klang *Malaysia* 3°2N 101°26E **39** L3
Klappan ➤ *Canada* 58°0N 129°43W **70** B3
Klarälven ➤ *Sweden* 59°23N 13°32E **9** G15
Klatovy *Czech Rep.* 49°23N 13°18E **16** D7
Klawer *S. Africa* 31°44S 18°36E **56** E2
Klazienaveen *Neths.* 52°44N 7°0E **15** B6
Kleena Kleene *Canada* 52°0N 124°59W **70** C4
Klein-Karas *Namibia* 27°33S 18°7E **56** D2
Klerksdorp *S. Africa* 26°53S 26°38E **56** D4
Kletsk = Klyetsk *Belarus* 53°5N 26°45E **17** B14
Kletskiy *Russia* 49°16N 43°11E **19** E7
Klickitat *U.S.A.* 45°49N 121°9W **76** D3
Klickitat ➤ *U.S.A.* 45°42N 121°17W **78** E5
Klidhes *Cyprus* 35°42N 34°36E **25** D13
Klinaklini ➤ *Canada* 51°21N 125°40W **70** C3
Klip ➤ *S. Africa* 27°3S 29°3E **57** D4
Klipdale *S. Africa* 34°19S 19°57E **56** E2
Klipplaat *S. Africa* 33°1S 24°22E **56** E3
Kłodzko *Poland* 50°28N 16°38E **17** C9
Klong Wang Chao △
　Thailand 16°20N 99°9E **38** D2
Klouto *Togo* 6°57N 0°44E **50** G6
Kluane △ *Canada* 60°45N 139°30W **70** A1
Kluane L. *Canada* 61°15N 138°40W **68** C6
Kluang *Malaysia* 2°3N 103°18E **39** L4
Kluczbork *Poland* 50°58N 18°12E **17** C10
Klukwan *U.S.A.* 59°24N 135°54W **70** B1
Klungkung *Indonesia* 8°32S 115°24E **37** K18
Klyetsk *Belarus* 53°5N 26°45E **17** B14
Klyuchevskaya, Gora
　Russia 55°50N 160°30E **29** D17
Klyuchi *Russia* 56°18N 160°51E **29** D17
Knaresborough *U.K.* 54°1N 1°28W **12** C6
Knee L. *Man., Canada* 55°3N 94°45W **72** A1
Knee L. *Sask., Canada* 55°51N 107°0W **71** B7
Knight Inlet *Canada* 50°45N 125°40W **70** C3
Knighton *U.K.* 52°21N 3°3W **13** E4
Knights Ferry *U.S.A.* 37°50N 120°40W **78** H6
Knights Landing
　U.S.A. 38°48N 121°43W **78** G5
Knob, C. *Australia* 34°32S 119°16E **61** F2
Knock *Ireland* 53°48N 8°55W **10** C3
Knockmealdown Mts.
　Ireland 52°14N 7°56W **10** D4

Knokke-Heist *Belgium* 51°21N 3°17E **15** C3
Knossos *Greece* 35°16N 25°10E **25** D7
Knowlton *Canada* 45°13N 72°31W **83** A12
Knox *U.S.A.* 41°18N 86°37W **80** E10
Knox Coast *Antarctica* 66°30S 108°0E **5** C8
Knoxville *Iowa, U.S.A.* 41°19N 93°6W **80** E7
Knoxville *Pa., U.S.A.* 41°57N 77°27W **82** E7
Knoxville *Tenn., U.S.A.* 35°58N 83°55W **85** D13
Knud Rasmussen Land
　Greenland 78°0N 60°0W **4** A5
Knysna *S. Africa* 34°2S 23°2E **56** E3
Ko Kha *Thailand* 18°11N 99°24E **38** C2
Ko Tarutao △ *Thailand* 6°31N 99°26E **39** J2
Ko Yao *Thailand* 8°7N 98°35E **39** a
Koartac = Quaqtaq
　Canada 60°55N 69°40W **69** C13
Koba *Indonesia* 6°37S 134°37E **37** F8
Kobarid *Slovenia* 46°15N 13°30E **16** E7
Kobayashi *Japan* 31°56N 130°59E **31** J5
Kōbe *Japan* 34°41N 135°13E **31** G7
København *Denmark* 55°40N 12°26E **9** J15
Kōbi-Sho *Japan* 25°56N 123°41E **31** M1
Koblenz *Germany* 50°21N 7°36E **16** C4
Kobryn *Belarus* 52°15N 24°22E **17** B13
Kocaeli *Turkey* 40°45N 29°50E **19** F4
Kočani *Macedonia* 41°55N 22°25E **23** D10
Koch Bihar *India* 26°22N 89°29E **41** F16
Kochas *India* 25°15N 83°56E **43** G10
Kochi = Cochin *India* 9°58N 76°20E **40** Q10
Kōchi *Japan* 33°30N 133°35E **31** H6
Kōchi □ *Japan* 33°40N 133°30E **31** H6
Kochiu = Gejiu *China* 23°20N 103°10E **32** D5
Kodarma *India* 24°28N 85°36E **43** G11
Kodiak *U.S.A.* 57°47N 152°24W **74** a
Kodiak I. *U.S.A.* 57°30N 152°45W **74** a
Kodinar *India* 20°46N 70°46E **42** J4
Kodinsk *Russia* 58°40N 99°10E **29** D10
Koedoesberge *S. Africa* 32°40S 20°11E **56** E3
Koes *Namibia* 26°0S 19°15E **56** D2
Koffiefontein *S. Africa* 29°30S 25°0E **56** D4
Kofiau *Indonesia* 1°11S 129°50E **37** E8
Koforidua *Ghana* 6°3N 0°17W **50** G5
Kōfu *Japan* 35°40N 138°30E **31** G9
Koga *Japan* 36°11N 139°43E **31** F9
Kogaluc ➤ *Canada* 56°12N 61°44W **73** A7
Køge *Denmark* 55°27N 12°11E **9** J15
Kogon *Uzbekistan* 39°43N 64°33E **28** F7
Koh-i-Khurd *Afghan.* 33°30N 65°59E **42** C1
Koh-i-Maran *Pakistan* 29°18N 66°50E **42** E2
Kohat *Pakistan* 33°40N 71°29E **42** C4
Kohima *India* 25°35N 94°10E **41** G19
Kohkīlūyeh va Būyer Aḥmadi □
　Iran 31°30N 50°30E **45** D6
Kohler Ra. *Antarctica* 77°0S 110°0W **5** D15
Kohlu *Pakistan* 29°54N 69°15E **42** E3
Kohtla-Järve *Estonia* 59°20N 27°20E **9** G22
Koi Sanjaq *Iraq* 36°5N 44°38E **44** B5
Koillismaa *Finland* 65°44N 28°36E **8** D23
Koin *N. Korea* 40°28N 126°18E **35** D14
Koillismaa *Finland* 65°44N 28°36E **8** D23
Kojō *N. Korea* 38°58N 127°58E **35** E14
Kojonup *Australia* 33°48S 117°10E **61** F2
Kojūr *Iran* 36°23N 51°43E **45** B6
Kokand = Qŭqon
　Uzbekistan 40°31N 70°56E **28** E8
Kokas *Indonesia* 2°42S 132°26E **37** E8
Kokchetav = Kökshetaū
　Kazakhstan 53°20N 69°25E **28** D7
Kokemäenjoki ➤
　Finland 61°32N 21°44E **8** F19
Kokkola *Finland* 63°50N 23°8E **8** E20
Koko Kyunzu *Burma* 14°10N 93°25E **41** M18
Kokomo *U.S.A.* 40°29N 86°8W **80** E10
Koksan *N. Korea* 38°46N 126°40E **35** E14
Kökshetaū *Kazakhstan* 53°20N 69°25E **28** D7
Koksoak ➤ *Canada* 58°30N 68°10W **69** D13
Kokstad *S. Africa* 30°32S 29°29E **57** E4
Kokubu *Japan* 31°44N 130°46E **31** J5
Kola *Indonesia* 5°35S 134°30E **37** F8
Kola *Russia* 68°45N 33°8E **8** B25
Kola Pen. = Kolskiy Poluostrov
　Russia 67°30N 38°0E **18** A6
Kolachi ➤ *Pakistan* 27°8N 67°2E **42** F2
Kolahoi *India* 34°12N 75°22E **43** B6
Kolaka *Indonesia* 4°3S 121°46E **37** E6
Kolar *India* 13°12N 78°15E **40** N11
Kolar Gold Fields *India* 12°58N 78°16E **40** N11
Kolaras *India* 25°14N 77°36E **42** G6
Kolari *Finland* 67°20N 23°48E **8** C20
Kolayat *India* 27°50N 72°50E **42** F5
Kolda *Senegal* 12°55N 14°57W **50** F3
Kolding *Denmark* 55°30N 9°29E **9** J13
Kolepom = Dolak, Pulau
　Indonesia 8°0S 138°30E **37** F9
Kolguyev, Ostrov *Russia* 69°20N 48°30E **18** A8
Kolhapur *India* 16°43N 74°15E **40** L9
Kolimbia *Greece* 36°15N 28°10E **25** C10
Kolín *Czech Rep.* 50°2N 15°9E **16** C8
Kolkas rags *Latvia* 57°46N 22°37E **9** H20
Kolkata *India* 22°34N 88°21E **43** H13
Kollam = Quilon *India* 8°50N 76°38E **40** Q10
Kollum *Neths.* 53°17N 6°10E **15** A6
Kolmanskop *Namibia* 26°45S 15°14E **56** D2
Köln *Germany* 50°56N 6°57E **16** C4
Koło *Poland* 52°14N 18°40E **17** B10
Kołobrzeg *Poland* 54°10N 15°35E **16** A8
Kolomna *Russia* 55°8N 38°45E **18** C6
Kolomyya *Ukraine* 48°31N 25°2E **17** D13
Kolonodale *Indonesia* 2°0S 121°19E **37** E6
Kolosib *India* 24°15N 92°45E **41** G18
Kolpashevo *Russia* 58°20N 83°5E **28** D9
Kolpino *Russia* 59°44N 30°39E **18** C5
Kolskiy Poluostrov
　Russia 67°30N 38°0E **18** A6
Kolskiy Zaliv *Russia* 69°23N 34°0E **8** B26
Kolwezi
　Dem. Rep. of the Congo 10°40S 25°25E **55** E2
Kolyma ➤ *Russia* 69°30N 161°0E **29** C17

Kolymskoye Nagorye
　Russia 63°0N 157°0E **29** C16
Kôm Ombo *Egypt* 24°25N 32°52E **51** D12
Komandorskie Is. =
　Komandorskiye Ostrova
　Russia 55°0N 167°0E **29** D17
Komandorskiye Ostrova
　Russia 55°0N 167°0E **29** D17
Komárno *Slovak Rep.* 47°49N 18°5E **17** E10
Komatipoort *S. Africa* 25°25S 31°55E **57** D5
Komatou Yialou *Cyprus* 35°25N 34°8E **25** D13
Komatsu *Japan* 36°25N 136°30E **31** F8
Komatsushima *Japan* 34°0N 134°35E **31** H7
Komi *Cyprus* 35°24N 34°0E **25** D13
Komi □ *Russia* 64°0N 55°0E **18** B10
Kommunarsk = Alchevsk
　Ukraine 48°30N 38°45E **19** E6
Kommunizma, Pik = imeni Ismail
　Samani, Pik *Tajikistan* 39°0N 72°2E **28** F8
Komodo *Indonesia* 8°37S 119°20E **37** F5
Komoran, Pulau
　Indonesia 8°18S 138°45E **37** F9
Komoro *Japan* 36°19N 138°26E **31** F9
Komotini *Greece* 41°9N 25°26E **23** D11
Kompasberg *S. Africa* 31°45S 24°32E **56** E3
Kompong Cham
　Cambodia 12°0N 105°30E **39** G5
Kompong Chhnang = Kampong
　Chhnang *Cambodia* 12°20N 104°35E **39** F5
Kompong Chikreng
　Cambodia 13°5N 104°18E **38** F5
Kompong Kleang
　Cambodia 13°6N 104°8E **38** F5
Kompong Luong
　Cambodia 11°49N 104°48E **39** G5
Kompong Pranak
　Cambodia 13°35N 104°55E **38** F5
Kompong Som = Kampong Saom
　Cambodia 10°38N 103°30E **39** G4
Kompong Som, Chhung =
　Kampong Saom, Chaak
　Cambodia 10°50N 103°32E **39** G4
Kompong Speu
　Cambodia 11°26N 104°32E **39** G5
Kompong Sralau
　Cambodia 14°5N 105°46E **38** E5
Kompong Thom
　Cambodia 12°35N 104°51E **38** F5
Kompong Trabeck
　Cambodia 13°6N 105°14E **38** F5
Kompong Trabeck
　Cambodia 11°9N 105°28E **39** G5
Kompong Trach
　Cambodia 11°25N 105°48E **39** G5
Kompong Tralach
　Cambodia 11°54N 104°47E **39** G5
Komrat = Comrat
　Moldova 46°18N 28°40E **17** E15
Komsberg *S. Africa* 32°40S 20°45E **56** E3
Komsomolets, Ostrov
　Russia 80°30N 95°0E **29** A10
Komsomolsk-na-Amure
　Russia 50°30N 137°0E **33** A8
Kon Tum *Vietnam* 14°24N 108°0E **38** E7
Kon Tum, Plateau du
　Vietnam 14°30N 108°30E **38** E7
Konar □ *Afghan.* 34°30N 71°3E **40** B7
Konārī *Iran* 28°13N 51°36E **45** D6
Konch *India* 26°0N 79°10E **43** G8
Konde *Tanzania* 4°57S 39°45E **54** C4
Kondinin *Australia* 32°34S 118°8E **61** F2
Kondoa *Tanzania* 4°55S 35°50E **54** C4
Kondopaga *Russia* 62°12N 34°17E **18** B5
Kondratyevo *Russia* 57°22N 98°15E **29** D10
Köneürgench
　Turkmenistan 42°19N 59°10E **28** E6
Konevo *Russia* 62°8N 39°20E **18** B6
Kong = Khong ➤
　Cambodia 13°32N 105°58E **38** F5
Kong, Koh *Cambodia* 11°20N 103°0E **39** G4
Kong Christian IX Land
　Greenland 68°0N 36°0W **4** C6
Kong Christian X Land
　Greenland 74°0N 29°0W **4** B6
Kong Frederik IX Land
　Greenland 67°0N 52°0W **4** C5
Kong Frederik VI Kyst
　Greenland 63°0N 43°0W **4** C5
Kong Frederik VIII Land
　Greenland 78°30N 26°0W **4** B6
Kong Oscar Fjord
　Greenland 72°20N 24°0W **4** B6
Konglu *Burma* 27°13N 97°57E **41** F20
Kongola *Namibia* 17°45S 23°20E **56** B3
Kongolo *Kasai-Or.,
　Dem. Rep. of the Congo* 5°26S 24°49E **54** D1
Kongolo *Katanga,
　Dem. Rep. of the Congo* 5°22S 27°0E **54** D2
Kongsberg *Norway* 59°39N 9°39E **9** G13
Kongsvinger *Norway* 60°12N 12°2E **9** F15
Kongur Shan *China* 38°34N 75°18E **32** C2
Kongwa *Tanzania* 6°11S 36°26E **54** D4
Koni
　Dem. Rep. of the Congo 10°40S 27°11E **55** E2
Koni, Mts.
　Dem. Rep. of the Congo 10°36S 27°10E **55** E2
Konin *Poland* 52°12N 18°15E **17** B10
Konjic *Bos.-H.* 43°42N 17°58E **23** C7
Konkiep *Namibia* 26°49S 17°15E **56** D2
Konosha *Russia* 61°0N 40°5E **18** B7
Kōnosu *Japan* 36°3N 139°31E **31** F9
Konotop *Ukraine* 51°12N 33°7E **19** D5
Konqi He ➤ *China* 41°0N 86°0E **32** B3
Końskie *Poland* 51°15N 20°23E **17** C11
Konstanz *Germany* 47°40N 9°10E **16** E5
Kont *Iran* 26°55N 61°50E **45** E9

Kontagora Nigeria 10°23N 5°27E 50 F7
Kontiolahti Finland 62°46N 29°50E 8 E23
Kontokali Greece 39°38N 19°51E 25 A3
Konya Turkey 37°52N 32°35E 44 B2
Konza Kenya 1°45S 37°7E 54 C4
Koocanusa, L. Canada 49°20N 115°15W 76 B6
Kookynie Australia 29°17S 121°22E 61 E3
Koolyanobbing Australia 30°48S 119°36E 61 F2
Koonibba Australia 31°54S 133°25E 63 E1
Koorawatha Australia 34°2S 148°33E 63 E4
Koorda Australia 30°48S 117°35E 61 F2
Kooskia U.S.A. 46°9N 115°59W 76 C6
Kootenay → U.S.A. 49°19N 117°39W 70 D5
Kootenay △ Canada 51°0N 116°0W 70 C5
Kootenay L. Canada 49°45N 116°50W 76 B5
Kootjieskolk S. Africa 31°15S 20°21E 56 E3
Kopaonik Serbia 43°10N 20°50E 23 C9
Kópavogur Iceland 64°6N 21°55W 8 D3
Koper Slovenia 45°31N 13°44E 16 F7
Kopervik Norway 59°17N 5°17E 9 G11
Kopet Dagh Asia 38°0N 58°0E 45 B8
Kopi Australia 33°24S 135°40E 63 E2
Köping Sweden 59°31N 16°3E 9 G17
Koppeh Dāgh = Kopet Dagh
Asia 38°0N 58°0E 45 B8
Koppies S. Africa 27°20S 27°30E 57 D4
Koprivnica Croatia 46°12N 16°45E 22 A7
Köprülü △ Turkey 37°20N 31°5E 44 B1
Kopychyntsi Ukraine 49°7N 25°58E 17 D13
Kora △ Kenya 0°14S 38°44E 54 C4
Korab Macedonia 41°44N 20°40E 23 D9
Koral India 21°50N 73°12E 42 J5
Korba India 22°20N 82°45E 43 H10
Korbu, G. Malaysia 4°41N 101°18E 39 K3
Korçë Albania 40°37N 20°50E 23 D9
Korčula Croatia 42°56N 16°57E 22 C7
Kord Kūy Iran 36°48N 54°7E 45 B7
Kord Sheykh Iran 28°31N 52°53E 45 D7
Kordestān □ Iran 36°0N 47°0E 44 C5
Kordofān Sudan 13°0N 29°0E 51 F11
Korea, North ■ Asia 40°0N 127°0E 35 E14
Korea, South ■ Asia 36°0N 128°0E 35 G15
Korea Bay Korea 39°0N 124°0E 35 E13
Korea Strait Asia 34°0N 129°30E 35 H15
Korets Ukraine 50°40N 27°5E 17 C14
Korhogo Ivory C. 9°29N 5°28W 50 G4
Korinthiakos Kolpos
Greece 38°16N 22°30E 23 E10
Korinthos Greece 37°56N 22°55E 23 F10
Korissia, L. Greece 39°27N 19°53E 25 B3
Köriyama Japan 37°24N 140°23E 30 F10
Korla China 41°45N 86°4E 32 B3
Kormakiti, C. Cyprus 35°23N 32°56E 25 D11
Korneshty = Corneşti
Moldova 47°21N 28°1E 17 E15
Koro Fiji 17°19S 179°23E 59 a
Koro Ivory C. 8°32N 7°30W 50 G4
Koro Sea Fiji 17°30S 179°45W 59 a
Korogwe Tanzania 5°5S 38°25E 54 D4
Korolevu Fiji 18°12S 177°46E 59 a
Koronadal Phil. 6°12N 125°1E 37 C6
Koror Palau 7°20N 134°28E 64 G5
Körös → Hungary 46°43N 20°12E 17 E11
Korosten Ukraine 50°54N 28°36E 17 C15
Korostyshev Ukraine 50°19N 29°4E 17 C15
Korovou Fiji 17°47S 178°32E 59 a
Koroyanitu △ Fiji 17°40S 177°35E 59 a
Korraraika, Helodranon' i
Madag. 17°45S 43°57E 57 B7
Korsakov Russia 46°36N 142°42E 29 E15
Korshunovo Russia 58°37N 110°10E 29 D12
Korsør Denmark 55°20N 11°9E 9 J14
Kortrijk Belgium 50°50N 3°17E 15 D3
Korwai India 24°7N 78°5E 42 G8
Koryakskoye Nagorye
Russia 61°0N 171°0E 29 C18
Kos Greece 36°50N 27°15E 23 F12
Kosan N. Korea 38°52N 127°25E 35 E14
Koschagyl Kazakhstan 46°40N 54°0E 19 E9
Kościan Poland 52°5N 16°40E 17 B9
Kosciusko U.S.A. 33°4N 89°35W 85 E10
Kosciuszko, Mt.
Australia 36°27S 148°16E 63 F4
Kosha Sudan 20°50N 30°30E 51 D12
K'oshih = Kashi China 39°30N 76°2E 32 C2
Koshiki-Rettō Japan 31°45N 129°49E 31 J4
Kosi India 27°48N 77°29E 42 F7
Kosi → India 28°41N 78°57E 43 E8
Košice Slovak Rep. 48°42N 21°15E 17 D11
Koskinou Greece 36°23N 28°13E 25 C10
Koslan Russia 63°34N 49°14E 18 B8
Kosŏng N. Korea 38°40N 128°22E 35 E15
Kosovo □ Serbia 42°30N 21°0E 23 C9
Kosovska Mitrovica
Serbia 42°54N 20°52E 23 C9
Kossou, L. de Ivory C. 6°59N 5°31W 50 G4
Koster S. Africa 25°52S 26°54E 56 D4
Kôsti Sudan 13°8N 32°43E 51 F12
Kostopil Ukraine 50°51N 26°22E 17 C14
Kostroma Russia 57°50N 40°58E 18 C7
Kostrzyn Poland 52°35N 14°39E 16 B8
Koszalin Poland 54°11N 16°8E 16 A9
Kot Addu Pakistan 30°30N 71°0E 42 D4
Kot Kapura India 30°35N 74°50E 42 D6
Kot Moman Pakistan 32°13N 73°0E 42 C5
Kot Sultan Pakistan 30°46N 70°56E 42 D4
Kota India 25°14N 75°49E 42 G6
Kota Barrage India 25°6N 75°51E 42 G6
Kota Belud Malaysia 6°21N 116°26E 36 C5
Kota Bharu Malaysia 6°7N 102°14E 39 J4
Kota Kinabalu Malaysia 6°0N 116°4E 36 C5
Kota Tinggi Malaysia 1°44N 103°53E 39 M4
Kotaagung Indonesia 5°38S 104°29E 36 F2
Kotabaru Indonesia 3°20S 116°20E 36 E5
Kotabumi Indonesia 4°49S 104°54E 36 E2
Kotamobagu Indonesia 0°57N 124°31E 37 D6

Kotapinang Indonesia 1°53N 100°5E 39 M3
Kotcho L. Canada 59°7N 121°12W 70 B4
Kotdwara India 29°45N 78°32E 43 E8
Kotelnich Russia 58°22N 48°24E 18 C8
Kotelnikovo Russia 47°38N 43°8E 19 E7
Kotelnyy, Ostrov
Russia 75°10N 139°0E 29 B14
Kothari → India 25°20N 75°4E 42 G6
Kothi Chhattisgarh, India 23°21N 82°3E 43 H10
Kothi Mad. P., India 24°45N 80°40E 43 G9
Kotiro Pakistan 26°17N 67°13E 42 F2
Kotka Finland 60°28N 26°58E 8 F22
Kotlas Russia 61°17N 46°43E 18 B8
Kotli Pakistan 33°30N 73°55E 42 C5
Kotma India 23°12N 81°58E 43 H9
Kotor Montenegro 42°25N 18°47E 23 C8
Kotovsk Ukraine 47°45N 29°35E 17 E15
Kotputli India 27°43N 76°12E 42 F7
Kotri Pakistan 25°22N 68°22E 42 G3
Kotto → C.A.R. 4°14N 22°2E 52 D4
Kotturu India 14°45N 76°10E 40 M10
Kotu Group Tonga 20°0S 174°45W 59 c
Kotuy → Russia 71°54N 102°6E 29 B11
Kotzebue U.S.A. 66°53N 162°39W 74 a
Kotzebue Sound U.S.A. 66°20N 163°0W 66 C3
Kouchibouguac △
Canada 46°50N 65°0W 73 C6
Koudougou Burkina Faso 12°10N 2°20W 50 F5
Koufonisi Greece 34°56N 26°8E 25 E8
Kougaberge S. Africa 33°48S 23°50E 56 E3
Kouilou → Congo 4°10S 12°5E 52 E2
Koula Moutou Gabon 1°15S 12°25E 52 E2
Koulen = Kulen
Cambodia 13°50N 104°40E 38 F5
Kouloura Greece 39°42N 19°54E 25 A3
Koumala Australia 21°38S 149°15E 62 C4
Koumra Chad 8°50N 17°35E 51 G9
Kountze U.S.A. 30°22N 94°19W 84 F7
Kouris → Cyprus 34°38N 32°54E 25 E11
Kourou Fr. Guiana 5°9N 52°39W 93 B8
Kouroussa Guinea 10°45N 9°45W 50 F4
Kousséri Cameroon 12°0N 14°55E 51 F8
Koutiala Mali 12°25N 5°23W 50 F4
Kouvola Finland 60°52N 26°43E 8 F22
Kovdor Russia 67°34N 30°24E 8 C24
Kovel Ukraine 51°11N 24°38E 17 C13
Kovrov Russia 56°25N 41°25E 18 C7
Kowanyama Australia 15°29S 141°44E 62 B3
Kowloon China 22°19N 114°11E 33 G11
Kowôn N. Korea 39°26N 127°14E 35 E14
Koyampattur = Coimbatore
India 11°2N 76°59E 40 P10
Köyceğiz Turkey 36°57N 28°40E 23 F13
Koyukuk → U.S.A. 64°55N 157°32W 66 C4
Koza = Okinawa Japan 26°19N 127°46E 31 L3
Kozan Turkey 37°35N 35°50E 44 B2
Kozani Greece 40°19N 21°47E 23 D9
Kozhikode = Calicut
India 11°15N 75°43E 40 P9
Kozhva Russia 65°10N 57°0E 18 A10
Kozyatyn Ukraine 49°45N 28°50E 17 D15
Kozyrevsk Russia 56°3N 159°51E 29 D16
Kpalimé Togo 6°57N 0°44E 50 G6
Kra, Isthmus of = Kra, Kho Khot
Thailand 10°15N 99°30E 39 G2
Kra, Kho Khot Thailand 10°15N 99°30E 39 G2
Kra Buri Thailand 10°22N 98°46E 39 G2
Kraai → S. Africa 30°40S 26°45E 56 E4
Krabi Thailand 8°4N 98°55E 39 H2
Kracheh Cambodia 12°32N 106°10E 38 F6
Kragan Indonesia 6°43S 111°38E 37 G14
Kragerø Norway 58°52N 9°25E 9 G13
Kragujevac Serbia 44°2N 20°56E 23 B9
Krakatau = Rakata, Pulau
Indonesia 6°10S 105°20E 36 F3
Krakatoa = Rakata, Pulau
Indonesia 6°10S 105°20E 36 F3
Krakor Cambodia 12°32N 104°12E 38 F5
Kraków Poland 50°4N 19°57E 17 C10
Kralanh Cambodia 13°35N 103°25E 38 F4
Kraljevo Serbia 43°44N 20°41E 23 C9
Kramatorsk Ukraine 48°50N 37°30E 19 E6
Kramfors Sweden 62°55N 17°48E 8 E17
Kranj Slovenia 46°16N 14°22E 16 E8
Krankskop S. Africa 28°0S 30°47E 57 D5
Krasavino Russia 60°58N 46°29E 18 B8
Kraskino Russia 42°44N 130°48E 30 C5
Kraśnik Poland 50°55N 22°15E 17 C12
Krasnoarmeysk Russia 51°0N 45°42E 28 D5
Krasnodar Russia 45°5N 39°0E 19 E6
Krasnokamensk Russia 50°3N 118°0E 29 D12
Krasnokamsk Russia 58°4N 55°48E 18 C10
Krasnoperekopsk Ukraine 46°0N 33°54E 19 E5
Krasnorechenskiy
Russia 44°41N 135°14E 30 B7
Krasnoselkup Russia 65°20N 82°10E 28 C9
Krasnoturinsk Russia 59°46N 60°12E 18 C11
Krasnoufimsk Russia 56°36N 57°38E 18 C10
Krasnouralsk Russia 58°21N 60°3E 18 C11
Krasnovishersk Russia 60°23N 57°3E 18 B10
Krasnoyarsk Russia 56°8N 93°0E 29 D10
Krasnyy Kut Russia 50°50N 47°0E 19 D8
Krasnyy Luch Ukraine 48°13N 39°0E 19 E6
Krasnyy Yar Russia 46°43N 48°23E 19 E8
Kratie = Kracheh
Cambodia 12°32N 106°10E 38 F6
Krau Indonesia 3°19S 140°5E 37 E10
Kravanh, Chuor Phnum
Cambodia 12°0N 103°32E 39 G4
Krefeld Germany 51°20N 6°33E 16 C4
Kremen Croatia 44°28N 15°53E 16 F8
Kremenchuk Ukraine 49°5N 33°25E 19 E5
Kremenchuksk Vdskh.
Ukraine 49°20N 32°30E 19 E5
Kremenets Ukraine 50°8N 25°43E 17 C13
Kremmling U.S.A. 40°4N 106°24W 76 F10
Krems Austria 48°25N 15°36E 16 D8

Kretinga Lithuania 55°53N 21°15E 9 J19
Kribi Cameroon 2°57N 9°56E 52 D1
Krichev = Krychaw
Belarus 53°40N 31°41E 17 B16
Kril'on, Mys Russia 45°53N 142°5E 30 B11
Krios, Akra Greece 35°13N 23°34E 25 D5
Krishna → India 15°57N 80°59E 41 M12
Krishnanagar India 23°24N 88°33E 43 H13
Kristiansand Norway 58°8N 8°1E 9 G13
Kristianstad Sweden 56°2N 14°9E 9 H16
Kristiansund Norway 63°7N 7°45E 8 E12
Kristiinankaupunki
Finland 62°16N 21°21E 8 E19
Kristinehamn Sweden 59°18N 14°7E 9 G16
Kristinestad =
Kristiinankaupunki
Finland 62°16N 21°21E 8 E19
Kriti Greece 35°15N 25°0E 25 D7
Kritsa Greece 35°10N 25°41E 25 D7
Krivoy Rog = Kryvyy Rih
Ukraine 47°51N 33°20E 19 E5
Krk Croatia 45°8N 14°40E 16 F8
Krokodil = Umgwenya →
Mozam. 25°14S 32°18E 57 D5
Krong Kaoh Kong
Cambodia 11°37N 102°59E 39 G4
Kronprins Olav Kyst
Antarctica 69°0S 42°0E 5 C5
Kronprinsesse Märtha Kyst
Antarctica 73°30S 10°0W 5 D2
Kronshtadt Russia 59°57N 29°51E 18 B4
Kroonstad S. Africa 27°43S 27°19E 56 D4
Kropotkin Russia 45°28N 40°28E 19 E7
Krosno Poland 49°42N 21°46E 17 D11
Krotoszyn Poland 51°42N 17°23E 17 C9
Krousonas Greece 35°13N 24°59E 25 D6
Kruger △ S. Africa 24°50S 26°10E 57 C5
Krugersdorp S. Africa 26°5S 27°46E 57 D4
Kruisfontein S. Africa 33°59S 24°43E 56 E3
Krung Thep = Bangkok
Thailand 13°45N 100°35E 38 F3
Krupki Belarus 54°19N 29°8E 17 A15
Kruševac Serbia 43°35N 21°28E 23 C9
Krychaw Belarus 53°40N 31°41E 17 B16
Krymskiy Poluostrov = Krymskyy
Pivostriv Ukraine 45°0N 34°0E 19 F5
Krymskyy Pivostriv
Ukraine 45°0N 34°0E 19 F5
Kryvyy Rih Ukraine 47°51N 33°20E 19 E5
Ksar el Kebir Morocco 35°0N 6°0W 50 B4
Ksar es Souk = Er Rachidia
Morocco 31°58N 4°20W 50 B5
Kuah Malaysia 6°19N 99°51E 39 J2
Kuala Belait Malaysia 4°35N 114°11E 36 D4
Kuala Berang Malaysia 5°5N 103°1E 39 K4
Kuala Dungun = Dungun
Malaysia 4°45N 103°25E 39 K4
Kuala Kangsar Malaysia 4°46N 100°56E 39 K3
Kuala Kelawang Malaysia 2°56N 102°5E 39 L4
Kuala Kerai Malaysia 5°30N 102°12E 39 K4
Kuala Kerian Malaysia 5°10N 100°25E 39 c
Kuala Kubu Bharu
Malaysia 3°34N 101°39E 39 L3
Kuala Lipis Malaysia 4°10N 102°3E 39 K4
Kuala Lumpur Malaysia 3°9N 101°41E 39 L3
Kuala Nerang Malaysia 6°16N 100°37E 39 J3
Kuala Pilah Malaysia 2°45N 102°15E 39 L4
Kuala Rompin Malaysia 2°49N 103°29E 39 L4
Kuala Selangor Malaysia 3°20N 101°15E 39 L3
Kuala Sepetang
Malaysia 4°49N 100°28E 39 K3
Kuala Terengganu
Malaysia 5°20N 103°8E 39 K4
Kualajelai Indonesia 2°58S 110°46E 36 E4
Kualakapuas Indonesia 2°55S 114°20E 36 E4
Kualakurun Indonesia 1°10S 113°50E 36 E4
Kualapembuang
Indonesia 3°14S 112°38E 36 E4
Kualasimpang Indonesia 4°17N 98°3E 36 D1
Kuancheng China 40°37N 118°30E 35 D10
Kuandang Indonesia 0°56N 123°1E 37 D6
Kuandian China 40°45N 124°45E 35 D13
Kuangchou = Guangzhou
China 23°6N 113°13E 33 D6
Kuantan Malaysia 3°49N 103°20E 39 L4
Kuba = Quba Azerbaijan 41°21N 48°32E 19 F8
Kuban → Russia 45°20N 37°30E 19 E6
Kubokawa Japan 33°12N 133°8E 31 H6
Kubutambahan
Indonesia 8°16S 115°35E 37 J18
Kucar, Tanjung
Indonesia 8°39S 114°34E 37 K18
Kuchaman India 27°13N 74°47E 42 F6
Kuchinda India 21°44N 84°21E 43 J11
Kuching Malaysia 1°33N 110°25E 36 D4
Kuchino-eruba-Jima
Japan 30°28N 130°12E 31 J5
Kuchino-Shima Japan 29°57N 129°55E 31 K4
Kuchinotsu Japan 32°36N 130°11E 31 H5
Kucing = Kuching
Malaysia 1°33N 110°25E 36 D4
Kud → Pakistan 26°5N 66°20E 42 F2
Kuda India 23°10N 71°15E 42 H4
Kudat Malaysia 6°55N 116°55E 36 C5
Kudus Indonesia 6°48S 110°51E 37 G14
Kudymkar Russia 59°1N 54°39E 18 C9
Kueiyang = Guiyang
China 26°32N 106°40E 32 D5
Kufra Oasis = Al Kufrah
Libya 24°17N 23°15E 51 D10
Kufstein Austria 47°35N 12°11E 16 E7
Kugaaruk = Pelly Bay
Canada 68°38N 89°50W 69 C11
Kugluktuk Canada 67°50N 115°5W 68 C8
Kugong I. Canada 56°18N 79°50W 72 A4
Kūh Dasht Iran 33°32N 47°36E 44 C5

Kūh-e-Jebāl Bārez Iran 29°0N 58°0E 45 D8
Kūhak Iran 27°12N 63°10E 45 E9
Kuhan Pakistan 28°19N 67°14E 42 E2
Kūhbonān Iran 31°23N 56°19E 45 D8
Kūhestak Iran 26°47N 57°2E 45 E8
Kuhin Iran 36°22N 49°40E 45 B6
Kūhīrī Iran 26°55N 61°2E 45 E9
Kuhmo Finland 64°7N 29°31E 8 D23
Kūhpāyeh Eşfahan, Iran 32°44N 52°20E 45 C7
Kūhpāyeh Kermān, Iran 30°35N 57°15E 45 D8
Kūhrān, Kūh-e Iran 26°46N 58°12E 45 E8
Kui Buri Thailand 12°3N 99°52E 39 F2
Kuichong China 22°38N 114°25E 33 F11
Kuiseb → Namibia 22°59S 14°31E 56 C1
Kuito Angola 12°22S 16°55E 53 G3
Kuiu I. U.S.A. 57°45N 134°10W 70 B2
Kujang N. Korea 39°57N 126°1E 35 E14
Kuji Japan 40°11N 141°46E 30 D10
Kujū-San Japan 33°5N 131°15E 31 H5
Kukës Albania 42°5N 20°27E 23 C9
Kukup Malaysia 1°20N 103°27E 39 d
Kukup, Pulau Malaysia 1°18N 103°25E 39 d
Kula Turkey 38°32N 28°40E 23 E13
K'ula Shan Bhutan 28°14N 90°36E 32 C4
Kulachi Pakistan 31°56N 70°27E 42 D4
Kulai Malaysia 1°44N 103°35E 39 M4
Kulasekarappattinam
India 8°20N 78°5E 40 Q11
Kuldīga Latvia 56°58N 21°59E 9 H19
Kulen Cambodia 13°50N 104°40E 38 F5
Kulgam India 33°36N 75°2E 43 C6
Kulgera Australia 25°50S 133°18E 62 D1
Kulim Malaysia 5°22N 100°34E 39 K3
Kulin Australia 32°40S 118°2E 61 F2
Kulkayu = Hartley Bay
Canada 53°25N 129°15W 70 C3
Kullu India 31°58N 77°6E 42 D7
Külob Tajikistan 37°55N 69°50E 28 F7
Kulsary = Qulsary
Kazakhstan 46°59N 54°1E 19 E9
Kulti India 23°43N 86°50E 43 H12
Kulunda Russia 52°35N 78°57E 28 D8
Kulungar Afghan. 34°0N 69°2E 42 C3
Külvand Iran 31°21N 54°35E 45 D7
Kulwin Australia 35°2S 142°42E 63 F3
Kulyab = Külob
Tajikistan 37°55N 69°50E 28 F7
Kuma → Russia 44°55N 47°0E 19 F8
Kumaganum Nigeria 13°8N 10°38E 51 F8
Kumagaya Japan 36°9N 139°22E 31 F9
Kumai Indonesia 2°44S 111°43E 36 E4
Kumamba, Kepulauan
Indonesia 1°36S 138°45E 37 E9
Kumamoto Japan 32°45N 130°45E 31 H5
Kumamoto □ Japan 32°55N 130°55E 31 H5
Kumara N.Z. 42°37S 171°12E 59 E3
Kumarina Roadhouse
Australia 24°41S 119°32E 61 D2
Kumasi Ghana 6°41N 1°38W 50 G5
Kumba Cameroon 4°36N 9°24E 52 D1
Kumbakonam India 10°58N 79°25E 40 P11
Kumbarilla Australia 27°15S 150°55E 63 D5
Kumbhraj India 24°22N 77°3E 42 G7
Kumbia Australia 26°41S 151°39E 63 D5
Kŭmch'ŏn N. Korea 38°10N 126°29E 35 E14
Kumdok India 33°32N 78°10E 43 C8
Kumertau Russia 52°45N 55°57E 18 D10
Kumharsain India 31°19N 77°27E 42 D7
Kumi Uganda 1°30N 33°58E 54 B3
Kumo Nigeria 10°1N 11°12E 51 F8
Kumo älv = Kokemäenjoki →
Finland 61°32N 21°44E 8 F19
Kumon Bum Burma 26°30N 97°15E 41 F20
Kumtag Shamo China 39°40N 92°0E 32 C4
Kunashir, Ostrov Russia 44°0N 146°0E 29 E15
Kunda Estonia 59°30N 26°34E 9 G22
Kunda India 25°43N 81°31E 43 G9
Kundar → Pakistan 31°56N 69°19E 42 D3
Kundelungu △
Dem. Rep. of the Congo 10°30S 27°40E 55 E2
Kundelungu Ouest △
Dem. Rep. of the Congo 9°55S 27°17E 55 D2
Kundian Pakistan 32°27N 71°28E 42 C4
Kundla India 21°21N 71°25E 42 J4
Kung, Ao Thailand 8°5N 98°24E 39 a
Kunga → Bangla. 21°46N 89°30E 43 J13
Kunghit I. Canada 52°6N 131°3W 70 C2
Kungrad = Qŭnghirot
Uzbekistan 43°2N 58°50E 28 E6
Kungsbacka Sweden 57°30N 12°5E 9 H15
Kungur Russia 57°25N 56°57E 18 C10
Kungurri Australia 21°4S 148°45E 62 K6
Kunhar → Pakistan 34°20N 73°30E 43 B5
Kuningan Indonesia 6°59S 108°29E 37 G13
Kunlong Burma 23°20N 98°50E 41 H21
Kunlun Shan Asia 36°0N 86°30E 32 C3
Kunming China 25°1N 102°41E 32 D5
Kununurra Australia 15°40S 128°50E 60 C4
Kunwari → India 26°26N 79°11E 43 F8
Kunya-Urgench = Köneürgench
Turkmenistan 42°19N 59°10E 28 E6
Kuopio Finland 62°53N 27°35E 8 E22
Kupa → Croatia 45°28N 16°24E 16 F9
Kupang Indonesia 10°19N 123°39E 37 G6
Kupreanof I. U.S.A. 56°50N 133°30W 70 B2
Kupyansk-Uzlovoi
Ukraine 49°40N 37°43E 19 E6
Kuqa China 41°35N 82°30E 32 B3
Kür → Azerbaijan 39°29N 49°15E 19 G8
Kür Dili Azerbaijan 39°3N 49°13E 45 B6
Kura = Kür →
Azerbaijan 39°29N 49°15E 19 G8
Kuranda Australia 16°48S 145°35E 62 B4
Kuranga India 22°4N 69°10E 42 H3
Kurashiki Japan 34°40N 133°50E 31 G6

Kurayn Si. Arabia 27°39N 49°50E 45 E6
Kurayoshi Japan 35°26N 133°50E 31 G6
Kürchatov Kazakhstan 50°45N 78°32E 28 D8
Kŭrdzhali Bulgaria 41°38N 25°21E 23 D11
Kure Japan 34°14N 132°32E 31 G6
Kuressaare Estonia 58°15N 22°30E 9 G20
Kurgan Russia 55°26N 65°18E 28 D7
Kuri India 26°37N 70°43E 42 F4
Kuria Maria Is. = Ḩallāniyat,
Jazā'ir al Oman 17°30N 55°58E 47 D6
Kuridala Australia 21°16S 140°29E 62 C3
Kurigram Bangla. 25°49N 89°39E 41 G16
Kurikka Finland 62°36N 22°24E 8 E20
Kuril Basin Pac. Oc. 47°0N 150°0E 4 E15
Kuril Is. = Kurilskiye Ostrova
Russia 45°0N 150°0E 29 E16
Kuril-Kamchatka Trench
Pac. Oc. 44°0N 153°0E 64 C7
Kurilsk Russia 45°14N 147°53E 29 E15
Kurilskiye Ostrova
Russia 45°0N 150°0E 29 E16
Kurino Japan 31°57N 130°43E 31 J5
Kurinskaya Kosa = Kür Dili
Azerbaijan 39°3N 49°13E 45 B6
Kurnool India 15°45N 78°0E 40 M11
Kuro-Shima Kagoshima,
Japan 30°50N 129°57E 31 J4
Kuro-Shima Okinawa,
Japan 24°14N 124°1E 31 M2
Kurow N.Z. 44°44S 170°29E 59 F3
Kurram → Pakistan 32°36N 71°20E 42 C4
Kurri Kurri Australia 32°50S 151°28E 63 E5
Kurrimine Australia 17°47S 146°6E 62 B4
Kurshskiy Zaliv Russia 55°9N 21°6E 9 J19
Kursk Russia 51°42N 36°11E 18 D6
Kuruman S. Africa 39°39N 38°29E 44 B3
Kuruktag China 41°0N 89°0E 32 B3
Kuruman S. Africa 27°28S 23°28E 56 D3
Kuruman → S. Africa 26°56S 20°39E 56 D3
Kurume Japan 33°15N 130°30E 31 H5
Kurunegala Sri Lanka 7°30N 80°23E 40 R12
Kurya Russia 61°42N 57°9E 18 B10
Kus Gölü Turkey 40°10N 27°55E 23 D12
Kuşadası Turkey 37°52N 27°15E 23 F12
Kusamba Indonesia 8°34S 115°27E 37 K18
Kusatsu Japan 36°37N 138°36E 31 F9
Kusawa L. Canada 60°20N 136°13W 70 A1
Kushalgarh India 23°10N 74°27E 42 H6
Kushikino Japan 31°44N 130°16E 31 J5
Kushima Japan 31°29N 131°14E 31 J5
Kushimoto Japan 33°28N 135°47E 31 H7
Kushiro Japan 43°0N 144°25E 30 C12
Kushiro-Gawa →
Japan 42°59N 144°23E 30 C12
Kushiro Shitsugen △
Japan 43°9N 144°26E 30 C12
Kūshk Iran 28°46N 56°51E 45 D8
Kushka = Serhetabat
Turkmenistan 35°20N 62°18E 45 C9
Kushol India 33°40N 76°36E 43 C7
Kushtia Bangla. 23°55N 89°5E 41 H16
Kushva Russia 58°18N 59°45E 18 C10
Kuskokwim → U.S.A. 60°5N 162°25W 66 C3
Kuskokwim B. U.S.A. 59°45N 162°25W 74 a
Kusmi India 23°17N 83°55E 43 H10
Kusŏng N. Korea 39°59N 125°15E 35 E13
Kussharo-Ko Japan 43°38N 144°21E 30 C12
Kustanay = Qostanay
Kazakhstan 53°20N 63°35E 28 D7
Kut, Ko Thailand 11°40N 102°35E 39 G4
Kuta Indonesia 8°43S 115°11E 37 K18
Kütahya Turkey 39°30N 30°2E 19 G5
Kutaisi Georgia 42°19N 42°40E 19 F7
Kutaraja = Banda Aceh
Indonesia 5°35N 95°20E 36 C1
Kutch, Gulf of = Kachchh, Gulf of
India 22°50N 69°15E 42 H3
Kutch, Rann of = Kachchh, Rann
of India 24°0N 70°0E 42 H4
Kutiyana India 21°36N 70°2E 42 J4
Kutno Poland 52°15N 19°23E 17 B10
Kutse Botswana 21°7S 22°16E 56 C3
Kuttabul Australia 21°1S 148°54E 62 K6
Kutu Dem. Rep. of the Congo 2°40S 18°11E 52 E3
Kutum Sudan 14°10N 24°40E 51 F10
Kuujjuaq Canada 58°6N 68°15W 69 F18
Kuujjuarapik Canada 55°20N 77°35W 72 A4
Kuusamo Finland 65°57N 29°8E 8 D23
Kuusankoski Finland 60°55N 26°38E 8 F22
Kuwait = Al Kuwayt
Kuwait 29°30N 48°0E 44 D5
Kuwait ■ Asia 29°30N 47°30E 44 D5
Kuwana Japan 35°5N 136°43E 31 G8
Kuwana → India 26°25N 83°15E 43 F10
Kuybyshev = Samara
Russia 53°8N 50°6E 18 D9
Kuybyshev Russia 55°27N 78°19E 28 D8
Kuybyshevskoye Vdkhr.
Russia 55°2N 49°30E 18 C8
Kuye He → China 38°23N 110°46E 34 E6
Küyeh Iran 38°45N 47°57E 44 B5
Kuyto, Ozero Russia 65°6N 31°20E 8 D24
Kuzey Anadolu Dağları
Turkey 41°0N 36°45E 19 F6
Kuznetsk Russia 53°12N 46°40E 18 D8
Kuzomen Russia 66°22N 36°50E 18 A6
Kvænangen Norway 70°5N 21°15E 8 A19
Kvaløya Norway 69°40N 18°30E 8 B18
Kvarner Croatia 44°50N 14°10E 16 F8
Kvarnerič Croatia 44°43N 14°37E 16 F8
Kwabhaca S. Africa 30°51S 29°0E 57 E4
Kwakoegron Suriname 5°25N 55°25W 93 B7
Kwakwani Guyana 5°12N 58°29W 92 B7
Kwale Kenya 4°15S 39°31E 54 C4
KwaMashu S. Africa 29°45S 30°58E 57 D5

Kwando → Africa 18°27S 23°32E 56 B3
Kwangchow = Guangzhou
China 23°6N 113°13E 33 D6
Kwango →
Dem. Rep. of the Congo 3°14S 17°22E 52 E3
Kwangsi-Chuang = Guangxi
Zhuangzu Zizhiqu □
China 24°0N 109°0E 33 D5
Kwangtung = Guangdong □
China 23°0N 113°0E 33 D6
Kwataboahegan →
Canada 51°9N 80°50W 72 B3
Kwatisore Indonesia 3°18S 134°50E 37 E8
KwaZulu Natal □ S. Africa 29°0S 30°0E 57 D5
Kweichow = Guizhou □
China 27°0N 107°0E 32 D5
Kwekwe Zimbabwe 18°58S 29°48E 55 F2
Kwidzyn Poland 53°44N 18°55E 17 B10
Kwilu →
Dem. Rep. of the Congo 3°22S 17°22E 52 E3
Kwinana Australia 32°15S 115°47E 61 F2
Kwoka Indonesia 0°31S 132°27E 37 E8
Kwun Tong China 22°19N 114°13E 33 G11
Kyabra Cr. → Australia 25°36S 142°55E 63 D3
Kyabram Australia 36°19S 145°4E 63 F4
Kyaikto Burma 17°20N 97°3E 38 D1
Kyakhta Russia 50°30N 106°25E 29 D11
Kyambura △ Uganda 0°7S 30°9E 54 C3
Kyancutta Australia 33°8S 135°33E 63 E2
Kyaukpadaung Burma 20°52N 95°8E 41 J19
Kyaukpyu Burma 19°28N 93°30E 41 K18
Kyaukse Burma 21°36N 96°10E 41 J20
Kyburz U.S.A. 38°47N 120°18W 78 G6
Kyelang India 32°35N 77°2E 42 C7
Kyenjojo Uganda 0°40N 30°37E 54 B3
Kyle Canada 50°50N 108°2W 71 C7
Kyle Dam Zimbabwe 20°15S 31°0E 55 G3
Kyle of Lochalsh U.K. 57°17N 5°44W 11 D3
Kymijoki → Finland 60°30N 26°55E 8 F22
Kymmene älv = Kymijoki →
Finland 60°30N 26°55E 8 F22
Kyneton Australia 37°10S 144°29E 63 F3
Kynuna Australia 21°37S 141°55E 62 C3
Kyō-ga-Saki Japan 35°45N 135°15E 31 G7
Kyoga, L. Uganda 1°35N 33°0E 54 B3
Kyogle Australia 28°40S 153°0E 63 D5
Kyŏngju = Gyeongju
S. Korea 35°51N 129°14E 35 G15
Kyŏngsŏng N. Korea 41°35N 129°36E 35 D15
Kyonpyaw Burma 17°12N 95°10E 41 L19
Kyōto Japan 35°0N 135°45E 31 G7
Kyōto □ Japan 35°15N 135°45E 31 G7
Kyparissovouno Cyprus 35°19N 33°10E 25 D12
Kyperounda Cyprus 34°56N 32°58E 25 E11
Kypros = Cyprus ■ Asia 35°0N 33°0E 25 E12
Kyrenia Cyprus 35°20N 33°20E 25 D12
Kyrgyzstan ■ Asia 42°0N 75°0E 28 E8
Kyro älv = Kyrönjoki →
Finland 63°14N 21°45E 8 E19
Kyrönjoki → Finland 63°14N 21°45E 8 E19
Kystatyam Russia 67°20N 123°10E 29 C13
Kythira Greece 36°8N 23°0E 23 F10
Kythréa Cyprus 35°15N 33°29E 25 D12
Kyunhla Burma 23°25N 95°15E 41 H19
Kyūshū □ Japan 33°0N 131°0E 31 H5
Kyūshū □ Japan 33°0N 131°0E 31 H5
Kyushu-Palau Ridge
Pac. Oc. 20°0N 136°0E 64 E5
Kyūshū-Sanchi Japan 32°35N 131°17E 31 H5
Kyustendil Bulgaria 42°16N 22°41E 23 C10
Kyusyur Russia 70°19N 127°30E 29 B13
Kyyiv Ukraine 50°30N 30°28E 17 C16
Kyyiv Vdskh.
Ukraine 51°0N 30°25E 17 C16
Kyzyl Russia 51°50N 94°30E 32 A4
Kyzyl Kum Uzbekistan 42°30N 65°0E 28 E7
Kyzyl Kyya Kyrgyzstan 40°16N 72°8E 28 E8
Kyzyl Orda = Qyzylorda
Kazakhstan 44°48N 65°28E 28 E7

L

La Alcarria Spain 40°31N 2°45W 21 B4
La Amistad △ Cent. Amer. 9°28N 83°18W 88 E3
La Asunción Venezuela 11°2N 63°53W 92 A6
La Baie Canada 48°19N 70°53W 73 C5
La Banda Argentina 27°45S 64°10W 94 B3
La Barca Mexico 20°17N 102°34W 86 C4
La Barge U.S.A. 42°16N 110°12W 76 E8
La Barra Nic. 12°54N 83°33W 88 D3
La Belle U.S.A. 26°46N 81°26W 85 H14
La Biche → Canada 59°57N 123°50W 70 B4
La Biche, L. Canada 54°50N 112°3W 70 C6
La Brea Trin. & Tob. 10°15N 61°37W 93 K15
La Calera Chile 32°50S 71°10W 94 C1
La Campana △ Chile 32°58S 71°14W 94 C1
La Canal = Sa Canal
Spain 38°51N 1°23E 24 C7
La Carlota Argentina 33°30S 63°20W 94 C3
La Ceiba Honduras 15°40N 86°50W 88 C2
La Chaux-de-Fonds Switz. 47°7N 6°50E 20 C7
La Chorrera Panama 8°53N 79°47W 88 E4
La Cocha Argentina 27°50S 65°40W 94 B2
La Concepción Panama 8°31N 82°37W 88 E3
La Concordia Mexico 16°5N 92°38W 87 D6
La Coruña = A Coruña
Spain 43°20N 8°25W 21 A1
La Crescent U.S.A. 43°50N 91°18W 80 D8
La Crete Canada 58°11N 116°24W 70 B5
La Crosse Kans., U.S.A. 38°32N 99°18W 80 F4
La Crosse Wis., U.S.A. 43°48N 91°15W 80 D8
La Cruz Costa Rica 11°4N 85°39W 88 D2
La Cruz Mexico 23°55N 106°54W 86 C3
La Désirade Guadeloupe 16°18N 61°3W 88 b
La Digue Seychelles 4°20S 55°51E 53 b

La Esperanza Cuba 22°46N 83°44W 88 B3
La Esperanza Honduras 14°15N 88°10W 88 D2
La Estrada = A Estrada
Spain 42°43N 8°27W 21 A1
La Fayette U.S.A. 34°42N 85°17W 85 D12
La Fé Cuba 22°2N 84°15W 88 B3
La Follette U.S.A. 36°23N 84°7W 85 C12
La Grande U.S.A. 45°20N 118°5W 76 D4
La Grande → Canada 53°50N 79°0W 72 B5
La Grande 3, Rés.
Canada 53°40N 75°10W 72 B4
La Grande 4, Rés. Canada 54°0N 73°15W 72 B5
La Grange Calif., U.S.A. 37°42N 120°27W 78 H6
La Grange Ga., U.S.A. 33°2N 85°2W 85 E12
La Grange Ky., U.S.A. 38°24N 85°22W 81 F11
La Grange Tex., U.S.A. 29°54N 96°52W 84 G6
La Guaira Venezuela 10°36N 66°56W 92 A5
La Habana Cuba 23°8N 82°22W 88 B3
La Independencia Mexico 16°15N 92°1W 87 D6
La Isabela Dom. Rep. 19°58N 71°2W 89 C5
La Junta U.S.A. 37°59N 103°33W 76 H12
La Laguna Canary Is. 28°28N 16°18W 24 F3
La Libertad = Puerto Libertad
Mexico 29°55N 112°43W 86 B2
La Libertad Guatemala 16°47N 90°7W 88 C1
La Ligua Chile 32°30S 71°16W 94 C1
La Línea de la Concepción
Spain 36°15N 5°23W 21 D3
La Loche Canada 56°29N 109°26W 71 B7
La Louvière Belgium 50°27N 4°10E 15 D4
La Lune Trin. & Tob. 10°3N 61°22W 93 K15
La Malbaie Canada 47°40N 70°10W 73 C5
La Malinche △ Mexico 19°15N 98°3W 87 D5
La Mancha Spain 39°10N 2°54W 21 C4
La Martre, L. Canada 63°15N 117°55W 70 A5
La Mesa Mexico 32°30N 116°57W 79 N10
La Mesa U.S.A. 32°46N 117°1W 79 N9
La Mesilla U.S.A. 32°16N 106°48W 77 K10
La Misión Mexico 32°6N 116°53W 86 A1
La Moure U.S.A. 46°21N 98°18W 80 B4
La Negra Chile 23°46S 70°18W 94 A1
La Oliva Canary Is. 28°36N 13°57W 24 F6
La Orotava Canary Is. 28°22N 16°31W 24 F3
La Oroya Peru 11°32S 75°54W 92 F3
La Palma Canary Is. 28°40N 17°50W 24 F2
La Palma Panama 8°15N 78°0W 88 E4
La Palma del Condado
Spain 37°21N 6°38W 21 D2
La Paloma Chile 30°35S 71°0W 94 C1
La Pampa □ Argentina 36°50S 66°0W 94 D2
La Paragua Venezuela 6°50N 63°20W 92 B6
La Paz Entre Ríos,
Argentina 30°50S 59°45W 94 C4
La Paz San Luis,
Argentina 33°30S 67°20W 94 C2
La Paz Bolivia 16°20S 68°10W 92 G5
La Paz Honduras 14°20N 87°47W 88 D2
La Paz Mexico 24°10N 110°18W 86 C2
La Paz Centro Nic. 12°20N 86°41W 88 D2
La Pedrera Colombia 1°18S 69°43W 92 D5
La Pérade Canada 46°35N 72°12W 73 C5
La Perla Mexico 28°18N 104°32W 86 B4
La Perouse Str. Asia 45°40N 142°0E 30 B11
La Pesca Mexico 23°46N 97°47W 87 C5
La Piedad Mexico 20°21N 102°0W 86 C4
La Pine U.S.A. 43°40N 121°30W 76 E3
La Plata Argentina 35°0S 57°55W 94 D4
La Pocatière Canada 47°22N 70°2W 73 C5
La Porte U.S.A. 29°40N 95°1W 84 G7
La Purísima Mexico 26°10N 112°4W 86 B2
La Push U.S.A. 47°55N 124°38W 78 C2
La Quiaca Argentina 22°5S 65°35W 94 A2
La Restinga Canary Is. 27°38N 17°59W 24 G2
La Rioja Argentina 29°20S 67°0W 94 B2
La Rioja □ Argentina 29°30S 67°0W 94 B2
La Rioja □ Spain 42°20N 2°20W 21 A4
La Robla Spain 42°50N 5°41W 21 A3
La Roche-en-Ardenne
Belgium 50°11N 5°35E 15 D5
La Roche-sur-Yon France 46°40N 1°25W 20 C3
La Rochelle France 46°10N 1°9W 20 C3
La Roda Spain 39°13N 2°15W 21 C4
La Romaine Canada 50°13N 60°40W 73 B7
La Romana Dom. Rep. 18°27N 68°57W 89 C6
La Ronge Canada 55°5N 105°20W 71 B7
La Rumorosa Mexico 32°34N 116°6W 79 N10
La Sabina = Sa Savina
Spain 38°44N 1°25E 24 C7
La Salle U.S.A. 41°20N 89°6W 80 E9
La Santa Canary Is. 29°5N 13°40W 24 E6
La Sarre Canada 48°45N 79°15W 72 C4
La Scie Canada 49°57N 55°36W 73 C8
La Selva Beach U.S.A. 36°56N 121°51W 78 J5
La Serena Chile 29°55S 71°10W 94 B1
La Seu d'Urgell Spain 42°22N 1°23E 21 A6
La Seyne-sur-Mer France 43°7N 5°52E 20 E6
La Soufrière St. Vincent 13°20N 61°11W 89 D7
La Spézia Italy 44°7N 9°50E 20 D8
La Tagua Colombia 0°3N 74°40W 92 C4
La Tortuga Venezuela 11°0N 65°22W 89 D6
La Trinité Martinique 14°43N 60°58W 88 c
La Tuque Canada 47°30N 72°50W 72 C5
La Unión Chile 40°10S 73°0W 96 E2
La Unión El Salv. 13°20N 87°50W 88 D2
La Unión Mexico 17°58N 101°49W 86 D4
La Urbana Venezuela 7°8N 66°56W 92 B5
La Vache Pt.
Trin. & Tob. 10°47N 61°28W 93 K15
La Vall d'Uixó Spain 39°49N 0°15W 21 C5
La Vega Dom. Rep. 19°20N 70°30W 89 C5
La Vela de Coro
Venezuela 11°27N 69°34W 92 A5
La Venta Mexico 18°5N 94°3W 87 D6
La Vergne U.S.A. 36°1N 86°35W 85 C11
La Villa Joiosa = Villajoyosa
Spain 38°30N 0°12W 21 C5
Laascaanood Somali Rep. 8°26N 47°19E 47 F4

Labasa Fiji 16°30S 179°27E 59 a
Labdah = Leptis Magna
Libya 32°40N 14°12E 51 B8
Labe = Elbe → Europe 53°50N 9°0E 16 B5
Labé Guinea 11°24N 12°16W 50 F3
Laberge, L. Canada 61°11N 135°12W 70 A1
Labinsk Russia 44°40N 40°48E 19 F7
Labis Malaysia 2°22N 103°2E 39 L4
Laborie St. Lucia 13°45N 61°2W 89 f
Labrador Canada 53°20N 61°0W 73 B7
Labrador City Canada 52°57N 66°55W 73 B6
Labrador Sea Atl. Oc. 57°0N 54°0W 69 D14
Lábrea Brazil 7°15S 64°51W 92 E6
Labuan Malaysia 3°45S 103°30E 36 E2
Labuan, Pulau Malaysia 5°21N 115°13E 36 C5
Labuha Indonesia 0°30S 127°30E 37 E7
Labuhan Indonesia 6°22S 105°50E 37 G11
Labuhanbajo Indonesia 8°28S 119°54E 37 F6
Labuhanbilik Indonesia 2°31N 100°10E 39 L3
Labuk, Telok Malaysia 6°10N 117°50E 36 C5
Labyrinth, L. Australia 30°40S 135°11E 63 E2
Labytnangi Russia 66°39N 66°21E 28 C7
Lac-Bouchette Canada 48°16N 72°11W 73 C5
Lac Brochet Canada 57°53N 101°40W 71 B8
Lac Édouard Canada 47°40N 72°16W 72 C5
Lac La Biche Canada 54°45N 111°58W 70 C6
Lac la Martre = Wha Ti
Canada 63°8N 117°16W 68 C8
Lac La Ronge △ Canada 55°9N 104°41W 71 B7
Lac-Mégantic Canada 45°35N 70°53W 73 C5
Lac Thien Vietnam 12°25N 108°11E 38 F7
Lacanau France 44°58N 1°5W 20 D3
Lacantún → Mexico 16°36N 90°39W 87 D6
Laccadive Is. = Lakshadweep Is.
India 10°0N 72°30E 3 D13
Lacepede B. Australia 36°40S 139°40E 63 F2
Lacepede Is. Australia 16°55S 122°0E 60 C3
Lacerdónia Mozam. 18°3S 35°35E 55 F4
Lacey U.S.A. 47°7N 122°49W 78 C4
Lachania Greece 35°58N 27°54E 25 D9
Lachhmangarh India 27°50N 75°4E 42 F6
Lachi Pakistan 33°25N 71°20E 42 C4
Lachine Canada 45°26N 73°42W 72 C5
Lachlan → Australia 34°22S 143°55E 63 E3
Lachute Canada 45°39N 74°21W 72 C5
Lackagh Hills Ireland 54°16N 8°10W 10 B3
Lackawanna U.S.A. 42°50N 78°50W 82 D6
Lackawaxen U.S.A. 41°29N 74°59W 83 E10
Lacolle Canada 45°5N 73°22W 83 A11
Lacombe Canada 52°30N 113°44W 70 C6
Lacona U.S.A. 43°39N 76°10W 83 C8
Laconia U.S.A. 43°32N 71°28W 83 C13
Ladakh Ra. India 34°0N 78°0E 43 C8
Ladismith S. Africa 33°28S 21°15E 56 E3
Lādīz Iran 28°55N 61°15E 45 D9
Ladnun India 27°38N 74°25E 42 F6
Ladoga, L. = Ladozhskoye Ozero
Russia 61°15N 30°30E 8 F24
Ladozhskoye Ozero
Russia 61°15N 30°30E 8 F24
Lady Elliott I. Australia 24°7S 152°42E 62 C5
Lady Grey S. Africa 30°43S 27°13E 56 E4
Ladybrand S. Africa 29°9S 27°29E 56 D4
Ladysmith Canada 49°0N 123°49W 78 B3
Ladysmith S. Africa 28°32S 29°46E 57 D4
Ladysmith U.S.A. 45°28N 91°12W 80 C8
Lae Papua N. G. 6°40S 147°2E 58 B7
Laem Hin Khom Thailand 9°25N 99°56E 39 b
Laem Khat Thailand 8°6N 98°26E 39 a
Laem Nga Thailand 7°55N 98°27E 39 a
Laem Ngop Thailand 12°10N 102°26E 39 F4
Laem Phan Wa Thailand 7°47N 98°25E 39 a
Laem Pho Thailand 6°55N 101°19E 39 J3
Laem Phrom Thep Thailand 7°45N 98°19E 39 a
Laem Riang Thailand 8°7N 98°27E 39 a
Laem Sam Rong Thailand 9°35N 100°4E 39 b
Laem Son Thailand 7°59N 98°16E 39 a
Laem Yamu Thailand 7°59N 98°26E 39 a
Laerma Greece 36°9N 27°57E 25 C9
Læsø Denmark 57°15N 11°5E 9 H14
Lafayette Ind., U.S.A. 40°25N 86°54W 80 E10
Lafayette La., U.S.A. 30°14N 92°1W 84 F8
Lafayette Tenn., U.S.A. 36°31N 86°2W 85 C11
Laferte → Canada 61°53N 117°44W 70 A5
Lafia Nigeria 8°30N 8°34E 50 G7
Lafleche Canada 49°45N 106°40W 71 D7
Lagan → U.K. 54°36N 5°55W 10 B6
Lagarfljót → Iceland 65°40N 14°18W 8 D6
Lagdo, Rés. de Cameroon 8°40N 14°0E 51 G8
Lågen → Oppland, Norway 61°8N 10°25E 8 F14
Lågen → Vestfold, Norway 59°3N 10°3E 9 G14
Lages Brazil 27°48S 50°0W 95 B5
Laghouat Algeria 33°50N 2°59E 50 B6
Lagoa do Peixe △ Brazil 31°12S 50°55W 95 C5
Lagoa Vermelha Brazil 28°13S 51°32W 95 B5
Lagonoy G. Phil. 13°35N 123°50E 37 B6
Lagos Nigeria 6°25N 3°27E 50 G6
Lagos Portugal 37°5N 8°41W 21 D1
Lagos de Moreno
Mexico 21°21N 101°55W 86 C4
Lagrange = Bidyadanga
Australia 18°45S 121°43E 60 C3
Lagrange B. Australia 18°38S 121°42E 60 C3
Laguna Brazil 28°30S 48°50W 95 B6
Laguna U.S.A. 35°2N 107°25W 77 J10
Laguna, Sa. de la
Mexico 23°35N 109°55W 86 C3
Laguna Beach U.S.A. 33°33N 117°47W 79 M9
Laguna de la Restinga △
Venezuela 10°58N 64°0W 89 D6
Laguna de Lachuá △
Guatemala 15°55N 90°40W 88 C1
Laguna del Laja △ Chile 37°27S 71°20W 94 D1
Laguna del Tigre △
Guatemala 17°32N 90°56W 88 C1
Laguna Limpia
Argentina 26°32S 59°45W 94 B4

Lagunas Chile 21°0S 69°45W 94 A2
Lagunas Peru 5°10S 75°35W 92 E3
Lagunas de Chacahua △
Mexico 16°0N 97°43W 87 D5
Lagunas de Montebello △
Mexico 16°4N 91°42W 87 D6
Lahad Datu Malaysia 5°0N 118°20E 37 D5
Lahad Datu, Telok
Malaysia 4°50N 118°20E 37 D5
Lahan Sai Thailand 14°25N 102°52E 38 E4
Lahanam Laos 16°16N 105°16E 38 D5
Lahar India 26°12N 78°57E 43 F8
Laharpur India 27°43N 80°56E 43 F9
Lahat Indonesia 3°45S 103°30E 36 E2
Lahewa Indonesia 1°22N 97°12E 36 D1
Lāhījān Iran 37°10N 50°6E 45 B6
Lahn → Germany 50°19N 7°37E 16 C4
Laholm Sweden 56°30N 13°2E 9 H15
Lahore Pakistan 31°32N 74°22E 42 D6
Lahri Pakistan 29°11N 68°13E 42 E3
Lāhrūd Iran 38°30N 47°52E 44 B5
Lahti Finland 60°58N 25°40E 8 F21
Lahtis = Lahti Finland 60°58N 25°40E 8 F21
Laï Chad 9°25N 16°18E 51 G9
Lai Chau Vietnam 22°5N 103°3E 38 A4
Laila = Layla Si. Arabia 22°10N 46°40E 47 C4
Laingsburg S. Africa 33°9S 20°52E 56 E3
Lainioälven → Sweden 67°35N 22°40E 8 C20
Lairg U.K. 58°2N 4°24W 11 C4
Laisamis Kenya 1°36N 37°48E 54 B4
Laishui China 39°23N 115°45E 34 E8
Laiwu China 36°15N 117°40E 35 F9
Laixi China 36°50N 120°31E 35 F11
Laiyang China 36°59N 120°45E 35 F11
Laiyuan China 39°20N 114°40E 34 E8
Laizhou China 37°8N 119°57E 35 F10
Laizhou Wan China 37°30N 119°30E 35 F10
Laja → Mexico 20°55N 100°46W 86 C4
Lajamanu Australia 18°23S 130°38E 60 C5
Lak Sao Laos 18°11N 104°59E 38 C5
Lakaband Pakistan 31°2N 69°15E 42 D3
Lake U.S.A. 44°33N 110°24W 76 D8
Lake Alpine U.S.A. 38°29N 120°0E 78 G7
Lake Andes U.S.A. 43°9N 98°32W 80 D4
Lake Arthur U.S.A. 30°5N 92°41W 84 F8
Lake Bindegolly △
Australia 28°0S 144°12E 63 D3
Lake Cargelligo
Australia 33°15S 146°22E 63 E4
Lake Charles U.S.A. 30°14N 93°13W 84 F8
Lake City Colo., U.S.A. 38°2N 107°19W 76 G10
Lake City Fla., U.S.A. 30°11N 82°38W 85 F13
Lake City Mich., U.S.A. 44°20N 85°13W 81 C11
Lake City Minn., U.S.A. 44°27N 92°16W 80 C7
Lake City Pa., U.S.A. 42°1N 80°21W 82 D4
Lake City S.C., U.S.A. 33°52N 79°45W 85 E15
Lake Cowichan Canada 48°49N 124°3W 70 D4
Lake District △ U.K. 54°30N 3°21W 12 C4
Lake Elsinore U.S.A. 33°38N 117°20W 79 M9
Lake Eyre △ Australia 28°40S 137°31E 63 D2
Lake Gairdner △
Australia 31°41S 135°51E 63 E2
Lake George U.S.A. 43°26N 73°43W 83 C11
Lake Grace Australia 33°7S 118°28E 61 F2
Lake Harbour = Kimmirut
Canada 62°50N 69°50W 69 C13
Lake Havasu City
U.S.A. 34°27N 114°22W 79 L12
Lake Hughes U.S.A. 34°41N 118°26W 79 L8
Lake Isabella U.S.A. 35°38N 118°28W 79 K8
Lake Jackson U.S.A. 29°3N 95°27W 84 G7
Lake King Australia 33°5S 119°45E 61 F2
Lake Lenore Canada 52°24N 104°59W 71 C8
Lake Louise Canada 51°30N 116°10W 70 C5
Lake Malawi △ Malawi 14°2S 34°53E 55 E3
Lake Mburo △ Uganda 0°33S 30°56E 54 C3
Lake Mead △ U.S.A. 36°30N 114°22W 79 K12
Lake Meredith △
U.S.A. 35°50N 101°50W 84 D4
Lake Mills U.S.A. 43°25N 93°32W 80 D7
Lake Nakura △ Kenya 0°21S 36°8E 54 C4
Lake Placid U.S.A. 44°17N 73°59W 83 B11
Lake Pleasant U.S.A. 43°28N 74°25W 83 C10
Lake Providence U.S.A. 32°48N 91°10W 84 E9
Lake Roosevelt △
U.S.A. 48°5N 118°14W 76 B4
Lake St. Peter Canada 45°18N 78°2W 82 A6
Lake Superior △ Canada 47°45N 84°45W 72 C3
Lake Torrens △
Australia 30°55S 137°40E 63 E2
Lake Village U.S.A. 33°20N 91°17W 84 E9
Lake Wales U.S.A. 27°54N 81°35W 85 H14
Lake Worth U.S.A. 26°37N 80°3W 85 H14
Lakeba Fiji 18°13S 178°47E 59 a
Lakeba Passage Fiji 18°0S 178°45W 59 a
Lakefield Canada 44°25N 78°16W 82 B6
Lakefield △ Australia 15°24S 144°26E 62 B3
Lakehurst U.S.A. 40°1N 74°19W 83 F10
Lakeland Australia 15°49S 144°57E 62 B3
Lakeland U.S.A. 28°3N 81°57W 85 G14
Lakeport Calif., U.S.A. 39°3N 122°55W 78 F4
Lakeport Mich., U.S.A. 43°7N 82°30W 82 C2
Lakes Entrance Australia 37°50S 148°0E 63 F4
Lakeside Calif., U.S.A. 32°52N 116°55W 79 N10
Lakeside Nebr., U.S.A. 42°3N 102°26W 80 D2
Lakeview U.S.A. 42°11N 120°21W 76 E3
Lakeville U.S.A. 44°39N 93°14W 80 C7
Lakewood Colo., U.S.A. 39°42N 105°6W 76 G11
Lakewood N.J., U.S.A. 40°6N 74°13W 83 F10
Lakewood N.Y., U.S.A. 42°6N 79°19W 82 D5
Lakewood Ohio, U.S.A. 41°28N 81°47W 82 E3
Lakewood Wash.
U.S.A. 47°11N 122°32W 78 C4
Lakha India 26°9N 70°54E 42 F4
Lakhimpur India 27°57N 80°46E 43 F9
Lakhisarai India 25°11N 86°5E 43 G12

Lakhnadon India 22°36N 79°36E 43 H8
Lakhnau = Lucknow
India 26°50N 81°0E 43 F9
Lakhonpheng Laos 15°54N 105°34E 38 E5
Lakhpat India 23°48N 68°47E 42 H3
Lakin U.S.A. 37°57N 101°15W 80 G3
Lakitusaki → Canada 54°21N 82°25W 72 B3
Lakki Greece 35°24N 23°57E 25 D5
Lakki Pakistan 32°36N 70°55E 42 C4
Lakonikos Kolpos
Greece 36°40N 22°40E 23 F10
Lakor Indonesia 8°15S 128°17E 37 F7
Lakota Ivory C. 5°50N 5°30W 50 G4
Lakota U.S.A. 48°2N 98°21W 80 A4
Laksefjorden Norway 70°45N 26°50E 8 A22
Lakselv Norway 70°2N 25°0E 8 A21
Lakshadweep Is. India 10°0N 72°30E 3 D13
Lakshmanpur India 22°58N 83°3E 43 H10
Lakshmikantapur India 22°5N 88°20E 43 H13
Lala Musa Pakistan 32°40N 73°57E 42 C5
Lalaghat India 24°30N 92°40E 41 G18
Lalago Tanzania 3°28S 33°58E 54 C3
Lalapanzi Zimbabwe 19°20S 30°15E 55 F3
L'Albufera Spain 39°20N 0°27W 21 C5
Lalganj India 25°52N 85°13E 43 G11
Lalgola India 24°25N 88°15E 43 G13
Lālī Iran 32°21N 49°6E 45 C6
Lalibela Ethiopia 12°3N 39°0E 47 E2
Lalín China 45°12N 127°0E 35 B14
Lalín Spain 42°40N 8°5W 21 A1
Lalín He → China 45°32N 125°40E 35 B13
Lalitapur Nepal 27°40N 85°20E 43 F11
Lalitpur India 24°42N 78°28E 43 G8
Lalkua India 29°5N 79°31E 43 E8
Lam Pao Res. Thailand 16°50N 103°15E 38 D4
Lamae Malaysia 9°51N 99°5E 39 H2
Lamaing Burma 15°25N 97°53E 38 E1
Lamar Colo., U.S.A. 38°5N 102°37W 76 G12
Lamar Mo., U.S.A. 37°30N 94°16W 80 G6
Lamas Peru 6°28S 76°31W 92 E3
Lamayuru India 34°18N 76°46E 43 B7
Lamayuru Jammu & Kashmir,
India 34°35N 76°56E 43 B7
Lambaréné Gabon 0°41S 10°12E 52 E2
Lambasa = Labasa Fiji 16°30S 179°27E 59 a
Lambay I. Ireland 53°29N 6°1W 10 C5
Lambert's Bay S. Africa 32°5S 18°17E 56 E2
Lambeth Canada 42°54N 81°18W 82 D3
Lambomakondro
Madag. 22°41S 44°44E 57 C7
Lambton Shores Canada 43°10N 81°56W 82 C3
Lame Deer U.S.A. 45°37N 106°40W 76 D10
Lamego Portugal 41°5N 7°52W 21 B2
Lameque Canada 47°45N 64°38W 73 C7
Lameroo Australia 35°19S 140°33E 63 F3
Lamesa U.S.A. 32°44N 101°58W 84 E4
Lamia Greece 38°55N 22°26E 23 E10
Lamington △ Australia 28°13S 153°12E 63 D5
Lamma I. China 22°12N 114°7E 33 G11
Lammermuir Hills U.K. 55°50N 2°40W 11 F6
Lamoille → U.S.A. 44°38N 73°13W 83 B11
Lamon B. Phil. 14°30N 122°20E 37 B6
Lamont Canada 53°46N 112°50W 70 C6
Lamont Calif., U.S.A. 35°15N 118°55W 79 K8
Lamont Wyo., U.S.A. 42°13N 107°29W 76 E10
Lampa Peru 15°22S 70°22W 92 G4
Lampang Thailand 18°16N 99°32E 38 C2
Lampasas U.S.A. 31°4N 98°11W 84 F5
Lampazos de Naranjo
Mexico 27°1N 100°31W 86 B4
Lampedusa Medit. S. 35°36N 12°40E 22 G5
Lampeter U.K. 52°7N 4°4W 13 E3
Lampione Medit. S. 35°33N 12°20E 22 G5
Lampman Canada 49°25N 102°50W 71 D8
Lampung □ Indonesia 5°30S 104°30E 36 F2
Lamta India 22°8N 80°7E 43 H9
Lamu Kenya 2°16S 40°55E 54 C5
Lamy U.S.A. 35°29N 105°53W 77 J11
Lan Xian China 38°15N 111°35E 34 E6
Lāna'i U.S.A. 20°50N 156°55W 74 b
Lanak La China 34°27N 79°32E 43 B8
Lanak'o Shank'ou = Lanak La
China 34°27N 79°32E 43 B8
Lanark Canada 45°1N 76°22W 83 A8
Lanark U.K. 55°40N 3°47W 11 F5
Lanbi Kyun Burma 10°50N 98°20E 39 G2
Lancang Jiang →
China 21°40N 101°10E 32 D5
Lancashire □ U.K. 53°50N 2°48W 12 D5
Lancaster Canada 45°10N 74°30W 83 A10
Lancaster U.K. 54°3N 2°48W 12 C5
Lancaster Calif., U.S.A. 34°42N 118°8W 79 L8
Lancaster Ky., U.S.A. 37°37N 84°35W 81 G11
Lancaster N.H., U.S.A. 44°29N 71°34W 83 B13
Lancaster Ohio, U.S.A. 39°43N 82°36W 81 F12
Lancaster Pa., U.S.A. 40°2N 76°19W 83 F8
Lancaster S.C., U.S.A. 34°43N 80°46W 85 D14
Lancaster Sd. Canada 74°13N 84°0W 69 B11
Lancelin Australia 31°0S 115°18E 61 F2
Lanchow = Lanzhou
China 36°1N 103°52E 34 F2
Lanciano Italy 42°14N 14°23E 22 C6
Lancun China 36°25N 120°10E 35 F11
Land Between the Lakes △
U.S.A. 36°25N 88°0W 85 C11
Landeck Austria 47°9N 10°34E 16 E6
Lander U.S.A. 42°50N 108°44W 76 E9
Lander → Australia 22°0S 132°0E 60 D5
Landes France 44°0N 1°0W 20 D3
Landi Kotal Pakistan 34°7N 71°6E 42 B4
Landisburg U.S.A. 40°21N 77°19W 82 F7
Landmannalaugar Iceland 63°59N 19°4W 8 E4
Land's End U.K. 50°4N 5°44W 13 G2
Landsborough Cr. →
Australia 22°28S 144°35E 62 C3

Landshut Germany 48°32N 12°8E **16** D7
Lanesboro U.S.A. 41°57N 75°34W **83** E9
Lanett U.S.A. 32°52N 85°12W **85** E12
Lang Shan China 41°0N 106°30E **34** D4
Lang Son Vietnam 21°52N 106°42E **38** B6
Lang Suan Thailand 9°57N 99°4E **39** H2
La'nga Co China 30°45N 81°15E **43** D9
Langar Iran 35°23N 60°25E **45** C9
Langara I. Canada 54°14N 133°1W **70** C2
Langarūd Iran 37°11N 50°8E **45** B6
Langdon U.S.A. 48°45N 98°22W **80** A4
Langeberg S. Africa 33°55S 21°0E **56** E3
Langeberge S. Africa 28°15S 22°33E **56** D3
Langeland Denmark 54°56N 10°48E **9** J14
Langenburg Canada 50°51N 101°43W **71** C8
Langholm U.K. 55°9N 3°0W **11** F5
Langjökull Iceland 64°39N 20°12W **8** D3
Langkawi, Pulau
  Malaysia 6°25N 99°45E **39** J2
Langklip S. Africa 28°12S 20°20E **56** D3
Langkon Malaysia 6°30N 116°40E **36** C5
Langley Canada 49°7N 122°39W **78** A4
Langøya Norway 68°45N 14°50E **8** B16
Langreo Spain 43°18N 5°40W **21** A3
Langres France 47°52N 5°20E **20** C6
Langres, Plateau de France 47°45N 5°3E **20** C6
Langsa Indonesia 4°30N 97°57E **36** D1
Langtang △ Nepal 28°10N 85°30E **43** E11
Langtry U.S.A. 29°49N 101°34W **84** G4
Langu Thailand 6°53N 99°47E **39** J2
Languedoc France 43°58N 3°55E **20** E5
Langwang China 27°38N 113°27E **33** F9
Langxiangzhen China 39°43N 116°8E **34** E9
Lanigan Canada 51°51N 105°2W **71** C7
Lankao China 34°48N 114°50E **34** G8
Länkäran Azerbaijan 38°48N 48°52E **45** B6
Lannion France 48°46N 3°29W **20** B2
L'Annonciation Canada 46°25N 74°55W **72** C5
Lansdale U.S.A. 40°14N 75°17W **83** F9
Lansdowne Australia 31°48S 152°30E **63** E5
Lansdowne Canada 44°24N 76°1W **83** B8
Lansdowne India 29°50N 78°41E **43** E8
Lansdowne House = Neskantaga
  Canada 52°14N 87°53W **72** B2
L'Anse U.S.A. 46°45N 88°27W **80** B9
L'Anse au Loup Canada 51°32N 56°50W **73** B8
L'Anse aux Meadows
  Canada 51°36N 55°32W **73** B8
L'Anse la Raye St. Lucia 13°55N 61°3W **89** f
Lansford U.S.A. 40°50N 75°53W **83** F9
Lansing U.S.A. 42°44N 84°33W **81** D11
Lanta Yai, Ko Thailand 7°35N 99°3E **39** J2
Lantau I. China 22°15N 113°56E **33** G10
Lantian China 34°11N 109°20E **34** G5
Lanus Argentina 34°42S 58°23W **94** C4
Lanusei Italy 39°52N 9°34E **22** E3
Lanzarote Canary Is. 29°0N 13°40W **24** F6
Lanzarote ✈ (ACE)
  Canary Is. 28°57N 13°40W **24** F6
Lanzhou China 36°1N 103°52E **34** F2
Lao Bao Laos 16°35N 106°30E **38** D6
Lao Cai Vietnam 22°30N 103°57E **38** A4
Laoag Phil. 18°7N 120°34E **37** A6
Laoang Phil. 12°32N 125°8E **37** B7
Laoha He → China 43°25N 120°35E **35** C11
Laois ☐ Ireland 52°57N 7°36W **10** D4
Laon France 49°33N 3°35E **20** B5
Laona U.S.A. 45°34N 88°40W **80** C9
Laos ■ Asia 17°45N 105°0E **38** D5
Lapa Brazil 25°46S 49°44W **95** B6
Lapeer U.S.A. 43°3N 83°19W **81** D12
Lapithos Cyprus 35°21N 33°11E **25** D12
Lapland = Lappland
  Europe 68°7N 24°0E **8** B21
LaPorte Ind., U.S.A. 41°36N 86°43W **80** E10
Laporte Pa., U.S.A. 41°25N 76°30W **83** E8
Lappeenranta Finland 61°3N 28°12E **8** F23
Lappland Europe 68°7N 24°0E **8** B21
Lappo = Lapua Finland 62°58N 23°0E **8** E20
Laprida Argentina 37°34S 60°45W **94** D3
Lâpseki Turkey 40°20N 26°41E **23** D12
Laptev Sea Russia 76°0N 125°0E **29** B13
Lapua Finland 62°58N 23°0E **8** E20
L'Áquila Italy 42°22N 13°22E **22** C5
Lār Iran 27°40N 54°14E **45** E7
Laramie U.S.A. 41°19N 105°35W **76** F11
Laramie Mts. U.S.A. 42°0N 105°30W **76** F11
Laranjeiras do Sul Brazil 25°23S 52°23W **95** B5
Larantuka Indonesia 8°21S 122°55E **37** F6
Larat Indonesia 7°0S 132°0E **37** F8
Larde Mozam. 16°28S 39°43E **55** F4
Larder Lake Canada 48°5N 79°40W **72** C4
Lardos Greece 36°6N 28°1E **25** C10
Lardos, Akra = Lindos, Akra
  Greece 36°4N 28°10E **25** C10
Lardos, Ormos Greece 36°4N 28°2E **25** C10
Lare Kenya 0°20N 37°56E **54** C4
Laredo U.S.A. 27°30N 99°30W **84** H5
Laredo Sd. Canada 52°30N 128°53W **70** C3
Largo U.S.A. 27°54N 82°47W **85** H13
Largs U.K. 55°47N 4°52W **11** F4
Lariang Indonesia 1°26S 119°17E **37** E5
Larimore U.S.A. 47°54N 97°38W **80** B5
Larisa Greece 39°36N 22°27E **23** E10
Larkana Pakistan 27°32N 68°18E **42** F3
Larnaca Cyprus 34°55N 33°38E **25** E12
Larnaca Bay Cyprus 34°53N 33°45E **25** E12
Larne U.K. 54°51N 5°51W **10** B6
Larned U.S.A. 38°11N 99°6W **80** F4
Larose U.S.A. 29°34N 90°23W **85** G9
Larrimah Australia 15°35S 133°12E **60** C5
Larsen Ice Shelf Antarctica 67°0S 62°0W **5** C17
Larvik Norway 59°4N 10°2E **9** G14
Las Animas U.S.A. 38°4N 103°13W **76** G12
Las Anod = Laascaanood
  Somali Rep. 8°26N 47°19E **47** F4
Las Breñas Argentina 27°5S 61°7W **94** B3

Las Cañadas del Teide △
  Canary Is. 28°15N 16°37W **24** F3
Las Cejas Argentina 26°53S 64°44W **96** B4
Las Chimeneas Mexico 32°8N 116°5W **79** N10
Las Cruces U.S.A. 32°19N 106°47W **77** K10
Las Flores Argentina 36°10S 59°7W **94** D4
Las Heras Argentina 32°51S 68°49W **94** C2
Las Lajas Argentina 38°30S 70°25W **96** D2
Las Lomitas Argentina 24°43S 60°35W **94** A3
Las Palmas Argentina 27°8S 58°45W **94** B4
Las Palmas Canary Is. 28°7N 15°26W **24** F4
Las Palmas → Mexico 32°31N 116°58W **79** N10
Las Palmas ✈ (LPA)
  Canary Is. 27°55N 15°25W **24** G4
Las Piedras Uruguay 34°44S 56°14W **95** C4
Las Pipinas Argentina 35°30S 57°19W **94** D4
Las Plumas Argentina 43°40S 67°15W **96** E3
Las Rosas Argentina 32°30S 61°35W **94** C3
Las Tablas Panama 7°49N 80°14W **88** E3
Las Toscas Argentina 28°21S 59°18W **94** B4
Las Truchas Mexico 17°57N 102°13W **86** D4
Las Tunas Cuba 20°58N 76°59W **88** B4
Las Varillas Argentina 31°50S 62°50W **94** C3
Las Vegas N. Mex.,
  U.S.A. 35°36N 105°13W **77** J11
Las Vegas Nev., U.S.A. 36°10N 115°8W **79** J11
Las Vegas McCarran Int. ✈ (LAS)
  U.S.A. 36°5N 115°9W **79** J11
Lascano Uruguay 33°35S 54°12W **95** C5
Lash-e Joveyn Afghan. 31°45N 61°30E **40** D2
Lashburn Canada 53°10N 109°40W **71** C7
Lashio Burma 22°56N 97°45E **41** H20
Lashkar India 26°10N 78°10E **42** F8
Lasithi Greece 35°11N 25°31E **25** D7
Lasithi ☐ Greece 35°5N 25°50E **25** D7
Lāsjerd Iran 35°24N 53°4E **45** C7
Lassen Pk. U.S.A. 40°29N 121°30W **76** F3
Lassen Volcanic △
  U.S.A. 40°30N 121°20W **76** F3
Last Mountain L.
  Canada 51°5N 105°14W **71** C7
Lastchance Cr. →
  U.S.A. 40°2N 121°15W **78** E5
Lastoursville Gabon 0°55S 12°38E **52** E2
Lastovo Croatia 42°46N 16°55E **22** C7
Lat Yao Thailand 15°45N 99°48E **38** E2
Latacunga Ecuador 0°50S 78°35W **92** D3
Latakia = Al Lādhiqiyah
  Syria 35°30N 35°45E **44** C2
Latchford Canada 47°20N 79°50W **72** C4
Late Tonga 18°48S 174°39W **59** c
Latehar India 23°45N 84°30E **43** H11
Latham Australia 29°44S 116°20E **61** E2
Lathi India 27°43N 71°23E **42** F4
Lathrop Wells U.S.A. 36°39N 116°24W **79** J10
Latina Italy 41°28N 12°52E **22** D5
Latium = Lazio ☐ Italy 42°10N 12°30E **22** C5
Laton U.S.A. 36°26N 119°41W **78** J7
Latouche Treville, C.
  Australia 18°27S 121°49E **60** C3
Latrobe Australia 41°14S 146°30E **63** G4
Latrobe U.S.A. 40°19N 79°23W **82** F5
Latvia ■ Europe 56°50N 24°0E **9** H21
Lau Fau Shan China 22°28N 113°59E **33** G10
Lau Group Fiji 17°0S 178°30W **59** a
Lauchhammer Germany 51°29N 13°47E **16** C7
Laughlin U.S.A. 35°10N 114°34W **77** J6
Laukaa Finland 62°24N 25°56E **8** E21
Launceston Australia 41°24S 147°8E **63** G4
Launceston U.K. 50°38N 4°22W **13** G3
Laune → Ireland 52°7N 9°47W **10** D2
Launglon Bok Burma 13°50N 97°54E **38** F1
Laura Australia 15°32S 144°32E **62** B3
Laurel Miss., U.S.A. 31°41N 89°8W **85** F10
Laurel Mont., U.S.A. 45°40N 108°46W **76** D9
Laurel Hill U.S.A. 40°14N 79°6W **82** F5
Laurencekirk U.K. 56°50N 2°28W **11** E6
Laurens U.S.A. 34°30N 82°1W **85** D13
Laurentian Plateau
  Canada 52°0N 70°0W **73** B6
Lauria Italy 40°2N 15°50E **22** E6
Laurie L. Canada 56°35N 101°57W **71** B8
Laurinburg U.S.A. 34°47N 79°28W **85** D15
Laurium U.S.A. 47°14N 88°27W **80** B9
Lausanne Switz. 46°32N 6°38E **20** C7
Laut Indonesia 4°45N 108°0E **36** D3
Laut, Pulau Indonesia 3°40S 116°10E **36** E5
Laut Kecil, Kepulauan
  Indonesia 4°45S 115°40E **36** E5
Lautoka Fiji 17°37S 177°27E **59** a
Lava Beds △ U.S.A. 41°40N 121°30W **76** F3
Lavagh More Ireland 54°46N 8°6W **10** B3
Laval France 48°4N 0°48W **20** B3
Laval-des-Rapides
  Canada 45°33N 73°42W **72** C5
Lavalle Argentina 28°15S 65°15W **94** B2
Lāvān Iran 26°48N 53°22E **45** E7
Lavant Canada 45°3N 76°42E **83** A8
Lavras Brazil 21°20S 45°0W **95** A7
Lavrio Greece 37°40N 24°4E **23** F11
Lavris Greece 35°25N 24°40E **25** D6
Lavumisa Swaziland 27°20S 31°55E **57** D5
Lavushi Manda △ Zambia 12°46S 31°0E **55** E3
Lawaki Fiji 17°38S 178°35E **59** a
Lawas Malaysia 4°55N 115°25E **36** D5
Lawele Indonesia 5°13S 122°57E **37** F6
Lawn Hill = Boodjamulla △
  Australia 18°15S 138°6E **62** B2
Lawqah Si. Arabia 29°49N 42°45E **44** D4
Lawrence N.Z. 45°55S 169°41E **59** F2
Lawrence Ind., U.S.A. 39°50N 86°2W **80** F10
Lawrence Kans., U.S.A. 38°58N 95°14W **80** F6
Lawrence Mass., U.S.A. 42°43N 71°10W **83** D13
Lawrenceburg Ind.,
  U.S.A. 39°6N 84°52W **81** F11

Lawrenceburg Tenn.,
  U.S.A. 35°14N 87°20W **85** D11
Lawrenceville Ga.,
  U.S.A. 33°57N 83°59W **85** E13
Lawrenceville Pa., U.S.A. 41°59N 77°8W **82** E7
Laws U.S.A. 37°24N 118°20W **78** H8
Lawton U.S.A. 34°37N 98°25W **84** H5
Lawu Indonesia 7°40S 111°13E **37** G14
Laxford, L. U.K. 58°24N 5°6W **11** C3
Layla Si. Arabia 22°10N 46°40E **47** C4
Laylān Iraq 35°18N 44°31E **44** C5
Layton U.S.A. 41°4N 111°58W **76** F8
Laytonville U.S.A. 39°41N 123°29W **76** G2
Lazarev Russia 52°13N 141°30E **29** D15
Lazarev Sea S. Ocean 67°30S 3°0W **5** C2
Lazaro Madag. 23°54S 44°59E **57** C7
Lázaro Cárdenas
  Mexico 17°55N 102°11W **86** D4
Lazio ☐ Italy 42°10N 12°30E **22** C5
Lazo Russia 43°25N 133°55E **30** C6
Le Bic Canada 48°20N 68°41W **73** C6
Le Creusot France 46°48N 4°24E **20** C6
Le François Martinique 14°38N 60°57W **88** c
Le Gosier Guadeloupe 16°14N 61°29W **88** b
Le Gris Gris Mauritius 20°31S 57°32E **53** d
Le Havre France 49°30N 0°5E **20** B4
Le Lamentin Martinique 14°35N 61°2W **88** c
Le Mans France 48°0N 0°10E **20** C4
Le Marin Martinique 14°27N 60°55W **88** c
Le Mars U.S.A. 42°47N 96°10W **80** D5
Le Mont-St-Michel
  France 48°40N 1°30W **20** B3
Le Moule Guadeloupe 16°20N 61°22W **88** b
Le Moyne, L. Canada 56°45N 68°47W **73** A6
Le Port Réunion 20°56S 55°18E **53** a
Le Prêcheur Martinique 14°50N 61°12W **88** c
Le Puy-en-Velay France 45°3N 3°52E **20** D5
Le Raysville U.S.A. 41°50N 76°10W **83** E8
Le Robert Martinique 14°40N 60°56W **88** c
Le Roy U.S.A. 42°58N 77°59W **82** D7
Le St-Esprit Martinique 14°34N 60°56W **88** c
Le Sueur U.S.A. 44°28N 93°55W **80** C7
Le Tampon Réunion 21°16S 55°32E **53** c
Le Thuy Vietnam 17°14N 106°49E **38** D6
Le Touquet-Paris-Plage
  France 50°30N 1°36E **20** A4
Le Tréport France 50°3N 1°20E **20** A4
Le Verdon-sur-Mer France 45°33N 1°4W **20** D3
Lea → U.K. 51°31N 0°1E **13** F8
Leach Cambodia 12°21N 103°46E **39** F4
Lead U.S.A. 44°21N 103°46W **80** C2
Leader Canada 50°50N 109°30W **71** C7
Leadville U.S.A. 39°15N 106°18W **76** G10
Leaf → U.S.A. 30°59N 88°44W **85** F10
Leaf Rapids Canada 56°30N 99°59W **71** B9
Leamington Canada 42°3N 82°36W **82** D2
Leamington U.S.A. 39°32N 112°17W **76** G7
Leamington Spa = Royal
  Leamington Spa U.K. 52°18N 1°31W **13** E6
Leandro Norte Alem
  Argentina 27°34S 55°15W **95** B4
Leane, L. Ireland 52°2N 9°32W **10** D2
Learmonth Australia 22°13S 114°10E **60** D1
Leask Canada 53°5N 106°45W **71** C7
Leatherhead U.K. 51°18N 0°20W **13** F7
Leavenworth Kans.,
  U.S.A. 39°19N 94°55W **80** F6
Leavenworth Wash.,
  U.S.A. 47°36N 120°40W **76** C3
Leawood U.S.A. 38°58N 94°37W **80** F6
Lebak Phil. 6°32N 124°5E **37** C6
Lebam U.S.A. 46°34N 123°33W **78** D3
Lebanon Ind., U.S.A. 40°3N 86°28W **80** E10
Lebanon Kans., U.S.A. 39°49N 98°34W **80** F4
Lebanon Ky., U.S.A. 37°34N 85°15W **81** G11
Lebanon Mo., U.S.A. 37°41N 92°40W **80** G7
Lebanon N.H., U.S.A. 43°39N 72°15W **83** C12
Lebanon Oreg., U.S.A. 44°32N 122°55W **76** D2
Lebanon Pa., U.S.A. 40°20N 76°26W **83** F8
Lebanon Tenn., U.S.A. 36°12N 86°18W **85** D11
Lebanon ■ Asia 34°0N 36°0E **46** B5
Lebec U.S.A. 34°51N 118°52W **79** L8
Lebel-sur-Quévillon
  Canada 49°3N 76°59W **72** C4
Lebomboberge S. Africa 24°30S 32°0E **57** C5
Lebork Poland 54°33N 17°46E **17** A9
Lebrija Spain 36°53N 6°5W **21** D2
Lebu Chile 37°40S 73°47W **94** D1
Lecce Italy 40°23N 18°11E **23** D8
Lecco Italy 45°51N 9°23E **20** D8
Lech → Germany 48°43N 10°56E **16** D6
Lecontes Mills U.S.A. 41°5N 78°17W **82** E6
Ledong China 18°41N 109°5E **38** C7
Leduc Canada 53°15N 113°30W **70** C6
Lee U.S.A. 42°19N 73°15W **83** D11
Lee → Ireland 51°53N 8°56W **10** E3
Lee Vining U.S.A. 37°58N 119°7W **78** H7
Leech L. U.S.A. 47°10N 94°24W **80** B6
Leechburg U.S.A. 40°37N 79°36W **82** F5
Leeds U.K. 53°48N 1°33W **12** D6
Leeds U.S.A. 33°33N 86°33W **85** E11
Leek Neths. 53°10N 6°24E **15** A6
Leek U.K. 53°7N 2°1W **12** D5
Leeman Australia 29°57S 114°58E **61** E1
Leeper U.S.A. 41°22N 79°18W **82** E5
Leer Germany 53°13N 7°26E **16** B4
Leesburg U.S.A. 28°49N 81°53W **85** G14
Leesville U.S.A. 31°8N 93°16W **84** F8
Leeton Australia 34°33S 146°23E **63** E4
Leetonia U.S.A. 40°53N 80°45W **82** F4
Leeu Gamka S. Africa 32°47S 21°59E **56** E3
Leeuwarden Neths. 53°15N 5°48E **15** A5
Leeuwin, C. Australia 34°20S 115°9E **61** F2
Leeuwin Naturaliste △
  Australia 34°6S 115°3E **61** F2
Leeward Is. Atl. Oc. 16°30N 63°30W **89** C7

Lefka Cyprus 35°6N 32°51E **25** D11
Lefkada Greece 38°40N 20°43E **23** E9
Lefkimi Greece 39°25N 20°3E **25** B4
Lefkimis, Akra Greece 39°29N 20°4E **25** B4
Lefkoniko Cyprus 35°18N 33°44E **25** D12
Lefroy Canada 44°16N 79°34W **82** B5
Lefroy, L. Australia 31°21S 121°40E **61** F3
Leganés Spain 40°19N 3°45W **21** B4
Legazpi Phil. 13°10N 123°45E **37** B6
Legendre I. Australia 20°22S 116°55E **60** D2
Leghorn = Livorno Italy 43°33N 10°19E **22** C4
Legionowo Poland 52°25N 20°50E **17** B11
Legnago Italy 45°11N 11°18E **22** B4
Legnica Poland 51°12N 16°10E **16** C9
Leh India 34°9N 77°35E **43** B7
Lehigh Acres U.S.A. 26°36N 81°39W **85** H14
Lehighton U.S.A. 40°50N 75°43W **83** F9
Lehututu Botswana 23°54S 21°55E **56** C3
Leiah Pakistan 30°58N 70°58E **42** D4
Leicester U.K. 52°38N 1°8W **13** E6
Leicester City ☐ U.K. 52°38N 1°8E **13** E6
Leicestershire ☐ U.K. 52°41N 1°17W **13** E6
Leichhardt → Australia 17°35S 139°48E **62** B2
Leichhardt Ra. Australia 20°46S 147°40E **62** C4
Leiden Neths. 52°9N 4°30E **15** B4
Leie → Belgium 51°2N 3°45E **15** C3
Leimus Nic. 14°40N 84°3W **88** D3
Leine → Germany 52°43N 9°36E **16** B5
Leinster Australia 27°51S 120°36E **61** E3
Leinster ☐ Ireland 53°3N 7°8W **10** C4
Leinster, Mt. Ireland 52°37N 6°46W **10** D5
Leipzig Germany 51°18N 12°22E **16** C7
Leiria Portugal 39°46N 8°53W **21** C1
Leirvik Norway 59°47N 5°28E **9** G11
Leisler, Mt. Australia 23°23S 129°20E **60** D4
Leith U.K. 55°59N 3°11W **11** F5
Leith Hill U.K. 51°11N 0°22W **13** F7
Leitrim Ireland 54°0N 8°5W **10** B3
Leitrim ☐ Ireland 54°8N 8°0W **10** B4
Leizhou Bandao China 21°0N 110°0E **33** D6
Lek → Neths. 51°54N 4°35E **15** C4
Leka Norway 65°5N 11°35E **8** D14
Leland Mich., U.S.A. 45°1N 85°45W **81** C11
Leland Miss., U.S.A. 33°24N 90°54W **85** E9
Leleque Argentina 42°28S 71°0W **96** E2
Lelystad Neths. 52°30N 5°25E **15** B5
Léman, L. Europe 46°26N 6°30E **20** C7
Lembar Indonesia 8°45S 116°4E **37** K19
Lembuak Indonesia 8°36S 116°11E **37** K19
Lemera
  Dem. Rep. of the Congo 3°0S 28°55E **54** C2
Lemhi Ra. U.S.A. 44°0N 113°0W **76** D7
Lemmer Neths. 52°51N 5°43E **15** B5
Lemmon U.S.A. 45°57N 102°10W **80** C2
Lemon Grove U.S.A. 32°44N 117°1W **79** N9
Lemoore U.S.A. 36°18N 119°46W **78** J7
Lemvig Denmark 56°33N 8°20E **9** H13
Lena → Russia 72°52N 126°40E **29** B13
Lenadoon Pt. Ireland 54°18N 9°3W **10** B2
Lenc Australia 52°2N 9°32W **10** D2
Lenggong Malaysia 5°6N 100°58E **39** K3
Lengua de Vaca, Pta.
  Chile 30°14S 71°38W **94** C1
Lengwe △ Malawi 16°14S 34°45E **55** F3
Leninogorsk Kazakhstan 50°20N 83°30E **28** D9
Leninsk Russia 48°40N 45°15E **19** E8
Leninsk-Kuznetskiy
  Russia 54°44N 86°10E **28** D9
Lenkoran = Länkäran
  Azerbaijan 38°48N 48°52E **45** B6
Lenmalu Indonesia 1°45S 130°15E **37** E8
Lennox U.S.A. 43°21N 96°53W **80** D5
Lennoxville Canada 45°22N 71°51W **83** A13
Lenoir U.S.A. 35°55N 81°32W **85** D14
Lenoir City U.S.A. 35°48N 84°16W **85** D12
Lenore L. Canada 52°30N 104°59W **71** C8
Lenox U.S.A. 42°22N 73°17W **83** D11
Lens France 50°26N 2°50E **20** A5
Lensk Russia 60°48N 114°55E **29** C12
Lentas Greece 34°56N 24°56E **25** E6
Lentini Italy 37°17N 15°0E **22** F6
Lenwood U.S.A. 34°53N 117°7W **79** L9
Lenya Burma 11°33N 98°57E **39** G2
Leoben Austria 47°22N 15°5E **16** E8
Leodhas = Lewis U.K. 58°9N 6°40W **11** C2
Leola U.S.A. 45°43N 98°56W **80** C4
Leominster U.K. 52°14N 2°43W **13** E5
Leominster U.S.A. 42°32N 71°46W **83** D13
León Mexico 21°6N 101°41W **86** C4
León Nic. 12°20N 86°51W **88** D2
León Spain 42°38N 5°34W **21** A3
León → Spain 40°44N 93°45W **80** E7
León → U.S.A. 31°14N 97°28W **84** F6
León, Montes de Spain 42°30N 6°18W **21** A2
Leonardtown U.S.A. 38°17N 76°38W **81** F15
Leonardville Namibia 23°29S 18°49E **56** C2
Leone Amer. Samoa 14°23S 170°48W **59** b
Leongatha Australia 38°30S 145°58E **63** F4
Leonora Australia 28°49S 121°19E **61** E3
Leopoldina Brazil 21°28S 42°40W **95** A7
Leopoldsburg Belgium 51°7N 5°13E **15** C5
Leoti U.S.A. 38°29N 101°21W **80** F3
Leova Moldova 46°28N 28°15E **17** E15
Leoville Canada 53°39N 107°33W **71** C7
Lepel = Lyepyel Belarus 54°50N 28°40E **9** J23
Lépo, L. do Angola 17°0S 19°0E **56** B2
Leppävirta Finland 62°29N 27°46E **8** E22
Leptis Magna Libya 32°40N 14°12E **51** B8
Leribe Lesotho 28°51S 28°3E **57** D4
Lérida = Lleida Spain 41°37N 0°39E **21** B6
Lerwick U.K. 60°9N 1°9W **11** A7
Les Cayes Haiti 18°15N 73°46W **89** C5
Les Coteaux Canada 45°15N 74°13W **83** A10
Les Escoumins Canada 48°21N 69°24W **73** C6
Les Sables-d'Olonne
  France 46°30N 1°45W **20** C3
Lesbos Greece 39°10N 26°20E **23** E12
Leshan China 29°33N 103°41E **32** D5

Leshukonskoye Russia 64°54N 45°46E **18** B8
Leshwe △
  Dem. Rep. of the Congo 12°45S 29°30E **55** E2
Leskov I. Antarctica 56°0S 28°0W **5** B1
Leskovac Serbia 43°0N 21°58E **23** C9
Lesopilnoye Russia 46°44N 134°20E **30** A7
Lesotho ■ Africa 29°40S 28°0E **57** D4
Lesozavodsk Russia 45°30N 133°29E **30** B6
Lesse → Belgium 50°15N 4°54E **15** D4
Lesse et Lomme △ Belgium 50°8N 5°9E **15** D5
Lesser Antilles W. Indies 15°0N 61°0W **89** D7
Lesser Slave L. Canada 55°30N 115°25W **70** B5
Lesser Sunda Is. Indonesia 8°0S 120°0E **37** F6
Lessines Belgium 50°42N 3°50E **15** D3
Lester B. Pearson Int., Toronto ✈
  (YYZ) Canada 43°46N 79°35W **82** C5
Lestock Canada 51°19N 103°59W **71** C8
Lesuer I. Australia 13°50S 127°17E **60** B4
Lesueur △ Australia 30°11S 115°10E **61** F2
Lésvos = Lesbos Greece 39°10N 26°20E **23** E12
Leszno Poland 51°50N 16°30E **16** C9
Letaba S. Africa 23°59S 31°50E **57** C5
Letchworth U.K. 51°59N 0°13W **13** F7
Lethbridge Canada 49°45N 112°45W **70** D6
Lethem Guyana 3°20N 59°50W **92** C7
Leti, Kepulauan Indonesia 8°10S 128°0E **37** F7
Leti Is. = Leti, Kepulauan
  Indonesia 8°10S 128°0E **37** F7
Letiahau → Botswana 21°16S 24°0E **56** C3
Leticia Colombia 4°9S 70°0W **92** D5
Leting China 39°23N 118°55E **35** E10
Letjiesbos S. Africa 32°34S 22°16E **56** E3
Letlhakane Botswana 21°27S 25°30E **56** C4
Letlhakeng Botswana 24°0S 24°59E **56** C3
Letpadan Burma 17°45N 95°45E **41** L19
Letpan Burma 19°28N 94°10E **41** K19
Letsôk-aw Kyun Burma 11°30N 98°25E **39** G2
Letterkenny Ireland 54°57N 7°45W **10** B4
Leucadia U.S.A. 33°4N 117°18W **79** M9
Leuchars U.K. 56°24N 2°53W **11** E6
Leuser, G. Indonesia 3°46N 97°12E **36** D1
Leuven Belgium 50°52N 4°42E **15** D4
Leuze-en-Hainaut
  Belgium 50°36N 3°37E **15** D3
Levanger Norway 63°45N 11°19E **8** E14
Levelland U.S.A. 33°35N 102°23W **84** E3
Leven U.K. 56°12N 3°0W **11** E6
Leven, L. U.K. 56°12N 3°22W **11** E5
Leven, Toraka Madag. 12°30S 47°45E **57** A8
Leveque C. Australia 16°20S 123°0E **60** C3
Levice Slovak Rep. 48°13N 18°35E **17** D10
Levin N.Z. 40°37S 175°18E **59** D5
Lévis Canada 46°48N 71°9W **73** C5
Levis, L. Canada 62°37N 117°58W **70** A5
Levittown N.Y., U.S.A. 40°44N 73°31W **83** F11
Levittown Pa., U.S.A. 40°9N 74°51W **83** F10
Levka Oros Greece 35°18N 24°3E **25** D6
Levkás = Lefkada Greece 38°40N 20°43E **23** E9
Levkôsia = Nicosia
  Cyprus 35°10N 33°25E **25** D12
Levskigrad = Karlovo
  Bulgaria 42°38N 24°47E **23** C11
Levuka Fiji 17°34S 179°0E **59** a
Lewes U.K. 50°52N 0°1E **13** G8
Lewes U.S.A. 38°46N 75°9W **81** F16
Lewis U.K. 58°9N 6°40W **11** C2
Lewis → U.S.A. 45°51N 122°48W **78** E4
Lewis, Butt of U.K. 58°31N 6°16W **11** C2
Lewis Ra. Australia 20°3S 128°50E **60** D4
Lewis Range U.S.A. 48°5N 113°5W **76** B7
Lewis Run U.S.A. 41°52N 78°40W **82** E6
Lewisburg Pa., U.S.A. 40°58N 76°54W **82** F8
Lewisburg Tenn., U.S.A. 35°27N 86°48W **85** D11
Lewisburg W. Va.,
  U.S.A. 37°48N 80°27W **81** G13
Lewisporte Canada 49°15N 55°3W **73** C8
Lewiston Idaho, U.S.A. 46°25N 117°1W **76** C5
Lewiston Maine, U.S.A. 44°6N 70°13W **81** C18
Lewiston N.Y., U.S.A. 43°11N 79°3W **82** C5
Lewistown Mont., U.S.A. 47°4N 109°26W **76** C9
Lewistown Pa., U.S.A. 40°36N 77°34W **82** F7
Lexington Ill., U.S.A. 40°39N 88°47W **80** E9
Lexington Ky., U.S.A. 38°3N 84°30W **81** F11
Lexington Mich., U.S.A. 43°16N 82°32W **82** C2
Lexington Mo., U.S.A. 39°11N 93°52W **80** F7
Lexington N.C., U.S.A. 35°49N 80°15W **85** D14
Lexington Nebr., U.S.A. 40°47N 99°45W **80** E4
Lexington Ohio, U.S.A. 40°41N 82°35W **82** F2
Lexington Tenn., U.S.A. 35°39N 88°24W **85** D10
Lexington Va., U.S.A. 37°47N 79°27W **81** G14
Lexington Park U.S.A. 38°16N 76°27W **81** F15
Leyburn U.K. 54°19N 1°48W **12** C6
Leyland U.K. 53°42N 2°43W **12** D5
Leyte ☐ Phil. 11°0N 125°0E **37** B7
Leyte Gulf Phil. 10°50N 125°25E **37** B7
Lezhë Albania 41°47N 19°39E **23** D8
Lhasa China 29°25N 90°58E **32** D4
Lhazê China 29°5N 87°38E **32** D3
Lhokkruet Indonesia 4°55N 95°24E **36** D1
Lhokseumawe Indonesia 5°10N 97°10E **36** C1
L'Hospitalet de Llobregat
  Spain 41°21N 2°6E **21** B7
Li Thailand 17°48N 98°57E **38** D2
Li Xian Gansu, China 34°10N 105°5E **34** G3
Li Xian Hebei, China 38°30N 115°35E **34** E8
Liancourt Rocks = Tokdo
  Asia 37°15N 131°52E **31** F5
Lianga Phil. 8°38N 126°6E **37** C7
Liangcheng Nei Monggol Zizhiqu,
  China 40°28N 112°25E **34** D7
Liangcheng Shandong,
  China 35°32N 119°37E **35** G10
Liangdang China 33°56N 106°18E **34** H4
Liangpran Indonesia 1°4N 114°23E **36** D4
Lianshanguan China 40°53N 123°43E **35** D12
Lianshui China 33°42N 119°20E **35** H10

Lianyungang China 34°40N 119°11E 35 G10
Liao He → China 41°0N 121°50E 35 D11
Liaocheng China 36°28N 115°58E 34 F8
Liaodong Bandao China 40°0N 122°30E 35 E12
Liaodong Wan China 40°20N 121°10E 35 D11
Liaoning □ China 41°40N 122°30E 35 D12
Liaotung, G. of = Liaodong Wan China 40°20N 121°10E 35 D11
Liaoyang China 41°15N 122°58E 35 D12
Liaoyuan China 42°58N 125°2E 35 C13
Liaozhong China 41°23N 122°50E 35 D12
Liapades Greece 39°42N 19°40E 25 A3
Liard → Canada 61°51N 121°18W 70 A4
Liard River Canada 59°25N 126°5W 70 B3
Liari Pakistan 25°37N 66°30E 42 G2
Libau = Liepāja Latvia 56°30N 21°0E 9 H19
Libby U.S.A. 48°23N 115°33W 76 B6
Libenge Dem. Rep. of the Congo 3°40N 18°55E 52 D3
Liberal U.S.A. 37°3N 100°55W 80 G3
Liberec Czech Rep. 50°47N 15°7E 16 C8
Liberia Costa Rica 10°40N 85°30W 88 D2
Liberia ■ W. Afr. 6°30N 9°30W 50 G4
Libertador □ Chile 34°15S 70°45W 94 C1
Liberty Mo., U.S.A. 39°15N 94°25W 80 F6
Liberty N.Y., U.S.A. 41°48N 74°45W 83 E10
Liberty Pa., U.S.A. 41°34N 77°6W 82 E7
Liberty Tex., U.S.A. 30°3N 94°48W 84 F7
Liberty-Newark Int. ✈ (EWR) U.S.A. 40°42N 74°10W 83 F10
Lîbîya, Sahrâ' Africa 25°0N 25°0E 51 C10
Libobo, Tanjung Indonesia 0°54S 128°28E 37 E7
Libode S. Africa 31°33S 29°2E 57 E4
Libong, Ko Thailand 7°15N 99°23E 39 J2
Libourne France 44°55N 0°14W 20 D3
Libramont Belgium 49°55N 5°23E 15 E5
Libreville Gabon 0°25N 9°26E 52 D1
Libya ■ N. Afr. 27°0N 17°0E 51 C9
Libyan Desert = Lîbîya, Sahrâ' Africa 25°0N 25°0E 51 C10
Libyan Plateau = Ed Déffa Egypt 30°40N 26°30E 51 B11
Licantén Chile 35°55S 72°0W 94 D1
Licata Italy 37°6N 13°56E 22 F5
Licheng China 36°28N 113°20E 34 F7
Lichfield U.K. 52°41N 1°49W 13 E6
Lichinga Mozam. 13°13S 35°11E 55 E4
Lichtenburg S. Africa 26°8S 26°8E 56 D4
Licking → U.S.A. 39°6N 84°30W 81 F11
Licungo → Mozam. 17°40S 37°15E 55 F4
Lida Belarus 53°53N 25°15E 17 B13
Lidköping Sweden 58°31N 13°7E 9 G15
Liebig, Mt. Australia 23°18S 131°22E 60 D5
Liechtenstein ■ Europe 47°8N 9°35E 20 C8
Liège Belgium 50°38N 5°35E 15 D5
Liège □ Belgium 50°32N 5°35E 15 D5
Liegnitz = Legnica Poland 51°12N 16°10E 16 C9
Lieksa Finland 63°18N 30°2E 8 E24
Lienart Dem. Rep. of the Congo 3°3N 25°31E 54 B2
Lienyünchiangshih = Lianyungang China 34°40N 119°11E 35 G10
Lienz Austria 46°50N 12°46E 16 E7
Liepāja Latvia 56°30N 21°0E 9 H19
Lier Belgium 51°7N 4°34E 15 C4
Lietuva = Lithuania ■ Europe 55°30N 24°0E 9 J21
Lièvre → Canada 45°31N 75°26W 72 C4
Liffey → Ireland 53°21N 6°13W 10 C5
Lifford Ireland 54°51N 7°29W 10 B4
Lifudzin Russia 44°21N 134°58E 30 B7
Lightning Ridge Australia 29°22S 148°0E 63 D4
Ligonha → Mozam. 16°54S 39°9E 55 F4
Ligonier U.S.A. 40°15N 79°14W 82 F5
Liguria □ Italy 44°30N 8°50E 20 D8
Ligurian Sea Medit. S. 43°20N 9°0E 22 C3
Lihou Reefs and Cays Australia 17°25S 151°40E 62 B5
Lihue U.S.A. 21°59N 159°23W 74 b
Lihué Calel △ Argentina 38°0S 65°10W 94 D2
Lijiang China 26°55N 100°20E 32 D5
Likasi Dem. Rep. of the Congo 10°55S 26°48E 55 E2
Likoma I. Malawi 12°3S 34°45E 55 E3
Likumburu Tanzania 9°43S 35°8E 55 D4
L'Île-Rousse France 42°38N 8°57E 20 E8
Lille France 50°38N 3°3E 20 A5
Lille Bælt Denmark 55°20N 9°45E 9 J13
Lillehammer Norway 61°8N 10°30E 8 F14
Lillesand Norway 58°15N 8°23E 9 G13
Lillian Pt. Australia 27°40S 126°6E 61 E4
Lillooet Canada 50°44N 121°57W 70 C4
Lillooet → Canada 49°15N 121°57W 70 D4
Lilongwe Malawi 14°0S 33°48E 55 E3
Liloy Phil. 8°4N 122°39E 37 C6
Lim → Europe 43°45N 19°15E 23 C8
Lim Chu Kang Singapore 1°26N 103°43E 39 d
Lima Indonesia 3°39S 127°58E 37 E7
Lima Peru 12°3S 77°2W 92 F3
Lima Mont., U.S.A. 44°38N 112°36W 76 D7
Lima N.Y., U.S.A. 42°54N 77°36W 82 D7
Lima Ohio, U.S.A. 40°44N 84°6W 81 E11
Lima → Portugal 41°41N 8°50W 21 B1
Liman Indonesia 7°48S 111°45E 37 G14
Limassol Cyprus 34°42N 33°1E 25 E12
Limavady U.K. 55°3N 6°56W 10 A5
Limay → Argentina 39°0S 68°0W 96 D3
Limay Mahuida Argentina 37°10S 66°45W 94 D2
Limbang Brunei 4°42N 115°6E 36 D5
Limbaži Latvia 57°31N 24°42E 9 H21
Limbdi India 22°34N 71°51E 42 H4
Limbe Cameroon 4°1N 9°10E 52 D1
Limburg Germany 50°22N 8°4E 16 C5
Limburg □ Belgium 51°2N 5°25E 15 C5
Limburg □ Neths. 51°20N 5°55E 15 C5
Limeira Brazil 22°35S 47°28W 95 A6
Limerick Ireland 52°40N 8°37W 10 D3
Limerick U.S.A. 43°41N 70°48W 83 C14
Limerick □ Ireland 52°30N 8°50W 10 D3
Limestone U.S.A. 42°2N 78°38W 82 D6
Limestone → Canada 56°31N 94°7W 71 B10
Limfjorden Denmark 56°55N 9°0E 9 H13
Limia = Lima → Portugal 41°41N 8°50W 21 B1
Limingen Norway 64°48N 13°35E 8 D15
Limmen Bight Australia 14°40S 135°35E 62 A2
Limmen Bight → Australia 15°7S 135°44E 62 B2
Limnos Greece 39°50N 25°5E 23 E11
Limoges Canada 45°20N 75°16W 83 A9
Limoges France 45°50N 1°15E 20 D4
Limón Costa Rica 10°0N 83°2W 88 E3
Limon U.S.A. 39°16N 103°41W 76 G12
Limousin □ France 45°30N 1°30E 20 D4
Limoux France 43°4N 2°12E 20 E5
Limpopo □ S. Africa 24°5S 29°0E 57 C4
Limpopo → Africa 25°5S 33°30E 57 D5
Limuru Kenya 1°2S 36°35E 54 C4
Lin Xian China 37°57N 110°58E 34 F6
Linares Chile 35°50S 71°40W 94 D1
Linares Mexico 24°52N 99°34W 87 C5
Linares Spain 38°10N 3°40W 21 C4
Lincang China 23°58N 100°1E 32 D5
Lincheng China 37°25N 114°30E 34 F8
Lincoln = Beamsville Canada 43°12N 79°28W 82 C5
Lincoln Argentina 34°55S 61°30W 94 C3
Lincoln N.Z. 43°38S 172°30E 59 E4
Lincoln U.K. 53°14N 0°32W 12 D7
Lincoln Calif., U.S.A. 38°54N 121°17W 78 G5
Lincoln Ill., U.S.A. 40°9N 89°22W 80 E9
Lincoln Kans., U.S.A. 39°3N 98°9W 80 F4
Lincoln Maine, U.S.A. 45°22N 68°30W 81 C19
Lincoln N.H., U.S.A. 44°3N 71°40W 83 B13
Lincoln N. Mex., U.S.A. 33°30N 105°23W 77 K11
Lincoln Nebr., U.S.A. 40°49N 96°41W 80 E5
Lincoln City U.S.A. 44°57N 124°1W 76 D1
Lincoln Hav = Lincoln Sea Arctic 84°0N 55°0W 66 A14
Lincoln Sea Arctic 84°0N 55°0W 66 A14
Lincolnshire □ U.K. 53°14N 0°32W 12 D7
Lincolnshire Wolds U.K. 53°26N 0°13W 12 D7
Lincolnton U.S.A. 35°29N 81°16W 85 D14
Lind U.S.A. 46°58N 118°37W 76 C4
Linda U.S.A. 39°8N 121°34W 78 F5
Lindeman I. Australia 20°27S 149°3E 62 J7
Linden Guyana 6°0N 58°10W 92 B7
Linden Ala., U.S.A. 32°18N 87°48W 85 E11
Linden Calif., U.S.A. 38°1N 121°5W 78 G5
Linden Tex., U.S.A. 33°1N 94°22W 84 E7
Lindenhurst U.S.A. 40°41N 73°23W 83 F11
Lindesnes Norway 57°58N 7°3E 9 H12
Lindi Tanzania 9°58S 39°38E 55 D4
Lindi □ Tanzania 9°40S 38°30E 55 D4
Lindi → Dem. Rep. of the Congo 0°33N 25°5E 54 B2
Lindley U.S.A. 42°1N 77°8W 82 D7
Lindos Greece 36°6N 28°4E 25 C10
Lindos, Akra Greece 36°4N 28°10E 25 C10
Lindsay Canada 44°22N 78°43W 82 B6
Lindsay Calif., U.S.A. 36°12N 119°5W 78 J7
Lindsay Okla., U.S.A. 34°50N 97°38W 84 D6
Lindsborg U.S.A. 38°35N 97°40W 80 F5
Line Islands Pac. Oc. 7°0N 160°0W 65 H12
Linesville U.S.A. 41°39N 80°26W 82 E4
Linfen China 36°3N 111°30E 34 F6
Ling Xian China 37°22N 116°30E 34 F9
Lingao China 19°56N 109°42E 38 C7
Lingayen Phil. 16°1N 120°14E 37 A6
Lingayen G. Phil. 16°10N 120°15E 37 A6
Lingbi China 33°33N 117°33E 35 H9
Lingchuan China 35°45N 113°12E 34 G7
Lingding Yang China 22°25N 113°44E 33 G10
Lingen Germany 52°31N 7°19E 16 B4
Lingga Indonesia 0°12S 104°37E 36 E2
Lingga, Kepulauan Indonesia 0°10S 104°30E 36 E2
Lingga Arch. = Lingga, Kepulauan Indonesia 0°10S 104°30E 36 E2
Lingle U.S.A. 42°8N 104°21W 76 E11
Lingqiu China 39°28N 114°22E 34 E8
Lingshi China 36°48N 111°48E 34 F6
Lingshou China 38°20N 114°20E 34 E8
Lingshui China 18°27N 110°0E 38 C8
Lingtai China 35°0N 107°40E 34 G4
Linguère Senegal 15°25N 15°5W 50 E2
Lingwu China 38°6N 106°20E 34 E4
Lingyuan China 41°10N 119°15E 35 D10
Linhai China 28°50N 121°8E 33 D7
Linhares Brazil 19°25S 40°4W 93 G10
Linhe China 40°48N 107°20E 34 D4
Linjiang China 41°50N 127°0E 35 D14
Linköping Sweden 58°28N 15°36E 9 G16
Linkou China 45°15N 130°18E 35 B16
Linnhe, L. U.K. 56°36N 5°25W 11 E3
Linosa Medit. S. 35°51N 12°50E 22 G5
Linqi China 35°45N 113°52E 34 G7
Linqing China 36°50N 115°42E 34 F8
Linqu China 36°25N 118°30E 35 F10
Linru China 34°11N 112°52E 34 G7
Lins Brazil 21°40S 49°44W 95 A6
Linstead Jamaica 18°8N 77°2W 88 a
Linta → Madag. 25°2S 44°5E 57 D7
Linton Ind., U.S.A. 39°2N 87°10W 80 F10
Linton N. Dak., U.S.A. 46°16N 100°14W 80 B3
Lintong China 34°20N 109°10E 34 G5
Linwood Canada 43°35N 80°43W 82 C4
Linxi China 43°36N 118°2E 35 C10
Linxia China 35°36N 103°10E 32 C5
Linyanti → Africa 17°50S 25°5E 56 B4
Linyi China 35°5N 118°21E 35 G10
Linz Austria 48°18N 14°18E 16 D8
Linzhenzhen China 36°30N 109°59E 34 F5
Linzi China 36°50N 118°20E 35 F10
Lion, G. du France 43°10N 4°0E 20 E6
Lionárisso Cyprus 35°28N 34°8E 25 D13
Lions, G. of = Lion, G. du France 43°10N 4°0E 20 E6
Lion's Den Zimbabwe 17°15S 30°5E 55 F3
Lion's Head Canada 44°58N 81°15W 82 B3
Lipa Phil. 13°57N 121°10E 37 B6
Lipali Mozam. 15°50S 35°50E 55 F4
Lípari Italy 38°26N 14°58E 22 E6
Lípari, Is. = Eólie, Ís. Italy 38°30N 14°57E 22 E6
Lipcani Moldova 48°14N 26°48E 17 D14
Liperi Finland 62°31N 29°24E 8 E23
Lipetsk Russia 52°37N 39°35E 18 D6
Lipkany = Lipcani Moldova 48°14N 26°48E 17 D14
Lipovets Ukraine 49°12N 29°1E 17 D15
Lippe → Germany 51°39N 6°36E 16 C4
Lipscomb U.S.A. 36°14N 100°16W 84 C4
Liptrap, C. Australia 38°50S 145°55E 63 F4
Lira Uganda 2°17N 32°57E 54 B3
Liria = Lliria Spain 39°37N 0°35W 21 C5
Lisala Dem. Rep. of the Congo 2°12N 21°38E 52 D4
Lisboa Portugal 38°42N 9°8W 21 C1
Lisbon = Lisboa Portugal 38°42N 9°8W 21 C1
Lisbon N. Dak., U.S.A. 46°27N 97°41W 80 B5
Lisbon N.H., U.S.A. 44°13N 71°55W 83 B13
Lisbon N.Y., U.S.A. 44°43N 75°19W 83 B9
Lisbon Ohio, U.S.A. 40°46N 80°46W 82 F4
Lisbon Falls U.S.A. 44°0N 70°4W 81 D18
Lisburn U.K. 54°31N 6°3W 10 B5
Lisburne, C. U.S.A. 68°53N 166°13W 4 C17
Liscannor B. Ireland 52°55N 9°24W 10 D2
Lisdoonvarna Ireland 53°2N 9°18W 10 C2
Lishi China 37°31N 111°8E 34 F6
Lishu China 43°20N 124°18E 35 C13
Lisianski I. U.S.A. 26°2N 174°0W 64 E10
Lisichansk = Lysychansk Ukraine 48°55N 38°30E 19 E6
Lisieux France 49°10N 0°12E 20 B4
Liski Russia 51°3N 39°30E 19 D6
Lismore Australia 28°44S 153°21E 63 D5
Lismore Ireland 52°8N 7°55W 10 D4
Lista Norway 58°7N 6°39E 9 G12
Lister, Mt. Antarctica 78°0S 162°0E 5 D11
Liston Australia 28°39S 152°6E 63 D5
Listowel Canada 43°44N 80°58W 82 C4
Listowel Ireland 52°27N 9°29W 10 D2
Litani → Lebanon 33°20N 35°15E 46 B4
Litchfield Calif., U.S.A. 40°24N 120°23W 78 E6
Litchfield Conn., U.S.A. 41°45N 73°11W 83 E11
Litchfield Ill., U.S.A. 39°11N 89°39W 80 F9
Litchfield Minn., U.S.A. 45°8N 94°32W 80 C6
Litchfield △ Australia 13°14S 131°1E 60 B5
Lithgow Australia 33°25S 150°8E 63 E5
Líthino, Akra Greece 34°55N 24°44E 25 E6
Lithuania ■ Europe 55°30N 24°0E 9 J21
Lititz U.S.A. 40°9N 76°18W 83 F8
Litoměřice Czech Rep. 50°33N 14°10E 16 C8
Little Abaco Bahamas 26°50N 77°30W 88 A4
Little Barrier I. N.Z. 36°12S 175°8E 59 B5
Little Belt Mts. U.S.A. 46°40N 110°45W 76 C8
Little Bighorn Battlefield ⌂ U.S.A. 45°34N 107°25W 76 D10
Little Blue → U.S.A. 39°42N 96°41W 80 F5
Little Buffalo → Canada 61°0N 113°46W 70 A6
Little Cayman Cayman Is. 19°41N 80°3W 88 C3
Little Churchill → Canada 57°30N 95°22W 71 B9
Little Colorado → U.S.A. 36°12N 111°48W 77 H8
Little Current Canada 45°55N 82°0W 72 C3
Little Current → Canada 50°57N 84°36W 72 B3
Little Falls Minn., U.S.A. 45°59N 94°22W 80 C6
Little Falls N.Y., U.S.A. 43°3N 74°51W 83 C10
Little Fork → U.S.A. 48°31N 93°35W 80 A7
Little Grand Rapids Canada 52°0N 95°29W 71 C9
Little Humboldt → U.S.A. 41°1N 117°43W 76 F5
Little Inagua I. Bahamas 21°40N 73°50W 89 B5
Little Karoo S. Africa 33°45S 21°0E 56 E3
Little Khingan Mts. = Xiao Hinggan Ling China 49°0N 127°0E 33 B7
Little Lake U.S.A. 35°56N 117°55W 79 K9
Little Laut Is. = Laut Kecil, Kepulauan Indonesia 4°45S 115°40E 36 E5
Little Mecatina = Petit-Mécatina → Canada 50°40N 59°30W 73 B8
Little Minch U.K. 57°35N 6°45W 11 D2
Little Missouri → U.S.A. 47°36N 102°25W 80 B2
Little Ouse → U.K. 52°22N 1°12E 13 E9
Little Rann India 23°25N 71°25E 42 H4
Little Red → U.S.A. 35°11N 91°27W 84 D9
Little River N.Z. 43°45S 172°49E 59 E4
Little Rock U.S.A. 34°45N 92°17W 84 D8
Little Ruaha → Tanzania 7°57S 37°53E 54 D4
Little Sable Pt. U.S.A. 43°38N 86°33W 80 D10
Little Sioux → U.S.A. 41°48N 96°4W 80 E5
Little Smoky → Canada 54°44N 117°11W 70 C5
Little Snake → U.S.A. 40°27N 108°26W 76 F9
Little Tobago Trin. & Tob. 11°18N 60°30W 93 J16
Little Valley U.S.A. 42°15N 78°48W 82 D6
Little Wabash → U.S.A. 37°55N 88°5W 80 G9
Little White → U.S.A. 43°40N 100°40W 80 D3
Little Zab = Zāb aş Şaghīr → Iraq 35°17N 43°29E 44 C4
Littlefield U.S.A. 33°55N 102°20W 84 E3
Littlehampton U.K. 50°49N 0°32W 13 G7
Littleton U.S.A. 44°18N 71°46W 83 B13
Liu He → China 40°55N 121°35E 35 D11
Liuba China 33°38N 106°55E 34 H4
Liugou China 40°57N 118°15E 35 D10
Liuhe China 42°17N 125°43E 35 C13
Liukang Tenggaja = Sabalana, Kepulauan Indonesia 6°45S 118°50E 37 F5
Liuli Tanzania 11°3S 34°38E 55 E3
Liupanshui China 26°38N 104°48E 32 D5
Liuwa Plain Zambia 14°20S 22°30E 53 G4
Liuzhou China 24°22N 109°22E 33 D5
Liuzhuang China 33°12N 120°18E 35 H11
Livadhia Cyprus 34°57N 33°38E 25 E12
Livadia Greece 38°27N 22°54E 23 E10
Live Oak Calif., U.S.A. 39°17N 121°40W 78 F5
Live Oak Fla., U.S.A. 30°18N 82°59W 85 F13
Lively Canada 46°26N 81°9W 81 B13
Liveras Cyprus 35°23N 32°57E 25 D11
Livermore U.S.A. 37°41N 121°47W 78 H5
Livermore, Mt. U.S.A. 30°38N 104°11W 84 F2
Livermore Falls U.S.A. 44°29N 70°11W 81 C18
Liverpool Australia 33°54S 150°58E 63 B5
Liverpool Canada 44°5N 64°41W 73 D7
Liverpool U.K. 53°25N 3°0W 12 D4
Liverpool U.S.A. 43°6N 76°13W 83 C8
Liverpool Bay U.K. 53°30N 3°20W 12 D4
Liverpool Ra. Australia 31°50S 150°30E 63 E5
Livingston Guatemala 15°50N 88°50W 88 C2
Livingston U.K. 55°54N 3°30W 11 F5
Livingston Ala., U.S.A. 32°35N 88°11W 85 E10
Livingston Calif., U.S.A. 37°23N 120°43W 78 H6
Livingston Mont., U.S.A. 45°40N 110°34W 76 D8
Livingston S.C., U.S.A. 33°38N 81°7W 85 E14
Livingston Tenn., U.S.A. 36°23N 85°19W 85 C12
Livingston Tex., U.S.A. 30°43N 94°56W 84 F7
Livingston, L. U.S.A. 30°50N 95°10W 84 F7
Livingston Manor U.S.A. 41°54N 74°50W 83 E10
Livingstone Zambia 17°46S 25°52E 55 F2
Livingstone Mts. Tanzania 9°40S 34°20E 55 D3
Livingstonia Malawi 10°38S 34°5E 55 E3
Livny Russia 52°30N 37°30E 18 D6
Livonia Mich., U.S.A. 42°23N 83°23W 81 D12
Livonia N.Y., U.S.A. 42°49N 77°40W 82 D7
Livorno Italy 43°33N 10°19E 22 C4
Livramento Brazil 30°55S 55°30W 95 C4
Liwale Tanzania 9°48S 37°58E 55 D4
Liwonde △ Malawi 14°48S 35°20E 55 E4
Lizard I. Australia 14°42S 145°30E 62 A4
Lizard Pt. U.K. 49°57N 5°13W 13 H2
Ljubljana Slovenia 46°4N 14°33E 16 E8
Ljungan → Sweden 62°18N 17°23E 8 E17
Ljungby Sweden 56°49N 13°55E 9 H15
Ljusdal Sweden 61°46N 16°3E 8 F17
Ljusnan → Sweden 61°12N 17°8E 8 F17
Ljusne Sweden 61°13N 17°7E 8 F17
Llancanelo, Salina Argentina 35°40S 69°8W 94 D2
Llandeilo U.K. 51°53N 3°59W 13 F4
Llandovery U.K. 51°59N 3°48W 13 F4
Llandrindod Wells U.K. 52°14N 3°22W 13 E4
Llandudno U.K. 53°19N 3°50W 12 D4
Llanelli U.K. 51°41N 4°10W 13 F3
Llanes Spain 43°25N 4°50W 21 A3
Llangollen U.K. 52°58N 3°11W 12 E4
Llanidloes U.K. 52°27N 3°31W 13 E4
Llano U.S.A. 30°45N 98°41W 84 F5
Llano → U.S.A. 30°39N 98°26W 84 F5
Llano Estacado U.S.A. 33°30N 103°0W 84 E3
Llanos S. Amer. 5°0N 71°35W 92 C4
Llanos de Challe △ Chile 28°8S 71°1W 94 B1
Llanquihue, L. Chile 41°10S 72°50W 96 E1
Llanwrtyd Wells U.K. 52°7N 3°38W 13 E4
Llebeig, C. des Spain 39°33N 2°18E 24 B9
Lleida Spain 41°37N 0°39E 21 B6
Llentrisca, C. Spain 38°52N 1°15E 24 C7
Llera de Canales Mexico 23°19N 99°1W 87 C5
Lleyn Peninsula U.K. 52°51N 4°36W 12 E3
Llico Chile 34°46S 72°5W 94 C1
Lliria Spain 39°37N 0°35W 21 C5
Llobregat → Spain 41°19N 2°5E 21 B7
Lloret de Mar Spain 41°41N 2°53E 21 B7
Lloseta Spain 39°43N 2°52E 24 B9
Lloyd B. Australia 12°45S 143°27E 62 A3
Lloyd L. Canada 57°22N 108°57W 71 B7
Lloydminster Canada 53°17N 110°0W 71 C7
Llubí Spain 39°42N 3°0E 24 B10
Llucmajor Spain 39°29N 2°53E 24 B9
Llullaillaco, Volcán S. Amer. 24°43S 68°30W 94 A2
Llullaillaco △ Chile 24°50S 68°51W 94 A2
Lo → Vietnam 21°18N 105°25E 38 B5
Loa U.S.A. 38°24N 111°39W 76 G8
Loa → Chile 21°26S 70°41W 94 A1
Loaita I. S. China Sea 10°41N 114°25E 36 B4
Loange → Dem. Rep. of the Congo 4°17S 20°2E 52 E4
Lobatse Botswana 25°12S 25°40E 56 D4
Lobería Argentina 38°10S 58°40W 94 D4
Lobito Angola 12°18S 13°35E 53 G2
Lobos Argentina 35°10S 59°0W 94 D4
Lobos, I. Mexico 27°20N 110°36W 86 B2
Lobos, I. de Canary Is. 28°45N 13°50W 24 F6
Loc Binh Vietnam 21°46N 106°54E 38 B6
Loc Ninh Vietnam 11°50N 106°34E 39 G6
Locarno Switz. 46°10N 8°47E 20 C8
Loch Baghasdail = Lochboisdale U.K. 57°9N 7°20W 11 D1
Loch Garman = Wexford Ireland 52°20N 6°28W 10 D5
Loch Lomond and the Trossachs △ U.K. 56°10N 4°40W 11 E4
Loch Nam Madadh = Lochmaddy U.K. 57°36N 7°10W 11 D1
Lochaber U.K. 56°59N 5°1W 11 E3
Locharbriggs U.K. 55°7N 3°35W 11 F5
Lochboisdale U.K. 57°9N 7°20W 11 D1
Loche, L. La Canada 56°30N 109°30W 71 B7
Lochem Neths. 52°9N 6°26E 15 B6
Loches France 47°7N 1°0E 20 C4
Lochgilphead U.K. 56°2N 5°26W 11 E3
Lochinvar △ Zambia 15°55S 27°15E 55 F2
Lochinver U.K. 58°9N 5°14W 11 C3
Lochmaddy U.K. 57°36N 7°10W 11 D1
Lochnagar Australia 23°33S 145°38E 62 C4
Lochnagar U.K. 56°57N 3°15W 11 E5
Lochy, L. U.K. 57°0N 4°53W 11 E4
Lock Australia 33°34S 135°46E 63 E2
Lock Haven U.S.A. 41°8N 77°28W 82 E7
Lockeford U.S.A. 38°10N 121°9W 78 G5
Lockeport Canada 43°47N 65°4W 73 D6
Lockerbie U.K. 55°7N 3°21W 11 F5
Lockhart U.S.A. 29°53N 97°40W 84 G6
Lockhart, L. Australia 33°15S 119°3E 61 F2
Lockhart River Australia 12°58S 143°30E 62 A3
Lockney U.S.A. 34°7N 101°27W 84 D4
Lockport U.S.A. 43°10N 78°42W 82 C6
Lod Israel 31°57N 34°54E 46 D3
Lodeinoye Pole Russia 60°44N 33°33E 18 B5
Lodge Bay Canada 52°14N 55°51W 73 B8
Lodge Grass U.S.A. 45°19N 107°22W 76 D10
Lodhran Pakistan 29°32N 71°30E 42 E4
Lodi Italy 45°19N 9°30E 20 D8
Lodi Calif., U.S.A. 38°8N 121°16W 78 G5
Lodi Ohio, U.S.A. 41°2N 82°1W 82 E3
Lodja Dem. Rep. of the Congo 3°30S 23°23E 54 C1
Lodwar Kenya 3°7N 35°36E 54 B4
Łódź Poland 51°45N 19°27E 17 C10
Loei Thailand 17°29N 101°35E 38 D3
Loengo Dem. Rep. of the Congo 4°48S 26°30E 54 C2
Loeriesfontein S. Africa 31°0S 19°26E 56 E2
Lofoten Norway 68°30N 14°0E 8 B16
Logan Iowa, U.S.A. 41°39N 95°47W 80 E6
Logan Ohio, U.S.A. 39°32N 82°25W 81 F12
Logan Utah, U.S.A. 41°44N 111°50W 76 F8
Logan W. Va., U.S.A. 37°51N 81°59W 81 G13
Logan, Mt. Canada 60°34N 140°23W 68 C5
Logandale U.S.A. 36°36N 114°29W 79 J12
Logansport Ind., U.S.A. 40°45N 86°22W 80 E10
Logansport La., U.S.A. 31°58N 94°0W 84 F8
Logone → Chad 12°6N 15°2E 51 F9
Logroño Spain 42°28N 2°27W 21 A4
Lohardaga India 23°27N 84°45E 43 H11
Loharia India 23°45N 74°14E 42 H6
Loharu India 28°27N 75°49E 42 E6
Lohri Wah → Pakistan 27°27N 67°37E 42 F2
Loi-kaw Burma 19°40N 97°17E 41 K20
Loimaa Finland 60°50N 23°5E 8 F20
Loir → France 47°33N 0°32W 20 C3
Loire → France 47°16N 2°10W 20 C2
Loja Ecuador 3°59S 79°16W 92 D3
Loja Spain 37°10N 4°10W 21 D3
Loji = Kawasi Indonesia 1°38S 127°28E 37 E7
Lokandu Dem. Rep. of the Congo 2°30S 25°45E 54 C2
Lokeren Belgium 51°6N 3°59E 15 C3
Lokgwabe Botswana 24°10S 21°50E 56 C3
Lokichar Kenya 2°23N 35°39E 54 B4
Lokichokio Kenya 4°19N 34°13E 54 B3
Lokitaung Kenya 4°12N 35°48E 54 B4
Lokkan tekojärvi Finland 67°55N 27°35E 8 C22
Lokoja Nigeria 7°47N 6°45E 50 G7
Lokolo → Dem. Rep. of the Congo 1°43S 18°23E 52 E3
Lola, Mt. U.S.A. 39°26N 120°22W 78 F6
Lolgorien Kenya 1°14S 34°48E 54 C3
Loliondo Tanzania 2°2S 35°39E 54 C4
Lolland Denmark 54°45N 11°30E 9 J14
Lolo U.S.A. 46°45N 114°5W 76 C6
Lom Bulgaria 43°48N 23°12E 23 C10
Lom Kao Thailand 16°53N 101°14E 38 D3
Lom Sak Thailand 16°47N 101°15E 38 D3
Loma U.S.A. 47°56N 110°30W 76 C8
Loma Linda U.S.A. 34°3N 117°16W 79 L9
Lomaloma Fiji 17°17S 178°59W 59 a
Lomami → Dem. Rep. of the Congo 0°46N 24°16E 54 B1
Lomas de Zamora Argentina 34°45S 58°24W 94 C4
Lombadina Australia 16°31S 122°54E 60 C3
Lombárdia □ Italy 45°40N 9°30E 20 D8
Lombardy = Lombárdia □ Italy 45°40N 9°30E 20 D8
Lomblen Indonesia 8°30S 123°32E 37 F6
Lombok Indonesia 8°45S 116°30E 36 F5
Lombok, Selat Indonesia 8°30S 115°50E 37 K18
Lomé Togo 6°9N 1°20E 50 G6
Lomela Dem. Rep. of the Congo 2°19S 23°15E 52 E4
Lomela → Dem. Rep. of the Congo 0°15S 20°40E 52 E4
Lommel Belgium 51°14N 5°19E 15 C5
Lomond Canada 50°24N 112°36W 70 C6
Lomond, L. U.K. 56°8N 4°38W 11 E4
Lomonosov Ridge Arctic 88°0N 140°0E 4 A
Lomphat Cambodia 13°30N 106°59E 38 F6
Lompobatang Indonesia 5°24S 119°56E 37 F5
Lompoc U.S.A. 34°38N 120°28W 79 L6
Łomża Poland 53°10N 22°2E 17 B12
Lon, Ko Thailand 7°47N 98°23E 39 a
Loncoche Chile 39°20S 72°50W 96 D2
Londa India 15°30N 74°30E 40 M9
Londiani Kenya 0°10S 35°33E 54 C4
London Canada 42°59N 81°15W 82 D3
London U.K. 51°30N 0°3W 13 F7
London Ky., U.S.A. 37°8N 84°5W 81 G11
London Ohio, U.S.A. 39°53N 83°27W 81 F12
London, Greater □ U.K. 51°36N 0°5W 13 F7

138 London Gatwick
INDEX TO WORLD MAPS

London Gatwick ✈ (LGW) U.K. 51°10N 0°11W 13 F7
London Heathrow ✈ (LHR) U.K. 51°28N 0°27W 13 F7
London Stansted ✈ (STN) U.K. 51°54N 0°14E 13 F8
Londonderry U.K. 55°0N 7°20W 10 B4
Londonderry □ U.K. 55°0N 7°20W 10 B4
Londonderry, C. Australia 13°45S 126°55E 60 B4
Londonderry, I. Chile 55°0S 71°0W 96 H2
Londres Argentina 27°43S 67°7W 96 B3
Londrina Brazil 23°18S 51°10W 95 A5
Lone Pine U.S.A. 36°36N 118°4W 78 J8
Lonely Mine Zimbabwe 19°30S 28°49E 57 B4
Long B. U.S.A. 33°35N 78°45W 85 E15
Long Beach Calif., U.S.A. 33°46N 118°11W 79 M8
Long Beach N.Y., U.S.A. 40°35N 73°39W 83 F11
Long Beach Wash., U.S.A. 46°21N 124°3W 78 D2
Long Branch U.S.A. 40°18N 74°0W 83 F11
Long Creek U.S.A. 44°43N 119°6W 76 D4
Long Eaton U.K. 52°53N 1°15W 12 E6
Long I. Australia 20°22S 148°51E 62 J6
Long I. Bahamas 23°20N 75°10W 89 B4
Long I. Canada 54°50N 79°20W 72 B4
Long I. Ireland 51°30N 9°34W 10 E2
Long I. U.S.A. 40°45N 73°30W 83 F11
Long Island Sd. U.S.A. 41°10N 73°0W 83 E12
Long L. Canada 49°30N 86°50W 72 C2
Long L. U.S.A. 44°0N 74°23W 83 C10
Long Lake U.S.A. 43°58N 74°25W 83 C10
Long Point Canada 42°34N 80°25W 82 D4
Long Point B. Canada 42°40N 80°10W 82 D4
Long Prairie U.S.A. 45°59N 94°52W 80 C6
Long Prairie → U.S.A. 46°20N 94°36W 80 B6
Long Pt. Ont., Canada 42°35N 80°2W 82 D4
Long Pt. Ont., Canada 43°56N 76°53W 83 C8
Long Range Mts. Canada 49°30N 57°30W 73 C8
Long Reef Australia 14°1S 125°48E 60 B4
Long Sault Canada 45°2N 74°53W 83 A10
Long Str. = Longa, Proliv Russia 70°0N 175°0E 29 C18
Long Thanh Vietnam 10°47N 106°57E 39 G6
Long Xian China 34°55N 106°55E 34 G4
Long Xuyen Vietnam 10°19N 105°28E 39 G5
Longa, Proliv Russia 70°0N 175°0E 29 C18
Longbenton U.K. 55°1N 1°31W 12 B6
Longboat Key U.S.A. 27°23N 82°39W 85 H13
Longde China 35°30N 106°20E 34 G4
Longford Australia 41°32S 147°3E 63 G4
Longford Ireland 53°43N 7°49W 10 C4
Longford □ Ireland 53°42N 7°45W 10 C4
Longhua Guangdong, China 22°39N 114°0E 33 F11
Longhua Hebei, China 41°18N 117°45E 35 D9
Longido Tanzania 2°43S 36°42E 54 C4
Longiram Indonesia 0°5S 115°45E 36 E5
Longkou China 37°40N 120°18E 35 F11
Longlac Canada 49°45N 86°25W 72 C2
Longmeadow U.S.A. 42°3N 72°34W 83 D12
Longmont U.S.A. 40°10N 105°6W 76 F11
Longnawan Indonesia 1°51N 114°55E 36 D4
Longreach Australia 23°28S 144°14E 62 C3
Longueuil Canada 45°31N 73°29W 83 A11
Longview Tex., U.S.A. 32°30N 94°44W 84 E7
Longview Wash., U.S.A. 46°8N 122°57W 78 D4
Longxi China 34°53N 104°40E 34 G3
Longxue Dao China 22°41N 113°38E 33 F10
Longyearbyen Svalbard 78°13N 15°40E 4 B8
Lonoke U.S.A. 34°47N 91°54W 84 D9
Lonquimay Chile 38°26S 71°14W 96 D2
Lons-le-Saunier France 46°40N 5°31E 20 C6
Looe U.K. 50°22N 4°28W 13 G3
Lookout, C. Canada 55°18N 83°56W 72 A3
Lookout, C. U.S.A. 34°35N 76°32W 85 D16
Loolmalasin Tanzania 3°0S 35°53E 54 C4
Loon → Alta., Canada 57°8N 115°3W 70 B5
Loon → Man., Canada 55°53N 101°59W 71 B8
Loon Lake Canada 54°2N 109°10W 71 C7
Loongana Australia 30°52S 127°5E 61 F4
Loop Hd. Ireland 52°34N 9°56W 10 D2
Lop China 37°3N 80°11E 32 C3
Lop Buri Thailand 14°48N 100°37E 38 E3
Lop Nor = Lop Nur China 40°20N 90°10E 32 B4
Lop Nur China 40°20N 90°10E 32 B4
Lopatina, Gora Russia 50°47N 143°10E 29 D15
Lopatka, Mys Russia 50°52N 156°40E 29 D16
Lopez U.S.A. 41°27N 76°20W 83 E8
Lopez, C. Gabon 0°47S 8°40E 52 E1
Lopphavet Norway 70°27N 21°15E 8 A19
Lora → Afghan. 31°35N 66°32E 40 D4
Lora, Hāmūn-i- Pakistan 29°38N 64°58E 40 E4
Lora Cr. → Australia 28°10S 135°22E 63 D2
Lora del Río Spain 37°39N 5°33W 21 D3
Lorain U.S.A. 41°28N 82°11W 82 E2
Loralai Pakistan 30°20N 68°41E 42 D3
Lorca Spain 37°41N 1°42W 21 D5
Lord Howe I. Pac. Oc. 31°33S 159°6E 58 E8
Lord Howe Rise Pac. Oc. 30°0S 162°30E 64 L8
Lordsburg U.S.A. 32°21N 108°43W 77 K9
Lorestān □ Iran 33°30N 48°40E 45 C6
Loreto Brazil 7°5S 45°10W 93 E9
Loreto Mexico 26°0N 111°21W 86 B2
Lorient France 47°45N 3°23W 20 C2
Lormi India 22°17N 81°41E 43 H9
Lorn U.K. 56°26N 5°10W 11 E3
Lorn, Firth of U.K. 56°20N 5°40W 11 E3
Lorne Australia 38°33S 143°59E 63 F3
Lorovouno Cyprus 35°8N 32°36E 25 D11
Lorraine □ France 48°53N 6°0E 20 B7
Los Alamos Calif., U.S.A. 34°44N 120°17W 79 L6
Los Alamos N. Mex., U.S.A. 35°53N 106°19W 77 J10
Los Altos U.S.A. 37°23N 122°7W 78 H4
Los Andes Chile 32°50S 70°40W 94 C1
Los Angeles Chile 37°28S 72°23W 94 D1
Los Angeles U.S.A. 34°4N 118°15W 79 M8
Los Angeles, Bahia de Mexico 28°56N 113°34W 86 B2
Los Angeles Aqueduct U.S.A. 35°22N 118°5W 79 K9
Los Angeles Int. ✈ (LAX) U.S.A. 33°57N 118°25W 79 M8
Los Banos U.S.A. 37°4N 120°51W 78 H6
Los Blancos Argentina 23°40S 62°30W 94 A3
Los Cardones △ Argentina 25°8S 65°55W 94 B2
Los Chiles Costa Rica 11°2N 84°43W 88 D3
Los Cristianos Canary Is. 28°3N 16°42W 24 F3
Los Gatos U.S.A. 37°14N 121°59W 78 H5
Los Haïtises △ Dom. Rep. 19°4N 69°36W 89 C6
Los Hermanos Is. Venezuela 11°45N 64°25W 89 D7
Los Islotes Canary Is. 29°4N 13°44W 24 E6
Los Llanos de Aridane Canary Is. 28°38N 17°54W 24 F2
Los Loros Chile 27°50S 70°6W 94 B1
Los Lunas U.S.A. 34°48N 106°44W 77 J10
Los Mochis Mexico 25°45N 108°57W 86 B3
Los Olivos U.S.A. 34°40N 120°7W 79 L6
Los Palacios Cuba 22°35N 83°15W 88 B3
Los Queñes Chile 35°1S 70°48W 94 D1
Los Reyes de Salgado Mexico 19°35N 102°29W 86 D4
Los Roques Is. Venezuela 11°50N 66°45W 89 D6
Los Teques Venezuela 10°21N 67°2W 92 A5
Los Testigos, Is. Venezuela 11°23N 63°6W 92 A6
Los Vilos Chile 32°10S 71°30W 94 C1
Lošinj Croatia 44°30N 14°30E 16 F8
Loskop Dam S. Africa 25°23S 29°20E 57 D4
Lossiemouth U.K. 57°42N 3°17W 11 D5
Lostwithiel U.K. 50°24N 4°41W 13 G3
Lot → France 44°18N 0°20E 20 D4
Lota Chile 37°5S 73°10W 94 D1
Loṭfābād Iran 37°32N 59°20E 45 B8
Lothair S. Africa 26°22S 30°27E 57 D5
Lotta → Europe 68°42N 31°6E 8 B24
Loubomo Congo 4°9S 12°47E 52 E2
Loudonville U.S.A. 40°38N 82°14W 82 F2
Louga Senegal 15°45N 16°5W 50 E2
Loughborough U.K. 52°47N 1°11W 12 E6
Lougheed I. Canada 77°26N 105°6W 69 B9
Loughrea Ireland 53°12N 8°33W 10 C3
Loughros More B. Ireland 54°48N 8°32W 10 B3
Louis Trichardt S. Africa 23°1S 29°43E 57 C4
Louis XIV, Pte. Canada 54°37N 79°45W 72 B4
Louisa U.S.A. 38°7N 82°36W 81 F12
Louisbourg Canada 45°55N 60°0W 73 C8
Louisburgh Ireland 53°46N 9°49W 10 C2
Louise I. Canada 52°55N 131°50W 70 C2
Louiseville Canada 46°20N 72°56W 72 C5
Louisiade Arch. Papua N. G. 11°10S 153°0E 58 C8
Louisiana U.S.A. 39°27N 91°3W 80 F8
Louisiana □ U.S.A. 30°50N 92°0W 84 F9
Louisville Ky., U.S.A. 38°15N 85°46W 81 F11
Louisville Miss., U.S.A. 33°7N 89°3W 85 E10
Louisville Ohio, U.S.A. 40°50N 81°16W 82 F3
Louisville Ridge Pac. Oc. 31°0S 172°30W 64 L10
Loulé Portugal 37°9N 8°0W 21 D1
Loup City U.S.A. 41°17N 98°58W 80 E4
Loups Marins, Lacs des Canada 56°30N 73°45W 72 A5
Lourdes France 43°6N 0°3W 20 E3
Lourdes-de-Blanc-Sablon Canada 51°24N 57°12W 73 B8
Louroujina Cyprus 35°0N 33°28E 25 E12
Louth Australia 30°30S 145°8E 63 E4
Louth Ireland 53°58N 6°32W 10 C5
Louth U.K. 53°22N 0°1W 12 D7
Louth □ Ireland 53°56N 6°34W 10 C5
Louvain = Leuven Belgium 50°52N 4°42E 15 D4
Louwsburg S. Africa 27°37S 31°7E 57 D5
Lovech Bulgaria 43°8N 24°42E 23 C11
Loveland U.S.A. 40°24N 105°5W 76 F11
Lovell U.S.A. 44°50N 108°24W 76 D9
Lovelock U.S.A. 40°11N 118°28W 76 F4
Loviisa Finland 60°28N 26°12E 8 F22
Loving U.S.A. 32°17N 104°6W 77 K11
Lovington U.S.A. 32°57N 103°21W 77 K12
Lovisa = Loviisa Finland 60°28N 26°12E 8 F22
Low, L. Canada 52°29N 76°17W 72 B4
Low Pt. Australia 32°25S 127°25E 61 F4
Low Tatra = Nízké Tatry Slovak Rep. 48°55N 19°30E 17 D10
Lowa Dem. Rep. of the Congo 1°25S 25°47E 54 C2
Lowa → Dem. Rep. of the Congo 1°24S 25°51E 54 C2
Lowell U.S.A. 42°38N 71°19W 83 D13
Lowellville U.S.A. 41°2N 80°32W 82 E4
Löwen → Namibia 26°51S 18°17E 56 D2
Lower Alkali L. U.S.A. 41°16N 120°2W 76 F3
Lower Arrow L. Canada 49°40N 118°5W 70 D5
Lower California = Baja California Mexico 31°10N 115°12W 86 A1
Lower Hutt N.Z. 41°10S 174°55E 59 D5
Lower Lake U.S.A. 38°55N 122°37W 78 G4
Lower Manitou L. Canada 49°15N 93°0W 71 D10
Lower Post Canada 59°58N 128°30W 70 B3
Lower Red L. U.S.A. 47°58N 95°0W 80 B6
Lower Saxony = Niedersachsen □ Germany 52°50N 9°0E 16 B5
Lower Tunguska = Tunguska, Nizhnyaya → Russia 65°48N 88°4E 29 C9
Lower Zambezi △ Zambia 15°25S 29°40E 55 F2
Lowestoft U.K. 52°29N 1°45E 13 E9
Lowgar □ Afghan. 34°0N 69°0E 40 B6
Łowicz Poland 52°6N 19°55E 17 B10
Lowville U.S.A. 43°47N 75°29W 83 C9
Loxton Australia 34°28S 140°31E 63 E3
Loxton S. Africa 31°30S 22°22E 56 E3
Loyalton U.S.A. 39°41N 120°14W 78 F6
Loyalty Is. = Loyauté, Îs. N. Cal. 20°50S 166°30E 58 D9
Loyang = Luoyang China 34°40N 112°26E 34 G7
Loyauté, Îs. N. Cal. 20°50S 166°30E 58 D9
Loyev = Loyew Belarus 51°56N 30°46E 17 C16
Loyew Belarus 51°56N 30°46E 17 C16
Loyoro Uganda 3°22N 34°14E 54 B3
Lu Wo China 22°33N 114°6E 33 F11
Luachimo Angola 7°23S 20°48E 52 F4
Luajan → India 24°44N 85°1E 43 G11
Lualaba → Dem. Rep. of the Congo 0°26N 25°20E 54 B2
Luampa Zambia 15°4S 24°20E 55 F1
Luan Chau Vietnam 21°38N 103°24E 38 B4
Luan He → China 39°20N 119°5E 35 E10
Luan Xian China 39°40N 118°40E 35 E10
Luancheng China 37°53N 114°40E 34 F8
Luanda Angola 8°50S 13°15E 52 F2
Luang, Thale Thailand 7°30N 100°15E 39 J3
Luang Prabang Laos 19°52N 102°10E 38 C4
Luangwa Zambia 15°35S 30°16E 55 F3
Luangwa → Zambia 14°25S 30°25E 55 E3
Luangwa Valley Zambia 13°30S 31°30E 55 E3
Luanne China 40°55N 117°40E 35 D9
Luanping China 40°53N 117°23E 35 D9
Luanshya Zambia 13°3S 28°28E 55 E2
Luapula □ Zambia 11°0S 29°0E 55 E2
Luapula → Africa 9°26S 28°33E 55 D2
Luarca Spain 43°32N 6°32W 21 A2
Luashi Dem. Rep. of the Congo 10°50S 23°36E 55 E1
Luau Angola 10°40S 22°10E 52 G4
Lubana, Ozero = Lubānas Ezers Latvia 56°45N 27°0E 9 H22
Lubānas Ezers Latvia 56°45N 27°0E 9 H22
Lubang Is. Phil. 13°50N 120°12E 37 B6
Lubango Angola 14°55S 13°30E 53 G2
Lubao Dem. Rep. of the Congo 5°17S 25°42E 54 D2
Lubbock U.S.A. 33°35N 101°51W 84 E4
Lübeck Germany 53°52N 10°40E 16 B6
Lubefu Dem. Rep. of the Congo 4°47S 24°27E 54 C1
Lubefu → Dem. Rep. of the Congo 4°10S 23°0E 54 C1
Lubero = Luofu Dem. Rep. of the Congo 0°10S 29°15E 54 C2
Lubicon L. Canada 56°23N 115°56W 70 B5
Lubilash → Dem. Rep. of the Congo 6°2S 23°45E 52 F4
Lubin Poland 51°24N 16°11E 16 C9
Lublin Poland 51°12N 22°38E 17 C12
Lubnān = Lebanon ■ Asia 34°0N 36°0E 46 B5
Lubnān, Jabal Lebanon 33°45N 35°40E 46 B4
Lubny Ukraine 50°3N 32°58E 28 D4
Lubongola Dem. Rep. of the Congo 2°35S 27°50E 54 C2
Lubudi Dem. Rep. of the Congo 9°57S 25°58E 52 F5
Lubudi → Dem. Rep. of the Congo 9°0S 25°35E 55 D2
Lubuklinggau Indonesia 3°15S 102°55E 36 E2
Lubuksikaping Indonesia 0°10N 100°15E 36 D2
Lubumbashi Dem. Rep. of the Congo 11°40S 27°28E 55 E2
Lubunda Dem. Rep. of the Congo 5°12S 26°41E 54 D2
Lubungu Zambia 14°35S 26°24E 55 E2
Lubutu Dem. Rep. of the Congo 0°45S 26°30E 54 C2
Luc An Chau Vietnam 22°6N 104°43E 38 A5
Lucan Canada 43°11N 81°24W 82 C3
Lucania, Mt. Canada 61°1N 140°27W 68 C5
Lucas Channel = Main Channel Canada 45°21N 81°45W 82 A3
Lucca Italy 43°50N 10°29E 22 C4
Luce Bay U.K. 54°45N 4°48W 11 G4
Lucea Jamaica 18°27N 78°10W 88 a
Lucedale U.S.A. 30°56N 88°35W 85 F10
Lucena Phil. 13°56N 121°37E 37 B6
Lucena Spain 37°27N 4°31W 21 D3
Lučenec Slovak Rep. 48°18N 19°42E 17 D10
Lucerne = Luzern Switz. 47°3N 8°18E 20 C8
Lucerne U.S.A. 39°6N 122°48W 78 F4
Lucerne Valley U.S.A. 34°27N 116°57W 79 L10
Lucero Mexico 30°49N 106°30W 86 A3
Lucheng China 36°20N 113°11E 34 F7
Lucheringo → Mozam. 11°43S 36°17E 55 E4
Lucia U.S.A. 36°2N 121°33W 78 J5
Lucinda Australia 18°32S 146°20E 62 B4
Luckenwalde Germany 52°5N 13°10E 16 B7
Luckhoff S. Africa 29°44S 24°43E 56 D3
Lucknow Canada 43°57N 81°31W 82 C3
Lucknow India 26°50N 81°0E 43 F9
Lüda = Dalian China 38°50N 121°40E 35 E11
Lüderitz Namibia 26°41S 15°8E 56 D2
Lüderitzbaai Namibia 26°36S 15°8E 56 D2
Ludhiana India 30°57N 75°56E 42 D6
Ludington U.S.A. 43°57N 86°27W 80 D10
Ludlow U.K. 52°22N 2°42W 13 E5
Ludlow Calif., U.S.A. 34°43N 116°10W 79 L10
Ludlow Pa., U.S.A. 41°43N 78°56W 82 E6
Ludlow Vt., U.S.A. 43°24N 72°42W 83 C12
Ludvika Sweden 60°8N 15°14E 9 F16
Ludwigsburg Germany 48°53N 9°11E 16 D5
Ludwigshafen Germany 49°29N 8°26E 16 D5
Lueki Dem. Rep. of the Congo 3°20S 25°48E 54 C2
Luena Dem. Rep. of the Congo 9°28S 25°43E 55 D2
Luena Zambia 10°40S 30°25E 55 E3
Luena Flats Zambia 14°47S 23°17E 53 G4
Luenha = Ruenya → Africa 16°24S 33°48E 55 F3
Lüeyang China 33°22N 106°10E 34 H4
Lufira → Dem. Rep. of the Congo 9°30S 27°0E 55 D2
Lufkin U.S.A. 31°21N 94°44W 84 F7
Lufupa Dem. Rep. of the Congo 10°37S 24°56E 55 E1
Luga Russia 58°40N 29°55E 9 G23
Lugano Switz. 46°1N 8°57E 20 C8
Lugansk = Luhansk Ukraine 48°38N 39°15E 19 E6
Lugard's Falls Kenya 3°6S 38°41E 54 C4
Lugela Mozam. 16°25S 36°43E 55 F4
Lugenda → Mozam. 11°25S 38°33E 55 E4
Lugh Ganana = Luuq Somali Rep. 3°48N 42°34E 47 G3
Lugnaquillia Ireland 52°58N 6°28W 10 D5
Lugo Italy 44°25N 11°54E 22 B4
Lugo Spain 43°2N 7°35W 21 A2
Lugoj Romania 45°42N 21°57E 17 F11
Lugovoy = Qulan Kazakhstan 42°55N 72°43E 28 E8
Luhansk Ukraine 48°38N 39°15E 19 E6
Lui → Angola 8°21S 17°33E 52 F3
Luiana Angola 17°25S 22°59E 56 B3
Luiana → Angola 17°24S 23°3E 53 H4
Luichow Pen. = Leizhou Bandao China 21°0N 110°0E 33 D6
Luimneach = Limerick Ireland 52°40N 8°37W 10 D3
Luing U.K. 56°14N 5°39W 11 E3
Luís Correia Brazil 3°0S 41°35W 93 D10
Luitpold Coast Antarctica 78°30S 32°0W 5 D1
Luiza Dem. Rep. of the Congo 7°40S 22°30E 52 F4
Luizi Dem. Rep. of the Congo 6°0S 27°25E 54 D2
Luján Argentina 34°45S 59°5W 94 C4
Lukanga Swamp Zambia 14°30S 27°40E 55 E2
Lukenie → Dem. Rep. of the Congo 3°0S 18°50E 52 E3
Lukolela Dem. Rep. of the Congo 5°23S 24°32E 54 D1
Lukosi Zimbabwe 18°30S 26°30E 55 F2
Łuków Poland 51°55N 22°23E 17 C12
Lukusuzi △ Zambia 12°43S 32°36E 55 E3
Luleå Sweden 65°35N 22°10E 8 D20
Luleälven → Sweden 65°35N 22°10E 8 D20
Lüleburgaz Turkey 41°23N 27°22E 23 D12
Luling U.S.A. 29°41N 97°39W 84 G6
Lulong China 39°53N 118°51E 35 E10
Lulonga → Dem. Rep. of the Congo 1°0N 18°10E 52 D3
Lulua → Dem. Rep. of the Congo 4°30S 20°30E 52 E4
Luma Amer. Samoa 14°16S 169°33W 59 b
Lumajang Indonesia 8°8S 113°13E 37 H15
Lumbala N'guimbo Angola 14°18S 21°18E 53 G4
Lumberton U.S.A. 34°37N 79°0W 85 D15
Lumsden Canada 50°39N 104°52W 71 C8
Lumsden N.Z. 45°44S 168°27E 59 F2
Lumut Malaysia 4°13N 100°37E 39 K3
Lumut, Tanjung Indonesia 3°50S 105°58E 36 E3
Luna India 23°43N 69°16E 42 H3
Lunavada India 23°8N 73°37E 42 H5
Lund Sweden 55°44N 13°12E 9 J15
Lundazi Zambia 12°20S 33°7E 55 E3
Lundi → Zimbabwe 21°43S 32°34E 55 G3
Lundu Malaysia 1°40N 109°50E 36 D3
Lundy U.K. 51°10N 4°41W 13 F3
Lune → U.K. 54°0N 2°51W 12 C5
Lüneburg Germany 53°15N 10°24E 16 B6
Lüneburg Heath = Lüneburger Heide Germany 53°10N 10°12E 16 B6
Lüneburger Heide Germany 53°10N 10°12E 16 B6
Lunenburg Canada 44°22N 64°18W 73 D7
Lunéville France 48°36N 6°30E 20 B7
Lunga → Zambia 14°34S 26°25E 55 E2
Lunga Lunga Kenya 4°33S 39°7E 54 C4
Lunglei India 22°55N 92°45E 41 H18
Luni India 26°0N 73°6E 42 G5
Luni → India 24°41N 71°14E 42 G4
Luninets = Luninyets Belarus 52°15N 26°50E 17 B14
Luning U.S.A. 38°30N 118°11W 76 G4
Luninyets Belarus 52°15N 26°50E 17 B14
Lunkaransar India 28°29N 73°44E 42 E5
Lunsemfwa → Zambia 14°54S 30°12E 55 E3
Lunsemfwa Falls Zambia 14°30S 29°6E 55 E2
Luo He → China 34°35N 110°20E 34 G6
Luochuan China 35°45N 109°26E 34 G5
Luofu Dem. Rep. of the Congo 0°10S 29°15E 54 C2
Luohe China 33°32N 114°2E 34 H8
Luonan China 34°5N 110°10E 34 G6
Luoning China 34°35N 111°40E 34 G6
Luoyang China 34°40N 112°26E 34 G7
Luozigou China 43°42N 130°18E 35 C16
Lupilichi Mozam. 11°47S 35°13E 55 E4
Luque Paraguay 25°19S 57°25W 94 B4
Luquillo, Sierra de Puerto Rico 18°20N 65°47W 89 d
Luray U.S.A. 38°40N 78°28W 81 F14
Lurgan U.K. 54°28N 6°19W 10 B5
Lusaka Zambia 15°28S 28°16E 55 F2
Lusaka □ Zambia 15°30S 29°0E 55 F2
Lusambo Dem. Rep. of the Congo 4°58S 23°28E 54 C1
Lusangaye Dem. Rep. of the Congo 4°54S 26°0E 54 C2
Luseland Canada 52°5N 109°24W 71 C7
Lusenga Plain △ Zambia 9°22S 29°14E 55 D2
Lushan China 33°45N 112°55E 34 H7
Lushi China 34°3N 111°3E 34 G6
Lushnjë Albania 40°55N 19°41E 23 D8
Lushoto Tanzania 4°47S 38°20E 54 C4
Lüshun China 38°45N 121°15E 35 E11
Lusk U.S.A. 42°46N 104°27W 76 E11
Lūt, Dasht-e Iran 31°30N 58°0E 45 D8
Luta = Dalian China 38°50N 121°40E 35 E11
Lutherstadt Wittenberg Germany 51°53N 12°39E 16 C7
Luton U.K. 51°53N 0°24W 13 F7
Luton □ U.K. 51°53N 0°24W 13 F7
Łutsel K'e Canada 62°24N 110°44W 71 A6
Lutsk Ukraine 50°50N 25°15E 17 C13
Lutto = Lotta → Europe 68°42N 31°6E 8 B24
Lützow Holmbukta Antarctica 69°10S 37°30E 5 C4
Lutzputs S. Africa 28°3S 20°40E 56 D3
Luuq Somali Rep. 3°48N 42°34E 47 G3
Luverne Ala., U.S.A. 31°43N 86°16W 85 F11
Luverne Minn., U.S.A. 43°39N 96°13W 80 D5
Luvua Dem. Rep. of the Congo 8°48S 25°17E 55 D2
Luvua → Dem. Rep. of the Congo 6°50S 27°30E 54 D2
Luvuvhu → S. Africa 22°25S 31°18E 57 C5
Luwegu → Tanzania 8°31S 37°23E 55 D4
Luwuk Indonesia 0°56S 122°47E 37 E6
Luxembourg Lux. 49°37N 6°9E 15 E6
Luxembourg □ Belgium 49°58N 5°30E 15 E5
Luxembourg ■ Europe 49°45N 6°0E 15 E5
Luxembourg ✈ (LUX) Lux. 49°37N 6°10E 15 E6
Luxi China 24°27N 98°36E 32 D4
Luxor = El Uqsur Egypt 25°41N 32°38E 51 C12
Luyi China 33°50N 115°35E 34 H8
Luza Russia 60°39N 47°10E 18 B8
Luzern Switz. 47°3N 8°18E 20 C8
Luzhou China 28°52N 105°20E 32 D5
Luziânia Brazil 16°20S 48°0W 93 G9
Luzon Phil. 16°0N 121°0E 37 A6
Lviv Ukraine 49°50N 24°0E 17 D13
Lvov = Lviv Ukraine 49°50N 24°0E 17 D13
Lyakhavichy Belarus 53°2N 26°32E 17 B14
Lyakhovskiye, Ostrova Russia 73°40N 141°0E 29 B15
Lyal I. Canada 44°57N 81°24W 82 B3
Lybster U.K. 58°18N 3°15W 11 C5
Lycksele Sweden 64°38N 18°40E 8 D18
Lydda = Lod Israel 31°57N 34°54E 46 D3
Lyddan I. Antarctica 74°0S 21°0W 5 D2
Lydenburg S. Africa 25°10S 30°29E 57 D5
Lydia Turkey 38°48N 28°19E 23 E13
Lyell N.Z. 41°48S 172°4E 59 D4
Lyell I. Canada 52°40N 131°35W 70 C2
Lyepyel Belarus 54°50N 28°40E 9 J23
Lykens U.S.A. 40°34N 76°42W 83 F8
Lyman U.S.A. 41°20N 110°18W 76 F8
Lyme B. U.K. 50°42N 2°53W 13 G4
Lyme Regis U.K. 50°43N 2°57W 13 G5
Lymington U.K. 50°45N 1°32W 13 G6
Łyna → Poland 54°37N 21°14E 17 A11
Lynchburg U.S.A. 37°25N 79°9W 81 G14
Lynd → Australia 16°28S 143°18E 62 B3
Lynd Ra. Australia 25°30S 149°20E 63 D4
Lynden Canada 43°14N 80°9W 82 C4
Lynden U.S.A. 48°57N 122°27W 78 B4
Lyndhurst Australia 30°15S 138°18E 63 E2
Lyndon → Australia 23°29S 114°6E 61 D1
Lyndonville N.Y., U.S.A. 43°20N 78°23W 82 C6
Lyndonville Vt., U.S.A. 44°31N 72°1W 83 B12
Lyngen Norway 69°45N 20°30E 8 B19
Lynher Reef Australia 15°27S 121°55E 60 C3
Lynn U.S.A. 42°28N 70°57W 83 D14
Lynn Haven U.S.A. 30°15N 85°39W 85 F12
Lynn Lake Canada 56°51N 101°3W 71 B8
Lynnwood U.S.A. 47°49N 122°18W 78 C4
Lynton U.K. 51°13N 3°50W 13 F4
Lyntupy Belarus 55°4N 26°23E 9 J22
Lynx L. Canada 62°25N 106°15W 71 A7
Lyon France 45°46N 4°50E 20 D6
Lyonnais France 45°45N 4°15E 20 D6
Lyons = Lyon France 45°46N 4°50E 20 D6
Lyons Ga., U.S.A. 32°12N 82°19W 85 E13
Lyons Kans., U.S.A. 38°21N 98°12W 80 F4
Lyons N.Y., U.S.A. 43°5N 77°0W 82 C8
Lyons → Australia 25°2S 115°9E 61 E2
Lyons Falls U.S.A. 43°37N 75°22W 83 C9
Lys = Leie → Belgium 51°2N 3°45E 15 C3
Lysi Cyprus 35°6N 33°41E 25 D12
Lysva Russia 58°7N 57°49E 18 C10
Lysychansk Ukraine 48°55N 38°30E 19 E6
Lytham St. Anne's U.K. 53°45N 3°0W 12 D4
Lyttelton N.Z. 43°35S 172°44E 59 E4
Lytton Canada 50°13N 121°31W 70 C4
Lyubertsy Russia 55°40N 37°51E 18 C6
Lyuboml Ukraine 51°11N 24°4E 17 C13

M

Ma → Vietnam 19°47N 105°56E 38 C5
Ma'adaba Jordan 30°43N 35°47E 46 E4
Maamba Zambia 17°17S 26°28E 56 B4
Ma'ān Jordan 30°12N 35°44E 46 E4
Ma'ān □ Jordan 30°0N 36°0E 46 F5
Maanselkä Finland 63°52N 28°32E 8 E23
Ma'anshan China 31°44N 118°29E 33 C6
Maarianhamina = Mariehamn Finland 60°5N 19°55E 9 F18
Ma'arrat an Nu'mān Syria 35°43N 36°43E 44 C3
Maas → Neths. 51°45N 4°32E 15 C4
Maaseik Belgium 51°6N 5°45E 15 C5
Maasin Phil. 10°8N 124°50E 37 B6
Maastricht Neths. 50°50N 5°40E 15 D5
Maave Mozam. 21°4S 34°47E 57 C5
Mababe Depression Botswana 18°50S 24°15E 56 B3

Mabalane *Mozam.* 23°37S 32°31E **57 C5**
Mabel L. *Canada* 50°35N 118°43W **70 C5**
Mabenge
  Dem. Rep. of the Congo 4°15N 24°12E **54 B1**
Maberly *Canada* 44°50N 76°32W **83 B8**
Mablethorpe *U.K.* 53°20N 0°15E **12 D8**
Maboma
  Dem. Rep. of the Congo 2°30N 28°10E **54 B2**
Mabuasehube △
  Botswana 25°5S 21°10E **56 D3**
Mac Bac *Vietnam* 9°46N 106°7E **39 H6**
Macachín *Argentina* 37°10S 63°43W **94 D3**
Macaé *Brazil* 22°20S 41°43W **95 A7**
McAlester *U.S.A.* 34°56N 95°46W **84 D7**
McAllen *U.S.A.* 26°12N 98°14W **84 H5**
MacAlpine L. *Canada* 66°32N 102°45W **68 C9**
Macamic *Canada* 48°45N 79°0W **72 C4**
Macao = Macau *China* 22°12N 113°33E **33 G10**
Macapá *Brazil* 0°5N 51°4W **93 C8**
Macarao △ *Venezuela* 10°22N 67°7W **89 D6**
McArthur → *Australia* 15°54S 136°40E **62 B2**
McArthur, Port *Australia* 16°4S 136°23E **62 B2**
Macau *Brazil* 5°15S 36°40W **93 E11**
Macau *China* 22°12N 113°33E **33 G10**
McBride *Canada* 53°20N 120°19W **70 C4**
McCall *U.S.A.* 44°55N 116°6W **76 D5**
McCamey *U.S.A.* 31°8N 102°14W **84 F3**
McCammon *U.S.A.* 42°39N 112°12W **76 E7**
McCarran Int., Las Vegas ✈ (LAS)
  U.S.A. 36°5N 115°9W **79 J11**
McCauley I. *Canada* 53°40N 130°15W **70 C2**
McCleary *U.S.A.* 47°3N 123°16W **78 C3**
McClennan *U.S.A.* 30°17N 82°7W **85 F13**
Macclesfield *U.K.* 53°15N 2°8W **12 D5**
M'Clintock Chan. *Canada* 72°0N 102°0W **68 B9**
McClintock Ra.
  Australia 18°44S 127°38E **60 C4**
McCloud *U.S.A.* 41°15N 122°8W **76 F2**
McCluer I. *Australia* 11°5S 133°0E **60 B5**
McClure *U.S.A.* 40°42N 77°19W **82 F7**
McClure, L. *U.S.A.* 37°35N 120°16W **78 H6**
M'Clure Str. *Canada* 75°0N 119°0W **69 B8**
McClusky *U.S.A.* 47°29N 100°27W **80 B3**
McComb *U.S.A.* 31°15N 90°27W **85 F9**
McCook *U.S.A.* 40°12N 100°38W **80 E3**
McCreary *Canada* 50°47N 99°29W **71 C9**
McCullough Mt.
  U.S.A. 35°35N 115°13W **79 K11**
McCusker → *Canada* 55°32N 108°39W **71 B7**
McDermitt *U.S.A.* 41°59N 117°43W **76 F5**
McDonald *U.S.A.* 40°22N 80°14W **82 F4**
McDonald Is. *Ind. Oc.* 53°0S 73°0E **3 G13**
MacDonnell Ranges
  Australia 23°40S 133°0E **60 D5**
MacDowell L. *Canada* 52°15N 92°45W **72 B1**
Macduff *U.K.* 57°40N 2°31W **11 D6**
Macedonia *U.S.A.* 41°19N 81°31W **82 E3**
Macedonia □ *Greece* 40°39N 22°0E **23 D10**
Macedonia ■ *Europe* 41°53N 21°40E **23 D9**
Maceió *Brazil* 9°40S 35°41W **93 E11**
Macerata *Italy* 43°18N 13°27E **22 C5**
McFarland *U.S.A.* 35°41N 119°14W **79 K7**
McFarlane → *Canada* 59°12N 107°58W **71 B7**
Macfarlane, L. *Australia* 32°0S 136°40E **63 E2**
McGehee *U.S.A.* 33°38N 91°24W **84 E9**
McGill *U.S.A.* 39°23N 114°47W **76 G6**
Macgillycuddy's Reeks
  Ireland 51°58N 9°45W **10 E2**
McGraw *U.S.A.* 42°36N 76°8W **83 D8**
McGregor *U.S.A.* 43°1N 91°11W **80 D8**
McGregor Ra. *Australia* 27°0S 142°45E **63 D3**
McGuire, Mt. *Australia* 29°18S 148°23E **62 J6**
Mach *Pakistan* 29°50N 67°20E **42 E2**
Māch Kowr *Iran* 25°48N 61°28E **45 E9**
Machado = Jiparaná →
  Brazil 8°3S 62°52W **92 E6**
Machagai *Argentina* 26°56S 60°2W **94 B3**
Machakos *Kenya* 1°30S 37°15E **54 C4**
Machanga *Mozam.* 20°59S 35°0E **57 C6**
Machattie, L. *Australia* 24°50S 139°48E **62 C2**
Machava *Mozam.* 25°54S 32°28E **57 D5**
Macheke *Zimbabwe* 18°5S 31°51E **57 B5**
Machhu → *India* 23°6N 70°46E **42 H4**
Machiara △ *Pakistan* 34°40N 73°30E **42 B5**
Machias *Maine, U.S.A.* 44°43N 67°28W **81 C20**
Machias *N.Y., U.S.A.* 42°25N 78°29W **82 D6**
Machichi → *Canada* 57°3N 92°6W **71 B10**
Machico *Madeira* 32°43N 16°44W **24 D3**
Machilipatnam *India* 16°12N 81°8E **41 L12**
Machiques *Venezuela* 10°4N 72°34W **92 A4**
Machu Picchu *Peru* 13°8S 72°30W **92 F4**
Machynlleth *U.K.* 52°35N 3°50W **13 E4**
Macia *Mozam.* 25°2S 33°8E **57 D5**
McIlwraith Ra.
  Australia 13°50S 143°20E **62 A3**
McInnes L. *Canada* 52°13N 93°45W **71 C10**
McIntosh *U.S.A.* 45°55N 101°21W **80 C3**
McIntosh L. *Canada* 55°45N 105°0W **71 B8**
Macintyre → *Australia* 27°39S 125°32E **61 E4**
Macintyre → *Australia* 28°37S 150°47E **63 D5**
Mackay *Australia* 21°8S 149°11E **62 K7**
Mackay *U.S.A.* 43°55N 113°37W **76 E7**
Mackay, L. *Australia* 22°30S 129°0E **60 D4**
McKay Ra. *Australia* 23°0S 122°30E **60 D3**
McKeesport *U.S.A.* 40°20N 79°51W **82 F5**
McKellar *Canada* 45°30N 79°55W **82 A5**
McKenna *U.S.A.* 46°56N 122°33W **78 D4**
Mackenzie *Canada* 55°20N 123°5W **70 B4**
McKenzie *U.S.A.* 36°8N 88°31W **85 C10**
Mackenzie → *Australia* 23°38S 149°46E **62 C4**
Mackenzie → *Canada* 69°10N 134°20W **68 C6**
McKenzie → *U.S.A.* 44°7N 123°6W **76 D2**
Mackenzie Bay *Canada* 69°0N 137°30W **66 C6**

Mackenzie City = Linden
  Guyana 6°0N 58°10W **92 B7**
Mackenzie King I.
  Canada 77°45N 111°0W **69 B8**
Mackenzie Mts. *Canada* 64°0N 130°0W **68 C7**
Mackinaw City *U.S.A.* 45°47N 84°44W **81 C11**
McKinlay *Australia* 21°16S 141°18E **62 C3**
McKinlay → *Australia* 20°50S 141°28E **62 C3**
McKinley, Mt. *U.S.A.* 63°4N 151°0W **74 a**
McKinley Sea *Arctic* 82°0N 0°0 **4 A7**
McKinney *U.S.A.* 33°12N 96°37W **84 E6**
Mackinnon Road *Kenya* 3°40S 39°1E **54 C4**
McKittrick *U.S.A.* 35°18N 119°37W **79 K7**
Macklin *Canada* 52°20N 109°56W **71 C7**
Macksville *Australia* 30°40S 152°56E **63 E5**
McLaughlin *U.S.A.* 45°49N 100°49W **80 C3**
Maclean *Australia* 29°26S 153°16E **63 D5**
McLean *U.S.A.* 35°14N 100°36W **84 D4**
McLeansboro *U.S.A.* 38°6N 88°32W **80 F9**
Maclear *S. Africa* 31°2S 28°23E **57 E4**
Maclear, C. *Malawi* 13°58S 34°49E **55 E3**
Macleay → *Australia* 30°56S 153°0E **63 E5**
McLennan *Canada* 55°42N 116°50W **70 B5**
McLeod → *Canada* 54°9N 115°44W **70 C5**
McLeod, L. *Australia* 24°9S 113°47E **61 D1**
McLeod Lake *Canada* 54°58N 123°0W **70 C4**
McLoughlin, Mt.
  U.S.A. 42°27N 122°19W **76 E2**
McMechen *U.S.A.* 39°57N 80°44W **82 G4**
McMinnville *Oreg.,*
  U.S.A. 45°13N 123°12W **76 D2**
McMinnville *Tenn.,*
  U.S.A. 35°41N 85°46W **85 D12**
McMurdo *Antarctica* 77°0S 140°0E **5 D11**
McMurdo Sd. *Antarctica* 77°0S 170°0E **5 D11**
McMurray = Fort McMurray
  Canada 56°44N 111°7W **70 B6**
McMurray *U.S.A.* 48°19N 122°14W **78 B4**
Macodoene *Mozam.* 23°32S 35°5E **57 C6**
Macomb *U.S.A.* 40°27N 90°40W **80 E8**
Mâcon *France* 46°19N 4°50E **20 C6**
Macon *Ga., U.S.A.* 32°51N 83°38W **85 E13**
Macon *Miss., U.S.A.* 33°7N 88°34W **85 E10**
Macon *Mo., U.S.A.* 39°44N 92°28W **80 F7**
Macossa *Mozam.* 17°55S 33°56E **55 F3**
Macoun L. *Canada* 56°32N 103°40W **71 B8**
Macovane *Mozam.* 21°30S 35°2E **57 C6**
McPherson *U.S.A.* 38°22N 97°40W **80 F5**
McPherson Pk. *U.S.A.* 34°53N 119°53W **79 L7**
McPherson Ra.
  Australia 28°15S 153°15E **63 D5**
Macquarie → *Australia* 30°7S 147°24E **63 E4**
Macquarie Harbour
  Australia 42°15S 145°23E **63 G4**
Macquarie Is. *Pac. Oc.* 54°36S 158°55E **64 N7**
Macquarie Ridge *S. Ocean* 57°0S 159°0E **5 B10**
MacRobertson Land
  Antarctica 71°0S 64°0E **5 D6**
Macroom *Ireland* 51°54N 8°57W **10 E3**
MacTier *Canada* 45°8N 79°47W **82 A5**
Macubela *Mozam.* 16°53S 37°49E **55 F4**
Macuira △ *Colombia* 12°9N 71°21W **89 D5**
Macuiza *Mozam.* 18°7S 34°29E **55 F3**
Macumba → *Australia* 27°52S 137°12E **63 D2**
Macuro *Venezuela* 10°42N 61°55W **93 K15**
Macusani *Peru* 14°4S 70°29W **92 F4**
Macuse *Mozam.* 17°45S 37°10E **55 F4**
Macuspana *Mexico* 17°46N 92°36W **87 D6**
Macusse *Angola* 17°48S 20°23E **56 B3**
Ma'dabā □ *Jordan* 31°43N 35°47E **46 D4**
Madadeni *S. Africa* 27°43S 30°3E **57 D5**
Madagascar ■ *Africa* 20°0S 47°0E **57 C8**
Madā'in Sālih *Si. Arabia* 26°46N 37°57E **44 E3**
Madama *Niger* 22°0N 13°40E **51 D8**
Madame, I. *Canada* 45°30N 60°58W **73 C7**
Madang *Papua N. G.* 5°12S 145°49E **58 B7**
Madaripur *Bangla.* 23°19N 90°15E **41 H17**
Madauk *Burma* 17°56N 96°52E **41 L20**
Madawaska *Canada* 45°30N 78°0W **82 A7**
Madawaska → *Canada* 45°27N 76°21W **82 A7**
Madaya *Burma* 22°12N 96°10E **41 H20**
Maddalena *Italy* 41°16N 9°23E **22 D3**
Madeira *Atl. Oc.* 32°50N 17°0W **24 D3**
Madeira → *Brazil* 3°22S 58°45W **92 D7**
Madeleine, Îs. de la
  Canada 47°30N 61°40W **73 C7**
Madera *Mexico* 29°12N 108°7W **86 B3**
Madera *Calif., U.S.A.* 36°57N 120°3W **78 J6**
Madera *Pa., U.S.A.* 40°49N 78°26W **82 F6**
Madha *India* 18°0N 75°30E **40 L9**
Madhavpur *India* 21°15N 69°58E **42 J3**
Madhepura *India* 26°11N 86°23E **43 F12**
Madhubani *India* 26°21N 86°7E **43 F12**
Madhupur *India* 24°16N 86°39E **43 G12**
Madhya Pradesh □ *India* 22°50N 78°0E **42 J8**
Madidi → *Bolivia* 12°32S 66°52W **92 F5**
Madikeri *India* 12°30N 75°45E **40 N9**
Madikwe △ *S. Africa* 27°38S 32°15E **57 D5**
Madill *U.S.A.* 34°6N 96°46W **84 D6**
Madimba
  Dem. Rep. of the Congo 4°58S 15°5E **52 E3**
Ma'din *Syria* 35°45N 39°36E **44 C3**
Madinat al Malik Khālid al
  Askarīyah *Si. Arabia* 25°24N 45°31E **44 E5**
Madingou *Congo* 4°10S 13°33E **52 E2**
Madirovalo *Madag.* 16°26S 46°32E **57 B8**
Madison *Calif., U.S.A.* 38°41N 121°59W **78 G5**
Madison *Fla., U.S.A.* 30°28N 83°25W **85 F13**
Madison *Ind., U.S.A.* 38°44N 85°23W **81 F11**
Madison *Nebr., U.S.A.* 41°50N 97°27W **80 E5**
Madison *Ohio, U.S.A.* 41°46N 81°3W **82 E3**
Madison *S. Dak., U.S.A.* 44°0N 97°7W **80 C5**
Madison *Wis., U.S.A.* 43°4N 89°24W **80 D9**
Madison → *U.S.A.* 45°56N 111°31W **76 D8**
Madison Heights *U.S.A.* 37°25N 79°8W **81 G14**
Madisonville *Ky.,*
  U.S.A. 37°20N 87°30W **80 G10**

Madisonville *Tex.,*
  U.S.A. 30°57N 95°55W **84 F7**
Madista *Botswana* 21°15S 25°6E **56 C4**
Madiun *Indonesia* 7°38S 111°32E **37 G14**
Mado Gashi *Kenya* 0°44N 39°10E **54 B4**
Madoc *Canada* 44°30N 77°28W **82 B7**
Madona *Latvia* 56°53N 26°5E **9 H22**
Madrakah, Ra's al *Oman* 19°0N 57°50E **47 D6**
Madras = Chennai *India* 13°8N 80°19E **40 N12**
Madras = Tamil Nadu □
  India 11°0N 77°0E **40 P10**
Madras *U.S.A.* 44°38N 121°8W **76 D3**
Madre, L. *U.S.A.* 25°15N 97°30W **84 J6**
Madre, Sierra *Phil.* 17°0N 122°0E **37 A6**
Madre de Dios → *Bolivia* 10°59S 66°8W **92 F5**
Madre de Dios, I. *Chile* 50°20S 75°10W **96 G1**
Madre Occidental, Sierra
  Mexico 27°0N 107°0W **86 B3**
Madre Oriental, Sierra
  Mexico 25°0N 100°0W **86 C5**
Madre del Sur, Sierra
  Mexico 17°30N 100°0W **87 D5**
Madri *India* 24°16N 73°32E **42 G5**
Madrid *Spain* 40°24N 3°42W **21 B4**
Madrid *U.S.A.* 44°45N 75°8W **83 B9**
Madura *Australia* 31°55S 127°0E **61 F4**
Madura *Indonesia* 7°30S 114°0E **37 G15**
Madura, Selat *Indonesia* 7°30S 113°20E **37 G15**
Madurai *India* 9°55N 78°10E **40 Q11**
Madurantakam *India* 12°30N 79°50E **40 N11**
Mae Chan *Thailand* 20°9N 99°52E **38 B2**
Mae Hong Son *Thailand* 19°16N 97°56E **38 C2**
Mae Khlong → *Thailand* 13°24N 100°0E **38 F3**
Mae Phrik *Thailand* 17°27N 99°7E **38 D2**
Mae Ping △ *Thailand* 17°37N 98°51E **38 D2**
Mae Ramat *Thailand* 16°58N 98°31E **38 D2**
Mae Rim *Thailand* 18°54N 98°57E **38 C2**
Mae Sai *Thailand* 20°20N 99°55E **38 B2**
Mae Sot *Thailand* 16°43N 98°34E **38 D2**
Mae Suai *Thailand* 19°39N 99°33E **38 C2**
Mae Tha *Thailand* 18°28N 99°8E **38 C2**
Mae Wong △ *Thailand* 15°54N 99°12E **38 E2**
Mae Yom △ *Thailand* 18°43N 100°15E **38 C3**
Maebashi *Japan* 36°24N 139°4E **31 F9**
Maesteg *U.K.* 51°36N 3°40W **13 F4**
Maestra, Sierra *Cuba* 20°15N 77°0W **88 B4**
Maevatanana *Madag.* 16°56S 46°49E **57 B8**
Mafeking = Mafikeng
  S. Africa 25°50S 25°38E **56 D4**
Mafeking *Canada* 52°40N 101°10W **71 C8**
Mafeteng *Lesotho* 29°51S 27°15E **56 D4**
Maffra *Australia* 37°53S 146°58E **63 F4**
Mafia I. *Tanzania* 7°45S 39°50E **54 D4**
Mafikeng *S. Africa* 25°50S 25°38E **56 D4**
Mafra *Brazil* 26°10S 49°55W **95 B6**
Mafra *Portugal* 38°55N 9°20W **21 C1**
Mafungabusi Plateau
  Zimbabwe 18°30S 29°8E **55 F2**
Magadan *Russia* 59°38N 150°50E **29 D16**
Magadi *Kenya* 1°54S 36°19E **54 C4**
Magadi, L. *Kenya* 1°54S 36°19E **54 C4**
Magaliesburg *S. Africa* 26°0S 27°32E **57 D4**
Magallanes, Estrecho de
  Chile 52°30S 75°0W **96 G2**
Magangué *Colombia* 9°14N 74°45W **92 B4**
Magdagachi *Russia* 53°27N 125°48E **29 D13**
Magdalen Is. = Madeleine, Îs. de la
  Canada 47°30N 61°40W **73 C7**
Magdalena *Argentina* 35°5S 57°30W **94 D4**
Magdalena *Bolivia* 13°13S 63°57W **92 F6**
Magdalena *U.S.A.* 34°7N 107°15W **77 J10**
Magdalena → *Colombia* 11°6N 74°51W **92 A4**
Magdalena → *Mexico* 30°40N 112°25W **86 A2**
Magdalena, B. *Mexico* 24°35N 112°0W **86 C2**
Magdalena, I. *Mexico* 24°40N 112°15W **86 C2**
Magdalena, Llano de
  Mexico 25°0N 111°25W **86 C2**
Magdalena de Kino
  Mexico 30°38N 110°57W **86 A2**
Magdeburg *Germany* 52°7N 11°38E **16 B6**
Magdelaine Cays
  Australia 16°33S 150°18E **62 B5**
Magee *U.S.A.* 31°52N 89°44W **85 F10**
Magelang *Indonesia* 7°29S 110°13E **37 G14**
Magellan's Str. = Magallanes,
  Estrecho de *Chile* 52°30S 75°0W **96 G2**
Magenta, L. *Australia* 33°30S 119°2E **61 F2**
Magerøya *Norway* 71°3N 25°40E **8 A21**
Maggiore, Lago *Italy* 45°57N 8°39E **20 D8**
Maggotty *Jamaica* 18°9N 77°46W **88 a**
Maghâgha *Egypt* 28°38N 30°50E **51 C12**
Magherafelt *U.K.* 54°45N 6°37W **10 B5**
Maghreb *N. Afr.* 32°0N 4°0W **50 B5**
Magistralnyy *Russia* 56°16N 107°36E **29 D11**
Magnetic Pole (North)
  Canada 82°42N 114°24W **69 B9**
Magnetic Pole (South)
  Antarctica 64°8S 138°8E **5 C9**
Magnitogorsk *Russia* 53°27N 59°4E **18 D10**
Magnolia *Ark., U.S.A.* 33°16N 93°14W **84 E8**
Magnolia *Miss., U.S.A.* 31°9N 90°28W **85 F9**
Mago *Fiji* 17°26S 179°9W **59 a**
Magoro *Uganda* 1°45N 34°12E **54 B3**
Magoša = Famagusta
  Cyprus 35°8N 33°55E **25 D12**
Magoye *Zambia* 16°1S 27°50E **55 F2**
Magpie, L. *Canada* 51°0N 64°41W **73 B7**
Magrath *Canada* 49°25N 112°50W **70 D6**
Maguarinho, C. *Brazil* 0°15S 48°30W **93 D9**
Magude *Mozam.* 25°2S 32°40E **57 D5**
Māgusa = Famagusta
  Cyprus 35°8N 33°55E **25 D12**
Maguse L. *Canada* 61°37N 95°10W **71 A9**
Maguse Pt. *Canada* 61°20N 93°50W **71 A10**
Magvana *India* 23°13N 69°22E **42 H3**

Magwe *Burma* 20°10N 95°0E **41 J19**
Magyarország = Hungary ■
  Europe 47°20N 19°20E **17 E10**
Maha Sarakham
  Thailand 16°12N 103°16E **38 D4**
Mahābād *Iran* 36°50N 45°45E **44 B5**
Mahabharat Lekh *Nepal* 28°30N 82°0E **43 E10**
Mahabo *Madag.* 20°23S 44°40E **57 C7**
Mahadeo Hills *India* 22°20N 78°30E **43 H8**
Mahaffey *U.S.A.* 40°53N 78°44W **82 F6**
Mahagi
  Dem. Rep. of the Congo 2°20N 31°0E **54 B3**
Mahajamba → *Madag.* 15°33S 47°8E **57 B8**
Mahajamba, Helodranon' i
  Madag. 15°24S 47°5E **57 B8**
Mahajan *India* 28°48N 73°56E **42 E5**
Mahajanga *Madag.* 15°40S 46°25E **57 B8**
Mahajanga □ *Madag.* 17°0S 47°0E **57 B8**
Mahajilo → *Madag.* 19°42S 45°22E **57 B8**
Mahakam → *Indonesia* 0°35S 117°17E **36 E5**
Mahalapye *Botswana* 23°1S 26°51E **56 C4**
Mahale Mts. *Tanzania* 6°20S 30°0E **54 D3**
Mahale Mts. △ *Tanzania* 6°10S 29°50E **54 D2**
Maḩallāt *Iran* 33°55N 50°30E **45 C6**
Māhān *Iran* 30°5N 57°18E **45 D8**
Mahan → *India* 23°30N 82°50E **43 H10**
Mahanadi → *India* 20°20N 86°25E **41 J15**
Mahananda → *India* 25°12N 87°52E **43 G12**
Mahanoro *Madag.* 19°54S 48°48E **57 B8**
Mahanoy City *U.S.A.* 40°49N 76°9W **83 F8**
Maharashtra □ *India* 20°30N 75°30E **40 J9**
Mahasham, W. →
  Egypt 30°15N 34°10E **46 E3**
Mahasoa *Madag.* 22°12S 46°6E **57 C8**
Mahasolo *Madag.* 19°7S 46°22E **57 B8**
Mahattat ash Shīdīyah
  Jordan 29°55N 35°55E **46 F4**
Mahattat 'Unayzah
  Jordan 30°30N 35°47E **46 E4**
Mahavavy → *Madag.* 15°57S 45°54E **57 B8**
Mahaxay *Laos* 17°22N 105°12E **38 D5**
Mahbubnagar *India* 16°45N 77°59E **40 L10**
Maḩdah *Oman* 24°24N 55°59E **45 E7**
Mahdia *Tunisia* 35°28N 11°0E **51 A8**
Mahe *India* 33°10N 78°32E **43 C8**
Mahé *Seychelles* 5°0S 55°30E **53 b**
Mahé (SEZ) *Seychelles* 4°40S 55°31E **53 b**
Mahébourg *Mauritius* 20°24S 57°42E **53 d**
Mahendragarh *India* 28°17N 76°14E **42 E7**
Mahendranagar *Nepal* 28°55N 80°20E **43 E9**
Mahenge *Tanzania* 8°45S 36°41E **55 D4**
Maheno *N.Z.* 45°10S 170°50E **59 F3**
Mahesana *India* 23°39N 72°26E **42 H5**
Maheshwar *India* 22°11N 75°35E **42 H6**
Mahgawan *India* 26°29N 78°37E **43 F8**
Mahi → *India* 22°15N 72°55E **42 H5**
Mahia Pen. *N.Z.* 39°9S 177°55E **59 C6**
Mahilyow *Belarus* 53°55N 30°18E **17 B16**
Mahina *Tahiti* 17°30S 149°27W **59 d**
Mahinerangi, L. *N.Z.* 45°50S 169°56E **59 F2**
Mahmud Kot *Pakistan* 30°16N 71°0E **42 D4**
Mahnomen *U.S.A.* 47°19N 95°58W **80 B6**
Mahoba *India* 25°15N 79°55E **43 G8**
Mahón = Maó *Spain* 39°53N 4°16E **24 B11**
Mahone Bay *Canada* 44°27N 64°23W **73 D7**
Mahopac *U.S.A.* 41°22N 73°45W **83 E11**
Mahuva *India* 21°5N 71°48E **42 J4**
Mai-Ndombe, L.
  Dem. Rep. of the Congo 2°0S 18°20E **52 E3**
Mai Thon, Ko *Thailand* 7°40N 98°28E **39 a**
Maicuru → *Brazil* 2°14S 54°17W **93 D8**
Maidan Khula *Afghan.* 33°36N 69°50E **42 C3**
Maidenhead *U.K.* 51°31N 0°42W **13 F7**
Maidstone *Canada* 53°5N 109°20W **71 C7**
Maidstone *U.K.* 51°16N 0°32E **13 F8**
Maiduguri *Nigeria* 12°0N 13°20E **51 F8**
Maihar *India* 24°16N 80°45E **43 G9**
Maiji *Bangla.* 22°48N 91°10E **41 H17**
Maikala Ra. *India* 22°0N 81°0E **41 J12**
Maiko △
  Dem. Rep. of the Congo 0°30S 27°50E **54 C2**
Mailani *India* 28°17N 80°21E **43 E9**
Mailsi *Pakistan* 29°48N 72°15E **42 E5**
Main → *Germany* 50°0N 8°18E **16 C5**
Main → *U.K.* 54°48N 6°18W **10 B5**
Main Channel *Canada* 45°21N 81°45W **82 A3**
Main Range △
  Australia 28°11S 152°27E **63 D5**
Main Ridge *Trin. & Tob.* 11°16N 60°40W **93 J16**
Maine *France* 48°20N 0°15W **20 C3**
Maine □ *U.S.A.* 45°20N 69°0W **81 C19**
Maine → *Ireland* 52°9N 9°45W **10 D2**
Maine, G. of *U.S.A.* 43°0N 68°30W **81 D19**
Maingkwan *Burma* 26°15N 96°37E **41 F20**
Mainit, L. *Phil.* 9°31N 125°30E **37 C7**
Mainland *Orkney, U.K.* 58°59N 3°8W **11 C5**
Mainland *Shet., U.K.* 60°15N 1°22W **11 A7**
Mainoru *Australia* 14°0S 134°6E **62 A1**
Mainpuri *India* 27°18N 79°4E **43 F8**
Maintirano *Madag.* 18°3S 44°1E **57 B7**
Mainz *Germany* 50°1N 8°14E **16 C5**
Maio *C. Verde Is.* 15°10N 23°10W **50 b**
Maipú *Argentina* 36°52S 57°50W **94 D4**
Maiquetía *Venezuela* 10°36N 66°57W **92 A5**
Mairabari *India* 26°30N 92°22E **41 F18**
Maisí *Cuba* 20°17N 74°9W **89 B5**
Maisí, Pta. de *Cuba* 20°10N 74°10W **89 B5**
Maitland *N.S.W.,*
  Australia 32°33S 151°36E **63 E5**
Maitland *S. Austral.,*
  Australia 34°23S 137°40E **63 E2**
Maitland → *Canada* 43°45N 81°43W **82 C3**
Maitri *Antarctica* 70°0S 3°0W **5 D3**
Maíz, Is. del *Nic.* 12°15N 83°4W **88 D3**
Maizuru *Japan* 35°25N 135°22E **31 G7**
Majalengka *Indonesia* 6°50S 108°13E **37 G13**
Majene *Indonesia* 3°38S 118°57E **37 E5**

Majete △ *Malawi* 15°54S 34°34E **55 F3**
Majorca = Mallorca
  Spain 39°30N 3°0E **24 B10**
Majuro *Marshall Is.* 7°9N 171°12E **64 G9**
Maka *Senegal* 13°40N 14°10W **50 F3**
Makaha *Zimbabwe* 17°20S 32°39E **57 B5**
Makalamabedi *Botswana* 20°19S 23°51E **56 C3**
Makale *Indonesia* 3°6S 119°51E **37 E5**
Makalu-Barun △ *Nepal* 27°45N 87°10E **43 F12**
Makamba *Burundi* 4°8S 29°49E **54 C2**
Makarikari = Makgadikgadi Salt
  Pans *Botswana* 20°40S 25°45E **56 C4**
Makarov Basin *Arctic* 87°0N 150°0W **4 A**
Makarovo *Russia* 57°40N 107°45E **29 D11**
Makasar = Ujung Pandang
  Indonesia 5°10S 119°20E **37 F5**
Makasar, Selat *Indonesia* 1°0S 118°20E **37 E5**
Makasar, Str. of = Makasar, Selat
  Indonesia 1°0S 118°20E **37 E5**
Makat = Maqat
  Kazakhstan 47°39N 53°19E **19 E9**
Makedonija = Macedonia ■
  Europe 41°53N 21°40E **23 D9**
Makeni *S. Leone* 8°55N 12°5W **50 G3**
Makeyevka = Makiyivka
  Ukraine 48°0N 38°0E **19 E6**
Makgadikgadi △
  Botswana 20°27S 24°47E **56 C3**
Makgadikgadi Salt Pans
  Botswana 20°40S 25°45E **56 C4**
Makhachkala *Russia* 43°0N 47°30E **19 F8**
Makhado = Louis Trichardt
  S. Africa 23°1S 29°43E **57 C4**
Makham, Ao *Thailand* 7°51N 98°25E **39 a**
Makhfar al Buşayyah
  Iraq 30°0N 46°10E **44 D5**
Makhmūr *Iraq* 35°46N 43°35E **44 C4**
Makian *Indonesia* 0°20N 127°20E **37 D7**
Makindu *Kenya* 2°18S 37°50E **54 C4**
Makīnsk *Kazakhstan* 52°37N 70°26E **28 D8**
Makira = San Cristóbal
  Solomon Is. 10°30S 161°0E **58 C9**
Makiyivka *Ukraine* 48°0N 38°0E **19 E6**
Makkah *Si. Arabia* 21°30N 39°54E **47 C2**
Makkovik *Canada* 55°10N 59°10W **73 A8**
Makó *Hungary* 46°14N 20°33E **17 E11**
Makogai *Fiji* 17°28S 179°0E **59 a**
Makokou *Gabon* 0°40N 12°50E **52 D2**
Makongo
  Dem. Rep. of the Congo 3°25N 26°17E **54 B2**
Makoro
  Dem. Rep. of the Congo 3°10N 29°59E **54 B2**
Makrai *India* 22°2N 77°0E **42 H7**
Makran Coast Range
  Pakistan 25°40N 64°0E **40 G4**
Makrana *India* 27°2N 74°46E **42 F6**
Makrigialos *Greece* 35°2N 25°59E **25 D7**
Mākū *Iran* 39°15N 44°31E **44 B5**
Makunda *Botswana* 22°30S 20°7E **56 C3**
Makurazaki *Japan* 31°15N 130°20E **31 J5**
Makurdi *Nigeria* 7°43N 8°35E **50 G7**
Makwassie *S. Africa* 27°17S 26°0E **56 D4**
Makwiro *Zimbabwe* 17°58S 30°25E **57 B5**
Mal B. *Ireland* 52°50N 9°30W **10 D2**
Mala, Pta. *Panama* 7°28N 80°2W **88 E3**
Malabar Coast *India* 11°0N 75°0E **40 P9**
Malacca, Straits of
  Indonesia 3°0N 101°0E **39 L3**
Malad City *U.S.A.* 42°12N 112°15W **76 E7**
Maladzyechna *Belarus* 54°20N 26°50E **17 A14**
Málaga *Spain* 36°43N 4°23W **21 D3**
Malagarasi *Tanzania* 5°5S 30°50E **54 D3**
Malagarasi → *Tanzania* 5°12S 29°47E **54 D2**
Malagasy Rep. = Madagascar ■
  Africa 20°0S 47°0E **57 C8**
Malahide *Ireland* 53°26N 6°9W **10 C5**
Malaimbandy *Madag.* 20°20S 45°36E **57 C8**
Malaita *Solomon Is.* 9°0S 161°0E **58 B9**
Malakāl *Sudan* 9°33N 31°40E **51 G12**
Malakand *Pakistan* 34°40N 71°55E **42 B4**
Malakula *Vanuatu* 16°15S 167°30E **58 C9**
Malakwal *Pakistan* 32°34N 73°13E **42 C5**
Malamala *Indonesia* 3°21S 120°55E **37 E6**
Malanda *Australia* 17°22S 145°35E **62 B4**
Malang *Indonesia* 7°59S 112°45E **37 G15**
Malanga *Mozam.* 13°28S 36°7E **55 E4**
Malangen *Norway* 69°24N 18°37E **8 B18**
Malanje *Angola* 9°36S 16°17E **52 F3**
Mälaren *Sweden* 59°30N 17°10E **9 G17**
Malargüe *Argentina* 35°32S 69°30W **94 D2**
Malartic *Canada* 48°9N 78°9W **72 C4**
Malaryta *Belarus* 51°50N 24°3E **17 C13**
Malatya *Turkey* 38°25N 38°20E **44 B3**
Malawi ■ *Africa* 11°55S 34°0E **55 E3**
Malawi, L. *Africa* 12°30S 34°30E **55 E3**
Malay Pen. *Asia* 7°25N 100°0E **39 J3**
Malaya Vishera *Russia* 58°55N 32°25E **18 C5**
Malaybalay *Phil.* 8°5N 125°7E **37 C7**
Malāyer *Iran* 34°19N 48°51E **45 C6**
Malaysia ■ *Asia* 5°0N 110°0E **39 K4**
Malazgirt *Turkey* 39°10N 42°33E **44 B4**
Malbon *Australia* 21°5S 140°17E **62 C3**
Malbooma *Australia* 30°41S 134°11E **63 E1**
Malbork *Poland* 54°3N 19°1E **17 B10**
Malcolm *Australia* 28°51S 121°25E **61 E3**
Malcolm, Pt. *Australia* 33°48S 123°45E **61 F3**
Maldah *India* 25°2N 88°9E **43 G13**
Maldegem *Belgium* 51°14N 3°26E **15 C3**
Malden *Mass., U.S.A.* 42°26N 71°3W **83 D13**
Malden *Mo., U.S.A.* 36°34N 89°57W **80 G9**
Malden I. *Kiribati* 4°3S 155°1W **65 H12**
Maldives ■ *Ind. Oc.* 5°0N 73°0E **26 H9**
Maldon *U.K.* 51°44N 0°42E **13 F8**
Maldonado *Uruguay* 34°59S 55°0W **95 C5**
Maldonado, Pta. *Mexico* 16°20N 98°33W **87 D5**
Malé Karpaty *Slovak Rep.* 48°30N 17°20E **17 D9**

140 Maleas, Akra INDEX TO WORLD MAPS

Maleas, Akra Greece 36°28N 23°7E 23 F10
Malebo, Pool Africa 4°17S 15°20E 52 E3
Malegaon India 20°30N 74°38E 40 J9
Malei Mozam. 17°12S 36°58E 55 F4
Malek Kandī Iran 37°9N 46°6E 44 B5
Malela Dem. Rep. of the Congo 4°22S 26°8E 54 C2
Malema Mozam. 14°57S 37°20E 55 E4
Maleme Greece 35°31N 23°49E 25 D5
Malerkotla India 30°32N 75°58E 42 D6
Males Greece 35°6N 25°35E 25 D7
Malgomaj Sweden 64°40N 16°30E 8 D17
Malha Sudan 15°8N 25°10E 51 E11
Malhargarh India 24°17N 74°59E 42 G6
Malheur → U.S.A. 44°4N 116°59W 76 D5
Malheur L. U.S.A. 43°20N 118°48W 76 E4
Mali ■ Africa 17°0N 3°0W 50 E5
Mali → Burma 25°42N 97°30E 41 G20
Mali Kyun Burma 13°0N 98°20E 38 F2
Malia Greece 35°17N 25°32E 25 D7
Malia, Kolpos Greece 35°19N 25°27E 25 D7
Malibu U.S.A. 34°2N 118°41W 79 L8
Maliku Indonesia 0°39S 123°16E 37 E6
Malili Indonesia 2°42S 121°6E 37 E6
Malimba, Mts. Dem. Rep. of the Congo 7°30S 29°30E 54 D2
Malin Hd. Ireland 55°23N 7°23W 10 A4
Malin Pen. Ireland 55°20N 7°17W 10 A4
Malindi Kenya 3°12S 40°5E 54 C5
Malines = Mechelen Belgium 51°2N 4°29E 15 C4
Malino Indonesia 1°0N 121°0E 37 D6
Malinyi Tanzania 8°56S 36°0E 55 D4
Malita Phil. 6°19N 125°39E 37 C7
Maliwun Burma 10°17N 98°40E 39 G2
Maliya India 23°5N 70°46E 42 H4
Malka Mari △ Kenya 4°11N 40°46E 54 B5
Malkara Turkey 40°53N 26°53E 23 D12
Mallacoota Inlet Australia 37°34S 149°40E 63 F4
Mallaig U.K. 57°0N 5°50W 11 D3
Mallawan India 27°4N 80°12E 43 F9
Mallawi Egypt 27°44N 30°44E 51 C12
Mallicolo = Malakula Vanuatu 16°15S 167°30E 58 C9
Mallorca Spain 39°30N 3°0E 24 B10
Mallorytown Canada 44°29N 75°53W 83 B9
Mallow Ireland 52°8N 8°39W 10 D3
Malmberget Sweden 67°11N 20°40E 8 C19
Malmédy Belgium 50°25N 6°2E 15 D6
Malmesbury S. Africa 33°28S 18°41E 56 E2
Malmivaara = Malmberget Sweden 67°11N 20°40E 8 C19
Malmö Sweden 55°36N 12°59E 9 J15
Malolo Fiji 17°45S 177°11E 59 a
Malolos Phil. 14°50N 120°49E 37 B6
Malolotja ⌂ Swaziland 26°4S 31°6E 57 D5
Malombe L. Malawi 14°40S 35°15E 55 E4
Malone U.S.A. 44°51N 74°18W 83 B10
Måløy Norway 61°57N 5°6E 8 F11
Malpaso Canary Is. 27°43N 18°3W 24 G1
Malpaso, Presa = Netzahualcóyotl, Presa Mexico 17°8N 93°35W 87 D6
Malpelo, I. de Colombia 4°3N 81°35W 92 C2
Malpur India 23°21N 73°27E 42 H5
Malpura India 26°17N 75°23E 42 F6
Malta Idaho, U.S.A. 42°18N 113°22W 76 E7
Malta Mont., U.S.A. 48°21N 107°52W 76 B10
Malta ■ Europe 35°55N 14°26E 25 D2
Maltahöhe Namibia 24°55S 17°0E 56 C2
Malton Canada 43°42N 79°38W 82 C5
Malton U.K. 54°8N 0°49W 12 C7
Maluku Indonesia 1°0S 127°0E 37 E7
Maluku ☐ Indonesia 3°0S 128°0E 37 E7
Maluku Sea = Molucca Sea Indonesia 0°0 125°0E 37 E6
Malvan India 16°2N 73°30E 40 L8
Malvern U.S.A. 34°22N 92°49W 84 D8
Malvern Hills U.K. 52°0N 2°19W 13 E5
Malvinas, Is. = Falkland Is. ☒ Atl. Oc. 51°30S 59°0W 96 G5
Malya Tanzania 3°5S 33°38E 54 C3
Malyn Ukraine 50°46N 29°3E 17 C15
Malyy Lyakhovskiy, Ostrov Russia 74°7N 140°36E 29 B15
Malyy Taymyr, Ostrov Russia 78°6N 107°15E 29 B11
Mama Russia 58°18N 112°54E 29 D12
Mamanguape Brazil 6°50S 35°4W 93 E11
Mamanuca Group Fiji 17°35S 177°5E 59 a
Mamarr Mitlā Egypt 30°2N 32°54E 46 E1
Mamasa Indonesia 2°55S 119°20E 37 E5
Mambasa Dem. Rep. of the Congo 1°22N 29°3E 54 B2
Mamberamo → Indonesia 2°0S 137°50E 37 E9
Mambilima Falls Zambia 10°31S 28°45E 55 E2
Mambirima Dem. Rep. of the Congo 11°25S 27°33E 55 E2
Mambo Tanzania 4°52S 38°22E 54 C4
Mambrui Kenya 3°5S 40°5E 54 C5
Mamburao Phil. 13°13N 120°39E 37 B6
Mameigwess L. Canada 52°35N 87°50W 72 B2
Mammoth U.S.A. 32°43N 110°39W 77 K8
Mammoth Cave △ U.S.A. 37°8N 86°13W 80 G10
Mamoré → Bolivia 10°23S 65°53W 92 F5
Mamou Guinea 10°15N 12°0W 50 F3
Mamoudzou Mayotte 12°48S 45°14E 53 a
Mampikony Madag. 16°6S 47°38E 57 B8
Mamuju Indonesia 2°41S 118°50E 37 E5
Mamuno Botswana 22°16S 20°1E 56 C3
Man Ivory C. 7°30N 7°40W 50 G4
Man, I. of U.K. 54°15N 4°30W 12 C3
Man-Bazar India 23°4N 86°39E 43 H12
Man Na Burma 23°27N 97°19E 41 H20
Mana → Fr. Guiana 5°45N 53°55W 93 B8
Mana Pools △ Zimbabwe 15°56S 29°25E 55 F2
Manaar, G. of = Mannar, G. of Asia 8°30N 79°0E 40 Q11
Manacapuru Brazil 3°16S 60°37W 92 D6
Manacor Spain 39°34N 3°13E 24 B10
Manado Indonesia 1°29N 124°51E 37 D6
Managua Nic. 12°6N 86°20W 88 D2
Managua, L. de Nic. 12°20N 86°30W 88 D2
Manakara Madag. 22°8S 48°1E 57 C8
Manali India 32°16N 77°10E 42 C7
Manama = Al Manāmah Bahrain 26°10N 50°30E 45 E6
Manambao → Madag. 17°35S 44°0E 57 B7
Manambato Madag. 13°43S 49°7E 57 A8
Manambolo → Madag. 19°18S 44°22E 57 B7
Manambolosy Madag. 16°2S 49°40E 57 B8
Mananara Madag. 16°10S 49°46E 57 B8
Mananara → Madag. 23°21S 47°42E 57 C8
Mananara ⌂ Madag. 16°14S 49°45E 57 B8
Mananjary Madag. 21°13S 48°20E 57 C8
Manantenina Madag. 24°17S 47°19E 57 C8
Manaos = Manaus Brazil 3°0S 60°0W 92 D7
Manapire → Venezuela 7°42N 66°7W 92 B5
Manapouri N.Z. 45°34S 167°39E 59 F1
Manapouri, L. N.Z. 45°32S 167°32E 59 F1
Manār, Jabal Yemen 14°2N 44°17E 47 E3
Manaravolo Madag. 23°59S 45°39E 57 C8
Manas China 44°17N 85°56E 32 B3
Manas → India 26°12N 90°40E 41 F17
Manas He → China 45°38N 85°12E 32 B3
Manaslu Nepal 28°33N 84°33E 43 E11
Manasquan U.S.A. 40°8N 74°3W 83 F10
Manassa U.S.A. 37°11N 105°56W 77 H11
Manatí Puerto Rico 18°26N 66°29W 89 d
Manaung Burma 18°45N 93°40E 41 K18
Manaus Brazil 3°0S 60°0W 92 D7
Manawan L. Canada 55°24N 103°14W 71 B8
Manbij Syria 36°31N 37°57E 44 B3
Manchegorsk Russia 67°54N 32°58E 28 C4
Manchester U.K. 53°29N 2°12W 12 D5
Manchester Calif., U.S.A. 38°58N 123°41W 78 G3
Manchester Conn., U.S.A. 41°47N 72°31W 83 E12
Manchester Ga., U.S.A. 32°51N 84°37W 85 E12
Manchester Iowa, U.S.A. 42°29N 91°27W 80 D8
Manchester Ky., U.S.A. 37°9N 83°46W 81 G12
Manchester N.H., U.S.A. 42°59N 71°28W 83 D13
Manchester N.Y., U.S.A. 42°56N 77°16W 82 D7
Manchester Pa., U.S.A. 40°4N 76°43W 83 F8
Manchester Tenn., U.S.A. 35°29N 86°5W 85 D11
Manchester Vt., U.S.A. 43°10N 73°5W 83 C11
Manchester Int. ✕ (MAN) U.K. 53°21N 2°17W 12 D5
Manchester L. Canada 61°28N 107°29W 71 A7
Manchhar L. Pakistan 26°25N 67°39E 42 F2
Manchuria = Dongbei China 45°0N 125°0E 30 A5
Manchurian Plain China 47°0N 124°0E 26 D14
Mand → India 21°42N 83°15E 43 J10
Mand → Iran 28°20N 52°30E 45 D7
Manda Ludewe, Tanzania 10°30S 34°40E 55 E3
Manda Mbeya, Tanzania 7°58S 32°29E 54 D3
Manda Mbeya, Tanzania 8°30S 32°49E 55 D3
Mandabé Madag. 21°0S 44°55E 57 C7
Mandaguari Brazil 23°32S 51°42W 95 A5
Mandah = Töhöm Mongolia 44°27N 108°2E 34 B5
Mandal Norway 58°2N 7°25E 9 G12
Mandala, Puncak Indonesia 4°44S 140°20E 37 E10
Mandalay Burma 22°0N 96°4E 41 J20
Mandale = Mandalay Burma 22°0N 96°4E 41 J20
Mandalgarh India 25°12N 75°6E 42 G6
Mandalgovĭ Mongolia 45°45N 106°10E 34 B4
Mandalī Iraq 33°43N 45°28E 44 C5
Mandan U.S.A. 46°50N 100°54W 80 B3
Mandar, Teluk Indonesia 3°35S 119°15E 37 E5
Mandaue Phil. 10°20N 123°56E 37 B6
Mandera Kenya 3°55N 41°53E 54 B5
Mandeville Jamaica 18°2N 77°31W 88 a
Mandi India 31°39N 76°58E 42 D7
Mandi Burewala Pakistan 30°9N 72°41E 42 D5
Mandi Dabwali India 29°58N 74°42E 42 E6
Mandimba Mozam. 14°20S 35°40E 55 E4
Mandioli Indonesia 0°40S 127°20E 37 E7
Mandla India 22°39N 80°30E 43 H9
Mandorah Australia 12°32S 130°42E 60 B5
Mandoto Madag. 19°34S 46°17E 57 B8
Mandra Pakistan 33°23N 73°12E 42 C5
Mandrare → Madag. 25°10S 46°30E 57 D8
Mandritsara Madag. 15°50S 48°49E 57 B8
Mandronarivo Madag. 21°7S 45°38E 57 C8
Mandsaur India 24°3N 75°8E 42 G6
Mandurah Australia 32°36S 115°48E 61 F2
Mandvi India 22°51N 69°22E 42 H3
Mandya India 12°30N 77°0E 40 N10
Mandzai Pakistan 30°55N 67°6E 42 D2
Maneh Iran 37°39N 57°7E 45 B8
Manera Madag. 22°55S 44°20E 57 C7
Maneroo Cr. → Australia 23°21S 143°53E 62 C3
Manfalût Egypt 27°20N 30°52E 51 C12
Manfredónia Italy 41°38N 15°55E 22 D6
Mangabeiras, Chapada das Brazil 10°0S 46°30W 93 F9
Mangaia Cook Is. 21°55S 157°55W 65 K12
Mangalia Romania 43°50N 28°35E 17 G15
Mangalore India 12°55N 74°47E 40 N9
Mangan India 27°31N 88°32E 43 F13
Mangaon India 18°15N 73°20E 40 K8
Mangawan India 24°41N 81°33E 43 G9
Mangaweka N.Z. 39°48S 175°47E 59 C5
Manggar Indonesia 2°50S 108°10E 36 E3
Manggawitu Indonesia 4°8S 133°32E 37 E8
Mangghystaū Tübegi Kazakhstan 44°30N 52°30E 28 E6
Manggis Indonesia 8°29S 115°31E 37 J18
Mangindrano Madag. 14°17S 48°58E 57 A8
Mangkalihat, Tanjung Indonesia 1°2N 118°59E 37 D5
Mangla Pakistan 33°7N 73°39E 42 C5
Mangla Dam Pakistan 33°9N 73°44E 43 C5
Manglaur India 29°44N 77°49E 42 E7
Mangnai China 37°52N 91°43E 32 C4
Mangnai Zhen China 38°24N 90°14E 32 C4
Mango Togo 10°20N 0°30E 50 F6
Mango Tonga 20°17S 174°29W 59 c
Mangoche Malawi 14°25S 35°16E 55 E4
Mangoky → Madag. 21°29S 43°41E 57 C7
Mangole Indonesia 1°50S 125°55E 37 E6
Mangombe Dem. Rep. of the Congo 1°20S 26°48E 54 C2
Mangonui N.Z. 35°1S 173°32E 59 A4
Mangoro → Madag. 20°0S 48°45E 57 B8
Mangrol Mad. P., India 21°7N 70°7E 42 J4
Mangrol Raj., India 25°20N 76°31E 42 G6
Mangueira, L. da Brazil 33°0S 52°50W 95 C5
Mangum U.S.A. 34°53N 99°30W 84 D5
Manguri Australia 28°58S 134°22E 63 A1
Mangyshlak, Poluostrov = Mangghystaū Tübegi Kazakhstan 44°30N 52°30E 28 E6
Manhattan U.S.A. 39°11N 96°35W 80 F5
Manhiça Mozam. 25°23S 32°49E 57 D5
Mania → Madag. 19°42S 45°22E 57 B8
Manica Mozam. 18°58S 32°59E 57 B5
Manica ☐ Mozam. 19°10S 33°45E 57 B5
Manicaland ☐ Zimbabwe 19°0S 32°30E 55 F3
Manicoré Brazil 5°48S 61°16W 92 E6
Manicouagan → Canada 49°30N 68°30W 73 C6
Manicouagan, Rés. Canada 51°5N 68°40W 73 B6
Maniema ☐ Dem. Rep. of the Congo 3°0S 26°0E 54 C2
Manīfah Si. Arabia 27°44N 49°0E 45 E6
Manifold, C. Australia 22°41S 150°50E 62 C5
Manigotagan Canada 51°6N 96°18W 71 C9
Manigotagan → Canada 51°7N 96°20W 71 C9
Manihari India 25°21N 87°38E 43 G12
Manihiki Cook Is. 10°24S 161°1W 65 J11
Manihiki Plateau Pac. Oc. 11°0S 164°0W 65 J11
Manika, Plateau de la Dem. Rep. of the Congo 10°0S 25°5E 55 E2
Manikpur India 25°4N 81°7E 43 G9
Manila Phil. 14°35N 120°58E 37 B6
Manila U.S.A. 40°59N 109°43W 76 F9
Manila B. Phil. 14°40N 120°35E 37 B6
Manilla Australia 30°45S 150°43E 63 E5
Maningrida Australia 12°3S 134°13E 62 A1
Manipur ☐ India 25°0N 94°0E 41 G19
Manipur → Burma 23°45N 94°20E 41 H19
Manisa Turkey 38°38N 27°30E 23 E12
Manistee U.S.A. 44°15N 86°19W 80 C10
Manistee → U.S.A. 44°15N 86°21W 80 C10
Manistique U.S.A. 45°57N 86°15W 80 C10
Manitoba ☐ Canada 53°30N 97°0W 71 B9
Manitoba, L. Canada 51°0N 98°45W 71 C9
Manitou Canada 49°15N 98°32W 71 D9
Manitou, L. Canada 50°55N 65°17W 73 B6
Manitou Is. U.S.A. 45°8N 86°0W 81 C10
Manitou L. Canada 52°43N 109°43W 71 C7
Manitou Springs U.S.A. 38°52N 104°55W 76 G11
Manitoulin I. Canada 45°40N 82°30W 72 C3
Manitouwadge Canada 49°8N 85°48W 72 C2
Manitowoc U.S.A. 44°5N 87°40W 80 C10
Manizales Colombia 5°5N 75°32W 92 B3
Manja Madag. 21°26S 44°20E 57 C7
Manjacaze Mozam. 24°45S 34°0E 57 C5
Manjakandriana Madag. 18°55S 47°47E 57 B8
Manjhand Pakistan 25°50N 68°10E 42 G3
Manjimup Australia 34°15S 116°6E 61 F2
Manjra → India 18°49N 77°52E 40 K10
Mankato Kans., U.S.A. 39°47N 98°13W 80 F4
Mankato Minn., U.S.A. 44°10N 94°0W 80 C6
Mankayane Swaziland 26°40S 31°4E 57 D5
Mankera Pakistan 31°23N 71°26E 42 D4
Mankota Canada 49°25N 107°5W 71 D7
Manlay = Üydzin Mongolia 44°9N 107°0E 34 B4
Manmad India 20°18N 74°28E 40 J9
Mann Ranges Australia 26°6S 130°5E 61 E5
Manna Indonesia 4°25S 102°55E 36 E2
Mannahill Australia 32°25S 140°0E 63 E3
Mannar Sri Lanka 9°1N 79°54E 40 Q11
Mannar, G. of Asia 8°30N 79°0E 40 Q11
Mannar I. Sri Lanka 9°5N 79°45E 40 Q11
Mannheim Germany 49°29N 8°29E 16 D5
Manning Canada 56°53N 117°39W 70 B5
Manning Oreg., U.S.A. 45°45N 123°13W 78 E3
Manning S.C., U.S.A. 33°42N 80°13W 85 E14
Mannum Australia 34°50S 139°20E 63 E2
Manoharpur India 22°23N 85°12E 43 H11
Manokwari Indonesia 0°54S 134°0E 37 E8
Manombo Madag. 22°57S 43°28E 57 C7
Manono Dem. Rep. of the Congo 7°15S 27°25E 54 D2
Manono Samoa 13°50S 172°5W 59 b
Manorhamilton Ireland 54°18N 8°9W 10 B3
Manosque France 43°49N 5°47E 20 E6
Manotick Canada 45°13N 75°41W 83 A9
Manouane → Canada 49°30N 71°10W 73 C5
Manouane, L. Canada 50°45N 70°45W 73 B5
Manp'o N. Korea 41°6N 126°24E 35 D14
Manpojin = Manp'o N. Korea 41°6N 126°24E 35 D14
Manpur Chhattisgarh, India 23°17N 83°35E 43 H10
Manpur Mad. P., India 22°26N 75°37E 42 H6
Manresa Spain 41°48N 1°50E 21 B6
Mansa Gujarat, India 23°27N 72°45E 42 H5
Mansa Punjab, India 30°0N 75°27E 42 E6
Mansa Zambia 11°13S 28°55E 55 E2
Mansehra Pakistan 34°20N 73°15E 42 B5
Mansel I. Canada 62°0N 80°0W 69 C12
Mansfield Australia 37°4S 146°6E 63 F4
Mansfield U.K. 53°9N 1°11W 12 D6
Mansfield La., U.S.A. 32°2N 93°43W 84 E8
Mansfield Mass., U.S.A. 42°2N 71°13W 83 D13
Mansfield Ohio, U.S.A. 40°45N 82°31W 82 F2
Mansfield Pa., U.S.A. 41°48N 77°5W 82 E7
Mansfield Tex., U.S.A. 32°33N 97°8W 84 E6
Mansfield, Mt. U.S.A. 44°33N 72°49W 83 B12
Manson Creek Canada 55°37N 124°32W 70 B4
Manta Ecuador 1°0S 80°40W 92 D2
Mantadia △ Madag. 18°54S 48°21E 57 B8
Mantalingajan, Mt. Phil. 8°55N 117°45E 36 C5
Mantare Tanzania 2°42S 33°13E 54 C3
Manteca U.S.A. 37°48N 121°13W 78 H5
Manteo U.S.A. 35°55N 75°40W 85 D17
Mantes-la-Jolie France 48°58N 1°41E 20 B4
Manthani India 18°40N 79°35E 40 K11
Manti U.S.A. 39°16N 111°38W 76 G8
Mantiqueira, Serra da Brazil 22°0S 44°0W 95 A7
Manton U.S.A. 44°25N 85°24W 81 C11
Mántova Italy 45°9N 10°48E 22 B4
Mänttä Finland 62°3N 24°40E 8 E21
Mantua = Mántova Italy 45°9N 10°48E 22 B4
Manú Peru 12°10S 70°51W 92 F4
Manú → Peru 12°16S 70°55W 92 F4
Manu'a Is. Amer. Samoa 14°13S 169°35W 59 b
Manuel Alves → Brazil 11°19S 48°28W 93 F9
Manui Indonesia 3°35S 123°5E 37 E6
Manukau N.Z. 37°0S 174°52E 59 B5
Manuripi → Bolivia 11°6S 67°36W 92 F5
Many U.S.A. 31°34N 93°29W 84 F8
Manyani Kenya 3°5S 38°30E 54 C4
Manyara, L. Tanzania 3°40S 35°50E 54 C4
Manych-Gudilo, Ozero Russia 46°24N 42°38E 19 E7
Manyonga → Tanzania 4°10S 34°15E 54 C3
Manyoni Tanzania 5°45S 34°55E 54 D3
Manzai Pakistan 32°12N 70°15E 42 C4
Manzanar ⌂ U.S.A. 36°44N 118°9W 78 J7
Manzanares Spain 39°2N 3°22W 21 C4
Manzanillo Cuba 20°20N 77°31W 88 B4
Manzanillo Mexico 19°3N 104°20W 86 D4
Manzanillo, Pta. Panama 9°30N 79°40W 88 E4
Manzano Mts. U.S.A. 34°40N 106°20W 77 J10
Manzarīyeh Iran 34°53N 50°50E 45 C6
Manzhouli China 49°35N 117°25E 33 B6
Manzini Swaziland 26°30S 31°25E 57 D5
Manzur Vadisi △ Turkey 39°10N 39°30E 44 B3
Mao Chad 14°4N 15°19E 51 F9
Maó Spain 39°53N 4°16E 24 B11
Maoke, Pegunungan Indonesia 3°40S 137°30E 37 E9
Maolin China 43°58N 123°30E 35 C12
Maoming China 21°50N 110°54E 33 D6
Maoxing China 45°28N 124°40E 35 B13
Mapam Yumco China 30°45N 81°28E 43 D9
Mapastepec Mexico 15°26N 92°54W 87 D6
Maphrao, Ko Thailand 7°56N 98°26E 39 a
Mapia, Kepulauan Indonesia 0°50N 134°20E 37 D8
Mapimí Mexico 25°49N 103°51W 86 B4
Mapimí, Bolsón de Mexico 27°0N 104°15W 86 B4
Mapinga Tanzania 6°40S 39°12E 54 D4
Mapinhane Mozam. 22°20S 35°0E 57 C6
Maple Creek Canada 49°55N 109°29W 71 D7
Maple Valley U.S.A. 47°25N 122°3W 78 C4
Mapleton U.S.A. 44°2N 123°52W 76 D2
Mapuera → Brazil 1°5S 57°2W 92 D7
Mapulanguene Mozam. 24°29S 32°6E 57 C5
Mapungubwe △ S. Africa 22°12S 29°22E 55 G2
Maputo Mozam. 25°58S 32°32E 57 D5
Maputo ☐ Mozam. 26°0S 32°25E 57 D5
Maputo, B. de Mozam. 25°50S 32°45E 57 D5
Maputo ⌂ Mozam. 26°23S 32°48E 57 D5
Maqat Kazakhstan 47°39N 53°19E 19 E9
Maqên China 34°24N 100°6E 32 C5
Maqiaohe China 44°40N 130°30E 35 B16
Maqnā Si. Arabia 28°25N 34°50E 44 D2
Maqteïr Mauritania 21°50N 11°40W 50 D3
Maquan He = Brahmaputra → Asia 23°40N 90°35E 43 H13
Maquela do Zombo Angola 6°0S 15°15E 52 F3
Maquinchao Argentina 41°15S 68°50W 96 E3
Maquoketa U.S.A. 42°4N 90°40W 80 D8
Mar Canada 44°49N 81°12W 82 B3
Mar, Serra do Brazil 25°30S 49°0W 95 B6
Mar Chiquita, L. Argentina 30°40S 62°50W 94 C3
Mar del Plata Argentina 38°0S 57°30W 94 D4
Mar Menor Spain 37°40N 0°45W 21 D5
Mara Tanzania 1°30S 34°32E 54 C3
Mara ☐ Tanzania 1°45S 34°20E 54 C3
Maraã Brazil 1°52S 65°25W 92 D5
Maraa Tahiti 17°46S 149°34W 59 d
Marabá Brazil 5°20S 49°5W 93 E9
Maraboon, L. Australia 23°41S 148°0E 62 C4
Maracá, I. de Brazil 2°10N 50°30W 93 C8
Maracaibo Venezuela 10°40N 71°37W 92 A4
Maracaibo, L. de Venezuela 9°40N 71°30W 92 B4
Maracaju Brazil 21°38S 55°9W 95 A4
Maracas Bay Village Trin. & Tob. 10°46N 61°28W 93 K15
Maracay Venezuela 10°15N 67°28W 92 A5
Marādah Libya 29°15N 19°15E 51 C9
Maradi Niger 13°29N 7°20E 50 F7
Marāgheh Iran 37°30N 46°12E 44 B5
Marāh Si. Arabia 25°0N 45°35E 44 E5
Marajó, I. de Brazil 1°0S 49°30W 93 D9
Marākand Iran 38°51N 45°16E 44 B5
Marakele △ S. Africa 32°14S 25°27E 57 E4
Maralal Kenya 1°0N 36°38E 54 B4
Maralinga Australia 30°13S 131°32E 61 F5
Marambio Antarctica 64°0S 56°0W 5 C18
Maran Malaysia 3°35N 102°45E 39 L4
Marana U.S.A. 32°27N 111°13W 77 K8
Maranboy Australia 14°40S 132°39E 60 B5
Marand Iran 38°30N 45°45E 44 B5
Marang Malaysia 5°12N 103°13E 39 K4
Maranguape Brazil 3°55S 38°50W 93 D11
Maranhão = São Luís Brazil 2°39S 44°15W 93 D10
Maranhão ☐ Brazil 5°0S 46°0W 93 E9
Maranoa → Australia 27°50S 148°37E 63 D4
Marañón → Peru 4°30S 73°35W 92 D4
Marão Mozam. 24°18S 34°2E 57 C5
Maraş = Kahramanmaraş Turkey 37°37N 36°53E 44 B3
Marathasa Cyprus 34°59N 32°51E 25 E11
Marathon Australia 20°51S 143°32E 62 C3
Marathon Canada 48°44N 86°23W 72 C2
Marathon N.Y., U.S.A. 42°27N 76°2W 83 D8
Marathon Tex., U.S.A. 30°12N 103°15W 84 F3
Marathóvouno Cyprus 35°13N 33°37E 25 D12
Maratua Indonesia 2°10N 118°35E 37 D5
Maraval Trin. & Tob. 10°42N 61°31W 93 K15
Maravatío Mexico 19°54N 100°27W 86 D4
Marāwih U.A.E. 24°18N 53°18E 45 E7
Marbella Spain 36°30N 4°57W 21 D3
Marble Bar Australia 21°9S 119°44E 60 D2
Marble Falls U.S.A. 30°35N 98°16W 84 F5
Marblehead Mass., U.S.A. 42°29N 70°51W 83 D14
Marblehead Ohio, U.S.A. 41°32N 82°44W 82 E2
Marburg Germany 50°47N 8°46E 16 C5
Marca, Pta. Da Angola 16°31S 11°43E 53 H2
March U.K. 52°33N 0°5E 13 E8
Marche France 46°5N 1°20E 20 C4
Marche-en-Famenne Belgium 50°14N 5°19E 15 D5
Marchena Spain 37°18N 5°23W 21 D3
Marco Island U.S.A. 25°58N 81°44W 85 J14
Marcos Juárez Argentina 32°42S 62°5W 94 C3
Marcus I. = Minami-Tori-Shima Pac. Oc. 24°20N 153°58E 64 E7
Marcy, Mt. U.S.A. 44°7N 73°56W 83 B11
Mardan Pakistan 34°20N 72°0E 42 B5
Mardin Turkey 37°20N 40°43E 44 B4
Maree, L. U.K. 57°40N 5°26W 11 D3
Mareeba Australia 16°59S 145°28E 62 B4
Mareetsane S. Africa 26°9S 25°25E 56 D4
Marek = Stanke Dimitrov Bulgaria 42°17N 23°9E 23 C10
Marengo U.S.A. 41°48N 92°4W 80 E7
Marerano Madag. 21°23S 44°52E 57 C7
Marfa U.S.A. 30°19N 104°1W 84 F2
Marfa Pt. Malta 35°59N 14°19E 25 D1
Margaret → Australia 18°9S 125°41E 60 C4
Margaret Bay Canada 51°20N 127°35W 70 C3
Margaret L. Canada 58°56N 115°25W 70 B5
Margaret River Australia 33°57S 115°4E 61 F2
Margarita, I. de Venezuela 11°0N 64°0W 92 A6
Margaritovo Russia 43°25N 134°45E 30 C7
Margate S. Africa 30°50S 30°20E 57 E5
Margate U.K. 51°23N 1°23E 13 F9
Margherita Pk. Uganda 0°22N 29°51E 54 B3
Marghilon Uzbekistan 40°27N 71°42E 28 E8
Mārgow, Dasht-e Afghan. 30°40N 62°30E 40 D3
Marguerite Canada 52°30N 122°25W 70 C4
Mari El ☐ Russia 56°30N 48°0E 18 C8
Mari Indus Pakistan 32°57N 71°34E 42 C4
Mari Republic = Mari El ☐ Russia 56°30N 48°0E 18 C8
María de la Salut Spain 39°40N 3°5E 24 B10
María Elena Chile 22°18S 69°40W 94 A2
María Grande Argentina 31°45S 59°55W 94 C4
Maria I. N. Terr., Australia 14°52S 135°45E 62 A2
Maria I. Tas., Australia 42°35S 148°0E 63 G4
Maria Island △ Australia 42°38S 148°5E 63 G4
Maria van Diemen, C. N.Z. 34°29S 172°40E 59 A4
Mariakani Kenya 3°50S 39°27E 54 C4
Mariala △ Australia 25°57S 145°2E 63 D4
Marian Australia 21°9S 148°57E 62 K6
Marian L. Canada 63°0N 116°15W 70 A5
Mariana Trench Pac. Oc. 13°0N 145°0E 64 F6
Marianna Ark., U.S.A. 34°46N 90°46W 85 D9
Marianna Fla., U.S.A. 30°46N 85°14W 85 F12
Marias → U.S.A. 47°56N 110°30W 76 C8
Marías, Islas Mexico 21°25N 106°28W 86 C3
Mariato, Punta Panama 7°12N 80°52W 88 E3
Maribor Slovenia 46°36N 15°40E 16 E8
Marico → Africa 23°35S 26°57E 56 C4
Maricopa Ariz., U.S.A. 33°4N 112°3W 77 K7
Maricopa Calif., U.S.A. 35°4N 119°24W 79 K7
Marié → Brazil 0°27S 66°26W 92 D5
Marie Byrd Land Antarctica 79°30S 125°0W 5 D14
Marie-Galante Guadeloupe 15°56N 61°16W 88 b
Mariecourt = Kangiqsujuaq Canada 61°30N 72°0W 69 C12
Mariehamn Finland 60°5N 19°55E 9 F18
Mariembourg Belgium 50°6N 4°31E 15 D4
Mariental Namibia 24°36S 18°0E 56 C2
Marienville U.S.A. 41°28N 79°8W 82 E5
Mariestad Sweden 58°43N 13°50E 9 G15
Marietta Ga., U.S.A. 33°57N 84°33W 85 E12
Marietta Ohio, U.S.A. 39°25N 81°27W 81 F13
Marieville Canada 45°26N 73°10W 83 A11
Mariinsk Russia 56°10N 87°20E 28 D9
Marijampolė Lithuania 54°33N 23°19E 9 J20

Marília Brazil 22°13S 50°0W 95 A6
Marín Spain 42°23N 8°42W 21 A1
Marina U.S.A. 36°41N 121°48W 78 J5
Marinduque Phil. 13°25N 122°0E 37 B6
Marine City U.S.A. 42°43N 82°30W 82 D2
Marinette U.S.A. 45°6N 87°38W 80 C10
Maringá Brazil 23°26S 52°2W 95 A5
Marion Ala., U.S.A. 32°38N 87°19W 85 E11
Marion Ill., U.S.A. 37°44N 88°56W 80 G9
Marion Ind., U.S.A. 40°32N 85°40W 81 E11
Marion Iowa, U.S.A. 42°2N 91°36W 80 D8
Marion Kans., U.S.A. 38°21N 97°1W 80 F5
Marion N.C., U.S.A. 35°41N 82°1W 85 D13
Marion Ohio, U.S.A. 40°35N 83°8W 81 E12
Marion Va., U.S.A. 36°50N 81°31W 81 G13
Marion, L. U.S.A. 33°28N 80°10W 85 E14
Mariposa U.S.A. 37°29N 119°58W 78 H7
Mariscal Estigarribia Paraguay 22°3S 60°40W 94 A3
Maritime Alps = Maritimes, Alpes Europe 44°10N 7°10E 20 D7
Maritimes, Alpes Europe 44°10N 7°10E 20 D7
Maritsa = Evros ~ Greece 41°40N 26°34E 23 D12
Maritsa Greece 36°22N 28°8E 25 C10
Mariupol Ukraine 47°5N 37°31E 19 E6
Mariusa ~ Venezuela 9°24N 61°27W 89 E7
Marīvān Iran 35°30N 46°25E 44 C5
Marj 'Uyūn Lebanon 33°21N 35°34E 46 B4
Marka Somali Rep. 1°48N 44°50E 47 G3
Markam China 29°42N 98°38E 32 D4
Markdale Canada 44°19N 80°39W 82 B4
Marked Tree U.S.A. 35°32N 90°25W 85 D9
Market Drayton U.K. 52°54N 2°29W 12 E5
Market Harborough U.K. 52°29N 0°55W 13 E7
Market Rasen U.K. 53°24N 0°20W 12 D7
Markham Canada 43°52N 79°16W 82 C5
Markham, Mt. Antarctica 83°0S 164°0E 5 E11
Markleeville U.S.A. 38°42N 119°47W 78 G7
Markovo Russia 64°40N 170°24E 29 C17
Marks Russia 51°45N 46°50E 18 D8
Marksville U.S.A. 31°8N 92°4W 84 F8
Marla Australia 27°19S 133°33E 63 D1
Marlbank Canada 44°26N 77°6W 82 B7
Marlboro U.S.A. 41°36N 73°59W 83 E11
Marlborough Australia 22°46S 149°52E 62 C4
Marlborough U.K. 51°25N 1°43W 13 F6
Marlborough U.S.A. 42°21N 71°33W 83 D13
Marlborough Downs U.K. 51°27N 1°53W 13 F6
Marlin U.S.A. 31°18N 96°54W 84 F6
Marlow U.K. 51°34N 0°46W 13 F7
Marlow U.S.A. 34°39N 97°58W 84 H6
Marmagao India 15°25N 73°56E 40 M8
Marmara Turkey 40°35N 27°34E 23 D12
Marmara, Sea of = Marmara Denizi Turkey 40°45N 28°15E 23 D13
Marmara Denizi Turkey 40°45N 28°15E 23 D13
Marmaris Turkey 36°50N 28°14E 23 F13
Marmion, Mt. Australia 29°16S 119°50E 61 E2
Marmion L. Canada 48°55N 91°20W 72 C1
Marmolada, Mte. Italy 46°26N 11°51E 22 A4
Marmora Canada 44°28N 77°41W 82 B7
Marne ~ France 48°47N 2°29E 20 B5
Maroala Madag. 15°23S 47°59E 57 B8
Maroantsetra Madag. 15°26S 49°44E 57 B8
Maroelaboom Namibia 19°15S 18°53E 56 B2
Marofandilia Madag. 20°7S 44°34E 57 C7
Marolambo Madag. 20°2S 48°7E 57 C8
Maromandia Madag. 14°13S 48°5E 57 A8
Maromokotro Madag. 14°0S 49°0E 57 A8
Marondera Zimbabwe 18°5S 31°42E 55 F3
Maroni ~ Fr. Guiana 5°30N 54°0W 93 B8
Maroochydore Australia 26°29S 153°5E 63 D5
Maroona Australia 37°27S 142°54E 63 F3
Marosakoa Madag. 15°26S 46°38E 57 B8
Maroseranana Madag. 18°32S 48°51E 57 B8
Marotandrano Madag. 16°10S 48°50E 57 B8
Marotaolano Madag. 12°47S 49°15E 57 A8
Maroua Cameroon 10°40N 14°20E 51 F8
Marovato Madag. 15°48S 48°5E 57 B8
Marovoay Madag. 16°6S 46°39E 57 B8
Marquard S. Africa 28°40S 27°28E 56 D4
Marquesas Fracture Zone Pac. Oc. 9°0S 125°0W 65 H15
Marquesas Is. = Marquises, Îs. French Polynesia 9°30S 140°0W 65 H14
Marquette U.S.A. 46°33N 87°24W 80 B10
Marquis St. Lucia 14°2N 60°54W 89 f
Marquises, Îs. French Polynesia 9°30S 140°0W 65 H14
Marra, Djebel Sudan 13°10N 24°22E 51 F10
Marracuene Mozam. 25°45S 32°35E 57 D5
Marrakech Morocco 31°9N 8°0W 50 B4
Marrawah Australia 40°55S 144°42E 63 G3
Marree Australia 29°39S 138°1E 63 D2
Marrero U.S.A. 29°53N 90°6W 85 G9
Marrimane Mozam. 22°58S 33°34E 57 C5
Marromeu Mozam. 18°15S 36°25E 57 B6
Marromeu ~ Mozam. 19°0S 36°0E 57 B6
Marrowie Cr. ~ Australia 33°23S 145°40E 63 E4
Marrubane Mozam. 18°0S 37°0E 55 F4
Marrupa Mozam. 13°8S 37°30E 55 E4
Mars Hill U.S.A. 46°31N 67°52W 81 B20
Marsá 'Alam Egypt 25°5N 34°54E 47 B11
Marsá Matrûh Egypt 31°19N 27°9E 51 B11
Marsá Susah Libya 32°52N 21°59E 51 B10
Marsabit Kenya 2°18N 38°0E 54 B4
Marsabit △ Kenya 2°23N 37°56E 54 B4
Marsala Italy 37°48N 12°26E 22 F5
Marsalforn Malta 36°4N 14°16E 25 C1
Marsden Australia 33°47S 147°32E 63 E4
Marseille France 43°18N 5°23E 20 E6

Marseilles = Marseille France 43°18N 5°23E 20 E6
Marsh I. U.S.A. 29°34N 91°53W 84 G9
Marshall Ark., U.S.A. 35°55N 92°38W 84 D8
Marshall Mich., U.S.A. 42°16N 84°58W 81 D11
Marshall Minn., U.S.A. 44°27N 95°47W 80 C6
Marshall Mo., U.S.A. 39°7N 93°12W 80 F7
Marshall Tex., U.S.A. 32°33N 94°23W 84 E7
Marshall ~ Australia 22°59S 136°59E 62 C2
Marshall Is. ■ Pac. Oc. 9°0N 171°0E 58 A10
Marshalltown U.S.A. 42°3N 92°55W 80 D7
Marshbrook Zimbabwe 18°33S 31°9E 57 B5
Marshfield Mo., U.S.A. 37°15N 92°54W 80 G7
Marshfield Vt., U.S.A. 44°20N 72°20W 83 B12
Marshfield Wis., U.S.A. 44°40N 90°10W 80 C8
Marshūn Iran 36°19N 49°23E 45 B6
Märsta Sweden 59°37N 17°52E 9 G17
Mart U.S.A. 31°33N 96°50W 84 F6
Martaban Burma 16°30N 97°35E 41 L20
Martaban, G. of Burma 16°5N 96°30E 41 L20
Martapura Kalimantan, Indonesia 3°22S 114°47E 36 E4
Martapura Sumatera, Indonesia 4°19S 104°22E 36 E2
Marte R. Gómez, Presa Mexico 26°10N 99°0W 87 B5
Martelange Belgium 49°49N 5°43E 15 E5
Martha's Vineyard U.S.A. 41°25N 70°38W 83 E14
Martigny Switz. 46°6N 7°3E 20 C7
Martigues France 43°24N 5°4E 20 E6
Martin Slovak Rep. 49°6N 18°58E 17 D10
Martin S. Dak., U.S.A. 43°11N 101°44W 80 D3
Martin Tenn., U.S.A. 36°21N 88°51W 85 C10
Martin L. U.S.A. 32°41N 85°55W 85 E12
Martina Franca Italy 40°42N 17°20E 22 D7
Martinborough N.Z. 41°14S 175°29E 59 D5
Martinez Calif., U.S.A. 38°1N 122°8W 78 G4
Martinez Ga., U.S.A. 33°31N 82°5W 85 E13
Martinique ☑ W. Indies 14°40N 61°0W 88 c
Martinique Passage W. Indies 15°15N 61°0W 89 C7
Martinópolis Brazil 22°11S 51°12W 95 A5
Martin's Bay Barbados 13°12N 59°29W 89 g
Martins Ferry U.S.A. 40°6N 80°44W 82 F4
Martinsburg Pa., U.S.A. 40°19N 78°20W 82 F6
Martinsburg W. Va., U.S.A. 39°27N 77°58W 81 F15
Martinsville Ind., U.S.A. 39°26N 86°25W 80 F10
Martinsville Va., U.S.A. 36°41N 79°52W 81 G14
Marton N.Z. 40°4S 175°23E 59 D5
Martos Spain 37°44N 3°58W 21 D4
Marudi Malaysia 4°11N 114°19E 36 D4
Maruf Afghan. 31°30N 67°6E 40 D5
Marugame Japan 34°15N 133°40E 31 G6
Marunga Angola 17°28S 20°2E 56 B3
Marungu, Mts. Dem. Rep. of the Congo 7°30S 30°0E 54 D3
Marv Dasht Iran 29°50N 52°40E 45 D7
Marvast Iran 30°30N 54°15E 45 D7
Marvel Loch Australia 31°28S 119°29E 61 F2
Marwar India 25°43N 73°45E 42 G8
Mary Turkmenistan 37°40N 61°50E 45 B9
Maryborough = Port Laoise Ireland 53°2N 7°18W 10 C4
Maryborough Queens., Australia 25°31S 152°37E 63 D5
Maryborough Vic., Australia 37°3S 143°44E 63 F3
Maryfield Canada 49°50N 101°35W 71 D8
Maryland ☐ U.S.A. 39°0N 76°30W 81 F15
Maryland Junction Zimbabwe 17°45S 30°31E 55 F3
Maryport U.K. 54°44N 3°28W 12 C4
Mary's Harbour Canada 52°18N 55°51W 73 B8
Marystown Canada 47°10N 55°10W 73 C8
Marysville Calif., U.S.A. 39°9N 121°35W 78 F5
Marysville Kans., U.S.A. 39°51N 96°39W 80 F5
Marysville Mich., U.S.A. 42°54N 82°29W 82 D2
Marysville Ohio, U.S.A. 40°14N 83°22W 81 E12
Marysville Wash., U.S.A. 48°3N 122°11W 78 B4
Maryville Mo., U.S.A. 40°21N 94°52W 80 E6
Maryville Tenn., U.S.A. 35°46N 83°58W 85 D13
Marzūq Libya 25°53S 13°57E 51 C8
Marzūq, Idehan Libya 24°50N 13°51E 51 D8
Masada Israel 31°15N 35°20E 46 D4
Masahunga Tanzania 2°6S 33°18E 54 C3
Masai Malaysia 1°29N 103°55E 39 d
Masai Mara △ Kenya 1°25S 35°5E 54 C4
Masai Steppe Tanzania 4°30S 36°30E 54 C4
Masaka Uganda 0°21S 31°45E 54 C3
Masalembo, Kepulauan Indonesia 5°35S 114°30E 36 F4
Masalima, Kepulauan Indonesia 5°4S 117°5E 36 F5
Masamba Indonesia 2°30S 120°15E 37 E6
Masan S. Korea 35°11N 128°32E 35 G15
Masandam, Ra's Oman 26°30N 56°30E 45 E8
Masasi Tanzania 10°45S 38°52E 55 E4
Masaya Nic. 12°0N 86°7W 88 D2
Masbate Phil. 12°21N 123°36E 37 B6
Mascara Algeria 35°26N 0°6E 50 A6
Mascota Mexico 20°32N 104°49W 86 C4
Masela Indonesia 8°9S 129°51E 37 F7
Maseru Lesotho 29°18S 27°30E 56 D4
Mashaba Zimbabwe 20°2S 30°29E 55 G3
Mashābih Si. Arabia 25°35N 36°30E 44 E3
Mashatu △ Botswana 22°5S 29°5E 57 C4
Masherbrum Pakistan 35°38N 76°18E 43 B7
Mashhad Iran 36°20N 59°35E 45 B8
Mashiz Iran 29°56N 56°37E 45 D8
Māshkel, Hāmūn-i- Pakistan 28°20N 62°56E 45 D9
Māshki Chāh Pakistan 29°5N 62°30E 40 E3
Mashonaland Zimbabwe 16°30S 31°0E 53 H6
Mashonaland Central ☐ Zimbabwe 17°30S 31°0E 57 B5

Mashonaland East ☐ Zimbabwe 18°0S 32°0E 57 B5
Mashonaland West ☐ Zimbabwe 17°30S 29°30E 57 B4
Mashrakh India 26°7N 84°48E 43 F11
Masi Manimba Dem. Rep. of the Congo 4°40S 17°54E 52 E3
Masindi Uganda 1°40N 31°43E 54 B3
Masindi Port Uganda 1°43N 32°2E 54 B3
Maşīrah Oman 21°0N 58°50E 47 C6
Maşīrah, Khalīj Oman 20°10N 58°10E 47 C6
Masisi Dem. Rep. of the Congo 1°23S 28°49E 54 C2
Masjed Soleyman Iran 31°55N 49°18E 45 D6
Mask, L. Ireland 53°36N 9°22W 10 C2
Maskin Oman 23°44N 56°52E 45 F8
Masoala, Tanjon' i Madag. 15°59S 50°13E 57 B9
Masoarivo Madag. 19°3S 44°19E 57 B7
Masohi = Amahai Indonesia 3°20S 128°55E 37 E7
Masomeloka Madag. 20°17S 48°37E 57 C8
Mason Nev., U.S.A. 38°56N 119°8W 78 G4
Mason Tex., U.S.A. 30°45N 99°14W 84 F5
Mason City U.S.A. 43°9N 93°12W 80 D7
Maspalomas Canary Is. 27°46N 15°35W 24 G4
Maspalomas, Pta. Canary Is. 27°43N 15°36W 24 G4
Masqat Oman 23°37N 58°36E 47 C6
Massa Italy 44°1N 10°9E 20 D9
Massachusetts ☐ U.S.A. 42°30N 72°0W 83 D13
Massachusetts B. U.S.A. 42°25N 70°50W 83 D14
Massakory Chad 13°0N 15°49E 51 F8
Massanella Spain 39°48N 2°51E 24 B9
Massangena Mozam. 21°34S 33°0E 57 C5
Massango Angola 8°2S 16°21E 52 F3
Massawa = Mitsiwa Eritrea 15°35N 39°25E 47 D2
Massena U.S.A. 44°56N 74°54W 83 B10
Massénya Chad 11°21N 16°9E 51 F9
Masset Canada 54°2N 132°10W 70 C2
Massiah Street Barbados 13°9N 59°29W 89 g
Massif Central France 44°55N 3°0E 20 D5
Massillon U.S.A. 40°48N 81°32W 82 F3
Massinga Mozam. 23°15S 35°22E 57 C6
Massingir Mozam. 23°51S 32°4E 57 C5
Masson-Angers Canada 45°32N 75°25W 83 A9
Masson I. Antarctica 66°10S 93°20E 5 C7
Mastanli = Momchilgrad Bulgaria 41°33N 25°23E 23 D11
Masterton N.Z. 40°56S 175°39E 59 D5
Mastic U.S.A. 40°47N 72°54W 83 F12
Mastung Pakistan 29°50N 66°56E 40 E5
Masty Belarus 53°27N 24°38E 17 B13
Masuda Japan 34°40N 131°51E 31 G5
Masurian Lakes = Mazurski, Pojezierze Poland 53°50N 21°0E 17 B11
Masvingo Zimbabwe 20°8S 30°49E 55 G3
Masvingo ☐ Zimbabwe 21°0S 31°30E 55 G3
Maswa △ Tanzania 2°58S 34°19E 54 C3
Maşyāf Syria 35°4N 36°20E 44 C3
Mata-au = Clutha ~ N.Z. 46°20S 169°49E 59 G2
Matabeleland Zimbabwe 18°0S 27°0E 53 H5
Matabeleland North ☐ Zimbabwe 19°0S 28°0E 57 B4
Matabeleland South ☐ Zimbabwe 21°0S 29°0E 55 G2
Matachewan Canada 47°56N 80°39W 72 C3
Matadi Dem. Rep. of the Congo 5°52S 13°31E 52 F2
Matagalpa Nic. 13°0N 85°58W 88 D2
Matagami Canada 49°45N 77°34W 72 C4
Matagami, L. Canada 49°50N 77°40W 72 C4
Matagorda B. U.S.A. 28°40N 96°12W 84 G6
Matagorda I. U.S.A. 28°15N 96°30W 84 G6
Mataiea Tahiti 17°46S 149°25W 59 d
Matak Indonesia 3°18N 106°16E 36 D3
Matala Greece 34°59N 24°45E 25 E6
Matam Senegal 15°34N 13°17W 50 E3
Matamoros Campeche, Mexico 18°50N 90°50W 87 D6
Matamoros Coahuila, Mexico 25°32N 103°15W 86 B4
Matamoros Tamaulipas, Mexico 25°53N 97°30W 87 B5
Ma'ţan as Sarra Libya 21°45N 22°0E 51 D10
Matandu ~ Tanzania 8°45S 34°19E 55 D3
Matane Canada 48°50N 67°33W 73 C6
Matanomadh India 23°33N 68°57E 42 H3
Matanzas Cuba 23°0N 81°40W 88 B3
Matapa Botswana 23°11S 24°39E 56 C3
Matapan, C. = Tenaro, Akra Greece 36°22N 22°27E 23 F10
Matapédia Canada 48°0N 66°59W 73 C6
Matapo △ Zimbabwe 20°30S 29°40E 55 G2
Matara Sri Lanka 5°58N 80°30E 40 S12
Mataram Indonesia 8°35S 116°7E 37 K19
Matarani Peru 17°0S 72°10W 92 G4
Mataranka Australia 14°55S 133°4E 60 B5
Matarma, Râs Egypt 30°27N 32°44E 46 E1
Mataró Spain 41°32N 2°29E 21 B7
Matatiele S. Africa 30°20S 28°49E 57 E4
Mataura N.Z. 46°11S 168°51E 59 G2
Matavai, B. de Tahiti 17°30S 149°23W 59 d
Matehuala Mexico 23°39N 100°39W 86 C4
Mateke Hills Zimbabwe 21°48S 31°0E 55 G3
Matelot Trin. & Tob. 10°50N 61°7W 93 K15
Matera Italy 40°40N 16°36E 22 D7
Matetsi Zimbabwe 18°12S 26°0E 55 F2
Mathis U.S.A. 28°6N 97°50W 84 G6
Mathraki Greece 39°48N 19°31E 25 A3
Mathura India 27°30N 77°40E 42 F7

Mati Phil. 6°55N 126°15E 37 C7
Matiali India 26°56N 88°49E 43 F13
Matías Romero Mexico 16°53N 95°2W 87 D5
Matibane Mozam. 14°49S 40°45E 55 E5
Matiri Ra. N.Z. 41°38S 172°20E 59 D4
Matla ~ India 21°40N 88°40E 43 J13
Matlamanyane Botswana 19°33S 25°57E 56 B4
Matli Pakistan 25°2N 68°39E 42 G3
Matlock U.K. 53°9N 1°33W 12 D6
Mato Grosso ☐ Brazil 14°0S 55°0W 93 F8
Mato Grosso, Planalto do Brazil 15°0S 55°0W 93 G8
Mato Grosso do Sul ☐ Brazil 18°0S 55°0W 93 G8
Matobo = Matapo △ Zimbabwe 20°30S 29°40E 55 G2
Matochkin Shar, Proliv Russia 73°23N 55°12E 28 B6
Matopo Hills Zimbabwe 20°36S 28°20E 55 G2
Matopos Zimbabwe 20°20S 28°29E 55 G2
Matosinhos Portugal 41°11N 8°42W 21 B1
Matroosberg S. Africa 33°23S 19°40E 56 E2
Maţruh Oman 23°37N 58°30E 47 C6
Matsue Japan 35°25N 133°10E 31 G6
Matsumae Japan 41°26N 140°7E 30 D10
Matsumoto Japan 36°15N 138°0E 31 F9
Matsusaka Japan 34°34N 136°32E 31 G8
Matsuura Japan 33°20N 129°49E 31 H4
Matsuyama Japan 33°45N 132°45E 31 H6
Mattagami ~ Canada 50°43N 81°29W 72 B3
Mattancheri India 9°50N 76°15E 40 Q10
Mattawa Canada 46°20N 78°45W 72 C4
Matterhorn Switz. 45°58N 7°39E 20 D7
Matthew Town Bahamas 20°57N 73°40W 89 B5
Matthews Ridge Guyana 7°37N 60°10W 92 B6
Mattice Canada 49°40N 83°20W 72 C3
Mattituck U.S.A. 40°59N 72°32W 83 F12
Mattō Japan 36°31N 136°34E 31 F8
Mattoon U.S.A. 39°29N 88°23W 80 F9
Matuba Mozam. 24°28S 32°49E 57 C5
Matucana Peru 11°55S 76°25W 92 F3
Matuku Fiji 19°10S 179°44E 59 a
Matūn = Khowst Afghan. 33°22N 69°58E 42 C3
Matura B. Trin. & Tob. 10°39N 61°1W 93 K15
Maturín Venezuela 9°45N 63°11W 92 B6
Matusadona △ Zimbabwe 16°58S 28°42E 55 F2
Mau Mad. P., India 26°17N 78°41E 43 F8
Mau Ut. P., India 25°56N 83°33E 43 G10
Mau Ut. P., India 25°17N 81°23E 43 G9
Mau Escarpment Kenya 0°40S 36°0E 54 C4
Mau Ranipur India 25°16N 79°8E 43 G8
Maubeuge France 50°17N 3°57E 20 A6
Maubin Burma 16°44N 95°39E 41 L19
Maud, Pt. Australia 23°6S 113°45E 60 D1
Maud Rise S. Ocean 66°0S 3°0E 5 C3
Maude Australia 34°29S 144°18E 63 E3
Maudin Sun Burma 16°0N 94°30E 41 M19
Maués Brazil 3°20S 57°45W 92 D7
Mauganj India 24°50N 81°55E 43 G9
Maughold Hd. I. of Man 54°18N 4°18W 12 C3
Maui U.S.A. 20°48N 156°20W 74 b
Maulamyaing = Moulmein Burma 16°30N 97°40E 41 L20
Maule ☐ Chile 36°5S 72°30W 94 D1
Maumee U.S.A. 41°34N 83°39W 81 E12
Maumee ~ U.S.A. 41°42N 83°28W 81 E12
Maumere Indonesia 8°38S 122°13E 37 F6
Maun Botswana 20°0S 23°26E 56 B3
Mauna Kea U.S.A. 19°50N 155°28W 74 b
Mauna Loa U.S.A. 19°30N 155°35W 74 b
Maungmagan Kyunzu Burma 14°0N 97°48E 38 E1
Maungu Kenya 3°33S 38°45E 54 C4
Maupin U.S.A. 45°11N 121°5W 76 D3
Maurepas, L. U.S.A. 30°15N 90°30W 85 F9
Maurice, L. Australia 29°30S 131°0E 61 E5
Mauricie △ Canada 46°45N 73°0W 72 C5
Mauritania ■ Africa 20°50N 10°0W 50 E3
Mauritius ■ Ind. Oc. 20°0S 57°0E 53 d
Mauston U.S.A. 43°48N 90°5W 80 D8
Mavli India 24°45N 73°55E 42 G5
Mavuradonha Mts. Zimbabwe 16°30S 31°30E 55 F3
Mawa Dem. Rep. of the Congo 2°45N 26°40E 54 B2
Mawai India 22°30N 81°4E 43 H9
Mawana India 29°6N 77°58E 42 E7
Mawand Pakistan 29°33N 68°38E 42 E3
Mawjib, W. al ~ Jordan 31°28N 35°36E 46 D4
Mawk Mai Burma 20°14N 97°37E 41 J20
Mawlaik Burma 23°40N 94°26E 41 H19
Mawlamyine = Moulmein Burma 16°30N 97°40E 41 L20
Mawson Base Antarctica 67°30S 62°53E 5 C6
Mawson Coast Antarctica 68°30S 63°0E 5 C6
Max U.S.A. 47°49N 101°18W 80 B3
Maxcanú Mexico 20°35N 90°0W 87 C6
Maxesibeni S. Africa 30°49S 29°23E 57 E4
Maxhamish L. Canada 59°50N 123°17W 70 B4
Maxixe Mozam. 23°54S 35°17E 57 C6
Maxville Canada 45°17N 74°51W 83 A10
Maxwell U.S.A. 39°17N 122°11W 78 F4
Maxwelton Australia 20°43S 142°41E 62 C3
May, C. U.S.A. 38°56N 74°58W 81 F16
May Pen Jamaica 17°58N 77°15W 88 a
Maya ~ Russia 60°28N 134°28E 29 D14
Maya Mts. Belize 16°30N 89°0W 87 D7
Mayaguana Bahamas 22°30N 72°44W 89 B5
Mayagüez Puerto Rico 18°12N 67°9W 89 d
Mayāmey Iran 36°24N 55°42E 45 B7

Mayanup Australia 33°57S 116°27E 61 F2
Mayapán Mexico 20°29N 89°11W 87 C7
Mayarí Cuba 20°40N 75°41W 89 B4
Mayaro B. Trin. & Tob. 10°14N 60°59W 93 K16
Maybell U.S.A. 40°31N 108°5W 76 F9
Maybole U.K. 55°21N 4°42W 11 F4
Maydän Iraq 34°55N 45°37E 44 C5
Maydena Australia 42°45S 146°30E 63 G4
Mayenne ~ France 47°30N 0°32W 20 C3
Mayer U.S.A. 34°24N 112°14W 77 J7
Mayerthorpe Canada 53°57N 115°8W 70 C5
Mayfield Ky., U.S.A. 36°44N 88°38W 80 G9
Mayfield N.Y., U.S.A. 43°6N 74°16W 83 C10
Mayhill U.S.A. 32°53N 105°29W 77 K11
Maykop Russia 44°35N 40°10E 19 F7
Maymyo Burma 22°2N 96°28E 38 A1
Maynard Mass., U.S.A. 42°26N 71°27W 83 D13
Maynard Wash., U.S.A. 47°59N 122°55W 78 C4
Maynard Hills Australia 28°28S 119°49E 61 E2
Mayne ~ Australia 23°40S 141°55E 62 C3
Maynooth Canada 45°13N 77°56W 82 A7
Maynooth Ireland 53°23N 6°34W 10 C5
Mayo Canada 63°38N 135°57W 68 C6
Mayo ☐ Ireland 53°53N 9°3W 10 C2
Mayon Volcano Phil. 13°15N 123°41E 37 B6
Mayor I. N.Z. 37°16S 176°17E 59 B6
Mayotte ☑ Ind. Oc. 12°50S 45°10E 53 a
Maysān ☐ Iraq 31°55N 47°15E 44 D5
Maysville U.S.A. 38°39N 83°46W 81 F12
Mayu Indonesia 1°30N 126°30E 37 D7
Mayville N. Dak., U.S.A. 47°30N 97°20W 80 B5
Mayville N.Y., U.S.A. 42°15N 79°30W 82 D5
Mazabuka Zambia 15°52S 27°44E 55 F2
Mazagán = El Jadida Morocco 33°11N 8°17W 50 B4
Mazagão Brazil 0°7S 51°16W 93 D8
Mazán Peru 3°30S 73°0W 92 D4
Māzandarān ☐ Iran 36°30N 52°0E 45 B7
Mazapil Mexico 24°39N 101°34W 86 C4
Mazar China 36°32N 77°1E 32 C2
Mazara del Vallo Italy 37°39N 12°35E 22 F5
Mazarrón Spain 37°38N 1°19W 21 D5
Mazaruni ~ Guyana 6°25N 58°35W 92 B7
Mazatán Mexico 29°0N 110°8W 86 B2
Mazatenango Guatemala 14°35N 91°30W 88 D1
Mazatlán Mexico 23°13N 106°25W 86 C3
Mažeikiai Lithuania 56°20N 22°20E 9 H20
Māzhān Iran 32°30N 59°0E 45 C8
Mazīnān Iran 36°19N 56°56E 45 B8
Mazoe Mozam. 16°42S 33°7E 55 F3
Mazoe ~ Mozam. 16°20S 33°30E 55 F3
Mazowe Zimbabwe 17°28S 30°58E 55 F3
Mazurski, Pojezierze Poland 53°50N 21°0E 17 B11
Mazyr Belarus 51°59N 29°15E 17 B15
Mba Fiji 17°33S 177°41E 59 a
Mbabane Swaziland 26°18S 31°6E 57 D5
Mbaïki C.A.R. 3°53N 18°1E 52 D3
Mbala Zambia 8°46S 31°24E 55 D3
Mbalabala Zimbabwe 20°27S 29°3E 57 C4
Mbale Uganda 1°8N 34°12E 54 B3
Mbalmayo Cameroon 3°33N 11°33E 52 D2
Mbamba Bay Tanzania 11°13S 34°49E 55 E3
Mbandaka Dem. Rep. of the Congo 0°1N 18°18E 52 D3
Mbanza Congo Angola 6°18S 14°16E 52 F2
Mbanza Ngungu Dem. Rep. of the Congo 5°12S 14°53E 52 F2
Mbarangandu Tanzania 10°11S 36°48E 55 D4
Mbarara Uganda 0°35S 30°40E 54 C3
Mbengga = Beqa Fiji 18°23S 178°8E 59 a
Mbenkuru ~ Tanzania 9°25S 39°50E 55 D4
Mberengwa Zimbabwe 20°29S 29°57E 55 G2
Mberengwa, Mt. Zimbabwe 20°37S 29°55E 55 G2
Mbesuma Zambia 10°0S 32°2E 55 E3
Mbeya Tanzania 8°54S 33°29E 55 D3
Mbeya ☐ Tanzania 8°15S 33°30E 55 D3
Mbhashe ~ S. Africa 32°15S 28°54E 57 E4
Mbinga Tanzania 10°50S 35°0E 55 E4
Mbini = Río Muni ☐ Eq. Guin. 1°30N 10°0E 52 D2
Mbour Senegal 14°22N 16°54W 50 F2
Mbuji-Mayi Dem. Rep. of the Congo 6°9S 23°40E 54 D1
Mbulu Tanzania 3°45S 35°30E 54 C4
Mburucuyá Argentina 28°1S 58°14W 94 B4
Mburucuyá △ Argentina 28°1S 58°12W 94 B4
Mchinja Tanzania 9°44S 39°45E 55 D4
Mchinji Malawi 13°47S 32°58E 55 E3
Mdantsane S. Africa 32°56S 27°46E 57 E4
Mead, L. U.S.A. 36°0N 114°44W 79 J12
Meade U.S.A. 37°17N 100°20W 80 G3
Meadow Lake Canada 54°10N 108°26W 71 C7
Meadow Lake △ Canada 54°27N 109°0W 71 C7
Meadow Valley Wash ~ U.S.A. 36°40N 114°34W 79 J12
Meadville U.S.A. 41°39N 80°9W 82 E4
Meaford Canada 44°36N 80°35W 82 B4
Mealpaeg L. Canada 48°20N 56°30W 73 C8
Mealy Mts. Canada 53°10N 58°0W 73 B8
Meander River Canada 59°2N 117°42W 70 B5
Meares, C. U.S.A. 45°37N 124°0W 76 D1
Mearim ~ Brazil 3°4S 44°35W 93 D10
Meath ☐ Ireland 53°40N 6°57W 10 C5
Meath Park Canada 53°27N 105°22W 71 C7
Meaux France 48°58N 2°50E 20 B5
Mebechi-Gawa ~ Japan 40°31N 141°31E 30 D10
Mebulu, Tanjung Indonesia 8°50S 115°0E 37 K18
Mecanhelas Mozam. 15°12S 35°54E 55 F4
Mecca = Makkah Si. Arabia 21°30N 39°54E 47 C2
Mecca U.S.A. 33°34N 116°5W 79 M10
Mechanicsburg U.S.A. 40°13N 77°1W 82 F8
Mechanicville U.S.A. 42°54N 73°41W 83 D11

142 Mechelen
INDEX TO WORLD MAPS

Mechelen *Belgium* 51°2N 4°29E **15** C4
Mecheria *Algeria* 33°35N 0°18W **50** B5
Mecklenburg *Germany* 53°33N 11°40E **16** B7
Mecklenburger Bucht *Germany* 54°20N 11°40E **16** A6
Meconta *Mozam.* 14°59S 39°50E **55** E4
Medan *Indonesia* 3°40N 98°38E **36** D1
Médanos de Coro △ *Venezuela* 11°35N 69°44W **89** D6
Medanosa, Pta. *Argentina* 48°8S 66°0W **96** F3
Médéa *Algeria* 36°12N 2°50E **50** A6
Medellín *Colombia* 6°15N 75°35W **92** B3
Medelpad *Sweden* 62°33N 16°30E **8** E17
Medemblik *Neths.* 52°46N 5°8E **15** B5
Medford *Mass., U.S.A.* 42°25N 71°7W **83** D13
Medford *Oreg., U.S.A.* 42°19N 122°52W **76** E2
Medford *Wis., U.S.A.* 45°9N 90°20W **80** C8
Medgidia *Romania* 44°15N 28°19E **17** F15
Media Agua *Argentina* 31°58S 68°25W **94** C2
Media Luna *Argentina* 34°45S 66°44W **94** C2
Medianeira *Brazil* 25°17S 54°5W **95** B5
Mediaş *Romania* 46°9N 24°22E **17** E13
Medicine Bow *U.S.A.* 41°54N 106°12W **76** F10
Medicine Bow Mts. *U.S.A.* 40°40N 106°0W **76** F10
Medicine Bow Pk. *U.S.A.* 41°21N 106°19W **76** F10
Medicine Hat *Canada* 50°0N 110°45W **71** D6
Medicine Lake *U.S.A.* 48°30N 104°30W **76** B11
Medicine Lodge *U.S.A.* 37°17N 98°35W **80** G4
Medina = Al Madīnah *Si. Arabia* 24°35N 39°52E **44** E3
Medina *N. Dak., U.S.A.* 46°54N 99°18W **80** B4
Medina *N.Y., U.S.A.* 43°13N 78°23W **82** C6
Medina *Ohio, U.S.A.* 41°8N 81°52W **82** E3
Medina → *U.S.A.* 29°16N 98°29W **84** G5
Medina del Campo *Spain* 41°18N 4°55W **21** B3
Medina L. *U.S.A.* 29°32N 98°56W **84** G5
Medina Sidonia *Spain* 36°28N 5°57W **21** D3
Medinipur *India* 22°25N 87°21E **43** H12
Mediterranean Sea *Europe* 35°0N 15°0E **6** H7
Médoc *France* 45°10N 0°50W **20** D3
Medveditsa → *Russia* 49°35N 42°41E **19** E7
Medvezhi, Ostrava *Russia* 71°0N 161°0E **29** B17
Medvezhyegorsk *Russia* 63°0N 34°25E **18** B5
Medway □ *U.K.* 51°25N 0°32E **13** F8
Medway → *U.K.* 51°27N 0°46E **13** F8
Meekatharra *Australia* 26°32S 118°29E **61** E2
Meeker *U.S.A.* 40°2N 107°55W **76** F10
Meerut *India* 29°1N 77°42E **42** E7
Meeteetse *U.S.A.* 44°9N 108°52W **76** D9
Mega *Ethiopia* 3°57N 38°19E **47** G2
Megara *Greece* 37°58N 23°22E **23** F10
Megasini *India* 21°38N 86°21E **43** J12
Meghalaya □ *India* 25°50N 91°0E **41** G17
Meghna → *Bangla.* 22°50N 90°50E **41** H17
Megion *Russia* 61°3N 76°6E **28** C8
Mégiscane, L. *Canada* 48°35N 75°55W **72** C4
Meharry, Mt. *Australia* 22°59S 118°35E **60** D2
Mehlville *U.S.A.* 38°31N 90°19W **80** F8
Mehndawal *India* 26°58N 83°5E **43** F10
Mehr Jān *Iran* 33°50N 55°6E **45** C7
Mehrābād *Iran* 36°53N 47°55E **44** B5
Mehrān *Iran* 33°7N 46°10E **44** C5
Mehrān → *Iran* 26°45N 55°26E **45** E7
Mehrgarh *Pakistan* 29°30N 67°30E **42** E2
Mehrīz *Iran* 31°35N 54°28E **45** D7
Mei Xian *China* 34°18N 107°55E **34** G4
Meighen I. *Canada* 80°0N 99°30W **69** B10
Meihekou *China* 42°32N 125°40E **35** C13
Meiktila *Burma* 20°53N 95°54E **41** J19
Meissen *Germany* 51°9N 13°29E **16** C7
Meizhou *China* 24°16N 116°6E **33** D6
Meja *India* 25°9N 82°7E **43** G10
Mejillones *Chile* 23°10S 70°30W **94** A1
Mekele *Ethiopia* 13°33N 39°30E **47** E2
Mekerghene, Sebkra *Algeria* 26°21N 1°30E **50** C6
Mekhtar *Pakistan* 30°30N 69°15E **40** D6
Meknès *Morocco* 33°57N 5°33W **50** B4
Mekong → *Asia* 9°30N 106°15E **39** H6
Mekongga *Indonesia* 3°39S 121°15E **37** E6
Mekvari = Kür → *Azerbaijan* 39°29N 49°15E **19** G8
Melagiri Hills *India* 12°20N 77°30E **40** N10
Melaka *Malaysia* 2°15N 102°15E **39** L4
Melalap *Malaysia* 5°10N 116°5E **36** C5
Melambes *Greece* 35°8N 24°40E **25** D6
Melanesia *Pac. Oc.* 4°0S 155°0E **64** H7
Melanesian Basin *Pac. Oc.* 0°5N 160°35E **64** G8
Melaya *Indonesia* 8°17S 114°30E **37** J17
Melbourne *Australia* 37°48S 144°58E **63** F4
Melbourne *U.S.A.* 28°5N 80°37W **85** G14
Melchor Múzquiz *Mexico* 27°53N 101°31W **86** B4
Melchor Ocampo *Mexico* 24°51N 101°39W **86** C4
Mélèzes → *Canada* 57°40N 69°29W **72** A5
Melfort *Canada* 52°50N 104°37W **71** C8
Melfort *Zimbabwe* 18°0S 31°25E **55** F3
Melhus *Norway* 63°17N 10°18E **8** E14
Melilla *N. Afr.* 35°21N 2°57W **21** E4
Melipilla *Chile* 33°42S 71°15W **94** C1
Melissa *Canada* 45°24N 79°14W **82** A5
Melissa, Akra *Greece* 35°6N 24°33E **25** D6
Melita *Canada* 49°15N 101°0W **71** D8
Melitopol *Ukraine* 46°50N 35°22E **19** E6
Melk *Austria* 48°13N 15°20E **16** D8
Mellansel *Sweden* 63°26N 18°19E **8** E18
Mellen *U.S.A.* 46°20N 90°40W **80** B8
Mellerud *Sweden* 58°41N 12°28E **9** G15
Mellette *U.S.A.* 45°9N 98°30W **80** C4
Mellieha *Malta* 35°57N 14°22E **25** D1
Melo *Uruguay* 32°20S 54°10W **95** C5
Melolo *Indonesia* 9°53S 120°40E **37** F6
Melouprey *Cambodia* 13°48N 105°16E **38** F5
Melrhir, Chott *Algeria* 34°13N 6°30E **50** B7
Melrose *Australia* 32°42S 146°57E **63** E4
Melrose *U.K.* 55°36N 2°43W **11** F6
Melrose *Minn., U.S.A.* 45°40N 94°49W **80** C6
Melrose *N. Mex., U.S.A.* 34°26N 103°38W **77** J12
Melstone *U.S.A.* 46°36N 107°52W **76** C10
Melton Mowbray *U.K.* 52°47N 0°54W **12** E7
Melun *France* 48°32N 2°39E **20** B5
Melville *Canada* 50°55N 102°50W **71** C8
Melville, C. *Australia* 14°11S 144°30E **62** A3
Melville, L. *Canada* 53°30N 60°0W **73** B8
Melville B. *Australia* 12°0S 136°45E **62** A2
Melville I. *Australia* 11°30S 131°0E **60** B5
Melville I. *Canada* 75°30N 112°0W **69** B8
Melville Pen. *Canada* 68°0N 84°0W **69** C11
Melvin, Lough *Ireland* 54°26N 8°10W **10** B3
Memba *Mozam.* 14°11S 40°30E **55** E5
Memboro *Indonesia* 9°30S 119°30E **37** F5
Memel = Klaipėda *Lithuania* 55°43N 21°10E **9** J19
Memel *S. Africa* 27°38S 29°36E **57** D4
Memmingen *Germany* 47°58N 10°10E **16** E6
Mempawah *Indonesia* 0°30N 109°5E **36** D3
Memphis *Mich., U.S.A.* 42°54N 82°46W **82** D2
Memphis *Tenn., U.S.A.* 35°8N 90°2W **85** D9
Memphis *Tex., U.S.A.* 34°44N 100°33W **84** D4
Memphrémagog, L. *N. Amer.* 45°8N 72°17W **83** B12
Mena *U.S.A.* 34°35N 94°15W **84** D7
Menai Strait *U.K.* 53°11N 4°13W **12** D3
Ménaka *Mali* 15°59N 2°18E **50** E6
Menan = Chao Phraya → *Thailand* 13°40N 100°31E **38** F3
Menarandra → *Madag.* 25°17S 44°30E **57** D7
Menard *U.S.A.* 30°55N 99°47W **84** F5
Menard Fracture Zone *Pac. Oc.* 43°0S 97°0W **65** M18
Mendaña Fracture Zone *Pac. Oc.* 16°0S 91°0W **65** J18
Mendawai → *Indonesia* 3°30S 113°0E **36** E4
Mende *France* 44°31N 3°30E **20** D5
Mendeleyev Ridge *Arctic* 80°0N 178°0W **4** B17
Mendhar *India* 33°35N 74°10E **43** C6
Mendip Hills *U.K.* 51°17N 2°40W **13** F5
Mendocino *U.S.A.* 39°19N 123°48W **76** G2
Mendocino, C. *U.S.A.* 40°26N 124°25W **76** F1
Mendocino Fracture Zone *Pac. Oc.* 40°0N 142°0W **65** D13
Mendota *Calif., U.S.A.* 36°45N 120°23W **78** J6
Mendota *Ill., U.S.A.* 41°33N 89°7W **80** E9
Mendoyo *Indonesia* 8°23S 114°42E **37** J17
Mendoza *Argentina* 32°50S 68°52W **94** C2
Mendoza □ *Argentina* 33°0S 69°0W **94** C2
Mene Grande *Venezuela* 9°49N 70°56W **92** B4
Menemen *Turkey* 38°34N 27°3E **23** E12
Menen *Belgium* 50°47N 3°7E **15** D3
Menggala *Indonesia* 4°30S 105°15E **36** E3
Mengjin *China* 34°55N 112°45E **34** G7
Mengyin *China* 35°40N 117°58E **35** G9
Mengzi *China* 23°20N 103°22E **32** D5
Menihek *Canada* 54°28N 56°36W **73** B6
Menihek L. *Canada* 54°0N 67°0W **73** B6
Menin = Menen *Belgium* 50°47N 3°7E **15** D3
Menindee *Australia* 32°20S 142°25E **63** E3
Menindee L. *Australia* 32°20S 142°25E **63** E3
Meningie *Australia* 35°50S 139°18E **63** F2
Menjangan, Pulau *Indonesia* 8°7S 114°31E **37** J17
Menlo Park *U.S.A.* 37°27N 122°12W **78** H4
Menominee *U.S.A.* 45°6N 87°37W **80** C10
Menominee → *U.S.A.* 45°6N 87°35W **80** C10
Menomonie *U.S.A.* 44°53N 91°55W **80** C8
Menongue *Angola* 14°48S 17°52E **53** G3
Menorca *Spain* 40°0N 4°0E **24** B11
Mentakab *Malaysia* 3°29N 102°21E **39** L4
Mentawai, Kepulauan *Indonesia* 2°0S 99°0E **36** E1
Menton *France* 43°50N 7°29E **20** E7
Mentor *U.S.A.* 41°40N 81°21W **82** E3
Menzelinsk *Russia* 55°47N 53°11E **18** C9
Menzies *Australia* 29°40S 121°2E **61** E3
Meob B. *Namibia* 24°25S 14°34E **56** C1
Me'ona *Israel* 33°1N 35°15E **46** B4
Meoqui *Mexico* 28°17N 105°29W **86** B3
Mepaco *Mozam.* 15°57S 30°48E **55** F3
Meppel *Neths.* 52°42N 6°12E **15** B6
Merak *Indonesia* 6°10N 106°26E **37** F12
Meramangye, L. *Australia* 28°25S 132°13E **61** E5
Meran = Merano *Italy* 46°40N 11°9E **22** A4
Merano *Italy* 46°40N 11°9E **22** A4
Merauke *Indonesia* 8°29S 140°24E **37** F10
Merbein *Australia* 34°10S 142°2E **63** E3
Merbuk, Gunung *Indonesia* 8°13S 114°39E **37** J17
Merca = Marka *Somali Rep.* 1°48N 44°50E **47** G3
Merced *U.S.A.* 37°18N 120°29W **78** H6
Merced → *U.S.A.* 37°21N 120°59W **78** H6
Merced Pk. *U.S.A.* 37°36N 119°24W **78** H7
Mercedes *B. Aires, Argentina* 34°40S 59°30W **94** C4
Mercedes *Corrientes, Argentina* 29°10S 58°5W **94** B4
Mercedes *San Luis, Argentina* 33°40S 65°21W **94** C2
Mercedes *Uruguay* 33°12S 58°0W **94** C4
Merceditas *Chile* 28°20S 70°35W **94** B1
Mercer *N.Z.* 37°16S 175°5E **59** B5
Mercer *U.S.A.* 41°14N 80°15W **82** E4
Mercer Island *U.S.A.* 47°34N 122°13W **78** C4
Mercury *U.S.A.* 36°40N 115°59W **79** J11
Mercy, C. *Canada* 65°0N 63°30W **69** C13
Mere *U.K.* 51°6N 2°16W **13** F5
Meredith, C. *Falk. Is.* 52°15S 60°40W **96** G4
Meredith, L. *U.S.A.* 35°43N 101°33W **84** D4
Mergui *Burma* 12°26N 98°34E **38** F2
Mergui Arch. = Myeik Kyunzu *Burma* 11°30N 97°30E **39** G1
Mérida *Mexico* 20°58N 89°37W **87** C7
Mérida *Spain* 38°55N 6°25W **21** C2
Mérida *Venezuela* 8°24N 71°8W **92** B4
Mérida, Cord. de *Venezuela* 9°0N 71°0W **92** B4
Meriden *U.K.* 52°26N 1°38W **13** E6
Meriden *U.S.A.* 41°32N 72°48W **83** E12
Meridian *Calif., U.S.A.* 39°9N 121°55W **78** F5
Meridian *Idaho, U.S.A.* 43°37N 116°24W **76** E5
Meridian *Miss., U.S.A.* 32°22N 88°42W **85** E10
Merinda *Australia* 20°2S 148°11E **62** C4
Merir *Pac. Oc.* 4°10N 132°30E **37** D8
Merirumã *Brazil* 1°15N 54°50W **93** C8
Merkel *U.S.A.* 32°28N 100°1W **84** E4
Mermaid Reef *Australia* 17°6S 119°36E **60** C2
Merredin *Australia* 31°28S 118°18E **61** F2
Merrick *U.K.* 55°8N 4°28W **11** F4
Merrickville *Canada* 44°55N 75°50W **83** B9
Merrill *Oreg., U.S.A.* 42°1N 121°36W **76** E3
Merrill *Wis., U.S.A.* 45°11N 89°41W **80** C9
Merrimack → *U.S.A.* 42°49N 70°49W **83** D14
Merriman *U.S.A.* 42°55N 101°42W **80** D3
Merritt *Canada* 50°10N 120°45W **70** C4
Merritt Island *U.S.A.* 28°21N 80°42W **85** G14
Merriwa *Australia* 32°6S 150°22E **63** E5
Merry I. *Canada* 55°29N 77°31W **72** A4
Merryville *U.S.A.* 30°45N 93°33W **84** F8
Mersch *Lux.* 49°44N 6°7E **15** E6
Mersea I. *U.K.* 51°47N 0°58E **13** F8
Merseburg *Germany* 51°22N 11°59E **16** C6
Mersey → *U.K.* 53°25N 3°1W **12** D4
Merseyside □ *U.K.* 53°31N 3°2W **12** D4
Mersin = İçel *Turkey* 36°51N 34°36E **44** B2
Mersing *Malaysia* 2°25N 103°50E **39** L4
Merta *India* 26°39N 74°4E **42** F6
Merta Road *India* 26°43N 73°55E **42** F5
Merthyr Tydfil *U.K.* 51°45N 3°22W **13** F4
Merthyr Tydfil □ *U.K.* 51°46N 3°21W **13** F4
Merti *Kenya* 1°4N 38°40E **54** B4
Mértola *Portugal* 37°40N 7°40W **21** D2
Mertzon *U.S.A.* 31°16N 100°49W **84** F4
Meru *Kenya* 0°3N 37°40E **54** B4
Meru *Tanzania* 3°15S 36°46E **54** C4
Meru △ *Kenya* 0°5N 38°10E **54** B4
Mesa *U.S.A.* 33°25N 111°50W **77** K8
Mesa Verde △ *U.S.A.* 37°11N 108°29W **77** H9
Mesanagros *Greece* 36°1N 27°49E **25** C9
Mesaoría *Cyprus* 35°12N 33°14E **25** D12
Mesgouez, L. *Canada* 51°20N 75°0W **72** B5
Meshed = Mashhad *Iran* 36°20N 59°35E **45** B8
Meshgīn Shahr *Iran* 38°30N 47°45E **44** B5
Meshoppen *U.S.A.* 41°36N 76°3W **83** E8
Mesilinka → *Canada* 56°6N 124°30W **70** B4
Mesologi *Greece* 38°21N 21°28E **23** E9
Mesongi *Greece* 39°29N 19°56E **25** B3
Mesopotamia = Al Jazirah *Iraq* 33°30N 44°0E **44** C5
Mesopotamia *U.S.A.* 41°27N 80°57W **82** E4
Mesquite *U.S.A.* 36°48N 114°4W **77** H6
Messaad *Algeria* 34°8N 3°30E **50** B6
Messalo → *Mozam.* 12°25S 39°15E **55** E4
Messara, Kolpos *Greece* 35°6N 24°47E **25** D6
Messina = Musina *S. Africa* 22°20S 30°5E **57** C5
Messina *Italy* 38°11N 15°34E **22** E6
Messina, Str. di *Italy* 38°15N 15°35E **22** F6
Messini *Greece* 37°4N 22°1E **23** F10
Messiniakos Kolpos *Greece* 36°45N 22°5E **23** F10
Mesta → *Bulgaria* 40°54N 24°49E **23** D11
Meta → *S. Amer.* 6°12N 67°28W **92** B5
Meta Incognita Pen. *Canada* 62°45N 68°30W **69** C13
Metabetchouan *Canada* 48°26N 71°52W **73** C5
Metairie *U.S.A.* 29°59N 90°9W **85** G9
Metaline Falls *U.S.A.* 48°52N 117°22W **76** B5
Metán *Argentina* 25°30S 65°0W **94** B3
Metangula *Mozam.* 12°40S 34°50E **55** E3
Metcalfe *Canada* 45°14N 75°28W **83** A9
Metema *Ethiopia* 12°58N 36°12E **47** E2
Metengobalame *Mozam.* 14°49S 34°30E **55** E3
Methven *N.Z.* 43°38S 171°40E **59** E3
Metil *Mozam.* 16°24S 39°0E **55** F4
Metlakatla *U.S.A.* 55°8N 131°35W **68** D6
Metropolis *U.S.A.* 37°9N 88°44W **80** G9
Metropolitana □ *Chile* 33°30S 70°50W **94** C1
Metu *Ethiopia* 8°18N 35°35E **47** F2
Metz *France* 49°8N 6°10E **20** B7
Meulaboh *Indonesia* 4°11N 96°3E **36** D1
Meureudu *Indonesia* 5°19N 96°10E **36** C1
Meuse → *Europe* 50°45N 5°41E **15** D5
Mexia *U.S.A.* 31°41N 96°29W **84** F6
Mexiana, I. *Brazil* 0°0 49°30W **93** D9
Mexicali *Mexico* 32°40N 115°30W **79** N11
Mexican Plateau *Mexico* 25°0N 104°0W **66** G9
Mexican Water *U.S.A.* 36°57N 109°32W **77** H9
México *Mexico* 19°24N 99°9W **87** D5
Mexico *Maine, U.S.A.* 44°34N 70°33W **83** B14
Mexico *Mo., U.S.A.* 39°10N 91°53W **80** F8
Mexico *N.Y., U.S.A.* 43°28N 76°14W **83** C8
México □ *Mexico* 19°20N 99°30W **87** D5
Mexico ■ *Cent. Amer.* 25°0N 105°0W **86** C4
México, Ciudad de *Mexico* 19°24N 99°9W **87** D5
Mexico, G. of *Cent. Amer.* 25°0N 90°0W **87** C7
Mexico B. *U.S.A.* 43°35N 76°20W **83** C8
Meydān-e Naftūn *Iran* 31°56N 49°18E **45** D6
Meydani, Ra's-e *Iran* 25°24N 59°6E **45** E8
Meyers Chuck *U.S.A.* 55°45N 132°15W **70** B2
Meymaneh *Afghan.* 35°53N 64°38E **40** B4
Mezen *Russia* 65°50N 44°20E **18** A7
Mezen → *Russia* 65°44N 44°22E **18** A7
Mézenc, Mt. *France* 44°54N 4°11E **20** D6
Mezhdurechensk *Russia* 53°41N 88°3E **28** D9
Mezhdurechenskiy *Russia* 59°36N 65°56E **28** D7
Mezőkövesd *Hungary* 47°49N 20°35E **17** E11
Mezőtúr *Hungary* 47°1N 20°41E **17** E11
Mezquital *Mexico* 23°29N 104°23W **86** C4
Mfolozi → *S. Africa* 28°25S 32°26E **57** D5
Mgeta *Tanzania* 8°22S 36°6E **55** D4
Mhlaba Hills *Zimbabwe* 18°30S 30°30E **55** F3
Mhow *India* 22°33N 75°50E **42** H6
Miahuatlán *Mexico* 16°20N 96°36W **87** D5
Miami *Fla., U.S.A.* 25°46N 80°11W **85** J14
Miami *Okla., U.S.A.* 36°53N 94°53W **84** C7
Miami *Tex., U.S.A.* 35°42N 100°38W **84** D4
Miami Beach *U.S.A.* 25°47N 80°7W **85** J14
Mian Xian *China* 33°10N 106°32E **34** H4
Mianchi *China* 34°48N 111°48E **34** G6
Mīāndarreh *Iran* 35°37N 53°39E **45** C7
Mīāndowāb *Iran* 37°0N 46°5E **44** B5
Miandrivazo *Madag.* 19°31S 45°29E **57** B8
Mīāneh *Iran* 37°30N 47°40E **44** B5
Mianwali *Pakistan* 32°38N 71°28E **42** C4
Mianyang *China* 31°22N 104°47E **32** C5
Miarinarivo *Antananarivo, Madag.* 18°57S 46°55E **57** B8
Miarinarivo *Toamasina, Madag.* 16°38S 48°15E **57** B8
Miariravaratra *Madag.* 20°13S 47°31E **57** C8
Miass *Russia* 54°59N 60°6E **18** D11
Mica *S. Africa* 24°10S 30°48E **57** C5
Michalovce *Slovak Rep.* 48°47N 21°58E **17** D11
Michigan □ *U.S.A.* 44°0N 85°0W **81** C11
Michigan, L. *U.S.A.* 44°0N 87°0W **80** D10
Michigan City *U.S.A.* 41°43N 86°54W **80** E10
Michipicoten I. *Canada* 47°40N 85°40W **72** C2
Michoacán □ *Mexico* 19°10N 101°50W **86** D4
Michurin *Bulgaria* 42°9N 27°51E **23** C12
Michurinsk *Russia* 52°58N 40°27E **18** D7
Micoud *St. Lucia* 13°49N 60°54W **89** f
Micronesia *Pac. Oc.* 11°0N 160°0E **64** G7
Micronesia, Federated States of ■ *Pac. Oc.* 9°0N 150°0E **58** A8
Mid-Pacific Seamounts *Pac. Oc.* 18°0N 177°0W **64** F10
Midai *Indonesia* 3°0N 107°47E **36** D3
Midale *Canada* 49°25N 103°20W **71** D8
Middelburg *Neths.* 51°30N 3°36E **15** C3
Middelburg *Eastern Cape, S. Africa* 31°30S 25°0E **56** E4
Middelburg *Mpumalanga, S. Africa* 25°49S 29°28E **57** D4
Middelpos *S. Africa* 31°55S 20°13E **56** E3
Middelwit *S. Africa* 24°51S 27°3E **56** C4
Middle Alkali L. *U.S.A.* 41°27N 120°5W **76** F3
Middle America Trench = Guatemala Trench *Pac. Oc.* 14°0N 95°0W **66** H10
Middle Bass I. *U.S.A.* 41°41N 82°48W **82** E2
Middle East *Asia* 35°0N 40°0E **26** E5
Middle Fork Feather → *U.S.A.* 38°33N 121°30W **78** F5
Middle I. *Australia* 34°6S 123°11E **61** F3
Middle Loup → *U.S.A.* 41°17N 98°24W **80** E4
Middleboro *U.S.A.* 41°54N 70°55W **83** E14
Middleburg *Fla., U.S.A.* 30°4N 81°52W **85** F14
Middleburg *Pa., U.S.A.* 40°47N 77°3W **82** F7
Middleburgh *U.S.A.* 42°36N 74°20W **83** D10
Middlebury *U.S.A.* 44°1N 73°10W **83** B11
Middlefield *U.S.A.* 41°27N 81°4W **82** E3
Middlemount *Australia* 22°50S 148°40E **62** C4
Middleport *N.Y., U.S.A.* 43°13N 78°29W **82** C6
Middleport *Ohio, U.S.A.* 39°0N 82°3W **81** F12
Middlesboro *U.S.A.* 36°36N 83°43W **81** G12
Middlesbrough *U.K.* 54°35N 1°13W **12** C6
Middlesbrough □ *U.K.* 54°28N 1°13W **12** C6
Middlesex *Belize* 17°2N 88°31W **88** C2
Middlesex *N.J., U.S.A.* 40°36N 74°30W **83** F10
Middlesex *N.Y., U.S.A.* 42°42N 77°16W **82** D7
Middleton *Australia* 22°22S 141°32E **62** C3
Middleton *Canada* 44°57N 65°4W **73** D6
Middleton Cr. → *Australia* 22°35S 141°51E **62** C3
Middletown *U.K.* 54°17N 6°51W **10** B5
Middletown *Calif., U.S.A.* 38°45N 122°37W **78** G4
Middletown *Conn., U.S.A.* 41°34N 72°39W **83** E12
Middletown *N.Y., U.S.A.* 41°27N 74°25W **83** E10
Middletown *Ohio, U.S.A.* 39°31N 84°24W **81** F11
Middletown *Pa., U.S.A.* 40°12N 76°44W **83** F8
Midge Point *Australia* 20°39S 148°43E **62** J6
Midhurst *Canada* 44°26N 79°43W **82** B5
Midhurst *U.K.* 50°59N 0°44W **13** G7
Midi, Canal du → *France* 43°45N 1°21E **20** E4
Midland *Australia* 31°54S 116°1E **61** F2
Midland *Canada* 44°45N 79°50W **82** B5
Midland *Calif., U.S.A.* 33°52N 114°48W **79** M12
Midland *Mich., U.S.A.* 43°37N 84°14W **81** D11
Midland *Pa., U.S.A.* 40°39N 80°27W **82** F4
Midland *Tex., U.S.A.* 32°0N 102°3W **84** F3
Midlands □ *Zimbabwe* 19°40S 29°0E **55** F2
Midleton *Ireland* 51°55N 8°10W **10** E3
Midlothian □ *U.K.* 55°51N 3°5W **11** F5
Midongy, Tangorombohitr' i *Madag.* 23°30S 47°0E **57** C8
Midongy Atsimo *Madag.* 23°35S 47°1E **57** C8
Midway Is. *Pac. Oc.* 28°13N 177°22W **64** E10
Midway Wells *U.S.A.* 32°41N 115°7W **79** N11
Midwest *U.S.A.* 42°0N 90°0W **75** B9
Midwest *Wyo., U.S.A.* 43°25N 106°16W **76** E10
Midwest City *U.S.A.* 35°27N 97°24W **84** D6
Midyat *Turkey* 37°25N 41°23E **44** B4
Midžor *Bulgaria* 43°24N 22°40E **23** C10
Mie □ *Japan* 34°30N 136°10E **31** G8
Międzychód *Poland* 52°35N 15°53E **16** B8
Międzyrzec Podlaski *Poland* 51°58N 22°45E **17** C12
Mielec *Poland* 50°15N 21°25E **17** C11
Mienga *Angola* 17°12S 19°48E **56** B2
Miercurea-Ciuc *Romania* 46°21N 25°48E **17** E13
Mieres *Spain* 43°18N 5°48W **21** A3
Mifflintown *U.S.A.* 40°34N 77°24W **82** F7
Mifraz Ḥefa *Israel* 32°52N 35°0E **46** C4
Migori *Kenya* 1°4S 34°28E **54** C3
Miguel Alemán, Presa *Mexico* 18°15N 96°32W **87** D5
Mihara *Japan* 34°24N 133°5E **31** G6
Mikese *Tanzania* 6°48S 37°55E **54** D4
Mikhaylovgrad = Montana *Bulgaria* 43°27N 23°16E **23** C10
Mikhaylovka *Russia* 50°3N 43°5E **19** D7
Mikines *Greece* 37°43N 22°46E **23** F10
Mikkeli *Finland* 61°43N 27°15E **8** F22
Mikkwa → *Canada* 58°25N 114°46W **70** B6
Míkonos = Mykonos *Greece* 37°30N 25°25E **23** F11
Mikumi *Tanzania* 7°26S 37°0E **54** D4
Mikumi △ *Tanzania* 7°35S 37°15E **54** D4
Mikun *Russia* 62°20N 50°0E **18** B9
Milaca *U.S.A.* 45°45N 93°39W **80** C7
Milagro *Ecuador* 2°11S 79°36W **92** D3
Milan = Milano *Italy* 45°28N 9°10E **20** D8
Milan *Mo., U.S.A.* 40°12N 93°7W **80** E7
Milan *Tenn., U.S.A.* 35°55N 88°46W **85** D10
Milange *Mozam.* 16°3S 35°45E **55** F4
Milano *Italy* 45°28N 9°10E **20** D8
Milanoa *Madag.* 13°35S 49°47E **57** A8
Milâs *Turkey* 37°20N 27°50E **23** F12
Milatos *Greece* 35°18N 25°34E **25** D7
Milazzo *Italy* 38°13N 15°15E **22** E6
Milbank *U.S.A.* 45°13N 96°38W **80** C5
Milbanke Sd. *Canada* 52°19N 128°33W **70** C3
Milden *Canada* 51°29N 107°32W **71** C7
Mildenhall *U.K.* 52°21N 0°32E **13** E8
Mildmay *Canada* 44°3N 81°7W **82** B3
Mildura *Australia* 34°13S 142°9E **63** E3
Miles *Australia* 26°40S 150°9E **63** D5
Miles City *U.S.A.* 46°25N 105°51W **76** C11
Milestone *Canada* 49°59N 104°31W **71** D8
Miletus *Turkey* 37°30N 27°18E **23** F12
Milford *Calif., U.S.A.* 40°10N 120°22W **78** E6
Milford *Conn., U.S.A.* 41°14N 73°3W **83** E11
Milford *Del., U.S.A.* 38°55N 75°26W **81** F16
Milford *Mass., U.S.A.* 42°8N 71°31W **83** D13
Milford *N.H., U.S.A.* 42°50N 71°39W **83** D13
Milford *N.Y., U.S.A.* 42°35N 74°56W **83** D10
Milford *Pa., U.S.A.* 41°19N 74°48W **83** E10
Milford *Utah, U.S.A.* 38°24N 113°1W **76** G7
Milford Haven *U.K.* 51°42N 5°7W **13** F2
Milford Sd. *N.Z.* 44°41S 167°47E **59** F1
Milford Sound *N.Z.* 44°41S 167°55E **59** F1
Milḥ, Baḥr al = Razāzah, Buḥayrat ar *Iraq* 32°40N 43°35E **44** C4
Milikapiti *Australia* 11°26S 130°40E **60** B5
Miling *Australia* 30°30S 116°17E **61** F2
Milk River *Canada* 49°10N 112°5W **70** D6
Mill → *U.S.A.* 42°57N 83°23W **82** D1
Mill I. *Antarctica* 66°0S 101°30E **5** C8
Mill Valley *U.S.A.* 37°54N 122°32W **78** H4
Millau *France* 44°8N 3°4E **20** D5
Millbridge *Canada* 44°41N 77°36W **82** B7
Millbrook *Canada* 44°10N 78°29W **82** B6
Millbrook *Ala., U.S.A.* 32°29N 86°22W **85** E11
Millbrook *N.Y., U.S.A.* 41°47N 73°42W **83** E11
Mille Lacs, L. des *Canada* 48°45N 90°35W **72** C1
Mille Lacs L. *U.S.A.* 46°15N 93°39W **80** B7
Milledgeville *U.S.A.* 33°5N 83°14W **85** E13
Millen *U.S.A.* 32°48N 81°57W **85** E14
Millennium I. = Caroline I. *Kiribati* 9°58S 150°13W **65** H12
Miller *U.S.A.* 44°31N 98°59W **80** C4
Miller Lake *Canada* 45°6N 81°26W **82** A3
Millersburg *Ohio, U.S.A.* 40°33N 81°55W **82** F3
Millersburg *Pa., U.S.A.* 40°32N 76°58W **82** F8
Millerton *U.S.A.* 41°57N 73°31W **83** E11
Millerton L. *U.S.A.* 37°1N 119°41W **78** J7
Millet *St. Lucia* 13°55N 60°59W **89** f
Millheim *U.S.A.* 40°54N 77°29W **82** F7
Millicent *Australia* 37°34S 140°21E **63** F3
Millington *U.S.A.* 35°20N 89°53W **85** D10
Millinocket *U.S.A.* 45°39N 68°43W **81** C19
Millmerran *Australia* 27°53S 151°16E **63** D5
Millom *U.K.* 54°13N 3°16W **12** C4
Mills L. *Canada* 61°30N 118°20W **70** A5
Millsboro *U.S.A.* 40°0N 80°0W **82** G5
Millstream Chichester △ *Australia* 21°35S 117°6E **60** D2
Millstreet *Ireland* 52°4N 9°4W **10** D2
Milltown Malbay *Ireland* 52°52N 9°24W **10** D2
Millville *N.J., U.S.A.* 39°24N 75°2W **81** F16
Millville *Pa., U.S.A.* 41°7N 76°32W **83** E8
Millwood L. *U.S.A.* 33°42N 93°58W **84** E8
Milne → *Australia* 21°10S 137°33E **62** C2
Milo *U.S.A.* 45°15N 68°59W **81** C19
Milon, Akra *Greece* 36°15N 28°11E **25** C10
Milos *Greece* 36°44N 24°25E **23** F11
Milparinka *Australia* 29°46S 141°57E **63** D3
Milpitas *U.S.A.* 37°26N 121°55W **78** H5
Milton *N.S., Canada* 44°4N 64°45W **73** D7
Milton *Ont., Canada* 43°31N 79°53W **82** C5
Milton *N.Z.* 46°7S 169°59E **59** G2
Milton *Calif., U.S.A.* 38°3N 120°51W **78** G6
Milton *Fla., U.S.A.* 30°38N 87°3W **85** F11
Milton *Pa., U.S.A.* 41°1N 76°51W **82** F8
Milton *Vt., U.S.A.* 44°38N 73°7W **83** B11
Milton-Freewater *U.S.A.* 45°56N 118°23W **76** D4
Milton Keynes *U.K.* 52°1N 0°44W **13** E7
Milton Keynes □ *U.K.* 52°1N 0°44W **13** E7
Milverton *Canada* 43°34N 80°55W **82** C4
Milwaukee *U.S.A.* 43°2N 87°54W **80** D10
Milwaukee Deep *Atl. Oc.* 19°50N 68°0W **89** C6
Milwaukie *U.S.A.* 45°26N 122°38W **78** E4
Min Jiang → *Fujian, China* 26°0N 119°35E **33** D6

Min Jiang → *Sichuan,*
  China 28°45N 104°40E **32** D5
Min Xian *China* 34°25N 104°5E **34** G3
Minā' Jabal 'Alī *U.A.E.* 25°2N 55°8E **45** E7
Mina Pirquitas
  Argentina 22°40S 66°30W **94** A2
Mīnā Su'ud *Si. Arabia* 28°45N 48°28E **45** D6
Mīnā'al Aḥmadī *Kuwait* 29°5N 48°10E **45** D6
Minago → *Canada* 54°33N 98°59W **71** C9
Minaki *Canada* 49°59N 94°40W **71** D10
Minamata *Japan* 32°10N 130°30E **31** H5
Minami-Arapusa △
  Japan 35°30N 138°9E **31** G9
Minami-Tori-Shima
  Pac. Oc. 24°20N 153°58E **64** E7
Minas *Uruguay* 34°20S 55°10W **95** C4
Minas, Sierra de las
  Guatemala 15°9N 89°31W **88** C2
Minas Basin *Canada* 45°20N 64°12W **73** C7
Minas Gerais □ *Brazil* 18°50S 46°0W **93** G9
Minatitlán *Mexico* 17°59N 94°31W **87** D6
Minbu *Burma* 20°10N 94°52E **41** J19
Minchinabad *Pakistan* 30°10N 73°34E **42** D5
Mindanao *Phil.* 8°0N 125°0E **37** C7
Mindanao Sea = Bohol Sea
  Phil. 9°0N 124°0E **37** C6
Mindanao Trench
  Pac. Oc. 12°0N 126°6E **37** B7
Mindelo *C. Verde Is.* 16°24N 25°0W **50** b
Minden *Canada* 44°55N 78°43W **82** B6
Minden *Germany* 52°17N 8°55E **16** B5
Minden *La., U.S.A.* 32°37N 93°17W **84** E8
Minden *Nev., U.S.A.* 38°57N 119°46W **78** G7
Mindibungu = Billiluna
  Australia 19°37S 127°41E **60** C4
Mindiptana *Indonesia* 5°55S 140°22E **37** F10
Mindoro *Phil.* 13°0N 121°0E **37** B6
Mindoro Str. *Phil.* 12°30N 120°30E **37** B6
Mine *Japan* 34°12N 131°7E **31** G5
Minehead *U.K.* 51°12N 3°29W **13** F4
Mineola *N.Y., U.S.A.* 40°44N 73°38W **83** F11
Mineola *Tex., U.S.A.* 32°40N 95°29W **84** E7
Mineral King *U.S.A.* 36°27N 118°36W **78** J8
Mineral Wells *U.S.A.* 32°48N 98°7W **84** E5
Miners Bay *Canada* 44°49N 78°46W **82** B6
Minersville *U.S.A.* 40°41N 76°16W **83** F8
Minerva *N.Y., U.S.A.* 43°47N 73°59W **83** C11
Minerva *Ohio, U.S.A.* 40°44N 81°6W **82** F3
Minetto *U.S.A.* 43°24N 76°28W **83** C8
Minfeng *China* 37°4N 82°46E **32** C3
Mingäçevir Su Anbarı
  Azerbaijan 40°57N 46°50E **19** F8
Mingan *Canada* 50°20N 64°0W **73** B7
Mingechaurskoye Vdkhr. =
  Mingäçevir Su Anbarı
  Azerbaijan 40°57N 46°50E **19** F8
Mingela *Australia* 19°52S 146°38E **62** B4
Mingenew *Australia* 29°12S 115°21E **61** E2
Mingera Cr. →
  Australia 20°38S 137°45E **62** C2
Mingin *Burma* 22°50N 94°30E **41** H19
Mingo Junction *U.S.A.* 40°19N 80°37W **82** F4
Mingora *Pakistan* 34°48N 72°22E **43** B5
Mingteke Daban = Mintaka Pass
  Pakistan 37°0N 74°58E **43** A6
Mingyuegue *China* 43°2N 128°50E **35** C15
Minho → = Miño → *Spain* 41°52N 8°40W **21** A2
Minho *Portugal* 41°25N 8°20W **21** B1
Minidoka *U.S.A.* 42°45N 113°29W **76** E7
Minigwal, L. *Australia* 29°31S 123°14E **61** E3
Minilya → *Australia* 23°45S 114°0E **61** D1
Minilya Roadhouse
  Australia 23°55S 114°0E **61** D1
Minipi L. *Canada* 52°25N 60°45W **73** B7
Mink L. *Canada* 61°54N 117°40W **70** A5
Minna *Nigeria* 9°37N 6°30E **50** G7
Minneapolis *Kans., U.S.A.* 39°8N 97°42W **80** F5
Minneapolis *Minn.,*
  U.S.A. 44°57N 93°16W **80** C8
Minnedosa *Canada* 50°14N 99°50W **71** C9
Minnesota □ *U.S.A.* 46°0N 94°15W **80** B6
Minnesota → *U.S.A.* 44°54N 93°9W **80** C7
Minnewaukan *U.S.A.* 48°4N 99°15W **80** A4
Minnipa *Australia* 32°51S 135°9E **63** E2
Mino *Japan* 35°32N 136°55E **31** G8
Miño → *Spain* 41°52N 8°40W **21** A2
Minorca = Menorca *Spain* 40°0N 4°0E **24** B11
Minot *U.S.A.* 48°14N 101°18W **80** A3
Minqin *China* 38°38N 103°20E **34** E2
Minsk *Belarus* 53°52N 27°30E **17** B14
Mińsk Mazowiecki
  Poland 52°10N 21°33E **17** B11
Mintabie *Australia* 27°15S 133°7E **63** D1
Mintaka Pass *Pakistan* 37°0N 74°58E **43** A6
Minto *Canada* 46°5N 66°5W **73** C6
Minto, L. *Canada* 57°13N 75°0W **72** A5
Minton *Canada* 49°10N 104°35W **71** D8
Minturn *U.S.A.* 39°35N 106°26W **76** G10
Minudasht *Iran* 37°17N 56°7E **45** B8
Minusinsk *Russia* 53°43N 91°20E **29** D10
Minutang *India* 28°15N 96°30E **41** E20
Minvoul *Gabon* 2°9N 12°8E **52** D2
Minzhong *China* 22°37N 113°30E **33** F10
Miquelon *Canada* 49°25N 76°27W **72** C4
Miquelon *St-P. & M.* 47°8N 56°22W **73** C8
Mīr Kūh *Iran* 26°22N 58°55E **45** E8
Mīr Shahdād *Iran* 26°15N 58°29E **45** E8
Mira *Italy* 45°26N 12°8E **22** B5
Mira por vos Cay
  Bahamas 22°9N 74°30W **89** B5
Mirador-Río Azul △
  Guatemala 17°45N 89°50W **88** C2
Miraj *India* 16°50N 74°45E **40** L9
Miram Shah *Pakistan* 33°0N 70°2E **42** C4
Miramar *Argentina* 38°15S 57°50W **94** D4

Miramar *Mozam.* 23°50S 35°35E **57** C6
Miramichi *Canada* 47°2N 65°28W **73** C6
Miramichi B. *Canada* 47°15N 65°0W **73** C7
Miranda *Brazil* 20°10S 56°15W **93** H7
Miranda → *Brazil* 19°25S 57°20W **92** D2
Miranda de Ebro *Spain* 42°41N 2°57W **21** A4
Miranda do Douro
  Portugal 41°30N 6°16W **21** B2
Mirandópolis *Brazil* 21°9S 51°6W **95** A5
Mirango *Malawi* 13°32S 34°58E **55** E3
Mirani *Australia* 21°8S 148°53E **62** K6
Mirassol *Brazil* 20°46S 49°28W **95** A6
Mirbāţ *Oman* 17°0N 54°45E **47** D5
Mires *Greece* 35°4N 24°56E **25** D6
Miri *Malaysia* 4°23N 113°59E **36** D4
Miriam Vale *Australia* 24°20S 151°33E **62** C5
Mirim, L. *S. Amer.* 32°45S 52°50W **95** C5
Mīrjāveh *Iran* 29°1N 61°30E **45** D9
Mirny *Antarctica* 66°50S 92°30E **5** C14
Mirnyy *Russia* 62°33N 113°53E **29** C12
Mirokhan *Pakistan* 27°46N 68°6E **42** F3
Mirond L. *Canada* 55°6N 102°47W **71** B8
Mirpur *Pakistan* 33°32N 73°56E **43** C5
Mirpur Batoro *Pakistan* 24°44N 68°16E **42** G3
Mirpur Bibiwari *Pakistan* 28°33N 67°44E **42** E2
Mirpur Khas *Pakistan* 25°30N 69°0E **42** G3
Mirpur Sakro *Pakistan* 24°33N 67°41E **42** G2
Mirs Bay = Tai Pang Wan
  China 22°33N 114°24E **33** F11
Mirtağ *Turkey* 38°23N 41°56E **44** B4
Mirtoo Sea *Greece* 37°0N 23°20E **23** F10
Miryang *S. Korea* 35°31N 128°44E **35** G15
Mirzapur *India* 25°10N 82°34E **43** G10
Mirzapur-cum-Vindhyachal =
  Mirzapur *India* 25°10N 82°34E **43** G10
Misantla *Mexico* 19°56N 96°50W **87** D5
Misawa *Japan* 40°41N 141°24E **30** D10
Miscou I. *Canada* 47°57N 64°31W **73** C7
Mish'āb, Ra's al
  Si. Arabia 28°15N 48°43E **45** D6
Mishan *China* 45°37N 131°48E **30** B5
Mishawaka *U.S.A.* 41°40N 86°11W **80** E10
Mishima *Japan* 35°10N 138°52E **31** G9
Misión *Mexico* 32°6N 116°53W **79** N10
Misiones □ *Argentina* 27°0S 55°0W **95** B5
Misiones □ *Paraguay* 27°0S 56°0W **94** B4
Miskah *Si. Arabia* 24°49N 42°56E **44** E4
Miskitos, Cayos *Nic.* 14°26N 82°50W **88** D3
Miskolc *Hungary* 48°7N 20°50E **17** D11
Misoke
  Dem. Rep. of the Congo 0°42S 28°2E **54** C2
Misool *Indonesia* 1°52S 130°10E **37** E8
Miṣr = Egypt ■ *Africa* 28°0N 31°0E **51** C12
Miṣrātah *Libya* 32°24N 15°3E **51** B9
Missanabie *Canada* 48°20N 84°6W **72** C3
Missinaibi → *Canada* 50°43N 81°29W **72** B3
Missinaibi L. *Canada* 48°23N 83°40W **72** C3
Mission *Canada* 49°10N 122°15W **70** D4
Mission *S. Dak., U.S.A.* 43°18N 100°39W **80** D3
Mission *Tex., U.S.A.* 26°13N 98°20W **84** H5
Mission Beach *Australia* 17°53S 146°6E **62** B4
Mission Viejo *U.S.A.* 33°36N 117°40W **79** M9
Missisa L. *Canada* 52°20N 85°7W **72** B2
Missisicabi → *Canada* 51°14N 79°31W **72** B4
Mississagi → *Canada* 46°15N 83°9W **72** C3
Mississauga *Canada* 43°32N 79°35W **82** C5
Mississippi □ *U.S.A.* 33°0N 90°0W **85** E10
Mississippi → *U.S.A.* 29°9N 89°15W **85** G10
Mississippi L. *Canada* 45°5N 76°10W **83** A8
Mississippi River Delta
  U.S.A. 29°10N 89°15W **85** G10
Mississippi Sd. *U.S.A.* 30°20N 89°0W **85** F10
Missoula *U.S.A.* 46°52N 114°1W **76** C6
Missouri □ *U.S.A.* 38°25N 92°30W **80** F7
Missouri → *U.S.A.* 38°49N 90°7W **80** F8
Missouri City *U.S.A.* 29°37N 95°32W **84** G7
Missouri Valley *U.S.A.* 41°34N 95°53W **80** E6
Mist *U.S.A.* 45°59N 123°15W **78** E3
Mistassibi → *Canada* 48°53N 72°13W **73** B5
Mistassini *Canada* 48°53N 72°12W **73** C5
Mistassini → *Canada* 48°42N 72°20W **73** C5
Mistassini, L. *Canada* 51°0N 73°30W **72** B5
Mistastin L. *Canada* 55°57N 63°20W **73** A7
Mistinibi, L. *Canada* 55°56N 64°17W **73** A7
Mistissini *Canada* 48°53N 72°12W **73** C5
Misty L. *Canada* 58°53N 101°40W **71** B8
Misurata = Miṣrātah
  Libya 32°24N 15°3E **51** B9
Mitchell *Australia* 26°29S 147°58E **63** D4
Mitchell *Canada* 43°28N 81°12W **82** C3
Mitchell *Nebr., U.S.A.* 41°57N 103°49W **80** E2
Mitchell *Oreg., U.S.A.* 44°34N 120°9W **76** D3
Mitchell *S. Dak., U.S.A.* 43°43N 98°2W **80** D4
Mitchell → *Australia* 15°12S 141°35E **62** B3
Mitchell, Mt. *U.S.A.* 35°46N 82°16W **85** D13
Mitchell-Alice Rivers △
  Australia 15°28S 142°5E **62** B3
Mitchell Ra. *Australia* 12°49S 135°36E **62** A2
Mitchelstown *Ireland* 52°15N 8°16W **10** D3
Mitha Tiwana *Pakistan* 32°13N 72°6E **42** C5
Mithi *Pakistan* 24°44N 69°48E **42** G3
Mithrao *Pakistan* 27°28N 69°40E **42** F3
Mitilíni *Greece* 39°6N 26°35E **23** E12
Mitla Pass = Mamarr Mitla
  Egypt 30°2N 32°54E **46** E1
Mito *Japan* 36°20N 140°30E **31** F10
Mitrovica = Kosovska Mitrovica
  Serbia 42°54N 20°52E **23** C9
Mitsamiouli *Comoros Is.* 11°20S 43°16E **53** a
Mitsinjo *Madag.* 16°1S 45°52E **57** B8
Mitsiwa *Eritrea* 15°35N 39°25E **47** D2
Mitsukaidō *Japan* 36°1N 139°59E **31** F9
Mittagong *Australia* 34°28S 150°29E **63** E5
Mittimatalik = Pond Inlet
  Canada 72°40N 77°0W **69** B12
Mitú *Colombia* 1°15N 70°13W **92** C4
Mitumba *Tanzania* 7°8S 31°2E **54** D3

Mitumba, Mts.
  Dem. Rep. of the Congo 7°0S 27°30E **54** D2
Mitwaba
  Dem. Rep. of the Congo 8°2S 27°17E **55** D2
Mityana *Uganda* 0°23N 32°2E **54** B3
Mixteco → *Mexico* 18°11N 98°30W **87** D5
Miyagi □ *Japan* 38°15N 140°45E **30** E10
Miyah, W. el → *Syria* 34°44N 39°57E **44** C3
Miyako *Japan* 39°40N 141°59E **30** E10
Miyako-Jima *Japan* 24°45N 125°20E **31** M2
Miyako-Rettō *Japan* 24°24N 125°0E **31** M2
Miyakonojō *Japan* 31°40N 131°5E **31** J5
Miyani *India* 21°50N 69°26E **42** J3
Miyanoura-Dake *Japan* 30°20N 130°31E **31** J5
Miyazaki *Japan* 31°56N 131°30E **31** J5
Miyazaki □ *Japan* 32°30N 131°30E **31** H5
Miyazu *Japan* 35°35N 135°10E **31** G7
Miyet, Bahr el = Dead Sea
  Asia 31°30N 35°30E **46** D4
Miyoshi *Japan* 34°48N 132°51E **31** G6
Miyun *China* 40°28N 116°50E **34** D9
Miyun Shuiku *China* 40°30N 117°0E **35** D9
Mizdah *Libya* 31°30N 13°0E **51** B8
Mizen Hd. *Cork, Ireland* 51°27N 9°50W **10** E2
Mizen Hd. *Wicklow, Ireland* 52°51N 6°4W **10** D5
Mizhi *China* 37°47N 110°12E **34** F6
Mizoram □ *India* 23°30N 92°40E **41** H18
Mizpe Ramon *Israel* 30°34N 34°49E **46** E3
Mizusawa *Japan* 39°8N 141°8E **30** E10
Mizusawa *Antarctica* 70°30S 41°0E **5** D5
Mjölby *Sweden* 58°20N 15°10E **9** G16
Mjøsa *Norway* 60°40N 11°0E **8** F14
Mkata *Tanzania* 5°45S 38°20E **54** D4
Mkhaya △ *Swaziland* 26°34S 31°45E **57** D5
Mkhuze △ *S. Africa* 27°25S 29°30E **57** D4
Mkokotoni *Tanzania* 5°55S 39°15E **54** D4
Mkomazi *Tanzania* 4°40S 38°7E **54** C4
Mkomazi → *S. Africa* 30°12S 30°50E **57** E5
Mkomazi △ *Tanzania* 4°4S 30°2E **54** C3
Mkulwe *Tanzania* 8°37S 32°20E **55** D3
Mkushi *Zambia* 14°25S 29°15E **55** E2
Mkushi River *Zambia* 13°32S 29°45E **55** E2
Mkuze *S. Africa* 27°10S 32°0E **57** D5
Mladá Boleslav
  Czech Rep. 50°27N 14°53E **16** C8
Mlala Hills *Tanzania* 6°50S 31°40E **54** D3
Mlange = Mulanje, Mt.
  Malawi 16°2S 35°33E **55** F4
Mława *Poland* 53°9N 20°25E **17** B11
Mlawula △ *Swaziland* 26°12S 32°2E **57** D5
Mljet *Croatia* 42°43N 17°30E **22** C7
Mmabatho *S. Africa* 25°49S 25°30E **56** D4
Mo i Rana *Norway* 66°20N 14°7E **8** C16
Moa *Cuba* 20°40N 74°56W **89** B4
Moa *Indonesia* 8°0S 128°0E **37** F7
Moa → *S. Leone* 6°59N 11°36W **50** G3
Moab *U.S.A.* 38°35N 109°33W **76** G9
Moala *Fiji* 18°36S 179°53E **59** a
Moama *Australia* 36°7S 144°46E **63** F3
Moamba *Mozam.* 25°36S 32°15E **57** D5
Moapa *U.S.A.* 36°40N 114°37W **79** J12
Moate *Ireland* 53°24N 7°44W **10** C4
Moba *Dem. Rep. of the Congo* 7°0S 29°48E **54** D2
Mobārakābād *Iran* 28°24N 53°20E **45** D7
Mobaye *C.A.R.* 4°25N 21°5E **52** D4
Mobayi
  Dem. Rep. of the Congo 4°15N 21°8E **52** D4
Moberly *U.S.A.* 39°25N 92°26W **80** F7
Moberly Lake *Canada* 55°50N 121°44W **70** B4
Mobile *U.S.A.* 30°41N 88°3W **85** F10
Mobile B. *U.S.A.* 30°30N 88°0W **85** F11
Mobridge *U.S.A.* 45°32N 100°26W **80** C3
Moc Chau *Vietnam* 20°50N 104°38E **38** B5
Moc Hoa *Vietnam* 10°46N 105°56E **39** G5
Mocabe Kasari
  Dem. Rep. of the Congo 9°58S 26°12E **55** D2
Moçambique = Mozambique ■
  Africa 19°0S 35°0E **55** F4
Moçambique *Mozam.* 15°3S 40°42E **55** F5
Mocanaqua *U.S.A.* 41°9N 76°8W **83** E8
Moce *Fiji* 18°40S 178°29W **59** a
Mochima △ *Venezuela* 10°30N 64°5W **89** D7
Mochos *Greece* 35°16N 25°27E **25** D7
Mochudi *Botswana* 24°27S 26°7E **56** C4
Mocimboa da Praia
  Mozam. 11°25S 40°20E **55** E5
Moclips *U.S.A.* 47°14N 124°13W **78** C2
Mocoa *Colombia* 1°7N 76°35W **92** C3
Mococa *Brazil* 21°28S 47°0W **95** A6
Mocorito *Mexico* 25°29N 107°55W **86** B3
Moctezuma *Mexico* 29°48N 109°42W **86** B3
Moctezuma → *Mexico* 21°59N 98°34W **87** C5
Mocuba *Mozam.* 16°54S 36°57E **55** F4
Modane *France* 45°12N 6°40E **20** D7
Modasa *India* 23°30N 73°21E **42** H5
Modder → *S. Africa* 29°2N 24°37E **56** D3
Modderrivier *S. Africa* 29°2S 24°38E **56** D3
Módena *Italy* 44°40N 10°55E **22** B4
Modesto *U.S.A.* 37°39N 121°0W **78** H6
Módica *Italy* 36°52N 14°46E **22** F6
Modimolle *S. Africa* 24°42S 28°22E **57** C4
Modjadjiskloof *S. Africa* 23°42S 30°10E **57** C5
Moe *Australia* 38°12S 146°19E **63** F4
Moebase *Mozam.* 17°3S 38°41E **55** F4
Moengo *Suriname* 5°45N 54°20W **93** B8
Moffat *U.K.* 55°21N 3°27W **11** F5
Moga *India* 30°48N 75°8E **42** D6
Mogadishu = Muqdisho
  Somali Rep. 2°2N 45°25E **47** G4
Mogador = Essaouira
  Morocco 31°32N 9°42W **50** B4
Mogalakwena →
  S. Africa 22°38S 28°40E **57** C4
Mogami-Gawa →
  Japan 38°45N 140°0E **30** E10

Mogán *Canary Is.* 27°53N 15°43W **24** G4
Mogaung *Burma* 25°20N 97°0E **41** G20
Mogi das Cruzes *Brazil* 23°31S 46°11W **95** A6
Mogi-Guaçu → *Brazil* 20°53S 48°10W **95** A6
Mogi-Mirim *Brazil* 22°29S 47°0W **95** A6
Mogilev = Mahilyow
  Belarus 53°55N 30°18E **17** B16
Mogilev-Podolskiy = Mohyliv-
  Podilskyy *Ukraine* 48°26N 27°48E **17** D14
Mogincual *Mozam.* 15°35S 40°25E **55** F5
Mogocha *Russia* 53°40N 119°50E **29** D12
Mogok *Burma* 23°0N 96°40E **41** H20
Mogollon Rim *U.S.A.* 34°10N 110°50W **77** J8
Mogumber *Australia* 31°2S 116°3E **61** F2
Mogwadi → *S. Africa* 23°4S 29°36E **57** C4
Mohács *Hungary* 45°58N 18°41E **17** F10
Mohales Hoek *Lesotho* 30°7S 27°26E **56** E4
Mohall *U.S.A.* 48°46N 101°31W **80** A3
Mohammadābād *Iran* 37°52N 59°5E **45** B8
Mohammedia *Morocco* 33°44N 7°21W **50** B4
Mohana → *India* 24°43N 85°0E **43** G11
Mohanlalganj *India* 26°41N 80°58E **43** F9
Mohave, L. *U.S.A.* 35°12N 114°34W **79** K12
Mohawk → *U.S.A.* 42°47N 73°41W **83** D11
Mohéli *Comoros Is.* 12°20S 43°40E **53** a
Mohenjodaro *Pakistan* 27°19N 68°7E **42** F3
Moher, Cliffs of *Ireland* 52°58N 9°27W **10** D2
Mohicanville Res. *U.S.A.* 40°45N 82°9W **82** F2
Mohns Ridge *Arctic* 72°30N 5°0W **4** B7
Mohoro *Tanzania* 8°6S 39°8E **54** D4
Mohsenābād *Iran* 36°40N 59°35E **45** B8
Mohyliv-Podilskyy
  Ukraine 48°26N 27°48E **17** D14
Moidart, L. *U.K.* 56°47N 5°52W **11** E3
Moira → *Canada* 44°21N 77°24W **82** B7
Moisaküla *Estonia* 58°3N 25°12E **9** G21
Moisie *Canada* 50°12N 66°1W **73** B6
Moisie → *Canada* 50°14N 66°5W **73** B6
Mojave *U.S.A.* 35°3N 118°10W **79** K8
Mojave → *U.S.A.* 35°7N 115°32W **79** K11
Mojave Desert *U.S.A.* 35°0N 116°30W **79** L10
Mojo *Bolivia* 21°48S 65°33W **94** A2
Mojokerto *Indonesia* 7°28S 112°26E **37** G15
Mokai *N.Z.* 38°32S 175°56E **59** C5
Mokambo
  Dem. Rep. of the Congo 12°25S 28°20E **55** E2
Mokameh *India* 25°24N 85°55E **43** G11
Mokau *N.Z.* 38°42S 174°39E **59** C5
Mokelumne → *U.S.A.* 38°13N 121°28W **78** G5
Mokelumne Hill
  U.S.A. 38°18N 120°43W **78** G6
Mokhotlong *Lesotho* 29°22S 29°2E **57** D4
Mokokchung *India* 26°15N 94°30E **41** F19
Mokolo → *S. Africa* 23°14S 27°43E **57** C4
Mokopane *S. Africa* 24°10S 28°55E **57** C4
Mokpo *S. Korea* 34°50N 126°25E **35** G14
Mokra Gora *Europe* 42°50N 20°30E **23** C9
Mol *Belgium* 51°11N 5°5E **15** C5
Molchanovo *Russia* 57°40N 83°50E **28** D9
Mold *U.K.* 53°9N 3°8W **12** D4
Moldavia = Moldova ■
  Europe 47°0N 28°0E **17** E15
Moldavia *Romania* 46°30N 27°0E **17** E14
Molde *Norway* 62°45N 7°9E **8** E12
Moldova ■ *Europe* 47°0N 28°0E **17** E15
Moldoveanu, Vf.
  Romania 45°36N 24°45E **17** F13
Mole → *U.K.* 51°24N 0°21W **13** F7
Mole Creek *Australia* 41°34S 146°24E **63** G4
Molepolole *Botswana* 24°28S 25°28E **56** C4
Molfetta *Italy* 41°12N 16°36E **22** D7
Moline *U.S.A.* 41°30N 90°31W **80** E8
Molinos *Argentina* 25°28S 66°15W **94** B2
Moliro
  Dem. Rep. of the Congo 8°12S 30°30E **54** D3
Mollendo *Peru* 17°0S 72°0W **92** G4
Mollerin, L. *Australia* 30°30S 117°35E **61** F2
Molo *Kenya* 0°15S 35°44E **54** C4
Molodechno = Maladzyechna
  Belarus 54°20N 26°50E **17** A14
Molodezhnaya *Antarctica* 67°40S 45°51E **5** C9
Moloka'i *U.S.A.* 21°8N 157°0W **74** b
Molokai Fracture Zone
  Pac. Oc. 28°0N 125°0W **65** E15
Molong *Australia* 33°5S 148°54E **63** E4
Molopo → *Africa* 28°30S 20°12E **56** D3
Molson L. *Canada* 54°22N 96°40W **71** C9
Molteno *S. Africa* 31°22S 26°22E **56** E4
Molu *Indonesia* 6°45S 131°40E **37** F8
Molucca Sea *Indonesia* 0°0 125°0E **37** E6
Moluccas = Maluku
  Indonesia 1°0S 127°0E **37** E7
Moma
  Dem. Rep. of the Congo 1°35S 23°52E **54** C1
Moma *Mozam.* 16°47S 39°4E **55** F4
Mombasa *Kenya* 4°3S 39°40E **54** C4
Mombetsu *Japan* 44°21N 143°22E **30** B11
Momchilgrad *Bulgaria* 41°33N 25°23E **23** D11
Momi *Dem. Rep. of the Congo* 1°42S 27°0E **54** C2
Mompós *Colombia* 9°14N 74°26W **92** B4
Møn *Denmark* 54°57N 12°20E **9** J15
Mon □ *Burma* 16°0N 97°30E **41** L20

Monashee Mts. *Canada* 51°0N 118°43W **70** C5
Monasterevin *Ireland* 53°8N 7°4W **10** C4
Monastir = Bitola
  Macedonia 41°1N 21°20E **23** D9
Monastir *Tunisia* 35°50N 10°49E **51** A8
Moncayo, Sierra del
  Spain 41°48N 1°50W **21** B5
Monchegorsk *Russia* 67°54N 32°58E **8** C25
Mönchengladbach
  Germany 51°11N 6°27E **16** C4
Monchique *Portugal* 37°19N 8°38W **21** D1
Moncks Corner *U.S.A.* 33°12N 80°1W **85** E14
Monclova *Mexico* 26°54N 101°25W **86** B4
Moncton *Canada* 46°7N 64°51W **73** C7
Mondego → *Portugal* 40°9N 8°52E **21** B1
Mondeodo *Indonesia* 3°34S 122°9E **37** E6
Mondoví *Italy* 44°23N 7°49E **20** D7
Mondrain I. *Australia* 34°9S 122°14E **61** F3
Moneague *Jamaica* 18°16N 77°7W **88** a
Moneron, Ostrov
  Russia 46°15N 141°16E **30** A10
Monessen *U.S.A.* 40°9N 79°54W **82** F5
Monett *U.S.A.* 36°55N 93°55W **80** G7
Moneymore *U.K.* 54°41N 6°40W **10** B5
Monforte de Lemos *Spain* 42°31N 7°33W **21** A2
Mong Cai *Vietnam* 21°27N 107°54E **38** B6
Mong Hsu *Burma* 21°54N 98°30E **41** J21
Mong Kung *Burma* 21°35N 97°35E **41** J20
Mong Nai *Burma* 20°32N 97°46E **41** J20
Mong Pawk *Burma* 22°4N 99°16E **41** H21
Mong Ton *Burma* 20°17N 98°45E **41** J21
Mong Wa *Burma* 21°26N 100°27E **41** J22
Mong Yai *Burma* 22°21N 98°3E **41** H21
Mongalla *Sudan* 5°8N 31°42E **51** G12
Mongers, L. *Australia* 29°25S 117°5E **61** E2
Monghyr = Munger
  India 25°23N 86°30E **43** G12
Mongibello = Etna *Italy* 37°50N 14°55E **22** F6
Mongo *Chad* 12°14N 18°43E **51** F9
Mongolia ■ *Asia* 47°0N 103°0E **32** B5
Mongolia, Plateau of
  Asia 45°0N 105°0E **26** D12
Mongu *Zambia* 15°16S 23°12E **53** H4
Môngua *Angola* 16°43S 15°20E **56** B2
Monifieth *U.K.* 56°30N 2°48W **11** E6
Monkey Bay *Malawi* 14°7S 35°1E **55** E4
Monkey Mia *Australia* 25°48S 113°43E **61** E1
Monkey River *Belize* 16°22N 88°29W **87** D7
Monkland *Canada* 45°11N 74°52W **83** A10
Monkoto
  Dem. Rep. of the Congo 1°38S 20°35E **52** E4
Monkton *Canada* 43°35N 81°5W **82** C3
Monmouth *U.K.* 51°48N 2°42W **13** F5
Monmouth *Ill., U.S.A.* 40°55N 90°39W **80** E8
Monmouth *Oreg.,*
  U.S.A. 44°51N 123°14W **76** D2
Monmouthshire □ *U.K.* 51°48N 2°54W **13** F5
Mono → *Canada* 44°0N 80°30W **82** B3
Mono L. *U.S.A.* 38°1N 119°1W **78** H7
Monolith *U.S.A.* 35°7N 118°22W **79** K8
Monolithos *Greece* 36°7N 27°45E **25** C9
Monongahela *U.S.A.* 40°12N 79°56W **82** F5
Monópoli *Italy* 40°57N 17°18E **22** D7
Monos I. *Trin. & Tob.* 10°42N 61°44W **93** K15
Monroe *Ga., U.S.A.* 33°47N 83°43W **85** E13
Monroe *La., U.S.A.* 32°30N 92°7W **84** E8
Monroe *Mich., U.S.A.* 41°55N 83°24W **81** E12
Monroe *N.C., U.S.A.* 34°59N 80°33W **85** D14
Monroe *N.Y., U.S.A.* 41°20N 74°11W **83** E10
Monroe *Utah, U.S.A.* 38°38N 112°7W **76** G7
Monroe *Wash., U.S.A.* 47°51N 121°58W **78** C5
Monroe *Wis., U.S.A.* 42°36N 89°38W **80** D9
Monroe City *U.S.A.* 39°39N 91°44W **80** F8
Monroeton *U.S.A.* 41°43N 76°29W **83** E8
Monroeville *Ala.,*
  U.S.A. 31°31N 87°20W **85** F11
Monroeville *Pa., U.S.A.* 40°26N 79°45W **82** F5
Monrovia *Liberia* 6°18N 10°47W **50** G3
Mons *Belgium* 50°27N 3°58E **15** D3
Monse *Indonesia* 4°0S 123°10E **37** E6
Mont-de-Marsan *France* 43°54N 0°31W **20** E3
Mont-Joli *Canada* 48°37N 68°10W **73** C6
Mont-Laurier *Canada* 46°35N 75°30W **72** C4
Mont-Louis *Canada* 49°15N 65°44W **73** C6
Mont-St-Michel, Le
  France 48°40N 1°30W **20** B3
Mont-Tremblant △
  Canada 46°30N 74°30W **72** C5
Montagne d'Ambre △
  Madag. 12°37S 49°8E **57** A8
Montagu *S. Africa* 33°45S 20°8E **56** E3
Montagu I. *Antarctica* 58°25S 26°20W **5** B1
Montague *Canada* 46°10N 62°39W **73** C7
Montague, I. *Mexico* 31°45N 114°48W **86** A2
Montague Ra. *Australia* 27°15S 119°30E **61** E2
Montague Sd. *Australia* 14°28S 125°20E **60** B4
Montalbán *Spain* 40°50N 0°45W **21** B5
Montalvo *U.S.A.* 34°15N 119°12W **79** L7
Montana *Bulgaria* 43°27N 23°16E **23** C10
Montaña *Peru* 6°0S 73°0W **92** E4
Montana □ *U.S.A.* 47°0N 110°0W **76** C9
Montana Clara, I.
  Canary Is. 29°17N 13°33W **24** E6
Montargis *France* 47°59N 2°43E **20** C5
Montauban *France* 44°2N 1°21E **20** D4
Montauk *U.S.A.* 41°3N 71°57W **83** E13
Montauk Pt. *U.S.A.* 41°4N 71°51W **83** E13
Montbéliard *France* 47°31N 6°48E **20** C7
Montceau-les-Mines
  France 46°40N 4°23E **20** C6
Montclair *U.S.A.* 40°49N 74°12W **83** F10
Monte Albán *Mexico* 17°2N 96°46W **87** D5
Monte Alegre *Brazil* 2°0S 54°0W **93** D8
Monte Azul *Brazil* 15°9S 42°53W **93** G10
Monte-Carlo *Monaco* 43°44N 7°25E **20** E7
Monte Caseros
  Argentina 30°10S 57°50W **94** C4

Monte Comán *Argentina* 34°40S 67°53W **94** C2
Monte Crísti *Dom. Rep.* 19°52N 71°39W **89** C5
Monte Lindo →
  Paraguay 23°56S 57°12W **94** A4
Monte Patria *Chile* 30°42S 70°58W **94** C1
Monte Quemado
  Argentina 25°53S 62°41W **94** B3
Monte Rio *U.S.A.* 38°28N 123°0W **78** G4
Monte Santu, C. di *Italy* 40°5N 9°44E **22** D3
Monte Vista *U.S.A.* 37°35N 106°9W **77** H10
Monteagudo *Argentina* 27°14S 54°8W **95** B5
Montebello *Canada* 45°40N 74°55W **72** C5
Montebello Is. *Australia* 20°30S 115°45E **60** D2
Montecarlo *Argentina* 26°34S 54°47W **95** B5
Montecito *U.S.A.* 34°26N 119°40W **79** L7
Montecristo *Italy* 42°20N 10°19E **22** C4
Montego Bay *Jamaica* 18°28N 77°55W **88** a
Montélimar *France* 44°33N 4°45E **20** D6
Montello *U.S.A.* 43°48N 89°20W **80** D9
Montemorelos *Mexico* 25°12N 99°49W **87** B5
Montenegro *Brazil* 29°39S 51°29W **95** B5
Montenegro ■ *Europe* 42°40N 19°20E **23** C8
Montepuez *Mozam.* 13°8S 38°59E **55** E4
Montepuez → *Mozam.* 12°32S 40°27E **55** E5
Monterey *U.S.A.* 36°37N 121°55W **78** J5
Monterey B. *U.S.A.* 36°45N 122°0W **78** J5
Montería *Colombia* 8°46N 75°53W **92** B3
Monteros *Argentina* 27°11S 65°30W **94** B2
Monterrey *Mexico* 25°40N 100°19W **86** B4
Montes Azules △ *Mexico* 16°21N 91°3W **87** D6
Montes Claros *Brazil* 16°30S 43°50W **93** G10
Montesano *U.S.A.* 46°59N 123°36W **78** D3
Montesilvano *Italy* 42°29N 14°8E **22** C6
Montevideo *Uruguay* 34°50S 56°11W **95** C4
Montevideo *U.S.A.* 44°57N 95°43W **80** C6
Montezuma *U.S.A.* 41°35N 92°32W **80** E7
Montezuma Castle △
  U.S.A. 34°39N 111°45W **77** J8
Montgomery *U.K.* 52°34N 3°8W **13** E4
Montgomery *Ala.,*
  U.S.A. 32°23N 86°19W **85** E11
Montgomery *Pa., U.S.A.* 41°10N 76°53W **82** E8
Montgomery *W. Va.,*
  U.S.A. 38°11N 81°19W **81** F13
Montgomery City
  U.S.A. 38°59N 91°30W **80** F8
Monticello *Ark., U.S.A.* 33°38N 91°47W **84** E9
Monticello *Fla., U.S.A.* 30°33N 83°52W **85** F13
Monticello *Ind., U.S.A.* 40°45N 86°46W **80** E10
Monticello *Iowa, U.S.A.* 42°15N 91°12W **80** D8
Monticello *Ky., U.S.A.* 36°50N 84°51W **81** G11
Monticello *Minn., U.S.A.* 45°18N 93°48W **80** C7
Monticello *Miss., U.S.A.* 31°33N 90°7W **85** F9
Monticello *N.Y., U.S.A.* 41°39N 74°42W **83** E10
Monticello *Utah, U.S.A.* 37°52N 109°21W **77** H9
Montijo *Portugal* 38°41N 8°54W **21** C1
Montilla *Spain* 37°36N 4°40W **21** D3
Montluçon *France* 46°22N 2°36E **20** C5
Montmagny *Canada* 46°58N 70°34W **73** C5
Montmartre *Canada* 50°14N 103°27W **71** C8
Montmorillon *France* 46°26N 0°50E **20** C4
Monto *Australia* 24°52S 151°6E **62** C5
Montongbuwoh
  Indonesia 8°33S 116°4E **37** K19
Montoro *Spain* 38°1N 4°27W **21** C3
Montour Falls *U.S.A.* 42°21N 76°51W **82** D8
Montoursville *U.S.A.* 41°15N 76°55W **82** E8
Montpelier *Idaho,*
  U.S.A. 42°19N 111°18W **76** E8
Montpelier *Vt., U.S.A.* 44°16N 72°35W **83** B12
Montpellier *France* 43°37N 3°52E **20** E5
Montréal *Canada* 45°30N 73°33W **83** A11
Montreal → *Canada* 47°14N 84°39W **72** C3
Montréal L. *Canada* 50°14N 105°45W **71** C7
Montreal Lake *Canada* 54°3N 105°46W **71** C7
Montreux *Switz.* 46°26N 6°55E **20** C7
Montrose *U.K.* 56°44N 2°27W **11** E6
Montrose *Colo., U.S.A.* 38°29N 107°53W **76** G10
Montrose *Pa., U.S.A.* 41°50N 75°53W **83** E9
Monts, Pte. des *Canada* 49°20N 67°12W **73** C6
Montserrat ☑ *W. Indies* 16°40N 62°10W **89** C7
Montuiri *Spain* 39°34N 2°59E **24** B9
Monywa *Burma* 22°7N 95°11E **41** H19
Monza *Italy* 45°35N 9°16E **20** D8
Monze *Zambia* 16°17S 27°29E **55** F2
Monze, C. *Pakistan* 24°47N 66°37E **42** G2
Monzón *Spain* 41°52N 0°10E **21** B6
Mooers *U.S.A.* 44°58N 73°35W **83** B11
Mooi → *S. Africa* 28°45S 30°34E **57** D5
Mooi River *S. Africa* 29°13S 29°50E **57** D4
Moomba *Australia* 28°6S 140°12E **63** A3
Moonah → *Australia* 22°3S 138°33E **62** C2
Moonda, L. *Australia* 25°52S 140°25E **62** D3
Moonie *Australia* 27°46S 150°20E **63** D5
Moonie → *Australia* 29°19S 148°43E **63** D4
Moonta *Australia* 34°6S 137°32E **63** E2
Moora *Australia* 30°37S 115°58E **61** F2
Moorcroft *U.S.A.* 44°16N 104°57W **76** D11
Moore → *Australia* 31°22S 115°30E **61** F2
Moore, L. *Australia* 29°50S 117°35E **61** E2
Moore Falls *Canada* 44°48N 78°48W **82** B6
Moore Park *Australia* 24°43S 152°17E **62** C5
Moore Res. *U.S.A.* 44°20N 71°53W **83** B13
Moore River △ *Australia* 31°7S 115°39E **61** F2
Moorea *French Polynesia* 17°30S 149°50W **59** d
Moorefield *U.S.A.* 39°4N 78°58W **81** F14
Moorfoot Hills *U.K.* 55°44N 3°8W **11** F5
Moorhead *U.S.A.* 46°53N 96°45W **80** B5
Moorpark *U.S.A.* 34°17N 118°53W **79** L8
Mooreesburg *S. Africa* 33°6S 18°38E **56** E2
Moorrinya △ *Australia* 21°42S 144°58E **62** C3
Moose → *Canada* 51°20N 80°25W **72** B3
Moose → *U.S.A.* 43°38N 75°24W **83** C9
Moose Creek *Canada* 45°15N 74°58W **83** A10
Moose Factory *Canada* 51°16N 80°32W **72** B3
Moose Jaw *Canada* 50°24N 105°30W **71** C7
Moose Jaw → *Canada* 50°34N 105°18W **71** C7

Moose Lake *Canada* 53°46N 100°8W **71** C8
Moose Lake *U.S.A.* 46°27N 92°46W **80** B7
Moose Mountain △
  Canada 49°48N 102°25W **71** D8
Moosehead L. *U.S.A.* 45°38N 69°40W **81** C19
Mooselookmeguntic L.
  U.S.A. 44°55N 70°49W **83** B14
Moosilauke, Mt. *U.S.A.* 44°3N 71°40W **83** B13
Moosomin *Canada* 50°9N 101°40W **71** C8
Moosonee *Canada* 51°17N 80°39W **72** B3
Moosup *U.S.A.* 41°43N 71°53W **83** E13
Mopane *S. Africa* 22°37S 29°52E **57** C4
Mopeia Velha *Mozam.* 17°30S 35°40E **55** F4
Mopipi *Botswana* 21°6S 24°55E **56** C3
Mopoi *C.A.R.* 5°6N 26°54E **54** A2
Mopti *Mali* 14°30N 4°0W **50** F5
Moqor *Afghan.* 32°50N 67°42E **42** C2
Moquegua *Peru* 17°15S 70°46W **92** G4
Mora *Sweden* 61°2N 14°38E **8** F16
Mora *Minn., U.S.A.* 45°53N 93°18W **80** C7
Mora *N. Mex., U.S.A.* 35°58N 105°20W **77** J11
Moradabad *India* 28°50N 78°50E **43** E8
Morafenobe *Madag.* 17°50S 44°53E **57** B7
Moramanga *Madag.* 18°56S 48°12E **57** B8
Moran *Kans., U.S.A.* 37°55N 95°10W **80** G6
Moran *Wyo., U.S.A.* 43°50N 110°31W **76** E8
Moranbah *Australia* 22°1S 148°6E **62** C4
Morant Bay *Jamaica* 17°53N 76°25W **88** a
Morant Cays *Jamaica* 17°22N 76°0W **88** a
Morant Pt. *Jamaica* 17°55N 76°12W **88** a
Morar *India* 26°14N 78°14E **42** F8
Morar, L. *U.K.* 56°57N 5°40W **11** E3
Moratuwa *Sri Lanka* 6°45N 79°55E **40** R11
Morava → *Serbia* 44°36N 21°4E **23** B9
Morava → *Slovak Rep.* 48°10N 16°59E **17** D9
Moravia *U.S.A.* 42°43N 76°25W **83** D8
Moravian Hts. = Českomoravská
  Vrchovina *Czech Rep.* 49°30N 15°40E **16** D8
Morawa *Australia* 29°13S 116°0E **61** E2
Morawhanna *Guyana* 8°30N 59°40W **92** B7
Moray □ *U.K.* 57°31N 3°18W **11** D5
Moray Firth *U.K.* 57°40N 3°52W **11** D5
Morbi *India* 22°50N 70°42E **42** H4
Morden *Canada* 49°15N 98°10W **71** D9
Mordovian Republic =
  Mordvinia □ *Russia* 54°20N 44°30E **18** D7
Mordvinia □ *Russia* 54°20N 44°30E **18** D7
Moreau → *U.S.A.* 45°18N 100°43W **80** C3
Morebeng *S. Africa* 23°30S 29°55E **57** C4
Morecambe *U.K.* 54°5N 2°52W **12** C5
Morecambe B. *U.K.* 54°7N 3°0W **12** C5
Moree *Australia* 29°28S 149°54E **63** D4
Morehead *U.S.A.* 38°11N 83°26W **81** F12
Morehead City *U.S.A.* 34°43N 76°43W **85** D16
Morel → *India* 26°13N 76°36E **42** F7
Morelia *Mexico* 19°42N 101°7W **86** D4
Morella *Australia* 23°0S 143°52E **62** C3
Morella *Spain* 40°35N 0°5W **21** B5
Morelos *Mexico* 26°42N 107°40W **86** B3
Morelos □ *Mexico* 18°45N 99°0W **87** D5
Moremi △ *Botswana* 19°18S 23°10E **56** B3
Morena *India* 26°30N 78°4E **42** F8
Morena, Sierra *Spain* 38°20N 4°0W **21** C3
Moreno Valley *U.S.A.* 33°56N 117°14W **79** M10
Moresby I. *Canada* 52°30N 131°40W **70** C2
Moreton I. *Australia* 27°10S 153°25E **63** D5
Moreton Island △
  Australia 27°2S 153°24E **63** D5
Morgan *U.S.A.* 41°2N 111°41W **76** F8
Morgan City *U.S.A.* 29°42N 91°12W **84** G9
Morgan Hill *U.S.A.* 37°8N 121°39W **78** H5
Morganfield *U.S.A.* 37°41N 87°55W **80** G10
Morganton *U.S.A.* 35°45N 81°41W **85** D14
Morgantown *U.S.A.* 39°38N 79°57W **81** F14
Morgenzon *S. Africa* 26°45S 29°36E **57** D4
Morghak *Iran* 29°7N 57°54E **45** D8
Mori *Japan* 42°6N 140°35E **30** C10
Moriarty *U.S.A.* 34°59N 106°3W **77** J10
Morice L. *Canada* 53°50N 127°40W **70** C3
Morinville *Canada* 53°49N 113°41W **70** C6
Morioka *Japan* 39°45N 141°8E **30** E10
Moris *Mexico* 28°10N 108°32W **86** B3
Morlaix *France* 48°36N 3°52W **20** B2
Mornington *Australia* 38°15S 145°5E **63** F4
Mornington, I. *Chile* 49°50S 75°30W **96** F1
Mornington I. *Australia* 16°30S 139°30E **62** B2
Moro *Pakistan* 26°40N 68°0E **42** F2
Moro → *Pakistan* 29°42N 67°22E **42** E2
Moro G. *Phil.* 6°30N 123°0E **37** C6
Morocco ■ *N. Afr.* 32°0N 5°50W **50** B4
Morogoro *Tanzania* 6°50S 37°40E **54** D4
Morogoro □ *Tanzania* 8°0S 37°0E **54** D4
Moroleón *Mexico* 20°8N 101°12W **86** C4
Morombe *Madag.* 21°45S 43°22E **57** C7
Moron *Argentina* 34°39S 58°37W **94** C4
Morón *Cuba* 22°8N 78°39W **88** B4
Mörön *Mongolia* 49°38N 100°9E **32** B4
Morón de la Frontera
  Spain 37°6N 5°28W **21** D3
Morona → *Peru* 4°40S 77°10W **92** D3
Morondava *Madag.* 20°17S 44°17E **57** C7
Morongo Valley *U.S.A.* 34°3N 116°37W **79** L10
Moroni *Comoros Is.* 11°40S 43°16E **53** a
Moroni *U.S.A.* 39°32N 111°35W **76** G8
Morotai *Indonesia* 2°10N 128°30E **37** D7
Moroto *Uganda* 2°28N 34°42E **54** B3
Moroto, Mt. *Uganda* 2°30N 34°43E **54** B3
Morpeth *Canada* 42°23N 81°50W **82** D3
Morpeth *U.K.* 55°10N 1°41W **12** B6
Morphou *Cyprus* 35°12N 32°59E **25** D11
Morphou Bay *Cyprus* 35°15N 32°50E **25** D11
Morrilton *U.S.A.* 35°9N 92°44W **84** D8
Morrinhos *Brazil* 17°45S 49°10W **93** G9
Morrinsville *N.Z.* 37°40S 175°32E **59** B5
Morris *Canada* 49°25N 97°22W **71** D9
Morris *Ill., U.S.A.* 41°22N 88°26W **80** E9

Morris *Minn., U.S.A.* 45°35N 95°55W **80** C6
Morris *N.Y., U.S.A.* 42°33N 75°15W **83** D9
Morris *Pa., U.S.A.* 41°35N 77°17W **82** E7
Morris, Mt. *Australia* 26°9S 131°4E **61** E5
Morris Jesup, Kap
  Greenland 83°40N 34°0W **66** A16
Morrisburg *Canada* 44°55N 75°7W **83** B9
Morristown *Ariz.,*
  U.S.A. 33°51N 112°37W **77** K7
Morristown *N.J., U.S.A.* 40°48N 74°29W **83** F10
Morristown *N.Y., U.S.A.* 44°35N 75°39W **83** B9
Morristown *Tenn.,*
  U.S.A. 36°13N 83°18W **85** C13
Morrisville *N.Y., U.S.A.* 42°53N 75°35W **83** D9
Morrisville *Pa., U.S.A.* 40°13N 74°47W **83** F11
Morrisville *Vt., U.S.A.* 44°34N 72°36W **83** B12
Morro, Pta. *Chile* 27°6S 71°0W **94** B1
Morro Bay *U.S.A.* 35°22N 120°51W **78** K6
Morro del Jable *Canary Is.* 28°3N 14°23W **24** F5
Morro Jable, Pta. de
  Canary Is. 28°2N 14°20W **24** F5
Morrocoy △ *Venezuela* 10°48N 68°13W **89** D6
Morrosquillo, G. de
  Colombia 9°35N 75°40W **88** E4
Morrumbene *Mozam.* 23°31S 35°16E **57** C6
Morshansk *Russia* 53°28N 41°50E **18** D7
Morteros *Argentina* 30°50S 62°0W **94** C3
Mortlach *Canada* 50°27N 106°4W **71** C7
Mortlake *Australia* 38°5S 142°50E **63** F3
Morton *Tex., U.S.A.* 33°44N 102°46W **84** B3
Morton *Wash., U.S.A.* 46°34N 122°17W **78** D4
Moruga *Trin. & Tob.* 10°4N 61°16W **93** K15
Morundah *Australia* 34°57S 146°19E **63** E4
Moruya *Australia* 35°58S 150°3E **63** F5
Morvan *France* 47°5N 4°3E **20** C6
Morven *Australia* 26°22S 147°5E **63** D4
Morvern *U.K.* 56°38N 5°44W **11** E3
Morwell *Australia* 38°10S 146°22E **63** F4
Morzhovets, Ostrov
  Russia 66°44N 42°35E **18** A7
Moscos Is. *Burma* 14°0N 97°30E **38** F1
Moscow = Moskva
  Russia 55°45N 37°37E **18** C6
Moscow *Idaho, U.S.A.* 46°44N 117°0W **76** C5
Moscow *Pa., U.S.A.* 41°20N 75°31W **83** E9
Mosel → *Europe* 50°22N 7°36E **20** A7
Moselle = Mosel →
  Europe 50°22N 7°36E **20** A7
Moses Lake *U.S.A.* 47°8N 119°17W **76** C4
Mosgiel *N.Z.* 45°53S 170°21E **59** F3
Moshaweng → *S. Africa* 26°35S 22°50E **56** D3
Moshchnyy, Ostrov
  Russia 60°1N 27°50E **9** F22
Moshi *Tanzania* 3°22S 37°18E **54** C4
Moshupa *Botswana* 24°46S 25°29E **56** C4
Mosjøen *Norway* 65°51N 13°12E **8** D15
Moskenesøya *Norway* 67°58N 13°0E **8** C15
Moskenstraumen
  Norway 67°47N 12°45E **8** C15
Moskva *Russia* 55°45N 37°37E **18** C6
Mosomane *Botswana* 24°2S 26°19E **56** C4
Mosonmagyaróvár
  Hungary 47°52N 17°18E **17** E9
Mosquera *Colombia* 2°35N 78°24W **92** C3
Mosquero *U.S.A.* 35°47N 103°58W **77** J12
Mosquitia *Honduras* 15°20N 84°10W **88** C3
Mosquito Coast = Mosquitia
  Honduras 15°20N 84°10W **88** C3
Mosquito Creek L.
  U.S.A. 41°18N 80°46W **82** E4
Mosquito L. *Canada* 62°35N 103°20W **71** A8
Mosquitos, G. de los
  Panama 9°15N 81°10W **88** E3
Moss *Norway* 59°27N 10°40E **9** G14
Moss Vale *Australia* 34°32S 150°25E **63** E5
Mossaka *Congo* 1°15S 16°45E **52** E3
Mossbank *Canada* 49°56N 105°56W **71** D7
Mossburn *N.Z.* 45°41S 168°15E **59** F2
Mosselbaai *S. Africa* 34°11S 22°8E **56** E3
Mossendjo *Congo* 2°55S 12°42E **52** E2
Mossgiel *Australia* 33°15S 144°5E **63** E3
Mossman *Australia* 16°21S 145°15E **62** B4
Mossoró *Brazil* 5°10S 37°15W **93** E11
Mossuril *Mozam.* 14°58S 40°42E **55** E5
Most *Czech Rep.* 50°31N 13°38E **16** C7
Mosta *Malta* 35°55N 14°26E **25** D1
Mostaganem *Algeria* 35°54N 0°5E **50** A6
Mostar *Bos.-H.* 43°22N 17°50E **23** C7
Mostardas *Brazil* 31°2S 50°51W **95** C5
Mostiska = Mostyska
  Ukraine 49°48N 23°4E **17** D12
Mosty = Masty *Belarus* 53°27N 24°38E **17** B13
Mostyska *Ukraine* 49°48N 23°4E **17** D12
Mosul = Al Mawşil *Iraq* 36°15N 43°5E **44** B4
Motagua → *Guatemala* 15°44N 88°14W **88** C2
Motala *Sweden* 58°32N 15°1E **9** G16
Motaze *Mozam.* 24°48S 32°52E **57** C5
Moth *India* 25°43N 78°57E **43** G8
Motherwell *U.K.* 55°47N 3°58W **11** F5
Motihari *India* 26°30N 84°55E **43** F11
Motozintla de Mendoza
  Mexico 15°22N 92°14W **87** D6
Motril *Spain* 36°31N 3°37W **21** D4
Mott *U.S.A.* 46°23N 102°20W **80** B2
Motueka *N.Z.* 41°7S 173°1E **59** D4
Motueka → *N.Z.* 41°5S 173°1E **59** D4
Motul *Mexico* 21°6N 89°17W **87** C7
Mouchalagane →
  Canada 50°56N 68°41W **73** B6
Moudros *Greece* 39°50N 25°18E **23** E11
Mouila *Gabon* 1°50S 11°0E **52** E2
Moulamein *Australia* 35°3S 144°1E **63** F3
Moule à Chique, C.
  St. Lucia 13°43N 60°57W **89** f
Mouliana *Greece* 35°10N 25°59E **25** D7
Moulins *France* 46°35N 3°19E **20** C5
Moulmein *Burma* 16°30N 97°40E **41** L20

Moulouya, O. → *Morocco* 35°5N 2°25W **50** B5
Moultrie *U.S.A.* 31°11N 83°47W **85** F13
Moultrie, L. *U.S.A.* 33°20N 80°5W **85** E14
Mound City *Mo., U.S.A.* 40°7N 95°14W **80** E6
Mound City *S. Dak.,*
  U.S.A. 45°44N 100°4W **80** C3
Moundou *Chad* 8°40N 16°10E **51** G9
Moundsville *U.S.A.* 39°55N 80°44W **82** G4
Moung *Cambodia* 12°46N 103°27E **38** F4
Mount Airy *U.S.A.* 36°31N 80°37W **85** C14
Mount Albert *Canada* 44°8N 79°19W **82** B5
Mount Aspiring △ *N.Z.* 44°19S 168°47E **59** F2
Mount Barker *S. Austral.,*
  Australia 35°5S 138°52E **63** F2
Mount Barker *W. Austral.,*
  Australia 34°38S 117°40E **61** F2
Mount Bellew Bridge
  Ireland 53°28N 8°31W **10** C3
Mount Brydges *Canada* 42°54N 81°29W **82** D3
Mount Burr *Australia* 37°34S 140°26E **63** F3
Mount Carmel = Ha Karmel △
  Israel 32°45N 35°5E **46** C4
Mount Carmel *Ill.,*
  U.S.A. 38°25N 87°46W **80** F10
Mount Carmel *Pa.,*
  U.S.A. 40°47N 76°26W **83** F8
Mount Clemens *U.S.A.* 42°35N 82°53W **82** D2
Mount Coolon *Australia* 21°25S 147°25E **62** C4
Mount Darwin *Zimbabwe* 16°47S 31°38E **55** F3
Mount Desert I. *U.S.A.* 44°21N 68°20W **81** C19
Mount Dora *U.S.A.* 28°48N 81°38W **85** G14
Mount Edziza △
  Canada 57°30N 130°45W **70** B2
Mount Elgon △ *E. Afr.* 1°4N 34°42E **54** B3
Mount Field △ *Australia* 42°39S 146°35E **63** G4
Mount Fletcher *S. Africa* 30°40S 28°30E **57** E4
Mount Forest *Canada* 43°59N 80°43W **82** C4
Mount Frankland △
  Australia 31°47S 116°37E **60** F2
Mount Gambier
  Australia 37°50S 140°46E **63** F3
Mount Garnet *Australia* 17°37S 145°6E **62** B4
Mount Holly *U.S.A.* 39°59N 74°47W **83** G10
Mount Holly Springs
  U.S.A. 40°7N 77°12W **82** F7
Mount Hope *N.S.W.,*
  Australia 32°51S 145°51E **63** E4
Mount Hope *S. Austral.,*
  Australia 34°7S 135°23E **63** E2
Mount Isa *Australia* 20°42S 139°26E **62** C2
Mount Jewett *U.S.A.* 41°44N 78°39W **82** E6
Mount Kaputar △
  Australia 30°16S 150°10E **63** E5
Mount Kenya △ *Kenya* 0°7S 37°21E **54** C4
Mount Kilimanjaro △
  Tanzania 3°2S 37°19E **54** C4
Mount Kisco *U.S.A.* 41°12N 73°44W **83** E11
Mount Laguna *U.S.A.* 32°52N 116°25W **79** N10
Mount Larcom
  Australia 23°48S 150°59E **62** C5
Mount Lofty Ranges
  Australia 34°35S 139°5E **63** E2
Mount Magnet *Australia* 28°2S 117°47E **61** E2
Mount Maunganui
  N.Z. 37°40S 176°14E **59** B6
Mount Molloy *Australia* 16°42S 145°20E **62** B4
Mount Morgan
  Australia 23°40S 150°25E **62** C5
Mount Morris *U.S.A.* 42°44N 77°52W **82** D7
Mount Pearl *Canada* 47°31N 52°47W **73** C9
Mount Penn *U.S.A.* 40°20N 75°54W **83** F9
Mount Perry *Australia* 25°13S 151°42E **63** D5
Mount Pleasant *Iowa,*
  U.S.A. 40°58N 91°33W **80** E8
Mount Pleasant *Mich.,*
  U.S.A. 43°36N 84°46W **81** D11
Mount Pleasant *Pa.,*
  U.S.A. 40°9N 79°33W **82** F5
Mount Pleasant *S.C.,*
  U.S.A. 32°47N 79°52W **85** E15
Mount Pleasant *Tenn.,*
  U.S.A. 35°32N 87°12W **85** D11
Mount Pleasant *Tex.,*
  U.S.A. 33°9N 94°58W **84** E7
Mount Pleasant *Utah,*
  U.S.A. 39°33N 111°27W **76** G8
Mount Pocono *U.S.A.* 41°7N 75°22W **83** E9
Mount Rainier △
  U.S.A. 46°55N 121°50W **78** D5
Mount Revelstoke △
  Canada 51°5N 118°30W **70** C5
Mount Robson △ *Canada* 53°0N 119°0W **70** C5
Mount St. Helens △
  U.S.A. 46°14N 122°11W **78** D4
Mount Selinda *Zimbabwe* 20°24S 32°43E **57** C5
Mount Shasta *U.S.A.* 41°19N 122°19W **76** F2
Mount Signal *U.S.A.* 32°39N 115°37W **79** N11
Mount Sterling *Ill.,*
  U.S.A. 39°59N 90°45W **80** F8
Mount Sterling *Ky.,*
  U.S.A. 38°4N 83°56W **81** F12
Mount Surprise
  Australia 18°10S 144°17E **62** B3
Mount Union *U.S.A.* 40°23N 77°53W **82** F7
Mount Upton *U.S.A.* 42°26N 75°23W **83** D9
Mount Vernon *Ill.,*
  U.S.A. 38°19N 88°55W **80** F9
Mount Vernon *Ind.,*
  U.S.A. 37°56N 87°54W **80** G10
Mount Vernon *N.Y.,*
  U.S.A. 40°55N 73°49W **83** F11
Mount Vernon *Ohio,*
  U.S.A. 40°23N 82°29W **82** F2
Mount Vernon *Wash.,*
  U.S.A. 48°25N 122°20W **78** B4
Mount William △
  Australia 40°56S 148°14E **63** G4

Mountain Ash *U.K.* 51°40N 3°23W **13** F4
Mountain Center
  U.S.A. 33°42N 116°44W **79** M10
Mountain City *Nev.,*
  U.S.A. 41°50N 115°58W **76** F6
Mountain City *Tenn.,*
  U.S.A. 36°29N 81°48W **85** C14
Mountain Dale *U.S.A.* 41°41N 74°32W **83** E10
Mountain Grove *U.S.A.* 37°8N 92°16W **80** G7
Mountain Home *Ark.,*
  U.S.A. 36°20N 92°23W **84** C8
Mountain Home *Idaho,*
  U.S.A. 43°8N 115°41W **76** E6
Mountain Iron *U.S.A.* 47°32N 92°37W **80** B7
Mountain Pass *U.S.A.* 35°29N 115°35W **79** K11
Mountain View *Ark.,*
  U.S.A. 35°52N 92°7W **84** D8
Mountain View *Calif.,*
  U.S.A. 37°23N 122°5W **78** H4
Mountain View *Hawai'i,*
  U.S.A. 19°33N 155°7W **74** b
Mountain Zebra △
  S. Africa 32°14S 25°27E **56** E4
Mountainair *U.S.A.* 34°31N 106°15W **77** J10
Mountlake Terrace
  U.S.A. 47°47N 122°18W **78** C4
Mountmellick *Ireland* 53°7N 7°20W **10** C4
Mountrath *Ireland* 53°0N 7°28W **10** C4
Moura *Australia* 24°35S 149°58E **62** C4
Moura *Brazil* 1°32S 61°38W **92** D6
Moura *Portugal* 38°7N 7°30W **21** C2
Mourdi, Dépression du
  Chad 18°10N 23°0E **51** E10
Mourilyan *Australia* 17°35S 146°3E **62** B4
Mourne → *U.K.* 54°52N 7°26W **10** B4
Mourne Mts. *U.K.* 54°10N 6°0W **10** B5
Mournies *Greece* 35°29N 24°1E **25** D6
Mouscron *Belgium* 50°45N 3°12E **15** D3
Moussoro *Chad* 13°41N 16°35E **51** F9
Moutong *Indonesia* 0°28N 121°13E **37** D6
Movas *Mexico* 28°10N 109°25W **86** B3
Moville *Ireland* 55°11N 7°3W **10** A4
Moy → *Ireland* 54°8N 9°8W **10** B2
Moya *Comoros Is.* 12°18S 44°18E **53** a
Moyale *Kenya* 3°30N 39°0E **54** B4
Moyen Atlas *Morocco* 33°0N 5°0W **50** B4
Moyo *Indonesia* 8°10S 117°40E **36** F5
Moyobamba *Peru* 6°0S 77°0W **92** E3
Moyyero → *Russia* 68°44N 103°42E **29** C11
Moyynqum *Kazakhstan* 44°12N 71°0E **32** B2
Moyynty *Kazakhstan* 47°10N 73°18E **28** E8
Mozambique = Moçambique
  Mozam. 15°3S 40°42E **55** F5
Mozambique ■ *Africa* 19°0S 35°0E **55** F4
Mozambique Chan.
  Africa 17°30S 42°30E **57** B7
Mozdok *Russia* 43°45N 44°48E **19** F7
Mozdūrān *Iran* 36°9N 60°35E **45** B9
Mozhnābād *Iran* 34°7N 60°6E **45** C9
Mozyr = Mazyr *Belarus* 51°59N 29°15E **17** B15
Mpanda *Tanzania* 6°23S 31°1E **54** D3
Mphoengs *Zimbabwe* 21°10S 27°51E **57** C4
Mpika *Zambia* 11°51S 31°25E **55** E3
Mpulungu *Zambia* 8°51S 31°5E **55** D3
Mpumalanga *S. Africa* 29°50S 30°33E **57** D5
Mpumalanga □ *S. Africa* 26°0S 30°0E **57** D5
Mpwapwa *Tanzania* 6°23S 36°30E **54** D4
Mqanduli *S. Africa* 31°49S 28°45E **57** E4
Msaken *Tunisia* 35°49N 10°33E **51** A8
Msambansovu *Zimbabwe* 15°50S 30°3E **55** F3
M'sila → *Algeria* 35°30N 4°29E **50** A6
Msoro *Zambia* 13°35S 31°50E **55** E3
Mstislavl = Mstsislaw
  Belarus 54°0N 31°50E **17** A16
Mstsislaw *Belarus* 54°0N 31°50E **17** A16
Mtama *Tanzania* 10°17S 39°21E **55** E4
Mtamvuna = Mthamvuna →
  S. Africa 31°6S 30°12E **57** E5
Mthamvuna → *S. Africa* 31°6S 30°12E **57** E5
Mthatha *S. Africa* 31°36S 28°49E **57** E4
Mtilikwe → *Zimbabwe* 21°9S 31°30E **55** G3
Mtito Andei *Kenya* 2°41S 38°10E **54** C4
Mtubatuba *S. Africa* 28°30S 32°8E **57** D5
Mtwalume *S. Africa* 30°30S 30°38E **57** E5
Mtwara-Mikindani
  Tanzania 10°20S 40°20E **55** E5
Mu Gia, Deo *Vietnam* 17°40N 105°47E **38** D5
Mu Ko Chang △
  Thailand 11°59N 102°22E **39** G4
Mu Us Shamo *China* 39°0N 109°0E **34** E5
Muang Chiang Rai = Chiang Rai
  Thailand 19°52N 99°50E **38** C2
Muang Khong *Laos* 14°7N 105°51E **38** E5
Muang Lamphun
  Thailand 18°40N 99°2E **38** C2
Muang Mai *Thailand* 8°5N 98°21E **39** a
Muang Pak Beng *Laos* 19°54N 101°8E **38** C3
Muar *Malaysia* 2°3N 102°34E **39** L4
Muarabungo *Indonesia* 1°28S 102°52E **36** E2
Muaraenim *Indonesia* 3°40S 103°50E **36** E2
Muarajuloi *Indonesia* 0°12S 114°3E **36** E4
Muarakaman *Indonesia* 0°2S 116°45E **36** E5
Muaratebo *Indonesia* 1°30S 102°26E **36** E2
Muaratembesi *Indonesia* 1°42S 103°8E **36** E2
Muaratewe *Indonesia* 0°58S 114°52E **36** E4
Mubarakpur *India* 26°6N 83°18E **43** F10
Mubarraz = Al Mubarraz
  Si. Arabia 25°30N 49°40E **45** E6
Mubende *Uganda* 0°33N 31°22E **54** B3
Mubi *Nigeria* 10°18N 13°16E **51** F8
Mucajaí → *Brazil* 2°25N 60°52W **92** C6
Muchachos, Roque de los
  Canary Is. 28°44N 17°52W **24** F2
Muchinga Mts. *Zambia* 11°30S 31°30E **55** E3
Muck *U.K.* 56°50N 6°15W **11** E2
Muckadilla *Australia* 26°35S 148°23E **63** D4

Muckle Flugga U.K. 60°51N 0°54W 11 A8
Mucuri Brazil 18°0S 39°36W 93 G11
Mucusso Angola 18°1S 21°25E 56 B3
Muda Canary Is. 28°34N 13°57W 24 F6
Mudanjiang China 44°38N 129°30E 35 B15
Mudanya Turkey 40°25N 28°50E 23 D13
Muddy Cr. → U.S.A. 38°24N 110°42W 76 G8
Mudgee Australia 32°32S 149°31E 63 E4
Mudjatik → Canada 56°1N 107°36W 71 B7
Muecate Mozam. 14°55S 39°40E 55 E4
Mueda Mozam. 11°36S 39°28E 55 E4
Mueller Ranges Australia 18°18S 126°46E 60 C4
Muende Mozam. 14°28S 33°0E 55 E3
Muerto, Mar Mexico 16°10N 94°10W 87 D6
Mufulira Zambia 12°32S 28°15E 55 E2
Mufumbiro Range Africa 1°25S 29°30E 54 C2
Mughal Sarai India 25°18N 83°7E 43 G10
Mughayrā' Si. Arabia 29°17N 37°41E 44 D3
Mugi Japan 33°40N 134°25E 31 H7
Mugila, Mts. Dem. Rep. of the Congo 7°0S 28°50E 54 D2
Muğla Turkey 37°15N 28°22E 23 F13
Mugu Nepal 29°45N 82°30E 43 E10
Muhammad, Râs Egypt 27°44N 34°16E 44 E2
Muhammad Qol Sudan 20°53N 37°9E 51 D13
Muhammadabad India 26°4N 83°25E 43 F10
Muhesi → Tanzania 7°0S 35°20E 54 D4
Mühlhausen Germany 51°12N 10°27E 16 C6
Mühlig Hofmann fjell Antarctica 72°30S 5°0E 5 D3
Muhos Finland 64°47N 25°59E 8 D21
Muhu Estonia 58°36N 23°11E 9 G20
Muhutwe Tanzania 1°35S 31°45E 54 C3
Mui Wo China 22°16N 113°59E 33 G10
Muine Bheag Ireland 52°42N 6°58W 10 D5
Muir, L. Australia 34°30S 116°40E 61 F2
Muir of Ord U.K. 57°32N 4°28W 11 D4
Mujeres, I. Mexico 21°13N 86°43W 88 B2
Mujnak = Muynak Uzbekistan 43°44N 59°10E 28 E6
Muka, Tanjung Malaysia 5°28N 100°11E 39 c
Mukacheve Ukraine 48°27N 22°45E 17 D12
Mukachevo = Mukacheve Ukraine 48°27N 22°45E 17 D12
Mukah Malaysia 2°55N 112°5E 36 D4
Mukandwara India 24°49N 75°59E 42 G6
Mukawwa, Geziret Egypt 23°55N 35°53E 44 F2
Mukdahan Thailand 16°32N 104°43E 38 D5
Mukden = Shenyang China 41°48N 123°27E 35 D12
Mukerian India 31°57N 75°37E 42 D6
Mukinbudin Australia 30°55S 118°5E 61 F2
Mukishi Dem. Rep. of the Congo 8°30S 24°44E 55 D1
Mukomuko Indonesia 2°30S 101°10E 36 E2
Mukomwenze Dem. Rep. of the Congo 6°49S 27°15E 54 D2
Muktsar India 30°30N 74°30E 42 D6
Mukur = Moqor Afghan. 32°50N 67°42E 42 C2
Mukutuwa → Canada 53°10N 97°24W 71 C9
Mukwela Zambia 17°0S 26°40E 55 F2
Mula Spain 38°3N 1°33W 21 C5
Mula → Pakistan 27°57N 67°36E 42 F2
Mulange Dem. Rep. of the Congo 3°40S 27°10E 54 C2
Mulanje, Mt. Malawi 16°2S 35°33E 55 F4
Mulchén Chile 37°45S 72°20W 94 D1
Mulde → Germany 51°53N 12°15E 16 C7
Mule Creek Junction U.S.A. 43°23N 104°13W 76 E11
Muleba Tanzania 1°50S 31°37E 54 C3
Mulegé Mexico 26°53N 111°59W 86 B2
Muleshoe U.S.A. 34°13N 102°43W 84 D3
Mulgrave Canada 45°38N 61°31W 73 C7
Mulhacén Spain 37°4N 3°20W 21 D4
Mulhouse France 47°40N 7°20E 20 C7
Mulifanua Samoa 13°50S 171°59W 59 b
Muling China 44°35N 130°10E 35 B16
Mull U.K. 56°25N 5°56W 11 E3
Mull, Sound of U.K. 56°30N 5°50W 11 E3
Mullaittivu Sri Lanka 9°15N 80°49E 40 Q12
Mullen U.S.A. 42°3N 101°1W 80 D3
Mullens U.S.A. 37°35N 81°23W 81 G13
Muller, Pegunungan Indonesia 0°30N 113°30E 36 D4
Mullet Pen. Ireland 54°13N 10°2W 10 B1
Mullewa Australia 28°29S 115°30E 61 E2
Mulligan → Australia 25°0S 139°0E 62 D2
Mullingar Ireland 53°31N 7°21W 10 C4
Mullins U.S.A. 34°12N 79°15W 85 D15
Mullumbimby Australia 28°30S 153°30E 63 D5
Mulobezi Zambia 16°45S 25°7E 55 F2
Mulonga Plain Zambia 16°20S 22°40E 53 H4
Mulroy B. Ireland 55°15N 7°46W 10 A4
Multan Pakistan 30°15N 71°36E 42 D4
Mulumbe, Mts. Dem. Rep. of the Congo 8°40S 27°30E 55 D2
Mulungushi Dam Zambia 14°48S 28°48E 55 E2
Mulvane U.S.A. 37°29N 97°15W 80 G5
Mumbai India 18°56N 72°50E 40 K8
Mumbwa Zambia 15°0S 27°0E 55 F2
Mumias Kenya 0°20N 34°29E 54 C4
Mun → Thailand 15°19N 105°30E 38 E5
Muna Indonesia 5°0S 122°30E 37 F6
Munabao India 25°45N 70°17E 42 G4
Munamagi Estonia 57°43N 27°4E 9 H22
Muncan Indonesia 8°34S 115°11E 37 K18
Muncar Indonesia 8°26S 114°20E 37 J17
München Germany 48°8N 11°34E 16 D6
Munchen-Gladbach = Mönchengladbach Germany 51°11N 6°27E 16 C4
Muncho Lake Canada 59°0N 125°50W 70 B3
Munch'ŏn N. Korea 39°14N 127°19E 35 E14
Muncie U.S.A. 40°12N 85°23W 81 E11
Muncoonie L. West Australia 25°12S 138°40E 62 D2
Mundabbera Australia 25°36S 151°18E 63 D5
Munday U.S.A. 33°27N 99°38W 84 E5
Münden Germany 51°25N 9°38E 16 C5
Mundiwindi Australia 23°47S 120°9E 60 D3
Mundo Novo Brazil 11°50S 40°29W 93 F10
Mundra India 22°54N 69°48E 42 H3
Mundrabilla Australia 31°52S 127°51E 61 F4
Mungallala Australia 26°28S 147°34E 63 D4
Mungallala Cr. → Australia 28°53S 147°5E 63 D4
Mungana Australia 17°8S 144°27E 62 B3
Mungaoli India 24°24N 78°7E 42 G8
Mungari Mozam. 17°12S 33°30E 55 F3
Mungbere Dem. Rep. of the Congo 2°36N 28°28E 54 B2
Mungeli India 22°4N 81°41E 43 H9
Munger India 25°23N 86°30E 43 G12
Mungerannie Australia 28°1S 138°39E 63 A2
Mungkan Kandju △ Australia 13°35S 142°52E 62 A3
Munich = München Germany 48°8N 11°34E 16 D6
Munising U.S.A. 46°25N 86°40W 80 B10
Munku-Sardyk Russia 51°45N 100°20E 29 D11
Munnsville U.S.A. 42°58N 75°35W 83 D9
Muñoz Gamero, Pen. Chile 52°30S 73°5W 96 G2
Munroe L. Canada 59°13N 98°35W 71 B9
Munsan S. Korea 37°51N 126°48E 35 F14
Münster Germany 51°58N 7°37E 16 C4
Munster □ Ireland 52°18N 8°44W 10 D3
Muntadgin Australia 31°45S 118°33E 61 F2
Muntok Indonesia 2°5S 105°10E 36 E3
Munyama Zambia 16°5S 28°31E 55 F2
Muong Beng Laos 20°23N 101°46E 38 B3
Muong Boum Vietnam 22°24N 102°49E 38 A4
Muong Et Laos 20°49N 104°1E 38 B5
Muong Hai Laos 21°3N 101°49E 38 B3
Muong Hiem Laos 20°5N 103°22E 38 B4
Muong Houn Laos 20°8N 101°23E 38 B3
Muong Hung Vietnam 20°56N 103°53E 38 B4
Muong Kau Laos 15°6N 105°47E 38 E5
Muong Khao Laos 19°38N 103°32E 38 C4
Muong Khoua Laos 21°5N 102°31E 38 B4
Muong Liep Laos 18°29N 101°40E 38 C3
Muong May Laos 14°49N 106°56E 38 E6
Muong Ngeun Laos 20°36N 101°3E 38 B3
Muong Ngoi Laos 20°43N 102°41E 38 B4
Muong Nhie Vietnam 22°12N 102°28E 38 A4
Muong Nong Laos 16°22N 106°30E 38 D6
Muong Ou Tay Laos 22°7N 101°48E 38 A3
Muong Oua Laos 18°18N 101°20E 38 C3
Muong Peun Laos 20°13N 103°52E 38 B4
Muong Phalane Laos 16°39N 105°34E 38 D5
Muong Phieng Laos 19°6N 101°32E 38 C3
Muong Phine Laos 16°32N 106°2E 38 D6
Muong Sai Laos 20°42N 101°59E 38 B3
Muong Saiapoun Laos 18°24N 101°31E 38 C3
Muong Sen Vietnam 19°24N 104°8E 38 C5
Muong Sing Laos 21°11N 101°9E 38 B3
Muong Son Laos 20°27N 103°19E 38 B4
Muong Soui Laos 19°33N 102°52E 38 C4
Muong Va Laos 21°53N 102°19E 38 B4
Muong Xia Vietnam 20°19N 104°50E 38 B5
Muonio Finland 67°57N 23°40E 8 C20
Muonio älv = Muonionjoki → Finland 67°11N 23°34E 8 C20
Muonioälven = Muonionjoki → Finland 67°11N 23°34E 8 C20
Muonionjoki → Finland 67°11N 23°34E 8 C20
Muping China 37°22N 121°36E 35 F11
Muqdisho Somali Rep. 2°2N 45°25E 47 G4
Mur → Austria 46°18N 16°52E 17 E9
Murakami Japan 38°14N 139°29E 30 E9
Murallón, Cerro Chile 49°48S 73°30W 96 F2
Muranda Rwanda 1°52S 29°20E 54 C2
Murang'a Kenya 0°45S 37°9E 54 C4
Murashi Russia 59°30N 49°0E 18 C8
Murat → Turkey 38°46N 40°0E 19 G7
Muratlı Turkey 41°10N 27°29E 23 D12
Murayama Japan 38°30N 140°25E 30 E10
Murchison → Australia 27°45S 114°0E 61 E1
Murchison, Mt. Antarctica 73°25S 166°20E 5 D11
Murchison Falls Uganda 2°15N 31°30E 54 B3
Murchison Falls △ Uganda 2°17N 31°48E 54 B3
Murchison Ra. Australia 20°0S 134°10E 62 C1
Murchison Rapids Malawi 15°55S 34°35E 55 F3
Murchison Roadhouse Australia 27°39S 114°14E 61 E1
Murcia Spain 38°5N 1°10W 21 D5
Murcia □ Spain 37°50N 1°30W 21 D5
Murdo U.S.A. 43°53N 100°43W 80 D3
Murdoch Pt. Australia 14°37S 144°55E 62 A3
Mureş → Romania 46°15N 20°13E 17 E11
Mureşul = Mureş → Romania 46°15N 20°13E 17 E11
Murewa Zimbabwe 17°39S 31°47E 57 B5
Murfreesboro N.C., U.S.A. 36°27N 77°6W 85 C16
Murfreesboro Tenn., U.S.A. 35°51N 86°24W 85 D11
Murgap Tajikistan 38°10N 74°2E 28 F8
Murgap → Turkmenistan 38°18N 61°12E 45 B9
Murgenella Australia 11°34S 132°56E 60 B5
Murgha Kibzai Pakistan 30°44N 69°25E 42 D3
Murghob = Murgap Tajikistan 38°10N 74°2E 28 F8
Murgon Australia 26°15S 151°54E 63 D5
Muri India 23°22N 85°52E 43 H11
Muria Indonesia 6°36S 110°53E 37 G14
Muriaé Brazil 21°8S 42°23W 95 A7
Muriel Mine Zimbabwe 17°14S 30°40E 55 F3
Müritz Germany 53°25N 12°42E 16 B7
Murliganj India 25°54N 86°59E 43 G12
Murmansk Russia 68°57N 33°10E 8 B25
Murmashi Russia 68°47N 32°42E 8 B25
Muro Spain 39°44N 3°3E 24 B10
Murom Russia 55°35N 42°3E 18 C7
Muroran Japan 42°25N 141°0E 30 C10
Muroto Japan 33°18N 134°9E 31 H7
Muroto-Misaki Japan 33°15N 134°10E 31 H7
Murphy U.S.A. 43°13N 116°33W 76 E5
Murphys U.S.A. 38°8N 120°28W 78 G6
Murray Ky., U.S.A. 36°37N 88°19W 80 G9
Murray Utah, U.S.A. 40°40N 111°53W 76 F8
Murray → Australia 35°20S 139°22E 63 F2
Murray, L. U.S.A. 34°3N 81°13W 85 D14
Murray Bridge Australia 35°6S 139°14E 63 F2
Murray Fracture Zone Pac. Oc. 35°0N 130°0W 65 D14
Murray Harbour Canada 46°0N 62°28W 73 C7
Murray River △ Australia 34°23S 140°32E 63 E3
Murraysburg S. Africa 31°58S 23°47E 56 E3
Murree Pakistan 33°56N 73°28E 42 C5
Murrieta U.S.A. 33°33N 117°13W 79 M9
Murrumbidgee → Australia 34°43S 143°12E 63 E3
Murrumburrah Australia 34°32S 148°22E 63 E4
Murrurundi Australia 31°42S 150°51E 63 E5
Murshidabad India 24°11N 88°19E 43 G13
Murtle L. Canada 52°8N 119°38W 70 C5
Murtoa Australia 36°35S 142°28E 63 F3
Murungu Tanzania 4°12S 31°10E 54 C3
Mururoa French Polynesia 21°52S 138°55W 65 K14
Murwara India 23°46N 80°28E 43 H9
Murwillumbah Australia 28°18S 153°27E 63 D5
Mürzzuschlag Austria 47°36N 15°41E 16 E8
Muş Turkey 38°45N 41°30E 44 B4
Mûsa, Gebel Egypt 28°33N 33°59E 44 D2
Musa Khel Pakistan 30°59N 69°52E 42 D3
Mūsa Qal'eh Afghan. 32°20N 64°50E 40 C4
Musafirkhana India 26°22N 81°48E 43 F9
Musala Bulgaria 42°13N 23°37E 23 C10
Musala Indonesia 1°41N 98°28E 36 D1
Musan N. Korea 42°12N 129°12E 35 C15
Musangu Dem. Rep. of the Congo 10°28S 23°55E 55 E1
Musasa Tanzania 3°25S 31°30E 54 C3
Musay'īd Qatar 25°0N 51°33E 45 E6
Muscat = Masqat Oman 23°37N 58°36E 47 C6
Muscatine U.S.A. 41°25N 91°3W 80 E8
Muscle Shoals U.S.A. 34°45N 87°40W 85 D11
Musengezi = Unsengedsi → Zimbabwe 15°43S 31°14E 55 F3
Musgrave Harbour Canada 49°27N 53°58W 73 C9
Musgrave Ranges Australia 26°0S 132°0E 61 E5
Mushie Dem. Rep. of the Congo 2°56S 16°55E 52 E3
Musi → Indonesia 2°20S 104°56E 36 E2
Musina S. Africa 22°20S 30°5E 57 C5
Muskeg → Canada 60°20N 123°20W 70 A4
Muskegon U.S.A. 43°14N 86°16W 80 D10
Muskegon → U.S.A. 43°14N 86°21W 80 D10
Muskegon Heights U.S.A. 43°12N 86°16W 80 D10
Muskogee U.S.A. 35°45N 95°22W 84 D7
Muskoka, L. Canada 45°0N 79°25W 82 B5
Muskoka Falls Canada 44°59N 79°17W 82 B5
Muskwa → Canada 58°47N 122°48W 70 B4
Muslīmiyah Syria 36°19N 37°12E 44 B3
Musofu Zambia 13°30S 29°0E 55 E2
Musoma Tanzania 1°30S 33°48E 54 C3
Musquaro, L. Canada 50°38N 61°5W 73 B7
Musquodoboit Harbour Canada 44°50N 63°9W 73 D7
Musselburgh U.K. 55°57N 3°2W 11 F5
Musselshell → U.S.A. 47°21N 107°57W 76 C10
Mussende Angola 10°32S 16°5E 52 G3
Mussoorie India 30°27N 78°6E 42 D8
Mussuco Angola 17°2S 19°3E 56 B2
Mustafakemalpaşa Turkey 40°2N 28°24E 23 D13
Mustang Nepal 29°10N 83°55E 43 E10
Musters, L. Argentina 45°20S 69°25W 96 F3
Musudan N. Korea 40°50N 129°43E 35 D15
Muswellbrook Australia 32°16S 150°56E 63 E5
Mût Egypt 25°28N 28°58E 51 C11
Mut Turkey 36°40N 33°28E 44 B2
Mutanda Mozam. 21°0S 33°34E 57 C5
Mutanda Zambia 12°24S 26°13E 55 E2
Mutare Zimbabwe 18°58S 32°38E 55 F3
Mutawintji △ Australia 31°10S 142°30E 63 E3
Mutha Kenya 1°48S 38°26E 54 C4
Muting Indonesia 7°23S 140°20E 37 F10
Mutki = Mirtağ Turkey 38°23N 41°56E 44 B4
Mutoko Zimbabwe 17°24S 32°13E 57 B5
Mutomo Kenya 1°51S 38°12E 54 C4
Mutoray Russia 60°56N 101°0E 29 C11
Mutsamudu Comoros Is. 12°10S 44°25E 53 a
Mutshatsha Dem. Rep. of the Congo 10°35S 24°20E 55 E1
Mutsu Japan 41°5N 140°55E 30 D10
Mutsu-Wan Japan 41°5N 140°55E 30 D10
Muttaburra Australia 22°38S 144°29E 62 C3
Mutton I. Ireland 52°49N 9°32W 10 D2
Mutuáli Mozam. 14°55S 37°0E 55 E4
Muweilih Egypt 30°42N 34°19E 46 E3
Muy Muy Nic. 12°39N 85°36W 88 D2
Muyinga Burundi 3°14S 30°33E 54 C3
Muynak Uzbekistan 43°44N 59°10E 28 E6
Muyunkum, Peski = Moyynqum Kazakhstan 44°12N 71°0E 32 B2
Muz Tag China 36°25N 87°25E 32 C3
Muzaffarabad Pakistan 34°25N 73°30E 43 B5
Muzaffargarh Pakistan 30°5N 71°14E 42 D4
Muzaffarnagar India 29°26N 77°40E 42 E7
Muzaffarpur India 26°7N 85°23E 43 F11
Muzafirpur Pakistan 30°58N 69°9E 42 D3
Muzhi Russia 65°25N 64°40E 18 A11
Muztagh-Ata China 38°17N 75°7E 32 C2
Mvuma Zimbabwe 19°16S 30°30E 55 F3
Mvurwi Zimbabwe 17°0S 30°57E 55 F3
Mwabvi ⌂ Malawi 16°42S 35°0E 55 F3
Mwadui Tanzania 3°26S 33°32E 54 C3
Mwali = Mohéli Comoros Is. 12°20S 43°40E 53 a
Mwambo Tanzania 10°30S 40°22E 55 E5
Mwandi Zambia 17°30S 24°51E 55 F1
Mwanza Dem. Rep. of the Congo 7°55S 26°43E 54 D2
Mwanza Tanzania 2°30S 32°58E 54 C3
Mwanza Zambia 16°58S 24°28E 55 F1
Mwanza □ Tanzania 2°0S 33°0E 54 C3
Mwaya Tanzania 9°32S 33°55E 55 D3
Mweelrea Ireland 53°39N 9°49W 10 C2
Mweka Dem. Rep. of the Congo 4°50S 21°34E 52 E4
Mwene-Ditu Dem. Rep. of the Congo 6°35S 22°27E 52 F4
Mwenezi Zimbabwe 21°15S 30°48E 55 G3
Mwenezi → Mozam. 22°40S 31°50E 55 G3
Mwenga Dem. Rep. of the Congo 3°1S 28°28E 54 C2
Mweru, L. Zambia 9°0S 28°40E 55 D2
Mweru Wantipa △ Zambia 8°39S 29°25E 55 D2
Mweza Range Zimbabwe 21°0S 30°0E 55 G3
Mwilambwe Dem. Rep. of the Congo 8°7S 25°5E 54 D2
Mwimbi Tanzania 8°38S 31°39E 55 D3
Mwingi Kenya 0°56S 38°4E 54 C4
Mwinilunga Zambia 11°43S 24°25E 55 E1
My Tho Vietnam 10°29N 106°23E 39 G6
Myajlar India 26°15N 70°20E 42 F4
Myanaung Burma 18°18N 95°22E 41 K19
Myanmar = Burma ■ Asia 21°0N 96°30E 41 J20
Myaungmya Burma 16°30N 94°40E 41 L19
Mycenæ = Mikines Greece 37°43N 22°46E 23 F10
Myeik Kyunzu Burma 11°30N 97°30E 39 G1
Myerstown U.S.A. 40°22N 76°19W 83 F8
Myingyan Burma 21°30N 95°20E 41 J19
Myitkyina Burma 25°24N 97°26E 41 G20
Mykines Færoe Is. 62°7N 7°35W 8 E9
Mykolayiv Ukraine 46°58N 32°0E 19 E5
Mykonos Greece 37°30N 25°25E 23 F11
Mymensingh Bangla. 24°45N 90°24E 41 G17
Mynydd Du U.K. 51°52N 3°50W 13 F4
Mýrdalsjökull Iceland 63°40N 19°6W 8 E4
Myrtle Beach U.S.A. 33°42N 78°53W 85 E15
Myrtle Creek U.S.A. 43°1N 123°17W 76 E2
Myrtle Point U.S.A. 43°4N 124°8W 76 E1
Myrtou Cyprus 35°18N 33°4E 25 D12
Mysia Turkey 39°50N 27°0E 23 E12
Mysore = Karnataka □ India 13°15N 77°0E 40 N10
Mysore India 12°17N 76°41E 40 N10
Mystic U.S.A. 41°21N 71°58W 83 E13
Myszków Poland 50°45N 19°22E 17 C10
Mytishchi Russia 55°50N 37°50E 18 C6
Mývatn Iceland 65°36N 17°0W 8 D5
Mzimba Malawi 11°55S 33°39E 55 E3
Mzimkulu → S. Africa 30°44S 30°28E 57 E5
Mzimvubu → S. Africa 31°38S 29°33E 57 E4
Mzuzu Malawi 11°30S 33°55E 55 E3

N

Na Hearadh = Harris U.K. 57°50N 6°55W 11 D2
Na Noi Thailand 18°19N 100°43E 38 C3
Na Phao Laos 17°35N 105°44E 38 D5
Na Sam Vietnam 22°3N 106°37E 38 A6
Na San Vietnam 21°12N 104°2E 38 B5
Na Thon Thailand 9°32N 99°56E 39 b
Naab → Germany 49°1N 12°2E 16 D6
Naantali Finland 60°29N 22°2E 9 F20
Naas Ireland 53°12N 6°40W 10 C5
Nababeep S. Africa 29°36S 17°46E 56 D2
Nabadwip = Navadwip India 23°34N 88°20E 43 H13
Nabawa Australia 28°30S 114°48E 61 E1
Nabberu, L. Australia 25°50S 120°30E 61 E3
Naberezhnyye Chelny Russia 55°42N 52°19E 18 C9
Nabeul Tunisia 36°30N 10°44E 51 A8
Nabha India 30°26N 76°14E 42 D7
Nabīd Iran 29°40N 57°38E 45 D8
Nabire Indonesia 3°15S 135°26E 37 E9
Nabisar Pakistan 25°8N 69°40E 42 G3
Nabisipi → Canada 50°14N 62°13W 73 B7
Nabiswera Uganda 1°27N 32°15E 54 B3
Nāblus = Nābulus West Bank 32°14N 35°15E 46 C4
Naboomspruit S. Africa 24°32S 28°40E 57 C4
Nabouwalu Fiji 17°0S 178°45E 59 a
Nābulus West Bank 32°14N 35°15E 46 C4
Nacala-Velha Mozam. 14°32S 40°34E 55 E5
Nacaome Honduras 13°31N 87°30W 88 D2
Nacaroa Mozam. 14°22S 39°56E 55 E4
Naches U.S.A. 46°44N 120°42W 76 C3
Naches → U.S.A. 46°38N 120°31W 78 D6
Nachicapau, L. Canada 56°40N 68°5W 73 A6
Nachingwea Tanzania 10°23S 38°49E 55 E4
Nachna India 27°34N 71°41E 42 F4
Nacimiento, L. U.S.A. 35°46N 120°53W 78 K6
Naco Mexico 31°19N 109°56W 86 A3
Nacogdoches U.S.A. 31°36N 94°39W 84 F7
Nácori Chico Mexico 29°40N 108°57W 86 B3
Nacozari de García Mexico 30°25N 109°38W 86 A3
Nacula Fiji 16°54S 177°27E 59 a
Nådendal = Naantali Finland 60°29N 22°2E 9 F20
Nadi Fiji 17°42S 177°20E 59 a
Nadiad India 22°41N 72°56E 42 H5
Nador Morocco 35°14N 2°58W 50 B5
Nadur Malta 36°2N 14°18E 25 C1
Nadūshan Iran 32°2N 53°35E 45 C7
Nadvirna Ukraine 48°37N 24°30E 17 D13
Nadvoitsy Russia 63°52N 34°14E 18 B5
Nadvornaya = Nadvirna Ukraine 48°37N 24°30E 17 D13
Nadym Russia 65°35N 72°42E 28 C8
Nadym → Russia 66°12N 72°0E 28 C8
Nærbø Norway 58°40N 5°39E 9 G11
Næstved Denmark 55°13N 11°44E 9 J14
Nafpaktos Greece 38°24N 21°50E 23 E9
Nafplio Greece 37°33N 22°50E 23 F10
Naft-e Safīd Iran 31°40N 49°17E 45 D6
Naftshahr Iran 34°0N 45°30E 44 C5
Nafud Desert = An Nafūd Si. Arabia 28°15N 41°0E 44 D4
Naga Phil. 13°38N 123°15E 37 B6
Nagagami Canada 50°23N 84°20W 72 B3
Nagahama Japan 35°23N 136°16E 31 G8
Nagai Japan 38°6N 140°2E 30 E10
Nagaland □ India 26°0N 94°30E 41 G19
Nagano Japan 36°40N 138°10E 31 F9
Nagano □ Japan 36°15N 138°0E 31 F9
Nagaoka Japan 37°27N 138°51E 31 F9
Nagappattinam India 10°46N 79°51E 40 P11
Nagar → Bangla. 24°27N 89°12E 43 G13
Nagar Parkar Pakistan 24°28N 70°46E 42 G4
Nagasaki Japan 32°47N 129°50E 31 H4
Nagasaki □ Japan 32°50N 129°40E 31 H4
Nagato Japan 34°19N 131°5E 31 G5
Nagaur India 27°15N 73°45E 42 F5
Nagda India 23°27N 75°25E 42 H6
Nagercoil India 8°12N 77°26E 40 Q10
Nagina India 29°30N 78°30E 43 E8
Nagīneh Iran 34°20N 57°15E 45 C8
Nagir Pakistan 36°12N 74°42E 43 A6
Nagles Mts. Ireland 52°8N 8°30W 10 D3
Nagod India 24°34N 80°36E 43 G9
Nagoorin Australia 24°17S 151°15E 62 C5
Nagorno-Karabakh □ Azerbaijan 39°55N 46°45E 44 B5
Nagornyy Russia 55°58N 124°57E 29 D13
Nagoya Japan 35°10N 136°50E 31 G8
Nagpur India 21°8N 79°10E 40 J11
Nagua Dom. Rep. 19°23N 69°50W 89 C6
Naguabo Puerto Rico 18°13N 65°44W 89 d
Nagykanizsa Hungary 46°28N 17°0E 17 E9
Nagykőrös Hungary 47°5N 19°48E 17 E10
Naha Japan 26°13N 127°42E 31 L3
Nahan India 30°33N 77°18E 42 D7
Nahanni △ Canada 61°36N 125°41W 70 A4
Nahanni Butte Canada 61°2N 123°31W 70 A4
Nahargarh Mad. P., India 24°10N 75°14E 42 G6
Nahargarh Raj., India 24°55N 76°50E 42 G7
Nahariyya Israel 33°1N 35°5E 44 C2
Nahāvand Iran 34°10N 48°22E 45 C6
Nahuel Huapi, L. Argentina 41°0S 71°32W 96 E2
Nahuelbuta △ Chile 37°44S 72°57W 94 D1
Nai Yong Thailand 8°14N 98°22E 39 a
Naicá Mexico 27°53N 105°31W 86 B3
Naicam Canada 52°30N 104°30W 71 C8
Naikoon ⌂ Canada 53°55N 131°55W 70 C2
Naimisharanya India 27°21N 80°30E 43 F9
Naimona'nyi Feng Nepal 30°26N 81°18E 43 D9
Nain Canada 56°34N 61°40W 73 A7
Nā'īn Iran 32°54N 53°0E 45 C7
Naini Tal India 29°30N 79°30E 43 E8
Nainpur India 22°30N 80°10E 43 H9
Nainwa India 25°46N 75°51E 42 G6
Nairai Fiji 17°49S 179°15E 59 a
Nairn U.K. 57°35N 3°53W 11 D5
Nairobi Kenya 1°17S 36°48E 54 C4
Nairobi △ Kenya 1°22S 36°50E 54 C4
Naissaar Estonia 59°34N 24°29E 9 G21
Naitaba Fiji 17°0S 179°16W 59 a
Naivasha Kenya 0°40S 36°30E 54 C4
Naivasha, L. Kenya 0°48S 36°20E 54 C4
Najaf = An Najaf Iraq 32°3N 44°15E 44 C5
Najafābād Iran 32°40N 51°15E 45 C6
Najd Si. Arabia 26°30N 42°0E 47 B3
Najibabad India 29°40N 78°20E 42 E8
Najin N. Korea 42°12N 130°15E 35 C16
Najmah Si. Arabia 26°42N 50°6E 45 E6
Najrān Si. Arabia 17°34N 44°18E 47 D3
Naju S. Korea 35°3N 126°43E 35 G14
Nakadōri-Shima Japan 32°57N 129°4E 31 H4
Nakalagba Dem. Rep. of the Congo 2°50N 27°58E 54 B2
Nakaminato Japan 36°21N 140°36E 31 F10
Nakamura Japan 32°59N 132°56E 31 H6
Nakano Japan 36°45N 138°22E 31 F9
Nakano-Shima Japan 29°51N 129°52E 31 K4
Nakashibetsu Japan 43°33N 144°59E 30 C12
Nakfa Eritrea 16°40N 38°32E 47 D2
Nakha Yai, Ko Thailand 8°3N 98°28E 39 a
Nakhichevan = Naxçıvan Azerbaijan 39°12N 45°15E 44 B5
Nakhichevan Rep. = Naxçıvan □ Azerbaijan 39°25N 45°26E 44 B5
Nakhl Egypt 29°55N 33°43E 46 F2
Nakhl-e Taqī Iran 27°28N 52°36E 45 E7
Nakhodka Russia 42°53N 132°54E 30 C6
Nakhon Nayok Thailand 14°12N 101°13E 38 E3
Nakhon Pathom Thailand 13°49N 100°3E 38 F3

Nakhon Phanom Thailand 17°23N 104°43E 38 D5
Nakhon Ratchasima Thailand 14°59N 102°12E 38 E4
Nakhon Sawan Thailand 15°35N 100°10E 38 E3
Nakhon Si Thammarat Thailand 8°29N 100°0E 39 H3
Nakhon Thai Thailand 17°5N 100°44E 38 D3
Nakhtarana India 23°20N 69°15E 42 H3
Nakina Canada 50°10N 86°40W 72 B2
Nakodar India 31°8N 75°31E 42 D6
Naktong → S. Korea 35°7N 128°57E 35 G15
Nakuru Kenya 0°15S 36°4E 54 C4
Nakuru, L. Kenya 0°23S 36°5E 54 C4
Nakusp Canada 50°20N 117°45W 70 C5
Nal Pakistan 27°40N 66°12E 42 F2
Nal → Pakistan 25°20N 65°30E 42 G1
Nalázi Mozam. 24°3S 33°20E 57 C5
Nalchik Russia 43°30N 43°33E 19 F7
Nalgonda India 17°6N 79°15E 40 L11
Nalhati India 24°17N 87°52E 43 G12
Naliya India 23°16N 68°50E 42 H3
Nallamalai Hills India 15°30N 78°50E 40 M11
Nalubaale Dam Uganda 0°30N 33°5E 54 B3
Nam Can Vietnam 8°46N 104°59E 39 H5
Nam-ch'on N. Korea 38°15N 126°26E 35 E14
Nam Co China 30°30N 90°45E 32 C4
Nam Dinh Vietnam 20°25N 106°5E 38 B6
Nam Du, Hon Vietnam 9°41N 104°21E 39 H5
Nam Nao △ Thailand 16°44N 101°32E 38 D3
Nam Ngum Res. Laos 18°35N 102°34E 38 C4
Nam-Phan Vietnam 10°30N 106°0E 39 G6
Nam Phong Thailand 16°42N 102°52E 38 D4
Nam Tha Laos 20°58N 101°30E 38 B3
Nam Tok Thailand 14°21N 99°4E 38 E2
Namacunde Angola 17°18S 15°50E 56 B2
Namacurra Mozam. 17°30S 36°50E 57 B6
Namak, Daryācheh-ye Iran 34°30N 52°0E 45 C7
Namak, Kavir-e Iran 34°30N 57°30E 45 C8
Namakzār, Daryācheh-ye Iran 34°0N 60°30E 45 C9
Namaland Namibia 26°0S 17°0E 56 C2
Namanga Kenya 2°33S 36°47E 54 C4
Namangan Uzbekistan 41°0N 71°40E 28 E8
Namapa Mozam. 13°43S 39°50E 55 E4
Namaqualand S. Africa 30°0S 17°25E 56 E2
Namasagali Uganda 1°2N 33°0E 54 B3
Namber Indonesia 1°2S 134°49E 37 E8
Nambour Australia 26°32S 152°58E 63 D5
Nambouwalu = Nabouwalu Fiji 17°0S 178°45E 59 a
Nambucca Heads Australia 30°37S 153°0E 63 E5
Nambung △ Australia 30°30S 115°5E 61 F2
Namcha Barwa China 29°40N 95°10E 32 D4
Namche Bazar Nepal 27°51N 86°47E 43 F12
Namchonjŏm = Nam-ch'on N. Korea 38°15N 126°26E 35 E14
Namecunda Mozam. 14°54S 37°37E 55 E4
Namenalala Fiji 17°8S 179°9E 59 a
Nameponda Mozam. 15°50S 39°50E 55 F4
Nametil Mozam. 15°40S 39°21E 55 F4
Namew L. Canada 54°14N 101°56W 71 C8
Namgia India 31°48N 78°40E 43 D8
Namib Desert Namibia 22°30S 15°0E 56 C2
Namib-Naukluft ⌂ Namibia 24°40S 15°16E 56 C2
Namibe Angola 15°7S 12°11E 53 H2
Namibe □ Angola 16°35S 12°30E 56 B1
Namibia ■ Africa 22°0S 18°9E 56 C2
Namibwoestyn = Namib Desert Namibia 22°30S 15°0E 56 C2
Namlea Indonesia 3°18S 127°5E 37 E7
Namoi → Australia 30°12S 149°30E 63 E4
Nampa U.S.A. 43°34N 116°34W 76 E5
Namp'o N. Korea 38°52N 125°10E 35 E13
Nampō-Shotō Japan 32°0N 140°0E 31 J10
Nampula Mozam. 15°6S 39°15E 55 F4
Namrole Indonesia 3°46S 126°46E 37 E7
Namse Shankou China 30°0N 82°25E 43 E10
Namsen → Norway 64°28N 11°37E 8 D14
Namsos Norway 64°29N 11°30E 8 D14
Namtok Chat Trakan △ Thailand 17°17N 100°40E 38 D3
Namtok Mae Surin △ Thailand 18°55N 98°2E 38 C2
Namtsy Russia 62°43N 129°37E 29 C13
Namtu Burma 23°5N 97°28E 41 H20
Namtumbo Tanzania 10°30S 36°4E 55 E4
Namu Canada 51°52N 127°50W 70 C3
Namuka-i-Lau Fiji 18°53S 178°37W 59 a
Namur Belgium 50°27N 4°52E 15 D4
Namur □ Belgium 50°17N 5°0E 15 D4
Namuruputh Kenya 4°34N 35°57E 54 B4
Namutoni Namibia 18°49S 16°55E 56 B2
Namwala Zambia 15°44S 26°30E 55 F2
Namwon S. Korea 35°23N 127°23E 35 G14
Namyang N. Korea 42°57N 129°52E 35 C15
Nan Thailand 18°48N 100°46E 38 C3
Nan → Thailand 15°42N 100°9E 38 E3
Nan-ch'ang = Nanchang China 28°42N 115°55E 33 D6
Nanaimo Canada 49°10N 124°0W 70 D4
Nanam N. Korea 41°44N 129°40E 35 D15
Nanango Australia 26°40S 152°0E 63 D5
Nanao Japan 37°0N 137°0E 31 F8
Nanchang China 28°42N 115°55E 33 D6
Nanching = Nanjing China 32°2N 118°47E 33 C6
Nanchong China 30°43N 106°2E 32 C5
Nancy France 48°42N 6°12E 20 B7
Nanda Devi India 30°23N 79°59E 43 D8
Nanda Devi △ India 30°30N 79°50E 43 D8
Nanda Kot India 30°17N 80°5E 43 D9
Nandan Japan 34°10N 134°42E 31 G7
Nanded India 19°10N 77°20E 40 K10
Nandewar Ra. Australia 30°15S 150°35E 63 E5
Nandi = Nadi Fiji 17°42S 177°20E 59 a
Nandigram India 22°1N 87°58E 43 H12
Nandurbar India 21°20N 74°15E 40 J9
Nandyal India 15°30N 78°30E 40 M11
Nang Rong Thailand 14°38N 102°48E 38 E4
Nanga-Eboko Cameroon 4°41N 12°22E 52 D2
Nanga Parbat Pakistan 35°10N 74°35E 43 B6
Nangade Mozam. 11°5S 39°36E 55 E4
Nangapinoh Indonesia 0°20S 111°44E 36 E4
Nangarhār □ Afghan. 34°20N 70°0E 40 B7
Nangatayap Indonesia 1°32S 110°34E 36 E4
Nangeya Mts. Uganda 3°30N 33°30E 54 B3
Nangong China 37°23N 115°22E 34 F8
Nanhuang China 36°58N 121°48E 35 F11
Nanjeko Zambia 15°31S 23°30E 55 F1
Nanjing China 32°2N 118°47E 33 C6
Nanjirinji Tanzania 9°41S 39°5E 55 D4
Nankana Sahib Pakistan 31°27N 73°38E 42 D5
Nanking = Nanjing China 32°2N 118°47E 33 C6
Nankoku Japan 33°39N 133°44E 31 H6
Nanlang China 22°30N 113°32E 33 G10
Nanning China 22°48N 108°20E 32 D5
Nannup Australia 33°59S 115°48E 61 F2
Nanpara India 27°52N 81°33E 43 F9
Nanpi China 38°2N 116°45E 34 E9
Nanping China 26°38N 118°10E 33 D6
Nanripe Mozam. 13°52S 38°52E 55 E4
Nansei-Shotō = Ryūkyū-rettō Japan 26°0N 126°0E 31 M3
Nansen Basin Arctic 84°0N 50°0E 4 A10
Nansen Sd. Canada 81°0N 91°0W 69 A10
Nansha China 22°45N 113°34E 33 F10
Nanshan I. S. China Sea 10°45N 115°49E 36 B5
Nansio Tanzania 2°3S 33°4E 54 C3
Nantes France 47°12N 1°33W 20 C3
Nanticoke U.S.A. 41°12N 76°0W 83 E8
Nanton Canada 50°21N 113°46W 70 C6
Nantong China 32°1N 120°52E 33 C7
Nantou China 22°32N 113°55E 33 F10
Nantucket U.S.A. 41°17N 70°6W 81 E18
Nantucket I. U.S.A. 41°16N 70°5W 81 E18
Nantwich U.K. 53°4N 2°31W 12 D5
Nanty Glo U.S.A. 40°28N 78°50W 82 F6
Nanuku Passage Fiji 16°45S 179°15W 59 a
Nanuque Brazil 17°50S 40°21W 93 G10
Nanusa, Kepulauan Indonesia 4°45N 127°1E 37 D7
Nanutarra Roadhouse Australia 22°32S 115°30E 60 D2
Nanyang China 33°11N 112°30E 34 H7
Nanyuki Kenya 0°2N 37°4E 54 B4
Nao, C. de la Spain 38°44N 0°14E 21 C6
Naococane, L. Canada 52°50N 70°45W 73 B5
Napa U.S.A. 38°18N 122°17W 78 G4
Napa → U.S.A. 38°10N 122°19W 78 G4
Napanee Canada 44°15N 77°0W 82 B8
Napanoch U.S.A. 41°44N 74°22W 83 E10
Nape Laos 18°18N 105°6E 38 C5
Nape Pass = Keo Neua, Deo Vietnam 18°23N 105°10E 38 C5
Napier N.Z. 39°30S 176°56E 59 C6
Napier Broome B. Australia 14°2S 126°37E 60 B4
Napier Pen. Australia 12°4S 135°43E 62 A2
Napierville Canada 45°11N 73°25W 83 A11
Naples = Nápoli Italy 40°50N 14°15E 22 D6
Naples U.S.A. 26°8N 81°48W 85 H14
Napo → Peru 3°20S 72°40W 92 D4
Napoleon N. Dak., U.S.A. 46°30N 99°46W 80 B4
Napoleon Ohio, U.S.A. 41°23N 84°8W 81 E11
Nápoli Italy 40°50N 14°15E 22 D6
Napopo Dem. Rep. of the Congo 4°15N 28°0E 54 B2
Naqadeh Iran 36°57N 45°23E 44 B5
Naqb, Ra's an Jordan 29°48N 35°44E 46 F4
Naqqāsh Iran 35°40N 49°6E 45 C6
Nara Japan 34°40N 135°49E 31 G7
Nara Mali 15°10N 7°20W 50 E4
Nara □ Japan 34°30N 136°0E 31 G8
Nara Canal Pakistan 24°30N 69°20E 42 G3
Nara Visa U.S.A. 35°37N 103°6W 77 J12
Naracoorte Australia 36°58S 140°45E 63 F3
Naradhan Australia 33°34S 146°17E 63 E4
Naraini India 25°11N 80°29E 43 G9
Naranjos Mexico 21°21N 97°41W 87 C5
Narasapur India 16°26N 81°40E 41 L12
Narathiwat Thailand 6°30N 101°48E 39 J3
Narayanganj Bangla. 23°40N 90°33E 41 H17
Narayanpet India 16°45N 77°30E 40 L10
Narberth U.K. 51°47N 4°44W 13 F3
Narbonne France 43°11N 3°0E 20 E5
Nardīn Iran 37°3N 55°59E 45 B7
Nardò Italy 40°11N 18°2E 23 D8
Narembeen Australia 32°7S 118°24E 61 F2
Narendranagar India 30°10N 78°18E 42 D8
Nares Str. Arctic 80°0N 70°0W 66 A13
Naretha Australia 31°0S 124°45E 61 F3
Narew → Poland 52°26N 20°41E 17 B11
Nari → Pakistan 28°0N 67°40E 42 E2
Narin Afghan. 36°5N 69°0E 40 A6
Narindra, Helodranon' i Madag. 14°55S 47°30E 57 A8
Narita Japan 35°47N 140°19E 31 G10
Nariva Swamp Trin. & Tob. 10°26N 61°4W 93 K15
Narmada → India 21°38N 72°36E 42 J5
Narnaul India 28°5N 76°11E 42 E7
Narodnaya Russia 65°5N 59°58E 18 A10
Narok Kenya 1°55S 35°52E 54 C4
Narooma Australia 36°14S 150°4E 63 F5
Narowal Pakistan 32°6N 74°52E 42 C6
Narrabri Australia 30°19S 149°46E 63 E4
Narran → Australia 28°37S 148°12E 63 D4
Narrandera Australia 34°42S 146°31E 63 E4
Narrogin Australia 32°58S 117°14E 61 F2
Narromine Australia 32°12S 148°12E 63 E4
Narrow Hills ⌂ Canada 54°0N 104°37W 71 C8
Narsimhapur India 22°54N 79°14E 43 H8
Narsinghgarh India 23°45N 76°40E 42 H7
Naruto Japan 34°11N 134°37E 31 G7
Narva Estonia 59°23N 28°12E 18 C4
Narva → Russia 59°27N 28°2E 9 G23
Narva Bay = Narva Laht Estonia 59°35N 27°35E 9 G22
Narva Laht Estonia 59°35N 27°35E 9 G22
Narvik Norway 68°28N 17°26E 8 B17
Narwana India 29°39N 76°6E 42 E7
Naryan-Mar Russia 67°42N 53°12E 18 A9
Narym Russia 59°0N 81°30E 28 D9
Naryn Kyrgyzstan 41°26N 75°58E 28 E8
Naryn Qum Kazakhstan 47°30N 49°0E 28 E5
Nasa Norway 66°29N 15°23E 8 C16
Nasau Fiji 17°19S 179°27E 59 a
Nasca = Nazca Peru 14°50S 74°57W 92 F4
Naseby N.Z. 45°1S 170°10E 59 F3
Naselle U.S.A. 46°22N 123°49W 78 D3
Naser, Buheirat en Egypt 23°0N 32°30E 51 D12
Nashua Mont., U.S.A. 48°8N 106°22W 76 B10
Nashua N.H., U.S.A. 42°45N 71°28W 83 D13
Nashville Ark., U.S.A. 33°57N 93°51W 84 E8
Nashville Ga., U.S.A. 31°12N 83°15W 85 F13
Nashville Tenn., U.S.A. 36°10N 86°47W 85 C11
Nasik India 19°58N 73°50E 40 K8
Nasirabad India 26°15N 74°45E 42 F6
Nasirabad Pakistan 28°23N 68°24E 42 E3
Nasiri = Ahvāz Iran 31°20N 48°40E 45 D6
Nasiriyah = An Nāşirīyah Iraq 31°0N 46°15E 44 D5
Naskaupi → Canada 53°47N 60°51W 73 B7
Naşrābād Iran 34°8N 51°26E 45 C6
Naşriān-e Pā'īn Iran 32°52N 46°52E 44 C5
Nass → Canada 55°0N 129°40W 70 C3
Nassau Bahamas 25°5N 77°20W 88 A4
Nassau U.S.A. 42°31N 73°37W 83 D11
Nassau, B. Chile 55°20S 68°0W 96 H3
Nasser, L. = Naser, Buheirat en Egypt 23°0N 32°30E 51 D12
Nässjö Sweden 57°39N 14°42E 9 H16
Nastapoka → Canada 56°55N 76°33W 72 A4
Nastapoka, Is. Canada 56°55N 76°50W 72 A4
Nata Botswana 20°12S 26°12E 56 C4
Nata → Botswana 20°14S 26°10E 56 C4
Natal Brazil 5°47S 35°13W 93 E11
Natal Indonesia 0°35N 99°7E 36 D1
Natal Drakensberg ⌂ S. Africa 29°27S 29°30E 57 D4
Naţanz Iran 33°30N 51°55E 45 C6
Natashquan Canada 50°14N 61°46W 73 B7
Natashquan → Canada 50°7N 61°50W 73 B7
Natchez U.S.A. 31°34N 91°24W 84 F9
Natchitoches U.S.A. 31°46N 93°5W 84 F8
Natewa B. Fiji 16°35S 179°40E 59 a
Nathalia Australia 36°1S 145°13E 63 F4
Nathdwara India 24°55N 73°50E 42 G5
Nati, Pta. Spain 40°3N 3°50E 24 A10
Natimuk Australia 36°42S 142°0E 63 F3
Nation → Canada 55°30N 123°32W 70 B4
National City U.S.A. 32°40N 117°5W 79 N9
Natitingou Benin 10°20N 1°26E 50 F6
Natividad, I. Mexico 27°52N 115°11W 86 B1
Natkyizin Burma 14°57N 97°59E 38 E1
Natron, L. Tanzania 2°20S 36°0E 54 C4
Natrona Heights U.S.A. 40°37N 79°44W 82 F5
Natukanaoka Pan Namibia 18°40S 15°45E 56 B2
Natuna Besar, Kepulauan Indonesia 4°0N 108°15E 36 D3
Natuna Is. = Natuna Besar, Kepulauan Indonesia 4°0N 108°15E 36 D3
Natuna Selatan, Kepulauan Indonesia 2°45N 109°0E 36 D3
Natural Bridge U.S.A. 44°5N 75°30W 83 B9
Natural Bridges ⌂ U.S.A. 37°36N 110°0W 77 H9
Naturaliste, C. Tas., Australia 40°50S 148°15E 63 G4
Naturaliste, C. W. Austral., Australia 33°32S 115°0E 61 F2
Naturaliste Plateau Ind. Oc. 34°0S 112°0E 64 L3
Nau Qala Afghan. 34°5N 68°5E 42 B3
Naugatuck U.S.A. 41°30N 73°3W 83 E11
Naujaat = Repulse Bay Canada 66°30N 86°30W 69 C11
Naumburg Germany 51°9N 11°47E 16 C6
Nauru ■ Pac. Oc. 1°0S 166°0E 58 B9
Naushahra = Nowshera Pakistan 34°0N 72°0E 40 C8
Naushahro Pakistan 26°50N 68°7E 42 F3
Naushon I. U.S.A. 41°29N 70°45W 83 E14
Nausori Fiji 18°2S 178°32E 59 a
Nauta Peru 4°31S 73°35W 92 D4
Nautanwa India 27°20N 83°25E 43 F10
Naute ⌂ Namibia 26°55S 17°57E 56 D2
Nautla Mexico 20°13N 96°47W 87 C5
Nava Mexico 28°25N 100°45W 86 B4
Navadwip India 23°34N 88°20E 43 H13
Navahrudak Belarus 53°40N 25°50E 17 B13
Navajo Res. U.S.A. 36°48N 107°36W 77 H10
Navalmoral de la Mata Spain 39°52N 5°33W 21 C3
Navan = An Uaimh Ireland 53°39N 6°41W 10 C5
Navarin, Mys Russia 62°15N 179°5E 29 C18
Navarino, I. Chile 55°0S 67°40W 96 H3
Navarra □ Spain 42°40N 1°40W 21 A5
Navarre U.S.A. 40°43N 81°31W 82 F3
Navarro → U.S.A. 39°11N 123°45W 78 F3
Navasota U.S.A. 30°23N 96°5W 84 F6
Navassa I. W. Indies 18°30N 75°0W 89 C5
Naver → U.K. 58°32N 4°14W 11 C4
Navibandar India 21°26N 69°48E 42 J3
Navidad Chile 33°57S 71°50W 94 C1
Naviraí Brazil 23°8S 54°13W 95 A5
Naviti Fiji 17°7S 177°15E 59 a
Navlakhi India 22°58N 70°28E 42 H4
Năvodari Romania 44°19N 28°36E 17 F15
Navoi Uzbekistan 40°9N 65°22E 28 E7
Navojoa Mexico 27°6N 109°26W 86 B3
Navolato Mexico 24°47N 107°42W 86 C3
Navsari India 20°57N 72°59E 40 J8
Navua Fiji 18°12S 178°11E 59 a
Nawa Kot Pakistan 28°21N 71°24E 42 E4
Nawab Khan Pakistan 30°17N 69°12E 42 D3
Nawabganj Ut. P., India 26°56N 81°14E 43 F9
Nawabganj Ut. P., India 28°32N 79°40E 43 E8
Nawabshah Pakistan 26°15N 68°25E 42 F3
Nawada India 24°50N 85°33E 43 G11
Nawakot Nepal 27°55N 85°10E 43 F11
Nawalgarh India 27°50N 75°15E 42 F6
Nawanshahr India 32°33N 74°48E 43 C6
Nawar, Dasht-i- Afghan. 33°52N 68°0E 42 C3
Nawoiy = Navoi Uzbekistan 40°9N 65°22E 28 E7
Naxçıvan Azerbaijan 39°12N 45°15E 44 B5
Naxçıvan □ Azerbaijan 39°25N 45°26E 44 B5
Naxos Greece 37°8N 25°25E 23 F11
Nay, Mui Vietnam 12°55N 109°23E 36 B3
Nāy Band Būshehr, Iran 27°20N 52°40E 45 E7
Nāy Band Khorāsān, Iran 32°20N 57°34E 45 C8
Nayakhan Russia 61°56N 159°0E 29 C16
Nayarit □ Mexico 22°0N 105°0W 86 C4
Nayau Fiji 18°6S 178°10E 59 a
Nayoro Japan 44°21N 142°28E 30 B11
Naypyidaw Burma 19°44N 96°12E 38 C1
Nayyāl, W. → Si. Arabia 28°35N 39°4E 44 D3
Nazaré Brazil 13°2S 39°0W 93 F11
Nazareth = Nazerat Israel 32°42N 35°17E 46 C4
Nazareth U.S.A. 40°44N 75°19W 83 F9
Nazarovo Russia 57°2N 90°40E 29 D10
Nazas Mexico 25°14N 104°8W 86 B4
Nazas → Mexico 25°12N 104°12W 86 B4
Nazca Peru 14°50S 74°57W 92 F4
Nazca Ridge Pac. Oc. 20°0S 80°0W 65 K19
Naze Japan 28°22N 129°27E 31 K4
Naze, The U.K. 51°53N 1°18E 13 F9
Nazerat Israel 32°42N 35°17E 46 C4
Nāzīk Iran 39°1N 45°4E 44 B5
Nazilli Turkey 37°55N 28°15E 23 F13
Nazko Canada 53°1N 123°37W 70 C4
Nazko → Canada 53°7N 123°34W 70 C4
Nazret Ethiopia 8°32N 39°22E 47 F2
Nchanga Zambia 12°30S 27°49E 55 E2
Ncheu Malawi 14°50S 34°47E 55 E3
Ndala Tanzania 4°45S 33°15E 54 C3
Ndalatando Angola 9°12S 14°48E 52 F2
Ndareda Tanzania 4°12S 35°30E 54 C4
Ndélé C.A.R. 8°25N 20°36E 52 C4
Ndjamena Chad 12°10N 14°59E 51 F8
Ndola Zambia 13°0S 28°34E 55 E2
Ndomo ⌂ S. Africa 26°52S 32°15E 57 D5
Ndoto Mts. Kenya 2°0N 37°0E 54 B4
Nduguti Tanzania 4°18S 34°41E 54 C3
Neagh, Lough U.K. 54°37N 6°25W 10 B5
Neah Bay U.S.A. 48°22N 124°37W 78 B2
Neale, L. Australia 24°15S 130°0E 60 D5
Neales → Australia 28°8S 136°47E 63 D2
Neapoli Greece 35°15N 25°37E 25 D7
Near Is. U.S.A. 52°30N 174°0E 74 a
Neath U.K. 51°39N 3°48W 13 F4
Neath Port Talbot □ U.K. 51°42N 3°45W 13 F4
Nebine Cr. → Australia 29°27S 146°56E 63 D4
Nebitdag = Balkanabat Turkmenistan 39°30N 54°22E 45 B7
Nebo Australia 21°42S 148°42E 62 C4
Nebraska □ U.S.A. 41°30N 99°30W 80 E4
Nebraska City U.S.A. 40°41N 95°52W 80 E6
Nébrodi, Monti Italy 37°54N 14°35E 22 F6
Necedah U.S.A. 44°2N 90°4W 80 C8
Nechako → Canada 53°55N 122°42W 70 C4
Neches → U.S.A. 29°58N 93°51W 84 G8
Neckar → Germany 49°27N 8°29E 16 D5
Necochea Argentina 38°30S 58°50W 94 D4
Nederland = Netherlands ■ Europe 52°0N 5°30E 15 C5
Needles Canada 49°53N 118°7W 70 D5
Needles U.S.A. 34°51N 114°37W 79 L12
Needles, The U.K. 50°39N 1°35W 13 G6
Neembucú □ Paraguay 27°0S 58°0W 94 B4
Neemuch = Nimach India 24°30N 74°56E 42 G6
Neenah U.S.A. 44°11N 88°28W 80 C9
Neepawa Canada 50°15N 99°30W 71 C9
Neftçala Azerbaijan 39°19N 49°12E 45 B6
Neftegorsk Russia 53°1N 142°58E 29 D15
Neftekumsk Russia 44°46N 44°50E 19 F7
Nefteyugansk Russia 61°5N 72°42E 28 C8
Nefyn U.K. 52°56N 4°31W 12 E3
Negapatam = Nagappattinam India 10°46N 79°51E 40 P11
Negara Indonesia 8°22S 114°37E 37 J17
Negaunee U.S.A. 46°30N 87°36W 80 B10
Negele Ethiopia 5°20N 39°36E 47 F2
Negev Desert = Hanegev Israel 30°50N 35°0E 46 E4
Negombo Sri Lanka 7°12N 79°50E 40 R11
Negotin Serbia 44°16N 22°37E 23 B10
Negra, Pta. Mauritania 22°54N 16°18W 50 D2
Negra, Pta. Peru 6°6S 81°10W 92 E2
Negrais, C. = Maudin Sun Burma 16°0N 94°30E 41 M19
Negril Jamaica 18°22N 78°20W 88 a
Negro → Argentina 41°2S 62°47W 96 E4
Negro → Brazil 3°0S 60°0W 92 D7
Negro → Uruguay 33°24S 58°22W 94 C4
Negros Phil. 9°30N 122°40E 37 C6
Neguac Canada 47°15N 65°5W 73 C6
Nehalem → U.S.A. 45°40N 123°56W 78 E3
Nehāvand Iran 35°56N 49°31E 45 C6
Nehbandān Iran 31°35N 60°5E 45 D9
Nei Monggol Zizhiqu □ China 42°0N 112°0E 34 D7
Neiafu Tonga 18°39S 173°59W 59 c
Neiges, Piton des Réunion 21°5S 55°29E 53 c
Neijiang China 29°35N 104°55E 32 D5
Neilingding Dao China 22°25N 113°48E 33 G10
Neillsville U.S.A. 44°34N 90°36W 80 C8
Neilton U.S.A. 47°25N 123°53W 76 C2
Neiqiu China 37°15N 114°30E 34 F8
Neiva Colombia 2°56N 75°18W 92 C3
Neixiang China 33°10N 111°52E 34 H6
Nejanilini L. Canada 59°33N 97°48W 71 B9
Nejd = Najd Si. Arabia 26°30N 42°0E 47 B3
Nekā Iran 36°39N 53°19E 45 B7
Nekemte Ethiopia 9°4N 36°30E 47 F2
Neksø Denmark 55°4N 15°8E 9 J16
Nelia Australia 20°39S 142°12E 62 C3
Neligh U.S.A. 42°8N 98°2W 80 D4
Nelkan Russia 57°40N 136°4E 29 D14
Nellore India 14°27N 79°59E 40 M11
Nelson Canada 49°30N 117°20W 70 D5
Nelson N.Z. 41°18S 173°16E 59 D4
Nelson U.K. 53°50N 2°13W 12 D5
Nelson Ariz., U.S.A. 35°31N 113°19W 77 J7
Nelson Nev., U.S.A. 35°42N 114°49W 79 K12
Nelson → Canada 54°33N 98°2W 71 C9
Nelson, C. Australia 38°26S 141°32E 63 F3
Nelson, Estrecho Chile 51°30S 75°0W 96 G2
Nelson Forks Canada 59°30N 124°0W 70 B4
Nelson House Canada 55°47N 98°51W 71 B9
Nelson L. Canada 55°48N 100°7W 71 B8
Nelson Lakes △ N.Z. 41°55S 172°44E 59 D4
Nelspoort S. Africa 32°7S 23°0E 56 E3
Nelspruit S. Africa 25°29S 30°59E 57 D5
Néma Mauritania 16°40N 7°15W 50 E4
Neman = Nemunas → Lithuania 55°25N 21°10E 9 J19
Nemeiben L. Canada 55°20N 105°20W 71 B7
Nemiscau Canada 51°18N 76°54W 72 B4
Nemiscau, L. Canada 51°25N 76°40W 72 B4
Nemunas → Lithuania 55°25N 21°10E 9 J19
Nemuro Japan 43°20N 145°35E 30 C12
Nemuro-Kaikyō Japan 43°30N 145°30E 30 C12
Nen Jiang → China 45°28N 124°30E 35 B13
Nenagh Ireland 52°52N 8°11W 10 D3
Nenasi Malaysia 3°9N 103°23E 39 L4
Nene → U.K. 52°49N 0°11E 13 E8
Nenjiang China 49°10N 125°10E 33 B7
Neno Malawi 15°25S 34°40E 55 F3
Neodesha U.S.A. 37°25N 95°41W 80 G6
Neora Valley △ India 27°0N 88°45E 43 F13
Neosho U.S.A. 36°52N 94°22W 80 G6
Neosho → U.S.A. 36°48N 95°18W 84 C7
Nepal ■ Asia 28°0N 84°30E 43 F11
Nepalganj Nepal 28°5N 81°40E 43 E9
Nepalganj Road India 28°1N 81°41E 43 E9
Nephi U.S.A. 39°43N 111°50W 76 G8
Nephin Ireland 54°1N 9°22W 10 B2
Nephin Beg Range Ireland 54°0N 9°40W 10 C2
Neptune U.S.A. 40°13N 74°2W 83 F10
Neqāb Iran 36°42N 57°25E 45 B8
Nerang Australia 27°58S 153°20E 63 D5
Nerastro, Sarîr Libya 24°20N 20°37E 51 D10
Nerchinsk Russia 52°0N 116°39E 29 D12
Néret, L. Canada 54°45N 70°44W 73 B5
Neretva → Croatia 43°1N 17°27E 23 C7
Neringa Lithuania 55°20N 21°5E 9 J19
Neris → Lithuania 55°8N 24°16E 9 J21
Neryungri Russia 57°38N 124°28E 29 D13
Nescopeck U.S.A. 41°3N 76°12W 83 E8
Neskantaga Canada 52°14N 87°53W 72 B2
Ness, L. U.K. 57°15N 4°32W 11 D4
Ness City U.S.A. 38°27N 99°54W 80 F4
Nesterov Ukraine 50°4N 23°58E 17 C12
Nesvizh = Nyasvizh Belarus 53°14N 26°38E 17 B14
Netanya Israel 32°20N 34°51E 46 C3
Netarhat India 23°29N 84°16E 43 H11
Nete → Belgium 51°7N 4°14E 15 C4
Netherdale Australia 21°10S 148°33E 62 K6
Netherlands ■ Europe 52°0N 5°30E 15 C5
Netherlands Antilles ☑ W. Indies 12°15N 69°0W 92 A5
Netrang India 21°39N 73°21E 42 J5
Nettilling L. Canada 66°30N 71°0W 69 C12
Netzahualcóyotl, Presa Mexico 17°8N 93°35W 87 D6
Neubrandenburg Germany 53°33N 13°15E 16 B7
Neuchâtel Switz. 47°0N 6°55E 20 C7
Neuchâtel, Lac de Switz. 46°53N 6°50E 20 C7
Neufchâteau Belgium 49°50N 5°25E 15 E5
Neumayer Antarctica 71°0S 68°30W 5 D17
Neumünster Germany 54°4N 9°58E 16 A5
Neunkirchen Germany 49°20N 7°9E 16 D4
Neuquén Argentina 38°55S 68°0W 96 D3
Neuquén □ Argentina 38°0S 69°50W 94 D2
Neuruppin Germany 52°55N 12°48E 16 B7
Neuse → U.S.A. 35°6N 76°29W 85 D16
Neusiedler See Austria 47°50N 16°47E 17 E9
Neustrelitz Germany 53°21N 13°4E 16 B7
Neva → Russia 59°56N 30°20E 18 C5
Nevada Iowa, U.S.A. 42°1N 93°27W 80 D7
Nevada Mo., U.S.A. 37°51N 94°22W 80 G6
Nevada □ U.S.A. 39°0N 117°0W 76 G5
Nevada City U.S.A. 39°16N 121°1W 78 F6
Nevado, Cerro Argentina 35°30S 68°32W 94 D2
Nevado de Colima = Volcán de Colima △ Mexico 19°30N 103°40W 86 D4
Nevado de Tres Cruces △ Chile 27°13S 69°5W 94 B2
Nevel Russia 56°0N 29°55E 18 C4

Nevelsk *Russia* 46°40N 141°51E **29** E15
Nevers *France* 47°0N 3°9E **20** C5
Nevertire *Australia* 31°50S 147°44E **63** E4
Neville *Canada* 49°58N 107°39W **71** D7
Nevinnomyssk *Russia* 44°40N 42°0E **19** F7
Nevis *St. Kitts & Nevis* 17°0N 62°30W **89** C7
Nevşehir *Turkey* 38°33N 34°40E **44** B2
Nevyansk *Russia* 57°30N 60°13E **18** C11
New → *U.S.A.* 38°10N 81°12W **81** F13
New Aiyansh *Canada* 55°12N 129°4W **70** B3
New Albany *Ind.,*
  U.S.A. 38°18N 85°49W **81** F11
New Albany *Miss.,*
  U.S.A. 34°29N 89°0W **85** D10
New Albany *Pa., U.S.A.* 41°36N 76°27W **83** E8
New Amsterdam *Guyana* 6°15N 57°36W **92** B7
New Angledool *Australia* 29°5S 147°55E **63** D4
New Baltimore *U.S.A.* 42°41N 82°44W **82** D2
New Bedford *U.S.A.* 41°38N 70°56W **83** E14
New Berlin *N.Y., U.S.A.* 42°37N 75°20W **83** D9
New Berlin *Pa., U.S.A.* 40°50N 76°57W **82** F8
New Bern *U.S.A.* 35°7N 77°3W **85** D16
New Bethlehem *U.S.A.* 41°0N 79°20W **82** F5
New Bight *Bahamas* 24°19N 75°24W **89** B4
New Bloomfield *U.S.A.* 40°25N 77°11W **82** F7
New Boston *U.S.A.* 33°28N 94°25W **84** E7
New Braunfels *U.S.A.* 29°42N 98°8W **84** G5
New Brighton *N.Z.* 43°29S 172°43E **59** E4
New Brighton *U.S.A.* 40°42N 80°19W **82** F4
New Britain *Papua N. G.* 5°50S 150°20E **58** B8
New Britain *U.S.A.* 41°40N 72°47W **83** E12
New Brunswick *U.S.A.* 40°30N 74°27W **83** F10
New Brunswick □
  Canada 46°50N 66°30W **73** C6
New Caledonia ☑ *Pac. Oc.* 21°0S 165°0E **58** D9
New Caledonia Trough
  Pac. Oc. 30°0S 165°0E **64** L8
New Castile = Castilla-La
  Mancha □ *Spain* 39°30N 3°30W **21** C4
New Castle *Ind., U.S.A.* 39°55N 85°22W **81** F11
New Castle *Pa., U.S.A.* 41°0N 80°21W **82** F4
New City *U.S.A.* 41°9N 73°59W **83** E11
New Concord *U.S.A.* 39°59N 81°54W **82** G3
New Cumberland
  U.S.A. 40°30N 80°36W **82** F4
New Cuyama *U.S.A.* 34°57N 119°38W **79** L7
New Delhi *India* 28°36N 77°11E **42** D10
New Denver *Canada* 50°0N 117°25W **70** D5
New Don Pedro Res.
  U.S.A. 37°43N 120°24W **78** H6
New England *U.S.A.* 43°0N 71°0W **75** B12
New England *N. Dak.,*
  U.S.A. 46°32N 102°52W **80** B2
New England Ra.
  Australia 30°20S 151°45E **63** E5
New Forest △ *U.K.* 50°53N 1°34W **13** G6
New Galloway *U.K.* 55°5N 4°9W **11** F4
New Glasgow *Canada* 45°35N 62°36W **73** C7
New Guinea *Oceania* 4°0S 136°0E **58** B6
New Hamburg *Canada* 43°23N 80°42W **82** C4
New Hampshire □
  U.S.A. 44°0N 71°30W **83** C13
New Hampton *U.S.A.* 43°3N 92°19W **80** D7
New Hanover *S. Africa* 29°22S 30°31E **57** D5
New Hartford *U.S.A.* 43°4N 75°18W **83** D9
New Haven *Conn.,*
  U.S.A. 41°18N 72°55W **83** E12
New Haven *Mich.,*
  U.S.A. 42°44N 82°48W **82** D2
New Haven *N.Y., U.S.A.* 43°28N 76°18W **83** C8
New Hazelton *Canada* 55°20N 127°30W **70** B3
New Hebrides = Vanuatu ■
  Pac. Oc. 15°0S 168°0E **58** C9
New Holland *U.S.A.* 40°6N 76°5W **83** F8
New Iberia *U.S.A.* 30°1N 91°49W **84** F9
New Ireland *Papua N. G.* 3°20S 151°50E **58** B8
New Jersey □ *U.S.A.* 40°0N 74°30W **81** F16
New Kensington *U.S.A.* 40°34N 79°46W **82** F5
New Lexington *U.S.A.* 39°43N 82°13W **81** F12
New Liskeard *Canada* 47°31N 79°41W **72** C4
New London *Conn.,*
  U.S.A. 41°22N 72°6W **83** E12
New London *Ohio, U.S.A.* 41°5N 82°24W **82** E2
New London *Wis.,*
  U.S.A. 44°23N 88°45W **80** C9
New Madrid *U.S.A.* 36°36N 89°32W **80** G9
New Martinsville
  U.S.A. 39°39N 80°52W **81** F13
New Meadows *U.S.A.* 44°58N 116°18W **76** D5
New Melones L. *U.S.A.* 37°57N 120°31W **78** H6
New Mexico □ *U.S.A.* 34°30N 106°0W **77** J11
New Milford *Conn.,*
  U.S.A. 41°35N 73°25W **83** E11
New Milford *Pa., U.S.A.* 41°52N 75°44W **83** E9
New Moore I. *Ind. Oc.* 21°37N 89°10E **43** J13
New Norcia *Australia* 30°57S 116°13E **61** F2
New Norfolk *Australia* 42°46S 147°2E **63** G4
New Orleans *U.S.A.* 29°57N 90°4W **85** G9
New Philadelphia
  U.S.A. 40°30N 81°27W **82** F3
New Plymouth *N.Z.* 39°4S 174°5E **59** C5
New Plymouth *U.S.A.* 43°58N 116°49W **76** E5
New Port Richey
  U.S.A. 28°16N 82°43W **85** G13
New Providence
  Bahamas 25°25N 78°35W **88** A4
New Quay *U.K.* 52°13N 4°21W **13** E3
New Radnor *U.K.* 52°15N 3°9W **13** E4
New Richmond *Canada* 48°15N 65°45W **73** C6
New Richmond *U.S.A.* 45°7N 92°32W **80** C7
New River Gorge △
  U.S.A. 37°53N 81°5W **81** G13
New Roads *U.S.A.* 30°42N 91°26W **84** F9
New Rochelle *U.S.A.* 40°55N 73°46W **83** F11
New Rockford *U.S.A.* 47°41N 99°8W **80** B4
New Romney *U.K.* 50°59N 0°57E **13** G8
New Ross *Ireland* 52°23N 6°57W **10** D5

New Salem *U.S.A.* 46°51N 101°25W **80** B3
New Scone = Scone *U.K.* 56°25N 3°24W **11** E5
New Siberian I. = Novaya Sibir,
  Ostrov *Russia* 75°10N 150°0E **29** B16
New Siberian Is. = Novosibirskiye
  Ostrova *Russia* 75°0N 142°0E **29** B15
New Smyrna Beach
  U.S.A. 29°1N 80°56W **85** G14
New South Wales □
  Australia 33°0S 146°0E **63** E4
New Tecumseth = Alliston
  Canada 44°9N 79°52W **82** B5
New Town *U.S.A.* 47°59N 102°30W **80** B2
New Tredegar *U.K.* 51°44N 3°16W **13** F4
New Ulm *U.S.A.* 44°19N 94°28W **80** C6
New Waterford *Canada* 46°13N 60°4W **73** C7
New Westminster
  Canada 49°13N 122°55W **78** A4
New York *U.S.A.* 40°43N 74°0W **83** F11
New York □ *U.S.A.* 43°0N 75°0W **83** D9
New York J.F. Kennedy Int. ✈
  (JFK) *U.S.A.* 40°38N 73°47W **83** F11
New Zealand ■ *Oceania* 40°0S 176°0E **59** D6
Newaj → *India* 24°24N 76°49E **42** G7
Newala *Tanzania* 10°58S 39°18E **55** E4
Newark *Del., U.S.A.* 39°41N 75°46W **81** F16
Newark *N.J., U.S.A.* 40°44N 74°10W **83** F10
Newark *N.Y., U.S.A.* 43°3N 77°6W **82** C7
Newark *Ohio, U.S.A.* 40°3N 82°24W **82** F2
Newark Liberty Int. ✈ (EWR)
  U.S.A. 40°42N 74°10W **83** F10
Newark-on-Trent *U.K.* 53°5N 0°48W **12** D7
Newark Valley *U.S.A.* 42°14N 76°11W **83** D8
Newberg *U.S.A.* 45°18N 122°58W **76** D2
Newberry *Mich., U.S.A.* 46°21N 85°30W **81** B11
Newberry *S.C., U.S.A.* 34°17N 81°37W **85** D14
Newberry Springs
  U.S.A. 34°50N 116°41W **79** L10
Newboro L. *Canada* 44°38N 76°20W **83** B8
Newbridge = Droichead Nua
  Ireland 53°11N 6°48W **10** C5
Newburgh *Canada* 44°19N 76°52W **82** B8
Newburgh *U.S.A.* 41°30N 74°1W **83** E10
Newbury *U.K.* 51°24N 1°20W **13** F6
Newbury *N.H., U.S.A.* 43°19N 72°3W **83** B12
Newbury *Vt., U.S.A.* 44°5N 72°4W **83** B12
Newburyport *U.S.A.* 42°49N 70°53W **83** D14
Newcastle *Australia* 33°0S 151°46E **63** E5
Newcastle *N.B., Canada* 47°1N 65°38W **73** C6
Newcastle *Ont., Canada* 43°55N 78°35W **72** D4
Newcastle *S. Africa* 27°45S 29°58E **57** D4
Newcastle *U.K.* 54°13N 5°54W **10** B6
Newcastle *Calif., U.S.A.* 38°53N 121°8W **78** G5
Newcastle *Wyo.,*
  U.S.A. 43°50N 104°11W **76** E11
Newcastle Emlyn *U.K.* 52°2N 4°28W **13** E3
Newcastle Ra. *Australia* 15°45S 130°15E **60** C5
Newcastle-under-Lyme
  U.K. 53°1N 2°14W **12** D5
Newcastle-upon-Tyne
  U.K. 54°58N 1°36W **12** C6
Newcastle Waters
  Australia 17°30S 133°28E **62** B1
Newcastle West *Ireland* 52°27N 9°3W **10** D2
Newcomb *U.S.A.* 43°58N 74°10W **83** C10
Newcomerstown *U.S.A.* 40°16N 81°36W **82** F3
Newdegate *Australia* 33°6S 119°0E **61** F2
Newell *Australia* 16°20S 145°16E **62** B4
Newell *U.S.A.* 44°43N 103°25W **80** C3
Newfane *U.S.A.* 43°17N 78°43W **82** C6
Newfield *U.S.A.* 42°18N 76°33W **83** D8
Newfound L. *U.S.A.* 43°40N 71°47W **83** C13
Newfoundland *Canada* 49°0N 55°0W **73** C8
Newfoundland *U.S.A.* 41°18N 75°19W **83** E9
Newfoundland & Labrador □
  Canada 53°0N 58°0W **73** B8
Newhaven *U.K.* 50°47N 0°3E **13** G8
Newkirk *U.S.A.* 36°53N 97°3W **84** C6
Newlyn *U.K.* 50°6N 5°34W **13** G2
Newman *Australia* 23°18S 119°45E **60** D2
Newman *U.S.A.* 37°19N 121°1W **78** H5
Newmarket *Canada* 44°3N 79°28W **82** B5
Newmarket *Ireland* 52°13N 9°0W **10** D2
Newmarket *U.K.* 52°15N 0°25E **13** E8
Newmarket *U.S.A.* 43°5N 70°56W **83** C14
Newnan *U.S.A.* 33°23N 84°48W **85** E12
Newport *Ireland* 53°53N 9°33W **10** C2
Newport *I. of W., U.K.* 50°42N 1°17W **13** G6
Newport *Newport, U.K.* 51°35N 3°0W **13** F5
Newport *Ark., U.S.A.* 35°37N 91°16W **84** D9
Newport *Ky., U.S.A.* 39°5N 84°29W **81** F11
Newport *N.H., U.S.A.* 43°22N 72°10W **83** C12
Newport *N.Y., U.S.A.* 43°11N 75°1W **83** C9
Newport *Oreg., U.S.A.* 44°39N 124°3W **76** D1
Newport *Pa., U.S.A.* 40°29N 77°8W **82** F7
Newport *R.I., U.S.A.* 41°29N 71°19W **83** E13
Newport *Tenn., U.S.A.* 35°58N 83°11W **85** D13
Newport *Vt., U.S.A.* 44°56N 72°13W **83** B12
Newport *Wash., U.S.A.* 48°11N 117°3W **76** B5
Newport *U.K.* 52°46N 2°22W **12** E5
Newport Beach *U.S.A.* 33°37N 117°56W **79** M9
Newport News *U.S.A.* 36°58N 76°25W **81** G15
Newport Pagnell *U.K.* 52°5N 0°43W **13** E7
Newquay *U.K.* 50°25N 5°6W **13** G2
Newry *U.K.* 54°11N 6°21W **10** B5
Newton *Ill., U.S.A.* 38°59N 88°10W **80** F9
Newton *Iowa, U.S.A.* 41°42N 93°3W **80** E7
Newton *Kans., U.S.A.* 38°3N 97°21W **80** F5
Newton *Mass., U.S.A.* 42°21N 71°12W **83** D13
Newton *Miss., U.S.A.* 32°19N 89°10W **85** E10
Newton *N.C., U.S.A.* 35°40N 81°13W **85** D14
Newton *N.J., U.S.A.* 41°3N 74°45W **83** E10
Newton *Tex., U.S.A.* 30°51N 93°46W **84** F8
Newton Abbot *U.K.* 50°32N 3°37W **13** G4
Newton Aycliffe *U.K.* 54°37N 1°34W **12** C6
Newton Falls *N.Y.,*
  U.S.A. 44°12N 74°59W **83** B10

Newton Falls *Ohio,*
  U.S.A. 41°11N 80°59W **82** E4
Newton Stewart *U.K.* 54°57N 4°30W **11** G4
Newtonmore *U.K.* 57°4N 4°8W **11** D4
Newtown *U.K.* 52°31N 3°19W **13** E4
Newtownabbey *U.K.* 54°40N 5°56W **10** B6
Newtownards *U.K.* 54°36N 5°42W **10** B6
Newtownbarry = Bunclody
  Ireland 52°39N 6°40W **10** D5
Newtownstewart *U.K.* 54°43N 7°23W **10** B4
Newville *U.S.A.* 40°10N 77°24W **82** F7
Neya *Russia* 58°21N 43°49E **18** C7
Neyrīz *Iran* 29°15N 54°19E **45** D7
Neyshābūr *Iran* 36°10N 58°50E **45** B8
Nezperce *U.S.A.* 46°14N 116°14W **76** C5
Ngabang *Indonesia* 0°23N 109°55E **36** D3
Ngabordamlu, Tanjung
  Indonesia 6°56S 134°11E **37** F8
N'Gage *Angola* 7°46S 15°15E **52** F3
Ngami Depression
  Botswana 20°30S 22°46E **56** C3
Ngamo *Zimbabwe* 19°3S 27°32E **55** F2
Nganglong Kangri *China* 33°0N 81°0E **43** C9
Ngao *Thailand* 18°46N 99°59E **38** C2
Ngaoundéré *Cameroon* 7°15N 13°35E **52** C2
Ngapara *N.Z.* 44°57S 170°46E **59** F3
Ngara *Tanzania* 2°29S 30°40E **54** C3
Ngawi *Indonesia* 7°24S 111°26E **37** G14
Ngcobo *S. Africa* 31°37S 28°0E **57** E4
Nghia Lo *Vietnam* 21°33N 104°28E **38** B5
Ngoma *Malawi* 13°8S 33°45E **55** E3
Ngomahura *Zimbabwe* 20°26S 30°43E **55** G3
Ngomba *Tanzania* 8°20S 32°53E **55** D3
Ngomeni, Ras *Kenya* 2°59S 40°14E **54** C5
Ngong *Kenya* 1°22S 36°39E **54** C4
Ngoring Hu *China* 34°55N 97°5E **32** C4
Ngorongoro *Tanzania* 3°11S 35°32E **54** C4
Ngorongoro △ *Tanzania* 2°40S 35°30E **54** C4
Ngozi *Burundi* 2°54S 29°50E **54** C2
Ngudu *Tanzania* 2°58S 33°25E **54** C3
Nguigmi *Niger* 14°20N 13°20E **51** F8
Nguiu *Australia* 11°46S 130°38E **60** B5
Ngukurr *Australia* 14°44S 134°44E **62** A1
Ngunga *Tanzania* 3°37S 33°37E **54** C3
Nguru *Nigeria* 12°56N 10°29E **51** F8
Nguru Mts. *Tanzania* 6°0S 37°30E **54** D4
Nguyen Binh *Vietnam* 22°39N 105°56E **38** A5
Nha Trang *Vietnam* 12°16N 109°10E **39** F7
Nhacoongo *Mozam.* 24°18S 35°14E **57** C6
Nhamaabué *Mozam.* 17°25S 35°5E **55** F4
Nhamundá → *Brazil* 2°12S 56°41W **93** D7
Nhangulaze, L. *Mozam.* 24°0S 34°30E **57** C5
Nhill *Australia* 36°18S 141°40E **63** F3
Nho Quan *Vietnam* 20°18N 105°45E **38** B5
Nhulunbuy *Australia* 12°10S 137°20E **62** A2
Nia-nia
  Dem. Rep. of the Congo 1°30N 27°40E **54** B2
Niagara *Canada* 43°7N 79°5W **82** C5
Niagara Falls *U.S.A.* 43°5N 79°4W **82** C6
Niagara-on-the-Lake
  Canada 43°15N 79°4W **82** C5
Niah *Malaysia* 3°58N 113°46E **36** D4
Niamey *Niger* 13°27N 2°6E **50** F6
Niangara
  Dem. Rep. of the Congo 3°42N 27°50E **54** B2
Niantic *U.S.A.* 41°20N 72°11W **83** E12
Nias *Indonesia* 1°0N 97°30E **36** D1
Niassa □ *Mozam.* 13°30S 36°0E **55** E4
Niassa △ *Mozam.* 12°4S 36°57E **55** E4
Nibāk *Si. Arabia* 24°25N 50°50E **45** E7
Nicaragua ■
  Cent. Amer. 11°40N 85°30W **88** D2
Nicaragua, L. de *Nic.* 12°0N 85°30W **88** D2
Nicastro *Italy* 38°59N 16°19E **22** E7
Nice *France* 43°42N 7°14E **20** E7
Niceville *U.S.A.* 30°31N 86°30W **85** F11
Nichicun, L. *Canada* 53°5N 71°0W **73** B5
Nichinan *Japan* 31°38N 131°23E **31** J5
Nicholás, Canal *W. Indies* 23°30N 80°5W **88** B3
Nicholasville *U.S.A.* 37°53N 84°34W **81** G11
Nichols *U.S.A.* 42°1N 76°22W **83** D8
Nicholson *Australia* 18°2S 128°54E **60** C4
Nicholson *U.S.A.* 41°37N 75°47W **83** E9
Nicholson → *Australia* 17°31S 139°36E **62** B2
Nicholson L. *Canada* 62°40N 102°40W **71** A8
Nicholson Ra. *Australia* 27°15S 116°45E **61** E2
Nicholville *U.S.A.* 44°41N 74°39W **83** B10
Nicobar Is. *Ind. Oc.* 8°0N 93°30E **27** H11
Nicola *Canada* 50°12N 120°40W **70** C4
Nicolls Town *Bahamas* 25°8N 78°0W **88** A4
Nicosia *Cyprus* 35°10N 33°25E **25** D12
Nicoya *Costa Rica* 10°9N 85°27W **88** D2
Nicoya, G. de *Costa Rica* 10°0N 85°0W **88** E3
Nicoya, Pen. de
  Costa Rica 9°45N 85°40W **88** E2
Nidd → *U.K.* 53°59N 1°23W **12** D6
Niedersachsen □ *Germany* 52°50N 9°0E **16** B5
Niekerkshoop *S. Africa* 29°19S 22°51E **56** D3
Niemba
  Dem. Rep. of the Congo 5°58S 28°24E **54** D2
Niemen = Nemunas →
  Lithuania 55°25N 21°10E **9** J19
Nienburg *Germany* 52°39N 9°13E **16** B5
Nieu Bethesda *S. Africa* 31°51S 24°34E **56** E3
Nieuw Amsterdam
  Suriname 5°53N 55°5W **93** B7
Nieuw Nickerie *Suriname* 6°0N 56°59W **93** B7
Nieuwoudtville *S. Africa* 31°23S 19°7E **56** E2
Nieuwpoort *Belgium* 51°8N 2°45E **15** C2
Nieves, Pico de las
  Canary Is. 27°57N 15°35W **24** G4
Niğde *Turkey* 37°58N 34°40E **44** B2
Nigel *S. Africa* 26°27S 28°25E **57** D4
Niger ■ *W. Afr.* 17°30N 10°0E **50** E7
Niger → *W. Afr.* 5°33N 6°33E **50** G7
Nigeria ■ *W. Afr.* 8°30N 8°0E **50** G7

Nighasin *India* 28°14N 80°52E **43** E9
Nightcaps *N.Z.* 45°57S 168°2E **59** F2
Nihon = Japan ■ *Asia* 36°0N 136°0E **31** G8
Nii-Jima *Japan* 34°20N 139°15E **31** G9
Niigata *Japan* 37°58N 139°0E **30** F9
Niigata □ *Japan* 37°15N 138°45E **31** F9
Niihama *Japan* 33°55N 133°16E **31** H6
Ni'ihau *U.S.A.* 21°54N 160°9W **74** b
Niimi *Japan* 34°59N 133°28E **31** G6
Niitsu *Japan* 37°48N 139°7E **30** F9
Nijil *Jordan* 30°32N 35°33E **46** E4
Nijkerk *Neths.* 52°13N 5°30E **15** B5
Nijmegen *Neths.* 51°50N 5°52E **15** C5
Nijverdal *Neths.* 52°22N 6°28E **15** B6
Nīk Pey *Iran* 36°50N 48°10E **45** B6
Nikel *Russia* 69°24N 30°13E **8** B24
Nikiniki *Indonesia* 9°49S 124°30E **37** F6
Nikkō *Japan* 36°45N 139°35E **31** F9
Nikkō △ *Japan* 36°50N 139°35E **31** F9
Nikolayev = Mykolayiv
  Ukraine 46°58N 32°0E **19** E5
Nikolayevsk *Russia* 50°0N 45°35E **19** E8
Nikolayevsk-na-Amur
  Russia 53°8N 140°44E **29** D15
Nikolskoye *Russia* 55°12N 166°0E **29** D17
Nikopol *Ukraine* 47°35N 34°25E **19** E5
Nikshahr *Iran* 26°15N 60°10E **45** E9
Nikšić *Montenegro* 42°50N 18°57E **23** C8
Nîl, Nahr en → *Africa* 30°10N 31°6E **51** B12
Nîl el Abyad → *Sudan* 15°38N 32°31E **51** E12
Nîl el Azraq → *Sudan* 15°38N 32°31E **51** E12
Nila *Indonesia* 6°44S 129°31E **37** F7
Niland *U.S.A.* 33°14N 115°31W **79** M11
Nile = Nîl, Nahr en →
  Africa 30°10N 31°6E **51** B12
Niles *Mich., U.S.A.* 41°50N 86°15W **80** E10
Niles *Ohio, U.S.A.* 41°11N 80°46W **82** E4
Nim Ka Thana *India* 27°44N 75°48E **42** F6
Nimach *India* 24°30N 74°56E **42** G6
Nimbahera *India* 24°37N 74°45E **42** G6
Nîmes *France* 43°50N 4°23E **20** E6
Nimfaíon, Ákra = Pines, Akra
  Greece 40°5N 24°20E **23** D11
Nimmitabel *Australia* 36°29S 149°15E **63** F4
Nīnawā *Iraq* 36°25N 43°10E **44** B4
Nīnawā □ *Iraq* 36°15N 43°0E **44** B4
Nindigully *Australia* 28°21S 148°50E **63** D4
Ninepin Group *China* 22°16N 114°21E **33** G11
Nineveh = Nīnawā *Iraq* 36°25N 43°10E **44** B4
Ning Xian *China* 35°30N 107°58E **34** G4
Ningaloo △ *Australia* 22°23S 113°32E **60** D1
Ning'an *China* 44°22N 129°20E **35** B15
Ningbo *China* 29°51N 121°28E **33** D7
Ningcheng *China* 41°32N 119°53E **35** D10
Ningjin *China* 37°35N 114°57E **34** F8
Ningjing Shan *China* 30°0N 98°20E **32** C4
Ningling *China* 34°25N 115°22E **34** G8
Ningpo = Ningbo *China* 29°51N 121°28E **33** D7
Ningqiang *China* 32°47N 106°15E **34** H4
Ningshan *China* 33°21N 108°21E **34** H5
Ningsia Hui A.R. = Ningxia Huizu
  Zizhiqu □ *China* 38°0N 106°0E **34** F4
Ningwu *China* 39°0N 112°18E **34** E7
Ningxia Huizu Zizhiqu □
  China 38°0N 106°0E **34** F4
Ningyang *China* 35°47N 116°45E **34** G9
Ninh Binh *Vietnam* 20°15N 105°55E **38** B5
Ninh Giang *Vietnam* 20°44N 106°24E **38** B6
Ninh Hoa *Vietnam* 12°30N 109°7E **38** F7
Ninh Ma *Vietnam* 12°48N 109°21E **38** F7
Ninove *Belgium* 50°51N 4°2E **15** D4
Nioaque *Brazil* 21°5S 55°50W **95** A4
Niobrara *U.S.A.* 42°45N 98°2W **80** D4
Niobrara → *U.S.A.* 42°46N 98°3W **80** D4
Nioro du Sahel *Mali* 15°15N 9°30W **50** E4
Niort *France* 46°19N 0°29W **20** C3
Nipawin *Canada* 53°20N 104°0W **71** C8
Nipigon *Canada* 49°0N 88°17W **72** C2
Nipigon, L. *Canada* 49°50N 88°30W **72** C2
Nipishish L. *Canada* 54°12N 60°45W **73** B7
Nipissing, L. *Canada* 46°20N 80°0W **72** C4
Nipomo *U.S.A.* 35°3N 120°29W **79** K6
Nippon = Japan ■ *Asia* 36°0N 136°0E **31** G8
Nipton *U.S.A.* 35°28N 115°16W **79** K11
Niquelândia *Brazil* 14°33S 48°23W **93** F9
Nīr *Iran* 38°2N 47°59E **44** B5
Nirasaki *Japan* 35°42N 138°27E **31** G9
Nirmal *India* 19°3N 78°20E **40** K11
Nirmali *India* 26°20N 86°35E **43** F12
Niš *Serbia* 43°19N 21°58E **23** C9
Nişāb *Si. Arabia* 29°11N 44°43E **44** D5
Nişāb *Yemen* 14°25N 46°29E **47** E4
Nisbet → *Canada* 56°29N 88°9W **72** A2
Nisi → *Greece* 39°43N 19°52E **25** A3
Nissum Bredning
  Denmark 56°40N 8°20E **9** H13
Nistru = Dnister →
  Europe 46°18N 30°17E **17** E16
Nisutlin → *Canada* 60°14N 132°34W **70** A2
Nitchequon *Canada* 53°10N 70°58W **73** B5
Niterói *Brazil* 22°53S 43°7W **95** A7
Nith → *Canada* 43°12N 80°23W **82** C4
Nith → *U.K.* 55°14N 3°33W **11** F5
Nitmiluk △ *Australia* 14°6S 132°15E **60** B5
Nitra *Slovak Rep.* 48°19N 18°4E **17** D10
Nitra → *Slovak Rep.* 47°46N 18°10E **17** E10
Niue *Pac. Oc.* 19°2S 169°54W **65** J11
Niut *Indonesia* 0°55N 110°6E **36** D4
Niuzhuang *China* 40°58N 122°28E **35** D12
Nivala *Finland* 63°56N 24°57E **8** E21
Nivelles *Belgium* 50°35N 4°20E **15** D4
Nivernais *France* 47°15N 3°30E **20** C5
Niverville *Canada* 49°36N 97°3W **71** D9
Niwas *India* 23°3N 80°26E **43** H9

Nixa *U.S.A.* 37°3N 93°18W **80** G7
Nixon *U.S.A.* 29°16N 97°46W **84** G6
Nizamabad *India* 18°45N 78°7E **40** K11
Nizamghat *India* 28°20N 95°45E **41** E19
Nizhne Kolymsk
  Russia 68°34N 160°55E **29** C17
Nizhnekamsk *Russia* 55°38N 51°49E **18** C9
Nizhneudinsk *Russia* 54°54N 99°3E **29** D10
Nizhnevartovsk *Russia* 60°56N 76°38E **28** C8
Nizhniy Bestyakh
  Russia 61°57N 129°54E **29** C13
Nizhniy Novgorod *Russia* 56°20N 44°0E **18** C7
Nizhniy Tagil *Russia* 57°55N 59°57E **18** C10
Nizhyn *Ukraine* 51°5N 31°55E **19** D5
Nizip *Turkey* 37°5N 37°50E **44** B3
Nízké Tatry *Slovak Rep.* 48°55N 19°30E **17** D10
Nizwá *Oman* 22°56N 57°32E **47** C6
Njakwa *Malawi* 11°1S 33°56E **55** E3
Njanji *Zambia* 14°25N 31°46E **55** E3
Njazidja = Grande Comore
  Comoros Is. 11°35S 43°20E **53** a
Njinjo *Tanzania* 8°48S 38°54E **55** D4
Njombe *Tanzania* 9°20S 34°50E **55** D3
Njombe → *Tanzania* 6°56S 35°6E **54** D4
Nkana *Zambia* 12°50S 28°8E **55** E2
Nkawkaw *Ghana* 6°36N 0°49W **50** G5
Nkayi *Zimbabwe* 19°41S 29°20E **55** F2
Nkhotakota *Malawi* 12°56S 34°15E **55** E3
Nkhotakota △ *Malawi* 12°50S 34°0E **55** E3
Nkongsamba *Cameroon* 4°55N 9°55E **52** D1
Nkurenkuru *Namibia* 17°42S 18°32E **56** B2
Nmai → *Burma* 25°30N 97°25E **41** G20
Noakhali = Maijdi
  Bangla. 22°48N 91°10E **41** H17
Nobel *Canada* 45°25N 80°6W **82** A4
Nobeoka *Japan* 32°36N 131°41E **31** H5
Noblesville *U.S.A.* 40°3N 86°1W **80** E10
Noboribetsu *Japan* 42°24N 141°6E **30** C10
Noccundra *Australia* 27°50S 142°36E **63** D3
Nocera Inferiore *Italy* 40°44N 14°38E **22** D6
Nocona *U.S.A.* 33°47N 97°44W **84** E6
Noda *Japan* 35°56N 139°52E **31** G9
Nogales *Mexico* 31°19N 110°56W **86** A2
Nogales *U.S.A.* 31°21N 110°56W **77** L8
Nōgata *Japan* 33°48N 130°44E **31** H5
Noggerup *Australia* 33°32S 116°5E **61** F2
Noginsk *Russia* 64°30N 90°50E **29** C10
Nogliki *Russia* 51°50N 143°10E **29** D15
Nogoa → *Australia* 23°40S 147°55E **62** C4
Nogoyá *Argentina* 32°24S 59°48W **94** C4
Nohar *India* 29°11N 74°49E **42** E6
Nohta *India* 23°40N 79°34E **43** H8
Noires, Mts. *France* 48°11N 3°40W **20** B2
Noirmoutier, Î. de *France* 46°58N 2°10W **20** C2
Nojane *Botswana* 23°15S 20°14E **56** C3
Nojima-Zaki *Japan* 34°54N 139°53E **31** G9
Nok Kundi *Pakistan* 28°50N 62°45E **40** E3
Nok Ta Phao, Ko *Thailand* 9°23N 99°40E **39** b
Nokaneng *Botswana* 19°40S 22°17E **56** B3
Nokia *Finland* 61°30N 23°30E **8** F20
Nokomis *Canada* 51°35N 105°0W **71** C8
Nokomis L. *Canada* 57°0N 103°0W **71** B8
Nola *C.A.R.* 3°35N 16°4E **52** D3
Noma Omuramba →
  Namibia 18°52S 20°53E **56** B3
Nombre de Dios *Panama* 9°34N 79°28W **88** E4
Nome *U.S.A.* 64°30N 165°25W **74** a
Nomo-Zaki *Japan* 32°35N 129°44E **31** H4
Nomuka *Tonga* 20°17S 174°48W **59** c
Nomuka Group *Tonga* 20°20S 174°48W **59** c
Nonacho L. *Canada* 61°42N 109°40W **71** A7
Nonda *Australia* 20°40S 142°28E **62** C3
Nong Chang *Thailand* 15°23N 99°51E **38** E2
Nong Het *Laos* 19°29N 103°59E **38** C4
Nong Khai *Thailand* 17°50N 102°46E **38** D4
Nong'an *China* 44°25N 125°5E **35** B13
Nongoma *S. Africa* 27°58S 31°35E **57** D5
Nongsa *Indonesia* 1°11N 104°8E **39** d
Nonoava *Mexico* 27°28N 106°44W **86** B3
Nonthaburi *Thailand* 13°50N 100°29E **38** F3
Noonamah *Australia* 12°40S 131°4E **60** B5
Noondie, L. *Australia* 28°30S 119°30E **61** E2
Noord Brabant □ *Neths.* 51°40N 5°0E **15** C5
Noord Holland □ *Neths.* 52°30N 4°45E **15** B5
Noordbeveland *Neths.* 51°35N 3°50E **15** C3
Noordoostpolder *Neths.* 52°45N 5°45E **15** B5
Noordwijk *Neths.* 52°14N 4°26E **15** B4
Noosa Heads *Australia* 26°25S 153°6E **63** D5
Nootka I. *Canada* 49°32N 126°42W **70** D3
Nopiming △ *Canada* 50°30N 95°37W **71** C9
Noralee *Canada* 53°59N 126°26W **70** C3
Noranda = Rouyn-Noranda
  Canada 48°20N 79°0W **72** C4
Norco *U.S.A.* 33°56N 117°33W **79** M9
Nord-Kivu □
  Dem. Rep. of the Congo 1°0S 29°0E **54** C2
Nord-Ostsee-Kanal
  Germany 54°12N 9°32E **16** A5
Nordaustlandet *Svalbard* 79°14N 23°0E **4** B9
Nordegg *Canada* 52°29N 116°5W **70** C5
Norderney *Germany* 53°42N 7°9E **16** B4
Norderstedt *Germany* 53°42N 10°1E **16** B5
Nordfjord *Norway* 61°55N 5°30E **8** F11
Nordfriesische Inseln
  Germany 54°40N 8°20E **16** A5
Nordhausen *Germany* 51°30N 10°47E **16** C6
Norðoyar *Færoe Is.* 62°17N 6°35W **8** E9
Nordkapp *Norway* 71°10N 25°50E **8** A22
Nordkapp *Svalbard* 80°31N 20°0E **4** A9
Nordkinnhalvøya
  Norway 70°55N 27°40E **8** A22
Nordrhein-Westfalen □
  Germany 51°45N 7°30E **16** C4
Nordvik *Russia* 74°2N 111°32E **29** B12
Nore → *Ireland* 52°25N 6°58W **10** D4
Noreland *Canada* 44°43N 78°48W **82** B6

Norfolk = Simcoe
  Canada 42°50N 80°23W **82 D4**
Norfolk N.Y., U.S.A. 44°48N 74°59W **83 B10**
Norfolk Nebr., U.S.A. 42°2N 97°25W **80 D5**
Norfolk Va., U.S.A. 36°50N 76°17W **81 G15**
Norfolk □ U.K. 52°39N 0°54E **13 E8**
Norfolk Broads △ U.K. 52°45N 1°30E **13 E9**
Norfolk I. Pac. Oc. 28°58S 168°3E **58 D9**
Norfolk L. U.S.A. 36°15N 92°14W **84 C8**
Norge = Norway ■ Europe 63°0N 11°0E **8 E14**
Norilsk Russia 69°20N 88°6E **29 C9**
Norma, Mt. Australia 20°55S 140°42E **62 C3**
Normal U.S.A. 40°31N 88°59W **80 E9**
Norman U.S.A. 35°13N 97°26W **84 D6**
Norman → Australia 19°18S 141°51E **62 B3**
Norman Wells Canada 65°17N 126°51W **68 C7**
Normanby → Australia 14°23S 144°10E **62 A3**
Normandie France 48°45N 0°10E **20 B4**
Normandin Canada 48°49N 72°31W **72 C5**
Normandy = Normandie
  France 48°45N 0°10E **20 B4**
Normanhurst, Mt.
  Australia 25°4S 122°30E **61 E3**
Normanton Australia 17°40S 141°10E **62 B3**
Normétal Canada 49°0N 79°22W **72 C4**
Norquay Canada 51°53N 102°5W **71 C8**
Norquinco Argentina 41°51S 70°55W **96 E2**
Norrbottens län □
  Sweden 66°50N 20°0E **8 C19**
Norris Point Canada 49°31N 57°53W **73 C8**
Norristown U.S.A. 40°7N 75°21W **83 F9**
Norrköping Sweden 58°37N 16°11E **9 G17**
Norrland Sweden 62°15N 15°45E **8 E16**
Norrtälje Sweden 59°46N 18°42E **9 G18**
Norseman Australia 32°8S 121°43E **61 F3**
Norsk Russia 52°30N 130°5E **29 D14**
Norte, Pta. del Canary Is. 27°51N 17°57W **24 G2**
Norte, Serra do Brazil 11°20S 59°0W **92 F7**
North, C. Canada 47°2N 60°20W **73 C7**
North Adams U.S.A. 42°42N 73°7W **83 D11**
North America 40°0N 100°0W **66 F10**
North Arm Canada 62°0N 114°30W **70 A5**
North Augusta U.S.A. 33°30N 81°59W **85 E14**
North Australian Basin
  Ind. Oc. 14°30S 116°30E **64 J3**
North Ayrshire □ U.K. 55°45N 4°44W **11 F4**
North Bass I. U.S.A. 41°40N 82°56W **82 E2**
North Battleford
  Canada 52°50N 108°17W **71 C7**
North Bay Canada 46°20N 79°30W **72 C4**
North Belcher Is. Canada 56°50N 79°50W **72 A4**
North Bend Oreg.,
  U.S.A. 43°24N 124°14W **76 E1**
North Bend Pa., U.S.A. 41°20N 77°42W **82 E7**
North Bend Wash.,
  U.S.A. 47°30N 121°47W **78 C5**
North Bennington
  U.S.A. 42°56N 73°15W **83 D11**
North Berwick U.K. 56°4N 2°42W **11 E6**
North Berwick U.S.A. 43°18N 70°44W **83 C14**
North Bruce Canada 44°22N 81°26W **82 B3**
North C. Canada 47°5N 64°0W **73 C7**
North C. N.Z. 34°23S 173°4E **59 A4**
North Canadian →
  U.S.A. 35°22N 95°37W **84 D7**
North Canton U.S.A. 40°53N 81°24W **82 F3**
North Cape = Nordkapp
  Norway 71°10N 25°50E **8 A21**
North Caribou L.
  Canada 52°50N 90°40W **72 B1**
North Carolina □
  U.S.A. 35°30N 80°0W **85 D15**
North Cascades △
  U.S.A. 48°45N 121°10W **76 B3**
North Channel Canada 46°0N 83°0W **72 C3**
North Channel U.K. 55°13N 5°52W **11 F3**
North Charleston
  U.S.A. 32°53N 79°58W **85 E15**
North Chicago U.S.A. 42°19N 87°51W **80 D10**
North Collins U.S.A. 42°35N 78°56W **82 D6**
North Creek U.S.A. 43°42N 73°59W **83 C11**
North Dakota □
  U.S.A. 47°30N 100°15W **80 B3**
North Downs U.K. 51°19N 0°21E **13 F8**
North East U.S.A. 42°13N 79°50W **82 D5**
North East Frontier Agency =
  Arunachal Pradesh □
  India 28°0N 95°0E **41 F19**
North East Lincolnshire □
  U.K. 53°34N 0°2W **12 D7**
North Eastern □ Kenya 1°30N 40°0E **54 B5**
North Esk → U.K. 56°46N 2°24W **11 E6**
North European Plain
  Europe 55°0N 25°0E **6 E10**
North Foreland U.K. 51°22N 1°28E **13 F9**
North Fork U.S.A. 37°14N 119°21W **78 H7**
North Fork American →
  U.S.A. 38°57N 120°59W **78 G5**
North Fork Feather →
  U.S.A. 38°33N 121°30W **78 F5**
North Fork Grand →
  U.S.A. 45°47N 102°16W **80 C2**
North Fork Red →
  U.S.A. 34°24N 99°14W **84 D5**
North Frisian Is. = Nordfriesische
  Inseln Germany 54°40N 8°20E **16 A5**
North Gower Canada 45°8N 75°43W **83 A9**
North Hd. U.S.A. 30°14S 114°59E **61 F1**
North Henik L. Canada 61°45N 97°40W **71 A9**
North Highlands
  U.S.A. 38°40N 121°23W **78 G5**
North Horr Kenya 3°20N 37°8E **54 B4**
North I. Kenya 4°5N 36°5E **54 B4**
North I. N.Z. 38°0S 175°0E **59 C5**
North I. Seychelles 4°25S 55°13E **53 b**
North Kingsville U.S.A. 41°54N 80°42W **82 E4**
North Kitui △ Kenya 0°15S 38°29E **54 C4**

North Knife → Canada 58°53N 94°45W **71 B10**
North Koel → India 24°45N 83°50E **43 G10**
North Korea ■ Asia 40°0N 127°0E **35 E14**
North Lakhimpur India 27°14N 94°7E **41 F19**
North Lanarkshire □
  U.K. 55°52N 3°56W **11 F5**
North Las Vegas U.S.A. 36°11N 115°7W **79 J11**
North Lincolnshire □
  U.K. 53°36N 0°30W **12 D7**
North Little Rock
  U.S.A. 34°45N 92°16W **84 D8**
North Loup → U.S.A. 41°17N 98°24W **80 E4**
North Luangwa △ Zambia 11°49S 32°9E **55 E3**
North Magnetic Pole
  Canada 82°42N 114°24W **69 B9**
North Mankato U.S.A. 44°10N 94°2W **80 C6**
North Minch U.K. 58°5N 5°55W **11 C3**
North Moose L. Canada 54°4N 100°12W **71 C8**
North Myrtle Beach
  U.S.A. 33°48N 78°42W **85 E15**
North Nahanni →
  Canada 62°15N 123°20W **70 A4**
North Olmsted U.S.A. 41°25N 81°56W **82 E3**
North Ossetia □ Russia 43°30N 44°30E **19 F7**
North Pagai, I. = Pagai Utara,
  Pulau Indonesia 2°35S 100°0E **36 E2**
North Palisade U.S.A. 37°6N 118°31W **78 H8**
North Platte U.S.A. 41°8N 100°46W **80 E3**
North Platte → U.S.A. 41°7N 100°42W **80 E3**
North Pole Arctic 90°0N 0°0E **4 A**
North Portal Canada 49°0N 102°33W **71 D8**
North Powder U.S.A. 45°2N 117°55W **76 D5**
North Pt. Barbados 13°20N 59°37W **89 g**
North Pt. Trin. & Tob. 11°21N 60°31W **93 J16**
North Rhine Westphalia =
  Nordrhein-Westfalen □
  Germany 51°45N 7°30E **16 C4**
North River Canada 53°49N 57°6W **73 B8**
North Ronaldsay U.K. 59°22N 2°26W **11 B6**
North Saskatchewan →
  Canada 53°15N 105°5W **71 C7**
North Sea Europe 56°0N 4°0E **6 D6**
North Seal → Canada 58°50N 98°7W **71 B9**
North Somerset □ U.K. 51°24N 2°45W **13 F5**
North Sydney Canada 46°12N 60°15W **73 C7**
North Syracuse U.S.A. 43°8N 76°7W **83 C8**
North Taranaki Bight
  N.Z. 38°50S 174°15E **59 C5**
North Thompson →
  Canada 50°40N 120°20W **70 C4**
North Tonawanda
  U.S.A. 43°2N 78°53W **82 C6**
North Troy U.S.A. 45°0N 72°24W **83 B12**
North Twin I. Canada 53°20N 80°0W **72 B4**
North Tyne → U.K. 55°0N 2°8W **12 B5**
North Uist U.K. 57°40N 7°15W **11 D1**
North Vancouver
  Canada 49°19N 123°4W **78 A3**
North Vernon U.S.A. 39°0N 85°38W **81 F11**
North Wabasca L.
  Canada 56°0N 113°55W **70 B5**
North Walsham U.K. 52°50N 1°22E **12 E9**
North West = Severo-Zapadnyy □
  Russia 65°0N 40°0E **28 C4**
North-West □ S. Africa 27°0S 25°0E **56 D4**
North West C. Australia 21°45S 114°9E **60 D1**
North West Frontier □
  Pakistan 34°0N 72°0E **42 C4**
North West Highlands
  U.K. 57°33N 4°58W **11 D4**
North West River
  Canada 53°30N 60°10W **73 B7**
North Western □ Zambia 13°30S 25°30E **55 E2**
North Wildwood U.S.A. 39°0N 74°48W **81 F16**
North York Moors U.K. 54°23N 0°53W **12 C7**
North York Moors △
  U.K. 54°27N 0°51W **12 C7**
North Yorkshire □ U.K. 54°15N 1°25W **12 C6**
Northallerton U.K. 54°20N 1°26W **12 C6**
Northam Australia 31°35S 116°42E **61 F2**
Northam S. Africa 24°56S 27°18E **57 C4**
Northampton Australia 28°27S 114°33E **61 E1**
Northampton U.K. 52°15N 0°53W **13 E7**
Northampton Mass.,
  U.S.A. 42°19N 72°38W **83 D12**
Northampton Pa.,
  U.S.A. 40°41N 75°30W **83 F9**
Northamptonshire □
  U.K. 52°16N 0°55W **13 E7**
Northbridge U.S.A. 42°9N 71°39W **83 D13**
Northbrook Canada 44°44N 77°9W **82 B7**
Northcliffe Australia 34°39S 116°7E **61 F2**
Northeast Pacific Basin
  Pac. Oc. 32°0N 145°0W **65 D13**
Northeast Providence Chan.
  W. Indies 26°0N 76°0W **88 A4**
Northern = Limpopo □
  S. Africa 24°5S 29°0E **57 C4**
Northern □ Malawi 11°0S 34°0E **55 E3**
Northern □ Zambia 10°30S 31°0E **55 E3**
Northern Areas □
  Pakistan 36°30N 73°0E **43 A5**
Northern Cape □ S. Africa 30°0S 20°0E **56 D3**
Northern Circars India 17°30N 82°30E **41 L13**
Northern Indian L.
  Canada 57°20N 97°20W **71 B9**
Northern Ireland □ U.K. 54°45N 7°0W **10 B5**
Northern Lau Group
  Fiji 17°30S 178°59W **59 a**
Northern Light L.
  Canada 48°15N 90°39W **72 C1**
Northern Marianas ☑
  Pac. Oc. 17°0N 145°0E **64 F6**
Northern Province □
  S. Africa 24°0S 29°0E **57 C4**
Northern Range
  Trin. & Tob. 10°46N 61°15W **93 K15**

Northern Sporades
  Greece 39°15N 23°30E **23 E10**
Northern Territory □
  Australia 20°0S 133°0E **60 D5**
Northfield Minn., U.S.A. 44°27N 93°9W **80 C7**
Northfield Vt., U.S.A. 44°9N 72°40W **83 B12**
Northgate Canada 49°0N 102°16W **71 D8**
Northland □ N.Z. 35°30S 173°30E **59 A4**
Northome U.S.A. 47°52N 94°17W **80 B6**
Northport Ala., U.S.A. 33°14N 87°35W **85 E11**
Northport Wash.,
  U.S.A. 48°55N 117°48W **76 B5**
Northumberland □ U.K. 55°12N 2°0W **12 B6**
Northumberland, C.
  Australia 38°5S 140°40E **63 F3**
Northumberland Is.
  Australia 21°30S 149°50E **62 C4**
Northumberland Str.
  Canada 46°20N 64°0W **73 C7**
Northville U.S.A. 43°13N 74°11W **83 C10**
Northwest Pacific Basin
  Pac. Oc. 32°0N 165°0E **64 D8**
Northwest Providence Channel
  W. Indies 26°0N 78°0W **88 A4**
Northwest Territories □
  Canada 63°0N 118°0W **68 C8**
Northwich U.K. 53°15N 2°31W **12 D5**
Northwood Iowa, U.S.A. 43°27N 93°13W **80 D7**
Northwood N. Dak.,
  U.S.A. 47°44N 97°34W **80 B5**
Norton U.S.A. 39°50N 99°53W **80 F4**
Norton Zimbabwe 17°52S 30°40E **55 F3**
Norton Sd. U.S.A. 63°50N 164°0W **74 a**
Norwalk Calif., U.S.A. 33°54N 118°4W **79 M8**
Norwalk Conn., U.S.A. 41°7N 73°22W **83 E11**
Norwalk Iowa, U.S.A. 41°29N 93°41W **80 E7**
Norwalk Ohio, U.S.A. 41°15N 82°37W **82 E2**
Norway Maine, U.S.A. 44°13N 70°32W **81 C18**
Norway Mich., U.S.A. 45°47N 87°55W **80 C10**
Norway ■ Europe 63°0N 11°0E **8 E14**
Norway House Canada 53°59N 97°50W **71 C9**
Norwegian B. Canada 77°30N 90°0W **69 B11**
Norwegian Basin Atl. Oc. 68°0N 2°0W **4 C7**
Norwegian Sea Atl. Oc. 66°0N 1°0E **6 B6**
Norwich Canada 42°59N 80°36W **82 D4**
Norwich U.K. 52°38N 1°18E **13 E9**
Norwich Conn., U.S.A. 41°31N 72°5W **83 E12**
Norwich N.Y., U.S.A. 42°32N 75°32W **83 D9**
Norwood Canada 44°23N 77°59W **82 B7**
Norwood U.S.A. 44°45N 75°0W **83 B10**
Nosappu-Misaki Japan 45°26N 141°39E **30 C12**
Noshiro Japan 40°12N 140°0E **30 D10**
Noşratābād Iran 29°55N 60°0E **45 D8**
Noss Hd. U.K. 58°28N 3°3W **11 C5**
Nossob → S. Africa 26°55S 20°45E **56 D3**
Nosy Barren Madag. 18°25S 43°40E **53 H8**
Nosy Bé Madag. 13°25S 48°15E **53 G9**
Nosy Boraha Madag. 16°50S 49°55E **57 B8**
Nosy Lava Madag. 14°33S 47°36E **57 A8**
Nosy Varika Madag. 20°35S 48°32E **57 C8**
Noteć → Poland 52°44N 15°26E **16 B8**
Notikewin → Canada 57°2N 117°38W **70 B5**
Notodden Norway 59°35N 9°17E **9 G13**
Notre Dame B. Canada 49°45N 55°30W **73 C8**
Notre-Dame-de-Koartac =
  Quaqtaq Canada 60°55N 69°40W **69 C13**
Notre-Dame-des-Bois
  Canada 45°24N 71°4W **83 A13**
Notre-Dame-d'Ivugivic = Ivujivik
  Canada 62°24N 77°55W **69 C12**
Notre-Dame-du-Nord
  Canada 47°36N 79°30W **72 C4**
Nottawasaga B. Canada 44°35N 80°15W **82 B4**
Nottaway → Canada 51°22N 78°55W **72 B4**
Nottingham U.K. 52°58N 1°10W **12 E6**
Nottingham, City of □
  U.K. 52°58N 1°10W **12 E6**
Nottingham I. Canada 63°20N 77°55W **69 C12**
Nottinghamshire □ U.K. 53°10N 1°3W **12 D6**
Nottoway → U.S.A. 36°33N 76°55W **81 G15**
Notwane → Botswana 23°35S 26°58E **56 C4**
Nouâdhibou Mauritania 20°54N 17°0W **50 D2**
Nouâdhibou, Râs
  Mauritania 20°50N 17°0W **50 D2**
Nouakchott Mauritania 18°9N 15°58E **50 E2**
Nouméa N. Cal. 22°17S 166°30E **58 D9**
Noupoort S. Africa 31°10S 24°57E **56 E3**
Nouveau Comptoir = Wemindji
  Canada 53°0N 78°49W **72 B4**
Nouvelle Amsterdam, Î.
  Ind. Oc. 38°30S 77°30E **3 F13**
Nouvelle-Calédonie = New
  Caledonia □ Pac. Oc. 21°0S 165°0E **58 D9**
Nova Esperança Brazil 23°8S 52°24W **95 A5**
Nova Friburgo Brazil 22°16S 42°30W **95 A7**
Nova Iguaçu Brazil 22°45S 43°28W **95 A7**
Nova Iorque Brazil 7°0S 44°5W **93 E10**
Nova Lamego
  Guinea-Biss. 12°19N 14°11W **50 F3**
Nova Lima Brazil 19°59S 43°51W **93 G10**
Nova Lusitânia Mozam. 19°50S 34°34E **55 F3**
Nova Mambone Mozam. 21°0S 35°3E **57 C6**
Nova Scotia □ Canada 45°10N 63°0W **73 C7**
Nova Sofala Mozam. 20°7S 34°42E **57 C6**
Nova Venécia Brazil 18°45S 40°24W **93 G10**
Nova Zagora Bulgaria 42°32N 26°1E **23 C11**
Novar Canada 45°27N 79°15W **82 A5**
Novara Italy 45°28N 8°38E **20 D8**
Novato U.S.A. 38°6N 122°35W **78 G4**
Novaya Ladoga Russia 60°7N 32°16E **18 B5**
Novaya Lyalya Russia 59°4N 60°45E **18 C11**
Novaya Sibir, Ostrov
  Russia 75°10N 150°0E **29 B16**
Novaya Zemlya Russia 75°0N 56°0E **28 B6**
Nové Zámky Slovak Rep. 47°59N 18°11E **17 D10**
Novgorod Russia 58°30N 31°25E **18 C5**
Novgorod-Seversky = Novhorod-
  Siverskyy Ukraine 52°2N 33°10E **18 D5**

Novhorod-Siverskyy
  Ukraine 52°2N 33°10E **18 D5**
Novi Lígure Italy 44°46N 8°47E **20 D8**
Novi Pazar Serbia 43°12N 20°28E **23 C9**
Novi Sad Serbia 45°18N 19°52E **23 B8**
Novo Hamburgo Brazil 29°37S 51°7W **95 B5**
Novo Mesto Slovenia 45°47N 15°12E **22 B6**
Novoaltaysk Russia 53°30N 84°0E **28 D9**
Novocherkassk Russia 47°27N 40°15E **19 E7**
Novodvinsk Russia 64°25N 40°42E **28 C5**
Novogrudok = Navahrudak
  Belarus 53°40N 25°50E **17 B13**
Novohrad-Volynskyy
  Ukraine 50°34N 27°35E **17 C14**
Novokachalinsk Russia 45°5N 132°0E **30 B5**
Novokuybyshevsk Russia 53°7N 49°58E **18 D8**
Novokuznetsk Russia 53°45N 87°10E **28 D9**
Novolazarevskaya
  Antarctica 71°0S 12°0E **5 D3**
Novomoskovsk Russia 54°5N 38°15E **18 D6**
Novorossiysk Russia 44°43N 37°46E **19 F6**
Novorybnoye Russia 72°50N 105°50E **29 B11**
Novoselytsya Ukraine 48°14N 26°15E **17 D14**
Novoshakhtinsk Russia 47°46N 39°58E **19 E6**
Novosibirsk Russia 55°0N 83°5E **28 D9**
Novosibirskiye Ostrova
  Russia 75°0N 142°0E **29 B15**
Novotroitsk Russia 51°10N 58°15E **18 D10**
Novouzensk Russia 50°32N 48°17E **19 D8**
Novovolynsk Ukraine 50°45N 24°4E **17 C13**
Novoska Croatia 45°19N 17°0E **22 B7**
Novvy Urengoy Russia 66°48N 76°52E **28 C8**
Novyy Bor Russia 66°43N 52°19E **18 A9**
Novyy Port Russia 67°40N 72°30E **28 C8**
Nowa Sól Poland 51°48N 15°44E **16 C8**
Nowata U.S.A. 36°42N 95°38W **84 C7**
Nowbarān Iran 35°8N 49°42E **45 C6**
Nowghāb Iran 33°53N 59°4E **45 C8**
Nowgong Assam, India 26°20N 92°50E **41 F18**
Nowgong Mad. P., India 25°4N 79°27E **43 G8**
Nowra Australia 34°53S 150°35E **63 E5**
Nowshera Pakistan 34°0N 72°0E **40 C8**
Nowy Sącz Poland 49°40N 20°41E **17 D11**
Nowy Targ Poland 49°29N 20°2E **17 D11**
Nowy Tomyśl Poland 52°19N 16°10E **16 B9**
Noxen U.S.A. 41°25N 76°4W **83 E8**
Noyabr'sk Russia 64°34N 76°21E **28 C8**
Noyon France 49°34N 2°59E **20 B5**
Noyon Mongolia 43°2N 102°4E **34 C2**
Nqutu S. Africa 28°13S 30°32E **57 D5**
Nsanje Malawi 16°55S 35°12E **55 F4**
Nsawam Ghana 5°50N 0°24W **50 G5**
Nsomba Zambia 10°45S 29°51E **55 E2**
Nu Jiang → China 29°58N 97°25E **32 D4**
Nu Shan China 26°0N 99°20E **32 D4**
Nuba Mts. = Nubah, Jibalan
  Sudan 12°0N 31°0E **51 F12**
Nubah, Jibalan Sudan 12°0N 31°0E **51 F12**
Nubia Africa 21°0N 32°0E **48 D7**
Nubian Desert = Nûbîya, Es Sahrâ
  en Sudan 21°30N 33°30E **51 D12**
Nûbîya, Es Sahrâ en
  Sudan 21°30N 33°30E **51 D12**
Nuboai Indonesia 2°10S 136°30E **37 E9**
Nubra → India 34°35N 77°35E **43 B7**
Nueces → U.S.A. 27°51N 97°30W **84 H6**
Nueltin L. Canada 60°30N 99°30W **71 A9**
Nuestra Señora del Rosario de
  Caá-Catí Argentina 27°45S 57°36W **94 B4**
Nueva Ciudad Guerrero
  Mexico 26°34N 99°12W **87 B5**
Nueva Gerona Cuba 21°53N 82°49W **88 B3**
Nueva Palmira Uruguay 33°52S 58°20W **94 C4**
Nueva Rosita Mexico 27°57N 101°13W **86 B4**
Nueva San Salvador
  El Salv. 13°40N 89°18W **88 D2**
Nuéve de Julio Argentina 35°30S 61°0W **94 D3**
Nuevitas Cuba 21°30N 77°20W **88 B4**
Nuevo, G. Argentina 43°0S 64°30W **96 E4**
Nuevo Casas Grandes
  Mexico 30°25N 107°55W **86 A3**
Nuevo Laredo Mexico 27°30N 99°31W **87 B5**
Nuevo León □ Mexico 25°20N 100°0W **86 C5**
Nuevo Rocafuerte
  Ecuador 0°55S 75°27W **92 D3**
Nugget Pt. N.Z. 46°27S 169°50E **59 G2**
Nuhaka N.Z. 39°3S 177°45E **59 C6**
Nukey Bluff Australia 32°26S 135°29E **63 E2**
Nukhayb Iraq 32°4N 42°3E **44 C4**
Nuku Hiva
  French Polynesia 8°54S 140°6W **65 H13**
Nuku'alofa Tonga 21°10S 175°12W **59 c**
Nukus Uzbekistan 42°27N 59°41E **28 E6**
Nullagine Australia 21°53S 120°7E **60 D3**
Nullagine → Australia 21°20S 120°20E **60 D3**
Nullarbor Australia 31°28S 130°55E **61 F5**
Nullarbor △ Australia 32°39S 130°0E **61 F5**
Nullarbor Plain Australia 31°10S 129°0E **61 F4**
Numalla, L. Australia 28°43S 144°20E **63 D3**
Numan Nigeria 9°29N 12°3E **51 G8**
Numata Japan 36°45N 139°4E **31 F9**
Numaykoos Lake △
  Canada 57°52N 95°58W **71 B9**
Numazu Japan 35°7N 138°51E **31 G9**
Numbulwar Australia 14°15S 135°45E **62 A2**
Numfoor Indonesia 1°0S 134°50E **37 E8**
Numurkah Australia 36°5S 145°26E **63 F4**
Nunakasaluk I. Canada 55°49N 60°20W **73 A7**
Nunap Isua Greenland 59°48N 43°55W **66 D15**
Nunavut □ Canada 66°0N 85°0W **69 C11**
Nunda U.S.A. 42°35N 77°56W **82 D7**
Nuneaton U.K. 52°32N 1°27E **13 E6**
Nungarin Australia 31°12S 118°6E **61 F2**
Nungo Mozam. 13°23S 37°43E **55 E4**
Nungwe Tanzania 2°48S 32°2E **54 C3**
Nunivak I. U.S.A. 60°10N 166°30W **74 a**
Nunkun India 33°57N 76°2E **43 C7**
Núoro Italy 40°20N 9°20E **22 D3**

Nūr Iran 36°33N 52°1E **45 B7**
Nūrābād Hormozgān, Iran 27°47N 57°12E **45 E8**
Nūrābād Lorestān, Iran 34°4N 47°58E **44 C5**
Nuremberg = Nürnberg
  Germany 49°27N 11°3E **16 D6**
Nuri Mexico 28°5N 109°22W **86 B3**
Nuriootpa Australia 34°27S 139°0E **63 E2**
Nūristān □ Afghan. 35°20N 71°0E **40 B7**
Nurmes Finland 63°33N 29°10E **8 E23**
Nürnberg Germany 49°27N 11°3E **16 D6**
Nurpur Pakistan 31°53N 71°54E **42 D4**
Nurran, L. = Terewah, L.
  Australia 29°52S 147°35E **63 D4**
Nurrari Lakes Australia 29°1S 130°5E **61 E5**
Nusa Barung Indonesia 8°30S 113°30E **37 H15**
Nusa Dua Indonesia 8°48S 115°14E **37 K18**
Nusa Kambangan
  Indonesia 7°40S 108°10E **37 G13**
Nusa Tenggara Barat □
  Indonesia 8°50S 117°30E **36 F5**
Nusa Tenggara Timur □
  Indonesia 9°30S 122°0E **37 F6**
Nusaybin Turkey 37°3N 41°10E **19 G7**
Nushki Pakistan 29°35N 66°0E **42 E2**
Nuuk Greenland 64°10N 51°35W **67 C14**
Nuupere, Pte. Moorea 17°36S 149°47W **59 d**
Nuwakot Nepal 28°10N 83°55E **43 E10**
Nuwayb'ī, W. an →
  Si. Arabia 29°18N 34°57E **46 F3**
Nuweiba' Egypt 28°59N 34°39E **44 D2**
Nuwerus S. Africa 31°8S 18°24E **56 E2**
Nuweveldberge S. Africa 32°10S 21°45E **56 E3**
Nuyts, Pt. Australia 35°4S 116°38E **61 G2**
Nuyts Arch. Australia 32°35S 133°20E **63 E1**
Nxai Pan △ Botswana 19°50S 24°46E **56 B3**
Nxau-Nxau Botswana 18°57S 21°4E **56 B3**
Nyabing Australia 33°33S 118°9E **61 F2**
Nyack U.S.A. 41°5N 73°55W **83 E11**
Nyagan Russia 62°30N 65°38E **28 C7**
Nyahanga Tanzania 2°20S 33°37E **54 C3**
Nyahua Tanzania 5°25S 33°23E **54 D3**
Nyahururu Kenya 0°2N 36°27E **54 B4**
Nyaingêntanglha Shan
  China 30°0N 90°0E **32 D3**
Nyakanazi Tanzania 3°2S 31°10E **54 C3**
Nyâlâ Sudan 12°2N 24°58E **51 F10**
Nyamandhlovu
  Zimbabwe 19°55S 28°16E **55 F2**
Nyambiti Tanzania 2°48S 33°27E **54 C3**
Nyamira Kenya 0°36S 34°52E **54 B4**
Nyamwaga Tanzania 1°27S 34°33E **54 C3**
Nyandekwa Tanzania 3°57S 32°32E **54 C3**
Nyandoma Russia 61°40N 40°12E **18 B7**
Nyanga △ Zimbabwe 18°17S 32°46E **55 F3**
Nyangana Namibia 18°0S 20°40E **56 B3**
Nyanguge Tanzania 2°30S 33°12E **54 C3**
Nyanza Rwanda 2°20S 29°42E **54 C2**
Nyanza □ Kenya 0°10S 34°15E **54 C3**
Nyanza-Lac Burundi 4°21S 29°36E **54 C2**
Nyasa, L. = Malawi, L.
  Africa 12°30S 34°30E **55 E3**
Nyasvizh Belarus 53°14N 26°38E **17 B14**
Nyazepetrovsk Russia 56°3N 59°36E **18 C10**
Nyazura Zimbabwe 18°40S 32°16E **55 F3**
Nyazwidzi → Zimbabwe 20°0S 31°17E **55 G3**
Nybro Sweden 56°44N 15°55E **9 H16**
Nyda Russia 66°40N 72°58E **28 C8**
Nyeri Kenya 0°23S 36°56E **54 C4**
Nyika △ Malawi 10°30S 33°53E **55 E3**
Nyíregyháza Hungary 47°58N 21°47E **17 E11**
Nyiru, Mt. Kenya 2°8N 36°50E **54 B4**
Nykarleby = Uusikaarlepyy
  Finland 63°32N 22°31E **8 E20**
Nykøbing Nordjylland,
  Denmark 56°48N 8°51E **9 H13**
Nykøbing Sjælland,
  Denmark 54°56N 11°52E **9 J14**
Nykøbing Sjælland,
  Denmark 55°55N 11°40E **9 J14**
Nyköping Sweden 58°45N 17°1E **9 G17**
Nylstroom = Modimolle
  S. Africa 24°42S 28°22E **57 C4**
Nymagee Australia 32°7S 146°20E **63 E4**
Nymboida △ Australia 29°38S 152°26E **63 D5**
Nynäshamn Sweden 58°54N 17°57E **9 G17**
Nyngan Australia 31°30S 147°8E **63 E4**
Nyoma Rap India 33°10N 78°40E **43 C8**
Nyoman = Nemunas →
  Lithuania 55°25N 21°10E **9 J19**
Nysa Poland 50°30N 17°22E **17 C9**
Nysa → Europe 52°4N 14°46E **16 B8**
Nyslott = Savonlinna
  Finland 61°52N 28°53E **8 F23**
Nyssa U.S.A. 43°53N 117°0W **76 E5**
Nystad = Uusikaupunki
  Finland 60°47N 21°25E **8 F19**
Nyunzu
  Dem. Rep. of the Congo 5°57S 27°58E **54 D2**
Nyurba Russia 63°17N 118°28E **29 C12**
Nzega Tanzania 4°10S 33°12E **54 C3**
Nzérékoré Guinea 7°49N 8°48W **50 G4**
Nzeto Angola 7°10S 12°52E **52 F2**
Nzilo, Chutes de
  Dem. Rep. of the Congo 10°18S 25°27E **55 E2**
Nzubuka Tanzania 4°45S 32°50E **54 C3**
Nzwani = Anjouan
  Comoros Is. 12°15S 44°20E **53 a**

O

O Le Pupū Pu'e △
  Samoa 13°59S 171°43W **59 b**
Ō-Shima Hokkaidō,
  Japan 41°30N 139°22E **30 D9**
Ō-Shima Shizuoka, Japan 34°44N 139°24E **31 G9**
Oa, Mull of U.K. 55°35N 6°20W **11 F2**

Oacoma U.S.A. 43°48N 99°24W 80 D4
Oahe, L. U.S.A. 44°27N 100°24W 80 C3
Oahe Dam U.S.A. 44°27N 100°24W 80 C3
O'ahu U.S.A. 21°28N 157°58W 74 b
Oak Harbor U.S.A. 48°18N 122°39W 78 B4
Oak Hill U.S.A. 37°59N 81°9W 81 G13
Oak Island U.S.A. 33°55N 78°10W 85 E15
Oak Ridge U.S.A. 36°1N 84°16W 85 C12
Oak View U.S.A. 34°24N 119°18W 79 L7
Oakdale Calif., U.S.A. 37°46N 120°51W 78 H6
Oakdale La., U.S.A. 30°49N 92°40W 84 F8
Oakes U.S.A. 46°8N 98°6W 80 B4
Oakesdale U.S.A. 47°8N 117°15W 76 C5
Oakey Australia 27°25S 151°43E 63 D5
Oakfield U.S.A. 43°4N 78°16W 82 C6
Oakham U.K. 52°40N 0°43W 13 E7
Oakhurst U.S.A. 37°19N 119°40W 78 H7
Oakland Calif., U.S.A. 37°48N 122°18W 78 H4
Oakland Pa., U.S.A. 41°57N 75°36W 83 E9
Oakley Idaho, U.S.A. 42°15N 113°53W 76 E7
Oakley Kans., U.S.A. 39°8N 100°51W 80 F3
Oakover → Australia 21°0S 120°40E 60 D3
Oakridge U.S.A. 43°45N 122°28W 76 E2
Oakville Canada 43°27N 79°41W 82 C5
Oakville U.S.A. 46°51N 123°14W 78 D3
Oamaru N.Z. 45°5S 170°59E 59 F3
Oasis Calif., U.S.A. 37°29N 117°55W 78 H9
Oasis Calif., U.S.A. 33°28N 116°6W 79 M10
Oates Land Antarctica 69°0S 160°0E 5 C11
Oatlands Australia 42°17S 147°21E 63 G4
Oatman U.S.A. 35°1N 114°19W 79 K12
Oaxaca Mexico 17°3N 96°43W 87 D5
Oaxaca □ Mexico 17°0N 96°30W 87 D5
Ob → Russia 66°45N 69°30E 28 C7
Oba Canada 49°4N 84°7W 72 C3
Obama Japan 35°30N 135°45E 31 G7
Oban U.K. 56°25N 5°29W 11 E3
Oberá Argentina 27°21S 55°2W 95 B4
Oberhausen Germany 51°28N 6°51E 16 C4
Oberlin Kans., U.S.A. 39°49N 100°32W 80 F3
Oberlin La., U.S.A. 30°37N 92°46W 84 F8
Oberlin Ohio, U.S.A. 41°18N 82°13W 82 E2
Oberon Australia 33°45S 149°52E 63 E4
Obi, Kepulauan Indonesia 1°23S 127°45E 37 E7
Óbidos Brazil 1°50S 55°30W 93 D7
Obihiro Japan 42°56N 143°12E 30 C11
Obilatu Indonesia 1°25S 127°20E 37 E7
Obluchye Russia 49°1N 131°4E 29 E14
Obo C.A.R. 5°20N 26°32E 54 A2
Oboyan Russia 51°15N 36°21E 28 D4
Obozerskaya = Obozerskiy Russia 63°34N 40°21E 18 B7
Obozerskiy Russia 63°34N 40°21E 18 B7
Observatory Inlet Canada 55°10N 129°54W 70 B3
Obshchi Syrt Russia 52°0N 53°0E 6 E16
Obskaya Guba Russia 69°0N 73°0E 28 C8
Obuasi Ghana 6°17N 1°40W 50 G5
Ocala U.S.A. 29°11N 82°8W 85 G13
Ocampo Chihuahua, Mexico 28°11N 108°23W 86 B3
Ocampo Tamaulipas, Mexico 22°50N 99°20W 87 C5
Ocaña Spain 39°55N 3°30W 21 C4
Occidental, Cordillera Colombia 5°0N 76°0W 92 C3
Occidental, Grand Erg Algeria 30°20N 1°0E 50 B6
Ocean City Md., U.S.A. 38°20N 75°5W 81 F16
Ocean City N.J., U.S.A. 39°17N 74°35W 81 F16
Ocean City Wash., U.S.A. 47°4N 124°10W 78 C2
Ocean Falls Canada 52°18N 127°48W 70 C3
Ocean I. = Banaba Kiribati 0°45S 169°50E 64 H8
Ocean Park U.S.A. 46°30N 124°3W 78 D2
Oceano U.S.A. 35°6N 120°37W 79 K6
Oceanport U.S.A. 40°19N 74°3W 83 F10
Oceanside U.S.A. 33°12N 117°23W 79 M9
Ochil Hills U.K. 56°14N 3°40W 11 E5
Ocho Rios Jamaica 18°24N 77°6W 88 a
Ocilla U.S.A. 31°36N 83°15W 85 F13
Ocmulgee → U.S.A. 31°58N 82°33W 85 F13
Ocniţa Moldova 48°25N 27°30E 17 D14
Oconee → U.S.A. 31°58N 82°33W 85 F13
Oconomowoc U.S.A. 43°7N 88°30W 80 D9
Oconto U.S.A. 44°53N 87°52W 80 C10
Oconto Falls U.S.A. 44°52N 88°9W 80 C9
Ocosingo Mexico 16°53N 92°6W 87 D6
Ocotal Nic. 13°41N 86°31W 88 D2
Ocotlán Jalisco, Mexico 20°21N 102°46W 86 C4
Ocotlán Oaxaca, Mexico 16°48N 96°40W 87 D5
Ōda Japan 35°11N 132°30E 31 G6
Ódáðahraun Iceland 65°5N 17°0W 8 D5
Odate Japan 40°16N 140°34E 30 D10
Odawara Japan 35°20N 139°6E 31 G9
Odda Norway 60°3N 6°35E 9 F12
Odei → Canada 56°6N 96°54W 71 B9
Ödemiş Turkey 38°15N 28°0E 23 E13
Odendaalsrus S. Africa 27°48S 26°45E 56 D4
Odense Denmark 55°22N 10°23E 9 J14
Oder → Europe 53°33N 14°38E 16 B8
Odesa Ukraine 46°30N 30°45E 19 E5
Odessa = Odesa Ukraine 46°30N 30°45E 19 E5
Odessa Canada 44°17N 76°43W 83 B8
Odessa Tex., U.S.A. 31°52N 102°23W 84 F3
Odessa Wash., U.S.A. 47°20N 118°41W 76 C4
Odiakwe Botswana 20°12S 25°17E 56 C4
Odienné Ivory C. 9°30N 7°34W 50 G4
Odintsovo Russia 55°40N 37°16E 18 C6
O'Donnell U.S.A. 32°58N 101°50W 84 E4
O'Donnell Pt. Canada 45°5N 80°5W 82 A4
Odorheiu Secuiesc Romania 46°21N 25°21E 17 E13
Odra = Oder → Europe 53°33N 14°38E 16 B8

Odzi Zimbabwe 19°0S 32°20E 57 B5
Odzi → Zimbabwe 19°45S 32°23E 57 B5
Oeiras Brazil 7°0S 42°8W 93 E10
Oelrichs U.S.A. 43°11N 103°14W 80 D2
Oelwein U.S.A. 42°41N 91°55W 80 D8
Oeno I. Pac. Oc. 24°0S 131°0W 65 K14
Oenpelli = Gunbalanya Australia 12°20S 133°4E 60 B5
Ofanto → Italy 41°22N 16°13E 22 D7
Offa Nigeria 8°13N 4°42E 50 G6
Offaly □ Ireland 53°15N 7°30W 10 C4
Offenbach Germany 50°6N 8°44E 16 C5
Offenburg Germany 48°28N 7°56E 16 D4
Officer Cr. → Australia 27°46S 132°30E 61 E5
Ofolanga Tonga 19°38S 174°27W 59 c
Ofotfjorden Norway 68°27N 17°0E 8 B17
Ofu Amer. Samoa 14°11S 169°41W 59 b
Ōfunato Japan 39°4N 141°43E 30 E10
Oga Japan 39°55N 139°50E 30 E9
Oga-Hantō Japan 39°58N 139°47E 30 E9
Ogaden Ethiopia 7°30N 45°30E 47 F3
Ōgaki Japan 35°21N 136°37E 31 G8
Ogallala U.S.A. 41°8N 101°43W 80 E3
Ogasawara Gunto Pac. Oc. 27°0N 142°0E 27 F16
Ogbomosho Nigeria 8°1N 4°11E 50 G6
Ogden U.S.A. 41°13N 111°58W 76 F8
Ogdensburg U.S.A. 44°42N 75°30W 83 B9
Ogea Driki Fiji 19°12S 178°27W 59 a
Ogea Levu Fiji 19°8S 178°24W 59 a
Ogeechee → U.S.A. 31°50N 81°3W 85 F14
Oglio → Italy 45°2N 10°39E 22 B4
Ogmore Australia 22°37S 149°35E 62 C4
Ogoki Canada 51°38N 85°58W 72 B2
Ogoki → Canada 51°38N 85°57W 72 B2
Ogoki L. Canada 50°50N 87°10W 72 B2
Ogoki Res. Canada 50°45N 88°15W 72 B2
Ogowe = Ogooué → Gabon 1°0S 9°0E 52 E1
Ogre Latvia 56°49N 24°36E 9 H21
Ogurchinskiy, Ostrov Turkmenistan 38°55N 53°2E 45 B7
Ohai N.Z. 45°55S 168°0E 59 F2
Ohakune N.Z. 39°24S 175°24E 59 C5
Ohata Japan 41°24N 141°10E 30 D10
Ohau, L. N.Z. 44°15S 169°53E 59 F2
Ohio □ U.S.A. 40°15N 82°45W 82 F2
Ohio → U.S.A. 36°59N 89°8W 80 G9
Ohře → Czech Rep. 50°30N 14°10E 16 C8
Ohrid Macedonia 41°8N 20°52E 23 D9
Ohridsko Jezero Macedonia 41°8N 20°52E 23 D9
Ohrigstad S. Africa 24°39S 30°36E 57 C5
Oiapoque Brazil 3°50N 51°50W 93 C8
Oikou China 38°35N 117°42E 35 E9
Oil City U.S.A. 41°26N 79°42W 82 E5
Oil Springs Canada 42°47N 82°7W 82 D2
Oildale U.S.A. 35°25N 119°1W 79 K7
Oise → France 49°0N 2°4E 20 B5
Oistins Barbados 13°4N 59°33W 89 g
Oistins B. Barbados 13°4N 59°33W 89 g
Ōita Japan 33°14N 131°36E 31 H5
Ōita □ Japan 33°15N 131°30E 31 H5
Oiticica Brazil 5°3S 41°5W 93 E10
Ojai U.S.A. 34°27N 119°15W 79 L7
Ojinaga Mexico 29°34N 104°25W 86 B4
Ojiya Japan 37°18N 138°48E 31 F9
Ojo Caliente Mexico 21°53N 102°15W 86 C4
Ojos del Salado, Cerro Argentina 27°0S 68°40W 94 B2
Oka → Russia 56°20N 43°59E 18 C7
Okaba Indonesia 8°6S 139°42E 37 F9
Okahandja Namibia 22°0S 16°59E 56 C2
Okanagan L. Canada 50°0N 119°30W 70 D5
Okandja Gabon 0°35S 13°45E 52 E2
Okanogan U.S.A. 48°22N 119°35W 76 B4
Okanogan → U.S.A. 48°6N 119°44W 76 B4
Okanogan Range N. Amer. 49°0N 119°55W 70 D5
Okapi △ Dem. Rep. of the Congo 2°30N 27°20E 54 B2
Okaputa Namibia 20°5S 17°0E 56 C2
Okara Pakistan 30°50N 73°31E 42 D5
Okaukuejo Namibia 19°10S 16°0E 56 B2
Okavango Delta Botswana 18°45S 22°45E 56 B3
Okavango Swamp = Okavango Delta Botswana 18°45S 22°45E 56 B3
Okaya Japan 36°5N 138°10E 31 F9
Okayama Japan 34°40N 133°54E 31 G6
Okayama □ Japan 35°0N 133°50E 31 G6
Okazaki Japan 34°57N 137°10E 31 G8
Okeechobee U.S.A. 27°15N 80°50W 85 H14
Okeechobee, L. U.S.A. 27°0N 80°50W 85 H14
Okefenokee △ U.S.A. 30°45N 82°18W 85 F13
Okefenokee Swamp U.S.A. 30°40N 82°20W 85 F13
Okehampton U.K. 50°44N 4°0W 13 G4
Okha India 22°27N 69°4E 42 H3
Okha Russia 53°40N 143°0E 29 D15
Okhotsk Russia 59°20N 143°10E 29 D15
Okhotsk, Sea of Asia 55°0N 145°0E 29 D15
Okhotskiy Perevoz Russia 61°52N 135°35E 29 C14
Okhtyrka Ukraine 50°25N 35°0E 19 D5
Oki-Shotō Japan 36°5N 133°15E 31 F6
Okinawa Japan 26°19N 127°46E 31 L3
Okinawa □ Japan 26°40N 128°0E 31 L4
Okinawa-Guntō Japan 26°40N 128°0E 31 L4
Okinawa-Jima Japan 26°32N 128°0E 31 L4
Okino-erabu-Shima Japan 27°21N 128°33E 31 L4
Oklahoma □ U.S.A. 35°20N 97°30W 84 D6
Oklahoma City U.S.A. 35°30N 97°30W 84 D6
Okmulgee U.S.A. 35°37N 95°58W 84 D7

Oknitsa = Ocniţa Moldova 48°25N 27°30E 17 D14
Okolo Uganda 2°37N 31°8E 54 B3
Okolona U.S.A. 34°0N 88°45W 85 E10
Okombahe Namibia 21°23S 15°22E 56 C2
Okotoks Canada 50°43N 113°58W 70 C6
Oksibil Indonesia 4°59S 140°35E 37 E10
Oksovskiy Russia 62°33N 39°57E 18 B6
Oktyabrsk = Qandyaghash Kazakhstan 49°28N 57°25E 19 E10
Oktyabrskiy = Aktsyabrski Belarus 52°38N 28°53E 17 B15
Oktyabrskiy Bashkortostan, Russia 54°28N 53°28E 18 D9
Oktyabrskiy Kamchatka, Russia 52°39N 156°14E 29 D16
Oktyabrskoy Revolyutsii, Ostrov Russia 79°30N 97°0E 29 B10
Okuru N.Z. 43°55S 168°55E 59 E2
Okushiri-Tō Japan 42°15N 139°30E 30 C9
Okwa → Botswana 22°30S 23°0E 56 C3
Ola Russia 59°35N 151°17E 29 D16
Ola U.S.A. 35°2N 93°13W 84 D8
Ólafsfjörður Iceland 66°4N 18°39W 8 C4
Ólafsvík Iceland 64°53N 23°43W 8 D2
Olancha U.S.A. 36°17N 118°1W 79 J8
Olancha Pk. U.S.A. 36°16N 118°7W 79 J8
Olanchito Honduras 15°30N 86°30W 88 C2
Öland Sweden 56°45N 16°38E 9 H17
Olary Australia 32°18S 140°19E 63 E3
Olascoaga Argentina 35°15S 60°39W 94 D3
Olathe U.S.A. 38°53N 94°49W 80 F6
Olavarría Argentina 36°55S 60°20W 94 D3
Oława Poland 50°57N 17°20E 17 C9
Ólbia Italy 40°55N 9°31E 22 D3
Olcott U.S.A. 43°20N 78°42W 82 C6
Old Bahama Chan. = Bahama, Canal Viejo de W. Indies 22°10N 77°30W 88 B4
Old Baldy Pk. = San Antonio, Mt. U.S.A. 34°17N 117°38W 79 L9
Old Bridge U.S.A. 40°25N 74°22W 83 F10
Old Castile = Castilla y Leon □ Spain 42°0N 5°0W 21 B3
Old Crow Canada 67°30N 139°55W 68 C6
Old Dale U.S.A. 34°8N 115°47W 79 L11
Old Forge N.Y., U.S.A. 43°43N 74°58W 83 C10
Old Forge Pa., U.S.A. 41°22N 75°45W 83 E9
Old Perlican Canada 48°5N 53°1W 73 C9
Old Shinyanga Tanzania 3°33S 33°27E 54 C3
Old Speck Mt. U.S.A. 44°34N 70°57W 83 B14
Old Town U.S.A. 44°56N 68°39W 81 C19
Old Washington U.S.A. 40°2N 81°27W 82 F3
Old Wives L. Canada 50°5N 106°0W 71 C7
Oldbury U.K. 51°38N 2°33E 13 F5
Oldcastle Ireland 53°46N 7°10W 10 C4
Oldeani Tanzania 3°22S 35°35E 54 C4
Oldenburg Germany 53°9N 8°13E 16 B5
Oldenzaal Neths. 52°19N 6°53E 15 B6
Oldham U.K. 53°33N 2°7W 12 D5
Oldman → Canada 49°57N 111°42W 70 D6
Oldmeldrum U.K. 57°20N 2°19W 11 D6
Olds Canada 51°50N 114°10W 70 C6
Olduvai Gorge Tanzania 2°58S 35°23E 54 C4
Oldziyt Mongolia 44°40N 109°1E 34 B5
Olean U.S.A. 42°5N 78°26W 82 D6
Olekma → Russia 60°22N 120°42E 29 C13
Olekminsk Russia 60°25N 120°30E 29 C13
Oleksandriya Ukraine 50°37N 26°19E 17 C14
Olema U.S.A. 38°3N 122°47W 78 G4
Olenegorsk Russia 68°9N 33°18E 8 B25
Olenek Russia 68°28N 112°18E 29 C12
Olenek → Russia 73°0N 120°10E 29 B13
Oléron, Î. d' France 45°55N 1°15W 20 D3
Oleśnica Poland 51°13N 17°22E 17 C9
Olevsk Ukraine 51°12N 27°39E 17 C14
Olga, L. Canada 49°47N 77°15W 72 C4
Olgas, The = Kata Tjuta Australia 25°20S 130°50E 61 E5
Ölgiy Mongolia 48°56N 89°57E 32 B3
Olhão Portugal 37°3N 7°48W 21 D2
Olifants = Elefantes → Africa 24°10S 32°40E 57 C5
Olifants → Namibia 25°30S 19°30E 56 C2
Olifantshoek S. Africa 27°57S 22°42E 56 D3
Ólimbos, Óros = Olympos Oros Greece 40°6N 22°23E 23 D10
Olímpia Brazil 20°44S 48°54W 95 A6
Olinda Brazil 8°1S 34°51W 93 E12
Oliva Argentina 32°0S 63°38W 94 C3
Olivares, Cerro los Argentina 30°18S 69°55W 94 C2
Olive Branch U.S.A. 34°57N 89°49W 85 D10
Olivehurst U.S.A. 39°6N 121°34W 78 F5
Olivenza Spain 38°41N 7°9W 21 C2
Oliver Canada 49°13N 119°37W 70 D5
Oliver L. Canada 56°56N 103°22W 71 B8
Ollagüe Chile 21°15S 68°10W 94 A2
Olmaliq Uzbekistan 40°50N 69°35E 28 E7
Olney Ill., U.S.A. 38°44N 88°5W 80 F9
Olney Tex., U.S.A. 33°22N 98°45W 84 E5
Oloitokitok Kenya 2°56S 37°30E 54 C4
Olomane → Canada 50°14N 60°37W 73 B7
Olomouc Czech Rep. 49°38N 17°12E 17 D9
Olonets Russia 61°0N 32°54E 18 B5
Olongapo Phil. 14°50N 120°18E 37 B6
Olosega Amer. Samoa 14°10S 169°37W 59 b
Olosenga = Swains I. Amer. Samoa 11°11S 171°4W 65 J11
Olot Spain 42°11N 2°30E 21 A7
Olovyannaya Russia 50°58N 115°35E 29 D12
Oloy → Russia 66°29N 159°29E 29 C16
Olsztyn Poland 53°48N 20°29E 17 B11
Olt → Romania 43°43N 24°51E 17 G13
Olteniţa Romania 44°7N 26°42E 17 F14
Olton U.S.A. 34°11N 102°8W 84 D3
Olympos Cyprus 35°21N 33°45E 25 D12

Olymbos Oros Greece 40°6N 22°23E 23 D10
Olympia Greece 37°39N 21°39E 23 F9
Olympia U.S.A. 47°3N 122°53W 78 D4
Olympic △ U.S.A. 47°45N 123°43W 78 C3
Olympic Dam Australia 30°30S 136°55E 63 E2
Olympic Mts. U.S.A. 47°55N 123°45W 78 C3
Olympus Cyprus 34°56N 32°52E 25 E11
Olympus, Mt. = Olympos Oros Greece 40°6N 22°23E 23 D10
Olympus, Mt. = Uludağ Turkey 40°4N 29°13E 23 D13
Olympus, Mt. U.S.A. 47°48N 123°43W 78 C3
Olyphant U.S.A. 41°27N 75°36W 83 E9
Olyutorskiy, Mys Russia 59°55N 170°27E 29 D18
Om → Russia 54°59N 73°22E 28 D8
Om Koi Thailand 17°48N 98°22E 38 D2
Ōma Japan 41°45N 141°5E 30 D10
Ōmachi Japan 36°30N 137°50E 31 F8
Omae-Zaki Japan 34°36N 138°14E 31 G9
Ōmagari Japan 39°27N 140°29E 30 E10
Omagh U.K. 54°36N 7°19W 10 B4
Omagh □ U.K. 54°35N 7°15W 10 B4
Omaha U.S.A. 41°17N 95°58W 80 E6
Omak U.S.A. 48°25N 119°31W 76 B4
Omalos Greece 35°19N 23°55E 25 D5
Oman ■ Asia 23°0N 58°0E 47 C6
Oman, G. of Asia 24°30N 58°30E 45 E8
Omaruru Namibia 21°26S 16°0E 56 C2
Omaruru → Namibia 22°7S 14°15E 56 C1
Omate Peru 16°45S 71°0W 92 G4
Ombai, Selat Indonesia 8°30S 124°50E 37 F6
Omboué Gabon 1°35S 9°15E 52 E1
Ombrone → Italy 42°42N 11°5E 22 C4
Omdurmân Sudan 15°40N 32°28E 51 E12
Omemee Canada 44°18N 78°33W 82 B6
Omeonga Dem. Rep. of the Congo 3°40S 24°22E 54 C1
Ometepe, I. de Nic. 11°32N 85°35W 88 D2
Ometepec Mexico 16°41N 98°25W 87 D5
Ominato Japan 41°17N 141°10E 30 D10
Omineca → Canada 56°3N 124°16W 70 B4
Omineca Mts. Canada 56°30N 125°30W 70 B3
Omitara Namibia 22°16S 18°2E 56 C2
Ōmiya = Saitama Japan 35°54N 139°38E 31 G9
Ommen Neths. 52°31N 6°26E 15 B6
Ömnögovi □ Mongolia 43°15N 104°0E 34 C3
Omo → Ethiopia 6°25N 36°10E 47 F2
Omodhos Cyprus 34°51N 32°48E 25 E11
Omolon → Russia 68°42N 158°36E 29 C16
Omono-Gawa → Japan 39°46N 140°3E 30 E10
Ompha Canada 45°0N 76°50W 83 B8
Omsk Russia 55°0N 73°12E 28 D8
Omsukchan Russia 62°32N 155°48E 29 C16
Ōmu Japan 44°34N 142°58E 30 B11
Omul, Vf. Romania 45°27N 25°29E 17 F13
Ōmura Japan 32°56N 129°57E 31 H4
Omuramba Omatako → Namibia 17°45S 20°25E 56 B2
Omuramba Ovambo → Namibia 18°45S 16°59E 56 B2
Ōmuta Japan 33°5N 130°26E 31 H5
Onaga U.S.A. 39°29N 96°10W 80 F5
Onalaska U.S.A. 43°53N 91°14W 80 D8
Onancock U.S.A. 37°43N 75°45W 81 G16
Onang Indonesia 3°2S 118°49E 37 E5
Onangue, L. Gabon 0°57S 10°4E 52 E2
Onaping L. Canada 47°3N 81°30W 72 C3
Onavas Mexico 28°31N 109°35W 86 B3
Onawa U.S.A. 42°2N 96°6W 80 D5
Oncócua Angola 16°30S 13°25E 56 B1
Onda Spain 39°55N 0°17W 21 C5
Ondangwa Namibia 17°57S 16°4E 56 B2
Ondjiva Angola 16°48S 15°50E 56 B2
Öndörhaan Mongolia 47°19N 110°39E 33 B6
Öndörshil Mongolia 45°13N 108°5E 34 B5
Öndverðarnes Iceland 64°52N 24°0W 8 D2
One Tree Australia 34°11S 144°43E 63 E3
Oneata Fiji 18°26S 178°25W 59 a
Onega Russia 64°0N 38°10E 18 B6
Onega → Russia 63°58N 38°2E 18 B6
Onega, G. of = Onezhskaya Guba Russia 64°24N 36°38E 18 B6
Onega, L. = Onezhskoye Ozero Russia 61°44N 35°22E 18 B6
Oneida U.S.A. 43°6N 75°39W 83 C9
Oneida L. U.S.A. 43°12N 75°54W 83 C9
O'Neill U.S.A. 42°27N 98°39W 80 D4
Onekotan, Ostrov Russia 49°25N 154°45E 29 E16
Onema Dem. Rep. of the Congo 4°35S 24°30E 54 C1
Oneonta U.S.A. 42°27N 75°4W 83 D9
Oneşti Romania 46°17N 26°47E 17 E14
Onezhskaya Guba Russia 64°24N 36°38E 18 B6
Onezhskoye Ozero Russia 61°44N 35°22E 18 B6
Ongarue N.Z. 38°42S 175°19E 59 C5
Ongea Levu = Ogea Levu Fiji 19°8S 178°24W 59 a
Ongers → S. Africa 31°4S 23°13E 56 E3
Ongerup Australia 33°58S 118°28E 61 F2
Ongjin N. Korea 37°56N 125°21E 35 F13
Ongkharak Thailand 14°8N 101°1E 38 E3
Ongniud Qi China 43°0N 118°38E 35 C10
Ongoka Dem. Rep. of the Congo 1°20S 26°0E 54 C2
Ongole India 15°33N 80°2E 40 M12
Ongon = Havirga Mongolia 45°41N 113°5E 34 B7
Onida U.S.A. 44°42N 100°4W 80 C3
Onilahy → Madag. 23°34S 43°45E 57 C7
Onitsha Nigeria 6°6N 6°42E 50 G7
Ono Fiji 18°55S 178°29E 59 a
Onoda Japan 33°59N 131°11E 31 G5
Onslow Australia 21°40S 115°12E 60 D2
Onslow B. U.S.A. 34°20N 77°15W 85 D16

Ontake-San Japan 35°53N 137°29E 31 G8
Ontario Calif., U.S.A. 34°4N 117°39W 79 L9
Ontario Oreg., U.S.A. 44°2N 116°58W 76 D5
Ontario □ Canada 48°0N 83°0W 72 B2
Ontario, L. N. Amer. 43°20N 78°0W 82 C7
Ontonagon U.S.A. 46°52N 89°19W 80 B9
Onyx U.S.A. 35°41N 118°14W 79 K8
Oodnadatta Australia 27°33S 135°30E 63 D2
Ooldea Australia 30°27S 131°50E 61 F5
Oombulgurri Australia 15°15S 127°45E 60 C4
Oorindi Australia 20°40S 141°1E 62 C3
Oost-Vlaanderen □ Belgium 51°5N 3°50E 15 C3
Oostende Belgium 51°15N 2°54E 15 C2
Oosterhout Neths. 51°39N 4°47E 15 C4
Oosterschelde → Neths. 51°33N 4°0E 15 C4
Oosterwolde Neths. 53°0N 6°17E 15 B6
Ootacamund = Udagamandalam India 11°30N 76°44E 40 P10
Ootsa L. Canada 53°50N 126°2W 70 C3
Op Luang △ Thailand 18°12N 98°32E 38 C2
Opala Dem. Rep. of the Congo 0°40S 24°20E 54 C1
Opanake Sri Lanka 6°35N 80°40E 40 R12
Opasatika Canada 49°30N 82°50W 72 C3
Opasquia △ Canada 53°33N 93°5W 72 B1
Opava Czech Rep. 49°57N 17°58E 17 D9
Opelika U.S.A. 32°39N 85°23W 85 E12
Opelousas U.S.A. 30°32N 92°5W 84 F8
Opémisca, L. Canada 49°56N 74°52W 72 C5
Opheim U.S.A. 48°51N 106°24W 76 B10
Ophthalmia Ra. Australia 23°15S 119°30E 60 D2
Opinaca → Canada 52°15N 78°2W 72 B4
Opinaca, Rés. Canada 52°39N 76°20W 72 B4
Opinnagau → Canada 54°12N 82°25W 72 B3
Opiscotéo, L. Canada 53°10N 68°10W 73 B6
Opobo Nigeria 4°35N 7°34E 50 H7
Opole Poland 50°42N 17°58E 17 C9
Oponono L. Namibia 18°8S 15°45E 56 B2
Oporto = Porto Portugal 41°8N 8°40W 21 B1
Opotiki N.Z. 38°1S 177°19E 59 C6
Opp U.S.A. 31°17N 86°16W 85 F11
Oppdal Norway 62°35N 9°41E 8 E13
Opportunity U.S.A. 47°39N 117°15W 76 C5
Opua N.Z. 35°19S 174°9E 59 A5
Opunake N.Z. 39°26S 173°52E 59 C4
Opuwo Namibia 18°3S 13°45E 56 B1
Ora Cyprus 34°51N 33°12E 25 E12
Oracle U.S.A. 32°37N 110°46W 77 K8
Oradea Romania 47°2N 21°58E 17 E11
Öræfajökull Iceland 64°2N 16°39W 8 D5
Orai India 25°58N 79°30E 43 G8
Oral = Zhayyq → Kazakhstan 47°0N 51°48E 19 E9
Oral Kazakhstan 51°20N 51°20E 19 D9
Oran Algeria 35°45N 0°39W 50 A5
Orange Australia 33°15S 149°7E 63 E4
Orange France 44°8N 4°47E 20 D6
Orange Calif., U.S.A. 33°47N 117°51W 79 M9
Orange Mass., U.S.A. 42°35N 72°19W 83 D12
Orange Tex., U.S.A. 30°6N 93°44W 84 F8
Orange Va., U.S.A. 38°15N 78°7W 81 F14
Orange → S. Africa 28°41S 16°28E 56 D2
Orange, C. Brazil 4°20N 51°30W 93 C8
Orange Cove U.S.A. 36°38N 119°19W 78 J7
Orange Free State = Free State □ S. Africa 28°30S 27°0E 56 D4
Orange Grove U.S.A. 27°58N 97°56W 84 H6
Orange Walk Belize 18°6N 88°33W 87 D7
Orangeburg U.S.A. 33°30N 80°52W 85 E14
Orangeville Canada 43°55N 80°5W 82 C4
Orango Guinea-Biss. 11°5N 16°0W 50 F2
Oranienburg Germany 52°45N 13°14E 16 B7
Oranje = Orange → S. Africa 28°41S 16°28E 56 D2
Oranjemund Namibia 28°38S 16°29E 56 D2
Oranjerivier S. Africa 29°40S 24°12E 56 D3
Oranjestad Aruba 12°32N 70°2W 89 D5
Orapa Botswana 21°15S 25°30E 53 J5
Oras Phil. 12°9N 125°28E 37 B7
Orbetello Italy 42°27N 11°13E 22 C4
Orbisonia U.S.A. 40°15N 77°54W 82 F7
Orbost Australia 37°40S 148°29E 63 F4
Orcadas Antarctica 60°44S 44°37W 5 C18
Orcas I. U.S.A. 48°42N 122°56W 78 B4
Orchard City U.S.A. 38°50N 107°58W 76 G10
Orchard Homes U.S.A. 46°55N 114°4W 76 C6
Orchila, I. Venezuela 11°48N 66°10W 89 D6
Orchilla, Pta. Canary Is. 27°42N 18°10W 24 G1
Orcutt U.S.A. 34°52N 120°27W 79 L6
Ord U.S.A. 41°36N 98°56W 80 E4
Ord → Australia 15°33S 128°15E 60 C4
Ord, Mt. Australia 17°20S 125°34E 60 C4
Ord Mts. U.S.A. 34°39N 116°45W 79 L10
Orderville U.S.A. 37°17N 112°38W 77 H7
Ordos = Mu Us Shamo China 39°0N 109°0E 34 E5
Ordu Turkey 40°55N 37°53E 19 F6
Ordway U.S.A. 38°13N 103°46W 76 G12
Ore Dem. Rep. of the Congo 3°17N 29°30E 54 B2
Ore Mts. = Erzgebirge Germany 50°27N 12°55E 16 C7
Örebro Sweden 59°20N 15°18E 9 G16
Oregon U.S.A. 42°1N 89°20W 80 D9
Oregon □ U.S.A. 44°0N 121°0W 76 E3
Oregon City U.S.A. 45°21N 122°36W 78 E4
Oregon Dunes △ U.S.A. 43°40N 124°10W 76 E1
Orekhovo-Zuyevo Russia 55°50N 38°55E 18 C6
Orel Russia 52°57N 36°3E 18 D6
Orem U.S.A. 40°19N 111°42W 76 F8
Ören Turkey 37°3N 27°57E 23 F12
Orenburg Russia 51°45N 55°6E 18 D10
Orense = Ourense Spain 42°19N 7°55W 21 A2
Orepuki N.Z. 46°19S 167°46E 59 G1

Orestes Pereyra *Mexico* 26°30N 105°39W **86** B3
Orestiada *Greece* 41°30N 26°33E **23** D12
Orfanos Kolpos *Greece* 40°33N 24°0E **23** D11
Orford Ness *U.K.* 52°5N 1°35E **13** E9
Organ Pipe Cactus △
  U.S.A. 32°0N 112°52W **77** K7
Organos, Pta. de los
  Canary Is. 28°12N 17°17W **24** F2
Orgaz *Spain* 39°39N 3°53W **21** C4
Orgeyev = Orhei
  Moldova 47°24N 28°50E **17** E15
Orhaneli *Turkey* 39°54N 28°59E **23** E13
Orhangazi *Turkey* 40°29N 29°18E **23** D13
Orhei *Moldova* 47°24N 28°50E **17** E15
Orhon Gol → *Mongolia* 50°21N 106°0E **32** A5
Oriental, Cordillera
  Colombia 6°0N 73°0W **92** B4
Oriental, Grand Erg *Algeria* 30°0N 6°30E **50** B7
Orientale □
  Dem. Rep. of the Congo 2°20N 26°0E **54** B2
Oriente *Argentina* 38°44S 60°37W **94** D3
Orihuela *Spain* 38°7N 0°55W **21** C5
Orillia *Canada* 44°40N 79°24W **82** B5
Orinoco → *Venezuela* 9°15N 61°30W **92** B6
Orion *Canada* 49°27N 110°49W **71** D6
Oriskany *U.S.A.* 43°10N 75°20W **83** C9
Orissa □ *India* 20°0N 84°0E **41** K14
Orissaare *Estonia* 58°34N 23°5E **9** G20
Oristano *Italy* 39°54N 8°36E **22** E3
Oristano, G. di *Italy* 39°50N 8°29E **22** E3
Orizaba *Mexico* 18°51N 97°6W **87** D5
Orizaba, Pico de *Mexico* 18°58N 97°15W **87** D5
Orkanger *Norway* 63°18N 9°52E **8** E13
Orkla → *Norway* 63°18N 9°51E **8** E13
Orkney *S. Africa* 26°58S 26°40E **56** D4
Orkney □ *U.K.* 59°2N 3°13W **11** B5
Orkney Is. *U.K.* 59°0N 3°0W **11** B6
Orland *U.S.A.* 39°45N 122°12W **78** F4
Orlando *U.S.A.* 28°32N 81°22W **85** G14
Orléanais *France* 48°0N 2°0E **20** C5
Orléans *France* 47°54N 1°52E **20** C4
Orleans *U.S.A.* 44°49N 72°12W **83** B12
Orléans, Î. d' *Canada* 46°54N 70°58W **73** C5
Ormara *Pakistan* 25°16N 64°33E **40** G4
Ormoc *Phil.* 11°0N 124°37E **37** B6
Ormond *N.Z.* 38°33S 177°56E **59** C6
Ormond Beach *U.S.A.* 29°17N 81°3W **85** G14
Ormskirk *U.K.* 53°35N 2°54W **12** D5
Ormstown *Canada* 45°8N 74°0W **83** A11
Örnsköldsvik *Sweden* 63°17N 18°40E **8** E18
Oro *N. Korea* 40°1N 127°27E **35** D14
Oro → *Mexico* 25°35N 105°2W **86** B3
Oro Grande *U.S.A.* 34°36N 117°20W **79** L9
Oro Valley *U.S.A.* 32°26N 110°58W **77** K8
Orocué *Colombia* 4°48N 71°20W **92** C4
Orofino *U.S.A.* 46°29N 116°15W **76** C5
Orohena, Mt. *Tahiti* 17°37S 149°28W **59** d
Orol Dengizi = Aral Sea
  Asia 44°30N 60°0E **28** E7
Oromocto *Canada* 45°54N 66°29W **73** C6
Orono *Canada* 43°59N 78°37W **82** C6
Orono *U.S.A.* 44°53N 68°40W **81** C19
Oronsay *U.K.* 56°1N 6°15W **11** E2
Oroqen Zizhiqi *China* 50°34N 123°43E **33** A7
Oroquieta *Phil.* 8°32N 123°44E **37** C6
Orosei *Italy* 40°23N 9°42E **22** D3
Orosháza *Hungary* 46°32N 20°42E **17** E11
Orotukan *Russia* 62°16N 151°42E **29** C16
Oroville *Calif., U.S.A.* 39°31N 121°33W **78** F5
Oroville *Wash., U.S.A.* 48°56N 119°26W **76** B4
Oroville, L. *U.S.A.* 39°33N 121°29W **78** F5
Orroroo *Australia* 32°43S 138°38E **63** E2
Orrville *U.S.A.* 40°50N 81°46W **82** F3
Orsha *Belarus* 54°30N 30°25E **18** D5
Orsk *Russia* 51°12N 58°34E **28** D6
Orșova *Romania* 44°41N 22°25E **17** F12
Ortaca *Turkey* 36°49N 28°45E **23** F13
Ortegal, C. *Spain* 43°43N 7°52W **21** A2
Orthez *France* 43°29N 0°48W **20** E3
Ortigueira *Spain* 43°40N 7°50W **21** A2
Orting *U.S.A.* 47°6N 122°12W **78** C4
Ortles *Italy* 46°31N 10°33E **20** C9
Ortón → *Bolivia* 10°50S 67°0W **92** F5
Ortonville *U.S.A.* 45°19N 96°27W **80** C5
Orūmīyeh *Iran* 37°40N 45°0E **44** B5
Orūmīyeh, Daryācheh-ye
  Iran 37°50N 45°30E **44** B5
Oruro *Bolivia* 18°0S 67°9W **92** G5
Orust *Sweden* 58°10N 11°40E **9** G14
Oruzgān □ *Afghan.* 33°0N 66°0E **40** C5
Orvieto *Italy* 42°43N 12°7E **22** C5
Orwell *N.Y., U.S.A.* 43°35N 75°50W **83** C9
Orwell *Ohio, U.S.A.* 41°32N 80°52W **82** E4
Orwell → *U.K.* 51°59N 1°18E **13** F9
Orwigsburg *U.S.A.* 40°38N 76°6W **83** F8
Oryakhovo *Bulgaria* 43°40N 23°57E **23** C10
Osa *Russia* 57°17N 55°26E **18** C10
Osa, Pen. de *Costa Rica* 8°0N 84°0W **88** E3
Osage *U.S.A.* 43°17N 92°49W **80** D7
Osage → *U.S.A.* 38°36N 91°57W **80** F8
Osage City *U.S.A.* 38°38N 95°50W **80** F6
Ōsaka *Japan* 34°42N 135°30E **31** G7
Osan *S. Korea* 37°11N 127°4E **35** F14
Osawatomie *U.S.A.* 38°31N 94°57W **80** F7
Osborne *U.S.A.* 39°26N 98°42W **80** F4
Osceola *Ark., U.S.A.* 35°42N 89°58W **85** D10
Osceola *Iowa, U.S.A.* 41°2N 93°46W **80** E7
Oscoda *U.S.A.* 44°26N 83°20W **82** B1
Ösel = Saaremaa *Estonia* 58°30N 22°30E **9** G20
Osgoode *Canada* 45°8N 75°36W **83** A9
Oshakati *Namibia* 17°45S 15°40E **53** H3
Oshawa *Canada* 43°50N 78°50W **82** C6
Oshigambo *Namibia* 17°45S 16°5E **56** B2
Oshkosh *Nebr., U.S.A.* 41°24N 102°21W **80** E2
Oshkosh *Wis., U.S.A.* 44°1N 88°33W **80** C9
Oshmyany = Ashmyany
  Belarus 54°26N 25°52E **17** A13

Oshnovīyeh *Iran* 37°2N 45°6E **44** B5
Oshogbo *Nigeria* 7°48N 4°37E **50** G6
Oshtorīnān *Iran* 34°1N 48°38E **45** C6
Oshwe
  Dem. Rep. of the Congo 3°25S 19°28E **52** E3
Osijek *Croatia* 45°34N 18°41E **23** B8
Osipovichi = Asipovichy
  Belarus 53°19N 28°33E **17** B15
Osiyan *India* 26°43N 72°55E **42** F5
Osizweni *S. Africa* 27°49S 30°7E **57** D5
Oskaloosa *U.S.A.* 41°18N 92°39W **80** E7
Oskarshamn *Sweden* 57°15N 16°27E **9** H17
Oskélanéo *Canada* 48°5N 75°15W **72** C4
Öskemen *Kazakhstan* 50°0N 82°36E **28** E9
Oslo *Norway* 59°54N 10°43E **9** G14
Oslofjorden *Norway* 59°20N 10°35E **9** G14
Osmanabad *India* 18°5N 76°10E **40** K10
Osmaniye *Turkey* 37°5N 36°10E **44** B3
Osnabrück *Germany* 52°17N 8°3E **16** B5
Osório *Brazil* 29°53S 50°17W **95** B5
Osorno *Chile* 40°25S 73°0W **96** E2
Osorno, Vol. *Chile* 41°0S 72°30W **96** D2
Osoyoos *Canada* 49°0N 119°30W **70** D5
Osøyro *Norway* 60°9N 5°30E **8** F11
Ospika → *Canada* 56°20N 124°0W **70** B4
Osprey Reef *Australia* 13°52S 146°36E **62** A4
Oss *Neths.* 51°46N 5°32E **15** C5
Ossa, Mt. *Australia* 41°52S 146°3E **63** G4
Ossa, Oros *Greece* 39°47N 22°42E **23** E10
Ossabaw I. *U.S.A.* 31°50N 81°5W **85** F14
Ossining *U.S.A.* 41°10N 73°55W **83** E11
Ossipee *U.S.A.* 43°41N 71°7W **83** C13
Ossokmanuan L. *Canada* 53°25N 65°0W **73** B7
Ossora *Russia* 59°20N 163°13E **29** D17
Ostend = Oostende
  Belgium 51°15N 2°54E **15** C2
Oster *Ukraine* 50°57N 30°53E **17** C16
Österbotten = Pohjanmaa
  Finland 62°58N 22°50E **8** E20
Osterburg *U.S.A.* 40°16N 78°31W **82** F6
Österdalälven *Sweden* 61°30N 13°45E **8** F15
Österdalen *Norway* 61°40N 10°50E **8** F14
Östermyra = Seinäjoki
  Finland 62°40N 22°51E **8** E20
Österreich = Austria ■
  Europe 47°0N 14°0E **16** E8
Östersund *Sweden* 63°10N 14°38E **8** E16
Ostfriesische Inseln
  Germany 53°42N 7°0E **16** B4
Ostrava *Czech Rep.* 49°51N 18°18E **17** D10
Ostróda *Poland* 53°42N 19°58E **17** B10
Ostroh *Ukraine* 50°20N 26°30E **17** C14
Ostrołęka *Poland* 53°4N 21°32E **17** B11
Ostrów Mazowiecka
  Poland 52°50N 21°51E **17** B11
Ostrów Wielkopolski
  Poland 51°36N 17°44E **17** C9
Ostrowiec-Świętokrzyski
  Poland 50°55N 21°22E **17** C11
Ostuni *Italy* 40°44N 17°35E **23** D7
Ōsumi-Kaikyō *Japan* 30°55N 131°0E **31** J5
Ōsumi-Shotō *Japan* 30°30N 130°0E **31** J5
Osuna *Spain* 37°14N 5°8W **21** D3
Oswegatchie → *U.S.A.* 44°42N 75°30W **83** B9
Oswego *U.S.A.* 43°27N 76°31W **83** C8
Oswego → *U.S.A.* 43°27N 76°30W **83** C8
Oswestry *U.K.* 52°52N 3°3W **12** E4
Oświęcim *Poland* 50°2N 19°11E **17** C10
Otago □ *N.Z.* 45°15S 170°0E **59** F2
Otago Harbour *N.Z.* 45°47S 170°42E **59** F3
Otahaiti B. *Trin. & Tob.* 10°15N 61°30W **93** K15
Ōtake *Japan* 34°12N 132°13E **31** G6
Otaki *N.Z.* 40°45S 175°10E **59** D5
Otaru *Japan* 43°10N 141°0E **30** C10
Otaru-Wan = Ishikari-Wan
  Japan 43°25N 141°1E **30** C10
Otavalo *Ecuador* 0°13N 78°20W **92** C3
Otavi *Namibia* 19°40S 17°24E **56** B2
Otchinjau *Angola* 16°30S 13°56E **56** B1
Otego *U.S.A.* 42°23N 75°10W **83** D9
Otelnuk, L. *Canada* 56°9N 68°12W **73** A6
Othello *U.S.A.* 46°50N 119°10W **76** C4
Otish, Mts. *Canada* 52°18N 70°37W **73** B5
Otjiwarongo *Namibia* 20°30S 16°33E **56** C2
Oto Tolu Group *Tonga* 20°21S 174°32W **59** c
Otoineppu *Japan* 44°44N 142°16E **30** B11
Otorohanga *N.Z.* 38°12S 175°14E **59** C5
Otoskwin → *Canada* 52°13N 88°6W **72** B2
Otra → *Norway* 58°9N 8°1E **9** G13
Otranto *Italy* 40°9N 18°28E **23** D8
Otranto, C. d' *Italy* 40°7N 18°30E **23** D8
Otranto, Str. of *Italy* 40°15N 18°40E **23** D8
Otse *S. Africa* 25°2S 25°45E **56** D4
Otsego L. *U.S.A.* 42°45N 74°53W **83** D10
Ōtsu *Japan* 35°0N 135°50E **31** G7
Ōtsuki *Japan* 35°36N 138°57E **31** G9
Ottawa = Outaouais →
  Canada 45°27N 74°8W **72** C5
Ottawa *Canada* 45°26N 75°42W **83** A9
Ottawa *Ill., U.S.A.* 41°21N 88°51W **80** E9
Ottawa *Kans., U.S.A.* 38°37N 95°16W **80** F6
Ottawa Is. *Canada* 59°35N 80°10W **69** D11
Otter Cr. → *U.S.A.* 44°13N 73°17W **83** B11
Otter Lake *Canada* 45°17N 79°56W **82** A5
Otterville *Canada* 42°55N 80°36W **82** D4
Ottery St. Mary *U.K.* 50°44N 3°17W **13** G4
Otto Beit Bridge
  Zimbabwe 15°59S 28°56E **55** F2
Ottosdal *S. Africa* 26°46S 25°59E **56** D4
Ottumwa *U.S.A.* 41°1N 92°25W **80** E7
Oturkpo *Nigeria* 7°16N 8°8E **50** G7
Otway, B. *Chile* 53°30S 74°0W **96** G2
Otway, C. *Australia* 38°52S 143°30E **63** F3
Otwock *Poland* 52°5N 21°20E **17** B11
Ou → *Laos* 20°4N 102°13E **38** B4
Ou Neua *Laos* 22°18N 101°48E **38** A3
Ou-Sammyaku *Japan* 39°20N 140°35E **30** E10

Ouachita → *U.S.A.* 31°38N 91°49W **84** F9
Ouachita, L. *U.S.A.* 34°34N 93°12W **84** H8
Ouachita Mts. *U.S.A.* 34°30N 94°30W **84** D7
Ouagadougou
  Burkina Faso 12°25N 1°30W **50** F5
Ouahigouya *Burkina Faso* 13°31N 2°25W **50** F5
Ouahran = Oran *Algeria* 35°45N 0°39W **50** A5
Ouallene *Algeria* 24°41N 1°11E **50** D6
Ouarâne *Mauritania* 21°0N 10°30W **50** D3
Ouargla *Algeria* 31°59N 5°16E **50** B7
Ouarra → *C.A.R.* 5°5N 24°26E **52** C4
Ouarzazate *Morocco* 30°55N 6°50W **50** B4
Oubangi →
  Dem. Rep. of the Congo 0°30S 17°50E **52** E3
Ouddorp *Neths.* 51°50N 3°57E **15** C3
Oude Rijn → *Neths.* 52°12N 4°24E **15** B4
Oudenaarde *Belgium* 50°50N 3°37E **15** D3
Oudtshoorn *S. Africa* 33°35S 22°14E **56** E3
Ouessant, Î. d' *France* 48°28N 5°6W **20** B1
Ouesso *Congo* 1°37N 16°5E **52** D3
Ouest, Pte. de l' *Canada* 49°42N 64°40W **73** C7
Ouezzane *Morocco* 34°51N 5°35W **50** B4
Oughter, L. *Ireland* 54°1N 7°28W **10** B4
Oughterard *Ireland* 53°26N 9°18W **10** C2
Ouidah *Benin* 6°25N 2°0E **50** G6
Oujda *Morocco* 34°41N 1°55W **50** B5
Oulainen *Finland* 64°17N 24°47E **8** D21
Oulu *Finland* 65°1N 25°29E **8** D21
Oulujärvi *Finland* 64°25N 27°15E **8** D22
Oulujoki → *Finland* 65°1N 25°30E **8** D21
Oum Chalouba *Chad* 15°48N 20°46E **51** E10
Oum Hadjer *Chad* 13°18N 19°41E **51** F9
Ounasjoki → *Finland* 66°31N 25°40E **8** C21
Ounguati *Namibia* 22°0S 15°46E **56** C2
Ounianga Kébir *Chad* 19°4N 20°29E **51** E10
Our → *Lux.* 49°55N 6°5E **15** E6
Ouray *U.S.A.* 38°1N 107°40W **77** G10
Ourense *Spain* 42°19N 7°55W **21** A2
Ouricuri *Brazil* 7°53S 40°5W **93** E10
Ourinhos *Brazil* 23°0S 49°54W **95** A6
Ouro Fino *Brazil* 22°16S 46°25W **95** A6
Ouro Prêto *Brazil* 20°20S 43°30W **95** A7
Ourthe → *Belgium* 50°29N 5°35E **15** D5
Ouse → *E. Sussex, U.K.* 50°47N 0°4E **13** G8
Ouse → *N. Yorks., U.K.* 53°44N 0°55W **12** D7
Outaouais → *Canada* 45°27N 74°8W **72** C5
Outardes → *Canada* 49°24N 69°30W **73** C6
Outer Hebrides *U.K.* 57°30N 7°40W **11** D1
Outjo *Namibia* 20°5S 16°7E **56** C2
Outlook *Canada* 51°30N 107°0W **71** C7
Outokumpu *Finland* 62°43N 29°1E **8** E23
Ouyen *Australia* 35°1S 142°22E **63** F3
Ovalau *Fiji* 17°40S 178°48E **59** a
Ovalle *Chile* 30°33S 71°18W **94** C1
Ovamboland *Namibia* 18°30S 16°0E **56** B2
Ovar *Portugal* 40°51N 8°40W **21** B1
Overflakkee *Neths.* 51°44N 4°10E **15** C4
Overijssel □ *Neths.* 52°25N 6°35E **15** B6
Overland Park *U.S.A.* 38°58N 94°40W **80** F6
Overton *U.S.A.* 36°33N 114°27W **79** J12
Övertorneå *Sweden* 66°23N 23°38E **8** C20
Ovid *U.S.A.* 42°41N 76°49W **83** D8
Oviedo *Spain* 43°25N 5°50W **21** A3
Oviši *Latvia* 57°33N 21°44E **9** H19
Ovoot *Mongolia* 45°21N 113°45E **34** B7
Övör Hangay □
  Mongolia 45°0N 102°30E **34** B2
Øvre Årdal *Norway* 61°19N 7°48E **8** F12
Ovruch *Ukraine* 51°25N 28°45E **17** C15
Owaka *N.Z.* 46°27S 169°40E **59** G2
Owambo = Ovamboland
  Namibia 18°30S 16°0E **56** B2
Owasco L. *U.S.A.* 42°50N 76°31W **83** D8
Owase *Japan* 34°7N 136°12E **31** G8
Owatonna *U.S.A.* 44°5N 93°14W **80** C7
Owbeh *Afghan.* 34°28N 63°10E **40** B3
Owego *U.S.A.* 42°6N 76°16W **83** D8
Owen Falls Dam = Nalubaale
  Dam *Uganda* 0°30N 33°5E **54** B3
Owen Sound *Canada* 44°35N 80°55W **82** B4
Owen Stanley Ra.
  Papua N. G. 8°30S 147°0E **58** B7
Oweniny → *Ireland* 54°8N 9°34W **10** B2
Owens → *U.S.A.* 36°32N 117°59W **78** J9
Owens L. *U.S.A.* 36°26N 117°57W **79** J9
Owensboro *U.S.A.* 37°46N 87°7W **80** G10
Owo *Nigeria* 7°10N 5°39E **50** G7
Owosso *U.S.A.* 43°0N 84°10W **81** D11
Owyhee *U.S.A.* 41°57N 116°6W **76** F5
Owyhee → *U.S.A.* 43°49N 117°2W **76** E5
Owyhee, L. *U.S.A.* 43°38N 117°14W **76** E5
Ox Mts. = Slieve Gamph
  Ireland 54°6N 9°0W **10** B3
Öxarfjörður *Iceland* 66°15N 16°45W **8** C5
Oxbow *Canada* 49°14N 102°10W **71** D8
Oxelösund *Sweden* 58°43N 17°15E **9** G17
Oxford *N.Z.* 43°18S 172°11E **59** E4
Oxford *U.K.* 51°46N 1°15W **13** F6
Oxford *Mass., U.S.A.* 42°7N 71°52W **83** D13
Oxford *Miss., U.S.A.* 34°22N 89°31W **85** D10
Oxford *N.C., U.S.A.* 36°19N 78°35W **85** G15
Oxford *N.Y., U.S.A.* 42°27N 75°36W **83** D9
Oxford *Ohio, U.S.A.* 39°31N 84°45W **81** F11
Oxfordshire □ *U.K.* 51°48N 1°16W **13** F6
Oxnard *U.S.A.* 34°12N 119°11W **79** L7
Oxus = Amudarya →
  Uzbekistan 43°58N 59°34E **28** E6
Oya *Malaysia* 2°55N 111°55E **36** D4
Oyama *Japan* 36°18N 139°48E **31** F9
Oyem *Gabon* 1°34N 11°31E **52** D2
Oyen *Canada* 51°22N 110°28W **71** C6
Oykel → *U.K.* 57°56N 4°26W **11** D4
Oymyakon *Russia* 63°25N 142°44E **29** C15
Oyo *Nigeria* 7°46N 3°56E **50** G6
Oyster Bay *U.S.A.* 40°52N 73°32W **83** F11
Öyübari *Japan* 43°1N 142°5E **30** C11
Ozamiz *Phil.* 8°15N 123°50E **37** C6

Ozark *Ala., U.S.A.* 31°28N 85°39W **85** F12
Ozark *Ark., U.S.A.* 35°29N 93°50W **84** D8
Ozark *Mo., U.S.A.* 37°1N 93°12W **80** G7
Ozark Plateau *U.S.A.* 37°20N 91°40W **80** G8
Ozarks, L. of the *U.S.A.* 38°12N 92°38W **80** F7
Ózd *Hungary* 48°14N 20°15E **17** D11
Ozernovskiy *Russia* 51°30N 156°31E **29** D16
Ozette, L. *U.S.A.* 48°6N 124°38W **78** B2
Ozieri *Italy* 40°35N 9°0E **22** D3
Ozona *U.S.A.* 30°43N 101°12W **84** F4
Ozuluama *Mexico* 21°40N 97°51W **87** C5

P

Pa-an *Burma* 16°51N 97°40E **41** L20
Pa Mong Dam *Thailand* 18°0N 102°22E **38** D4
Pa Sak → *Thailand* 15°30N 101°0E **38** E3
Paamiut *Greenland* 62°0N 49°43W **4** C5
Paarl *S. Africa* 33°45S 18°56E **56** E2
Pab Hills *Pakistan* 26°30N 66°45E **42** F2
Pabbay *U.K.* 57°46N 7°14W **11** D1
Pabianice *Poland* 51°40N 19°20E **17** C10
Pabna *Bangla.* 24°1N 89°18E **41** G16
Pabo *Uganda* 3°1N 32°10E **54** B3
Pacaja → *Brazil* 1°56S 50°50W **93** D8
Pacaraima, Sa. *S. Amer.* 4°0N 62°30W **92** C6
Pacasmayo *Peru* 7°20S 79°35W **92** E3
Pachitea → *Peru* 8°46S 74°33W **92** E4
Pachmarhi *India* 22°28N 78°26E **43** H8
Pachpadra *India* 25°58N 72°10E **42** G5
Pachuca *Mexico* 20°7N 98°44W **87** C5
Pacific Antarctic Ridge
  Pac. Oc. 43°0S 115°0W **5** B13
Pacific Grove *U.S.A.* 36°38N 121°56W **78** J5
Pacific Ocean 10°0N 140°0W **65** G14
Pacific Rim △ *Canada* 48°40N 124°45W **78** B2
Pacifica *U.S.A.* 37°37N 122°27W **78** H4
Pacitan *Indonesia* 8°12S 111°7E **37** H14
Packwood *U.S.A.* 46°36N 121°40W **78** D5
Padaido, Kepulauan
  Indonesia 1°15S 136°30E **37** E9
Padang *Riau, Indonesia* 1°30N 102°30E **39** M4
Padang *Sumatera Barat,
  Indonesia* 1°0S 100°20E **36** E2
Padang Endau *Malaysia* 2°40N 103°38E **39** L4
Padangpanjang
  Indonesia 0°40S 100°20E **36** E2
Padangsidempuan
  Indonesia 1°30N 99°15E **36** D1
Paddle Prairie *Canada* 57°57N 117°29W **70** B5
Paderborn *Germany* 51°42N 8°45E **16** C5
Padma *India* 24°12N 85°22E **43** G11
Pádova *Italy* 45°25N 11°53E **22** B4
Padra *India* 22°15N 73°7E **42** H5
Padrauna *India* 26°54N 83°59E **43** F10
Padre I. *U.S.A.* 27°10N 97°25W **84** H6
Padre Island △ *U.S.A.* 27°0N 97°25W **84** H6
Padstow *U.K.* 50°33N 4°58W **13** G3
Padua = Pádova *Italy* 45°25N 11°53E **22** B4
Paducah *Ky., U.S.A.* 37°5N 88°37W **80** G9
Paducah *Tex., U.S.A.* 34°1N 100°18W **84** D4
Paea *Tahiti* 17°41S 149°35W **59** d
Paeroa *N.Z.* 37°23S 175°41E **59** B5
Pafúri *Mozam.* 22°28S 31°17E **57** C5
Pag *Croatia* 44°25N 15°3E **16** F8
Pagadian *Phil.* 7°55N 123°30E **37** C6
Pagai Selatan, Pulau
  Indonesia 3°0S 100°15E **36** E2
Pagai Utara, Pulau
  Indonesia 2°35S 100°0E **36** E2
Pagalu = Annobón *Atl. Oc.* 1°25S 5°36E **49** G4
Pagara *India* 24°22N 80°1E **43** G9
Pagastikos Kolpos
  Greece 39°15N 23°0E **23** E10
Pagatan *Indonesia* 3°33S 115°59E **36** E5
Page *U.S.A.* 36°57N 111°27W **77** H8
Paget, Mt. *S. Georgia* 54°26S 36°31W **96** G9
Pago Pago *Amer. Samoa* 14°16S 170°43W **59** b
Pagosa Springs *U.S.A.* 37°16N 107°1W **77** H10
Pagwa River *Canada* 50°2N 85°14W **72** B2
Pāhala *U.S.A.* 19°12N 155°29W **74** b
Pahang → *Malaysia* 3°30N 103°9E **39** L4
Pahiatua *N.Z.* 40°27S 175°50E **59** D5
Pahokee *U.S.A.* 26°50N 80°40W **85** H14
Pahrump *U.S.A.* 36°12N 115°59W **79** J11
Pahute Mesa *U.S.A.* 37°20N 116°45W **78** H10
Pai *Thailand* 19°19N 98°27E **38** C2
Paicines *U.S.A.* 36°44N 121°17W **78** J5
Paide *Estonia* 58°53N 25°33E **9** G21
Paignton *U.K.* 50°26N 3°35W **13** G4
Päijänne *Finland* 61°30N 25°30E **8** F21
Pailani *India* 25°45N 80°26E **43** G9
Pailin *Cambodia* 12°46N 102°36E **38** F4
Painan *Indonesia* 1°21S 100°34E **36** E2
Painesville *U.S.A.* 41°43N 81°15W **82** E3
Paint Hills = Wemindji
  Canada 53°0N 78°49W **72** B4
Paint L. *Canada* 55°28N 97°57W **71** B9
Painted Desert *U.S.A.* 36°0N 111°0W **77** J8
Paintsville *U.S.A.* 37°49N 82°48W **81** G12
País Vasco □ *Spain* 42°50N 2°45W **21** A4
Paisley *Canada* 44°18N 81°16W **82** B3
Paisley *U.K.* 55°50N 4°25W **11** F4
Paita *Peru* 5°11S 81°9W **92** E2
Pajares, Puerto de *Spain* 42°58N 5°46W **21** A3
Pak Lay *Laos* 18°15N 101°27E **38** C3
Pak Phanang *Thailand* 8°21N 100°12E **39** H3
Pak Sane *Laos* 18°22N 103°39E **38** C4
Pak Song *Laos* 15°11N 106°14E **38** E6
Pak Suong *Laos* 19°58N 102°14E **38** C4
Pak Tam Chung *China* 22°24N 114°19E **33** a
Pakaur *India* 24°38N 87°51E **43** G12
Pakch'ŏn *N. Korea* 39°44N 125°35E **35** E13
Pakenham *Canada* 45°18N 76°18W **83** A8

Pakhuis *S. Africa* 32°9S 19°5E **56** E2
Pakistan ■ *Asia* 30°0N 70°0E **42** E4
Pakkading *Laos* 18°19N 103°59E **38** C4
Pakokku *Burma* 21°20N 95°0E **41** J19
Pakowki L. *Canada* 49°20N 111°0W **71** D6
Pakpattan *Pakistan* 30°25N 73°27E **42** D5
Paktīā □ *Afghan.* 33°30N 69°15E **40** C6
Paktīkā □ *Afghan.* 32°30N 69°0E **40** C6
Pakwach *Uganda* 2°28N 31°27E **54** B3
Pakxe *Laos* 15°5N 105°52E **38** E5
Pala *Chad* 9°25N 15°5E **51** G9
Pala *Dem. Rep. of the Congo* 6°45S 29°30E **54** D2
Pala *U.S.A.* 33°22N 117°5W **79** M9
Palabek *Uganda* 3°22N 32°33E **54** B3
Palacios *U.S.A.* 28°42N 96°13W **84** G6
Palagruža *Croatia* 42°24N 16°15E **22** C7
Palam *India* 19°0N 77°0E **40** K10
Palampur *India* 32°10N 76°30E **42** C7
Palana *Australia* 39°45S 147°55E **63** F4
Palana *Russia* 59°10N 159°59E **29** D16
Palanan *Phil.* 17°8N 122°29E **37** A6
Palanan Pt. *Phil.* 17°17N 122°30E **37** A6
Palandri *Pakistan* 33°42N 73°40E **43** C5
Palanga *Lithuania* 55°58N 21°3E **9** J19
Palangkaraya *Indonesia* 2°16S 113°56E **36** E4
Palani Hills *India* 10°14N 77°33E **40** P10
Palanpur *India* 24°10N 72°25E **42** G5
Palapye *Botswana* 22°30S 27°7E **56** C4
Palas *Pakistan* 35°4N 73°14E **43** B5
Palasponga *India* 21°47N 85°34E **43** J11
Palatka *Russia* 60°6N 150°54E **29** C16
Palatka *U.S.A.* 29°39N 81°38W **85** G14
Palau ■ *Palau* 7°30N 134°30E **58** A6
Palauk *Burma* 13°10N 98°40E **38** F2
Palawan *Phil.* 9°30N 118°30E **36** C5
Palayankottai *India* 8°45N 77°45E **40** Q10
Paldiski *Estonia* 59°23N 24°9E **9** G21
Paleleh *Indonesia* 1°10N 121°50E **37** D6
Palembang *Indonesia* 3°0S 104°50E **36** E2
Palencia *Spain* 42°1N 4°34W **21** A3
Palenque *Mexico* 17°39N 91°58W **87** D6
Paleochora *Greece* 35°16N 23°39E **25** D5
Paleokastritsa *Greece* 39°40N 19°41E **25** A3
Paleometokho *Cyprus* 35°7N 33°11E **25** D12
Palermo *Italy* 38°7N 13°22E **22** E5
Palermo *U.S.A.* 39°26N 121°33W **78** F5
Palestina *Chile* 23°50S 69°47W **96** A3
Palestine *Asia* 32°0N 35°0E **46** D4
Palestine *U.S.A.* 31°46N 95°38W **84** F7
Paletwa *Burma* 21°10N 92°50E **41** J18
Palghat *India* 10°46N 76°42E **40** P10
Palgrave, Mt. *Australia* 23°22S 115°58E **60** D2
Pali *India* 25°50N 73°20E **42** G5
Palikir *Micronesia* 6°55N 158°9E **64** G7
Paliouri, Ákra *Greece* 39°57N 23°45E **23** E10
Palisades Res. *U.S.A.* 43°20N 111°12W **76** E8
Paliseul *Belgium* 49°54N 5°8E **15** E5
Palitana *India* 21°32N 71°49E **42** J4
Palizada *Mexico* 18°15N 92°8W **87** D6
Palk Bay *Asia* 9°30N 79°15E **40** Q11
Palk Strait *Asia* 10°0N 79°45E **40** Q11
Palkānbará *Iraq* 35°49N 44°26E **44** C5
Palkot *India* 22°53N 84°39E **43** H11
Pallanza = Verbánia *Italy* 45°56N 8°33E **20** D8
Pallarenda *Australia* 19°12S 146°46E **62** B4
Pallinup → *Australia* 34°27S 118°50E **61** F2
Pallisa *Uganda* 1°12N 33°43E **54** B3
Pallu *India* 28°59N 74°14E **42** E6
Palm Bay *U.S.A.* 28°2N 80°35W **85** G14
Palm Beach *U.S.A.* 26°43N 80°2W **85** H14
Palm Coast *U.S.A.* 29°35N 81°12W **85** G14
Palm Desert *U.S.A.* 33°43N 116°22W **79** M10
Palm Is. *Australia* 18°40S 146°35E **62** B4
Palm Springs *U.S.A.* 33°50N 116°33W **79** M10
Palma *Mozam.* 10°46S 40°29E **55** E5
Palma, B. de *Spain* 39°30N 2°39E **24** B9
Palma Soriano *Cuba* 20°15N 76°0W **88** B4
Palmanova *Spain* 39°32N 2°34E **24** B9
Palmares *Brazil* 8°41S 35°28W **93** E11
Palmas *Brazil* 26°29S 52°0W **95** B5
Pálmas, G. di *Italy* 39°0N 8°30E **22** E3
Palmdale *U.S.A.* 34°35N 118°7W **79** L8
Palmeira das Missões
  Brazil 27°55S 53°17W **95** B5
Palmeira dos Índios
  Brazil 9°25S 36°37W **93** E11
Palmer *Antarctica* 64°35S 65°0W **5** C17
Palmer *U.S.A.* 61°36N 149°7W **68** C5
Palmer → *Australia* 16°0S 142°26E **62** B3
Palmer Arch. *Antarctica* 64°15S 65°0W **5** C17
Palmer Lake *U.S.A.* 39°7N 104°55W **76** G11
Palmer Land *Antarctica* 73°0S 63°0W **5** D18
Palmerston *Australia* 12°31S 130°59E **60** B5
Palmerston *Canada* 43°50N 80°51W **82** C4
Palmerston *N.Z.* 45°29S 170°43E **59** F3
Palmerston North *N.Z.* 40°21S 175°39E **59** D5
Palmetto *U.S.A.* 27°31N 82°34W **85** H13
Palmi *Italy* 38°21N 15°51E **22** E6
Palmira *Argentina* 32°59S 68°34W **94** C2
Palmira *Colombia* 3°32N 76°16W **92** C3
Palmyra = Tudmur
  Syria 34°36N 38°15E **44** C3
Palmyra *Mo., U.S.A.* 39°48N 91°32W **80** F8
Palmyra *N.J., U.S.A.* 40°0N 75°1W **83** F9
Palmyra *N.Y., U.S.A.* 43°5N 77°18W **82** C7
Palmyra *Pa., U.S.A.* 40°18N 76°36W **83** F8
Palmyra Is. *Pac. Oc.* 5°52N 162°5W **65** G11
Palo Alto *U.S.A.* 37°27N 122°10W **78** H4
Palo Seco *Trin. & Tob.* 10°4N 61°36W **93** K15
Palo Verde *U.S.A.* 33°26N 114°44W **79** M12

Palo Verde △ Costa Rica 10°21N 85°21W 88 D2
Palomar Mt. U.S.A. 33°22N 116°50W 79 M10
Palopo Indonesia 3°0S 120°16E 37 E6
Palos, C. de Spain 37°38N 0°40W 21 D5
Palos Verdes, Pt. U.S.A. 33°46N 118°25W 79 M8
Palos Verdes Estates U.S.A. 33°48N 118°23W 79 M8
Palu Indonesia 1°0S 119°52E 37 E5
Palu Turkey 38°45N 40°0E 44 B3
Palwal India 28°8N 77°19E 42 E7
Pamanukan Indonesia 6°16S 107°49E 37 G12
Pamekasan Indonesia 7°10S 113°28E 37 G15
Pamenang Indonesia 8°24S 116°6E 37 J19
Pamiers France 43°7N 1°39E 20 E4
Pamir Tajikistan 37°40N 73°0E 28 F8
Pamlico → U.S.A. 35°20N 76°28W 85 D16
Pamlico Sd. U.S.A. 35°20N 76°0W 85 D17
Pampa U.S.A. 35°32N 100°58W 84 D4
Pampa de las Salinas Argentina 32°1S 66°58W 94 C2
Pampanua Indonesia 4°16S 120°8E 37 E6
Pampas Argentina 35°0S 63°0W 94 D3
Pampas Peru 12°20S 74°50W 92 F4
Pamplona Colombia 7°23N 72°39W 92 B4
Pamplona-Iruña Spain 42°48N 1°38W 21 A5
Pampoenpoort S. Africa 31°3S 22°40E 56 E3
Pan de Azúcar Chile 24°5S 68°10W 94 A2
Pan de Azúcar △ Chile 26°0S 70°40W 94 B1
Pana U.S.A. 39°23N 89°5W 80 F9
Panaca U.S.A. 37°47N 114°23W 77 H6
Panaitan Indonesia 6°36S 105°12E 37 G11
Panaji India 15°25N 73°50E 40 M8
Panamá Panama 9°0N 79°25W 88 E4
Panama ■ Cent. Amer. 8°48N 79°55W 88 E4
Panamá, G. de Panama 8°4N 79°20W 88 E4
Panama, Isthmus of Cent. Amer. 9°0N 79°0W 66 J12
Panama Basin Pac. Oc. 5°0N 83°30W 65 G19
Panama Canal Panama 9°10N 79°37W 88 E4
Panama City U.S.A. 30°10N 85°40W 85 F12
Panamint Range U.S.A. 36°20N 117°20W 79 J9
Panamint Springs U.S.A. 36°20N 117°28W 79 J9
Panão Peru 9°55S 75°55W 92 E3
Panare Thailand 6°51N 101°30E 39 J3
Panay Phil. 11°10N 122°30E 37 B6
Panay, G. Phil. 11°0N 122°30E 37 B6
Panayarvi △ Russia 66°16N 30°10E 8 C24
Pančevo Serbia 44°52N 20°41E 23 B9
Panda Mozam. 24°2S 34°45E 57 C5
Pandan Malaysia 1°32N 103°46E 39 d
Pandan Phil. 11°45N 122°10E 37 B6
Pandan, Selat Singapore 1°15N 103°44E 39 d
Pandan Tampoi = Tampoi Malaysia 1°30N 103°39E 39 d
Pandegelang Indonesia 6°25S 106°5E 37 G12
Pandhana India 21°42N 76°13E 42 J7
Pandharpur India 17°41N 75°20E 40 L9
Pando Uruguay 34°44S 56°0W 95 C4
Pando, L. = Hope, L. Australia 28°24S 139°18E 63 D2
Pandokratoras Greece 39°45N 19°50E 25 A3
Pandora Costa Rica 9°43N 83°3W 88 E3
Panevėžys Lithuania 55°42N 24°25E 9 J21
Pang-Long Burma 23°11N 98°45E 41 H21
Pang Sida △ Thailand 14°5N 102°17E 38 E4
Pang-Yang Burma 22°7N 98°48E 41 H21
Panga Dem. Rep. of the Congo 1°52N 26°18E 54 B2
Pangalanes, Canal des = Ampangalana, Lakandranon' Madag. 22°48S 47°50E 57 C8
Pangani Tanzania 5°25S 38°58E 54 D4
Pangani → Tanzania 5°26S 38°58E 54 D4
Pangfou = Bengbu China 32°58N 117°20E 35 H9
Pangil Dem. Rep. of the Congo 3°10S 26°35E 54 C2
Pangkah, Tanjung Indonesia 6°51S 112°33E 37 G15
Pangkajene Indonesia 4°46S 119°34E 37 E5
Pangkalanbrandan Indonesia 4°1N 98°20E 36 D1
Pangkalanbuun Indonesia 2°41S 111°37E 36 E4
Pangkalpinang Indonesia 2°0S 106°0E 36 E3
Pangkor, P. Malaysia 4°13N 100°34E 39 K3
Pangnirtung Canada 66°8N 65°43W 69 C13
Pangody Russia 65°52N 74°27E 28 C8
Panguitch U.S.A. 37°50N 112°26W 77 H7
Pangutaran Group Phil. 6°18N 120°34E 37 C6
Panhandle U.S.A. 35°21N 101°23W 84 D4
Pani Mines India 22°29N 73°50E 42 H5
Pania-Mutombo Dem. Rep. of the Congo 5°11S 23°51E 54 D1
Panikota I. India 20°46N 71°21E 42 J4
Panipat India 29°25N 77°2E 42 E7
Panjal Range = Pir Panjal Range India 32°30N 76°50E 42 C7
Panjang, Hon Vietnam 9°20N 103°28E 39 H4
Panjgur Pakistan 27°0N 64°5E 40 F4
Panjim = Panaji India 15°25N 73°50E 40 M8
Panjin China 41°3N 122°2E 35 D12
Panjnad → Pakistan 28°57N 70°30E 42 E4
Panjnad Barrage Pakistan 29°22N 71°15E 42 E4
Panjwai Afghan. 31°26N 65°27E 42 D1
Panmunjŏm N. Korea 37°59N 126°38E 35 F14
Panna India 24°40N 80°15E 43 G9
Panna △ India 24°40N 80°0E 43 G8
Panna Hills India 24°40N 81°15E 43 G9
Pannawonica Australia 21°39S 116°19E 60 D2
Pannga, Tanjung Indonesia 8°54S 116°2E 37 K19
Pannirtuuq = Pangnirtung Canada 66°8N 65°43W 69 C13
Pano Akil Pakistan 27°51N 69°7E 42 F3
Pano Lefkara Cyprus 34°53N 33°20E 25 E12
Pano Panayia Cyprus 34°55N 32°38E 25 E11
Panorama Brazil 21°21S 51°51W 95 A5
Panormos Greece 35°25N 24°41E 25 D6
Pansemal India 21°39N 74°42E 42 J6
Panshan = Panjin China 41°3N 122°2E 35 D12
Panshi China 42°58N 126°5E 35 C14
Pantanal Brazil 17°30S 57°40W 92 H7
Pantanos de Centla ⌂ Mexico 18°25N 92°25W 87 D6
Pantar Indonesia 8°28S 124°10E 37 F6
Pante Macassar E. Timor 9°30S 123°58E 37 F6
Pantelleria Italy 36°50N 11°57E 22 F4
Pánuco Mexico 22°3N 98°10W 87 C5
Panzhihua China 26°33N 101°44E 32 D5
Paola Malta 35°52N 14°30E 25 D2
Paola U.S.A. 38°35N 94°53W 80 F6
Paonia U.S.A. 38°52N 107°36W 76 G10
Paopao Moorea 17°30S 149°49W 59 d
Paoting = Baoding China 38°50N 115°28E 34 E8
Paot'ou = Baotou China 40°32N 110°2E 34 D6
Paoua C.A.R. 7°9N 16°20E 52 C3
Pápa Hungary 47°22N 17°30E 17 E9
Papa Stour U.K. 60°20N 1°42W 11 A7
Papa Westray U.K. 59°20N 2°55W 11 B6
Papagayo → Mexico 16°46N 99°43W 87 D5
Papagayo, G. de Costa Rica 10°30N 85°50W 88 D2
Papakura N.Z. 37°4S 174°59E 59 B5
Papantla Mexico 20°27N 97°19W 87 C5
Papar Malaysia 5°45N 116°0E 36 C5
Papara Tahiti 17°43S 149°31W 59 d
Paparoa △ N.Z. 42°7S 171°26E 59 E3
Papeete Tahiti 17°32S 149°34W 59 d
Papenoo Tahiti 17°30S 149°25W 59 d
Papenoo → Tahiti 17°30S 149°25W 59 d
Papetoai Moorea 17°29S 149°52W 59 d
Paphos Cyprus 34°46N 32°25E 25 E11
Paposo Chile 25°0S 70°30W 94 B1
Papoutsa Cyprus 34°54N 33°4E 25 E12
Papua □ Indonesia 4°0S 137°0E 37 E9
Papua, G. of Papua N. G. 9°0S 144°50E 58 B7
Papua New Guinea ■ Oceania 8°0S 145°0E 58 B7
Papudo Chile 32°29S 71°27W 94 C1
Papun Burma 18°2N 97°30E 41 K20
Papunya Australia 23°15S 131°54E 60 D5
Pará = Belém Brazil 1°20S 48°30W 93 D9
Pará □ Brazil 3°20S 52°0W 93 D8
Paraburdoo Australia 23°14S 117°32E 60 D2
Paracatu Brazil 17°10S 46°50W 93 G9
Paracel Is. S. China Sea 15°50N 112°0E 36 A4
Parachilna Australia 31°10S 138°21E 63 E2
Parachinar Pakistan 33°55N 70°5E 42 C4
Paradip India 20°15N 86°35E 41 J15
Paradise Calif., U.S.A. 39°46N 121°37W 78 F5
Paradise Nev., U.S.A. 36°5N 115°8W 79 J11
Paradise → Canada 53°27N 57°19W 73 B8
Paradise Hill Canada 53°32N 109°28W 71 C7
Paradise River Canada 53°27N 57°17W 73 B8
Paradise Valley U.S.A. 41°30N 117°32W 76 F5
Paradisi Greece 36°18N 28°7E 25 C10
Parado Indonesia 8°42S 118°30E 37 F5
Paragould U.S.A. 36°3N 90°29W 85 C9
Paragua → Venezuela 6°55N 62°55W 92 B6
Paraguaçú → Brazil 12°45S 38°54W 93 F11
Paraguaçu Paulista Brazil 22°22S 50°35W 95 A5
Paraguaná, Pen. de Venezuela 12°0N 70°0W 92 A5
Paraguarí Paraguay 25°36S 57°0W 94 B4
Paraguarí □ Paraguay 26°0S 57°10W 94 B4
Paraguay ■ S. Amer. 23°0S 57°0W 94 A4
Paraguay → Paraguay 27°18S 58°38W 94 B4
Paraíba = João Pessoa Brazil 7°10S 34°52W 93 E12
Paraíba □ Brazil 7°0S 36°0W 93 E11
Paraíba do Sul → Brazil 21°37S 41°3W 95 A7
Parainen Finland 60°18N 22°18E 9 F20
Paraíso Mexico 18°24N 93°14W 87 D6
Parak Iran 27°38N 52°25E 45 E7
Parakou Benin 9°25N 2°40E 50 G6
Paralimni Cyprus 35°2N 33°58E 25 D12
Paramaribo Suriname 5°50N 55°10W 93 B7
Páramos del Batallón y La Negra △ Venezuela 8°2N 71°55W 89 E5
Paramushir, Ostrov Russia 50°24N 156°0E 29 D16
Paran → Israel 30°20N 35°10E 46 E4
Paraná Argentina 31°45S 60°30W 94 C3
Paraná Brazil 12°30S 47°48W 93 F9
Paraná □ Brazil 24°30S 51°0W 95 A5
Paraná → Argentina 33°43S 59°15W 94 C4
Paranaguá Brazil 25°30S 48°30W 95 B6
Paranaíba Brazil 19°40S 51°11W 93 G8
Paranaíba → Brazil 20°6S 51°4W 93 H8
Paranapanema → Brazil 22°40S 53°9W 95 A5
Paranapiacaba, Serra do Brazil 24°31S 48°35W 95 A6
Paranavaí Brazil 23°4S 52°56W 95 A5
Parang Maguindanao, Phil. 7°23N 124°16E 37 C6
Parang Sulu, Phil. 5°55N 120°54E 37 C6
Parângul Mare, Vf. Romania 45°20N 23°37E 17 F12
Paraparaumu N.Z. 40°57S 175°3E 59 D5
Parbati → Mad. P., India 25°50N 76°30E 42 G7
Parbati → Raj., India 26°54N 77°53E 42 F7
Parbhani India 19°8N 76°52E 40 K10
Parchim Germany 53°26N 11°52E 16 B6
Pardes Hanna-Karkur Israel 32°28N 34°57E 46 C3
Pardo → Bahia, Brazil 15°40S 39°0W 93 G11
Pardo → Mato Grosso, Brazil 21°46S 52°9W 95 A5
Pardoo Roadhouse Australia 20°6S 119°3E 60 D2
Pardubice Czech Rep. 50°3N 15°45E 16 C8
Pare Indonesia 7°43S 112°12E 37 G15
Pare Mts. Tanzania 4°0S 37°45E 54 C4
Parecis, Serra dos Brazil 13°0S 60°0W 92 F7
Paren Russia 62°30N 163°15E 29 C17
Parent Canada 47°55N 74°35W 72 C5
Parent, L. Canada 48°31N 77°1W 72 C4
Parepare Indonesia 4°0S 119°40E 37 E5
Parga Greece 39°15N 20°29E 23 E9
Pargas = Parainen Finland 60°18N 22°18E 9 F20
Pargo, Pta. do Madeira 32°49N 17°17W 24 D2
Parham Canada 44°39N 76°43W 83 B8
Paria → U.S.A. 36°52N 111°36W 77 H8
Paria, G. de Venezuela 10°20N 62°0W 93 K14
Pariaguán Venezuela 8°51N 64°34W 92 B6
Paricutín, Cerro Mexico 19°28N 102°15W 86 D4
Parigi Indonesia 0°50S 120°5E 37 E6
Parika Guyana 6°50N 58°20W 92 B7
Parikkala Finland 61°33N 29°31E 8 F23
Parima, Serra Brazil 2°30N 64°0W 92 C6
Parinari Peru 4°35S 74°25W 92 D4
Pariñas, Pta. S. Amer. 4°30S 82°0W 90 D2
Parintins Brazil 2°40S 56°50W 93 D7
Pariparit Kyun Burma 14°55N 93°45E 41 M18
Paris Canada 43°12N 80°25W 82 C4
Paris France 48°53N 2°20E 20 B5
Paris Idaho, U.S.A. 42°14N 111°24W 76 E8
Paris Ky., U.S.A. 38°13N 84°15W 81 F11
Paris Tenn., U.S.A. 36°18N 88°19W 85 C10
Paris Tex., U.S.A. 33°40N 95°33W 84 E7
Parish U.S.A. 43°25N 76°8W 83 C8
Parishville U.S.A. 44°38N 74°49W 83 B10
Park U.S.A. 48°45N 122°18W 78 B4
Park City U.S.A. 37°48N 97°20W 80 G5
Park Falls U.S.A. 45°56N 90°27W 80 C8
Park Head Canada 44°36N 81°9W 82 B3
Park Hills U.S.A. 37°51N 90°51W 80 G8
Park Range U.S.A. 40°41N 106°41W 76 F10
Park Rapids U.S.A. 46°55N 95°4W 80 B6
Park River U.S.A. 48°24N 97°45W 80 A5
Park Rynie S. Africa 30°25S 30°45E 57 E5
Parkā Bandar Iran 25°55N 59°35E 45 E8
Parkano Finland 62°1N 23°0E 8 E20
Parker Ariz., U.S.A. 34°9N 114°17W 79 L12
Parker Pa., U.S.A. 41°5N 79°41W 82 E5
Parker Dam U.S.A. 34°18N 114°8W 79 L12
Parkersburg U.S.A. 39°16N 81°34W 81 F13
Parkes Australia 33°9S 148°11E 63 E4
Parkfield U.S.A. 35°54N 120°26W 78 K6
Parkhill Canada 43°15N 81°38W 82 C3
Parkland U.S.A. 47°9N 122°26W 78 C4
Parkston U.S.A. 43°24N 97°59W 80 D5
Parksville Canada 49°20N 124°21W 70 D4
Parkway U.S.A. 38°32N 121°26W 78 G5
Parla Spain 40°14N 3°46W 21 B4
Parma Italy 44°48N 10°20E 20 D9
Parma Idaho, U.S.A. 43°47N 116°57W 76 E5
Parma Ohio, U.S.A. 41°24N 81°43W 82 E3
Parnaguá Brazil 10°10S 44°38W 93 F10
Parnaíba Brazil 2°54S 41°47W 93 D10
Parnaíba → Brazil 3°0S 41°50W 93 D10
Parnassos Greece 38°35N 22°30E 23 E10
Pärnu Estonia 58°28N 24°33E 9 G21
Paro Dzong Bhutan 27°32N 89°53E 43 F13
Paroo → Australia 31°28S 143°32E 63 E3
Paroo-Darling △ Australia 31°32S 144°0E 63 E3
Paros Greece 37°5N 25°12E 23 F11
Parowan U.S.A. 37°51N 112°50W 77 H7
Parral Chile 36°10S 71°52W 94 D1
Parramatta Australia 33°48S 151°1E 63 B5
Parras Mexico 25°25N 102°11W 86 B4
Parrett → U.K. 51°12N 3°1W 13 F4
Parris I. U.S.A. 32°20N 80°41W 85 E14
Parrsboro Canada 45°30N 64°25W 73 C7
Parry I. Canada 45°18N 80°10W 82 A4
Parry Is. Canada 77°0N 110°0W 69 B9
Parry Sound Canada 45°20N 80°0W 82 A5
Parsaloi Kenya 1°16N 36°51E 54 B4
Parsnip → Canada 55°10N 123°2W 70 B4
Parsons U.S.A. 37°20N 95°16W 80 G6
Parsons Ra. Australia 13°30S 135°15E 62 A2
Partinico Italy 38°3N 13°7E 22 E5
Partizansk Russia 43°8N 133°9E 30 C6
Partridge I. Canada 55°59N 87°37W 72 A2
Partry Mts. Ireland 53°40N 9°28W 10 C2
Paru → Brazil 1°33S 52°38W 93 D8
Parvān □ Afghan. 35°0N 69°0E 40 B6
Parvatipuram India 18°50N 83°25E 41 K13
Parvatsar India 26°52N 74°49E 42 F6
Parys S. Africa 26°52S 27°29E 56 D4
Pas, Pta. des Spain 38°46N 1°26E 24 C7
Pas, The Canada 53°45N 101°15W 71 C8
Pasadena Canada 49°1N 57°36W 73 C8
Pasadena Calif., U.S.A. 34°9N 118°8W 79 L8
Pasadena Tex., U.S.A. 29°43N 95°13W 84 G7
Pasaje → Argentina 25°39S 63°56W 94 B3
Pasar Indonesia 8°27S 114°54E 37 J17
Pascagoula U.S.A. 30°21N 88°33W 85 F10
Pascagoula → U.S.A. 30°23N 88°37W 85 F10
Paşcani Romania 47°14N 26°45E 17 E14
Pasco U.S.A. 46°14N 119°6W 76 C4
Pasco, Cerro de Peru 10°45S 76°10W 92 F3
Pasco I. Australia 20°57S 115°20E 60 D2
Pascoag U.S.A. 41°57N 71°42W 83 E13
Pascua, I. de Chile 27°7S 109°23W 65 K17
Pasfield L. Canada 58°24N 105°20W 71 B7
Pasir Mas Malaysia 6°2N 102°8E 39 J4
Pasir Panjang Singapore 1°18N 103°46E 39 d
Pasir Putih Malaysia 5°50N 102°24E 39 K4
Pasirian Indonesia 8°13S 113°8E 37 H15
Pasirkuning Indonesia 0°30S 104°33E 36 E2
Paskūh Iran 27°34N 61°39E 45 E9
Pasley, C. Australia 33°52S 123°35E 61 F3
Pašman Croatia 43°58N 15°20E 16 G8
Pasni Pakistan 25°15N 63°27E 40 G3
Paso Bravo △ Paraguay 22°32S 57°5W 94 A4
Paso Cantinela Mexico 32°33N 115°47W 79 N11
Paso de Indios Argentina 43°55S 69°0W 96 E3
Paso de los Libres Argentina 29°44S 57°10W 94 B4
Paso de los Toros Uruguay 32°45S 56°30W 94 C4
Paso Robles U.S.A. 35°38N 120°41W 78 K6
Paspébiac Canada 48°3N 65°17W 73 C6
Pasrur Pakistan 32°16N 74°43E 42 C6
Passage East Ireland 52°14N 7°0W 10 D5
Passage West Ireland 51°52N 8°21W 10 E3
Passaic U.S.A. 40°51N 74°7W 83 F10
Passau Germany 48°34N 13°28E 16 D7
Passero, C. Italy 36°41N 15°10E 22 F6
Passo Fundo Brazil 28°10S 52°20W 95 B5
Passos Brazil 20°45S 46°37W 93 H9
Pastavy Belarus 55°4N 26°50E 9 J22
Pastaza → Peru 4°50S 76°52W 92 D3
Pasto Colombia 1°13N 77°17W 92 C3
Pasuruan Indonesia 7°40S 112°44E 37 G15
Patagonia Argentina 45°0S 69°0W 96 F3
Patagonia U.S.A. 31°33N 110°45W 77 L8
Patambar Iran 29°45N 60°17E 45 D9
Patan = Lalitapur Nepal 27°40N 85°20E 43 F11
Patan India 23°54N 72°14E 42 H5
Patani Indonesia 0°20N 128°50E 37 D7
Pataudi India 28°18N 76°48E 42 E7
Patchewollock Australia 35°22S 142°12E 63 F3
Patchogue U.S.A. 40°46N 73°1W 83 F11
Pate Kenya 2°10S 41°0E 54 C5
Patea N.Z. 39°45S 174°30E 59 C5
Patensie S. Africa 33°46S 24°49E 56 E3
Paternò Italy 37°34N 14°54E 22 F6
Pateros U.S.A. 48°3N 119°54W 76 B4
Paterson U.S.A. 40°54N 74°9W 83 F10
Paterson Ra. Australia 21°45S 122°10E 60 D3
Pathankot India 32°18N 75°45E 42 C6
Pathein = Bassein Burma 16°45N 94°30E 41 L19
Pathfinder Res. U.S.A. 42°28N 106°51W 76 E10
Pathiu Thailand 10°42N 99°19E 39 G2
Pathum Thani Thailand 14°1N 100°32E 38 E3
Pati Indonesia 6°45S 111°1E 37 G14
Patía → Colombia 2°13N 78°40W 92 C3
Patiala Punjab, India 30°23N 76°26E 42 D7
Patiala Ut. P., India 27°43N 79°1E 43 F8
Patkai Bum India 27°0N 95°30E 41 F19
Patmos Greece 37°21N 26°36E 23 F12
Patna India 25°35N 85°12E 43 G11
Pato Branco Brazil 26°13S 52°40W 95 B5
Patong, Ao Thailand 7°54N 98°17E 39 a
Patonga Uganda 2°45N 33°15E 54 B3
Patos Brazil 6°55S 37°16W 93 E11
Patos, L. dos Brazil 31°20S 51°0W 95 C5
Patos, Río de los → Argentina 31°18S 69°25W 94 C2
Patos de Minas Brazil 18°35S 46°32W 93 G9
Patquía Argentina 30°2S 66°55W 94 C2
Patra Greece 38°14N 21°47E 23 E9
Patraikos Kolpos Greece 38°17N 21°30E 23 E9
Patras = Patra Greece 38°14N 21°47E 23 E9
Patriot Hills Antarctica 82°20S 81°25W 5 E16
Patrocínio Brazil 18°57S 47°0W 93 G9
Pattani Thailand 6°48N 101°15E 39 J3
Pattaya Thailand 12°52N 100°55E 38 F3
Patten U.S.A. 46°0N 68°38W 81 B19
Patterson Calif., U.S.A. 37°28N 121°8W 78 H5
Patterson La., U.S.A. 29°42N 91°18W 84 G9
Patterson, Mt. U.S.A. 38°29N 119°20W 78 G7
Patti Punjab, India 31°17N 74°54E 42 D6
Patti Ut. P., India 25°55N 82°12E 43 G10
Pattoki Pakistan 31°5N 73°52E 42 D5
Patton U.S.A. 40°38N 78°39W 82 F6
Patuakhali Bangla. 22°20N 90°25E 41 H17
Patuanak Canada 55°55N 107°43W 71 B7
Patuca → Honduras 15°50N 84°18W 88 C3
Patuca, Punta Honduras 15°49N 84°14W 88 C3
Patuca △ Honduras 14°30N 85°30W 88 D2
Patvinsuo △ Finland 63°7N 30°45E 8 E24
Pátzcuaro Mexico 19°31N 101°38W 86 D4
Pau France 43°19N 0°25W 20 E3
Paudash Canada 44°59N 77°58W 82 B7
Pauk Burma 21°27N 94°30E 41 J19
Paul I. Canada 56°30N 61°20W 73 A7
Paul Smiths U.S.A. 44°26N 74°15W 83 B10
Paulatuk Canada 69°25N 124°0W 68 C7
Paulding Bay S. Ocean 66°0S 118°0E 5 C8
Paulistana Brazil 8°9S 41°9W 93 E10
Paulo Afonso Brazil 9°21S 38°15W 93 E11
Paulpietersburg S. Africa 27°23S 30°50E 57 D5
Pauls Valley U.S.A. 34°44N 97°13W 84 D6
Pauma Valley U.S.A. 33°16N 116°58W 79 M10
Pauri India 30°9N 78°47E 43 D8
Pāveh Iran 35°3N 46°22E 44 C5
Pavia Italy 45°7N 9°8E 20 D8
Pavilion U.S.A. 42°52N 78°1W 82 D6
Pāvilosta Latvia 56°53N 21°14E 9 H19
Pavlodar Kazakhstan 52°33N 77°0E 28 D8
Pavlograd = Pavlohrad Ukraine 48°30N 35°52E 19 E6
Pavlohrad Ukraine 48°30N 35°52E 19 E6
Pavlovo Russia 55°58N 43°5E 18 C7
Pavlovsk Russia 50°26N 40°5E 19 D7
Pavlovskaya Russia 46°17N 39°47E 19 E6
Pawai, Pulau Singapore 1°11N 103°44E 39 d
Pawayan India 28°4N 80°6E 43 E9
Pawhuska U.S.A. 36°40N 96°20W 84 C6
Pawling U.S.A. 41°34N 73°36W 83 E11
Pawnee U.S.A. 36°20N 96°48W 84 C6
Pawnee City U.S.A. 40°7N 96°9W 80 E5
Pawtucket U.S.A. 41°53N 71°23W 83 E13
Paxi Greece 39°14N 20°12E 23 E9
Paximadia Greece 35°0N 24°35E 25 E6
Paxton U.S.A. 40°27N 88°6W 80 E9
Payakumbuh Indonesia 0°20S 100°35E 36 E2
Payette U.S.A. 44°5N 116°56W 76 D5
Payne Bay = Kangirsuk Canada 60°0N 70°0W 69 D13
Payne L. Canada 59°30N 74°30W 69 D12
Paynes Find Australia 29°15S 117°42E 61 E2
Paynesville U.S.A. 45°23N 94°43W 80 C6
Paysandú Uruguay 32°19S 58°8W 94 C4
Payson Ariz., U.S.A. 34°14N 111°20W 77 J8
Payson Utah, U.S.A. 40°3N 111°44W 76 F8
Paz → Guatemala 13°44N 90°10W 88 D1
Paz, B. de la Mexico 24°9N 110°25W 86 C2
Pāzanān Iran 30°35N 49°59E 45 D6
Pazardzhik Bulgaria 42°12N 24°20E 23 C11
Pe Ell U.S.A. 46°34N 123°18W 78 D3
Peabody U.S.A. 42°31N 70°56W 83 D14
Peace → Canada 59°0N 111°25W 70 B6
Peace Point Canada 59°7N 112°27W 70 B6
Peace River Canada 56°15N 117°18W 70 B5
Peach Springs U.S.A. 35°32N 113°25W 77 J7
Peachland Canada 49°47N 119°45W 70 D5
Peachtree City U.S.A. 33°25N 84°35W 85 E12
Peak, The = Kinder Scout U.K. 53°24N 1°52W 12 D6
Peak Charles △ Australia 32°42S 121°10E 61 F3
Peak District △ U.K. 53°24N 1°46W 12 D6
Peak Hill N.S.W., Australia 32°47S 148°11E 63 E4
Peak Hill W. Austral., Australia 25°35S 118°43E 61 E2
Peak Ra. Australia 22°50S 148°20E 62 C4
Peake Cr. → Australia 28°2S 136°7E 63 D2
Peale, Mt. U.S.A. 38°26N 109°14W 76 G9
Pearblossom U.S.A. 34°30N 117°55W 79 L9
Pearl → U.S.A. 30°11N 89°32W 85 F10
Pearl City U.S.A. 21°24N 157°59W 74 b
Pearl Harbor U.S.A. 21°21N 157°57W 74 b
Pearl River U.S.A. 41°4N 74°2W 83 E10
Pearsall U.S.A. 28°54N 99°6W 84 G5
Pearson Int. Toronto ✈ (YYZ) Canada 43°46N 79°35W 82 C5
Peary Land Greenland 82°40N 33°0W 4 A6
Pease → U.S.A. 34°12N 99°2W 84 D5
Peawanuck Canada 55°15N 85°12W 72 A2
Pebane Mozam. 17°10S 38°8E 55 F4
Pebas Peru 3°10S 71°46W 92 D4
Pebble Beach U.S.A. 36°34N 121°57W 78 J5
Peć Serbia 42°40N 20°17E 23 C9
Pechenga Russia 69°29N 31°4E 8 B24
Pechenizhyn Ukraine 48°30N 24°48E 17 D13
Pechiguera, Pta. Canary Is. 28°51N 13°53W 24 F6
Pechora Russia 65°10N 57°11E 18 A10
Pechora → Russia 68°13N 54°15E 18 A9
Pechorskaya Guba Russia 68°40N 54°0E 18 A9
Pechory Russia 57°48N 27°40E 9 H22
Pecos N. Mex., U.S.A. 35°35N 105°41W 77 J11
Pecos Tex., U.S.A. 31°26N 103°30W 84 F3
Pecos → U.S.A. 29°42N 101°22W 84 G4
Pécs Hungary 46°5N 18°15E 17 E10
Pedasí Panama 7°32N 80°2W 88 E3
Pedder, L. Australia 42°55S 146°10E 63 G4
Peddie S. Africa 33°14S 27°7E 57 E4
Pedernales Dom. Rep. 18°2N 71°44W 89 C5
Pedieos → Cyprus 35°10N 33°54E 25 D12
Pedirka Australia 26°40S 135°14E 63 D2
Pedirka Desert Australia 26°47S 134°11E 63 A1
Pedra Azul Brazil 16°2S 41°17W 93 G10
Pedra Lume C. Verde Is. 16°40N 22°52W 50 b
Pedreiras Brazil 4°32S 44°40W 93 D10
Pedro Afonso Brazil 9°0S 48°10W 93 E9
Pedro Cays Jamaica 17°5N 77°48W 88 C4
Pedro de Valdivia Chile 22°55S 69°38W 94 A2
Pedro Juan Caballero Paraguay 22°30S 55°40W 95 A4
Pee Dee = Great Pee Dee → U.S.A. 33°21N 79°10W 85 E15
Peebinga Australia 34°52S 140°57E 63 E3
Peebles U.K. 55°40N 3°11W 11 F5
Peekskill U.S.A. 41°17N 73°55W 83 E11
Peel I. of Man 54°13N 4°40W 12 C3
Peel → Australia 30°50S 150°29E 63 E5
Peel → Canada 67°0N 135°0W 68 C6
Peel Sd. Canada 73°0N 96°0W 68 B10
Peera Peera Poolanna L. Australia 26°30S 138°0E 63 D2
Peerless Lake Canada 56°37N 114°40W 70 B6
Peers Canada 53°40N 116°0W 70 C5
Pegasus Bay N.Z. 43°20S 173°10E 59 E4
Pegu Burma 17°20N 96°29E 41 L20
Pegu Yoma Burma 19°0N 96°0E 41 K20
Pehuajó Argentina 35°45S 62°0W 94 D3
Pei Xian = Pizhou China 34°44N 116°55E 34 G9
Peine Chile 23°45S 68°8W 94 A2
Peine Germany 52°19N 10°14E 16 B6
Peip'ing = Beijing China 39°53N 116°21E 34 E9
Peipus, L. = Chudskoye, Ozero Russia 58°13N 27°30E 9 G22
Peixe Brazil 12°0S 48°40W 93 F9
Peixe → Brazil 21°31S 51°58W 93 H8
Pekalongan Indonesia 6°53S 109°40E 37 G13
Pekan Malaysia 3°30N 103°25E 39 L4
Pekan Nenas Malaysia 1°31N 103°31E 39 d
Pekanbaru Indonesia 0°30N 101°15E 36 D2
Pekin U.S.A. 40°35N 89°40W 80 E9
Peking = Beijing China 39°53N 116°21E 34 E9
Pekutatan Indonesia 8°25S 114°49E 37 J17
Pelabuhan Klang Malaysia 3°0N 101°23E 39 L3
Pelabuhan Ratu, Teluk Indonesia 7°5S 106°30E 37 G12
Pelabuhanratu Indonesia 7°0S 106°32E 37 G12
Pelagie, Is. Italy 35°39N 12°33E 22 G5

Pelaihari *Indonesia* 3°55'S 114°45'E **36 E4**
Peleaga, Vf. *Romania* 45°22'N 22°55'E **17 F12**
Pelée, Mt. *Martinique* 14°48'N 61°10'W **88 c**
Pelee, Pt. *Canada* 41°54'N 82°31'W **72 D3**
Pelee I. *Canada* 41°47'N 82°40'W **82 E2**
Pelekech *Kenya* 3°52'N 35°8'E **54 B4**
Peleng *Indonesia* 1°20'S 123°30'E **37 E6**
Pelentong *Malaysia* 1°32'N 103°49'E **39 d**
Pelican *U.S.A.* 57°58'N 136°14'W **70 B1**
Pelican L. *Canada* 52°28'N 100°20'W **71 C8**
Pelican Narrows
 Canada 55°10'N 102°56'W **71 B8**
Pelješac *Croatia* 42°55'N 17°25'E **22 C7**
Pelkosenniemi *Finland* 67°6'N 27°28'E **8 C22**
Pella *S. Africa* 29°1'S 19°6'E **56 D2**
Pella *U.S.A.* 41°25'N 92°55'W **80 E7**
Pello *Finland* 66°47'N 23°59'E **8 C20**
Pelly → *Canada* 62°47'N 137°19'W **70 A1**
Pelly Bay *Canada* 68°38'N 89°50'W **69 C11**
Peloponnese □ *Greece* 37°10'N 22°0'E **23 F10**
Pelorus Sd. *N.Z.* 40°59'S 173°59'E **59 D4**
Pelotas *Brazil* 31°42'S 52°23'W **95 C5**
Pelotas → *Brazil* 27°28'S 51°55'W **95 B5**
Pelvoux, Massif du
 France 44°52'N 6°20'E **20 D7**
Pemalang *Indonesia* 6°53'S 109°23'E **37 G13**
Pemanggil, Pulau
 Malaysia 2°37'N 104°21'E **39 L5**
Pematangsiantar *Indonesia* 2°57'N 99°5'E **36 D1**
Pemba *Mozam.* 12°58'S 40°30'E **55 E5**
Pemba *Zambia* 16°30'S 27°28'E **55 F2**
Pemba Channel *Tanzania* 5°0'S 39°37'E **54 D4**
Pemba I. *Tanzania* 5°0'S 39°45'E **54 D4**
Pemberton *Australia* 34°30'S 116°0'E **61 F2**
Pemberton *Canada* 50°25'N 122°50'W **70 C4**
Pembina → *Canada* 54°45'N 114°17'W **70 C6**
Pembroke *Canada* 45°50'N 77°7'W **72 C4**
Pembroke *U.K.* 51°41'N 4°55'W **13 F3**
Pembrokeshire □ *U.K.* 51°52'N 4°56'W **13 F3**
Pembrokeshire Coast △
 U.K. 51°50'N 5°2'W **13 F2**
Pen-y-Ghent *U.K.* 54°10'N 2°14'W **12 C5**
Penal *Trin. & Tob.* 10°9'N 61°29'W **93 K15**
Penang = Pinang
 Malaysia 5°25'N 100°15'E **39 c**
Penápolis *Brazil* 21°30'S 50°0'W **95 A6**
Peñarroya-Pueblonuevo
 Spain 38°19'N 5°16'W **21 C3**
Penarth *U.K.* 51°26'N 3°11'W **13 F4**
Peñas, C. de *Spain* 43°42'N 5°52'W **21 A3**
Peñas, G. de *Chile* 47°0'S 75°0'W **96 F2**
Peñas del Chache
 Canary Is. 29°6'N 13°33'W **24 E6**
Pench △ *India* 21°45'N 79°20'E **43 J8**
Pench'i = Benxi *China* 41°20'N 123°48'E **35 D12**
Pend Oreille → *U.S.A.* 49°4'N 117°37'W **76 B5**
Pend Oreille, L. *U.S.A.* 48°10'N 116°21'W **76 B5**
Pendembu *S. Leone* 9°7'N 11°14'W **50 G3**
Pender B. *Australia* 16°45'S 122°42'E **60 C3**
Pendleton *U.S.A.* 45°40'N 118°47'W **76 D4**
Pendra *India* 22°46'N 81°57'E **43 H9**
Penedo *Brazil* 10°15'S 36°36'W **93 F11**
Penelokan *Indonesia* 8°17'S 115°22'E **37 J18**
Penetanguishene
 Canada 44°50'N 79°55'W **82 B5**
Penfield *U.S.A.* 41°13'N 78°35'W **82 E6**
Peng Chau *China* 22°17'N 114°2'E **33 G11**
Pengalengan *Indonesia* 7°9'S 107°30'E **37 G12**
Penge Kasai-Or.,
 Dem. Rep. of the Congo 5°30'S 24°33'E **54 D1**
Penge Sud-Kivu,
 Dem. Rep. of the Congo 4°27'S 28°25'E **54 C2**
Penglai *China* 37°48'N 120°42'E **35 F11**
Penguin *Australia* 41°8'S 146°6'E **63 G4**
Penhalonga *Zimbabwe* 18°52'S 32°40'E **55 F3**
Peniche *Portugal* 39°19'N 9°22'W **21 C1**
Penicuik *U.K.* 55°50'N 3°13'W **11 F5**
Penida, Nusa *Indonesia* 8°45'S 115°30'E **37 K18**
Peninsular Malaysia □
 Malaysia 4°0'N 102°0'E **39 L4**
Penitente, Serra do *Brazil* 8°45'S 46°20'W **93 E9**
Penkridge *U.K.* 52°44'N 2°6'W **12 E5**
Penmarch, Pte. de *France* 47°48'N 4°22'W **20 C1**
Penn Hills *U.S.A.* 40°28'N 79°52'W **82 F5**
Penn Yan *U.S.A.* 42°40'N 77°3'W **82 D7**
Pennant *Canada* 50°32'N 108°14'W **71 C7**
Penner → *India* 14°35'N 80°10'E **40 M12**
Pennines *U.K.* 54°45'N 2°27'W **12 C5**
Pennington *U.S.A.* 39°15'N 121°47'W **78 F5**
Pennsburg *U.S.A.* 40°23'N 75°29'W **83 F9**
Pennsylvania □ *U.S.A.* 40°45'N 77°30'W **81 E15**
Penny *Canada* 53°51'N 121°20'W **70 C4**
Penny Str. *Canada* 76°30'N 97°0'W **69 B8**
Penobscot → *U.S.A.* 44°30'N 68°48'W **81 C19**
Penobscot B. *U.S.A.* 44°35'N 68°50'W **81 C19**
Penola *Australia* 37°25'S 140°48'E **63 F3**
Penong *Australia* 31°56'S 133°1'E **61 F5**
Penonomé *Panama* 8°31'N 80°21'W **88 E3**
Penrhyn *Cook Is.* 9°0'S 158°0'W **65 H12**
Penrith *Australia* 33°43'S 150°38'E **63 E5**
Penrith *U.K.* 54°40'N 2°45'W **12 C5**
Penryn *U.K.* 50°9'N 5°7'W **13 G2**
Pensacola *U.S.A.* 30°25'N 87°13'W **85 F11**
Pensacola Mts. *Antarctica* 84°0'S 40°0'W **5 E1**
Pense *Canada* 50°25'N 104°59'W **71 C8**
Penshurst *Australia* 37°49'S 142°20'E **63 F3**
Penticton *Canada* 49°30'N 119°38'W **70 D5**
Pentland *Australia* 20°32'S 145°25'E **62 C4**
Pentland Firth *U.K.* 58°43'N 3°10'W **11 C5**
Pentland Hills *U.K.* 55°48'N 3°25'W **11 F5**
Pentland Hills △ *U.K.* 55°51'N 3°15'W **11 F5**
Penza *Russia* 53°15'N 45°5'E **18 D8**
Penzance *U.K.* 50°7'N 5°33'W **13 G2**
Penzhino *Russia* 63°30'N 167°55'E **29 C17**
Penzhinskaya Guba
 Russia 61°30'N 163°0'E **29 C17**

Peoria *Ill., U.S.A.* 40°42'N 89°36'W **80 E9**
Pepacton Res. *U.S.A.* 42°5'N 74°58'W **83 D10**
Pepani → *S. Africa* 25°49'S 22°47'E **56 D3**
Pera Hd. *Australia* 12°55'S 141°37'E **62 A3**
Perabumilih *Indonesia* 3°27'S 104°15'E **36 E2**
Perak → *Malaysia* 4°0'N 100°50'E **39 K3**
Perama *Kerkyra, Greece* 39°34'N 19°54'E **25 A3**
Perama *Kriti, Greece* 35°20'N 24°40'E **25 D6**
Perancak *Indonesia* 8°24'S 114°37'E **37 J17**
Peräpohjola *Finland* 66°16'N 26°10'E **8 C22**
Percé *Canada* 48°31'N 64°13'W **73 C7**
Perche, Collines du
 France 48°30'N 0°40'E **20 B4**
Percival Lakes *Australia* 21°25'S 125°0'E **60 D4**
Percy Is. *Australia* 21°39'S 150°16'E **62 C5**
Perdido, Mte. *Spain* 42°40'N 0°5'E **21 A6**
Perdu, Mt. = Perdido, Mte.
 Spain 42°40'N 0°5'E **21 A6**
Pereira *Colombia* 4°49'N 75°43'W **92 C3**
Perenjori *Australia* 29°26'S 116°16'E **61 E2**
Pereyaslav-Khmelnytskyy
 Ukraine 50°3'N 31°28'E **19 D5**
Pérez, I. *Mexico* 22°24'N 89°42'W **87 C7**
Pergamino *Argentina* 33°52'S 60°30'W **94 C3**
Pergau → *Malaysia* 5°23'N 102°2'E **39 K3**
Perham *U.S.A.* 46°36'N 95°34'W **80 B6**
Perhentian, Kepulauan
 Malaysia 5°54'N 102°42'E **39 K4**
Péribonca → *Canada* 48°45'N 72°5'W **73 C5**
Péribonca, L. *Canada* 50°1'N 71°10'W **73 B5**
Perico *Argentina* 24°20'S 65°5'W **94 A2**
Pericos *Mexico* 25°3'N 107°42'W **86 B3**
Périgueux *France* 45°10'N 0°42'E **20 D4**
Perijá, Sierra de *Colombia* 9°30'N 73°3'W **92 B4**
Perijá □ *Venezuela* 9°30'N 72°55'W **89 E5**
Peristerona → *Cyprus* 35°8'N 33°5'E **25 D12**
Perito Moreno *Argentina* 46°36'S 70°56'W **96 F2**
Perkasie *U.S.A.* 40°22'N 75°18'W **83 F9**
Perlas, Arch. de las
 Panama 8°41'N 79°7'W **88 E4**
Perlas, Punta de *Nic.* 12°30'N 83°30'W **88 D3**
Perm *Russia* 58°0'N 56°10'E **18 C10**
Pernambuco = Recife
 Brazil 8°0'S 35°0'W **93 E12**
Pernambuco □ *Brazil* 8°0'S 37°0'W **93 E11**
Pernatty Lagoon
 Australia 31°30'S 137°12'E **63 E2**
Pernik *Bulgaria* 42°35'N 23°2'E **23 C10**
Peron Is. *Australia* 13°9'S 130°4'E **60 B5**
Peron Pen. *Australia* 26°0'S 113°10'E **61 E1**
Perow *Canada* 54°35'N 126°10'W **70 C3**
Perpignan *France* 42°42'N 2°53'E **20 E5**
Perris *U.S.A.* 33°47'N 117°14'W **79 M9**
Perry *Fla., U.S.A.* 30°7'N 83°35'W **85 F13**
Perry *Ga., U.S.A.* 32°28'N 83°44'W **85 E13**
Perry *Iowa, U.S.A.* 41°51'N 94°6'W **80 E6**
Perry *N.Y., U.S.A.* 42°42'N 78°0'W **82 D7**
Perry *Okla., U.S.A.* 36°17'N 97°14'W **84 C6**
Perryton *U.S.A.* 36°24'N 100°48'W **84 C4**
Perryville *U.S.A.* 37°43'N 89°52'W **80 G10**
Persepolis *Iran* 29°55'N 52°50'E **45 D7**
Pershotravensk *Ukraine* 50°13'N 27°40'E **17 C14**
Persia = Iran ■ *Asia* 33°0'N 53°0'E **45 C7**
Persian Gulf *Asia* 27°0'N 50°0'E **45 E6**
Perth *Australia* 31°57'S 115°52'E **61 F2**
Perth *Canada* 44°55'N 76°15'W **83 B8**
Perth *U.K.* 56°24'N 3°26'W **11 E5**
Perth & Kinross □ *U.K.* 56°45'N 3°55'W **11 E5**
Perth Amboy *U.S.A.* 40°30'N 74°15'W **83 F10**
Perth-Andover *Canada* 46°44'N 67°42'W **73 C6**
Perth Basin *Ind. Oc.* 30°0'S 108°0'E **64 L2**
Peru *Ind., U.S.A.* 40°45'N 86°4'W **80 E10**
Peru *N.Y., U.S.A.* 44°35'N 73°32'W **83 B11**
Peru ■ *S. Amer.* 4°0'S 75°0'W **92 D4**
Peru Basin *Pac. Oc.* 20°0'S 95°0'W **65 J18**
Peru-Chile Trench
 Pac. Oc. 20°0'S 72°0'W **92 G3**
Perúgia *Italy* 43°7'N 12°23'E **22 C5**
Pervomaysk *Ukraine* 48°10'N 30°46'E **19 E5**
Pervouralsk *Russia* 56°59'N 59°59'E **18 C10**
Pésaro *Italy* 43°54'N 12°55'E **22 C5**
Pescara *Italy* 42°28'N 14°13'E **22 C6**
Peshawar *Pakistan* 34°2'N 71°37'E **42 B4**
Peshkopi *Albania* 41°41'N 20°25'E **23 D9**
Peshtigo *U.S.A.* 45°3'N 87°45'W **80 C10**
Pesqueira *Brazil* 8°20'S 36°42'W **93 E11**
Petah Tiqwa *Israel* 32°6'N 34°53'E **46 C3**
Petaling Jaya *Malaysia* 3°4'N 101°42'E **39 L3**
Petaloudes *Greece* 36°18'N 28°5'E **25 C10**
Petaluma *U.S.A.* 38°14'N 122°39'W **78 G4**
Pétange *Lux.* 49°33'N 5°55'E **15 E5**
Petaro *Pakistan* 25°31'N 68°18'E **42 G3**
Petatlán *Mexico* 17°31'N 101°16'W **86 D4**
Petauke *Zambia* 14°14'S 31°20'E **55 E3**
Petawawa *Canada* 45°54'N 77°17'W **72 C4**
Petén Itzá, L. *Guatemala* 16°58'N 89°50'W **88 C2**
Peter I. *Br. Virgin Is.* 18°22'N 64°35'W **89 e**
Peter I. Øy *Antarctica* 69°0'S 91°0'W **5 C16**
Peter Pond L. *Canada* 55°55'N 108°44'W **71 B7**
Peterbell *Canada* 48°36'N 83°21'W **72 C3**
Peterborough *Australia* 32°58'S 138°51'E **63 E2**
Peterborough *Canada* 44°20'N 78°20'W **82 B6**
Peterborough *U.K.* 52°35'N 0°15'W **13 E7**
Peterborough *U.S.A.* 42°53'N 71°57'W **83 D13**
Peterborough □ *U.K.* 52°35'N 0°15'W **13 E7**
Peterculter *U.K.* 57°6'N 2°16'W **11 D6**
Peterhead *U.K.* 57°31'N 1°48'W **11 D7**
Peterlee *U.K.* 54°47'N 1°20'W **12 C6**
Petermann Ranges
 Australia 26°0'S 130°30'E **61 E5**
Petersburg *Alaska,*
 U.S.A. 56°48'N 132°58'W **68 D6**
Petersburg *Pa., U.S.A.* 40°34'N 78°3'W **82 F6**
Petersburg *Va., U.S.A.* 37°14'N 77°24'W **81 G15**
Petersburg *W. Va., U.S.A.* 39°1'N 79°5'W **81 F14**
Petersfield *U.K.* 51°1'N 0°56'W **13 F7**
Petit-Canal *Guadeloupe* 16°25'N 61°31'W **88 b**

Petit Goâve *Haiti* 18°27'N 72°51'W **89 C5**
Petit Lac Manicouagan
 Canada 51°25'N 67°40'W **73 B6**
Petit-Mécatina →
 Canada 50°40'N 59°30'W **73 B8**
Petit-Mécatina, Î. du
 Canada 50°30'N 59°25'W **73 B8**
Petit Piton *St. Lucia* 13°51'N 61°5'W **89 f**
Petit-Saguenay *Canada* 48°15'N 70°4'W **73 C5**
Petitcodiac *Canada* 45°57'N 65°11'W **73 C6**
Petite Terre, Îles de la
 Guadeloupe 16°13'N 61°9'W **88 b**
Petitot → *Canada* 60°14'N 123°29'W **70 A4**
Petitsikapau L. *Canada* 54°37'N 66°25'W **73 B6**
Petlad *India* 22°30'N 72°45'E **42 H5**
Peto *Mexico* 20°8'N 88°55'W **87 C7**
Petone *N.Z.* 41°13'S 174°53'E **59 D5**
Petorca *Chile* 32°15'S 70°56'W **94 C1**
Petoskey *U.S.A.* 45°22'N 84°57'W **81 C11**
Petra *Jordan* 30°20'N 35°22'E **46 E4**
Petra *Spain* 39°37'N 3°6'E **24 B10**
Petra, Ostrova *Russia* 76°15'N 118°30'E **29 B12**
Petra Velikogo, Zaliv
 Russia 42°40'N 132°0'E **30 C6**
Petre, Pt. *Canada* 43°50'N 77°9'W **82 C7**
Petrich *Bulgaria* 41°24'N 23°13'E **23 D10**
Petrified Forest △ *U.S.A.* 35°0'N 109°30'W **77 J9**
Petrikov = Pyetrikaw
 Belarus 52°11'N 28°29'E **17 B15**
Petrolândia *Brazil* 9°5'S 38°20'W **93 E11**
Petrolia *Canada* 42°54'N 82°9'W **82 D2**
Petrolina *Brazil* 9°24'S 40°30'W **93 E10**
Petropavl *Kazakhstan* 54°53'N 69°13'E **28 D7**
Petropavlovsk = Petropavl
 Kazakhstan 54°53'N 69°13'E **28 D7**
Petropavlovsk-Kamchatskiy
 Russia 53°3'N 158°43'E **29 D16**
Petrópolis *Brazil* 22°33'S 43°9'W **95 A7**
Petroşani *Romania* 45°28'N 23°20'E **17 F12**
Petrovaradin *Serbia* 45°16'N 19°55'E **23 B8**
Petrovsk *Russia* 52°22'N 45°19'E **18 D8**
Petrovsk-Zabaykalskiy
 Russia 51°20'N 108°55'E **29 D11**
Petrozavodsk *Russia* 61°41'N 34°20'E **18 B5**
Petrus Steyn *S. Africa* 27°38'S 28°8'E **57 D4**
Petrusburg *S. Africa* 29°4'S 25°26'E **56 D4**
Peumo *Chile* 34°21'S 71°12'W **94 C1**
Peureulak *Indonesia* 4°48'N 97°45'E **36 D1**
Pevek *Russia* 69°41'N 171°19'E **29 C18**
Pforzheim *Germany* 48°52'N 8°41'E **16 D5**
Pha Taem △ *Thailand* 15°32'N 105°30'E **38 E5**
Phaestos *Greece* 35°2'N 24°50'E **25 D6**
Phagwara *India* 31°10'N 75°40'E **42 D6**
Phala *Botswana* 23°45'S 26°50'E **56 C4**
Phalera = Phulera *India* 26°52'N 75°16'E **42 F6**
Phalodi *India* 27°12'N 72°24'E **42 F5**
Phaluai, Ko *Thailand* 9°32'N 99°41'E **39 b**
Phan *Thailand* 19°28'N 99°43'E **38 C2**
Phan Rang *Vietnam* 11°34'N 109°0'E **39 G7**
Phan Ri = Hoa Da
 Vietnam 11°16'N 108°40'E **39 G7**
Phan Si Pan *Vietnam* 22°18'N 103°46'E **38 A4**
Phan Thiet *Vietnam* 11°1'N 108°9'E **39 G7**
Phanat Nikhom
 Thailand 13°27'N 101°11'E **38 F3**
Phangan, Ko *Thailand* 9°45'N 100°0'E **39 H3**
Phangnga *Thailand* 8°28'N 98°30'E **39 H2**
Phangnga, Ao *Thailand* 8°16'N 98°33'E **39 a**
Phanom Sarakham
 Thailand 13°45'N 101°21'E **38 F3**
Phaphund *India* 26°36'N 79°28'E **43 F8**
Pharenda *India* 27°5'N 83°17'E **43 F10**
Pharr *U.S.A.* 26°12'N 98°11'W **84 H5**
Phatthalung *Thailand* 7°39'N 100°6'E **39 J3**
Phayao *Thailand* 19°11'N 99°55'E **38 C2**
Phelps *U.S.A.* 42°58'N 77°3'W **82 D7**
Phelps L. *Canada* 59°15'N 103°15'W **71 B8**
Phenix City *U.S.A.* 32°28'N 85°0'W **85 E12**
Phet Buri *Thailand* 13°1'N 99°55'E **38 F2**
Phetchabun *Thailand* 16°25'N 101°8'E **38 D3**
Phetchabun, Thiu Khao
 Thailand 16°0'N 101°20'E **38 E3**
Phetchaburi = Phet Buri
 Thailand 13°1'N 99°55'E **38 F2**
Phi Phi, Ko *Thailand* 7°45'N 98°46'E **39 J2**
Phiafay *Laos* 14°48'N 106°0'E **38 E6**
Phibun Mangsahan
 Thailand 15°14'N 105°14'E **38 E5**
Phichai *Thailand* 17°22'N 100°10'E **38 D3**
Phichit *Thailand* 16°26'N 100°22'E **38 D3**
Philadelphia *Miss.,*
 U.S.A. 32°46'N 89°7'W **85 E10**
Philadelphia *N.Y., U.S.A.* 44°9'N 75°43'W **83 B9**
Philadelphia *Pa., U.S.A.* 39°57'N 75°9'W **83 G9**
Philip *U.S.A.* 44°2'N 101°40'W **80 C3**
Philippeville *Belgium* 50°12'N 4°33'E **15 D4**
Philippi *U.S.A.* 39°9'N 80°3'W **81 F13**
Philippi L. *Australia* 24°20'S 138°55'E **62 C2**
Philippine Basin *Pac. Oc.* 17°0'N 130°0'E **64 F5**
Philippine Sea *Pac. Oc.* 18°0'N 125°0'E **64 F4**
Philippine Trench = Mindanao
 Trench *Pac. Oc.* 12°0'N 126°6'E **37 B7**
Philippines ■ *Asia* 12°0'N 123°0'E **37 B6**
Philippolis *S. Africa* 30°15'S 25°16'E **56 E4**
Philippopolis = Plovdiv
 Bulgaria 42°8'N 24°44'E **23 C11**
Philipsburg *Canada* 45°2'N 73°5'W **83 A11**
Philipsburg *Mont.,*
 U.S.A. 46°20'N 113°18'W **76 C7**
Philipsburg *Pa., U.S.A.* 40°54'N 78°13'W **82 F6**
Philipstown = Daingean
 Ireland 53°18'N 7°17'W **10 C4**
Philipstown *S. Africa* 30°28'S 24°30'E **56 E3**
Phillip I. *Australia* 38°30'S 145°12'E **63 F4**
Phillips *U.S.A.* 45°42'N 90°24'W **80 C8**
Phillipsburg *Kans.,*
 U.S.A. 39°45'N 99°19'W **80 F4**

Phillipsburg *N.J., U.S.A.* 40°42'N 75°12'W **83 F9**
Philmont *U.S.A.* 42°15'N 73°39'W **83 D11**
Philomath *U.S.A.* 44°32'N 123°22'W **76 D2**
Phimai *Thailand* 15°13'N 102°30'E **38 E4**
Phitsanulok *Thailand* 16°50'N 100°12'E **38 D3**
Phnom Dangrek
 Thailand 14°20'N 104°0'E **38 E5**
Phnom Kulen △
 Cambodia 13°38'N 104°15'E **38 F5**
Phnom Penh *Cambodia* 11°33'N 104°55'E **39 G5**
Phnom Penh = Phnom Penh
 Cambodia 11°33'N 104°55'E **39 G5**
Phoenicia *U.S.A.* 42°5'N 74°14'W **83 D10**
Phoenix *Mauritius* 20°17'S 57°30'E **53 d**
Phoenix *Ariz., U.S.A.* 33°26'N 112°4'W **77 K7**
Phoenix *N.Y., U.S.A.* 43°14'N 76°18'W **83 C8**
Phoenix Is. *Kiribati* 3°30'S 172°0'W **64 H10**
Phoenixville *U.S.A.* 40°8'N 75°31'W **83 F9**
Phon *Thailand* 15°49'N 102°30'E **38 E4**
Phon Tiou *Laos* 17°53'N 104°37'E **38 D5**
Phong → *Thailand* 16°23'N 102°56'E **38 D4**
Phong Saly *Laos* 21°42'N 102°9'E **38 A4**
Phong Tho *Vietnam* 22°32'N 103°21'E **38 A4**
Phonhong *Laos* 18°30'N 102°25'E **38 C4**
Phonum *Thailand* 8°49'N 98°48'E **39 H2**
Phosphate Hill *Australia* 21°53'S 139°58'E **62 C2**
Photharam *Thailand* 13°41'N 99°51'E **38 F2**
Phra Nakhon Si Ayutthaya
 Thailand 14°25'N 100°30'E **38 E3**
Phra Thong, Ko *Thailand* 9°5'N 98°17'E **39 H2**
Phrae *Thailand* 18°7'N 100°9'E **38 C3**
Phrom Phiram *Thailand* 17°2'N 100°12'E **38 D3**
Phu Bia *Laos* 19°10'N 103°0'E **38 C4**
Phu Dien *Vietnam* 18°58'N 105°31'E **38 C5**
Phu Hin Rang Kla △
 Thailand 16°59'N 100°54'E **38 D3**
Phu Krading △ *Thailand* 17°2'N 101°44'E **38 D3**
Phu Loi *Laos* 20°14'N 103°14'E **38 B4**
Phu Luang △ *Thailand* 17°15'N 101°29'E **38 D3**
Phu Ly *Vietnam* 20°35'N 105°50'E **38 B5**
Phu Phan △ *Thailand* 17°0'N 103°56'E **38 D4**
Phu Quoc, Dao *Vietnam* 10°20'N 104°0'E **39 G4**
Phu Tho *Vietnam* 21°24'N 105°13'E **38 B5**
Phu Wiang △ *Thailand* 16°39'N 102°23'E **38 D4**
Phuc Yen *Vietnam* 21°16'N 105°45'E **38 B5**
Phuket *Thailand* 7°53'N 98°24'E **39 a**
Phuket, Ko *Thailand* 8°0'N 98°22'E **39 a**
Phul *India* 30°19'N 75°14'E **42 D6**
Phulad *India* 25°38'N 73°49'E **42 G5**
Phulchari *Bangla.* 25°11'N 89°37'E **43 G13**
Phulera *India* 26°52'N 75°16'E **42 F6**
Phulpur *India* 25°31'N 82°49'E **43 G10**
Phun Phin *Thailand* 9°7'N 99°12'E **39 H2**
Phuntsholing *Bhutan* 26°51'N 89°23'E **43 F13**
Piacenza *Italy* 45°1'N 9°40'E **20 D8**
Piai, Tanjung *Malaysia* 1°17'N 103°30'E **39 d**
Pian Cr. → *Australia* 30°2'S 148°12'E **63 E4**
Pian-Upe △ *Uganda* 1°44'N 34°20'E **54 B3**
Pianosa *Italy* 42°35'N 10°5'E **22 C4**
Piapot *Canada* 49°59'N 109°8'W **71 D7**
Piatra Neamţ *Romania* 46°56'N 26°21'E **17 E14**
Piauí □ *Brazil* 7°0'S 43°0'W **93 E10**
Piauí → *Brazil* 6°38'S 42°42'W **93 E10**
Piave → *Italy* 45°32'N 12°44'E **22 B5**
Pibor Post *Sudan* 6°47'N 33°3'E **51 G12**
Picardie □ *France* 49°50'N 3°0'E **20 B5**
Picardy = Picardie □
 France 49°50'N 3°0'E **20 B5**
Picayune *U.S.A.* 30°32'N 89°41'W **85 F10**
Pichhor *India* 25°58'N 78°20'E **43 G8**
Pichilemu *Chile* 34°22'S 72°0'W **94 C1**
Pichor *India* 25°11'N 78°11'E **42 G8**
Pickerel L. *Canada* 48°40'N 91°25'W **72 C1**
Pickering *U.K.* 54°15'N 0°46'W **12 C7**
Pickering, Vale of *U.K.* 54°14'N 0°45'W **12 C7**
Pickle Lake *Canada* 51°30'N 90°12'W **72 B1**
Pickwick L. *U.S.A.* 35°4'N 88°15'W **85 D10**
Pico *Azores* 38°28'N 28°20'W **50 a**
Pico Bonito △ *Honduras* 15°34'N 86°48'W **88 C2**
Pico Truncado *Argentina* 46°40'S 68°0'W **96 F3**
Picos *Brazil* 7°5'S 41°28'W **93 E10**
Picton *Australia* 34°12'S 150°34'E **63 E5**
Picton *Canada* 44°1'N 77°9'W **82 B7**
Picton *N.Z.* 41°18'S 174°3'E **59 D5**
Pictou *Canada* 45°41'N 62°42'W **73 C7**
Picture Butte *Canada* 49°55'N 112°45'W **70 D6**
Pictured Rocks △
 U.S.A. 46°30'N 86°30'W **80 B10**
Picún Leufú *Argentina* 39°30'S 69°5'W **96 D3**
Pidurutalagala *Sri Lanka* 7°10'N 80°50'E **40 R12**
Piedmont = Piemonte □
 Italy 45°0'N 8°0'E **20 D7**
Piedmont *Ala., U.S.A.* 33°55'N 85°37'W **85 E12**
Piedmont *S.C., U.S.A.* 34°42'N 82°28'W **85 D13**
Piedras Negras *Mexico* 28°42'N 100°31'W **86 B4**
Pieksämäki *Finland* 62°18'N 27°10'E **8 E22**
Pielinen *Finland* 63°15'N 29°40'E **8 E23**
Piemonte □ *Italy* 45°0'N 8°0'E **20 D7**
Pienaarsrivier *S. Africa* 25°15'S 28°18'E **57 D4**
Piercefield *U.S.A.* 44°13'N 74°35'W **83 B10**
Pierceland *Canada* 54°20'N 109°46'W **71 C7**
Pierpont *U.S.A.* 41°45'N 80°34'W **82 E4**
Pierre *U.S.A.* 44°22'N 100°21'W **80 C3**
Pierrefonds *Canada* 45°29'N 73°51'W **83 A11**
Pierreville *Trin. & Tob.* 10°16'N 61°0'W **93 K16**
Piet Retief *S. Africa* 27°1'S 30°50'E **57 D5**
Pietarsaari *Finland* 63°40'N 22°43'E **8 E20**
Pietermaritzburg
 S. Africa 29°35'S 30°25'E **57 D5**
Pietersburg = Polokwane
 S. Africa 23°54'S 29°25'E **57 C4**
Pietrosul, Vf. *Maramureş,*
 Romania 47°35'N 24°43'E **17 E13**
Pietrosul, Vf. *Suceava,*
 Romania 47°12'N 25°18'E **17 E13**

Pigeon L. *Canada* 44°27'N 78°30'W **82 B6**
Piggott *U.S.A.* 36°23'N 90°11'W **85 C9**
Pigüe *Argentina* 37°36'S 62°25'W **94 D3**
Pihani *India* 27°36'N 80°15'E **43 F9**
Pihlajavesi *Finland* 61°45'N 28°45'E **8 F23**
Pihlajavesi *Finland* 61°45'N 28°45'E **8 F23**
Pijijiapan *Mexico* 15°42'N 93°14'W **87 D6**
Pikangikum *Canada* 51°49'N 94°0'W **71 C10**
Pikes Peak *U.S.A.* 38°50'N 105°3'W **76 G11**
Piketberg *S. Africa* 32°55'S 18°40'E **56 E2**
Pikeville *U.S.A.* 37°29'N 82°31'W **81 G12**
Pikou *China* 39°18'N 122°22'E **35 E12**
Pikwitonei *Canada* 55°35'N 97°9'W **71 B9**
Piła *Poland* 53°10'N 16°48'E **17 B9**
Pilanesberg △ *S. Africa* 25°15'S 27°4'E **56 D4**
Pilani *India* 28°22'N 75°33'E **42 E6**
Pilar *Paraguay* 26°50'S 58°20'W **94 B4**
Pilaya → *Bolivia* 20°55'S 64°4'W **92 H6**
Pilcomayo → *Paraguay* 25°21'S 57°42'W **94 B4**
Pilgrim's Rest *S. Africa* 24°55'S 30°44'E **57 C5**
Pilibhit *India* 28°40'N 79°50'E **43 E8**
Pilica → *Poland* 51°52'N 21°17'E **17 C11**
Pilipinas = Philippines ■
 Asia 12°0'N 123°0'E **37 B6**
Pilkhawa *India* 28°43'N 77°42'E **42 E7**
Pilliga *Australia* 30°21'S 148°54'E **63 E4**
Pilos *Greece* 36°55'N 21°42'E **23 F9**
Pilot Mound *Canada* 49°15'N 98°54'W **71 D9**
Pilot Point *U.S.A.* 33°24'N 96°58'W **84 E6**
Pilot Rock *U.S.A.* 45°29'N 118°50'W **76 D4**
Pima *U.S.A.* 32°54'N 109°50'W **77 K9**
Pimba *Australia* 31°18'S 136°46'E **63 E2**
Pimenta Bueno *Brazil* 11°35'S 61°10'W **92 F6**
Pimentel *Peru* 6°45'S 79°55'W **92 E3**
Pin Valley △ *India* 31°50'N 77°50'E **42 D7**
Pinang *Malaysia* 5°25'N 100°15'E **39 c**
Pinar, C. des *Spain* 39°53'N 3°12'E **24 B10**
Pinar del Río *Cuba* 22°26'N 83°40'W **88 B3**
Pınarhisar *Turkey* 41°37'N 27°30'E **23 D12**
Pinatubo, Mt. *Phil.* 15°8'N 120°21'E **37 A6**
Pinawa *Canada* 50°9'N 95°50'W **71 C9**
Pincher Creek *Canada* 49°30'N 113°57'W **70 D6**
Pinchi L. *Canada* 54°38'N 124°30'W **70 C4**
Pinckneyville *U.S.A.* 38°5'N 89°23'W **80 F9**
Pińczów *Poland* 50°32'N 20°32'E **17 C11**
Pindar *Australia* 28°30'S 115°47'E **61 E2**
Pindi Gheb *Pakistan* 33°14'N 72°21'E **42 C5**
Pindos Oros *Greece* 40°0'N 21°0'E **23 E9**
Pindus Mts. = Pindos Oros
 Greece 40°0'N 21°0'E **23 E9**
Pine → *B.C., Canada* 56°8'N 120°43'W **70 B4**
Pine → *Sask., Canada* 58°50'N 105°38'W **71 B7**
Pine Bluff *U.S.A.* 34°13'N 92°1'W **84 D8**
Pine Bluffs *U.S.A.* 41°11'N 104°4'W **76 F11**
Pine City *U.S.A.* 45°50'N 92°59'W **80 C7**
Pine Cr. → *U.S.A.* 41°10'N 77°16'W **82 E7**
Pine Creek *Australia* 13°50'S 131°50'E **60 B5**
Pine Falls *Canada* 50°34'N 96°11'W **71 C9**
Pine Flat L. *U.S.A.* 36°50'N 119°20'W **78 J7**
Pine Grove *U.S.A.* 40°33'N 76°23'W **83 F8**
Pine Hill *Australia* 23°38'S 146°57'E **62 C4**
Pine Pass *Canada* 55°25'N 122°42'W **70 B4**
Pine Point *Canada* 60°50'N 114°28'W **70 A6**
Pine Ridge *U.S.A.* 43°2'N 102°33'W **80 D2**
Pine River *Canada* 51°45'N 100°30'W **71 C8**
Pine River *U.S.A.* 46°43'N 94°24'W **80 B6**
Pine Valley *U.S.A.* 32°50'N 116°32'W **79 N10**
Pinecrest *U.S.A.* 38°12'N 120°1'W **78 G6**
Pinedale *Calif., U.S.A.* 36°50'N 119°48'W **78 J7**
Pinedale *Wyo., U.S.A.* 42°52'N 109°52'W **76 E9**
Pinega → *Russia* 64°30'N 44°19'E **18 B8**
Pinehouse L. *Canada* 55°32'N 106°35'W **71 B7**
Pineimuta → *Canada* 52°8'N 88°33'W **72 B1**
Pinerolo *Italy* 44°53'N 7°21'E **20 D7**
Pines, Akra *Greece* 40°5'N 24°20'E **23 D11**
Pinetop-Lakeside *U.S.A.* 34°9'N 109°58'W **77 J9**
Pinetown *S. Africa* 29°48'S 30°54'E **57 D5**
Pineview *U.S.A.* 31°19'N 92°26'W **84 F8**
Ping → *Thailand* 15°42'N 100°9'E **38 E3**
Pingaring *Australia* 32°40'S 118°32'E **61 F2**
Pingding *China* 37°47'N 113°38'E **34 F7**
Pingdingshan *China* 33°43'N 113°27'E **34 H7**
Pingdong *Taiwan* 22°39'N 120°30'E **33 F13**
Pingdu *China* 36°42'N 119°59'E **35 F10**
Pingelly *Australia* 32°32'S 117°5'E **61 F2**
Pingliang *China* 35°35'N 106°31'E **34 G4**
Pinglu *China* 39°31'N 112°30'E **34 E7**
Pingluo *China* 38°52'N 106°30'E **34 E4**
Pingquan *China* 41°1'N 118°37'E **35 D10**
Pingrup *Australia* 33°32'S 118°29'E **61 F2**
P'ingtung *Taiwan* 22°38'N 120°30'E **33 D7**
Pingwu *China* 32°25'N 104°30'E **34 H3**
Pingxiang *China* 22°6'N 106°46'E **32 D5**
Pingyao *China* 37°12'N 112°10'E **34 F7**
Pingyi *China* 35°30'N 117°35'E **35 G9**
Pingyin *China* 36°20'N 116°25'E **34 F9**
Pingyuan *China* 37°10'N 116°22'E **34 F9**
Pinhal *Brazil* 22°10'S 46°46'W **95 A6**
Pinheiro *Brazil* 2°31'S 45°5'W **93 D9**
Pinheiro Machado
 Brazil 31°34'S 53°23'W **95 C5**
Pinhel *Portugal* 40°50'N 7°1'W **21 B2**
Pini *Indonesia* 0°10'N 98°40'E **36 D1**
Pinios → *Greece* 39°55'N 22°41'E **23 E10**
Pinjarra *Australia* 32°37'S 115°52'E **61 F2**
Pink Mountain *Canada* 57°3'N 122°52'W **70 B4**
Pinnacles △ *U.S.A.* 36°33'N 121°19'W **78 J5**
Pinnaroo *Australia* 35°17'S 140°53'E **63 F3**
Pinon Hills *U.S.A.* 34°26'N 117°39'W **79 L9**
Pinos *Mexico* 22°18'N 101°34'W **86 C4**
Pinos, Mt. *U.S.A.* 34°49'N 119°8'W **79 L7**
Pinos Pt. *U.S.A.* 36°38'N 121°57'W **77 H3**
Pinrang *Indonesia* 3°46'S 119°41'E **37 E5**
Pins, Pte. aux *Canada* 42°15'N 81°51'W **82 D3**
Pinsk *Belarus* 52°10'N 26°1'E **17 B14**
Pintados *Chile* 20°35'S 69°40'W **92 H5**
Pinyug *Russia* 60°5'N 48°0'E **18 B8**

Pioche U.S.A. 37°56N 114°27W **77** H6
Piombino Italy 42°55N 10°32E **22** C4
Pioner, Ostrov Russia 79°50N 92°00E **29** B10
Piopiotaki = Milford Sd.
  N.Z. 44°41S 167°47E **59** F1
Piorini, L. Brazil 3°15S 62°35W **92** D6
Piotrków Trybunalski
  Poland 51°23N 19°43E **17** C10
Pīp Iran 26°45N 60°10E **45** E9
Pipar India 26°25N 73°31E **42** F5
Pipar Road India 26°27N 73°27E **42** F5
Piparia Mad. P., India 22°45N 78°23E **42** H8
Piparia Mad. P., India 21°49N 77°37E **42** J7
Pipestone U.S.A. 44°0N 96°19W **80** D5
Pipestone → Canada 52°53N 89°23W **72** B2
Pipestone Cr. →
  Canada 49°38N 100°15W **71** D8
Piplan Pakistan 32°17N 71°21E **42** C4
Piploda India 23°37N 74°56E **42** H6
Pipmuacan, Rés. Canada 49°45N 70°30W **73** C5
Pippingarra Australia 20°27S 118°42E **60** D2
Piqua U.S.A. 40°9N 84°15W **81** E11
Piquiri → Brazil 24°3S 54°14W **95** A5
Pir Panjal Range India 32°30N 76°50E **42** C7
Pīr Sohrāb Iran 25°44N 60°54E **45** E9
Piracicaba Brazil 22°45S 47°40W **95** A6
Piracuruca Brazil 3°50S 41°50W **93** D10
Pirae Tahiti 17°31S 149°32W **59** d
Piraéus = Piraís Greece 37°57N 23°42E **23** F10
Piraiévs = Piraís Greece 37°57N 23°42E **23** F10
Pirajuí Brazil 21°59S 49°29W **95** A6
Piram I. India 21°36N 72°21E **42** J5
Pirané Argentina 25°42S 59°6W **94** B4
Pīranshahr Iran 36°41N 45°8E **44** B5
Pirapora Brazil 17°20S 44°56W **93** G10
Pirawa India 24°10N 76°2E **42** G7
Pireas Greece 37°57N 23°42E **23** F10
Pirgos Greece 37°40N 21°27E **23** F9
Piribebuy Paraguay 25°26S 57°2W **94** B4
Pirimapun Indonesia 6°20S 138°24E **37** F9
Pirin Planina Bulgaria 41°40N 23°30E **23** D10
Pirineos = Pyrénées
  Europe 42°45N 0°18E **20** E4
Piripiri Brazil 4°15S 41°46W **93** D10
Pirlangimpi Australia 11°24S 130°26E **60** B5
Pirmasens Germany 49°12N 7°36E **16** D4
Pirot Serbia 43°9N 22°33E **23** C10
Piru Indonesia 3°4S 128°12E **37** E7
Piru U.S.A. 34°25N 118°48W **79** L8
Pisa Italy 43°43N 10°23E **22** C4
Pisagua Chile 19°40S 70°15W **92** G4
Pisco Peru 13°50S 76°12W **92** F3
Pisek Czech Rep. 49°19N 14°10E **16** D8
Pishan China 37°30N 78°33E **32** C2
Pīshīn Iran 26°6N 61°47E **45** E9
Pishin Pakistan 30°35N 67°0E **42** D2
Pishin Lora → Pakistan 29°9N 64°5E **42** E1
Pising Indonesia 5°8S 121°53E **37** F6
Pismo Beach U.S.A. 35°9N 120°38W **79** K6
Pissis, Cerro Argentina 27°45S 68°48W **94** B2
Pissouri Cyprus 34°40N 32°42E **25** E11
Pistóia Italy 43°55N 10°54E **22** C4
Pistol B. Canada 62°25N 92°37W **71** A10
Pisuerga → Spain 41°33N 4°52W **21** B3
Pit → U.S.A. 40°47N 122°6W **76** F2
Pitarpunga L. Australia 34°24S 143°30E **63** E3
Pitcairn I. Pac. Oc. 25°5S 130°5W **65** K14
Pitch I. Trin. & Tob. 10°12N 61°39W **93** K15
Piteå Sweden 65°20N 21°25E **8** D19
Piteälven → Sweden 65°20N 21°25E **8** D19
Pitești Romania 44°52N 24°54E **17** F13
Pithapuram India 17°10N 82°15E **41** L13
Pithara Australia 30°20S 116°35E **61** F2
Pithoro India 29°35N 80°13E **43** E9
Pithoro Pakistan 25°31N 69°23E **42** G3
Pitlochry U.K. 56°42N 3°44W **11** E5
Pitsilia Cyprus 34°55N 33°0E **25** E12
Pitt I. Canada 53°30N 129°50W **70** C3
Pittsburg Calif., U.S.A. 38°2N 121°53W **78** G5
Pittsburg Kans., U.S.A. 37°25N 94°42W **80** G6
Pittsburg Tex., U.S.A. 33°0N 94°59W **84** E7
Pittsburgh U.S.A. 40°26N 79°58W **82** F5
Pittsfield Ill., U.S.A. 39°36N 90°49W **80** F8
Pittsfield Maine, U.S.A. 44°47N 69°23W **81** C19
Pittsfield Mass., U.S.A. 42°27N 73°15W **83** D11
Pittsfield N.H., U.S.A. 43°18N 71°20W **83** C13
Pittston U.S.A. 41°19N 75°47W **83** E9
Pittsworth Australia 27°41S 151°37E **63** D5
Pituri → Australia 22°35S 138°30E **62** C2
Piura Peru 5°15S 80°38W **92** E2
Pixley U.S.A. 35°58N 119°18W **78** K7
Pizhou China 34°44N 116°55E **34** G9
Placentia Canada 47°20N 54°0W **73** C9
Placentia B. Canada 47°0N 54°40W **73** C9
Placerville U.S.A. 38°44N 120°48W **78** G6
Placetas Cuba 22°15N 79°44W **88** B4
Plainfield N.J., U.S.A. 40°37N 74°25W **83** F10
Plainfield Ohio, U.S.A. 40°13N 81°43W **82** F3
Plainfield Vt., U.S.A. 44°17N 72°26W **83** B12
Plains Mont., U.S.A. 47°28N 114°53W **76** C6
Plains Tex., U.S.A. 33°11N 102°50W **84** E3
Plainview Nebr., U.S.A. 42°21N 97°47W **80** D5
Plainview Tex., U.S.A. 34°11N 101°43W **84** D4
Plainwell U.S.A. 42°27N 85°38W **81** D11
Plaistow U.S.A. 42°50N 71°6W **83** D13
Plaka, Ákra Greece 35°11N 26°19E **25** D8
Plana Cays Bahamas 22°38N 73°30W **89** B5
Planada U.S.A. 37°16N 120°19W **78** H6
Plano U.S.A. 33°1N 96°42W **84** E6
Plant City U.S.A. 28°1N 82°7W **85** G13
Plaquemine U.S.A. 30°17N 91°14W **84** F9
Plasencia Spain 40°3N 6°8W **21** B2
Plaster City U.S.A. 32°47N 115°51W **79** N11
Plaster Rock Canada 46°53N 67°22W **73** C6
Plastun Russia 44°45N 136°19E **30** B8
Plata, Río de la →
  S. Amer. 34°45S 57°30W **94** C4

Plátani → Italy 37°23N 13°16E **22** F5
Platanos Greece 35°28N 23°33E **25** D5
Platte U.S.A. 43°23N 98°51W **80** D4
Platte → Mo., U.S.A. 39°16N 94°50W **80** F6
Platte → Nebr., U.S.A. 41°4N 95°53W **80** E6
Platteville U.S.A. 42°44N 90°29W **80** D8
Plattsburgh U.S.A. 44°42N 73°28W **83** B11
Plattsmouth U.S.A. 41°1N 95°53W **80** E6
Plauen Germany 50°30N 12°8E **16** C7
Plavinas Latvia 56°35N 25°46E **9** H21
Playa Blanca Canary Is. 28°55N 13°37W **24** F6
Playa Blanca Sur
  Canary Is. 28°51N 13°50W **24** F6
Playa de las Americas
  Canary Is. 28°5N 16°43W **24** F3
Playa de Mogán
  Canary Is. 27°48N 15°47W **24** G4
Playa del Carmen Mexico 20°37N 87°4W **87** C7
Playa del Inglés
  Canary Is. 27°45N 15°33W **24** G4
Playa Esmerelda
  Canary Is. 28°8N 14°16W **24** F5
Playgreen L. Canada 54°0N 98°15W **71** C9
Pleasant Bay Canada 46°51N 60°48W **73** C7
Pleasant Hill U.S.A. 37°57N 122°4W **78** H4
Pleasant Mount U.S.A. 41°44N 75°26W **83** E9
Pleasanton Calif.,
  U.S.A. 37°39N 121°52W **78** H5
Pleasanton Tex., U.S.A. 28°58N 98°29W **84** G5
Pleasantville N.J.,
  U.S.A. 39°24N 74°32W **81** F16
Pleasantville Pa., U.S.A. 41°35N 79°34W **82** E5
Plei Ku Vietnam 13°57N 108°0E **38** F7
Plenty → Australia 23°25S 136°31E **62** C2
Plenty, B. of N.Z. 37°45S 177°0E **59** B6
Plentywood U.S.A. 48°47N 104°34W **76** B11
Plesetsk Russia 62°43N 40°20E **18** B7
Plessisville Canada 46°14N 71°47W **73** C5
Plétipi, L. Canada 51°44N 70°6W **73** B5
Pleven Bulgaria 43°26N 24°37E **23** C11
Plevlja Montenegro 43°21N 19°21E **23** C8
Plevna Canada 44°58N 76°59W **82** B8
Płock Poland 52°32N 19°40E **17** B10
Plöckenstein Germany 48°46N 13°51E **16** D7
Ploiești Romania 44°57N 26°5E **17** F14
Plonge, Lac la Canada 55°8N 107°20W **71** B7
Plovdiv Bulgaria 42°8N 24°44E **23** C11
Plover Cove Res. China 22°28N 114°15E **33** G11
Plum U.S.A. 40°29N 79°47W **82** F5
Plum I. U.S.A. 41°11N 72°12W **83** E12
Plumas U.S.A. 39°45N 120°4W **78** F6
Plummer U.S.A. 47°20N 116°53W **76** C5
Plumtree Zimbabwe 20°27S 27°55E **55** G2
Plungė Lithuania 55°53N 21°59E **9** J19
Plymouth Trin. & Tob. 11°14N 60°48W **93** J16
Plymouth U.K. 50°22N 4°10W **13** G3
Plymouth Calif., U.S.A. 38°29N 120°51W **78** G6
Plymouth Ind., U.S.A. 41°21N 86°19W **80** E10
Plymouth Mass., U.S.A. 41°57N 70°40W **83** E14
Plymouth N.C., U.S.A. 35°52N 76°43W **85** D16
Plymouth N.H., U.S.A. 43°46N 71°41W **83** C13
Plymouth Pa., U.S.A. 41°14N 75°57W **83** E9
Plymouth Wis., U.S.A. 43°45N 87°59W **80** D10
Plympton-Wyoming = Wyoming
  Canada 42°57N 82°7W **82** D2
Plynlimon = Pumlumon Fawr
  U.K. 52°28N 3°46W **13** E4
Plyusa Russia 58°28N 29°27E **9** G23
Plzeň Czech Rep. 49°45N 13°22E **16** D7
Po → Italy 44°57N 12°4E **22** B5
Po Hai = Bo Hai China 39°0N 119°0E **35** E10
Po Toi China 22°10N 114°16E **33** G11
Pobeda Russia 65°12N 146°12E **29** C15
Pobedy, Pik Kyrgyzstan 42°0N 79°58E **32** B2
Pocahontas Ark., U.S.A. 36°16N 90°58W **84** C9
Pocahontas Iowa, U.S.A. 42°44N 94°40W **80** D6
Pocatello U.S.A. 42°52N 112°27W **76** E7
Pocomoke City U.S.A. 38°5N 75°34W **81** F16
Poços de Caldas Brazil 21°50S 46°33W **95** A6
Podgorica Montenegro 42°30N 19°19E **23** C8
Podilska Vysochyna
  Ukraine 49°0N 28°0E **17** D14
Podolsk Russia 55°25N 37°30E **18** C6
Podporozhye Russia 60°55N 34°2E **18** B5
Pofadder S. Africa 29°10S 19°22E **56** D2
Pogranichnyy Russia 44°25N 131°24E **30** B5
Poh Indonesia 0°46S 122°51E **37** E6
Pohang S. Korea 36°1N 129°23E **35** F15
Pohjanmaa Finland 62°58N 22°50E **8** E20
Pohnpei Micronesia 6°55N 158°10E **64** G7
Pohri India 25°32N 77°22E **42** G6
Poinsett, C. Antarctica 65°42S 113°18E **5** C8
Point Arena U.S.A. 38°55N 123°41W **78** G3
Point Baker U.S.A. 56°21N 133°37W **70** B2
Point Fortin
  Trin. & Tob. 10°10N 61°42W **93** K15
Point Hope U.S.A. 68°21N 166°47W **74** a
Point L. Canada 65°15N 113°4W **68** E8
Point Lisas Industrial Estate
  Trin. & Tob. 10°24N 61°29W **93** K15
Point Pedro Sri Lanka 9°50N 80°15E **40** Q12
Point Pelee △ Canada 41°57N 82°31W **82** E2
Point Pleasant N.J.,
  U.S.A. 40°5N 74°4W **83** F10
Point Pleasant W. Va.,
  U.S.A. 38°51N 82°8W **81** F12
Point Reyes △ U.S.A. 38°10N 122°55W **78** G2
Pointe-à-Pitre Guadeloupe 16°10N 61°32W **88** b
Pointe-au-Pic = La Malbaie
  Canada 47°40N 70°10W **73** C5
Pointe-Claire Canada 45°26N 73°50W **83** A11
Pointe-Gatineau Canada 45°27N 75°41W **83** A9
Pointe-Noire Congo 4°48S 11°53E **52** E2
Pointe-Noire Guadeloupe 16°14N 61°47W **88** b
Poipet Cambodia 13°39N 102°33E **38** F4
Poisonbush Ra.
  Australia 22°30S 121°30E **60** D3

Poissonnier Pt.
  Australia 19°57S 119°10E **60** C2
Poitiers France 46°35N 0°20E **20** C4
Poitou France 46°40N 0°10W **20** C3
Pojoaque U.S.A. 35°54N 106°1W **77** J10
Pokaran India 27°0N 71°50E **42** F4
Pokataroo Australia 29°30S 148°36E **63** D4
Pokhara Nepal 28°14N 83°58E **43** E10
Poko Dem. Rep. of the Congo 3°7N 26°52E **54** B2
Pokrovsk Russia 61°29N 129°0E **29** C13
Pola = Pula Croatia 44°54N 13°57E **16** F7
Polacca U.S.A. 35°50N 110°23W **77** J8
Polan Iran 25°30N 61°10E **45** E9
Poland ■ Europe 52°0N 20°0E **17** C10
Polar Bear △ Canada 55°0N 83°45E **72** A2
Polatsk Belarus 55°30N 28°50E **9** J23
Polcura Chile 37°17S 71°43W **94** D1
Polesye = Pripet Marshes
  Europe 52°10N 28°10E **17** B15
Polevskoy Russia 56°26N 60°11E **18** C11
Police Poland 53°33N 14°33E **16** B8
Police, Pte. Seychelles 4°51S 55°32E **53** b
Poligiros Greece 40°23N 23°25E **23** D10
Polillo Is. Phil. 14°56N 122°0E **37** B6
Polis Cyprus 35°2N 32°26E **25** D11
Polk U.S.A. 41°22N 79°56W **82** E5
Pollachi India 10°35N 77°0E **40** P10
Pollença Spain 39°54N 3°1E **24** B10
Pollença, B. de Spain 39°53N 3°8E **24** B10
Polnovat Russia 63°50N 65°54E **28** C7
Polokwane S. Africa 23°54S 29°25E **57** C4
Polokwane → S. Africa 22°25S 30°5E **57** C5
Polonne Ukraine 50°6N 27°30E **17** C14
Polonnoye = Polonne
  Ukraine 50°6N 27°30E **17** C14
Polson U.S.A. 47°41N 114°9W **76** C6
Poltava Ukraine 49°35N 34°35E **19** E5
Pöltsamaa Estonia 58°39N 25°58E **9** G21
Polunochnoye Russia 60°52N 60°25E **28** C7
Põlva Estonia 58°3N 27°3E **9** G22
Polyarny Russia 69°8N 33°20E **8** B25
Polyarnyye Zori Russia 67°22N 32°30E **8** C25
Polynesia Pac. Oc. 10°0S 162°0W **65** F11
Polynésie française = French
  Polynesia ☑ Pac. Oc. 20°0S 145°0W **65** J13
Pombal Portugal 39°55N 8°40W **21** C1
Pombia Greece 35°0N 24°51E **25** E6
Pomene Mozam. 22°53S 35°33E **57** C6
Pomeroy Ohio, U.S.A. 39°2N 82°2W **81** F12
Pomeroy Wash., U.S.A. 46°28N 117°36W **76** C5
Pomézia Italy 41°40N 12°30E **22** D5
Pomona Australia 26°22S 152°52E **63** D5
Pomona U.S.A. 34°4N 117°45W **79** L9
Pomorskie, Pojezierze
  Poland 53°40N 16°37E **17** B9
Pomos Cyprus 35°9N 32°33E **25** D11
Pomos, C. Cyprus 35°10N 32°33E **25** D11
Pompano Beach U.S.A. 26°14N 80°7W **85** H14
Pompeys Pillar U.S.A. 45°59N 107°57W **76** D10
Pompeys Pillar △
  U.S.A. 46°0N 108°0W **76** D10
Pompton Lakes U.S.A. 41°0N 74°17W **83** F10
Ponape = Pohnpei
  Micronesia 6°55N 158°10E **64** G7
Ponask L. Canada 54°0N 92°41W **72** B1
Ponca U.S.A. 42°34N 96°43W **80** D5
Ponca City U.S.A. 36°42N 97°5W **84** C6
Ponce Puerto Rico 18°1N 66°37W **89** d
Ponchatoula U.S.A. 30°26N 90°26W **85** F9
Poncheville, L. Canada 50°10N 76°55W **72** B4
Pond U.S.A. 35°43N 119°20W **79** K7
Pond Inlet Canada 72°40N 77°0W **69** B12
Pondicherry = Puducherry
  India 11°59N 79°50E **40** P11
Ponds, I. of Canada 53°27N 55°52W **73** B8
Ponferrada Spain 42°32N 6°35W **21** A2
Ponnani India 10°45N 75°59E **40** P9
Ponoka Canada 52°42N 113°40W **70** C6
Ponorogo Indonesia 7°52S 111°27E **37** G14
Ponoy Russia 67°0N 41°13E **18** A7
Ponoy → Russia 66°59N 41°17E **18** A7
Ponta Delgada Azores 37°44N 25°40W **50** a
Ponta do Sol Madeira 32°42N 17°7W **24** D2
Ponta Grossa Brazil 25°7S 50°10W **95** B5
Ponta Porã Brazil 22°20S 55°35W **95** A4
Pontarlier France 46°54N 6°20E **20** C7
Pontchartrain, L. U.S.A. 30°5N 90°5W **85** F9
Ponte do Pungué
  Mozam. 19°30S 34°33E **55** F3
Ponte Nova Brazil 20°25S 42°54W **95** A7
Ponteix Canada 49°46N 107°29W **71** D7
Pontevedra Spain 42°26N 8°40W **21** A1
Pontiac Ill., U.S.A. 40°53N 88°38W **80** E9
Pontiac Mich., U.S.A. 42°38N 83°18W **81** D12
Pontian Kechil Malaysia 1°29N 103°23E **39** d
Pontianak Indonesia 0°3S 109°15E **36** E3
Pontine Is. = Ponziane, Ísole
  Italy 40°55N 12°57E **22** D5
Pontine Mts. = Kuzey Anadolu
  Dağları Turkey 40°0N 36°45E **19** F6
Pontivy France 48°5N 2°58W **20** B2
Pontoise France 49°3N 2°5E **20** B5
Ponton → Canada 58°27N 116°11W **70** B5
Pontypool Canada 44°6N 78°38W **82** B6
Pontypool U.K. 51°42N 3°2W **13** F4
Pontypridd U.K. 51°36N 3°20W **13** F4
Ponziane, Ísole Italy 40°55N 12°57E **22** D5
Poochera Australia 32°43S 134°51E **63** E1
Poole U.K. 50°43N 1°59W **13** G6
Poole □ U.K. 50°43N 1°59W **13** G6
Poona = Pune India 18°29N 73°57E **40** K8
Pooncarie Australia 33°22S 142°31E **63** E3
Poopelloe L. Australia 31°40S 144°0E **63** E3
Poopó, L. de Bolivia 18°30S 67°35W **92** G5
Popayán Colombia 2°27N 76°36W **92** C3
Poperinge Belgium 50°51N 2°42E **15** D2
Popiltah L. Australia 33°10S 141°42E **63** E3

Popio L. Australia 33°10S 141°52E **63** E3
Poplar U.S.A. 48°7N 105°12W **76** B11
Poplar → Canada 53°0N 97°19W **71** C9
Poplar Bluff U.S.A. 36°46N 90°24W **80** G8
Poplarville U.S.A. · 30°51N 89°32W **85** F10
Popocatépetl, Volcán
  Mexico 19°2N 98°38W **87** D5
Popokabaka
  Dem. Rep. of the Congo 5°41S 16°40E **52** F3
Poprad Slovak Rep. 49°3N 20°18E **17** D11
Porali → Pakistan 25°58N 66°26E **42** G2
Porbandar India 21°44N 69°43E **42** J3
Porcher I. Canada 53°50N 130°30W **70** C2
Porcupine → Canada 59°11N 104°46W **71** B8
Porcupine → U.S.A. 66°34N 145°19W **74** a
Porcupine Gorge △
  Australia 20°22S 144°26E **62** C3
Pordenone Italy 45°57N 12°39E **22** B5
Pori Finland 61°29N 21°48E **8** F19
Porkhov Russia 57°45N 29°38E **9** H23
Porlamar Venezuela 10°57N 63°51W **92** A6
Pormpuraaw Australia 14°59S 141°26E **62** A3
Poronaysk Russia 49°13N 143°0E **29** E15
Poroshiri-Dake Japan 42°41N 142°52E **30** C11
Poroto Mts. Tanzania 9°0S 33°30E **55** D3
Porpoise B. Antarctica 66°0S 127°0E **5** C9
Porreres Spain 39°31N 3°2E **24** B10
Porsangerfjorden
  Norway 70°40N 25°40E **8** A21
Porsgrunn Norway 59°10N 9°40E **9** G13
Port Alberni Canada 49°14N 124°50W **70** D4
Port Alfred S. Africa 33°36S 26°55E **56** E4
Port Alice Canada 50°20N 127°25W **70** C3
Port Allegany U.S.A. 41°48N 78°17W **82** E6
Port Allen U.S.A. 30°27N 91°12W **84** F9
Port Alma Australia 23°38S 150°53E **62** C5
Port Alma Canada 42°10N 82°14W **82** D2
Port Angeles U.S.A. 48°7N 123°27W **78** B3
Port Antonio Jamaica 18°10N 76°26W **88** a
Port Aransas U.S.A. 27°50N 97°4W **84** H6
Port Arthur Australia 43°7S 147°50E **63** G4
Port Arthur U.S.A. 29°54N 93°56W **84** G8
Port au Choix Canada 50°43N 57°22W **73** B8
Port au Port B. Canada 48°40N 58°50W **73** C8
Port-au-Prince Haiti 18°40N 72°20W **89** C5
Port Augusta Australia 32°30S 137°50E **63** E2
Port Austin U.S.A. 44°3N 83°1W **82** B2
Port Bell Uganda 0°18N 32°35E **54** B3
Port Bergé Vaovao
  Madag. 15°33S 47°40E **57** B8
Port Blandford Canada 48°20N 54°10W **73** C9
Port Bradshaw
  Australia 12°30S 137°20E **62** A2
Port Broughton
  Australia 33°37S 137°56E **63** E2
Port Bruce Canada 42°39N 81°0W **82** D4
Port Burwell Canada 42°40N 80°48W **82** D4
Port Canning India 22°23N 88°40E **43** H13
Port Carling Canada 45°7N 79°35W **82** A5
Port-Cartier Canada 50°2N 66°50W **73** B6
Port Chalmers N.Z. 45°49S 170°30E **59** F3
Port Charlotte U.S.A. 26°59N 82°6W **85** H13
Port Chester U.S.A. 41°0N 73°40W **83** F11
Port Clements Canada 53°40N 132°10W **70** C2
Port Clinton U.S.A. 41°31N 82°56W **81** E12
Port Colborne Canada 42°50N 79°10W **82** D5
Port Coquitlam Canada 49°15N 122°45W **78** A4
Port Credit Canada 43°33N 79°35W **82** C5
Port Curtis Australia 23°57S 151°20E **62** C5
Port d'Alcúdia Spain 39°50N 3°7E **24** B10
Port Dalhousie Canada 43°13N 79°16W **82** C5
Port d'Andratx Spain 39°32N 2°23E **24** B9
Port Darwin Australia 12°24S 130°45E **60** B5
Port Darwin Falk. Is. 51°50S 59°0W **96** G5
Port Davey Australia 43°16S 145°55E **63** G4
Port-de-Paix Haiti 19°50N 72°50W **89** C5
Port de Pollença Spain 39°54N 3°4E **24** B10
Port de Sóller Spain 39°48N 2°42E **24** B9
Port Dickson Malaysia 2°30N 101°49E **39** L3
Port Douglas Australia 16°30S 145°30E **62** B4
Port Dover Canada 42°47N 80°12W **82** D4
Port Edward Canada 54°12N 130°10W **70** C2
Port Elgin Canada 44°25N 81°25W **82** B3
Port Elizabeth S. Africa 33°58S 25°40E **56** E4
Port Ellen U.K. 55°38N 6°11W **11** F2
Port Erin I. of Man 54°5N 4°45W **12** C3
Port Essington Australia 11°15S 132°10E **60** B5
Port Ewen U.S.A. 41°54N 73°59W **83** E11
Port Fairy Australia 38°22S 142°12E **63** F3
Port Gamble U.S.A. 47°51N 122°34W **78** C4
Port-Gentil Gabon 0°40S 8°50E **52** E1
Port Germein Australia 33°1S 138°1E **63** E2
Port Ghalib Egypt 25°20N 34°50E **44** E2
Port Gibson U.S.A. 31°58N 90°59W **84** F9
Port Glasgow U.K. 55°56N 4°41W **11** F4
Port Harcourt Nigeria 4°40N 7°10E **50** H7
Port Hardy Canada 50°41N 127°30W **70** C3
Port Harrison = Inukjuak
  Canada 58°25N 78°15W **69** D12
Port Hawkesbury
  Canada 45°36N 61°22W **73** C7
Port Hedland Australia 20°25S 118°35E **60** D2
Port Henry U.S.A. 44°3N 73°28W **83** B11
Port Hood Canada 46°0N 61°32W **73** C7
Port Hope Canada 43°56N 78°20W **82** C6
Port Hope U.S.A. 43°57N 82°43W **82** C2
Port Hope Simpson
  Canada 52°33N 56°18W **73** B8
Port Hueneme U.S.A. 34°7N 119°12W **79** L7
Port Huron U.S.A. 42°58N 82°26W **82** D2
Port Jefferson U.S.A. 40°57N 73°3W **83** F11
Port Jervis U.S.A. 41°22N 74°41W **83** E10
Port Kelang = Pelabuhan Klang
  Malaysia 3°0N 101°23E **39** L3
Port Kenny Australia 33°10S 134°41E **63** E1
Port Lairge = Waterford
  Ireland 52°15N 7°8W **10** D4

Port Laoise Ireland 53°2N 7°18W **10** C4
Port Lavaca U.S.A. 28°37N 96°38W **84** G6
Port Leyden U.S.A. 43°35N 75°21W **83** C9
Port Lincoln Australia 34°42S 135°52E **63** E2
Port Loko S. Leone 8°48N 12°46W **50** G3
Port-Louis Guadeloupe 16°28N 61°32W **88** b
Port Louis Mauritius 20°10S 57°30E **53** d
Port MacDonnell
  Australia 38°5S 140°48E **63** F3
Port McNeill Canada 50°35N 127°6W **70** C3
Port Macquarie
  Australia 31°25S 152°25E **63** E5
Port Maria Jamaica 18°22N 76°54W **88** a
Port Matilda U.S.A. 40°48N 78°3W **82** F6
Port McNicoll Canada 44°44N 79°48W **82** B5
Port Mellon Canada 49°32N 123°31W **78** A3
Port-Menier Canada 49°51N 64°15W **73** C7
Port Moody Canada 49°17N 122°51W **78** A4
Port Morant Jamaica 17°54N 76°19W **88** a
Port Moresby Papua N. G. 9°24S 147°8E **58** B7
Port Musgrave
  Australia 11°55S 141°50E **62** A3
Port Neches U.S.A. 30°0N 93°59W **84** G8
Port Nolloth S. Africa 29°17S 16°52E **56** D2
Port Nouveau-Québec =
  Kangiqsualujjuaq
  Canada 58°30N 65°59W **69** D13
Port of Climax Canada 49°10N 108°20W **71** D7
Port of Coronach
  Canada 49°7N 105°31W **71** D7
Port of Spain
  Trin. & Tob. 10°40N 61°31W **89** D7
Port Orange U.S.A. 29°9N 80°59W **85** G14
Port Orchard U.S.A. 47°32N 122°38W **78** C4
Port Orford U.S.A. 42°45N 124°30W **76** E1
Port Pegasus N.Z. 47°12S 167°41E **59** G1
Port Perry Canada 44°6N 78°56W **82** B6
Port Phillip B. Australia 38°10S 144°50E **63** F3
Port Pirie Australia 33°10S 138°1E **63** E2
Port Renfrew Canada 48°30N 124°20W **78** B2
Port Roper Australia 14°45S 135°25E **62** A2
Port Rowan Canada 42°40N 80°30W **82** D4
Port Safaga = Bûr Safâga
  Egypt 26°43N 33°57E **44** E2
Port Said = Bûr Sa'îd
  Egypt 31°16N 32°18E **51** B12
Port St. Joe U.S.A. 29°49N 85°18W **85** G12
Port St. Johns = Umzimvubu
  S. Africa 31°38S 29°33E **57** E4
Port St. Lucie U.S.A. 27°18N 80°21W **85** H14
Port Sanilac U.S.A. 43°26N 82°33W **82** C2
Port Severn Canada 44°48N 79°43W **82** B5
Port Shepstone S. Africa 30°44S 30°28E **57** E5
Port Simpson Canada 54°30N 130°20W **70** C2
Port Stanley = Stanley
  Falk. Is. 51°40S 59°51W **96** G5
Port Stanley Canada 42°40N 81°10W **82** D3
Port Sudan = Bûr Sûdân
  Sudan 19°32N 37°9E **51** E13
Port Sulphur U.S.A. 29°29N 89°42W **85** G10
Port Talbot U.K. 51°35N 3°47W **13** F4
Port Townsend U.S.A. 48°7N 122°45W **78** B4
Port-Vendres France 42°32N 3°8E **20** E5
Port Vila Vanuatu 17°45S 168°18E **58** C9
Port Vladimir Russia 69°25N 33°6E **8** B25
Port Wakefield Australia 34°12S 138°10E **63** E2
Port Washington
  U.S.A. 43°23N 87°53W **80** D10
Porta Orientalis Romania 45°6N 22°18E **17** F12
Portacloy Ireland 54°20N 9°46W **10** B2
Portadown U.K. 54°25N 6°27W **10** B5
Portaferry U.K. 54°23N 5°33W **10** B6
Portage Pa., U.S.A. 40°23N 78°41W **82** F6
Portage Wis., U.S.A. 43°33N 89°28W **80** D9
Portage la Prairie
  Canada 49°58N 98°18W **71** D9
Portageville U.S.A. 36°26N 89°42W **80** G9
Portalegre Portugal 39°19N 7°25W **21** C2
Portales U.S.A. 34°11N 103°20W **77** J12
Portarlington Ireland 53°9N 7°14W **10** C4
Portbou Spain 42°25N 3°9E **21** A7
Porter L. N.W.T., Canada 61°41N 108°5W **71** A7
Porter L. Sask., Canada 56°20N 107°20W **71** B7
Porterville S. Africa 33°0S 19°0E **56** E2
Porterville U.S.A. 36°4N 119°1W **78** J8
Porthcawl U.K. 51°29N 3°42W **13** F4
Porthill U.S.A. 48°59N 116°30W **76** B5
Porthmadog U.K. 52°55N 4°8W **12** E3
Portile de Fier Europe 44°44N 22°30E **17** F12
Portimão Portugal 37°8N 8°32W **21** D1
Portishead U.K. 51°29N 2°46W **13** F5
Portknockie U.K. 57°42N 2°51W **11** D6
Portland N.S.W.,
  Australia 33°20S 150°0E **63** E5
Portland Vic., Australia 38°20S 141°35E **63** F3
Portland Canada 44°42N 76°12W **83** B8
Portland Conn., U.S.A. 41°34N 72°38W **83** E12
Portland Maine, U.S.A. 43°39N 70°16W **81** D18
Portland Mich., U.S.A. 42°52N 84°54W **81** D11
Portland Oreg., U.S.A. 45°32N 122°37W **78** E4
Portland Pa., U.S.A. 40°55N 75°6W **83** F9
Portland Tex., U.S.A. 27°53N 97°20W **84** H6
Portland, I. of U.K. 50°33N 2°26W **13** G5
Portland B. Australia 38°15S 141°45E **63** F3
Portland Bight Jamaica 17°52N 77°5W **88** a
Portland Bill U.K. 50°31N 2°28W **13** G5
Portland Canal U.S.A. 55°56N 130°0W **70** B2
Portland Int. ✈ (PDX)
  U.S.A. 45°35N 122°36W **78** E4
Portland Pt. Jamaica 17°42N 77°11W **88** a
Portmadoc = Porthmadog
  U.K. 52°55N 4°8W **12** E3
Portmore Jamaica 17°53N 76°53W **88** a
Porto France 42°16N 8°42E **20** E8
Porto Portugal 41°8N 8°40W **21** B1
Pôrto Alegre Brazil 30°5S 51°10W **95** C5
Porto Colom Spain 39°26N 3°15E **24** B10

Porto Cristo Spain 39°33N 3°20E **24 B10**
Porto de Moz Brazil 1°41S 52°13W **93 D8**
Porto Empédocle Italy 37°17N 13°32E **22 F5**
Porto Esperança Brazil 19°37S 57°29W **92 G7**
Porto Franco Brazil 6°20S 47°24W **93 E9**
Porto Inglês C. Verde Is. 15°21N 23°10W **50 b**
Porto Mendes Brazil 24°30S 54°15W **95 A5**
Porto Moniz Madeira 32°52N 17°11W **24 D2**
Porto Murtinho Brazil 21°45S 57°55W **92 H7**
Porto Nacional Brazil 10°40S 48°30W **93 F9**
Porto-Novo Benin 6°23N 2°42E **50 G6**
Porto Primavera, Represa Brazil 22°10S 52°45W **95 A5**
Porto Santo, I. de Madeira 33°45N 16°25W **50 B2**
Porto São José Brazil 22°43S 53°10W **95 A5**
Porto Seguro Brazil 16°26S 39°5W **93 G11**
Porto Tórres Italy 40°50N 8°24E **22 D3**
Porto União Brazil 26°10S 51°10W **95 B5**
Porto-Vecchio France 41°35N 9°16E **20 F8**
Pôrto Velho Brazil 8°46S 63°54W **92 E6**
Porto Walter Brazil 8°15S 72°40W **92 E4**
Portobelo Panama 9°35N 79°42W **88 E4**
Portoferráio Italy 42°48N 10°20E **22 C4**
Portola U.S.A. 39°49N 120°28W **78 F6**
Portopetro Spain 39°22N 3°13E **24 B10**
Portoscuso Italy 39°12N 8°24E **22 E3**
Portoviejo Ecuador 1°7S 80°28W **92 D2**
Portpatrick U.K. 54°51N 5°7W **11 G3**
Portree U.K. 57°25N 6°12W **11 D2**
Portrush U.K. 55°12N 6°40W **10 A5**
Portsmouth Dominica 15°34N 61°27W **89 C7**
Portsmouth U.K. 50°48N 1°6W **13 G6**
Portsmouth N.H., U.S.A. 43°5N 70°45W **83 C14**
Portsmouth Ohio, U.S.A. 38°44N 82°57W **81 F12**
Portsmouth R.I., U.S.A. 41°36N 71°15W **83 E13**
Portsmouth Va., U.S.A. 36°58N 76°23W **81 G15**
Portsmouth □ U.K. 50°48N 1°6W **13 G6**
Portsoy U.K. 57°41N 2°41W **11 D6**
Portstewart U.K. 55°11N 6°43W **10 A5**
Porttipahdan tekojärvi Finland 68°5N 26°40E **8 B22**
Portugal ■ Europe 40°0N 8°0W **21 C1**
Portumna Ireland 53°6N 8°14W **10 C3**
Portville U.S.A. 42°3N 78°20W **82 D6**
Porvenir Chile 53°10S 70°16W **96 G2**
Posadas Argentina 27°30S 55°50W **95 B4**
Posht-e Badam Iran 33°2N 55°23E **45 C7**
Poso Indonesia 1°20S 120°55E **37 E6**
Posse Brazil 14°4S 46°18W **93 F9**
Possession I. Antarctica 72°4S 172°0E **5 D11**
Possum Kingdom L. U.S.A. 32°52N 98°26W **84 E5**
Post U.S.A. 33°12N 101°23W **84 E4**
Post Falls U.S.A. 47°43N 116°57W **76 C5**
Postavy = Pastavy Belarus 55°4N 26°50E **9 J22**
Poste-de-la-Baleine = Kuujjuarapik Canada 55°20N 77°35W **72 A4**
Postmasburg S. Africa 28°18S 23°5E **56 D3**
Postojna Slovenia 45°46N 14°12E **16 F8**
Poston U.S.A. 34°0N 114°24W **79 M12**
Postville Canada 54°54N 59°47W **73 B8**
Posyet Russia 42°39N 130°48E **30 C5**
Potchefstroom S. Africa 26°41S 27°7E **56 D4**
Poteau U.S.A. 35°3N 94°37W **84 D7**
Poteet U.S.A. 29°2N 98°35W **84 G5**
Potenza Italy 40°38N 15°48E **22 D6**
Poteriteri, L. N.Z. 46°5S 167°10E **59 G1**
Potgietersrus = Mokopane S. Africa 24°10S 28°55E **57 C4**
Poti Georgia 42°10N 41°38E **19 F7**
Potiskum Nigeria 11°39N 11°2E **51 F8**
Potomac → U.S.A. 38°0N 76°23W **81 F14**
Potosí Bolivia 19°38S 65°50W **92 G5**
Potosi Mt. U.S.A. 35°57N 115°29W **79 K11**
Pototan Phil. 10°54N 122°38E **37 B6**
Potrerillos Chile 26°30S 69°30W **94 B2**
Potsdam Germany 52°23N 13°3E **16 B7**
Potsdam U.S.A. 44°40N 74°59W **83 B10**
Pottersville U.S.A. 43°43N 73°50W **83 C11**
Pottstown U.S.A. 40°15N 75°39W **83 F9**
Pottsville U.S.A. 40°41N 76°12W **83 F8**
Pottuvil Sri Lanka 6°55N 81°50E **40 R12**
Pouce Coupé Canada 55°40N 120°10W **70 B4**
Poughkeepsie U.S.A. 41°42N 73°56W **83 E11**
Poulaphouca Res. Ireland 53°8N 6°30W **10 C5**
Poulsbo U.S.A. 47°44N 122°38W **78 C4**
Poultney U.S.A. 43°31N 73°14W **83 C11**
Poulton-le-Fylde U.K. 53°51N 2°58W **12 D5**
Pouso Alegre Brazil 22°14S 45°57W **95 A6**
Pouthisat Cambodia 12°34N 103°50E **38 F4**
Považská Bystrica Slovak Rep. 49°8N 18°27E **17 D10**
Povenets Russia 62°50N 34°50E **18 B5**
Poverty B. N.Z. 38°43S 178°2E **59 C7**
Póvoa de Varzim Portugal 41°25N 8°46W **21 B1**
Povorotnyy, Mys Russia 42°40N 133°2E **30 C6**
Povungnituk = Puvirnituq Canada 60°2N 77°10W **69 C12**
Powassan Canada 46°5N 79°25W **72 C4**
Poway U.S.A. 32°58N 117°2W **79 N9**
Powder → U.S.A. 46°45N 105°26W **76 C11**
Powder River U.S.A. 43°2N 106°59W **76 E10**
Powell U.S.A. 44°45N 108°46W **76 D9**
Powell, L. U.S.A. 36°57N 111°29W **77 H8**
Powell River Canada 49°50N 124°35W **70 D4**
Powers U.S.A. 45°41N 87°32W **80 C10**
Pownal U.S.A. 42°45N 73°14W **83 D11**
Powys □ U.K. 52°20N 3°20W **13 E4**
Poyang Hu China 29°5N 116°20E **33 D6**
Poyarkovo Russia 49°36N 128°41E **29 E13**
Poza Rica Mexico 20°33N 97°27W **87 C5**
Požarevac Serbia 44°35N 21°18E **23 B9**
Poznań Poland 52°25N 16°55E **17 B9**

Pozo U.S.A. 35°20N 120°24W **79 K6**
Pozo Almonte Chile 20°10S 69°50W **92 H5**
Pozo Colorado Paraguay 23°30S 58°45W **94 A4**
Pozoblanco Spain 38°23N 4°51W **21 C3**
Pozzuoli Italy 40°49N 14°7E **22 D6**
Prachin Buri Thailand 14°0N 101°25E **38 F3**
Prachuap Khiri Khan Thailand 11°49N 99°48E **39 G2**
Prado Brazil 17°20S 39°13W **93 G11**
Prague = Praha Czech Rep. 50°4N 14°25E **16 C8**
Praha Czech Rep. 50°4N 14°25E **16 C8**
Praia C. Verde Is. 15°2N 23°34W **50 b**
Prainha Brazil 1°45S 53°30W **93 D8**
Prainha Nova Brazil 7°10S 60°30W **92 E6**
Prairie Australia 20°50S 144°35E **62 C3**
Prairie City U.S.A. 44°28N 118°43W **76 D4**
Prairie Dog Town Fork Red → U.S.A. 34°34N 99°58W **84 D5**
Prairie du Chien U.S.A. 43°3N 91°9W **80 D8**
Prairies, L. of the Canada 51°16N 101°32W **71 C8**
Pran Buri Thailand 12°23N 99°55E **38 F2**
Prapat Indonesia 2°41N 98°58E **36 D1**
Praslin Seychelles 4°18S 55°45E **53 b**
Prasonisi, Akra Greece 35°42N 27°46E **25 D9**
Prata Brazil 19°25S 48°54W **93 G9**
Pratabpur India 23°28N 83°15E **43 H10**
Pratapgarh Raj., India 24°2N 74°40E **42 G6**
Pratapgarh Ut. P., India 25°56N 81°59E **43 G9**
Prato Italy 43°53N 11°6E **22 C4**
Pratt U.S.A. 37°39N 98°44W **84 C4**
Prattville U.S.A. 32°28N 86°29W **85 E11**
Pravia Spain 43°30N 6°12W **21 A2**
Praya Indonesia 8°39S 116°17E **36 F5**
Preble U.S.A. 42°44N 76°8W **83 D8**
Precipice △ Australia 25°18S 150°5E **63 D5**
Precordillera Argentina 30°0S 69°1W **94 C2**
Preeceville Canada 51°57N 102°40W **71 C8**
Preiļi Latvia 56°18N 26°43E **9 H22**
Premont U.S.A. 27°22N 98°7W **84 H5**
Prentice U.S.A. 45°33N 90°17W **80 C8**
Preobrazheniye Russia 42°54N 133°54E **30 C6**
Preparis North Channel Ind. Oc. 15°27N 94°5E **41 M18**
Preparis South Channel Ind. Oc. 14°33N 93°30E **41 M18**
Přerov Czech Rep. 49°28N 17°27E **17 D9**
Prescott Canada 44°45N 75°30W **83 B9**
Prescott Ariz., U.S.A. 34°33N 112°28W **77 J7**
Prescott Ark., U.S.A. 33°48N 93°23W **84 E8**
Prescott Valley U.S.A. 34°40N 112°18W **77 J7**
Preservation Inlet N.Z. 46°8S 166°35E **59 G1**
Presho U.S.A. 43°54N 100°3W **80 D3**
Presidencia de la Plaza Argentina 27°0S 59°50W **94 B4**
Presidencia Roque Saenz Peña Argentina 26°45S 60°30W **94 B3**
Presidente Epitácio Brazil 21°56S 52°6W **93 H8**
Presidente Hayes □ Paraguay 24°0S 59°0W **94 A4**
Presidente Prudente Brazil 22°5S 51°25W **95 A5**
Presidio Mexico 29°29N 104°23W **86 B4**
Presidio U.S.A. 29°34N 104°22W **84 G2**
Prešov Slovak Rep. 49°0N 21°15E **17 D11**
Prespa, L. = Prespansko Jezero Macedonia 40°55N 21°0E **23 D9**
Prespansko Jezero Macedonia 40°55N 21°0E **23 D9**
Presque I. U.S.A. 42°10N 80°6W **82 D4**
Presque Isle U.S.A. 46°41N 68°1W **81 B19**
Prestatyn U.K. 53°20N 3°24W **12 D4**
Presteigne U.K. 52°17N 3°0W **13 E5**
Preston Canada 43°23N 80°21W **82 C4**
Preston U.K. 53°46N 2°42W **12 D5**
Preston Idaho, U.S.A. 42°6N 111°53W **76 E8**
Preston Minn., U.S.A. 43°40N 92°5W **80 D7**
Preston, C. Australia 20°51S 116°12E **60 D2**
Prestonsburg U.S.A. 37°40N 82°47W **81 G12**
Prestwick U.K. 55°29N 4°37W **11 F4**
Pretoria S. Africa 25°44S 28°12E **57 D4**
Preveza Greece 38°57N 20°45E **23 E9**
Prey Veng Cambodia 11°35N 105°29E **39 G5**
Pribilof Is. U.S.A. 57°0N 170°0W **74 a**
Příbram Czech Rep. 49°41N 14°2E **16 D8**
Price U.S.A. 39°36N 110°49W **76 G8**
Price I. Canada 52°23N 128°41W **70 C3**
Prichard U.S.A. 30°44N 88°5W **85 F10**
Priekule Latvia 56°26N 21°35E **9 H19**
Prienai Lithuania 54°38N 23°57E **9 J20**
Prieska S. Africa 29°40S 22°42E **56 D3**
Priest → U.S.A. 48°35N 116°52W **76 B5**
Priest River U.S.A. 48°11N 116°55W **76 B5**
Priest Valley U.S.A. 36°10N 120°39W **78 J6**
Prievidza Slovak Rep. 48°46N 18°36E **17 D10**
Prikaspiyskaya Nizmennost = Caspian Depression Eurasia 47°0N 48°0E **19 E8**
Prilep Macedonia 41°21N 21°32E **23 D9**
Priluki = Pryluky Ukraine 50°30N 32°24E **19 D5**
Prime Seal I. Australia 40°3S 147°43E **63 G4**
Primo Tapia Mexico 32°16N 116°54W **79 N10**
Primorskiy Kray □ Russia 45°0N 135°0E **30 B7**
Primrose L. Canada 54°55N 109°45W **71 C7**
Prince Albert Canada 53°15N 105°50W **71 C7**
Prince Albert S. Africa 33°12S 22°2E **56 E3**
Prince Albert △ Canada 54°0N 106°25W **71 C7**
Prince Albert Mts. Antarctica 76°0S 161°30E **5 D11**
Prince Albert Pen. Canada 72°30N 116°0W **68 B8**
Prince Albert Sd. Canada 70°25N 115°0W **68 B8**
Prince Alfred, C. Canada 74°20N 124°40W **69 B7**

Prince Charles I. Canada 67°47N 76°12W **69 C12**
Prince Charles Mts. Antarctica 72°0S 67°0E **5 D6**
Prince Edward Fracture Zone Ind. Oc. 46°0S 35°0E **5 A4**
Prince Edward I. □ Canada 46°20N 63°20W **73 C7**
Prince Edward Is. Ind. Oc. 46°35S 38°0E **3 G11**
Prince George Canada 53°55N 122°50W **70 C4**
Prince Gustaf Adolf Sea Canada 78°30N 107°0W **69 B9**
Prince of Wales, C. U.S.A. 65°36N 168°5W **66 C3**
Prince of Wales I. Australia 10°40S 142°10E **62 A3**
Prince of Wales I. Canada 73°0N 99°0W **68 B10**
Prince of Wales I. U.S.A. 55°47N 132°50W **68 D6**
Prince Patrick I. Canada 77°0N 120°0W **69 B8**
Prince Regent Inlet Canada 73°0N 90°0W **4 B3**
Prince Rupert Canada 54°20N 130°20W **70 C2**
Princes Town Trin. & Tob. 10°16N 61°23W **93 K15**
Princess Charlotte B. Australia 14°25S 144°0E **62 A3**
Princess Elizabeth Trough S. Ocean 64°10S 83°0E **5 C7**
Princess May Ranges Australia 15°30S 125°30E **60 C4**
Princess Royal I. Canada 53°0N 128°40W **70 C3**
Princeton Canada 49°27N 120°30W **70 D4**
Princeton Calif., U.S.A. 39°24N 122°1W **78 F4**
Princeton Ill., U.S.A. 41°23N 89°28W **80 E9**
Princeton Ind., U.S.A. 38°21N 87°34W **80 F10**
Princeton Ky., U.S.A. 37°7N 87°53W **80 G10**
Princeton Mo., U.S.A. 40°24N 93°35W **80 E7**
Princeton N.J., U.S.A. 40°21N 74°39W **83 F10**
Princeton W. Va., U.S.A. 37°22N 81°6W **81 G13**
Príncipe São Tomé & Príncipe 1°37N 7°25E **48 F4**
Príncipe da Beira Brazil 12°20S 64°30W **92 F6**
Prineville U.S.A. 44°18N 120°51W **76 D3**
Prins Harald Kyst Antarctica 70°0S 35°1E **5 D4**
Prinsesse Astrid Kyst Antarctica 70°45S 12°30E **5 D3**
Prinsesse Ragnhild Kyst Antarctica 70°15S 27°30E **5 D4**
Prinzapolca Nic. 13°20N 83°35W **88 D3**
Priozersk Russia 61°2N 30°7E **8 F24**
Pripet = Prypyat → Europe 51°20N 30°15E **17 C16**
Pripet Marshes Europe 52°10N 28°10E **17 B15**
Pripyat Marshes = Pripet Marshes Europe 52°10N 28°10E **17 B15**
Pripyats = Prypyat → Europe 51°20N 30°15E **17 C16**
Priština Serbia 42°40N 21°13E **23 C9**
Privas France 44°45N 4°37E **20 D6**
Privolzhskaya Vozvyshennost Russia 51°0N 46°0E **19 D8**
Privolzhskiy □ Russia 56°0N 50°0E **28 D6**
Prizren Serbia 42°13N 20°45E **23 C9**
Probolinggo Indonesia 7°46S 113°13E **37 G15**
Proctor U.S.A. 43°40N 73°2W **83 C11**
Proddatur India 14°45N 78°30E **40 M11**
Prodhromos Cyprus 34°57N 32°50E **25 E11**
Profilia Greece 36°5N 27°51E **25 C9**
Profondeville Belgium 50°23N 4°52E **15 D4**
Progreso Coahuila, Mexico 27°28N 100°59W **86 B4**
Progreso Yucatán, Mexico 21°20N 89°40W **87 C7**
Progress Antarctica 66°22S 76°22E **5 C12**
Progress Russia 49°45N 129°37E **29 E13**
Prokopyevsk Russia 54°0N 86°48E **28 D9**
Prokuplje Serbia 43°16N 21°36E **23 C9**
Prome Burma 18°49N 95°13E **41 K19**
Prophet → Canada 58°48N 122°40W **70 B4**
Prophet River Canada 58°6N 122°43W **70 B4**
Propriá Brazil 10°13S 36°51W **93 F11**
Propriano France 41°41N 8°52E **20 F8**
Proserpine Australia 20°21S 148°36E **62 J6**
Prosna → Poland 52°6N 17°44E **17 B9**
Prospect U.S.A. 43°18N 75°9W **83 C9**
Prosser U.S.A. 46°12N 119°46W **76 C4**
Prostějov Czech Rep. 49°30N 17°9E **17 D9**
Proston Australia 26°8S 151°32E **63 D5**
Provence France 43°40N 5°46E **20 E6**
Providence Ky., U.S.A. 37°24N 87°46W **80 G10**
Providence R.I., U.S.A. 41°49N 71°24W **83 E13**
Providence Bay Canada 45°41N 82°15W **72 C3**
Providence Mts. U.S.A. 35°10N 115°15W **79 K11**
Providencia, I. de Colombia 13°25N 81°26W **88 D3**
Providenyia Russia 64°23N 173°18W **29 C19**
Provincetown U.S.A. 42°3N 70°11W **81 D18**
Provins France 48°33N 3°15E **20 B5**
Provo U.S.A. 40°14N 111°39W **76 F8**
Provost Canada 52°25N 110°20W **71 C6**
Prudhoe Bay U.S.A. 70°18N 148°22W **74 a**
Prudhoe I. Australia 21°19S 149°41E **62 C4**
Prud'homme Canada 52°20N 105°54W **71 C7**
Pruszków Poland 52°9N 20°49E **17 B11**
Prut → Romania 45°28N 28°10E **17 F15**
Pruzhany Belarus 52°33N 24°28E **17 B13**
Prydz B. Antarctica 69°0S 74°0E **5 C6**
Pryluky Ukraine 50°30N 32°24E **19 D5**
Pryor U.S.A. 36°19N 95°19W **84 C7**
Prypyat → Europe 51°20N 30°15E **17 C16**
Przemyśl Poland 49°50N 22°45E **17 D12**
Przhevalsk = Karakol Kyrgyzstan 42°30N 78°20E **32 B2**
Psara Greece 38°37N 25°38E **23 E11**
Psíloritis, Oros Greece 35°15N 24°45E **25 D6**
Psira Greece 35°12N 25°52E **25 D7**
Pskov Russia 57°50N 28°25E **9 H23**

Ptich = Ptsich → Belarus 52°9N 28°52E **17 B15**
Ptichia = Vidos Greece 39°38N 19°55E **25 A3**
Ptolemaida Greece 40°30N 21°43E **23 D9**
Ptsich → Belarus 52°9N 28°52E **17 B15**
Pu Xian China 36°24N 111°6E **34 F6**
Pua Thailand 19°11N 100°55E **38 C3**
Puán Argentina 37°30S 62°45W **94 D3**
Pu'apu'a Samoa 13°34S 172°9W **59 b**
Pucallpa Peru 8°25S 74°30W **92 E4**
Puch'on = Bucheon S. Korea 37°28N 126°45E **35 F14**
Pudasjärvi Finland 65°23N 26°53E **8 D22**
Pudozh Russia 61°48N 36°32E **18 B6**
Puducherry India 11°59N 79°50E **40 P11**
Pudukkottai India 10°28N 78°47E **40 P11**
Puebla Mexico 19°3N 98°12W **87 D5**
Puebla □ Mexico 18°50N 98°0W **87 D5**
Pueblo U.S.A. 38°16N 104°37W **76 G11**
Puelches Argentina 38°5S 65°51W **94 D2**
Puelén Argentina 37°32S 67°38W **94 D2**
Puente Alto Chile 33°32S 70°35W **94 C1**
Puente-Genil Spain 37°22N 4°47W **21 D3**
Puerca, Pta. Puerto Rico 18°13N 65°36W **89 d**
Puerco → U.S.A. 34°22N 107°50W **77 J10**
Puerto Aisén Chile 45°27S 73°0W **96 F2**
Puerto Ángel Mexico 15°40N 96°29W **87 D5**
Puerto Arista Mexico 15°56N 93°48W **87 D6**
Puerto Armuelles Panama 8°20N 82°51W **88 E3**
Puerto Ayacucho Venezuela 5°40N 67°35W **92 B5**
Puerto Barrios Guatemala 15°40N 88°32W **88 C2**
Puerto Bermejo Argentina 26°55S 58°34W **94 B4**
Puerto Bermúdez Peru 10°20S 74°58W **92 F4**
Puerto Bolívar Ecuador 3°19S 79°55W **92 D3**
Puerto Cabello Venezuela 10°28N 68°1W **92 A5**
Puerto Cabezas Nic. 14°0N 83°30W **88 D3**
Puerto Cabo Gracias á Dios Nic. 15°0N 83°10W **88 D3**
Puerto Carreño Colombia 6°12N 67°22W **92 B5**
Puerto Castilla Honduras 16°0N 86°0W **88 C2**
Puerto Chicama Peru 7°45S 79°20W **92 E3**
Puerto Coig Argentina 50°54S 69°15W **96 G3**
Puerto Cortés Honduras 15°51N 88°0W **88 C2**
Puerto Cumarebo Venezuela 11°29N 69°30W **92 A5**
Puerto de Alcudia = Port d'Alcúdia Spain 39°50N 3°7E **24 B10**
Puerto de Cabrera Spain 39°8N 2°56E **24 B9**
Puerto de Gran Tarajal Canary Is. 28°13N 14°1W **24 F5**
Puerto de la Cruz Canary Is. 28°24N 16°32W **24 F3**
Puerto de los Angeles △ Mexico 23°39N 105°45W **86 C3**
Puerto de Pozo Negro Canary Is. 28°19N 13°55W **24 F6**
Puerto de Sóller = Port de Sóller Spain 39°48N 2°42E **24 B9**
Puerto del Carmen Canary Is. 28°55N 13°38W **24 F6**
Puerto del Rosario Canary Is. 28°30N 13°52W **24 F6**
Puerto Deseado Argentina 47°55S 66°0W **96 F3**
Puerto Escondido Mexico 15°50N 97°3W **87 D5**
Puerto Heath Bolivia 12°34S 68°39W **92 F5**
Puerto Inírida Colombia 3°53N 67°52W **92 C5**
Puerto Juárez Mexico 21°11N 86°49W **87 C7**
Puerto La Cruz Venezuela 10°13N 64°38W **92 A6**
Puerto Leguízamo Colombia 0°12S 74°46W **92 D4**
Puerto Lempira Honduras 15°16N 83°46W **88 C3**
Puerto Libertad Mexico 29°55N 112°43W **86 B2**
Puerto Limón Colombia 3°23N 73°30W **92 C4**
Puerto Lobos Argentina 42°0S 65°3W **96 E3**
Puerto Madryn Argentina 42°48S 65°4W **96 E3**
Puerto Maldonado Peru 12°30S 69°10W **92 F5**
Puerto Manatí Cuba 21°22N 76°50W **88 B4**
Puerto Montt Chile 41°28S 73°0W **96 E2**
Puerto Morazán Nic. 12°51N 87°11W **88 D2**
Puerto Morelos Mexico 20°50N 86°52W **87 C7**
Puerto Natales Chile 51°45S 72°15W **96 G2**
Puerto Oscuro Chile 31°24S 71°35W **94 C1**
Puerto Padre Cuba 21°13N 76°35W **88 B4**
Puerto Páez Venezuela 6°13N 67°28W **92 B5**
Puerto Peñasco Mexico 31°20N 113°33W **86 A2**
Puerto Pinasco Paraguay 22°36S 57°50W **94 A4**
Puerto Plata Dom. Rep. 19°48N 70°45W **89 C5**
Puerto Pollensa = Port de Pollença Spain 39°54N 3°4E **24 B10**
Puerto Princesa Phil. 9°46N 118°45E **37 C5**
Puerto Quepos Costa Rica 9°29N 84°6W **88 E3**
Puerto Rico Canary Is. 27°47N 15°42W **24 G4**
Puerto Rico ☑ W. Indies 18°15N 66°45W **89 d**
Puerto Rico Trench Atl. Oc. 19°50N 66°0W **89 C6**
Puerto San Julián Argentina 49°18S 67°43W **96 F3**
Puerto Santa Cruz Argentina 50°0S 68°32W **96 G3**
Puerto Sastre Paraguay 22°2S 57°55W **94 A4**
Puerto Suárez Bolivia 18°58S 57°52W **92 G7**
Puerto Vallarta Mexico 20°37N 105°15W **86 C3**
Puerto Varas Chile 41°19S 72°59W **96 E2**
Puerto Wilches Colombia 7°21N 73°54W **92 B4**
Puerto Yerrdón, L. Argentina 44°20S 72°0W **96 E2**
Puertollano Spain 38°43N 4°7W **21 C3**
Pueu Tahiti 17°44S 149°13W **59 d**
Puffin I. Ireland 51°50N 10°24W **10 E1**
Pugachev Russia 52°0N 48°49E **18 D8**
Pugal India 28°30N 72°48E **42 E5**

Puge Tanzania 4°45S 33°11E **54 C3**
Puget Sound U.S.A. 47°50N 122°30W **76 C2**
Pugŏdong N. Korea 42°5N 130°0E **35 C16**
Pugu Tanzania 6°55S 39°4E **54 D4**
Pügünzï Iran 25°49N 59°10E **45 E8**
Puig Major Spain 39°48N 2°47E **24 B9**
Puigcerdà Spain 42°24N 1°50E **21 A6**
Puigpunyent Spain 39°38N 2°32E **24 B9**
Pujon-ho N. Korea 40°35N 127°35E **35 D14**
Pukaki, L. N.Z. 44°4S 170°1E **59 F2**
Pukapuka Cook Is. 10°53S 165°49W **65 J11**
Pukaskwa △ Canada 48°20N 86°0W **72 C2**
Pukatawagan Canada 55°45N 101°20W **71 B8**
Pukchin N. Korea 40°12N 125°45E **35 D13**
Pukch'ŏng N. Korea 40°14N 128°10E **35 D15**
Pukekohe N.Z. 37°12S 174°55E **59 B5**
Pukhrayan India 26°14N 79°51E **43 F8**
Pula Croatia 44°54N 13°57E **16 F7**
Pulacayo Bolivia 20°25S 66°41W **92 H5**
Pulai Malaysia 1°20N 103°31E **39 d**
Pulandian China 39°25N 121°58E **35 E11**
Pulaski N.Y., U.S.A. 43°34N 76°8W **83 C8**
Pulaski Tenn., U.S.A. 35°12N 87°2W **85 D11**
Pulaski Va., U.S.A. 37°3N 80°47W **81 G13**
Pulau → Indonesia 5°50S 138°15E **37 F9**
Puławy Poland 51°23N 21°59E **17 C11**
Pulga U.S.A. 39°48N 121°29W **78 F5**
Pulicat L. India 13°40N 80°15E **40 N12**
Pullman U.S.A. 46°44N 117°10W **76 C5**
Pulog, Mt. Phil. 16°40N 120°50E **37 A6**
Pultusk Poland 52°43N 21°6E **17 B11**
Pumlumon Fawr U.K. 52°28N 3°46W **13 E4**
Puná, I. Ecuador 2°55S 80°5W **92 D2**
Punaauia Tahiti 17°37S 149°34W **59 d**
Punakaiki N.Z. 42°7S 171°20E **59 E3**
Punakha Dzong Bhutan 27°42N 89°52E **41 F16**
Punasar India 27°6N 73°6E **42 F5**
Punata Bolivia 17°32S 65°50W **92 G5**
Punch India 33°48N 74°4E **43 C6**
Punch → Pakistan 33°12N 73°40E **42 C5**
Punda Maria S. Africa 22°40S 31°5E **57 C5**
Pune India 18°29N 73°57E **40 K8**
P'ungsan N. Korea 40°50N 128°9E **35 D15**
Pungue, Ponte de Mozam. 19°0S 34°0E **55 F3**
Punjab □ India 31°0N 76°0E **42 D7**
Punjab □ Pakistan 32°0N 72°30E **42 E6**
Puno Peru 15°55S 70°3W **92 G4**
Punpun → India 25°31N 85°18E **43 G11**
Punta, Cerro de Puerto Rico 18°10N 66°37W **89 d**
Punta Alta Argentina 38°53S 62°4W **96 D4**
Punta Arenas Chile 53°10S 71°0W **96 G2**
Punta del Díaz Chile 28°0S 70°45W **94 B1**
Punta del Hidalgo Canary Is. 28°33N 16°19W **24 F3**
Punta Gorda Belize 16°10N 88°45W **87 D7**
Punta Gorda U.S.A. 26°56N 82°3W **85 H13**
Punta Prieta Mexico 28°58N 114°17W **86 B2**
Punta Prima Spain 39°48N 4°16E **24 B11**
Puntarenas Costa Rica 10°0N 84°50W **88 E3**
Puntland Somali Rep. 8°0N 49°0E **47 F4**
Punto Fijo Venezuela 11°50N 70°13W **92 A4**
Punxsatawney U.S.A. 40°57N 78°59W **82 F6**
Pupuan Indonesia 8°19S 115°0E **37 J18**
Puquio Peru 14°45S 74°10W **92 F4**
Pur → Russia 67°31N 77°55E **28 C8**
Puracé, Vol. Colombia 2°21N 76°23W **92 C3**
Puralia = Puruliya India 23°17N 86°24E **43 H12**
Puranpur India 28°31N 80°9E **43 E9**
Purbeck, Isle of U.K. 50°39N 1°59W **13 G5**
Purcell U.S.A. 35°1N 97°22W **84 D6**
Purcell Mts. Canada 49°55N 116°15W **70 D5**
Purdy Canada 45°19N 77°44W **82 A7**
Puri India 19°50N 85°58E **41 K14**
Purmerend Neths. 52°32N 4°58E **15 B4**
Purnia India 25°45N 87°31E **43 G12**
Purnululu △ Australia 17°20S 128°20E **60 C4**
Pursat = Pouthisat Cambodia 12°34N 103°50E **38 F4**
Purukcahu Indonesia 0°35S 114°35E **36 E4**
Puruliya India 23°17N 86°24E **43 H12**
Purus → Brazil 3°42S 61°28W **92 D6**
Puruvesi Finland 61°50N 29°30E **8 F23**
Purvis U.S.A. 31°9N 89°25W **85 F10**
Purwa India 26°28N 80°47E **43 F9**
Purwo, Tanjung Indonesia 8°44S 114°21E **37 K18**
Purwodadi Indonesia 7°7S 110°55E **37 G14**
Purwokerto Indonesia 7°25S 109°14E **37 G13**
Puryŏng N. Korea 42°5N 129°43E **35 C15**
Pusa India 25°59N 85°41E **43 G11**
Pusan = Busan S. Korea 35°5N 129°0E **35 G15**
Pushkin Russia 59°45N 30°25E **9 C6**
Pushkino Russia 51°16N 47°0E **18 D8**
Put-in-Bay U.S.A. 41°39N 82°49W **82 E2**
Putao Burma 27°28N 97°30E **41 F20**
Putaruru N.Z. 38°2S 175°50E **59 C5**
Putignano Italy 40°51N 17°7E **22 D7**
Putorana, Gory Russia 69°0N 95°0E **29 C10**
Putrajaya Malaysia 2°55N 101°40E **39 L3**
Puttalam Sri Lanka 8°1N 79°55E **40 Q11**
Puttgarden Germany 54°30N 11°10E **16 A6**
Putumayo → S. Amer. 3°7S 67°58W **92 D5**
Putussibau Indonesia 0°50N 112°56E **36 D4**
Puvirnituq Canada 60°2N 77°10W **69 C12**
Puy-de-Dôme France 45°46N 2°57E **20 D5**
Puyallup U.S.A. 47°12N 122°18W **78 C4**
Puyang China 35°40N 115°1E **34 G8**
Püzeh Rig Iran 27°20N 58°40E **45 E8**
Pwani □ Tanzania 7°0S 39°0E **54 D4**
Pweto Dem. Rep. of the Congo 8°25S 28°51E **55 D2**

Pwllheli U.K. 52°53N 4°25W 12 E3
Pyaozero, Ozero Russia 66°5N 30°58E 8 C24
Pyapon Burma 16°20N 95°40E 41 L19
Pyasina → Russia 73°30N 87°0E 29 B9
Pyatigorsk Russia 44°2N 43°6E 19 F7
Pyè = Prome Burma 18°49N 95°13E 41 K19
Pyeongtaek S. Korea 37°1N 127°4E 35 F14
Pyetrikaw Belarus 52°11N 28°29E 17 B15
Pyhäjoki Finland 64°28N 24°14E 8 D21
Pyinmana Burma 19°45N 96°12E 41 K20
Pyla, C. Cyprus 34°56N 33°51E 25 E12
Pymatuning Res. U.S.A. 41°30N 80°28W 82 E4
Pyŏktong N. Korea 40°50N 125°50E 35 D13
Pyŏnggang N. Korea 38°24N 127°17E 35 E14
P'yŏngsong N. Korea 39°14N 125°52E 35 E13
P'yŏngyang N. Korea 39°0N 125°30E 35 E13
Pyote U.S.A. 31°32N 103°8W 84 F3
Pyramid L. U.S.A. 40°1N 119°35W 76 F4
Pyramid Pk. U.S.A. 36°25N 116°37W 79 J10
Pyramids Egypt 29°58N 31°9E 51 C12
Pyrénées Europe 42°45N 0°18E 20 E4
Pyu Burma 18°30N 96°28E 41 K20

Q

Qaanaaq Greenland 77°40N 69°0W 4 B4
Qachasnek S. Africa 30°6S 28°42E 57 E4
Qa'el Jafr Jordan 30°20N 36°25E 46 E5
Qa'emābād Iran 31°44N 60°2E 45 D9
Qā'emshahr Iran 36°30N 52°53E 45 B7
Qagan Nur China 43°30N 114°55E 34 C8
Qahar Youyi Zhongqi China 41°12N 112°40E 34 D7
Qahremānshahr = Kermānshāh Iran 34°23N 47°0E 44 C5
Qaidam Pendi China 37°0N 95°0E 32 C4
Qajarīyeh Iran 31°1N 48°22E 45 D6
Qala, Ras il Malta 36°2N 14°20E 25 C1
Qala-i-Jadid = Spīn Būldak Afghan. 31°1N 66°25E 42 D2
Qala Point = Qala, Ras il Malta 36°2N 14°20E 25 C1
Qala Viala Pakistan 30°49N 67°17E 42 D2
Qala Yangi Afghan. 34°20N 66°30E 42 B2
Qal'at al Akhḑar Si. Arabia 28°4N 37°9E 44 E3
Qal'at Dīzah Iraq 36°11N 45°7E 44 B5
Qal'at Şāliḩ Iraq 31°31N 47°16E 44 D5
Qal'at Sukkar Iraq 31°51N 46°5E 44 D5
Qamani'tuaq = Baker Lake Canada 64°20N 96°3W 68 C10
Qamdo China 31°15N 97°6E 32 C4
Qamea Fiji 16°45S 179°45W 59 a
Qamruddin Karez Pakistan 31°45N 68°20E 42 D3
Qandahār = Kandahār Afghan. 31°32N 65°43E 40 D4
Qandahār = Kandahār □ Afghan. 31°0N 65°0E 40 D4
Qandyaghash Kazakhstan 49°28N 57°25E 19 E10
Qapān Iran 37°40N 55°47E 45 B7
Qapshaghay Kazakhstan 43°51N 77°14E 28 E8
Qaqortoq Greenland 60°43N 46°0W 4 C5
Qara Qash → China 35°0N 78°30E 43 B8
Qarabutaq Kazakhstan 49°59N 60°14E 28 E7
Qaraghandy Kazakhstan 49°50N 73°10E 28 E8
Qaraghayly Kazakhstan 49°26N 76°0E 28 E8
Qārah Si. Arabia 29°55N 40°3E 44 D4
Qarataū Kazakhstan 43°30N 69°30E 28 E7
Qarataū Zhambyl, Kazakhstan 43°10N 70°28E 28 E8
Qarazhal Kazakhstan 48°2N 70°49E 28 E8
Qardho Somali Rep. 9°30N 49°6E 47 F4
Qareh → Iran 39°25N 47°22E 44 B5
Qareh Tekān Iran 36°38N 49°29E 45 B6
Qarnein U.A.E. 24°56N 52°52E 45 E7
Qarqan He → China 39°30N 88°30E 32 C3
Qarqaraly Kazakhstan 49°26N 75°30E 28 E8
Qarshi Uzbekistan 38°53N 65°48E 28 F7
Qartabā Lebanon 34°4N 35°50E 46 A4
Qārūh Kuwait 28°49N 48°46E 45 D6
Qaryat al Gharab Iraq 31°27N 44°48E 44 D5
Qaryat al 'Ulyā Si. Arabia 27°33N 47°42E 44 E5
Qasr 'Amra Jordan 31°48N 36°35E 44 D3
Qaşr-e Qand Iran 26°15N 60°45E 45 E9
Qaşr-e Shīrīn Iran 34°31N 45°35E 44 C5
Qasr Farâfra Egypt 27°0N 28°1E 51 C11
Qatanā Syria 33°26N 36°4E 46 B5
Qatar ■ Asia 25°30N 51°15E 45 E6
Qatlīsh Iran 37°50N 57°19E 45 B8
Qattâra, Munkhafed el Egypt 29°30N 27°30E 51 C11
Qattâra Depression = Qattâra, Munkhafed el Egypt 29°30N 27°30E 51 C11
Qausiuittuq = Resolute Canada 74°42N 94°54W 69 B10
Qawām al Ḩamzah = Al Ḩamzah Iraq 31°43N 44°58E 44 D5
Qāyen Iran 33°40N 59°10E 45 C8
Qazaqstan = Kazakhstan ■ Asia 50°0N 70°0E 28 E8
Qazımämmäd Azerbaijan 40°3N 49°0E 45 A6
Qazvīn Iran 36°15N 50°0E 45 B6
Qazvīn □ Iran 36°20N 50°0E 45 B6
Qena Egypt 26°10N 32°43E 51 C12
Qeqertarsuaq Greenland 69°15N 53°38W 4 C5
Qeqertarsuaq Greenland 69°45N 53°30W 66 C14
Qeshlāq Iran 34°55N 46°28E 44 C5
Qeshm Iran 26°55N 56°10E 45 E8
Qeys Iran 26°32N 53°58E 45 E7
Qezel Owzen → Iran 36°45N 49°22E 45 B6
Qezi'ot Israel 30°52N 34°26E 46 E3
Qi Xian China 34°40N 114°48E 34 G8
Qian Gorlos China 45°5N 124°42E 35 B13
Qian Hai China 22°32N 113°54E 33 F10
Qian Xian China 34°31N 108°15E 34 G5
Qianshan China 22°15N 113°31E 33 G10
Qianyang China 34°40N 107°8E 34 G4
Qi'ao China 22°25N 113°39E 33 G10
Qi'ao Dao China 22°25N 113°38E 33 G10
Qiemo China 38°8N 85°32E 32 C3
Qijiaojing China 43°28N 91°36E 32 B4
Qikiqtarjuaq Canada 67°33N 63°0W 69 C13
Qila Saifullāh Pakistan 30°45N 68°17E 42 D3
Qilian Shan China 38°30N 96°0E 32 C4
Qin He → China 35°1N 113°22E 34 G7
Qin Ling = Qinling Shandi China 33°50N 108°10E 34 H5
Qin'an China 34°48N 105°40E 34 G3
Qing Xian China 38°35N 116°45E 34 E9
Qingcheng China 37°15N 117°40E 35 F9
Qingdao China 36°5N 120°20E 35 F11
Qingfeng China 35°52N 115°8E 34 G8
Qinghai □ China 36°0N 98°0E 32 C4
Qinghai Hu China 36°40N 100°10E 32 C5
Qinghecheng China 41°28N 124°15E 35 D13
Qinghemen China 41°48N 121°25E 35 D11
Qingjian China 37°8N 110°8E 34 F6
Qingjiang = Huaiyin China 33°30N 119°2E 35 H10
Qingshui China 34°48N 106°8E 34 G4
Qingshuihe China 39°55N 111°35E 34 E6
Qingtongxia Shuiku China 37°50N 105°58E 34 F3
Qingxu China 37°34N 112°22E 34 F7
Qingyang China 36°2N 107°55E 34 F4
Qingyuan China 42°10N 124°55E 35 C13
Qingyun China 37°45N 117°20E 35 F9
Qinhuangdao China 39°56N 119°30E 35 E10
Qinling Shandi China 33°50N 108°10E 34 H5
Qinshui China 35°40N 112°8E 34 G7
Qinyang = Jiyuan China 35°7N 112°57E 34 G7
Qinyuan China 36°29N 112°20E 34 F7
Qinzhou China 21°58N 108°38E 32 D5
Qionghai China 19°15N 110°26E 38 C8
Qiongzhou Haixia China 20°10N 110°15E 38 B8
Qiqihar China 47°26N 124°0E 33 B7
Qira China 37°0N 80°48E 32 C3
Qiraîya, W. → Egypt 30°27N 34°0E 46 E3
Qiryat Ata Israel 32°47N 35°6E 46 C4
Qiryat Gat Israel 31°32N 34°46E 46 D3
Qiryat Mal'akhi Israel 31°44N 34°44E 46 D3
Qiryat Shemona Israel 33°13N 35°35E 46 B4
Qiryat Yam Israel 32°51N 35°4E 46 C4
Qishan China 34°25N 107°38E 34 G4
Qitai China 44°2N 89°35E 32 B3
Qitaihe China 45°48N 130°51E 30 B5
Qixia China 37°17N 120°52E 35 F11
Qızılağac Körfäzi Azerbaijan 39°9N 49°0E 45 B6
Qojūr Iran 36°12N 47°55E 44 B5
Qom Iran 34°40N 51°0E 45 C6
Qom □ Iran 34°40N 51°0E 45 C6
Qomolangma Feng = Everest, Mt. Nepal 28°5N 86°58E 43 E12
Qomsheh Iran 32°0N 51°55E 45 D6
Qoqek = Tacheng China 46°40N 82°58E 32 B3
Qoqon = Qŭqon Uzbekistan 40°31N 70°56E 28 E8
Qoraqalpoghistan □ Uzbekistan 43°0N 58°0E 28 E6
Qorveh Iran 35°10N 47°48E 44 C5
Qostanay Kazakhstan 53°10N 63°35E 28 D7
Quabbin Res. U.S.A. 42°20N 72°20W 83 D12
Quairading Australia 32°0S 117°21E 61 F2
Quakertown U.S.A. 40°26N 75°21W 83 F9
Qualicum Beach Canada 49°22N 124°26W 70 D4
Quambatook Australia 35°49S 143°34E 63 F3
Quambone Australia 30°57S 147°53E 63 E4
Quamby Australia 20°22S 140°17E 62 C3
Quan Long = Ca Mau Vietnam 9°7N 105°8E 39 H5
Quanah U.S.A. 34°18N 99°44W 84 D5
Quang Ngai Vietnam 15°13N 108°58E 38 E7
Quang Tri Vietnam 16°45N 107°13E 38 D6
Quang Yen Vietnam 20°56N 106°52E 38 B6
Quantock Hills U.K. 51°8N 3°10W 13 F4
Quanzhou China 24°55N 118°34E 33 D6
Qu'Appelle → Canada 50°33N 103°53W 71 C8
Quaqtaq Canada 60°55N 69°40W 69 C13
Quarai Brazil 30°15S 56°20W 94 C4
Quartu Sant'Èlena Italy 39°15N 9°10E 22 E3
Quartzsite U.S.A. 33°40N 114°13W 79 M12
Quatre Bornes Mauritius 20°15S 57°28E 53 d
Quatsino Sd. Canada 50°25N 127°58W 70 C3
Quba Azerbaijan 41°21N 48°32E 19 F8
Qūchān Iran 37°10N 58°27E 45 B8
Queanbeyan Australia 35°17S 149°14E 63 F4
Québec Canada 46°52N 71°13W 73 C5
Québec □ Canada 48°0N 74°0W 73 C6
Quebrada del Condorito △ Argentina 31°49S 64°40W 94 C3
Queen Alexandra Ra. Antarctica 85°0S 170°0E 5 E11
Queen Charlotte City Canada 53°15N 132°2W 70 C2
Queen Charlotte Is. Canada 53°20N 132°10W 70 C2
Queen Charlotte Sd. Canada 51°0N 128°0W 70 C3
Queen Charlotte Strait Canada 50°45N 127°10W 70 C3
Queen Elizabeth △ Uganda 0°0 30°0E 54 C3
Queen Elizabeth ⌂ U.K. 56°7N 4°30W 11 E4
Queen Elizabeth Is. Canada 76°0N 95°0W 69 B10
Queen Mary Land Antarctica 70°0S 95°0E 5 D7
Queen Maud G. Canada 68°15N 102°30W 68 C9
Queen Maud Land = Dronning Maud Land Antarctica 72°30S 12°0E 5 D3
Queen Maud Mts. Antarctica 86°0S 160°0W 5 E13
Queens Channel Australia 15°0S 129°30E 60 C4
Queenscliff Australia 38°16S 144°39E 63 F3
Queensland □ Australia 22°0S 142°0E 62 C3
Queenstown Australia 42°4S 145°35E 63 G4
Queenstown N.Z. 45°1S 168°40E 59 F2
Queenstown Singapore 1°18N 103°48E 39 d
Queenstown S. Africa 31°52S 26°52E 56 E4
Queets U.S.A. 47°32N 124°19W 78 C2
Queguay Grande → Uruguay 32°9S 58°9W 94 C4
Queimadas Brazil 11°0S 39°38W 93 F11
Quelimane Mozam. 17°53S 36°58E 55 F4
Quellón Chile 43°7S 73°37W 96 E2
Quelpart = Jeju-do S. Korea 33°29N 126°34E 35 H14
Quemado N. Mex., U.S.A. 34°20N 108°30W 77 J9
Quemado Tex., U.S.A. 28°56N 100°37W 84 G4
Quemú-Quemú Argentina 36°3S 63°36W 94 D3
Quequén Argentina 38°30S 58°30W 94 D4
Querétaro Mexico 20°36N 100°23W 86 C4
Querétaro □ Mexico 21°0N 99°55W 86 C5
Queshan China 32°55N 114°2E 34 H8
Quesnel Canada 53°0N 122°30W 70 C4
Quesnel → Canada 52°58N 122°29W 70 C4
Quesnel L. Canada 52°30N 121°20W 70 C4
Questa U.S.A. 36°42N 105°36W 77 H11
Quetico ⌂ Canada 48°30N 91°45W 72 C1
Quetta Pakistan 30°15N 66°55E 42 D2
Quezaltenango Guatemala 14°50N 91°30W 88 D1
Quezon City Phil. 14°37N 121°2E 37 B6
Qufār Si. Arabia 27°26N 41°37E 44 E4
Qui Nhon Vietnam 13°40N 109°13E 38 F7
Quibala Angola 10°46S 14°59E 52 G2
Quibaxe Angola 8°24S 14°27E 52 F2
Quibdó Colombia 5°42N 76°40W 92 B3
Quiberon France 47°29N 3°9W 20 C2
Quiet L. Canada 61°5N 133°5W 70 A2
Quiindy Paraguay 25°58S 57°14W 94 B4
Quilá Mexico 24°23N 107°13W 86 C3
Quilán, C. Chile 43°15S 74°30W 96 E2
Quilcene U.S.A. 47°49N 122°53W 78 C4
Quilimarí Chile 32°5S 71°30W 94 C1
Quilino Argentina 30°14S 64°29W 94 C3
Quillabamba Peru 12°50S 72°50W 92 F4
Quillagua Chile 21°40S 69°40W 94 A2
Quillota Chile 32°54S 71°16W 94 C1
Quilmes Argentina 34°43S 58°15W 94 C4
Quilon India 8°50N 76°38E 40 Q10
Quilpie Australia 26°35S 144°11E 63 D3
Quilpué Chile 33°5S 71°33W 94 C1
Quilua Mozam. 16°17S 39°54E 55 F4
Quimilí Argentina 27°40S 62°30W 94 B3
Quimper France 48°0N 4°9W 20 B1
Quimperlé France 47°53N 3°33W 20 C2
Quinault → U.S.A. 47°21N 124°18W 78 C2
Quincy Calif., U.S.A. 39°56N 120°57W 78 F6
Quincy Fla., U.S.A. 30°35N 84°34W 85 F12
Quincy Ill., U.S.A. 39°56N 91°23W 80 F8
Quincy Mass., U.S.A. 42°14N 71°0W 83 D14
Quincy Wash., U.S.A. 47°14N 119°51W 76 C4
Quines Argentina 32°13S 65°48W 94 C2
Quinga Mozam. 15°49S 40°15E 55 F5
Quintana Roo □ Mexico 19°40N 88°30W 87 D7
Quintanar de la Orden Spain 39°36N 3°5W 21 C4
Quintero Chile 32°45S 71°30W 94 C1
Quirihue Chile 36°15S 72°35W 94 D1
Quirimbas ⌂ Mozam. 12°30S 40°15E 55 E5
Quirindi Australia 31°28S 150°40E 63 E5
Quirinópolis Brazil 18°32S 50°30W 93 G8
Quissanga Mozam. 12°24S 40°28E 55 E5
Quissico Mozam. 24°42S 34°44E 57 C5
Quitilipi Argentina 26°50S 60°13W 94 B3
Quitman U.S.A. 30°47N 83°34W 85 F13
Quito Ecuador 0°15S 78°35W 92 D3
Quixadá Brazil 4°55S 39°0W 93 D11
Quixaxe Mozam. 15°17S 40°4E 55 F5
Qulan Kazakhstan 42°55N 72°43E 28 E8
Qul'ân, Jazâ'ir Egypt 24°22N 35°31E 44 E2
Qulsary Kazakhstan 46°59N 54°1E 19 E9
Qumbu S. Africa 31°10S 28°48E 57 E4
Quneitra Syria 33°7N 35°48E 46 B4
Qŭnghirot Uzbekistan 43°2N 58°50E 28 E6
Quoin I. Australia 14°54S 129°32E 60 B4
Quoin Pt. S. Africa 34°46S 19°37E 56 E2
Quorn Australia 32°25S 138°5E 63 E2
Qŭqon Uzbekistan 40°31N 70°56E 28 E8
Qurnat as Sawdā' Lebanon 34°18N 36°6E 46 A5
Quşaybā' Si. Arabia 26°53N 43°35E 44 E4
Qusaybah Iraq 34°24N 40°59E 44 C4
Quseir Egypt 26°7N 34°16E 44 E2
Qūshchī Iran 37°59N 45°3E 44 B5
Quthing Lesotho 30°25S 27°36E 57 E4
Qūţīābād Iran 35°47N 48°30E 45 C6
Quwo China 35°38N 111°25E 34 G6
Quyang China 38°35N 114°40E 34 E8
Quynh Nhai Vietnam 21°49N 103°33E 38 B4
Quyon Canada 45°31N 76°14W 83 A8
Quzhou China 28°57N 118°54E 33 D6
Quzi China 36°20N 107°20E 34 F4
Qyzylorda Kazakhstan 44°48N 65°28E 28 E7

R

Ra, Ko Thailand 9°13N 98°16E 39 H2
Raahe Finland 64°40N 24°28E 8 D21
Raalte Neths. 52°23N 6°16E 15 B6
Raasay U.K. 57°25N 6°4W 11 D2
Raasay, Sd. of U.K. 57°30N 6°8W 11 D2
Raba Indonesia 8°36S 118°55E 37 F5
Rába → Hungary 47°38N 17°38E 17 E9
Rabai Kenya 3°50S 39°31E 54 C4
Rabat = Victoria Malta 36°3N 14°14E 25 C1
Rabat Malta 35°53N 14°24E 25 D1
Rabat Morocco 34°2N 6°48W 50 B4
Rabaul Papua N. G. 4°24S 152°18E 58 B8
Rabbit Flat Australia 20°11S 130°1E 60 D5
Rabbit Lake Mine Canada 58°4N 104°5W 71 B8
Rabi Fiji 16°30S 179°59W 59 a
Rābigh Si. Arabia 22°50N 39°5E 47 C2
Râbniţa Moldova 47°45N 29°0E 17 E15
Rābor Iran 29°17N 56°55E 45 D8
Rabwah = Chenab Nagar Pakistan 31°45N 72°55E 42 D5
Race, C. Canada 46°40N 53°5W 73 C9
Rach Gia Vietnam 10°5N 105°5E 39 G5
Rachid Mauritania 18°45N 11°35W 50 E3
Racibórz Poland 50°7N 18°18E 17 C10
Racine U.S.A. 42°44N 87°47W 80 D10
Rackerby U.S.A. 39°26N 121°22W 78 F5
Radama, Nosy Madag. 14°0S 47°47E 57 A8
Radama, Saikanosy Madag. 14°16S 47°53E 57 A8
Rădăuţi Romania 47°50N 25°59E 17 E13
Radcliff U.S.A. 37°51N 85°57W 81 G11
Radekhiv Ukraine 50°25N 24°32E 17 C13
Radekhov = Radekhiv Ukraine 50°25N 24°32E 17 C13
Radford U.S.A. 37°8N 80°34W 81 G13
Radhanpur India 23°50N 71°38E 42 H4
Radhwa, Jabal Si. Arabia 24°34N 38°18E 44 E3
Radisson Qué., Canada 53°47N 77°37W 72 B4
Radisson Sask., Canada 52°30N 107°20W 71 C7
Radium Hot Springs Canada 50°35N 116°2W 70 C5
Radnor Forest U.K. 52°17N 3°10W 13 E4
Radom Poland 51°23N 21°12E 17 C11
Radomsko Poland 51°5N 19°28E 17 C10
Radomyshl Ukraine 50°30N 29°12E 17 C15
Radstock, C. Australia 33°12S 134°20E 63 E1
Raduzhnyy Russia 62°5N 77°28E 28 C8
Radviliškis Lithuania 55°49N 23°33E 9 J20
Radville Canada 49°30N 104°15W 71 D8
Rae Canada 62°50N 116°3W 70 A5
Rae Bareli India 26°18N 81°20E 43 F9
Rae Isthmus Canada 66°40N 87°30W 69 C11
Raeren Belgium 50°41N 6°7E 15 D6
Raeside, L. Australia 29°20S 122°0E 61 E3
Raetihi N.Z. 39°25S 175°17E 59 C5
Rafaela Argentina 31°10S 61°30W 94 C3
Rafah Gaza Strip 31°18N 34°14E 46 D3
Rafai C.A.R. 4°59N 23°58E 54 B1
Rafḩā Si. Arabia 29°35N 43°35E 44 D4
Rafsanjān Iran 30°30N 56°5E 45 D8
Raft Pt. Australia 16°4S 124°26E 60 C3
Râgâ Sudan 8°28N 25°41E 51 G11
Ragachow Belarus 53°8N 30°5E 17 B16
Ragama Sri Lanka 7°0N 79°50E 40 R11
Ragged, Mt. Australia 33°27S 123°25E 61 F3
Ragged Pt. Barbados 13°10N 59°26W 89 g
Raghunathpalli India 22°14N 84°48E 43 H11
Raghunathpur India 23°33N 86°40E 43 H12
Raglan N.Z. 37°55S 174°55E 59 B5
Ragusa Italy 36°55N 14°44E 22 F6
Raha Indonesia 4°55S 123°0E 37 E6
Rahaeng = Tak Thailand 16°52N 99°8E 38 D2
Rahatgarh India 23°47N 78°22E 43 H8
Rahimyar Khan Pakistan 28°30N 70°25E 42 E4
Rāhjerd Iran 34°22N 50°22E 45 C6
Rahole ⌂ Kenya 0°5N 38°57E 54 B4
Rahon India 31°3N 76°7E 42 D7
Raiatéa, Î. French Polynesia 16°50S 151°25W 65 J12
Raichur India 16°10N 77°20E 40 L10
Raiganj India 25°37N 88°10E 43 G13
Raigarh India 21°56N 83°25E 41 J13
Raijua Indonesia 10°37S 121°36E 37 F6
Raikot India 30°41N 75°42E 42 D6
Railton Australia 41°25S 146°28E 63 G4
Rainbow Bridge ⌂ U.S.A. 37°5N 110°58W 77 H8
Rainbow Lake Canada 58°30N 119°23W 70 B5
Rainier U.S.A. 46°53N 122°41W 78 D4
Rainier, Mt. U.S.A. 46°52N 121°46W 78 D5
Rainy L. Canada 48°42N 93°10W 71 D10
Rainy River Canada 48°43N 94°29W 71 D10
Raippaluoto Finland 63°13N 21°14E 8 E19
Raipur India 21°17N 81°45E 41 J12
Raisen India 23°20N 77°48E 42 H8
Raisio Finland 60°28N 22°11E 9 F20
Raj Nandgaon India 21°5N 81°5E 41 J12
Raj Nilgiri India 21°28N 86°46E 43 J12
Raja, Ujung Indonesia 3°40N 96°25E 36 D1
Raja Ampat, Kepulauan Indonesia 0°30S 130°0E 37 E8
Rajahmundry India 17°1N 81°48E 41 L12
Rajaji △ India 30°10N 78°20E 42 D8
Rajang → Malaysia 2°30N 112°0E 36 D4
Rajanpur Pakistan 29°6N 70°19E 42 E4
Rajapalaiyam India 9°25N 77°35E 40 Q10
Rajasthan □ India 26°45N 73°30E 42 F5
Rajasthan Canal = Indira Gandhi Canal India 28°0N 72°0E 42 F5
Rajauri India 33°25N 74°21E 43 C6
Rajgarh Mad. P., India 24°2N 76°45E 42 G7
Rajgarh Raj., India 27°14N 76°38E 42 F7
Rajgarh Raj., India 28°40N 75°25E 42 E6
Rajgir India 25°2N 85°25E 43 G11
Rajkot India 22°15N 70°56E 42 H4
Rajmahal Hills India 24°30N 87°30E 43 G12
Rajpipla India 21°50N 73°30E 40 J8
Rajpur India 22°18N 74°21E 42 H6
Rajpura India 30°25N 76°32E 42 D7
Rajshahi Bangla. 24°22N 88°39E 41 G16
Rajshahi □ Bangla. 25°0N 89°0E 43 G13
Rajula India 21°3N 71°26E 42 J4
Rakaia N.Z. 43°45S 172°1E 59 E4
Rakaia → N.Z. 43°36S 172°15E 59 E4
Rakan, Ra's Qatar 26°10N 51°20E 45 E6
Rakaposhi Pakistan 36°10N 74°25E 43 A6
Rakata, Pulau Indonesia 6°10S 105°20E 36 F3
Rakhiv Ukraine 48°3N 24°12E 17 D13
Rakhni Pakistan 30°4N 69°56E 42 D3
Rakhni → Pakistan 29°31N 69°36E 42 E3
Rakiraki Fiji 17°22S 178°11E 59 a
Rakitnoye Russia 45°36N 134°17E 30 B7
Rakiura △ N.Z. 47°0S 167°50E 59 G1
Rakops Botswana 21°1S 24°28E 56 C3
Rakvere Estonia 59°20N 26°25E 9 G22
Raleigh U.S.A. 35°47N 78°39W 85 D15
Ralik Chain Pac. Oc. 8°0N 168°0E 64 G8
Ralls U.S.A. 33°41N 101°24W 84 E4
Ralston U.S.A. 41°30N 76°57W 82 E8
Ram → Canada 62°1N 123°41W 70 A4
Rām Allāh West Bank 31°55N 35°10E 46 D4
Rama Nic. 12°9N 84°15W 88 D3
Ramakona India 21°43N 78°50E 43 J8
Rāmallāh = Rām Allāh West Bank 31°55N 35°10E 46 D4
Raman Thailand 6°29N 101°18E 39 J3
Ramanathapuram India 9°25N 78°55E 40 Q11
Ramanetaka, B. de Madag. 14°13S 47°52E 57 A8
Ramanujganj India 23°48N 83°42E 43 H10
Ramat Gan Israel 32°4N 34°48E 46 C3
Ramatlhabama S. Africa 25°37S 25°33E 56 D4
Ramban India 33°14N 75°12E 43 C6
Rambi = Rabi Fiji 16°30S 179°59W 59 a
Rambipuji Indonesia 8°12S 113°37E 37 H15
Rame Hd. Australia 37°47S 149°30E 63 F4
Ramechhap Nepal 27°25N 86°10E 43 F12
Ramganga → India 27°5N 79°58E 43 F8
Ramgarh Jharkhand, India 23°40N 85°35E 43 H11
Ramgarh Raj., India 27°16N 75°14E 42 F6
Ramgarh Raj., India 27°30N 70°36E 42 F4
Rāmhormoz Iran 31°15N 49°35E 45 D6
Ramīān Iran 37°3N 55°16E 45 B7
Ramingining Australia 12°19S 135°3E 62 A2
Ramla Israel 31°55N 34°52E 46 D3
Ramm = Rum Jordan 29°39N 35°26E 46 F4
Ramm, Jabal Jordan 29°35N 35°24E 46 F4
Ramnad = Ramanathapuram India 9°25N 78°55E 40 Q11
Ramnagar Jammu & Kashmir, India 32°47N 75°18E 43 C6
Ramnagar Uttarakhand, India 29°24N 79°7E 43 E8
Râmnicu Sărat Romania 45°26N 27°3E 17 F14
Râmnicu Vâlcea Romania 45°9N 24°21E 17 F13
Ramona U.S.A. 33°2N 116°52W 79 M10
Ramore Canada 48°30N 80°25W 72 C3
Ramotswa Botswana 24°50S 25°52E 56 C4
Rampur H.P., India 31°26N 77°43E 42 D7
Rampur Mad. P., India 23°25N 73°53E 42 H5
Rampur Ut. P., India 28°50N 79°5E 43 E8
Rampur Hat India 24°10N 87°50E 43 G12
Rampura India 24°30N 75°27E 42 G6
Ramrama Tola India 21°52N 79°55E 43 J8
Ramree I. Burma 19°0N 93°40E 41 K19
Rāmsar Iran 36°53N 50°41E 45 B6
Ramsey I. of Man 54°20N 4°22W 12 C3
Ramsey U.S.A. 41°4N 74°9W 83 E10
Ramsey L. Canada 47°13N 82°15W 72 C3
Ramsgate U.K. 51°20N 1°25E 13 F9
Ramtek India 21°20N 79°15E 40 J11
Ramu Kenya 3°55N 41°10E 54 B5
Rana Pratap Sagar Dam India 24°58N 75°38E 42 G6
Ranaghat India 23°15N 88°35E 43 H13
Ranahu Pakistan 25°55N 69°45E 42 G3
Ranau Malaysia 6°2N 116°40E 36 C5
Rancagua Chile 34°10S 70°50W 94 C1
Rancheria → Canada 60°13N 129°7W 70 A3
Ranchester U.S.A. 44°54N 107°10W 76 D10
Ranchi India 23°19N 85°27E 43 H11
Rancho Cordova U.S.A. 38°36N 121°18W 78 G5
Rancho Cucamonga U.S.A. 34°10N 117°30W 79 L9
Randalstown U.K. 54°45N 6°19W 10 B5
Randers Denmark 56°29N 10°1E 9 H14
Randfontein S. Africa 26°8S 27°45E 57 D4
Randle U.S.A. 46°32N 121°57W 78 D5
Randolph Mass., U.S.A. 42°10N 71°2W 83 D13
Randolph N.Y., U.S.A. 42°10N 78°59W 82 D6
Randolph Utah, U.S.A. 41°40N 111°11W 76 F8
Randolph Vt., U.S.A. 43°55N 72°40W 83 C12
Randsburg U.S.A. 35°22N 117°39W 79 K9
Råneälven → Sweden 65°50N 22°20E 8 D20
Rangae Thailand 6°19N 101°44E 39 J3
Rangaunu B. N.Z. 34°51S 173°15E 59 A4
Range, The Zimbabwe 19°2S 31°2E 55 F3
Rangeley U.S.A. 44°58N 70°39W 83 B14
Rangeley L. U.S.A. 44°55N 70°43W 83 B14
Rangely U.S.A. 40°5N 108°48W 76 F9
Ranger U.S.A. 32°28N 98°41W 84 E5
Rangia India 26°28N 91°38E 41 F17
Rangiora N.Z. 43°19S 172°36E 59 E4
Rangitaiki → N.Z. 37°54S 176°49E 59 B6
Rangitata → N.Z. 43°45S 171°15E 59 E3
Rangitoto ke te tonga = D'Urville I. N.Z. 40°50S 173°55E 59 D4
Rangkasbitung Indonesia 6°21S 106°15E 37 G12
Rangon → Burma 16°28N 96°40E 41 L20
Rangoon Burma 16°45N 96°20E 41 L20
Rangpur Bangla. 25°42N 89°22E 41 G16
Rangsang Indonesia 1°20N 103°30E 39 M4
Rangsit Thailand 13°59N 100°37E 38 F3
Ranibennur India 14°35N 75°30E 40 M9
Raniganj Ut. P., India 27°3N 82°13E 43 F9
Raniganj W. Bengal, India 23°40N 87°5E 41 H15

Ranikhet India 29°39N 79°25E **43 E8**
Raniwara India 24°50N 72°10E **42 G5**
Rāniyah Iraq 36°15N 44°53E **44 B5**
Ranka India 23°59N 83°47E **43 H10**
Ranken → Australia 20°31S 137°36E **62 C2**
Rankin U.S.A. 31°13N 101°56W **84 F4**
Rankin Inlet Canada 62°30N 93°0W **68 C10**
Rankins Springs
  Australia 33°49S 146°14E **63 E4**
Rannoch, L. U.K. 56°41N 4°20W **11 E4**
Rannoch Moor U.K. 56°38N 4°48W **11 E4**
Ranobe, Helodranon' i
  Madag. 23°3S 43°33E **57 C7**
Ranohira Madag. 22°29S 45°24E **57 C8**
Ranomafana Toamasina,
  Madag. 18°57S 48°50E **57 B8**
Ranomafana Toliara,
  Madag. 24°34S 47°0E **57 C8**
Ranomafana △ Madag. 21°16S 47°25E **57 C8**
Ranomena Madag. 23°25S 47°17E **57 C8**
Ranong Thailand 9°56N 98°40E **39 H2**
Ranotsara Nord Madag. 22°48S 46°36E **57 C8**
Rānsa Iran 33°39N 48°18E **45 C6**
Ransiki Indonesia 1°30S 134°10E **37 E8**
Rantabe Madag. 15°42S 49°39E **57 B8**
Rantauprapat Indonesia 2°15N 99°50E **36 D1**
Rantemario Indonesia 3°15S 119°57E **37 E5**
Ranthambore △ India 26°1N 76°30E **42 F7**
Rantoul U.S.A. 40°19N 88°9W **80 E9**
Raohe China 46°47N 134°0E **30 A7**
Raoyang China 38°15N 115°45E **34 E8**
Rap, Ko Thailand 9°19N 99°58E **39 b**
Rapa French Polynesia 27°35S 144°20W **65 K13**
Rapa Nui = Pascua, I. de
  Chile 27°7S 109°23W **65 K17**
Rapallo Italy 44°21N 9°14E **20 D8**
Rapar India 23°34N 70°38E **42 H4**
Rāpch Iran 25°40N 59°15E **45 E8**
Rapel, Lago Chile 34°20S 71°14W **94 C1**
Raper, C. Canada 69°44N 67°6W **69 C13**
Rapid City U.S.A. 44°5N 103°14W **80 C2**
Rapid River U.S.A. 45°55N 86°58W **80 C10**
Rapla Estonia 59°1N 24°52E **9 G21**
Rapti → India 26°18N 83°41E **43 F10**
Raquette → U.S.A. 45°0N 74°42W **83 B10**
Raquette Lake U.S.A. 43°49N 74°40W **83 C10**
Rara △ Nepal 29°30N 82°10E **43 E10**
Rarotonga Cook Is. 21°30S 160°0W **65 K12**
Ra's al 'Ayn Syria 36°45N 40°12E **44 B4**
Ra's al Khaymah U.A.E. 25°50N 55°59E **45 E7**
Ra's at Tib Tunisia 37°1N 11°2E **22 F4**
Rasa, Pta. Argentina 36°20S 56°41W **94 D4**
Rasca, Pta. de la
  Canary Is. 27°59N 16°41W **24 G3**
Raseiniai Lithuania 55°25N 23°5E **9 J20**
Rashmi India 25°4N 74°22E **42 G6**
Rasht Iran 37°20N 49°40E **45 B6**
Rasi Salai Thailand 15°20N 104°9E **38 E5**
Rason L. Australia 28°45S 124°25E **61 E3**
Rasra India 25°50N 83°50E **43 G10**
Rasul Pakistan 32°42N 73°34E **42 C5**
Rat → Canada 49°35N 97°10W **71 D9**
Rat Buri Thailand 13°30N 99°54E **38 F2**
Rat Islands U.S.A. 52°0N 178°0E **74 a**
Rat L. Canada 56°10N 99°40W **71 B9**
Ratak Chain Pac. Oc. 1°0N 170°0E **64 G8**
Ratangarh India 28°5N 74°35E **42 E6**
Raṭāwī Iraq 30°38N 47°13E **44 D5**
Rath India 25°36N 79°37E **43 G8**
Rath Luirc Ireland 52°21N 8°40W **10 D3**
Rathangan Ireland 53°13N 7°1W **10 C4**
Rathdrum Ireland 52°56N 6°14W **10 D5**
Rathenow Germany 52°37N 12°19E **16 B7**
Rathkeale Ireland 52°32N 8°56W **10 D3**
Rathlin I. U.K. 55°18N 6°14W **10 A5**
Rathmelton Ireland 55°2N 7°38W **10 A4**
Ratibor = Racibórz
  Poland 50°7N 18°18E **17 C10**
Ratlam India 23°20N 75°0E **42 H6**
Ratnagiri India 16°57N 73°18E **40 L8**
Ratodero Pakistan 27°48N 68°18E **42 F3**
Raton U.S.A. 36°54N 104°24W **77 H11**
Rattaphum Thailand 7°8N 100°16E **39 J3**
Rattray Hd. U.K. 57°38N 1°50W **11 D7**
Ratz, Mt. Canada 57°23N 132°12W **70 B2**
Raub Malaysia 3°47N 101°52E **39 L3**
Rauch Argentina 36°45S 59°5W **94 D4**
Raudales Mexico 17°27N 93°39W **87 D6**
Raufarhöfn Iceland 66°27N 15°57W **8 C6**
Raufoss Norway 60°44N 10°37E **8 F14**
Raukumara Ra. N.Z. 38°5S 177°55E **59 C6**
Rauma Finland 61°10N 21°30E **8 F19**
Raumo = Rauma
  Finland 61°10N 21°30E **8 F19**
Raung, Gunung Indonesia 8°8S 114°3E **37 J17**
Raurkela India 22°14N 84°50E **43 H11**
Rausu-Dake Japan 44°4N 145°7E **30 B12**
Rava-Ruska Ukraine 50°15N 23°42E **17 C12**
Rava Russkaya = Rava-Ruska
  Ukraine 50°15N 23°42E **17 C12**
Ravalli U.S.A. 47°17N 114°11W **76 C6**
Ravānsar Iran 34°43N 46°40E **44 C5**
Rāvar Iran 31°20N 56°51E **45 D8**
Ravena U.S.A. 42°28N 73°49W **83 D11**
Ravenna Italy 44°25N 12°12E **22 B5**
Ravenna Nebr., U.S.A. 41°1N 98°55W **80 E4**
Ravenna Ohio, U.S.A. 41°9N 81°15W **82 E3**
Ravensburg Germany 47°46N 9°36E **16 E5**
Ravenshoe Australia 17°37S 145°29E **62 B4**
Ravensthorpe Australia 33°35S 120°2E **61 F3**
Ravenswood Australia 20°6S 146°54E **62 C4**
Ravenswood U.S.A. 38°57N 81°46W **81 F13**
Ravi → Pakistan 30°35N 71°49E **42 D4**
Rawalpindi Pakistan 33°38N 73°8E **42 C5**
Rawang Malaysia 3°20N 101°35E **39 L3**
Rawene N.Z. 35°25S 173°32E **59 A4**
Rawlinna Australia 30°58S 125°28E **61 F4**

Rawlins U.S.A. 41°47N 107°14W **76 F10**
Rawlinson Ra. Australia 24°40S 128°30E **61 D4**
Rawson Argentina 43°15S 65°5W **96 E3**
Raxaul India 26°59N 84°51E **43 F11**
Ray, C. Canada 47°33N 59°15W **73 C8**
Raya Ring, Ko Thailand 8°18N 98°29E **39 a**
Rayadurg India 14°40N 76°50E **40 M10**
Rayagada India 19°15N 83°20E **41 K13**
Raychikhinsk Russia 49°46N 129°25E **29 E13**
Rāyen Iran 29°34N 57°26E **45 D8**
Rayleigh U.K. 51°36N 0°37E **13 F8**
Raymond Canada 49°30N 112°35W **70 D6**
Raymond Calif., U.S.A. 37°13N 119°54W **78 H7**
Raymond N.H., U.S.A. 43°2N 71°11W **83 C13**
Raymond Wash.,
  U.S.A. 46°41N 123°44W **78 D3**
Raymondville U.S.A. 26°29N 97°47W **84 H6**
Raymore Canada 51°25N 104°31W **71 C8**
Rayón Mexico 29°43N 110°35W **86 B2**
Rayong Thailand 12°40N 101°20E **38 F3**
Raystown L. U.S.A. 40°25N 78°5W **82 F6**
Rayville U.S.A. 32°29N 91°46W **84 E9**
Raz, Pte. du France 48°2N 4°47W **20 C1**
Razan Iran 35°23N 49°2E **45 C6**
Razāzah, Buḥayrat ar
  Iraq 32°40N 43°35E **44 C4**
Razazah, L. = Razāzah, Buḥayrat
  ar Iraq 32°40N 43°35E **44 C4**
Razdel'naya = Rozdilna
  Ukraine 46°50N 30°2E **17 E16**
Razdolnoye Russia 43°30N 131°52E **30 C5**
Razeh Iran 32°47N 48°9E **45 C6**
Razgrad Bulgaria 43°33N 26°34E **23 C12**
Razim, Lacul Romania 44°50N 29°0E **17 F15**
Razmak Pakistan 32°45N 69°50E **42 C3**
Re, Cu Lao Vietnam 15°22N 109°8E **38 E7**
Ré, Î. de France 46°12N 1°30W **20 C3**
Reading U.K. 51°27N 0°58W **13 F7**
Reading U.S.A. 40°20N 75°56W **83 F9**
Reading □ U.K. 51°27N 0°58W **13 F7**
Realicó Argentina 35°0S 64°15W **94 D3**
Ream Cambodia 10°34N 103°39E **39 G4**
Ream △ Cambodia 10°30N 103°45E **39 G4**
Reay Forest U.K. 58°22N 4°55W **11 C4**
Rebecca, L. Australia 30°0S 122°15E **61 F3**
Rebi Indonesia 6°23S 134°7E **37 F8**
Rebiana Libya 24°12N 22°10E **51 D10**
Rebiana, Sahrâ' Libya 24°30N 21°0E **51 D10**
Reboly Russia 63°49N 30°47E **8 E24**
Rebun-Tō Japan 45°23N 141°2E **30 B10**
Recherche, Arch. of the
  Australia 34°15S 122°50E **61 F3**
Rechna Doab Pakistan 31°35N 73°30E **42 D5**
Rechytsa Belarus 52°21N 30°24E **17 B16**
Recife Brazil 8°0S 35°0W **93 E12**
Recife Seychelles 4°36S 55°42E **53 b**
Recklinghausen Germany 51°37N 7°12E **15 C7**
Reconquista Argentina 29°10S 59°45W **94 B4**
Recreo Argentina 29°25S 65°10W **94 B2**
Red → U.S.A. 31°1N 91°45W **84 F9**
Red Bank U.S.A. 40°21N 74°5W **83 F10**
Red Bay Canada 51°44N 56°25W **73 B8**
Red Bluff U.S.A. 40°11N 122°15W **76 F2**
Red Bluff Res. U.S.A. 31°54N 103°55W **77 L12**
Red Cliffs Australia 34°19S 142°11E **63 E3**
Red Cloud U.S.A. 40°5N 98°32W **80 E4**
Red Creek U.S.A. 43°14N 76°45W **83 C8**
Red Deer Canada 52°20N 113°50W **70 C6**
Red Deer → Alta.,
  Canada 50°58N 110°0W **71 C7**
Red Deer → Man.,
  Canada 52°53N 101°1W **71 C8**
Red Deer L. Canada 52°55N 101°20W **71 C8**
Red Hook U.S.A. 41°55N 73°53W **83 E11**
Red Indian L. Canada 48°35N 57°0W **73 C8**
Red L. Canada 51°3N 93°49W **71 C10**
Red Lake Canada 51°3N 93°49W **71 C10**
Red Lake Falls U.S.A. 47°53N 96°16W **80 B5**
Red Lake Road Canada 49°59N 93°25W **71 C10**
Red Lodge U.S.A. 45°11N 109°15W **76 D9**
Red Mountain U.S.A. 35°37N 117°38W **79 K9**
Red Oak U.S.A. 41°1N 95°14W **80 E6**
Red River of the North →
  N. Amer. 49°0N 97°15W **80 A5**
Red Rock Canada 48°55N 88°15W **72 C2**
Red Rock, L. U.S.A. 41°22N 92°59W **80 E7**
Red Rocks Pt. Australia 32°13S 127°32E **61 F4**
Red Sea Asia 25°0N 36°0E **47 C2**
Red Slate Mt. U.S.A. 37°31N 118°52W **78 H8**
Red Sucker L. Canada 54°9N 93°40W **72 B1**
Red Tower Pass = Turnu Roşu, P.
  Romania 45°24N 24°15E **17 F13**
Red Wing U.S.A. 44°34N 92°31W **80 C7**
Redang Malaysia 5°49N 103°2E **39 K4**
Redange Lux. 49°46N 5°52E **15 E5**
Redcar U.K. 54°37N 1°4W **12 C6**
Redcar & Cleveland □
  U.K. 54°29N 1°0W **12 C7**
Redcliff Canada 50°10N 110°50W **76 A8**
Redcliffe Australia 27°12S 153°0E **63 D5**
Redcliffe, Mt. Australia 28°30S 121°30E **61 E3**
Reddersburg S. Africa 29°41S 26°10E **56 D4**
Redding U.S.A. 40°35N 122°24W **76 F2**
Redditch U.K. 52°18N 1°55W **13 E6**
Redfield U.S.A. 44°53N 98°31W **80 C4**
Redford U.S.A. 44°38N 73°48W **83 B11**
Redhead Trin. & Tob. 10°44N 60°58W **93 K16**
Redlands U.S.A. 34°4N 117°11W **79 M9**
Redmond Oreg., U.S.A. 44°17N 121°11W **76 D3**
Redmond Wash., U.S.A. 47°40N 122°7W **78 C4**
Redon France 47°40N 2°6W **20 C2**
Redonda Antigua & B. 16°58N 62°19W **89 C7**
Redondela Spain 42°15N 8°38W **21 A1**
Redondo Beach U.S.A. 33°50N 118°23W **79 M8**
Redruth U.K. 50°14N 5°14W **13 G2**
Redvers Canada 49°35N 101°40W **71 D8**

Redwater Canada 53°55N 113°6W **70 C6**
Redwood U.S.A. 44°18N 75°48W **83 B9**
Redwood △ U.S.A. 41°40N 124°5W **76 F1**
Redwood City U.S.A. 37°30N 122°15W **78 H4**
Redwood Falls U.S.A. 44°32N 95°7W **80 C6**
Ree, L. Ireland 53°35N 8°0W **10 C3**
Reed City U.S.A. 43°53N 85°31W **81 D11**
Reed L. Canada 54°38N 100°30W **71 C8**
Reedley U.S.A. 36°36N 119°27W **78 J7**
Reedsburg U.S.A. 43°32N 90°0W **80 D8**
Reedsport U.S.A. 43°42N 124°6W **76 E1**
Reedsville U.S.A. 40°39N 77°35W **82 F7**
Reefton N.Z. 42°6S 171°51E **59 E3**
Refugio U.S.A. 28°18N 97°17W **84 G6**
Regana, C. de Spain 39°25N 2°43E **24 B9**
Regensburg Germany 49°1N 12°6E **16 D7**
Reggâne = Zaouiet Reggâne
  Algeria 26°32N 0°3E **50 C6**
Réggio di Calábria Italy 38°6N 15°39E **22 E6**
Réggio nell'Emília Italy 44°43N 10°36E **22 B4**
Reghin Romania 46°46N 24°42E **17 E13**
Regina Canada 50°27N 104°35W **71 C8**
Regina Beach Canada 50°47N 105°0W **71 C8**
Registro Brazil 24°29S 47°49W **95 A6**
Rehar → India 23°55N 82°40E **43 H10**
Rehli India 23°38N 79°5E **43 H8**
Rehoboth Namibia 23°15S 17°4E **56 C2**
Rehovot Israel 31°54N 34°48E **46 D3**
Reichenbach Germany 50°37N 12°17E **16 C7**
Reid Australia 30°49S 128°26E **61 F4**
Reidsville U.S.A. 36°21N 79°40W **85 C15**
Reigate U.K. 51°14N 0°12W **13 F7**
Reims France 49°15N 4°1E **20 B6**
Reina Adelaida, Arch.
  Chile 52°20S 74°0W **96 G2**
Reina Sofía, Tenerife ✈ (TFS)
  Canary Is. 28°3N 16°33W **24 F3**
Reindeer → Canada 55°36N 103°11W **71 B8**
Reindeer I. Canada 52°30N 98°0W **71 C9**
Reindeer L. Canada 57°15N 102°15W **71 B9**
Reinga, C. N.Z. 34°25S 172°43E **59 A4**
Reinosa Spain 43°2N 4°15W **21 A3**
Reitz S. Africa 27°48S 28°29E **57 D4**
Reivilo S. Africa 27°36S 24°8E **56 D3**
Reliance Canada 63°0N 109°20W **71 A7**
Remanso Brazil 9°41S 42°4W **93 E10**
Remarkable, Mt.
  Australia 32°48S 138°10E **63 E2**
Rembang Indonesia 6°42S 111°21E **37 G14**
Remedios Panama 8°15N 81°50W **88 E3**
Remeshk Iran 26°55N 58°50E **45 E8**
Remich Lux. 49°32N 6°22E **15 E6**
Ren Xian China 37°8N 114°40E **34 F8**
Rendang Indonesia 8°26S 115°25E **37 J18**
Rendsburg Germany 54°17N 9°39E **16 A5**
Renfrew Canada 45°30N 76°40W **83 A8**
Renfrewshire □ U.K. 55°49N 4°38W **11 F4**
Rengat Indonesia 0°30S 102°45E **36 E2**
Rengo Chile 34°24S 70°50W **94 C1**
Reni Ukraine 45°28N 28°15E **17 F15**
Renmark Australia 34°11S 140°43E **63 E3**
Rennell Sd. Canada 53°23N 132°35W **70 C2**
Renner Springs
  Australia 18°20S 133°47E **62 B1**
Rennes France 48°7N 1°41W **20 B3**
Rennick Glacier
  Antarctica 70°30S 161°45E **5 D21**
Rennie L. Canada 61°32N 105°35W **71 A7**
Reno U.S.A. 39°31N 119°48W **78 F7**
Reno → Italy 44°38N 12°16E **22 B5**
Renovo U.S.A. 41°20N 77°45W **82 E7**
Renqiu China 38°43N 116°5E **34 E9**
Rensselaer Ind., U.S.A. 40°57N 87°9W **80 E10**
Rensselaer N.Y., U.S.A. 42°38N 73°45W **83 D11**
Renton U.S.A. 47°28N 122°12W **78 C4**
Reotipur India 25°33N 83°45E **43 G10**
Republic Mo., U.S.A. 37°7N 93°29W **80 G7**
Republic Wash., U.S.A. 48°39N 118°44W **76 B4**
Republican → U.S.A. 39°4N 96°48W **80 F5**
Repulse B. Australia 20°35S 148°46E **62 J6**
Repulse Bay Canada 66°30N 86°30W **69 C11**
Requena Peru 5°5S 73°52W **92 E4**
Requena Spain 39°30N 1°4W **21 C5**
Reserve U.S.A. 33°43N 108°45W **77 K9**
Resht = Rasht Iran 37°20N 49°40E **45 B6**
Resistencia Argentina 27°30S 59°0W **94 B4**
Reşiţa Romania 45°18N 21°53E **17 F11**
Reso = Raisio Finland 60°28N 22°11E **9 F20**
Resolute Canada 74°42N 94°54W **69 B10**
Resolution I. Canada 61°30N 65°0W **69 C13**
Resolution I. N.Z. 45°40S 166°40E **59 F1**
Ressano Garcia Mozam. 25°25S 32°0E **57 D5**
Reston Canada 49°33N 101°6W **71 D8**
Retalhuleu Guatemala 14°33N 91°46W **88 D1**
Retenue, L. de
  Dem. Rep. of the Congo 11°0S 27°0E **55 E2**
Retford U.K. 53°19N 0°56W **12 D7**
Rethímnon Greece 35°18N 24°30E **25 D6**
Rethímno □ Greece 35°23N 24°28E **25 D6**
Reti Pakistan 28°5N 69°48E **42 E3**
Réunion ☑ Ind. Oc. 21°0S 56°0E **53 c**
Reus Spain 41°10N 1°5E **21 B6**
Reutlingen Germany 48°29N 9°12E **16 D5**
Reval = Tallinn Estonia 59°22N 24°48E **9 G21**
Revda Russia 56°48N 59°57E **18 C10**
Revelganj India 25°50N 84°40E **43 G11**
Revelstoke Canada 51°0N 118°10W **70 C5**
Reventazón Peru 6°10S 80°58W **92 E2**
Revillagigedo, Is. de
  Pac. Oc. 18°40N 112°0W **86 D2**
Revuè → Mozam. 19°50S 34°0E **55 F3**
Rewa India 24°33N 81°25E **43 G9**
Rewari India 28°15N 76°40E **42 E7**
Rexburg U.S.A. 43°49N 111°47W **76 E8**
Rey Iran 35°35N 51°25E **45 C6**

Rey, I. del Panama 8°20N 78°30W **88 E4**
Rey, L. del Mexico 27°1N 103°26W **86 B4**
Rey Malabo Eq. Guin. 3°45N 8°50E **52 D1**
Reyðarfjörður Iceland 65°2N 14°13W **8 D6**
Reyes, Pt. U.S.A. 38°0N 123°0W **78 H3**
Reykjahlið Iceland 65°40N 16°55W **8 D5**
Reykjanes Iceland 63°48N 22°40W **8 E2**
Reykjavík Iceland 64°10N 21°57E **8 D3**
Reynolds Ra. Australia 22°30S 133°0E **60 D5**
Reynoldsville U.S.A. 41°6N 78°53W **82 E6**
Reynosa Mexico 26°7N 98°18W **87 B5**
Rēzekne Latvia 56°30N 27°17E **9 H22**
Rezvān Iran 27°34N 56°6E **45 E8**
Rhayader U.K. 52°18N 3°29W **13 E4**
Rhein → Europe 51°52N 6°2E **15 C6**
Rhein-Main-Donau-Kanal
  Germany 49°1N 11°27E **16 D6**
Rheine Germany 52°17N 7°26E **16 B4**
Rheinland-Pfalz □ Germany 50°0N 7°0E **16 C4**
Rhin = Rhein → Europe 51°52N 6°2E **15 C6**
Rhine = Rhein → Europe 51°52N 6°2E **15 C6**
Rhinebeck U.S.A. 41°56N 73°55W **83 E11**
Rhineland-Palatinate =
  Rhineland-Pfalz □
  Germany 50°0N 7°0E **16 C4**
Rhinelander U.S.A. 45°38N 89°25W **80 C9**
Rhinns Pt. U.K. 55°40N 6°29W **11 F2**
Rhino Camp Uganda 3°0N 31°22E **54 B3**
Rhir, Cap Morocco 30°38N 9°54W **50 B4**
Rhode Island □ U.S.A. 41°40N 71°30W **83 E13**
Rhodes Greece 36°15N 28°10E **25 C10**
Rhodope Mts. = Rhodopi Planina
  Bulgaria 41°40N 24°20E **23 D11**
Rhodopi Planina
  Bulgaria 41°40N 24°20E **23 D11**
Rhön Germany 50°24N 9°58E **16 C5**
Rhondda U.K. 51°39N 3°31W **13 F4**
Rhondda Cynon Taff □
  U.K. 51°42N 3°27W **13 F4**
Rhône → France 43°28N 4°42E **20 E6**
Rhum U.K. 57°0N 6°20W **11 E2**
Rhyl U.K. 53°20N 3°29W **12 D4**
Riachão Brazil 7°20S 46°37W **93 E9**
Riasi India 33°10N 74°50E **43 C6**
Riau □ Indonesia 0°0 102°35E **36 E2**
Riau, Kepulauan
  Indonesia 0°30N 104°20E **36 D2**
Riau Arch. = Riau, Kepulauan
  Indonesia 0°30N 104°20E **36 D2**
Ribadeo Spain 43°35N 7°5W **21 A2**
Ribas do Rio Pardo
  Brazil 20°27S 53°46W **93 H8**
Ribauè Mozam. 14°57S 38°17E **55 E4**
Ribble → U.K. 53°52N 2°25W **12 D5**
Ribe Denmark 55°19N 8°44E **9 J13**
Ribeira Brava Madeira 32°41N 17°4W **24 D2**
Ribeira Grande C. Verde Is. 17°0N 25°4W **50 b**
Ribeirão Prêto Brazil 21°10S 47°50W **95 A6**
Riberalta Bolivia 11°0S 66°0W **92 F5**
Riccarton N.Z. 43°32S 172°37E **59 E4**
Rice L. Canada 44°12N 78°10W **82 B6**
Rice Lake U.S.A. 45°30N 91°44W **80 C8**
Rich, C. Canada 44°43N 80°38W **82 B4**
Richards Bay S. Africa 28°48S 32°6E **57 D5**
Richardson → Canada 58°25N 111°14W **71 B6**
Richardson Lakes
  U.S.A. 44°46N 70°58W **81 C18**
Richardson Springs
  U.S.A. 39°51N 121°46W **78 F5**
Riche, C. Australia 34°36S 118°47E **61 F2**
Richey U.S.A. 47°39N 105°4W **76 C11**
Richfield U.S.A. 38°46N 112°5W **76 G7**
Richfield Springs
  U.S.A. 42°51N 74°59W **83 D10**
Richford U.S.A. 45°0N 72°40W **83 B12**
Richibucto Canada 46°42N 64°54W **73 C7**
Richland Ga., U.S.A. 32°5N 84°40W **85 E12**
Richland Wash., U.S.A. 46°17N 119°18W **76 C4**
Richland Center U.S.A. 43°21N 90°23W **80 D8**
Richlands U.S.A. 37°6N 81°48W **81 G13**
Richmond Australia 20°43S 143°8E **62 C3**
Richmond N.Z. 41°20S 173°12E **59 D4**
Richmond U.K. 54°25N 1°43W **12 C6**
Richmond Calif., U.S.A. 37°56N 122°21W **78 H4**
Richmond Ind., U.S.A. 39°50N 84°53W **81 F11**
Richmond Ky., U.S.A. 37°45N 84°18W **81 G11**
Richmond Mich., U.S.A. 42°49N 82°45W **82 D2**
Richmond Mo., U.S.A. 39°17N 93°58W **80 F8**
Richmond Tex., U.S.A. 29°35N 95°46W **84 G7**
Richmond Utah, U.S.A. 41°56N 111°48W **76 F8**
Richmond Vt., U.S.A. 44°24N 72°59W **83 B12**
Richmond Hill Canada 43°52N 79°27W **82 C5**
Richmond Ra. Australia 29°0S 152°45E **63 D5**
Richmondville U.S.A. 42°38N 74°33W **83 D10**
Richtersveld △ S. Africa 28°15S 17°10E **56 D2**
Richville U.S.A. 38°14N 80°32W **81 F13**
Richwood U.S.A. 40°9N 78°15W **82 F6**
Ridder = Leninogorsk
  Kazakhstan 50°20N 83°30E **28 D9**
Riddlesburg U.S.A. 21°0S 56°0E **53 c**
Ridgecrest U.S.A. 35°38N 117°40W **79 K9**
Ridgefield Conn., U.S.A. 41°17N 73°30W **83 E11**
Ridgefield Wash.,
  U.S.A. 45°49N 122°45W **78 E4**
Ridgeland Miss., U.S.A. 32°26N 90°8W **85 E9**
Ridgeland S.C., U.S.A. 32°29N 80°59W **85 E14**
Ridgetown Canada 42°26N 81°52W **82 D3**
Ridgewood U.S.A. 40°59N 74°7W **83 F10**
Ridgway U.S.A. 41°25N 78°44W **82 E6**
Riding Mountain △
  Canada 50°50N 100°0W **71 C9**
Ridley, Mt. Australia 33°12S 122°7E **61 F3**
Riebeek-Oos S. Africa 33°10S 26°10E **56 E4**
Ried Austria 48°14N 13°30E **16 D7**
Riesa Germany 51°17N 13°17E **16 C7**

Riet → S. Africa 29°0S 23°54E **56 D3**
Rietbron S. Africa 32°54S 23°10E **56 E3**
Rietfontein Namibia 21°58S 20°58E **56 C3**
Rieti Italy 42°24N 12°51E **22 C5**
Rif = Er Rif Morocco 35°1N 4°1W **50 A5**
Riffe L. U.S.A. 46°32N 122°26W **78 D4**
Rifle U.S.A. 39°32N 107°47W **76 G10**
Rift Valley Africa 7°0N 30°0E **48 G7**
Rift Valley □ Kenya 0°20N 36°0E **54 B4**
Riga Latvia 56°53N 24°8E **9 H21**
Riga, G. of Latvia 57°40N 23°45E **9 H20**
Rīgān Iran 28°37N 58°58E **45 D8**
Rīgas Jūras Līcis = Riga, G. of
  Latvia 57°40N 23°45E **9 H20**
Rigaud Canada 45°29N 74°18W **83 A10**
Rigby U.S.A. 43°40N 111°55W **76 E8**
Rīgestān Afghan. 30°15N 65°0E **40 D4**
Riggins U.S.A. 45°25N 116°19W **76 D5**
Rigolet Canada 54°10N 58°23W **73 B8**
Rihand Dam India 24°9N 83°2E **43 G10**
Riihimäki Finland 60°45N 24°48E **8 F21**
Riiser-Larsen-halvøya
  Antarctica 68°0S 35°0E **5 C4**
Riiser-Larsen Ice Shelf
  S. Ocean 74°0S 19°0W **5 D2**
Riiser-Larsen Sea S. Ocean 67°30S 22°0E **5 C4**
Rijeka Croatia 45°20N 14°21E **16 F8**
Rijssen Neths. 52°19N 6°31E **15 B6**
Rikuchū-Kaigan △
  Japan 39°20N 142°0E **30 E11**
Rikuzentakada Japan 39°0N 141°40E **30 E10**
Riley U.S.A. 43°32N 119°28W **76 E4**
Rima → Nigeria 13°4N 5°10E **50 F7**
Rimah, Wadi ar →
  Si. Arabia 26°5N 41°30E **44 E4**
Rimau, Pulau Malaysia 5°15N 100°16E **39 c**
Rimbey Canada 52°35N 114°15W **70 C6**
Rimersburg U.S.A. 41°3N 79°30W **82 E5**
Rímini Italy 44°3N 12°33E **22 B5**
Rimouski Canada 48°27N 68°30W **73 C6**
Rimrock U.S.A. 46°40N 121°7W **78 D5**
Rinca Indonesia 8°45S 119°35E **37 F5**
Rincón de Romos
  Mexico 22°14N 102°18W **86 C4**
Rinconada Argentina 22°26S 66°10W **94 A2**
Rind → India 25°53N 80°33E **43 G9**
Ringas India 27°21N 75°34E **42 F6**
Ringgold Is. Fiji 16°15S 179°25W **59 a**
Ringkøbing Denmark 56°5N 8°15E **9 H13**
Ringvassøya Norway 69°56N 19°15E **8 B18**
Ringwood U.S.A. 41°7N 74°15W **83 E10**
Rinjani Indonesia 8°24S 116°28E **36 F5**
Río Branco Brazil 9°58S 67°49W **92 E5**
Río Branco Uruguay 32°40S 53°40W **95 C5**
Río Bravo △ N. Amer. 29°2N 102°45W **86 B4**
Río Bravo del Norte →
  Mexico 25°57N 97°9W **87 B5**
Río Brilhante Brazil 21°48S 54°33W **95 A5**
Río Claro Brazil 22°19S 47°35W **95 A6**
Río Claro Trin. & Tob. 10°20N 61°25W **89 D7**
Río Colorado Argentina 39°0S 64°0W **96 D4**
Río Cuarto Argentina 33°10S 64°25W **94 C3**
Río das Pedras Mozam. 23°8S 35°28E **57 C6**
Río de Janeiro Brazil 22°54S 43°12W **95 A7**
Río de Janeiro □ Brazil 22°50S 43°0W **95 A7**
Río do Sul Brazil 27°13S 49°37W **95 B6**
Río Dulce △ Guatemala 15°43N 88°50W **88 C2**
Río Gallegos Argentina 51°35S 69°15W **96 G3**
Río Grande Argentina 53°50S 67°45W **96 G3**
Río Grande Brazil 32°0S 52°20W **95 C5**
Río Grande Mexico 23°50N 103°2W **86 C4**
Río Grande Puerto Rico 18°23N 65°50W **89 d**
Río Grande → N. Amer. 25°58N 97°9W **84 N6**
Río Grande City U.S.A. 26°23N 98°49W **84 H5**
Río Grande de Santiago →
  Mexico 21°36N 105°26W **86 C3**
Río Grande do Norte □
  Brazil 5°40S 36°0W **93 E11**
Río Grande do Sul □
  Brazil 30°0S 53°0W **95 C5**
Río Hato Panama 8°22N 80°10W **88 E3**
Río Lagartos Mexico 21°36N 88°10W **87 C7**
Río Largo Brazil 9°28S 35°50W **93 E11**
Río Mulatos Bolivia 19°40S 66°50W **92 G5**
Río Muni □ Eq. Guin. 1°30N 10°0E **52 D2**
Río Negro Brazil 26°0S 49°55W **95 B6**
Río Pardo Brazil 30°0S 52°30W **95 C5**
Río Pilcomayo △
  Argentina 25°5S 58°5W **94 B4**
Río Platano △ Honduras 15°45N 85°0W **88 C3**
Río Rancho U.S.A. 35°14N 106°41W **77 J10**
Río Segundo Argentina 31°40S 63°59W **94 C3**
Río Tercero Argentina 32°15S 64°8W **94 C3**
Río Verde Brazil 17°50S 51°0W **93 G8**
Río Verde Mexico 21°56N 99°59W **87 C5**
Río Vista U.S.A. 38°10N 121°42W **78 G5**
Ríobamba Ecuador 1°50S 78°45W **92 D3**
Ríohacha Colombia 11°33N 72°55W **92 A4**
Ríosucio Colombia 7°27N 77°7W **92 B3**
Riou L. Canada 59°7N 106°25W **71 B7**
Ripley Calif., U.S.A. 33°32N 114°39W **79 M12**
Ripley N.Y., U.S.A. 42°16N 79°43W **82 D5**
Ripley Tenn., U.S.A. 35°45N 89°32W **85 D10**
Ripley W. Va., U.S.A. 38°49N 81°43W **81 F13**
Ripon U.K. 54°9N 1°31W **12 C6**
Ripon Calif., U.S.A. 37°44N 121°7W **78 H5**
Ripon Wis., U.S.A. 43°51N 88°50W **80 D9**
Rishā', W. ar → Si. Arabia 25°33N 44°5E **44 E5**
Rishiri-Rebun-Sarobetsu △
  Japan 45°26N 141°30E **30 B10**
Rishiri-Tō Japan 45°11N 141°15E **30 B10**
Rishon le Ziyyon Israel 31°58N 34°48E **46 D3**
Rison U.S.A. 33°58N 92°11W **84 E8**
Risør Norway 58°43N 9°13E **9 G13**
Rita Blanca Cr. →
  U.S.A. 35°40N 102°29W **84 D3**

Ritter, Mt. U.S.A. 37°41N 119°12W 78 H7
Rittman U.S.A. 40°58N 81°47W 82 F3
Ritzville U.S.A. 47°8N 118°23W 76 C4
Riva del Garda Italy 45°53N 10°50E 22 B4
Rivadavia B. Aires, Argentina 35°29S 62°59W 94 D3
Rivadavia Mendoza, Argentina 33°13S 68°30W 94 C2
Rivadavia Salta, Argentina 24°5S 62°54W 94 A3
Rivadavia Chile 29°57S 70°35W 94 B1
Rivas Nic. 11°30N 85°50W 88 D2
Rivash Iran 35°28N 58°26E 45 C8
River Cess Liberia 5°30N 9°32W 50 G4
River Jordan Canada 48°26N 124°3W 78 E2
Rivera Argentina 37°12S 63°14W 94 D3
Rivera Uruguay 31°0S 55°50W 95 C4
Riverbank U.S.A. 37°44N 120°56W 78 H6
Riverdale U.S.A. 36°26N 119°52W 78 J7
Riverhead U.S.A. 40°55N 72°40W 83 F12
Riverhurst Canada 50°55N 106°50W 71 C7
Rivers Canada 50°2N 100°14W 71 C8
Rivers Inlet Canada 51°42N 127°15W 70 C3
Riversdale Canada 44°5N 81°20W 82 B3
Riversdale S. Africa 34°7S 21°15E 56 E3
Riverside U.S.A. 33°59N 117°22W 79 M9
Riverton Australia 34°10S 138°46E 63 E2
Riverton Canada 51°1N 97°0W 71 C9
Riverton N.Z. 46°21S 168°0E 59 G2
Riverton U.S.A. 43°2N 108°23W 76 E9
Riviera U.S.A. 35°4N 114°35W 79 K12
Riviera di Levante Italy 44°15N 9°30E 20 D8
Riviera di Ponente Italy 44°10N 8°20E 20 D8
Rivière-au-Renard Canada 48°59N 64°23W 73 C7
Rivière-du-Loup Canada 47°50N 69°30W 73 C6
Rivière-Pentecôte Canada 49°57N 67°1W 73 C6
Rivière-Pilote Martinique 14°26N 60°53W 88 c
Rivière-St-Paul Canada 51°28N 57°45W 73 B8
Rivière-Salée Martinique 14°31N 61°0W 88 c
Rivne Ukraine 50°40N 26°10E 17 C14
Rívoli Italy 45°3N 7°31E 20 D7
Rivoli B. Australia 37°32S 140°3E 63 F3
Riyadh = Ar Riyāḍ Si. Arabia 24°41N 46°42E 44 E5
Riyadh al Khabrā' Si. Arabia 26°2N 43°33E 44 E4
Rize Turkey 41°0N 40°30E 19 F7
Rizhao China 35°25N 119°30E 35 G10
Rizokarpaso Cyprus 35°36N 34°23E 25 D13
Rizzuto, C. Italy 38°53N 17°5E 22 E7
Rjukan Norway 59°54N 8°33E 9 G13
Road Town Br. Virgin Is. 18°27N 64°37W 89 e
Roan Plateau U.S.A. 39°20N 109°20W 76 G9
Roanne France 46°3N 4°4E 20 C6
Roanoke Ala., U.S.A. 33°9N 85°22W 85 E12
Roanoke Va., U.S.A. 37°16N 79°56W 81 G14
Roanoke → U.S.A. 35°57N 76°42W 85 D16
Roanoke I. U.S.A. 35°53N 75°39W 85 D17
Roanoke Rapids U.S.A. 36°28N 77°40W 85 C16
Roatán Honduras 16°18N 86°35W 88 C2
Robāt Sang Iran 35°35N 59°10E 45 C8
Robāṭkarīm Iran 35°25N 50°59E 45 C6
Robbins I. Australia 40°42S 145°0E 63 G4
Robe → Australia 21°42S 116°15E 60 D2
Robert Bourassa, Rés. Canada 53°40N 76°55W 72 B4
Robert Lee U.S.A. 31°54N 100°29W 84 F4
Robertsdale U.S.A. 40°11N 78°6W 82 F6
Robertsganj India 24°44N 83°4E 43 G10
Robertson S. Africa 33°46S 19°50E 56 E2
Robertson I. Antarctica 65°15S 59°30W 5 C18
Robertson Ra. Australia 23°15S 121°0E 60 D3
Robertstown Australia 33°58S 139°5E 63 E2
Roberval Canada 48°32N 72°15W 73 C5
Robeson Chan. N. Amer. 82°0N 61°30W 4 A4
Robesonia U.S.A. 40°21N 76°8W 83 F8
Robinson U.S.A. 39°0N 87°44W 80 F10
Robinson → Australia 16°3S 137°16E 62 B2
Robinson Crusoe I. Pac. Oc. 33°38S 78°52W 90 F2
Robinson Ra. Australia 25°40S 119°0E 61 E2
Robinvale Australia 34°40S 142°45E 63 E3
Roblin Canada 51°14N 101°21W 71 C8
Roboré Bolivia 18°10S 59°45W 92 G7
Robson, Mt. Canada 53°10N 119°10W 70 C5
Robstown U.S.A. 27°47N 97°40W 84 H6
Roca, C. da Portugal 38°40N 9°31W 21 C1
Roca Partida, I. Mexico 19°1N 112°2W 86 D2
Rocas, I. Brazil 4°0S 34°1W 93 D12
Rocha Uruguay 34°30S 54°25W 95 C5
Rochdale U.K. 53°38N 2°9W 12 D5
Rochefort Belgium 50°9N 5°12E 15 D5
Rochefort France 45°56N 0°57W 20 D3
Rochelle U.S.A. 41°56N 89°4W 80 E9
Rocher River Canada 61°23N 112°44W 70 A6
Rochester U.K. 51°23N 0°31E 13 F8
Rochester Ind., U.S.A. 41°4N 86°13W 80 E10
Rochester Minn., U.S.A. 44°1N 92°28W 80 C7
Rochester N.H., U.S.A. 43°18N 70°59W 83 C14
Rochester N.Y., U.S.A. 43°10N 77°37W 82 C7
Rock → Canada 60°7N 127°7W 70 A3
Rock, The Australia 35°15S 147°2E 63 F4
Rock Creek U.S.A. 41°40N 80°52W 82 E4
Rock Falls U.S.A. 41°47N 89°41W 80 E9
Rock Hill U.S.A. 34°56N 81°1W 85 D14
Rock Island U.S.A. 41°30N 90°34W 80 E8
Rock Port U.S.A. 40°25N 95°31W 80 E6
Rock Rapids U.S.A. 43°26N 96°10W 80 D5
Rock Sound Bahamas 24°54N 76°12W 88 B4
Rock Springs Mont., U.S.A. 46°49N 106°15W 76 C10
Rock Springs Wyo., U.S.A. 41°35N 109°14W 76 F9
Rock Valley U.S.A. 43°12N 96°18W 80 D5
Rockall Atl. Oc. 57°37N 13°42W 6 D3
Rockdale Tex., U.S.A. 30°39N 97°0W 84 F6
Rockdale Wash., U.S.A. 47°22N 121°28W 78 C5

Rockeby = Mungkan Kandju △ Australia 13°35S 142°52E 62 A3
Rockefeller Plateau Antarctica 76°0S 130°0W 5 E14
Rockford U.S.A. 42°16N 89°6W 80 D9
Rockglen Canada 49°11N 105°57W 71 D7
Rockhampton Australia 23°22S 150°32E 62 C5
Rockingham Australia 32°15S 115°38E 61 F2
Rockingham N.C., U.S.A. 34°57N 79°46W 85 D15
Rockingham Vt., U.S.A. 43°11N 72°29W 83 C12
Rockingham B. Australia 18°5S 146°10E 62 B4
Rocklake U.S.A. 48°47N 99°15W 80 A4
Rockland Canada 45°33N 75°17W 83 A9
Rockland Idaho, U.S.A. 42°34N 112°53W 76 E7
Rockland Maine, U.S.A. 44°6N 69°7W 81 C19
Rockland Mich., U.S.A. 46°44N 89°11W 80 B9
Rocklin U.S.A. 38°48N 121°14W 78 G5
Rockly B. Trin. & Tob. 11°9N 60°46W 93 J16
Rockmart U.S.A. 34°0N 85°3W 85 D12
Rockport Mass., U.S.A. 42°39N 70°37W 83 D14
Rockport Tex., U.S.A. 28°2N 97°3W 84 G6
Rocksprings U.S.A. 30°1N 100°13W 84 F4
Rockville Conn., U.S.A. 41°52N 72°28W 83 E12
Rockville Md., U.S.A. 39°5N 77°9W 81 F15
Rockwall U.S.A. 32°56N 96°28W 84 E6
Rockwell City U.S.A. 42°24N 94°38W 80 D6
Rockwood Canada 43°37N 80°8W 82 C4
Rockwood Maine, U.S.A. 45°41N 69°45W 81 C19
Rockwood Tenn., U.S.A. 35°52N 84°41W 85 D12
Rocky Ford U.S.A. 38°3N 103°43W 76 G12
Rocky Gully Australia 34°30S 116°57E 61 F2
Rocky Harbour Canada 49°36N 57°55W 73 C8
Rocky Island L. Canada 46°55N 83°0W 72 C3
Rocky Lane Canada 58°31N 116°22W 70 B5
Rocky Mount U.S.A. 35°57N 77°48W 85 D16
Rocky Mountain △ U.S.A. 40°25N 105°45W 76 F11
Rocky Mountain House Canada 52°22N 114°55W 70 C6
Rocky Mts. N. Amer. 49°0N 115°0W 76 B6
Rocky Point Namibia 19°3S 12°30E 56 B2
Rod Pakistan 28°10N 63°5E 40 E3
Roda Greece 39°48N 19°46E 25 A3
Rødbyhavn Denmark 54°39N 11°22E 9 J14
Roddickton Canada 50°51N 56°8W 73 B8
Rodez France 44°21N 2°33E 20 D5
Ródhos = Rhodes Greece 36°15N 28°10E 25 C10
Rodia Greece 35°22N 25°1E 25 D7
Rodney Canada 42°34N 81°41W 82 D3
Rodney, C. N.Z. 36°17S 174°50E 59 B5
Rodopos Greece 35°34N 23°45E 25 D5
Rodriguez Ind. Oc. 19°45S 63°20E 3 E13
Roe → U.K. 55°6N 6°59W 10 A5
Roebling U.S.A. 40°7N 74°47W 83 F10
Roebourne Australia 20°44S 117°9E 60 D2
Roebuck B. Australia 18°5S 122°20E 60 C3
Roermond Neths. 51°12N 6°0E 15 C6
Roes Welcome Sd. Canada 65°0N 87°0W 69 C11
Roeselare Belgium 50°57N 3°7E 15 D3
Rogachev = Ragachow Belarus 53°8N 30°5E 17 B16
Rogagua, L. Bolivia 13°43S 66°50W 92 F5
Rogatyn Ukraine 49°24N 24°36E 17 D13
Rogers U.S.A. 36°20N 94°7W 84 C7
Rogers City U.S.A. 45°25N 83°49W 81 C12
Rogersville Canada 46°44N 65°26W 73 C6
Roggan → Canada 54°24N 79°25W 72 B4
Roggan L. Canada 54°8N 77°50W 72 B4
Roggeveen Basin Pac. Oc. 31°30S 95°30W 65 L18
Roggeveldberge S. Africa 32°10S 20°10E 56 E3
Rogoaguado, L. Bolivia 13°0S 65°30W 92 F5
Rogojampi Indonesia 8°19S 114°17E 37 J17
Rogue → U.S.A. 42°26N 124°26W 76 E1
Rohnert Park U.S.A. 38°16N 122°40W 78 G4
Rohri Pakistan 27°45N 68°51E 42 F3
Rohri Canal Pakistan 26°15N 68°27E 42 F3
Rohtak India 28°55N 76°43E 42 E7
Roi Et Thailand 16°4N 103°40E 38 D4
Roja Latvia 57°29N 22°43E 9 H20
Rojas Argentina 34°10S 60°45W 94 C3
Rojo, C. Mexico 21°33N 97°20W 87 C5
Rokan → Indonesia 2°0N 100°50E 36 D2
Rokiškis Lithuania 55°55N 25°35E 9 J21
Rolândia Brazil 23°18S 51°23W 95 A5
Rolla Mo., U.S.A. 37°57N 91°46W 80 G8
Rolla N. Dak., U.S.A. 48°52N 99°37W 80 A4
Rolleston Australia 24°28S 148°35E 62 C4
Rollingstone Australia 19°2S 146°24E 62 B4
Roma Australia 26°32S 148°49E 63 D4
Roma Italy 41°54N 12°28E 22 D5
Roma Sweden 57°32N 18°26E 9 H18
Roma-Los Saenz U.S.A. 26°24N 99°1W 84 H5
Romain, C. U.S.A. 33°0N 79°22W 85 E15
Romaine → Canada 50°18N 63°47W 73 B7
Roman Romania 46°57N 26°55E 17 E14
Romang Indonesia 7°30S 127°20E 37 F7
Români Egypt 30°59N 32°38E 46 E1
Romania ■ Europe 46°0N 25°0E 17 F12
Romano, Cayo Cuba 22°0N 77°30W 88 B4
Romans-sur-Isère France 45°3N 5°3E 20 D6
Romblon Phil. 12°33N 122°17E 37 B6
Rome = Roma Italy 41°54N 12°28E 22 D5
Rome Ga., U.S.A. 34°15N 85°10W 85 D12
Rome N.Y., U.S.A. 43°13N 75°27W 83 D9
Rome Pa., U.S.A. 41°51N 76°21W 83 E8
Romney U.S.A. 39°21N 78°45W 81 F14
Romney Marsh U.K. 51°2N 0°54E 13 F8
Rømø Denmark 55°10N 8°30E 9 J13
Romorantin-Lanthenay France 47°21N 1°45E 20 C4

Romsdalen Norway 62°25N 7°52E 8 E12
Romsey U.K. 51°0N 1°29W 13 G6
Ron Vietnam 17°53N 106°27E 38 D6
Rona U.K. 57°34N 5°59W 11 D3
Ronan U.S.A. 47°32N 114°6W 76 C6
Roncador, Cayos Colombia 13°32N 80°4W 88 D3
Roncador, Serra do Brazil 12°30S 52°30W 93 F8
Ronda Spain 36°46N 5°12W 21 D3
Rondane Norway 61°57N 9°50E 8 F13
Rondônia □ Brazil 11°0S 63°0W 92 F6
Rondonópolis Brazil 16°28S 54°38W 93 G8
Rondu Pakistan 35°32N 75°10E 43 B6
Rong, Koh Cambodia 10°45N 103°15E 39 G4
Rong, L. la Canada 55°6N 105°17W 71 B7
Rønne Denmark 55°6N 14°43E 9 J16
Ronne Ice Shelf Antarctica 77°30S 60°0W 5 D18
Ronsard, C. Australia 24°46S 113°10E 61 D1
Ronse Belgium 50°45N 3°35E 15 D3
Roodepoort S. Africa 26°11S 27°54E 57 D4
Roof Butte U.S.A. 36°28N 109°5W 77 H9
Rooiboklaagte → Namibia 20°50S 21°0E 56 C3
Rooniu, Mt. Tahiti 17°49S 149°12W 59 d
Roorkee India 29°52N 77°59E 42 E7
Roosendaal Neths. 51°32N 4°29E 15 C4
Roosevelt U.S.A. 40°18N 109°59W 76 F9
Roosevelt → Brazil 7°35S 60°20W 92 E6
Roosevelt, Mt. Canada 58°26N 125°20W 70 B3
Roosevelt I. Antarctica 79°30S 162°0W 5 D12
Roper → Australia 14°43S 135°27E 62 A2
Roper Bar Australia 14°44S 134°44E 62 A1
Roque Pérez Argentina 35°25S 59°24W 94 D4
Roquetas de Mar Spain 36°46N 2°36W 21 D4
Roraima □ Brazil 2°0N 61°30W 92 C6
Roraima, Mt. Venezuela 5°10N 60°40W 92 B6
Røros Norway 62°35N 11°23E 8 E14
Rosa Zambia 9°33S 31°15E 55 D3
Rosa, Monte Europe 45°57N 7°53E 20 D7
Rosalia U.S.A. 47°14N 117°22W 76 C5
Rosamond U.S.A. 34°52N 118°10W 79 L8
Rosario Argentina 33°0S 60°40W 94 C3
Rosário Brazil 3°0S 44°15W 93 D10
Rosario Baja Calif., Mexico 30°0N 115°50W 86 B1
Rosario Sinaloa, Mexico 22°58N 105°53W 86 C3
Rosario Paraguay 24°30S 57°35W 94 A4
Rosario de la Frontera Argentina 25°50S 65°0W 94 B3
Rosario de Lerma Argentina 24°59S 65°35W 94 A2
Rosario del Tala Argentina 32°20S 59°10W 94 C4
Rosário do Sul Brazil 30°15S 54°55W 95 C5
Rosarito Mexico 32°20N 117°2W 79 N9
Roscoe U.S.A. 41°56N 74°55W 83 E10
Roscommon Ireland 53°38N 8°11W 10 C3
Roscommon □ Ireland 53°49N 8°23W 10 C3
Roscrea Ireland 52°57N 7°49W 10 D4
Rose → Australia 14°16S 135°45E 62 A2
Rose, L. Bahamas 21°0N 73°30W 89 B5
Rose Belle Mauritius 20°24S 57°36E 53 d
Rose Blanche Canada 47°38N 58°45W 73 C8
Rose Hill Mauritius 20°14S 57°27E 53 d
Rose Pt. Canada 54°11N 131°39W 70 C2
Rose Valley Canada 52°19N 103°49W 71 C8
Roseau Dominica 15°17N 61°24W 89 C7
Roseau U.S.A. 48°51N 95°46W 80 A6
Rosebery Australia 41°46S 145°33E 63 G4
Rosebud S. Dak., U.S.A. 43°14N 100°51W 80 D3
Rosebud Tex., U.S.A. 31°4N 96°59W 84 F6
Roseburg U.S.A. 43°13N 123°20W 76 E2
Rosedale U.S.A. 33°51N 91°2W 85 E9
Rosehearty U.K. 57°42N 2°7W 11 D6
Roseires Res. Sudan 11°51N 34°23E 51 F12
Roseland U.S.A. 38°25N 122°43W 78 G4
Rosemary Canada 50°46N 112°5W 70 C6
Rosenberg U.S.A. 29°34N 95°49W 84 L7
Rosenheim Germany 47°51N 12°7E 16 E7
Roses, G. de Spain 42°10N 3°15E 21 A7
Rosetown Canada 51°35N 107°59W 71 C7
Roseville Calif., U.S.A. 38°45N 121°17W 78 G5
Roseville Mich., U.S.A. 42°30N 82°56W 82 D2
Roseville Pa., U.S.A. 41°51N 76°57W 83 E8
Rosewood Australia 27°38S 152°36E 63 D5
Roshkhvār Iran 34°58N 59°37E 45 C8
Rosignano Maríttimo Italy 43°24N 10°28E 22 C4
Rosignol Guyana 6°15N 57°30W 92 B7
Roşiori de Vede Romania 44°9N 25°0E 17 F13
Roskilde Denmark 55°38N 12°3E 9 J15
Roslavl Russia 53°57N 32°55E 18 D5
Rosmead S. Africa 31°29S 25°8E 56 E4
Ross Australia 42°2S 147°30E 63 G4
Ross N.Z. 42°53S 170°49E 59 E3
Ross Dependency Antarctica 76°0S 170°0W 5 D12
Ross I. Antarctica 77°30S 168°0E 5 D11
Ross Ice Shelf Antarctica 80°0S 180°0E 5 E12
Ross L. U.S.A. 48°44N 121°4W 78 B5
Ross-on-Wye U.K. 51°54N 2°34W 13 F5
Ross River Australia 23°44S 134°30E 62 C1
Ross River Canada 62°30N 131°30W 70 A2
Ross Sea Antarctica 74°0S 178°0E 5 D11
Rossall Pt. U.K. 53°55N 3°3W 12 D4
Rossan Pt. Ireland 54°42N 8°47W 10 B3
Rossano Italy 39°36N 16°39E 22 E7
Rossburn Canada 50°40N 100°49W 71 C8
Rosseau Canada 45°16N 79°39W 82 A5
Rosseau, L. Canada 45°10N 79°35W 82 A5
Rosses, The Ireland 55°2N 8°20W 10 A3
Rossignol, L. Canada 52°43N 73°40W 72 B5
Rossignol L. Canada 44°12N 65°10W 73 D6
Rossiya = Russia ■ Eurasia 62°0N 105°0E 29 C11

Rossland Canada 49°6N 117°50W 70 D5
Rosslare Ireland 52°17N 6°24W 10 D5
Rosslare Harbour Ireland 52°15N 6°20W 10 D5
Rossmore Canada 44°8N 77°23W 82 B7
Rosso Mauritania 16°40N 15°45W 50 E2
Rossosh Russia 50°15N 39°28E 19 D6
Rossvatnet Norway 65°45N 14°5E 8 D16
Røst Norway 67°32N 12°0E 8 C15
Rosthern Canada 52°40N 106°20W 71 C7
Rostock Germany 54°5N 12°8E 16 A7
Rostov Don, Russia 47°15N 39°45E 19 E6
Rostov Yaroslavl, Russia 57°14N 39°25E 18 C6
Roswell Ga., U.S.A. 34°2N 84°22W 85 D12
Roswell N. Mex., U.S.A. 33°24N 104°32W 77 K11
Rotan U.S.A. 32°51N 100°28W 84 E4
Rother → U.K. 50°59N 0°45E 13 G8
Rotherham U.K. 53°26N 1°20W 12 D6
Rothes U.K. 57°32N 3°13W 11 D5
Rothesay Canada 45°23N 66°0W 73 C6
Rothesay U.K. 55°50N 5°3W 11 F3
Roti Indonesia 10°50S 123°0E 37 F6
Roto Australia 33°0S 145°30E 63 E4
Rotondo, Mte. France 42°14N 9°8E 20 E8
Rotoroa, L. N.Z. 41°55S 172°39E 59 D4
Rotorua N.Z. 38°9S 176°16E 59 C6
Rotorua, L. N.Z. 38°5S 176°18E 59 C6
Rotterdam Neths. 51°55N 4°30E 15 C4
Rotterdam U.S.A. 42°48N 74°1W 83 D10
Rottnest I. Australia 32°0S 115°27E 61 F2
Rottumeroog Neths. 53°33N 6°34E 15 A6
Rottweil Germany 48°9N 8°37E 16 D5
Rotuma Fiji 12°25S 177°5E 58 C10
Roubaix France 50°40N 3°10E 20 A5
Rouen France 49°27N 1°4E 20 B4
Rouleau Canada 50°10N 104°56W 71 C8
Round I. Mauritius 19°51S 57°45E 53 d
Round Mountain U.S.A. 38°43N 117°4W 76 G5
Round Mt. Australia 30°26S 152°16E 63 E5
Round Rock U.S.A. 30°31N 97°41W 84 F6
Roundup U.S.A. 46°27N 108°33W 76 C9
Rousay U.K. 59°10N 3°2W 11 B5
Rouses Point U.S.A. 44°59N 73°22W 83 B11
Rouseville U.S.A. 41°28N 79°42W 82 E5
Rousse = Ruse Bulgaria 43°48N 25°59E 23 C12
Roussillon France 42°30N 2°35E 20 E5
Rouxville S. Africa 30°25S 26°50E 56 E4
Rouyn-Noranda Canada 48°20N 79°0W 72 C4
Rovaniemi Finland 66°29N 25°41E 8 C21
Rovereto Italy 45°53N 11°3E 22 B4
Rovigo Italy 45°4N 11°47E 22 B4
Rovinj Croatia 45°5N 13°40E 16 F7
Rovno = Rivne Ukraine 50°40N 26°10E 17 C14
Rovuma = Ruvuma → Tanzania 10°29S 40°28E 55 E5
Row'an Iran 35°8N 48°51E 45 C6
Rowena Australia 29°48S 148°55E 63 D4
Rowley Shoals Australia 17°30S 119°0E 60 C2
Roxas Phil. 11°36N 122°49E 37 B6
Roxboro U.S.A. 36°24N 78°59W 85 C15
Roxborough Trin. & Tob. 11°15N 60°35W 93 J16
Roxburgh N.Z. 45°33S 169°19E 59 F2
Roxbury N.Y., U.S.A. 42°17N 74°33W 83 D10
Roxbury Pa., U.S.A. 40°6N 77°39W 82 F7
Roxby Downs Australia 30°43S 136°46E 63 E2
Roy Mont., U.S.A. 47°20N 108°58W 76 C9
Roy N. Mex., U.S.A. 35°57N 104°12W 77 J11
Roy Utah, U.S.A. 41°10N 112°2W 76 F7
Royal Bardia △ Nepal 28°20N 81°20E 43 E9
Royal Canal Ireland 53°30N 7°13W 10 C4
Royal Chitawan △ Nepal 26°30N 84°30E 43 F11
Royal Leamington Spa U.K. 52°18N 1°31W 13 E6
Royal Natal △ S. Africa 28°43S 28°51E 57 D4
Royal Tunbridge Wells U.K. 51°7N 0°16E 13 F8
Royale, Isle U.S.A. 48°0N 88°54W 80 B9
Royan France 45°37N 1°2W 20 D3
Royston U.K. 52°3N 0°0 13 E7
Rozdilna Ukraine 46°50N 30°2E 17 E16
Rozhyshche Ukraine 50°54N 25°15E 17 C13
Rtishchevo Russia 52°18N 43°46E 18 D7
Ruacaná Namibia 17°27S 14°21E 56 B1
Ruaha △ Tanzania 7°41S 34°30E 54 D3
Ruahine Ra. N.Z. 39°55S 176°2E 59 C6
Ruapehu N.Z. 39°17S 175°35E 59 C6
Ruapuke I. N.Z. 46°46S 168°31E 59 G2
Ruâq, W. → Egypt 30°0N 33°49E 46 F2
Rub' al Khālī Si. Arabia 19°0N 48°0E 47 D4
Rubeho Mts. Tanzania 6°50S 36°25E 54 D4
Rubh a' Mhail U.K. 55°56N 6°8W 11 F2
Rubha Hunish U.K. 57°42N 6°20W 11 D2
Rubha Robhanais = Lewis, Butt of U.K. 58°31N 6°16W 11 C2
Rubicon → U.S.A. 38°53N 121°4W 78 G5
Rubio Venezuela 7°43N 72°22W 92 B4
Rubondo △ Tanzania 2°18S 31°58E 54 C3
Rubtsovsk Russia 51°30N 81°10E 28 D9
Ruby L. U.S.A. 40°10N 115°28W 76 F6
Ruby Mts. U.S.A. 40°30N 115°20W 76 F6
Rubyvale Australia 23°25S 147°42E 62 C4
Rūd Sar Iran 37°8N 50°18E 45 B6
Rudall Australia 33°43S 136°17E 63 E2
Rudall River △ Australia 22°38S 122°30E 60 D3
Rudbar Iran 36°8N 49°23E 45 B6
Rudewa Tanzania 10°7S 34°40E 55 E3
Rudnya Kazakhstan 52°57N 63°7E 28 D7
Rudolfa, Ostrov Russia 81°45N 58°30E 28 A6
Rudyard U.S.A. 46°14N 84°36W 81 B11

Rufiji → Tanzania 7°50S 39°15E 54 D4
Rufino Argentina 34°20S 62°50W 94 C3
Rufunsa Zambia 15°4S 29°34E 55 F2
Rugby U.K. 52°23N 1°16W 13 E6
Rugby U.S.A. 48°22N 100°0W 80 A4
Rügen Germany 54°22N 13°24E 16 A7
Ruhengeri Rwanda 1°30S 29°36E 54 C2
Ruhnu Estonia 57°48N 23°15E 9 H20
Ruhr → Germany 51°27N 6°43E 16 C4
Ruhuhu → Tanzania 10°31S 34°34E 55 E3
Ruidoso U.S.A. 33°20N 105°41W 77 K11
Ruivo, Pico Madeira 32°45N 16°56W 24 D3
Rujm Tal'at al Jamā'ah Jordan 30°24N 35°30E 46 E4
Ruk Pakistan 27°50N 68°42E 42 F3
Rukhla Pakistan 32°27N 71°57E 42 C4
Ruki → Dem. Rep. of the Congo 0°5N 18°17E 52 E3
Rukwa □ Tanzania 7°0S 31°30E 54 D3
Rukwa, L. Tanzania 8°0S 32°20E 54 D3
Rulhieres, C. Australia 13°56S 127°22E 60 B4
Rum = Rhum U.K. 57°0N 6°20W 11 E2
Rum Jordan 29°39S 35°26E 46 F4
Rum Cay Bahamas 23°40N 74°58W 89 B5
Rum Jungle Australia 13°0S 130°59E 60 B5
Ruma △ Kenya 0°39S 34°18E 54 C3
Rumāḥ Si. Arabia 25°29N 47°10E 44 E5
Rumania = Romania ■ Europe 46°0N 25°0E 17 F12
Rumaylah Iraq 30°47N 47°37E 44 D5
Rumbêk Sudan 6°54N 29°37E 51 G11
Rumford U.S.A. 44°33N 70°33W 83 B14
Rumia Poland 54°37N 18°25E 17 A10
Rumoi Japan 43°56N 141°39E 30 C10
Rumonge Burundi 3°59S 29°26E 54 C2
Rumson U.S.A. 40°23N 74°0W 83 F11
Rumuruti Kenya 0°17N 36°32E 54 B4
Runan China 33°0N 114°30E 34 H8
Runanga N.Z. 42°25S 171°15E 59 E3
Runaway, C. N.Z. 37°32S 177°59E 59 B6
Runaway Bay Jamaica 18°27N 77°20W 88 a
Runcorn U.K. 53°21N 2°44W 12 D5
Rundu Namibia 17°52S 19°43E 56 B2
Rungwa Tanzania 6°55S 33°32E 54 D3
Rungwa → Tanzania 7°36S 31°50E 54 D3
Rungwa △ Tanzania 6°53S 34°2E 54 D3
Rungwe Tanzania 9°11S 33°32E 55 D3
Rungwe, Mt. Tanzania 9°8S 33°40E 52 F6
Runton Ra. Australia 23°31S 123°6E 60 D3
Ruo Shui → China 41°0N 100°16E 32 B5
Ruokolahti Finland 61°17N 28°50E 8 F23
Ruoqiang China 38°55N 88°10E 32 C3
Rupa India 27°15N 92°21E 41 F18
Rupar India 31°2N 76°38E 42 D7
Rupat Indonesia 1°45N 101°40E 36 D2
Rupen → India 23°28N 71°31E 42 H4
Rupert U.S.A. 42°37N 113°41W 76 E7
Rupert → Canada 51°29N 78°45W 72 B4
Rupert B. Canada 51°35N 79°0W 72 B4
Rupert House = Waskaganish Canada 51°30N 78°40W 72 B4
Rupsa India 21°37N 87°1E 43 J12
Rurrenabaque Bolivia 14°30S 67°32W 92 F5
Rusambo Zimbabwe 16°30S 32°4E 55 F3
Rusape Zimbabwe 18°35S 32°8E 55 F3
Ruschuk = Ruse Bulgaria 43°48N 25°59E 23 C12
Ruse Bulgaria 43°48N 25°59E 23 C12
Rush Ireland 53°31N 6°6W 10 C5
Rushan China 36°56N 121°30E 35 F11
Rushden U.K. 52°18N 0°35W 13 E7
Rushmore, Mt. U.S.A. 43°53N 103°28W 80 D2
Rushville Ill., U.S.A. 40°7N 90°34W 80 E8
Rushville Ind., U.S.A. 39°37N 85°27W 81 F11
Rushville Nebr., U.S.A. 42°43N 102°28W 80 D2
Russas Brazil 4°55S 37°50W 93 D11
Russell Canada 50°50N 101°20W 71 C8
Russell Kans., U.S.A. 38°54N 98°52W 80 F4
Russell N.Y., U.S.A. 44°27N 75°9W 83 B9
Russell Pa., U.S.A. 41°56N 79°8W 82 E5
Russell Cave △ U.S.A. 34°59N 85°49W 85 D12
Russell I. Man., Canada 56°15N 101°30W 71 B8
Russell L. N.W.T., Canada 63°5N 115°44W 70 A5
Russellkonda India 19°57N 84°42E 41 K14
Russellville Ala., U.S.A. 34°30N 87°44W 85 D11
Russellville Ark., U.S.A. 35°17N 93°8W 84 D8
Russellville Ky., U.S.A. 36°51N 86°53W 80 G10
Russia ■ Eurasia 62°0N 105°0E 29 C11
Russian → U.S.A. 38°27N 123°8W 78 G3
Russkoye Ustye Russia 71°0N 149°0E 4 B15
Rustam Pakistan 34°25N 72°13E 42 B5
Rustam Shahr Pakistan 26°58N 66°6E 42 F2
Rustavi Georgia 41°30N 45°0E 19 F8
Rustenburg S. Africa 25°41S 27°14E 56 D4
Ruston U.S.A. 32°32N 92°38W 84 E8
Rutana Burundi 3°55S 30°0E 54 C3
Ruteng Indonesia 8°35S 120°30E 37 F6
Ruth U.S.A. 38°26N 122°24W 78 G4
Rutherford U.S.A. 38°26N 122°24W 78 G4
Rutland U.S.A. 43°37N 72°58W 83 C12
Rutland Water U.K. 52°38N 0°40W 13 E7
Rutledge → Canada 61°4N 112°0W 71 A6
Rutledge L. Canada 61°33N 110°47W 71 A6
Rutog China 33°27N 79°42E 32 C2
Rutshuru Dem. Rep. of the Congo 1°13S 29°25E 54 C2
Ruvu Tanzania 6°49S 38°43E 54 D4
Ruvu → Tanzania 6°23S 38°52E 54 D4
Ruvuma □ Tanzania 10°20S 36°0E 55 E4
Ruvuma → Tanzania 10°29S 40°28E 55 E5
Ruvuba △ Burundi 3°3S 29°33E 54 C2
Ruwais U.A.E. 24°5N 52°50E 45 E7
Ruwenzori Africa 0°30N 29°55E 54 B2
Ruwenzori △ Uganda 0°20N 30°0E 54 B2
Ruya → Zimbabwe 16°27S 32°5E 57 B5

Ruyigi *Burundi* 3°29S 30°15E 54 C3
Ružomberok *Slovak Rep.* 49°3N 19°17E 17 D10
Rwanda ■ *Africa* 2°0S 30°0E 54 C3
Ryan, L. *U.K.* 55°0N 5°2W 11 G3
Ryazan *Russia* 54°40N 39°40E 18 D6
Ryazhsk *Russia* 53°45N 40°3E 18 D7
Rybachiy Poluostrov *Russia* 69°43N 32°0E 8 B25
Rybachye = Balykchy *Kyrgyzstan* 42°26N 76°12E 32 B2
Rybinsk *Russia* 58°5N 38°50E 18 C6
Rybinskoye Vdkhr. *Russia* 58°30N 38°25E 18 C6
Rybnitsa = Râbniţa *Moldova* 47°45N 29°0E 17 E15
Rycroft *Canada* 55°45N 118°40W 70 B5
Ryde *U.K.* 50°43N 1°9W 13 G6
Ryderwood *U.S.A.* 46°23N 123°3W 78 D3
Rye *U.K.* 50°57N 0°45E 13 G8
Rye → *U.K.* 54°11N 0°44W 12 C7
Rye Bay *U.K.* 50°52N 0°49E 13 G8
Rye Patch Res. *U.S.A.* 40°28N 118°19W 76 F4
Ryegate *U.S.A.* 46°18N 109°15W 76 C9
Ryley *Canada* 53°17N 112°26W 70 C6
Rylstone *Australia* 32°46S 149°58E 63 E4
Ryn Peski = Naryn Qum *Kazakhstan* 47°30N 49°0E 28 E5
Ryōtsu *Japan* 38°5N 138°26E 30 E9
Rypin *Poland* 53°3N 19°25E 17 B10
Ryūgasaki *Japan* 35°54N 140°11E 31 G10
Ryukyu Is. = Ryūkyū-rettō *Japan* 26°0N 126°0E 31 M3
Ryūkyū-rettō *Japan* 26°0N 126°0E 31 M3
Rzeszów *Poland* 50°5N 21°58E 17 C11
Rzhev *Russia* 56°20N 34°20E 18 C5

S

Sa *Thailand* 18°34N 100°45E 38 C3
Sa Cabaneta *Spain* 39°37N 2°45E 24 B9
Sa Canal *Spain* 38°51N 1°23E 24 C7
Sa Conillera *Spain* 38°59N 1°13E 24 C7
Sa Dec *Vietnam* 10°20N 105°46E 39 G5
Sa Dragonera *Spain* 39°35N 2°19E 24 B9
Sa Kaeo *Thailand* 13°49N 102°4E 38 F4
Sa Mesquida *Spain* 39°55N 4°16E 24 B11
Sa Pa *Vietnam* 22°20N 103°47E 38 A4
Sa Savina *Spain* 38°44N 1°25E 24 C7
Sa'ādatābād *Fārs, Iran* 30°10N 53°5E 45 D7
Sa'ādatābād *Hormozgān, Iran* 28°3N 55°53E 45 D7
Sa'ādatābād *Kermān, Iran* 29°40N 55°51E 45 D7
Saale → *Germany* 51°56N 11°54E 16 C6
Saalfeld *Germany* 50°38N 11°21E 16 C6
Saanich *Canada* 48°29N 123°26W 78 B3
Saar → *Europe* 49°41N 6°32E 15 E6
Saarbrücken *Germany* 49°14N 6°59E 16 D4
Saaremaa *Estonia* 58°30N 22°30E 9 G20
Saarijärvi *Finland* 62°43N 25°16E 8 E21
Saariselkä *Finland* 68°16N 28°15E 8 B23
Sab 'Ābar *Syria* 33°46N 37°41E 44 C3
Saba *W. Indies* 17°38N 63°14W 89 C7
Šabac *Serbia* 44°48N 19°42E 23 B8
Sabadell *Spain* 41°28N 2°7E 21 B7
Sabah □ *Malaysia* 6°0N 117°0E 36 C5
Sabak *Malaysia* 3°46N 100°58E 39 L3
Sabalān, Kūhhā-ye *Iran* 38°15N 47°45E 44 B5
Sabalana, Kepulauan *Indonesia* 6°45S 118°50E 37 F5
Sábana de la Mar *Dom. Rep.* 19°7N 69°24W 89 C6
Sábanalarga *Colombia* 10°38N 74°55W 92 A4
Sabang *Indonesia* 5°50N 95°15E 36 C1
Sabará *Brazil* 19°55S 43°46W 93 G10
Sabarmati → *India* 22°18N 72°22E 42 H5
Sabattis *U.S.A.* 44°6N 74°40W 83 B10
Saberania *Indonesia* 2°5S 138°18E 37 E9
Sabhā *Libya* 27°9N 14°29E 51 C8
Sabi → *India* 28°29N 76°44E 42 E7
Sabie *S. Africa* 25°10S 30°48E 57 D5
Sabinal *Mexico* 30°57N 107°30W 86 A3
Sabinal *U.S.A.* 29°19N 99°28W 84 G5
Sabinas *Mexico* 27°51N 101°7W 86 B4
Sabinas → *Mexico* 27°37N 100°42W 86 B4
Sabinas Hidalgo *Mexico* 26°30N 100°10W 86 B4
Sabine → *U.S.A.* 29°59N 93°47W 84 G8
Sabine L. *U.S.A.* 29°53N 93°51W 84 G8
Sabine Pass *U.S.A.* 29°44N 93°54W 84 G8
Sablayan *Phil.* 12°50N 120°50E 37 B6
Sable *Canada* 55°30N 68°21W 73 A6
Sable, C. *Canada* 43°29N 65°38W 73 D6
Sable, C. *U.S.A.* 25°9N 81°8W 88 A3
Sable I. *Canada* 44°0N 60°0W 73 D8
Sabrina Coast *Antarctica* 68°0S 120°0E 5 C9
Sabulubbek *Indonesia* 1°36S 98°40E 36 E1
Sabzevār *Iran* 36°15N 57°40E 45 B8
Sabzvārān *Iran* 28°45N 57°50E 45 D8
Sac City *U.S.A.* 42°25N 95°0W 80 D6
Săcele *Romania* 45°37N 25°41E 17 F13
Sacheon *S. Korea* 35°0N 128°6E 35 G15
Sachigo → *Canada* 55°6N 88°58W 72 A2
Sachigo, L. *Canada* 53°50N 92°12W 72 B1
Sachimbo *Angola* 9°14S 20°16E 52 F4
Sachsen □ *Germany* 50°55N 13°10E 16 C7
Sachsen-Anhalt □ *Germany* 52°0N 12°0E 16 C7
Sackets Harbor *U.S.A.* 43°57N 76°7W 83 C8
Sackville *Canada* 45°54N 64°22W 73 C7
Saco *Maine, U.S.A.* 43°30N 70°27W 83 C14
Saco *Mont., U.S.A.* 48°28N 107°21W 76 B10
Sacramento *U.S.A.* 38°35N 121°29W 78 G5
Sacramento → *U.S.A.* 38°3N 121°56W 78 G5
Sacramento Mts. *U.S.A.* 32°30N 105°30W 77 K11
Sacramento Valley *U.S.A.* 39°30N 122°0W 78 G5
Sada-Misaki *Japan* 33°20N 132°5E 31 H6
Sadabad *India* 27°27N 78°3E 42 F8
Sadani *Tanzania* 5°58S 38°35E 54 D4
Sadao *Thailand* 6°38N 100°26E 39 J3
Sadd el Aali *Egypt* 23°54N 32°54E 51 D12
Saddle Mt. *U.S.A.* 45°58N 123°41W 78 E3
Sadimi *Dem. Rep. of the Congo* 9°25S 23°32E 55 D1
Sado *Japan* 38°0N 138°25E 30 F9
Sadra *India* 23°21N 72°43E 42 H5
Sadri *India* 25°11N 73°26E 42 G5
Sæby *Denmark* 57°21N 10°30E 9 H14
Saegertown *U.S.A.* 41°43N 80°9W 82 E4
Şafājah *Si. Arabia* 26°25N 39°0E 44 E3
Safata B. *Samoa* 14°0S 171°50W 59 b
Säffle *Sweden* 59°8N 12°55E 9 G15
Safford *U.S.A.* 32°50N 109°43W 77 K9
Saffron Walden *U.K.* 52°1N 0°16E 13 E8
Safi *Morocco* 32°18N 9°20W 50 B4
Şafīābād *Iran* 36°45N 57°58E 45 B8
Safīd Dasht *Iran* 33°27N 48°11E 45 C6
Safīd Kūh *Afghan.* 34°45N 63°0E 40 B3
Safīd Rūd → *Iran* 37°23N 50°11E 45 B6
Safipur *India* 26°44N 80°21E 43 F9
Şāfītā *Syria* 34°48N 36°7E 44 C3
Safune *Samoa* 13°25S 172°21W 59 b
Şafwān *Iraq* 30°7N 47°43E 44 D5
Sag Harbor *U.S.A.* 41°0N 72°18W 83 F12
Saga *Japan* 33°15N 130°16E 31 H5
Saga □ *Japan* 33°15N 130°20E 31 H5
Sagae *Japan* 38°22N 140°17E 30 E10
Sagaing *Burma* 21°52N 95°59E 41 J19
Sagamore *U.S.A.* 40°46N 79°14W 82 F5
Saganaga L. *Canada* 48°14N 90°52W 80 A8
Sagar *Karnataka, India* 14°14N 75°6E 40 M9
Sagar *Mad. P., India* 23°50N 78°44E 43 H8
Sagara, L. *Tanzania* 5°20S 31°0E 54 D3
Sagarmatha = Everest, Mt. *Nepal* 28°5N 86°58E 43 E12
Sagarmatha △ *Nepal* 27°55N 86°45E 43 F12
Saginaw *U.S.A.* 43°26N 83°56W 81 D12
Saginaw B. *U.S.A.* 43°50N 83°40W 81 D12
Saglouc = Salluit *Canada* 62°14N 75°38W 69 C12
Sagone *France* 42°7N 8°42E 20 E8
Sagua la Grande *Cuba* 22°50N 80°10W 88 B3
Saguache *U.S.A.* 38°5N 106°8W 76 G10
Saguaro △ *U.S.A.* 32°12N 110°38W 77 K8
Saguenay → *Canada* 48°22N 71°0W 73 C5
Sagunt *Spain* 39°42N 0°18W 21 C5
Sagunto = Sagunt *Spain* 39°42N 0°18W 21 C5
Sagwara *India* 23°41N 74°1E 42 H6
Sahagún *Spain* 42°18N 5°2W 21 A3
Saḩam al Jawlān *Syria* 32°45N 35°55E 46 C4
Sahamandrevo *Madag.* 23°15S 45°35E 57 C8
Sahand, Kūh-e *Iran* 37°44N 46°27E 44 B5
Sahara *Africa* 23°0N 5°0E 50 D6
Saharan Atlas = Saharien, Atlas *Algeria* 33°30N 1°0E 50 B6
Saharanpur *India* 29°58N 77°33E 42 E7
Saharien, Atlas *Algeria* 33°30N 1°0E 50 B6
Saharsa *India* 25°53N 86°36E 43 G12
Sahasinaka *Madag.* 21°49S 47°49E 57 C8
Sahaswan *India* 28°5N 78°45E 43 E8
Saheira, W. el → *Egypt* 30°5N 33°25E 46 E2
Sahel *Africa* 16°0N 5°0E 50 E5
Sahibganj *India* 25°12N 87°40E 43 G12
Sāḩilīyah *Iraq* 33°43N 42°42E 44 C4
Sahiwal *Pakistan* 30°45N 73°8E 42 D5
Şaḩneh *Iran* 34°29N 47°41E 44 C5
Sahrawi = Western Sahara ■ *Africa* 25°0N 13°0W 50 D3
Sahuaripa *Mexico* 29°3N 109°14W 86 B3
Sahuarita *U.S.A.* 31°57N 110°58W 77 L8
Sahuayo de Díaz *Mexico* 20°4N 102°43W 86 C4
Sai → *India* 25°39N 82°47E 43 G10
Sai Buri *Thailand* 6°43N 101°45E 39 J3
Sai Kung *China* 22°23N 114°16E 33 G11
Sai Twong △ *Thailand* 15°56N 101°10E 38 E3
Sai Yok △ *Thailand* 14°25N 98°40E 38 E2
Sa'id Bundâs *Sudan* 8°24N 24°48E 51 G10
Sa'īdābād = Sīrjān *Iran* 29°30N 55°45E 45 D7
Sa'īdābād *Iran* 36°8N 54°11E 45 B7
Sa'īdīyeh *Iran* 36°20N 48°55E 45 B6
Saidpur *Bangla.* 25°48N 89°0E 41 G16
Saidpur *India* 25°33N 83°11E 43 G10
Saidu Sharif *Pakistan* 34°43N 72°24E 43 B5
Saigō *Japan* 36°12N 133°20E 31 F6
Saigon = Thanh Pho Ho Chi Minh *Vietnam* 10°58N 106°40E 39 G6
Saijō *Japan* 33°55N 133°11E 31 H6
Saikai △ *Japan* 33°12N 129°36E 31 H4
Saikanosy Masoala *Madag.* 15°45S 50°10E 57 B9
Saikhoa Ghat *India* 27°50N 95°40E 41 F19
Saiki *Japan* 32°58N 131°51E 31 H5
Şā'īl *Si. Arabia* 27°28N 41°45E 44 E4
Sailana *India* 23°28N 74°55E 42 H6
Sailolof *Indonesia* 1°15S 130°46E 37 E8
Saimaa *Finland* 61°15N 28°15E 8 F23
Saimen = Saimaa *Finland* 61°15N 28°15E 8 F23
Şa'in Dezh *Iran* 36°40N 46°25E 44 B5
St. Abb's Head *U.K.* 55°55N 2°8W 11 F6
St. Alban's *Canada* 47°51N 55°50W 73 C8
St. Albans *U.K.* 51°45N 0°19W 13 F7
St. Albans *Vt., U.S.A.* 44°49N 73°5W 83 B11
St. Albans *W. Va., U.S.A.* 38°23N 81°50W 81 F13
St. Alban's Head *U.K.* 50°34N 2°4W 13 G5
St. Albert *Canada* 53°37N 113°32W 70 C6
St-André *Réunion* 20°57S 55°39E 53 c
St. Andrew's *Canada* 47°45N 59°15W 73 C8
St. Andrews *U.K.* 56°20N 2°47W 11 E6
St-Anicet *Canada* 45°8N 74°22W 83 A10
St. Annes *Canada* 49°40N 96°39W 71 D9
St. Anns B. *Canada* 46°22N 60°25W 73 C7
St. Ann's Bay *Jamaica* 18°26N 77°12W 88 a
St. Anthony *Canada* 51°22N 55°35W 73 B8
St. Anthony *U.S.A.* 43°58N 111°41W 76 E8
St-Antoine *Canada* 46°22N 64°45W 73 C7
St. Arnaud *Australia* 36°40S 143°16E 63 F3
St-Augustin *Canada* 51°13N 58°38W 73 B8
St-Augustin → *Canada* 51°16N 58°40W 73 B8
St. Augustine *U.S.A.* 29°54N 81°19W 85 G14
St. Austell *U.K.* 50°20N 4°47W 13 G3
St. Barbe *Canada* 51°12N 56°46W 73 B8
St-Barthélemy *W. Indies* 17°50N 62°50W 89 C7
St. Bees Hd. *U.K.* 54°31N 3°38W 12 C4
St. Bees I. *Australia* 20°56S 149°26E 62 J7
St-Benoît *Réunion* 21°2S 55°43E 53 c
St. Bride's *Canada* 46°56N 54°10W 73 C9
St. Brides B. *U.K.* 51°49N 5°9W 13 F2
St-Brieuc *France* 48°30N 2°46W 20 B2
St. Catharines *Canada* 43°10N 79°15W 82 C5
St. Catherines I. *U.S.A.* 31°40N 81°10W 85 F14
St. Catherine's Pt. *U.K.* 50°34N 1°18W 13 G6
St-Chamond *France* 45°28N 4°31E 20 D6
St. Charles *Ill., U.S.A.* 41°54N 88°19W 80 E9
St. Charles *Md., U.S.A.* 38°36N 76°56W 81 F15
St. Charles *Mo., U.S.A.* 38°47N 90°29W 80 F8
St. Charles *Va., U.S.A.* 36°48N 83°4W 81 G12
St. Christopher-Nevis = St. Kitts & Nevis ■ *W. Indies* 17°20N 62°40W 89 C7
St. Clair *Mich., U.S.A.* 42°50N 82°30W 82 D2
St. Clair *Pa., U.S.A.* 40°43N 76°12W 83 F8
St. Clair → *U.S.A.* 42°38N 82°31W 82 D2
St. Clair, L. *N. Amer.* 42°27N 82°39W 82 D2
St. Clairsville *U.S.A.* 40°5N 80°54W 82 F4
St. Claude *Canada* 49°40N 98°20W 71 D9
St. Clears *U.K.* 51°49N 4°31W 13 F3
St-Clet *Canada* 45°21N 74°13W 83 A10
St. Cloud *Fla., U.S.A.* 28°15N 81°17W 85 G14
St. Cloud *Minn., U.S.A.* 45°34N 94°10W 80 C6
St. Cricq, C. *Australia* 25°17S 113°6E 61 E1
St. Croix *U.S. Virgin Is.* 17°45N 64°45W 89 C7
St. Croix → *U.S.A.* 44°45N 92°48W 80 C7
St. Croix Falls *U.S.A.* 45°24N 92°38W 80 C7
St. David's *Canada* 48°12N 58°52W 73 C8
St. David's *U.K.* 51°53N 5°16W 13 F2
St. David's Head *U.K.* 51°54N 5°19W 13 F2
St-Denis *France* 48°56N 2°20E 20 B5
St-Denis *Réunion* 20°52S 55°27E 53 c
St-Denis ✈ (RUN) *Réunion* 20°53S 55°32E 53 c
St-Dizier *France* 48°38N 4°56E 20 B6
St. Elias, Mt. *U.S.A.* 60°18N 140°56W 68 C5
St. Elias Mts. *N. Amer.* 60°33N 139°28W 70 A1
St-Étienne *France* 45°27N 4°22E 20 D6
St. Eugène *Canada* 45°30N 74°28W 83 A10
St. Eustatius *W. Indies* 17°20N 63°0W 89 C7
St-Félicien *Canada* 48°40N 72°25W 72 C5
St-Flour *France* 45°2N 3°6E 20 D5
St. Francis *U.S.A.* 39°47N 101°48W 80 F3
St. Francis → *U.S.A.* 34°38N 90°36W 85 D9
St. Francis, C. *S. Africa* 34°14S 24°49E 56 E3
St. Francisville *U.S.A.* 30°47N 91°23W 84 F9
St-François, L. *Canada* 45°10N 74°22W 83 A10
St-Gabriel *Canada* 46°17N 73°24W 72 C5
St. Gallen = Sankt Gallen *Switz.* 47°26N 9°22E 20 C8
St-Gaudens *France* 43°6N 0°44E 20 E4
St. George *Australia* 28°1S 148°30E 63 D4
St. George *N.B., Canada* 45°11N 66°50W 73 C6
St. George *Ont., Canada* 43°15N 80°15W 82 C4
St. George *S.C., U.S.A.* 33°11N 80°35W 85 E14
St. George *Utah, U.S.A.* 37°6N 113°35W 77 H7
St. George, C. *Canada* 48°30N 59°16W 73 C8
St. George, C. *U.S.A.* 29°40N 85°5W 85 G12
St. George Ra. *Australia* 18°40S 125°0E 60 C4
St. George's *Canada* 48°26N 58°31W 73 C8
St-Georges *Canada* 46°8N 70°40W 73 C5
St. George's *Grenada* 12°5N 61°43W 89 D7
St. George's B. *Canada* 48°24N 58°53W 73 C8
St. Georges Basin *N.S.W., Australia* 35°7S 150°36E 63 F5
St. Georges Basin *W. Austral., Australia* 15°23S 125°2E 60 C4
St. George's Channel *Europe* 52°0N 6°0W 10 E6
St. Georges Hd. *Australia* 35°12S 150°42E 63 F5
St. Gotthard P. = San Gottardo, P. del *Switz.* 46°33N 8°33E 20 C8
St. Helena *Atl. Oc.* 15°58S 5°42W 48 H3
St. Helena *U.S.A.* 38°30N 122°28W 76 G2
St. Helena, Mt. *U.S.A.* 38°40N 122°36W 78 G4
St. Helena B. *S. Africa* 32°40S 18°10E 56 E2
St. Helens *Australia* 41°20S 148°15E 63 G4
St. Helens *U.K.* 53°27N 2°44W 12 D5
St. Helens *U.S.A.* 45°52N 122°48W 78 E4
St. Helens, Mt. *U.S.A.* 46°12N 122°12W 78 D4
St. Helier *U.K.* 49°10N 2°7W 13 H5
St-Hubert *Belgium* 50°2N 5°23E 15 D5
St-Hubert *Canada* 45°29N 73°25W 83 A11
St-Hyacinthe *Canada* 45°40N 72°58W 72 C5
St. Ignace *U.S.A.* 45°52N 84°44W 81 C11
St. Ignace I. *Canada* 48°45N 88°0W 72 C2
St. Ignatius *U.S.A.* 47°19N 114°6W 76 C6
St. Ives *Cambs., U.K.* 52°20N 0°4W 13 E7
St. Ives *Corn., U.K.* 50°12N 5°30W 13 G2
St. James *U.S.A.* 43°59N 94°38W 80 D6
St-Jean → *Canada* 50°17N 64°20W 73 B7
St-Jean, L. *Canada* 48°40N 72°0W 73 C5
St-Jean-Port-Joli *Canada* 47°15N 70°13W 73 C5
St-Jean-sur-Richelieu *Canada* 45°20N 73°20W 83 A11
St-Jérôme *Canada* 45°47N 74°0W 72 C5
St. John *Canada* 45°20N 66°8W 73 C6
St. John *U.S.A.* 38°0N 98°46W 80 F4
St. John → *N. Amer.* 45°12N 66°5W 81 C20
St. John, C. *Canada* 50°0N 55°32W 73 C8
St. John I. *U.S. Virgin Is.* 18°20N 64°42W 89 e
St. John's *Antigua & B.* 17°6N 61°51W 89 C7
St. John's *Canada* 47°35N 52°40W 73 C9
St. Johns *Ariz., U.S.A.* 34°30N 109°22W 77 J9
St. Johns *Mich., U.S.A.* 43°0N 84°33W 81 D11
St. Johns → *U.S.A.* 30°24N 81°24W 85 F14
St. John's Pt. *Ireland* 54°34N 8°27W 10 B3
St. Johnsbury *U.S.A.* 44°25N 72°1W 83 B12
St. Johnsville *U.S.A.* 43°0N 74°43W 83 C10
St. Joseph *Canada* 43°24N 81°42W 82 C3
St-Joseph *Martinique* 14°39N 61°4W 88 c
St-Joseph *Réunion* 21°22S 55°37E 53 c
St. Joseph *La., U.S.A.* 31°55N 91°14W 84 F9
St. Joseph *Mo., U.S.A.* 39°46N 94°50W 80 F6
St. Joseph → *U.S.A.* 42°7N 86°29W 80 D10
St. Joseph, I. *Canada* 46°12N 83°58W 72 C3
St. Joseph, L. *Canada* 51°10N 90°35W 72 B1
St-Jovite *Canada* 46°8N 74°38W 72 C5
St. Kilda *U.K.* 57°49N 8°34W 14 C2
St. Kitts & Nevis ■ *W. Indies* 17°20N 62°40W 89 C7
St. Laurent *Canada* 50°25N 97°58W 71 C9
St. Lawrence *Australia* 22°16S 149°31E 62 C4
St. Lawrence *Canada* 46°54N 55°23W 73 C8
St. Lawrence → *Canada* 49°30N 66°0W 73 C6
St. Lawrence, Gulf of *Canada* 48°25N 62°0W 73 C7
St. Lawrence I. *U.S.A.* 63°30N 170°30W 74 a
St. Lawrence Islands △ *Canada* 44°27N 75°52W 83 B9
St. Léonard *Canada* 47°12N 67°58W 73 C6
St-Leu *Réunion* 21°9S 55°18E 53 c
St. Lewis → *Canada* 52°26N 56°11W 73 B8
St-Lô *France* 49°7N 1°5W 20 B3
St-Louis *Guadeloupe* 15°56N 61°19W 88 b
St-Louis *Réunion* 21°16S 55°25E 53 c
St. Louis *Senegal* 16°8N 16°27W 50 E2
St. Louis *U.S.A.* 38°37N 90°11W 80 F8
St. Louis → *U.S.A.* 46°44N 92°9W 80 B7
St-Luc *Canada* 45°22N 73°18W 83 A11
St. Lucia ■ *W. Indies* 14°0N 60°57W 89 f
St. Lucia, L. *S. Africa* 28°5S 32°30E 57 D5
St. Lucia Channel *W. Indies* 14°15N 61°0W 89 D7
St. Maarten ⊠ *W. Indies* 18°0N 63°5W 89 C7
St. Magnus B. *U.K.* 60°25N 1°35W 11 A7
St-Malo *France* 48°39N 2°1W 20 B2
St-Marc *Haiti* 19°10N 72°41W 89 C5
St. Maries *U.S.A.* 47°19N 116°35W 76 C5
St-Martin ⊠ *W. Indies* 18°0N 63°0W 89 C7
St-Martin, C. *Martinique* 14°52N 61°14W 88 c
St. Martin, L. *Canada* 51°40N 98°30W 71 C9
St. Martins *Barbados* 13°5N 59°28W 89 g
St. Mary Pk. *Australia* 31°32S 138°34E 63 E2
St. Marys *Australia* 41°35S 148°11E 63 G4
St. Marys *Canada* 43°20N 81°10W 82 C3
St. Mary's *Corn., U.K.* 49°55N 6°18W 13 H1
St. Mary's *Orkney, U.K.* 58°54N 2°54W 11 C6
St. Marys *Ga., U.S.A.* 30°44N 81°33W 85 F14
St. Marys *Pa., U.S.A.* 41°26N 78°34W 82 E6
St. Mary's, C. *Canada* 46°50N 54°12W 73 C9
St. Mary's B. *Canada* 46°50N 53°50W 73 C9
St. Marys Bay *Canada* 44°25N 66°10W 73 D6
St-Mathieu, Pte. *France* 48°20N 4°45W 20 B1
St. Matthew I. *U.S.A.* 60°24N 172°42W 74 a
St-Maurice → *Canada* 46°21N 72°31W 72 C5
St. Mawes *U.K.* 50°10N 5°2W 13 G2
St-Nazaire *France* 47°17N 2°12W 20 C2
St. Neots *U.K.* 52°14N 0°15W 13 E7
St-Niklaas *Belgium* 51°10N 4°8E 15 C4
St-Omer *France* 50°45N 2°15E 20 A5
St-Pamphile *Canada* 46°58N 69°48W 73 C6
St-Pascal *Canada* 47°32N 69°48W 73 C6
St. Paul *Canada* 54°0N 111°17W 70 C6
St-Paul *Réunion* 20°59S 55°17E 53 c
St. Paul *Minn., U.S.A.* 44°56N 93°5W 80 C7
St. Paul *Nebr., U.S.A.* 41°13N 98°27W 80 E4
St-Paul → *Canada* 51°27N 57°42W 73 B8
St. Paul, I. *Ind. Oc.* 38°55S 77°34E 3 F13
St. Paul I. *Canada* 47°12N 60°9W 73 C7
St. Peter *U.S.A.* 44°20N 93°57W 80 C7
St. Peter Port *U.K.* 49°26N 2°33W 13 H5
St. Peters *N.S., Canada* 45°40N 60°53W 73 C7
St. Peters *P.E.I., Canada* 46°25N 62°35W 73 C7
St. Petersburg = Sankt-Peterburg *Russia* 59°55N 30°20E 9 G24
St. Petersburg *U.S.A.* 27°46N 82°40W 85 H13
St-Phillippe *Réunion* 21°21S 55°44E 53 c
St-Pie *Canada* 45°30N 72°54W 83 A12
St-Pierre *Martinique* 14°45N 61°10W 88 c
St-Pierre *Réunion* 21°19S 55°28E 53 c
St-Pierre *St-P. & M.* 46°46N 56°12W 73 C8
St-Pierre, L. *Canada* 46°12N 72°52W 72 C5
St-Pierre-et-Miquelon ⊠ *N. Amer.* 46°55N 56°10W 73 C8
St-Quentin *Canada* 47°30N 67°23W 73 C6
St-Quentin *France* 49°50N 3°16E 20 B5
St. Regis *U.S.A.* 47°18N 115°6W 76 C6
St. Regis Falls *U.S.A.* 44°40N 74°32W 83 B10
St. Sebastien, Tanjon' i *Madag.* 12°26S 48°44E 57 A8
St-Siméon *Canada* 47°51N 69°54W 73 C6
St. Simons I. *U.S.A.* 31°12N 81°15W 85 F14
St. Simons Island *U.S.A.* 31°9N 81°22W 85 F14
St. Stephen *Canada* 45°16N 67°17W 73 C6
St. Thomas *Canada* 42°45N 81°10W 82 D3
St. Thomas I. *U.S. Virgin Is.* 18°20N 64°55W 89 e
St-Tite *Canada* 46°45N 72°34W 72 C5
St-Tropez *France* 43°17N 6°38E 20 E7
St-Troud = St. Truiden *Belgium* 50°48N 5°10E 15 D5
St. Truiden *Belgium* 50°48N 5°10E 15 D5
St. Vincent = São Vicente *C. Verde Is.* 17°0N 25°0W 50 b
St. Vincent, G. *Australia* 35°0S 138°0E 63 F2
St. Vincent & the Grenadines ■ *W. Indies* 13°0N 61°10W 89 D7
St. Vincent Passage *W. Indies* 13°30N 61°0W 89 D7
St-Vith *Belgium* 50°17N 6°9E 15 D6
St. Walburg *Canada* 53°39N 109°12W 71 C7
Ste-Agathe-des-Monts *Canada* 46°3N 74°17W 72 C5
Ste-Anne *Guadeloupe* 16°13N 61°24W 88 b
Ste-Anne *Seychelles* 4°36S 55°31E 53 b
Ste-Anne, L. *Canada* 50°0N 67°42W 73 B6
Ste-Anne-des-Monts *Canada* 49°8N 66°30W 73 C6
Ste. Genevieve *U.S.A.* 37°59N 90°2W 80 G8
Ste-Marguerite → *Canada* 50°9N 66°36W 73 B6
Ste-Marie *Canada* 46°26N 71°0W 73 C5
Ste-Marie *Martinique* 14°48N 61°1W 88 c
Ste-Marie *Réunion* 20°53S 55°33E 53 c
Ste-Marie, Ile = Nosy Boraha *Madag.* 16°50S 49°55E 57 B8
Ste-Rose *Guadeloupe* 16°20N 61°45W 88 b
Ste-Rose *Réunion* 21°8S 55°45E 53 c
Ste. Rose du Lac *Canada* 51°4N 99°30W 71 C9
Saintes *France* 45°45N 0°37W 20 D3
Saintes, Îs. des *Guadeloupe* 15°50N 61°35W 88 b
Saintfield *U.K.* 54°28N 5°49W 10 B6
Saintonge *France* 45°40N 0°50W 20 D3
Saipan *N. Marianas* 15°12N 145°45E 64 F6
Sairang *India* 23°50N 92°45E 41 H18
Sairecábur, Cerro *Bolivia* 22°43S 67°54W 94 A2
Saitama *Japan* 35°54N 139°38E 31 G9
Saitama □ *Japan* 36°25N 139°30E 31 F9
Saiyid *Pakistan* 33°7N 73°2E 42 C5
Sajama *Bolivia* 18°7S 69°0W 92 G5
Sajószentpéter *Hungary* 48°12N 20°44E 17 D11
Sajum *India* 33°20N 79°0E 43 C8
Sak → *S. Africa* 30°52S 20°25E 56 E3
Saka *Kenya* 0°9S 39°20E 54 B4
Sakai *Japan* 34°34N 135°27E 31 G7
Sakaide *Japan* 34°19N 133°50E 31 G6
Sakaiminato *Japan* 35°38N 133°11E 31 G6
Sakākah *Si. Arabia* 30°0N 40°8E 44 D4
Sakakawea, L. *U.S.A.* 47°30N 101°25W 80 B3
Sakami → *Canada* 53°40N 76°40W 72 B4
Sakami, L. *Canada* 53°15N 77°0W 72 B4
Sakania *Dem. Rep. of the Congo* 12°43S 28°30E 55 E2
Sakaraha *Madag.* 22°55S 44°32E 57 C7
Sakartvelo = Georgia ■ *Asia* 42°0N 43°0E 19 F7
Sakarya *Turkey* 40°48N 30°25E 19 F5
Sakashima-Guntō *Japan* 24°46N 124°0E 31 M2
Sakata *Japan* 38°55N 139°50E 30 E9
Sakchu *N. Korea* 40°23N 125°2E 35 D13
Sakeny → *Madag.* 20°0S 45°25E 57 C8
Sakha □ *Russia* 66°0N 130°0E 29 C14
Sakhalin *Russia* 51°0N 143°0E 29 D15
Sakhalinskiy Zaliv *Russia* 54°0N 141°0E 29 D15
Šakiai *Lithuania* 54°59N 23°2E 9 J20
Sakon Nakhon *Thailand* 17°10N 104°9E 38 D5
Sakrand *Pakistan* 26°10N 68°15E 42 F3
Sakri *India* 26°13N 86°5E 43 F12
Sakrivier *S. Africa* 30°54S 20°28E 56 E3
Sakti *India* 22°2N 82°58E 43 H10
Sakuma *Japan* 35°3N 137°49E 31 G8
Sakurai *Japan* 34°30N 135°51E 31 G7
Sal *C. Verde Is.* 16°45N 22°55W 50 b
Sal Rei *C. Verde Is.* 16°11N 22°53W 50 b
Sala *Sweden* 59°58N 16°35E 9 G17
Sala Consilina *Italy* 40°23N 15°35E 22 D6
Sala-y-Gómez *Pac. Oc.* 26°28S 105°28W 65 K17
Sala y Gómez Ridge *Pac. Oc.* 25°0S 98°0W 65 K18
Salaberry-de-Valleyfield *Canada* 45°15N 74°8W 83 A10
Salada, L. *Mexico* 32°20N 115°40W 77 K6
Saladas *Argentina* 28°15S 58°40W 94 B4
Saladillo *Argentina* 35°40S 59°55W 94 D4
Salado → *B. Aires, Argentina* 35°44S 57°22W 94 D4
Salado → *La Pampa, Argentina* 37°30S 67°0W 96 D3
Salado → *Santa Fe, Argentina* 31°40S 60°41W 94 C3
Salado → *Mexico* 26°52N 99°19W 84 H5
Salaga *Ghana* 8°31N 0°31W 50 G5
Şalāh *Syria* 32°40N 36°45E 46 C5
Şalāḩ ad Dīn □ *Iraq* 34°35N 43°35E 44 C4
Salakos *Greece* 36°17N 27°57E 25 C9
Salālah *Oman* 16°56N 53°59E 47 D5
Salamanca *Chile* 31°46S 70°59W 94 C1
Salamanca *Spain* 40°58N 5°39W 21 B3
Salamanca *U.S.A.* 42°10N 78°43W 82 D6
Salāmatābād *Iran* 35°39N 47°50E 44 C5
Salamina *Greece* 37°56N 23°30E 23 F10
Salamis *Cyprus* 35°11N 33°54E 25 D12
Salar de Atacama *Chile* 23°30S 68°25W 94 A2
Salar de Uyuni *Bolivia* 20°30S 67°45W 92 H5
Salatiga *Indonesia* 7°19S 110°30E 37 G14
Salavat *Russia* 53°21N 55°55E 18 D10
Salaverry *Peru* 8°15S 79°0W 92 E3
Salawati *Indonesia* 1°7S 130°52E 37 E8
Salaya *India* 22°19N 69°35E 42 H3
Salayar *Indonesia* 6°7S 120°30E 37 F6
S'Albufera *Spain* 39°47N 3°7E 24 B10
Salcombe *U.K.* 50°14N 3°47W 13 G4
Saldanha *S. Africa* 33°0S 17°58E 56 E2
Saldanha B. *S. Africa* 33°6S 18°0E 56 E2
Saldus *Latvia* 56°38N 22°30E 9 H20
Sale *Australia* 38°6S 147°6E 63 F4
Salé *Morocco* 34°3N 6°48W 50 B4
Sale *U.K.* 53°26N 2°19W 12 D5
Salekhard *Russia* 66°30N 66°35E 28 C7
Salelologa *Samoa* 13°41S 172°11W 59 b
Salem *India* 11°40N 78°11E 40 P11
Salem *Ill., U.S.A.* 38°38N 88°57W 80 F9

Salem *Ind., U.S.A.* 38°36N 86°6W **80** F10
Salem *Mass., U.S.A.* 42°31N 70°53W **83** D14
Salem *Mo., U.S.A.* 37°39N 91°32W **80** G8
Salem *N.H., U.S.A.* 42°45N 71°12W **83** D13
Salem *N.J., U.S.A.* 39°34N 75°28W **81** F16
Salem *N.Y., U.S.A.* 43°10N 73°20W **83** C11
Salem *Ohio, U.S.A.* 40°54N 80°52W **82** F4
Salem *Oreg., U.S.A.* 44°56N 123°2W **76** D2
Salem *S. Dak., U.S.A.* 43°44N 97°23W **80** D6
Salem *Va., U.S.A.* 37°18N 80°3W **81** G13
Salerno *Italy* 40°41N 14°47E **22** D6
Salford *U.K.* 53°30N 2°18W **12** D5
Salgótarján *Hungary* 48°5N 19°47E **17** D10
Salgueiro *Brazil* 8°4S 39°6W **93** E11
Salibabu *Indonesia* 3°51N 126°40E **37** D7
Salida *U.S.A.* 38°32N 106°0W **74** C5
Salihli *Turkey* 38°28N 28°8E **23** E13
Salihorsk *Belarus* 52°51N 27°27E **17** B14
Salima *Malawi* 13°47S 34°28E **53** G6
Salina *Italy* 38°34N 14°50E **22** E6
Salina *Kans., U.S.A.* 38°50N 97°37W **80** F6
Salina *Utah, U.S.A.* 38°58N 111°51W **76** G8
Salina Cruz *Mexico* 16°10N 95°12W **87** D5
Salinas *Brazil* 16°10S 42°10W **93** G10
Salinas *Ecuador* 2°10S 80°58W **92** D2
Salinas *U.S.A.* 36°40N 121°39W **78** J5
Salinas → *Guatemala* 16°28N 90°31W **87** D6
Salinas → *U.S.A.* 36°45N 121°48W **78** J5
Salinas, B. de *Nic.* 11°4N 85°45W **88** D2
Salinas, Pampa de las
 Argentina 31°58S 66°42W **94** C2
Salinas Ambargasta
 Argentina 29°0S 65°0W **94** B3
Salinas de Hidalgo
 Mexico 22°38N 101°43W **86** C4
Salinas Grandes *Argentina* 30°0S 65°0W **94** C3
Salinas Pueblo Missions △
 U.S.A. 34°6N 106°4W **77** J10
Salinas Valley *U.S.A.* 36°15N 121°15W **78** J5
Saline → *Ark., U.S.A.* 33°10N 92°8W **84** E8
Saline → *Kans., U.S.A.* 38°52N 97°30W **80** F5
Salines, C. de ses *Spain* 39°16N 3°4E **24** B10
Salinópolis *Brazil* 0°40S 47°20W **93** D9
Salisbury *Australia* 34°46S 138°38E **63** E2
Salisbury *U.K.* 51°4N 1°47W **13** F6
Salisbury *Md., U.S.A.* 38°22N 75°36W **81** F16
Salisbury *N.C., U.S.A.* 35°40N 80°29W **85** D5
Salisbury I. *Canada* 63°30N 77°0W **69** C12
Salisbury Plain *U.K.* 51°14N 1°55W **13** F6
Salkhad *Syria* 32°29N 36°43E **46** C5
Salla *Finland* 66°50N 28°49E **8** C23
Salliq = Coral Harbour
 Canada 64°8N 83°10W **69** C11
Sallisaw *U.S.A.* 35°28N 94°47W **84** D7
Salluit *Canada* 62°14N 75°38W **69** C12
Salmãs *Iran* 38°11N 44°47E **44** B5
Salmo *Canada* 49°10N 117°20W **70** D5
Salmon *U.S.A.* 45°11N 113°54W **76** D7
Salmon → *Canada* 54°3N 122°40W **70** C4
Salmon → *U.S.A.* 45°51N 116°47W **76** D5
Salmon Arm *Canada* 50°40N 119°15W **70** C5
Salmon Gums *Australia* 32°59S 121°38E **61** F3
Salmon Pt. *Canada* 43°52N 77°15W **82** C7
Salmon River Mts.
 U.S.A. 44°50N 115°30W **76** D6
Salmon River Res.
 U.S.A. 43°32N 75°55W **83** C9
Salome *U.S.A.* 33°47N 113°37W **79** M13
Salon *India* 26°2N 81°27E **43** F9
Salon-de-Provence *France* 43°39N 5°6E **20** E6
Salonica = Thessaloníki
 Greece 40°38N 22°58E **23** D10
Salonta *Romania* 46°49N 21°42E **17** E11
Salpausselkä *Finland* 61°3N 26°15E **8** F22
Salsacate *Argentina* 31°20S 65°5W **94** C2
Salsk *Russia* 46°28N 41°30E **19** E7
Salso → *Italy* 37°6N 13°57E **22** F5
Salt → *Canada* 60°0N 112°25W **70** B6
Salt → *U.S.A.* 33°23N 112°19W **77** K7
Salt Fork Red → *U.S.A.* 34°27N 99°23W **84** H5
Salt L. *Australia* 30°6S 142°8E **63** E3
Salt Lake City *U.S.A.* 40°45N 111°53W **76** F8
Salt Range *Pakistan* 32°30N 72°25E **42** C5
Salta *Argentina* 24°57S 65°25W **94** A2
Salta □ *Argentina* 24°48S 65°30W **94** A2
Saltash *U.K.* 50°24N 4°14W **13** G3
Saltburn by the Sea *U.K.* 54°35N 0°58W **12** C7
Saltcoats *U.K.* 55°38N 4°47W **11** F4
Saltee Is. *Ireland* 52°7N 6°37W **10** D5
Saltfjellet *Norway* 66°40N 15°15E **8** C16
Saltfjorden *Norway* 67°15N 14°10E **8** C16
Saltillo *Mexico* 25°25N 101°0W **86** B4
Salto *Argentina* 34°20S 60°15W **94** C3
Salto *Uruguay* 31°27S 57°50W **94** C4
Salto → *Italy* 42°26N 12°25E **22** C5
Salto del Guairá *Paraguay* 24°3S 54°17W **95** A5
Salton City *U.S.A.* 33°18N 115°57W **79** M11
Salton Sea *U.S.A.* 33°15N 115°45W **79** M11
Saltsburg *U.S.A.* 40°29N 79°27W **82** F5
Saluda → *U.S.A.* 34°1N 81°4W **85** D14
Salûm *Egypt* 31°31N 25°7E **51** B11
Salur *India* 18°27N 83°18E **41** K13
Salvador *Brazil* 13°0S 38°30W **93** F11
Salvador *Canada* 52°10N 109°32W **71** C7
Salvador, El ■
 Cent. Amer. 13°50N 89°0W **88** D2
Salvador, L. *U.S.A.* 29°43N 90°15W **85** G9
Salween → *Burma* 16°31N 97°37E **41** L20
Salyan *Azerbaijan* 39°33N 48°59E **45** B6
Salybia *Trin. & Tob.* 10°43N 61°2W **93** K15
Salzach → *Austria* 48°12N 12°56E **16** D7
Salzburg *Austria* 47°48N 13°2E **16** E7
Salzgitter *Germany* 52°9N 10°19E **16** B6
Salzwedel *Germany* 52°52N 11°10E **16** B6

Salem *Ind., U.S.A.*
Sam *India* 26°50N 70°31E **42** F4
Sam Neua *Laos* 20°29N 104°5E **38** B5
Sam Ngao *Thailand* 17°18N 99°0E **38** D2
Sam Rayburn Res. *U.S.A.* 31°4N 94°5W **84** F7
Sam Son *Vietnam* 19°44N 105°54E **38** C5
Sam Teu *Laos* 19°59N 104°38E **38** C5
Sama de Langreo = Langreo
 Spain 43°18N 5°40W **21** A3
Samagaltay *Russia* 50°36N 95°3E **29** D10
Samales Group *Phil.* 6°0N 122°0E **37** C6
Samana *India* 30°10N 76°13E **42** D7
Samana Cay *Bahamas* 23°3N 73°45W **89** B5
Samanga *Tanzania* 8°20S 39°13E **55** D4
Samangān □ *Afghan.* 36°15N 68°3E **40** B3
Samangwa
 Dem. Rep. of the Congo 4°23S 24°10E **54** C1
Samani *Japan* 42°7N 142°56E **30** C11
Samar *Phil.* 12°0N 125°0E **37** B7
Samara *Russia* 53°8N 50°6E **18** D9
Samaria = Shōmrōn
 West Bank 32°15N 35°13E **46** C4
Samaria △ *Greece* 35°17N 23°58E **25** D5
Samarinda *Indonesia* 0°30S 117°9E **36** E5
Samarkand = Samarqand
 Uzbekistan 39°40N 66°55E **28** F7
Samarqand *Uzbekistan* 39°40N 66°55E **28** F7
Sāmarrā *Iraq* 34°12N 43°52E **44** C4
Samastipur *India* 25°50N 85°50E **43** G11
Samba
 Dem. Rep. of the Congo 4°38S 26°22E **54** C2
Samba *India* 32°32N 75°10E **43** C6
Sambalpur *India* 21°28N 84°4E **41** J14
Sambar, Tanjung
 Indonesia 2°59S 110°19E **36** E4
Sambas *Indonesia* 1°20N 109°20E **36** D3
Sambava *Madag.* 14°16S 50°10E **57** A9
Sambawizi *Zimbabwe* 18°24S 26°13E **55** F2
Sambhal *India* 28°35N 78°37E **43** E8
Sambhar *India* 26°52N 75°6E **42** F6
Sambhar L. *India* 26°55N 75°12E **42** F6
Sambiase *Italy* 38°58N 16°17E **22** E7
Sambir *Ukraine* 49°30N 23°10E **17** D12
Sambor *Cambodia* 12°46N 106°0E **38** F6
Samborombón, B.
 Argentina 36°5S 57°20W **94** D4
Samburu □ *Kenya* 0°37N 37°31E **54** B4
Samcheok *S. Korea* 37°30N 129°10E **35** F15
Same *Tanzania* 4°2S 37°38E **54** C4
Samfya *Zambia* 11°22S 29°31E **55** E2
Samnah *Si. Arabia* 25°10N 37°15E **44** E3
Samo Alto *Chile* 30°22S 71°0W **94** C1
Samokov *Bulgaria* 42°18N 23°35E **23** C10
Samos *Greece* 37°45N 26°50E **23** F12
Samothráki = Mathráki
 Greece 39°48N 19°31E **25** A3
Samothráki *Greece* 40°28N 25°28E **23** D11
Sampacho *Argentina* 33°20S 64°50W **94** C3
Sampalan *Indonesia* 8°41S 115°34E **37** K18
Sampang *Indonesia* 7°11S 113°13E **37** G15
Sampit *Indonesia* 2°34S 113°0E **36** E4
Sampit, Teluk *Indonesia* 3°5S 113°3E **36** E4
Samrong *Cambodia* 14°15N 103°30E **38** E4
Samrong *Thailand* 15°10N 100°40E **38** E3
Samsø *Denmark* 55°50N 10°35E **9** J14
Samsun *Turkey* 41°15N 36°22E **19** F6
Samui, Ko *Thailand* 9°30N 100°0E **39** b
Samusole
 Dem. Rep. of the Congo 10°2S 24°0E **55** E1
Samut Prakan *Thailand* 13°32N 100°40E **38** F3
Samut Songkhram
 Thailand 13°24N 100°1E **38** F3
Samwari *Pakistan* 28°30N 66°46E **42** E2
San Mali 13°15N 4°57W **50** F5
San → *Cambodia* 13°32N 105°57E **38** F5
San → *Poland* 50°45N 21°51E **17** C11
San Agustin, C. *Phil.* 6°20N 126°13E **37** C7
San Agustín de Valle Fértil
 Argentina 30°35S 67°30W **94** C2
San Ambrosio *Pac. Oc.* 26°28S 79°53W **90** F3
San Andres, I. de
 Caribbean 12°42N 81°46W **88** D3
San Andres Mts.
 U.S.A. 33°0N 106°30W **77** K10
San Andrés Tuxtla
 Mexico 18°27N 95°13W **87** D5
San Angelo *U.S.A.* 31°28N 100°26W **84** F4
San Anselmo *U.S.A.* 37°59N 122°34W **78** H4
San Antonio *Belize* 16°15N 89°2W **87** D7
San Antonio *Chile* 33°40S 71°40W **94** C1
San Antonio *N. Mex.,*
 U.S.A. 33°55N 106°52W **77** K10
San Antonio *Tex.,*
 U.S.A. 29°25N 98°29W **84** G5
San Antonio → *U.S.A.* 28°30N 96°54W **84** G6
San Antonio, C.
 Argentina 36°15S 56°40W **94** D4
San Antonio, C. de *Cuba* 21°50N 84°57W **88** B3
San Antonio, Mt.
 U.S.A. 34°17N 117°38W **79** L9
San Antonio de los Baños
 Cuba 22°54N 82°31W **88** B3
San Antonio de los Cobres
 Argentina 24°10S 66°17W **94** A2
San Antonio Oeste
 Argentina 40°40S 65°0W **96** E4
San Ardo *U.S.A.* 36°1N 120°54W **78** J6
San Agustín *Canary Is.* 27°47N 15°32W **24** G4
San Augustine *U.S.A.* 31°32N 94°7W **84** F7
San Bartolomé
 Canary Is. 28°59N 13°37W **24** F6
San Bartolomé de Tirajana
 Canary Is. 27°54N 15°34W **24** G4
San Benedetto del Tronto
 Italy 42°57N 13°53E **22** C5
San Benedicto, I.
 Mexico 19°18N 110°49W **86** D2

San Benito *U.S.A.* 26°8N 97°38W **84** H6
San Benito → *U.S.A.* 36°53N 121°34W **78** J5
San Benito Mt. *U.S.A.* 36°22N 120°37W **78** J6
San Bernardino *U.S.A.* 34°7N 117°19W **79** L9
San Bernardino Mts.
 U.S.A. 34°10N 116°45W **79** L10
San Bernardino Str. *Phil.* 13°0N 125°0E **37** B7
San Bernardo *Chile* 33°40S 70°50W **94** C1
San Bernardo, I. de
 Colombia 9°45N 75°50W **92** B3
San Blas *Mexico* 26°5N 108°46W **86** B3
San Blas, Arch. de
 Panama 9°50N 78°31W **88** E4
San Blas, Cordillera de
 Panama 9°15N 78°30W **88** E4
San Blas, C. *U.S.A.* 29°40N 85°21W **85** G12
San Borja *Bolivia* 14°50S 66°52W **92** F5
San Buenaventura = Ventura
 U.S.A. 34°17N 119°18W **79** L7
San Buenaventura
 Mexico 27°5N 101°32W **86** B4
San Carlos = Sant Carles
 Spain 39°3N 1°34E **24** B8
San Carlos *Argentina* 33°50S 69°0W **94** C2
San Carlos *Chile* 36°10S 72°0W **94** D1
San Carlos *Baja Calif. S.,*
 Mexico 24°47N 112°7W **86** C2
San Carlos *Coahuila,*
 Mexico 29°1N 100°51W **86** B4
San Carlos *Nic.* 11°12N 84°50W **88** D3
San Carlos *Phil.* 10°29N 123°25E **37** B6
San Carlos *Uruguay* 34°46S 54°58W **95** C5
San Carlos *U.S.A.* 33°21N 110°27W **77** K8
San Carlos *Venezuela* 9°40N 68°36W **92** B5
San Carlos de Bariloche
 Argentina 41°10S 71°25W **96** E2
San Carlos de Bolívar
 Argentina 36°15S 61°6W **94** D3
San Carlos del Zulia
 Venezuela 9°1N 71°55W **92** B4
San Carlos L. *U.S.A.* 33°11N 110°32W **77** K8
San Clemente *Chile* 35°30S 71°29W **94** D1
San Clemente *U.S.A.* 33°26N 117°37W **79** M9
San Clemente I. *U.S.A.* 32°53N 118°29W **79** N8
San Cristóbal = Es Migjorn Gran
 Spain 39°57N 4°3E **24** B11
San Cristóbal *Argentina* 30°20S 61°10W **94** C3
San Cristóbal *Dom. Rep.* 18°25N 70°6W **89** C5
San Cristóbal *Solomon Is.* 10°30S 161°0E **58** C9
San Cristóbal *Venezuela* 7°46N 72°14W **92** B4
San Cristóbal de las Casas
 Mexico 16°45N 92°38W **87** D6
San Diego *Calif., U.S.A.* 32°42N 117°9W **79** N9
San Diego *Tex., U.S.A.* 27°46N 98°14W **84** H5
San Diego, C. *Argentina* 54°40S 65°10W **96** G3
San Diego de la Unión
 Mexico 21°28N 100°52W **86** C4
San Diego Int. ✈ (SAN)
 U.S.A. 32°44N 117°11W **79** N9
San Dimitri, Ras *Malta* 36°4N 14°11E **25** C1
San Dimitri Point = San Dimitri,
 Ras *Malta* 36°4N 14°11E **25** C1
San Estanislao *Paraguay* 24°39S 56°26W **94** A4
San Felipe *Chile* 32°43S 70°42W **94** C1
San Felipe *Mexico* 31°1N 114°52W **86** A2
San Felipe *Venezuela* 10°20N 68°44W **92** A5
San Felipe → *U.S.A.* 33°10N 115°49W **79** M11
San Félix *Chile* 28°56S 70°28W **94** B1
San Félix *Pac. Oc.* 26°23S 80°0W **90** F2
San Fernando = Sant Ferran
 Spain 38°42N 1°28E **24** C7
San Fernando *Chile* 34°30S 71°0W **94** C1
San Fernando *Mexico* 24°51N 98°10W **87** C5
San Fernando *La Union,*
 Phil. 16°40N 120°23E **37** A6
San Fernando *Pampanga,*
 Phil. 15°5N 120°37E **37** A6
San Fernando *Spain* 36°28N 6°17W **21** D2
San Fernando
 Trin. & Tob. 10°16N 61°28W **89** D7
San Fernando *U.S.A.* 34°17N 118°26W **79** L8
San Fernando de Apure
 Venezuela 7°54N 67°15W **92** B5
San Fernando de Atabapo
 Venezuela 4°3N 67°42W **92** C5
San Francisco *Argentina* 31°30S 62°5W **94** C3
San Francisco *U.S.A.* 37°46N 122°23W **78** H4
San Francisco →
 U.S.A. 32°59N 109°22W **77** K9
San Francisco, C. de
 Colombia 6°18N 77°29W **90** C3
San Francisco, Paso de
 S. Amer. 27°0S 68°0W **94** B2
San Francisco de Macorís
 Dom. Rep. 19°19N 70°15W **89** C5
San Francisco del Monte de Oro
 Argentina 32°36S 66°8W **94** C2
San Francisco del Oro
 Mexico 26°52N 105°51W **86** B3
San Francisco Int. ✈ (SFO)
 U.S.A. 37°37N 122°22W **78** H4
San Francisco Javier = Sant
 Francesc de Formentera
 Spain 38°42N 1°26E **24** C7
San Gabriel *Chile* 33°47S 70°15W **94** C1
San Gabriel Chilac
 Mexico 18°19N 97°21W **87** D5
San Gabriel Mts.
 U.S.A. 34°17N 117°38W **79** L9
San Gavino Monreale
 Italy 39°33N 8°47E **22** E3
San German *Puerto Rico* 18°4N 67°4W **89** d
San Gorgonio Mt.
 U.S.A. 34°6N 116°50W **79** L10
San Gottardo, P. del
 Switz. 46°33N 8°33E **20** C8
San Gregorio *Uruguay* 32°37S 55°40W **95** C4
San Gregorio *U.S.A.* 37°20N 122°23W **78** H4
San Guillermo △
 Argentina 27°50S 69°45W **94** B2

San Ignacio *Belize* 17°10N 89°5W **87** D7
San Ignacio *Bolivia* 16°20S 60°55W **92** G6
San Ignacio *Mexico* 27°27N 112°51W **86** B2
San Ignacio *Paraguay* 26°52S 57°3W **94** B4
San Ignacio, L. *Mexico* 26°54N 113°13W **86** B2
San Ildefonso, C. *Phil.* 16°0N 122°1E **37** A6
San Isidro *Argentina* 34°29S 58°31W **94** C4
San Jacinto *U.S.A.* 33°47N 116°57W **79** M10
San Jaime = Sant Jaume
 Spain 39°54N 4°4E **24** B11
San Javier *Misiones,*
 Argentina 27°55S 55°5W **95** B4
San Javier *Santa Fe,*
 Argentina 30°40S 59°55W **94** C4
San Javier *Bolivia* 16°18S 62°30W **92** G6
San Javier *Chile* 35°40S 71°45W **94** D1
San Jerónimo Taviche
 Mexico 16°44N 96°35W **87** D5
San Joaquin *U.S.A.* 36°36N 120°11W **78** J6
San Joaquin → *U.S.A.* 38°4N 121°51W **78** G5
San Joaquin Valley
 U.S.A. 37°20N 121°0W **78** J6
San Jon *U.S.A.* 35°6N 103°20W **77** J12
San Jordi = Sant Jordi
 Spain 39°33N 2°46E **24** B9
San Jorge *Argentina* 31°54S 61°50W **94** C3
San Jorge, B. *Mexico* 31°20N 113°20W **86** A2
San Jorge, G. *Argentina* 46°0S 66°0W **96** F3
San Jose = San Josep
 Spain 38°55N 1°18E **24** C7
San José *Argentina* 32°12S 58°15W **94** C4
San José *Costa Rica* 9°55N 84°2W **88** E3
San José *Guatemala* 14°0N 90°50W **88** D1
San Jose *Mind. Occ., Phil.* 12°27N 121°4E **37** B6
San Jose *Nueva Ecija,*
 Phil. 15°45N 120°55E **37** A6
San Jose *U.S.A.* 37°20N 121°53W **78** H5
San Jose → *U.S.A.* 34°25N 106°45W **77** J10
San José, I. *Mexico* 25°0N 110°38W **86** C2
San Jose de Buenavista
 Phil. 10°45N 121°56E **37** B6
San José de Chiquitos
 Bolivia 17°53S 60°50W **92** G6
San José de Feliciano
 Argentina 30°26S 58°46W **94** C4
San José de Jáchal
 Argentina 30°15S 68°46W **94** C2
San José de Mayo
 Uruguay 34°27S 56°40W **94** C4
San José del Cabo
 Mexico 23°3N 109°41W **86** C3
San José del Guaviare
 Colombia 2°35N 72°38W **92** C4
San Josep *Spain* 38°55N 1°18E **24** C7
San Juan *Argentina* 31°30S 68°30W **94** C2
San Juan *Puerto Rico* 18°28N 66°7W **89** d
San Juan *Trin. & Tob.* 10°39N 61°29W **93** K15
San Juan □ *Argentina* 31°9S 69°0W **94** C2
San Juan → *Argentina* 32°20S 67°25W **94** C2
San Juan → *Nic.* 10°56N 83°42W **88** D3
San Juan → *U.S.A.* 37°16N 110°26W **77** H8
San Juan Bautista = Sant Joan de
 Labritja *Spain* 39°5N 1°31E **24** B8
San Juan Bautista
 Paraguay 26°37S 57°6W **94** B4
San Juan Bautista
 U.S.A. 36°51N 121°32W **78** J5
San Juan Capistrano
 U.S.A. 33°30N 117°40W **79** M9
San Juan Cr. → *U.S.A.* 35°40N 120°22W **78** J5
San Juan de Guadalupe
 Mexico 24°38N 102°44W **86** C4
San Juan de la Costa
 Mexico 24°20N 110°41W **86** C2
San Juan de los Lagos
 Mexico 21°15N 102°18W **86** C4
San Juan de los Morros
 Venezuela 9°55N 67°21W **92** B5
San Juan del Norte *Nic.* 10°58N 83°40W **88** D3
San Juan del Norte, B. de
 Nic. 11°0N 83°40W **88** D3
San Juan del Río *Mexico* 20°23N 100°0W **87** C5
San Juan del Sur *Nic.* 11°20N 85°51W **88** D2
San Juan I. *U.S.A.* 48°32N 123°5W **78** B3
San Juan Island △
 U.S.A. 48°35N 123°8W **78** B4
San Juan Mts. *U.S.A.* 37°30N 107°0W **77** H10
San Justo *Argentina* 30°47S 60°30W **94** C3
San Kamphaeng *Thailand* 18°45N 99°8E **38** C2
San Lázaro, C. *Mexico* 24°50N 112°18W **86** C2
San Leandro *U.S.A.* 37°44N 122°9W **78** H4
San Lorenzo = Sant Llorenç des
 Cardassar *Spain* 39°37N 3°17E **24** B10
San Lorenzo *Argentina* 32°45S 60°45W **94** C3
San Lorenzo *Ecuador* 1°15N 78°50W **92** C3
San Lorenzo *Paraguay* 25°20S 57°32W **94** B4
San Lorenzo → *Mexico* 24°15N 107°24W **86** C3
San Lorenzo, I. *Mexico* 28°38N 112°51W **86** B2
San Lorenzo, Mte.
 Argentina 47°40S 72°20W **96** F2
San Lucas = Cabo San Lucas
 Mexico 22°53N 109°54W **86** C3
San Lucas *Bolivia* 20°5S 65°7W **92** H5
San Lucas *Mexico* 27°10N 112°14W **86** B2
San Lucas *U.S.A.* 36°8N 121°1W **78** J5
San Lucas, C. *Mexico* 22°52N 109°53W **86** C3
San Luis *Argentina* 33°20S 66°20W **94** C2
San Luis *Cuba* 22°17N 83°46W **88** B3
San Luis *Guatemala* 16°14N 89°27W **88** C2
San Luis *Ariz., U.S.A.* 32°29N 114°47W **79** N6
San Luis *Colo., U.S.A.* 37°12N 105°25W **77** H11
San Luis □ *Argentina* 34°0S 66°0W **94** C2
San Luis, I. *Mexico* 29°58N 114°26W **86** B2
San Luis, Sierra de
 Argentina 32°30S 66°10W **94** C2
San Luis de la Paz
 Mexico 21°18N 100°31W **86** C4

San Luis Obispo *U.S.A.* 35°17N 120°40W **79** K6
San Luis Potosí *Mexico* 22°9N 100°59W **86** C4
San Luis Potosí □ *Mexico* 22°9N 100°59W **86** C4
San Luis Res. *U.S.A.* 37°4N 121°5W **78** H5
San Luis Río Colorado
 Mexico 32°29N 114°58W **86** A2
San Manuel *U.S.A.* 32°36N 110°38W **77** K8
San Marcos *Guatemala* 14°59N 91°52W **88** D1
San Marcos *Calif.,*
 U.S.A. 33°9N 117°10W **79** M9
San Marcos *Tex., U.S.A.* 29°53N 97°56W **84** G6
San Marcos, I. *Mexico* 27°13N 112°6W **86** B2
San Marino *San Marino* 43°55N 12°30E **16** G7
San Marino ■ *Europe* 43°56N 12°25E **22** C5
San Martín *Antarctica* 68°11S 67°0W **5** C17
San Martín *Argentina* 33°5S 68°28W **94** C2
San Martín → *Bolivia* 13°8S 63°43W **92** F6
San Martín, L. *Argentina* 48°50S 72°50W **96** F2
San Martín de los Andes
 Argentina 40°10S 71°20W **96** E2
San Mateo = Sant Mateu
 Spain 39°3N 1°23E **24** B7
San Mateo *U.S.A.* 37°34N 122°19W **78** H4
San Matías *Bolivia* 16°25S 58°20W **92** G7
San Matías, G. *Argentina* 41°30S 64°0W **96** E4
San Miguel = Sant Miquel
 Spain 39°3N 1°26E **24** B7
San Miguel *El Salv.* 13°30N 88°12W **88** D2
San Miguel *Panama* 8°27N 78°55W **88** E4
San Miguel *U.S.A.* 35°45N 120°42W **78** K6
San Miguel → *Bolivia* 13°52S 63°56W **92** F6
San Miguel de Tucumán
 Argentina 26°50S 65°20W **94** B2
San Miguel del Monte
 Argentina 35°23S 58°50W **94** C4
San Miguel I. *U.S.A.* 34°2N 120°23W **79** L6
San Nicolás *Canary Is.* 27°58N 15°47W **24** G4
San Nicolás de los Arroyos
 Argentina 33°25S 60°10W **94** C3
San Nicolas I. *U.S.A.* 33°15N 119°30W **79** M7
San Onofre *U.S.A.* 33°22N 117°34W **79** M9
San Pablo *Bolivia* 21°43S 66°38W **94** A2
San Pablo *U.S.A.* 37°58N 122°21W **78** H4
San Pedro *B. Aires,*
 Argentina 33°40S 59°40W **94** C4
San Pedro *Misiones,*
 Argentina 26°30S 54°10W **95** B5
San Pedro *Chile* 33°54S 71°28W **94** C1
San Pedro *Ivory C.* 4°50N 6°33W **50** H4
San Pedro *Mexico* 23°55N 110°17W **86** C3
San Pedro □ *Paraguay* 24°0S 57°0W **94** A4
San Pedro → *Chihuahua,*
 Mexico 28°20N 106°10W **86** B3
San Pedro → *Nayarit,*
 Mexico 21°45N 105°30W **86** C3
San Pedro → *U.S.A.* 32°59N 110°47W **77** K8
San Pedro, Pta. *Chile* 25°30S 70°38W **94** B1
San Pedro Channel
 U.S.A. 33°30N 118°25W **79** M8
San Pedro de Atacama
 Chile 22°55S 68°15W **94** A2
San Pedro de Jujuy
 Argentina 24°12S 64°55W **94** A3
San Pedro de las Colonias
 Mexico 25°45N 102°59W **86** B4
San Pedro de Macorís
 Dom. Rep. 18°30N 69°18W **89** C6
San Pedro del Norte *Nic.* 13°4N 84°33W **88** D3
San Pedro del Paraná
 Paraguay 26°43S 56°13W **94** B4
San Pedro Mártir, Sierra
 Mexico 31°0N 115°30W **86** A1
San Pedro Mártir △
 Mexico 31°0N 115°21W **86** A1
San Pedro Ocampo = Melchor
 Ocampo *Mexico* 24°51N 101°39W **86** C4
San Pedro Pochutla
 Mexico 15°44N 96°28W **87** D5
San Pedro Sula *Honduras* 15°30N 88°0W **88** C2
San Pedro Tututepec
 Mexico 16°9N 97°38W **87** D5
San Pietro *Italy* 39°8N 8°17E **22** E3
San Rafael *Argentina* 34°40S 68°21W **94** C2
San Rafael *Calif., U.S.A.* 37°58N 122°32W **78** H4
San Rafael *N. Mex.,*
 U.S.A. 35°7N 107°53W **77** J10
San Rafael Mt. *U.S.A.* 34°41N 119°52W **79** L7
San Rafael Mts. *U.S.A.* 34°40N 119°50W **79** L7
San Ramón de la Nueva Orán
 Argentina 23°10S 64°20W **94** A3
San Remo *Italy* 43°49N 7°46E **20** E7
San Roque *Argentina* 28°25S 58°45W **94** B4
San Roque *Spain* 36°17N 5°21E **21** D3
San Rosendo *Chile* 37°16S 72°43W **94** D1
San Saba *U.S.A.* 31°12N 98°43W **84** F5
San Salvador *El Salv.* 13°40N 89°10W **88** D2
San Salvador de Jujuy
 Argentina 24°10S 64°48W **94** A3
San Salvador I. *Bahamas* 24°0N 74°40W **89** B5
San Sebastián = Donostia-San
 Sebastián *Spain* 43°17N 1°58W **21** A5
San Sebastián *Argentina* 53°10S 68°30W **96** G3
San Sebastián *Puerto Rico* 18°20N 66°59W **89** d
San Sebastián de la Gomera
 Canary Is. 28°5N 17°7W **24** F2
San Serra = Son Serra
 Spain 39°43N 3°13E **24** B10
San Severo *Italy* 41°41N 15°23E **22** D6
San Simeon *U.S.A.* 35°39N 121°11W **78** K5
San Simon *U.S.A.* 32°16N 109°14W **77** K9
San Telmo = Sant Elm
 Spain 39°35N 2°21E **24** B9
San Telmo *Mexico* 30°58N 116°6W **86** A1
San Tiburcio *Mexico* 24°8N 101°32W **86** C4
San Valentin, Mte. *Chile* 46°30S 73°30W **96** F2
San Vicente de Cañete
 Peru 13°8S 76°30W **92** F3

160 San Vicente de la Barquera
INDEX TO WORLD MAPS

San Vicente de la Barquera
Spain 43°23N 4°29W 21 A3
San Vito Costa Rica 8°50N 82°58W 88 E3
Sana' Yemen 15°27N 44°12E 47 D3
Sana → Bos.-H. 45°3N 16°23E 16 F9
Sanae IV Antarctica 70°20S 9°0W 5 D2
Sanaga → Cameroon 3°35N 9°38E 52 D1
Sanaloa, Presa Mexico 24°50N 107°20W 86 C3
Sanana Indonesia 2°4S 125°58E 37 E7
Sanand India 22°59N 72°25E 42 H5
Sanandaj Iran 35°18N 47°1E 44 C5
Sanandita Bolivia 21°40S 63°45W 94 A3
Sanawad India 22°11N 76°5E 42 H7
Sancellas = Sencelles
Spain 39°39N 2°54E 24 B9
Sanchahe China 44°50N 126°2E 35 B14
Sánchez Dom. Rep. 19°15N 69°36W 89 C6
Sanchor India 24°45N 71°55E 42 G4
Sancti Spíritus Cuba 21°52N 79°33W 88 B4
Sancy, Puy de France 45°32N 2°50E 20 D5
Sand = Polokwane →
S. Africa 22°25S 30°5E 57 C5
Sand Hills U.S.A. 42°10N 101°30W 80 D3
Sand Lakes ⌂ Canada 57°51N 98°32W 71 B9
Sand Springs U.S.A. 36°9N 96°7W 84 C6
Sanda Japan 34°53N 135°14E 31 G7
Sandakan Malaysia 5°53N 118°4E 36 C5
Sandan = Sambor
Cambodia 12°46N 106°0E 38 F6
Sandanski Bulgaria 41°35N 23°16E 23 D10
Sanday U.K. 59°16N 2°31W 11 B6
Sandefjord Norway 59°10N 10°15E 9 G14
Sanders U.S.A. 35°13N 109°20W 77 J9
Sanderson U.S.A. 30°9N 102°24W 84 F3
Sandersville U.S.A. 32°59N 82°48W 85 E13
Sandfire Roadhouse
Australia 19°45S 121°15E 60 C3
Sandfly L. Canada 55°43N 106°6W 71 B7
Sandfontein Namibia 23°48S 19°1E 56 C2
Sandheads, The India 21°10N 88°20E 43 J13
Sandía Peru 14°10S 69°30W 92 F5
Sandila India 27°5N 80°31E 43 F9
Sandnes Norway 58°50N 5°45E 9 G11
Sandnessjøen Norway 66°2N 12°38E 8 C15
Sandoa
Dem. Rep. of the Congo 9°41S 23°0E 52 F4
Sandomierz Poland 50°40N 21°43E 17 C11
Sandover → Australia 21°43S 136°32E 62 C2
Sandoway = Thandwe
Burma 18°20N 94°30E 41 K19
Sandoy Færoe Is. 61°52N 6°46W 8 F9
Sandpoint U.S.A. 48°17N 116°33W 76 B5
Sandray U.K. 56°53N 7°31W 11 E1
Sandringham U.K. 52°51N 0°31E 12 E8
Sandstone Australia 27°59S 119°16E 61 E2
Sandusky Mich., U.S.A. 43°25N 82°50W 82 C2
Sandusky Ohio, U.S.A. 41°27N 82°42W 82 E2
Sandveld Namibia 21°25S 20°0E 56 C3
Sandviken Sweden 60°38N 16°46E 8 F17
Sandwich, C. Australia 18°14S 146°18E 62 B4
Sandwich B. Canada 53°40N 57°15W 73 B8
Sandwich B. Namibia 23°25S 14°20E 56 C1
Sandy Oreg., U.S.A. 45°24N 122°16W 78 E4
Sandy Pa., U.S.A. 41°6N 78°46W 82 E6
Sandy Utah, U.S.A. 40°32N 111°50W 76 F8
Sandy Bay Canada 55°31N 102°19W 71 B8
Sandy Bight Australia 33°50S 123°20E 61 F3
Sandy C. Queens.,
Australia 24°42S 153°15E 62 C5
Sandy C. Tas., Australia 41°25S 144°45E 63 G3
Sandy Cay Bahamas 23°13N 75°18W 89 B4
Sandy Cr. → U.S.A. 41°51N 109°47W 76 F9
Sandy Creek U.S.A. 43°38N 76°5W 83 C8
Sandy L. Canada 53°2N 93°0W 72 B1
Sandy Lake Canada 53°0N 93°15W 72 B1
Sandy Valley U.S.A. 35°49N 115°38W 79 K11
Sanford Fla., U.S.A. 28°48N 81°16W 85 G14
Sanford Maine, U.S.A. 43°27N 70°47W 83 C14
Sanford N.C., U.S.A. 35°29N 79°10W 85 D15
Sanford → Australia 27°22S 115°53E 61 E2
Sanford, Mt. U.S.A. 62°13N 144°8W 68 C5
Sang-i-Masha Afghan. 33°8N 67°27E 42 C2
Sanga Mozam. 12°22S 35°21E 55 E4
Sanga → Congo 1°5S 17°0E 52 E3
Sangamner India 19°37N 74°15E 40 K9
Sangān Iran 34°23N 60°15E 45 C9
Sangar Afghan. 32°56N 65°30E 42 C1
Sangar Russia 64°2N 127°31E 29 C13
Sangar Sarai Afghan. 34°27N 70°35E 42 B4
Sangarh → Pakistan 30°43N 70°44E 42 D4
Sangay Ecuador 2°0S 78°20W 92 D3
Sange
Dem. Rep. of the Congo 6°58S 28°21E 54 D2
Sangeang Indonesia 8°12S 119°6E 37 F5
Sanger U.S.A. 36°42N 119°33W 78 J7
Sangerhausen Germany 51°28N 11°18E 16 C6
Sanggan He → China 38°12N 117°15E 34 E9
Sanggau Indonesia 0°5N 110°30E 36 D4
Sanghar Pakistan 26°2N 68°57E 42 F3
Sangihe, Kepulauan
Indonesia 3°0N 125°30E 37 D7
Sangihe, Pulau Indonesia 3°35N 125°30E 37 D7
Sangju S. Korea 36°25N 128°10E 35 F15
Sangkapura Indonesia 5°52S 112°40E 36 F4
Sangkhla Buri Thailand 14°57N 98°28E 38 E2
Sangkulirang Indonesia 0°59N 117°58E 36 D5
Sangla Pakistan 31°43N 73°23E 42 D5
Sangli India 16°55N 74°33E 40 L9
Sangmélima Cameroon 2°57N 12°1E 52 D2
Sangod India 24°55N 76°17E 42 G7
Sangre de Cristo Mts.
U.S.A. 37°30N 105°20W 77 H11
Sangre Grande
Trin. & Tob. 10°35N 61°8W 93 K15
Sangrur India 30°14N 75°50E 42 D6
Sangudo Canada 53°50N 114°54W 70 C6
Sangue → Brazil 11°1S 58°39W 92 F7
Sanibel U.S.A. 26°27N 82°1W 85 H13
Sanikluaq Canada 56°32N 79°14W 72 A4
Sanin-Kaigan Δ Japan 35°39N 134°37E 31 G7
Sanirajak Canada 68°46N 81°12W 69 C11
Sanjawi Pakistan 30°17N 68°21E 42 D3
Sanje Uganda 0°49S 31°30E 54 C3
Sanjo Japan 37°37N 138°57E 30 F9
Sankh → India 22°15N 84°48E 43 H11
Sankt Gallen Switz. 47°26N 9°22E 20 C8
Sankt Michel = Mikkeli
Finland 61°43N 27°15E 8 F22
Sankt Moritz Switz. 46°30N 9°51E 20 C8
Sankt-Peterburg Russia 59°55N 30°20E 9 G24
Sankt Pölten Austria 48°12N 15°38E 16 D8
Sankuru →
Dem. Rep. of the Congo 4°17S 20°25E 52 E4
Sanliurfa Turkey 37°12N 38°50E 44 B3
Sanlúcar de Barrameda
Spain 36°46N 6°21W 21 D2
Sanmenxia China 34°47N 111°12E 34 G6
Sanming China 26°15N 117°40E 33 D6
Sannicandro Gargánico
Italy 41°50N 15°34E 22 D6
Sânnicolau Mare
Romania 46°5N 20°39E 17 E11
Sannieshof S. Africa 26°30S 25°47E 56 D4
Sannīn, J. Lebanon 33°57N 35°52E 46 B4
Sanniquellie Liberia 7°19N 8°38W 50 G4
Sanok Poland 49°35N 22°10E 17 D12
Sanquhar U.K. 55°22N 3°54W 11 F5
Sans Souci Trin. & Tob. 10°50N 61°0W 93 K16
Sant Antoni de Portmany
Spain 38°59N 1°19E 24 C7
Sant Carles Spain 39°3N 1°34E 24 B8
Sant Elm Spain 39°35N 2°21E 24 B9
Sant Feliu de Guíxols Spain 41°45N 3°1E 21 B7
Sant Ferran Spain 38°42N 1°28E 24 C7
Sant Francesc de Formentera
Spain 38°42N 1°26E 24 C7
Sant Jaume Spain 39°54N 4°4E 24 B11
Sant Joan Spain 39°36N 3°4E 24 B10
Sant Joan de Labritja Spain 39°5N 1°31E 24 B8
Sant Jordi Ibiza, Spain 38°53N 1°24E 24 C7
Sant Jordi Mallorca, Spain 39°33N 2°46E 24 B9
Sant Jordi, G. de Spain 40°53N 1°2E 21 B6
Sant Llorenç des Cardassar
Spain 39°37N 3°17E 24 B10
Sant Mateu Spain 39°3N 1°23E 24 B7
Sant Miquel Spain 39°3N 1°26E 24 B7
Sant Salvador Spain 39°27N 3°11E 24 B10
Santa Agnés Spain 39°3N 1°21E 24 B7
Santa Ana Bolivia 13°50S 65°40W 92 F5
Santa Ana El Salv. 14°0N 89°31W 88 D2
Santa Ana Mexico 30°33N 111°7W 86 A2
Santa Ana U.S.A. 33°46N 117°52W 79 M9
Sant' Antioco Italy 39°4N 8°27E 22 E3
Santa Bárbara Chile 37°40S 72°1W 94 D1
Santa Bárbara Honduras 14°53N 88°14W 88 D2
Santa Bárbara Mexico 26°48N 105°49W 86 B3
Santa Barbara U.S.A. 34°25N 119°42W 79 L7
Santa Barbara Channel
U.S.A. 34°15N 120°0W 79 L7
Santa Barbara I. U.S.A. 33°29N 119°2W 79 M7
Santa Catalina, Gulf of
U.S.A. 33°10N 117°50W 79 N9
Santa Catalina, I.
Mexico 25°40N 110°47W 86 B2
Santa Catalina I.
U.S.A. 33°23N 118°25W 79 M8
Santa Catarina □ Brazil 27°25S 48°30W 95 B6
Santa Catarina, I. de
Brazil 27°30S 48°40W 95 B6
Santa Cecília Brazil 26°56S 50°18W 95 B5
Santa Clara Cuba 22°20N 80°0W 88 B4
Santa Clara Calif.,
U.S.A. 37°21N 121°57W 78 H5
Santa Clara N.Y.,
U.S.A. 44°38N 74°27W 83 B10
Santa Clara Utah, U.S.A. 37°8N 113°39W 77 H7
Santa Clara de Olimar
Uruguay 32°50S 54°54W 95 C5
Santa Clara Valley
U.S.A. 36°50N 121°30W 78 J5
Santa Clarita U.S.A. 34°24N 118°33W 79 L8
Santa Clotilde Peru 2°33S 73°45W 92 D4
Santa Coloma de Gramenet
Spain 41°27N 2°13E 21 B7
Santa Cruz Bolivia 17°43S 63°10W 92 G6
Santa Cruz Chile 34°38S 71°27W 94 C1
Santa Cruz Costa Rica 10°15N 85°35W 88 D2
Santa Cruz Madeira 32°42N 16°46W 24 D3
Santa Cruz Phil. 14°20N 121°24E 37 B6
Santa Cruz U.S.A. 36°58N 122°1W 78 J4
Santa Cruz → Argentina 50°10S 68°20W 96 G3
Santa Cruz de la Palma
Canary Is. 28°41N 17°46W 24 F2
Santa Cruz de la Palma ✈ (SPC)
Canary Is. 28°40N 17°45W 24 F2
Santa Cruz de Tenerife
Canary Is. 28°28N 16°15W 24 F3
Santa Cruz del Norte
Cuba 23°9N 81°55W 88 B3
Santa Cruz del Sur Cuba 20°44N 78°0W 88 B4
Santa Cruz do Rio Pardo
Brazil 22°54S 49°37W 95 A6
Santa Cruz do Sul Brazil 29°42S 52°25W 95 B5
Santa Cruz I. U.S.A. 34°1N 119°43W 79 M7
Santa Cruz Is. Solomon Is. 10°30S 166°0E 58 C9
Santa Cruz Mts. Jamaica 17°58N 77°43W 88 a
Santa Domingo, Cay
Bahamas 21°25N 75°15W 88 B4
Santa Elena Argentina 30°58S 59°47W 94 C4
Santa Elena, C.
Costa Rica 10°54N 85°56W 88 D2
Santa Eulària des Riu
Spain 38°59N 1°32E 24 C8
Santa Fé Argentina 31°35S 60°41W 94 C3
Santa Fe U.S.A. 35°41N 105°57W 77 J11
Santa Fé □ Argentina 31°50S 60°55W 94 C3
Santa Fé do Sul Brazil 20°13S 50°56W 93 H8
Santa Filomena Brazil 9°6S 45°50W 93 E9
Santa Gertrudis Spain 39°0N 1°26E 24 C7
Santa Inês Brazil 13°17S 39°48W 93 F11
Santa Inés, I. Chile 54°0S 73°0W 96 G2
Santa Isabel Argentina 36°10S 66°54W 94 D2
Santa Isabel do Morro
Brazil 11°34S 50°40W 93 F8
Santa Lucía Corrientes,
Argentina 28°58S 59°5W 94 B4
Santa Lucía San Juan,
Argentina 31°30S 68°30W 94 C2
Santa Lucía Uruguay 34°27S 56°24W 94 C4
Santa Lucia Range
U.S.A. 36°0N 121°20W 78 K5
Santa Luzia C. Verde Is. 16°50N 24°35W 50 b
Santa Margalida Spain 39°42N 3°6E 24 B10
Santa Margarita
Argentina 38°28S 61°35W 94 D3
Santa Margarita
U.S.A. 35°23N 120°37W 78 K6
Santa Margarita →
U.S.A. 33°13N 117°23W 79 M9
Santa Margarita, I.
Mexico 24°27N 111°50W 86 C2
Santa María Argentina 26°40S 66°0W 94 B2
Santa Maria Azores 36°58N 25°6W 50 a
Santa Maria Brazil 29°40S 53°48W 95 B5
Santa Maria C. Verde Is. 16°31N 22°53W 50 b
Santa Maria U.S.A. 34°57N 120°26W 79 L6
Santa María → Mexico 31°0N 107°14W 86 A3
Santa María, B. de
Mexico 25°4N 108°6W 86 B3
Santa Maria da Vitória
Brazil 13°24S 44°12W 93 F10
Santa María del Camí
Spain 39°38N 2°47E 24 B9
Santa Maria di Léuca, C.
Italy 39°47N 18°22E 23 E8
Santa Marta Colombia 11°15N 74°13W 92 A4
Santa Marta, Sierra Nevada de
Colombia 10°55N 73°50W 92 A4
Santa Marta Grande, C.
Brazil 28°43S 48°50W 95 B6
Santa Maura = Lefkada
Greece 38°40N 20°43E 23 E9
Santa Monica U.S.A. 34°1N 118°29W 79 M8
Santa Monica Mts. ⌂
U.S.A. 34°4N 118°44W 79 L8
Santa Paula U.S.A. 34°21N 119°4W 79 L7
Santa Ponça Spain 39°30N 2°28E 24 B9
Santa Rosa La Pampa,
Argentina 36°40S 64°17W 94 D3
Santa Rosa San Luis,
Argentina 32°21S 65°10W 94 C2
Santa Rosa Brazil 27°52S 54°29W 95 B5
Santa Rosa Calif.,
U.S.A. 38°26N 122°43W 78 G4
Santa Rosa N. Mex.,
U.S.A. 34°57N 104°41W 77 J11
Santa Rosa and San Jacinto
Mts. ⌂ U.S.A. 33°28N 116°20W 79 M10
Santa Rosa de Copán
Honduras 14°47N 88°46W 88 D2
Santa Rosa de Río Primero
Argentina 31°8S 63°20W 94 C3
Santa Rosa del Sara
Bolivia 17°7S 63°35W 92 G6
Santa Rosa I. Calif.,
U.S.A. 33°58N 120°6W 79 M6
Santa Rosa I. Fla.,
U.S.A. 30°20N 86°50W 85 F11
Santa Rosa Range
U.S.A. 41°45N 117°40W 76 F5
Santa Rosalía Mexico 27°19N 112°17W 86 B2
Santa Sylvina Argentina 27°50S 61°10W 94 B3
Santa Tecla = Nueva San
Salvador El Salv. 13°40N 89°18W 88 D2
Santa Teresa Argentina 33°25S 60°47W 94 C3
Santa Teresa Australia 24°8S 134°22E 62 C1
Santa Teresa Mexico 25°17N 97°51W 87 B5
Santa Teresa Δ Uruguay 33°57S 53°31W 95 C5
Santa Teresita Argentina 36°32S 56°41W 94 D4
Santa Vitória do Palmar
Brazil 33°32S 53°25W 95 C5
Santa Ynez → U.S.A. 34°41N 120°36W 79 L6
Santa Ynez Mts. U.S.A. 34°30N 120°0W 79 L6
Santa Ysabel U.S.A. 33°7N 116°40W 79 M10
Santai China 31°5N 104°58E 32 C5
Santana Madeira 32°48N 16°52W 24 D3
Santana, Coxilha de
Brazil 30°50S 55°35W 95 C4
Santana do Livramento
Brazil 30°55S 55°30W 95 C4
Santander Spain 43°27N 3°51W 21 A4
Santander Jiménez
Mexico 24°13N 98°28W 87 C5
Santanilla, Is. Honduras 17°22N 83°57W 88 C3
Santanyí Spain 39°20N 3°5E 24 B10
Santaquin U.S.A. 39°59N 111°47W 76 G8
Santarém Brazil 2°25S 54°42W 93 D8
Santarém Portugal 39°12N 8°42W 21 C1
Santaren Channel
W. Indies 24°0N 79°30W 88 B4
Santee U.S.A. 32°50N 116°58W 79 N10
Santee → U.S.A. 33°7N 79°17W 85 E15
Santiago = Río Grande de
Santiago → Mexico 21°36N 105°26W 86 C3
Santiago = São Tiago
C. Verde Is. 15°0N 23°40W 50 b
Santiago Brazil 29°11S 54°52W 95 B5
Santiago Canary Is. 28°2N 17°12W 24 F2
Santiago Chile 33°26S 70°40W 94 C1
Santiago Panama 8°0N 81°0W 88 E3
Santiago → Peru 4°27S 77°38W 92 D3
Santiago de Compostela
Spain 42°52N 8°37W 21 A1
Santiago de Cuba Cuba 20°0N 75°49W 88 C4
Santiago de los Caballeros
Dom. Rep. 19°30N 70°40W 89 C5
Santiago del Estero
Argentina 27°50S 64°15W 94 B3
Santiago del Estero □
Argentina 27°40S 63°15W 94 B3
Santiago del Teide
Canary Is. 28°17N 16°48W 24 F3
Santiago Ixcuintla
Mexico 21°49N 105°13W 86 C3
Santiago Jamiltepec
Mexico 16°17N 97°49W 87 D5
Santiago Papasquiaro
Mexico 25°3N 105°25W 86 C3
Santiago Pinotepa Nacional
Mexico 16°19N 98°1W 87 D5
Santiaguillo, L. de
Mexico 24°48N 104°48W 86 C4
Santo Amaro Brazil 12°30S 38°43W 93 F11
Santo Anastácio Brazil 21°58S 51°39W 95 A5
Santo André Brazil 23°39S 46°29W 95 A6
Santo Ângelo Brazil 28°15S 54°15W 95 B5
Santo Antão C. Verde Is. 16°52N 25°10W 50 b
Santo Antônio do Içá
Brazil 3°5S 67°57W 92 D5
Santo Antônio do Leverger
Brazil 15°52S 56°5W 93 G7
Santo Domingo
Dom. Rep. 18°30N 69°59W 89 C6
Santo Domingo Baja Calif.,
Mexico 30°43N 116°2W 86 A1
Santo Domingo Baja Calif. S.,
Mexico 25°29N 111°55W 86 B2
Santo Domingo Nic. 12°14N 84°59W 88 D3
Santo Domingo de los Colorados
Ecuador 0°15S 79°9W 92 D3
Santo Domingo Pueblo
U.S.A. 35°31N 106°22W 77 J10
Santo Tomás Mexico 31°33N 116°24W 86 A1
Santo Tomás Peru 14°26S 72°8W 92 F4
Santo Tomé Argentina 28°40S 56°5W 95 B4
Santo Tomé de Guayana = Ciudad
Guayana Venezuela 8°0N 62°30W 92 B6
Santoña Spain 43°29N 3°27W 21 A4
Santorini Greece 36°23N 25°27E 23 F11
Santos Brazil 24°0S 46°20W 95 A6
Santos Dumont Brazil 22°55S 43°10W 95 A7
Santuario de Aves Laguna
Colorada Δ Bolivia 22°10S 67°45W 94 A2
Sanur Indonesia 8°41S 115°15E 37 K18
Sanwer India 22°59N 75°50E 42 H6
Sanxiang China 22°21N 113°25E 33 G9
Sanya China 18°14N 109°29E 38 C7
Sanyuan China 34°35N 108°58E 34 G5
São Bernardo do Campo
Brazil 23°45S 46°34W 95 A6
São Borja Brazil 28°39S 56°0W 95 B4
São Carlos Brazil 22°0S 47°50W 95 A6
São Cristóvão Brazil 11°1S 37°15W 93 F11
São Domingos Brazil 13°25S 46°19W 93 F9
São Filipe C. Verde Is. 15°2N 24°30W 50 b
São Francisco Brazil 16°0S 44°50W 93 G10
São Francisco →
Brazil 10°30S 36°24W 93 F11
São Francisco do Sul
Brazil 26°15S 48°36W 95 B6
São Gabriel Brazil 30°20S 54°20W 95 C5
São Gonçalo Brazil 22°48S 43°5W 95 A7
São Hill Tanzania 8°20S 35°12E 55 D4
São João da Boa Vista
Brazil 22°0S 46°52W 95 A6
São João da Madeira
Portugal 40°54N 8°30W 21 B1
São João del Rei Brazil 21°8S 44°15W 95 A7
São João do Araguaia
Brazil 5°23S 48°46W 93 E9
São João do Piauí Brazil 8°21S 42°15W 93 E10
São Joaquim Brazil 28°18S 49°56W 95 B6
São Joaquim Δ Brazil 28°12S 49°37W 95 B6
São Jorge Azores 38°38N 28°3W 50 a
São Jorge, Pta. de
Madeira 32°50N 16°53W 24 D3
São José Brazil 27°38S 48°39W 95 B5
São José do Norte Brazil 32°1S 52°3W 95 C5
São José do Rio Preto
Brazil 20°50S 49°20W 95 A6
São José dos Campos
Brazil 23°7S 45°52W 95 A6
São Leopoldo Brazil 29°50S 51°10W 95 B5
São Lourenço Brazil 22°7S 45°3W 95 A6
São Lourenço → Brazil 17°53S 57°27W 93 G7
São Lourenço, Pta. de
Madeira 32°44N 16°39W 24 D3
São Lourenço do Sul
Brazil 31°22S 51°58W 95 C5
São Luís Brazil 2°39S 44°15W 93 D10
São Luís Gonzaga Brazil 28°25S 55°0W 95 B5
São Marcos → Brazil 18°15S 47°37W 93 G9
São Marcos, B. de Brazil 2°0S 44°0W 93 D10
São Mateus Brazil 18°44S 39°50W 93 G11
São Mateus do Sul
Brazil 25°52S 50°23W 95 B5
São Miguel Azores 37°47N 25°30W 50 a
São Miguel do Oeste
Brazil 26°45S 53°34W 95 B5
São Nicolau C. Verde Is. 16°20N 24°20W 50 b
São Paulo Brazil 23°32S 46°38W 95 A6
São Paulo □ Brazil 22°0S 49°0W 95 A6
São Paulo de Olivença
Brazil 3°27S 68°48W 92 D5
São Roque Madeira 32°46N 16°48W 24 D3
São Roque, C. de Brazil 5°30S 35°16W 93 E11
São Sebastião, I. de
Brazil 23°50S 45°18W 95 A6
São Sebastião do Paraíso
Brazil 20°54S 46°59W 95 A6
São Tiago C. Verde Is. 15°0N 23°40W 50 b
São Tomé
São Tomé & Príncipe 0°10N 6°39E 48 F4
São Tomé, C. de Brazil 22°0S 40°59W 95 A7
São Tomé & Príncipe ■
Africa 0°12N 6°39E 49 F4
São Vicente Brazil 23°57S 46°23W 95 A6
São Vicente C. Verde Is. 17°0N 25°0W 50 b
São Vicente Madeira 32°48N 17°3W 24 D2
São Vicente, C. de Portugal 37°0N 9°0W 21 D1
Saona, I. Dom. Rep. 18°10N 68°40W 89 C6
Saône → France 45°44N 4°50E 20 D6
Saonek Indonesia 0°22S 130°55E 37 E8
Sapam, Ao Thailand 8°0N 98°26E 39 a
Saparua Indonesia 3°33S 128°40E 37 E7
Sapele Nigeria 5°50N 5°40E 50 G7
Sapelo I. U.S.A. 31°25N 81°12W 85 F14
Sapi ⌂ Zimbabwe 15°48S 29°42E 55 F2
Saposoa Peru 6°55S 76°45W 92 E3
Sapphire Australia 23°28S 147°43E 62 C4
Sappho U.S.A. 48°4N 124°16W 78 B2
Sapporo Japan 43°0N 141°21E 30 C10
Sapulpa U.S.A. 35°59N 96°5W 84 D6
Saqqez Iran 36°15N 46°20E 44 B5
Sar Dasht Āzarbāyjān-e Gharbī,
Iran 36°9N 45°28E 44 B5
Sar Dasht Khuzestān, Iran 32°32N 48°52E 45 C6
Sar-e Pol □ Afghan. 36°20N 65°50E 40 B4
Sar Gachīneh = Yāsūj
Iran 30°31N 51°31E 45 D6
Sar Planina Macedonia 42°0N 21°0E 23 C9
Sara Buri = Saraburi
Thailand 14°30N 100°55E 38 E3
Sarāb Iran 37°55N 47°40E 44 B5
Sarābādī Iraq 33°1N 44°48E 44 C5
Saraburi Thailand 14°30N 100°55E 38 E3
Saradiya India 21°34N 70°2E 42 J4
Saragossa = Zaragoza
Spain 41°39N 0°53W 21 B5
Saraguro Ecuador 3°35S 79°16W 92 D3
Sarahs Turkmenistan 36°32N 61°13E 45 B9
Sarai Naurang Pakistan 32°50N 70°47E 42 C4
Saraikela India 22°42N 85°56E 43 H11
Sarajevo Bos.-H. 43°52N 18°26E 23 C8
Sarakhs = Sarahs
Turkmenistan 36°32N 61°13E 45 B9
Saran, Gunung Indonesia 0°30S 111°25E 36 E4
Saranac Lake U.S.A. 44°20N 74°10W 83 B10
Saranac Lakes U.S.A. 44°20N 74°28W 83 B10
Saranda Tanzania 5°45S 34°59E 54 D3
Sarandí del Yí Uruguay 33°18S 55°38W 95 C4
Sarandí Grande
Uruguay 33°44S 56°20W 94 C4
Sarangani B. Phil. 6°0N 125°13E 37 C7
Sarangani Is. Phil. 5°25N 125°25E 37 C7
Sarangarh India 21°30N 83°5E 41 J13
Saransk Russia 54°10N 45°10E 18 D8
Sarapul Russia 56°28N 53°48E 18 C9
Sarasota U.S.A. 27°20N 82°32W 85 H13
Saratoga Calif., U.S.A. 37°16N 122°2W 78 H4
Saratoga Wyo., U.S.A. 41°27N 106°49W 76 F10
Saratoga ⌂ U.S.A. 43°0N 73°38W 83 D11
Saratoga L. U.S.A. 43°1N 73°44W 83 C11
Saratoga Springs U.S.A. 43°5N 73°47W 83 C11
Saratok Malaysia 1°55N 111°17E 36 D4
Saratov Russia 51°30N 46°2E 19 D8
Sarāvān Iran 27°25N 62°15E 45 E9
Saravane Laos 15°43N 106°25E 38 E6
Sarawak □ Malaysia 2°0N 113°0E 36 D4
Saray Turkey 41°26N 27°55E 23 D12
Sarayköy Turkey 37°55N 28°54E 23 F13
Sarbāz Iran 26°38N 61°19E 45 E9
Sarbīsheh Iran 32°30N 59°40E 45 C8
Sarda → India 27°21N 81°23E 43 F9
Sardarshahr India 28°30N 74°29E 42 E6
Sardegna □ Italy 40°0N 9°0E 22 D3
Sardhana India 29°9N 77°39E 42 E7
Sardina, Pta. Canary Is. 28°9N 15°44W 24 F4
Sardinia = Sardegna □
Italy 40°0N 9°0E 22 D3
Sardis Turkey 38°28N 27°58E 23 E12
Sārdūīyeh = Dar Mazār
Iran 29°14N 57°20E 45 D8
Saren Indonesia 8°26S 115°34E 37 J18
S'Arenal Spain 39°30N 2°45E 24 B9
Sarera, G. of Indonesia 2°0S 135°0E 58 B6
Sargasso Sea Atl. Oc. 27°0N 72°0W 66 G13
Sargodha Pakistan 32°10N 72°40E 42 C5
Sarh Chad 9°5N 18°23E 51 G9
Sārī Iran 36°30N 53°4E 45 B7
Saria India 21°38N 83°22E 43 J10
Sariab Pakistan 30°6N 66°59E 42 D2
Sarıgöl Turkey 38°14N 28°41E 23 E13
Sarikei Malaysia 2°8N 111°30E 36 D4
Sarila India 25°46N 79°41E 43 G8
Sarina Australia 21°22S 149°13E 62 C4
Sarita U.S.A. 27°13N 97°47W 84 H6
Sariwŏn N. Korea 38°31N 125°46E 35 E13
Sarju → India 27°21N 81°23E 43 F9
Sark U.K. 49°25N 2°22W 13 H5
Sarkari Tala India 27°39N 70°52E 42 F4
Şarköy Turkey 40°36N 27°6E 23 D12
Sarlat-la-Canéda France 44°54N 1°13E 20 D4
Sarmi Indonesia 1°49S 138°44E 37 E9
Sarmiento Argentina 45°35S 69°5W 96 F3
Särna Sweden 61°41N 13°8E 8 F15
Sarnia Canada 42°58N 82°23W 82 D2
Sarolangun Indonesia 2°19S 102°42E 36 E2
Saronikos Kolpos
Greece 37°45N 23°45E 23 F10
Saros Körfezi Turkey 40°30N 26°15E 23 D12
Sarpsborg Norway 59°16N 11°7E 9 G14
Sarqan Kazakhstan 45°24N 79°55E 32 B2
Sarre = Saar → Europe 49°41N 6°32E 15 E6
Sarreguemines France 49°5N 7°4E 20 B7

Sarthe → *France* 47°33N 0°31W **20** C3
Saruna → *Pakistan* 26°31N 67°7E **42** F2
Sarvar *India* 26°4N 75°0E **42** F6
Sarvestān *Iran* 29°20N 53°10E **45** D7
Sary-Tash *Kyrgyzstan* 39°44N 73°15E **28** F8
Saryshaghan *Kazakhstan* 46°12N 73°38E **28** E8
Sasan Gir *India* 21°10N 70°36E **42** J4
Sasaram *India* 24°57N 84°5E **43** G11
Sasebo *Japan* 33°10N 129°43E **31** H4
Saser Kangri *India* 34°50N 77°50E **43** B7
Saskatchewan ☐
  Canada 54°40N 106°0W **71** C7
Saskatchewan →
  Canada 53°37N 100°40W **71** C8
Saskatoon *Canada* 52°10N 106°38W **71** C7
Saskylakh *Russia* 71°55N 114°1E **29** B12
Saslaya △ *Nic.* 13°45N 85°4W **88** D2
Sasolburg *S. Africa* 26°46S 27°49E **57** D4
Sasovo *Russia* 54°25N 41°55E **18** D7
Sassandra *Ivory C.* 4°55N 6°8W **50** H4
Sassandra → *Ivory C.* 4°58N 6°5W **50** H4
Sássari *Italy* 40°43N 8°34E **22** D3
Sassnitz *Germany* 54°29N 13°39E **16** A7
Sassuolo *Italy* 44°33N 10°47E **22** B4
Sasyk, Ozero *Ukraine* 45°45N 29°20E **17** F15
Sata-Misaki *Japan* 31°0N 130°40E **31** J5
Satadougou *Mali* 12°25N 11°25W **50** F3
Satakunda = Satakunta
  Finland 61°45N 23°0E **8** F20
Satakunta *Finland* 61°45N 23°0E **8** F20
Satara *India* 17°44N 73°58E **40** L8
Satara *S. Africa* 24°29S 31°47E **57** C5
Satbarwa *India* 23°55N 84°16E **43** H11
Satevó *Mexico* 27°57N 106°7W **86** B3
Satilla → *U.S.A.* 30°59N 81°29W **85** F14
Satka *Russia* 55°3N 59°1E **18** C10
Satmala Hills *Andhra Pradesh,*
  India 19°45N 78°45E **40** K11
Satmala Hills *Maharashtra,*
  India 20°15N 74°40E **40** J9
Satna *India* 24°35N 80°50E **43** G9
Sátoraljaújhely
  Hungary 48°25N 21°41E **17** D11
Satpura △ *India* 22°40N 78°15E **42** J7
Satpura Ra. *India* 21°25N 76°10E **40** J10
Satsuna-Shotō *Japan* 30°0N 130°0E **31** K5
Sattahip *Thailand* 12°41N 100°54E **38** F3
Satu Mare *Romania* 47°46N 22°55E **17** E12
Satui *Indonesia* 3°50S 115°27E **36** E5
Satun *Thailand* 6°43N 100°2E **39** J2
Satupa'itea *Samoa* 13°45S 172°18W **59** b
Saturnina → *Brazil* 12°15S 58°10W **92** F7
Sauce *Argentina* 30°5S 58°46W **94** C4
Sauceda *Mexico* 25°46N 101°19W **86** B4
Saucillo *Mexico* 28°1N 105°17W **86** B3
Sauda *Norway* 59°40N 6°20E **9** G12
Sauðárkrókur *Iceland* 65°45N 19°40W **8** D4
Saudi Arabia ■ *Asia* 26°0N 44°0E **44** B3
Sauerland *Germany* 51°12N 7°59E **16** C4
Saugeen → *Canada* 44°30N 81°22W **82** B3
Saugerties *U.S.A.* 42°5N 73°57W **83** D11
Saugus *U.S.A.* 34°25N 118°32W **79** L8
Sauk Centre *U.S.A.* 45°44N 94°57W **80** C6
Sauk Rapids *U.S.A.* 45°35N 94°10W **80** C6
Sault Ste. Marie *Canada* 46°30N 84°20W **72** C3
Sault Ste. Marie *U.S.A.* 46°30N 84°21W **81** B11
Saumlaki *Indonesia* 7°55S 131°20E **37** F8
Saumur *France* 47°15N 0°5W **20** C3
Saunders, C. *N.Z.* 45°53S 170°45E **59** F3
Saunders I. *Antarctica* 57°48S 26°28W **5** B1
Saunders Pt. *Australia* 27°52S 125°38E **61** E4
Saurimo *Angola* 9°40S 20°12E **52** F4
Sausalito *U.S.A.* 37°51N 122°29W **78** H4
Savá *Honduras* 15°32N 86°15W **88** C2
Sava → *Serbia* 44°50N 20°26E **23** B9
Savage *U.S.A.* 47°27N 104°21W **76** C11
Savage I. = Niue
  Pac. Oc. 19°2S 169°54W **65** J11
Savage River *Australia* 41°31S 145°14E **63** G4
Savalou *Benin* 7°57N 1°58E **50** G6
Savane *Mozam.* 19°37S 35°8E **55** F4
Savanna *U.S.A.* 42°5N 90°8W **80** D8
Savanna-la-Mar *Jamaica* 18°10N 78°10W **88** a
Savannah *Ga., U.S.A.* 32°5N 81°6W **85** E14
Savannah *Mo., U.S.A.* 39°56N 94°50W **80** F6
Savannah *Tenn., U.S.A.* 35°14N 88°15W **85** D10
Savannah → *U.S.A.* 32°2N 80°53W **85** E14
Savannakhet *Laos* 16°30N 104°49E **38** D5
Savant L. *Canada* 50°16N 90°44W **72** B1
Savant Lake *Canada* 50°14N 90°40W **72** B1
Save → *Mozam.* 21°16S 34°0E **57** C5
Sāveh *Iran* 35°2N 50°20E **45** C6
Savelugu *Ghana* 9°38N 0°54W **50** G5
Savo *Finland* 62°45N 27°30E **8** E22
Savoie ☐ *France* 45°26N 6°25E **20** D7
Savolax = Savo *Finland* 62°45N 27°30E **8** E22
Savona *Italy* 44°17N 8°30E **20** D8
Savona *U.S.A.* 42°17N 77°13W **82** D7
Savonlinna *Finland* 61°52N 28°53E **8** F23
Savoy = Savoie ☐ *France* 45°26N 6°25E **20** D7
Savur *Turkey* 37°34N 40°53E **44** B4
Savusavu *Fiji* 16°34S 179°15E **59** a
Savusavu B. *Fiji* 16°45S 179°15E **59** a
Sawahlunto *Indonesia* 0°40S 100°52E **36** E2
Sawai *Indonesia* 3°0S 129°5E **37** E7
Sawai Madhopur *India* 26°0N 76°25E **42** G7
Sawaleke *Fiji* 17°59S 179°18E **59** a
Sawang Daen Din
  Thailand 17°28N 103°28E **38** D4
Sawankhalok *Thailand* 17°19N 99°50E **38** D2
Sawara *Japan* 35°55N 140°30E **31** G10
Sawatch Range *U.S.A.* 39°0N 106°30W **76** G10
Sawel Mt. *U.K.* 54°50N 7°2W **10** B4
Sawi *Thailand* 10°14N 99°5E **39** G2
Sawmills *Zimbabwe* 19°30S 28°2E **55** F2
Sawtooth △ *U.S.A.* 44°0N 114°50W **76** D6

Sawtooth Range *U.S.A.* 44°3N 114°58W **76** D6
Sawu *Indonesia* 10°35S 121°50E **37** F6
Sawu Sea *Indonesia* 9°30S 121°50E **37** F6
Saxby → *Australia* 18°25S 140°53E **62** B3
Saxmundham *U.K.* 52°13N 1°30E **13** E9
Saxony = Sachsen ☐
  Germany 50°55N 13°10E **16** C7
Saxony, Lower =
  Niedersachsen ☐
  Germany 52°50N 9°0E **16** B5
Saxton *U.S.A.* 40°13N 78°15W **82** F6
Sayabec *Canada* 48°35N 67°41W **73** C6
Sayaboury *Laos* 19°15N 101°45E **38** C3
Sayán *Peru* 11°8S 77°12W **92** F3
Sayan, Vostochnyy
  Russia 54°0N 96°0E **29** D10
Sayan, Zapadnyy *Russia* 52°30N 94°0E **32** A4
Sayanogorsk *Russia* 53°5N 91°23E **29** D10
Saydā *Lebanon* 33°35N 35°25E **46** B4
Sayhandulaan = Oldziyt
  Mongolia 44°40N 109°1E **34** B5
Sayḥūt *Yemen* 15°12N 51°10E **47** D5
Saylac *Somali Rep.* 11°21N 43°30E **47** E3
Saynshand = Buyant-Uhaa
  Mongolia 44°55N 110°11E **33** B6
Sayre *Okla., U.S.A.* 35°18N 99°38W **84** D5
Sayre *Pa., U.S.A.* 41°59N 76°32W **83** E8
Sayreville *U.S.A.* 40°28N 74°22W **83** F10
Sayula *Mexico* 19°52N 103°36W **86** D4
Sayward *Canada* 50°21N 125°55W **70** C3
Sazanit *Albania* 40°30N 19°20E **23** D8
Sazin *Pakistan* 35°35N 73°30E **43** B5
Sázava → *Czech Rep.* 49°53N 14°24E **16** D8
Scafell Pike *U.K.* 54°27N 3°14W **12** C4
Scalloway *U.K.* 60°9N 1°17W **11** A7
Scalpay *U.K.* 57°18N 6°0W **11** D3
Scandia *Canada* 50°20N 112°2W **70** C6
Scandicci *Italy* 43°45N 11°11E **22** C4
Scandinavia *Europe* 64°0N 12°0E **8** E15
Scapa Flow *U.K.* 58°53N 3°3W **11** C5
Scappoose *U.S.A.* 45°45N 122°53W **78** E4
Scarba *U.K.* 56°11N 5°43W **11** E3
Scarborough
  Trin. & Tob. 11°11N 60°42W **89** D7
Scarborough *U.K.* 54°17N 0°24W **12** C7
Scariff I. *Ireland* 51°44N 10°15W **10** E1
Scarp *U.K.* 58°1N 7°8W **11** C1
Scebeli = Shabeelle →
  Somali Rep. 2°0N 44°0E **47** G3
Schaffhausen *Switz.* 47°42N 8°39E **20** C8
Schagen *Neths.* 52°49N 4°48E **15** B4
Schaghticoke *U.S.A.* 42°54N 73°35W **83** D11
Schefferville *Canada* 54°48N 66°50W **73** B6
Schelde → *Belgium* 51°15N 4°16E **15** C4
Schell Creek Ra. *U.S.A.* 39°25N 114°40W **76** G6
Schellsburg *U.S.A.* 40°3N 78°39W **82** F6
Schenectady *U.S.A.* 42°49N 73°57W **83** D11
Schenevus *U.S.A.* 42°33N 74°50W **83** D10
Schiedam *Neths.* 51°55N 4°25E **15** C4
Schiermonnikoog *Neths.* 53°30N 6°15E **15** A6
Schio *Italy* 45°43N 11°21E **22** B4
Schiphol, Amsterdam ✈ (AMS)
  Neths. 52°18N 4°45E **15** B4
Schleswig *Germany* 54°31N 9°34E **16** A5
Schleswig-Holstein ☐
  Germany 54°30N 9°30E **16** A5
Schœlcher *Martinique* 14°36N 61°7W **88** c
Schoharie *U.S.A.* 42°40N 74°19W **83** D10
Schoharie Cr. →
  U.S.A. 42°57N 74°18W **83** D10
Scholls *U.S.A.* 45°24N 122°56W **78** E4
Schouten I. *Australia* 42°20S 148°20E **63** G4
Schouten Is. = Supiori
  Indonesia 1°0S 136°0E **37** E9
Schouwen *Neths.* 51°43N 3°45E **15** C3
Schreiber *Canada* 48°45N 87°20W **72** C2
Schroffenstein *Namibia* 27°11S 18°42E **56** D2
Schroon Lake *U.S.A.* 43°50N 73°46W **83** C11
Schuler *Canada* 50°20N 110°6W **71** C6
Schumacher *Canada* 48°30N 81°16W **72** C3
Schurz *U.S.A.* 38°57N 118°49W **76** G4
Schuyler *U.S.A.* 41°27N 97°4W **80** E5
Schuylerville *U.S.A.* 43°6N 73°35W **83** C11
Schuylkill → *U.S.A.* 39°53N 75°12W **83** G9
Schuylkill Haven *U.S.A.* 40°37N 76°11W **83** F8
Schwäbische Alb
  Germany 48°20N 9°30E **16** D5
Schwaner, Pegunungan
  Indonesia 1°0S 112°30E **36** E4
Schwarzrand *Namibia* 25°37S 16°50E **56** D2
Schwarzwald *Germany* 48°30N 8°20E **16** D5
Schwedt *Germany* 53°3N 14°16E **16** B8
Schweinfurt *Germany* 50°3N 10°14E **16** C6
Schweiz = Switzerland ■
  Europe 46°30N 8°0E **20** C8
Schweizer-Reneke
  S. Africa 27°11S 25°18E **56** D4
Schwenningen = Villingen-
  Schwenningen *Germany* 48°3N 8°26E **16** D5
Schwerin *Germany* 53°36N 11°22E **16** B6
Schwyz *Switz.* 47°2N 8°39E **20** C8
Sciacca *Italy* 37°31N 13°3E **22** F5
Scilla *Italy* 38°15N 15°43E **22** E6
Scilly, Isles of *U.K.* 49°56N 6°22W **13** H1
Scioto → *U.S.A.* 38°44N 83°1W **81** F12
Scituate *U.S.A.* 42°12N 70°44W **83** D14
Scobey *U.S.A.* 48°47N 105°25W **76** B11
Scone *Australia* 32°5S 150°52E **63** E5
Scone *U.K.* 56°25N 3°24W **11** E5
Scoresbysund = Ittoqqortoormiit
  Greenland 70°20N 23°0W **4** B6
Scotia *Calif., U.S.A.* 40°29N 124°6W **76** F1
Scotia *N.Y., U.S.A.* 42°50N 73°58W **83** D11
Scotia Sea *Antarctica* 56°5S 56°0W **5** B18
Scotland *Canada* 43°1N 80°22W **82** C4
Scotland ☐ *U.K.* 57°0N 4°0W **11** E5
Scott *Antarctica* 77°0S 165°0E **5** D11

Scott, C. *Australia* 13°30S 129°49E **60** B4
Scott City *U.S.A.* 38°29N 100°54W **80** F3
Scott Glacier *Antarctica* 66°15S 100°5E **5** C8
Scott I. *Antarctica* 67°0S 179°0E **5** C11
Scott Is. *Canada* 50°48N 128°40W **70** C3
Scott L. *Canada* 59°55N 106°18W **71** B7
Scott Reef *Australia* 14°0S 121°50E **60** B3
Scottburgh *S. Africa* 30°15S 30°47E **57** E5
Scottdale *U.S.A.* 40°6N 79°35W **82** F5
Scottish Borders ☐ *U.K.* 55°35N 2°50W **11** F6
Scotts Valley *U.S.A.* 37°3N 122°1W **78** H4
Scottsbluff *U.S.A.* 41°52N 103°40W **80** E2
Scottsboro *U.S.A.* 34°40N 86°2W **85** D11
Scottsburg *U.S.A.* 38°41N 85°47W **81** F11
Scottsdale *Australia* 41°9S 147°31E **63** G4
Scottsdale *U.S.A.* 33°40N 111°53W **77** K8
Scottsville *Ky., U.S.A.* 36°45N 86°11W **80** G10
Scottsville *N.Y., U.S.A.* 43°2N 77°47W **82** C7
Scottville *U.S.A.* 43°58N 86°17W **80** D10
Scranton *U.S.A.* 41°25N 75°40W **83** E9
Scugog, L. *Canada* 44°10N 78°55W **82** B6
Scunthorpe *U.K.* 53°36N 0°39W **12** D7
Scutari = Shkodër
  Albania 42°4N 19°32E **23** C8
Sea Is. *U.S.A.* 31°30N 81°7W **85** F14
Seabrook, L. *Australia* 30°55S 119°40E **61** F2
Seaford *U.K.* 50°47N 0°7E **13** G8
Seaford *U.S.A.* 38°39N 75°37W **81** F16
Seaforth *Australia* 20°55S 148°57E **62** J6
Seaforth *Canada* 43°35N 81°25W **82** C3
Seaforth, L. *U.K.* 57°52N 6°36W **11** D2
Seagraves *U.S.A.* 32°57N 102°34W **84** E3
Seaham *U.K.* 54°50N 1°20W **12** C6
Seal → *Canada* 59°4N 94°48W **71** B10
Seal L. *Canada* 54°20N 61°30W **73** B7
Sealy *U.S.A.* 29°47N 96°9W **84** G6
Searchlight *U.S.A.* 35°28N 114°55W **79** K12
Searcy *U.S.A.* 35°15N 91°44W **84** D9
Searles L. *U.S.A.* 35°44N 117°21W **79** K9
Seascale *U.K.* 54°24N 3°29W **12** C4
Seaside *Calif., U.S.A.* 36°37N 121°50W **78** J5
Seaside *Oreg., U.S.A.* 46°0N 123°56W **78** E3
Seaspray *Australia* 38°25S 147°15E **63** F4
Seattle *U.S.A.* 47°36N 122°19W **78** C4
Seattle-Tacoma Int. ✈ (SEA)
  U.S.A. 47°27N 122°18W **78** C4
Seaview Ra. *Australia* 18°40S 145°45E **62** B4
Sebago L. *U.S.A.* 43°52N 70°34W **83** C14
Sebago Lake *U.S.A.* 43°51N 70°34W **83** C14
Sebastián Vizcaíno, B.
  Mexico 28°0N 114°30W **86** B2
Sebastopol = Sevastopol
  Ukraine 44°35N 33°30E **19** F5
Sebastopol *U.S.A.* 38°24N 122°49W **78** G4
Sebewaing *U.S.A.* 43°44N 83°27W **81** D12
Sebha = Sabhā *Libya* 27°9N 14°29E **51** C8
Şebinkarahisar *Turkey* 40°22N 38°28E **19** F6
Sebring *Fla., U.S.A.* 27°30N 81°27W **85** H14
Sebring *Ohio, U.S.A.* 40°55N 81°2W **82** F3
Sebringville *Canada* 43°24N 81°4W **82** C3
Sebta = Ceuta *N. Afr.* 35°52N 5°18W **21** E3
Sebuku *Indonesia* 3°30S 116°25E **36** E5
Sebuku, Teluk *Malaysia* 4°0N 118°10E **36** D5
Sechelt *Canada* 49°25N 123°42W **70** D4
Sechura, Desierto de *Peru* 6°0S 80°30W **92** E2
Secretary I. *N.Z.* 45°15S 166°56E **59** F1
Secunderabad *India* 17°28N 78°30E **40** L11
Security *U.S.A.* 38°45N 104°45W **76** G11
Sedalia *U.S.A.* 38°42N 93°14W **80** F7
Sedan *France* 49°43N 4°57E **20** B6
Sedan *U.S.A.* 37°8N 96°11W **80** G5
Sedbergh *U.K.* 54°20N 2°31W **12** C5
Seddon *N.Z.* 41°40S 174°7E **59** D5
Seddonville *N.Z.* 41°33S 172°1E **59** D4
Sedé Boqér *Israel* 30°52N 34°47E **46** E3
Sedeh *Fārs, Iran* 30°45N 52°11E **45** D7
Sedeh *Khorāsān, Iran* 33°20N 59°14E **45** C8
Séderot *Israel* 31°32N 34°37E **46** D3
Sédhiou *Senegal* 12°44N 15°30W **50** F2
Sedley *Canada* 50°10N 104°0W **71** C8
Sedona *U.S.A.* 34°52N 111°46W **77** J8
Sedro-Woolley *U.S.A.* 48°30N 122°14W **78** B4
Seeheim *Namibia* 26°50S 17°45E **56** D2
Seeis *Namibia* 22°28S 17°39E **56** C2
Seekoei → *S. Africa* 30°18S 25°1E **56** E4
Seeley's Bay *Canada* 44°29N 76°14W **83** B8
Seferihisar *Turkey* 38°10N 26°50E **23** E12
Seg-ozero *Russia* 63°20N 33°46E **18** B5
Segamat *Malaysia* 2°30N 102°50E **39** L4
Segesta *Italy* 37°56N 12°50E **22** F5
Seget *Indonesia* 1°24S 130°58E **37** E8
Segezha *Russia* 63°44N 34°19E **18** B5
Ségou *Mali* 13°30N 6°16W **50** F4
Segovia = Coco →
  Cent. Amer. 15°0N 83°8W **88** D3
Segovia *Spain* 40°57N 4°10W **21** B3
Segre → *Spain* 41°40N 0°43E **21** B6
Séguéla *Ivory C.* 7°55N 6°40W **50** G4
Seguin *U.S.A.* 29°34N 97°58W **84** G6
Segundo → *Argentina* 30°53S 62°44W **94** C3
Segura → *Spain* 38°3N 0°44W **21** C5
Seh Konj, Kūh-e *Iran* 30°6N 57°30E **45** D8
Seh Qal'eh *Iran* 33°40N 58°24E **45** C8
Sehitwa *Botswana* 20°30S 22°30E **56** C3
Sehlabathebe △ *Lesotho* 29°53S 29°7E **57** D4
Sehore *India* 23°10N 77°5E **42** H7
Sehwan *Pakistan* 26°28N 67°53E **42** F2
Seikan Tunnel *Japan* 41°28N 140°10E **30** D10
Seil *U.K.* 56°18N 5°38W **11** E3
Seiland *Norway* 70°25N 23°15E **8** A20
Seiling *U.S.A.* 36°9N 98°56W **84** C5
Seinäjoki *Finland* 62°40N 22°51E **8** E20
Seine → *France* 49°26N 0°26E **20** B4
Seine, B. de la *France* 49°40N 0°30W **20** B3
Seistan = Sīstān *Asia* 30°50N 61°0E **45** D9
Seistan, Daryācheh-ye = Sīstān,
  Daryācheh-ye *Iran* 31°0N 61°0E **45** D9

Sekayu *Indonesia* 2°51S 103°51E **36** E2
Seke *Tanzania* 3°20S 33°31E **54** C3
Sekenke *Tanzania* 4°18S 34°11E **54** C3
Sekondi-Takoradi *Ghana* 4°58N 1°45W **50** H5
Sekudai *Malaysia* 1°32N 103°39E **39** d
Sekuma *Botswana* 24°36S 23°50E **56** C3
Selah *U.S.A.* 46°39N 120°32W **76** C3
Selama *Malaysia* 5°12N 100°42E **39** K3
Selaru *Indonesia* 8°9S 131°0E **37** F8
Selatan, Selat *Malaysia* 5°15N 100°20E **39** c
Selby *U.K.* 53°47N 1°5W **12** D6
Selby *U.S.A.* 45°31N 100°2W **80** C3
Selçuk *Turkey* 37°56N 27°22E **23** F12
Selden *U.S.A.* 39°33N 100°34W **80** F3
Sele → *Italy* 40°29N 14°56E **22** D6
Selebi-Phikwe *Botswana* 21°58S 27°48E **57** C4
Selemdzha → *Russia* 51°42N 128°53E **29** D13
Selenga = Selenge Mörön →
  Asia 52°16N 106°16E **32** A5
Selenge Mörön → *Asia* 52°16N 106°16E **32** A5
Seletan, Tanjung
  Indonesia 4°10S 114°40E **36** E4
Sélibabi *Mauritania* 15°10N 12°15W **50** E3
Selîma, El Wâhât el
  Sudan 21°22N 29°19E **51** D11
Selinda Spillway →
  Botswana 18°35S 23°10E **56** B3
Selinsgrove *U.S.A.* 40°48N 76°52W **82** F8
Selkirk *Man., Canada* 50°10N 96°55W **71** C9
Selkirk *Ont., Canada* 42°49N 79°56W **82** D5
Selkirk *U.K.* 55°33N 2°50W **11** F6
Selkirk I. = Horse I.
  Canada 53°20N 99°6W **71** C9
Selkirk Mts. *Canada* 51°15N 117°40W **68** D8
Sellafield *U.K.* 54°25N 3°29W **12** C4
Sellía *Greece* 35°12N 24°23E **25** D6
Sells *U.S.A.* 31°55N 111°53W **77** L8
Selma *Ala., U.S.A.* 32°25N 87°1W **85** E11
Selma *Calif., U.S.A.* 36°34N 119°37W **78** J7
Selma *N.C., U.S.A.* 35°32N 78°17W **85** D15
Selmer *U.S.A.* 35°10N 88°36W **85** D10
Selous △ *Tanzania* 8°37S 37°42E **55** D4
Selowandoma Falls
  Zimbabwe 21°15S 31°50E **55** G3
Selpele *Indonesia* 0°1S 130°5E **37** E8
Selsey Bill *U.K.* 50°43N 0°47W **13** G7
Seltso *Russia* 53°22N 34°4E **18** D5
Selu *Indonesia* 7°32S 130°55E **37** F8
Selva *Argentina* 29°50S 62°0W **94** B3
Selva *Spain* 39°46N 2°54E **24** B9
Selva Lancandona = Montes
  Azules △ *Mexico* 16°21N 91°3W **87** D6
Selvagens, Ilhas *Madeira* 30°5N 15°55W **50** B2
Selvas *Brazil* 6°30S 67°0W **92** E5
Selwyn L. *Canada* 60°0N 104°30W **71** B8
Selwyn Mts. *Canada* 63°0N 130°0W **68** C6
Selwyn Ra. *Australia* 21°10S 140°0E **62** C3
Seman → *Albania* 40°47N 19°30E **23** D8
Semarang *Indonesia* 7°0S 110°26E **37** G14
Sembabule *Uganda* 0°4S 31°25E **54** C3
Sembawang *Singapore* 1°27N 103°50E **39** d
Sembung *Indonesia* 8°28S 115°11E **37** J18
Semenanjung Blambangan
  Indonesia 8°42S 114°29E **37** K17
Semeru *Indonesia* 8°4S 112°55E **37** H15
Semey *Kazakhstan* 50°30N 80°10E **28** D9
Seminoe Res. *U.S.A.* 42°9N 106°55W **76** E10
Seminole *Okla., U.S.A.* 35°14N 96°41W **84** D6
Seminole *Tex., U.S.A.* 32°43N 102°39W **84** E3
Seminole Draw →
  U.S.A. 32°27N 102°20W **84** E3
Semipalatinsk = Semey
  Kazakhstan 50°30N 80°10E **28** D9
Semirara Is. *Phil.* 12°0N 121°20E **37** B6
Semitau *Indonesia* 0°29N 111°57E **36** D4
Semmering P. *Austria* 47°41N 15°45E **16** E8
Semnān *Iran* 35°40N 53°23E **45** C7
Semnān ☐ *Iran* 36°0N 54°0E **45** C7
Semporna *Malaysia* 4°30N 118°33E **37** D5
Semuda *Indonesia* 2°51S 112°58E **36** E4
Sen → *Cambodia* 12°32N 104°28E **38** F5
Senā *Iran* 28°27N 51°36E **45** D6
Sena *Mozam.* 17°25S 35°0E **55** F4
Sena Madureira *Brazil* 9°5S 68°45W **92** E5
Senador Pompeu *Brazil* 5°40S 39°20W **93** E11
Senang, Pulau *Singapore* 1°11N 103°52E **39** d
Senanga *Zambia* 16°7S 23°16E **53** H4
Senatobia *U.S.A.* 34°37N 89°58W **85** D10
Sencelles *Spain* 39°39N 2°54E **24** B9
Sendai *Kagoshima, Japan* 31°50N 130°20E **31** J5
Sendai *Miyagi, Japan* 38°15N 140°53E **30** E10
Sendai-Wan *Japan* 38°15N 141°0E **30** E10
Sendhwa *India* 21°41N 75°6E **42** J6
Seneca *U.S.A.* 33°41N 82°57W **85** D13
Seneca Falls *U.S.A.* 42°55N 76°48W **83** D8
Seneca L. *U.S.A.* 42°40N 76°54W **82** D8
Senecaville L. *U.S.A.* 39°55N 81°25W **82** G3
Senegal ■ *W. Afr.* 14°30N 14°30W **50** F3
Sénégal → *W. Afr.* 15°48N 16°32W **50** E2
Senegambia *Africa* 12°45N 12°0W **48** E2
Senekal *S. Africa* 28°20S 27°36E **57** D4
Senga Hill *Zambia* 9°19S 31°11E **55** D3
Senge Khambab = Indus →
  Pakistan 24°20N 67°47E **42** G2
Sengua → *Zimbabwe* 17°7S 28°5E **55** F2
Senhor-do-Bonfim
  Brazil 10°30S 40°10W **93** F10
Senigállia *Italy* 43°43N 13°13E **22** C5
Senj *Croatia* 45°0N 14°58E **16** F8
Senja *Norway* 69°25N 17°30E **8** B17
Senkaku-Shotō
  E. China Sea 25°45N 123°30E **31** M1
Senkuang *Indonesia* 1°11N 104°2E **39** d
Senlis *France* 49°13N 2°35E **20** B5
Senmonorom *Cambodia* 12°27N 107°12E **38** F6
Senneterre *Canada* 48°25N 77°15W **72** C4

Seno *Laos* 16°35N 104°50E **38** D5
Sens *France* 48°11N 3°15E **20** B5
Senta *Serbia* 45°55N 20°3E **23** B9
Sentery = Lubao
  Dem. Rep. of the Congo 5°17S 25°42E **54** D2
Sentinel *U.S.A.* 32°52N 113°13W **77** K7
Sentosa *Singapore* 1°16N 103°50E **39** d
Seo de Urgel = La Seu d'Urgell
  Spain 42°22N 1°23E **21** A6
Seogwipo *S. Korea* 33°13N 126°34E **35** H14
Seohara *India* 29°15N 78°33E **43** E8
Seonath → *India* 21°44N 82°28E **43** J10
Seondha *India* 26°9N 78°48E **43** F8
Seongnam *S. Korea* 37°26N 127°8E **35** F14
Seoni *India* 22°5N 79°30E **43** H8
Seoni Malwa *India* 22°27N 77°28E **42** H8
Seonsan *S. Korea* 36°14N 128°17E **35** F15
Seosan *S. Korea* 36°47N 126°27E **35** F14
Seoul *S. Korea* 37°31N 126°58E **35** F14
Sepīdān *Iran* 30°20N 52°5E **45** D7
Sepo'o *N. Korea* 38°57N 127°25E **35** E14
Sepone *Laos* 16°45N 106°13E **38** D6
Sept-Îles *Canada* 50°13N 66°22W **73** B6
Sequim *U.S.A.* 48°5N 123°6W **78** B3
Sequoia △ *U.S.A.* 36°30N 118°30W **78** J8
Seraing *Belgium* 50°35N 5°32E **15** D5
Serakhis → *Cyprus* 35°13N 32°55E **25** D11
Seram *Indonesia* 3°10S 129°0E **37** E7
Seram Sea *Indonesia* 2°30S 128°30E **37** E7
Serang *Indonesia* 6°8S 106°10E **37** G12
Serangoon *Singapore* 1°23N 103°54E **39** d
Serasan *Indonesia* 2°29N 109°4E **36** D3
Serbia ☐ *Serbia* 43°30N 21°0E **23** C9
Serbia ■ *Europe* 43°20N 20°0E **23** B9
Serdar *Turkmenistan* 39°4N 56°23E **45** B8
Serdobsk *Russia* 52°28N 44°10E **18** D7
Seremban *Malaysia* 2°43N 101°53E **39** L3
Serengeti △ *Tanzania* 2°11S 35°0E **54** C3
Serengeti Plain *Tanzania* 2°40S 35°0E **54** C3
Serenje *Zambia* 13°14S 30°15E **55** E3
Sereth = Siret →
  Romania 45°24N 28°1E **17** F14
Sergeya Kirova, Ostrova
  Russia 77°30N 90°0E **29** B10
Sergino *Russia* 62°25N 65°12E **28** C7
Sergipe ☐ *Brazil* 10°30S 37°30W **93** F11
Sergiyev Posad *Russia* 56°20N 38°10E **18** C6
Serhetabat *Turkmenistan* 35°20N 62°18E **45** C9
Seria *Brunei* 4°37N 114°23E **36** D4
Serian *Malaysia* 1°10N 110°31E **36** D4
Seribu, Kepulauan
  Indonesia 5°36S 106°33E **36** F3
Sericho *Kenya* 1°5N 39°5E **54** B4
Serifos *Greece* 37°9N 24°30E **23** F11
Sérigny → *Canada* 56°47N 66°0W **73** A6
Seringapatam Reef
  Australia 13°38S 122°5E **60** B3
Seririt *Indonesia* 8°12S 114°56E **37** J17
Sermata *Indonesia* 8°15S 128°50E **37** F7
Sermersuaq *Greenland* 79°30N 62°0W **4** B4
Serov *Russia* 59°29N 60°35E **18** C11
Serowe *Botswana* 22°25S 26°43E **56** C4
Serpentine Lakes
  Australia 28°30S 129°10E **61** E4
Serpent's Mouth = Sierpe, Bocas
  de la *Venezuela* 10°0N 61°30W **93** L15
Serpukhov *Russia* 54°55N 37°28E **18** D6
Serra do Navio *Brazil* 0°59N 52°3W **93** C8
Serranía San Luís △
  Paraguay 22°35S 57°22W **94** A4
Serranía San Rafael △
  Paraguay 26°30S 56°0W **95** B4
Serres *Greece* 41°5N 23°31E **23** D10
Serrezuela *Argentina* 30°40S 65°20W **94** C2
Serrinha *Brazil* 11°39S 39°0W **93** F11
Sertanópolis *Brazil* 23°4S 51°2W **95** A5
Serua *Indonesia* 6°18S 130°1E **37** F8
Serui *Indonesia* 1°53S 136°10E **37** E9
Serule *Botswana* 21°57S 27°20E **56** C4
Ses Salines *Spain* 39°21N 3°3E **24** B10
Sese Is. *Uganda* 0°20S 32°20E **54** C3
Sesepe *Indonesia* 1°30S 127°59E **37** E7
Sesfontein *Namibia* 19°7S 13°39E **56** B1
Sesheke *Zambia* 17°29S 24°13E **56** B3
S'Espalmador *Spain* 38°47N 1°26E **24** C7
S'Espardell *Spain* 38°48N 1°29E **24** C7
S'Estanyol *Spain* 39°22N 2°54E **24** B9
Setana *Japan* 42°26N 139°51E **30** C9
Sète *France* 43°25N 3°42E **20** E5
Sete Lagoas *Brazil* 19°27S 44°16W **93** G10
Sétif *Algeria* 36°9N 5°26E **50** A7
Seto *Japan* 35°14N 137°6E **31** G8
Setonaikai *Japan* 34°20N 133°30E **31** G6
Setonaikai △ *Japan* 34°15N 133°15E **31** G6
Settat *Morocco* 33°0N 7°40W **50** B4
Setting L. *Canada* 55°0N 98°38W **71** C9
Settle *U.K.* 54°5N 2°16W **12** C5
Settlement, The
  Br. Virgin Is. 18°43N 64°22W **89** e
Settlers *S. Africa* 25°2S 28°30E **57** C4
Setúbal *Portugal* 38°30N 8°58W **21** C1
Setúbal, B. de *Portugal* 38°40N 8°56W **21** C1
Seul, Lac *Canada* 50°20N 92°30W **72** B1
Sevan, Ozero = Sevana Lich
  Armenia 40°30N 45°20E **44** A5
Sevana Lich *Armenia* 40°30N 45°20E **44** A5
Sevastopol *Ukraine* 44°35N 33°30E **19** F5
Seven Sisters *Canada* 54°56N 128°10W **70** C3
Severn → *Canada* 56°2N 87°36W **72** A2
Severn → *U.K.* 51°35N 2°40W **13** F5
Severnaya Zemlya
  Russia 79°0N 100°0E **29** B11
Severnyye Uvaly *Russia* 60°0N 50°0E **18** C8
Severo-Kurilsk *Russia* 50°40N 156°8E **29** D16
Severo-Yeniseyskiy
  Russia 60°22N 93°1E **29** C10

Severo-Zapadnyy □ Russia 65°0N 40°0E 28 C4
Severobaykalsk
  Russia 55°39N 109°19E 29 D11
Severodvinsk Russia 64°27N 39°58E 18 B6
Severomorsk Russia 69°5N 33°27E 8 B25
Severouralsk Russia 60°9N 59°57E 18 B10
Seversk Russia 56°36N 84°49E 28 D9
Sevier → U.S.A. 39°4N 113°6W 76 G7
Sevier Desert U.S.A. 39°40N 112°45W 76 G7
Sevier L. U.S.A. 38°54N 113°9W 76 G7
Sevilla Spain 37°23N 5°58W 21 D2
Seville = Sevilla Spain 37°23N 5°58W 21 D2
Sevlievo Bulgaria 43°2N 25°6E 23 C11
Sewani India 28°58N 75°39E 42 E6
Seward Alaska, U.S.A. 60°7N 149°27W 68 C5
Seward Nebr., U.S.A. 40°55N 97°6W 80 E5
Seward Pa., U.S.A. 40°25N 79°1W 82 F7
Seward Peninsula U.S.A. 65°30N 166°0W 74 a
Sewell Chile 34°10S 70°23W 94 C1
Sewer Indonesia 5°53S 134°40E 37 F8
Seychelles ■ Ind. Oc. 5°0S 56°0E 53 b
Seyðisfjörður Iceland 65°16N 13°57W 8 D7
Seydişehir Turkey 37°25N 31°51E 19 G5
Seydvān Iran 38°34N 45°2E 44 B5
Seyhan → Turkey 36°43N 34°53E 44 B2
Seym → Ukraine 51°27N 32°34E 19 D5
Seymour Australia 37°2S 145°10E 63 F4
Seymour S. Africa 32°33S 26°46E 57 E4
Seymour Conn., U.S.A. 41°24N 73°4W 83 E11
Seymour Ind., U.S.A. 38°58N 85°53W 81 F11
Seymour Tex., U.S.A. 33°35N 99°16W 84 E5
Sfântu Gheorghe
  Romania 45°52N 25°48E 17 F13
Sfax Tunisia 34°49N 10°48E 51 B8
Sha Tau Kok China 22°33N 114°13E 33 F11
Sha Tin China 22°23N 114°12E 33 G11
Shaanxi □ China 35°0N 109°0E 34 G5
Shaba = Katanga □
  Dem. Rep. of the Congo 8°0S 25°0E 54 D2
Shaba △ Kenya 0°38N 37°48E 54 B4
Shabeelle → Somali Rep. 2°0N 44°0E 47 G3
Shabogamo L. Canada 53°15N 66°30W 73 B6
Shabunda
  Dem. Rep. of the Congo 2°40S 27°16E 54 C2
Shache China 38°20N 77°10E 32 C2
Shackleton Fracture Zone
  S. Ocean 60°0S 60°0W 5 B18
Shackleton Ice Shelf
  Antarctica 66°0S 100°0E 5 C8
Shackleton Inlet
  Antarctica 83°0S 160°0E 5 E11
Shādegān Iran 30°40N 48°38E 45 D6
Shadi India 33°24N 77°14E 43 C7
Shadrinsk Russia 56°5N 63°32E 28 D7
Shadyside U.S.A. 39°58N 80°45W 82 G4
Shafter U.S.A. 35°30N 119°16W 79 K7
Shaftesbury U.K. 51°0N 2°11W 13 F5
Shaftsbury U.S.A. 43°0N 73°11W 83 D11
Shagram Pakistan 36°24N 72°20E 43 A5
Shah Alam Malaysia 3°5N 101°32E 39 L3
Shah Alizai Pakistan 29°25N 66°33E 42 E2
Shah Bunder Pakistan 24°13N 67°56E 42 G2
Shahabad Punjab, India 30°10N 76°55E 42 D7
Shahabad Raj., India 25°15N 77°11E 42 G7
Shahabad Ut. P., India 27°36N 79°56E 43 F8
Shahadpur Pakistan 25°55N 68°35E 42 G3
Shahbā' Syria 32°52N 36°38E 46 C5
Shahdād Iran 30°30N 57°40E 45 D8
Shahdād, Namakzār-e
  Iran 30°20N 58°20E 45 D8
Shahdadkot Pakistan 27°50N 67°55E 42 F2
Shahdol India 23°19N 81°26E 43 H9
Shahe China 37°0N 114°32E 34 F8
Shahganj India 26°3N 82°44E 43 F10
Shahgarh India 27°15N 69°50E 42 F3
Shahjahanpur India 27°54N 79°57E 43 F8
Shahpur = Salmās Iran 38°11N 44°47E 44 B5
Shahpur India 22°12N 77°58E 42 H7
Shahpur Baluchistan,
  Pakistan 28°46N 68°27E 42 E3
Shahpur Punjab, Pakistan 32°17N 72°26E 42 C5
Shahpur Chakar Pakistan 26°9N 68°39E 42 F3
Shahpura Mad. P., India 23°10N 80°45E 43 H9
Shahpura Raj., India 25°38N 74°56E 42 G6
Shahr-e Bābak Iran 30°7N 55°9E 45 D7
Shahr-e Kord Iran 32°15N 50°55E 45 C6
Shāhrakht Iran 33°38N 60°16E 45 C9
Shahrezā = Qomsheh
  Iran 32°0N 51°55E 45 D6
Shahrig Pakistan 30°15N 67°40E 42 D2
Shāhrūd = Emāmrūd
  Iran 36°30N 55°0E 45 B7
Shahukou China 40°20N 112°18E 34 D7
Shaikhabad Afghan. 34°2N 68°45E 42 B3
Shajapur India 23°27N 76°21E 42 H7
Shajing China 22°44N 113°48E 33 F10
Shakargarh Pakistan 32°17N 75°10E 42 C6
Shakawe Botswana 18°28N 21°49E 56 B3
Shaker Heights U.S.A. 41°28N 81°32W 82 E3
Shakhtersk Russia 49°10N 142°8E 29 E15
Shakhty Russia 47°40N 40°16E 19 E7
Shakhunya Russia 57°40N 46°46E 18 C8
Shaki Nigeria 8°41N 3°21E 50 G6
Shaksam Valley Asia 36°0N 76°20E 43 A6
Shallow Lake Canada 44°36N 81°5W 82 B3
Shalqar Kazakhstan 47°48N 59°39E 28 E6
Shaluli Shan China 30°40N 99°55E 32 C4
Shām Iran 26°39N 57°21E 45 E8
Shām, Bādiyat ash Asia 32°0N 40°0E 44 C3
Shamâl Sînî □ Egypt 30°0N 34°0E 46 E2
Shamattawa Canada 55°51N 92°5W 72 A1
Shamattawa → Canada 55°1N 85°23W 72 A2
Shamīl Iran 29°32N 56°55E 45 D8
Shāmkūh Iran 35°47N 57°50E 45 C8
Shamli India 29°32N 77°18E 42 E7

Shammar, Jabal Si. Arabia 27°40N 41°0E 44 E4
Shamo = Gobi Asia 44°0N 110°0E 34 C6
Shamo, L. Ethiopia 5°45N 37°30E 47 F2
Shamokin U.S.A. 40°47N 76°34W 83 F8
Shamrock Canada 45°23N 76°50W 83 A8
Shamrock U.S.A. 35°13N 100°15W 84 D4
Shamva Zimbabwe 17°20S 31°32E 55 F3
Shan □ Burma 21°30N 98°30E 41 J21
Shan Xian China 34°50N 116°5E 34 G9
Shanchengzhen China 42°20N 125°20E 35 C13
Shāndak Iran 28°28N 60°27E 45 D9
Shandon U.S.A. 35°39N 120°23W 78 K6
Shandong □ China 36°0N 118°0E 35 G10
Shandong Bandao China 37°0N 121°0E 35 F11
Shandur Pass Pakistan 36°4N 72°31E 43 A5
Shang Xian = Shangzhou
  China 33°50N 109°58E 34 H5
Shangalowe
  Dem. Rep. of the Congo 10°50S 26°30E 55 E2
Shangani Zimbabwe 19°41S 29°20E 57 B4
Shangani → Zimbabwe 18°41S 27°10E 55 F2
Shangbancheng China 40°50N 118°1E 35 D10
Shangdu China 41°30N 113°30E 34 D7
Shanghai China 31°15N 121°26E 33 C7
Shanghe China 37°20N 117°10E 35 F9
Shangnan China 33°32N 110°50E 34 H6
Shangqiu China 34°26N 115°36E 34 G8
Shangrao China 28°25N 117°59E 33 D6
Shangshui China 33°42N 114°35E 33 C6
Shangzhi China 45°22N 127°56E 35 B14
Shangzhou China 33°50N 109°58E 34 H5
Shanhetun China 44°33N 127°15E 35 B14
Shanklin U.K. 50°38N 1°11W 13 G6
Shannon N.Z. 40°33S 175°25E 59 D5
Shannon → Ireland 52°35N 9°30W 10 D2
Shannon ✈ (SNN)
  Ireland 52°42N 8°57W 10 D3
Shannon, Mouth of the
  Ireland 52°30N 9°55W 10 D2
Shannon △ Australia 34°35S 116°25E 61 F2
Shannonbridge Ireland 53°17N 8°3W 10 C3
Shansi = Shanxi □ China 37°0N 112°0E 34 F7
Shantipur India 23°17N 88°25E 43 H13
Shantou China 23°18N 116°40E 33 D6
Shantung = Shandong □
  China 36°0N 118°0E 35 G10
Shanxi □ China 37°0N 112°0E 34 F7
Shanyang China 33°31N 109°55E 34 H5
Shanyin China 39°25N 112°56E 34 E7
Shaoguan China 24°48N 113°35E 33 D6
Shaoxing China 30°0N 120°35E 33 D7
Shaoyang China 27°14N 111°25E 33 D6
Shap U.K. 54°32N 2°40W 12 C5
Shapinsay U.K. 59°3N 2°51W 11 B6
Shaqra' Si. Arabia 25°15N 45°16E 44 E5
Shaqra' Yemen 13°22N 45°44E 47 E4
Sharafkhāneh Iran 38°11N 45°29E 44 B5
Sharbot Lake Canada 44°46N 76°41W 83 B8
Shari Japan 43°55N 144°40E 30 C12
Sharjah = Ash Shāriqah
  U.A.E. 25°23N 55°26E 45 E7
Shark B. Australia 25°30S 113°32E 61 E1
Shark Bay △ Australia 25°30S 113°30E 61 E1
Sharm el Sheikh Egypt 27°53N 34°18E 51 C12
Sharon Canada 44°6N 79°26E 82 B5
Sharon Mass., U.S.A. 42°7N 71°11W 83 D13
Sharon Pa., U.S.A. 41°14N 80°31W 82 E4
Sharon Springs Kans.,
  U.S.A. 38°54N 101°45W 80 F3
Sharon Springs N.Y.,
  U.S.A. 42°48N 74°37W 83 D10
Sharp Pt. Australia 10°58S 142°43E 62 A3
Sharpe L. Canada 54°24N 93°40W 72 B1
Sharpsville U.S.A. 41°15N 80°29W 82 E4
Sharqi, Al Jabal ash
  Lebanon 33°40N 36°10E 46 B5
Sharya Russia 58°22N 45°20E 18 C8
Shashemene Ethiopia 7°13N 38°33E 47 F2
Shashi Botswana 21°15S 27°27E 57 C4
Shashi China 30°25N 112°14E 33 C6
Shashi → Africa 21°14S 29°20E 55 G2
Shasta, Mt. U.S.A. 41°25N 122°12W 76 F2
Shasta L. U.S.A. 40°43N 122°25W 76 F2
Shatsky Rise Pac. Oc. 34°0N 157°0E 64 D7
Shatt al Arab Asia 29°57N 48°34E 45 D6
Shaunavon Canada 49°35N 108°25W 71 D7
Shaver L. U.S.A. 37°9N 119°18W 78 H7
Shaw → Australia 20°21S 119°17E 60 D2
Shaw I. Australia 20°30S 149°2E 62 J7
Shawanaga Canada 45°31N 80°17W 82 A4
Shawangunk Mts.
  U.S.A. 41°35N 74°30W 83 E10
Shawano U.S.A. 44°47N 88°36W 80 C9
Shawinigan Canada 46°35N 72°50W 72 C5
Shawmari, J. ash Jordan 30°35N 36°35E 46 E5
Shawnee U.S.A. 35°20N 96°55W 84 D6
Shay Gap Australia 20°30S 120°10E 60 D3
Shaybārā Si. Arabia 25°26N 36°47E 44 E3
Shaykh, J. ash Lebanon 33°25N 35°50E 46 B4
Shaykh Miskīn Syria 32°49N 36°9E 46 C5
Shaykh Sa'd Iraq 32°34N 46°17E 44 C5
Shāzand Iran 33°56N 49°24E 45 C6
She Xian China 36°30N 113°40E 34 F7
Shebele = Shabeelle →
  Somali Rep. 2°0N 44°0E 47 G3
Sheboygan U.S.A. 43°46N 87°45W 80 D10
Shediac Canada 46°14N 64°32W 73 C7
Sheelin, L. Ireland 53°48N 7°20W 10 C4
Sheep Haven Ireland 55°11N 7°52W 10 A4
Sheep Range U.S.A. 36°35S 115°15W 79 J11
Sheerness U.K. 51°26N 0°47E 13 F8
Sheet Harbour Canada 44°56N 62°31W 73 D7
Sheffield U.K. 53°23N 1°28W 12 D6
Sheffield Ala., U.S.A. 34°46N 87°41W 85 D11

Sheffield Mass., U.S.A. 42°5N 73°21W 83 D11
Sheffield Pa., U.S.A. 41°42N 79°3W 82 E5
Sheikhpura India 25°9N 85°53E 43 G11
Shekhupura Pakistan 31°42N 73°58E 42 D5
Shekou China 22°30N 113°55E 33 G10
Shelburne N.S., Canada 43°47N 65°20W 73 D6
Shelburne Ont., Canada 44°4N 80°15W 82 B4
Shelburne U.S.A. 44°23N 73°14W 83 B11
Shelburne B. Australia 11°50S 142°50E 62 A3
Shelburne Falls U.S.A. 42°36N 72°45W 83 D12
Shelby Mich., U.S.A. 43°37N 86°22W 80 D10
Shelby Miss., U.S.A. 33°57N 90°46W 85 E9
Shelby Mont., U.S.A. 48°30N 111°51W 76 B8
Shelby N.C., U.S.A. 35°17N 81°32W 85 D14
Shelby Ohio, U.S.A. 40°53N 82°40W 82 F2
Shelbyville Ill., U.S.A. 39°24N 88°48W 80 F9
Shelbyville Ind., U.S.A. 39°31N 85°47W 81 F11
Shelbyville Ky., U.S.A. 38°13N 85°14W 81 F11
Shelbyville Tenn.,
  U.S.A. 35°29N 86°28W 85 D11
Sheldon U.S.A. 43°11N 95°51W 80 D6
Sheldrake Canada 50°20N 64°51W 73 B7
Shelikhova, Zaliv
  Russia 59°30N 157°0E 29 D16
Shell Lakes Australia 29°20S 127°30E 61 E4
Shellbrook Canada 53°13N 106°24W 71 C7
Shellharbour Australia 34°31S 150°51E 63 E5
Shelter I. U.S.A. 41°4N 72°20W 83 E12
Shelton Conn., U.S.A. 41°19N 73°5W 83 E11
Shelton Wash., U.S.A. 47°13N 123°6W 78 C3
Shen Xian China 36°15N 115°40E 34 F8
Shenandoah Iowa,
  U.S.A. 40°46N 95°22W 80 E6
Shenandoah Pa., U.S.A. 40°49N 76°12W 83 F8
Shenandoah Va.,
  U.S.A. 38°29N 78°37W 81 F14
Shenandoah → U.S.A. 39°19N 77°44W 81 F15
Shenandoah △ U.S.A. 38°35N 78°22W 81 F14
Shenchi China 39°8N 112°10E 34 E7
Shendam Nigeria 8°49N 9°30E 50 G7
Shendi Sudan 16°46N 33°22E 51 E12
Shengfang China 39°3N 116°42E 34 E9
Shenjingzi China 44°40N 124°30E 35 B13
Shenmu China 38°50N 110°29E 34 E6
Shenqiu China 33°25N 115°5E 34 H8
Shensi = Shaanxi □
  China 35°0N 109°0E 34 G5
Shenyang China 41°48N 123°27E 35 D12
Shenzhen China 22°32N 114°5E 33 F10
Shenzhen ✈ (SZX)
  China 22°41N 113°49E 33 F10
Shenzhen Shuiku China 22°34N 114°8E 33 F11
Shenzhen Wan China 22°27N 113°55E 33 G10
Sheo India 26°11N 71°15E 42 F4
Sheopur Kalan India 25°40N 76°40E 42 G7
Shepetivka Ukraine 50°10N 27°10E 17 C14
Shepparton Australia 36°23S 145°26E 63 F4
Sheppey, I. of U.K. 51°25N 0°48E 13 F8
Shepton Mallet U.K. 51°11N 2°33W 13 F5
Sheqi China 33°12N 112°57E 34 H7
Sher Dira Pakistan 36°7N 74°2E 43 A6
Sherborne U.K. 50°57N 2°31W 13 G5
Sherbro I. S. Leone 7°30N 12°40W 50 G3
Sherbrooke N.S., Canada 45°8N 61°59W 73 C7
Sherbrooke Qué.,
  Canada 45°28N 71°57W 83 A13
Sherburne U.S.A. 42°41N 75°30W 83 D9
Shergarh India 26°20N 72°18E 42 F5
Sherghati India 24°34N 84°47E 43 G11
Sheridan Ark., U.S.A. 34°19N 92°24W 84 D8
Sheridan Wyo., U.S.A. 44°48N 106°58W 76 D10
Sheringham U.K. 52°56N 1°13E 12 E9
Sherkin I. Ireland 51°28N 9°26W 10 E2
Sherkot India 29°22N 78°35E 43 E8
Sherlovaya Gora
  Russia 50°34N 116°15E 29 D12
Sherman N.Y., U.S.A. 42°9N 79°35W 82 D5
Sherman Tex., U.S.A. 33°38N 96°36W 84 E6
Sherpur India 25°34N 83°47E 43 G10
Sherridon Canada 55°8N 101°5W 71 B8
Sherwood Forest U.K. 53°6N 1°7W 12 D6
Sherwood Park Canada 53°31N 113°19W 70 C6
Sheslay → Canada 58°48N 132°5W 70 B2
Shethanei L. Canada 58°48N 97°50W 71 B9
Shetland □ U.K. 60°30N 1°30W 11 A7
Shetland Is. U.K. 60°30N 1°30W 11 A7
Shetrunji → India 21°19N 72°7E 42 J5
Sheung Shui China 22°31N 114°7E 33 F11
Shey-Phoksundo △
  Nepal 29°30N 82°45E 43 E10
Sheyenne → U.S.A. 47°2N 96°50W 80 B5
Shiashkotan, Ostrov
  Russia 48°49N 154°6E 29 E16
Shibām Yemen 15°59N 48°36E 47 D4
Shibata Japan 37°57N 139°20E 30 F9
Shibecha Japan 43°17N 144°36E 30 C12
Shibetsu Japan 44°10N 142°23E 30 B11
Shibogama L. Canada 53°35N 88°15W 72 B2
Shibushi Japan 31°25N 131°8E 31 J5
Shickshinny U.S.A. 41°9N 76°9W 83 E8
Shickshock Mts. = Chic-Chocs,
  Mts. Canada 48°55N 66°0W 73 C6
Shidao China 36°50N 122°25E 35 F12
Shido Japan 34°19N 134°10E 31 G7
Shiel, L. U.K. 56°48N 5°34W 11 E3
Shield, C. Australia 13°20S 136°20E 62 A2
Shīeli Kazakhstan 44°20N 66°15E 28 E7
Shiga □ Japan 35°20N 136°0E 31 G8
Shiguaigou China 40°52N 110°15E 34 D6
Shihchiachuangi = Shijiazhuang
  China 38°2N 114°28E 34 E8
Shihezi China 44°15N 86°2E 32 B3
Shijiazhuang China 38°2N 114°28E 34 E8
Shikarpur India 28°17N 78°7E 42 E8
Shikarpur Pakistan 27°57N 68°39E 42 F3
Shikohabad India 27°6N 78°36E 43 F8
Shikoku □ Japan 33°30N 133°30E 31 H6

Shikoku-Sanchi Japan 33°30N 133°30E 31 H6
Shikotan, Ostrov Asia 43°47N 146°44E 29 E15
Shikotsu-Ko Japan 42°45N 141°25E 30 C10
Shikotsu-Tōya △ Japan 44°4N 145°8E 30 C10
Shiliguri India 26°45N 88°25E 41 F16
Shiliu = Changjiang
  China 19°20N 108°55E 38 C7
Shilka Russia 52°0N 115°55E 29 D12
Shilka → Russia 53°20N 121°26E 29 D13
Shillelagh Ireland 52°45N 6°32W 10 D5
Shillington U.S.A. 40°18N 75°58W 83 F9
Shillong India 25°35N 91°53E 41 G17
Shilo West Bank 32°4N 35°18E 46 C4
Shilou China 37°0N 110°48E 34 F6
Shimabara Japan 32°48N 130°20E 31 H5
Shimada Japan 34°49N 138°10E 31 G9
Shimane □ Japan 35°0N 132°30E 31 G6
Shimanovsk Russia 52°15N 127°30E 29 D13
Shimizu Japan 35°0N 138°30E 31 G9
Shimla India 31°2N 77°9E 42 D7
Shimodate Japan 36°20N 139°55E 31 F9
Shimoga India 13°57N 75°32E 40 N9
Shimoni Kenya 4°38S 39°20E 54 C4
Shimonoseki Japan 33°58N 130°55E 31 H5
Shimpuru Rapids
  Namibia 17°45S 19°55E 56 B2
Shin, L. U.K. 58°5N 4°30W 11 C4
Shinano-Gawa →
  Japan 36°50N 138°30E 31 F9
Shināş Oman 24°46N 56°28E 45 E8
Shindand Afghan. 33°12N 62°8E 40 C3
Shinglehouse U.S.A. 41°58N 78°12W 82 E6
Shingū Japan 33°40N 135°55E 31 H7
Shingwidzi S. Africa 23°5S 31°25E 57 C5
Shinjō Japan 38°46N 140°18E 30 E10
Shinkolobwe
  Dem. Rep. of the Congo 11°10S 26°40E 52 G5
Shinshār Syria 34°36N 36°43E 46 A5
Shinyanga Tanzania 3°45S 33°27E 54 C3
Shinyanga □ Tanzania 3°50S 34°0E 54 C3
Shio-no-Misaki Japan 33°25N 135°45E 31 H7
Shiogama Japan 38°19N 141°1E 30 E10
Shiojiri Japan 36°6N 137°58E 31 F8
Shipchenski Prokhod
  Bulgaria 42°45N 25°15E 23 C11
Shiping China 23°45N 102°23E 32 D5
Shippagan Canada 47°45N 64°45W 73 C7
Shippensburg U.S.A. 40°3N 77°31W 82 F7
Shippenville U.S.A. 41°15N 79°28W 82 E5
Shiprock U.S.A. 36°47N 108°41W 77 H9
Shiqma, N. → Israel 31°37N 34°30E 46 D3
Shiquan China 33°5N 108°15E 34 H5
Shiquan He = Indus →
  Pakistan 24°20N 67°47E 42 G2
Shīr Kūh Iran 31°39N 54°3E 45 D7
Shiragami-Misaki
  Japan 41°24N 140°12E 30 D10
Shirakawa Fukushima,
  Japan 37°7N 140°13E 31 F10
Shirakawa Gifu, Japan 36°17N 136°56E 31 F8
Shirane-San Gumma,
  Japan 36°48N 139°22E 31 F9
Shirane-San Yamanashi,
  Japan 35°42N 138°9E 31 G9
Shiraoi Japan 42°33N 141°21E 30 C10
Shīrāz Iran 29°42N 52°30E 45 D7
Shire → Africa 17°42S 35°19E 55 F4
Shiretoko-Misaki
  Japan 44°21N 145°20E 30 B12
Shirinab → Pakistan 30°15N 66°28E 42 D2
Shiriya-Zaki Japan 41°25N 141°30E 30 D10
Shiroishi Japan 38°0N 140°37E 30 F10
Shirshov Ridge Pac. Oc. 58°0N 170°0E 64 B8
Shīrvān Iran 37°30N 57°50E 45 B8
Shirwa, L. = Chilwa, L.
  Malawi 15°15S 35°40E 55 F4
Shivpuri India 25°26N 77°42E 42 G7
Shixian China 43°5N 129°50E 35 C15
Shiyan China 32°42N 113°56E 33 F10
Shiyan Shuiku China 22°42N 113°54E 33 F10
Shizuishan China 39°15N 106°50E 34 E4
Shizuoka Japan 34°57N 138°24E 31 G9
Shizuoka □ Japan 35°15N 138°40E 31 G9
Shklov = Shklow
  Belarus 54°16N 30°15E 17 A16
Shklow Belarus 54°16N 30°15E 17 A16
Shkodër Albania 42°4N 19°32E 23 C8
Shkumbini → Albania 41°2N 19°31E 23 D8
Shmidta, Ostrov Russia 81°0N 91°0E 29 A10
Shō-Gawa → Japan 36°47N 137°4E 31 F8
Shoal L. Canada 49°33N 95°1W 71 D9
Shoal Lake Canada 50°30N 100°35W 71 C8
Shōdo-Shima Japan 34°30N 134°15E 31 G7
Sholapur = Solapur
  India 17°43N 75°56E 40 L9
Shomron West Bank 32°15N 35°13E 46 C4
Shoreham U.S.A. 43°53N 73°18W 83 C11
Shoreham by Sea U.K. 50°50N 0°16W 13 G7
Shori → Pakistan 28°29N 69°44E 42 E3
Shorkot Road Pakistan 30°47N 72°15E 42 D5
Shoshone Calif.,
  U.S.A. 35°58N 116°16W 79 K10
Shoshone Idaho, U.S.A. 42°56N 114°25W 76 E6
Shoshone L. U.S.A. 44°22N 110°43W 76 D8
Shoshone Mts. U.S.A. 39°20N 117°25W 76 G5
Shoshong Botswana 22°56S 26°31E 56 C4
Shoshoni U.S.A. 43°14N 108°7W 76 E9
Shouguang China 37°52N 118°45E 35 F10
Shouyang China 37°54N 113°8E 34 F7
Show Low U.S.A. 34°15N 110°2W 77 J8
Shqipëria = Albania ■
  Europe 41°0N 20°0E 23 D9
Shreveport U.S.A. 32°31N 93°45W 84 E8
Shrewsbury U.K. 52°43N 2°45W 13 E5
Shri Mohangarh India 27°17N 71°18E 42 F4

Shrirampur India 22°44N 88°21E 43 H13
Shropshire □ U.K. 52°36N 2°45W 13 E5
Shū Kazakhstan 43°36N 73°42E 28 E8
Shuangcheng China 45°20N 126°15E 35 B14
Shuanggou China 34°2N 117°30E 35 G9
Shuangliao China 43°29N 123°30E 35 C12
Shuangshanzi China 40°20N 119°8E 35 D10
Shuangyang China 43°28N 125°40E 35 C13
Shuangyashan China 46°28N 131°5E 33 B8
Shuguri Falls Tanzania 8°33S 37°22E 55 D4
Shuiye China 36°7N 114°8E 34 F8
Shujalpur India 23°18N 76°46E 42 H7
Shukpa Kunzang India 34°22N 78°22E 43 B8
Shulan China 44°28N 127°0E 35 B14
Shule China 39°25N 76°3E 32 C2
Shule He → China 40°20N 92°50E 32 B4
Shumagin Is. U.S.A. 55°7N 160°30W 74 a
Shumen Bulgaria 43°18N 26°55E 23 C12
Shumikha Russia 55°10N 63°15E 28 D7
Shuo Xian = Shuozhou
  China 39°20N 112°33E 34 E7
Shuozhou China 39°20N 112°33E 34 E7
Shūr → Fārs, Iran 28°30N 55°0E 45 D7
Shūr → Kermān, Iran 30°52N 57°37E 45 D8
Shūr → Yazd, Iran 31°45N 55°15E 45 D7
Shūr Āb Iran 34°23N 51°11E 45 C6
Shūr Gaz Iran 29°10N 59°20E 45 D8
Shūrāb Iran 33°43N 56°29E 45 C8
Shūrjestān Iran 31°24N 52°25E 45 D7
Shurugwi Zimbabwe 19°40S 30°0E 55 F3
Shūsf Iran 31°50N 60°5E 45 D9
Shūshtar Iran 32°0N 48°50E 45 D6
Shuswap L. Canada 50°55N 119°3W 70 C5
Shuyang China 34°10N 118°42E 35 G10
Shūzū Iran 29°52N 54°30E 45 D7
Shwebo Burma 22°30N 95°45E 41 H19
Shwegu Burma 24°15N 96°26E 41 G20
Shweli → Burma 23°45N 96°45E 41 H20
Shymkent Kazakhstan 42°18N 69°36E 28 E7
Shyok India 34°13N 78°12E 43 B8
Shyok → Pakistan 35°13N 75°53E 43 B6
Si Kiang = Xi Jiang →
  China 22°5N 113°20E 33 D6
Si Lanna △ Thailand 19°17N 99°12E 38 C2
Si Nakarin Res. Thailand 14°35N 99°0E 38 E2
Si Prachan Thailand 14°37N 100°9E 38 E3
Si Racha Thailand 13°10N 100°48E 38 F3
Si Xian China 33°30N 117°50E 35 H9
Siachen Glacier Asia 35°20N 77°30E 43 B7
Siahaf → Pakistan 29°3N 68°57E 42 E3
Siahan Range Pakistan 27°30N 64°40E 40 F4
Siaksriindrapura
  Indonesia 0°51N 102°0E 36 D2
Sialkot Pakistan 32°32N 74°30E 42 C6
Siam = Thailand ■ Asia 16°0N 102°0E 38 E4
Sian = Xi'an China 34°15N 109°0E 34 G5
Sian Ka'an △ Mexico 19°35N 87°40W 87 D7
Siantan Indonesia 3°10N 106°15E 36 D3
Siäreh Iran 28°5N 60°14E 45 D9
Siargao I. Phil. 9°52N 126°3E 37 C7
Siari Pakistan 34°55N 76°40E 43 B7
Siasi Phil. 5°34N 120°50E 37 C6
Siau Indonesia 2°50N 125°25E 37 D7
Šiauliai Lithuania 55°56N 23°15E 9 J20
Sibâi, Gebel el Egypt 25°45N 34°10E 44 E2
Sibang Indonesia 8°34S 115°13E 37 K18
Sibay Russia 52°42N 58°39E 18 D10
Sibayi, L. S. Africa 27°20S 32°45E 57 D5
Šibenik Croatia 43°48N 15°54E 22 C6
Siberia = Sibirskiy □
  Russia 58°0N 90°0E 29 D10
Siberia Russia 60°0N 100°0E 4 D13
Siberut Indonesia 1°30S 99°0E 36 E1
Sibi Pakistan 29°30N 67°54E 42 E2
Sibil = Oksibil Indonesia 4°59S 140°35E 37 E10
Sibiloi △ Kenya 4°0N 36°20E 54 B4
Sibirskiy □ Russia 58°0N 90°0E 29 D10
Sibirtsevo Russia 44°12N 132°26E 30 B5
Sibiti Congo 3°38S 13°19E 52 E2
Sibiu Romania 45°45N 24°9E 17 F13
Sibley U.S.A. 43°24N 95°45W 80 D6
Sibolga Indonesia 1°42N 98°45E 36 D1
Siborongborong Indonesia 2°13N 98°59E 39 L2
Sibsagar India 27°0N 94°36E 41 F19
Sibu Malaysia 2°18N 111°49E 36 D4
Sibuco Phil. 7°20N 122°10E 37 C6
Sibuguey B. Phil. 7°50N 122°45E 37 C6
Sibut C.A.R. 5°46N 19°10E 52 C3
Sibutu Phil. 4°45N 119°30E 37 D5
Sibutu Passage E. Indies 4°50N 120°0E 37 D5
Sibuyan I. Phil. 12°25N 122°40E 37 B6
Sibuyan Sea Phil. 12°30N 122°20E 37 B6
Sicamous Canada 50°49N 119°0W 70 C5
Siccus → Australia 31°55S 139°17E 63 E2
Sichon Thailand 9°0N 99°54E 39 H2
Sichuan □ China 30°30N 103°0E 32 C5
Sicilia Italy 37°30N 14°30E 22 F6
Sicily = Sicilia Italy 37°30N 14°30E 22 F6
Sicily, Str. of Medit. S. 37°35N 11°56E 22 F4
Sico → Honduras 15°58N 84°58W 88 C3
Sicuani Peru 14°21S 71°10W 92 F4
Sidari Greece 39°47N 19°41E 25 A3
Siddhapur India 23°56N 72°25E 42 H5
Siddipet India 18°5N 78°51E 40 K11
Sideros, Akra Greece 35°19N 26°19E 25 D8
Sidhauli India 27°17N 80°50E 43 F9
Sidhi India 24°25N 81°53E 43 G9
Sidi-bel-Abbès Algeria 35°13N 0°39W 50 A5
Sidi Ifni Morocco 29°29N 10°12W 50 C3
Sidikalang Indonesia 2°45N 98°19E 39 L2
Sidlaw Hills U.K. 56°32N 3°2W 11 E5
Sidley, Mt. Antarctica 77°2S 126°2W 5 D14
Sidmouth U.K. 50°40N 3°15W 13 G4
Sidmouth, C. Australia 31°55S 139°17E 63 E2
Sidney Canada 48°39N 123°24W 78 B3
Sidney Mont., U.S.A. 47°43N 104°9W 76 C11

Sidney *N.Y., U.S.A.* 42°19N 75°24W **83** D9
Sidney *Nebr., U.S.A.* 41°8N 102°59W **80** E2
Sidney *Ohio, U.S.A.* 40°17N 84°9W **81** E11
Sidney Lanier, L. *U.S.A.* 34°10N 84°4W **85** D12
Sidoarjo *Indonesia* 7°27S 112°43E **37** G15
Sidon = Saydā *Lebanon* 33°35N 35°25E **46** B4
Sidra, G. of = Surt, Khalīj
  Libya 31°40N 18°30E **51** B9
Siedlce *Poland* 52°10N 22°20E **17** B12
Sieg → *Germany* 50°46N 7°6E **16** C4
Siegen *Germany* 50°51N 8°0E **16** C5
Siem Pang *Cambodia* 14°7N 106°23E **38** E6
Siem Reap = Siemreab
  Cambodia 13°20N 103°52E **38** F4
Siemreab *Cambodia* 13°20N 103°52E **38** F4
Siena *Italy* 43°19N 11°21E **22** C4
Sieradz *Poland* 51°37N 18°41E **17** C10
Sierpe, Bocas de la
  Venezuela 10°0N 61°30W **93** L15
Sierra Blanca *U.S.A.* 31°11N 105°22W **84** F2
Sierra Blanca Peak
  U.S.A. 33°23N 105°49W **77** K11
Sierra City *U.S.A.* 39°34N 120°38W **78** F6
Sierra Colorada
  Argentina 40°35S 67°50W **96** E3
Sierra de Agalta △
  Honduras 15°1N 85°48W **88** C2
Sierra de Bahoruco △
  Dom. Rep. 18°10N 71°25W **89** C5
Sierra de La Culata △
  Venezuela 8°45N 71°10W **89** E5
Sierra de Lancandón △
  Guatemala 16°59N 90°23W **88** C1
Sierra de las Quijadas △
  Argentina 32°29S 67°5W **94** C2
Sierra de San Luis △
  Venezuela 11°20N 69°43W **89** D6
Sierra de San Pedro Mártir,
  Parque Nacional △
  Mexico 31°10N 115°30W **86** A1
Sierra Gorda *Chile* 22°50S 69°15W **94** A2
Sierra Leone ■ *W. Afr.* 9°0N 12°0W **50** D3
Sierra Madre *Mexico* 16°0N 93°0W **87** D6
Sierra Madre Occidental
  Mexico 27°0N 107°0W **86** B3
Sierra Madre Oriental
  Mexico 25°0N 100°0W **86** C5
Sierra Mojada *Mexico* 27°18N 103°41W **86** B4
Sierra Nevada *Spain* 37°3N 3°15W **21** D4
Sierra Nevada *U.S.A.* 39°0N 120°30W **78** H4
Sierra Nevada △
  Venezuela 8°35N 70°45W **89** E5
Sierra Nevada de Santa Marta △
  Colombia 10°56N 73°36W **89** D5
Sierra Vista *U.S.A.* 31°33N 110°18W **77** L8
Sierraville *U.S.A.* 39°36N 120°22W **78** F6
Sifnos *Greece* 37°0N 24°45E **23** F11
Sifton *Canada* 51°21N 100°8W **71** C8
Sifton Pass *Canada* 57°52N 126°15W **70** B3
Sig *Algeria* 35°32N 0°12W **50** A5
Sigatoka *Fiji* 18°8S 177°32E **59** a
Sighetu-Marmaţiei
  Romania 47°57N 23°52E **17** E12
Sighişoara *Romania* 46°12N 24°50E **17** E13
Sigli *Indonesia* 5°25N 96°0E **36** C1
Siglufjörður *Iceland* 66°12N 18°55W **8** C4
Signal de Botrang *Belgium* 50°29N 6°4E **15** D6
Signal Pk. *U.S.A.* 32°30N 114°2W **79** M12
Signy I. *Antarctica* 60°43S 45°36W **5** C18
Sigsig *Ecuador* 3°0S 78°50W **92** D3
Sigüenza *Spain* 41°3N 2°40W **21** B4
Siguiri *Guinea* 11°31N 9°10W **50** F4
Sigulda *Latvia* 57°10N 24°55E **9** H21
Sihora *India* 23°29N 80°6E **43** H9
Siikajoki → *Finland* 64°50N 24°43E **8** D21
Siilinjärvi *Finland* 63°4N 27°39E **8** E22
Sijarira Ra. = Chizarira
  Zimbabwe 17°36S 27°45E **55** F2
Sika *India* 22°26N 69°47E **42** H3
Sikanni Chief →
  Canada 57°47N 122°15W **70** B4
Sikao *Thailand* 7°34N 99°21E **39** J2
Sikar *India* 27°33N 75°10E **42** F6
Sikasso *Mali* 11°18N 5°35W **50** F4
Sikeston *U.S.A.* 36°53N 89°35W **80** G9
Sikhote Alin, Khrebet
  Russia 45°0N 136°0E **30** B8
Sikhote Alin Ra. = Sikhote Alin,
  Khrebet *Russia* 45°0N 136°0E **30** B8
Sikinos *Greece* 36°40N 25°8E **23** F11
Sikkim □ *India* 27°50N 88°30E **41** F16
Sil → *Spain* 42°27N 7°43W **21** A2
Silacayoapan *Mexico* 17°30N 98°9W **87** D5
Silawad *India* 21°54N 74°54E **42** J6
Silchar *India* 24°49N 92°48E **41** G18
Siler City *U.S.A.* 35°44N 79°28W **85** D15
Silesia = Śląsk *Poland* 51°0N 16°30E **16** C9
Silgarhi Doti *Nepal* 29°15N 81°0E **43** E9
Silghat *India* 26°35N 93°0E **41** F18
Silhouette *Seychelles* 4°29S 55°12E **53** b
Silifke *Turkey* 36°22N 33°58E **44** B2
Siliguri = Shiliguri *India* 26°45N 88°25E **41** F16
Siling Co *China* 31°50N 89°20E **32** C3
Silistra *Bulgaria* 44°6N 27°19E **23** B12
Silivri *Turkey* 41°4N 28°14E **23** D13
Siljan *Sweden* 60°55N 14°45E **8** F16
Silkeborg *Denmark* 56°10N 9°32E **9** H13
Silkwood *Australia* 17°45S 146°2E **62** B4
Sillajhuay, Cordillera
  Chile 19°46S 68°40W **92** G5
Sillamäe *Estonia* 59°24N 27°45E **9** G22
Silloth *U.K.* 54°52N 3°23W **12** C4
Siloam Springs *U.S.A.* 36°11N 94°32W **84** C7
Silopi *Turkey* 37°15N 42°27E **44** B4
Šilutė *Lithuania* 55°21N 21°33E **9** J19
Silvan *Turkey* 38°7N 41°2E **44** B4

Silvani *India* 23°18N 78°25E **43** H8
Silver City *U.S.A.* 32°46N 108°17W **77** K9
Silver Cr. → *U.S.A.* 43°16N 119°13W **76** E4
Silver Creek *U.S.A.* 42°33N 79°10W **82** D5
Silver L. *U.S.A.* 38°39N 120°6W **78** G6
Silver Lake *Calif.,*
  U.S.A. 35°21N 116°7W **79** K10
Silver Lake *Oreg., U.S.A.* 43°8N 121°3W **76** E3
Silvermine Mts. *Ireland* 52°47N 8°15W **10** D3
Silverton *Colo., U.S.A.* 37°49N 107°40W **77** H10
Silverton *Tex., U.S.A.* 34°28N 101°19W **84** D4
Silvies → *U.S.A.* 43°34N 119°2W **76** E4
Simaltala *India* 24°43N 86°33E **43** G12
Simanggang = Sri Aman
  Malaysia 1°15N 111°32E **36** D4
Simard, L. *Canada* 47°40N 78°40W **72** C4
Simav *Turkey* 39°4N 28°58E **23** E13
Simav → *Turkey* 40°24N 28°31E **23** D12
Simba *Tanzania* 2°10S 37°36E **54** C4
Simbirsk = Ulyanovsk
  Russia 54°20N 48°25E **18** D8
Simbo *Tanzania* 4°51S 29°41E **54** C2
Simcoe *Canada* 42°50N 80°20W **82** D4
Simcoe, L. *Canada* 44°25N 79°20W **82** B5
Simdega *India* 22°37N 84°31E **43** H11
Simeria *Romania* 45°51N 23°1E **17** F12
Simeulue *Indonesia* 2°45N 95°45E **36** D1
Simferopol *Ukraine* 44°55N 34°3E **19** F5
Simi *Greece* 36°35N 27°50E **23** F12
Simi Valley *U.S.A.* 34°16N 118°47W **79** L8
Simikot *Nepal* 30°0N 81°50E **43** E9
Simla = Shimla *India* 31°2N 77°9E **42** D7
Simlipal △ *India* 21°45N 86°30E **43** J12
Simmie *Canada* 49°56N 108°6W **71** D7
Simmler *U.S.A.* 35°21N 119°59W **79** K7
Simo älv = Simojoki →
  Finland 65°35N 25°1E **8** D21
Simojoki → *Finland* 65°35N 25°1E **8** D21
Simojovel *Mexico* 17°12N 92°38W **87** D6
Simonette → *Canada* 55°9N 118°15W **70** B5
Simonstown *S. Africa* 34°14S 18°26E **56** E2
Simpang Empat *Malaysia* 5°27N 100°29E **39** c
Simplonpass *Switz.* 46°15N 8°3E **20** C8
Simpson Desert *Australia* 25°0S 137°0E **62** D2
Simpson Desert △
  Australia 24°59S 138°21E **62** C2
Simpson Pen. *Canada* 68°34N 88°45W **69** C11
Simrishamn *Sweden* 55°33N 14°22E **9** J16
Simsbury *U.S.A.* 41°53N 72°48W **83** E12
Simushir, Ostrov
  Russia 46°50N 152°30E **29** E16
Sin Cowe I. *S. China Sea* 9°53N 114°19E **36** C4
Sina Dhago *Somali Rep.* 5°50N 47°0E **47** F4
Sinabang *Indonesia* 2°30N 96°24E **36** D1
Sinai = Es Sînâ' *Egypt* 29°0N 34°0E **46** F3
Sinai, Mt. = Mûsa, Gebel
  Egypt 28°33N 33°59E **44** D2
Sinaloa □ *Mexico* 25°0N 107°30W **86** C3
Sinaloa de Leyva
  Mexico 25°50N 108°14W **86** B3
Sinarades *Greece* 39°34N 19°51E **25** A3
Sincelejo *Colombia* 9°18N 75°24W **92** B3
Sinch'ang *N. Korea* 40°7N 128°28E **35** D15
Sinch'ŏn *N. Korea* 38°17N 125°21E **35** E13
Sinclair *U.S.A.* 41°47N 107°7W **76** F10
Sinclair Mills *Canada* 54°5N 121°40W **70** C4
Sinclair's B. *U.K.* 58°31N 3°5W **11** C5
Sinclairville *U.S.A.* 42°16N 79°16W **82** D5
Sincorá, Serra do *Brazil* 13°30S 41°0W **93** F10
Sind = Sindh □ *Pakistan* 26°0N 69°0E **42** G3
Sind → *Jammu & Kashmir,*
  India 34°18N 74°45E **43** B6
Sind → *Mad. P., India* 26°26N 79°13E **43** F8
Sind Sagar Doab *Pakistan* 32°0N 71°30E **42** D4
Sindangan *Phil.* 8°10N 123°5E **37** C6
Sindangbarang *Indonesia* 7°27S 107°1E **37** G12
Sinde *Zambia* 17°28S 25°51E **55** F2
Sindh = Indus →
  Pakistan 24°20N 67°47E **42** G2
Sindh □ *Pakistan* 26°0N 69°0E **42** G3
Sindri *India* 23°45N 86°42E **43** H12
Sines *Portugal* 37°56N 8°51W **21** D1
Sines, C. de *Portugal* 37°58N 8°53W **21** D1
Sineu *Spain* 39°38N 3°1E **24** B10
Sing Buri *Thailand* 14°53N 100°25E **38** E3
Singa *Sudan* 13°10N 33°57E **51** F12
Singalila △ *India* 27°10N 88°5E **43** F13
Singapore ■ *Asia* 1°17N 103°51E **39** d
Singapore, Straits of *Asia* 1°15N 104°0E **39** d
Singapore Changi ✈ (SIN)
  Singapore 1°23N 103°59E **39** M4
Singaraja *Indonesia* 8°7S 115°6E **37** J18
Singatoka = Sigatoka *Fiji* 18°8S 177°32E **59** a
Singida *Tanzania* 4°49S 34°48E **54** C3
Singida □ *Tanzania* 6°0S 34°30E **54** D3
Singkaling Hkamti
  Burma 26°0N 95°39E **41** G19
Singkang *Indonesia* 4°8S 120°1E **37** E6
Singkawang *Indonesia* 1°0N 108°57E **36** D3
Singkep *Indonesia* 0°30S 104°25E **36** E2
Singkil *Indonesia* 2°17N 97°49E **39** L1
Singleton *Australia* 32°33S 151°0E **63** E5
Singleton, Mt. *N. Terr.,*
  Australia 22°0S 130°46E **60** D5
Singleton, Mt. *W. Austral.,*
  Australia 29°27S 117°15E **61** E2
Singoli *India* 25°0N 75°22E **42** G6
Singora = Songkhla
  Thailand 7°13N 100°37E **39** J3
Sinhung *N. Korea* 40°11N 127°34E **35** D14
Siniscóla *Italy* 40°34N 9°41E **22** D3
Sinjai *Indonesia* 5°7S 120°20E **37** F6
Sinjār *Iraq* 36°19N 41°52E **44** B4
Sinkat *Sudan* 18°55N 36°49E **51** E13
Sinkiang = Xinjiang Uygur
  Zizhiqu □ *China* 42°0N 86°0E **32** C3
Sinmak *N. Korea* 38°25N 126°14E **35** E14
Sinmi-do *N. Korea* 39°33N 124°53E **35** E13

Sinnamary *Fr. Guiana* 5°25N 53°0W **93** B8
Sinni → *Italy* 40°8N 16°41E **22** D7
Sinop *Turkey* 42°1N 35°11E **19** F6
Sinor *India* 21°55N 73°20E **42** J5
Sinp'o *N. Korea* 40°0N 128°13E **35** E15
Sinsk *Russia* 61°8N 126°48E **29** C13
Sintang *Indonesia* 0°5N 111°35E **36** D4
Sinton *U.S.A.* 28°2N 97°31W **84** G6
Sintra *Portugal* 38°47N 9°25W **21** C1
Sinŭiju *N. Korea* 40°5N 124°24E **35** D13
Siocon *Phil.* 7°40N 122°10E **37** C6
Siófok *Hungary* 46°54N 18°3E **17** E10
Sion *Switz.* 46°14N 7°20E **20** C7
Sion Mills *U.K.* 54°48N 7°29W **10** B4
Sioux Center *U.S.A.* 43°5N 96°11W **80** D5
Sioux City *U.S.A.* 42°30N 96°24W **80** D5
Sioux Falls *U.S.A.* 43°33N 96°44W **80** D5
Sioux Lookout *Canada* 50°10N 91°50W **72** B1
Sioux Narrows *Canada* 49°25N 94°10W **71** D10
Sipadan *Malaysia* 7°6N 118°38E **37** D5
Siparia *Trin. & Tob.* 10°8N 61°31W **93** K15
Siping *China* 43°8N 124°21E **35** C13
Sipiwesk L. *Canada* 55°5N 97°35W **71** B9
Siple *Antarctica* 75°0S 74°0W **5** D7
Sipura *Indonesia* 2°18S 99°40E **36** E1
Siquia → *Nic.* 12°10N 84°20W **88** D3
Siquijor *Phil.* 9°12N 123°35E **37** C6
Siquirres *Costa Rica* 10°6N 83°30W **88** D3
Şīr Abu Nu'ayr *U.A.E.* 25°20N 54°20E **45** E7
Şīr Banī Yās *U.A.E.* 24°19N 52°37E **45** E7
Sir Edward Pellew Group
  Australia 15°40S 137°10E **62** B2
Sir Graham Moore Is.
  Australia 13°53S 126°34E **60** B4
Sir James MacBrien, Mt.
  Canada 62°7N 127°41W **68** C7
Sira → *Norway* 58°23N 6°34E **9** G12
Siracusa *Italy* 37°4N 15°17E **22** F6
Sirajganj *Bangla.* 24°25N 89°47E **43** G13
Sirathu *India* 25°39N 81°19E **43** G9
Sīrdān *Iran* 36°39N 49°12E **45** B6
Siren *U.S.A.* 45°47N 92°24W **80** C7
Sirer *Spain* 38°56N 1°22E **24** C7
Siret → *Romania* 45°24N 28°1E **17** F14
Sirghāyā *Syria* 33°51N 36°8E **46** B5
Sirinat △ *Thailand* 8°6N 98°17E **39** a
Sīrjān *Iran* 29°30N 55°45E **45** D7
Sirmaur *India* 24°51N 81°23E **43** G9
Sirohi *India* 24°52N 72°53E **42** G5
Sironj *India* 24°5N 77°39E **42** G7
Síros = Syros *Greece* 37°28N 24°57E **23** F11
Sirr, Nafud as *Si. Arabia* 25°33N 44°35E **44** E5
Sirretta Pk. *U.S.A.* 35°56N 118°19W **79** K8
Sīrrī *Iran* 25°55N 54°32E **45** E7
Sirsa *India* 29°33N 75°4E **42** E6
Sirsa → *India* 26°51N 79°4E **43** F8
Sisak *Croatia* 45°30N 16°21E **16** F9
Sisaket *Thailand* 15°8N 104°23E **38** E5
Sishen *S. Africa* 27°47S 22°59E **56** D3
Sishui *Henan, China* 34°48N 113°15E **34** G7
Sishui *Shandong, China* 35°42N 117°18E **35** G9
Sisipuk L. *Canada* 55°45N 101°50W **71** B8
Sisophon *Cambodia* 13°38N 102°59E **38** F4
Sisseton *U.S.A.* 45°40N 97°3W **80** C5
Sīstān *Asia* 30°50N 61°0E **45** D9
Sīstān, Daryācheh-ye *Iran* 31°0N 61°0E **45** D9
Sīstān va Balūchestān □
  Iran 27°0N 62°0E **45** E9
Sisters *U.S.A.* 44°18N 121°33W **76** D3
Sisters, The *Seychelles* 4°16S 55°52E **53** b
Siswa Bazar *India* 27°9N 83°46E **43** F10
Sitamarhi *India* 26°37N 85°30E **43** F11
Sitampiky *Madag.* 16°41S 46°6E **57** B8
Sitapur *India* 27°38N 80°45E **43** F9
Siteki *Swaziland* 26°32S 31°58E **57** D5
Sitges *Spain* 41°17N 1°47E **21** B6
Sitia *Greece* 35°13N 26°6E **25** D8
Sitito-Ozima Ridge
  Pac. Oc. 23°0N 143°0E **64** E6
Sitka *U.S.A.* 57°3N 135°20W **70** B1
Sitoti *Botswana* 23°15S 23°40E **56** C3
Sittang Myit → *Burma* 17°20N 96°45E **41** L20
Sittard *Neths.* 51°0N 5°52E **15** C5
Sittingbourne *U.K.* 51°21N 0°45E **13** F8
Sittoung = Sittang Myit →
  Burma 17°20N 96°45E **41** L20
Sittwe *Burma* 20°18N 92°45E **41** J18
Situbondo *Indonesia* 7°42S 114°0E **37** G16
Si'umu *Samoa* 14°1S 171°48W **59** b
Siuna *Nic.* 13°37N 84°45W **88** D3
Siuri *India* 23°50N 87°34E **43** H12
Sīvand *Iran* 30°5N 52°55E **45** D7
Sivas *Turkey* 39°43N 36°58E **44** B3
Siverek *Turkey* 37°50N 39°19E **44** B3
Sivomaskinskiy *Russia* 66°40N 62°35E **18** A11
Sivrihisar *Turkey* 39°30N 31°35E **19** G5
Sîwa *Egypt* 29°11N 25°31E **51** C11
Sîwa, El Wâhât es *Egypt* 29°10N 25°30E **48** D6
Siwa Oasis = Sîwa, El Wâhât es
  Egypt 29°10N 25°30E **48** D6
Siwalik Range *Nepal* 28°0N 83°0E **43** F10
Siwan *India* 26°13N 84°21E **43** F11
Siwana *India* 25°38N 72°25E **42** G5
Six Cross Roads *Barbados* 13°7N 59°28W **89** g
Sixmilebridge *Ireland* 52°44N 8°46W **10** D3
Sixth Cataract *Sudan* 16°20N 32°42E **51** E12
Siyah Kuh, Kavīr-e *Iran* 32°55N 53°55E **45** C7
Siziwang Qi *China* 41°25N 111°40W **34** D6
Sizewell *U.K.* 52°12N 1°38E **13** E9
Sjælland *Denmark* 55°30N 11°30E **9** J14
Sjumen = Shumen
  Bulgaria 43°18N 26°55E **23** C12
Skadarsko Jezero *Europe* 42°10N 19°20E **23** C8
Skaftafell *Iceland* 64°1N 17°0W **8** D5
Skaftafell △ *Iceland* 64°9N 16°50W **8** D5
Skagafjörður *Iceland* 65°54N 19°35W **8** D3
Skagastølstindane
  Norway 61°28N 7°52E **8** F12

Skagaströnd *Iceland* 65°50N 20°19W **8** D3
Skagen *Denmark* 57°43N 10°35E **9** H14
Skagerrak *Denmark* 57°30N 9°0E **9** H13
Skagit → *U.S.A.* 48°23N 122°22W **78** B4
Skagway *U.S.A.* 59°28N 135°19W **68** F4
Skala-Podilska *Ukraine* 48°50N 26°15E **17** D14
Skalat *Ukraine* 49°23N 25°55E **17** D13
Skåne *Sweden* 55°59N 13°30E **9** J15
Skaneateles *U.S.A.* 42°57N 76°26W **83** D8
Skaneateles L. *U.S.A.* 42°51N 76°22W **83** D8
Skardu *Pakistan* 35°20N 75°44E **43** B6
Skarżysko-Kamienna
  Poland 51°7N 20°52E **17** C11
Skeena → *Canada* 54°9N 130°5W **70** C2
Skeena Mts. *Canada* 56°40N 128°30W **70** B3
Skegness *U.K.* 53°9N 0°20E **12** D8
Skeldon = Corriverton
  Guyana 5°55N 57°20W **92** B7
Skeleton Coast *Namibia* 20°0S 13°0E **53** J2
Skeleton Coast △ *Namibia* 20°0S 13°20E **56** C1
Skellefteå *Sweden* 64°45N 20°50E **8** D19
Skellefteälven →
  Sweden 64°45N 21°10E **8** D19
Skelleftehamn *Sweden* 64°40N 21°9E **8** D19
Skerries, The *U.K.* 53°25N 4°36W **12** D3
Ski *Norway* 59°43N 10°52E **9** G14
Skiathos *Greece* 39°12N 23°30E **23** E10
Skibbereen *Ireland* 51°33N 9°16W **10** E2
Skiddaw *U.K.* 54°39N 3°9W **12** C4
Skidegate *Canada* 53°15N 132°1W **70** C2
Skien *Norway* 59°12N 9°35E **9** G13
Skierniewice *Poland* 51°58N 20°10E **17** C11
Skihist, Mt. *Canada* 50°12N 121°54W **70** C4
Skikda *Algeria* 36°50N 6°58E **50** A7
Skilloura *Cyprus* 35°14N 33°10E **25** D12
Skipton *U.K.* 53°58N 2°3W **12** D5
Skirmish Pt. *Australia* 11°59S 134°17E **62** A1
Skiros *Greece* 38°55N 24°34E **23** E11
Skive *Denmark* 56°33N 9°2E **9** H13
Skjálfandafljót → *Iceland* 65°59N 17°25W **8** D5
Skjálfandi *Iceland* 66°5N 17°30W **8** C5
Skole *Ukraine* 49°3N 23°30E **17** D12
Skopelos *Greece* 39°9N 23°47E **23** E10
Skopi *Greece* 35°11N 26°2E **25** D8
Skopje *Macedonia* 42°1N 21°26E **23** C9
Skovorodino *Russia* 54°0N 124°0E **29** D13
Skowhegan *U.S.A.* 44°46N 69°43W **81** C19
Skull *Ireland* 51°32N 9°34W **10** E2
Skunk → *U.S.A.* 40°42N 91°7W **80** E8
Skuodas *Lithuania* 56°16N 21°33E **9** H19
Skvyra *Ukraine* 49°44N 29°40E **17** D15
Skye *U.K.* 57°15N 6°10W **11** D2
Skykomish *U.S.A.* 47°42N 121°22W **76** C3
Skyros = Skiros *Greece* 38°55N 24°34E **23** E11
Slade *Pa., Australia* 21°5S 149°13E **62** K7
Slættaratindur *Faroe Is.* 62°18N 7°1W **8** E9
Slagelse *Denmark* 55°23N 11°19E **9** J14
Slamet *Indonesia* 7°16S 109°8E **37** G13
Slane *Ireland* 53°42N 6°33W **10** C5
Slaney → *Ireland* 52°26N 6°33W **10** D5
Slangberge *S. Africa* 31°32S 20°48E **56** E3
Śląsk *Poland* 51°0N 16°30E **16** C9
Slate Is. *Canada* 48°40N 87°0W **72** C2
Slatina *Romania* 44°28N 24°22E **17** F13
Slaton *U.S.A.* 33°26N 101°39W **84** E4
Slave → *Canada* 61°18N 113°39W **70** A6
Slave Coast *W. Afr.* 6°0N 2°30E **50** G6
Slave Lake *Canada* 55°17N 114°43W **70** B6
Slave Pt. *Canada* 61°11N 115°56W **70** A5
Slavgorod *Russia* 53°1N 78°37E **28** D8
Slavonski Brod *Croatia* 45°11N 18°1E **23** B8
Slavuta *Ukraine* 50°15N 27°2E **17** C14
Slavyanka *Russia* 42°53N 131°21E **30** C5
Slavyansk = Slovyansk
  Ukraine 48°55N 37°36E **19** E6
Slawharad *Belarus* 53°27N 31°0E **17** B16
Sleaford *U.K.* 53°0N 0°24W **12** D7
Sleaford B. *Australia* 34°55S 135°45E **63** E2
Sleat, Sd. of *U.K.* 57°5N 5°47W **11** D3
Sleeper Is. *Canada* 58°30N 81°0W **69** D11
Sleeping Bear Dunes △
  U.S.A. 44°50N 86°5W **80** C10
Sleepy Eye *U.S.A.* 44°18N 94°43W **80** C6
Slemon L. *Canada* 63°13N 116°4W **70** A5
Slide Mt. *U.S.A.* 42°0N 74°25W **83** E10
Slidell *U.S.A.* 30°17N 89°47W **85** F10
Sliema *Malta* 35°55N 14°30E **25** D2
Slieve Aughty *Ireland* 53°4N 8°30W **10** C3
Slieve Bloom *Ireland* 53°4N 7°40W **10** C4
Slieve Donard *U.K.* 54°11N 5°55W **10** B6
Slieve Gamph *Ireland* 54°6N 9°0W **10** B3
Slieve Gullion *U.K.* 54°7N 6°26W **10** B5
Slieve League *Ireland* 54°40N 8°42W **10** B3
Slieve Mish *Ireland* 52°12N 9°50W **10** D2
Slievenamon *Ireland* 52°25N 7°34W **10** D4
Sligeach = Sligo *Ireland* 54°16N 8°28W **10** B3
Sligo *Ireland* 54°16N 8°28W **10** B3
Sligo *U.S.A.* 41°6N 79°29W **82** E5
Sligo □ *Ireland* 54°8N 8°42W **10** B3
Sligo B. *Ireland* 54°18N 8°40W **10** B3
Slippery Rock *U.S.A.* 41°4N 80°3W **82** E4
Slite *Sweden* 57°42N 18°48E **9** H18
Sliven *Bulgaria* 42°42N 26°19E **23** C12
Sloan *U.S.A.* 35°57N 115°13W **79** K11
Sloansville *U.S.A.* 42°45N 74°22W **83** D10
Slobodskoy *Russia* 58°40N 50°6E **18** C9
Slobozia *Romania* 44°34N 27°23E **17** F14
Slocan *Canada* 49°48N 117°28W **70** D5
Slonim *Belarus* 53°4N 25°19E **17** B13
Slough *U.K.* 51°30N 0°36W **13** F7
Slough □ *U.K.* 51°30N 0°36W **13** F7
Sloughhouse *U.S.A.* 38°26N 121°12W **78** G5
Slovak Rep. ■ *Europe* 48°30N 20°0E **17** D10
Slovakia = Slovak Rep. ■

Slovakian Ore Mts. = Slovenské
  Rudohorie *Slovak Rep.* 48°45N 20°0E **17** D10
Slovenia ■ *Europe* 45°58N 14°30E **16** F8
Slovenija = Slovenia ■
  Europe 45°58N 14°30E **16** F8
Slovenská = Slovak Rep. ■
  Europe 48°30N 20°0E **17** D10
Slovenské Rudohorie
  Slovak Rep. 48°45N 20°0E **17** D10
Slovyansk *Ukraine* 48°55N 37°36E **19** E6
Sluch → *Ukraine* 51°37N 26°38E **17** C14
Sluis *Neths.* 51°18N 3°23E **15** C3
Słupsk *Poland* 54°30N 17°3E **17** A9
Slurry *S. Africa* 25°49S 25°42E **56** D4
Slutsk *Belarus* 53°2N 27°31E **17** B14
Slyne Hd. *Ireland* 53°25N 10°10W **10** C1
Slyudyanka *Russia* 51°40N 103°40E **29** D11
Småland *Sweden* 57°15N 15°25E **9** H16
Smalltree L. *Canada* 61°0N 105°0W **71** A8
Smallwood Res. *Canada* 54°5N 64°30W **73** B7
Smarhon *Belarus* 54°20N 26°24E **17** A14
Smartt Syndicate Dam
  S. Africa 30°45S 23°10E **56** E3
Smartville *U.S.A.* 39°13N 121°18W **78** F5
Smeaton *Canada* 53°30N 104°49W **71** C8
Smederevo *Serbia* 44°40N 20°57E **23** B9
Smerwick Harbour
  Ireland 52°12N 10°23W **10** D1
Smethport *U.S.A.* 41°49N 78°27W **82** E6
Smidovich *Russia* 48°36N 133°49E **29** E14
Smith *Canada* 55°10N 114°0W **70** B6
Smith Center *U.S.A.* 39°47N 98°47W **80** F4
Smith River *U.S.A.* 41°55N 124°9W **76** F1
Smithburne → *Australia* 17°3S 140°57E **62** B3
Smithers *Canada* 54°45N 127°10W **70** C3
Smithfield *S. Africa* 30°9S 26°30E **56** E4
Smithfield *N.C., U.S.A.* 35°31N 78°21W **85** D15
Smithfield *Utah, U.S.A.* 41°50N 111°50W **76** F8
Smiths Falls *Canada* 44°55N 76°0W **83** B9
Smithton *Australia* 40°53S 145°6E **63** G4
Smithville *Canada* 43°6N 79°33W **82** C5
Smithville *U.S.A.* 30°1N 97°10W **84** F6
Smoke Creek Desert
  U.S.A. 40°30N 119°40W **76** F4
Smoky → *Canada* 56°10N 117°21W **70** B5
Smoky Bay *Australia* 32°22S 134°13E **63** E1
Smoky Hill → *U.S.A.* 39°4N 96°48W **80** F5
Smoky Hills *U.S.A.* 39°15N 99°30W **80** F4
Smoky Lake *Canada* 54°10N 112°30W **70** C6
Smøla *Norway* 63°23N 8°3E **8** E13
Smolensk *Russia* 54°45N 32°5E **18** D5
Smolikas, Oros *Greece* 40°9N 20°58E **23** D9
Smolyan *Bulgaria* 41°36N 24°38E **23** D11
Smooth Rock Falls
  Canada 49°17N 81°37W **72** C3
Smoothstone L. *Canada* 54°40N 106°50W **71** C7
Smorgon = Smarhon
  Belarus 54°20N 26°24E **17** A14
Smyrna = İzmir *Turkey* 38°25N 27°8E **23** E12
Smyrna *U.S.A.* 39°18N 75°36W **81** F16
Snæfell *Iceland* 64°48N 15°34W **8** D6
Snaefell *I. of Man* 54°16N 4°27W **12** C3
Snæfellsjökull *Iceland* 64°49N 23°46W **8** D2
Snake → *U.S.A.* 46°12N 119°2W **76** C4
Snake I. *Australia* 38°47S 146°33E **63** F4
Snake Range *U.S.A.* 39°0N 114°20W **76** G6
Snake River Plain
  U.S.A. 42°50N 114°0W **76** E7
Snåsavatnet *Norway* 64°12N 12°0E **8** D15
Sneek *Neths.* 53°2N 5°40E **15** A5
Sneem *Ireland* 51°50N 9°54W **10** E2
Sneeuberge *S. Africa* 31°46S 24°20E **56** E3
Snelling *U.S.A.* 37°31N 120°26W **78** H6
Snežka *Europe* 50°41N 15°50E **16** C8
Snihurivka *Ukraine* 47°2N 32°49E **19** E5
Snizort, L. *U.K.* 57°33N 6°28W **11** D2
Snøhetta *Norway* 62°19N 9°16E **8** E13
Snohomish *U.S.A.* 47°55N 122°6W **78** C4
Snoqualmie Pass
  U.S.A. 47°25N 121°25W **78** C5
Snoul *Cambodia* 12°4N 106°26E **39** F6
Snover *U.S.A.* 43°27N 82°58W **82** C2
Snow Hill *U.S.A.* 38°11N 75°24W **81** F16
Snow Lake *Canada* 54°52N 100°3W **71** C8
Snow Mt. *Calif., U.S.A.* 39°23N 122°45W **78** F4
Snow Mt. *Maine, U.S.A.* 45°18N 70°48W **83** A14
Snow Shoe *U.S.A.* 41°2N 77°57W **82** E7
Snowbird L. *Canada* 60°45N 103°0W **71** A8
Snowdon *U.K.* 53°4N 4°5W **12** D3
Snowdonia △ *U.K.* 53°7N 3°59W **12** D4
Snowdrift = Lutsel K'e
  Canada 62°24N 110°44W **71** A6
Snowdrift → *Canada* 62°24N 110°44W **71** A6
Snowflake *U.S.A.* 34°30N 110°5W **77** J8
Snowshoe Pk. *U.S.A.* 48°13N 115°41W **76** B6
Snowtown *Australia* 33°46S 138°14E **63** E2
Snowville *U.S.A.* 41°58N 112°43W **76** F7
Snowy → *Australia* 37°46S 148°30E **63** F4
Snowy Mt. *U.S.A.* 43°42N 74°23W **83** C10
Snowy Mts. *Australia* 36°30S 148°20E **63** F4
Snug Corner *Bahamas* 22°33N 73°52W **89** B5
Snug Harbour *Canada* 45°22N 80°17W **82** A4
Snyatyn *Ukraine* 48°27N 25°38E **17** D13
Snyder *Okla., U.S.A.* 34°40N 98°57W **84** D5
Snyder *Tex., U.S.A.* 32°44N 100°55W **84** E4
Soahanina *Madag.* 18°42S 44°13E **57** B7
Soalala *Madag.* 16°6S 45°20E **57** B8
Soaloka *Madag.* 18°32S 45°15E **57** B8
Soamanonga *Madag.* 24°43S 44°47E **57** C7
Soan → *Pakistan* 33°1N 71°44E **42** C4
Soanierana-Ivongo
  Madag. 16°55S 49°35E **57** B8
Soanindrariny *Madag.* 19°54S 47°14E **57** B8
Soavina *Madag.* 19°9S 46°45E **57** B8
Soavinandriana *Madag.* 19°9S 46°45E **57** B8
Sobat, Nahr → *Sudan* 9°22N 31°33E **51** G12
Sobhapur *India* 22°47N 78°17E **42** H8
Sobradinho, Represa de
  Brazil 9°30S 42°0W **93** E10

Sobral *Brazil* 3°50S 40°20W **93** D10
Soc Giang *Vietnam* 22°54N 106°1E **38** A6
Soc Trang *Vietnam* 9°37N 105°50E **39** H5
Socastee *U.S.A.* 33°41N 78°59W **85** E15
Soch'e = Shache *China* 38°20N 77°10E **32** C2
Sochi *Russia* 43°35N 39°40E **19** F6
Société, Îs. de la
   French Polynesia 17°0S 151°0W **65** J12
Society Is. = Société, Îs. de la
   French Polynesia 17°0S 151°0W **65** J12
Socompa, Portezuelo de
   Chile 24°27S 68°18W **94** A2
Socorro *N. Mex., U.S.A.* 34°4N 106°54W **77** J10
Socorro *Tex., U.S.A.* 31°39N 106°18W **84** F1
Socorro, I. *Mexico* 18°45N 110°58W **86** D2
Socotra *Yemen* 12°30N 54°0E **47** E5
Soda L. *India* 35°10N 116°4W **77** J5
Soda Plains *India* 35°30N 79°0E **43** B8
Soda Springs *U.S.A.* 42°39N 111°36W **76** E8
Sodankylä *Finland* 67°29N 26°40E **8** C22
Söderhamn *Sweden* 61°18N 17°10E **8** F17
Söderköping *Sweden* 58°31N 16°20E **9** G17
Södermanland *Sweden* 58°56N 16°55E **9** G17
Södertälje *Sweden* 59°12N 17°39E **9** G17
Sodiri *Sudan* 14°27N 29°0E **51** F11
Sodus *U.S.A.* 43°14N 77°4W **82** C7
Sodwana Bay △ *S. Africa* 27°35S 32°43E **57** D5
Soekmekaar = Morebeng
   S. Africa 23°30S 29°55E **57** C4
Soest *Neths.* 52°9N 5°19E **15** B5
Sofala □ *Mozam.* 19°30S 34°30E **57** B5
Sofia = Sofiya *Bulgaria* 42°45N 23°20E **23** C10
Sofia → *Madag.* 15°27S 47°23E **57** B8
Sofiya *Bulgaria* 42°45N 23°20E **23** C10
Sōfu-Gan *Japan* 29°49N 140°21E **31** K10
Sogamoso *Colombia* 5°43N 72°56W **92** B4
Sogār *Iran* 25°53N 58°6E **45** E8
Sogndalsfjøra *Norway* 61°14N 7°5E **8** F12
Søgne *Norway* 58°5N 7°48E **9** G12
Sognefjorden *Norway* 61°10N 5°50E **8** F11
Soh *Iran* 33°26N 51°27E **45** C6
Sohâg *Egypt* 26°33N 31°43E **51** C12
Sohagpur *India* 22°42N 78°12E **42** H8
Soignies *Belgium* 50°35N 4°5E **15** D4
Soissons *France* 49°25N 3°19E **20** B5
Sōja *Japan* 34°40N 133°45E **31** G6
Sojat *India* 25°55N 73°45E **42** G5
Sokal *Ukraine* 50°31N 24°15E **17** C13
Sokcho *S. Korea* 38°12N 128°36E **35** E15
Söke *Turkey* 37°48N 27°28E **23** F12
Sokelo
   Dem. Rep. of the Congo 9°55S 24°36E **55** D1
Sokhumi *Georgia* 43°0N 41°0E **19** F7
Soko Is. *China* 22°10N 113°54E **33** G10
Sokodé *Togo* 9°0N 1°11E **50** G6
Sokol *Russia* 59°30N 40°5E **18** C7
Sokółka *Poland* 53°25N 23°30E **17** B12
Sokołów Podlaski
   Poland 52°25N 22°15E **17** B12
Sokoto *Nigeria* 13°2N 5°16E **50** F7
Sol Iletsk *Russia* 51°10N 55°0E **18** D10
Solai *Kenya* 0°2N 36°12E **54** B4
Solan *India* 30°55N 77°7E **42** D7
Solana Beach *U.S.A.* 32°58N 117°16W **79** N9
Solander I. *N.Z.* 46°34S 166°54E **59** G1
Solano *Phil.* 16°31N 121°15E **37** A6
Solapur *India* 17°43N 75°56E **40** L9
Soldotna *U.S.A.* 60°29N 151°3W **68** C4
Soléa *Cyprus* 35°5N 33°4E **25** D12
Soledad *Colombia* 10°55N 74°46W **92** A4
Soledad *U.S.A.* 36°26N 121°20W **78** J5
Soledad *Venezuela* 8°10N 63°34W **92** B6
Solent, The *U.K.* 50°45N 1°25W **13** G6
Solfonntaggen *Norway* 60°2N 6°57E **9** F12
Solhan *Turkey* 38°57N 41°3E **44** B4
Soligalich *Russia* 59°5N 42°10E **18** C7
Soligorsk = Salihorsk
   Belarus 52°51N 27°27E **17** B14
Solihull *U.K.* 52°26N 1°47W **13** E6
Solikamsk *Russia* 59°38N 56°50E **18** C10
Solila *Madag.* 21°25S 46°37E **57** C8
Solimões = Amazonas →
   S. Amer. 0°5S 50°0W **93** D8
Solingen *Germany* 51°10N 7°5E **16** C4
Sollefteå *Sweden* 63°12N 17°20E **8** E17
Sóller *Spain* 39°46N 2°43E **24** B9
Solo → *Indonesia* 6°47S 112°22E **37** G15
Sologne *France* 47°40N 1°45E **20** C4
Solok *Indonesia* 0°45S 100°40E **36** E2
Sololá *Guatemala* 14°49N 91°10W **88** D1
Sololo *Kenya* 3°33N 38°39E **54** B4
Solomon, N. Fork →
   U.S.A. 39°29N 98°26W **80** F4
Solomon, S. Fork →
   U.S.A. 39°25N 99°12W **80** F4
Solomon Is. ■ *Pac. Oc.* 6°0S 155°0E **58** B8
Solomon Rise *Pac. Oc.* 1°0N 157°0E **64** G7
Solon *China* 46°32N 121°10E **33** B7
Solon Springs *U.S.A.* 46°22N 91°49W **80** B8
Solor *Indonesia* 8°27S 123°0E **37** F6
Solothurn *Switz.* 47°13N 7°32E **20** C7
Šolta *Croatia* 43°24N 16°15E **22** C7
Solṭānābād *Khorāsān,*
   Iran 34°13N 59°58E **45** C8
Solṭānābād *Khorāsān, Iran* 36°29N 58°5E **45** B8
Solunska Glava
   Macedonia 41°44N 21°31E **23** D9
Solvang *U.S.A.* 34°36N 120°8W **79** L6
Solvay *U.S.A.* 43°3N 76°13W **82** C8
Sölvesborg *Sweden* 56°5N 14°35E **9** H16
Solvychegodsk *Russia* 61°21N 46°56E **18** B8
Solway Firth *U.K.* 54°49N 3°35W **12** C4
Solwezi *Zambia* 12°11S 26°21E **55** E2
Sōma *Japan* 37°40N 140°50E **30** F10
Soma *Turkey* 39°10N 27°35E **23** E12
Somabhula *Zimbabwe* 19°42S 29°40E **57** B4

Somali Pen. *Africa* 7°0N 46°0E **48** F8
Somali Rep. ■ *Africa* 7°0N 47°0E **47** F4
Somalia = Somali Rep. ■
   Africa 7°0N 47°0E **47** F4
Somaliland □ *Somali Rep.* 9°0N 46°0E **47** F4
Sombor *Serbia* 45°46N 19°9E **23** B8
Sombra *Canada* 42°43N 82°29W **82** D2
Sombrerete *Mexico* 23°38N 103°39W **86** C4
Sombrero *Anguilla* 18°37N 63°30W **89** C7
Somdari *India* 25°47N 72°38E **42** G5
Somers *U.S.A.* 48°5N 114°13W **76** B6
Somerset *Ky., U.S.A.* 37°5N 84°36W **81** G11
Somerset *Mass., U.S.A.* 41°47N 71°8W **83** E13
Somerset *Pa., U.S.A.* 40°1N 79°5W **82** F5
Somerset □ *U.K.* 51°9N 3°0W **13** F5
Somerset East *S. Africa* 32°42S 25°35E **56** E4
Somerset I. *Canada* 73°30N 93°0W **68** B10
Somerset West *S. Africa* 34°8S 18°50E **56** E2
Somersworth *U.S.A.* 43°16N 70°52W **83** C14
Somerton *U.S.A.* 32°36N 114°43W **77** K6
Somerville *U.S.A.* 40°35N 74°38W **83** F10
Someş → *Romania* 47°49N 22°43E **17** D12
Somme → *France* 50°11N 1°38E **20** A4
Somnath *India* 20°53N 70°22E **42** J4
Somosierra, Puerto de
   Spain 41°4N 3°35W **21** B4
Somosomo *Fiji* 16°47S 179°58W **59** a
Somosomo Str. *Fiji* 16°0S 180°0E **59** a
Somoto *Nic.* 13°28N 86°37W **88** D2
Somport, Tunnel de
   Spain 42°48N 0°31W **20** E3
Son → *India* 25°42N 84°52E **43** G11
Son Ha *Vietnam* 15°3N 108°34E **38** E7
Son Hoa *Vietnam* 13°2N 108°58E **38** F7
Son La *Vietnam* 21°20N 103°50E **38** B4
Son Morrell *Spain* 39°44N 3°20E **24** B10
Son Rapinya *Spain* 39°35N 2°37E **24** B9
Son Sardina *Spain* 39°37N 2°40E **24** B9
Son Serra *Spain* 39°43N 3°13E **24** B10
Son Tay *Vietnam* 21°8N 105°30E **38** B5
Soná *Panama* 8°0N 81°20W **88** E3
Sonamarg *India* 34°18N 75°21E **43** B6
Sonamukhi *India* 23°18N 87°27E **43** H12
Sonar → *India* 24°24N 79°56E **43** G8
Sönch'ŏn *N. Korea* 39°48N 124°55E **35** E13
Sondags → *S. Africa* 33°44S 25°51E **56** E4
Sondar *India* 33°28N 75°56E **43** C6
Sønderborg *Denmark* 54°55N 9°49E **9** J13
Sóndrio *Italy* 46°10N 9°52E **20** C8
Sone *Mozam.* 17°23S 34°55E **55** F3
Sonepur *India* 20°55N 83°50E **41** J13
Song *Thailand* 18°28N 100°11E **38** C3
Song Cau *Vietnam* 13°27N 109°18E **38** F7
Song Hong → *Vietnam* 22°0N 104°0E **32** D5
Song Xian *China* 34°12N 112°8E **34** G7
Songan *Indonesia* 8°13S 115°24E **37** J18
Songea *Tanzania* 10°40S 35°40E **55** E4
Songgang *China* 22°46N 113°50E **33** F10
Songhua Hu *China* 43°35N 126°50E **35** C14
Songhua Jiang →
   China 47°45N 132°30E **33** B8
Songimvelo ⌂ *S. Africa* 25°50S 31°2E **57** D5
Sŏngjin = Kimch'aek
   N. Korea 40°40N 129°10E **35** D15
Songkhla *Thailand* 7°13N 100°37E **39** J3
Songnim *N. Korea* 38°45N 125°39E **35** E13
Songo *Mozam.* 15°34S 32°38E **55** F3
Songo *Sudan* 9°47N 24°21E **51** G10
Songpan *China* 32°40N 103°30E **32** C5
Songwe
   Dem. Rep. of the Congo 3°20S 26°16E **54** C2
Songwe → *Africa* 9°44S 33°58E **55** D3
Sonhat *India* 23°29N 82°31E **43** H10
Sonid Youqi *China* 42°45N 112°48E **34** C7
Sonipat *India* 29°0N 77°5E **42** E7
Sonkach *India* 22°59N 76°21E **42** H7
Sonmiani *Pakistan* 25°25N 66°40E **42** G2
Sonmiani B. *Pakistan* 25°15N 66°30E **42** G2
Sono → *Brazil* 9°58S 48°11W **93** E9
Sonoma *U.S.A.* 38°18N 122°28W **78** G4
Sonora *Calif., U.S.A.* 37°59N 120°23W **78** H6
Sonora *Tex., U.S.A.* 30°34N 100°39W **84** F4
Sonora □ *Mexico* 29°20N 110°40W **86** B2
Sonora → *Mexico* 29°5N 110°55W **86** B2
Sonoran Desert
   U.S.A. 33°40N 113°30W **79** L12
Sonoyta *Mexico* 31°51N 112°50W **86** A2
Sonsonate *El Salv.* 13°43N 89°44W **88** D2
Soochow = Suzhou
   China 31°19N 120°38E **33** C7
Sooke *Canada* 48°13N 123°43W **78** B3
Soomaaliya = Somali Rep. ■
   Africa 7°0N 47°0E **47** F4
Sop Hao *Laos* 20°33N 104°27E **38** B5
Sop Prap *Thailand* 17°53N 99°20E **38** D2
Sopi *Indonesia* 2°34N 128°28E **37** D7
Sopot *Poland* 54°27N 18°31E **17** A10
Sopron *Hungary* 47°45N 16°32E **17** E9
Sopur *India* 34°18N 74°27E **43** B6
Sør-Rondane *Antarctica* 72°0S 25°0E **5** D4
Sorah *Pakistan* 27°13N 68°56E **42** F3
Soraon *India* 25°37N 81°51E **43** G9
Sorel *Canada* 46°0N 73°10W **72** C5
Sórgono *Italy* 40°1N 9°6E **22** D3
Soria *Spain* 41°43N 2°32W **21** B4
Soriano *Uruguay* 33°24S 58°19W **94** C4
Sorkh, Kuh-e *Iran* 35°40N 58°30E **45** C8
Soroca *Moldova* 48°8N 28°12E **17** D15
Sorocaba *Brazil* 23°31S 47°27W **95** A6
Sorochinsk *Russia* 52°26N 53°10E **18** D9
Soroki = Soroca *Moldova* 48°8N 28°12E **17** D15
Sorong *Indonesia* 0°55S 131°15E **37** E8
Soroni *Greece* 36°21N 28°1E **25** C10
Soroti *Uganda* 1°43N 33°35E **54** B3
Sørøya *Norway* 70°40N 22°30E **8** A20
Sørøysundet *Norway* 70°25N 23°0E **8** A20
Sorrell *Australia* 42°47S 147°34E **63** G4

Sorrento *Italy* 40°37N 14°22E **22** D6
Sorsele *Sweden* 65°31N 17°30E **8** D17
Sorsogon *Phil.* 13°0N 124°0E **37** B6
Sortavala *Russia* 61°42N 30°41E **8** F24
Sortland *Norway* 68°42N 15°25E **8** B16
Soscumica, L. *Canada* 50°15N 77°27W **72** B4
Sosnogorsk *Russia* 63°37N 53°51E **18** B9
Sosnowiec *Poland* 50°20N 19°10E **17** C10
Sossus Vlei *Namibia* 24°40S 15°23E **56** C2
Sŏsura *N. Korea* 42°16N 130°36E **35** C16
Sot → *India* 27°27N 79°37E **43** F8
Sotavento *C. Verde Is.* 15°0N 25°0W **50** b
Sotik *Kenya* 0°41S 35°7E **54** C4
Sotkamo *Finland* 64°8N 28°23E **8** D23
Soto la Marina *Mexico* 23°46N 98°13W **87** C5
Soto la Marina →
   Mexico 23°45N 97°45W **87** C5
Sotuta *Mexico* 20°36N 89°1W **87** C7
Souanké *Congo* 2°10N 14°3E **52** D2
Souda *Greece* 35°29N 24°4E **25** D6
Soudas, Ormos *Greece* 35°25N 24°10E **25** D6
Souderton *U.S.A.* 40°19N 75°19W **83** F9
Soufrière *Guadeloupe* 16°5N 61°40W **88** b
Soufrière *St. Lucia* 13°51N 61°3W **89** f
Soufrière Bay *Dominica* 15°13N 61°22W **89** f
Soukhouma *Laos* 14°38N 105°48E **38** E5
Sŏul = Seoul *S. Korea* 37°31N 126°58E **35** F14
Sound, The *U.K.* 50°20N 4°10W **13** G3
Sources, Mt. aux *Lesotho* 28°45S 28°50E **57** D4
Soure *Brazil* 0°35S 48°30W **93** D9
Souris *Man., Canada* 49°40N 100°20W **71** D8
Souris *P.E.I., Canada* 46°21N 62°15W **73** C7
Souris → *N. Amer.* 49°40N 99°34W **80** A4
Sousa *Brazil* 6°45S 38°10W **93** E11
Sousse *Tunisia* 35°50N 10°38E **51** A8
Sout → *S. Africa* 31°35S 18°24E **56** E2
South Africa ■ *Africa* 32°0S 23°0E **56** E3
South America 10°0S 60°0W **90** E5
South Aulatsivik I.
   Canada 56°45N 61°30W **73** A7
South Australia □
   Australia 32°0S 139°0E **63** E2
South Australian Basin
   Ind. Oc. 38°0S 126°0E **64** L4
South Ayrshire □ *U.K.* 55°18N 4°41W **11** F4
South Baldy Pk. *U.S.A.* 34°6N 107°11W **77** J10
South Bass I. *U.S.A.* 41°39N 82°49E **82** E2
South Bend *Ind., U.S.A.* 41°41N 86°15W **80** E10
South Bend *Wash.,*
   U.S.A. 46°40N 123°48W **78** D3
South Boston *U.S.A.* 36°42N 78°54W **81** G14
South Branch *Canada* 47°55N 59°2W **73** C8
South Brook *Canada* 49°26N 56°5W **73** C8
South Bruny I. *Australia* 43°20S 147°15E **63** G4
South Carolina □ *U.S.A.* 34°0N 81°0W **85** E14
South Charleston
   U.S.A. 38°22N 81°44W **81** F13
South China Sea *Asia* 10°0N 113°0E **36** C4
South Cumberland Is. △
   Australia 20°42S 149°11E **62** J7
South Dakota □ *U.S.A.* 44°15N 100°0W **80** C4
South Dayton *U.S.A.* 42°15N 79°3W **82** D5
South Deerfield *U.S.A.* 42°29N 72°37W **83** D12
South Downs *U.K.* 50°52N 0°25W **13** G7
South East C. *Australia* 43°40S 146°50E **63** G4
South East Is. *Australia* 34°17S 123°30E **61** F3
South Esk → *U.K.* 56°43N 2°31W **11** E6
South Fiji Basin *Pac. Oc.* 26°0S 175°0E **64** K9
South Foreland *U.K.* 51°8N 1°24E **13** F9
South Fork American →
   U.S.A. 38°57N 120°59W **78** G5
South Fork Feather →
   U.S.A. 39°17N 121°36W **78** F5
South Fork Grand →
   U.S.A. 45°43N 102°17W **80** C2
South Fork Milk →
   U.S.A. 48°4N 106°19W **76** B10
South Fork Republican →
   U.S.A. 40°3N 101°31W **80** E3
South Georgia *Antarctica* 54°30S 37°0W **96** G9
South Gloucestershire □
   U.K. 51°32N 2°28W **13** F5
South Hadley *U.S.A.* 42°16N 72°35W **83** D12
South Haven *U.S.A.* 42°24N 86°16W **80** D10
South Henik L. *Canada* 61°30N 97°20W **71** A9
South Horr *Kenya* 2°12N 36°56E **54** B4
South I. *Kenya* 2°35N 36°35E **54** B4
South I. *N.Z.* 44°0S 170°0E **59** F3
South Indian Lake
   Canada 56°47N 98°56W **71** B9
South Invercargill *N.Z.* 46°26S 168°23E **59** G2
South Island △ *Kenya* 2°39N 36°35E **54** B4
South Kitui △ *Kenya* 1°48S 38°46E **54** C4
South Knife → *Canada* 58°55N 94°37W **71** B10
South Koel → *India* 22°32N 85°14E **43** H11
South Korea ■ *Asia* 36°0N 128°0E **35** G15
South Lake Tahoe
   U.S.A. 38°57N 119°59W **78** G6
South Lanarkshire □
   U.K. 55°37N 3°53W **11** F5
South Loup → *U.S.A.* 41°4N 98°39W **80** E4
South Luangwa △ *Zambia* 13°0S 31°20E **55** E3
South Magnetic Pole
   Antarctica 64°8S 138°8E **5** C9
South Milwaukee
   U.S.A. 42°55N 87°52W **80** D10
South Molton *U.K.* 51°1N 3°51W **13** F4
South Moose L. *Canada* 53°49N 100°1W **71** C8
South Nahanni →
   Canada 61°3N 123°21W **70** A4
South Nation → *Canada* 45°34N 75°6W **83** A9
South Natuna Is. = Natuna
   Selatan, Kepulauan
   Indonesia 2°45N 109°0E **36** D3
South Negril Pt. *Jamaica* 18°16N 78°22W **88** a
South Orkney Is.
   Antarctica 63°0S 45°0W **5** C18

South Ossetia □ *Georgia* 42°21N 44°2E **19** F7
South Otselic *U.S.A.* 42°38N 75°46W **83** D9
South Pagai, I. = Pagai Selatan,
   Pulau *Indonesia* 3°0S 100°15E **36** E2
South Paris *U.S.A.* 44°14N 70°31W **83** B14
South Pittsburg *U.S.A.* 35°1N 85°42W **85** D12
South Platte → *U.S.A.* 41°7N 100°42W **80** E3
South Pole *Antarctica* 90°0S 0°0 **5** E
South Porcupine *Canada* 48°30N 81°12W **72** C3
South Portland *U.S.A.* 43°38N 70°15W **81** D18
South Pt. *Barbados* 13°2N 59°32W **89** g
South Pt. *U.S.A.* 44°52N 83°19W **82** B1
South River *Canada* 45°52N 79°23W **82** A5
South River *U.S.A.* 40°27N 74°23W **83** F10
South Ronaldsay *U.K.* 58°48N 2°58W **11** C6
South Sandwich Is.
   Antarctica 57°0S 27°0W **5** B1
South Sandwich Trench
   Atl. Oc. 56°0S 24°0W **5** B1
South Saskatchewan →
   Canada 53°15N 105°5W **71** C7
South Seal → *Canada* 58°48N 98°8W **71** B9
South Shetland Is.
   Antarctica 62°0S 59°0W **5** C18
South Shields *U.K.* 55°0N 1°25W **12** C6
South Sioux City *U.S.A.* 42°28N 96°24W **80** D5
South Sister *Canada* 41°21N 121°51W **76** D3
South Talpatti = New Moore I.
   Ind. Oc. 21°37N 89°10E **43** J13
South Taranaki Bight
   N.Z. 39°40S 174°5E **59** C5
South Tasman Rise
   S. Ocean 48°0S 146°0E **5** A10
South Thompson →
   Canada 50°40N 120°20W **70** C4
South Twin I. *Canada* 53°7N 79°52E **72** B4
South Tyne → *U.K.* 54°59N 2°8W **12** C5
South Uist *U.K.* 57°20N 7°15W **11** D1
South Valley *U.S.A.* 35°1N 106°41W **77** J10
South Wellesley Is.
   Australia 16°58S 139°17E **62** B2
South West C. *Australia* 43°34S 146°3E **63** G4
South West C. *N.Z.* 47°17S 167°28E **59** G1
South Williamsport
   U.S.A. 41°13N 77°0W **82** E8
South Yorkshire □ *U.K.* 53°27N 1°36W **12** D6
Southampton *Canada* 44°30N 81°25W **82** B3
Southampton *U.K.* 50°54N 1°23W **13** G6
Southampton *U.S.A.* 40°53N 72°23W **83** F12
Southampton I. *Canada* 64°30N 84°0W **69** C11
Southaven *U.S.A.* 34°59N 90°0W **85** D9
Southbank *Canada* 54°2N 125°46W **70** C3
Southbridge *N.Z.* 43°48S 172°16E **59** E4
Southbridge *U.S.A.* 42°5N 72°2W **83** D12
Southend *Canada* 56°19N 103°22W **71** B8
Southend-on-Sea *U.K.* 51°32N 0°44E **13** F8
Southend-on-Sea □ *U.K.* 51°32N 0°44E **13** F8
Southern = Yuzhnyy □
   Russia 44°0N 40°0E **28** E5
Southern □ *Malawi* 15°0S 35°0E **55** F4
Southern □ *Zambia* 16°20S 26°20E **55** F2
Southern Alps *N.Z.* 43°41S 170°11E **59** E3
Southern Cross
   Australia 31°12S 119°15E **61** F2
Southern Indian L.
   Canada 57°10N 98°30W **71** B9
Southern Lau Group
   Fiji 18°40S 178°40W **59** a
Southern Ocean *Antarctica* 62°0S 60°0E **5** C6
Southern Pines *U.S.A.* 35°11N 79°24W **85** D15
Southern Uplands *U.K.* 55°28N 3°52W **11** F5
Southington *U.S.A.* 41°36N 72°53W **83** E12
Southland □ *N.Z.* 45°30S 168°0E **59** F1
Southold *U.S.A.* 41°4N 72°26W **83** E12
Southport *Australia* 27°58S 153°25E **63** D5
Southport *U.K.* 53°39N 3°0W **12** D4
Southport *U.S.A.* 33°29N 78°1W **85** E15
Southwest △ *Australia* 43°8S 146°5E **63** G4
Southwest Pacific Basin
   Pac. Oc. 40°0S 140°0W **5** A12
Southwold *U.K.* 52°20N 1°41E **13** E9
Southwood △ *Australia* 27°48S 150°8E **63** D5
Soutpansberg *S. Africa* 23°0S 29°30E **57** C4
Sovetsk *Kaliningrad, Russia* 55°6N 21°50E **9** J19
Sovetsk *Kirov, Russia* 57°38N 48°53E **18** C8
Sovetskaya Gavan
   Russia 48°58N 140°18E **29** E15
Soweto *S. Africa* 26°14S 27°54E **57** D4
Sowma'eh Sarā *Iran* 37°17N 49°18E **45** B6
Sōya-Kaikyō = La Perouse Str.
   Asia 45°40N 142°0E **30** B11
Sōya-Misaki *Japan* 45°30N 141°55E **30** B10
Soyo *Angola* 6°13S 12°20E **52** F2
Sozh → *Belarus* 51°57N 30°48E **17** B16
Spa *Belgium* 50°29N 5°53E **15** D5
Spain ■ *Europe* 39°0N 4°0W **21** B4
Spalding *Australia* 33°30S 138°37E **63** E2
Spalding *U.K.* 52°48N 0°9W **12** E7
Spanaway *U.S.A.* 47°6N 122°26W **78** C4
Spangler *U.S.A.* 40°39N 78°48W **82** F6
Spanish *Canada* 46°12N 82°20W **72** C3
Spanish Fork *U.S.A.* 40°7N 111°39W **76** F8
Spanish Town
   Br. Virgin Is. 18°27N 64°26W **89** e
Spanish Town *Jamaica* 18°0N 76°57W **88** a
Sparks *U.S.A.* 39°32N 119°45W **78** F7
Sparta = Sparti *Greece* 37°5N 22°25E **23** F10
Sparta *Mich., U.S.A.* 43°10N 85°42W **81** D11
Sparta *N.J., U.S.A.* 41°2N 74°38W **83** E10
Sparta *Wis., U.S.A.* 43°56N 90°49W **80** D8
Spartanburg *U.S.A.* 34°56N 81°57W **85** D14
Sparti *Greece* 37°5N 22°25E **23** F10
Spartivento, C. *Calabria,*
   Italy 37°55N 16°4E **22** F7
Spartivento, C. *Sard., Italy* 38°53N 8°50E **22** E3
Sparwood *Canada* 49°44N 114°53W **70** D6

Spassk Dalniy *Russia* 44°40N 132°48E **30** B6
Spatha, Akra *Greece* 35°42N 23°43E **25** D5
Spatsizi → *Canada* 57°42N 128°7W **70** B3
Spatsizi Plateau Wilderness ⌂
   Canada 57°40N 128°0W **70** B3
Spean → *U.K.* 56°55N 4°59W **11** E4
Spearfish *U.S.A.* 44°30N 103°52W **80** C2
Spearman *U.S.A.* 36°12N 101°12W **84** C4
Speculator *U.S.A.* 43°30N 74°22W **83** C10
Speightstown *Barbados* 13°15N 59°39W **89** g
Speke Gulf *Tanzania* 2°20S 32°50E **54** C3
Spence Bay = Taloyoak
   Canada 69°32N 93°32W **68** C10
Spencer *Idaho, U.S.A.* 44°22N 112°11W **76** D7
Spencer *Iowa, U.S.A.* 43°9N 95°9W **80** D6
Spencer *N.Y., U.S.A.* 42°13N 76°30W **83** D8
Spencer *Nebr., U.S.A.* 42°53N 98°42W **80** D4
Spencer, C. *Australia* 35°20S 136°53E **63** F2
Spencer B. *Namibia* 25°30S 14°47E **56** D1
Spencer G. *Australia* 34°0S 137°20E **63** E2
Spencerville *Canada* 44°51N 75°33W **83** B9
Spences Bridge *Canada* 50°25N 121°20W **70** C4
Spennymoor *U.K.* 54°42N 1°36W **12** C6
Spenser Mts. *N.Z.* 42°15S 172°45E **59** E4
Sperrin Mts. *U.K.* 54°50N 7°0W **10** B5
Spey → *U.K.* 57°40N 3°6W **11** D5
Speyer *Germany* 49°29N 8°25E **16** D5
Spezand *Pakistan* 29°59N 67°0E **42** E2
Spiddle *Ireland* 53°15N 9°18W **10** C2
Spili *Greece* 35°13N 24°31E **25** D6
Spīn Būldak *Afghan.* 31°1N 66°25E **42** D2
Spinalonga *Greece* 35°18N 25°44E **25** D7
Spirit Lake *U.S.A.* 46°15N 122°9W **78** D4
Spirit River *Canada* 55°45N 118°50W **70** B5
Spiritwood *Canada* 53°24N 107°33W **71** C7
Spithead *U.K.* 50°45N 1°10W **13** G6
Spitzbergen = Svalbard
   Arctic 78°0N 17°0E **4** B8
Spjelkavik *Norway* 62°28N 6°22E **8** E12
Split *Croatia* 43°31N 16°26E **22** C7
Split L. *Canada* 56°8N 96°15W **71** B9
Split Lake *Canada* 56°8N 96°15W **71** B9
Spofford *U.S.A.* 29°10N 100°25W **84** G4
Spokane *U.S.A.* 47°40N 117°24W **76** C5
Spoleto *Italy* 42°44N 12°44E **22** C5
Spooner *U.S.A.* 45°50N 91°53W **80** C8
Sporyy Navolok, Mys
   Russia 75°50N 68°40E **28** B7
Sprague *U.S.A.* 47°18N 117°59W **76** C5
Spratly I. *S. China Sea* 8°38N 111°55E **36** C4
Spratly Is. *S. China Sea* 8°20N 112°0E **36** C4
Spray *U.S.A.* 44°50N 119°48W **76** D4
Spree → *Germany* 52°32N 13°12E **16** B7
Spring City *U.S.A.* 40°11N 75°33W **83** F9
Spring Creek *U.S.A.* 40°44N 115°35W **76** F6
Spring Garden *U.S.A.* 39°52N 120°47W **78** F6
Spring Hall *Barbados* 13°18N 59°36W **89** g
Spring Hill *U.S.A.* 28°27N 82°41W **85** G13
Spring Mts. *U.S.A.* 36°0N 115°45W **79** J11
Spring Valley *Calif.,*
   U.S.A. 32°44N 116°59W **79** N10
Spring Valley *Nev.,*
   U.S.A. 36°6N 115°14W **79** J11
Springbok *S. Africa* 29°42S 17°54E **56** D2
Springboro *U.S.A.* 41°48N 80°22W **82** E4
Springdale *Canada* 49°30N 56°6E **73** C8
Springdale *U.S.A.* 36°11N 94°8W **84** C7
Springer *U.S.A.* 36°22N 104°36W **77** H11
Springerville *U.S.A.* 34°8N 109°17W **77** J9
Springfield *Canada* 42°50N 80°56W **82** D4
Springfield *N.Z.* 43°19S 171°56E **59** E3
Springfield *Colo.,*
   U.S.A. 37°24N 102°37W **77** H12
Springfield *Ill., U.S.A.* 39°48N 89°39W **80** F10
Springfield *Mass., U.S.A.* 42°6N 72°35W **83** D12
Springfield *Mo., U.S.A.* 37°13N 93°17W **80** G7
Springfield *Ohio, U.S.A.* 39°55N 83°49W **81** F12
Springfield *Oreg., U.S.A.* 44°3N 123°1W **76** D2
Springfield *Tenn.,*
   U.S.A. 36°31N 86°53W **85** C11
Springfield *Vt., U.S.A.* 43°18N 72°29W **83** C12
Springfontein *S. Africa* 30°15S 25°40E **56** E4
Springhill *Canada* 45°40N 64°4W **73** C7
Springhill *U.S.A.* 33°0N 93°28W **84** E8
Springhouse *Canada* 51°56N 122°7W **70** C4
Springs *S. Africa* 26°13S 28°25E **57** D4
Springsure *Australia* 24°8S 148°6E **62** C4
Springvale *U.S.A.* 43°28N 70°48W **83** C14
Springville *Calif., U.S.A.* 36°8N 118°49W **78** J8
Springville *N.Y., U.S.A.* 42°31N 78°40W **82** D6
Springville *Utah, U.S.A.* 40°10N 111°37W **76** F8
Springwater *U.S.A.* 42°38N 77°35W **82** D7
Spruce-Creek *U.S.A.* 40°36N 78°9W **82** F6
Spruce Knob-Seneca Rocks ⌂
   U.S.A. 38°50N 79°30W **81** F14
Spruce Mt. *U.S.A.* 44°12N 72°19W **83** B12
Sprucedale *Canada* 45°29N 79°28W **82** A5
Spur *U.S.A.* 33°28N 100°52W **84** E4
Spurn Hd. *U.K.* 53°35N 0°8E **12** D8
Spuzzum *Canada* 49°37N 121°23W **70** D4
Squam L. *U.S.A.* 43°45N 71°32W **83** C13
Squamish *Canada* 49°45N 123°10W **70** D4
Square Islands *Canada* 52°47N 55°47W **73** B8
Squires, Mt. *Australia* 26°14S 127°28E **61** E4
Srbija = Serbia ■ *Europe* 43°20N 20°0E **23** B9
Sre Ambel *Cambodia* 11°8N 103°46E **39** G4
Sre Khtum *Cambodia* 12°10N 106°52E **39** F6
Sre Umbell = Sre Ambel
   Cambodia 11°8N 103°46E **39** G4
Srebrenica *Bos.-H.* 44°6N 19°18E **23** B8
Sredinny Ra. = Sredinnyy Khrebet
   Russia 57°0N 160°0E **29** D17
Sredinnyy Khrebet
   Russia 57°0N 160°0E **29** D17
Sredinnyy Khrebet
   Russia 57°0N 160°0E **29** D17
Srednekolymsk *Russia* 67°27N 153°40E **29** C16
Šrem *Poland* 52°6N 17°2E **17** B9

Sremska Mitrovica
  Serbia 44°59N 19°38E 23 B8
Srepok → Cambodia 13°33N 106°16E 38 F6
Sretensk Russia 52°10N 117°40E 29 D12
Sri Aman Malaysia 1°15N 111°32E 36 D4
Sri Lanka ■ Asia 7°30N 80°50E 40 R12
Srikakulam India 18°14N 83°58E 41 K13
Srinagar India 34°5N 74°50E 43 B6
Srono Indonesia 8°24S 114°16E 37 J17
Staaten → Australia 16°24S 141°17E 62 B3
Staaten River △
  Australia 16°15S 142°40E 62 B3
Stade Germany 53°35N 9°29E 16 B5
Stadskanaal Neths. 53°4N 6°55E 15 A6
Staffa U.K. 56°27N 6°21W 11 E2
Stafford U.K. 52°49N 2°7W 12 E5
Stafford U.S.A. 37°58N 98°36W 80 G4
Stafford Springs U.S.A. 41°57N 72°18W 83 E12
Staffordshire □ U.K. 52°53N 2°10W 12 E5
Staines U.K. 51°26N 0°29W 13 F7
Stakhanov Ukraine 48°35N 38°40E 19 E6
Stalida Greece 35°17N 25°25E 25 D7
Stalowa Wola Poland 50°34N 22°3E 17 C12
Stalybridge U.K. 53°28N 2°3W 12 D5
Stamford Australia 21°15S 143°46E 62 C3
Stamford U.K. 52°39N 0°29W 13 E7
Stamford Conn., U.S.A. 41°3N 73°32W 83 E11
Stamford N.Y., U.S.A. 42°25N 74°38W 83 D10
Stamford Tex., U.S.A. 32°57N 99°48W 84 E5
Stampriet Namibia 24°20S 18°28E 56 C2
Stamps U.S.A. 33°22N 93°30W 84 E8
Standerton S. Africa 26°55S 29°7E 57 D4
Standish U.S.A. 43°59N 83°57W 81 D12
Stanford S. Africa 34°26S 19°29E 56 E2
Stanford U.S.A. 47°9N 110°13W 76 C8
Stanger S. Africa 29°27S 31°14E 57 D5
Stängseläsen = Salpausselkä
  Finland 61°3N 26°15E 8 F22
Stanislaus → U.S.A. 37°40N 121°14W 78 H5
Stanke Dimitrov
  Bulgaria 42°17N 23°9E 23 C10
Stanley Australia 40°46S 145°19E 63 G4
Stanley China 22°13N 114°12E 33 G11
Stanley Falk. Is. 51°40S 59°51W 96 G5
Stanley U.K. 54°53N 1°41W 12 C6
Stanley Idaho, U.S.A. 44°13N 114°56W 76 D6
Stanley N. Dak., U.S.A. 48°19N 102°23W 80 A2
Stanley N.Y., U.S.A. 42°48N 77°6W 82 D7
Stanley Mission
  Canada 55°25N 104°33W 71 B8
Stannards U.S.A. 42°5N 77°55W 82 D7
Stanovoy Khrebet
  Russia 55°0N 130°0E 29 D14
Stanovoy Ra. = Stanovoy Khrebet
  Russia 55°0N 130°0E 29 D14
Stansmore Ra. Australia 21°23S 128°33E 60 D4
Stansted, London ✈ (STN)
  U.K. 51°54N 0°14E 13 F8
Stanthorpe Australia 28°36S 151°59E 63 D5
Stanton U.S.A. 32°8N 101°48W 84 E4
Stanwood U.S.A. 48°15N 122°23W 78 B4
Staples Canada 42°10N 82°35W 82 D2
Staples U.S.A. 46°21N 94°48W 80 B6
Stapleton U.S.A. 41°29N 100°31W 80 E3
Star City Canada 52°50N 104°20W 71 C8
Star Lake U.S.A. 44°10N 75°2W 83 B9
Stara Planina Bulgaria 43°15N 23°0E 23 C10
Stara Zagora Bulgaria 42°26N 25°39E 23 C11
Starachowice Poland 51°3N 21°2E 17 C11
Staraya Russa Russia 57°58N 31°23E 18 C5
Starbuck I. Kiribati 5°37S 155°55W 65 H12
Starcke △ Australia 14°56S 145°2E 62 A4
Stargard Szczeciński
  Poland 53°20N 15°0E 16 B8
Staritsa Russia 56°33N 34°55E 18 C5
Starke U.S.A. 29°57N 82°7W 85 G13
Starkville U.S.A. 33°28N 88°49W 85 E10
Starogard Gdański
  Poland 53°59N 18°30E 17 B10
Starokonstantinov =
  Starokonstyantyniv
  Ukraine 49°48N 27°10E 17 D14
Starokonstyantyniv
  Ukraine 49°48N 27°10E 17 D14
Start Pt. U.K. 50°13N 3°39W 13 G4
Staryy Chartoriysk
  Ukraine 51°15N 25°54E 17 C13
Staryy Oskol Russia 51°19N 37°55E 19 D6
State College U.S.A. 40°48N 77°52W 82 F7
Stateline U.S.A. 38°57N 119°56W 78 G7
Staten, I. = Estados, I. de Los
  Argentina 54°40S 64°30W 96 G4
Staten I. U.S.A. 40°35N 74°9W 83 F10
Statesboro U.S.A. 32°27N 81°47W 85 E14
Statesville U.S.A. 35°47N 80°53W 85 D14
Statia = St. Eustatius
  W. Indies 17°20N 63°0W 89 C7
Stauffer U.S.A. 34°45N 119°3W 79 L7
Staunton Ill., U.S.A. 39°1N 89°47W 80 F9
Staunton Va., U.S.A. 38°9N 79°4W 81 F14
Stavanger Norway 58°57N 5°40E 9 G11
Staveley N.Z. 43°40S 171°32E 59 E3
Stavelot Belgium 50°23N 5°55E 15 D5
Stavern Norway 59°0N 10°1E 9 G14
Stavoren Neths. 52°53N 5°22E 15 B5
Stavropol Russia 45°5N 42°0E 19 E7
Stavros Cyprus 35°1N 32°38E 25 D11
Stavros Greece 35°12N 24°45E 25 D6
Stavros, Akra Greece 35°26N 24°58E 25 D6
Stawell Australia 37°5S 142°47E 63 F3
Stawell → Australia 20°20S 142°55E 62 C3
Stayner Canada 44°25N 80°5W 82 B4
Stayton U.S.A. 44°48N 122°48W 76 D2
Steamboat Springs
  U.S.A. 40°29N 106°50W 76 F10
Steele U.S.A. 46°51N 99°55W 80 B4
Steelton U.S.A. 40°14N 76°50W 82 F8

Steen River Canada 59°40N 117°12W 70 B5
Steens Mt. U.S.A. 42°35N 118°40W 76 E4
Steenwijk Neths. 52°47N 6°7E 15 B6
Steep Pt. Australia 26°8S 113°8E 61 E1
Steep Rock Canada 51°30N 98°48W 71 C9
Stefanie L. = Chew Bahir
  Ethiopia 4°40N 36°50E 47 G2
Stefansson Bay Antarctica 67°20S 59°8E 5 C5
Steiermark □ Austria 47°26N 15°0E 16 E8
Steilacoom U.S.A. 47°10N 122°36W 78 C4
Steilrandberge Namibia 17°45S 13°20E 56 B1
Steinbach Canada 49°32N 96°40W 71 D9
Steinhausen Namibia 21°49S 18°20E 56 C2
Steinkjer Norway 64°1N 11°31E 8 D14
Steinkopf S. Africa 29°18S 17°43E 56 D2
Stellarton Canada 45°32N 62°30W 73 C7
Stellenbosch S. Africa 33°58S 18°50E 56 E2
Stendal Germany 52°36N 11°53E 16 B6
Steornabhaigh = Stornoway
  U.K. 58°13N 6°23W 11 C2
Stepanakert = Xankändi
  Azerbaijan 39°52N 46°49E 44 B5
Stephens Creek
  Australia 31°50S 141°30E 63 E3
Stephens I. Canada 54°10N 130°45W 70 C2
Stephens L. Canada 56°32N 95°0W 71 B9
Stephenville Canada 48°31N 58°35W 73 C8
Stephenville U.S.A. 32°13N 98°12W 84 E5
Steppe Asia 50°0N 50°0E 26 C7
Sterkstroom S. Africa 31°32S 26°32E 56 E4
Sterling Colo., U.S.A. 40°37N 103°13W 76 F12
Sterling Ill., U.S.A. 41°48N 89°42W 80 E9
Sterling Kans., U.S.A. 38°13N 98°12W 80 F4
Sterling City U.S.A. 31°51N 101°0W 84 F4
Sterling Heights U.S.A. 42°35N 83°2W 81 D12
Sterling Run U.S.A. 41°25N 78°12W 82 E6
Sterlitamak Russia 53°40N 56°0E 18 D10
Sternes Greece 35°30N 24°9E 25 D6
Stettin = Szczecin Poland 53°27N 14°27E 16 B8
Stettiner Haff Germany 53°47N 14°15E 16 B8
Stettler Canada 52°19N 112°40W 70 C6
Steubenville U.S.A. 40°22N 80°37W 82 F4
Stevenage U.K. 51°55N 0°13W 13 F7
Stevens Point U.S.A. 44°31N 89°34W 80 C9
Stevenson U.S.A. 45°42N 121°53W 78 E5
Stevenson → Australia 27°6S 135°33E 63 D2
Stevenson L. Canada 53°55N 96°0W 71 C9
Stevensville U.S.A. 46°30N 114°5W 76 C6
Stewart Canada 55°56N 129°57W 70 B3
Stewart U.S.A. 39°5N 119°46W 78 F7
Stewart → Canada 63°19N 139°26W 68 C6
Stewart, C. Australia 11°57S 134°56E 62 A1
Stewart, I. Chile 54°50S 71°15W 96 G2
Stewart I. N.Z. 46°58S 167°54E 59 G1
Stewarts Point U.S.A. 38°39N 123°24W 78 G3
Stewartville U.S.A. 43°51N 92°29W 80 D7
Stewiacke Canada 45°9N 63°22W 73 C7
Steynsburg S. Africa 31°15S 25°49E 56 E4
Steyr Austria 48°3N 14°25E 16 D8
Steytlerville S. Africa 33°17S 24°19E 56 E3
Stigler U.S.A. 35°15N 95°8W 84 D7
Stikine → Canada 56°40N 132°30W 70 B2
Stilfontein S. Africa 26°51S 26°50E 56 D4
Stillwater N.Z. 42°27S 171°20E 59 E3
Stillwater N.Y., U.S.A. 42°55N 73°41W 83 D11
Stillwater Okla., U.S.A. 36°7N 97°4W 84 C6
Stillwater Range U.S.A. 39°50N 118°5W 76 G4
Stillwater Res. U.S.A. 43°54N 75°3W 83 C9
Stilwell U.S.A. 35°49N 94°38W 84 D7
Stînga Nistrului □
  Moldova 47°20N 29°15E 17 E15
Ştip Macedonia 41°42N 22°10E 23 D10
Stirling Canada 44°18N 77°33W 82 B7
Stirling U.K. 56°8N 3°57W 11 E5
Stirling Ra. Australia 34°23S 118°0E 61 F2
Stirling Range △
  Australia 34°26S 118°20E 61 F2
Stittsville Canada 45°15N 75°55W 83 A9
Stjernøya Norway 70°20N 22°40E 8 A20
Stjørdalshalsen Norway 63°29N 10°51E 8 E14
Stockerau Austria 48°24N 16°12E 16 D9
Stockholm Sweden 59°19N 18°4E 9 G18
Stockport U.K. 53°25N 2°9W 12 D5
Stockton Calif., U.S.A. 37°58N 121°17W 78 H5
Stockton Kans., U.S.A. 39°26N 99°16W 80 F4
Stockton Mo., U.S.A. 37°42N 93°48W 80 G7
Stockton-on-Tees U.K. 54°35N 1°19W 12 C6
Stockton-on-Tees □
  U.K. 54°35N 1°19W 12 C6
Stockton Plateau
  U.S.A. 30°30N 102°30W 84 F3
Stoeng Treng Cambodia 13°31N 105°58E 38 F5
Stoer, Pt. of U.K. 58°16N 5°23W 11 C3
Stoke-on-Trent U.K. 53°1N 2°11W 12 D5
Stoke-on-Trent □ U.K. 53°1N 2°11W 12 D5
Stokes △ Australia 33°45S 121°11E 61 F3
Stokes Bay Canada 45°0N 81°28W 82 B3
Stokes Pt. Australia 40°10S 143°56E 63 G3
Stokes Ra. Australia 15°50S 130°50E 60 C5
Stokksnes Iceland 64°14N 14°58W 8 D6
Stokmarknes Norway 68°34N 14°54E 8 B16
Stolac Bos.-H. 43°5N 17°59E 23 C7
Stolbovoy, Ostrov
  Russia 74°44N 135°14E 29 B14
Stolbtsy = Stowbtsy
  Belarus 53°30N 26°43E 17 B14
Stolin Belarus 51°53N 26°50E 17 C14
Stomio Greece 35°21N 23°32E 25 D5
Stone U.K. 52°55N 2°9W 12 E5
Stoneboro U.S.A. 41°20N 80°7W 82 E4
Stonehaven U.K. 56°59N 2°12W 11 E6
Stonehenge Australia 24°22S 143°17E 62 C3
Stonehenge U.K. 51°9N 1°45W 13 F6
Stonewall Canada 50°10N 97°19W 71 C9
Stony L. Man., Canada 58°51N 98°40W 71 B9

Stony L. Ont., Canada 44°30N 78°5W 82 B6
Stony Point U.S.A. 41°14N 73°59W 83 E11
Stony Pt. U.S.A. 43°50N 76°18W 83 C8
Stony Rapids Canada 59°16N 105°50W 71 B7
Stony Tunguska = Tunguska,
  Podkamennaya →
  Russia 61°50N 90°13E 29 C10
Stonyford U.S.A. 39°23N 122°33W 78 F4
Stora Lulevatten Sweden 67°10N 19°30E 8 C18
Storavan Sweden 65°45N 18°10E 8 D18
Stord Norway 59°52N 5°23E 9 G11
Store Bælt Denmark 55°20N 11°0E 9 J14
Storm B. Australia 43°10S 147°30E 63 G4
Storm Lake U.S.A. 42°39N 95°13W 80 D6
Stormberge S. Africa 31°16S 26°17E 56 E4
Stormsrivier S. Africa 33°59S 23°52E 56 E3
Stornoway U.K. 58°13N 6°23W 11 C2
Storozhinets = Storozhynets
  Ukraine 48°14N 25°45E 17 D13
Storozhynets Ukraine 48°14N 25°45E 17 D13
Storrs U.S.A. 41°49N 72°15W 83 E12
Storsjön Sweden 63°9N 14°30E 8 E16
Storuman Sweden 65°5N 17°10E 8 D17
Storuman, L. Sweden 65°13N 16°50E 8 D17
Stouffville Canada 43°58N 79°15W 82 C5
Stoughton Canada 49°40N 103°0W 71 D8
Stour → Dorset, U.K. 50°43N 1°47W 13 G6
Stour → Kent, U.K. 51°18N 1°22E 13 F9
Stour → Suffolk, U.K. 51°57N 1°4E 13 F9
Stourbridge U.K. 52°28N 2°8W 13 E5
Stout L. Canada 52°0N 94°40W 71 C10
Stove Pipe Wells Village
  U.S.A. 36°35N 117°11W 79 J9
Stow U.S.A. 41°10N 81°27W 82 E3
Stowbtsy Belarus 53°30N 26°43E 17 B14
Stowmarket U.K. 52°12N 1°0E 13 E9
Strabane U.K. 54°50N 7°27W 10 B4
Strahan Australia 42°9S 145°20E 63 G4
Stralsund Germany 54°18N 13°4E 16 A7
Strand S. Africa 34°9S 18°48E 56 E2
Stranda Møre og Romsdal,
  Norway 62°19N 6°58E 8 E12
Stranda Nord-Trøndelag,
  Norway 63°33N 10°14E 8 E14
Strangford L. U.K. 54°30N 5°37W 10 B6
Stranorlar Ireland 54°48N 7°46W 10 B4
Stranraer U.K. 54°54N 5°1W 11 G3
Strasbourg Canada 51°4N 104°55W 71 C8
Strasbourg France 48°35N 7°42E 20 B7
Stratford Canada 43°23N 81°0W 82 C3
Stratford N.Z. 39°20S 174°19E 59 C5
Stratford Calif., U.S.A. 36°11N 119°49W 78 J7
Stratford Conn., U.S.A. 41°12N 73°8W 83 E11
Stratford Tex., U.S.A. 36°20N 102°4W 84 C3
Stratford-upon-Avon
  U.K. 52°12N 1°42W 13 E6
Strath Spey U.K. 57°9N 3°49W 11 D5
Strathalbyn Australia 35°13S 138°53E 63 F2
Strathaven U.K. 55°40N 4°5W 11 F4
Strathcona △ Canada 49°38N 125°40W 70 D3
Strathmore Canada 51°5N 113°18W 70 C6
Strathmore U.K. 56°37N 3°7W 11 E5
Strathmore U.S.A. 36°9N 119°4W 78 J7
Strathnaver Canada 53°20N 122°33W 70 C4
Strathpeffer U.K. 57°35N 4°32W 11 D4
Strathroy Canada 42°58N 81°38W 82 D3
Strathy Pt. U.K. 58°36N 4°1W 11 C4
Strattanville U.S.A. 41°12N 79°19W 82 E5
Stratton U.S.A. 45°8N 70°26W 83 A14
Stratton Mt. U.S.A. 43°4N 72°55W 83 C12
Straubing Germany 48°52N 12°34E 16 D7
Straumnes Iceland 66°26N 23°8W 8 C2
Strawberry → U.S.A. 40°10N 110°24W 76 F8
Streaky B. Australia 32°48S 134°13E 63 E1
Streaky Bay Australia 32°51S 134°18E 63 E1
Streator U.S.A. 41°8N 88°50W 80 E9
Streetsboro U.S.A. 41°14N 81°21W 82 E3
Streetsville Canada 43°35N 79°42W 82 C5
Streng → Cambodia 13°12N 103°37E 38 F4
Strezhevoy Russia 60°42N 77°34E 28 C8
Strimonas → Greece 40°46N 23°51E 23 D10
Strokestown Ireland 53°46N 8°7W 10 C3
Stroma U.K. 58°41N 3°7W 11 C5
Strómboli Italy 38°47N 15°13E 22 E6
Stromeferry U.K. 57°21N 5°33W 11 D3
Stromness U.K. 58°58N 3°17W 11 C5
Stromsburg U.S.A. 41°7N 97°36W 80 E5
Strömstad Sweden 58°56N 11°10E 9 G14
Strömsund Sweden 63°51N 15°33E 8 E16
Strongsville U.S.A. 41°19N 81°50W 82 E3
Stronsay U.K. 59°7N 2°35W 11 B6
Stroud U.K. 51°45N 2°13W 13 F5
Stroud Road Australia 32°18S 151°57E 63 E5
Stroudsburg U.S.A. 40°59N 75°12W 83 F9
Stroumbi Cyprus 34°53N 32°29E 25 E11
Struer Denmark 56°30N 8°35E 9 H13
Strugi Krasnyye Russia 58°21N 29°1E 9 G23
Strumica Macedonia 41°28N 22°41E 23 D10
Struthers Canada 48°41N 85°51W 72 C2
Struthers U.S.A. 41°4N 80°39W 82 E4
Stryker U.S.A. 48°41N 114°46W 76 B6
Stryy Ukraine 49°16N 23°48E 17 D12
Strzelecki Cr. →
  Australia 29°37S 139°59E 63 D2
Strzelecki Desert
  Australia 29°30S 140°0E 63 D3
Stuart Fla., U.S.A. 27°12N 80°15W 85 H14
Stuart Nebr., U.S.A. 42°36N 99°8W 80 D4
Stuart → Canada 54°0N 123°35W 70 C4
Stuart Bluff Ra.
  Australia 22°50S 131°52E 60 D5
Stuart L. Canada 54°30N 124°30W 70 C4
Stuart Ra. Australia 29°10S 134°56E 63 D1
Stull L. Canada 54°24N 92°34W 72 B1
Stung Treng = Stoeng Treng
  Cambodia 13°31N 105°58E 38 F5

Stupart → Canada 56°0N 93°25W 72 A1
Sturgeon B. Canada 52°0N 97°50W 71 C9
Sturgeon Bay U.S.A. 44°50N 87°23W 80 C10
Sturgeon Falls Canada 46°25N 79°57W 72 C4
Sturgeon L. Alta., Canada 55°6N 117°32W 70 B5
Sturgeon L. Ont., Canada 50°0N 90°45W 72 C1
Sturgeon L. Ont., Canada 44°28N 78°43W 82 B6
Sturgis Canada 51°56N 102°36W 71 C8
Sturgis Mich., U.S.A. 41°48N 85°25W 81 E11
Sturgis S. Dak., U.S.A. 44°25N 103°31W 80 C2
Sturt △ Australia 27°17S 141°37E 63 D3
Sturt Cr. → Australia 19°8S 127°50E 60 C4
Sturt Stony Desert
  Australia 28°30S 141°0E 63 D3
Stutterheim S. Africa 32°33S 27°28E 56 E4
Stuttgart Germany 48°48N 9°11E 16 D5
Stuttgart U.S.A. 34°30N 91°33W 84 D9
Stuyvesant U.S.A. 42°23N 73°45W 83 D11
Stykkishólmur Iceland 65°2N 22°40W 8 D2
Styria = Steiermark □
  Austria 47°26N 15°0E 16 E8
Su Xian = Suzhou
  China 33°41N 116°59E 34 H9
Suakin Sudan 19°8N 37°20E 51 E13
Suan N. Korea 38°42N 126°22E 35 E14
Suar India 29°2N 79°3E 43 E8
Şubā Si. Arabia 27°10N 35°40E 44 E2
Subang Indonesia 6°34S 107°45E 37 G12
Subansiri → India 26°48N 93°50E 41 F18
Subarnarekha → India 22°34N 87°24E 43 H12
Subayhah Si. Arabia 30°2N 38°50E 44 D3
Subi Indonesia 2°58N 108°50E 36 D3
Subotica Serbia 46°6N 19°39E 23 A8
Suceava Romania 47°38N 26°16E 17 E14
Suchan = Partizansk
  Russia 43°8N 133°9E 30 C6
Suchil Mexico 23°38N 103°55W 86 C4
Suchou = Suzhou
  China 31°19N 120°38E 33 C7
Süchow = Xuzhou
  China 34°18N 117°10E 35 G9
Suck → Ireland 53°17N 8°3W 10 C3
Sucre Bolivia 19°0S 65°15W 92 G5
Sucuriú → Brazil 20°47S 51°38W 93 H8
Sud, Pte. du Canada 49°3N 62°14W 73 C7
Sud-Kivu □
  Dem. Rep. of the Congo 3°0S 28°30E 54 C2
Sud-Ouest, Pte. Canada 49°23N 63°36W 73 C7
Sud Ouest, Pte. Mauritius 20°28S 57°18E 53 d
Sudan ■ Africa 15°0N 30°0E 51 E11
Sudbury Canada 46°30N 81°0W 72 C3
Sudbury U.K. 52°2N 0°45E 13 E8
Sûdân Sudan 8°20N 30°0E 51 G12
Sudeten Mts. = Sudety
  Europe 50°20N 16°45E 17 C9
Sudety Europe 50°20N 16°45E 17 C9
Sudi Tanzania 10°11S 39°57E 55 E4
Sudirman, Pegunungan
  Indonesia 4°30S 137°0E 37 E9
Sudong, Pulau Singapore 1°13N 103°44E 39 d
Sueca Spain 39°12N 0°21W 21 C5
Suemez I. U.S.A. 55°15N 133°20W 70 B2
Suez = El Suweis Egypt 29°58N 32°31E 51 C12
Suez, G. of = Suweis, Khalig el
  Egypt 28°40N 33°0E 51 C12
Suez Canal = Suweis, Qanâ es
  Egypt 31°0N 32°20E 51 B12
Suffield Canada 50°12N 111°10W 70 C6
Suffolk U.S.A. 36°44N 76°35W 81 G15
Suffolk □ U.K. 52°16N 1°0E 13 E9
Sugar Grove U.S.A. 41°59N 79°20W 82 E5
Sugarcreek U.S.A. 41°25N 79°52W 82 E5
Sugarive → India 26°16N 86°24E 43 F12
Sugluk = Salluit
  Canada 62°14N 75°38W 69 C12
Suḩār Oman 24°20N 56°40E 45 E8
Sühbaatar Mongolia 50°17N 106°10E 32 A5
Sühbaatar □ Mongolia 45°30N 114°0E 34 B8
Suhl Germany 50°36N 10°42E 16 C6
Sui Pakistan 28°37N 69°19E 42 E3
Sui Xian China 34°25N 115°2E 34 G8
Suide China 37°30N 110°12E 34 F6
Suifenhe China 44°25N 131°10E 35 B16
Suihua China 46°32N 126°55E 33 B7
Suining Jiangsu, China 33°56N 117°58E 35 H9
Suining Sichuan, China 30°26N 105°35E 32 C5
Suiping China 33°10N 113°59E 34 H7
Suir → Ireland 52°16N 7°9W 10 D4
Suisse = Switzerland ■
  Europe 46°30N 8°0E 20 C8
Suisun City U.S.A. 38°15N 122°2W 78 G4
Suiyang China 44°30N 130°56E 35 B16
Suizhong China 40°21N 120°20E 35 D11
Sujangarh India 27°42N 74°31E 42 F6
Sukabumi Indonesia 6°56S 106°50E 37 G12
Sukadana Indonesia 1°10S 110°0E 36 E4
Sukagawa Japan 37°17N 140°23E 31 F10
Sukaraja Indonesia 2°28S 110°25E 36 E4
Sukawati Indonesia 8°35S 115°17E 37 K18
Sukch'ŏn N. Korea 39°22N 125°35E 35 E13
Sukhona → Russia 61°15N 46°39E 18 C8
Sukhothai Thailand 17°1N 99°49E 38 D2
Sukhumi = Sokhumi
  Georgia 43°0N 41°0E 19 F7
Sukkur Pakistan 27°42N 68°54E 42 F3
Sukkur Barrage Pakistan 27°40N 68°54E 42 F3
Sukri → India 25°4N 71°43E 42 G4
Sukumo Japan 32°56N 132°44E 31 H6
Sukunka → Canada 55°45N 121°15W 70 B4
Sula, Kepulauan Indonesia 1°45S 125°0E 37 E7
Sulaco → Honduras 15°2N 87°44W 88 C2
Sulaiman Range
  Pakistan 30°30N 69°50E 42 D3
Sülär Iran 31°53N 51°54E 45 D6
Sulawesi Indonesia 2°0S 120°0E 37 E6

Sulawesi Barat □ Indonesia 3°0S 119°0E 37 E5
Sulawesi Sea = Celebes Sea
  Indonesia 3°0N 123°0E 37 D6
Sulawesi Selatan □
  Indonesia 2°0S 120°0E 37 E6
Sulawesi Tengah □
  Indonesia 1°0S 121°0E 37 E6
Sulawesi Tenggara □
  Indonesia 3°50S 122°0E 37 E6
Sulawesi Utara □ Indonesia 1°0N 124°0E 37 D6
Sulima S. Leone 6°58N 11°32W 50 G3
Sulina Romania 45°10N 29°40E 17 F15
Sulitjelma Norway 67°9N 16°3E 8 C17
Sullana Peru 4°52S 80°39W 92 D2
Sullivan Ill., U.S.A. 39°36N 88°37W 80 F9
Sullivan Ind., U.S.A. 39°6N 87°24W 80 F10
Sullivan Mo., U.S.A. 38°13N 91°10W 80 F8
Sullivan Bay Canada 50°55N 126°50W 70 C3
Sullivan I. = Lanbi Kyun
  Burma 10°50N 98°20E 39 G2
Sullom Voe U.K. 60°27N 1°20W 11 A7
Sulphur La., U.S.A. 30°14N 93°23W 84 F8
Sulphur Okla., U.S.A. 34°31N 96°58W 84 D6
Sulphur Pt. Canada 60°56N 114°48W 70 A6
Sulphur Springs U.S.A. 33°8N 95°36W 84 E7
Sultan Canada 47°36N 82°47W 72 C3
Sultan U.S.A. 47°52N 121°49W 78 C5
Sultan Hamud Kenya 2°1S 37°22E 54 C4
Sultanābād = Arāk Iran 34°0N 49°40E 45 C6
Sultanpur Mad. P., India 23°9N 77°56E 42 H8
Sultanpur Punjab, India 31°13N 75°11E 42 D6
Sultanpur Ut. P., India 26°18N 82°4E 43 F10
Sulu Arch. Phil. 6°0N 121°0E 37 C6
Sulu Sea E. Indies 8°0N 120°0E 37 C6
Suluq Libya 31°44N 20°14E 51 B10
Sulzberger Ice Shelf
  Antarctica 78°0S 150°0W 5 E13
Sumalata Indonesia 1°0N 122°31E 37 D6
Sumampa Argentina 29°25S 63°29W 94 B3
Sumatera Indonesia 0°40N 100°20E 36 D2
Sumatera Barat □
  Indonesia 1°0S 101°0E 36 E2
Sumatera Utara □
  Indonesia 2°30N 98°0E 36 D1
Sumatra = Sumatera
  Indonesia 0°40N 100°20E 36 D2
Sumba Indonesia 9°45S 119°35E 37 F5
Sumba, Selat Indonesia 9°0S 118°40E 37 F5
Sumbawa Indonesia 8°26S 117°30E 36 F5
Sumbawa Besar
  Indonesia 8°30S 117°26E 36 F5
Sumbawanga □ Tanzania 8°0S 31°30E 52 F6
Sumbe Angola 11°10S 13°48E 52 G2
Sumbu □ Zambia 8°43S 30°22E 55 D3
Sumburgh Hd. U.K. 59°52N 1°17W 11 B7
Sumdeo India 31°26N 78°44E 43 D8
Sumdo China 35°6N 78°41E 43 B8
Sumedang Indonesia 6°52S 107°55E 37 G12
Šumen = Shumen
  Bulgaria 43°18N 26°55E 23 C12
Sumenep Indonesia 7°1S 113°52E 37 G15
Sumgait = Sumqayıt
  Azerbaijan 40°34N 49°38E 19 F8
Summer L. U.S.A. 42°50N 120°45W 76 E3
Summerland Canada 49°32N 119°41W 70 D5
Summerside Canada 46°24N 63°47W 73 C7
Summersville U.S.A. 38°17N 80°51W 81 F13
Summerville Ga.,
  U.S.A. 34°29N 85°21W 85 D12
Summerville S.C., U.S.A. 33°1N 80°11W 85 E14
Summit Lake Canada 54°20N 122°40W 70 C4
Summit Peak U.S.A. 37°21N 106°42W 77 H10
Sumner Iowa, U.S.A. 42°51N 92°6W 80 D7
Sumner Wash., U.S.A. 47°12N 122°14W 78 C4
Sumoto Japan 34°21N 134°54E 31 G7
Šumperk Czech Rep. 49°59N 16°59E 17 D9
Sumqayıt Azerbaijan 40°34N 49°38E 19 F8
Sumter U.S.A. 33°55N 80°21W 85 E14
Sumy Ukraine 50°57N 34°50E 19 D5
Sun City S. Africa 25°17S 27°3E 56 D4
Sun City Ariz., U.S.A. 33°35N 112°16W 77 K7
Sun City Calif., U.S.A. 33°42N 117°11W 79 M9
Sun City Center U.S.A. 27°43N 82°21W 85 H13
Sun Lakes U.S.A. 33°10N 111°52W 77 K8
Sun Valley U.S.A. 43°42N 114°21W 76 E6
Sunagawa Japan 43°29N 141°55E 30 C10
Sunan N. Korea 39°15N 125°40E 35 E13
Sunart, L. U.K. 56°42N 5°43W 11 E3
Sunburst U.S.A. 48°53N 111°55W 76 B8
Sunbury Australia 37°35S 144°44E 63 F3
Sunbury U.S.A. 40°52N 76°48W 83 F8
Sunchales Argentina 30°58S 61°35W 94 C3
Suncheon S. Korea 34°52N 127°31E 35 G14
Suncho Corral Argentina 27°55S 63°27W 94 B3
Sunch'on N. Korea 39°25N 125°56E 35 E13
Suncook U.S.A. 43°8N 71°27W 83 C13
Sunda, Selat Indonesia 6°20S 105°30E 36 F3
Sunda Is. Indonesia 5°0S 105°0E 64 H2
Sunda Str. = Sunda, Selat
  Indonesia 6°20S 105°30E 36 F3
Sunda Trench = Java Trench
  Ind. Oc. 9°0S 105°0E 64 H3
Sundance Canada 56°32N 94°4W 71 B10
Sundance U.S.A. 44°24N 104°23W 76 D11
Sundar Nagar India 31°32N 76°53E 42 D7
Sundarbans Asia 22°0N 89°0E 41 J16
Sundarbans △ India 22°0N 88°45E 43 J13
Sundargarh India 22°4N 84°5E 41 H14
Sundays = Sondags →
  S. Africa 33°44S 25°51E 56 E4
Sunderland Canada 44°16N 79°4W 82 B5
Sunderland U.K. 54°55N 1°23W 12 C6
Sundown △ Australia 28°49S 151°38E 63 D5
Sundre Canada 51°49N 114°38W 70 C6
Sundsvall Sweden 62°23N 17°17E 8 E17
Sung Hei Vietnam 10°20N 106°2E 39 G6
Sungai Acheh Malaysia 5°8N 100°30E 39 c

Sungai Kolok Thailand 6°2N 101°58E 39 J3
Sungai Lembing Malaysia 3°55N 103°3E 39 L4
Sungai Petani Malaysia 5°37N 100°30E 39 K3
Sungaigerong Indonesia 2°59S 104°52E 36 E2
Sungailiat Indonesia 1°51S 106°8E 36 E3
Sungaipenuh Indonesia 2°1S 101°20E 36 E2
Sungari = Songhua Jiang →
   China 47°45N 132°30E 33 B8
Sunghua Chiang = Songhua
   Jiang → China 47°45N 132°30E 33 B8
Sunland Park U.S.A. 31°50N 106°40W 77 L10
Sunndalsøra Norway 62°40N 8°33E 8 E13
Sunnyside U.S.A. 46°20N 120°0W 76 C4
Sunnyvale U.S.A. 37°23N 122°2W 78 H4
Sunrise Manor U.S.A. 36°12N 115°4W 79 J11
Suntar Russia 62°15N 117°30E 29 C12
Suomenselkä Finland 62°52N 24°0E 8 E21
Suomi = Finland ■ Europe 63°0N 27°0E 8 E22
Suomussalmi Finland 64°54N 29°10E 8 D23
Suoyarvi Russia 62°3N 32°20E 18 B5
Supai U.S.A. 36°15N 112°41W 77 H7
Supaul India 26°10N 86°40E 43 F12
Superior Ariz., U.S.A. 33°18N 111°6W 77 K8
Superior Mont., U.S.A. 47°12N 114°53W 76 C6
Superior Nebr., U.S.A. 40°1N 98°4W 80 E4
Superior Wis., U.S.A. 46°44N 92°6W 80 B7
Superior, L. N. Amer. 47°0N 87°0W 72 C2
Suphan Buri Thailand 14°14N 100°10E 38 E3
Suphan Dağı Turkey 38°54N 42°48E 44 B4
Supiori Indonesia 1°0S 136°0E 37 E9
Supung Shuiku China 40°35N 124°50E 35 D13
Süq ash Shuyūkh Iraq 30°53N 46°28E 44 D5
Süq Suwayq Si. Arabia 24°23N 38°27E 44 E3
Suqian China 33°54N 118°8E 35 H10
Suquţra = Socotra Yemen 12°30N 54°0E 47 E5
Şūr Lebanon 33°19N 35°16E 46 B4
Şūr Oman 22°34N 59°32E 47 C6
Sur, Pt. U.S.A. 36°18N 121°54W 78 J5
Sura → Russia 56°6N 46°0E 18 C8
Surab Pakistan 28°25N 66°15E 42 E2
Surabaja = Surabaya
   Indonesia 7°17S 112°45E 37 G15
Surabaya Indonesia 7°17S 112°45E 37 G15
Surakarta Indonesia 7°35S 110°48E 37 G14
Surat Australia 27°10S 149°6E 63 D4
Surat India 21°12N 72°55E 40 J8
Surat Thani Thailand 9°6N 99°20E 39 H2
Suratgarh India 29°18N 73°55E 42 E5
Şuraymilā Si. Arabia 25°7N 46°7E 44 E5
Surendranagar India 22°45N 71°40E 42 H4
Surf U.S.A. 34°41N 120°36W 79 L6
Surfers Paradise
   Australia 28°0S 153°25E 63 D5
Surgut Russia 61°14N 73°20E 28 C8
Suriapet India 17°10N 79°40E 40 L11
Surigao Phil. 9°47N 125°29E 37 C7
Surin Thailand 14°50N 103°34E 38 E4
Surin Nua, Ko Thailand 9°30N 97°55E 39 H1
Surinam = Suriname ■
   S. Amer. 4°0N 56°0W 93 C7
Suriname ■ S. Amer. 4°0N 56°0W 93 C7
Suriname → Suriname 5°50N 55°15W 93 B7
Sūrmaq Iran 31°3N 52°48E 45 D7
Surrey Canada 49°7N 122°45W 78 A4
Surrey □ U.K. 51°15N 0°31W 13 F7
Sursand India 26°39N 85°43E 43 F11
Sursar → India 26°14N 87°3E 43 F12
Surt Libya 31°11N 16°39E 51 B9
Surt, Khalīj Libya 31°40N 18°30E 51 B9
Surtanahu Pakistan 26°22N 70°0E 42 F4
Surtsey Iceland 63°20N 20°30W 8 E3
Suruga-Wan Japan 34°45N 138°30E 31 G9
Susaki Japan 33°22N 133°17E 31 H6
Süsangerd Iran 31°35N 48°6E 45 D6
Susanville U.S.A. 40°25N 120°39W 76 F3
Susner India 23°57N 76°5E 42 H7
Susquehanna U.S.A. 41°57N 75°36W 83 E9
Susquehanna → U.S.A. 39°33N 76°5W 83 G8
Susques Argentina 23°35S 66°25W 94 A2
Sussex Canada 45°45N 65°37W 73 C6
Sussex U.S.A. 41°13N 74°37W 83 E10
Sussex, E. □ U.K. 51°0N 0°20E 13 G8
Sussex, W. □ U.K. 51°0N 0°30W 13 G7
Sustut → Canada 56°20N 127°30W 70 B3
Susuman Russia 62°47N 148°10E 29 C15
Susunu Indonesia 3°7S 133°39E 37 E8
Susurluk Turkey 39°54N 28°8E 23 E13
Sutay Uul Asia 46°35N 93°38E 32 B4
Sutherland S. Africa 32°24S 20°40E 56 E3
Sutherland U.K. 58°12N 4°50W 11 C4
Sutherland U.S.A. 41°10N 101°8W 80 E3
Sutherland Falls N.Z. 44°48S 167°46E 59 F1
Sutherlin U.S.A. 43°23N 123°19W 76 E2
Suthri India 23°3N 68°55E 42 H3
Sutlej → Pakistan 29°23N 71°3E 42 E4
Sutter U.S.A. 39°10N 121°45W 78 F5
Sutter Buttes U.S.A. 39°12N 121°49W 78 F5
Sutter Creek U.S.A. 38°24N 120°48W 78 G6
Sutton Canada 45°6N 72°37W 83 A12
Sutton Nebr., U.S.A. 40°36N 97°52W 80 E6
Sutton W. Va., U.S.A. 38°40N 80°43W 81 F13
Sutton → Canada 55°15N 83°45W 72 A3
Sutton Coldfield U.K. 52°35N 1°49W 13 E6
Sutton in Ashfield U.K. 53°8N 1°16W 12 D6
Sutton L. Canada 54°15N 84°42W 72 B3
Suttor → Australia 21°36S 147°2E 62 C4
Suttsu Japan 42°48N 140°14E 30 C10
Suva Fiji 18°6S 178°30E 59 a
Suva Planina Serbia 43°10N 22°5E 23 C10
Suvorov Is. = Suwarrow Is.
   Cook Is. 13°15S 163°5W 65 J11
Suwałki Poland 54°8N 22°59E 17 A12
Suwana Indonesia 8°44S 115°36E 37 K18
Suwannaphum
   Thailand 15°33N 103°47E 38 E4
Suwannee → U.S.A. 29°17N 83°10W 85 G13
Suwanose-Jima Japan 29°38N 129°43E 31 K4

Suwarrow Is. Cook Is. 13°15S 163°5W 65 J11
Suweis, Khalīg el Egypt 28°40N 33°0E 51 C12
Suweis, Qanâ es Egypt 31°0N 32°20E 51 B12
Suwon S. Korea 37°17N 127°1E 35 F14
Suzdal Russia 56°29N 40°26E 18 C7
Suzhou Anhui, China 33°41N 116°59E 34 H9
Suzhou Jiangsu, China 31°19N 120°38E 33 C7
Suzu Japan 37°25N 137°17E 31 F8
Suzu-Misaki Japan 37°31N 137°21E 31 F8
Suzuka Japan 34°55N 136°36E 31 G8
Svalbard Arctic 78°0N 17°0E 4 B8
Svalbard Radio = Longyearbyen
   Svalbard 78°13N 15°40E 4 B8
Svappavaara Sweden 67°40N 21°3E 8 C19
Svartisen Norway 66°40N 13°50E 8 C15
Svay Chek Cambodia 13°48N 102°58E 38 F4
Svay Rieng Cambodia 11°9N 105°45E 39 G5
Svealand □ Sweden 60°20N 15°0E 9 F16
Sveg Sweden 62°2N 14°21E 8 E16
Svendborg Denmark 55°4N 10°35E 9 J14
Sverdlovsk Chan. Canada 75°56N 96°25W 69 B10
Sverdrup Is. Canada 79°0N 97°0W 69 B10
Sverige = Sweden ■
   Europe 57°0N 15°0E 9 H16
Svetlaya Russia 46°33N 138°18E 30 A9
Svetlogorsk = Svyetlahorsk
   Belarus 52°38N 29°46E 17 B15
Svir → Russia 60°30N 32°48E 18 B5
Svishtov Bulgaria 43°36N 25°23E 23 C11
Svislach Belarus 53°3N 24°2E 17 B13
Svizzera = Switzerland ■
   Europe 46°30N 8°0E 20 C8
Svobodnyy Russia 51°20N 128°0E 29 D13
Svolvær Norway 68°15N 14°34E 8 B16
Svyetlahorsk Belarus 52°38N 29°46E 17 B15
Swabian Alps = Schwäbische Alb
   Germany 48°20N 9°30E 16 D5
Swaffham U.K. 52°39N 0°42E 13 E8
Swains I. Amer. Samoa 11°11S 171°4W 65 J11
Swainsboro U.S.A. 32°36N 82°20W 85 E13
Swakop → Namibia 22°38S 14°36E 56 C2
Swakopmund Namibia 22°37S 14°30E 56 C1
Swale → U.K. 54°5N 1°20W 12 C6
Swan → Australia 32°3S 115°45E 61 F2
Swan → Canada 52°30N 100°45W 71 C8
Swan Hill Australia 35°20S 143°33E 63 F3
Swan Hills Canada 54°43N 115°24W 70 C5
Swan Is. = Santanilla, Is.
   Honduras 17°22N 83°57W 88 C3
Swan L. Man., Canada 52°30N 100°40W 71 C8
Swan L. Ont., Canada 54°16N 91°11W 72 B1
Swan Ra. U.S.A. 48°0N 113°45W 76 C7
Swan River Canada 52°10N 101°16W 71 C8
Swanage U.K. 50°36N 1°58W 13 G6
Swansea Australia 42°8S 148°4E 63 G4
Swansea Canada 43°38N 79°28W 82 C5
Swansea U.K. 51°37N 3°57W 13 F4
Swansea □ U.K. 51°38N 4°3W 13 F3
Swartberge S. Africa 33°20S 22°0E 56 E3
Swartmodder S. Africa 28°1S 20°32E 56 D3
Swartnossob → Namibia 23°8S 18°42E 56 C2
Swartruggens S. Africa 25°39S 26°42E 56 D4
Swastika Canada 48°7N 80°6W 72 C3
Swatow = Shantou
   China 23°18N 116°40E 33 D6
Swaziland ■ Africa 26°30S 31°30E 57 D5
Sweden ■ Europe 57°0N 15°0E 9 H16
Sweet Grass U.S.A. 48°59N 111°58W 76 B8
Sweet Home U.S.A. 44°24N 122°44W 76 D2
Sweetwater Nev., U.S.A. 38°27N 119°9W 78 G7
Sweetwater Tenn.,
   U.S.A. 35°36N 84°28W 85 D12
Sweetwater Tex.,
   U.S.A. 32°28N 100°25W 84 E4
Sweetwater → U.S.A. 42°31N 107°2W 76 E10
Swellendam S. Africa 34°1S 20°26E 56 E3
Świdnica Poland 50°50N 16°30E 17 C9
Świdnik Poland 51°13N 22°39E 17 C12
Świebodzin Poland 52°15N 15°31E 16 B8
Świecie Poland 53°25N 18°30E 17 B10
Swift Current Canada 50°20N 107°45W 71 C7
Swift Current →
   Canada 50°38N 107°44W 71 C7
Swilly, L. Ireland 55°12N 7°33W 10 A4
Swindon U.K. 51°34N 1°46W 13 F6
Swindon □ U.K. 51°34N 1°46W 13 F6
Swinemünde = Świnoujście
   Poland 53°54N 14°16E 16 B8
Swinford Ireland 53°57N 8°58W 10 C3
Świnoujście Poland 53°54N 14°16E 16 B8
Switzerland ■ Europe 46°30N 8°0E 20 C8
Swords Ireland 53°28N 6°13W 10 C5
Swoyerville U.S.A. 41°18N 75°53W 83 E9
Sydenham → Canada 42°33N 82°25W 82 D2
Sydney Australia 33°52S 151°12E 63 E5
Sydney Canada 46°7N 60°7W 73 C7
Sydney L. Canada 50°41N 94°25W 71 C10
Sydney Mines Canada 46°18N 60°15W 73 C7
Sydprøven = Alluitsup Paa
   Greenland 60°30N 45°35W 4 C5
Sydra, G. of = Surt, Khalīj
   Libya 31°40N 18°30E 51 B9
Sykesville U.S.A. 41°3N 78°50W 82 E6
Syktyvkar Russia 61°45N 50°40E 18 B10
Sylacauga U.S.A. 33°10N 86°15W 85 E11
Sylarna Sweden 63°2N 12°13E 8 E15
Sylhet Bangla. 24°54N 91°52E 41 G17
Sylhet □ Bangla. 24°50N 91°10E 41 G17
Sylt Germany 54°54N 8°22E 16 A5
Sylvan Beach U.S.A. 43°12N 75°44W 83 C9
Sylvan Lake Canada 52°20N 114°3W 70 C6
Sylvania U.S.A. 32°45N 81°38W 85 E14
Sylvania Ohio, U.S.A. 41°43N 83°42W 81 E12
Sylvester U.S.A. 31°32N 83°50W 85 F13
Sym Russia 60°20N 88°18E 28 C9
Synnot Ra. Australia 16°30S 125°20E 60 C4

Syowa Antarctica 68°50S 12°0E 5 C5
Syracuse Kans., U.S.A. 37°59N 101°45W 80 G3
Syracuse N.Y., U.S.A. 43°3N 76°9W 83 C8
Syracuse Nebr., U.S.A. 40°39N 96°11W 80 E5
Syrdarya → Kazakhstan 46°3N 61°0E 28 E7
Syria ■ Asia 35°0N 38°0E 44 C3
Syrian Desert = Shām, Bādiyat
   ash Asia 32°0N 40°0E 44 C3
Syros Greece 37°28N 24°57E 23 F11
Syzran Russia 53°12N 48°30E 18 D8
Szczecin Poland 53°27N 14°27E 16 B8
Szczecinek Poland 53°43N 16°41E 17 B9
Szczeciński, Zalew = Stettiner Haff
   Germany 53°47N 14°15E 16 B8
Szczytno Poland 53°33N 21°0E 17 B11
Szechwan = Sichuan □
   China 30°30N 103°0E 32 C5
Szeged Hungary 46°16N 20°10E 17 E11
Székesfehérvár Hungary 47°15N 18°25E 17 E10
Szekszárd Hungary 46°22N 18°42E 17 E10
Szentes Hungary 46°39N 20°21E 17 E11
Szolnok Hungary 47°10N 20°15E 17 E11
Szombathely Hungary 47°14N 16°38E 17 E9

T

Ta Khli Thailand 15°15N 100°21E 38 E3
Ta Khli Khok Thailand 15°18N 100°20E 38 E3
Ta Lai Vietnam 11°24N 107°23E 39 G6
Tabacal Argentina 23°15S 64°15W 94 A3
Tabaco Phil. 13°22N 123°44E 37 B6
Tabanan Indonesia 8°32S 115°8E 37 K18
Tabas Khorāsān, Iran 32°48N 60°12E 45 C9
Ṭabas Yazd, Iran 33°35N 56°55E 45 C8
Tabasará, Serranía de
   Panama 8°35N 81°40W 88 E3
Tabasco □ Mexico 18°0N 92°40W 87 D6
Tabāsīn Iran 31°12N 57°54E 45 D8
Tabatinga, Serra da
   Brazil 10°30S 44°0W 93 F10
Taber Canada 49°47N 112°8W 70 D6
Tablas Phil. 12°25N 122°2E 37 B6
Table B. Canada 53°40N 56°25W 73 B8
Table B. S. Africa 33°35S 18°25E 56 E2
Table Mt. S. Africa 33°58S 18°26E 56 E2
Table Rock L. U.S.A. 36°36N 93°19W 84 D7
Tabletop, Mt. Australia 23°24S 147°11E 62 C4
Tábor Czech Rep. 49°25N 14°39E 16 D8
Tabora Tanzania 5°2S 32°50E 54 D3
Tabora □ Tanzania 5°0S 33°0E 54 D3
Tabou Ivory C. 4°30N 7°20W 50 H4
Tabrīz Iran 38°7N 46°20E 44 B5
Tabuaeran Kiribati 3°51N 159°22W 65 G12
Tabūk Si. Arabia 28°23N 36°8E 44 D3
Tabūk □ Si. Arabia 27°40N 36°50E 44 E3
Tacámbaro de Codallos
   Mexico 19°14N 101°28W 86 D4
Tacheng China 46°40N 82°58E 32 B3
Tach'ing Shan = Daqing Shan
   China 40°40N 111°0E 34 D6
Tacloban Phil. 11°15N 124°58E 37 B6
Tacna Peru 18°0S 70°20W 92 G4
Tacoma U.S.A. 47°14N 122°26W 78 C4
Tacuarembó Uruguay 31°45S 56°0W 95 C4
Tademaït, Plateau du
   Algeria 28°30N 2°30E 50 C6
Tadjoura Djibouti 11°50N 42°55E 47 E3
Tadmor N.Z. 41°27S 172°45E 59 D4
Tadoule L. Canada 58°36N 98°20W 71 B9
Tadoussac Canada 48°11N 69°42W 73 C6
Tadzhikistan = Tajikistan ■
   Asia 38°30N 70°0E 28 F8
Taegu = Daegu
   S. Korea 35°50N 128°37E 35 G15
Taegwan N. Korea 40°13N 125°12E 35 D13
Taejŏn = Daejeon
   S. Korea 36°20N 127°28E 35 F14
Taen, Ko Thailand 9°22N 99°57E 39 b
Tafalla Spain 42°30N 1°41W 21 A5
Tafelbaai = Table B.
   S. Africa 33°35S 18°25E 56 E2
Tafermaar Indonesia 6°47S 134°10E 37 F8
Tafi Viejo Argentina 26°43S 65°17W 94 B2
Tafihān Iran 29°25N 52°39E 45 D7
Tafresh Iran 34°45N 49°57E 45 C6
Taft Iran 31°45N 54°14E 45 D7
Taft Phil. 11°57N 125°30E 37 B7
Taft U.S.A. 35°8N 119°28W 79 K7
Taftan Pakistan 29°0N 61°30E 40 E2
Taftān, Kūh-e Iran 28°40N 61°0E 45 D9
Taga Dzong Bhutan 27°5N 89°55E 41 F16
Taganrog Russia 47°12N 38°50E 19 E6
Tagbilaran Phil. 9°39N 123°51E 37 C6
Tagish Canada 60°19N 134°16W 70 A2
Tagish L. Canada 60°10N 134°20W 70 A2
Tagliamento → Italy 45°38N 13°6E 22 B5
Tagomago Spain 39°2N 1°39E 24 B8
Taguatinga Brazil 12°25S 46°22W 93 F10
Tagum Phil. 7°33N 125°53E 37 C7
Tagus = Tejo → Europe 38°40N 9°24W 21 C1
Tahakopa N.Z. 46°30S 169°23W 59 G2
Tahan, Gunung
   Malaysia 4°34N 102°17E 39 K4
Tahat Algeria 23°18N 5°33E 50 D7
Tāherī Iran 27°43N 52°20E 45 E7
Tahiti French Polynesia 17°37S 149°27W 59 d
Tahiti, I. Tahiti 17°37S 149°27W 59 d
Tahlequah U.S.A. 35°55N 94°58W 84 D7
Tahoe, L. U.S.A. 39°6N 120°2W 78 G6
Tahoe City U.S.A. 39°10N 120°9W 78 F6
Tahoka U.S.A. 33°10N 101°48W 84 E4
Taholah U.S.A. 47°21N 124°17W 78 C2
Tahoua Niger 14°57N 5°16E 50 F7

Tahrūd Iran 29°26N 57°49E 45 D8
Tahsis Canada 49°55N 126°40W 70 D3
Tahta Egypt 26°44N 31°32E 51 C12
Tahulandang Indonesia 2°27N 125°23E 37 D7
Tahuna Indonesia 3°38N 125°30E 37 D7
Tai Au Mun China 22°18N 114°17E 33 G11
Tai Mo Shan China 22°25N 114°7E 33 G11
Tai O China 22°15N 113°52E 33 G10
Tai Pang Wan China 22°33N 114°24E 33 F11
Tai Po China 22°27N 114°10E 33 G11
Tai Rom Yen △ Thailand 8°45N 99°30E 39 H2
Tai Shan China 36°25N 117°20E 35 F9
Tai Yue Shan = Lantau I.
   China 22°15N 113°56E 33 G10
Tai'an China 36°12N 117°8E 35 F9
Taiarapu, Presqu'île de
   Tahiti 17°47S 149°14W 59 d
Taibei = T'aipei Taiwan 25°4N 121°29E 33 D7
Taibique Canary Is. 27°42N 17°58W 24 G2
Taibus Qi China 41°54N 115°22E 34 D8
T'aichung Taiwan 24°9N 120°37E 33 D7
Taieri → N.Z. 46°3S 170°12E 59 G3
Taigu China 37°28N 112°30E 34 F7
Taihang Shan China 36°0N 113°30E 34 G7
Taihape N.Z. 39°41S 175°48E 59 C5
Taihe China 33°20N 115°42E 34 H8
Taikang China 34°5N 114°50E 34 G8
Tailem Bend Australia 35°12S 139°29E 63 F2
Taimyr Peninsula = Taymyr,
   Poluostrov Russia 75°0N 100°0E 29 B11
Tain U.K. 57°49N 4°4W 11 D4
T'ainan Taiwan 23°0N 120°10E 33 D7
Taipa China 22°10N 113°35E 33 G10
T'aipei Taiwan 25°4N 121°29E 33 D7
Taiping Malaysia 4°51N 100°44E 39 K3
Taipingzhen China 33°35N 111°42E 34 H6
Tairbeart = Tarbert U.K. 57°54N 6°49W 11 D2
Taita Hills Kenya 3°25S 38°15E 54 C4
Taitao, Pen. de Chile 46°30S 75°0W 96 F2
T'aitung Taiwan 22°43N 121°4E 33 D7
Taivalkoski Finland 65°33N 28°12E 8 D23
Taiwan ■ Asia 23°30N 121°0E 33 D7
Taiyiba Israel 32°36N 35°27E 46 C4
Taiyuan China 37°52N 112°33E 34 F7
Taizhong = T'aichung
   Taiwan 24°9N 120°37E 33 D7
Ta'izz Yemen 13°35N 44°2E 47 E3
Tājābād Iran 30°2N 54°24E 45 D7
Tajikistan ■ Asia 38°30N 70°0E 28 F8
Tajima Japan 37°12N 139°46E 31 F9
Tajo = Tejo → Europe 38°40N 9°24W 21 C1
Tajrīsh Iran 35°48N 51°25E 45 C6
Tak Thailand 16°52N 99°8E 38 D2
Takāb Iran 36°24N 47°7E 44 B5
Takachiho Japan 32°42N 131°18E 31 H5
Takachu Botswana 22°37S 21°58E 56 C3
Takada Japan 37°7N 138°15E 31 F9
Takahagi Japan 36°43N 140°45E 31 F10
Takaka N.Z. 40°51S 172°50E 59 D4
Takamaka Seychelles 4°50S 55°30E 53 b
Takamatsu Japan 34°20N 134°5E 31 G7
Takaoka Japan 36°47N 137°0E 31 F8
Takapuna N.Z. 36°47S 174°47E 59 B5
Takasaki Japan 36°20N 139°0E 31 F9
Takatsuki Japan 34°51N 135°37E 31 G7
Takaungu Kenya 3°38S 39°52E 54 C4
Takayama Japan 36°18N 137°11E 31 F8
Take-Shima Japan 30°49N 130°26E 31 J5
Takefu Japan 35°50N 136°10E 31 G8
Takengon Indonesia 4°45N 96°50E 36 D1
Takeo Japan 33°12N 130°1E 31 H5
Takeshima = Tokdo
   Asia 37°15N 131°52E 31 F5
Taketa Japan 32°58N 131°24E 31 H5
Takev Cambodia 10°59N 104°47E 39 G5
Takh India 33°6N 77°32E 43 C7
Takhmau Cambodia 11°29N 104°57E 39 G5
Takht-Sulaiman
   Pakistan 31°40N 69°58E 42 D3
Takikawa Japan 43°33N 141°54E 30 C10
Takla L. Canada 55°15N 125°45W 70 B3
Takla Landing Canada 55°30N 125°50W 70 B3
Takla Makan China 38°0N 83°0E 32 C3
Taklamakan Shamo = Takla
   Makan China 38°0N 83°0E 32 C3
Taksimo Russia 56°20N 114°52E 29 D12
Taku → Canada 58°30N 133°50W 70 B2
Takua Pa Thailand 8°52N 98°21E 39 H2
Takua Thung Thailand 8°24N 98°27E 39 a
Tal Halāl Iran 27°35N 52°45E 45 D7
Tala Uruguay 34°21S 55°46W 95 C4
Talagang Pakistan 32°55N 72°25E 42 C5
Talagante Chile 33°40S 70°50W 94 C1
Talamanca, Cordillera de
   Cent. Amer. 9°20N 83°20W 88 E3
Talampaya △ Argentina 29°43S 67°42W 94 B2
Talara Peru 4°38S 81°18W 92 D2
Talas Kyrgyzstan 42°30N 72°13E 28 E8
Talâta Morocco 29°0N 10°12W 50 C3
Talaud, Kepulauan
   Indonesia 4°30N 126°50E 37 D7
Talaud Is. = Talaud, Kepulauan
   Indonesia 4°30N 126°50E 37 D7
Talavera de la Reina
   Spain 39°55N 4°46W 21 C3
Talbandh India 23°18N 86°20E 43 H12
Talbot, C. Australia 13°48S 126°43E 60 B4
Talbragar → Australia 32°12S 148°37E 63 E4
Talca Chile 35°28S 71°40W 94 D1
Talcahuano Chile 36°40S 73°10W 94 D1
Talcher India 21°0N 85°18E 41 J14
Taldy Kurgan = Taldyqorghan
   Kazakhstan 45°10N 78°45E 28 E8
Taldyqorghan
   Kazakhstan 45°10N 78°45E 28 E8

Tālesh Iran 37°58N 48°58E 45 B6
Tālesh, Kūhhā-ye Iran 37°42N 48°55E 45 B6
Tali Post Sudan 5°55N 30°44E 51 G12
Taliabu Indonesia 1°50S 125°0E 37 E6
Talibon Phil. 10°9N 124°20E 37 B6
Talihina U.S.A. 34°45N 95°3W 84 D7
Taliwang Indonesia 8°50S 116°55E 36 F5
Tall 'Afar Iraq 36°22N 42°27E 44 B4
Tall Kalakh Syria 34°41N 36°15E 46 A5
Talladega U.S.A. 33°26N 86°6W 85 E11
Tallahassee U.S.A. 30°27N 84°17W 85 F12
Tallangatta Australia 36°15S 147°19E 63 F4
Tallering Pk. Australia 28°6S 115°37E 61 E2
Talli Pakistan 29°32N 68°8E 42 E3
Tallinn Estonia 59°22N 24°48E 9 G21
Tallmadge U.S.A. 41°6N 81°27W 82 E3
Tallulah U.S.A. 32°25N 91°11W 84 E9
Talnakh Russia 69°29N 88°22E 29 C9
Taloyoak Canada 69°32N 93°32W 68 C10
Talpa de Allende
   Mexico 20°23N 104°51W 86 C4
Talparo Trin. & Tob. 10°30N 61°17W 93 K15
Talsi Latvia 57°10N 22°30E 9 H20
Taltal Chile 25°23S 70°33W 94 B1
Taltson → Canada 61°24N 112°46W 70 A6
Talwood Australia 28°29S 149°29E 63 D4
Talyawalka Cr. →
   Australia 32°28S 142°22E 63 E3
Tam Ky Vietnam 15°34N 108°29E 38 E7
Tam Quan Vietnam 14°35N 109°3E 38 E7
Tama U.S.A. 41°58N 92°35W 80 E7
Tamale Ghana 9°22N 0°50W 50 G5
Taman Negara △
   Malaysia 4°38N 102°26E 39 K4
Tamano Japan 34°29N 133°59E 31 G6
Tamanrasset Algeria 22°50N 5°30E 50 D7
Tamaqua U.S.A. 40°48N 75°58W 83 F9
Tamar → U.K. 50°27N 4°15W 13 G3
Tamarin Mauritius 20°19S 57°20E 53 d
Tamashima Japan 34°32N 133°40E 31 G6
Tamatave = Toamasina
   Madag. 18°10S 49°25E 57 B8
Tamaulipas □ Mexico 24°0N 98°45W 87 C5
Tamaulipas, Sierra de
   Mexico 23°30N 98°20W 87 C5
Tamazula Mexico 24°57N 106°57W 86 C3
Tamazunchale Mexico 21°16N 98°47W 87 C5
Tambach Kenya 0°36N 35°31E 54 B4
Tambacounda Senegal 13°45N 13°40W 50 F3
Tambelan, Kepulauan
   Indonesia 1°0N 107°30E 36 D3
Tambellup Australia 34°4S 117°37E 61 F2
Tambo Australia 24°54S 146°14E 62 C4
Tambo de Mora Peru 13°30S 76°8W 92 F3
Tambohorano Madag. 17°30S 43°58E 57 B7
Tambora Indonesia 8°12S 118°5E 36 F5
Tambov Russia 52°45N 41°28E 18 D7
Tambuku Indonesia 7°8S 113°40E 37 G15
Tâmega → Portugal 41°5N 8°21W 21 B1
Tamenglong India 25°0N 93°35E 41 G18
Tamiahua, L. de Mexico 21°35N 97°35W 87 C5
Tamil Nadu □ India 11°0N 77°0E 40 P10
Tamluk India 22°18N 87°58E 43 H12
Tammerfors = Tampere
   Finland 61°30N 23°50E 8 F20
Tammisaari Finland 60°0N 23°26E 9 G20
Tamo Abu, Banjaran
   Malaysia 3°10N 115°5E 36 D5
Tampa U.S.A. 27°56N 82°27W 85 H13
Tampa, Tanjung
   Indonesia 8°55S 116°12E 37 K19
Tampa B. U.S.A. 27°50N 82°30W 85 H13
Tampere Finland 61°30N 23°50E 8 F20
Tampico Mexico 22°13N 97°51W 87 C5
Tampin Malaysia 2°28N 102°13E 39 L4
Tampoi Malaysia 1°30N 103°39E 39 d
Tamu Burma 24°13N 94°12E 41 G19
Tamworth Australia 31°7S 150°58E 63 E5
Tamworth Canada 44°29N 77°0W 82 B8
Tamworth U.K. 52°39N 1°41W 13 E6
Tan An Vietnam 10°32N 106°25E 39 G6
Tan Chau Vietnam 10°48N 105°12E 39 G5
Tan-Tan Morocco 28°0N 11°0W 50 C3
Tana → Kenya 2°32S 40°31E 54 C5
Tana → Norway 70°30N 28°14E 8 A23
Tana, L. Ethiopia 13°5N 37°30E 47 E2
Tana River Primate △
   Kenya 1°55S 40°7E 54 C5
Tanabe Japan 33°44N 135°22E 31 H7
Tanafjorden Norway 70°45N 28°25E 8 A23
Tanahbala Indonesia 0°30S 98°30E 36 E1
Tanahgrogot Indonesia 1°55S 116°15E 36 E5
Tanahjampea Indonesia 7°10S 120°35E 37 F6
Tanahmasa Indonesia 0°12S 98°39E 36 E1
Tanahmerah Indonesia 6°5S 140°16E 37 F10
Tanakpur India 29°5N 80°7E 43 E9
Tanakura Japan 37°10N 140°20E 31 F10
Tanami Desert Australia 18°50S 132°0E 60 C5
Tanami Mine Australia 19°59S 129°43E 60 C4
Tananarive = Antananarivo
   Madag. 18°55S 47°31E 57 B8
Tánaro → Italy 44°55N 8°40E 20 D8
Tancheng China 34°25N 118°20E 35 G10
Tanch'ŏn N. Korea 40°27N 128°54E 35 D15
Tanda Ut. P., India 26°33N 82°35E 43 F9
Tanda Ut. P., India 28°57N 78°56E 43 E8
Tandag Phil. 9°4N 126°9E 37 C7
Tandaué Angola 16°58S 18°5E 56 B2
Tandil Argentina 37°15S 59°6W 94 D4
Tandil, Sa. del Argentina 37°30S 59°0W 94 D4
Tandlianwala Pakistan 31°3N 73°9E 42 D5
Tando Adam Pakistan 25°45N 68°40E 42 G3
Tando Allahyar Pakistan 25°28N 68°43E 42 G3
Tando Bago Pakistan 24°47N 68°58E 42 G3
Tando Mohommed Khan
   Pakistan 25°8N 68°32E 42 G3

Tandou L. *Australia* 32°40S 142°5E **63** E3
Tandoureh △ *Iran* 37°50N 59°0E **44** B8
Tandragee *U.K.* 54°21N 6°24W **10** B5
Tane-ga-Shima *Japan* 30°30N 131°0E **31** J5
Taneatua *N.Z.* 38°4S 177°1E **59** C6
Tanen Tong Dan = Dawna Ra.
　Burma 16°30N 98°30E **38** D2
Tanezrouft *Algeria* 23°9N 0°11E **50** D6
Tang, Koh *Cambodia* 10°16N 103°7E **39** G4
Tang, Ra's-e *Iran* 25°21N 59°52E **45** E8
Tang Krasang *Cambodia* 12°34N 105°3E **38** F5
Tanga *Tanzania* 5°5S 39°2E **54** D4
Tanga □ *Tanzania* 5°20S 38°0E **54** D4
Tanganyika, L. *Africa* 6°40S 30°0E **54** D3
Tanger *Morocco* 35°50N 5°49W **50** A4
Tangerang *Indonesia* 6°11S 106°37E **37** G12
Tanggu *China* 39°2N 117°40E **35** E9
Tanggula Shan *China* 32°40N 92°10E **32** C4
Tanggula Shankou
　China 32°42N 92°27E **32** C4
Tanghe *China* 32°47N 112°50E **34** H7
Tanghla Range = Tanggula Shan
　China 32°40N 92°10E **32** C4
Tangier = Tanger
　Morocco 35°50N 5°49W **50** A4
Tangjia *China* 22°22N 113°35E **33** G10
Tangjia Wan *China* 22°21N 113°36E **33** G10
Tangorin *Australia* 21°47S 144°12E **62** C3
Tangorombohitr'i Makay
　Madag. 21°0S 45°15E **57** C8
Tangra Yumco *China* 31°0N 86°38E **32** C3
Tangshan *China* 39°38N 118°10E **35** E10
Tangtou *China* 35°28N 118°30E **35** G10
Tanimbar, Kepulauan
　Indonesia 7°30S 131°30E **37** F8
Tanimbar Is. = Tanimbar,
　Kepulauan *Indonesia* 7°30S 131°30E **37** F8
Taninthari = Tenasserim
　Burma 12°6N 99°3E **39** F2
Tanjay *Phil.* 9°30N 123°5E **37** C6
Tanjong Malim *Malaysia* 3°42N 101°31E **39** L3
Tanjong Pelepas *Malaysia* 1°21N 103°33E **39** d
Tanjore = Thanjavur
　India 10°48N 79°12E **40** P11
Tanjung *Indonesia* 8°21S 116°9E **37** J19
Tanjung *Phil.* 2°10S 115°25E **36** E5
Tanjung Tokong *Malaysia* 5°28N 100°18E **39** c
Tanjungbalai *Indonesia* 2°55N 99°44E **36** D1
Tanjungbatu *Indonesia* 2°23N 118°3E **36** D5
Tanjungkarang Telukbetung =
　Bandar Lampung
　Indonesia 5°20S 105°10E **36** F3
Tanjungpandan
　Indonesia 2°43S 107°38E **36** E3
Tanjungpinang *Indonesia* 1°5N 104°30E **36** D2
Tanjungredeb *Indonesia* 2°9N 117°29E **36** D5
Tanjungselor *Indonesia* 2°55N 117°25E **36** D5
Tank *Pakistan* 32°14N 70°25E **42** C4
Tankhala *India* 21°58N 73°47E **42** J5
Tankwa-Karoo △
　S. Africa 32°14S 19°50E **56** E2
Tannersville *U.S.A.* 41°3N 75°18W **83** E9
Tannu Ola *Asia* 51°0N 94°0E **29** D10
Tannum Sands
　Australia 23°57S 151°22E **62** C5
Tanout *Niger* 14°50N 8°55E **50** F7
Tanta *Egypt* 30°45N 30°57E **51** B12
Tantoyuca *Mexico* 21°21N 98°14W **87** C5
Tantung = Dandong
　China 40°10N 124°20E **35** D13
Tanunda *Australia* 34°30S 139°0E **63** E2
Tanzania ■ *Africa* 6°0S 34°0E **54** D3
Tanzhou *China* 22°16N 113°28E **33** G9
Tanzilla → *Canada* 58°8N 130°43W **70** B2
Tao, Ko *Thailand* 10°5N 99°52E **39** G2
Tao'an = Taonan
　China 45°22N 122°40E **35** B12
Tao'er He → *China* 45°45N 124°5E **35** B13
Taolanaro *Madag.* 25°2S 47°0E **57** D8
Taole *China* 38°48N 106°40E **34** E4
Taonan *China* 45°22N 122°40E **35** B12
Taos *U.S.A.* 36°24N 105°35W **77** H11
Taoudenni *Mali* 22°40N 3°55W **50** D5
Tapa *Estonia* 59°15N 25°50E **9** G21
Tapa Shan = Daba Shan
　China 32°0N 109°0E **33** C5
Tapachula *Mexico* 14°54N 92°17W **87** E6
Tapah *Malaysia* 4°12N 101°15E **39** K3
Tapajós → *Brazil* 2°24S 54°41W **93** D8
Tapaktuan *Indonesia* 3°15N 97°10E **36** D1
Tapanahoni → *Suriname* 4°20N 54°25W **93** C8
Tapanui *N.Z.* 45°56S 169°18E **59** F2
Tapauá → *Brazil* 5°40S 64°21W **92** E6
Tapes *Brazil* 30°40S 51°23W **95** C5
Tapeta *Liberia* 6°29N 8°52W **50** G4
Taphan Hin *Thailand* 16°13N 100°26E **38** D3
Tapirapecó, Serra
　Venezuela 1°10N 65°0W **92** C6
Tapo-Capara △ *Venezuela* 7°55N 71°15W **89** E5
Tapti → *India* 21°8N 72°41E **40** J8
Tapuae-o-Uenuku *N.Z.* 42°0S 173°39E **59** E4
Tapul Group *Phil.* 5°35N 120°50E **37** C6
Tapurucuará *Brazil* 0°24S 65°2W **92** D5
Ţaqtaq *Iraq* 35°53N 44°35E **44** C5
Taquara *Brazil* 29°36S 50°46W **95** B5
Taquari → *Brazil* 19°15S 57°17W **92** G7
Tara *Australia* 27°17S 150°31E **63** D5
Tara *Canada* 44°28N 81°9W **82** B3
Tara *Russia* 56°55N 74°24E **28** D8
Tara *Zambia* 16°58S 26°45E **55** F2
Tara → *Montenegro* 43°21N 18°51E **23** C8
Tarābulus *Lebanon* 34°31N 35°50E **46** A4
Tarābulus *Libya* 32°49N 13°7E **51** B8
Taradehi *India* 23°18N 79°21E **43** H8
Tarajalejo *Canary Is.* 28°12N 14°7W **24** F5
Tarakan *Indonesia* 3°2N 117°35E **36** D5

Tarakit, Mt. *Kenya* 2°2N 35°10E **54** B4
Tarama-Jima *Japan* 24°39N 124°42E **31** M2
Taran, Mys *Russia* 54°56N 19°59E **9** J18
Taranagar *India* 28°43N 74°50E **42** E6
Taranaki □ *N.Z.* 39°25S 174°30E **59** C5
Taranaki, Mt. *N.Z.* 39°17S 174°5E **59** C5
Tarancón *Spain* 40°1N 3°1W **21** B4
Tarangire △ *Tanzania* 4°21S 36°7E **54** C4
Taransay *U.K.* 57°54N 7°0W **11** D1
Táranto *Italy* 40°28N 17°14E **22** D7
Táranto, G. di *Italy* 40°8N 17°20E **22** D7
Tarapacá *Colombia* 2°56S 69°46W **92** D5
Tarapacá □ *Chile* 20°45S 69°30W **94** A2
Tarapoto *Peru* 6°30S 76°20W **92** E3
Tararua Ra. *N.Z.* 40°45S 175°25E **59** D5
Tarashcha *Ukraine* 49°30N 30°31E **17** D16
Tarauacá *Brazil* 8°6S 70°48W **92** E4
Tarauacá → *Brazil* 6°42S 69°48W **92** E5
Taravao *Tahiti* 17°43S 149°18W **59** d
Taravao, Isthme de
　Tahiti 17°43S 149°19W **59** d
Tarawa *Kiribati* 1°30N 173°0E **64** G9
Tarawera *N.Z.* 39°2S 176°36E **59** C6
Tarawera, L. *N.Z.* 38°13S 176°27E **59** C6
Taraz *Kazakhstan* 42°54N 71°22E **28** E8
Tarazona *Spain* 41°55N 1°43W **21** B5
Tarbagatay, Khrebet
　Kazakhstan 48°0N 83°0E **28** E9
Tarbat Ness *U.K.* 57°52N 3°47W **11** D5
Tarbela Dam *Pakistan* 34°8N 72°52E **42** B5
Tarbert *Ireland* 52°34N 9°22W **10** D2
Tarbert *Argyll & Bute,*
　U.K. 55°52N 5°25W **11** F3
Tarbert *W. Isles, U.K.* 57°54N 6°49W **11** D2
Tarbes *France* 43°15N 0°3E **20** E4
Tarboro *U.S.A.* 35°54N 77°32W **85** D16
Tarcoola *Australia* 30°44S 134°36E **63** E1
Tarcoon *Australia* 30°15S 146°43E **63** E4
Taree *Australia* 31°50S 152°30E **63** E5
Tarfaya *Morocco* 27°55N 12°55W **50** C3
Târgoviște *Romania* 44°55N 25°27E **17** F13
Târgu Jiu *Romania* 45°5N 23°19E **17** F12
Târgu Mureş *Romania* 46°31N 24°38E **17** E13
Ţarif *U.A.E.* 24°3N 53°46E **45** E7
Tarifa *Spain* 36°1N 5°36W **21** D3
Tarija *Bolivia* 21°30S 64°40W **94** A3
Tarija □ *Bolivia* 21°30S 63°30W **94** A3
Tariku → *Indonesia* 2°55S 138°26E **37** E9
Tarim Basin = Tarim Pendi
　China 40°0N 84°0E **32** B3
Tarim He → *China* 39°30N 88°30E **32** C3
Tarim Pendi *China* 40°0N 84°0E **32** B3
Taritatu → *Indonesia* 2°54S 138°27E **37** E9
Tarka → *S. Africa* 32°10S 26°0E **56** E4
Tarka La *Bhutan* 27°12N 89°44E **43** F13
Tarkastad *S. Africa* 32°0S 26°16E **56** E4
Tarkhankut, Mys
　Ukraine 45°25N 32°30E **19** E5
Tarko Sale *Russia* 64°55N 77°50E **28** C8
Tarkwa *Ghana* 5°20N 2°0W **50** G5
Tarlac *Phil.* 15°29N 120°35E **37** A6
Tarma *Peru* 11°25S 75°45W **92** F3
Tarn □ *France* 44°5N 1°6E **20** E4
Tarn → *France* 44°5N 1°6E **20** D4
Târnăveni *Romania* 46°19N 24°13E **17** E13
Tarnobrzeg *Poland* 50°35N 21°41E **17** C11
Tarnów *Poland* 50°3N 21°0E **17** C11
Tarnowskie Góry
　Poland 50°27N 18°54E **17** C10
Ţārom *Iran* 28°11N 55°46E **45** D7
Taroom *Australia* 25°36S 149°48E **63** D4
Taroudannt *Morocco* 30°30N 8°52W **50** B4
Tarpon Springs *U.S.A.* 28°9N 82°45W **85** G13
Tarrafal *C. Verde Is.* 15°18N 23°39W **50** b
Tarragona *Spain* 41°5N 1°17E **21** B6
Tarraleah *Australia* 42°17S 146°26E **63** G4
Tarrasa = Terrassa *Spain* 41°34N 2°1E **21** B7
Tarrytown *U.S.A.* 41°4N 73°52W **83** E11
Tarshiha = Me'ona *Israel* 33°1N 35°15E **46** B4
Tarsus *Turkey* 36°58N 34°55E **44** B2
Tartagal *Argentina* 22°30S 63°50W **94** A3
Tartu *Estonia* 58°20N 26°44E **9** G22
Ţarţūs *Syria* 34°55N 35°55E **44** C2
Tarumizu *Japan* 31°29N 130°42E **31** J5
Tarutao = Ko Tarutao △
　Thailand 6°31N 99°26E **39** J2
Tarutao, Ko *Thailand* 6°33N 99°40E **39** J2
Tarutung *Indonesia* 2°0N 98°54E **36** D1
Taseko → *Canada* 52°8N 123°45W **70** C4
Tash-Kömür *Kyrgyzstan* 41°40N 72°10E **28** E8
Tash-Kumyr = Tash-Kömür
　Kyrgyzstan 41°40N 72°10E **28** E8
Tashauz = Dashoguz
　Turkmenistan 41°49N 59°58E **28** E6
Tashi Chho Dzong = Thimphu
　Bhutan 27°31N 89°45E **41** F16
Tashk, Daryācheh-ye
　Iran 29°45N 53°35E **45** D7
Tashkent = Toshkent
　Uzbekistan 41°20N 69°10E **28** E7
Tashtagol *Russia* 52°47N 87°53E **28** D9
Tasiilaq *Greenland* 65°40N 37°20W **4** C6
Tasik Kenyir *Malaysia* 5°5N 102°45E **39** K4
Tasikmalaya *Indonesia* 7°18S 108°12E **37** G13
Tåsjön *Sweden* 64°15N 15°40E **8** D16
Taskan *Russia* 62°59N 150°20E **29** C16
Tasman B. *N.Z.* 40°59S 173°25E **59** D4
Tasman Basin *Pac. Oc.* 46°0S 158°0E **64** M7
Tasman Mts. *N.Z.* 41°3S 172°25E **59** D4
Tasman Pen. *Australia* 43°10S 148°0E **63** G4
Tasman Sea *Pac. Oc.* 36°0S 160°0E **58** E9
Tasmania □ *Australia* 42°0S 146°30E **63** G4
Tasmanian Wilderness World
　Heritage Area △
　Australia 43°0S 146°0E **63** G4
Tassili n' Ajjer *Algeria* 25°47N 8°1E **50** C7
Tassili-Oua-n-Ahaggar
　Algeria 20°41N 5°30E **50** D7

Tat Ton △ *Thailand* 15°57N 102°2E **38** E4
Tata *Morocco* 29°46N 7°56W **50** C4
Tatabánya *Hungary* 47°32N 18°25E **17** E10
Tatahouine *Tunisia* 32°56N 10°27E **51** B8
Tataouine *Tunisia* 32°57N 10°29E **51** B8
Tatar Republic = Tatarstan □
　Russia 55°30N 51°30E **18** C9
Tatarsk *Russia* 55°14N 76°0E **28** D8
Tatarskiy Proliv *Russia* 50°0N 141°0E **29** E15
Tatarstan □ *Russia* 55°30N 51°30E **18** C9
Tatatua, Pte. *Tahiti* 17°44S 149°8W **59** d
Tateyama *Japan* 35°0N 139°50E **31** G9
Tathlina L. *Canada* 60°33N 117°39W **70** A5
Tathra *Australia* 36°44S 149°59E **63** F4
Tatinnai L. *Canada* 60°55N 97°40W **71** A9
Tatla Lake *Canada* 52°0N 124°20W **70** C4
Tatnam, C. *Canada* 57°16N 91°0W **71** B10
Tatra = Tatry *Slovak Rep.* 49°20N 20°0E **17** D11
Tatry *Slovak Rep.* 49°20N 20°0E **17** D11
Tatshenshini →
　Canada 59°28N 137°45W **70** B1
Tatsuno *Japan* 34°52N 134°33E **31** G7
Tatta *Pakistan* 24°42N 67°55E **42** G2
Tatuı̄ *Brazil* 23°25S 47°53W **95** A6
Tat'ung = Datong *China* 40°6N 113°18E **34** D7
Tatvan *Turkey* 38°31N 42°15E **44** B4
Ta'ū *Amer. Samoa* 14°15S 169°30W **59** b
Taubaté *Brazil* 23°0S 45°36W **95** A6
Tauern *Austria* 47°15N 12°40E **16** E7
Taumarunui *N.Z.* 38°53S 175°15E **59** C5
Taumaturgo *Brazil* 8°54S 72°51W **92** E4
Taung *S. Africa* 27°33S 24°47E **56** D3
Taungdwingyi *Burma* 20°1N 95°40E **41** J19
Taunggyi *Burma* 20°50N 97°0E **41** J20
Taungup *Burma* 18°51N 94°14E **41** K19
Taunsa *Pakistan* 30°42N 70°39E **42** D4
Taunsa Barrage *Pakistan* 30°42N 70°50E **42** D4
Taunton *U.K.* 51°1N 3°5W **13** F4
Taunton *U.S.A.* 41°54N 71°6W **83** E13
Taunus *Germany* 50°13N 8°34E **16** C5
Taupo *N.Z.* 38°41S 176°7E **59** C6
Taupo, L. *N.Z.* 38°46S 175°55E **59** C5
Tauragė *Lithuania* 55°14N 22°16E **9** J20
Tauranga *N.Z.* 37°42S 176°11E **59** B6
Tauranga Harb. *N.Z.* 37°30S 176°5E **59** B6
Taureau, Rés. *Canada* 46°46N 73°50W **72** C5
Taurianova *Italy* 38°21N 16°1E **22** E7
Taurus Mts. = Toros Dağları
　Turkey 37°0N 32°30E **44** B2
Tautira *Tahiti* 17°44S 149°9W **59** d
Tauyskaya Guba
　Russia 59°20N 150°20E **29** D16
Tavan Bogd Uul
　Mongolia 49°10N 87°49E **32** B3
Tavastehus = Hämeenlinna
　Finland 61°0N 24°28E **8** F21
Tavda *Russia* 58°7N 65°8E **28** D7
Tavda → *Russia* 57°47N 67°18E **28** D7
Taveta *Kenya* 3°23S 37°37E **54** C4
Taveuni *Fiji* 16°51S 179°58W **59** a
Tavira *Portugal* 37°8N 7°40W **21** D2
Tavistock *Canada* 43°19N 80°50W **82** C4
Tavistock *U.K.* 50°33N 4°9W **13** G3
Tavoy *Burma* 14°2N 98°12E **38** E2
Tavrichanka *Russia* 43°18N 131°59E **30** C5
Tavua *Fiji* 17°37S 177°5E **59** a
Tavuki *Fiji* 19°7S 178°8E **59** a
Taw → *U.K.* 51°4N 4°4W **13** F3
Tawa → *India* 22°48N 77°48E **42** H8
Tawas City *U.S.A.* 44°16N 83°31W **81** C12
Tawau *Malaysia* 4°20N 117°55E **36** D5
Tawi-Tawi *Phil.* 5°10N 120°15E **37** C6
Taxco *Mexico* 18°33N 99°36W **87** D5
Taxila *Pakistan* 33°42N 72°52E **42** C5
Taxkorgan Tajik Zizhixian
　China 37°49N 75°14E **32** C2
Tay → *U.K.* 56°37N 3°38W **11** E5
Tay, Firth of *U.K.* 56°25N 3°8W **11** E5
Tay, L. *Australia* 32°55S 120°48E **61** F3
Tay, L. *U.K.* 56°32N 4°8W **11** E4
Tay △ *U.K.* 56°43N 3°59W **11** E5
Tay Ninh *Vietnam* 11°20N 106°5E **39** G6
Tayabamba *Peru* 8°15S 77°16W **92** E3
Taygetos Oros *Greece* 37°0N 22°23E **23** F10
Taylakova *Russia* 59°13N 74°0E **28** D8
Taylor *Canada* 56°13N 120°40W **70** B4
Taylor *Nebr., U.S.A.* 41°46N 99°23W **80** E4
Taylor *Pa., U.S.A.* 41°23N 75°43W **83** E9
Taylor *Tex., U.S.A.* 30°34N 97°25W **84** F6
Taylor, Mt. *U.S.A.* 35°14N 107°37W **77** J10
Taylorville *U.S.A.* 39°33N 89°18W **80** F10
Taymā *Si. Arabia* 27°35N 38°45E **44** E3
Taymyr, Oz. *Russia* 74°20N 102°0E **29** B11
Taymyr, Poluostrov
　Russia 75°0N 100°0E **29** B11
Tayport *U.K.* 56°27N 2°52W **11** E6
Tayrona □ *Colombia* 11°20N 74°2W **89** D5
Tayshet *Russia* 55°58N 98°1E **29** D10
Taytay *Phil.* 10°45N 119°30E **37** B5
Ţāyyebād *Iran* 34°45N 60°45E **45** C9
Ţāyyebād □ *Iran* 34°44N 60°44E **45** C9
Taz → *Russia* 67°32N 78°40E **28** C8
Taza *Morocco* 34°16N 4°6W **50** B5
Tāza Khurmātū *Iraq* 35°18N 44°20E **44** C5
Tazawa-Ko *Japan* 39°43N 140°40E **30** E10
Tazin → *Canada* 59°48N 109°55W **71** B7
Tazin L. *Canada* 59°44N 108°42W **71** B7
Tazovskiy *Russia* 67°30N 78°44E **28** C8
Tbilisi *Georgia* 41°43N 44°50E **19** F7
Tchad = Chad ■ *Africa* 15°0N 17°15E **51** F8
Tchad, L. *Chad* 13°30N 14°30E **51** F8
Tch'eng-tou = Chengdu
　China 30°38N 104°2E **32** C5
Tchentlo L. *Canada* 55°15N 125°0W **70** B4

Tchibanga *Gabon* 2°45S 11°0E **52** E2
Tch'ong-k'ing = Chongqing
　China 29°35N 106°25E **32** D5
Tczew *Poland* 54°8N 18°50E **17** A10
Te Anau, L. *N.Z.* 45°15S 167°45E **59** F1
Te Aroha *N.Z.* 37°32S 175°44E **59** B5
Te Awamutu *N.Z.* 38°1S 175°20E **59** C5
Te Ika a Maui = North I.
　N.Z. 38°0S 175°0E **59** C5
Te Kuiti *N.Z.* 38°20S 175°11E **59** C5
Te Puke *N.Z.* 37°46S 176°22E **59** B6
Te Waewae B. *N.Z.* 46°13S 167°33E **59** G1
Te Wai Pounamu = South I.
　N.Z. 44°0S 170°0E **59** F3
Teague *U.S.A.* 31°38N 96°17W **84** F6
Teahupoo *Tahiti* 17°50S 149°16W **59** d
Teapa *Mexico* 17°33N 92°57W **87** D6
Tebakang *Malaysia* 1°6N 110°30E **36** D4
Teberu *Malaysia* 1°30N 103°42E **39** d
Tébessa *Algeria* 35°22N 8°8E **50** A7
Tebicuary → *Paraguay* 26°36S 58°16W **94** B4
Tebingtinggi *Riau,*
　Indonesia 1°0N 102°45E **36** E2
Tebingtinggi *Sumatera Utara,*
　Indonesia 3°20N 99°9E **36** D1
Tecate *Mexico* 32°34N 116°38W **79** N10
Tecka *Argentina* 43°29N 70°48W **96** E2
Tecomán *Mexico* 18°55N 103°53W **86** D4
Tecopa *U.S.A.* 35°51N 116°13W **79** K10
Tecoripa *Mexico* 28°37N 109°57W **86** B3
Tecuala *Mexico* 22°23N 105°27W **86** C3
Tecuci *Romania* 45°51N 27°27E **17** F14
Tecumseh *Canada* 42°19N 82°54W **82** D2
Tecumseh *Mich., U.S.A.* 42°0N 83°57W **81** D12
Tecumseh *Okla., U.S.A.* 35°15N 96°56W **84** D6
Tedzhen = Tejen
　Turkmenistan 37°23N 60°31E **28** F7
Tees → *U.K.* 54°37N 1°10W **12** C6
Tees B. *U.K.* 54°40N 1°9W **12** C6
Teeswater *Canada* 43°59N 81°17W **82** C3
Tefé *Brazil* 3°25S 64°50W **92** D6
Tegal *Indonesia* 6°52S 109°8E **37** G13
Tegallalang *Indonesia* 8°27S 115°17E **37** J18
Tegalsari *Indonesia* 8°25S 114°8E **37** J17
Tegid, L. = Bala, L. *U.K.* 52°53N 3°37W **12** E4
Tegucigalpa *Honduras* 14°5N 87°14W **88** D2
Tehachapi *U.S.A.* 35°8N 118°27W **79** K8
Tehachapi Mts. *U.S.A.* 35°0N 118°30W **79** L8
Teheran = Tehrān *Iran* 35°41N 51°25E **45** C6
Tehoru *Indonesia* 3°23S 129°30E **37** E7
Tehrān *Iran* 35°41N 51°25E **45** C6
Tehrān □ *Iran* 35°30N 51°30E **45** C6
Tehri *India* 30°23N 78°29E **43** D8
Tehuacán *Mexico* 18°27N 97°23W **87** D5
Tehuantepec *Mexico* 16°21N 95°13W **87** D5
Tehuantepec, G. de
　Mexico 15°50N 95°12W **87** D5
Tehuantepec, Istmo de
　Mexico 17°15N 94°30W **87** D6
Teide, Pico de *Canary Is.* 28°15N 16°38W **24** F3
Teifi → *U.K.* 52°5N 4°41W **13** E3
Teign → *U.K.* 50°32N 3°32W **13** G4
Teignmouth *U.K.* 50°33N 3°31W **13** G4
Tejakula *Indonesia* 8°8S 115°20E **37** J18
Tejam *India* 29°57N 80°11E **43** E9
Tejen *Turkmenistan* 37°23N 60°31E **28** F7
Tejen → *Turkmenistan* 37°24N 60°38E **45** B9
Tejo → *Europe* 38°40N 9°24W **21** C1
Tejon Pass *U.S.A.* 34°49N 118°53W **79** L8
Tekamah *U.S.A.* 41°47N 96°13W **80** E5
Tekapo, L. *N.Z.* 43°53S 170°33E **59** E3
Tekax *Mexico* 20°12N 89°17W **87** C7
Tekeli *Kazakhstan* 44°50N 79°0E **28** E8
Tekirdağ *Turkey* 40°58N 27°30E **23** D12
Tekkali *India* 18°37N 84°15E **41** K14
Tekoa *U.S.A.* 47°14N 117°4W **76** C5
Tekong Besar, Pulau
　Singapore 1°25N 104°3E **39** d
Tel Aviv ✈ (TLV) *Israel* 32°5N 34°49E **46** C3
Tel Aviv-Yafo *Israel* 32°4N 34°48E **46** C3
Tel Lakhish *Israel* 31°34N 34°51E **46** D3
Tel Megiddo *Israel* 32°35N 35°11E **46** C4
Tela *Honduras* 15°40N 87°28W **88** C2
Telanaipura = Jambi
　Indonesia 1°38S 103°30E **36** E2
Telavi *Georgia* 42°0N 45°30E **19** F8
Telde *Canary Is.* 27°59N 15°25W **24** G4
Telegraph Creek *Canada* 58°0N 131°10W **70** B2
Telekhany = Tsyelyakhany
　Belarus 52°30N 25°46E **17** B13
Telemark *Norway* 59°15N 7°40E **9** G12
Telén *Argentina* 36°15S 65°31W **94** D2
Teleng *Iran* 25°47N 61°3E **45** E9
Teles Pires → *Brazil* 7°21S 58°3W **92** E7
Telescope Pk. *U.S.A.* 36°10N 117°5W **79** J9
Telfer Mine *Australia* 21°40S 122°12E **60** D3
Telford *U.K.* 52°40N 2°27W **13** E5
Telford and Wrekin □
　U.K. 52°45N 2°27W **12** E5
Telkwa *Canada* 54°41N 127°5W **70** C3
Tell City *U.S.A.* 37°57N 86°46W **80** G10
Tellicherry *India* 11°45N 75°30E **40** P9
Telluride *U.S.A.* 37°56N 107°49W **77** H10
Teloloapán *Mexico* 18°21N 99°51W **87** D5
Telpos Iz *Russia* 63°16N 59°13E **18** B10
Telsen *Argentina* 42°30S 66°50W **96** E3
Telšiai *Lithuania* 55°59N 22°14E **9** J20
Teluk Anson = Teluk Intan
　Malaysia 4°3N 101°0E **39** K3
Teluk Bahang *Malaysia* 5°27N 100°12E **39** K3
Teluk Betung = Bandar Lampung
　Indonesia 5°20S 105°10E **36** F3
Teluk Intan *Malaysia* 4°3N 101°0E **39** K3
Teluk Kumbar *Malaysia* 5°18N 100°14E **39** c
Telukbutun *Indonesia* 4°13N 108°12E **36** D3
Telukdalam *Indonesia* 0°33N 97°50E **36** D1
Tema *Ghana* 5°41N 0°0 **50** G5

Temagami, L. *Canada* 47°0N 80°10W **72** C3
Temax *Mexico* 21°9N 88°56W **87** C7
Temba *S. Africa* 25°20S 28°17E **57** D4
Tembagapura *Indonesia* 4°20S 137°0E **37** E9
Tembe
　Dem. Rep. of the Congo 0°16S 28°14E **54** C2
Tembe △ *S. Africa* 26°51S 32°24E **57** D5
Temblor Range *U.S.A.* 35°20N 119°50W **79** K7
Teme → *U.K.* 52°11N 2°13W **13** E5
Temecula *U.S.A.* 33°30N 117°9W **79** M9
Temengor, Tasik
　Malaysia 5°24N 101°18E **39** K3
Temerloh *Malaysia* 3°27N 102°25E **39** L4
Teminabuan *Indonesia* 1°26S 132°1E **37** E8
Temir *Kazakhstan* 49°1N 57°14E **19** E10
Temirtau *Kazakhstan* 50°5N 72°56E **32** A2
Temirtau *Russia* 53°10N 87°30E **28** D9
Témiscamie → *Canada* 50°59N 73°5W **73** B5
Témiscaming *Canada* 46°44N 79°5W **72** C4
Témiscamingue, L.
　Canada 47°10N 79°25W **72** C4
Temosachic *Mexico* 28°57N 107°51W **86** B3
Tempe *U.S.A.* 33°24N 111°54W **77** K8
Tempiute *U.S.A.* 37°39N 115°38W **78** H11
Temple *U.S.A.* 31°6N 97°21W **84** F6
Temple B. *Australia* 12°15S 143°3E **62** A3
Templemore *Ireland* 52°47N 7°51W **10** D4
Templeton *U.S.A.* 35°33N 120°42W **78** K6
Templeton → *Australia* 21°0S 138°40E **62** C2
Tempoal de Sánchez
　Mexico 21°31N 98°23W **87** C5
Temuco *Chile* 38°45S 72°40W **96** D2
Temuka *N.Z.* 44°14S 171°17E **59** F3
Tenabo *Mexico* 20°3N 90°14W **87** C6
Tenaha *U.S.A.* 31°57N 94°15W **84** F7
Tenakee Springs
　U.S.A. 57°47N 135°13W **70** B1
Tenali *India* 16°15N 80°35E **41** L12
Tenancingo de Degollado
　Mexico 18°58N 99°36W **87** D5
Tenango del Valle
　Mexico 19°7N 99°33W **87** D5
Tenaro, Akra *Greece* 36°22N 22°27E **23** F10
Tenasserim *Burma* 12°6N 99°3E **39** F2
Tenasserim □ *Burma* 14°0N 98°30E **38** F2
Tenby *U.K.* 51°40N 4°42W **13** F3
Tenda, Colle di *France* 44°7N 7°36E **20** D7
Tendaho *Ethiopia* 11°48N 40°54E **47** E3
Tendukhera *India* 23°24N 79°33E **43** H8
Teneguía, Volcanes de
　Canary Is. 28°28N 17°51W **24** F2
Ténéré, Erg du *Niger* 17°35N 10°55E **51** E8
Tenerife *Canary Is.* 28°15N 16°35W **24** F3
Tenerife, Pico *Canary Is.* 27°43N 18°1W **24** G1
Tenerife Norte ✈ (TFN)
　Canary Is. 28°28N 16°17W **24** F3
Tenerife Sur ✈ (TFS)
　Canary Is. 28°3N 16°33W **24** F3
Teng Xian *China* 35°5N 117°10E **35** G9
Tengah, Kepulauan
　Indonesia 7°5S 118°15E **36** F5
Tengchong *China* 25°0N 98°28E **32** D4
Tengchowfu = Penglai
　China 37°48N 120°42E **35** F11
Tenggarong *Indonesia* 0°24S 116°58E **36** E5
Tengger Shamo *China* 38°0N 104°0E **32** D5
Tenggol, Pulau *Malaysia* 4°48N 103°41E **39** K4
Tengiz Köli *Kazakhstan* 50°30N 69°0E **32** A1
Teniente Enciso △
　Paraguay 21°5S 61°8W **94** A3
Teniente Rodolfo Marsh
　Antarctica 62°30S 58°0W **5** C18
Tenino *U.S.A.* 46°51N 122°51W **78** D4
Tenkasi *India* 8°55N 77°20E **40** Q10
Tenke *Katanga,*
　Dem. Rep. of the Congo 11°22S 26°40E **55** E2
Tenke *Katanga,*
　Dem. Rep. of the Congo 10°32S 26°7E **55** E2
Tennant Creek
　Australia 19°30S 134°15E **62** B1
Tennessee □ *U.S.A.* 36°0N 86°30W **85** D11
Tennessee → *U.S.A.* 37°4N 88°34W **85** C10
Teno, Pta. de *Canary Is.* 28°21N 16°55W **24** F3
Tenom *Malaysia* 5°4N 115°57E **36** C5
Tenosique *Mexico* 17°29N 91°26W **87** D6
Tenryū-Gawa → *Japan* 35°39N 137°48E **31** G8
Tenterden *U.K.* 51°4N 0°42E **13** F8
Tenterfield *Australia* 29°0S 152°0E **63** D5
Teófilo Otoni *Brazil* 17°50S 41°30W **93** G10
Tepa *Indonesia* 7°52S 129°31E **37** F7
Tepalcatepec →
　Mexico 18°35N 101°59W **86** D4
Tepehuanes *Mexico* 25°21N 105°44W **86** B3
Tepetongo *Mexico* 22°28N 103°9W **86** C4
Tepic *Mexico* 21°30N 104°54W **86** C4
Teplice *Czech Rep.* 50°40N 13°48E **16** C7
Tepoca, C. *Mexico* 30°20N 112°25W **86** A2
Tequila *Mexico* 20°54N 103°47W **86** C4
Ter → *Spain* 42°2N 3°12E **21** A7
Ter Apel *Neths.* 52°53N 7°5E **15** B7
Téra *Niger* 14°0N 0°45E **50** F6
Teraina *Kiribati* 4°43N 160°25W **65** G12
Téramo *Italy* 42°39N 13°42E **22** C5
Terang *Australia* 38°15S 142°55E **63** F3
Terang, Teluk *Indonesia* 8°45S 116°0E **37** K19
Terceira *Azores* 38°43N 27°13W **50** a
Tercero → *Argentina* 32°58S 61°47W **94** C3
Terebovlya *Ukraine* 49°18N 25°44E **17** D13
Terek → *Russia* 44°0N 47°30E **19** F8
Terepaima △ *Venezuela* 9°58N 69°17W **89** E6
Teresina *Brazil* 5°9S 42°45W **93** E10
Terewah, L. *Australia* 29°52S 147°35E **63** D4
Teridgerie Cr. →
　Australia 30°25S 148°50E **63** E4
Termas de Río Hondo
　Argentina 27°29S 64°52W **94** B3
Termez = Termiz
　Uzbekistan 37°15N 67°15E **28** F7

Términi Imerese *Italy* 37°59N 13°42E **22 F5**
Términos, L. de *Mexico* 18°37N 91°33W **87 D6**
Termiz *Uzbekistan* 37°15N 67°15E **28 F7**
Térmoli *Italy* 42°0N 15°0E **22 C6**
Ternate *Indonesia* 0°45N 127°25E **37 D7**
Terneuzen *Neths.* 51°20N 3°50E **15 C3**
Terney *Russia* 45°3N 136°37E **30 B8**
Terni *Italy* 42°34N 12°37E **22 C5**
Ternopil *Ukraine* 49°30N 25°40E **17 D13**
Ternopol = Ternopil
  Ukraine 49°30N 25°40E **17 D13**
Terowie *Australia* 33°8S 138°55E **63 E2**
Terra Bella *U.S.A.* 35°58N 119°3W **79 K7**
Terra Nova △ *Canada* 48°33N 53°55W **73 C9**
Terrace *Canada* 54°30N 128°35W **70 C3**
Terrace Bay *Canada* 48°47N 87°5W **72 C2**
Terracina *Italy* 41°17N 13°15E **22 D5**
Terralba *Italy* 39°43N 8°39E **22 E3**
Terre Haute *U.S.A.* 39°28N 87°25W **81 F10**
Terrebonne B. *U.S.A.* 29°5N 90°35W **85 G9**
Terrell *U.S.A.* 32°44N 96°17W **84 E6**
Terrenceville *Canada* 47°40N 54°44W **73 C9**
Terry *U.S.A.* 46°47N 105°19W **76 C11**
Terryville *U.S.A.* 41°41N 73°3W **83 E11**
Terschelling *Neths.* 53°25N 5°20E **15 A5**
Teruel *Spain* 40°22N 1°8W **21 B5**
Tervola *Finland* 66°6N 24°49E **8 C21**
Teryaweynya L.
  Australia 32°18S 143°22E **63 E3**
Teshio *Japan* 44°53N 141°44E **30 B10**
Teshio-Gawa → *Japan* 44°53N 141°45E **30 B10**
Tesiyn Gol → *Mongolia* 50°40N 93°20E **32 A4**
Teslin *Canada* 60°10N 132°43W **70 A2**
Teslin → *Canada* 61°34N 134°35W **70 A2**
Teslin L. *Canada* 60°15N 132°57W **70 A2**
Tessalit *Mali* 20°12N 1°0E **50 D6**
Tessaoua *Niger* 13°47N 7°56E **50 F7**
Test → *U.K.* 50°56N 1°29W **13 G6**
Testigos, Is. Los *Venezuela* 11°23N 63°7W **89 D7**
Tetachuck L. *Canada* 53°18N 125°55W **70 C3**
Tetas, Pta. *Chile* 23°31S 70°38W **94 A1**
Tete *Mozam.* 16°13S 33°33E **55 F3**
Tete □ *Mozam.* 15°15S 32°40E **55 F3**
Teterev → *Ukraine* 51°1N 30°5E **17 C16**
Teteven *Bulgaria* 42°58N 24°17E **23 C11**
Tethul → *Canada* 60°35N 112°12W **70 A6**
Tetiyev *Ukraine* 49°22N 29°38E **17 D15**
Teton → *U.S.A.* 47°56N 110°31W **76 C8**
Tétouan *Morocco* 35°35N 5°21W **50 A4**
Tetovo *Macedonia* 42°1N 20°59E **23 C9**
Tetufera, Mt. *Tahiti* 17°40S 149°26W **59 d**
Teuco → *Argentina* 25°35S 60°11W **94 B3**
Teulon *Canada* 50°23N 97°16W **71 C9**
Teun *Indonesia* 6°59S 129°8E **37 F7**
Teuri-Tō *Japan* 44°26N 141°19E **30 B10**
Teutoburger Wald
  Germany 52°5N 8°22E **16 B5**
Tevere → *Italy* 41°44N 12°14E **22 D5**
Teverya *Israel* 32°47N 35°32E **46 C4**
Teviot → *U.K.* 55°29N 2°38W **11 F6**
Tewantin *Australia* 26°27S 153°3E **63 D5**
Tewkesbury *U.K.* 51°59N 2°9W **13 F5**
Texada I. *Canada* 49°40N 124°25W **70 D4**
Texarkana *Ark., U.S.A.* 33°26N 94°2W **84 E7**
Texarkana *Tex., U.S.A.* 33°26N 94°3W **84 E7**
Texas *Australia* 28°49S 151°9E **63 D5**
Texas □ *U.S.A.* 31°40N 98°30W **84 F5**
Texas City *U.S.A.* 29°24N 94°54W **84 G7**
Texel *Neths.* 53°5N 4°50E **15 A4**
Texline *U.S.A.* 36°23N 103°2W **84 E3**
Texoma, L. *U.S.A.* 33°50N 96°34W **84 E6**
Teyateyaneng *Lesotho* 29°7S 27°34E **53 K5**
Tezin *Afghan.* 34°24N 69°30E **42 B3**
Teziutlán *Mexico* 19°49N 97°21W **87 D5**
Tezpur *India* 26°40N 92°45E **41 F18**
Tezzeron L. *Canada* 54°43N 124°30W **70 C4**
Tha-anne → *Canada* 60°31N 94°37W **71 A10**
Tha Deua *Laos* 17°57N 102°53E **38 D4**
Tha Deua *Laos* 19°26N 101°50E **38 C3**
Tha Li *Thailand* 17°37N 101°25E **38 D3**
Tha Pla *Thailand* 17°48N 100°32E **38 D3**
Tha Rua *Thailand* 14°34N 100°44E **38 E3**
Tha Sala *Thailand* 8°40N 99°56E **39 H2**
Tha Song Yang *Thailand* 17°34N 97°55E **38 D1**
Thaba Putsoa *Lesotho* 29°45S 28°0E **57 D4**
Thabana Ntlenyana
  Lesotho 29°30S 29°16E **57 D4**
Thabazimbi *S. Africa* 24°40S 27°21E **57 C4**
Thādiq *Si. Arabia* 25°18N 45°52E **44 E5**
Thai Binh *Vietnam* 20°35N 106°1E **38 B6**
Thai Muang *Thailand* 8°24N 98°16E **39 H2**
Thai Nguyen *Vietnam* 21°35N 105°55E **38 B5**
Thailand ■ *Asia* 16°0N 102°0E **38 E4**
Thailand, G. of *Asia* 11°30N 101°0E **39 G3**
Thakhek *Laos* 17°25N 104°45E **38 D5**
Thal *Pakistan* 33°28N 70°33E **42 C4**
Thal Desert *Pakistan* 31°10N 71°30E **42 D4**
Thala La = Hkakabo Razi
  Burma 28°25N 97°23E **41 E20**
Thalabarivat *Cambodia* 13°33N 105°57E **38 F5**
Thallon *Australia* 28°39S 148°49E **63 D4**
Thalu, Ko *Thailand* 9°26N 99°54E **39 b**
Thames *N.Z.* 37°7S 175°34E **59 B5**
Thames → *Canada* 42°20N 82°25W **82 D2**
Thames → *U.K.* 51°29N 0°34E **13 F8**
Thames Estuary *U.K.* 51°29N 0°52E **13 F8**
Thamesford *Canada* 43°4N 81°0W **82 C4**
Thamesville *Canada* 42°33N 81°59W **82 D3**
Than *India* 22°34N 71°11E **42 H4**
Than Uyen *Vietnam* 22°0N 103°54E **38 B4**
Thana Gazi *India* 27°25N 76°19E **42 F7**
Thandla *India* 23°0N 74°34E **42 H6**
Thandwe *Burma* 18°20N 94°30E **41 K19**
Thane *India* 19°12N 72°59E **40 K8**
Thanesar *India* 30°1N 76°52E **42 D7**

Thanet, I. of *U.K.* 51°21N 1°20E **13 F9**
Thangool *Australia* 24°38S 150°42E **62 C5**
Thanh Hoa *Vietnam* 19°48N 105°46E **38 C5**
Thanh Hung *Vietnam* 9°55N 105°43E **39 H5**
Thanh Pho Ho Chi Minh
  Vietnam 10°58N 106°40E **39 G6**
Thanh Thuy *Vietnam* 22°55N 104°51E **38 A5**
Thanjavur *India* 10°48N 79°12E **40 P11**
Thano Bula Khan
  Pakistan 25°22N 67°50E **42 G2**
Thaolintoa L. *Canada* 61°30N 96°25W **71 A9**
Thap Lan △ *Thailand* 14°15N 102°16E **38 E4**
Thap Sakae *Thailand* 11°30N 99°37E **39 G2**
Thap Than *Thailand* 15°27N 99°54E **38 E2**
Thar Desert *India* 28°0N 72°0E **42 F5**
Tharad *India* 24°30N 71°44E **42 G4**
Thargomindah
  Australia 27°58S 143°46E **63 D3**
Tharp Fracture Zone
  S. Ocean 54°0S 135°0W **5 B14**
Tharrawaddy *Burma* 17°38N 95°48E **41 L19**
Tharthār, Buḩayrat ath
  Iraq 34°0N 43°15E **44 C4**
Tharthar, L. = Tharthār,
  Buḩayrat ath *Iraq* 34°0N 43°15E **44 C4**
Tharthār, W. ath → *Iraq* 34°32N 43°4E **44 C4**
Thasos *Greece* 40°40N 24°40E **23 D11**
That Khe *Vietnam* 22°16N 106°28E **38 A6**
Thatcher *Ariz., U.S.A.* 32°51N 109°46W **77 K9**
Thatcher *Colo., U.S.A.* 37°33N 104°7W **77 H11**
Thaton *Burma* 16°55N 97°22E **41 L20**
Thaungdut *Burma* 24°30N 94°40E **41 G19**
Thayer *U.S.A.* 36°31N 91°33W **80 G8**
Thayetmyo *Burma* 19°20N 95°10E **41 K19**
Thazi *Burma* 21°0N 96°5E **41 J20**
Thbeng Meanchey
  Cambodia 13°49N 104°58E **38 F5**
The Broads *U.K.* 52°45N 1°30E **12 E9**
The Everglades *U.S.A.* 25°50N 81°0W **85 J14**
The Gulf = Persian Gulf
  Asia 27°0N 50°0E **45 E6**
The Hague = 's-Gravenhage
  Neths. 52°7N 4°17E **15 B4**
The Pas *Canada* 53°45N 101°15W **71 C8**
The Wash *U.K.* 52°58N 0°20E **12 E8**
The Weald *U.K.* 51°4N 0°20E **13 F8**
Thebes = Thiva *Greece* 38°19N 23°19E **23 E10**
Thebes *Egypt* 25°40N 32°35E **51 C12**
Thedford *U.S.A.* 41°59N 100°35W **80 E3**
Theebine *Australia* 25°57S 152°34E **63 D5**
Thekulthili L. *Canada* 61°3N 110°0W **71 A7**
Thelon → *Canada* 64°16N 96°4W **71 A8**
Theodore *Australia* 24°55S 150°3E **62 C5**
Theodore *Canada* 51°26N 102°55W **71 C8**
Theodore *U.S.A.* 30°33N 88°10W **85 F10**
Theodore Roosevelt △
  U.S.A. 47°0N 103°25W **80 B2**
Theodore Roosevelt L.
  U.S.A. 33°40N 111°10W **77 K8**
Thepha *Thailand* 6°52N 100°58E **39 J3**
Theresa *U.S.A.* 44°13N 75°48W **83 B9**
Thermopolis *U.S.A.* 43°39N 108°13W **76 E9**
Thermopylae *Greece* 38°48N 22°35E **23 E10**
Thessalon *Canada* 46°20N 83°30W **72 C3**
Thessalonica, Gulf of =
  Thessaloniki Kolpos
  Greece 40°15N 22°45E **23 D10**
Thessaloniki *Greece* 40°38N 22°58E **23 D10**
Thessaloniki Kolpos
  Greece 40°15N 22°45E **23 D10**
Thetford *U.K.* 52°25N 0°45E **13 E8**
Thetford Mines *Canada* 46°8N 71°18W **73 C5**
Theun → *Laos* 18°19N 104°0E **38 C5**
Theunissen *S. Africa* 28°26S 26°43E **56 D4**
Thevenard *Australia* 32°9S 133°38E **63 E1**
Thibodaux *U.S.A.* 29°48N 90°49W **85 G9**
Thicket Portage *Canada* 55°19N 97°42W **71 B9**
Thief River Falls *U.S.A.* 48°7N 96°10W **80 A5**
Thiel Mts. *Antarctica* 85°15S 91°0W **5 E16**
Thiers *France* 45°52N 3°33E **20 D5**
Thiès *Senegal* 14°50N 16°51W **50 F2**
Thika *Kenya* 1°1S 37°5E **54 C4**
Thimphu *Bhutan* 27°31N 89°45E **41 F16**
Thina → *S. Africa* 31°18S 29°13E **57 E4**
Þingvallavatn *Iceland* 64°11N 21°9W **8 D3**
Thionville *France* 49°20N 6°10E **20 B7**
Thira = Santorini
  Greece 36°23N 25°27E **23 F11**
Third Cataract *Sudan* 19°42N 30°20E **51 E12**
Thirsk *U.K.* 54°14N 1°19W **12 C6**
Thiruvananthapuram =
  Trivandrum *India* 8°41N 77°0E **40 Q10**
Thisted *Denmark* 56°58N 8°40E **9 H13**
Thistle I. *Australia* 35°0S 136°8E **63 F2**
Thiva *Greece* 38°19N 23°19E **23 E10**
Þjórsá → *Iceland* 63°47N 20°48W **8 E3**
Thlewiaza → *Canada* 60°29N 94°40W **71 A10**
Thmar Puok *Cambodia* 13°57N 103°4E **38 F4**
Tho Vinh *Vietnam* 19°16N 105°42E **38 C5**
Thoa → *Canada* 60°31N 109°47W **71 A7**
Thoen *Thailand* 17°43N 99°41E **38 D2**
Thoeng *Thailand* 19°41N 100°12E **38 C3**
Thohoyandou *S. Africa* 22°58S 30°29E **53 J6**
Tholdi *Pakistan* 35°5N 76°6E **43 B7**
Thomas *U.S.A.* 35°45N 98°45W **84 D5**
Thomas, L. *Australia* 26°4S 137°58E **63 D2**
Thomaston *U.S.A.* 32°53N 84°20W **85 E12**
Thomasville *Ala.,*
  U.S.A. 31°55N 87°44W **85 F11**
Thomasville *Ga., U.S.A.* 30°50N 83°59W **85 F13**
Thomasville *N.C., U.S.A.* 35°53N 80°5W **85 D14**
Thompson *Canada* 55°45N 97°52W **71 B9**
Thompson *U.S.A.* 41°52N 75°31W **83 E9**
Thompson → *Canada* 50°15N 121°24W **70 C4**
Thompson → *U.S.A.* 39°46N 93°37W **80 F7**
Thompson Falls *U.S.A.* 47°36N 115°21W **76 C6**

Thompson Pk. *U.S.A.* 41°0N 123°2W **76 F2**
Thompson Springs
  U.S.A. 38°58N 109°43W **76 G9**
Thompsontown *U.S.A.* 40°33N 77°14W **82 F7**
Thomson *U.S.A.* 33°28N 82°30W **85 E13**
Thomson → *Australia* 25°11S 142°53E **62 C3**
Thong Yang *Thailand* 9°28N 99°56E **39 b**
Þórisvatn *Iceland* 64°20N 18°55W **8 D4**
Thornaby on Tees *U.K.* 54°33N 1°18W **12 C6**
Thornbury *Canada* 44°34N 80°26W **82 B4**
Thorne *U.K.* 53°37N 0°57W **12 D7**
Thornton *Canada* 44°16N 79°43W **82 B5**
Thornton *U.S.A.* 39°52N 104°58W **76 G11**
Thorold *Canada* 43°7N 79°12W **82 C5**
Þórshöfn *Iceland* 66°12N 15°20W **8 C6**
Thouin, C. *Australia* 20°20S 118°10E **60 D2**
Thousand Islands *U.S.A.* 44°20N 76°0W **83 B9**
Thousand Oaks *U.S.A.* 34°10N 118°50W **79 L8**
Thrace *Turkey* 41°0N 27°0E **23 D12**
Three Forks *U.S.A.* 45°54N 111°33W **76 D8**
Three Hills *Canada* 51°43N 113°15W **70 C6**
Three Hummock I.
  Australia 40°25S 144°55E **63 G3**
Three Pagodas Pass *Asia* 15°20N 98°30E **38 E2**
Three Points, C. *Ghana* 4°42N 2°6W **50 H5**
Three Rivers *Calif.,*
  U.S.A. 36°26N 118°54W **78 J8**
Three Rivers *Tex.,*
  U.S.A. 28°28N 98°11W **84 G5**
Three Springs *Australia* 29°32S 115°45E **61 E2**
Throssell, L. *Australia* 27°33S 124°10E **61 E3**
Throssell Ra. *Australia* 22°3S 121°43E **60 D3**
Thrushton △ *Australia* 27°47S 147°40E **63 D4**
Thua → *Kenya* 1°31S 39°30E **54 C4**
Thuan Hoa *Vietnam* 8°58N 105°30E **39 H5**
Thubun Lakes *Canada* 61°30N 112°0W **71 A6**
Thuin *Belgium* 50°20N 4°17E **15 D4**
Thule = Qaanaaq
  Greenland 77°40N 69°0W **4 B4**
Thule Air Base = Uummannaq
  Greenland 77°28N 69°13W **4 B4**
Thun *Switz.* 46°45N 7°38E **20 C7**
Thunder B. *U.S.A.* 45°0N 83°20W **82 B1**
Thunder Bay *Canada* 48°20N 89°15W **72 C2**
Thung Salaeng Luang △
  Thailand 16°43N 100°50E **38 D3**
Thung Song *Thailand* 8°10N 99°40E **39 H2**
Thunkar *Bhutan* 27°55N 91°0E **41 F17**
Thuong Tra *Vietnam* 16°2N 107°42E **38 D6**
Thüringer Wald *Germany* 50°35N 11°0E **16 C6**
Thurles *Ireland* 52°41N 7°49W **10 D4**
Thurrock □ *U.K.* 51°31N 0°23E **13 F8**
Thursday I. *Australia* 10°30S 142°3E **62 A3**
Thurso *Canada* 45°36N 75°15W **72 C4**
Thurso *U.K.* 58°36N 3°32W **11 C5**
Thurso → *U.K.* 58°36N 3°32W **11 C5**
Thurston I. *Antarctica* 72°0S 100°0W **5 D16**
Thutade L. *Canada* 57°0N 126°55W **70 B3**
Thyolo *Malawi* 16°7S 35°5E **55 F4**
Ti-Tree *Australia* 22°5S 133°22E **62 C1**
Tian Shan *Asia* 40°30N 76°0E **32 B3**
Tianjin *China* 39°7N 117°12E **35 E9**
Tianshifu *China* 41°17N 124°22E **35 D13**
Tianshui *China* 34°32N 105°40E **34 G3**
Tianyar *Indonesia* 8°12S 115°30E **37 J18**
Tianzhen *China* 40°24N 114°5E **34 D8**
Tianzhuangtai *China* 40°43N 122°5E **35 D12**
Tiarei *Tahiti* 17°32S 149°20E **59 d**
Tiaret *Algeria* 35°20N 1°21E **50 A6**
Tibagi *Brazil* 24°30S 50°24W **95 A5**
Tibagi → *Brazil* 22°47S 51°1W **95 A5**
Tibastī, Sarīr *Libya* 22°50N 18°30E **51 D9**
Tibati *Cameroon* 6°22N 12°30E **52 C2**
Tiber = Tevere → *Italy* 41°44N 12°14E **22 D5**
Tiber Res. *U.S.A.* 48°19N 111°6W **76 B8**
Tiberias = Teverya *Israel* 32°47N 35°32E **46 C4**
Tiberias, L. = Yam Kinneret
  Israel 32°45N 35°35E **46 C4**
Tibesti *Chad* 21°0N 17°30E **51 D9**
Tibet = Xizang Zizhiqu □
  China 32°0N 88°0E **32 C3**
Tibet, Plateau of *Asia* 32°0N 86°0E **26 E10**
Tibnī *Syria* 35°36N 39°50E **44 C3**
Tibooburra *Australia* 29°26S 142°1E **63 D3**
Tiburón, I. *Mexico* 29°0N 112°25E **86 B2**
Ticino → *Italy* 45°9N 9°14E **20 D8**
Ticonderoga *U.S.A.* 43°51N 73°26W **83 C11**
Ticul *Mexico* 20°24N 89°32W **87 C7**
Tidaholm *Sweden* 58°12N 13°58E **9 G15**
Tiddim *Burma* 23°28N 93°45E **41 H18**
Tidioute *U.S.A.* 41°41N 79°24W **82 E5**
Tidjikja *Mauritania* 18°29N 11°35W **50 E3**
Tidore *Indonesia* 0°40N 127°25E **37 D7**
Tiefa *China* 42°28N 123°26E **35 C12**
Tiegang Shuiku *China* 22°37N 113°53E **33 F10**
Tiel *Neths.* 51°53N 5°26E **15 C5**
Tieling *China* 42°20N 123°55E **35 C12**
Tielt *Belgium* 51°0N 3°20E **15 C3**
Tien Shan = Tian Shan
  Asia 40°30N 76°0E **32 B3**
Tien-tsin = Tianjin
  China 39°7N 117°12E **35 E9**
Tien Yen *Vietnam* 21°20N 107°24E **38 B6**
Tienching = Tianjin
  China 39°7N 117°12E **35 E9**
Tienen *Belgium* 50°48N 4°57E **15 D4**
Tientsin = Tianjin *China* 39°7N 117°12E **35 E9**
Tieri *Australia* 23°2S 148°21E **62 C4**
Tierra Amarilla *Chile* 27°28S 70°18W **94 B1**
Tierra Amarilla
  U.S.A. 36°42N 106°33W **77 H10**
Tierra Colorada *Mexico* 17°11N 99°32W **87 D5**
Tierra de Campos *Spain* 42°10N 4°50W **21 A3**
Tierra del Fuego, I. Grande de
  Argentina 54°0S 69°0W **96 G3**
Tiétar → *Spain* 39°50N 6°1W **21 C3**
Tieté → *Brazil* 20°40S 51°35W **95 A5**

Tiffin *U.S.A.* 41°7N 83°11W **81 E12**
Tifton *U.S.A.* 31°27N 83°31W **85 F13**
Tifu *Indonesia* 3°39S 126°24E **37 E7**
Tighina *Moldova* 46°50N 29°30E **17 E15**
Tigil *Russia* 57°49N 158°40E **29 D16**
Tigre → *Peru* 4°30S 74°10W **92 D4**
Tigre → *Venezuela* 9°20N 62°30W **92 B6**
Tigris = Dijlah, Nahr →
  Asia 31°0N 47°25E **44 D5**
Tigyaing *Burma* 23°45N 96°10E **41 H20**
Tihāmah *Asia* 15°3N 41°55E **47 D3**
Tijara *India* 27°56N 76°31E **42 F7**
Tijuana *Mexico* 32°32N 117°1W **79 N9**
Tikal *Guatemala* 17°13N 89°24W **88 C2**
Tikal △ *Guatemala* 17°23N 89°34W **88 C2**
Tikamgarh *India* 24°44N 78°50E **43 G8**
Tikhoretsk *Russia* 45°56N 40°5E **19 E7**
Tikhvin *Russia* 59°35N 33°30E **18 C5**
Tikirarjuaq = Whale Cove
  Canada 62°10N 92°34W **71 A10**
Tikrīt *Iraq* 34°35N 43°37E **44 C4**
Tiksi *Russia* 71°40N 128°45E **29 B13**
Tilamuta *Indonesia* 0°32N 122°23E **37 D6**
Tilburg *Neths.* 51°31N 5°6E **15 C5**
Tilbury *Canada* 42°17N 82°23W **82 D2**
Tilbury *U.K.* 51°27N 0°22E **13 F8**
Tilcara *Argentina* 23°36S 65°23W **94 A2**
Tilden *U.S.A.* 42°3N 97°50W **80 D5**
Tilhar *India* 28°0N 79°45E **43 F8**
Tilichiki *Russia* 60°27N 166°5E **29 C17**
Tilissos *Greece* 35°20N 25°1E **25 D7**
Till → *U.K.* 55°41N 2°13W **12 B5**
Tillamook *U.S.A.* 45°27N 123°51W **76 D2**
Tillsonburg *Canada* 42°53N 80°44W **82 D4**
Tillyeria *Cyprus* 35°6N 32°40E **25 D11**
Tilos *Greece* 36°27N 27°27E **23 F12**
Tilpa *Australia* 30°57S 144°24E **63 E3**
Tilt → *U.K.* 56°46N 3°51W **11 E5**
Tiltonsville *U.S.A.* 40°10N 80°41W **82 F4**
Timanfaya △ *Canary Is.* 29°0N 13°46W **24 F6**
Timanskiy Kryazh *Russia* 65°58N 50°5E **18 A9**
Timaru *N.Z.* 44°23S 171°14E **59 F3**
Timau *Kenya* 0°4N 37°15E **54 B4**
Timbaki *Greece* 35°4N 24°45E **25 D6**
Timber Creek *Australia* 15°40S 130°29E **60 C5**
Timber Lake *U.S.A.* 45°26N 101°5W **80 C3**
Timber Mt. *U.S.A.* 36°58N 116°28W **78 H10**
Timbuktu = Tombouctou
  Mali 16°50N 3°0W **50 E5**
Timi *Cyprus* 34°44N 32°31E **25 E11**
Timimoun *Algeria* 29°14N 0°16E **50 C6**
Timiris, Râs *Mauritania* 19°21N 16°30W **50 E2**
Timiskaming, L. =
  Témiscamingue, L..
  Canada 47°10N 79°25W **72 C4**
Timișoara *Romania* 45°43N 21°15E **17 F11**
Timmins *Canada* 48°28N 81°25W **72 C3**
Timok → *Serbia* 44°10N 22°40E **23 B10**
Timoleague *Ireland* 51°39N 8°46W **10 E3**
Timor *Asia* 9°0S 125°0E **37 F7**
Timor Leste = East Timor ■
  Asia 8°50S 126°0E **37 F7**
Timor Sea *Ind. Oc.* 12°0S 127°0E **60 B4**
Tin Can Bay *Australia* 25°56S 153°0E **63 D5**
Tin Mt. *U.S.A.* 36°50N 117°10W **78 J9**
Tina = Thina → *S. Africa* 31°18S 29°13E **57 E4**
Tîna, Khalîg el *Egypt* 31°10N 32°40E **46 D1**
Tinaca Pt. *Phil.* 5°30N 125°25E **37 C7**
Tinajo *Canary Is.* 29°4N 13°42W **24 E6**
Tindal *Australia* 14°31S 132°22E **60 B5**
Tindouf *Algeria* 27°42N 8°10W **50 C4**
Tinfunque △ *Paraguay* 23°55S 60°17W **94 A3**
Tinggi, Pulau *Malaysia* 2°18N 104°7E **39 L5**
Tingo María *Peru* 9°10S 75°54W **92 E3**
Tingrela *Ivory C.* 10°27N 6°25W **50 F4**
Tinh Bien *Vietnam* 10°36N 104°57E **39 G5**
Tinian *N. Marianas* 15°0N 145°38E **64 F6**
Tinnevelly = Tirunelveli
  India 8°45N 77°45E **40 Q10**
Tinogasta *Argentina* 28°5S 67°32W **94 B2**
Tinos *Greece* 37°33N 25°8E **23 F11**
Tinpahar *India* 24°59N 87°44E **43 G12**
Tintina *Argentina* 27°2S 62°45W **94 B3**
Tintinara *Australia* 35°48S 140°2E **63 F3**
Tioga *N. Dak., U.S.A.* 48°24N 102°56W **80 A2**
Tioga *Pa., U.S.A.* 41°55N 77°8W **82 E7**
Tioman, Pulau *Malaysia* 2°50N 104°10E **39 L5**
Tionesta *U.S.A.* 41°30N 79°28W **82 E5**
Tipperary *Ireland* 52°28N 8°10W **10 D3**
Tipperary □ *Ireland* 52°37N 7°55W **10 D4**
Tipton *Calif., U.S.A.* 36°4N 119°19W **78 J7**
Tipton *Iowa, U.S.A.* 41°46N 91°8W **80 E8**
Tipton Mt. *U.S.A.* 35°32N 114°12W **79 K12**
Tiptonville *U.S.A.* 36°23N 89°29W **85 C10**
Tīrān *Iran* 32°45N 51°8E **45 C6**
Tiranë *Albania* 41°18N 19°49E **23 D8**
Tirari Desert *Australia* 28°22S 138°6E **63 D2**
Tiraspol *Moldova* 46°55N 29°35E **17 E15**
Tire *Turkey* 38°5N 27°45E **23 E12**
Tirebolu *Turkey* 40°58N 38°45E **19 F6**
Tiree *U.K.* 56°31N 6°55W **11 E2**
Tiree, Passage of *U.K.* 56°30N 6°30W **11 E2**
Tîrgovişte = Târgovişte
  Romania 44°55N 25°27E **17 F13**
Tîrgu Jiu = Târgu Jiu
  Romania 45°5N 23°19E **17 F12**
Tîrgu Mureş = Târgu Mureş
  Romania 46°31N 24°38E **17 E13**
Tirich Mir *Pakistan* 36°15N 71°55E **40 A7**
Tiritiri o te Moana = Southern
  Alps *N.Z.* 43°41S 170°11E **59 E3**
Tirnavos *Greece* 39°45N 22°18E **23 E10**
Tirodi *India* 21°40N 79°44E **40 J11**
Tirol □ *Austria* 47°3N 10°43E **16 E6**
Tirso → *Italy* 39°53N 8°32E **22 E3**

Tiruchchirappalli *India* 10°45N 78°45E **40 P11**
Tirunelveli *India* 8°45N 77°45E **40 Q10**
Tirupati *India* 13°39N 79°25E **40 N11**
Tiruppur *India* 11°5N 77°22E **40 P10**
Tiruvannamalai *India* 12°15N 79°5E **40 N11**
Tisa → *India* 32°50N 76°9E **42 C7**
Tisa → *Serbia* 45°15N 20°17E **23 B9**
Tisdale *Canada* 52°50N 104°0W **71 C8**
Tishomingo *U.S.A.* 34°14N 96°41W **84 D6**
Tisza = Tisa → *Serbia* 45°15N 20°17E **23 B9**
Tit-Ary *Russia* 71°55N 127°2E **29 B13**
Tithwal *Pakistan* 34°21N 73°50E **43 B5**
Titicaca, L. *S. Amer.* 15°30S 69°30W **92 G5**
Titiwa *Nigeria* 12°14N 12°53E **51 F8**
Titule
  Dem. Rep. of the Congo 3°15N 25°31E **54 B2**
Titusville *Fla., U.S.A.* 28°37N 80°49W **85 G14**
Titusville *Pa., U.S.A.* 41°38N 79°41W **82 E5**
Tivaouane *Senegal* 14°56N 16°45W **50 F2**
Tiverton *Canada* 44°16N 81°32W **82 B3**
Tiverton *U.K.* 50°54N 3°29W **13 G4**
Tívoli *Italy* 41°58N 12°45E **22 D5**
Tizi-Ouzou *Algeria* 36°42N 4°3E **50 A6**
Tizimín *Mexico* 21°9N 88°9W **87 C7**
Tiznit *Morocco* 29°48N 9°45W **50 C4**
Tjeggelvas *Sweden* 66°37N 17°45E **8 C17**
Tjieggelvas = Tjeggelvas
  Sweden 66°37N 17°45E **8 C17**
Tjirebon = Cirebon
  Indonesia 6°45S 108°32E **37 G13**
Tjluring *Indonesia* 8°25S 114°13E **37 J17**
Tjörn *Sweden* 58°0N 11°35E **9 H14**
Tlacotalpan *Mexico* 18°37N 95°40W **87 D5**
Tlahualilo de Zaragoza
  Mexico 26°7N 103°27W **86 B4**
Tlaquepaque *Mexico* 20°39N 103°19W **86 C4**
Tlaxcala *Mexico* 19°19N 98°14W **87 D5**
Tlaxcala □ *Mexico* 19°30N 98°20W **87 D5**
Tlaxiaco *Mexico* 17°25N 97°35W **87 D5**
Tlemcen *Algeria* 34°52N 1°21W **50 B5**
To Bong *Vietnam* 12°45N 109°16E **38 F7**
Toa Payoh *Singapore* 1°20N 103°51E **39 d**
Toad → *Canada* 59°25N 124°57W **70 B4**
Toad River *Canada* 58°51N 125°14W **70 B3**
Toamasina *Madag.* 18°10S 49°25E **57 B8**
Toamasina □ *Madag.* 18°0S 49°0E **57 B8**
Toay *Argentina* 36°43S 64°38W **94 D3**
Toba *Japan* 34°30N 136°51E **31 G8**
Toba, Danau *Indonesia* 2°30N 97°30E **36 D1**
Toba Kakar *Pakistan* 31°30N 69°0E **42 D3**
Toba Tek Singh *Pakistan* 30°55N 72°25E **42 D5**
Tobago *Trin. & Tob.* 11°10N 60°30W **89 D7**
Tobelo *Indonesia* 1°45N 127°56E **37 D7**
Tobermory *Canada* 45°12N 81°40W **82 A3**
Tobermory *U.K.* 56°38N 6°5W **11 E2**
Tobin, L. *Australia* 21°45S 125°49E **60 D4**
Tobin L. *Canada* 53°35N 103°30W **71 C8**
Toboali *Indonesia* 3°0S 106°25E **36 E3**
Tobol → *Russia* 58°10N 68°12E **28 D7**
Toboli *Indonesia* 0°38S 120°5E **37 E6**
Tobolsk *Russia* 58°15N 68°10E **28 D7**
Tobruk = Ţubruq *Libya* 32°7N 23°55E **51 B10**
Tobyhanna *U.S.A.* 41°11N 75°25W **83 E9**
Tobyl = Tobol → *Russia* 58°10N 68°12E **28 D7**
Tocantinópolis *Brazil* 6°20S 47°25W **93 E9**
Tocantins □ *Brazil* 10°0S 48°0W **93 F9**
Tocantins → *Brazil* 1°45S 49°10W **93 D9**
Toccoa *U.S.A.* 34°35N 83°19W **85 D13**
Tochi → *Pakistan* 32°49N 70°41E **42 C4**
Tochigi *Japan* 36°25N 139°45E **31 F9**
Tochigi □ *Japan* 36°45N 139°45E **31 F9**
Toco *Trin. & Tob.* 10°49N 60°57W **93 K16**
Toconao *Chile* 23°11S 68°1W **94 A2**
Tocopilla *Chile* 22°5S 70°10W **94 A1**
Tocumwal *Australia* 35°51S 145°31E **63 F4**
Tocuyo → *Venezuela* 11°3N 68°23W **92 A5**
Todd → *Australia* 24°52S 135°48E **62 C2**
Todeli *Indonesia* 1°40S 124°29E **37 E6**
Todenyang *Kenya* 4°35N 35°56E **54 B4**
Todgarh *India* 25°42N 73°58E **42 G5**
Todos os Santos, B. de
  Brazil 12°48S 38°38W **93 F11**
Todos Santos *Mexico* 23°26N 110°13W **86 C2**
Toe Hd. *U.K.* 57°50N 7°8W **11 D1**
Tofield *Canada* 53°25N 112°40W **70 C6**
Tofino *Canada* 49°11N 125°55W **70 D3**
Tofua *Tonga* 19°45S 175°5W **59 c**
Tōgane *Japan* 35°33N 140°22E **31 G10**
Togian, Kepulauan
  Indonesia 0°20S 121°50E **37 E6**
Togliatti *Russia* 53°32N 49°24E **18 D8**
Togo ■ *W. Afr.* 8°30N 1°35E **50 G6**
Togtoh *China* 40°15N 111°10E **34 D6**
Tohiea, Mt. *Moorea* 17°33S 149°49W **59 d**
Tōhoku □ *Japan* 39°50N 141°45E **30 E10**
Töhöm *Mongolia* 44°27N 108°2E **34 B5**
Toinya *Sudan* 6°17N 29°46E **51 G11**
Toiyabe Range *U.S.A.* 39°30N 117°0W **76 G5**
Tojikiston = Tajikistan ■
  Asia 38°30N 70°0E **28 F8**
Tojo *Indonesia* 1°20S 121°15E **37 E6**
Tōjō *Japan* 34°53N 133°16E **31 G6**
Tok *U.S.A.* 63°20N 142°59E **68 C5**
Tokachi-Dake *Japan* 43°17N 142°5E **30 C11**
Tokachi-Gawa →
  Japan 42°44N 143°42E **30 C11**
Tokala *Indonesia* 1°30S 121°40E **37 E6**
Tōkamachi *Japan* 37°8N 138°43E **31 F9**
Tokanui *N.Z.* 46°34S 168°56E **59 G2**
Tokara-Rettō *Japan* 29°37N 129°43E **31 K4**
Tokarahi *N.Z.* 44°56S 170°39E **59 F3**
Tokashiki-Shima *Japan* 26°11N 127°21E **31 L3**
Tokat *Turkey* 40°22N 36°35E **19 F6**
Tokdo *Asia* 37°15N 131°52E **31 F5**
Tokch'ŏn *N. Korea* 39°45N 126°18E **35 E14**

Tokeland U.S.A. 46°42N 123°59W 78 D3
Tokelau Is. Pac. Oc. 9°0S 171°45W 64 H10
Tokmak Kyrgyzstan 42°49N 75°15E 28 E8
Toko Ra. Australia 23°5S 138°20E 62 C2
Tokoro-Gawa → Japan 44°7N 144°5E 30 B12
Toku Tonga 18°10S 174°11W 59 c
Tokuno-Shima Japan 27°56N 128°55E 31 L4
Tokushima Japan 34°4N 134°34E 31 G7
Tokushima □ Japan 33°55N 134°0E 31 H7
Tokuyama Japan 34°3N 131°50E 31 G5
Tōkyō Japan 35°43N 139°45E 31 G9
Tolaga Bay N.Z. 38°21S 178°20E 59 C7
Tolbukhin = Dobrich
  Bulgaria 43°37N 27°49E 23 C12
Toledo Brazil 24°44S 53°45W 95 A5
Toledo Spain 39°50N 4°2W 21 C3
Toledo Ohio, U.S.A. 41°39N 83°33W 81 E12
Toledo Oreg., U.S.A. 44°37N 123°56W 76 D2
Toledo Wash., U.S.A. 46°26N 122°51W 76 C2
Toledo, Montes de Spain 39°33N 4°20W 21 C3
Toledo Bend Res. U.S.A. 31°11N 93°34W 84 F8
Tolga Australia 17°15S 145°29E 62 B4
Toliara Madag. 23°21S 43°40E 57 C7
Toliara □ Madag. 21°0S 45°0E 57 C8
Tolima Colombia 4°40N 75°19W 92 C3
Tolitoli Indonesia 1°5N 120°50E 37 D6
Tollhouse U.S.A. 37°1N 119°24W 78 H7
Tolmachevo Russia 58°56N 29°51E 9 G23
Tolo, Teluk Indonesia 2°20S 122°10E 37 E6
Tolo Harbour China 22°27N 114°12E 33 G11
Toluca Mexico 19°17N 99°40W 87 D5
Tom Burke S. Africa 23°5S 28°0E 57 C4
Tom Price Australia 22°40S 117°48E 60 D2
Tomah U.S.A. 43°59N 90°30W 80 D8
Tomahawk U.S.A. 45°28N 89°44W 80 C9
Tomakomai Japan 42°38N 141°36E 30 C10
Tomales U.S.A. 38°15N 122°53W 78 G4
Tomales B. U.S.A. 38°15N 123°58W 78 G3
Tomanivi Fiji 17°37S 178°1E 59 a
Tomar Portugal 39°36N 8°25W 21 C1
Tomaszów Mazowiecki
  Poland 51°30N 20°2E 17 C10
Tomatlán Mexico 19°56N 105°15W 86 D3
Tombador, Serra do Brazil 12°0S 58°0W 92 F7
Tombigbee → U.S.A. 31°8N 87°57W 85 F11
Tombouctou Mali 16°50N 3°0W 50 E5
Tombstone U.S.A. 31°43N 110°4W 77 L8
Tombua Angola 15°55S 11°55E 56 B1
Tomé Chile 36°36S 72°57W 94 D1
Tomelloso Spain 39°10N 3°2W 21 C4
Tomini Indonesia 0°30N 120°30E 37 D6
Tomini, Teluk Indonesia 0°10S 121°0E 37 E6
Tomintoul U.K. 57°15N 3°23W 11 D5
Tomkinson Ranges
  Australia 26°11S 129°5E 61 E4
Tommot Russia 59°4N 126°20E 29 D13
Tomnop Ta Suos
  Cambodia 11°20N 104°15E 39 G5
Tomo → Colombia 5°20N 67°48W 92 B5
Toms Place U.S.A. 37°34N 118°41W 78 H8
Toms River U.S.A. 39°58N 74°12W 83 G10
Tomsk Russia 56°30N 85°5E 28 D9
Tonalá Chiapas, Mexico 16°4N 93°45W 87 D6
Tonalá Jalisco, Mexico 20°37N 103°14W 86 C4
Tonasket U.S.A. 48°42N 119°26W 76 B4
Tonawanda U.S.A. 43°1N 78°53W 82 D6
Tonb Iran 26°15N 55°15E 45 E7
Tonbridge U.K. 51°11N 0°17E 13 F8
Tondano Indonesia 1°35N 124°54E 37 D6
Tondoro Namibia 17°45S 18°50E 56 B2
Tone → Australia 34°25S 116°25E 61 F2
Tone-Gawa → Japan 35°44N 140°51E 31 F9
Tonekābon Iran 36°45N 51°12E 45 B6
Tong Xian China 39°55N 116°35E 34 E9
Tong-Yeong S. Korea 34°50N 128°20E 35 G15
Tonga ■ Pac. Oc. 19°50S 174°30W 59 c
Tonga Trench Pac. Oc. 18°0S 173°0W 64 J10
Tongaat S. Africa 29°33S 31°9E 57 D5
Tongareva = Penrhyn
  Cook Is. 9°0S 158°0W 65 H12
Tongariro △ N.Z. 39°8S 175°33E 59 C5
Tongatapu Tonga 21°10S 175°10W 59 c
Tongatapu Group Tonga 21°0S 175°0W 59 c
Tongchuan China 35°6N 109°3E 34 G5
Tongeren Belgium 50°47N 5°28E 15 D5
Tonggu Jiao China 22°22N 113°37E 33 G10
Tongguan China 34°40N 110°25E 34 G6
Tonghua China 41°42N 125°58E 35 D13
Tongjosŏn Man
  N. Korea 39°30N 128°0E 35 E15
Tongking, G. of = Tonkin, G. of
  Asia 20°0N 108°0E 38 C7
Tongliao China 43°38N 122°18E 35 C12
Tongling China 30°55N 117°48E 33 C6
Tongobory Madag. 23°32S 44°20E 57 C7
Tongoy Chile 30°16S 71°31W 94 C1
Tongres = Tongeren
  Belgium 50°47N 5°28E 15 D5
Tongsa Dzong Bhutan 27°31N 90°31E 41 F17
Tongue U.K. 58°29N 4°25W 11 C4
Tongue → U.S.A. 46°25N 105°52W 76 C11
Tongwei China 35°0N 105°5E 34 G3
Tongxin China 36°59N 105°58E 34 F3
Tongyang N. Korea 39°9N 126°53E 35 E14
Tongyu China 44°45N 123°4E 35 B12
Tonj Sudan 7°20N 28°44E 51 G11
Tonk India 26°6N 75°54E 42 F6
Tonkawa U.S.A. 36°41N 97°18W 84 C6
Tonkin = Bac Phan
  Vietnam 22°0N 105°0E 38 B5
Tonkin, G. of Asia 20°0N 108°0E 38 C7
Tonle Sap Cambodia 13°0N 104°0E 38 F5
Tono Japan 39°19N 141°32E 30 E10
Tonopah U.S.A. 38°4N 117°14W 77 G5
Tonosí Panama 7°20N 80°20W 88 E3

Tons → Haryana, India 30°30N 77°39E 42 D7
Tons → Ut. P., India 26°1N 83°33E 43 F10
Tønsberg Norway 59°19N 10°25E 9 G14
Tonto → U.S.A. 33°39N 111°7W 77 K8
Tonumea Tonga 20°30S 174°30W 59 c
Toobanna Australia 18°42S 146°9E 62 B4
Toodyay Australia 31°34S 116°28E 61 F2
Tooele U.S.A. 40°32N 112°18W 76 F7
Toompine Australia 27°15S 144°19E 63 D3
Toora Australia 38°39S 146°23E 63 F4
Toora-Khem Russia 52°28N 96°17E 29 D10
Toowoomba Australia 27°32S 151°56E 63 D5
Top Springs Australia 16°37S 131°51E 60 C5
Topaz U.S.A. 38°41N 119°30W 78 G7
Topeka U.S.A. 39°3N 95°40W 80 F6
Topley Canada 54°49N 126°18W 70 C3
Topocalma, Pta. Chile 34°10S 72°2W 94 C1
Topock U.S.A. 34°46N 114°29W 79 L12
Topol'čany Slovak Rep. 48°35N 18°12E 17 D10
Topolobampo Mexico 25°36N 109°3W 86 B3
Topozero, Ozero Russia 65°35N 32°0E 8 D25
Toppenish U.S.A. 46°23N 120°19W 76 C3
Toraka Vestale Madag. 16°20S 43°58E 57 B7
Torata Peru 17°23S 70°1W 92 G4
Torbalı Turkey 38°10N 27°21E 23 E12
Torbat-e Heydārīyeh
  Iran 35°15N 59°12E 45 C8
Torbat-e Jām Iran 35°16N 60°35E 45 C9
Torbay Canada 47°40N 52°42W 73 C9
Torbay U.K. 50°26N 3°31W 13 G4
Tordesillas Spain 41°30N 5°0W 21 B3
Torfaen □ U.K. 51°43N 3°3W 13 F4
Torgau Germany 51°34N 13°0E 16 C7
Torhout Belgium 51°5N 3°7E 15 C3
Tori-Shima Japan 30°29N 140°19E 31 J10
Torino Italy 45°3N 7°40E 20 D7
Torit Sudan 4°27N 32°31E 51 H12
Torkamān Iran 37°35N 47°23E 44 B5
Tormes → Spain 41°18N 6°29W 21 B2
Tornado Mt. Canada 49°55N 114°40W 70 D6
Torneå = Tornio Finland 65°50N 24°12E 8 D21
Torneälven → Europe 65°50N 24°12E 8 D21
Torneträsk Sweden 68°24N 19°15E 8 B18
Tornio Finland 65°50N 24°12E 8 D21
Tornionjoki = Torneälven →
  Europe 65°50N 24°12E 8 D21
Tornquist Argentina 38°8S 62°15W 94 D3
Toro Spain 39°59N 4°8E 24 B11
Toro, Cerro del Chile 29°10S 69°50W 94 B2
Toro △ Uganda 1°5N 30°22E 54 C3
Toro Pk. U.S.A. 33°34N 116°24W 79 M10
Toronto Canada 43°39N 79°20W 82 C5
Toronto U.S.A. 40°28N 80°36W 82 F4
Toronto Lester B. Pearson Int. ✈
  (YYZ) Canada 43°49N 79°35W 82 C5
Toropets Russia 56°30N 31°40E 18 C5
Tororo Uganda 0°45N 34°12E 54 B3
Toros Dağları Turkey 37°0N 32°30E 44 B2
Torpa India 22°57N 85°6E 43 H11
Torquay U.K. 50°27N 3°32W 13 G4
Torrance U.S.A. 33°50N 118°20W 79 M8
Torre de Moncorvo
  Portugal 41°12N 7°8W 21 B2
Torre del Greco Italy 40°47N 14°22E 22 D6
Torrejón de Ardoz Spain 40°27N 3°29W 21 B4
Torrelavega Spain 43°20N 4°5W 21 A3
Torremolinos Spain 36°38N 4°30W 21 D3
Torrens, L. Australia 31°0S 137°50E 63 E2
Torrens Cr. → Australia 22°23S 145°9E 62 C4
Torrens Creek Australia 20°48S 145°3E 62 C4
Torrent Spain 39°27N 0°28W 21 C5
Torreón Mexico 25°33N 103°26W 86 B4
Torres Brazil 29°21S 49°44W 95 B5
Torres Mexico 28°46N 110°47W 86 B2
Torres Strait Australia 9°50S 142°20E 58 B7
Torres Vedras Portugal 39°5N 9°15W 21 C1
Torrevieja Spain 37°59N 0°42W 21 D5
Torrey U.S.A. 38°18N 111°25W 76 G8
Torridge → U.K. 51°0N 4°13W 13 G3
Torridon, L. U.K. 57°35N 5°50W 11 D3
Torrington Conn., U.S.A. 41°48N 73°7W 83 E11
Torrington Wyo.,
  U.S.A. 42°4N 104°11W 76 E11
Tórshavn Færoe Is. 62°5N 6°56W 8 E9
Tortola Br. Virgin Is. 18°19N 64°45W 89 e
Tortosa Spain 40°49N 0°31E 21 B6
Tortosa, C. Spain 40°41N 0°52E 21 B6
Tortue, Î. de la Haiti 20°5N 72°57W 89 B5
Tortuguero △ Costa Rica 10°31N 83°29W 88 D3
Ţorūd Iran 35°25N 55°5E 45 C7
Toruń Poland 53°2N 18°39E 17 B10
Tory Hill Canada 44°58N 78°16W 82 B6
Tory I. Ireland 55°16N 8°14W 10 A3
Tosa Japan 33°24N 133°23E 31 H6
Tosa-Shimizu Japan 32°52N 132°58E 31 H6
Tosa-Wan Japan 33°15N 133°30E 31 H6
Toscana □ Italy 43°25N 11°0E 22 C4
Toshka Lakes Egypt 22°50N 31°0E 51 D12
Toshkent Uzbekistan 41°20N 69°10E 28 E7
Tostado Argentina 29°15S 61°50W 94 B3
Tostón, Pta. de Canary Is. 28°42N 14°2W 24 F5
Tosu Japan 33°22N 130°31E 31 H5
Toteng Botswana 20°22S 22°58E 56 C3
Totma Russia 60°0N 42°40E 18 C7
Totnes U.K. 50°26N 3°42W 13 G4
Totness Suriname 5°53N 56°19W 93 B7
Totonicapán Guatemala 14°58N 91°12W 88 D1
Totoya, I. Fiji 18°57S 179°50W 59 a
Totten Glacier Antarctica 66°45S 116°10E 5 C8
Tottenham Australia 32°14S 147°21E 63 E4
Tottenham Canada 44°1N 79°49W 82 B5
Tottori Japan 35°30N 134°15E 31 G7
Tottori □ Japan 35°30N 134°12E 31 G7
Toubkal, Djebel Morocco 31°0N 8°0W 50 B4
Tougan Burkina Faso 13°11N 2°58W 50 F5
Touggourt Algeria 33°6N 6°4E 50 B7
Toul France 48°40N 5°53E 20 B6

Toulon France 43°10N 5°55E 20 E6
Toulouse France 43°37N 1°27E 20 E4
Toummo Niger 22°45N 14°8E 51 D8
Toungoo Burma 19°0N 96°30E 41 K20
Touraine France 47°20N 0°30E 20 C4
Tourcoing France 50°42N 3°10E 20 A5
Touriñán, C. Spain 43°3N 9°18W 21 A1
Tournai Belgium 50°35N 3°25E 15 D3
Tournon-sur-Rhône
  France 45°4N 4°50E 20 D6
Tours France 47°22N 0°40E 20 C4
Toussoro, Mt. C.A.R. 9°7N 23°14E 52 C4
Touwrivier S. Africa 33°20S 20°2E 56 E3
Touws → S. Africa 33°45S 21°11E 56 E3
Touwsrivier S. Africa 33°20S 20°2E 56 E3
Towada Japan 40°37N 141°13E 30 D10
Towada-Hachimantai △
  Japan 40°20N 140°55E 30 D10
Towada-Ko Japan 40°28N 140°55E 30 D10
Towanda U.S.A. 41°46N 76°27W 83 E8
Tower U.S.A. 47°48N 92°17W 80 B7
Towerhill Cr. →
  Australia 22°28S 144°35E 62 C3
Towner U.S.A. 48°21N 100°25W 80 A3
Townsend U.S.A. 46°19N 111°31W 76 C8
Townshend I. Australia 22°10S 150°31E 62 C5
Townsville Australia 19°15S 146°45E 62 B4
Towraghondī Afghan. 35°13N 62°16E 40 B3
Towson U.S.A. 39°24N 76°36W 81 F15
Towuti, Danau Indonesia 2°45S 121°32E 37 E6
Toya-Ko Japan 42°35N 140°51E 30 C10
Toyama Japan 36°40N 137°15E 31 F8
Toyama □ Japan 36°45N 137°30E 31 F8
Toyama-Wan Japan 37°0N 137°30E 31 F8
Toyapakeh Indonesia 8°41S 115°29E 37 K18
Toyohashi Japan 34°45N 137°25E 31 G8
Toyokawa Japan 34°48N 137°27E 31 G8
Toyonaka Japan 34°46N 135°28E 31 G7
Toyooka Japan 35°35N 134°48E 31 G7
Toyota Japan 35°3N 137°7E 31 G8
Tozeur Tunisia 33°56N 8°0E 50 B7
Trá Li = Tralee Ireland 52°16N 9°42W 10 D2
Tra On Vietnam 9°58N 105°55E 39 H5
Trabzon Turkey 41°0N 39°45E 19 F6
Tracadie Canada 47°30N 64°55W 73 C7
Tracy Canada 46°1N 73°9W 72 C5
Tracy Calif., U.S.A. 37°44N 121°26W 78 H5
Tracy Minn., U.S.A. 44°14N 95°37W 80 C6
Trafalgar, C. Spain 36°10N 6°2W 21 D2
Trail Canada 49°5N 117°40W 70 D5
Trainor L. Canada 60°24N 120°17W 70 A4
Trakai △ Lithuania 54°30N 25°10E 9 J21
Trákhonas Cyprus 35°12N 33°21E 25 D12
Tralee Ireland 52°16N 9°42W 10 D2
Tralee B. Ireland 52°17N 9°55W 10 D2
Tramore Ireland 52°10N 7°10W 10 D4
Tramore B. Ireland 52°9N 7°10W 10 D4
Tramuntana, Serra de
  Spain 39°48N 2°54E 24 B9
Tran Ninh, Cao Nguyen
  Laos 19°30N 103°10E 38 C4
Tranås Sweden 58°3N 14°59E 9 G16
Trancas Argentina 26°11S 65°20W 94 B2
Trang Thailand 7°33N 99°38E 39 J2
Trangahy Madag. 19°7S 44°31E 57 B7
Trangan Indonesia 6°40S 134°20E 37 F8
Trangie Australia 32°4S 148°0E 63 E4
Trani Italy 41°17N 16°25E 22 D7
Tranoroa Madag. 24°42S 45°4E 57 C8
Tranqueras Uruguay 31°13S 55°45W 95 C4
Transantarctic Mts.
  Antarctica 85°0S 170°0W 5 E12
Transilvania Romania 46°30N 24°0E 17 E12
Transilvanian Alps = Carpații
  Meridionali Romania 45°30N 25°0E 17 F13
Transnistria = Stînga Nistrului □
  Moldova 47°20N 29°15E 17 E15
Transylvania = Transilvania
  Romania 46°30N 24°0E 17 E12
Trápani Italy 38°1N 12°29E 22 E5
Trapper Pk. U.S.A. 45°54N 114°18W 76 D6
Traralgon Australia 38°12S 146°34E 63 F4
Trasimeno, L. Italy 43°8N 12°6E 22 C5
Trat Thailand 12°14N 102°33E 39 F4
Tratani → Pakistan 29°19N 68°20E 42 E3
Traun Austria 48°14N 14°15E 16 D8
Travellers L. Australia 33°20S 142°0E 63 E3
Travemünde Germany 53°57N 10°52E 16 B6
Travers, Mt. N.Z. 42°1S 172°45E 59 E4
Traverse City U.S.A. 44°46N 85°38W 81 C11
Travis, L. U.S.A. 30°24N 97°55W 84 F6
Travnik Bos.-H. 44°17N 17°39E 23 B7
Trawbreaga B. Ireland 55°20N 7°25W 10 A4
Trébbia → Italy 45°4N 9°41E 20 D8
Třebíč Czech Rep. 49°14N 15°55E 16 D8
Trebinje Bos.-H. 42°44N 18°22E 23 C8
Trebonne Australia 18°37S 146°5E 62 B4
Tregaron U.K. 52°14N 3°56W 13 E4
Tregrosse Is. Australia 17°41S 150°43E 62 B5
Treherne Canada 49°38N 98°42W 71 D9
Treinta y Tres Uruguay 33°16S 54°17W 95 C5
Trelawney Zimbabwe 17°30S 30°30E 57 B5
Trelew Argentina 43°10S 65°20W 96 E3
Trelleborg Sweden 55°20N 13°10E 9 J15
Tremadog Bay U.K. 52°51N 4°18W 12 E3
Tremonton U.S.A. 41°43N 112°10W 76 F7
Tremp Spain 42°10N 0°52E 21 A6
Trenche → Canada 47°46N 72°53W 72 C5
Trenčín Slovak Rep. 48°52N 18°4E 17 D10
Trenggalek Indonesia 8°3S 111°43E 37 H14
Trenque Lauquen
  Argentina 36°5S 62°45W 94 D3
Trent → Canada 44°6N 77°34W 82 B7
Trent → U.K. 53°41N 0°42W 12 D7
Trento Italy 46°4N 11°8E 22 A4
Trenton Canada 44°10N 77°34W 82 B7
Trenton Mo., U.S.A. 40°5N 93°37W 80 E7
Trenton N.J., U.S.A. 40°14N 74°46W 83 F10

Trenton Nebr., U.S.A. 40°11N 101°1W 80 E3
Trepassey Canada 46°43N 53°25W 73 C9
Tres Arroyos Argentina 38°26S 60°20W 94 D3
Três Corações Brazil 21°44S 45°15W 95 A6
Três Lagoas Brazil 20°50S 51°43W 93 H8
Tres Lomas Argentina 36°27S 62°51W 94 D3
Tres Montes, C. Chile 46°50S 75°30W 96 F1
Tres Pinos U.S.A. 36°48N 121°19W 78 J5
Três Pontas Brazil 21°23S 45°29W 95 A6
Tres Puentes Chile 27°50S 70°15W 94 B1
Tres Puntas, C. Argentina 47°0S 66°0W 96 F3
Três Rios Brazil 22°6S 43°15W 95 A7
Tres Valles Mexico 18°15N 96°8W 87 D5
Tresco U.K. 49°57N 6°20W 13 H1
Treviso Italy 45°40N 12°15E 22 B5
Triabunna Australia 42°30S 147°55E 63 G4
Trianda Greece 36°25N 28°10E 25 C10
Triangle Zimbabwe 21°2S 31°28E 57 C5
Tribal Areas □ Pakistan 33°0N 70°0E 42 C4
Tribulation, C. Australia 16°5S 145°29E 62 B4
Tribune U.S.A. 38°28N 101°45W 80 F3
Trichinopoly = Tiruchchirappalli
  India 10°45N 78°45E 40 P11
Trichur India 10°30N 76°18E 40 P10
Trida Australia 33°1S 145°1E 63 E4
Trier Germany 49°45N 6°38E 16 D4
Trieste Italy 45°40N 13°46E 22 B5
Triglav Slovenia 46°21N 13°50E 16 E7
Trikala Greece 39°34N 21°47E 23 E9
Trikomo Cyprus 35°17N 33°52E 25 D12
Trikora, Puncak
  Indonesia 4°15S 138°45E 37 E9
Trim Ireland 53°33N 6°48W 10 C5
Trimmu Dam Pakistan 31°10N 72°8E 42 D5
Trincomalee Sri Lanka 8°38N 81°15E 40 Q12
Trindade Brazil 16°40S 49°30W 93 G9
Trindade, I. Atl. Oc. 20°20S 29°50W 2 F8
Trinidad Bolivia 14°46S 64°50W 92 F6
Trinidad Cuba 21°48N 80°0W 88 B4
Trinidad Trin. & Tob. 10°30N 61°15W 89 D7
Trinidad Uruguay 33°30S 56°50W 94 C4
Trinidad U.S.A. 37°10N 104°31W 77 H11
Trinidad → Mexico 17°49N 95°9W 87 D5
Trinidad & Tobago ■
  W. Indies 10°30N 61°20W 89 D7
Trinity Canada 48°59N 53°55W 73 C9
Trinity U.S.A. 30°57N 95°22W 84 F7
Trinity → Calif., U.S.A. 41°11N 123°42W 76 F2
Trinity → Tex., U.S.A. 29°45N 94°43W 84 G7
Trinity B. Canada 48°20N 53°10W 73 C9
Trinity Hills Trin. & Tob. 10°7N 61°7W 93 K15
Trinity Is. U.S.A. 56°33N 154°25W 74 a
Trinity Range U.S.A. 40°10N 118°40W 76 F4
Trinkitat Sudan 18°45N 37°51E 51 E13
Trinway U.S.A. 40°9N 82°1W 82 F2
Triolet Mauritius 20°4S 57°32E 53 d
Tripoli = Tarābulus
  Lebanon 34°31N 35°50E 46 A4
Tripoli = Tarābulus Libya 32°49N 13°7E 51 B8
Tripoli Greece 37°31N 22°25E 23 F10
Tripolitania = Tarābulus
  N. Afr. 31°0N 13°0E 51 B8
Tripura □ India 24°0N 92°0E 41 H18
Tripylos Cyprus 34°59N 32°41E 25 E11
Tristan da Cunha Atl. Oc. 37°6S 12°20W 49 K2
Trisul India 30°19N 79°47E 43 D8
Trivandrum India 8°41N 77°0E 40 Q10
Trnava Slovak Rep. 48°23N 17°35E 17 D9
Trochu Canada 51°50N 113°13W 70 C6
Trodely I. Canada 52°15N 79°26W 72 B4
Troglav Croatia 43°56N 16°36E 22 C7
Troilus, L. Canada 50°50N 74°35W 72 B5
Trois-Pistoles Canada 48°5N 69°10W 73 C6
Trois-Rivières Canada 46°25N 72°34W 72 C5
Trois-Rivières Guadeloupe 15°57N 61°40W 88 b
Troitsk Russia 54°10N 61°35E 28 D7
Troitsko Pechorsk
  Russia 62°40N 56°10E 18 B10
Trölladyngja Iceland 64°54N 17°16W 8 D5
Trollhättan Sweden 58°17N 12°20E 9 G15
Trollheimen Norway 62°46N 9°1E 8 E13
Trombetas → Brazil 1°55S 55°35W 93 D7
Tromsø Norway 69°40N 18°56E 8 B18
Tron Thailand 17°28N 100°7E 38 D3
Trona U.S.A. 35°46N 117°23W 79 K9
Tronador, Mte.
  Argentina 41°10S 71°50W 96 E2
Trøndelag Norway 64°17N 11°50E 8 D14
Trondheim Norway 63°36N 10°25E 8 E14
Trondheimsfjorden
  Norway 63°35N 10°30E 8 E14
Troodos Cyprus 34°55N 32°52E 25 E11
Troon U.K. 55°33N 4°39W 11 F4
Tropic U.S.A. 37°37N 112°5W 77 H7
Trostan U.K. 55°3N 6°10W 10 A5
Trou Gras Pt. St. Lucia 13°51N 60°53W 89 f
Trout → Canada 61°19N 119°51W 70 A5
Trout L. N.W.T., Canada 60°40N 121°14W 70 A4
Trout L. Ont., Canada 51°20N 93°15W 71 C10
Trout Lake Canada 56°30N 114°32W 70 B6
Trout Lake U.S.A. 46°0N 121°32W 78 E5
Trout River U.S.A. 44°53N 74°41W 83 B10
Trout Run U.S.A. 41°23N 77°3W 82 E7
Trouville-sur-Mer France 49°21N 0°5E 20 B4
Trowbridge U.K. 51°18N 2°12W 13 F5
Troy Turkey 39°57N 26°12E 23 E12
Troy Ala., U.S.A. 31°48N 85°58W 85 F12
Troy Kans., U.S.A. 39°47N 95°5W 80 F6
Troy Mo., U.S.A. 38°59N 90°59W 80 F8
Troy Mont., U.S.A. 48°28N 115°53W 76 B6
Troy N.Y., U.S.A. 42°44N 73°41W 83 D11
Troy Ohio, U.S.A. 40°2N 84°12W 81 E11
Troyes France 48°19N 4°3E 20 B6
Truchas Pk. U.S.A. 35°58N 105°39W 77 J11
Trucial States = United Arab
  Emirates ■ Asia 23°50N 54°0E 45 F7

Truckee U.S.A. 39°20N 120°11W 78 F6
Trudovoye Russia 43°17N 132°5E 30 C6
Trujillo Honduras 16°0N 86°0W 88 C2
Trujillo Peru 8°6S 79°0W 92 E3
Trujillo Spain 39°28N 5°55W 21 C3
Trujillo U.S.A. 35°32N 104°42W 77 J11
Trujillo Venezuela 9°22N 70°38W 92 B4
Truk Micronesia 7°25N 151°46E 64 G7
Trumann U.S.A. 35°41N 90°31W 85 D9
Trumansburg U.S.A. 42°33N 76°40W 83 D8
Trumbull, Mt. U.S.A. 36°25N 113°19W 77 H7
Trundle Australia 32°53S 147°35E 63 E4
Trung-Phan = Annam
  Vietnam 16°0N 108°0E 38 E7
Truro Canada 45°21N 63°14W 73 C7
Truro U.K. 50°16N 5°4W 13 G2
Truskavets Ukraine 49°17N 23°30E 17 D12
Trutch Canada 57°44N 122°57W 70 B4
Truth or Consequences
  U.S.A. 33°8N 107°15W 77 K10
Trutnov Czech Rep. 50°37N 15°54E 16 C8
Tryonville U.S.A. 41°42N 79°48W 82 E5
Tsandi Namibia 17°42S 14°50E 56 B1
Tsaratanana Madag. 16°47S 47°39E 57 B8
Tsaratanana, Mt. de =
  Maromokotro Madag. 14°0S 49°0E 57 A8
Tsaratanana △ Madag. 13°57S 48°52E 57 A8
Tsau Botswana 20°8S 22°22E 56 C3
Tsavo Kenya 2°59S 38°28E 54 C4
Tsavo East △ Kenya 2°44S 38°47E 54 C4
Tsavo West △ Kenya 3°19S 37°57E 54 C4
Tsentralnyy □ Russia 52°0N 40°0E 28 D4
Tses Namibia 25°58S 18°8E 56 D2
Tsetserleg Mongolia 47°36N 101°32E 32 B5
Tsévié Togo 6°25N 1°20E 50 G6
Tshabong Botswana 26°2S 22°29E 56 D3
Tshane Botswana 24°5S 21°54E 56 C3
Tshela
  Dem. Rep. of the Congo 4°57S 13°4E 52 E2
Tshesebe Botswana 21°51S 27°32E 57 C4
Tshibeke
  Dem. Rep. of the Congo 2°40S 28°35E 54 C2
Tshibinda
  Dem. Rep. of the Congo 2°23S 28°43E 54 C2
Tshikapa
  Dem. Rep. of the Congo 6°28S 20°48E 52 F4
Tshilenge
  Dem. Rep. of the Congo 6°17S 23°48E 54 D1
Tshinsenda
  Dem. Rep. of the Congo 12°20S 28°0E 55 E2
Tshofa
  Dem. Rep. of the Congo 5°13S 25°16E 54 D2
Tshwane = Pretoria
  S. Africa 25°44S 28°12E 57 D4
Tshwane Botswana 22°24S 22°1E 56 C3
Tsigara Botswana 20°22S 25°54E 56 C4
Tsihombe Madag. 25°10S 45°41E 57 D8
Tsiigehtchic Canada 67°15N 134°0W 68 C6
Ts'il-os △ Canada 51°9N 123°59W 70 C4
Tsimlyansk Res. = Tsimlyanskoye
  Vdkhr. Russia 48°0N 43°0E 19 E7
Tsimlyanskoye Vdkhr.
  Russia 48°0N 43°0E 19 E7
Tsinan = Jinan China 36°38N 117°1E 34 F9
Tsineng S. Africa 27°5S 23°5E 56 D3
Tsing Yi China 22°21N 114°6E 33 G11
Tsinghai = Qinghai □
  China 36°0N 98°0E 32 C4
Tsingtao = Qingdao
  China 36°5N 120°20E 35 F11
Tsingy de Bemaraha △
  Madag. 18°35S 45°25E 57 B8
Tsingy de Namoroka △
  Madag. 16°29S 45°25E 57 B8
Tsinjoarivo Madag. 19°37S 47°40E 57 B8
Tsinjomitondraka Madag. 15°40S 47°8E 57 B8
Tsirigo = Kythira Greece 36°8N 23°0E 23 F10
Tsiroanomandidy Madag. 18°46S 46°2E 57 B8
Tsitondroina Madag. 21°19S 46°0E 57 C8
Tsitsikamma △ S. Africa 34°3S 23°40E 56 E3
Tsivory Madag. 24°4S 46°5E 57 C8
Tskhinvali Georgia 42°14N 44°1E 19 F7
Tsna → Russia 54°55N 41°58E 18 D7
Tso Moriri, L. India 32°50N 78°20E 43 C8
Tsobis Namibia 19°27S 17°30E 56 B2
Tsodilo Hill Botswana 18°49S 21°43E 56 B3
Tsogttsetsiy = Baruunsuu
  Mongolia 43°43N 105°35E 34 C3
Tsolo S. Africa 31°18S 28°37E 57 E4
Tsomo S. Africa 32°0S 27°42E 57 E4
Tsu Japan 34°45N 136°25E 31 G8
Tsu L. Canada 60°40N 111°52W 70 A6
Tsuchiura Japan 36°5N 140°15E 31 F10
Tsuen Wan China 22°22N 114°6E 33 G11
Tsugaru-Kaikyō Japan 41°35N 141°0E 30 D10
Tsumeb Namibia 19°9S 17°44E 56 B2
Tsumis Namibia 23°39S 17°29E 56 C2
Tsuruga Japan 35°45N 136°2E 31 G8
Tsurugi-San Japan 33°51N 134°6E 31 H7
Tsuruoka Japan 38°44N 139°50E 30 E9
Tsushima Gifu, Japan 35°10N 136°43E 31 G8
Tsushima Nagasaki,
  Japan 34°20N 129°20E 31 G4
Tsuyama Japan 35°3N 134°0E 31 G7
Tsyelyakhany Belarus 52°30N 25°46E 17 B13
Tual Indonesia 5°38S 132°44E 37 F8
Tualatin U.S.A. 45°23N 122°45W 78 E4
Tuam Ireland 53°31N 8°51W 10 C3
Tuamotu, Îs.
  French Polynesia 17°0S 144°0W 65 J13
Tuamotu Arch. = Tuamotu, Îs.
  French Polynesia 17°0S 144°0W 65 J13
Tuamotu Ridge Pac. Oc. 20°0S 138°0W 65 K14
Tuan Giao Vietnam 21°35N 103°25E 38 B4
Tuao Phil. 17°55N 121°22E 37 A6
Tuapse Russia 44°5N 39°10E 19 F6
Tuas Singapore 1°19N 103°39E 39 d

Tuatapere *N.Z.* 46°8S 167°41E **59** G1
Tuba City *U.S.A.* 36°8N 111°14W **77** H8
Tuban *Indonesia* 6°54S 112°3E **37** G15
Tubani *Botswana* 24°46S 24°18E **56** C3
Tubarão *Brazil* 28°30S 49°0W **95** B6
Tûbâs *West Bank* 32°20N 35°22E **46** C4
Tübingen *Germany* 48°31N 9°4E **16** D5
Tubou *Fiji* 18°13S 178°48W **59** a
Tubruq *Libya* 32°7N 23°55E **51** B10
Tubuaï, Îs.
 French Polynesia 25°0S 150°0W **65** K13
Tuc Trung *Vietnam* 11°1N 107°12E **39** G6
Tucacas *Venezuela* 10°48N 68°19W **92** A5
Tuchitua *Canada* 60°55N 129°13W **70** A3
Tuchodi → *Canada* 58°17N 123°42W **70** B4
Tuckanarra *Australia* 27°7S 118°5E **61** E2
Tucson *U.S.A.* 32°13N 110°58W **77** K8
Tucumán □ *Argentina* 26°48S 66°2W **94** B2
Tucumcari *U.S.A.* 35°10N 103°44W **77** J12
Tucupita *Venezuela* 9°2N 62°3W **92** B6
Tucuruí *Brazil* 3°42S 49°44W **93** D9
Tucuruí, Represa de
 Brazil 4°0S 49°30W **93** D9
Tudela *Spain* 42°4N 1°39W **21** A5
Tudmur *Syria* 34°36N 38°15E **44** C3
Tudor, L. *Canada* 55°50N 65°25W **73** A6
Tuen Mun *China* 22°24N 113°59E **33** G10
Tugela → *S. Africa* 29°14S 31°30E **57** D5
Tuguegarao *Phil.* 17°35N 121°42E **37** A6
Tugur *Russia* 53°44N 136°45E **29** D14
Tui *Spain* 42°3N 8°39W **21** A1
Tuineje *Canary Is.* 28°19N 14°3W **24** F5
Tukangbesi, Kepulauan
 Indonesia 6°0S 124°0E **37** F6
Tukarak I. *Canada* 56°15N 78°45W **72** A4
Tukayyid *Iraq* 29°47N 45°36E **44** D5
Tuktoyaktuk *Canada* 69°27N 133°2W **68** C6
Tukums *Latvia* 56°58N 23°10E **9** H20
Tukuyu *Tanzania* 9°17S 33°35E **55** D3
Tula *Hidalgo, Mexico* 20°3N 99°21W **87** C5
Tula *Tamaulipas, Mexico* 23°0N 99°43W **87** C5
Tula *Russia* 54°13N 37°38E **18** D6
Tulancingo *Mexico* 20°5N 98°22W **87** C5
Tulare *U.S.A.* 36°13N 119°21W **78** J7
Tulare Lake Bed *U.S.A.* 36°0N 119°48W **78** K7
Tularosa *U.S.A.* 33°5N 106°1W **77** K10
Tulbagh *S. Africa* 33°16S 19°6E **56** E2
Tulcán *Ecuador* 0°48N 77°43W **92** C3
Tulcea *Romania* 45°13N 28°46E **17** F15
Tulchyn *Ukraine* 48°41N 28°49E **17** D15
Tüleh *Iran* 34°35N 52°33E **45** C7
Tulemalu L. *Canada* 62°58N 99°25W **71** A9
Tuli *Zimbabwe* 21°58S 29°13E **55** G2
Tulia *U.S.A.* 34°32N 101°46W **84** D4
Tulita *Canada* 64°57N 125°30W **68** C7
Tülkarm *West Bank* 32°19N 35°2E **46** C4
Tulla *Ireland* 52°53N 8°46W **10** D3
Tullahoma *U.S.A.* 35°22N 86°13W **85** D11
Tullamore *Australia* 32°39S 147°36E **63** E4
Tullamore *Ireland* 53°16N 7°31W **10** C4
Tulle *France* 45°16N 1°46E **20** D4
Tullow *Ireland* 52°49N 6°45W **10** D5
Tully *Australia* 17°56S 145°55E **62** B4
Tully *U.S.A.* 42°48N 76°7W **83** D8
Tulsa *U.S.A.* 36°10N 95°55W **84** C7
Tulsequah *Canada* 58°39N 133°35W **70** B2
Tuluá *Colombia* 4°6N 76°11W **92** C3
Tulun *Russia* 54°32N 100°35E **29** D11
Tulungagung *Indonesia* 8°5S 111°54E **37** H14
Tuma → *Russia* 54°44N 84°35W **88** D3
Tumaco *Colombia* 1°50N 78°45W **92** C3
Tumatumari *Guyana* 5°20N 58°55W **92** B7
Tumba *Sweden* 59°12N 17°48E **9** G17
Tumba, L.
 Dem. Rep. of the Congo 0°50S 18°0E **52** E3
Tumbarumba *Australia* 35°44S 148°0E **63** F4
Tumbaya *Argentina* 23°50S 65°26W **94** A2
Tumbes *Peru* 3°37S 80°27W **92** D2
Tumbler Ridge *Canada* 55°8N 121°0W **70** B4
Tumbwe
 Dem. Rep. of the Congo 11°25S 27°15E **55** E2
Tumby Bay *Australia* 34°21S 136°8E **63** E2
Tumd Youqi *China* 40°30N 110°30E **34** D6
Tumen *China* 43°0N 129°50E **30** C4
Tumen Jiang → *China* 42°20N 130°35E **35** C16
Tumeremo *Venezuela* 7°18N 61°30W **92** B6
Tumkur *India* 13°18N 77°6E **40** N10
Tump *Pakistan* 26°7N 62°16E **40** F3
Tumpat *Malaysia* 6°11N 102°10E **39** J4
Tumu *Ghana* 10°56N 1°56W **50** F5
Tumucumaque, Serra
 Brazil 2°0N 55°0W **93** C8
Tumut *Australia* 35°16S 148°13E **63** F4
Tumwater *U.S.A.* 47°1N 122°54W **78** C4
Tuna *India* 22°59N 70°5E **42** H4
Tunapuna *Trin. & Tob.* 10°38N 61°24W **93** K15
Tunas de Zaza *Cuba* 21°39N 79°34W **88** B4
Tunbridge Wells = Royal
 Tunbridge Wells *U.K.* 51°7N 0°16E **13** F8
Tuncurry *Australia* 32°17S 152°29E **63** E5
Tundla *India* 27°12N 78°17E **42** F8
Tunduru *Tanzania* 11°8S 37°25E **55** E4
Tundzha → *Bulgaria* 41°40N 26°35E **23** C11
Tung Chung *China* 22°17N 113°57E **33** G10
Tung Lung Chau
 China 22°15N 114°17E **33** G11
Tungabhadra → *India* 15°57N 78°15E **40** M11
Tungla *Nic.* 13°24N 84°21W **88** D3
Tungsten *Canada* 61°57N 128°16W **70** A3
Tunguska, Nizhnyaya →
 Russia 65°48N 88°4E **29** C9
Tunguska, Podkamennaya →
 Russia 61°50N 90°13E **29** C10
Tunica *U.S.A.* 34°41N 90°23W **85** D9
Tunis *Tunisia* 36°50N 10°11E **51** A7

Tunisia ■ *Africa* 33°30N 9°10E **51** A7
Tunja *Colombia* 5°33N 73°25W **92** B4
Tunkhannock *U.S.A.* 41°32N 75°57W **83** E9
Tunliu *China* 36°13N 112°52E **34** F7
Tunnel Creek △
 Australia 17°41S 125°18E **60** C4
Tunnsjøen *Norway* 64°45N 13°25E **8** D15
Tunungayualok I. *Canada* 56°0N 61°0W **73** A7
Tunuyán *Argentina* 33°35S 69°0W **94** C2
Tunuyán → *Argentina* 33°33S 67°30W **94** C2
Tuolumne *U.S.A.* 37°58N 120°15W **78** H6
Tuolumne → *U.S.A.* 37°36N 121°13W **78** H5
Tûp Āghāj *Iran* 36°3N 47°50E **44** B5
Tupã *Brazil* 21°57S 50°28W **95** A5
Tupelo *U.S.A.* 34°16N 88°43W **85** D10
Tupinambarana, Ilha
 Brazil 3°0S 58°0W **92** D7
Tupiza *Bolivia* 21°30S 65°40W **94** A2
Tupman *U.S.A.* 35°18N 119°21W **79** K7
Tupper *Canada* 55°32N 120°1W **70** B4
Tupper L. *U.S.A.* 44°10N 74°32W **83** B10
Tupper Lake *U.S.A.* 44°14N 74°28W **83** B10
Tupungato, Cerro
 S. Amer. 33°15S 69°50W **94** C2
Tuquan *China* 45°18N 121°38E **35** B11
Túquerres *Colombia* 1°5N 77°37W **92** C3
Tura *Russia* 64°20N 100°17E **29** C11
Turabah *Si. Arabia* 28°20N 43°15E **44** D4
Tûrān *Iran* 35°39N 56°42E **45** C8
Turan *Russia* 51°55N 94°0E **29** D10
Ţuraýf *Si. Arabia* 31°41N 38°39E **44** D3
Turda *Romania* 46°34N 23°47E **17** E12
Turek *Poland* 52°3N 18°30E **17** B10
Turfan = Turpan *China* 43°58N 89°10E **32** B3
Turfan Basin = Turpan Pendi
 China 42°40N 89°25E **32** B3
Turfan Depression = Turpan
 Pendi *China* 42°40N 89°25E **32** B3
Turgeon → *Canada* 50°0N 78°56W **72** C4
Tŭrgovishte *Bulgaria* 43°17N 26°38E **23** C12
Turgutlu *Turkey* 38°30N 27°43E **23** E12
Turgwe → *Zimbabwe* 21°31S 32°15E **57** C5
Turia → *Spain* 39°27N 0°19W **21** C5
Turiaçu *Brazil* 1°40S 45°19W **93** D9
Turiaçu → *Brazil* 1°36S 45°19W **93** D9
Turin = Torino *Italy* 45°3N 7°40E **20** D7
Turkana, L. *Africa* 3°30N 36°5E **54** B4
Turkestan = Türkistan
 Kazakhstan 43°17N 68°16E **28** E7
Turkey ■ *Eurasia* 39°0N 36°0E **19** G6
Turkey Creek = Warmun
 Australia 17°2S 128°12E **60** C4
Türkistan *Kazakhstan* 43°17N 68°16E **28** E7
Türkmenabat
 Turkmenistan 39°6N 63°34E **45** B9
Türkmenbashi
 Turkmenistan 40°5N 53°5E **45** A7
Turkmenistan ■ *Asia* 39°0N 59°0E **28** F6
Turks Island Passage
 W. Indies 21°30N 71°30W **89** B5
Turku *Finland* 60°30N 22°19E **9** F20
Turkwel → *Kenya* 3°6N 36°6E **54** B4
Turlock *U.S.A.* 37°30N 120°51W **78** H6
Turnagain → *Canada* 59°12N 127°35W **70** B3
Turnagain, C. *N.Z.* 40°28S 176°38E **59** D6
Turneffe Is. *Belize* 17°20N 87°50W **87** D7
Turner *U.S.A.* 48°51N 108°24W **76** B9
Turner Pt. *Australia* 11°47S 133°32E **62** A1
Turner Valley *Canada* 50°40N 114°17W **70** C6
Turners Falls *U.S.A.* 42°36N 72°33W **83** D12
Turnhout *Belgium* 51°19N 4°57E **15** C4
Turnor L. *Canada* 56°35N 108°35W **71** B7
Türnovo = Veliko Tŭrnovo
 Bulgaria 43°5N 25°41E **23** C11
Turnu Măgurele
 Romania 43°46N 24°56E **17** G13
Turnu Roşu, P.
 Romania 45°33N 24°17E **17** F13
Turpan *China* 43°58N 89°10E **32** B3
Turpan Pendi *China* 42°40N 89°25E **32** B3
Turriff *U.K.* 57°32N 2°27W **11** D6
Tursãq *Iraq* 33°27N 45°47E **44** C5
Turtle Head I. *Australia* 10°56S 142°37E **62** A3
Turtle L. *Canada* 53°36N 108°38W **71** C7
Turtle Lake *U.S.A.* 47°31N 100°53W **80** B4
Turtleford *Canada* 53°23N 108°57W **71** C7
Turuépano △ *Venezuela* 10°34N 62°43W **89** D7
Turukhansk *Russia* 65°21N 88°5E **29** C9
Tuscaloosa *U.S.A.* 33°12N 87°34W **85** E11
Tuscany = Toscana □
 Italy 43°25N 11°0E **22** C4
Tuscarawas → *U.S.A.* 40°24N 81°25W **82** F3
Tuscarora Mt. *U.S.A.* 40°55N 77°55W **82** F7
Tuscola *Ill., U.S.A.* 39°48N 88°17W **80** F9
Tuscola *Tex., U.S.A.* 32°12N 99°48W **84** E5
Tuscumbia *U.S.A.* 34°44N 87°42W **85** D11
Tuskegee *U.S.A.* 32°25N 85°42W **85** E12
Tuticorin *India* 8°50N 78°12E **40** Q11
Tutóia *Brazil* 2°45S 42°20W **93** D10
Tutrakan *Bulgaria* 44°2N 26°40E **23** B11
Tuttle Creek L. *U.S.A.* 39°15N 96°36W **80** F5
Tuttlingen *Germany* 47°58N 8°48E **16** E5
Tutuala *E. Timor* 8°25S 127°15E **37** F7
Tutuila *Amer. Samoa* 14°19S 170°50W **59** b
Tutume *Botswana* 20°30S 27°5E **53** J5
Tuul Gol → *Mongolia* 48°30N 104°25E **32** B5
Tuva □ *Russia* 51°30N 95°0E **29** D10
Tuvalu ■ *Pac. Oc.* 8°0S 178°0E **58** B10
Tuvuca *Fiji* 17°40S 178°48W **59** a
Tuxpan *Mexico* 20°57N 97°24W **87** C5
Tuxtla Gutiérrez *Mexico* 16°45N 93°7W **87** D6
Tuy = Tui *Spain* 42°3N 8°39W **21** A1
Tuy An *Vietnam* 13°17N 109°16E **38** F7
Tuy Duc *Vietnam* 12°15N 107°27E **39** F6
Tuy Hoa *Vietnam* 13°5N 109°10E **38** F7

Tuy Phong *Vietnam* 11°14N 108°43E **39** G7
Tuya L. *Canada* 59°7N 130°35W **70** B2
Tuyen Hoa *Vietnam* 17°50N 106°10E **38** D6
Tuyen Quang *Vietnam* 21°50N 105°10E **38** B5
Tûysarkān *Iran* 34°33N 48°27E **45** C6
Tuz Gölü *Turkey* 38°42N 33°18E **19** G5
Tūz Khurmātū *Iraq* 34°56N 44°38E **44** C5
Tuzigoot △ *U.S.A.* 34°46N 112°2W **77** J7
Tuzla *Bos.-H.* 44°34N 18°41E **23** B8
Tver *Russia* 56°55N 35°55E **18** C6
Twain *U.S.A.* 40°1N 121°3W **78** E5
Twain Harte *U.S.A.* 38°2N 120°14W **78** G6
Tweed *Canada* 44°29N 77°19W **82** B7
Tweed → *U.K.* 55°45N 2°0W **11** F6
Tweed Heads *Australia* 28°10S 153°31E **63** D5
Tweedsmuir △ *Canada* 53°0N 126°20W **70** C3
Twentynine Palms
 U.S.A. 34°8N 116°3W **79** L10
Twillingate *Canada* 49°42N 54°45W **73** C9
Twin Bridges *U.S.A.* 45°33N 112°20W **76** D7
Twin Falls *Canada* 53°30N 64°32W **73** B7
Twin Falls *U.S.A.* 42°34N 114°28W **76** E6
Twin Valley *U.S.A.* 47°16N 96°16W **80** B5
Twinsburg *U.S.A.* 41°19N 81°26W **82** E3
Twitchell Res. *U.S.A.* 34°59N 120°19W **79** L6
Two Harbors *U.S.A.* 47°2N 91°40W **80** B8
Two Hills *Canada* 53°43N 111°52W **70** C6
Two Rivers *U.S.A.* 44°9N 87°34W **80** C10
Two Rocks *Australia* 31°30S 115°35E **61** F2
Twofold B. *Australia* 37°8S 149°59E **63** F4
Tyachiv *Ukraine* 48°1N 23°35E **17** D12
Tychy *Poland* 50°9N 18°59E **17** C10
Tyler *Minn., U.S.A.* 44°17N 96°8W **80** C5
Tyler *Tex., U.S.A.* 32°21N 95°18W **84** E7
Tynda *Russia* 55°10N 124°43E **29** D13
Tyndall *U.S.A.* 43°0N 97°50W **80** D5
Tyne → *U.K.* 54°59N 1°32W **12** C6
Tyne & Wear □ *U.K.* 55°6N 1°17W **12** B6
Tynemouth *U.K.* 55°1N 1°26W **12** B6
Tyre = Sûr *Lebanon* 33°19N 35°16E **46** B4
Tyrifjorden *Norway* 60°2N 10°8E **9** F14
Tyrol = Tirol □ *Austria* 47°3N 10°43E **16** E6
Tyrone *U.S.A.* 40°40N 78°14W **82** F6
Tyrone □ *U.K.* 54°38N 7°11W **10** B4
Tyrrell → *Australia* 35°26S 142°51E **63** F3
Tyrrell, L. *Australia* 35°20S 142°50E **63** F3
Tyrrell L. *Canada* 63°7N 105°27W **71** A7
Tyrrhenian Sea *Medit.* 40°0N 12°30E **22** E5
Tysfjorden *Norway* 68°7N 16°25E **8** B17
Tyulgan *Russia* 52°22N 56°12E **18** D10
Tyumen *Russia* 57°11N 65°29E **28** D7
Tywi → *U.K.* 51°48N 4°21W **13** F3
Tywyn *U.K.* 52°35N 4°5W **13** E3
Tzaneen *S. Africa* 23°47S 30°9E **57** C5
Tzermiado *Greece* 35°12N 25°29E **25** D7
Tzukong = Zigong
 China 29°15N 104°48E **32** D5

U

U.S.A. = United States of
 America ■ *N. Amer.* 37°0N 96°0W **74** C7
U.S. Virgin Is. ☑ *W. Indies* 18°20N 65°0W **89** e
Uanle Uen = Wanleweyne
 Somali Rep. 2°37N 44°54E **47** G3
Uatumã → *Brazil* 2°26S 57°37W **92** D7
Uaupés *Brazil* 0°8S 67°5W **92** D5
Uaupés → *Brazil* 0°2N 67°16W **92** C5
Uaxactún *Guatemala* 17°25N 89°29W **88** C2
Ubá *Brazil* 21°8S 43°0W **95** A7
Ubaitaba *Brazil* 14°18S 39°20W **93** F11
Ubangi = Oubangi →
 Dem. Rep. of the Congo 0°30S 17°50E **52** E3
Ubauro *Pakistan* 28°15N 69°45E **42** E3
Ubayyiḍ, W. al → *Iraq* 32°34N 43°48E **44** C4
Ube *Japan* 33°56N 131°15E **31** H5
Úbeda *Spain* 38°3N 3°23W **21** C4
Uberaba *Brazil* 19°50S 47°55W **93** G9
Uberlândia *Brazil* 19°0S 48°20W **93** G9
Ubin, Pulau *Singapore* 1°24N 103°57E **39** d
Ubly *U.S.A.* 43°42N 82°55W **82** C2
Ubolratna Res. *Thailand* 16°45N 102°30E **38** D4
Ubombo *S. Africa* 27°31S 32°4E **57** D5
Ubon Ratchathani
 Thailand 15°15N 104°50E **38** E5
Ubondo
 Dem. Rep. of the Congo 0°55S 25°42E **54** C2
Ubort → *Belarus* 52°6N 28°30E **17** B15
Ubud *Indonesia* 8°30S 115°16E **37** J18
Ubundu
 Dem. Rep. of the Congo 0°22S 25°30E **54** C2
Ucayali → *Peru* 4°30S 73°30W **92** D4
Uchab *Namibia* 19°47S 17°42E **56** B2
Uchiura-Wan *Japan* 42°25N 140°40E **30** C10
Uchquduq *Uzbekistan* 41°50N 62°50E **28** E7
Uchur → *Russia* 58°48N 130°35E **29** D14
Ucluelet *Canada* 48°57N 125°32W **70** D3
Uda → *Russia* 54°42N 135°14E **29** D14
Udachnyy *Russia* 66°25N 112°24E **29** C12
Udagamandalam *India* 11°30N 76°44E **40** P10
Udaipur *India* 24°36N 73°44E **42** G5
Udaipur Garhi *Nepal* 27°0N 86°35E **43** F12
Udala *India* 21°35N 86°34E **43** J12
Uddevalla *Sweden* 58°21N 11°55E **9** G14
Uddjaure *Sweden* 65°56N 17°49E **8** D17
Uden *Neths.* 51°40N 5°37E **15** C5
Udgir *India* 18°25N 77°5E **40** K10
Udhampur *India* 33°0N 75°5E **43** C6
Údine *Italy* 46°3N 13°14E **22** A5
Udintsev Fracture Zone
 S. Ocean 55°0S 145°0W **5** B13
Udmurtia □ *Russia* 57°30N 52°30E **18** C9
Udon Thani *Thailand* 17°29N 102°46E **38** D4
Udong *Cambodia* 11°48N 104°45E **39** G5
Udskaya Guba *Russia* 54°50N 135°45E **29** D14

Udu Pt. *Fiji* 16°9S 179°57W **59** a
Udupi *India* 13°25N 74°42E **40** N9
Udzungwa △ *Tanzania* 7°52S 36°35E **54** D4
Udzungwa Range
 Tanzania 9°30S 35°10E **55** D4
Ueda *Japan* 36°24N 138°16E **31** F9
Uedineniya, Os. *Russia* 78°0N 85°0E **4** B12
Uele →
 Dem. Rep. of the Congo 3°45N 24°45E **52** D4
Uelen *Russia* 66°10N 170°0W **29** C19
Uelzen *Germany* 52°57N 10°32E **16** B6
Ufa *Russia* 54°45N 55°55E **18** D10
Ufa → *Russia* 54°40N 56°0E **18** D10
Ugab → *Namibia* 20°55S 13°30E **56** C1
Ugalla → *Tanzania* 5°8S 30°42E **54** D3
Ugalla River △ *Tanzania* 5°50S 31°54E **54** D3
Uganda ■ *Africa* 2°0N 32°0E **54** B3
Ugie *S. Africa* 31°10S 28°13E **57** E4
Uglegorsk *Russia* 49°5N 142°2E **29** E15
Ugljan *Croatia* 44°12N 15°10E **16** F8
Ugolnye Kopi *Russia* 64°44N 177°42E **29** C18
Uhlenhorst *Namibia* 23°45S 17°55E **56** C2
Uhrichsville *U.S.A.* 40°24N 81°21W **82** F3
Uibhist a Deas = South Uist
 U.K. 57°20N 7°15W **11** D1
Uibhist a Tuath = North Uist
 U.K. 57°40N 7°15W **11** D1
Uig *U.K.* 57°35N 6°21W **11** D2
Uíge *Angola* 7°30S 14°40E **52** F2
Uiha *Tonga* 19°54S 174°25W **59** c
Uijeongbu *S. Korea* 37°44N 127°2E **35** F14
Úijũ *N. Korea* 40°15N 124°35E **35** D13
Uinta Mts. *U.S.A.* 40°45N 110°30W **76** F8
Uis *Namibia* 21°8S 14°49E **56** C1
Uiseong *S. Korea* 36°21N 128°45E **35** F15
Uitenhage *S. Africa* 33°40S 25°28E **56** E4
Uithuizen *Neths.* 53°24N 6°41E **15** A6
Ujh → *India* 32°10N 75°18E **42** C6
Ujhani *India* 28°0N 79°6E **43** F8
Uji-guntō *Japan* 31°15N 129°25E **31** J4
Ujjain *India* 23°9N 75°43E **42** H6
Ujung Pandang *Indonesia* 5°10S 119°20E **37** F5
Uka *Russia* 57°50N 162°0E **29** D17
Ukara I. *Tanzania* 1°50S 33°0E **54** C3
Uke-Shima *Japan* 28°2N 129°14E **31** K4
Ukerewe I. *Tanzania* 2°0S 33°0E **54** C3
Ukhrul *India* 25°10N 94°25E **41** G19
Ukhta *Russia* 63°34N 53°41E **18** B9
Ukiah *U.S.A.* 39°9N 123°13W **78** F3
Ukmergė *Lithuania* 55°15N 24°45E **9** J21
Ukraine ■ *Europe* 49°0N 32°0E **19** E5
Ukwi *Botswana* 23°29S 20°30E **56** C3
Ulaan-Uul *Mongolia* 44°13N 111°10E **34** B6
Ulaanbaatar *Mongolia* 47°55N 106°53E **32** B5
Ulaangom *Mongolia* 50°5N 92°10E **32** A4
Ulaanjirem *Mongolia* 45°5N 105°30E **34** B3
Ulamba
 Dem. Rep. of the Congo 9°3S 23°38E **55** D1
Ulan Bator = Ulaanbaatar
 Mongolia 47°55N 106°53E **32** B5
Ulan Ude *Russia* 51°45N 107°40E **29** D11
Ulaya *Morogoro, Tanzania* 7°3S 36°55E **54** D4
Ulaya *Tabora, Tanzania* 4°25S 33°30E **54** C3
Ulcinj *Montenegro* 41°58N 19°10E **23** D8
Ulco *S. Africa* 28°21S 24°15E **56** D3
Ule älv = Oulujoki →
 Finland 65°1N 25°30E **8** D21
Ule träsk = Oulujärvi
 Finland 64°25N 27°15E **8** D22
Uleåborg = Oulu *Finland* 65°1N 25°29E **8** D21
Ulefoss *Norway* 59°17N 9°16E **9** G13
Ulhasnagar *India* 19°15N 73°10E **40** K8
Uliastay *Mongolia* 47°56N 97°28E **32** B4
Uljin *S. Korea* 36°59N 129°24E **35** F15
Ulladulla *Australia* 35°21S 150°29E **63** F5
Ullapool *U.K.* 57°54N 5°9W **11** D3
Ulleungdo *S. Korea* 37°30N 130°30E **31** F5
Ullswater *Canada* 45°12N 79°29W **82** A5
Ullswater *U.K.* 54°34N 2°52W **12** C5
Ulm *Germany* 48°23N 9°58E **16** D5
Ulmarra *Australia* 29°37S 153°4E **63** D5
Ulonguè *Mozam.* 14°37S 34°19E **55** E3
Ulricehamn *Sweden* 57°46N 13°26E **9** H15
Ulsan *S. Korea* 35°20N 129°15E **35** G15
Ulsta *U.K.* 60°30N 1°9W **11** A7
Ulster □ *U.K.* 54°35N 6°30W **10** B5
Ulubat Gölü *Turkey* 40°9N 28°35E **23** D13
Uludağ *Turkey* 40°4N 29°13E **23** D13
Uluguru Mts. *Tanzania* 7°15S 37°40E **54** D4
Ulungur He → *China* 47°1N 87°24E **32** B3
Ulungur Hu *China* 47°20N 87°10E **32** B3
Uluru *Australia* 25°23S 131°5E **61** E5
Uluru-Kata Tjuta △
 Australia 25°19S 131°1E **61** E5
Ulutau *Kazakhstan* 48°39N 67°1E **28** E7
Uluwatu *Indonesia* 8°50S 115°5E **37** K18
Ulva *U.K.* 56°29N 6°13W **11** E2
Ulverston *U.K.* 54°13N 3°5W **12** C4
Ulverstone *Australia* 41°11S 146°11E **63** G4
Ulya *Russia* 59°10N 142°0E **29** D15
Ulyanovsk *Russia* 54°20N 48°25E **18** D8
Ulyasutay = Uliastay
 Mongolia 47°56N 97°28E **32** B4
Ulysses *Kans., U.S.A.* 37°35N 101°22W **80** G3
Ulysses *Pa., U.S.A.* 41°54N 77°46W **82** E7
Ulysses, Mt. *Canada* 57°20N 124°5W **70** B4
Umala *Bolivia* 17°25S 68°5W **92** G5
'Umān = Oman ■ *Asia* 23°0N 58°0E **47** C6
Uman *Ukraine* 48°40N 30°12E **17** D16
Umaria *India* 23°35N 80°50E **43** H9
Umarkot *Pakistan* 25°15N 69°40E **42** G3
Umarpada *India* 21°27N 73°30E **42** J5
Umatilla *U.S.A.* 45°55N 119°21W **76** D4
Umba *Russia* 66°42N 34°11E **18** A5
Umbagog L. *U.S.A.* 44°46N 71°3W **83** B13
Umbakumba *Australia* 13°47S 136°50E **62** A2
Umbrella Mts. *N.Z.* 45°35S 169°5E **59** F2

Umeå *Sweden* 63°45N 20°20E **8** E19
Umeälven → *Sweden* 63°45N 20°20E **8** E19
Umera *Indonesia* 0°12S 129°37E **37** E7
Umfuli → *Zimbabwe* 17°30S 29°23E **55** F2
Umgusa *Zimbabwe* 19°29S 27°52E **55** F2
Umgwenya → *Mozam.* 25°14S 32°18E **57** D5
Umiujaq *Canada* 56°33N 76°33W **72** A4
Umkomaas *S. Africa* 30°13S 30°48E **57** E5
Umlazi *S. Africa* 29°59S 30°54E **53** L6
Umm ad Daraj, J. *Jordan* 32°18N 35°48E **46** C4
Umm al Qaywayn
 U.A.E. 25°30N 55°35E **45** E7
Umm al Qittayn *Jordan* 32°18N 36°40E **46** C5
Umm Bâb *Qatar* 25°12N 50°48E **45** E6
Umm Durman = Omdurmân
 Sudan 15°40N 32°28E **51** E12
Umm el Fahm *Israel* 32°31N 35°9E **46** C4
Umm Keddada *Sudan* 13°33N 26°35E **51** F11
Umm Lajj *Si. Arabia* 25°0N 37°23E **44** E3
Umm Qasr *Iraq* 30°1N 47°58E **44** D5
Umm Ruwaba *Sudan* 12°50N 31°20E **51** F12
Umnak I. *U.S.A.* 53°15N 168°20W **74** a
Umniati → *Zimbabwe* 16°49S 28°45E **55** F2
Umpqua → *U.S.A.* 43°40N 124°12W **76** E1
Umreth *India* 22°41N 73°4E **42** H5
Umtata = Mthatha
 S. Africa 31°36S 28°49E **57** E4
Umuarama *Brazil* 23°45S 53°20W **95** A5
Umvukwe Ra. *Zimbabwe* 16°45S 30°45E **55** F3
Umzimvubu *S. Africa* 31°38S 29°33E **57** E4
Umzingwane →
 Zimbabwe 22°12S 29°56E **55** G2
Umzinto = eMuziwezinto
 S. Africa 30°15S 30°45E **57** E5
Una *India* 20°46N 71°8E **42** J4
Una → *Bos.-H.* 45°0N 16°20E **16** F9
Unadilla *U.S.A.* 42°20N 75°19W **83** D9
Unalakleet *U.S.A.* 63°52N 160°47W **74** a
Unalaska *U.S.A.* 53°53N 166°32W **74** a
Unalaska I. *U.S.A.* 53°35N 166°50W **74** a
'Unayzah, Si. Arabia 26°6N 43°58E **44** E4
'Unayzah, J. *Asia* 32°12N 39°18E **44** C3
Uncía *Bolivia* 18°25S 66°40W **92** G5
Uncompahgre Peak
 U.S.A. 38°4N 107°28W **76** G10
Uncompahgre Plateau
 U.S.A. 38°20N 108°15W **76** G9
Undara Volcanic △
 Australia 18°14S 144°41E **62** B3
Underbool *Australia* 35°10S 141°51E **63** F3
Underwood *Canada* 44°18N 81°29W **82** B3
Ungarie *Australia* 33°38S 146°56E **63** E4
Ungarra *Australia* 34°12S 136°2E **63** E2
Ungava, Pén. d' *Canada* 60°0N 74°0W **69** D12
Ungava B. *Canada* 59°30N 67°30W **69** D13
Ungeny = Ungheni
 Moldova 47°11N 27°51E **17** E14
Unggi *N. Korea* 42°16N 130°28E **35** C16
Ungheni *Moldova* 47°11N 27°51E **17** E14
Ungwana B. *Kenya* 2°45S 40°20E **54** C5
União da Vitória *Brazil* 26°13S 51°5W **95** B5
Unimak I. *U.S.A.* 54°45N 164°0W **74** a
Union *Miss., U.S.A.* 32°34N 89°7W **85** E10
Union *Mo., U.S.A.* 38°27N 91°0W **80** F8
Union *S.C., U.S.A.* 34°43N 81°37W **85** D14
Union City *Calif., U.S.A.* 37°36N 122°1W **78** H4
Union City *N.J., U.S.A.* 40°45N 74°2W **83** F10
Union City *Pa., U.S.A.* 41°54N 79°51W **82** E5
Union City *Tenn., U.S.A.* 36°26N 89°3W **85** C10
Union Dale *U.S.A.* 41°43N 75°29W **83** E9
Union Gap *U.S.A.* 46°33N 120°28W **76** C3
Union Springs *Ala.,*
 U.S.A. 32°9N 85°43W **85** E12
Union Springs *N.Y.,*
 U.S.A. 42°50N 76°41W **83** D8
Uniondale *S. Africa* 33°39S 23°7E **56** E3
Uniontown *U.S.A.* 39°54N 79°44W **81** F14
Unionville *U.S.A.* 40°29N 93°1W **80** E7
United Arab Emirates ■
 Asia 23°50N 54°0E **45** F7
United Kingdom ■ *Europe* 53°0N 2°0W **14** E6
United States of America ■
 N. Amer. 37°0N 96°0W **74** C7
Unity *Canada* 52°30N 109°5W **71** C7
University Park
 U.S.A. 32°17N 106°45W **77** K10
University Place *U.S.A.* 47°14N 122°33W **78** C4
Unjha *India* 23°46N 72°24E **42** H5
Unnao *India* 26°35N 80°30E **43** F9
Unsengedsi → *Zimbabwe* 15°43S 31°14E **55** F3
Unst *U.K.* 60°44N 0°53W **11** A8
Unuk → *Canada* 56°5N 131°3W **70** B2
Unzen-Amakusa △
 Japan 32°15N 130°10E **31** H5
Uozu *Japan* 36°48N 137°24E **31** F8
Upata *Venezuela* 8°1N 62°24W **92** B6
Upemba, L.
 Dem. Rep. of the Congo 8°30S 26°20E **55** D2
Upemba △
 Dem. Rep. of the Congo 9°0S 26°35E **55** D2
Upernavik *Greenland* 72°49N 56°20W **4** B5
Upington *S. Africa* 28°25S 21°15E **56** D3
Upleta *India* 21°46N 70°16E **42** J4
'Upolu *Samoa* 13°58S 172°0W **59** b
Upper Alkali L. *U.S.A.* 41°47N 120°8W **76** F3
Upper Arrow L. *Canada* 50°30N 117°50W **70** C5
Upper Darby *U.S.A.* 39°55N 75°16W **81** F16
Upper Foster L. *Canada* 56°47N 105°20W **71** B7
Upper Hutt *N.Z.* 41°8S 175°5E **59** D5
Upper Klamath L.
 U.S.A. 42°25N 121°55W **76** E3
Upper Lake *U.S.A.* 39°10N 122°54W **78** F4
Upper Liard *Canada* 60°3N 128°54W **70** A3
Upper Manzanilla
 Trin. & Tob. 10°31N 61°4W **93** K15
Upper Missouri Breaks △
 U.S.A. 47°50N 109°55W **76** C9

Upper Musquodoboit
  Canada   45°10N 62°58W **73** C7
Upper Red L. *U.S.A.*   48°8N 94°45W **80** A6
Upper Sandusky
  U.S.A.   40°50N 83°17W **81** E12
Upper Volta = Burkina Faso ■
  Africa   12°0N 1°0W **50** F5
Uppland *Sweden*   59°59N 17°48E **9** G17
Uppsala *Sweden*   59°53N 17°38E **9** G17
Upshi *India*   33°48N 77°52E **43** C7
Upstart, C. *Australia*   19°41S 147°45E **62** B4
Upton *U.S.A.*   44°6N 104°38W **76** D11
Uqsuqtuuq = Gjoa Haven
  Canada   68°38N 95°53W **68** C10
Ur *Iraq*   30°55N 46°25E **44** D5
Urad Qianqi *China*   40°40N 108°30E **34** D5
Urakawa *Japan*   42°9N 142°47E **30** C11
Ural = Uralskiy □ *Russia* 64°0N 70°0E **28** C7
Ural = Zhayyq ⇢
  Kazakhstan   47°0N 51°48E **19** E9
Ural *Australia*   33°21S 146°12E **63** E4
Ural Mts. = Uralskie Gory
  Eurasia   60°0N 59°0E **18** C10
Uralla *Australia*   30°37S 151°29E **63** E5
Uralsk = Oral *Kazakhstan* 51°20N 51°20E **19** D9
Uralskie Gory *Eurasia*   60°0N 59°0E **18** C10
Uralskiy □ *Russia*   64°0N 70°0E **28** C7
Urambo *Tanzania*   5°4S 32°0E **54** D3
Urandangi *Australia*   21°32S 138°14E **62** C2
Uranium City *Canada*   59°34N 108°37W **71** B7
Urapuntja = Utopia
  Australia   22°14S 134°33E **62** C1
Uraricoera ⇢ *Brazil*   3°2N 60°30W **92** C6
Urasoe *Japan*   26°15N 127°43E **31** L3
Urawa = Saitama *Japan*   35°54N 139°38E **31** G9
Uray *Russia*   60°5N 65°15E **28** C7
'Uray'irah *Si. Arabia*   25°57N 48°53E **45** E6
Urbana *Ill., U.S.A.*   40°7N 88°12W **80** E1
Urbana *Ohio, U.S.A.*   40°7N 83°45W **81** E12
Urbandale *U.S.A.*   41°38N 93°43W **80** E7
Urbino *Italy*   43°43N 12°38E **22** C5
Urbión, Picos de *Spain* 42°1N 2°52W **21** A4
Urcos *Peru*   13°40S 71°38W **92** F4
Urdinarrain *Argentina*   32°37S 58°52W **94** C4
Ure ⇢ *U.K.*   54°5N 1°20W **12** C6
Urengoy *Russia*   65°58N 78°22E **28** C8
Ures *Mexico*   29°26N 110°24W **86** B2
Urewera △ *N.Z.*   38°29S 177°7E **59** C6
Urfa = Sanliurfa *Turkey* 37°12N 38°50E **44** B3
Urganch = Urgench
  Uzbekistan   41°40N 60°41E **28** E7
Ürgüp *Turkey*   38°38N 34°56E **44** B2
Uri *India*   34°8N 74°2E **43** B6
Uribia *Colombia*   11°43N 72°16W **92** A4
Uriondo *Bolivia*   21°41S 64°41W **94** A3
Urique *Mexico*   27°13N 107°55W **86** B3
Urique ⇢ *Mexico*   26°29N 107°58W **86** B3
Urk *Neths.*   52°39N 5°36E **15** B5
Urla *Turkey*   38°20N 26°47E **23** E12
Urmia = Orūmīyeh *Iran*   37°40N 45°0E **44** B5
Uroševac *Serbia*   42°23N 21°10E **23** C9
Uroyan, Montanas de
  Puerto Rico   18°12N 67°0W **89** d
Uruaçu *Brazil*   14°30S 49°10W **93** F9
Uruapan *Mexico*   19°24N 102°3W **86** D4
Urubamba ⇢ *Peru*   10°43S 73°48W **92** F4
Urucará *Brazil*   2°32S 57°45W **92** D7
Uruçuí *Brazil*   7°20S 44°28W **93** E10
Uruguai ⇢ *Brazil*   26°0S 53°30W **95** B5
Uruguaiana *Brazil*   29°50S 57°0W **94** B4
Uruguay ■ *S. Amer.*   32°30S 56°30W **94** C4
Uruguay ⇢ *S. Amer.*   34°12S 58°18W **94** C4
Urumchi = Ürümqi
  China   43°45N 87°45E **32** B3
Ürümqi *China*   43°45N 87°45E **32** B3
Urup, Ostrov *Russia*   46°0N 151°0E **29** E16
Ürzhar *Kazakhstan*   47°5N 81°38E **28** E9
Usa ⇢ *Russia*   66°16N 59°49E **18** A10
Uşak *Turkey*   38°43N 29°28E **19** G4
Usakos *Namibia*   21°54S 15°31E **56** C2
Usedom *Germany*   53°55N 14°2E **16** B8
Useless Loop *Australia* 26°8S 113°23E **61** E1
Ushakova, Ostrov *Russia* 82°0N 80°0E **29** A8
Ushant = Ouessant, Î. d'
  France   48°28N 5°6W **20** B1
Ushashi *Tanzania*   1°59S 33°57E **54** C3
'Ushayrah *Si. Arabia*   25°35N 45°47E **44** E5
Ushibuka *Japan*   32°11N 130°1E **31** H5
Üshtöbe *Kazakhstan*   45°16N 78°0E **28** E8
Ushuaia *Argentina*   54°50S 68°23W **96** G3
Ushumun *Russia*   52°47N 126°32E **29** D13
Usinsk *Russia*   65°57N 57°27E **28** C6
Usk *Canada*   54°38N 128°26W **70** C3
Usk ⇢ *U.K.*   51°33N 2°58W **13** F5
Uska *India*   27°12N 83°7E **43** F10
Usman *Russia*   52°5N 39°48E **18** D6
Usoke *Tanzania*   5°8S 32°24E **54** D3
Usolye-Sibirskoye
  Russia   52°48N 103°40E **29** D11
Uspallata, P. de
  Argentina   32°37S 69°22W **94** C2
Ussuriysk *Russia*   43°48N 131°59E **30** C5
Ussurka *Russia*   45°12N 133°31E **30** B6
Ust-Chaun *Russia*   68°47N 170°30E **29** C18
Ust-Ilimsk *Russia*   58°3N 102°39E **29** D11
Ust-Ishim *Russia*   57°45N 71°10E **28** D8
Ust-Kamchatsk *Russia* 56°10N 162°28E **29** D17
Ust-Kamenogorsk = Öskemen
  Kazakhstan   50°0N 82°36E **28** E9
Ust-Khayryuzovo
  Russia   57°15N 156°45E **29** D16
Ust-Kut *Russia*   56°50N 105°42E **29** D11
Ust-Kuyga *Russia*   70°1N 135°43E **29** B14
Ust-Maya *Russia*   60°30N 134°28E **29** C14
Ust-Mil *Russia*   59°40N 133°11E **29** D14
Ust-Nera *Russia*   64°35N 143°15E **29** C15

Ust-Nyukzha *Russia*   56°34N 121°37E **29** D13
Ust-Olenek *Russia*   73°0N 120°5E **29** B12
Ust-Omchug *Russia*   61°9N 149°38E **29** C15
Ust-Port *Russia*   69°40N 84°26E **28** C9
Ust-Tsilma *Russia*   65°28N 52°11E **18** A9
Ust-Urt = Ustyurt Plateau
  Asia   44°0N 55°0E **28** E6
Ust-Usa *Russia*   66°2N 56°57E **18** A10
Ust-Vorkuta *Russia*   67°24N 64°0E **18** A11
Ústí nad Labem *Czech Rep.* 50°41N 14°3E **16** C8
Ústica *Italy*   38°42N 13°11E **22** E5
Ustinov = Izhevsk
  Russia   56°51N 53°14E **18** C9
Ustyurt Plateau *Asia*   44°0N 55°0E **28** E6
Usu *China*   44°27N 84°40E **32** B3
Usuki *Japan*   33°8N 131°49E **31** H5
Usulután *El Salv.*   13°25N 88°28W **88** D2
Usumacinta ⇢ *Mexico*   18°24N 92°38W **87** D6
Usumbura = Bujumbura
  Burundi   3°16S 29°18E **54** C2
Usure *Tanzania*   4°40S 34°22E **54** C3
Usutuo ⇢ *Mozam.*   26°48S 32°7E **57** D5
Uta *Indonesia*   4°33S 136°0E **37** E9
Utah □ *U.S.A.*   39°20N 111°30W **76** G8
Utah L. *U.S.A.*   40°12N 111°48W **76** F8
Utara, Selat *Malaysia*   5°28N 100°20E **39** c
Utarni *India*   26°5N 71°58E **42** F4
Utatlan *Guatemala*   15°2N 91°11W **88** C1
Ute Creek ⇢ *U.S.A.*   35°21N 103°50W **77** J12
Utena *Lithuania*   55°27N 25°40E **9** J21
Utete *Tanzania*   8°0S 38°45E **54** D4
Uthai Thani *Thailand*   15°22N 100°3E **38** E3
Uthal *Pakistan*   25°44N 66°40E **42** G2
Utiariti *Brazil*   13°0S 58°10W **92** F7
Utica *N.Y., U.S.A.*   43°6N 75°14W **83** C9
Utica *Ohio, U.S.A.*   40°14N 82°27W **82** F2
Utikuma L. *Canada*   55°50N 115°30W **70** B5
Utila *Honduras*   16°6N 86°56W **88** C2
Utopia *Australia*   22°14S 134°33E **62** C1
Utraula *India*   27°19N 82°25E **43** F10
Utrecht *Neths.*   52°5N 5°8E **15** B5
Utrecht □ *Neths.*   52°6N 5°7E **15** B5
Utrera *Spain*   37°12N 5°48W **21** D3
Utsjoki ⇢ *Finland*   69°51N 26°59E **8** B22
Utsunomiya *Japan*   36°30N 139°50E **31** F9
Uttar Pradesh □ *India*   27°0N 80°0E **43** F9
Uttaradit *Thailand*   17°36N 100°5E **38** D3
Uttarakhand □ *India*   30°0N 79°30E **43** D8
Utterson *Canada*   45°12N 79°19W **82** A5
Uttoxeter *U.K.*   52°54N 1°52W **12** E6
Utuado *Puerto Rico*   18°16N 66°42W **89** d
Uummannaq *Avannaarsua,
  Greenland*   77°28N 69°13W **4** B4
Uummannaq *Kitaa,
  Greenland*   70°58N 52°17W **4** B5
Uummannarsuaq = Nunap Isua
  Greenland   59°48N 43°55W **66** D15
Uusikaarlepyy *Finland*   63°32N 22°31E **8** E20
Uusikaupunki *Finland*   60°47N 21°25E **8** F19
Uva *Russia*   56°59N 52°13E **18** C9
Uvalde *U.S.A.*   29°13N 99°47W **84** G5
Uvat *Russia*   59°5N 68°50E **28** D7
Uvinza *Tanzania*   5°5S 30°24E **54** D3
Uvira *Dem. Rep. of the Congo* 3°22S 29°3E **54** C2
Uvs Nuur *Mongolia*   50°20N 92°30E **32** A4
'Uwairidh, Ḥarrat al
  Si. Arabia   26°50N 38°0E **44** E3
Uwajima *Japan*   33°10N 132°35E **31** H6
Uwanda △ *Tanzania*   7°46S 32°0E **54** D3
Uweinat, Jebel *Sudan*   21°54N 24°58E **51** D10
Uxbridge *Canada*   44°6N 79°7W **82** B5
Uxin Qi *China*   38°50N 109°5E **34** E5
Uxmal *Mexico*   20°22N 89°46W **87** C7
Uydzin *Mongolia*   44°9N 107°0E **34** B4
Uyo *Nigeria*   5°1N 7°53E **50** G7
Uyûn Mûsa *Egypt*   29°53N 32°40E **46** F1
Uyuni *Bolivia*   20°28S 66°47W **92** H5
Uzbekistan ■ *Asia*   41°30N 65°0E **28** E7
Uzboy ⇢ *Turkmenistan*   39°30N 55°0E **45** B7
Uzen, Bolshoi = Uzen, Mal ⇢
  Kazakhstan   49°4N 49°44E **19** E8
Uzen, Mal ⇢ *Kazakhstan* 49°4N 49°44E **19** E8
Uzerche *France*   45°25N 1°34E **20** D4
Uzh ⇢ *Ukraine*   51°15N 30°12E **17** C16
Uzhgorod = Uzhhorod
  Ukraine   48°36N 22°18E **17** D12
Uzhhorod *Ukraine*   48°36N 22°18E **17** D12
Užice *Serbia*   43°55N 19°50E **23** C8
Uzunköprü *Turkey*   41°16N 26°43E **23** D12

V

Vaal ⇢ *S. Africa*   29°4S 23°38E **56** D3
Vaal Dam *S. Africa*   27°0S 28°14E **57** D4
Vaalbos △ *S. Africa*   28°22S 24°20E **56** D3
Vaalwater *S. Africa*   24°15S 28°8E **57** C4
Vaasa *Finland*   63°6N 21°38E **8** E19
Vác *Hungary*   47°49N 19°10E **17** E10
Vacaria *Brazil*   28°31S 50°52W **95** B5
Vacata *Fiji*   17°15S 179°31W **59** a
Vacaville *U.S.A.*   38°21N 121°59W **78** G5
Vach = Vakh ⇢ *Russia*   60°45N 76°45E **28** C8
Vache, Î. à *Haiti*   18°2N 73°35W **89** C5
Vacoas *Mauritius*   20°18S 57°29E **53** d
Vadnagar *India*   23°47N 72°40E **42** H5
Vadodara *India*   22°20N 73°10E **42** H5
Vadsø *Norway*   70°3N 29°50E **8** A23
Vaduz *Liech.*   47°8N 9°31E **20** C8
Værøy *Norway*   67°40N 12°40E **8** C15
Vágar *Færoe Is.*   62°5N 7°15W **8** E9
Vagia, Akra *Greece*   36°15N 28°11E **25** C10
Vågsfjorden *Norway*   68°50N 16°50E **8** B17
Váh ⇢ *Slovak Rep.*   47°43N 18°7E **17** D9

Váhtjer = Gällivare
  Sweden   67°9N 20°40E **8** C19
Vaï *Greece*   35°15N 26°18E **25** D8
Vaihiria, L. *Tahiti*   17°40S 149°25W **59** d
Vail *U.S.A.*   39°40N 106°20W **74** C5
Vairao *Tahiti*   17°47S 149°17W **59** d
Vaisali ⇢ *India*   26°28N 78°53E **43** F8
Vaitogi *Amer. Samoa*   14°24S 170°44W **59** b
Vakh ⇢ *Russia*   60°45N 76°45E **28** C8
Val-d'Or *Canada*   48°7N 77°47W **72** C4
Val Marie *Canada*   49°15N 107°45W **71** D7
Valaam *Russia*   61°22N 30°57E **8** F24
Valahia *Romania*   44°35N 25°0E **17** F13
Valatie *U.S.A.*   42°24N 73°40W **83** D11
Valcheta *Argentina*   40°40S 66°8W **96** E3
Valdai Hills = Valdayskaya
  Vozvyshennost *Russia* 57°0N 33°30E **18** C5
Valdepeñas *Spain*   38°43N 3°25W **21** C4
Valdés, Pen. *Argentina* 42°30S 63°45W **96** E4
Valdez *U.S.A.*   61°7N 146°16W **68** C5
Valdivia *Chile*   39°50S 73°14W **96** D2
Valdivia Abyssal Plain
  S. Ocean   62°30S 70°0E **5** C6
Valdosta *U.S.A.*   30°50N 83°17W **85** F13
Valdres *Norway*   61°5N 9°5E **8** F13
Vale of Glamorgan □
  U.K.   51°28N 3°25W **13** F4
Valemount *Canada*   52°50N 119°15W **70** C5
Valença *Brazil*   13°20S 39°5W **93** F11
Valença do Piauí *Brazil* 6°20S 41°45W **93** E10
Valence *France*   44°57N 4°54E **20** D6
Valencia *Spain*   39°27N 0°23W **21** C5
Valencia *Trin. & Tob.*   10°39N 61°11W **93** K15
Valencia *Venezuela*   10°11N 68°0W **92** A5
Valencia □ *Spain*   39°20N 0°40E **21** C5
Valencia, G. de *Spain*   39°30N 0°20E **21** C6
Valencia de Alcántara
  Spain   39°25N 7°14W **21** C2
Valencia I. *Ireland*   51°54N 10°22W **10** E1
Valenciennes *France*   50°20N 3°34E **20** A5
Valentim, Sa. do *Brazil* 6°0S 43°30W **93** E10
Valentin *Russia*   43°8N 134°17E **30** C7
Valentine *Nebr., U.S.A.* 42°52N 100°33W **80** D3
Valentine *Tex., U.S.A.* 30°35N 104°30W **84** F2
Valera *Venezuela*   9°19N 70°37W **92** B4
Valga *Estonia*   57°47N 26°2E **9** H22
Valier *U.S.A.*   48°18N 112°16W **76** B7
Valjevo *Serbia*   44°18N 19°53E **23** B8
Valka *Latvia*   57°46N 26°3E **9** H22
Valkeakoski *Finland*   61°16N 24°2E **8** F21
Valkenswaard *Neths.*   51°21N 5°29E **15** C5
Vall de Uxó = La Vall d'Uixó
  Spain   39°49N 0°15W **21** C5
Valladolid *Mexico*   20°41N 88°12W **87** C7
Valladolid *Spain*   41°38N 4°43W **21** B3
Valldemossa *Spain*   39°43N 2°37E **24** B9
Valle de la Pascua
  Venezuela   9°13N 66°0W **92** B5
Valle de las Palmas
  Mexico   32°20N 116°43W **79** N10
Valle de Santiago
  Mexico   20°23N 101°12W **86** C4
Valle de Zaragoza
  Mexico   27°25N 105°50W **86** B3
Valle Fértil, Sierra del
  Argentina   30°20S 68°0W **94** C2
Valle Gran Rey *Canary Is.* 28°5N 17°20W **24** F2
Valle Hermoso *Mexico*   25°35N 97°40W **87** B5
Valle Nacional *Mexico*   17°47N 96°18W **87** D5
Valledupar *Colombia*   10°29N 73°15W **92** A4
Vallehermoso *Canary Is.* 28°10N 17°15W **24** F2
Vallejo *U.S.A.*   38°7N 122°14W **78** G4
Vallenar *Chile*   28°30S 70°50W **94** B1
Valletta *Malta*   35°54N 14°31E **25** D2
Valley Center *U.S.A.*   33°13N 117°2W **79** M9
Valley City *U.S.A.*   46°55N 98°0W **80** B5
Valley Falls *Oreg.,
  U.S.A.*   42°29N 120°17W **76** E3
Valley Falls *R.I., U.S.A.* 41°54N 71°24W **83** E13
Valley of Flowers △
  India   30°50N 79°40E **43** D8
Valley Springs *U.S.A.*   38°12N 120°50W **78** G6
Valley View *U.S.A.*   40°39N 76°33W **83** F8
Valley Wells *U.S.A.*   35°27N 115°46W **79** K11
Valleyview *Canada*   55°5N 117°17W **70** B5
Vallimanca, Arroyo
  Argentina   35°40S 59°10W **94** D4
Valls *Spain*   41°18N 1°15E **21** B6
Valmiera *Latvia*   57°37N 25°29E **9** H21
Valognes *France*   49°30N 1°28W **20** B3
Valona = Vlorë *Albania* 40°32N 19°28E **23** D8
Valozhyn *Belarus*   54°3N 26°30E **17** A14
Valparaíso *Chile*   33°2S 71°40W **94** C1
Valparaíso *Mexico*   22°46N 103°34W **86** C4
Valparaíso *U.S.A.*   41°28N 87°4W **80** E2
Valparaíso □ *Chile*   33°2S 71°40W **94** C1
Vals ⇢ *S. Africa*   27°23S 26°30E **56** D4
Vals, Tanjung *Indonesia* 8°26S 137°25E **37** F9
Valsad *India*   20°40N 72°58E **40** J8
Valverde *Canary Is.*   27°48N 17°55W **24** G2
Valverde del Camino
  Spain   37°35N 6°47W **21** D2
Vammala *Finland*   61°20N 22°54E **8** F20
Vamos *Greece*   35°24N 24°13E **25** D6
Van *Turkey*   38°30N 43°20E **44** B4
Van, L. = Van Gölü
  Turkey   38°30N 43°0E **44** B4
Van Alstyne *U.S.A.*   33°25N 96°35W **84** E6
Van Blommestein Meer
  Surinam   4°45N 55°5W **93** C7
Van Buren *Canada*   47°10N 67°55W **73** C6
Van Buren *Ark., U.S.A.* 35°26N 94°21W **84** D7

Van Buren *Maine,
  U.S.A.*   47°10N 67°58W **81** B20
Van Buren *Mo., U.S.A.*   37°0N 91°1W **80** G8
Van Canh *Vietnam*   13°37N 109°0E **38** F7
Van Diemen, C. *N. Terr.,
  Australia*   11°9S 130°24E **60** B5
Van Diemen, C. *Queens.,
  Australia*   16°30S 139°46E **62** B2
Van Diemen G. *Australia* 11°45S 132°0E **60** B5
Van Gölü *Turkey*   38°30N 43°0E **44** B4
Van Horn *U.S.A.*   31°3N 104°50W **84** F2
Van Ninh *Vietnam*   12°42N 109°14E **38** F7
Van Rees, Pegunungan
  Indonesia   2°35S 138°15E **37** E9
Van Wert *U.S.A.*   40°52N 84°35W **81** E11
Van Yen *Vietnam*   21°4N 104°42E **38** B5
Vanadzor *Armenia*   40°48N 44°30E **19** F7
Vanavara *Russia*   60°22N 102°16E **29** C11
Vancouver *Canada*   49°15N 123°7W **78** A3
Vancouver *U.S.A.*   45°38N 122°40W **78** E4
Vancouver, C. *Australia* 35°2S 118°11E **61** G2
Vancouver I. *Canada*   49°50N 126°0W **78** B2
Vancouver Int. ✈ (YVR)
  Canada   49°10N 123°10W **78** A3
Vanda = Vantaa *Finland* 60°18N 24°56E **9** F21
Vandalia *Ill., U.S.A.*   38°58N 89°6W **80** F9
Vandalia *Mo., U.S.A.*   39°19N 91°29W **80** F8
Vandenberg Village
  U.S.A.   34°43N 120°28W **79** L6
Vanderbijlpark *S. Africa* 26°42S 27°54E **57** D4
Vandergrift *U.S.A.*   40°36N 79°34W **82** F5
Vanderhoof *Canada*   54°0N 124°0W **70** C4
Vanderkloof Dam
  S. Africa   30°4S 24°40E **56** E3
Vanderlin I. *Australia* 15°44S 137°2E **62** B2
Vänern *Sweden*   58°47N 13°30E **9** G15
Vänersborg *Sweden*   58°26N 12°19E **9** G15
Vang Vieng *Laos*   18°58N 102°32E **38** C4
Vanga *Kenya*   4°35S 39°12E **54** C4
Vangaindrano *Madag.*   23°21S 47°36E **57** C8
Vanguard *Canada*   49°55N 107°20W **71** D7
Vanino *Russia*   48°50N 140°5E **29** E15
Vankleek Hill *Canada*   45°32N 74°40W **83** A10
Vännäs *Sweden*   63°58N 19°48E **8** E18
Vannes *France*   47°40N 2°47W **20** C2
Vannøya *Norway*   70°6N 19°50E **8** A18
Vanrhynsdorp *S. Africa* 31°36S 18°44E **56** E2
Vansbro *Sweden*   60°32N 14°15E **9** F16
Vansittart B. *Australia* 14°3S 126°17E **60** B4
Vantaa *Finland*   60°18N 24°56E **9** F21
Vanua Balavu *Fiji*   17°12S 178°59W **59** a
Vanua Levu *Fiji*   16°33S 179°15E **59** a
Vanua Vatu *Fiji*   18°22S 179°15W **59** a
Vanuatu ■ *Pac. Oc.*   15°0S 168°0E **58** C9
Vanwyksvlei *S. Africa*   30°18S 21°49E **56** E3
Vanzylsrus *S. Africa*   26°52S 22°4E **56** D3
Vapnyarka *Ukraine*   48°32N 28°45E **17** D15
Var ⇢ *France*   43°39N 7°12E **20** E7
Varámín *Iran*   35°20N 51°39E **45** C6
Varanasi *India*   25°22N 83°0E **43** G10
Varangerfjorden *Norway* 70°3N 29°25E **8** A23
Varangerhalvøya
  Norway   70°25N 29°30E **8** A23
Varaždin *Croatia*   46°20N 16°20E **16** E9
Varberg *Sweden*   57°6N 12°20E **9** H15
Vardak □ *Afghan.*   34°0N 68°0E **40** B6
Vardar = Axios ⇢
  Greece   40°57N 22°35E **23** D10
Varde *Denmark*   55°38N 8°29E **9** J13
Vardø *Norway*   70°23N 31°5E **8** A24
Varella, Mui *Vietnam*   12°54N 109°26E **38** F7
Varéna *Lithuania*   54°12N 24°30E **9** J21
Varese *Italy*   45°48N 8°50E **20** D8
Varginha *Brazil*   21°33S 45°25W **95** A6
Varkaus *Finland*   62°19N 27°50E **8** E22
Varna *Bulgaria*   43°13N 27°56E **23** C12
Värnamo *Sweden*   57°10N 14°3E **9** H16
Vars *Canada*   45°21N 75°21W **83** A9
Varysburg *U.S.A.*   42°46N 78°19W **82** D6
Varzaneh *Iran*   32°25N 52°40E **45** C7
Vasa = Vaasa *Finland*   63°6N 21°38E **8** E19
Vasa Barris ⇢ *Brazil*   11°10S 37°10W **93** F11
Vascongadas = País Vasco
  Spain   42°50N 2°45W **21** A4
Vasht = Khāsh *Iran*   28°15N 61°15E **45** D9
Vasilevichi *Belarus*   52°15N 29°50E **17** B15
Vasilkov = Vasylkiv
  Ukraine   50°7N 30°15E **17** C16
Vaslui *Romania*   46°38N 27°42E **17** E14
Vassar *Canada*   49°10N 95°55W **71** D9
Vassar *U.S.A.*   43°22N 83°35W **81** D12
Västerås *Sweden*   59°37N 16°38E **9** G17
Västerbotten *Sweden*   64°36N 20°4E **8** D18
Västerdalälven ⇢ *Sweden* 60°30N 14°7E **8** F16
Västervik *Sweden*   57°43N 16°33E **9** H17
Västmanland *Sweden*   59°45N 16°20E **9** G16
Vasto *Italy*   42°8N 14°40E **22** C6
Vasylkiv *Ukraine*   50°7N 30°15E **17** C16
Vatersay *U.K.*   56°55N 7°32W **11** E1
Vati *Greece*   36°3N 27°53E **25** D9
Vatican City ■ *Europe*   41°54N 12°27E **22** D5
Vatili *Cyprus*   35°6N 33°40E **25** D12
Vatiu = Atiu *Cook Is.*   20°0S 158°10W **65** J12
Vatnajökull *Iceland*   64°30N 16°48W **8** D5
Vatoa *Fiji*   19°50S 178°13W **59** a
Vatólakkos *Greece*   35°27N 23°53E **25** D5
Vatoloha *Madag.*   17°52S 48°48E **57** B8
Vatomandry *Madag.*   19°20S 48°59E **57** B8
Vatra-Dornei *Romania*   47°22N 25°22E **17** E13
Vatrak ⇢ *India*   23°9N 73°2E **42** H5
Vättern *Sweden*   58°25N 14°30E **9** G16
Vatu Vara *Fiji*   17°26S 179°31W **59** a
Vatulele *Fiji*   18°33S 177°37E **59** a
Vaudreuil-Dorion
  Canada   45°23N 74°3W **83** A10
Vaughn *Mont., U.S.A.*   47°33N 111°33W **76** C8

Vaughn *N. Mex.,
  U.S.A.*   34°36N 105°13W **77** J11
Vaujours L. *Canada*   55°27N 74°15W **72** A5
Vaupés = Uaupés ⇢
  Brazil   0°2N 67°16W **92** C5
Vaupés □ *Colombia*   1°0N 71°0W **92** C4
Vauxhall *Canada*   50°5N 112°9W **70** C6
Vav *India*   24°22N 71°31E **42** G4
Vavatenina *Madag.*   17°28S 49°12E **57** B8
Vava'u *Tonga*   18°36S 174°0W **59** c
Vava'u Group *Tonga*   18°40S 174°0W **59** c
Vawkavysk *Belarus*   53°9N 24°30E **17** B13
Växjö *Sweden*   56°52N 14°50E **9** H16
Vaygach, Ostrov *Russia* 70°0N 60°0E **28** C7
Veaikevárri = Svappavaara
  Sweden   67°40N 21°3E **8** C19
Vechte ⇢ *Neths.*   52°34N 6°6E **15** B6
Vedea ⇢ *Romania*   43°42N 25°41E **17** G13
Vedia *Argentina*   34°30S 61°31W **94** C3
Veendam *Neths.*   53°5N 6°52E **15** A6
Veenendaal *Neths.*   52°2N 5°34E **15** B5
Vefsna ⇢ *Norway*   65°48N 13°10E **8** D15
Vega *Norway*   65°40N 11°55E **8** D14
Vega *U.S.A.*   35°15N 102°26W **84** D3
Vega Baja *Puerto Rico*   18°27N 66°23W **89** d
Vegreville *Canada*   53°30N 112°5W **70** C6
Vejer de la Frontera
  Spain   36°15N 5°59W **21** D3
Vejle *Denmark*   55°43N 9°30E **9** J13
Velas, C. *Costa Rica*   10°21N 85°52W **88** D2
Velasco, Sierra de
  Argentina   29°20S 67°10W **94** B2
Velddrif *S. Africa*   32°42S 18°11E **56** E2
Velebit Planina *Croatia* 44°50N 15°20E **16** F8
Veles *Macedonia*   41°46N 21°47E **23** D9
Vélez-Málaga *Spain*   36°48N 4°5W **21** D3
Vélez Rubio *Spain*   37°41N 2°5W **21** D4
Velhas ⇢ *Brazil*   17°13S 44°49W **93** G10
Velika Kapela *Croatia*   45°10N 15°5E **16** F8
Velikaya ⇢ *Russia*   57°48N 28°10E **18** C4
Velikaya Kema *Russia*   45°30N 137°12E **30** B8
Veliki Ustyug *Russia*   60°47N 46°20E **18** B8
Velikiye Luki *Russia*   56°25N 30°32E **18** C5
Veliko Tǔrnovo *Bulgaria* 43°5N 25°41E **23** C11
Velikonda Range *India* 14°45N 79°10E **40** M11
Velletri *Italy*   41°41N 12°47E **22** D5
Vellore *India*   12°57N 79°10E **40** N11
Velsk *Russia*   61°10N 42°5E **18** B7
Veluwezoom △ *Neths.*   52°5N 6°0E **15** B6
Velva *U.S.A.*   48°4N 100°56W **80** A4
Venado *Mexico*   22°56N 101°6W **86** C4
Venado Tuerto *Argentina* 33°50S 62°0W **94** C3
Vendée □ *France*   46°50N 1°35W **20** C3
Vendôme *France*   47°47N 1°3E **20** C4
Venézia *Italy*   45°27N 12°21E **22** B5
Venézia, G. di *Italy*   45°15N 13°0E **22** B5
Venezuela ■ *S. Amer.*   8°0N 66°0W **92** B5
Venezuela, G. de
  Venezuela   11°30N 71°0W **92** A4
Vengurla *India*   15°53N 73°45E **40** M8
Venice = Venézia *Italy* 45°27N 12°21E **22** B5
Venice *U.S.A.*   27°6N 82°27W **85** H13
Venkatapuram *India*   18°20N 80°30E **41** K12
Venlo *Neths.*   51°22N 6°11E **15** C6
Vennachar Junction
  Canada   45°5N 77°14W **82** A7
Vennesla *Norway*   58°15N 7°59E **9** G12
Venray *Neths.*   51°31N 6°0E **15** C6
Ventana, Punta de la
  Mexico   24°4N 109°48W **86** C3
Ventana, Sa. de la
  Argentina   38°0S 62°30W **94** D3
Ventersburg *S. Africa*   28°7S 27°9E **56** D4
Venterstad *S. Africa*   30°47S 25°48E **56** E4
Ventnor *U.K.*   50°36N 1°12W **13** G6
Ventotene *Italy*   40°47N 13°25E **22** D5
Ventspils *Latvia*   57°25N 21°32E **9** H19
Ventuarí ⇢ *Venezuela*   3°58N 67°2W **92** C5
Ventucopa *U.S.A.*   34°50N 119°29W **79** L7
Ventura *U.S.A.*   34°17N 119°18W **79** L7
Vénus, Pte. *Tahiti*   17°29S 149°29W **59** d
Venus B. *Australia*   38°40S 145°42E **63** F4
Venustiano Carranza
  Mexico   30°25N 115°53W **86** A1
Vera *Argentina*   29°30S 60°20W **94** B3
Vera *Spain*   37°15N 1°51W **21** D5
Veracruz *Mexico*   19°11N 96°8W **87** D5
Veracruz □ *Mexico*   19°0N 96°15W **87** D5
Veraval *India*   20°53N 70°27E **42** J4
Verbánia *Italy*   45°56N 8°33E **20** D8
Vercelli *Italy*   45°19N 8°25E **20** D8
Verdalsøra *Norway*   63°48N 11°30E **8** E14
Verde ⇢ *Argentina*   41°56S 65°5W **96** E3
Verde ⇢ *Goiás, Brazil*   18°1S 50°14W **93** G8
Verde ⇢ *Mato Grosso do Sul,
  Brazil*   21°25S 52°20W **93** H8
Verde ⇢ *Chihuahua,
  Mexico*   26°29N 107°58W **86** B3
Verde ⇢ *Oaxaca, Mexico* 15°59N 97°50W **87** D5
Verde ⇢ *Veracruz,
  Mexico*   21°10N 102°50W **86** C4
Verde ⇢ *Paraguay*   23°9S 57°37W **94** A4
Verde ⇢ *U.S.A.*   33°33N 111°40W **77** K8
Verde, Cay *Bahamas*   23°0N 75°5W **88** B4
Verden *Germany*   52°55N 9°14E **16** B5
Verdi *U.S.A.*   39°31N 119°59W **78** F7
Verdun *France*   49°9N 5°24E **20** B6
Vereeniging *S. Africa*   26°38S 27°57E **57** D4
Verga, C. *Guinea*   10°30N 14°10W **50** F3
Vergara *Uruguay*   32°56S 53°57W **95** C5
Vergemont Cr. ⇢
  Australia   24°16S 143°16E **62** C3
Vergennes *U.S.A.*   44°10N 73°15W **83** B11
Veria *Greece*   40°34N 22°12E **23** D10
Verín *Spain*   41°57N 7°27W **21** B2
Verkhnetulomskoye Vdkhr.
  Russia   68°36N 31°12E **8** B24

Verkhnevilyuysk
Russia 63°27N 120°18E **29** C13
Verkhniy Baskunchak
Russia 48°14N 46°44E **19** E8
Verkhoyansk Russia 67°35N 133°25E **29** C14
Verkhoyansk Ra. =
Verkhoyanskiy Khrebet
Russia 66°0N 129°0E **29** C13
Verkhoyanskiy Khrebet
Russia 66°0N 129°0E **29** C13
Vermilion Canada 53°20N 110°50W **71** C6
Vermilion U.S.A. 41°25N 82°22W **82** E2
Vermilion → Canada 53°22N 110°51W **71** C6
Vermilion B. U.S.A. 29°42N 92°0W **84** G9
Vermilion Bay Canada 49°51N 93°34W **71** D10
Vermilion L. U.S.A. 47°53N 92°26W **80** B7
Vermillion U.S.A. 42°47N 96°56W **80** D6
Vermillion → Canada 47°38N 72°56W **72** C5
Vermont □ U.S.A. 44°0N 73°0W **83** C12
Vernadsky Antarctica 65°0S 64°0W **5** C17
Vernal U.S.A. 40°27N 109°32W **76** F9
Vernalis U.S.A. 37°36N 121°17W **78** H5
Verner Canada 46°25N 80°8W **72** C3
Verneukpan S. Africa 30°0S 21°0E **56** E3
Vernon Canada 50°20N 119°15W **70** C5
Vernon U.S.A. 34°9N 99°17W **84** D5
Vernonia U.S.A. 45°52N 123°11W **78** E3
Vero Beach U.S.A. 27°38N 80°24W **85** H14
Véroia = Veria Greece 40°34N 22°12E **23** D10
Verona Canada 44°29N 76°42W **83** B8
Verona Italy 45°27N 10°59E **22** B4
Versailles France 48°48N 2°7E **20** B5
Vert, C. Senegal 14°45N 17°30W **50** F2
Verulam S. Africa 29°38S 31°2E **57** D5
Verviers Belgium 50°37N 5°52E **15** D5
Veselovskoye Vdkhr.
Russia 46°58N 41°25E **19** E7
Vesoul France 47°40N 6°11E **20** C7
Vesterålen Norway 68°45N 15°0E **8** B16
Vestfjorden Norway 67°55N 14°0E **8** C16
Vestmannaeyjar Iceland 63°27N 20°15W **8** E3
Vestspitsbergen Svalbard 78°40N 17°0E **4** B8
Vestvågøy Norway 68°18N 13°50E **8** B15
Vesuvio Italy 40°49N 14°26E **22** D6
Vesuvius, Mt. = Vesuvio
Italy 40°49N 14°26E **22** D6
Veszprém Hungary 47°8N 17°57E **17** E9
Vetlanda Sweden 57°24N 15°3E **9** H16
Vetlugu → Russia 56°36N 46°4E **18** C8
Vettore, Mte. Italy 42°49N 13°16E **22** C5
Veurne Belgium 51°5N 2°40E **15** C2
Veys Iran 31°30N 49°0E **45** D6
Vezhen Bulgaria 42°50N 24°20E **23** C11
Vi Thanh Vietnam 9°42N 105°26E **39** H5
Viacha Bolivia 16°39S 68°18W **92** G5
Viamão Brazil 30°5S 51°0W **95** C5
Viana Brazil 3°13S 44°55W **93** D10
Viana do Alentejo
Portugal 38°17N 7°59W **21** C2
Viana do Castelo Portugal 41°42N 8°50W **21** B1
Vianden Lux. 49°56N 6°12E **15** E6
Viangchan = Vientiane
Laos 17°58N 102°36E **38** D4
Vianópolis Brazil 16°40S 48°35W **93** G9
Vianos Greece 35°2N 25°21E **25** D7
Viaréggio Italy 43°52N 10°14E **22** C4
Vibo Valéntia Italy 38°40N 16°6E **22** E7
Viborg Denmark 56°27N 9°23E **9** H13
Vic Spain 41°58N 2°19E **21** B7
Vicenza Italy 45°33N 11°33E **22** B4
Vich = Vic Spain 41°58N 2°19E **21** B7
Vichada → Colombia 4°55N 67°50W **92** C5
Vichy France 46°9N 3°26E **20** C5
Vicksburg Ariz.,
U.S.A. 33°45N 113°45W **79** M13
Vicksburg Miss., U.S.A. 32°21N 90°53W **85** E9
Victor India 21°0N 71°30E **42** J4
Victor Harbor Australia 35°30S 138°37E **63** F2
Victoria Argentina 32°40S 60°10W **94** C3
Victoria Canada 48°30N 123°25W **78** B3
Victoria Chile 38°13S 72°20W **96** D2
Victoria China 22°17N 114°9E **33** G1
Victoria Malta 36°3N 14°14E **25** C1
Victoria Seychelles 4°38S 55°28E **53** b
Victoria Kans., U.S.A. 38°52N 99°9W **80** F4
Victoria Tex., U.S.A. 28°48N 97°0W **84** G6
Victoria □ Australia 37°0S 144°0E **63** F3
Victoria → Australia 15°10S 129°40E **60** C4
Victoria, Grand L.
Canada 47°31N 77°30W **72** C4
Victoria, L. Africa 1°0S 33°0E **54** C3
Victoria, L. Australia 33°57S 141°15E **63** E3
Victoria, Mt. Burma 21°14N 93°55E **41** J18
Victoria Beach Canada 50°40N 96°35W **71** C9
Victoria de Durango = Durango
Mexico 24°3N 104°39W **86** C4
Victoria de las Tunas = Las Tunas
Cuba 20°58N 76°59W **88** B4
Victoria Falls Zimbabwe 17°58S 25°52E **55** F2
Victoria Harbour
Canada 44°45N 79°45W **82** B5
Victoria I. Canada 71°0N 111°0W **68** B8
Victoria L. Canada 48°20N 57°27W **73** C8
Victoria Ld. Antarctica 75°0S 160°0E **5** D11
Victoria Nile → Uganda 2°14N 31°26E **54** B3
Victoria Pk. Belize 16°48N 88°37W **87** D7
Victoria River Australia 16°25S 131°0E **60** C5
Victoria Str. Canada 69°31N 100°30W **68** B9
Victoria West S. Africa 31°25S 23°4E **56** E3
Victoriaville Canada 46°4N 71°56W **73** C5
Victorica Argentina 36°20S 65°30W **94** D2
Victorville U.S.A. 34°32N 117°18W **79** L9
Vicuña Chile 30°0S 70°50W **94** C1
Vicuña Mackenna
Argentina 33°53S 64°25W **94** C3
Vidal U.S.A. 34°7N 114°31W **79** L12
Vidal Junction U.S.A. 34°11N 114°34W **79** L12

Vidalia U.S.A. 32°13N 82°25W **85** E13
Vidin Bulgaria 43°59N 22°50E **23** C10
Vidisha India 23°28N 77°53E **42** H7
Vidos Greece 39°38N 19°55E **25** A3
Vidzy Belarus 55°23N 26°37E **9** J22
Viedma Argentina 40°50S 63°0W **96** E4
Viedma, L. Argentina 49°30S 72°30W **96** F2
Vielsalm Belgium 50°17N 5°54E **15** D5
Vieng Pou Kha Laos 20°41N 101°4E **38** B3
Vienna = Wien Austria 48°12N 16°22E **16** D9
Vienna Canada 42°41N 80°48W **82** D4
Vienna Ill., U.S.A. 37°25N 88°54W **80** G9
Vienna Mo., U.S.A. 38°11N 91°57W **80** F8
Vienne France 45°31N 4°53E **20** D6
Vienne → France 47°13N 0°5E **20** C4
Vientiane Laos 17°58N 102°36E **38** D4
Vientos, Paso de los
Caribbean 20°0N 74°0W **89** C5
Vieques Puerto Rico 18°8N 65°25W **89** d
Vierge Pt. St. Lucia 13°49N 60°53W **89** f
Vierzon France 47°13N 2°5E **20** C5
Viet Tri Vietnam 21°18N 105°25E **38** B5
Vietnam ■ Asia 19°0N 106°0E **38** C6
Vieux Fort St. Lucia 13°46N 60°58W **89** f
Vigan Phil. 17°35N 120°28E **37** A6
Vigévano Italy 45°19N 8°51E **20** D8
Vigia Brazil 0°50S 48°5W **93** D9
Viglas, Akra Greece 35°54N 27°51E **25** D9
Vigo Spain 42°12N 8°41W **21** A1
Vihowa Pakistan 31°8N 70°30E **42** D4
Vihowa → Pakistan 31°8N 70°41E **42** D4
Vijayawada India 16°31N 80°39E **41** L12
Vijosë → Albania 40°37N 19°24E **23** D8
Vík Iceland 63°25N 19°1W **8** E4
Vikeke = Viqueque
E. Timor 8°52S 126°23E **37** F7
Viking Canada 53°7N 111°50W **70** C6
Vikna Norway 64°55N 10°58E **8** D14
Vila da Maganja Mozam. 17°18S 37°30E **55** F4
Vila da Ribeira Brava
C. Verde Is. 16°32N 24°25W **50** b
Vila do Bispo Portugal 37°5N 8°53W **21** D1
Vila Franca de Xira
Portugal 38°57N 8°59W **21** C1
Vila Gamito Mozam. 14°12S 33°0E **55** E3
Vila Gomes da Costa
Mozam. 24°20S 33°37E **57** C5
Vila Machado Mozam. 19°15S 34°14E **55** F3
Vila Mouzinho Mozam. 14°48S 34°25E **55** E3
Vila Nova de Gaia Portugal 41°8N 8°37W **21** B1
Vila Real Portugal 41°17N 7°48W **21** B2
Vila-Real Spain 39°55N 0°3W **21** C5
Vila Real de Santo António
Portugal 37°10N 7°28W **21** D2
Vila Vasco da Gama
Mozam. 14°54S 32°14E **55** E3
Vila Velha Brazil 20°20S 40°17W **95** A7
Vilagarcía de Arousa
Spain 42°34N 8°46W **21** A1
Vilaine → France 47°30N 2°27W **20** C2
Vilanandro, Tanjona
Madag. 16°11S 44°27E **57** B7
Vilanculos Mozam. 22°1S 35°17E **57** C6
Vilanova i la Geltrú Spain 41°13N 1°40E **21** B6
Vilcheka, Ostrov Russia 80°0N 58°31E **28** B6
Vilcheka, Zemlya Russia 80°30N 60°30E **4** A11
Vileyka Belarus 54°30N 26°53E **17** A14
Vilhelmina Sweden 64°35N 16°39E **8** D17
Vilhena Brazil 12°40S 60°5W **92** F6
Viliya = Neris →
Lithuania 55°8N 24°16E **9** J21
Viljandi Estonia 58°28N 25°30E **9** G21
Vilkitskogo, Proliv
Russia 78°0N 103°0E **29** B11
Vilkovo = Vylkove
Ukraine 45°28N 29°32E **17** F15
Villa Abecia Bolivia 21°0S 68°18W **94** A2
Villa Ana Argentina 28°28S 59°40W **94** B4
Villa Angela Argentina 27°34S 60°45W **94** B3
Villa Bella Bolivia 10°25S 65°22W **92** F5
Villa Cañás Argentina 34°0S 61°35W **94** C3
Villa Constitución
Argentina 33°15S 60°20W **94** C3
Villa de Arriaga Mexico 21°56N 101°20W **86** C4
Villa de María Argentina 29°55S 63°43W **94** B3
Villa de Méndez Mexico 25°7N 98°34W **87** B5
Villa Dolores Argentina 31°58S 65°15W **94** C2
Villa Frontera Mexico 26°56N 101°27W **86** B4
Villa Gesell Argentina 37°15S 56°55W **94** D4
Villa Guillermina
Argentina 28°15S 59°29W **94** B4
Villa Hayes Paraguay 25°5S 57°20W **94** B4
Villa Hidalgo Mexico 21°40N 99°26W **87** C5
Villa Iris Argentina 38°12S 63°12W **94** D3
Villa María Argentina 32°20S 63°10W **94** C3
Villa Mazán Argentina 28°40S 66°30W **94** B2
Villa Montes Bolivia 21°10S 63°30W **94** A3
Villa Ocampo Argentina 28°30S 59°20W **94** B4
Villa Ocampo Mexico 26°27N 105°31W **86** B3
Villa Ojo de Agua
Argentina 29°30S 63°44W **94** B3
Villa San Martín
Argentina 28°15S 64°9W **94** B3
Villa Unión Mexico 23°12N 106°14W **86** C3
Villacarlos Spain 39°53N 4°17E **24** B11
Villacarrillo Spain 38°7N 3°3W **21** C4
Villach Austria 46°37N 13°51E **16** E7
Villafranca de Bonany
Spain 39°34N 3°5E **24** B10
Villagrán Mexico 24°29N 99°29W **87** C5
Villaguay Argentina 32°0S 59°0W **94** C4
Villahermosa Mexico 17°59N 92°55W **87** D6
Villajoyosa Spain 38°30N 0°12W **21** C5
Villalba Spain 43°26N 7°40W **21** A2
Villanueva U.S.A. 35°16N 105°22W **77** J11
Villanueva de la Serena
Spain 38°59N 5°50W **21** C3

Villanueva y Geltrú = Vilanova i
la Geltrú Spain 41°13N 1°40E **21** B6
Villarreal = Vila-Real
Spain 39°55N 0°3W **21** C5
Villarrica Chile 39°15S 72°15W **96** D2
Villarrica Paraguay 25°40S 56°30W **94** B4
Villarrobledo Spain 39°18N 2°36W **21** C4
Villavicencio Argentina 32°28S 69°0W **94** C2
Villavicencio Colombia 4°9N 73°37W **92** C4
Villaviciosa Spain 43°32N 5°27W **21** A3
Villazón Bolivia 22°0S 65°35W **94** A2
Ville-Marie Canada 47°20N 79°30W **72** C4
Ville Platte U.S.A. 30°41N 92°17W **84** F8
Villena Spain 38°39N 0°52W **21** C5
Villeneuve-d'Ascq France 50°38N 3°9E **20** A5
Villeneuve-sur-Lot France 44°24N 0°42E **20** D4
Villiers S. Africa 27°2S 28°36E **57** D4
Villingen-Schwenningen
Germany 48°3N 8°26E **16** D5
Villmanstrand = Lappeenranta
Finland 61°3N 28°12E **8** F23
Vilna Canada 54°7N 111°55W **70** C6
Vilnius Lithuania 54°38N 25°19E **9** J21
Vilvoorde Belgium 50°56N 4°26E **15** D4
Vilyuchinsk Russia 52°55N 158°24E **29** D16
Vilyuy → Russia 64°24N 126°26E **29** C13
Vilyuysk Russia 63°40N 121°35E **29** C13
Viña del Mar Chile 33°0S 71°30W **94** C1
Vinarós Spain 40°30N 0°27E **21** B6
Vincennes U.S.A. 38°41N 87°32W **80** F10
Vincennes Bay S. Ocean 66°0S 109°0E **5** C8
Vincent U.S.A. 34°33N 118°11W **79** L8
Vinchina Argentina 28°45S 68°15W **94** B2
Vindelälven → Sweden 63°55N 19°50E **8** E18
Vindeln Sweden 64°12N 19°43E **8** D18
Vindhya Ra. India 22°50N 77°0E **42** H7
Vineland U.S.A. 39°29N 75°2W **81** F16
Vinh Vietnam 18°45N 105°38E **38** C5
Vinh Linh Vietnam 17°4N 107°2E **38** D6
Vinh Long Vietnam 10°16N 105°57E **39** G5
Vinh Yen Vietnam 21°21N 105°35E **38** B5
Vinita U.S.A. 36°39N 95°9W **84** C7
Vinkovci Croatia 45°19N 18°48E **23** B8
Vinnitsa = Vinnytsya
Ukraine 49°15N 28°30E **17** D15
Vinnytsya Ukraine 49°15N 28°30E **17** D15
Vinson Massif Antarctica 78°35S 85°25W **5** D16
Vinton Calif., U.S.A. 39°48N 120°10W **78** F6
Vinton Iowa, U.S.A. 42°10N 92°1W **80** D7
Vinton La., U.S.A. 30°11N 93°35W **84** F8
Viqueque E. Timor 8°52S 126°23E **37** F7
Virac Phil. 13°30N 124°20E **37** B6
Virachey Cambodia 13°59N 106°49E **38** E6
Virachey → Cambodia 14°14N 106°55E **38** E6
Virago Sd. Canada 54°0N 132°30W **70** C2
Viramgam India 23°5N 72°0E **42** H5
Virananşehir Turkey 37°13N 39°45E **44** B3
Virawah Pakistan 24°31N 70°46E **42** G4
Virden Canada 49°50N 100°56W **71** D8
Vire France 48°50N 0°53W **20** B3
Vírgenes, C. Argentina 52°19S 68°21W **96** G3
Virgin → U.S.A. 36°28N 114°21W **77** H6
Virgin Gorda Br. Virgin Is. 18°30N 64°26W **89** e
Virgin Is. (British) ☑
W. Indies 18°30N 64°30W **89** e
Virgin Is. (U.S.) ☑
W. Indies 18°20N 65°0W **89** e
Virgin Islands △
U.S. Virgin Is. 18°21N 64°43W **89** C7
Virginia S. Africa 28°8S 26°55E **56** D4
Virginia U.S.A. 47°31N 92°32W **80** B7
Virginia □ U.S.A. 37°30N 78°45W **81** G14
Virginia Beach U.S.A. 36°49N 76°9W **81** F16
Virginia City Mont.,
U.S.A. 45°18N 111°56W **76** D8
Virginia City Nev.,
U.S.A. 39°19N 119°39W **78** F7
Virginia Falls Canada 61°38N 125°42W **70** A3
Virginiatown Canada 48°9N 79°36W **72** C4
Viroqua U.S.A. 43°34N 90°53W **80** D8
Virovitica Croatia 45°51N 17°21E **22** B7
Virpur India 21°51N 70°42E **42** J4
Virton Belgium 49°35N 5°32E **15** E5
Virudunagar India 9°30N 77°58E **40** Q10
Virunga △
Dem. Rep. of the Congo 0°5N 29°38E **54** B2
Vis Croatia 43°4N 16°10E **22** C7
Visalia U.S.A. 36°20N 119°18W **78** J7
Visayan Sea Phil. 11°30N 123°30E **37** B6
Visby Sweden 57°37N 18°18E **9** H18
Viscount Melville Sd.
Canada 74°10N 108°0W **69** B9
Visé Belgium 50°44N 5°41E **15** D5
Vise, Ostrov Russia 79°33N 76°50E **28** B8
Višegrad Bos.-H. 43°47N 19°17E **23** C8
Viseu Brazil 1°10S 46°5W **93** D9
Viseu Portugal 40°40N 7°55W **21** B2
Vishakhapatnam India 17°45N 83°20E **41** L13
Vishnupur India 23°45N 72°32E **42** H5
Viso, Mte. Italy 44°38N 7°5E **20** D7
Visokoi I. Antarctica 56°43S 27°15W **5** B1
Vistula = Wisła →
Poland 54°22N 18°55E **17** A10
Vitebsk = Vitsyebsk
Belarus 55°10N 30°15E **18** C5
Viterbo Italy 42°25N 12°6E **22** C5
Viti Levu Fiji 17°30S 177°30E **59** a
Vitigudino Spain 41°1N 6°26W **21** B2
Vitim Russia 59°28N 112°35E **29** D12
Vitim → Russia 59°26N 112°34E **29** D12
Vitória Brazil 20°20S 40°22W **93** H10
Vitória da Conquista
Brazil 14°51S 40°51W **93** F10
Vitória de São Antão
Brazil 8°10S 35°20W **93** E11
Vitoria-Gasteiz Spain 42°50N 2°41W **21** A4

Vitsyebsk Belarus 55°10N 30°15E **18** C5
Vittória Italy 36°57N 14°32E **22** F6
Vittório Véneto Italy 45°59N 12°18E **22** B5
Viveiro Spain 43°39N 7°38W **21** A2
Vivian U.S.A. 32°53N 93°59W **84** E8
Viwa Fiji 17°10S 177°58E **59** a
Vizcaíno, Desierto de
Mexico 27°30N 113°45W **86** B2
Vizcaíno, Sierra Mexico 27°30N 114°0W **86** B2
Vize Turkey 41°34N 27°45E **23** D12
Vizianagaram India 18°6N 83°30E **41** K13
Vizinada Croatia 45°20N 13°46E **22** b
Vlaardingen Neths. 51°55N 4°21E **15** C4
Vladikavkaz Russia 43°0N 44°35E **19** F7
Vladimir Russia 56°15N 40°30E **18** C7
Vladimir Volynskiy = Volodymyr-
Volynskyy Ukraine 50°50N 24°18E **17** C13
Vladivostok Russia 43°10N 131°53E **30** C5
Vlieland Neths. 53°16N 4°55E **15** A4
Vlissingen Neths. 51°26N 3°34E **15** C3
Vlorë Albania 40°32N 19°28E **23** D8
Vltava → Czech Rep. 50°21N 14°30E **16** D8
Voe U.K. 60°21N 1°16W **11** A7
Vogelkop = Doberai, Jazirah
Indonesia 1°25S 133°0E **37** E8
Vogelsberg Germany 50°31N 9°12E **16** C5
Voghera Italy 44°59N 9°1E **20** D8
Vohibinany Madag. 18°49S 49°4E **57** B8
Vohilava Madag. 21°4S 48°0E **57** C8
Vohimarina = Iharana
Madag. 13°25S 50°0E **57** A9
Vohimena, Tanjon' i
Madag. 25°36S 45°8E **57** D8
Vohipeno Madag. 22°22S 47°51E **57** C8
Voi Kenya 3°25S 38°32E **54** C4
Voiron France 45°22N 5°35E **20** D6
Voisey B. Canada 56°15N 61°50W **73** A7
Vojmsjön Sweden 65°0N 16°24E **8** D17
Vojvodina □ Serbia 45°20N 20°0E **23** B9
Volborg U.S.A. 45°51N 105°41W **76** D11
Volcán de Colima △
Mexico 19°30N 103°40W **86** D4
Volcano Is. = Kazan-Rettō
Pac. Oc. 25°0N 141°0E **64** E6
Volcans △ Rwanda 1°30S 29°26E **54** C2
Volda Norway 62°9N 6°5E **8** E12
Volga = Privolzhskiy □
Russia 56°0N 50°0E **28** D6
Volga → Russia 46°0N 48°30E **19** E8
Volga Hts. = Privolzhskaya
Vozvyshennost Russia 51°0N 46°0E **19** D8
Volgodonsk Russia 47°33N 42°5E **19** E7
Volgograd Russia 48°40N 44°25E **19** E7
Volgogradskoye Vdkhr.
Russia 50°0N 45°20E **19** D8
Volkhov → Russia 60°8N 32°20E **18** B5
Volkovysk = Vawkavysk
Belarus 53°9N 24°30E **17** B13
Volksrust S. Africa 27°24S 29°53E **57** D4
Volochanka Russia 71°0N 94°28E **29** B10
Volodarsk Russia 56°12N 43°15E **18** C7
Volodymyr-Volynskyy
Ukraine 50°50N 24°18E **17** C13
Vologda Russia 59°10N 39°45E **18** C6
Volos Greece 39°24N 22°59E **23** E10
Volosovo Russia 59°27N 29°32E **9** G23
Volovets Ukraine 48°43N 23°11E **17** D12
Volozhin = Valozhyn
Belarus 54°3N 26°30E **17** A14
Volsk Russia 52°5N 47°22E **18** D8
Volta → Ghana 5°46N 0°41E **48** F4
Volta, L. Ghana 7°30N 0°0 **50** G6
Volta Redonda Brazil 22°31S 44°5W **95** A7
Voltaire, C. Australia 14°16S 125°35E **60** B4
Volterra Italy 43°24N 10°51E **22** C4
Volturno → Italy 41°1N 13°55E **22** D5
Volzhskiy Russia 48°56N 44°46E **19** E7
Vomo Fiji 17°30S 177°15E **59** a
Vondrozo Madag. 22°49S 47°20E **57** C8
Vopnafjörður Iceland 65°45N 14°50W **8** D6
Vorkuta Russia 67°48N 64°20E **18** A11
Vormsi Estonia 59°1N 23°13E **9** G20
Voronezh Russia 51°40N 39°10E **18** D6
Vorts Järv Estonia 58°16N 26°3E **9** G22
Võru Estonia 57°48N 26°54E **9** H22
Vosges France 48°20N 7°10E **20** B7
Vostok Antarctica 78°30S 106°50E **5** D8
Vostok I. Kiribati 10°5S 152°23W **65** J12
Votkinsk Russia 57°0N 53°55E **18** C9
Votkinskoye Vdkhr.
Russia 57°22N 55°12E **18** C10
Votsuri-Shima Japan 25°45N 123°29E **31** M1
Vouga → Portugal 40°41N 8°40W **21** B1
Vouxa, Akra Greece 35°37N 23°32E **25** D5
Voyageurs △ U.S.A. 48°32N 93°0W **80** A7
Voynitsa Russia 65°10N 30°20E **8** D24
Voyvozh Russia 62°56N 54°56E **18** B10
Vozhe, Ozero Russia 60°45N 39°0E **18** B6
Voznesensk Ukraine 47°35N 31°21E **19** E5
Voznesenye Russia 61°0N 35°28E **18** B6
Vrangel Russia 42°43N 133°5E **30** C6
Vrangelya, Ostrov
Russia 71°0N 180°0E **29** B18
Vranje Serbia 42°34N 21°54E **23** C9
Vratsa Bulgaria 43°15N 23°30E **23** C10
Vrbas → Bos.-H. 45°8N 17°29E **22** B7
Vrede S. Africa 27°24S 29°6E **57** D4
Vredefort S. Africa 27°0S 27°22E **56** D4
Vredenburg S. Africa 32°56S 18°0E **56** E2
Vredendal S. Africa 31°41S 18°35E **56** E2
Vrindavan India 27°37N 77°40E **42** F7
Vrises Greece 35°23N 24°13E **25** D6
Vršac Serbia 45°8N 21°20E **23** B9
Vryburg S. Africa 26°55S 24°45E **56** D3
Vryheid S. Africa 27°45S 30°47E **57** D5
Vu Liet Vietnam 18°43N 105°23E **38** C5
Vukovar Croatia 45°21N 18°59E **23** B8

Vuktyl Russia 63°52N 57°20E **28** C6
Vulcan Canada 50°25N 113°15W **70** C6
Vulcan Romania 45°23N 23°17E **17** F12
Vulcaneşti Moldova 45°41N 28°18E **17** F15
Vulcano Italy 38°24N 14°58E **22** E6
Vulkaneshty = Vulcaneşti
Moldova 45°41N 28°18E **17** F15
Vunduzi → Mozam. 18°56S 34°1E **55** F3
Vung Tau Vietnam 10°21N 107°4E **39** G6
Vunidawa Fiji 17°50S 178°21E **59** a
Vunisea Fiji 19°3S 178°10E **59** a
Vwaza △ Malawi 10°58S 33°25E **55** E3
Vyartsilya Russia 62°8N 30°45E **8** E24
Vyatka = Kirov Russia 58°35N 49°40E **18** C8
Vyatka → Russia 55°37N 51°28E **18** C9
Vyatskiye Polyany Russia 56°14N 51°5E **18** C9
Vyazemskiy Russia 47°32N 134°45E **29** E14
Vyazma Russia 55°10N 34°15E **18** C5
Vyborg Russia 60°43N 28°47E **8** F23
Vychegda → Russia 61°18N 46°36E **18** B8
Vychodné Beskydy
Europe 49°20N 22°0E **17** D11
Vyg-ozero Russia 63°47N 34°29E **18** B5
Vylkove Ukraine 45°28N 29°32E **17** F15
Vynohradiv Ukraine 48°9N 23°2E **17** D12
Vyrnwy, L. U.K. 52°48N 3°31W **12** E4
Vyshniy Volochek
Russia 57°30N 34°30E **18** C5
Vyshzha = imeni 26 Bakinskikh
Komissarov
Turkmenistan 39°22N 54°10E **45** B7
Vyškov Czech Rep. 49°17N 17°0E **17** D9
Vytegra Russia 61°0N 36°27E **18** B6

W

W.A.C. Bennett Dam
Canada 56°2N 122°6W **70** B4
Wa Ghana 10°7N 2°25W **50** F5
Waal → Neths. 51°37N 5°0E **15** C5
Waalwijk Neths. 51°42N 5°4E **15** C5
Wabakimi △ Canada 50°43N 89°29W **72** B2
Wabana Canada 47°40N 53°0W **73** C9
Wabasca → Canada 58°22N 115°20W **70** B5
Wabasca-Desmarais
Canada 55°57N 113°56W **70** B6
Wabash U.S.A. 40°48N 85°49W **81** E11
Wabash → U.S.A. 37°48N 88°2W **80** G9
Wabigoon L. Canada 49°44N 92°44W **71** D10
Wabowden Canada 54°55N 98°38W **71** C9
Wabuk Pt. Canada 55°20N 85°5W **72** A2
Wabush Canada 52°55N 66°52W **73** B6
Waco U.S.A. 31°33N 97°9W **84** F6
Waconichi, L. Canada 50°8N 74°0W **72** B5
Wad Hamid Sudan 16°30N 32°45E **51** E12
Wad Medanî Sudan 14°28N 33°30E **51** F12
Wad Thana Pakistan 27°22N 66°23E **42** F2
Wadai Africa 12°0N 19°0E **48** E5
Wadayama Japan 35°19N 134°52E **31** G7
Waddeneilanden Neths. 53°25N 5°10E **15** A5
Waddenzee Neths. 53°6N 5°10E **15** A5
Waddington Canada 44°52N 75°12W **83** B9
Waddington, Mt.
Canada 51°23N 125°15W **70** C3
Waddy Pt. Australia 24°58S 153°21E **63** C5
Wadebridge U.K. 50°31N 4°51W **13** G3
Wadena Canada 51°57N 103°47W **71** C8
Wadena U.S.A. 46°26N 95°8W **80** B6
Wadeye Australia 14°28S 129°52E **60** B4
Wadhams Canada 51°30N 127°30W **70** C3
Wadhwan India 22°42N 71°41E **42** H4
Wādī as Sīr Jordan 31°56N 35°49E **46** D4
Wadi Halfa Sudan 21°53N 31°19E **51** D12
Wadi Rum △ Jordan 29°30N 35°20E **46** F4
Wadsworth Nev.,
U.S.A. 39°38N 119°17W **76** G4
Wadsworth Ohio, U.S.A. 41°2N 81°44W **82** E3
Waegwan S. Korea 35°59N 128°23E **35** G15
Wafangdian China 39°38N 121°58E **35** E11
Wafrah Kuwait 28°33N 47°56E **44** D5
Wageningen Neths. 51°58N 5°40E **15** C5
Wager B. Canada 65°26N 88°40W **69** C11
Wagga Wagga Australia 35°7S 147°24E **63** F4
Waghete Indonesia 4°10S 135°50E **37** E9
Wagin Australia 33°17S 117°25E **61** F2
Wagner U.S.A. 43°5N 98°18W **80** D4
Wagon Mound U.S.A. 36°1N 104°42W **77** H11
Wagoner U.S.A. 35°58N 95°22W **84** D7
Wah Pakistan 33°45N 72°40E **42** C5
Wahai Indonesia 2°48S 129°35E **37** E7
Wahiawā U.S.A. 21°30N 158°2W **74** b
Wâhid Egypt 30°48N 32°21E **46** E1
Wahnai Afghan. 32°40N 65°50E **42** C1
Wahoo U.S.A. 41°13N 96°37W **80** E5
Wahpeton U.S.A. 46°16N 96°36W **80** B5
Waiau → N.Z. 42°47N 173°22E **59** E4
Waibeem Indonesia 0°30S 132°59E **37** E8
Waigeo Indonesia 0°20S 130°40E **37** E8
Waihi N.Z. 37°23S 175°52E **59** B5
Waihou → N.Z. 37°15S 175°40E **59** B5
Waika
Dem. Rep. of the Congo 2°22S 25°42E **54** C2
Waikabubak Indonesia 9°45S 119°25E **37** F5
Waikaremoana, L. N.Z. 38°49S 177°9E **59** C6
Waikari N.Z. 42°58S 172°41E **59** E4
Waikato → N.Z. 37°23S 174°43E **59** B5
Waikerie Australia 34°9S 140°0E **63** E3
Waikokopu N.Z. 39°3S 177°52E **59** C6
Waikouaiti N.Z. 45°36S 170°41E **59** F3
Wailingding Dao China 22°6N 114°2E **33** G10
Wailuku U.S.A. 20°53N 156°30W **74** b
Waimakariri → N.Z. 43°24S 172°42E **59** E4
Waimate N.Z. 44°45S 171°3E **59** F3
Wainganga → India 18°50N 79°55E **40** K11
Waingapu Indonesia 9°35S 120°11E **37** F6
Waini → Guyana 8°20N 59°50W **92** B7

Wainwright _Canada_ 52°50N 110°50W **71** C6
Waiouru _N.Z._ 39°28S 175°41E **59** C5
Waipara _N.Z._ 43°3S 172°46E **59** E4
Waipawa _N.Z._ 39°56S 176°38E **59** C6
Waipiro _N.Z._ 38°2S 178°22E **59** C7
Waipoua Forest _N.Z._ 35°39S 173°33E **59** A4
Waipu _N.Z._ 35°59S 174°29E **59** A5
Waipukurau _N.Z._ 40°1S 176°33E **59** D6
Wairakei _N.Z._ 38°37S 176°6E **59** C6
Wairarapa, L. _N.Z._ 41°14S 175°15E **59** D5
Wairoa _N.Z._ 39°3S 177°25E **59** C6
Waitaki → _N.Z._ 44°56S 171°7E **59** F3
Waitangi _N.Z._ 35°16S 174°5E **59** A5
Waitara _N.Z._ 38°59S 174°15E **59** C5
Waitomo Caves _N.Z._ 38°16S 175°7E **59** C5
Waitsburg _U.S.A._ 46°16N 118°9W **76** C4
Waiuku _N.Z._ 37°15S 174°45E **59** B5
Wajima _Japan_ 37°30N 137°0E **31** F8
Wajir _Kenya_ 1°42N 40°5E **54** B5
Wakasa _Japan_ 35°20N 134°24E **31** G7
Wakasa-Wan _Japan_ 35°40N 135°30E **31** G7
Wakatipu, L. _N.Z._ 45°5S 168°33E **59** F2
Wakaw _Canada_ 52°39N 105°44W **71** C7
Wakaya _Fiji_ 17°37S 179°0E **59** a
Wakayama _Japan_ 34°15N 135°15E **31** G7
Wakayama □ _Japan_ 33°50N 135°30E **31** G7
Wake Forest _U.S.A._ 35°59N 78°30W **85** D15
Wake I. _Pac. Oc._ 19°18N 166°36E **64** F8
WaKeeney _U.S.A._ 39°1N 99°53W **80** F4
Wakefield _Jamaica_ 18°26N 77°42W **88** a
Wakefield _N.Z._ 41°24S 173°5E **59** D4
Wakefield _U.K._ 53°41N 1°29W **12** D6
Wakefield _Mass., U.S.A._ 42°30N 71°5W **83** D13
Wakefield _Mich., U.S.A._ 46°29N 89°56W **80** B9
Wakkanai _Japan_ 45°28N 141°35E **30** B10
Wakool _Australia_ 35°28S 144°23E **63** F3
Wakool → _Australia_ 35°5S 143°33E **63** F3
Wakre _Indonesia_ 0°19S 131°5E **37** E8
Wakuach, L. _Canada_ 55°34N 67°32W **73** A6
Walamba _Zambia_ 13°30S 28°42E **55** E2
Wałbrzych _Poland_ 50°45N 16°18E **16** C9
Walbury Hill _U.K._ 51°21N 1°28W **13** F6
Walcha _Australia_ 30°55S 151°31E **63** E5
Walcheren _Neths._ 51°30N 3°35E **15** C3
Walcott _U.S.A._ 41°46N 106°51W **76** F10
Walcz _Poland_ 53°17N 16°27E **16** B9
Waldburg Ra. _Australia_ 24°40S 117°35E **61** D2
Walden _Colo., U.S.A._ 40°44N 106°17W **76** F10
Walden _N.Y., U.S.A._ 41°34N 74°11W **83** E10
Waldport _U.S.A._ 44°26N 124°4W **76** D1
Waldron _U.S.A._ 34°54N 94°5W **84** D7
Walebing _Australia_ 30°41S 116°13E **61** F2
Wales □ _U.K._ 52°19N 4°43W **13** E3
Walgett _Australia_ 30°0S 148°5E **63** E4
Walgreen Coast _Antarctica_ 75°15S 105°0W **5** D15
Walker _U.S.A._ 47°6N 94°35W **80** B6
Walker, L. _Canada_ 50°20N 67°11W **73** B6
Walker L. _Canada_ 54°42N 95°57W **71** C9
Walker L. _U.S.A._ 38°42N 118°43W **76** G4
Walkerston _Australia_ 21°11S 149°8E **62** K7
Walkerton _Canada_ 44°10N 81°10W **82** B3
Wall _U.S.A._ 44°0N 102°8W **80** C2
Walla Walla _U.S.A._ 46°4N 118°20W **76** C4
Wallace _Idaho, U.S.A._ 47°28N 115°56W **76** C6
Wallace _N.C., U.S.A._ 34°44N 77°59W **85** D16
Wallaceburg _Canada_ 42°34N 82°23W **82** D2
Wallachia = Valahia _Romania_ 44°35N 25°0E **17** F13
Wallal _Australia_ 26°32S 146°7E **63** D4
Wallam Cr. → _Australia_ 28°40S 147°20E **63** D4
Wallambin, L. _Australia_ 30°57S 117°35E **61** F2
Wallangarra _Australia_ 28°56S 151°58E **63** D5
Wallaroo _Australia_ 33°56S 137°39E **63** E2
Wallenpaupack, L. _U.S.A._ 41°25N 75°15W **83** E9
Wallingford _Conn., U.S.A._ 41°27N 72°50W **83** E12
Wallingford _Vt., U.S.A._ 43°28N 72°58W **83** C12
Wallis & Futuna, Is. _Pac. Oc._ 13°18S 176°10W **58** C11
Wallowa _U.S.A._ 45°34N 117°32W **76** D5
Wallowa Mts. _U.S.A._ 45°20N 117°30W **76** D5
Walls _U.K._ 60°14N 1°33W **11** A7
Walls of Jerusalem △ _Australia_ 41°56S 146°15E **63** G4
Wallula _U.S.A._ 46°5N 118°54W **76** C4
Wallumbilla _Australia_ 26°33S 149°9E **63** D4
Walmsley L. _Canada_ 63°25N 108°36W **71** A7
Walney, I. of _U.K._ 54°6N 3°15W **12** C4
Walnut Canyon △ _U.S.A._ 35°15N 111°20W **77** J8
Walnut Creek _U.S.A._ 37°54N 122°4W **78** H4
Walnut Ridge _U.S.A._ 36°4N 90°57W **85** C9
Walpole _Australia_ 34°58S 116°44E **61** F2
Walpole _U.S.A._ 42°9N 71°15W **83** D13
Walpole-Nornalup △ _Australia_ 35°0S 116°45E **61** G2
Walsall _U.K._ 52°35N 1°58W **13** E6
Walsenburg _U.S.A._ 37°38N 104°47W **77** H11
Walsh _U.S.A._ 37°23N 102°17W **77** H12
Walsh → _Australia_ 16°31S 143°42E **62** B3
Walsingham _Canada_ 42°40N 80°31W **82** D4
Walter F. George Res. _U.S.A._ 31°38N 85°4W **85** F12
Walterboro _U.S.A._ 32°55N 80°40W **85** E14
Walters _U.S.A._ 34°22N 98°19W **84** D5
Waltham _U.S.A._ 42°23N 71°14W **83** D13
Waltman _U.S.A._ 43°4N 107°12W **76** E10
Walton _U.S.A._ 42°10N 75°8W **83** D9
Walton-on-the-Naze _U.K._ 51°51N 1°17E **13** F9
Walvis Bay _Namibia_ 23°0S 14°28E **56** C1
Walvisbaai = Walvis Bay _Namibia_ 23°0S 14°28E **56** C1
Wamba _Dem. Rep. of the Congo_ 2°10N 27°57E **54** B2

Wamba _Kenya_ 0°58N 37°19E **54** B4
Wamego _U.S.A._ 39°12N 96°18W **80** F5
Wamena _Indonesia_ 4°4S 138°57E **37** E9
Wampsville _U.S.A._ 43°4N 75°42W **83** C9
Wamsutter _U.S.A._ 41°40N 107°58W **76** F10
Wamulan _Indonesia_ 3°27S 126°7E **37** E7
Wan Xian _China_ 38°47N 115°7E **34** E8
Wana _Pakistan_ 32°20N 69°32E **42** C3
Wanaaring _Australia_ 29°38S 144°9E **63** D3
Wanaka _N.Z._ 44°42S 169°9E **59** F2
Wanaka, L. _N.Z._ 44°33S 169°7E **59** F2
Wanapitei L. _Canada_ 46°45N 80°40W **72** C3
Wandel Sea = McKinley Sea _Arctic_ 82°0N 0°0 **4** A7
Wanderer _Zimbabwe_ 19°36S 30°1E **55** F3
Wandhari _Pakistan_ 27°42N 66°48E **42** F2
Wandoan _Australia_ 26°5S 149°55E **63** D4
Wanfu _China_ 40°8N 122°38E **35** D12
Wang → _Thailand_ 17°8N 99°2E **38** D2
Wang Noi _Thailand_ 14°13N 100°44E **38** E3
Wang Saphung _Thailand_ 17°18N 101°46E **38** D3
Wang Thong _Thailand_ 16°50N 100°26E **38** D3
Wanga _Dem. Rep. of the Congo_ 2°58N 29°12E **54** B2
Wangal _Indonesia_ 6°8S 134°9E **37** F8
Wanganella _Australia_ 35°6S 144°49E **63** F3
Wanganui _N.Z._ 39°56S 175°3E **59** C5
Wangaratta _Australia_ 36°21S 146°19E **63** F4
Wangary _Australia_ 34°35S 135°29E **63** E2
Wangdu _China_ 38°40N 115°7E **34** E8
Wangerooge _Germany_ 53°47N 7°54E **16** B4
Wangiwangi _Indonesia_ 5°22S 123°37E **37** F6
Wangqing _China_ 43°12N 129°42E **35** C15
Wankaner _India_ 22°35N 71°0E **42** H4
Wanless _Canada_ 54°11N 101°21W **71** C8
Wanleweyne _Somali Rep._ 2°37N 44°54E **47** G3
Wanneroo _Australia_ 31°42S 115°46E **61** F2
Wanning _China_ 18°48N 110°22E **38** C8
Wanon Niwat _Thailand_ 17°38N 103°46E **38** D4
Wanqinsha _China_ 22°43N 113°33E **33** F10
Wanquan _China_ 40°50N 114°40E **34** D8
Wanrong _China_ 35°25N 110°50E **34** G6
Wanshan Qundao _China_ 21°57N 113°45E **33** G10
Wantage _U.K._ 51°35N 1°25W **13** F6
Wanxian _China_ 30°42N 108°20E **32** C5
Wanzai _China_ 22°12N 113°31E **33** G10
Wapakoneta _U.S.A._ 40°34N 84°12W **81** E11
Wapato _U.S.A._ 46°27N 120°25W **76** C3
Wapawekka L. _Canada_ 54°55N 104°40W **71** C8
Wapikopa L. _Canada_ 52°56N 87°53W **72** B2
Wapiti → _Canada_ 55°5N 118°18W **70** B5
Wappingers Falls _U.S.A._ 41°36N 73°55W **83** E11
Wapsipinicon → _U.S.A._ 41°44N 90°19W **80** E8
Wapusk △ _Canada_ 57°46N 93°22W **71** B10
Warangal _India_ 17°58N 79°35E **40** L11
Waraseoni _India_ 21°45N 80°2E **43** J9
Waratah _Australia_ 41°30S 145°30E **63** G4
Waratah B. _Australia_ 38°54S 146°5E **63** F4
Warburton _Vic., Australia_ 37°47S 145°42E **63** F4
Warburton _W. Austral., Australia_ 26°8S 126°35E **61** E4
Warburton → _Australia_ 28°4S 137°28E **63** D2
Warburton Ra. _Australia_ 25°55S 126°28E **61** E4
Ward _N.Z._ 41°49S 174°11E **59** D5
Ward → _Australia_ 26°28S 146°6E **63** D4
Ward Mt. _U.S.A._ 37°12N 118°54W **78** H8
Warden _S. Africa_ 27°50S 29°0E **57** D4
Wardha _India_ 20°45N 78°39E **40** J11
Wardha → _India_ 19°57N 79°11E **40** K11
Wardsville _Canada_ 42°39N 81°45W **82** D3
Ware _U.K._ 51°49N 0°0 **13** F8
Ware _U.S.A._ 42°16N 72°14W **83** D12
Waregem _Belgium_ 50°53N 3°27E **15** D3
Wareham _U.S.A._ 41°46N 70°43W **83** E14
Waremme _Belgium_ 50°43N 5°15E **15** D5
Warialda _Australia_ 29°29S 150°33E **63** D5
Wariap _Indonesia_ 1°30S 134°5E **37** E8
Warin Chamrap _Thailand_ 15°12N 104°53E **38** E5
Warkopi _Indonesia_ 1°12S 134°9E **37** E8
Warm Springs _U.S.A._ 38°10N 116°20W **77** G5
Warman _Canada_ 52°19N 106°30W **71** C7
Warmbad = Bela Bela _S. Africa_ 24°51S 28°19E **57** C4
Warmbad _Namibia_ 28°25S 18°42E **56** D2
Warminster _U.K._ 51°12N 2°10W **13** F5
Warminster _U.S.A._ 40°12N 75°6W **83** F9
Warmun _Australia_ 17°2S 128°12E **60** C4
Warner Mts. _U.S.A._ 41°40N 120°15W **76** F3
Warner Robins _U.S.A._ 32°37N 83°36W **85** E13
Waroona _Australia_ 32°50S 115°58E **61** F2
Warracknabeal _Australia_ 36°9S 142°26E **63** F3
Warragul _Australia_ 38°10S 145°58E **63** F4
Warrego → _Australia_ 30°24S 145°21E **63** E4
Warrego Ra. _Australia_ 24°58S 146°0E **62** C4
Warren _Australia_ 31°42S 147°51E **63** E4
Warren _Ark., U.S.A._ 33°37N 92°4W **84** E8
Warren _Mich., U.S.A._ 42°28N 83°1W **81** D12
Warren _Minn., U.S.A._ 48°12N 96°46W **80** A5
Warren _Ohio, U.S.A._ 41°14N 80°49W **82** E4
Warren _Pa., U.S.A._ 41°51N 79°9W **82** E5
Warrenpoint _U.K._ 54°6N 6°15W **10** B5
Warrensburg _Mo., U.S.A._ 38°46N 93°44W **80** F7
Warrensburg _N.Y., U.S.A._ 43°29N 73°46W **83** C11
Warrenton _S. Africa_ 28°9S 24°47E **56** D3
Warrenton _U.S.A._ 46°10N 123°56W **78** D3
Warri _Nigeria_ 5°30N 5°41E **50** G7
Warrina _Australia_ 28°12S 135°50E **63** D2
Warrington □ _U.K._ 53°24N 2°35W **12** D5
Warrington _U.S.A._ 30°23N 87°17W **85** F11

Warrington □ _U.K._ 53°24N 2°35W **12** D5
Warrnambool _Australia_ 38°25S 142°30E **63** F3
Warroad _U.S.A._ 48°54N 95°19W **80** A6
Warruwi _Australia_ 11°36S 133°20E **62** A1
Warsa _Indonesia_ 0°47S 135°55E **37** E9
Warsak Dam _Pakistan_ 34°11N 71°19E **42** B4
Warsaw = Warszawa _Poland_ 52°14N 21°0E **17** B11
Warsaw _Ind., U.S.A._ 41°14N 85°51W **81** E11
Warsaw _N.Y., U.S.A._ 42°45N 78°8W **82** D6
Warsaw _Ohio, U.S.A._ 40°20N 82°0W **82** F3
Warszawa _Poland_ 52°14N 21°0E **17** B11
Warta → _Poland_ 52°35N 14°39E **16** B8
Warthe = Warta → _Poland_ 52°35N 14°39E **16** B8
Waru _Indonesia_ 3°30S 130°36E **37** E8
Warwick _Australia_ 28°10S 152°1E **63** D5
Warwick _U.K._ 52°18N 1°35W **13** E6
Warwick _N.Y., U.S.A._ 41°16N 74°22W **83** E10
Warwick _R.I., U.S.A._ 41°42N 71°28W **83** E13
Warwickshire □ _U.K._ 52°14N 1°38W **13** E6
Wasaga Beach _Canada_ 44°31N 80°1W **82** B4
Wasagaming _Canada_ 50°39N 99°58W **71** C9
Wasatch Ra. _U.S.A._ 40°0N 111°30W **76** F8
Wasbank _S. Africa_ 28°15S 30°9E **57** D5
Wasco _Calif., U.S.A._ 35°36N 119°20W **79** K7
Wasco _Oreg., U.S.A._ 45°36N 120°42W **76** D3
Waseca _U.S.A._ 44°5N 93°30W **80** C7
Wasekamio L. _Canada_ 56°45N 108°45W **71** B7
Wash, The _U.K._ 52°58N 0°20E **12** E8
Washago _Canada_ 44°45N 79°20W **82** B5
Washburn _N. Dak., U.S.A._ 47°17N 101°2W **80** B3
Washburn _Wis., U.S.A._ 46°40N 90°54W **80** B8
Washim _India_ 20°3N 77°0E **40** J10
Washington _U.K._ 54°55N 1°30W **12** C6
Washington _D.C., U.S.A._ 38°53N 77°2W **81** F15
Washington _Ga., U.S.A._ 33°44N 82°44W **85** E13
Washington _Ind., U.S.A._ 38°40N 87°10W **80** F10
Washington _Iowa, U.S.A._ 41°18N 91°42W **80** E8
Washington _Mo., U.S.A._ 38°33N 91°1W **80** F8
Washington _N.C., U.S.A._ 35°33N 77°3W **85** D16
Washington _N.J., U.S.A._ 40°46N 74°59W **83** F10
Washington _Pa., U.S.A._ 40°10N 80°15W **82** F4
Washington _Utah, U.S.A._ 37°8N 113°31W **77** H7
Washington □ _U.S.A._ 47°30N 120°30W **76** C3
Washington, Mt. _U.S.A._ 44°16N 71°18W **83** B13
Washington Court House _U.S.A._ 39°32N 83°26W **81** F12
Washington I. _U.S.A._ 45°23N 86°54W **80** C10
Washougal _U.S.A._ 45°35N 122°21W **78** E4
Washpool △ _Australia_ 29°22S 152°20E **63** D5
Wasian _Indonesia_ 1°47S 133°19E **37** E8
Wasilla _U.S.A._ 61°35N 149°26W **68** C5
Wasior _Indonesia_ 2°43S 134°30E **37** E8
Wāsiṭ □ _Iraq_ 32°50N 45°54E **44** C5
Waskaganish _Canada_ 51°30N 78°40W **72** B4
Waskaiowaka L. _Canada_ 56°33N 96°23W **71** B9
Waskesiu Lake _Canada_ 53°55N 106°5W **71** C7
Wasserkuppe _Germany_ 50°29N 9°55E **16** C5
Waswanipi _Canada_ 49°40N 76°29W **72** C4
Waswanipi, L. _Canada_ 49°35N 76°40W **72** C4
Watampone _Indonesia_ 4°29S 120°25E **37** E6
Watamu _Kenya_ 3°23S 40°0E **54** C5
Watarrka △ _Australia_ 24°20S 131°30E **60** D5
Water Park Pt. _Australia_ 22°56S 150°47E **62** C5
Water Valley _U.S.A._ 34°10N 89°38W **85** D10
Waterberg Plateau △ _Namibia_ 20°25S 17°18E **56** C2
Waterberge _S. Africa_ 24°10S 28°0E **57** C4
Waterbury _Conn., U.S.A._ 41°33N 73°3W **83** E11
Waterbury _Vt., U.S.A._ 44°20N 72°46W **83** B12
Waterbury L. _Canada_ 58°10N 104°22W **71** B8
Waterdown _Canada_ 43°20N 79°53W **82** C5
Waterford _Canada_ 42°56N 80°17W **82** D4
Waterford _Ireland_ 52°15N 7°8W **10** D4
Waterford _Calif., U.S.A._ 37°38N 120°46W **78** H6
Waterford _Pa., U.S.A._ 41°57N 79°59W **82** E5
Waterford □ _Ireland_ 52°10N 7°40W **10** D4
Waterford Harbour _Ireland_ 52°8N 6°58W **10** D5
Waterhen L. _Canada_ 52°10N 99°40W **71** C9
Waterloo _Belgium_ 50°43N 4°25E **15** D4
Waterloo _Ont., Canada_ 43°30N 80°32W **82** C4
Waterloo _Qué., Canada_ 45°22N 72°32W **83** A12
Waterloo _Ill., U.S.A._ 38°20N 90°9W **80** F8
Waterloo _Iowa, U.S.A._ 42°30N 92°21W **80** D7
Waterloo _N.Y., U.S.A._ 42°54N 76°52W **82** D7
Watersmeet _U.S.A._ 46°16N 89°11W **80** B9
Waterton Lakes △ _Canada_ 48°45N 115°0W **70** D6
Watertown _Conn., U.S.A._ 41°36N 73°7W **83** E11
Watertown _N.Y., U.S.A._ 43°59N 75°55W **83** C9
Watertown _S. Dak., U.S.A._ 44°54N 97°7W **80** C5
Watertown _Wis., U.S.A._ 43°12N 88°43W **80** D9
Waterval-Boven _S. Africa_ 25°40S 30°18E **57** D5
Waterville _Canada_ 45°16N 71°54W **83** A13
Waterville _Maine, U.S.A._ 44°33N 69°38W **81** C19
Waterville _N.Y., U.S.A._ 42°56N 75°23W **83** D9
Waterville _Pa., U.S.A._ 41°19N 77°21W **82** E7
Waterville _Wash., U.S.A._ 47°39N 120°4W **76** C3
Watford _Canada_ 42°57N 81°53W **82** D3
Watford _U.K._ 51°40N 0°24W **13** F7

Watford City _U.S.A._ 47°48N 103°17W **80** B2
Wathaman → _Canada_ 57°16N 102°59W **71** B8
Wathaman L. _Canada_ 56°58N 103°44W **71** B8
Watheroo _Australia_ 30°15S 116°5E **61** F2
Watheroo △ _Australia_ 30°19S 115°48E **61** F2
Wating _China_ 35°40N 106°38E **34** G4
Watkins Glen _U.S.A._ 42°23N 76°52W **82** D8
Watling I. = San Salvador I. _Bahamas_ 24°0N 74°40W **89** B5
Watonga _U.S.A._ 35°51N 98°25W **84** D5
Watrous _Canada_ 51°40N 105°25W **71** C7
Watrous _U.S.A._ 35°48N 104°59W **77** J11
Watsa _Dem. Rep. of the Congo_ 3°4N 29°30E **54** B2
Watseka _U.S.A._ 40°47N 87°44W **80** E10
Watson _Canada_ 52°10N 104°30W **71** C8
Watson Lake _Canada_ 60°6N 128°49W **70** A3
Watsontown _U.S.A._ 41°5N 76°52W **82** E8
Watsonville _U.S.A._ 36°55N 121°45W **78** J5
Wattiwarriganna Cr. → _Australia_ 28°57S 136°10E **63** D2
Watuata = Batuata _Indonesia_ 6°12S 122°42E **37** F6
Watubela, Kepulauan _Indonesia_ 4°28S 131°35E **37** E8
Watubela Is. = Watubela, Kepulauan _Indonesia_ 4°28S 131°35E **37** E8
Wau = Wâw _Sudan_ 7°45N 28°1E **51** G11
Waubamik _Canada_ 45°27N 80°1W **82** A4
Waubay _U.S.A._ 45°20N 97°18W **80** C5
Wauchope _N.S.W., Australia_ 31°28S 152°45E **63** E5
Wauchope _N. Terr., Australia_ 20°36S 134°15E **62** C1
Wauchula _U.S.A._ 27°33N 81°49W **85** H14
Waukarlycarly, L. _Australia_ 21°18S 121°56E **60** D3
Waukegan _U.S.A._ 42°22N 87°50W **80** D10
Waukesha _U.S.A._ 43°1N 88°14W **80** D9
Waukon _U.S.A._ 43°16N 91°29W **80** D8
Waupaca _U.S.A._ 44°21N 89°5W **80** C9
Waupun _U.S.A._ 43°38N 88°44W **80** D9
Waurika _U.S.A._ 34°10N 98°0W **84** D6
Wausau _U.S.A._ 44°58N 89°38W **80** C9
Wautoma _U.S.A._ 44°4N 89°18W **80** C9
Wauwatosa _U.S.A._ 43°2N 88°0W **80** D9
Wave Hill = Kalkarindji _Australia_ 17°30S 130°47E **60** C5
Wave Rock △ _Australia_ 32°26S 118°53E **61** F2
Waveney → _U.K._ 52°35N 1°39E **13** E9
Waverley _N.Z._ 39°46S 174°37E **59** C5
Waverly _Iowa, U.S.A._ 42°44N 92°29W **80** D7
Waverly _N.Y., U.S.A._ 42°1N 76°32W **83** E8
Wavre _Belgium_ 50°43N 4°38E **15** D4
Wâw _Sudan_ 7°45N 28°1E **51** G11
Wâw al Kabir _Libya_ 25°20N 16°43E **51** C9
Wawa _Canada_ 47°59N 84°47W **72** C3
Wawanesa _Canada_ 49°36N 99°40W **71** D9
Wawona _U.S.A._ 37°32N 119°39W **78** H7
Waxahachie _U.S.A._ 32°24N 96°51W **84** E6
Way, L. _Australia_ 26°45S 120°16E **61** E3
Waycross _U.S.A._ 31°13N 82°21W **85** F13
Wayland _U.S.A._ 42°34N 77°35W **82** D7
Wayne _Nebr., U.S.A._ 42°14N 97°1W **80** D5
Wayne _W. Va., U.S.A._ 38°13N 82°27W **81** F12
Waynesboro _Ga., U.S.A._ 33°6N 82°1W **85** E13
Waynesboro _Miss., U.S.A._ 31°40N 88°39W **85** F10
Waynesboro _Pa., U.S.A._ 39°45N 77°35W **81** F15
Waynesboro _Va., U.S.A._ 38°4N 78°53W **81** F14
Waynesburg _U.S.A._ 39°54N 80°11W **81** F13
Waynesville _U.S.A._ 35°28N 82°58W **85** D13
Waynoka _U.S.A._ 36°35N 98°53W **84** C5
Wazirabad _Pakistan_ 32°30N 74°8E **42** C6
We _Indonesia_ 5°51N 95°18E **36** C1
Weald, The _U.K._ 51°4N 0°20E **13** F8
Wear → _U.K._ 54°55N 1°23W **12** C6
Weatherford _Okla., U.S.A._ 35°32N 98°43W **84** D5
Weatherford _Tex., U.S.A._ 32°46N 97°48W **84** E6
Weaverville _U.S.A._ 40°44N 122°56W **76** F2
Webb City _U.S.A._ 37°9N 94°28W **80** G6
Webequie _Canada_ 52°59N 87°21W **72** B2
Webster _Mass., U.S.A._ 42°3N 71°53W **83** D13
Webster _N.Y., U.S.A._ 43°13N 77°26W **82** C7
Webster _S. Dak., U.S.A._ 45°20N 97°31W **80** C5
Webster City _U.S.A._ 42°28N 93°49W **80** D7
Webster Springs _U.S.A._ 38°29N 80°25W **81** F13
Weda _Indonesia_ 0°21N 127°50E **37** D7
Weda, Teluk _Indonesia_ 0°20N 128°0E **37** D7
Weddell Abyssal Plain _S. Ocean_ 65°0S 20°0W **5** C2
Weddell I. _Falk. Is._ 51°50S 61°0W **96** G4
Weddell Sea _Antarctica_ 72°30S 40°0W **5** D1
Wedderburn _Australia_ 36°26S 143°33E **63** F3
Wedgeport _Canada_ 43°44N 65°59W **73** D6
Wedza _Zimbabwe_ 18°40S 31°33E **55** F3
Wee Waa _Australia_ 30°11S 149°26E **63** E4
Weed _U.S.A._ 41°25N 122°23W **76** F2
Weed Heights _U.S.A._ 38°59N 119°13W **78** G7
Weedsport _U.S.A._ 43°2N 76°33W **83** C8
Weedville _U.S.A._ 41°17N 78°30W **82** E6
Weenen _S. Africa_ 28°48S 30°7E **57** D5
Weert _Neths._ 51°15N 5°43E **15** C5
Wei He → _Hebei, China_ 36°10N 115°45E **34** F8
Wei He → _Shaanxi, China_ 34°38N 110°15E **34** G6
Weichang _China_ 41°58N 117°49E **35** D9
Weichuan _China_ 34°20N 113°59E **34** G7
Weiden _Germany_ 49°41N 12°10E **16** D7
Weifang _China_ 36°44N 119°7E **35** F10
Weihai _China_ 37°30N 122°6E **35** F12
Weimar _Germany_ 50°58N 11°19E **16** C6
Weinan _China_ 34°31N 109°29E **34** G5
Weipa _Australia_ 12°40S 141°50E **62** A3

Weir → _Australia_ 28°20S 149°50E **63** D4
Weir → _Canada_ 56°54N 93°21W **71** B10
Weir River _Canada_ 56°49N 94°6W **71** B10
Weirton _U.S.A._ 40°24N 80°35W **82** F4
Weiser _U.S.A._ 44°15N 116°58W **76** D5
Weishan _China_ 34°47N 117°5E **35** G9
Weiyuan _China_ 35°7N 104°10E **34** G3
Wejherowo _Poland_ 54°35N 18°12E **17** A10
Wekusko L. _Canada_ 54°40N 99°50W **71** C9
Welch _U.S.A._ 37°26N 81°35W **81** G13
Welford △ _Australia_ 25°5S 143°16E **62** C3
Welkom _S. Africa_ 28°0S 26°46E **56** D4
Welland _Canada_ 43°0N 79°15W **82** D5
Welland → _U.K._ 52°51N 0°5W **13** E7
Wellesley Is. _Australia_ 16°42S 139°30E **62** B2
Wellingborough _U.K._ 52°19N 0°41W **13** E7
Wellington _Australia_ 32°35S 148°59E **63** E4
Wellington _Canada_ 43°57N 77°20W **82** C7
Wellington _N.Z._ 41°19S 174°46E **59** D5
Wellington _S. Africa_ 33°38S 19°1E **56** E2
Wellington _Somst., U.K._ 50°58N 3°13W **13** G4
Wellington _Telford & Wrekin, U.K._ 52°42N 2°30W **13** E5
Wellington _Colo., U.S.A._ 40°42N 105°0W **76** F11
Wellington _Kans., U.S.A._ 37°16N 97°24W **80** G5
Wellington _Nev., U.S.A._ 38°45N 119°23W **78** G7
Wellington _Ohio, U.S.A._ 41°10N 82°13W **82** E2
Wellington _Tex., U.S.A._ 34°51N 100°13W **84** D4
Wellington, I. _Chile_ 49°30S 75°0W **96** F2
Wellington, L. _Australia_ 38°6S 147°20E **63** F4
Wellington Chan. _Canada_ 75°0N 93°0W **69** B10
Wells _U.K._ 51°13N 2°39W **13** F5
Wells _Maine, U.S.A._ 43°20N 70°35W **83** C14
Wells _N.Y., U.S.A._ 43°24N 74°17W **83** C10
Wells _Nev., U.S.A._ 41°7N 114°58W **76** F6
Wells, L. _Australia_ 26°44S 123°15E **61** E3
Wells, Mt. _Australia_ 17°25S 127°8E **60** C4
Wells Gray △ _Canada_ 52°30N 120°15W **70** C4
Wells-next-the-Sea _U.K._ 52°57N 0°51E **12** E8
Wells River _U.S.A._ 44°9N 72°4W **83** B12
Wellsboro _U.S.A._ 41°45N 77°18W **82** E7
Wellsburg _U.S.A._ 40°16N 80°37W **82** F4
Wellsville _N.Y., U.S.A._ 42°7N 77°57W **82** D7
Wellsville _Ohio, U.S.A._ 40°36N 80°39W **82** F4
Wellsville _Utah, U.S.A._ 41°38N 111°56W **76** F8
Wellton _U.S.A._ 32°40N 114°8W **77** K6
Wels _Austria_ 48°9N 14°1E **16** D8
Welshpool _U.K._ 52°39N 3°8W **13** E4
Welwyn Garden City _U.K._ 51°48N 0°12W **13** F7
Wem _U.K._ 52°52N 2°44W **12** E5
Wembere → _Tanzania_ 4°10S 34°15E **54** C3
Wemindji _Canada_ 53°0N 78°49W **72** B4
Wemyss _Canada_ 44°52N 76°23W **83** B8
Wen Xian _China_ 34°55N 113°5E **34** G7
Wenatchee _U.S.A._ 47°25N 120°19W **76** C3
Wenchang _China_ 19°38N 110°42E **38** C8
Wenchi _Ghana_ 7°46N 2°8W **50** G5
Wenchow = Wenzhou _China_ 28°0N 120°38E **33** D7
Wenden _U.S.A._ 33°49N 113°33W **79** M13
Wendeng _China_ 37°15N 122°5E **35** F12
Wendesi _Indonesia_ 2°30S 134°17E **37** E8
Wendover _U.S.A._ 40°44N 114°2W **76** F6
Wenlock → _Australia_ 12°2S 141°55E **62** A3
Wenshan _China_ 23°20N 104°18E **32** D5
Wenshang _China_ 35°45N 116°30E **34** G9
Wenshui _China_ 37°26N 112°1E **34** F7
Wensleydale _U.K._ 54°17N 2°0W **12** C6
Wensu _China_ 41°15N 80°10E **32** B3
Wensum → _U.K._ 52°40N 1°15E **12** E8
Wentworth _Australia_ 34°2S 141°54E **63** E3
Wentzel L. _Canada_ 59°2N 114°28W **70** B6
Wenut _Indonesia_ 3°11S 133°19E **37** E8
Wenxi _China_ 35°20N 111°10E **34** G6
Wenxian _China_ 32°43N 104°36E **34** H3
Wenzhou _China_ 28°0N 120°38E **33** D7
Weott _U.S.A._ 40°20N 123°55W **78** F2
Wepener _S. Africa_ 29°42S 27°3E **56** D4
Werda _Botswana_ 25°24S 23°15E **56** D3
Weri _Indonesia_ 3°10S 132°38E **37** E8
Werra → _Germany_ 51°24N 9°39E **16** C5
Werrimull _Australia_ 34°25S 141°38E **63** E3
Werris Creek _Australia_ 31°18S 150°38E **63** E5
Weser → _Germany_ 53°36N 8°28E **16** B5
Wesiri _Indonesia_ 7°30S 126°30E **37** F7
Weslaco _U.S.A._ 26°10N 97°58W **84** H6
Weslemkoon L. _Canada_ 45°2N 77°25W **82** A7
Wesleyville _Canada_ 49°9N 53°33W **73** C9
Wesleyville _U.S.A._ 42°9N 80°1W **82** D4
Wessel, C. _Australia_ 10°59S 136°46E **62** A2
Wessel Is. _Australia_ 11°10S 136°45E **62** A2
Wessington Springs _U.S.A._ 44°5N 98°34W **80** C4
West _U.S.A._ 31°48N 97°6W **84** F6
West → _U.S.A._ 42°52N 72°33W **83** D12
West Allis _U.S.A._ 43°1N 88°0W **80** D9
West Antarctica _Antarctica_ 80°0S 90°0W **5** D15
West Baines → _Australia_ 15°38S 129°59E **60** C4
West Bank ■ _Asia_ 32°6N 35°13E **46** C4
West Bend _U.S.A._ 43°25N 88°11W **80** D9
West Bengal □ _India_ 23°0N 88°0E **43** H13
West Berkshire □ _U.K._ 51°25N 1°17W **13** F6
West Beskids = Západné Beskydy _Europe_ 49°30N 19°0E **17** D10
West Branch _U.S.A._ 44°17N 84°14W **81** C11
West Branch Susquehanna → _U.S.A._ 40°53N 76°48W **83** F8
West Bromwich _U.K._ 52°32N 1°59W **13** E6
West Burra _U.K._ 60°5N 1°21W **11** A7
West Canada Cr. → _U.S.A._ 43°1N 74°58W **83** C10
West Caroline Basin _Pac. Oc._ 4°0N 138°0E **64** G5

West Chazy U.S.A. 44°49N 73°28W **83 B11**
West Chester U.S.A. 39°58N 75°36W **83 G9**
West Coast △ Namibia 21°53S 14°14E **56 C1**
West Coast △ S. Africa 33°13S 18°0E **56 E2**
West Columbia U.S.A. 29°9N 95°39W **84 G7**
West Covina U.S.A. 34°4N 117°54W **79 L9**
West Des Moines U.S.A. 41°35N 93°43W **80 E7**
West Dunbartonshire □
U.K. 55°59N 4°30W **11 F4**
West End Bahamas 26°41N 78°58W **88 A4**
West Falkland Falk. Is. 51°40S 60°0W **96 G4**
West Fargo U.S.A. 46°52N 96°54W **80 B5**
West Fiji Basin Pac. Oc. 17°0S 173°0E **64 J9**
West Fjord = Vestfjorden
Norway 67°55N 14°0E **8 C16**
West Fork Trinity →
U.S.A. 32°48N 96°54W **84 E6**
West Frankfort U.S.A. 37°54N 88°55W **80 G9**
West Grand L. U.S.A. 45°14N 67°51W **81 C20**
West Hartford U.S.A. 41°45N 72°44W **83 E12**
West Haven U.S.A. 41°17N 72°57W **83 E12**
West Hazleton U.S.A. 40°58N 76°0W **83 F9**
West Helena U.S.A. 34°33N 90°38W **85 D9**
West Hurley U.S.A. 41°59N 74°7W **83 E10**
West Ice Shelf Antarctica 67°0S 85°0E **5 C7**
West Indies Cent. Amer. 15°0N 65°0W **89 D7**
West Jordan U.S.A. 40°36N 111°56W **76 F8**
West Lamma Channel
China 22°14N 114°4E **33 G11**
West Linn U.S.A. 45°21N 122°36W **78 E4**
West Lorne Canada 42°36N 81°36W **82 D3**
West Lothian □ U.K. 55°54N 3°36W **11 F5**
West Lunga → Zambia 13°6S 24°39E **55 E1**
West MacDonnell △
Australia 23°38S 132°59E **60 D5**
West Mariana Basin
Pac. Oc. 15°0N 137°0E **64 F5**
West Memphis U.S.A. 35°8N 90°10W **85 D9**
West Midlands □ U.K. 52°26N 2°0W **13 E6**
West Mifflin U.S.A. 40°21N 79°52W **82 F5**
West Milford U.S.A. 41°8N 74°22W **83 E10**
West Milton U.S.A. 41°1N 76°50W **82 E8**
West Monroe U.S.A. 32°31N 92°9W **84 E8**
West Newton U.S.A. 40°14N 79°46W **82 F5**
West Nicholson Zimbabwe 21°2S 29°20E **55 G2**
West Odessa U.S.A. 31°50N 102°30W **84 F3**
West Palm Beach
U.S.A. 26°43N 80°3W **85 H14**
West Plains U.S.A. 36°44N 91°51W **80 G8**
West Point Miss.,
U.S.A. 33°36N 88°39W **85 E10**
West Point N.Y., U.S.A. 41°24N 73°58W **83 E11**
West Point Nebr., U.S.A. 41°51N 96°43W **80 E5**
West Point Va., U.S.A. 37°32N 76°48W **81 G15**
West Point L. U.S.A. 33°8N 85°0W **85 E12**
West Pt. = Ouest, Pte. de l'
Canada 49°52N 64°40W **73 C7**
West Pt. Australia 35°1S 135°56E **63 F2**
West Road → Canada 53°18N 122°53W **70 C4**
West Rutland U.S.A. 43°36N 73°3W **83 C11**
West Schelde = Westerschelde →
Neths. 51°25N 3°25E **15 C3**
West Seneca U.S.A. 42°51N 78°48W **82 D6**
West Siberian Plain Russia 62°0N 75°0E **26 B9**
West Sussex □ U.K. 50°55N 0°30W **13 G7**
West-Terschelling Neths. 53°22N 5°13E **15 A5**
West Valley City U.S.A. 40°42N 111°58W **76 F8**
West Virginia □ U.S.A. 38°45N 80°30W **81 F13**
West-Vlaanderen □
Belgium 51°0N 3°0E **15 D2**
West Walker → U.S.A. 38°54N 119°9W **78 G7**
West Wyalong Australia 33°56S 147°10E **63 E4**
West Yellowstone
U.S.A. 44°40N 111°6W **76 D8**
West Yorkshire □ U.K. 53°45N 1°40W **12 D6**
Westall, Pt. Australia 32°55S 134°4E **63 E1**
Westbrook U.S.A. 43°41N 70°22W **81 D18**
Westbury Australia 41°30S 146°51E **63 G4**
Westby U.S.A. 48°52N 104°3W **76 B11**
Westend U.S.A. 35°42N 117°24W **79 K9**
Westerland Germany 54°54N 8°17E **16 A5**
Westerly U.S.A. 41°22N 71°50W **83 E13**
Western □ Kenya 0°30N 34°30E **54 B3**
Western □ Zambia 15°0S 24°4E **55 F1**
Western Australia □
Australia 25°0S 118°0E **61 E2**
Western Cape □ S. Africa 34°0S 20°0E **56 E3**
Western Dvina = Daugava →
Latvia 57°4N 24°3E **9 H21**
Western Ghats India 14°0N 75°0E **40 N9**
Western Isles □ U.K. 57°30N 7°10W **11 D1**
Western Sahara ■ Africa 25°0N 13°0W **50 D3**
Western Samoa = Samoa ■
Pac. Oc. 14°0S 172°0W **59 b**
Western Sierra Madre = Madre
Occidental, Sierra
Mexico 27°0N 107°0W **86 B3**
Westernport U.S.A. 39°29N 79°3W **81 F14**
Westerschelde → Neths. 51°25N 3°25E **15 C3**
Westerwald Germany 50°38N 7°56E **16 C4**
Westfield Mass., U.S.A. 42°7N 72°45W **83 D12**
Westfield N.Y., U.S.A. 42°20N 79°35W **82 D5**
Westfield Pa., U.S.A. 41°55N 77°32W **82 E7**
Westhill U.K. 57°9N 2°19W **11 D6**
Westhope U.S.A. 48°55N 101°1W **80 A3**
Westland △ N.Z. 43°16S 170°16E **59 E2**
Westland Bight N.Z. 42°55S 170°5E **59 E3**
Westlock Canada 54°9N 113°55W **70 C6**
Westmar Australia 27°55S 149°44E **63 D4**
Westmeath □ Ireland 53°33N 7°34W **10 C4**
Westminster Calif.,
U.S.A. 33°45N 118°0W **79 M8**
Westminster Colo.,
U.S.A. 39°50N 105°2W **76 G11**
Westminster Md.,
U.S.A. 39°34N 76°59W **81 F15**
Westmont U.S.A. 40°19N 78°58W **82 F6**

Westmoreland Barbados 13°13N 59°37W **89 g**
Westmorland U.S.A. 33°2N 115°37W **79 M11**
Weston Oreg., U.S.A. 45°49N 118°26W **76 D4**
Weston W. Va., U.S.A. 39°2N 80°28W **81 F13**
Weston I. Canada 52°33N 79°36W **72 B4**
Weston-super-Mare U.K. 51°21N 2°58W **13 F5**
Westover U.S.A. 40°45N 78°40W **82 F6**
Westport Canada 44°40N 76°25W **83 B8**
Westport Ireland 53°48N 9°31W **10 C2**
Westport N.Z. 41°46S 171°37E **59 D3**
Westport N.Y., U.S.A. 44°11N 73°26W **83 B11**
Westport Oreg., U.S.A. 46°8N 123°23W **78 D3**
Westport Wash., U.S.A. 46°53N 124°6W **78 D2**
Westray Canada 53°36N 101°24W **71 C8**
Westray U.K. 59°18N 3°0W **11 B5**
Westree Canada 47°26N 81°34W **72 C3**
Westville U.S.A. 39°8N 120°42W **78 F6**
Westwood U.S.A. 40°18N 121°0W **76 F3**
Wetar Indonesia 7°48S 126°30E **37 F7**
Wetaskiwin Canada 52°55N 113°24W **70 C6**
Wete Tanzania 5°4S 39°43E **52 F7**
Wetherby U.K. 53°56N 1°23W **12 D6**
Wethersfield U.S.A. 41°42N 72°40W **83 E12**
Wetteren Belgium 51°0N 3°53E **15 D3**
Wetzlar Germany 50°32N 8°31E **16 C5**
Wewoka U.S.A. 35°9N 96°30W **84 D6**
Wexford Ireland 52°20N 6°28W **10 D5**
Wexford □ Ireland 52°20N 6°25W **10 D5**
Wexford Harbour Ireland 52°20N 6°25W **10 D5**
Weyburn Canada 49°40N 103°50W **71 D8**
Weymouth Canada 44°30N 66°1W **73 D6**
Weymouth U.K. 50°37N 2°28W **13 G5**
Weymouth U.S.A. 42°13N 70°58W **83 D14**
Weymouth, C. Australia 12°37S 143°27E **62 A3**
Wha Ti Canada 63°8N 117°16W **68 C8**
Whakaari = White I.
N.Z. 37°30S 177°13E **59 B6**
Whakatane N.Z. 37°57S 177°1E **59 B6**
Whale → Canada 58°15N 67°40W **73 A6**
Whale Cove Canada 62°10N 92°34W **71 A10**
Whales, B. of Antarctica 78°0S 160°0W **5 D12**
Whalsay U.K. 60°22N 0°59W **11 A8**
Whangamata N.Z. 37°12S 175°53E **59 B5**
Whangamomona N.Z. 39°8S 174°44E **59 C5**
Whanganui △ N.Z. 39°17S 174°53E **59 C5**
Whangarei N.Z. 35°43S 174°21E **59 A5**
Whangarei Harb. N.Z. 35°45S 174°28E **59 A5**
Wharekauri = Chatham Is.
Pac. Oc. 44°0S 176°40W **64 M10**
Wharfe → U.K. 53°51N 1°9W **12 D6**
Wharfedale U.K. 54°6N 2°1W **12 C5**
Wharton N.J., U.S.A. 40°54N 74°35W **83 F10**
Wharton Pa., U.S.A. 41°31N 78°1W **82 E6**
Wharton Tex., U.S.A. 29°19N 96°6W **84 G6**
Wharton Basin Ind. Oc. 22°0S 92°0E **64 K11**
Wheatland Calif., U.S.A. 39°1N 121°25W **78 F5**
Wheatland Wyo.,
U.S.A. 42°3N 104°58W **76 E11**
Wheatley Canada 42°6N 82°27W **82 D2**
Wheaton Md., U.S.A. 39°3N 77°3W **81 F15**
Wheaton Minn., U.S.A. 45°48N 96°30W **80 C5**
Wheelbarrow Pk.
U.S.A. 37°26N 116°5W **78 H10**
Wheeler Oreg., U.S.A. 45°41N 123°53W **76 D2**
Wheeler Tex., U.S.A. 35°27N 100°16W **84 D4**
Wheeler → Canada 57°2N 67°13W **73 A6**
Wheeler L. U.S.A. 34°48N 87°23W **85 D11**
Wheeler Pk. N. Mex.,
U.S.A. 36°34N 105°25W **77 H11**
Wheeler Pk. Nev.,
U.S.A. 38°57N 114°15W **76 G6**
Wheeler Ridge U.S.A. 35°0N 118°57W **79 L8**
Wheelersburg U.S.A. 38°44N 82°51W **81 F12**
Wheeling U.S.A. 40°4N 80°43W **82 F4**
Whernside U.K. 54°14N 2°24W **12 C5**
Whiddy I. Ireland 51°41N 9°31W **10 E2**
Whim Creek Australia 20°50S 117°49E **60 D2**
Whiskey Jack L.
Canada 58°23N 101°55W **71 B8**
Whiskeytown-Shasta-Trinity △
U.S.A. 40°45N 122°15W **76 F2**
Whistleduck Cr. →
Australia 20°15S 135°18E **62 C2**
Whistler Canada 50°7N 122°58W **70 C4**
Whitby Canada 43°52N 78°56W **82 C6**
Whitby U.K. 54°29N 0°37W **12 C7**
White → Ark., U.S.A. 33°57N 91°5W **84 E9**
White → Ind., U.S.A. 38°25N 87°45W **80 F10**
White → S. Dak., U.S.A. 43°42N 99°27W **80 D4**
White → Tex., U.S.A. 33°14N 100°56W **84 E4**
White → Utah, U.S.A. 40°4N 109°41W **76 F9**
White → Vt., U.S.A. 43°37N 72°20W **83 C12**
White → Wash., U.S.A. 47°12N 122°15W **78 C4**
White, L. Australia 21°9S 128°56E **60 D4**
White B. Canada 50°0N 56°35W **73 C8**
White Bird U.S.A. 45°46N 116°18W **76 D5**
White Butte U.S.A. 46°23N 103°18W **80 B2**
White City U.S.A. 42°26N 122°51W **76 E2**
White Cliffs Australia 30°50S 143°10E **63 E3**
White Hall U.S.A. 39°26N 90°24W **80 F9**
White Haven U.S.A. 41°4N 75°47W **83 E9**
White Horse, Vale of
U.K. 51°37N 1°30W **13 F6**
White I. N.Z. 37°30S 177°13E **59 B6**
White L. Canada 45°18N 76°31W **83 A8**
White L. U.S.A. 29°44N 92°30W **84 G8**
White Lake Canada 45°21N 76°29W **83 A8**
White Mountain Peak
U.S.A. 37°38N 118°15W **77 H4**
White Mts. Calif.,
U.S.A. 37°30N 118°15W **78 H8**
White Mts. N.H.,
U.S.A. 44°15N 71°15W **83 B13**
White Mts. △ Australia 20°43S 145°12E **62 C4**
White Nile = Nîl el Abyad →
Sudan 15°38N 32°31E **51 E12**
White Otter L. Canada 49°5N 91°55W **72 C1**

White Pass U.S.A. 46°38N 121°24W **78 D5**
White Plains U.S.A. 41°2N 73°46W **83 E11**
White River Canada 48°35N 85°20W **72 C2**
White River S. Africa 25°20S 31°0E **57 D5**
White River U.S.A. 43°34N 100°45W **80 D3**
White Rock Canada 49°2N 122°48W **78 A4**
White Rock U.S.A. 35°50N 106°12W **77 J10**
White Russia = Belarus ■
Europe 53°30N 27°0E **17 B14**
White Sands △ U.S.A. 32°46N 106°20W **77 K10**
White Sea = Beloye More
Russia 66°30N 38°0E **8 C25**
White Sulphur Springs Mont.,
U.S.A. 46°33N 110°54W **76 C8**
White Sulphur Springs W. Va.,
U.S.A. 37°48N 80°18W **81 G13**
White Swan U.S.A. 46°22N 120°44W **78 D6**
Whitecliffs N.Z. 43°26S 171°55E **59 E3**
Whitecourt Canada 54°10N 115°45W **70 C5**
Whiteface Mt. U.S.A. 44°22N 73°54W **83 B11**
Whitefield U.S.A. 44°23N 71°37W **83 B13**
Whitefish U.S.A. 48°25N 114°20W **76 B6**
Whitefish B. U.S.A. 46°40N 84°55W **72 C3**
Whitefish L. Canada 62°41N 106°48W **71 A7**
Whitefish Pt. U.S.A. 46°45N 84°59W **81 B11**
Whitegull, L. = Goélands, L. aux
Canada 55°27N 64°17W **73 A7**
Whitehall Mich., U.S.A. 43°24N 86°21W **80 D10**
Whitehall Mont., U.S.A. 45°52N 112°6W **76 D7**
Whitehall N.Y., U.S.A. 43°33N 73°24W **83 C11**
Whitehall Wis., U.S.A. 44°22N 91°19W **80 C8**
Whitehaven U.K. 54°33N 3°35W **12 C4**
Whitehorse Canada 60°43N 135°3W **70 A1**
Whitemark Australia 40°7S 148°3E **63 G4**
Whiteriver U.S.A. 33°50N 109°58W **77 K9**
Whitesand → Canada 60°9N 115°45W **70 A5**
Whitesands S. Africa 34°23S 20°50E **56 E3**
Whitesboro N.Y., U.S.A. 43°7N 75°18W **83 C9**
Whitesboro Tex., U.S.A. 33°39N 96°54W **84 E6**
Whiteshell △ Canada 50°0N 95°40W **71 D9**
Whiteville U.S.A. 34°20N 78°42W **85 D15**
Whitewater U.S.A. 42°50N 88°44W **80 D9**
Whitewater Baldy
U.S.A. 33°20N 108°39W **77 K9**
Whitewater L. Canada 50°50N 89°10W **72 B2**
Whitewood Australia 21°28S 143°30E **62 C3**
Whitewood Canada 50°20N 102°20W **71 C8**
Whithorn U.K. 54°44N 4°26W **11 G4**
Whitianga N.Z. 36°47S 175°41E **59 B5**
Whitman U.S.A. 42°5N 70°56W **83 D14**
Whitney Canada 45°31N 78°14W **82 A6**
Whitney, Mt. U.S.A. 36°35N 118°18W **78 J8**
Whitney Point U.S.A. 42°20N 75°58W **83 D9**
Whitstable U.K. 51°21N 1°3E **13 F9**
Whitsunday I. Australia 20°15S 149°4E **62 J7**
Whitsunday Islands △
Australia 20°15S 149°0E **62 J7**
Whitsunday Passage
Australia 20°16S 148°51E **62 J6**
Whittier U.S.A. 33°58N 118°2W **79 M8**
Whittlesea Australia 37°27S 145°9E **63 F4**
Wholdaia L. Canada 60°43N 104°20W **71 A8**
Whyalla Australia 33°2S 137°30E **63 E2**
Wiang Kosai △ Thailand 17°54N 99°29E **38 D2**
Wiang Sa Thailand 18°34N 100°45E **38 C3**
Wiarton Canada 44°40N 81°10W **82 B3**
Wiay U.K. 57°24N 7°13W **11 D1**
Wibaux U.S.A. 46°59N 104°11W **76 C11**
Wichian Buri Thailand 15°39N 101°7E **38 E3**
Wichita U.S.A. 37°42N 97°20W **80 G5**
Wichita Falls U.S.A. 33°54N 98°30W **84 E5**
Wick U.K. 58°26N 3°5W **11 C5**
Wickenburg U.S.A. 33°58N 112°44W **77 K7**
Wickepin Australia 32°50S 117°30E **61 F2**
Wickham Australia 20°42S 117°11E **60 D2**
Wickham, C. Australia 39°35S 143°57E **63 F3**
Wickliffe U.S.A. 41°36N 81°28W **82 E3**
Wicklow Ireland 52°59N 6°3W **10 D5**
Wicklow □ Ireland 52°57N 6°25W **10 D5**
Wicklow Hd. Ireland 52°58N 6°0W **10 D6**
Wicklow Mts. Ireland 52°58N 6°26W **10 C5**
Wicklow Mts. △ Ireland 53°6N 6°21W **10 C5**
Widgeegoara Cr. →
Australia 28°51S 146°34E **63 D4**
Widgiemooltha
Australia 31°30S 121°34E **61 F3**
Widnes U.K. 53°23N 2°45W **12 D5**
Wieluń Poland 51°15N 18°34E **17 C10**
Wien Austria 48°12N 16°22E **16 D9**
Wiener Neustadt Austria 47°49N 16°16E **16 E9**
Wiesbaden Germany 50°4N 8°14E **16 C5**
Wigan U.K. 53°33N 2°38W **12 D5**
Wiggins Colo., U.S.A. 40°14N 104°4W **76 F11**
Wiggins Miss., U.S.A. 30°51N 89°8W **85 F10**
Wight, I. of U.K. 50°41N 1°17W **13 G6**
Wigston U.K. 52°35N 1°6W **13 E6**
Wigton U.K. 54°50N 3°10W **12 C4**
Wigtown U.K. 54°53N 4°27W **11 G4**
Wigtown B. U.K. 54°46N 4°15W **11 G4**
Wilber U.S.A. 40°29N 96°58W **80 E6**
Wilberforce Canada 45°2N 78°13W **82 A6**
Wilberforce, C. Australia 11°54S 136°35E **62 A2**
Wilburton U.S.A. 34°55N 95°19W **84 D7**
Wilcannia Australia 31°30S 143°26E **63 E3**
Wilcox U.S.A. 41°35N 78°41W **82 E6**
Wildrose U.S.A. 36°14N 117°11W **79 J9**
Wildspitze Austria 46°53N 10°53E **16 E6**
Wilge → S. Africa 27°3S 28°20E **57 D4**
Wilhelm II Coast Antarctica 68°0S 90°0E **5 C7**
Wilhelm, Mt. Papua N. G. see below
Wilhelmshaven Germany 53°31N 8°7E **16 B5**
Wilhelmstal Namibia 21°58S 16°21E **56 C2**
Wilkes-Barre U.S.A. 41°15N 75°53W **83 E9**
Wilkes Land Antarctica 69°0S 120°0E **5 D9**
Wilkie Canada 52°27N 108°42W **71 C7**
Wilkinsburg U.S.A. 40°26N 79°52W **82 F5**
Wilkinson Lakes
Australia 29°40S 132°39E **61 E5**

Willandra Creek →
Australia 33°22S 145°52E **63 E4**
Willapa B. U.S.A. 46°40N 124°0W **76 C1**
Willapa Hills U.S.A. 46°35N 123°25W **78 D3**
Willard U.S.A. 41°3N 82°44W **82 E2**
Willcox U.S.A. 32°15N 109°50W **77 K9**
Willemstad Neth. Ant. 12°5N 68°55W **89 D6**
William → Canada 59°8N 109°19W **71 B7**
William 'Bill' Dannelly Res.
U.S.A. 32°6N 87°24W **85 E11**
William Creek Australia 28°58S 136°22E **63 D2**
Williams Australia 33°2S 116°52E **61 F2**
Williams Ariz., U.S.A. 35°15N 112°11W **77 J7**
Williams Calif., U.S.A. 39°9N 122°9W **78 F4**
Williams Harbour
Canada 52°33N 55°47W **73 B8**
Williams Lake Canada 52°10N 122°10W **70 C4**
Williamsburg Ky.,
U.S.A. 36°44N 84°10W **81 G11**
Williamsburg Pa.,
U.S.A. 40°28N 78°12W **82 F6**
Williamsburg Va.,
U.S.A. 37°16N 76°43W **81 G15**
Williamson N.Y., U.S.A. 43°14N 77°11W **82 C7**
Williamson W. Va.,
U.S.A. 37°41N 82°17W **81 G12**
Williamsport U.S.A. 41°15N 77°1W **82 E7**
Williamston U.S.A. 35°51N 77°4W **85 D16**
Williamstown Australia 37°51S 144°52E **63 F3**
Williamstown Ky.,
U.S.A. 38°38N 84°34W **81 F11**
Williamstown Mass.,
U.S.A. 42°43N 73°12W **83 D11**
Williamstown N.Y.,
U.S.A. 43°26N 75°53W **83 C9**
Willimantic U.S.A. 41°43N 72°13W **83 E12**
Willingboro U.S.A. 40°3N 74°54W **81 E16**
Williston S. Africa 31°20S 20°53E **56 E3**
Williston Fla., U.S.A. 29°23N 82°27W **85 G13**
Williston N. Dak., U.S.A. 48°9N 103°37W **80 A2**
Williston L. Canada 56°0N 124°0W **70 B4**
Willits U.S.A. 39°25N 123°21W **76 G2**
Willmar U.S.A. 45°7N 95°3W **80 C6**
Willmore Wilderness △
Canada 53°45N 119°30W **70 C5**
Willoughby U.S.A. 41°39N 81°24W **82 E3**
Willow Bunch Canada 49°20N 105°35W **71 D7**
Willow L. Canada 62°10N 119°8W **70 A5**
Willow Wall, The China 42°10N 122°0E **35 C12**
Willowick U.S.A. 41°38N 81°28W **82 E3**
Willowlake → Canada 62°42N 123°8W **70 A4**
Willowmore S. Africa 33°15S 23°30E **56 E3**
Willows U.S.A. 39°31N 122°12W **78 F4**
Willowvale = Gatyana
S. Africa 32°16S 28°31E **57 E4**
Wills, L. Australia 21°25S 128°51E **60 D4**
Wills Cr. → Australia 22°43S 140°2E **62 C3**
Willsboro U.S.A. 44°21N 73°24W **83 B11**
Willunga Australia 35°15S 138°30E **63 F2**
Wilmette U.S.A. 42°4N 87°42W **80 D10**
Wilmington Australia 32°39S 138°7E **63 E2**
Wilmington Del.,
U.S.A. 39°45N 75°33W **81 F16**
Wilmington N.C.,
U.S.A. 34°14N 77°55W **85 D16**
Wilmington Ohio,
U.S.A. 39°27N 83°50W **81 F12**
Wilmington Vt., U.S.A. 42°52N 72°52W **83 D12**
Wilpena Cr. →
Australia 31°25S 139°29E **63 E2**
Wilsall U.S.A. 45°59N 110°38W **76 D8**
Wilson N.C., U.S.A. 35°44N 77°55W **85 D16**
Wilson N.Y., U.S.A. 43°19N 78°50W **82 C6**
Wilson Pa., U.S.A. 40°41N 75°15W **83 F9**
Wilson → Australia 16°48S 128°16E **60 C4**
Wilson Bluff Australia 31°41S 129°0E **61 F4**
Wilson Inlet Australia 35°0S 117°22E **61 G2**
Wilsons Promontory
Australia 38°59S 146°23E **63 F4**
Wilton U.S.A. 47°10N 100°47W **80 B3**
Wilton → Australia 14°45S 134°33E **62 A1**
Wiltshire □ U.K. 51°18N 1°53W **13 F6**
Wiltz Lux. 49°57N 5°55E **15 E5**
Wiluna Australia 26°36S 120°14E **61 E3**
Wimborne Minster U.K. 50°48N 1°59W **13 G6**
Wimmera → Australia 36°8S 141°56E **63 F3**
Winam G. Kenya 0°20S 34°15E **54 C3**
Winburg S. Africa 28°30S 27°2E **56 D4**
Winchendon U.S.A. 42°41N 72°3W **83 D12**
Winchester U.K. 51°4N 1°18W **13 F6**
Winchester Conn.,
U.S.A. 41°53N 73°9W **83 E11**
Winchester Idaho,
U.S.A. 46°14N 116°38W **76 C5**
Winchester Ind., U.S.A. 40°10N 84°59W **81 E11**
Winchester Ky., U.S.A. 37°59N 84°11W **81 G11**
Winchester N.H.,
U.S.A. 42°46N 72°23W **83 D12**
Winchester Nev., U.S.A. 36°7N 115°7W **79 J11**
Winchester Tenn.,
U.S.A. 35°11N 86°7W **85 D11**
Winchester Va., U.S.A. 39°11N 78°10W **81 F15**
Wind → U.S.A. 43°12N 108°12W **76 E9**
Wind Cave △ U.S.A. 43°32N 103°17W **80 D2**
Wind River Range
U.S.A. 43°0N 109°30W **76 E9**
Windau = Ventspils
Latvia 57°25N 21°32E **9 H19**
Windber U.S.A. 40°14N 78°50W **82 F6**
Winder U.S.A. 34°0N 83°45W **85 D13**
Windhoek Namibia 22°35S 17°4E **56 C2**
Windia Gorge △
Australia 17°51S 125°0E **60 C3**
Windom U.S.A. 43°52N 95°7W **80 D6**
Windorah Australia 25°24S 142°36E **62 D3**

Window Rock U.S.A. 35°41N 109°3W **77 J9**
Windrush → U.K. 51°43N 1°24W **13 F6**
Windsor Australia 33°37S 150°50E **63 E5**
Windsor N.S., Canada 44°59N 64°5W **73 D7**
Windsor Ont., Canada 42°18N 83°0W **82 D2**
Windsor U.K. 51°29N 0°36W **13 F7**
Windsor Calif., U.S.A. 38°33N 122°49W **78 G4**
Windsor Colo., U.S.A. 40°29N 104°54W **76 F11**
Windsor Conn., U.S.A. 41°50N 72°39W **83 E12**
Windsor Mo., U.S.A. 38°32N 93°31W **80 F7**
Windsor N.Y., U.S.A. 42°5N 75°37W **83 D9**
Windsor Vt., U.S.A. 43°29N 72°24W **83 C12**
Windsor & Maidenhead □
U.K. 51°29N 0°40W **13 F7**
Windsorton S. Africa 28°16S 24°44E **56 D3**
Windward Is. W. Indies 13°0N 61°0W **89 D7**
Windward Passage = Vientos,
Paso de los Caribbean 20°0N 74°0W **89 C5**
Winefred L. Canada 55°30N 110°30W **71 B6**
Winfield U.S.A. 37°15N 96°59W **80 G5**
Wingate Mts. Australia 14°25S 130°40E **60 B5**
Wingham Australia 31°48S 152°22E **63 E5**
Wingham Canada 43°55N 81°20W **82 C3**
Winisk → Canada 55°17N 85°5W **72 A2**
Winisk L. Canada 52°55N 87°22W **72 B2**
Wink U.S.A. 31°45N 103°9W **84 F3**
Winkler Canada 49°10N 97°56W **71 D9**
Winlock U.S.A. 46°30N 122°56W **78 D4**
Winneba Ghana 5°25N 0°36W **50 G5**
Winnebago, L. U.S.A. 44°0N 88°26W **80 D9**
Winnecke Cr. →
Australia 18°35S 131°34E **60 C5**
Winnemucca U.S.A. 40°58N 117°44W **76 F5**
Winnemucca L. U.S.A. 40°7N 119°21W **76 F4**
Winner U.S.A. 43°22N 99°52W **80 D4**
Winnett U.S.A. 47°0N 108°21W **76 C9**
Winnfield U.S.A. 31°56N 92°38W **84 F8**
Winnibigoshish, L.
U.S.A. 47°27N 94°13W **80 B6**
Winnipeg Canada 49°54N 97°9W **71 D9**
Winnipeg → Canada 50°38N 96°19W **71 C9**
Winnipeg, L. Canada 52°0N 97°0W **71 C9**
Winnipeg Beach Canada 50°30N 96°58W **71 C9**
Winnipegosis Canada 51°39N 99°55W **71 C9**
Winnipegosis L. Canada 52°30N 100°0W **71 C9**
Winnipesaukee, L.
U.S.A. 43°38N 71°21W **83 C13**
Winnisquam L. U.S.A. 43°33N 71°31W **83 C13**
Winnsboro La., U.S.A. 32°10N 91°43W **84 E9**
Winnsboro S.C., U.S.A. 34°23N 81°5W **85 D14**
Winnsboro Tex., U.S.A. 32°58N 95°17W **84 E7**
Winokapau, L. Canada 53°15N 62°50W **73 B7**
Winona Minn., U.S.A. 44°3N 91°39W **80 C8**
Winona Miss., U.S.A. 33°29N 89°44W **85 E10**
Winooski U.S.A. 44°29N 73°11W **83 B11**
Winooski → U.S.A. 44°32N 73°17W **83 B11**
Winschoten Neths. 53°9N 7°3E **15 A7**
Winsford U.K. 53°12N 2°31W **12 D5**
Winslow = Bainbridge Island
U.S.A. 47°38N 122°32W **78 C4**
Winslow U.S.A. 35°2N 110°42W **77 J8**
Winsted U.S.A. 41°55N 73°4W **83 E11**
Winston-Salem U.S.A. 36°6N 80°15W **85 C14**
Winter Garden U.S.A. 28°34N 81°35W **85 G14**
Winter Haven U.S.A. 28°1N 81°44W **85 G14**
Winter Park U.S.A. 28°36N 81°20W **85 G14**
Winterhaven U.S.A. 32°44N 114°38W **79 N12**
Winters U.S.A. 38°32N 121°58W **78 G5**
Winterset U.S.A. 41°20N 94°1W **80 E6**
Wintersville U.S.A. 40°23N 80°42W **82 F4**
Winterswijk Neths. 51°58N 6°43E **15 C6**
Winterthur Switz. 47°30N 8°44E **20 C8**
Winthrop U.S.A. 48°28N 120°10W **76 B3**
Winton Australia 22°24S 143°3E **62 C3**
Winton N.Z. 46°8S 168°20E **59 G2**
Wirrulla Australia 32°24S 134°31E **63 E1**
Wisbech U.K. 52°41N 0°9E **13 E8**
Wisconsin □ U.S.A. 44°45N 89°30W **80 C9**
Wisconsin → U.S.A. 43°0N 91°15W **80 D8**
Wisconsin Rapids
U.S.A. 44°23N 89°49W **80 C9**
Wisdom U.S.A. 45°37N 113°27W **76 D7**
Wishaw U.K. 55°46N 3°54W **11 F5**
Wishek U.S.A. 46°16N 99°33W **80 B4**
Wisła → Poland 54°22N 18°55E **17 A10**
Wismar Germany 53°54N 11°29E **16 B6**
Wisner U.S.A. 41°59N 96°55W **80 E6**
Witbank = eMalahleni
S. Africa 25°51S 29°14E **57 D4**
Witdraai S. Africa 26°58S 20°48E **56 D3**
Witham U.K. 51°48N 0°40E **13 F8**
Witham → U.K. 52°59N 0°2W **12 E7**
Withernsea U.K. 53°44N 0°1E **12 D8**
Witjira △ Australia 26°22S 135°37E **63 D2**
Witless Bay Canada 47°17N 52°50W **73 C9**
Witney U.K. 51°48N 1°28W **13 F6**
Witnossob → Namibia 23°55S 18°45E **56 D3**
Wittenberge Germany 53°0N 11°45E **16 B6**
Wittenoom Australia 22°15S 118°20E **60 D2**
Witu Namibia 2°23S 40°26E **54 C5**
Witvlei Namibia 22°23S 18°32E **56 C2**
Wiwon N. Korea 40°54N 126°3E **35 D14**
Wkra → Poland 52°27N 20°44E **17 B11**
Wlingi Indonesia 8°5S 112°25E **37 H15**
Włocławek Poland 52°40N 19°3E **17 B10**
Włodawa Poland 51°33N 23°31E **17 C13**
Woburn U.S.A. 42°29N 71°9W **83 D13**
Wodian China 32°50N 112°35E **34 H7**
Wodonga Australia 36°5S 146°50E **63 F4**
Wokam Indonesia 5°45S 134°28E **37 F8**
Woking U.K. 51°19N 0°34W **13 F7**
Wokingham □ U.K. 51°24N 0°49W **13 F7**
Wokingham U.K. 51°25N 0°51W **13 F7**
Wolf → Canada 60°17N 132°33W **70 A2**
Wolf Creek U.S.A. 47°0N 112°4W **76 C7**
Wolf L. Canada 60°24N 131°40W **70 A2**
Wolf Point U.S.A. 48°5N 105°39W **76 B11**

Wolfe I. *Canada* 44°N 76°20W **83** B8
Wolfeboro *U.S.A.* 43°35N 71°13W **83** C13
Wolfsberg *Austria* 46°50N 14°52E **16** E8
Wolfsburg *Germany* 52°25N 10°48E **16** B6
Wolin *Poland* 53°50N 14°37E **16** B8
Wollaston, Is. *Chile* 55°40S 67°30W **96** H3
Wollaston L. *Canada* 58°7N 103°10W **71** B8
Wollaston Lake *Canada* 58°3N 103°33W **71** B8
Wollaston Pen. *Canada* 69°30N 115°0W **68** B8
Wollongong *Australia* 34°25S 150°54E **63** E5
Wolmaransstad *S. Africa* 27°12S 25°59E **56** D4
Wolseley *S. Africa* 33°26S 19°7E **56** E2
Wolsey *U.S.A.* 44°25N 98°28W **80** C4
Wolstenholme, C.
Canada 62°35N 77°30W **66** C12
Wolvega *Neths.* 52°52N 6°0E **15** B6
Wolverhampton *U.K.* 52°35N 2°7W **13** E5
Wondai *Australia* 26°20S 151°49E **63** D5
Wongalarroo L. *Australia* 31°32S 144°0E **63** E3
Wongan Hills *Australia* 30°51S 116°37E **61** F2
Wonju *S. Korea* 37°22N 127°58E **35** F14
Wonosari *Indonesia* 7°58S 110°36E **37** G14
Wonosobo *Indonesia* 7°22S 109°54E **37** G13
Wonowon *Canada* 56°44N 121°48W **70** B4
Wonthaggi *Australia* 38°37S 145°37E **63** F4
Wood Buffalo △ *Canada* 59°0N 113°41W **70** B6
Wood Is. *Australia* 16°24S 123°19E **60** C3
Wood L. *Canada* 55°17N 103°17W **71** B8
Woodah, I. *Australia* 13°27S 136°10E **62** A2
Woodbourne *U.S.A.* 41°46N 74°36W **83** E10
Woodbridge *Canada* 43°47N 79°36W **82** C5
Woodbridge *U.K.* 52°6N 1°20E **13** E9
Woodburn *U.S.A.* 45°9N 122°51W **76** D2
Woodenbong *Australia* 28°24S 152°39E **63** D5
Woodend *Australia* 37°20S 144°33E **63** F3
Woodford *Australia* 26°58S 152°47E **63** D5
Woodfords *U.S.A.* 38°47N 119°50W **78** G7
Woodlake *U.S.A.* 36°25N 119°6W **78** J7
Woodland Calif., *U.S.A.* 38°41N 121°46W **78** G5
Woodland Maine, *U.S.A.* 45°9N 67°25W **81** C20
Woodland *Pa., U.S.A.* 41°0N 78°21W **82** F6
Woodland *Wash.,*
U.S.A. 45°54N 122°45W **78** E4
Woodland Caribou △
Canada 51°0N 94°45W **71** C10
Woodlands *Singapore* 1°26N 103°46E **39** d
Woodlands, The *U.S.A.* 30°9N 95°29W **84** F7
Woodonga *Australia* 36°10S 146°50E **63** F4
Woodridge *Canada* 49°20N 96°9W **71** D9
Woodroffe, Mt.
Australia 26°20S 131°45E **61** E5
Woods, L. *Australia* 17°50S 133°30E **62** B1
Woods, L. of the
Canada 49°15N 94°45W **71** D10
Woods Bay *Canada* 45°8N 79°59W **82** A5
Woodstock *Australia* 19°35S 146°50E **62** B4
Woodstock *N.B., Canada* 46°11N 67°37W **73** C6
Woodstock *Ont., Canada* 43°10N 80°45W **82** C4
Woodstock *U.K.* 51°51N 1°20W **13** F6
Woodstock *Ill., U.S.A.* 42°19N 88°27W **80** D9
Woodstock *N.Y., U.S.A.* 42°2N 74°7W **83** D10
Woodstock *Vt., U.S.A.* 43°37N 72°31W **83** C12
Woodsville *U.S.A.* 44°9N 72°2W **83** B13
Woodview *Canada* 44°35N 78°8W **82** B6
Woodville *N.Z.* 40°20S 175°53E **59** D5
Woodville *Miss., U.S.A.* 31°6N 91°18W **84** F9
Woodville *Tex., U.S.A.* 30°47N 94°25W **84** F7
Woodward *U.S.A.* 36°26N 99°24W **84** C5
Woody *U.S.A.* 35°42N 118°50W **79** K8
Woody → *Canada* 52°31N 100°51W **71** C8
Woolacombe *U.K.* 51°10N 4°13W **13** F3
Woolamai, C. *Australia* 38°30S 145°23E **63** F4
Wooler *U.K.* 55°33N 2°1W **12** B5
Woolgoolga *Australia* 30°6S 153°11E **63** E5
Woomera *Australia* 31°5S 136°50E **63** E2
Woonsocket *R.I., U.S.A.* 42°0N 71°31W **83** E13
Woonsocket *S. Dak.,*
U.S.A. 44°3N 98°17W **80** C4
Wooramel → *Australia* 25°47S 114°10E **61** E1
Wooramel Roadhouse
Australia 25°45S 114°17E **61** E1
Wooroonooran △
Australia 16°25S 146°1E **62** B4
Wooster *U.S.A.* 40°48N 81°56W **82** F3
Worcester *S. Africa* 33°39S 19°27E **56** E2
Worcester *U.K.* 52°11N 2°12W **13** E5
Worcester *Mass.,*
U.S.A. 42°16N 71°48W **83** D13
Worcester *N.Y., U.S.A.* 42°36N 74°45W **83** D10
Worcestershire □ *U.K.* 52°13N 2°10W **13** E5
Workington *U.K.* 54°39N 3°33W **12** C4
Worksop *U.K.* 53°18N 1°7W **12** D6
Workum *Neths.* 52°59N 5°26E **15** B5
Worland *U.S.A.* 44°1N 107°57W **76** D10
Worms *Germany* 49°37N 8°21E **16** D5
Worsley *Canada* 56°31N 119°8W **70** B5
Wortham *U.S.A.* 31°47N 96°28W **84** F6
Worthing *Barbados* 13°5N 59°35W **89** g
Worthing *U.K.* 50°49N 0°21W **13** G7
Worthington *Minn.,*
U.S.A. 43°37N 95°36W **80** D6
Worthington *Pa., U.S.A.* 40°50N 79°38W **82** F5
Wosi *Indonesia* 0°15S 128°0E **37** E7
Wote *Kenya* 1°47S 37°38E **54** C4
Wou-han = Wuhan
China 30°31N 114°18E **33** C6
Wousi = Wuxi *China* 31°33N 120°18E **33** C7
Wowoni *Indonesia* 4°5S 123°5E **37** E6
Wrangel I. = Vrangelya, Ostrov
Russia 71°0N 180°0E **29** B18
Wrangell *U.S.A.* 56°28N 132°23W **70** B2
Wrangell Mts. *U.S.A.* 61°30N 142°0W **68** C5
Wrath, C. *U.K.* 58°38N 5°1W **11** C3
Wray *U.S.A.* 40°5N 102°13W **76** F12
Wrekin, The *U.K.* 52°41N 2°32W **13** E5
Wrens *U.S.A.* 33°12N 82°23W **85** E13

Wrexham *U.K.* 53°3N 3°0W **12** D4
Wrexham □ *U.K.* 53°1N 2°58W **12** D5
Wright *Fla., U.S.A.* 30°27N 86°38W **85** F11
Wright *Wyo., U.S.A.* 43°45N 105°28W **76** E11
Wright Pt. *Canada* 43°48N 81°44W **82** C3
Wrightson, Mt. *U.S.A.* 31°42N 110°51W **77** L8
Wrightwood *U.S.A.* 34°22N 117°38W **79** L9
Wrigley *Canada* 63°16N 123°37W **68** C7
Wrocław *Poland* 51°5N 17°5E **17** C9
Września *Poland* 52°21N 17°36E **17** B9
Wu Jiang → *China* 29°40N 107°20E **32** D5
Wu Kau Tang *China* 22°30N 114°14E **33** F11
Wu'an *China* 36°40N 114°15E **34** F8
Wubin *Australia* 30°6S 116°37E **61** F2
Wubu *China* 37°28N 110°42E **34** F6
Wuchang *China* 44°55N 127°5E **35** B14
Wucheng *China* 37°12N 116°20E **34** F9
Wuchuan *China* 41°5N 111°28E **34** D6
Wudi *China* 37°40N 117°35E **35** F9
Wuding He → *China* 37°2N 110°23E **34** F6
Wudinna *Australia* 33°0S 135°22E **63** E2
Wudu *China* 33°22N 104°54E **34** H3
Wuguishan *China* 22°25N 113°25E **33** G9
Wugullar = Beswick
Australia 14°34S 132°53E **60** B5
Wuhai *China* 39°47N 106°52E **32** C5
Wuhan *China* 30°31N 114°18E **33** C6
Wuhe *China* 33°10N 117°50E **35** H9
Wuhsi = Wuxi *China* 31°33N 120°18E **33** C7
Wuhu *China* 31°22N 118°21E **33** C6
Wukari *Nigeria* 7°51N 9°42E **50** G7
Wulajie *China* 44°6N 126°33E **35** B14
Wulanbulang *China* 41°5N 110°55E **34** D6
Wular L. *India* 34°20N 74°30E **43** B6
Wulian *China* 35°40N 119°12E **35** G10
Wuliaru *Indonesia* 7°27S 131°0E **37** F8
Wulumuchi = Ürümqi
China 43°45N 87°45E **32** B3
Wundanyi *Kenya* 3°24S 38°22E **54** C4
Wunnummin L. *Canada* 52°55N 89°10W **72** B2
Wuntho *Burma* 23°55N 95°45E **41** H19
Wupatki △ *U.S.A.* 35°35N 111°20W **77** J8
Wuppertal *Germany* 51°16N 7°12E **16** C4
Wuppertal *S. Africa* 32°13S 19°12E **56** E2
Wuqing *China* 39°23N 117°4E **35** E9
Wurtsboro *U.S.A.* 41°35N 74°29W **83** E10
Würzburg *Germany* 49°46N 9°55E **16** D5
Wushan *China* 34°43N 104°53E **34** G3
Wushi *China* 41°9N 79°13E **32** B2
Wutai *China* 38°40N 113°12E **34** E7
Wuting = Huimin
China 37°27N 117°28E **35** F9
Wutonghaolai *China* 42°50N 120°5E **35** C11
Wutongqiao *China* 29°22N 103°50E **32** D5
Wuwei *China* 37°57N 102°34E **32** C5
Wuxi *China* 31°33N 120°18E **33** C7
Wuxiang *China* 36°49N 112°50E **34** F7
Wuyang *China* 33°25N 113°35E **34** H7
Wuyi *China* 37°46N 115°56E **34** F8
Wuyi Shan *China* 27°0N 117°0E **33** D6
Wuyuan *China* 41°2N 108°20E **34** D5
Wuzhai *China* 38°54N 111°48E **34** E6
Wuzhi Shan *China* 18°45N 109°45E **38** C7
Wuzhong *China* 38°2N 106°12E **34** E4
Wuzhou *China* 23°30N 111°18E **33** D6
Wyaaba Cr. →
Australia 16°27S 141°35E **62** B3
Wyalkatchem *Australia* 31°8S 117°22E **61** F2
Wyalusing *U.S.A.* 41°40N 76°16W **83** E8
Wyandra *Australia* 27°12S 145°56E **63** D4
Wyangala, L. *Australia* 33°54S 149°0E **63** E4
Wyara, L. *Australia* 28°42S 144°14E **63** D3
Wycheproof *Australia* 36°5S 143°17E **63** F3
Wycliffe Well *Australia* 20°48S 134°14E **62** C1
Wye → *U.K.* 51°38N 2°40W **13** F5
Wyemandoo *Australia* 28°28S 118°29E **61** E2
Wymondham *U.K.* 52°35N 1°7E **13** E9
Wymore *U.S.A.* 40°7N 96°40W **80** E6
Wyndham *Australia* 15°33S 128°3E **60** C4
Wyndham *N.Z.* 46°20S 168°51E **59** G2
Wynne *U.S.A.* 35°14N 90°47W **84** D9
Wynyard *Australia* 41°5S 145°44E **63** G4
Wynyard *Canada* 51°45N 104°10W **71** C8
Wyola L. *Australia* 29°8S 130°17E **61** E5
Wyoming *Canada* 42°57N 82°7W **82** D2
Wyoming □ *U.S.A.* 43°0N 107°30W **76** E10
Wyomissing *U.S.A.* 40°20N 75°59W **83** F9
Wyong *Australia* 33°14S 151°24E **63** E5
Wytheville *U.S.A.* 36°57N 81°5W **81** G13

X

Xaafuun *Somali Rep.* 10°25N 51°16E **47** E5
Xaafuun, Ras *Somali Rep.* 10°27N 51°24E **47** E5
Xaçmaz *Azerbaijan* 41°31N 48°42E **19** F8
Xai-Xai *Mozam.* 25°6S 33°31E **57** D5
Xainza *China* 30°58N 88°35E **32** D3
Xalapa *Mexico* 19°32N 96°55W **87** D5
Xangongo *Angola* 16°45S 15°5E **56** B2
Xankändi *Azerbaijan* 39°52N 46°49E **44** B5
Xanthi *Greece* 41°10N 24°58E **23** D11
Xanxerê *Brazil* 26°53S 52°23W **95** B5
Xapuri *Brazil* 10°35S 68°35W **92** F5
Xar Moron He →
China 43°25N 120°35E **35** C11
Xátiva *Spain* 38°59N 0°32W **21** C5
Xau, L. *Botswana* 21°15S 24°44E **56** C3
Xavantina *Brazil* 21°15S 52°48W **95** A5
Xenia *U.S.A.* 39°41N 83°56W **81** F12
Xeropotamos →
Cyprus 34°42N 32°33E **25** E11
Xhora *S. Africa* 31°55S 28°38E **57** E4
Xhumo *Botswana* 21°7S 24°35E **56** C3
Xi Jiang → *China* 22°5N 113°20E **33** D6
Xi Xian *China* 36°41N 110°58E **34** F6

Xia Xian *China* 35°8N 111°12E **34** G6
Xiachengzi *China* 44°40N 130°18E **35** B16
Xiaguan *China* 25°32N 100°16E **32** D5
Xiajin *China* 36°56N 116°0E **34** F9
Xiamen *China* 24°25N 118°4E **33** D6
Xi'an *China* 34°15N 109°0E **34** G5
Xian Xian *China* 38°12N 116°6E **34** E9
Xiang Jiang → *China* 28°55N 112°50E **33** D6
Xiangcheng *Henan,*
China 33°29N 114°52E **34** H8
Xiangcheng *Henan,*
China 33°50N 113°27E **34** H7
Xiangfan *China* 32°2N 112°8E **33** C6
Xianggang = Hong Kong □
China 22°11N 114°14E **33** G11
Xianghuang Qi *China* 42°2N 113°50E **34** C7
Xiangning *China* 35°58N 110°50E **34** G6
Xiangquan *China* 36°30N 113°1E **34** F7
Xiangquan He = Sutlej →
Pakistan 29°23N 71°3E **42** E4
Xiangshui *China* 34°12N 119°33E **35** G10
Xiangtan *China* 27°51N 112°54E **33** D6
Xiao Hinggan Ling *China* 49°0N 127°0E **33** B7
Xiao Xian *China* 34°15N 116°55E **34** G9
Xiaoyi *China* 37°8N 111°48E **34** F6
Xiawa *China* 42°35N 120°38E **35** C11
Xiayi *China* 34°15N 116°10E **34** G9
Xichang *China* 27°51N 102°19E **32** D5
Xichuan *China* 33°0N 111°30E **34** H6
Xieng Khouang *Laos* 19°17N 103°25E **38** C4
Xifei He → *China* 32°45N 116°40E **34** H9
Xifeng *Gansu, China* 35°40N 107°40E **34** G4
Xifeng *Liaoning, China* 42°42N 124°45E **35** C13
Xifengzhen = Xifeng
China 35°40N 107°40E **34** G4
Xigazê *China* 29°5N 88°45E **32** D3
Xihe *China* 34°2N 105°20E **34** G3
Xihua *China* 33°45N 114°30E **34** H8
Xili Shuiku *China* 22°36N 113°57E **33** F10
Xiliao He → *China* 43°32N 123°35E **35** C12
Xilinhot *China* 43°52N 116°2E **34** C9
Ximana *Mozam.* 19°24S 33°58E **55** F3
Xin Xian = Xinzhou
China 38°22N 112°46E **34** E7
Xinavane *Mozam.* 25°2S 32°47E **57** D5
Xinbin *China* 41°40N 125°2E **35** D13
Xincun *China* 38°15N 117°45E **35** E9
Xing Xian *China* 38°27N 111°7E **34** E6
Xing'an *China* 25°38N 110°40E **33** D6
Xingcheng *China* 40°40N 120°45E **35** D11
Xinghe *China* 40°55N 113°55E **34** D7
Xinghua *China* 32°58N 119°48E **35** H10
Xinglong *China* 40°25N 117°30E **35** D9
Xingping *China* 34°20N 108°28E **34** G5
Xingtai *China* 37°3N 114°32E **34** F8
Xingu → *Brazil* 1°30S 51°53W **93** D8
Xingyang *China* 34°45N 112°52E **34** G7
Xinhe *China* 37°30N 115°15E **34** F8
Xining *China* 36°34N 101°40E **32** C5
Xinjiang *China* 35°34N 111°11E **34** G6
Xinjiang Uygur Zizhiqu □
China 42°0N 86°0E **32** C3
Xinjin = Pulandian
China 39°25N 121°58E **35** E11
Xinkai He → *China* 43°32N 123°35E **35** C12
Xinken *China* 22°39N 113°36E **33** F10
Xinle *China* 38°25N 114°40E **34** E8
Xinlitun *China* 42°0N 122°8E **35** D12
Xinmin *China* 41°59N 122°50E **35** D12
Xintai *China* 35°55N 117°45E **35** G9
Xinwan *China* 22°47N 113°40E **33** F10
Xinxiang *China* 35°18N 113°50E **34** G7
Xinzhan *China* 43°50N 127°18E **35** C14
Xinzheng *China* 34°20N 113°45E **34** G7
Xinzhou *Hainan, China* 19°43N 109°17E **38** C7
Xinzhou *Shanxi, China* 38°22N 112°46E **34** E7
Xiongyuecheng *China* 40°12N 122°5E **35** D12
Xiping *Henan, China* 33°22N 114°5E **34** H8
Xiping *Henan, China* 33°25N 111°8E **34** H6
Xique-Xique *Brazil* 10°50S 42°40W **93** F10
Xisha Qundao = Paracel Is.
S. China Sea 15°50N 112°0E **36** A4
Xiuyan *China* 40°18N 123°11E **35** D12
Xixabangma Feng
China 28°20N 85°40E **43** E11
Xixia *China* 33°25N 111°29E **34** H6
Xixiang *China* 33°0N 107°44E **33** F10
Xixón = Gijón *Spain* 43°32N 5°42W **21** A3
Xiyang *China* 37°38N 113°38E **34** F7
Xizang Zizhiqu □ *China* 32°0N 88°0E **32** C3
Xlendi *Malta* 36°1N 14°12E **25** C1
Xochob *Mexico* 19°21N 89°48W **87** D7
Xuan Loc *Vietnam* 10°56N 107°14E **39** G6
Xuanhua *China* 40°40N 115°2E **34** D8
Xuchang *China* 34°2N 113°48E **34** G7
Xun Xian *China* 35°42N 114°33E **34** G8
Xunyang *China* 32°48N 109°22E **34** H5
Xunyi *China* 35°8N 108°20E **34** G5
Xúquer → *Spain* 39°5N 0°10W **21** C5
Xushui *China* 39°2N 115°40E **34** E8
Xuyen Moc *Vietnam* 10°34N 107°25E **39** G6
Xuzhou *China* 34°18N 117°10E **35** G9
Xylophagou *Cyprus* 34°54N 33°51E **25** E12

Y

Ya Xian = Sanya *China* 18°14N 109°29E **38** C7
Yaamba *Australia* 23°8S 150°22E **62** C5
Yaapeet *Australia* 35°45S 142°3E **63** F3
Yablonovyy Khrebet
Russia 53°0N 114°0E **29** D12
Yablonovvy Ra. = Yablonovyy
Khrebet *Russia* 53°0N 114°0E **29** D12
Yabrai Shan *China* 39°40N 103°0E **34** E2
Yabrūd *Syria* 33°58N 36°39E **46** B5

Yabucoa *Puerto Rico* 18°3N 65°53W **89** d
Yacambú △ *Venezuela* 9°42N 69°27W **89** E6
Yacheng *China* 18°22N 109°6E **38** C7
Yacuiba *Bolivia* 22°0S 63°43W **94** A3
Yacuma → *Bolivia* 13°38S 65°23W **92** F5
Yadgir *India* 16°45N 77°5E **40** L10
Yadkin → *U.S.A.* 35°23N 80°4W **85** D14
Yadua *Fiji* 16°49S 178°18E **59** a
Yagasa Cluster *Fiji* 18°57S 178°28W **59** a
Yagodnoye *Russia* 62°33N 149°40E **29** C15
Yahila
Dem. Rep. of the Congo 0°13N 24°28E **54** B1
Yahk *Canada* 49°6N 116°10W **70** D5
Yahuma
Dem. Rep. of the Congo 1°0N 23°10E **52** D4
Yaita *Japan* 36°48N 139°56E **31** F9
Yaiza *Canary Is.* 28°57N 13°46W **24** F6
Yakima *U.S.A.* 46°36N 120°31W **76** C3
Yakima → *U.S.A.* 46°15N 119°14W **76** C4
Yakishiri-Jima *Japan* 44°26N 141°25E **30** B10
Yakobi I. *U.S.A.* 58°0N 136°30W **70** D1
Yakovlevka *Russia* 44°26N 133°28E **30** B6
Yaku-Shima *Japan* 30°20N 130°30E **31** J5
Yakumo *Japan* 42°15N 140°16E **30** C10
Yakutat *U.S.A.* 59°33N 139°44W **68** D6
Yakutia = Sakha □
Russia 66°0N 130°0E **29** C14
Yakutsk *Russia* 62°5N 129°50E **29** C13
Yala *Thailand* 6°33N 101°18E **39** J3
Yalboroo *Australia* 20°50S 148°40E **62** J6
Yale *U.S.A.* 43°8N 82°48W **82** C2
Yalgoo *Australia* 28°16S 116°39E **61** E2
Yalgorup △ *Australia* 32°39S 115°38E **61** F2
Yalinga *C.A.R.* 6°33N 23°10E **52** C4
Yalkabul, Pta. *Mexico* 21°32N 88°37W **87** C7
Yalleroi *Australia* 24°3S 145°42E **62** C4
Yalobusha → *U.S.A.* 33°33N 90°10W **85** E9
Yalong Jiang → *China* 26°40N 101°55E **32** D5
Yalova *Turkey* 40°41N 29°15E **23** D13
Yalta *Ukraine* 44°30N 34°10E **19** F5
Yalu Jiang → *China* 39°55N 124°19E **35** E13
Yam Ha Melah = Dead Sea
Asia 31°30N 35°30E **46** D4
Yam Kinneret *Israel* 32°45N 35°35E **46** C4
Yamada *Japan* 33°33N 130°49E **31** H5
Yamagata *Japan* 38°15N 140°15E **30** E10
Yamagata □ *Japan* 38°30N 140°0E **30** E10
Yamaguchi *Japan* 34°10N 131°32E **31** G5
Yamaguchi □ *Japan* 34°20N 131°40E **31** G5
Yamal, Poluostrov *Russia* 71°0N 70°0E **28** B8
Yamal Pen. = Yamal, Poluostrov
Russia 71°0N 70°0E **28** B8
Yamanashi □ *Japan* 35°40N 138°40E **31** G9
Yamanie Falls △
Australia 18°29S 146°9E **62** B4
Yamantau, Gora *Russia* 54°15N 58°6E **18** D10
Yamato Ridge
Sea of Japan 39°20N 135°0E **30** E7
Yamba *Australia* 29°26S 153°23E **63** D5
Yambarran Ra.
Australia 15°10S 130°25E **60** C5
Yâmbiô *Sudan* 4°35N 28°16E **51** H11
Yambol *Bulgaria* 42°30N 26°30E **23** C12
Yamburg *Russia* 68°21N 77°8E **28** C8
Yamdena *Indonesia* 7°45S 131°20E **37** F8
Yame *Japan* 33°13N 130°35E **31** H5
Yamethin *Burma* 20°29N 96°18E **41** J20
Yamma Yamma, L.
Australia 26°16S 141°20E **63** D3
Yamoussoukro *Ivory C.* 6°49N 5°17W **50** G4
Yampa → *U.S.A.* 40°32N 108°59W **76** F9
Yampi Sd. *Australia* 16°8S 123°38E **60** C3
Yampil *Moldova* 48°15N 28°15E **17** D15
Yampol = Yampil
Moldova 48°15N 28°15E **17** D15
Yamuna → *India* 25°30N 81°53E **43** G9
Yamunanagar *India* 30°7N 77°17E **42** D7
Yamzho Yumco *China* 28°48N 90°35E **32** D4
Yana → *Russia* 71°30N 136°0E **29** B14
Yanagawa *Japan* 33°10N 130°24E **31** H5
Yanai *Japan* 33°58N 132°7E **31** H6
Yan'an *China* 36°35N 109°26E **34** F5
Yanaul *Russia* 56°25N 55°0E **18** C10
Yanco Cr. → *Australia* 35°14S 145°35E **63** F4
Yandicoogina *Australia* 22°49S 119°12E **60** D2
Yandoon *Burma* 17°0N 95°40E **41** L19
Yang Xian *China* 33°15N 107°30E **34** H4
Yang-yang *S. Korea* 38°4N 128°38E **35** E15
Yangambi
Dem. Rep. of the Congo 0°47N 24°24E **54** B1
Yangcheng *China* 35°28N 112°22E **34** G7
Yangch'ü = Taiyuan
China 37°52N 112°33E **34** F7
Yanggao *China* 40°21N 113°55E **34** D7
Yangliuqing *China* 39°2N 117°5E **35** E9
Yangon = Rangoon
Burma 16°45N 96°20E **41** L20
Yangpingguan *China* 32°58N 106°5E **34** H4
Yangquan *China* 37°58N 113°31E **34** F7
Yangtse = Chang Jiang →
China 31°48N 121°10E **33** C7
Yangtze Kiang = Chang Jiang →
China 31°48N 121°10E **33** C7
Yangyuan *China* 40°1N 114°10E **34** D8
Yangzhou *China* 32°21N 119°26E **33** C6
Yanji *China* 42°59N 129°30E **35** C15
Yankton *U.S.A.* 42°53N 97°23W **80** D5
Yanonge
Dem. Rep. of the Congo 0°35N 24°38E **54** B1

Yanqi *China* 42°5N 86°35E **32** B3
Yanqing *China* 40°30N 115°58E **34** D8
Yanshan *China* 38°4N 117°22E **35** E9
Yanshou *China* 45°28N 128°22E **35** B15
Yantai *China* 37°34N 121°22E **35** F11
Yantian *China* 22°35N 114°16E **33** F11
Yanzhou *China* 35°35N 116°49E **34** G9
Yao Noi, Ko *Thailand* 8°7N 98°37E **39** a
Yao Xian *China* 34°55N 108°59E **34** G5
Yao Yai, Ko *Thailand* 8°0N 98°35E **39** a
Yaoundé *Cameroon* 3°50N 11°35E **52** D2
Yaowan *China* 34°15N 118°3E **35** G10
Yap *Pac. Oc.* 9°30N 138°10E **64** G5
Yapen *Indonesia* 1°50S 136°0E **37** E9
Yapen, Selat *Indonesia* 1°20S 136°10E **37** E9
Yapero *Indonesia* 4°59S 137°11E **37** E9
Yappar → *Australia* 18°22S 141°16E **62** B3
Yaqaga *Fiji* 16°35S 178°36E **59** a
Yaqui → *Mexico* 27°37N 110°39W **86** B2
Yar-Sale *Russia* 66°50N 70°50E **28** C8
Yaraka *Australia* 24°53S 144°3E **62** C3
Yaransk *Russia* 57°22N 47°49E **18** C8
Yare → *U.K.* 52°35N 1°38E **13** E9
Yaremcha *Ukraine* 48°27N 24°33E **17** D13
Yarensk *Russia* 62°11N 49°15E **18** B8
Yarí → *Colombia* 0°20S 72°20W **92** D4
Yarkand = Shache
China 38°20N 77°10E **32** C2
Yarkant He → *China* 40°26N 80°59E **32** B3
Yarker *Canada* 44°23N 76°46W **83** B8
Yarkhun → *Pakistan* 36°17N 72°30E **43** A5
Yarlung Ziangbo Jiang =
Brahmaputra →
Asia 23°40N 90°35E **43** H13
Yarmouth *Canada* 43°50N 66°7W **73** D6
Yarmūk → *Syria* 32°42N 35°40E **46** C4
Yaroslavl *Russia* 57°35N 39°55E **18** C6
Yarqa, W. → *Egypt* 30°0N 33°49E **46** F2
Yarra Yarra Lakes
Australia 29°40S 115°45E **61** E2
Yarram *Australia* 38°29S 146°39E **63** F4
Yarraman *Australia* 26°50S 152°0E **63** D5
Yarras *Australia* 31°25S 152°20E **63** E5
Yarrie *Australia* 20°40S 120°12E **60** D3
Yartsevo *Russia* 60°20N 90°0E **29** C10
Yarumal *Colombia* 6°58N 75°24W **92** B3
Yasawa *Fiji* 16°47S 177°31E **59** a
Yasawa Group *Fiji* 17°0S 177°23E **59** a
Yaselda *Belarus* 52°7N 26°28E **17** B14
Yasin *Pakistan* 36°24N 73°23E **43** A5
Yasinski, L. *Canada* 53°16N 77°35W **72** B4
Yasinya *Ukraine* 48°16N 24°21E **17** D13
Yasothon *Thailand* 15°50N 104°10E **38** E5
Yass *Australia* 34°49S 148°54E **63** E4
Yassük *Iran* 30°31N 51°31E **45** D6
Yatağan *Turkey* 37°20N 28°10E **23** F13
Yates Center *U.S.A.* 37°53N 95°44W **80** G6
Yathkyed L. *Canada* 62°40N 98°0W **71** A9
Yatsushiro *Japan* 32°30N 130°40E **31** H5
Yatta Plateau *Kenya* 2°0S 38°0E **54** C4
Yauco *Puerto Rico* 18°2N 66°51W **89** d
Yavari → *Peru* 4°21S 70°2W **92** D4
Yávaros *Mexico* 26°42N 109°31W **86** B3
Yavatmal *India* 20°20N 78°15E **40** J11
Yavne *Israel* 31°52N 34°45E **46** D3
Yavoriv *Ukraine* 49°55N 23°20E **17** D12
Yavorov = Yavoriv
Ukraine 49°55N 23°20E **17** D12
Yawatahama *Japan* 33°27N 132°24E **31** H6
Yawri B. *S. Leone* 8°22N 13°0W **50** G3
Yazd = Sanya *China* 18°14N 109°29E **38** C7
Yazd *Iran* 31°55N 54°27E **45** D7
Yazd □ *Iran* 32°0N 55°0E **45** D7
Yazd-e Khvāst *Iran* 31°31N 52°7E **45** D7
Yazman *Pakistan* 29°8N 71°45E **42** E4
Yazoo → *U.S.A.* 32°22N 90°54W **85** E9
Yazoo City *U.S.A.* 32°51N 90°25W **85** E9
Ybycuí △ *Paraguay* 26°5S 56°46W **94** B4
Ybytyruzú △ *Paraguay* 25°51S 56°11W **95** B4
Ye *Burma* 15°15N 97°15E **38** E1
Ye Xian *China* 33°35N 113°25E **34** H7
Yebyu *Burma* 14°15N 98°13E **38** E2
Yecheng *China* 37°54N 77°26E **32** C2
Yecheon *S. Korea* 36°39N 128°27E **35** F15
Yecla *Spain* 38°35N 1°5W **21** C5
Yécora *Mexico* 28°20N 108°58W **86** B3
Yedintsy = Edineţ
Moldova 48°9N 27°18E **17** D14
Yegros *Paraguay* 26°20S 56°25W **94** B4
Yehbuah *Indonesia* 8°23S 114°45E **37** J17
Yehuda, Midbar *Israel* 31°35N 35°15E **46** D4
Yei *Sudan* 4°9N 30°40E **51** H12
Yekaterinburg *Russia* 56°50N 60°30E **28** D7
Yelarbon *Australia* 28°33S 150°38E **63** D5
Yelets *Russia* 52°40N 38°30E **18** D6
Yelizavetgrad = Kirovohrad
Ukraine 48°35N 32°20E **19** E5
Yelizovo *Russia* 53°11N 158°23E **29** D16
Yell *U.K.* 60°35N 1°5W **11** A7
Yell Sd. *U.K.* 60°33N 1°15W **11** A7
Yellow = Huang He →
China 37°55N 118°50E **35** F10
Yellow Sea *China* 35°0N 123°0E **35** G12
Yellowhead Pass
Canada 52°53N 118°25W **70** C5
Yellowknife *Canada* 62°27N 114°29W **70** A6
Yellowknife → *Canada* 62°31N 114°19W **70** A6
Yellowstone →
U.S.A. 47°59N 103°59W **76** C12
Yellowstone △ *U.S.A.* 44°40N 110°30W **76** D8
Yellowstone L. *U.S.A.* 44°27N 110°22W **76** D8
Yelsk *Belarus* 51°50N 29°10E **17** C15
Yemen ■ *Asia* 15°0N 44°0E **47** E3
Yen Bai *Vietnam* 21°42N 104°52E **38** B5
Yenangyaung *Burma* 20°30N 95°0E **41** J19

Yenbo = Yanbu 'al Baḥr
Si. Arabia 24°0N 38°5E **44** F3
Yenda *Australia* 34°13S 146°14E **63** E4
Yeni Erenköy = Yialousa
Cyprus 35°32N 34°10E **25** D13
Yenice *Turkey* 39°55N 27°17E **23** E12
Yenisey → *Russia* 71°50N 82°40E **28** B9
Yeniseysk *Russia* 58°27N 92°13E **29** D10
Yeniseyskiy Zaliv *Russia* 72°20N 81°0E **28** B9
Yenyuka *Russia* 57°57N 121°15E **29** D13
Yeo → *U.K.* 51°2N 2°49W **13** G5
Yeo, L. *Australia* 28°0S 124°30E **61** E3
Yeo I. *Canada* 45°24N 81°48W **82** A3
Yeoju *S. Korea* 37°20N 127°35E **35** F14
Yeola *India* 20°2N 74°30E **40** J9
Yeong-wol *S. Korea* 37°11N 128°28E **35** F15
Yeongcheon *S. Korea* 35°58N 128°56E **35** G15
Yeongdeok *S. Korea* 36°24N 129°22E **35** F15
Yeongdeungpo
S. Korea 37°31N 126°54E **35** F14
Yeongdong *S. Korea* 36°10N 127°46E **35** F14
Yeongju *S. Korea* 36°50N 128°40E **35** F15
Yeosu *S. Korea* 34°47N 127°45E **35** G14
Yeovil *U.K.* 50°57N 2°38W **13** G5
Yeppoon *Australia* 23°5S 150°47E **62** C5
Yerbent *Turkmenistan* 39°30N 58°50E **28** F6
Yerbogachen *Russia* 61°16N 108°0E **29** C11
Yerevan *Armenia* 40°10N 44°31E **44** A5
Yerington *U.S.A.* 38°59N 119°10W **76** G4
Yermak *Kazakhstan* 52°2N 76°55E **28** D8
Yermo *U.S.A.* 34°54N 116°50W **79** L10
Yerólakkos *Cyprus* 35°11N 33°15E **25** D12
Yeropol *Russia* 65°15N 168°40E **29** C17
Yeroskipos *Cyprus* 34°46N 32°28E **25** E11
Yershov *Russia* 51°23N 48°27E **19** D8
Yerushalayim = Jerusalem
Israel/West Bank 31°47N 35°10E **46** D4
Yes Tor *U.K.* 50°41N 4°0W **13** G4
Yesan *S. Korea* 36°41N 126°51E **35** F14
Yeso *U.S.A.* 34°26N 104°37W **77** J11
Yessey *Russia* 68°29N 102°10E **29** C11
Yetman *Australia* 28°56S 150°48E **63** D5
Yeu, Î. d' *France* 46°42N 2°20W **20** C2
Yevpatoriya *Ukraine* 45°15N 33°20E **19** E5
Yeysk *Russia* 46°40N 38°12E **19** E6
Yezd = Yazd *Iran* 31°55N 54°27E **45** D7
Ygatimí *Paraguay* 24°5S 55°40W **95** A4
Yhati *Paraguay* 25°45S 56°35W **94** B4
Yhú *Paraguay* 25°0S 56°0W **95** B4
Yí → *Uruguay* 33°7S 57°8W **94** C4
Yi 'Allaq, G. *Egypt* 30°21N 33°31E **46** E2
Yi He → *China* 34°10N 118°8E **35** G10
Yi Xian *Hebei, China* 39°20N 115°30E **34** E8
Yi Xian *Liaoning, China* 41°30N 121°22E **35** D11
Yialiás → *Cyprus* 35°9N 33°44E **25** D12
Yialousa *Cyprus* 35°32N 34°10E **25** D13
Yibin *China* 28°45N 104°32E **32** D5
Yichang *China* 30°40N 111°20E **33** C6
Yicheng *China* 35°42N 111°40E **34** G6
Yichuan *China* 36°2N 110°10E **34** F6
Yichun *China* 47°44N 128°52E **33** B7
Yidu *China* 36°43N 118°28E **35** F10
Yijun *China* 35°28N 109°8E **34** G5
Yıldız Dağları *Turkey* 41°48N 27°36E **23** D12
Yilehuli Shan *China* 51°20N 124°20E **33** A7
Yimianpo *China* 45°7N 128°2E **35** B15
Yinchuan *China* 38°30N 106°15E **34** E4
Yindarlgooda, L.
Australia 30°40S 121°52E **61** F3
Ying He → *China* 32°30N 116°30E **34** H9
Ying Xian *China* 39°32N 113°10E **34** E7
Yingkou *China* 40°37N 122°18E **35** D12
Yining *China* 43°58N 81°10E **32** B3
Yinmabin *Burma* 22°10N 94°55E **41** H19
Yirga Alem *Ethiopia* 6°48N 38°22E **47** F2
Yirrkala *Australia* 12°14S 136°56E **62** A2
Yishan *China* 24°28N 108°38E **32** D5
Yishui *China* 35°47N 118°30E **35** G10
Yishun *Singapore* 1°26N 103°51E **39** d
Yitong *China* 43°13N 125°20E **35** C13
Yixing *China* 31°21N 119°48E **33** C6
Yiyang *Henan, China* 34°27N 112°10E **34** G7
Yiyang *Hunan, China* 28°35N 112°18E **33** D6
Yli-Kitka *Finland* 66°8N 28°30E **8** C23
Ylitornio *Finland* 66°19N 23°39E **8** C20
Ylivieska *Finland* 64°4N 24°28E **8** D21
Yoakum *U.S.A.* 29°17N 97°9W **84** G6
Yog Pt. *Phil.* 14°6N 124°12E **37** B6
Yogyakarta *Indonesia* 7°49S 110°22E **37** G14
Yogyakarta □ *Indonesia* 7°48S 110°22E **37** G14
Yoho △ *Canada* 51°25N 116°30W **70** C5
Yojoa, L. de *Honduras* 14°53N 88°0W **88** D2
Yok Don △ *Vietnam* 12°50N 107°40E **38** F6
Yokadouma *Cameroon* 3°35N 14°55E **52** D2
Yokkaichi *Japan* 34°55N 136°38E **31** G8
Yoko *Cameroon* 5°32N 12°20E **52** C2
Yokohama *Japan* 35°27N 139°28E **31** G9
Yokosuka *Japan* 35°20N 139°40E **31** G9
Yokote *Japan* 39°20N 140°30E **30** E10
Yola *Nigeria* 9°10N 12°29E **51** G8
Yolaina, Cordillera de
Nic. 11°30N 84°0W **88** D3
Yólöten *Turkmenistan* 37°18N 62°21E **45** B9
Yom → *Thailand* 15°35N 100°1E **38** E3
Yonago *Japan* 35°25N 133°19E **31** G6
Yonaguni-Jima *Japan* 24°27N 123°0E **31** M1
Yonan N. *Korea* 37°55N 126°11E **35** F14
Yonezawa *Japan* 37°57N 140°4E **30** F10
Yong Peng *Malaysia* 2°0N 103°3E **39** M4
Yong Sata *Thailand* 7°8N 99°41E **39** J2
Yongamp'o N. *Korea* 39°56N 124°23E **35** E13
Yongcheng *China* 33°55N 116°20E **34** H9
Yongdeng *China* 36°38N 103°25E **34** F2
Yonghe *China* 36°46N 110°38E **34** F6
Yŏnghŭng *N. Korea* 39°31N 127°18E **35** E14
Yongji *China* 34°52N 110°28E **34** G6
Yongnian *China* 36°47N 114°29E **34** F8
Yongning *China* 38°15N 106°14E **34** E4

Yongqing *China* 39°25N 116°28E **34** E9
Yonibana *S. Leone* 8°30N 12°19W **50** G3
Yonkers *U.S.A.* 40°56N 73°52W **83** F11
Yonne → *France* 48°23N 2°58E **20** B5
York *Australia* 31°52S 116°47E **61** F2
York *U.K.* 53°58N 1°6W **12** D6
York *Ala., U.S.A.* 32°29N 88°18W **85** E10
York *Nebr., U.S.A.* 40°52N 97°36W **80** E5
York *Pa., U.S.A.* 39°58N 76°44W **81** F15
York, C. *Australia* 10°42S 142°31E **62** A3
York, City of □ *U.K.* 53°58N 1°6W **12** D6
York, Kap *Greenland* 75°55N 66°25W **4** B4
York, Vale of *U.K.* 54°15N 1°25W **12** C6
York Sd. *Australia* 15°0S 125°5E **60** C4
Yorke Pen. *Australia* 34°50S 137°40E **63** E2
Yorkshire Dales △ *U.K.* 54°12N 2°10W **12** C5
Yorkshire Wolds *U.K.* 54°8N 0°31W **12** C7
Yorkton *Canada* 51°11N 102°28W **71** C8
Yorkville *U.S.A.* 38°52N 123°13W **78** G3
Yoro *Honduras* 15°9N 87°7W **88** C2
Yoron-Jima *Japan* 27°2N 128°26E **31** L4
Yos Sudarso, Pulau = Dolak,
Pulau *Indonesia* 8°0S 138°30E **37** F9
Yosemite △ *U.S.A.* 37°45N 119°40W **78** H7
Yosemite Village
U.S.A. 37°45N 119°35W **78** H7
Yoshino-Kumano △
Japan 34°12N 135°55E **31** H8
Yoshkar Ola *Russia* 56°38N 47°55E **18** C8
Yotvata *Israel* 29°55N 35°2E **46** F4
Youbou *Canada* 48°53N 124°13W **78** B2
Youghal *Ireland* 51°56N 7°52W **10** E4
Youghal B. *Ireland* 51°55N 7°49W **10** E4
Young *Australia* 34°19S 148°18E **63** E4
Young *Canada* 51°47N 105°45W **71** C7
Young *Uruguay* 32°44S 57°36W **94** C4
Younghusband, L.
Australia 30°50S 136°5E **63** E2
Younghusband Pen.
Australia 36°0S 139°25E **63** F2
Youngstown *Canada* 51°35N 111°10W **71** C6
Youngstown *N.Y., U.S.A.* 43°15N 79°3W **82** C5
Youngstown *Ohio, U.S.A.* 41°6N 80°39W **82** E4
Youngsville *U.S.A.* 41°51N 79°19W **82** E5
Youngwood *U.S.A.* 40°14N 79°34W **82** F5
Youyu *China* 40°10N 112°20E **34** D7
Yozgat *Turkey* 39°51N 34°47E **19** G5
Ypacaraí △ *Paraguay* 25°18S 57°19W **94** B4
Ypané → *Paraguay* 23°29S 57°19W **94** A4
Ypres = Ieper *Belgium* 50°51N 2°53E **15** D2
Yreka *U.S.A.* 41°44N 122°38W **76** F2
Ystad *Sweden* 55°26N 13°50E **9** J15
Ysyk-Köl = Balykchy
Kyrgyzstan 42°26N 76°12E **32** B2
Ysyk-Köl *Kyrgyzstan* 42°25N 77°15E **28** E8
Ythan → *U.K.* 57°19N 1°59W **11** D7
Ytyk-Kyuyel *Russia* 62°30N 133°45E **29** C14
Yu Jiang → *China* 23°22N 110°3E **33** D6
Yu Xian = Yuzhou
China 34°10N 113°28E **34** G7
Yu Xian *Hebei, China* 39°50N 114°35E **34** E8
Yu Xian *Shanxi, China* 38°5N 113°20E **34** E7
Yuan Jiang → *China* 28°55N 111°50E **33** D6
Yuanqu *China* 35°18N 111°40E **34** G6
Yuanyang *China* 35°3N 113°58E **34** G7
Yuba → *U.S.A.* 39°8N 121°36W **78** F5
Yuba City *U.S.A.* 39°8N 121°37W **78** F5
Yūbari *Japan* 43°4N 141°59E **30** C10
Yūbetsu *Japan* 44°13N 143°50E **30** B11
Yucatán □ *Mexico* 21°30N 86°30W **87** C7
Yucatán, Canal de
Caribbean 22°0N 86°30W **88** B2
Yucatán, Península de
Mexico 19°30N 89°0W **66** H11
Yucatan Basin *Cent. Amer.* 19°0N 86°0W **87** D7
Yucatan Channel = Yucatán,
Canal de *Caribbean* 22°0N 86°30W **88** B2
Yucca *U.S.A.* 34°52N 114°9W **79** L12
Yucca Valley *U.S.A.* 34°8N 116°27W **79** L10
Yucheng *China* 36°55N 116°32E **34** F9
Yuci *China* 37°42N 112°46E **34** F7
Yuen Long *China* 22°26N 114°2E **33** G11
Yuendumu *Australia* 22°16S 131°49E **60** D5
Yugorenok *Russia* 59°47N 137°40E **29** D14
Yugoslavia = Serbia ■
Europe 43°20N 20°0E **23** B9
Yukon □ *U.S.A.* 35°31N 97°45W **84** D6
Yukon → *U.S.A.* 62°32N 163°54W **74** a
Yukon Territory □
Canada 63°0N 135°0W **68** C6
Yukta *Russia* 63°26N 105°42E **29** C11
Yukuhashi *Japan* 33°44N 130°59E **31** H5
Yulara *Australia* 25°10S 130°55E **61** E5
Yule → *Australia* 20°41S 118°17E **60** D2
Yuleba *Australia* 26°37S 149°24E **63** D4
Yulin *Hainan, China* 18°10N 109°31E **38** C7
Yulin *Shaanxi, China* 38°20N 109°30E **34** E5
Yuma *Ariz., U.S.A.* 32°43N 114°37W **79** N12
Yuma *Colo., U.S.A.* 40°8N 102°43W **76** F12
Yuma, B. de *Dom. Rep.* 18°20N 68°35W **89** C6
Yumbe *Uganda* 3°28N 31°15E **54** B3
Yumbi
Dem. Rep. of the Congo 1°12S 26°15E **54** C2
Yumen *China* 39°50N 97°30E **32** C4
Yun Xian *China* 32°50N 110°46E **34** H6
Yuncheng *Henan, China* 35°36N 115°57E **34** G8
Yuncheng *Shanxi, China* 35°2N 111°0E **34** G6
Yungas *Bolivia* 17°0S 66°0W **92** G5
Yungay *Chile* 37°10S 72°5W **94** D1
Yunnan □ *China* 25°0N 102°0E **32** D5
Yunta *Australia* 32°34S 139°36E **63** E2
Yunxi *China* 33°0N 110°22E **34** H6
Yupanqui Basin *Pac. Oc.* 19°0S 101°0W **65** H18
Yurga *Russia* 55°42N 84°51E **28** D9
Yurimaguas *Peru* 5°55S 76°7W **92** E3
Yurubí △ *Venezuela* 10°26N 68°42W **89** D6
Yuscarán *Honduras* 13°58N 86°45W **88** D2

Yushe *China* 37°4N 112°58E **34** F7
Yushu *Jilin, China* 44°43N 126°38E **35** B14
Yushu *Qinghai, China* 33°5N 96°55E **32** C4
Yutai *China* 35°0N 116°45E **34** G9
Yutian *Hebei, China* 39°53N 117°45E **35** E9
Yutian *Sinkiang-Uigur,
China* 36°52N 81°42E **32** C3
Yuxarı Qarabağ =
Nagorno-Karabakh □
Azerbaijan 39°55N 46°45E **44** B5
Yuxi *China* 24°30N 102°35E **32** D5
Yuzawa *Japan* 39°10N 140°30E **30** E10
Yuzhno-Kurilsk *Russia* 44°1N 145°51E **29** E15
Yuzhno-Sakhalinsk
Russia 46°58N 142°45E **29** E15
Yuzhnyy □ *Russia* 44°0N 40°0E **28** E5
Yuzhou *China* 34°10N 113°28E **34** G7
Yvetot *France* 49°37N 0°44E **20** B4

Z

Zaanstad *Neths.* 52°27N 4°50E **15** B4
Zāb al Kabīr → *Iraq* 36°1N 43°24E **44** B4
Zāb aş Şaghīr → *Iraq* 35°17N 43°29E **44** C4
Zābol *Iran* 31°0N 61°32E **45** D9
Zābol □ *Afghan.* 32°0N 67°0E **40** D5
Zābolī *Iran* 27°10N 61°35E **45** E9
Zabrze *Poland* 50°18N 18°50E **17** C10
Zacapa *Guatemala* 14°59N 89°31W **88** D2
Zacapu *Mexico* 19°50N 101°43W **86** D4
Zacatecas *Mexico* 22°47N 102°35W **86** C4
Zacatecas □ *Mexico* 23°0N 103°0W **86** C4
Zacatecoluca *El Salv.* 13°29N 88°51W **88** D2
Zachary *U.S.A.* 30°39N 91°9W **84** F9
Zacoalco de Torres
Mexico 20°14N 103°35W **86** C4
Zacualtipán *Mexico* 20°39N 98°36W **87** C5
Zadar *Croatia* 44°8N 15°14E **16** F8
Zadetkyi Kyun *Burma* 10°0N 98°25E **39** G2
Zafarqand *Iran* 33°11N 52°29E **45** C7
Zafra *Spain* 38°26N 6°30W **21** C2
Żagań *Poland* 51°39N 15°22E **16** C8
Zagaoua *Chad* 15°30N 22°24E **51** E10
Zagazig *Egypt* 30°40N 31°30E **51** B12
Zāgheh *Iran* 33°30N 48°42E **45** C6
Zagreb *Croatia* 45°50N 15°58E **16** F9
Zāgros, Kūhhā-ye *Iran* 33°45N 48°5E **45** C6
Zagros Mts. = Zāgros, Kūhhā-ye
Iran 33°45N 48°5E **45** C6
Zahamena △ *Madag.* 17°37S 48°49E **57** B8
Zāhedān *Fārs, Iran* 28°46N 53°52E **45** D7
Zāhedān *Sīstān va Balūchestān,
Iran* 29°30N 60°50E **45** D9
Zahlah *Lebanon* 33°52N 35°50E **46** B4
Zaïre = Congo → *Africa* 6°4S 12°24E **52** F2
Zaječar *Serbia* 43°53N 22°18E **23** C10
Zaka *Zimbabwe* 20°20S 31°29E **57** C5
Zakamensk *Russia* 50°23N 103°17E **29** D11
Zakhodnaya Dzvina =
Daugava → *Latvia* 57°4N 24°3E **9** H21
Zākhū *Iraq* 37°10N 42°50E **44** B4
Zakinthos = Zakynthos
Greece 37°47N 20°54E **23** F9
Zakopane *Poland* 49°18N 19°57E **17** D10
Zakros *Greece* 35°6N 26°10E **25** D8
Zakynthos *Greece* 37°47N 20°54E **23** F9
Zalaegerszeg *Hungary* 46°53N 16°47E **17** E9
Zalari *Russia* 53°33N 102°30E **29** D11
Zalău *Romania* 47°12N 23°3E **17** E12
Zaleshchiki = Zalishchyky
Ukraine 48°45N 25°45E **17** D13
Zalew Wiślany *Poland* 54°20N 19°50E **17** A10
Zalishchyky *Ukraine* 48°45N 25°45E **17** D13
Zama L. *Canada* 58°45N 119°5W **70** B5
Zambeke
Dem. Rep. of the Congo 2°8N 25°17E **54** B2
Zambeze → *Africa* 18°35S 36°20E **55** F4
Zambezi = Zambeze →
Africa 18°35S 36°20E **55** F4
Zambezi *Zambia* 13°30S 23°15E **53** G4
Zambezi → *Zimbabwe* 17°54S 25°41E **55** F2
Zambézia □ *Mozam.* 16°15S 37°30E **55** F4
Zambia ■ *Africa* 15°0S 28°0E **55** F2
Zamboanga *Phil.* 6°59N 122°3E **37** C6
Zamora *Mexico* 19°59N 102°16W **86** D4
Zamora *Spain* 41°30N 5°45W **21** B3
Zamość *Poland* 50°43N 23°15E **17** C12
Zanda *China* 31°32N 79°50E **32** C2
Zandvoort *Neths.* 52°22N 4°32E **15** B4
Zanesville *U.S.A.* 39°56N 82°1W **82** G2
Zangābād *Iran* 38°26N 46°44E **44** B5
Zangue → *Mozam.* 17°50S 35°21E **55** F4
Zanjān *Iran* 36°40N 48°35E **45** B6
Zanjān □ *Iran* 37°20N 49°30E **45** B6
Zanjān → *Iran* 37°8N 47°47E **45** B6
Zante = Zakynthos
Greece 37°47N 20°54E **23** F9
Zanthus *Australia* 31°2S 123°34E **61** F3
Zanzibar *Tanzania* 6°12S 39°12E **54** D4
Zaouiet El-Kala = Bordj Omar
Driss *Algeria* 28°10N 6°40E **50** C7
Zaouiet Reggâne *Algeria* 26°32N 0°3E **50** C6
Zaozhuang *China* 34°50N 117°35E **35** G9
Zap Suyu = Zāb al Kabīr →
Iraq 36°1N 43°24E **44** B4
Zapadnaya Dvina = Daugava →
Latvia 57°4N 24°3E **9** H21
Západné Beskydy *Europe* 49°30N 19°0E **17** D10
Zapala *Argentina* 39°0S 70°5W **96** D2
Zapaleri, Cerro *Bolivia* 22°49S 67°11W **94** A2
Zapata *U.S.A.* 26°55N 99°16W **84** H5
Zapolyarnyy *Russia* 69°26N 30°51E **8** B24
Zapopán *Mexico* 20°43N 103°24W **86** C4
Zaporozhye = Zaporizhzhya
Ukraine 47°50N 35°10E **19** E6

Zara *Turkey* 39°58N 37°43E **44** B3
Zaragoza *Coahuila,
Mexico* 28°29N 100°55W **86** B4
Zaragoza *Nuevo León,
Mexico* 23°58N 99°46W **87** C5
Zaragoza *Spain* 41°39N 0°53W **21** B5
Zarand *Kermān, Iran* 30°46N 56°34E **45** D8
Zarand *Markazī, Iran* 35°18N 50°25E **45** C6
Zaranj *Afghan.* 30°55N 61°55E **40** D2
Zārate *Argentina* 34°7S 59°0W **94** C4
Zard, Kūh-e *Iran* 32°22N 50°4E **45** C6
Zāreh *Iran* 35°7N 49°9E **45** C6
Zaria *Nigeria* 11°0N 7°40E **50** F7
Zarneh *Iran* 33°55N 46°10E **44** C5
Zaros *Greece* 35°8N 24°54E **25** D6
Zarqā', Nahr az →
Jordan 32°10N 35°37E **46** C4
Zarrīn *Iran* 32°46N 54°37E **45** C7
Zaruma *Ecuador* 3°40S 79°38W **92** D3
Zāry *Poland* 51°37N 15°10E **16** C8
Zarzis *Tunisia* 33°31N 11°2E **51** B8
Zaskar → *India* 34°13N 77°20E **43** B7
Zaskar Mts. *India* 33°15N 77°30E **43** C7
Zastron *S. Africa* 30°18S 27°7E **56** E4
Zavāreh *Iran* 33°29N 52°28E **45** C7
Zave *Zimbabwe* 17°6S 30°1E **57** B5
Zavitinsk *Russia* 50°10N 129°20E **29** D13
Zavodovski, I. *Antarctica* 56°0S 27°45W **5** B1
Zawiercie *Poland* 50°30N 19°24E **17** C10
Zāwiyat al Bayḍā = Al Bayḍā
Libya 32°50N 21°44E **51** B10
Zāyā *Iraq* 33°33N 44°13E **44** C5
Zāyandeh → *Iran* 32°35N 52°0E **45** C7
Zaysan *Kazakhstan* 47°28N 84°52E **32** B3
Zaysan Köli *Kazakhstan* 48°0N 83°0E **28** E9
Zayü *China* 28°48N 97°27E **32** D4
Zazafotsy *Madag.* 21°11S 46°21E **57** C8
Zbarazh *Ukraine* 49°43N 25°44E **17** D13
Zdolbuniv *Ukraine* 50°30N 26°15E **17** C14
Zduńska Wola *Poland* 51°37N 18°59E **17** C10
Zeballos *Canada* 49°59N 126°50W **70** D3
Zebediela *S. Africa* 24°20S 29°17E **57** C4
Zeebrugge *Belgium* 51°19N 3°12E **15** C3
Zeehan *Australia* 41°52S 145°25E **63** G4
Zeeland □ *Neths.* 51°30N 3°50E **15** C3
Zeerust *S. Africa* 25°31S 26°4E **56** D4
Zefat *Israel* 32°58N 35°29E **46** C4
Zehak *Iran* 30°53N 61°42E **45** D9
Zeil, Mt. *Australia* 23°30S 132°23E **60** D5
Zeila = Saylac
Somali Rep. 11°21N 43°30E **47** E3
Zeist *Neths.* 52°5N 5°15E **15** B5
Zeitz *Germany* 51°2N 12°7E **16** C7
Zelenogorsk *Russia* 60°12N 29°43E **8** F23
Zelenograd *Russia* 56°1N 37°12E **18** C6
Zelienople *U.S.A.* 40°48N 80°8W **82** F4
Zémio *C.A.R.* 5°2N 25°5E **54** A2
Zempoala *Mexico* 19°27N 96°23W **87** D5
Zemun *Serbia* 44°51N 20°25E **23** B9
Zenica *Bos.-H.* 44°10N 17°57E **23** B7
Zevenaar *Neths.* 51°56N 6°5E **15** C6
Zeya *Russia* 53°48N 127°14E **29** D13
Zeya → *Russia* 51°42N 128°53E **29** D13
Zêzere → *Portugal* 39°28N 8°20W **21** C1
Zghartā *Lebanon* 34°21N 35°53E **46** A4
Zgorzelec *Poland* 51°10N 15°0E **16** C8
Zhabinka *Belarus* 52°13N 24°2E **17** B13
Zhambyl = Taraz
Kazakhstan 42°54N 71°22E **28** E8
Zhangaqazaly *Kazakhstan* 45°48N 62°6E **28** E7
Zhangbei *China* 41°10N 114°45E **34** D8
Zhangguangcai Ling
China 45°0N 129°0E **35** B15
Zhangjiabian *China* 22°33N 113°28E **33** F9
Zhangjiagang *China* 31°55N 120°30E **37** B13
Zhangjiakou *China* 40°48N 114°55E **34** D8
Zhangwu *China* 42°43N 123°52E **35** C12
Zhangye *China* 38°50N 100°23E **32** C5
Zhangzhou *China* 24°30N 117°35E **33** D6
Zhanhua *China* 37°40N 118°8E **35** F10
Zhanjiang *China* 21°15N 110°20E **33** D6
Zhannetty, Ostrov
Russia 76°43N 158°0E **29** B16
Zhanyi *China* 25°38N 103°48E **32** D5
Zhanyu *China* 44°30N 122°30E **35** B12
Zhao Xian *China* 37°43N 114°45E **34** F8
Zhaocheng *China* 36°22N 111°38E **34** F6
Zhaotong *China* 27°20N 103°44E **32** D5
Zhaoyuan *Heilongjiang,
China* 45°27N 125°0E **35** B13
Zhaoyuan *Shandong,
China* 37°20N 120°23E **35** F11
Zhari Namco *China* 31°6N 85°36E **32** C3
Zharkent *Kazakhstan* 44°10N 80°0E **28** E9
Zhashkiv *Ukraine* 49°15N 30°5E **17** D16
Zhashui *China* 33°40N 109°8E **34** H5
Zhayylma *Kazakhstan* 51°37N 61°33E **28** D7
Zhayyq → *Kazakhstan* 47°0N 51°48E **19** E9
Zhdanov = Mariupol
Ukraine 47°5N 37°31E **19** E6
Zhecheng *China* 34°7N 115°20E **34** G8
Zhejiang □ *China* 29°0N 120°0E **33** D7
Zheleznodorozhnyy
Russia 62°35N 50°55E **18** B9
Zheleznogorsk-Ilimskiy
Russia 56°34N 104°8E **29** D11
Zhen'an *China* 33°27N 109°9E **34** H5
Zhengding *China* 38°8N 114°32E **34** E8
Zhengzhou *China* 34°45N 113°34E **34** G7
Zhenlai *China* 45°50N 123°5E **35** B12
Zhenping *China* 33°10N 112°16E **34** H7
Zhenyuan *China* 35°35N 107°30E **34** G4
Zhetiqara *Kazakhstan* 52°11N 61°12E **28** D7
Zhezqazghan *Kazakhstan* 47°44N 67°40E **28** E7
Zhidan *China* 36°48N 108°48E **34** F5
Zhigansk *Russia* 66°48N 123°27E **29** C13

Zhilinda *Russia* 70°0N 114°20E **29** C12
Zhitomir = Zhytomyr
Ukraine 50°20N 28°40E **17** C15
Zhlobin *Belarus* 52°55N 30°0E **17** B16
Zhob *Pakistan* 31°20N 69°31E **42** D3
Zhob → *Pakistan* 32°4N 69°50E **42** C3
Zhodzina *Belarus* 54°5N 28°17E **17** A15
Zhokhova, Ostrov
Russia 76°4N 152°40E **29** B16
Zhongdian *China* 27°48N 99°42E **32** D4
Zhongning *China* 37°29N 105°40E **34** F3
Zhongshan *Antarctica* 69°0S 39°50E **5** C6
Zhongshan *China* 22°26N 113°20E **33** G9
Zhongshankong *China* 22°35N 113°29E **33** G10
Zhongtiao Shan *China* 35°0N 111°10E **34** G6
Zhongwei *China* 37°30N 105°12E **34** F3
Zhongyang *China* 37°20N 111°11E **34** F6
Zhosaly *Kazakhstan* 45°29N 64°4E **28** E7
Zhoucun *China* 36°47N 117°48E **35** F9
Zhouzhi *China* 34°10N 108°12E **34** G5
Zhuanghe *China* 39°40N 123°0E **35** E12
Zhucheng *China* 36°0N 119°27E **35** G10
Zhugqu *China* 33°40N 104°30E **34** H3
Zhuhai *China* 22°17N 113°34E **33** G10
Zhujiang Kou *China* 22°20N 113°45E **33** G10
Zhumadian *China* 32°59N 114°2E **34** H8
Zhuo Xian = Zhuozhou
China 39°28N 115°58E **34** E8
Zhuolu *China* 40°20N 115°12E **34** D8
Zhuozhou *China* 39°28N 115°58E **34** E8
Zhuozi *China* 41°0N 112°25E **34** D7
Zhytomyr *Ukraine* 50°20N 28°40E **17** C15
Ziarat *Pakistan* 30°25N 67°49E **42** D2
Zibo *China* 36°47N 118°3E **35** F10
Zichang *China* 37°18N 109°40E **34** F5
Zidi = Wandhari
Pakistan 27°42N 66°48E **42** F2
Zielona Góra *Poland* 51°57N 15°31E **16** C8
Zierikzee *Neths.* 51°40N 3°55E **15** C3
Zigong *China* 29°15N 104°48E **32** D5
Ziguéy *Chad* 14°43N 15°50E **51** F9
Ziguinchor *Senegal* 12°35N 16°20W **50** F2
Zihuatanejo *Mexico* 17°39N 101°33W **86** D4
Žilina *Slovak Rep.* 49°12N 18°42E **17** D10
Zillah *Libya* 28°30N 17°33E **51** C9
Zima *Russia* 54°0N 102°5E **29** D11
Zimapán *Mexico* 20°45N 99°21W **87** C5
Zimba *Zambia* 17°20S 26°11E **55** F2
Zimbabwe *Zimbabwe* 20°16S 30°54E **55** G3
Zimbabwe ■ *Africa* 19°0S 30°0E **55** F3
Zimnicea *Romania* 43°40N 25°22E **17** G13
Zinave △ *Mozam.* 21°35S 33°40E **57** C5
Zinder *Niger* 13°48N 9°0E **50** F7
Zinga *Tanzania* 9°16S 38°49E **54** D4
Zion △ *U.S.A.* 37°15N 113°5W **77** H7
Ziros *Greece* 35°5N 26°8E **25** D8
Zirreh, Gowd-e *Afghan.* 29°45N 62°0E **40** E3
Zitácuaro *Mexico* 19°24N 100°22W **86** D4
Zitundo *Mozam.* 26°48S 32°47E **57** D5
Ziwa Magharibia = Kagera □
Tanzania 2°0S 31°30E **54** C3
Ziway, L. *Ethiopia* 8°0N 38°50E **47** F2
Ziyang *China* 32°32N 108°31E **34** H5
Zlatograd *Bulgaria* 41°22N 25°7E **23** D11
Zlatoust *Russia* 55°10N 59°40E **18** C10
Zlín *Czech Rep.* 49°14N 17°40E **17** D9
Zmeinogorsk *Kazakhstan* 51°10N 82°13E **28** D9
Znojmo *Czech Rep.* 48°50N 16°2E **16** D9
Zobeyrī *Iran* 34°10N 46°40E **44** C5
Zobia *Dem. Rep. of the Congo* 3°0N 25°59E **54** B2
Zoetermeer *Neths.* 52°3N 4°30E **15** B4
Zohreh → *Iran* 30°16N 51°15E **45** D6
Zolochiv *Ukraine* 49°45N 24°51E **17** D13
Zomba *Malawi* 15°22S 35°19E **55** F4
Zongo
Dem. Rep. of the Congo 4°20N 18°35E **52** D3
Zonguldak *Turkey* 41°28N 31°50E **19** F5
Zonqor Pt. *Malta* 35°52N 14°34E **25** D2
Zorritos *Peru* 3°43S 80°40W **92** D2
Zou Xiang *China* 35°30N 116°58E **34** G9
Zouar *Chad* 20°30N 16°32E **51** D9
Zouérate = Zouîrât
Mauritania 22°44N 12°21W **50** D3
Zouîrât *Mauritania* 22°44N 12°21W **50** D3
Zoutkamp *Neths.* 53°20N 6°18E **15** A6
Zrenjanin *Serbia* 45°22N 20°23E **23** B9
Zufār *Oman* 17°40N 54°0E **47** D5
Zug *Switz.* 47°10N 8°31E **20** C8
Zugspitze *Germany* 47°25N 10°59E **16** E6
Zuid-Holland □ *Neths.* 52°0N 4°35E **15** C4
Zuidbeveland *Neths.* 51°30N 3°50E **15** C3
Zuidhorn *Neths.* 53°15N 6°23E **15** A6
Zula *Eritrea* 15°17N 39°40E **47** D2
Zumbo *Mozam.* 15°35S 30°26E **55** F3
Zumpango *Mexico* 19°48N 99°6W **87** D5
Zunhua *China* 40°18N 117°58E **35** D9
Zuni Pueblo *U.S.A.* 35°4N 108°51W **77** J9
Zunyi *China* 27°42N 106°53E **32** D5
Zurbāṭīyah *Iraq* 33°9N 46°3E **44** C5
Zürich *Switz.* 47°22N 8°32E **20** C8
Zutphen *Neths.* 52°9N 6°12E **15** B6
Zuurberg △ *S. Africa* 33°12S 25°32E **56** E4
Zuwārah *Libya* 32°58N 12°1E **51** B8
Zūzan *Iran* 34°22N 59°53E **45** C8
Zvishavane *Zimbabwe* 20°17S 30°2E **55** G3
Zvolen *Slovak Rep.* 48°33N 19°10E **17** D10
Zwettl *Austria* 48°35N 15°9E **16** D8
Zwickau *Germany* 50°44N 12°30E **16** C7
Zwolle *Neths.* 52°31N 6°6E **15** B6
Zwolle *U.S.A.* 31°38N 93°39W **84** F8
Żyrardów *Poland* 52°3N 20°28E **17** B11
Zyryan *Kazakhstan* 49°43N 84°20E **28** E9
Zyryanka *Russia* 65°45N 150°51E **29** C16
Zyryanovsk = Zyryan
Kazakhstan 49°43N 84°20E **28** E9
Żywiec *Poland* 49°42N 19°10E **17** D10